ARARAT

n Sea

Tigris River

Rages •

Nineveh

ASSYRIA

Ashur •

Mari •

MARI

*Euphrates
River*

ELAM

• Susa

• Babylon

BABYLONIA

ARABIAN
DESERT

• Ur

*Ancient
coastline*

Persian
Gulf

• Dumah

| 0 | 100 | 200 | 300 mi |

| 0 | 200 | 400 km |

Andrews Bible Commentary

Light. Depth. Truth.

Andrews Bible Commentary

Light. Depth. Truth.

General Editor

Ángel Manuel Rodríguez

Associate Editors

Daniel Kwame Bediako
Carl P. Cosaert
Gerald A. Klingbeil

OLD TESTAMENT

Andrews
University Press

Berrien Springs, Michigan

Andrews University Press
Sutherland House
8360 W. Campus Circle Dr.
Berrien Springs, MI 49104–1700
Telephone: 269–471–6134
Fax: 269–471–6224
Email: aupo@andrews.edu
Website: http://universitypress.andrews.edu

ISBN: 978–1–936337–21–7

Printed in the United States of America
26 25 24 23 22   2 3 4 5 6

Library of Congress Cataloging-in-Publication Data

Names: Rodríguez, Ángel Manuel, 1945– editor. | Bediako, Daniel Kwame,
  1976– editor. | Cosaert, Carl P., 1968– editor. | Klingbeil, Gerald A., 1964– editor.
Title: Andrews Bible commentary. Old Testament / general editor, Ángel
  Manuel Rodríguez ; associate editors, Daniel Kwame Bediako, Carl P.
  Cosaert, Gerald A. Klingbeil.
Description: Berrien Springs, Michigan : Andrews University Press, [2020] |
Identifiers: LCCN 2019059294 | ISBN 9781936337217 (hardcover)
Subjects: LCSH: Bible. Old Testament--Commentaries.
Classification: LCC BS1151.52 .A64 2020 | DDC 221.7--dc23
LC record available at https://lccn.loc.gov/2019059294

CONTENTS

Poetry and Wisdom Books

Prophetic Books

PUBLISHER'S PREFACE

You hold in your hands a work unique in the history of the vibrant faith community that has sponsored its publication. This volume marks another, perhaps inevitable, step in the searching for and unfolding of truth that is a hallmark of the Reformation and the Advent movement.

Commentaries on the Bible, from many faith traditions and perspectives, have been an important part of serious Bible study for centuries. Seventh-day Adventists have always placed the Bible alone as authoritative above all human opinion on what it says. At the same time, we have been blessed by the insights of many scholars through various Bible commentaries from these faith traditions, even while holding some significant differences in interpretation on several of the grandest and most vital themes of Scripture.

In the 1950s, the publication of the multivolume, verse-by-verse *Seventh-day Adventist Bible Commentary* met with an enthusiastic reception within the Adventist world far beyond all initial expectations. Its influence on biblical understanding in our community of faith has been profound. It has served the church well for more than sixty years.

In 2008, Andrews University was honored to be asked to produce another major landmark in the history of Adventist engagement with Scripture. The *Andrews Study Bible*, originally produced in the New King James Version (2010) and now also in the New International Version (2019), contains thousands of study notes written by prominent and thoughtful Adventist scholars. It also includes a unique linked reference system highlighting the greatest themes of the Bible. It was published with sponsorship and funding by the General Conference of Seventh-day Adventists and has been identified as the most comprehensive one-volume Bible study resource in the Adventist world.

Led by Niels-Erik Andreasen, then president of Andrews University, planning began almost immediately after the release of the *Andrews Study Bible* to next produce a concise, full-featured Bible commentary as a companion to the *Andrews Study Bible*. With sponsorship and funding again from the General Conference, Andrews University authorized a worldwide team of some sixty scholars and Bible teachers, under the leadership of Ángel Manuel Rodríguez, to produce this landmark work which you now hold in your hands. As former director of the General Conference Biblical Research Institute, Dr. Rodríguez was uniquely qualified for this work because of his expertise in biblical studies, his personal acquaintance with scores of scholars, and his worldwide reputation for faithfulness in effectively communicating the message and mission of the Bible as understood by Seventh-day Adventists.

It is our intent that the *Andrews Bible Commentary* complement the *Andrews Study Bible*. We believe that together these two great works form a complete, ready-reference resource for every believer.

The earnest desire of the publishers is that the *Andrews Bible Commentary* may inspire your deeper engagement with God's word and increase your fervent expectation of the Advent Hope.

Andrea Luxton
President, Andrews University
Executive Publisher, *Andrews Bible Commentary*

PROJECT COMMITTEE

As delegated by the Andrews University Press Board, production and publication of the *Andrews Bible Commentary* has been guided by an oversight Project Committee that met in 2012. The members are listed below with the professional responsibilities they held at the time that the Project Committee conducted its work. This committee supervised the development of the purpose and concept, arranged for funding, selected the General Editor, and approved the team of contributors.

Niels-Erik A. Andreasen, President, Andrews University

Lisa M. Beardsley-Hardy, Director, Department of Education, General Conference of Seventh-day Adventists

Shawn Boonstra, Director, Voice of Prophecy Ministry

Mark Finley, Assistant to the President, General Conference of Seventh-day Adventists

Denis Fortin, Dean, Seventh-day Adventist Theological Seminary, Andrews University

Ernő Gyéresi, Associate Director, Andrews University Press

Willie E. Hucks II, Associate Editor, *Ministry,* General Conference of Seventh-day Adventists

Greg A. King, Dean of the School of Religion, Southern Adventist University

Gerald A. Klingbeil, Associate Editor, *Adventist Review/Adventist World,* General Conference of Seventh-day Adventists

Bill Knott, Editor, *Adventist Review/Adventist World,* General Conference of Seventh-day Adventists

Ronald A. Knott, Director, Andrews University Press

John K. McVay, President, Walla Walla University

Jerry N. Page, Secretary, Ministerial Association, General Conference of Seventh-day Adventists

Juan R. Prestol, Treasurer, General Conference of Seventh-day Adventists

Ángel Manuel Rodríguez, Former Director, Biblical Research Institute

Benjamin D. Schoun, General Vice President, General Conference of Seventh-day Adventists

Ella Smith Simmons, General Vice President, General Conference of Seventh-day Adventists

Artur A. Stele, General Vice President, General Conference of Seventh-day Adventists

Alberto R. Timm, Associate Director, Ellen G. White Estate

Ted N. C. Wilson, President, General Conference of Seventh-day Adventists

E. Edward Zinke, Treasurer, Adventist Theological Society

EDITORS

General Editor

Ángel Manuel Rodríguez, ThD
Former Director
Part-time Associate Director
Biblical Research Institute

Associate Editors

Daniel Kwame Bediako, PhD
Vice Chancellor
Associate Professor of Old Testament
Valley View University

Carl P. Cosaert, PhD
Dean of the School of Theology
Professor of Biblical Studies: Greek and New Testament
Walla Walla University

Gerald A. Klingbeil, DLitt
Associate Editor, Adventist Review Ministries
Research Professor of Old Testament and Ancient Near Eastern Studies
Andrews University

CONTRIBUTORS

The *Andrews Bible Commentary* has been made possible by the contributions of biblical scholars and theologians from around the world. Under the leadership of the General Editor, these men and women provided the original material for the articles, book introductions, and commentaries. As part of the normal publication process, their writing benefited from several lines of evaluation, critical review, and editing. Thus, the published work may differ from the writers' contributions. The publisher is solely responsible for all content. The titles and institutional affiliations are listed as they were either at the time of writing or at the time of publication.

Merling Alomía, PhD
Daniel
Professor Emeritus
Universidad Peruana Unión

Niels-Erik A. Andreasen, PhD
Obadiah
Professor of Old Testament and
    President Emeritus
Andrews University

Roberto David Badenas, PhD
Paul, the Law, and Salvation
Professor Emeritus of New Testament
Sagunto Adventist College

Delbert W. Baker, PhD
Philemon
Professor and Vice Chancellor
Adventist University of Africa

L. S. Baker Jr., PhD
Archaeology and the Bible
Old Testament Timeline
A Chronology Following the Internal Timeline
    of the Bible
Associate Director
Andrews University Press

Daniel Kwame Bediako, PhD
Joshua
Associate Professor of Old Testament and
    Vice Chancellor
Valley View University

Daniel Berchie, PhD
2 Corinthians
Associate Professor of Religion
Valley View University

Brant Berglin, PhD Candidate
Introduction to the New Testament Epistles
Associate Professor of Biblical Studies
Walla Walla University

Ernest Bursey, PhD
Romans
Professor of Religion
AdventHealth University

Lael O. Caesar, PhD
Job
Associate Editor
Adventist Review/Adventist World

Aecio E. Cairus, PhD
1 Chronicles, 2 Chronicles
Professor of Systematic Theology
Adventist International Institute of
    Advanced Studies

Félix Cortez, PhD
1 Timothy
Associate Professor of New Testament
Andrews University

Carl P. Cosaert, PhD
1 Corinthians, Galatians
Historical Introduction to the New Testament
Professor of Biblical Studies: Greek and
    New Testament
Walla Walla University

Jo Ann Davidson, PhD
Ruth
Professor of Systematic Theology
Andrews University

Richard M. Davidson, PhD
Song of Songs, Hosea
Introduction to the Pentateuch
J. N. Andrews Professor of Old Testament
    Interpretation
Andrews University

Hyunsok John Doh, PhD
1 Corinthians
Professor of New Testament Studies
Southern Adventist University

Jacques B. Doukhan, ThD
Ecclesiastes
Professor Emeritus of Hebrew and Old
    Testament Exegesis
Andrews University

Denis Fortin, PhD
2 Timothy
Professor of Historical Theology
Andrews University

Mathilde Frey, PhD
Deuteronomy
Associate Professor of Theology
Walla Walla University

Erhard Gallos, PhD
James, Jude
Assistant Professor of Religion
Andrews University

Constance E. C. Gane, PhD
Nahum
Associate Professor of Archaeology and
    Old Testament
Andrews University

L. James Gibson, PhD
Faith and Science
Director
Geoscience Research Institute

Michael G. Hasel, PhD
Exodus
Professor of Near Eastern Studies and
    Archaeology
Southern Adventist University

William G. Johnsson, PhD
Hebrews
Former Editor
Adventist Review/Adventist World

Gerald A. Klingbeil, DLitt
Genesis, Ezra, Nehemiah
*Introduction to the Old Testament Historical
    Books*
Research Professor of Old Testament and
    Ancient Near Eastern Studies
Andrews University

Martin G. Klingbeil, DLitt
Psalms
*Introduction to Hebrew Poetry and
    Wisdom Books*
Professor of Biblical Studies and Archaeology
Southern Adventist University

Donn Walter Leatherman, PhD
Zechariah
Professor Emeritus of Religion
Southern Adventist University

Richard P. Lehmann, PhD
Acts
Professor Emeritus of Theology
Adventist University of France

Tarsee Li, PhD
Proverbs
Professor of Religion
Oakwood University

Robert K. McIver, PhD
Matthew
Senior Lecturer in Biblical Studies
Avondale University

John K. McVay, PhD
Colossians
Introduction to the New Testament Historical
  Books
Professor of Theology and President
Walla Walla University

Richard W. Medina, PhD Candidate
Amos
Director, Public Campus Ministries
Israel Field

Jiří Moskala, ThD, PhD
Habakkuk
Professor of Old Testament Exegesis and
  Theology
Andrews University

Ekkehardt Mueller, ThD, DMin
1 John, 2 John, 3 John
Associate Director
Biblical Research Institute

Rubén Muñoz-Larrondo, PhD
1 Corinthians
Associate Professor of Biblical Studies
Andrews University

Paluku Mwendambio, PhD
Numbers
Rector
Adventist University of Goma

Daegeuk Nam, PhD
Zephaniah
Professor and President Emeritus
Sahmyook University

Gudmundur Olafsson, PhD
Lamentations
Professor Emeritus of Old Testament and
  Biblical Languages
Newbold College of Higher Education

Kim Papaioannou, PhD
1 Peter
Pastor, Trans-European Division of
  Seventh-day Adventists

Wilson Paroschi, PhD
John
Professor of New Testament Studies
Southern Adventist University

Roberto Pereyra, PhD
Philippians
Professor Emeritus of New Testament Studies
Universidad Adventista del Plata

Paul B. Petersen, PhD
Malachi
Professor of Religion
Andrews University

Gerhard Pfandl, PhD
Judges, Daniel
Interpreting Biblical Apocalyptic Prophecies
Former Associate Director
Biblical Research Institute

Martin Pröbstle, PhD
Micah
Professor of Old Testament
Seminar Schloss Bogenhofen

Teresa L. Reeve, PhD
2 Peter
Associate Professor of New Testament Contexts
Andrews University

Ángel Manuel Rodríguez, ThD
Leviticus, Judges, Daniel
Hope and the Advent of God
Revelation and Inspiration of the Bible
Formation of the Biblical Canon
Biblical Interpretation
Interpreting Biblical Apocalyptic Prophecies
Former Director
Part-time Associate Director
Biblical Research Institute

Richard Sabuin, PhD
Ephesians
Director of Education
Northern Asia-Pacific Division of Seventh-
    day Adventists

Thomas R. Shepherd, PhD
Mark
Senior Research Professor of New Testament
Andrews University

Jerome L. Skinner, PhD
Ezekiel
Introduction to the Prophetic Books
Assistant Professor of Exegesis and Theology
Andrews University

Michael Sokupa, PhD, DTh
Titus
Associate Director
Ellen G. White Estate

Elias Brasil de Souza, PhD
Joel
Director
Biblical Research Institute

Ranko Stefanovic, PhD
2 Thessalonians, Revelation
Professor of New Testament
Andrews University

Zdravko Stefanovic, PhD
1 Samuel, 2 Samuel
Professor of Religion
AdventHealth University

David Tasker, PhD
1 Kings, 2 Kings
Senior Lecturer
Avondale University

Laurence A. Turner, PhD
Jonah
Professor Emeritus of Theological Studies
Newbold College of Higher Education

Efraín Velázquez, PhD
Haggai
Professor of Ancient Near Eastern
    Archaeology/Hebrew Bible and President
Inter-American Adventist Theological Seminary

Cedric Vine, PhD
1 Thessalonians
Associate Professor of New Testament
Andrews University

Clinton Wahlen, PhD
Luke
Associate Director
Biblical Research Institute

A. Rahel Wells, PhD
Esther
Associate Professor of Biblical Studies
Andrews University

Bertil Wiklander, ThD
Isaiah, Jeremiah
Former President, Trans-European Division
    of Seventh-day Adventists

PUBLICATION

Executive Publisher   Andrea **Luxton**, President, Andrews University, and Chair, Scholarly Publications and Andrews University Press Board

Project Director   Ronald A. **Knott**, Director, Andrews University Press

Managing Editor   L. S. **Baker Jr.**, Associate Director, Andrews University Press

Editorial Director   Deborah L. **Everhart**, Editor, Andrews University Press

Editorial Assistance
(Theology, Biblical Languages)   Timothy Arena

Editorial Assistance
(General)
Nathon Hilton
Yusuf Imam
Jasmine Logan
Kenneth Logan
Uriel Garcia Millan
Samuel Pagan
Keldie Paroschi
Dwaine Vaughn
Kevin Wiley

Copyediting and Proofreading
Rodelinde Abrecht
Charissa Boyd
Rose Decaen
Samantha Mero
Jonathan Stefanovic
Lois G. Stück
Debra West Smith

Interior Design   Diane Myers

Typesetting   Daniel Gordan

Cover Design   Types & Symbols

ESSAYS, TABLES, AND CHARTS

Hosea

Joel

Jonah

Habakkuk

Haggai

ABBREVIATIONS

General

ABC-NT	*Andrews Bible Commentary* (New Testament)
ABC-OT	*Andrews Bible Commentary* (Old Testament)
A.D.	*anno Domini,* in the year of the Lord
ANE	ancient Near East(ern)
approx.	approximately
Arab.	Arabic
Aram.	Aramaic
B.C.	before Christ
Bg.	the Heb. OT published by Daniel Bomberg (1524–1525)
ca.	*circa,* about, approximately
cf.	*confer,* compare
chap./chaps.	chapter/chapters
cm	centimeters
DH	Deuteronomic History
DSS	Dead Sea Scrolls
E	east
e.g.	*exempli gratia,* for example
esp.	especially
ESV	English Standard Version of the Bible
etc.	*et cetera,* and so forth
ff.	and following
ft.	foot/feet
g	gram/grams
gal.	gallon/gallons
Gr.	Greek
Heb.	Hebrew
i.e.	*id est,* that is
in.	inch/inches
kg	kilogram/kilograms
KJV	King James Version of the Bible
km	kilometer/kilometers

Kt.	*kethib*, the written Heb. OT preserved by the Masoretes (see Qr. below)
L	liter/liters
Lat.	Latin
lb.	pound/pounds
lit.	literally
LXX	Septuagint, an ancient translation of the OT into Greek
M	Majority Text
m	meter/meters
mi.	mile/miles
ms./mss.	manuscript/manuscripts
MT	Masoretic Text, the traditional Hebrew OT
N	north
NIV	New International Version of the Bible
NKJV	New King James Version of the Bible
NRSV	New Revised Standard Version of the Bible
NT	New Testament
NU	the Gr. NT published in the Nestle-Aland Greek New Testament, 27th ed. (N) and in the United Bible Societies' Greek New Testament, 4th ed. (U)
OT	Old Testament
oz.	ounce/ounces
pt.	pint
Qr.	*qere*, certain words read aloud that differ from the written words in the Masoretic Heb. OT (see Kt. above)
qt.	quart
S	south
SW	southwest
Syr.	Syriac
t	teaspoon
Tg.	Targum, an Aramaic paraphrase of the OT
tn.	ton/tons
v./vv.	verse/verses
Vg.	Vulgate, an ancient translation of the Bible into Latin (Jerome, trans. and ed.)
W	west
yd.	yard/yards

Books of the Bible

Gen.	1 Kin.	Eccl.	Obad.	Mark	Col.	2 Pet.
Ex.	2 Kin.	Song	Jon.	Luke	1 Thess.	1 John
Lev.	1 Chr.	Is.	Mic.	John	2 Thess.	2 John
Num.	2 Chr.	Jer.	Nah.	Acts	1 Tim.	3 John
Deut.	Ezra	Lam.	Hab.	Rom.	2 Tim.	Jude
Josh.	Neh.	Ezek.	Zeph.	1 Cor.	Titus	Rev.
Judg.	Esth.	Dan.	Hag.	2 Cor.	Philem.	
Ruth	Job	Hos.	Zech.	Gal.	Heb.	
1 Sam.	Ps./Pss.	Joel	Mal.	Eph.	James	
2 Sam.	Prov.	Amos	Matt.	Phil.	1 Pet.	

Books by Ellen G. White

AA	*The Acts of the Apostles*
CD	*Counsels on Diet and Foods*
CT	*Counsels to Parents, Teachers, and Students*
CTr	*Christ Triumphant*
DA	*The Desire of Ages*
EW	*Early Writings*
GC	*The Great Controversy*
MB	*Thoughts from the Mount of Blessing*
PK	*Prophets and Kings*
PP	*Patriarchs and Prophets*
SC	*Steps to Christ*
SL	*The Sanctified Life*
SP	*The Spirit of Prophecy* (4 vols.)
ST	*Signs of the Times*
1T	*Testimonies for the Church*, vol. 1
TM	*Testimonies to Ministers and Gospel Workers*

INTRODUCTION

The *Andrews Bible Commentary* is a concise exposition of Scripture written by Adventist scholars as a companion to the *Andrews Study Bible*. It is a valuable Bible study tool for lay readers, pastors, students, and teachers living in expectation of the Advent Hope. It is a confessional commentary only in the sense that the authors are Adventists, who carefully listened to the biblical text to unfold its significance and meaning for its readers, paying particular attention to the topic of biblical hope. The methodology used in the exposition of the biblical text is the historical-grammatical method. In preparing the comments on the biblical text, contributors to the *Andrews Bible Commentary* have made use of a wide range of literature, including other commentaries. This literature has helped to enrich and sharpen our understanding of the biblical text. While the format does not allow space to engage with the writings of other scholars, essential questions of current interest about the meaning of the text are addressed.

Special Features

There are a number of important features in this work that together make this a unique commentary on the Bible and that will hopefully facilitate its usefulness for general reading and comprehension.

Unique Emphasis. The key distinctive feature of the *Andrews Bible Commentary* is its emphasis on the biblical topic of hope. The first article unveils some of the main theological dimensions of biblical hope, and the commentaries identify its presence and significance in each biblical book from a theological and historical perspective. This overarching topic, as well as others, provides theological unity to the commentary.

Articles. A number of articles will prepare readers to use the commentary. There is a rich collection of articles at the front of the work that helps provide background material before readers engage with the biblical books themselves. Each block of biblical books (e.g., the Pentateuch, the historical books) is introduced by an article that provides a general overview of the content of the books that constitute that particular block. The articles help the readers see what holds those books together historically and theologically. Some of the articles provide a general discussion of some of the historical background for both the Old and New Testaments.

Essays. Short essays on topics of relevance to the textual commentary are placed close to the biblical passages to which the topics are relevant. In addition to dealing with what appear to be problematic passages, these essays also develop or clarify significant theological issues and analyze important doctrinal passages in conjunction with other biblical texts.

Introduction to Biblical Books. In the introduction to the commentary for each book, the reader will find background information that is useful and, in some cases, indispensable for a proper understanding of the book. These introductory materials deal with questions related to authorship, date of composition, the book's historical setting, some of its main theological themes, and some of the literary features that characterize the book.

Block Commentary. With a few exceptions, the commentary generally does not provide a detailed exegesis of each biblical passage. The exposition is organized according to the blocks of passages or sections that constitute a unity by themselves. The comments show how each section is related to the other, identify the flow of the message of the text, develop some of the main theological concepts running throughout the biblical book, and clarify the meaning of the block of material. There are also personal applications of the message of the text to the present life of the believer. Sometimes it is necessary to linger a little longer on a particular passage by discussing the meaning of biblical terms or grammatical issues that have an impact on the interpretation of the passage.

Use of Ellen G. White. The readers will find occasional quotes from the writings of Ellen White or references in parenthesis to some of her writings. Adventists believe that she received from the Lord the gift of prophecy, through which He led the development of the Seventh-day Adventist Church and its institutions. Her writings contain significant theological insights on biblical topics, and the authors were encouraged to use them when contextually pertinent. The commentary, however, is based on the meaning of the biblical text and not on her writings. She is not part of the biblical canon and her writings, as she herself indicated, are to be judged by the Scriptures.

How to Use the Commentary

The *Andrews Bible Commentary* should function as a guide in the personal study of the Bible. In other words, the main interest of the reader should be to gain a better understanding of the Bible. Consequently, the Bible should be the starting point of the study. If the reader is interested in studying a particular book, it would be well to prayerfully read the entire book before consulting the commentary. In this way, the mind of the reader will be imbued with the thoughts from the Bible, making it easier to follow and even evaluate the exposition of the text provided in the commentary. If a person is interested in reading the biblical text and the commentary together, it would be better to read first the particular section of the Bible and then the commentary on that block of material. Priority should always be given to the biblical text.

Since backgrounds are so important in the interpretation of the Bible, it is useful to read the articles and even the introduction to particular books in order to gain a broad perspective of the times when the biblical writers and their audiences lived. Such information will provide a better understanding of the biblical text by placing it within a particular historical moment in the divine-human interaction. The essays found throughout the commentary can also be helpful in supplementing personal study of the Bible. Readers interested in a particular biblical subject can find some of the essays useful as introductions to the topic. Reading a specific essay may also help them realize the need to delve deeper into the subject through a more detailed personal study of the Bible.

Since this commentary does not repeat the information found in the *Andrews Study Bible,* readers will find it valuable to deepen their knowledge by consulting it at the same time. The combination of these two tools will provide a wealth of information that will enrich and broaden the reader's understanding of the exposition of the biblical text.

Gratitude

A project like this would not have been possible without the involvement of many individuals. The idea of producing a one-volume Bible commentary written by Adventist scholars originated in conversations between John McVay, president of Walla Walla University in College Place, Washington, and Greg King, dean of the School of Religion at Southern Adventist University in Collegedale, Tennessee. When Niels-Erik Andreasen, then president of Andrews University, showed an interest in the project, they both considered Andrews University Press to be the ideal publisher. John and Greg initially became associate editors of the commentary, but their multiple responsibilities made it impossible for them to provide leadership to the project. We are grateful to them for their contribution. The writers of the commentary for the biblical books come from around the world, representing, in a sense, the worldwide nature of the Seventh-day Adventist Church. They wrote while carrying heavy teaching or administrative responsibilities, and the final result is the volume that you have in your hands. We are grateful to them for their sacrifice and enthusiasm and for their willingness to be part of this project.

We appreciate the strong support of the administrations of Andrews University and the General Conference of Seventh-day Adventists, both of which provided specific funding allocations to make this project possible. We also are particularly grateful to the board and staff of Andrews University Press for entrusting to us the privilege of serving as editors in the production of the commentary and for their patience as they had to wait a little longer than anticipated for the closure of the project. The involvement of the staff of Andrews University Press—Ronald Knott, L. S. Baker Jr., and Deborah Everhart—significantly enhanced the final form of the commentary by providing valuable evaluations of the manuscripts and suggesting important changes. It has been a pleasure for us to work with them.

Finally, we are grateful to the Lord, who gave us the Bible and who, through the work of the Spirit, guides us in its interpretation. What we offer to the readers is a beginning in their study of the Bible, and we pray that the Lord will assist them in gaining a deeper knowledge of the love of Christ for us as revealed in His Word.

Ángel Manuel Rodríguez, ThD
Daniel Kwame Bediako, PhD
Carl P. Cosaert, PhD
Gerald A. Klingbeil, DLitt

GENERAL ARTICLES

HOPE AND THE ADVENT OF GOD

Hope may not be the center of a biblical theology, but it certainly belongs to the inner circle of that theology. In this Bible commentary, we seek to highlight the presence of this concept throughout the biblical text and underscore its potential impact on the thinking and life of human beings. The almost hopeless condition of human existence, or at least the disorientation that characterizes it, makes this task indispensable. In what follows, we offer some of the main aspects of biblical hope. The biblical terminology for hope emphasizes the elements of expectation and trust and is grounded in the fact that human existence is rooted in time—past, present, and future. The presence of the concept of hope in the biblical text is not limited to the use of certain vocabulary, and it is found in varying contexts, including narratives, rituals, and exhortations. If hope is primarily living in expectation and in anticipation of the future and what it will bring, then we are by nature creatures of hope; hope is at the very core of being human. According to the Scriptures, true hope is found only in God and in His Son.

HOPE IN THE OLD TESTAMENT

As humans came from the hands of the Creator, they were placed within the flow of time—within the sixth day of the Creation week anticipating the coming of the seventh day (Gen. 1:27, 31; 2:1). They were created standing before the future, and therefore they existed in the expectation of what that future would be like. This expectation was free from apprehension and fear because its realization was in the loving hands of the Creator. Elements of that future were made clear to Adam and Eve. So, for instance, they would rule the natural world and multiply themselves, filling the earth with their descendants (Gen. 1:26, 28). This future was masterminded by the Lord and offered to them as a gift. They simply were to look forward in expectation to its realization. They accepted it as part of their self-realization.

But the future could also present them with an element of danger, a threat to their harmonious experience and inner peace. Evil found its way into the Garden through a corrupting power represented by the serpent (Gen. 3:1; Is. 14:12–15; Ezek. 28:13–16; Rev. 12:7–9). Adam and Eve were offered an alternate future, and surprisingly, they accepted it. They were offered a future existence free from the alleged restraints imposed on them by God, in which it would be possible for them to obtain a new mode of existence—becoming like God (Gen. 3:1–3). This was an exhilarating expectation, something they had never before thought about. The "promise" of the serpent instilled in them a new hope. But it was a false hope—the "hope" of a hopeless future. Consequently, fear of the future crept into the human heart, and since then it has remained there, defining human existence to a large extent.

When humans found themselves in fear and without a future, and therefore without hope, God intervened and out of grace offered them a new future and a renewed hope. This new hope was grounded on the divine promise of the *coming/advent* of the Seed of the woman, who would permanently overcome the evil power represented by the deceptive serpent (Gen. 3:15; Gal. 3:16). Since then, hope has been grounded on God's promises to the human race and their expected fulfillment within history in a context of conflict. Hope, then, presupposes a need that should be supplied. The patriarchal narratives reaffirm the universal hope of restoration and blessing by extending it to all the nations of the earth through the descendants of Abraham (Gen. 12:1–3). Biblical hope is by nature universal (cf. Is. 42:4; 51:9).

HOPE AND CONFLICT

The moral and spiritual corruption of the human race is the basis for both divine judgment and the offer of hope. The judgment of a universal flood was announced together with a hope of salvation (Gen. 6:11–14). But the hope of survival was available only inside Noah's ark to those who would trust in the Lord. Hope was realized in the midst of judgment in the survival of a faithful remnant awaiting the fulfillment of God's promises. This pattern of spiritual decay, divine judgment, and trust in a hopeful promise of salvation is found throughout the OT. It reached its pinnacle in the preexilic rebellion of the people of God against the covenant Lord through idolatry and social injustices. The moment finally came when divine judgment was inevitable—Israel and later Judah would go into exile (e.g., Jer. 4:5–9; 6:1–5; Amos 9:1–6). Although this divine pronouncement was the end of hope for His people (Ezek. 37:11), the Lord graciously announced yet another new future (Jer. 29:11), a hope of salvation for a faithful remnant (e.g., Is. 10:20–23; Jer. 31:17; Amos 9:8, 13–15). The attempts of the enemy of God to destroy His people were frustrated by the divine preservation of a remnant through whom the Lord was to fulfill His saving will.

Even when the nations, moved by their own expansionistic desires, threatened God's people with extinction or oppression, it was hope based on faith in the Lord that sustained His servants (e.g., 2 Kin. 18:17—19:37). Under those and similar circumstances, hope and faith were severely tested, but the divine call was to trust in God. The conflict within which hope was usually present required the individual to pray for and anticipate deliverance (Pss. 33:18–19; 130:7–8), healing (Is. 40:31), and salvation (e.g., Pss. 14:7; 39:7–8; Is. 51:5), to trust in the Lord when facing trials (Pss. 27:14; 34:18–22; 130:5), and to rely on His loving-kindness in the midst of hopelessness (Ps. 147:11). In the final analysis God, and no one else, was the hope of His people (Pss. 39:7; 71:5). It is in the context of the suffering of the innocent that the strength of hope surfaces in the midst of struggle and it is finally victorious (Ps. 25:19–21). Job's suffering was so intense that he could foresee only death—the end of hope (Job 7:6–10). But even in that almost hopeless situation, he was able to affirm his *yahel* ("trust" or "hope") in God despite being "slain" by Him (Job 13:15; cf. Is. 8:17). This is a hope that is firmly grounded on the reliability of God (cf. Ps. 33:20–22; Jer. 14:22).

This hope is also related to the future of the nation. The OT looks forward to the Day of the Lord, a time when the nations will gather to fight against Israel but the Lord will permanently defeat them, bringing deliverance and salvation to His people (e.g., Joel 3:1–2, 12). This hope nurtured the life of God's people in the OT and enabled them to look forward to the future in full confidence. They knew that the future was in the hands of the Lord and that their hope would be actualized in the advent of the Lord (Is. 25:9).

HOPE AND GOD'S SANCTUARY/TEMPLE

Hope in a divine intervention that would bring salvation to God's people was expressed through the Israelite sacrificial and priestly systems. God instituted the sanctuary services in order to deal with the spiritual needs and challenges of His people. The sacrificial system was a means by which God's people worshiped Him, expressed gratitude to Him, sought His presence (Pss. 27:6; 107:22; 116:17), and asked for forgiveness of sin, hoping in faith that it would be granted to them (Ps. 65:3–5; cf. Lev. 4:20, 26, 31). The sanctuary/temple was a place where the sinner could find hope because the hope of Israel dwelt there (cf. Jer. 14:8; 17:13). The hope of the people was manifested through the vows they made to the Lord in anticipation of the fulfillment of a divine promise (Pss. 66:13–14; 116:17–19). The fulfillment of God's promises strengthened the faith and hope of the people because it revealed that God is trustworthy. By dwelling among them in the sanctuary/temple, He was near to them to bless and sustain them and to provide for them a means of atonement (Ps. 24:3–5; cf. Lev. 4:13–21).

Human sin, like that of Adam and Eve, could separate the Israelites from God, leaving them in a state of hopelessness. The relationship, broken or altered by sin, was restored through the sacrificial victims that died in place of the repentant sinners, bearing their sin (Lev. 17:11). The daily ministry of the priest in the Holy Place assured the people that atoning blood was available for the forgiveness of their sins. The annual Day of Atonement ministry of the high priest pointed to a future time when God, through His work of judgment, would cleanse the world from sin and impurity, thus restoring it to its original condition (Lev. 16:29–33; Dan. 8:13–14; Zech. 3:1–9). Thus God illustrated for them what He would do through the coming Savior who would die for them, bearing their sins and being their High Priest and the Mediator of reconciliation and judgment (Is. 52:13—53:12).

HOPE AND THE WORK OF THE PROPHETS

The prophets' messages of judgment and salvation pointed to a proclamation of a new future that was to be apprehended by the people as a reliable word of hope coming from the Lord. The promise of the Son, through whom the divine promise of salvation was to be realized, was reaffirmed (Is. 7:14; 11:1–5). The prophets announced a new future shaped by a new covenant (Jer. 31:31–34) that would bring with it a new heaven and a new earth (Is. 65:17; 66:22), the transformation of nature (e.g., Is. 11:6–9; 65:25) and social life, and the final victory over God's enemies, including death itself (e.g., Is. 25:7–8; 26:19; Dan. 12:2).

The realization of this hope would be possible through the coming/advent of the Lord in power and glory (Is. 35). This hope reminded God's people that the present configuration of what they saw and experienced was not final. Something greater and better was coming, and it was theirs in their present existence in the form of a divine promise.

HOPE AND THE MESSIAH

The institution of kingship was requested by the Israelites as a result of their concern about the future (1 Sam. 8:3–5). In the absence of a strong hope in the Lord, humans usually attempt to take their future into their own hands. But the Lord took this institution and adjusted and incorporated it into His plan for the human race. Most of the kings of the OT decided to create their own view of the future by setting aside the divine plan for them, the hope that God had offered His people. The result was the collapse of the nation and the Babylonian Exile. But the divine ideal of kingship, according to which the king was God's servant, was embodied in the person of David, who became a symbol or a type of the future Messiah ("Anointed One"; e.g., Ezek. 34:23). He would be a descendant of Abraham through the tribe of Judah (Gen. 49:8–11; cf. Gen. 17:16; Num. 24:17), God's Son in a unique way (Ps. 2:6–8; cf. Is. 7:14), His Anointed One (Ps. 2:2; cf. Dan. 9:25–26), who would sit on the throne of David (Is. 9:6–7). Micah indicated that from Bethlehem would come the Ruler of Israel (Mic. 5:2). He would be the victorious King who would reign forever over God's people and to whom the nations of the earth would be subjected (Dan. 7:13–14). He would bring war to an end (Is. 2:4; Zech. 9:10). But this most majestic King would also be a priest who would solve the serious problem of sin. He would do this by giving His life for His people, thus effecting full and final atonement. By dying in their place, He would save them from sin and from their estrangement from God (Is. 52:13—53:12; cf. 61:1). He would be installed not only as King but also as Mediator in the eschatological sanctuary (Dan. 9:24; cf. Ex. 30:26–29).

The OT closes filled with hope. In our mind's eye, we can perhaps see God's people looking up, reaching up, straining every nerve in eager anticipation of the glorious realization of their hope in the coming messianic King.

HOPE IN THE NEW TESTAMENT

In the NT, the messianic expectations of the OT find their fulfillment: the arrival of the Seed of the woman (Matt. 1:22–23; Gal. 4:4; Rev. 12:5). Jesus was the promised messianic King (John 20:31), the sacrificial victim who died in place of sinners (2 Cor. 5:21), the High Priest prefigured in the sanctuary services now ministering for us in the heavenly sanctuary (Heb. 8:1–6), and the ultimate Prophet of hope (e.g., John 14:1–4; Acts 3:19–23; cf. Deut. 18:15–19). The life, ministry, death, resurrection, and mediation of Jesus infuse human existence with unprecedented meaning and hope. The community of faith that He created was grounded on the saving message and efficacy of the cross while anticipating with great expectation the consummation of salvation at the Second Coming of the Lord. Existence in the present was understood by the church to be characterized by a longing or yearning for the real physical presence of the Lord at His advent in glory. This sense of expectation determined everything they did, and it had a direct impact on their daily lives.

PROMISE AND HOPE

As in the OT, hope now found its point of departure in the trustworthiness and reliability of God (Heb. 10:23). The fact that the salvific promises of God, recorded in the OT, have become a reality in Christ demonstrated in a unique way that God was able to deliver what He promised (Acts 26:6; 28:20). The permanent interlocking of promise and hope is determined by their common divine origin and contributes to enrich the content of each other. They both reach us through Scripture. Theologically speaking, we can suggest that before hope actualizes itself in human history, it exists in the form of a divine promise. The Scripture, as the bearer of God's promises, becomes our source of hope in the shape of a promise and links hope to our faith and confidence in God (Rom. 15:4; Gal. 5:5).

If hope grounds itself in the reliability of God's promises, then Christian hope is the most reliable hope humans can find because God, in an unparalleled way, demonstrated through the ministry, death, and resurrection of Jesus that He fulfilled His most audacious promise to us: salvation through the sacrificial death of His Son. The NT establishes a firm connection between the saving death of Jesus and the hope of His Second Coming (Titus 2:13–14). That connection provides a historical and theological foundation for Christian hope that flows from the reliability of the promises of God and the trustworthiness of His character (cf. Heb. 6:17–19). Such a hope is a gift of divine grace to those who desperately need it (2 Thess. 2:16). The absence of this hope in the human heart leaves human existence in a state of hopelessness (Eph. 2:12).

THE CERTAINTY OF HOPE

The expectation of the return of the Lord in glory, and everything that it entails, was never conceived by Christians as wishful thinking devoid of certainty or as an illusion. The Christian hope is a "living hope" in the sense that it is related to the resurrection of Jesus (1 Pet. 1:3). The linkage of hope with Jesus is so strong that hope is identified with Him. He is "our hope" (1 Tim. 1:1). The God of hope in the OT is now Jesus the Christ (the Anointed One). The implications of this aspect of hope are extremely significant and theologically rich. Hope is not something that at the present time exists only in the human mind as a dream and as an expectation. The Christian hope is a reality outside us that in the near future will irrupt with power into our time and space, radically changing the present human condition and its habitat. For now, it is in heaven (Col. 1:5), but it is there as an objective reality.

What we are saying is that what we expect, what we eagerly wait for, is already a reality in Jesus Christ. In other words, the NT provides for us a Christological understanding of hope. Our hope is embodied in the person of Christ. Perhaps a few examples will illustrate the idea.

- The Christian hope looks forward to the resurrection of the dead at the Second Coming (Acts 24:15), but the resurrection already took place in one human being, the Son of God (Acts 2:32). He came out of the tomb alive and in the process defeated the power of death. The resurrection of Jesus anticipated and assures our future resurrection (1 Thess. 4:14, 16).
- Jesus ascended to heaven, to the heavenly sanctuary, as our precursor, and we look forward to the moment when we will also ascend to heaven (Acts 1:9–11; 1 Thess. 4:17; Heb. 6:20).
- Jesus was born in union with God and never broke that union, and we look forward to the moment when our union with God will be fully manifested in the presence of our Savior (John 17:22).
- We hope for our glorification at the return of our Lord (Rom. 5:2), totally assured that it will happen because God resurrected Jesus and glorified Him (Rom. 8:17; 1 Pet. 1:21). He is now our "hope of glory" (Col. 1:27).
- Christ was installed as King of the universe, and He has promised that we will reign with Him in glory (Rev. 3:21).
- The content of the apostolic hope includes eternal life (Titus 1:2; 3:7). Although at the present time we have it by faith, the fullness of that life is hidden with Christ in God, and when Christ our Life appears, we will appear with Him in glory (Col. 3:3–4).
- We look forward to a new creation, but Jesus already introduced this new creation to those who are in Him. In the future the new creation will be revealed in power and glory (2 Cor. 5:17; 1 Pet. 1:3; 2 Pet. 3:13; Rev. 21:1).

The content of our hope is an objective reality in Christ and in the work that He has done and is still doing for us. He is, in a very real and concrete way, our only hope (1 Tim. 1:1) and our living hope (1 Pet. 1:3). Biblical hope does not belong to the field of human dreams or wishes but is firmly grounded in the work and person of the Son of God. The cross of Christ created a new future for the human race that is ours through His work of mediation before the Father in the heavenly temple.

HOPE AND THE CHRISTIAN LIFE

Hope is by nature oriented toward the future as the place from which God will unveil it to us within our history. But this hope makes a difference in the present conditions of human existence. Biblical hope does not detach itself from the realities of the present; it boldly addresses them. It does this at a personal and collective level and in the social interaction of believers with the world at large. This idea is communicated in the NT by associating the concept of hope with other important aspects of the Christian life.

Hope, Faith, and Love

In 1 Corinthians 13:13 Paul refers to the endurance of faith, hope, and love—and love is the greatest of these. Hope is not incompatible with love and faith but coexists with both of them in the Christian life (1 Thess. 1:3). It may be right to say that the three are inseparable because, on the one hand, hope orients faith toward the future and challenges it to perse-vere, and on the other hand, love challenges hope to action in the present. Hope does not allow love to become so obsessed with its immediate object as to forget the consummation of salvation. But love takes the future eschatological existence, characterized by freedom from selfishness and suffering, and makes its presence felt in the here and now in selfless care for others (Heb. 6:10–11). The model for this type of life is Jesus Himself, who con-stantly proclaimed the coming of the kingdom of God as an eschatological expectation while at the same time caring for the poor and needy (e.g., Matt. 4:23). Elements of the eschatological expectation were made present in His ministry in order to illustrate the quality of life in God's kingdom. Like faith and hope, agape-love—a totally unselfish com-mitment to the service of God and others—is not natural to humans. It was poured into the human heart through the Spirit, and this assures us that our hope will not disappoint us; it will be fulfilled (Rom. 5:5).

Hope and Spiritual Growth

The expectation of the soon return of Christ conjoins hope and holiness in an unbroken bond of unity. Thus it is indicated that hope should be constantly influencing the life of believers (1 John 3:3). Hope is so deeply woven into the core of the life of believers that it sanctifies them while they are eagerly waiting for its realization. John defines this hope as the expectation of being like Jesus and seeing Him at the advent (1 John 3:2). The implica-tion is that in order to see the Pure One, we should also be pure (Matt. 5:8). Hope impacts the present and begins, through the Spirit, to transform us into the likeness of the Son of God. We are becoming now what we will become at the end, when we will be changed (1 Cor. 15:52) and when we will see Him (1 John 3:2). Therefore the connection between hope and holiness is not only about our spiritual life but also about the ethical significance of the Christian hope (1 Thess. 5:5–8). Peter, in his discussion of the Second Coming of the Lord, refers to the importance of living holy and godly lives as we look forward to the Day of the Lord (2 Pet. 3:11). The ethical and moral lives of those who have placed their hope in Jesus reflect that of their Master. They humbly submit themselves to God's will as revealed in His law and particularly in His Son.

Hope and Perseverance

Hope also impacts the quality of our inner life, our character, by giving us consistency of action and courage to endure. Hope exists in the context of conflict and can be challenged by a hostile environment, but it is precisely in that setting that hope inspires endurance (1 Thess. 1:3). What we eagerly wait for—the return of Jesus in glory—is such a wonderful event that it moves us to be patient and to endure. The Greek word *hupomonē* ("endurance, perseverance") expresses the idea of remaining faithful to the Lord, holding on to hope by resisting oppression, affliction, and temptation while waiting for His intervention (Rom. 5:3; 2 Thess. 1:4; Rev. 14:12). The strength of hope is such that it could make us immovable in our commitment to the Lord and to the hope that He has set before us (Col. 1:23). The inner strength that hope provides for believers testifies about its reality and its significance in their present pilgrimage.

Hope and Joy

If hopelessness brings with it fear and anguish, the Christian hope fills the life of believers with joy. Paul exhorts believers to exult in the hope of the glory of God (Rom. 5:2) and to live joyfully in hope (Rom. 12:12). There is an inexpressible *something* about the Christian hope such that when believers meditate on this hope and anticipate its fulfillment, they are filled with joy. Hope brings elements of the future into the present, and we begin to experience now the joy that will be ours when we see our Lord coming in glory. Joy in the Bible is what defines the nature of eternal life in the presence of God, and that will permanently replace suffering, sorrow, and the oppression of death (Jude 24; Rev. 19:7; 21:3–40; cf. Is. 35; Jer. 31:13). Hope looks forward to that moment and gives us a foretaste of it in the present.

Hope and Mission

The richness and beauty of the Christian hope cannot be selfishly embraced as the exclusive possession of a few. Hope is universal because the human need for it is also universal. Humans are by nature without hope in a world of sin and death (Eph. 2:12), but God in His grace wants everyone to enjoy fullness of hope. Those who have received by grace and through the work of the Spirit the hope of the consummation of eternal salvation at the advent are impelled by that hope to proclaim it to the world. They have been chosen by God to reveal the glorious riches of the mystery among the Gentiles (nations): "Christ in you, the hope of glory" (Col. 1:27). The Christian hope instills in the heart the urgency of sharing it with those who are drifting in an ocean of hopelessness. Believers are called to be constantly prepared to give a defense of the hope within us to anyone who asks (1 Pet. 3:15). But this is to be done with kindness and respect in order for hope to be winsome.

CONCLUSION

The eschatological expectation of the return of Christ in glory, promised in the OT through the prophecies of the advent of God to establish His universal kingdom, continues to enrich the lives of millions around the world who are constantly anticipating this most glorious event. This hope has radically altered their lives, filling it with meaning and transforming them into messengers of hope. For them, the constant human search for a hope that could bring healing to the human heart filled with fear and anxiety has ended. They are pilgrims of hope in whom the richness of this hope has been embodied in acts of love and kindness modeled after the One who is in fact their hope, Jesus Christ.

They eagerly wait for the moment when they will see God. The full realization of that hope begins at the moment of the advent of Christ. They anticipate the moment when the Day of the Lord, announced by the prophets of the OT, will irrupt into our time and space with unparalleled majesty and glory. Then they will see their Savior and Lord dressed in the majesty of His divinity (Matt. 16:27; 24:30). The event will be of a global nature, filling every segment of our space with the glory of the presence of the Son of God (Rev. 1:7). He will come in judgment against the forces of evil that denied the value of the hope, and they will be forced to witness its realization (Rev. 6:15–17). But He also will come to consummate the redemption He accomplished on the cross of Calvary (Heb. 9:28). He will descend accompanied by the angelic host and by the powerful sound of the trumpet, calling to life those who went into the darkness of the tomb firmly holding on to the blessed hope (1 Thess. 4:14–17). His people will be transformed by the power of His presence and will be permanently removed from the sphere of death and suffering (1 Cor. 15:51–55; Rev. 21:4–5). The universal gathering will occur, and they will be reunited with the risen Lord to be with Him and their loved ones through eternal ages (Matt. 24:30–31; John 14:1–3; 1 Thess. 4:17). We can only continue to anticipate with great expectation and joy what such a life will be like.

REVELATION
AND INSPIRATION OF THE BIBLE

God communicates with His created beings through speech. Immediately after He is first introduced to us in the Scriptures, we hear His voice freely expressing Himself through the spoken word. God's speech or word reveals His inner thoughts, plans, attitudes, feelings, and emotions. God created humans in His own image and endowed them with the ability to speak and therefore to engage Him in dialogue using their own language skills. Speech is the primary means of communication among humans and contributes to the actualization of their social nature. The God who speaks is a social being, the Creator, who wants to be known.

The doctrine of revelation and inspiration is an exposition of the way God has made Himself known to His creatures. With respect to the Scriptures, *revelation* has been traditionally understood as the process by which God, through the Holy Spirit, reaches the minds of some individuals, called prophets, and mysteriously shares with them a specific message. *Inspiration* is usually understood as the work of the prophet in sharing with others that revelation through the spoken or written word.

GENERAL AND SPECIAL REVELATION

Theologians distinguish between a special revelation, preserved in the Holy Scriptures, and a general revelation of God outside the Bible, accessible to all but limited in scope. The distinction is important in that it shows that God wants to be known and is constantly doing what He can to achieve His purpose. He does not want to be the unknown God.

General Revelation

General revelation assumes that God uses other avenues in addition to the spoken word to reveal Himself. He reaches out to humans wherever they happen to be, in and through different means, but particularly through His actions. Probably the most impressive activity of God, apart from the act of redemption, is His work of creation. Only the most powerful, intelligent, and wise God could have brought into existence the majestic cosmos that we are barely beginning to understand. His creation is a vehicle through which He reveals to human beings His glory (Ps. 19:1), His wisdom (Prov. 3:19), and His eternal power and divine attributes (Rom. 1:20). This divine revelation is accessible to all who are willing to listen to its testimony. But due to its present damaged condition, creation cannot display the full expression of the loving character of God and His identity.

God also reveals Himself to humans through their intuitive awareness of the divine. This awareness is sometimes suppressed by the fall of humans from the divine ideal (Gen. 3), but it remains there reminding us that our very life is a witness to the existence of a divine being. Belief in God or some supernatural being is a universal phenomenon. We are by nature religious beings seeking to satisfy our need for God in different ways, and this need is evident even in the denial of Him. We still have a vague sense of what is good, even if we ultimately embrace what is wrong. The inner voice of our very nature tells us about God in spite of humanity's attempts to silence it through philosophical arguments and so-called scientific facts. This revelation of God is also general in that it does not reveal the full nature and works of God.

History could also be considered a means of divine, general revelation in the sense that humans may be able to detect in it God's activity on their behalf. Divine providence is perceptible to humans as they analyze their experiences in life. It is God who provides rain to both the righteous and unrighteous (Matt. 5:45), and He provides life, breath, and providential interaction for the purpose of drawing people to seek Him in return (Acts 17:25–27). God continues to be active in human affairs, and we continue to benefit from His work within history and experience.

General revelation is limited in its content, and because of the damaging presence of evil in the world, it may be misunderstood or even totally ignored. By itself it does not have salvific power. Consequently, the Lord provided for His people a special revelation through which He revealed His character and His purposes to the human race.

Special Revelation

God's special revelation was given to humans through prophets and apostles but reached its ultimate expression in the incarnation of the Son of God. It has been preserved for the human race in the Holy Scriptures. God revealed Himself to prophets and apostles in various ways (Heb. 1:1). At times He spoke to them in dreams, as was the case of Solomon while in Gibeon (1 Kin. 3:5), and also through visions while the prophets were awake, causing them to see what no one else could see (Gen. 15:1; Dan. 8:1; cf. Num. 12:6). In some cases God appeared to His prophets and spoke to them (theophanies; Gen. 17:1; Ex. 3:2–4). Quite often He simply spoke to them and they heard His voice or the voice of His messenger (auditions; e.g., Gen. 22:1). Through these means God shared with the prophets certain information that was meaningful to them and to their audiences. Revelation is not only an encounter with God but also an encounter in which God provides information in the form of promises and judgments that reveal Himself and His plan for the salvation of humanity. The information was to be shared with God's people through oral messages delivered in private or public settings.

The most important revelation of God was made available to humans when God became a human being and lived among us (John 1:14). Christ became the new expression of God's word in a unique modality—in human form. God's self-revelation to the prophets was limited to what the prophets could receive from Him. In God's Son we have God Himself speaking to us. The Son did not bring to us a revelation from God; He was God's most sublime revelation of Himself. In the final analysis, only God is able to tell us who He is, and He did it through the incarnated Word. In Him we come to understand the past, the present, and the future of humanity. In Him we see a loving God who created and then redeemed us at a very high cost to Himself—a sacrificial death. It is through the love revealed to us through the death of the Son that the sin problem, the cosmic conflict itself, will find ultimate and final closure.

The revelation of God to the prophets pointed forward to Christ, and the revelation to the apostles pointed back to Him. The body of that revelation has been preserved for us in written form, the Holy Scriptures. It is the most reliable revelation of God that we have, and consequently, it is good for us to listen to it. Through the power of the Holy Spirit, the written word is still alive, and through it God continues to speak to us with power and conviction in order to make Himself known to us and to invite us to choose Him in the context of a cosmic conflict.

SELF-TESTIMONY OF THE BIBLE

The Bible itself speaks about its origin and nature, and we should seek to understand this information as much as possible. Two of the most important passages that discuss the nature of biblical inspiration are 2 Timothy 3:16–17 and 2 Peter 1:19–21. We should examine these two passages and others as we proceed to understand the biblical teaching about revelation and inspiration.

Revelation and Inspiration: Definitions

It may surprise some to realize that, strictly speaking, the Bible does not separate revelation and inspiration—the reception of the message (revelation) and the moment the prophet embodies it in language to deliver it in oral form or to preserve it in written form (inspiration). The act of revelation includes within itself the activity of the human mind in the embodiment of it in words. Peter states that prophecy—a term he uses to emphasize that the Scriptures were written by prophets—comes from God and continues to be under the guidance of God when the prophets share it with others (2 Pet. 1). This does not mean that we should use only one word (i.e., either "revelation" or "inspiration") when dealing with the topic. It is indeed good to distinguish between revelation and inspiration to facilitate the analysis and discussion of the theme, but we should always be aware of the fact that they are in reality inseparable. Perhaps it would be better to speak about the divine process of revelation-inspiration.

Origin: God

The Scriptures clearly identify God as the originator of the content of biblical revelation. Peter makes it clear that the Scriptures are not the results of human will; that is to say, they do not originate as an impulse or even an intuition of the human mind, but they come from God (2 Pet. 1:21). Paul establishes this point as well in 2 Timothy 3:16. The significant term used here is the Greek *theopneustos* ("God-breathed," from *theos* ["God"] and *pneo* ["to breathe"]). What does "God-breathed" mean? No one knows what it specifically designates, but we can comment on its metaphorical meaning, which in fact sheds very little light on the revelation-inspiration process. The term reminds us of the activity of God during the creation of humans and the cosmos. It was through the breath of God that Adam became a living being (Gen. 2:7) and all the hosts of heaven were formed (Ps. 33:6). Metaphorically speaking, Paul seems to be using the term "God-breathed" to articulate the conviction that the Scriptures are the result of God's creative power. The creative power God employed when creating the world is the same power He used in the creation of the Scriptures. This is a unique way of stating that the Scriptures originated or came into being through divine activity. God is their ultimate author.

The conviction that the Bible is the "word of God" is found throughout its pages. The prophets testified that the word of the Lord came to them (e.g., Jer. 1:11–13; Joel 1:1; Mic. 1:1), and at times they introduced or concluded their messages by stating that the Lord had spoken (Is. 7:7; Amos 1:3; Hag. 1:7). We also find them calling people to hear the word of the Lord (e.g., Ezek. 6:3; Amos 3:1). The prophets understood that the very source of what they were communicating to the people and their leaders was God, and it was not the result of their religious, social, or political preferences. The Lord Himself stated that He would punish anyone who would not listen to (i.e., obey) His words that would be spoken in His name by the Prophet (i.e., Christ) who was like Moses (Deut. 18:18–19; Acts 3:22; Heb. 3:2). The word comes from the Lord and is authoritative, and the prophet communicates it to others on behalf of the Lord.

We find in the NT the same emphasis on the divine origin of the revelation that the apostles communicated to others. The "word" is now the teachings of Jesus (Mark 4:33; John 5:24; 8:31) and the person of Jesus, who is "the Word of God" (Rev. 19:13). The word of Jesus is as authoritative as the OT (John 2:22). He told the Jewish leaders that they could not listen to Him or understand Him because He was from God and they were not (John 8:43, 47). The word of Jesus is then summarized in the message of the gospel of salvation (Acts 15:7) that Jesus brought to the human race and that was to be proclaimed by the church (Acts 10:36–43). His teachings and His own person are the revelation of God to humanity. Paul, who was not at first one of the disciples of Jesus, received the gospel through a revelation from God (Gal. 1:12–13). In fact, it would be proper to say that all of the apostles received the gospel as a revelation coming from the incarnated God, Jesus Christ.

Extent of the Inspired Scriptures

Paul states that all Scripture is God-breathed and inspired (2 Tim. 3:16). Most probably the primary reference of the phrase "all Scripture" is to the totality of the Scriptures that form the OT (cf. 1 Tim. 5:18). All of it originated from God and was given to the prophets under divine inspiration. Paul's statement means that in the content of the Bible, there is no gradation or hierarchy of inspiration, with some documents being less inspired than others;

they are all inspired by God. It also demonstrates that any attempt to search the Scriptures in order to identify what is inspired and what is not is to search in vain. In that sense, the biblical understanding of inspiration is plenary—it applies to everything in the Bible. Humans are not to identify what is inspired in the Bible because the Lord explicitly stated that all of it is inspired.

The claim that "all Scripture" is inspired by God also applies to the writings of the apostles preserved in the NT. What they taught was what the Lord had commanded them to teach (1 Cor. 14:37). As apostles, their exposition of the gospel was an inspired oral or written expression of it, and consequently, it was authoritative (cf. 2 Thess. 2:15). The Spirit of the Lord was operative in their experience as they wrote the Gospels and the letters of the NT, and as apostles they were aware of this phenomenon. Paul wrote to the Thessalonians that they had accepted and believed the message that they had heard from the apostles not as a merely human word but as the word of God (1 Thess. 2:13; cf. 1 Cor. 2:12–13; 14:37). Like the prophets of the OT, they proclaimed to the people the word of God. We also find the explicit statement that the apostles proclaimed the gospel "by the Holy Spirit" (1 Pet. 1:12). Peter himself considered the writings of Paul to belong to the inspired Scriptures (2 Pet. 3:16). This should not surprise us for, as we saw, the apostles received their message from the Lord though divine revelation. This idea is clearly expressed by John when he writes that he received the content of the book of Revelation through a revelation from God through Jesus Christ (Rev. 1:1–2).

The Human Element

The process of revelation-inspiration includes the involvement of humans chosen by God, as Peter indicates (2 Pet. 1:21). The prophets and prophetesses received the messages from the Lord and then, still under the guidance of the Spirit, communicated to others the content of the revelation in a trustworthy way. The implication is that in the production of the Scriptures we find the human and the divine working together. However, the content of Scripture did not originate with humans. They were the spokespersons of God, and as such they embodied the content of the revelation in their language and expressions. God guided them in using their literary skills and linguistic expertise as they were wording the revelation received. Thus, they spoke in their own language as God's representatives and were not simply His public address system. God did not override their individuality through mystical experience.

The presence of the human element in the revelation-inspiration process is demonstrable in several ways. In the OT, the prophets wrote in Hebrew or in Aramaic because these were the languages they and their audiences knew. Some of them were excellent storytellers, and the Lord used their skills to preserve His message in the form of biblical historical narratives. He also gave messages to prophets and used them to write down the revelation in poetic form or as proverbs and other types of sayings. There were prophets skilled in the composition of psalms, and God used them to write the psalms now preserved in the Holy Scriptures. The writing style of the prophets is identifiable through the study of their books.

In the NT, the Lord used the Greek language to preserve in written form the messages He gave to the apostles, and their writings show their knowledge of Greek grammar, syntax, and vocabulary. The presence of four Gospels in the NT, each one written from a particular point of view and style, shows the human element in the revelation and inspiration process. One Gospel could not contain the fullness of the revelation brought to us by Jesus. Many of the epistles of the NT reveal the excellent rhetorical skills of the apostles, while others are less elegant and complex. One of the obvious conclusions that we can derive from this discussion is that God did not dictate to the prophets and the apostles the content of Scripture, except when He instructed them to quote Him directly. We will return to this topic later.

REVELATION-INSPIRATION AND THE EXPERIENCE OF THE PROPHET

The revelation-inspiration process is fundamentally a mystery not totally revealed to us, but there are some aspects of it that we can and should seek to understand based on the study of the Bible. As we approach the Scriptures we find different ways in which God communicated with the prophets and apostles.

Modes of Divine Revelation-Inspiration

The first way, which we have already mentioned, is a direct communication from God through dreams, visions, auditions, and theophanies. In most of these cases God directly accessed the minds of the prophets and shared with them some specific information. In such cases, the supernatural element of the revelation-inspiration process is at the forefront of the experience of the prophet. Among believers this is the most common understanding of the way God communicated with the prophets during the revelation-inspiration process. The experience of the prophets was a deeply emotional one throughout the whole process. Even at the moment of the call, it was common for them to feel unworthy of the call (Jer. 1:4–10) or even threatened by the majesty of God (Is. 6:5). At times the revelation from God overwhelmed them (e.g., Ezek. 3:15) and emotions came to expression in bodily reactions: John fell as though dead (Rev. 1:17) and wept (Rev. 5:4); Daniel was terrified and fell prostrate on his face (Dan. 8:17). There were also strong emotional experiences when delivering the message to the person or to the people. The indifference of the people to the message was painful to the prophets, who knew very well what the future would bring to the people (e.g., Jer. 4:19; Hab. 3:16). In a sense, part of the call of the prophet was an invitation to feel emotions analogous to those that God experiences as He views the experience and the reaction of humans to His message of judgment and salvation.

The second way God revealed His message to the prophets and apostles was through research. He impressed in their minds the need to collect historical information and to organize it in certain ways in order for Him to communicate a specific message to His people. Because this information was available to them, the Lord guided them in finding and using it. The best example of this phenomenon is found in Luke 1:1–4, where Luke describes in detail the reason why he wrote his Gospel. There are several important details in these verses that deserve brief attention. First, others before Luke wrote on the ministry and teachings of Jesus. This means that from very early in the apostolic church there was a serious interest in preserving the teachings and narrative of the life of Jesus for future generations. Second, Luke mentions that there were eyewitnesses who preserved in some form (orally or in written form) aspects of the story of Jesus. Third, Luke seems to have benefitted in his writing from what others had written and from the testimony and teachings of eyewitnesses.

Luke did his research to the best of his abilities under the guidance of the Spirit. We can without any hesitation apply to the experience of Luke what Peter said about prophets: Luke was a holy man of God who spoke/wrote as he was led by the Holy Spirit (2 Pet. 1:21). The revelation-inspiration process is from beginning to end the result of the activity of the Spirit as He works through the person of the prophets. In the case of Luke we have evidence from the NT that he carefully copied down the words of Jesus, preserving them for future generations in his own Gospel. This can be seen not only in the way he appears to have carefully incorporated material from Mark's and Matthew's earlier Gospels into his own, but also in his use of other sayings of Jesus in circulation at the time (e.g., 1 Cor. 11:24–25). Paul recounts one of these early sayings of Jesus along with an OT quotation (Deut. 25:4) in 1 Timothy 5:18. The quotation of Jesus was recorded by Luke (Luke 10:7). Since it is unlikely that Luke's Gospel existed at this early stage in the history of the church, this indicates Luke's careful use of sayings of Jesus that were known among early Christians, as indicated by Paul in this letter to Timothy. This passage also reveals that Christians placed the same level of authority on the words of Jesus as they did on the OT.

The third way God revealed His message to the prophets was by leading them in the selection of material already available to them that was then incorporated in their inspired writings. A few examples may suffice. In Proverbs we find a small collection of proverbs written by Agur, who was probably a non-Israelite (Prov. 30:1–33). The whole of Proverbs 31, or at least vv. 1–9, was written by the mother of King Lemuel, a non-Israelite king. Were these persons inspired by the Lord when composing the proverbs? Collections of proverbs similar to the ones we find in the biblical books were very common throughout the ANE and Egypt and there is evidence indicating that the biblical writers may have copied from some of them. Although we do not consider the original authors to have been inspired by God, we can ascertain that the biblical writers were moved by the Spirit to select and incorporate these writings into their inspired collection of proverbs. Thus the Spirit guided the prophet in the selection of proverbs from outside Israel that summarized concepts compatible with the will of God for His people. In such cases, revelation and inspiration are inseparable and consist of a process of selection of materials done under the direct influence of the Spirit.

The Scripture as the End Product

The end product of revelation-inspiration is the written word of God. It is during this process that the human element is most active. What went on within the person of the prophets as the Lord communicated with them and during the preservation of that revelation in written form has been a matter of discussion among Bible students. There are two extreme views. The first view is usually called the *dictation theory* of inspiration. According to it, God to a large extent dictated His message to the prophets and they wrote it down. Therefore, the Scripture is in a very literal form the word of God. We argue that this is not the case because, as mentioned above, the biblical books show the distinct writing abilities and styles of their authors.

The second view on revelation-inspiration is called *encounter revelation*, and it is the prevailing view among liberal scholars. It teaches that when the Lord approached the prophets, they experienced His presence in a deep and personal way. This experience was so sublime that the revelation itself was an encounter with God that transcended words. Therefore, God did not reveal to the prophets anything except Himself. There was no exchange of information about who He was or about His will and plans for His people. In other words, there is nothing in the Scriptures that comes to us from God. What we have in the Bible is the feeble attempt of the prophets to explain to us what the experience they had with God meant to them in their own cultural context. Therefore the content of the Scriptures is culturally determined and conditioned. It is a book like any other book. This also is not a satisfactory understanding. We have shown above that God's revelation to His prophets was cognitive; that is to say, during the divine-human encounter God spoke to the prophets and gave them a body of knowledge about Him, His will, and His plans for the human race. The end product of the revelation-inspiration process is called in the Bible the "word of God" or "the word of truth" (2 Tim. 2:15).

Since God shared information with the prophets, it is proper to conclude that in the revelation-inspiration process God accessed their minds and placed there the thoughts, concepts, or ideas that He wanted them to communicate to His people. This was an act of divine condescension in that God's thoughts were being adapted to the human way of thinking and speaking in order to make them intelligible to His creatures. The Infinite Mind was contacting and communicating with a finite mind. As we have shown above, in the revelation-inspiration process the prophets embodied the divine thoughts in human words, using their own words. Since Peter indicates that the prophets spoke as they were led by the Spirit (2 Pet. 1:21), we conclude that He continued to accompany and guide them as they incarnated the divine message in human words. God was interested in preserving the integrity and trustworthiness of the message He gave to the prophets. There are some cases in the Bible where, after the prophets received a message from the Lord, He asked them, "What do you see?" (i.e., He asked them to tell what they saw using their own words). And after they summarized what they saw, the Lord responded that they had seen accurately (Jer. 1:11–12). In such instances, God was verifying that the divine message that the prophets were to pass on to others in human words would be trustworthy. The words of the prophet became the word of God.

Working under the biblical assumptions that God did not dictate His message to the prophets and that He did not abandon them when they wrote it down, we can affirm that the guidance of the Spirit assisted the prophets in using their language skills, spoken or written, to the best of their abilities. Since the words were those of the prophets, we cannot affirm that the words were inspired, but we can affirm that the message from God, expressed through their words, was passed on to others in a trustworthy and reliable form. This was possible because they spoke through the guidance of the Holy Spirit (2 Pet. 1:21).

The special connection between God, the Spirit, and the prophets should not be interpreted to mean that a prophet reached a state of divine perfection in the reception and preservation of the messages from God. We have cases in the Bible where a prophet received a revelation from God but did not understand it. In the case of Daniel, the Lord sent an angel to explain to him a prophecy that he did not understand (Dan. 8:27; 9:22). Peter was confused as a result of a vision he had (Acts 10:17), but he gained a clear understanding during the three days that it took him to get to the house of Cornelius (Acts 10:19, 28). In this case, an angel was not sent to explain the vision to him. Since the prophets remained human beings, it should not surprise us to find in the Bible some minor and inconsequential discrepancies. Their inconsequential nature does not undermine the trustworthiness of the Bible. The Scriptures continue to be the inspired word of God and the infallible revelation of His will.

PURPOSE OF THE HOLY SCRIPTURES

The revelation of God preserved in the Holy Scriptures unveils to its readers a drama of love and sacrifice of cosmic dimensions. The drama is about the Creator God, who was unwilling to abandon His creatures to themselves in spite of their rebellion against Him. From among the heavenly beings created by God, a cherub rebelled against a loving Creator and charged Him with selfishness and arbitrariness in the administration of the universe (Gen. 3:1-5; Job 1:9-11; Is. 14:13-15; Ezek. 28:13-19). The conflict in heaven was so intense that rebellious angels had to be cast out from the presence of God to pursue their own selfish interests (Rev. 12:7-10). When humans joined the rebellion (Gen. 3:6-13), God out of His grace offered them the possibility of returning to an alliance with Him (3:15).

Other parts of the Scriptures are about the cosmic conflict as it has played out within human history, in which every person is a participant. In the Scriptures we find a cosmic disclosure of the true character of God and His final victory over the forces of evil. Beginning with Genesis, God introduces in human history the hope of a coming Redeemer who will demonstrate to the cosmos that the charges of the fallen cherub were totally unfounded. Divine love, grace, and mercy were constantly manifested in the lives of the patriarchs and in God's dealing with Israel and the nations of the world in the midst of a conflict that threatened the spiritual life of God's people and even their own existence. The prophets proclaimed to the people the coming of the Redeemer, who would give His life for God's people by dying as a sacrificial victim for them (e.g., Is. 52:12—53:12).

The ministry and person of the Son of God, who became human in order to manifest to the cosmos the deepness and unfathomable nature of the love of God (John 1:14; 3:16), represents the center of the Scriptures. In Him the prophetic proclamation found its fulfillment. He became human and offered His life as an unblemished sacrifice for sinners (1 Pet. 1:19). He took on Himself what was theirs in order for them to receive as a gift of grace what was His (2 Cor. 5:21; 8:9). The cross of Christ displayed the inscrutable nature of His loving character in an unparalleled way, thus unmasking the evilness of all rebellious powers in the universe. The sacrificial love of God took Him to the realm of death, to a dark tomb, from which He came out alive!

It is part of the function of the Bible to tell us that during the Christian era the conflict will still go on but that the consummation of the salvation brought to us through Christ will result in the final extermination of evil powers (Rev. 13:1-8). It also tells us that God is willing to use human beings who join in the proclamation of God's redeeming love to the world manifested on the cross of Christ (Matt. 28:10-20). These are individuals who were transformed by the power of the Spirit of the Lord and now manifest in their own lives the love of God in selfless service to others. They constitute the church of Christ. The church will suffer while on earth, and toward the end the conflict will intensify (Rev. 13:13-18), but the victory belongs to Christ and His faithful people (17:14). The ultimate resolution of the cosmic conflict will occur when every creature in the universe unites in acknowledging the goodness of God and praising His loving character (Phil. 2:11; Rev. 15:3-4).

It is the purpose of the Scriptures to announce the coming of a new world free from suffering, death, and the presence of evil, where God's redeemed will rejoice forever (Is. 35:10; Rev. 21:1-4). The focus of the Bible is on the sacrificial death of the Son of God, through whom all of this was made possible. Since the most fundamental purpose of the Scriptures is to introduce us to such a loving God, manifested in the person and ministry of His Son, we should indeed study the word of God to come to know Him better and to be transformed into His likeness.

FORMATION OF THE BIBLICAL CANON

The work of the Spirit of the Lord in the edification of God's people did not end with the revelation of God's message through the prophets and its communication in oral or written form. The preservation of that revelation for future generations was as important as the revelation itself in that it kept alive the divine plan for humanity in the form of a messianic hope of cosmic proportions. The most effective way of transmitting God's message to other generations throughout the ages has been by faithful copying and recopying of God's revealed word. Many books were written during both the OT and NT times, but not all of them became part of the biblical canon. What made the biblical books unique, and what forces set them apart to constitute them into the Holy Scriptures?

The history of the formation of the biblical canon is complex and difficult, and at times it distracts the researcher from what is probably the most important and perhaps obvious aspect of the canon, namely, its gratuitous nature. It was from the very first steps—from the moment when the divine word reached the first prophet—a gift from God to His people and through them, particularly through the Messiah, to the world. It is a gift in which the gift and the Giver are inseparable.

THE CANON OF SCRIPTURE

We will provide an introduction to the topic of the biblical canon that will highlight some of the most important biblical and historical evidence used to trace its history. While it would be impossible, within the confines of this introduction, to elaborate in a detailed manner on most of the information provided, the general contours of the formation of the canon should be clear to the reader.

Definitions and Concepts

The English word *canon* is derived from the Greek noun *kanōn*, meaning "reed," "measuring rod," or "rule." It is a loan word from the Hebrew noun *qaneh*, which also means "reed," "rod," or "measuring unit" (see 1 Kin. 14:15; Job 40:21). The term designates a standard to be followed when measuring, leading to the meaning of a rule or guide. The term *kanōn* was well known and utilized in Hellenistic Greek. In fact, the ancient world was full of "canons" that guided different aspects of human activity. In Galatians 6:16, Paul utilizes the term in the sense of a measure of Christian conduct that can be verified. However, in Scripture it does not designate the biblical canon itself. The term *kanōn* was used in a variety of ways in the earliest days of Christianity. Around A.D. 96, Clement of Rome used it in reference to the

Christian "tradition." Nearly a century later, Clement of Alexandria (ca. 150–215) referred to the canon of faith. It was not until the middle of the fourth century and onward that *kanōn* was used to designate the collection of sacred writings of both the OT and the NT.

The biblical canon is recognized by Christians to be authoritative for the church in terms of faith, practice, and mission. What constituted these books into a collection of authoritative books, a canon? The biblical answer is surprisingly simple but most effective: the books that now constitute the canon were considered authoritative by the community of believers (Israel and the Christian church) because of their divine origin. Their authority is deeply grounded in their nature as a gift from God that reaches us through divine revelation and inspiration. The self-authentication of these books is affirmed in both the OT and the NT. Consequently, their authority rests not upon the alleged fact that some person or group of individuals included them in the canon but upon the fact that they were recognized by their religious community as having authority because of their divine origin; that is, their gratuitous nature. It was as a result of that conviction that the books were preserved in the canon. The books were recognized as canonical and holy because of their intrinsic nature, not merely because they were declared to be such.

HISTORY OF THE OLD TESTAMENT CANON

The Biblical Evidence

The concept of a canon has its roots in the Bible itself. The OT provides valuable information concerning the existence of authoritative written documents that were recognized as coming from the Lord through His prophets. We begin at Mount Sinai, where God first gave His covenant instructions to His people audibly (Ex. 19:1—20:21). Afterward, Moses was specifically commanded to write down all of these principles, which provided a written narrative framework for them (cf. Ex. 17:14; 24:3–4; Num. 33:2). It was written in the book of the covenant and read to the people, who responded by affirming that they would obey everything the Lord had commanded (Ex. 24:7). Here we have the indispensable elements of a religious authoritative document: God spoke (divine origin), the revelation was preserved in written form (the book of the covenant), and the people acknowledged the authority of the document and promised to order their lives on the basis of its content. The written word was to be read on a regular basis to the people so that they would obey all the words of the law (Deut. 31:12).

The canonical authority of the law and Moses's instructions, as preserved in the Pentateuch, are recognized again and again throughout the OT, beginning with Joshua (Josh. 1:8), as well as in Judges (Judg. 1:20), the book of Kings (1 Kin. 2:3; 2 Kin. 14:6; 23:3), and others (2 Chr. 25:4; 34:32; 35:12; Ezra 3:2; 6:18; Neh. 8:1, 14; Dan. 9:11, 13; Mal. 4:4). The Pentateuch is foundational for the rest of the OT (see "Introduction to the Pentateuch," p. 120). A particularly interesting case is found in Nehemiah 8:9, in which Ezra read the law to the exiles who had returned from Babylon to Jerusalem, showing that its authority was recognized by all. The covenant relationship between God and His people was determined by their adherence to the word of the Lord preserved in written form. This collection was considered to be not of human origin but based on God's self-revelation.

Some scholars have noted that many of the books of the OT are interconnected, and have pointed to their essential unity. This is particularly true with the Pentateuch, which clearly connects Genesis and Exodus as the continuation of the same narrative. Exodus concludes with the construction of the sanctuary and God taking residence inside it, and Leviticus begins with God speaking to Moses from the tabernacle. After the covenant law is given and the sanctuary with its services is established, Numbers continues the narrative from Sinai to the promised land. Deuteronomy recapitulates the experiences of Israel in the wilderness, emphasizing the need for Israel to obey the covenant law in Canaan and concluding with the death of Moses. It is most logical to conclude that the connections between these books are the work of the author of the Pentateuch and serve to indicate that in this collection of books the readers found an authoritative revelation of God for them.

The book of Joshua is directly related to Deuteronomy by reporting the death of Moses and the new role of Joshua (Deut. 34:1–11), whose leadership is portrayed in the book that bears his name. In fact, Joshua is directly linked to Genesis and Exodus by referring to the bones of Joseph (Josh. 24:32), mentioned for the first time in Genesis 50:24–26 (cf. Ex. 13:19). Judges begins with a reference to the death of Joshua (Judg. 1:1), narrated in Joshua 24:29. While Joshua concludes by summarizing the faithfulness of the people during the time of Joshua and the elders who followed him (Josh. 24:31), Judges begins by affirming the faithfulness of the people (Judg. 1:1–26), followed by their spiritually unstable relationship with the Lord during the time of the Judges. Ruth is connected to the book of Judges by the very first phrase of the book: "In the days when the judges ruled" (Ruth 1:1). It closes with a genealogy that introduces David (Ruth 4:16–22), thus preparing the way for the monarchy and the important role of David in the book of Samuel. The book of Kings is an obvious continuation of the history of the monarchy, beginning with the ascension of Solomon and concluding with the fall and captivity of Judah during the Exile. The book of Chronicles retells or recapitulates the story of the monarchy from a particular God-centered perspective and connects it to universal history by taking the reader back to Genesis and the creation of Adam—an excellent way of closing the canon. It concludes with a reference to the work of Cyrus on behalf of God's people, as announced by Isaiah (Isa. 44:28). The book of Ezra begins the way 2 Chronicles closes, with a reference to Cyrus (2 Chron. 36:22; Ezra 1:1) and the people returning from exile. Esther provides a door of access to the life in exile and God's care for His people.

When we examine the prophetic books, we find them deeply connected to the history of God's people. In their introductions practically all of the authors relate their ministry to specific kings in Israel and Judah. The books are all part of the overarching story that finds its beginning in the Pentateuch. The prophets received revelations from God for His people within very specific historical moments. Some of them were acquainted with the ministry of other prophets and acknowledged their authority (e.g., Is. 8:16–20; 34:16; Jer. 26:17–18; 28:8–9; Dan. 9:2; cf. 2 Chr. 20:20).

Everything in the OT is related to that overarching story. For instance, the book of Proverbs is connected to Solomon and Hezekiah; Ecclesiastes and Song of Songs are also connected to Solomon. The biblical canon places these books within the history of God's people at a particular point. Even Job is connected to the patriarchal period. The book of Psalms is inseparable from the temple, and many of the psalms are connected to the experiences of different individuals in Israel, particularly David. The book itself groups the psalms in thematic blocks related to the history of God's people (see Psalms: Introduction).

What we find in the OT is a collection of books that are deeply interconnected, not only to each other but particularly to the Pentateuch, and that tell a history of the interaction of God and His people. It is not just history, but history narrated from the perspective of God revealed to and written by His prophets. It is an authoritative narrative that reveals the disastrous results of the violation of God's covenant law, embedded at the same time in a glorious messianic promise of hope. Who put this divine narrative together? It could be argued that later editors put it together, but the biblical evidence, if taken seriously, points in a different direction. The interlocking of the books is the result of the authors themselves who, under divine inspiration, were guiding God's people from beginning to end and moving from one historical moment to the next, thus affirming God's constant presence among His people. Who put the books together as a collection to constitute them into one canon?

Historical Evidence

As we close the OT, we are left with a large number of books recognized by God's people as authoritative because they contain a revelation from God. It could be that before the Exile some people may have had questions about the prophetic ministry of some of the prophets (e.g., Jeremiah), but after the Exile, seeing all their prophecies fulfilled, there was no room left for any further doubts. We do not know the specific order in which all these books were organized—for example, the place of the wisdom books within the collection. For this, we look for extrabiblical information.

The earliest datable extrabiblical reference pointing to a particular order of books is found in the prologue of the apocryphal book of Jesus Ben Sirach (Ecclesiasticus; ca. 195 B.C.). His grandson translated it from Hebrew into Greek (ca. 132 B.C.) and added to it a prologue in which he mentions three times the three main parts of the OT books: the Law, the Prophets, and the rest of the books of the fathers. In other words, it appears to point to a threefold division of the OT. The "Law" would be the Pentateuch, the "Prophets" most probably the historical and prophetic books, and the other books would designate the rest of the OT. What is particularly important in this case is that Ben Sirach is not defining the order or the content of the canon for the first time but using what was apparently well known. A similar collection, although perhaps more controversial, is mentioned in 2 Maccabees 2:13–15 (ca. 104–63 B.C.).

Evidence coming from the Dead Sea Scrolls found in Qumran is very informative and important. First, complete scrolls and fragments of all the books in the Hebrew canon, except Esther, were found there (although Esther is quoted in other Dead Sea Scrolls). This is significant since the majority of the scrolls are dated between the third century B.C. and A.D. 73. Therefore, virtually all books generally connected to the Jewish canon of the OT already existed as copies in the second to first centuries B.C., and commentaries had been written on some of them, confirming their authority. Second, the Qumran library contained many other books, but the evidence indicates that those books did not have the same authority as those that constitute the canon. Third, the Qumran community seems to have been familiar with the threefold division that was mentioned in the prologue of Ben Sirach in the second century B.C., called the books of Moses and the books of the prophets and David. This same classification is found in Luke 24:44 and implied in Matthew 23:35 (see also Luke 11:51).

Mention should be made of Philo (20 B.C.–A.D. 40), an Alexandrian Jew who sought to show the superiority of Jewish thinking over Hellenistic thinking. He mentions the laws, the oracles given by the prophets, the Psalms, and other books that, according to him, were useful for knowledge and piety. The last group of books refers probably to those outside the canon. In Philo, the Psalms refers not exclusively to the book of Psalms but to a collection that included at least Proverbs and Job, which he quotes as Scripture (e.g., "as the Holy Word says").

Josephus (A.D. 37–100), a Jewish historian, knew about the threefold division of the OT and was the first to provide a fixed number of books of the OT collection. He identifies a total of twenty-two books constituted by the five books of Moses (the Law), the thirteen books of the Prophets, and four books of Hymns and Precepts for the conduct of life. Josephus considered this collection to be a closed list of books to which nothing was to be added. He did not identify the books by name under each category, but it could easily correspond to the list we have today when we remember that some of the books at that time were combinations of books that we have today: *Law*—Genesis, Exodus, Leviticus, Numbers, and Deuteronomy (five); the *Prophets*—Joshua, Judges-Ruth, 1–2 Samuel, 1–2 Kings, 1–2 Chronicles, Ezra-Nehemiah, Esther, Job, Isaiah, Jeremiah-Lamentations, Ezekiel, Daniel, the book of the Minor Prophets (thirteen); *Hymns and Precepts*—Psalms, Proverbs, Ecclesiastes, and Song of Songs (four). Josephus's quotations from the OT in his writings seem to support this list of specific books. The list of the twenty-two books was known to Christian writers such as Origen (A.D. 185–254) and Jerome (A.D. 347–419). Other Jewish sources mention twenty-four books, instead of twenty-two, probably by counting Ruth and Lamentations as separate books; this number became the traditional number of the books in the Hebrew Bible.

The apocryphal book of 2 Esdras, written around A.D. 100, mentions that the OT contains twenty-four books, plus another seventy hidden books (the writer distinguishes between the two numbers). Melito, bishop of Sardis (ca. A.D. 170), published a list of books belonging to the OT that includes all the books in the modern canon, except possibly Esther.

Originally the books were written on independent scrolls, but once the codex (the precursor of modern bound books) was invented and became the standard format of writing (ca. A.D. 300), it was easier to arrange them in a fixed order. Today the Hebrew Bible organizes the books in a threefold order as follows:

Law (Heb. *torah*)	**Prophets** (Heb. *nebi'im*)	**Writings** (Heb. *ketubim*)
Genesis	Joshua	Psalms
Exodus	Judges	Proverbs
Leviticus	1–2 Samuel	Job
Numbers	1–2 Kings	Song of Songs
Deuteronomy	Isaiah	Ruth
	Jeremiah	Lamentations
	Ezekiel	Ecclesiastes
	The Twelve Prophets	Esther
	(Hosea, Joel, Amos, Obadiah,	Daniel
	Jonah, Micah, Nahum,	Ezra-Nehemiah
	Habakkuk, Zephaniah, Haggai,	1–2 Chronicles
	Zechariah, Malachi)	

In this arrangement the canon begins with Genesis and concludes with 1–2 Chronicles. This order of books appears to be the oldest witnessed in Jewish literature.

The crucial question that divides modern scholarship is whether the OT had already been standardized by the time of Jesus (or before) or whether this occurred only in the first century A.D. or perhaps even later in the second century A.D. A brief comment is necessary on some rabbinic debates about the canon. Among the Jews there were some disputed books, like Esther, in which the name of God is not mentioned. Some scholars have suggested that it was in the so-called council of Jamnia that final decisions were made concerning the books that would constitute the OT canon. Jamnia, located on the Mediterranean coast of Israel, hosted both a rabbinical school and a legal court established during the period of A.D. 70–135. In the school there were discussions on the extent of the sacred Scriptures and on many other topics. However, such discussions were not unusual, for rabbis had discussed these matters at least in the previous generation and also several times long after the Jamnia period. It is clear that these rabbinical discussions were not formative for the OT canon. The belief that there was a council in Jamnia where the OT canon was finally fixed is not historically reliable. Above all, the witness of Jesus is extraordinarily important for the fixing of the canon.

Jesus and the Old Testament Canon

When we examine the Gospels we find that Jesus confirmed the scope and divisions of the OT canon. In a discussion about the fate of prophets in the hands of the leaders of the people, He referred to the OT martyrs and held the leaders responsible for "the righteous blood [that has been] shed on the earth, from the blood of righteous Abel to the blood of Zechariah, son of Berechiah, whom you murdered between the temple and the altar" (Matt. 23:35; cf. Luke 11:51). Here Jesus was referring to the martyrdom of Zechariah recorded in 2 Chronicles 24:20–21, and He thus affirmed the canonical order of the OT books by choosing the first martyr mentioned in Genesis and the last martyr mentioned in the *last canonical* book, 2 Chronicles (*chronologically* Zechariah was not the last martyr of the OT; see Jer. 26:20–23). These boundaries of the canon used by Jesus indicate that in His day the canon was already closed. Jesus also confirmed the threefold division of the canon, which closed with 2 Chronicles, when He spoke about the fulfillment of everything written about Him in the Law of Moses, the Prophets, and the Psalms (Luke 24:44). Earlier in the chapter Luke wrote that Jesus had begun with "Moses and all the Prophets," as He used "all the Scriptures" to discuss matters regarding Himself (Luke 24:27). The shorter form is another way of designating the threefold order of the OT books (cf. Matt. 7:12; Luke 16:16), as it acknowledged the existence of divisions in a particular order with the Writings being the last. Mentioning only the first two of the three divisions was also the practice among other Jewish writers.

How were all the authoritative books of the OT collected and organized in a threefold order? There is no final answer to this question. Although most scholars have rejected the possibility that it was the work of Ezra and Nehemiah after the Exile, the possibility should not be ruled out. Three arguments give some credibility to this traditional proposal without demonstrating that this was the case. First, Ezra is depicted in the Bible as a man who knew the Hebrew Scriptures well and taught them to the people. Second, there is a Jewish tradition according to which Nehemiah collected books and founded a library. Obviously it is impossible to determine which books he collected, but the tradition suggests that Nehemiah and Ezra were interested in the religious books of the people of God. Third, there is another Jewish tradition that seems to have been affirmed also by some early church fathers, according to which prophecy ceased with Malachi, a contemporary of Nehemiah. The cessation of prophecy would be a way of suggesting that the canon of the OT was closed—nothing else could be added to it. Whether that was the case is impossible to establish beyond any doubt, but for Christians the fact that Jesus acknowledged the existence of a closed OT canon is of great significance and in fact becomes the historical center of the Christian canon.

HISTORY OF THE NEW TESTAMENT CANON

The canon of the Christian church is constituted by both the canon of the OT and the apostolic writings called the NT. This suggests that we should start by examining the OT canon of the Christian church. A good transition to this analysis is a discussion of the translation of the OT into Greek called the Septuagint (abbreviated as LXX).

The Old Testament Canon and the Septuagint

The Greek translation of the OT Scriptures is called "the Septuagint" because of a legend according to which the Ptolemaic king of Egypt Ptolemy II wanted a copy of the Hebrew

Scriptures for his Alexandrian library. He supposedly ordered seventy Jewish scholars to each translate the Pentateuch into Greek on the pain of death. As the legend maintains, after they had finished their independent work, the translation of each one of them miraculously and perfectly corresponded to that of all the others. The more likely situation is that the Septuagint was originally a Jewish project, which was produced from the third century B.C. onward and began with the translation of the Pentateuch. Whatever the case, the Septuagint became, during the first few centuries of the Christian era, the Christian Bible, and, in fact, Christians were also the first to call it the LXX.

As far as it can be ascertained, the Septuagint originally comprised the translation of the twenty-four books of the OT. The Gospels and the Epistles of the NT often use the Septuagint when quoting from the OT. Jewish writers distinguished the OT canonical books from other books written during the Second Temple period that were also highly regarded by the Jews. Christians usually referred to these books as the apocryphal or deuterocanonical books. The term *apocrypha* is of Greek origin and means "hidden things," probably used to indicate that such books lacked canonical status. When Christians made the Septuagint their Bible, the Jews stopped using it and produced other Greek translations of the OT (e.g., Theodotion, Aquila), but they finally returned to the Hebrew Bible.

The Apocrypha

Significant differences exist between the Hebrew canon and the canon preserved in the oldest codices of the Septuagint. The oldest codex containing the complete Greek Bible is the Codex Vaticanus (fourth century A.D.) and includes the apocryphal books of Tobit, Judith, Wisdom, Ecclesiasticus (Sirach), Baruch, and the Letter of Jeremiah, as well as additions to the books of Esther and Daniel (e.g., Susanna and Bel and the Dragon)—works written between 200 B.C. and A.D. 132 but absent from the Hebrew canon. The larger canon of the Septuagint should probably be understood in terms of confrontations and tensions between Judaism and the growth of the Christian church, already manifested in the NT. Although the Septuagint, as indicated, originated as a Jewish project, its rapid adoption and authority in the Christian community as an important tool for evangelizing the Roman world led to a definite rejection of it by the Jews early in the second century A.D. Therefore, it seems reasonable to argue that these monumental codices (that came into use only from the fourth century A.D. onward) exhibit influences prevalent in the early Christian church, which at that time struggled to define its identity against the background of rabbinic Judaism.

It must be noted that the early Christian church did not always accept the additional books as authoritative and canonical. Both Athanasius (ca. A.D. 296–373) and Jerome (ca. A.D. 345–420) mention the apocryphal books but clearly distinguish them from the OT canonical books. Jerome insisted on a return to the Hebrew canon and rejected the use of apocryphal books in doctrinal discussions. Neither the NT writers nor most patristic writers accepted the Apocrypha as authoritative and as belonging to the recognized OT canon. The larger canon of the Septuagint continued in use, but the discussion came to a climax during the Protestant Reformation. Protestants acknowledged only the Hebrew canon as authoritative and rejected the apocryphal books. In a sense this led the Catholic Church to officially accept, during the Council of Trent (A.D. 1546), the larger canon of the Septuagint, now found in the Latin Vulgate and in the canon of the Orthodox churches. The Orthodox churches have added some other apocryphal books (e.g., 1–2 Esdras, 3 Maccabees, the Prayer of Manasseh, and Psalm 151).

The Old Testament Canon and Jesus and His Disciples

The Gospels provide clear evidence indicating that Jesus used the OT Hebrew canon and considered it authoritative. A few examples illustrate His respect for the OT. Jesus spoke about the importance of complying with OT regulations (e.g., Matt. 5:17–19), thus indicating the binding nature of the inspired and written Scripture. He referred to the OT commands, promises, and other stories in the context of the declaration "it is written" (e.g., Matt. 4:4, 7, 10; 11:10; Mark 7:6), which always appears as a conclusive argument in His discussions. However, there is no evidence that Jesus ever used the Apocrypha or that He assigned canonical status to it.

Some NT books may refer to apocryphal works, the best example being Jude 14–15, which contains a quote from 1 Enoch. The apostle found in this quote content that was compatible with the Scriptures (see Gen. 6–9; Deut. 33:2; Is. 15–16; Jer. 25:30–31; Dan. 7:10, 18, 23, 25). In other words, he found in the text a good expression or summary of what he intended to say and decided to use it. This by no means demonstrates an authorization of this work as canonical. In several instances Paul quotes Greek thinkers (e.g., Acts 17:29; Titus 1:12) without necessarily making them canonical or authoritative. In this sense, a possible reference or allusion to an apocryphal book may be made without canonizing it. The OT text is quoted or alluded to again and again in the NT to teach or support arguments, and it is considered to be divinely inspired.

This same attitude toward the binding authority of the OT is reflected in the apostolic church as well. The Bereans checked the OT Scriptures daily to verify Paul's teachings (Acts 17:11). Paul utilizes the strength of the OT in his arguments on vengeance being the sole prerogative of God (Rom. 12:19–20) and on the universality of sin (3:10–13). Peter argues for a lifestyle of holiness on the basis of the OT (1 Pet. 2:4–6). This sample of the evidence points to the OT as an authoritative, inspired body of texts. This same attitude toward the OT determined its canonicity for the Christian church. Unfortunately, and for reasons not totally clear, the church through a slow process came to accept the Apocrypha as canonical. It must be remembered that apocryphal books contain some theological concepts not supported by the Holy Scriptures. Among them we find praying for the dead (2 Maccabees 12:43–45); the preexistence of the human soul (Wisdom 9:15); martyrdom as a means of atonement (2 Maccabees 7:37–38; 4 Maccabees 17:21–22); human works as a contribution to salvation (Tobit 4:7–11); and the intercession of dead saints for living ones (2 Maccabees 15:13–14). The fact that for Christ, the apostles, and the early Christian church the Hebrew canon was recognized as part of Christian canon (cf. 2 Pet. 3:16) reveals the deep continuity between the church and the Israel of faith in the NT. They have in common a fundamental messianic message of salvation and hope.

The New Testament Canon and Jesus and the Apostles

The Christian canon includes not only the Hebrew OT but also the writings of the apostles. Here again the identification of the canon as a gift of God is evident. The origin of the content of the NT canon is located in the person, work, and teachings of Jesus Christ, in the unique revelation of God that He brought to the world. The OT Messiah, the Prophet like Moses, arrived (Deut. 18:18–19; Acts 3:19–26), and His teachings, rooted in the OT, brought light and life to the human race. This revelation is to be preserved and proclaimed to the world (Matt. 28:18–20). The revelation from God that Jesus shared with His disciples is absolutely authoritative; all the nations of the earth should learn about it and submit to it. He brought to them the gift of the word of God. Jesus is therefore the historical as well as the theological center of the biblical canon in that in Him the authority of the canon of the OT and its fullness are confirmed and in that He provided the authoritative content of the NT canon. There seems to be a Christological component in the formation of the biblical canon.

At the time of the great commission, the authoritative body of Jesus's teachings had not been written down. For many years it was passed on to others through the spoken word, although aspects of His teachings and ministry were probably soon written down (cf. Luke 1:1). The task of passing on this revelation to others was entrusted by Jesus to His disciples and, in order to make sure that they would preserve His teachings accurately, He promised them the presence and guidance of the Holy Spirit, who would teach them and bring to their memory Jesus's teachings (John 14:26). Empowered by the Spirit, the disciples witnessed for Jesus because they had been with Him from the beginning of His public ministry (15:27). The disciples were made responsible for the trustworthy proclamation and preservation of the content of the NT canon.

Soon the life and teachings of Jesus began to be written down as Scripture for future generations. This happened, as in the OT, in the context of a narrative that is part of the biblical metanarrative of the cosmic conflict. As the church was growing, there was the need to instruct members concerning the deeper content of the gospel and its implications for the lives of the believers in the specific cultural and social settings in which they found themselves. The content of the NT Epistles is clearly identified by the apostles as the word of Jesus, not simply of the apostles, and as trustworthy and authoritative for the life and convictions of all the followers of Christ. The apostolic writings were recognized as authoritative and as Scripture (see "Revelation and Inspiration of the Bible," p. 11). The Gospels preserve the teachings of Jesus that rejected nonbiblical traditions in order for the light from God to fully shine on His followers. His ministry, as narrated in the Gospels, revealed the immensity of His saving sacrifice and the love of God. His teachings and work were being preserved in a trustworthy way in written form.

The Christian audiences who first received the written documents recognized them as authoritative and useful for ordering their lives. They contained a revelation from Jesus Christ for them through the apostles; that is to say, those who had been with Him from the beginning and to whom He entrusted His revelation. The NT canon, whose content was determined by Jesus, was from its very beginning directly connected to the work of the apostles.

It is difficult to determine how widespread the use of the apostolic writings was within the church, but the apostolic teaching was well known. When confronted by heresies, Christian writers began to summarize the apostolic teachings in what they called the "rule [canon] of faith" and used it to expose the falsehood of the heretics, thus revealing the authority of the apostolic teachings in oral and written forms.

The New Testament Canon and the Early Church

If what we have described is to be taken into serious consideration in any discussion of the origin of the canon of the NT, then the writings of the apostles must have been recognized as part of the Christian canon, together with the OT, very early in the history of the church (cf. 2 Pet. 3:16). Scholars are divided on the date the NT canon was closed, some arguing for a late second century date and others for the fourth or fifth century. Evidence from the early church fathers suggests that by the close of the first and beginning of the second century A.D. there was a collection of written Christian documents that enjoyed authoritative status within the church. Irenaeus (ca. A.D. 130–200) speaks about the writings of the apostles as the Scriptures that contain the message of salvation. This suggests that apostolic writings were considered Scripture even before Irenaeus's days.

In a document called the Muratorian Fragment, usually dated around A.D. 180, there is what could be called a canonical list of the books of the NT that includes the four Gospels, Acts, the Pauline Epistles (thirteen), 2 Johannine Epistles, Jude, and Revelation; but Hebrews, James, 1–2 Peter, and one of the Johannine Epistles are not mentioned. While some books are absent, it is significant that at this early date virtually the entire NT was recognized as authoritative Scripture. Clement of Alexandria (ca. A.D. 150–215) included Hebrews among Paul's letters. It seems that Papias (ca. A.D. 60–130), bishop in Asia Minor, was acquainted with 1 John, 1 Peter, and Revelation. In 1 Clement, a nonapostolic Christian letter written ca. A.D. 96 by an unknown author, the author uses 1 Corinthians, Romans, and Hebrews and probably knew about Galatians, Ephesians, Philippians, and Titus. The controversies with the Gnostics and their literature, such as the Gospel of Truth by Valentinus (ca. A.D. 135–140), illustrated the comprehensive use of the canonical writings in the Christian church and thus suggests that by that time the canon had already been standardized. The evidence summarized here suggests that at the beginning of the second century the Christian canon was practically in place and perhaps largely fixed. The earliest surviving list of all twenty-seven of the books within the NT canon dates to A.D. 367 in an Easter letter written by Athanasius, bishop of Alexandria, Egypt.

It is true that during the fourth and fifth century A.D. it was debated in some circles whether Revelation and Hebrews should be part of the canon, but the reasons for this are not totally clear. Perhaps for some the Epistle to the Hebrews sounded very Jewish, and the book of Revelation may have been considered quite different from other NT writings. As indicated above, during the second century both books were acknowledged to be part of the authoritative writings of the apostles. It could be that the growth of the church was not accompanied by a wide circulation of these books and consequently their canonicity was not then obvious. Nevertheless, they were received as canonical books. Several synods and church councils dealt with the issue of the canon of the NT, but they did not determine the canonicity of the NT writings; instead, they ratified earlier practices. The result was the canon of the NT that we now possess.

Criteria for Canonicity

The information related to the historical origin of the canon does not provide an explicit list of the criteria used to identify the canonical books. As we look back at that history, we can identify some implicit elements that contributed and determined whether a book was to be acknowledged as canonical. As we have pointed out, in the OT the revelation and inspiration of a written document was what invested it with authority, and consequently the author had to be a prophet. This is exemplified by the conviction that with the cessation of prophecy among the Jews, no more books could be added to the canon. Perhaps another criterion was that the message of the prophet should not undermine the message God gave to previous prophets—the issue of continuity and consistency within the canon.

When we come to the NT, the basic criterion for canonicity was probably the apostolicity of the written documents. Apostolicity assured the church that the message of Jesus Christ, His teachings, was being communicated in a trustworthy way by those whom the Lord taught, and with whom He entrusted His saving message. Since the apostles received the Spirit to help them remember the teachings of Jesus and to guide them in the proclamation and exposition of the message, the written form of the revelation was considered by the church to be the word of God. The divine inspiration of the apostles was important. Apostolicity was also credited to the writings of those who were not apostles in the technical sense of the word but who had been traveling companions of the apostles and who, under their influence and probably supervision, wrote down their teachings. This includes, for instance, Luke and Mark, whose writings were considered to be apostolic and are part of the canon of the NT. Another criterion was the content of the apostolic message itself, as indicated by the fact that it was used to identify heresies and to exclude written documents that some may have claimed to be canonical. This helped establish the concept of orthodoxy in the sense that congruence and continuity with the apostolic teaching was indispensable. In this case, the criterion served to exclude spurious documents and therefore to set limits to the canon.

THE CHURCH AND THE CANON

The canon and the church should not be separated from each other, not so much because the canon needs the church but mainly because the church needs the canon in order to be what it should be. The debate on this particular topic has been whether the church is the mother of the canon or the canon the mother of the church. According to Catholic tradition, the church defined and established the canon of the Christian church—including the selection of canonical books and the moment when the canon became closed. Therefore, it is claimed, the church has authority over the canon. One of the arguments used in this dispute is that it was the church that determined which books would be part of the canon of the OT for the Christian church by including in it a number of apocryphal books. In other words, the church had the authority to reject the Hebrew canon and create its own OT canon.

Behind this debate lies the question of the extent of the authority of the church or its limits. Unquestionably, the Lord entrusted authority to the church to perform the task He assigned it to do, but in our case the concern is whether the canon is outside the sphere of the authority of the church and, if so, how we should understand the authority of the canon. First, we should go back to Jesus, who both founded the church and gave to it the message it should proclaim. The church did not originate out of spontaneous generation but as the intended result of the work of the incarnated Creator. It was through the apostles that the risen Lord entrusted to the church the content of the biblical canon, thus indicating that the church is not the mother of the canon but a servant of it.

Second, although at first the content of the canon was preserved in oral form, it was protected from corruption by the gift of the Spirit, promised by Jesus to His disciples, until it was embodied by them in the documents and letters found in the NT. The question of the connection between canon and tradition should not cloud the priority of the canon over tradition. One of the most important functions of the written canon, if not the most important one, is to preserve the teachings of Christ and the apostles in a totally reliable and trustworthy form for the church. This was a nonrepeatable event in the life of the church and made it unnecessary to listen to an oral tradition that was not grounded in the teachings preserved now in their authoritative writings: the canon of the NT. The history of the church has made it abundantly obvious that the tradition of apostolic succession has not protected the Christian church from incorporating into its message teachings that reside outside the biblical canon. Tradition must submit to the authority of the canon.

Third, the validation of the church and its authority is not self-validation but comes to it from the outside—from the canon. The church finds in the canon its origin, its mission, its faith, and its way of life in a world that opposes it. These are all elements that display the nature of the canon as a gift from the Lord. Without the canon the church would be a faceless social phenomenon as disoriented as the world itself. One could rightly say that the church cannot define itself except through submission to the will of the Lord as preserved in the biblical canon. Therefore it is the canon that establishes the extent and the limits of the authority of the church and that functions as the rule that measures the church's faithfulness to the message of Jesus. The church did not define and establish the canon, but the canon continues to define and establish the church.

Fourth, the history of the canon indicates that the canon of the church, comprising the OT and the NT, was simply received by the church. Early in church history the received canon was identified as the Prophets (the OT), the Lord (the Gospels), and the Apostles (the Epistles; see 2 Pet. 3:2, 16). We also find a fourfold list: Law and Prophets (the OT), and

Gospels and Apostles (the NT). This body of holy and authoritative writings was received by the church as the canon. It is only late in the history of the church that we read about votes taken to define aspects of the biblical canon. The apostolic and early church had no need for such official decisions because they found in the apostolic teachings and writings the word of God, and they received the writings as holy and authoritative books to rule over their lives (e.g., 1 Thess. 2:13; 2 Pet. 3:15–16).

Finally, since the canon is the shaper of the church, the church should constantly make it the center of its concern and interest and the source for the formulation of doctrine, theology, and the Christian way of life. This means the believers must explore the totality of the canon in seeking to understand the will of the Lord for us individually and for the church. In this setting there is no room for the idea that there is a canon within the canon that is more authoritative than the collection of books of the canon itself. Some have argued that the true canon is Christ and that anything within the biblical books that testifies about Him should be considered truly canonical; hence the canon within the canon. In this approach the individual stands over the biblical canon using a critical tool to determine what is or is not canonical. The Scriptures have not entrusted such authority to any individual or group of individuals. To separate the Christ of the Scriptures from the Scriptures themselves in order to set limits to the authority of the canon is human hubris. The spiritual and missiological strengths of the church are directly correlated with the appropriation of the biblical message by those who have accepted the *Jesus/Christ of the Scriptures* as their Savior and Lord and who are being transformed by His grace. The biblical canon in its totality speaks to the church about its very foundation—Christ and the apostles (Eph. 2:20)—and about the willingness of the church to constantly listen to these holy writings during its pilgrimage on earth while waiting for the realization of the hope embraced by its members and sharing this hope with a world in crisis and despair.

BIBLICAL INTERPRETATION

Humans by nature seek to understand the world around them, including their own actions and those of others. When we see or hear something, we begin the process of interpretation: "What was that sound?" "Did you see that?" We want to understand, to find meaning, and we engage others in the search for understanding. In some cases we know the meaning and we simply move on: "No, that was not a gunshot; there is a crew working on the road, and one of the tools they use emitted that sound." We use previous knowledge to interpret the phenomenon. Although often we can interpret many of our experiences rather easily, in some cases we do not have all of the information needed and usually seek help. For instance, when we want to understand who we are, where we come from, and where we are heading, we need help because relying only on our limited knowledge we cannot answer these questions. Christians believe that the answers for such questions are ultimately found in the Scriptures.

The Holy Scriptures, written by many authors over a long period of time in cultures different from ours, need to be interpreted to understand and appreciate the profound message. The task of interpreting the Bible is called *hermeneutics*, from the Greek word *hermeneuein*, used to refer to the interpretation of utterance and even to translation from one language to another. Among its many usages, the term *hermeneutics* now designates the rules and principles to be used in the interpretation of the Bible. These principles are provided by and grounded in the nature of the Bible.

APPROACHING THE HOLY SCRIPTURES

Christians are called to interpret a written text, the Holy Scriptures, originally written mostly in Hebrew in the OT and Greek in the NT. The original text written by the biblical authors is no longer available to us, but copies were made of their writings. Fortunately, we have many of those manuscripts. When the manuscripts were compared one with another, scholars occasionally detected some different readings, but none of them has a negative impact on any biblical teaching and doctrine. Knowing the biblical languages is helpful in the task of interpreting the Bible, but laypeople can gain a deep understanding of the Bible without learning Hebrew and Greek.

Most Bible translations are good enough to be used for serious Bible study, though some are better than others. There are three main types of Bible translations from which the interpreter can choose. The first type is called a *formal translation*. These translations seek to stay as close as possible to the original biblical text, providing an almost word-for-word rendering of the original, making them ideal for serious Bible study. Such translations tend to preserve ambiguities that might be present in the original text and at times include in the margins alternative translations of a word or a phrase that provide the reader with additional information for contextual analysis. Some of the most popular formal Bible translations include the New King James Version (NKJV), the English Standard Version (ESV), the New American Standard Bible (NASB), and the New English Translation (NET).

The second type of Bible translation is a *dynamic translation*. These are versions of the Bible where translators do not emphasize word-for-word equivalence but attempt to transfer from one language to another the thoughts and ideas found in the original text, working phrase by phrase. The result is a version of the Bible that is easy to read and elegant in expression. The main challenge with this type of Bible is that the translators must decide for the reader what the biblical writer is saying more broadly than do the translators of the formal translation. In other words, they provide in the translation an interpretation of the biblical text to a greater degree than those who translate word for word. The problem for Bible students using this type of translation is that they need to distinguish between what was in the original text and what is the translator's interpretation, something that is much easier to do in a formal translation. Examples of this kind of dynamic Bible translation include the New International Version (NIV), the New Living Translation (NLT), and the New Century Version (NCV).

The third type of Bible translation is a *paraphrase*. This refers to a much more free reflection of the general ideas in the original language than that of the dynamic translations. It takes the ideas of the original text and restates them as it attempts to explain or clarify their meaning, similar to a commentary. Some paraphrases work with the original text and some work off of already translated material. This type of translation can be valuable for personal devotional readings. A paraphrase could be useful in that it reveals possible meanings of the text that the interpreter needs to evaluate through her or his own reading of the Bible. This also applies to *dynamic* translations. Usually the introductory section of a Bible translation informs the reader about the nature and purpose of that translation. Some of the most popular paraphrase versions of the Bible include the New International Reader's Version (NIRV), the Contemporary English Version (CEV), and The Message (MSG).

Claims of the Bible

As we open and read the Holy Scriptures, we soon realize that it makes some claims about itself that set it apart from any other books. First, Scripture claims to be a revelation of God to the human race (2 Tim. 3:16). We are instructed that in it we can hear the voice of God speaking to human beings (see "Revelation and Inspiration of the Bible," p. 11). Second, it claims to reveal the origin of everything, including human life, through the creative power of God. Thus the Bible answers questions that humans by themselves are unable to answer. Humans were created for love and fellowship with God, which could be developed throughout eternity. Third, Scripture teaches that humans chose to join the forces of evil in the cosmic conflict, breaking away from the Creator and bringing sin, suffering, and death into the world. Fourth, Scripture claims that God resolved the problem of the human race through the incarnation, ministry, death, resurrection, and Second Coming of His Son, Jesus Christ. Jesus is at the heart of Scripture, and every portion of it testifies in one way or another about Him.

Since the Bible originates with God, who is its ultimate Author, it makes two essential claims. First, *the Bible is authoritative*. This claim of ultimate authority is grounded in the fact that God is the Creator and the Redeemer and that in His omniscience He knows what is good for human beings and for the totality of His creation. Humans are challenged to decide how they will relate to the loving will of the Creator and Redeemer revealed in Scripture. Any attempt to remain indifferent to God's will is equivalent to a rejection of both the message of the Bible and God. Second, *the Bible is a unity*. Although the Bible is a collection of books written by different authors over a period of 1,500 years, and God is its ultimate Author, the unity of the Bible can be affirmed. It is His voice that speaks through each of its inspired authors. Thus, while the human aspect of the Bible can be seen in the different literary styles, vocabulary, and emotions of its individual authors, the divinity of the Bible is strikingly evident in its overall thematic harmony. The consistency of the divine mind speaking to us through the Bible does not allow for a message that is in conflict with itself, contradicting in one place what God states in another. In the Bible we find God's spoken word giving one message for the whole human race.

Since the Bible contains God's revealed will for humans, it is the ultimate source for the teachings of the church and the conduct of believers. In the Scriptures we read about God, His plan for us, and His invitation to live a life worth living in service to God and others. The Bible alone (Lat. *sola scriptura*) contains all we need to know for salvation and faith (2 Tim. 3:16–17).

Preparing to Study the Bible

As we open the Bible, a proper personal preparation is needed. First, we should acknowledge the need for divine guidance. The ultimate interpreter of the Bible is the Holy Spirit, to whom Jesus assigned the task of guiding us in understanding His message (John 16:13). This guidance is necessary because sin has damaged the human mind and filled it with self-sufficiency and pride (Jer. 17:9; 2 Tim. 3:2–3). Humans cannot by themselves gain a proper and full understanding of the Bible (cf. Eccl. 3:11; Is. 55:8–9). Spiritual things can be understood only through the Spirit (1 Cor. 2:11, 14). The meaning of the biblical text is not determined by the interpreters but is received by them under the influence and guidance of the spirit of the Lord.

Second, interpreters should be humble, honest, and willing to submit to the will of God as expressed in the Bible (Ps. 119:34). These qualities can be placed in the human heart only by the Spirit. Therefore, sincere Bible students have found in Jesus their only Savior and have surrendered their life to Him; they have experienced conversion. Third, in the heart of such persons there is a disposition to solicit, through prayer, the guidance of the Spirit as they open the Scriptures (Ps. 119:33). While in prayer, the human mind "touches" the divine mind, and the Spirit begins to enlighten and illuminate the human mind as it exposes itself to the word of God.

The spiritual preparation of the biblical interpreter does not mean that the meaning of the text will be accessed in a mystical and subjective experience with God or through intuitions. God expects students of His word to apply the mental abilities He has given to them in the study of the Bible. They need to employ proper methods of interpretation that may be used by others to verify whether the interpretation of the text given by someone is reliable and loyal to the intention of the biblical author. The principles of interpretation are drawn from the Bible itself. The divine Author has provided in His word the principles to be used to interpret it.

PRINCIPLES OF INTERPRETATION

That interpreters must follow certain principles of interpretation when studying the Bible does not mean that understanding it is a difficult task assigned only to a few. The content and meaning of the word of God are clear and accessible to any person who carefully and prayerfully reads it. Readers are encouraged to study the divine word for themselves (e.g., Deut. 30:11–14; Acts 17:10–11). The general meaning of the text is usually accessible by keeping in mind that the literal sense should predominate unless the context points to a figurative or symbolic meaning.

The Bible Interprets Itself

The very nature of the Bible requires from its readers the attitude of learners who are willing to open up their minds and hearts to the message of the Holy Scriptures. The axiom that the Bible interprets itself means, first, that readers will let the content of the Scriptures judge their personal ideas and convictions. For instance, if someone believes that everything we see today is the result of natural evolution, the biblical understanding of divine creation recorded in Genesis 1 will challenge that conviction, calling the interpreter to set aside his or her own personal views.

Second, the belief that the Bible interprets itself means that one portion of Scripture can and should be used to interpret another. This is based on the principle of the unity of the Bible, as discussed above. In order for this internal interpretation to occur, students of the Bible must become well acquainted with it by studying and reading it again and again. The more we read it, the easier it becomes to understand it and to appropriate its message. We are also able to perceive connections between one passage and another from a different section of the Bible, thus facilitating the interpretation of the first passage. For instance, when John writes of Jesus, the Word, becoming flesh in the incarnation and dwelling among us (John 1:14), it would immediately remind an attentive interpreter of Exodus 25:8, where God showed His willingness to dwell in a sanctuary among His people. Jesus is now God's dwelling "place" on earth because Jesus is the incarnated Son of God. The language used by John associates or connects His statement with what the Bible says in another place using similar language or concepts.

Third, in order to allow the Bible to interpret itself, we need to use clear texts to interpret difficult ones dealing with the same topic. One of the best examples to illustrate this principle is the gift of tongues discussed by Paul in 1 Corinthians 14. Establishing the nature of the gift in this chapter is a difficult task and different possibilities have been offered. Finding another passage in which the gift of tongues is discussed and its nature clearly stated would be helpful in the interpretation of the gift in 1 Corinthians 14. We find such a passage in Acts 2, the first manifestation of the gift of tongues. According to Acts 2, the gift of tongues consists of being enabled by the Spirit to speak in a foreign human language. The clear passage should be used to clarify the less clear one.

Fourth, the Bible interpreting itself means that we should study everything the Bible says on a particular topic in order to gain a truthful and reliable understanding of it. The best example of this practice is provided by Jesus Himself during His conversation with the two disciples on the road to Emmaus when He directed their minds to "all the Scriptures" that address everything about His life and mission (Luke 24:27). The unity of the Scriptures is presupposed in this type of study. In this particular case, that unity is grounded on the promise of the coming Messiah found throughout the OT.

Analysis of the Context

It is practically impossible to provide a correct interpretation of a biblical passage if its context is ignored. Taking into consideration the context is one of the most important principles in biblical interpretation; it provides the starting point for the task. The importance of the context cannot be overemphasized. There are different types of context that we should take into consideration as we attempt to comprehend the word of God.

First, there is the context of the words used in the text. Each word (a noun, a verb, a preposition, etc.) in the biblical text must be taken into consideration. Often words have different meanings and consequently the specific meaning is determined by the context within which it is used. The Greek term *parousia* may mean "coming," "arrival," or "presence," but the context will indicate which one of these meanings fits best. For instance, the *arrival* of Titus comforted Paul (2 Cor. 7:6), and the physical *presence* of Paul appeared to be weak (2 Cor. 2:10). The most important usage of this term is in reference to the *coming* of Christ in glory (e.g., 1 Cor. 15:32; 1 Thess. 4:15; 5:23). But it is also used to refer to the coming of the eschatological antichrist (2 Thess. 2:9). Only the context determines the specific meaning and usage of a word.

Second, each word is part of a sentence or a phrase, and its grammatical function can reveal its immediate significance. John says that "God is love" (1 John 4:8). In this phrase, something is being said about God, and consequently "love" functions as a predicate. Therefore, "love" is not being *equated* with "God." Thus, it would be incorrect to say that love is God because God would be identified merely as an abstract concept or quality.

Third, the interpreter should also explore the context of the sentence, namely, the section in which it is located. For instance, after one of Jesus's discussions with the Pharisees, Mark refers to Jesus's words in connection with the cleansing or purification of all foods (Mark 7:1–23). Is Mark declaring that the law of clean and unclean animals was abolished by Christ? To answer this question, we need to read the statement carefully and pay attention to the context. The discussion of food must be understood within the Jewish setting of the story—the participants in the story are Jews. Food in that context refers to the food Jews ate. Also, the sentence is part of a discussion about eating with unclean/unwashed hands that, according to the Pharisees, made the food God had given them to eat ritually unclean—and therefore forbidden to eat—a regulation that is not found in the OT. Thus the context shows that Jesus was rejecting the traditions of the Jewish elders regarding defilement (Mark 7:3). He was declaring that the otherwise clean food they claimed to be defiled by unwashed hands was still clean. He was not declaring to be clean those foods that the Levitical dietary laws had identified as unclean.

Fourth, it is important to examine the context of the section—that is, the whole book or Epistle. This specific step in the interpretation of the Bible requires students to read the entire book several times, taking notes, and outlining the development of the thoughts of the biblical writer. This is the moment when a study of the literary structure of the book can be useful. Identifying the literary structure of a block of material or even a book is time-consuming, as it requires paying careful attention to the use of similar terminology or synonyms and to the repetition of similar ideas within the passage or book. The primary point here is that very often the study of the entire book can help the reader to understand a section of it. For instance, any attempt to fully understand Hebrews 2:17 (or incorrect conclusions that might be drawn about the human nature of Christ) would require a careful study of the entire Epistle to the Hebrews.

Fifth, the ultimate context of a word or sentence is the totality of the Bible. There are cases that could require gaining a general biblical knowledge of a concept or practice before explaining a verse. The meaning of the term *nepesh* (sometimes translated as "soul") in Genesis 35:18 requires a clear understanding of the Hebrew term *nepesh*, translated here as "soul," as well as the biblical understanding of the nature of human beings. The Bible teaches that humans are an indivisible unity of life and body without an independent soul that goes on existing without a body (a Greek idea). Humans do not have a soul, but they are a soul in the sense that they are mortal, physical living beings (e.g., Gen. 2:7).

Sixth, it is good for the interpreter to know about the historical background of the biblical book that is being studied. This helps to understand veiled references to historical events found in the text. Often a biblical book (e.g., 1–2 Kin.; 1–2 Chr.) provides important historical information that frames the biblical narrative. In other cases a book provides a short historical statement to date the ministry of the prophet (e.g., Is. 1:1; Jer. 1:1–3; Hos. 1:1). Concerning the OT, it is good to have a general knowledge of the Egyptian, Assyrian,

Babylonian, Medo-Persian, and Greek empires. In the NT some knowledge of the history of the Jews and the Greco-Roman world would be valuable. In this commentary, a historical background is provided in the introduction to each of the biblical books. A Bible dictionary is also a good reference source for such information.

Finally, an understanding of the religious and cultural backgrounds of the OT in its ANE setting and of the NT in its Greco-Roman world is also useful in the interpretation of the Bible. Since God chose to reveal Himself in human history, the more we can know about the world within which He acted is helpful. This does not mean, however, that we cannot understand the basic meaning of the text without such historical knowledge. Knowledge of the religious and cultural backgrounds of the ancient world simply allows us to appreciate the biblical account even more fully. In the final analysis, what determines the meaning of the Bible is the Bible itself.

STUDYING DIFFERENT GENRES OF BIBLICAL TEXTS

In the Bible we find different literary genres, and it is important to use hermeneutical principles that apply specifically to each one. Here we will mention some of them.

Historical Narrative

In the Scriptures we find a significant amount of narratives—stories told for the edification of the people of God. In many cases reading the stories is easy and enjoyable, but in others the narrative is more challenging. When analyzing a narrative, we should first pay particular attention to the plot of the story. Most stories have a beginning, a development, a climax, and a resolution of the plot. Keeping these elements in mind helps the interpreter to gain a deeper understanding of the narrative.

Second, it is helpful to look carefully for the purpose of the story. The biblical narrator is using the narrative to convey to the readers a particular message or ideology, and this is commonly done through comments made during the telling of the story. For instance, in Genesis 22:1 the narrator (Moses) introduces the narrative by mentioning God's testing of Abraham. This is something that the narrator knows and is sharing with the readers to help them understand the story but that, at this point in the narrative, Abraham does not know. The attentive reader will find here an element of suspense that in fact will run throughout this narrative.

Third, the Bible student will do well to pay particular attention to the characters involved in the plot of the narrative and their specific roles within the account. Some characters remain the same while others change as the story develops, providing clues to readers about the significance of the narrative for their own lives. Sometimes there is an interaction between the good person and the evil one, allowing us to witness a chapter in the cosmic conflict (e.g., Esth. 4–7; Dan. 6). We should keep in mind that sometimes the inspired authors are "omniscient" in the sense that God reveals to them the deepest thoughts and secrets of the characters to help the readers understand the attributes of one of the protagonists.

For instance, in the story of Elisha and his servant Gehazi, the narrator shares the inner dialogue of the servant with himself (2 Kin. 5:20), revealing to us important aspects of the character of Gehazi.

Fourth, in reading the narrative, keep in mind that the narrator is in fact sharing with us the divine perspective with respect to the narrative, its plot, and its characters. The story may be used by the Lord to tell the readers, among many other things, something about true worship, ethical values, correct leadership, or the damaging effects of wickedness. In the process, the narrative is speaking to us by helping us decide whose character reflects ours and what changes, if any, need to be made in our lives.

Parables

Another type of literature that occurs in the Bible is the parable. In a parable a known reality is compared to a lesser-known one in order to share or gain new knowledge and understanding. For instance, Jesus compared the "kingdom of heaven" (something less known to His hearers) with a hidden treasure in a field (something more familiar to them; Matt. 13:44). The task of the interpreter is, first, to look for the purpose of the parable. In general, it could be said that the purpose of a particular parable is to move the listeners or the readers to make decisions for the Lord and to take a stand for what is right. The interpreter should read the parable carefully in order to ascertain the specific divine intention embedded in it. The parable of Lazarus and the Rich Man, based on a well-known story in the time of Jesus (Luke 16:19–31), is used by some to support the belief in the immortality of the soul. The purpose of the parable, however, is to teach that it is in this life that we prepare for life in the kingdom of God; there is not a second chance (Luke 16:29–31). Its purpose is not to teach that the wicked go to Hades and the righteous to heaven.

Second, since parables are usually based on the experience of the original listeners, it is helpful if interpreters are acquainted with what life was like in biblical times. Bible dictionaries are a good source of such information, although a close reading of the parable is in most cases enough to understand it. Third, it is important to remember that not every detail in a parable conveys a particular meaning. We need to read the parable carefully to discern what is meaningful and what is not in order to avoid speculating or reading too much into the use of words, characters, and images. In the parable of the Wise and Foolish Virgins, for example, sellers of oil are mentioned to increase suspense in the parable; it is unnecessary to find a particular figurative meaning for their role (Matt. 25:9).

Types

Sometimes the Bible infuses historical events, institutions, and persons with a future significance that goes beyond their immediate expression or manifestation. These are called *types,* and the fulfillments are *antitypes.* God designed a type to prefigure an eschatological antitypical fulfillment in the ministry and work of Christ. As we will see, the antitype is more encompassing and glorious than the type. In this case, the first question that the interpreter confronts is identifying a type. Here the best rule, based on the principle that the Bible interprets itself, is to allow the Bible to identify the type. The NT writers identify historical events, institutions, and persons that prefigured the work of Christ. If we carefully study the Scriptures, we can find these types. For example, the Exodus from Egypt, a historical event, is identified as a type of the new exodus through Christ (Matt. 2:14-15; 1 Cor. 10:1-5, 11). In the book of Hebrews, the Israelite sanctuary is seen as a type of the heavenly sanctuary (Heb. 8:5; 9:11); the priesthood of the OT, a religious institution, is a type of the priesthood of Christ in the heavenly sanctuary (Heb. 8:1); the sacrificial system was a type of the sacrifice of Christ (Heb. 10:1-4; see also John 1:29). In Romans, Paul identifies Adam (the first human) as a type of Christ, who was the second Adam (Rom. 5:14).

Second, the study of the type and its antitype should reveal a similarity of meaning between the two. For instance, the priests in the OT ministered on behalf of the people, representing God before them and them before God. The antitypical fulfillment in Christ reveals that He is the exclusive mediator between the people and God and between God and the people (Heb. 4:14-16). The foundation of Christ's superiority is located, among others, in the fact that He is divine and human (Heb. 2:14-18). The earthly sanctuary is a type of the real and yet superior heavenly sanctuary (Heb. 9:11-12, 24). In other words, the type cannot stand for something that is absolutely different from it; there is always a connection between type and antitype.

Third, the fulfillment of some types does not necessarily exhaust the meaning of the type, for it may still point to another antitypical fulfillment identified by the Bible itself. The Exodus from Egypt was a type of the redemptive power of the cross of Christ, but it also points to the moment of the Second Coming of Christ when God's people leave this world of sin to be forever with the Lord (Luke 2:15-16; Rev. 15:1-3). The type-antitype correspondence found in the Bible illustrates and confirms the consistency of the divine plan to save humans through divine grace.

For the interpretation of prophecy, apocalyptic prophecy, wisdom literature, poetic literature, and the Gospels and the Epistles, see the corresponding introductory articles in this commentary.

METHODS FOR THE STUDY OF THE SCRIPTURES

In order to take as much advantage as possible in the study of the Bible, we should select a particular way of reading it with some specific goals in mind. There are several ways of doing this.

Book by Book

The first step is to select a particular book for study. At first it may be better to select a short biblical book because a long one, like Isaiah, will take a long time to analyze and could easily discourage the reader. Second, the student should read the book several times, listening to its content, taking notes of passages, and writing down ideas that seem important. It could be that all we want is to get well acquainted with the content and overall message of the book, and such a reading will accomplish that purpose. We may find that some books have a single overriding theme and others have a cluster of theological topics that enrich our spiritual life and mind. Third, it is better to have a specific purpose for the study of a book. For instance, we may study the book of Psalms to find out what it teaches about the sanctuary and its services. We then need to read it to identify and set apart the passages in which the sanctuary, the sacrifices, the priests, and the festivals are mentioned, with the intention of spending more time with such passages. In the book of Proverbs, one could read it pulling together all the passages dealing with the wise or the fool, work, the use of words, or other topics.

Section by Section

If studying a single book requires too much time, then it is better to select a smaller portion of the Bible to study and reflect on. This could be a short narrative, a parable, a section from the NT Epistles or the Gospels, a psalm, or a passage from the prophetic books. The reader would then apply the steps of biblical interpretation discussed above to unpack the divine message found in the text and to apply it to his or her spiritual life. In selecting a portion of the Scriptures for study, we must ensure that we are taking a group of passages that can stand by themselves as a unity. We must then read the context of the passage to establish its extent or simply use the natural divisions of the text as indicated in the versions of the Bible we are studying.

Topical Study

The topical study of the Bible is also very rewarding and will enlarge one's understanding of the biblical text. We have already mentioned thematic studies on specific biblical books. Here the emphasis is on topical studies based in the whole Bible. The purpose is to bring together everything the Bible teaches on a particular subject. This is a good Bible study project that could last for several years. Among the many possible subjects, one could choose God's mercy, divine promises, redemption, salvation, the Messiah, the law, animal life, natural phenomena, family relations, the Sabbath, and the Second Coming. The list of topics can be extensive. When approaching the topic, one has to decide whether to follow the canonical order of the Bible—from Genesis to Revelation—or to start with blocks of books—for example the prophetic books, the Pentateuch, or the Gospels. In any case, it would be better to study the topic first in each specific book of the Bible and then to integrate the findings into a summary.

A useful topical study could consist in exploring what the Bible teaches on the doctrines of the church, taking each doctrine as a topic by itself. In this case, as well as in the study of words, the use of a concordance is significantly useful. A concordance lists all the biblical passages in which a particular subject is mentioned, thus saving the Bible student considerable time. Each passage must be studied within its own context before bringing different passages together. Topical studies reveal the unity of the Bible and the intention of the divine mind for us. The real purpose of these studies is to strengthen our relationship with the Lord and not to satisfy human curiosity. The results of our study should make us humble as we serve others.

We have identified some of the key elements of faithful Bible study. Finally, it is always good to seek the opinion of others who know the Scriptures and to listen to what they may have to say about our interpretation of particular passages. The interpretation of the Bible ultimately is a collective work in which the Spirit is always present in the body of believers. Realizing that the content of the Bible is deeper than any individual can fully comprehend, we should depend on God in a spirit of true humility.

INTERPRETING BIBLICAL APOCALYPTIC PROPHECIES

The term *apocalyptic* comes from the Greek *apokalypsis*, meaning "revelation," "disclosure," "unveiling." It is used in the Greek title of the book of Revelation—*Apokalypsis Ioannou* ("The Apocalypse/Revelation of John"). The term is employed to designate the books of Daniel and Revelation and some Jewish books that are not part of the biblical canon (e.g., Ethiopic Enoch, 4 Ezra, 2–3 Baruch, Apocalypse of Abraham). The term *apocalyptic* is usually employed to refer to a type of literature as well as to a worldview. We will examine both usages and the nature and role of the year-day principle in the interpretation of apocalyptic books of Daniel and Revelation.

NATURE OF APOCALYPTIC PROPHECY

It is not difficult to distinguish biblical narratives, poetic books, the Gospels, and even prophetic books from biblical apocalyptic literature.

First, this type of literature consists of messages from God communicated to the prophet through an angelic mediator, in most cases using visions and/or dreams and incorporating highly complex symbols (e.g., animals, composite beasts, elements from the natural world, time periods).

Second, the content of the prophecy covers the time from the days of the prophet to the very end of history, usually culminating with the kingdom of God, thus providing a brief summary of human history from the divine perspective.

Third, it is common to find in the apocalyptic prophecy long prophetic time periods (e.g., 1,260 days; 42 months; 2,300 days).

Fourth, the prophecies are given in visionary or discourse cycles (e.g., four kingdoms [Dan. 2, 7]; three kingdoms and a little horn [Dan. 8]; seven seals [Rev. 6]; seven trumpets [Rev. 8–9]), recapitulating the content of the previous cycle and enlarging its content with new insights from a new perspective. The parallelism of the content of the cycles is helpful in their interpretation.

Fifth, apocalyptic prophecy reveals God's plans for humanity and consequently is not conditional. In general, biblical prophets functioned within God's covenant with Israel, and their prophecies of judgment or salvation were directly related to the faithfulness or disobedience of the people to the covenant law. The prophecies of judgment would not be fulfilled if the people returned to God as the covenant Lord. Apocalyptic prophecy is based on God's foreknowledge and sovereignty and manifests His unchangeable plan for the resolution of the sin problem.

Sixth, although in nonbiblical apocalypses pseudonyms are used for the authors of the books, in the Bible the prophets who received the revelation are clearly identified—Daniel and John.

WORLDVIEW OF APOCALYPTIC PROPHECY

Apocalyptic prophecy offers to its readers a very specific worldview based on a theological perspective of cosmic proportions. It is a way of interpreting the human predicament and the divine plan to resolve it. We will briefly review some of the most important aspects of apocalyptic thought.

First, it assumes that there is a cosmic struggle between God and evil powers and that this conflict is now taking place in the arena of human history and existence (cf. Dan. 5:18–21; 10:13–14; 12:1–3; Rev. 12:2–4, 10–12). Every person is involved in the conflict and must make a decision concerning allegiance: Who is the true object of worship (cf. Rev. 13:8; 14:7)? In their struggle against God, evil powers misrepresent Him, oppress humans—in particular God's people—and will plan a final attack against God's kingdom.

Second, the resolution of the cosmic conflict includes a final intervention of God in human affairs that will end the corrupted social, political, and religious structures of this world (cf. Dan. 12:1; Rev. 6:12–17). This final manifestation of the power of God will address the very root of the problem, the very source of evil and oppression in the world—Satan and his evil angels—bringing them to an end. God's people are warned against the deceptive power of demons and the miracles they will perform aimed at deceiving God's people and the whole world (cf. Rev. 13:13–14; 17:13–14).

Third, the topic of the final judgment plays a significant role in apocalyptic prophecies (cf. Dan. 7:9–10, 26–27; Rev. 14:7; 20:11–15). The resolution of the problem of evil will not be the result of evil simply destroying itself. Neither will it be an arbitrary, vindictive action on God's part. Rather, it will be the result of a cosmic judgment. In the resolution of the problem, God's justice and love will prevail. In that judgment, objective evidence will be presented and analyzed that will demonstrate beyond any doubt that it is right to remove from the universe the disturbing and menacing presence of evil powers.

Fourth, in apocalyptic prophecies the presence of a mediator before God, in His heavenly dwelling, plays a key role in the deliverance of the saints and the restoration of cosmic harmony. This mediator Figure, the Messiah/Christ, ministers on behalf of God's people during the final judgment and condemns all evil powers to eternal extinction. Consequently, the heavenly sanctuary and the throne of God, as the center of divine government in the universe, are constantly in view (e.g., Dan. 8:10–14; Rev. 8:2–5; 11:19; 13:6; 15:8; 16:1; 21:3). It is there that the final resolution of the cosmic controversy will be determined on the basis of the experience of the sacrificial sufferings of the Messiah as the Lamb of God (cf. Dan. 9:26; Rev. 5:6, 9–10).

Fifth, apocalyptic thought operates within a particular understanding of history, according to which history is moving toward a specific goal preestablished by God (cf. Dan. 2:20–21; Rev. 4:1; 17:17; 21:1). The divine plan develops within the flow of time, and this is indicated by the use of prophetic time periods and the symbolic description of the events that will take place within those periods. This segmentation of history encourages the people of God in that they are able to locate themselves within the flow of history from the perspective of apocalyptic expectation. They are also able to observe God's constant activity within history as the different signs of His coming are manifested. The particular view of history found in apocalyptic thought emphasizes a strong view of divine sovereignty. There is nothing human beings or evil powers can do to alter God's plan for His people or His determination to extinguish evil and evil powers from His universe. Because of this important element, apocalyptic prophecies are not conditional. The coming of the Messiah at the end of the seventy weeks happened as God intended it to happen; the kingdoms of Babylon, Medo-Persia, and Greece have fallen; the fourth kingdom was divided, and so forth. God in His sovereignty expressed His will toward the kingdoms of this world, and that cannot be altered or defeated by any of His creatures. In God's foreknowledge He has predicted the development of historical events and determined in advance the final destiny of history and of those who will join the Lord or the forces of evil. The call to repentance found in biblical apocalyptic literature indicates that everyone must decide by himself or herself which of the two destinies, determined by God, he or she will choose.

Finally, apocalyptic thought projects itself into the distant future and depicts for us the final restoration of cosmic harmony (cf. Dan. 2:44; 7:26–27; Rev. 21). The peace and perfect harmony instituted by God in our world during Creation week are fully restored. In Christian apocalyptic literature this is initiated by the return in glory of the Messiah to consummate the salvation He obtained for all at the cross. At that time His people will be liberated from the presence and power of sin in their own existence and a new environment will be provided for them where they will be freed from the presence of evil.

Although apocalyptic thought contains pessimistic elements, it is fundamentally positive in its outlook. It is characterized by hope. If there is any pessimism, it is related to the inescapable judgment against social, political, and apostate religious institutions. They are described as instruments of oppression employed by evil powers to persecute the people of God. The condition of these institutions and of those who support them is such that they are all totally corrupted. God can only exterminate them. But such extermination has the purpose of creating a new world free from the oppressing presence of evil powers, in which God's people will be able to achieve their most cherished dreams in the company of loved ones, their Redeemer, and their God. Apocalyptic thought is, therefore, optimistic and hopeful, and points to a future of joy and glory rather than sadness and darkness.

HISTORICISM

In the interpretation of Daniel and Revelation scholars have used various methods. Today the prevailing methods are *futurism* and *preterism* (see Daniel: Introduction). Preterists generally date Daniel to the second century B.C. and consider the content of the book to be historical accounts given in the guise of prophecy (the technical phrase is *vaticinia ex eventu* or "prophecies [given] after the event"). In other words, an anonymous writer in the second century B.C. relates the historical events that occurred from the sixth century to the second century as though his writings are predictions made in the sixth century by a prophet called Daniel. Similarly, they teach that the book of Revelation is not about the future of the church but about events that had already taken place in the church's experience during the first century A.D. Futurists generally date Daniel to the sixth century B.C. but do not interpret the antichrist as the papacy. They apply it to a personal antichrist who will appear after the rapture of the church for a period of three and a half years before the Second Coming of Christ. They believe that from Revelation 4:1 onward the prophecies of the book are about the future to be fulfilled after the rapture of the church during seven years prior to the Second Coming. Both of these methods, with some variances, were formulated by Catholic interpreters to oppose the Reformers' understanding of the apocalyptic prophecies as anticipating the rise of apostate Christianity during the Middle Ages.

Adventists use the *historicist* approach because they are persuaded that this is the methodology that the biblical text itself provides for us. Historicists believe that Daniel, as the book itself demonstrates, was written in the sixth century B.C. by the prophet Daniel. They also believe that God has full knowledge of the future and that He can reveal to His prophets events that will take place in the distant future. This is clearly found in Daniel, who received from God a sketch of major historical events that will take place from the time of the prophet to the time when God's kingdom will be established on earth.

Witness of Daniel

When we examine the book of Daniel, it is obvious that the book is to be interpreted along the lines of historicism. In Daniel 2, neither the king nor Daniel knew how to interpret the dream. It is through a divine revelation that Daniel gains a full understanding of it. He indicates to the king that the dream is about what God will do in the time of the end (Dan. 2:28). The different parts of the image are interpreted as representing kingdoms, beginning with the kingdom of Babylon, represented by its king (v. 38). There will be four kingdoms and then at the latter days God will establish His everlasting kingdom (v. 44). Three of the four kingdoms will be identified by the angel interpreter as Babylon, Medo-Persia (cf. 5:30–31; 8:20), and Greece (8:21), and Jesus will indicate that the fourth is Rome (see Matt. 24:15–16; cf. Luke 21:20).

In Daniel 7 we have the same sequence of four kingdoms, represented by four beasts (v. 17), and the establishment of the kingdom of God (v. 18), but new information is added relating to the ten horns of the fourth beast and its little horn. The angel clarifies that the fourth kingdom (Rome) will be divided and then the little horn (the historical antichrist) will arise. The approach to the interpretation of the prophecy that we found in Daniel 2 is also the approach used by the angel interpreter to clarify the vision in Daniel 7. Again, this is the case in Daniel 8 where the ram and the goat represent Medo-Persia and Greece, respectively, and the little horn stands primarily for what happened after the division of the Roman Empire. In other words, we are dealing with prophecies that cover a significant amount of history and that will require long periods of time for their fulfillment.

Witness of Jesus and Paul

In Matthew 24 Jesus announces what will take place from the time of the destruction of Jerusalem to the moment of His Second Coming, following the pattern of apocalyptic prophecies found in Daniel. He specifically refers to the prophecy of Daniel 9, the destruction of the city announced by the prophet, and places it in the future (Dan. 9:15–16), connecting it to the Romans. The same approach is used by Paul in 2 Thessalonians 2:1–10 when discussing the coming of the antichrist predicted by Daniel. According to Paul, a number of historical events will take place before the coming of Christ, and he concentrates on the figure of the antichrist. For him, aspects of the prophecy of Daniel have not yet been fulfilled, but they will be fulfilled in the future before the Second Coming of Christ.

Witness of John

John uses the same approach found in Daniel. The best example is Revelation 12, where we can identify a sequence of events from the first century to the final attack against the remnant. The vision begins with the coming of the Messiah as a child, includes the attempt of the dragon to destroy Him (Rev. 12:4), His ascension to heaven (v. 5), and His ultimate sovereignty over the nations (v. 5). The experience of the dragon begins with his rebellion in heaven (vv. 7–8) and moves to the earth where he enters into conflict with the Messiah. This is followed by his attack against the church for 1,260 days and concludes with his final attack against the remnant (v. 17). The people of God are represented by a woman expecting the birth of the Messiah and who, after the ascension of the Messiah, becomes the object of attack of the dragon. At the time of the end, the dragon prepares to oppose God's remnant. The progression is clear: the arrival of the Messiah is followed by the historical period of the Christian church; the dragon persecutes the Christian church but is unable to destroy it; and at the time of the end there is an eschatological remnant threatened by the dragon (Rev. 12:17; 13:14–15), who will be defeated again at the return of Christ (cf. Rev. 17:14). The prophecy moves from the time of Jesus to the moment of the Second Coming, covering a long period of history that outlines the experience of the church within the cosmic conflict.

Witness of the Early Church and the Reformation

The historicist method was used by some of the early church fathers to interpret the prophecies of Daniel. Some of them identified the fourth beast as Rome, the ten horns as the division of the empire, and the little horn as the future antichrist. The approach was used by the early church fathers up to the fifth century A.D., at which time a significant shift in prophetic interpretation took place when Augustine spiritualized the millennium, making it a symbol of the Christian era (amillennialism). It was the Reformers who restored historicism as the method to be used in the interpretation of Daniel and Revelation and identified the papacy as a manifestation of the antichrist predicted in these books.

As already indicated, it was the Counter-Reformation that developed a new system of prophetic interpretation that came to be known as preterism. This method was developed by a Spanish Jesuit named Luis de Alcazar (died A.D. 1613). Preterism was later adopted by some Protestants and became the prevailing method of apocalyptic prophetic interpretation among critical scholars. Futurism, also of Catholic origin, is used by most dispensationalists.

Limitations of Historicism

Probably the main challenge historicists confront is identifying the historical events represented in the apocalyptic prophecies. In Daniel we find historical applications as part of the revelatory experience. The angel interpreter tells the prophet that four kingdoms will rise on earth and the fifth one will be the kingdom of God. As we indicated, three of those are identified in Daniel (Babylon, Medo-Persia, Greece) and the fourth by Jesus. As long as we follow the biblical text, we are on safe ground. But we still have other symbols not interpreted by the angel, such as the ten horns, the little horn, the beast from the sea, the beast from the earth, and Babylon (Rev. 13). How are we to identify the prophetic fulfillment of these symbols? Herein lies the challenge.

We can speak with certainty only in terms of the broad outline of the history depicted in those prophecies. Which controls should we use to identify that broad outline? We have to move from what is clearly revealed in the prophecies themselves to what is left historically undefined. It is useful, first, to pay particular attention to the chronology of events described in the prophecy itself. Second, it is also necessary to examine historical events, taking into consideration the prophetic line of thought and its historical perspective.

In Daniel 7 we find the most important outline of apocalyptic prophecy in both Daniel and Revelation. The prophetic backbone found there, together with the explanations given by the angel interpreter, provide the indispensable historical outline or skeleton to be used in fitting other apocalyptic prophecies and their fulfillment within history. The angel interpreter explains to Daniel that there will be four important kingdoms: Babylon, Medo-Persia, Greece, and a fourth one. This fourth one will be divided into many smaller kingdoms, but a particular horn (kingdom) will establish itself as the most influential one. This little horn is a political and also a religious power that opposes God and His people. It will exercise its power for 1,260 days, and at the end of that period the heavenly court will sit to judge (i.e., vindicate) God's people and to bring the power of the little horn to an end. After that, the kingdom of God will be established on earth.

YEAR-DAY PRINCIPLE

One of the interesting and even enigmatic characteristics of apocalyptic prophecies is the inclusion of long periods of time within the prophecies themselves. We read about time, times, and half a time (Dan. 7:25; 12:7; Rev. 12:14); 1,260 days (Rev. 11:3; 12:6); 42 months (Rev. 11:2; 13:5); 2,300 evenings/mornings or days (Dan. 8:14); 1,290 days (Dan. 12:11); and 1,335 days (Dan. 12:12). Historicist interpreters, utilizing the year-day principle, have taken these time periods to be symbolic for years. The Bible provides enough evidence to support the use of this principle.

Day Stands for Year

It is a common practice in poetic literature to use the term *day* in parallel with the word *year*, making these terms synonymous (Job 36:11; Pss. 77:11; 78:33; 90:15). In these verses *days* and *years* refer to the same general time period. But there are cases in which the Hebrew has the specific number of years of a person also designated as days (Gen. 5:5; see also vv. 8, 11, 14, 17, 20, 27, 31). In the case of Genesis 5:5, the days stand for 930 years.

Day-Year in an Early Prophecy

Interestingly, we find a correlation of days and years in the first-time prophecy recorded in the Bible (Gen. 6:3). No specific number of days is explicitly given, but instead we are told the specific number of years that the use of the term *days* intended to communicate. *Days* stand for the number of years granted by God to the antediluvians as probationary time. We can easily detect here the foundation of what later will become the year-day principle in apocalyptic prophecies. This last usage, together with the previous one, indicates that it was natural for the Hebrews to use the two terms interchangeably in their daily speech.

Cases of Year-Day Principle

There are some cases outside apocalyptic prophecies where we can see days being clearly and intentionally used to designate years. The first case is found in the law of the sabbatical year (Lev. 25:1–7). During the seventh year the land will rest, that is to say it will enjoy a Sabbath rest. The law is modeled after the regular week with its literal seventh-day Sabbath rest, but the sabbatical rest does not stand for a literal day but for a full year (Lev. 25:4–5). Both the weekly Sabbath and the sabbatical year were referred to by the same terms (Lev. 23:3; 25:4–5). The clear implication of the sabbatical legislation is that a day can represent a year.

Even closer to the point is Leviticus 25:8, concerning the day of Jubilee. Each day of the week is equated to a year, including the Sabbath, which stands for the seventh year. The Jubilee is calculated using the principle that a day stands for a year resulting in a period of seven years that are to be counted seven times bringing the total to forty-nine years. In order to arrive at the date for the Jubilee, the seven days of a week are to be interpreted as years (see Dan. 9:24–27). A future event is to be dated using the year-day principle.

Another passage in which the year-day principle is present is Numbers 14:34. This is a prophecy of judgment against rebellious Israelites. The forty days the spies spent exploring the land are used to determine the number of years the people will have to bear their sins. The same terminology is used in Ezekiel 4:4–6, when the Lord commands the prophet to lie on his two sides for a total of 430 days. The days are then identified as the years of grace the Lord granted the people before the destruction of the city and the experience of the Exile. The language used is very clear: "a day for each year." Although these cases are not found in apocalyptic prophecies, they provide the biblical background needed to justify identifying the use of the year-day principle in apocalyptic prophecies.

Symbolism of Apocalyptic Prophecies

The symbolism of the prophetic time periods is contextually supported by the abundant presence of apocalyptic symbols. For instance, human kingdoms are represented by metals (Dan. 2:31–33), animals (Dan. 7:3–7; 8:3–7; Rev. 13:1, 11), or horns (Dan. 7:8; 8:8–9; Rev. 17:12). The people of God are depicted as a pure woman (Rev. 12:1), while the false people of God are represented by the symbol of a prostitute (Rev. 17:4). Jesus is the Lamb (Rev. 6:1; cf. 5:5), and Satan is a dragon (Rev. 12:9). There is no question that apocalyptic prophecy is by definition rich in the use of symbols. Even the use of smaller numbers is usually interpreted as representing something other than literal numbers. For instance, seven is the number of completion or perfection; four stands for the universal; ten expresses completeness; and twelve is taken to represent the diversity of the people of God. It is within the context of the use of symbols that large prophetic time periods are introduced and discussed.

Even the language used to refer to prophetic time periods suggests a symbolic usage of the periods. For instance, the phrase "a time, [and] times, and half a time" (Dan. 7:25) cannot be taken as designating a literal three and a half years because the natural biblical way of expressing that literal time period is three years and six months (Luke 4:25; James 5:17; cf. 2 Sam. 2:11; Acts 8:11). Particularly interesting is that in apocalyptic prophecies days, weeks, and months are mentioned but not years. Symbolically the day stands for the year. Within the specific symbolic context of the time periods, it is hermeneutically sound, even required, to interpret the large time periods as symbolic. It is also hermeneutically sound to use the year-day principle to interpret the large numbers because it is, as we have demonstrated, a principle provided by the Bible itself.

Self-Authentication of the Year-Day Principle

The application of the year-day principle to apocalyptic prophecies is not a decision arbitrarily made by the interpreter, but one that flows from and is authenticated by the prophecy itself. For instance, as we have indicated, the apocalyptic discussion of four kingdoms leading to the kingdom of God covers the time from the days of the prophet to the end of sinful human history at the Second Coming of Christ. The time period of 1,260 days that covers the history of the little horn, representing apostate Christianity during the Middle Ages and the struggles of the dragon against God's people during that same time (Dan 7:25; Rev. 12:6), could not designate literal days but years (A.D. 538–1798), as the history of the Christian church shows.

The self-authentication of the year-day principle is most clearly manifested in the apocalyptic prophecy of Daniel 8 (see commentary on Dan. 8:1–27). Daniel received a vision (Dan. 8:1; Heb. *khazon*) from the Lord that covered the time period from the Persian Empire to the time of Papal Rome. The question is asked, "How long will the vision [*khazon*] be?"—that is to say, how long will it take for the whole vision to be fulfilled. Daniel is told that it will take 2,300 evenings and mornings and then the sanctuary would be *nitsdaq* (lit. "justified," variously translated as "cleansed" [LXX], "restored," or "reconsecrated"; Dan.

8:14). A literal reading of the time period would not cover such a long historical period and, therefore, would not be a correct answer to the question asked in the text. The prophecy itself indicates that the year-day principle is operative and that it is required of the interpreter to use the principle in order to correctly understand it.

The self-authentication of the year-day principle is also found in Daniel 9:24–27 (see commentary on Dan. 9:24–27). The interpreter angel tells Daniel that from the going out of the decree (lit. "word") to restore and rebuild Jerusalem (in 457 B.C.) until the coming of the Messiah ("the Anointed"), the Prince Ruler (A.D. 27), there would be seven weeks and sixty-two weeks, plus another week during which the Messiah will die (A.D. 31), for a total of seventy weeks (ending in A.D. 34). It is obvious that the prophecy is using the year-day principle because it requires for its fulfillment a span of hundreds of years. Some translate the Hebrew word for week (*shabua´*) as "sevens (of years)" and interpret it to refer to literal time (seven years in each week), thus practically excluding the use of the year-day principle. The weakness in this approach is that this word *shabua´* never means "seven"; it means "week." Besides, the prophetic period in Daniel is based on the sabbatical year and the Jubilee, according to which each day of the week represents a year. Therefore, the seventy weeks stand for a period of 490 days/years.

What we have seen in our discussion is that the year-day principle is solidly based on the Scriptures and that the Lord employed it in the revelations He gave to Daniel. The long historical span covered by the visions demonstrates that the principle was operative in them, thus self-authenticating its presence in the visions.

Year-Day Principle in History

As far as we can tell, apart from the Bible itself, the earliest evidence for the year-day principle can be found in the *Book of Jubilees*, a Jewish work from the intertestamental period, dated to the second century B.C. It uses the word *week* to refer to seven years. Each period of seven years is referred to as a week of years or simply as a week. The seventh of such "weeks of years" (i.e., the forty-ninth year) is designated as a Jubilee year.

A number of other Jewish sources also interpret the expression *seventy weeks* in Daniel 9:24 to mean 490 years (seventy weeks of years). They count seventy years from the destruction of the first temple to the restoration of the temple under Darius (Hag. 1:1–8) and another 420 years to the destruction of the second temple. This adds up to 490 years, although these figures do not harmonize with the actual dates in history (586 B.C. to A.D. 70).

Some church fathers who wrote commentaries on the book of Daniel interpreted it along historicist lines with Rome as the fourth power in Daniel 2 and 7. The seventy weeks in Daniel 9:24 were seen as 490 years, but the time prophecies in Daniel 7, 8, and 12 were placed as literal days either in the past, in the time of the Roman emperors, or in the future, in the time of the final antichrist. They did not yet have a clear understanding of the time periods, probably because they could not anticipate the passing of hundreds of years before the coming of Christ. The year-day principle, therefore, did not play an important role in the early centuries, though it was not unknown.

The first Christian interpreter to apply the year-day principle outside of the seventy weeks was probably Tichonius (late fourth century) from North Africa, who interpreted the three and a half days of the slaying of the witnesses (Rev. 11:11) to be three and a half years. Following Tichonius, we find throughout church history a number of Jewish and Christian interpreters who used the year-day principle, including Benjamin ben Moses Nahawendi (mid-ninth century), Joachim of Floris (A.D. 1130–1202), and Protestant Reformer Philipp Melanchthon (A.D. 1497–1560). But during the eighteenth and nineteenth centuries, at the time when the 1,260-, 1,290-, 1,335-, and 2,300-day prophecies were being fulfilled, the number of interpreters who used the year-day principle increased enormously (cf. Dan. 12:4).

Babylon

Medo-Persia

Greece

Rome

Division
of Rome

Little Horn
(1,260 days/years)

Judgment

**Kingdom
of God**

APOCALYPTIC HISTORICAL CHRONOLOGY

The angel interpreter does not identify the historical entities represented by the fourth kingdom or the little horn. It is at this point that we move from the known to the unknown, to the dangerous zone of human speculation. Finding proper controls is not impossible. The best we can do is to use the same procedure employed by the angel. It is obvious that in the historical outline he provided for us he was describing the succession of ancient empires. The one that destroyed the previous kingdom established itself as the new kingdom. Therefore, we can use that same idea to identify the fourth kingdom: the kingdom that overcame Greece and established itself as the new kingdom was Rome. In our identification of the fourth beast, we have simply followed the same procedure employed by the angel interpreter to identify the historical powers represented by the three previous beasts.

Our interpretation of the fourth kingdom is supported by the NT, particularly by Jesus, who, as indicated already, suggested that the fourth kingdom was Rome. Consequently, the horns would represent the division of the Roman Empire. What about the little horn? Already in around A.D. 200, Hippolytus interpreted the fourth beast as the Roman Empire and the little horn as the antichrist. Christian interpreters early in the Christian era continued to use the system of interpretation employed by the angel interpreter to identify the historical fulfillment of apocalyptic prophecies. This was also done by the Reformers. Adventists locate themselves within this approach to the interpretation of apocalyptic prophecies. We also keep in mind that we begin to gain a better understanding of the fulfillment of these prophecies after they are fulfilled. Nevertheless, such prophecies should be studied because they are a revelation from God to His church to guide it and to nurture hope while waiting for the return of the Lord.

CONCLUSION

Today historicism is not the predominant method used by scholars interpreting apocalyptic prophecies. Rationalism's rejection of divine intervention in human affairs, and of God's willingness to reveal to His prophets events that will occur in the distant future, has had a major impact on Christian theology. Liberal theologians prefer to find in Daniel and Revelation the situation of the people of God when the books were written, thus eliminating their predictive role. Our study shows that historicism is the only valid approach to apocalyptic prophecy simply because this is the method that the Bible itself offers. It accepts that Daniel was written in the sixth century B.C. and that there is such a thing as predictive prophecy that covers the whole span of time from the days of the prophet to the establishment of the kingdom of God. One of the key components of this hermeneutical focus is the year-day principle. The biblical evidence in favor of this principle is clear and decisive and is presupposed by the apocalyptic books themselves. In fact, these books authenticate the principle itself.

FAITH AND SCIENCE

Much has been written about the relationship between faith and science as two different ways of determining what is true. Authors generally agree that the question is important, but they often come to radically different conclusions in trying to construct an answer. What is it about the topic of faith and science that generates such different responses? There are several reasons, one of which can be seen by comparing their definitions.

FAITH AND SCIENCE: DEFINITIONS AND SCOPE

Faith

Christian faith is confident trust in God and His word demonstrated by action. Abraham is often used as an example of faith (Heb. 11:8–12). When God called Abraham to leave his home for an unknown location, he revealed his faith by obeying and leaving (Gen. 12:1, 4). When God called on Abraham to sacrifice his son Isaac as a burnt offering, he revealed his faith by laying Isaac on the altar. God intervened to spare Abraham the grief of losing his son and commended him for demonstrating his complete trust in God's word.

A combination of factors contribute to developing trust in Scripture. One factor is the appeal to our intellect. Fulfilled prophecy, archeological confirmation of biblical historical details, and internal consistency all contribute to increase one's confidence in the reliability of Scripture (e.g., John 13:19). A second factor is actual life experience. We may have found God's word trustworthy in the past. This may include events in our lives such as perceived acts of providence, answered prayers, and changed habits (e.g., John 10:38). These two factors are important in building our faith, but they are incomplete on their own. The internal testimony of the Holy Spirit impresses us of the truths of the Bible and solidifies our faith. Thus, faith is a divine gift (Eph. 2:10; John 16:13).

A key aspect of faith is that it goes beyond any direct evidence. Empirical evidence plays an indirect role here by establishing the credibility of the source on which faith rests, but faith extends that confidence to instances beyond the empirical evidence. People of faith choose to believe what the Bible says about the physical world because they have found Scripture to be reliable in their personal experience. Their conclusion may be corroborated by the experiences of other believers, adding to their confidence.

Science

Philosophers of science have been unable to provide a universally satisfactory definition of science, although most people have a fairly good idea of what it is. Two definitions of science are commonly used. Historically, science has been understood broadly as the search to understand how the world works. Using this definition, science could include almost any systematized body of knowledge, regardless of its philosophical underpinnings.

On the other hand, many scientists prefer to define science more narrowly, as a systematic search for the physical mechanisms that produce the regularities observed in the natural world, ideally expressed in mathematical terms. This definition gives science an implicitly atheistic approach, since it rejects any reference to God or any other supernatural agent. The exclusion of God from science is commonly called *methodological naturalism*.

Methodological naturalism does not necessarily require a denial of God's existence, but it does imply that everything in nature can be explained without reference to God. In effect, there is no difference between methodological naturalism and philosophical materialism in the practice of science. The naturalistic bias of science narrowly defined is a key factor in its tension with faith.

The legitimate scope of science depends on which of the two definitions is intended. Science defined narrowly applies to a more restricted scope of inquiry. This type of science is properly applied to events that follow frequently observed regularities in nature. Science that considers only physical mechanisms still in operation today will never find a true explanation for one-time events (miracles, singularities) caused by supernatural agents. Supernatural actions, by definition, are beyond the scope of this type of science.

In contrast, science defined in a general sense as an attempt to understand the world through systematic study can be applied to any aspect of reality that is accessible to human investigation. No potential explanation is excluded *a priori*, leaving the investigator open to any rational explanation, including the possibility of divine activity.

Role of Faith in Science

Faith is often considered strictly a religious idea, and indeed, faith is at the core of Christian belief and practice. It is impossible to please God without faith (Heb. 11:6). Trust is a necessary part of everyday life. Everyone has to act in situations where empirical evidence is incomplete. We may trust that another person is acting "in good faith," meaning we believe the person will honor his or her word, even when there is no written contract. We trust that our automobile will carry us to an appointment on time, even though we know there is a risk involved. Trust, or faith, cannot operate without risk, but it is a calculated risk where the perceived likelihood of failure is low enough to justify the action. Thus, faith in a generic sense is not strictly a religious idea but rather a universal experience that is present in all human activities.

Science is often considered superior to Christian faith because its claims are supposedly objective and verifiable by anyone with the proper training and equipment. Materialists often criticize faith because it is based on personal experience and cannot be independently verified. This perception is not entirely true, because many Christians have reported similar faith experiences, such as a sense of the divine presence, unexplained providences, and answered prayers. However, it is true that specific personal experience cannot be shared by another person.

Ironically, the situation in science is similar. No scientist can "share the experience" by personally verifying every scientific report. We tend to accept specific conclusions of scientists because other conclusions have so often been corroborated. This gives us confidence in science, and rightly so, but our confidence should be informed by times in the history of scientific revolutions when what everyone "knew" to be true turned out to be false or, at best, incomplete (see "Examples of Faith and Science in Tension," p. 61). In this sense, our understandings of both science and faith are subject to limitations in our ability to personally confirm the claims made by others.

The distinction between faith and science is not the presence or absence of empirical evidence, but the role of different types of evidence in drawing conclusions. Empirical evidence is also valued by faith. The Apostle John appealed to empirical evidence from his own experience as the basis for his testimony (1 John 1:1–3). However, science insists on clear physical evidence, whereas faith goes beyond the physical evidence to trusting God's word.

Reason

Reason is the use of our intellect to evaluate the logical and empirical implications of a statement, observation, or experience. A common misconception is the claim that conflict between faith and science is really a conflict between reason (science) and blind belief (Christian faith).

It is true that one cannot reason one's way to faith, any more than one can discover scientific truth purely by reason, but reason is necessary for both faith and science. We use our reason when we accept that what someone tells us is true because we have confidence in that person, even when we have no other evidence of the truth of the particular facts we are told by that person. We apply our reason as we evaluate the sometimes-conflicting claims of different sources of knowledge. It is incorrect to claim that reason is applied in science but not in faith. In both cases, we use our reason to analyze our experience, either with Scripture or with science or with both. Reason is absolutely necessary, although not sufficient, in both endeavors.

Misuse/Distortions

Both faith and science can be misused. One misuse of faith is to assume that God is acting directly in nature solely on the basis of our lack of explanations for various phenomena. This is called the *God-of-the-gaps fallacy*. Although now infrequently encountered, this has been a problem in the past. For example, the ancients did not know how blood flowed from the arteries to the veins. This lack of knowledge was used as a basis to conclude that God somehow miraculously guided the blood. When capillaries were discovered to connect the arteries and the veins, the idea that God was guiding the blood was discarded. As scientific knowledge increased, this type of experience was repeated several times until scholars discounted the whole idea of God acting directly in nature. As a result, He virtually disappeared from science.

Science also may be misused. The success of science in refuting many erroneous beliefs and discovering many aspects of nature has led some to extrapolate its successes far beyond the evidence. Some scholars claim science is the only way to obtain knowledge. This idea is known as *scientism*, and it is widely accepted in modern society, sometimes without awareness of its implications. Scientism is logically self-contradictory because the claim that there are no supernatural events is based not on scientific evidence but on a philosophical commitment to exclude God.

FAITH AND SCIENCE IN HISTORY

Faith and science are frequently regarded as hostile to each other, but the conflict is often overstated. In the history of modern science, many of the pioneers of science openly interpreted their scientific inquiries as attempts to understand how God acts in the world. At present, science is dominated by a materialistic bias, but this has not always been the case, nor is it necessary.

Most branches of modern science were founded by scientists of Christian faith. John Ray (1627–1705), considered the father of modern biology, chose to title his book *The Wisdom of God Manifested in the Works of Creation*. In this book Ray described the features of living organisms as evidence of God's actions in designing the creation.

Isaac Newton (1642–1726), probably the most influential scientist in history, made significant contributions to physics, mathematics, and other areas. It is said that Newton wrote more about the Bible than about science, but Newton's Christian faith did not interfere with his science. Robert Boyle (1627–1691), the father of modern chemistry, was a devout Christian who established a series of lectures dedicated to the study of God's handiwork in nature. Other pioneering scientists who regarded science as the study of God's works include Johannes Kepler, Blaise Pascal, Michael Faraday, James Clerk Maxwell, William Thompson (Lord Kelvin), Gregor Mendel, Antonie van Leewenhoek, and many others.

Science has contributed greatly to faith by expanding our knowledge of God's creation. Scripture tells us that God is all-powerful and all-knowing, but science has illustrated these points in ways that we would otherwise have no way of discovering. For example, scientific discoveries of the immense size and finely tuned structure of the universe have improved our understanding of God's infinite power and wisdom exercised in creating and sustaining it. Scientific discoveries of the astounding complexity of even the "simplest" living organism have increased our appreciation for God's engineering genius. Scientific discoveries of the fitness of our world for sustaining human life have added to our appreciation of His wonderful providence in designing an environment in which we can survive and thrive. These examples illustrate that science and faith can cooperate in productive partnership.

It should be emphasized that much, probably most, of science does not conflict at all with Christian faith. Instead, the two sources of knowledge are widely complementary. For example, there is no conflict over the physical constants of the universe, the structure of the atom, the principles of chemistry, cellular and organismal anatomy and physiology, ecological relationships, and a host of other aspects of science. There is no conflict between Christian faith and scientific experiments, except when the experiment is unethical, such as some experimentation on humans.

EXAMPLES OF FAITH AND SCIENCE IN TENSION

Some of the most dramatic examples of conflict between faith and science have come as the result of the corruption of faith by the incorporation of ideas from science that everyone "knew" at the time but that turned out to be incorrect. Probably the most famous examples of conflict between faith and science are the conflicts over a geocentric universe and the fixity of species.

Galileo and the Solar System

The experience of Galileo (and, by implication, Copernicus) is widely used as an example of what happens to faith when it opposes science, with the implication that faith must retreat in the face of science. There is an important lesson in this story, but it is quite different from the one usually proposed. The Galileo story is not nearly as simplistic as is sometimes claimed. There was indeed a conflict involving Galileo and some church leaders, but it was complicated by Galileo's abrasive attitude and intemperate language and the fact that his arguments were not that compelling and included some errors. There were scientists and theologians on both sides of the debate. Nevertheless, it is true that the Catholic Church was embroiled in the conflict and suffered a great loss of prestige as a result.

What is often overlooked is how the church got into that situation initially. Biblical texts are often invoked to claim that the Bible teaches a geocentric universe. However, the true origin of that idea comes from the Greek philosophers, whose ideas were organized and systematized about A.D. 150 by Ptolemy in Alexandria, Egypt. The geocentric system is known as the Ptolemaic system because Ptolemy systematized the thinking of previous philosophers into the theory that bears his name. In attempting to show that science confirms the Bible, early church fathers incorporated this Greek idea into their theology. Texts that use phenomenological words (describing an event in the language of appearance) were interpreted as literal descriptions of proven scientific reality. We still use phenomenological language when we refer to "sunrise" and "sunset," describing them as they appear, although we know that the earth's turning on its axis only creates the appearance.

Ironically, modern astrophysics tells us that any point, including the earth, can be taken as the center of the universe, as it is all relative. The advantage of taking the sun rather than the earth to be the center of the solar system is that the mathematics are much simpler.

The real lesson we need to learn from the Galileo incident is that it is inappropriate to incorporate scientific conclusions into our theology, even when "everyone knows they are true." Science is tentative, and scientific conclusions should never be given the status of biblical truths because it is likely the science will change in the future and leave the person of faith embarrassed.

Darwin and the Fixity of Species

The second example from history of a conflict between faith and science is the matter of the fixity of species. This came to the forefront with the work of Charles Darwin, who proposed that species are not fixed, contrary to what he was taught in his theology course at Cambridge. Instead, species can change and adapt to different habitats. Darwin's observations made a solid case that species can change. Unfortunately, he extrapolated the potential degree of change far beyond the evidence. The ensuing conflict with Christian faith continues to this day, and many Christians have abandoned the Creation story and accepted some form of Darwin's ideas of common ancestry. Again, the church was embarrassed in its conflict with "science."

One may ask how the church got into this predicament. Where did the idea come from that species cannot change? The answer, again, is that the idea came from the ancient Greeks, specifically from Plato's ideas of unchanging "types," further developed by Neoplatonic thinkers. Once more, church leaders took a secular, Greek idea that "everyone knew was true" and incorporated it into their theology. When science advanced and showed that the ancient Greeks were wrong, the church was wrong by association. As with the Galileo incident, the important lesson here is to resist attempts to incorporate "scientific" ideas that "everyone knows are true" into Christian theology. No scientific idea should be regarded as absolute; there is always a likelihood science will change.

CONTEMPORARY ISSUES IN FAITH AND SCIENCE

God and Nature

As already noted, Christian faith affirms that God actively created the universe, our world, and all that exists, continues to maintain its existence, and occasionally acts to accomplish specific purposes. In contrast, modern science generally endorses *methodological naturalism*, which is the claim that science can discover how nature works without any reference to God or any other supernatural agent. According to this thinking, the laws of nature are fixed, and if God acts in nature, He is constrained to follow natural law, and this means all events in nature can be explained by the "fixed laws of nature."

These differences between the presuppositions of faith and of science play out mainly in questions of origins and other events identified biblically as miraculous. The contemporary issues of greatest significance are the questions of deep time, the nature of humans, and intelligent design.

Deep Time

Those who postulate production of living organisms by natural law realize this is highly improbable and cannot be expected to occur without immense periods of time and vast numbers of chance events. Long ages of time are needed in hopes they can somehow fill the gap in natural law. George Wald, a Nobel-prize-winning chemist, noted the dependence on long ages of time for the materialistic origin of life, arguing that what humans consider impossible to happen in the natural world will happen if given enough time (two billion years). According to him, time performs miracles. But the logic of the statement does not work when the event is in fact impossible, and the origin of life by natural processes is, by all available evidence, truly impossible.

Scientists have searched for methods of measuring the expected long ages of time needed by materialistic science. They believe they have found such a method in the system of radioisotope dating. Radioisotope dating is based on the observation that certain atoms (radioactive isotopes) are unstable and break down by nuclear reactions to form a different kind of atom. The rate at which this breakdown occurs can be expressed in a mathematical formula, and the amount of time required for any specific amount of material to break down can be calculated. The amount of material thought to have broken down can be precisely measured in rocks. The results of such calculations are interpreted to show that different kinds of plants and animals have existed at different times of earth history, extending over a period exceeding 500 million years.

Creationists hold a different view of God's activity in nature. Because of God's supernatural power and intelligence, He can accomplish His purposes without any constraint of time. Scripture describes the creation of our world and its inhabitants within a single week of time. This is no problem for God, because He created nature and its laws. He is not limited by the laws of nature but uses them to accomplish His purposes in any period of time He chooses.

Because the Creation story is foundational to the message of the entire Bible, and Christians have found the Bible to be reliable in their personal lives, they can have faith to believe that the biblical Creation story is true and that Creation did not occupy long ages of time. Creationists point to evidence that indicates a shorter chronology, such as in the widespread preservation of fossil biomolecules, the evidence for catastrophic deposition of many of the sedimentary layers, layers missing without evidence of erosion, and other lines of evidence that do not fit easily with the long-age timescale.

Creationists do not yet have a satisfactory explanation for radioisotope dating, but they believe that such an explanation is possible and are working toward improving their understanding. There is no logical need to replace the biblical description of Creation with processes acting over long ages; the existence of a Creator God makes the short-age model entirely reasonable.

Human Nature

The Bible teaches that humans were created by God separately from any other form of life, endowed with the image of God, and given dominion over the other creatures. Thus, humans are qualitatively different from other creatures.

The uniqueness of humans can be observed in human capacities, which include a sense of morality and spirituality; awareness of one's self and one's relationship to the rest of creation;

and the ability to conceptualize abstract ideas and create new forms, plan for future events, compose and appreciate music, and conceptualize abstract mathematical concepts.

Humans also have numerous genes not found in other species. These so-called orphan genes may be responsible for some of the unique characteristics of humans, such as the expanded brain and reasoning capacity. Creationists endorse the biblical teaching that humans are created separately from ordinary animals.

Scientists who deny God's activity in nature have searched for natural mechanisms to explain the existence of humans and their unique qualities. The theory of evolution through random variation and natural selection has been offered as an explanation for the origin of humans and other types of creatures. There is widespread acceptance that natural selection can help species adapt to different local environments (microevolution). However, new types of organisms are not produced by gradual modification of existing species, and many scientists have concluded that evolutionary theory does not explain how new types of organisms might arise (macroevolution). Despite the empirical short-comings of evolution, there really is no other alternative except special creation, and this they refuse to accept.

Many fossils of humans and humanlike organisms (hominids) have been found. Some of these, such as Neanderthal Man and the "erectines" (*Homo erectus* and similar fossils) seem related to humans living today ("anatomically modern humans"). Some, such as most of the australopithecines, are clearly apelike. Some fossils appear to have a mosaic of human and apelike traits.

Proponents of evolutionary theory have pointed to these fossils, especially those with a mosaic of human and apelike traits, as transitional fossils that show the evolution of humans from apelike ancestors. Many attempts have been made to construct an evolution-ary tree linking all these different forms together, but a steady stream of new discoveries continues to upset the theories. Despite the unstable nature of the proposed evolutionary trees, the existence of these curious fossils has been used to oppose the biblical story of the separate creation of humans.

Very few creationists have pursued the training needed to critically analyze the hominid fossil evidence. It is obvious that the data are sparse, as seen by the frequent upset of pro-posed evolutionary relationships, but creationists would like to know how these fossils fit with their viewpoint.

Many of the fossil hominids appear to be degenerate, perhaps from inbreeding in iso-lated small groups soon after the biblical Flood. The extent of variation among the human-like fossils may be similar to the variation seen in other species. Considerable variation of genes and body form is seen in most living animal groups that have been examined. Among the many examples are dogs, horses, pigs, cattle, chickens, and carp. There is no reason to doubt that humans may have, or once had, a similar potential for variation that could include the Neanderthals and erectines.

The apelike fossils may represent an extinct type of ape, again with the ordinary variation in form that would encompass the entire australopithecine group. The mosaic fossils may represent corruption of the originally created species through degeneration, some type of genetic intermixing, or other unknown factors. Some have suggested the mosaic specimens are actually a mixture of human and apelike individuals, but this is difficult to evaluate without more data. Whatever the details, the hominid fossil record does not disprove the biblical record that humans were specially created apart from any other type of creature.

INTELLIGENT DESIGN IN NATURE: A CONTEMPORARY ISSUE

There is much debate over the possibility that evidence of God's activity can be seen in nature. Everyone recognizes that nature has a design that makes it possible for life to survive and flourish on the earth. The debate is whether this design comes from within nature itself (chance and natural law) or whether it has been crafted by an intelligent mind. As a result, there are two ways to explore this issue: establishing the complexity of design and then establishing the nature of design. With design as the hub, we can think of this as studies leading up to design and studies leading from design.

The Argument *to* Design

The claim here is that the apparent design in nature can be attributed to an intelligent cause, and not to a combination of chance and natural law, due to its complexity. This argument *to* design is the theme of the *intelligent design movement*. The identity of the designer is not a necessary part of this argument, although most people conclude it is probably the Creator God recognized by Christians and also by many non-Christians. Some examples of the argument to design are described below.

Intelligent Design in the Structure of the Universe. The origin, orderliness, and fine-tuning of the universe appear to be the result of intelligent design. Before the discovery of the cosmic redshift and the cosmic microwave background, materialists chose to believe the universe was eternal. Hence its origin needed no explanation. The new discoveries were interpreted to indicate that the universe had a beginning and was not eternal. Thus, an explanation was needed. Despite almost heroic efforts, materialists have not developed any plausible theory that explains the origin of the universe. Many see creation as the best explanation for the origin of the universe and also see it as an example of intelligent design.

The order observed in the universe is another feature that points to intelligent design in nature. The second law of thermodynamics is one of the most well-established regularities observed in nature, and it states that disorder increases over time in a closed system. What, then, is the origin of the order seen in the universe? If the universe exhibits order now, it must have been more orderly in the past. This implies the universe is not a closed system but has received input from an intelligent designer who acted to arrange order in the universe at its creation and possibly afterward.

A third feature of the universe that points to intelligent design is the fine-tuning problem. The structure of the universe is highly sensitive to the exact values of a multitude of physical constants and the fundamental forces. There are numerous physical constants, such as the charges and masses of the atomic particles, the speed of light, and Planck's constant. The four fundamental forces (electromagnetic force, weak nuclear force, strong nuclear force, and gravitational force) are responsible for interactions among atomic particles and different bodies of matter. Remarkably, the physical constants and fundamental forces have the precise values that are needed in order for the universe to be suitable for living organisms. In most cases, the slightest change would mean the universe would be unsuitable for life. It is difficult indeed to avoid the conclusion that the fine-tuning of the universe is purposeful, the result of design by an intelligent and omnipotent Creator.

Intelligent Design in the Living Cell. Living organisms provide an excellent example of intelligent design. The "simplest" living organisms are bacteria, each composed of a single cell. Bacteria are less complex than humans, but they are not at all simple. A single cell includes thousands of molecular machines that interact in chemical-mechanical pathways to produce materials that otherwise would never form in nature. Those molecular machines that have been investigated are extraordinarily complex, and it is highly probable that this is true for all the cellular machinery.

Living cells come only from other living cells and are never observed to form spontaneously from chemicals outside a living cell. Cells cannot form gradually through evolutionary processes, but a complete set of components must be in place for the cell to be alive. Thus, a living cell is irreducibly complex, meaning it cannot be constructed one step at a time through evolutionary processes. There is no plausible mechanism for the origin of living cells other than creation by an intelligent mind.

Irreducible complexity does not exclude the use of the components in other applications. Neither does it mean that there is no redundancy in the cellular components, as some opponents have pointed out. What it means is that an irreducibly complex system cannot be constructed stepwise by gradual evolutionary processes but must be assembled by an intelligent agent. The irreducible complexity of the cell, many of its interacting molecular systems, and a large number of its component parts all support the hypothesis of an active intelligent designer.

Other Examples of Intelligent Design. Intelligent design can also be seen in many other aspects of the creation. The information content of DNA and the molecules associated with its function is not explained by chance or by natural law. Information is stored in the sequence of nucleotides found in the DNA. The sequence is not determined by the laws of chemistry as we know them, and it is too specific and improbable to be explained as the result of chance. It does, however, have similarities with information codes produced by humans and thus bears the marks of intelligent design.

Numerous factors contribute to the fitness of our earth to support life. These include the distance of the earth from the sun, the type and amount of energy output by the sun, the mass of the earth and the moon, the speed of rotation of the earth, the composition of the atmosphere, the abundance of water, with its special properties, the earth's magnetic field, and more. Any single factor may seem unremarkable, but the combination of all these factors, both necessary and sufficient for life, is best explained by intelligent design.

Other examples could be described, such as the components of the nitrogen cycle, the ecological interdependence of plants and animals, the amazing migratory ability of birds, the human mind, the wonderful variety of plants and animals, and the striking mathematical nature of the creation. Any single example is a strong indicator of intelligent design and even more so when they are considered collectively.

The argument to design implies that the materialistic bias that pervades modern science is inappropriate. Because of this implication, materialistic scientists find it philosophically necessary to try to refute the evidence for intelligent design, attributing it to chance or the laws of nature. Their outspoken criticism has contributed to the perceived tension between faith and science, but, ironically, it has helped advocates of intelligent design sharpen their arguments, making the evidence for intelligent design even more compelling.

The Argument *from* Design

The argument *from* design is the argument that the intelligent designer whose works are seen in the creation must be the Creator God described in Scripture. This is certainly the biblical view, as, for example, in Psalm 19:1. Nature displays the glory of God. Many other texts affirm that God is the Creator of our world and all that is in it.

The biblical position is confirmed by many Christians in their own experiences. Many have had confirmation of the activity of God in their own personal lives and have experienced the guidance of the Holy Spirit.

Human Personality. The personal nature of humans provides evidence that the designer of the universe is a person and not an impersonal force. Human beings have personality, free will, self-consciousness, and, normally, an inborn sense of morality. These characteristics are not derived from natural laws but are best explained as the result of design by a Creator having similar characteristics. The biblical explanation is that humans were created in the image of the Creator, and this remains the best explanation.

Purpose in Nature. Purpose is another evidence that the world was designed by an intelligent Person and not by impersonal forces. Purpose requires the ability to arrange events in such a way as to produce a desired result. Impersonal forces do not have purpose but merely act according to natural law or randomly. Purpose may be seen in a general sense in the structure of the universe, the fitness of the environment, and the irreducible complexity of life. It may be seen more specifically in the actions of humans as they go about their daily lives and even in the lives of animals as they seek food, shelter, and mates. Purpose is a mark of a personal intelligence, in this case a supernatural intelligence—the Creator God.

The argument to design and the argument from design combine to affirm the view that the world was created by God, who is a Person and who continues to act to uphold His creation.

This claim results in tension between faith and science that is based on the fundamental difference between the two and what each can and cannot accomplish. There is also a tension between the faith bias and the materialistic bias of all practitioners of modern science. Science itself, which is dependent on neither, is used by both sides.

REASONS FOR TENSION BETWEEN FAITH AND SCIENCE

According to the Bible, God is both the Author of Scripture and the Creator of nature. Thus the expectation is that faith and science will be in harmony when properly interpreted. And yet sometimes there is tension, as has been described in previous paragraphs. Examining the philosophical underpinnings of science can help explain the basis of the tension.

Everyone makes some assumptions about the meaning of their existence and how they choose to live. These assumptions are not determined scientifically but are philosophical in nature. Among the most important of these are the relationship of God and nature (part of metaphysics), how one obtains knowledge (epistemology), and how one should behave (ethics). All these questions are related to one's beliefs about origins, and it is here that much of the tension between faith and science is grounded.

Different Worldviews

Collectively, these philosophical assumptions form our worldview, which shapes the way we interpret our experiences and the world about us. Having a worldview is not optional—everyone has one, whether or not they realize it. We generally take our worldview for granted and believe it represents the truth about our world. There are many different worldviews, but most of them fall into one of three categories: theism, pantheism, and materialism.

Theism is the view that God created the universe and is active in it. Matter and energy are created entities under the control of the Creator. People who accept this worldview believe their lives have meaning and purpose because God created them for a purpose. Theists ultimately expect harmony between faith and science and believe tension results from incomplete knowledge. Christians, Jews, and Muslims generally hold worldviews in this category.

Pantheism is the view that God and the universe are the same thing. Matter and energy are manifestations of eternal, impersonal spirit. People who accept this worldview generally believe their bodies are temporary vehicles for eternal spirit and this life is only a phase of existence. Pantheist thought varies, but many adherents do not consider the relationship between faith and science to be important because all truth is relative. Hindus, most animists, Daoists, some New Agers, and many Buddhists hold pantheistic beliefs.

The third worldview category is *materialism*, also called naturalism. In this view, matter and energy comprise all of reality, and no spiritual entities exist. People who accept this worldview generally believe they are merely complex forms of matter, and there is no spiritual reality or afterlife. Materialists do not expect to find harmony between faith and science because they believe faith is entirely subjective and science is the best way to find truth. Advocates of this position include secular humanists, many atheists, and many of the prominent voices in science.

Deism is another worldview that has an important influence on the relation of faith and science. It does not fit easily into any of the three categories described above, but it combines elements of theism and materialism. Deists accept the existence of a Creator God, a theistic concept, but they deny any supernatural activity in nature, a materialistic principle. In the context of science, there is little if any practical distinction between deists and materialists.

Contradictory Presuppositions in Worldviews

Different worldviews make contradictory assumptions about reality. The most important source of tension between faith and science may be the different presuppositions regarding the relationship of God and nature. Christians of faith affirm that a personal God has been, and continues to be, active in nature. In contrast, science is dominated by the materialistic assumption that there is no God active in nature, while pantheists see only impersonal forces. Thus tension exists on issues such as Creation and the Flood not necessarily because of the empirical evidence but because of philosophical preferences.

Another major philosophical factor underlying the tension between faith and science is their different ways of determining what is accepted as truth. Christian faith affirms the value of special revelation in Scripture, while materialistic scientists consider only physical evidence and only known natural laws. Materialism easily leads to scientism—the belief that science is the only pathway to knowledge. If science is defined materialistically but is applied to events with supernatural causes, tension is to be expected.

Another factor in the tension between faith and science is the tentative nature of scientific conclusions compared to the expectation that faith is based on eternal truths. This becomes a problem when scientific ideas are absorbed into religious faith, as discussed earlier. Science has experienced many revolutions in thought, in which ideas that everyone believed to be true were found to be faulty and replaced by newer ideas. If a scientific idea has been incorporated into religious faith and given the status of eternal truth, any change in the science will produce a crisis of faith.

Tension Related to Historical Questions

The conflict between faith and science primarily comes when we try to reconstruct past events. This is because one's worldview presuppositions have a much stronger influence on interpreting the evidence for historical questions than when dealing with events that can be replicated and analyzed repeatedly. For example, faith and science propose conflicting explanations (supernatural as opposed to naturalistic) for the origin of the universe, the origin of life, the origins of biodiversity, the origin of humans and human consciousness, and so on. These are all historical questions. It is much easier to analyze an event for which the initial conditions are known than to try to reconstruct a past event based only on the evidence left from that event.

When we find conflict regarding these historical questions, this should alert us to the likelihood that the event in question has a supernatural element that is not taken into account by the scientist with materialistic presuppositions. We would be wise to recognize that human efforts cannot access all of reality, and *there is more to nature than science can discover*.

DEALING WITH TENSION BETWEEN FAITH AND SCIENCE

The incompleteness of our knowledge makes tension between faith and science understandable. One's interpretation of the nature of faith and science and one's reaction to the tensions will be shaped by one's philosophical presuppositions. Those with different presuppositions will react to the tension in different ways. The major ways of dealing with the tension are described below.

Neglecting the Issue

Some are simply unaware that there is an issue here. Children would naturally be in this category until they reach a certain age or educational level, usually by the time they reach secondary school. Some avoid the issue by refusing to dwell on the idea or by keeping themselves so preoccupied with other issues that they never spend time thinking about faith and science. Many seem to think that the question is resolved and no further consideration is warranted.

This approach is unsatisfactory because the issues are central to our understanding of ourselves, the people around us, our environment, and our future. It is difficult to live in modern society very long without being confronted with questions of the relationship between faith and science.

Faith and Science as Inherently Contradictory

The takeover of science by scholars with a militantly materialistic worldview is a major factor in the perception that faith and science are enemies. The theism of faith and atheism/materialism that is imposed into the neutral processes of science pose an irreconcilable conflict, and since faith deals with the unseen and science with the seen, the choice is often made to reject faith, accept the materialism of many of the practitioners of science, and call that materialism itself *science*.

For those who deny God's activity in nature, the evidence for intelligent design is a nagging problem. The vehemence of the opposition to the apparently benign claim of intelligent design betrays the depth of the struggle to resist theism despite the evidence. Hopefully, the evidence, together with the impressions of the Holy Spirit, may help many to make the transition from materialism to theism.

Faith and Science as Isolated

One strategy to deal with tension between faith and science is to mentally isolate them from each other. One popular form of this approach is called NOMA (Non-Overlapping MAgesteria). In this view, science and faith deal with two separate, independent aspects of reality. Science deals with the physical world, while faith deals with spiritual issues such as feelings and morals. There is no possibility of conflict because the two sources are "non-overlapping"—they do not deal with the same topics.

It has been rightly pointed out that it is disingenuous to claim that faith and science do not overlap in scope. In fact, Christian faith has much to say about the world, its origins, its operations, and its future. If one accepts the claims of NOMA that faith deals only with feelings and emotions and not with the physical world, one has ceded to science the entire realm of physical reality, leaving only the subjective churnings of mental states to the realm of faith. This is essentially a materialistic position and faces the same problem of evidence for intelligent design that so threatens materialistic philosophy.

Science as Foundational for Faith

The concept of science as the foundation for faith suggests that the Bible describes God's interactions with His people but it is not intended to teach us about the physical world. That task is allegedly the work of science. This proposal is commonly associated with statements such as "the Bible is not a textbook of science." This phrase is commonly used to justify the proposition that we should look to science to learn about the origins and history of our world and let science determine the validity of what Scripture says about the natural world.

Theistic evolution probably fits into this category, as it holds that God exists but does not act in nature in detectable ways, implying that science is the only reliable way to learn the truth about our world. Theistic evolution fails for several reasons. Philosophically, one may ask what evidence there is for a God who does not act in nature and why anyone should accept that proposition. Scientifically, the evidence for intelligent design described above and elsewhere falsifies the assumption that God does not act in nature. This helps explain the outspoken antagonism of theistic evolutionists to the claims of intelligent design. Theologically, theistic evolution is inconsistent with the God of the Bible, who abhors suffering and opposes death. Death and replacement are required for evolution to proceed. Why would God oppose the very means He allegedly used to create? The relationship described here results in a view of faith and science that differs little from the materialistic view and is untenable in the light of biblical revelation.

Natural theology is the attempt to use science as the basis for theology. The natural theologian accepts that God is active in nature and uses that as the basis for inferring God's character. This approach is highly problematic. While it is true that we can see evidence of God's power in the creation, it is only in the Bible that we can clearly see God's grace, justice, mercy, love, and so on. Nature does not provide a clear picture of what God is like.

The attempt to infer what God is like by studying nature runs headlong into the problem of *natural evil*. Natural evil includes the destructive effects of earthquakes, floods, famine, and fire; along with suffering from cancer, genetic diseases, and infections; venomous animals; the violence of predation, and the like. If one constructs a picture of God based only on nature, it will be a God of both good and evil, not the compassionate Redeemer and Healer described in the Gospels.

The proper method for developing an understanding of God's character is to study the Bible, especially the life and teachings of Jesus Christ, who was and is the Creator. The Scriptures reveal that there is an enemy, Satan, who introduced evil into this world and is engaged in a great controversy with Christ. Nature has been affected by the curse of Satan's activities so that it does not present an accurate picture of the Creator. Jesus showed us what God is really like.

Concordism: Compromising Faith with Science

Concordism is the attempt to combine elements from both science and the Bible into a theory of origins. Where there is conflict, conclusions about the physical world are shaped by the teachings of science, while conclusions about divine activity are derived from Scripture. In practical terms, this means combining the discrete acts of special creation from the Bible with the long ages of deep time taken from geology. Two examples of concordism are described here.

The Day-Age Theory. This theory proposes that the days of Creation were each long ages of time, not a single week as described in Genesis. This theory has declined in popularity but still has many followers. Unfortunately for the theory, there are major discrepancies between the fossil sequence and the Creation week sequence. The most glaring of these are the fruit trees. Fruit trees and grains are among the first group of organisms created during Creation week, before any animals were created. In the fossil record, fruit trees and grains do not appear until after many fossil layers of both land and aquatic animals were deposited. Another discrepancy is that land animals were created after flying animals during Creation week, but land animals appear below (i.e., before) flying creatures in the fossil record.

Progressive Creation. This theory proposes that God created in discrete events, as described in Genesis, but the time of these events is expanded to millions of years in order to fit the geological time scale. In essence, the theory takes the fossil sequence as the sequence of creation rather than the sequence of burial and preservation. The creation sequence of Genesis is discarded, avoiding the problem of trying to match it to the fossil sequence. The days of Creation week are discarded and replaced by a long, indefinite period of time, avoiding the problem of trying to make it fit into a Creation week. All that is left of Genesis is the idea that God created the various elements of our world in discrete acts. Some similar theories discard special creation altogether and replace it with divinely guided evolution.

Progressive creation intends to resolve some of the conflicts between faith and science, but it does so by stripping the biblical Creation story of its content. The costs of this approach include the integrity of the Bible, the logical coherence of the gospel, and the basis for the seventh-day Sabbath. The gospel story tells us that Jesus died to save us from death, which was the result of Adam's sin. Progressive creation implies that death is not the result of Adam's sin, but that violence and suffering were part of nature for millions of years before humans were created. The seventh-day Sabbath is undermined by denial of God's six days of work and seventh day of rest as a basis for our weekly cycle.

Scientifically, this theory is entirely ad hoc. There is no scientific evidence that God created living organisms in the sequence recorded in the fossil record. It would be just as reasonable, and far more consistent with Scripture, to propose that God caused the various types of creatures to be buried in the sequence observed in the fossil record during the Flood.

Concordism may be based on good intentions, but it ends up placing science over Scripture. In the process, it undermines the gospel and the reliability of Scripture. It denies the evolutionary story but has neither biblical nor scientific support for its distinctive claims. It produces "just-so stories" with little reason for anyone to endorse them.

BIBLICAL FOUNDATION FOR RELATING FAITH AND SCIENCE

The approach recommended here is to regard the revelation of God's actions in Scripture as the foundation on which the natural world can be understood. To explore this idea, we will address the question of how God's activities in nature might affect the practice of science.

God Is Active in Nature

The Bible records many examples of God's action in our world. God created the world and filled it with living creatures (Gen. 1–2); He sent a flood to destroy the corrupted world (Gen. 6–8); He showered Sodom and Gomorrah with fire and brimstone (Gen. 19); He opened a path through the Red Sea for the Israelites to escape the Egyptians (Ex. 14); He caused the walls of Jericho to collapse (Josh. 6); He sent fire down from heaven to burn up the stones of Elijah's altar (1 Kin. 18); He created the heavens by His word (Ps. 33); He laid the foundation of the earth and spread out the heavens (Is. 48); He set up kings and removed them, revealed secrets, and gave wisdom (Dan. 2); and He caused a host of healings and other supernatural events. Any theory that denies God's activities in nature is incompatible with Scripture.

The reality of divine activity in nature means that a true history of our world must be grounded on special revelation. It invites us to faith in the revealed description of God's activities, including a creation in one literal week in which (1) the world was formed and provided with plants and animals in harmonious ecological relationships, (2) humans were created in God's image and given responsibility for the created world, and (3) death, violence, and suffering were absent.

Types of Divine Activities

God's actions in nature can be tentatively classified into three types: Creation, directing special events, and sustaining the creation. God's work in Creation is a past event, unobservable in the present, unrepeatable in the laboratory, and not subject to scientific analysis. God's work in directing special events is occasional and is likely to be regarded as a "miracle." Such events may leave effects that are subject to scientific analysis, but their causes are likely to be beyond the scope of science. God's work in sustaining the world must be consistent to maintain stability, and the regularities are observable in the present and can be tested in the laboratory and analyzed scientifically. Thus, science works well for analyzing the consistent patterns of God's activities in maintaining nature, but not for studying God's special actions in creation and other miraculous events.

Laws of Nature

In the biblical view, God is sovereign over all of nature. This means that what we call the "laws of nature" are God's tools for managing the world, not rules that limit His power or activities. Natural laws are not inherent properties of matter but merely describe how God exercises control over His creation. They are descriptive, not prescriptive.

Science and God's Activities

A common objection to the claim that God is active in nature is the claim that if God were active in the physical world, His activities would interfere with our ability to practice science. We could not depend on getting the same experimental results at different times or in different places because God might intervene at any moment. This is a misunderstanding of God's role in nature.

Theists do not fear that God's activity will spoil the experiment. They realize that they could not conduct scientific investigations if it were not for God's consistent actions in sustaining the universe. Without this consistency, there would be no regularities to discover in the physical world, and science would be impossible. Thus, it is false to claim that being open to God's activity in nature inhibits scientific discovery. Scientists should embrace the fact of God's activity in nature, not deny it.

Science applies well to studying God's consistent activities in sustaining the universe, but it is not equipped to analyze divine acts of creation. This leaves miraculous events, including the Creation, beyond the scope of science, but this is to be expected. Expertise in how a system operates is not the same thing as understanding how it originated. An auto mechanic may be able to take a car apart and put it back together again, but that does not qualify him to design an automobile manufacturing plant. We are still free to inquire into any topic and to use the power of science to enhance our quality of life and improve our ability to wisely manage our environment. However, we cannot expect that science will provide answers to all our questions.

Science Is Worthwhile

The biblical view of creation is that it is God's handiwork, made for our benefit. Although damaged by our sin and carelessness, it remains our responsibility to take care of. This requires an intelligent understanding of nature that comes from scientific study. Thus science is a good and worthwhile activity that can enhance our quality of life and improve our ability to cope with the responsibilities of overseeing the creation.

The New Creationists

The name "New Creationists" refers to a group of creationist scholars who are attempting to understand nature in the light of the biblical record. They include biologists, geologists, cosmologists, chemists, physicists, and others. Although their numbers are small, they have already made important discoveries in understanding the world from a biblical viewpoint.

One example of creationist research is the work done by several creationist scientists study-ing the "fossil forests" of Yellowstone National Park in the United States. Many layers of fossilized logs are preserved, including some trees that are standing upright. These were interpreted by scientists as a succession of forests growing in place over tens of thousands of years. Examination of the fossilized "soil" associated with the layers showed sorting of the particles, indicating that the leaves and "soil" had been washed into place, not formed in place. Several additional lines of evidence were pursued, resulting in the conclusion that these trees were transported from somewhere else and are not preserved where they grew. This conclusion supports the hypothesis of a catastrophic flood.

Numerous footprints and trackways are found in the Coconino Sandstone of the Grand Canyon, in the United States. Careful study of the footprints showed they were depos-ited under water, and not on dry sand dunes as had been thought. Since the layers below and above the Coconino Sandstone were deposited in water, it makes more sense that the Coconino Sandstone was also deposited under water and not in a desert, again supporting the hypothesis of a catastrophic flood.

Creationist scientists are also studying a series of rock layers in Utah. These layers are separated by distinct boundaries where the grain size changes abruptly. Ordinarily, bottom-dwelling animals burrow through the deposits on the seafloor and mix the sediments thor-oughly so that layers with abrupt boundaries do not form. Sequences of distinct layers indicate that deposition was too rapid for burrowing animals to mix the sediments. Such rapid deposition of layers suggests catastrophic processes at work.

As more creationists engage in the study of geology and other sciences, we can expect more progress in developing a creation-based understanding of nature, guided and facilitated by the Creator Himself. Perhaps some who are reading this will join in that endeavor.

CONCLUSIONS

What then can we conclude about the relationship between faith and science? First, we should recognize that the present tension between faith and science is largely determined by philosoph-ical assumptions and their influence on the practice of science. If science is defined as materi-alistic in approach, then it is inappropriate to try to apply it to events with supernatural causes. It is important to match the scope of science with its definition. Faith and science are rarely in conflict except when attempting to reconstruct historical events associated with divine activity.

Second, we should resist efforts to incorporate scientific "facts" into faith, even if "ev-eryone knows they are true." We should learn from the historical examples of conflict in-volving Galileo and Darwin and resist attempts to adjust our faith to accommodate the materialistic claims of deep time and animal ancestry of humans. The scientific path to truth is often slow and marked by many detours. The present state of knowledge is not the final destination, nor is it a safe guide for Christian faith.

Finally, we must affirm that both faith and science have value. We should give glory to God for the wonderful benefits that science has provided from the study of the created world and for the amazing complexity of life that reveals something of the power and wisdom of the Creator. We should encourage and support those who choose to prepare themselves academically and spiritually for engaging the world of science in order to present a creation-based understanding of the universe and our place in it.

ARCHAEOLOGY AND THE BIBLE

Archaeologists do not dig up dinosaurs. Archaeologists are not treasure hunters. Archaeologists study human antiquity, focusing on buried architecture and the material culture of everyday life associated with it. They need the context of buildings and even the soil in which an object is found in order to understand the significance of an object. Thus, in a way, archaeologists are like ancient crime scene investigators, recording even the minutest of details in order to reconstruct as much of the ancient past as is possible. Consequently, archaeology is a discovery science as opposed to an experimental science, although there is a field of study within archaeology that attempts to test archaeological theory by endeavoring to replicate ancient processes. Microstructural analysis, art criticism, and other such activities fall under the broad umbrella of archaeology, but exploration, excavation, and research are the traditional activities of archaeologists.

To understand the value of each discovery, archaeologists often conduct interdisciplinary studies. Cooperation with other branches of science helps to interpret what is discovered. The area of biblical studies can be used to interpret evidence established through archaeological activities.

ARCHAEOLOGY'S RELATIONSHIP TO THE BIBLE

The earliest archaeological efforts in Mesopotamia, the Levant (known more commonly as the Holy Land), Egypt, Turkey, Greece, Rome, and other parts of the Mediterranean world in the 1800s up through the mid-1900s were conducted with a general understanding that sections of the Bible were meant to reflect actual historical events, places, and persons. Many renowned archaeologists even felt it necessary to compare what was being discovered with statements contained in the biblical text. But in the 1970s and early 1980s most of these early scholars had passed away and were largely replaced by proponents of the "New Archaeology" theory. No longer was archaeology done solely for historical reasons, and therefore the connection to ancient texts (including the Bible) was no longer necessary. Today, many archaeologists avoid referencing the Bible in publications, even when it is obvious or necessary that this should be done. An understanding of both what the Bible can and cannot do and what archaeology can and cannot do should help demonstrate that this separation was unwise.

The Bible and Archaeologists

The Bible seems to arouse feelings of distrust for many scholars. This is probably a reaction to the well-meaning work of some religious adherents to prove the historical sections of the

Bible in order to justify cherished theological convictions. In the process, some archaeological discoveries have been misrepresented, and evidence that may contradict a cherished view is sometimes ignored, leading the adherent to reinterpret the biblical text in an effort to maintain a particular view. Such practices have unfortunately left many scholars outside of biblical studies (and some on the inside) with little use for the Bible. This includes the vast majority of archaeologists who are not trained in the methods of biblical studies. They dismiss the Bible and do not attempt to connect their work with it.

The Bible was written to instruct on several intellectual and spiritual levels. It contains history, but it is not merely a record of history. The majority of the supposed discrepancies critics often point out are due to hermeneutical presuppositions rather than any fault with the biblical text itself. Only a small portion of these discrepancies seem associated with scribal errors. And when given the benefit of the doubt, these discrepancies can be reconciled satisfactorily (for more, see "Revelation and Inspiration of the Bible," p. 11). Archaeology has played a significant role in helping to understand some of these discrepancies.

Archaeology and Bible Readers

Archaeologists discover evidence. This evidence needs to be interpreted. There has not been a significant archaeological discovery that has contradicted any historical element in the Bible, but there are many interpretations of evidence that contradict the Bible. This distinction is important. Misunderstanding this distinction has wrecked many sincere people's faith in the reliability of the Bible. Often it is the interpreter's presuppositions that provide the contradictory interpretation.

Lack of sufficient data can also result in contradictory interpretations of a piece of data. Most archaeological sites are only partially excavated. It has been the practice of archaeologists through the decades to purposely not excavate an entire site down to bedrock, knowing that better methods of excavation and recording will be developed in the future. As a result, it is estimated that only one-tenth of one percent of all known archaeological sites have been excavated. Further, more sites are being discovered each year and some are yet to be excavated due in large part to a lack of funding. Consequently, a significant amount of data lies waiting to be recovered. Because of this, it is common for archaeologists to discover evidence in an excavation that shifts previous understandings of the site, even from one year to the next. Thus, any dogmatic conclusion by archaeologists should be understood as zeal rather than incontrovertible fact.

A Proper Relationship

There are few, mostly minor, variants of the biblical text. It is always the hope that more manuscripts will be found, but it is doubtful that any will be discovered that will change the text as we currently have it in any consequential way. As a result, new information related to the Bible is most likely to come through archaeological discoveries.

Readers today are separated from the world of the Bible most directly by time, culture, language, and landscape. Archaeological data have the ability to provide the reader with a window in time and space through which they can glimpse the various cultures operating within the historical milieu of a given passage of Scripture. In this way, archaeology provides the modern reader with information that is not immediately apparent from a study of the text itself and that can shed light on the biblical text.

Since archaeologists are scientists and not theologians, their main interest is in providing trustworthy data that can be used by others in a study of the ancient world. The Bible is valuable for the work of archaeologists because it is an ancient document that contains information regarding life in the ancient past (be that geographical, topographical, political, or migrational). However, some secular archaeologists dismiss the value of the Bible partly because of the irresponsible interpretation of some who feel the need to "prove" the Bible to be true. Impatient with the perceived slowness by which archaeology discovers evidence, some pseudo-archaeologists publish documents, give lectures, or produce documentaries that fail to do the hard, slow work of archaeology and, instead, present their "proof" as groundbreaking. This does more damage than good.

Archaeologists, in a way, are at the mercy of elements beyond their control. They cannot control what is found, and what is found through the limited excavations may be an accident of survival following deliberate destructions, natural decay, lootings, and unfriendly environments. Organic materials, for example, do not survive well in damp environments, so any cloth, wood, parchment, paper, or organic substance has a low chance of survival in civilizations that were close to water sources. What material has survived war, natural catastrophe, and natural, organic decay also had to have survived looting through the millennia. Beyond that, it also has to be in an accessible location (i.e., not below a modern dwelling or city, in a war zone, or below water) so it can be found. And an item that has survived all of these still needs to actually be found by someone who knows how to record its context in a professionally responsible way. Putting together a picture of the ancient world, then, has been likened to trying to see life with only a few pieces of a puzzle of unknown size that comes in a box without a photograph of the completed puzzle.

Since archaeology discovers rather than experiments, archaeological findings are not controlled. And because only a small fraction of the available data has been discovered, archaeology is not well equipped to answer the question "Did it happen?" This means that aside from a fortuitous spade full of dirt that might turn up something that supports some aspect of what is contained in the Bible, the best questions that archaeology can answer are "Could it have happened?" and "Is the event, location, or person possible?"

Even when texts are discovered that seem to confirm an event from the biblical record (e.g., the Merenptah Stele; see p. 85), skeptics will not necessarily be persuaded. This is because some would suggest that the author of the text intentionally meant to mislead his audience or intended for the record to be understood as myth or legend. Some would, more kindly, propose that the author thought that he was recording an event that in reality did not happen. In the end, the interpretation of evidence allows for a broad range of views and, as a result, does not constitute proof one way or another.

The message of the Bible is believed through faith, not science. The Bible presents God as unchanging (Heb. 13:8). How He treated people in the past is how He treats people in the present and future. Archaeology helps us to better understand those who lived in the past. This understanding then also allows us to better see how God interacted with those people in the past and then, as a result, to gain a better understanding of how He will interact with us today. This is how archaeology can best help to strengthen faith. And while archaeology can help strengthen faith, the absence of archaeological evidence in relation to some biblical texts or narratives should also not lead anyone to distrust the Bible.

HISTORY OF ARCHAEOLOGY

The word *archaeology* comes from two Greek words: *archaios* ("ancient") and *logos* ("study of" or "word"). In this way, archaeology means the study of, or a word about, the ancient world. Although it is true that some ancients engaged in activities that resemble aspects of archaeological work, archaeology as a field of scientific study has been practiced for only about two hundred years. Due to its relatively young age, there is still some discussion within the discipline on the goals and aims of archaeology as a science, but nearly all agree that studying, preserving, and presenting material culture from the ancient world is what archaeologists do.

Following Napoleon's expedition to Egypt (from 1798 to 1801), in which 167 scholars and scientists accompanied him to record and study that ancient civilization, the world was captivated by archaeology and Egyptomania was born. A few decades later, as the Bible came under increasing attacks by source critical scholars, Bible believers financially supported archaeological efforts in the hope of confirming and better understanding the biblical record. Part of the original mission statement of the Palestinian Exploration Fund illustrates this well: "That the Biblical Scholar may yet receive assistance in illustrating the sacred text from careful observers of the manner and habits of the people in of the Holy Land." Likewise, the Egyptian Exploration Fund stated as one of its original purposes "to make surveys, [and] explorations...for the purpose of elucidating or illustrating the Old Testament narrative, or any part thereof, insofar as the same is in any way connected with Egypt."

In the early years, collecting objects was the primary objective of archaeology. Mysticism, prestige, and curiosity inspired scholars and laypersons alike to collect curio objects from the ancient world. The idea that the ancients had more understanding of the workings of the universe than modern humanity drove many to romanticize the potential knowledge behind even the most mundane objects. Some even ground up mummies and drank the powder thinking that they would attain some health benefit. Eventually, the first real professionals began to emerge and systematized the collection of data for the reconstruction of the historical past and a better understanding of life in the ancient world.

Sir Flinders Petrie recognized that certain pottery types were found in a specific sequence as seen from site to site. This realization resulted in the systemization of pottery as a method of dating. Although refined through the years, this system is still the standard used for dating related objects, walls, and dirt layers. His meticulous attention to detail and record keeping also became the good practice standard among archaeologists. William Foxwell Albright was instrumental in refining Petrie's ceramic typological work in the Holy Land. He became known as the father of biblical archaeology because of his insistence that all the historical aspects of the Bible were confirmed by archaeological finds. Although his premises were later challenged and his methods refined, his work inspired generations.

As criticism of the biblical text increased, two general lines of thought emerged. Those who considered the historical information in the early portions of the Bible up to the time of Ahab (ca. 874 B.C.) to have only minimal authenticity are called *minimalists. Maximalists,* on the other hand, argue that a maximum portion of the historical parts of the early portion of the Bible are authentic. Obviously not all minimalists agree with each other, and neither do all maximalists. Scholars of both positions have largely adjusted some terminology to avoid supporting positions of faith or political issues.

As archaeology as a discipline has become more codified, some changes of terminology have been introduced. One change that is common in publication is the practice of using B.C.E. ("before Common Era") and C.E. ("Common Era") rather than B.C. ("before Christ") and A.D. ("anno Domini" or "year of our Lord"), which has obvious Christian ties and thus can be awkward when engaged in research in modern non-Christian cultures. The numbers associated with these remain the same so that 1447 B.C. and 1447 B.C.E. are the same date. In the same way, A.D. 31 and C.E. 31 are the same date. While not all agree with the need for the change or use these new terms, it is important to understand them. As noted elsewhere, this commentary retains the dating system that acknowledges Christ's incarnation as the hinge-point of human history (for more, see "Old Testament Timeline," p. 94).

There have also been changes in the names used to describe the Holy Land. "Palestine" and "Israel" have been replaced as geographic terms in favor of "the southern Levant." (The term *Levant* comes from an Italian word adopted by the French referring to the rising of the sun and thus was applied to the western coast of the Mediterranean because it is a land east of Italy and France, from which the sun appears to rise.) This change was felt necessary by some to avoid seeming to side with either modern political entity (Israel or Palestine). Obviously, the modern world is divided up politically differently than the ancient world was, and archaeologists working in the region might need to work in territories governed by either Israeli or Palestinian authorities when researching an ancient civilization. To offend one or the other governments by terminology that suggests they are taking a side in a political disagreement does not seem wise. For similar reasons archaeologists also refer to the land in the southern Levant on the west side of the Jordan (modern-day Israel and Palestine) as

"Cisjordan" and that on the east (modern-day Jordan) as "Transjordan." In most places in this commentary, the more traditional term "Holy Land" is used for the entire region of the southern Levant.

Adventists have been conducting and joining archaeological digs in the Holy Land for decades. Siegfried Horn was the first to lead an Adventist dig in 1968 at Tal Hisban in Transjordan. This site was selected based on the similarity of the name with a site mentioned in the Bible (Heshbon; Num. 21:21–32). Since that time Adventist archaeologists have led digs or participated in the excavation of many other sites.

WHAT WE KNOW NOW

A tremendous number of discoveries have been made in the world of archaeology. A significant number of these provide information on some aspect of the Bible. Some of the more recent interpretations of discoveries are still waiting to be widely accepted.

Patriarchs

Abraham was called out of his homeland in Ur to travel to an unknown location (which turned out to be the Holy Land). In 1854 a great ziggurat (pyramid-shaped temple) was excavated at Ur. It had been built by Ur-Nammu to the moon god Nanna (also called Sin) during the approximate period that Abraham left the city. It was 210 feet (64 m) long by 148 feet (45 m) wide and 98 feet (30 m) tall. Many centuries later Nabonidus, the last king of the Babylonian Empire, restored it during his reign. In 1927 Leonard Woolley uncovered the ancient city of Ur itself. Several temples, private houses, tombs, and other buildings were excavated. One of the most impressive of these is the Great Death Pit where sixty-eight women dressed in fine clothing and six men (thought to be guards) surrounded by valuable objects were buried in a large mass grave. These objects still dazzle museum visitors today. The most famous of these are the twin Ram Caught in a Thicket statues that probably held a bowl between them. The rams are intricately decorated with shell, lapis lazuli, silver, and red limestone and have reminded scholars of both the story of the sacrifice of Isaac and the success Jacob had shepherding Laban's flock. However, these objects illustrate the pastoral element that was closely associated with the lives of even the very rich of this period rather than suggesting any association with a particular Bible story. These excavations and the literature in and about Ur have helped reconstruct the world Abraham left in order to follow God. We now understand that he was leaving the best civilization had to offer to live in a tent among strangers.

Abraham, and his family after him, entered into covenants and treaties with those who occupied the lands he moved through and lived in (e.g., Gen. 14:13; 21:25–32; 26:26–33; 31:43–54). Tablets discovered at Mari (on the Euphrates River) and dated to the first half of the second millennium B.C. reveal that such treaties were common between those living in urban centers and those living in tents around them. Tablets discovered at Nuzi (on the Tigris River) reveal that adoption of a servant in the absence of a legitimate heir was a cultural custom (Gen. 15:2). The tablets also reveal that if a woman could not produce children, it was her duty to provide a surrogate for her husband, a similar situation to what we see described in Genesis 16:2; 30:3–8. The law code of Hammurabi suggests that should an heir be produced by the original wife after providing a surrogate, the sons should split the inheritance, unless the slave and her son were released and allowed to go free (cf. Gen. 21:10). These findings help Bible scholars to have some historical background for the seemingly strange customs of Abraham and his family.

Exodus

A number of discoveries have helped us understand the world during the time of the Exodus event. For example, archaeologists are almost certain now of the locations of the supply cities Pithom and Raamses built by the Hebrews (Ex. 1:11). The locations of both have been a matter of debate for a long time. However, because of careful and persistent excavation in the delta region, the locations of both have now been established with a high degree of certainty. In the process, scholarly errors in this regard have been corrected.

Previously, it was thought that Raamses was located at Tanis in the northeast delta. This was because conclusions were prematurely reached after architectural materials dating to the time of Ramesses II were discovered there. Now we know that these building materials were robbed out of a location a bit further to the south at Qantir, where Seti I and Ramesses II (of the nineteenth dynasty) had established their capital city. Qantir had been selected for the capital (that was named Pi-Ramesses) because it was where the ruling family was from and also because a site more than half a mile (1 km) further to the south (at Tal ed-Dab'a) had been the northern capital in the eighteenth dynasty and the fifteenth dynasty before that.

During the fifteenth dynasty (seventeenth and sixteenth centuries B.C.), Semites (the Hyksos) from the southern Levant (the Holy Land) invaded and conquered Egypt. They set up a capital at Tal ed-Dab'a because it was a natural location for a harbor. This is likely the time when Joseph was in Egypt, although some scholars place him in Egypt approximately two centuries earlier (see "Old Testament Timeline," p. 94). After the Egyptians regained control of their country from the Hyksos (beginning the eighteenth dynasty, in the sixteenth century) this capital was renamed Perunefer (and possibly Raamses). The rulers of the eighteenth dynasty used Tal ed-Dab'a as one of two supply cities for the Egyptian military's excursions into what became the Holy Land. In fact, excavation has revealed that significant storage facilities and large military camps were constructed prior to the building of a large thirteen-acre palace at Tal ed-Dab'a illustrating where the priorities lay.

A similar error was made in the initial misidentification of Tal el-Maskhuta as Pithom. Excavations, as well as advances in ceramic typology, have demonstrated that Tal el-Maskhuta was not occupied in a significant way until the Persian period. Just as had happened with Tanis, building material had been robbed out of a location further west at Tal er-Retabeh. Tal er-Retabeh had a temple to Atum, one of the creator gods. Inscriptions with the name Pi-Atum (meaning "the domain of Atum") have been found. Linguistically, Pi-Atum is a match with Pithom. Tal er-Retabeh (i.e., Pi-Atum), in the western Wadi Tumilat, was constructed in the early eighteenth dynasty as a frontier fortress to supply the military's excursions into the Sinai, just at the time when the Hebrews were put into slavery. Consequently, both Tal er-Retabeh (Pi-Atum or Pithom) and Tal ed-Dab'a (Raamses) were constructed at the same time for the same purpose. A massive enclosure wall and western gate at Tal er-Retabeh made it nearly impossible to breach. It is likely that Tal er-Retabeh was the city that kept the Hebrews from leaving Egypt, which is why they needed permission from the king. Thus, Tal ed-Dab'a/Qantir is certainly Raamses and Tal er-Retabeh is Pithom.

The story of Aaron's rod changing to a serpent before Pharaoh and his court is a remarkable demonstration of the power of God. However, it may have had significance beyond just the obvious. Texts recovered in excavations in Egypt reveal that the Egyptians had more than 1,500 gods and goddesses. Two of these were considered protectors of the two lands of Egypt. Nekhbet, the vulture goddess, protected the narrow Nile valley of Upper Egypt, and Wadjet, the cobra goddess, protected the broad Nile delta region of Lower Egypt. Both appeared on the crown of Pharaoh, where Wadjet was called the Uraeus. Thus, the use of a serpent to demonstrate God's power would have clearly signaled that God was Master of the delta region, where His people lived and worked as slaves (the northern part of Egypt), and of the king himself. The use of the word *tomorrow* (Ex. 8:23; 9:5, 18–19; 10:4) when setting time designations for the plagues seems to indicate that the plagues affected Egypt for only about a one-day's journey in all directions, as that is the only territory that God's warning message could have reached and likely why He didn't connect any signs to the vulture goddess of the south.

But the Egyptians also had a god named Nehebu-kau (meaning "he who harnesses the spirits"), who had been worshiped since the time of the pyramids of the Old Kingdom. Nehebu-kau was a serpent god who was considered to have great power because he swallowed seven cobras. It is certain that every Egyptian in that room where Aaron's rod turned into a serpent would have immediately understood the significance of Aaron's serpent swallowing the serpents of the magicians. God was communicating to the Egyptians in a language that they would clearly understand, before any plague fell, that He had ultimate power over Egypt's gods. Pharaoh, who denied knowing God, was introduced to God in a way that could not have been misunderstood.

The golden calf narrative is another example of a story that has more meaning with backgrounds discovered in texts through archaeological efforts. The Bible describes Aaron as using an engraving tool to make the molded calf (Ex. 32:4). Later he said that he simply tossed the gold into the fire and a calf came out (Ex. 32:24). Although a clear misrepresentation of the process, this does describe the basic elements needed to make the calf. Statues of metal were often carved out of wax, then surrounded by clay, which was baked to harden into a mold (the wax melting and easily being poured out, leaving a hollow center). The metal was then put inside the clay mold to harden. Once the metal was cool, the clay mold was broken and out came the statue. It is certain that the calf was made in this way regardless of how Aaron minimized his participation in an effort to claim a miracle and remove himself from responsibility. What has not been as readily apparent is why a calf of gold was used to represent the God who brought them out of the land of Egypt. The Sinai region was the land of Hathor, the mother cow goddess, who is often represented as providing nourishment. In fact, Amenhotep II (one of the candidates for the pharaoh of the Exodus) is famously depicted as drinking milk right from her udder. Hathor was a favorite patron deity of Hatshepsut (the most likely candidate for the adopted mother of Moses). Hathor was worshiped by performing that act between a man and a woman that causes a woman to become a mother. Great festivals were held where social boundaries were eliminated so that a commoner could unite with a princess. These festivals were accompanied with frivolity and excess, singing, dancing, shouting, and the clanging of metal sistra (similar to a rattle). It is likely that this was the sound that Joshua heard and mistook for war but that Moses, who was much more familiar with it, was able to recognize for the evil it was (Ex. 32:17–18). However, God was not represented as the mother cow but rather an offspring. Hesat, another cow goddess, was the divine nurse who was also the mother of the new king. Her son, the new king, was represented as a golden calf. It is very likely that Hesat and Hathor were both being worshiped at Sinai because of their similarities. God was likely depicted as their son, the golden calf, the new King who had brought the Hebrews to His mountain and had given them nourishment in the form of manna only after they arrived in the Sinai. Syncretistic worship of the gods was common in Egypt. The people certainly considered that they were worshiping the God who had brought them out of the land of Egypt by worshiping the golden calf (Ex. 32:1, 4).

A few objects also help with the dating of the Exodus. The Merenptah Stele (now in the Cairo museum), which is over ten feet high and over five feet wide, contains the earliest mention of Israel outside of the Bible, with the possible exception of the more controversial Berlin Pedestal. Found by Sir Flinders Petrie in western Thebes, the Merenptah Stele describes Pharaoh Merenptah's successful attack on the Libyans in his fifth year. Toward the end of the account, the enemies of Egypt, including Israel, are listed as also being subdued. This is significant as it places Israel as a people group in the southern Levant (the Holy Land) just five years after the death of Merenptah's father, Ramesses II (in the thirteenth century B.C.), who is often identified incorrectly as the pharaoh of the Exodus. Since the biblical account of the Exodus describes a forty-year period between the Exodus and the conquest of the Holy Land, the Hebrews could not have been a people group living in the promised land when Merenptah attacked in his fifth year. And thus, Ramesses II could not have been the pharaoh of the Exodus.

Conquest of the Promised Land

Because of her stellar reputation as a responsible and trustworthy scholar, English archaeologist Kathleen Kenyon shocked the world when she announced that the walls of Jericho did not come tumbling down and, additionally, that Jericho was not even occupied when Israel was supposed to have conquered the promised land. Nearly fifty years earlier, Ernst

Sellin and Carl Watzinger had excavated Jericho. They felt that the evidence did reflect the biblical account. In the early 1930s, John Garstang excavated Jericho and came to the same conclusion. But Kenyon, who excavated in the mid-1950s, felt that they were wrong, stating so publicly, though she never published her findings.

Reexaminations of her notes by Bryant Wood and others reveal that she only dug a trench across the site and based all her conclusions on what was found in this trench. Subsequent excavations discovered evidence of Late Bronze Age occupation (roughly 1400 B.C.), a heavy burnt layer (cf. Josh. 6:24), a double-walled fortification that had fallen outward, as if in an earthquake (Josh. 6:20), large quantities of grain (Josh. 2:6; 3:15; 5:10–12), and grain that was left by the invaders that showed signs of being burnt, as if it had been only a short siege but the conquerors did not take anything (Josh. 6:17–18). Further, a portion of the wall did not collapse (Josh. 2:18–19; 6:22–23).

Kenyon was looking for occupation during the nineteenth dynasty when Ramesses II reigned (thirteenth century B.C.). During this time, Jericho was abandoned. Since Kenyon was not a Bible scholar and had only the academic opinion of Bible scholars to go by, she made their mistakes hers. Bible chronology places the conquest of Jericho around 1400 B.C., and the Bible clearly says that Jericho was abandoned until the reign of King Ahab (1 Kin. 16:34). By the 1200s, the period Kenyon was assuming for the conquest, no one lived there. In this Kenyon was right.

The Period of the Monarchy

The existence and reign of David has been challenged in recent times by minimalist scholars who would like to deny the historicity of David and any earlier biblical history. However, in 1993 archaeologists discovered a stone inscription at Tel Dan in northern Israel that had been reused as fill in the eastern wall of the outer gate. This stele is now called the Tel Dan inscription. The author of the inscription claimed that Hadad (the storm god) made him king and boasted of killing Jehoram of Israel and Ahaziah of the house of David. There is some discussion as to the identification of the author. What is most significant, however, is the reference to the "house of David" in the text, indicating that there was a historical person named David who founded the line of kings in the Southern Kingdom of Judah.

Large six-chamber gates, built as part of a strengthening of wall fortifications at Gezer, Hazor, and Megiddo, match in design and come from the period of Solomon's reign. This work was probably referenced in 1 Kings 9:15. Similarly, excavations in Jerusalem below the Temple Mount have revealed monumental buildings that have been suggested to be the palace of David and later Solomon. In 2010, part of a wall with a gate house was found and has been associated with Solomon's fortifications. Large buildings from the tenth century B.C. in Khirbet Qeiyafa, houses built onto casemate (double) walls typical of Judean construction techniques (and not found in neighboring countries at that time), also suggest a strong centralized government at this time, and these have also been associated with David and Solomon. The twin gates (four chambers each) may help with the identification of this site as biblical "Shaaraim" (meaning "two gates"; 1 Sam. 17:52) that guarded the Valley of Elah route between Bethlehem (north route) and Hebron (south route) to Gath in the west. However, further confirmation beyond the existence of architecture is needed before they can be associated with confidence to David and Solomon. In the meantime, the best that can be said is that these findings make a kingdom, like the one described for David and Solomon in the Bible, possible.

Another Bible story that has more credibility because of an archaeological discovery is Joram's attack against Mesha, king of Moab (2 Kin. 3). In August of 1868 a stele was shown by local tribespeople at Dhiban to a German missionary who immediately recognized its importance and informed the authorities in Jerusalem about what he had seen. Having heard about it, the French epigrapher Charles Simon Clermont-Ganneau obtained a paper squeeze of the inscription. The stone was eventually broken apart (stories vary at this point, so it is unclear what the motivation was), but the paper squeeze, together with the pieces of the stone that were salvaged, revealed that it was a stele commemorating Mesha's victory over Israel. It refers to the same battle mentioned in the Bible (2 Kin. 3:26–27) but offers the Moabite perspective and contains the earliest known reference to Yahweh outside of the Bible.

Aside from describing events in the Bible, sometimes ancient stelae provide information on events that are about Bible characters. Jehu is depicted in the Black Obelisk of Shalmaneser III, discovered at Nimrud (ancient Calah) in 1846 by Sir Austen Henry Layard. The obelisk has four sides. On each side are five panels depicting tribute being brought to the Assyrian king. Significantly, the top panel reveals Jehu bringing tribute and kissing the ground before this king. It is the earliest picture of a king of Israel or Judah. Unfortunately, it shows him submitting to Assyria rather than to God.

The presence and activities of the Assyrians is well documented archaeologically. On one occasion (2 Chr. 32) they invaded Judah. Hanging on walls in a room in the British Museum are twelve panels recovered from room 36 in the Assyrian palace at Nineveh. These reliefs depict Sennacherib's conquest of Lachish, which is recorded in 2 Kings 18:13–16. By themselves they reveal much more about the battle than is recorded in the Bible, so a fuller understanding of that Bible story is gained. Excavations at Lachish reveal that the depictions are accurate. The panels show the Assyrians attacking the city using siege ramps with siege machines on both sides of the gate. Excavations have found the siege ramps right where the panels seem to depict them. This allows archaeologists to construct a three-dimensional understanding of the two-dimensional panel reliefs and thus understand the Bible story more clearly.

Prior to the Assyrians besieging Jerusalem, Hezekiah had constructed a tunnel to allow the city to have fresh water during an inevitable siege (2 Kin. 20:20; 2 Chr. 32:30). In 1838 Edward Robinson discovered a rock-cut tunnel beneath Jerusalem's City of David. In 1880 a group of boys playing in this tunnel discovered an inscription. In 1890 this inscription was chiseled out and stolen. Eventually most of it was recovered on the black market. It describes how Hezekiah had two teams tunneling from both ends toward each other, and they were able to meet—a remarkable engineering feat.

Exile

Although the Assyrians did not succeed in taking Judah into exile as they had Israel (2 Kin. 17–19), the Babylonians did a short time later (2 Kin. 24–25). "Babylon" is the Greek rendering of the Hebrew word "Babel." In this way, both the tower (Gen. 11) and the city ruled by Nebuchadnezzar (in Daniel) are known as "Babel," demonstrating that the Hebrew authors recognized the parallel. In fact, inscriptions bear testimony that Nebuchadnezzar considered the large ziggurat in Babylon to be a renovation of the tower.

The Ishtar Gate and the Processional Way of Babylon are now housed in the Pergamon Museum in Berlin, but only the smaller of the two gates is reconstructed for visitors to experience. In 1899 Koldeway rediscovered the Babylon that flourished under the kings Nabopolassar and his son Nebuchadnezzar II (famous from the book of Daniel). Over the next fourteen years, work continued until the outbreak of World War I. Since that time, nothing approaching the significance of this excavation has occurred there, although small excavations and clean-up efforts have taken place.

Babylon existed on both sides of the Euphrates River. It was circled by double walls—the larger wall being 20 feet (ca. 6 m) thick or more and possibly 100 feet (ca. 30 m) tall. A moat surrounded the walls which varied in width from 65 to 250 feet (ca. 20 to 76 m). Eight double gates (only four have been excavated) allowed entrance into the city, the Ishtar gate being the most remarkable one yet excavated. The Ishtar Gate on the north side of the city connected the palace and temple district with the bridge that crossed the Euphrates via the Processional Way. Both the gate and the way had walls lined with glazed tiles of blue, yellow, white, and brown decorated with lions, bulls, and dragons. The pavement was also decorated with white limestone and red breccia blocks. The Processional Way was about 62 feet (ca. 19 m) wide and extended for about 600 feet (ca. 182 m).

The enormous palace (that presumably contained the hanging gardens), the gigantic temple of Marduk (the Esagila), and the towering ziggurat Etemenanki were colossal in scale and were designed to wow visitors, filling them with a sense of their insignificance. It is this that Daniel and his friends would have encountered as they first entered Babylon and throughout their life in the palace. What has been excavated sufficiently demonstrates the source of Nebuchadnezzar's pride (Dan. 4:30).

Nebuchadnezzar is well attested by archaeology. Belshazzar, on the other hand, has not been. For most of the modern era, Belshazzar, king of Babylon (Dan. 5), was unknown outside the Bible. All Babylonian king lists claim that Nabonidus was the last king of Babylon, with no reference to Belshazzar. Then in 1854, excavations at the ziggurat in Ur revealed a piece of history that had been lost. At each of the corners of the last stage of the ziggurat, small clay cylinders were placed. Each cylinder contains the same inscription. Nabonidus, who renovated that ziggurat, gave instructions on these cylinders for the construction of this temple. Each ends with a prayer for his son, Belshazzar.

It turns out, based on cuneiform inscriptions, that Belshazzar was left in charge of the city of Babylon while his father relocated to Tema, in Arabia, for the final ten years of his reign. Although still technically the king of Babylon, and thus its last king, Nabonidus left his son in charge. This is apparently why Belshazzar offered Daniel the position of third ruler over Babylon (Dan. 5:29), as Belshazzar himself was second in rank.

Intertestamental Period

One of the most significant archaeological discoveries related to the Bible happened in 1946 or 1947 when shepherds from the Ta'amireh Bedouin tribe stumbled upon a cave near the Dead Sea containing jars with scrolls in them. Over the next decade, a total of eleven caves were found and more than 800 manuscripts, dating from the third century B.C. to the first century A.D. The scrolls were mostly written on parchment (animal skin), with some on papyrus (paper) and one (in two parts) on copper.

About half of the Dead Sea Scrolls (a little more than 400 manuscripts) discovered so far are classified as Jewish literature, which had previously been available only in ancient translation but now is available in the original Hebrew and Aramaic. About a fourth of the scrolls represent previously unknown texts linked to the religious community of Qumran. Scrolls containing portions of biblical books make up the remaining fourth of texts recovered, reflecting all books of the Bible except Esther (which is referenced in other Dead Sea Scrolls). The manuscripts were only made available to the public in 1992 and now can be studied online.

Most significantly, the scrolls have provided an enormous amount of information about Jewish sects during the Second Temple period (including the time of history recorded in the NT). They also provided textual scholars with Hebrew manuscripts that are over a thousand years older than the ninth century A.D. Masoretic manuscript (the Leningrad Codex) that had been the basis for the Hebrew text of the OT. Scholars have recognized that the Masoretic Text appears to have been remarkably stable in transmission over these one thousand years.

On either side of the Dead Sea stood two major mountaintop fortresses, both containing a palace of Herod the Great. Masada, on the western shore of the Dead Sea, was the larger of the two. Machaerus, on the eastern shore of the Dead Sea, is the location where John the Baptist was imprisoned and later beheaded. Both fortresses were occupied by rebels in the Jewish War (A.D. 66). Both also have the remains of Roman siege ramps and camps still visible to visitors today. Machaerus was conquered by Rome in A.D. 72 and Masada in A.D. 73.

The third largest palace/fortress in the Roman world was constructed by Herod on a hill three miles southeast of Bethlehem. It is probable that the soldiers who killed all of the boys under the age of two (Matt. 2:16) were deployed from this fortress. Josephus wrote that Herod was buried halfway up the Herodium. In 2007 archaeologists discovered the burial site (robbed out in antiquity). In recent years some have challenged this identification. Regardless, the size and grandeur of the Herodium provides significant information about Herod.

Gospels

In 1968 Capernaum was fully excavated. Twelve simple homes were discovered around a first-century synagogue. In the largest of these homes, a few fish hooks were discovered along with simple ceramic lamps, jars, pots, and bowls. This large house, unlike the other smaller ones, had its floor covered repeatedly over time with crushed and beaten limestone, and the walls had been successively plastered and decorated. This suggests that it was more than just a simple fisherman's home at some point after the fisherman had lived there. Nothing is known for certain about the identity of the occupants or the use of the building other than this. However, based on early church documents, it is known that Peter's house in Capernaum was turned into an early church. By the Byzantine period, a basilica was erected above this large house to venerate it as the house of Peter. While the identity of Peter's house remains uncertain, the first century A.D. fisherman's home offers an authentic backdrop to the story of Jesus.

In the drought of 1985–1986, the water level of the Sea of Galilee dropped significantly, exposing parts of the sea floor that had not been seen before. Two brothers, looking for relics, stumbled upon a fishing boat from the first century A.D. Because it was waterlogged, great care was taken in preserving this object that now can be seen and studied. The boat, currently in a small museum on the shore of Galilee not far from where it was found, shows that it was repaired many times. A small deck at the stern and possibly another at the bow would have helped the fishermen haul in the nets and steer. Jesus would have slept on or under one of these decks on His boat during the stormy night described in Matthew 8:23–27; Mark 4:35–41; and Luke 8:22–25.

Many of the stories in the Gospels revolved around a pool, and quite a number of pools have been discovered in and around Jerusalem. Some were used for purification before entering the temple, others for water storage. A pool was discovered by the Sheep Gate (John 5:2) north of the Temple Mount that has been identified with the pool of Bethesda. The pool of Siloam was more difficult to identify. Since most of the modern Old City Jerusalem is built above the ancient iterations of Jerusalem, it is difficult to discover sites. For some time the pool at the end of Hezekiah's tunnel was thought to be the pool of Siloam. However, archaeological evidence suggested that this was used only from the Byzantine period onward. Then in 2004 workers digging to install pipes unexpectedly unearthed large ancient blocks. Archaeologists were called in and a massive pool was found with three landings before the bottom of the pool. Five steps descend to each landing and then to the bottom of the pool. The complete pool has not been excavated since much of it rests under the Orthodox church's orchard. However, pottery and coins discovered in the plaster of the pool confirm that it was dug in the first century B.C. and was most likely the pool of Siloam in the time of Jesus.

Also found around Jerusalem and other areas of the Holy Land are rolling stone tombs, although no two are exactly alike. Typically, they were owned by wealthy families (poorer families had rock-cut tombs but without the rolling stone). They usually had a stone bench upon which the body was prepared, carved resting places where the body would decompose, and sometimes there was a ledge where a box (called an ossuary) with the collected bones could sit so the resting place could be reused. The rolling stone itself was typically large and required several people to move. It was placed in a carved trench that allowed it to roll forward to cover the entrance and back to open the entrance. Excavation below the Church of the Holy Sepulcher has found a rock quarry, which had been abandoned in the first century, where new tombs were dug. It is likely that this abandoned rock quarry resembled a skull (John 19:17). This site (enclosed by the Jerusalem city wall in A.D. 41 and commemorated as the site of the crucifixion and burial until A.D. 66) was intentionally filled in by Hadrian ca. A.D. 135 and dedicated to a temple to Aphrodite in order to religiously "contaminate" it. In A.D. 325 it was excavated and has been associated with the death and burial of Jesus ever since. An alternate site was proposed by Charles Gordon in 1883 north of the city due to the appearance of a skull in the recently cut rock quarry. Ninth through seventh century B.C. tombs were discovered nearby that had been reused by the Byzantines. The Garden Tomb (as it is known today) provides a more authentic experience than does the Church of the Holy Sepulcher, even though the church is almost certainly the site of the death and burial of Jesus. The tombs that had been freshly dug at the abandoned rock quarry during the time of Jesus match the "new tomb" description found in John 19:41. The fact that this was a new tomb indicates that it was being reserved for the head of the family, Joseph, to die and that no other body had been placed inside (i.e., "new"). In this way, we can understand that Joseph gave up his right of first burial to Jesus.

In 1961 a fragmented stone dating to A.D. 26–36 with an inscription was recovered in an archaeological site at Caesarea Maritima. The lower portion of the inscription is missing, but what remains clearly says that Pontius Pilate was the prefect of Judea. The stone probably contained a dedication to a temple built for Tiberius. The stone had been reused in a set of stairs for a Herodian theater in the fourth century A.D. From Josephus and Philo we learn that Pilate had difficulty maintaining peace in Judea, particularly because he seemed to be insensitive to Jewish customs. On a number of occasions his actions caused near-insurrections. These incidents included allowing images of Caesar to be brought into Jerusalem, setting up gold shields to honor Tiberius (this time without an image but still despised by the Jews), using money from the temple to build an aqueduct, and slaughtering Samaritans. From these accounts a picture of Pilate begins to form of a man who had been reprimanded by Rome for his judgment on a few occasions, who cared little for the lives of those he ruled, and who certainly could not risk another riot during Passover.

Early Church

Jesus predicted the destruction of the temple of Jerusalem, which at the time seemed a nearly impossible task. Archaeological excavation around the Temple Mount over the decades has been ongoing to such a degree that most of us forget the accuracy of what He predicted. The scale of the blocks used in the construction reveals why His prediction was scoffed at.

When Herod rebuilt the Temple Mount, he did so on a grand scale. The structure covered 172,000 square yards (approx. 144,000 square meters), making it the largest temple precinct in the ancient world at that time. A staircase ran almost a half mile uphill to bring worshipers to the temple. Ritual immersion pools have been discovered along the route for worshipers to purify themselves before entering. An inscribed stone has been found instructing the priests where to stand when they blew the Sabbath trumpet.

Ancient quarries reveal that massive stones, tens to hundreds of tons each (the largest stone still at the quarry is 26 feet [or 8.5 m] long), were moved to the temple site. One of the foundation stones used in the temple wall was 45 feet (15 m) long, 11.6 feet (4 m) high, and 14–16 feet (approx. 5 m) wide and weighed almost 600 tons. The pedestrian street, discovered near the temple wall, has buckled from the weight of the stones tossed down when the Romans dismantled the temple.

Another site that was glorious but lies in ruins is Ephesus. Archaeological work began there in the nineteenth century. Because of this work we now know that Ephesus was the fourth largest city in the ancient Roman Empire. Ephesus was home to a temple dedicated to the Egyptian goddess Isis but was primarily known as the home of the goddess Artemis (who was later equated with the Roman goddess Diana). Her temple was one of the seven wonders of the ancient world. Archaeological evidence demonstrates that there was a building boom in Ephesus in the first century A.D. that included a new stadium, a larger agora (or open marketplace), a new theater that sat 25,000 people, and a complex to house the Olympic games. Temples to the Caesars, a concert hall, a library, a council chamber, baths, a communal latrine, and luxurious terraced houses complete with indoor plumbing, heating, water storage, and magnificent artistic paintings demonstrate the opulence of the upper class. In A.D. 262 an earthquake destroyed much of the city and the Goths attacked in the next year, leaving Ephesus in ruins.

Fake Discoveries

Some notable items of interest have not been found in spite of sensational claims otherwise. The search for Noah's ark continues. Most of the activity in this search centers around a large mountain called Greater Ararat in modern Iraq. Major expeditions took place in 1949, the 1980s, the 1990s, and the 2000s, but they were not led by recognized, professional archaeologists. The most recent claim was by a Turkish–Hong Kong expedition. Nothing found yet has satisfied archaeologists.

The ark of the covenant also has not been found. Ethiopians claim to have it, but this has been disputed with evidence that shows that what they have is a replica. Some have claimed to have found it under the Temple Mount, but this claim has not been verified. Others claim that it is on Mount Sinai or Mount Nebo. Archaeologists nearly universally do not recognize any of these as verified.

The Tower of Babel also has not been found. It is likely that the great ziggurat of Babylon was built on its ruins, but excavation was not extensive enough to confirm or disprove this. At the moment this is mere speculation based on Nebuchadnezzar's claims.

THE FUTURE OF ARCHAEOLOGY AND THE BIBLE

There remains a massive amount of work yet to be done. Each archaeology field report contains crucial information about some aspect of life in the ancient world. Most of this information languishes in the world's libraries for want of scholars trained to recognize its significance. Nearly all archaeological sites are underfunded and left dormant for large parts of the year. Many are not being excavated at all. Museums are filled with objects still needing to be studied and written about. And while there are experts in nearly every aspect of archaeology, few believe in the Bible or have any interest in using the knowledge of archaeology to help illuminate the ancient world presented in the Bible.

The biggest problem is funding for projects and recruiting new generations of archaeologists. One ray of hope is the advancement of technology. Remote imaging has allowed archaeologists to see entire buried cities in Egypt via infrared satellite images. LIDAR (an acronym for LIght Detection And Ranging) and drones have also provided very helpful images from above. Magnetometry, electric resistivity, and ground-penetrating radar allow archaeologists to see below the ground and dig more surgically, thus reducing costs. Computer modeling and Internet tools are allowing excavations to be reexamined and promote collaboration among experts across the globe. The importance of managing an archaeological site even after excavation ends has become a priority. Involving the local population in digs and project management helps them to gain a feeling of ownership that protects sites. Antiquities departments are discovering the value of tourism and are adding more security to certain sites.

Archaeology is a window into the past that allows us to better understand the world of the Bible. When we understand the world that God interacted with in the long-ago past, we better understand how He interacts with us today.

OLD TESTAMENT TIMELINE

The OT generally follows a time sequence from beginning to end such that, with a few exceptions, the further one reads through the biblical text the closer in history to the Roman period one travels. However, because the canon is not always presented in chronological order, it is necessary to understand the timeline in order to also understand the relationship of each part to the others. All of the elements that make up the OT (i.e., stories, laws, wisdom writings, and prophecies) hang upon chronological statements that place these elements along a timeline that the biblical authors often appear to assume the reader is familiar with. This understood timeline is not always clear to the modern reader.

It is important, then, for the modern reader to become familiar with this timeline, for it gives relational meaning to each passage by tying one text to another and one event to another. Modern readers can most easily see the timeline through the chronological statements of the Bible. The primary value of a study of these chronological statements (i.e., the visible portions of the timeline) is that it provides deeper insights into the text by recognizing these relationships. Understanding the statements also opens further comprehension of the invisible portion of the timeline (i.e. the understood timeline that is not explicitly mentioned).

Time is a fixed phenomenon that cannot be seen, but it can be measured. Ancient scholars throughout history found their own ways to measure it. And although there are multiple ways to measure time, time itself is unchanged by these efforts. In this way the natural timeline is unseen, and attempts to measure it, in a sense, endeavor to make portions of it visible. This article will begin by briefly reviewing some of the methods ancient scholars used to measure time and providing a brief history of those who have studied these methods in modern times. This will serve as important background to a study of the biblical timeline from Jesus back to Adam.

OVERVIEW OF CHRONOLOGY

Forces beyond human control were often deified in the ancient world. These natural forces were studied in an attempt to find patterns that could bring order to life and were often used to manipulate people for religious or political purposes. Patterns were identified in daily, monthly, and yearly periods through the movement of heavenly bodies (sun, moon, and stars) and the coming and going of identifiable seasons. The ebb and flow of the cycle of life also provided measurable patterns. Religions and the governments that supported them were built around these measurements, which were systematized into calendars.

Some of these calendars were built around the movement of the moon. The Hebrews, Assyrians, Babylonians, Greeks, and early Romans developed versions of this lunar calendar. This had an immediate value in daily life. However, the basic problem with the lunar calendar was that over time it gradually lost its synchronization with the seasons. Each lunar-based civilization had its own way of dealing with this problem.

Other civilizations, such as the Egyptians and later Romans, crafted a solar calendar. This system did not lose its synchronization with the seasons as quickly as did the lunar calendar, so it took generations to identify the weaknesses of the solar calendar and then make adjustments. Today, we have largely adopted the solar calendar while maintaining some aspects of the lunar calendar for specific purposes. Our modern solution for the problems of a strict solar calendar is based in large part on the Julian calendar system that Augustus introduced in 22 B.C., in which an extra day was added to the calendar every fourth year (known as a leap year).

Another complication was the start to the new year. The Egyptians began their year when Sirius, the most prominent star in the night sky, first became visible, which corresponded roughly to the flooding of the Nile in mid-to-late July. The Assyrians, Babylonians, and Persians celebrated the beginning of their new year at the first new moon after the vernal equinox in late March or early April. God instructed the Hebrews before the Exodus event to begin their new year in the month that they left Egypt (which also corresponded to the vernal equinox). Later, the new year was shifted to line up better with agriculture so that the time of sowing marked the beginning of the year around mid-September. Understanding when and where this shift in the Hebrew calendar took place is vital to understanding some of the chronological statements in the OT and will be discussed where appropriate below. The Romans originally also timed their new year to the vernal equinox but eventually shifted it to January 1, a practice that is in wide, but not universal, use around the world today.

Relative versus Absolute

We do not know how much time passed between the creation of humans and our era. The most common modern system of numbering years increases from a point in time that was associated with the coming of Christ into the world. This system, built around the Christian religion, called all years from year one onward *anno domini*, the year of our Lord (abbreviated as A.D.). The advantage to this system is that all years before A.D. 1 are numbered in reverse order so that the further back in time one goes the higher the year number, allowing for a variety of chronological schemes to be developed and tested. These years are called B.C. (before Christ). Ironically, a mistake was made when this system was invented so that Christ was actually born somewhere between 6 and 4 B.C. (see below, pp. 101–102).

Recently, there has been a shift in scholarship away from using the Christian-influenced labels, particularly in areas of the world where they might be offensive. Instead of A.D. and B.C., which are based on the advent of Christ, the designations C.E. (common era) and B.C.E. (before common era) are used. The numbers for the years remain exactly the same so that A.D. 1 is the same as 1 C.E. This commentary will retain the A.D./B.C. labels.

A major mistake was made when this system was devised, leaving out the year zero. The result is that when using arithmetic to calculate how many years passed from a B.C. date to an A.D. date, an extra year must be added to the sum. An extra year must be subtracted for the same exercise in reverse. For example, if we wanted to start at 457 B.C. to discover when a period of 490 years ended (the seventy-week prophecy of Daniel 9), we would need to cross between B.C. and A.D. Since B.C. numbers decrease through time, we add 490 (years) to negative 457 (or 457 B.C.), with a sum of 33 (or A.D. 33). However, our integer system uses a zero, which the calendar system does not. Since the span of time between 1 B.C. and A.D. 1 was one year and not two, we must account for that missing year by adding one more year to the sum of our calculation. In this way, 490 years spans the time between 457 B.C. and A.D. 34.

An alternate dating system exists that attempts to calculate time from Creation forward. This system is called *anno mundi* (A.M.), meaning "in the year of the world" (or "year after Creation"). Many have worked on a system that could be used universally, but since there is not a consensus on when Creation took place, there is no widely accepted standard system. The Eastern Orthodox Church during the Byzantine period used the dates in the Septuagint to arrive at a date equivalent to September 1, 5509 B.C. to begin their A.M. calendar system. The Jewish community in the Middle Ages used the Masoretic Text to come up with a date equivalent to October 6, 3761 B.C. to begin their A.M. system.

The ancient people did not use any of these methods to measure time. Most ancient civilizations primarily dated events by connecting them in a relative way to other events that were well established. We call them *anchor events* because these established events were used to anchor other dates to the timeline. The reign of a king was often the anchor event. Sometimes the anchor event was a natural disaster, such as an earthquake, famine, flood, or volcano eruption. Sometimes it was a war. In all ancient civilizations, astronomical phenomena such as eclipses and the movements of planets were noted and often tied to the reign of monarchs. These phenomena are useful in establishing absolute dates and setting chronological anchors. It is upon these anchor events that the secular historic chronology is largely based. For example, approximately 1,600 cuneiform texts dealing with astronomy have been recovered from the city of Babylon alone. About 300 of these were mathematical tables used for calculating the positions of various heavenly bodies. The remaining 1,300 texts were observational diaries, general yearly records, records that tracked individual planets, and records of lunar eclipses. Modern astronomers are able to work backward from known astronomical positions today to establish absolute dates that correspond to these observations.

Statements in the OT often use these anchor events to date other events, such as "In the third year of Cyrus…" (Dan. 10:1). It is up to modern chronologists to link the anchor event to a date in an absolute reckoning system (such as A.D./B.C. or A.M.). When this is done, we can know that an event that took place in the third year of Cyrus (Dan. 10:1) happened by our absolute reckoning system in 536 B.C. because we have calculated from other sources the exact absolute dates, according to our system, of the reign of Cyrus.

Archaeology is one area of research that provides absolute dates for these relative anchor events. When an absolute date is associated with an anchor event in OT history, we have an anchor date along the OT timeline. In the discussion of the OT timeline below, these anchor dates will be identified along with the archaeological data that allowed it to be assigned a date. In turn, the anchor date can be used to help understand the relative relationship of a number of other events; the most enlightening are often those from other books of the Bible.

Chronology versus Genealogy

Debate concerning the OT timeline often results from lack of data. Wherever an educated guess is the best that can be offered, there is debate. Sometimes theories are used to support a debated point. Often these theories are themselves educated guesses. And since it is not possible (due to the lack of data) to resolve all of the debates, these theories linger. Over time, unproven but not yet discredited theories become cherished by scholars who have used them. In some cases, when data later emerges that should have clarified the original debate, it is not allowed to do so because of the cherished theory. Students of chronology should always keep this in mind and seek to resolve debate rather than maintain a theory.

The concepts of chronology and genealogy often get confused. Chronology deals with statements of time. Genealogy deals with generations of family relations. It is common to find both of these in the same OT passage. However, genealogy does not follow any given time sequence and thus is immeasurable in absolute time and often unhelpful for debates on chronology. This is because certain numerical factors vary from case to case. These varying factors may be age when married, age of parents at procreation, gender of offspring, and quantity of offspring.

This is clearly seen in the family of Abraham. Before Isaac was born, Abraham's nephew had children (Gen. 18–19), producing three generations in Abraham's brother's line but only two in Abraham's. Thus, because Isaac was born late in Abraham's life, he was essentially contemporaneous with his uncle's grandchildren, rather than his uncle's children, his first cousins. Thus, when Abraham's family is compared to his brother's, a generation was essentially skipped. Without the details of the story, we would have assumed (from a genealogical list that included only names) that Isaac was in the same generation as his cousin, Abraham's brother's son. This generation disparity is further highlighted when we note that Isaac married his own cousin's daughter (Gen. 22:20–23).

Sometimes, disparate facts from different places in one or more scriptural narratives can help us identify generational relationships. Jacob, like Abraham, did not have children until late in life. We know this because his son Joseph was thirty when he rose to power in Egypt (Gen. 41:46). Jacob came to Egypt after seven years of plenty and two years of famine (Gen. 45:11), at which point he was 130 years old (Gen. 47:9). Thus, we can calculate that Joseph was born when Jacob was ninety-one years old. Joseph was also born in the last year of the second set of seven years that Jacob worked for his two wives (Gen. 30:25–26; 31:41), so Jacob was eighty-four when he married Leah and Rachel, one week apart (29:28), and seventy-seven when he fled home (Gen. 27:41—28:5). In this way, chronology helps illustrate how generations are not parallel, even among brothers (his twin, Esau, was married several times by that point and had sons of his own).

HISTORICAL OVERVIEW

The earliest attempts to reconcile biblical events with the history of secular nations were undertaken by Josephus, Africanus, and Eusebius. Josephus was a Jew living in the first century A.D. during the last days before the Romans destroyed Jerusalem and caused the second Diaspora (A.D. 70). It is evident that Josephus wanted the Romans to appreciate the long history of his people, going back to antiquity, and so he wrote his famous work, the *Antiquities*. Julius Africanus was a Christian writer who lived in the southern Levant at the end of the second and beginning of the third centuries A.D. He wrote *Chronography* in five volumes. Eusebius of Caesarea lived toward the end of the third and beginning of the fourth centuries A.D. and wrote *Chronicle*. All three quoted from ancient sources. Unfortunately, their writings do not all agree chronologically. For example, one source was the writings of an Egyptian priest named Manetho, who wrote a history of ancient Egypt. Manetho's work no longer exists as an independent work. Selected quotes, found in these three sources, are all that remain. Unfortunately, the quotes that these writers attribute to Manetho do not agree with each other. This has made modern attempts to use these sources difficult. It has been necessary to find additional data to help reconcile the inconsistencies and fill in the gaps from ancient writers such as these.

Early Attempts

In 1625, James Ussher was appointed archbishop of Armagh, making him the head of the Anglican Church of Ireland. He spent the next few decades writing on theology before publishing a treatise on the calendar in 1648. Two years later, in 1650, his most famous work, *Annales veteris testamenti, a prima mundi origine deducti* (Annals of the Old Testament, Deduced from the Beginning of the World), was published. In it, he traced the chronology of the Bible back to Creation, which he thought was the evening of October 22, 4004 B.C.

Although he died six years later, Ussher's chronology lived long after him. His A.M. dates were adopted for use as margin dates in many Bibles. The first was a French Catholic Latin Bible in 1662. The best-known Bible to include Ussher's dates in the margins, the King James Version (KJV), did not originally have them. Bishop William Lloyd adjusted Ussher's dates from A.M. to B.C./A.D. in the London edition of the Oxford Bible in 1701. In 1950, the KJV replaced them with an updated set of dates based on new knowledge. By the 1970s most Bibles had removed dates altogether from margins as it was becoming clear that the dates were problematic.

Thiele's Breakthrough

Edwin Thiele, Seventh-day Adventist professor of antiquities, did his doctoral work at the University of Chicago on the chronology of the kings of Judah and Israel. Kings rarely, if ever, died conveniently on the last day of the calendar year so that their successor could begin ruling on New Year's Day. As a result, the remaining days of a calendar year in which the former king died (or was removed from office) was the accession year of the next king. Thiele discovered that the Northern Kingdom of Israel counted the accession year (remaining time in the last year of the previous king) as year one of the new king (essentially counting the same year twice; termed nonaccession- or regnal-year system), while the Southern Kingdom of Judah counted the accession year as his year zero, making the regnal year (first full year of a new king) year one (termed accession-year system).

He also discovered that the two kingdoms considered the new year to begin at different points in the calendar year. Israel (in the north) began its new year in the spring (the month of Nisan), and Judah (in the south) began its new year in the fall (the month of Tishri). Armed with these two pieces of data, Thiele was able to demonstrate that most of the chronological statements in the OT regarding the kings lined up very well. Later scholars added the possibility of coregencies (where a son ruled with his father for a period immediately prior to the father's death). The addition of coregency to Thiele's discoveries reconciled nearly all of the chronological issues for the period of the kings, although some scholars still debate minor points. These discoveries proved vital in a more accurate understanding of how related chronological statements should be understood, not just among books but also within books and particularly the prophecies of Daniel.

TIMELINE AND ISSUES

The review of the OT timeline that follows will work from known to unknown. Most anchor dates are in the more recent past. The further back in time a civilization existed, the fewer archaeological records there are to be recovered. This results in less information for the older civilizations that would enable chronologists to create anchor dates.

Most of the dates from the Roman period back to the Babylonian civilization are firm. As a result, the first section will briefly review anchor dates from Nebuchadnezzar to Jesus (Babylon to early Rome). It will become clear that even with anchor dates, there is still room for debate around events that are not firmly fixed on the OT timeline. The sections that follow this will likewise mark time from one important figure to another until Creation. All dates in these sections are to indicate relationships between chronological statements in the Bible and should not be read as absolutely definitive. They are simply a point of reference. However, one system of interpretation needed to be followed for consistency, and so the one that required the least amount of subjectivity in regard to the biblical text was the method selected. Along the way, prominent areas of disagreement will be briefly examined.

Nebuchadnezzar to Jesus

Jehoiachin Released from Prison. The length of the captivity of Jehoiachin, one of the last kings of Judah, needs some chronological explanation. He was taken captive by the Babylonians when the city of Jerusalem fell on March 16, 597 B.C. For the Babylonians, a new calendar year began on April 13, 597 B.C., about one month later. Two ways were used to record that one month. One way was to ignore it (or wrap it into the next full calendar year). The other was to count it as a separate year altogether. The modern researcher cannot always be sure which system was used.

Jehoiachin was released from prison in the twelfth month on either the twenty-seventh day (2 Kin. 25:27) or the twenty-fifth day (Jer. 52:31), which would have been either March 23 or 21 (respectively), 560 B.C. This is a little more than thirty-seven years after being taken captive (2 Kin. 25:27) but almost a year and a half after Evil (Awcl)-Merodach (Marduk, also Amel Marduk) became king. However, 2 Kings 25:27 records that Jehoiachin was released from prison by Evil (Awel)-Merodach in the year that he rose to power. Nebuchadnezzar died in early October 562 B.C. (likely on October 8), making 562/561 B.C. the accession year of Evil (Awel)-Merodach. So his rise to power happened thirty-five years, not thirty-seven years after Jehoiachin was taken captive. The problem is resolved in the translation of the phrase related to Evil (Awel)-Merodach becoming king.

The statement in 2 Kings 25:27, "in the year that he began to reign" or "in the year [he] became king" must be a reference to his first regnal year (561/560), not his accession year. Without this information we might believe that Jehoiachin was released almost immediately after Nebuchadnezzar's death, rather than almost a year later. Understanding this helps us to realize that Jehoiachin's imprisonment was not immediately on the mind of Evil (Awel)-Merodach but appears to have been an issue that came up after he had taken the necessary time to secure his throne. This also demonstrates that a year in ancient (including biblical) texts does not always mean one full calendar year.

The Cyrus Decree to Release Jews. Nabonidus (Nabunaid) was the last king of the Babylonian Empire. The Nabonidus Chronicle records the fall of the city of Babylon. Based on the chronology presented in the Nabonidus Chronicle, the Persian forces of Cyrus the Great captured Sippar on October 10, 539 B.C., Babylon on October 12, 539 B.C., and Arahsamnu on October 29, 539 B.C. Having vanquished all his immediate enemies, Cyrus was able to begin the first year of his reign as king of Babylonia the following spring, with the new year in April of 538 B.C., making this the year the decree was made to release the Jewish exiles (2 Chron. 36:22; Ezra 1:1; 6:3).

Decree to Restore and Rebuild Jerusalem. One anchor date from the NT that affects the OT timeline is found in Luke 3:1, 23. This links the beginning of the ministry of Jesus (at about thirty years of age, following His baptism) to the fifteenth year of Tiberius Caesar, which is commonly believed to have been in A.D. 27 (although there is some discussion on this date). Remembering that there was no year zero, the prophecy given to Daniel (Dan. 9:25) can be calculated to have begun in 457 B.C., the year the command was given to restore and rebuild Jerusalem by Artaxerxes I in the seventh year of his reign (Ezra 7:8–26).

An important factor in correlating anchor dates given by different writers is the new-year reckoning system (spring or autumn) used by the audience those writers were addressing.

Daniel used the Babylonian system (spring) when writing about a Babylonian government event in the narrative portion of his book. Jeremiah, writing about the same event (from the Jewish perspective), used the autumn system (which was used in the Southern Kingdom of Judah at the time; see "Thiele's Breakthrough," pp. 98–99). On the other hand, Daniel's prophecies later in his book, written for a Jewish audience in captivity, also appear to use the autumn system of reckoning.

The Greek to Roman Transition. Alexander the Great crossed the Hellespont in 334 B.C. and defeated Darius in 333 B.C. In 332 B.C. he defeated the city of Tyre and marched into Egypt, establishing Alexandria. He marched into Mesopotamia and defeated Darius again in 331 B.C. On either June 10 or 11, 323 B.C., Alexander died in Babylon after having extended his kingdom into India.

Seleucus, former commander of the cavalry, emerged as ruler of Babylon in 312 B.C. In 301 B.C. Seleucus took control of Anatolia and Syria. Wars with other generals would mark this entire dynasty. Pompey killed the last Seleucid princes and established the Holy Land as a Roman province in 63 B.C. Hasmonean kings reigned there until Herod the Great (with the blessing of Rome) defeated the last of them in 37 B.C. and ascended to the throne.

Meanwhile, in either 305 or 304 B.C., the Ptolemaic Kingdom was established in Greece under Ptolemy I, former general and satrap of Egypt. Eventually the last (and famous) Cleopatra (the seventh) began to rule in 51 B.C. Julius Caesar, who had defeated Pompey, become emperor of Rome, and formed an alliance with Cleopatra, died on March 15, 44 B.C. His adopted son, Octavian, became emperor. In 37 B.C., the same year that Herod began ruling in Judea, Mark Antony married Cleopatra. Herod allied himself with Antony and named the Antonia Fortress just north of the Temple Mount in his honor. When Octavian defeated Cleopatra and Antony, Herod re-allied himself with Octavian, whose name was later changed to Caesar Augustus (Luke 2:1). Herod built a new port city (to replace Joppa) and named it Caesarea (Marittima) to honor his new patron.

Birth of Jesus. Luke 3:23 states that Jesus was "about thirty years of age" in A.D. 27. "About" could reasonably mean one to two years on either side of thirty (meaning that He could have been slightly younger or older than thirty at the time). Thirty years prior to A.D. 27 is 4 B.C. (remembering that there was no year zero in this system). Herod the Great died (Matt. 2:19–20) about 4 B.C.

Early church authors (Clement of Alexandria, Julius Africanus, Origen of Alexandria, Eusebius of Caesarea, Epiphanius, Tertullian, and others) record the tradition that Jesus was born anywhere from A.D. 1 to 4 B.C. Herod was named king by the Roman Senate in late 40 B.C. but not named king in Jerusalem until the summer or fall of 37 B.C. after defeating the last Hasmonean king. His reign ended after his thirty-fourth year in Judea, which was 4 B.C. (He died in Jericho but was buried at the Herodium, southeast of Bethlehem.) Both Origen and Eusebius relate the tradition that Jesus was about two years old when the wise men visited and that He was in Egypt for about two years, which fits the information in Matthew 2.

How trustworthy any of these early church traditions are (since they do not all agree) is still a matter of debate. Since Jesus spent some time in Egypt and was less than two years old when they traveled to Egypt (Matt. 2:16), it seems likely that He was not born before 6 B.C. and more likely sometime in 5 B.C.

Solomon to Nebuchadnezzar

Divided Monarchy Chronology. At some point following the death of Solomon, the years of the reigns of the kings of Judah (the Southern Kingdom) were recorded in Scripture using the accession-year system (essentially counting the remaining parts of the rest of the last year of the previous king as a year zero of the new king). The years of the reigns of the kings of Israel (the Northern Kingdom) were recorded by the regnal-year system (or nonaccession; making the last year of the previous king the first year of the new king, essentially counting the same year twice). Combining this piece of information with the understanding of coregencies of certain kings provides a solution to most chronological issues of the Hebrew kings (see "Thiele's Breakthrough," pp. 98–99).

Two archaeological objects provide the most important anchor dates that can be applied to the internal chronology to give the OT timeline absolute dates during the time of the divided monarchy. Corroborating archaeological evidence supports these dates. Shalmaneser III's Monolith Inscription records the defeat of a coalition of forces from the Levant at Qarqar that included "Ahab, the Israelite." This battle is believed to have taken place in 853 B.C. (based on the dating in the inscription) but is not recorded in Scripture. Soon after, in the same year (according to the chronology of the reigns of the kings in the Bible), Ahab died at Ramoth-Gilead, an event that is recorded in Scripture (1 Kin. 22:3, 35) and can thus be dated with confidence. The Black Obelisk shows Shalmaneser III receiving tribute in 841 B.C. from many peoples and regions, including Jehu, king of Israel. Scripture does not record this event, but it records the year in which Jehu began to reign in Israel. These two events, twelve years apart, are anchor dates in the chronology of the kings of Israel in the OT timeline.

There has been some debate regarding the date of the division of the kingdom. Alternative dates include 926 and 922 B.C. The year 922 B.C. is based on a citation of Menander of Ephesus by Josephus regarding a kings list of Tyre and not by a calculation of dates backward from Ahab. However, Josephus was wrong in his dates and also with his math. Thus, based on the anchor dates of Ahab and Jehu and on the reigns of the kings of the Northern Kingdom as given in Scripture, the date 926 B.C. is generally regarded as the correct one.

Other Anchor Dates. In an inscription, Tiglath-Pileser III of Assyria claims to have received tribute from Azariah/Uzziah of Judah in 743 B.C. This does not match with any account in Scripture, but it does fit within the chronology. Another inscription describes the defeat of Rezon by Tiglath-Pileser III in 732 B.C. (an account probably associated with 2 Kin. 16:7–9) around the time of Hoshea's rise to the throne in Israel (2 Kin. 17:1). This provides another anchor date.

A Babylonian chronicle that dates to about 500 B.C. records that Shalmaneser V destroyed Samaria in 722 B.C. (2 Kin. 17:3) in the last year of his reign. This is an anchor date. This was also the accession year of Sargon II. He also claimed in his own inscriptions to have destroyed Samaria in 722 B.C., probably because he participated in the battle before officially becoming king.

The annals of Sennacherib record that in his third campaign, dated to 701 B.C., he laid siege to Jerusalem. This is no doubt the same event that is recorded in Scripture (2 Kin. 18:13; Is. 36:1), which occurred during Hezekiah's fourteenth year as king. This is an anchor date.

Rise of Babylon. Cuneiform tablets help us pinpoint the exact dates and make sense of the chronology in the closing years of the kingdom of Judah. On November 23, 626 B.C., Nabopolassar began to reign in Babylon, according to a cuneiform tablet in the British Museum (BM 25127). He was the father of Nebuchadnezzar II (who appears in the book of Daniel). Jeremiah's ministry, then, began in the year before this event (627 B.C.). In other words, God had already begun to predict the fall of Jerusalem by a conqueror from the north (Jer. 1:14) in the year before Nebuchadnezzar's father even began to reign and while Babylon was still part of the Assyrian Empire.

Nabopolassar, king of Babylon, joined forces with the king of Media. Together they attacked and defeated Nineveh. According to a cuneiform tablet in the British Museum (BM 21901), this was in July or August of 612 B.C. That same tablet also indicates that Nabopolassar attacked the remnant of the Assyrian empire under Ashuruballit II, taking Haran in 610 B.C. The next year (609 B.C.) a large army from Egypt tried to capture Haran to assist the Assyrian king. This is almost surely what was referenced in 2 Kings 23:29 (2 Chr. 35:20–21) when Josiah died. This is an anchor date.

The Egyptians under Necho II took Kimuhu, a Babylonian fortress, in 606 B.C. according to a cuneiform tablet in the British Museum (BM 22047). The next year, 605 B.C., another tablet (BM 21946) says Nabopolassar sent his son Nebuchadnezzar to meet the Egyptians at Carchemish, where he crushed them. Nebuchadnezzar chased the Egyptians into the southern Levant and, in the process, conquered Jerusalem. This is an anchor date.

Nabopolassar died on August 15, 605 B.C. On September 7, 605 B.C., Nebuchadnezzar was made king of Babylon (making 605 B.C. his accession year). On April 2, 604 B.C., Nebuchadnezzar began his first regnal year as king of Babylon.

Dating the First Conquest of Jerusalem. Jeremiah wrote that the battle at Carchemish took place in the fourth year of Jehoiakim (Jer. 46:2). The kings of Judah, at least from the time of Josiah to the fifth year of Jehoiakim, reckoned their year from fall to fall (rather than spring to spring as they had from the Exodus at least through Solomon's reign). The book of the law was found during the eighteenth year of the reign of Josiah (2 Kin. 22:3, 8) and Passover was celebrated (because they wanted to do what the book of the law said) also in the eighteenth year (2 Kin. 23:23). Josiah died in May or June of 609 B.C. at the battle at Megiddo. Jehoahaz reigned for only three months, and thus his reign ended in either July or

August of 609 B.C. Pharaoh Necho II deposed Jehoahaz and installed another son of Josiah, Jehoiakim (changing his name from Eliakim), who reigned for eleven years (2 Kin. 23:36). Jehoiakim, therefore, took the throne in July or August of 609 B.C. with only a month left in that accession year. His first regnal year began in September of 609 B.C. and the battle of Carchemish occurred four years later, as Jeremiah said. Jeremiah also connected this event to the beginning of the reign of Nebuchadnezzar (Jer. 25:1). However, the phrase that is sometimes translated as "first year" should more accurately be understood to mean "beginning year" (or "accession year"). Because the Hebrews reckoned the regnal year from September (when Nebuchadnezzar was put on the throne), Nebuchadnezzar began his regnal year not from April of 604 B.C. (as the Babylonians reckoned) but from September of 605 B.C., as reckoned by those in Judah. Thus, it is still accurate from the perspective of Judah to call 605 B.C. Nebuchadnezzar's first year.

Exactly the reverse reckoning is seen in Daniel 1:1. Daniel recorded that Nebuchadnezzar attacked Jerusalem in the third year of Jehoiakim. But Nebuchadnezzar attacked Jerusalem after the battle of Carchemish, which, as just was said, took place in Jehoiakim's fourth year. This has been explained by simply understanding that Daniel was writing from Babylon, in which the regnal year began in April, not September, and so appears to have reflected the Babylonian government's system of reckoning. In later prophecies when writing about his people, Daniel's method appears to have used the autumn to autumn reckoning system. From the Babylonian perspective (as the first chapter of Daniel is written), the accession year of Jehoiakim ended not in September of 609 B.C. but in April of 608 B.C. Therefore, from the Babylonian way of reckoning, the battle of Carchemish, and thus the fall of Jerusalem in 605 B.C., took place in the third year of Jehoiakim, not his fourth. This does not affect the seventy-year prophecy of Jeremiah (Jer. 25:11–12; 29:10), as he was writing based on the Jewish way of reckoning. This amply illustrates the ever-present difficulty when comparing chronologies of unrelated ancient cultures. The chronologist must always remember from what perspective the information was recorded.

End of Judah. Nebuchadnezzar returned to the Levant (which the Babylonians called "Hatti-land") in May or June of 604 B.C. to receive tribute from those he had conquered the year before. It seems that when Jehoiakim became his vassal (2 Kin. 24:1), he also adopted the Babylonian calendar and returned to counting the years from spring to spring. From the perspective of those in Judah, Jehoiakim's fifth year was seventeen months long rather than the normal twelve. This explains how the ninth month of his fifth year fell in the winter (Jer. 36:9, 22).

In this way, Jehoiakim's eighth year was at this point the same as Nebuchadnezzar's fourth year. A cuneiform tablet in the British Museum (BM 21946) records that in Nebuchadnezzar's fourth year he was defeated on the border of Egypt. This most likely explains why Jehoiakim rebelled after serving Nebuchadnezzar for three years (2 Kin. 24:1).

Three years later (Jehoiakim's eleventh year; 2 Kin. 23:36; 2 Chr. 36:5) Nebuchadnezzar returned. A cuneiform tablet in the British Museum (BM 21946) says that he camped against the city of Judah in his seventh year. This tablet dates the beginning of the siege to December 18, 598 B.C. and the end to March 16, 597 B.C., which is the exact date of the fall of Jerusalem. Since 2 Kings 24:5-6 makes it clear that Jehoiakim died and his son Jehoiachin ascended to the throne and ruled for three months and ten days (2 Chr. 36:9) before Nebuchadnezzar replaced him after the siege, Jehoiakim must have died and Jehoiachin must have taken the throne on December 9, 598 B.C., just before the siege began.

Mattaniah, Jehoiachin's uncle, was made king by Nebuchadnezzar, who changed his name to Zedekiah (2 Kin. 24:17) immediately after the end of the siege, which was before the end of the regnal year in April. So the remainder of that year was his accession year. His first regnal year began on April 13, 597 B.C., corresponding to Nebuchadnezzar's eighth regnal year.

Zedekiah reigned for eleven years (2 Kin. 24:18), putting the fall of Judah in 587/586 B.C., which is dated to the nineteenth year of Nebuchadnezzar's reign (Jer. 52:12-14). The siege had begun in the ninth year on the tenth day of the tenth month of the reign of Zedekiah (2 Kin. 25:1; Jer. 39:1). This means that the siege began on January 15, 588 B.C. Zedekiah's eleventh (and last) year as king began on April 23, 587 B.C. On the ninth day of the fourth month of that year, the walls were breached (2 Kin. 25:3-4), which was July 29, 587 B.C. Then on either the seventh day (2 Kin. 25:8-9) or on the tenth day (Jer. 52:12-13) of the fifth month, which would have been either August 25 or August 28, 587 B.C., Nebuzaradan burned the temple, the palace, and all the houses of Jerusalem. If Jeremiah was using the old way of calculating the start of the year (meaning in the fall) and not the Babylonian way, then the fall of Jerusalem was in the spring of 586 B.C. instead. This is likely the case, which is why many Bible chronologies, including this one, list 586 B.C. as the date for the fall of Jerusalem.

The wealth of data available in this period of history demonstrates what could be possible in understanding biblical chronology and the events associated with it in earlier periods if more data were available to work with.

Moses to Solomon

Dating the Exodus Event. Working from known historical dates that connect with stated biblical events, anchor dates were established that can be used to apply absolute dating to the relative dating statements in Scripture. As a result, working backward in time, Solomon died in 931 B.C. after reigning for forty years (1 Kin. 11:42). Thus, he began his reign in 971 B.C. First Kings 6:1 reads that the construction of the temple began in the second month (month of Ziv) in Solomon's fourth year. The mention of the month of Ziv reminds readers that at that time the Hebrews were still reckoning their new year in the spring. Thus, the construction of the temple began in what we call April/May of 967 B.C. This is important for dating the Exodus event because 1 Kings 6:1 also links the building of the temple to the Exodus event, 480 years earlier. According to this reckoning, the Exodus event would have taken place in March/April of 1447 B.C.

There has been an attempt to push Solomon's reign back a few years due to his coregency with David, resulting in an Exodus date of around 1450 B.C. Solomon would have reigned (as coregent and later as sole king) for forty-three or forty-four years. Other conservative scholars propose 1446 or 1445 B.C. as the date of the Exodus by rounding down. A very different approach has been suggested by those who argue that the 480 years are representative of generations and should not be understood as actual years. This is proposed in an effort to shorten the duration of the period to allow for Ramesses II (who ruled in the thirteenth century B.C.) to be associated with the Exodus event, which is not possible if the 480 years are taken as literal years. If understood literally, the 480 years allows for a ca. 1407 B.C. destruction of Jericho (it was not occupied in the thirteenth century B.C.) and a full 300 years from that date to the time of Jephthah (Judg. 11:26).

Forty Years Wandering. The Hebrews left Egypt on the fourteenth day of the first month (Ex. 12:2, 6, 31). Three months later they reached Sinai (Ex. 19:1). They left Sinai nearly eleventh months later (Num. 10:11–13), a little over a year after the Exodus event. Aaron died on the first day of the fifth month in the fortieth year, when he was 123 years old (Num. 33:38–39). On the first day of the eleventh month of the fortieth year, Moses recited Deuteronomy to the Hebrews, who had already killed Sihon and Og and were camped across from Jericho (Deut. 1:3–4). Moses died shortly thereafter on Mount Nebo, when he was 120 years old (Deut. 34:1, 7). These statements are in harmony with the age gap given in Exodus and also confirm that the forty years spoken of were counted from the Exodus event (Ex. 7:7) and not from the rejection of God by the Hebrews following the report of the scouts (Num. 14:33). They also confirm that there were only thirty-eight years from the pronouncement of the penalty until they began to fight for the land that they would later inhabit (Deut. 2:14). Understanding this helps us to understand God's mercy. The forty-year penalty included time already spent in the wilderness at Sinai.

Reign of Saul. There is a chronological statement regarding the reign of Saul (1 Sam. 13:1), the first king of Israel, that is difficult to understand because it appears that the Masoretic Text has left some words out. The Septuagint provides the possible missing information that likely appeared in other Hebrew manuscripts that are now lost but were reflected in the statement in Acts 13:21. Saul likely ruled for forty or forty-two years and may have been thirty years old when he began to reign. This information gives us some insights into the timeline of the story. Since David was thirty years old when he began to reign (2 Sam. 5:4), Saul had ruled for about ten years before David's birth.

Genealogy of David. There is a very short genealogical list between Perez, son of Judah by Tamar (Gen. 38), and the birth of David (Ruth 4:18–22), but it is consistent with other genealogical lists (1 Chr. 2:3–15; Matt. 1:3–6; Luke 3:31–33). Aaron (from the tribe of Levi) had married Nahshon's sister (from the tribe of Judah), Elisheba (Ex. 6:23). Nahshon was the leader of the tribe of Judah in the Exodus event (Num. 1:7; 2:3). His son Salmon married Rahab (Josh. 6; Matt. 1:5). Their son, Boaz, married Ruth (Ruth 4:13; Matt. 1:5), even though she was much younger than he was (Ruth 3:10). Their son, Obed, was the grandfather of David, who was the youngest son of eight (1 Sam. 17:12–14), although it looks like one son might have died early and was not counted in later genealogies (1 Chr. 2:15). Since these genealogies do not give chronological statements, there is no reason not to trust that they are complete. However, if they are complete and there were 480 years (1 Kin. 6:1) between the Exodus and David's son Solomon's fourth year of rule, then most of these genealogical links must have also been unusual, such as marriages between those who were of different generations within a family (see Isaac and Rebekah below) and births to parents late in their lives (see Abraham and Isaac below). This is likely here since it appears that at least one of the marriages was late in life (Boaz and Ruth), at least one involved a youngest son (David), and at least one involved a son born when a parent was old (Solomon; 2 Sam. 11:1; cf. 2 Sam. 21:15–17; 1 Kin. 1:1).

Abraham to Moses

From this point back to Creation, the archaeological record is highly fragmented and has suffered data loss to such a degree that dates can be reckoned only by chronological statements. As a result, there are no more anchor dates that can be determined confidently using extrabiblical data. Thus, we move into a time when there is much uncertainty in regard to how biblical events line up with secular ones.

Call of Abram. It is clear that Abram was seventy-five years old when he left Haran following the death of Terah (Gen. 12:4), but it appears that the call (Gen. 12:1–3) came while the family was still in Ur. There is no chronological statement to allow us to know how much time expired between that call and the death of Terah, but it is likely to have been two to three years if the entire 430 years of the sojourn (Ex. 12:40–41) included time in Canaan beginning with Abram's call (see below).

Some scholars have suggested that Amraphel, king of Shinar (Gen. 14:1), is another name for Hammurabi, king of Babylon. There are three chronological schemes that are used by scholars to date kings of ancient Babylon. Each scheme is named based on the length of the chronology so that there is a long chronology, a middle chronology, and a short chronology. Because there is not sufficient data, there is no way to determine confidently which scheme is correct. However, it is not possible that Hammurabi was the same person as the biblical Amraphel since all three of the chronological schemes appear to place Hammurabi more in the lifetime of Isaac or Jacob than early Abraham.

Birth of Jacob's Sons. It is common to think of Joseph as much younger than his other brothers. However, chronological statements make it clear that all eleven brothers were born within a seven-year period (Gen. 30:25; cf. 31:41). In order for this to be possible and each of the four mothers to receive at least two months of recovery time before becoming pregnant again, some of the mothers were pregnant at the same time.

Sojourn and Exodus 6. One area that remains unsettled in scholarship is the length of the sojourn. The term *sojourn* means "temporary stay" and refers to a length of time either from Abraham until the Exodus or from Joseph until the Exodus. Exodus 12:40–41 says that the length of the time Israel lived temporarily (without a permanent home) was 430 years. The Masoretic Text reads that the entire 430 years were spent in Egypt. The Septuagint and the Samaritan Pentateuch read that the 430 years includes time spent in both Canaan and Egypt. This latter reading seems to reflect a Hebrew manuscript that no longer exists but was referenced by Paul (Gal. 3:16–17), who claims that there were 430 years between the call of Abraham and the Law given at Mount Sinai (three months after the Exodus and thus in the same year as the Exodus; Ex. 19:1). Exodus 6 also seems to support the understanding.

Exodus 6:13–16 recounts the names of the family members who moved to Egypt and follows the list in Genesis 46:8–11. None of the other brothers are listed because the point is to explain who Aaron and Moses were (Ex. 6:26–27). In vv. 17–25 all of the sons born in Egypt to the family of Levi are listed. Also listed is the age at death for each of those in the line of Aaron and Moses (Ex. 6:16, 18, 20). Moses and Aaron's ages are also listed (Ex. 7:7). However, because the age of the father when his son was born is not listed (as the chronologies of Genesis 5 and 11 do), there is no way to link the chronology of Jacob to Moses directly. This has allowed for both sojourn theories (Abraham until the Exodus or Joseph until the Exodus) to be debated. That said, there either have to be hidden generations (not mentioned in Exodus 6) or the time in Egypt was much shorter than 430 years. This is because the total listed years from Kohath to Moses equal only 350 years ($133 + 137 + 80 = 350$). However, this would mean that Kohath was only a newborn in Canaan and that all of his 133 years of life were spent in Egypt. It would also mean that he fathered his son, Amram, in the year he died (at the age of 133). It would likewise mean that Amram fathered Moses, his youngest son, in the year he died (at age 137). These scenarios are unlikely. It is also not clear where the hidden generations are supposed to be inserted to accommodate more time in Egypt, since the biblical text is clear that Kohath was born in Canaan (Gen. 46:11), that Amram married Levi's daughter/Kohath's sister (Ex. 2:1; 6:20), and that Moses was Amram's son (Ex. 2:1–10). This illustrates the difficulty of placing the Hebrews in Egypt for all 430 years of the "sojourn" (for more on this debate, see "The Four-Hundred-Thirty-Year Sojourn," p. 211).

Noah to Abraham

Flood Chronology. The Flood was tied to the age of Noah so that it began when he was 600 years old (Gen. 7:6). It ended when Noah was 601 (Gen. 8:13), although the family and animals (except for a few birds) did not leave the ark for nearly two more months (Gen. 8:14). There are chronological markers throughout the story to inform the reader when the rain stopped, when the waters started to diminish, when the tops of trees could be seen, and a few other events. This is important when discussing the event. Most events take place on a single day or within a relatively short period of time. Noah's family was in the ark well over an entire calendar year.

Dating Post-Flood Patriarchs. Because Genesis 11 provides chronological detail with the genealogy, it is possible to gain some insights into the patriarchs who lived after the Flood. There was a clear drop-off in age between Eber (who lived 464 years) and his son Peleg (who lived 239 years—only about half as long). Because the cryptic phrase about the dividing of earth is attached to the days of Peleg, some have theorized that this could be a reference to the Tower of Babel event and that it may have involved physiological changes rather than just a simple language confusion. Others have wondered if there was a physical division of the earth beyond what had happened during the Flood. Another drop in life span is noticeable between Serug (who lived 230 years) and his son Nahor (who lived 148 years). It is not clear what caused these drops in life span.

Also, because of these two major drops, a study of the chronology reveals that some of the patriarchs were alive for most of this period. Noah died two years before Abram was born. Shem died ten years after Isaac and Rebekah's wedding. This has led some to theorize that Shem may have been Melchizedek because he was the oldest living patriarch at the time. Arphaxad died two years after Ishmael was born. Shelah died only nineteen years before Sarah. And Eber (after whom the Hebrews were named) lived for 464 years and for all but sixteen years of Abraham's life.

Adam to Noah

Date of Creation. Ussher calculated his A.M. (*anno mundi*) 1 date to be equal with 4004 B.C. This was based on his understanding of Bible chronology that set Jehoiachin's release from prison in the year 562 B.C. (2 Kin. 25:27). He considered that since the Sabbath is Saturday, then the Creation week began on Sunday. Using the *Rudolphine Tables*, he thought that the autumnal equinox should match with the creation of the heavenly bodies on the fourth day of Creation, which helped him set the start of Creation to the evening of October 22.

A chronology that considers the 430-year sojourn (see above, pp. 107–108) to include time from Abram's call to Mount Sinai (Gal. 3:16–17) could calculate the Creation event as being equal to 3958 B.C. One who determines the 430 years to have been only time in Egypt might pinpoint the Creation to about 4173 B.C. Some Christian scholars allow for the Creation event to be dated as far back as 10,000 B.C. with the understanding that, since the Bible is basically a book with the purpose of teaching lessons, perhaps there are further gaps in the chronology that are not apparent in the text itself. There are enough variables in the record that no one can know with any certainty the date when Creation week began.

Dating Pre-Flood Patriarchs. Even a cursory glance at the chronological statements given in Genesis 5 reveals that the life span of humans after the Fall but before the Flood were on average somewhat less than one thousand years each, with two major exceptions. Enoch did not die (Gen. 5:21–24) but appears to have lived a life that included delivering warning messages to the pre-Flood world (Jude 14–15) before being taken to heaven (Heb. 11:5), as Elijah later was (2 Kin. 2:11; cf. Matt. 17:3). The other life span anomaly was Noah's father, Lamech, who lived only 777 years. This has led some scholars to speculate that he may have died of other causes than old age. Methuselah, who lived to an age older than any other recorded human, 969 (Gen. 5:27), died in the same year as the Flood, causing some to wonder if he died in the Flood or just before it. Altogether, the Masoretic Text lists 1,656 years between Creation and the beginning of the Flood.

CONCLUSION

A study of chronology has led some to misuse it. One way that it is misused is in the setting of future dates. One of the most common theories is the notion that since there are six days in a week and then a seventh-day Sabbath, perhaps the thousand-year millennium (Rev. 20:3) is a seventh part of the history of sin (2 Pet. 3:8). The theory postulates that the six thousand years that precede the seventh will end with the Second Advent of Christ.

Ussher predicted that the six thousand years would end in the year A.D. 2000. Many others have set other dates. All have been wrong. A chronology that saw Creation as occurring in 4173 would have expected the six thousand years to have ended in A.D. 1828. A chronology that dated Creation to 3958 B.C. would expect the Second Coming in A.D. 2043.

However, these theories need to take into account that there is no prophecy toward this end in Scripture. Also, the dates presented here rely heavily on the current understanding of archaeology, which is always open to revision due to new discoveries and excavations. Further, some of these dates are tied to eclipses, and as more precise astronomical information is collected, those dates may also be adjusted, which would shift the dates in the OT timeline. As a result, theoretical speculation regarding end-of-time date setting should be avoided.

The Bible is a document intended to teach its readers how to form a loving, healthy relationship with God. It records history, but not every part is intended to be a record of history as many events are skipped. Understanding how all of its parts are related requires a study of chronology. The OT timeline provides a line that connects these parts.

A CHRONOLOGY FOLLOWING THE INTERNAL TIMELINE OF THE BIBLE

The Bible writers followed ancient methods of marking time by linking events in a relational way to other events, usually referred to as relative dating. This sometimes makes it difficult for us today to quickly understand when these biblical events took place in regard to unrelated events. We solve that problem with absolute dating. This method assigns fixed year numbers that, by their very nature, provide the relationship for unrelated events.

Because of the relative dating method found in Scripture, modern scholars use different systems to understand how these relative dates should be reinterpreted as absolute dates. Here we provide a chronology that follows one of these systems, as reflected throughout this commentary. These dates begin with the most recent and move backward toward the beginning of biblical chronology. The dates given here should not be taken as the final word on the matter. This chronology is presented as a reference tool. Major events are highlighted with bold text. Biblical references are provided for entries based on chronological statements or statements about the event in the text.

Although several modern scientific dating systems are at conflict with some of the earlier dates in this chronology, the relative happenings of these events are seen by assigning them dates as indicated in the internal timeline of the Bible.

A.D. 98	John dies	A.D. 79	Titus reigns in Rome	ca. A.D. 65	Paul writes Titus
A.D. 96	John writes his Gospel	A.D. 77	Josephus writes *Jewish War*	A.D. 65	Paul writes 1 Timothy (or A.D. 65–66)
A.D. 96	Nerva ends official persecution	A.D. 73	Masada falls to the Romans	A.D. 65	Peter dies
ca. A.D. 95	John writes Revelation	**A.D. 70**	**Titus destroys Jerusalem**	ca. A.D. 64	Paul writes Hebrews (or early- to mid-60s)
A.D. 93	Josephus writes *Jewish Antiquities*	A.D. 70	John leaves Judea	ca. A.D. 64	Peter writes 2 Peter
ca. A.D. 90	John writes his epistles	A.D. 69	Year of the Four Emperors	A.D. 64	Nero persecutes Christians
A.D. 80	Colosseum is dedicated in Rome	A.D. 68	Nero dies	A.D. 63	Peter writes 1 Peter
A.D. 79	Pompeii is destroyed by Vesuvius	ca. A.D. 67	Paul dies	ca. A.D. 62	Luke writes Acts
		A.D. 66	Jews revolt		
		A.D. 66	Paul writes 2 Timothy		

A.D. 62	James, brother of Jesus, killed	A.D. 51	Gallio becomes proconsul in Achaia (Acts 18:12)	**A.D. 34**	**Stephen is stoned/gospel goes to the Gentiles (Acts 7:57–60; Dan. 9:24)**
ca. A.D. 61	Luke writes his Gospel	A.D. 51	Paul writes 2 Thessalonians (or A.D. 50–51)	A.D. 31	Falling of the early rain at Pentecost
ca. A.D. 61	Paul writes Colossians	ca. A.D. 50	Matthew writes his Gospel	A.D. 31	Jesus ascends to heaven
A.D. 61	Paul is acquitted of charges and released	A.D. 50	Paul writes 1 Thessalonians (or A.D. 50–51)	A.D. 31	Jesus is resurrected
A.D. 61	Paul writes Philemon	ca. A.D. 49	James writes his epistle	**A.D. 31**	**Jesus is crucified (Matt. 26:17; John 19:14; Dan. 9:27)**
A.D. 61	Paul writes Philippians	A.D. 49	Paul writes Galatians		
A.D. 61	Paul writes Ephesians	A.D. 49	Paul begins his second journey	A.D. 31	Jesus cleanses the temple again (John 13:1)
ca. A.D. 60	John Mark writes his Gospel	A.D. 49	Christian community rises in Philippi	A.D. 30	Jesus performs His last Judean ministry (John 6:4)
ca. A.D. 60	Jude writes his epistle	A.D. 49	Jerusalem Council meets	A.D. 29	Jesus performs His Galilean ministry
A.D. 60	Paul is taken from Caesarea	A.D. 49	Claudius expels Jews from Rome	A.D. 28	Jesus cleanses the temple (John 2:13)
A.D. 59	Festus governs Judea	A.D. 47	Ananias serves as high priest	**A.D. 27**	**Jesus is baptized (Luke 3:1–2; Dan. 9:25)**
A.D. 58	Paul is taken to Caesarea	A.D. 47	Paul ends his first journey		
A.D. 58	Paul ends his third journey	A.D. 45	Paul begins his first journey	A.D. 18	Caiaphas becomes high priest
ca. A.D. 56–57	Paul writes Romans	A.D. 44	Herod Agrippa dies (Acts 12:23)	A.D. 14	Tiberius reigns in Rome
A.D. 56	Paul writes 2 Corinthians in Macedonia	ca. A.D. 43	Barnabas seeks Saul in Tarsus (Acts 11:25)	ca. A.D. 8	Jesus amazes scholars in the temple (Luke 2:41–42)
A.D. 56	Paul arrives in Corinth in the winter	A.D. 42	Paul's vision in Tarsus (2 Cor. 12:1–2)	A.D. 6	Annas becomes high priest
ca. A.D. 55	Paul writes 1 Corinthians	A.D. 41	Herod Agrippa reigns in Judea	ca. 4 B.C.	Herod the Great dies
A.D. 54	Jews return to Rome	A.D. 41	Claudius reigns in Rome	ca. 5 B.C.	Jesus is born[1] (Matt. 2:1, 9–11, 16; Luke 2:1–7; 3:23)
A.D. 54	Nero reigns in Rome	A.D. 37	Caligula reigns in Rome		
A.D. 53	Paul begins his third journey	A.D. 37	Saul visits Jerusalem (Acts 9:26)		
A.D. 52	Paul ends his second journey	A.D. 36	Pilate loses his position		
A.D. 52	Felix becomes procurator of Judea				

19 B.C.	Herod begins building the temple	336 B.C.	Alexander the Great rises to power in Macedonia (Dan. 2:39; 7:6; 8:7, 21; 11:3)	520 B.C.	Darius issues the decree (Ezra 6:1–12)
27 B.C.	Augustus reigns in Rome	345 B.C.	Persians destroy Sidon	522 B.C.	Darius reigns in Persia
27 B.C.	Corinth made capital of Achaia	**408 B.C.**	**Jerusalem is rebuilt (Dan. 9:25)**	530 B.C.	Cyrus dies
30 B.C.	The last Greek kingdom falls to Rome	ca. 440 B.C.	Ezra writes his book	536 B.C.	Daniel receives the final vision (Dan. 10:1)
37 B.C.	Herod reigns in Judea	444 B.C.	Nehemiah leads the return to Jerusalem	537 B.C.	Zerubbabel leads the return to Jerusalem (Ezra 2:1–2)
42 B.C.	Philippi is established as a Roman colony	444 B.C.	Artaxerxes issues a second decree (Neh. 1:1)	537 B.C.	Cyrus issues a decree to return to Jerusalem (Ezra 1:1; Dan. 9:25)
44 B.C.	Julius Caesar is assassinated	457 B.C.	Ezra leads the return to Jerusalem (Ezra 7:7)	539 B.C.	Daniel receives the seventy-week vision (Dan. 9:1; 11:1)
44 B.C.	Rome rebuilds Corinth	**457 B.C.**	**Artaxerxes's command leads to the rebuilding of Jerusalem (Ezra 7:7, 12–26; Dan. 8:14; 9:25)**	539 B.C.	Darius the Mede reigns in Babylon (Dan. 5:30; 11:1)
47 B.C.	Julius Caesar reigns in Rome				
63 B.C.	Pompey conquers Judea (Dan. 11:20)	465 B.C.	Artaxerxes rules	**539 B.C.**	**Cyrus conquers Babylon (Dan. 2:39; 5:30; 7:5; 8:5)**
164 B.C.	Antiochus Epiphanes dies in the Levant	465 B.C.	Xerxes dies		
165 B.C.	The temple is rededicated (Hanukkah)	479 B.C.	Esther becomes Queen (Esth. 2:16)	548 B.C.	Daniel sees the ram and goat vision (Dan. 8:1)
168 B.C.	Rome begins war on Greek kingdoms (Dan. 2:40; 7:7)	483 B.C.	Xerxes dismisses Queen Vashti (Esth. 1:3)	550 B.C.	Daniel sees the four-beast vision (Dan. 7:1)
175 B.C.	Antiochus Epiphanes rules the Levant	486 B.C.	Ahasuerus/Xerxes rules	550 B.C.	Belshazzar co-reigns in Babylon
305 B.C.	Seleucus Nicator rules the Levant	**515 B.C.**	**The temple is rebuilt in Jerusalem (Ezra 6:15)**	555 B.C.	Nabonidus reigns in Babylon
305 B.C.	Ptolemy Soter rules Egypt	520 B.C.	Zechariah's ministry begins (Zech. 1:1)	559 B.C.	Cyrus rises to power in Persia
323 B.C.	Alexander the Great dies (Dan. 7:6; 8:8; 11:4)	520 B.C.	Haggai's ministry begins (Hag. 1:1)	562 B.C.	Jehoiachin is released in Babylon (2 Kin. 25:27–30)
332 B.C.	Alexander the Great destroys Tyre				
333 B.C.	Alexander the Great destroys Sidon				

562 B.C.	Nebuchad-nezzar dies
568 B.C.	The Babylonian invasion of Egypt fails
572 B.C.	Babylon conquers Tyre
585 B.C.	Babylon lays siege to Tyre
586 B.C.	Ishmael murders Gedaliah (Jer. 41)
586 B.C.	**Nebuchad-nezzar destroys the temple (2 Kin. 25:2, 8–9; Jer. 39:2; Dan. 1:2; 5:2)**
586 B.C.	Zedekiah is taken to Babylon (2 Kin. 25:7)
586 B.C.	Ezekiel gives an oracle for Tyre (Ezek. 26:1)
587 B.C.	Jeremiah buys a field (Jer. 32)
588 B.C.	Egypt forces the Babylo-nians to retreat from Jerusalem (Jer. 37:5)
588 B.C.	Babylon begins siege on Jerusalem (2 Kin. 25:1; Jer. 39:1)
590 B.C.	Ezekiel is visited by the elders (Ezek. 20:1)
592 B.C.	Ezekiel's min-istry begins (Ezek. 1:1–2)
597 B.C.	Zedekiah reigns in Judah (2 Kin. 24:17–18; 2 Chr. 36:11)
597 B.C.	Jehoaichin is taken to Babylon (2 Kin. 24:12)

597 B.C.	Babylon conquers Jerusalem (Jer. 24:1; 29:1)
598 B.C.	Jehoiachin reigns in Judah (2 Kin. 24:8; 2 Chr. 36:9)
ca. 599 B.C.	Babylon invades the Levant (Jer. 49:28)
601 B.C.	The Babylo-nian invasion of Egypt fails
603 B.C.	Nebuchad-nezzar has the image dream (Dan. 2:1)
605 B.C.	**Nebuchad-nezzar rises to power in Babylon**
605 B.C.	**Daniel is taken to Babylon (Dan. 1:1; 1:3–6)**
605 B.C.	Babylon conquers Jerusalem (2 Kin. 24:1; Dan. 1:1)
605 B.C.	The Carche-mish battle occurs (Jer. 46:2)
609 B.C.	Jehoiakim reigns in Judah (2 Kin. 23:34, 36; 2 Chr. 36:5)
609 B.C.	Jehoahaz is chained in Riblah (2 Kin. 23:33)
609 B.C.	Jehoahaz reigns in Judah (2 Kin. 23:31; 2 Chr. 36:2)
610 B.C.	Necho reigns in Egypt
612 B.C.	Nineveh is conquered by Babylon and Media

622 B.C.	Josiah renovates the temple (2 Chr. 34:8; 2 Kin. 22:3;)
627 B.C.	Jeremiah's ministry begins (Jer. 1:1–3)
629 B.C.	Josiah purges Judah of idols (2 Chr. 34:3)
641 B.C.	**Josiah reigns in Judah (2 Kin. 22:1; 2 Chr. 34:1)**
643 B.C.	Amon reigns in Judah (2 Kin. 21:19; 2 Chr. 33:21)
ca. 681 B.C.	Isaiah dies
687 B.C.	Hezekiah dies
697 B.C.	Manasseh co-reigns in Judah (2 Kin. 21:1; 2 Chr. 33:1)
ca. 700 B.C.	Hezekiah expands Jerusalem
701 B.C.	**Sennacherib invades Judah (2 Kin. 18:13; 2 Chr. 32:1; Is. 36:1)**
716 B.C.	**Hezekiah reigns in Judah (2 Kin. 18:1–2; 2 Chr. 29:1)**
722 B.C.	**Assyria conquers Israel (2 Kin. 17:6, 23)**
722 B.C.	Hoshea is taken to Assyria (2 Kin. 17:4)
725 B.C.	Hosea's ministry ends
732 B.C.	Hoshea reigns in Israel from Samaria (2 Kin. 17:1)
732 B.C.	Jotham dies

732 B.C.	Tiglath-Pileser conquers Damascus (2 Kin. 16:9)
734 B.C.	Israel and Syria attack Judah (2 Kin. 16:5)
735 B.C.	Ahaz co-reigns in Judah (2 Kin. 16:1–2; 2 Chr. 28:1)
740 B.C.	Pekah solely reigns in Israel from Samaria (2 Kin. 15:27)
740 B.C.	Pekah assassinates Pekahiah (2 Kin. 15:27)
740 B.C.	Azariah/Uzziah dies
742 B.C.	Pekahiah reigns in Israel from Samaria (2 Kin. 15:23)
750 B.C.	Hosea's ministry begins (Hos. 1:1)
750 B.C.	Jotham co-reigns in Judah (2 Kin. 15:32–33; 2 Chr. 27:1, 8)
752 B.C.	Pekah reigns in Israel from Gilead[2] (2 Kin. 15:32; 16:1)
752 B.C.	Menahem reigns in Israel from Samaria (2 Kin. 15:17)
752 B.C.	Shallum reigns in Israel from Samaria (2 Kin. 15:13)
753 B.C.	Zechariah reigns in Israel from Samaria (2 Kin. 15:8)
ca. 760 B.C.	Earthquake happens in the Levant
767 B.C.	Amaziah dies

782 B.C.	Jehoash/Joash of Israel dies
792 B.C.	Azariah/Uzziah co-reigns in Judah (2 Kin. 15:1–2; 2 Chr. 26:1, 3)
793 B.C.	Jeroboam II co-reigns in Israel from Samaria (2 Kin. 14:23)
796 B.C.	Amaziah reigns in Judah (2 Kin. 14:1–2; 2 Chr. 25:1, 25)
796 B.C.	Jehoash/Joash of Judah dies
798 B.C.	Jehoash/Joash reigns in Israel from Samaria (2 Kin. 13:10)
814 B.C.	Jehoahaz reigns in Israel from Samaria (2 Kin. 13:1)
835 B.C.	Jehoash/Joash reigns in Judah (2 Kin. 12:1; 2 Chr. 24:1)
841 B.C.	Athaliah reigns in Judah (2 Kin. 11:1–4; 2 Chr. 22:10—23:1)
841 B.C.	Ahaziah reigns in Judah (2 Kin. 8:25–26; 2 Chr. 22:2)
841 B.C.	Jehu reigns in Israel from Samaria (2 Kin. 10:36)
848 B.C.	Jehoshaphat dies
852 B.C.	Jehoram/Joram reigns in Israel from Samaria (2 Kin. 3:1)
853 B.C.	Jehoram/Joram co-reigns with Jehoshaphat in Judah (2 Kin. 8:16–17; 2 Chr. 21:5, 20)

853 B.C.	Ahaziah reigns in Israel from Samaria (1 Kin. 22:51)
869 B.C.	Jehoshaphat sends teachers to cities in Judah (2 Chr. 17:7)
870 B.C.	Asa dies
872 B.C.	Jehoshaphat co-reigns with Asa in Judah (1 Kin. 22:41–42; 2 Chr. 17:1; 20:31)
874 B.C.	**Ahab reigns in Israel from Samaria (1 Kin. 16:29)**
879 B.C.	Omri builds and reigns from Samaria (1 Kin. 16:23–24)
880 B.C.	Tibni dies
885 B.C.	Omri reigns in Israel from Tirzah (1 Kin. 16:23)
885 B.C.	Tibni reigns in Israel (1 Kin. 16:21)
885 B.C.	Zimri reigns in Israel from Tirzah (1 Kin. 16:15)
886 B.C.	Elah reigns in Israel from Tirzah (1 Kin. 16:8)
909 B.C.	Baasha reigns in Israel from Tirzah (1 Kin. 15:33)
910 B.C.	Nadab reigns in Israel from Shechem (1 Kin. 15:25)
911 B.C.	Asa reigns in Judah (1 Kin. 15:9–10; 2 Chr. 14:1; 16:13)

913 B.C.	Abijam/Abijah reigns in Judah (1 Kin. 15:1–2; 2 Chr. 13:1–2)
926 B.C.	Shishak invades Judah (1 Kin. 14:25)
928 B.C.	Jeroboam makes gold calves (1 Kin. 12:25–33; 2 Chr. 11:17)
931 B.C.	Jeroboam reigns in Israel from Shechem (1 Kin. 12:20, 25)
931 B.C.	**Israel's kingdom is divided (1 Kin. 12:1–24)**
931 B.C.	Rehoboam reigns (1 Kin. 11:43; 14:21; 2 Chr. 9:31)
931 B.C.	Solomon dies (1 Kin. 11:42; 2 Chr. 9:30)
947 B.C.	Solomon completes the palace (1 Kin. 9:10; 2 Chr. 8:1)
ca. 950 B.C.	Solomon writes Song of Songs
960 B.C.	Solomon completes the temple (1 Kin. 6:38)
967 B.C.	**Temple construction begins (1 Kin. 6:1)**
971 B.C.	Solomon's solo reign begins (1 Kin. 1:38–40; 2:11)
971 B.C.	David dies (2 Sam. 5:4; 1 Kin. 2:11)
972 B.C.	Rehoboam is born (1 Kin. 14:21)

1004 B.C.	David reigns from Jerusalem (2 Sam. 5:5)
1009 B.C.	Ish-Bosheth is murdered (2 Sam. 2:10; 4:7)
1011 B.C.	**David reigns from Hebron (2 Sam. 2:11; 5:4–5)**
1011 B.C.	Ish-Bosheth reigns from Mahanaim (2 Sam. 2:10)
1011 B.C.	Saul dies (1 Sam. 13:1; 31:4)
1041 B.C.	David is born (2 Sam. 5:4)
ca. 1050 B.C.	Philistines destroy Shiloh
1051 B.C.	Ish-Bosheth is born (2 Sam. 2:10)
1053 B.C.	Saul reigns from Gibeah[3] (1 Sam. 13:1; Acts 13:21)
1083 B.C.	Saul is born[4] (1 Sam. 13:1)
ca. 1107 B.C.	Jephthah makes a case to the Ammonites[5] (Judg. 11:26)
1401 B.C.	Caleb inherits Hebron (Josh. 14:10)
1407 B.C.	**Jericho falls to the Israelites (Josh. 1:2; 6:1–27)**
1407 B.C.	Moses dies (Deut. 34:7)
1407 B.C.	Aaron dies (Num. 33:38–39)
1407 B.C.	Miriam dies (Num. 20:1)
1446 B.C.	Spies are sent to Canaan (Num. 10:11; 13:1—14:38; Josh. 14:7)

1447 B.C.	Sanctuary construction begins (Ex. 19:1)
1447 B.C.	**The Exodus occurs[6] (Ex. 7:7; 1 Kin. 6:1; Acts 7:23, 30)**
1486 B.C.	Caleb is born (Josh. 14:7)
1487 B.C.	Moses flees from Egypt (Ex. 2:11–15; Acts 7:23)
1527 B.C.	Moses is born (Ex. 2:2; 7:7)
1530 B.C.	Aaron is born (Ex. 7:7)
1566 B.C. (1781)	Levi dies[7] (Ex. 6:16)
1589 B.C. (1804)	Joseph dies (Gen. 50:26)
1643 B.C. (1858)	Jacob dies (Gen. 47:28)
1660 B.C. (1875)	**Israel dwells in Egypt (Gen. 45:6; 47:9, 28)**
1662 B.C. (1877)	Years of famine begin (Gen. 41:30)
1669 B.C. (1884)	Years of great abundance begin (Gen. 41:29)
1669 B.C. (1884)	**Joseph is promoted by Pharaoh (Gen. 41:46)**
1670 B.C. (1885)	Isaac dies (Gen. 35:28)
1671 B.C. (1886)	The butler receives a dream (Gen. 41:1)
1682 B.C. (1897)	**Joseph is sold into slavery (Gen. 37:2, 28)**
1693 B.C. (1908)	Jacob leaves Laban (Gen. 31:38, 41)
1699 B.C. (1914)	Joseph is born (Gen. 29:20, 30; 30:25–26)

1705 B.C. (1920)	Reuben is born (Gen. 29:32)
1706 B.C. (1921)	Jacob marries Leah and Rachel (Gen. 29:20–30)
1713 B.C. (1928)	Jacob leaves home[8] (Gen. 28:5)
1727 B.C. (1942)	Ishmael dies (Gen. 25:17)
1750 B.C. (1965)	Esau marries Hittite women (Gen. 26:34)
1771 B.C. (1986)	**Eber dies (Gen. 11:16–17)**
1775 B.C. (1990)	**Abraham dies (Gen. 25:7)**
1790 B.C. (2005)	Jacob and Esau are born (Gen. 25:26)
1800 B.C. (2015)	**Shem dies (Gen. 11:10–11)**
1810 B.C. (2025)	Isaac marries Rebekah (Gen. 25:20)
1813 B.C. (2028)	Sarah dies (Gen. 23:1)
1832 B.C. (2047)	Salah/Shelah dies (Gen. 11:14–15)
1847 B.C. (2062)	**The 400-year affliction begins (Gen. 15:13; 21:8–9; Acts 7:6)**
1850 B.C. (2065)	Isaac is born (Gen. 21:5)
1851 B.C. (2066)	**Abram is circumcised (Gen. 17:24–25)**
1862 B.C. (2077)	Arphaxad dies (Gen. 11:12–13)
1864 B.C. (2079)	Ishmael is born (Gen. 16:16)

1875 B.C. (2090)	Abram leaves Har[r]an[9] (Gen. 12:4)
1875 B.C. (2090)	Terah dies (Gen. 11:32)
1877 B.C. (2092)	**The 430-year sojourn begins (Gen. 12:1; Ex. 12:40; Gal. 3:16–17)**
1909 B.C. (2124)	Serug dies (Gen. 11:22–23)
1932 B.C. (2147)	Reu dies (Gen. 11:20–21)
1940 B.C. (2155)	Sarai (Sarah) is born (Gen. 23:1)
1950 B.C. (2165)	**Abram (Abraham) is born (Gen. 11:32; 12:1, 4)**
1952 B.C. (2167)	**Noah dies (Gen. 9:28–29)**
1961 B.C. (2176)	Nahor dies (Gen. 11:24–25)
1962 B.C. (2177)	Peleg dies (Gen. 11:18–19)
2010 B.C. (2225)	Tereh's eldest is born (Gen. 11:26)
2080 B.C. (2295)	Terah is born (Gen. 11:24)
2109 B.C. (2324)	Nahor is born (Gen. 11:22)
2139 B.C. (2354)	Serug is born (Gen. 11:20)
2171 B.C. (2386)	Reu is born (Gen. 11:18)
ca. 2201 B.C. (2416)	**People are scattered from the Tower of Babel[10] (Gen. 11:9)**
2201 B.C. (2416)	Peleg is born (Gen. 11:16)
2235 B.C. (2450)	Eber is born (Gen. 11:14)

2265 B.C. (2480)	Salah/Shelah is born (Gen. 11:12)
2300 B.C. (2515)	Arphaxad is born[11] (Gen. 11:11)
2301 B.C. (2516)	The Flood ends (Gen. 8:13)
2302 B.C. (2517)	**The Flood begins[12] (Gen. 7:6)**
2302 B.C. (2517)	Methuselah dies (Gen. 5:27)
2307 B.C. (2522)	Lamech dies (Gen. 5:31)
2400 B.C. (2615)	Shem is born (Gen. 11:10)
2402 B.C. (2617)	Japheth is born (Gen. 5:32; 10:21)
2422 B.C. (2637)	**Work on the Ark begins (Gen. 6:3)**
2536 B.C. (2751)	Jared dies (Gen. 5:20)
2668 B.C. (2883)	Mahalalel dies (Gen. 5:17)
2723 B.C. (2938)	Cainan/Kenan dies (Gen. 5:14)
2818 B.C. (3033)	Enosh dies (Gen. 5:11)
2902 B.C. (3117)	**Noah is born[13] (Gen. 5:28)**
2916 B.C. (3131)	Seth dies (Gen. 5:8)
2971 B.C. (3186)	**Enoch is translated (Gen. 5:23)**
3028 B.C. (3243)	**Adam dies (Gen. 5:5)**
3084 B.C. (3299)	Lamech is born (Gen. 5:25)
3271 B.C. (3486)	Methuselah is born (Gen. 5:21)
3336 B.C. (3551)	Enoch is born (Gen. 5:18)
3498 B.C. (3713)	Jared is born (Gen. 5:15)

3563 B.C. Mahalalel is	3723 B.C. Enosh is born	**3958 B.C. Beginning**
(3778) born	(3938) (Gen. 5:6)	**(4173) of human**
(Gen. 5:12)		**chronology**
	3828 B.C. Seth is born	**with Adam**
3633 B.C. Cainan/Kenan	(4043) (Gen. 5:3)	**and Eve[14]**
(3848) is born		**(Gen. 5:5)**
(Gen. 5:9)		

1 If Jesus was about thirty years old when His ministry began (Luke 3:23), He would have been born ca. 5 B.C. However, "about thirty" could reasonably be plus or minus two to three years, which would shift this date.

2 The Northern Kingdom appears to have been split at this time (Hos. 5:5), which is reflected in the chronological reckoning.

3 The Septuagint provides missing information from the Masoretic text in 1 Samuel 13:1.

4 All dates from the birth of Saul to the Babylonian captivity are tied to dates related to Nebuchadnezzar, working backward through the chronological data related to the kings.

5 All dates from Jephthah back to the Exodus are based on the date of the Exodus and would move proportionally with that date, were it to shift.

6 This date reflects simple arithmetic from 1 Kings 6:1. Conservative scholars allow for an Exodus date between 1445 and 1452 B.C.

7 This reflects a 430-year sojourn in Canaan and Egypt (from the call of Abraham to the giving of the Law at Sinai; Gal. 3:16–17). Should the 430-year sojourn consist entirely of time spent in Egypt (Ex. 12:40; Masoretic text), all dates from Levi's death backward should be moved earlier by approximately 215 years. These alternate dates are provided in parentheses.

8 This date is deduced by moving backward through the chronological details found in Genesis 45:6.

9 Twenty-five of the thirty years between the beginning of the sojourn and the affliction are accounted for from Har[r]an to Isaac's birth. The remaining five years are split in a way that cannot be entirely known between the time between Ur and Haran and the time between Isaac's birth and the weaning party (the beginning of the affliction). The later period could not have been more than three years. If they were fewer than three years, the time in Haran would increase from two years proportionally and all dates from Levi's death backward would shift by that same number (a potential shift of one to two years).

10 Scripture does not provide a chronological statement for this event. The date reflects a statement connected with Peleg's birth (Gen. 10:25).

11 If Genesis 11:10 is a reference to the end of the Flood event (when Noah's family left the ark) rather than the beginning of the actual Flood itself, all dates before this would move back one year.

12 The date of this event depends on the accuracy of the chronology in Genesis 10 and 11 (compare Luke 3:35–36).

13 All antediluvian dates are based on Noah's age at the Flood moving backward (except the birth of Shem).

14 This date is extrapolated from simple arithmetic applied to the plain data in Genesis 5 and based on a trusted chronological system. This result is not meant to be the final word on the matter (for more, see "Old Testament Timeline," pp. 109–110). Some scholars allow for this date to be as far back as ca. 10,000 B.C. The Bible is not explicit regarding whether the chronology of Adam and Eve began at the Creation or at the Fall.

PENTATEUCH

INTRODUCTION
TO THE PENTATEUCH

The term *Pentateuch* refers to the first five books of the Bible. It is a two-part Greek word, *penta* ("five") plus *teuchos* (a case for carrying scrolls and later the scroll itself), and it goes back at least to the second century A.D. when the church father Tertullian spoke of the *pentateuchos biblios*, the "five-scrolled book." The oldest designation of the Pentateuch is the Hebrew word *torah*. Although usually translated "law," this term also more broadly refers to "instruction" and even "story."

AUTHORSHIP

There is abundant evidence throughout Scripture (and early Jewish/Christian testimony) that Moses was the author of the Pentateuch.

Evidence from within the Pentateuch

The Hebrew phrase "God spoke to Moses" is found more than 235 times in the Pentateuch. Numerous passages refer to Moses as writing parts of the Pentateuch, and these include all three major types of writing in the Pentateuch: history/narrative, legal material, and poetry (see Ex. 17:14; 24:4; Num. 33:2; Deut. 31:9, 22, 24). Deuteronomy 31:24 mentions that Moses wrote all the words of "this *torah*" on a scroll. This verse may refer primarily to the book of Deuteronomy, but in light of the other references in the Pentateuch to Moses's writing, it ultimately applies to the whole Torah.

Even though the book of Genesis does not itself explicitly mention Moses as the author, internal evidence of the Pentateuch points strongly toward this conclusion. The opening word of Exodus contains a grammatical construction (the word "and" as a *waw* conjunction) that links it with what comes before (i.e., the book of Genesis) and thus the two books are viewed together as a unity. The book of Genesis also has numerous Egyptian loan words, giving evidence that the author was well acquainted with the Egyptian language and customs, as was the case with Moses. Finally, various linguistic peculiarities of the Pentateuch are found only in Genesis and the other four books of the Torah.

Testimony of Joshua

After Moses's death, God appeared to Joshua, Moses's successor, and exhorted him to be strong, very courageous, and dedicated to obeying all of the Torah, which His servant Moses had given to him. Indeed, Joshua was instructed to continually speak of and think about the whole Torah in order to obey it and prosper (Josh. 1:7–8). Immediately after Moses completed the writing of the Torah, it was to be regarded as "canonical," the foundation of divine revelation to God's people.

Testimony of Later Old Testament Writers

Numerous passages in the OT refer to Moses as the author of the Pentateuch. Preexilic testimony includes Joshua 8:31–32, 34; 22:5; 23:6; Judges 1:20; 1 Kings 2:3; 2 Kings 14:6; 23:25. Exilic and postexilic testimony includes 2 Chronicles 23:18; 25:4; 30:16; 35:12; Ezra 3:2; 6:18; Nehemiah 8:1, 14; 13:1; Daniel 9:11, 13; and Malachi 4:4.

Testimony of Christ and the Gospel Writers

The Gospels cite the Pentateuch more than sixty times, often explicitly describing it as "the law of Moses" (e.g., Luke 2:22; 24:44; John 7:23) and using terms like "Moses wrote" (Mark 12:19; Luke 20:28; John 5:46) or simply "Moses" (Luke 24:27; John 5:45). In John 5:46, Jesus referred specifically to Moses's writings, noting that he had written about Him.

Testimony of Acts and the Apostles

The book of Acts cites the Pentateuch more than twenty times and contains several references to the "law (*nomos*—the Greek word used for the Torah) of Moses" (Acts 13:39; 15:5; 28:23) and other expressions implying authorship of the Torah to Moses (Acts 3:22–23; 6:11, 14; 15:21; 21:21; 26:22). The apostles quote the Pentateuch more than sixty times, often referring to Moses as the author (e.g., Rom. 10:5 says "Moses writes," citing Lev. 18:5; cf. Rom. 10:19; 1 Cor. 9:9; 2 Cor. 3:15; Heb. 10:28; 12:21).

Testimony of Early Jewish and Christian Sources and Ellen G. White

The historian Josephus (c.a. A.D. 37–100) states that "five are the books of Moses." The Babylonian Talmud likewise affirms that "Moses wrote the Pentateuch and Job." The early Christian church fathers consistently refer to the Pentateuch as written by Moses. Ellen White identifies Moses as the author of the Pentateuch, including the book of Genesis. She indicates that Moses wrote Genesis and Job in the wilderness of Midian (ST Feb 19, 1880; cf. PP 251). Other statements indicate her acceptance of Moses as the author of the Pentateuch (e.g., GC 434; PP 343, 364, 463).

Affirmation of Moses as the author of the Pentateuch does not eliminate the possibility that Moses himself used other written sources (see Gen. 5:1 and Num. 21:14) and that some explanatory phrases or updating of place-names may have been added for clarity in a later historical setting (e.g., the mention of Dan in Gen. 14:14 [cf. the original name Laish, Judg. 18:29]; the reference to the Canaanites in Gen. 12:6). The last eight verses of Deuteronomy, recording Moses's death, were apparently written by Joshua.

CRITICAL THEORIES OF AUTHORSHIP

Throughout Judeo-Christian history until the rise of higher criticism in the time of the Enlightenment, the Pentateuch was almost universally recognized as written by Moses, under the inspiration of God. But with the rise of the Enlightenment, which elevated human reason over divine revelation, questions regarding the authorship of the Torah began to be seriously entertained. Starting with the Jewish philosopher Benedict Spinoza in the seventeenth century and the French court physician Jean Astruc in the eighteenth century, scholars gradually began to reject Moses's authorship of the Pentateuch.

Especially in German scholarship, various hypotheses of multiple sources (excluding Moses's authorship) were proposed and came to be called the *Documentary Hypothesis*. During the latter half of the nineteenth century, the New Documentary Hypothesis, developed by K. H. Graf, Abraham Kuenen, and Julius Wellhausen, began to dominate over the earlier theories, and it still holds sway in much of higher critical scholarship to the present day. Wellhausen was largely responsible for giving classical expression to and popularizing this New Documentary Hypothesis (1878). According to this theory, there were four main sources for the Pentateuch:

- J (Jahwist): written about 850 B.C. in the Southern Kingdom of Judah
- E (Elohist): written about 750 B.C. in the Northern Kingdom of Israel (a redactor [R^{JE}] combined these sources about 650 B.C.)
- D (Deuteronomist): the core of the present book of Deuteronomy, produced in the time of Josiah (a redactor [R^D] added the D source to JE about 550 B.C.)
- P (Priestly): written between 536 B. C. and 450 B.C. (a redactor [R^P] incorporated the P source into the JED sources and completed the Pentateuch about 400 B.C.)

Since the time of Wellhausen, some modifications have been suggested regarding the dating of these and additional sources. But the basic schema of Wellhausen's Documentary Hypothesis is still widely defended in critical scholarship.

The basic pillars of the Documentary Hypothesis (also known as source criticism) were originally derived from the work of German classical literary critics studying the German fairy tales collected by the Grimm brothers and published in seven expanding editions from 1819 to 1857. In the spirit of the Enlightenment, it was assumed that the stories of the Pentateuch, like the Grimm stories, were myths or fairy tales and thus the techniques of literary source criticism common to the times could similarly be used for understanding the development of the Pentateuch.

The five basic pillars of the classical Documentary Hypothesis include: (1) use of different divine names (Yahweh and Elohim); (2) duplications and repetitions (double names like Jethro/Reuel, Ishmael/Midian, and Sinai/Horeb; repetitions like Abraham's two denials that Sarah was his wife [Gen. 12 and 20], and Hagar's two departures [Gen. 16 and 21]); (3) variations of style and language (such as different genres together—narrative, poetry, laws, etc.); (4) contradictions/anachronisms (e.g., the mention of domesticated camels and use of iron in the time of the patriarchs; the reference to the Hittite Empire; existence of codified laws); and (5) other signs of composite authorship (e.g., shifts and breaks in the narratives).

It must be noted that all of the basic pillars of the nineteenth-century literary-critical study of the German fairy tales and other Western folk literature have long since been abandoned, yet many biblical literary critics still continue to defend the results of scholarship based on these very pillars for supporting the composite authorship of the Pentateuch. Many of them simply ignore questions of authorship and focus on the final form of the text, called the New Literary Criticism.

Furthermore, all of the pillars of Wellhausen's Documentary Hypothesis have now been shown to be suspect when compared to other ANE literature discovered since the time of Wellhausen. (1) Numerous ancient documents with unquestioned unity use double names for the gods (e.g., Baal/Hadad in Ugaritic literature; Osiris/Wennofer in Egyptian literature; multiple epithets for God in the Code of Hammurabi). (2) Duplicates and repetitions like those in the Pentateuch can be seen in many Egyptian and Mesopotamian double names of individuals and geographical localities (e.g., the Assyrian King Tiglath-Pileser III/Pul; two names for Egypt in Merenptah's Israelite Stela). Documents and monuments with duplicate accounts, as in Genesis 1–2 (containing a general summary outline and then a more detailed account), are found throughout the ANE materials (e.g., the dual descriptions of Thutmose III on the Karnak Stela). (3) There are many ANE documents where variations of style/genre occur in the same context (e.g., the Biography of Uni [ca. 2400 B.C.] contains narrative, summary, hymns, and refrains). (4) Many of the supposed contradictions/anachronisms have now been shown to fit precisely into the times claimed for the patriarchal period: extensive evidence for the early domestication of camels and use of iron has been found; the existence of a vast Hittite Empire, unknown in the time of Wellhausen, has now come to light through archaeological excavations; various patriarchal customs described in the Pentateuch are illustrated in the Nuzi and Mari tablets from this very time; and major ANE law codes have been discovered from this period of history. Finally, (5) the supposed signs of composite authorship (e.g., narrative shifts/breaks) have been found throughout ancient literature, representing the literary style of the times. There is simply no ANE example for the kind of editorial method proposed by source critics.

Source criticism of the Pentateuch is undergirded by several specific presuppositions: (1) skepticism of the historicity of the recorded narratives; (2) an evolutionary model of Israel's development from primitive to advanced forms; (3) the rejection of supernatural activity in this evolutionary development; and (4) the assumption that the sources were human products of the life setting of the communities that produced them. Later techniques of higher criticism applied to the Pentateuch employ the same naturalistic presuppositions. This includes *form criticism* (pioneered by Hermann Gunkel in the 1920s), which focuses on the preliterary stage of oral traditions behind the written sources; and *tradition history* (pioneered by Gerhard von Rad in the 1930s), which attempts to trace the entire history of the pentateuchal tradition, from precompositional oral traditions, to written sources, to final shaping by the creative redactor.

The methodology underlying all of these approaches is that of the historical critical method (also called *higher criticism*). The central principle of this method is what scholars call the principle of *criticism* (the Cartesian principle of methodological doubt), which affirms the supremacy of reason as the ultimate criterion for truth. Nothing is accepted authoritatively at face value; everything must be verified or corrected by rationally reexamining the evidence; the Bible is always open to correction, and therefore the human interpreter is the final determiner of truth, and his or her reason is the final test of the authenticity of a passage. The basic steps of the higher critical method used on the Pentateuch involve (1) breaking down the text into sections, (2) inferring an original life setting that may have given rise to the text, and (3) reconstruction of the process in which the various stages of the tradition reached its final form.

Already at the turn of the century, Ellen White warned of the dangers of this method: "The work of *higher criticism*, in *dissecting, conjecturing, reconstructing*, is destroying faith in the Bible as a divine revelation. It is robbing God's word of power to control, uplift, and inspire human lives" (AA 474, italics added). This method is opposed to the basic biblical principle of *sola Scriptura*, the Bible and the Bible only as our rule of faith and practice (e.g., Is. 8:20). Even a modified use of the historical critical method, which retains the principle of criticism and subordinates the Bible to human reason or experience, is unacceptable to those who maintain the biblical principle of *sola Scriptura*. The biblical approach to interpreting the Pentateuch rejects the principle of criticism; it *analyzes* but refuses to *critique* the Bible; it accepts the text of Scripture at face value as true and refuses to engage in the threefold process of dissection, conjecture, and hypothetical reconstruction (often contrary to the claims of the text) that is at the heart of all historical critical analysis. The biblical approach accepts what Scripture itself claims about the authorship of the Pentateuch: that it was written by Moses under the inspiration of God.

DATE AND PLACE OF WRITING

According to 1 Kings 6:1, Solomon began to build the temple in the fourth year of his reign, which was 480 years after Israel's Exodus from Egypt. The fourth year of Solomon's reign is dated to 967 B.C., and thus 480 years earlier yields circa 1447 B.C. as the date of the Exodus (see "Old Testament Timeline," p. 94). Moses was eighty years old at the time of the Exodus (Ex. 7:7), after having spent forty years in the wilderness of Midian (Acts 7:30), during which period of time he wrote the book of Genesis (see pp. 120–121). Moses died at the age of 120 (Deut. 34:7), shortly after completing the writing of the Torah (31:24). Thus the Pentateuch was written during the fifteenth century B.C., with Genesis being written by Moses sometime between circa 1487 and 1447 B.C., while he was in the wilderness of Midian, and the rest of the Pentateuch between circa 1447 and 1407 B.C., during the wilderness sojourn of Israel between Egypt and the borders of the promised land.

UNITY OF THE PENTATEUCH

Historical Unity

The five books of Moses present a coherent and seamless history of the origins of this world and humankind and of the birth and development of the people of Israel as a nation. Genesis 1–11 chronicles the universal history of this world, including the accounts of the Creation and Fall of humankind and the history of the antediluvian world and the global Flood. Genesis 12–50 narrates the call of Abraham and pivotal events in the life of Abraham and Sarah and their descendants to the fourth generation of the covenant line—Isaac (and Rebekah), Jacob (and his wives), and the twelve sons of Jacob, with a spotlight on the life of Joseph, and Israel's entry into Egypt.

Exodus continues the story of the covenant line, focusing on God's presence with Israel in Egypt, delivering them from bondage to the Egyptians (Ex. 1–13), and God's presence with Israel in the wilderness and at Mount Sinai, delivering them from the bondage of sin (chaps. 14–40). At Mount Sinai, God revealed the Law to them, entered into a covenant with His people, and gave to Moses detailed instructions regarding the building of the sanctuary. After the people's sin of idolatry with the golden calf, God renewed His covenant with them. Israel, out of gratitude for God's forgiving grace, built the sanctuary according to divine instructions, and the glory of God filled the completed tabernacle. God's interaction with and revelation of His laws to Israel at Sinai occupied a period of almost a year and is described in Exodus 19–40, the entire book of Leviticus, and Numbers 1:1—10:10.

The rest of Numbers describes Israel's journey to the plains of Moab at the border of the promised land. This journey includes Israel's departure from Sinai and their rebellion at Kadesh Barnea; the forty years of wandering in the wilderness, interspersed with the giving of various laws; and Balaam's futile attempt to curse Israel, followed by Israel's apostasy at the Jordan. In the final book of the Pentateuch, Moses delivers his farewell address to the people of Israel, presented in a covenant renewal structure. The aged leader reviews God's leading of Israel and His covenant stipulations, and he encourages Israel to be faithful to God. The book of Deuteronomy and the Torah as a whole conclude with the account of the death of Moses and the transfer of leadership to Joshua, who would lead them into the promised land. It is a unified story, providing a connected history from the Creation of the world to the death of Moses.

In broad overview, the main story line of the Pentateuch may be summarized by highlighting the main contribution of each book. This story line actually constitutes a microcosm of the unfolding of the entire sweep of salvation history for the world:

Genesis: Humanity *created* in God's image but *ruined* through sin (the book of Genesis ends with the words "a coffin in Egypt")

Exodus: Humanity (God's people) *redeemed* from bondage

Leviticus: Humanity (God's people) *worshiping* God

Numbers: Humanity (God's people) in *pilgrimage* toward the promised land

Deuteronomy: Humanity (God's people) experiencing *covenant renewal* with God while poised at the borders of the promised land

Literary Unity: Macrostructure of the Pentateuch

The Pentateuch is composed of four major literary types: narrative, poetry, law, and genealogy. While the genealogies provide structure to the earlier sections of the Pentateuch, especially Genesis, they do not serve to structure the Pentateuch as a whole. Likewise, the legal portions of the Pentateuch are clustered in the center of the Pentateuch, especially Leviticus, but these collections of laws are not the means for shaping the Pentateuch as a whole. The whole of the Pentateuch is structured by the juxtaposition of the two remaining literary genres: narrative and poetry.

Already in the opening chapters of Genesis, a threefold literary sequence may be observed: narrative, poetic speech, and epilogue. The Creation account of Genesis 1:1—2:22 is narrative, followed by the poetic speech of Adam (2:23) and a short epilogue (2:24). Likewise, the account of the Fall (3:1–13) is a narrative, followed by a divine poetic speech (3:14–19) and an epilogue (3:20–24). There are numerous other examples of this technique in the microstructures of the Pentateuch (Gen. 4:1–26; 6:5—9:17; 9:18–29; 14:1–24; 16:1–16; 24:1–67; 25:1–26; 27:1–45; 37:1—48:22).

The fact that the threefold structuring sequence of narrative/poetic speech/epilogue is found so frequently in the Pentateuch on the microstructural level suggests the possibility that this same technique is perhaps employed in structuring the Pentateuch as a whole. OT scholar John Sailhamer has shown that indeed such is the case. The major blocks of narrative in the Pentateuch are punctuated by four major sections of poetic speech, each then followed by an epilogue. First, the patriarchal narratives of Genesis are concluded by a major block of poetic text in Genesis 49 followed by an epilogue (Gen. 50). Second, the Exodus narrative block (Ex. 1–14) is capped off by another major poetic text (Moses's and Miriam's songs in Ex. 15:1–21) followed by an epilogue (Ex. 15:22–27). Third, the narrative block of Israel's experience in the wilderness (Num. 1–22) is climaxed by the poetic oracles of Balaam (Num. 23–24) and an epilogue (Num. 25). Finally, the pattern embraces the whole of the Pentateuch, as the overarching narrative of the Pentateuch, which stretches from Genesis 1 through Deuteronomy, is concluded by the poetic Song of Moses (Deut. 32–33) and the epilogue of chapter 34.

In three of these macrostructural junctures in the Pentateuch (Gen. 49; Num. 24; and Deut. 31) the material that connects the poetic sections to the preceding narrative sections contains similar terminology and motifs. In each there is:

- a central narrative figure (Jacob, Balaam, Moses), who
- calls together an audience in the imperative (Gen. 49:1; Num. 24:14; Deut. 31:28),
- to proclaim (Gen. 49:1; Num. 24:14; Deut. 31:28)
- what will happen (Gen. 49:1; Num. 24:14; Deut. 31:29)
- *be'akharit hayyamim* ("in the end of the days" or "in the days to come"; Gen. 49:1; Num. 24:14; Deut. 31:29).

This final phrase provides an indication that the poetic passages are eschatological—the passages point to an indefinite future time, which also embraces the ultimate end-time windup of the plan of salvation. By placing the eschatological poetic speeches after the narrative sections, Moses is also highlighting the point that the narratives are likewise to be seen as ultimately having end-time significance. The narrative texts describing God's dealings with His people in the past may be seen to foreshadow the end-time divine acts of salvation.

The three poetic seams coming at the three macrostructural junctures in the pentateuchal narratives (Gen. 49, Num. 23–24, and Deut. 32–33) not only refer to the last days but also highlight the coming of the Messiah. These passages reveal that the very heart of the eschatological focus in the Torah is on the coming Messiah. In the first poetic passage (Gen. 49), Jacob's last words of blessing are introduced as being given to his twelve sons individually (v. 1), but the conclusion of the blessing reveals that Jacob also had in mind "the twelve tribes of Israel," not just the individual sons (v. 28). Among the blessings on each tribe, two tribes are singled out by Jacob for extended blessings: Judah and Joseph. Close reading of these two extended blessings indicates that both point beyond the tribe to a future messianic figure who will come in the last days. The Messiah will be a royal figure from the tribe of Judah, Shiloh ("Provider of peace/prosperity [Heb. *sh-l-h*]"; Gen. 49:10–12) and a divine, suffering servant, the antitypical Joseph (Gen. 49:22–26); note especially the motif of suffering in v. 23 and the abrupt aside referring to the divinity of the Messiah in v. 24, the Shepherd and Stone/Rock of Israel.

Deuteronomy 32–33, the last of the major pentateuchal poetic passages, contains a second blessing of the twelve tribes, paralleling that of Genesis 49, but this time given by Moses before his death. This blessing also occurs in the context of the "end of the days" (Deut. 31:22), which points to the indefinite future but also ultimately includes the messianic age to come. In his blessing Moses (like Jacob) singles out two tribes for extended attention, Joseph again but also Levi (not Judah as in Gen. 49). Again, close reading of these two extended blessings indicates that both point beyond the tribe to a future messianic figure who will come in the last days. The Messiah will be the new (antitypical) Joseph (Deut. 33:8–11) and also the antitypical Levitical priest (Deut. 33:13–17). Thus Genesis 49 and Deuteronomy 32–33 form a pair of poetic passages in the Pentateuch, both comprising blessings upon the twelve tribes, and both emphasizing the last days and the coming of the Messiah.

In a similar way, the Song of Moses (Ex. 15) and the Oracles of Balaam (Num. 23–24) form a pair of poetic passages, highlighting the eschatological future and the role of the Messiah in the New Exodus. The oracles of Balaam portray the Messiah as a future King bringing a new eschatological Exodus, recapitulating in His life the events of historical Israel in their Exodus from Egypt and conquest of their enemies. Note how Numbers 23:22 speaks of Israel's past Exodus and how God was bringing *them* out of Egypt. Numbers 24:8 repeats the exact same line in Hebrew, except with singular forms, applying it to the future King introduced in v. 7: God was bringing *Him* out of Egypt (note that some translations continue to use the plural forms in v. 8). The identity of the "Him" as conquering King is further clarified in vv. 8b–9 with the description of Him conquering His enemies, the nations. The fact that Numbers 24:17 takes place in the last days (v. 14) confirms the Messiah's eschatological royal reign and victory over the forces of evil (v. 17).

Exodus 15 does not contain the same eschatological phrase as the other three poetic passages located at the macrostructural junctures of the Pentateuch. But whereas Genesis 49 and Deuteronomy 32–33 form an *outer* pair of poetic passages, both comprising blessings on the twelve tribes, Exodus 15 and Numbers 23–24 comprise an *inner* pair of poetic passages with a common theme: the Exodus. Exodus 15 is the Song of Moses, celebrating the Exodus of Israel from Egypt and deliverance from their enemies at the Red Sea. Already in Exodus 15, the Exodus is open-ended toward the future, with a description of a future safe passage of Israel through the midst of their enemies instead of the expected portrayal of passage through the Red Sea (vv. 14–17). Next it climaxes with a description of the reign of Yahweh (ultimately the Messiah) "forever and ever" (v. 18). This forward-reaching movement in the Song of Moses finds its counterpart in the Balaam oracles, where the Exodus of Israel from Egypt is viewed as prefiguring the exodus of the messianic King and His conquest of His enemies. When viewed together, the Song of Moses (Ex. 15) and the Oracles of Balaam (Num. 23–24) form a pair highlighting the eschatological future and the role of the Messiah.

Thus the four poetic passages that form macrostructural seams in the Pentateuch are all eschatological in nature, and together they point to the Messiah at the heart of the last-days fulfillment. The four poetic passages are framed in a chiastic arrangement, ABBA, with the matching outer pair focusing on the motif of blessing the twelve tribes, and the matching inner pair focusing on the motif of the Exodus/New Exodus:

A Blessing of the Twelve Tribes: Judah and Joseph (Gen. 49)
  B Exodus and New Exodus (Ex. 15)
  B′ Exodus and New Exodus (Num. 22–24)
A′ Blessing of the Tribes: Joseph and Levi (Deut. 33)

Taken together, all of these poetic passages, placed after blocks of narrative, indicate that the preceding narrative portions are also to be seen as prefiguring the eschatological future. Thus, in the compositional strategy of Moses, under the inspiration of God, the large narrative blocks of the Pentateuch as well as the poetic seams are juxtaposed so as to be read eschatologically, and the eschatology ultimately focuses on the Messiah. The narrative portions of the Pentateuch, along with their poetic seams, may therefore be regarded as Christ-centered eschatology.

What about the major block of the Pentateuch that is not predominantly narrative/poetry, namely, the large section of legal material in the central portion of the Torah? A closer look reveals that in the compositional strategy of Moses, inspired by God, the legal portions of the Pentateuch clustered in its center, the book of Leviticus, are also framed to highlight Christ-centered eschatology.

The book of Leviticus is organized in a chiastic structure (see Leviticus: Introduction). The chiastic climax of Leviticus (and of the whole Pentateuch) is Leviticus 16, the chapter dealing with Yom Kippur, the Day of Atonement. The Day of Atonement came at the end of the Hebrew ritual year. Its more accurate name (from Scripture) is not *Yom Kippur* but *Yom Lippurim*—the "Day of Atonements" (plural), which in Hebrew syntax implies the "Day of Complete or Final/Ultimate Atonement" (Lev. 23:28). All during the year, atonement was made for sins, but this day was the climax of the yearly ritual, in which the high priest made final atonement for all the sins of Israel (Lev. 16:16) and for the entire sanctuary that had been defiled during the year. On the holiest day of the year (Day of Final Atonement) the holiest person on earth (the high priest) went into the holiest spot on earth (the Most Holy Place of the sanctuary) to conduct the holiest work of the year (the work of "ultimate atonement").

The high priest is a type of Christ (see Heb. 8:1–5), and this final cleansing work in its antitypical fulfillment takes place at the time of the end (see Dan. 7:9–14; 8:14). The eschatological nature of Leviticus 16 is already implied in the passage itself in the usage of the Hebrew verb *kalah* ("to finish," "make an end"; Lev. 16:20). Only in this one occurrence in the Pentateuch is there said to be an "end" of atoning work. The Hebrew ritual year is a compacted typology foreshadowing the entire sweep of salvation history, and the Day of Atonement represents the eschatological climax of salvation history, focused on the day of final judgment. This eschatological day of judgment, centered in the work of Jesus in the heavenly sanctuary, is further developed in the books of Daniel (chaps. 7–8), Hebrews (10:25–30), and Revelation (11:19—20:15).

It may be concluded, therefore, that Moses, under divine inspiration, had a compositional strategy that cast the entire Pentateuch into an eschatological framework, with the person and work of the coming Messiah at the heart of that eschatological frame. In a sense, then, the Pentateuch as a whole, from beginning to end, may be seen as messianic eschatology.

It is not known in detail all that Jesus said to the two disciples on the way to Emmaus on Resurrection Sunday, but when Luke records that He began with Moses and *diermēneuō* ("explained," "expounded") to them the materials in *all* the Scriptures concerning Himself (Luke 24:27), this may not be hyperbole after all. On the road to Emmaus Jesus's principle of interpretation, His "hermeneutic"—for that is the word used in this verse, *diermēneuō*—may not have been different, after all, than the original eschatological, messianic hermeneutic of Moses. The entire Pentateuch is centered in Christ.

Theological Unity: The Grand Central Theme

In recent decades scholars have increasingly recognized that Genesis 1–3 is set apart from the rest of the Pentateuch, constituting a kind of prologue or introduction. These opening chapters of the Torah are now widely regarded as providing the interpretive foundation for the rest of the Pentateuch. A close reading of Genesis 1–3 allows a multifaceted theological center of the Pentateuch to emerge. Like seven facets of a beautiful diamond, there are seven interrelated themes that comprise the grand central theme of the Pentateuch.

1. *Creation and God's Design for His Creatures.* As one opens the first pages of the Pentateuch, the overriding theme of divine creation becomes immediately apparent. Not only

creation per se but also God's original design for His creation is demonstrated. For humans this included God's provision for their home, their work, their diet, their day of rest and worship (the Sabbath), their social relationship with each other, their relationship with the animals, and so on. God also established a creation covenant with humans, who were made in His image, which involved the multiple covenant blessings of descendants, dominion, land, and a personal relationship with their Creator (Gen. 1:27–28; 2:1–3, 8–17), as well as one covenant curse/sanction (not to eat of the tree of knowledge of good and evil on pain of death; Gen. 2:17). So Creation and God's covenant provisions for His creation is an obvious first facet of the multifaceted diamond that comprises the theological center at the beginning of the Pentateuch.

The creation theme continues throughout the Pentateuch, often appearing in subtle ways. The Flood was a process of cosmic de-creation and re-creation of the earth. Abram swore an oath by the Creator of heaven and earth (Gen. 14:22). The plagues against the Egyptians were another de-creation (Ex. 7–12). At the end of the Pentateuch, coming full circle with its beginning, one encounters creation language echoing Genesis 1:1–3. God created again (Deut. 32:6, 10–11). This time He is described as the One who "made" (Heb. 'asah, Deut. 32:6; cf. Gen. 1:7, 11–12, 16, 25–26, 31, etc.) the people of Israel into a nation, finding them in the waste places (Heb. tohu, Deut. 32:10; cf. Gen. 1:2) and hovering (Heb. rakhap, v. 11; cf. Gen. 1:2) over His people as the Spirit did at Creation. The divine provisions for human needs given at Creation are expanded throughout the Pentateuch, including legislation regarding work, diet, Sabbath, marriage/family/sexuality, care of animals, and so on.

2. *The Character of the Creator.* A close reading of Genesis 1–2 reveals an even deeper underlying issue than the work of creation: the character of the Creator. In portraying creation week in Genesis 1 (which actually continues through Gen. 2:4a), Moses identifies the Creator as "God," using the Hebrew *elohim*; but in the rest of Genesis 2, the complementary Creation account, Moses adds the name of God, which in Hebrew is *yahweh* (represented in English as "Lord"). Critical scholars have claimed that this gives evidence of two different sources, but in so doing they have missed the profound central issue portrayed in Genesis 1–2. This two-part Creation narrative does not contain different conjectured sources but rather forms a unity composed by a single author. In Genesis 1 and 2, Moses is not only portraying the divine act of Creation and God's original design for humankind but also eloquently highlighting the character of the Creator.

In Genesis 1, God appears as *elohim*. This is the generic word for God; *el* in Hebrew means "mighty one," and the plural probably serves as a superlative, meaning "the Mightiest One." He is the omnipotent God; He speaks and it is done. He is the transcendent One, totally separate from and above His creation. He is the infinite One, the all-powerful sovereign Creator. He is *elohim*. In Genesis 2 the name *yahweh* (usually appearing in English as "Lord") is introduced alongside *elohim*. *Yahweh* is the personal, covenant name of God. He is the Self-Existent, Intimate One, who comes down to be present with His creatures, who bends down over a lump of clay and blows into Adam's nostrils the breath of life, who takes one of Adam's ribs and architecturally designs and builds a beautiful creature to be his companion. He is the intimate, caring God. The two methods of representing God reveal a dual portrayal of the character of God.

Throughout the Pentateuch the character of God is repeatedly revealed by the use of one or the other (and sometimes both) of these names for God, depending on which aspect of God's character is being emphasized. Various other names for God are also employed, highlighting other attributes of the divine character:

- *adonai*: "Lord" or "Sovereign" (e.g., Gen. 15:2)
- *'el 'elyon*: "God Most High" (Gen. 14:18–22; Num. 24:16; Deut. 32:8)
- *'el ro'i*: "the God Who Sees" (Gen. 16:13)
- *'el shaddai*: "God Almighty" (Gen. 17:1; Ex. 6:3; Num. 24:4)
- *'el 'olam*: "Eternal/Everlasting God" (e.g., Gen. 21:33)
- *pakhad yitskhaq:* "the Fear of Isaac" (Gen. 31:42)
- *'abid ya'aqob*: "Mighty One/God of Jacob" (Gen. 49:24)
- *tsur*: "Rock" (Deut. 32:4, 15, 18, 31)
- *'ab*: "Father" (Deut. 32:6)

Looking schematically at the Pentateuch, each of the five books may be seen to emphasize one major character trait of God: (1) Genesis presents God's *sovereignty* as Creator; (2) Exodus reveals God's *redeeming* power; (3) Leviticus emphasizes God's *holiness*; (4) Numbers traces God's *justice and mercy* (goodness and severity) in dealing with Israel during their wilderness pilgrimage; and (5) Deuteronomy highlights God's *covenant faithfulness* (Heb. *khesed*) toward His people.

3. *The Rise of the Moral Conflict.* Why was it so important to emphasize the character of the Creator at the beginning of the Pentateuch? Because only against this background can the central issue in Genesis 3 be properly grasped. Genesis 3 describes the rise of a moral conflict on earth over the issue of the character of God. The presence of the serpent, clearly identified in Revelation 12 as the devil or Satan who was cast out of heaven (Rev. 12:9), indicates the *cosmic* nature of this conflict that had already begun in heaven (Is. 14:12–15; Ezek. 28:12–19; Rev. 12:7–9). The serpent called into question the goodness of the Creator with his insinuations to Eve. Eve and Adam believed the lies of the serpent, they fell from innocence, and the floodgates of woe were opened upon the world.

Thus, the third facet of the Pentateuch's theological center is the rise of the moral controversy, and this conflict rages over the issue of the character of God. The first part of Genesis 3:15 records God's promise that He would put enmity between the serpent and the woman, and between his descendants and hers. Here is the prediction of the continued moral conflict down through history between the spiritual descendants of Satan and the spiritual descendants of Eve.

The remainder of the Pentateuch traces this continued moral conflict in the history of the world and in the history of Abraham and his descendants, the people of Israel. The paradigm of this Great Controversy outside the Garden is first illustrated in the moral conflict between Cain and Abel, and the conflict is highlighted throughout the book of Genesis: the genealogy of Cain (Gen. 4) versus the genealogy of Seth (Gen. 5); the "sons/daughters of men" versus the "sons of God" (Gen. 6:1–4); the wicked antediluvian world versus the righteous remnant saved in the ark during the Flood (Gen. 6–9); and the history of the covenant line through Abraham versus the attempts from both human and supernatural enemies to derail the onward progress of the covenant. Throughout this continued conflict the issue of theodicy—the trustworthiness of God's character—emerges over and over.

In the book of Exodus the cosmic moral conflict is concentrated in the clash of deities—the true and living God of Israel versus the gods of Egypt (Ex. 12:12)—played out on the human level in God's deliverance of His people from the oppressive power of Egypt. The moral conflict continues throughout the narratives of the Pentateuch, as Israel's experience alternates between obedience to God (all too infrequently) and rebellion/murmuring against Him in the wilderness, including apostasy with the golden calf at Sinai and with Baal Peor on the borders of the promised land. Throughout these episodes the trustworthiness of the living God is the core issue. Israel's worship—either of the true and living God Yahweh or of the false gods, such as Baal—reveals what they regard as the worthiness of the One they chose to worship.

4. *The Gospel Covenant Promise Centered in the Person of the Messianic Seed.* Genesis 3:15 also reveals a fourth pillar of the theological foundation of the Pentateuch. The enmity described in v. 15 is not a natural hatred. After Adam and Eve sinned, there was no longer natural enmity between them and the serpent. They had sold themselves to the serpent, and their hearts had become depraved and bent toward evil, just like the serpent's. But in this verse, God Himself promises to implant enmity between Eve and the serpent and between their spiritual descendants (collective *zer'a*, "seed," "offspring").

The structure of the narrative of the Fall, found in the third chapter of Genesis, is symmetrical (chiastic), and exactly in the center, at the apex of the chiasm (vv. 14–15) is found what theologians call "the first Gospel promise." The middle part of Genesis 3:15 goes to the heart of this promise and shows that it is centered in a Person. God told the serpent that *He* would *shup* ("crush," "bruise," "strike") the serpent's head and the serpent would *shup* ("crush," "bruise," "strike") *His* heel. In this verse the conflict narrows from many descendants (a collective "seed") in the first part of the verse to a masculine singular pronoun in the last part of the verse—"He"—fighting against the serpent. Elsewhere in Scripture whenever the term "seed" is modified by a singular pronoun, it is a single individual who is in view. Likewise, in this verse God promises victory centered in a Person. "He"—the ultimate representative Seed of the woman, later to be revealed as the Messiah—shall bruise your head, Satan, and you shall bruise His heel. This is the fourth facet of the Pentateuch's theological center: the promise of redemption centered in the Person of the messianic Offspring/Seed. In the examination of the literary macrostructure in a previous section, it became evident how this messianic theme structures and permeates the entire Pentateuch.

Covenant terminology is implicit in the context of Genesis 3:15, indicating that this messianic promise is actually the first pronouncement of the everlasting covenant between the Father and the Son, announcing that a solution to the cosmic moral conflict will be forthcoming. This covenant theme figures prominently throughout the rest of the Pentateuch, including the Noahic covenant (Gen. 6:18; 9:9–17), the Abrahamic covenant (Gen. 12, 15, 17), and the Sinaitic covenant (Ex. 19:5; 24; 34). The covenant promises originally given to humankind (Gen. 1:28)—seed/descendants, land, dominion, and divine-human intimacy— are repeated to Abram (Gen. 12:1–3, 7; 17:6–8) and to Israel at Sinai (Ex. 19, 24, 34). So the fourth facet of the Pentateuch's theological center is the Gospel covenant promise of a solution to the moral conflict, centered in the messianic Offspring/Seed.

5. *Substitutionary Atonement Worked Out by the Messianic Offspring/Seed.* Visualize what is depicted in Genesis 3:15: the Seed/Offspring, Christ, takes off His sandal, as it were, bares His heel, and steps voluntarily on a venomous viper. It is a picture of the Seed/Offspring voluntarily giving up His life to slay the serpent. Christ volunteered to consciously step on the head of the most deadly viper in the universe, the serpent Satan himself, knowing full well that it would cost Him His life. Here is a powerful portrait of the substitutionary sacrifice of Christ on our behalf. Here is the fifth facet of the Pentateuch's theological center: the substitutionary atonement, as our representative Seed/Offspring would die on behalf of the fallen human race. This facet is further highlighted in Genesis 3:21, where Adam and Eve are covered with the skins of a slain animal, intimating their being covered by the robe of righteousness of their Substitute, the Lamb of God (cf. Isa. 61:10).

The theme of substitutionary atonement is developed throughout the Pentateuch: in the drama of Abraham and Isaac on Mount Moriah, with the ram dying in Isaac's place (Gen. 22); in the instructions for the first Passover service, where God passed over the homes covered by the blood of the Passover lamb (Ex. 12:12–13); and in numerous divine instructions regarding the Levitical sacrificial system elsewhere in the Pentateuch, particularly in the book of Leviticus. For example, Leviticus 1:4 points to the meaning of substitution. The sacrificial animal was a substitute, representing the repentant sinner who brought it. Leviticus 17:11 describes the meaning of the blood in the sacrificial system: the life is in the blood, and the blood of the sacrifice makes atonement for the *nepesh*—a term meaning various things but here meaning "soul" or "life." The key phrase in this passage regarding this atonement can be rendered, "in exchange for the person." This highlights the concept of substitution that is involved in the sacrifice, pointing to the substitutionary death of Christ on the cross (see also Lev. 4 and 16).

6. *The End of the Cosmic Conflict.* The sixth facet of this theological jewel of the Pentateuch is also found in Genesis 3:15. Here is predicted the resolution of the cosmic conflict at the close of earth's history when evil and the serpent will come to an end. In New (mixed with Old) Testament terms, Christ's heel would be bruised at Calvary, but this was only a wound to the heel. Later revelation, including pentateuchal prefigurations in the typology of the sanctuary (e.g., the waving of the wave sheaf on the third day after the Passover sacrifice;

Lev. 23:10–11), makes clear that though the Messiah would die, on the third day He would come back to life. But Satan would be crushed in the head, a mortal wound with no hope of recovery. The great cosmic conflict will not go on forever (see Lev. 16). Romans 16:20 alludes to Genesis 3:15, as Paul describes the end of the cosmic conflict when the God of peace will crush Satan under our feet. Satan's head was mortally wounded at Calvary and will receive the final crushing at the end of time. So the sixth facet of the Pentateuch's theological center is the predicted final end of the moral conflict as the serpent's head is crushed.

7. *The Sanctuary Setting of the Moral Conflict.* A seventh, and last, facet of the multi-faceted theological center of the Pentateuch is implied throughout Genesis 1–3. There are in Genesis 2–3 theological concepts that later will be at the heart of the theology of the sanctuary as found in Exodus and Leviticus and other places in the Bible. This incipient theology of the sanctuary is expressed through what later on will be sanctuary terminology and concepts. Although Eden is the home of Adam and Eve, it is also the place where God comes and meets with them and where an investigative judgment takes place (Gen. 3:8–19) and grace is made available through the promised Messiah and His sacrificial death (Gen. 3:15, 21). After Adam and Eve are expelled from the Garden, God placed two cherubim by the *eastern* entrance of the Garden—pointing to the future eastern entrance to the sanctuary, where humans came to worship the Lord.

In the time of the patriarchs after the Flood, the basic features of the sanctuary were represented by the altars that the patriarchs built wherever they sojourned. After Israel was delivered from Egyptian bondage at the Red Sea, the Song of Moses predicted that God would establish His sanctuary in the promised land (Ex. 15:17). In the remainder of the Pentateuch, the sanctuary becomes the locus of attention as the place where God comes to dwell in the midst of the people (Ex. 25:8) and also as the battleground of the moral conflict. At the sanctuary the people of Israel expressed loyalty to Yahweh in their worship, and conversely at the sanctuary God's people and their leaders often showed their disloyalty and even rebellion against God (e.g., Nadab and Abihu; Lev. 10) and their failure to avail themselves of the provisions of the sanctuary services (e.g., Lev. 23:29–30). Thus the sanctuary is the seventh facet of the pentateuchal theological diamond, the center of the great controversy over the character of God, as well as the center of God's work of redemption for His people.

From its opening pages the Torah's seven-faceted theological center emerges and is unfolded in the remainder of the Pentateuch. This center is not an "organizing principle" into which all the other themes, motifs, and concepts of the Pentateuch are to be forced to fit. Instead, this center serves as an *orientation point* in light of which the other themes of the Pentateuch make ultimate sense.

IMPORTANCE OF THE PENTATEUCH

The Pentateuch constitutes the foundational revelation for the rest of Scripture. This becomes apparent in several ways.

The Torah Is Foundational for Later Blocks of Hebrew Scripture

The Hebrew Bible is divided into three sections: Torah, Prophets (Former and Latter/Major and Minor, beginning with Joshua), and Writings (beginning with the book of Psalms). These major blocks of inspired material were juxtaposed in the final canonical form of the Hebrew Bible (perhaps by Ezra; see "Formation of the Biblical Canon," p. 21). They are organized so that at the seam of each of these sections is an evident pattern that presents a consistent call to focus on the Torah.

It has already been pointed out above how the book of Joshua begins with the divine charge to study, consider, speak, and perform everything written in the law (Torah) of Moses (Josh. 1:8). At the end of the Prophets, in the final chapter of its last book, Malachi, God gives a similar charge to remember the law (Torah) of Moses, His servant (Mal. 4:4). And positioned immediately thereafter, as presented in the Hebrew Bible, is the book of Psalms, which begins with a Torah psalm, echoing Joshua 1 and offering a blessing upon the one whose delight and daily meditation is focused on Torah (Ps. 1:2).

The order of books in the Septuagint, organized thematically by the Greek translators and generally followed by modern versions, likewise highlights the Torah in the way the major blocks are seamed together. Immediately after the Torah come the Historical Books, beginning with Joshua with its divine call to meditate on the Torah (Josh. 1:6–8). Then comes the collection of Hymnic-Wisdom Literature, commencing with Psalm 1, in which the person is blessed who meditates day and night on the Torah (Ps. 1:3). Finally come the Prophets, concluding with Malachi, with its last chapter exhorting us to remember the Torah of Moses (Mal. 4:4).

Later Blocks of Hebrew Scripture Reveal a Dependence on the Torah

The later writers of the Hebrew Scriptures show their great indebtedness to the Torah by references and allusions to the books of Moses. In the historical books of the Former Prophets there are references to the curses of the law (Torah; i.e., Lev. 26; Deut. 28) that would fall upon Israel for disobedience (e.g., Josh. 8:34; 23:6–13) and narratives revealing how these curses did in fact fall upon the nation in their apostasy. As another example, the promise to David that his son would build a house for God's name (2 Sam. 7:13) is intertextually linked with the original promise in Deuteronomy 12:5. Again, at the end of David's reign, his final words to his son Solomon stressed the need for him and the nation to follow the will of God as set forth in the Torah (1 Kin. 2:3). As a final example, later kings of Judah (Hezekiah and Josiah) followed the Lord in accordance with the words of the Torah given by Moses (2 Kin. 18:6; 23:25).

The greatest impact of the Torah is found in the Latter Prophets. Both Major Prophets and Minor Prophets (the Book of the Twelve) give evidence of heavy dependence on the contents of the Torah. For example, the frequent covenant lawsuits of the OT prophets (e.g., Is. 1:2–20; Jer. 2:4–13), with their call to "heaven and earth" as witnesses, allude back to the covenant lawsuit of Deuteronomy 32. In these lawsuits there are also references to the covenant stipulations of the Torah that have been violated (e.g., Ps. 50:16–21; Jer. 2:10–11; Hos. 4:1–2; Mic.

6:9–12) and the covenant curses of the Torah that have already fallen or will fall upon those who are disobedient (e.g., Is. 1:5–6, alluding to Deut. 28:51–52; Hos. 4:3; and Mic. 6:13–16). Numerous other passages in the Prophets show direct dependence upon the Torah.

In the Writings, several psalms are devoted to extolling the Torah (Pss. 1, 19, 119). In the most unsuspected places of the wisdom literature appear references to the Pentateuch. In the Song of Songs, for example, subtle allusions to the events of Israel's Exodus from Egypt occur, which were long ago recognized by various Jewish authors. As noted above in the section on Mosaic authorship of the Pentateuch, Ezra and Nehemiah make numerous references to the "law of Moses," and Daniel and Chronicles refer to the covenant curses of the Torah that have come upon the people of Israel for their rebellion against God.

Numerous New Testament Citations of the Pentateuch

The Pentateuch is quoted by NT writers at least 148 times. Genesis is cited thirty-four times, Exodus forty-four times, Leviticus seventeen times, Numbers three times, and Deuteronomy fifty times. Deuteronomy is the third most cited book in the OT, after Psalms and Isaiah (cited seventy-nine and sixty-six times respectively). Often these citations from the Pentateuch form the basis for major theological arguments. For example, Paul's message in Romans and Galatians about righteousness by faith without the works of the law depends heavily on the story of Abram and Moses's foundational statement about this paragon of faith—that is, that Abram believed in the Lord and He credited/accounted it to him for/as righteousness (Gen. 15:6).

New Testament Use of the Pentateuch in Typological Readings

Beyond explicit NT citations of the Pentateuch, various historical realities of the Pentateuch—persons, events, and institutions—are recognized as types (1 Cor. 10:6, 11) that find antitypical fulfillment in Jesus and the Gospel realities brought about by Him. A few of these pentateuchal types identified as such include Adam (Rom. 5:14); Noah and the Flood (1 Pet. 3:20–21; 2 Pet. 3:5–7); Melchizedek (Heb. 7:1–17); the destruction of Sodom and Gomorrah (2 Pet. 2:6–10; Jude 7); Hagar and Sarah (Gal. 4:24–31); Isaac, Abraham's Seed/Offspring (Gal. 3:16, 18, 29), especially in his experience on Mount Moriah (Rom. 9:7); Israel's Exodus from Egypt (Gr. *exodos*; Matt. 2:14–15; Luke 9:31); Israel's "baptism" in the Red Sea (1 Cor. 10:1–2); Israel's wilderness wandering and temptations (1 Cor. 10:1–11), especially the water from the rock (John 7:37; 1 Cor. 10:4), the giving of manna (John 6:32–58), and the brazen serpent of Numbers 21:9 (John 3:14–15); Moses the prophet (Deut. 18:15–19; John 6:14; 8:40; Heb. 3:1–6; cf. Matt. 5–7; Luke 6:20–49); the sanctuary and its services (Matt. 12:6; John 1:14; 2:21; 1 Cor. 3:16–17; 2 Cor. 6:16; Heb. 8–10; Rev. 3:12; 7:15; 11:19; 21:3, 16, 22); and the priesthood (Heb. 3:1; 6:20; 8:1; 1 Pet. 2:5, 9; Rev. 1:5–6; 5:10; 20:6). As evidenced from this representative sample, whole swaths of NT theology and practical lessons of Christian living are built upon or illustrated by typology taken from the Pentateuch.

New Testament Doctrines and the Pentateuch

Almost all of the NT doctrines are already summarized in Genesis, even in the first three chapters of Genesis. There is a growing consensus among scholars, whether liberal or conservative, that Genesis 1–3 forms the interpretative foundation for the rest of Scripture. All of the major biblical doctrinal themes—Creation, covenant, the cosmic conflict, law, the Sabbath, God and His attributes/character, Christ, the Holy Spirit, the nature of humanity, sin, salvation, righteousness by faith, the sanctuary, atonement, eschatology, the remnant, marriage and sexuality, etc.—may be traced, at least embryonically, to the opening pages of the Bible in Genesis 1–3 and are developed in Genesis and the rest of the Pentateuch. Without this foundation in the Pentateuch, many of these doctrines would be incomprehensible or at least unclear.

For these and many other reasons, the Pentateuch may be regarded as the foundation of present truth, waiting to be explored by the earnest Bible student. Every new Spirit-led examination of the jewels found in the Pentateuch will make them shine with new luster, and the Christ to whom they ultimately point will become ever more precious to the attentive reader whose heart will be filled with hope.

Ultimately, the Pentateuch's foundational nature and its all-encompassing, God-centered worldview remind us of God's intimate engagement in this world and in the lives of His people. While readers throughout the ages have been able to discern innumerable pillars of magnificent truths, they have also been encouraged by the realization of God's unfathomable grace as manifested in the ups and downs of human history. In the midst of the Pentateuch's realistic depiction of dysfunctional families, failed leadership, and rebellious mobs, interrupted by sparks of human faithfulness and stubborn reliance on God's unwavering promises, we can see grace at work. This grace is taken hold of by frail human faith, engendering hope in a future when sin will be no more and eternity will become a present reality. That will truly be Eden restored.

GENESIS

INTRODUCTION

Title and Authorship. The book starts with the Hebrew term *bere'shit* ("in the beginning") which, following ancient conventions, is also its title. The English name comes from *geneseos*, meaning "origins," the title taken from the Greek Septuagint and adapted by the Latin Vulgate. The book of Genesis does not explicitly state who its author was. However, Moses is recognized as the author of the Pentateuch by many authors of the NT (Matt. 8:4; 19:7–8; 22:24; Mark 7:10; 12:19, 26; Luke 2:22; 16:29; 24:27, 44; John 1:17, 45; 5:46; 7:22–23; 8:5; Acts 3:22; 13:39), who themselves lived with the tradition that he was the author.

Date. From the early centuries A.D. until only recently, most Christian interpreters have understood Moses to have written the Pentateuch sometime in the fifteenth century B.C. Jewish interpreters have had this understanding much longer. However, beginning with the rise of rationalism in the mid-1800s, this consensus began to be questioned by scholars using the historical-critical method. These scholars suggested that the Pentateuch was written not by a single hand but by many through a complex editorial process. They proposed at least four different sources written by anonymous authors between the tenth and the fifth centuries B.C. Although no external evidence has ever surfaced for the existence of any of these proposed sources, most academic work done today assumes this theory to be true. Key arguments of critical scholarship include the use of differing divine names as an indication of multiple sources, the large numbers mentioned in the Pentateuch (esp. regarding the number of Israelites leaving Egypt), doublets and repetition (e.g., the wife/sister incidents in Abraham's and Isaac's lives [Gen. 12, 20, 26]), supposed anachronisms (such as the appearance of camels), and so forth. Some of these challenges to the authenticity of Mosaic authorship will be dealt with in the notes of this commentary (see "Introduction to the Pentateuch," p. 120). However, the heart of the issue concerns one's understanding of what makes a text historically reliable. First, it is important to remember that the theological, biographical, selective, and interpretive nature of biblical stories does not automatically disqualify them from being historical. Rather, these characteristics highlight the important cultural differences between a twenty-first-century (often Western) audience and the biblical authors whose Eastern and holistic worldview left space for a God, who actively intervenes in human history. Considering biblical chronology as a whole as well as the internal evidence of Genesis, it is likely that the book was indeed written by Moses during his sojourn in Midian prior to the Exodus. Moses himself may have had access to archival documents that were marked by the recurring *toledot* formula (see p. 139) while other material was received by direct divine revelation (see "Introduction to the Pentateuch," p. 120).

Backgrounds. The narrative flow of Genesis moves from Creation to the arrival of the Hebrews in Egypt. Genesis 1:1—11:26 is an overview of human history that serves as an introduction to the entire Bible. This overview includes the creation of the cosmos, the creation of humanity during the creation of life on this planet, humanity's fall into sin, a universal Flood, and the confusion of the languages. From Genesis 11:27 to the end of the book, the narrative slows down as it focuses on God's promises to Abram, particularly the promise of a "Son," and the struggles, mistakes, and faithfulness in the generations of Abraham, Isaac, and Jacob during their journey through the promised land and their final arrival in Egypt.

Genealogies play a significant role in the structure of Genesis. Ancient cultures placed great importance on genealogies because they provided a link to the past, explained origins, established kinship links, demonstrated the legitimacy of people or people groups (such as priests or kings), and highlighted continuity. The Hebrew phrase *'elleh toledot* ("these are the generations," or, using a more generic translation, "this is the genealogy") appears eleven times throughout the book (2:4; 5:1; 6:9; 10:1; 11:10; 11:27; 25:12; 25:19; 36:1; 36:9; 37:2). Based on comparative ANE data, scholars have understood the phrase as either a title or a summary statement. While many of these genealogies move the story forward or act as transitions between key scenes, others seem unimportant and disconnected from the bigger covenantal picture (e.g., 25:12 contains a brief genealogy of Ishmael, and 36:1, 9 contain genealogies related to Esau, both of whom are not part of the covenant line). While they do not provide a symmetrical or clear structural layout for Genesis, their presence throughout the book suggests unity and an attempt at creating structure. The author used a collection of similar documents to tell an important story, and the distinction between primordial and patriarchal histories is one not of historical reliability but of focus. This emphasis on name lists and their relations can become monotonous or boring to modern readers, who may find their significance difficult to understand. The genealogies in Genesis point toward the future: following the first pronouncement of the good news in Genesis 3:15, generation after generation wonders about the One who would bring salvation from the curse of sin.

Theology and Purpose. Genesis provides the foundation upon which all other authors in Scripture wrote and thus lays the groundwork for understanding and interpreting the entire Bible. Key topics, including theology (studies regarding God as Creator and Savior), anthropology (studies regarding humanity's creation from dust and its return to dust), sociology (studies regarding the family, marriage, and community), cosmology (studies regarding the origins of the cosmos), and soteriology (studies regarding the plan of salvation in the context of Creation and the Fall), all have their beginning in Genesis. This is why one will never accurately understand the remainder of Scripture without grasping Genesis's introductory theological themes.

1. In the Beginning. Genesis is built around beginnings. Light and darkness, earth and heaven, animals and plants, humanity, marriage, the Sabbath, the covenant family, sin and salvation—all are topics that will be further developed throughout the rest of Scripture. Genealogical notes are carefully positioned to emphasize the importance of beginnings (births) and continuity. Creation was a movement from seeming disorder to awesome order. Genesis 1:2 describes the earth as a mass of disorganized raw material, out of which the divine word created order in a systematic manner—forming, filling, and separating the physical and temporal environments. At the apex of Creation week, the seventh-day Sabbath ordered and sanctified life. In summary, Genesis is a reminder that in regard to order, true beginnings require a divine word. It is the creative word straight from the mouth of God that produced light, plants, animals, and life and that also sanctified the seventh day. In the prologue to his Gospel, the NT writer John reveals that this creative and divine Word arrived on earth with a mission of re-creation—and His name was Jesus (John 1:1–14).

2. The Disruption of Creation. Although Genesis begins with a description of the grand scheme of things, it soon becomes relational. A perfect creation was marred by the doubt and decisions made by humanity's first ancestors, which in turn led to the loss of paradise. The entrance of sin into this world, as told in the Fall narrative of Genesis 3, reversed the initial Creation order and resulted in disorder. It affected man and woman (3:12) and the rest of creation (3:15, 17–19). The pain of separation from God was palpable when Adam and Eve had to leave the Garden (3:23–24). Disorder was further exemplified when brother slayed brother (4:8). When humanity's downward trend toward wickedness reached a nadir, disorder became so irreversible that God decided to purify the world by a universal Flood (6:1–7). However, it wasn't long before disorder reigned supreme after the Flood as well. The confusion of languages, causing the dispersion of humanity (11:1–9), serves as a good example.

3. Promises and Hope. Promises play an important role in the book of Genesis. Without prompting, God promised a resolution to the conflict (Gen. 3:15). Immediately following the Flood, He offered another promise (8:21—9:1). In the selection of Abraham, Isaac, and Jacob, God made additional promises (12:1–3, 7; 13:15–17; 15:7–21; 17:4–8; 22:16–18; 26:2–4; 28:13–14) that were crucial to the development of the story in the rest of the Pentateuch and laid the foundation for further promises at its end (Deut. 28–32). The promises found in Genesis center on God.

The blessings pronounced in them deal with the growth of family, the settlement of land, and the result of both of these being a blessing to those who lived around them.

Genesis reveals that in the midst of evil and separation and pain, there was hope grounded in divine promises. Hope that the One who would crush the head of the serpent (3:15) would come as a descendent of the woman. Hope that God would provide a way to survive a universal Flood. Hope that God's elected would become a blessing to all the nations of the world (12:1–3). This hope recognized the Creator but longed for the Savior. While it is, at times, veiled, it reappears at key moments in the narrative and previews the blessed hope that has moved and transformed millions since. Ultimately, the last book of Scripture, Revelation, provides the balancing counterpart to Genesis. A new creation reverses the fallen creation. The Alpha and the Omega has been recognized as the One who was slain for the sins of humanity. Instead of a garden, there is a city, a new Jerusalem that becomes the home of re-created humanity.

4. Personal Piety. The first book of Scripture is not only a source of significant theology and crucial narratives for developing an understanding of origin and destiny. It is also a book permeated by prayer. Personal devotion and prayer are presented in Genesis as crucial to a life of piety. This can be seen in Abraham's prayers. He prayed for a son (15:1–3), for the cities doomed to destruction (18:16–33), and for foreign kings (20:7, 17–18). God answered the prayer of Abraham's servant (24:12–14, 26–27, 42–44) and Isaac's prayer for his wife (25:21). Prayer was significant in the life not only of the men of Genesis. Women are also shown as having had prayers answered: Hagar's desperate cry for help (21:16–21), Leah's prayer for children and the love of her husband (29:32–33; 30:17), and Rachel's prayer for children (30:22). People called upon the name of the Lord (e.g., 12:8; 13:4; 21:33; 26:25) in worship, praise, perplexity, and desperation—and God heard and acted in His time. The God of Genesis is a God who answers prayers and interacts with His creation—a critical message in the face of uncertainties, pain, loss, and hopelessness. Those who hope also pray.

5. Cosmic Theology. Genesis encourages the reader to step back to see the larger picture of a controversy with cosmic dimensions. Creation and the Fall were followed by tangible examples of God's involvement in this world and in the lives of His people and offer helpful insights into God's character. The God who searched for fallen humanity is also the God who planted the gospel seed found in Genesis 3:15. With the conflict moving from heaven to earth (Rev. 12), the entire universe could witness the divine plan that would bring salvation, rest, and restoration to a fallen world (1 Cor. 4:9).

COMMENTARY

1:1—11:26

PRIMORDIAL HISTORY: GOD'S DEALING WITH HUMANITY

Genesis 1:1—11:26 focuses on ancient history and describes the origins of humanity (including the creation of this planet, the Fall, a universal Flood, and the division of people).

Days of Creation

The phrase "evening and morning" in the Creation narrative indicates that the days of Creation should be understood as literal days. This is reinforced by the fact that the term "day" is accompanied by a numeral (e.g., "first," "second"), and in such cases, the term "day" designates a literal day. From a biological perspective, aside from supernatural intervention, vegetation and natural life would require a short cycle of darkness and light indicated by a literal day in order to be preserved. Besides, the Sabbath commandment demonstrates that the seven days are to be understood as literal days. While the Hebrew term for "day" can indicate a period of time longer than a twenty-four-hour day (e.g., it is possible that the Day of the Lord [Is. 2:12; Jer. 46:10; Joel 3:14] does not always refer to a 24-hour day), it does so in combination with other linguistic elements (such as prepositions, prepositional phrases, or compound constructions) but never when used with an ordinal or cardinal number.

An appropriate comprehension and appreciation of these first chapters is foundational for understanding the rest of Scripture.

1:1—2:25
God's Perfect Creation

After the general outline of Creation in chapter 1, chapter 2 focuses more closely on the creation of humanity. Genesis 1 and 2 are written in prose yet exhibit a wonderful rhythmic cadence while factually recording God's creative activity. The text is interested in the *who*, the *how*, and *the result* of God's creation.

1:1–2. Introductory Statement. The first two verses appear to function as a title or summary statement for the rest of the chapter. Scripture states right from the outset that the universe did not come into existence by itself but that it was the result of the creative activity of God. Before this beginning, there was only God, the uncreated One. In Hebrew thinking, the portrayal of the result often precedes the description of the process. God, standing above and outside of creation, created the heavens and the earth (v. 1), perhaps pointing to the planet with its atmospheric heaven surrounding it, even though it could also be interpreted as a reference to the creation of the larger universe. John's "in the beginning" (John 1:1) may point to the latter possibility, emphasizing the eternal existence of the Word. While this is possible, it is important to keep in mind that Genesis is primarily interested in God's relation to earth and its inhabitants. The verb "created" (*bara'*) is always linked to divine creative activity (Ps. 33:6, 9; Amos 4:13) but does not always refer to creation out of nothing (Is. 65:17).

The description in v. 2 does not refer to chaos but to the condition of the planet before the raw materials were constituted by the Creator into the proper habitat for human existence (cf. Is. 34:11; Jer. 4:23). The spirit of God is mentioned, without any introduction, as being active in the work of creation in anticipation of the Creation week. This is the same spirit of God mentioned in other parts of the Bible (e.g., Gen. 41:38; Ex. 31:3; Pss. 51:11; 143:10; Is. 63:10). The members of the Godhead all participated in Creation, as highlighted by John's description of the creative power of the living Word in John 1. John 1:1–3 describes the handiwork of the Word that became flesh, picking up on the divine word in Genesis 1 and linking it to the important concepts of the Jewish *memra'* ("word") that appeared in intertestamental Judaism and the Greek *logos* ("word"; see notes on John 1).

1:3—2:4a. The Creation of Earth. God created the various elements and environments, as well as the creatures that would inhabit them and benefit from them—a process sometimes referred to as "forming and filling." The speech for each Creation day includes an announcement, a command, the fulfillment of the command, an assessment, a separation, a summary of the components, and the number of the day.

The creation of light on the first day (1:3–5) established the format of the other days of Creation. While the sun and moon signaling times and seasons (1:14–19) appeared specifically during the fourth day, the reference to light on the first day perhaps indicates that God created some unidentified source of light. Some believe that the sun was created on the first day but given purpose on the fourth. The phrase "evening and morning" on the first day does indicate that the light was functioning in the same way that the sun would function. The author of Genesis purposefully avoided naming the celestial lights in 1:16, instead opting to call them the "greater light" and "lesser light." While contemporary Ugarit texts from the second millennium B.C. mention a "great light" in reference to the sun, there is no equivalent phrase for the moon. When Moses penned these timeless words during the second half of the second millennium B.C., the sun and moon were the major deities in the ANE. Genesis 1 establishes their rightful place: they were created, nameless entities that do not deserve human worship. They are in the Creator's hand—like plants, animals, and humanity. There is an apparent parallelism between v. 4 and v. 18. God *badal* ("separated" or "divided") the light from the darkness (v. 4), and the luminaries divided the light from the darkness (v. 18; see 2 Cor. 4:1–6). Creation by separation established boundaries and structured the transformation of raw materials into an ordered creation propitious for life. In the Bible, God's law regulated boundaries and made possible proper social and religious interaction. In the building of the Israelite sanctuary, separation would also play an important role, indicating that its construction was an act of creation (see "Creation, Sabbath, and the Sanctuary," p. 231).

The final element of each Creation day involved God's observation and declaration of goodness, followed by naming. Scripture often links God's "seeing" to other decisive activities

(Gen. 6:12–13). In Genesis 1, God saw each Creation day activity and then declared it good (1:4, 10, 18, 21, 25) or even very good, as He did at the end of the sixth day (1:31). The Hebrew notion of "good" is more comprehensive than the common definition in English. In addition to a functional dimension ("it works"), the Hebrew *tob* refers also to aesthetic beauty, especially when associated with seeing (cf. 6:2; 24:16; 1 Sam. 16:12; 1 Kin. 1:6; Dan. 1:4), as well as to ethical uprightness (Is. 7:15). Following each creative act, God named the phenomenon or being. The divine act of naming marked divine sovereignty.

The account of the second day of Creation (1:6–8) describes the creation of the firmament. God made the expanse or the atmosphere of the planet. The text utilizes a verb that is often associated with the work of an artisan (e.g., a potter in Jer. 18:3–4). Again, God spoke and then made the sky, separating the atmosphere surrounding the earth and establishing the crucial water cycle—though described in prescientific phenomenological language.

On the third day of Creation (1:9–13), the water was separated from the dry land, and vegetation was created. Twice God called His creation "good" on the third day. The preparatory act of

Scripture and Science

The relationship between Scripture and science has been debated heatedly since the Enlightenment in the eighteenth century. Up to that time, most scholars had presupposed the existence of God and the veracity of the Bible. Science was the handmaid of theology. This relationship changed dramatically when rationalism and materialism became the underlying philosophical presuppositions of science. Reason, logic, and matter were elevated as the all-encompassing building blocks of knowledge and truth. Since God's existence and His interventions could not be rationally demonstrated or explained, scholars began to exclude God from science. They suggested that the distinction between faith and science made science more objective, and faith became a private matter. In recent decades, scientists have begun to recognize that objectivity is impossible—due to the human factor. Yet the goal of achieving objectivity still remains a high priority for modern scientists. Scripture, on the other hand, begins with an assumption: *In the beginning—there was God*. Creation, albeit described in the first chapters of Genesis in phenomenological language, had God as its cause and agent. He spoke and it was.

Christian interaction with science can be classified using three different models. The first model suggests that science and religion should remain *isolated* from each other and should be considered separate entities. A search for truth—wherever the evidence leads—would argue against this model. The second model could be described as *parallel yet separate*. Both religion and science are recognized as sources of truth, yet they should not cross-pollinate. This model is the philosophical framework of theistic evolution, a theory that seeks to combine evolution and divine revelation by suggesting that God used evolution and its mechanisms (including natural selection) to "create" this world. One particular problem with this model is the existence of death and pain—as evidenced in the fossil record of the geologic column. While equality between the two sources of truth is postulated, science actually seems to play the first fiddle.

The third model calls for *interaction* between science and religion yet gives God (and His revelation) priority in the search for truth. Christians are not hostile to science but recognize God as the ultimate Creator of natural laws and seek to understand creation based on this premise. This model recognizes a higher Being as the true source of knowledge and wisdom and gives priority to Scripture in situations that require a choice between science and faith. It recognizes the transitory nature of scientific theories (some of the assured results of science that have been disproved by later generations of scientists) and gives priority to divine revelation. This model truly seeks to integrate *all relevant data* in a holistic manner because it acknowledges God not only as the Revelator but also as the Creator who established the laws of nature that engages and intrigues scientists (for more discussion, see "Faith and Science," p. 57).

dividing the dry land and the water created the environment that was needed for fauna, flora, and the human inhabitants of the earth. Water was subject to divine command and was not an independent divine agent as in many creation accounts found around the world. Water could also become an agent of divine judgment (cf. Gen. 6–8). Once dry land had been established, God adorned the land with grass, bushes, and trees.

A possible translation of v. 14 would be "let the lights in the expanse be for separating." This is held up by some as support for the notion that the sun had already been created on the first day but was only given its purpose and function on the fourth day. Either way, similar to v. 5, light was to play a key role in determining time and marking the distinction between day and night and different seasons by the position of these two heavenly bodies.

Day five witnessed the creation of fish and birds (1:20–23), who are described as *nepesh khayyah* (translated sometimes as "living souls" or "living creatures"). This phrase is also used with respect to humans (2:7). The biblical text reflects the abundance of life and life-forms that filled both water and sky, including the great sea creatures (cf. Job 3:8; Ps. 74:13–17; Is. 27:1). In ANE myths, these creatures represented primeval monsters; in the biblical text, they are part of a list of living creatures that derived their existence from an all-powerful Creator. Each species of animal and flora (1:11) was created according to its kind and followed God's divine master plan and purpose (1:21). Through the command to be fruitful and multiply (or increase), God identified the means by which the earth would be filled with fauna and flora.

The Hebrew text distinguishes between cattle (i.e., livestock or domesticated animals), creeping things (i.e., animals moving on the ground), and beasts of the earth (i.e., wild animals). God made each animal species according to its kind. However, in the creation of human beings, God did something that He had not done before. He used a plural to refer to Himself. This suggests that within the mystery of the one God, there was a plurality, something that had already been indicated in the reference to the spirit of God in v. 2. While plants and animals were made according to their various kinds, humans were created in God's image, with the capacity to interact with Him and to represent Him as free, rational moral agents. Their exhibition of their divine origin was reflected not only in the beauty and symmetry of their outward appearance but also in the holiness and purity of their characters (Ps. 8:5; 2 Cor. 3:18; Col. 3:10). Several English translations recognize v. 27 from the Hebrew as the first line of poetry in Scripture, emphasizing further the significant difference between the origin of humanity and the rest of creation. The distinction between male and female in humanity's creation points to the complementary nature of the two sexes. They were both the expression of God's image while at the same time being differentiated by gender. This gender distinction would be a vehicle to transform the divine blessing into reality (v. 28). God's blessing involved not only filling the earth but also representing the Creator as stewards. God gave to both Adam and Eve the privilege of participating in God's loving and caring dominion over creation. They became stewards of the Lord.

God also took care of the dietary needs of His creatures and assigned to them a vegetarian diet (1:29). Meat would become part of the human diet only after the Flood (9:3). God has always been interested in the well-being of His creatures, and this is shown here through His concern for what they should eat (see Lev. 11). The Lord created human beings as physical entities; matter is not evil. Scripture's resounding "it was very good" (1:31) provides a fitting summary of God's forming and filling activities. Order and structure point toward a Creator who enjoys a multiplicity of life.

The work of Creation climaxed on the Sabbath (Gen. 2:1–3) and consisted in the establishment of a time for communion with the Creator. He separated and sanctified the Sabbath for holy use. Although God is described as resting, He Himself does not need rest (Is. 40:28), but He did so to model for humans the importance of working six days and resting on the seventh day. This biblical passage provides for the reader the true origin of the seventh-day Sabbath rest. God instituted it during Creation week. Since God sanctified it, no human being has the right to desecrate it or appoint a substitute for it. The rest motif pointed beyond the Sabbath. In a post-Fall world, salvation rest is closely linked to Sabbath rest, without substituting for it (Heb. 4:1–10). Humanity can truly rest in God's grace, not in its own works, and look expectantly toward the ultimate rest with the Creator and Savior.

2:4b–25. Humanity in the Garden. Many scholars commenting on the Creation account of Genesis 1–2 have suggested the existence of multiple sources, distinguishing two Creation accounts that are, at times, at odds with each other. However, a careful reading of the literary design of the first two chapters of Genesis presents a different picture. Following the general outline of Creation in chapter 1, Genesis 2:4–25 focuses more closely on the creation of humanity and the living conditions of their garden home (note the subtle shift from heavens and earth [1:1] to earth and heavens [2:4]). The chapters complement and supplement each other. On a small scale, the relationship between Genesis 1 and 2 illustrates the larger move of Genesis from the universal to the personal, from the creation of a planet to the creation of a people, beginning with a family.

God is described by a new name in Genesis 2:4. While Genesis 1 used the generic *'elohim*, "God," throughout, chapter 2 uses the combination "the LORD God."

Genesis 2:4–6 is parallel to 1:1–3 and includes an important description stating that the Lord God formed Adam from the dust of the ground and breathed life into him (2:7). The Hebrew word *'asah* ("formed" or "made") used here designates the work of an artisan (Is. 29:16; Jer. 18:4–6). This human being or "man" (*'adam*) did not originate in the divine Being, but he was formed from the dust of the earth (Heb. *'adamah*), and because of sin, he would return to it (Gen. 3:19). God's life-giving breath transformed the dust into a creature made in the image of God who was to depend constantly on Him (Job 27:3; cf. Ezek. 37:9–10). Both animals and humans are described as *khayyah* ("living"; Gen. 1:20–21, 24, 30; 2:7, 19), but only the life of humankind was directly created through the divine breath.

The man was put in a garden (2:8), the future residence of both Adam and Eve. It would become the place where God met with them, and in that sense, the Garden expressed elements of the sanctuary (3:8; Ex. 25:8). The Garden of "Eden" (conveying the ideas of "pleasure" and "delight") connotes a beautiful location filled with fertile vegetation. Notice that by mentioning Gihon, Cush, Hiddekel/Tigris, and Euphrates, the biblical writer is using geographical terms (toponyms) known to the readers. However, the pre-Flood topography of earth (and thus the probable geographic location of Eden) was markedly different from the post-Flood topography, a transformation likely caused by major tectonic changes and continental shifts (cf. Gen. 10:25).

Genesis 2:8–17 describes God as a gardener placing humans in Eden. Two specific trees are mentioned in v. 9: the "tree of life," referred to in other places in the Bible (Prov. 3:18; 11:30; 13:12; 15:4; Rev. 2:7; 22:1–2, 14, 19), and the "tree of the knowledge of good and evil," found only in Genesis 2–3. The phrase "knowledge of good and evil" is employed in other places to express the idea of independence. Children, who do not know good and evil, depend on their parents for wisdom (Deut. 1:39). Therefore, to know good and evil is to claim and act in total independence from God. Following the description of the bounty and beauty of Eden, the Lord made a home for humanity in the Garden (2:15). They would *'abad* ("work" or "serve") and *shamar* ("guard" or "tend") their new home. This is how their dominion over nature would express itself. As noted, the verb *shamar* implies guarding, which suggests the possibility of danger (cf. 3:1). The two verbs are used together to define the work of the Levites in the sanctuary, indicating that God gave them "dominion over" the sanctuary and its services (Num. 3:7–8; 18:7).

Following the positioning of humanity, God's first command involving the tree of the knowledge of good and evil was issued as a positive expression of God's goodness (Gen. 2:16–17). God's permission to eat from all other trees of the Garden (v. 16) was later twisted by the cunning serpent to emphasize the prohibition (3:1). This was a test of human obedience (cf. Gen. 22) that must be understood in the context of a cosmic conflict. Who would own the allegiance of humanity—God or the not-yet-identified opponent whose voice would be heard through the words of the serpent in Genesis 3? The issue of human allegiance and obedience is still crucial and will play a significant role in end-time events (Rev. 14:6–12).

God's Name: The Tetragrammaton

The Hebrew divine name YHWH (most likely pronounced as Yahweh), also known as the tetragrammaton (Greek meaning "four letters"), appears first in Genesis 2:4. Recognizing God's immense holiness, modern Jews do not pronounce this name but read instead the term Adonai ("my Lord") whenever the name appears in the OT. Yahweh is most likely derived from the Hebrew verb "to be" and points to God's eternal existence and covenant relationship (cf. Ex. 3:13–15). The use of Yahweh emphasizes God's personal relationship with humanity.

Genesis 2:18 contains a surprising twist. Something in God's creation, recognized by the Creator Himself as "very good" (1:31), was "not good." Creation was not complete until Adam met Eve. Until a love relationship was established, Creation was unfinished. Humankind was to replicate (on a different scale) the divine love that gives and gives—and gives more. God designed Eve to be *kenegdo*—variously translated as "suitable," "comparable," "as his complement," "as his partner"—to Adam, yet she was also different. Creation in God's image and likeness (1:26–28) required both man and woman—only together did they reflect the ideal divine image. Sovereign God caused Adam to fall into a deep sleep, emphasizing the fact that man did not contribute anything to the creation of his soul mate. Woman was as much God's creature as man was. The verb used in 2:22 to describe Eve's creation means "fashioned" or "built." This verb marked the deliberate construction of the woman out of material taken from man—a fact that is recognized in the second piece of poetry included in the Creation account in 2:23. "Bone of my bones," "flesh of my flesh" marks the acknowledgment of correspondence: "She is like me!" was Adam's refrain after the Lord God had brought Eve to him in the first marriage to take place on earth. Notice that the Hebrew term for man (*'ish*) sounds very similar to the one for woman (*'ishah*) again suggesting closeness. They were joined in the oneness of marriage (v. 24), complementing each other, experiencing sexual union, and enjoying each other in their daily existence.

Living Soul or Living Being?

The phrase *nepesh khayyah* is at times translated as "living soul." While the word *nepesh* can mean various things in the Hebrew Bible, including "emotions," "thoughts," "mental faculties," "desires" (especially in poetic passages; e.g., Job 24:12; Pss. 6:3; 13:2; 31:9; 42:4–6; Ezek. 24:25), and even sometimes "dead body" (e.g., Num. 5:2; 9:6), it often, as here in Genesis 2:7, means "life" or "person"; never does it refer to an eternal, separate, conscious entity. God formed humans from dust and then breathed life into them. Death is the reverse process—when people breathe their last, their bodies return to dust (Eccl. 12:7). The concept of a soul as a separate, eternal entity is completely foreign to Scripture and based on Greek philosophy.

Genesis 2:25 functions as an important bridge to the Fall narrative in chapter 3. Man and woman were naked yet felt no shame. The term "naked" refers here to not being clothed in a normal manner (cf. 1 Sam. 19:24). Psalm 104:1–2 suggests that God's garments include splendor/honor, majesty, and light. The fact that humans were not dressed in a normal manner yet had been created in God's image and likeness (1:26–27) suggests that they reflected God's light and glory (cf. PP 45). This would change following the Fall, when Adam and Eve were suddenly ashamed of their nakedness after their eyes had been opened (3:10–11).

3:1–24
Humanity's Fall

The chapter tells the tragic story of humanity's temptation and Fall, followed by divine judgment and the introduction of the plan of salvation.

3:1–7. The Choice: Temptation and Fall. The initial *waw* conjunction at the beginning of v. 1 (usually translated as "now") captures well the link between the Creation narrative and the story of the Fall. This conjunction is used to highlight this important connection and is typical of Hebrew narratives. The unsuspecting reader expects, after the account of Creation, another story full of "good" or "very good" things. However, a creature more *'arum* ("cunning," "crafty," "prudent," or "intelligent") than any other animal became the mouthpiece of the tempter and antagonist of God. This word *'arum* can hold both negative and positive connotations in the OT (Prov. 12:16, 23; 13:16). In this context, the use suggests a negative meaning.

Hebrew readers would catch the wordplay between the "cunningness" (*'arum*) of the serpent and "naked" (*'arumim*; 2:25), the human experience that resulted from listening to the creature. The serpent demonstrated its cleverness by its ability to speak and the craftiness of its language. Throughout the ANE, serpents were used as mythological figures acting in opposition to the creator. The Bible identifies the serpent in the Garden with Satan (Rev. 12:9; 20:2), who also challenged God at the beginning of the cosmic conflict in heaven (Is. 14:12–14). The serpent's question did not contradict God's command outright but only added the negative "not," which suddenly transformed God's loving command into an absolute prohibition. It sounded similar yet communicated something entirely different—this is a good reminder of the power of words.

By entering into a dialogue with the serpent, Eve placed herself on dangerous ground. She was appointed together with Adam to guard the Garden and to have dominion over all the animals, but she was beginning to lose that dominion. She was the one who introduced the topic of death (v. 3), and the serpent took immediate advantage of it, arguing that death did not exist. It was God who, by threatening them with death, was setting limits on their potential. At first, the serpent's statement appeared to be true because after eating the fruit, the couple did not immediately die. Instead, what they experienced was spiritual death, and consequently, they were destined to disappear forever. The serpent demonstrated himself to be in open conflict with the Creator. Eve was fascinated by the prospect of opened eyes that the serpent offered her. The opening phrase of Genesis 3:6 mimics Genesis 1, where God saw that what He created was good. This implies that Eve was usurping the Creator's role in determining what was good. Suspicion of an all-powerful God, limited understanding, and selfish interest still warp humanity's ability to distinguish between good and evil (Is. 5:20). Eve's attraction affected three key areas: taste, vision, and intellect (cf. James 1:14–15). The Hebrew term *khamad* (usually translated as "desirable," as in v. 6) expresses the same idea of covetousness as expressed in the Ten Commandments (Ex. 20:17). Eve ate and became an instrument of the serpent in leading Adam to eat of the fruit of the tree. He was not deceived but voluntarily chose death over life (1 Tim. 2:14). As a result of their eyes being opened, both Adam and Eve "knew," yet this knowledge involved shame. They immediately set out to cover themselves with fig leaves (v. 7)—the first illustration of righteousness by works.

3:8–24. God's Questions and Judgment. The biblical text does not give any clue about the time span between Adam and Eve's recognition of shame and the hearing of God's voice. The reference in v. 8 to the "cool of the day"/"the time of the evening breeze" (lit. "the wind of the day"; *ruakh* can be translated as "wind" or "spirit") likely indicates a habitual meeting time. Adam and Eve heard the sound of God walking in the Garden, and instead of welcoming Him they hid from His presence. Ironically, the Hebrew word translated as "heard" can also mean "obey," which was precisely what both humans did *not* do. What followed was the first scene of divine investigation and judgment recorded in the Bible. God's approach was redemptive and began with a number of questions. "Where are you?" (v. 9) invited Adam and Eve to reflect on their relation to God. It was not a divine call for a precise geographical location. Obviously, God knew. "Who told you?" (v. 11) looked at the bigger picture, pointing the reader beyond the serpent to the antagonist whose rebellion had begun the cosmic conflict. "Have you eaten…?" (v. 11) reviewed the *what* of the transgression. All three questions were directed at Adam ("you" is singular), who immediately began pointing fingers (v. 12). Sin had changed forever the relationship between God and humanity and between husband and wife. Eve, in turn, pointed to the serpent as the source of her deception (v. 13). Indirectly, both Adam and Eve insinuated that God was responsible for sin.

The divine verdict was first pronounced against the serpent, then Eve, and finally Adam. The Lord did not leave them in total darkness to face the death that would follow their rebellion and their claim of independence from Him. Where there was no future for humanity, God provided one for them in Genesis 3:15—the first promise of redemption found in the Bible. The "seed" or "offspring" of the woman would overcome the serpent and would bring to an end enmity by restoring full *shalom* between humans and God. The "seed" (Heb. *zera'*) of the woman is singular and can refer to an immediate offspring (4:25; 15:3), a distant descendant, or a large group of descendants. David was guaranteed a *zera'* (2 Sam. 7:12). Paul applies the Abrahamic *zera'* promise to Jesus Christ but also includes the church in Christ as Abraham's seed (Gal. 3:16, 29). The Hebrew term appears repeatedly in the contexts of genealogies, leaving the reader wondering when *the* seed would finally appear. The male seed would bruise or crush the head of the serpent while the serpent would bruise or strike His heel. Since the Hebrew term is the same for both actions, the verb communicates similar enmity between both opponents—yet with different results, due to the nature of the organs involved. Judgment on Eve reflected the entrance of pain and struggle and death in birth and family relations. God is not the author of pain. Both death and pain are due to humanity's sin, and God's judgment is a result. The punishment involving "desire" and "rule" described in v. 16 involved a struggle for control, something that would become even clearer in 4:7, where both terms appear together again. Judgment on Adam involved the means of supporting life. The text refers five times to eating and to the increased struggle to provide food (vv. 17–19). Life separated from the Creator meant

toil, struggle, and constant conflict—and ultimately death (v. 19). Adam's naming of Eve (v.
20) has been interpreted as an indication of man's
headship, yet the name paradoxically also marks
the beginning of hope. Eve's name (Heb. *khawah*)
is related to the Hebrew words for "living" (*khay*),
"to live" (*khayah*), and "declaring" (*khawah*). In
naming her, Adam expressed confidence in the
coming of the seed/offspring (vv. 15–16).

Following this glimmer of hope, God concealed
the nakedness of the couple. Dressing them was
an act of investiture implying acceptance and a
new status. God provided for them the skin of an
animal, thus removing their shame. The plan of
salvation was prefigured: the innocent had to die
for the guilty in order to atone for sin. Finally, vv.
22–24 describe the expulsion of humanity from the
immediate presence of God. The language of vv.
23–24 is strong: God sent them away, banished
them, and drove them out. This is the language of
exile. Cherubim were stationed at the entrance to
Eden to prevent access to the tree of life (3:24). The
biblical text points to the direction of the eviction:
eastward movement marked increasing separation
from the Lord (4:14–16; 11:2; 25:6).

4:1–26

The Entrance of Death

The first human death soon followed the expulsion from Eden, yet the chapter ends on a hopeful
note: another son was born.

4:1–15. The First Death: Cain Murders Abel. Eve
expressed awe following the first human birth.
Even though neither Adam nor Eve "created" in
the divine sense, they shared in the creative act
that God had established. In the Hebrew of v. 1,
the verb *yada'* ("to know") is used as a euphemism for sexual intimacy. This underlines the
closeness of sexual love and, in this case, the joy
of the arrival of a child. Humans exhibited excitement in the midst of sadness. Eve's exclamation
regarding Cain (v. 1) is significant. The Hebrew
particle *'et* has caused translators significant difficulty. Most translations convey the idea that Eve
recognized God had helped her give birth. In that
case, the *'et* means "with"—"I have brought forth
a man with the Lord" (i.e., with His help). However, another translation is possible—one that is
in line with the nature of the promise of 3:15 and
that is plausible in the Hebrew grammar. It would
read: "I have acquired [or received] a man-child—
the Lord." Here the particle *'et* is translated as a
sign of the direct object and suggests that Adam
and Eve expected Cain to be the Savior.

Right from the outset, the biblical texts describe two basic (and, historically, often conflicting) human activities: Abel was a shepherd
while Cain had chosen to be a farmer (4:2).
Both Cain and Abel presented an offering to
the Lord that reflected their vocations (4:3–5).
The text does not provide details concerning
the performance of the ritual, but it does state
that God accepted Abel's offering from the firstborn of his flock but did not accept that of Cain
from the fruit of the ground (vv. 4–5). Assuming that when God dressed Adam and Eve with
the skins of animals, He also instructed them
concerning the importance of atoning sacrificial blood, one can find in Cain's offering a
lack of respect for God and His instructions
concerning atoning blood. Abel's bloody sacrifice, offered in faith (Heb. 11:4), indicates
his dependence on the promised Savior. Cain
refused to bring a sacrifice that would have
atoned for sin (cf. PP 71).

Cain's response to the rejection of his offering was rage, expressed in a similar way as the
fury and anger that led Jacob's sons to massacre
the city of Shechem after they had heard of the
rape of their sister (Gen. 34:7). The expression
referring to Cain's (lit.) "fallen face" (translated
variously as "downcast," "despondent," or "re-
sentful") reiterates the anger and frustration
boiling in Cain's heart. Part of this was a reaction
against God and the preference shown to Abel.
This jealousy was fueled by resentment over the
fact that his younger brother had not deferred to
his judgment. In spite of Cain's strong reaction,
God reached out and interacted directly with His
wayward creature, using pedagogical questions
to draw him out. He also indicated a path for
Cain to overcome his anger—he could change
his course and follow the Lord's plan (v. 7). This
suggests that Cain knew the difference between
right and wrong and between appropriate and
inappropriate offerings. The idea of *rabats* ("to
lie down") can convey the image of someone,
an animal or an evil power, waiting by the door
to attack (cf. 49:9). Another way to understand
this passage is to consider the term translated as
"sin" (*khatta't*) in v. 7 to mean "sin offering" (as
it does in much of the OT usages) rather than
"sin." The idea thus would be that God told
Cain to accept and present the "sin offering"
that was "at the door"—which may be understood as a reference to the worship that Adam
and his posterity offered at the Garden of Eden's
guarded gate. Two key words in 4:7 echo directly
the Fall narrative in Genesis 3. Sin had a desire
(*teshuqah*) for Cain yet needed to be mastered

(*mashal*). In 3:16, the woman's desire (*teshuqah*) would be for her husband, and he would rule (*mashal*) over her. While 3:16 represents a curse, God's admonition in 4:7 showed the way to life.

In spite of God's direct intervention, Cain murdered his brother Abel. The biblical author does not provide a specific reason or cause. Cain talked with Abel. In some ancient versions, it is written that Cain said to Abel, "Let's go out to the field." But in other manuscripts, no further details are given. Then brother rose against brother, and Abel was killed. The Hebrew term used here, *harag*, indicates "slaughter" and "murder" and is distinct from the verb used in the Ten Commandments (Ex. 20:13). Death entered human society and made explicit what had only been implicit in God's description of a world governed by sin.

In 4:9–15 the reader is privy to a second dialogue between the Lord and Cain, in which the Lord again sought to lead to the recognition of sin by using questions (a type of investigative judgment, as was the case with Adam and Eve). Clearly, God knew what had happened to Abel, so the issue here is not information but recognition and repentance (cf. 3:9–19). The first reference to blood in the Bible is found in v. 10, where it is personified as crying for justice to the Lord (cf. Rev. 6:9–10). Cain did not recognize the gravity of his action. Instead of repenting, he bewailed the punishment (v. 13). However, God's mercy was still at work and included protection from human recrimination (cf. Ex. 12:13). God's mark showed both guilt and protection and prefigured other marks (or "signs" as the Hebrew word can also be translated) in future narratives (Ex. 12:13; Josh. 2:12; Rev. 13:17; 16:2; 19:20; etc.).

Minkhah in the Old Testament

The term denoting "offering" used in this story is *minkhah*, representing a more generic term for an offering or a gift. In Leviticus 2, as part of a larger section dealing with different sacrifices, the term is used to describe a grain offering. In other instances, it can refer to food offerings in general (Is. 57:6; Ezek. 45:17) though it is usually translated as "grain offering." In Genesis 32:13, it describes a gift Jacob presented to his brother while in 1 Samuel 10:27, it refers to a gift for a king. Similar to its use in this story, it can also be employed to describe animal sacrifices involving the shedding of blood (1 Sam. 2:12–17).

4:16–24. Increasing Distance: Cain's Family Line and Lamech's Boast. The history of Cain's descendants (his wife was clearly one of his sisters, a daughter of Adam; 5:4) shows that they had an ever-increasing distance from God which culminated in Lamech's boastful challenge. Cain left the presence of the Lord and settled in the land of Nod (Heb. *nod*). A Hebrew audience would have immediately appreciated the wordplay employing the verb *nud*, referring to living as a vagabond or wanderer (vv. 12, 14). The juxtaposition conjured a picture of a vagabond living in the land of vagabonds. Cain's genealogy, the first in the Bible, includes not only names but also significant human accomplishments (vv. 17b, 20b, 21, 22) and concludes with Lamech's proud song (4:23–24). The founding of cities, the playing of musical instruments, and the introduction of animal husbandry and metalworking were all part of this human lineage. The section also includes the first reference to polygamy (v. 19), something that indicates further distance from the Edenic ideal of a monogamous union of a man and a woman in marriage partnership. Notably, the genealogy includes seven generations from Adam to Lamech, which reminds the reader of the importance of the number seven in Genesis. While Cain requested divine protection, Lamech, using poetic language, proudly claimed to be the ruler of his own life by using the motif of seven. While God had threatened sevenfold vengeance against anyone who harmed Cain (4:15), Lamech threatened a vengeance eleven times greater: seventy-seven (4:24). He did not rely on God's protection but sought to be his own master. Lamech was the perfect example of human hubris, self-reliance, pride, vindictiveness, and self-sufficiency.

4:25–26. Hope Never Dies: A Child Is Born. However, all was not lost. There was a faithful lineage. In two verses, the biblical author reinserts hope into a cold and desperate world. Eve gave birth to another son, Seth, who in turn had Enosh, whose name means "man," echoing Adam's name. Enosh, perhaps symbolic of a new Adam, represented a new line of faithful followers of the Lord, which would ultimately culminate in Jesus, the "second Adam" (see Rom. 5:12–21; 1 Cor. 15:45). The term Eve used to describe her new child, Seth, was very specific: *zera'* (lit. "seed," "offspring"; v. 25). It points directly and significantly back to Genesis 3:15. The birth of Seth marked another stride toward the fulfillment of God's famous promise and was characterized by reliance on God, recognition of His goodness, and worship of the Creator. The phrase referring to "calling on the name of the LORD" (4:26) is repeatedly used in Genesis in connection with the construction of an altar, the offering of sacrifices, and ultimately worship (12:8; 13:4; 21:33; 26:25). While Cain's family line was noteworthy for music, nomadism, herding, metalworking, and establishing cities, Seth's line was noteworthy for its worship. There was nothing intrinsically wrong with the ingenuity and invention of Cain's line; the problem was that they did not acknowledge God as the Giver of all of their gifts. In all of their accomplishments, there was a distinct lack of worship. In this way, the cosmic battle between Satan and God had come to earth, and humanity was choosing sides.

5:1–32
Bridging the Gap: Genealogy from Adam to Noah

Chapter 5 contains a linear genealogy of faithful descent, linking Adam to Noah. Genesis 5:1 is the only place in the book in which *toledot* ("genealogy," "family records," "generations"; see Genesis: Introduction) is associated with the word *seper* ("document" or "book"), which suggests a written document. God created humans in His image, but this is recalled here in the context of the rebellion of Cain and Lamech. Yet the descendants of Seth, the worshipers of the Lord, would preserve the image of God although it had been extremely damaged by sin.

The genealogy follows a common pattern, beginning with the name of the person, his age when the first child was born, the name of the child, the years he lived after the arrival of the firstborn, and his age at death. Adam could not create descendants in the exact image of God; Seth was born in Adam's own likeness and image (v. 3). Unfortunately, Seth's likeness was further removed from God's original image. Yet each child was named by a progenitor, marking another important connection to God's activity in Genesis 1. Human procreation was God's way of passing on the remnants of the divine image from parents to children—even after the Fall had almost entirely eradicated it.

Ancient versions (or translations) of this passage have resulted in differences in the chronology of Genesis 1–11. For example, the Samaritan Pentateuch (established at least from the first century B.C.), a text that was maintained by the Samaritans, tallies 1,307 years from Creation to the Flood, while the Masoretic Text (MT, established at least from the ninth century A.D., the text on which most modern versions of the OT are based) asserts there were 1,656. The Septuagint (LXX, established at least from the third century B.C.), the Greek translation of the OT, maintains 2,242 years for the same period. Some of these differences can be explained as variants resulting from textual errors. Others may suggest the use of a different chronological system. However, the system of the MT appears to be the most reliable since, by its reckoning, all of Noah's ancestors died before the Flood.

ANE genealogies are manifold and come in different shapes and forms. One of the most famous, the third-millennium-B.C. Sumerian King List, has often been connected to Genesis 5. The list contains the names and cities of Sumerian kings before and after the Flood. While it is primarily interested in kingship (thus having a focus distinct from Gen. 5) and contains ludicrously high numbers for royal reigns, one can note a similar pattern in longevity when compared to the genealogy of Genesis 5. Before the Flood, the reigns of the Sumerian kings were exceedingly long (e.g., King Emmenluanna reigned 43,200 years) while after the Flood, the number of years decreased drastically.

The importance of the number seven is evident in the genealogy of the faithful lineage of Adam's descendants. Enoch, the seventh member of that line, walked with God (v. 24), an expression not found in the other genealogical records. The metaphor "to walk with God" suggests intimate communion with God, is reminiscent of Adam and Eve's experience in the Garden (3:8), and would characterize the life of Noah (6:9), the only other human to whom this phrase was applied. In the Psalms, walking before God means life and prosperity (Pss. 56:13; 116:9); the prophets use the expression to highlight proper ethical choices (Is. 30:21; Jer. 18:15; Mic. 4:5). The author of Hebrews associates it with pleasing God through a life of faith, believing that God exists and that He rewards those who seek Him diligently (Heb. 11:5-6). Because of Enoch's close walk with God, He "took" him (Gen. 5:24). The Hebrew *laqakh* denotes physical activity but is also used metaphorically for death or for being saved from it. Life could be "taken" by God (1 Kin. 19:10, 14). Notably, the verb is also used to describe Elijah's ascension to heaven (2 Kin. 2:3, 10–11). Enoch's life did not end in death but in translation. For the pre-Flood generations, he represented a tangible expression of God's promise of redemption. Enoch appears in later biblical texts that extol his faith (Heb. 11:5) and his prophetic ministry (Jude 14), and he was also a famous figure in noncanonical texts.

The wish of Lamech (not the Lamech of Gen. 4) expressed at the birth of Noah (5:29) connected Noah's name with comfort. This illustrates how names and their sounds in the OT were often creatively linked to significant ideas or concepts. The genealogy of Seth splits into the three sons of Noah, thus preparing the way for the narrative of Noah (5:32).

6:1—9:29
Flood and Covenant

This section describes divine judgment by universal Flood and God's plan to fulfill His promise of salvation by ultimately renewing the covenant between the Creator and His creation. Noah, the tenth from Creation, became another type of the second Adam (see notes on 4:25–26), the first following the Flood. The text is organized in the literary form of a chiasm, pointing the reader to the most important element at its center. This chiastic structure is surrounded by two narratives that diagnose and narrate wickedness *before* and *after* the Flood (6:1–8 and 9:18–29).

A Noah and his three sons (6:9–10)
  B Violence in God's creation (6:11–12)
    C Resolution to destroy (6:13–22)
      D Command to enter the ark (7:1–10)
        E Beginning of the Flood (7:11–16)
          F The rising floodwaters (7:17–24)
            GOD REMEMBERED NOAH (8:1a)
          F' The receding floodwaters (8:1b–5)
        E' The drying of the earth (8:6–14)
      D' Command to leave the ark (8:15–19)
    C' God's resolution to preserve order (8:20–22)
  B' Covenant blessing and peace (9:1–17)
A' Noah and his three sons (9:18–19)

6:1–8. Divine Diagnosis: Increasing Wickedness. The initial words of 6:1 indicate narrative continuity in the typical Hebrew manner. While the text makes reference to multiplication (which, after all, corresponds to a divine command; cf. 1:22), the distinction between the "sons of God" and "daughters of men/humankind" prefigures conflict. Many different explanations for these two groups have been suggested (for example, angelic celestial beings, human rulers, or godly men), yet the most convincing contextual interpretation appears to be the correlation of the sons of God with the descendants of Seth (Gen. 5) and the daughters of humankind with the descendants of Cain. The faithful servants of God are occasionally identified as children of God (e.g., Deut. 14:1; Is. 43:6) although in some contexts the phrase suggests angelic or divine beings (Job 1:6; 2:1; Dan. 3:25). When the sons of God saw the beauty (lit. "good") of the daughters of humankind, they married (lit. "took wives") for themselves. The language employed in 6:2 clearly echoes the Fall narrative in 3:6, where Eve "saw" that the fruit was "good" and then "took" it. These actions led to divine judgment (6:3). Life spans were restricted, and God declared the withdrawal of His Spirit, most likely a reference to the life-giving power of God in 2:7. The duration of "forever" (Heb. *'olam*) in biblical texts is always linked to the subject the term describes. When associated with human beings, it marks a limited time span: several hundred years prior to the Flood and 120 years following the Flood (6:3). The word *don* is a difficult term, as suggested by the two main translations usually given: "contend/strive," or "abide/remain." It appears only once in the OT, and in this context, it could mean "remain" or "abide."

Another difficult term is *nepilim*. Some opt to transliterate it "Nephilim", while other translators use "giants" or "fallen ones." The former translation is based on the LXX rendering, which may have been influenced by the occurrence of the term in Numbers 13:33 (where it clearly refers to men of great stature, the children of *'anaq*; Num. 13:32–33). In identifying these same men elsewhere in the Bible, the term *repa'im* is used (Deut. 2:11, 20; 3:11, 13), a term later utilized to refer to Goliath and his brothers (2 Sam. 21:16, 18, 20, 22; 1 Chr. 20:4, 6, 8). In the context of the Flood, the *nepilim* could refer to both the "extraordinary ones" (thus suggesting mighty heroes) and the "ones who have fallen" (or "ones who have fallen upon"). Since Genesis 6:1–4 describes the conditions of pre-Flood humanity, the reference to the *nepilim* is another way of depicting the wickedness of the ante-diluvian world and the corrupting influence of marriages with unbelievers. This leads to an important moment in the narrative describing divine action. When God saw, He acted (cf. 29:31; Deut. 32:19; Is. 59:15–16)—either as Judge or as Savior. God saw human wickedness, including the intent and inclination of the heart (6:5). This description highlights the importance of motivation and attitudes. In response, the Lord was sorry and was disturbed. This confirms how seriously God takes human actions and how they impact Him. Some versions have "repent" here, but this is potentially misleading when referring to God because it suggests the idea of remorse for wrongdoing. God changes only in response to human repentance. God's determination to destroy (Heb. *makhah*) expresses the idea of "wiping out," a term that implies that the judgment was universal. Although there did not seem to be any hope for the human race, Noah found *khen* ("favor" or "grace") in the eyes of the Lord.

6:9—8:22. Judgment Call: A Universal Flood. Genesis 6:11–12 repeats some of the diagnostics of vv. 5–6. However, the focus is not on humanity alone but includes the entire system. That the earth was "corrupt" suggests that the divine order established at Creation was no long operative. All life on earth was characterized by a violence that paid no respect to social justice and spiritual integrity. The universal corruption of humanity required for its correction a judgment of universal extent—a global Flood.

The next section (6:13–22) contains detailed divine instructions regarding the construction of the ark. It is introduced by a phrase that is significant in biblical theology, namely, "the end of all people" (lit. "flesh"; v. 13). Intriguingly, Ezekiel 7 describes the destruction of Jerusalem in similar terms (including key words such as "end," "violence," "coming," "is full"), suggesting that the end of Jerusalem and its temple was perceived to be as existentially disturbing as the cataclysmic end of the antediluvian world. Since the Hebrew *qets* ("end") often has eschatological connotations (Dan. 8:17, 19; 12:13), the Flood provides a show-and-tell laboratory for eschatological realities.

The ark was a very large structure of 450 feet (137 m) long, 75 feet (23 m) wide, and 45 feet (14 m) high, built according to the instructions that God gave to Noah. The sentence structure of v. 17 is very emphatic: God Himself was going to generate floodwaters on the earth. Divine judgment was as personal as divine creation and divine salvation. This was not merely the result of God withdrawing His protection and allowing nature to take its course, as some have suggested. Genesis 6:18 marks the first occurrence of the term "covenant" (Heb. *berit*) in Scripture, which is employed here to refer to a unilateral decision on the part of God based on His grace and expectation of a response of faith from humans.

God gave Noah specific instructions about the construction of the ark and explained His intention to use the boat to rescue Noah, his family, and all living things. Genesis 6 concludes with a brief completion formula that prefigures a similar formula found at the conclusion of the construction of the sanctuary (cf. Ex. 40:16; Lev. 8:4, 9, 13, 17, 21, 29, 36): Noah listened, he obeyed (v. 22), and he trusted that what he had heard had

The Biblical Flood Story and Extrabiblical Flood Stories

Flood narratives have been found throughout the world with significant variations. For biblical scholars, the most important stories come from Mesopotamia because they show interesting similarities to the biblical tale. They are called the Gilgamesh and Atrahasis epics, dated to second-millennium sources. When compared to the biblical narrative, there are some significant differences, two of which are worth mentioning. First, in the Bible, God was in complete control of the waters and did not feel threatened by them while in the Mesopotamian stories, the gods were afraid when they saw the waters rising uncontrollably. Second, while in the Babylonian story, the reason for the flood was an emotional reaction to human noise that made it difficult for the gods to rest, in the Bible, the Flood was a divine response to moral evil. One could speculate that Moses was acquainted with the Mesopotamian flood stories, but by offering a reliable account of what took place, he was undermining the pagan version of the event and discrediting the characters of their gods.

indeed been God's voice preparing him for an unprecedented phenomenon—a Flood.

Noah and his household entered the ark in obedience to God's command without ever having experienced rain (7:1–9). He stepped out in faith, trusting the One who does not fail (Heb. 11:7). The biblical text clearly distinguishes between clean and unclean animals here: God ordered Noah to take both types of animals into the ark (7:2–3, 9). The Hebrew text remains unclear as to whether there were one or two pairs of unclean animals. Different Bible translations handle this discrepancy differently. The distinction between clean and unclean highlights the ritual classification of animals, already known in Noah's time, that was later explicitly included in laws governing the dietary practices of the covenant people (Lev. 11:1–47; Deut. 14:3–21). Here, however, the distinction seems to prepare the reader for the sacrificial offering Noah and his family prepare after disembarking from the ark (8:20). Only clean animals were offered; this underlines divine holiness and separation. Furthermore, up to this point, God's diet for humanity had been a strictly vegetarian one (Gen. 1:29).

Echoing the larger literary design of 6:9—9:19 that highlights God's remembering of Noah (and his family), chapters 7–8 exhibit a similar chiastic design based on time markers associated with the Flood narrative.

> **7 days** of waiting for the Flood (7:4)
> > **7 days** of waiting for the Flood (7:10)
> > > **40 days** of rain (7:17)
> > > > **150 days** of water rising (7:24)
> > > > > **CENTER: God remembered Noah**
> > > > **150 days** of waters receding (8:3)
> > > **40 days** of waiting for dry land (8:6)
> > **7 days** of waiting for the return of first bird (8:10)
> **7 days** of waiting for the return of second bird (8:12)

Genesis 7:10–24 describes the catastrophic Flood that covers everything. Every living being outside the ark perished (7:21–23), except, of course, the inhabitants of the sea, a fact that highlights the divine diagnostic of 6:5, 7, 13, referring to the earth. The destructive water came from on high and from below (7:11). The reference to the "fountains" or "springs of the great deep" involves the use of the Hebrew term *tehom* ("sea," "deep," or "abyss") that is used in the description of the earth prior to God's creation (1:2).

The destructive waters of the great deep corresponded to the great wickedness of humanity leading to the Flood (6:5). Isaiah 51:10 uses the same phrase to describe God's destruction of the Egyptian armies during the Exodus. To accomplish this, the windows/floodgates of heaven were opened (Gen. 7:11). The rain (Gen. 1:6–8) fell to the earth like mighty waterfalls, and that which lay beneath the earth shot up in jets. In this way, God was returning the earth to its pre-creation state.

The biblical text provides a very specific time reference, namely, the six hundredth year of Noah's life, in the second month, on the seventeenth day. One year and eleven days later, the earth had finally dried up enough to support life (8:14). "On that day" (or, in this case, on the "very same day"; 7:13) is often used in the OT to emphasize a significant event. For example, "this day" marked the arrival of Israel at the Wilderness of Sinai (Ex. 19:1). The identical phrase found here in 7:13 (*be'etsem hayyom*, "the same day") is used to tie the Festivals of Unleavened Bread and the Passover to the first night of the Exodus (Ex. 12:17, 41, 51) and to link Moses's speech to the moment of his death (Deut. 32:48–50).

While Noah was singled out, he was not saved alone. Noah's household—including his wife (whose name is not mentioned); his sons Japheth, Shem, and Ham; and their wives (whose names are also not mentioned)—was likewise part of God's rescue plan. The miraculous entry of wild and domesticated animals into the ark must have caused quite a stir to the observing onlookers. After all had entered, the Lord sealed the door of the ark (Gen. 7:16). This highlighted God's commitment to Noah and those inside the ark. Humanity's survival was due to divine grace, not human effort. In the Mesopotamian flood narratives, the heroes shut the door themselves.

The following verses describe the immensity of the Flood. The ark was at this point moving in the waters that covered the mountains by 15 cubits, or approximately 22 feet (7 m; 7:20). All *basar* (lit. "flesh"), meaning all living things with the breath of life in their nostrils (7:22), animals and humans, died in this cataclysmic event (7:21–23); only Noah and those who had sought refuge in the ark remained alive. Here, the biblical text introduces a significant theological concept—the remnant. It is found here in Genesis and also in Revelation (12:17). In the midst of total upheaval, God is always willing and able to preserve a remnant through whom He continues to demonstrate His saving purpose for the human race.

As already indicated, God remembered Noah and all who were with him (8:1). The meaning is not that God had forgotten but that He was caring for and acting on behalf of His servants (e.g., 30:22; Ex. 2:24; 6:5). As the waters receded, the ark settled on firm ground. The might of the subterranean water and seemingly endless rain from above must have resulted in immense changes to the earth's surface, including newly created continents, mountains, deep canyons, twisted rock folds, and rugged riverbeds. The location of the mountains of Ararat (8:4) is not quite clear. Assyrian records link Ararat to ancient Urartu, covering southeast Turkey, southern Russia, and northwest Iran. Yet no specific location can be ascertained from the biblical text, particularly considering the completely changed geography of the post-Flood world.

Noah's opening of a window of the ark (8:6) was not prompted explicitly by a divine command. He released first a raven (v. 7), followed by a dove (v. 8). While the raven, which could eat carrion and was a stronger bird, did not return to the ark, the dove found no place to land or rest (v. 9). Ancient mariners often used birds to ascertain proximity to land; Noah may have used them to confirm his visual impressions after he had opened the window of the ark. The verb used to describe Noah's sending (*shalakh*) of the birds is also used to describe the sending of the spies into Canaan (Num. 13:3; Josh. 2:1) and God sending Adam and Eve from the Garden (Gen. 3:23). The image of the returning dove, holding a freshly plucked olive leaf, has become a symbol of peace and safety in contemporary culture. Here it is merely an indication of the existence of growing vegetation, resulting in Noah's removal of the covering of the ark (8:13). Only then did God speak again to Noah. The divine order was clear and echoed the order of 1:28, "Be fruitful" (8:17).

After having been inside the ark for over a year, Noah's initial action involved the construction of an altar (8:20). This is the first explicit mention of an altar and a burnt offering, even though 3:21 and 4:3–5 may implicitly refer to an altar. The burnt offering was taken from among the clean animals. The anthropomorphic phrase stating that the Lord smelled a soothing or pleasing aroma is language found in the context of the sanctuary services and communicates the idea that God accepts the sacrifice and the offerer (see Lev. 1:9). Here, it is an expression of God's grace conveyed in the poetic declaration of 8:22. The promise guaranteed God's continued preservation of the earth and its ecology until the final judgment (2 Pet. 2:5–12).

9:1–17. God's Covenant with Noah and His Descendants. The following section represents the first formal covenant ritual in the OT and starts off with a number of divine instructions (9:1–7). Importantly, God's blessing preceded any instruction. The command of 9:1 to be fruitful echoed chapters 1 and 2. After the Flood there was, so to speak, a new creation and a new beginning. Following the order to fill the earth, the passage contains detailed instructions concerning diet and cultic purity involving the use of blood (anticipating Lev. 17:10–14). Even more important, beginning in v. 5, God gives specific directions as to the sacredness of human life. Whoever shed human blood would have to answer to the Creator because life belongs to Him (v. 6). The text foreshadows the *lex talionis* ("eye for eye" [Ex. 21:24; Lev. 24:20; Deut. 19:21]), which required that the punishment for a crime correspond to the nature of the crime. Shedding blood is another way of referring to murder (Gen. 37:22; 1 Kin. 2:31; Ezek. 22:4). The taking of life required death because it was a violation of the image of God (1:27). Later legislation underlined the importance of societal punishment (over individual revenge), tempered with regulations such as the cities of refuge that governed accidental manslaughter (Num. 35:9–15; Deut. 4:41–43; 19:1–13).

God's covenant (cf. 6:18) included Noah and his descendants, as well as every living creature with him (9:9–10). It was based on the grace of God, who took the initiative to reach out to sinners and restore their fractured relationship. God's covenant sign was public and highly visible (9:12–13). The Hebrew word *qeshet* in v. 13 is sometimes translated as "rainbow" here, but it is the same word used for a warrior's bow in the OT. Part of the implication is that further conflict with God was needless. The bow was an offer of peace and a covenant sign. The context indicates that this bow "in the cloud" was a rainbow. The same word is used in Ezekiel 1:28, where "rainbow" is again evidently intended. In Revelation 4:3 and 10:1, the rainbow is associated with God's throne room in a vision. Following God's remembering of Noah (8:1), God promised twice to remember the covenant (Gen. 9:15–16). He did not forget Noah, his family, or any living creature in the ark, and neither would He forget His promises.

9:18–29. Noah's Curse and Blessings. Following the assurance of divine acceptance and protection, the focus changes from Noah to Noah's three sons. Would the future be different from the past, considering the terrifying experience of the Flood still fresh in the minds of Noah's sons?

The section opens with a description of three generations, including also a reference to Canaan, the son of Ham (9:18–19), who was the only grandchild mentioned in the genealogy. Genesis 9:20 contains the first reference to viticulture in the OT. Whether by innocent accident or carelessness, Noah's drunkenness led to his shameful condition. Nudity is, in most cases in the Bible, considered shameful and humiliating. Prisoners of war were displayed naked to humiliate them and as a sign of victory over them (for more on the idea of uncovering oneself, see Ex. 20:26; Deut. 23:13–14; cf. Hab. 2:16). In this case, nakedness was associated with the consumption of alcohol. Several passages of Scripture point to the damaging effects of alcohol on humans (cf. Lev. 10:9; Prov. 21:17; 23:20–21; 29–31; Is. 5:22). What Ham did to his father was also ignoble because, instead of covering him, he passed on the information to his brothers and thus dishonored his father.

Scripture does not reveal precisely how Noah ascertained what Ham had done; yet his curse, expressed in poetic lines, was unequivocal. The curse of Canaan (9:25) represents a surprising twist in a problematic story. Why would Canaan be cursed when his father had committed the sin? Was this not an affront to divine justice? Commentators have struggled with this verse. However, a look at the larger context of the first eleven chapters of Genesis may provide a hint. Adam and Eve's decisions to heed the voice of the tempter resulted in their expulsion from Eden and the entrance of death—affecting all future generations. The wickedness of the sons of God in Genesis 6:1–7 resulted in the Flood and the destruction of almost all human and animal life. In line with the language of the commandments, sin shatters relationships and affects both the one committing the sin as well as future generations (cf. Ex. 20:5–6). However, later generations may have emphasized this reality to such an extreme that the Hebrew prophets argued against using this concept fatalistically to avoid personal responsibility (cf. Jer. 31:29; Ezek. 18:2). Canaan's punishment was to be subservient to his brothers. The curse language is similar to 3:14, but this time it was uttered by a human being. The curse of Canaan was balanced by the blessings of Shem and Japheth (9:26) and did not exclude his descendants (e.g., Rahab and the Gibeonites) from being part of the people of God.

10:1—11:26
Dispersion of the Nations

This section describes, in geographical terms, God's interest in the nations of the world. Taking as its point of departure one family, it chronicles divine blessings (i.e., multiplication) in response to the divine command, followed by dispersion and the focus upon the line of Shem.

10:1–32. Peoples: The Table of Nations. The presence of the many genealogies in chapters 1–11 underlines their importance. In this case, the list of the nations prepares the way for the call of Abram and the divine promise to make of him a new nation by which the other nations of the earth would be blessed (12:1–3). None of these early nations could be used by the Lord to accomplish His purpose to save sinful human beings.

Japheth was likely the eldest son of Noah (10:21), although Shem is often named first since it was through his descendants that the family of Abraham came. Japheth's offspring essentially represented Indo-European people groups who populated the region covering India, Asia Minor, and southern Europe. Seven sons of Japheth are included in this list, followed by further descendants of his first two sons (10:2–5). Throughout the table of nations, it is not always clear if a name represents solely an individual or a people. Furthermore, the table seems to be based on authentic ancient data since Israel's neighbors (such as the Moabites, Ammonites, and Edomites), known from later sources (and biblical texts) dating to the first millennium B.C., are not explicitly mentioned. The final note of 10:5 mentions the peoples on the coast who were separated (or "divided") into their lands, anticipating 11:8.

The sons of Ham represented the peoples of northeastern Africa and the Levant (10:6–20). Cush (Ethiopia), Mizraim (Egypt), Put (possibly Libya or Somalia), and Canaan (the Levant) were direct sons of Ham and had names known from other biblical texts. Genesis 10:8–12 describes in further details the exploits of Nimrod, the son of Cush. Geographically, Nimrod was associated with prominent cities in Mesopotamia that impacted Israel's history (e.g., Babel and Nineveh; cf. Mic. 5:6) and is described as a "mighty hunter before the LORD" (v. 9). The description "before the LORD" is often used to indicate priestly service (Ex. 16:9; 27:21; etc.), but here it seems to simply highlight the fact that even this mighty warrior was not outside of God's control and vision. Interestingly, later in the narrative, Esau is also described as a skill-ful hunter (25:27) and thus his (infamous) story becomes linked to Nimrod's story. Nimrod's name can be translated as "we shall rebel," and his kingdom and city building anticipated the huge construction project of Babel's tower in Genesis 11. The description of Nimrod as a mighty or heroic figure (v. 8) uses the same He-brew term as in the description of the mighty ones of 6:4 prior to the Flood. While Nimrod built cities and an empire by sheer aggression and power (vv. 10–11), Abraham built altars to worship the One who led him to the promised land (12:7–8; 13:18; 22:9; etc.). Much later, the humble carpenter from Nazareth exemplified and taught the same principle: lasting change and the kingdom of God can be built only upon love, service, and community.

The reference to Casluhim (some transla-tions read "Kasluhites") in 10:14 includes an additional note introducing the Philistines. During the early history following Israel's ar-rival in the Holy Land, the Philistines repre-sented an important reference point in biblical history. A few hundred years after the Exodus, waves of people began to immigrate to the southern Levant (and even tried to settle in northern Egypt). These peoples are referred to as the "Sea Peoples." Some associate them with the later Philistines of the late Judges and early monarchy period. The question then is: *Who are the Philistines mentioned in the patri-archal narratives?* Different answers have been given to this question. It is possible that the migrants, these "Sea Peoples," assimilated into the people group already known to the He-brews as Philistines (21:32–34; 26:1–33). It is also conceivable that the term "Philistines" was added anachronistically by later scribes since the people with whom the patriarchs interacted lived in the same location as the Phi-listines from the time of the early monarchy (see "The Philistines," p. 407).

Canaan's descendants (10:15–19) included later city-states and tribal groups. At the end of 10:15, the term *khet* is mentioned. Some take this to refer to early Hittites, the famous em-pire in Anatolia, but others suggest that this term could also indicate a different group. In the patriarchal period, the Hittites lived in Ca-naan around Hebron (cf. Gen. 23). In stark disregard for his parents' views about eligible marriage partners for their sons, Esau inter-married with the Hittites (26:34–35; 27:46). The final summary statement of Ham's descen-dants involves families, languages, clans, and peoples (similar to 10:5, 31–32). The reference to languages anticipates 11:1.

Genesis 10:21–31 lists Shem's descendants. This was the group from which God's covenant people would emerge. Shem's descendants in-cluded four tiers, for a total of twenty-six names. Attention is given to the offspring of Arphaxad and then Joktan. The name of one of Eber's sons, Peleg (v. 25), was associated with an event that was apparently so significant that it is included in the genealogy. The name Peleg means "divide" and is associated here with the division of the earth. Many have speculated on what this might mean. Most likely it is a refer-ence to the dividing of the earth into nations at the Tower of Babel. Other suggestions include a major earthquake or even the continental shift. Shem's genealogy is not complete by 10:31 and will be continued in 11:10–26. The final state-ment (10:32) echoes the first verse of this chap-ter. This appears to form some type of literary bracket (also called an "*inclusio*").

11:1–9. The Tower of Babel and the Disper-sion of Humanity. This story describes two diametrically opposed movements: human-ity's desire and ill-conceived attempt to reach heaven (11:4) and God's coming down in re-sponse (11:5). The story is sandwiched between two lines of the descendants of Shem. One line ends in confusion and Babylon (Babel), the other in a promise and covenant leading to the promised land.

The Tower of Babel in Comparative Perspective

While no direct parallel has been found, Mesopotamian texts contain references to the origin of the diversity of languages (e.g., the Sumerian Enmerkar and the Lord of Aratta) and the desire of humans to reach heaven, which belongs to the gods (a Mesopotamian proverb). There are also references to humanity's intention to build a structure that would extend to heaven in order to indicate their supremacy (the Enuma Elish epic). The religious con-notations of the tower can also be linked to Sumerian ziggurats, or temple towers, which represented an artificial mountain with a temple at its peak. However, while some ideas are shared, the texts them-selves are completely distinct from the biblical narrative.

Language is one of the most fundamental characteristics of being human. The confusion created by the multiplicity of languages made it more difficult to communicate; this damaged the possibility of peaceful existence. But perhaps this is not only about language but also about the beginning of significant cultural distinctions in the population of the earth.

Human pride resulted in the rejection of the divine promise, and this was accompanied by an attempt for self-preservation. They built a tower in order to make a name for themselves (11:4). They did not seem to know that making a name for someone is the work of God (see 12:2). Clearly, they wanted to be self-sufficient and independent from God—attitudes that are closely associated with the unfathomable origin of sin (cf. Is. 14:12–14). The desire to be independent from the Creator and Lord of the universe is not only a problem in this narrative; it represents an important theological theme found in Scripture. Humans habitually seek control over their own lives and often reject the Creator's lordship.

Genesis 11:5 describes God as "coming down" to pronounce a legal verdict. Sometimes the appearance of God is for salvation or to instruct His people, but here His coming down is also a reminder of His justice. God's descent did not mean that He was unaware of what was going on. He knows all things and is omnipresent (1 Kin. 8:27; Ps. 139:1–4, 7; Is. 46:10; Jer. 23:24). In fact, the text indicates that He knew what would have happened had He not intervened to disrupt the tower builders. Rather than showing a lack of knowledge, the anthropomorphic language used here is evocative of God's justice having been displayed. God is shown as having investigated the case before executing judgment. God once again spoke within the mystery of His being, using a plural pronoun as He did in 1:26, but this time the result was judgment in the form of confusion. The Babylonians called the city *bab-ili* ("gate of the gods"), but for the Hebrews, it was *balal* ("confusion"). The irony of this is highly significant, especially in view of the later importance of Babylon in Scripture. While Babylon (Babel) considered itself to be the gateway to the gods, it produced only confusion. As a result of God having confused the ability of the builders to freely communicate, the city (and the tower) could not be completed. The builders were scattered (v. 8); this resulted in the state that the builders had intended to avoid (v. 4).

11:10–26. The Righteous Family Line from Shem to Abram. The narrative moves almost imperceptibly from concerns of a universal nature to matters related to one single family: the descendants of Shem. The list of Shem's faithful descendants includes ten individuals—a description that echoes the list of the ten descendants of Adam (5:1–32). While the first eleven chapters of Genesis contained a number of important promises, the opening verses of chapter 12 add more that would become highly significant for God's redemptive plan. God was on the move again and was preparing an individual and his family to step out in faith.

11:27—50:26

PATRIARCHAL HISTORY: GOD'S CALL OF A FAMILY TO BE A BLESSING

Genesis 11:27—50:26 represents the second major division of the book of beginnings. Having painted in broad strokes the vast picture of Creation, the Fall, and the Flood, in order to briefly explain where Abraham came from, the text now shifts to the story of one family—Abraham's—and how that family came to live in Egypt. The history of this family with its victories and setbacks is the nucleus of God's hands-on plan of redemption. A cursory examination of these chapters may lead the reader, at times, to wonder about God's covenant people, but their struggles and God's patience highlight the nature of the kingdom. Abraham, Isaac, Jacob, and all their descendants (including the later sons and daughters of the promise) could not lay exclusive claim to God's blessings or even argue that they deserved it exclusively. God's blessings have always been available, not because humans have a claim to them but because of His abundant grace.

11:27—25:18
Abraham

The story of Abraham brings a new tone to the biblical narrative. The earlier descriptive and genealogical material of the first eleven chapters of Genesis are complemented by the multiple facets of the story of an individual and his family. Abraham's story of faith, failure, and forgiveness provides a valuable backdrop for understanding the travails and victories of God's elect through the ages. It represents another beginning for humanity and is a reminder that the God of Genesis (and Scripture) was a God of new beginnings.

11:27—12:9. God Calls Abram. Genesis 11:27–32, as part of the genealogy of Shem's righteous line, introduces the family of the man who will be the subject of the next fourteen chapters of Genesis. The mention of Abram's and Nahor's wives, and particularly the infertility of Sarai, in the genealogy prepares the reader for what is coming (11:29–30).

Ur was an important Sumerian city-state in Mesopotamia at the end of the third millennium B.C., which corresponds to the time of Abram. The city boasted an important religious center (including a towering ziggurat), as well as sophisticated public and private buildings. The Ur that Terah and his family left was a center of the arts, science, and literature, and included many of the conveniences of city life.

God spoke at Creation (2:18) and following the Fall (3:13–14, 22); He also spoke with Cain (4:6, 9) and Noah (6:13–21; 7:1–4; 8:15–17; 9:1–17). Here He spoke again. The Lord first called Abram in Ur, before the first stage of his journey with his family described at the end of chapter 11 (see Acts 7:2–5). Abram's family had been idolatrous (Josh. 24:2), but they were willing to leave Ur with him at Yahweh's command. Perhaps the start of 12:1, *vayyo'mer*, should be translated and understood (as it has been by some commentators and translators) as, "Now the Lord *had* said to Abram." In this case, 12:1 describes God's call to Abram that had led to his family's departure from Ur as described in 11:31, and the mention of leaving Haran in 12:4 is a continuation of the previous description. On the other hand, it could also be the case that Abram received two calls—one in Ur, and one to leave Haran, which was a renewal of the first. In both cases, it could be said that Abram was leaving his house, his family, and more—in the first case, because he was leaving his homeland, friends, and extended family, and in the second case, because 12:5 indicates that Abram left Haran with only part of his family (Lot) though he was accompanied by people who had joined his household in Haran. God's call to Abram was succinct and definitive: the divine command is to *halakh*: "Go!" Some translations emphasize the separation from everything known and thus read "Get out." Abram's obedient and trusting response is described in 12:4—he went, leaving country, family, and his father's house behind. The sequence marked the different spheres of ancient society, even though "country" should not be confused with the modern notion of a nation. Important layers of patriarchal society included the family, the larger clan, and the tribe.

Even though Abram was not aware of his destination (Heb. 11:8), nor did he have an heir (cf. 11:30), God promised three specific blessings associated with this call: (1) Abram would become a great nation, (2) he would receive God's blessings, and (3) God would make his name great (in contrast to 11:4 where the builders wanted to make a name for themselves). Blessings and curses were closely linked to Abram's relationship with God. Ultimately, Abram was to bless all the *mishpekhot* ("families," "clans," "peoples") of the earth (12:3). This highlights the global dimension of God's call. God did not simply select an individual at random in order to bless him and his descendants. His mission was much larger: God wanted to reach and transform the entire world through this one family.

Abram left Haran and obeyed God's word and promise (12:4). Abram's family included not only his own large household but also the household of Lot, his nephew and the son of Abram's brother Haran (11:27). Lot's choices and interactions with his uncle would play an important role in later chapters. When Abram left Haran, he was seventy-five years old (v. 4) and did not have even *one* son—yet God promised the improbable. Canaan is mentioned as the destination following Abram's departure from Haran (cf. 11:31). The term describes a land that was somewhere on the eastern shore of the Mediterranean, comprised of parts of modern Lebanon, Syria, and most of the southern Levant west of the Jordan River. Abram's first address in Canaan was in Shechem, at the terebinth or oak tree of Moreh (12:6). Ancient Shechem was located between Mounts Ebal and Gerizim, the location where, hundreds of years later, Joshua renewed the covenant between the Lord and Israel's tribes (Josh. 24:1–25). Following the conquest of Canaan, Shechem would also be designated as a city of refuge for the central part of the Holy Land (Josh. 20:7).

The Lord then appeared to Abram, marking the first specific reference to a theophany in Genesis (cf. Gen. 17:1; 18:1; 26:2, 24; Deut. 31:15), and in response to this revelation, Abram built an altar to Him (Gen. 12:7–8; 13:18; 22:9). These altar construction references represent, in a condensed form, patriarchal worship. The altars focused the attention of the family upon the God who had called them to live as foreigners, and they also served as a public witness to the tribes living near the patriarchs. While no explicit reference to sacrifices is included, the altar suggests them. Genesis 12:8 hints at an additional dimension of patriarchal worship: calling on the name of the Lord, which is a clear reference to prayer (Ps. 116:4).

In reference to the divine promise of land, the word *zera'* ("seed" or "offspring") is used again. The Hebrew term is singular, and even though the noun can be used in a collective sense, it is an echo of the *zera'* referred to in 3:15, where the singular "He" is clearly and emphatically indicated. The theology of land in the OT is deeply rooted in God's ownership of the earth and His promise to Abram. In an agricultural society, land meant security, food, and a future.

Abram's travel log references three locations: Shechem (v. 6), a site between Bethel and Ai (v. 8), and the South (or the *negev* in Hebrew; v. 9), the region bordering the southern limit of Canaan. As a foreigner, he lived a seminomadic existence, always contending for grazing lands and water.

12:10–20. Abram's Egyptian Sojourn. Famine drove Abram's household to Egypt, anticipating similar moves by his son Isaac (26:1) and his grandson Jacob (41:54; 43:1; cf. Ruth 1:1). As a result of poor judgment, Abram failed this test of faith. Yet God did not fail him. The beauty of Sarai must have been stunning—even considering her advanced age of about sixty-five years (see 17:17). Abram felt vulnerable as a foreigner and prepped Sarai to state a half-truth (both Sarai and Abram had the same father; cf. 20:12)—that is, to refer to herself before the Egyptians as his sister (v. 13). Abram's fears were well founded, and Sarai was taken to Pharaoh's house (v. 15). In line with ANE customs, Pharaoh paid the bridal price, including slaves and a variety of animals (v. 16), to the bride's family (cf. 34:12).

The question of whether Pharaoh actually had sexual intercourse with Sarai is difficult to answer. That Sarai was taken into his house (or palace; v. 15) may not indicate that sexual intercourse took place (cf. 20:2, 6), even though the phrase is ambiguous. The Hebrew *laqakh* ("take") is used to indicate marriage and thus sexual intercourse (6:2; 11:29), but similar episodes in Genesis add additional information that usually follows sequentially once a woman had been "taken" (e.g., 34:2, 38:2). Pharaoh's strong response highlighted the fact that adultery was a serious offense in the ANE, as many law codes suggest. This episode was different from the later one with Abimelech (20:3), in which God communicated directly to the offending king. The link between the Lord and the afflictions in Pharaoh's palace (12:17) was not immediately obvious to the king. Yet he recognized the superior power of Abram's

God and had Abram's household escorted to the borders of his kingdom. There are noticeable narrative parallels between this story and that of the Exodus: Abram and Israel were both welcomed in Egypt at first but later faced challenges, they were rescued by means of plagues, and in both cases, they left Egypt with increased wealth and returned to Canaan.

13:1–18. Abram and Lot Separate. The conflict between the servants of Abram and those of Lot was a dispute that could be resolved through dialogue. The Hebrew word *rib*, used to describe the quarrel, is sometimes employed in the context of legal arguments and prosecution (cf. Gen. 26:20–22; Ex. 17:2, 7; 23:2–3, 6; Job 31:35; 40:2; Hos. 4:1; Mic. 6:2). In the patriarchal narratives, Lot's actions often contrast with Abram's, thus shining a spotlight on the latter's faithfulness. Lot, as the younger man, ignored custom by actually accepting Abram's generous offer to allow Lot to choose first (13:10) and selected Sodom and the cities of the plain (v. 11). With this, he moved east (cf. notes on 11:2). Clearly, his choices were motivated by economic factors (v. 10). The author of Genesis adds an important explanatory postscript to Lot's choice in v. 13 and diagnoses Sodom's inhabitants as extremely wicked and sinful. Several examples of lexical imagery exist between Lot's poor choice and Eve's fateful decision. This suggests that Lot was moving in the wrong direction (see "Common Imagery Associated with Lot's and Eve's Choices," p. 159).

The description of Sodom's wickedness anticipates Genesis 18 and 19. The evil inhabitants of Sodom were sinning against the Lord (13:13). This is a reminder to the reader that the Lord is not a parochial or regional deity like the other deities of the ANE. God's jurisdiction and sovereignty went beyond the land—even the promised land. Just as He judged an Egyptian pharaoh and the anonymous tower builders at Babel, He also knew what was happening in Sodom.

Lot's departure, most likely disheartening to Abram, was followed by an affirmation of the divine promises (13:14–17). The Lord spoke and revealed the future to Abram. The assurance of land for him and his descendants (v. 15) represented an expansion on the original promise of 12:7. When God invited him to walk through the land (v. 17), He was asking Abram to possess it and was anticipating the filling of the land by his descendants. This land promise was partially fulfilled in Joshua's time (Josh. 21:43–45;

but note 13:1–7). Later generations saw another partial fulfillment (in the time of David and Solomon; see 1 Kin. 4:20–25); but due to Israel's unfaithfulness, the promise was never completely fulfilled, except ultimately through Christ (Rom. 4:13; Gal. 3:16). Abram's next destination was Hebron, the town with the highest elevation in the southern Levant and located at 3,050 feet (930 m) above sea level. Hebron was strategically located between Jerusalem and Beersheba. Here Abram built another altar and affirmed his commitment to the God of the promise (v. 18; see notes on 12:7, 8).

14:1–24. Abram Rescues Lot. The exciting story of the rescue of Lot and the people of Sodom by Abram and his allies seems to interrupt a narrative that is concerned with God's plan for His chosen people and not really interested in the ups and downs of regional power games. However, this story is another reminder that God is not a regional or parochial God but is interested in blessing all those who willingly receive His benedictions.

The names of the four kings who threatened the Jordan Valley city-states suggest an ethnically diverse coalition including Elamite, Amorite, Hurrian, and Hittite groups (14:1). The biblical record of these regional city-states controlling other city-states fits well into the known historical landscape of the last part of the third millennium B.C. The five city-states of the Jordan Valley (Sodom, Gomorrah, Admah, Zeboim, and Zoar) could not withstand the attack of the Mesopotamian coalition, which had previously received tribute from the Jordan Valley inhabitants for twelve years (v. 4). Chedorlaomer (Kedorlaomer), the king of Elam, located in modern Persia, seems to have been the leader of the coalition (vv. 4–5). While no individual of this name has been attested in surviving texts from this period, the two elements comprising his name are authentically Elamite. The itinerary of the attacking eastern coalition and their victories (vv. 5–7) underlined the army's north-south movement along the so-called King's Highway (Num. 20:17; 21:22), which followed the Transjordanian plateau on the eastern shores of the Jordan and Dead Sea. In order to stop the approach of the eastern coalition, the five city-states of the Jordan Valley engaged them in battle (Gen. 14:8).

This chapter contains five explanatory notes suggesting that the biblical author may have used an older account that required updating so that the readers could understand it appropriately. The notes always commence with "that is." For example, Bela apparently was the ancient name for Zoar (vv. 2, 8). The Valley of Siddim was the Valley of the Salt Sea (or the Dead Sea Valley; v. 3) and was also the location of the battle between the two armies (v. 8). En Mishpat was later known as Kadesh (v. 7), and the king of Sodom met Abram and his people at the Valley of Shaveh—that is, the King's Valley (v. 17).

The asphalt or tar pits in the vicinity of the Dead Sea favored the eastern coalition. The kings of Sodom and Gomorrah and their disintegrating armies became stuck in the pits when they tried to flee to the mountains surrounding the low-lying plains (v. 10). The Hebrew term describing Abram's trained army (*khanik*; v. 14) occurs only here in the Hebrew Bible, but it can be found in a nineteenth-century-B.C. Egyptian text and in a fifteenth-century-B.C. letter from Taanak, written in cuneiform. This locates the story in time. The size of Abram's household was significant. Abram was not a poor shepherd but a powerful clan leader who had established important ties with the surrounding clans.

Whereas the king of Sodom wanted to talk business (vv. 21–24), the meeting was interrupted by the appearance of the king of Salem. Encountering Melchizedek signified a divine

Common Imagery Associated with Lot's and Eve's Choices

Concept	Lot (Gen. 13)	Eve (Gen. 2 and 3)
eyes	v. 10	3:6–7
saw	v. 10	3:6
watered	v. 10	2:6, 10
garden	v. 10	2:8
east	v. 11	3:24

blessing since he was the priest of God Most High (v. 18). Bread and wine could signify a lavish meal, perhaps even a banquet (1 Sam. 16:20). In later parts of Scripture, these items are connected with covenant and sacrifices (cf. Num. 15:2, 10; 1 Sam. 1:24; Matt. 26:26–29).

Melchizedek's blessing is written in poetic form and refers twice to "God Most High." The Hebrew is *'el 'elyon*. This divine epithet functions here as a personal name highlighting the power of God. Verse 19 includes the Hebrew term *qoneh*, which is sometimes translated as "Possessor" because it comes from the verb "to own" or "to purchase." However, based on parallels in other Semitic languages and the use of the verb in some OT texts (e.g., 4:1; Deut. 32:6; Ps. 139:13), another possible translation would be "Creator." Melchizedek's blessings would thus include two key statements about God: He is both Creator and Deliverer. Both elements are also central to a biblical Sabbath theology and the God of the Sabbath.

The person of Melchizedek would be used as a type of Jesus, the real Priest-King (Heb. 7:1–16). Abram, in response to the blessing received from the Lord, gave a tithe (or a tenth) to God's representative. The law of tithing preceded the Levitical legislation (Lev. 27:30–33). Here the practice was established on the theological idea that God is the Creator of the universe and the One who blesses humans. Giving the tithe to Him is not only a duty but also a deep expression of gratitude.

Abram's interaction with the king of Sodom was brief but poignant (Gen. 14:21–24). Abram rejected the customary practice of retaining the bounty and agreed to return the people to their cities of origin (v. 21). Framed as part of an oath, Abram affirmed his reliance on the Lord and echoed terminology and characteristics of Melchizedek's earlier blessing (vv. 19–20, 22). Abram's faith journey involved waiting upon God's timing, not his own timing or careful geopolitical plotting. The Hiphil form of the verb *'ashar* ("to make someone rich") constitutes a wordplay on "tenth" (*ma'aser*). Abram's wealth was attributed to the Lord's blessings (24:35), and he accepted only the provisions that his allies had already consumed on the campaign (14:24).

15:1–21. God's Covenant with Abram. After Abram experienced divine blessings during the daring rescue mission of Lot and his family in chapter 14, God reminded him of his future and his mission and affirmed the covenant.

Significant events begin with "the word of the LORD" (v. 1). In this case the divine intention for Abram was introduced by the assurance that he did not need to be afraid. The dialogue between God and Abram suggests intimacy and a close relationship. Abram was even ready to question God— Abram's concerns were presented to God, and He responded to him! God's promise involved protection and blessings, something that Abram had already experienced in different circumstances. However, he still has no offspring.

Abram's servant Eliezer is described as a servant born in his house and Abram's designated heir. This reflects an ancient custom where a childless couple adopted a son as their heir (vv. 2–3). In fact, Abram had already been assured a son three times (12:2, 7; 13:16), but the promise had yet to be fulfilled. God's response to Abram's question was unequivocal (15:4–5): He emphatically indicated that Eliezer would not be Abram's heir and that His plan would involve no shortcuts or alternative routes. Again, the promise was renewed by an object lesson (counting the stars in the sky) and a divine proclamation (v. 5). Echoing the futile attempt to count the dust of the earth (13:16), the impossibility of counting all the stars in a bright night sky emphasizes that only God can do the impossible. Faith is defined here as belief, in the sense of placing absolute trust in God's power to fulfill His promise. This response of profound faith in God was accounted to him for righteousness. He was declared to be so not because of his superior works but on the basis of his faith (v. 6; cf. Rom. 4:3–4, 9, 22–25; Gal. 3:6–9). God then reminded Abram of His saving action in bringing him out of Ur, employing words that anticipated God's liberation of Israel from Egypt (v. 7; Ex. 20:2; Deut. 5:6). The phrase is part of a brief historical review that precedes the account of the covenant ritual. It also reminded Abram of the fact that the promise included not only offspring but also land. The covenant was ratified through a ritual that required that the sacrificial animal, unlike a regular sacrifice, be cut in two halves. The covenant ritual apparently lasted a significant amount of time since vultures tried to feed on the split carcasses and were driven away by Abram (v. 11).

At sunset, a deep sleep and a thick and terrifying darkness overcame Abram (15:12). Both seem to have been divinely induced, which is suggested by the fact that Adam's deep sleep in 2:21 is described using the same Hebrew term. The Hebrew word for the horror described in

15:12 is the same word used when God promised to send terror before Israel when they entered Canaan (Ex. 23:27; Josh. 2:9). God spoke to Abram in his deep sleep, and His communication was significant. What He said was certain, as the construct *yadoaʻ teda*ʻ (lit. "knowing, know"), an idiom for "know certainly," suggests (v. 13; on the four hundred years mentioned in v. 13, see "The Four-Hundred-Thirty-Year Sojourn," p. 211). Abram's descendants would be strangers (Heb. *ger*) in a foreign land. Readers should immediately notice the link to Egypt, considering that Abram's sojourn in Egypt is described using the same root (12:10). The Amorites mentioned in v. 16 represent all the inhabitants of Canaan.

The description of the smoking pot and burning torch that passed through the animals in v. 17 is emblematically significant. Fire is often a symbol of God's presence, and walking between the two parts of the animal was a declaration that what happened to the sacrificial victim would be the fate of the violator of the covenant (cf. Jer. 34:18).

16:1–16. Hagar and Ishmael. The prototype of faith was struggling with the practical implications of faith. In this chapter, Abram does not hear from God. However, God talks to Hagar (16:8–14).

The biblical text reminds the reader of the barrenness of Sarai right from the outset (v. 1). What appears to be a sad fact in a Western context becomes a tragedy in a biblical (and Eastern) context. Barrenness encompassed every aspect of a woman's life in biblical times and brought pain and stigma (cf. 1 Sam. 1:5–6). It not only endangered the very survival and future of a family, but it also suggested possible divine displeasure. Sarai, the main protagonist of this chapter, decided to be proactive and resolve her barrenness by turning to the practice of surrogate motherhood, which was well known in the ANE from the third to the first millennium B.C. Both Abram and her maidservant Hagar submitted to Sarai's proposal. Surprisingly (and tellingly), the end of v. 2 in the Hebrew echoes Genesis 3:17, where the same phrase is used with different names when Adam decided to eat the forbidden fruit: Abram listened to Sarai as Adam listened to Eve. Careful readers will anticipate conflict and additional verbal links and motifs that connect this story to the Fall narrative (e.g., "took" [3:6; 16:3]).

Sarah's reasoning in v. 2 is revealing: the fact that God had prevented her thus far from having children (similar also in 20:18) was suggested as a rationale for attempting the logical solution. While Hagar appears to be a tool in Sarai's hands, Hagar's pregnancy changed everything in Abram's household (vv. 4–6). Hagar came to despise (*qalal*) her mistress (v. 4). The Hebrew term used here, which Sarai repeats in v. 5, is the same as the one describing Michal's reaction to David's ritual procession in 2 Samuel 6:20. Sarai's position in the household was in danger. She complained to Abram and seemed to suggest his guilt in the matter (v. 5). The Hebrew term *khamas* ("wrong" or "violence") is strong and is later used by the Hebrew prophets to indicate social injustice (Amos 3:10; Hab. 1:3; cf. the use of the term in the Flood story in Gen. 6:11, 13). Sarai concluded her complaint by appealing to a higher authority, the Lord, to be the Judge (Gen. 16:5).

In response to Sarai's complaint, Abram confirmed Sarai's position in the household (v. 6). Once Sarai's position was validated, Sarai dealt harshly (*ʻanah*) with Hagar (cf. 31:50, where the same verb is used). Interestingly, this verb is also used to describe the Egyptian mistreatment of the Israelites (Ex. 1:12). As a result of Sarai's harsh treatment, Hagar fled from the family's home settlement.

The next seven verses describe the dialogue between the Lord and Hagar. Hagar's recognition, in v. 13, of a divine presence suggests that the Angel of the Lord was God Himself in this context. Surprisingly, the Angel of the Lord addressed Hagar by name (v. 8). This is the only known instance in ANE literature where a Deity addresses a woman by name.

Hagar was addressed not only by name but also as Sarai's servant, which reminded the runaway servant of her relationships and obligations. This is the first time in the Bible that a child was named before birth (v. 11). The child would be an expression of God's concern for a woman in suffering. Ishmael ("God hears") would be a reminder to her and to others that God indeed listens to those who pray to Him. As was the case with other important sites of God encounters during the patriarchal period, the place where Hagar encountered the Lord was commemorated by name.

The chapter concludes with Hagar's return to Abram's encampment and the birth of Ishmael, who was named by his father and was thus legitimized (vv. 15–16). Abram was, at this point, eighty-six years old and had been traversing Canaan for more than eleven years (v. 16). Had God's promises been realized in Ishmael's birth?

17:1–27. The Covenant Sign: Name Change and Circumcision. Following the covenant ritual described in chapter 15 and the Hagar episode, God's silence lasted for thirteen years. God spoke again in this chapter and emphasized the renewal of the already-established covenant and the institution of a specific covenant sign. God confirmed again the promises of descendants and land to Abram (cf. 12:1–3; 13:14–17; 15:4–5, 18–21). He identified Himself with the name *'el shaddai* (v. 1). The phrase appears five other times in Genesis (28:3; 35:11; 43:14; 48:3; 49:25) and thirty-one times in Job. Jewish interpreters understood the name as "He who is sufficient" while others have suggested "God of the mountain." Both possibilities emphasize power and strength. The all-powerful God offered His blessings to His elect. God also reminded Abram of the fact that the covenant relationship required his devoted response of "walking" (i.e., living) before Him and being *tam* ("sound," "blameless," "perfect"). To be *tam* is to live a life entirely committed to God rather than to sinless moral perfection (Job 1:1, 8; for the use of the phrase in a sacrificial context, see Lev. 1:3).

God changed the name of Abram ("exalted father") to Abraham ("father of many nations"; v. 5). This essentially proclaimed the promise as if it were already fulfilled. The covenant (vv. 4, 7, 9–10, 14) that is mentioned is actually part of the everlasting covenant (v. 7). Note the difference between the essence of the eternal covenant and the sign of the covenant—that is, circumcision. God's covenant with humanity is eternal.

Circumcision became the sign of the covenant (vv. 10–11) and was required from all male members of the household. Those unwilling to participate would be cut off from among God's people. This punishment was normally applied to acts of commission (e.g., eating blood [Lev. 7:27; 17:10, 14], eating sacrificial fat [7:25], eating the peace or fellowship offering while unclean [Lev. 7:20], eating what is unclean [Lev. 7:21], etc.). Being "cut off" may refer to the death penalty (as in Ex. 31:14–15; Num. 15:31; 1 Sam. 28:9) or to being separated from God's covenant community. This is the fourth account in Genesis that mentions the importance of a sign (*'ot*; v. 11). In 1:14, the luminaries served as signs of the seasons. In 4:15, God's sign on Cain signified divine protection. Following the Flood, God placed a rainbow in the sky as a sign to remind Himself and the world of His promise to Noah (9:8–17). Circumcision was also practiced by other people groups in the ANE though mostly as a puberty

rite and not on the eighth day following birth (17:12). Other biblical passages clarify the fact that true circumcision is circumcision of the heart (e.g., Lev. 26:41; Deut. 10:16).

Following the introduction of circumcision as the covenant sign, God changed Sarai's name to Sarah ("princess"), another form of the earlier Sarai. While the new name is not explicitly explained (as was the case for Abraham's name change; cf. v. 5), a name change suggests a change of destiny. Divine blessings would finally transform Sarah into a mother of nations (v. 16). Abraham's reaction to this divine promise is surprising. Falling on his face, he laughed (v. 17) and rightly wondered how a one-hundred-year-old man and a ninety-year-old woman could have a son. The first act suggests worship; the second is sometimes taken as implying doubt and is replicated in 18:12–15 (and in 21:6 by Sarah). However, Abraham's question was a practical one. Without divine intervention, birthing a child was impossible. The father of John the Baptist had a similar question (Luke 1:18) and was reprimanded for unbelief (Luke 1:20), perhaps because he had the example of God's involvement in Abraham's case. Not surprisingly, Isaac's name ("he laughs") echoes the surprised reaction of his parents to God's promise. Yet God did the impossible, and doubt became joyous laughter. Finally, Abraham pled for Ishmael, the son by Sarah's maidservant Hagar. Abraham's prayer for Ishmael in Genesis 21:18 was both an expression of doubt and an appeal for blessing. The man of faith (15:6) could not predict God's solution.

God promised to bless Ishmael but also made it clear that the son of Sarah would be the son of the promise (vv. 19, 21). Finally, the promise had a name, and the clock was ticking. The reference to the time (Heb. *mo'ed*, "appointed time," "next year") is a cipher for the birth of a child following a regular pregnancy lasting nine months (cf. the promise to Abraham in 18:10 and to the Shunammite woman given Elisha's prophecy in 2 Kin. 4:16, where a similar phrase appears). This indicates that Abraham and Sarah had to act on the promise for it to come true. The final verses of the chapter report the execution of the divine order, involving Abraham himself, Ishmael, and all the male members of Abraham's household (Gen. 17:23–27). The response was immediate—twice it is mentioned that the rite was carried out that same day (vv. 23, 26). The stage was set for the son of the promise to appear; yet prior to his coming, Abraham's faith, compassion, and character needed to grow even more.

18:1-15. Abraham Entertains Three Messengers from Heaven. Even though Abraham did not immediately recognize the heavenly visitors, his generous hospitality provided another opportunity for God to affirm the future reality of the seemingly impossible.

The language of 18:1 recalls earlier theophanies (12:7; 17:1), yet Abraham himself was seemingly not initially aware of his heavenly visitors. However, it is true that he bowed down to the ground (v. 2), an act that often indicated worship (e.g., Ex. 20:5). Abraham saw three men; one turned out to be the Lord (vv. 2, 22), and two were possibly angels (19:1). Yet Abraham spoke only with the One who ostensibly stood out: Abraham's address in 18:3 uses a second-person-singular grammatical form in Hebrew. As was customary, Abraham provided his visitors with water (for washing their feet) and food (vv. 4-5).

The following verses (18:6-8) describe a household that sprang into action to prepare a meal for their guests, according to the usual customs of hospitality. The narrative then turns to the Guest's prophecy of what lies in store for Sarah. By verbalizing Sarah's private thoughts (v. 13) after she overheard the promise and laughed, the Lord showed Himself omniscient. The rhetorical question of whether anything is too difficult for the Lord (v. 14; cf. Jer. 32:17, 27) implies a negative answer. Sarah was not punished for unbelief, which indicates that, like Abraham's, her question was of a practical nature. She had long since passed the childbearing age, and she had not been able to have children, even when she was younger. In support of this, Hebrews 11:11 highlights Sarah's belief in the famous parade of faith.

18:16-33. Abraham Intercedes for Sodom. As a good host, Abraham accompanied his guests on the first leg of their onward journey (18:16). He literally walked with God (cf. Enoch in 5:24 and Noah in 6:9). Overlooking Sodom from the heights of the Judean mountains, the Lord revealed to Abraham His intentions (v. 17-19; cf. Amos 3:7). The divine rationale for this was the fact that Abraham's descendants would be a great, mighty, powerful nation (v. 18) that would bless the entire population of the earth. In other words, God wanted Abraham to develop compassion and the capacity to bless others, beginning with his household and his descendants (v. 19). "To keep the way of the Lord" involves doing what is right and just and indicates metaphorically right behavior leading

to right destiny based on a right relationship with the Lord.

The "outcry against Sodom and Gomorrah" (v. 20; the cities are usually mentioned together in biblical texts) stood in direct contrast to Abraham's righteousness (v. 19). In Hebrew, the words for outcry (*ze'aqah*) and righteousness (*tsedaqah*) sound very similar. Isaiah uses the same wordplay in the famous prophetic vineyard song in relation to God's chosen people (Is. 5:7). The Lord intended to go down (see notes on Gen. 11:5, 7) and see whether the outcry against Sodom and Gomorrah was warranted (v. 21). This language does not imply any lack of omniscience or foreknowledge on God's part—these attributes were strikingly evident in the detailed prophecies of the preceding chapters (e.g., 15:13-21; 17:5-8, 15-21) as well as the preceding verses, which indicate that God anticipated that Abraham would faithfully instruct his children and that the world would be blessed through his progeny (vv. 17-19). Instead, the use of this anthropomorphic language was indicative of a legal case, an investigation, and judgment.

Genesis 18:22 contains a textual note preserved by the Masoretes, the Jewish scholars who transmitted the biblical text. It suggests that the original reading of this verse was inverted to indicate that Abraham was standing before the Lord, whereas the original had indicated that the Lord was standing before Abraham. This change was most likely motivated by theological reasons, since "standing before" was the position of a servant and indicated social status (Gen. 41:46; Lev. 9:5). The theological implications are staggering and foreshadow God's willingness to serve humanity—even unto death (Matt. 20:28). God's attitude of service invited Abraham to become an intercessor.

Here Abraham entered the conversation and based his plea on God's righteousness (Gen. 18:25). Indiscriminate punishment is not divine judgment. Abraham did not question God's ability or jurisdiction for judgment—"all the earth" included every location and people group—but he appealed to God's justice. God punishes the guilty (Ezek. 14:12-20) and spares the repentant (cf. Rahab in Josh. 2 and Nineveh in Jon. 3-4).

When the Lord concluded the dialogue with Abraham, His justice and righteousness had been established beyond the shadow of a doubt. God investigated the accusations (18:21) carefully, included in the deliberation two objective witnesses as well as the faithful, and offered a way to salvation. The pattern in 18:16–33 provides a blueprint for future judgments and foreshadows the activities associated with the millennium following the Second Coming of Jesus as Judge of all the earth (Rev. 20).

19:1–38. Sodom's Destruction and Lot's Rescue. The dramatic story involving Sodom provides another example of divine judgment in response to human sin. The location of Sodom and Gomorrah is debatable. Some have suggested that they were located on the southeastern side of the Dead Sea, the areas of Bab-edh-Dhra and Numeria. A geographical text from Ebla in Syria from the same period mentions *sa-dam* as a city located in the region of Bab-edh-Dhra, close to the Dead Sea. However, Lot chose to live in the Jordan River Valley (Gen. 13:10; north of the Dead Sea). Certainly, the general region of the Lower Jordan River Valley and the Dead Sea (called "Salt Sea" in the OT) was the location of these cities (Gen. 19:25).

The following verses (Gen. 19:4–9) graphically highlight the evilness of Sodom's inhabitants (cf. 13:13), a description that provides clear justification for the coming judgment. The Hebrew verb *yada'* (lit. "to know") used at the end of the verse implies sexual activity (cf. 4:1) and is accordingly translated in some versions as "have sex" or "have relations." This exhibits the depravity of the misguided sexuality exhibited by the men of the city (v. 4) and suggests homosexual practices. The biblical text specifically indicates that this was not an isolated group of degenerate people—both old and young, and people from every section of the city, surrounded Lot's home (v. 4). Considering the important cultural value of hospitality in Eastern cultures (including also ancient Canaan), the complete corruption of basic human values that this intended sexual abuse represented becomes immediately clear, even for readers who did not worship Yahweh. Sexual predators justified the coming judgment by their utterly immoral action. Lot was rightly concerned with his guests' well-being, something that, as already indicated, was highly valued in his ANE culture. However, the offer of his daughters to the mob also reveals, on the one hand, that Sodom had affected his inner moral core (vv. 4–9) and, on the other, that girls were of very little value at that time. Ironically, Lot's daughters later abused their father sexually, resulting in competing lineages (vv. 36–38; the Moabites and Ammonites). While Lot was a "righteous person," in the sense that he had not

completely allowed himself to be absorbed into the evils of these cities and was still disturbed by the people's conduct (2 Pet. 2:7), his grasp of moral principles was seriously diminished by his association with Sodom's residents. It was out of divine grace that he and his family were preserved.

Instead of ten righteous people (Gen. 18:32), only four people were left (and the righteousness of these is in serious doubt), some of whom the angels had to drag out of the city (19:16). God's mercy often involves a painful separation from the things and people that keep His children in "Sodom." Thankfully, salvation is based entirely on divine grace (Titus 3:5) and not on human performance.

In the face of an imminent inferno, Lot began to negotiate with his angelic companions. Lot's hesitation (Gen. 19:16), his objections, and his wife's ultimate destiny, as well as the later abusive ploy of Lot's daughters, suggest that even though the family had been saved physically, their hearts and minds carried the seed of Sodom with them to safety. Instead of trusting in divine protection in the mountains (v. 19), Lot longed for the urban safety and security of nearby Zoar, a name derived from the size of the city (v. 20). Hopefully, a little city would have little sin in it. Lot's bargaining (vv. 18–20) echoes lexically Abraham's intercession for Sodom and its inhabitants (18:22–33). The angels conceded, and at sunrise, Lot finally entered Zoar, one of the five cities of the plain (14:8).

The description of the destruction of Sodom and Gomorrah uses flood language (*himtir* ["rained"] in v. 24 and *mamtir* ["caused to rain"] in 7:4 make use of the same Hebrew root). The mention of fire and brimstone (or burning sulfur; 19:24) could be a reference to a firestorm caused by the breaking up of the surface of the earth, accompanied by strong tremors that resulted in major destruction of the beautiful region. The repeated use of forms of *hapak* ("overthrow," lit. "to turn upside down"; 19:21, 25, 29), may suggest the breaking up of the earth's crust. The nature of the fire from heaven is not defined in the text but could have been meteorites, resembling bolts or balls of fire. The biblical author makes it very clear that this judgment was not the result of a natural catastrophe; twice the Lord is identified as the originator of the cities' destruction. Later prophets considered this event to be *the* symbol of destruction (Amos 4:11). In the NT, it is used as an illustration of the eschatological judgment against the wicked (Luke 17:28–30; 2 Pet. 2:6–9). Tragically, Lot lost not only his home and property but also his wife, who, in direct disregard for the command of the angels in v. 17, looked back and became a pillar of salt (Gen. 19:26). It is possible that she belonged to a Sodomite family since she was mentioned prior to Genesis 19. In Luke 17:31–32, Jesus admonishes His audience to not look back, as did Lot's wife, when the time of the end comes, for those who strive to keep their lives will lose them (v. 33).

The dramatic action was observed by Abraham from the place where he had stood before the Lord (see commentary on Gen. 18:16–33). The mediator had become a spectator, yet God remembered him (v. 29). Often in Scripture, to remember is to act on behalf of the person in need (see 8:1).

The final verses of this chapter include the last references to Lot (19:30–38), who fled further away from Abraham and his spiritual values. His story would include alcohol use, incest, and the birth of two sons whose descendants would become two enemies of Israel, the Moabites and the Ammonites.

20:1–18. Abraham and Abimelech at Gerar. The man who would be remembered forever because of his faith in God here failed another test of faith for a second time, in the same way he failed before (Gen. 12:10–20). Unbeknownst to him, an even more severe test (Gen. 22) still awaited him. Abraham's move to Gerar, a town located halfway between Beersheba and Gaza that marked the southern border of Canaan, was not motivated by a famine (12:10). Yet in brief, terse phrases, the drama of chapter 12 was repeated: Abraham publicly declared Sarah to be his sister; in response, Abimelech (also Abimelek), king of Gerar, sent for and "took" Sarah (20:2). Genesis 21:32, 34 (see also Gen. 26) link Abimelech to the Philistines (for more on the Philistines, see "The Philistines," p. 407).

God spoke to the king of Gerar in a dream (v. 3) in order to avert a grave iniquity. Dreams were believed to be important means of divine communication (cf. 28:12; 40:8; Num. 22:9, 20). Adultery was considered a serious sin among many peoples of the ANE, as can be seen in Ugaritic and Egyptian marriage contracts (cf. Deut. 22:22). Abimelech's defense (vv. 4–5) was reasonable and also emphasized that no sexual intercourse had taken place. God's response acknowledged that no sexual relations had occurred but adds an important concept: God kept Abimelech from sinning against Him (v. 6). God's restraint of the evil actions of humanity (e.g., 1 Sam. 25:39; Ps. 19:13) is another facet of His grace and mercy.

God demanded from Abimelech full restoration of Sarah to her husband (Gen. 20:7). The reference to Abraham as a prophet, the first time this technical term (*nabi'*) is used in the OT, emphasizes the intercessory role of a prophet (v. 7). Following the divine orders, Abimelech summoned his household and court and confessed publicly. The ensuing dialogue between Abraham and Abimelech echoes Pharaoh's interaction with the patriarch (12:18–19). The question "What have you done?" (20:9) recalls the rhetorical question in 3:13. Abraham's response, while plausible, lacked an important ingredient: faith in the God who called him to be a blessing. Abraham did not expect Abimelech to exhibit high moral values (20:11) and thus decided to use his old ruse.

Abimelech's response was overwhelming and included a comprehensive list of special gifts (Gen. 20:14–15), free access to the land of Gerar, as well as an "honor fee" of one thousand shekels (v. 16)—a huge sum, considering that Babylonian laborers earned half a shekel per month and a slave could be bought for a mere twenty shekels (37:28). This payment to Abraham vindicated Sarah and represented a public exoneration—particularly in view of the following chapter that describes the birth of Isaac. The phrase at the end of v. 16 is literally "a covering of the eyes." Some have suggested that this phrase signifies that she was to be veiled so as to avoid further incident—that is, that she was "rebuked," as some translations indicate. Others suggest that this means that any suspicions of adultery were covered by Abimelech's gift, signifying that her honor was vindicated, as noted in other translations. Surprisingly, the Lord, in response to the intercession of Abraham, restored the fertility of the women in the household of Abimelech. He would certainly do the same for Sarah.

21:1–21. Birth of Isaac and Expulsion of Ishmael. God's promise finally became a reality, yet joy over its fulfillment was mingled with pain over past mistakes and their effects on many lives. The chapter opens with a magnificent statement: the Lord *paqad* (lit. "visited") Sarah, and the son of the promise was born. This verb (*paqad*) often conveys the idea of "caring for"; accordingly, some translate the verb as "was gracious to," "came to help" or "took note of." Considering the long wait and ensuing complications, the description of the birth of

Isaac is very brief and emphasizes God's faithfulness (vv. 1–2, 6). The mention of the *mo'ed* ("appointed time") in v. 2 points back to 17:21 and 18:14. The bottom line of this important theological motif is significant: God always fulfills His promises—at the right time (cf. also in regard to the Messiah; Gal. 4:4). As is customary in the Abraham narrative, the age of the patriarch is mentioned at key moments in his life. At the birth of Isaac, Abraham was one hundred years old (21:5); this was twenty-five years after he had been called by God and had been promised descendants.

Yet not all is well. Unfortunately, human designs often clash with divinely ordained plans (21:8–21). Isaac's weaning, a significant rite of passage that accompanied the transition from infancy to childhood, marked the beginning of the affliction (Gen. 15:16). ANE texts uniformly indicate that weaning normally occurred after three years. The scorning of Isaac by Ishmael (who was half Egyptian), a teenager of seventeen years, is represented by a term (*tsakhaq*) difficult to translate (some read "mocking," others read "playing"). It comes from the same Hebrew root (*tsakhaq*) as Isaac's name (*yitskhaq*), meaning "to laugh." Sometimes it expresses the idea of being superior (laughing at or mocking others) and may also indicate laughter that is occasionally associated with sexual acts (e.g., Gen. 26:8; 39:14, 17). Its use here should be understood as mocking Isaac, expressing disdain and a sense of superiority. Sarah's response was immediate: she told Abraham to banish Hagar and Ishmael (Gen. 21:10), which meant that Ishmael would lose his inheritance. Abraham was distressed because Ishmael was his son (v. 11). However, Sarah based her demand on moral and legal grounds. For example, the Mesopotamian Lipit-Ishtar code (ca. 1875 B.C.) stipulated that if a master granted freedom to a slave and her children, the children of the slave should not share the estate with the children of their master. God endorsed Sarah's request but included a special blessing for Ishmael (vv. 12–13).

The expulsion of Hagar and Ishmael echoes the earlier story of Genesis 16. For a second time, Hagar found herself alone, despondent, and out of options. Yet God sustained her again. The first woman in Scripture whom God addressed by name (16:8) received another important visitor. In response to Ishmael's cries, God promised Hagar an unexpected blessing. The admonition to not be afraid (v. 17) always introduces God's special blessings (Is. 41:13–14; 43:1; Dan. 10:19). God not only spoke to Hagar but also opened her eyes (v. 19; cf. 22:13; 2 Kin. 6:17). Hagar's experience prefigured Abraham's encounter with God on Mount Moriah (Gen. 22) in many ways (a journey, provisions, a child about to die, divine intervention, a solution, and a promise).

21:22–34. Abraham's Covenant with Abimelech. After assuring the future of Abraham's family physically, the text now describes Abraham's place in society and his survival as a foreigner within an unpredictable political context. Due to the importance of water, Abraham came to an agreement with Abimelech concerning the use of wells (see Isaac's similar action later in 26:15–18), yet the covenant was much broader in scope, allowing Abraham's family to stay in the land of the Philistines for an extended period of time (21:34). The covenant ritual was sealed by the giving of gifts (vv. 27–28) and a solemn oath (v. 31). This is a classic example of a bilateral covenant involving mutual obligations from two parties. Abraham planted a tree at the well (most likely as a sign) and "called on the name of the LORD" (v. 33; 12:8; 13:4; 26:25), who had opened the way for a new alliance. God's description as the Everlasting/Eternal God (v. 33) underlines His omnipotence and power.

22:1–19. The Gospel to Abraham: The Binding of Isaac. The ultimate test of Abraham's faith involved the most precious gift the patriarch had received from the Lord—his long-awaited son. Yet while Abraham's faith is on display, it is ultimately God's character that shines through this chapter. The binding of Isaac has been an object of reflection for centuries.

Verse 1 represents, in typical Hebrew fashion, a summary as part of the introduction. The testing of Abraham consisted of creating a situation within which the faith and commitment of Abraham to the Lord would be manifested. The divine command—to take Isaac, his beloved son, and offer him as a burnt offering—is shocking (Gen. 22:2). What is missing in most English versions is the translation of a Hebrew term (*na'*) meaning "please," at the beginning of the sentence. The imperative to offer Isaac creates a theological conundrum. Why would God, who hates human sacrifices (Lev. 18:21; Deut. 12:31; 18:10), demand such an offering? The reference to testing invites the reader to reserve judgment. More than what meets the eye is at play here. The location of the offering was in the land of Moriah, most likely an area around Jerusalem (2 Chr. 3:1). The distance from Beersheba to

Jerusalem was about 50 miles (80 km), corresponding to three days' travel (22:4). Mention of Abraham's early rising and departure marks the patriarch's immediate and deliberate response. Taking with him two servants, a donkey, Isaac, and firewood, Abraham set off toward the place to which God had directed him.

On the third day (v. 4) of the journey, the party finally arrived. The third day is often when a decisive moment takes place in biblical stories (Gen. 31:22; 34:25; Ex. 19:11; Judg. 20:30; Esth. 5:1). One wonders how Abraham lived through these days, knowing that he would be required to sacrifice his only son. Abraham's comment that "we will come back," however, was not simply a reassuring reply to the slightly suspicious members of his household. It was a desperate expression of faith, similar to his answer to Isaac's question in v. 8. It anticipated the later struggle of Abraham's grandson, who pled for a blessing from the One who had wrestled with him at Jabbok (32:26). Faith can struggle, but faith holds on. The book of Hebrews confirms that Abraham believed that God could raise Isaac from the dead (Heb. 11:19). This was quite extraordinary because there is no record of anyone ever having been raised from the dead before that time.

The crucial dialogue between father and son (22:7–8) underlines the fact that Isaac's role was not passive. He could have run away from his father. Abraham's statement of faith—God would provide a lamb—was the answer to Isaac's question. They both went together (vv. 6, 8), one in obedience to God and the other in obedience to the father.

The New Testament and the *Aqedah*

The Hebrew term *aqedah* is used for the "binding" of Isaac as a sacrificial victim in Genesis 22 and has been employed in Jewish literature as a name for the story. This particular narrative plays a significant role in explaining God's work of salvation through Christ in the NT. Hebrews 11:17–19 and James 2:21–23 explicitly refer to Abraham's faith and obedience while the wording of Romans 8:32 ("He who did not spare His own Son") highlights God's willingness to offer Jesus in substitution for humanity and creates a clear link to the well-known story of Isaac's binding and Abraham's faith.

Following the construction of the altar, Abraham bound Isaac (marked by the important designation "his son") and laid him on the altar (v. 9). The following sequence reads as a slow-motion description of Abraham's most heart-wrenching moment. Yet at the right moment, the Angel of the Lord intervened (regarding the nature and identity of the Angel of the Lord, see 16:8–14 and Judg. 2:1–5). The Angel's twofold exclamation expressed the urgency of the instruction. A ram caught in a thicket (v. 13) became the substitutionary sacrifice on Mount Moriah—it was offered "instead of his son." The experience of Abraham was, in a very limited sense, a revelation of the experience of God through Jesus Christ, His Son, when He offered Himself as an expiatory lamb for sinful human beings (Mark 10:45; John 1:29, 36; 2 Cor. 5:17–21; 1 Pet. 1:18–19).

Following the climax of the narrative, God reaffirmed His promises to Abraham (12:2–3; 13:16; 15:5; 17:5–6). Abraham's obedience is one of the key themes of this chapter. Isaac is not explicitly mentioned in the report of Abraham's return, even though the phrase "they went together to Beersheba" may indicate he was included in the return party (cf. the similar phrase in vv. 6, 8). Since this chapter is primarily focused on the characters of Abraham and God, the absence of Isaac's name should not surprise the reader.

The final section of Genesis 22:20–24 functions as a bridge to what follows. Notably, the text mentions twelve sons of Nahor (by his wife and a concubine), corresponding to the twelve sons of Israel (49:28) or the twelve sons of Ishmael (25:12–15). The names of Nahor's descendants have been associated with locations in northern Mesopotamia and Transjordan. For example, "Uz" in v. 21 has been linked to Edom (cf. 10:23; 36:28). The location is also mentioned in Job 1:1 even though some translations have transcribed the Hebrew name as "Huz" in Genesis and as "Uz" in Job—in fact, a more phonetically precise transliteration is *'uts*.

23:1–20. Sarah's Death and Burial. When Sarah died, Abraham succeeded in procuring a piece of property for her burial. While still a stranger, Abraham legally owned a piece of the land that in the future would belong to his descendants. Similar to Jeremiah's purchase of a field in the face of the impending Babylonian captivity (Jer. 32:6–15), Abraham's purchase was another expression of faith.

Sarah died at the age of 127 in Hebron, twenty miles (32 km) south of Jerusalem (23:1–2).

This marked the beginning of the end of an era and slowly shifted the focus of the biblical narrative from Abraham's family to Isaac, the son of the promise. Hebron played an important role in the early reign of David (2 Sam. 2:1–4). Abraham came to mourn and to weep for Sarah (v. 2). This generally involved certain mourning rites, such as tearing garments, wearing sackcloth, shaving one's beard, and loud weeping. The presence of death in Genesis at crucial intersections of the narrative serves as a brutal reminder of the loss of immortality and paradise.

The bulk of the chapter describes the important negotiations for a burial site (Gen. 23:3–16). Keywords include *natan* ("give" or, as some translate contextually here, "sell" or "pay"; vv. 4, 9, 11, 13) and *shama'* ("listen," "hear"; vv. 6, 8, 11, 13, 15), which represent operative words in ANE negotiations and were used instead of "buy" and "sell." The identity of the sons of Heth (also called Hittites) in 23:3 is unclear, as is their relationship to the well-known Hittites from Anatolia (modern Turkey) that dominated the ANE more than half a millennium later. The Semitic names of the sons of Heth in chapter 23 may suggest a different group from the later Indo-European Hittites.

Since Abraham was a foreigner (v. 4), he did not own land that he could use as a burial ground for his family. He had to negotiate with the landowners, and this took place at the gate of the city, which was a center for business and legal decisions (cf. Deut. 21:18–20; Ruth 4:1–11). The negotiation was marked by courteous interaction and demonstrations of respect (e.g., Abraham stood and bowed repeatedly). Note that Abraham did not address Ephron directly but requested the leadership of Hebron to intercede on his behalf. This presence of an intercessor was another important feature of ANE culture.

Ephron the Hittite finally suggested an amount (v. 15) for the purchase of the field that also included a burial cave. Burial practices during the time of Abraham included cave tombs that were often used for an entire family. Following the decomposition of the body of the deceased several months or years after the burial, the bones and other grave gifts were often collected in a big vessel or ossuary, which was then placed in a niche in one section of the cave. The cave of Machpelah was not only the burial place for Sarah but also the location where Abraham, Isaac, Rebekah, Leah, and Jacob were later buried (Gen. 49:30–32; 50:13). Four hundred shekels of silver, or 10 pounds (4.5 kg; v. 15),

represented a significant investment. Although later in history, "shekel" was the name of a particular denomination of coinage, at this time, coins had not yet been invented. Thus, shekel here is in reference to the weight (v. 16). The weight of silver was what merchants in this period used for transactions. Cross period comparisons are always difficult, but Jeremiah purchased his field for only seventeen shekels (Jer. 32:9) while Omri paid six thousand shekels for the entire site of Samaria (1 Kin. 16:24). In any case, Abraham was able to pay what was required for the sale. We should remember that during the time of Abraham a "shekel" was not a denomination of coinage; coins had not yet been invented. It was a weight of silver used by merchants for transactions. The final summary statement of the legal and public transaction as well as the burial of Sarah (23:17–20) highlights Abraham's faith in God's promises. Abraham invested in a future he could not see.

24:1–67. Finding a Suitable Wife for Isaac. Isaac's future and the assurance of God's promise were important concerns for Abraham, recently widowed and conscious of his age; the text introduces the patriarch as quite old (Gen. 24:1). Yet in order to secure the future of his family, Isaac needed a wife. Since parents did the matchmaking in OT times, Abraham made his chief servant swear an oath, which forms a frame around the dialogue. These are the last recorded words of Abraham.

The oath was ratified by Eliezer's symbolic act of putting his hand under Abraham's thigh (v. 9). The legal function of this symbolic act was to commit the oath-taker to fulfilling the pledge (cf. 47:29). Notably, Eliezer is never mentioned by name in the entire chapter—rather he is called the servant (or the oldest servant of his house; v. 2), and his name, presuming this is the same person, is known only from Abraham's earlier dialogue with the Lord in 15:2. The intimate nature of the symbolic gesture underlines the solemnity of the oath. Abraham made two important requests that were in line with the larger issue of the divine promise to his family: (1) the future wife of Isaac should not be from the daughters of the Canaanites (v. 3), and (2) Isaac should not return to the land of his ancestors in the north (vv. 6–8).

A brief travel log linking Canaan to Aram Naharaim in northern Syria introduces the next scene (vv. 10–27). Eliezer prayed and asked God for a sign (vv. 12–14). The decision he would make would have important repercussions for Isaac and his future. The hospitality of the young girl was impressive, as was her physical strength—providing water for ten camels was no small matter. The servant's requests for God's kindness shows dependability and trust in the Lord (24:12, 14, 26–27, 52). Additionally, v. 16 also notes that Rebekah was very beautiful, of marriageable age, but not married. Rebekah passed the test of kindness and offered to give water to the camels, as the servant looked on silently (vv. 16–21). Finally, after the hard work had been done, the servant presented her with abundant gifts (v. 22). Jewelry was often representative of financial security when given to a woman in this context.

Bethuel was Isaac's cousin (v. 24; cf. 22:23), and thus met the first of the two requirements stipulated by Abraham. Rebekah's speedy return to her mother's household may be an indication that Bethuel had more than one wife or that they were living as an extended family (v. 28). Laban's reaction was probably motivated by selfishness (v. 30; cf. 29:1–30).

Meals were important events in ancient cultures because they brought people together and provided a space for negotiations. The drawn-out marriage negotiations began (24:33–51) with a report of divine guidance by Abraham's servant (vv. 34–49), who also included hints as to Abraham's riches (v. 35). The role of Laban in the story suggests that Bethuel was old by this time and that Laban had become the leader of the clan. Alternatively, it could also reflect a local custom involving the eminence of the brother in marriage negotiations, as attested in Old and Neo-Babylonian period documents.

Abraham's servant then offered a prayer of thanksgiving and presented the bride-price to the family. The request for a quick departure the following morning was met with mixed reception. The amount of time requested in v. 55 is literally "days or ten," which could mean few days or years. In order to settle this issue, the bride-to-be was, for the first time, actively involved in the process and was asked personally whether she would go with Abraham's servant. Rebekah's concise, affirmative answer (one word in Hebrew) settled the issue (v. 58). Prior to her departure, Rebekah received the family blessing (v. 60), which was written in poetry in Hebrew and which invoked the promise of numerous descendants and power. The blessing echoed the earlier blessing to Abraham on Mount Moriah (22:17).

The final scene of the unique love story was located in Canaan, the place of God's particular blessings. Isaac lived in the south (or Negev) and went out to *suakh* (24:62–63). This is an obscure Hebrew term that appears only once in the OT. Most versions understand it as referring to some type of activity involving prayer or meditation (LXX, Vg., Tg.). Others have suggested the translation "roaming." The point of the story is that Isaac and Rebekah met outside the camp. Following the customs of her time, Rebekah covered herself with a veil while Eliezer (still described as the servant) informed Isaac about the marriage negotiations (vv. 64–66). The next verse describes a formal marriage ceremony. Isaac brought Rebekah into his mother's tent and *laqakh*—"took" Rebekah (the technical term for marriage), which resulted in Rebekah becoming his wife (v. 67). The final statement, that Isaac loved her and was comforted after his mother's death, connects the narrative to the bigger story. Scripture highlights the special relationship between Isaac and Rebekah. On the occasion of their marriage, she would become the matriarch of the clan. By this time, Abraham would have been 140 years old (see 17:17; 25:20).

25:1–18. Abraham's Death and Ishmael's Family Line.

The final wrap-up of Abraham's story brought his sons together at the grave of the patriarch. Both were sons of the friend of God (James 2:23), but only one was the son of the blessing, whose line would ultimately see the divine promise of land and offspring realized.

Following Isaac's marriage to Rebekah, Abraham took another wife (v. 1), who may also be described as a concubine (v. 6). Her ethnicity and family heritage are not mentioned. Neither the text nor the context is clear concerning the question of whether Abraham married Keturah while Sarah was still alive or whether it was after her death, though the term *pilegesh*, "concubine," might imply the former. Abraham's sons from Keturah warrant a brief genealogy, and yet, aside from Midian, they are irrelevant within the larger scheme (v. 6). At the ripe age of 175 years, Abraham breathed his last and died (25:8). The description denotes not only age but also contentment. Abraham was ready to rest in his grave, having experienced God's presence, forgiveness, and vindication of his faith. The expression used at his death, that he "was gathered to his people," is not about the survival of an immortal soul but about the reality of human mortality. This is a term used in reference to being buried in a common tomb. The equivalent is "rested," "slept," or "lay down" (*shakhab*). He was not in heaven with his ancestors/fathers (e.g., Gen. 47:30; Deut. 31:16; 1 Kin. 2:10). All are sooner or later gathered to those who preceded them; all will die (cf. 25:17; 35:29; 49:33; Deut. 32:50).

Genesis 25:11 introduces the important continuation of the story of divine blessings for Abraham's family. The verse reads like the passing of the baton, highlighting God's special blessing for Isaac, whose story would continue in 25:19. The brief genealogy of Ishmael (vv. 12–18), also described as Abraham's son, underlines the fulfillment of the promises to Hagar (16:10) and Abraham (17:20). Ishmael's twelve sons foreshadowed the later tribal units of Israel (35:22–26). The summary statement of Ishmael's life (25:17) is very similar to Abraham's (25:8) and links father and son in death. The final verse of this genealogical summary includes a brief geographical note as to the whereabouts of Ishmael's descendants as well as the obscure final phrase *al pene kol 'ekhaiw napal* (v. 18). The Hebrew text literally reads, "And upon all the faces of his brothers he fell." Some translations have viewed this as a reference to his death in the presence of his brothers, but it can also be viewed as suggesting the hostility mentioned in 16:12.

25:19—26:35
Isaac's Story

Isaac's limited role in the patriarchal stories is reflected in the space allotted to the description of his life and activities. While some have included Jacob and Esau's story as part of Isaac's family record, it may be better to recognize the quiet and unobtrusive presence of Isaac, the son of the promise, on his own terms. He represented another link in the chain of promises, and readers are privy to his struggles involving faith, trust in the God of his father, and ultimately, personal victory.

25:19–34. Birth and Rivalry of Esau and Jacob. Following the programmatic reference to Isaac's genealogy (v. 19), using the technical marker *toledot* (see Genesis: Introduction), the text focuses on Rebekah's barrenness and the birth of her twin sons in response to Isaac's intercessory prayer and God's miraculous intervention.

Isaac's story begins with his birth (v. 19), followed by a brief recap of the facts involving his marriage to Rebekah (v. 20), whose barrenness of twenty years (cf. 25:26) must have been a continuous source of stress in the patriarch's

marriage. However, unlike his parents, Isaac did not succumb to the "quick solutions" of concubinage. Isaac's proactive intercessory prayer sheds a different light on Isaac, who often appears to be passive. The Hebrew term referring to Isaac's entreaty in v. 21 (*'atar*) appears repeatedly in the Exodus narrative, where it describes Moses's appeal to God to remove the plagues (Ex. 8:8–9, 28–30). The lack of time markers (when did God grant Isaac's plea?) emphasizes the powerful intercessory ministry of Isaac, as the sequence of prayer, divine response, and conception seemingly followed one after the other.

Yet all is not well. The mention of the children struggling in Rebekah's womb introduces the theme of conflict and strife into the Isaac narrative. The Hebrew word used for their conflict (*ratsats*) is a strong term, referring to "crushing" (Deut. 28:33; Judg. 9:53). Conflict began in the womb, occurred during delivery (Gen. 25:26), is highlighted by the different professions chosen by the sons (v. 27), and ultimately is reflected in the opposing preferences of the parents (v. 28). Rebekah desired to hear from the Lord, so she went to inquire of Him (v. 22; cf. 2 Kin. 8:7–15). Usually this phrase in the OT is reserved for requesting divine guidance from a prophet (Ex. 18:15; 1 Sam. 9:9). The divine reply was expressed in a poetic, four-line response that underlines the conflict between the two sons of Isaac and highlights divine election over and against established traditions (i.e., the rights of the firstborn). The statement about the older (lit. the "greater") serving the younger (Gen. 25:23) contains a wordplay between "shall serve" (*ya'abod*) and Jacob's name (*ya'aqob*). Jacob's election was based on divine sovereignty, grace, and foreknowledge (cf. Rom. 8:29–30; 9:11–12), not on his upright character.

The biblical text briefly relates how Jacob and Esau developed distinctly different personas (Gen. 25:27–28). Esau, the skillful hunter, was loved by Isaac, while Jacob, who lived in the fields, was loved by Rebekah. The Hebrew adjective *tam* (translated variously as "mild," "peaceful," "quiet," or "plain") is based on a root indicating completion or perfection. It can also be translated as "full of integrity," "complete," "flawless," "clean," "blameless," or "perfect" (cf. Gen. 6:9; 17:1 [where the similar *tamim* is used]; 20:5–6; Job 1:1; Ps. 7:8; Song 5:2; 6:9). In the present context, this word, used to describe Jacob, seems to suggest the idea of an amiable and pious person.

The stage was set for more conflict within Isaac's family. Genesis 25:29–34 illustrates the personalities of both sons. Jacob, calculating and astute, won the birthright in exchange for a meal. He sought to outsmart tradition and "assist" God, whose prophecy he must have heard from his doting mother. Esau's shortsightedness and disdain (Heb. 12:16–17) for the birthright is clearly illustrated by the speed with which he made the transaction, consumed the food, and went on his way. The *bekorah* ("birthright") refers to the rights of the firstborn in biblical times. The firstborn held a position of honor within the family (Gen. 43:33) and the right of succession (2 Chr. 21:3), or as in the case of Abraham's family, the covenant. The pentateuchal laws stipulated that the firstborn should receive a double portion of his father's inheritance (Deut. 21:17). Israel as a people was considered God's firstborn among the nations (Ex. 4:22; Jer. 2:3).

26:1–33. Isaac and Abimelech. Isaac's encounter with Abimelech contains many echoes of earlier episodes in Abraham's life. It is the first story focusing exclusively on Isaac. Genesis 25 and 26 are not ordered chronologically but thematically. Since there is no mention of children in chapter 26, it is possible that the events described in the chapter happened during the first twenty years of Isaac's marriage to Rebekah. The Philistines who recognized her beauty would have noticed her nursing or raising her children had they already been born.

Genesis 26:1 sounds like a repeat of 12:10. A famine in the land led Isaac to move to Gerar, the territory of Abimelech, king of the Philistines. Several decades separated Abraham's move to Gerar (Gen. 20) from Isaac's visit. The repetition of the same name for Gerar's king, Abimelech, is most likely due to its use as a dynastic name (something that was common in other ANE cultures; i.e., Egypt). Isaac obeyed God's direct command not to go to Egypt, given during the divine appearance (26:2). God reiterated four key promises to Isaac (vv. 3–4), including (1) the special divine presence and blessing, (2) ownership of the promised land, (3) countless descendants, and (4) the blessing of the nations through his descendants. The final verse of the divine promise, introduced by "because," reminded Isaac of the conditionality of the blessings. Obedience to the divine principles and instructions were central to the promises to Abraham as well as to Isaac (v. 5).

Unfortunately, Isaac repeated some of his father's mistakes (Gen. 12:10–20; 20:1–18). Out of a fear similar to his father's, he told a lie. The "long time" referenced in v. 8 suggests that Isaac's fears were baseless. Instead, the king saw Isaac showing affection to Rebekah. The Hebrew term used here (*tsakhaq*, "to laugh") includes the same consonants that are present in Isaac's name. There is thus here a wordplay that appears repeatedly in the Abraham narrative: Sarah *tsakhaq* in unbelief at the announcement of Isaac's birth (18:12–15) but eventually *tsakhaq* for joy at his birth (21:6). Later, Ishmael *tsakhaq* (cf. notes on 21:9) when Isaac was weaned, and then Isaac (26:8) *tsakhaq* with his wife (here the nuance of the verb is more like "to play with" or "to caress"; cf. Ex. 32:6, indicating more of a sexual playfulness). Abimelech's critique was stern, and he recognized the potential for grave sin that would have affected an entire community (v. 10).

Genesis 26:12 marks the first reference to a patriarch working in agriculture. Isaac enjoyed tremendous divine blessings and reaped a hundredfold. Gerar's inhabitants envied him (v. 14), and the resulting conflict suggested it was time to relocate. Farming and animal husbandry both required secure access to water. Three times Isaac's servants reopened a well that Abraham had dug (and that had been stopped up by the Philistines). Each time Isaac renamed the well and thus laid claim to its water (vv. 15–22). The tenuous interactions between Isaac's clan and the inhabitants of the land were mirrored by the different names given to the three wells: Esek (i.e., "quarrel" or "dispute" in v. 20), then Sitnah (i.e., "hostility" in v. 21), and finally Rehoboth (or "open space" in v. 22), which in the OT is often associated with prosperity or salvation (Is. 54:2–3).

The second theophany reminded Isaac of the true source of power in his life: God's declarations that He was the God of his father, that he should not be afraid, and that He was with him and would bless him and fulfill His promises to Abraham through his descendants dispelled any challenge he might face (Gen. 26:24). These words continue to have deep meaning for Abraham's seed (Gal. 3:29) on the other side of the cross. In response, Isaac, for the first time, built an altar and worshiped the Lord—echoing earlier responses of his father (v. 25; cf. 12:7–8; 13:18).

The final section of the narrative describes another covenant-making ceremony involving a patriarch and Abimelech, who represented the inhabitants of Gerar (Gen. 26:26–31). Initially, Isaac, because of the earlier hostilities, does not seem to be cordial toward the king (v. 27). Accordingly, he did not offer the king food, but he was probably anticipating an agreement, after which he prepared a covenant meal to seal the agreement (v. 30).

26:34–35. Esau's Foreign Wives. The final verses of Genesis 26 seem to be completely disconnected from the earlier narrative of Isaac's sojourn in Gerar and his faith-building experiences. Featuring Esau's foreign wives, they function as a bridge to move the spotlight upon Jacob, beginning in 27:1. Together with 28:6–9, they form a frame for the crucial story of how Jacob stole Esau's blessing.

Esau erred on two accounts: first, he entered into a polygamous relationship; second, he had not learned anything from his grandfather's search to find Isaac an appropriate wife, a bride who not only had a similar ethnic and cultural background but, more importantly, shared the family's commitment to the Lord. Both wives are described as Hittites (26:34), which was greatly distressing to Esau's parents. The last phrase can be literally translated as "they were bitterness of spirit to Isaac and Rebekah," and may be related to the better-known expression *marat nepesh* (lit. "bitter in soul"; 1 Sam. 1:10; Job 7:11; 10:1). The exact nature of Isaac and Rebekah's bitterness and grief is unclear; however, Isaac should have recognized that Esau was unfit to receive the blessing of the firstborn. Isaac's poor judgment is an appropriate introduction to Jacob's story.

27:1—35:29
Jacob's Story

Conflict, tension, faith, and finally, reconciliation are key themes in Jacob's story. Caught between a father committed to following tradition (while avoiding careful Spirit-guided judgment) and a mother who had heard God's voice and schemed to help God along, the son of the blessing experienced numerous mountaintop and valley experiences as he grew into the man who would become Israel.

27:1–28:5. Jacob Steals Esau's Blessing. Forms of the root "bless" appear twenty times in this suspense-filled story, representing the key word of the narrative. The ill-gotten blessing of the firstborn revealed that Rebekah's plan did not agree with that of her husband.

Isaac is described as old and suffering from eye trouble (27:1). He seemed to have been aware of his decline because, in his instructions to Esau, he asserted that he wished to bless him

before he died (v. 4). In contrast to other OT figures who called their families to their side in anticipation of death (Gen. 47:29; 50:24), Isaac did not include Jacob and Rebekah.

Rebekah overheard Isaac's command to his favorite son, Esau, and immediately set in motion a plan to secure the blessing for her favorite son, Jacob (27:5–10). Note the clear distinction between his son (Esau) and her son (Jacob) in vv. 5–6. Isaac's family was a family with divided loyalties. Rebekah's words to Jacob (v. 8) were another way of saying, "Do what I tell you. I know better." Individuals should take responsibility for their own moral decision-making—even if the guidance of others appears to be pure. Rebekah's reply to Jacob's concerns suggested a possible curse (v. 13).

The word *mat'ammim* ("savory/tasty foods" or "delicacies"; vv. 4, 7, 9, 14, 17, 31) appears only twice outside of this chapter—in Proverbs 23:3 and 6. Food played an important role in Jacob's acquisition of both the birthright (*bekorah*) and the blessing (*berakah*) in 25:29–34 and 27:1–29. Following the preparation of the choice meal, Rebekah masked Jacob with Esau's clothes and wrapped the skin of young goats around her son's hands and neck (v. 16). Jacob was camouflaged—but would the ruse work?

Jacob's first words, "my father," resulted in an immediate query regarding his identity. Jacob's reply represented the first of his spoken lies. In response to Isaac's question about his son's quick return, Jacob credited God's special blessings during the hunt (vv. 19–20). The reader can sense Isaac's unease as he invited Jacob to come closer so that he could touch his skin (vv. 21–22). The deception had been successful, yet Isaac remained puzzled: it seemed to him that the voice was Jacob's but the hands were Esau's (v. 22).

Finally, Isaac finished his meal and blessed Jacob. This entailed divine gifts of fertile land as well as dominion over peoples (Gen. 27:27b–29). The land blessings, more relevant for a farmer than for a hunter, alluded to Israel's settlement of the land of the promise. The final promise is later repeated in Balaam's blessing of Israel as a nation—albeit in inverted sequence (Num. 24:9).

Following Isaac's blessing and Jacob's immediate departure, Esau entered the scene. Isaac's question, "Who are you?" (v. 32), echoed the earlier question to Jacob (v. 18) and suggested a completely bewildered Isaac. In response to Esau's answer, Isaac trembled uncontrollably (v.

33). The text describes Isaac as more animated than he is described anywhere else in Genesis, and the reason for his animation was intense fear. Esau wept in anger and begged for his father's blessing (v. 38), but what resulted was a make-shift "anti-blessing" that contained many negative statements. The words of Isaac to Esau (v. 39) began in the same way as part of the blessing of Jacob (v. 28), but translators and commentators disagree concerning whether they mean the same thing. The difficulty lies in the Hebrew preposition *min*, which can mean "with" or "in," but also "away from." Thus, some suggest that here *min* means that Isaac was proclaiming that Esau would live "away from" the fertile ground and the dew of heaven. Others suggest that the same words should have the same meaning in both verses and that the prophecy concerning Esau (which includes some bleak elements in v. 40) need not be entirely negative. The prophetic final line of the blessing in v. 40 was fulfilled during the time of the reign of Jehoram of Judah, when Edom revolted against Judah and crowned its own king (2 Kin. 8:20, 22).

Clearly beaten, Esau's hatred for Jacob smoldered dangerously underneath the surface of a dysfunctional family life. Esau's determination to kill his brother Jacob (v. 41) identified him as the seed of the serpent, following the pattern of Cain and Lamech (Gen. 3:15; 4:8, 23; John 8:44). Rebekah's dense network within the camp kept her informed of Esau's threats, and consequently, she commanded Jacob (cf. v. 8) to flee to her clan's home in Haran (v. 43). However, while she intended for her son to stay there only a short time (v. 44), the sojourn lasted twenty years (31:41), and Jacob never saw his mother again following his departure to Haran.

The last verse of this chapter contains one of the few dialogues between Isaac and Rebekah. Again, Rebekah took the initiative, shaping her request for Jacob to travel to Haran within the context of a bridal search. In response, Isaac called Jacob, blessed him, and admonished him to abstain from marrying a Canaanite (28:1; cf. 24:3–4). Then he sent Jacob away (v. 5), but not before he blessed him a second time. Isaac's second blessing echoes Abraham's earlier blessings (vv. 3–4; cf. 12:2–3, 7; 13:15, 17; 22:17). Jacob left for the homeland of his mother. Padan (Paddan) Aram (v. 5) may be linked to the Akkadian *paddanu*, "highway."

28:6–9. Esau Marries Ishmael's Daughter. The use of the Hebrew verb *ra'ah* ("to see"; 28:6, 8) suggests not only observation but

also mental assimilation and thought; hence, some translate it in these verses as "learned" or "realized." The disappointment over the lost birthright, the stolen blessing, and the impossibility of revenge compelled Esau to change his strategy. Esau went to his uncle Ishmael, who had married an Egyptian (21:21), and married (again, the Hebrew verb here is lit. "took") Ishmael's daughter Mahalath as his third wife (v. 9). Esau forgot that the divine promises were to be fulfilled through the descendants of Isaac, not Ishmael. His partial obedience to his father's command was not good enough (v. 8).

28:10–22. Jacob's Dream at Bethel. A dream encouraged and guided Jacob on his way to Haran. His encounter with the God of his forefathers marked a definitive moment in his life, prefiguring another important encounter many years later on his return from Haran (Gen. 32:22–32). Following the commands of his parents, Jacob was en route from Beersheba, in southern Israel, to Haran, in modern-day Syria. The journey covered about 550 miles (885 km) and must have taken weeks. Reaching "a certain place" (Gen. 28:11), the fugitive prepared for another night on the road. The word "place" reappears several times in the passage (vv. 11, 16, 17, 19) and is significant for the identification and naming of Bethel. In some instances, the term is used to indicate a cultic place of worship (Deut. 12:5). The basic meaning of the verb *paga'*, appearing at the outset of v. 11 and translated as "reached" or "came to," is literally "to meet" or "to encounter" and reappears in 32:1 when Jacob is met by God's angels on his return trip. The presence of the verb, together with other elements, suggests a close link between chapters 28 and 32.

Jacob encountered God in a dream in which he saw angels ascending and descending a ladder with the Lord at the top of it. The movement of angels on the ladder underlines the important link between heaven and earth and is later referred to by Jesus describing Himself as the true link between God and humanity (John 1:51). God's self-description as the Lord God of Abraham his father and the God of Isaac (v. 13) emphasizes covenant continuity. In line with other patriarchs, Jacob received affirmation of previous promises of land, descendants, and the role of mediator of blessings to the world (cf. 12:3, 7; 13:15; 17:4–6; 18:18; 22:17–18). Then God spoke to Jacob's current needs: He promised to be with him and *shamar* ("keep," "watch over") him (v. 15; cf. the same promise given to Isaac in 26:3).

Jacob's response recognized God's presence and his own lack of perception (vv. 16–17). Jacob then used two phrases to describe "this place" adequately (28:17). The "house of God" (Heb. "Bethel") became an idolatrous sanctuary during the time of the divided kingdom (1 Kin. 12:28–31). The "gate of heaven" is reminiscent of Mesopotamian language linked to ziggurats (cf. notes on Gen. 11:6–7).

Following the naming, the pillow stone became a pillar stone (28:18), a memorial to Jacob's experience with the Lord in this place. He consecrated the stone by offering a libation offering of oil on top of it (v. 18). Later legislation would condemn the erection of pillars because of their function in the religions of Israel's neighbors (Ex. 23:24; 34:13; Lev. 26:1; Deut. 16:22).

Jacob's final response to the dream was a vow (Gen. 28:20)—the longest formulated vow in Scripture. Vows include conditions involving God's blessings. Some misunderstand Jacob to have been exhibiting a wrongful spirit of bargaining by using the word "if," as if he were in doubt of God's promise and would obey Him only contingently. The context (vv. 16–19; 32:9–12, 22–32), however, indicates that this was not the case. He was responding in faith and commitment to the assurance that he had just received. The "if" is best understand as "because" or "since." Jacob's pledge of a tenth in v. 22 is the second reference in Genesis (cf. 14:20) to tithing prior to the formulation of the specific law (Lev. 27:30–33; Deut. 14:22–29). Clearly, the patriarchs were aware of and practiced tithing.

29:1–14. Jacob's Safe Arrival at Haran.
Jacob's arrival at his destination is marked by a change in scenery. The reader encounters a pastoral scene instead of dark nights and lonely locales. As an outsider who did not know the geography of the place, Jacob realized only later in the dialogue that he had finally arrived at Haran—safe at last. The chapter opens with a typical betrothal-type scene (see 24:10–61; Ex. 2:15–21).

Jacob's journey ended in a country populated by Eastern peoples. No specific location is mentioned, but he must have felt relief when he finally saw a well (Gen. 29:2). The stone covering of the well represented a well-known strategy of water preservation. The ensuing dialogue between the shepherds and Jacob was terse. Jacob's questions regarding location and his relations were met with one- or two-word answers in Hebrew. This changed only when the shepherds announced the arrival of Laban's

daughter Rachel. At the appearance of Rachel, the text has a particle of interjection (*hinneh*), variously translated as "behold," "and look," and then "here comes his daughter Rachel." The use of this word is an indication to the reader that this is a crucial moment requiring attention.

Jacob saw Rachel and then went to the well, rolled the stone from its mouth, and watered the flock of his uncle Laban. Was Jacob showing off, or was he overcome by sheer relief at having reached his destination? Most likely both, as his strong emotional reaction in v. 11 suggests—he kissed Rachel and wept aloud. Different from Abraham's servant, who prior to accomplishing his purpose committed himself and the purpose of his visit to God in prayer (24:12–14), Jacob, the man of action, was on his way to marital bliss. At least that must have been on his mind as the conversation with Laban in vv. 15–19, following his arrival at the household, suggests. Laban likely anticipated that the arrival of a member of Abraham's family would bring with him a valuable bride-price but was frustrated by what he saw, namely, a young man without any possessions. Laban recognized Jacob's kinship by referring to him as his flesh and bone (or, in more contemporary terms, "flesh and blood"; this description echoes Gen. 2:23, where the same phrase occurs. Cf. Judg. 9:2; 2 Sam. 5:1; 19:13). The formula may indicate more than blood relations and point to a larger covenant agreement.

29:15–30. Jacob Marries Leah and Rachel.
The suggestion of another successful marriage agreement (see Gen. 24) was dashed when Laban outsmarted Jacob. This dispute is programmatic and links this section to the larger theological motif of conflict in the households of Isaac and Jacob.

This brief section describes the service-in-lieu-of-a-bride-price agreement between Laban and Jacob (seven years of service). The key words "work"/"serve" and "pay"/"wages" reappear repeatedly in the following three chapters (29:18, 20, 25, 27, 30; 30:16, 18, 26, 28–29, 32–33; 31:6–7, 41). Laban's initial question regarding Jacob's wages is followed by a description of the main characteristics of Laban's two eligible daughters (29:16–17). The oldest daughter, Leah (most likely meaning "cow"), had eyes that were *rak* ("tender," "delicate"). Some translate this term as "weak" or "ordinary." However, this adjective has a wide spectrum of meaning depending on the context. Thus, either she had weak eyes, or her eyes were an attractive and captivating part of her. In comparison, Rachel (whose name means "ewe") is described as being beautiful in appearance and *to'ar* ("form" or "figure"; v. 17). Jacob loved Rachel (v. 18), and this was shown in the depth and single-mindedness of Jacob's commitment and his willingness to serve for seven years in exchange for her hand.

Deceived by Laban, Jacob completed the bridal week with Leah, and then immediately married Rachel, the one he indeed loved. The result of this polygamous relationship can be seen in the record of chronic family conflict and jealousy. This underscores the fact that such a practice was not part of God's plan for human families.

29:31—30:24. A Promise Fulfilled: Jacob's Wives and Children.

The story of Jacob's wives, concubines, and children is a story of fulfilled divine promises and challenging family conflicts. Similar to Abraham's experience with Sarah and Hagar, Jacob was to suffer the consequences of a polygamous household where jealousy reigned supreme. Yet in the midst of tension, jealousy, and conflict, God showed Himself sovereign and fulfilled His promises.

In a tight sequence of seemingly never-ending pregnancies and birth announcements, the section describes the birth of eleven of Jacob's sons, plus the arrival of one daughter, Dinah (30:21), all within seven years (30:26). Dinah's presence among the birth announcements echoes the earlier inclusion of Rebekah in Nahor's genealogy (22:23). God was intricately involved in giving children—in line with other OT references that clearly link children to divine intervention and blessings.

The text also suggests God's care for His children's emotional well-being. The introduction to the first sequence of four birth announcements reveals that God was concerned about Leah being less loved than Rachel (29:31). The Hebrew word here (*sane'*) can mean "hate" but also "less loved" or "unloved." The text need not imply that Jacob detested Leah (since all of her children were begotten of Jacob). God was not passive. He enabled her to have a child (v. 31), the first reference to divine activity since Jacob's encounter at Bethel. A son was born, and Leah called him Reuben (v. 32), whose name can be translated as "See, a son!" He was Jacob's firstborn. As this story illustrates, God cares for the brokenhearted.

The naming of each son by either Leah or Rachel emphasized the substitutionary function of the two maidservants Bilhah (30:3–8) and Zilpah (30:9–13), who each bore two sons to Jacob. Both Leah and Rachel used sexuality and childbearing to outmaneuver and gain dominance over the rival wife while Jacob appeared essentially passive in the midst of the conflict.

30:25–43. Divine Blessing: Jacob's Wealth Increases.

The compressed story detailing the birth of Jacob's children is followed by another recounting of divine blessings—how Jacob acquired his riches. The narrative is full of strange symbolic acts, yet it is not Jacob's cleverness or astuteness but God's hidden hand that ultimately is in control of the natural world and human hearts.

In response to Jacob's request to return home (v. 25), Laban publicly recognized God's special blessing, but he also stated that this recognition had been acquired by *nakhash* (v. 27). This word usually means "to divine." Divination often attempted to gain wisdom from the gods through ritual performances and the observation of signs. It was widely practiced in the ANE but strictly forbidden in Israel years later (Lev. 19:26; Deut. 18:10, 14). Some have taken the word to mean that Laban learned "by experience" or observation that the Lord had blessed him through his relationship with Jacob. This interpretation is highly unlikely, for the verbal root always refers to divination through means other than this. A better alternative, based on an Akkadian verbal root, is a Hebrew verbal root spelled the same way as *nakhash* meaning "to become rich." In that case, Laban would be saying "I have become rich/prospered for the Lord has blessed me on account of you." Laban finally offered a wage contract that would guarantee Jacob the possibility of acquiring his own herds while taking care of Laban's (v. 28).

Jacob's request for the speckled and spotted sheep and goats as his wage must have seemed very minimal to Laban, who immediately took the offer without any haggling (v. 35). Laban knew that goats were normally black or dark brown while sheep were white. Contemporary records set the wages for hired shepherds at around 20 percent of the newborn animals. Because of the relative rarity of speckled and spotted animals, Jacob was apparently settling for a potential wage much lower than that of a typical shepherd. Laban knew he had secured an advantageous arrangement; furthermore, he made sure that Jacob's wages would be even lower by removing the speckled and spotted animals from his herds and giving them to his sons (v. 35). Later, Jacob claimed that Laban had changed his wages ten times (31:41).

However, Jacob became exceedingly prosperous (v. 43) after an additional six years of service for Laban. Different translations present different purposes for the rods Jacob laid before his flocks (vv. 37–42): (1) to encourage more breeding or (2) to actually affect the appearance of the animals. The context indicates that the increase in livestock was the result of God blessing Jacob (31:8–12) and not the result of Jacob's unusual ideas about breeding and genetics. Jacob's riches included not only goats and sheep but also servants, camels, and donkeys (v. 43).

31:1–55. Jacob's Flight and a New Covenant. At the end of twenty years full of tension, conflict, and treachery, Jacob finally decided to relocate his large household to his homeland. Pursued by Laban and his kinsmen, Jacob experienced divine protection and reassurance (31:1–3). The charge of Laban's sons that Jacob had taken everything from their father was at least partially true. God had blessed Jacob so abundantly that his possessions surpassed those of Laban. God's commanded Jacob to return to Canaan—that is, the land of his fathers and his relatives (v. 3). Both land and community had been part of God's promise to Abraham.

The next scene involved clandestine meetings, and for the first time, Rachel and Leah agreed on a plan of action. Jacob shared his perception that their living situation had changed, following a visit from the Angel of God, called in other places the Angel of the Lord (see Judg. 2:1–5). Here He is the Angel of "God" because He identified Himself as the "God" who spoke to Jacob at Bethel (cf. Gen. 16:7–8; 22:11–18; 32:30; cf. Ex. 23:20–22; Judg. 13; Hos. 12:4). The divine "I have seen" (v. 12) is repeatedly used in Scripture to indicate God's compassion for those suffering (cf. Gen. 16:13; 29:31; 31:42; Ex. 3:7, 9; 4:31). When God sees, things begin to happen. God also identified Himself as the God of Bethel (v. 13)—that is, the God who had already appeared to Jacob and who had heard Jacob's vow. Interestingly, the brief, summarized version of God's communication to Jacob in v. 3 is expanded in the fuller description in vv. 10–13. Rachel and Leah's response was unanimous; in fact, they disassociated themselves from their father's house, utilizing terminology involving outsiders and slaves (v. 15).

With his wives in agreement, Jacob moved quickly and departed from Laban's household while Laban was away shearing his sheep (v. 19). Camels were used as means of transport for the growing family (v. 17) and had already been mentioned in 12:16 and 24:10. Critical scholarship has questioned the historicity of camel domestication in the time of the patriarchs. However, archaeological evidence confirms that the camel was domesticated in the second millennium B.C.

Rachel's theft of the family household idols (or teraphim) was her reaction to Laban retaining her bridal price (vv. 14–16), which was paid to him to be held in trust for her. Teraphim were generally portable idols, often associated with the gods of the ancestors. Rachel's thievery was not discovered because she hid the teraphim in her saddle and claimed (probably falsely) that she could not rise from it due to her menstruation (vv. 33–35). The "Fear of Isaac" is used as a surprising divine epithet or title (vv. 42, 53). Data from the third-millennium-B.C. Ebla texts support the rendering of the Hebrew *pakhad* as "dread," suggesting the translation "the Dreaded One of Isaac." Dread often befalls Israel's enemies (e.g., Ex. 15:16; Deut. 2:25; 11:25; Esth. 8:17). It should be taken into consideration that *pakhad* is also used to describe a proper awe and respect for God (e.g., 2 Chr. 19:7; Ps. 119:120; Prov. 28:14; Hos. 3:5). Also the LXX translation of *pakhad* here is *phobos*, which is also used throughout the OT and NT to refer to an appropriate reverence (e.g., Ex. 20:20; 2 Cor. 7:1; Eph. 5:21; cf. Heb. 12:28–29).

Finally, Jacob and Laban entered into a covenant (v. 44), bringing resolution to the tension between them. Pillars of stones were set up as witnesses to the covenant (v. 52). The use of Aramaic and Hebrew terms for the pillars suggests that Laban's primary language may have been Aramaic, an element that underlines the separation between the distinct families. Jacob then offered a sacrifice (v. 54), followed by a covenant meal ratifying the agreement. Laban's departure the next morning included a kiss for his grandchildren and daughters but none for Jacob (cf. 29:13). Twenty years had taken their toll on Laban and Jacob's relationship.

32:1–32. Jacob Wrestles with God. Fear is one of the threads running through this key chapter of Jacob's biography. Wrestling with the divine Messenger, Jacob finally reached the end of himself. Fear, pain, and dread fell away as he overcame and was overcome. Jacob was ready to meet his brother, Esau.

Genesis 32:1–2 describes an angelic encounter, one which was probably intended to encourage Jacob on his journey home. Mahanaim means "two camps." In order to prepare for the encounter with Esau, Jacob sent messengers ahead of his caravan (32:3–5). The report that these messengers brought back, however, was ambiguous and increased Jacob's anxiety. The prayer of Jacob expressed his fears (v. 11) and claimed divine promises (v. 12). The God of Abraham and Isaac had become the God of Jacob (v. 9). God was becoming real and personal in this chapter—in more ways than Jacob could have imagined.

Following his prayer, Jacob sent a significant gift ahead for his brother, Esau. He referred to Esau as "my lord" and himself as "your servant," which implied that Jacob honored Esau and did not seek to flaunt his birthright status. Jacob's reference to his attempt to appease or pacify his brother in 32:20 is related to the Hebrew term translated in other places as "ransom" (e.g., Ex. 21:30; Ps. 49:8).

Having divided his camp, Jacob found himself alone (v. 24). The careful reader recalls an earlier night spent alone in the fields around Bethel (28:11–22). Suddenly, a Man appeared and wrestled with Jacob in the darkness. The Hebrew verb for "wrestled" occurs only in this chapter and sounds similar to the Hebrew *yabboq*. It has been linked to a comparable Hebrew verb meaning "embrace" (29:13; 33:4). However, this was no friendly embrace. The identity of the Attacker was at first unknown, but Hosea would call Him the Angel (12:4) while Jacob would acknowledge Him to be God (32:30; cf. Hos. 12:5; see notes on Gen. 16:7–8; 31:9–12). Jacob was defeated by a simple touch, and this led him to ask for a blessing. He had finally realized that the blessing was a divine gift.

The ensuing dialogue between Jacob and the unidentified Assailant centered on the issue of names (vv. 27–28). Jacob received a new name, Israel, the future name of the covenant nation. Jacob also wanted to know his Attacker's name (v. 29). Knowing the name of another person provides access to that person. Yet Jacob's Opponent did not want to provide this information; instead, He blessed him. Even though Jacob may have only sensed the true identity of his Attacker, *this* was the blessing he had sought for years. This was the real thing. His declaration that he had seen God "face-to-face" forms the basis for the place name Peniel—that is, "face of God" (v. 30). However, "face-to-face" emphasizes more the intimacy of the encounter and not necessarily visual contact. As Jacob limped into a new morning, he walked with a constant reminder of the divine Presence—in this sense, the divine touch that had caused the limp functioned as an object lesson. He could face the coming encounters with Esau and his parents with hope. Jacob had been transformed. The dietary restriction based on this encounter was a perpetual reminder; "to this day" (v. 32) reflects the perspective of the author.

33:1–20. The Reunion of Jacob and Esau. The encounter at Jabbok changed many things for Jacob, but it did not immediately change Jacob's relationship with Esau. However, vertical transformation affects horizontal relationships. Again, God was working behind the scenes. As He did for Israel during their sojourn in the wilderness many centuries later, God went ahead of Jacob and prepared the way for reconciliation. Jacob preceded his household (v. 3) instead of staying behind them (32:17, 19, 21). The Hebrew term used here ('*abar*) is also the root of the name "Hebrew." Jacob crossed over the Jabbok, but his move from rearguard to vanguard also marked profound changes in his character. Seven times Jacob bowed to the ground before Esau. This was a common practice of vassals toward their overlords, documented in the second-millennium-B.C. Amarna correspondence. The four-hundred-man fighting force (see 32:6) behind Esau must have appeared formidable. Yet God had done another miracle and had prepared Esau's heart and blessed him (33:9). While the biblical text does not mention any direct divine intervention, as was the case during Laban's pursuit (cf. 31:29), Esau's intent on hearing of the arrival of his brother and calling up four hundred fighting men must have been hostile. The sequence of Esau's actions represents a complete reversal of what the reader expects: Esau ran to meet Jacob, embraced him, fell on his neck, and kissed him—and then both wept (33:4). A comparable scene, using similar language, is described by Jesus in Luke 15:20. This was palpable grace. Instead of attacking and hurting one another, the two estranged brothers embraced, which is described by a Hebrew term (*khabaq*) that sounds similar to the one describing Jacob's wrestling with God ('*abaq*; 32:24–25).

The ensuing dialogue repeatedly reflected the vassal-overlord motif introduced by Jacob's seven bows. Jacob referred to himself as "your servant" (33:5) and provided expensive gifts that he urged Esau to accept (v. 10). Esau's changed attitude was reflected in the kisses he bestowed on his brother. His reaction seems to indicate forgiveness (2 Sam. 14:33), recognition of Jacob as his brother (Gen. 33:9), and acceptance of the blessing (v. 11; in reference to the gifts in v. 10 and a conscious echo of the stolen blessing).

Yet all was not well—Jacob's responses to Esau's invitation to accompany his household suggest some hesitation (vv. 12–17). Jacob's delicate replies underlined his reliance on God; thus, he avoided offending his brother (vv. 12–15). Following Esau's departure to Seir (cf. 36:8), Jacob journeyed (again using a term marking nomadic travel) to Succoth (or Sukkoth), which is the Hebrew word for "shelters" or "booths." Succoth was located on the eastern side of the Jordan River Valley in territory that was later given to the tribe of Gad (Josh. 13:24–27). This is the fourth location that Jacob named (Bethel, Mahanaim, Peniel, and Succoth), each marking significant events in his journeys with the Lord.

Finally, Jacob entered Canaan proper and settled near Shechem, where he bought a parcel of land for his camp (Gen. 33:17–20). There he built his first altar, providing an important link to Abraham and Isaac (12:7–8; 13:18; 22:9–10; 26:25; 35:7). The final verses of Genesis 33 function as a bridge to the story of Dinah.

34:1–31. The Dinah Incident. Peace and reconciliation, so marvelously illustrated in the previous chapter, did not last long. There were major tensions between the residents of Shechem and the sons of Jacob, and they would lead to disaster, involving the rape of Dinah. The problems had to do with dissimilar values and matters of honor and shame.

Dinah, introduced as Leah's daughter (34:1), "went out to see," or visit with, the daughters of the Hivites that lived in Shechem. When Shechem, the son of Hamor (Hebrew for "male donkey"), "saw her," he raped her (v. 2). This verbal sequence (*ra'ah, laqakh, shakav, 'anah*) is telling and deliberate. Seeing (the first verb) led to taking (the second; cf. Eve in Gen. 3:6, with no sexual connotations). "To lay with" or "have sex with" is the third verb, which is combined with the fourth in some translations as "raped" or "lay with her by force." This is because the last of these verbs (*'anah*) comes from a Hebrew root meaning "humiliated, afflicted." This was not consensual sex but blatant rape. Yet Shechem thought he was in love. The biblical text states that he loved her and spoke kindly/tenderly to her. This last phrase is literally "he spoke upon the heart," which appears several times in the OT, in less than perfect contexts where there is often a sense of guilt or repentance (e.g., Judg. 19:3;

1 Sam. 1:13; 2 Sam. 19:7; 2 Chr. 30:22). Shechem endeavored to right a wrong and asked his father to request Dinah's hand in marriage (Gen. 34:4), initiating customary marriage negotiations. Consequently, the chapter contains a number of elaborate speeches designed to convince the opposing party.

It is unclear how Jacob heard the news, but it appeared to be public knowledge and thus brought shame upon his family. Jacob's role in this narrative was very passive—most of the talking was done by Shechem, Hamor, and the sons of Jacob. When the sons heard the news, they were disturbed and extremely angry because of the *nebalah* ("disgraceful," "senseless") act that Shechem had done (v. 7). The term *'atsav*, which is one of the words used to describe the grief, shock, and anger of Jacob's sons, had been used earlier in Genesis to describe God's response to Noah's pre-Flood generation (6:6). Interestingly, decades later, Joseph's response to his brothers' speechlessness after he had disclosed his identity employed the same two terms (45:5). *Nebalah* is a serious term, appearing thirteen times in the OT, eight of which describe sexual crimes (e.g., Deut. 22:21; Josh. 7:15; Judg. 20:6, 10; 2 Sam. 13:12).

The invitation to unite in marriages with the people of the city (v. 9) utilizes a technical term marking intermarriage, which was later forbidden in Mosaic law (Deut. 7:3). One of the key elements of marriage involved religious loyalties. While there were instances of Canaanites, Moabites, or others who married into Israel and became part of the covenant people (e.g., Tamar, Rahab, Ruth), intermarriage in general was forbidden by law (cf. Ezra 9–10; Neh. 13:23–29).

The negotiations with Shechem and Hamor were managed by Jacob's sons, who were deceptive in their dealings (Gen. 34:13). The theme of deceit and betrayal, so prevalent in Jacob's earlier story (27:35; 29:25), continued in the lives of his sons, who insisted on circumcision as a prerequisite for a marriage agreement (vv. 14–15). Jacob's sons "used" the covenant sign (17:9–14; cf. Ex. 12:43–49) and voided it of any spiritual implication. Jacob later disassociated himself completely from the two ringleaders of the massacre, Simeon and Levi (49:5–6).

Hamor and Shechem brought the proposal to the city gate (v. 20), the place of official deliberations and decisions (Gen. 19:1; 23:18; Ruth 4:1). Nowhere in their speech (34:21–23) did Hamor and Shechem explain the true reason for their request to circumcise the male population of the city. Instead, they emphasized the point that if they joined with Jacob's family, all of the patriarch's possessions (livestock, property, and animals) would be shared (or taken over; v. 23). Two cycles of deceit and duplicity are at work in this narrative. In response to their convincing counsel, every male was circumcised (v. 24).

Finally, Jacob spoke his mind (v. 30). He reproved his sons strongly. He said that their actions had made him *ba'ash* (lit. "to stink") sometimes translated here as "obnoxious." This refers metaphorically to behavior that leads to reprisal and revenge (Ex. 5:21; 1 Sam. 13:4; 2 Sam. 10:6). Jacob feared complete annihilation (v. 30; 2 Sam. 21:5). Jacob's fear was palpable, yet no reference to Dinah's painful experience is included. The lack of respect in the reply of Jacob's sons anticipated future conflict. "Our sister" instead of "your daughter" emphasizes deeper rifts in Jacob's family (v. 31). The final rhetorical question remains unanswered in the narrative and leaves the reader to genuinely speculate about Jacob, the state of his family, and the blessing he was meant to be.

35:1-29. Jacob Returns to Bethel. Following the tragic disaster at Shechem, God was on the move again. Spiritual revival and worship characterized Jacob's journey and arrival at Bethel. Finally, the patriarch could fulfill his vow.

This chapter begins with God's all-powerful voice and the command to return to Bethel. Jacob, unlike Abram (12:1-3), knew his direction and destination. God's directions were even more specific: Jacob was commanded to build an altar. An altar indicated worship and was a witness to others of Jacob's commitment and dedication to the Lord (12:7-8; 13:18; 22:9-10; 26:25).

Jacob's response reveals a need for spiritual renewal. First, he commanded his household to dispense with their foreign gods (v. 2). The imperative appears in similar revivals elsewhere in the OT (Josh. 24:14, 23; Judg. 10:16; 1 Sam. 7:3-4; 2 Chr. 33:15). The exact nature of the foreign gods is not further described. They may have included figurines, amulets, and the family teraphim that Rachel had stolen from Laban (Gen. 31:30-35). Together with the gods, the family gathered their earrings, and everything was hidden under a tree (35:4). The hiding or burying is not expressed by the regular verb denoting burial (*qabar*) but by the rare verb *taman*—possibly an indication of a descent into oblivion (cf. Job 3:16 and its reference to a miscarriage using the same verb). The gods whom Rachel had sat upon and allegedly tarnished

with menstrual blood (31:30-35) were finally being discarded. Furthermore, Jacob ordered his household to purify themselves (v. 2). Purification required ritual activities and, together with the change of garments, was an important element of the priestly ordination ritual (Ex. 29:4-9; Lev. 8:6-9, 13). The cultic language of the passage suggests the notion that Jacob's household was to be a "priestly" household, prefiguring Exodus 19:6. Because Abraham, Isaac, and Jacob had all been called to be God's special people, they were to be holy and mission-driven (cf. 1 Pet. 2:5-9).

As Jacob's household journeyed toward Bethel, the terror of God fell on the inhabitants of Canaan (Gen. 35:5), enabling Jacob to travel safely through an increasingly hostile environment (cf. Ex. 15:14-15). Luz was the ancient name of Bethel (v. 6; cf. 28:19). This update suggests some type of later contextualization of the biblical text in the earlier story of Abram (13:3), for in Abram's time, the city was still called Luz. The construction of the altar seems to have functioned as a symbol of the complete fulfillment of Jacob's vow—even though the text does not elaborate further.

Genesis 35:8 contains the surprising death of someone who had not appeared by name in the story before. Deborah, Rebekah's nurse (cf. 24:59), died at Bethel and was buried under the terebinth or oak tree (the definite article, "the," indicates that this was one of the landmarks of Bethel). Her presence may have been due to Rebekah's absence. Genesis does not provide a death notice for Rebekah.

The next section (35:9-15) affirms Jacob's name change (cf. 32:28) and blessing. The mention of God having appeared to Jacob (35:9) reminds the reader that God is never far off. This covenant renewal is a powerful reminder of God's presence and care in the face of death.

The notice of the departure from Bethel (v. 16) is surprising—especially in view of the fact that Jacob's favorite wife, Rachel, was pregnant and at the point of giving birth. However, what appeared to be another blessing, fulfilling the ideal family size of twelve sons, turned out to be an experience of grief and pain. Rachel died while giving birth to her second son, whom she named Ben-Oni, "son of my sorrow" (v. 18; cf. the irony of Rachel's clamor to Jacob in 30:1, that he should give her children or else she would die). Jacob renamed his son Benjamin, "son of the right hand." The text mentions Rachel's *nepesh* (see "Living Soul or Living Being?" on p. 145). In this case, it seems evident that the meaning is simply "life"—her life was ending (lit. "going out"). This is an illustrative description of Rachel's death rather than evidence that her eternal "soul" was returning to heaven (as some have claimed). There is no evidence in Scripture for the idea of an eternal, conscious entity that survives the death of the body. The explanatory note in v. 19 clarifies the statement in 35:18. Rachel was buried in Bethlehem, about 15 miles (24 km) south of Bethel. Another pillar marked this significant place (v. 20).

Signs of further fragmentation and disunity in the family soon followed. Reuben had sex with Bilhah, his father's concubine (v. 22). Bilhah, the maidservant of Rachel and the mother of Dan and Naphtali, after having lost Rachel's protection, represented a prized target for power-hungry Reuben. His disturbing action (one that rabbinical traditions considered offensive enough to prohibit its translation in the synagogue) was meant to assert his leadership over the clan and establish his rights as the firstborn. This anticipated Absalom's later similar act (2 Sam. 16:22; cf. 2 Sam. 3:7; 1 Kin. 2:22). As one of Leah's sons, Reuben may have also detested Jacob's disdain for his mother Leah. Similar to the Dinah incident, Jacob heard about what Reuben had done but did not do anything (Gen. 35:22). The text gives the impression of an old and broken man, unable or unwilling to discipline or even engage with his family. The moral fiber of Jacob's clan became increasingly brittle.

The brief notice of Isaac's death concludes the stories of Isaac and Jacob (vv. 27–29). Isaac died at the age of 180 years. Esau and Jacob (listed in the order of their birth; 35:29) buried him. Similar to Isaac and Ishmael at the grave of Abraham (25:9), the brothers were united by the death of their father.

36:1–43. The Family of Esau. The genealogy of Esau demonstrates that God had fulfilled His promise of making Abraham the father of many nations (17:5–6, 16). Similar to the manner in which the account of Ishmael's descendants separated the family histories of Abraham and Isaac (25:12–18), this description of Esau's line acts as an interjection between Jacob's family story and Joseph's, which resumes in chapter 37.

The lists contain seventy personal names and mark an overall sociopolitical movement from extended family (vv. 1–8), to tribal organization (vv. 15–19), and ultimately to a monarchy (vv. 31–39)—a description that anticipates Israel's own historical development. The record opens with a list of Esau's wives, including his two Canaanite wives, Adah and Aholibamah, plus Basemath, the daughter of Ishmael. When compared to the earlier references to Esau's wives (26:34; 28:6–9), there is only one name, Basemath, that appears in all references, even though in 26:34, Basemath is the daughter of Elon the Hittite while in 36:3 she is the daughter of Ishmael. All three references agree that the first two wives were Canaanite (or Hittite/Hivite) while the third wife was more closely related, a daughter of Ishmael. There is no easy solution to this puzzle. The apparent mix-up in names may have been due to problems in the textual transmission, even though there is little indication of that. Perhaps the wives had more than one name.

Woven among the names of Esau's wives are the names of his five sons. The author of Genesis includes this information purposefully in this location as a contrast to the listing of Jacob's twelve sons by two wives and two concubines (35:22b–26) that anticipates the notice of Isaac's death. Children illustrate numerically the blessings and the promise of the covenant.

Esau's decision to move out of the promised land was likely motivated by an abundance of (divine) blessings. Their possessions (referring to Jacob's and Esau's clans) were too numerous (36:7) for the land to sustain them both. Unlike the situation described in Genesis 28, Jacob and Esau's separation did not involve hostilities or conflict. The land simply "could not support them." The final clause of this section, which equates Esau with Edom, is programmatic; it links Edom to Mount Seir (Deut. 2:4–6, 12, 22; Josh. 24:4), and it thus reminds the reader of postpatriarchal geopolitical realities. Esau is more precisely characterized as the father of the Edomites (36:9). "Father" can also be understood as "ancestor" (Ex. 13:5; Deut. 26:5; Josh. 24:3; etc.). Esau's grandchildren (from only two sons, Eliphaz and Reuel) were ten in number, including Amalek, the son of Eliphaz's concubine Timna (36:12). The Amalekites later became bitter enemies of Israel (Ex. 17:8–16) and became a distinct people separate from the Edomites (Deut. 25:17–19).

The next section (Gen. 36:15–19) names the chiefs of the sons of Edom. The Hebrew term can also be translated as "clans," but "chief" appears to be the better translation here as the reference is to tribal units identified by their leader.

Verse 19 underlines the important links between Esau's sons and Edom's sociopolitical structure.

The following section (vv. 20–30) records the sons of Seir, the Horite. According to Deuteronomy 2:12 and 22, the Horites (perhaps Hurrians?) were the original inhabitants of the hill country of Seir but were later dispossessed by Esau's descendants. Their inclusion in the list provides a snapshot of the populations that Esau's family encountered. While Deuteronomy 2:12 and 22 suggest that Esau's descendants destroyed the Horites, some names in the list also appear as spouses or in-laws of Esau's family (including Anah [v. 20, 25; cf. vv. 2, 14], Timna [v. 22, cf. v. 12], Aholibamah [v. 25, cf. v. 2]). This suggests that the Horites were absorbed into Esau's family line. As with other genealogies in Genesis, sometimes a noteworthy event or an accomplishment of an individual is included. Genesis 36:24 includes such a note for Anah, who was possibly a father-in-law of Esau (cf. vv. 2, 14). Some translations describe him as the one who found water in the wilderness. The translation of the Hebrew word *yemim* is uncertain. The Latin Vulgate reads "hot springs," which is followed by some translations. One of the targums (Pseudo Jonathan) suggests that "mules" is the correct meaning, and this rendering is followed by some other translations.

The next section lists the kings of Edom (vv. 31–39). Eight kings are listed in the linear sequence of Edomite kings before there were any kings in Israel (v. 31). Some kings are associated with specific cities while others are mentioned in connection with specific events. Hadad is reported to have struck down Midian in the field of Moab (v. 35). Hadad is the name of the Semitic storm god who is also identified with Baal. The chapter concludes with another list of chiefs, cataloging eleven names, seven of which appear for the first time. The exact relationship to the first list of chiefs or clans (vv. 15–19) is not clear. It may be that the latter list represented later chiefs of Edom, some of which used names already employed by their predecessors. The final line of v. 43 forms a frame with v. 9 that brackets the genealogies proper of Genesis 36.

37:1—50:26
Joseph's Story

The final section of Genesis, introduced by another *toledot* (see Introduction), focuses on Joseph, Jacob's first son by Rachel. It revisits many themes from earlier patriarchal history (including sibling rivalry, famine and survival, deceit, divine blessings, etc.), yet it concludes in a different location. While Abraham, Isaac, and Jacob all returned to Canaan toward the ends of their lives, Joseph and his family died in Egypt. Thus, Joseph's story anchors the Exodus narrative many centuries later.

37:1–36. Joseph's Dreams and Slavery. Joseph's story is not told in isolation. As Jacob's son, he was only one of twelve, yet his life affected his entire family—and beyond. Like many patriarchal narratives, Joseph's story begins with a dream, followed by much trouble. Throughout the narrative, Joseph experiences divine silence but not divine absence. God works behind the scenes in the flow of the narrative and in the heart of the protagonist of the story, preparing a great deliverance.

The characterization of seventeen-year-old Joseph is nuanced: Joseph worked as a shepherd alongside his half brothers, yet he was apparently no team player since he brought Jacob a "bad report" about them. The phrase "Israel loved Joseph" (v. 3) anticipates the undercurrent of envy and hatred in the family. Considering the divided household of Isaac, Israel should have remembered the disastrous effects of having a favorite child. Instead, he made Joseph a tunic of many colors. Israel's skills as a tailor may have pointed back to the depiction of him in 25:27 as one who lived in tents. The Hebrew term for Joseph's robe is puzzling, and its translation is based on ancient versions. Egyptian contemporary tomb paintings of Beni Hassan (dated to the nineteenth century B.C.) show Semitic merchants doing business with Egyptians and wearing multicolored wraparound knee-length tunics. Clothing signaled status and played a major role in Joseph's story (37:3, 23; 39:12; 41:14, 42). The reaction of Joseph's brothers to his preferential treatment is candidly described by the author—they hated him and could not speak to him peacefully or kindly (37:4). Hebrew grammar allows for two interpretations of the object of their hatred, with "him" referring to either Jacob or Joseph. Most likely, the brothers hated both and treated them accordingly. Yet more hatred was to come (vv. 5, 8).

Joseph was not only the favorite. He was also a dreamer. Up to this point in Genesis, God has been the source of all dreams. While v. 5 does not explicitly specify God as the dream-giver, this is silently assumed since dreams were considered to be messages from the gods in the ANE. The term translated "bowed" (v. 7) reappears significantly in 42:6 when the brothers bowed to the Egyptian governor they did not recognize as their brother Joseph. Jacob recognized the potential explosiveness of the reversal of social order (v. 10), yet he kept this dream in mind as a revelation of Joseph's future (cf. Luke 2:19; 51).

Pastoral serenity is suggested at the opening of the next scene. Joseph's brothers went to feed the family's flock in Shechem (v. 12). The location is an ominous harbinger of disaster to readers of Genesis (cf. Gen. 34). However, the brothers had moved from Shechem to Dothan, about 13 miles (21 km) northwest of Shechem. All in all, Joseph traveled 65 miles (104 km) from Hebron to find his brothers. The reader may wonder why they had pastured the animals so far from the family home. Distance and location in Genesis are often used to indicate proximity to divine blessings—Joseph's brothers surely were keeping their distance. The appearance of Joseph in the distance triggered an evil scheme in the minds of the brothers, and they *nakal*, "plotted" or "conspired," to kill him (v. 18). The Hebrew term appears only three more times in the OT and marks deceitful action (Num. 25:18; Ps. 105:25; Mal. 1:14). The description of Joseph as a dreamer (lit. "the lord of dreams") was a sarcastic one (v. 19). The plan to kill their brother was a collective decision (v. 20). However, Reuben, Jacob's firstborn, intervened to rescue him (v. 21). The language of deliverance used here (*natsal*) is often linked to divine intervention (Ex. 18:4, 8; 1 Sam. 26:24), yet Reuben's impotence soon became apparent (Gen. 37:26–28).

Joseph was stripped of his robe, the symbol of his preferred status and then thrown into a *bor* ("pit" or "cistern"), which was most likely a dry well that had been dug to collect rainwater for use during the dry season (vv. 23–24). The callous nature of Joseph's brothers became evident when they sat down to eat a meal while Joseph was left terrified in the pit nearby. Next, a caravan of Ishmaelites appeared on the scene (v. 25). Ishmaelites and Midianites (v. 28) were related to Abraham (Midianites through Keturah [25:1–2]; Ishmaelites through Hagar). Joseph was sold for twenty shekels (v. 28), which seems to have been a traditional price for a slave (cf. Lev. 27:5).

The final scene returns the focus to Joseph's garment, which was presented as evidence of his death to Jacob (Gen. 37:31–35). Meanwhile, unbeknown to Jacob, Joseph had been sold in Egypt by the Midianites to Potiphar, a high official at Pharaoh's court. The name Potiphar means "he whom Ra has given" and is one that is known from Egyptian texts.

38:1–30. Judah and Tamar. The phrase "at that time" (38:1) locates the chapter within the Joseph narrative even though it does not provide clear chronological information. Judah's departure from his family recalls Eve's separation from Adam and Lot's move toward the lush plain of the Jordan (13:11). Judah saw a certain Canaanite woman and married (lit. "took") her, against all previous counsel (24:3; 26:35; 27:46). This same verbal sequence was used earlier to describe action in opposition to God's guidance (3:6; 6:2; 12:15; 34:2). Shua conceived three times, and she and Judah had three sons. Judah took Tamar as a wife for his firstborn, Er (v. 6). The biblical text does not provide further information as to Er's wickedness, yet the divine judgment is immediate; the Lord killed Er (v. 7). This is the first reference to God putting an individual to death (cf. v. 10).

After Judah's second son was struck down by God, Judah refused to give Tamar his third son to be her husband. When Judah's wife died, he had sexual relations with Tamar (although he did not know it was her). Three months after the sexual encounter, Judah was told that Tamar was pregnant by means of prostitution (v. 24). Later law required adulterers to be put to death (Lev. 20:10; Deut. 22:22). The Mosaic law prescribed public stoning for some sexual sins (Deut. 22:21, 24) while other crimes were punishable by burning (Lev. 20:14; 21:9). Some scholars consider the sentence for adultery a two-level procedure, according to which the involved parties were first stoned and then burned.

The dialogue between Tamar and Judah focused upon the pledge items (sources of identification) that Judah had left with the supposed prostitute. Judah admitted that Tamar was more in the right than he was (v. 26). Judah's relative righteousness contrasted with God's absolute righteousness (cf. Jer. 33:15; Rom. 3:25–26). The focus of the chapter is on what motivated Tamar—the fulfillment of the Levirate law—rather than on her actions. Levirate marriage required the brother of a deceased Israelite to produce a son with the widow of the deceased brother (Deut. 25:5–10) in order to assure an heir and the future of that family line. The practice is also known from Hittite and Middle Assyrian laws, the main difference being that in biblical law, the brother-in-law was responsible for providing an heir. Tamar, a

Canaanite woman, became part of the messianic line (Ruth 4:12, 18–22; Matt. 1:3–6). The birth of male twins (Gen. 38:27–30) compensated Tamar for her forced barrenness (cf. 25:22–26).

39:1–23. Joseph in Potiphar's House. Giving a glimpse of divine righteousness in a surprising way, 39:1 picks up the story line from 37:36. Joseph had arrived in Egypt and had been sold. The chapter reminds the reader that God is in control, and yet mountains and valleys are part of the Christian's daily journey with the Creator and Savior of the universe.

In spite of miserable circumstances, the Lord was with Joseph (39:2)—a statement that becomes the refrain of Joseph's story. Joseph undoubtedly felt alone many times in his suffering, but God was always close to him, as He is with all of those who suffer, to strengthen them. *Tsalakh* ("to prosper," "to be successful") is one of the key words in this story, and it is always connected to God's presence (vv. 2–3, 23). Potiphar is described as an officer of Pharaoh and captain of the guard (37:36; 39:1). The Hebrew term *saris* ("official" or "officer") appears over forty times in the OT and has been translated "eunuch," "court official," and "chamberlain" (1 Sam. 8:15; Is. 56:3–5; etc.). Clearly, in Potiphar's case, the classic sense of "eunuch" would not apply since he was married. Rather, he was a high official in Pharaoh's court. The second title, captain of the guard, is also a generic title that could be applied to a number of Egyptian offices.

Responding to Potiphar's trust, Joseph worked faithfully for him (39:4). The Hebrew term here denotes personal service instead of the generic word for a servant (Ex. 24:13; 1 Kin. 19:21). As the parallel texts suggest, this type of service involved grooming for leadership. Potiphar's household was blessed by the Lord because of Joseph (v. 5). The reference to blessing would serve

to remind the reader of a key element of God's covenant with Abraham (12:3), as well as a key theme of Genesis. God blesses people in order for them to be a blessing to others (see v. 5).

God blessed Joseph with success and an attractive physical appearance (39:5–6). The words used to describe Joseph's handsome form are uniquely applied to a male here (cf. 1 Sam. 16:18). It is naturally assumed that this combination made him desirable to Potiphar's wife (39:7), although the text does not explicitly say this. The context of the story suggests that there was some evil power tempting Joseph to sin, not only against Potiphar but also, more importantly, against God. Had he fallen into temptation, the narrative would have taken an unexpected turn, and perhaps the story of Joseph would never have been written. Wrong decisions can alter one's life in radical ways.

Potiphar's wife's continual pressure for Joseph to lie with her demonstrates Joseph's absolute commitment to God's moral values, even under great temptation. The garment left behind as a sign of refusal was used by the woman to construct a story aimed at destroying the one who refused her (Gen. 39:11–19). Joseph had gone into the house to do his work—not to invite temptation (v. 11). Potiphar's wife caught him, described with a verb (*tapas*) implying violence (Deut. 9:17; 22:28; 1 Kin. 11:30). Upon the return of her husband, she accused Joseph of attempted sexual assault. Her reference to Joseph's ethnicity (Gen. 39:17) implied a racial slur, not only to inflame racial tensions but to defend herself from any accusation of sexually provoking this particular foreign man. Her implication was that her husband was ultimately responsible for this "travesty." This is only the second time in Genesis that a member of Abraham's family is described as Hebrew (14:13).

Potiphar's response was rapid. He threw Joseph into Pharaoh's prison (v. 20). Yet in spite

Joseph in Egypt

There are two main theories regarding the time period when Joseph was in Egypt. One suggests that he was in Egypt during the Middle Kingdom (approx. 20th–17th centuries B.C.) and the other that he was there during the Second Intermediate Period (approx. 17th–16th centuries B.C.), a difference of approximately two hundred years.

1. Origin of the Theories. The Middle Kingdom theory (hereafter, MK) exists primarily because the Masoretic version of Exodus 12:40 pushes the Joseph narrative back to that period. Most modern translations of the Bible reflect this in the text. The Second Intermediate Period theory (hereafter, 2IP) exists primarily because the Septuagint and

Samaritan Pentateuch versions of Exodus 12:40 include time lived in Canaan before coming to Egypt. Most modern translations of the Bible include this option in the margin notes. Other chronological statements in the Bible (Ex. 6:14–25; 7:7; Gal. 3:16–17) seem to reflect this although there is debate on the issue.

2. *Semitic People in Egypt.* During the MK, a single ruler mostly controlled all of Egypt from the capital, first in the south at Thebes and later in the north near the Faiyum region at Itjtawy. During the 2IP, which followed the MK, more than one person claimed to be king, partly because armies of Semitic people invaded the land. Due to their more advanced weapon technology (compound bow, chariot, and battle-ax) and use of horses (apparently not in Egypt before this period), the Semitic people conquered the north and set up their capital at Avaris, while Egyptians ruled from the south at Thebes. The southern Egyptian rulers eventually pushed the northern Semitics out of Egypt, unifying the country in a new period call the New Kingdom (approx. 16th–11th centuries B.C.), which was the time of the Exodus.

3. *Key Issues in the Debate.* The two possible time periods during which Joseph may have resided in Egypt, according to these two theories, are about two hundred years apart. The two periods represent very different cultural realities in Egypt that affect one's understanding of the story in a number of key areas.

A. *Location of the Land of Goshen.* Joseph stated that his family would live near to him (Gen. 45:10). It can be assumed that Joseph's seat of authority was near the royal court. The MK theory puts that court in the south. The 2IP theory puts it in the north. If the land of Goshen is in the northeastern delta, as is generally believed, Joseph's claim that they would be near to him can be interpreted to support either theory. "Near" could mean that his family was at least in the same country that he was, as opposed to still living in the Holy Land (MK), or it could mean literal geographic closeness to the royal court in the north (2IP).

B. *Horses and Chariots.* Joseph was given a chariot to ride in, and horses were part of the livestock exchanged for food (Gen. 41:43; 46:29; 47:17). The MK theory argues that these details were later editorial additions

that were not actually part of the reality of the story but were added for other reasons or that archaeological evidence for horses is simply incomplete (MK). The 2IP theory argues that these details were actually part of the story and help to place it historically according to the available archaeological evidence.

C. *Abominable Shepherds.* Joseph instructed his brothers to tell Pharaoh that they were shepherds so he could put them in a part of Egypt removed from the rest of the Egyptian population because shepherds were abominable to Egyptians (46:34). Archaeologists have discovered that the ancient Egyptians were prejudiced against foreigners. However, there were Egyptians who owned flocks and herds (47:16–17; Ex. 9:1–7; 19–21). The MK theory argues that this statement by Joseph (46:34) means that *foreign* shepherds only were detested. The 2IP theory argues that there was a foreign ruling class Joseph's brothers would have been prejudicially associated with that all owned flocks and herds (47:6), and thus Pharaoh would have understood their need for separation (2IP).

4. *Further Elements in the Debate.* Beyond these three main interpretive issues, the debate continues. Supporters of the MK theory point to Semitic names on papyri from the MK—a canal dug in the MK that today is called Bar Yoseph, suggesting a potential memory—and records of officials from the MK who helped people during times of famine.

Supporters of the 2IP theory point to the change in land ownership from the *people* in the MK to the *king* in the New Kingdom as evidence that something happened during the 2IP famine to facilitate the switch (possibly the events of Gen. 47:18–26); archaeological evidence of Semitic people moving in to the Wadi Tumilat (the area generally accepted to be the land of Goshen) during the 2IP and various statements in Scripture can be interpreted to mean that Semitic people were ruling at the time (Gen. 39:1, 7, 14; 40:1, 22; 42:8; 43:32; 44:5; 45:2).

The difference between the two theories (approximately two hundred years) affects one's understanding of biblical chronology, particularly as it relates to interpreting other biblical statements about the length of time the Hebrews were in captivity (see "The Four-Hundred-Thirty-Year Sojourn," p. 211).

of his anger (v. 19), one gets the impression that he actually wanted to get Joseph out of harm's way (i.e., out of his wife's way). Biblical (and Egyptian) law demanded that a convicted rapist should be executed (Deut. 22:23–27), particularly in a situation involving distinct social classes, such as those of Joseph and Potiphar's wife. As the captain of the guard, Potiphar still controlled Joseph's destiny (or so he may have thought). The fact that the keeper of the prison committed all prisoners into Joseph's care (Gen. 39:21–23) may ultimately suggest Potiphar's influence over the prison, which was also under his jurisdiction. Yet neither Potiphar nor any other person controlled Joseph's life. The Lord was with Joseph and showed him *khesed* ("mercy," "kindness," "covenant faithfulness"; v. 21). In the midst of injustice and persecution, God's presence lightens even the darkest prison cell.

40:1–23. Joseph Interprets the Dreams of Pharaoh's Servants. The next chapter opens to a different scene, detailing the positive and negative turns in Joseph's story. From slave to second-in-command of Potiphar's house to prisoner to right hand of the prison warden was a journey that required longsuffering and inner strength. Joseph's interpretation of the dreams of two high court officials opened the way for God to save not only Joseph and his family but also Egypt and its neighboring countries. The two officials placed in prison were to be served and attended to by Joseph (40:1–4). Both the chief butler (or cupbearer) and the chief baker would have been responsible for preparing Pharaoh's food and protecting him from poisoning. These positions formed part of the inner circle of ancient kings. The biblical text does not contain any indications as to the cause of Pharaoh's anger (v. 2). But their roles in relationship to food and the penalty for failure to protect the pharaoh suggest that they may have been charged with a crime related to the food of the king, even attempted murder.

Dreams and their interpretation, an important ingredient of Joseph's story, reappear at this point (cf. 37:5–11). Both high-ranking prisoners had dreams and shared them with Joseph, who, in turn, interpreted them. The question "Do not interpretations belong to God?" was in itself a polemic against the Egyptian methods of interpreting dreams. Joseph was stating that only God, his God, could provide accurate interpretations of dreams (41:16, 25, 28; Dan. 2:22, 28, 47). Following the retelling of the dreams by both

officials, Joseph quickly offered their meaning. The biblical text does not specifically mention a time of prayer (as in Dan. 2:18). Joseph's admonition to the chief cupbearer to remember him (v. 14) indicated his confidence in the interpretation and represented the first expression of frustration on Joseph's part. Up to this point, Joseph had been quiet in the face of injustice and displayed a distinct character change from the self-important seventeen-year-old from Canaan (Gen. 37).

While the interpretation of the butler's dream promised restoration, the interpretation of the baker's dream suggested complete disaster. His execution was described in terms that an Egyptian would consider to indicate death without an afterlife, the worst that could happen to the baker. A brief summary statement (vv. 20–22) describes the fulfillment of the dreams and confirms Joseph's interpretation (on the importance of the third day, see 22:3–6). Egyptian sources provide no evidence for the celebration of the birthdays of pharaohs before the first millennium B.C. However, it may be possible that the "day of birth" refers to Pharaoh's ascension to the throne, a celebration that is evidenced in contemporary sources. In spite of the fact that the chief butler forgot Joseph (v. 23), God continued to work behind the scenes.

41:1–36. Joseph Interprets Pharaoh's Dreams. Two additional dreams marked the pivotal point of Joseph's life. Pharaoh's need for reliable interpretation required a capable interpreter. Joseph, long forgotten by the chief butler, was brought before Pharaoh and provided the interpretation of the two dreams. Joseph's unsolicited counsel paved the way for the great reversal. No prison, no chief butler, and no pharaoh could obstruct God's plans.

Pharaoh's two dreams disturbed the Egyptian king—particularly because no one could interpret them (v. 8; cf. Job 7:14; Dan 2:1, 3, 10; 4:5, 19). Unlike Nebuchadnezzar many centuries later, Pharaoh at least described his dreams to his magicians. Double dreams appear in other ANE contexts (e.g., Gilgamesh epic, Gudea of Lagash). This repetition heightened the importance of the dream's content. Pharaoh's dreams (Gen. 41:1–7) first involved seven healthy-looking, well-fed cows being devoured by seven ugly and gaunt cows. In the second dream, seven plump and ripe heads of grain were devoured by seven thin and scorched heads of grain. Pharaoh's dream was bizarre. Even in ancient Egypt, cows did not eat cows, and heads of grain did not devour other heads of grain.

In this dramatic moment, the chief butler remembered (cf. 40:14) his error (lit. "sins") in forgetting Joseph, and he came to recall Joseph's skill as a dream interpreter (41:9–13). The main point of his concise summary of chapter 40 is that Joseph's interpretation came to pass just as he had said it would (41:13). From the butler's perspective, Joseph was someone who truly knew the art and the science of dream interpretation.

Pharaoh's reaction was quick and immediate: Joseph was brought into the royal presence after he had shaved and changed into clean clothing. Male Egyptians usually shaved their faces and sometimes also their heads while Asiatics (or Semites) wore beards. The implied washing, shaving, and clothing rites often marked the transition from one state to another (e.g., the sons of Aaron during the priestly ordination ritual [Lev. 8:6–13]). Joseph's reply to Pharaoh's question was bold, considering the fact that the pharaohs were considered gods (v. 16). Joseph's denial that he could interpret dreams on his own was a clear indication of the divine source of Joseph's capability (cf. 40:8; Dan. 2:27–28; 2 Cor. 3:5). Joseph averred that "God" would give the answer (v. 16), and thus he introduced the Egyptian ruler to *'elohim*, the God of Abraham, Isaac, and Jacob. Joseph seems to have used a generic term for God in an effort to speak in a manner that Pharaoh could relate to. The story is an excellent blueprint for missiologically sound communication.

Following Pharaoh's retelling of the two dreams (41:17–24), Joseph began his point-by-point interpretation with another statement of faith: he declared that in these dreams, God had shown Pharaoh what He was about to do (41:25). Pharaoh needed to know that his country was under the domain of Joseph's God and part of a larger plan that involved Egypt's survival through its connection to the covenant family. Both dreams communicated the same reality of seven years of plenty, followed by seven years of famine and hunger (41:25–32). In both dreams, the fat and plentiful were devoured by the lean and famished. The Nile flooded every year, depositing rich silt from upriver on the fields of Egypt. This natural fertilizer resulted in an excess of produce. However, if the annual Nile flooding was too high or too low, a famine was sure to follow. Too much water, and the rich silt would be washed downriver into the Mediterranean Sea. Too little, and the water carrying the silt would not reach the fields. It is not clear which was the case during this period.

Joseph's unsolicited counsel was fronted by the particle *'atah*, "now," which is sometimes used to introduce a new idea or section (41:33–36). It is also often used in the OT to introduce the lesson of a story (cf. Is. 5:3, 5). Here the particle introduces the new ideas that Joseph would offer to Pharaoh. Confronted with the magicians' inability to interpret the dreams, Pharaoh realized that he did not have a "discerning and wise man" (41:33; cf. Deut. 4:6; Prov. 10:13; 14:33; 16:21; Hos. 14:9). In order to face this extraordinary drought, Pharaoh needed someone whom he could trust.

41:37–57. Joseph's Rise to Power. Joseph's rise to power was unprecedented and functioned as an illustration of divine deliverance. Thirteen years after his arrival in Egypt (41:46), Joseph's life had gone from slave to supervisor and from prisoner to second-in-command in Egypt. From a human standpoint, this was something that would have been unimaginable if the ruling class were made up of Egyptians. It is slightly more possible if they were also Semitic (i.e., the Hyksos), as Joseph was. Whichever group was then in power, God's providence was advancing Joseph's standing.

Joseph's counsel (lit. "word") was well received by Pharaoh and his court (v. 37). Pharaoh's rhetorical question emphasized the presence of the spirit of God in Joseph (v. 38). Pharaoh's observation recognized Joseph's premise—that is, that he had not relied on his own intelligence to interpret Pharaoh's dreams. The reference to Pharaoh's house/palace (v. 40) marks the third "house" that Joseph supervised (Potiphar's house, the prison, and then a palace). The exact nature of Joseph's title has been debated, but it appears that it was not that of vizier. Perhaps Pharaoh created a new position—something that the court would undoubtedly be more tolerant of than the demotion of an existing official. That Joseph was set over the entire "land" of Egypt (v. 41) might serve to highlight the agricultural focus of Joseph's service. A signet ring, new clothing, a gold chain, and the right to ride in the second chariot (see "Joseph in Egypt," p. 183) all functioned as markers of Joseph's new status (vv. 42–43). It was common in the ANE to have servants precede a dignitary to draw attention to his presence (cf. 2 Sam. 15:1; 1 Kin. 1:5; Esth. 6:9). The term *abrek* (v. 43) is a rare Hebrew term that may be related to an Egyptian term indicating homage, and it is translated variously as "bow the knee," "make way" or "attention." A name change indicated authority and also a new identity (Dan 1:7). Joseph used this Egyptian name, but the available evidence in Genesis points toward his retention of his faith in God.

The seven years of plenty were also reflected in Joseph's personal life (Gen. 41:46–52): he married the daughter of an influential official and had two sons. The high priest of On (Heliopolis in Greek and Iunu in Egyptian, the cult center for the worship of Ra) held the title "Greatest of Seers." Together with Memphis and Thebes, On was one of the most revered cities of ancient Egypt. While previous children had been named by the family matriarchs, Joseph named his boys himself (vv. 51–52). That Joseph was fruitful (v. 52) marked God's partial fulfillment of His promise to the patriarchs (17:6, 20; 28:3). The text does not indicate whether Joseph influenced his wife to become a believer in Yahweh, but given Joseph's overall faithfulness to God, it is possible.

According to schedule, the years of plenty ended (41:53). The divine prediction, given to the pharaoh in a dream and interpreted by Joseph, was finally fulfilled, but Egypt had an abundance of food, thanks to the wisdom God had given to His servant. The stage was set for the encounter with Joseph's brothers.

42:1–38. Jacob's Sons Buy Grain in Egypt. After the great bounty followed the great hunger. Jacob's sons came to Egypt in search of food and, without recognizing him, encountered their brother Joseph. The chapter describes people in transition and their relationships to one another.

This is the first appearance of Jacob following the loss of Joseph. Though old and bereaved, Jacob was still the head of his household. He discovered (lit. "saw," 42:1, and "heard," v. 2) that Egypt had grain and ordered his sons to go down to buy food in order to assure the family's survival. The last part of v. 1 contains a perplexing phrase. Most translations read something like, "Why are you looking at each other?" The root ra'ah, "to see," is well known; however, the verbal form used here means elsewhere "to meet in combat" or "face one another in battle" (2 Kin. 14:8, 11; 2 Chr. 25:17, 21). The author may have used the phrase to highlight the continued strife in Jacob's household. Jacob sent only ten brothers and kept Benjamin at home.

Joseph's introduction as governor (v. 6) explains why the brothers bowed down to him (in partial fulfillment of 37:7–10). The Hebrew term *shallit*, which is usually translated as "governor," is very rare and may reflect the author's challenge to find an appropriate Hebrew equivalent for Joseph's position in Egypt. Joseph pretended not to know them and spoke brusquely to the brothers (vv. 7, 30). Speaking through an interpreter in a different language (v. 23), the adult Joseph was in an unexpected position of power. He saw his brothers and recognized them immediately while they did *not* recognize him (cf. 37:32–33; see "Joseph in Egypt," p. 183). About twenty-one years had passed since they had sold him into slavery, when all of them had been in their late teens and early twenties. In their late thirties and early forties by this point, all had changed significantly. Joseph was dressed as an Egyptian leader speaking to them in the Egyptian language. Recognizing somebody or something is a key concept in this chapter (42:7–8). Joseph not only recognized his brothers. He also remembered the dreams God had given him about them (v. 9). He knowingly tested the moral fiber of the hapless brothers.

Joseph's charge that his brothers were spies (v. 9) was a serious accusation, but it provided the occasion for the brothers of Joseph to give him information he wanted about the family. The brothers were then put into prison for three days to await a final decision. On the third day, Joseph modified his plan: he would detain only one of the brothers, but they would be required to return with their youngest brother to demonstrate the truthfulness of their account. Joseph introduced an important element in the tense conversation. He mentioned that his fear of God (v. 18) was the rationale for his changed plan. Invoking God reassured his brothers and also introduced God into the conversation. The brothers then talked amongst themselves about their guilt; they imagined their current situation to be a punishment for their treatment of Joseph (v. 21). This realization was theologically significant because it highlighted a clear relationship between guilt (or sin) and punishment. Time had not taken away their guilt but had only amplified it.

Upon hearing their conversation, Joseph turned away and wept (v. 24). The brothers' confession of guilt moved him. The text did not provide an explicit rationale for the selection of Simeon (v. 24) as the hostage. However, since Reuben as the firstborn had sought to intervene on Joseph's behalf (v. 22), the second oldest son was to stand surety. Simeon had also been one of two leaders in the cruel revenge on the Shechemites (34:25; cf. 49:5–7).

On their return trip, the brothers found their payment (lit. "silver") in their grain sacks (42:25–28). This may have been a conscious nod to their earlier greed, selling Joseph for twenty shekels (in weight) of silver (37:28). Upon their arrival in Jacob's camp in Canaan, the brothers reported all that had happened to Jacob. His reaction revealed his pain, and he felt bereaved because he assumed that Joseph was dead and that Simeon might die too (or remain in prison), and he thus refused to allow Benjamin to be lost also (v. 36). His resolute rejection of the idea of Reuben's two sons (v. 37) or Benjamin going to Egypt was accompanied by the observation that Benjamin was the only one of Rachel's sons left (v. 38). It was not a secret in the family that Rachel was the favored wife and that hers were the favored sons. Jacob's family remained divided and in need of healing.

43:1-34. Benjamin Travels with His Brothers to Egypt.

Facing an increasingly devastating drought, Jacob finally agreed to allow Benjamin to travel with his brothers to Egypt as their only chance of survival. In Egypt, Joseph's encounter with his brothers culminated in a feast. The extensive dialogues in this chapter form the backdrop to the coming final test of Joseph's brothers in chapter 44.

Surviving the severe (lit. "heavy") famine (cf. 41:56-57) in Canaan (i.e., the land) required a concerted effort. However, unlike his response in 42:1, Jacob was not proactive (cf. 43:10-11). He wavered. The dialogue between Judah and Jacob revisited the known facts (vv. 3-10): in order to demonstrate their integrity, the brothers could return to Egypt only with Benjamin in tow. Israel seems to have concluded that his sons had given information to the Egyptian man that he had not requested from them, namely, that they had another brother. In doing this, they had increased his fears. Judah clarified that the man specifically asked them whether they had another brother, making it impossible for them to hide the fact. Judah offered himself as surety (Gen. 43:9), willing to carry the blame. In this exchange, Judah revealed his deepening character transformation; his tribe would become prominent among Israel's sons (49:8-10) and would include the Messiah (Matt. 1:1-16; Luke 3:23-38).

Finally, Israel agreed to let Benjamin travel with his brothers to Egypt (vv. 11-14)—with a gift in hand (Heb. minkhah; cf. 32:13 and sidebar on 4:3-5). Judah referred to Benjamin as a na'ar (43:8). This word can encompass a whole range of ages, from a boy to a young man. Based on the internal chronology of Genesis, Benjamin must have been in his twenties since he was born prior to Joseph's trip to Egypt (Gen. 37)

yet after the family dwelt in and fled from Shechem (Gen. 34-35; cf. 30:25-43; 31:41). Jacob sent the brothers with the prayer that 'el shaddai (17:1) would grant them mercy from the ruler of Egypt.

The "men" (not "the brothers" or "the sons") went to Egypt and appeared before Joseph (43:15). Joseph was most interested in the presence of his brother Benjamin, not the gift or the returned payment, and he ordered his steward to prepare a feast in his home (vv. 15-17). Joseph's brothers immediately recognized this as an abnormality and were afraid (v. 18); they decided to make a clean slate regarding the return of their payment (vv. 19-22). Unbeknownst to them, they had passed a character test. The Egyptian steward, a foreigner, ultimately affirmed the God of Jacob's sons: he said that God had given them "treasure" (v. 23; cf. Job 3:21; Prov. 2:4; Is. 45:3) in their sacks. The opening phrase is shalom lakem—"peace to you" (translated contextually in this verse variously as "be at ease," "it is alright," "rest assured," etc.). These Hebrew words are a typical Eastern greeting. The word shalom is another significant key word in this section (cf. its appearance in vv. 27-28) and implies more than the absence of war. Finally, Simeon was released to his brothers—all seemed well.

Verses 26-30 include an important dialogue between Joseph and his (unsuspecting) brothers after they had given him their gifts and bowed down (vv. 26, 28; cf. 37:7-10). Moved by the sight of Benjamin and the good news about his father's well-being, Joseph slipped out and wept (v. 30). The opening words of v. 30—that Joseph hurried away because kamar rakhamim—literally mean that his "compassion/mercy warmed" toward his brother. This phrase is used elsewhere to describe a mother's feeling for her dying child (1 Kin. 3:26), which demonstrates the deeply emotional nature of the interaction.

The seating arrangements at the meal included three groups: (1) the brothers, seated in their birth order; (2) Joseph seated alone; and (3) the Egyptians, who also ate by themselves. To eat with Hebrews was considered to be a to'ebah ("an abomination," "detestable," "loathsome"; v. 32; see "Joseph in Egypt," p. 183). This comment both anticipated the changed relationship between Hebrews and Egyptians in Exodus 1 and, at the same time, emphasized the fact that Israel would not be absorbed and integrated into Egyptian society. Benjamin's fivefold portion did not result in envy—the brothers thus passed another character test (v. 34).

**44:1–34. Joseph's Cup and Judah's Interven-
tion.** Prior to reconciliation, there is conflict.
Crises bring out the best (and the worst) in
people—as exemplified in Genesis 44. Judah's
transformation was illustrated in his speech
and represented the change in the characters of
Joseph's brothers.

The idyllic meal concluded with the ultimate
test of genuineness: Joseph's silver cup. The Hebrew term suggests a large vessel; there is another
word for a smaller "cup" (Ex. 25:31, 33–34). In
Mesopotamia, divination was performed by observing liquids being mixed in a large cup (e.g.,
oil poured into water or milk is one example
from Mesopotamian sources; cf. Lev. 19:26; Deut.
18:10 for the biblical prohibition of divination). In
Egypt, gods were consulted in other ways. Divination by cup is not indicated in the archaeological record in Egypt, but this does not exclude its
practice. It would seem unlikely that Joseph actually practiced divination, but the cup may have
been designed for that purpose, even if Joseph
did not use it in this way.

Judah's increasing preeminence among the
brothers is highlighted in 44:14, where he is
mentioned first in the list. The description of the
brothers' prostration before Joseph employs a
stronger term (*napal*) than the one used in 43:26,
one that expresses complete submission. Joseph's
rhetorical question in 44:15 highlighted the hopelessness of the situation for Jacob's sons: they
were foreigners without any rights caught stealing the divination cup of the second-in-command
of Egypt. Judah's response included an acknowledgment of their desperate situation, leading to
a theologically important moment in the Joseph
narrative: Judah declared that God had disclosed
their guilt (v. 16). It is possible that this comment
points to an admission of earlier guilt. Judah's
recognition underlined the biblical notion that
sin is foremost an affront to God (Is. 59:2), as
Joseph's earlier reply to Potiphar's wife indicated
(39:9). Both Judah and Joseph had reached the
same point independently in moments of crisis.
Judah's offer of collective slavery was rejected by
Joseph (44:17), using oath language (cf. v. 7).

Judah's speech not only effectively communicated the grief and mourning of the father but
also represented a high point in the transformation of Judah himself from a selfish man into
one who was ready to take the place of another
in suffering.

45:1–28. Joseph's Encounters in Egypt. Reconciliation and forgiveness are the key words of this
chapter. Joseph's self-disclosure created tension

and fear in his brothers that was ultimately alleviated by locating everything within the greater
picture of God's actions (often behind the scenes
of history) for His covenant people.

The tension that had built up in the Joseph narrative was about to be released. Genesis 45 is the
theological center of the story. Following Judah's
moving speech, Joseph could no longer contain
himself (v. 1). While he had been able to show restraint in 43:31, this time he was unable to do so.
Once the Egyptian attendants had been ushered
out, it was time to make himself known to his
brothers. Men become brothers when grace and
mercy are extended (cf. 44:1, 3). Joseph's weeping (cf. 42:24; 43:30) was heard even by Pharaoh's household (45:2; see "Joseph in Egypt,"
p. 183)—a significant detail picked up in v. 16,
anticipating the official resolution involving the
settlement of Jacob's family.

The shocking and staccato "I am Joseph" (a
nominal sentence lit. translated "I Joseph") was
followed by the seemingly superfluous question
about whether Jacob was still alive (v. 3; cf.
43:27–28; 44:18–34). "Your father" (43:27) becomes "my father." However, his brothers could
not answer him, for they were quite fearful.
Joseph's second self-disclosure contained the
apposition "your brother" (Gen. 45:4) as well as
the one piece of information (that he had been
"sold into Egypt") that only his brothers would
have known.

"God sent me" (v. 5), a phrase expressed three
times in varied forms, represents the theological
center of Joseph's story (vv. 7, 8; cf. 50:19–21;
Acts 7:9–10). The term *shalakh*, "sent," is used
to describe somebody sent on a specific mission
(Gen. 28:5; Deut. 34:11; Neh. 6:5; Jer. 19:14).
It speaks in a unique way about divine providence in the life of His servants. They may not
hear His voice, but He is constantly present,
leading them in His wisdom according to what
is best for them. Joseph's ability to provide a
safe haven for God's covenant people for the remaining five years of severe famine (v. 6) was
part of God's design.

Joseph's next imperatives in v. 9 emphasized
both his longing as well as the seriousness of the
situation. Joseph's affirmation that it was God
who had made him lord of Egypt (v. 9) reminded
the brothers, and reminds the reader, of the God
of history who was and is active in the affairs of
this planet. Similar to the earlier detailed instruction to the steward (44:4–5), Joseph sent a very
specific message to his father (45:9). After his
speech, Joseph embraced his brothers and kissed
them—two important activities expressing love

and concern in Eastern cultures. Only then did his brothers converse with him (v. 15).

Once Pharaoh heard the report (lit. the "sound" or "voice") concerning the presence of Joseph's brothers in Egypt, he supported Joseph's plans (vv. 16–20). The "fat [*kheleb*] of the land" (cf. Is. 1:19) metaphorically describes the ideal conditions of the richness of the land (*kheleb* is often used to describe the best produce or animals; cf. Num. 18:12; Deut. 32:14). Carts (Gen. 45:19) refer most likely to wagons used for transporting goods and drawn by oxen. The reference to clothing (v. 22) completes the transformation of Joseph's brothers and links this section to the opening of the Joseph story. Benjamin's five garments, as well as the three hundred shekels in weight of silver that Joseph gave him, apparently did not generate the same jealous response from the brothers as the robe of many colors (37:3) so many years before. The final instruction in v. 24 from Joseph was to not *ragaz*. This has been variously translated as "become troubled," "quarrel," "worry," or "be angry." This is the only occurrence of the verb in Genesis. Elsewhere, its more literal meaning involves shaking—in fear (Ex. 15:14) or in rage (Prov. 29:9). The final verses of the chapter mark a wonderful contrast to the two previous returns of Jacob's sons, which had caused grief and heartache (37:33–35; 42:36–38). Jacob's reaction is described in terms of physical phenomena. Verse 26 reads literally that "his heart became numb," and v. 27 refers to his spirit (*ruakh*, the same word for "breath") being revived. The final words of the story are Jacob's. The transformation of Joseph's brothers was significant: their first word to their father was concerning Joseph (and not about the gifts, invitation, etc.).

46:1—47:12. Jacob and His Family Move to Egypt. This account of Jacob's journey to Egypt also includes a detailed listing of the names of his male descendants who accompanied him to Goshen. Before initiating the travel to Egypt, sacrifices were offered, and God's voice was heard again. In a night vision (v. 2; 15:5, 12; 20:6; 26:24: 28:12; etc.), God addressed the patriarch using his original name. The usage of the two names Israel and Jacob in this section reminds the reader of the weakness of human design as well as God's power to transform a situation. The Lord's declaration, "I am God" (46:3), provided Jacob with the credentials needed to assure him that God's divine presence would accompany the family to Egypt. The imagery here is of a bodyguard guaranteeing protection and

the fulfillment of earlier promises. The prediction that Joseph's hand would be on his father's eyes (v. 4) was a divine promise of a peaceful death.

Following divine encouragement, there was human engagement. Jacob left Beersheba and, together with the entire family, was carried in the carts to Egypt (vv. 5–7). The mention of Jacob's daughters (v. 7) in the list of people going to Egypt suggests that Jacob had more than one daughter (besides Dinah). The migration of Jacob's household included all his descendants.

Verses 8–27 list the names of Jacob's offspring up to the third generation, thus identifying all who went into Egypt. The mention of the children of Israel (lit. "sons of Israel"; v. 8) anticipates Exodus 1:7, where the people had grown into a nation whose size threatened Egypt. Leah's children and grandchildren are listed first (vv. 8–15), followed by Zilpah's (vv. 16–18), Rachel's (vv. 19–22), and finally Bilhah's (vv. 23–25). Ohad, a son of Simeon, is not included in the lists of Num. 26:12 and 1 Chr. 4:24—it is possible that he died without leaving any descendants. In the list of Judah's offspring, Er and Onan are still included (Gen. 46:12) even though they had already died in Canaan (38:6–10; 46:12). The final two verses of this section include relative and grand totals (vv. 26–27). In total, sixty-six descendants (two of them female) born to Jacob and his sons traveled to Egypt. Seventy (Ex. 1:5) represents the grand total, which includes the three living mothers and Jacob himself. Stephen in Acts (Acts 7:14) stated that the total was seventy-five, which may reflect the Septuagint, which has that number both here and in Exodus 1:5. Joseph and his two sons were not counted in the seventy but may have been counted in the seventy-five. The remaining two could be the two sons of Judah who had died (Gen. 46:12). The Septuagint in 46:20, 27 speaks about other sons of Joseph, who could have been added to the list in the Hebrew text to reach the number seventy.

The final section, describing the emotional encounter between father and long-lost son, as well as the presentation of the members of Joseph's family before Pharaoh, concludes most of the action in Joseph's story (46:28—47:12). Joseph took his chariot to meet his father, Israel (see "Joseph in Egypt," p. 183), which marked his high status. Father and son embraced, and Joseph wept on his father's neck (46:29). Joseph's repeated reference to the historic occupation of his family captured the Egyptian distrust of Semitic seminomadic people (46:34). The benefit of a clear separation between Jacob's family and the Egyptians was twofold: first, by maintaining their distinct lifestyle and expertise, Israel would remain a foreign people group (cf. Gen. 15:13; 17:8; Deut. 10:19; 26:5; Ps. 105:23) and would not assimilate into the Egyptian culture; second, it would help Israel remember the divine promises involving Canaan. Egypt was not their land.

Joseph presented five (unnamed) brothers as well as his father to Pharaoh (Gen. 47:1–10). He particularly emphasized the fact that they had arrived with their flocks and their herds (v. 1) and had moved to Goshen (cf. 45:10; 46:34). Pharaoh's first question involved the occupation of the brothers (47:3). The brothers' reply, that they were shepherds, was different from the description that Joseph had suggested (46:34)—that is, that they worked with livestock. They used the exact term that had earlier been identified as abhorrent to the Egyptians. Pharaoh told them that the land of Egypt was before them (47:6). This represented an open invitation to choose the land that was best suited for the needs of Joseph's family. Pharaoh's search for competent men for his livestock (see "Joseph in Egypt," p. 183) was another open door and offered Joseph's brothers legal protection. Pharaoh's hospitality was based on his high regard for Joseph. Finally, Jacob was brought before Pharaoh, who showed great respect to the aged man, who was, at this point, 130 years old. Jacob blessed Pharaoh. Jacob's reference to his "pilgrimage" made use of the same Hebrew root that marks sojourning as a foreigner (e.g., 12:10; 47:4). Abraham, Isaac, Jacob, and Joseph were all foreigners and pilgrims waiting to see the fulfillment of God's promises (cf. Heb. 11:8–16). The summary clause of this section describes how Joseph provided his family with property, or a possession (a legal title to a piece of ground; v. 11). God had promised Abraham possession of Canaan (17:8). The inclusion of the name of the land of Rameses (v. 11) as another term for Goshen occurs only here (when they arrived in the land) and in Exodus 12:37 (when they left). In Exodus 1:11, the Hebrews built a supply city with a similar name. In Hebrew, the spelling of the name of the supply city (Ex. 1:11) is different than the spelling of the name of the land (Gen. 47:11; Ex. 12:37), and they were certainly not in the same location. Jacob and his family did not live in the city that later generations of Hebrews built.

47:13–26. Joseph's Wise Administration of the Famine. From Goshen's relative safety and comfort, the reader's view is directed to the larger picture of the massive famine. Joseph's astute management made it possible for the Egyptians to use their silver (vv. 13–14), their herds (vv. 15–17), and their land rights (vv. 18–26) to buy back the grain they had been required to pay as a tax during the years of plenty. Horses are mentioned (v. 17) as one type of animal that Joseph was willing to trade for food. The archaeological record does not indicate that horses were in Egypt before the Second Intermediate Period (17th to 16th centuries B.C.), when they appeared in burials. After this (in the New Kingdom [16th to 11th centuries B.C.] and following), horses are represented in iconography with the Egyptian military and as a status symbol for kings. The horse was associated with nobility, so this indicates that even those of status were in need of food.

There are two possible ways of translating Genesis 47:21. The Hebrew text reads, "He removed them to the cities," perhaps meaning that Joseph reorganized the population, probably temporarily, according to the cities in which the grain was stored. The Septuagint and the Samaritan Pentateuch read, "He made them slaves," meaning that the people were indebted to or working for the pharaoh. The difference can be explained by a scribal error confusing two Hebrew consonants that look very much alike.

The tax exemption of the powerful Egyptian priestly class (v. 22) highlighted their importance and corresponded to known periods from Egyptian history where the Egyptian crown did not tax priestly estates (the most famous is recorded on the Rosetta Stone from the Ptolemaic Period). The 20 percent tax rate on the produce of the land was the same during the famine as it had been during the years of plenty (v. 24; cf. 41:34). Joseph readily acknowledged "buying" both the people and their land (v. 23). Thus, despite the huge economic shift away from private ownership by the people to ownership by the government, the people expressed gratitude to Joseph for saving their lives (47:25; cf. 45:7; 50:20). This highlighted the severity of the crisis and Joseph's effective management of it. Thus, the picture of the people becoming Pharaoh's slaves/servants must be understood in the framework of ancient societies: the patronage system provided protection and security in an interconnected world.

47:27–31. Jacob Prepares for His Death. A description of seventeen years of peaceful living in Egypt (47:28) is followed by Jacob's preparation for his death.

The description of Israel's growth (v. 27) utilizes creation language (Gen. 1:28; cf. notes on Ex. 1:7). The death of Jacob is mentioned several times and brings to an end the patriarchal narrative (47:28–31; 48:21–22; 49:29–32). This section functions as the introductory summary statement, prior to more detailed descriptions. Note the distinction between Israel, the people, (47:27) and Jacob, the patriarch (v. 28). God's promises had been fulfilled: Jacob had seen his family safely established in Egypt, and they were multiplying greatly (v. 27), which is later highlighted in the transition chapter of Exodus 1 (Ex. 1:7, 12, 20).

48:1–22. Jacob Blesses Joseph and His Sons. The visit of Joseph and his two sons marks the beginning of the end. Jacob was settling his affairs and preparing for the important final blessings. A historic review is often part of rituals involving blessings or covenants.

Jacob's adoption of the two sons of Joseph was unexpected (v. 5). Reuben and Simeon, although mentioned, would lose their prominence among the descendants of Jacob (Gen. 49:3–7). Joseph, who was the firstborn of Jacob's favorite wife (although his eleventh son), received the double blessing of the birthright by the inclusion of his two sons. In the adoption process, children were placed upon or close to one's knees to symbolize giving birth. To remind all that Joseph was considered his firstborn and thus received the birthright, Jacob recalled the death of his beloved favorite wife Rachel.

"Who are these?" (48:8) was not only a question stemming from Jacob's poor eyesight but was also most likely an expression related to the adoption process. The practice may have required the verbal identification of those being adopted. Joseph's response was part of the official adoption ritual, leading to Jacob's blessing. The scene contains clear echoes of the earlier scene in which Jacob "stole" Esau's blessing from his father, Isaac (cf. Gen. 27). Common elements include an introductory question (27:18; 48:8), the reference to eye trouble (27:1; 48:10), and the embrace and kiss that is part of the blessing (27:27; 48:10). However, while Isaac had blessed Jacob unwittingly, Jacob's blessing was deliberate. Joseph's response to his father's blessing (he bowed down; v. 12) reflected his respect and love.

Jacob, contrary to Joseph's expectation, placed the right hand not on the firstborn but on Ephraim while Joseph himself received the blessing of his father as the firstborn of Rachel. The practice of assigning the blessing of the firstborn to the second son appears several times in Genesis and reveals God's freedom to elect whomever He wants according to His purpose. Jacob's blessing was prophetically significant. Ephraim did become more prominent than Manasseh. His tribe came to represent the whole northern kingdom (Is. 7:2, 5; Hos. 9:13). Jacob's blessing highlights two important divine characteristics. Because God had fed Jacob (using a verb associated with shepherding) and redeemed him, He would do the same for Joseph's two sons (vv. 15–16). The reference to redemption or deliverance is the first occurrence of this theologically important term (*go'el*), one which is used repeatedly to refer to God's redemptive activity (cf. Ruth 4:1, 6, 8; Ps. 71:4; Jer. 31:10–11).

Joseph reacted to Jacob's apparent error, and his attempt to correct the order was met by strong insistence. While Joseph was displeased, Jacob refused to surrender his prerogative and choice (48:17–20). Distinct from the Genesis 27 story, God's will is not specifically made clear in the narrative.

49:1–28. Jacob's Final Words to His Sons. Jacob's last words are in the form of a testament to his sons written in poetry. It is prophetic in nature. See "The Sons of Jacob and His Final Blessing" (p. 193) for a summary of the most important facts of this testament.

Most of the testaments are comprised of one or two verses. However, the extent and content of Jacob's final words emphasized the importance of two sons in particular—Judah (vv. 8–12) and Joseph (vv. 22–26). While not the firstborn, Judah's character transformation, described in the previous chapters in the Joseph narrative, had prepared him for a more significant leadership role. This, combined with the fact that Reuben (Gen. 35:22; 49:3–4) and Simeon and Levi (Gen. 34:25, 30; 49:5) had all been found wanting, left Judah as the next in line. Although he made poor choices early in life (Gen. 37:26; 38:1–18), he allowed the Tamar incident (Gen. 38:24–26) to humble and transform him. Jesus's messianic title of "the Lion of the tribe of Judah" (Rev. 5:5) is based on this text and the fact that lions were symbols of kingship in the ANE. The scepter (*shebet*) of the first line of v. 10 is parallel to the *mekhoqeq* (variously rendered as "lawgiver," "ruler's staff," "prince") in the second line of the verse. Overall, the text of 49:10 represents a challenge for translators, particularly the phrase mentioning Shiloh. Some render it as "until Shiloh comes."

Other suggested translations include "until he to whom it belongs shall come" or (based on a textual change) "until tribute comes to him." The Hebrew term is the same as the place name Shiloh but seems to hint at a future powerful leader of Judah. The text is practically quoted in Ezekiel 21:27 to describe a Davidic King. The passage in Genesis announces the arrival of a future king from Judah and points beyond David to Christ as the true messianic King (see "Introduction to the Pentateuch," p. 120).

The imagery of the even longer section describing the blessing of Joseph is varied and includes images denoting agricultural fertility (v. 22) and military prowess (vv. 23–24). The divine epithet *'abir*, "mighty," appears repeatedly in the OT (Ps. 132:2, 5; Is. 49:26; 60:16) and is followed by two additional metaphors: the Shepherd (cf. Gen. 48:15; Pss. 23:1; 80:1; Heb. 13:20) and the unique "Stone of Israel," which is distinct from the more often used "Rock" (Heb. *tsor*) of Israel (Deut. 32:15, 18, 30–31). Jacob's God had many characteristics and metaphorical names, but ultimately, He was the familiar God of his father (v. 25; cf. Gen. 49:25).

49:29—50:14. Jacob's Death and Burial. Following Jacob's final words, this section describes Jacob's death and interment in Canaan. The final scene recounting Jacob's death echoes his final words of admonition regarding his burial place (cf. 47:29–30). Interestingly, this death scene is referred to in the list of faith heroes in Hebrews 11:21. Jacob's expression of faith involved his blessings as well as his worship. He recognized that the land of God's promise was not in Egypt but in Canaan. After he had finished instructing his sons, he drew his feet up and died. Breathing one's last breath and being gathered to one's people is

The Sons of Jacob and His Final Blessing

Mother	Son (birth order)	Meaning of name	Birth reference	Order within blessing	Keyword(s) of blessing	Blessing reference
Leah	Reuben	"Behold, a son"	29:32	1	*pakhaz* (reckless, unstable)	49:3–4
	Simeon	"Hearing"	29:33	2	*'ap* (anger) and *qashah* (cruel)	49:5–7
	Levi	"Attachment"	29:34	3	*'ap* (anger) and *qashah* (cruel)	49:5–7
	Judah	"Praise"	29:35	4	*'aryeh* (lion)	49:8–12
Bilhah	Dan	"Judgment"	30:6	7	*nakhash* (serpent or snake)	49:16–18
	Naphtali	"Wrestle"	30:8	10	*'ayyalah* (deer or doe)	49:21
Zilpah	Gad	"Good fortune"	30:11	8	*gud* (attack)	49:19
	Asher	"Happy"	30:13	9	*shamen lekhem* (rich food)	49:20
Leah	Issachar	"Reward"	30:18	6	*khamod gerem* (strong donkey)	49:14–15
	Zebulun	"Abode"	30:20	5	*'aniyyah* (ship)	49:13
Rachel	Joseph	"May He add"	30:24	11	*parah* (bear fruit)	49:22–26
	Benjamin	"Son of the right hand"	35:18	12	*ze'eb* (wolf)	49:27

a formulaic expression marking death in Genesis (cf. 25:8, 17; 35:29). Jacob's fetal-like position reflects Scripture's understanding of death as sleep (e.g., Pss. 6:5; 115:17; Eccl. 9:5; Dan. 12:2; John 11:11–13).

At Jacob's death, Joseph collapsed onto his father, wept over him, and kissed him (Gen. 50:1). The strength of the emotional bond between Joseph and his father is highlighted by the minimal role that Joseph's brothers played. They first appear in v. 8, describing the large procession that traveled to Canaan for Jacob's burial. Joseph's order to embalm his father (v. 2) reflected the high status of Joseph's family in Egyptian society. Jacob was treated as nobility. Ancient Egyptians believed that to have eternal life, one needed to retain the body, which is why they practiced mummification. In Jacob's case, embalming was required for his journey to his burial site in Canaan. The physicians (lit. "those who healed") needed forty days to complete their task (v. 3)—a time period that appears repeatedly in the OT (Gen. 7:17; Ex. 24:18; 34:28; Deut. 9:9; 1 Kin. 19:8). Following the forty days of embalming was a thirty-day period of mourning, for a total of seventy days. The nation of Israel, much later, grieved the deaths of Aaron and Moses for thirty days (Num. 20:29; Deut. 34:8). The mourning period would eventually involve only seven days (1 Sam. 31:13).

Authorized by Pharaoh, Joseph, his brothers, and a number of officials of Pharaoh traveled to Canaan to bury Jacob. He had requested to be placed in the tomb he had made for himself (v. 5). Joseph's unusual use of messengers when communicating with Pharaoh may have been a clear recognition of his state of impurity following his contact with a corpse (vv. 4–5; cf. similarly Esth. 4:2). The military presence (marked by the reference to chariots and horsemen in Gen. 50:9) was a harbinger of future events associated with the Exodus, using similar language (Ex. 14:9, 17–18, 23, 26, 28).

The seven days of mourning at the threshing floor of Atad (Gen. 50:10) is an example of an important Israelite ritual practice (e.g., Ex. 12:15; Lev. 13:4–5; 14:8) and is associated with mourning rites elsewhere in Scripture (1 Sam. 31:13; Job 2:13). The recognition of Jacob's burial party as Egyptian (Gen. 50:11) by the local Canaanites highlighted the adaptation of Joseph's family in Egypt and was a marker of irony, considering the opening verses of Exodus, describing a completely different reality. The Egyptian entourage and the fact that Jacob's

sons were probably wearing Egyptian clothing would have led those looking at the mourning ritual from a distance to identify them as Egyptians. The location was renamed Abel Mizraim (lit. "mourning of Egypt"), which reechoed the grievous sorrow that Jacob had felt earlier over his loss of Joseph (37:35).

50:15–21. Joseph Assures His Brothers. The need for the assurance of Joseph's forgiveness highlights the challenge of true reconciliation. Seventeen years (Gen. 47:9, 28) after the emotional reunion between Joseph and his brothers, a lingering doubt remained. This illustrates the common struggle to accept God's grace, compassion, and pardon.

When the brothers twice reported to Joseph their father's plea that Joseph would forgive them (v. 17), Joseph reciprocated by twice encouraging his brothers not to be afraid (vv. 19, 21). Joseph had recognized God's involvement in his personal history, as well as the history of the people surrounding him (cf. 45:5–8). The full significance of Jacob's death weighed upon Joseph's brothers following their return to Egypt (50:15), and they projected malevolent motives on Joseph. Joseph's reaction reflected concern and empathy. He spoke kindly and reassuringly to them (50:21; lit. "he spoke to their hearts"; cf. 34:3); he had recognized their evil intent (50:20), but God had meant it for good. Genuine forgiveness toward others is grounded in God's forgiveness (Eph. 4:32).

50:22–26. Joseph's Death. Joseph's death set the stage for a new chapter in God's story. Israel's slavery and liberation from Egypt (Ex. 1) was not yet on the horizon, but Joseph's last words referring to Israel's return to Canaan represent the introduction to God's story of redemption.

There is a general decrease in the longevity of the patriarchs, culminating with Joseph at the end of Genesis. Joseph's age was considered the ideal age in Egyptian sources, but his decreased life span (when compared to his ancestors) underscores an important theme in Genesis: following the Fall, life on earth has been on a downward trajectory, moving further and further away from the Creator's ideal for humanity. Yet, God was on the move. Joseph said that God would surely *paqad* ("take care of," "come to aid"; lit. "visit") them (50:24–25). This word appears twice in Joseph's final statement and later reappears in a similar context in Exodus 3:16, 4:31, and 13:19. He also promised that God would bring them out of Egypt. The word here is a verbal form of *'alah*, used forty-two times in the OT to describe Israel's rescue from Egypt; the phrase functions as an important bridge to God's future acts of salvation. God's oath (v. 24) suggested the assurance of the fulfillment of His promises. Similarly, the oath of Joseph's brothers to bring Joseph's bones back to Canaan (v. 25) would ultimately be fulfilled during the time of Joshua (Ex. 13:19; Josh. 24:32).

Genesis began with the fullness of life: human life to be enjoyed in fellowship with God. It closes with a corpse: the embalmed body of Joseph. The bones were a symbol not only of death but also of hope (Ezek. 37:11–14). In this case, their presence anticipated a journey to Canaan. The story was not finished. It would continue to unfold throughout the rest of Scripture and will lead to everlasting hope for those who wait for the heavenly Canaan.

EXODUS

INTRODUCTION

Title and Authorship. The name "Exodus" derives from the LXX translation, abbreviated from a fuller title "The Exodus of the Children of Israel from Egypt" and adopted by the Latin Vulgate as "Exodus." The original Hebrew name is *we'elleh shemot*, "and these are the names of" (or simply *shemot*, "names"), taken from the opening words of the Hebrew text, as was customary for the books of the Pentateuch.

The author is identified as Moses in several explicit statements where he was told by God to write certain things down in a scroll (sometimes translated as "book") so they could be remembered (Ex. 17:14; 24:4; cf. 34:27). It is also stated that he read to the people from the covenant scroll (book) that he had written (24:7). The authorship by Moses is confirmed in later OT books where reference is made to the "law of Moses" (Josh. 8:31–32; 1 Kin. 2:3; 2 Kin. 14:6; 21:8; Ezra 6:18; Neh. 13:1; Dan. 9:11–13; Mal. 4:4). In the NT, Jesus specifically referred to Moses as the author of Exodus 3:6 (Mark 12:26) and the Torah (John 5:46–47; 7:19), as did also the apostles (Acts 3:22; Rom. 10:5).

The internal evidences of the book attest that the author was someone who was well acquainted with the language and customs of Egypt, was a contemporary eyewitness of the wilderness wanderings, and possessed a high level of education and literary skill. Moses, who received the highest education and military training in the court of Pharaoh, possessed these characteristics.

Date. If the biblical premise that Moses was the author of Exodus is accepted, then the date of the event of the Exodus provides the date for its composition. That date is evidenced by several key chronological passages (Judg. 11:26; 1 Kin. 6:1) and the nineteen generations enumerated between Korah and Solomon in 1 Chronicles 6:33–37.

These internal chronological data together with the Jubilee cycle recorded in the Talmud point to a date in the fifteenth century B.C.

Backgrounds. Genesis provides a foundational setting, encompassing God's Creation, the Flood and dispersal of nations, the specific call of Abraham, and the covenant promise to establish great nations through his descendants. The book establishes how, in God's providence, a faithful Joseph, followed by his father and brothers, was saved in the land of Egypt in the historical turmoil of hardship and famine. Exodus continues this history of God's people in Egypt. It spans the gap from the death of Joseph to the birth of Moses, Moses's exile and return, the miraculous events leading up to the deliverance of the Hebrews from Egypt in the event of the Exodus, the codification of the law, the construction of the sanctuary, and culminates in God's divine presence entering into the wilderness tabernacle upon its completion.

The chronology of Egyptian kings of the Eighteenth Dynasty has not yet been firmly established, but based on the internal biblical evidence and its approximate correlation with Egyptian history, the events of the first two chapters correspond to the beginning of that dynasty. Many have suggested that Thutmose I might have issued the death decree for all the Hebrew male children and that his daughter Hatshepsut could have been the princess who rescued Moses from the Nile River. While names of the royal family are not given in the Pentateuch, this theory is made more plausible by the dynastic crisis that enveloped the royal family in the first several generations because no male heir was born to the chief queens. After the death of her father, Thutmose I, and the short reign of her husband Thutmose II, Hatshepsut assumed kingship over Egypt as coregent with her half brother and nephew, Thutmose III. In this correlation of events, it would have been from Thutmose III that Moses fled after killing the Egyptian taskmaster. During Moses's forty years in the wilderness of Sinai, not only did Thutmose III conduct a record sixteen military campaigns in the territory of Canaan, perhaps partly in search of Moses, but his stepmother Hatshepsut died a few years after Moses fled. Moses would have returned to face either Thutmose III or his son Amenhotep II. The systematic proscription (destruction) of all records of Hatshepsut at the end of Thutmose III's or the beginning of Amenhotep II's reign suggests the threat of a rival and corresponds to the return of Moses.

Historical records of the early Eighteenth Dynasty hint at the plagues, the Exodus, and the death of the Egyptian army in the Red Sea, but these are few. The Egyptians of the New Kingdom who left vivid pictorial and historical records of their military campaigns never recorded a defeat, only victories. There is no reason to expect that the administration of Egypt would record on its temple walls a history of the most devastating series of judgments on Egypt and its gods or the defeat of their army in the Red Sea (Ps. 78:43–51; 105:26–36; 135:8–9; 136:10–15).

Theology and Purpose. The book of Exodus is theologically very rich and diverse, making it difficult to identify a particular theme as its center. The following survey identifies the theology of God's presence as one of the most important refrains in Exodus. The narrative is focused upon God's desire and willingness to dwell among His people, and the book closes when God is, in fact, dwelling among them in the sanctuary.

1. God's Presence in the Midst of Affliction. The book opens with a reminder to the reader that only seventy Israelites had descended to Egypt and that they had all died there. But the intention is to contrast the past with the present. While in Egypt, the people had been blessed by the Lord and, in fulfillment of the promises He made to Abraham, they multiplied considerably. God was with them, making them fruitful and transforming twelve small tribes into a people. The divine blessing was opposed by Pharaoh, who tried to control the population growth through the oppression of excessive work and then by asking the Hebrew midwives to kill newborn male children. Both attempts failed because the Lord was with His people, and in a special way, He blessed the midwives who disobeyed Pharaoh. The silent presence of God with His people in Egypt preserved them and

caused them to grow. It was through His protective care that the life of the child Moses was preserved and he became the son of the daughter of Pharaoh.

2. God and Moses Descend to Egypt. After leaving Egypt and perhaps feeling abandoned by God, Moses met the Lord at the base of Mount Sinai. The divine presence revealed itself for the first time in the book of Exodus to one person, Moses, and in a strange form: "In a flame of fire from the midst of a bush" (3:2). Very often in the Bible, the manifestation of God's presence is accompanied by fire to indicate that God is unapproachable to humans. God remains the transcendental God. The divine presence is holy, unique, distinct, and should be approached with reverence (3:3–5). God expressed to Moses His concern for what was happening to the Israelites in Egypt (v. 7). This divine interest is dynamic and expresses itself in salvific action: God wanted Moses to go with Him to Egypt. God was searching for an instrument through whom He would accomplish His plan. He told Moses that He would be with him (v. 12). The Lord was going down to Egypt, to the place of enslavement, to the place where His people were.

God's visit to Egypt had two main purposes. First, He was going to destroy the Egyptians' sources of security, which were the powers of their gods and the economic production of the country. Through the ten plagues, the Lord brought Egypt to its knees and left the country in economic ruin. The situation became so desperate that Pharaoh's officials told him to let the Israelites go because the land was destroyed (10:7). The Egyptians had used the Israelites for their own benefit, but now the presence of the Israelites' God devastated them. God's judgment was also against the Egyptian gods (12:12). These gods, whom the Egyptians believed would protect them from plagues, were impotent before the Lord.

The second reason for God going down to Egypt was to redeem His people from the powerful hand of Pharaoh (3:8, 17). This redemption was possible through the blood of a lamb (Ex. 12). The Passover lamb was a reminder to the Israelites that their redemption from Egypt was possible through a bloody sacrifice. The life of the Passover lamb substituted for the life of the firstborn. During the plagues, God's presence among His people protected them, and He finally led them out of Egypt.

3. God's Presence during the Exodus. Moses received a very specific assignment from the Lord: "When you have brought the people out of

Egypt, you [pl.] should serve God on this mountain" (3:12). God made an appointment with the people of Israel. In Egypt, He would speak to them through Moses, but on Sinai, He would speak to them personally, and they would experience God's majestic presence in a unique way.

After leaving Egypt, God's presence became visible, powerful, and providential. It was visible in a pillar of cloud during the day and in a pillar of fire during the night (13:22). He mysteriously hid Himself in order to reveal Himself. The cloud and the fire represented the mystery of God's constant presence and His transcendence—there is a natural distance between the Creator and His creatures. The divine presence was also powerful. He protected His people and overcame their enemies (14:4). The Egyptian armies drew near to attack Israel, but the Lord fought for them and sheltered His people (v. 19). The Lord looked down from the pillar of cloud and destroyed their enemies, forcing the Egyptians to confess that the Lord was fighting against them (v. 25). God's presence among His people was also providential. During the Israelites' trek through the wilderness, He supplied water (15:23–25) and bread for them (16:4). The Israelites saw the glory of the Lord through His provision of food for them (16:10–13). The wilderness was a place of danger for the people, but there they were learning to depend exclusively on the power of the divine presence among them.

4. *God's Presence in the Tabernacle.* Approaching the next climax of their journey, the Israelites reached Mount Sinai to meet with the Lord (cf. 3:12). In preparation for the meeting, they were to consecrate themselves to Him, and then Moses was to lead them to the foot of Mount Sinai to meet with God (19:17). The Lord descended on Mount Sinai with power accompanied by thunder, lightning, a thick cloud, and the sound of a trumpet (19:16, 18). Yahweh and His people met together in the most glorious experience of God's presence and nearness the Israelites would ever have. This event transformed Sinai into the first Israelite sanctuary. According to the instructions God gave to Moses, the people were not to have access to the mountain (19:12) because it had become holy through God's presence. A fence was placed around the mountain to avoid any violation of its holiness.

At the foot of the mountain, an altar was built (24:4), and only a limited group of young men could approach the altar to offer sacrifices (24:5; similar to the court of the sanctuary). Access to the mountain was limited to Moses, Aaron, Nadab, Abihu, and the seventy elders (24:1). They could go up to the mountain only after the covenant had been ratified (24:6–8), to worship the Lord "from afar" (24:1; equivalent to the Holy Place). Only Moses was allowed to approach the Lord (24:2) at the top of the mountain (the Most Holy Place). There the glory of the Lord was revealed to him in a special way, and there he received from the Lord the Ten Commandments (24:12). Sinai indeed became a sanctuary. Later the Lord told Moses that Sinai was not His permanent dwelling place and that He wanted to dwell among His people. They were to build a sanctuary so that He could dwell among them (25:8).

Sanctuary theology plays an important role in Exodus. First, according to this theology, access to the sanctuary presupposes redemption. God redeemed Israel from Egypt, entered into a covenant with them, and then asked them to build Him a sanctuary. The divine intention was, from the very beginning of the narrative, for God to be near them by dwelling among them (29:45–46). As already indicated, the book looks forward to that moment and ends when that goal is achieved (40:34–38). This suggests that access to the sanctuary assumes harmony between God and the worshipers. Sin is alien to the divine dwelling.

Second, the sanctuary theology of Exodus reveals that God's presence in the sanctuary was a manifestation of divine condescension. During their journey to the promised land, every Israelite resided in a tent. Similarly, the Lord wanted to make His home in a tent—to be among His people. He chose this dwelling not because He had physical needs that they could satisfy but in order to identify with His people. The sacrifices were not food for Him; when the Israelites adopted the pagan idea that the sacrifices were food for the gods, He rejected their offerings (Ps. 50:7–15). They had nothing with which to enrich or bribe Him. Rather, it was Yahweh who was the giver. His presence among them blessed Israel by providing for them a religious and national identity (33:16). Through the sanctuary, the Lord gave Himself to Israel, revealing His nature as a loving and just God who should be worshiped. The sanctuary was the expression of a divine longing: His desire to be near and among His people.

Third, the sanctuary was a meeting place. Mount Sinai was the first Israelite sanctuary where God met with His people (3:12), and what happened there was to be perpetuated in the tabernacle. The sanctuary would be the place where God would connect with His children, a place made holy by His glory (29:43). The structure inside the courtyard was called the tent or tabernacle of meeting because it was the meeting place for God and His people. Their coming together had the purpose of revealing to the Israelites that Yahweh was their God (29:45–46).

Fourth, the theology of the sanctuary in Exodus indicates that the sanctuary is the center of divine activity. It was located in the heart of the camp as a place where God *revealed His will* to His people. On Sinai, He proclaimed to Israel the Ten Commandments of the covenant (20:1–20) and later, the law would be located in the Most Holy Place. From there the Lord would continue to reveal His will to the people (25:22). In the sanctuary, God *reigned as king* over the entire world. There was a divine movement from this central location to all the earth. The Lord as a warrior (15:3) fought for His people and caused the nations of Canaan to be afraid of Him (15:14, 15). The sanctuary was also the place from which *God blessed* (20:24) and *guided Israel* (40:36–38). For the Israelites, it was the source of life for individuals as well as the nation and where they could go to express their gratitude to God.

Fifth, the sanctuary is a place of forgiveness. Although the sanctuary and sin were incompatible, the incident of the golden calf indicated that the merciful God who would soon dwell there dispensed forgiveness from His dwelling place. The worship of the golden calf was a violation of the covenant, and the Lord treated it as such. His presence was unable to coexist with sin and threatened to consume His rebellious people (32:9, 10). When God appeared to Moses in the midst of the bush, the bush was burning, and yet it was not burned up (3:2) because the presence of the Lord sanctified it. But at Sinai, because of Israel's sin, they were imperiled by God's presence.

It was only because of the mediation of Moses that God, from His dwelling place, decided to reveal His loving and merciful character by forgiving His people. He, not Moses (32:32–33), would bear the sins of the people in order for them to remain in His presence (34:7). Forgiveness was granted, and the covenant was renewed. Moses went to the top of Sinai, and there he heard the voice of the Lord proclaiming not the law but His willingness to forgive His people for their sins, rebellions, and iniquities. He was willing to bear their sins. The sanctuary became not only the meeting place for Yahweh and His redeemed people but also a place of atonement. God was willing to deal with the sin problem from His own dwelling place. There, He and the repentant sinner could meet in order for Him to remove the sin from His presence but not the sinner.

5. The Earthly and Heavenly Dwellings. According to Exodus, the Israelite sanctuary points to a greater heavenly one. The Lord showed Moses a model of the sanctuary he was going to build (e.g., 25:9, 40). Most likely, Moses saw the heavenly sanctuary (the original) and/or a miniature model of it adapted to the needs of the Israelites. There are several reasons to support this suggestion. First, according to ANE religions, the earthly temples of the gods were considered to be a representation of the heavenly temple. Second, the OT itself indicates that there is a temple in heaven, in which Yahweh dwells. There was a connection between this earthly dwelling and the heavenly one. According to 1 Kings 8:30, when God's people pray in the earthly sanctuary/temple, God will hear their prayers in the heavenly one. The Psalms also testify about a heavenly temple where God listens to our prayers (18:6) and from where He descends to help us (vv. 9–10). God is clearly perceived in the OT as dwelling in a heavenly temple (e.g., Ps. 11:4; 102:18, 19; Mic. 1:2–3). It is this dwelling that served as a pattern for the earthly one.

Third, the biblical concept of a heavenly sanctuary is also found in the NT. Hebrews argues, referring back to Exodus 25:9, that the earthly sanctuary was a copy/model of the heavenly one and, therefore, the heavenly is superior to the earthly (8:1–2, 5). The same applies to the description of the sanctuary in the book of Revelation (e.g., 11:19; 15:5, 8).

The book of Exodus indicates that behind the Israelites' sanctuary there was a sublime reality—God's heavenly abode. This is the place in heaven where God dwells among His creation. From there, He rules over creation, blesses and judges His creatures, and reveals His will to them. It is the center of worship in the universe. This is also the place where God applies the benefit of the atonement to repentant sinners, made possible through the mediation of Christ, and where the mystery of atonement will reach its consummation, resulting in the cleansing of the universe (cf. Dan. 8:14; Heb. 9:23; for more on the theology of the sanctuary in Exodus, see "Sanctuary, Covenant, Worship, and Forgiveness" (p. 226) and "Creation, Sabbath, and the Sanctuary" (p. 231).

COMMENTARY

1:1—18:27

DELIVERANCE FROM EGYPT

The Exodus is the most remembered divine act of deliverance recorded in Scripture. In this first section of the book of Exodus, the historical events leading to Israel's departure from Egypt are described, from their suffering at the hands of Pharaoh to their arrival at Mount Sinai. Chapters 1–4 describe the sojourn in Egypt and the birth of Moses, his rescue from the Nile River, his youth and eventual exile from Egypt. Taking things into one's own hands, without trusting in the timing of God, never works out well. But Moses grew into a person God could use, and He spoke to him from the burning bush, calling him to prophetic leadership. Chapters 5:1—15:21 recount Moses's journey back to Goshen, God's miraculous judgments of salvation in the ten plagues, and the Exodus from Egypt, culminating in the crossing of the Red Sea. With God all things are possible, and what He says will come to pass. Chapters 15:22—18:27 provide the itinerary and challenges the Hebrews faced as they traveled to Sinai, recounting the miraculous care of a loving God who provided fresh water to drink, manna from heaven, and victory over the Amalekites.

1:1–22

Condition of the People in Egypt

The first chapter of Exodus serves as a transition from the death of Jacob and Joseph in Genesis to the generations in the period of the sojourn and their descent into slavery. God had not forsaken His people. Just as God's providence had provided salvation through the faithfulness of Joseph, the birth of Moses ushered in a new chapter for the descendants of Abraham.

1:1–6. Sojourn in Egypt. The length of time between the entrance of Israel into Egypt (Gen. 46) and the return of Moses to Egypt ahead of the Exodus event—the period of the Egyptian sojourn—has been a matter of debate, with two lines of thought concerning how this should be understood (see "The Four-Hundred-Thirty-Year Sojourn," p. 211). In Exodus 1, the movement from those years when the people were favored by the king of Egypt to those years when they suffered under a Pharaoh who did

not know Joseph (Ex. 1:8) reminds us of the changing circumstances in life that are often beyond one's control.

1:7–14. God's Blessing in the Midst of Slavery. God blessed Jacob's descendants in Egypt—they were fruitful and grew strong and numerous (Ex. 1:7). The three verbs used here are taken from Genesis 1:21, 22, and 28 and emphasize the rapid growth of the tribe of Jacob under the blessings and presence of the Creator. Even though Joseph and his brothers had died, God was faithful to His promise and blessed their descendants. This king who was unfamiliar with Joseph probably refers to a king of the newly established Eighteenth Dynasty of Egypt. The previous generation of Asiatic Hyksos rulers who had infiltrated the ranks of the Egyptians had been expelled. This dynasty instilled a fear of foreigners and built on a general disdain for other ethnicities that had existed since Egypt's earliest history. This included the Hebrews.

If Joseph lived during the Twelfth Dynasty of the Middle Kingdom, his contribution to saving Egypt from the seven-year famine would have long been forgotten. If he lived during the Fifteenth Dynasty of the Second Intermediate Period under the Asiatic Hyksos, the events might still be in the collective memory but simply ignored. Accordingly, some translators render the Hebrew *lo' yada'* as "meant nothing" instead of "did not know"; *yada'* can refer to relationships that transcend mere intellectual knowledge (e.g., Gen. 4:1). Either way, the new king would not have had a relationship with Joseph that tied the king to any previous administration's goodwill. The new king, once subjugated by the Asiatic Hyksos, became the oppressor of the Hebrews. This reflects the human condition. If given a chance, the oppressed often becomes the oppressor. The cities that the Hebrews built, Pithom and Raamses (v. 11), were storage cities made out of mud brick, as all cities in ancient Egypt were. It is nearly certain that Raamses was located at modern Tal ed-Dab'a/Qantir (for more information, see "Archaeology and the Bible," p. 77). Here, construction of a major city began in the period of the Hyksos and continued into the early Eighteenth Dynasty before it was abandoned in the first part of Amenhotep II's reign. Construction began again in the late Eighteenth Dynasty and continued into the early Nineteenth Dynasty. It is theorized that the name was later updated to reflect the location of a major palace there in the time of Ramesses II (see commentary on Gen. 46:1—47:12 for a discussion of the land with a similar name). While this slavery aimed at controlling population, the subjugation of the Hebrews did not put an end to the divine blessing. God strengthens His children in the midst of their weakness (2 Cor. 12:9-10).

1:15-22. God's Blessing and the Threat of Genocide. The Pharaoh, possibly Thutmose I, resorted to ordering the extermination of all newborn males. In this case, genocide was used for population control (Ex. 1:15-20). He began by ordering the Hebrew midwives to execute the babies at childbirth, but the Bible reports that the women feared God (v. 17) and honored the sanctity of life. The fact that the term "midwives" is mentioned seven times and their names are recorded while the king of Egypt remains nameless testifies to the power of moral right over civil might. God honored these women and provided for their basic needs. Pharaoh finally commanded his people to cast every Hebrew male infant into the river. One cannot help but be reminded of the command by Herod the Great when he sent his soldiers to Bethlehem over 1,500 years later (Matt. 2:16-18). Neither decree could keep God from fulfilling His ultimate plan of raising up a deliverer.

2:1—4:31
The Birth, Life, and Call of Moses

Considering the internal biblical chronology, Moses was born around 1527 B.C., the youngest son of Amram and Jochebed. He was born into slavery under a death decree, but God would dramatically alter history by ensuring his rescue and subsequent training in the court of Pharaoh. God is always sovereign, regardless of the plans of the enemy of God's people (epitomized here by Pharaoh).

2:1-10. Hidden for the Service of God. Following his birth, Moses was first kept at home quietly for three months until another means for his safety could be planned. The Hebrew terminology for the box in which Moses was placed is *tebat* (construct form of *tebah*) *gome'*. These are Egyptian loanwords describing a basket made from the papyrus plant. Papyrus was often employed to construct small water vessels used along the Nile (which can be seen depicted in Egyptian paintings). The term *sup* is also an Egyptian word that is used to refer to the reeds where Moses was placed. This is the second and only other use of the Hebrew term *tebah*, which first appeared in the Flood story in Genesis 6,

where it is used seven times (6:14 [2x], 15, 16, [2x], 18, 19). The use of this unique word reminds the reader of God's providence and salvation during the universal Flood and anticipates Moses's rescue. In both cases, God used *tebat* to protect His people from water and guarantee their survival. Under the watchful eye of his sister Miriam, Moses was placed in the marshy tracts of the Nile (2:1-5).

The princess who rescued Moses is not named, but she may well have been Hatshepsut, who some twenty years later would become Pharaoh over Egypt due to the dynastic crisis surrounding the lack of a male heir. Archaeological evidence indicates that two palaces along the Pelusaic branch of the Nile near Avaris, known later as Pi-Ramesses, were built at the beginning of the Eighteenth Dynasty and may have been the location from which the princess went out to bathe. The Nile was sanctified as the Egyptian god *Hapi*, who unified Upper and Lower Egypt, and was the source of life for the nation. It may well have been that the daughter of Pharaoh, knowing that there was no male heir, perceived this child to be a gift of the Nile god to solve Egypt's dilemma of dynastic succession. Later, after Moses had been brought up by his mother until the age of twelve (cf. PP 244) and presented at the palace, his adoptive mother named him Moses because she drew him out of the water.

Moses is an Egyptian name, *mes* or *mesi* meaning "son of" or "the one born of." This was appropriate for a dynasty where the kings were named Ka-mose ("son of Ka"), Ah-mose ("son of Akh"), and Thut-mose ("son of Thoth")— each portrayed as the son of one of the gods of Egypt. Moses refused the divine element of his name when he ultimately rejected the crown (Heb. 11:24-25). He modified his Egyptian name and rendered it in Hebrew as *mosheh*, which is from the verb meaning "to draw out." Pharaoh's daughter snatched him from death so that he might accomplish God's plan for his life.

2:11-15. Not by Human Strength. Moses was forty years of age when he slew the Egyptian taskmaster and buried his body in the sand (Acts 7:23). Groomed and educated to be the next king of Egypt (PP 245), he saw what was taking place and had compassion for his brothers, just as the princess who rescued him was moved to compassion for him. He confronted the oppressor and took the side of the enslaved and destitute. Moses believed that the Hebrews would declare him their new leader (Acts 7:25), but instead, they turned on him. The enslaved did not realize their plight and were not ready for freedom. How often do those enslaved by sin prefer their dark situation over the freedom offered by the Deliverer!

Which pharaoh attempted to have Moses killed? It is unlikely to have been Hatshepsut, Moses's adoptive mother, who reigned as full regent. In the dynastic crisis that followed the death of her husband Thutmose II, his son Thutmose III was declared king, but being too young to rule, Hatshepsut had taken power on his behalf and later usurped all authority from him. When Thutmose III did come of age, Hatshepsut retained that position as full regent and declared that because she was the daughter of Thutmose I she was his rightful heir. The temple at Deir el-Bahri declared her to be the divine daughter of Amun and Hathor. She took on royal titles and became the first female ruler of the New Kingdom of Egypt. It is not difficult to imagine the rivalry and jealousy that must have developed between Thutmose III and Moses. Moses's slaying of the Egyptian taskmaster and his subsequent flight from Egypt gave Thutmose III the opportunity to become the sole heir of the mightiest power on earth.

As this earthly struggle for power was taking place, there was another controversy taking place in the heart of Moses. To be king of Egypt meant to be inducted into the rituals of Egypt—to accept that he was a son of the gods, the divine pharaoh, Horus incarnate. He wrestled with issues of allegiance and loyalty. This was a test of faith. He did not flee for his life in fear of the king's anger (Heb. 11:27). He understood that his act had ruined his opportunity to free his people by his own mighty hand (cf. Ex. 3:19; 4:13; Acts 7:22). By faith, he was led by God into the wilderness where he could unlearn the sophisticated and mysterious refinements of Egyptian court life. Moses was not yet prepared to lead the people out of Egypt. He needed to learn to rely not on himself but solely on God, who would accomplish the deliverance of Israel through His own power and strength. For Moses, this would take another forty years. The exercise of daily self-denial and constant dependence on God remains a challenge for all Christians.

2:16–22. God Provides. Eventually, Moses arrived in Midian. In this period of history, the Midianites lived as nomads and moved between the territories to the east of the Gulf of Aqaba (modern Jordan and Saudi Arabia) and to the west (the Sinai Peninsula). It is to Sinai

where Moses fled, and he eventually arrived at a well in Midian (see 3:1; cf. PP 247). It is customary still today for Bedouin women, not men, to draw water for their flocks. Here Moses once again delivered the weak from the hand of the strong—the Midianite priest's daughters from the shepherds—but this time he took the role of a servant and watered the women's flocks for them, an act unusual both then and today. Notice that he was identified by Reuel's daughters as an Egyptian. Perhaps on account of his dress, hairstyle, demeanor, and speech, Moses appeared to be Egyptian, but he was, in fact, their distant relative. Moses agreed to dwell with Reuel and subsequently entered into marriage with Zipporah. The name of their son Gershom means "banishment," an expression of how Moses felt living in the wilderness, separated from his people and the land that he had known.

2:23–25. God and the Suffering of Israel. For Moses, the time of banishment was a period of approximately forty years (Acts 7:30). He would be eighty years of age when he returned to Egypt (7:7). All this time, he lived as a shepherd in the desert, removed from the temples and palaces created by the Egyptians and surrounded by the majestic mountains and open plains of his Creator. During this time, the king of Egypt died (2:23). Some have suggested that it was Thutmose III (who died ca. 1450 B.C.), who had sought to kill Moses (4:19). Others have suggested it was Hatshepsut (who died ca. 1482 B.C.). After the death of the pharaoh, the exploitation of the children of Israel became even more severe. But God was still with His people—He heard their cry for deliverance, saw them, and recognized their plight (2:25). The Hebrew term used in v. 25, *yada* ("to know"), suggests that God experienced and understood their suffering in a relational way (cf. 1:8). God remembered His covenant with Abraham, Isaac, and Jacob and acted accordingly. He is a God who initiates and remains faithful to His covenant. This covenant would become the major focus of God's interaction with Israel in Exodus 19–24 and is the central motivation for God to commence a rescue plan for His people.

3:1—4:17. God Calls Moses. God's call was dramatic and arrested Moses's attention. The Angel of the Lord appeared to him when he came to Horeb, the mountain of God (v. 1). "Horeb" means literally "dry place" and appears also in Exodus 17:6 and 33:6. God's mountain was also known as Sinai (Ex. 19:1, 18, 20, 23; 24:16). Both names may have been associated with the same larger mountain range.

The Being that appeared in a flame of fire placed in the midst of a bush that would not be consumed was none other than Yahweh, the Lord God. The three terms (Angel, Yahweh, God) are used interchangeably in this passage to describe the One who appeared and spoke to Moses (see Gen. 18; 22:11–18; 23:20–23; 31:11–13; Judg. 2:1–5; 13:2–23; Hos. 12:3–5; Mal. 3:1 ["messenger" is a translation of the same Hebrew word for "angel"]). The ground was made holy by the presence of God, and Moses was instructed to remove his sandals (v. 5). By removing his sandals and hiding his face, Moses honored the God of the covenant with awe and reverence. This passage is reminiscent of the seraphim who stand by the throne of God. Each has six wings: two covering their faces, two covering their feet, and two used for flying (Is. 6:2). Here Moses's actions are a demonstration of the honor, awe, and reverence due to the God of the universe.

God would reveal to Moses His plan for the deliverance of His people from Egypt (3:7–12). In fulfillment of the covenant promise made to Abram (Gen. 13:15), God would "come down" to deliver Israel and bring them to a "good and large land" (v. 8). Compared with the area of Goshen, the land of Israel would be enormous. While Israel today includes some desert areas, most of the land west of the peaks of the central hill country is lush, supporting extensive agriculture. The north has flowing rivers from Mount Hermon, which fill the Sea of Galilee, emptying into the Dead Sea via the Jordan River. Here there are waterfalls and rapids. The Carmel Mountains in the north central part of the country contain springs of water. The term "milk and honey" refers to the pastoralist (goat milk) and agricultural (fruit bearing) land and to the lifestyle of the future inhabitants of Canaan. Moses's objection, "Who am I?" (v. 11), is set in contrast to his earlier high position in the palace of Pharaoh. By this time, he was a lowly shepherd and filled with self-distrust. But God assured Moses that He would certainly be with him (v. 12). When God calls people to overwhelming tasks, He always enables them to accomplish His purpose.

Moses asked God to tell him what response should be given if the Israelites were to ask for His name. In response, God revealed Himself to Moses as "I AM WHO I AM," alternatively rendered as "I WILL BE WHAT I WILL BE" (v. 14). The sentence expresses "being" not as "pure being" in the Greek philosophical sense but as "active being," in terms of revelation. God has been in the past, is in the present, and will be in the future. The great I AM was sending Moses. The eternal, self-existent One (John 8:58; cf. DA 469) would accompany him. The derived form "Yahweh" is the sacred covenant name of God who makes Himself known through the act of redemption. He set Israel free from bondage, made them His special covenant people, and provided the means for them to remain His covenant people through His grace and enabling power.

To encourage Moses, Yahweh told him that He would stretch out His hand and strike Egypt with "wonders" (v. 20). The mention of stretching out the hand is a direct reference to a phrase in Egyptian used often to describe the pharaoh, who is said "to stretch out his hand" against his enemies in battle. But Moses, like most human beings, asked for evidence that appealed to his senses, and God provided him with three proofs so that the people would know that he was the Lord's representative (4:1–9). Perhaps in the back of his mind, Moses remembered the accusation of his fellow Israelites when they tauntingly asked him who had appointed him to be their ruler (or "prince," Heb. *sar*) and judge (2:14). The rod would be a symbol of God's power in the hands of Moses (7:15; 17:5) and Aaron (7:9; 8:5; 8:16). As Creator, God could fashion a serpent out of the rod and use the rod to perform wonders. The second sign indicated that Moses's hand would be empowered by God to perform His actions. The third sign gave evidence of God's authority over life and death. Moses was simply to be God's servant and rely on His strength.

Moses provided another reason for not wanting to return to Egypt, namely, that he was slow of speech (4:10–17). After forty years, had he forgotten the Egyptian language? Moses later repeated the response in part when he referred to his *'arel*—literally "uncircumcised" lips (6:12)—which contextually referred to his lacking eloquence. Other prophets (Jer. 1:6) and apostles like Paul (2 Cor. 10:10) would make similar statements. God's response is clear: when He calls individuals to deliver a message, He who created their mouths will give them the words to say (vv. 11–12). The reality is that Moses simply did not want to go. This speaks to Christians today who are called to witness for the One who saved them. They should remember that the God who spoke to Moses will always go before them.

4:18–31. Back to Egypt. When the time arrived for Moses to return to Egypt, God reassured him that it was safe—everyone who had sought his life was dead (4:19). As Moses set out, God explained his mission: to display the wonders that had been revealed to him (v. 21) and to speak the words God would give him (vv. 22–23). The hardening of Pharaoh's heart (v. 21) must be understood concretely in the idiomatic sense of Hebrew thought. In the Hebrew way of thinking, whatever God allows, He does. God predicted that He would harden Pharaoh's heart through the course of the ten plagues (which are also described as "signs" or "works" of God [7:3; 8:19; 10:1–2], "wonders" [4:21; 7:3; 11:9–10], and "extraordinary deeds/wonders" [15:11; 34:10]). This is something the Lord discerned because of His foreknowledge. But this did not remove Pharaoh's freedom of choice. Ten times during the initial five plagues where the phrase is used, Pharaoh is said to have hardened his own heart (e.g., 8:15, 32; 9:34). Rather than allowing God to soften his heart, the king became more determined and resolute with every demonstration of God's power. This was a deliberate decision on his part. During the last five plagues, God is said to have hardened Pharaoh's heart (e.g., 9:12; 11:10; 14:8). God provided the circumstances and the occasion for Pharaoh to be forced into making a decision. God was the instigator and initiator of the dilemma, but He was not the author of Pharaoh's defiance.

Moses had to spiritually and physically prepare his family for his mission (4:24–26). The sign of the Lord's covenant with Israel was shown through the rite of circumcision (Gen. 17:10–14). One son, presumably Gershom, the eldest, had been circumcised, but the younger son Eliezer had not been (cf. PP 256). This duty needed to be carried out before Moses could act as leader of the covenant people. The immediate act of circumcision evidently satisfied the Lord, and they were allowed to continue on their journey. Soon Moses met Aaron and told him all that the Lord had done (Ex. 4:27–28), and they traveled on to Goshen together. Faithful to God's assignment to act as Moses's spokesman, Aaron related Moses's experience to the elders of the people. The three signs were performed by God in their midst, and they bowed their heads in belief and reverence and worshiped God (vv. 29–31).

5:1—7:13
Judgment on Egypt and the Deliverance of Israel

Moses's journey of forty years transformed him from a self-sufficient and confident prince of Egypt (Acts 7:22) to a humble shepherd, dependent on God. The people of Israel changed from being passive slaves to crying out to the Lord for deliverance. The circumstances in Egypt had also changed, and the men who had sought Moses's life were dead, which would have included Pharaoh himself (Ex. 2:15; 23). The prophecy related to the affliction of the descendants of Abraham (Gen. 15:13) was coming to a close. God had a plan, which He set in motion at the proper time. Even though followers of God may not always see the end from the beginning, they are called to trust Him patiently. The justice of God, longed for by the Israelites for so many years, would be meted out, not only in their deliverance and salvation but also in the judgment and punishment of their oppressors. These judgments preceded deliverance and anticipated God's judgment at Christ's return in the eschaton.

5:1—6:13. Confrontations with Pharaoh. Moses was instructed by God to confront the king of Egypt. Perhaps this was what Moses feared most, given his former background. How would the king view the former successor to the throne? As a threat? As a laughing stock, given his new life as a shepherd? But the controversy that was about to unfold was not about Moses. It was about God's presence in Egypt and His demonstration of sovereignty, power, and judgment upon the nation. God chose people as His instruments to confront evil. God's love for the Egyptians had been demonstrated by sending Joseph to witness about a holy God who knows the future and is able to save a nation from famine. But several generations later, Egypt, so long steeped in pagan religious practices, had finally rejected the God of Israel and Joseph. Left to their own designs for power and supremacy, they had sunk deeper into darkness over the ensuing centuries. God desired to reach the great nation by humbling their self-reliance and challenging their worship of false gods, revealing to them His power and majesty.

Moses and Aaron entered the courts of Pharaoh as the ambassadors of the Lord (5:1–5). Moses identifies himself as a representative of the Lord God of Israel, a title that challenged the very core of the king's authority. Pharaoh's sarcastic response was a direct challenge to God: "Who is the Lord?" (v. 2). Bringing up the God of an enslaved people as a challenge to Pharaoh's absolute position as a son of the gods must have seemed absurd. The confidence of Moses and Aaron stemmed from their knowledge of who

God is while the king's sarcasm resulted from his ignorance. Notice the contrast in Moses's response when receiving the call from God: "Who am I?" (3:11) rather than "Who is the Lord?"

Pharaoh's response was to require the Israelites to construct their bricks without the government supply of straw (5:6–13). Not only did the king refuse Moses's request, but he also added to the burden of the Israelites—requiring them to obtain their own straw while still meeting the same quota of bricks. After the enlightenment, scholars questioned whether bricks were made with straw in Egypt—they were not in Europe and the Americas—and many doubted the historical accuracy of this statement. However, Egyptian texts and tomb paintings illustrating that the process involved the use of straw have since been discovered. Bricks from the Ramesseum in Thebes still have straw preserved in them after 3,200 years. The technology has not changed, for along the Nile, Egyptians still build their houses of sun-dried bricks made with straw.

Pharaoh had made the work of the Israelites almost impossible, and the result was conflict among them (5:14–21). The people cried out that God should judge Moses and Aaron for making them *ba'ash*—"abhorrent" or "odious," literally "to stink"—before the king (v. 21). The officials of Israel thought they were doomed to die under the new workload and blamed Moses and Aaron, a pattern that began here and would continue throughout their wanderings. Moses talked to God, seeking answers (vv. 22–23). To Moses, the situation seemed to be deteriorating because he had been rejected not only by Pharaoh but also by his own people. Moses did not realize that the difficulties he was facing would prepare him for some greater manifestation of God's strength.

In His response to Moses, God used the phrase "I am the LORD [Yahweh]" four times (6:1–13). His discourse was foundational in His continued self-revelation to Moses and the generations reading the story. He was the One who established the covenant. He is the One who hears and responds, the One who redeems with great judgment. From here on, the Lord would be the One to "remember" the covenant. In these verses, there is no reference to a three-day journey for the purpose of worshiping God; this time, their departure from Egypt would be permanent.

6:14—7:13. Moses's Genealogy and His Return to Pharaoh. In the middle of the narrative is the genealogy of Moses. It is provided in order to establish his credentials as a legitimate leader of Israel. The genealogy indicates that Israel was

organized under tribes and that record of their divisions and subdivisions was kept. This genealogy concentrates on the tribe of Levi (v. 16), Moses's tribe. Therefore, it progresses quickly to the family of Aaron and Moses (v. 20). Since Aaron was the older of the two, he is mentioned first several times (vv. 20, 23, 26). But by the end, when the narrative resumes, Moses is mentioned first to identify him as God's chosen leader (v. 27).

When God ordered Moses to go back to Pharaoh, Moses showed self-distrust. The term *'aral sepatayim*—literally "uncircumcised lips," which is used here to express Moses's lack of speaking ability (6:12, 30)—is similar to that found in Exodus 4:10: "slow of speech." This time God overcame Moses's deficiency by telling him that He would make him like God to Pharaoh. Pharaoh assumed he himself was God, but Moses, as the representative of Yahweh, would be superior to the king. He would appear before Pharaoh with greater authority, and Aaron would function as his prophet. This authority was demonstrated in the miracle of the rod becoming a serpent (7:9–12). In Egypt, the uraeus-goddess Wadjet personified the cobra and represented all strength, power, and sovereignty over Lower Egypt. Pharaoh was imbued with the power of the goddess and was, thereby, able to rule over all the land. Wadjet appeared on his crown, at his forehead, as a cobra spitting venom at the enemies of Pharaoh. The cobra became the emblem of the pharaoh's power. In death, it was the serpent that guided the deceased king into the afterlife. The power of the serpent was observed in all aspects of Egyptian life and death.

For Moses's rod to have become a serpent and to have devoured all the other serpents before Pharaoh not only manifested the supremacy of Yahweh but also challenged the sorcery and magic of Egypt. The Egyptians loved to manipulate serpents, but Moses and Aaron could "create" (through the power of God) the serpent that devoured the Egyptian counterfeits (cf. PP 264). Finally, Moses and Aaron cast down to the ground the very symbol that gave Pharaoh power, and they were able to take it up again as a rod. But Pharaoh's heart was hardened, and he rejected this sign.

7:14—12:30
The Ten Plagues

God initiated His request for the deliverance of His people with the simple command to let His people go (5:1; 7:16). Not only were the words rejected, but their Source was scoffed at as well. God knew that this would be Pharaoh's response (3:19–20), and He determined to use it to show Pharaoh who He is by demonstrating His power through the ten plagues (see below, "The Ten Plagues and the Religion of Egypt").

7:14–25. First Plague: Water to Blood. Herodotus, a Greek historian in the fifth century B.C., called Egypt "the gift of the Nile." The annual inundation of the Nile, caused by floodwaters deep in the heart of Africa, added richness to the soil that was indispensable for agriculture. Moses did not tell Pharaoh that the Nile would appear to be red like blood but that the Nile would be turned into blood. When this happened, the contamination spread not only through their water supply but also to one of their main food sources—fish. The Nile lost its capacity to sustain Egypt. But this was not limited to the Nile. The references to this plague affecting other bodies of water (v. 19) indicate an accurate knowledge of Egypt, where tributaries of the Nile, artificial canals, and reservoirs were also affected. The text also indicates that this was not some "red tide" or algae affecting only the river. All of the water of the Egyptians turned to blood. Khnum, the creator god, who was guardian of the Nile, could not change what Moses had commanded. The plague demonstrated that all sustenance comes from the Lord who spoke water and fish into existence, not the deities of Egypt. In desperation, the Egyptians dug for water. No mention is made here of the Israelites, suggesting that this plague did not affect them or their families. This is a repeated pattern:

the plagues fell on the Egyptians but not on the land of Goshen. This is another indication that these were miraculous judgments of God specifically for Egypt.

8:1–15. Second Plague: Frogs. As water was restored by the God of heaven, not Khnum, the protector of the Nile, the next plague was a polemic against Khnum's spouse Hekhet, one of the primary deities of Egypt, who was depicted as a female with a frog's head. While Khnum formed human bodies on the potter's wheel, Hekhet was the goddess of childbirth, who gave life to those bodies. As a result of this plague, the lives of the Egyptians were made miserable by the frogs they worshiped, and consequently they despised and hated them. After the plague, the putrid stench of dead frogs testified against the supposed life-giving "breath" that Hekhet was thought to provide.

8:16–32. Third and Fourth Plagues: Lice and Biting Flies. The next two pestilences that were brought on by the Lord involved insects. The first (*ken*) has been interpreted as either lice or gnats. Since they were found on both people and animals, lice may be a better explanation. The second was *'arob*, which was an insect with a venomous bite that inflicted great pain (PP 266). These plagues could have been a polemic against the self-generating god of the resurrection, Kheper, who was depicted in Egyptian reliefs as the dung or scarab beetle. The female scarab beetle was worshiped because it formed

The Ten Plagues and the Religion of Egypt

The plagues were an attack against the Egyptian source of power. The Egyptians had deified nature to such an extent that their religion had become a type of pantheism with a pantheon of about two thousand gods and goddesses. In a sense, the plagues were successive acts of divine de-creation, the undoing of the creation order and of the people's understanding of the origin of Egypt. For the Egyptians, the concept of ma'at ("truth," "justice," and "order") portrayed the universe as the harmonious coexistence of all elements. Pharaoh himself was given responsibility by the gods to maintain this universal order. This was accomplished by subduing the forces of chaos. The Egyptian concept of ma'at was thrown into chaos during the ten

plagues as a direct challenge to the authority and ability of the king of Egypt.

Before nearly every plague, Moses was instructed to relate to Pharaoh the exact manner and effects of what would take place. He did this for two reasons: (1) to give the king the opportunity to avert the consequences, and (2) to make it impossible for the king to deny that the plagues had come from the Lord (PP 263). The plagues began with the most powerful force of life in Egypt (i.e., water) but had the least devastating impact on Egypt. As each plague came upon Egypt, the effects on the land and the people would become more severe. It was through this manifestation of His divine presence and power that God hoped to reveal the deficiencies of the religious beliefs of Egypt and draw the people to worship and honor Him.

The theory that the plagues could be explained as natural disasters rather than divine interventions is not supported by the biblical text. God announced that He would bring these wonders upon Egypt (Ex. 3:20), and they took place as He stated. In no instance was one plague the source of the next one. The hail of the seventh plague had no relationship to the boils of plague six. The tenth plague had no link to the previous plagues. The plagues are related in direct historical narrative and are not to be understood as metaphor or simple literary creations.

with its front legs a perfect sphere of dung, where it placed its eggs, and eventually life sprang forth spontaneously as the eggs hatched. The Egyptians believed this sphere represented the life-giving sun, which Kheper gave rise to in the morning and pushed from the east across the horizon. The Egyptian magicians could not reproduce this miracle and identified it as "the finger of God" (v. 19). This recognition is not necessarily an expression of faith by the magicians, but rather it highlights the divine origins of the plague (cf. 31:18; Deut. 9:10). Miraculously, the fourth plague did not affect the land of Goshen (cf. Gen. 45:9–13).

9:1–7. Fifth Plague: Livestock Diseased. The pestilence that fell on the domesticated animals struck at the property of the Egyptians—their livelihood. It included camels, donkeys, cattle, and horses, which had been introduced to Egypt by the Asiatic Hyksos (v. 3). Again, the livestock of Israel were spared (v. 4). Cattle were worshiped in two ways in Egypt. The bull cult included the worship of Apis, who epitomized the virility of life-giving strength. In Memphis, he was represented by Ptah, the divine father of Pharaoh. His consort was Hathor, the goddess embodied as a cow. Hatshepsut was depicted at her temple at Deir el-Bahri nursing from the cow Hathor, who was being led by her consort Amun-Re. The fifth plague struck at the heart of the divine origin of the king. Pharaoh set out to determine whether it was true that none of the Israelite livestock had died. Even when faced with the truth, his heart was hardened.

9:8–12. Sixth Plague: Boils. The exact nature of the disease that next fell on the Egyptians is not precisely known. Perhaps this was a boil that broke forth in blisters when fine dust fell on the skin. Even the magicians abandoned Pharaoh and fled to their homes in misery. Sekhmet was the most important of Egypt's cat deities, represented by a woman's body with the head of a lioness. She had the power to ward off pestilence and was a healing goddess, "the mistress of life." While some Egyptian texts describe the scattering of ashes as a means to end pestilence, here God used the same method to cause it.

9:13–35. Seventh Plague: Hail. In this long discourse of God with Moses, explicit detail is given regarding the hail and fire that would fall on Egypt and God's reason for not already destroying Pharaoh—namely, that as a result of the plagues, His name would be known in all the earth (v. 16). The hail destroyed man, beast, and every herb of the field, but the land of Goshen was spared (vv. 23–26). Hail is often associated with divine judgment (Is. 28:2, 17; 30:30–31; Ezek. 13:11–13; 38:22–23). This polemic was aimed against the celestial deities Nut, the goddess of the sky; Shu, the supporter of the heavens; and Tefnut, the goddess of moisture. Intriguingly, the biblical text indicates a polarization of Egyptian society: those who began to take the Lord seriously (perhaps some of those Egyptians, mentioned in Ex. 12:38, who went with the Israelites) and prepared for the plague and those who did not. The plague was directed against Egypt so that Pharaoh would know that the earth belongs to the Lord (v. 29). For the first time, the king admitted that he had sinned, that the Lord is righteous, and that he and his people were wrong (v. 27). But after the storm was called off, he hardened his heart (v. 34).

10:1–20. Eighth Plague: Locusts. Locusts were always a threat in the Mediterranean region. They could eat their own body weight in one day and could swarm in by the millions, consuming everything in their path (on locusts, see Joel 1:1–12). This was the next peril facing Egypt if Pharaoh did not let the people go. What vegetation was left after the storm would be devoured. The locusts came with an east wind from the territory of Arabia. The Tanis stele of Taharqa reads, "A fine field, which the gods protected against grasshoppers." This may suggest that this was the function of many gods, not merely one god. Pharaoh's servants tried to convince him to let the people go—Egypt was already destroyed. The persistence of the king's stubbornness would ultimately bring about Egypt's ruin. This is one of the reasons for the plagues—that they might be a testimony for generations signifying that He is indeed the Lord.

10:21-29. Ninth Plague: Darkness. The chief deity of the Egyptians was the sun god, Re. The rising of Re in the east symbolized new life and resurrection—the cyclical nature of rejuvenated life. When the sun set in the west, it entered the underworld, representing death, before it was reborn in the morning. In a land where there were rarely clouds, the sun was the constant source of life-giving power. The king's titles included "son of Re." Even during the reign of Amenhotep IV—who limited the worship of the Egyptians to the Aten sun-disk, changed his name to Akhenaten, and relocated to a newly built capital all in Aten's honor—the sun was the primary deity of Egypt. When Re was hidden by the might of Yahweh, Pharaoh's realm and, by extension, all of Egypt were plunged into symbolic death and nothingness. A deep foreboding settled over the land. Nothing like this had ever happened in the history of Egypt. What did it mean? The Lord, who had created the greater and lesser lights in the heaven on the fourth day, had never intended that they be worshiped, and He demonstrated once again that He alone is the source of light and life (cf. John 1:1-4). The darkness was so thick that it could be felt by the inhabitants of Egypt. But the children of Israel had light in their homes. No matter how dark the circumstances may become, how oppressing the situation may be, the Creator will supply light to those who trust in Him.

11:1-3. Israel Will Be Compensated. God announced to His people that they would soon leave Egypt, fully compensated for the years of slave labor they had provided to the Egyptians. God had foretold this future event to Abraham—that after the oppression of his descendants, the oppressing nation would be judged and that Israel would come out with great possessions (Gen. 15:14). The Hebrews had labored for the Egyptians for generations. They had been subjected to brutality and injustice, compelled to build Egypt's public works while receiving minimal remuneration. The time had come to ask the Egyptians for their rightful payment. The inhabitants of Egypt, so overcome by the devastating plagues, paid their debt to the Israelites and urged them to leave the land (Ex. 12:35-36). Moses had obtained great respect as the messenger of the God through whom He performed such great signs. The Lord thus communicated to Moses that all their needs would be supplied through His power.

11:4-10. Announcement of Death of the Firstborn. Moses announced to Pharaoh the final judgment of death to the firstborn. Because the king did not let God's firstborn son, Israel (Ex. 4:22-23), depart from the land, God would strike the firstborn of all Egypt. This would occur at midnight, in the darkest moment of night, marked by vulnerability and defenselessness. Moses predicted that this would be the final blow, causing all Egypt to beg for Israel's departure. Moses turned to leave in anger (11:8), frustrated perhaps at the needless judgment of death that would soon take place because of Pharaoh's stubborn heart yet triumphantly certain that the trials of Egypt would soon come to an end.

12:1-28. Institution of Passover. Once again, as in the previous judgments against Egypt, the Lord made provision for the salvation of His people. The ordinance of the Passover came prior to the plague directed against the firstborn of Egypt. The people were to take a lamb *without blemish* (v. 5). Animals that had not experienced injury, were perfect in shape, and had simple coloring without complex spots or other markings were later required as the offerings of Israel (Lev. 22:20-23; Mal. 1:8). The Passover lamb was to be a type of the Promised One, who though without sin (Heb. 4:15), would die as the Lamb of God who takes away the sins of the world (John 1:29).

The sacrifice was to take place at twilight or in the evening (v. 6), or "between the two evenings," a literal translation of the Hebrew phrase. In Egypt, this would have been done before the night of the tenth plague. So, when was Passover kept throughout history? Based on Leviticus 23:5 and Numbers 9:3, which refer to Passover on the date of Nisan 14, it seems likely that Passover lambs were slain in the late afternoon, after the sun began to visibly settle in the horizon but before sunset. This time lines up well with the death of the antitypical "Lamb of God," who died on the cross at the ninth hour (Matt. 27:46-50; Mark 15:34-37).

The instruction to take some of the blood (v. 7) is a reminder that it is only the "blood of the Lamb" that saves and provides redemption (1 Pet. 1:18-19) and by which the Christian might overcome (Rev. 12:11). The blood is life (Lev. 17:11). The unleavened bread (v. 8) is significant because yeast caused the dough to ferment and came to represent corruption. Jesus applied the two Passover symbols of unleavened bread and unfermented wine (grape juice) to Himself when He said, "Take, eat; this is My body" and "Drink from it, all of you. For this is My blood of the new covenant, which is shed for many for the remission of sins" (Matt. 26:26–28). For this reason, the Passover became a day to remember (v. 14), which pointed back to the great day of deliverance in Egypt and pointed forward to the great event when the "firstborn Son" of Mary (Matt. 1:25; Luke 2:7), indeed "the firstborn over all creation" (Col. 1:15) and "the firstborn from the dead" (Rev. 1:5), would shed His innocent blood that all might have eternal life (John 3:16). The divine "passing over" is not based on human efforts (even though it requires obedience) but, rather, on God's active protection and grace (Ex. 12:23, 27).

12:29–30. Tenth Plague: Death of the Firstborn. The death of the firstborn was the final blow to Egypt's dynastic legacy. Pharaoh was the son of Re, and his heir too would one day lead Egypt. The one who was groomed to be king was slain. The successor of Amenhotep II was not his firstborn son. Amenhotep II was likely placed as coregent to his father Thutmose III a few years prior to the king's death, suggesting that Thutmose III wanted to avoid a dynastic crisis at the end of his reign. Hatshepsut's image was erased from many of her monuments throughout Egypt, suggesting that there might have been a rival to the throne. Could it be that Moses, arriving in Egypt after forty years in the wilderness, was perceived as one reclaiming his right to the throne? Why else would Thutmose III have waited so long to have Hatshepsut's image removed? The intrigue surrounding the succession indicates that something unusual was taking place in Egypt. Extraordinary measures were taken in order to secure Egypt's future.

12:31—15:21
The Exodus and Red Sea Crossing

The miraculous judgments of God on Egyptian ideology found their final expression in the deliverance of the children of Israel through the Red Sea and the destruction of Pharaoh's armies. Under the Eighteenth Dynasty, Egypt had developed into one of the world's most advanced military powers. Through the sixteen campaigns of Thutmose III into the Holy Land, the army of Egypt, with its chariots and horses, its infantry and navy, had been tactically refined. In Egyptian military records, Egypt was always victorious, given success by Amun-Re, the god of Thebes and divine father of the king. Israel would face this formidable force in a final showdown between the powers of Egypt and the God of heaven.

12:31–42. Exodus from Egypt. Urged by Pharaoh and the Egyptians to leave with haste, the Israelites were not even able to finish baking their bread. The total number of Israelites given is about six hundred thousand men on foot, besides women and children (v. 37; see "The Number of Israelites Who Left Egypt," p. 210). The *'ereb rab*—variously translated as "mixed multitude," "many other people," or the "ethnically diverse crowd" (v. 38)—that accompanied Israel witnessed the power of the plagues and the protection of Israel and decided to put their trust in God and the leadership of Moses. At this point, Egypt was devastated, and little remained for them in the land of the pharaohs.

12:43–51. Further Passover Regulations. The Passover was to be observed only by Israel and their future generations. Strangers, non-Hebrew servants, and hirelings who desired to become part of this covenant community did so through the act of circumcision. Only then could they take part in the Passover. The command to not break the bones of the paschal lamb (v. 46) was typologically fulfilled in Jesus (John 19:36). The consecration of the firstborn would remind the Israelites of the redemption of grace that they had experienced during the Passover in Egypt (13:1–2). They were the firstborn of God (Ex. 4:22–23), and as such, they belonged to God because of His saving grace.

13:3–16. Festival of Unleavened Bread. This festival would be a memorial of the day when Israel left Egypt in haste. It was to be passed down from generation to generation as a reminder of the historical event. The instruction to wear the story as a sign on the hand and as a reminder between the eyes has been applied in a very literal way by Jews of the first century onward. A box or phylactery with passages from Exodus and Deuteronomy are placed on the forehead, between the eyes, and bound with black leather strips. Likewise, these are also bound around the arms during prayer. This literal interpretation was not the intention of the text, and even Jesus seemed to have criticized the motives behind the outward display of this application (Matt. 23:5). Celebrating the festival would remind the people to serve the Lord who had brought them out of Egypt with a powerful hand (v. 9). It would also be a memorial between their eyes that would orient their journey through life by reminding them of what God had done for them in the past. Consequently, they would often speak of the law of the Lord. In Revelation 14:9, the hand and the mind become the focus of true worship because one's actions and decisions determine whether a person remains faithful to God's commands or follows human inventions.

All the firstborn of the animals were to be allocated for the Lord (v. 12). If they were clean sacrificial animals, they could be offered as sacrifices to God (v. 12). Unclean animals (e.g., donkeys) and firstborn sons were to be redeemed with a lamb (v. 13; cf. Lev. 27:26–27). This ritual commemorated the salvation experienced in Egypt at the Passover when the firstborn sons of Israel were spared.

The Number of Israelites Who Left Egypt

Numbers are common in the Bible, and in most cases, they are not a matter of serious concern. Questions are raised with respect to large numbers, such as the ones given for the Exodus from Egypt. The matter is somewhat complex, and the numbers have been interpreted in different ways. Here only two of them will be mentioned.

1. Consistency of the Numbers. The number of people who left Egypt under the leadership of Moses is given in several places and is consistent. Exodus 12:37 reports that there were about 600,000 men on foot, besides women and children (see also Num. 11:21, where the same number is given). This number of people is confirmed in Exodus 38:25–26, when the number of men (age twenty and above) who gave half a shekel to the sanctuary is listed as 603,550. The census taken before leaving Mount Sinai, which did not include the Levites, indicated that the number of all those at least twenty years old who were able to go to war was 603,550 (Num. 1:45–46). This is a military census, and the 603,550 were men who could still function as soldiers, implying that there were other older male Israelites, besides the Levites, not included in the number. This could also be the case with respect to the number given in Exodus 12:37, where about 600,000 are identified as "men on foot," or infantry. Shortly before entering Canaan, after the previous generation had died during the forty years between censuses, another military census was taken and the number given was 601,730 (Num. 26:2, 51). One has to conclude that the numbers are significantly consistent. Therefore, a nonliteral interpretation would require new evidence that, at present, does not seem to be available (cf. PP 334, 410).

2. A Smaller Number. In spite of the information discussed above, some still argue that the number of Israelites who left Egypt was not that large. It is suggested that the term "thousand" is sometimes used to refer to large military units and is not to be taken literally. However, this explanation is not able to solve the computational difficulties of Exodus 38 and Numbers 1 and 26. Some scholars propose that Deuteronomy can be understood to suggest that Israel was not "more in number than any other people," but rather that they "were the least [the fewest] of all peoples" (Deut. 7:7). To this is added that the Israelites considered the nations of Canaan to be greater than them and, therefore, difficult to dispossess (Deut. 7:17, 22). Besides, if the Lord were to drive out the people of Canaan, there would not be enough Israelites to inhabit the land. It would then become desolate, and the wild animals would become too numerous for them. Accordingly, God promised to drive out the Canaanites gradually (Ex. 23:29–30). Additional concerns about survival conditions in the wilderness are often raised, but one should take into consideration God's miraculous interventions. Although these arguments are worth reflection, the main challenge to this approach to the question is the consistent use of the number 600,000 in the Bible.

13:17—14:20. The Journey Begins. The Israelites were to avoid the area where the Philistines lived—v. 17 (called the "Ways of Horus" by the Egyptians and later the *Via Maris*). The Lord did not want the Israelites to be discouraged by the Egyptian garrisons that lined the shortest route to Canaan. He sent them around by way of the wilderness of the Red Sea (v. 18) to the south instead of along the northern trade and campaign route. Sometimes, God sends His children the "long way" around situations, an approach that often seems illogical. God's ultimate goal is to build up their faith through their experience of His mighty works.

The Israelites went up from Egypt in organized military formation (v. 18; cf. 12:51). The original Hebrew verb in 13:18 derives from the number five and could be translated "and the

The Four-Hundred-Thirty-Year Sojourn

The chronology of the sojourn for the people of Israel has been a matter of debate. Part of the problem is that the Bible presents two different but related numbers of years: 400 years of affliction, according to Genesis 15:13 and Acts 7:6, and 430 years of sojourn, according to Exodus 12:40–41 and Galatians 3:16–17. If both ended in the same year as the Exodus event, when did both time periods begin?

1. *Chronology of Exodus.* The Masoretic texts of Exodus 12:40–41 give the impression that the 430 years covered the time from Jacob's migration to Egypt until the Exodus. This would mean that the people of Israel lived in Egypt a total of 430 years. Those who hold this view argue that 400 is simply a round number and that the distinction between affliction and sojourn is a matter of semantics, thus allowing 430 years for the fulfillment of the prophecy.

2. *Contribution of Paul.* Paul discusses the connection between God's promises to Abraham and the giving of the law at Sinai (Gal. 3:16–17), which was three months after the Exodus event (Ex. 19:1). Paul totals the years between the two occurrences at 430, the same number as Exodus 12:40–41. The promises are those of the covenant God, made to Abraham based on his faith. Consequently, the law, added 430 years later, does not change the promises received by faith. Although Paul is not dealing here with the chronology of the 430 years, he does provide for us the historical event that initiates the time period. It is the moment when God made and ratified His covenant with Abram as recorded in Genesis 15, which itself was promised in Ur some years earlier (Gen. 11:31—12:3). The only existing texts today that reflect this understanding are the Septuagint and the Samaritan Pentateuch. Both state that the 430 years were split between Canaan and Egypt.

3. *Proposed Solutions.* Looking a little more carefully at the chronological details, one notes that Abram was called by the Lord to leave Ur (Gen. 11:31—12:1) sometime before he was 75 years old (his age when he left Haran; Gen. 12:4). This was the beginning of the 430 years, according to Paul (Gal. 3:16–17). Isaac was born when Abraham was 100 years old (Gen. 21:5). The Bible mentions that during the celebration of Isaac's weaning, he was despised by Hagar (an Egyptian) and her son Ishmael. As a result of the conflict (Gen. 21:8–12), Isaac was confirmed as the true seed of Abraham, and Hagar and her son were cast out. Weaning generally happened three years after birth. Thus, it is reasonable to expect that there were about thirty years between Abram's call in Ur and the weaning of Isaac. This would make the weaning celebration the beginning of the 400-year affliction of Abraham's descendants (through Sarah) by the Egyptians (Ishmael was half-Egyptian).

Isaac was 60 years old when Jacob and Esau were born (Gen. 25:26), and Jacob was 130 years old when he migrated to Egypt and referred to his years as a sojourn/pilgrimage (Gen. 47:9). The patriarchal period that began when Abram left Haran lasted 215 years (25 + 60 + 130 = 215). If this is a correct reading of the biblical text, then the Israelites were in Egypt a total of about 215 years, beginning with Jacob's migration to Egypt and ending with the Exodus. Although the biblical text seems to lean toward a shorter sojourn, it is best to avoid being dogmatic about whatever position is taken.

sons of Israel went up in fives"—that is, the people were divided into five major divisions. The Bible does not indicate the size of the divisions or the way in which they were organized, but it is important to remember that Moses, who was a prince of Egypt, was militarily trained and would have known how to organize a large group in military formation (PP 245). The same term is used in Joshua 1:14 and 4:12 to describe the organization of Israel before crossing the Jordan River to take possession of the promised land.

The location for the crossing of the sea that fits the biblical descriptions (see below, "The Route of the Exodus and Mount Sinai") places the crossing at the Gulf of Suez where Jebel 'Ataqah reaches down to the gulf. According to Numbers 33:7, the Israelites moved from Etham and turned back to Pi-Hahiroth (Ex. 14:1–9).

This could mean that they first moved down and camped southeast of the northern tip of the Gulf of Suez. Later realizing that they were trapped by the massive mountain range, they turned back to go around Pi-Hahiroth—"the mouth of the water"—toward the Sinai.

The Egyptian army was mobilized with chariots led by their king. The chariot was one of the most effective war machines, one which led to Egyptian supremacy throughout Asia. During the sixteen military campaigns of Thutmose III, innovators had perfected the lightweight and thereby easily maneuverable chariot, and these would be hastened to meet the Israelites.

As the Israelites made preparations to turn back from their dead-end position, they suddenly saw the army of Pharaoh and were terrified. But Moses encouraged them and told them to not be

The Route of the Exodus and Mount Sinai

The route of the Exodus and the location of Mount Sinai have been debated for centuries. The fact remains that Mount Sinai has never been positively identified. What follows is a review and evaluation of four of the major proposals made for the location of the Red Sea crossing.

1. *Balah Lakes (South Central Route)*. The first proposal interprets the Hebrew phrase *yam sup* as "Reed Sea" instead of "Red Sea" (10:19; 13:18; 15:4, 22; 23:31). This is based on four arguments. First, the term *sup* derives from the Egyptian *twf(y)*, "papyrus reeds." Second, *sup*, when used alone without *yam*, refers to "reeds" (2:3). Third, reeds only grow along marshy freshwater banks, not at the Red Sea. Fourth, *sup* does not mean "red," which was a mistranslation in the LXX. While it is true that *sup* when used alone means "reed," recent studies have shown that when the OT refers to *yam sup* as a combined designation, it consistently refers to the Red Sea, as all modern translations of the Bible attest. Solomon refers to a fleet of his ships being stationed at Elath on the shore of the *yam sup* near Edom (1 Kin. 9:26), or the northern tip of the Gulf of Aqaba. Moses likewise refers to the Gulf of Aqaba as the Red Sea in Deuteronomy 1:40 and 2:1. These three biblical texts make it certain that the Red Sea was understood as the two fingers or gulfs of Suez and Aqaba

and not a lake system on the border of Egypt.

The origin point of the Red Sea crossing is specified with geographical designations: Pi Hahiroth, between Migdol and the sea, opposite Baal-Zephon (Ex. 14:2; Num. 33:7). These locations have been difficult to identify. Some have suggested that these points refer to actual Egyptian place names located in the north, near the beginning of the "Ways of Horus," where the term *migdol*, "tower," appears with a toponym later in the Nineteenth Dynasty reliefs of Seti I. But there remain several problems. (1) If the Red Sea and not the Reed Sea is meant, then the crossing must have been at either the Gulf of Suez or the Gulf of Aqaba. (2) The journey from Rameses (Ex. 12:37) took the children of Israel to Succoth, which is identified as *Tjaru*, the Egyptian border town near the el-Balah lake district in the north. (3) According to Exodus 13:17–18, God did not lead them by the "way of the Philistines," the biblical equivalent to the "Ways of Horus," but sent Israel around by the wilderness of the Red Sea to the south, where they camped at Etham. (4) Crossing at the el-Balah lakes would have been the logical and shortest route, but the Lord told Moses that Pharaoh, noting the circuitous route of the Israelites, would conclude that they were confused by the land and had become enclosed by the wilderness (14:3). The route south and to the west of the Red Sea better fits this description.

2. *Mediterranean (Northern Route).* An extreme northern crossing over the spit of land separating the Mediterranean Sea from Lake Sirbonis has been suggested in connection with a natural tide of waters that would have swallowed the Egyptian army. But there are complications with this suggestion as well. (1) The route lies too close to the "Ways of Horus," which the Lord told Israel to avoid. (2) Deuteronomy 1:2 states that Kadesh-barnea was an eleven-day march from Mount Sinai. This would suggest a location for Mount Sinai in the south, further from Kadesh-barnea. (3) This is the shortest route to Canaan, but the Israelites were expressly told to take a different route.

3. *Gulf of Aqaba (East Central Route).* Another theory is that the Israelites wandered across the Sinai Peninsula and crossed the Gulf of Aqaba into the Arabian Desert, where Mount Sinai was located at Gebel el-Lawz. Some proponents maintain that the Sinai belonged to Egypt and that Israel could not have wandered there because the text says they had left Egypt. Others claim they have located an underwater shelf from Nuweiba beach in Sinai extending across the gulf, and this was where the Israelites crossed. This theory is unlikely for several reasons. (1) The purported underwater shelf between Sinai and Arabia does not exist, according to soundings of the British Admiralty. (2) Chariot wheels in the Gulf of Aqaba have not been confirmed. (3) The distances between Succoth, Etham, and the Red Sea indicate a three-day journey, but the Israelites could not have covered 180 miles (290 km) to reach the Gulf of Aqaba in three days. (4) The biblical account clearly locates Mount Sinai/Horeb in the Sinai,

not in Midian or Arabia (3:12; 19:1–2). To use the Galatians 4:25 reference to identify Mount Sinai as being in Arabia and to extend the understanding of geography in NT times back to the second millennium B.C. ignores the fact that in Paul's time, Arabia included the Sinai Peninsula. (5) Although Egypt had copper mining activities at locations like Serabit el-Khadem, in the Sinai, the border of Egypt was at Tjaru/Succoth. The Egyptians did not consider Sinai as part of their territory in the Eighteenth or Nineteenth dynasties.

4. *Gulf of Suez (Southern Route).* Others have suggested a southern route that took the Israelites west of the Gulf of Suez. They understand the terms Pi Hahiroth, Migdol, and Baal Zephon as geographical or topographical features. Pi Hahiroth may refer to the "opening/mouth of the canal or water," according to one etymology. The term *migdol*, "tower," could refer to a mountain, as could Baal Zephon. If this is the case, then Pi Hahiroth may designate the opening mouth of the northern tip of the Gulf of Suez. If the Israelites camped to the east of the mountain range of Jebel 'Ataqah, perhaps designated *migdol* as these were the closest mountains to the Nile delta to the south (Num. 33:7), their camp would have been located in between the mountains and the sea. As one writer observed, "The Hebrews were encamped beside the sea, whose waters presented a seemingly impassible barrier before them, while on the south a rugged mountain obstructed further progress" (PP 283–84). This description corresponds well with the location southwest of Suez and seems to be the best option. On the other hand, there are no mountains in the north around the el-Balah lake system or the "Ways of Horus," which rules out the northern locations.

afraid (v. 13). Was not the pillar of cloud-encased fire with them (13:21–22; 14:19–20)? Was not the Angel of the Lord moving between them and the armies of Egypt (14:19; 23:20–23; 33:2)? Moses adjured the people to stand firmly still (v. 13). How often do followers of Christ fail to stand still but instead try to work out their own salvation? God instructs, "Be still and know that I am God" (Ps. 46:10a). Moses reassured the Israelites that the Lord would fight for them and that they

should simply be silent (v. 14). The Christian can have a true sense of *shalom*—"peace," "health," "well-being"—even amid the greatest threats and trials, for God is stronger than any opponent.

14:21–30. The Parting of the Sea. A way is made as the sea is divided, or split open (v. 21). The verb *baqa'* here indicates a violent, sudden action, such as splitting wood (Eccl. 10:9) or splitting a rock (Judg. 15:19). The waters were walls on their right hand and on their left (v. 22). It is unclear how high these walls of water were, but a natural explanation does not seem to fit the violent description of the "split" or "cleaved" waters and the resulting walls. The Lord then caused a strong east wind to dry a passage through the sea.

As the pillar of cloud-encased fire followed the Israelites into the sea, the Egyptians followed them. The terms used here are comprehensive: the text mentions that all of Pharaoh's horses, chariots, and horsemen (v. 23) pursued the Israelites. If true to Egyptian military practice, Pharaoh would have led the pursuit up to the point of attack, at which point he would have held back. Egyptian armies consistently appear in Egyptian art in perfect order and symmetry while their enemies are in disarray. But suddenly, the roles were reversed (v. 24). Charioteers veered off to the right and left as chariot wheels fell off (v. 25). Horses stumbled. The God who ordered creation was fighting for Israel, as Israel moved on in martial array. The Egyptians attempted to turn and run. Moses raised his hand once again, and the waters surged back over the Egyptians (v. 27). Not one Egyptian who entered the Red Sea survived, and not one Israelite was lost (vv. 28–29). The emphasis in vv. 30–31 is that Israel "saw"; they witnessed the destruction of their feared enemy. The final triumph of the Lord over Egypt was at that point accomplished. Pharaoh, the god-king, was defeated (Ps. 136:15). So it will be at the close of the cosmic conflict, when all evil powers will be overcome and the enemy will be defeated. God saves those who trust His word and fear Him.

15:1–19. Song of Moses. This song is the poetic recounting of God's saving act at the Red Sea. The people could not have helped but sing and make a joyful noise after God's miraculous intervention. This is the earliest song recorded in Scripture and consists of three stanzas. Each stanza begins with praises to the Lord and ends with the reasons for praising the Lord. The Lord is praised because He is our salvation (v. 2). His name is powerful, and by that power, Pharaoh's armies are no more (v. 4). Though the forces of evil may plot the destruction of God's children, God's right hand delivers them, overthrowing their enemies. The motif of the right hand of Pharaoh as that which delivers Egypt's enemy is often found in Egyptian texts. Here, this image is contrasted with the right hand of the Lord, which is glorious and majestic in power (v. 6).

The certainty of this redemptive act of God in history assures us that we have nothing to fear for the future. The last stanza focuses on future enemies who would be faced in the conquest of Canaan. Because of God's powerful "arm," they would be "as still as a stone" (v. 16). When we face certain impossibilities, when we feel cornered and do not know which way to turn, we can find assurance in "The Song of Moses," for it commemorates a great event in the history of God's people. God's past intervention in our lives assures us that He will carry us and plant us on the "mountain of His inheritance," where the Lord reigns forever and ever (vv. 17–18). Women participated in the singing (vv. 20–21). Miriam prophesied to the women, and the women responded in a refrain with dances and timbrels. Dancing was an expression of holy joy (Ps. 149:3; 150:4), not to be confused with the

Crossing the Sea

The logistics of leading two million Israelites across the Red Sea in one night are not difficult to conceive. The Israelites were not an unorganized group of men, women, and children moving through the desert in a haphazard manner. They were organized in martial array, perhaps in five divisions (13:18). It should not be assumed that they left Egypt in single file. The width of the dry land God created in the midst of the sea is not known, but given Israel's formation, it might have been one mile (1.6 km) wide. Divided into five divisions, the Israelites may have stood 600 abreast, which would have been less than half a mile (.8 km) wide. Thus, each of the five divisions of 402,000 (600 abreast and 670 deep) could have occupied less than four miles (in length, adding another mile (1.6 km) for flocks and herds. Given that the rate of walking would not have exceeded more than thirty minutes for one mile (1.6 km), and the length of the sea crossing at that location was about ten miles (16 km), the crossing could have been accomplished within eight hours, or in one night.

licentious dancing of Herodias's daughter before Herod (Matt. 14:6; Mark 6:22). This song points to the one that will be sung by all those who, in the final day of deliverance, will stand on the sea of glass with Jesus (Rev. 15:3).

15:22—18:27
The Journey to Sinai

The deliverance of Israel from Pharaoh's army at the Red Sea indicated that the people were free from the threat of Egypt at last. After the plagues, this marked the final victory of God over the gods and powers of Egypt. From this moment on, Israel would journey with God as their King. Under this theocracy, God wanted Israel to learn total dependence upon Him and to walk by faith. The journey to Sinai was marked by the itinerary described in Exodus 15 and elaborated upon in more detail in Numbers 33. Moses kept meticulous records of the camping locations until they reached Mount Sinai/Horeb. Egyptian texts suggest that this type of record-keeping was practiced during this period by scribes recording Egyptian military campaigns. Over the course of time, many of these oases have disappeared, making it very difficult to reconstruct the journey precisely. Taking into consideration the rate of travel per day, it seems most likely that Mount Sinai/Horeb was located in the southern part of the Sinai Peninsula (see "The Route of the Exodus and Mount Sinai," p. 212).

15:22—17:16. Miracles of Deliverance. By leading them through the wilderness, God was teaching Israel to trust in Him. The Red Sea seemed to be immovable obstacle, but they would face further impossibilities to test their faith. Each time, God would show them that He could and would supply their needs.

First, God provided water for them (vv. 22–27). For a large group of people, donkeys, cattle, and sheep in a parched desert, water was vital, and after three days it was running out. The first oasis Israel came to after traveling for some forty-seven miles (75 km) south of Suez may have been *'Ain Hawdrah,* although the exact itinerary is not certain. Its water is still bitter today, a fact which (if this is the same location) indicates that the miracle of God through Moses was not of a permanent nature. When the people tasted the water, they grumbled to Moses (v. 24). How typical of human nature! God had just delivered Israel from the Red Sea less than forty-eight hours before, and when faced with the first test, they complained. Interestingly, the Hebrew word referring to God's "test" of the people in v. 25 can also mean "trained" (cf. notes on Gen. 22:1). There is potential for growth in adversity.

Moses was instructed to find a tree and throw it into the water. This was a miracle from God, who used the tree to do what a tree by itself could not achieve. This experience illustrates the correlation between serving the Lord and health. If the people of Israel would have listened to Him by doing what was right in His estimation, God promised to keep them from all the diseases of the Egyptians, for He is the God who heals (v. 26). This promise underlines the significant concern for health visible in the Pentateuchal laws. A similar promise is repeated on the border to Canaan (Deut. 32:39).

The Miracle of the Manna

Some commentators have suggested a natural explanation for the manna, such as the gum secretions of the tamarisk bush. However, there are many indications that the provision of the manna was, in fact, a supernatural act of God. (1) The tamarisk bush only makes these secretions in June and July, while the manna was continuous for forty years. (2) The timing of delivery of the manna was unique. It was provided six days a week, and on the sixth day, twice as much was available. The double portion of manna from the sixth day would not spoil but would be preserved until the seventh day. On any other day, the manna would spoil if saved overnight. On the seventh-day Sabbath, no manna would fall. These specific sequences suggest a miraculous event. (3) The gift of the manna was so significant that Moses commanded Aaron to place an omer of manna in the ark of the covenant. (4) In the NT, Paul calls manna a supernatural food (1 Cor. 10:3). (5) Jesus compared the miraculous gift of Himself as the bread of life with manna that had come down from heaven (John 6:31–63).

God desired to save Israel, not only from Egyptian servitude but also from the diseases of the Egyptians (Deut. 7:15; 28:27, 35). Forensic studies of ancient Egyptian mummies indicate that the upper classes of Egyptian society suffered from the same diseases that plague the affluent today. If a mummy recently identified as Hatshepsut is genuine, then later in life she was obese, suffering from clogged arteries and diabetes. God had previously demonstrated His desire to save His people during the plagues, when disease fell on the Egyptians and their domesticated animals, but Israel and their livestock were protected. In this same manner, God here shared His plan to promote the Israelites' future health. Had they obeyed, they might have given both spiritual and physical light to the nations in truth and well-being (cf. PP 378).

Second, God provided food for the people (16:1–21). The people said *man hu'* ("What is it?"). This became the name of the food—*man* in Hebrew and *manna* in the Greek LXX and NT. The manna was similar to white coriander seed with a taste like honey, flaky, and as fine as frost (16:14, 31; Num. 11:8). It could be ground into a kind of flour, boiled, or made into cakes. It is often described as "heaven's grain" (Deut. 8:3, 16; Neh. 9:20; Ps. 78:24; see "The Miracle of the Manna," p. 215). Through this miracle, God demonstrated to Israel—as well as to future believers—crucial lessons for their journey to the promised land. He will abundantly provide for the needs of His children according to what He knows is best. The human tendency is to long for and return to familiar habits, and Israel was no exception. God indulged their desires but worked out a better plan that would train them to trust and depend on Him. He would provide them with sustenance for their bodies that was superior to the diet of Egypt, which included meat.

Third, God reaffirmed the importance of rest (16:22–30). The daily gift of manna served to train the Israelites concerning proper Sabbath observance. The instruction to gather what they needed in the first days of the week and the miracle of a double provision on the sixth day were given to test them in regard to whether they would follow His *torah*—"law" or "instruction" (vv. 4–5). The text clearly suggests that the Sabbath had been observed since the creation of the world and did not originate during the giving of the law at Sinai. Despite those who did not follow God's instructions, His plan for the Sabbath did not change but became normative throughout their journeys. God provides for His children according to their needs. It is easy to worry about the future, but God's care is sufficient for each day, teaching constant reliance on Him (Matt. 6:11).

Fourth, God wanted the people to remember His blessings (vv. 31–36). The manna was to be kept as a perpetual reminder of God's deliverance and to be put before the Lord, to be kept for subsequent generations (v. 33).

Fifth, God provided water for a second time (17:1–7). After the provision of the manna, there arose another crisis of faith over water. The Lord was teaching His children total dependence on Him. The question raised by Moses is notable: What should I do with these people (v. 4)? During his forty years of exile from Egypt, Moses had learned implicit confidence in the One who had led him from pasture to pasture with his flocks. His question demonstrates the exemplary posture of a leader of God's people. Rather than depend on his own abilities, Moses asked, "What shall I do?" When humanity solicits God's help, He intervenes. In providing the water from the rock at Rephidim, God demonstrated His sovereignty before the elders of Israel so that they could then go and witness to the people. Just as the manna was a type for Christ (John 6:31–63), so also was the water (John 4:14).

Sixth, God blessed the people with victory over their enemies (Ex. 17:8–16). The battle with the Amalekites, the descendants of Esau, initiated a feud that would last through the generations to the establishment of the monarchy under Saul (1 Sam. 15:2–3). This was the first battle Israel was to fight against another nation and would test their reliance on God. The Amalekites used guerilla tactics, fighting the Israelites from behind, where the weak and feeble were easy prey (Deut. 25:18). Joshua appeared here for the first time and commanded the forces against the enemy while Moses stood upon the mountain with the rod of God outstretched. Moses once again demonstrated his absolute dependence on God; however, he did not act alone—he was assisted by others. Here lies a lesson for the Christian today. One cannot prevail in the battles of this life without trusted companions for support. Moses was in earnest prayer on behalf of God's people, supported by Aaron and Hur (vv. 10–13).

18:1–27. Visit of Jethro. The visit of Jethro marked an important development in Moses's leadership effectiveness and Israel's organizational structure. Through the wise counsel of Jethro, God was able to preserve the energies of His chosen leader. Moses had sent Zipporah and their sons back to her father for safety before his confrontations with Pharaoh in Egypt, and the time had come for them to be reunited. Jethro escorted Moses's family to Mount Sinai/Horeb. Jethro's response on hearing about God's deliverance of the Hebrews from Egypt demonstrated that he was truly a righteous man who recognized the uniqueness of the Lord and His superiority to all other gods (v. 11).

As godly priest of Midian, Jethro offered Moses sage advice as he watched a day in the life of God's chosen leader. From morning until evening, people came to Moses with complaints or problems to resolve (v. 14). Why not delegate his burdens by establishing leadership positions over groups of a thousand, groups of a hundred, groups of fifty, and groups of ten? These rulers were not merely judges but heads over their companies in times of peace and war. Their positions involved both civil and military aspects. These men were to be competent, God-fearing, honest men who were not greedy (v. 21). Under God's approval, Moses would be able to endure and serve His people more effectively. Moses did everything Jethro advised (v. 24). Effective leadership cannot be accomplished by one person alone. Responsibilities must be delegated. Courageous servant-leaders share their duties with others and work in harmony to bring about the ultimate goal, namely, that of entering the promised land.

19:1—24:18

GOD ESTABLISHES HIS COVENANT PEOPLE

This central section of Exodus describes the arrival of the people at Sinai (19:1–9) and their meeting with the Lord (19:10–25). In preparation for entering into a covenant with His people, God majestically promulgated the Ten Commandments (20:1–17), gave additional laws—the book of the covenant (20:22—23:19)—and called the people to covenant faithfulness (23:20–33). The covenant was formally made between God and His people (24:1–8), and the section concludes with a meeting between Moses and the Lord on the mountain (24:9–18).

This section reveals that the invincible God who was active in salvation is a God who was also willing to dwell close to His people and who wanted to formalize His relationship with them. The Sinai covenant was decisive for both Israel and for humanity as a whole

(see "Covenant," p. 905). It was essentially a continuation, enlargement, and particularization of God's earlier covenants, containing, in essence, the same design, purpose, and goal of redemption for the human race. The Sinai covenant was *not* a covenant of works aimed at teaching the Israelites salvation through obedience to the law. Like the covenant that God made with Abraham and the other patriarchs, this one was also a covenant of grace. Surely it demanded obedience, but this obedience was not a way to gain salvation. It was a way to express gratitude to God for the salvation already provided and experienced—redemption from Egypt.

19:1–25
Arrival at Sinai

As Israel established camp at the base of Mount Sinai, the God who had revealed Himself in judgments against Egypt would reveal Himself to His redeemed people as the covenant Lord. The giving of the law is one of the major focal points of the Torah, if not the entire OT. Although the law was recognized in Genesis (PP 363), here it would be formally written by God's own finger for the children of Israel.

19:1–8. A Peculiar People. The journey of the Israelites through the wilderness took them to the mountain of God, located in the wilderness of Sinai. This is in agreement with other passages that locate Mount Sinai/Horeb in the Sinai Peninsula (3:12; Num. 10:12). The journey may have taken about forty-five days, which suggests that they camped for considerable time at certain locations before moving to the place where they would remain for the remaining events recounted in the book. At Mount Sinai, the Lord revealed His plan and purpose for Israel (vv. 3–8). This was the first time that God personally (through Moses) instructed Israel since carrying them on eagles' wings from Egypt (v. 4; Deut. 32:11–12). Three unique statements were made concerning God's covenant people.

First, they were to become God's own possession, a special treasure (v. 5). In contrast to other types of possessions, such as real estate, Israel became God's personally obtained and privately owned treasure because of His love and affection (cf. Deut. 7:6; 14:2; 26:18, 19), which implies deep value and a special relationship. Second, they were set apart as a kingdom of priests (v. 6). This phrase is found only here in the entire OT. God's particular choice of one people had universal implications. While not every Israelite was a priest, as a nation they were to function, in one way or another, as God's priestly agents, to bless all the nations of the world. Third, Israel was to become a holy nation, specially dedicated to God (cf. 1 Pet. 2:9). Again, this phrase is used only once in the OT although the modified expression "holy people" can be found a number of times in Deuteronomy (Deut. 7:6; 14:2, 21; 26:19; 28:9). It was God's promise and design to make them holy by separating them from all other nations. The Israel of the covenant was to be primarily a religious entity (see Lev. 19:2; Ezek. 36:25–28).

Obedience to God's commandments, included in the terms of the covenant, made the holiness of the people visible. The Lord planned to establish Israel as His own holy people (Deut. 28:9; cf. 7:6–9), and to that end, He called them to keep His commandments. In fulfillment of His covenant promises, He made obedience possible by dwelling among them. In this sense, holiness is not something humans can achieve through their own strength but rather something received and reflected in a life of faith and obedience. The response of the people to God's gracious offer, grounded in their redemption from Egypt, is clear: they promised to do everything the Lord had said (v. 8; cf. Ex. 24:7). But the eagerness of the people to do so is ironic when compared with their subsequent failures.

19:9–25. Meeting a Holy God. God gave specific instructions for how Israel should prepare to meet Him. They were to sanctify themselves through outward ritual purification reflecting inner conviction. This included washing their garments (v. 14; cf. Num. 8:21), abstaining from sexual relations as part of the purification required (v. 15; cf. Lev. 15:18), and building a fence around the mountain (v. 12). The Lord's presence made the mountain holy. There is hardly any reason to believe that the mountain was volcanic and that God's presence caused an eruption. This naturalistic interpretation should not be imposed on a supernatural event. Throughout the OT, theophanies or powerful manifestations of God coming down to earth are associated with earthquakes (Ps. 77:18; Is. 29:6; Amos 8:8; Nah. 1:4), lightning (Zech. 9:14), and smoke or clouds (Is. 6:4; 19:1). The Second Coming will likewise be accompanied by an earthquake, lightning, and Jesus riding on a cloud (Matt. 24:27; Luke 21:27; Rev. 14:14; 16:18) together with a voice and the sound of a trumpet (Matt. 24:31; 1 Cor. 15:52; Rev. 4:1).

Moses and Aaron were called up to the mountain to speak with God, but the priests and the people were to stay within the boundaries (v. 24; see the section on Theology in the Introduction). Order is part of the nature of God's people. They were to stand within the camp and not cross the boundaries, for if they did, death would ensue (v. 12). As the Lord came down, Moses went up (v. 20). It was only because God came down that Moses was able to approach.

20:1–21
The Ten Commandments

Here is found the most important piece of legislation in human history. The law came out of the mouth of the Lord and was written by His own finger; therefore, this religious/moral code is immovable and unchangeable. It determines how humans should relate to God and to each other (see "The Decalogue in Deuteronomy and Exodus," p. 322). There is no evidence in the OT or the NT that God intended to modify or abolish the Ten Commandments. Submission to them constitutes a joy and a pleasure for Christian believers.

20:1–2. Preamble. The Ten Commandments, or ten words, are located within the context of God's redeeming grace that freed His people from the bondage of Egypt. God revealed Himself in this tangible demonstration of love—not in abstract or philosophical terms, but as a God who acts in history. Only love can produce a response of love and obedience (Deut. 5:6). The experience and memory of redemption brings together gospel and law. Only the Redeemer can call His people to love Him with all their hearts (Deut. 6:5; cf. Ps. 18:1; Jer. 2:2; Matt. 22:37). Thus, the first four commandments focus on our worship of God (Rev. 14:7), for it is only in the context of loving worship that we will be able to live in harmony with those around us. The law then defines our relationship with God on the vertical level and our relationship with humanity on the horizontal. The last six commandments are summarized in the words "Love your neighbor as yourself" (Lev. 19:18; Matt. 19:19). Jesus revealed the relational nature of the Decalogue when He said that those who love Him will obey His commands (John 14:15).

Eight of the Ten Commandments are often interpreted as being negative: "Do not...." But in the context of the introduction, which reveals God as the great deliverer, these may also be interpreted in the following way: "Because I am the Lord who brought you out of the land of Egypt.... You will have no other gods before me." This reveals the reason for keeping the commandments—out of love and devotion for the One who created and redeemed humanity. The Hebrew negative term *lo'*—"do not"—is to be understood not only as a prohibition but also as an enabling promise.

20:3. First Commandment. Although Israel came out of the polytheistic world of ancient Egypt and would enter the polytheistic world of Canaan, they were set apart to worship the one true and living God. The Lord who made heaven and earth will not share worship with any other, for there is no other (see Is. 37:19). In fashioning for themselves gods, the surrounding nations came to worship nature and themselves. Little has changed in the modern scientific age, which is focused on autonomous reason and experience. Humanity is placed at the center of the universe, and we degrade ourselves when we worship nature and the works of our minds and hands (Rom. 1:22–25).

20:4–6. Second Commandment. The ancient Egyptians believed that by following the activities portrayed on tomb reliefs, images, and statues, the soul of the deceased could experience the afterlife. They deified all aspects of nature, such as the sun and the moon "in heaven above," the animals and trees "on earth beneath," and the Nile River, which was the sea of "water beneath." These images lowered humanity's conception of God (PP 373). Idolatry was a phenomenon practiced not only in the ancient world but also throughout human history, even in modern times. Paul was greatly disturbed when he observed the pervasive idolatry in Athens (Acts 17:16). Paul's message to the Areopagus, the philosophical leaders of Athens, was that God cannot be reduced to a mere object.

The Lord God, the Creator of all things, alone deserves worship and honor. By worshiping nature rather than the Creator, humanity places itself under the control of demonic deception. We are not to attempt to fashion God's image, we are to be restored to God's image. It is in this context that many OT passages equate Israel to a harlot, or an unfaithful wife, for pursuing foreign gods (Ex. 34:15–16; Jer. 3:1; Hos. 2:5). We are called to be exclusively faithful to God, who longs to show us His divine mercy and love (v. 6). The commandment states that unfaithfulness to God will impact the third and fourth

generations. Through hereditary tendencies and the imitation of parents and culture, the sin is passed down. Today, idols can be anything to which we assign the priority and commitment that belong only to God. In popular culture, movie stars, athletes, and musicians receive the honor, respect, and admiration that only God deserves, as our Redeemer. Furthermore, time spent in the use of contemporary means of communication bombards the senses with the unimportant and desensitizes the mind. The focus has shifted away from the infinite God who created the universe. God's word alone provides an accurate image of who He is and what He has done for us.

20:7. Third Commandment. The name of the Lord is to be respected, honored, and revered. It should not be spoken carelessly. It should not be invoked in a dishonest oath. The name of the Lord is awesome in significance. It is by His name that He reveals Himself (3:13; 33:19) and by invoking His name that people are blessed (Num. 6:27). His name is to be praised (Ps. 145:2), for it is exalted (Ps. 148:13). Engaging in false worship profanes His name (Lev. 20:3; 21:6). Those who enter into a covenant relationship with the Lord are also called by His name. If they are known as followers of God but do not live as followers of God, then their witness (James 1:26) and their worship are in vain (Is. 1:11; Matt. 15:7–9). Believers represent God in every aspect of their lives.

20:8–11. Fourth Commandment. The Sabbath is a gift from God to humanity, instituted at Creation (see "The Sabbath Commandment in Deuteronomy," p. 323). This commandment stands at the center of the ten words as a reminder of God's creative act and His relational nature in our lives. It is the longest commandment. It has a distinct syntactic structure and specifies the *what, when, how,* and *why* of Sabbath observation. First, we are instructed *what* to do. We are to remember the Sabbath day. There is a double meaning here. On the one hand, we are pointed back to Creation week to recall what God accomplished. We are also reminded to keep the Sabbath holy. We are to sanctify it, or set it apart for holy use. Thus, by remembering that on the seventh day of Creation God blessed and made holy the Sabbath, setting it for communion with Him, we continue worshiping the One who is the giver of all life.

Second, the commandment specifies *when* we are to remember: the seventh day is a Sabbath of our God (v. 10). The seven-day cycle of the week was instituted at Creation. The week was not related to any other natural order (the earth rotating on its axis for a 24-hour day, or revolving around the sun for the year). This measurement of time was ordained by the Creator, and we are invited to commemorate this great event with Him every week on the seventh day. That God Himself rested on the Sabbath (Gen. 2:2) and that the Sabbath was observed by the Israelites in their weekly collection of manna (Ex. 16:23–26) demonstrates that the commandment of the seventh-day Sabbath was established and known long before Sinai.

Third, the commandment describes *how* we are to keep the Sabbath. We are to do no work (v. 10; cf. Ex. 23:12), "to desist," "to cease" (which is what the verb form *shabat*—a term related to the noun *shabbat*—means) from our daily labor. We work during the first six days of the week, but the seventh day is a divinely instituted time reserved for God. The command to rest extends to the entire household. The whole family, as well as servants, livestock, and guests, are to enjoy the peace of the Sabbath. The extended household also should enjoy the rejuvenation of resting in the Lord as part of the family of God.

Finally, the commandment tells us *why* we are to keep the Sabbath. "In six days the LORD made the heavens and the earth, the sea, and all that is in them." Then He rested on the seventh day, as an example to us (v. 11). But He also spent that day enjoying the fellowship of Adam and Eve. Therefore, He blessed the Sabbath day and sanctified it, or made it holy (v. 11; cf. Gen. 2:3). It is blessed because this relational God desires communion with us. It is holy because He set it apart for us. Spending time with our Creator renews us spiritually and physically. Calling the world to worship the Creator (Rev. 14:7) and to keep His commandments will be a special characteristic of the remnant living just before Jesus returns (Rev. 12:17; 14:12; see "Creation, Sabbath, and the Sanctuary," p. 231).

20:12. Fifth Commandment. Our relationship with God, as prescribed in the first four commandments, is here brought to bear on the single most important relational unit on earth— the family. Both the fourth and fifth commandments begin with positive injunctions. God's plan for preserving the family is foundational to the church and society. Here, children receive their first instruction in obedience, courtesy, respect, and honor. All of life's most important lessons are to be initially taught in the home.

God emphasizes this relationship with the words "Honor your father and your mother." This honor and respect for properly instituted authority will spill over into the way we relate to society.

Here, the verb "to honor" (Heb. *kabed*) implies a continuous action and attitude, indicating that to honor one's parents is not a onetime event. As long as one's parents are alive, they are worthy of honor. "Honor" also means "heavy" or "weighty" and is the word used when God is given glory. How we honor our parents is a very weighty matter. Fathers and mothers carry the authority of governance in the home. How do children give their parents honor? By caring for them and obeying them "in all things, for this is well pleasing to the Lord" (Col. 3:20; cf. Eph. 6:1).

There is a promise associated with honor and obedience. The children of Israel had just come out of Egypt and were entering a new land. God promised them that if they honored their parents, their days would be long in the new land of Canaan. This promise is also for us. Even though disobedience to parents is one of the characteristics of people living in the last days (Rom. 1:30; 2 Tim. 3:2), there will also be those who remain in an honorable relationship with their parents, willing to listen to their instruction in the ways of God, His love, and His salvation. They too will enjoy a long life in the heavenly kingdom.

20:13. Sixth Commandment. Honoring the life of our neighbor is one of the sacred duties of humanity (Gen. 9:5–6). Jesus extended this commandment to incorporate not only the physical act of murder but also anger (Matt. 5:21–22). John the apostle included hatred (1 John 3:14–15). The story of Cain and Abel indicates not only how rapidly sin infected the first family of God but also how anger toward a brother can lead to murder (Gen. 4:5–8). Our thoughts and words must be guarded and focused on the respect and honor due to others because they were also created in the image of God.

20:14. Seventh Commandment. Instituted at Creation, marriage is the most sacred trust instituted by God between man and woman (Gen. 1:27–28; 2:21–23). The union between husband and wife forms the bond that holds the family together (Gen. 2:24) and exemplifies the union between Christ and the church (Eph. 5:31–32). This commandment protects marriage and trust, which adultery destroys. The commandment also extends to other forms of sexual immorality, such as premarital sex (called "fornication"; 1 Cor. 6:13–17; Eph. 5:3–4). Sexual purity is a matter of the heart. Jesus warns against the lust of the flesh and committing adultery in one's heart (Matt. 5:28). In our media-driven society, sexual immorality has become a multibillion-dollar industry. Faithful vigilance on the part of Christians protects not only the sacred bonds of marriage but also their own souls (cf. Prov. 6:32–33), or their connection to God and the salvation it brings (1 Cor. 6:9–10). As far-reaching as the impact of sexual sin is, the grace of God offers the sinner redemption (1 Cor. 6:11) as well as the power to leave sin behind (John 8:11).

20:15. Eighth Commandment. Faithful stewardship and selfless giving are essential to the life of a follower of God and greatly impact relationships between neighbors and with God. Stealing breaks these relationships. When we take what is not ours, we exhibit a lack of trust in God to care for our needs, and we deprive our neighbors of God's providence for them. Stealing does not simply involve property theft but also extends to other practices in society. Greed has led companies to cheat employees by downsizing their workforces and forcing the remaining employees to do more work than they are being paid for. It has led employees to help themselves to office supplies and cheat on their time cards. This commandment protects people from being the victim of theft and from acting the part of the perpetrator. Our time and talents are gifts from God. We are accountable not only to God but also to our families and employers. Whenever we seek to gain from the loss of others or are more devoted to our private advantage than to equity, we infringe on the government of God.

One of the great responsibilities God gave humanity at Creation was the stewardship of the world (Gen. 1:26, 28). Good stewardship requires hard work and dedication (Prov. 6:10–11) to maintaining and increasing our God-given gifts and talents (Matt. 25:14–30). It shapes our characters into the likeness of God, who is the most sublime Giver. Everything we own belongs to Him, and we have been called to share it with those who are less fortunate than we are (Deut. 10:18; Acts 6:1–2). The rich young ruler was instructed by Jesus to give all that he had to the poor, to take up the cross and follow Him (Mark 10:21). When we find joy in giving, we will be less inclined to take or hoard what ultimately belongs to God.

20:16. Ninth Commandment. Honesty and integrity, or truthfulness, is the basis for trust in human relationships and is the core of God's character. He is truth (Deut. 32:4; Ps. 31:5), and everything He does is true and faithful (Heb. *'emunah*; Ps. 33:4). The entirety of His word is truth (Ps. 119:160; John 17:17), and His truth or fidelity (*'emunah*) continues throughout all generations (Ps. 100:5; cf. 117:2). Jesus is the way, the truth, and the life (John 14:6), and He sent His Spirit, who would guide us into all truth (John 16:13). Because the followers of Christ are to be transformed into His likeness, Paul urges Christians to be honest with one another—for we are members of each other in the same body (Eph. 4:25)—and to learn truth (1 Tim. 2:4).

The commandment addresses perjury in a court of law (23:1) but applies to speaking falsely about others, damaging their character, or slandering their reputation through falsehood and gossip (Ps. 31:13; 101:5; Prov. 10:18). Focusing on an individual's faults, having a critical attitude, or gossiping can give one a sense of superiority, but it essentially destroys another person for the sake of one's own ego. Character assassination does not foster positive relationships, nor does it draw the individual or neighbor closer to God. Remaining silent when others take part in these actions, rather than standing up for the individual, is also being dishonest, for it allows lies and deceit to go unchecked. The suppression of truth is not worthy of a disciple of the God who is truth.

20:17. Tenth Commandment. This commandment stands at the root of the other nine because it addresses the heart, where thoughts determine actions. Most other ancient laws dealt with actions, but not the motives behind those actions. God sees the heart (Gen. 6:5; 1 Sam. 16:7; Heb. 4:13), and it is upon our hearts that God desires to place His character (2 Cor. 3:3). Desiring that which is not ours, whether a neighbor's property, wife, servants, or anything that we do not possess, can lead us to break the preceding commandments. We are called to be content with what God gives us and employ those gifts to honor Him for the glory of His kingdom. In a world that is obsessed with materialism, the challenge for the believer is to be fully content in Him. True contentment requires submission and obedience to His will (1 Tim. 6:6–10).

20:18–20. The People's Response. God's presence on the mountain impressed the people with its power and magnificence. They were terrified at the sights and sounds coming from the mountain. The Lord had spoken directly to them, and the experience was terrifying, partly because they recognized that they were sinners. Their sense of wretchedness in the presence of God's holiness caused them to tremble (cf. Is. 6:4–5). But Moses instructed them not to be afraid or to forget this experience because this had happened so that reverence for God would keep them from sin (v. 20). How often humans become arrogant and sin boldly, forgetting the almighty power of the Creator who is able, through His everlasting love, to empower us to live holy lives!

20:22—23:19
The Book of the Covenant

There are several legal sections in the Pentateuch, built upon the principles of the Decalogue, that serve to instruct God's people regarding the application of the law of God in daily life. Many of these laws could be referred to as law cases, where God deals with issues that His people are likely to face. In the next three chapters, some of these situations are described in what is called the "book of the covenant" (24:7). In contrast to the Ten Commandments, these were given to Moses privately, to be communicated to the people. These laws provided the new nation of Israel with God's perspective on many issues, such as the sanctity of life, marriage, commemorative holy days, the Sabbath, and personal rights. Through these laws, God created within the covenant a social and religious order—one that, if followed, would result in a righteous society with its members at peace with God and each other.

20:22–26. Law of the Altar. Verses 22 and 23 serve as a transition to the new regulations. God spoke to the people from heaven without being seen; therefore, they were not to make any image of Him. How should they worship Him? At this point, the Lord asked them to worship Him by offering sacrifices to Him on an altar made of earth. It would be a place of meeting for God and His people, chosen by Him, where He would bless them. In the ancient world, there were many types of altars and associated modes of worship. Excavations have revealed altars dating back to the earliest periods of history. God instructed that if the altars were made of stone, they were not to be finished with tools but were to be built of unhewn stone so that the craftsmanship would not become an object of worship. The focus would remain on God and

the sacrificial victim that pointed to Christ. In order to preserve proper decorum, there should not be many steps leading up to the altar.

21:1. Ordinances Set before Them. Some have suggested that many of the laws in Exodus 21–23 and other parts of the Pentateuch were borrowed from ancient extrabiblical law codes (Eshnunna, Hammurabi, Hittite, and Assyrian). Although similarities may be expected since most societies have legislation against murder, theft, and other crimes, comparisons must also take into account the differences between these sources. No other law code was based on a covenant relationship between a god or gods and a people. Additionally, all the other known law codes were produced by a particular culture, whereas Hebrew legislation came through divine revelation. Further comparisons suggest that biblical laws were less harsh in the treatment of women and servants.

21:2–11. Rights of Slaves. Israel had come out of slavery from Egypt, and they were here given strict laws that protected slaves from the cruelty they themselves had experienced. Sometimes poverty forced people to sell themselves or their children into slavery. Debtors were sold by their creditors, but under no circumstances were Hebrew slaves to serve in perpetuity against their will; they were to be released after six years (v. 2). Only if servants wished to continue serving their masters would they be allowed to do so (vv. 5–6). The rights given to servants under these circumstances protected them from injustice.

21:12–32. Laws Concerning Physical Violence and Lex Talionis. These law cases parallel the fifth and sixth commandments. Dishonoring parents by physically striking them was a most serious capital offense (Deut. 21:18–21). Cursing parents was equated with blaspheming God (Lev. 24:16). This law reflects the honor and dignity due to parents, who stand before their children in the place of God (cf. PP 308). Murderers were to be punished based on intentionality. Premeditated murder was punishable by death (v. 14), but asylum in the "cities of refuge" was offered in cases that were not premeditated (v. 13; Num. 35:9–28; Deut. 19:1–13). Slaves or servants in the ANE were the sole property of their owners, who had complete control in decisions of life and death. Biblical legislation gave slaves certain legal rights. Justice and mercy were demonstrated in these legislations. The principle of "an eye for an eye" is found throughout vv. 23–32 and in two additional passages in the Pentateuch (Lev. 24:17–22; Deut. 19:15–21), and Jesus also referred to it (Matt. 5:38–41). The action itself was never carried out literally in the Bible (the exception being "a life for a life"). The principle implied is that punishment for injuries done to a person or an animal is to be commensurate with the harm done. Revenge, which often escalated a situation and led to more harm, was forbidden. The punishment for children and adults was the same, underlining the high level of value placed on children (vv. 22–25).

21:33—22:15. Laws Concerning Property. In an agricultural economy, where animals were considered indispensable to the landowner, this category of property was especially protected in the cases of accidental harm, injury, or loss. According to the circumstances, the appropriate compensation was specified. The specific law cases dealing with theft indicate how seriously the offense is regarded by God. The owner was to be compensated fivefold for a stolen ox, fourfold for a lamb (22:1), and twofold if the thief were caught within twenty-four hours with the stolen animal (v. 4). The restitution was comparable to the value of the animal and, in the latter case, how long the offender had deprived the owner from the service of the animal.

Property damage to fields, either by animals or fire, was to be fully compensated by those responsible (22:5–6). The person owning the animal causing the damage or responsible for starting the fire was to make restitution, even if the act was unintentional or due to negligence.

Before there were lockable storage facilities or banks, it was common in the ancient world to entrust property to a neighbor, friend, or relative (vv. 7–15). This set of legislation deals with cases where silver or gold, animals, clothing, or other valuable items were stolen, lost, damaged or hurt in some way while in the trusted possession of someone other than the owner. In situations of theft, the thief had to repay double what was stolen. In the case of inadvertent loss or death by wild animal, an oath was given of no ill intent, the owner was to accept that oath, and no restitution was required.

22:16–17. Laws Concerning Seduction. The honor of young women was protected by legislation dealing with enticement. The Hebrew verb *patah* can mean "to seduce" or "allure" and indicates that both participants consent to a sexual act. The law required that a man who seduced a virgin must marry her, with her father's permission. The right of the father to refuse her hand in marriage remained, but in that case, the woman was to be compensated by a full bride-price, or dowry, to support her future. These laws were meant to govern proper acts of courtship, marriage, and sex, and the order in which they were to take place. Even if both individuals were equally guilty, the man was to marry the woman because they had acted as if they were married by having premarital sex. The father was to make the final verdict because he was obliged to protect his daughter from decisions that could permanently damage her future.

22:18–20. Three Capital Crimes. These death penalties were legislated for abhorrent crimes that challenged the order of God's creation. Each also involved false worship. The first addressed witchcraft and sorcery. God's people were not to allow a sorceress, a woman who practiced magic, among them. Both men and women involved in the occult were to be put to death (Lev. 20:27). Practices such as fortune-telling, conjuring spells, attempted communication with the dead, acting as a medium, or participating in other magical occupations were strictly forbidden (Deut. 18:9–14). God's plan and purposes would not be manipulated. The second abhorrent crime was bestiality, or intercourse with an animal. Such an act defied God's created order in nature and defiled God's image in creating humanity as man and woman. This was attested in Canaanite religious practice where deities were worshiped in the form of animals. The third capital offense was offering up sacrifices to pagan deities. Each of these violations was extremely serious in the eyes of God. Today, these activities are becoming increasingly more common. Best-selling books and media for children and teens are saturated with the occult. In Europe and America, there are a growing number of Wiccan practitioners, and in Africa and Asia, ancestor worship remains prevalent. In some places in the Caribbean and South America, macumba, voodoo, and other African religious traditions are popular and are even integrated into certain branches of Christianity. The text reminds us that God detests such practices.

22:21–27. Laws Involving Social Obligations. The laws concerning strangers, widows, orphans, and the poor revealed God's concern for the vulnerable in society. The foreigner or stranger was not to be mistreated but was to be honored because the children of Israel knew what it was like to live as strangers in the land of Egypt (v. 21). The alien was to be loved (Deut. 10:19) and treated like those who were native born (Lev. 19:34). Oppression of the weak was a trademark of Egypt in Scripture and found its strongest expression in the enslavement of the Israelites. Widows and orphans were to be cared for and not abandoned. They were to be protected and provided with clothing and food (vv. 22–24; Deut. 10:18). Those who have been in these situations, as Israel was in Egypt, will understand how important the church is in providing a sense of family and home to those who have neither. We are not to take advantage of the poor by making a profit from their misfortune (v. 25). God's passion for the disadvantaged is visible in the usage of "I" or "me" in this section. The mission of God's people is to ease the suffering of the world.

22:28—23:9. Religious and Social Obligations. Proper respect was to be shown to God and to the leaders of the people, applying concepts contained in the third commandment (v. 28; 20:7). Speaking in a way that insulted, blasphemed, or applied the prerogatives of God to oneself was not permitted. God instructed Israel to give the first and best of their agricultural and animal products to Him (vv. 29–30). This included the redemption of the firstborn son by a money payment (13:13; Num. 3:46–48). Israel was to be a holy people unto God (v. 31; Ex. 19:6; Lev. 11:44–45; 19:2; Deut. 7:6), which was connected to food prohibitions here and elsewhere (Deut. 14:21).

Living a life of honesty and integrity is an application of the ninth commandment (Ex. 20:16; 23:1). Peer pressure must be avoided when seeking justice (23:2). Sympathy toward the poor is not to distort justice when the person has committed a crime. The reason given is that God Himself will not justify the wicked (v. 7), for ultimately, all will face His judgment.

23:10–19. Sabbatical Laws and the Festivals. The fourth commandment (20:8–11) was the focus of law cases dealing with the sabbatical year and the seventh-day Sabbath. During the sabbatical year, landowners were instructed to let the land rest by not plowing it—a beneficial agricultural practice. There was also a social interest in the legislation: the practice provided food for the poor and for the animals. Orchards, vineyards, and fields were not to be harvested, allowing those in need to take what they required

for sustenance (23:11). It is reiterated here that the seventh day was for rest, not work (v. 12; cf. 16:22–30; 20:9; Deut. 5:13–14). This rest means "to cease" from work for the benefit of animals, servants, and strangers. It is God's desire that all have this seventh day to rest.

23:20–33. Divine Guidance and Obedience. God ratified the covenant by sending His Angel, His Son Jesus Christ (Mal. 3:1; cf. PP 352, 366), for only Christ was able to pardon transgressions (v. 21). God declares, "My Name is in Him," which indicates that He is coequal with God (John 1:1–31; Col. 1:13–19; Heb. 1:8). God through His Son is always the initiator of the covenant relationship, but this covenant—like the ones in Genesis—was conditional: it depended on whether the people would obey Him and do all that He instructed them (v. 22). If the people upheld their part of the covenant, then God would fulfill His promises and provide blessings. God promised to drive out the inhabitants of the land of Canaan using fear, confusion, and hornets (vv. 27–28), but this would take longer than a year, in order to preserve the ecological balance of the land (v. 29). This is what might have been had this generation believed in the promises of God rather than the report of the ten spies who returned from Canaan (Num. 13:26–33; see "The Extermination of the Canaanites" [p. 330] and "Holy Warfare" [p. 372]). God stipulated that His covenant was between Him and His people, not with other nations (v. 32).

24:1–18. Covenant and the Tablets of Stone. God wrote the Ten Commandments with His finger, and Moses transcribed all the words of the book of the covenant (v. 4) before reading them to the people (v. 7). The Hebrew terms found in conjunction here (*karat* and *berit*) literally mean to "cut a covenant." In the ancient world, it was a common practice in treaty-making to kill and "cut" an animal or animals in order to establish or ratify a covenant. The covenant with Abram in Genesis 15:7–21 was ratified by cutting animals in two. Then God, represented by the smoke/cloud and torch, passed between the divided pieces. Moses requested that young Israelite men sacrifice oxen as burnt and peace or fellowship offerings to the Lord, and he sprinkled the blood on the altar and on the people (vv. 6, 8). This represented the establishment of a covenant relationship between God and Israel. Israel declared that they would do everything the Lord had said to do.

Thus, they affirmed their commitment to the conditions (see Ex. 19:5–8).

Moses ascended the mountain once more to receive from the Lord the tablets of stone and the statutes. The tablets of stone were written by God for the purpose of instructing them (v. 12). The word *torah*, "law," means, in its broadest sense, "teaching" or "instruction" and refers to all the revealed will of God. Here it is used in its narrow sense to designate the Ten Commandments. Their all-inclusive purpose was to govern the covenant between God and the people. Moses stayed with God on the mountain for forty days and forty nights (v. 18). This foreshadowed Christ's experience immediately after His baptism, before beginning His earthly ministry that would bring reconciliation and the establishment of a new covenant (Matt. 4:2; Luke 4:1–2).

25:1—40:38
THE SANCTUARY: GOD'S PRESENCE AMONG HIS PEOPLE

The main topic of Exodus 25–40 is the sanctuary and its construction and significance. The chapters could be divided into three sections: instructions related to the building of all key aspects of the sanctuary (25.1—31:18), the episode of the golden calf (32:1—34:35), and the construction of the sanctuary and its inauguration (35:1–40:38). The instructions given to Moses for the creation of the sanctuary, its tabernacle, its furniture, the courtyard, the incense and oil, and the clothing and implements of the priests underlined the significance of having the covenant Lord dwelling among them and the seriousness of that privilege. The explicit attention to detail also highlights the importance that God places on worship and how it is to take place. Since the later construction account (chaps. 35–40) closely parallels the wording of the initial one (chaps. 25–31), they will be treated together here, as indicated with parentheses in each relevant heading.

25:1—31:18
Instructions for the Construction of the Sanctuary

The instructions given for the building of the sanctuary begin with the ark of the covenant (25:10–22), where God's divine presence would reside, then move to two of the articles of furniture in the Holy Place (25:23–40). This is followed by the construction of the tabernacle (26:1–37), one of the articles of furniture in the courtyard

(27:1–8), and the courtyard itself (27:9–19). Directions are also provided for the care of the lampstand (27:20–21). The clothing for the priests and their consecration, along with offerings, are then described (chaps. 28–29). Finally, the altar of incense, the issue of ransom money, the laver (also called the basin), and recipes for the oil and incense are discussed (chap. 30). The instruction ends with guidelines for the artisans and a review of the Sabbath law (chap. 31). This systematic presentation indicates the structure and order of God's design (for a discussion of the literary structure of this section and its significance, see "Creation, Sabbath, and the Sanctuary," p. 231).

25:1–9. Make Me a Sanctuary. The construction of the sanctuary would require the people to provide resources in the form of an offering to the Lord. Their offerings were to be given, presumably, from the plunder that the defeated Egyptians had conferred on them when leaving Egypt (Ex. 12:36) as back pay for their years of labor. Offerings then and today are to spring from a thankful and responsive heart (v. 2; 2 Cor. 9:6–7), otherwise they lack true spiritual value. Part of worship is returning to God a portion of the many blessings He has given us. Every member of the community was, in this way, a participant in the construction of the sanctuary. The response of the people was so overwhelming that they were restrained from giving more (Ex. 35:21–29; 36:3–7).

From the time of Creation, when He walked in the Garden with Adam and Eve, God has always been interested in being close to humans, even dwelling with them. The sanctuary provided the means by which God could dwell among the Israelites. The term *mishkan* means "tabernacle" or "dwelling." This is expressed in other places as well (Lev. 15:31; 26:11). It points to the incarnation of Christ, when the Word became flesh and made His dwelling among us (John 1:14). This theme of God's nearness anticipates the new earth, where God's dwelling and tabernacle will be with His people (Rev. 21:3; see "Sanctuary, Covenant, Worship, and Forgiveness," p. 226).

While on the mountain, God presented Moses with the pattern of the sanctuary and its furnishings (v. 9), and Moses was directed to follow the divine instructions. The Hebrew term for "pattern" (*tabnit*) can also be translated as "model" (2 Kin. 16:10) or "plan" (1 Chr. 28:19). A functional model of the heavenly sanctuary was to be used in the construction of the earthly sanctuary. God dwells in the original heavenly sanctuary, where Christ mediates for us (Acts 7:44; Heb. 8:2; 9:23–24).

25:10–22 (37:1–9). The Ark of the Covenant.
The ark of the covenant, with its cherubim, was the focal point of the sanctuary, representing the throne of God. The ark was made of acacia wood overlaid with gold. It would contain the tablets of stone and, eventually, the budding rod of Aaron and a bowl of manna. Above the ark was the mercy seat, or "atonement cover," serving as the resting place of the Shekinah glory of God. Its position over the ark and the Ten Commandments indicated that mercy and justice are inseparable from each other (Ps. 85:10; 89:14)—mercy and justice perfectly reflect God's character. Thus, the blood sprinkled on the mercy seat on the Day of Atonement symbolized God's mediation of mercy toward the sinner who had transgressed the law (Rom. 3:25; 8:34; Heb. 7:25).

The cherubim fashioned of solid gold stood on either side of the throne of God as guardians of holiness and perfection (Gen. 3:24; Is. 6:2; Ezek. 1:11) and were intimately connected with the heavenly sanctuary, from where angels

Sanctuary, Covenant, Worship, and Forgiveness

Most of the second half of the book of Exodus concerns itself with the wilderness sanctuary, detailing the instructions from God to Moses and the implementation of those instructions in its construction and services. The narrative is interrupted by the worship of the golden calf and its implications. There are several important concepts related to the sanctuary that would be useful to explore.

1. A Place of Meeting. The sanctuary remained central throughout the history of Israel concerning the covenant. Within the covenant relationship, it was essential for the Lord to be close to His people. The central purpose of the sanctuary was to provide a particular place for God to dwell among them. In fact, the Hebrew term for "tabernacle" (*mishkan*) is related to Shekinah, God's glorious presence (Ex. 25:8). Divine love moved God to dwell in a tent, among His people. As Messiah, He became human and dwelt among us (John 1:14; see the section on Theology in the Introduction).

2. Redemption, Covenant, and Tabernacle. The construction of the sanctuary was preceded by a divine act of redemption, namely, the deliverance of Israel from the enslaving power of Egypt. This, in turn, was followed by God's willingness to enter into a permanent covenant relationship with His people. He would be their God, and they would become His people (Ex. 6:7). The way they would relate to Him and to each other was defined by the covenant law. The tabernacle was indeed a place of meeting, a place where God and humans came together. It was only after redemption and the establishment of a permanent union with God through the covenant that the people had access to God in His dwelling place.

3. The Tabernacle, Worship, and Forgiveness. Through the sacrificial services, Israel would express to the covenant Lord, who dwelled among them, their love, gratitude, devotion, and joy, thus strengthening the covenant relationship. But the sanctuary would also be the place where, in cases of covenant violations, the people could find reconciliation and forgiveness of sin by bringing to the covenant Lord a sacrificial victim. The sanctuary was the place where the sin problem was resolved through sacrificial blood and the priestly work on behalf of the people. It was through the daily and annual services performed in the sanctuary courtyard outside of the tabernacle that the problem of sin and impurity was resolved and the covenant relationship preserved or reestablished.

It was through the blood of the innocent sacrificial animal that sin was expiated (Lev. 17:11). The sanctuary services illustrate God's plan of redemption, the symbols and shadows pointing to the sinless Redeemer who one day would come to offer His life as a sacrifice and substitute for the sins of the world (Is. 53; John 3:16). He would also become our High Priest, who ministers in the heavenly sanctuary as our Mediator before the Father (Heb. 7:25; 9:11–12). The Israelite sanctuary and its services encapsulate a complete system of divinely-revealed truth, connected and harmonious, illuminating the plan of redemption and the mission and message of God's people to the world (cf. GC 23).

The Current Location of the Ark of the Covenant

What happened to the ark of the covenant? The last mention of the ark is after the refurbishing of the temple, when Josiah instructs the Levites to bring it into the temple (2 Chr. 35:3). It is never mentioned again. Today, there are at least fifteen theories about the location of the ark, with possible whereabouts ranging from Babylon to Egypt, Ethiopia to Mount Nebo, and multiple sites in and around Jerusalem. The apocryphal book 2 Maccabees 2:4–8 states that the ark was hidden by Jeremiah on Mount Nebo. But the book was written 500 years after the event. Ellen White provides the insight that the ark was hidden in a cave by the priests just before the Babylonian destruction of the temple and that it remains there today (PK 453). While many claims have been made concerning the discovery of the ark, these claims have not been verified by credible archaeological investigation and remain uncertain.

minister to God's people on earth (cf. PP 345). With one set of wings, they covered their bodies, representing humility and reverence, and their other wings were raised toward the center above the mercy seat.

25:23–30 (37:10–16). The Table of Showbread. This is the table where "the bread of the presence" or "showbread" was placed. This terminology was used because the bread was placed before God in the Holy Place. As one entered the tabernacle, it would have been on the right side, to the north (Ex. 40:22). Like the ark, the table was made of acacia wood covered with hammered gold. Twelve loaves of showbread were set upon the table every Sabbath and were to be eaten by the priests (Lev. 24:5–9). The bread represented the twelve tribes of Israel and pointed toward Christ, "the bread of life" (John 6:35).

25:31–40 (37:17–24). The Seven-branched Candle. The lampstand (v. 31) was called a "menorah," formed from the noun *ner*, "light," and *nur*, "to shine, blaze." It was built of solid gold, weighing a talent, which is about 75.38 pounds (34.19 kg), and was engraved with almond blossoms. The almond was the first tree to blossom in the springtime, thus exemplifying

Christ, the first fruit of the resurrection. Christ, who is also the light of the world (John 1:4; 8:12; 12:46), is represented as standing at the center of the lampstand, whose lamps represented the people of God disseminating His light to the world (see Rev. 1:12, 20). The lamp oil symbolized the power of the Holy Spirit to illuminate His truth through the church (Zech. 4:2–6).

26:1–37 (36:8–38). The Furnishings of the Tabernacle and the Veil. The tabernacle was to be a portable building that could be moved as the people journeyed from Sinai to Canaan. For this reason, it was made of individual parts that could be disassembled and reassembled. The ten curtains, two rows of five, were made of linen and colored thread (gold/blue/purple/scarlet). They were intricately woven by skilled craftsmen and embroidered with cherubim (Ex. 36:8). This was the layer that could be seen from inside the tabernacle by the priests who ministered there. The workmanship style reported in the Hebrew text involving the tabernacle and the priestly clothing corresponds to grades of holiness. The high priest's clothing was more elaborate than that of the other priests, just as the designs and the curtain of the Most Holy Place were more elaborate than those in other parts of the sanctuary.

The roofing was composed of a layer of goat hair coverings, then ram skins, followed by an outer layer. The outer layer was made of *takhash* (v. 14), which has been interpreted and translated variously as "badger skins," "goatskins," or "porpoise skins" from the dugong or sea cow. These durable leathers were used to make the outer layer waterproof. The Red Sea is still heavily populated with sea cows today, and porpoises would also have been available at that time. These curtains were fastened together with gold rings. The combined effect would have made the interior very dark. The frames of the tabernacle were made of acacia wood, covered in gold (v. 15). These planks would have been heavy to transport, so Moses instructed four wagons and eight oxen to be given to the sons of Merari of the Levites for their transport (Num. 7:7–8).

The veil separating the Holy Place from the Most Holy Place was made of the same material as the curtains—blue, purple, and scarlet, with embroidered cherubim. The veil in the Jerusalem temple was torn at the moment of Christ's death on Calvary, which symbolized the end of the sacrificial system (Matt. 27:51; Heb. 9). The curtain covering the entrance was made of similar woven materials and hung on pillars (Ex. 36:37–38).

27:1–8 (38:1–7). Altar of Burnt Offering. This altar was located in the courtyard and measured 7 feet, 4 inches (2.22 m) square by 4 feet, 5 inches (1.33 m) high. It was made from acacia wood and bronze, an alloy of tin and copper. It was probably hollow, which allowed for easier transport. The Hebrew term *qeren*, "horn," symbolized strength and power (Ps. 75:10). These horns have been found on altars in many archaeological contexts, including the Judean sites of Arad and Beersheba and the northern site of Dan. The horns protruded outward from the four square corners of the altar. The priests dipped their fingers in blood and applied it on the horns during the atonement process (Lev. 8:15; 9:9). Criminals seeking refuge in the temple would cling to them (1 Kin. 1:50–51). The blood of the burnt offering represented the atoning blood of Jesus Christ for sin (Is. 53:4–7; Eph. 1:5–7; 1 Pet. 1:18; Rev. 5:9). Tools were fashioned for use in offering sacrifices on the altar—shovels to remove the ash, three-pronged forks to arrange the pieces of the offering on the altar, and fire pans to dispense the coals from the fire (Ex. 27:3).

27:9–19 (38:9–17). Outer Court. It was in the court that the altar of burnt offering and the laver (or basin) were located. The outer court measured about 150 feet (44.45 m) in length and 75 feet (22.86 m) wide. The hangings or curtains surrounding the court were 7 feet, 4 inches (3.46 m) high, half the height of the tabernacle, so that it was clearly visible from outside the enclosure. They were hung from pillars of bronze (vv. 10–11) surrounding the tabernacle. The entryway to the court faced east and had a screen that was composed of the same materials as the veil separating the Most Holy Place from the Holy Place (v. 16) although the quality was not as refined as that of the tabernacle veil. The courtyard represented the death of Christ on the cross.

27:20–21. Oil for the Lamp. The oil was to be supplied by the people. Here there is a shift in focus from the apportionments of the tabernacle and the description of its furniture to the people. The subject addressed here is their obligation and involvement in the sanctuary services. Clear, pure oil of olives was collected, the olives having been beaten with a mortar rather than crushed in a press (v. 20). This provided the finest fuel. The lamps of the menorah were to be kept burning by Aaron and his sons from evening until morning or continually (v. 21). The priest was required to reside in the sanctuary throughout the twenty-four-hour period. The light represented God's

eternal presence, reciprocated by the priest's continual worship. Perhaps this imagery was what Christ had in mind in his parable of the ten virgins when he admonished his followers, "Keep your lamps burning" (Luke 12:35).

28:1–6 (39:1). The Priests: Aaron and His Sons. The priesthood was not a position that Aaron and his sons aspired to; it was ordained by God. To minister as priests required being set apart for their duties by God (see 1 Sam. 2:28a). God chooses whom He will appoint. One recalls, in contrast, Jeroboam's appointment of his own priests, including himself, to serve in the apostate high places of Dan and Bethel in the northern kingdom of Israel (1 Kin. 12:32; 13:33; 2 Chr. 11:14). The results of this decision led to widespread apostasy and finally defeat and exile at the hand of the Assyrians. Just as the priests kept the lamps trimmed in the Holy Place, they were to approach God continuously, wearing unique clothes that God designated for their high office.

28:7–30 (39:1–21). The Ephod and Breastplate. The ephod was the symbol of the high office of the priest. The ephod is described in more detail than any other article of clothing. This emphasizes its significance. It was made of fine linen by skilled craftsmen who wove in the colors and threads used for the veil (v. 6). It was worn as an apron or vest. Two semiprecious onyx stones were fixed on the shoulders of the ephod (v. 9). The names of the twelve tribes of Israel inscribed on these stones signified the high priest's intercessory role (v. 12). When the high priest entered the tabernacle, he stood before the Lord as the representative of the twelve tribes whose names he bore.

The breastplate was attached to the ephod by strands of gold cord (v. 24). It was made of similar cloth as the ephod but measured about 10 inches (25.4 cm) square (v. 16), for placement over the heart of the high priest (v. 29). Twelve precious stones, each engraved with the name of a tribe of Israel, were fastened to the breastplate (vv. 17–20). Whereas the two onyx stones were placed on the shoulders (vv. 9–12), the twelve stones were positioned over the heart, the main organ of life. The instruction to place it over the heart was repeated three times for emphasis (vv. 29–30). It is interesting that in Egyptian embalming practices, the heart was never removed from the corpse. It was the heart that was evaluated in the judgment and weighed in the balances. The heart was considered the place where decisions between right and wrong were made. The Urim and Thummim were placed on either side of the breastplate. God's will was made known to the people through these stones (1 Sam. 23:9–12; 30:7–8). The Urim illuminated by light indicated divine approval while a cloud over the Thummim denoted disapproval (cf. PP 351). The twelve stones placed over the heart of the high priest probably pointed to the heart relationship Christ desires to have with His people, exemplified in both the old and new covenants (Deut. 6:5–6; Jer. 31:33).

28:31–43 (39:22–31). The Clothing of Aaron and His Sons. The text here shifts from the most important element of the priestly vestments, the ephod, to the clothing underneath. A fine robe of blue linen was to offset the brilliant colors of the ephod and its precious stones (v. 31). The color blue may have symbolized the law. The people wore garments fringed with tassels in blue to remind them of the law of God (Num. 15:37–40), and the high priest was completely covered in blue, signifying submission to God's will. It was to be made without seam, indicating its perfection. Later, the redeemed are described as being dressed in robes of righteousness, worn by the faithful who have been cleansed in the blood of Christ (cf. Zech. 3:4). Pomegranates were to hang from the hem of the robe, interspersed with bells of pure gold (vv. 33–34). The pomegranate signified life and fertility. The priest standing in the presence of God represented the lives of those he interceded for. The bells rang constantly while the high priest carried out his work. The sounds from his ornaments were constant reminders of the need for the people to be in prayer and worship during his ministration on their behalf.

The gold-plated inscription with the words HOLINESS (or HOLY) TO THE LORD indicated the most sacred task of the priesthood. It was to be placed on the high priest's forehead so all could be reminded of who God was and their relationship to Him as sinners. Only through the work of their Redeemer could the penalty of sin be atoned for. The symbolism of the priestly garments provided significant types pointing to a high priest whose messianic mission is a superior ministry because He is the Mediator of a better covenant established upon better promises (Heb. 8:6).

29:1–37. Ordination of the Priests. This passage begins with a list of items needed for the service: a young bull, two rams, and three types of flatbread (vv. 1–2). They were to be brought with Aaron and his sons to the entrance of the tabernacle (v. 4). Aaron and his sons were not allowed to enter the tabernacle until their consecration had been completed. Three rituals were performed, namely, rituals of cleansing, clothing, and anointing. The instruction to wash the men (v. 4) implied cleansing. The Hebrew term *rakhats* suggests a complete submersion or bath in water, not a mere sprinkling (Ex. 30:18–20; 40:30–32). Ritual bathing became an important representation of cleansing from sin and impurities. Standing in the presence of God as mediator required purity. After the priests were cleansed by Moses, who acted as God's representative (Ex. 4:16; 7:1), they were clothed in their holy vestments (vv. 5–6). Finally, the priests were anointed with oil, an act that probably signified consecration to their function through the Holy Spirit. The same anointing oil was also used to consecrate the tabernacle and its utensils during the ordination ritual, reflecting the unity of sacred space and personnel (see Lev. 8–9). A similar pattern is seen with Christ, who was baptized in the Jordan and anointed by the Holy Spirit descending as a dove over Him (Matt. 3:17; 2 Pet. 1:17).

A series of offerings was required to complete the consecration. The first was the sin offering (v. 14), which the high priest and his sons presented every day for seven days. Typically, a bull was offered for the congregation or for the high priest (Lev. 4:1–12). Smaller animals, such as female goats, were offered for individuals (Lev. 4:28). On the Day of Atonement, the high priest would lay both hands on the goat and confess the sins of the people over it (Lev. 16; see "The Laying On of Hands," p. 243). Aaron and his sons placed their hands on the sacrificial victim, and the blood of the bull was placed on the horns of the altar, purifying the high priest (v. 12). The second offering was the ram for a burnt offering (vv. 15–18; cf. Lev. 1), a sweet aroma or pleasing fragrance before the Lord (v. 18). This was a gift offering and was therefore pleasing to God. The third offering was the ordination or consecration offering (v. 22). The blood of this offering was applied to the right ears of the priests, that they might hear the instructions of the Lord, upon their right thumbs, that they might perform the work of the Lord, and upon their rights toes, that they might go in the way of the Lord (v. 20). The final step was for Aaron and his sons to eat the bread and the flesh of the ram to consecrate and sanctify themselves (vv. 32–33). In this way, Aaron and his sons were to be set apart to do the work of priests, teaching and leading God's people in truth and righteousness (Mal. 2:6-7).

29:38—30:10 (37:25-28). The Continual Burnt Offering and the Altar of Incense. The burnt offering was to take place in the evenings and the mornings (v. 39), perhaps in connection with the trimming of the menorah and the burning of the incense (30:1-10). A yearling lamb was to be placed on the altar first in the morning and then in the evening, left to burn throughout the night. Although two sacrificial victims are mentioned, one offered in the evening and the other in the morning, the two constitute one single sacrifice called the continual burnt offering (see Num. 28:3, 6). God promised that He would meet with His people at the altar, suggesting that it was a symbol of His presence and accessibility to the people in the courtyard. The Hebrew term *tamid*, continual or regular (v. 38), pointed to the continual or daily mediation of Christ in the heavenly sanctuary (see Lev. 6:8-13; Heb. 7:25; see also notes on Heb. 7:23-25).

The altar of incense was to be placed before the veil separating the Most Holy Place from the Holy Place. It was to be centered between the menorah and the table of showbread and, like them, was made of acacia wood covered in pure gold with horns. Incense was to be burned on it, morning and evening, before the Lord. The incense represented the prayers of the people ascending to God, mingled with the merits of Christ, the perfect sacrifice. The heavenly altar of incense was seen by John in his visions (Rev. 8:3-4).

30:11-16. The Half-Shekel of Atonement. The Lord required from the people a specific sum to be used for the maintenance and upkeep of the sanctuary. The same amount was required from the rich and the poor alike. This tax was to be a ransom for their lives. The Hebrew term *koper*, ransom (v. 12), and the phrase *kesep hakkipurim*, "atonement money" (v. 16), seem to indicate the importance of this tax. It was brought so that there would be no plague when the census was conducted. It was a legal way of counting the people and of reminding them that their lives could be preserved only by the Lord and not by their collective strength. This brings to mind the later consequences of David's census taken for reasons of personal interest and military gain (2 Sam. 24).

30:17-38 (37:29; 38:8; 40:7, 30). Bronze Laver (or Basin) and Anointing Oil. The laver (or basin) was placed in the courtyard between the altar of burnt offering and the entrance to the tabernacle. Its function was to provide water for the cleansing of the priests' hands and feet before they entered the tabernacle. On the Day of Atonement, this cleansing was also to take place upon completing the work (Lev. 16:24). The anointing oil was composed of specific ingredients (myrrh, cinnamon, cane or calamus, cassia, and olive oil) and was for the anointing of the priests, the tabernacle, and its furniture, for all generations (vv. 25-31). The incense was aromatic (Ex. 30:7) and composed of certain key ingredients. The importance of this composition is highlighted in the experience of Nadab and Abihu, who burned profane, unauthorized fire upon this altar (Lev. 10:1).

31:1-11 (35:30—36:7). The Artisans: Bezalel and Aholiab. The calling of these two individuals indicates that priests were not the only ones called by name to service. These two men were filled with the spirit of God, and God put the wisdom of skillful artistry in their hearts (vv. 3, 6). In highlighting this special calling, God established art and creativity as important ways to reflect His image. God then enumerated the types of abilities that Bezalel and Aholiab would be endowed with: wisdom, understanding, knowledge, and all kinds of craftsmanship (v. 3). Wisdom, knowledge, and understanding were to be combined with skill. All aspects were necessary for these men to accomplish their work. God did not simply call them to the task, but He also provided the means and abilities needed to fulfill His calling. All of these gifts were given for a specific purpose, namely, to honor God in building the sanctuary as a glorious place of worship. Thus, art is defined in Scripture as having a purpose: art is for God's sake. This stands in stark contrast to contemporary movements where "art is for art's sake." Everything that God does has a purpose and should draw others to Him. Thus, art as defined in these verses is for service.

31:12-18. Keeping the Sabbath Holy. This passage on the Sabbath concludes the instructions given for the building of the sanctuary. It also forms part of the chiastic structure that begins later with the renewal of the covenant and the actual construction of the sanctuary (see "Creation, Sabbath, and the Sanctuary," p. 231). While circumcision was given as an outward sign, the Sabbath was the internal sign of the heart (v. 13), indicating the loyalty of God's people to His covenant (see Ezek. 20:12, 20). The death penalty for its violation emphasized its holiness and functioned as a deterrent (v. 14). The nature of the Sabbath, on the seventh day, is emphasized by a reference back to the Creation week (v. 15). The permanence of the Sabbath is also emphasized in vv. 16–17. It is the longest of the commandments, and it was the only one repeated and emphasized just before Moses was given the two tablets of testimony (v. 18).

32:1—34:35
Violation of the Covenant: The Golden Calf

This account is placed after the instructions to build the sanctuary but before its actual construction because this was when the event took place. What follows is a description of an act of open rebellion against the covenant Lord, an offense that He took very seriously.

32:1–6. Back to Egypt. Moses's long stay on the mountain caused unrest among the people. Fearing the permanent absence of their leader, they fell back into the idolatry that perhaps many of them had practiced in Egypt. The Hebrews and the mixed multitude had come out of Egypt, where nature was worshiped in the form of hundreds of gods, within a complex, spiritualistic religion. In this moment of anxiety, they demanded a visual representation of that which their finite minds could not conceive: "Make us gods," they demanded (v. 1). The golden calf could have represented any number of Egyptian deities. The Apis bull was worshiped in Memphis as Ptah, the god of life. Hathor, the cow goddess, was worshiped in Thebes as the goddess of motherhood, beauty, love, and joy. The description of the activities of the people in vv. 6 and 25 contains clear sexual overtones that might be equated with the rituals surrounding Hathor worship. Aaron, their spiritual leader, who was to be inaugurated as high priest, even built an altar before the image and offered up burnt offerings and incense, proclaiming that this calf was the god who had brought them out of the land of Egypt (v. 4). When the kingdom of Israel later divided in 931/30 B.C., Jeroboam also made two calves, placed them in Dan and Bethel, and quoted the same phrase from Aaron to legitimize his actions (1 Kin. 12:28).

32:7–14. God's Reaction and Moses's Intercession. From the mountain, the Lord saw what was happening and told Moses that He was ready

Sabbath, Creation, and the Sanctuary

Scholars commonly find in the book of Exodus a connection between the construction of the sanctuary, Creation, and the Sabbath. This is indeed the case in the instructions to build the sanctuary and its actual construction.

1. Sanctuary and the Sabbath. It is significant that in the midst of the sanctuary narrative of Exodus, the Sabbath appears, the sign of the covenant relationship (Ex. 31:12–18). Not even the construction of a holy place for God (i.e., the sanctuary) would justify the violation of the Sabbath. Its violation would be an intolerable rebellion against the loving covenant relationship God had established with them. Such rebellion would indicate that the violators are no longer identifying themselves with the covenant community because of their rejection of the sign of the covenant. They would be excluded from the community and from having access to God's presence in the sanctuary. In this way, God was emphasizing the importance of faithfulness to Him in the context of the sanctuary and its services. The sanctuary in space (the tabernacle) did not replace the sanctuary in time (the Sabbath).

2. Sanctuary, Sabbath, and Forgiveness. Notice how the literary structure of Exodus 24–40 combines the sanctuary, the Sabbath, and forgiveness into a unified whole.

A Theophany/Moses goes up to the mountain (24:13–18)
  B Instructions for the construction of the sanctuary (25:1—31:11)
    C Sabbath (31:12–18)
      D Apostasy, forgiveness, covenant renewal (32–34)
    C' Sabbath (35:1–3)
  B' Construction of the sanctuary (35:4—40:33)
A' Theophany/Moses could not enter the tabernacle (40:34–48)

The narrative about the construction of the sanctuary is interrupted by the worship of the golden calf. The Sabbath commandment, which should have reminded the people to worship God as Creator, preceded and followed the act of idolatry. The people repented and God forgave them, thus restoring the people to the covenant relationship with God. The Sabbath was then reaffirmed in the context of the construction of the sanctuary.

3. *Sanctuary and the Garden of Eden.* The emphasis on the sanctuary, the Sabbath, and forgiveness of sin reminds us of the Garden of Eden. The Garden was not only the dwelling place of Adam and Eve (Gen. 2:8) but was also the place where God came to meet with them (3:8). This was where God instituted and gave the seventh-day Sabbath to humanity (2:1–2). In addition, it was the place where sin entered into the world (3:1–8), where an investigative judgment took place (3:9–19), and where God offered to humanity forgiveness of sin through the coming Seed of the woman (3:15), represented by the sacrificial victims (cf. 3:21). It would be correct to say that when the Israelites came to the holy sanctuary to worship God and to seek forgiveness, they were returning spiritually to the union and perfect harmony with the Creator that characterized the life of Adam and Eve in the Garden of Eden.

There is a connection between the construction of the sanctuary and the Creation narrative in Genesis. In Genesis there were seven days, and in Exodus there are seven divine speeches, introduced by the phrase "The Lord said to Moses" (25:1; 30:11, 17, 22, 34; 31:1, 12), that instructed Moses how to construct the sanctuary. The seventh speech is about the Sabbath and references Creation (31:1–12). The narrative regarding the actual construction of the sanctuary begins with the Sabbath commandment (35:1–3), and the phrase "as the Lord commanded" is used seven times to affirm compliance with God's will (40:17–33). It was in obedience to God's commands, to His word, that the sanctuary was built. In Genesis, God created by separating elements and assigning to them specific functions (Gen. 1:4, 6, 7, 14, 18). The same happened in the building of the tabernacle. For instance, the veil divided the Holy Place from the Most Holy Place (Ex. 26:33), and the priests were to separate or distinguish between the holy and the common, the clean and the unclean (Lev. 10:10). The emphasis on creation through separation and the cycle of seven, culminating with the Sabbath, indicates that the building of the sanctuary was a divine activity through which God was creating a holy space within a world of sin and uncleanness. There He would meet with His people to sanctify them. It could be suggested that the tabernacle was the beginning of a new creation that will reach a cosmic dimension. The original relationship between God and humans in the Garden of Eden was being restored, and this restoration would reach its climax on the Day of Atonement (see Lev. 16).

to consume the people on account of the violation of the covenant. God no longer referred to them as His people but as the people Moses had brought out of Egypt (v. 7). As intercessor, Moses reminded the Lord that He was the One who brought them out of Egypt and they were, in fact, His people (v. 11). God listened to Moses and did not destroy the people. After descending, Moses saw what was happening and broke the two tables of the law in recognition that the covenant had been broken (Deut. 9:17). Nevertheless, so deep was Moses's love for these people that he offered his life for theirs and asked that his name be blotted from the Book of Life (v. 32; cf. Rev. 3:5; 13:8; 20:12–15). But God rejected his offer because only His Son's death would be an acceptable substitution (see Is. 52:14—53:12).

33:1–6. Command to Leave Sinai. The Lord was willing to let the people leave Sinai to head to the promised land, but at a cost: He would not be with them. The sanctuary building project, which had not yet begun, was set aside during this crisis. Although the covenant had been broken, God would keep His promise to defeat the enemies of the people and grant them a new home in the promised land, but they would enter the land without Him. This raises a major question for Israel and for Christians today. Is anything worth doing without God's presence and blessing? He had brought them out of Egypt, but He would not go with them into Canaan. Canaan, the land flowing with milk and honey (v. 3), would be meaningless without God. This was the greatest moment of crisis for Israel. Even in Egypt, when the people were slaves, God had been attentive to their cries for help. But if they moved forward without God, their cries would go unheeded.

The reaction of the people was to strip themselves of their ornaments (v. 6). The Hebrew may imply that they did this at Mount Horeb or, as some translations indicate, that they removed their ornaments at Mount Horeb and did not don them again. In other words, the Israelites did not wear jewelry after this point. Why? There could be several reasons. (1) They were acting in obedience to what God had asked (v. 5). (2) Some of the jewelry had been used to make the golden calf (Ex. 32:2-4). (3) It was common in ancient Egypt for jewelry to be fashioned to resemble foreign gods. Jewelry could also include amulets, which were thought to carry inherent magic. (4) Or this was a sign of contrition, repentance, and humility. Judges 8:24 seems to indicate that, at that time, the Israelites were still not wearing earrings, in contrast to the custom of the Ishmaelites. During times of apostasy, Israelites again wore jewelry, and God warned the people He would remove their jewelry as part of His judgment (Is. 3:16-23). Paul and Peter affirm this position and encourage modesty, good actions, and the inward beauty of gentleness instead of jewelry (1 Tim. 2:9-10; 1 Pet. 3:3-4).

33:7-23. Moses Again Intercedes for the People. Since the sanctuary was not yet built, Moses placed the temporary tent of worship well outside the camp (v. 7). The people had removed themselves so far from God's will that, in His holiness, He could not dwell near them. But Moses could approach Him. The pillar of cloud descended, and the divine presence spoke face-to-face with Moses (vv. 9-11). This figure of speech does not mean that Moses saw God's face (see v. 20), but it emphasizes the direct communication Moses had with God. God had not completely forsaken the people. He was willing to speak to their leader, Moses. Sinners can find comfort in knowing that, in spite of their sin, their heavenly Mediator can approach the Father on their behalf. Therefore, Moses continued to intercede, asking God not

The Sanctuary/Temple and Ancient Near Eastern Parallels

The sanctuary and the subsequent temple are often compared with the long tradition of temple buildings in the various ANE cultures. Some critical scholars suggest that the tripartite design (courtyard–Holy Place–Most Holy Place) was copied directly from the Egyptian, Canaanite, or Assyrian world. Others further argue that the technologies and design of the sanctuary resembles Bronze Age Egyptian parallels. A number of parallels have been documented. However, there also exist three fundamental distinctions. (1) There was no representation of the deity in the Hebrew sanctuary/temple. The Lord was not to be depicted in images. (2) The sacrificial system with its goal of atonement for the individual and corporate body was unique to the Hebrew sanctuary/temple. (3) Dedicating a temple to one god alone was not practiced by the polytheistic nations surrounding Israel. Egyptian temples frequently depicted multiple gods interacting with the king. Canaanite temples could have been dedicated to any number of gods in the pantheon. Despite these major differences, why are there so many similarities between the sanctuary/temple and ANE temple designs? In Exodus 25:9, Moses was shown the sanctuary according to a heavenly pattern. Lucifer was once a covering cherub in the heavenly sanctuary before the throne of God (see Ezek. 28:14-17). He was cast down because of his pride and rebellion (Is. 14:12-14). His attempt ever since has been to counterfeit God's plan. Would it not be natural for him to imitate and adapt God's plan for salvation as taught through the sanctuary service? Could not Lucifer have inspired false worship in these "sanctuaries" of Egypt, Canaan, and Assyria while God inspired Moses and Solomon to remain faithful to the heavenly pattern? Worship and whom we worship are central to the conflict in Exodus and the rest of Scripture (e.g., Rev. 12, 14). This may be a possible reason for the similarities between the Hebrew sanctuary/temple and ANE parallels. It is at least worth considering by those who are well-acquainted with the biblical concept of the cosmic conflict.

to abandon His people but to go with them to Canaan (33:12–13). God agreed to go with Moses but not with the people (v. 14). Moses was not satisfied with this answer. In the end, the Lord pronounced that He would accompany the people—because of His relationship with Moses (v. 17). In order to confirm that the Lord would escort the people to Canaan, Moses requested God to allow him to see His glory (v. 18). This time, the Lord could not grant him the request, but He could let Moses see His love, goodness, and compassion (vv. 19–23).

34:1–9. Moses Goes Up to the Mountain. Moses was instructed to cut two tablets of stone identical to the first ones (v. 4) and to carry them to the top of the mountain. The Lord would again inscribe the Decalogue with His finger. These tablets would be placed in a box of acacia wood (Deut. 10:3–5) and later within the ark of the covenant (Ex. 37:1; 1 Kin. 8:9; 2 Chr. 5:10). When Moses reached the mountaintop, the Lord descended in a cloud (v. 5), revealing Himself as "the LORD, the LORD God" (v. 6), identifying Himself as Yahweh *'elohim* ("God"), the Creator and covenant God. On this occasion, He revealed to Moses seven aspects of His character. He is merciful and compassionate. He draws near to His children in sympathy and cares about their struggles. He is gracious, a word that describes undeserved mercy. He is longsuffering, slow to anger, and patient with them in their mistakes. He is abounding in (Heb.) *khesed*—"goodness," "loving-kindness," or "mercy" and overflows with *'emet*—"truth" and/or "faithfulness." His love and faithfulness are without bounds. His *khesed* (v. 7), repeated again for emphasis, is available to "thousands." Finally, He is forgiving of *'awon*—"iniquity" or "wickedness," *pesha'*—"transgression" or "rebellion," and sin. The Hebrew word *nasa'*—usually translated as "forgive"—also means literally "to lift up, to carry," which is what God does with the sins of His people. He lifts their burdens and casts them "into the depths of the sea" (Mic. 7:19). In legal contexts, the term *nasa'* also means to assume responsibility for sin. God forgives by assuming responsibility and taking sin upon Himself. He did this through Christ. Yet those who persistently reject Him will experience divine judgment. All of God's gracious, loving, merciful, and forgiving characteristics can only truly be appreciated by fallen, sinful beings in the context of God's just wrath against sin. All of us fully deserve eternal death if we are without Christ and His forgiveness.

34:10–35. Covenant Renewal. God had revealed Himself as a forgiving God, and this was shown in His pardon of the covenant violation of His people. His relationship with His people was restored: He promised to make a covenant with the same promises and conditions He had stated earlier (vv. 11–28; Ex. 23:10–33). He is a jealous God (v. 14) who demands sole worship and allegiance. He still requires from His covenant partners obedience to the covenant law. After descending from the mountain, with his face shining with the glory of the Lord, Moses reported to the people the divine decision. His shining face confirmed that he had been in the presence of God and that he was God's appointed leader.

35:1—40:38
The Building of the Sanctuary

The worship of the golden calf had nearly eliminated the divine assurance of God's dwelling among His people. Had it not been for a persistent leader and intercessor and for the gracious and longsuffering Redeemer, Israel would have entered the promised land alone and left to their own devices. The renewal of the covenant reminds us that we serve a God of second chances. Where we are unfaithful, He is faithful; where we are impatient, He is patient. Once the covenant relationship had been restored, this Holy God was ready to fulfill His promises and His ultimate desire to dwell with His people. The construction of the sanctuary was about to begin. (In this section, less detailed explanations will be provided because of the repetitive nature of Exodus 36–39, which mirrors much of Exodus 24–31. The reader will be referred back to the comments made previously.)

35:1–3. Sabbath Commandment. Moses then gathered or assembled the whole people of Israel. The Hebrew verb *qakhal*, "to gather, assemble" is used here and in 32:1, when the people demanded the golden calf from Aaron. But the contrast between the two gatherings is stark. The first assembly was a gathering of a people rising up against God. The second gathering was an attempt to lead the people to obediently follow God's instructions. In this new gathering, Moses emphasized the Sabbath (vv. 2–3), which would guide the people's focus back to the Creator. Previously, they worshiped a calf of their own creation, but this time, through the Sabbath, they would acknowledge the God who created all things. The Sabbath closed the chiasm of covenant broken and covenant restored, becoming a sign that the people were in fellowship and communion with the covenant Lord.

35:4—36:7. Offerings from the People. The overflow of the offering was an expression of their gratitude to God not only for saving them from Egypt but also for reconciling them to Himself after their idolatry. Everyone whose hearts were impressed to contribute came with willingness (v. 21). The construction of the greatest visual representation of God's plan of salvation was possible only through the gifts of these worshipers. The Holy Spirit not only filled Bezalel and Aholiab with wisdom and understanding to build the sanctuary (see Ex. 31:1–11) but also put in their hearts the ability to teach the other craftsmen and artisans who were to work under their supervision (35:34). Men and women who are given gifts to accomplish great things are to work together with others and teach them what God has given them for His honor and glory. It is significant that when God gives instructions, in this case for the construction of the sanctuary, He also provides the means to accomplish it. He does so by giving individuals the necessary skills and by providing, through His people, the needed materials and funds. The people wanted God to dwell among them and were willing to do whatever it took to make this happen. Eventually, the builders had more than enough, and the people had to be restrained from bringing any further donations. How refreshing to see such an outpouring of sacrificial love toward God! How different churches would be if believers would consistently give freely of themselves and the means at their disposal so that God's message could go out to the world!

36:8—39:31. Construction of the Sanctuary. The instructions given in Exodus 25–31 are largely repeated here in their execution, and some may wonder about this redundancy. In the Bible, repetitions are significant. In the Creation narrative of Genesis 1, God gives a command, and this is consistently followed by a description of how His command was enacted (e.g., Gen. 1:3). This was done to demonstrate that God does what He says. In Exodus 25–31, the instructions were given by God, according to the pattern shown to Moses, in explicit detail. After the disruption of the golden calf rebellion and the covenant renewal, this information is repeated to indicate what was done. Several purposes are accomplished within this narrative. First, this account serves to verify that Moses was faithful in delivering God's commands to the people. The phrase "as the Lord [had] commanded Moses" is repeated twelve times in Exodus 38–39. Second, this testimony highlights the fact that the Spirit-filled work of Bezalel, Aholiab, the craftsmen, and the people of Israel was an expression of God's wisdom and power. Third, this record indicates that what God predicts for the future will be fulfilled in every detail through the outworking of His Spirit. Finally, it emphasizes that when the people followed God's plan, they accomplished even more than they had ever imagined.

39:32—40:33. The Work Is Completed. In vv. 31–43, it is indicated three times in different ways that the people of Israel did everything according to the Lord's commands to Moses. This is repeated to signify that all was done according to God's will. The rebellion of the golden calf is here contrasted with the obedience in carrying out the plans of God. And Moses blessed them (v. 43). This is the only time in Exodus where Moses blesses anyone. Moses's anger at seeing the calf turned into a blessing at seeing the completed sanctuary. Previous curses because of a broken covenant were, at this point, turned to blessings in response to obedience to the covenant.

The tabernacle was next erected and anointed, and Aaron and his sons were ordained (40:1–16). All of the tabernacle and its furnishings were to be anointed with oil (v. 9). The altar of the burnt offering was to be set apart, consecrated, and made most holy, or "utterly holy" (v. 10). The priests were also to be anointed and consecrated (vv. 13–15), an activity that is described in more detail in Leviticus 8. The fact that this was an anointing for a continuous or eternal priesthood throughout the generations suggests that it was an ordination service with permanence as long as the sanctuary and later the temple services functioned in Israel (v. 15).

The tabernacle was erected on the first day of the first month of the second year, precisely one year since the Exodus from Egypt (Ex. 12:2) and nine months after Israel arrived at Sinai (Ex. 19:1). Moses and the people erected the tent of meeting (the tabernacle) and carefully placed the furniture in the designated locations. They finished their work faithfully.

40:34–38. God Descends to His Tabernacle. The filling of the tabernacle with the glory of the Lord was the ultimate reward for a work well done, but above all, it was the realization of

God's longing to be near His people. Moses and the people had done what the Lord had commanded, and as a result, God resided among them. These concluding verses recapitulate the Exodus theme. The covenant had been established, God was now dwelling among His people, and He would guide Israel in all their ways. The light of God's presence would be in the sight of all Israel (v. 38), reminding them that they were not an ordinary people but a God-led people. The promise of Exodus 25:9 was fulfilled. Their future journey would be with a God who would dwell among them. Their journey to the promised land was ready to begin. The hearts of the people throbbed with hope as they faced the future, knowing that the Lord was in their midst. The Christian reader also looks forward, knowing that Christ is present in the church and leading it in its journey toward the heavenly promised land (John 16:13–15; Heb. 12:1–2). The One who has begun a good work in us will bring it to completion (Phil. 1:6). This is the promise we embrace in hope.

LEVITICUS

INTRODUCTION

Title and Authorship. The English name of the third book of the Bible is based on the name of the book in the Latin Vulgate: *Liber Leviticus*. In fact, the name "Leviticus" goes back to the Greek translation of the OT (LXX), where the book is called *Leuitikon*. This suggests that, for the translators, the book was about matters related to the Levites. However, the Levites are rarely mentioned in the book. It could be that the title refers to the Levitical priests, and in that case, it would be closer to the truth. This idea is found in Jewish writings where the book is called "The Priest's Manual" or "Priestly Torah/Instructions" although the book is hardly a manual.

The Hebrew name is taken from the opening word of the book, *wayyiqra'* ("and He called"). It was a common ancient practice to name a book after its first words. In this particular case, the name corresponds well with the content of the book. *Wayyiqra'* introduces God as the speaker—"and He [God] called" Moses—and, as will be demonstrated, the book consists primarily of a series of divine speeches addressed to Moses, or to Aaron, and to the people. Moses has traditionally been identified as the author of the book, and there is no persuasive argument to the contrary. This is principally the case at a time when critical scholars are reexamining the origin and authorship of the Pentateuch (see "Introduction to the Pentateuch," p. 120). There is also the testimony of Jesus, who, when referencing Leviticus, identified Moses as the author (see Matt. 8:4; Mark 7:10; Luke 5:14).

Date. The book is a literary unit in itself, but it is part of the history of the Israelites during their sojourn near Mount Sinai. This helps date the book. The title "and/then He called" points back to Exodus 40:34–35, when God's glory descended on the tabernacle after it was built. At that moment, the Lord called on Moses and gave him instructions concerning the services to be performed in the sanctuary (Lev. 1:1). This suggests that the book was written in the fifteenth century B.C.

Theology and Purpose. When attempting to understand the theological message of Leviticus, its connection to the book of Exodus must not be overlooked. The construction of the sanctuary had just been completed, and the glory of the Lord had filled the place (Ex. 40:34; cf. 25:8). This sanctuary was defined as holy space, made holy by the presence of a holy God (Ex. 29:43).

1. Only God Is Holy. The concept of holiness is very prominent in Leviticus and conveys two basic ideas. First, the holy is not part of the world as such. There is only One who is by nature holy: the Lord (Lev. 11:44; see also 11:45; 19:2; 20:26). Since nothing else is holy in and of itself, holiness refers to God as He is in Himself. Holiness points to the uniqueness of God and to His incomparability, completely distinct from His creation. It points to the mystery of His nature. Simply put, there is nothing and no one like Him. Second, and almost paradoxically, God's holiness also speaks to His closeness to humans as their only source of life (17:11). He brought the Israelites out of Egypt (11:45) and made them His people (20:26). Therefore, divine holiness is demonstrated by God's uniqueness and His willingness to enter into a unique relationship with humans. In the midst of a world damaged by the presence of sin and evil, a holy God created a space to dwell among His people. Now the question is: How could sinful human beings, who are not holy by nature, relate to this majestic God who dwelled among them? It is this question that the sanctuary services, as described in Leviticus, seek to answer.

2. Sin, the Unclean, the Common, and the Clean. Since only God is holy, in what condition is His creation? According to Leviticus, the world is characterized by sin, the unclean or impure, the common or profane, and the clean or pure. Since nothing on earth is considered holy, everything is in a state of separation from God. The sanctuary services described God's way of ordering the world, similar to His actions at Creation (Gen. 1–2), by establishing distinctions and boundaries that the Israelites were to respect in order to exist in harmony with Him and with each other (see "Creation, Sabbath, and the Sanctuary," p. 231). At the center of this order was the Holy God of Israel. But as indicated, there were other forces at play in the world—sin, the unclean, the common, and the clean. The Israelites were to relate to these elements in certain ways in order to preserve the order established by God.

The unclean/impure signifies death and is, by nature, incompatible with the Holy One, the fountain of life. The common/profane was not to come into contact with the holy because it would profane the holy or make it common. However, the common, the clean, and even the unclean/impure were sanctified through cleansing and sanctification rituals.

It is correct to suggest that, in Leviticus, the world is fundamentally divided into two realms, namely, the holy and the sinful/impure. In other words, there was the divine realm of life and the sphere of sin and death. There was also the common and clean, indicating that not everything was under the absolute control of sin and impurity. There were to be clean places (4:12) and clean animals (chap. 11). Even the common was not necessarily evil unless it was improperly brought into contact with the holy (Ex. 3:2–5; Num. 18:15–18). But ultimately, all living creatures come under the power of the unclean by descending into the sphere of death; everyone and everything dies (cf. Eccl. 9:2–6). The ultimate source of death is not God but Azazel (see chap. 16). Leviticus appears to indicate that humans, in themselves, are in a state of sinfulness and impurity and are, therefore, in constant need of divine grace to be cleansed, forgiven, and sanctified. Within the divine order established by God are means to deal with this existential problem.

3. *God Shares His Holiness.* The holy God placed His dwelling in the midst of a world characterized by sin, the unclean, the common, and the clean. He sanctified the people of Israel by redeeming them from Egypt and by entering into a covenant relationship with them. Israel became holy in the sense of belonging to God, and therefore, they were a unique people—a holy nation and a kingdom of priests (Ex. 19:6). In this context, being holy means that the Lord had set them apart to be His people (Deut. 7:6;

14:2). This is the relational side of the covenant, but there is also an ethical side to it. They were also holy in the sense of being under God's jurisdiction through obedient service to Him and to His covenant law (see Lev. 11:44, 45; 20:6–8, 22–26). Holiness is a gift and, at the same time, a task. The Israelites were to be holy as God is holy (19:2). He is the model to be followed, the image to be reflected.

Within Israel, God also set apart (sanctified) priests and Levites for a particular purpose (8:12, 30; 21:8). Additionally, portions of time were consecrated by the Lord for specific service to Him: the Sabbath (23:3), the celebration of the festivals (23:4, 7, 8, 37), and the Jubilee (25:12). There were holy things, like offerings (see 2:3; 6:17; 7:1; 21:21–22), tithes (27:30), utensils (8:9, 11), clothing (16:4, 32), the altar (8:11, 15; 16:19), and the furniture of the sanctuary (8:10). The tabernacle, in particular, was a holy space, forming the center of the sanctuary with its Holy and Most Holy Places (16:2). All of these persons, things, and times were set apart for a divine purpose, and all of them were equally threatened by the incursion of sin and impurity. When the divine order was disrupted, death threatened the covenant relationship.

4. *Holiness and Covenant Violations.* Obedience to the covenant law was, in a sense, the ethical expression of the holiness of God in the life of the people. Therefore, the violation of the moral or ritual aspects of the law was a serious act that required the exclusion of the violator from the sphere of holiness and life. Such individuals found themselves in the sphere of death, moving inexorably toward destruction. The violation of the *laws of cleanliness* resulted in a state of impurity. To be unclean was to be alienated from God's dwelling and from others. Unclean persons were not in the sphere of fullness of life but under the influence and power of the sphere of death. This is suggested by the fact that the sources of impurity were associated with death. These sources include dead bodies (Num. 6:6, 7, 11), diseases (Lev. 13; 14), blood discharge (chap. 15), and semen (15:16; which could be called the "seed" of life). Impurity was associated with the realm of death and, as illustrated in the experience of the leper, the individuals were separated from God and others. They were considered to be under the power of death (Num. 12:9–12). These individuals were headed toward absolute alienation from the holy community and from God. Death was their final destination unless something was done to remove them from the fatal sphere.

Disobeying the *moral aspects of the covenant law*—that is, sinning against God and others—resulted in moral impurity, and the outcome was alienation from God. Sin was not a physical impurity but a burden that left sinners in a state of guilt (Lev. 5:1-2). The Hebrew *nasa' 'awon*—translated as "to bear guilt," "to bear iniquity," or "to be held responsible"—refers to a legal declaration, indicating that sinners were responsible for their specific sin and that they were liable to a punishment or penalty (see 5:1; 20:20; 24:14, 15; Ex. 28:42, 43; Num. 9:13). The ultimate result of this condition was death, which was suggested by the fact that in order to free sinners from this condition, a sacrificial victim was to die in their place (Lev. 5:1, 5, 6; 17:11).

God's holiness cannot peacefully coexist with sin or impurity (death). Even after God sanctified His people, the presence of impurity among them was not totally eradicated. Impurity was, in some instances, inevitable, as in the case of menstruation (15:25-27). Consequently, the Lord developed and established a system that addressed the needs of His people and that strengthened and preserved or restored their moral and ritual purity. In other words, God instituted a sacrificial, priestly, and atoning system that aimed at separating impurity and sin from His people in order for them to continue to exist in His holy presence, within the order He had established for their fellowship.

5. Holiness and Atonement. According to Leviticus, atonement is a divine gift through which God ransoms the life of repentant sinners, restoring them to covenant fellowship with Him. Leviticus 17:11 establishes a direct connection between sacrifices, the use of blood, and the atoning process. It assumes that because of sin and impurity, human life is endangered and needs deliverance, which God provided in the form of blood. The blood of the animal—that is to say, its life (17:14; Gen. 9:4; Deut. 12:23)—was to represent the life of the sinner. In His grace, God, as the proprietor of blood/life, accepted the life of the animal instead of the life of the sinner.

The Hebrew verb *kipper* ("to make atonement") expresses the idea of removing sin or impurity from people or objects ("to perform a rite of cleansing"). In the case of persons, *kipper* removes the obstacle that obstructs a proper relationship with the Lord and, thus, conveys a sense of expiation. The verb is probably derived from the noun *koper* ("ransom"), indicating that the barrier between God and humans is removed by giving "a ransom" for the endangered

life of the person. The concept of substitution is clearly indicated because the life of the sacrificial victim stands in for the life of the sinner (see Lev. 17:10-11). The process of atonement is seen in the verb *kipper*, which is directly associated with the sacrificial victim (5:10, 18; 7:7), the laying on of hands (1:4), the use of the blood (6:30; 8:15), the eating of the flesh of the sacrificial victim by the priest (10:19), and the Day of Atonement (16:16, 20). The atoning process consisted of two services, the daily and the annual (the Day of Atonement; chap. 16), during which different rituals were performed.

During the *daily services*, the Israelites were to approach the Lord to express their joy and gratitude, thus strengthening their communion with Him, but were also to seek cleansing and forgiveness. Two different atoning sacrifices were to be offered by the Israelites for violations of the covenant law: the sin/purification offering (Lev. 4) and the guilt offering (5:14—6:7). A specific, unblemished sacrificial victim was required, and the offerers were to lay their hands on the animal. Through the laying on of hands, the individuals were to identify themselves with the sacrificial victim, transferring onto it their sin/impurity (see "The Laying On of Hands," p. 243). After the animal was slaughtered, a complex application of the blood (ritual blood manipulation) was required. The blood, which belonged to the Lord, was to be given back to Him through the ritual process and would become a vehicle for transferring the sin/impurity from sinners to the sanctuary. There were two other important sacrifices, whose primary function was not expiatory: the burnt offering (chap. 1) and the peace/fellowship offering (chap. 3). In both sacrifices, the blood manipulation was simplified, indicating that their primary function was not to atone for sin/impurity. The burnt offering was to be offered to make atonement for a person (1:4). The use of the peace offering for atonement is not specified in Leviticus, but Ezekiel indicates that this offering also had an atoning function (Ezek. 45:15, 17). Besides, Leviticus 17:11 indicates that the blood of all sacrifices had an atoning purpose. The implication is that when God's people come before Him, they are always in need of divine cleansing and forgiveness.

The *annual service*, or the Day of Atonement (chap. 16), brought the circle of the process of atonement to its close. The rites that were to be performed on that day had the specific purpose of removing from the sanctuary the sins and impurities of the people of Israel that had accumulated there through the daily services over the course of the previous year (16:16). The Holy and Most Holy Places of the tabernacle, as well as the altar of burnt offering, were to be cleansed and reconsecrated; atonement was to be made for them (16:33). During the performance of the ritual, the true source of sin and impurity (Satan) was symbolically identified and made responsible (16:21–22). The Day of Atonement was a day of judgment (see "The Theology of the Day of Atonement," p. 264). It was not when the sins of the Israelites were forgiven but when their forgiveness was made complete or finished. For a brief period of time, holiness reigned in the absence of sin/impurity in Israel.

6. *The Work of Christ and Leviticus.* Christians have generally found in the Levitical sacrificial system and its priestly services a prefiguration or a type of the sacrifice and the high priestly ministry of Jesus. The NT uses the sacrificial system to interpret the meaning of the sacrificial death of Jesus. This is particularly the case in Ephesians 1:7, which states that Christ provides redemption and forgiveness of sins through His blood. Redemption, which is at the heart of atonement in the OT, is now the result of the death of Christ. As in Leviticus 4, this passage in Ephesians brings together redemption, blood, and divine forgiveness. Peter adds that this redemption was accomplished with "the precious blood of Christ," who is the Lamb without blemish (1 Pet. 1:19). Jesus Himself stated, "For even the Son of Man did not come to be served, but to serve, and to give His life a ransom for many" (Mark 10:45). Redemption is now a gift from God through Christ. In this particular passage, the idea of substitution is explicitly indicated through the use of the Greek preposition *anti* ("in place of" or "instead of"). This was to be the role of the Servant of the Lord in Isaiah (Is. 53:11–12; see "The Servant of the Lord in Isaiah," p. 885). The idea of substitution is even stronger in 1 Timothy 2:6: Jesus "gave Himself a ransom [*antilytron*, a "substitutive ransom"] for [*hyper*, "on behalf, for the benefit of"] all." Paul adds that Christ "redeemed us from the curse of the law" by having become "a curse for us" (Gal. 3:13). He took upon Himself what was ours—the curse—and freed us from it. He took our place and our death. It is only through the sacrificial death of Christ that atonement is possible for repentant sinners. There is no need for any other sacrifice because He accomplished what every sacrifice in the OT pointed to: redemption, reconciliation, forgiveness of sin, cleansing (Heb. 7:27; 9:14, 26, 28; 10:5–14).

Christ is now the believers' high priest before the Father: He is able to forever and completely (Gk. *panteles*) save those who come to God through Him, since He lives to intercede for them (Heb. 7:25; cf. Rom. 8:34; 1 Tim. 2:5; 1 John 2:1–2). He officiates, not in the earthly sanctuary but in the heavenly one (Heb. 8:1, 2, 5; 9:12, 24; 10:19, 20; Rev. 11:19; 14:17; 15:5; see also Psalms: Introduction). He began His priestly mediation after His ascension by asking the Father for the Holy Spirit on behalf of the disciples (John 14:16, 26; 15:26; Acts 1:4–5), and His request was granted (Acts 2:33). In fulfillment of the typological function of the daily services in the earthly sanctuary, Christ is interceding for His people by applying to them all the benefits of His saving sacrifice on the cross for their forgiveness, cleansing, and sanctification. The typological significance of the Day of Atonement is to be fulfilled in the consummation of the saving work of Christ before and at His Second Coming (Dan. 8:13–14; Heb. 9:23–28; Rev. 11:19). The ritual of the Day of Atonement was a day of judgment that proclaimed the coming of a day when the cosmos would be utterly free from the miasma of sin and death (impurity). The OT also anticipated a time when the holiness of God would be victorious (e.g., Zech. 14:20). Likewise, Christians look forward to the consummation of the redemptive work of Christ at the close of His priestly work before the Father in the heavenly sanctuary (see Dan. 8:14; Heb. 9:23).

Literary Features. There are four important literary features in Leviticus: divine speeches, literary structure, descriptions of rituals, and narratives. The book is chiefly made up of divine speeches given to Moses to instruct the people and the priests concerning the sanctuary services and their covenant responsibilities as a holy community. In some cases, the Lord gave private instructions to Moses (5:14; 6:1; 6:19; 8:1; 14:1; 23:26; 24:13) or to Aaron (10:8). He also spoke to Moses and Aaron together (11:1; 13:1; 14:33; 15:1). In most cases, God addressed Moses with directives for Aaron (16:1; 21:16; 22:1), for Aaron and his sons (6:8, 24; 21:1), and for all the Israelites (1:1; 4:1; 7:22, 28; 12:1; 15:1; 17:1; 18:1; 19:1; 20:1; 22:17; 23:1, 23, 33; 24:1, 25; 27:1). The only sections that are not divine speeches are the narratives. This literary feature emphasizes, in a particular way, the divine origin of the book, making absolutely clear its authoritative nature.

Overall, Leviticus is well structured. It opens with the Lord speaking to Moses, giving him instructions for the people of Israel (1:1–2), and closes with a summary statement that the book contains the instructions from the Lord to Israel at Mount Sinai (27:34). The book is a single literary unit. It is located at the center of the Pentateuch, flanked on each side by two books: Genesis/Exodus-Leviticus-Numbers/Deuteronomy. It places in the center of the five books of Moses the important topics of holiness and atonement. At the center of Leviticus itself is the chapter on the Day of Atonement (chap. 16)—a placement which accentuates its significance. The structure of the book chapters can be represented as follows:

A Laws Related to the People and the
     Sanctuary (1–7)
  B Laws Related to the Priesthood (8–10)
    C Laws Related to the Individual
         (11–15)
      D Day of Atonement (16)
    C' Laws Related to the Individual
         (17–20)
  B' Laws Related to the Priesthood (21–22)
A' Laws Related to the People and the
     Sanctuary (23–27)

Leviticus contains ritual laws and a handful of narratives. The narratives include the ordination of Aaron and his sons to the priesthood (chaps. 8–9), the experience of Nadab and Abihu (10:1–7), the incident between Moses and Eleazar and Ithamar (10:12–20), and the account of the blasphemer (24:10–14). The stories generate insight into some of the ritual laws and, in some cases, lead to the formulation of new legislation.

Most of the book is about rituals and their proper performance. In Leviticus, a ritual was basically an act of worship intended to strengthen or restore/renew the relationship between God, the individual, and the community. It usually resulted in ritual cleansing or in atonement. It was an *action* to be performed in a certain *place* (mainly in the courtyard of the sanctuary or inside of it), at a particular *moment* (daily, during festivals, once a year), and according to some specific *instructions* (bringing the offering to the Lord, laying on of hands, slaughtering, etc.). The ritual was intended to introduce *change* (such as forgiveness of sin or cleansing) or to *express* individual or communal feelings/convictions (joy, gratitude, faith) in a particular *situation* (after sinning, after an answer to prayer, after receiving a blessing, etc.).

The Christian ritual of the Lord's Supper illustrates how rituals function. Many conservative Christians gather together once every three months (*time*) inside the church (*place*) to partake of the bread and the grape juice (*action*). This is reverently done (following specific *instructions*) and is an individual and collective expression of our common union with the risen Lord (*expressing* religious convictions). Participants seek spiritual renewal (*change*), and this is done in obedience to the Lord (a particular *situation*).

Rituals are often formed by combining numerous rites. For instance, the Day of Atonement was a ritual that aimed at the cleansing of the sanctuary. But this ritual was formed by a number of rites: a cleansing rite for the high priest, another for the altar of burnt offering, and further cleansing rites for the Holy and Most Holy Places. The combination of these rites resulted in the ritual of the Day of Atonement. Rites carry symbolic meanings. For instance, the rite of sprinkling blood on the altar signified that the altar was being purified and sanctified (16:18–19). The symbolic meaning of a rite is not always clear. In order to uncover its meaning, the context, the nature of the ritual, and parallel passages need to be examined.

COMMENTARY

1:1—7:38
HOLINESS PRESERVED AND RESTORED

The first major division of Leviticus begins with a brief introduction, situating the book within the narrative flow of the Pentateuch (1:1–2a). The section contains instructions given to the people for worship through sacrifices and offerings that aimed at strengthening or preserving their relationship with the Lord (1:2b—3:17). There are also guidelines for how to restore a broken relationship with the Lord through required expiatory sacrifices (4:1—6:7). Further direction is given concerning the proper handling of the sacrificial offerings by the priests and the people (6:8—7:36). The section concludes with a brief summary (7:37–38). The first task of the book is to institute the sacrificial system, through which the order established by the Lord was strengthened, preserved, and, if broken, reestablished. The activities associated with this system took place in the presence of the holy God of Israel, who dwelled among His people.

1:1—3:17
Voluntary Offerings

The divine speech begins with instructions concerning the burnt (chap. 1), the grain (chap. 2), and the peace/fellowship offerings (chap. 3). These were voluntary offerings and, as such, expressed the willingness of the people to worship the Lord with thanksgivings and gratitude for His blessings. Bringing these offerings manifested the person's desire to enjoy fellowship with the covenant God and with others.

1:1–2a. Moses as Mediator. The Lord, who descended from Sinai to dwell in the sanctuary (Ex. 40:34–38), now addressed Moses from the tabernacle/tent of meeting. Two important ideas were being expressed. First, the tabernacle was by nature the dwelling place of God where His people would come to worship Him (e.g., Lev. 26:11, 12; Ex. 25:8; 29:45, 46; Ps. 132:7). He had become accessible to them in a unique way (Deut. 4:7). Second, the tabernacle was the place from which God spoke to Moses, giving him instructions to convey to the people of Israel (v. 2; cf. Ex. 25:22). Moses was God's messenger and the mediator between a holy God and humans damaged by sin and impurity. The sacrificial system itself had a mediatorial function. Through it, the Israelites expressed their inner feelings and needs to the Lord and sought forgiveness. The priestly system was established to provide an additional form of intercession between the people and their God (Lev. 8–9). The concept of mediation runs throughout Leviticus as a type of the mediation of Christ. God has spoken through Him to us in "these last days" and has appointed Him as our Mediator before the Father in the heavenly sanctuary (Heb. 1:2; 7:25; 8:6; 9:15; 12:24).

1:2b–17. Burnt Offering. The instructions for the burnt offering (Heb. *'olah*, "ascending/rising offering;" Gr. *holokautōma*, from which the word "holocaust" originated), are organized by the type of sacrificial victim: animals from the herd (vv. 3–9), animals from the flocks (vv. 10–13), and birds (vv. 14–17). The specific instruction is preceded by a statement about the animals to be brought to the Lord as an offering (*qorban*, "what is brought near" to the Lord, designates animal and nonanimal offerings). The sacrificial victim was to be from the herd or the flock (not a wild animal), and it was to be without blemish or physical defects and in good health (v. 3; cf. 22:20–25; Mal. 1:8–14). What was morally and spiritually expected from the people was to be a physical reality in the sacrificial animal (Deut.

18:13). Anyone (v. 2; Heb. *'adam*, "a person," used in a generic sense) could bring a burnt offering, but if it were from the herd, it had to be male—an expensive animal, demonstrating the person's willingness to give to the Lord the very best. The ritual took place in the space between the altar and the entrance to the courtyard in the presence of the Lord. The altar represented God's presence and was accessible to the common Israelites to grant them forgiveness and to accept their expressions of gratitude, joy, and worship (Ps. 43:4). The closest they could come to the Lord was to the altar. The burnt offering was to be voluntary and assumed that the occasion for the sacrifice was one of gladness and thankfulness. It was a votive offering to be brought after a vow was fulfilled (Lev. 22:18).

The ritual required the participation of the offerer and the priest according to a set of specific instructions. Worshipers were to firmly place their hands upon the head of the animal for it to be accepted and to make atonement on their behalf (v. 4; on the verb "to atone," see the section on Theology in Leviticus: Introduction). A profound relationship was to be established between the offerer and the sacrifice to the degree that when the Lord accepted the sacrifice, He was accepting the person (cf. Lev. 7:18; see "The Laying On of Hands," p. 243). The burnt offering operated under the assumption that humans are not holy by nature and, consequently, when they approach the Lord, even to express gratitude, joy, and thanksgiving, they are in need of forgiveness.

Next, the offerer was to kill the sacrifice. The verb *shakhat* ("kill") refers to slaughtering the victim by slitting the throat to reduce the pain and to let the animal bleed out and die. The priest was to gather and present the blood to the Lord and sprinkle or splash (Heb. *zaraq*, "to toss, throw") it around the sides of the altar (v. 5). Then the worshiper skinned the animal, cut it into pieces, and washed its entrails and legs with water (vv. 6, 9). The priests were to prepare the altar for the sacrifice, then place everything on it and burn the offering (vv. 7–9). By burning, the offering was permanently given to the Lord; it became irretrievable. This sacrifice was one of the most significant Israelite offerings in that all of it was given to the Lord, indicating the willingness of the offerer to surrender all to God in an act of worship.

The section concludes with a statement indicating the aim of the sacrifice: it was a burnt offering and an *'isheh*, which is usually rendered as "an offering made by fire" or "fire offering," but it probably means "gift" or "food gift," as suggested by the fact that the wine libation

(Num. 15:10) and the showbread (Lev. 24:7, 9) are called *'isheh*, but no portion of them was burned on the altar. The burnt offering is further defined as a sweet or pleasing aroma to the Lord (v. 9). This last phrase could mean that the sacrifice pleased the Lord, was pleasant to Him, or that it pacified/soothed Him by its "aroma" (e.g., Gen. 8:21; Ex. 29:18; 2 Cor. 2:15; Eph. 5:2). These ideas are not mutually exclusive. When God voluntarily "smelled the aroma" of the sacrifice, He was choosing to express His acceptance of the worshipers and not His wrath or rejection (Lev. 26:31). God chose to preserve a harmonious and peaceful relationship with them.

If the sacrifice were from the flocks (vv. 10–13), the animal was to be a male without blemish or defect (v. 10). The instructions are significantly shortened, which indicates that the procedure used was to be the same as in the previous verses. The animal was to be killed on the north side of the altar (v. 11), probably the location where all burnt offerings were killed. The section ends with an indication of the ultimate purpose for the ritual: it was a burnt offering, a gift, a sweet or pleasing aroma to the Lord (v. 13; see v. 9).

The poor could offer doves or young pigeons (vv. 14–17). No one was to be excluded from the benefits of the burnt offering. In this case, since the victim was a bird, particular instructions were given. The priest was to wring off the head of the bird, burn it on the altar, and then drain its blood at the side of the altar (v. 15). He also was to remove its crop and feathers and place them on the east side, where the ashes were (v. 16). In other words, these elements were not to be placed on the altar. Finally, the priests were to split the bird, without dividing it into two parts, and burn it on the altar (v. 17). The purpose of the burnt offering of birds was the same as in the other two cases.

In the NT, the burnt offering finds its fulfillment in the unblemished sacrifice of Christ (1 Pet. 1:19). Jesus gave His blood and flesh, His whole person, to the Lord (1 Cor. 11:23–25; Heb. 7:27) in order to cleanse us from sin, making it possible for us to approach the throne of God with joy and gratitude (Heb. 4:16). Jesus is indeed a sacrifice of pleasing aroma to God (Eph. 5:2). In the acceptance of the sacrifice of His Son, God accepts us as well. Christ's sacrifice also signals our need for sanctification (1 Thess. 5:23).

The Laying On of Hands

The Hebrew phrase *samak yad 'al* means "to press the hand on" the sacrificial victim and was used in the cultic (sanctuary services) and in some noncultic cases. It was required for the burnt (Lev. 1:4), peace/fellowship (3:2), sin (4:4, 15, 33), and guilt offerings (7:7); it was to be part of the ritual of ordination for Aaron and his sons (8:14, 18, 22); and Aaron was to take the same action on the Day of Atonement (16:21). This essay will examine both the cultic and noncultic passages.

1. Laying On of "Hand" or "Hands"? When an individual brought a sacrifice, he or she was to lay a "hand" on the animal (Lev. 1:4; 3:2, 8, 13; 4:4, 24, 29, 33), but when the subject is plural, the text reads "hands" (4:15; 8:14, 18, 22; Ex. 29:10, 15, 19; Num. 8:12; 2 Chr. 29:23). This has led some to conclude that there were two different rituals, one to be performed using one hand, to express the idea of ownership ("This is my animal"), the other to employ two hands, expressing the idea of transfer. Support for these two rituals is allegedly found in Leviticus 16:21, where Aaron placed two hands on the scapegoat

and transferred to it the sins and impurities of the people, and in Numbers 27:23 (cf. Deut. 34:9), when Moses transferred to Joshua the role of leader of the people of Israel. Several comments can be made in the evaluation of this theory.

First, the use of "hands" when the subject is plural is clearly ambiguous because it could designate one or two hands from each person. Second, in other contexts, the singular and the plural are sometimes used interchangeably to designate the same action. For instance, Moses raised his "hand" in prayer, but Aaron and Hur helped to hold up his "hands" (Ex. 17:11–12). In other words, the use of the plural or the singular is not especially important. Third, the phrase "to lay hands on" shows the same shift from the singular to the plural. According to Numbers 27:18, the Lord commanded Moses, "Lay your hand on him [Joshua]," but in v. 23, when Moses obeyed the Lord, the text states that "he laid his hands on him" (see Deut. 34:9). This suggests that the use of one or two hands was not significant. Fourth,

Leviticus 16:21 alone is not strong enough to prove the argument that there were two different rituals. The proposed existence of two rituals with two different meanings is a scholarly invention.

2. Nonsacrificial Use. The first nonsacrificial use of the ritual is found in Leviticus 24:14. Those who heard a person blaspheme the name of the Lord were to place their hands on the blasphemer before she or he was executed. The meaning of the ritual is not stated. It can be speculated that as witnesses, they were identifying the guilty one before the execution, but there seems to be more to it than mere identification. The individuals who heard the blasphemer were somehow implicated in the sin. This seems to be what Leviticus 5:1 is also suggesting. This passage has been understood as referring to cases in which people knew something about a crime or a sin and were adjured to tell the truth about the matter (as in a modern court trial, where witnesses testify under oath). If they knew something but did not testify, they would be also held responsible for the crime committed. Others believe that it refers more specifically to the type of case described here in Leviticus 24:14—if a person blasphemed, anyone who heard was to speak up; if not, the hearer would also be held responsible for the sin. In both cases, the crime committed impacted the person who knew about it, requiring that he or she expose the criminal. The case of the blasphemer demonstrates that, in such cases, those who witnessed what happened were to symbolically transfer to the criminal the guilt that otherwise would have permanently adhered to them.

The second case involves the ordination of Joshua. Moses laid hands on him to give to him some of Moses's authority (Num. 27:20). The idea of transfer is also present here, and since Joshua was taking Moses's role as leader, the idea of substitution is present.

The third case is recorded in Numbers 8:10. Representatives from the people were to lay hands on the Levites as they were set apart to officiate in the sanctuary. They were chosen by the Lord to serve Him in place of the firstborn of all the people of Israel (v. 16). We have here a delegation of responsibility and the concept of substitution. These cases demonstrate that, through the laying on of hands, a relationship was established between the subject and the object (witness-accused, leader-successor/substitute, firstborn-substitute), that something was transferred from one to the other, and that in some cases, the idea of substitution was present.

3. Meaning of the Ritual. With respect to sacrificial offerings, the meaning of the ritual is not explicitly stated, but there is enough information to postulate that it expresses at least the idea of transfer. First, the only place where the meaning of the laying on of hands is interpreted in a cultic setting is in Leviticus 16:20. It refers to the transfer of sin and impurity to an animal. It has been suggested that since the scapegoat was not a sacrifice, this meaning should not be assigned to sacrifices in general. But this is an arbitrary restriction because, as noted earlier, there are other passages in which the laying on of hands consistently expresses the idea of the transfer of something from a subject to an object. Obviously, the context establishes what was being transferred. With this biblical evidence at hand, one should feel safe to argue that Leviticus 16:21 serves as an interpretational link that connects the meaning of the ritual in noncultic passages with its practice in the Israelite cultus. This is supported by other biblical evidence.

Second, Leviticus establishes a deep connection between the laying on of hands, the sacrifice, and the offerers. Individuals were to bring the sacrifice and place their hand(s) on it, and the offering was to be accepted to make atonement on their behalf (lit. "for him"; 1:4). God's acceptance of this sacrifice was equivalent to His acceptance of the one who offered it (7:18). The connection was produced through the laying on of hands. It was through this action that the victim became the substitute onto which the sinfulness and deepest feelings of the worshiper were transferred in the case of the burnt and peace/fellowship offerings.

Third, those who brought an expiatory sacrifice had violated one of the commandments of the Lord (Lev. 4:2) and bore their sin or guilt (5:1–3). Through the atoning sacrifice, the sin they committed was removed from them (4:35; see also v. 26). In the case of impurity, the atoning sacrifice removed the uncleanness "from" the person (12:7). There was clearly a transfer from the repentant sinner to the sacrificial victim. The only rite that signaled the transfer was the laying on of hands. This implies that the expiatory sacrifices were likely rituals of elimination (removal of sin and impurity).

Fourth, the life of the unblemished sacrificial victim was directly associated with the endangered life of the sinner—one stood for the other in order to bring atonement/expiation through a ransom/substitute (see 17:10–14). Atonement occurred at the cost of the life of the animal that carried the sin, transferred to it by the laying on of hands, thus removing the person's sin and guilt.

Fifth, the sin of repentant sinners reached the horns of the altar (cf. Jer. 17:1). During the atonement process, the priest was to put some of the blood of the offering on the horns of the altar (Lev. 4:7, 25). The blood/life of the sacrifice stood for the blood/life of the repentant sinner, and it carried his or her sin. It was to be transferred to the altar, which represented the very presence of God (see 1:5). This explains why a garment on which the blood of a sin offering fell was to be washed (6:27).

Sixth, the rite in which the priests ate the flesh of the most holy offerings assumes that sin/impurity was transferred to the sacrificial victim. As part of the atoning process, the priest was to eat the flesh of the sacrifice in order to bear the sin of the people (see 10:12–20). Therefore, sin "moved" from the sinner to the sacrificial victim to the priest. Whenever the priest himself was in need of atonement, he was not to eat the flesh of his own sacrifice, but his sin was to be transferred to the tabernacle through the blood manipulation in the Holy Place, where he, as a priest, had access to God (4:6–7).

Seventh, the transfer of sin/impurity to the sacrificial victim, whose flesh was considered most holy, points to the paradoxical nature of the atonement process. The process brought into direct contact sin/impurity and holiness/life, and the result was atonement—that is, the removal of sin/impurity from the sinner. This was possible only because the Lord allowed for it to happen via the altar (17:10–11). Thus, the holy priest was to eat the most holy flesh of the sacrifice and yet, in so doing, was to bear the sin of the people (10:17). The flesh of the sin offering was most holy (6:24–30), but the fact that the person who burned

its flesh needed a purification bath shows that the most holy was bearing sin/impurity (4:12). The holy and the unclean stood together, but the holy was not damaged by it. This connection was broken or came to an end through the ritual of the Day of Atonement (Lev. 16), when all the sins and impurities of the children of Israel, transferred there through the daily sacrifices, were to be removed from the holy tabernacle (16:16). The modern reader cannot avoid noticing the parallels to Jesus, the Holy One (Luke 1:35), who was also the Lamb of God and who bore humanity's sins yet remained holy (John 1:29; 2 Cor. 5:21; Heb. 4:15).

Eighth, the idea of an innocent victim bearing the sins of others in order to atone for them is clearly found in Isaiah 52:13—53:12 (see "The Servant of the Lord in Isaiah," p. 885). The Servant of the Lord, a messianic figure, is described as the ultimate sacrificial victim (Is. 53:10), who gives His life as a substitute for the life of many (vv. 6, 11). The transfer of sin in the sacrificial system pointed typologically to Christ as the substitute sin-bearer.

4. Contamination of the Sanctuary. The transfer of sin/impurity to the sanctuary through the sacrificial system freed the person from spiritual corruption and resulted in forgiveness or cleansing. Not so for the person who contaminated the sanctuary through the violation of the covenant law. Such individuals bore their own sin and died for it. For example, the person who, after offering a son to Molech, contaminated the sanctuary was to be put to death (see Lev. 20:1–3; cf. 18:21). The sin of Nadab and Abihu was also resolved through their death and not through a sacrificial substitute (10:1–2). The priest who ate the holy offerings while unclean was to be put to death (22:2–9). The contamination of the temple by kings, priests, and the people shortly before the exile was removed by their destruction (see Ezek. 8:5–18). The only sin/impurity that was to be removed from the tabernacle was that which, through the laying on of hands, was transferred to the sacrificial offering and, ultimately, to the tabernacle itself. Thus was sin/impurity removed from the person according to God's will.

2:1–16. Grain Offering. The instructions related to the grain offering are organized on the basis of uncooked (2:1–3) and cooked grain (2:4–10, 14–15). Additional instructions are added in 2:11–13. The Hebrew name for this offering, *minkhah*, designates both grain and animal offerings (Judg. 6:18, 19; 1 Sam. 2:15–17). It refers to a gift or tribute given to a superior as an act of homage or gratitude (e.g., Gen. 32:13–21; 1 Sam. 26:19). In Leviticus, *minkhah* is a technical term designating a "grain offering" brought on different occasions as an act of homage to the covenant Lord (see Gen. 4:3). It was always to accompany the burnt (e.g., Num. 15:2–12, 28–29) and peace/fellowship offerings (e.g., Lev. 7:11–14; Num. 15:3). It was a voluntary offering that anyone (*nepesh*, "person") could bring to the court of the sanctuary. The uncooked offering (see 2:1–2) was to be made of fine flour, semolina of wheat (see Ex. 29:2), accompanied by olive oil and incense (made of a costly dried tree resin). These were all symbols of blessing, joy, gladness, and devotion to God (Deut. 11:14; Pss. 104:15; 141:2; Is. 61:3; Joel 2:24; Acts 10:4). The priest was to burn on the altar a handful of the flour mixed with oil and all the frankincense as a memorial on the altar (Lev. 2:2), which meant that the portion burned on the altar was a token portion of the totality of the offering given to the Lord. As a memorial, it could also be an act of remembrance—that is to say, the worshipers were indicating that they had not forgotten the Lord's goodness in providing food for them. They had not forgotten His grace. It is specifically called an *'isheh*, a "gift" or "food offering" offered as a pleasant aroma (vv. 2, 9; see 1:9). The rest of the flour and oil was to go to the priests to provide for their needs. The offering was most holy (v. 3), meaning that the Lord set it apart to be eaten only by the priests in the sanctuary, not by their family members at home.

The cooked grain offering was to be baked in an oven (v. 4) in the form of thick unleavened cakes made of semolina mixed with oil. It could also be in the form of thin wafers smeared with oil. A third possibility was to cook the offering on a flat pan or griddle, which produced a type of pancake that was then broken into pieces to facilitate the burning of a portion of it (v. 6; cf. 1:6). The fourth option was to deep-fry the semolina in a covered pan (v. 7). The cooked grain offering was to be given to the Lord through the mediation of the priest, who took it to the altar to burn a portion of it (vv. 8–9).

Two additional regulations were given. First, the use of leaven or honey (Heb. *debash*, "honey" or "fruit syrup") was forbidden (v. 11). These were fermenting agents associated with death and, therefore, incompatible with God's holiness. The exception was the offering of firstfruits (v. 12; Heb. *qarban re'shit*, "first offering"), but no portion of it was to go on the altar. The firstfruits refer to the first processed foods of the harvest (Num. 18:12–13), which the Lord assigned to the priests (Num. 15:19–21). Second, the grain offering, and in fact all offerings, were to be seasoned with salt (v. 13; cf. 2 Chr. 13:5). Since salt conveyed the idea of preservation or permanency (Num. 18:19), the salt emphasized the permanent nature of God's covenant. Adding salt to the offerings may have expressed covenant loyalty, thus strengthening the covenant relationship between God and the Israelites.

The last type of cooked grain offering consisted of the firstfruits (Heb. *bikkurim*, "first produce"; v. 12 uses a different Heb. term), probably barley (v. 14; cf. Ex. 9:31). In this particular case, the green head of the grain was to be roasted and crushed, with oil added to it and incense placed on it (vv. 14–15).

Leviticus 2 suggests some important theological and spiritual lessons. First, it demonstrates that God is the Lord of His people and that He abundantly provides for them. The offering was an act of joyful gratitude, homage, and adoration to the covenant Lord. Second, the uncooked grain was untouched by human hands. The people were to bring the grain to God as they received it from Him, without processing it, because it was in itself a revelation of His goodness. But they could also bring it cooked; that is to say, through the cooked grain, they were consecrating their work and service to God. Third, the exclusion of leaven and honey (used for fermentation) as symbols of death and sin (see Matt. 16:6, 11; 1 Cor. 5:6–8) symbolizes that God does not want spiritual fermenting agents to alter His children's relationship with Him. Fourth, this offering was a plant-based meal, a fact that is often ignored. It has been suggested that perhaps this offering was a reference to the original plant-based diet of humans (Gen. 1:29–30). In that case, it was pointing back to the Edenic ideal and to the future peaceful coexistence of humans and animals (see Is. 11:6–9; 65:25). Finally, since this is about grain, from which bread is made, it is a reminder of Jesus, the true Bread of Life, who nurtures our spiritual life and preserves our physical existence (John 6:35). He should therefore be the Lord of our lives.

3:1–16. Peace/Fellowship/Communion Offerings. This chapter could be divided into two main discussions regarding peace offerings: those from the herd (3:1–5) and those from the flock (3:6–16), subdivided into sheep and goats. The chapter concludes with a regulation about animal blood and fat (v. 17).

The proper translation of the Hebrew *zebakh shelamim* is debated. Some translate the term as "peace [or well-being] offering" and others as "fellowship offering." *Zebakh* means "to kill/slaughter" and could refer to sacrifices, as is the case here, or to the common killing of animals (Deut. 12:15) and even humans (2 Kin. 23:20). The term *shelamim* appears to be derived from *shalom*, "peace," and thus refers to a peace/well-being sacrifice that would include the ideas of communion and covenant fellowship. Accordingly, both "peace" and "fellowship" are appropriate translations. This sacrifice belongs to the category of voluntary sacrifices introduced in Leviticus 1:2.

If the sacrificial victim (male or female) came *from the herd* (v. 1), it was to be without blemish or defect (see Lev. 1:3). The sacrificial procedure was very similar to the burnt offering (see chap. 1), the main difference being that the sacrifice was not to be burned on the altar. Since it was a voluntary offering, no specific occasion is mentioned. The procedure was as follows: the offerer was to lay her or his hand on the head of the animal (see "The Laying On of Hands," p. 243) and slaughter it by the entrance to the courtyard, and the priest was to collect the blood and splash it around the altar (in regard to *'isheh* ["food offering" or "fire offering"] and the "aroma," see commentary on 1:2b–17). The fat of the inner organs and the kidneys (vv. 3–4; see v. 9) were to be given to the Lord, placed on the burnt offering of the daily sacrifice.

If the sacrifice was from the flock (sheep, ewes, goats, and she-goats), the requirements were the same as for the cattle (3:6–16). In the case of the sheep, the fatty tail was also to be placed on the altar. The large fat tail of the sheep was considered a delicacy, the most delicious part of the sheep (v. 9). In fact, the Hebrew term *kheleb* ("fat") is metaphorically used to designate "the best" (e.g., Num. 18:12; Deut. 32:14; for the possible connection between this legislation and health concerns, see "Health and Hygiene in Leviticus," p. 272). In giving it to the Lord, the offerer was giving to Him the very best. It is clear that the main emphasis was on the blood and fat of the sacrifice, as the closing

legislation illustrates (v. 17). They belonged to the Lord, and no one was to consume them (on blood, see Lev. 17).

The purpose of the peace offering is not explicitly stated in the text, but according to 7:11–20, it could be brought as an offering of gratitude (7:12–15; 22:29–30), a freewill offering (7:16–17; 22:17–23), and a votive offering (7:16–17). It was fundamentally understood to be a religious meal in which the food would not be consumed by God—the priest was given a portion of the meat (7:31–32), and the offerer was to eat the rest of it with relatives and friends in the presence of the Lord (7:15). It seems that the meal was to be an expression of fellowship with the covenant Lord and of the desire of the offerer to strengthen the covenant relationship with Him, as well as a deep expression of joy in the presence of God (Pss. 54:6; 107:22). Although Leviticus 3 does not speak about the atoning function of the peace offering, according to Leviticus 17:11 and Ezekiel 45:15, 17, it did have this function. Since its primary purpose was not expiatory, the blood manipulation, like that of the burnt offering, was significantly simpler than that of the sin offering. But the fact that blood was to be returned to the Lord via the altar suggests that whenever a person approached the Lord, cleansing/forgiveness was needed (see Leviticus: Introduction). The acceptance of the offering signified the acceptance of the offerer. The sacrifice finds its fulfillment in Jesus who, through His broken body, offers the bread of life to all who believe (Matt. 26:26; John 6:53–56) and grants them peace (John 14:27; Eph. 2:14).

4:1—6:7
Required Offerings

The required offerings were those that redressed violations of the covenant law, namely, the sin/purification offering (4:1—5:13) and the guilt offering (5:14–19). These offerings assumed that God's people wanted to preserve the covenant relationship with Him and that they occasionally violated it. The dilemma was resolved through expiatory sacrifices. The multiplicity of sacrifices points to the inadequacy of the system. There was no single sacrifice able to satisfy all the spiritual and emotional needs of the people. This would be possible only through the sacrifice of Christ.

4:1—5:13. Sin/Purification Offering. This section discusses the sin offering both for the inadvertent sins of the priest, the community, the ruler, and the individual (4:1–35) and for intentional offenses (5:1–13). In a sense, this is about accountability for sins based on a person's sphere of influence. The proper translation of the Hebrew term *khatta't* is still debated; some retain the traditional "sin offering" while others argue for "purification offering" or other terms. The first claim is based on the literal meaning of the Hebrew term, while the second is primarily based on the function of the offering. The second possibility is also acceptable as long as the sinner is recognized as the one who needed cleansing from sin or impurity.

The sin offering was to be brought when a person sinned unintentionally (*shagagah*) and violated any of the commands of the Lord (v. 2). The Hebrew term *shagagah* designated unintentional sin (Gen. 43:12) as well as consciously committed sins (1 Sam. 26:21). This is suggested by Leviticus 4:22–23 and 27–28, where sinners were to bring the sacrifice because they were guilty (vv. 22, 27) or because they came to know that they had sinned (vv. 23, 28). This type of sin was contrasted with open rebellion against God, which is called "high-handed sin," for which there was no atonement available (Num. 15:30–31). The term could then include the idea of sin as a result of human frailty.

Sin of the Priest and the Community (4:1–21). The phrase "the anointed priest" appears to designate the high priest, but since all priests were anointed and there is no other legislation dealing with the sin of a regular priest, it may be better to interpret the phrase as referring to any member of the priestly family (cf. Lev. 10:6–7). In this case, the priest was aware of his sin and brought the offering. The congregation, however, was not aware of their sin (4:13). Once they did become aware of their sin, they were to offer a sin offering (vv. 13–14). A sin of the congregation implicated the priest, for he was part of the congregation. Consequently, he could not eat of the flesh of the sacrificial victim. The priest and the congregation brought an unblemished and expensive young bull (or perhaps, "an animal from the herd") for the sin offering (vv. 3, 14; see 1:3). The rest of the ritual procedure was to be basically the same for both the priest and the community: (1) laying hands on the sacrificial animal (v. 4), (2) slaying the sacrifice (v. 4), (3) sprinkling the blood inside the tent (v. 6), (4) placing blood on the horns of the altar of incense (v. 7), (5) pouring out the blood at the base of the altar of burnt offering (v. 7), (6) burning the fat on the altar (vv. 8–10), and (7) burning the flesh of the

animal (v. 12). The laying on of hands indicates that sin was transferred to the sacrificial victim, and it died in place of the sinner (see "The Laying On of Hands," p. 243). The sin was to be transferred to the tabernacle by sprinkling blood seven times in the Holy Place toward the veil and by putting some of the blood on the horns of the altar (v. 7)—a place of refuge for sinners (1 Kin. 1:50–51; 2:28) and where their sin was recorded (Jer. 17:1). Notice that during the Day of Atonement, blood was applied to the horns of the altar to cleanse it, but a different phrase is used: literally "on the horns of the altar all around" (16:18), which, in Leviticus, always expresses the idea of cleansing. One could then suggest that placing *some blood* on the horns indicates transfer, while placing blood on the horns *all around* could mean cleansing; the last is the undoing of the first. The fat also belonged to God and was given to Him via the altar. Since the priests could not profit from their own atoning offerings, the rest of the flesh of the animal was burned (cf. Lev. 6:23, 29–30). According to 4:20, forgiveness is a divine prerogative and not the automatic result of the atoning ritual (also in vv. 26, 31, 35). The book of Hebrews argues that because the priests had to offer a sacrifice for their sins, they belonged to a defective priesthood to be superseded by Christ's. This is because Jesus did not have to offer a sacrifice for His sin; He was without sin (Heb. 4:14–16; 5:3). But the fact that even the most important spiritual leader in Israel was in need of atonement is a reminder that the need for Christ is universal.

Sin of the Leader and the Individual (4:22–35). The most important difference between the offering of the leader and that of the individual was the value of the victim—a more valuable male goat for the leader and a female goat or a female lamb for the individual (vv. 23, 28, 32). The term *nasi'* is vague but most likely refers to a civic, tribal representative (though it is used for the unique prince or king/priest figure of Ezek. 45–46). The most important difference between this sin offering and the one offered for the priest and congregation is that, in this case, no blood was to be taken inside the tent (vv. 25, 30, 34). Instead, the priest was to eat the flesh of the animal (6:26); he was not implicated in the sin of the leader. The meaning of the ritual of eating the flesh of the sin offering is given in 10:17: by eating it, the priests bore (*nasa'*) the guilt of the people. Sin was to be transferred to the tabernacle through the priest, who assumed responsibility for it. The burning of the fat of the animal is described as a sweet or pleasing aroma to the Lord (v. 31; see 1:9). This demonstrated that God was willing to accept both the offering and the offerer. This was possible because the offerer's sins had been removed. The text explicitly states that atonement would be made for both the offerer and his or her sin (vv. 26, 35). In v. 26, the Hebrew reads "from his sin," clarifying that the purpose of the atonement was to free the person "from" sin, indicating that this is an expiatory sacrifice. It was not the sanctuary that needed to be cleansed from sin but the repentant sinner (see also 5:6, 10; on the removal of impurity, see 12:7; 14:19).

The sin offering was a prefiguration of the sacrificial death of Christ, who offered Himself as a sin offering for humanity's sins: Romans 8:3 says that the Father sent Jesus "in the likeness of sinful flesh" (*peri hamaritias*, "because of/for sin" or, according to some translations, "as a sin offering"; *peri hamartias* was used in the LXX to translate the Hebrew *khatta't* ["sin offering"]). He took upon Himself our sins and voluntarily and vicariously accepted responsibility for them, dying in our place (2 Cor. 5:21). He is the Lamb of God who takes away the sins of the world (John 1:29; cf. Gal. 3:13; 1 Pet. 2:24). Through Christ, God provided the sin offering that cleanses all who seek Him (Rom. 3:25; Eph. 5:2). This is the ultimate sacrifice that cleanses humanity once and for all. The atoning work of Christ continues to be effective, even for postbaptismal sins committed as a result of human frailty (1 John 2:1-2). The proper response to such a display of love is loyalty and gratitude to Him.

Other Offenses (5:1-13). This section contains a list of sins, followed by the required sin offering. Four specific sins are mentioned, and the first and the last were definitively intentional, with the persons fully aware of what they had done. The first was the sin of someone who hears another person pronouncing a curse and does not report it (v. 1; see Prov. 29:24); that is to say, she or he ignores it. It is also possible to interpret the text as referring to the witness of a crime who is unwilling to testify when called or adjured to do so. The Hebrew text speaks about a person who sins by not testifying against someone whom they heard curse. By not reporting the crime, the person participates in it and is perhaps considered an accomplice (cf. Prov. 29:24) and bears the sin or iniquity. The Hebrew expression *nasa' 'awon*, usually translated "to bear iniquity," is

a legal phrase meaning "to be responsible for the crime and liable to punishment."

The second sin involved becoming unclean by touching the carcass of unclean animals (v. 2; see 11:8). Even if the offenders were unaware of their sin (lit. "it is hidden from him"), they were still considered unclean (lit. "and/but he is unclean") and guilty. The last verb is a legal statement expressing the same idea as *nasa' 'awon* (see v. 1). Since touching the unclean did not require a sin offering (11:24–28), something else must have happened after the person became unclean. The phrase referring to the individual being "unaware" is puzzling because the verb means "to hide" (lit. "it is hidden from him"). Many scholars prefer to translate it as "to forget," but the Hebrew verb does not appear to carry this meaning anywhere else in the Hebrew Bible. It is probable that the phrase "it is hidden from him" is an idiomatic expression that conveys the idea of hiding by choosing to ignore something or by being negligent (cf. Lev. 20:4; Deut. 22:1, 3–4; Is. 58:7). If this suggestion is accepted, the person who became unclean ignored the violation of the law of cleanness; and by not performing the required cleansing rite, his or her spiritual condition was compromised. Consequently, a sin offering was required.

The third case addressed coming into contact with human uncleanness (see Lev. 15), resulting in ritual contamination (v. 3). Once again, the text explains that this act "was hidden from him" (i.e., the person ignored his or her condition and did not perform the required cleansing rite). The end of the verse has been understood in various ways— for example, that the person becomes guilty upon realizing what had happened or (perhaps, as all major translations suggest) that the person has come to know or recognize her or his guilt after being initially unaware of it. A literal translation of the Hebrew text reads, "And he knows and is guilty." This is not a matter of ignorance but a case of knowingly violating the law of cleanness.

The fourth case concerned a person who uttered a promissory oath without seriously considering it first (v. 4). According to the law, the sin does not consist of making a thoughtless oath but of not fulfilling it (Deut. 23:22–24; Eccl. 5:3–5). Some Bible translations render the passage "and he is unaware of it—when he realizes it, then he shall be guilty." But such a translation and similar ones do not make sense within the context because a person who pronounces an oath is fully aware of what she or he is doing. In fact, the Hebrew text reads literally "and he knows." The only possible interpretation is that the person simply ignored the oath and did not fulfill it. This was not an involuntary violation of the law, so consequently it required a sin offering.

The resolution of the problem began with a confession of negligence due to intentionally ignoring the law (v. 5). Translators and commentators differ over how to translate the first part of v. 6. The Hebrew term 'asham could refer to a trespass offering (v. 15), but in this context, the topic is the sin offering (vv. 9, 11–12). 'Asham could also be translated "reparation, penalty" (i.e., the penalty/reparation for the violation of the law is a sin offering). The sacrificial victim chosen for the sin offering was based on the financial status of the person. Some were to bring a female from the flock or a lamb or a goat, and others two turtle doves, one for a sin offering and the other for a burnt offering (vv. 7–10; cf. Luke 2:22–24). Since the amount of blood from a bird was very small, the blood application was simplified. If the persons were very poor, they were to bring a meal offering as a sin offering (vv. 11–13). In this case, oil and incense were to be excluded (cf. 2:1), perhaps as a sign of contrition and to distinguish it from the regular meal offering. Obviously, not everything was cleansed through blood (Heb. 9:22). This exemption was made in order to assure those facing financial difficulties that God's atoning grace is for all.

The sacrifice required to atone for human sin would cost more than anyone could pay. But God supplied it through the "precious [*timios*, "costly, of incomparable value"] blood of Christ," the Lamb without blemish or defect (1 Pet. 1:19). Christ paid the full penalty for our sins by bearing them upon Himself, and therefore, if there is repentance, there is no sin that He cannot forgive through His gracious provision (Rom. 5:20).

5:14—6:7. Guilt/Reparation Offering. "Reparation offering" is becoming a more common way of referring to this sacrifice, but it does not correspond well to the case described in 5:17–19, in which reparation was not required. This legislation lists two main reasons for bringing a guilt offering but does not describe in detail the procedure to be followed. This is provided in 7:1–7, where it is stated that it was to be like the sin offering. The only difference is the blood manipulation of the guilt offering, which was to be dashed on the sides of the altar of the burnt offering. The atoning significance of the blood was probably less emphasized because there was to be restitution and a 20 percent

penalty given to the priest before the sacrifice was to be performed.

The first occasion for this offering was for cases of inadvertent sacrilege (v. 15). The misappropriation of God's property—sinning in regard to the holy things of the Lord—was an extremely serious matter (cf. Josh. 7). Such a sin included, for instance, eating the tithe after setting it apart for the Lord. Nothing is said about how the person realized that he or she sinned, which may suggest that the person was not totally unaware of what happened. In any case, three things were required: restitution of what was taken, paying an additional 20 percent of the value, and bringing a ram for the guilt offering. The person could bring the equivalent of the cost of the ram to the sanctuary to buy it from the priest (v. 18). As the mediator for the people, the priest was to perform the atoning ritual, and the sin was to be forgiven (see 4:21).

According to 5:17–19, the guilt offering was to be brought when a person suspected he or she had committed an unknown sin. Since the sin was never identified, the remedy was to treat it as a sacrilege. For this unknown sin, a guilt offering was required, but without restitution. God indeed cares for the psychological and spiritual well-being of His children. Verse 19 could perhaps be translated "It is a guilt offering; he is guilty to the Lord."

The second occasion for bringing a guilt offering was for deliberate misappropriation of human property aggravated by taking a false oath before the Lord (6:1–7). The offenses listed are deception in matters of deposit, investment, robbery, withholding goods, and finding something lost and lying about it. The charges were denied under a false oath that desecrated the name of the Lord. At some point, the person realizing or acknowledging her or his guilt was allowed to bring a guilt offering and make restitution (v. 5). This was a very atrocious sin that came very close to a high-handed sin, and surprisingly, it was forgivable. The most logical explanation is that the sinner, at a particular moment, realized that he or she was indeed guilty, found refuge in God's mercy, and brought a guilt offering. The legislation itself encouraged the person to do this.

6:8—7:38
Sacrifices, the Priests, and the People

This section of Leviticus supplements the legislations found in 1:2—6:7 and places a more specific emphasis on the role of the priests, the portions that belonged to them, and the responsibility of the people in preserving the holiness of the offerings. It is organized in terms of the laws related to the burnt offering (6:8–13), grain offering (6:14–23), sin offering (6:24–30), guilt offering (7:1–10), and peace offerings (7:11–21), with emphases on the prohibition against eating fat and blood (7:22–27) and the proper distribution of the flesh of the animal (7:28–36), concluding with a summary (vv. 37–38).

6:8–13. Law of the Burnt Offering. This legislation concentrated on the proper handling of the ashes of the burnt offering. The reference was to the daily burnt offering, which was to be kept burning all night (v. 9) and day (v. 12; see Ex. 29:38–42). The priest was to provide the wood to keep the fire burning. When removing the ashes from the altar, the priest was to put on his holy, priestly linen garments and underpants to prevent exposure of his genitalia when ascending the steps to the altar (Ex. 28:42–43). The ashes were to be placed beside the altar while the priest changed into his common clothes to go outside the sanctuary. He was to deposit the ashes in a clean place outside the camp. The fire was to be kept burning because it was originally ignited by the Lord (Lev. 9:24). The fat of the peace offering was also to be burned on it. The daily burnt offering (Heb. *tamid*) pointed to the peoples' constant dependence on God's forgiving grace that would be fully manifested through the blood of Christ (see Ex. 29:38).

6:14–23. Law of the Grain Offering. The legislation repeated part of what is found in chapter 2 but clarified who should eat the meal offering as well as the reason. It was declared to be most holy (v. 17), and therefore, only the priests (not their families) were to eat a portion of it, in a holy place in the courtyard of the sanctuary. When the grain offering was brought by the priest, no portion of it was to go to him, but it was to be wholly burned on the altar (cf. v. 30). The grain offering of the priests was to be offered every day from the moment of their anointing. For them, it was not voluntary. They were required to honor God personally, not solely through the sacrifices of the people. The end of v. 18 is understood in a variety of ways by translators and commentators. According to some, whatever or whoever (the Heb. *'asher* could be referring to either persons or objects) touched the grain offering *became holy*. According to others (and this is likely the more accurate interpretation),

only those who were *already holy* could touch the grain offering. In this case, the implication is that holiness is not transferable through touch.

6:24–30. Law of the Sin Offering. The law clarified some aspects of the sin offering not mentioned before, with particular emphasis on its holiness. First, it was to be killed, like the burnt offering, on the north side of the altar (1:11). No reason is given for this specific requirement. Again, the translations and commentaries differ over whether the meaning of the first part of v. 27 is that the person who touched the flesh became holy or that the person who did so must have been holy already—that is to say, a priest. Another option, again, is to render the phrase as "whatever [not whoever] touches its flesh will be [become] holy." The basic question is whether holiness is transferrable through contact. In the present context, it is explicitly said that only the holy priests were to handle the holy, implying that only holy persons or objects could come into contact with the holy. The ritual of the eating of the flesh was an important one (see 6:26; 10:17). It is again stated that when the priest was involved in the sin that was being expiated, he was not to eat of the meat of the sacrifice (6:30). If the blood of the offering spattered on a garment, the item was to be washed in a holy place (v. 27). Ritual washing was done to remove impurity, and if this were the case here, then the blood of the sin offering, by carrying the sin of the repentant person, transferred impurity, not holiness, by contact. If it were boiled in a clay pot, the pot was to be broken because washing was not enough to cleanse it—it was too porous. If boiled in a bronze pot, then washing was enough to remove contagion (v. 28).

7:1–10. Law of the Guilt Offering. Previously, the instructions about the guilt offering were about the sins expiated and the procedure (5:14–6:7). Here the interest is defining the portion of it that went to the priest. There is some repetition related to blood manipulation and the fat of the animal (vv. 3–4). It is further established that the ritual procedure for this offering was to be the same as for the sin offering with respect to the flesh of the animal, declared to be most holy and, therefore, belonging to the officiating priest only (v. 6). The priest was also to have for himself the skin of the sacrifice of the burnt offering (not mentioned in chap. 1) and the grain offering baked in the oven or prepared in a pan or griddle (vv.

8–9; see 2:4–7). Uncooked grain offerings were to belong to all the priests (v. 10).

7:11–21. Law of the Peace/Fellowship Offering. A specific distinction is made between the peace offering as thanksgiving and the peace offering as votive or freewill. The peace/fellowship offering involved thanksgiving, and it was to be brought with grains in the form of unleavened wafers/cakes and leavened bread. One cake was offered as a heave offering—a contribution set apart—to the Lord, and it went to the priest; the rest probably went to the offerer. The leavened bread was not to go to the altar (2:11). The flesh of the animal was to be eaten the same day it was brought to the Lord, but if it were brought for a vow or voluntary, whatever was left over could be eaten the next day (vv. 16–17). After that, it was not good for human consumption. Whatever remained was to be burned.

If any of the meat were eaten on the third day, the offering and the offerer were rejected by the Lord, and the benefits were not credited or imputed to the person. In fact, the person was responsible for the desecration and liable to punishment (see 5:1). Another reason for not eating the meat was if it had come into contact with the unclean. Only those who were in a state of cleanness were to partake of it (v. 19). But if by any chance the unclean person ate of it, then he or she was to be cut off from the people (vv. 20–21). This is the most severe penalty for sin in the OT because the person was permanently banished or excommunicated from the covenant people. The ultimate punishment was in God's hands, although, in a few cases, He used humans to accomplish His purpose (20:2; Ex. 31:14). But even when humans failed, God Himself still cut off the person (20:2–3), which suggests that the penalty impacted the afterlife.

7:22–27. Prohibition of Fat and Blood. This parenthesis is a development of the regulation against eating fat and blood (3:16–17). Since this was required from all, the divine speech was addressed to the people through Moses (7:22; in chaps. 1–5, the people were addressed, and in chaps. 6–7, the priests). The text establishes that the fat of sacrificial animals was not to be consumed, and neither was the fat of animals that die of natural causes or that have been killed by other animals. In the last two cases, the fat could be used for some other purpose (e.g., to polish or grease instruments) but not for food. The penalty for eating the fat of sacrifices was serious—the offender was to be cut

off from the people (v. 25; see v. 21). The prohibition against consuming blood applied to any kind of animal or bird, even at home, and the penalty was the same (vv. 26–27; see "Health and Hygiene in Leviticus," p. 272).

7:28–36. Meat Portions for the Priests. The main interest of this section is to identify the portion of the flesh that was to go to the priest. Offerings made by fire refer to the portions that were to be given to God as a gift from the worshiper (see 1:9). In this case, those offerings designate the fat that was to go to the altar and the breast of the animal that was to be "raised" (from the Heb. verb *nup*, not "waved") before the Lord as an "elevated offering" (*tenupah*) dedicated to Him (v. 30). The breast was to be for the priest, as was also the right thigh, set apart as a "contribution" (Heb. *terumah*) or "heave" (raised) offering (v. 32). These were considered the most valuable portions of the flesh that the Israelites gave to the Lord, and He, in turn, gave them to the priests as a permanent mandate (v. 34). The Lord required this same type of sacrifice from the Israelites when the priests were consecrated to minister in the sanctuary (v. 35; this prepares the way for chap. 8).

The section dealing with voluntary and required sacrifices closes with a summary stating that the previous discussion was about the burnt, the grain, the sin, the guilt, the consecration, and the peace offerings, concerning which the Lord instructed Moses on Mount Sinai (v. 38). A new offering is introduced that had not been mentioned before—the consecration or ordination offering (v. 37), which referred to the offerings brought during the consecration of the priests, to be discussed in chapter 8. These instructions were given to the people of Israel when they were ordered to bring their offerings to the Lord in the Sinai Desert (v. 38), which indicates that these sacrificial regulations were placed within a narrative, as indicated in 1:1. The meticulous instructions given by the Lord to the Israelites reveal how important order is in the eyes of the Lord. By being so specific, He was establishing boundaries that would contribute to the preservation of spiritual order in the life of His people. Order continues to be significant in the life of the church in the preservation of its unity and the fulfillment of its mission.

8:1—10:20

A HOLY PRIESTHOOD

Leviticus begins with a reference to the sanctuary that had just been built and progresses to the different types of sacrifices to be offered there. The most natural next step was to identify and enable those who would minister in the sanctuary. Chapter 8 outlines the complex ritual of the ordination of Aaron and his sons as priests and the anointing of the tabernacle itself (see Ex. 29:1-37). Chapter 9 describes the beginning of the priestly system. The narrative found in chapter 10 illustrates the serious responsibility of the priests as they operated within the sphere of holiness.

8:1-36

Anointing of Aaron, His Sons, and the Tabernacle

The priesthood in Israel was of divine origin. God selected and appointed Aaron and his sons to minister as priests on behalf of the people of Israel. This is emphasized throughout the text by the repetition of the compliance formula and its variations: "Moses did as the Lord commanded him" (vv. 4, 9, 13, 17, 21, 29, 31, 34, 35). Moses performed the priestly role before the priesthood was formally instituted. The anointing was a public meeting. It is likely that the representatives of the people were invited to be present. The ceremony was well organized: the first part had to do with the investiture of Aaron and his sons and the setting apart of Aaron and the sanctuary for God (vv. 6-13). This was followed by the offering of three sacrifices for the cleansing and consecration of the future priests (vv. 14-32). The anointing service was extended for seven days (vv. 33-36).

8:1-13. Investiture and Consecration. The complexity of the ritual was, in part, related to the fact that Aaron, his sons, and the sanctuary were in a state of transition as they moved from the sphere of the common to the sphere of the holy. They were not the subjects of the action but the objects—they were not yet priests. Later traditions indicate that there were specific areas within the courtyard, protected by a curtain, where the full washings took place. The change of clothing indicated a new status for Aaron; he was being invested as high priest (vv. 7-9; see Ex. 28). He was transitioning to a different role.

At this point in the narrative, the tabernacle, its furniture, and the altar were sprinkled with oil to set them apart for the Lord. Some oil was also poured out on Aaron's head (representing his whole person) to set him apart for the service of the tabernacle (vv. 10-12). Both personnel and location were finally ready for service because they had both been marked by the special

anointing oil, which exuded a fragrant aroma. This was another step in the process of transition. The section concludes with the investiture of the sons of Aaron as priests. Moses put on them a priestly dress that was less embellished in order to establish a difference in priestly functions. This was done in accordance with what the Lord commanded Moses to do. Later, oil was also placed on the sons (v. 30).

8:14-22. Sin and Burnt Offerings. Although Aaron and his sons had been set apart, they and the tabernacle needed to go through a cleansing ritual. This was the function of the sin offering (vv. 14-17). Since the tabernacle was not yet functioning and this offering was part of the anointing of the priests, it was different from the regular sin offerings (chap. 4). The ritual emphasized the use of the blood in connection to the altar and the disposition of the flesh of the sacrifice. Since it was an atoning sacrifice (Ex. 29:36), in this particular case, it cleansed the priests (through the laying on of hands) and the altar (blood was applied all around the horns; see 4:7). The altar seems to have stood for the cleansing of the whole sanctuary complex. Since no specific violation of the law of impurity is mentioned, it follows that anyone or anything that was to be in the service of God was, by nature, in need of purification. The burnt offering (vv. 18-21) was to follow the general procedure of a regular burnt offering (see Lev. 1). The sequence of this procedure was important. First, the sin offering cleansed. Second, the burnt offering expressed, along with atonement, the total dedication of Aaron and his sons to the Lord. Cleansing both precedes and accompanies true worship.

The consecration/ordination offering (lit. "filling [offering]"; v. 31) was unique. The literal translation is related to the phrase *mille'yad*, "to fill the hand" (which occurs in the Hebrew text of Ex. 29:9, 33, 35), and refers to an act by which a new status was given to someone—for example, consecration. In fact, parts of this offering were placed in the hands of Aaron and his sons (Lev. 8:27-29). Since their hands were filled, they could not use them to do anything else but the service of the Lord. Although the sacrifice was unique, it was similar to the peace offering and was to be accompanied by unleavened bread. The main difference was the complex use of the blood. Some of the blood was applied to the tip of the right ear (perhaps signaling a willingness to listen to/obey the Lord), on the thumb of the right hand (suggesting readiness to serve), and on the big toe of the right foot (indicating a desire to walk in the way of the Lord) of Aaron and his sons (vv. 23–24). This was probably an act of cleansing and dedication (cf. 14:14, 17, 25), similar to what was done to the altar (v. 15). The portions that were placed on the altar, together with the right thigh that was for the priests (7:32–33), were put into the hands or palms of Aaron and his sons and raised before the Lord as a wave offering (see 7:30); then the portions were incinerated (in regard to the aroma of the sacrifice, see notes on 1:9.) In this case, Moses received the breast of the animal (v. 29).

The oil and blood of the consecration sacrifice were mixed and sprinkled on Aaron, his sons, and their garments to contribute to their ordination (v. 30). The anointing oil was a symbol of consecration, and the blood suggested the idea of cleansing. Since the consecration offering was similar to the peace offering of thanksgiving (7:11–15), the priests could eat it as other Israelites would. Moses gave them the breast of the sacrifice that belonged to him and told them to eat it together with the unleavened bread within the precincts of the tabernacle. Whatever was left was to be immediately incinerated (vv. 31–32).

At the end of the day, the ritual of anointing was still unfinished. Aaron and his sons were required to stay by the entrance of the tabernacle for seven days in order for their consecration to be complete. Interestingly, all the elements of the consecration ritual performed during that day are interpreted or summarized as making atonement for Aaron and his sons (v. 34). The ordination ritual of the priests was a way of cleansing them in order to serve a holy God.

The complexity of the ritual of ordination illustrates the distance that exists between a holy God and beings that are in constant need of cleansing. One is almost led to ask, Who can approach the Holy One? The answer is found in the divine disposition to interact with humans and to draw them into the sphere of His holiness. He is constantly willing to remove that which impedes fellowship with Him, and consequently, He creates a way through the atoning sacrifice, which makes heaven accessible to all, not only to priests. This requires the Christian to go through a rite of transition—moving from the secular (the world) to the sphere of salvation in Christ. This takes place through the rite of baptism, which leads to life in harmony with God, a transition from a life of enslavement to sin to a new life of service to God and fellow human beings (Rom. 6:1–11). Christ indeed opened a way (Heb. 10:19–22).

9:1–24
Beginning of the Priestly Ministry

After seven days had elapsed, on the eighth day, Moses instructed Aaron and his sons about what to do as they began their priestly work and provided a list of the sacrifices to be offered. This was followed by the sin and burnt offerings of Aaron (vv. 8–14) and the sin, burnt, and peace offerings of the people (vv. 15–21). The section concludes with a double blessing and the manifestation of the glory of God (vv. 22–24).

9:1–14. Moses's Instructions and Aaron's Sacrifices. Moses informed Aaron that this day he would receive direct confirmation from God of his role as high priest: the glory of the Lord would appear to him (v. 6; see v. 4). The inauguration of the priestly ministry was also a public ceremony, and the elders were present. They were expected to provide animals for the sacrifices of the people. Moses also told Aaron that he should offer a sin and a burnt offering for himself as well as sin, burnt, grain, and peace offerings for the people. He clarified that the purpose of the sin and burnt offerings was to make atonement for all of them.

Verse 3 contains abbreviated instructions for the sin offering (cf. 4:3–12) and the burnt offering (1:3–9). The text emphasizes the expiatory function of both sacrifices. The cleansing rituals for Aaron and his sons performed during their ordination were intended to install them as priests, but here they went through another set of cleansing rituals as they began their priestly responsibilities. This reinforces the fact that uncleanness is practically a constant in human life and that humans never reach a moment when they can stand by themselves before God.

9:15–21. Sacrifices of the People. The inauguration of the worship system in Israel began with the cleansing of the people, suggesting that worship includes the need for atonement. The procedure for the different offerings brought by the people is not given in detail. It is simply stated that they were offered in the prescribed manner (v. 16). In this case, two sacrificial victims were brought for the burnt offering and two for the peace offering. The disposition of the fat of the peace offering is repeated in more detail to stress the importance of having given it to the Lord (v. 21).

After the sacrifices were offered, Aaron performed for the first time one of his most important responsibilities, namely, blessing the people (Num. 6:23; Deut. 21:5). He did this from the altar, and then he and Moses went into the tabernacle, perhaps to ask the Lord to accept the sacrifices. As they came out, they blessed the people (cf. 1 Kin. 8:14–21, 54–61). It was at this moment that the promised theophany occurred. The glory of the Lord appeared to all the people, and fire came out from the tabernacle and burned all the sacrifices that were on the altar. God provided the fire to demonstrate His acceptance of the sacrifices, thus inaugurating the sacrificial system and legitimizing Aaron's priestly ministry. As the consecration ceremony implies, the fire previously present on the altar was God's fire that officially inaugurated the sacrificial system, and from this moment on, no other fire would be accepted by the Lord. The people responded to the divine presence with a cry of joy and prostrated themselves before the Lord. Something wonderful and unique had occurred on earth. God had established a particular space to dwell among His creation, consecrated the place through cleansing rituals and through His presence, organized a priestly system to mediate the benefits of His presence among His people, and created a sacrificial system to strengthen and renew His covenant relationship with His people. This was the cosmic center from which God's presence would irradiate the world and restore order.

The priestly system, once established, would operate until the coming of the true High Priest, Jesus Christ, whose arrival was announced by the Lord through Daniel (Dan. 9:24–27). He offered the sacrifice on the cross and ascended to the Father, where He was installed as High Priest according to the order of Melchizedek (Heb. 6:19–20; 7:15–17) in the heavenly sanctuary (Heb. 9:11–22), and as a result of His mediation, the Spirit descended on the disciples in the form of fire (Acts 2:3, 33). He is High Priest in the heavenly sanctuary, offering before the Father the merits of His sacrificial death on behalf of humanity (Heb. 8:1–3; 9:11–12). Since Jesus Christ possesses life in Himself, He remains Priest forever (7:22–25). No other being can occupy His priestly role as Mediator between God and humans (1 Tim. 2:5–6). It will be from the heavenly sanctuary (Heb. 8–10) that He will come back to earth "a second time" to appear to those who have been relying on His work of mediation on their behalf before the Father and who are eagerly waiting for His return (Heb. 9:28).

10:1–20
Sacredness of the Priesthood

The main purpose of this narrative is to underline the sacred responsibility of the priests. It narrates the death of Nadab and Abihu (vv. 1–5), contains two prohibitions (vv. 6–11), and includes instructions about the consumption of holy flesh (vv. 12–20).

10:1–5. Death of Nadab and Abihu. This incident occurred on the day the priestly services were inaugurated (chap. 9). The two oldest sons of Aaron burned incense using unauthorized fire—that is, not from the altar. This likely took place in the courtyard of the sanctuary ("before the LORD," v. 1). God destroyed them with the same fire that had come from heaven and burned the sacrifices (9:24). The Lord, through Moses, interpreted for Aaron what had happened. God considered the priests to be servants of the Most High, responsible for revealing to others His holy character (or before whom He displayed His magnificent holiness; v. 3). God was glorified—acknowledged as right—by the people for punishing priests who did not respect His holiness (see Num. 20:13). Aaron's silence indicated that he accepted the justice of God. No atoning sacrifice was needed because they had borne their own sin and died for it.

10:6–10. Two Prohibitions. The first was given by Moses to Aaron and his sons: they were not to mourn for the death of Nadab and Abihu, possibly because this could be perceived as support for their conduct. Mourning rituals included tearing the garments; but in the case of the priests, this would have been sacrilegious and would have spiritually damaged the congregation because their garments had been sanctified by the Lord. The priests were to remain in their posts, officiating in the tabernacle (vv. 6–7). The Lord gave the second prohibition directly to Aaron. It forbade the priests to drink intoxicating beverages while officiating in the sanctuary. Such drinks would have clouded their judgment, and they would not have been able to distinguish between the holy and unholy (or common) or between the unclean and clean. They would not have been effective teachers of God's laws (v. 10). This is an excellent description of the damaging effects of alcohol.

10:11–20. Handling Holy and Most Holy Flesh. Perhaps another reason for asking the priests to continue to officiate was that their responsibilities for the day had not yet ended. They had to eat the grain offering, which is most holy. Moses reminded them that the flesh of the peace offerings was holy and they could eat it with the members of their families (for more on the heave contribution and wave offerings, see 7:30, 32). At first, Moses did not say anything about the flesh of the sin offering.

But when he realized that its flesh was incinerated instead of being eating by the priests, he became upset. For him, this was another violation of God's will. He reminded them that they should have eaten it, and in the process, he provided a valuable interpretation of the rite of eating the flesh of the sin offering: it was most holy, and God had given it to them to bear (*nasa'*) the guilt of the people of Israel and make atonement for them (v. 17; see 5:1).

The discussion is about the eating of the flesh of the sin offering and not about the atoning function of the sin offering as such. Therefore, the connection between the two phrases—"to bear guilt" and "to make atonement"—is significant and indicates that eating the flesh was part of the atoning ritual; it contributed to the removal of sin. It did so by transferring it to the priest. This explains why the priest could not eat the flesh of his own sin offering—he could not bear his own sin and at the same time atone for it. To bear sin means to be responsible for sin and liable to punishment. The person who came to the sanctuary bearing his or her sin (see 5:1) offered a sacrifice to which the sin was transferred, and by eating of its flesh, the priest became the one who bore it. This ritual capacity of the priest was symbolized by the plate of pure gold placed on the turban of the high priest, inscribed with the phrase, "HOLY [OR HOLINESS] TO THE LORD" (Ex. 28:36–37). Exodus 28:38 explains that this plate was to be on Aaron's forehead with the intention that he would bear all the iniquity ritually associated with the holy offerings of the Israelites and, thus, render the people acceptable to the Lord. Holiness is stronger than sin. Aaron could bear the iniquity of the people and not perish because he was shielded by God's holiness. It was through this process that sin in the person of the priest was transferred to the tabernacle. What is perhaps surprising is that the atoning process brought sin/impurity/death into contact with the holiness, purity, and life of God, and holiness remained undamaged by sin. It overcame everything (see "The Laying On of Hands," p. 243). This finds its ultimate expression in Christ, who became human and bore the world's sin, yet His holiness and purity were not compromised. He defeated sin and death and freed humanity from their enslaving power (see Is. 53:5–6; Col. 1:13–14, 19–22; 2:13–15).

11:1—17:16
HOLINESS AND CLEANNESS/UNCLEANNESS

The topic of clean and unclean was introduced in the previous chapter when God reminded Aaron that he should distinguish between the two (10:10–11). The topic is important because impurity brought people into the realm of death and separated them from access to the sanctuary. Unless a cleansing ritual were performed, the separation could have been permanent. Impurity is, in principle, a metaphor for death as that which separates individuals from God. The God who dwells among His people as the source of life expects them to be holy. The intention of the instructions was to teach the people how to avoid becoming unclean and what to do once a person became unclean. This section discusses clean and unclean animals (Lev. 11:1–47) and the uncleanness of childbirth (12:1–8), skin diseases (13:1—14:32), houses with mold and mildew (14:33–57), and bodily discharges (15:1–33). It culminates in the Day of Atonement, the center of the book of Leviticus (16:1–34). Chapter 17 is included in this section because it thematically deals with the question of blood while raising topics to be discussed in the following chapters.

11:1–47
Clean and Unclean Creatures

The introduction to the speech indicates that this was a dietary law (v. 2). This concern for diet reached back to the Garden of Eden (Gen. 1:29; 3:18). Using the categories and language of the Creation narrative in Genesis 1, the chapter discusses the allowance or prohibition of consuming certain land animals (vv. 2–8), sea creatures (vv. 9–12), flying creatures (vv. 13–19), winged insects (vv. 20–25), carcasses (vv. 24–40), and swarming land creatures (vv. 41–45; see "Clean and Unclean Animals," p. 257).

11:1–28. Criteria for Clean Animals. Clean (*tahor*, "clean, pure") land animals had cloven hooves and chew the cud. If they had only one of these characteristics, they were unclean (*tame'*, "to be unclean, impure") and, consequently, were not be eaten, and their carcasses were not to be touched (v. 8). The criteria for the category of clean sea creatures was fins and scales, while those without them were considered to be *sheqets*. The noun *sheqets* ("a detestable thing" or "an abomination") and its related verb (*shaqats*, "to detest") seem to express, in this chapter, the same ideas as the adjective *tame'* ("unclean, impure"; see Lev. 11:8, 11, 43; 7:21). These creatures were not to be eaten, and neither were their carcasses to be touched (vv. 9–12). With respect to flying creatures, no specific criteria are given, but instead, the text contains a list of those that should not be eaten—those considered to be unclean, or an abomination. Many of the Hebrew names for the birds are obscure, which makes it difficult to identify the specific creature (vv. 13–19). Most, if not all of them, were birds of prey, and this characteristic has traditionally been used to identify those that cannot be eaten. Flying insects with four feet and that walk on the earth were clean if they had jointed legs with which to jump (vv. 20–23). Among them were locusts and different types of grasshoppers. If they lacked these characteristics, they were not to be eaten; they were an unclean (detestable) abomination (v. 23).

The list is interrupted by a discussion of uncleanness through touch (vv. 24–28). Touching the carcass of any of the unclean animals made a person unclean until evening (the end of the day). But if the person also carried part of it, then the individual was unclean until the evening and had to wash his or her clothes to remove the impurity (cf. 13:6). Animals with paws were unclean, and touching or carrying their carcasses was also prohibited (vv. 27–28).

11:29–47. Swarming Land Creatures. These were mainly reptiles and small mammals that multiplied quickly. A list is provided, but in many of the cases, the meaning of the Hebrew term is not clear. Touching them when they were dead made the person unclean until evening (v. 31). When the carcass fell on clothing, skins, sacks, or anything made of wood, the item it touched became unclean and was to be put in water until evening. If the carcass fell into a clay vessel, what was inside the container became unclean, and the object was to be broken. The uncleanness is viewed as penetrating porous vessels, making it impossible to remove. If the carcass fell into a spring of water or a large cistern, the water remained clean (v. 36), probably because the body

of a small animal could not contaminate the entire body of water. The same happened if it fell on planting seed, perhaps inside a vessel, but if it fell on damp seed, the seed became unclean (vv. 37–38). Even clean animals became unclean after they died, and touching their carcasses made a person unclean until evening. Those who ate of their flesh or carried them were unclean until evening and had to wash their clothes (vv. 39–41). Since all these animals, to some extent, competed with humans for space, it was difficult to avoid impurity. Accordingly, it was necessary to develop ways to eliminate it from objects and humans. In most cases, these were minor impurities that were removed at the end of the day and did not require a sacrifice.

All creeping things were considered an abomination that could make God's people unclean. The reason provided for this law was that God is holy and they should be holy as He is holy (v. 44). This call to holiness was grounded in God's redemptive power, manifested in the liberation of the people from Egypt (v. 45). God invaded the world with His holiness, and He began to transform it by making His people holy. At the end, in a summary, it is stated that this law is about clean and unclean animals—animals that can and cannot be eaten (vv. 46–47; see below, "Clean and Unclean Animals").

12:1–8
Uncleanness and Childbirth

Leviticus moves now from the uncleanness of animals (chap. 11), to human uncleanness, beginning with the mystery of childbirth, which combines the start of a new life with the phenomenon of impurity as a symbol of death. The legislation deals first with impurity caused by childbirth and concludes with the atoning ritual.

Clean and Unclean Animals

The nature of the law of clean and unclean animals, as well as its purpose, continues to be debated among biblical interpreters. This commentary maintains the idea that it is primarily a health law and is still valid for God's people.

1. The Motivation Is Holiness. The reason provided by the biblical text to justify this unique regulation is holiness (11:44). The implicit contrast is between the unclean and

the holy. The unclean is a metaphor for the realm of death while, the holy is what belongs to God and is an appropriate expression of life. The law of clean and unclean animals sought to preserve the life of the people by keeping them as far as possible from the sphere of death, including the sphere of sickness and suffering.

2. Uniqueness of the Law. According to Leviticus, ritual uncleanness had two basic characteristics. First, it was acquired through the direct or perhaps indirect contact with the unclean (blood, a dead body, a carcass, etc.). Second, this type of impurity could be removed from the individual through the performance of a particular ritual (hence the designation "ritual uncleanness" that is sometimes used by commentators). Those two characteristics do not apply to the uncleanness of the unclean animals, which indicates that the nature of their impurity is essentially different from ritual impurity. First, the impurity of the animals was not acquired but was part of the very nature of the animal. They did not become unclean by coming into contact with a source of impurity. Since these animals were permanently unclean, there was no particular ritual capable of removing their uncleanness from them.

Second, the uncleanness of these animals was not transferable through contact. The Israelites could come into direct or indirect contact with an unclean animal without becoming unclean. In fact, they reared unclean animals and used them for a variety of tasks. For instance, they used donkeys, horses, and camels for transportation and to carry loads. The impurity of these animals did not affect the Israelites in any way. People became unclean only by eating the flesh of the animal, but no ritual was prescribed to remove this impurity from them. The Israelites were simply expected to obey the Lord and not eat unclean animals. Of course, an animal could become ritually unclean after it died, and this impurity was transferable through touch. Touching the carcass of a clean or unclean animal made a person unclean, and a ritual had to be performed in order to cleanse the individual. Here, the natural and ritual uncleanness of an animal are clearly distinguished.

3. The Distinction Clean/Unclean is Pre-Mosaic. The law classifying clean and unclean animals is mentioned for the first time in the Bible in the Flood narrative, *before there was an Israelite* (Gen. 7:2–3). In the context, a change in the human diet was introduced. While only two pairs of the unclean animals entered the ark, seven of each clean animal were preserved. This suggests that some of the clean animals were to be used for sacrifices, and any of them could be used as food by Noah and his family without the risk of extinguishing any particular species.

Therefore, the permission to eat all moving things that are alive in 9:3 is to be interpreted contextually as restricted to clean animals that neither died of natural causes nor were torn by wild beasts—in both instances, the animals' blood was not properly drained (cf. 7:2). The early biblical narratives indicate that the patriarchs consumed the flesh of clean animals only (e.g., Gen. 18:7; 25:27–28; 27:3–4, 9–10, 14, 30–31). This universal law was incorporated into the Israelite covenant law for preservation and as guidance for God's people.

4. Context of the Law in Deuteronomy 14. The fact that this law is recorded in Deuteronomy is significant because Deuteronomy (with its focus on the covenant) generally does not deal with ceremonial laws. In this particular passage, there is no contextual discussion of ritual uncleanness. Deuteronomy 13 is an exhortation to worship only the Lord, and the last part of chapter 14 deals with tithing laws. In between them is found the law of unclean animals. This implies that the law of unclean animals was not considered a ceremonial law but a dietary one.

5. It Is a Dietary Law. One should not ignore the fact that the law of clean/unclean animals regulated the animal flesh that the Israelites were allowed to consume as food and, as such, forms part of a long tradition of dietary regulations given by God to His people. God has always been interested in the diet of humans. To Adam and Eve, He gave seed-bearing plants or herbs—that is, fruits, vegetables, and grains (Gen. 1:29). After the Fall, He modified their diet to include what may have been cultivated vegetables (3:18). Finally, after the Flood, He allowed humans to eat the flesh of clean animals (9:3–4). Clean animals are relatively safer to eat than the unclean ones. The original plant-based diet continues to point to God's ideal for His people. God allowed humans to be partially responsible for the preservation of their lives but instructed them on how to preserve it to His glory (1 Cor. 10:31). The lordship of Christ includes our bodies because He is interested in both our physical and spiritual well-being (1 Cor. 6:19–20; 3 John 2). There is no evidence in the NT that indicates that Christ eliminated, through His sacrifice, the law of clean/unclean animals (see Mark 7; Acts 10).

It leads the reader from separation to full access to the holy in the sanctuary.

At the birth of a child, a woman would become unclean because of the blood flow that accompanied the birth (v. 7). If the child was male, the woman would be initially unclean for seven days (v. 2; cf. 15:19–24). The law was based on the understanding of blood as a physical expression of life. The loss of blood/life brought the person into contact with sphere of death, which separated her from full interaction with others and with God in the sanctuary. The seven days of impurity distanced her from other human beings, allowing her to recuperate from the experience of childbearing. Obviously, there was to be limited interaction with others at home who would also become unclean through touch, but her fellowship with God did not cease. The issue was not that sex or birth were inherently sinful but rather that because of Adam's sin, humans exist in a context in which the ugliness of death is always potentially present and occasionally touches us. In the ancient world, as well as in many places around the world today, at the moment of childbirth, death occasionally manifested itself in all its power and ended a human life. Death is an enemy, but this ritual reveals that there is a remedy for it.

After seven days, her impurity was no longer contagious—she could interact freely with others and with her husband. On the eighth day, the child was to be circumcised and, thus, officially declared a member of the covenant people of God. But the woman was to go through a longer period of purification before having access to the holy. She was to wait thirty-three days for her cleansing to be final. No reason is given for this long period, and scholars have speculated about it. The total period was forty days, perhaps suggesting new beginnings, as in other contexts (e.g., Ex. 24:18). In this case, the conclusion of this interval introduces the restoration of full access to the dwelling of the Lord.

If the child was female, the waiting period was to be extended to two weeks and sixty-six days (v. 5). There have been many attempts to explain the reason for doubling the time period in the case of a girl, but none has found wide acceptance. A more popular rationalization suggests that as a result of no longer receiving maternal hormones, a newborn girl often experiences vaginal bleeding, and this bleeding, together with that of the mother, would account for the double period of impurity. The only sure conclusion is that the birth of a girl blessed the mother with a longer period of rest!

The remaining uncleanness was to be removed through a burnt and a sin offering brought by the woman to the sanctuary. Her impurity had a contamination potential above minor impurities, which were removed through a ritual bath, and consequently, a sacrifice was required in order for her to have access to the sanctuary. Women could offer sacrifices in the sanctuary, as this legislation makes absolutely clear. The sacrifices were to be offered not to remove a sin committed but to remove physical uncleanness. As a result of the ritual, she was declared clean (v. 7). The issue was not that she had committed a specific misdeed, nor had she been sick. Rather, this uncleanness was a part of the sinful state of human life, but the Lord provided cleansing even for uncleanness over which they had no control. Humanity's struggle with death in this life will come to an end at the moment of the Second Coming (1 Cor. 15:54).

13:1—14:32
Uncleanness and Skin Diseases

This section of Leviticus deals with abnormal skin conditions or diseases. The Hebrew term translated "leprosy" (*tsara'at*) is now commonly understood to designate multiple types of skin diseases (e.g., psoriasis, ringworm). Although many scholars believe that the designation does not include leprosy (Hansen's disease), others have correctly argued that it does. The translation of the term could be "leprosy," as a generic term, or perhaps "skin disease." The purpose of the discussion was not so much to identify a disease and then provide medication for it but to identify it and control its spread. Therefore, the information on how to diagnose it remains the primary concern of the text. The outbreak was to be controlled by imposing quarantine and isolating the unclean person. The people knew that the disease was contagious. In the Bible, leprosy is associated with death, as suggested by the experience of Miriam (Num. 12:10–12). In fact, lepers identified themselves as under the power of death by dressing like a person in mourning (Lev. 13:45). Since they were in the sphere of death, they were unclean, separated from social interaction, and without access to the sanctuary.

13:2–46. Symptoms and Diagnosis. The priest was to provide a rational diagnosis based on the specific instructions the Lord had given him through Moses. The priest was to examine the condition and, in most cases, to quarantine the person until it could be ascertained that the person was clean or unclean. If diagnosed with leprosy, the person was to be declared unclean (v. 3).

The chapter is organized around eight cases: (1) suspected leprosy because of certain anomalous skin conditions (v. 2); (2) skin disease (vv. 9–11; most likely Hansen's disease); (3) a full body outbreak (vv. 12–17; possibly vitiligo); (4) a boil on the skin that had been healed and later developed a white swelling or reddish-white spot (v. 19); (5) a person whose skin had been burned and the raw flesh of the burn became a bright white or reddish-white spot (v. 24); (6) a person with a sore on the head or chin (v. 29); (7) white/bright patches on the skin (v. 38); and (8) a bald person with a reddish-white sore on the head (v. 42). In cases of leprosy, the persons' clothes were to be torn and their heads uncovered (or hair disheveled), as if in a state of mourning; they were in the realm of death. In order to not contaminate others, they were to shout "Unclean! Unclean!" (v. 45) and live outside the camp in isolation (v. 46). This was a living experience of death: separation from others and physical distance from the holy sanctuary. In practice, the relatives and friends of the sick person provided for them. The law did not discourage such expressions of love because touching them, perhaps by accident, was not a sin but a way of contracting impurity, which was redressed through a cleansing rite.

13:47–59. Infested Garments. The description of the phenomenon indicates that the text is describing a fungal infection, usually identified as mold or mildew. It was a "disease" that contaminated fabrics (clothing made of wool, linen) and leather. In this case, the term *tsara'at* refers to such fungal infections. If it were suspected that a piece of clothing was contaminated, it was brought to the priest for analysis. He examined it and quarantined it for seven days, after which he might be able to determine if it was clean or unclean. If he was uncertain, it was quarantined again. Washing the clothes was part of the process which ascertained their condition. If it was declared to be unclean, then the clothing was burned. The quarantine was a preventive measure that protected the owner of the cloth from becoming unclean.

14:1–32
Cleansing of the Leper

The ritual described here is not therapeutic because it was to be performed after the person was healed. It was to be a ritual of transition that led lepers from their place outside the camp to the camp, then to the sanctuary, and finally to full restoration. The ritual wonderfully illustrated God's plan for overcoming death and moral impurity and that it is realized in stages. The resolution of the cosmic conflict is complex, but it will be resolved. There is hope for lepers.

14:1–9. Heading to the Tabernacle. If a leper concluded that he or she had been healed, the priest was asked to perform an examination. The priest was to go to the leper to carry out the cleansing ritual—a beautiful portrait of Jesus, who approaches humanity in their uncleanness. It is likely that the leper's relatives provided the required elements for the ritual: two living clean birds, a stick of cedar wood, hyssop (a type of herb; cf. Ex. 12:22; Num. 19:6; Ps. 51:7), and a string of scarlet yarn, probably used to tie the wood and the hyssop together to create a sprinkling instrument. One of the two birds was to be killed over running water and its blood collected in a vessel. Perhaps water was added to the blood to facilitate sprinkling the blood (see v. 52). The living bird, together with the wood, the scarlet yarn, and the hyssop, was to be dipped into the blood and sprinkled seven times on the leper for cleansing. The living bird was to be set free in the open field (v. 7) as an elimination rite (see 14:49–53; 16:15, 21). Similar rituals found in some cultures in the ANE have expressed, at least in some cases, the idea of evil returning to its place of origin. Leviticus seems to be hinting at the idea that impurity found its ultimate origin outside the place where God had manifested Himself—the Israelite camp. But the symbolism could also point to the leper's movement from the sphere of death (leprosy) to the freedom of life (i.e., the "resurrection").

At this early stage in the ritual, the former lepers were clean but not completely clean. In order to enter the camp, they were to undergo a ritual bath, shave their bodies, and wash their clothes. They were allowed to enter the camp but not their place of residence (their tent) for seven days, probably to avoid contaminating it with the residual impurity. On the seventh day, after the they had shaved and washed their clothes and bodies, they were declared clean and were able to have full social interaction with others. On the eighth day, they were finally able to visit the tabernacle.

14:10–32. Final Cleansing in the Tabernacle. The priest, as the mediator of those needing cleansing, was to bring the former leper to the entrance of the tabernacle and offer guilt, sin, burnt, and grain offerings on behalf of the individual. The reason for the guilt offering was probably ignorant sin (see 5:17–19). In this case, the blood of the sacrifice was also to be applied to the right ear, the right thumb, and the right toe of the person, as was done to the priest during the anointing (8:23–24), to rededicate the person to the Lord. The oil was to be consecrated to the Lord and then applied to the same parts of the body, and the rest of it was to be placed on the head of the person. The sin offering was to be sacrificed to make atonement for the person— that is to say, to remove his or her impurity. This was to be followed by the burnt and grain offerings as expressions of gratitude and full dedication to the Lord. Allowance was made for a poor person who could not afford expensive sacrifices (vv. 21–32). The summary emphasizes the importance of atonement for cleansing (v. 20; cf. v. 31). Uncleanness will be overcome.

14:33–57. Leprous House. The noun *tsara'at* applies also to fungus- or mold-infested houses. This section is placed last because it describes what was to be done once the people had settled in the land of Canaan. The passage is composed of two main cases: a house that was condemned (vv. 33–47) and a house that was declared clean (vv. 48–53). The Lord had control over the situation (v. 34). The owner of the house who suspected an outbreak was to ask the priest to come and examine it. The priest was to order the house to be emptied because once he declared it unclean, the house and anything inside it would be unclean. If it were diagnosed as unclean, the house would be temporarily abandoned, and if at the end of the period, the fungus had spread, the damaged stones and the plaster of the walls were to be carried away to an unclean place and replaced by new stones and plaster. It is important to remember that the text does not suggest any magic- or spirit-driven impurity. If the plague returned, then the house was to be demolished. Entering, eating, or sleeping in the house while it was unclean would contaminate the person (vv. 46–48). If after the seven days quarantine, the plague had not spread, the priest was to perform a cleansing rite similar to that of the cleansing of the leper, using only the two birds (vv. 49–53). The uncleanness was to be sent away through the living bird.

The law of the *tsara'at* indicates that there is something wrong with the environment in which humans live. It is under the influence and power of death and brings with it separation and pain. It causes harm to humans, clothing, and even their houses or homes. No wonder Paul conceives of death as a power that rules over humanity because of Adam's sin and from which only Jesus

can deliver us (Rom. 5:12–21). We have been delivered from spiritual death through the life of Jesus (Rom. 6:5–7), but at the same time, we look forward to the moment when physical death will be vanquished forever (Rev. 21:1–4). It is this hope that the Day of Atonement announces in types and shadows (see Lev. 16).

15:1–33. Impurity and Bodily Discharges. Contamination here is the result of something that comes out of the human body, not something that enters the body. Four cases appear: abnormal male discharge (vv. 2–15), normal male discharge (vv. 16–18), normal female discharge (vv. 19–24), and abnormal female discharge (vv. 25–30). These are followed by a theological statement and a summary (vv. 30–33). The first case is that of a man with a genital infection that caused a flow from his penis (*basar*—"flesh" is a euphemism for penis), which may have included pus and blood. This was highly contagious, and anyone who touched him, his bed, or where he sat became unclean until evening, and a ritual washing of clothes and bathing was required. If he touched anyone after washing his hands, the person touched did not become unclean. Once the discharge was healed, the sick person was to wait for seven days, and then he was to wash his clothes and bathe. In order for the cleansing to be final, he was to bring two turtledoves or pigeons, one for a sin offering and the other for a burnt offering, to make atonement—that is to say, to remove the impurity and recommit him to God.

The emission of semen (lit. "laying of seed"; (v. 16) could have happened either during sleep or, as is commonly believed, during intercourse with a woman. There is also the possibility that the reference is to having an emission while sleeping next to a woman. In the first case of emission during sleep, the man was unclean, and in the second, both were unclean (vv. 16–18). They were unclean until evening, and a ritual bath was required. No reason is given for this legislation, but since the biblical term for semen, *zera'*, means "seed," it could be suggested that the loss of some of the seed of life resulted in the diminution of life. Again, this is in the context of the conceptual sphere of death, and death is a result of Adam and Eve's sin (Gen. 3; Rom. 5:12–21). Death and sin are closely connected. Besides, by considering semen a contaminating agent, a clear incompatibility was established between sexual activity and the worship of God in the sanctuary, thus condemning the practice of pagan fertility rites in pagan temples.

The blood issue resulting from a woman's menstrual cycle was also a contaminating substance (vv. 19–24). Sexual intercourse during menstruation was forbidden, but if it happened that during intercourse, both parties realized that the woman was menstruating, they both became unclean (see 18:19). There was nothing intrinsically wrong or sinful about menstruation, but coming into direct or indirect contact with blood brought one close to the realm of death (see 12:2). On a more positive note, because she was considered unclean for seven days following the beginning of her menstruation, she was able to rest at a time when she was in state of physical discomfort (see 20:18). No particular cleansing ritual was legislated, but one could assume that she washed herself at the end of the period (cf. 2 Sam. 11:2, 4). The case of abnormal female blood discharge was more severe (vv. 25–30). Like in the case of the man with abnormal discharge, after seven days, she was to bring to the priest two turtledoves or pigeons, one for a sin offering and the other for a burnt offering, to cleanse her from her uncleanness.

The closing verses (15:31–33) establish that the previous regulations intended to demonstrate how the Israelites should be cleansed from impurities that were unavoidable and natural in their lives. If the impurities were not removed, then they ran the risk of contaminating the tabernacle by approaching it in a state of impurity, and they could have died (see 20:4–5). From God's perspective, life and death cannot coexist peacefully. This connection with life suggests that throughout these legislations, there is a health concern to be taken into consideration (see "Health and Hygiene in Leviticus," p. 272). These legislations are a reminder that Jesus is the ultimate healer (Is. 53:5). Healing is needed because humans exist in a condition of impurity that can be avoided in some cases but not in others. After all, everyone will die.

16:1–34

Day of Atonement

The shift here is from the daily services to the annual, whose goal was to restore wholeness to the Israelite camp. At the pinnacle of the Israelite sacrificial and priestly services in the sanctuary is the moment that integrated all of the elements of the worship system. The tabernacle and the people were free from impurity and sin on the Day of Atonement, which ritually expressed an eschatological hope of cosmic extent. It pointed both back to the original harmony between God and humans and, typologically, to the restoration of that harmony after the consummation of the cleansing made possible through the blood of the Son of God. The chapter, placed at the center of the literary structure of the book (see Leviticus: Introduction), is carefully arranged, beginning with the statement "The LORD spoke to Moses" (v. 1) and concluding with a formula of completion: "The LORD commanded Moses" (v. 34). The literary structure of the chapter forms a chiasm:

A Limitations on Aaron's ability to enter the Most Holy Place (v. 2)

  B Aaron's sacrificial victim and vestments (vv. 3–4)

    C Sacrificial victims provided by the people (v. 5)

      D Aaron's bull, goat for the Lord, goat for Azazel (vv. 6–10)

        E Aaron's bull sacrificed as a sin offering (vv. 11–14)

          F Community's goat as sin offering (v. 15)

            G Atonement made (vv. 16–19)

            G' Atonement finished (v. 20a)

          F' Community's goat for Azazel sent to the wilderness (vv. 20b–22)

        E' Aaron's closing activities (vv. 23–25)

      D' Goat for Azazel, Aaron's bull, goat for sin offering (vv. 26–28)

    C' People rested and humbled themselves (vv. 29–31)

  B' Anointed priest officiated wearing special garments (vv. 29–33)

A' Anointed priest made atonement once a year (v. 34)

At the center of the structure, the high priest makes an all-encompassing atonement for the tabernacle, the altar, the people, and himself and his family. Here, the atoning work of the priest reached its climax and came to an end (v. 20a). The chapter has an introduction (vv. 3–5), a first development (vv. 6–10), a second development (vv. 11–22), concluding ritual acts (vv. 23–28), the institutionalization of the ritual (vv. 29–34), and concluding remarks (v. 34). It combines three rites into a large ritual: a *rite of entrance* that prepared Aaron to go into the Most Holy Place, a *cleansing rite* of total atonement, and the *elimination rite*, in which the goat for Azazel played a particular role.

16:2–10. Introduction and First Development. The *introduction* lists what Aaron was to bring in order to enter the Most Holy Place: for himself, a bull for a sin offering and a ram for a burnt offering, and for the people, two male goats for a sin offering and a ram for a burnt offering. He was to take a ritual bath and put on a common priestly tunic. The *first development* mentions the sacrifice of the sin offering for Aaron and his house but places the main emphasis on identifying the goat for Azazel and its purpose. The two goats to be brought by the people are identified as a sin offering. After lots were cast, only one was to be offered as the sin offering, chosen for the Lord (belonging to Him). The other was for Azazel (belonging to him). The parallelism suggests that since the Lord is a person, Azazel also stands for a person. The fact that Azazel is associated with sin and impurity identifies him as a demonic being. The goat for Azazel stood before the Lord alive, which indicates that it was not a sacrificial victim to be offered to Azazel. Verse 10 states that it was to be brought near the Lord first, then sent to Azazel, to the wilderness. The goat was not Azazel, but it was to be sent to him, and in a sense, it represented him who was already in the wilderness. At this point, no reason is given for sending the goat to him.

The mention of atonement to be made over the goat for Azazel (*kipper 'al*) has elicited much discussion. When the object of the verb is a person, the phrase *kipper 'al* is often used to mean "to make atonement on behalf of," but here the object was a goat. This is a unique usage of the phrase. This commentary has argued that making atonement meant to remove sin/impurity from the person or from the tabernacle to cleanse it (see the section on Theology in Leviticus: Introduction). This meaning is operative in v. 10 in the unique sense of removing sin/impurity by placing it upon the goat. In other words, this is the biblical way of referring to a rite of elimination. The phrase could then be translated "to perform an elimination/removal rite upon it" by placing sin/impurity upon the goat and sending it to Azazel (see vv. 21–22).

16:11–22. Second Development. Aaron was to offer the bull for the sin offering to atone for himself and his family. Absolutely nothing is said about laying hands on this sin offering, probably because its purpose was to remove sin/impurity from the tabernacle, not from the offerer. Its blood was to be transferred into the Most Holy Place. But first Aaron was to take incense and a censer with burning coals from the altar to the tabernacle, where he was to burn the incense, creating a cloud that would allow him to go into the Most Holy Place. The cloud of incense was to mediate his presence before the Lord lest he die by attempting to approach the Lord directly. The cloud must have reached the Most Holy Place before he did, to cover the mercy seat/atonement cover (v. 13), the golden slab that covered the ark of the covenant and the place God revealed His glory and forgiving grace.

Aaron was to bring the blood of his sin offering to the very presence of the Lord in the Most Holy Place, and surrounded by the cloud of incense, he was to sprinkle some of it once on the "mercy seat"/"atonement cover" (Heb. *kaporet*, "place of atonement") and seven times before it—a total of eight times, as a perfect or full cleansing. Next, Aaron was to kill the goat for the sin offering of the people and to repeat the blood rite in the Most Holy Place (v. 15), thus mixing its blood with that of his own sin offering. He was to use the blood in the same way in the Holy Place (the tabernacle/tent of meeting; v. 16), meaning that it was to be applied all around the horns of the altar of incense and sprinkled seven times in front of it (cf. Ex. 30:10). The high priest was to put some blood around the horns of the altar of burnt offering (see Lev. 4:7), sprinkle some blood seven times on the altar for cleansing (*taher*, "to pronounce clean, to purify"), and consecrate it from the uncleanness (*tum'ah*, "impurity") of the Israelites (v. 19). The meaning of the blood manipulation is explained in v. 16: (1) to make atonement for the people, the tabernacle, and Aaron and his family by removing from the tabernacle all their uncleanness (*tum'ah*, "impurity"), transgressions (*pesha'*, "crimes"), and sins (*khatta't*, "sin"), and (2) to cleanse and consecrate the altar. The terms for sin and impurity are common in Leviticus, with the exception of *pesha'* ("transgression," "crime"), which is found only in vv. 19 and 21. This term is never associated with high-handed sin. The purpose for this cluster of terms for sin is to show that all sins and impurities were removed from the sanctuary (cf. Ex. 34:7; Ps. 32:5; Is. 59:12; Jer. 14:20; see "The Theology of the Day of Atonement," p. 264). They were transferred to the tabernacle, to the very presence of God, through the ministry of the priests during the daily services. At the end of the year, God removed the sin and impurities from His residence, demonstrating that He was not the source of evil. Azazel was.

Consequently, that day Azazel assumed responsibility for sin and impurities as their ultimate originator or source. After the atoning and purifying rites were performed, Aaron was to place his hands on the head of the goat for Azazel, confess over it the iniquity (*'awon*) and transgressions (*pasha'*) and sins (*khatta't*), and transfer them to the goat that would transport all of them to the wilderness (v. 21). Once more the cluster of terms for sin indicates that all sins were to be transferred to the goat. "Uncleanness" is not mentioned, but the idea could be expressed through the term *'awon* (see Lev. 5:2; 7:18; 17:16; 18:25; 19:8; Is. 64:6; Ezek. 9:4, 9; Hos. 8:13). In fact, this term could summarize all the other sins, as suggested in v. 22 (cf. Dan. 9:13; Hos. 5:5; 14:2; Amos 3:2).

The goat for Azazel was to bear or carry all the *'awon* to a desolate place (v. 22). In this case, the "bearing" (*nasa'*) does not mean to accept responsibility for the sins of others and be liable to punishment. It means to take something from one place to another, to transfer something. The goat is described as a vehicle transporting all the iniquities of Israel to Azazel, who, it is implied, dwells in the wilderness, which was characterized by the absence of fullness of life.

16:23–34. Concluding Ritual and Institutionalization of the Day of Atonement. Aaron was to change clothes, wash himself, offer the two burnt offerings, and burn the fat of the sin offering on the altar (vv. 24–25). There were instructions for the person who was to release the goat in the wilderness and for the disposal of the flesh of the sin offerings. The ritual was to be performed once a year, on the tenth day of the seventh month. An important detail was added related to the attitude of the people during that day: they were to *te'annu* (from *'anah*, "to be afflicted, to be humbled") *'et napshotekhem* ("your souls"). This phrase has been translated various ways—for example, "afflict your souls," "humble your souls" "deny yourselves" (v. 29). This would traditionally have included fasting and other acts of humility, expressing their total dependence on God's cleansing power. The rest of the section summarizes the most important aspects of the ritual. There is a marked emphasis on removing all the sins of the people from the tabernacle.

The Theology of the Day of Atonement

Leviticus 16 prescribes a theologically rich ritual, introducing new insights in the study of the book that help to clarify the meaning of the sacrificial system and integrate it into a theological unity. It was fundamentally a day of judgment that anticipated the eschatological day of judgment.

1. Cosmic Scope. During the Day of Atonement, the ritual polarity of the holy and the impure reached cosmic dimensions, unveiling like never before the source of both. The ritual moved from the center of holiness and life to the distant space of sin/impurity and death—the wilderness. In biblical religious geography, the two places most distant from each other are the spheres of life/holiness and sin/impurity/death. In between these two poles are the common and the clean, and they could gravitate toward one or the other. In a unique theological turn, the Day of Atonement took the priest into the very center of holiness and life, the Most Holy Place, where the *kapporet*, "mercy seat" or place of atonement, was found. This was the earthly location that directly connected the people to the cosmic center, the heavenly sanctuary, and where God met with Aaron as He met with Moses. There was no place on earth like this because it was located within the residence of the Holy One of Israel. This sanctuary itself was not a cosmic temple but a cosmic center from which cosmic order was established, restored, and preserved.

Then there is the realm of sin and the impure, so distant from the holy that it is described as being located outside the camp, in the wilderness. This implied that the presence of sin/impurity within the camp was the result of the incursion of the sphere of death into the life of the people. They were not completely isolated from it. Yes, the people, through their violation of the covenant law, sinned and were touched by the sphere of death, but the ultimate source of sin and impurity was located in the demonic figure called Azazel. Implicit here is the concept of a cosmic conflict between God and His enemies. This conflict is illustrated in the experience of Adam and Eve and their encounter with a dark power who questioned the integrity of the character of God, the serpent (Gen. 3:1–7). Job also provides a behind the scene perspective of this cosmic conflict between God and Satan, who is finally defeated (1:6–12; 2:1–7; 42:7–17; see "Evil and the Fallen Cherub," p. 1008, and the Introduction to Job). The Day of Atonement pointed to the moment when the conflict will be resolved once and for all at a cosmic level.

2. Day of Judgment. The Day of Atonement could be described as a ritual or a typological expression of the final judgment. The attitude expected from the people was to demonstrate their total dependence on God as they faced the Judge of the earth. They were expected to humble themselves by, among other things, abstaining from any type of work, and, as later biblical and rabbinical sources confirm, fasting (16:29; cf. Is. 58:3, 5, 10). These two commands addressed one common concern, namely, total dependence on God by setting aside any activity that would signal self-reliance. The human concern for self-preservation finds expression in a particular way through work and food consumption. To discontinue these activities is to thrust oneself absolutely into God's care and redemption. This total reliance on God was examined during the Day of Atonement/day of judgment (Lev. 23:29–30). There was a law that was to be obeyed, and it required total dependence on God. The law was located inside the ark of the covenant, whose cover was the *kapporet* ("mercy seat," "place of atonement"; 16:13). The lives of the people were analyzed to uncover whether they were trusting in the Lord for their final deliverance from sin/impurity, and a legal verdict was pronounced against violators. For those who trusted in the Lord, there was deliverance through the work of the high priest on their behalf, but for the rebellious, there was permanent transfer to the realm of death. On this day, God called

for a separation between the faithful and the unfaithful (see Ezek. 8–9).

The connection between the Day of Atonement and the day of judgment is also found in the experience of Joshua, the high priest, and the Angel of the Lord (Zech. 3:1–5). This vision was related to the Day of Atonement through the use of similar terms and images. He was the high priest and bore the people's sin as their representative; the enemy of God (Satan) was present, but he was silenced by the Lord; the Lord removed the people's sins; and Joshua's priestly garments were changed. Unquestionably, the background is the Day of Atonement, and it is interpreted here as an experience of judgment.

We find a similar judgment scene in Daniel 7:9–10, 13–14, in which God was present, the legal records were opened, and a mediator approached, surrounded by the clouds of heaven, and was brought before God (Dan. 7:13). As a result of this apocalyptic judgment, the Son of Man received the kingdom. In Leviticus 16:12–13, the high priest was required to burn incense in order to draw near to the Lord. In both situations, the setting is a judgment, and the mediator approaches God in a cloud. The Son of Man is being described as a High Priest who, after the judgment, received a kingdom free from the presence of God's enemies. This scene of judgment parallels the scene of the sanctuary in Daniel 8:9–14. There the Commander and Prince of God's people performed the daily services while in conflict with a powerful enemy whom He would finally defeat during the Day of Atonement (see Dan. 8:12–14). There are many other places in the Bible where the judgment includes separating true worshipers of God from false ones (e.g., Ezek. 9) as well as the separation of God's people from the wicked of the earth (e.g., Joel 3:11–16). Jesus also associates the final judgment with the separation of the righteous from the unrighteous (Matt. 13:24–30, 47–50).

The judicial examination of God's people during the Day of Atonement resulted in their vindication by revealing that they had remained in a faith relationship with the Lord. Consequently, all their sins/impurities were removed from the sanctuary. During the year, they came to the tabernacle with expiatory sacrifices, through which sin/impurity was transferred to the sanctuary, and forgiveness and cleansing were granted to them. The Day of Atonement was a reaffirmation of the effectiveness of that daily cleansing. The tabernacle needed to be cleansed because it was defiled by the uncleanness and sins of the people (v. 16). The people's daily cleansing was consummated on the Day of Atonement (vv. 30, 33).

The ritual assumed that the sins of the people had been transferred to the tabernacle, thus justifying the need to remove the impurity, bringing to an end the process of atonement. Therefore, the cleansing of God's residence offered to the people a new beginning. For a day, they returned to life in the Garden of Eden, in perfect harmony with the order established by God at Creation, free from sin and impurity. The Day of Atonement anticipated the moment when the whole cosmos will be cleansed from the miasma of sin and set free from the contaminating power and influence of evil.

3. *Vindication of God.* The Day of Atonement was a theodicy (Gr. *theos* ["God"] and *dike* ["justice"]); that is to say, it was a declaration that God is just in spite of the presence of sin/impurity in the cosmos. First, the presence of the concept of judgment in Leviticus 16 suggests that the chapter is addressing the question of theodicy. A judgment seeks to uncover the truth in a situation in which it is not obviously accessible to the common observer. During the Day of Atonement, God functioned as Judge in order to demonstrate that the way He dealt with the sin/impurity of the people was legally justifiable and not an arbitrary decision on His part. He gave to each one what they legally deserved. The judgment ultimately reveals who in the cosmic conflict is right and who is wrong and will conclude with the cosmic recognition that God is indeed righteous. The NT captures this important theological concept when describing what will happen when God's righteousness is recognized by all (Phil. 2:10–11).

John saw the redeemed singing a song to the Lord and declaring His justice (Rev. 15:3–4). Angels are depicted as proclaiming God to be righteous and true in all His judgments (16:5, 7). At the revelation of God's judgment, a great multitude in heaven will proclaim this same reality (19:1–2). The final judgment will be a theodicy of the saving power of the cross on behalf of sinners that will reveal the justice and love of God at a cosmic level.

Second, the removal of sin/impurity from the dwelling of God revealed that, in spite of the fact that He allowed the people to transfer their sin to Him, God and sin are incompatible. Therefore, it was impossible for them to coexist permanently within the camp. The Day of Atonement reaffirmed the fact that when God assumed responsibility for sin/impurity in the tabernacle, He was bearing it as a manifestation of His forgiving grace and not because He was somehow directly and naturally connected to it (e.g., Ex. 34:7). His rendezvous with sin/impurity had a saving purpose and nothing else. During the Day of Atonement, the incompatibility between holiness and sin/impurity was graphically illustrated by removing the latter from the tabernacle and the camp and by sending it away into the wilderness.

Third, the rite of elimination—sending the goat to Azazel, loaded with sin/impurity—indicates that the Day of Atonement was essentially a theodicy. Without it, the significance of the expiatory sacrifices during the daily services could have been seriously misconstrued. By placing the Israelite expiatory sacrifices within their cultural context, the role of the Day of Atonement as a theodicy can perhaps be better understood. Similar elimination rites were practiced in the ANE with the purpose of removing evil and sickness from people by returning them to the place they came from, usually either to the camp of the enemy (in a military campaign) or to the underworld, the demonic realm. Without the Day of Atonement, it would have been easy to misunderstand the daily transference of sin/impurity to the tabernacle as a ritual return of wickedness and uncleanness to its place of origin, implying that the Lord was indeed the source of all evil. The rite of elimination, by pointing to a source of sin/impurity outside the camp, demonstrated that the origin of these most disturbing phenomena was not located in the Lord or His sanctuary, nor even in the camp of Israel, but in the wilderness—in Azazel. God could not be charged with sin. Within the context of the Pentateuch, the presence of evil in the world could not be assigned to God because He brought into existence a perfectly organized cosmos, but an enemy, Azazel, had been plotting to upset and even destroy the divine order. The people were not excused for their sins and impurities but were required to acknowledge them, repent, and bring a substitutive sacrifice to expiate them. The divine promise is that an eschatological Day of Atonement is coming when sin/impurity will be permanently removed from the cosmos.

Fourth, during the Day of Atonement and as part of the theodicy, God's sovereignty is powerfully proclaimed. The removal of sin/impurity from the tabernacle and the Israelite camp ritually proclaimed God's power and sovereignty over evil. It revealed that holiness was superior to sin/impurity. This was indeed a message of hope. Not even in the act of forgiving and cleansing His people was God tainted by sin/impurity. Yes, in the atonement, sin/impurity and holiness touched each other, but God's holiness remained absolutely undamaged, and He was amazingly able to restore holiness to His people (see "The Laying On of Hands," p. 243). During the Day of Atonement, God also proclaimed His sovereignty over Azazel. This character is introduced as the opposite of the Lord, but he remained in the shadows, in silence, unable to oppose the work of God during the Day of Atonement. His silence was the silence of the accused who, when confronted with the evidence against him or her, is left speechless, entirely unable to rebut it. His inactivity was not like the Sabbath rest enjoyed by the people but rather like the inactivity that characterizes the realm of death. The goat itself carried the sins and impurities of the people to Azazel in submission to God and under the guidance of His appointed instrument. One could perhaps venture to say that the silence of Azazel in the text was an acknowledgement of guilt. In this powerful display of His sovereignty, God restored things to the original order He had established. Creation through separation found its counterpart in God's work of re-creation through separation (see "Creation, Sabbath, and the Sanctuary," p. 231).

4. Reconciliation and Judgment. The work of Christ as High Priest consists of a work of reconciliation and judgment (see "The Cleansing of the Sanctuary and Judgment in Daniel," p. 1043). As a Sacrifice, He took upon Himself the sins of humanity, and as High Priest, He applies the benefits of His sacrifice to them. He provided cleansing from past sin, even those committed under the first covenant (Heb. 9:15), He continues to cleanse people from sin (Heb. 9:14), and He performs the cleansing of the antitypical Day of Atonement in the heavenly sanctuary (Heb. 9:23). After finishing His work as High Priest in the heavenly sanctuary, He will return for His people (Heb. 9:28). Satan, as the antitype of Azazel, will be left in the wilderness of a planet in chaos for a thousand years (Rev. 20:1–3), after which Christ will destroy the source of sin and impurity (20:11–15). This will be the beginning of true Jubilee. There will be a new creation, free from the miasma of sin and impurity—a return to Eden (21:1–5; 22:1–4).

17:1–16

The Question of Blood

This is a transitional chapter dealing with topics addressed in the previous chapters (e.g., blood, uncleanness), but it also points to topics found in the next chapters. It could as well be placed within the following major section of Leviticus. It consists of three main legislations dealing with the offering of sacrifices outside the sanctuary or to demons and idols (vv. 1–9), the consumption of blood (vv. 10–14), and the eating of animals that had died of natural causes or were killed by other animals (vv. 15–16). These three elements were included in the decision of the Jerusalem Council in the same order, along with another transgression found in Leviticus 18, namely, sexual immorality (Acts 15:28–29). These legislations were not only for the Israelites but also for foreigners residing in Israel.

17:1–9. Sanctuary and Sacrifices. The legislation forcefully established that the desire to eat animal flesh was not to be satisfied by killing an animal in the camp or outside as an offering to other spiritual powers but by bringing it to the Lord as a peace offering—a portion of its meat was to be given back to the offerer (see Lev. 3).

If the animal was not brought to the sanctuary as a sacrifice to the Lord, the person who killed it was to be charged with murder (v. 4) and was to be cut off from his or her people (v. 4; see 7:20–21). The animal's life had been taken illegally if its blood was not poured out at the base of the altar. The punishment could have been considered too severe; consequently, the Lord provided a rational for it—it functioned as a deterrent to offering sacrifices to demons (lit. "male goats"; v. 7). Male goats living in desolate places were considered symbols of demons; for example, the goat for Azazel, a demon, was sent to the wilderness (16:10; cf. 2 Chr. 11:15; Is. 13:21). Such sacrifices were an act of unfaithfulness to God, and He wanted to bring them to an end, hence the severity of the penalty. The requirement to bring a peace offering to the sanctuary was here extended to any other sacrifice the Israelites or the resident aliens may have wanted to offer. A most severe penalty was prescribed for failing to do this: being cut off from their people (v. 9; see v. 4).

17:10–14. Consuming Blood. Israelites or resident aliens who consumed blood were also to be cut off from their people. The reason given for the prohibition is theologically significant (v. 11). Three important statements were made. First, the life (*nepesh*) of the creature (lit. "flesh") was in the blood. There has been some debate about the proper translation of the phrase, but it is possible to render it "the life of the flesh/animal is the blood." The equation of both is stated in Deuteronomy 12:23 and is also affirmed in Leviticus 17:14. Blood is the tangible expression of life. Second, God gave it to the people in order for them to bring it to Him through the altar. In other words, blood belonged exclusively to God, but He gave it to the people with the understanding that they were to return it to Him via the altar of sacrifices. This was a wonderful gift in that the blood of the animal would now stand for the blood of repentant sinners. The text then proceeds to explain the significance of this ritual. Third, the purpose of returning to God, through the altar, the blood that He provided for them was to make atonement for the Israelites (*napeshotekem*, "your lives"; v. 11). In the process of returning the blood to God via the altar, atonement was made for their lives. The implication was that their lives were in danger, but God had found a way to preserve them. The phrase "to make atonement [*kipper*] for your souls/lives" is used in other places in conjunction with the noun "ransom" (*koper*), meaning

"to give a ransom [*kipper*] for your lives" (Ex. 30:11–16; cf. Num. 31:48–54). This confirms that in this particular passage, *kipper* means to atone in the sense of removing sin by "giving a ransom for your lives." The idea is that the blood/life of the sacrificial victim was given to God as a ransom/payment for the endangered life of the person. The association of the life of the animal with that of the sinner indicates that the first substituted for the second—human life was preserved through the death of the animal.

Fourth, the text indicates that it was the blood that made atonement for the soul (*nepesh*, "person, life"; v. 11). "For" suggests that what follows deals with what was said before, in this case emphasizing it: for it is the blood, as life, that serves as ransom/expiates. The "life" could be the life of the animal, as in the previous translation, or that of the person: "it is the blood that effects expiation/ransom in exchange for life." Either of these two translations would be theologically sound. One could even translate the phrase as "for the blood effects atonement by the life," but this would be done at the risk of implying that blood was an almost magical substance, able to bring about atonement because life was in it. In this case, God would be removed from the process of atonement, and blood, as the carrier of life, would be the focus.

What about the blood of clean animals or birds that were hunted for food (vv. 13–14)? In such cases, the blood was to be returned to God by pouring it on the ground and covering it with dust (earth). The reason for this legislation was the same as before: the life of every creature (lit. "flesh") was its blood (v. 14), and the penalty for its violation was the same. But what about a person who ate from an animal found dead or one that was torn by beasts? If individuals ate the flesh, which presumably still had blood in it, they were unclean until evening and were to wash their clothes and take a ritual bath. If this was not done, they were responsible and bore their guilt (v. 16; see 5:2–6).

The legislations found in Leviticus 17 are principally addressing the proper use of blood. The understanding of sacrificial blood present in the text is applied to all atoning sacrifices, and it is based on the conviction that since blood, as life, is God's property, it was to be returned to Him. But God did the unimaginable: He allowed the Israelites to send Him this blood/life, loaded with their sins and impurities, as a ransom for their lives. Thus, sin and impurity were transferred to His dwelling place through a substitute, making it necessary to remove them during the Day of Atonement. Although this chapter displays some health concerns, its main purpose is theological and it serves to point to the blood of Christ, who died as a substitute to ransom humanity from sin and who is the only means of atonement before the Lord.

18:1—27:34

HOLY PEOPLE

The presence of a holy God dwelling among His people required them to be holy. This was possible because God sanctified them and removed their sins and impurities from them through the sacrificial system (Lev. 1–17). Now, the gift of holiness became a task, and it revealed that holiness has an ethical component. The assignment was to separate from sin and impurity in order to model God's holiness. This section provides numerous instructions about sexuality (18:1–30; 20:1–27), with several laws related to morality and holiness interjected (19:1–37).

18:1–30
Holiness and Sexuality

18:1–17. Incest. The Lord spoke through Moses to the children of Israel and identified Himself as their covenant Lord, who was leading them to the land of Canaan. The laws were not given in order for them to earn the land but because their redeemer Lord was giving it to them and wanted them to retain it. Obedience to God's laws makes life enjoyable. Therefore, these laws served to organize life by establishing boundaries and differentiations, as the Lord did during Creation (Gen. 1). The repetition of the phrase "I am the LORD" firmly grounded the laws in His authority. The laws against incest are moral laws, not restricted to any particular time or nation, as is shown by the condemnation of their practice in Egypt and Canaan and by the clarification that even the resident alien living among the Israelites was to obey them (v. 26).

The legislation forbade sexual relations (lit. "to uncover nakedness") beginning with the near of kin or blood relatives (vv. 6–17; this includes one's daughter though daughters are not mentioned specifically in this particular list; see 20:2): mother (v. 7; some versions distinguish the nakedness of the father from that of the mother [the father or the mother], while others equate the nakedness of the father with that of the mother [the father "that

is to say" the mother], suggesting that having sexual relations with the mother [uncovering the nakedness of the mother] dishonors the father by uncovering his nakedness—that is, only the father should have access to the mother's sexuality); stepmother (v. 8); sister or half sister (v. 9); granddaughter (v. 10); stepsister or daughter of the woman the father married who was also from the same clan (v. 11); paternal aunt (v. 12); maternal aunt (v. 13); paternal uncle's wife (v. 14); daughter-in-law (v. 15); fraternal sister-in-law (v. 16); a mother and her daughter (v. 17); and a mother and her granddaughter (v. 17). Incest was condemned not only because it violates the boundary of consanguinity but also because it is wickedness (v. 17); that is to say, it is lewdness—the shameful immorality that characterized the people in Egypt and Canaan (v. 3). Sexual purity is directly related to the holiness that God expects from His people. Throughout history, women have been abused by men in power at home and in society. These laws set limits to male power in the family, and by extension in society, and placed female sexuality under the protection of God, with serious consequences for any violator.

18:18–30. Other Sexual Prohibitions and the Rationale. The cases listed here were not based on consanguinity. The first case has been interpreted as indicating that a man was not to marry the sister of his wife while the wife was living (v. 18). However, it could also be read as prohibiting polygamy. The mention of a woman as rival to her sister could be read as meaning one woman in addition to another (see, e.g., Ex. 16:15; lit. "a man to his brother"; see also Num. 14:4). This type of marriage was forbidden because it would destroy the wholeness of the home (see 1 Sam. 1:6).

Intentionally having sex with a woman during menstruation was forbidden (Lev. 18:19; see 15:24). In Leviticus 20:18, the man and the woman who had sexual intercourse during her period were both to be cut off from their people, indicating that both had consented to the act. But here, in the context of incest, the man was to be cut off from his people (18:29).

The prohibition against adultery is part of the Decalogue (v. 20; Ex. 20:14). What follows is a case of spiritual adultery or unfaithfulness: sacrificing children to Molech, probably an underworld deity (v. 21). The reason was that such an act profaned the name of God—He was treated not as holy but as a common pagan deity.

This association of His people with idolatry damaged His reputation.

Homosexuality was clearly rejected as a proper expression of any type of sexual intimacy. It was a moral defilement and a *to'ebah* ("abomination," "abhorrence," something "detestable"; v. 22; see 20:13); it was repugnant to God and incompatible with His character. It violated the order established by Him at Creation (Gen. 2:21–24; cf. Rom. 1:26–27).

Bestiality was condemned as a *tebel* ("perversion," "confusion") from the verb *balal* ("mix," "confuse"), a term that emphasizes even more the violation of divine order.

The chapter concludes with an admonition calling the people not to commit the discussed abominations, also identified as *'awon* ("iniquity," "sin," "rebellion"; 18:25; see 16:21) because these sins defiled the land and would lead the people to be removed from it, like the previous inhabitants. The language of impurity was used to refer to moral impurity (vv. 29–30). The same high moral standards are expected from those who today claim to walk with the Lord.

19:1–37
Explicit Call to Holiness

This chapter illustrates what the Lord meant when He told His people that they were to be holy because He, the Lord their God, is holy (v. 2). The laws flowed from the basic principles of the Decalogue and touched almost every aspect of the social life of the Israelites, interspersed with laws related to God.

19:1–18. Principles, Casuistic Laws, and Respect for Others. Three of the Ten Commandments are mentioned: respect parents, keep the Sabbath, and reject idolatry (vv. 3–4). These are followed by two case laws: (1) bringing a peace/fellowship offering (see 7:11–21)—the emphasis here is on the proper use of the flesh of the animal—and (2) providing food for the poor during the harvest (vv. 9–10) by leaving the gleanings in the field for them. The next section, dealing with justice and care for others, begins with a reference to the eighth commandment (v. 11; Ex. 20:15), supplemented by a command to be truthful and a reference to the third commandment (Ex. 20:7), which prohibits a false oath—possibly taken to hide one's sin—that would profane God's name (Lev. 19:12).

The next set of laws deals with caring for the underprivileged by not defrauding them through robbery (taking their property by force) or by withholding their wages at the end of a workday. The deaf and blind (v. 14) were to be treated with respect and not abused (cf. John 9). Cursing the deaf could mean belittling the person, and placing stumbling blocks before the blind would include the idea of misleading the person. The command to care for others is grounded in the fear of or respect for God, not in natural human goodness. This respect for God was to express itself in the judicial system (v. 15). Justice was to be impartial and not controlled by bribes. Neither was one to speak unjustly before the court against someone else. If someone's brother hurt him or her, the person who was hurt was not to be hypocritical by making the brother believe that he was loved when, in fact, he was secretly hated (v. 17). It was better to rebuke or reprove the brother (v. 17); perhaps he would repent. Neither was one to seek vengeance or hold a grudge against one's brother (v. 18). God expected His people to love their neighbors as themselves (v. 18) and to care for and respect others, at least in the same way that they would like others to care for them.

19:19–30. Principles, Casuistic Laws, and More Commands. This new section begins with an exhortation to keep the Lord's statutes, followed by a law against certain mixtures: of livestock, seeds (making the harvesting process difficult; see Deut. 22:9), and fabrics, such as in the garments worn by the priests (v. 19; cf. Ex. 28:5). The law sought to preserve the divine order of Creation and religious life by establishing proper boundaries. Another boundary was established through a case law related to a man who had sexual relations with a betrothed female slave (v. 20). Since she was still a slave, capital punishment was not to be enforced, but an inquiry was to be made to determine the facts and the punishment to be applied—the compensation to be paid. He misappropriated what was not his, thus compensation and a guilt offering (see 6:1–7) were required (assuming that he repented).

The second case law is related to agricultural practices in the land of Canaan (vv. 23–25). The fruits of newly planted trees were forbidden (lit. "uncircumcised") for three years—that is, not acceptable to the Lord or for human consumption (v. 23). They were "uncircumcised" for three years, and in the fourth year, the fruits were declared holy and given as praise to the Lord (v. 24) to express joyful gratitude to Him. This legislation vividly reminded the Israelites that the land and its fruits belonged to God.

They partook of its fruits according to His will, and they were to recognize this by rejoicing when consecrating the fruits to God. They were not owners but stewards of the land. The discussion of the relationship of the people to the land was followed by instructions regarding their relationship to the dead (vv. 26–28). Eating animals with (lit. "over") the blood either refers to the previous prohibition discussed in chapter 17 (cf. Gen. 9:4) or to the pagan practice of pouring out blood for the spirits into a pit and eating over the pit. They were not to consult the spirits for divination purposes. Humans have always been concerned about the future and have thought that by knowing what will happen, they could, to some extent, have control over it. Verses 27–28 describe pagan mourning rites aimed at pleasing and showing respect and care to the spirits of the ancestors. The text forbade them and affirmed the importance of showing respect to God by not damaging the human body. The realm of the spirits of the dead is the realm of demons (Deut. 32:17; Ps. 106:28). Christians should mourn for their dead relatives in ways that express their hope in the resurrection (John 11:25–26; 1 Thess. 4:13–18), since the dead are resting and do not know anything (see Pss. 6:5; 115:17; Eccl. 9:5–6; Isa. 38:18; Dan. 12.2–3, John 11:11–13).

Parents were to care for their children and were never to sell a daughter into harlotry, either for financial benefit or for pagan fertility rites (v. 29). Respect was to be shown to the Lord (who sanctified them through His presence in time and in the sanctuary) by keeping the Sabbath holy and by serving and worshiping Him only (v. 30; see v. 3). This was to be done instead of seeking mediums or necromancers (Heb. *yid'oni*; some versions have "familiar spirits," others have "spiritists"; v. 31). By entering the realm of death, they became unclean.

The people of God were commanded to show respect to the elderly—while they were still alive—out of respect to God. They were to care for strangers who dwelt among them in their land (vv. 32–33) by treating them well, even considering them fellow Israelites, and loving them as themselves (see v. 18). In other words, they were to not do to foreigners what had been done to them in Egypt. They were to also show respect and kindness in the business world by not deceiving or taking advantage of others—they were to use balanced weights and proper measures (vv. 35–36). This was firmly grounded in God's previous work of salvation for His people. The chapter closes with an emphatic exhortation to submit to God's loving will for them as their Lord (v. 37).

20:1–27
Laws and Penalties

Chapter 20 repeats many of the laws discussed first in chapter 18 but identifies specific penalties for their violation. It is organized by the type of penalty (death, vv. 9–16; exile, vv. 17–19; childlessness, vv. 20–21).

20:1–16. Introduction and Capital Punishment. Israelites or resident aliens who worshiped Molech were to be stoned (v. 2; see 18:21). If the people failed to perform the execution, then God Himself was to cut off the idolaters (see 7:20–21), as well as the members of the family who supported them, from their people (v. 5). They dishonored the character of God, committed spiritual harlotry, and could have contaminated the tabernacle by visiting it in a state of impurity (see 15:31). This is the way Ezekiel explains the contamination of the temple through the worship of Molech (23:38–39), providing a biblical explanation for this particular case. The death penalty applied also to those who committed spiritual adultery by consulting spirits (vv. 6, 27; see 19:31) and to those who cursed, dishonored, and abused their parents (v. 9; 19:3; see Ex. 21:17; Deut. 21:18–21; 27:16). Their blood would be upon them (v. 9)—that is, this was a case of capital punishment brought by the persons upon themselves.

The list mentions other cases involving capital punishment, including adultery (v. 10; 18:20, 29), sexual relations with the wife of one's father (v. 11; 18:8), lying with one's daughter-in-law—a *tebel* (an incestuous "perversion"; v. 12; see 18:15; cf. v. 23)—and homosexual intercourse, a *to'ebah* ("abomination" or "detestable thing"; v. 13; 18:22, 23). In the case of a man marrying both a woman and her mother ("a wicked act"; vv. 14; 18:17), they were all to be burned, which probably meant that the corpses were burned after they were executed (e.g., Josh. 7:15, 25). The list of sexual sins concludes with bestiality (vv. 15–16; 18:23). The reference to being put to death may have referred to stoning (cf. Deut. 22:23–24).

20:17–21. Noncapital Offenses. In the case of consensual sex between a man and his sister ("a disgraceful, wicked thing"; cf. 18:9), the penalty of being cut off publically may have referred to exiling the persons. The same penalty applied to a couple who had sex during menstruation (v. 18). The Hebrew term used here (*daweh*) conveys the idea of "weak" or "faint," implying a time of discomfort for the woman (see 15:33; 18:19), and does not necessarily imply that menstruation was an illness (though some translations render the word as "sickness"). With respect to consensual sexual intercourse with an aunt, no specific penalty is mentioned except that they were to bear their guilt (v. 19; 18:12–13; see 5:1). Perhaps the punishment was also exile. The penalty for sex with an aunt (wife of an uncle) or sister-in-law was to be infertility (vv. 20–21; 18:14–16); the family name would not be perpetuated.

The chapter closes with an exhortation to abide by God's will as expressed in His decrees and legal ordinances (v. 22). The law orders the cosmos and society by establishing distinctions in nature and roles. God was re-creating the land of Canaan by removing the cause of chaos and disorder and restoring it to order, giving it to a new people who would support His plan and preserve the distinctions He had established. He separated Israel from the nations, not on the basis of ethnic superiority but on the basis of moral regulations that were designed to instill God's values in humans. God's people were to be holy because He is holy. He separated them for Himself (v. 24) so that they would also separate themselves for Him. This is the way God organized their world, and they were not to upset that order. The law of clean/unclean animals is used here to illustrate the importance of being holy as God is holy. Holiness has to do with how we relate to God's will in our daily lives—what we eat and how we interact with others and with Him. The laws discussed in this chapter were not abolished by Jesus because they are directly related to a life of moral integrity. God continues to abhor (v. 23) the violation of these and other laws found in the Pentateuch (cf. Acts 15:19–20).

The last verse builds on v. 6, establishing the punishment for any person who was a leader in the promotion of spiritualism. Such persons were to be stoned (v. 27). This instruction was probably left for the end because such practices were a rejection of the power of God to lead and protect His people and showed allegiance to evil powers that opposed Him—the forces that attempted to destroy the order established by God at Creation.

Health and Hygiene in Leviticus

The laws of uncleanness were chiefly theological in nature, but they also contained hygienic principles. The unclean was associated with the realm of death, to which all were exposed, while the holy stood for life. Therefore, the theological and hygienic interests were complementary. Those who were sick lacked fullness of life and vibrancy. They had been touched by death; they were weak. In a sense, the sick were already within the sphere of death (Ps. 88), and unless they were healed, they would die. The biblical emphasis is not so much on healing but on preventing sickness, and this is clearly demonstrated through the laws regulating impurity.

1. Obedience to God. God was not only the Healer of Israel but also the One who protected them from diseases. The well-being of the people was directly associated with the covenant relationship and required their faithfulness to the covenant law. Obedience to it resulted in divine blessings and, more specifically, in protection from illness (Ex. 23:25–26). This exemplifies the biblical understanding of human nature as an integrated system in which the physical and the spiritual are inseparable components of one single person. The divine call to observe the Sabbath as a day of rest and spiritual renewal is probably one of the best examples of God's concern for the spiritual and physical well-being of His people (Ex. 20:8–11).

2. Avoiding the Unclean. Since uncleanness is related to the absence of life, the preservation of health required abstaining from and not coming into contact with any unclean sources. This is particularly the situation in cases related to blood flows (Lev. 15:2–30), carcasses of animals (11:24, 26, 31), dead persons (21:1–2; Num. 6:6–9; 19:11), and lepers (13:45–46). Sex during menstruation was forbidden (15:24; 18:18; 20:18). All of these were potential sources of disease. The fungi on the walls of a house could damage the health of its residents, particularly children, and would have made it necessary for the house to be renovated or demolished (14:33–47). These are extremely useful hygienic principles.

3. *The Practice of Quarantine.* In order to control the potential spread of diseases among the population, a period of quarantine was often required. The Lord instructed Moses to quarantine lepers, those with discharges, and those defiled by touching a dead body (Num. 5:2). The extent of the isolation varied, depending on the case, but in some situations, indefinite isolation was required until the person was healed. For instance, a house with suspected fungi was initially quarantined for seven days (Lev. 14:38), but persons with a blood discharge (15:13, 29) or leprosy (14:3–4) were required to wait to reintegrate until they had been healed and had gone through a cleansing ritual.

4. *Not Eating the Unclean.* The flesh of an animal which died from natural causes was not to be eaten (Lev. 17:15; Deut. 14:21). Consumption of blood or fat in meat (two potential sources of serious disease) was forbidden (Lev. 7:22–25, 27). Even eating utensils suspected of contamination were not to be used until they had been washed (11:32), and in some cases, they were destroyed (v. 33). These were important prophylactic measures that served to protect food and water from contaminating agents (vv. 31–38; see "Clean and Unclean Animals," p. 257).

5. *Use of Water.* Water played an important role as a hygienic agent in the discussions of uncleanness. The garment that came into contact with blood or on which semen fell was to be washed (Lev. 15:16–17). This was also the case with the garments of a person who carried the carcass of an animal (11:24–25). After emissions of semen, persons were to bathe (15:18). The man with a blood flow was to rinse his hands before touching another person (15:11), and if he spat on a clean person, that person was to wash his or her clothes and bathe (v. 8). Coming into contact with sources of impurity required washing the garments and bathing the body. This was a very effective way of controlling the spread of disease.

6. *Sexual Restrictions.* There are a number of laws dealing with incest intended to set limits on the physical, mental, and genetic deterioration of the people (Lev. 18:1–18).

Bestiality and homosexuality were strongly forbidden (18:22; 20:13) on the basis of morality. Furthermore, the laws would have prevented sexually-transmitted infections and other health problems threatening the well-being of God's people. The same applied to the practice of prostitution. The Israelites, particularly priests (21:9), were not to allow their daughters to become prostitutes (19:29).

7. *Healthy Environment.* Keeping the environment clean provided protection against infectious diseases. Instructions were given, in the context of military campaigns, for the proper disposition of human excrement. This was designed to prevent the spread of infectious diseases and odor pollutants (Deut. 23:12–14). God promised the Israelites a land that would contribute to their physical and emotional well-being (Lev. 26:4–6).

8. *Mental Health.* God is interested in the spiritual, physical, and mental health of His people. Very few actions upset the inner peace of human beings more than actions that damage their relationships with God and others. Guilt and shame rob humans of their inner peace. The Lord provided for the restoration of mental peace through the sacrificial system. Any Israelite who committed a sin against God or another Israelite was expected to bring a guilt or sin offering to the Lord in order for the priest to make atonement for him or her (Lev. 5; 6:24–29). Even in cases where individuals felt anxiety because they suspected that they had committed a sin which they could not recall or identify, the Lord invited them to bring a sacrifice in order to restore their inner peace (5:17–19). Divine forgiveness is the best medicine for a sense of unworthiness, regret, and guilt.

There are some important health principles present in the biblical legislations related to uncleanness. These principles are, in most cases, suggested by the text and not explicitly mentioned. The theological concern predominates, but this does not imply the exclusion of health concerns expressed in a setting in which the mechanism of infectious disease was unknown. Through these laws, God provided a way for them to prevent the inroad of disease. This demonstrates His care for the physical, mental, and spiritual health of His children.

21:1—22:33
Holiness of Priests and Sacrifices

The priests had unique access to God and were therefore called to a higher status of holiness in their lives and work than the common people. This section deals with the preservation of the holiness of the priests (vv. 2–24) and of the holiness of offerings (22:1–33). Those who served the Lord in special capacities were challenged to manifest in their lives His holiness and to become models for others while earning their respect. Whatever belonged to the Lord must be treated with respect and not dragged into a world of sin and death.

21:1–24. Holiness of the Priests. This divine speech was for the instruction of all God's people because caring for holiness is not for the priests alone. Since the common priest was holy, he was forbidden to come in contact with the dead, except for his nearest relatives (vv. 2–3). Through contamination, the priests profaned themselves. Neither were they allowed to practice pagan mourning rites, for this profaned the name of the Lord (v. 5). They were not to marry a harlot, or a defiled woman (perhaps a cultic prostitute), or a divorcée because holiness required wholeness in every form. The Israelites were to acknowledge and respect the holiness of the priest, but this holiness was to be particularly manifest within their own families. When the daughter of a priest profaned her own holiness by becoming sexually promiscuous, her conduct disqualified the priest from performing his ministry. Such a profanation of holiness was a capital offense, and she was to be burned (v. 9; see 20:14).

The holiness of the high priest was particularly important because God appointed him to unique responsibilities; he wore holy garments (v. 10). The requirements for the common priests applied to him as well, but with a few stringent additions. He was not to mourn or to defile himself by coming near a corpse, not even that of his father or mother (v. 11). In v. 11, the text literally refers to a prohibition against touching a *nepesh* (which could mean various things; see "Living Soul or Living Being?" p. 145)—in this case, a reference to a dead person. He was also forbidden to leave the sanctuary to engage in such acts. Death could not interrupt his life-preserving ministry. He was to marry only an Israelite virgin, a woman attuned to God's moral order, in order to not profane or defile his offspring/posterity (vv. 14–15)—that is to say, his

descendants, from whom the next high priest would be selected.

In order to preserve the holiness of the tabernacle, priests with certain infirmities—mainly physical imperfections or health problems—were disqualified from service (vv. 16–21). These were people whose bodies did not express fullness of life, so they were not allowed to minister before the Lord of life. Otherwise they would profane the tabernacle (by treating it as a common building). Nevertheless, they were allowed to eat from the holy and most holy offerings.

22:1–33. Preserving the Holiness of Offerings. It was the responsibility of the people to consecrate their offerings to the Lord and that of the priests to not desecrate them. Priests could desecrate the offerings by handling them while in a state of impurity, thus showing disrespect to the Lord. The cases of uncleanness which excluded priests included leprosy, a bodily discharge, and impurity contracted by touching a person who was unclean (v. 4; see also Lev. 11:24, 29–30; 15:15–18; Num. 19:10–12). If the impurity came through contact, the priest would be unclean until evening and could not eat from the holy things until he had washed his body (vv. 6–7). He was not to eat clean animals that had died of natural causes or had been killed by another beast (v. 8). The emphasis was on protecting the priests from coming into contact with the realm of death because they ministered before the Lord of life. The violation of these regulations was a capital offense; the priest was to bear his own sin and die for it (v. 9).

The holy offerings constituted the food of the priests and their families. It is here stipulated who within the household could eat this food (vv. 10–13). The Hebrew word *zar* in v. 12, which refers to the man to whom the priest's daughter was married, has been translated variously as "outsider," "layman," "stranger," and so forth, and has been generally understood to refer to an Israelite from a nonpriestly line. If someone in the household ate of the holy offerings unintentionally, a guilt offering and compensation were required (vv. 14–16; see 5:14–19).

The Israelites were also instructed concerning how to safeguard the sacredness of their offerings. The preservation of the holiness of the burnt offering, brought for vows or as a freewill offering (vv. 18–20), required the proper animal, without defect. Otherwise the offering would not be acceptable on the offerer's behalf (v. 20; cf. 1:3). If a peace offering were brought, the sacrificial victim was to be without defect—a list of imperfections was provided, similar to the imperfections of the priests excluded from service but more extensive (vv. 22–23; cf. 1:2). The exceptions were a bull or a lamb with a stunted or overgrown limb, to be offered only as a freewill offering. Perhaps this was because it was a completely voluntary offering. The imperfect animals described in this passage do not represent the spiritual condition that God expected from the offerers, for they manifested the impact of death on God's creation (vv. 24–25). But above all, they were not to be a type of Christ, "a lamb without blemish" (1 Pet. 1:19).

The next two laws demonstrated respect for animal life (vv. 27–29; cf. Ex. 22:30). The third reminded the people that a thanksgiving sacrifice was a freewill offering and the flesh of the animal was to be eaten on the same day (vv. 29–30; see 7:12–15). The chapter concludes with an exhortation to keep the commandments of God (v. 31) and not profane His holy name. The leaders were to sanctify the Lord in the eyes of the people because He sanctified the people (v. 32). The call to be holy was grounded in the fact that the Lord had redeemed the people from Egypt (v. 33).

23:1–44
Holy Times: The Festivals

Time flows on relentlessly, bringing change, often boredom, and it is a common human response to seek meaningful activity. The festivals were God's way of enriching time for His people by providing celebrations and reminders of His saving acts on their behalf. These were holy occasions that stopped the common flow of time to bring the community together in worship and celebration before the Lord. They pointed to God's mighty acts in the past and in the future and filled life with meaning and hope. They were called *miqra'e qodesh* ("sacred assemblies" or "holy convocations"), during which portions of time were set apart (*mo'adai* [plural of *mo'ed*] *yahweh*—"appointed times," "festivals," "seasons" of the Lord; v. 4) to worship God in a particular way, in some cases in the sanctuary and in others in the people's dwellings (v. 3). Three of the festivals were pilgrimage festivals, requiring the people to come to the sanctuary to worship (Unleavened Bread [vv. 6–8], Weeks [vv. 15–22], and Tabernacles [vv. 33–36, 39–43]; cf. Deut. 16:16).

Many sacrifices were offered during these celebrations (cf. Num. 28), including sin, burnt, grain/food, drink, and peace/fellowship offerings. These sacrifices conveyed the conviction that atonement was needed even when the people came to worship the Lord, to recommit themselves to Him, and to express joyful gratitude. The convocations included six days of partial rest (ceremonial sabbaths), during which "laborious work" was forbidden (vv. 7, 8, 21, 24–25, 35–36), and two of full rest—the Sabbath (v. 3) and Day of Atonement (v. 27).

23:1–3. The Sabbath. The divine speech here was directed to the people who would participate in the festivals that were to be proclaimed as holy convocations or sacred assemblies for worship. The convocations required a gathering of the people. God referred to them as His appointed times or festivals (v. 3). After this, the Sabbath is mentioned as a day of total rest (*shabbat shabbaton*, a superlative expression meaning "the most restful rest/*shabbat*") and is called a holy convocation or sacred assembly for worship. The Sabbath is never called a "festival" because its celebration is not controlled by the calendar but is based on a cycle of seven days, independent of the month or the year. As a matter of fact, in this passage, the Sabbath is not specifically called a *mo'ed* but is introduced in order to suggest that the holiness of the Sabbath is extended in a limited way to the festivals—the other sacred times. Immediately after the reference to the Sabbath, the introduction to the festivals is repeated again to preserve the uniqueness of the Sabbath (v. 4). Besides, at the end of the chapter, a distinction is drawn between Sabbaths and festivals (vv. 37–38). The Sabbath was instituted by God at Creation and entrusted to Adam and Eve (Gen. 2:1–3; Mark 2:27).

23:4–22. Spring Festivals. The Passover lamb was to be slain on the date of Abib 14 and eaten in the evening—that is to say, on the fifteenth of the month. It was to celebrate the departure of Israel from Egypt—the most magnificent act of divine redemption in the OT (Ex. 12; Num. 28:16–25). It was a type of the redemptive work of Christ, who became the definitive Passover sacrifice (1 Cor. 5:7), slain during the Passover season (19:14, 36; cf. Ex. 12:46, Num. 9:12, Ps. 34:20). He instituted the Lord's Supper as a memorial of His sacrifice (Matt. 26:26–29; 1 Cor. 11:23–26). The Festival of Unleavened Bread was closely related to the Passover because it started on the fifteenth of the month and lasted for seven days. The full period was sometimes called the Passover Festival. During those days, the Israelites ate only unleavened bread to remember the food they ate when leaving Egypt (Ex. 12:39). The bread pointed to the need for believers to remove spiritual leaven from their lives. It was on the day after the Sabbath, perhaps of the first harvest week or after the ceremonial sabbath (on Nisan 16), that the people were to bring a sheaf of the firstfruits of the barley harvest. This ceremony is interpreted in the NT as a type of the resurrection of Jesus, the firstfruits from the dead (1 Cor. 15:23).

Fifty days after the Sabbath preceding the presentation of the firstfruits, the Festival of Weeks/Pentecost was celebrated (Lev. 23:15-22) for the purpose of thanking God for the harvest of wheat (see Ex. 34:22). *Shabbaton* can refer to seven weeks or seven Sabbaths (Lev. 23:15). The outpouring of the Holy Spirit on the disciples occurred during the Festival of Pentecost (Acts 2:1-42). The Spirit, for believers, is the firstfruits of what God will provide (Rom. 8:23). It is a gift more glorious than the literal harvest of wheat.

23:23-44. Autumn Festivals. Two festivals were celebrated during the autumn, besides the Day of Atonement. On the first day of the seventh month, there was a partial day of rest and a *tiru'ah* (a blast, which implies the use of the *shopar* [ram's horn]). The sound of the horn was most likely a reminder that God is Creator and Judge of the world and was used in preparation for the Day of Atonement (cf. 47:5-7; 81:3; 98:6-9). The NT does not mention this festival, but Revelation mentions seven trumpets that sound before the consummation of salvation, reminding people that God is Creator and Judge (Rev. 8:7-9:21; 11:15-19). The trumpets signify God's judgment upon impenitent sinners within the flow of history, preparing the way for the final judgment. In Revelation, the trumpets also culminate with a sanctuary scene related to the Day of Atonement (11:19).

The Day of Atonement took place on the tenth day of the seventh month and was not, properly speaking, a festival (see Lev. 16; Num. 29:7-11). It was a day of judgment for the people that brought about total cleansing (see "The Theology of the Day of Atonement," p. 264). The last festival was the Festival of Tabernacles (Lev. 23:33-43; see Num. 29:12-14; Deut. 16:13-17). It was to be celebrated after the harvest and lasted seven days, with a conclusion on the eighth day. During the week, there was to be a daily procession, with people waving tree branches to express their joy before the Lord (Lev. 23:40). They were to dwell in booths (*sukkot*) and celebrate the Festival of Tabernacles (i.e., tents/booths) so as to remember the time when they had lived in tents in the wilderness after God had brought them out of Egypt (23:42-43; Deut. 16:12-15). Later prophets announced an eschatological Festival of Tabernacles to be celebrated after the cleansing of Jerusalem that would include the nations of the earth (Zech. 14:16-21). John saw an innumerable multitude of people from all nations standing before the throne and the Lamb with palm branches, praising God and the Lamb (Rev. 7:9).

At the end of Leviticus 23, the Lord identified the festivals as occasions to worship Him through sacrifices and offerings (v. 37). These festivals were to be celebrated in addition to the Sabbath. Thus, a distinction was established between the festivals and the Sabbath (v. 38). The festivals pointed to the past—to remind the people of the goodness of God in their lives—but at the same time, they pointed to the future redemptive work of the Lord. They revealed elements of God's plan for the salvation of humanity through Christ.

24:1-23
Holy Place and Holy Name

The subject of holiness continues by transitioning into the Holy Place of the tabernacle, the house of the Lord (vv. 1-9), and by presenting a case in which the holiness of God's name was violated (vv. 10-23). The common theme continues to be how one should handle that which belongs to the Lord.

24:1-9. Light and Bread. In the house of the Lord there were, among other pieces of furniture, a lampstand and a table (see Ex. 25:23-40). The light of the lamps was a symbol of the presence of the Lord in the tabernacle (Pss. 18:28; 27:1; 36:9; 90:8), and therefore, the lamps were to be kept burning all night long or continually (vv. 2-4; cf. Ex. 27:20-21). Maintaining the lamps was one of the activities to be performed by the priest on a regular basis (Heb. *tamid*, "daily," used here adverbially, suggesting that they were to be kept burning day and night; cf. PP 348). The lamp was also a symbol of the life (Zech. 4:1-14) available through the Holy Spirit. The oil was to be provided by the people to demonstrate that the presence of the Lord among them was of utmost importance.

The table's purpose was to present the show bread. Every Sabbath, the priest was to set out twelve cakes of fine flour, in two piles of six, with incense placed by their side. The bread was to be placed before the Lord (v. 6; cf. Num. 4:7), but He was not the One who was to eat it. His description is in human terms—living in a house, receiving bread—but He is not a human being; He is the holy, omnipresent Lord. He did not need bread to subsist, and therefore, He did not eat it but gave it to the priests as a most holy thing to enjoy (v. 9). The bread represented the people of Israel, who provided the flour and who lived in the presence of a holy God, but it also represented God as Creator and sustainer of life (for more information on the fire/food offering [v. 7], see notes on 1:9). Jesus identifies Himself with the Light (John 8:12) and Bread of God (6:48) as the Source and Preserver of life.

24:10–23. Holiness of God's Name. This narrative describes one of the most serious sins that a human being can commit. In this case, it was committed by the son of an Israelite woman and an Egyptian father (v. 10). In the midst of a fight with an Israelite, he cursed the Name, which refers to Yahweh, the Holy One (v. 11; 23:3; cf. Ex. 20:7) and the very source of holiness and life for Israel. The penalty to be inflicted on the man was stipulated in terms of the *lex talionis* (Lat. *lex* ["law"] and *talio* ["like"]), the law of equivalent retribution, which was used in cases of murder (Lev. 24:17, 20; see Ex. 21:23–24; Deut. 19:21)—the penalty should correspond to the crime. Cursing the Lord was treated as the equivalent of murdering a fellow Israelite and thus required the death penalty. Apparently the man wanted the God of Israel dead. This was a most violent attack (*qalal*, "to revile, to curse" [vv. 11, 15]; it is used to indicate that someone is destitute of his or her value) against God. Since the crime was committed in public, those who heard the man were considered polluted by it. Through the laying on of hands, they transferred their guilt to him (v. 14); otherwise, it would have permanently attached to them (cf. 5:1).

The text then proceeds to legislate what to do when someone killed a person or an animal. According to the law of exact retribution, the person who killed another should die, but when an animal was killed, the offender was to replace the animal (vv. 17, 21; lit. "life for life"). The value of a human life is higher than that of an animal because humans were created in the image of God (Gen. 1:26–27). Disfigurement is

the diminution of life, and the same was to be done to the criminal unless compensation was arranged (Lev. 24:19). These laws were also to be applied to resident aliens (v. 22). The chapter closes stating that the divine decision was implemented and the blasphemer was executed (v. 23). No sacrifice was required to expiate for the sin of cursing the Lord because the individuals were executed; they bore their own sin. Today, blasphemers in the church are not to be executed but are disfellowshipped from the community of believers in the hope that they will repent and return to the Lord (1 Tim. 1:20; cf. 1 Cor. 5:1–5). But in the eschatological judgment of God, those who refuse to repent will be excluded from the city of God (Rev. 13:5–6; 19:20).

25:1–55
Holy Times: Sabbatical Years and Jubilee

After dealing with the Holy Place and the holiness of God's name, there is a return to legislation addressing holy time. The sabbatical years (vv. 1–7) and the Jubilee (vv. 8–22) were not based on the calendar. The unifying topic is the land, and consequently, the legislation addresses property redemption (vv. 23–34), the poor, and slavery (vv. 35–55).

25:1–7. Sabbatical Years and Jubilee. The land was to enjoy its sabbath after six years of planting and harvesting. The seventh year was to be a sabbath of rest (*shabbat shabbaton*; see 23:3) for the land (v. 4). This meant that during that year, there would be no sowing, no pruning of vineyards, and no harvesting. The people, the laborers, the strangers, and the livestock would eat what grew by itself—the produce from the sabbath year (vv. 6–7; cf. Ex. 23:10–11; Neh. 10:31). Deuteronomy adds that during the seventh year, there was to be a cancellation of debts (15:1; *shemittah*, "release, remission"). This could refer to the seventh year after the person became a slave and not to the sabbatical year, or it could have also involved a moratorium imposed on collecting debts during the sabbatical year, when there was no sowing or harvesting. In any case, the Levitical law established that the land belonged to the Lord and that in the seventh year, He removed it from the hands of the people to let it rest. This allowed even the poor to benefit from what it produced under His blessing. It also demonstrates that human security does not exclusively depend on the productivity of the land but on the blessing of the Lord.

The Jubilee arrived after forty-nine years, was to be proclaimed on the tenth day of the seventh month (the Day of Atonement), and was to be celebrated in the fiftieth year (Lev. 25:10). Like the sabbatical year, it was to start in the autumn. During that year, slaves were set free to return to their properties and families (Lev. 25:10). When selling land to pay off debts, a person was to take into consideration how many years were left until the Jubilee in order to calculate a fair price (vv. 13–17). The Jubilee was treated as a sabbatical year, during which there was to be no sowing or harvesting (v. 11). The chronological connection between the sabbatical year and the Jubilee is best explained by looking at vv. 20–22: in the sixth year, under God's blessing, the land would yield enough produce for three years (the sixth, seventh, and eighth). Subsequently, in the eighth year, the year of Jubilee (fiftieth year), the people were to start planting and then harvest in the ninth year.

25:23–34. Redemption of Property and the Poor. The practice of freeing the land during the Jubilee was based on the theological conviction that the land belonged to the Lord (v. 23). If, as a result of poverty, it had been sold or leased, the original owner could redeem it in one of two ways. His closest relative (the *go'el*) could redeem it by buying it back for him. In the absence of a redeemer, he could buy it back after acquiring sufficient financial resources. Several other regulations were given to clarify under what circumstances houses were redeemable (vv. 29–34).

The Jubilee protected not only the land but also the poor, for whom there was specific legislation (vv. 35–38). They were to be treated with respect and not financially exploited (i.e., not charged interest). This too was based on the fact that God had redeemed them from Egypt and that He had given them the land. When Israelites had to sell themselves into debt-slavery, they were to be treated as hired servants, not as slaves (v. 40), until the Jubilee. The theological foundation is that the Israelites were the servants of the Lord and could not be treated as slaves (v. 42). Verses 44–46 establish that Israelites could purchase foreigners as slaves (in most cases, prisoners of war) or could purchase the children of foreigners who lived in Israel. These slaves were not to be released during the Jubilee. They were the permanent property of the owner, who could pass them on to his children as inheritance; the slaves' social status was permanent. However, this was not the way the Israelites were to treat their own brothers; this rigorous law did not apply to them (v. 46b). If Israelites sold themselves as debt-slaves to non-Israelites dwelling in the land with them, one of their relatives should redeem them, or if they had reached financial stability, they should redeem themselves (vv. 48–49). In setting the amount to be paid, the years left until Jubilee were to be taken into consideration. The strangers were expected to treat them as a yearly hired servant in the sight of the people of Israel (v. 53). In any case, they should be released in the year of Jubilee. The Israelites were God's servants whom He brought out of the land of Egypt (v. 55).

The legislation resonates with valuable principles and Christological insights. It teaches respect for the land/creation on the basis of the fact that God owns it. It should not be exploited because human survival is ultimately in the hands of the Lord, who provides for His children even when they cease from their work. What the land produces is for the benefit of all, not just for a few, and consequently, systems should be developed to ensure that others benefit from it. The poor should be treated with respect. Their dignity should not be undermined, and they should not be taken advantage of. Typologically, the law of the sabbatical year and the Jubilee awaken hope in the human heart for a land over which justice and love will rule forever—a new land. This eschatological expectation is a reality because we do have a *go'el*, a close relative who has acted as our Redeemer— Jesus Christ, who paid the price for our redemption (Mark 10:45). Isaiah announces that the Messiah would fulfill the Jubilee proclamation of freedom (61:1–3), and this was done by Jesus in Nazareth (Luke 4:16–30). Daniel uses the sabbatical year to establish the time for the coming of the Messiah—7 weeks of days x 7 (49) x 10 = 490 years (see Dan. 9:24–27). The typology of the Jubilee will find its consummation at the return of Jesus, when His people and the planet will be liberated from the oppressive power and presence of evil (Dan. 7:21–22; Rom. 8:20–23; 1 Cor. 15:55; cf. EW 35).

26:1–46
Blessings and Curses

This chapter brings to an end the speech that began in 25:1, while incorporating all the legislations found in the book of Leviticus into the covenant God made between Himself and Israel on Sinai (for more information on the topic of covenants in the ANE and the Bible, see Deuteronomy: Introduction). The call to a holy life closes with an exhortation to obey the laws of the covenant Lord because doing so would bring rich blessing to the people and to the land, while violating them would result in curses or the presence of disorder and chaos in the life of the covenant community (see Deut. 28). The law established divine order, and its rejection would upset and could even destroy that order by damaging or bringing to an end the relationship between the Lord and His people. This chapter, like Deuteronomy 28, establishes that a life shaped by the blessings/promises of the Lord is possible only within a covenant relationship with Him. A life outside that sphere would be characterized by curses/judgments. The chapter can be divided into four main sections: introduction (vv. 1–2), blessings (vv. 3–13), curses (vv. 14–39), and hope for the future (vv. 40–45).

26:1–13. Introduction and Blessings. The introduction summarizes the core of the relationship between God and His people: He wanted to be their exclusive God, and He wanted them to be His people (cf. v. 12). The emphasis is on the first, second, and fourth commandments of the Decalogue (Ex. 20:3, 4–6, 8–11). God would not tolerate idolatry or the representation of the Deity in physical form. The reference to engraved or carved stone in v. 1 probably refers to stones adorned with pagan symbols used for worship (cf. Num. 8:12; 33:52). Being God's holy people was expressed in keeping the Sabbath (Lev. 26:2) and in showing respect to Him as the Lord. In principle, any violation of the laws of the Lord was a rejection of Him as Creator and Redeemer (Ex. 20:8–11; Deut. 5:12–15) and an insult to the God who dwelt among them (cf. Lev. 26:12).

Six main blessings/promises are listed for those who were willing to submit to the covenant Lord: fertility of the land (vv. 4–5), peace and safety in the land (v. 6), military superiority (vv. 7–8), population growth (v. 9), abundance of food (v. 10), and God's permanent presence among them (vv. 11–12). These promises were the outworking of God's redemptive acts on behalf of Israel when He liberated them from Egypt (v. 13). All these blessings were conditional, depending on the commitment of the people to the covenant Lord.

26:14–39. Curses or Denunciations. The curses were much more abundant and specific than the blessings because they were intended to function as a deterrent. Several things could be said about them. First, they were avoidable contingent upon the faithfulness of the people (v. 14). Most of the prophecies of judgment in the Prophets were based on the covenant curses and are conditional (see "God's Judgment in the Prophets," p. 981). Second, the intensity of the judgment increased from terror (v. 16) to the dissolution of the covenant and the removal of the people from the land (vv. 34–39). This revealed God's patience and love for them (vv. 16, 23–24, 27–28). Third, the purpose of the curses was to prevent the people from rebelling against the Lord (v. 21) and to reform them (Heb. *yasar*, "to be disciplined," "to become wise"; v. 23). This was redemptive discipline that sought, under God's power, to bring something good out of a state of chaos. There were five main denunciations: panic as a result of the threat or reality of military defeat (vv. 14–17); famine in the land (vv. 18–20); decimation of humans and animals by wild beasts (vv. 21–22); war, with its accompanying epidemics and famines (vv. 23–26); and destruction and loss of the land (exile; vv. 27–39), preceded by cannibalism (see Lam. 2:20), profanation of cultic places (Lev. 26:30–31), desolation of the land (v. 32), and intensified psychological panic (vv. 36–39). Then the land was to enjoy its sabbatical years (vv. 34–35; cf. 2 Chr. 36:21).

26:40–46. Hope for the Future. Although the people might break the covenant, the Lord was unwilling to break it, and this fact introduces into these dark verses a door of hope. In response, the Lord expected the rebellious people to confess their iniquity, humble themselves, and acknowledge their guilt and that God was righteous in His judgments (vv. 40–41). His faithfulness to the covenant assured the people that He would not completely destroy them (v. 44); that is to say, He would be willing to renew the covenant with them (v. 42). He would also remember the land: during the time it enjoyed its sabbath rest, the people were to remain in exile. Hope is always at the disposal of God's people. Such hope anticipated the coming of the Messiah, who would take upon Himself humanity's curse (Gal. 3:10–14) and who, at the end, will remove the curse from the earth (Rev. 22:3). The chapter concludes by stating that the legislations found in Leviticus, as well as the promises and denunciations, were part of the covenant the Lord made with the people on Mount Sinai through the mediation of Moses.

27:1-34
Holy Vows and Tithes

The previous chapters have emphasized the importance of protecting the holy while becoming holy. This chapter closes Leviticus on a positive note and emphasizes the laws which regulated the legal desecration or redemption of persons, animals, and things. Humans, within certain limitations, could practice the redemption of the holy. The chapter examines the redemption of persons and animals (vv. 2-13) and houses and fields (vv. 14-25), along with a discussion of certain restrictions (vv. 26-29) and the practice of tithing (vv. 30-33).

27:1-13. Introduction and Redemption of Humans and Animals. The book begins and ends with a divine speech addressed, through Moses, to the children of Israel (1:2; 27:1-2). A vow is a voluntary promise made to the Lord that must be honored. Hannah's dedication of Samuel is one example of the consecration of a person to the Lord through a vow (1 Sam. 1:11). If the person was to be redeemed, the priest was to determine the amount of the redemption money based on age and gender. This was not about the intrinsic value of a person but about the estimated amount of productive work that a person could perform. The financial assessment took into consideration the economic status of the person who made the vow (v. 8). With respect to animals, if someone promised to bring a sacrifice to the Lord, there was no way of redeeming the animal (v. 9), and neither should the owner substitute it or exchange it for a different animal that was in better or worse condition. In a case where one animal was exchanged for another (presumably when they were essentially equivalent), both animals belonged to the Lord (v. 10). If the promised animal was unclean, then redemption of it would require one-fifth more added to its value (vv. 11-13). The uncleanness could be considered a legitimate desecration. In a sense, this law motivated the Israelites to be like the Lord, who makes and fulfills His promises (cf. Acts 5:1-11).

27:14-29. Houses, Fields, and Some Restrictions. The price for a house that had been dedicated to the Lord, in the sense of giving it to the sanctuary, was established by the priest (v. 14). To redeem the house, those who made the vow would need to add one-fifth to its price (v. 15). Concerning fields dedicated to the Lord, the priest assessed its value on the basis of the amount of seed planted in it (v. 16). Its value was

determined by taking into consideration the time left until the year of Jubilee. The redemption of the field required adding one-fifth to its value. The case mentioned in vv. 20-21 is puzzling, but it appears to refer, as suggested by some, to a person who, after selling a field and not redeeming it, decided to dedicate it to the Lord. In this case, the field would not return to the original owner in the year of Jubilee but would become the property of the sanctuary (*kherem*, "totally devoted to God"). When a person dedicated to the Lord a field that he had bought (leased) and that at Jubilee would return to its original owner (vv. 22-25), the field was not redeemable, and in the year of Jubilee, it would revert to its owner.

All the firstborn of animals belonged to the Lord, and no one was to dedicate them to Him. The firstborn of unclean animals were redeemable. Those things or people totally devoted (*kherem*) to the Lord were not redeemable, for they were most holy (vv. 26-29). The term *kherem* designates what was permanently assigned to the tabernacle or to be destroyed. A person had to be legally declared *kherem* (the sense of the term being, in this case, one set apart for destruction) before he or she was killed (v. 29; cf. Num. 21:2-3; Deut. 13:13-16; 1 Sam. 15:3; see "The Extermination of the Canaanites," p. 330, and "Holy Warfare," p. 372).

27:30-33. Tithe. The last section of Leviticus 27 addresses the redemption of tithe and reveals some important details. It is probably discussed last because it was related to humans, the produce of land, and animals. First, the nature of tithe is clearly established: it is holy to the Lord (v. 30). Humans are not to consecrate it to Him because it is already His. Second, since it is holy and belongs to the Lord, humans are to return it to Him as instructed. A tenth of the produce of the land, from the seeds or the fruits, and from the herds or the flocks, of whatever passed under the rod of the shepherd, belonged to Him and was placed out of the reach of humans. Third, the tithe of the animals was not to be manipulated by exchanging the animals—in which case, both animals were to be declared holy. The animals passing under the rod belonged to the Lord, whether they were in good condition or not. If the person wanted to redeem the tithe—perhaps to retain more food or seeds—the person was to add one-fifth to the value of the produce or the animal.

Based on the reading of Leviticus 27, it can be assumed that the people of God had a generous spirit and would voluntarily consecrate some of their blessings to Him out of gratitude. By motivating them to bring donations and the tithe, the Lord was helping them overcome the deep darkness of selfishness that lodges in the human heart. We too should find ways in our own cultural settings to express our love and gratitude to God for His constant care for us, particularly for what He has done for us through Christ. The tithe is not so much an offering but a moral responsibility that involves returning to the Lord what is His (Mal. 3:10). Jesus did not abolish this expression of love but affirmed it (Matt. 23:23).

The book of Leviticus closes with a reminder to the readers that its contents are an expression of the will of the Lord. The story ends with Israel camping by Mount Sinai. The covenant had been established, the tabernacle had been erected and consecrated, the priests had been anointed, and the sacrificial system had been instituted. All that remained was to leave Sinai on a journey of hope.

NUMBERS

INTRODUCTION

Title and Authorship. Numbers is the fourth book of the Pentateuch. In the Hebrew Bible, the book is entitled *bemidbar*, "in the wilderness" or "in the desert." This title is the translation of the fifth Hebrew word of the opening verse of the book—"And-the-Lord spoke to Moses in-the-wilderness" (1:1). The Greek translation (LXX) named the book *Arithmoi*, "Numbers," which the Latin Vulgate rendered as *Numeri*, "Numbers." The English title, "Numbers," is the translation of either the Greek *Arithmoi* or the Latin *Numeri*. While the title "Numbers" highlights the two censuses recorded in chapters 1 and 26 of the book, the Hebrew title "in the wilderness" seems more appropriate because it indicates the location of the events reported in the book. It is thus a reminder of the many experiences the Israelites had with God during their journey toward the promised land. During the long journey, they felt disappointment and hope, but God ultimately managed to bring them home.

Traditionally, scholars have credited the composition of the Pentateuch, including the book of Numbers, to Moses. While many modern scholars question the Mosaic authorship of Numbers (see "Introduction to the Pentateuch," p. 120), the following biblical elements indicate that Moses should be maintained as the author of the book.

(1) Numbers itself states that Moses recorded the stages of their journey (33:2), suggesting that Moses wrote at least portions of the book. While recording the itinerary of the journey, he also narrated events that took place in different sites. (2) The phrase "the Lord spoke to Moses," which occurs over fifty times in the book and is recurrent in other books of the Pentateuch, indicates that Moses received communication from God that he wrote down. He did not write the book of Numbers in keeping with his own will, but, like other prophets and men of God, he wrote under divine inspiration (2 Pet. 1:21).

(3) The testimony of the NT points to Mosaic authorship by citing a number of events from Numbers associated with him (John 3:14; 6:31, cf. Num. 21:9; 11:7; 1 Cor. 10:5, 8–10, cf. Num. 26:65; 25:1, 9; 21:6; 14:36–37; Heb. 3:2, 11, 17, cf. Num. 12:7; 14:21–23, 36–37; Jude 5, 11, cf. Num. 14:29; 22:7; 16:1–2). These NT references imply that Jesus and the apostles Paul and Jude considered Moses to be the author of Numbers.

Date. The book of Numbers is part of a larger literary whole (the Pentateuch), produced during the fifteenth century B.C. Its contents indicate that it continues the story of the Exodus of the Israelites from Egypt. Its direct connection with the Exodus story implies that it was written during the fifteenth century B.C.

Backgrounds. The book of Numbers continues the story already begun in the book of Exodus. In their journey from Egypt, the Israelites reached Sinai, where they stayed temporarily (Ex. 19:1). The book first describes some features related to their stay in the desert of Sinai (1:1—10:10). It then focuses on the history of their wanderings in the wilderness from Sinai to the plains of Moab (10:11—22:1). It finally describes their sojourn in the plains of Moab, where they prepared to enter the promised land (22:2—36:1-13). The journey from the desert of Sinai to the plains of Moab took about thirty-eight years, during which the first generation of freed Israelites—those who came out of Egypt—died in the wilderness because of their unfaithfulness (26:63–65). When they were ready to enter Canaan, they doubted God's promises. Their hope vanished, and therefore, they became wanderers in the wilderness. The new generation of Israelites, born in the wilderness, developed a strong bond of love with the Lord and believed that He would bring them into the promised land.

Theology and Purpose. The theme of Israel as the Lord's pilgrim people is a key motif in the book of Numbers. Numbers 33:1 states that the children of Israel went "out of the land of Egypt" in an orderly way. The terms *tseba'ot* ("armies"), *tseba'o* ("his army"), and *tsaba'* ("army" or "war") are altogether used more than fifty times in the book of Numbers in connection with the people of Israel. The image of an army is not used in Numbers to emphasize aggressive military action but to describe Israel as a well-organized group of pilgrims traveling under the leadership of the Lord in full commitment to Him and in opposition to the forces of evil that they will face during their journey. This image also serves to demonstrate that the people left Egypt victorious over the forces of Pharaoh.

1. God as Leader. In the description of Israel as the Lord's army, God is identified as the supreme leader of the people. He organized them after the censuses (1:1–46; 26:1–65) and gave instructions regarding leadership roles, camp layout, and marching formation (chaps. 2–4; 9:15–10:28). During their travels, God provided for their material, social, and spiritual needs and granted them shade, manna, quails, water (10:34; 11:6–7, 31–32; 20:2–13), security, and victory over the enemies they confronted (21:1–3, 21–35; 31:1–12). He blessed them with religious and social regulations and promised them the gift of the land (chaps. 27–30; 32–36). The headquarters of the Lord, His sanctuary, was placed in the center of the camp; He traveled with them. The terms *'ohel* ("tent") and *mishkan* ("tabernacle") occur more than ninety times in Numbers and refer to the dwelling place of God (i.e., the sanctuary from where God guided and communicated with His people; 1:1; 7:89). God even acted as the Judge of His people and settled legal disputes from the sanctuary (5:11–22; 6:9–12; 8:19; 11:16–23; 12:1–15; 14:10–12; 16:16–35; 17:1–9).

2. Dedicated Pilgrims. The metaphor of an army on a pilgrimage implies total separation and dedication to God's purpose under His leadership. The multitude who left Egypt were constituted as a people on a journey to the promised land. The book highlights obedience and faithfulness to God, the supreme leader, as prerequisites for their success. It also warns about the consequences of disobedience—in this case, the exclusion of many Israelites, including key leaders (Moses, Aaron, and Miriam), from entering the promised land (26:63–65). The breaking of God's covenant distances sinners from the Lord and deprives them of God's covenant blessings. Perseverance in hope and faith should have made the journey meaningful and even enjoyable in the presence of the Lord.

3. The Threat of Rebellion. As God's people, the Israelites were to remain loyal and in submission to Him. Whenever the order established by the Lord was upset on account of the rebellion of some, God intervened in order to enable His people to fulfill His plan for them (11:1, 4–6, 32–33; 12:1–15; chaps. 13–14; cf. Gen. 12:1–3). Finally, following the journey from Sinai to Kadesh, up to the plains of Moab, the book of Numbers tells how God faithfully worked out His plan to bring His fainthearted people to the promised land. Like the former Israel, "the church of Christ, enfeebled and defective as it may be, is the only object on earth on which He bestows His supreme regard" (TM 15). Despite the challenges God's people face, there is hope that God will take care of them and bring them safely into the heavenly kingdom.

Literary Features. The book contains diverse literary features, including lists (chaps. 1, 26), poetry (6:24–26; 10:35; 21:14–18, 27–30; 24:17, 20–25), travel logs (chap. 33), historical narratives, and legal material, which are sometimes interwoven. The structure of the book is difficult to delineate. However, most commentators seem to view the book as structured around the three major geographic locations or the two censuses. The first structure divides the book into three parts: (1) stay at Sinai (1:1—10:10), (2) wandering around Kadesh (10:11—20:21), and (3) journey from Kadesh to the plains of Moab (20:22—36:13). The second structure splits the book into two sections: (1) death of the old and rebellious generation in the wilderness (1:1—25:18) and (2) birth of the new generation (26:1—36:13). Although both are potential organizing structures, the first links Numbers to its preceding and following books, aligns well with the journey motif begun already in the call of Abram (Gen. 12:1–3), and fittingly portrays the larger picture of the book.

COMMENTARY

1:1—10:10

ISRAEL ENCAMPED AT SINAI

The first part of the book of Numbers (1:1—10:10) encompasses the organization of the people of Israel during their temporary stay at Sinai in preparation for the next step of their journey, which culminated in the conquest of the land of Canaan. The organization focused on various aspects, such as numbering of people, structuring the encampment and marching formation, and assigning tasks (1:1—4:49). We also find some legal material (5:1—6:27), matters related to the sanctuary (7:1—8:26), instructions concerning the Passover, a description of the cloud as divine guidance (9:17–23), and directions for the creation and function of the silver trumpets (9:1—10:10). The emphasis on organization was intended to unify God's people, shape their identity, and strengthen their relationship with God. Order and unity of action and purpose should always characterize God's people as they seek to participate in God's mission.

1:1—4:49
Numbering and Organization of Israel

Numbers 1–4 principally contains instructions concerning the census and the structure of the Israelite community during its sojourn in the wilderness. The section describes two censuses: (1) the general census of the children of Israel (except the tribe of Levi) and its purpose (chap. 1); and (2) the special census of the Levites, followed by an outline of their duties (chaps. 3–4). Between the two censuses, the author narrates how the Israelite community was organized around the sanctuary, which symbolized God's presence among them (chap. 2).

1:1–46. Numbering of Israel. The Lord spoke to Moses from the tabernacle/tent of meeting and ordered him to take a census of Israel (v. 2). The tabernacle/tent of meeting mentioned in the passage was a physical structure reflecting the model of the original sanctuary found in heaven (Ex. 25:8–9; 26:30; 35–40; Heb. 8:2, 5; 9:11; Rev. 4:5; 8:3; 11:19; see Exodus: Introduction). The earthly sanctuary served as God's headquarters from where He directed the affairs of His people (cf. 12:4–5). From there, He communicated with Moses from above the ark of the covenant/testimony (7:89). The census described in this section was commanded by the Lord, the supreme ruler of the people of Israel (1:1–2). In the ANE context, kings generally ordered a census to confirm their authority over the people being numbered. The census data also served to meet military, economic, religious, and political goals.

In the case of Israel, the census was used for conscripting men for military and religious service (1:3; 3:1–39; 1 Chr. 23:1–5), allotting land

in Canaan (Num. 26), assigning specific tasks (2 Chr. 2:17–18), and on occasion, strengthening a person's relationship with the Lord (Ex. 30:11–16). In the specific context of Numbers 1, the census was primarily held for a military purpose (1:2–3). The conquest of the Holy Land was a divine project, and the Israelites would accompany God as He fulfilled His purpose. The census revealed that God is indeed a God of order, as is indicated in the Creation account (Gen. 1) and here in the creation of a people through whom He would bless all the nations of the earth.

Moreover, the census could be seen as a confirmation of God's sovereignty over His people. It assumed the willingness of a people who had been redeemed from Egypt to embrace the divine plan and cooperate with God in its realization, with the knowledge that in the process, He would take care of them. They were to rely on Him as their King and Leader. This is also seen in the Eschaton. Revelation 7 provides numbers for the Israel of faith, represented by a unique list of the twelve tribes of Israel. They bear on their foreheads "the seal of the living God" (Rev. 7:3), belonging to Him, and He has made them victorious through the blood of the Lamb (12:11). They too ally themselves with the King of kings, support His plan, and anticipate His victory over rebellious powers.

The census of Numbers 1 is also useful in terms of the leadership principles it contains (e.g., planning, delegation, and the involvement of the youth). The text indicates that Moses counted people according to their families, as well as each individual male (1:2). He also chose assistants to help him conduct the census (1:1–17). These assistants were referred to as called or chosen, which can imply that they were recognized as respected, eminent, and able leaders (v. 16). The age criterion for the census was twenty years old and above (v. 3). The expression "twenty years old and above" is repeated fifteen times to identify who was eligible to go to war. The narrative suggests that accurate recording of statistical reports, delegation of authority, and the inclusion of youth in God's work should be important to the people of God. Numbers 1:46 indicates that the total number of those who were counted was 603,550. This large number is considered problematic by many people, but it is not necessarily so (see Ex. 12:31–42; see "The Number of Israelites Who Left Egypt," p. 210).

1:47–54. Levites Appointed over the Tabernacle. Levites constituted a special group that was not counted in the military census (1:46–49).

Their census is recorded in Numbers 3. Their exclusion from the census in chapter 1 is related to the sacred task assigned to them. The Levites were appointed by the Lord for the care and transportation of the tabernacle (1:50–51, 53); hence, their role was somewhat different from that of other Israelites. They were set apart to protect the sanctuary and, if necessary, to kill unauthorized persons who attempted to enter illegally (1:51). They were in charge of the security of God's holy headquarters. The details of the duties of the Levites are elaborated in chapters 3–4. However, one aspect can be highlighted here: the Levites were set apart to minister in the sanctuary so that God's wrath would not fall on the congregation (1:50, 53). The verb *sharat* ("to minister"), applied to the Levites (1:50), is the same term used for God's angels or the heavenly host (Ps. 103:21) and designates a special type of service that a subordinate renders to a superior. Intriguingly, the Hebrew term is also used to describe the unique relationship between Joshua and Moses (Ex. 24:13; 33:11; Num. 11:28; Josh. 1:1). This kind of service was not restricted to military or guard duties, however. The word may indicate that because the Levites took care of the sanctuary—the symbol of God's presence—they bore a great responsibility as God's official representatives before the people. Serving as guards, placed around the sanctuary to prevent all unauthorized individuals from accessing it, the Levites were protecting the people from God's wrath (v. 53). Numbers 1 closes by stating that the Israelites followed the Lord's instructions given through Moses (v. 54). The revelation of God's will for His people should always lead them to humble and grateful submission to Him.

2:1–34. Camps and Leaders of the Tribes.

Numbers 2 describes how the tribes of Israel were organized with respect to each other and around the sanctuary. They formed a square or rectangular camp, with three tribes on each side. Judah, Issachar, and Zebulun took positions on the east, where the entrance to the sanctuary was located; Reuben, Simeon, and Gad on the south; Ephraim, Manasseh, and Benjamin on the west; and Dan, Asher, and Naphtali on the north. On the east side, the tribe of Judah took the lead and broke camp first; to the south, it was the tribe of Reuben, and this group set out second; then on the west side, it was the tribe of Ephraim that led, breaking camp third; and finally, to the north, the tribe of Dan took preeminence and set out last. The tribe of Levi was placed around the

sanctuary (2:17) as a military guard to protect its holiness. Chapters 3 and 4 provide more details about their position and function.

The structure of the camp probably reflected the status of each tribe. Judah took the first position and thus replaced Reuben, the firstborn. This change was based on what the patriarch Jacob had foretold in Genesis 49:2–4 and 8–11. It is encouraging to know that Reuben was not excluded from God's people. God always seeks to keep His children close to Him. The arrangement of the Israelite camp reflected order and unity. It also indicates the place of God in the life of the Israelite community. Each tribe was related to the nearer tribes, and thus, all the tribes were tied together as one body. Each tribe was part of the larger whole (i.e., God's community). Tribes were interdependent and all depended on God, whose presence was evidenced by the sanctuary stationed in the middle of the camp. Without the Lord dwelling in their midst, they could not be a united community. His presence was at the center of all aspects of their lives. A similar idea is found in Revelation 21 in the description of the new Jerusalem. The city is without a temple because "the Lord God Almighty and the Lamb" dwell among their creation (v. 22). While believers still expect the future fulfillment of this marvelous event, they can now experience it by allowing Immanuel, Jesus Christ, to be at the center of their lives as individuals and as a community of faith.

3:1–39. Duties of the Levites.

While Numbers 1–2 centers mainly on the survey and organization of the twelve tribes in the camp, Numbers 3–4 focuses on the same activities specifically in regard to the tribe of Levi. This section (3:1–39) describes the anointing of the sons of Aaron for the priesthood (vv. 2–4), the duties of the Levites (vv. 5–10), and the numbering of the three Levite clans (vv. 14–39).

The priests and Levites were both descendants of Levi, the third son of Jacob (Gen. 29:34). The sons of Levi were Gershom, Kohath, and Merari (Gen. 46:11; Ex. 6:16). Aaron and Moses were descendants of Kohath (Ex. 6:16–20; 1 Chr. 6:2–3), and the priests were descendants of Aaron. They were given the exclusive task of offering sacrifices and presiding over the performance of sacred rituals in the sanctuary (Num. 4:5–15; 18:1–32). The other descendants of Levi formed the group of Levites who assisted the priests. Their major roles consisted of guarding, tending, transporting, and performing other holy activities for the sanctuary (Num. 3:21–37;

4:4-14; 1 Chr. 9:26-32; 15:16; 24:6; 26:29; 2 Chr. 23:7; Ezek. 44:11).

The censuses in Numbers 3:14-39 and 4:34-49 are mainly connected to religious service. Levites were to serve the community at the sanctuary, as well as protect, disassemble, transport, and reassemble the sanctuary during the journey to the promised land (1:50-51, 3:6-10). Each Levitical family had a specific task to perform in regard to the sanctuary (3:21-38) under the leadership of Aaron and his sons (3:9). This implies that the work of the Levites was carefully organized. The sanctuary was not primarily a public gathering place but the holy residence of God. It was a place where God's representatives (i.e., the priests) met with Him in order to mediate between God and His people. Moreover, the order to restrict unauthorized access to the sanctuary suggested that the holy presence of God should be strictly revered. Reverence or respect should always be a significant part of the worship of the Holy God. At the same time, the focus upon God's holiness was not intended to keep other Israelites away from the sanctuary. Instead, God's presence represented a constant invitation to worship and draw close to the Lord who had brought Israel out of Egypt with a "mighty hand and an outstretched arm" (Deut. 4:34). Grace, forgiveness, and hope were important elements of the sacrificial ritual of the sanctuary.

3:40-51. Levites and the Redemption of the Firstborn. As a separated group, the Levites also played the role of representing the rest of the Israelites before God. According to vv. 11-13 and 40-51, they substituted for all the firstborn of the Israelites. This substitution was related to the fact that during the Passover in Egypt, the Lord preserved the lives of the firstborn of the Israelites. From then on, they belonged to God (Ex. 13:2; 22:29; Lev. 27:26), and it seems that His plan was to appoint them to His service in the sanctuary.

At this point, however, the Levites were "wholly given" to God in place of all the firstborn of Israel in order to work on behalf of the Israelites in the sanctuary and to make atonement for them (Num. 3:7-8; 8:16, 19). In addition, the Lord required the Israelites to give Him all the firstborn of their animals and the first of their ripe produce (Ex. 13:2, 12; 22:29-30). The firstborn could be either sacrificed or redeemed. Hence, clean animals were sacrificed while unclean animals and humans were redeemed (Lev. 27:1-29; Num. 18:15). The firstborn could be considered the best or ideal gift that one could offer to God in recognition of His ownership of everything. As firstborn, the Levites were considered a precious gift to God, expected to serve Him wholeheartedly.

The text indicates that the total number of Israelites' firstborn was 22,273 (3:43). Out of this number, the Lord took 22,000 Levites as His own. The Lord commanded that the remaining 273 Levites should be ransomed with a payment of five shekels each. This money was to be given to Aaron and his sons (v. 48). The ransom money is twice referred to as "the sanctuary shekel" (vv. 47, 50). Since coins were not invented until the Persian period, the reference to shekel here is as a unit of weight used in payment or valuation. The weight and value of the shekel varied somewhat, according to time and place. The shekel of the sanctuary seems to have weighed more than the one used in the marketplace. The people could compare the value of the market shekel with that of the sanctuary shekel in order to pay an honest amount to God's treasury. Levites themselves could not debase it and were able to check if the offering had the required value. Five shekels could equate to about half a year's wages. The text does not reveal how the amount was used, but one may infer that it was devoted to God's work.

4:1-49. Tasks Assigned to the Levites. Numbers 4 returns to the census of the Levites and their duties. This census was a record of those who would do the work of the sanctuary (4:3, 23, 30, 35). As indicated, some of their responsibilities involved taking down and setting up the sanctuary, as well as its transportation. Moses numbered the Levites according to their assigned tasks and the items they were assigned to carry (4:49).

When the Israelites moved from one site to another, they bore the sanctuary with them. It was carefully dismantled by Aaron and his sons, not by the Levites (vv. 5, 15, cf., 1:51). The Levites were responsible for the transportation of tabernacle and furniture. Aaron and his sons disassembled the tabernacle, beginning with the veil (v. 5), moving from the Most Holy Place to the other parts of the tabernacle. The veil referred to in v. 5 separated the holy from the Most Holy Place of the tabernacle. The screen that was at the entrance of the tabernacle was carried by the Gershonites instead of the Kohathites, who were appointed specifically to carry items related to the Most Holy Place (3:25; 4:4-5). The holiness of the tabernacle needed to be protected, even during its disassembly.

After dismantling the tabernacle, Aaron and his sons packed the items and covered them (v. 15). The ark of the covenant was the first item to be covered (v. 5). Even Kohathite Levites were not allowed to touch or see the holy items while being packed (vv. 15, 20). Their duty was limited to transportation (v. 15). The Levites served between the ages of thirty and fifty (vv. 3, 23, 30, 35, 39, 43, 47; i.e., about twenty years of service). Numbers 8:23-26 brings the entire period of service to twenty-five years by stating that the Levites were to begin their work at the age of twenty-five. It is unclear whether the Levites began their service at thirty or twenty-five. A possible solution to this question is that they entered the service at twenty-five as apprentices, and at thirty, they were adequately skilled to carry out their official functions.

The text insists that Levites from thirty to fifty could enter into the work (vv. 3, 23, 30, 35, 39, 43, 47). The Hebrew term used here (*latsaba'*) suggests "warfare" or "army service." The Levitical service was equivalent to military service. Members were to be physically fit in order to fight and protect the tabernacle from trespassers (1:51, 53). The Levites were assigned to their roles based on the families of the three sons of Levi (3:17; 4:2, 22, 29). The Lord appointed the sons of Kohath (one of the three sons of Levi) for special duty (i.e., the transportation of articles related to the Most Holy Place of the tabernacle; 4:4, 15). The Kohathites were to carry their load on their shoulders (7:9) as indicated by the fact that poles were inserted into rings attached to the side of most of the holy furniture (4:6, 8, 11, 14). The sons of Gershom and Merari were given wagons for their duty because their load was heavier than that of the Kohathites (7:7-8).

5:1—6:27
Special Legislation

In the previous chapters, the emphasis is on the structure of the Israelite community. In the current section, the focus is on laws related to health and the social, moral, and religious lives of the Israelites. During their journey in the wilderness and at the time of their settlement in the promised land, God's people were to remember that the Holy God was living in their midst. Therefore, their camp was to be devoid of impurity (5:1-4); restitution was to be made in case of fraud (5:5-10); and cases of marital unfaithfulness were to be settled before God (5:11-31). People—other than Levites—were encouraged

to dedicate themselves to God's service (6:1-21), and the priests were to bless God's people (6:22-27). All these instructions were intended to enhance the relationship between God and His people. The principles expressed in these laws are still valid today because they have the power to enhance the lives of God's people.

5:1-4. Unclean Persons Sent outside the Camp. This section is part of a series of three prescriptions recorded in Numbers 5 concerning the preservation of purity in the Israelite community. Numbers 5:1-4 concerns the Israelites who became unclean because they had an infectious skin disease (perhaps leprosy or a similar skin disease), any kind of bodily discharge (particularly emission from sexual organs due to some disease or other reason), or contact with a dead body. These instructions were based on the legislation found in Leviticus 13-15. The two passages are complementary. While Leviticus focuses on the exclusion of unclean persons from the tabernacle to avoid illegal contact with God's dwelling place (Lev. 15:31), Numbers emphasizes their exclusion from the camp (Num. 5:3) to avoid contamination through touch.

The text indicates that people who were affected by one of these three impurities were sent outside the camp so that "they may not defile" it because the Lord was dwelling there among them (v. 3). While it is true that a hygienic aspect is underlined in Numbers 5:1-4, holiness is its major focus (see "Health and Hygiene in Leviticus," p. 272). Preventing the spread of disease among the vast multitude of Israelites living in the camp was imperative (as instances of large and densely populated refugee camps have confirmed). However, God desires purity that goes beyond hygiene (i.e., spiritual purity that enhances the quality of one's relationship with Him and with others). Besides, the impurities described in Numbers 5:1-4, like those in Leviticus, have in common the element of death. Death/the unclean and God/the Holy One are incompatible. Consequently, unclean individuals were removed from the community. By removing the unclean from the camp (v. 4), the Israelites rejected death and clung to life (see Leviticus: Introduction). The Israelites complied with this law throughout their sojourn in the wilderness.

God is interested in both the physical and spiritual well-being of His children. The call is to live a holy life before the Lord (cf. 1 Thess. 5:23). Those who look forward to a condition of absolute freedom from spiritual and moral uncleanness, to be consummated at the return of the Lord, will seek true spiritual health without disregarding physical health (3 John 2).

5:5-10. Restitution for Wrongs. This second regulation is a supplement to Leviticus 6:1-7 and addresses Israelites who wronged others by robbery or fraud and then denied it under oath. Scholars have suggested that the verb *ma'al*— "to be unfaithful" against God—designates a sacrilege that, in some cases, refers to the violation of an oath taken in the name of the Lord. The parallel with Leviticus indicates that here it means the violation of an oath. This was a case of willful sin, and consequently, the wrongdoer was to confess his or her sin and make restitution to the one to whom the wrong was done in order to restore peace/wholeness in the camp (v. 7). Since this was not only a sin against others but also against the Lord, a guilt/reparation offering was required to atone for the sin committed (v. 8; see Lev. 6:1-7). What was new in this law was that it legislated what should be done when no kinsman was available to receive the restitution; it was to be given to the Lord, who assigned it to the priest (v. 8). This decree was likely meant to encourage honesty in all exchanges. But beyond that, it inspired the offender to repent by pointing to God's willingness to forgive sins, even intentional ones. Addition or clarification to already established law can be found repeatedly in Numbers (cf. Num. 27:1-11 and the case of Zelophehad's daughters). In Numbers, God's law was applied to day-to-day issues faced in the Israelite camp, which, at times, raised new questions.

5:11-31. Ritual of Jealousy. This legislation focused on the procedure to be undertaken when a husband suspected his wife of adultery. If she had been unfaithful, the alleged adulterer would have been defiled (vv. 12-14, 19-20, 27-29). Such uncleanness would have polluted the moral, physical, and social life of the Israelite community. This was a serious threat that needed to be addressed by God Himself (vv. 16, 18, 21, 30). Ancient people used a variety of tests to resolve similar issues. Practices used by other cultures included throwing the accused in the river or making the accused drink a potion, retrieve a given item from boiling liquid, or touch, lick, walk upon, or carry a red-hot object. Today, in some parts of the world, women are still stoned to death if adultery is suspected. Contrary to other ANE people, to solve the issue of alleged marital unfaithfulness, the Israelites used a ritual that involved drinking water. This Israelite ritual was not a life-threatening ordeal like those practiced by the nations surrounding Israel (see "A Woman Suspected of Adultery," p. 289).

6:1-21. Nazirite Law. The Nazirite law can be divided into four parts: (1) forbidden activities (vv. 1-8), (2) responses to defilement (vv. 9-12), (3) the ritual marking the end of the vow (vv. 13-20), and (4) a concluding statement (v. 21). The term "Nazirite" is related to the Hebrew verb *nazar*, "to separate," which implies "to keep oneself away from" or "separated for," in the sense of consecration. Therefore, a Nazirite (male or female; v. 2) was a person who consecrated a specific length of time for a particular service to the Lord.

Although the priests and Levites were set apart in a very special way for God's work, all Israelites had the opportunity to voluntarily dedicate themselves to God as a Nazirite. In this case, they separated themselves from common affairs and were consecrated to God's service for a specific period. Like the priests and Levites, Nazirites were not allowed to drink wine, touch a corpse, or shave their heads (6:1-8; Lev. 10:9; 21:5, 11). Nazirites were common Israelites who were granted a status similar to that of a priest, particularly since they were entirely consecrated to the Lord, in some cases for life (e.g., Samuel; 1 Sam 1:11). The Nazirite was not to break the vow (vv. 9-12). If the vow were involuntarily broken, a purification ritual was performed. The ritual required shaving the individual's head (v. 9) and offering two turtledoves, one for a burnt offering and the other for a sin offering, to remove ritual contamination (vv. 10-11). Since the Nazirite's consecration was defiled, a guilt offering was also required (v. 11; see Lev. 5:5-6). At the end of the Nazirite period, the individual's hair was to be shaved and burned as an offering to God (vv. 18-19). In this particular case, long hair was considered a visible symbol of the consecration of the Nazirite to the Lord (v. 7).

The offerings required at the end of the period of consecration include animals (vv. 14, 19); grain, bread, and oil (v. 15); and the hair of the Nazirite (v. 18). These were to be offered as a burnt offering, sin offering, and peace/fellowship offering (v. 14; cf. Lev. 1-7). The burnt offering involved burning the entire sacrificial animal, and it was employed in a number of different types of ceremonies (Lev. 8:18-21; Ex. 29:15-18). In the context of the Nazirite law, the burnt offering represented the complete dedication of the

Nazirite to the Lord. No reason is given here for bringing a sin/purification offering, but it could have been for any sin committed in ignorance during the period of the vow or because anyone who approached God was sinful and in need of atonement (Lev. 4:2–4; Num. 15:22–29). The peace/fellowship offering involved burning part of the sacrificial animal. The rest of the sacrifice was eaten by the priest and the person who brought the offering (Lev. 3:11; 7:14). It served to strengthen the offerer's covenant relationship with the Lord. Through this offering, the Nazirite expressed joy and gratitude to God.

The grain offerings (v. 15) were accessory to animal offerings (lamb, ram), as required in the Israelite sacrificial system (Lev. 2; Num. 15:2–12).

A Woman Suspected of Adultery

The legislation addressing a woman suspected of adultery is unique in biblical jurisprudence and sounds strange to modern readers. It would be useful to explore this passage more carefully in order to understand its intention.

1. Role of the Husband. This was a case of suspected marital infidelity, in which the husband's suspicions were motivated by jealousy (Num. 5:12–14). The legislation removed the case from the jurisdiction of the husband and placed it in the hands of the priest, as a spiritual leader of the people. This decision protected the wife from the physical and/or psychological abuse that a jealous husband could inflict on her. It was, therefore, beneficial to her. The husband was required to bring to the sanctuary a grain offering on behalf of his wife.

2. Role of the Priest and the Community. Since the husband did not have any evidence acceptable in a human court of law, his only recourse was to bring his wife to the priest (vv. 15). The priest was to set the accused woman before the Lord (vv. 16–26) and mix dust from the floor of the tabernacle with sacred water. He stood before the woman, placed the grain offering in her hand, and put her under an oath of innocence or guilt that spelled out the results of the ritual. He would then write the content of the oath on a scroll and symbolically scrape the words of oath into the bitter water. Next, he would take the grain offering from her hands and offer it to the Lord. Lastly, the woman would drink the water. The community did not take any action against her; it simply served as a witness to what the Lord would reveal. On account of their limitations, all human participants (the husband, the priest, and the community) withdrew themselves from the case and left it between the suspected wife and the Lord. She was in good hands.

3. Role of the Lord. The process was a search for truth unavailable to humans. In such situations, only the Lord could reveal whether the woman was innocent or guilty and restore harmony to the home and society (vv. 27–28). The offering was brought by the husband to the Lord on behalf of the wife as a prayer asking the Lord to reveal the truth. It was called an offering of jealousy or iniquity, to indicate the occasion and the mental condition of the husband (v. 15). Offering on her behalf meant that, if innocent, she would benefit from it through the blessings of God. While most ancient ordeals considered the accused guilty until the deity could prove otherwise, in this case, the accused was considered innocent unless God revealed otherwise. Thus, the ritual favored the accused woman. She would not be stigmatized by society after she was vindicated by the Lord.

4. Role of the Woman. The voice of the woman was heard only once—when, after listening to the oath of culpability or exculpation, she was asked by the priest to say "Amen" (v. 22). There were several reasons a woman might be willing to participate in this examination. First, it would bring to an end all accusations by her husband. Second, if innocent, she would be cleared not only before the Lord but also in public; she had witnesses. Third, if she were found guilty, the penalty would be infertility, and her husband would divorce her. This was severe but better than if she had been caught in the act of adultery—that would have resulted in the death penalty. It would appear that, overall, the law was indeed beneficial to the suspected adulterer, and it revealed God's concern for her.

The Nazirite's hair, which was burned along with the peace offering (v. 18), could also be considered an offering. Nazirites expressed their commitment to God by offering a portion of their property (animal and food) but also a portion of themselves. This reinforced the seriousness of the dedication of their lives to God.

It can be observed that through the Nazirite ritual, the Israelite community was encouraged to serve God voluntarily with all their hearts. Just as all Israelites (men and women) could take the Nazirite vow, all believers today are called to offer themselves as living sacrifices to God (Rom. 12:1). Voluntary service implies a high understanding of Christian responsibility.

6:22–27. Priestly Blessing. The legal portion of Numbers (chaps. 5–6) ends with a blessing. This section (6:22–27) is usually referred to as the "priestly blessing." However, the text clearly indicates that the blessing comes from the Lord. In fact, the passage is introduced by the phrase "The Lord bless you" (v. 24) and ends with "I [the Lord] will bless them" (v. 27). The Lord is the ultimate source of blessing. The priest was merely the instrument mediating God's blessing to His people. Hence, the act of blessing (6:24–27) was not related to any kind of magical activity.

The reading of vv. 24–27 indicates that the blessing of the Lord is associated with "keeping" those blessed by Him (v. 24). In v. 24, the Hebrew verb *shamar*, "to keep," also means "to guard" or "to protect." It can refer to protection from physical harm and any sort of evil (Ps. 91:11). Thus, the divine act of blessing and keeping implied that the Lord would make His people prosperous (physically and spiritually). This blessing highlights the graciousness of God and the peace that only He can grant to His people. Notice the parallel lines in vv. 25–26. The first and third lines both reference the Lord's "face" or "countenance." Then in the second and fourth lines, there is another parallel: "And be gracious to you," "and give you peace." When the Lord makes His face shine upon His people, He looks straight at them, regards them favorably, and bestows on them His grace and peace. The grace of the Lord connotes His saving acts that bring genuine peace and goodness to the receiver (Ps. 31:16; 44:3; 67:1–2; 80:3, 7; 89:15). By contrast, at times God hides His face, which refers to the removal of His protection and to desolation (Is. 64:6–7). Since the people had been blessed by the Lord, they bore His name (v. 27); they belonged to Him. The name of God refers to His character, which is here revealed in

the blessing that constituted them as His people. God's blessed people are called to live holy lives that honor the Lord and are characterized by dependence on Him (Deut. 8:17–18).

7:1—8:26
Offerings, Lamps, and the Ordination of Levites

The current section records the tasks required for establishing the sanctuary services. This preparation at Sinai included offerings for the sanctuary (7:1–88), the setting of the lamps (7:89—8:4), and the ordination of the Levites (8:5–26). All these aspects were intended to foster a deep relationship between God and the people of Israel.

7:1–88. Offerings for the Sanctuary. The offerings described in this section are preceded by the anointing of the tabernacle and its furniture, especially the altar (vv. 1, 10, 84). The anointing functioned as an act of dedication. The tabernacle was set apart as a holy place from where the Lord revealed His will to the people. There they were drawn near to God through a variety of rituals. In addition, the text indicates that twelve princes, who were representatives of the Israelite community, brought offerings for twelve days—one prince each day (vv. 2–83).

The offerings for the sanctuary were divided into two categories. The first was comprised of offerings related to transportation—six wagons and twelve oxen in all (vv. 1–9). The Lord accepted these offerings and ordered that they should be given to the Levites who were to use them for the tabernacle service (vv. 5–8). They were to be used for the transportation of the sanctuary furnishings and materials, except for those items that were to be carried on the shoulders of the Kohath Levites (v. 9). The second category of offerings consisted of articles needed for worship—utensils, fine flour mixed with oil, incense, and animals (vv. 10–83). These offerings, which were contributions to support God's work, were brought by the leaders of the Israelite tribes (v. 2). The donations encouraged generosity and commitment among God's people. Through these offerings, the Israelites wholeheartedly dedicated themselves and their possessions to the Lord. The contributions were expensive. They included articles made of silver and gold, and there were also important plant products and animals (bulls, rams, lambs, goats) for the sacrifices. Although the individual contributions were similar, each leader brought his donation on a specific day, and record was made of every single offering. Individually and collectively, all children of God are responsible for doing His work.

All of this was done in the context of preparation for the next step of the journey, which would culminate in reaching the land of Canaan. The donations brought by the community demonstrate the depth of their motivation to fulfill God's mission. Taking the dedication of the Israelites as an example, God's people today are encouraged to use their resources for God's work. They are called to give their best in order to advance the kingdom of God (1 Cor. 16:1-4; 2 Cor. 8-9).

7:89—8:4. Arrangement of the Lamps. Before the lighting of the lamps, the Lord spoke to Moses inside the tabernacle from above the ark of the covenant (7:89; Ex. 25:22), commanding him to tell Aaron to set up the lamps so that they might give light (8:1-3). Thus, the sanctuary was inaugurated. The main purpose of the lamps was not only to illuminate the tabernacle but also to symbolize the light of God through Christ that illumines every human being (John 1:9; 8:12), as well as the knowledge or spiritual enlightenment that comes from the Holy Spirit (Zech. 4:1-14; Acts 2:1-4; Rev. 1:4; 4:5). The lighting of the lamps was one of the key daily activities in the tabernacle. The Lord ordered that the lamps should be kept burning continually (Ex. 27:20-21; Lev. 24:2-4). Therefore, they were to be maintained efficiently every day.

8:5-26. Ordination of the Levites. This portion can be divided into two parts: the cleansing of the Levites for service (vv. 5-22) and the age of Levitical service (vv. 23-26). The dedication of the tabernacle was followed by the consecration of those who should work in the sanctuary. The Levites were consecrated to serve in the sanctuary (vv. 6, 11) and were dedicated to the Lord as a wave offering (vv. 11, 13, 15, 21; see Lev. 7:30). They were taken from the community and were wholly dedicated to God as a living sacrifice. In their work in the sanctuary, they represented the people of God (Num. 8:19). Since the Levites were dedicated to God in place of the Israelites' firstborn, they, in a sense, became a permanent reminder of the deliverance God performed on behalf of the firstborn of Israel in Egypt (vv. 17-19).

Further, the Levites also reminded Israel of its identity as God's firstborn (Ex. 4:22-23). As such, the people were expected to obey the Lord and to serve the nations as a kingdom of priests (Ex. 19:5-6). The apostle Peter alluded to this

passage when he referred to God's church as a chosen people, a royal priesthood, and a holy nation (1 Pet. 2:9).

The consecration of the Levites included physical and spiritual cleansing (vv. 6-12) and the laying on of hands (v. 10). The laying on of hands in this passage expresses the idea of substitution: they were dedicated to God in place of the firstborn of the people of Israel (8:9-19). The ritual also emphasized the need for the removal of uncleanness from the Levites. They were to avoid any kind of ritual or moral defilement. As to the age of Levitical service, as already indicated, the Levites were to start their service at the age of twenty-five (v. 24) or thirty (see chap. 4) and retire at the age of fifty (v. 25).

9:1—10:10
Passover Regulations, the Cloud, and the Trumpets

As the departure from Sinai drew near, the Israelites celebrated the Passover (9:1-14), and the symbols of divine guidance were set in place (9:14—10:10).

9:1-14. Passover Regulations. The initial Passover served as a prelude to the departure of the Israelites from Egypt (Ex. 12). This second Passover was a prelude to the departure from the wilderness of Sinai, where the Israelites had stayed temporarily. It was celebrated at the appointed time, as required by the Lord (vv. 3-5). On this occasion, the Lord gave Israel additional regulations about its celebration. He specified two reasons for which someone could be exempt from celebrating the Passover at the regular appointed time. People defiled by a human corpse and those who were away on a distant journey were allowed to postpone the celebration (vv. 6-12). The Lord forbade defiled persons from partaking of His sacrifice. Whoever neglected this instruction was to be cut off from the people and thus assumed responsibility for the sin committed (v. 13; 15:30-31; see commentary on Lev. 7:11-21); no atoning sacrifice was available to such persons. Therefore, since anyone who touched a dead body remained unclean for seven days (Num. 19:11), the unclean people mentioned in the passage could not celebrate the Passover at the regular appointed time. They needed to be purified first and then celebrate the Passover later, as required by the Lord.

The Passover celebration was a reminder of Israel's redemption from Egypt and its beginning as a nation (Ex. 12:27). In a particular way, the Passover celebration of Numbers 9 reminded Israel that the Lord was still working out His plan to bring them into the land He had promised to them (Ex. 12:25). Hence, the Israelites started their journey from Sinai with confidence and hope. In addition to those who were Israelites by birth, the "sojourners" or "strangers" (that is, those who were non-Israelites by birth but committed to the Israelite faith and practice) were also allowed to celebrate the Passover (v. 14). God's blessings are not a matter of birth (Acts 10:34–35).

9:15–23. Cloud of Guidance. As the Lord was preparing His people for the next step of the journey, He provided the cloud as a means of guidance and as a sign of His presence. When the Israelites departed from Egypt, after the first Passover, the Lord went before them by day in a pillar of cloud, to lead the way, and by night in a pillar of fire, to give them light (Ex. 13:21). In Numbers 9:15, the appearance of the cloud on the tabernacle was a clear prelude to the coming journey. It reminded the Israelites that the Lord would continue to lead them toward the promised land. Moreover, the cloud indicated that God was dwelling in the tabernacle (Ex. 40:36–38). When the cloud rose from the tabernacle, the people marched, and when it settled, they encamped (Num. 9:17). No human being could predict or manipulate the movement of the cloud. The Lord alone was leading His people. The Lord's command is mentioned seven times in relation to the cloud (9:18 [x2]; 9:20 [x2]; 9:23 [x3]) to emphasize that not the cloud but the Lord Himself was the Leader of the pilgrimage. At His command, the people were to obey and act accordingly. In the Christian journey, it is important that believers fix their eyes upon Jesus—the author and finisher of their faith—by laying aside every sin that easily ensnares them. The promise of the pillar of cloud for Israel is similar to the NT promise of the Spirit for the church—God is present with His people, even until the end of the world (Matt. 28:20).

10:1–10. Silver Trumpets. The current passage ends the preparatory section. The silver trumpets were a supplementary means of guidance and communication. Although the people could see the cloud (Ex. 40:38), they needed an audible signal to commence or cease the march. These trumpets gave special signals, which the people understood and which directed their movements. The silver trumpets were used for different purposes: to summon the congregation to the door of the tent of meeting (vv. 3, 7), to call the tribal leaders to Moses (v. 4), to signal the breaking of camp and the beginning of the march (vv. 5–6), and to prepare the people for war or for the celebration of festivals (vv. 9–10). Trumpets facilitated clarity in communication as well as order and unity, characteristics God seeks among His people. God was and continues to be a God of order (cf. 1 Cor. 14:8–19, 33).

The text indicates that the silver trumpets were sounded during war so that the Lord would remember His people (i.e., "care for and attend to them"; cf. Gen. 8:1; 30:22; Ex. 2:24) and save them from their enemies (v. 9). The blowing of the trumpets could be considered a prayer offered to God for deliverance or a call to God to bring judgment on the enemies of His people. Similarly, Israel was encouraged to blow the trumpets to express joyful gratitude to God, as well as to mark religious festivals and sacred times (v. 10). The trumpets became a means to express dependency on God when threatened by enemies (vv. 9–10). This reinforced the people's confidence and hope in God's plan and in His power to fulfill His promises.

10:11—20:21

FROM SINAI TO KADESH

After the long preparatory stay at Sinai, the time came for God's people to continue the journey. They were expected to trust and submit to God as their effective leader. The journey from Sinai began on a note of obedience: when the cloud lifted up from above the tabernacle, the children of Israel departed (10:11–12). The text indicates that they followed the Lord's command given through Moses (10:13), but as the narrative develops, obedient Israel quickly became rebellious Israel (chaps. 11–20). Israel's rebellion highlights two important aspects: God's faithfulness and the tragic consequences of disobedience. Despite their insubordination, the Lord would fulfill His promises. He punished the rebellious generation and raised a new one willing to follow Him into Canaan.

10:11–36
Initiation of the Journey

The current section marks the beginning of the second phase of Israel's journey toward the promised land. It focuses on the obedience of Israel (vv. 11–28), the request Moses made to Hobab (vv. 29–32), and the attention given to the ark during the journey (vv. 33–36).

10:11-28. Obedient Israel. The children of Israel started their journey at the command of the Lord (v. 13). They marched according to their military subdivisions (vv. 14-28), following the directions given in Numbers 2 and 4. God's people were on the move. Order and discipline are not enemies to spirituality. God values obedience (see 1 Sam. 15:22; Is. 1:11-19) as an expression of a mature relationship with Him, not as mechanical submission to mere regulations.

10:29-32. Moses's Request to Hobab. During the journey, Moses asked Hobab to continue the journey with them and assured him that God would bless him. Thanks to his extensive knowledge of the wilderness, Hobab, Moses's brother-in-law, had been of valuable service to the Israelites. Moses held that Hobab's assistance was still needed. At first, Hobab declined the invitation (v. 30). However, it seems that he eventually agreed because his descendants were later found living in Canaan and sharing the land along with the Israelites (Judg. 1:16).

Moses's request to Hobab begs the question why additional human aid was needed when the Lord was leading the people by means of the cloud and through direct communication. Hobab's assistance indicates that the Lord accomplishes his plans not only in unique and miraculous ways but also with the assistance of human beings. In the Exodus account, God used Moses, Aaron, and other people, as well as the cloud, trumpets, and the ark of the covenant. The role of the cloud did not prevent the Israelites from thinking logically and putting their faith in action in order to work out the details of the journey (e.g., the encampment and its related aspects). Human beings worked in cooperation with God. Like Moses, current leaders of God's people should recognize and collaborate with valuable human resources that can advance the work of God.

10:33-36. The Role of the Ark. When the journey began, the ark of the covenant moved before the people (v. 33). The Levites were appointed to carry it. The ark and the cloud were not magical elements but physical things that the Lord used as symbols of His presence among His people. At a later time, some Israelites thought they could manipulate God's power through the ark, but their effort proved disastrous because God is not compelled by human schemes (1 Sam. 4).

The reference to the ark of the covenant of the Lord preceding the people (v. 33) seems puzzling at first because of previous instructions

to transport the sanctuary in the midst of the army (2:9-17; 10:11-21). Numbers 10:14 indicates that at the departure from Sinai, the tribe of Judah advanced first (cf. 2:9). Other tribes followed, along with some of the Levites (the sons of Gershon and Merari) carrying the tabernacle (i.e., its furniture, except the articles from the Most Holy Place; Num. 10:17; cf. 4:4, 15). Then came the Kohathite Levites carrying the holy things (10:21). The Gershon and Merari Levites preceded the Kohathites to facilitate the erection of the tabernacle before the arrival of the holy articles (v. 21). But there is a compelling solution to the puzzle: the Kohathites who followed the Gershon and Merari Levites did not carry the ark (10:21 does not specifically mention it) but rather left it for other Kohathites to carry out in front of the people (as is implied by vv. 35-36; see PP 375). The invocation of vv. 35-36 was an expression of absolute confidence in God's power to overcome the enemies of His people.

11:1—14:45
Rebellion and Its Suppression

This section introduces the struggle between God and Israel in the wilderness. The obedient and confident army of pilgrims (10:11-28) became insubordinate and discouraged. After three days' journey (10:33), the Israelites began to lose confidence in God's leadership, and eventually, the condition of their hearts became fully visible in their rebellion against God. As a result of disaffection, treason, and unfaithfulness to God's covenant, their entrance into Canaan was delayed for forty years (14:34). The rebellion developed slowly, with seven compounding complaints: misfortunes (11:1-3), food (11:4-35), Moses's leadership (12:1-16), the conditions in the promised land (13:1—14:45), Moses and Aaron's leadership (16:1—17:13), water (20:1-13), and further misfortunes (21:4-9). The grumbling escalated gradually from concerns about basic physical needs and expanded to social issues (leadership crises), finally culminating in deep spiritual trepidation (doubt about God's plan to bring Israel into Canaan). The ultimate origin of their complaints was distrust in God and rejection of His leadership (11:20). The Lord handled the multiple rebellions with much care.

11:1-3. Israel's Disaffection. This first complaint stirred up God's wrath, which was manifested in a burning fire (v. 1). Thanks to Moses's prayer of intercession, the fire ceased (v. 2).

The text does not mention the specific complaint. Apparently, this was a general objection to the hardships of life in the wilderness. Maybe the Israelites expected a short trip free of difficulties. The Lord did not ignore this internal unfaithfulness. God takes the attitudes of His people seriously and responds to them. One of the worst enemies of God's people is the discouragement that arises from within. Endurance in tribulation and confidence in God's promises should be a daily aspiration. The Lord is leading and promises to be with His children, even when they walk through the darkest of times (Ps. 23:4; 33:19; 56:3; 147:3; cf. Matt. 28:20). He also declares that the one who endures to the end will be saved (Matt. 24:13).

11:4–35. Rebellion Related to Food. Contrary to the unspecified complaint of vv. 1–3, here the grievance is clear. The concern was about food. As with the former complaint, this one was followed by Moses's prayer and God's response. The people grumbled about their diet, but their words concealed a deeper concern. The text specifies that they desired the fish they ate in Egypt (i.e., their mind went back to the Egyptian diet; v. 5), in rejection of the manna provided by the Lord (v. 6). The Lord understood that their true issue was distrust in Him (v. 20).

Although the complainers mentioned some vegetables and other vegetarian delicacies that they enjoyed in Egypt (vv.4–5), their major concern involved meat, including fish, which is repeated seven times in the narrative (vv. 4, 13 [x2], 18 [x3], 21). Requesting fish in the wilderness was futile because there were no rivers or lakes. Acquiring fish would require a return to Egypt. They preferred bondage over the Lord's freedom if freedom meant living without fish. They had forgotten Egypt's oppression, and they dared to say that they had lived better in Egypt (v. 18). Testing God in this way, similar to the incident at Meribah (Ex. 17:1–7), was a clear sign of unbelief and disobedience that needed to be dealt with (Ps. 95:9–11). This was an act of high treason; a rejection of the authority of the supreme Leader. In a military setting, this represents a criminal act, which called for a severe penalty.

Moses as a man of prayer consulted his superior, the Lord (vv. 10–15). But his prayer was also a complaint in itself, for out of frustration, he went so far as to request that God take his life (v. 15). Moses complained about his many responsibilities, which he could no longer bear alone, and about his inability to provide meat to the grumbling Israelites. But the Lord reminded Moses that He was in charge of the situation (v. 23). He appointed seventy elders to assist Moses (vv. 24–30) and provided quail (vv. 31–32) to feed the people. Like the apostles at the Pentecost, the seventy elders received the Spirit in order to perform their ministry. The Spirit they received belonged to the Lord, not to Moses (vv. 25, 29). The Lord provided quail to meet the demand of the complainers, but He punished their rebellion with a severe plague (vv. 33). The Israelites were overly worried about their material needs and had lost confidence in God's leadership. What was needed was temperance and trust in the Lord, the One who is always able to provide (Deut. 8:3; Matt. 4:4). God's children should not be overcome with the worries of life (Luke 21:34) but should remain confident in God.

12:1–16. Insubordination of Miriam and Aaron. The two earlier rebellions came from among the people while this one rose from among the leaders of the people. Miriam and Aaron, who were Moses's primary assistants (Mic. 6:4) as well as his own sister and brother, undermined his authority. Their grievance was twofold: (1) they were uncomfortable with Moses's marriage (v. 1), and (2) they objected to the unique relationship between Moses and God (v. 2). As in the preceding insurrection, Moses interceded for the errant leaders, and the Lord's response was swift (vv.13–16).

The text declares that Moses was a humble person (v. 3). The Hebrew word 'anaw ("bowed," "humble") denotes the state of someone who is in deep distress or need and humbly seeks help from God alone (Ps. 40:17; 102:1). It implies a trustful, unpretentious attitude. The account mentions that before Moses could do anything, the Lord "heard" (i.e., He took note of the complaint made against Moses; v. 2). This implies that in the face of unjust attack, Moses was ready to submit his fate. During Miriam and Aaron's revolt, he endured the attacks patiently and did not seek vindication for himself or his family. He left this to God.

Most Bible translations introduce this rebellious account by suggesting that both Miriam and Aaron spoke against Moses (v. 1). However, the Hebrew verb translated "to speak" is in the feminine form third person singular and can be rendered "and she spoke," which suggests that Miriam was the one who initiated the complaint; her name precedes that of Aaron. The grammatical structure suggests that Miriam spoke against Moses (i.e., rebelled against him), and Aaron supported her as an accomplice. This may explain why she was disciplined while Aaron was spared (v. 10). Furthermore, in this case, if Aaron had been punished with leprosy, as Miriam was, Israel would no longer have had a high priestly intercessor since priests could not enter the sanctuary when afflicted with leprosy. In fact, his punishment would not have corresponded to the crime; it arguably would have been too severe.

Miriam and Aaron's objection to Moses's wife seems to have been at least partially due to her ethnicity. Miriam was displeased with Moses because he had not married an Israelite woman but had instead taken a wife from a different ethnic group (v. 1). But it appears that the issue also went beyond ethnicity. Their contention was that the Lord had spoken through them, not only through Moses (v. 2). Miriam and Aaron challenged the uniqueness of Moses's status and apparently wanted to use their own position as leaders to augment their social position or influence among the Israelites. It is possible that they interpreted the influence of Moses's wife as diminishing their own leadership roles. Their discontent was evidently with the subordinate position they held in relationship to Moses. They were envious and arrogant, similar to Lucifer's transgression in heaven (Is. 14:12-14). God's established order was being questioned.

The narrative mentions that the Lord heard the complaint (v. 2) and intervened. The Lord summoned Moses, Aaron, and Miriam to the tent of meeting (v. 4) to settle the matter. In the course of events, the Lord vindicated Moses while the insubordinate leaders were rebuked (vv. 5-11). It is indeed from God's heavenly sanctuary that He judges and defends believers and condemns the wicked. Because of her sin, and as a ringleader of the rebellion, Miriam was punished. She suffered a severe skin disease, designated by the word *tsar'at*, a term that encompassed various malignant skin diseases, including leprosy (v. 10; see Lev. 13:1). Instead of being exalted, she was publicly disgraced. God's reaction demonstrated that He does not approve of ethnic hatred, jealousy, or insubordination among His people. Aaron was not physically punished but was humiliated through his association with Miriam. He requested to be spared from punishment (v. 11). As a high priest, instead of praying for Miriam, he asked Moses, whom he called "my lord," to intercede for her healing (vv. 11-12). Aaron confessed his sin and recognized the authority given to Moses by the Lord.

Dispute over position and influence is a permanent issue that generates dysfunctional relationships inside and outside the church. God's people are encouraged to learn from Miriam and Aaron's experience and to focus on humility and loyalty to their appointed leaders (Ps. 75:5-7; Phil. 2:5-8; Titus 3:1-2). At the same time, leaders should trust fully in God and humbly seek guidance from Him and from others who have also been appointed by God to lead His people. Moreover, securing power by using one's status, authority, and social or religious connections can endanger the mission of God's people. Each believer should promote unity and collaboration in the service of God and His people.

13:1—14:45. Report of the Spies and Rebellion. The people reached the edge of the promised land, but unfortunately, they became completely disoriented and lost hope. The spies entered the promised land and made an initial survey. Sadly, ten of them were unfaithful to God. As a result, they brought a *dibbah*—"bad report" (13:32)—that generated fear, despair, and distrust in the hearts of the Israelites. They questioned God's motives and, therefore, renounced His leadership. To ensure the success of their rebellion, they decided to select another leader who could take them back to Egypt (14:4). They broke the covenant made at Sinai, but God, in His great steadfast love, did not give them up; they were still His people. The section can be divided into five parts: (1) the sending of the spies (13:1-25), (2) the report of the spies (13:26-33), (3) the people's rebellion (14:1-10), (4) God's forgiveness and punishment (14:11-38), and (5) a false repentance and an unsuccessful battle (14:39-45).

The spies were sent, with God's approval (13:1-25), on a military mission. They were to determine whether the inhabitants of the land were weak or strong, few or many, and whether or not the cities were well fortified (vv. 17-19). Before leaving for their mission, Moses commanded them to *wehitkhazaqtem* (from *khazaq*)—"strengthen yourselves" or "be courageous"—and to bring back some fruit from the land (v. 20). Therefore, they returned to the camp with an excellent sample of the fruits of the land (v. 23). Unfortunately, the abundant natural fruit did not inspire the people to bear spiritual fruit (cf. John 15:1-8; Gal. 5:22-26).

The report of the spies (13:26-33) contained two elements: a depiction of the fruitfulness of the land (v. 27) and an exaggerated description of the strength of its inhabitants (vv. 28-29). Ten of the spies gave way to pessimism and insisted that it was impossible for the Israelites to conquer the land. They purposely exaggerated the truth by describing the land of Canaan as a land that devoured its inhabitants (i.e., a dangerous place to live; 13:32) though at the beginning of their report they called it a land flowing with milk and honey (i.e., a place where it was good to live; v. 27). Their report generated fear, leading to despair and insurrection. The other two spies, Joshua and Caleb, did not deny or downplay the challenges that the Canaanites presented, but they insisted that Israel would be able to overcome their foes through God's power (13:30; 14:6–9). Because of their unbelief, the people accepted the lie rather than the truth. The majority is not always right.

The apex of the rebellion is described in 14:1–10. The people wept in expression of their hopelessness and accused God of having malevolent plans for them (vv. 1–3). They wanted to return to Egypt, which in comparison, looked like a better option (vv. 3–4). They despaired, despite the presence of the Lord in their midst (v. 9). The Canaanites had already been deprived of divine protection and could have been defeated (v. 9), but the positive contribution of Joshua and Caleb was completely ignored (v. 10).

The Lord threatened to suppress the dangerous rebellion by destroying the entire nation except Moses, from whom He would raise a new community (vv. 11–38). But Moses interceded for his people, and the Lord revealed His grace and forgave them. However, the consequence of their rebellion remained. The unfaithful spies died (vv. 36–37) and the people became wanderers in the wilderness for forty years, unable to enter the land they despised (vv. 30–35). Some of the people attempted to challenge God's judgment (vv. 39–45). Despite expressing repentance, they sinned further by attempting to take the promised land by their own force rather than waiting for God's direction. The military attack they launched on the Canaanites without God's command resulted in utter disaster (14:45). The Lord would grant the old unfaithful generation what they requested—to die in the wilderness (14:2); they would not reach Canaan.

15:1–41
Additional Legislation

The laws described in this section are, in a certain way, connected to the context of the preceding rebellion. Despite the people's rejection of God's promise, the Lord gave them hope and reaffirmed His determination to give them the land (15:1–4). He insisted that the children of Israel would inhabit the promised land and that they would bring offerings to Him in that land (15:2, 18–19). They were to make tassels on the corners of their garments to remember all the commandments of the Lord and the importance of a holy life (15:38–39). God's purpose could not ultimately be defeated, even by His rebellious people.

15:1–31. Laws Concerning Offerings. The laws described in this section concern votive, thanksgiving, and purification offerings. The Lord instructed His people that once they occupied the promised land and were enjoying its produce, they were to offer the firstfruits of their labor to the Lord (vv. 1–21). Grain and libation offerings were to accompany every gift or burnt offering brought to the Lord, and He promised to accept their offerings, as well as those of the faithful strangers dwelling among them (vv. 8–10, 13–15). In Canaan, the people were also to offer to the Lord a heave or set-apart contribution offering of grain in the form of bread (vv. 17–21) as an expression of gratitude to God for providing bread from the land for them.

In addition, knowing that people are sinful by nature, the Lord allowed for the community to bring an offering for its unintentional sin (vv. 22–29; see Lev. 4:13–21); in this case, a burnt offering instead of a sin/purification offering. The function of the burnt offering was now enlarged. But if an individual, not the community, committed an unintentional sin, then the sin/purification offering would be required (Num. 15:27–29; cf. Lev. 4:1–12). The sacrificial ritual aimed at restoring a peaceful relationship with God. However, there was a type of sin for which the sacrificial system did not provide atonement. This was the case of the sin committed defiantly or presumptuously (lit. "with a high hand"; v. 30). This was considered to be premeditated defiance against the Lord, a sin committed with the full knowledge of one's action. No sacrificial victim could bear this sin, and consequently, the sinner would have to bear his or her own sin (v. 31). The perpetrator of such defiant sin was to be cut off from the people (v. 30; see Lev. 7:20); that is to say, he or she would be permanently excluded from being part of God's people. The sin described in the following section belongs to this category of defiant sin, for which sinners show no remorse. They have rejected God's grace.

15:32–36. Stoning of a Sabbath Breaker. The preceding passage (vv. 30–31) dealt with sins committed in open rebellion against the Lord. Now the case of a Sabbath breaker is given as an illustration of this type of sin. The prohibition of work on the Sabbath was extended to outlaw the act of lighting a fire in one's home (Ex. 35:2–3). The Lord ordered that during the sojourn in the wilderness, no fires were to be built on the Sabbath. This was probably based on the fact that the climate was warm. The prohibition appears to have been temporary; it would not be applied in the land of Canaan, where significant climate changes would render fire a necessity (cf. PP 408). The one who gathered wood on the Sabbath while sojourning in the wilderness did so as an open, defiant act against God's law. Since this was a violation of the Decalogue itself rather than the Levitical laws, there was no precedent or guidance regarding how the person should be punished. The Lord provided the needed legislation; the person would be put to death (vv. 35–36). Rejecting the Lord meant rejecting life.

15:37–41. Law of Tassels. A tassel is an ornament for clothing. God required the Israelites to attach fringes or tassels to the corners of their garments (Deut. 22:12). These would remind the Israelites to obey God's commandments instead of following their own desires (v. 39). The verb *zakar* ("to remember"), which also connotes "to think about or meditate upon," is used twice in the passage to highlight the role of the tassels (vv. 39–40). The tassels were intended to help the Israelites meditate upon God's commandments and to practice them in order to be holy for God (i.e., to be consecrated to Him; vv. 40–41). In other words, the tassels were a symbol of the consecration of the Israelites to the Lord; their adornment was to be a holy life (v. 40). The tassels identified them as worshipers of the Lord.

This instruction reminded the rebellious people that the Lord expected faithfulness and obedience to the covenant law. The blue thread or cord (v. 38) included in the tassels was significant because it was the same color used in the tabernacle and the clothing of the priests (Ex. 25:4; 26:1, 4, 31; 27:16; 39:1; etc.). Wearing tassels thus emphasized that each Israelite was a member of a kingdom of priests (Ex. 19:5–6), with specific privileges and responsibilities. In Revelation 3:18, believers are exhorted to acquire white garments (i.e., the gift of the righteousness of Jesus Christ, which covers their sinfulness and produces righteous deeds in their lives).

16:1—17:13
Rebellion and Its Suppression

In the previous insurrection (Num. 14), God's people clearly chose desertion. In their spirit of revolt, they declared that the Lord had brought them to Canaan in order for their wives and children to fall by the sword and that it would be better to return to Egypt (14:3). Driven by such interests, the Israelites multiplied reasons to give up the promised land. They lost their hope and commitment to God's plan. In the rebellion described in chapters 16–17, their insolence reached its highest and most dangerous point.

Korah, Dathan, and Abiram's rebellion was the worst in the history of the children of Israel. This rebellion, involving both common people and religious leaders, was an attempt to overthrow the Israelite political and religious system established by God. Similar to the rebellion of chapter 12, this one also rose from within the distinguished leaders of God's people and aimed to challenge the leadership system operated by Moses and Aaron. Korah, a Levite (and a close relative of Moses and Aaron), was displeased with his position and wanted Aaron's (16:10). Dathan and Abiram, descendants of Reuben, the firstborn of Israel, believed it was their natural right to claim the preeminence of the civil power held by Moses (16:1–3). Their dissatisfaction escalated from envy to all-out rebellion. The Lord suppressed the mutiny and reaffirmed the leadership He had appointed.

16:1–50. Rebellion and Suppression. The rebellion of Korah and his followers was a direct affront against God's appointed leaders. They considered the supremacy of Moses and Aaron unjustified in view of the fact that all Israelites were holy (v. 3). They justified the insurrection on the basis of the people's holiness. But Moses clarified that they were actually challenging the holiness of those chosen by the Lord to serve Him in a special way. He unambiguously declared to Korah and his supporters that the Lord would reveal to all Israel who was holy, who belonged to Him, and who was designated to come near to Him in the sanctuary (v. 5). Biblical references to coming near to God point to either the act of bringing an offering to God at His altar or the fact of being chosen by God to minister in His presence (Lev. 1:5, 13–14; Ex. 29:4; Num. 16:9, 40; 18:4). Verse 5 seems to contain both aspects. This verse implies that the person who was holy was someone chosen by the Lord to officiate in His presence.

According to Korah, each Israelite was holy—that is to say, fitted to do the same service performed by Aaron (v. 3). This could also mean that there was no need for a special priestly class among the Israelites because the Lord was in their midst. However, the judgment that fell on Korah and his followers (16:31–35) and the test related to the rod of Aaron (Num. 17) implied that holiness should be also understood in terms of degrees. Though all the Israelites were expected to be holy (Ex. 19:6; Lev. 20:26), Aaron was invested with a special degree of holiness in the sense that he was separated by the Lord for a specific work (16:40; Lev. 8). Moses told Korah and his followers that it was God's prerogative to decide who should come near to Him to minister on behalf of the people (v. 5). The leadership of Moses and Aaron was determined by the fact that the Lord appointed them to their functions. Korah probably understood the priesthood in terms of social power and self-exaltation rather than service for the benefit of others. In line with ANE practices, Moses insisted that all contenders undergo a test to indicate who was holy (v. 7).

In their rebellion, Dathan and Abiram derided God's plan concerning the promised land. They applied the expression "land flowing with milk and honey" to Egypt (v. 13) rather than to the place where the Lord was leading them. They thoroughly misrepresented the ways of God. They ultimately branded Moses as an impostor, deceiving people with false promises (vv. 13–14). Dathan and Abiram also argued that God's promises had not been fulfilled. When the Lord took the Israelites out of Egypt, He had promised to give them a blessed land (Ex. 3:8, 17; 33:3; Lev. 20:24). The insurgent leaders argued that this was simply an illusion (v. 14). They conveniently chose to forget that Moses had already brought them to the border of the promised land. They had failed to enter it on account of their own unfaithfulness and rebellious spirit (see Num. 13–14). In their despair, Dathan and Abiram regarded Moses as a kidnapper who had made a sophisticated plan to take the people hostage in the wilderness in order to rule over them (16:13). They insinuated that he intended to put out the eyes of the people so that they would not discern his scheme (v. 14).

Moses forcefully rejected all the accusations. He argued that he had neither harmed the people nor taken anything from them (v. 15). He committed the matter to the Lord through prayer by asking God not to respect or accept their offering (v. 15). The expression is reminiscent of Cain's experience, when God did not respect his offering (Gen. 4:5). Moses asked God to deny them favor or acceptance when they came into His presence. Filled with defiance, the rebels elected to offer incense to God as evidence of His approval of their ministry (v. 18). But the ringleaders were not accepted into God's presence. They were swallowed up by the earth, and their followers were devoured by fire (vv. 31–35). Instead of mourning for their complicity in Korah's rebellion, the people engaged in a much larger rebellion and might have been completely annihilated (vv. 45–46) if Aaron, at Moses's direction, had not rushed to intercede for them. Even so, 14,700 people died (vv. 47–49).

Aaron stood between the dead and the living to halt the devastating plague (v. 48). He stood in the transition point between death and life. Through his intercession, atonement was made for the people. In vv. 46–47, the verb *kapar* ("to make atonement," "to ransom") is used twice to express the work of Aaron on behalf of God's people. In the immediate context of the passage, this term conveys the idea of removing sin to avert punishment. In the Israelite sacrificial system, the more common means of expiation was blood (Lev. 17:11–14). The ritual of expiation of sin by blood was performed during the daily sacrificial service (Lev. 4:20) and especially on the Day of Atonement (Lev. 16). The sacrificial blood represented the life that was given on behalf of the penitent. It substituted for the sinner's blood (i.e., life). However, in the narrative of Numbers 16, atonement was made through the burning of incense (vv. 46–48). Incense could also be used by the high priest to make atonement for sin and thus avert God's anger. It is interesting to observe that the incense offered by the rebels brought wrath while that offered by Aaron, the divinely chosen high priest, brought relief (vv. 18, 35, 47–48). The incense itself had no supernatural power to effect atonement, but the Lord used it to reaffirm that He would work only through His appointed instruments.

The atonement performed by Aaron (vv. 46–48) prefigured the ministry of Jesus Christ on behalf of the human race. Jesus Christ, the true high priest, made atonement through offering His own blood (Heb. 2:2–17; 9:11–12). Today, through His ministry in the heavenly sanctuary, He applies the benefits of His expiatory death to all believers (Heb. 7:25; 10:22; Rev. 8:2–4).

The insurrection of Korah, Dathan, and Abiram resulted in a significant loss of human life. The ringleaders, their 250 closest associates, and their

14,700 accomplices perished (vv. 32, 35, 49). Why was the punishment so harsh? The core issue was that the rebels "rejected the Lord" (v. 30). The Hebrew verb *na'ats* (to "reject," "spurn," "disdain," "abhor") is used in v. 30 and previously in 14:23 to express the rebellious attitude of the people during the mutiny launched by the unfaithful spies. The use of this verb in v. 30 indicates that the rebels treated God disrespectfully; they rejected His authority and leadership and considered it devoid of any value. Such behavior was nothing less than a fundamental breaking of the covenant, a blasphemy that called for severe discipline and that placed the perpetrators outside the covenant blessings (Deut. 31:20–21). It was for such blasphemy that the Lord decreed that the old generation was banned from entering the promised land (Num. 14:28–33). The entire rebellion demonstrated that the Israelites did not want to remain on God's side. This was a serious crime, an act of treason. Hence, the Lord destroyed the insurgents and moved forward with the remnant of His people toward the promised land. Korah's rebellion should alert Christians to the fact that envy, discontent, insubordination, and greed promote the worst in humanity. The account of Korah also places a high value on the importance of the unity of God's people in their journey to the promised land.

17:1–13. Rod of Aaron. In order to reaffirm the election of Aaron, the Lord made the staff of Aaron to blossom. A staff symbolized the authority of a person. When Aaron's staff bloomed, his special call, anointing, and authority from God were confirmed, and the arguments ceased (vv. 5, 10). The almond was the earliest blossoming plant in the region; it could, therefore, signify the preeminence of Aaron's office. As highlighted in an interesting wordplay in Jeremiah, the sprouting of the almond branch (Heb. *shaqed*) also indicates that the Lord watches (Heb. *shaqad*) over His word and makes certain it is fulfilled (Jer. 1:11, 12). What He decides to do, He does.

18:1—19:22
Additional Legislation

In the previous chapters, Korah and his supporters challenged the exclusive leadership of Moses and Aaron, but the Lord intervened and revealed that the appointment of Aaron was not arbitrary. In chapter 18, He reaffirmed the privileges and responsibilities of the Levites and priests. In this section, the Lord instructed His people concerning the impurity resulting from contact with a corpse. (Perhaps this instruction is placed here because of the many people who died in Korah's rebellion; 19:1–22.)

18:1–32. Duties and Provision for the Levites and Priests. The current passage is a general summary of the responsibility of the Levites and their relationship to the priests, the descendants of Aaron (vv. 1–7). It also deals with the dues owed to the priests for their ministry (vv. 8–20) and the tithe that the Lord assigned to the Levites (vv. 21–24). In their turn, Levites were to give tithe to the priests (vv. 25–32).

The duties of Levites and priests were already described in chapters 1 and 3–4. The current section (18:1–7) insists on the importance of order in the service at the sanctuary. The Levites had the responsibility of guarding the sanctuary, preventing the approach of any unauthorized persons (v. 22), and performing the tasks assigned to them by the priests. Priests had the exclusive duty of ministering before the ark of the covenant and offering sacrifices. Thus, the issue over the priestly roles was settled in order to avoid another disastrous situation like that of Korah. The divine instruction that Aaron and his descendants should bear the iniquity related to the sanctuary or their priesthood (v. 1) indicates that the priests were fully responsible for matters related to the sanctuary and priesthood. If the sanctuary or the priesthood became inadvertently defiled, the priests and Levites should be held responsible. Thus the appointment to serve at the sanctuary carried with it a heavy responsibility.

In vv. 8–19, the Lord gave instructions about particular offerings that would go to Aaron and his sons as reward for their service at the sanctuary. The Lord pronounced that this practice would be considered a perpetual covenant of salt before the Lord (v. 19). In many ancient cultures, salt was understood as a symbol of preservation and was employed during alliances to underline the idea that the terms of the agreement would be long preserved. The covenant between God and the priests is said to be "of salt" because it was to be a permanent covenant (v. 19), for as long as the system was operative. The significance of the Levites' service was honored; the Lord assigned them the tithe (vv. 21, 23–24). The Israelites gave the tithe to the Lord, but the Lord gave it to the Levites for their service in the sanctuary. The Levites also gave a tithe from the tithe they received, and God assigned it to the priests (vv. 25–32). The system was based on the goodness of the Lord and the response of love and gratitude of the people. These same principles should continue to guide contemporary believers on matters related to tithe and offerings (cf. 1 Chr. 29:14).

19:1–22. Red Heifer Ritual. This was a ritual intended to remove impurity caused by contact with a dead body. The ritual aimed at the preservation of purity in the community and implied that God's purpose was to preserve the lives of His people. The description of the ritual and its ramifications can be divided into four sections: (1) the burning of the red heifer to make ashes (vv. 1–10), (2) the purification of someone who touched a corpse (vv. 11–13), (3) the process of cleansing those who became unclean (vv. 14–20), and (4) the uncleanness of the person who manipulated the water mixed with the ashes from the red heifer (vv. 21–22).

The unblemished red heifer was slaughtered and incinerated outside the camp by an Israelite, under the supervision of the priest, to produce the ashes (v. 3; cf. Lev. 4:11–12). During the burning of the animal, some cleansing agents were added to the fire (cedar wood, hyssop, and scarlet; see v. 6). These elements also appeared in other purification ceremonies, such as the cleansing of the leper (Lev. 14:4). Their usage in purification rituals was significant. The scarlet, for example, symbolized life by its red color, which recalled blood—a key element for a ritual that corrected a state of uncleanness and death. There was also hyssop, which the psalmist uses figuratively as a cleansing element from sin (Ps. 51:7) even though he clearly recognizes that the Lord is the one who blots out transgression (51:7), not the hyssop.

In the process of cleansing, the ashes were mixed with "living" or "fresh" water, usually translated as "running water" (v. 17). The flowing water used in the red heifer ritual worked as a symbol of purification and life, as in other biblical rituals (Ex. 29:4; Lev. 8:6; 14:5–7, 50–52; 15:13; 16:4, 24). The water, as well as other elements used in the ritual, pointed to the basic elements of life. The product (ashes plus flowing water) served for the purification of the uncleanness that resulted from touching a dead body or coming into contact with objects or places defiled by a corpse (vv. 9, 13, 17, 20). The Hebrew word *khatta't* ("sin"), used in v. 9, could designate either (1) sin (i.e., a moral failure) or (2) the offering brought for sin or impurity (Lev. 4:3). The sin offering was performed in response to immoral actions as well as physical impurities (Lev. 5:2–3, 6; 12:6–8). When the sin offering was brought

for physical impurity, its purpose was to decontaminate by removing impurity from the defiled person or object. In either case, the core issue was that of sin and its effects—death, defilement, and a state of sin.

The red heifer ritual dealt mainly with ceremonial uncleanness. It is mentioned that the person on whom the water of purification was applied remained defiled until nightfall or even for days afterward (Num. 19:10–12, 19). The ritual aimed at maintaining purity or life among God's people by cleansing them from physical defilement. It should be remembered that the Lord disapproves of impurity, whether moral or ceremonial. The text declares that an unclean person who voluntarily refused to make use of the water of purification was to be cut off from Israel (19:13, 20).

There is a paradox in the ritual of the red heifer in the fact that what cleansed the defiled person defiled the clean one. In fact, those who performed some roles, such as the burning of the red heifer or the manipulation of its ashes, became ceremonially unclean while those on whom the same ash was applied were purified (vv. 7–8, 10, 18–19, 21–22). The connection between impurity and death was established in order to instill in the Israelites the fundamental truth that life is found only in the Lord (see Leviticus: Introduction). Anything related to death was foreign to the Lord and His sanctuary. The ritual system suggested that the Lord has power over death and that He can remove it from His people. This was to take place through the death of the Son of God, who cleanses sinners from all impurity (Heb. 9:13–14; 1 John 1:7).

20:1–21
Final Events at Kadesh

Following the turbulence of Korah's rebellion, the children of Israel resumed their journey and arrived at Kadesh. Two remarkable events took place there, namely, the death of Miriam and another rebellion against the Lord involving the people as well as their key leaders (Moses and Aaron).

20:1–13. Death of Miriam and a New Rebellion. Numbers 20 begins with the death of Miriam (v. 1) and ends with the death of Aaron (v. 28). Miriam, one of the most influential leaders of Israel, died at Kadesh. Her death reminded the people of Israel that, as the Lord had declared, the unfaithful generation would not enter Canaan (14:35). Sadly, shortly after her death, the people launched a new rebellion (v. 2). At first, the issue appears to center on the lack of water (v. 2), but a deeper motivation is disclosed in vv. 3–5, where it is indicated that the people questioned God's plan to take them to the promised land.

Because of the lack of water at Kadesh, the children of Israel gathered together to oppose Moses and Aaron (v. 2). This expression denotes the idea of disaffection, a kind of aggressive attitude born out of despair and leading to riot (cf. 16:3, 19, 42). The text mentions that they had a *rib* with Moses (v. 3). This Hebrew verb generally expresses an idea of contending and quarreling, or in many OT contexts, it is a legal battle. In this context, it implies a struggle with words. Harsh words were addressed to Moses (vv. 3–5). The same verb is used in v. 13 to indicate that the whole rebellion was not directed against Moses but against the Lord Himself. The waters were called Meribah (quarrelling or contention) because the children of Israel contended or quarreled with the Lord (v. 13). The army rebelled against their Chief Commander—God Himself.

The people again gave the impression that Moses had taken them hostage, and they referred to the desert where they were as an "evil/terrible [Heb. *ra'*] place"—that is to say, a place of misfortune or calamity, a place deprived of food and water (vv. 4–5). They lost hope and confidence in God's guidance and providence and complained; they asked why Moses had brought them out of Egypt (v. 5). They had not learned from previous experience that the Lord was always able to provide for their basic needs. This time, the Lord did not punish them. He had compassion on them (Ps. 78:38).

In face of the new provocation, Moses became exceedingly frustrated and lost his patience. The Lord instructed Moses and Aaron to speak or command the rock to produce water (v. 8). Instead of speaking to the rock, Moses struck it twice (v. 11). The act of Moses and Aaron is referred to by the verb *marah*, "to rebel against" (i.e., a willful refusal to obey the Lord; Num. 20:24; 27:14). Rebellion had made its way into the hearts of the people and their leaders.

Psalm 106:32–33 indicates that Moses spoke rashly with his lips. This denotes that his statement in Numbers 20:10b was the root of the issue. By these words, Moses and Aaron failed to respect God in the eyes of Israel and thereby deprived Him of His due honor. Moreover, the sin of Moses gave the people occasion to question whether his past course of action was truly under God's control. They may have also thought that like Moses, they could excuse their own sins (cf. PP 417). Even though Moses and Aaron did not revere the Lord in the eyes of the children of Israel (v. 12), the narrative declares that God's holiness was ultimately validated (v. 13). God proved His holiness in His adherence to His promises (see Ezek. 20:41; 28:25; 39:27). Despite their insurrection, the Lord performed a miracle in their favor and manifested His faithfulness and power.

Moses and Aaron exercised significant influence over the people as their primary leaders. Their great responsibility and privilege required impeccable behavior as representatives of the Lord. The Lord could not ignore their sin without showing partiality and, therefore, a lack of integrity as a righteous God. As a result of Moses and Aaron's sin, the people learned that the Lord does not excuse any sin, not even that of leaders. In His dealings with Moses and Aaron, God showed Himself to be reliable and trustworthy.

This account of Moses's failure demonstrates the objectivity of the biblical narratives. Contrary to other ancient writings that highlight only the strong points of their protagonists, the Bible does not overlook the weaknesses of its great heroes. It narrates even the failings of God's honorable people. Christians are encouraged to learn from the mistakes of their predecessors and remain fully dependent on God. God is the only true hero of the Bible. It is on Him that all human beings must rely for their victory. The narrative also speaks to church leaders. To them also the Lord has given great privileges and responsibilities. Pressures and frustrations will not excuse rash actions or a lack of self-control. They must properly represent the Lord at all times before His people.

20:14–21. Edom Refuses Passage to Israel. The shortest route to the promised land lay through the land of Edom, but when the Israelites arrived there, they confronted opposition. Moses kindly appealed to the Edomites to allow passage through their land, but the Edomites refused the request. The people were obliged to turn around or fight against Edom. At this point, the Lord intervened and directed the Israelites to take a long detour around Edom. This time, the new generation of God's people quietly obeyed Him. Sometimes, in order for the Lord to lead His children to their spiritual, social, or professional destinations, He guides them along a detour. However, a detour with Him is preferable to a direct route without Him.

20:22—36:13

JOURNEY FROM KADESH
TO THE PLAINS OF MOAB

The last part of the book describes the journey of the Israelites from Kadesh to the plains of Moab. The Lord's people finally reached the border of the promised land. Over the course of the journey, the Israelites vacillated between hope and despair, trust and distrust, obedience and disobedience. Among them, there remained a significant number of the old generation who had escaped from Egypt. This explains why their victory over Arad was followed by a rebellion against God because of the lack of food and the long journey (21:1–9). Their victory over Sihon and Og was also followed by an act of idolatry and immorality at the border of the promised land (21:21–34; 25:1–18). Despite their deficiency, the Lord continued to lead them. Reaching the plains of Moab, the new generation was ready to inherit the land of Canaan. A new census was carried out (26:1–51), and additional instructions were given that pertained to the inheritance rights of daughters (27:1–11; 36:1–13), the calendar of festivals for regular celebration of God's goodness (28:1—29:40), the division of the land (32:1–42; 34:1–29), and the Levitical cities and cities of refuge (35:1–8; 35:9–34). The instructions renewed the hope of the children of God, for they pointed toward a bright future in the promised land.

20:22–29
Death of Aaron at Hor

The children of Israel went from Kadesh to Hor, where Aaron died. His death confirmed the temporary function of his priesthood, which was a type of the perpetual priesthood of Christ (Heb. 7:23–24). In Hebrews 7:25, the apostle Paul exalts the importance of the permanent and unchangeable priesthood of Christ based on the fact that He is alive; He will never die. Consequently, Christ is able to always intercede on behalf of those who come to God through Him. The apostle insists that since Christ was tempted in all points but did not sin, He is able to assist His children in their weaknesses and give them His grace (Heb. 4:15–16).

The death of Aaron, the high priest, meant that a new high priest had to be appointed (20:28). In obedience to God, Moses took Aaron and his son to Mount Hor, where Aaron would die. But before Aaron died, Moses removed the priestly vestments from him and put them on Eleazar,

his son. This was an act of investiture by which Eleazar, the priest, was installed as high priest among the people of Israel. This was not a pompous ceremony or celebration but a simple and silent transfer of responsibilities under the guidance of the Lord. The appointment of Eleazar indicated that the spiritual leadership was now being transferred to a new generation.

21:1–35
From Hor to the Plains of Moab

From Hor, the Israelites moved closer toward the promised land. Before reaching the plains of Moab, they experienced a prelude to God's victory over the unfaithful nations. With God's assistance, they defeated the Canaanites of Arad (21:1–3). But after the victory over Arad, they again became impatient and complained against God's leadership (vv. 4–9). Nevertheless, their complaints did not prevent God from leading them in their journey (vv. 10–20). The Israelites traveled as a victorious people and, as such, defeated King Sihon (vv. 21–32), and King Og (vv. 33–35).

21:1–3. Defeat of Arad. After the discouraging report of the spies thirty-eight years before, the Israelites attempted to conquer the land by their own efforts, but the Amalekites and the Canaanites who dwelt in Arad defeated them (14:39–45). Returning to this same location after their wilderness wanderings, the Israelites were once again attacked by Canaanites, and some of their people were captured. Instead of repeating their former mistake, the Israelites committed themselves to the Lord, and He "delivered up" or "gave" (Heb. *natan*) the Canaanites to them (vv. 2–3). This verb denotes the action of giving a thing or a person to someone. It is also used in the context of war when the Lord, in an act of judgment, gave or handed over unfaithful people to other nations (21:3; Deut. 2:33; Josh. 10:30–32; Judg. 1:4; 3:10; 11:21; 1 Sam. 14:10, 12; Dan. 1:2).

This text indicates that it was the Lord who gave or handed over the Canaanites to the Israelites, which implies that the Lord had authority over the Canaanites. The battle and the victory were the Lord's enterprise. This victory likely boosted morale among the Israelites. But it seems that the victory produced only short-term positive effects among some of the Israelites. The following narrative indicates that during the next phase of the journey, the Israelites were disheartened and renewed their complaints against God and Moses (21:4–5). Unlike the Israelites, believers today should consider each victory that God produces in our lives as a prelude to His ultimate victory over all the forces of evil.

21:4–9. More Complaints: Fiery Serpents.
When the Edomites forbade the Israelites from crossing their territory, the Israelites were forced to take a long detour past part of the Red Sea identified today as the Gulf of Aqaba (v. 4; Deut. 2:8) and around the land of the Edomites. Over the course of the journey, they became discouraged again and criticized both God and Moses (vv. 4–5). Their complaint, centered on the need for bread and water, was preceded by their recurrent insistence that Moses had brought them out of Egypt only to die in the wilderness (v. 5). This time, the Lord withdrew His protection from them, and fiery serpents (i.e., venomous snakes) attacked them (v. 6). The serpents were described as "fiery" because their poisonous bite caused violent inflammation. Many people died. In the midst of their suffering, those yet remaining recognized their sin and cried to the Lord for help (v. 7).

In response to the prayers of the people, the Lord asked Moses to make a serpent of bronze and lift it up on a pole so that whoever was bitten could look at it and be healed (vv. 8–9). There was no healing power in the bronze serpent. The serpent was neither an idol nor a magic artifact. The Lord Himself was the healer, and the serpent on the pole was a symbol of His healing power. Looking at the serpent was an expression of faith in God, the Healer. It also indicated that sinners cannot save themselves because salvation is from the Lord (Jon. 2:9). The serpent, a symbol of evil, pointed forward to the ministry of our Savior, Jesus Christ. He who knew no sin became sin for us (2 Cor. 5:21) and was lifted up on the cross as God's means of salvation for those who look to Him (John 3:14). Placing one's faith in Jesus Christ is indispensable for salvation (John 3:15–18, 36).

21:10–35. Defeat of Sihon and Og. The travel itinerary of the Israelites is carefully preserved in the text to indicate how the Lord cared for and guided them (vv. 10–20). Soon they would confront two more enemies. Under God's command, Israel would move from victory to victory on their way to the plains of Moab (22:1). Obedience to God's command and confidence in His leadership were important prerequisites for success (21:34). The territories of King Sihon and King Og were located in the Transjordan region.

This would serve as the Israelites' entrance point into the land of promise. As in the case with Edom, the Israelites requested passage from King Sihon, but he refused and engaged them in war (vv. 21–23). Sihon's army attacked, but Israel, empowered by the Lord, defeated them. The land of the Amorites became the first portion of the promised land taken by the Israelites (vv. 24–31; Deut. 2:26–31).

After the Israelites defeated Sihon, they were also attacked by King Og. But as He did with Arad, the Lord gave Og, his people, and his land to the Israelites (vv. 33–35). In preparation for the battle, the Lord told Moses not to be afraid of Og or his people because He had delivered or given them into Moses's hands (21:34). Later, Moses would remind his successor, Joshua, of the victory over Sihon and Og and reassure him that the Lord would similarly overcome the other inhabitants of the region. Then he exhorted Joshua not to be afraid because the Lord his God would fight for him (Deut. 3:21–22). During the conquest itself, Joshua confirmed that the God of Israel fought for His people (Josh. 10:14, 42). It seems that the victory over Sihon and Og was a significant one for Israel. The names of the two kings are repeated many times in the OT (Sihon [37 times]; Og [22 times]), probably because this was the first conquest in the land of Canaan (cf. Deut. 1:4; 3:1–13; 4:47; 29:7; 31:4; Josh. 2:10; 9:10; 1 Kin. 4:19).

The victory over Sihon and Og validated the word of God and the faithful speech that Caleb had given some thirty-eight years before. Caleb firmly believed that when God is with His people, they can overcome mighty enemies (14:8–9). The narrative of Numbers 21:1–3 and 21–35 demonstrates that the Amorites were powerless when confronted by the army of Israel under the command of the Lord.

22:1—36:13
Israel on the Plains of Moab

After the victory over Sihon and Og, the Israelites continued their journey and reached the plains of Moab, a steppe region located immediately north of the Dead Sea to the east of the Jordan River. During Israel's stay in the area, the Moabites attempted to destroy Israel through the influence of Balaam (22:1—25:18). A new census was taken (26:1–65), and God gave an additional law regarding the inheritance of land. It was on the plains of Moab that Joshua was appointed as the new leader of the people (27:1–23). Several laws were instituted concerning sacrificial offerings (28:1—29:40) and vows (30:1–16). The narrative continues with a report of the victory over the Midianites (31:1–54), an account of the tribes that settled down in East Jordan (32:1–42), and a final overview of the trip from Egypt (33:1–49). The book closes with instructions concerning the conquest of the land and laws related to life in Canaan (33:50—36:13).

22:1—24:25. Story of Balaam. After hearing about the defeat of Sihon and Og by the Israelites, Balak, king of the Moabites, became desperate and afraid as the Israelites approached his territory (22:2–3). Instead of launching a military attack against them, Balak decided to take what he thought would be a more effective route. He hired Balaam, an unfaithful prophet, to curse the Israelites (see see below, "God's Use of a Flawed Prophet"). The Bible identifies the homeland of Balaam, son of Beor, as "Pethor" (22:5; Deut. 23:4), a town located in northern Mesopotamia on the west bank of the Euphrates. It is possible that Balaam was Aramaean.

Some have seen a contradiction in 22:20–35 because God allowed Balaam to meet with Balak, but once Balaam was on his way, the Lord opposed him. Actually, God had already prohibited Balaam from going, and Balaam had informed Balak's messengers of that fact (v. 13). It was because of Balaam's insistence that the Lord finally gave him permission to go, but only if the messengers of Balak came to him in the morning and asked him to go with them. And if they did, Balaam could only speak what God told him to (v. 35). However, the messengers did not come to him in the morning. They left, and Balaam went after them. Therefore, it is not at all strange that after Balaam departed, God's anger was directed against him, and the Angel of the Lord stood in his way (v. 22). In any case, by trying to prevent him from going, God wanted Balaam to understand that it was not His intention to allow him to curse the Israelites.

So as to prevent Balaam from interfering with His plan, God enabled the donkey to speak. This certainly should have alarmed Balaam! But it did not. The seer did not see what the donkey saw. The narrative implicitly mocks Balaam. Balaam tried to serve his client well, but he failed, blessing Israel instead (22:41—24:24; for more information on the contribution of these oracles to the theological unity of the Pentateuch, see "Introduction to the Pentateuch," p. 120). God's determination to bless His people was unalterable (23:19),

God's Use of a Flawed Prophet

The figure of Balaam in the OT is unique and perplexing.

1. Archaeology and Balaam. There is some archaeological evidence that Balaam was a historical figure. In 1967, a plaster inscription containing the name Balaam was discovered in the Transjordanian site of Deir 'Alla in the ruins of a building dated to around the eighth century B.C. The plaster inscription mentions "Balaam son of Beor," a "seer of the gods" who received messages during the night concerning future things and reported them in the morning. We find in Numbers 22 and 24 some elements similar to those found in the inscription. For example, Numbers describes Balaam as a person who received messages from God through visions or dreams; he was a "seer" (22:8, 19; 24:4). In both documents, he had nocturnal visions (22:20), and in the morning, he shared them, in this case, with Balak's messengers (22:13). And in both instances, he is called Balaam, son of Beor. These similarities and others suggest that the Balaam mentioned in the inscription is the biblical Balaam.

2. He Was Used by God. In the story in Numbers, the connection between the Lord and Balaam is unusual. Was he a worshiper of Yahweh? One thing is clear—the spirit of the Lord came upon him, and he prophesied about the future of the people of God and the coming of the Messiah (Num. 24:1–9, 17–19). Although Balak, king of Moab, wanted Balaam to curse Israel, Balaam could speak only the words of God. Unquestionably, God used him and revealed to him His plan. It is unclear whether this was an isolated incident or the first time the Lord had used him as a prophet. But one thing is certain: Balaam declared to the messengers of Balak that he could not go beyond the word of the Lord his God in any way (22:18). When he identified the Lord as his God, he was obviously indicating that he knew Yahweh, the God of Israel, and worshiped Him. However, the narrative reveals a number of problems with Balaam's relationship with the Lord and implies an eventual full apostasy. Despite this reality, God still used Balaam as His prophet.

3. *Use of Pagan Rituals.* There are two details that contribute to Balaam's enigmatic reputation. First, he is in the service of a king who wanted him to curse Israel, the people of Yahweh. Second, in seeking a revelation from God, he used pagan practices. Pagans used various rituals to influence the gods and to predict the future. At some point in his life, Balaam combined the worship of God with pagan ritual practices and worshiped other gods. The inscription found in 1967 supports that conclusion. In the Bible, he is described as a diviner who receives divination fees or instruments used for divination purposes (Heb. *qesem* in 22:7 could refer to divination instruments or to fees). According to Numbers 24:1, before he pronounced his third oracle, he did not seek to use sorcery or divination as he had previously (Heb. *nakhash*, meaning "to call for an evil omen"; cf. 23:23), which implies that on the two previous occasions, he had practiced sorcery. The text does not specify the type of ritual he used to seek the omen. In any case, he was unable to coerce the Lord into supporting his efforts to curse Israel. His connection with polytheism suggests that, in principle, Balaam was not a faithful worshiper of the Lord of Israel.

4. *Goal of the Narrative.* The most important element of this story is not the information it provides about Balaam but what it reveals about the purpose and meaning of the story within the book of Numbers. First, the story reveals that there is no God like the God of Israel. Balaam was completely aware of the fact that Yahweh is unique and that, consequently, he would not be able to coerce Him. Balaam's sorcery was ineffective against Him. Several times, Balaam recognized that he could say only what Yahweh put in his mouth and that he was unable to go beyond it. By the third oracle, Balaam abandoned any attempt to influence God and placed himself at His disposal. It was then that the Spirit came upon him.

Second, the story demonstrates that the people of God are under special protection. The forces of evil cannot bring to fruition their purpose against those blessed by the Lord. In Numbers, God reveals Himself as the leader of His people, depicted as an army of pilgrims advancing victoriously toward the land of Canaan.

Third, through this narrative, God shared with the pagan world His plans for Israel. The vision of Balaam pointed to a time when, through the power of God, Israel would be victorious over all its enemies and would be at peace (24:8–9; see the Introduction to the Pentateuch). He foresaw an era in which the glorious king of Israel and His kingdom would be exalted (24:8, 17–19). The message of the story of Balaam applies with equal force to God's people today and should reaffirm their confidence in their Savior and Lord.

---

to the point that He was willing to forgive their sins (23:21). No human or demonic sorcery could alter God's will for them (v. 23).

The oracles of Balaam recorded in Numbers 24 are the most impressive of his prophecies and are recorded in poetry. In the third oracle, the Lord describes the camp of Israel as a garden planted by a river; it is a beautiful and fruitful paradise (24:5–7). Then the image transforms to that of a kingdom that is ruled by a king more powerful than Agag (v. 7), described metaphorically as a mighty wild ox (v. 8). While according to 23:22, God brought the Israelites out of Egypt, here God brings this king out of Egypt (a new Exodus), suggesting a powerful messianic figure who permanently overcomes His enemies. This messianic figure then lies down to rest like a powerful lion, whom no one dares to challenge (v. 9). The message is not only about the proclamation of the defeat of the nation of Balak, an enemy of God's people, but about the final defeat of all of God's enemies through God's Messiah, represented as an ox and a lion (see "Introduction to the Pentateuch," p. 120).

The final oracle is the high point (24:15–24). Balaam witnessed what would happen in the distant future, God's eschatological plan. The "He" mentioned in v. 8 is now identified as the future king, prophesied in Genesis 49:10, who was to come from the tribe of Judah. Balaam speaks about a star and scepter coming out of Jacob (v. 17), both symbols pointing to royalty. The NT applies the symbol of the star to Jesus, the messianic King (Rev. 22:16). The star would appear in order to guide the wise men/kings to the child Jesus, who himself was to be the Star that was to come out of Jacob (Matt. 2:1–11).

Finding here a reference to the Davidic Dynasty, from which the Messiah would come, is appropriate. David defeated the enemies of God, including Moab and Edom. But the eschatological emphasis of the text suggests that the ultimate significance of the passage is found in the coming Messiah, who was Himself the culmination of the dynasty (see Ps. 89:19–52; Isa. 11; 55:3; Jer. 23:5–6; 30:9; Ezek. 34:23–24; 37:24–25; Hos. 3:5; Amos 9:11; Matt. 1:1; Luke 1:32; 2 Tim. 2:8; Rev. 5:5). The nations mentioned in Numbers 24:17b–24 would symbolically represent all of God's enemies who would be defeated by the Messiah. Moab, Edom (see Is. 63:1–3), and Amalek would not be able to stand before the future King. The proud nations, like the Kenites, would be overpowered (vv. 21–22), even if God had to employ other nations in the process (e.g., Asshur; v. 22). Implicit in the passage is a future for God's people free from the threat of enemies. This last oracle of Balaam was an oracle of hope for Israel.

Israel later attacked the Midianites, and in the ensuing battle, Balaam was killed (31:8). Thus, Balaam died as a result of his sin. He fell from divine grace and tragically became an instrument in the hands of God's enemy. In spite of the imperfections of the Israelites in the wilderness, God was with them, protecting them from physical and spiritual forces. Israel did not discern what Balak and Balaam were attempting to do against them, but God knew and fought for them. He does the same for His people today.

25:1–18. Israel's Immorality and Idolatry. Despite a clear prelude of ultimate victory against the inhabitants of the land (see the victory over Sihon [21:21–25] and Og [21:33–35]), some Israelites remained spiritually vulnerable. When Balaam failed to curse God's people, he returned home, the place where he should have remained (24:25). But, overcome by greed, he revisited Balak with a strategy to overthrow Israel: to lead some among the people to violate God's covenant by committing harlotry with the women of Moab and worshiping their gods (25:1–2; 31:16; cf. 2 Pet. 2:15; Rev. 2:14). Balaam recognized that the formidable mix of immorality and idolatry would lead many Israelites astray.

As a result of the violation of the covenant, the people were immediately afflicted by a plague

from the Lord. God commanded Moses to hang the culprits (v. 4) as a way of bringing the plague to an end. It was particularly because of the intervention of the priest Eleazar, who made atonement on behalf of the people, that God's anger receded (vv. 7–8). The punishment inflicted on Zimri by Phinehas was not arbitrary. He was a leader in Israel and, through his behavior, could have influenced others to sin. Though we no longer live under a theocracy, immoral and sinful behavior in the church always requires a firm response from God's people (1 Cor. 5:1–5).

26:1–65. Second Numbering of Israel. Part of the preparation to conquer Canaan included a census of the new generation. After dealing with the disaster at Baal-Peor, the Lord ordered Moses and Eleazar to number the people (vv. 1–56) and the Levites (vv. 57–62). This was a new census because all those who were originally numbered in the wilderness of Sinai were already dead, except for Caleb, Joshua, and Moses (vv. 63–67), and Moses himself would die soon (27:12–14). The census was conducted according to the number of the Israelite tribes. For all the tribes except that of Levi, the census included male Israelites who were twenty years old and above and able to go to war (v. 2) and female Israelites in case of fathers who had no sons (v. 33). Concerning the Levites, the numbering involved all males older than one month of age (v. 62). In light of vv. 52–56, it appears that the census was to be used in the division of the land. The number of people in the tribe determined how much land a tribe would inherit. The Levites were not counted among their Israelite brethren because they had no land inheritance (v. 62). However, since the land could only be divided after its conquest, the census had a military purpose as well. Thus, the ability to go to war was one of the considerations (v. 2). The division of the land even before its conquest reassured the people that through God's power, they would conquer the land.

In vv. 9–10, the rebellion of Dathan, Abiram, and Korah is recalled as a sign (v. 10; i.e., a warning for others). This reminder to the new generation was important because they faced a genuine challenge in conquering the land, and their success required faithfulness to God. Unlike Dathan, Abiram, and Korah, who mocked God's plan by describing Egypt as the land flowing with milk and honey (16:13–14), the new generation needed to trust in God's leadership and develop strong hope in Him. The apostle Peter warned that in the last days, there would be scoffers who would view the promise of the Second Coming of Jesus with derision. But the children of God are encouraged to wait with hope for the fulfillment of His promise (2 Pet. 3:3-14).

27:1-11. Zelophehad's Daughters. The daughters of Zelophehad raised an issue concerning their father's property. Their situation was serious because the continued existence of someone's name was important to the Israelites, and the most enduring way to preserve a man's name was for his descendants to inherit his land. Because the matter was so complex, Moses referred the case to the Lord (v. 5).

The Lord answered that daughters have the right to inherit their father's property (vv. 6-9). He made it clear that the land of Canaan should be kept in small holdings and passed down along hereditary lines (vv. 9-11). Thus, the case of the daughters of Zelophehad facilitated the creation of a new law entitling women to be considered legal channels through which possession and inheritance of the land could be traced, as it was with sons. This was a revolutionary law that should inform contemporary society, especially cultures in which women still have lower status than men.

27:12-23. Joshua as the Successor of Moses. The current section focuses on the transfer of leadership from Moses to Joshua. The Lord informed Moses that the day of his death was drawing near. He would not enter Canaan because he had been disobedient to God and had not glorified Him at Kadesh (vv. 12-14). Instead of arguing with the Lord, Moses complied with His determination and displayed a deep sense of responsibility (vv. 15-17). Thinking about the welfare of his people, he requested that the Lord appoint a suitable leader, one who would go out and come in before the people (i.e., lead them in battle; v. 17). The Lord directed Moses to Joshua (one of the two faithful spies) and instructed him to lay his hands on Joshua, for the Spirit was in him (v. 18).

The laying on of hands denoted the transfer of power from one leader to another, with one taking the place of the other (Num. 8:10; cf. Lev. 16:21). By laying hands on Joshua, Moses consecrated him as the new leader of God's people (vv. 18-20, 23), the one who would guide them to Canaan. Aaron had given way to Eleazar, and Moses relinquished his position to Joshua. It was clear that the Lord, the ultimate leader of Israel, was in charge of the affairs of His people. He would not allow a leadership vacuum. The future of His work could not be jeopardized by the absence of appointed leaders.

Joshua, a man endowed by the Spirit with wisdom and authority, was installed as Moses's successor in the sight of the congregation while Moses was still alive (vv. 19, 22). This ensured that there would be no misunderstanding or uncertainty concerning leadership

---

The Status of Women in the Book of Numbers

Despite containing sparse data concerning the lives of women, the book of Numbers seems to indicate that there was a continuous effort to improve their status in Israelite society. Numbers 5-6, 12, 27, 30, and 36 provide some hints about a woman's position in the Israelite community. For example, in 5:1-4, whoever (man or woman) became unclean due to leprosy or corpse defilement was to be sent outside the camp, without discrimination. In 5:6-7, a man or a woman who did wrong to a fellow human being was considered guilty before the Lord and was required to repent. In the same chapter, the Lord indicated that no wife could be held guilty simply on the basis of her husband's suspicion. A wife was considered innocent until the Lord Himself proved her guilty (5:11-31). In relation to the Nazirite law, women as well as men were free to choose to be Nazirites (6:1-2). In addition to the Nazirite vow, women could also take other vows (Numbers 30). Moreover, the incident of Numbers 12 implies that Miriam was recognized as an important female leader in Israel. Furthermore, on the request of Zelophehad's daughters, a law about a daughter's inheritance was established in Israel. Though these illustrations are limited, they marked a step forward in the lives of women. Current society, and especially the church, is called to do better, particularly in the areas of women's education, leadership, and employment.

responsibilities after Moses's death. Joshua would cooperate with Eleazar in leading God's people (vv. 21–22). Eleazar was to consult the Lord with the Urim and Thummim to provide divine instructions to Joshua (v. 21). While Moses anticipated his death, he continued to instruct God's people.

At times, succession can be a source of conflict within religious organizations. But looking back at Moses's and Joshua's experiences, it is clear that the ability to serve and the endowment of wisdom from God should serve as key criteria in the transfer of leadership. The entire matter of succession should be submitted to the Lord, following the example of Moses. Moreover, once the decision is made, it must be reported to the public in an appropriate way. Joshua's collaboration with Eleazar would be important in order to effectively lead God's people into the promised land. God never directs one leader independently of His other chosen instruments.

28:1—29:40. Offerings in the Cultic Calendar. The offerings described in this section would be required at prescribed intervals in the promised land (see also Lev. 23). There were daily (vv. 3–8; not included in Lev. 23), weekly (vv. 9–10), and monthly sacrifices (vv. 11–15; not mentioned in Lev. 23), as well as offerings for the specific festivals (28:16—29:40). Four kinds of offerings were envisaged for the festivals: whole/burnt offerings, which consisted of burning the flesh of the whole animal; cereal/grain offerings (grain and oil); drink offerings or libations (wine); and sin/ purification offerings (29:39). The various offerings presented to God during the festivals were acts of faith through which the Israelites were to express their gratitude to God for His saving actions and for the successful harvests He provided for them. They were also an expression of their commitment to Him.

In other words, the performance of sacrifices at regular intervals, particularly the sin offering, should have reminded the Israelites that God dwelled permanently in their midst and that, consequently, they were in constant need of atonement and cleansing from sin. The sacrifices also developed within the people an attitude of thanksgiving to God, compliance with His covenant, and commitment to Him, as well as the conviction of being accepted by Him. The calendrical sacrifices functioned as constant reminders of God's presence, His holiness, His grace, and, above all, His acts of salvation within the history of His people.

There were several festivals in Israel: the Passover (28:16; cf. Lev. 23:5), the Festival of Unleavened Bread (28:17–25; cf. Lev. 23:6), the Festival of Harvest (28:26–31; cf. Lev. 23:15–21), the Festival of Trumpets (29:1–6; cf. Lev. 23:23–25), the Day of Atonement (29:7–11; cf. Lev. 23:26–32), and the Festival of Tabernacles (29:12–38; cf. Lev. 23:33–43). These different festivals were organized in the context of the agricultural year and the harvests. The Passover and the Festival of Unleavened Bread were scheduled during the barley harvest in spring. The Festival of Weeks or Harvest came during the wheat harvest around the month of June. The Festival of Trumpets and Tabernacles, as well as the Day of Atonement, were celebrated between September and October and corresponded with the ripening of grapes, figs, and olives. By celebrating these festivals at their appointed times, the Israelites expressed their gratitude to God for His provision of food, and they were protected from the influence of idolatrous and immoral pagan harvest festivals.

The festivals also aimed to reinforce relationships among the Israelites in the promised land. The festivals were intended to shape their identity, mission, and destiny, bolstering the idea that they were God's chosen people with one major purpose—namely, to be a blessing to other nations. Moreover, the celebrations would remind them of God's saving acts, His goodness, and His continuous care for them (see Lev. 23 for the typological significance of the festivals). Today, worship should also be centered on the goodness of God and His saving power, and it should be a time of joy and thanksgiving.

30:1–16. Legislation Regarding Vows. This section of Numbers records legislation regarding the seriousness of making a vow or swearing an oath to the Lord. The specific nature of the vow or the oath is not mentioned, except in one instance (v. 13). Five specific cases are discussed. First, if a man made a vow, he was not allowed to violate it (v. 2; see Deut. 23:21–23). Second, if a young woman still living in the house of her father made a vow, and her father knew about it but remained silent (v. 4), the vow was inviolable. But if her father overruled the vow when he learned about it, the Lord would *yislah* (from *salakh*) *lah*—"forgive or release her" (i.e., release her from fulfilling the vow; v. 5). Third, in the case of a young woman who had made a vow before getting married, her husband could annul the vow the moment he became aware of it, and the woman would be forgiven by the Lord. Otherwise the vow would be confirmed through his silence (vv. 6–8). Fourth, the case of a widow or divorced woman was like that of a man; she was bound to fulfill her vow (v. 9). Fifth, when a married woman made a vow, her husband could override it when he first heard of it. Otherwise, the vow would be binding. If, later on, the husband changed his mind and annulled the vow, the women was forgiven, but her husband would bear her guilt (i.e., be responsible/punishable for the violation of her vow; vv. 10–15).

The annulment of a vow by a father or husband could have been motivated by concerns about the family's limited economic resources or by other marital responsibilities (e.g., when the wife took an oath to humble or deny herself; lit. "humble the soul"; v. 13), which usually meant fasting (Is. 58:3, 5), but which may have included abstaining from sexual relations. What is significant here is that a woman was free to make a vow by herself, without the prior approval of her father or husband, and that it was valid. The potential annulment by the father or husband could be linked to the woman owning insufficient property to fulfill her vow. The object of a vow was often a sacrifice, but it could also have included becoming a Nazirite.

31:1–54. War against the Midianites. At the suggestion of Balaam, the Midianites led Israel into a grievous sin, which resulted in a plague in which twenty-four thousand Israelites died. The Lord spoke again to Moses and instructed him to take vengeance on the Midianites before he died (vv. 1–2; cf. 25:16–18). The time of retribution had arrived, and the Lord ordered the people to go to war. It was not a common thing in the ANE or even in the Bible for a deity to command a war; this was usually done by kings. In response to God's command, Moses organized a military expedition against the Midianites. The new generation of Israelites was ready to cooperate with God and obey His instructions. Hence, they put into practice some of the previous legislations, including the use of trumpets in the context of war (v. 6; cf. 10:9), the purification from corpse defilement (v. 19; cf. 19:1–22), and the support for priests and Levites (v. 47; cf. 18:1–32).

Moses asked Phinehas, the son of Eleazar, to accompany the army to battle and to take with him some holy articles (v. 6), perhaps the Urim and Thummim (27:21). Most armies in the ANE employed priests, diviners, and portable sacred objects when they went to war. The gods were considered responsible for the outcome of the war and would be consulted on the battlefield in an effort to be victorious. In the case of Israel, the company of God's representative, the priest Phinehas, would encourage the army in its mission. His presence, along with sacred articles, could imply that the battle was under God's control, and this would encourage the Israelite soldiers to keep fighting.

At God's command, the Israelites fought against the Midianites and killed the five kings of Midian and many of their people, including Balaam, the unfaithful prophet (vv. 2, 7–8). However, the Israelite army spared the women and children and took them captive (v. 9). This action vexed Moses (v. 14). He then commanded the soldiers to kill all of the women who had ever had sexual contact with men because they were among the key agents who led Israel to apostasy (vv. 16–17). Male children were also destroyed so that they would not become a military threat to Israel in the future (v. 17; see "The Extermination of the Canaanites," p. 330, and "Holy Warfare," p. 372).

Though the war against Midian was carried out at God's command, the text does not indicate that this should serve as basis for individuals to avenge themselves. It is important to note that Moses's army did not exterminate the Midianites. The context of Numbers 31 indicates that the Lord used the Israelites as an instrument to enact His judgment on the Midianites, who were a threat to His plan of bringing His people into Canaan. The command to fight the Midianites was limited to a particular space and time, in relation to the settling of the promised land.

After the battle, the soldiers cleansed themselves, along with the plunder they took (vv. 19–24). The plunder was divided according to certain regulations. One portion went for the maintenance of the sanctuary, another was given to the priests and Levites, still another belonged to the soldiers, and the remainder was taken by the congregation (vv. 25–47). The Lord granted the Midianites and their possessions to the Israelites. In turn, as a sign of gratitude, the Israelites presented an offering to the Lord (vv. 48–54). Thus, they recognized that the victory over the Midianites belonged to God. As with Israel in times long past, the Lord is still ready to give victory to His people today as they continue to trust in His promises, power, and lordship in their lives.

32:1–42. Settlement in the Transjordan. The tribes of Reuben and Gad and the half-tribe of Manasseh did not wait on God to designate their allotment. They requested the Transjordan land, which had already been conquered and which was well suited to their pastoral life (vv. 1–5). Their request was accepted, with the condition that they must participate in the conquest of the rest of the land. The agreement was recorded multiple times (vv. 25–27; 31–32; see Josh. 22:1–34).

The commitment of the tribes of Reuben and Gad and the half-tribe of Manasseh reinforced the sense of united purpose, mutual responsibility, and interdependence among God's people. At that time, the children of Israel worked together as one people and conquered the promised land. When God's people decide to unite and focus together on a common goal, they can do mighty things for the Lord.

33:1–49. Israel's Journey from Egypt to Canaan. In this section, Moses summarizes the journey of the people from Egypt to the plains of Moab. Many places mentioned in this passage have not yet been identified and may forever remain unknown. Place names as well as geographical environments are subject to change over time. However, the itinerary as it stands testifies that the Lord led His people progressively and in an organized manner from Egypt to the frontier of the promised land. They were about to leave the wilderness, which had been a place of rebellion and punishment, but it was also a place of divine care, grace, and love, and one where the relationship between God and the new generation of Israelites was finally solidified.

33:50—34:29. Division of the Promised Land. Before the Israelites conquered the land, the Lord assured them that it was theirs and that they could begin dividing it among themselves. But He reminded them that one of their major tasks would be to destroy the idolatry that prevailed in the land (v. 52). Failing to do this would make the Canaanites a constant threat to their physical and spiritual well-being (v. 55) and would make the Israelites candidates for destruction (v. 56). The size of the tribe was the key criterion in the partitioning of the land (v. 54). The land was to be divided among the nine and a half tribes since the others were allotted shares in the Transjordan territory (34:1–12). Though the land belonged to God, He involved the people in its division and apportionment. They were to allocate the land even before it was conquered, and thus rely completely on the promise that the Lord would indeed give it to them (34:16–29). The Israelites were to be stewards of God's land. As He had directed their liberation from Egypt and their subsequent journey, He also had full control of the division of the land. God wanted to plant His people in a safe place, where faith could grow free from the weeds of sin and rebellion.

35:1–34. Levitical Cities and Cities of Refuge. The Levites did not inherit any land (26:62). The Lord Himself was their share. He provided for them through the tithes and offerings that the people of Israel contributed. He also required the Israelite tribes to give to the Levites a number of cities and suburbs (35:1–3, 6). It should be noted that, similar to the previous instructions (33:50—34:29), these directives about Levitical cities and cities of refuge were given to the Israelites when they were still on the plains of Moab (i.e., before the conquest of the land; 35:1). The Lord was assuring them again that He would indeed fulfill His plan. There was no reason for them to despair. All they needed was faith and conviction regarding what is not seen (Heb. 11:1).

The Levitical cities would serve as dwelling places for God's servants. These cities were centers for religious instruction and aided the collection of revenue for God's work. Cities of refuge were places where persons who had committed unintentional homicide could seek safety. These cities prevented blood feuds and provided a safe haven to the accused person until the trial (v. 30). Moreover, since it was considered that the blood of the slain could only be expiated by another death, the death of the high priest eliminated the bloodguilt attached to the homicide. In other words, since the high priest was representative of the community at large, his death expiated accidental bloodshed (35:25, 28; Ex. 28:36–38; Lev. 16:16). Furthermore, in Israel, human life was of such high value that a murderer could not pay a ransom for the crime. He or she was to be put to death (35:31). This provision emphasizes the dignity and significance of human life in the sight of God.

This way of thinking short-circuited the common ANE custom of blood vengeance in which a person was obliged to avenge the death of a deceased relative by killing the guilty individual and even his or her family. In vv. 33–34, the Lord insisted that the land should be protected from all possible defilement, especially murder. The holy presence of the Lord in the land required the purity of its inhabitants.

36:1–13. Inheritance of Zelophehad's Daughters. This passage is a supplement to the law in 27:1–11, which allowed the daughters of Zelophehad to inherit the land of their father, who died without a male heir (27:3). The new legislation required women in this situation to marry men within their own tribe so that their inheritance would not be taken from their tribe and granted to another. In this way, the preservation of family property (land), which was one of the highest values in Israelite society, would not be jeopardized. Consequently, the additional law of Numbers 36 contributed to the stability of relationships within the community. The final statement of the book of Numbers (36:13) indicates that the commandments and the instructions that Moses received on the plains of Moab came from the Lord. These regulations were intended to prepare the Israelites for the conquest of the promised land and to clarify how they should live in it. To conquer Canaan, they needed to trust fully in God's leadership. They were to properly organize themselves by taking the census, dealing honestly with leadership succession, and fighting under God's command.

The Lord also instructed them that once they occupied the land, their priority should be true worship and the reinforcement of civil and social rights. On the plains of Moab, at the very border of the promised land, God's instructions strengthened the hope of the Israelites that they would inherit what God had promised them, despite their moments of despair. At this juncture, they stood before the land and anticipated the fulfillment of God's promises to their forefathers and to themselves. Christians too stand waiting, looking for a new heaven and a new earth where righteousness reigns (2 Pet. 3:13).

DEUTERONOMY

INTRODUCTION

Title. Deuteronomy is the final book of the Jewish Torah, also known as the Pentateuch—this name is based on the Greek title of the five books of Moses. In Hebrew the book is known as *seper debarim* ("Book of Words"), a title taken from its opening line, "These are the words..." (1:1). The Greek translation of the OT (LXX) sets the ground for the name *Deuteronomion* ("Second Law")—a designation derived from the instructions given for an eventual king of Israel, which stipulated that he would write for himself a copy of the law on a scroll (17:18). The book reiterates the Decalogue of Exodus 20 almost word for word in Deuteronomy 5, as well as many of the laws found in Exodus, Leviticus, and Numbers. However, because of this title, the reader of the book may get the wrong impression—unintended by the author—that Deuteronomy is only a series of speeches or sermons that review Israel's history, including the Exodus narrative and God's instructions to the people as they journeyed toward the promised land. However, the primary intention of these speeches was to motivate the people to remain faithful to God.

Authorship. Deuteronomy identifies Moses as the author of its content: "These are the words which Moses spoke to all Israel" (1:1). The thirty-eight occurrences of the name Moses, together with the use of the first-person pronoun, support the idea of Mosaic authorship. Also, the NT upholds Moses as the author of Deuteronomy: Jesus referred to Moses as the author of the law of divorce found in Deuteronomy 24:1–4 (cf. Matt. 19:7–8; Mark 10:3–4), and Stephen and Peter cite the prophetic word found in Deuteronomy 18:15–19 about the raising of a prophet likeas being spoken by Moses himself (cf. Acts 3:22; 7:37). An exception of Mosaic authorship, however,

is chapter 34, which narrates Moses's death. Joshua, the Israelite leader following Moses, may have recorded this chapter.

Date and Backgrounds. The traditional date for the book of Deuteronomy places the Exodus from Egypt in the fifteenth century (approx. 1447 B.C.). After forty years of desert wanderings, Israel's new generation arrived in the fields of Moab, where Moses spoke the words of Deuteronomy to them (Deut. 1:3).

With the rise of the Enlightenment, the prevailing consensus among Jewish and Christian scholars about the Mosaic authorship of Deuteronomy and its date of composition changed. Today, many critical scholars believe that the book of Deuteronomy was the scroll found in the Jerusalem temple during the reform of King Josiah in 622 B.C. (2 Kin. 22:8—23:3; 2 Chr. 34:14–33), and that the scroll had been only recently composed and placed in the temple. Others hold that Deuteronomy is the result of Josianic reform. In any case, critics view Deuteronomy as composed by Jewish scribes and fictionally attributed to Moses.

However, not all scholars are willing to date Deuteronomy late. Many still hold to an early date of composition based on the inner-biblical testimony. The use of archaic language and literary devices such as *inclusio*, chiasms, key words, and thematic links point to the cohesive literary structure of the book, which bears close resemblance to late, second millennium B.C. Hittite treaties. These features appear across the entire book of Deuteronomy and show evidence for the unity of authorship and an early date of composition.

Theology and Purpose. Deuteronomy is often regarded as "the theology book" of the OT. Similar to Romans in the NT, Deuteronomy reviews God's gracious acts toward Israel and lays the foundation for the messages of the prophets who followed Moses. The book consists of Moses's passionate farewell address to Israel, cast into the form of an ancient covenant document. Its content centers around God's faithfulness in fulfilling His promises to the patriarchs, which were manifested in Israel's miraculous Exodus and the instructions God gave them. Deuteronomy systematizes the accounts of Exodus through Numbers into a manifesto calling Israel to respond to God's grace with unreserved love and loyalty.

1. God's Faithfulness. The 120-year-old Moses addressed the new generation of Israelites who camped in the fields of Moab and reminded them of the promises God made to their ancestors (Deut. 2:14–15; Num. 13–14). Moses highlighted God's covenant faithfulness and exhorted the people to be faithful and obedient to Him as their covenant Lord. There would be blessings for such obedience, but curses for disobedience (Deut. 27–30). Deuteronomy's purpose was to prepare the new generation of the Lord's chosen people to be His kingdom representatives in the land He had promised in the Abrahamic covenant. Loyalty to God was to be grounded in the fulfillment of God's redemptive promises to them. The book portrays a reliable God who would deliver to the people the future He offered them through His wonderful promises. Deuteronomy's spiritual emphasis and its call to a total commitment to the Lord in worship and obedience inspired references to its message throughout the rest of Scripture. In particular, the Former Prophets division of the Hebrew Bible (Joshua, Judges, Samuel, Kings; see "Introduction to the Old Testament Historical Books," p. 350) is thoroughly imbued with the style, themes, and motifs of Deuteronomy. Among the Latter Prophets, Jeremiah also reflects a strong influence from this book.

2. God's Love. The reciprocal love of the Lord for His people, and that of the people for the Lord as their sovereign God, pervades the whole book. In fact, God's love seems to be Deuteronomy's main theological theme. The election of Israel was not based on the people's qualities, but solely on God's love toward a small and insignificant people. The deliverance of Israel from bondage in Egypt was a fundamental expression of His love as well as the fulfillment of His promises. Furthermore, because of His loving grace, God assigned them a home in a bounteous and fertile land. In response to all these benefits, it was the individual Israelite's duty to fear and to love the Lord. The love of God is portrayed as His full commitment to them and as an all-absorbing personal devotion of the people to Him. Love is the primary motivator for human

duty. The Israelite was to love God with undivided affection ("with all your heart and with all your soul," 6:5), thereby renouncing everything inconsistent with loyalty to Him.

3. Love as the Rejection of Idolatry. God's covenant with Israel (Ex. 19–24) constituted the backbone of the challenge to remain obedient to Him, especially in view of the temptations that they would face among the Canaanites. In order to motivate Israel to start anew in the promised land, Moses cast his speeches into the framework of a new covenant relationship between God and Israel that placed younger generations in their parents' footsteps when they encountered God at Mount Sinai. God called each Israelite to experience by faith the same redemptive events and respond to them with trust and obedience. Loyalty in the expression of love toward God would bring an earnest repudiation of all false gods and idolatrous rites and practices. This loyal love was also to express itself as a cheerful and ready acquiescence to the positive commandments that God had laid down. God repeatedly and emphatically warned Israel against the temptations of idolatry and of the perils of yielding to it. In this context, they would exterminate Canaan's heathen populations. No intermarriage or any other relationship with them was to be permitted, and their places of worship and religious symbols were to be completely destroyed. Israel was always to remember that they were a "holy" people to the Lord (Deut. 7:6; 14:2, 21; 26:19; 28:9). The Canaanite forms of divination and magic were not to be tolerated. While other nations relied upon oracles of fortune-tellers and soothsayers, Israel would rely on the Lord's prophets for divine counsel and guidance (28:9–19). Instruction was given regarding the worship of the true God so that Israel would not follow heathen rites. Part of this worship included the celebration of the three great annual festivals (the Festival of Unleavened Bread, the Festival of Weeks, and the Festival of Tabernacles), the offering of all sacrifices, and the performance of other religious duties at a single central sanctuary where God would put His name (12:5–7, 11, 14, 18, 26). Obedience to these commandments was to be sincere and from the heart, and would bring with it the blessing of the Lord. Disobedience, on the other hand, would end in national disasters and exile (6:14–15; 7:12–16; 8:19, and especially chap. 28).

4. Love and Practicing Justice. The practical expression of loving God was not confined to Israel's religious duties, but also embraced their social and domestic life. The laws included in chapters 12 to 26 contain details for the moral and social well-being of the community that every Israelite was to follow. Love of God translated into love of one's neighbor. Any act detrimental to a neighbor's welfare was to be avoided. The moral principles that the book insists on are justice, integrity, equity, philanthropy, and generosity. Judges were to be appointed in every city to administer justice with strict impartiality so that these principles were followed (26:18–20). Fathers were not to be condemned judicially for the crimes of their children, nor children for the crimes of their fathers (24:16). Just weights and measures were to be used in all commercial transactions (25:13–16). Grave moral offenses were punished severely. Death was the penalty not only for murder but also for the rebellious behavior of a son toward his parents, for unchastity, for adultery, and for kidnapping (21:18–21; 22:20–27; 24:7).

5. *Love and Caring for the Needy.* The governing motive of the laws of Deuteronomy was philanthropy—compassion and charity shown toward those in need and in difficult life situations. These included those in need of a loan (15:7–11), slaves at the time of manumission (15:13–15), fugitives (13:15–16), hired servants (14:14–15), strangers (i.e., foreign residents), orphans, and widows (cf. 14:29). The Israelites' own past as foreigners and slaves was evoked in order to promote gratitude and a sense of sympathy toward the needy (10:19; cf. 15:15; 16:12; 24:18, 22). Deuteronomy promotes a spirit of tolerance, equity, and regard for the welfare of others like no other book of the OT. Israel was to live within an atmosphere of generous devotion to God and large-hearted benevolence toward human beings. Following the principles found in this book would ennoble, elevate, and refine the entire life of the community.

6. *Love and Hope.* The strong concern in Deuteronomy for rightful living anticipated rightful living in the land that the Lord had promised to Israel. Previous residents had corrupted the land through their inhumane and idolatrous practices, and their future was removal from it. Israel was now ready to possess it and to make it a center for the worship of the Lord who had brought the people out of Egypt. While on the plains of Moab, Moses informed them about the future and the impact of their hope on the present. In terms of their loving commitment to the Lord and to each other, they were to live the way they would eventually live in the promised land. Their future, the realization of

hope, would depend to a large extent on that commitment. It could be characterized by blessings based on God's promises or by curses that would result from the rejection of God's promises. They could choose life or death, but the divine intention for them was life.

Literary Features. From a literary point of view, Deuteronomy's structure reflects the suzerain-vassal treaties of the ancient Near East, specifically Hittite and Assyrian treaties. The elements of such treaties are reflected in the book's division: (1) Preamble (1:1–5); (2) Historical Prologue (1:6—4:49); (3) Stipulations (chaps. 5–26); (4) Curses and Blessings, or Covenant Ratification (chaps. 27–30); and (5) Succession Arrangements or Covenant Continuity, which includes the invocation of witnesses and directions for the disposition and public reading of the treaty (chaps. 31–34).

The book consists of a series of speeches that correspond to treaty documents in which the suzerain orally proclaimed his terms and conditions at the covenant ceremony to the vassals. The treaty style of the book is reflected in the characteristic "I/thou" form that is found in ancient Near Eastern suzerainty treaties. In line with the oral proclamation of the covenant text was the response by the vassal during the covenant ceremony. An example of such a response appears in the text of King Esarhaddon of Assyria (681–669 B.C.), which was found in the royal city of Nimrud. The text contains a self-maledictory oath binding the vassal to the lord's stipulations and repeats a summary of these stipulations in the response. Likewise, Deuteronomy mentions the "Amen" that was to be uttered by the Israelites in the course of their ceremony (27:15–26; cf. 26:17–18; 29:12). Thus, the farewell speeches of Moses were the ceremonial words of a covenant ritual calling the people to accept the treaty offered to them by God. The formal structure of these speeches closely followed fixed ceremonial/legal traditions within the context of a passionate liturgical address.

The example that scholars cite as exhibiting the books's treaty pattern in a miniature format is Deuteronomy 4. This chapter has the following constitutive features: (1) the identification of the speaker (vv. 1–2, 5, 10); (2) the appeal to covenant history (e.g., vv. 10–12, 20–24); (3) the basic stipulation of undivided allegiance (e.g., vv. 15–18); (4) the blessing/curse sanctions (v. 27); (5) the invocation of witnesses (v. 26); and (6) the arrangements for the perpetuation of the covenant (vv. 9–10, 21–22). This brief passage stands as a reflection of the treaty pattern of Moses's speeches and signifies the unity of the book. It is also an interesting indication of how Moses viewed the occasion on the banks of the Jordan River. One might say that in his mind, Moses understood the entire ceremony not just as a passionate farewell speech but as a call for decision making, a solemn dedication service, and a sending ceremony of the younger generation under the protective and guiding governance of their supreme Lord. Moses himself had served the Lord, and he anticipated the same from Israel. The speeches were filled with exhortations recounting important historical events, prophetic utterances, and poetic orations.

COMMENTARY

1:1—4:43

MOSES'S FIRST DISCOURSE: REMEMBERING THE GRACE OF YAHWEH

Chapters 1–4 are often referred to as the "preamble" of Deuteronomy. Moses recalled key events that occurred during the forty years of wanderings in the desert after the Israelites left Sinai. He recapped the history of their journey for a couple of reasons: (1) this younger generation was not the group who experienced these significant events, and (2) he was reminding them of all that God had done to bring them to this historic point. To understand what is to come, we must understand what has gone before; both are indispensable to biblical hope.

This introduction mentions that Moses told the people everything that the Lord had commanded (1:3), and he also expressed his own emotion. He focused specifically on episodes difficult for him: when he needed help in managing such a large group of people, when the spies presented their negative report, and when he was punished. Moses was an old man who had carried a tremendous burden. Some commentators find contradictions with the original narrative in this review of past experiences. For example, Moses centered on his own role in the appointing of the leaders of thousands, hundreds, fifties, and tens, without addressing Jethro's as Exodus does (1:12–17; Ex. 18:17–23). Moses mentioned that the people suggested sending spies into Canaan before they took possession of it, whereas Numbers mentions only God's command (Num. 13:1–2). Yet these narratives are not contradictory, but rather

complementary: Moses commanded the people to do what Jethro had suggested, and God commanded Moses to do what the people had suggested. Most surprising of all is Moses's claim that it was due to God's anger over the Israelites' refusal to enter Canaan at Kadesh Barnea that he was refused entry as well (Deut. 1:37; cf. 3:26; 4:21). No mention is made of his own act of disobedience (Num. 20:8–12). These two events are closely associated in the biblical narrative. Here Moses is right in the sense that if they had entered Canaan when they were supposed to, those events would not have happened, and Moses would have entered the promised land. In the present context, Moses chose to highlight the rebellion of the people and its impact on his own life, which complemented what he wrote in Numbers. Thus, he accurately placed responsibility on the Israelites for not entering Canaan and for rebelling at Meribah.

In chapter 2, Moses recounts God's faithfulness and provisions (Deut. 2:7). There is an image of God as a gentle Guide who carefully directed Israel's steps. He told Moses when to pass by a nation peacefully and when to fight, and Israel followed His orders (2:37). Due to their faithfulness, God led them to military victory over the territory east of the Jordan River in preparation for their conquest of Canaan. Conversely, here God appears as a mighty warrior (3:22; cf. Ex. 14:14). Moses's speech of remembrance was meant to encourage the Israelites in what they were about to do. God led them to victory before, and He would do it again.

It is difficult to understand why Moses's account in the first chapters of Deuteronomy is so selective in its detail and condensed in scope. But we should understand that his address was meant to summarize forty years of history and personal experiences into a short period of time. Also, Moses was speaking to a crowd of millions of people and was possibly relying on others who shouted to those who were further back in the crowd. He had to be concise in order to avoid misunderstanding. This reminds us of Jesus's words in the Sermon on the Mount in Matthew 5. Jesus condensed God's laws, which were written in large parts of the OT, into eight statements, which we call the Beatitudes. Surely, He did that not for the sake of the disciples or for the learned among the people sitting in front of him, but for the crowds who had gathered around them. A speaker is always aware of his audience and chooses the right discourse for the occasion. Moses chose to focus on the events that he saw as significant and that pointed to one indisputable fact: the Israelites had made it to the promised land not because of their efforts, but because of God's faithfulness.

The first three chapters of Deuteronomy relate bittersweet memories for Moses. He stood before the people he loved, and this was his last chance to address them before he died. He was disappointed at not being able to enter the promised land, but he had spent his life following God's orders under all circumstances. He had been a loyal servant and shepherd. Through most of the journey, we see him as a strong leader who persevered through conditions that most of us would find intolerable. But that is why God had chosen him for this mission. He had the right attitude and was totally committed to do what God had set before him. Now, at the end, we get a much more human picture of Moses. He was a man with the same weaknesses all humans share. The difference is that his faith was unshakable. No matter how bad things became, Moses never questioned God's faithfulness or love. We can learn from his example. While our lives may not turn out exactly as we had hoped, we can trust that God makes all things work together for the good of those who love Him (Rom. 8:28). In Him, we are more than conquerors (Rom. 8:37).

1:1–5
Preamble to Moses's First Discourse

The first five verses give the time and place of the addresses that make up the book. What follows consists of the laws and teachings Moses addressed to the people in the land of Moab, shortly before they entered the land of Canaan. Critical scholars argue for a multiple authorship of the book on the basis of the three introductions to Moses's speech in vv. 1, 3, and 5. However, traditional commentators have made suggestions about their coherence, based on their chiastic design:

A The site of Moses's speeches—east of (lit. "across" or "beyond"—Heb. *'eber*) the Jordan (v. 1)

  B The foreshadowing of the first message of the first speech (v. 2)

    C The date when Moses began the speeches (v. 3)

  B' The foreshadowing of the second message of the first speech (v. 4)

A' The site where he delivered his speeches (v. 5)

The speaker of Deuteronomy was Moses himself, apart from a few connecting passages and the narrative about his last days. Moses reviewed the past forty years and prepared Israel for the future. He brought the laws together with the lessons learned and urged the people to keep both in mind.

Though the voice of God is heard only five times in the book of Deuteronomy (31:14b, 16b–21, 23b; 32:49–52; 34:4b), and the introduction alerts the reader to the voice of Moses, the authority behind the book was God (1:3). Moses served as the mediator of Yahweh's covenant with Israel and as a human conduit of divine revelation at Sinai. He was God's authoritative spokesperson.

Those addressed were "all Israel" and "the children of Israel" or "the Israelites" (1:1, 3). These two expressions are scattered throughout the book. The former suggests that Moses spoke to the community of faith; the latter highlights the nation's ethnic cohesion—they were the descendants of the patriarch Jacob, who was renamed Israel. The introduction gives the location of the speeches of Moses as *be'eber hayyarden*—a phrase variously translated as "beyond the Jordan," "east of the Jordan," or "on this side of the Jordan." More specifically, the text locates the speeches as being given in the land of Moab. The exact location seems to be at the northern edge of Moab (32:49; 34:1).

The time of Moses's address was in the fortieth year, on the first day of the eleventh month. The peoples' departure from Egypt appears to mark the beginning of Israel's history. On Mount Sinai, God constituted them into a holy nation (Ex. 19:6). This reference designates how much time had passed since the Exodus (Ex. 12:2). This chronological marker is synchronized with the rest of the Pentateuch (cf. Ex. 16:1; 19:1; 40:17; Num. 1:1; 9:1; 12:11; 33:38). A second chronological marker is that Moses delivered the speeches after the defeat of the two Amorite kings, Sihon and Og, who ruled east of the Jordan (Deut. 1:4). These victories provided concrete proof that when Israel was faithful to Yahweh, He would fight for them.

Moses proclaimed to the Israelites all that Yahweh had commanded him (v. 3). He functioned as an interpreter of the law (1:5), prophet (18:15; 34:10), and pastor (cf. Num. 27:17; Is. 63:11), delivering his final sermon before he passed from the scene. The use of the verb *ba'ar* ("make plain," "explain," or "expound") to designate Moses's activity refers to more than mere verbal exposition. The Hebrew word has links to the Akkadian notion of covenant making in the sense of confirming or putting a legal document into force. Through the exposition and the proclamation of the performance of the covenant renewal rituals implied in the book, the Israelite covenant ratified at Horeb was put into force for the new generation. In this sense, Moses was not just making plain the word of God, but confirming and legalizing it. The expression *hattorah hazzo't* ("this law") characterizes what follows as legal instruction. Moses taught the people (Deut. 4:5, 14; 5:31; 6:1; 31:19), and they learned the Torah (4:10; 5:1; 17:19; 31:12–13). The bulk of the book consists of instruction and exhortation, and when laws are cited, they are surrounded by exhortations.

Deuteronomy involves two kinds of Torah: oral and written. Deuteronomy 1:5 and 4:8 classify Moses's first address as oral. However, within the reports of Moses's second (6:6–9; 11:18–21; 17:18–20; 27:1–8; 28:58–61) and third (29:14–29; 30:8–11) addresses, we find numerous references to a written Torah, which is the transcribed version of his speeches. As if to dispel any doubt about the genre of the book, the introduction concludes with a verb of speech: "saying" (v. 5). Moses stood before the people as pastor, delivering his final sermon at the command of Yahweh and pleading with the Israelites to remain faithful to their God once they crossed the Jordan and settled down in the land promised to their ancestors.

1:6—4:40
Essence of Moses's First Discourse: The Grace of Calling

Moses's first discourse serves as a prologue to the book. Its description of historical events precedes the proclamation of the law in 4:44—28:68. Structurally, this speech is divided into two parts: a retrospective view (1:6–3:29), and an exhortation to obey God's laws (4:1–40). Complemented with a marked shift in style and tone, the transition to the second part is formally signaled by an exhortation to "hear/listen" (4:1). While 1:6—3:29 consists largely of historical collections, 4:1–40 bears a distinct sermonic style, as it is Moses's call for his people not to forsake the Lord and to go after other gods. They both emphasize the importance of obedience to God.

The two parts are linked by at least four theological themes: (1) Yahweh's presence (1:30–33, 42; 2:7; 4:9–14, 36–39) and (2) Yahweh's election of Israel. Although chapter 2 casts a broad vision in which Yahweh allotted

lands to the Edomites, Moabites, and Ammonites (2:5, 9, 19), Israel's title to the land was based on the election of the ancestors and the divine promise of land to them (1:8, 21, 35). The rescue of Israel from Egypt was the decisive proof of Israel's elect status (1:27, 30; 3:24; 4:32–33). (3) Obedience was the appropriate response to divine grace. In 1:19, 26–46, obedience means heading for and entering the land of Canaan; in chapter 4, obedience involves adherence to Yahweh's will as revealed at Horeb, especially to the prohibition of idolatry (vv. 1–8, 15–24, 40). (4) The land of Canaan was Yahweh's gracious grant to His chosen people (cf. 1:7–8, 20, 36; 2:29; 3:20, 24–28; and 4:1–5, 21–26, 38–40). To these features we should add Moses's personal references to his experience with the people (1:37; 3:26; 4:21). In developing these themes, Moses told Israel's story backwards in four stages: Yahweh's care and guidance of Israel from Horeb to the plains of Moab (1:6–3:29); Yahweh's revelation of His will (4:1–8); Yahweh's covenant relationship with Israel (4:9–31); and Yahweh's salvation of Israel from the slavery of Egypt (4:32–38). In 4:37, there is a fifth stage: Yahweh's love and election of their ancestors.

By recounting Israel's recent past and concluding with an impassioned appeal, Moses summoned Israel to not rebel like their ancestors (1:6—3:29). Instead, they should respond to Yahweh's amazing grace with wholehearted devotion. Only then would their future be secure (4:39–40).

1:6—2:1. Yahweh's Grace to the Exodus Generation. This passage can be divided into three sections (1:6–33; 1:34–41; and 1:42—2:1) that summarize the relationship between God and Israel from Mount Sinai to the border of the land of Canaan. The passage begins with God's command to Israel to proceed and possess the land of Canaan, His gracious gift to them. When they reached the border of the land, Moses also exhorted them to take possession, but the people disregarded the exhortations of God and Moses, refusing to possess the land because of fear at the report of the spies (1:6–33). This was one of the most grievous sins: the rebellion of the people against the loving grace of the covenant Lord. Consequently, God withdrew His promise to give the land to this rebellious generation of Israelites. He vowed that none of them, except Joshua and Caleb, would enter Canaan, and commanded the people to turn back to the wilderness. When they decided to enter the land of

Canaan and fight for it (1:34–41), God warned them against this plan and left them to their own designs. Without the presence of their covenant Lord, they were defeated by the Canaanites. Disgruntled, they decided to obey God's command and turned back to the wilderness. Their disobedience and lack of faith in God resulted in the refusal to accept and possess the divine gift of the land of Canaan (1:42—2:1). In a sense it could be said that God extended His grace to the Exodus generation by not destroying them immediately. By allowing them to live, God gave them the opportunity to repent before they died as a consequence of their sin.

2:2—3:29. Yahweh's Grace to the New Generation. In order to enter the land, the Israelites were to approach it from the east, which required passing through the territories of five tribal groups: Edom, Moab, Amon, and the Amorite kingdoms of Sihon and Og. Israel was commanded to not harass Moab (2:9). The Moabites and Ammonites were descendants of Lot, the nephew of Abraham (Gen. 19:36–38). Since they and the Edomites were relatives of Israel, and the Lord had given them their land, He did not permit the Israelites to attack them (cf. Deut. 2:4—7:19). Feeling threatened by the presence of the Israelites, the Moabites and the Midianites (also related to Israel, Gen. 25:2) came together and tried to destroy Israel (Num. 22–25). This time God fought for His people, made them victorious, and gave them the land of King Og, which was east of the Jordan, from Aroer to Gilead. Israel was already beginning to possess the promised land; prophecy was being fulfilled.

4:1–40. Yahweh's Grace with the Future in Mind. Moses described how Israel reached the border of Canaan and stressed that the future welfare of the new generation would depend on their obedience to God's Torah. In vv. 2–8, he explained why obedience to the Torah was crucial: (1) The Torah in itself is normative (v. 2), and nothing should be added or deleted from God's word; (2) Obedience to the Lord's word is a matter of life and death (vv. 3–4), as was demonstrated in the experience at Baal Peor when Israel worshiped Baal (Num 25:1–9). All who followed Baal were destroyed, but those who were alive and standing before Moses were those who held fast by making a decisive and irreversible commitment to the Lord. They were a living testimony to the importance of obedience to God's will. (3) Obedience to the Torah was a high privilege (vv. 6–8). It was not a burden imposed on the people; it was a special privilege that would make the surrounding nations envious. They would recognize Israel's status as a great nation. Interestingly, the nations would understand the greatness of Israel as coming from Yahweh, and not from its own qualities.

There was no other nation like Israel (vv. 6–8). Israel was unique because God was near His people, dwelling among them and answering their prayers. When the people who worshiped other gods prayed, their gods remained silent because they could not hear. While Israel's God was not represented by images set up in the temple or in homes, He was near and He heard the cries of His people whenever they cried to Him. Hearing was more important than seeing. Furthermore, the Israelites were privileged because they knew what their God expected of them—righteous living in obedience to laws that were just and righteous. Righteousness was not an abstract norm, but was related to concrete ethical acts that were directed toward the interests of others and that led to a harmony between the people and God. Though the Lord gave them an elevated status, they were not to boast of this, but were to become a blessing and a light to the nations.

In the major section of chapter 4 (vv. 9–31), Moses recollected three main aspects of God's dealing with His covenant people. He mentioned the word "covenant" three times (vv. 13, 23, 31), and this term provides the key to the main idea of this section and to the literary structure of the verses. Each occurrence of the word "covenant" alludes to a particular moment in the covenantal history of Israel with God: the origins of the covenant (vv. 9–14); the essence of the covenant (vv. 15–24); and the permanence of the covenant (vv. 25–31).

With regard to the *origins* of the covenant, the people heard the address of the Lord when they stood at the foot of Mount Sinai. He introduced them to His covenant, which means that He initiated the relationship with Israel. He also identified the covenant partners, defined the terms of the covenant, and determined the consequences for compliance and noncompliance. The difference between this covenant and the Hittite or Assyrian treaties was that the Sinai covenant was not imposed on Israel by an overlord upon a defeated vassal. Out of His great compassion, God had rescued Israel from an oppressive overlord to establish a loving relationship with the people for the sake of their well-being. He then asked the people to fear, or revere and respect, Him and to be in awe of His amazing and mighty saving power. This kind of fear or reverence is grounded in love, which encourages God's people to obey Him and discourages disobedience. John writes about this type of fear when he calls believers to love God as our Father and Friend, and not to fear His judgment (1 John 4:18).

The *essence* of the covenant with Israel is captured in Deuteronomy 4:15–24. Israel knew that God has no form (v. 15). There was no way that one could know how to make an idol that would be an accurate material representation of Him. Another religious perversion that Moses warned against was the worship of the sun, moon, and stars. Ancient Near Eastern people perceived these as representations of divine beings who governed the earth. Moses described five concepts of such worship: raising eyes heavenward, gazing at the heavenly array with devotion, being seduced into thinking that there is more to them than mere celestial bodies, prostrating before them, and submitting as vassals to the gods. The last clause of v. 19 is one of the most difficult in Deuteronomy. Some take it to mean that the Lord assigned heavenly bodies as objects of worship to the nations, while reserving Himself for Israel. First, this interpretation not only goes against the Lord's emphasis on worshiping Him only, but also assumes that the verb "to worship" is implied after the verb "to give/apportion." Second, the fact that the Lord gave them to all the nations means that their role was defined by the Lord. Third, this role is defined in the Creation account of Genesis 1:14–19. These heavenly bodies were not created to be worshiped, but to function as sources of light over the whole earth and to establish times and seasons. These divinely assigned functions are for the benefit of all the nations of the earth.

Verse 20 is the *center* point of the passage. It highlights Israel's special relationship with the Lord: (1) Israel was the product of the Lord's saving actions; (2) Israel was rescued from the iron furnace (used to smelt iron) of Egypt to be God's covenant partner; and (3) Yahweh claimed Israel as His own special possession. The text highlights the Lord's loving relationship with Israel. Verse 24 identifies the Lord's relationship using marital language. God is a "jealous God"—not envious, but jealous to protect His exclusively intimate, marriage-like covenant relationship with His people.

The covenant between God and Israel was to last into the future; it was to be *permanent*. Moses spoke (vv. 25–31) of the future, and his tone became pessimistic. The covenant relationship would disintegrate, and Israel would descend into idolatry. This recognition was so important that Moses called heaven and earth to witness against Israel (v. 26), using the language of a formal treaty/covenant between God and the Israelite nation. Other ancient Near Eastern treaty documents, such as those of Hittite kings, called upon various gods to serve as witnesses to hold treaty partners accountable. Since the Israelites believed in only one God (6:4), Moses instead personified and invoked heaven and earth (from which people could not escape) as witnesses.

Moses's speech was filled with irony and sarcasm as he spoke of the folly of idolatry: instead of the creature worshiping the Creator, the humans worshiped their own creations, idols formed by human hands. If they worshiped idols, the Israelites would face a total disintegration of the relationship between God, the nation, and the land. But suddenly the tone of the speech changed again. According to v. 29, Moses saw a change in the people's disposition. In Exile, when Israel would suffer and worship idols, the people would start to seek God, and He, amazingly, would let Himself be found. Unlike other deities, He is a God without a particular territory; He is the God of personal relationships. A reversal would take place out of distress. In the land of exile, the people would seek their God, He would listen, and they would find Him (vv. 29–30). They would turn back toward their God. Moses assured them that the Lord would not abandon Israel, would not destroy Israel, and would not forget His covenant with their ancestors (v. 31). These are powerful promises that gave shape to a hopeful future.

In vv. 32–40, Moses's first speech reaches its climax. God is incomparable and gracious beyond understanding in the revelation of His will (vv. 1–8) and in His invitation to the covenant relationship (vv. 9–31). Moses called the audience to engage in exhaustive historical research: Has anything like this great event (Israel's salvation) ever happened? Has anybody ever heard about such a thing? Has another nation ever heard the voice of God? If it had, did somebody live to tell about it? Has any other god done what Israel's God has done in taking a people for Himself from the midst of another nation?

Moses declared that Israel's rescue from Egypt was unique and unparalleled in history. Israel's God is unique. He revealed His acts and demonstrated that He alone is God. He chose Israel because He loved their ancestors (v. 37). Love is the basis of the covenant relationship. This was a revolutionary statement in the context of the divine/human covenant relationships of the ANE. Love was the foundation of the Sinai covenant, including the Ten Commandments. Moses appealed to the people to obey the will of God for their own good (v. 40).

4:41-43
Epilogue to Moses's First Discourse

These verses are not part of Moses's address, but are a narrative appendix about the assignment of three cities to provide asylum for those who committed accidental manslaughter. The specific law about the cities of refuge appears in 19:1-13 and Numbers 35:9-34. In Numbers 35:14, the six cities to be chosen included three in the Transjordan. Deuteronomy 4:42, therefore, seems to be an abridgement of 19:3-5.

4:44—29:1
MOSES'S SECOND DISCOURSE: EXPLAINING THE GRACE OF YAHWEH

Before Israel entered the promised land, Moses communicated the laws to the people (Deut. 4:44—28:69). This speech is preceded by a description of the contents of the discourse and its setting (4:44-49). Moses described the historical circumstances under which God gave him the laws to be communicated to Israel (chap. 5). In the preamble, Moses presented the ideological basis of the laws and appealed for their observance (6:1—11:19). He then presented the laws (chaps. 12-26), described the mutual commitments made by God and Israel (26:16-19), and prescribed ceremonies to reaffirm the covenant after they entered the promised land (chap. 27). He finally announced promises and warnings as the consequences for fulfilling or violating the covenant (28:1-68). A subscription concludes the discourse (29:1).

Moses referenced the covenant made at Mount Sinai at the beginning and at the end of the speech (5:2; 28:68). The text sandwiches the core of the discourse within framing passages. Moses preceded and followed the laws with instructions about the ceremonies, reaffirming the covenant (11:29-30; 27). He also repeated the heading to the laws at their conclusion (11:32—12:1; 26:16). Below is the chiastic structure of the second discourse (author's translations):

A "The LORD our God made a covenant with us at Horeb" (5:2)

B Ceremony at Mount Ebal and Gerizim (11:29-30)

C "Take care to observe all the laws and rules that I have set before you today. These are the laws and rules that you must carefully observe…" (11:32—12:1)

D The laws (12:2—26:15)

C' "The LORD your God commands you this day to observe these laws and rules; take care to observe them…" (26:16)

B' Ceremonies at Mount Ebal and Gerizim (27)

A' "The covenant which He had made with them at Horeb" (29:1)

4:44-49
Preamble to Moses's Second Discourse

In the speech's preamble, the reference to the Torah—including the testimonies, statutes, and ordinances—points to the covenant stipulations given at Sinai and other regulations delivered during the time in the wilderness. Verse 46 links the speech specifically to the defeat of the Amorite kings.

5:1—26:19
Essence of Moses's Second Discourse: The Grace of the Covenant

Moses's second discourse involved specific legal stipulations. It dealt first with the Ten Commandments (chaps. 5-11), followed by legislation concerning ordinances involved in worship and social interaction (chaps. 12-26). Its text in Deuteronomy is in two parts. The first is largely sermonic (5:1b—11:32), while parts of the second (12:1—29:1) are more formal, making more direct use of previously revealed prescriptions and concluding with covenant blessings and curses. However, Moses's pastoral voice runs throughout the speech. The exhortations were not inserted, as some critical scholars argue. These are vital in determining the genre of the book and are much more extensive in chapters 12-28 than is generally recognized. In the first address, there was a pastoral exhortation to covenant faith, and in the second, there were more detailed pastoral applications of covenant faith and life.

Chapters 5–11 subdivide into three parts, each of which begins with an exhortation to Israel to hear or listen (5:1b; 6:4; 9:1). By word count, these sections increase progressively in length: Deuteronomy 5:1b—6:3 consists of approximately 570 words; 6:4—8:20 has about 830 words; and 9:1—11:32 has approximately 1,150 words. Homiletically, these three parts represent three constituents of authoritative preaching: the Scripture lesson (5:1b—6:3), highlighting the foundations of covenant relationship; the theology arising from the Scripture (6:4—8:20), focusing on the essence of covenant relationship; and the appropriate response arising from that theology (9:1—11:32), demonstrating love for Yahweh as evidence of the covenant relationship. It is fitting that Moses begins this discourse on Yahweh's relationship with Israel by reciting the foundational covenant document, the Decalogue (cf. 4:13). This was the official statement of the covenant, and it fit that time's practice of covenant making. Since most of the younger generation of Israelites had grown up after the original revelation at Sinai, it was especially important for them to hear these words from Moses himself.

5:1–33. Principles of the Covenant Relationship. Moses's purpose in the first five verses was twofold: to challenge the generation he was addressing to take hold of what their parents failed to take hold of at Sinai and to highlight the importance of his teaching. His message was the same as what was revealed at Sinai, and he delivered it as the very message of God. With the opening summons calling Israel to hear/listen, Moses both challenged his hearers to listen and called for obedience to the will of the Suzerain. This summons also introduces the content of Moses's message: the revelation given by Yahweh through Moses at Sinai. As in 4:1, with this summons Moses also declared the goal of his address: the laws were to be learned and rigorously applied. The construction *shamartem la'asotam* ("keep by doing them") in 5:1 contrasts with 4:6, which used finite verbs for both "keep and do." This form in 5:1 occurs often in the book (e.g., 6:3, 25; 8:1) and is reminiscent of Genesis 18:19, where Yahweh calls on Abraham's descendants to keep (*shamar*) the way of Yahweh by doing (*'asah*) justice and righteousness.

Before Moses described the stipulations, he made an exceptional declaration: Yahweh did not make a covenant with their ancestors at Horeb, but with the people standing before Him (vv. 2–3). Verses 4 and 5 plainly state that it was to those present at his address, who were standing at the foot of the mountain, that the Lord spoke face to face. The modern reader may ask the question, "How could Yahweh make a covenant with this generation when some or most of them had not yet been born at the time of the Horeb/Sinai covenant?" Another question may arise concerning the reference in v. 3 to the ancestors. If Moses had in mind the former generation, his statement would seem to some to contradict Exodus 19–24, which clearly shows that God had made a covenant with the Israelites.

The ancestors could refer to the patriarchs, and in this case the contrast would be between the Horeb covenant and the covenant that God renewed with Abram in Genesis 15 (cf. Gen. 17). But Deuteronomy interprets the covenant rituals at Horeb and in Moab as the means by which the patriarchs' descendants were incorporated into the covenant that was originally made with them (cf. Gen. 17:7). It is natural to treat the reference to the ancestors ("fathers") as designating the Exodus generation. The association of the stipulations, decrees, and laws with the descendants of Israel who came out of Egypt (Deut. 4:45) suggests that this was how Moses understood the matter. The reason why this way of describing the covenant in 5:3 is not contradictory is because Moses was calling the new generation to identify itself with the events at Sinai. They were exhorted not to see what happened there as something that happened to their forefathers, the previous generation, but to view it as a covenant the Lord was making with them. They were invited to incorporate themselves into the redemptive history of Israel. Every new generation was to do this through covenant renewals because the covenant was made with Israel. By faith in God's redemptive power, they had been redeemed from Egypt. The new generation stood on the shoulders of the earlier generation, and God's previous speaking was relevant and applicable to them also.

Deuteronomy 5:6–21 recounts the Decalogue of Exodus 20:1–17, but it contains a number of differences and additions. These changes in the Deuteronomy version of the Decalogue were determined by the sermonic nature of the book and the contextualization of the Exodus text for the younger generation of Israelites standing at the border of the promised land (see "The Decalogue in Deuteronomy and Exodus," p. 322).

The Decalogue is foundational for later revelations in the OT. The prophets referred to the Ten Commandments and expounded their relevance when they admonished the people concerning their behavior toward God and each other. The Decalogue itself is cast as a complete entity in Exodus as well as in Deuteronomy. Its structure resembles ancient Near Eastern treaties, which were composed of distinct sections. The Deuteronomy document (as well as the Exodus one) includes its own formal introduction (v. 6), its own discrete number of stipulations (vv. 7–21), and an epilogue (v. 22).

5:6. Historical Prologue of the Decalogue. The prologue is a fundamental part of the covenant document, similar to ancient Near Eastern treaties in which the prologue introduces the suzerain and summarizes the history of the relationship between the two parties of the covenant. Unlike many ancient Near Eastern vassal treaties, however, the Decalogue document does not speak of the suzerain God as conquering and defeating Israel; it does not reflect a superior's military conquest of Israel. Rather, the foundation of this document lies in the gracious actions of a God who rescued His people from those who held them in bondage. In his discourse, Moses addressed the people of Israel as being God's own people by divine grace (v. 6). God's grace created an environment of

The Decalogue in Deuteronomy and Exodus

As already indicated, when Exodus 20:1–17 and Deuteronomy 5:6–21 are compared, a number of differences and additions to the Ten Commandments are evident.

1. Minor Differences. Leaving the Sabbath commandment aside for now, we find in the text minor differences. Among them are those that have to do with Hebrew vowels and the conjunction "and" (Heb. *waw*) that links the two clauses. These differences are not abundant and do not in any way affect the meaning of the text.

2. Significant Variations. There are a number of places where there are more significant variations between the two accounts, which to a certain extent alter or enrich the sense of the passage. First, Exodus 20:8 has the verb "remember" as the key verb, whereas Deuteronomy 5:12 has the verb "keep." The verb "remember" in Hebrew (*zakar*) has the sense of imprinting or impressing on something, while "keep, observe" (*shamar*) highlights care and stewardship. Second, Exodus 20:16 forbids giving "deceitful" testimony, while Deuteronomy 5:20 broadens this prohibition to "worthless" testimony. Third, there are several differences between Exodus 20:17 and Deuteronomy 5:21 in the prohibition about coveting what belongs to the neighbor. Exodus uses the same verb in both clauses: "desire, covet" (*khamad*). This verb indicates an emotional aspect—a desire or taking pleasure in something. It is sometimes used in a positive sense, but more commonly it suggests an inappropriate or uncontrolled,

selfish passion. Deuteronomy uses this verb for the first clause, but uses a different verb (Heb. *'awah*) for "desire" in the second clause. This verb can have a more calculating connotation to it. The other difference between Exodus 20:17 and Deuteronomy 5:21 is the order of items mentioned. Exodus places house first, followed by wife, manservant, maidservant, cattle, donkeys, and anything else. Conversely, Deuteronomy places wife first, followed by house, field, manservant, maidservant, cattle, donkeys, and anything else.

3. Additions to the Text. Additions to the Exodus version have resulted in a longer version of the Decalogue in Deuteronomy. Verse 12 (author's translation) contains the extra phrase "as Yahweh your God has commanded you." Verse 14 adds "your cattle or your donkeys" and "so that your male servant and your female servant may rest just like you." Verse 16 includes "as Yahweh your God has commanded you…in order that it may be well for you." And v. 21 contains the extra word "field."

Moses applied the Decalogue to the present and future life of the new generation. His additions were determined by the fact that they are part of a sermon in which he makes the Decalogue particularly relevant to the new generation. In the process, the content of the Decalogue was enriched and nothing was lost. Additionally, in some instances what is implicit in the Exodus text is made explicit in the Deuteronomy text.

benevolence toward Israel, expressing His desire for the people's well-being. The law was preceded by grace in the context of the gospel. Obedience to God's terms of well-being as outlined in the following commands represented a supreme response to grace, an act of worship in all aspects of life, involving reverential acts of submission and homage before the divine Sovereign.

5:7–21. Covenant Stipulations in the Decalogue. Moses's speech cast the terms of the covenant as second person singular commands without preconditions or consequences. Except for the Sabbath commandment and the command to honor parents, the stipulations were negative in form, and motive clauses were the exception rather than the rule. To interpret them as the law code for Israel alone would mean to fail in understanding their intention and meaning. They were cast in absolute, universal, and permanent terms. God's covenant document with Israel served to create a worldview intended to govern the relationship between the redeemed and their Redeemer, and between the members of the community. It has been correctly indicated that the Decalogue functioned as a type of constitution that provided the basis for later specifications of the laws as recorded in other parts of the Scriptures.

Furthermore, in Moses's discourse the Decalogue emphasized the responsibility of individuals before God and to each other. God claims exclusive allegiance and worship (vv. 7–10) and requires proper respect (v. 11). Respect is also expected toward one's household members (vv. 12–15), to one's parents (v. 16), and to one's neighbor and their property (vv.

17, 21b). Purity and fidelity in marriage are required (vv. 18, 21a), as well as respect for the property of others (v. 19), and the proper use of our words (v. 20). The first two commands (vv. 7–11) govern the vertical relationship of the Israelite with the Lord, and the last seven govern the horizontal relationship between the members of the community (vv. 16–21). Similar to the Exodus version of the Decalogue, here in Deuteronomy the Sabbath commandment receives prominent status by its central position and great quantity of words. Its theological content emphasizes a Sabbath rest designed for the entire household and is based on the Exodus experience of deliverance from bondage.

As argued previously, the modified formulations of the Deuteronomy version of the Decalogue should be understood on the basis of the sermonic aspect of the book and as a form of contextualization of the Exodus text for the young generation of Israelites standing at the border of the promised land. One of the most significant changes becomes apparent when one studies the Sabbath commandment (see below, "The Sabbath Commandment in Deuteronomy"). The expansion in Deuteronomy involves additions in vv. 12 and 14, concerning the list of all those who were to keep the Sabbath and be affected by Sabbath rest. At the end of v. 12, Moses added the very well-known fulfillment formula, "as the LORD your God commanded you." This formula occurs frequently in the Pentateuch and indicates the execution of a command given directly or indirectly by God. In Deuteronomy 5, the phrase appears three times (vv. 12, 15 [with slight variation], and 16). The three occurrences highlight the proclamation of the ten words.

The Sabbath Commandment in Deuteronomy

The greatest difference—one which has puzzled biblical scholars—between Exodus 20:8–11 and Deuteronomy 5:12–15 concerns the motivation clause for Sabbath observance. The Sabbath commandment in Deuteronomy 5:12–15 replaces the focus on Creation and God's rest on the seventh day (Ex. 20:11) with a focus on Israel's deliverance from Egypt (Deut. 5:15). Here, too, some speak about the changed historical situation of Israel, which was about to enter the promised land and needed to hear the law in applicable words.

1. The Deliverance Motivation. In the introduction to the Decalogue in Deuteronomy, Moses already focused on the applicability of the covenant and the covenant law to the new generation (Deut. 5:3). In addition, the deliverance motivation suggests that the Israelites were urged to observe the Sabbath because they were liberated from Egypt, which implies that they should give others the freedom to rest on this day. However, the deliverance motivation for the Sabbath also features prominently in the Sabbath commandment of the Covenant Code in Exodus 23:12. This text seems to be rooted in the Creation and contains the motif of God's compassionate interest in the liberation of the oppressed. Therefore, the deliverance motivation clause in Deuteronomy 5:14 does not contradict the Creation motive clause in Exodus 20:11. It appears to apply Creation themes such as rest, freedom, and equality to the actual life situation of the new generation of Israel.

2. Length of the Sabbath Commandment. The Sabbath commandment in Deuteronomy contains intricate parallelisms that show the correspondence between the Sabbath and the Exodus. Similar to the Sabbath commandment in Exodus 20, the commandment in Deuteronomy 5 is the longest, being about ten Hebrew words longer. Similar to the original version in Exodus 20, the first part of the Sabbath commandment in Deuteronomy 5 focuses on humanity (5:12–14), and the second part focuses on God, who liberated Israel from slavery (5:15).

The difference in length between the Exodus and Deuteronomy versions of the Sabbath commandment does not change its basic structure. Both versions are consistently marked by the twofold occurrence of the phrase "the Sabbath day" at the beginning and the end.

3. The Sabbath and the Individual. The text states that the Sabbath is given as an explicit command to the individual person. The personal meaning of the Sabbath is expressed four times by the second-person-singular suffix in the phrase "the LORD your God." The following parallel structure shows the importance of the Sabbath as a commandment of the personal God of each individual Israelite:

A "Observe the Sabbath day to keep it holy as the LORD your God [has] commanded you"

    B "The seventh day is a Sabbath to/of the LORD your God"

    B' "The LORD your God brought you out of/from there"—i.e., Egypt

A' "The LORD your God commanded you to make/celebrate the Sabbath day"

The fact that the phrase "the LORD your God" is used 308 times in the book of Deuteronomy testifies to its importance (the phrase occurs in Genesis only once, in Exodus twenty-seven times, in Leviticus twenty-six times, and in Numbers six times). Moreover, it is interesting to note that in the account of the Decalogue in Deuteronomy 5:6–21, the personal note is brought into view by the use of the phrase "the LORD your [singular] God," which occurs in this passage nine times: three times in the commandments that precede the Sabbath commandment (vv. 6, 9, 11) and two times in the commandment that follows the Sabbath commandment (v. 16). The cluster of four occurrences of the phrase "the LORD your God" in the Sabbath commandment demonstrates the importance that Moses placed upon the personal relationship between God and every Israelite, and shows the central position of this view, not only in the Sabbath command, but also in the Decalogue itself.

The two lines at the center of the parallel structure, B and B', draw attention to the heart of the Sabbath commandment: the Sabbath was given by "the LORD your God" who delivered each Israelite individually out of slavery, emphasized again by the second-person-singular suffix of the word He "brought you out" (v. 15). In this way, the commandment expressed the idea that the Sabbath functioned as a personal sign of personal deliverance from Egypt.

Included in the dynamic character of the Sabbath commandment may also be an allusion to the people's oppression as slaves in Egypt, recorded in Exodus 5:1–9. The presence of this allusion might be supported by the chiastic correspondence of the Sabbath and the Exodus event in the commandment, which is mentioned above. In Exodus 5:1–9, the narrative mentions that the people were not allowed to "cease" (*shabat*; Ex. 5:5) from their hard labor, but were afflicted with even more hard work (5:1–9) before God liberated them with "a mighty hand" and "outstretched arm" (Deut. 5:15; cf. Ex. 6:6; 13:9).

4. Sabbath and the Household. Further insight into the text of Deuteronomy 5:12–15 may be gained from its chiastic arrangement. The following chiastic structure displays the same characteristics as the Sabbath commandment in Exodus 20:8–11 with regard to its center focusing on the members of the Israelite household:

A God's command to keep the Sabbath holy

   B Work six days and rest on the seventh day

      C Do no work: you, your children, your male and female servants (mentioned twice), your ox, your donkey, your cattle, or your sojourner

   B′ Remember you were slaves in Egypt, and the Lord brought you out of there

A′ The Lord your God commanded you to keep the Sabbath day

A comparison of Deuteronomy 5:12–15 and Exodus 20:8–11 shows that the center of the chiasm is even more specific in Deuteronomy 5:14 (where the ox and donkey are mentioned) than in Exodus 20:10. This reference alludes to or may even be a verbatim quotation of Exodus 23:12, where the ox and the donkey were to rest because of the householder's Sabbath observance. Also, Sabbath "rest" (Heb. *nuakh*) is made more specific in Deuteronomy 5:14 by two references to the male servant and the female servant as equal beneficiaries of Sabbath rest together with the householder himself. Here, the significance of the matter of equality and justice within the Israelite household comes into view and shows the concern of this Sabbath commandment for the equality of each human being, regardless of his or her status in society (see below).

5. *Sabbath and Service.* The literary structure of the Sabbath commandment in Deuteronomy 5:12–15 emphasizes social and spiritual service. The root *'abad*, "to work, serve," is used four times and is the key word in its chiastic structure:

A You shall serve (v. 13)

   B Your male/female servant shall not do any work (v. 14)

   B′ Your male/female servant shall rest (v. 14)

A′ You were a servant (v. 15)

This arrangement shows the emphasis in the Sabbath commandment upon the act of serving. This emphasis occurs once in verbal form as part of the clause, "six days you shall labor," which corresponds to the reference about the Israelites serving as slaves in Egypt (A / A'). The center of the structure contains two references to the male/female servant and calls for them to not do any work on the Sabbath, which corresponds with resting on the Sabbath (B / B'). This parallel arrangement, built upon the word "serve," shows that the state of slavery in Egypt paralleled the six days of weekly labor. This suggests the interpretation of the Sabbath as a sign of deliverance from slavery. In other words, the Sabbath corresponded to the Exodus as an act of redemption. Because of this, every Israelite was called to service.

6. *"Remember" and "Keep/Observe" the Sabbath.* The verb that introduces the Sabbath commandment in Deuteronomy 5:12–15 has a variety of nuances in the Hebrew language: "watch, guard, observe, fulfill, keep, keep watch, spy out." Its grammatical form in Hebrew is an infinitive absolute (*shamor*), which is similar to the infinitive absolute of "remember" (*zakor*) in Exodus 20:8. Whereas "remember" connotes the commemoration of the Sabbath as a day of celebration and historical remembrance, "observe" is used for the fulfilling of obligations regarding the Sabbath in the context of obeying the law of the covenant. Moses changed the verbs because he was introducing a complementary motivation. The Exodus event is to be remembered as an act of divine deliverance. In Jewish understanding, the different verbs ("remember" in Exodus and "observe" in Deuteronomy) are linked to the different motivation clauses, but are not mutually exclusive. They serve different functions: the Exodus commandment explains the origin of the Sabbath so that the motivation is to remember our Creator, while the Deuteronomy commandment explains its aim to identify God as Redeemer and offers another motive for observing it.

One more insight in regard to the infinitive absolute form of the verb "to observe/keep" is that Deuteronomy contains only five infinitive absolute forms of the verb "observe." The first occurs in the Sabbath commandment in Deuteronomy 5:12, followed by two such forms complemented or intensified by the repetition of the same verb (a common way in Hebrew to emphasize an action). Thus in Deuteronomy 6:17 and 11:22, the Hebrew word can be translated as "observe diligently" (lit. "observe observing"); in these two cases the reference is to all of God's commandments. The fourth infinitive absolute of "observe" occurs in the Passover commandment in 16:1, and the fifth is about observing all of God's commandments (27:1). The significance of the usages of this particular verbal form is that out of the call to the Israelites to observe all the commandments, only two specific laws are singled out, namely, the Sabbath and the Passover, the latter directly related to the Exodus from Egypt. The great significance of Israel's redemption from Egypt would lend itself, on the lips of Moses, to be another reason for Sabbath observance.

The use of the infinitive absolute of the verb "to observe" in the book of Deuteronomy corresponds to the use of the same verbal form of the verb "to remember" in the book of Exodus. "To remember" is used in only two passages in Exodus, namely, for the Passover festival (Ex. 13:3) and for the Sabbath (20:8). Both events have to do with origins: the creation of everything and the liberation/creation of God's people. Both events are to be remembered through obedience to the Lord's law. While "remember" characterizes the Sabbath and the Passover festival of the Exodus from Egypt in terms of the covenant and its promises made to Israel's forefathers, the infinitive absolute of "observe" in Deuteronomy identifies and regulates the Sabbath and the Passover festival in terms of the law of the covenant. The new generation of Israelites is especially urged to observe the law of God out of love and total devotion to Him (Deut. 6:5–6; 11:13).

7. *Keep It Holy and Celebrate.* The Sabbath commandment in Deuteronomy 5:12–15 displays a parallelism between the specific verbs (also infinitives), "to keep it holy," "to make," or "to celebrate."

Deut. 5:12 — "Observe the Sabbath day *to keep it holy* as the LORD your God [has] commanded you."

Deut. 5:15 — "You shall remember…. Therefore the LORD your God commanded you *to celebrate/observe* the Sabbath day."

The parallelism between these two lines is substantiated by two identical clauses, "the Sabbath day" and "the LORD your God commanded you." The analogy between these two forms concerns a Sabbath observance that aims toward Sabbath holiness by remembering the Creator God who acted with "a mighty hand and an outstretched arm" (v. 15) when He brought Israel out of Egypt. "Therefore," the commandment continues, "you are la'asot (from 'asah, —"to do/make") the Sabbath." Contextually, 'asah expresses the idea of "observing" and "celebrating." The parallelism between the verbs "to sanctify" and "to observe/celebrate" alludes to their close relationship in the Sabbath text in Exodus 31:12–17. Here, the text also uses the verb 'asah in the same form and states that the sons of Israel are to make the Sabbath a day that is "holy to the Lord" in order to know that the Lord makes them holy. This text makes an even stronger point by suggesting that "observe/celebrate" the Sabbath has an existential meaning for human beings in a covenant relationship with God: whoever would profane the Sabbath would be put to death and be cut off from his people.

The analogy that exists between the verbs "sanctify" and "observe/celebrate" has further implications for differentiating the nature of the Sabbath and the Passover in the book of Deuteronomy. The Sabbath was to be observed by humans in order to keep it holy, and the Passover was to be observed and celebrated as well:

Sabbath — Observe to keep it holy by observing/celebrating (Deut. 5:12)

Passover — Observe and celebrate (Deut. 16:1)

While both festival days were to be observed and celebrated as a remembrance of God's deliverance, the intent of the Sabbath is emphasized by its holiness; for it was to be the day of a holy God, "the LORD your God."

8. *Sabbath and the New Creation.* The Sabbath commandment in Deuteronomy 5:12–15 addresses the individual Israelite as a human being delivered from slavery in Egypt and personally calls each one to remember his or her deliverance and therefore observe the Sabbath to keep it holy. The individual Israelite delivered from slavery experienced a new beginning marked by the gift of freedom and Sabbath rest. He or she was in a way a new creation, similar to the first created human being described in Genesis 1:26–29. The liberation of Israel from Egypt was the starting point of a new creation that parallels the creation of the human race in Genesis 1–2. Israel, as a liberated people, was God's new creation. This concept occurs frequently in the prophets and is often associated with the new creation after the Exile (cf. Is. 40:26; 42:5; 43:1, 7, 15; Mal. 2:10). This new creation is rooted in God's election of Abraham and his family (Gen. 12:1–3). In this sense, the Sabbath links the cosmic creation of the world to the establishment of a people who were to reflect the image and holiness of God (Ex. 19:6).

The Sabbath commandment addressed the individual Israelite (whether male or female) with the appeal of the law, which has its place in the heart and calls one to love the Lord with heart, soul, and strength (Deut. 6:5). This same law of the heart is a reminder and asks for obedience to all of God's commands, including a Sabbath observance aiming for Sabbath holiness. In following the law out of love for the Creator, the newly created human being will receive the gift of Sabbath rest and Sabbath holiness, and imitate the Creator's Sabbath observance, which testifies to the holiness of this day and to the sanctifying power of the God of the Sabbath.

9. *Sabbath, Gender, and Class Distinction.* The Sabbath carries high significance in regard to the question of gender and class distinction in Israelite society. In differentiating the household members by gender and social class, God placed each member at the same level in regard to the Sabbath, perhaps pointing to His ideal for the human race. His ways of dealing with distinctions in society have always been such as to mitigate their potential abuses, even while apparently tolerating some of those distinctions. This gender and class leveling during the Sabbath was highly significant, because it was given to a people who existed in a millennia-old world of hierarchical male dominance. In Exodus 20:10, seven household members are mentioned to make the house complete, with five categorized by their gender. With regard to the first "you"—a second person masculine singular—some have wondered why the wife is not part of the list.

A contextual reading of the Ten Commandments shows that they address each individual in Israel, including women and children, with a masculine singular "you." Otherwise it would mean that only males have to obey the Ten Commandments. One of the most important reasons for understanding the inclusion of the wife in the masculine "you" of the Sabbath keeper is the principle of embeddedness in Israelite society, which is based on the creation order of husband and wife to become "one flesh" (Gen. 2:24). This principle becomes visible in the Hebrew Bible by the free use of the masculine grammatical form without specification of gender unless it is used to refer to a definite, particular person.

The second and third gender defined household members in the Sabbath commandment are the son and daughter. It is truly revolutionary that God, giving the commandment, identified the children by gender, "your son...your daughter." Even more surprising is the fact that the slaves were also differentiated by gender: "your male servant...your female servant." God spoke of each as an individual in His Sabbath address. In speaking to a community that was shaped by the paradigm of hierarchical, patriarchal power, the Sabbath opened the mind of the Israelite man and woman, son and daughter, male and female servant to a diametrically opposed model—the Creator's prototype. For the Sabbath is the Lord's, and when male and female keep this day, they equally personify the "image and likeness" model established during the Creation week.

The Sabbath's significance for equality is even more emphatic in the Deuteronomy Sabbath commandment. It was reiterated by Moses after the establishment of the Levitical priesthood. The Sabbath commandment in Deuteronomy 5:12–15 contains a more detailed list than the one in Exodus 20:8–11 in that it distinguishes nine entities (you, your son, your daughter, your male servant, your female servant, your ox, your donkey, all your cattle, and your stranger) and places emphasis on the rest of the male and female servants through repetition (Deut. 5:14). The commandment shows that God's concern and kindness toward animals is to be imitated by the Israelites. Furthermore, the importance of this list lies in remembering that Israel was a nation saved from slavery. The worldly bonds of dominance and hierarchical power were broken, and Israel was called to witness to this event in its weekly Sabbath celebrations, with a message of equality and inclusion to all the surrounding living beings. The Sabbath told every Israelite man and woman that they were set free from the bonds of any kind of slavery. They existed as human beings in direct relation to God, and each individual was placed into relational bonds with others who had the same privileges, rights, status, and opportunities.

Over the course of millennia of slavery, hierarchical authority, and discrimination, the Sabbath has always carried its message forward and has remained God's standard for all cultures in all circumstances.

10. The Sabbath Is the Lord's Day. Finally, the Sabbath commandment reminds us that the day, in the sense of created time, belongs to the Creator God. Exodus 20:10a and Deuteronomy 5:14a are reminders of divine lordship and ownership, and point back to Creation. This insight has much to say to today's contemporary culture in which time is too often identified with accomplishments, and the individual is measured by his or her achievements. God has a different way of computing, measuring, and categorizing time. His Creation laws are recognized in rhythm of time that is distinct from our own perception and from life in a postmodern world. For Him the seventh day Sabbath is unique and imbued with rich blessings for those who keep it holy.

5:22–33. Epilogue. Based on a comparison with ancient treaties, many consider v. 22 to be the introduction to the next literary section that extends from 5:22 to 6:3. However, this verse is best understood as the conclusion to Moses's recitation of the Decalogue (cf. Ex. 24:12–18; 31:18). Moses mentioned the affirmative response of the people to God's grand revelation at Sinai, including their fear and the request for Moses to be their mediator (vv. 22–27). The Lord's voice was heard (vv. 28–31) accepting the people's commitment of obedience. Moses, the mediator, exhorted the covenant community to a life of obedience toward the Lord, the source of the commandments (vv. 32–33).

6:1—11:32
Proclaiming the Covenant Relationship

Chapter 6 continues Moses's second charge to the Israelites, in which he called them to acknowledge God as the teacher of the commands (6:1–2). He then discussed the third charge for the people to become doers of the commands. After reciting the Scripture in the form of the Decalogue, Moses launched into a theological exposition of that text. His primary goal in the first major part of the second address (6:4—11:32) was to impress on the people the privilege and the sheer grace of the special relationship

they enjoyed with Yahweh. This grace was not to be received casually, however; it was to be embraced with grateful and unreserved devotion to their Redeemer and covenant Lord.

6:1–25. The Centrality of Torah Study. Deuteronomy 6:4–25 is formed by four units: (a) 6:4–9, (b) 6:10–15, (c) 6:16–19, and (d) 6:20–25. Thematically, these paragraphs fall into a parallel pattern: paragraphs (a) and (d) reference teaching God's words and instructions to one's children; paragraphs (b) and (c) warn against forgetting God and His providence, and against testing His ability to provide. Paragraphs (c) and (d) emphasize the reward for obedience and the role of the laws in expressing and instilling reverence for God; they point to the introductory section in 6:1–3 and create a frame for the entire chapter.

6:4–9. The Shema. Verses 4 and 5 are identified to the core of the Shema, a name that is derived from the Hebrew word for "hear." The Shema is the sum total of all the statutes, which the Israelites were to abide by and teach to subsequent generations. This section displays a meaningful structure. First, there is a proclamation containing three words that apply to God's covenant stipulations: *mitswah*—"command," *khoq*—"decree" or "statute," and *mishpat*—"judgments," "rules," or "laws" (v. 1). These stipulations were given as a guarantee for a prolonged life. Then, Moses emphatically appealed to his people to listen and be careful (v. 3). The metaphorical words used to describe the land—as one that was flowing with milk and honey—capture the notion of a strong desire for a bountiful, lavish place, a place so different from the wilderness where the people had lived and wandered for forty years. The land that lay in front of them would overflow with blessings.

Scholars debate the grammar, syntax, and etymology of the words used in this passage. Unquestionably, these words aimed, according to the context, at the innermost being of the listeners—at their heart (vv. 4–6). From there the words would impact the world of the family, reaching far to the outmost limits (the gates; v. 9).

The term "gates" certainly does not set limits on the impact of these powerful words concerning the only God of Israel. For "your gates" were not the borderline for God; they were meeting places to enter into dialogue with other individuals. The gates were exits into the world for lovers of God and humans; they were entry points for outsiders to be drawn in and experience God's love. "Your gates" surely hold opportunities for God as well as challenges for the lovers of God.

The problem with v. 4 is that it contains two clauses without a verb, and translators are expected to supply one. Linguistic studies indicate that in such cases the verb "to be" is usually inserted. What follows represents the main translations proposed by scholars:

"Hear, O Israel, Yahweh our God; Yahweh is one."

"Hear, O Israel, Yahweh our God is one Yahweh."

"Hear, O Israel, Yahweh is our God; Yahweh is one."

"Hear, O Israel, Yahweh is our God; Yahweh is one/unique."

"Hear, O Israel, Yahweh is our God, Yahweh alone."

The Hebrew word for "one" used in the Shema is also used for man and woman in Genesis 2:24—they become "one flesh." This majestic proclamation emphasizes the essential oneness

of God. He had already been known to be the only God (cf. 4:35, 39). There are passages where the plurality of God is implied in the OT (e.g., the plural pronouns in Gen. 1:26–27). Also, there are passages where the Angel of the Lord is clearly a reference to a divine being who *is also* Yahweh (see Gen. 6:7–14; 22:11–18; 31:11–13; Ex. 3:2–6; 14:19; 23:20–23; Judg. 2:1–5; 13:2–23; Hos. 12:3–5; Mal. 3:1). Furthermore, the messianic prophecies imply the divinity of the Anointed One (e.g., Is. 9:6; Mic. 5:2). In the NT, the plurality of God is also clearly indicated or implied (Matt. 28:19–20; John 1:1–3; 14:16–18; Acts 5:3–4; Col. 1:15–20; Heb. 9:14). As a result, the unity and oneness of God mentioned here would not exclude the plurality of the holy Trinity of Father, Son, and Holy Spirit (see Matt. 28:19). This is the mystery of three persons who are yet one deity (cf. Col. 1:19; 2:9). The oneness of God would also include the idea that He is the only one for His people (cf. Zech. 14:9, for all peoples). This is the concept behind the First Commandment (Deut. 5:7; Ex. 20:3). Israel's worship of idols—as attested during the monarchy, and lamented and condemned by the prophets—is astonishing in light of their testimony to the monotheistic concept of God over the course of millennia.

The recitation of the Shema had legal implications. It enjoined the people to remain true to their calling. It was a committal to follow a declaration that was true and firmly established. It had the force of an oath solemnly affirming that the obligation just recited was valid and binding in every way. Furthermore, the Shema emphasized the response that God expects from his people. The first verb, the imperative "hear," occurred in a series of subsequent imperatives: love, impress or teach, talk, bind, and write. Its binding importance is reflected in the Gospels.

A scribe approached Jesus and asked which commandment was the greatest or most significant, and He responded quoting the Shema as well as Leviticus 19:34 (Mark 12:29–31). Jesus stated further that all the Law and the Prophets were based on these two commands. To love God with all the soul (v. 5) is the driving force behind obedience to all the statutes and ordinances given by Him for the welfare of His people. Jesus regarded the principles of love for God and for other human beings as the basis of Scripture. The Ten Commandments provide principles based on two kinds of love. The fact that love is foundational should not surprise us because the Bible expresses the character of God in terms of love (1 John 4:8).

The Shema is one of the most important identifications in Judaism. Its liturgical significance is reflected in the fact that it appears immediately after the Decalogue in the Nash Papyrus, a second-century B.C. liturgical text, and in a first-century phylactery text from Cave 8 at Qumran, where the Shema is written in a rectangle and surrounded by other texts. To this day, Orthodox Jews recite the Shema as part of their prayers when they wake up and before they fall asleep (cf. according to the instruction in v. 7). In so doing, they take "the yoke of the kingdom," which means that they place themselves under the sovereignty and kingship of Yahweh. Some Jewish groups take the command of v. 8 to mean that God's written laws should be literally bound to the body. Others have understood these instructions as a symbolic emphasis of the need to remember well the commands of God (as in Ex. 13:9, 16, on remembering the events of the Exodus). In any case, placing God's laws on the hand and head highlights the importance of doing and thinking about them (cf. Ezek. 9:4; Rev. 7:3; 13:16).

6:10—8:20. Challenges of Faith. In Deuteronomy 6:10 and 8:20, Moses forecast the challenges that his people would endure as a result of their loyal confession to God. Some scholars suggest that the structure of this section is developed on the basis of internal and external tests arranged according to an ABA order. The internal tests are in 6:10–25 and 8:1–20, and the external are in 7:1–26. Whereas 6:4–5 embodies the central idea of love for God, the rest of the section (chaps. 6–8) responds to the question, "What does it mean to be totally committed to God?" Moses presented his audience with the

challenges that come as a result of unreserved loyalty to God.

Deuteronomy 6:10–25 contains an internal test and the answer to it. Israel was warned not to forget their loyalty to the Lord once they entered into the prosperous land of Canaan. They were not to follow the gods of the people surrounding them. The solution to this potential test or temptation is given in vv. 20–25. In this passage, Moses tried in different ways to impress upon the people the importance of loyalty to God. Obedience to the different laws was to be firmly grounded in the Lord's saving acts. In other words, it was all predicated on His grace.

Deuteronomy 7:1–26 presents the external test that the people of Israel would face when they reached Canaan. The chapter describes the Gentile nations as the greatest danger to Israel's loyalty to God. The Israelites were forbidden to enter into covenantal relationships with the nations or to intermarry with them. They were commanded to eliminate the Canaanite population. This latter policy is known as the *kherem* ordinance and is based on the Hebrew word for "destroy, ban, devote for destruction" (see below, "The Extermination of the Canaanites"; see also "Holy Warfare," p. 372). Some find in it a reference to ritual sacredness and argue that *kharam* means "to reserve for divine service." This last meaning is far from certain. The regulation was intended to preserve both the Israelites' holiness and God's plan for them in a world of threatening idolatry and corruption.

Deuteronomy 8:1–20 contains the third challenge of faith that the Israelites would encounter in the promised land. The chiastic structure of this chapter highlights the importance of not forgetting to keep the commandments of the Lord when life is good and full of satisfaction. At that time, God would test His people to know what

The Extermination of the Canaanites

In their response to one of the most problematic texts in all of Scripture, the early church fathers tended to interpret Deuteronomy 7 allegorically. Modern scholars ascribe the chapter's harsh policies (cf. also chap. 20) to a primitive mindset that lacked the ethical and religious ideals preached by later prophets and that was inferior to those of Jesus in the NT (Matt. 5:44; Luke 6:27, 35). Other scholars hold to the concept of

progressive revelation in the sense that God adapted the prevailing practices of the time to His own agenda, which consisted of establishing a future society free from violence. This raises questions about divine consistency and seems to either support Marcion's heretical assertion that the God of Israel and the God of the NT were two different Gods, or that God is the same in both, flexible in desiring an idealistic universe, but working for the time being in the realistic universe of sin.

1. God as the Agent. It has been suggested, based on Exodus 23:20–33, that the destruction of the Canaanites was not a prescription for the Israelites, but was given as God's pledge that He Himself would exterminate the Canaanites. He would do this by sending His terror ahead of the people when they entered the promised land. He would confuse the Canaanites, make them run, send hornets ahead of Israel's army, drive out the Canaanite nations, and deliver them into the hands of Israel. All of these actions would not happen immediately, but would be implemented by God "little by little" (vv. 29–30; Deut. 7:22).

2. God as Indirect Agent. Furthermore, it is important to note that Exodus 23 does not use the word *kherem* to speak of the total destruction of the Canaanite nations, but employs another Hebrew word (*kakhad*) with the connotations of hiding, keeping something back, effacement, and nonexistence. This word occurs in Exodus 23:23 and is usually translated as "I will completely destroy them" or "I will cut them off." However, its grammatical form in Hebrew is causative (*hiphil*) and could denote God acting indirectly through afflictions that would cause the Canaanites to destroy themselves. The divine activities listed above support this latter reading. The reason for the legislation was given: the Canaanites would cause Israel to sin against God (23:33).

3. Israel as Agent. Deuteronomy 7, on the other hand, focuses on Israel's active partnership with God after they entered Canaan. In this instance, Moses placed much emphasis upon the reason for the Canaanites' destruction, namely to safeguard Israel's holiness and fidelity in regard to God. Ethnic purity was not at all in the purview of the legislation. However, the war policy of Deuteronomy 7 raises serious ethical questions, especially for a postmodern reader: How could a God who claims to be gracious and merciful command the extermination of whole populations?

Consideration of the biblical *kherem* policy needs to take into account that if Deuteronomy 7 is to be interpreted in terms of total annihilation, the Israelites should have been completely destroyed because their failure to enforce *kherem* meant its application to them (see vv. 4 and 26). But even in Deuteronomy,

Moses foresees the failure of Israel and indicates that they would not be completely destroyed, but that a remnant would survive God's judgment of the Exile (4:29–31; cf. 30:1–10). Total extermination does not necessarily mean the literal extermination of all.

4. Its Implementation in Joshua. The conquest narratives in the book of Joshua cause some to cast doubt on a literal interpretation of the *kherem* ordinance that would have required the total, not partial, extermination of the Canaanite population. The case of the Gibeonites is certainly unique, but remains a good example. Although they feared that the Israelites would execute the policies of Deuteronomy 20:15–18 (see Josh. 9), they were not exterminated because they abandoned their idolatry and converted to the Lord. Although they were Canaanites, the divine command to destroy the *idolatrous* Canaanites did not apply to them. The accounts in Joshua and Judges suggest that the *kherem* ordinance was carried out in only four places: Jericho (Josh. 6:24), Ai (8:28), Hazor (11:13–14), and Laish (Judg. 18:27; cf. Josh. 19:47). This accords with the archaeological record, which does not present evidence for a widespread destruction of Canaanite cities, and it accords with texts in Deuteronomy, which mention that the Israelites would inherit cities that they did not build—cities that were intact, great, and splendid (Deut. 6:10–11). The text also makes it clear that the Hebrews made a mistake by not driving out or exterminating all the idolatrous inhabitants of Canaan (Judg. 1:27—2:4).

5. Fundamental Principles. When dealing with this subject, we should first remember that the *kherem* policy was driven neither by hate for other nations nor by ethnic concerns. The reason for the policy was the elimination of all rivals to God, who holds supreme power over Israel. Under His authority there was no room for compromise with the gods of other nations. In addition, these nations were being destroyed because of their recalcitrance and wickedness. God had allowed hundreds of years of probationary time for the Canaanites to accept His love and forgiveness, but they would not (see Gen. 15:16; Deut. 9:4–5). The uncompromising nature of God had been declared in the command of the Shema (6:4–5) and in the first two of the Ten Commandments (5:6–9).

Second, the inheritance records and the farewell speech in the book of Joshua (Josh. 13–21, 23) testify to the concept put forth in Exodus 23:20–33 concerning the initiative and activity of God in freeing the land from the Canaanite nations (Josh. 23:3; and vv. 4–13). In addition, Joshua directly referred to Deuteronomy 7 (the religious concept of war, the prohibition of covenant making with the Canaanites, and intermarriage). In a theocracy, war and destruction took place in order to eliminate idols and their worship. Biblical theocracy strove toward a society that lived uncompromisingly under the government of the supreme God.

was in their hearts (v. 2). Notice the structure of the passage:

A Observe the commandments and prosper (v. 1)

  B The wilderness and the manna (vv. 2–4)

    C Observe the commandments in prosperity (vv. 6–10)

    C′ Do not forget the Lord in prosperity (vv. 11–14)

  B′ The wilderness and the manna (vv. 15–16)

A′ Remember and do not forget the Lord or you will perish (vv. 18–20)

The threat was to forget that goodness and well-being come from the Lord and not by chance. The gift of food and the sustenance of life are from the Creator God. Moses appealed five times to the people to keep alive the memory of Yahweh's miraculous actions in the wilderness (vv. 2, 11, 14, 18, 19). The remembrance of God's goodness in the past strengthens our hope and faith in the present. The notion of remembering played a key theological role in Moses's speech. The main charge was to keep the commands of Yahweh by walking in His ways and fearing Him (vv. 6, 11). Moses's dramatic descriptions of the Israelite experience in the wilderness heightened the nature of the test and called for a personal commitment to the Lord.

9:1—11:32. Disputations. The opening words, "Hear, O Israel!" (9:1), signal the beginning of the third major section (9:1–11:32) of Moses's second address to Israel (4:45—26:19). This large section can be divided according to its temporal vision, which shifts inconsecutively from Israel's future (9:1–6), to the past (9:7–10:11), to the present (10:12–11:1), back to the past (11:2–7), forward to the future (11:8–25), and ends at the present (11:26–32).

Deuteronomy 9:1—10:11 is a self-contained literary subunit featuring Moses looking forward to the crossing of the Jordan (9:1). He demonstrated that the future of Israel was grounded in the events of the past when Yahweh commanded him to lead the people away from Sinai/Horeb and toward the possession of the land He had promised to their ancestors (10:11). The appeal between these two events is composed of stories about Israel's time in the wilderness, their rebellions, the way the Lord handled their wayward actions, and their relationship with each other. All these parts of the text are held together by the temporal phrase "forty days and forty nights." This phrase occurs nine times in the OT and five times here: it took forty days and forty nights (1) for the Lord to deliver the Ten Commandments to Moses (9:9–10), (2) for the Israelites to prove the shallowness of their covenant commitment when they worshiped the golden calf (9:11–17), (3) for Moses to deal with the sin of the people and his own (9:18–21), (4) for Moses's plea before the Lord not to annihilate His people (9:25—10:5), and (5) to receive the assurance that the Lord would not destroy His people and to hear the order to march toward the promised land (10:10–11). It was a period of time that led to new beginnings—good or bad.

The elevated style of 10:12—11:1 suggests that Moses's second speech was nearing a climax. The use of *we 'attah*—"and now" (10:12) signals a climactic moment, similar to 4:1, when Moses introduced the section of commandments and statutes. With the words recorded in 10:12, Moses stressed the moral and spiritual implications of a covenant relationship with the Lord. He used the rhetorical marker "and now" before his opening question, "What does the LORD your God ask [or "require"] of you?" (10:12a). Moses answered (11:1), but also gave a preliminary answer (10:12b). It contained two main ideas: they were to fear the Lord, their God, and to serve Him with full heart and soul. In general, Moses provided three answers to the opening question:

(1) allegiance to the Lord expressed by a fundamental disposition to fear and love, followed by obedience to the God of the covenant; (2) circumcision of the heart as a true sign of the Israelites belonging to the Lord (not merely the outer sign of circumcision instituted in Genesis 17); and (3) unqualified devotion to the Lord. Moses then tied the three responses together in the final climactic response that linked it back to the Shema (11:1; cf. 6:5).

Deuteronomy 11:2–28 is a complex passage of historical recollections and theological expositions and exhortations. The text is characterized by frequent repetitions, interruptive appositions, and parenthetical comments. From Moses's preacher's perspective, this style was most suited to impress the audience with his message. From a structural point of view, the passage has a break between vv. 7 and 8 as Moses moved from recollections of history to exhortation.

Moses presented lessons from history (vv. 2–7) as he reviewed God's mighty acts against Pharaoh and what He did to Dathan and Abiram when the earth opened and swallowed them. Moses included in his speech references to the land (vv. 8–12) for which God constantly cared, as His eyes were continually on it (v. 12). The land was God's climactic gift to Israel; it was the fulfillment of His promise to their ancestors (Gen. 17:8; Ex. 3:6–8; 6:8). This gift challenged the people to remain faithful to God (Deut. 11:13–21), who provided for the fruitfulness of the land. If they were faithful to the Lord, they would possess the land from the wilderness to Lebanon, from the River Euphrates to the Mediterranean Sea (v. 24). But they would have to decide whether to receive the blessings or the curses that were embedded in the covenant relationship with the Lord (vv. 26–28).

Deuteronomy 11:29–32 closes this portion of Moses's second speech (8:1—11:32) with a reference to the covenant blessings and curses. This passage looks forward and anticipates the covenant ceremony that would take place with the reading of the blessings on Mount Gerizim, and with the reading of the curses on Mount Ebal. In his brief speech, Moses described the ceremony with only nine words in the Hebrew text (v. 29b). It would occur soon because, as Moses emphatically indicated, they would cross over the Jordan to enter and possess the land (v. 31). Moses concluded this section of his second speech with a most contemporary appeal: the laws and decrees were set before the Israelites "today": these decrees were to be obeyed.

12:1—26:19
Proclaiming the Dimensions of the Covenant Relationship

In this new section of the second speech, Moses dealt with the vertical and horizontal dimensions of the covenant obligations. The dominant theme recorded in Deuteronomy 12:2—14:21 is the vertical relationship with the Lord; the theme appearing in 15:19–16:21 is primarily about human concerns. These vertical/horizontal dimensions were to teach the people that the worship of God and everyday life are intertwined. To come before the Lord with offerings and sacrifices means nothing if familial or neighborly relationships are not cleared of all burdens and strains. Acceptable worship to the Lord asks for fidelity in horizontal relationships.

Deuteronomy 12:1 introduces a new section (12:1—26:19), which is composed of a formal series of laws, and 26:16-19 is its formal conclusion. The covenant obligations found here are very similar to those found in the Book of the Covenant (Ex. 20:22—23:19). They are similar in structure, and their opening and closing sections resemble each other. An outline of the material, based on the content of these two passages, helps the reader to grasp the flow of thought. A chiastic structure occurs in both law sections, with the principles of worship framing the different laws:

A Principles of worship highlighting Israel's cultic expression of devotion to Yahweh (Ex. 20:23–26; Deut. 12:2—16:17)

  B Casuistic and apodictic laws highlighting Israel's ethical expression of devotion to Yahweh (Ex. 21:1—23:9; Deut. 16:18—25:19)

A' Principles of worship highlighting Israel's cultic expression of devotion to Yahweh (Ex. 23:10–19; Deut. 26:1–15)

But these parallels, useful as they are, do not do complete justice to the extent and scope of the passage in Deuteronomy. The sermonic tone and style portray Moses as a preacher, as is also the case in chapters 6–11. While he drew on the specific laws and regulations that Israel received at Sinai, his aim was more pastoral than legislative.

In terms of the flow of this speech (Deut. 12–16), Moses began with the nation's direct obligations to the Lord (12:2—16:17). After presenting the vertical dimension—their relationship with the Lord—Moses moved to the horizontal dimension and gave instructions about the offices through which the Lord would exercise His kingship once the people settled in the promised land (16:18—21:9). Then, he included a section on the family (21:10—22:30), reminded the people of the boundaries of the covenant community (23:1–8), gave regulations regarding different aspects of Israelite life (23:9—25:19), and ended with instructions for worship, returning to the vertical dimension (26:1–15). By adopting the vertical/horizontal dimension and structuring his speeches accordingly, Moses, the pastor, taught his congregation that worship and daily life are intricately intertwined. Acceptable vertical expressions of covenant faithfulness are preconditioned by fidelity in horizontal relationships, which offer opportunities for the corporate celebration of the vertical.

12:2–14. Worship at the Sanctuary. The limitation of sacrificial worship to a single place is the most unique and far-reaching law in Deuteronomy. It affected the religious life of individuals, the sacrificial system, the way festivals were celebrated, the economic status of the Levites, and the judicial system of Israel. Aside from the triannual celebrations at the central sanctuary, religious activities such as prayer and study were to take place in people's lives throughout the year.

In his expositions about the obligations of the people to the Lord (12:2—16:17), Moses employed a positive and appealing strategy: he introduced the obligations by inviting the people to celebrate the presence of the Lord in the promised land (12:2–14). There were negative charges, like the command to purge the land from Canaanite idol worship (vv. 2–4, 8–9), interpolated with positive invitations and instructions to worship the Lord, (vv. 5–7, 10–12). The invitation that families were to gather and eat together in the place that the Lord would choose for worship is especially beautiful and brings out the meaning of ancient fellowship practices as the culmination of covenant making rituals (Gen. 31:54; Ex. 24:5–11). At Mount Horeb, only a small privileged leadership circle had the opportunity to eat in the presence of the Lord (Ex. 24:9, 11). Here, Moses opened the invitation to everyone. Worship is a joyful practice; it calls for celebration and communion among all participants.

Interestingly, Moses used language reminiscent of the Sabbath commandment to call the congregation to worship and joyful fellowship at the sanctuary (Deut. 12:12; cf. v. 18). The equality and inclusivity of the Sabbath in regard to social status and gender were placed at the forefront by Moses's use of this language. Male and female slaves were invited to worship together with sons and daughters and were to receive the same treatment. The Levites were not given higher authority or even a place of honor at the table, but they were to gather like the others to enjoy a meal before the Lord (Deut. 12:18).

For the contemporary readers of this text, Deuteronomy 12:1–14 offers some elements of a theology of worship: (1) The Lord, the Creator of heaven and earth, is the Redeemer of humankind and the only one who can legitimately receive our praises. All other objects are illegitimate, even abominable. (2) The purpose of worship is to please the Lord, and this is to happen with humility and awe before God in the course of the lives of the worshipers (Ps. 15; 24; Is. 1:2–17; Mic. 6:6–8). (3) The location of worship, important as it is, is less important than the presence of the divine host (cf. John 4:21–34). Fortunately, in Deuteronomy God selected the place where He would be present for worship. (4) True worship occurs in the presence of an awe-inspiring God and in communion with fellow believers. Deuteronomy emphasizes the inclusion of all; gifts of food would be shared not just with family members, but also with the marginalized (12:12). It would be correct to say, in agreement with others, that the hour of church worship is often the most segregated hour of the week. Deuteronomy stands against this and suggests that when churches split their services or differentiate on the basis of hierarchical status, social status, race, gender, age, musical tastes, or for any other reason, the house of God is divided. Consequently, God's goal for unity and fellowship in equality, inclusion, and the joy of worship is diminished.

12:15–28. Sacrifices. Moses proceeded to provide instructions about the sacrifices to be offered in the place of worship chosen by the Lord. This section has two parts, like a coin with two sides. On one side are the regulations for the regular slaughter of animals and meat eating (vv. 15–16, 20–25); on the other side are the instructions about sacred offerings at the sanctuary (vv. 17–19, 26–27). When Moses spoke about meat eating, his way of expression was remarkably positive and generous (vv. 15, 20–22). He highlighted the craving of the people to eat meat thrice daily (vv. 15, 20b, 21b) and then anticipated their expression of this craving (v. 20a). The response to the stress on craving meat is fourfold: (1) The people were permitted to slaughter animals and eat meat because of the Lord's blessing on the promised land (v. 15; cf. 16:17). (2) The people were allowed to slaughter animals and eat meat in their towns and in proportion to the Lord's blessing (vv. 15, 20–21). The regulation given in Leviticus 17:1–16, according to which the slaughtering of animals and eating their meat was only allowed in front of the tabernacle, would no longer be necessary in the land of Canaan. (3) Anyone, clean or unclean, was permitted to eat meat (vv. 15b, 22b). This included every person, even those who had touched a corpse or carcass, or were unclean because of a disease or a bodily discharge (Lev. 11–15; Num. 5; 19). (4) The people were allowed to eat the meat of clean domestic animals and of wild game (vv. 15b, 22).

The concession to eat meat does not exclude the concept of the value of animal life before God and neither does it eliminate the plant-based diet assigned to humans in the beginning (Gen. 1:29). During the journey of the people through the wilderness, the Lord initially provided vegetarian food for them (Ex. 16:1–4). The plant-based diet remained an ideal in the setting of an agrarian society. The concession to eat meat was regulated by the Lord. Slaughtering an animal to eat meat was commonly associated with the cult in the sanctuary, but it was not detached from God's perspective and the regulations about the proper treatment of animals. There was the demand to drain the blood (vv. 16, 23). The common slaughter of animals was to follow the same method used in sacrificial slaughter.

12:29—13:18. Warnings about Apostasy. Moses continued to warn his audience against idolatry as he discussed the temptations that Israel would encounter in the promised land. He placed four hypothetical circumstances before the people under which seduction toward the Canaanite gods might occur. The first might result from the work of a false prophet (13:1–5). This is the first time that Moses uses the word "prophet" (*nabi'*) in Deuteronomy. In the Old Testament, a prophet is one who is summoned or called by God to proclaim His messages (Ex. 7:1–2; Jer. 23:16–22). Moses's audience was not oblivious to the meaning and work of prophets. Abraham was regarded as a prophet of God (Gen. 20:7). The Israelites even knew of the prophetic ministry of a female prophet, Miriam. Moses, the leader himself, was regarded as a prophet in Israel, as was Aaron. There was also the incident with Balaam, the deceiving prophet (Num. 22–24; 31:8, 16; Deut. 23:4–5). Therefore, to discern between true and false prophets was of highest importance.

The second hypothetical cause of an apostasy was a dreamer (Deut. 13:1–5). Studies on ancient Near Eastern history reveal that divination through dreams (oneiromancy) was widespread. There are numerous texts from Egypt and Mesopotamia about such phenomena. Moses warned that such persons might provide a sign or wonder and then invite the people to follow other gods (13:2b [3b]). These "other gods" were ones they had not known, the gods of the Canaanites (12:29–30). The treatment of false prophets and dreamers who would try to entice Israel to follow other gods is unambiguous and absolute: they were to be put to death (13:5a). In the political arena, a person who tries to subvert allegiance to the king is sentenced to death; how much more would the death penalty apply to one who called God's people to abandon Him and worship idols?

The third hypothetical scenario of apostasy was related to a member of an Israelite family (13:6–11). Moses spoke about family members and close friends—a brother, a son, a daughter, a wife, and a friend—people who were loved and respected. The list heightens the threat of potential familial treachery. In cultures where family networks are close, this scenario involves the highest potential danger. The fourth scenario of apostasy involved anyone in Israel who was rumored to be enticing fellow citizens to desert the Lord in favor of other gods (13:12–18). Again, the seriousness of idolatry called for capital punishment.

14:1–21. Eating. Eating is connected to a holy life. Moses constructed this section as another chiasm:

A A holy people to the Lord their God (vv. 1–3)
  B Edible versus inedible animals (vv. 4–20)
A' A holy people to the Lord their God (v. 21)

There is a clear link to Leviticus 11 (see "Clean and Unclean Animals," p. 257). Moses emphasized the definition of kosher food instead of the abominable animals. In addition, vv. 1–3 build the foundation for the list of permitted and prohibited animals. Moses spoke of Israel as a holy people, possessing a unique covenant status with God. Without this foundation right at the beginning, the words spoken here would have sounded like those of a suzerain imposing his law on a vassal. The status and quality that God had placed upon His people marked them in all aspects of life, including eating and the treatment of the body. The latter was probably related to pagan rites of mourning for the dead.

14:22–29. The Economically Vulnerable. Although tithing was a well-known practice in the ancient world and is found elsewhere in the Torah, Deuteronomy provides legislation concerning a second tithe. Leviticus 27:30–33 proclaims the tithes on both produce and cattle as "holy to the LORD." This phrase normally indicated that tithes belonged to the priests and the Levites (cf. Lev. 22:10; 27:21). A farmer could redeem produce by paying its value plus an extra fifth. Numbers 18:21–32 indicates that all tithes were required to be given to the Lord, who then assigned it to the Levites, who were also to give a tithe of tithes to the priests. The Levites could then live off the rest of the tithes given to them. This was the first tithe, not to be confused with the second tithe mentioned in Deuteronomy. This second tithe was to be used for a family fellowship meal eaten in the sanctuary.

Deuteronomy 14:22–29 begins with an emphatic call to annually set aside an extra tenth of all that the fields produce. What follows is an invitation for celebration. The goal of the speech was reached when Moses expressed concern for the well-being of the economically vulnerable. From this perspective, a true covenant relationship with the Lord was to be demonstrated by active care for the poor. This commitment would reach its high point when the poor were invited to join in the celebration in the Lord's presence at the sanctuary.

Similar to the previous instruction about tithe, another highly significant insight Moses provided was about inclusion and equality (14:28–29; cf. 26:12–15). Every three years, the second tithe was to be used for the benefit of the poor and powerless in Israel (vv. 28–29). It seems that the beneficiaries of this tithe were those who had no inheritance in the land, that is to say, the widows, orphans, foreigners, and the Levites. The OT often lists the triad of widow, orphan, and foreigner as representing the poor, oppressed, and disempowered within a patriarchal society governed by a hierarchical order. They were the most easily marginalized and had no safety net; but God cared for their needs. This extra tithe that provided for the Levites and for the "disempowered triad" reveals God's concern for equality and justice.

15:1–23. Remission of Debts. The appeal to be generous toward the poor and disadvantaged found a climatic expression in the seventh year. Debts were to be canceled, and lost property was to be returned to the original owner. Creditors were not to pressure debt-slaves to pay off their loan before the arrival of the year of remission. When Moses began to speak about the different groups of disadvantaged people, he looked with a visionary eye into the future and stated that there would be no poor in Israel because of God's blessing, (v. 4). However, in order for them to arrive at this hope, an almost utopian future, Israel was called to have the greatest concern for the poor, the widows, the fatherless, and strangers. These were economically deprived and dependent on others for relief and survival. When he gave instructions on how to treat the poor, Moses used the term "brother" (or "fellow Israelite"; vv. 7, 9, 11); if the Israelites treated the poor badly and they cried out to the Lord, this treatment would be recognized as sin. There are definite warnings about hardheartedness and tightfistedness (v. 9), and there is a call to generosity toward the poor in the context of lending money to them, especially when there is little to no hope of repayment.

It was also important to establish humane laws concerning those who were bound to work for six years toward paying off a debt. Just because the debt was paid (by six years of labor) did not mean that the newly released man or woman was to leave without payment of their own (v. 13). Coinage was not invented until the Persian period (by Lydians or Greeks in the sixth or fifth centuries B.C.), so lending and payment at this time were done through foodstuff or flocks. Concerning the law of the firstborn (vv. 19–23), see Leviticus 27:26–27.

16:1–17. The Three Annual Festivals. For the celebration of three festivals, the Israelites were to travel to the place of worship that the Lord would choose for Himself in the promised land.

These three festivals were the Festival of Passover (vv. 1–8), the Festival of Weeks (vv. 9–12), and the Festival of Tabernacles (vv. 13–15). The Festival of Passover and the immediately following Festival of Unleavened Bread had their origin in the Exodus event and are described in detail in Exodus 12. In Exodus, the focus is on the festival's observance in the homes of the Israelites in Egypt; there was no centralized place of worship. In this speech in Deuteronomy, Moses envisioned and prophesied that God would choose for Himself a place of worship in the promised land; thus the locus of the celebration of the festival shifted, and it became more of a national celebration. Moses strongly charged the people to keep the Passover by using Sabbath language. The link with the Sabbath is made direct and clear by the use of the same word of command: "observe" is found in both passages (Deut. 5:12 and 16:1); likewise in Exodus, the word "remember" occurs in two passages, the Passover text in Exodus 13:3 and the Sabbath commandment in Exodus 20:8. Furthermore, a Sabbath link is also found in the reference to the six days during which the Israelites were to eat unleavened bread as a remembrance of the time of slavery in Egypt. On the seventh day, there was to be a solemn assembly before the Lord (Deut. 16:8).

The Festival of Weeks (vv. 9–12) brought the Sabbath even more to the forefront. While the Passover already showed its closeness to the Sabbath, it was the Festival of Weeks that had an even stronger connection through its counting of seven times seven days after Passover and the Festival of Unleavened Bread. Moreover, Sabbath inclusion was highly emphasized when Moses's words recalled the different members of the household (also mentioned in the Sabbath command) who were to celebrate and rejoice before the Lord. Then Moses continued with the list and added orphans, the fatherless, and widows (v. 11). The Festival of Tabernacles (vv. 13–15) was the final festival of the year, and the Levites were to sit together with everybody else to celebrate with people from all classes and both genders (v. 14). It seems that the festivals incorporated the Sabbath concern for equality and inclusion among the Israelites. A biblical Sabbath theology affects all parts of society, including the festivals, and emphasizes the importance of equality.

16:18—21:9. Offices of Justice. After the appeals for concern toward those in need among the worshiping congregation of Israel, Moses appropriately turned to the theme of justice (16:20). In this section, Moses described conditions that would apply directly to specific offices among the Israelites in Canaan. First, judges were to administer righteous justice (16:18—17:13), and then the future king of Israel was called to the highest moral order (17:14–20). The Israelites were to provide for priests and Levites (18:1–8), and the Levites were to care for each other. With the gift of prophecy (18:9–22), the future of the Israelites was ensured, so that standards of righteousness would be applied in all circumstances: in matters of life and death (19:1–21), when Israel's troops went to war (20:1–20), and even in cases of extreme incidents such as manslaughter and blood guilt (21:1–9).

16:18—17:13. Israel's Judge. God's pervasive concern for justice and righteousness is the focus of the section that discusses the judges in Israel. The central idea is not so much concerned with the administration of social justice by a judicial institution, but with the engagement of the entire community in living a life of righteousness as defined by the Torah. The emphatic call to righteousness in 16:20 demonstrates the passion of Moses. His words were not those of a legislator administering decrees, but were those of a passionate preacher who pleaded and strove for the real and deep need of his people.

Moses listed three examples of how righteousness could be violated. The first was spiritual syncretism. This involved a compromise between a legitimate and an illegitimate act (e.g., setting up an Asherah pole beside the altar of the Lord; v. 21). The second prohibition was against the setting up of pillars for Asherim (v. 22). This example may be understood as the Israelites erecting a symbol for Yahweh as the Canaanites did to celebrate the fertility rituals of Baal and Asherah. The third prohibition dealt with sacrifices that were defective. All three prohibitions spoke of the violation of righteousness having its roots in the breaking of the covenantal relationship with Israel's Suzerain.

The violation of the principle of doing what is right (16:20), which represented the vertical relationship, would lead to violations on the horizontal level. Deuteronomy 17:2–13 deals first with violations that could be resolved. These were to be investigated and judged by the courts of the judges in Israel, with the judicial process sometimes ending in execution. In the second part of this section, extreme cases that go beyond the power of the secular offices of the judges are discussed. Such cases were to be submitted to the sanctuary and its priests. The sanctuary was a place of judgment. Priestly judgment was to be "theocratic" in these cases. The oracles Urim and Thummim might have been involved, or there may have been a process such as the one involved with a jealous husband who was to bring his wife before the priest into the courtyard of the sanctuary because there were no witnesses to attest to her wrongdoing, and only God was in the position to judge her (see Num. 5:11–31).

17:14–20. Israel's King. In light of Moses's address, Israelite kingship was revolutionary in the ancient world. First, the desire for a king was societal. The lengthy temporal clause of direct speech that introduces the desire of the people (v. 14) shows that kingship was not necessary for Israel's society and economy to grow and flourish. The Lord was the reason for Israel's success in the land. Kingship was the result of the people's desire, which was based on what they saw among the nations. However, God legislated how kingship would function in Israel, and He would choose the king. Moses mentioned the first rule for the king: he was to be a native Israelite (v. 15). Moses then listed prohibitions unheard of in the annals of other nations: (1) the king was not to acquire many horses from Egypt (v. 16); (2) he was not to take many wives (v. 17); and (3) he was not to accumulate large amounts of wealth (v. 17). Following these prohibitions were positively formulated instructions: (1) Seated on the throne, the king was to copy the Torah for himself in the presence of the Levitical priests (v. 18). This was a sacred act showing the king's spiritual subordination to the holy book and the priests. In addition, the king did not issue the law; he received it from a higher authority. (2) The king was to keep the Torah close to himself; it would accompany him wherever he was. (3) He was to read the Torah for himself all the days of his life (v. 19). Moses used four purpose clauses to show what reading the Torah would mean for the king: (1) he was to learn to fear the Lord (v. 19); (2) he was to show a proper disposition toward his people and not consider himself superior (v. 20); (3) he was to remain faithful to the Lord and not turn in any other direction (v. 20); and (4) the reading of the Torah was the key to securing the future of Israel (v. 20).

One is amazed at such simple instructions for what was considered the highest office on earth. Each one contains lessons that run against human perceptions and operations, both at the time they were issued and in the contemporary world. Such lessons include the following: (1) Whereas leaders of the world gain power or usurp it at the expense of rivals and subjects, God's leaders are appointed by a divine call and without any need for human power. (2) Whereas leaders of the world are viewed as administrators of justice, God's leaders embody justice within a covenantal relationship with the Lord. (3) Whereas the leaders of the world codify laws to regulate standards under their government or to protect their own interests, God's leaders have no authority to issue laws. They themselves are subject to the laws of God. (4) Whereas the leaders of the world are elevated above their people, God's leaders are equals among their fellows.

18:1–22. Israel's Priest and Prophets. Israel's treatment of the Levites and priests was a barometer of their fidelity to the Lord and His standards of righteousness given in the Torah. Levites and priests were entitled to compensation, tithe, and food gifts because they would not be allotted land inheritance. The Lord was their inheritance (v. 2b).

Before speaking of Israel's prophetic ministry, Moses addressed the dangers of the occult practices that other nations used to communicate with their gods. The Israelites were forbidden to imitate the occult methods that the Canaanites used to seek guidance from their gods. Moses gave a long list of such methods and strictly forbade the Israelites to imitate them when they lived in the land together with the local inhabitants (vv. 10–11; cf. v. 14). The God of Israel detested idolatry and spiritual prostitution. Moreover, it was because of the very practice of these abominable things that God would drive out the Canaanite nations from the land.

Moses countered the occultism of Canaan with the ministry of a prophet chosen by the God of Israel to speak to His people (v. 15; see v. 18). Interestingly, the raising of a prophet was caused by the people's reaction to God's direct and awesome revelation at Mount Sinai (vv. 16–17). Moses had already referred to Exodus 20:18–21 in his first speech (Deut. 4:10–13). Here, in the context of contrasting the revelations of idolatrous gods with God's revelation to Israel, Moses reminded the people that they made the request for a mediator between them and God. Their fear of not being able to endure God's continual, direct, and overwhelming revelations became paradigmatic for a future succession of prophets in Israel.

According to Moses's speech, the contrast between a Canaanite diviner and a prophet of God was clear. However, prophets would come up among their own people and would show ambiguous signs. Moses drew lines and provided five signs in order for his people to be able to differentiate between a prophet speaking with presumptuous words and a true prophet of God. The true prophet would (1) be an Israelite (vv. 15, 18); (2) speak in the name of the Lord (vv. 16, 19–20) (death was to be the result for false claims; v. 20); (3) speak words that proved true (vv. 21–22); (4) perform miracles (13:1); and (5) give words and revelations that did not contradict previous certified revelations of God (13:1–18).

Still, for today's reader, the rejection of witchcraft, magic, or occultism is sometimes not clear. Why does God detest sorcery or necromancy? When looking at the Canaanite methods of occultism, one realizes that each practice was controlled by the power and authority of the one who performed it for another person. In order to establish, keep, or increase their power, the sorcerer or diviner would perform things meant to impress and frighten. Today, the spell of witchcraft not only spreads a fascination with a world that is thought to be governed by the spirits of the dead, but is actually led by demonic powers and therefore allows evil forces to have access to our lives. Occult practices have terrorizing effects; some put human life in danger or require the destruction of life.

God's ways of communicating with His people were completely different from those of the occultists. The prophet of God was His spokesperson and was called to speak words that show a deep concern for life. When Moses told the Israelites that there would be more prophets like himself (in their function and in terms of the content of their message), he placed himself as the paramount example for all future prophets. For the past forty years, his life and his words had been a testimony of one who deeply cared for his people. He did not exercise power to keep the people under his control. His care and love for his people especially stood out during Israel's greatest revolt, which was when they built the golden calf. Moses stood up for his people in a sacrificial way. Such a person would be the prophet whom the Lord would choose for His people. He would intercede before God for the sake of His people. At the same time, the prophet would speak only God's words. Again, Moses was the example. For a long time, the audience had listened to him speaking words of life and wisdom, words of warning and concern, words of compassion and enthusiasm.

The prophet Moses was willing to give his own life for the lives of his beloved people. The subsequent prophets in Israel all stood as witnesses of their sacrificial love for God and the people they served. For NT writers, the full actualization of God's promise to Moses came in the life, death, and resurrection of Jesus Christ (v. 18). When Philip encountered Nathanael, he alluded to Moses's prophecies in the law (John 1:45). After Jesus fed the five thousand, the people affirmed that He was "the Prophet" (John 6:14). Peter identified Jesus as the Prophet of whom Moses had prophesied (Acts 3:22–23), and in his apologetic before the Sanhedrin, Stephen declared that Jesus was the promised messianic Prophet to whom Moses had pointed (Acts 7:37–38). After Christ's death and resurrection, some may ask whether there is still a need for prophets in the church. An understanding of the NT indicates that God continues to raise up prophets to guide His people and assure the church of His presence (Acts 11:27; 13:1; 15:32; 1 Cor. 14:29; Eph. 2:20). God calls and appoints prophets according to the gifts imparted by the Spirit. Paul indicates that prophets are specifically appointed for the benefit of the church (1 Cor. 12:28–29; 14:4; Eph. 4:11–14). On the other hand, Paul, in line with Moses who once wished that every Israelite would be a prophet of God (Num. 11:29), wished that all church members would prophesy (1 Cor. 14:24–25).

19:1—21:9. Righteousness in Matters of Life and Death. This part of Moses's speech has links to Exodus 20:22—23:33. Moses spoke about everyday life as well as about extreme situations. He spoke of a provision for asylum for those who committed accidental manslaughter (19:1–14). In cases of false accusation, Moses assured the Israelites that God was in charge (19:15–21). The *lex talionis* ("law of retaliation") hindered disproportionate vengeance or malicious payback; its demand was that punishment be proportional to the crimes committed.

Righteousness was the standard in times of war (20:1–20). Since Moses knew that his people would soon be involved in war, he addressed the specific situation of corporate violence. He provides instructions for distant war campaigns (vv. 10–15). He also had instructions for how to deal with Canaanite towns and people on smaller local campaigns (vv. 16–18). The issue of the complete destruction of towns and people in vv. 16–18 brings the *kherem* policy back into discussion, which in scholarly and non-scholarly studies is often associated with the notion of "holy war." This is differentiated from ordinary warfare in the rest of Deuteronomy 20 (see "The Extermination of the Canaanites," p. 330, and "Holy Warfare," p. 372). It is important to notice that after dealing with the mustering of the troops, Moses gave a lengthy speech of encouragement. Obviously, Israel did not have trained military forces, so Moses spoke to the common people about the emotional crisis that they would experience at the sight of armed Canaanites in their fortified cities. "Do not be afraid" is the motto of the speech (vv. 1–9), an emphasis underlined by the use of three different expressions of the word "afraid" (*yare'*—"to be afraid," v. 1; *khapaz*—"to be alarmed," v. 3; *'arats*—"to be fearful," v. 3). The reason they were not to be afraid was that the Lord their God was with them to fight against their enemies and save them. The priests and other officials received direct instructions and words for the recruits. They were to provide assurance that Yahweh would be with the troops in battle.

There are several remarkable insights into military actions that prove a high ethical standard: (1) The fearful and the recently married were exempted from military activities (vv. 7–8). (2) Targeted cities were to be given the opportunity to surrender before an attack (vv. 10–11). (3) Israelites were prohibited from using the wood of fruit trees to make military machinery (v. 19). On the other hand, there were instructions to the troops about the complete destruction of towns and people. These instructions were built on the law of *kherem* as prescribed in chapter 7:

- The policy demanded the slaughter of the entire human population of Canaanite towns;
- The ordinance originated with Yahweh and not with military leaders or strategic planning;
- The people groups to be targeted were specifically identified;
- The policy was not driven by acts of hate and genocide, but by religious reasons—to punish the nations for their wickedness (9:4–5) and to keep Yahweh's people free from syncretism and idolatry (v. 18).

21:10—26:19. Righteousness in Everything. This section brings all of life under the principle of justice (16:20). The cases of women taken captive are discussed (20:10–14). They were to

be treated well when taken as wives, as well as in cases where they were not. Their dignity and rights were to be protected. There are two prohibitions issued for the Israelite husband in case he decided not to marry (or according to some, to divorce after marriage) his war bride: he was not allowed to sell her nor treat her as chattel. Moses promoted a compassionate treatment of war brides even in cases when they were not married or were sent away. As a captive, she was degraded; now, she was not to be humiliated again by being treated as property. These texts speak to today's crimes of the abuse of women and show that God did not allow this to happen even in the most extreme situations. God was concerned with the dignity of and respect for women, native or alien. He did not permit denying women their rights or treating them as property.

Deuteronomy 22 addresses care for domestic animals, wild animals, and the land. Deuteronomy 22:13–30 concerns righteousness in marital relations by addressing matters of sexual infidelity and misconduct. Contemporary readers of this passage have two alternatives: to interpret the text as a document of a time and culture that has no relevance today or to try to understand the values reflected and apply them to contemporary issues in marriage. With regard to the first choice, we may recognize that this passage reflects a high view of community, family, and human sexuality. This may run against our modern perspectives where individualism reigns, and human beings strive for independence and self-sufficiency. Sexual matters today are regarded as purely private. However, Moses taught that human sexuality is sacred, and that the purity of marriage is precious and needs to be defended. In a society where families disintegrate, and the rate of divorces among Christians is as high as among nonbelievers, Moses's call for the defense of the institution of marriage is highly needed.

The law concerning the exclusion of eunuchs from the assembly did not preclude them from worshiping God (Isa. 56:3–7). Therefore, it is likely that the term "assembly of the LORD" (Deut. 23:1–8) designated an administrative body within Israel. Because they represented the people of God, the wholeness of the physical body of its members was required—representing the absence of moral or spiritual defects. In the case of foreigners, they could participate after living in Israel for a number of generations; at which time they would have assimilated into the religious culture of the Hebrews and could make decisions more in line with God's will. This notion is reinforced in the laws concerning the holiness and cleanliness of the army that represented God (23:9–14). These laws of cleanliness not only had a theological aspect, but also contained valuable health principles (see "Health and Hygiene in Leviticus," p. 272).

The law concerning runaway slaves (Deut. 23:15–16) is thought to apply to the slaves of foreigners since Hebrew bondservants could expect their freedom after six years of work (15:12). Other cultures were not as generous in this regard. In Egypt, treaties were signed with other nations requiring the return of slaves that might have escaped to or from Egypt. In Mesopotamia, Hammurabi's Code had the penalty of death for anyone who harbored a runaway slave, and the Code rewarded the bounty hunter for finding and returning them.

Prostitution (23:17–18) was often associated with a temple or a cult as part of the way a god or goddess was worshiped. A price was paid (Gen. 38:15–23) for this service. In no instance was a Hebrew to participate in this practice, and no foreigner was allowed to bring the wages received from such service as a gift to God.

The remaining three laws in Deuteronomy 23 all address different aspects of honesty, especially when relating to another person in the community. This included interest, keeping vows, and taking advantage of neighborly generosity.

Deuteronomy 24:1–4 is often understood as the passage that regulates divorce. However, it is important to note what the passage says and what it does not say: (1) Only the husband could initiate the divorce, likely because in that culture (unlike in Egypt where the wife could initiate a divorce) only the man was able to act legally. (2) The husband found 'erwah, "nakedness of a word/thing" (Heb. dabar), in the wife and divorced her. The meaning of this Hebrew word is difficult to understand in this context. It is possible that the term can be understood as pointing to a physical rather than a moral problem. The physical problem may have been related to menstrual irregularity, which would make the woman unclean and uncapable of regular marital activities, including potential childbirth (cf. Lev. 15:19–30). A number of other interpretive options have been advanced, but none of them have clarified the question of the cause for divorce mentioned here. Ultimately, there is no explicit indication of what the "nakedness/thing" is (see Mark 10:1–12). (3) Moses did not speak primarily regarding the grounds for divorce, but focused on instruction for the conduct of the husband after the divorce. The husband was not allowed to reclaim her after she had married a second time, after her second husband died, or after her second husband also divorced her. (4) The husband who divorced his wife had to provide her with legal proof of the dissolution of the marriage. This document protected the woman from being forced to go back to the husband or from being accused of adultery when she married another man. Jesus clarified that the divorce document was only allowed for sexual immorality (Matt. 19:7–9), which by the time of Jeremiah included adultery (Jer. 3:8).

In the next part of his speech (Deut. 24:5—25:16), Moses addressed different aspects of life and demanded the implementation of righteousness. Each of these short laws contains some aspect of decentness toward one's neighbor.

Childbirth provided security in latter years, value in the esteem of their culture, and most importantly, a child to love, tend, and care for. Children brought happiness to a woman. Therefore, it was improper to give a woman to a man through marriage and not to provide her with the opportunity to become a mother (24:5), something that required the man to be around before risking his life as a soldier. To be a childless widow was pitiable in that culture.

Food processing was a daily task. The reason given for not taking a millstone implies that the same principle would apply to other forms of security that directly affected a person's ability to live (24:6).

A person could become a slave in different ways. Poor or indebted families sometimes sold family members into slavery to pay debts. Prisoners of war often became slaves. This law, however, particularly prohibited the evil of kidnapping Israelites for the purpose of selling them as slaves (24:7).

A community could easily be wiped out through poor hygiene, so if a person was suspected of having a communicable skin condition, he or she needed to be sent away from the community even if they were of high standing (24:8–9; cf. Lev. 13, 14).

It was the practice to pledge objects as collateral for a debt. The dignity of a person was not to be disregarded, regardless of the financial obligation (24:10–13). It was common to pay a worker each day. However, it is reasonable that an employer might want to pay wages on an accumulated basis. Thus, it needed to be stated that if the worker was not able to survive without the daily wages, the employer was required to pay them regardless of the business inconvenience (24:14–15).

The prohibition against punishing children for their parents' sins was directed at the magistrates—apparently only God was to decide when corporate punishments were to be applied (24:16). This law was cited as the reason why Amaziah did not kill the families of the men who assassinated his father (2 Kin. 14:6).

Historical memory was to motivate kindness and compassion for those less fortunate within the community. The protected class was to include widows, orphans, and the poor (Deut. 24:17-22). This principle was still emphasized in the early church (James 1:27). The minimal personal requirement was not to hoard every last portion of a harvest so that the protected class could glean and eat.

Even in receiving punishment, dignity was to be extended to the justly condemned person (Deut. 25:1-3). This was preceded by an impartial evaluation of the evidence by the judges. The physical punishment was to be inflicted in the presence of the judge to assure that the law was properly enforced, but in the process the judge was probably emotionally impacted by the execution of the sentence.

Those who worked were to receive wages for their work. This requirement was extended to the work of service animals (25:4). Oxen were used to pull threshing sledges across stocks of grain. These sledges were flat boards that often had small stones embedded on the underside. Those stones, combined with the hooves of an ox, were what helped to release the grain from the stocks.

Aged women were cared for by their children, particularly by their sons. For a wife to be widowed before she had a son was considered a tragedy. The levirate marriage law was designed to provide her with one and was not to be taken advantage of for the pleasure of the levirate brother (see Gen. 38:8-10). The best example of how this was to work comes from the story of Ruth where the closest kin refused to do his duty (Ruth 4), allowing the next nearest kin to do so. However, in that story, it is interesting that the son of Boaz and Ruth was never considered in the genealogies to be the son of her former husband (Ruth 4:21; Matt. 1:4).

Although the punishment of the woman who attempted to help her husband in a fight (Deut. 25:11-12) sounds harsh to our ears, it was designed to prevent sexual immodesty. There were ways to help her husband that did not require her coming in contact with the genitals of another man. Thus, this was a made choice. That part of the man's anatomy was to be regarded as untouchable, probably since it was his way to produce heirs. However, this is the only law that allowed for physical mutilation as the form of punishment, and it was better than death (the punishment for adultery, Deut. 22:22). It certainly was a powerful deterrent.

Because coins were not used until the Persian period, bartering was the only way to pay for goods or services. Often this required a way to measure what was exchanged, and scales were used. However, this required the weights to be accurate. A dishonest merchant could easily doctor his weights more or less than was proper. This was not to be allowed (Deut. 25:13-16).

The Amalekites, descendants of Esau (Gen. 36:12), have not been associated with any known archaeological material culture from Sinai (Exod. 17:8-13), the Negev (Num. 13:29; 14:25, 45; Judg. 6:3; 1 Sam. 30:1-20), or lands to the east (Judg. 3:13; 7:12). There is archaeological evidence of nomads in these regions at that time, but at this point it is impossible to associate any of that material with the Amalekites, perhaps in fulfillment of God's command to "blot out" any remembrance of Amalek (Deut. 25:19). That command (Deut. 25:17-19) restates a similar one from Exodus 17:14-16 that immediately followed an incident in Israel's victory over the Amalekites. This speech by Moses was given at the end of the forty years of wandering; whoever heard this speech when the Amalekites attacked would have been eighteen years old then. In the process of reminding this new generation, it is implied that the Amalekites knew better than to attack because they were aware that God would disapprove of their actions, and yet they did so anyway (Deut. 25:18), which was, in itself, a subtle warning to the Israelites to live as God would want. True to this command (v. 19), the Amalekites were later subdued by both Saul (1 Sam. 14:47-48) and David (2 Sam. 8:11-12), and in the time of Hezekiah they were completely destroyed (1 Chron. 4:41-43).

The Israelites were to remember that God gave them the land they were living in through two unique ways that dealt with their agricultural produce. First, they were to provide an offering for the Lord in the first year (Deut. 26:1-2, 10b-11), accompanied by a declaration that recognized God's providential hand in their own history (26:3-10a). Second, they were to give the third year's tithe to the protected class (Levites, foreigners, orphans, and widows; 26:12), accompanied by a declaration of covenant faithfulness and a plea for the blessing of the nation (26:13–15).

Moses concluded this section by picking up the theme of cultic worship and calling for a celebration of the Lord's faithfulness at the central sanctuary. Deuteronomy 26:16–19 summarizes the key theological issues in Moses's second speech. With the expression "this day" (v. 16), Moses refocused the attention of the audience and asked for their positive decision and a total commitment to the Lord. Furthermore, Moses reminded his congregation that while he was speaking, they actually heard the voice of the Lord their God.

27:1–26
Call for Covenantal Renewal in the Promised Land

Deuteronomy 27 seems to interrupt the flow between chapters 26 and 28, which are linked by common vocabulary and themes (an appeal to obedience and an announcement of blessings and curses). However, in the covenant call (Deut. 27), Moses specifically identified Mount Ebal and Mount Gerizim as the places where the covenant renewal was to take place after the Israelites had crossed over into Canaan. Furthermore, the Israelites were to erect inscribed stones (vv. 2–4), build an altar (vv. 5–7), and have witnesses present (vv. 12–13). Also, a speech was to be given (v. 14) with a series of curses (vv. 15–26). Moses formally charged the people and the elders to adhere to the obligations of the covenant with the Lord. In view of the fact that the congregation was gathered at the border of the promised land and was ready to enter it, this covenant underlined the triangle between God, the people, and the land. At their entrance into the land, the people were to erect stone monuments and write on them the law that Moses had spoken. If the stone monuments were inscribed in Hebrew with Moses's three Deuteronomy speeches, there would have been about twelve thousand words written on each stone. Evidence for such customs in the ancient world comes from the Code of Hammurabi, which was written on a seven-foot stela in syllabic cuneiform script.

The main part of the covenant renewal is composed of the imprecations listed in vv. 15–26. The use of the word "cursed" (Heb. 'arur) implies that covenantal righteousness would not be enforced merely by the Israelite courts. The response of the entire congregation with a solemn "Amen" at the end of each of the twelve curses bound the people

to God as the ultimate supervisor of moral order and placed the violators under divine sanction.

28:1—29:1
Blessings and Curses

Deuteronomy 28 is unevenly divided into two panels: blessings for those faithful to their covenant Lord (vv. 1–14) and curses for those persistently rebellious against Him (vv. 15–68).

28:1–14. Blessings. Before the expression of the blessings in seven principal clauses (vv. 7–14), Moses introduced them in the form of rhetorical declarations: town/country; fruit of the body (children)/fruit of the ground (crops)/fruit of the animals (the young from the livestock); basket/kneading bowl (trough); coming in/going out (vv. 3–6). Each of the following seven statements of blessing highlighted the Lord as the originator of blessings, so that Israel could not claim credit for anything that they would enjoy in the future. In the center of the material benefactions was Israel's special relationship with Yahweh (vv. 9–10). The ideal for Israel was to be a holy people, set apart and high above all nations; here, Moses envisioned the climax and fulfillment of all blessings. All the nations of the earth would recognize the name of Yahweh in Israel and that the well-being of the people was a gift of their divine Suzerain. Consequently, they would bring praise and honor to God. In these words, Israel represented all humanity in a microcosm; they were a people pointing back to the original creation order of the first human beings.

28:15—29:1. Curses and Epilogue. Moses began the curses with a series of blessing reversals (vv. 16–19), creating similarity by using the same words and concepts as in vv. 3–6, followed by a long list of curses (vv. 20–68). (1) As with the blessings, the Lord is the subject of all the actions stated in the text. (2) The preposition "until" ('ad) emphasizes the intent of the curses: the people would be destroyed (vv. 20, 24, 45, 51, 61). The covenantal triangle between God, Israel, and the land would be dissolved, and the entire nation would be wiped out. (3) Disasters would follow without relief. (4) Disasters and destruction would be caused by Israel's unfaithfulness to God. Deuteronomy 29:1 is the subscription that concludes the covenant made in the land of Moab. The reference to the words or terms of the covenant involve specific legal obligations and their stated consequences, and it applies to the laws, blessings, and curses of the preceding chapters (see "The Wrath of God," p. 918, and "God's Judgment in the Prophets," p. 981).

29:2—30:20
MOSES'S THIRD DISCOURSE: TRUSTING IN THE GRACE OF YAHWEH

Moses summoned the people to reaffirm the covenant they had with the Lord (4:44—26:19; and chap. 28). He emphasized that the covenant bound both the people who were present and about to enter the promised land, and those of future generations (29:9–14). He warned of exile as the consequence of disobeying the covenant (vv. 15–28); but sincere repentance would result in the restoration of God's favor (30:1–10). Consequently, Moses assured Israel that the terms of the covenant were not too difficult to fulfill (30:11–14). He concluded by making them an offer: choose between life and death (30:15–30).

In his third speech, Moses looked into Israel's past history (29:2–9), using the word *hayyom* ("today" or "this day" or "now") thirteen times to address the present generation, and provided visions of the future. The different temporal sections of the speech are arranged in an ABABA pattern, with the A sections addressing the immediate audience and the B sections looking into the future:

A Present generation (29:10–13)
  B Future generations (29:14–28)
A Present generation (29:29)
  B Future generations (30:1–10)
A Present generation (30:11–20)

The climax of the speech is in the call to choose life rather than death (30:19) by completely submitting to the will of God.

29:2—30:20
Essence of Moses's Third Discourse: The Grace of Covenant Renewal

The importance of the Exodus can never be overestimated. Moses looked back at this event and used similar words to those of God when He spoke to the Israelites at the foot of Mount Sinai (Ex. 19:4).

29:2–13. God's Guidance in the Past. Moses recapitulated the themes of his speech in Deuteronomy 1–4 and 8 and showed again how God supernaturally sustained Israel to teach them His full power. The eyes that saw the great events in Egypt were very young eyes (eighteen years old or younger). Close to a year and a half after the Exodus, the spies gave their report, and the people refused to enter the promised land (Num. 13–14). All those who were twenty years or older at that time died over the course of the next forty years (Num. 14:29–35). However, all of those living at the time of this speech had seen the more recent victories over Sihon king of Heshbon (Num. 21:21–32) and Og king of Bashan (Num. 21:33–35). In spite of this, Moses wanted them to know that they still had the same problem of the heart that their parents had when they rebelled (Deut. 29:4). They had witnessed great victories but had not been convicted. So Moses reminded them of a more recent personal experience: their clothes and sandals had not worn out (v. 5) over the course of forty years. These experiences could have enabled Israel to realize the wisdom of obeying God and the folly of disobeying Him. Deuteronomy 29:10–15 addresses both the present and future generations of Israel, and the covenant formula at the center is the same for all generations (v. 13).

29:14–28. Consequences. Moses then spoke about the consequences that would befall the individual, family, or tribe that was disloyal to the Lord because of idolatry. Such persons needed to know that the blessings of the covenant were not unconditionally guaranteed. Because of their defiant response to God, they would seal their fate and suffer the anger of Yahweh (vv. 18–21). In the second part of this section, Moses shifted the focus to the collective consequences of idolatry for all Israel (vv. 22–28). The curses of Yahweh would come over the people and the land with full fury, and all would be uprooted and destroyed. Most of this section is direct speech involving three different voices: (1) the descendants of the present generation of Israel (vv. 22–23); (2) the nations surrounding Israel (v. 24); and (3) unknown respondents to the previous voices (vv. 25–28). Verses 22–24 contain questions that fit the context of the ancient world in which devastated land was interpreted as evidence of divine fury: Why had the Lord done this to the land? Why did He have this great anger? (v. 24). The respondents would speak of Israel's treachery as the cause of their fate and of Yahweh's response to idolatry. The speech was filled with a series of unparalleled expressions of the fury of Yahweh: He (lit. in the Hebrew) "burned at the nose" (v. 23), an expression derived from the natural phenomenon of hot breath coming from the nose of an infuriated person or creature; Yahweh acted in rage (*khemah*, v. 22) and great wrath (v. 23). He had imposed all the curses written in this book (v. 27), uprooted all the population, and tossed them away from the land (v. 28; see "God's Judgment in the Prophets," p. 981).

30:1–20. Restoration. In his speech, Moses transitioned from the horrific image of a devastated land to the promise of restored grace. But before this, he placed before his audience a most enigmatic passage (29:29): the secret things belong to the Lord God, but the revealed things belong to His people and their children forever, so that they may follow everything in the law. That generation had received a clear understanding of the will of the Lord and the nature of His covenant. Because of His gracious presence among disloyal people, there was hope for renewal and restoration.

Moses brought his audience (Deut. 30) to the climax of the gospel that he had proclaimed in all his speeches. The tone of his words completely changed. He offered the assurance that if Israel would be exiled, God would reinstate the people based on their genuine repentance and their return to Him and His will. The chiasm below shows that the keyword in this section is the Hebrew word *shub*, "turn" or "return," which expresses both Israel's return to God and God's act of returning Israel to its prior state of well-being. In the Hebrew text, this word occurs in seven clauses in which the activity of a "return" by God and Israel appears in a chiastic pattern, as noted in this literal translation of the Hebrew text:

A When...you *return* them [these words] to your heart...and you *return* to the Lord your God...and obey Him with all your heart and soul (vv. 1–2)

  B Then the Lord will *return* you from captivity...He will *return* you from all the people where he has scattered you (v. 3)

    C The Lord your God will circumcise your heart and the heart of your descendants; love the Lord your God with all your heart and with all your soul, so that you may live (v. 6)

  B' You will *return* and obey the Lord... the Lord will *return* to rejoice over you (vv. 8–9)

A' If you *return* to the Lord your God with all your heart and soul (v. 10)

Moses made the core, the most important part, consist of Israel's and Yahweh's turning to each other and the returning of blessings: circumcision of the heart and love for God that comes from the heart (v. 6). He reintroduced a theme that he had already presented (10:16) when he called the Israelites to circumcise their hearts. Circumcision of the flesh became a metaphor for the removal of all the barriers that hinder a person from being totally committed to the Lord. As a result, devotion to the Lord would be evident in undivided love and obedience. Those whom the Lord would bring back from the Exile would have undergone a surgery of the heart, exposing radical actions of affection toward their divine covenant partner. Concomitant with the restoration of the former exiles would be the Lord's restoration of their place among the nations. The nations would suffer the punishments that they had inflicted upon Israel. They acted as God's agents against Israel, but they were also His enemies and He would address their evilness. Moses concluded his third discourse with a most urgent appeal to choose wisely between the two options that he had presented, namely, life and death (vv. 15–20).

31:1—34:12
THE DEATH OF MOSES

This portion of the book, the epilogue to both Deuteronomy and the entire Torah, is about the last days of Moses. It describes the final steps Moses took to prepare Israel for their future in the promised land. The reader will experience soaring moments in meditating on the song of Moses and contemplating the description of his final moments: his climb of Mount Nebo and his death. The actions described in this section are interwoven with lengthy poems, which show their importance to both the new beginnings of Israel as a covenant nation and the conclusion of Moses's life: (1) Moses announced his imminent departure and appointed Joshua as his successor (31:1-8, 14–15, 23). (2) He wrote a copy of the teaching in his three speeches, placed the copy in the care of the priests and elders, gave instructions for its regular public reading, and urged the people to observe it (31:9–13, 24–26; 32:45–47). (3) Moses orally taught the people a prophetic poem and deposited a copy of it with the priests (31:16–22, 27–30; 32:1–44). (4) He delivered a final blessing on the tribes (chap. 33). (5) Finally, he ascended Mount Nebo and died (32:48–52; 34).

31:1—32:52

Preparing for the Death of Moses

Deuteronomy 31 and 32 stand as a memorial to the covenant between God and Israel that was renewed on the plains of Moab. Deuteronomy 31–32 consists of eight sections. Scholars recognize in this section an alternating order of long speeches about the transcription of the Torah and shorter speeches dealing with the appointment of Joshua; in between these are two poetic sections.

31:1–29. New Leader. In these narrative sections, Yahweh committed to the people of Israel, and they responded to their supreme Lord. The repeated mention of witnesses and testimony (31:19, 21, 26, 28; 32) reinforces the ritual aspect of the covenant renewal. Moses's legacy lives on due to his inspired writings, which chronicle a life of dedication to the call that came to him in the wilderness when he stood barefoot before the burning bush in the awesome presence of the Lord. His never-ending, passionate concern for a people who so often disrespected him, speaks more of the man Moses and his love for the Lord than any pillar of stone that has been erected for the great leaders of the world. Another remarkable act of Moses was his appointment of his successor, Joshua. One might expect that Moses would perhaps hand over his mantle of leadership in the form of his staff, which had carried a symbolic meaning for the past forty years; yet all the text records is that Moses delivered a song. (For the eschatological content of v. 29, see "Introduction to the Pentateuch," p. 120.)

31:30—32:43. Song of Moses. The Song of Moses is a magnificent artwork and didactic poem. The style is typical of biblical Hebrew poetry. Each line consists of at least two phrases or clauses that are parallel, synonymous, antithetical, or complementary to each other. Scholars refer to the phrases or clauses as "colons," and to pairs and trios of colons as "bicolons" and "tricolons" (see "Introduction to Hebrew Poetry and Wisdom Books," p. 614).

The core of the poem shows God's faithfulness and Israel's betrayal of Him. Moses began the song by praising the name of God and ascribing all greatness to Him. He spoke (vv. 4–6) of the faithfulness of the Lord as being manifested in His numerous dealings with a corrupt and ungrateful nation. Looking back upon the past, the poet described God's providence, which had brought Israel safely through the wilderness.

With the word "remember" (v. 7), all attention turns even further into the days of old when God separated the peoples of the earth and set boundaries to them. There is an allusion to the story of Babel in which the nations were divided and separated all over the earth. Moses seems to have used the context of this story when singing about Israel's ancestor Jacob receiving the inheritance and portion of the Lord.

Verses 10–14 are an extravagant poem about God's care for Jacob (v. 9). The reader is reminded that just after the scattering of the nations who attempted to make themselves a name by building the tower of Babel, Abraham received God's divine call and promise to make a name for Abraham and bless him abundantly. In his song to the Israelites on the Plains of Moab, Moses cast these ancestral stories into words filled with passion and loving enthusiasm. The Lord's actions toward Jacob, the foundling in the wasteland, were twofold. First, Yahweh acted like an army encircling a village of defenseless, hungry people. He surrounded and protected them from the enemy, guarding them like a precious treasure, like the apple of His eye (v. 10). The following image in v. 11 is that of a mother eagle who encircles the nest of her young and hovers over the little eaglets to protect them from enemies and feed them out of her beak. When the birds are old enough to learn to fly, the mother spreads her wings and catches the young and carries them back into the safety of the nest for as long as they need this training.

Second, the song alludes to the beginnings of time and the primordial world as described in Genesis 1:1–2. There, the Spirit of God was "hovering over the waters" like the eagle mother over the nest with the young birds. The same verb used in Genesis 1:2 is used in Deuteronomy 32:11 to speak of the interest of the Spirit of God in a world that was to be filled with God's works of creation. Moses's song stresses the uniqueness of the relationship between God and a young Israel who knew of no other god (v. 12). He provided nourishment so that Israel would prosper. The metaphors of honey and oil that flowed from the land and rocks show the abundance that God gave.

The next stanza of the song portrays the very opposite image. Israel violated the supreme command by abandoning the Lord and pursuing other gods (vv. 15–18). Neglect of God, ingratitude, and perverse actions of idolatry committed by "Jeshurun"—a metaphor likely used in an ironic way because the name designates the "straight one"—resulted in the Lord threatening Israel with national disaster and bringing it almost to the verge of ruin (vv. 19–30). The imagery of v. 18 is especially interesting because Moses used a portrait of God that is often neglected: he spoke of God as a mother who gave birth to Israel and agonized in labor pains. Israel, the child, had forgotten God, her mother.

After a lengthy description of the evils that would come over Israel, vv. 31–43 describe the Lord's determination not to allow an unworthy foe to triumph over His people. In the ultimate sense of the poem, the underlying theme is the rescue of the people by an act of grace. Just as God found and rescued the baby dying in the wilderness, so would he save again in the very moment of imminent annihilation (cf. Ezek. 1–14). Moses returned to the theme of divine rescue in the face of despair with impassioned earnestness and great literary and artistic skill.

32:44–52. God's Address to Moses. In between the magnificent song chanted by the congregation and the grand blessing spoken over the tribes of Israel (chap. 33) is a unique paragraph: God spoke to Moses, the old leader, after Moses's three long speeches for the people of Israel. At first glance, the obvious difference in the style of the passage, with its narrations and direct speeches in between two highly artistic pieces, makes God's address to Moses seem awkwardly placed. The content of God's address to Moses is completely different from the content of the two poetic sections. While the two poetic panels tell of God's faithfulness, care, and blessing toward Israel, even in the times of Israel's apostasy, the insertion of God's address to Moses reminds readers of the most disappointing event in his life, which was when he disobeyed by striking, instead of speaking to, the rock. His disobedience was the reason why he was not allowed to enter the promised land. God used strong imperatives in all four verbs in vv. 49–50. Then He expressed the reason why Moses would not be allowed to enter into the promised land though he would be in sight of it (vv. 51–52).

The incident mentioned here is found in Numbers 20:2–13 and 27:12–14, conveying the reason why Moses could not go into the promised land. Moses mentioned this fateful event earlier in the book and told of how he pleaded with the Lord about going into the land, but the Lord remained firm on His prohibition (Deut. 3:23–27).

A look into the unusual form of God's speech reveals that the first pair of imperative verbs ("go up" and "look/view") harks back to Moses's own words in the beginning of his speeches to the Israelites (Deut. 1:21). The parallelism between God's speech to Moses and Moses's speech to the people should not be overlooked. Moses received the same command that he had given to his people: "Go up!" The sharp contrast is followed by a second pair of imperatives, which are not about taking possession of the land as Moses had told the people (see 1:21), but instead are about his dying. The combination of the verbs "die" and "be gathered" place Moses in a direct line with the patriarchs of old, all of whom died and were gathered to their dead: Abraham (Gen. 25:8), Ishmael (25:17), Isaac (35:29), and Aaron, Moses's brother (Deut. 32:50).

33:1–29
The Blessings

Deuteronomy 33 contains the blessings of Moses upon the Israelite tribes. The chapter is cast into elegant poetic Hebrew consisting of a series of benedictions, almost identical in size, for each tribe.

The poetic blessing in Genesis 49 that was spoken by Jacob to his sons before he died resembles Deuteronomy 33 most closely. However, the order of the tribes in Deuteronomy differs from Genesis 49, which lists the sons of Jacob in order of birth. Deuteronomy seems to list them in the geographical order of their territory in Canaan. The list begins with Reuben in the Transjordan and then moves west to Judah and ends with the northern tribes of the Galilee area. The list also seems to be organized according to their mothers. The first three that are listed are Leah's sons, then come Rachel's two sons, followed by Leah's last two sons. The last four are the sons of Jacob's concubines. Moses omits one son, Simeon, possibly because Simeon's territory was within that of Judah.

The three sections of the poem, the introduction, core, and conclusion, work together in a unifying way. The core of the poem is composed of the blessings on the individual tribes (vv. 6–25), with the sections on Levi and Joseph at the center. The introduction and the coda emphasize the ideal unity of the tribes as a single people and heighten their security and prosperity in the land by the chiastic repetition of key words that form an *inclusio* around the poem: the names "LORD" (YHWH), "Jacob," and "Jeshurun" appear in the introduction (vv. 2, 4, 5), and then in reverse order in the conclusion (vv. 26, 28, 29). Also, "people" and "Israel" appear in chiastic order in the introduction and conclusion (vv. 5, 28, 29).

The blessings of Moses begin with a majestic vision of the Lord coming from Sinai, rising up from Seir, and shining forth from Mount Paran (v. 2). The reference to His coming from Sinai seems to connect with God's revelation and the giving of the law, which is accompanied by the fiery phenomena and loud sounds that attended a solemn occasion. As the priestly tribe, the Levites were entrusted with the Urim and Thummim to find out God's will in specific situations (v. 8; Num. 27:21). These objects were kept in the breastplate (ephod) of the high priest (Ex. 28:30). The responsibilities of the Levites were twofold: to teach the law to Israel and to assist with the offerings (v. 10). The mediatory and instructive role of the Torah were foundational for the future of Israel as God's covenant people.

Moses had the longest blessing for Joseph, which was similar to Jacob's blessing in Genesis 49:22–26. In this blessing, Moses spoke about fertility and strength. Joseph received a double portion of territory, but was represented by his two sons, Ephraim and Manasseh (v. 17b; Josh. 14:2–4). Together, the two tribes received the largest portion of land. Their areas were some of the most fertile in the Transjordan territory and in all the promised land. In his wish for fruitfulness (vv. 13, 14, 15, 16), Moses mentioned all of God's creation as a source of blessing for Joseph: heaven, sun, moon, mountains, and earth. Moses expressed Joseph's power over the nations through the horns of a wild ox, a metaphor for strength (see various uses of a wild ox as a metaphor in v. 17; Num. 23:22; Job 39:9–12; Ps. 22:21).

The messianic language in the blessings for Levi and Joseph appears in the context of a visionary speech pointing to the end of days (Deut. 31:29; see "Introduction to the Pentateuch," p. 120, for a discussion of the messianic content of Deut. 32–33). The phrase "latter days/end of the days" may refer to the coming messianic age. In the blessing for Levi, Moses spoke of the *khasid*, "holy, faithful" One (33:8), which seems to allude to the Messiah as the antitypical Priest, who is a cultic Mediator and Offerer of sacrifices as well as the Teacher of Israel (v. 10). In the blessing on Joseph, the term *nazir* (33:16) contains the meaning "consecrated" or "separated," including a notion pointing to the royal and priestly line of the Messiah (some translations have "prince"). This suggests that Deuteronomy closes with a view of the near future, the conquest of the land, and a messianic perspective of hope.

34:1–12
Death of Moses

The record of Moses's death has a mysterious element in its description of the magnificent view of the promised land and in the suggestion that God Himself officiated at the burial of His precious servant (v. 6). During Jesus's transfiguration, He was accompanied by Elijah and Moses, which indicates that Moses had been resurrected by the Lord. Moses died in good health at the age of 120 years. The Israelites lost their greatest leader; a man used by God like no one else in the OT. His successor was Joshua the son of Nun, chosen by God because he was full of the spirit of wisdom (v. 9). Moses had placed his hands on him, thereby appointing Joshua as the leader of Israel. The book closes with the absence of Moses, but the people were ready to conquer the land in fulfillment of the divine promises and under the leadership of God's instrument. In reality, there was no change in leadership. The Lord was still leading His people through human instruments. Joshua and the people shared the same hope of victory.

HISTORICAL BOOKS

INTRODUCTION TO THE
OLD TESTAMENT HISTORICAL BOOKS

A large part of both testaments of Scripture include significant historical writing. Apart from the many historical sections contained in the Pentateuch, the OT books of Joshua, Judges, Ruth, 1 and 2 Samuel, 1 and 2 Kings, 1 and 2 Chronicles, Ezra, Nehemiah, and Esther are all almost exclusively presented as history. Their NT equivalents include the four Gospels, which tell the story of Jesus, and the Acts of the Apostles, which details the story of the early Christian community.

The organization of the Hebrew Bible, which is different in book order than our modern Christian Bible, included Joshua, Judges, 1 and 2 Samuel, and 1 and 2 Kings in the section titled Prophets (*nebi'im*), more precisely the Former Prophets, while Ruth, Ezra, Nehemiah, 1 and 2 Chronicles, and Esther were included in the Writings (*ketubim*), the last of three groups of books in the Hebrew canon—the Law, Prophets, and Writings (see "Formation of the Biblical Canon," p. 21).

HISTORY WRITING, HISTORIOGRAPHY, AND THEOLOGY

In order to appropriately understand this particular genre of the OT canon, it is helpful to consider the relationship between biblical history writing, historiography, and theology. While the first two elements are obviously related, the visible presence of theology and theological thinking in these texts has led critical scholars to discount the historical veracity of biblical texts detailing history. After all, how does God fit into a literary category that requires objective, nonpartisan, and dispassionate reporting?

If we want to understand this legitimate question, we need to remember that any writing, including biblical historical accounts, reflects the convictions and presuppositions of the author. We always bring our own experiences, beliefs, and perspectives to the text, and these are also reflected in the way information is communicated to us. Texts and images always reflect an angle and perspective and cannot be truly "objective" since they always involve human communicators.

Right from the outset, biblical history writing identifies its most foundational assumption. Based on its claims of divine revelation (2 Tim. 3:16–17; 2 Pet. 1:19–21), Scripture makes it very clear that God is always at the center of what we read. As Creator, Sustainer, and Redeemer, He is actively involved in human affairs. War is reported in terms of God's engagement; kings are evaluated based on their spiritual commitment to the covenant God made with David and his successors. Nations and individuals are participants and witnesses of God's interaction in history. While this may be a challenging concept for many Western twenty-first-century readers, the notion of divinely inspired texts, presenting history from God's perspective, was not unique to Israel in biblical times. Mesopotamian and Egyptian texts contained similar claims.

Historiography is the science of writing history. Biblical historiography includes several important characteristics that need to be acknowledged before one attempts to understand the text. First, OT authors writing historical reports were very *selective* in the choice of details they reported. The narratives in the book of Judges reflect this characteristic, as they do not provide a comprehensive and systematic list of leaders (or judges) governing Israel. Some judges included in the book seem to have led regional confederations, as Israel lacked a central government during that period. Furthermore, the tenure of a number of the judges may have overlapped with other judges governing in a different region. This is not always clearly indicated in the text of Judges, since the biblical text focuses on the response of Israel's tribes to God's call to covenant faithfulness.

Second, OT historiography is *theological and God-centered*. Events and people are evaluated in the light of their commitment to the revealed word and their relationship to the Creator God. The well-known formula "X did evil in the sight [or eyes] of the Lord" (e.g., 1 Kin. 11:6; 14:22; 2 Kin. 8:18, 27; 13:2; 2 Chr. 22:4) appears dozens of times and reminds the reader that Israel's God is not far removed but rather is intimately engaged in human history. This concept can also be found in contemporary ANE texts and would have been readily understood by ancient readers.

Third, OT historiography is unabashedly *interpretive*. The biblical text describes people and events not from a neutral, objective manner but from the vantage point of Yahweh, the covenant God. The authors emphasize what is important for salvation history, moving from Creation, the Fall, and the Flood to the ups and downs of a people called by God for a specific mission. The life of King Omri of Israel, the founder of an important dynasty in the Northern Kingdom of Israel, is summarized in only eight verses (1 Kin. 16:21–28), while the reign of his son Ahab is covered in seven long chapters (1 Kin. 16:29—22:40). This ancient characteristic of recording what is important to the purpose of the text is understood more clearly when we note that Ahab does make an appearance in Assyrian texts (e.g., in a stela erected by Assyrian King Shalmaneser III celebrating his supposed victory at Qarqar in 853 B.C. over a coalition of kings including Ahab). However, most references to Israel in these texts over the following century and a half include the Akkadian *bit ḫumria* ("the house of Omri") found in texts of Shalmaneser III, Adad-Nirari III, Tiglath-Pileser III, and Sargon II. Thus, for the Assyrian superpower, Omri himself, as the icon of his dynasty, must have played a much more significant role than suggested by his limited appearance in the biblical text.

Fourth, OT historical writing is *realistic*. While we would wish for stories that tell of perfection and excellence in the lives of God's people (including their kings), the stories told in the historical books of the OT offer us the real version without an idealized tint. In fact, compared to some other ancient texts that tell truly unbelievable stories, this trait of biblical history writing should give us more confidence in the authenticity of the material. King David, who looms large in biblical texts and whose name is the most referenced in the Bible, is not portrayed only as a fearless warrior and wise negotiator. The reader can also see his fierce and arrogant anger in his threat to avenge the disrespect from Nabal (1 Sam. 25) and his adulterous affair with Bathsheba and the eventual murder of her husband, which led to more death and pain in his family and Israel as a whole (2 Sam. 11; cf. 1 Kin. 15:5). The biblical author describes not only the extraordinary wisdom and riches of King Solomon but also his ungodly importation of Egyptian horses and chariots (1 Kin. 10:28–29; in violation of the divine command found in Deut. 17:16) and his waning commitment to the Lord due to his love for many foreign women (1 Kin. 11:1–8). A propagandist purpose would not have allowed the inclusion of these damaging facts. But the Bible includes them as lessons and examples of God's grace, forgiveness, transformation, and, at times, judgment.

People living in the world of the OT related well to stories, and history often has its best effect when it is presented in that way. This was as true then as it is today. Beyond the selective, theological, interpretive, and realistic nature of OT history writing, all these texts were given to tell the story of redemption again and again. Sometimes this happens through the vehicle of personal biographies or brief glimpses of key moments; at other times, the focus is more on the national storyline within the bigger context of a cosmic controversy. All of these stories, however, include a teaching component. In the NT, John 20:30–31 summarizes this focus by stating that John's book was written so that readers would believe that Jesus is the Christ/Messiah, the Son of God, and thus have life in His name. Ultimately, reading and hearing these stories help us to focus on the most foundational response of believing that the God who worked in the life of individuals and people is still at work today in the life of His church.

DEUTERONOMY AND THE HISTORICAL BOOKS OF THE OLD TESTAMENT

Scholars have noted a number of similarities between Deuteronomy and the first six historical books (Joshua, Judges, 1 and 2 Samuel, 1 and 2 Kings), involving terminology and the overall theological lens, characterized by a focus on the covenant. Consequently, these books have been labeled as belonging to a Deuteronomistic History (DH). Clearly, many of the specific commands and values found in these books reflect those included in Deuteronomy. However, since the concept of a DH is closely linked to the source-critical paradigm pioneered by German scholars K. H. Graf and Julius Wellhausen (see "Introduction to the Pentateuch," p. 120), it suffices to recognize the logical sequence of these books following the covenant renewal described in Deuteronomy at the border of the promised land. In this sequence of biblical history, Joshua describes the time immediately prior to the conquest of Canaan and continues until the death of that first generation of conquerors. Judges continues the narrative, relating the frequent ups and downs of Israel's tribes, who often forget their commitment to the covenant made with the God who saved them out of slavery. The books of Samuel and Kings tell the story of Israel's transition from a tribal, judge-led confederation of clans and people to a united monarchy under Saul, David, and Solomon.

While the historical books do not reflect the sermonic frame of Deuteronomy, the treaty elements using distinctive vocabulary and phraseology connected to the promised land appear repeatedly in these books and highlight the close connection. One of the crucial themes of Deuteronomy, the need and requirement for a specific, single place of worship (Deut. 12:5), appears again and again in the historical books. Prior to the construction of the temple in Jerusalem, this is focused on the location of the tabernacle and the constant battle to maintain the singularity of the worship of the Lord amid the turn to high places and rival sanctuaries. After the construction of the temple under Solomon's leadership, the struggle continued as high places and household cultic places threatened to distract people from worshiping God as the unique Creator of heaven and earth. They were tempted to forget the object-lesson quality of the sacrificial and temple service, which pointed forward to the true Lamb of God.

The emphasis on heart religion and commitment in Deuteronomy is echoed by the early prophetic voices heard in the historical books. Moses's call for Israel to love God with all their heart, soul, and strength (Deut. 6:5; cf. 10:12) is repeated again and again in the later books (e.g., Josh. 22:5; 24:23; 1 Sam. 12:20, 24; 1 Kin. 8:61).

EARLY PROPHECY AND THE HISTORICAL BOOKS

Throughout history, God has very often communicated with humanity through the ministry of prophets. According to the definition found in Scripture, a prophet is an individual who has been called by God to speak on God's behalf to God's people and the larger world (as exemplified in Moses; cf. Deut. 18:15–22). Beginning in the Pentateuch, prophets are God's instruments to invite individuals or peoples to turn around and commit themselves again to God.

There are several Hebrew terms describing prophets, and all of them are used in the historical books (e.g., "man of God" [1 Sam. 9:6]; "seer" [1 Sam. 9:9]; and "prophet" [1 Sam. 3:20], to mention a few). Prophets and prophetic ministry per se were also known in the cultures surrounding Israel, including Egypt, Mesopotamia, and Syria. Texts from Emar and Mari and other regions of the ANE illustrate this phenomenon. In most instances (and rather distinct from biblical prophecy), extrabiblical prophets spoke to kings and were mostly in the employ of royalty. Their ministry happened typically within the context of cultic, ritual, and priestly activities, while biblical prophets came mostly from families that were not of the priestly line (with some exceptions, such as Samuel or Jeremiah). Unlike the monarchic and priestly functions, there was no hereditary prophetic role in Israel. God called whom and when He liked.

Early biblical prophets include Enoch (based on Jude 14; cf. CTr 51), Noah (Gen. 9:24–27; PP 117), Abraham (Gen. 20:7), Miriam (Ex. 15:20–21), Balaam (Num. 22), Deborah (Judg. 4:4), and a number of anonymous prophets (Judg. 6:8; 1 Kin. 13:1–10).

Samuel played an important role in the late premonarchic and early monarchic periods in relation to the monarchy, similar to the ministries of Nathan and Gad, who faithfully and fearlessly communicated God's messages to King David, even if that potentially meant a death sentence (2 Sam. 12:1–15; 24:11–25; 1 Chr. 21:9–19). Elijah's and Elisha's ministries affected a significant number of Israelite and Judean kings, as well as their Syrian neighbors. Like later writing prophets, such as Micah, Isaiah, and Jeremiah, their messages often annoyed and ultimately challenged their people and leaders to take a stand for the Lord and remember the covenant that God had made with them. The description of Ahab's and Jehoshaphat's encounter with Micaiah, the son of Imlah, in 1 Kings 22 provides a telling illustration of the different ways that various kings related to prophets of Yahweh.

Ahab of Israel and Jehoshaphat of Judah, linked through the marriage of their children (2 Kin. 8:18), agreed to fight the Syrian regional power to regain control over Ramoth Gilead, which had originally belonged to Israel. Like other ANE kings, they required divine orientation. It appears that Ahab followed the normal custom of maintaining a large number of court-supported prophets and diviners. The biblical text reports that about 400 prophets were gathered by the king, and they noisily proclaimed a resounding victory (1 Kin. 22:6). Jehoshaphat's skeptical reaction (v. 7) highlights one of the characteristics of true prophecy: a prophet of the Lord speaks the word from the Lord—not a conveniently packaged message requested by a king willing to pay for the right words. Micaiah's first message was full of irony and echoed what Ahab wanted to hear. Ahab's reaction suggested that he caught the irony (v. 16), and when he demanded the truth in the name of the Lord, the prophet revealed the king's imminent death. Micaiah's incarceration is a good illustration of the fact that the message of biblical prophets was not always welcomed by national leaders and the people.

In the ninth century B.C., during the time of Elijah and Elisha, the biblical text also depicts the existence of schools of the prophets. Generally, their members were called "sons/company of the prophets" (e.g., 1 Kin. 20:35; 2 Kin. 2:3, 5, 7, 15). Some scholars consider them as groups of individuals who practiced asceticism and preferred communal living. The biblical data, however, suggests a more school-like institution whose members were often married (2 Kin. 4:1–7) and may have functioned as itinerant religious teachers following their studies (PP 592–94).

The OT includes a number of books written by prophets (beginning with Jonah in the eighth century B.C.) whose ministries affected both Israel and Judah and whose writings became part of the biblical canon. Biblical prophets continued to admonish, encourage, challenge, and call back God's people until the Exile and the destruction of Jerusalem. The prophetic gift continued to bless God's people even after the Exile, as can be noted in the Ezra-Nehemiah narrative where Haggai and Zechariah play key roles in encouraging the returnees to continue the reconstruction of the temple (Ezra 5:1; 6:14; cf. the reference in Ezra's prayer in Ezra 9:11 and the many references to past prophetic ministry in Neh. 9:26, 30, 32). Intriguingly, the text also describes false prophets who had been hired to discourage Jerusalem's leadership and people through their misguided ministry (Neh. 6:10–14). This brief review clearly highlights the enduring presence of God's prophets ministering to the needs of the covenant people as well as the larger world surrounding them. During the intertestamental period this prophetic voice essentially disappeared, but it rang out loud preceding the time of Jesus's ministry and in the foundational decades of the early Christian community.

MAIN HISTORICAL PERIODS COVERED IN THE HISTORICAL BOOKS

The historical books cover the period beginning with the conquest of Canaan (ca. 1400 B.C.) until the time of the return of the Jews to Jerusalem under the leadership of Ezra in the fifth century B.C. (ca. 450 B.C.), slightly less than a thousand years. This period comprises a significant part of Israel's history, beginning with the time of the judges, that was characterized by tribal division and near-constant conflict with local powers, until the return of the Jews to Jerusalem during the time of Artaxerxes II when the province of Yehud was under the control of the Persian Empire. Following is a brief review of the major divisions of Israelite history.

Period of the Judges (ca. 1407–1053 B.C.)

The total number of years reported in the book of Judges for individual judges, if added sequentially, significantly exceeds 450 years (in addition to the three fairly extensive periods for which the biblical text does not include explicit durations: the time that Joshua and the elders governed Israel [Judg. 2:7]; the period that Samgar led Israel [Judg. 3:31]; as well as the long period that Samuel served as a judge [1 Sam. 7:15]). This significantly surpasses the roughly 350 known years between the conquest (ca. 1407 B.C.) and the anointing of Saul (1053 B.C.). This discrepancy suggests that judges may have governed at the same time in different parts of the country. This suggestion is supported by the geography of Canaan, which may have led to the isolation of some of the tribes (e.g., the tribes living on the eastern side of the Jordan). The biblical text itself highlights the fact that not all tribes were always afflicted by the same enemy or participated in every fight for liberation (e.g., Judg. 6:35; 8:1; 12:1).

United Monarchy (1053–931 B.C.)

Three kings reigned during this period, separated by some years of strife and civil war. Luke suggests in Acts 13:21 that Saul's reign lasted for forty years, which may indicate a rounded number, in line with David's (1 Chron. 29:27) and Solomon's reigns (1 Kin. 11:42). The meaning of the text of 1 Samuel 13:1 is unclear, as can be seen in the many diverging modern versions ("Saul reigned one year; and when he had reigned two years over Israel" [NKJV]; "Saul was thirty years old when he became king, and he reigned over Israel forty-two years" [NIV]; "Saul was…years old when he began to reign; and he reigned…and two years over Israel" [NRSV]). The ancient versions reflect the difficult nature of the text: the translators of the Septuagint, the Greek translation of the Hebrew Bible, simply omitted the verse. In the Targums, the Aramaic translations of the Hebrew Bible, the text is paraphrased as "Saul was as innocent as a child of one year when he began to reign."

David's forty-year reign (1011–971 B.C.) is divided into two periods. David reigned for seven years in Hebron over Judah and Benjamin. He conquered Jerusalem and made it his capital (2 Sam. 5:6–10), and he reigned thirty-three years in Jerusalem as king of a united kingdom (1 Chr. 29:27). His military victories over the Philistines and other neighboring nations laid the foundation for a short period characterized by military strength, advances in the organization of the kingdom, and economic blessings. The biblical text draws a clear connection between David's faithfulness and God's divine blessings for the nation. Critical scholars have long doubted the very existence of King David. However, recent discoveries, including the ninth-century-B.C. Tel Dan inscription mentioning "the house of David," found in 1993, and the important contribution of the excavations of Khirbet Qeiyafa (possibly to be identified as the biblical Shaaraim, mentioned in 1 Sam. 17:52 as a border town separating Israel and Philistia), strongly suggest the existence of a central administrative power in the tenth century B.C. in Israel. These discoveries have put these doubts from critical scholarship to rest (for more, see "Archaeology and the Bible," p. 77).

Solomon's reign (971–931 B.C.) also covered forty years (1 Kin. 11:42) and represents the pinnacle of power, economic prowess, art, and architecture of Israel's united monarchy. At this time, Israel's territory extended from the Gulf of Aqaba in the south to the Euphrates in the north. Solomon's plea for divine wisdom (1 Kin. 3:1–15) was granted and his fame spread throughout the ANE. His marriage to Pharaoh's daughter (1 Kin. 3:1) underlines Solomon's elevated status within the context of ANE powers of the tenth century B.C. Solomon is well known for his construction of the first temple, but from a strategic position, his construction of a series of fortified cities for his standing army and his extensive chariot force (1 Kin. 4:26; 9:15–19; 10:26) hints at his political, economic, and military significance. Israel's crucial geographical location, connecting Africa (and Egypt) to Syria, Asia Minor, and Mesopotamia, gave Solomon serious control of key routes. Unfortunately, his huge harem and his agreement to the construction around Jerusalem of places of worship honoring scores of ANE deities for his wives set the stage for Israel's continuous struggle with idolatry over the following centuries (1 Kin. 11:1–8). Furthermore, his ambitious building projects and the complete administrative reorganization of the kingdom required that every Israelite had to contribute labor, leading to disquiet and challenging the agricultural production of the kingdom.

Divided Monarchy

Due to Rehoboam's unwise decision soon after his coronation to increase the forced labor requirements for his citizens, the ten northern tribes broke away from Judah and Benjamin. This resulted in the division of God's people into the kingdoms of Israel and Judah (1 Kin. 12:1–20). The following contains a brief summary of key kings and events during the following centuries.

Kingdom of Israel (931–722 B.C.)

Jeroboam I (931–910 B.C.) became Israel's first king (1 Kin. 12:19–20). During the reign of Solomon he had been part of the royal administration (1 Kin. 11:26–28), but following a prophetic oracle anticipating the division of the ten northern tribes from Judah and Benjamin, Jeroboam had to flee from Solomon to Egypt (1 Kin. 11:29–40). He later returned to Israel after the death of Solomon, and became king over the ten northern tribes when they rebelled against Rehoboam. Even though he had been called to reign over Israel by a prophet from God, Jeroboam built two temples and installed two golden calves in two crucial geographical locations of his kingdom: Bethel (marking the southern border) and Dan (marking the northern border). This was most likely for political reasons, as he sought to keep his people from traveling to the temple in Jerusalem to fulfill a requirement of the law (1 Kin. 12:27–30). He also appointed non-Levitical priests and established high places around his kingdom (v. 31). These became known as Jeroboam's sins that caused Israel to sin (e.g., 1 Kin. 14:16; 15:30; 2 Kin. 3:3; 10:29).

Jeroboam's form of worship was a beguiling mixture of true and false religion. Jeroboam was the first king of a line of twenty kings representing many dynasties. His son **Nadab** (910–909 B.C.) reigned for only two years (1 Kin. 15:25) and was assassinated by **Baasha** from the tribe of Issachar (1 Kin. 15:27). Baasha reigned for twenty-two years (909–886 B.C.) and fought a number of battles with Judah and also Syria to the north. His son **Elah** (886–885 B.C.) reigned for less than two years and was assassinated in his capital, Tirzah, by one of his generals, **Zimri** (885 B.C.), who made himself king but reigned for only seven days (1 Kin. 16:8–10, 15). In fulfillment of the message that the prophet Jehu had delivered to Baasha (1 Kin. 16:1–4), Zimri spent his very short-lived reign killing all the family members of the house of Baasha (1 Kin. 16:11–13). After Zimri's violent coup another of Elah's generals, **Omri**, was proclaimed king by the army of Israel and took the capital from Zimri, who committed suicide, after a short siege (vv. 16–18).

The biblical text reports that, for a while, Israel was ravaged by civil war between the followers of **Tibni** (885–880 B.C.) and Omri. The reign of Omri, who finally prevailed (1 Kin. 16:21–22), lasted twelve years (885–874 B.C.) and represents the beginning of the longest-reigning dynasty of Israel (four generations). According to the Moabite Mesha Stele, Omri subjugated Moab, and during the time of King Ahab, Omri's son, Moab paid him a yearly tribute of 100,000 lambs and 100,000 rams (2 Kin. 3:4). Omri also established Samaria as Israel's capital (1 Kin. 16:24). His son **Ahab** (874–853 B.C.) reigned for twenty-two years and, based on the evaluation of the biblical text, was one of the worst kings of the Northern Kingdom. His reign overlaps with the ministry of Elijah. His marriage to the Phoenician Queen Jezebel caused a major religious crisis in Israel (1 Kin. 18:4, 19). She introduced court-sponsored prophets and priests of Baal. First Kings 22:39 states that Ahab built an ivory house in Samaria. Excavations of the palace at Samaria found hundreds of artistic ivory fragments. His son **Ahaziah** (853–852 B.C.) reigned for only two years (1 Kin. 22:51–53) and followed in the footsteps of his father. He was followed by his son **Joram** (Jehoram; 852–841 B.C.), completing the fourth generation of the dynasty of Omri. Moab rebelled against Israel during his reign (2 Kin. 3:4–27).

Jehoram (sometimes also called Joram, cf. 2 Kin. 9:14–26) was assassinated by his general **Jehu** (841–814 B.C.), who had been anointed at Elisha's direction by one of the sons of the prophets (2 Kin. 9:1–10) and had been charged to completely destroy Ahab's descendants. Jehu's zealous fulfillment of this command resulted in the divine promise of the establishment of Jehu's dynasty until the fourth generation (2 Kin. 10:30), even though he ultimately did not help Israel to return to the Lord and continued in the worship at Dan and Bethel established by Jeroboam I (2 Kin. 10:31). His son **Jehoahaz** (814–798 B.C.) reigned for seventeen years (2 Kin. 13:1–2) but did not change the general downward course of Israel. During his reign Israel lost significant territory to the Syrians, led by Hazael and Ben-Hadad. Second Kings 13:7 states that Israel was left with only 50 horsemen, 10 chariots, and 10,000 foot soldiers. His son **Jehoash** (Joash; 798–782 B.C.) reigned for sixteen years and recovered some of the territory lost to the Syrians (or Arameans; 2 Kin. 13:25). He also won a battle against Judah at Beth-Shemesh and took hostages and booty from Jerusalem to Samaria (2 Kin. 14:8–14). It is likely that he coreigned with his son **Jeroboam II** (793–753 B.C.) for twelve years.

Jeroboam II's reign represents the golden age of the Northern Kingdom of Israel. Due to the weakness of the Assyrians and the Syrians, he was able to extend his reign and recover much of the territory that had been lost since the days of Solomon. While the seven verses describing his reign suggest political and economic stability and link his reign to the prophetic ministry of Jonah, he did not initiate true reformation (2 Kin. 14:23–29). Judging from the writing of Amos, a contemporary of Jeroboam II, it appears as if social injustice became an ever more pressing problem in Israelite society. His son **Zechariah** (753–752 B.C.) reigned for only six months and was assassinated by **Shallum** (752 B.C.), who in turn was killed a month later by **Menahem** (752–742 B.C.), who had to pay a high tribute to the Assyrian King Tiglath-Pileser III.

That turbulent period of Israelite history underlines the decay and diminishing importance of Israel (2 Kin. 15:8–22). The reign of Menahem's son **Pekahiah** (742–740 B.C.) was cut short when he was assassinated by **Pekah** (752–732 B.C.). Intriguingly, according to 2 Kings 15:27 Pekah reigned for twenty years, suggesting that he may have governed a small part of the kingdom during Menahem's reign. He rebelled against the Assyrian power and formed an alliance with Syrian city-states (cf. Is. 7:1–4 for more information). The last king of Israel, **Hoshea** (732–722 B.C.), killed his predecessor, Pekah, and had to pay heavy tribute to the Assyrians. He joined an anti-Assyrian alliance under the leadership of Pharaoh So of Egypt (2 Kin. 17:4), possibly Osorkon IV, who reigned in Tanis. Ten years into Hoshea's reign, Samaria and Israel ceased to exist and the people were deported by the Assyrian kings Shalmaneser V and Sargon II (2 Kin. 18:10).

Kingdom of Judah (931–586 B.C.)

Different from Israel, Judah's kings all belonged to the Davidic dynasty. **Rehoboam** (931–913 B.C.) suffered an attack and defeat by Pharaoh Sheshonq I of Egypt in his fifth year (1 Kin.

14:25–28). The temple was raided and its treasures taken. Unfortunately, like his father, Solomon, he had many wives and many concubines (2 Chr. 11:21). Judah fell more and more into idolatry (1 Kin. 14:22–24) during his reign. His son **Abijam** (913–911 B.C.) reigned for only three years and followed the general downward trend of his father. His son **Asa** (911–870 B.C.), however, is considered a good king by the biblical author because of his religious reforms (1 Kin. 15:9–15). He was one of the longest-reigning kings of Judah. Because of his lack of faith in God's power to save when Israel's Baasha attacked Judah, he was severely reprimanded by the prophet Hanani (2 Chr. 16:1–10). Asa's son **Jehoshaphat** (872–848 B.C.) reigned as coregent due to his father's ill health (2 Chr. 16:12–13). He continued his father's reforms but made an alliance by marriage with the dynasty of Omri when his son married Ahab's daughter (2 Kin. 8:18, 26). Unfortunately, this marriage opened Judah to Baal worship. He also fought alongside Ahab against the Arameans at Ramoth Gilead (2 Chr. 18–19:3).

Jehoshophat's son **Jehoram** (853–841 B.C.) reigned with his father from 853 B.C. onward. He should not be confused with Joram (Jehoram) of Israel, who reigned in the same period. Scripture's evaluation of his reign is entirely negative due to the influence of his wife, the daughter of Ahab (2 Kin. 8:16–18). Judah lost control over Edom and Libnah during his reign (2 Kin. 8:20–22). The reign of his son **Ahaziah** (841 B.C.) was cut short dramatically when he died from the injuries sustained during Jehu's rebellion in neighboring Israel (2 Kin. 9:14–28). His mother, **Athaliah**, reigned from 841 to 835 B.C. and secured her reign by killing all the royal heirs (2 Kin. 11:1) except for her grandson Joash, who was hidden by his aunt Jehosheba, who was married to the high priest Jehoiada (2 Kin. 11:2–3). Athaliah's reign of terror ended six years later when, under the leadership of Jehoiada, the army and the people of the land made Joash king of Judah and killed Athaliah.

The long reign of **Joash** (Jehoash; 835–796 B.C.), not to be confused with the king of Israel with a similar name, reflects both good and evil. Guided by his priestly uncle, Joash attempted a major religious reform, seeking to destroy the worship of Baal in the land (2 Kin. 12:1–16; 2 Chr. 24:1–14). Later on, however, he killed Jehoiada's son Zechariah, who had challenged Judah publicly (2 Chr. 24:15–22). Joash was killed by his servants, and his son **Amaziah** (796–767 B.C.) became king in Jerusalem (2 Chr. 25). God gave him a resounding victory over Edom (2 Chr. 25:5–12), but Amaziah became arrogant and challenged Jehoash of Israel, who won a great victory and marched into Jerusalem (2 Kin. 14:8–14) and took many spoils and hostages back to Samaria. Amaziah was also killed by his own servants, and his son Azariah was made king in his stead (2 Kin. 14:17–21). **Azariah** (Uzziah; 792–740 B.C.) is considered a good king, and he reigned for fifty-two years, coreigning with his father, Amaziah, at the end of his life. Judah avoided many of the dynastic struggles that Israel experienced by appointing future kings as coregents. Azariah is called Uzziah in Chronicles, perhaps reflecting a throne name. Parallel to the reign of Jeroboam II in Israel, Azariah's reign is characterized by peace and strong economic development (2 Chr. 26:10). He maintained a strong army (2 Chr. 26:11–15) and regained control over Elath at the Gulf of Aqaba (2 Kin. 14:22), thus giving him sea access and control over an important trade route. During his reign Judah experienced a major earthquake that is referenced in Scripture (Amos 1:1; Zech. 14:5). When the king attempted to enter the Holy Place and burn incense on its altar, he was struck with leprosy and had to live a secluded life in the palace (2 Chr. 26:16–21). His son **Jotham** (750–732 B.C.) reigned in his place and was a contemporary of the prophets Isaiah, Hosea, and Micah, who, most likely, were a good influence on him (2 Chr. 27:1–9). His son **Ahaz** (735–716 B.C.), however, represents one of the worst kings in Judah's history; he practiced idolatrous abominations, including sacrificing one of his sons (2 Kin. 16:3–4). Instead of trusting in the Lord, Ahaz sent a heavy tribute to the Assyrian king Tiglath-Pileser III, requesting his help against the alliance of Israel and Syria (2 Kin. 16:5–9; Is. 7:3–13). He also introduced an Assyrian altar into the temple in Jerusalem (2 Kin. 16:10–16).

Ahaz was succeeded by his son **Hezekiah** (716–687 B.C.), who initiated major religious reforms and also strengthened the national defenses (at Lachish and Jerusalem) in light of the Assyrian threat following the destruction of Samaria (2 Kin. 18:1–8; 2 Chr. 32:28–29). His name is associated with the 1,900-foot (ca. 582 m) tunnel connecting the Gihon Spring to a pool in the lower part of Jerusalem inside the city walls (2 Kin. 20:20; 2 Chr. 32:30; see "Archaeology and the Bible," p. 77). Lachish, the second-largest fortified city of Judah located south of Jerusalem, was destroyed by Sennacherib during his reign. God delivered Jerusalem from the Assyrian attack and killed a huge number of Assyrian soldiers (2 Kin. 18–19).

Manasseh (697–643 B.C.), Hezekiah's son, became one of the worst kings of the kingdom of Judah, reconstructing altars for Baal, practicing magic, sacrificing children, and worshiping the stars (2 Chr. 33:1–10). Consequently, he was taken to Mesopotamia as a prisoner of the Assyrian kings (2 Chr. 33:11). Chronicles reports that Manasseh repented and God forgave and restored him to his throne (2 Chr. 33:12–13). The damage done by his example, however, accelerated Judah's fall and soon-coming destruction. God's prophetic word announced that it was for the sins of Manasseh that Judah would go into captivity (2 Kin. 24:3). **Amon** (643–641 B.C.), Manasseh's son, reigned for only two years and was killed by his servants (2 Kin. 21:19–26; 2 Chr. 33:21–25). He was succeeded by Judah's last good king, **Josiah** (641–609 B.C.), who undertook a major reform at the age of fifteen or sixteen years (2 Chr. 34:3). In the eighteenth year of his reign (622 B.C.), the "book of the law" was found in the temple, which gave impetus for more reforms, including reinstating the celebration of the Passover (2 Kin. 22–23; 2 Chr. 34:6–7). Josiah died in the battle of Megiddo against Pharaoh Necho in 609 B.C. (2 Chr. 35:20–24) as he sought to delay the arrival of the Egyptian army on their way to support the remainder of the severely diminished army of the last Assyrian king. His son **Jehoahaz** (609 B.C.) reigned for three months and was deported by the Egyptian pharaoh, who put another son of Josiah, **Jehoiakim** (609–598 B.C.), on the throne.

When the Babylonian crown prince Nebuchadnezzar took Jerusalem for the first time in 605 B.C., Judah became a vassal of the new Babylonian superpower. Among the hostages taken by Nebuchadnezzar were Daniel and his three friends (Dan. 1:1–6). When another battle between Egypt and Babylon in 601 B.C. ended in heavy losses to the Babylonians, Jehoiakim thought that his time had come, and he rebelled against Nebuchadnezzar. He died in 598 B.C. before the Babylonian troops were able to take Jerusalem for a second time. His son **Jehoiachin** (598–597 B.C.) was made king of Judah following the sudden death of his father, but he reigned for only three months (2 Kin. 24:8–12) before Jerusalem fell for a second time to the Babylonians. He was taken as prisoner to Babylon but was released in the thirty-seventh year of his captivity by Babylonian King Evil-Merodach, a son of Nebuchadnezzar, who ruled Babylon from 562 to 560 B.C. (2 Kin. 25:27–30). Judah's final king's birth name was Mattaniah ("gift of Yahweh"), but he received the throne name **Zedekiah** ("justice of Yahweh"; 597–586 B.C.) from Nebuchadnezzar (2 Kin. 24:17). He was another son of Josiah but did not live as his father had lived. He traveled to Babylon in his fourth year (ca. 594/593 B.C.; Jer. 51:59) to swear allegiance to Nebuchadnezzar. That trip to Babylon may be connected to the story found in Daniel 3 when all the princes of the Babylonian Empire were required to worship the golden image that Nebuchadnezzar had built on the plain of Dura. Like some of the other kings before him, Zedekiah was persuaded by Egypt into another anti-Babylon alliance (Jer. 37:6–10) and rebelled in 590 B.C. Babylon's quick response led to the destruction of all fortified cities in Judah and, finally, in July of 586 B.C., to the fall of Jerusalem (2 Kin. 25:2; Jer. 39:2), resulting in the complete destruction of Jerusalem and its temple. Zedekiah was caught when he tried to leave the city prior to the fall, was blinded, and was taken to Babylon as a prisoner (2 Kin. 25:1–7). Nebuchadnezzar appointed Gedaliah as administrative overseer of the newly established Babylonian province, and Gedaliah resided in Mizpah (2 Kin. 25:22–24). Unfortunately, he was killed by Jewish rebels, who took many of the remaining Jews, including Jeremiah, to Egypt (2 Kin. 25:25–26; see Jer. 41–43).

Exile and Return (605–444 B.C.)

Judah's Exile lasted about seventy years, beginning with the first deportation in 605 B.C. and concluding after the fall of Babylon in 539 B.C. and the subsequent decree issued by the Medo-Persian King Cyrus (2 Chr. 36:22–23; Ezra 1:1–4). The first group of Jews returned to Jerusalem around 537 B.C. under the leadership of Sheshbazzar (most likely the Babylonian version of the Hebrew name Zerubbabel; cf. Ezra 1:5–11; 2:2; 3:2–8; Hag. 1:14–15). While the altar was immediately reestablished and the sacrificial worship began right after the arrival of the returnees, it took more than twenty years to complete the rebuilding of the temple itself (Ezra 6:15 gives the sixth year of King Darius I [515 B.C.] as the time when the newly rebuilt temple was dedicated). Ezra and Nehemiah describe three returns: the first under Zerrubabel/Sheshbazzar in 537 B.C.; the second under Ezra in 457 B.C. (the seventh year of Artaxerxes I; Ezra 7:8); and the third under Nehemiah, who had been appointed as the new governor of the province of Yehud that was part of the Medo-Persian Empire (in the twentieth year of Artaxerxes I, 444 B.C.; Neh. 2:1, 11).

Judah's provincial status within the satrapy Beyond the River suggests limited control over its destiny, which is also reflected in Ezra and Nehemiah (cf. Ezra 4). Restoration of the temple and return to the land did not automatically mean political restoration equivalent to the freedom Israel and Judah had enjoyed during the centuries of the united and divided monarchies. For the next centuries until the beginning of the NT period, Jerusalem and its surrounding territory were part of a sequence of empires that controlled its destiny. God's covenant people were called to affect the world and cultures surrounding them by their example and message. In many ways, this was a time of growing expectations, as the time of the Messiah, anticipated by Israel's prophets for centuries, was drawing closer and closer.

MAJOR THEOLOGICAL THEMES OF THE HISTORICAL BOOKS

God's engagement in human history is one of the key theological motifs shared by all of the historical books of the OT. In spite of unfaithfulness by His people and leaders, God is at work. He heard Joshua's plea for wisdom and strength before he had even expressed it verbally (Josh. 1:1–9). He heard Israel's repeated cries during the period of the judges as they experienced repeated oppression due to their poor choices (e.g., Judg. 3:9, 15; 4:3; 5:28). God hears when we lack hope or when we are burdened by our sins and bad choices. As we cry we also turn toward the only One who can offer us hope and liberation. This is the covenantal framework that runs like a golden thread through the historical books. God woos us into recognizing our distress, which causes us to turn to Him and repent. In turn, God provides a way out. Sometimes He uses other people (as illustrated by the stories told in Judges and Ruth); sometimes He intervenes directly, moving the hearts of princes and kings or sending His prophets to offer a way through a parched desert, which led to an unexpected victory (2 Kin. 3:9–24); sometimes He uses kings and courtiers to make a way (see Ezra 1), as when He stirred up the spirit of Cyrus and the hearts of His own people. He moves history forward and fills it with hope.

God's engagement in human history is central to the larger cosmic battle between good and evil. There is a purpose to God hearing the cries of His people and those who are afflicted and oppressed. Ultimately, it drives us to make a decision about whom we will trust. God's covenant blessings were a way of helping the larger world surrounding Israel and Judah to pay attention to the Lord, the God of Israel, who is not a local or regional deity made of stone, wood, or metal. This principle of establishing His people as witnesses (already anticipated in Gen. 12:1–3) is appropriately expressed in 1 Kings 10:1 when the queen of Sheba came to visit King Solomon and asked him questions because of his fame and the name of the Lord. Solomon's fame was related to "the name of the LORD"—shorthand for His character and qualities. Israel was to demonstrate to the world that God is the Creator and Sustainer of *all* the world. Intriguingly, most canonical prophets writing during this period included a significant number of messages and oracles directed to the nations surrounding Israel, illustrating perfectly the universal nature of God. In the NT the same principle is summarized so powerfully in John 3:16—God loved the whole world and gave His only Son to save us from eternal death and give eternal life to those who trust in Him. There is no partiality or partisanship in God's saving grace.

Another recurring motif found in the historical books involves *the power of leadership*. Faithful leaders inspire faithful followers; idolatrous leaders seduce people to more idolatry. This clear message can be easily documented in the annals of Israelite history. Great moments of national reformation are led by God-fearing kings, prophets, or priests who don't consider the cost of unpopular decisions (e.g., Joash's repair of the temple was inspired by the godly influence of the high priest Jehoiada [2 Kin. 12:1–16; 2 Chr. 24:1–14]; following the death of his mentor, Joash served wooden images and idols [2 Chr. 24:15–22]). Other examples include Asa, Jehoshaphat, Hezekiah, and Josiah from the kingdom of Judah. Their examples and leadership functioned as powerful initiators of national transformation, even though we can clearly see in the biblical text some of their weaknesses and bad choices.

When we consider the importance of leadership, we should not overlook the significance of the prophetic ministry. The role of the prophets in the historical books cannot be underestimated. Their divinely inspired messages often call God's people to return to Him or, in other moments, are a reminder of the fact that God is still in control and able and willing to save His people, thus offering them hope.

God's sovereignty and grace shines through the story again and again. He gave the land to Israel. He chose Jerusalem to be the location for His temple and His presence. He listened to the cries of His people and their leaders. He appointed and empowered kings—even though a human monarchy was not part of His ideal plan (1 Sam. 8). He gathered a remnant to return to Jerusalem. His ability to hear the prayers and cries of His people is not limited by time and space. He is the all-powerful, almighty, all-knowing, and all-caring God, even though Israel often forgot these foundational truths.

As we reach the end of OT history in the Chronicles and in Ezra and Nehemiah, we wonder about the Messiah, the One foretold by prophets and prefigured by some of Israel's leaders. When will He come? How will He come, and for whom will He come? As easily recognizable from the lack of recognition in the NT Gospel narratives, Israel was waiting for the Messiah but looked for the wrong kind. The Messiah's arrival would change the world forever and validate the hope of thousands who yearned to see Immanuel, God with us.

JOSHUA

INTRODUCTION

Title and Authorship. In the Jewish canon, the book of Joshua is the first of the section called "the Prophets." The title of the book is a personal name, *yehoshua'*, meaning "Yahweh saves." Joshua's name was originally *hoshea'*, "salvation," but Moses changed it by prefixing the abbreviated form of the divine name Yahweh (*yahweh + hoshua*; Num. 13:16). The English form "Joshua" abbreviates the Hebrew "Yehoshua," while the name Jesus derives from the Greek version. This means that the names Yehoshua, Joshua, and Jesus are one and the same. Both in name and work, Joshua was a type of Jesus Christ, the "Commander of the army of the Lord" (Josh. 5:13–15).

Internal evidence shows that the book was composed shortly after the conquest. Several examples can be cited. First, it is stated that Rahab was still living in Israel in the writer's lifetime ("to this day"; 6:25), which suggests that the writing of the book occurred during the lifetime of the generation that entered the Holy Land (cf. Judg. 2:10). Second, the author seems to have been an eyewitness to the conquest, not only because he uses a first-person pronoun (Josh. 5:6) but also because of the copious geographical and topographical details found throughout the book. Third, the references to Jerusalem (15:63) and Gezer (16:10) as being inhabited by the Jebusites and Canaanites, respectively, as well as the preeminence given to Sidon as opposed to Tyre (11:8; 13:4; 19:28), imply that the book was composed long before the reigns of David and Solomon (cf. 2 Sam. 5:6–11; 1 Kin. 7:13; 9:16). According to the text, Joshua was literate (Josh. 8:32; 24:26). He is also the dominant human character of the book, as is Moses in the Pentateuch. It is probable, therefore, that Joshua is the author of the book that bears his name, though his death account, as well as that of Eleazar (24:29–33), must have been added

by another inspired person(s). The internal evidence agrees with Jewish traditions that Joshua wrote chapters 1:1—24:28 while Eleazer and Phinehas added 24:29–32 and 24:33, respectively. Nonetheless, there are some later scribal modernizations intended to clarify the text for later generations (see 11:21; 15:13–15; 19:47). The reference to the book of Jasher (10:13; 2 Sam. 1:18) may be one of these later scribal additions. Such additions, however, do not affect the inspiration and authenticity of the book.

Date. The dating of the book of Joshua depends largely on the dating of the Exodus, since this book is a direct continuation of Genesis–Deuteronomy. Scripture supports the fifteenth-century-B.C. dating of the Exodus (see Judg. 2:10; 11:26; 1 Kin. 6:1; cf. Exodus: Introduction). Therefore, the conquest of the Holy Land must have begun about 1407 B.C. Caleb was forty years old when, along with Joshua, he was numbered among the spies (Josh. 14:7; Num. 13:6, 8). Caleb was eighty-five at the end of the conquest (Josh. 14:10), with at least thirty-eight of these years elapsing between Kadesh Barnea and the crossing of the Zered river in Transjordan (Deut. 2:14; cf. Num. 10:11–12; 33:38). The conquest then must have lasted for about seven years (i.e., between ca. 1407 and 1400 B.C.), with Joshua dying a few decades later (Josh. 23:1, 14; 24:29). As demonstrated above, the bulk of the book of Joshua was probably written by Joshua before his death. Consequently, this composition (including more than 24:29–33) was in the late fifteenth/early fourteenth century B.C.

Backgrounds. Genesis–Deuteronomy provides the background to the book of Joshua (1:1–9; 21:43–45). The call of Abram recorded in Genesis 12:1–3 highlights the universal hope of restoration and blessing. These verses sum up God's covenant with Abram (Gen. 15:7–21; 17:1–22). Abraham was promised that through him and his offspring God would bring salvation to all the people of the earth. He was also promised a land to be inherited by his descendants after a few centuries, which included the promise of an Exodus from Egypt to the Holy Land. The reason God saved Israel from Egypt was to relocate His people in the Holy Land as promised to Abraham (Ex. 6:2–6). The promise of land, therefore, was the immediate hope of Israel at the Exodus (1:11; 13:5–11; Lev. 25:38; Num. 14:8; Deut. 1:8, 21). The realization of this promise is the focus of the book of Joshua. If the Lord led Israel out of Egypt through Moses, He settled Israel in the Holy Land through Joshua.

Although scholarly debate surrounds the dating of the Exodus and the conquest, evidence from Scripture, as noted above, suggests that the time period covered by the book is between the last decade of the fifteenth century and the first quarter of the fourteenth century B.C. (ca. 1407–1357 B.C.). During this time, the Holy Land was probably nominally under Egyptian control, with the country divided into numerous independent city-states (e.g., Jericho, Ai, Bethel). The archaeological documents known as the Amarna Letters, written about 1400 B.C., reveal that during this time a people called *habiru* were invading the Holy Land, forcing Canaanite kings to send distress calls to Egypt for military assistance. In these letters, *habiru* may refer to the Israelites.

By failing to respond to the requests for reinforcements, the Egyptians seemed to have had little interest in the affairs of Syro-Palestine at that time. Also, due probably to either internal or external reasons, none of the other contemporary powers in the ANE (Hittites, Hurrians, Kassites, and Assyrians) was in a position to interfere with developments in the Holy Land. Similarly, the major wave of Philistine immigrants was not yet ready to form a barrier against the Israelite conquest. Finally, further evaluation of archaeological discoveries places the destruction of Canaanite cities such as Jericho and Hazor around 1400 B.C., thereby confirming the scriptural account. Archaeological research, though, has equally yielded conflicting results and questions relating to the conquest. While we may hope for more reliable findings, the internal claims of Scripture should always be the final arbiter.

The biblical text is clear that Israel actually conquered and settled in the land of promise (13:1—21:45), and other scriptural passages refer to this fact (see 2 Sam. 21:1–6; 1 Kin. 16:34; 2 Chr. 20:7). But what was the extent of this conquest? On the one hand, some texts use the language of totality in regard to the campaigns (Josh. 10:40–42; 11:16–23; 21:43–45). On the other hand, there are texts indicating that Joshua did not conquer the whole land (13:1–6; 17:12–13; 18:2–3; 23:4–5, 13). There is, however, no contradiction between these two sets of texts. The former texts, examined contextually, do not denote the whole land of promise but rather portions within the land. These texts emphasize that God was faithful in fulfilling the promise of land to Abraham (cf. 21:43–45). The second set of texts shows that parts of the Holy Land were yet to be possessed, though these too were divided among the tribes (23:4). In these texts, God promises to drive out the inhabitants of the land from before Israel (13:6; 23:5). This reiterates the earlier promise that God would drive out the inhabitants of the Holy Land "little by little," otherwise the land would be desolate and wild animals would be too numerous for Israel (Ex. 23:29–33; Deut. 7:22).

Theology and Purpose. The primary purpose of the book of Joshua is to describe Israel's entry into the land of promise, the conquest of the land, and its division among the tribes. This purpose underlines the message of the book, namely, the faithfulness of God in fulfilling the promise of land made to Abraham. The book emphasizes God's faithfulness to His covenant promises (Josh. 21:43–45).

1. Covenant Faithfulness. Obviously, the major theological theme of the book of Joshua is the covenant. The central element of the covenant is the promise of the Holy Land. As such, the book repeatedly emphasizes the Lord's faithfulness in fulfilling this promise (2:24; 3:10; 11:23; 21:43–45; 23:14). Israel was a covenant nation and thus was required to keep the covenant (Ex. 19–24). As enshrined in the covenant provisions, any deviation on the part of Israel was punishable

---

Habiru

Habiru, a people group, are mentioned in texts from various places in the ANE between 1750 and 1150 B.C. These were generally nomadic tribesmen or fugitives who had penetrated urbanized centers and were proving troublesome to native populations. While *habiru* could refer to any group of people "outside of the law," the *habiru* in the Amarna letters may refer to people groups including the Israelites. Moreover, *habiru* would be a fitting designation of the Hebrews (Israel) who were then invading the Holy Land.

(see Josh. 23:16), yet this was a means to protect the divine promise. This is the backdrop against which the destruction of Achan and his family is to be understood. Achan's sin constituted covenantal unfaithfulness on the part of Israel as a whole (7:1, 11). As a covenant community, Israel shared a corporate identity, so the sin of one member affected the whole community until it was purged (7:11–13). Similarly, by violating the covenant and thus bringing himself under the "curse," Achan damaged all who shared in his identity (7:12, 24–26). The importance of the covenant theme in Joshua is further highlighted by the several references to its renewal (5:2–9; 8:30–35; 24:1–28). Joshua's exhortation against disobedience, idolatry, and intermarriage with the Canaanites summarizes the covenantal demand on Israel (23:6–16; 24:14–27). The implication is that the continual possession of the land was contingent on Israel's obedience of the covenant law (23:16; Deut. 28:58–68).

2. God's Sovereignty. The book also places quite an emphasis on the sovereignty of God. The Lord is the "living God" whose promises do not fail (Josh. 3:10). The God of Israel is "the LORD [Yahweh]," "the Lord [Adonai] of all the earth," who is able to "cut off" the waters of the Jordan to make way for His people (3:13–17) and to command the sun and the moon to stand still till He claims victory for His people (10:12–14). It was this Sovereign Lord, El-Shaddai, who transferred the land of the Canaanites to Israel (cf. 3:10). He gave rest (23:1) to Israel by extirpating the Canaanites through the holy warfare strategy known as *kherem*, meaning to "ban" (see "Holy Warfare," p. 372). The Exodus and the conquest, therefore, demonstrate that the Sovereign Lord intervenes in history to accomplish His purposes for humanity.

3. Judgment and Salvation. The book also discusses judgment and salvation within the confines of the covenant. On the one hand, the circumcision ceremony in 5:2–8 reiterated that those who came out of Egypt died in the wilderness because of their unfaithfulness to the covenant. Achan and his family also were destroyed due to his violation of the covenant (7:24–25). On the other hand, those who sought refuge in the Lord by joining the covenant community found salvation. Rahab declared faith in the Lord, and this led to the salvation of her entire family (2:11; 6:25). The Gibeonites also joined the covenant community, though deceptively, and shared in the blessings thereof (9:3–27). As hinted in Genesis 12:1–3, the possession of the Holy Land was not an end in itself. Rather, Israel's settlement in the Holy Land was a means

to the ultimate realization of the divine promise, namely, the blessings of salvation to the world. Settled strategically at the crossroads of the ancient world, Israel was God's missionary, serving as a channel of the "blessed hope" to the world.

4. True Leadership. We also find in the book a theology of leadership. It is God who establishes leaders (Josh. 1:1–9). The leaders God appoints are prepared both physically (Ex. 17:8–16; 24:12–13; Num. 13:16) and spiritually (Num. 27:15–23; Deut. 34:9) for the task at hand. Courage, dynamism, promptness, dedication, a serving attitude, firmness, and reliance on the word of God are some of the qualities of good leaders. The transition from Moses to Joshua reveals that there was a succession plan—God's people always had a leader. Yet, the success of leaders depends on their total submission to the will of the Lord (Josh. 1:8; 11:15). By submitting himself to the leadership of the Lord, Joshua succeeded in leading Israel into the promised land. Joshua's leading of Israel into the promised inheritance anticipated the work of the Messiah, Jesus Christ (Is. 49:8; Eph. 1:11–14; Heb. 4:8–11; 9:15; cf. Matt. 5:5). Through the saving work of the Messiah, the promise of the land becomes the promise of a land that is free from evil and sin. It is a land recreated by the power of Christ for His people (Rev. 21:10).

Literary Features. The book is formed by a narrative telling the experience of the twelve tribes from the death of Moses to the death of Joshua. The covenant renewal ceremonies (Josh. 8:30–35; 24:1–27) and the ritual ceremonies (circumcision and Passover; 5:1–12) are embedded in the narrative. The book can be divided in two parts: the first dealing with the conquest (chaps. 1–12) and the second with the division of the land (chaps. 13–24).

COMMENTARY

1:1—12:24

A HOPE REALIZED:
CONQUEST OF THE HOLY LAND

The inheritance of the land of promise was a central element in God's covenant with Abram (Gen. 12:1–7; 15:7–21). In order to fulfill this covenant promise, God saved Israel from Egyptian slavery and led them into the promised land by His servants Moses and Joshua. Joshua 1:1—12:24 describes Israel's conquest of the Holy Land.

1:1–18

Joshua Succeeds Moses

Joshua 1:1–18 reports the commissioning of Joshua and his initial orders to the leaders of the congregation. While Moses was alive, Joshua served as his attendant (Ex. 24:13; 33:11; Num. 11:28), and this experience prepared him to succeed Moses.

1:1–9. Joshua's Commission. The phrase "after the death of Moses" connects the book of Joshua to the five books of Moses, especially Deuteronomy. Verses 1–2 recall the death of Moses recorded in Deuteronomy 34. The book of Joshua, therefore, continues from where Moses left off. Before Moses's death, the Lord had appointed Joshua and commissioned him as Moses's successor. Following the Lord's command, Moses laid his hands on Joshua and commissioned him, signaling to the entire nation the transfer of the mantle of leadership (Num. 27:18–23; Deut. 3:28; 31:1–23; 34:7–9). Not only was he a man of experience and strength, but he was also a man full of the "spirit of wisdom." Such are the qualities the leaders of God's people must demonstrate.

Joshua 1:2–9 constitutes a divine charge to Joshua, the thrust of which is to build confidence in the promises, to urge courage and obedience, and to assure victory. The opening of the book contains the excitement of knowing that the promises of God to the patriarchs were about to be fulfilled. The people would witness and be part of the fulfillment of prophecy—the promised land was becoming theirs. Although the land west of the Jordan was the allotted land for Israel, the influence of Israel would extend far beyond the Jordan (1:4; 22:19; Deut. 11:24; 12:10; 32:48–52; 34:4). God made two important promises to Joshua. The first was a promise of victory (Josh. 1:3, 5). The outcome of the battle was assured and therefore he, and consequently the people, would be invincible. Second, God promised to be with Joshua (v. 5). His invincibility was grounded in God's presence with him: God would be with Joshua; He would not leave or abandon him (v. 5). Yet, divine promises require human involvement. Two things were required of Joshua: strength and courage (vv. 6–7, 9). These two characteristics were important for Joshua to be an able military leader (v. 6), but they were also indispensable for him to remain loyal to the divine law (v. 7). Courageous and strong people remain faithful to God in the context of spiritual conflict. Such individuals are not afraid or dismayed when facing the enemy (v. 9). Joshua was expected to continually study the word of God to avoid any deviation from the covenant and to keep himself focused on the divine will (vv. 7–8). The instruction to meditate upon the law provides the platform for courage and obedience (v. 8). Through meditation and prayer, leaders draw on the divine resources. In sum, vv. 1–9 teach both that faith and obedience are inseparable ingredients for leadership and that success in leadership depends on the presence of God among His people and on the leader's relationship with Him and His word.

1:10–11. Getting Ready. God's charge to Joshua would certainly have encouraged and strengthened him (vv. 2–9). Following the charge, the officers conveyed to the people Joshua's instructions for preparing for crossing the Jordan. His communication to the people was both clear (i.e., indicating a definite plan of action) and appropriate (i.e., following a quick and effective chain of command). The people's response to this command revealed that he was both convinced of the divine promise and convincing in his rallying call to the people.

If the spying of Jericho is to be included, "three days" in v. 11 may denote "few days" rather than three literal days (cf. 2:16, 22; 3:2; 9:16). However, if the instruction in v. 11 was given after the return of the spies (2:1, 23), then the three days should be understood in a literal sense. The people were to take possession of the land that God was giving them (v. 11). The land was a gift, but it was also a task— it was to be possessed. God's gifts require a human response.

1:12–18. Rekindling the Commitment. The conquest of the Holy Land was a task to be undertaken by all Israel, including the tribes of Reuben, Gad, and half of Manasseh, who had already received their inheritance in the Transjordan (Num. 32:20–22). Joshua urged these tribes to join the others in battle until the Lord gave rest to all Israel (Josh. 1:12–15; cf. Deut. 3:18–20). Their response evinces total obedience to the Lord and to His chosen leader. They not only pledged to cross the Jordan to assist the other tribes in the battles but also confirmed Joshua as the chosen replacement of Moses by promising to punish anyone who rebeled against him (vv. 16–18). It is only when leaders and followers unite and cooperate in the Lord that they can accomplish the divine mission entrusted to them.

> ## Rest
>
> The concept of rest is important in Joshua (1:13–15; 21:44; 22:4; 23:1) and finds its spiritual type in Hebrews 4:1–11. The rest intended for Israel was both political and economic (Deut. 3:20; 28:12–13). It would serve as the substratum for the fulfillment of their spiritual mission—becoming a channel of blessings to the world.

2:1–24
Hope beyond the River

The sending of spies was a crucial part of warfare, as military morale and preparations for an impending battle largely depended on their reports (cf. Num. 13:31—14:5). The report of the two spies sent to Jericho inspired hope in the hearts of the Israelites.

2:1–7. Surveying Jericho. Israel encamped east of the Jordan, while Jericho was on the west. The city was a formidable fortress guarding the access routes leading to the central highland of the southern Levant; therefore, it was particularly important as the scene of Israel's first attack in the Holy Land. Joshua's sending of spies was not an act of unbelief but good military strategy. The promise of divine intervention does not rule out human responsibility. Knowledge of the enemy's strategy and conditions would strengthen the faith of Israel (Josh. 2:24).

Why seek shelter in a harlot's house? The spies did not engage Rahab's professional services (cf. v. 8). Subsequent events in the narrative will indicate that the Lord had already been working in the heart of this woman, and that He had providentially led His servants to her house. Besides, in Rahab's house the spies would not only be less detectable but would also find an easy escape since the house was part of the city's outer wall complex (v. 15). Moreover, she had the information the spies needed (vv. 9–11). The king of Jericho expected Rahab to cooperate in an intelligence activity, but she deceived the king in order to save the spies. She would rather side with God's chosen people (6:17). By sending the king's guard on a vain pursuit, Rahab successfully deflated any suspicion against her as well as any possible search of her house. It is clear that Rahab knew that her only salvation lay with the Hebrews and their God. The text does not condone lying but reveals the well-intentioned actions of someone who was only beginning to learn about God. Meanwhile, she had hidden the spies on the roof. In this period, houses had flat roofs that were used for drying grain or stalks, as well as for eating and sometimes sleeping. The bold decision of Rahab to hide the spies can be attributed only to her fear and faith in the God of Israel. Those who truly fear the Lord do not fear humans.

2:8–21. Refuge in the Lord. Rahab's recital of Israel's crossing of the Red Sea (Ex. 14) and their subjugation of Sihon and Og (Num. 21:21–35) testify that the Canaanites had fair knowledge about Israel's history and God's plans for them. What God had done for Israel at the Red Sea and in the land of the Amorites convinced Rahab that the Lord had given Israel the land of promise (Josh. 2:9). Her report of the great fear and panic that had befallen Jericho on account of Israel recalls Exodus 15:15–16. Perhaps, the high point of Joshua 2 is Rahab's confession of faith in v. 11: she recognized that the God of Israel (to whom she refers by using the covenant name of YHWH) was the God of both heaven and earth (v. 11). Following the confession, she sought refuge in the Lord by requiring an oath from the spies to save her extended family. An oath taken in the name of the Lord could not be broken with impunity. The reciprocal relationship of mutual trust that Rahab expected is expressed by the word *khesed* ("loving-kindness," "loyalty"). In delivering the spies from the king's officers, she showed that she had shifted loyalties. The spies granted her request on the conditions that she would keep the matter secret, tie a line of scarlet cord on the window, and bring her extended family into her house. These conditions would provide a way for Rahab's family to exercise faith in the God of Israel. Salvation comes by faith, but faith is expressed through obedience—a lesson Israel had already experienced during the tenth plague when the blood of the Passover lamb had to be painted upon the doorpost of every Israelite house. It seems that Rahab immediately tied the scarlet cord on the window as a symbol of her hope for salvation. The Hebrew *tiqwah*, usually translated as "line," means "hope." The references to the scarlet cord and the gathering of the family in the house have undertones of the Passover in Egypt (Ex. 12:21–23). By acknowledging the God of Israel and pleading for salvation from the impending doom, Rahab sought entry into the covenant community. The experience of this Canaanite prostitute testifies to the gracious saving purpose of the Lord, a grace that pardons and cleanses. The NT honors Rahab for her faith (Heb. 11:31) and good works (James 2:25).

2:22–24. Report of Hope. Rahab's loving-kindness (*khesed*) to the spies was proof of her faith in the Lord. Thanks to her testimony (Josh. 2:9–11) and direction (vv. 15–16, 22–23), the spies returned to Joshua with a message of hope. The spies went to see what the enemy was planning to do, but instead they witnessed what God was already doing in the camp and in the hearts of the enemy. He had planted fear in their hearts, and in this case fear preceded defeat. God had already given the land into Israel's hands (v. 24). Unlike the majority of the spies sent to the Holy Land by Moses (Num. 13:31—14:5), the spies sent to Jericho brought encouraging words to Joshua (Josh. 2:24). Israel was now poised to take over the land.

3:1—4:24
Crossing the River

Israel crossed two water bodies, and in both instances the Lord parted the waters before His people. The crossing of the Red Sea under Moses marked Israel's departure from Egypt, while the crossing of the Jordan under Joshua marked their entrance into the land of Canaan, which was the climax of the redemptive act that began in Egypt (cf. Ps. 114). By entering Canaan, the promise of land made to Abraham was being realized. Prophecy was being fulfilled.

3:1–13. Instructions for Crossing. From Shittim (or the Acacia Grove) Israel journeyed to the Jordan—a distance of about ten miles (16 km)—and encamped on the bank of the river. The instructions for the crossing of the Jordan were clear. The people were to wait for the ark, carried by the Levite priests, to lead the way and then follow after it. They were also to consecrate or sanctify themselves in anticipation of the wondrous works of the Lord on the following day (Josh 3:5). The Lord's holiness requires and makes possible the holiness of His people. In the context of the covenant, Israel's consecration in preparation to meet the Lord included bathing, washing of clothing, and abstaining from sexual activity (Ex. 19:14–15; cf. Gen. 35:1–2).

The miracle of the crossing of the Jordan both confirmed Joshua as the leader and demonstrated that the Lord was with him as He had been with Moses. One of Joshua's primary responsibilities was to exhort the people to trust in the Lord (Josh. 3:9–11). He assured the congregation of the certainty of the Lord's promise to deliver the inhabitants of Canaan to Israel. Joshua promised that the living God

among them would, without a doubt, drive out the inhabitants of the land before them (v. 10). God also promised to march in front of the Israelite army to defeat the enemy for them. He is the Lord of all the earth (v. 13). God's parting of the waters validated His sovereignty over the earth.

3:14–17. Crossing on a Dry Riverbed. The waters of the Jordan were cut off as soon as the feet of the priests carrying the ark touched the water, allowing the people to cross over on dry ground (vv. 13–17; 4:18–23). Like the crossing of the Red Sea, the crossing of the Jordan was a solemn religious event. It gave to the new generation of Israelites the opportunity to deeply ponder the wondrous things that God had done and was doing for them. The Lord, symbolized by the ark, was marching with His people to claim the land of Canaan. Although those who carried the ark in Joshua 3 are called priests, it was the Levites—the Kohathites—who were assigned that responsibility (Num. 4). The term "priest" is used here to include the Levites (cf. Josh. 3:3). Although the priests were commanded to carry the ark and cross over (3:6), the water did not stop flowing until they stepped into the river and touched the water (v. 13). Oftentimes, God waits for His people to go forward in faith before He opens a way for them. The crossing occurred when the Jordan was overflowing its banks due to the spring rains and the melting of snow on Mt. Hermon. By indicating that the Jordan was at flood stage (v. 15), the text clearly suggests it was impossible for Israel to cross over without the Lord's work (v. 5). He who commanded Israel to cross the river made the crossing possible.

4:1–24. Remembrance of the Crossing. During the crossing of the Jordan, the Israelites were ordered by the Lord to pick twelve stones from the dry riverbed as a memorial of this solemn act. That twelve men representing the twelve tribes picked the stones (3:12; 4:3–4) signifies that all Israel crossed the river into Canaan and that it was the responsibility of all tribal leaders to ensure that succeeding generations would not forget what the Lord had accomplished for them. The monument, set up at the camp in Gilgal, would provide concrete evidence to later generations and thus encourage faith in them that the waters of the Jordan had actually been "cut off" to make a passage for their ancestors. Scripture attests to the raising of stones as a memorial (see 7:26; 24:26–27; Gen. 28:18–22;

31:45–47; 1 Sam. 7:12). Remembering or celebrating the past deeds of the Lord is tantamount to participating in the blessings of those events. The Lord does not want us to forget His goodness. Joshua 4:9 possibly refers to another set of twelve stones placed where the priests bearing the ark had stood.

In Joshua 3:7, the Lord promised to exalt Joshua, and 4:14 reports a fulfillment of this promise—Israel stood in awe of Joshua as they had stood in awe of Moses. The basis of his exaltation was his humility and his obedience to the Lord. Joshua 4:19–24 reaffirms the miraculous crossing of the Jordan and the memorial function of the twelve stones. In the future, the monument would awaken the curiosity of children and would provide for their parents the opportunity to instruct them about the goodness of the Lord (vv. 21–24). Israel crossed the Jordan on the tenth day of the first month and encamped at Gilgal. Gilgal would become Israel's base of operations for the period of the conquest (10:15, 43; 14:6). God's salvific power was illustrated both in the crossing of the Red Sea by the previous generation and in the crossing of the Jordan by the present generation. Both of these supernatural events would lead the nations to acknowledge the power of Israel's God. Miracles serve to encourage faith. Historically, the crossings of the Red Sea and the Jordan marked Israel's washing away of the filth of bondage and their glorious entry into the Holy Land.

5:1–15
Preparing for the Conquest

In Joshua 5, we see the Israelites committing themselves to obedience to the covenant Lord (vv. 1–12) and to His word (vv. 13–15). The two covenantal ceremonies performed at Gilgal (namely, circumcision and Passover) prepared Israel for the conquest. Circumcision marked every male as a son of Abraham and a member of God's people (Gen. 17:10–11)—hence they were heirs of the covenant—and was a prerequisite for the Passover, which celebrated the redemption of Israel from Egypt (Ex. 12:48). Like baptism, circumcision marked one's entrance into the covenant community, and like the Lord's Supper, the Passover celebrated the salvific deeds of the Lord.

5:1. Demoralization of the Canaanites. The miraculous crossing of the Jordan was meant partly to move the nations to recognize the Lord as the only living God (Josh. 4:24). This purpose was achieved, and consequently the kings of the Amorites (west of the Jordan) and the kings of the Canaanites (east of the Jordan) got demoralized upon receiving the news of the crossing of the Jordan (v. 1). Rahab must have shared the conviction of many fellow Canaanites that the Lord had handed the land over to Israel (2:9). The demoralization of the Canaanites (5:1) was part of the covenantal blessings (Ex. 23:28). The fear expressed by the Canaanites must certainly have bolstered Israel up for the conquest.

5:2–9. Covenant Renewal. In the meantime, Israel had to renew the covenant to fully claim its blessings. Canaan was a covenantal land, and Israel could possess it only while maintaining their covenantal relationship with the Lord. The performance of the rite of circumcision before staging the conquest evoked and brought to fulfillment the covenantal promises made to Abraham (Gen. 17:10–11). The outward rite of circumcision represented the true circumcision of heart, demonstrating a life of faith and obedience (Deut. 30:6; Jer. 4:4; Rom. 2:29). A reconsecration to the Lord's service was necessary before Israel could undertake the Lord's warfare and take possession of the land.

The people were to be circumcised a second time with flint knives (v. 2). This may denote a renewal of the observance of the rite that had been discontinued for about forty years. But if mass circumcision took place in Egypt prior to the Passover celebration (cf. Ex. 12:43–49), then the second mass circumcision took place in Joshua 5. In any case, the command does not mean that there was a second circumcision of the same generation. All the males who came out of Egypt had been circumcised, but these died in the wilderness due to disobedience (vv. 4–7). Those who received circumcision at Gilgal were the second-generation males—sons born after the Exodus, all of whom had not been circumcised. Although metal knives were available, flint knives were probably more surgically efficient. The place-name gib'at-ha'aralot ("Hill of the Foreskins") shows that this was a mass circumcision. As a monument, this hill would remind Israel of the first renewal of the covenant upon entry into Canaan. The period after the circumcision was certainly a time when Israel would be militarily most vulnerable (cf. Gen. 34), but this act also demonstrated their faith in the Lord. Even though Israel was vulnerable, the presence of the Lord was all the people needed.

The place-name "Gilgal" derives from *galal*, "to roll away" (v. 9). The reference in this verse to "the reproach [or disgrace] of Egypt" lends itself to different interpretations. It could refer to the disgrace of the enslavement in Egypt, but it may also relate to the neglect of the rite of circumcision by the previous generation while in Egypt. It most probably refers to the people's forty years of wandering in the wilderness as a result of their rebellion, which led the Egyptians to say that God brought this people to the wilderness to kill them (see Ex. 32:12; Num. 14:13–16; Deut. 9:28). Now, finally, the people were ready to enter the promised land. The reproach of Egypt was proven to be unfounded. Within the context of the covenant, the foreskin signified opposition to God, and its removal meant dedication to Him (cf. Ex. 4:24–26). Gilgal, therefore, became a place where the nation was constituted anew as the people of God. Israel's constitution through the rite of circumcision meant that Egypt would have no basis to scorn her.

5:10–12. The Passover Event. These verses record the third celebration of the Passover (Ex. 12; Num. 9). The Passover marked Israel's redemption from Egyptian bondage. The previous generation had probably not celebrated the Passover in the wilderness, just as they had neglected circumcision. Since no uncircumcised male could celebrate the Passover (Ex. 12:43–49), the circumcision of the people before the celebration of Passover in Joshua 5 is significant. The Passover could be celebrated only by the covenant community, native or adopted, but a male person could not be a member of the covenant community without having undergone circumcision. By observing the Passover, Israel remembered the deliverance from bondage, even as the Lord's Supper is a remembrance of the death of Jesus Christ, which wrought salvation for the human race.

On the fifteenth day of the month—when the Festival of Unleavened Bread began (Ex. 12:14–20)—the Israelites ate of the produce of the land (Josh. 5:11). Consequently the "raining down" of manna ceased that same day (v. 12; cf. Deut. 8:2–4). The barley harvest took place during the first month. God provided manna to Israel during their journey in the wilderness, but now that they were in Canaan, they could eat of the fruit of the land. All instances of miraculous feeding in Scripture were only temporary; they were not intended to be regular sustenance. The unleavened bread was eaten for seven days following the Passover.

5:13–15. The Two Commanders Meet. The earthly and the heavenly commanders of the armies of the Lord met each other near Jericho in the darkness of the night. Realizing that He was his holy Lord, Joshua worshiped Him and in obedience to His command took the sandals off his feet (Josh. 5:15). Joshua was now ready to receive orders from the Commander of the heavenly army. This theophany convinced Joshua that the Lord Himself was at the head of the Israelite army, ready to conquer Canaan. With this Commander, defeat was an utter impossibility. But Joshua would soon learn from the incident involving Achan that the question was whether Israel was on God's side.

6:1–27
The Conquest of Jericho

Joshua 6 reports the destruction of Jericho and the salvation of Rahab. The destruction of all the inhabitants of Jericho indicates that the Lord judges sin, while the salvation of Rahab teaches that His grace extends to everyone willing to accept Him as Lord.

6:1–7. Instructions for the Conquest. Frozen in fear of Israel, the city was shut up inside out. This was a sure sign that the Lord had already defeated Jericho before Joshua's assault. The battle was already won; Israel only had to claim the victory (v. 16). While the victory had already been won for Israel, the army still had to follow certain instructions in order to claim that victory. It is probable that the heavenly Commander, after their brief conversation, proceeded to give Joshua instructions concerning the attack against Jericho (vv. 2–5). They were to work together. The army of the heavenly Commander would be in charge of the demolition of the wall, the most difficult part. The role of the people was to march around the city, to shout at the proper moment, and to charge against the city once the walls collapsed. The injunction to march around the city with the ark and with trumpets would teach the people that the ensuing battles were holy wars in which the Lord led the procession. Faith in the Lord, demonstrated by obedience to His word, was all that was required in order for Israel to claim the victory.

6:8–16. Blowing the Trumpets. The Lord is a God of order. In the wilderness, the Israelites marched in order (Num. 2). When crossing the Jordan, they marched in order (Josh. 3–4). Now, the army was instructed to march around Jericho in order. The six-day voiceless march, however senseless it might appear, was a requirement of faith. The wall would collapse at the shout of the marching army, yet the army was not to shout until the seventh day. At times faith may not appear to be scientifically or logically sound, but we act on it. Those who think that an earthquake was needed in order for the wall to tumble down forget that rocks obey the voice of the Lord (Ex. 17:5–7).

In the Bible, the number "seven" denotes perfection and completeness. During the march, the army was instructed to shout only during the seventh round on the seventh day. That the army had to march seven times on the seventh day meant that the land was theirs and that victory was complete. The blending of trumpet with voice would mark the fall of the city. The wall would obey the voice of the Lord. The strong shout was a war cry, which usually served to encourage the army and frighten the enemy. Given the size of Jericho (i.e., five or six acres [2–2.5 hectares] of land), Israel must have encircled the city with a number of columns of armed men. These columns could, therefore, charge simultaneously from all sides. Miraculously, Rahab's house was still standing after the collapse of the wall.

6:17–27. The Ban, Rahab, and Joshua. The injunction to destroy the city and its inhabitants, human and animal, is what is normally referred to as the "ban," translated from the Hebrew *kherem*, which denotes total annihilation (see below, "Holy Warfare"). Whatever was devoted to the Lord under this curse had to be destroyed (Josh. 6:17). In the case of Jericho, only Rahab and those of her family who sought refuge in her house were to be spared. Note that *kherem* did not include silver, gold, and bronze; these were consecrated to the

Lord and were to be brought to the treasury of the house of the Lord—the sanctuary (vv. 19, 24). Through a four-fold repetition of the term *kherem*, Joshua 6:18 provided a stern warning against violating the ban regulation. Israel shared a corporate identity and responsibility, so that even if only one person violated the ban regulation, the whole congregation was answerable.

Like the blood on the Israelite doorposts at the Passover, the scarlet cord on Rahab's window signaled her faith in the Lord and occasioned her deliverance. The decision of the spies to save Rahab was taken seriously not only by Joshua but also by the Lord. An oath, once taken in the name of the Lord, is irrevocable, and God honors such. Rahab and her family were placed outside the Israelite military camp, until the moment when she and her family were fully incorporated into the community.

The conquest of Jericho was among the firstfruits of the Lord's victory in the promised land. Joshua's curse (v. 26) was meant to deter future generations from rebuilding the city. The remains of Jericho would forever remind the Israelites of the Lord's miraculous destruction of the enemy. Being prophetic in nature, this curse was fulfilled in Hiel, whose two sons died because he rebuilt the city (1 Kin. 16:34). Although the city of Jericho was not rebuilt before the time of Hiel, there were still people living in the lands around it who were still called by its name (Josh. 18:21; Judg. 3:13–14; 2 Sam. 10:5).

The concluding verse records the fame of Joshua (Josh. 6:27). He was famous only because he allowed himself to be used by the Lord. In Scripture, success in leadership depends completely on the leader's reliance on the Lord. This verse testifies to the Lord's faithfulness in delivering on His promise to exalt Joshua before the nation (1:5; 3:7).

Holy Warfare

The extermination of the Canaanites has raised many questions among believers and nonbelievers. In what follows, we will discuss this matter from within the biblical text itself, hoping to shed some light on the practice of the "ban."

1. God as a Warrior. The book of Joshua portrays God as a Warrior (5:13–15; 6:2–5;

8:1–2; 10:14). He waged war against the Canaanites and gave rest to Israel in accordance with His promise (1:13; 14:15; 21:44; 23:1–3). During the conquest, He planned the attacks, developed the tactics, and handed over the enemy to Israel (see 6:3–5; 8:1–8). Because God is the Sovereign Warrior, nature stands at His command in battle—the walls of Jericho obeyed His voice (6:20), hailstones descended upon the enemy (10:11), and the sun and moon obeyed His word (10:12–14). These miracles, as well as the presence of the ark on the battlefield, confirmed the presence of God in the conquest. But more than these, the real Joshua, the Commander of the army, was at the head of the Israelite army, conquering Canaan with a drawn sword (5:13–15).

2. Meaning of the Term "Ban." The "ban" was central to holy warfare; it demanded the total extermination of the inhabitants of the promised land. This concept is based on the Hebrew term *kherem*, related to *kharam* ("give over," "devote for destruction," or "exterminate"), which in the context of warfare denotes what is irrevocably "devoted" or "dedicated" on oath for destruction (see Num. 21:2–3), be it animate or inanimate. Even outside of warfare, anything that was pronounced *kherem* could not be redeemed (cf. Lev. 27:28–29). By placing the inhabitants of Canaan under *kherem*, God required their complete annihilation (cf. Josh. 6:17–21; Deut. 7:1–11; 20:16–17). The policy of *kherem* as found in the book of Joshua has raised both hermeneutical and ethical questions. Why would God command the slaughter of all the Canaanites?

3. Seeking an Answer. A few points may be considered in an attempt to answer this question. First, in military contexts, *kherem* was applicable only to the conquest of Canaan; it did not apply to people outside of that land (Josh. 9:6–7; Deut. 7:26; 20:10–16). God does not desire the destruction of life (Ezek. 18:32; Jon. 4:11). Second, the destruction of the Canaanites was a fulfillment of earlier prophecy. The prophetic curse of Noah upon Canaan (Gen. 9:25–27), as well as God's covenant with Abraham (Gen. 15:7–21), foreshadowed the future displacement of the Canaanites from their territory by the Hebrews (Gen. 10:15–20; 15:18–21), who were the descendants of Shem through Eber and Abraham (Gen. 10:21; 11:14–26). Third, the Canaanites deserved destruction. While God promised to give Canaan to Abraham, He waited five to seven centuries, depending on the length of the sojourn of Israel in Egypt, until the sin of the Amorites was complete (Gen.

15:16; see "The Four-Hundred-Thirty-Year Sojourn," p. 211). In the meantime, He warned the Canaanites with the fire of Sodom and Gomorrah (Gen. 19:24), but they soon outlived the memories of such destruction from the "Judge of all the earth" (Gen. 18:25). At the time of the conquest, Canaan was at the peak of religious and moral degradation, hence ripe for judgment (Deut. 9:5; 12:29–31; 18:9–12). Fourth, God probably had to settle Israel strategically at the crossroads of the ancient world so that Israel would serve as the light and salt of the world (Matt. 5:13–16), proclaiming the salvation found in the Lord. The earth belongs to the Sovereign Lord (Josh. 2:11; 3:10; Ex. 9:29; Lev. 25:23), hence He could give it to anyone in accordance with His salvific purposes. Israel, too, would be removed from the land if they failed to live up to their calling and mission (Josh. 23:16; Deut. 28:58–68). Fifth, God's promise to drive out the inhabitants of Canaan using hornets (Josh. 24:12; Ex. 23:27–30; Deut. 7:20; cf. Josh. 13:6; 23:5) would seem to imply that the Canaanites did not have to come under the ban had they—upon receiving the miraculous news of the Exodus and the impending conquest—vacated the land so solemnly promised Israel (Josh. 2:9–11; 9:24). Finally, just as the family of Achan was destroyed in the ban because they shared in his identity, so were the Canaanites destroyed because they too shared in the identity of the Canaanite family. The conquest of Canaan was undertaken not only to secure the promised land but also to protect Israel from foreign practices and hegemony (Josh. 23:7–12; Deut. 7:3–6; 20:18). This required that all the inhabitants of the land be purged, together with their evil practices. The foregoing observations would require that the policy of the annihilation of the Canaanites be understood within the contexts of God's sovereignty, the plan of salvation, prophecies relating to the Canaanites, and corporate solidarity. To seek to unravel the problem posed by *kherem* merely on the basis of human ethics is to lose sight of the power, love, and grace of the supreme Source of morality in the cosmos, namely, the Lord. (For more on this topic, see "The Extermination of the Canaanites," p. 330).

7:1—8:35
The Conquest of Ai and Covenant Renewal

Joshua 7–8 reports the conquest of Ai (7:1—8:29) and the renewal of the covenant (8:30–35). The initial defeat of Israel by Ai indicated that Israel could not win its battles without the Lord. The renewal of the covenant was done in fulfillment of Moses's instruction (Deut. 11:26–30; 27:1–26).

7:1–5. Failure of First Attack. Joshua had warned the army against taking any of the things under the ban or curse of Jericho for themselves, lest they bring trouble upon the whole congregation (Josh. 6:17–19). Joshua 7:1–5 shows that despite this warning, Israel, in the person of Achan, violated the ban regulation. This act constituted a violation of the Lord's covenant, and hence incurred His anger (v. 1). Although only Achan did the stealing, the congregation of Israel was guilty of an egregiously rebellious sin, which deserved capital punishment (cf. Num. 15:30–36). Though Achan stole the items during the destruction of Jericho, the consequences for doing so came during the battle against Ai. God, in His mercy, had granted him enough probationary time to reflect and return the stolen objects.

Spies were sent out, and after returning they advised an attack on Ai with only a segment of the army because the inhabitants of Ai were small in number. Israel would soon realize that they were not on the side of the divine Commander in this battle against Ai. Here the Israelites experienced their first military defeat in the land of Canaan (v. 4). Their defeat was so severe that, like the inhabitants of Jericho, the hearts of the people "melted" and became like water (v. 5; see 2:9–11; 5:1). Whether then or now, the Lord is the only hope of victory. Had Joshua and the leaders consulted the Lord before engaging Ai, the congregation as a whole would not have reaped the consequences of Achan's sin. It is important to consult the Lord. Leaders are bound to fail if they lean on their own understanding (cf. 9:14; Prov. 3:5–6).

7:6–9. Joshua's Question. The killing of thirty-six Israelites was a great tragedy; it threw the congregation into a panic (Josh. 7:5). The tearing of clothes, falling down on the face, and putting dust on the head were vivid expressions in ancient times of sorrow and mourning. Even if Joshua did not consult the Lord before the battle, he now turned to Him in prayer. The words of v. 7 are not words of resignation, as if Joshua regretted crossing the Jordan.

Rather, he was simply unable to imagine Israel turning its back to the enemy. His prostration before the ark was a prayer of intercession. He shared with the Lord his own feelings and showed great concern for God's reputation (v. 9). He was certainly concerned about Israel's name being cut off from the earth, but more than that, he was concerned about the Lord's "great name" (v. 9). In Scripture, a name stands for the reputation of the one who bears it, so that if the name of Israel was cut off, the Lord, whose name Israel bore, would be equally disgraced (cf. Ex. 32:12–13; Num. 14:13–19).

7:10–15. The Lord's Answer. For the Lord this was not the time to feel frustrated but to stand and find out what happened. Israel, He said, was defeated because they had sinned. Stealing the things under the ban constituted a violation of the covenant, an outrageous sin that needed to be purged. Since Israel's inheritance of the land of Canaan was a covenantal promise, the conquest could not continue if they violated the covenant. The penalty for a deliberate and rebellious violation of the covenant was death. As noted in the comment on Joshua 6:19–21, Israel shared a strong sense of solidarity. Accordingly, the Lord pressed charges against Israel as if the whole congregation was involved (7:11).

While Achan became cursed for stealing the things under the ban, which were devoted to the Lord, the whole congregation was bound to suffer for his disobedience. It would be in the interest of the congregation to purge the one devoted to the curse of destruction (here *kherem* refers to Achan and the things he stole). The command to sanctify and bring the people, tribe by tribe, was meant to involve the whole congregation in the searching process. Whenever the congregation had to meet the Lord, they needed to sanctify themselves (cf. Josh. 3:5). The people were also to undergo a searching process in order to identify and punish the offender. What we do impacts others for good or evil. Although individual responsibility is not overlooked, believers share a corporate responsibility, so the sin of one member could affect others.

7:16–21. Finding the Culprit. God's omniscience is forcefully underscored in chapters 6–7. Achan successfully hid the cursed things from the congregation, but he could not hide them from the Omniscient One. The presentation of the people by tribes, clans, families, and individuals was not intended to inform God about the identity of the perpetrator. The search signaled to the people that nothing could be hidden from Him, and that the resolution of this act of rebellion involved the entire congregation. Whatever humans think they are hiding is actually already laid out in the open before the Lord (7:23). The searching process was probably carried out through the use of the Urim and Thummim (Ex. 28:29–30). "Give glory to the LORD" (Josh. 7:19) was the oath formula by which a person swore to honestly testify or confess in a law court that he or she was guilty as charged and that God was righteous in His decision (v. 20; cf. John 9:24). Achan had disobeyed the word of the Lord by coveting, stealing, and hiding the items (Josh. 7:21). Coveting involves direct opposition to the Lord (Gen. 3:6; Ex. 20:17). He should have taken the articles to the priests, as commanded by the Lord, but he chose to keep them for himself (Josh. 6:19). Unwilling confession, like Achan's, is devoid of repentance and feelings of remorse. Such confessions often come too late.

7:22–26. The Punishment. Achan deserved death because he defiantly violated the covenant (vv. 11–15) and brought trouble upon Israel (v. 25). God would have permanently withdrawn His presence from Israel if the sin of Achan were left unpunished (vv. 12, 26). By taking the cursed things devoted to the Lord, Achan brought himself and his family under the ban (cf. 6:18). It could be that his family knew what he had done and kept quiet; we do not know. But one thing is clear, human solidarity, particularly familial solidarity, causes others to suffer as a result of the evil actions of one person. One stroke of sin flares like brushfire, licking up everything that is around it. The destruction of Achan together with his family recalls that of Dathan and his company (Num. 16). Stoning was a form of capital punishment that quickly rendered the person unconscious (see Ex. 21:28–32; Lev. 20:2–5). Achan and his family were not only stoned; their corpses were burned. Burning his property was necessary because it had also been contaminated. The pile of stones over the remains of Achan would serve as a warning against similar rebellions. The stoning was done by all Israel—probably tribal representatives—signifying their corporate responsibility as a covenant community in dealing with rebellion (see Josh. 1:18). The Hebrew *'emeq 'akor* means "valley of trouble" (vv. 24–26). With the troubler of Israel (1 Chr. 2:7) destroyed in the valley of trouble, God relented of His wrath and granted Israel His favor. The Lord is able to transform the valley of trouble into a door of hope (Hos. 2:15).

8:1–9. Instructions for a Second Attack. Having purged the accursed from Israel, the Lord assured Joshua victory over Ai in the second attack. As always, Israel only claimed the victory that the Lord had already won. Ai was also brought under the ban. But while in the case of Jericho only silver, gold, and bronze were taken as booty (Josh. 6:19–21), in Ai both the spoils and the livestock were taken (vv. 2, 27). The requirement was that the spoils should be brought to the leaders to be shared proportionally (Num. 31:27). In the second attack, Israel was instructed to lay an ambush behind Ai. Ambush suggests a surprise attack from a concealed position; when a defending army withdrew from their post, the ambushing army would move behind them. The troops in ambush would set the city on fire to signal to Joshua and his troops that the city had been taken. This would also demoralize the defending army. There is an intertwining of the miraculous and human effort in the conquest narratives. While victory was assured, Israel needed to take active steps to realize that victory. The Lord taught Israel military tactics and decoy. Yet it was not Israel alone who fought these wars; the unseen army did it together with them (2 Kin. 6:17).

8:10–29. Victory with the Lord. To be a leader means to go before the people. Joshua and the elders led the army against Ai. Joshua spent the night in the valley, probably meditating and surveying the land in preparation for the battle. While in Joshua 8:3 the warriors who were set to ambush numbered thirty thousand, Joshua set only a five-thousand-man ambush (v. 12). It is possible that the figure in v. 3 refers to the size of the entire army that attacked Ai, while the figure in v. 12 is the ambush party. There was only one ambush party (vv. 14, 19, 21), and the ambush mentioned in v. 13 would refer to it. The nearby city of Bethel joined Ai in its attack against Israel. But in the haste of the pursuit, they left the city open behind them, offering an easy entrance for the Israelite ambush (v. 17). In the battle against Amalek, Moses held up the staff of God until victory was won (Ex. 17:8–12). Joshua's stretching forth of the spear was a sign that the Lord had given them victory; it also served as a signal to the ambush party to break out into the city (Josh. 8:18–19). Just as Moses did not let down his hand until Amalek was defeated, so Joshua did not draw back his spear until he destroyed Ai (v. 26). Once the enemy was engaged, there was no room for retreat. Victory comes from the Lord, but believers must engage the enemy as if they were fighting the battle (2 Chr. 20).

Through tactical deception and decoy, the Israelite army completely broke the power of the enemy (Josh. 8:20). Israel annihilated the inhabitants and burned the city (vv. 22–28). The hanging of Ai's king on a tree follows the instructions of Deuteronomy 21:22–23. A dead body was not supposed to be hung on a tree or pole throughout the night. The fight against Ai resulted in two heaps of stones, one for Achan and his possessions (Josh. 7:26), a symbol of rebellion and defeat, and the other for the king of Ai (8:28), a symbol of Israel's faithfulness and victory.

8:30–35. Covenant Renewed. Moses had commanded the people to build an altar on Mt. Ebal. Six tribes were to stand on Mt. Ebal and another six on Mt. Gerizim for the reading of the law and the recitation of the covenant blessings and curses (Deut. 11:26–30; 27:1–26). This ceremony was a covenant renewal during which the Lord, represented by the ark, was in the midst of Israel, witnessing the pledges of the congregation. As in Exodus 19, all Israel—men, women, and little ones, citizen or alien—was present. The covenant was meant for everyone in Israel, not just for the men. The building of an altar, the offering of sacrifices, congregational standing, the proclamation of blessings, and the reading of the law, were all central elements of worship. Burnt offerings and peace offerings represented devotion and fellowship, respectively. This was an appropriate time to celebrate the Lord's victory over their enemies. The renewal of the covenant was also timely, given Achan's rebellion and its consequences for Israel. The writing of the law on stones and its reading in the hearing of the people would create an indelible impression on Israel, both in sight and in heart. As Joshua read the law and they enjoyed the blessings of fellowship, they would also ponder the blessings or the curses that would follow obedience or disobedience to the law. Israel's possession and occupancy of the land of Canaan was contingent upon obedience to the covenant law. The law, as the transcript of God's character, was the basis of life in the land.

Joshua 8:31–34 affirms Moses as the author of the book of the law. Here, the "law of Moses" is the same as the "words of the law" that Joshua read to the people, namely, the blessings and curses "written in the Book of the Law." Since these instructions of Moses are found in Deuteronomy, we may conclude that the "Book of the Law" refers, at least, to Deuteronomy. Joshua 8:31–35 testify that Joshua carefully followed the instructions of Moses. The success of Joshua

and Israel was dependent upon their adherence to the law of God given through Moses. This lay at the heart of the covenant renewal ceremony.

9:1—10:43
The Conquest of the Southern Coalition

Chapters 9–10 demonstrate the centrality of the covenant in the book of Joshua. Israel's inheritance of the land of Canaan was a fulfillment of a covenant promise. In chapter 9, Gibeon established a covenant relationship with Israel through deception in order to remain in the land. Since Israel entered into this covenant by swearing on the name of the Lord, they were bound as a covenant suzerain (overlord) to protect the vassal (subordinate), Gibeon, from enemies such as the coalition of armies in 10:1–5. The covenant with Gibeon (chap. 9) was the immediate basis for Israel's battle and conquest of the southern coalition (chap. 10).

9:1–13. Reaction of the Canaanites and the Gibeonites. The city-states in the land of Canaan formed a coalition army to fight Israel following its conquests of Jericho and Ai. They ignored that Joshua, through the presence and power of the Lord, was invincible. Despite their knowledge of the miraculous deeds of the Lord among Israel, these Canaanites decided to oppose Him. Consequently, they would soon be swallowed up in their obstinate rebellion.

The Gibeonites sought a covenant with Israel for the preservation of their lives. This was based on their conviction that the Lord had given all the land to Israel (v. 24). The poor appearance of the Gibeonite delegation sent to Israel at Gilgal was intended to make Israel believe that they were coming from a far country. The dry and crumbly bread would also communicate the same message. Like the serpent in Genesis 3:1, the Gibeonites were truly crafty in deception. In Genesis 3:1, the serpent was 'arum, and in Joshua 9:4 the Gibeonites were 'armmah. Both of these words are related to the same root. Being cunning, they succeeded in trapping Israel into a covenant of peace. The word translated as "covenant" is berit, the same word which is used for the covenant between the Lord and Israel. The Gibeonites seemed to have known the rules of warfare, or they may have had some knowledge of the warfare regulations in Deuteronomy 20. Israel could proclaim an offer of peace to a far away country but not to the inhabitants of the promised land (Deut. 20:10–18). This explains why both the Gibeonites and the Israelites were concerned with distance (Josh. 9:6–7, 12–13). The Gibeonites also knew about the miraculous deeds of the Lord in Egypt and the subjugation of the two kings east of the Jordan. However, they seem intentionally to have left out mention of the destruction of Jericho and Ai (cf. v. 3). The delegation was probably sent soon after the destruction of these cities, but because they pretended to have come from a far away country, they craftily avoided mention of the destruction since the Israelites might question how this news could have reached them so soon. This too was part of the plot to convince Israel that Gibeon was a far away country. By appearing in worn-out clothes with worn-out provisions, the Gibeonites convinced the elders of Israel that Gibeon was a faraway country that merited the proclamation of peace. Moreover, by evoking the name of Israel's God and accepting His rulership over the land (v. 9), the Gibeonites theologically convinced Israel that they, like Rahab, sought real refuge in the Lord.

9:14–15. A Hasty Covenant. The Gibeonites were Hivites. Hivites were among the nations God had promised to drive out of the land (3:10). Their insistence that Israel make a covenant with them should have made the elders of the congregation more suspicious, for a truly distant country would naturally not be in desperate need of a covenant relation with Israel. Israelite leaders partook of the provisions of the Gibeonites as a covenant meal and entered into a covenant of peace by swearing in the name of the Lord to preserve their lives (cf. v. 18). By making peace with Gibeon on oath to the Lord, Israel was bound not only to desist from fighting them but also to protect them from their enemies. When they said, "We are your servants" (v. 8), they meant that they were ready to be a vassal nation to Israel, the suzerain. As in every suzerainty covenant (see commentary on 9:1—10:43), the suzerain promised on oath to protect the vassal. While Joshua and the elders of Israel made attempts to follow the divine instruction in Deuteronomy 20 and subsequently entered into a genuine covenant with Gibeon, they did not seek the guidance of the Lord (Josh. 9:14) in whose name they sealed that covenant. In other words, evidence and logical arguments were not enough to legitimize such an important decision. Any major Israelite decision with covenantal implication was supposed to be guided by the Lord. Both success and failure in leadership depend on the leaders' constant reliance on the Lord.

9:16–27. The Response to Deception. Once Israel had made the covenant with Gibeon in the name of the Lord, it could no longer be revoked. About three days later, the Israelites realized that the Gibeonites were their neighbors in the promised land, but by then they could not attack Gibeon. When leaders fail, the congregation complains. In this case the complaints of the congregation may have been justifiable, but they did not have the right to attack the Gibeonites. They apparently thought about it (v. 26). Israel's covenant with Gibeon would remain binding forever, for the Lord's name cannot be vainly misused (Ex. 20:7). And any attempt to revoke it would incur divine wrath (Josh. 9:20; 22:20). God's wrath fell on King Saul when he violated Israel's covenant with Gibeon (2 Sam. 21:1–9).

Deception and lies have adverse consequences, though. The Gibeonites successfully tricked Israel into a covenant of peace, but they had to bear the consequences. By telling Joshua to do to them what "seems good and right" (Josh. 9:25), the Gibeonites both reminded him of their covenant relationship and accepted the consequences of their deception. The penalty for their deception was the curse of slavery. As slaves, they would hew wood and draw water on behalf of the congregation for the Lord's altar (vv. 21, 23, 27; cf. Deut. 20:10–15). Interestingly, Gibeon was notable for its water supply (2 Sam. 2:13; Jer. 41:12). When Solomon became king, the sanctuary was at Gibeon (1 Kin. 3:4–5; 2 Chr. 1:3, 13). The proclamation of Joshua against the Gibeonites recalls partly the curse of Noah over Canaan (Gen. 9:25–27). The references to a curse, the service of slavery, and "the house of my God" (i.e., the God of Shem dwelling in the tent of Shem) strengthens this connection. Despite the consequences of their deception, however, the Gibeonites became members of the covenant community—hence they were partakers of the covenantal blessings (v. 27; cf. Ps. 84:10)—and shared in the service of the sanctuary, even though as menial servants. Thus, like Rahab, the Gibeonites sought and found refuge in Israel's God, the God whose salvific grace extends beyond Israel.

10:1–11. Fulfilling the Demands of the Covenant. According to Joshua 9:1–2, many Canaanite city-states formed a coalition to fight Israel, but Gibeon refused to join them and sought peace with Israel. It is the coalition of chapter 9 that Israel defeated in chapter 10. Gibeon was close to Jerusalem. The fear of Jerusalem's king was fueled both by Israel's conquests of Jericho and Ai and by its covenant with Gibeon. The defection of Gibeon gave Israel a military advantage and weakened any resistance of the city-states in the region. Gibeon is described as an important, large city—"like one of the royal cities" (v. 2).

The coalition of the five kings was formed with the intention to attack Gibeon and break its alliance with Israel. In view of the covenant relationship between Israel and Gibeon, any attack on Gibeon was an attack on Israel. All three parties of the covenant—Gibeon, Israel, and the Lord—fulfilled their covenantal obligations. On its part, Gibeon sent messengers to tell Israel not to abandon its new servants (v. 6), reminding Israel of its obligation to protect Gibeon. Joshua gathered an army of valiant warriors to rescue Gibeon. The Lord encouraged Joshua and promised victory (v. 8). While the immediate cause of Israel's attack on the Amorite kings was to protect Gibeon, the destruction of the city-states constituted a major part of the conquest of Canaan. The description of the battles mentioned in vv. 9–39 clearly shows that it was the Lord who fought for Israel. The Lord defeated the enemy both with hailstones and with Joshua's sword (vv. 10–11). Nature stands at the sovereign Warrior's command in battle. At Jericho, the wall obeyed His voice and tumbled down (6:20). At Gibeon, hailstones descended upon the enemy (10:11), and the sun and moon obeyed His word to prolong this day of great victory (vv. 12–14). As in all the battles of the conquest, victory was the Lord's.

10:12–15. The Long Day. On the chronology of chapter 10, see "Chronology in Joshua 10," p. 379. Based on the use of the verb *damam* ("be silent"), some think that Joshua asked only that the sun reduce its heat that day. However, v. 13 uses both *damam* ("be silent") and *'amad* ("stand" or "stop") for both the sun and the moon. The sun "stopped" (*'amad*) and did not go down for a whole day (v. 13). The stopping of the sun and the moon must not be considered "too hard" for the Lord (Gen. 18:14; Jer. 32:17). He who created daytime, the sun, and the moon, still had these objects under command. There have been various attempts to explain this miracle, but the truth is that it is beyond our understanding. Some have claimed that scientists have been able to establish a missing day in cosmic history. These claims have not been verified and remain in the realm of speculation. The context proves without a doubt that it was a divine miracle,

unprecedented and unsurpassed. Verse 14 shows that the Lord heeds the voice of His servants and fights their battles for them. These miracles were all meant to communicate this important truth. During the conquest, Gilgal was the main base of Israel's operations. The return of the army to Gilgal occurred after the slaughter of the enemy on that prolonged daytime (Josh. 10:15). The Book of Jashar referred to in v. 13 may have been a collection of battle narratives or heroic songs (cf. 2 Sam. 1:18).

10:16–27. Execution of the Coalition Kings. Joshua was in the camp at Gilgal when the report reached him that the five kings were hiding in a cave at Makkedah. Caves provided places of hiding and refuge in the Holy Land (see 1 Sam. 22:1). Joshua barricaded the cave to allow the army to pursue the enemy. These were probably the remaining armies of the five kings and the inhabitants of Makkedah (Josh. 10:19–20, 28). Since the Lord fought the battle, Israel suffered no casualties (v. 21). Like the king of Ai, the five kings were killed and then were hung until evening (see commentary on 8:10–29). By asking the captains of the warriors to place their feet on the necks of the five kings, Joshua reiterated and fulfilled the Lord's promise to put the enemy under the feet of Israel (cf. 1:3). This would then be a concrete expression of the enemy-under-foot motif (1 Kin. 5:3; Pss. 8:6; 110:1). This gesture served to encourage the Israelite warriors to fight on with the assurance that the Lord had already defeated their enemies. For the five kings, however, it meant total humiliation and subjection. The pile of stones over the cave was another monument to remind later generations of how the Lord had conquered the Amorites.

10:28–39. Capturing the Southern Cities. The events of vv. 29–39 occurred over a period of time. The reference to the king of Jericho in association with the capture of Libnah suggests that v. 29 begins a conquest narrative that starts at a different date, after the capture of Makkedah. Throughout these verses, *kherem* ("the ban"; see commentary on 6:17–27) is completely carried out; according to the divine command, Joshua annihilated all the inhabitants of the captured cities (cf. 11:15; Deut. 20). The "second day" in v. 32 refers to the second day of the siege of Lachish (Josh. 10:31), rather than the day following the prolonged day. In several places in the narrative, the word translated as "people" is the Hebrew *nepesh*, which is often rendered "soul" (see vv. 28–39; 11:11). In the OT, this word often represents the person as a whole; it never refers to an immaterial essence that is capable of conscious existence apart from the body. The same word is used for a dead body (Lev. 21:11).

10:40–43. Extent of the Southern Conquest. Verses 40–43 are mainly a summary of the conquest of the kings and cities narrated in 10:1–39. The *kol* ("all" or "whole") land that was conquered was not the whole of Canaan but all of the territories of the peoples defeated in vv. 1–39. This was a large area that included the central mountains of the Holy Land, the desert in the south, and the Shephelah or the western foothills. Goshen in Israel (v. 41) is not to be confused with the land of Goshen in Egypt (Ex. 8:22). For a further discussion of the extent of the conquest described in Joshua, see the section on Backgrounds in Joshua: Introduction. The Israelite army encamped temporarily at Makkedah for the subsequent battles (Josh. 10:21) and v. 43 records their return to the main camp at Gilgal. As in several other places, "all Israel" (v. 43) designates the warriors and not every Israelite. Although Israel took these portions of land during a single military campaign (v. 42), the length of time is not indicated. The conquest of these lands might have taken a couple of years (cf. *yamim rabbim,* "many days"; 11:18). Verses 40–43 stress the Lord's faithfulness in fighting for Israel and handing over the land as a covenantal gift. Now that Israel had gained a substantial foothold in Canaan, the hope of the Exodus, which was the inheritance of Canaan, was finally being realized.

11:1–15
The Conquest of the Northern Coalition

In 10:1–39, Joshua defeated the southern coalition. After this, Israel's attention turned to the northern coalition in 11:1–15. The conquest story in this chapter emphasizes the Lord's faithfulness in fulfilling His covenant promises. Joshua's obedience to the Lord and His word also stand out.

11:1–5. The Coalition. As usual, coalitions were formed because of the threat posed by Israel's victories. The northern coalition, led by the king of Hazor, was larger and perhaps stronger than the southern coalition. The armies of this coalition are compared to the sand. Its military strength is highlighted by its numerous horses and chariots (v. 4). A vast army with a large number of sophisticated weaponry thus gathered to battle Israel. Horses and chariots posed serious challenges to the Israelite army, which consisted of only foot soldiers with limited weaponry. Israel would soon be reminded, however, that the battle is not to the one who possesses chariots and horses but to the one who is on the Lord's side.

11:6. Encouragement and Instruction. The size and weapons of the coalition army might have caused alarm among Israelite soldiers, but the Lord's words in v. 6 encouraged Israel and assured them of victory. Even though Israel had to face this great and strong enemy, it was the Lord, the God of war, who would fight the battle and hand over the enemy to Israel. This divine assurance of victory breathed hope

---

Chronology in Joshua 10

The chronology of Joshua 10 is difficult to unravel. It appears that only vv. 10–15 constitute events of the prolonged day, while the events of vv. 16–43 occurred at other times. After the prolonged day, Joshua and the army returned to Gilgal (v. 15); but when the report came that the five kings were hiding in the cave of Makkedah, the army set out from Gilgal and encamped at Makkedah (v. 21). If Makkedah was farther than Azekah (vv. 10–11), it means that Israel did not reach Makkedah during the pursuit on the prolonged day—Israel stopped at Azekah while the five

kings sought refuge in the cave of Makkedah (v. 16). The slaughter of Makkedah "that day" (v. 28) must relate to vv. 16–28 rather than vv. 10–15. That the events of vv. 16–43 did not occur on the prolonged day is supported by references to "that day" (vv. 28, 35; cf. vv. 26–27), "second day" (v. 32), and a siege (vv. 31, 34). Within vv. 16–43, the events of vv. 16–28 might have taken one day, while those of vv. 29–43 occurred on different days. According to 11:18, the battles recorded in 10:40–42 (cf. 11:16–23) took a long time, probably a couple of years.

and comfort into the hearts of the Israelites. The word of the Lord was always the strength of Joshua. The horses and chariots, which might have scared Israel, would be good only for destruction. Horses were hamstrung by cutting a tendon on the hind legs, rendering them militarily ineffective. The Lord does not need horses and chariots to fight (cf. Deut. 17:16; 2 Sam. 8:4; Is. 31:1), and so He would not let Israel take these as booty.

11:7–15. The Victory. Joshua deployed surprise attacks during the conquest (cf. Josh. 10:9). Through surprise attacks, Israel caught the enemy unprepared and drove them into the mountains toward the north, where chariots could not be used. The Lord fulfilled His promise by delivering the enemy into the hand of the Israelite army, whose task was only to pursue a terrorized army to the slaughter. There is always a blend of divine and human effort in the conquest stories (see commentary on 8:1–9). Whether literally as in Joshua's day or spiritually as in the Christian's life, victory over the enemy results from this blend of divine and human effort. Victory is always a gift from God, but believers must claim it in faith and action.

Joshua annihilated all the inhabitants of the cities of the coalition army in accordance with the *kherem* policy (the "ban"; see commentary on 6:17–27). The destruction of Hazor marked a significant victory in the region, since it was the most impressive city in the land. Unlike other elevated cities, only Hazor was burnt during the northern campaign. This was probably done because of the atrocities associated with it. Since Hazor was completely burned, it is possible that Israel did not take booty from it. As the chief city-state, it might have been the epitome of Canaanite corruption, luxury, and paganism.

This section concludes by stressing Joshua's faithfulness to the *kherem* policy (extermination) as commanded through Moses (v. 15). Since *kherem* was the central warfare policy of the conquest, Joshua's obedience to this regulation is remarkable. In chapter 11, the word *kherem* and related words occur four times, showing that the ban is a major concern. The repeated references to the annihilation of the Canaanites emphasizes this point (vv. 16, 20–21). By stressing Joshua's obedience to Moses's command, the text suggests that Joshua was completing the work that Moses had begun.

11:16—12:24
Record of the Conquest

Joshua 11:16—12:24 is an inventory of Israelite conquests. In 11:16–23, the author summarizes the conquests of Joshua. Chapter 12 summarizes the conquests of Moses east of the Jordan (vv. 1–6) and those of Joshua west of the Jordan (vv. 7–24). This inventory prepares for the division of the land that begins in chapter 13.

11:16–23. Summary of Joshua's Conquest with Special Highlights. The use of the Hebrew word *kol* ("all," "whole," "entire") in vv. 16 and 23 does not refer to the whole land of Canaan but rather to the portions of land defined in vv. 16–17 (cf. 12:7–8). For more on the extent of the conquest, see the section on Backgrounds in Joshua: Introduction. The summary description of conquered land (11:16–18, 23) seems to cover all the portions of land taken by Joshua, including the territories of the southern campaign (10:43–45). We do not know how long Israel made war with these kings, but the entire conquest under Joshua may have taken about seven years (see the section on Date in Joshua: Introduction). In their battles against the Canaanites, the Israelites remained faithful to the divine rules of engagement, their only mistake being the covenant with Gibeon (10:19; Deut. 20:16–18).

While the Israelites were eager to conquer the land, they seem to have been slow in initiating the attack. Therefore, the Lord brought the battle to Israel by hardening the already stubborn hearts of the enemy to attack Israel. Thus were the enemies quickly destroyed (Josh. 11:20). When the Lord incites or allows the enemy to come against His people, He certainly intends the destruction of the enemy.

In Numbers 13–14, ten of the twelve spies discouraged Israel from entering Canaan because of the *'anakim* ("giants"). Caleb and Joshua, the two other spies, encouraged Israel to march into Canaan and to trust in the Lord's promise to drive out these giants. Joshua 11:21–22 and 15:13–14 record the victories of Joshua and Caleb over the *'anakim* in accordance with the Lord's promise. Joshua defeated all the *'anakim* except those in Gaza, Gath, and Ashdod (11:22). These were Philistine cities, and as we read in 13:2, the Philistines were not conquered during Joshua's time. The *'anakim* who remained in these cities were the ancestors of Goliath of Gath, whom David would kill (cf. 1 Sam. 17:4–7). The references to Israel and Judah, at a time when the nation was not yet divided, constitute an example of the scribal modernization of place-names rather than evidence of late authorship (Josh. 11:16, 21).

Joshua 11:23 concludes by highlighting key theological elements of the book. Joshua took the "land" and gave it to the tribes of Israel as "inheritance." The Lord had promised to give rest (*nuakh*) to Israel in 1:13, and 11:23 testifies that the land had rest (*shaqat*) from war. The rest denoted by *shaqat* is quietness from war (11:23; 14:15) and thus prepares the way for *nuakh*, which denotes settling down or repose (23:1; see commentary on 1:12–18). In 11:23, the conquest of Canaan is at least substantially complete.

12:1–24. Kings Defeated by Moses and Joshua. Verses 1–6 describe the territory east of the Jordan that Moses took from the two Amorite kings Sihon and Og (Num. 21:21–35; Deut. 2:26—3:11). The territory included the fertile lands of Gilead (i.e., the mountainous region east of the Jordan) and Bashan (i.e., the rich pastureland east of the Sea of Galilee). The two-and-a-half tribes (Reuben, Gad, and half of Manasseh) who inherited the lands of these Amorite kings owned large numbers of livestock, and Gilead and Bashan provided excellent pasturelands (Num. 32:1, 26–40).

Throughout the book, Joshua's work is portrayed as complementing that of Moses. Moses had conquered the land east of the Jordan, and Joshua continued the conquest west of the Jordan. As noted earlier, the summary of land conquered by Joshua in Josh. 11:16–18, 23 includes all the territories taken during the entire conquest west of the Jordan. This is supported by the summary description of Joshua's conquests in 12:7–8. Verse 8 lists the nations the Lord had promised to drive out of the land (3:10; Deut. 7:1), implying that Israel had carefully followed the divine command. Although as in 9:1 and 11:3 the Girgashites are omitted from the list of nations in 12:8, 24:11 records the fulfillment of the Lord's promise to drive out the seven nations. The list of kings, thirty-one in all, that follows (12:9–24) illustrates that Israel massively broke the power of the Canaanites and took the land. The list includes only defeated kings with their capital cities; it is not an inventory of all the towns taken in the conquest. Among other things, the vivid descriptions of the conquest of Canaan presented throughout the book leave no room for doubt regarding the historicity of the Exodus from Egypt and the conquest of Canaan.

13:1—24:33
A HOPE REALIZED:
DIVISION OF THE LAND

While the first half of the book (1–12) describes Israel's conquest of the land of Canaan, the second half (13–24) describes the division of the land among the tribes of Israel. The narrative of chapters 13–24 is fraught with geographical and topographical details that forcefully underline the historicity of the conquest and division of the land. The careful demarcation of territories enabled later generations to identify their tribal boundaries. The actual division of the land ends in chapter 21, and the remaining chapters relate to issues of unity, loyalty, and covenantal faithfulness. With the division of the land, Israel's hope of inheriting Canaan was realized (chaps. 13–21). But whether Israel would continue to receive God's blessings and thus become channels of the "blessed hope" depended on their faithfulness to the covenant (chaps. 22–24).

13:1–7
The Command to Divide the Land

Although significant conquests had been made, Joshua seemed to have delayed dividing the land. The conquest took about seven years (cf. 14:7 10; Num. 13). The Lord's promise was to conquer the land and divide it through Joshua (Josh. 1:6; Deut. 31:7), hence it was appropriate for the Lord to remind him to divide the land before he died. Verses 2–6 explain the last part of v. 1, which states that there was still much land to be possessed by Israel. Read superficially, vv. 1–6 seem to contradict earlier statements that Joshua took the whole land (Josh. 10:40–42; 11:16–23; see the section on Backgrounds in Joshua: Introduction). The portions of land yet to be taken were basically the lands of the Philistines and Sidonians (Phoenicians), who lived along the coast of the Great Sea and in Lebanon, respectively. The Philistines were not conquered during Joshua's time (13:2). This explains why the *'anakim* were still in Philistia (11:22).

While much of the land was yet to be possessed, the Lord bade Joshua to focus on his assigned task of apportioning the land, promising that He Himself would gradually drive out the Canaanites (cf. Ex. 23:28–29). In v. 6, the Hebrew *raq happileha* (lit. "only/surely cause it to fall") refers to the allocation of Israelite land into tribal divisions—this adds some urgency to the Lord's command. In later passages, it is revealed that the land of Canaan was to be divided by lots among nine and a half tribes (Josh. 18:6; 19:51). The casting of lots was probably done using the priestly Urim and Thummim and so placed the decision completely in God's hands (Ex. 28:30; Num. 27:21). Lot casting was a means of divine revelation.

13:8–33
Territory East of the Jordan

Joshua 13:8–33 describes the territories of Reuben, Gad, and half of Manasseh. These two and a half tribes received their inheritance east of the Jordan.

13:8–14. Extent of the Territory and the Levites. The land west of the Jordan was to be divided among nine and a half tribes because Moses had already given tribal allotments to two and a half tribes east of the Jordan. These were, namely, the lands over which Sihon and Og had ruled (see commentary on 12:1–24). The two and a half tribes failed to drive out some of the inhabitants of the land (13:13). This failure of Israel is a recurring theme in chapters 13–24 and anticipates the idolatrous practices that ensnare Israel in the book of Judges. The Levites were not given a tribal allotment since the Lord was their portion (v. 33). They received only forty-eight cities and their pastureland scattered throughout the land east and west of the Jordan. Being fully employed in the work of the Lord in His sanctuary, the priests and Levites were not to engage in farming or business activities. Since they did not possess land, it was the responsibility of the other tribes to provide for their needs through tithes, offerings, and other sacred donations.

13:15–28. Reuben and Gad. The Reubenites settled in the territory that had belonged to the kingdom of Sihon, south of Gilead and north of the Arnon River. The text mentions the slaughter of the Midianites (vv. 21–22) in the land of Moses's in-laws (Num. 31:8) and of Balaam the prophet, who unwillingly blessed Israel and subsequently entrapped them into sexual immorality and idolatry (Num. 25:1–3; 31:16). By rehearsing these incidents that took place in the Transjordan, the text indirectly warns God's people against sexual immorality and idolatry.

The Gadites shared the land of Gilead and part of the land of Ammon with the Reubenites. The Lord had commanded Israel not to conquer or claim the territory of Ammon (Deut. 2:19,

37). The reference to Ammon in Joshua 13:25 may refer to a portion of the Ammonite territory that had been conquered by Sihon before being taken over by Israel. This may provide a background to Judges 11:13–27.

13:29–33. Half-tribe of Manasseh. Half of the tribe of Manasseh settled in the land of Bashan, which Og had ruled, and Manasseh also shared the land of Gilead with Reuben and Gad. Machir (or, alternately, Makir) was the son of Manasseh and father of Gilead (Gen. 50:23; Num. 26:29). In v. 31, Machir is used to designate the tribe of Manasseh (cf. Judg. 5:14). Verse 32 summarily reasserts that Moses gave the conquered territory east of the Jordan as an inheritance to Israel. For v. 33, see commentary on 13:8–14.

14:1—19:51
Territory West of the Jordan

Joshua 14:1—19:51 describes the territories of the nine and a half tribes who settled west of the Jordan in the land of Canaan. In the division of the land, priority was given to the tribes of Judah and Joseph, probably because of their size and importance (see commentary on 15:20–16:4); these tribes were influential and would become the two major forces in Israel. The priority given to them was in agreement with the principle that the land was to be allocated based on the sizes of the tribes (Num. 26:52–56). As the Lord had commanded, Joshua divided the whole land of Canaan, including portions of the land that were yet to be conquered (Josh. 13:6).

14:1–5. Principles for the Division. The divine instruction was carefully followed in the allocation of the land. The principles outlined in vv. 1–5 suggest that the tribal territories were allocated under divine sanction and supervision. Eleazar the priest, Joshua, and the tribal heads administered the distribution. They divided the land through lot casting as commanded by Moses (on the use of lots, see comment on 13:1–7). Since two and a half tribes had already received their inheritance east of the Jordan, the land west of the Jordan was to be divided among nine and a half tribes. The Levites had no share since the Lord was their portion (18:7). By stating that the descendants of Joseph constituted two tribes (i.e., Ephraim and Manasseh), v. 4 explains why there were still nine and a half tribes even after excluding the tribe of Levi and the two and a half tribes who settled in the east.

14:6–15. Caleb. Some think that Caleb was not an Israelite because his father was a Kenizzite (cf. Num. 32:12), but in Joshua 14:6–7, Caleb seems to be included among the people of Judah. It seems that only the Judahite delegation accompanied Caleb as fellow tribesmen to claim his promised inheritance. Caleb had represented this tribe among the twelve spies (Num. 13:6). He probably would not have represented the tribe in such a capacity had he not been a direct descendant of Judah. He was probably considered a Kenizzite because his ancestor was named Kenaz (Josh. 14:14; 15:13, 17; cf. 1 Chr. 4:13–15).

Caleb reminded Joshua about the Lord's promise through Moses to give Caleb the land upon which his feet had walked as a reward for exercising bold faith and confidence in the Lord in his spy report. In his recounting of the incident of the twelve spies, Caleb noted that forty-five years had elapsed between the sending of the spies and the end of the conquest. This means that the conquest took about seven years, since thirty-eight years had passed between the time that Caleb returned from spying the land and their entrance into it (Deut. 2:14). The strength of Caleb was remarkable; even at the age of eighty-five he still could go to war (Josh. 14:10–11). But he seemed to praise his own strength in order to convince Joshua that he was strong enough to conquer Hebron if it were given to him. Caleb's request for Hebron was thus a fulfillment of the Lord's promise through Moses, who is here for the first time called "man of God" (v. 6). Hebron was noted for its warriors, greatness, and fortifications. The 'anakim lived in Hebron. Yet Caleb was convinced that since the Lord had promised him the land, He would be able to drive out these giants. Throughout the conquest, the Lord had been faithful in delivering the enemy into the hand of Israel as promised, and so Caleb had no doubt He would do the same with the 'anakim in Hebron (cf. Deut. 9:1–3).

In Joshua 11:21, Joshua is said to have driven the 'anakim out of Hebron, but in 15:13–14 it is Caleb who did this. It is possible that 11:21 is a summary of all the conquests, including Caleb's conquest of Hebron. In other words, Caleb's conquest of Hebron might have taken place as part of the southern campaign. The statement that "the land had rest from war" in 14:15, which also occurs in 11:23, strengthens this observation. Notice that there is no record of a battle in chapter 14, so v. 15 may be referring back to 11:23.

15:1–12. Judah. Judah was the first to receive its inheritance in the land of Canaan. Judah's territory was the southern part of the land, covering part of the central hill country. They shared borders with the Brook of Egypt (which flows from the Sinai Peninsula into the Great Sea), the Great Sea (i.e., Mediterranean Sea), Edom, and the Salt Sea (i.e., Dead Sea). While Jebus or Jerusalem proper was in Benjamin's territory (18:16, 28), its southern slope belonged to Judah (15:8, 63).

15:13–19. Caleb Claims Inheritance. As seen in 14:6–15, Joshua gave Hebron to Caleb in accordance with the Lord's promise. The three 'anakim named here appear in the report of the spies in Numbers 13:22. In bold confidence, Caleb had encouraged Israel to march into Canaan and possess the land because the Lord was with His people (Num. 14:9). With that same faith in the Lord, he won victory over the 'anakim. Thus Caleb, whose name may mean "dog," proved to be that "dog" who would not rest until he had chased out the enemy. That Caleb offered Debir (i.e., Kirjath [or Kiriath] Sepher) as the bride price for his daughter may be a hint that he was already fostering the next generation of leaders, since Othniel, Caleb's nephew and later his son-in-law, is the same Othniel who became a judge in Israel (Judg. 3:9).

15:20—16:4. Towns of Judah and Joseph's Territory. Judah's territory was the largest in the land of Canaan. Judah failed to drive out the Jebusites from Jerusalem, at least at the time the book was composed (cf. 2 Sam. 5:6–10). This failure of the Israelites is a significant refrain in the second half of the book. The recurrence of this refrain implies that at the division of the land the national wars of conquest were over; wars of occupation were now the responsibility of individual tribes.

Jacob had adopted Joseph's two sons (i.e., Manasseh and Ephraim), thereby giving Joseph the right to a double inheritance (Gen. 48:5–6, 22). Ephraim was the second born, but he received the blessings of a firstborn (Gen. 48:13–20). Unlike the other tribes west of the Jordan, the description of the territory of the tribes of Joseph does not contain a list of towns. The territory may have been thinly populated (cf. Josh. 17:14–18).

16:5–10. Ephraim. Ephraim's territory stretched from the Jordan to the Great Sea. It covered the central hill country of Israel. The Ephraimites had some cities within the territory of Manasseh (16:9; cf. 17:9). Like Judah, Ephraim failed to drive out some of the inhabitants of the Canaanite cities (e.g., Gezer), though they subjected them to forced labor. The result of this failure on Israel's part was interfaith marriages and religious syncretism (Judg. 2:1–3; 3:1–6; 10:6).

17:1–13. Half-Tribe of Manasseh. Even though Manasseh was the firstborn of Joseph, Jacob transferred the right of succession, which at that time usually belonged to the eldest son, to Ephraim (Gen. 48:13–20). On Machir, see commentary on Joshua 13:29–33. Some Manassites had received their inheritance east of the Jordan in Gilead and Bashan, though it is not possible to determine the specific clan(s). The reference to the "rest" of the people of Manasseh designates the other half of the tribe who settled west of the Jordan. On the inheritance of Zelophehad's daughters, see Numbers 27:1–11 and 36:1–12. Apparently, Zelophehad had only daughters. Traditionally, women would not have had a share in the division of the land, but the Lord granted the request of these women to inherit portions of the land alongside their father's brothers. The reason for the daughters' request was to preserve the name of their deceased father and thus ensure the future of the family among the tribes. Accordingly, they had to marry within their father's clan to keep the property within the clan and tribe (Num. 36:6–9). The territory of Manasseh in the land of Canaan shared borders with Asher, Zebulun, and Issachar (north), the Sea (west), the Jordan (east), and Ephraim (south). Ephraim had several towns within Manasseh (Josh. 16:9), and Manasseh had a few towns within Issachar and Asher (17:11). Manasseh also failed to completely drive out the Canaanites, even though Manasseh eventually subjected them to forced labor (see commentary on 15:20—16:4; 16:5–10).

17:14–18. Complaint of the House of Joseph. A quick look at a map of the tribal allotments reveals that Ephraim and Manasseh inherited a large territory. Moreover, their territory was the most fertile in all Israel. Thus, while it is true that the Lord had blessed the two tribes and made them a great and numerous people, it is not true that they had only one lot and one share (v. 14; cf. v. 5). Perhaps the people viewed their inheritance in terms of the number of cities and already-cleared farmlands ready for use and not in terms of the actual size of the allotments. By stating that they received only one lot and one share, the tribes of Joseph probably sought to remind Joshua of the prophetic blessing in Genesis 48, where Joseph was given the right of double inheritance. The tribes of Joseph may also have compared their allotment to that of Judah and may have reasoned that since Joshua was a fellow tribesman, he would reconfigure the division to their advantage. Ephraim and Manasseh requested more territory because they were a great and numerous people (v. 14). Joshua turned the argument around to challenge them to subdue the land already allotted to them. If these tribes were a great people as they claimed, they should have used their numerical strength to clear out more forest country and expand their territory (v. 15). The forest refers to the central mountainous region. The Perizzites were among the nations that the Lord promised to drive out before Israel (Deut. 7:1). *Repa'im* (sometimes translated as "giants"), like *'anakim*, were a people of unusually large stature (Deut. 2:11; 3:11).

Joshua's response in Joshua 17:15 reveals that what the tribes of Joseph needed was not more territory but rather a proper mind-set and faith in the Lord. Their response reveals that the real reason for their confrontation was an unwillingness to clear a place in the forest country as well as a fear of the Canaanite iron chariots (v. 16). Thus, they refused to see the hill country as theirs because it would be difficult to clear and settle in. They also felt unable to drive out the Canaanites in the lowlands because they possessed chariots of iron. Humanly speaking, the foot soldiers of Israel were no match for the Canaanite army with iron chariots, which were formidable implements of war. But the tribes of Joseph forgot that the conquest of the land of Canaan was the Lord's business. They seem to have forgotten that the divine Warrior has no regard for horses and chariots (11:6). If the Lord drove out the *'anakim* from Hebron before Caleb (15:13–14), Ephraim and Manasseh should well have known and believed that He would similarly drive out the *repa'im* and the Canaanites with their iron chariots (cf. 13:1–7).

In vv. 17–18, Joshua forcefully repeated his challenge to the two tribes. He was truly a transformational leader who sought to effect change in the mind-set of the people. As a good leader, he would not yield to a narrow or selfish request, nor would he succumb to a tribal wooing. Rather, he would challenge their faith in the Lord. Lack of faith and courage easily turns into rebellion. The tribes of Joseph should have realized that the division of the land was done under the direct supervision of the Lord, and if by any chance they charged Joshua with unfairness in the apportioning of the land, they were in fact murmuring against the Lord.

18:1–10. Allotting the Rest of the Land.
Gilgal had been the base of Israel's operations during the conquest. The tabernacle
was pitched there. After Gilgal, Shiloh became the next base and religious center (18:1;
see "Shiloh," p. 920). While at Gilgal, Judah,
Ephraim, and Manasseh (west) received their
inheritance, but the remaining seven tribes had
not yet received theirs (v. 2). Joshua reproved
the seven tribes for their apparent reluctance
in dividing and thus occupying the land. The
clause literally reads "they did not divide/
share." Throughout the book, the Israelites
carefully obeyed Joshua. At his command,
tribal representatives went and surveyed the
land, and returned with a map describing the
land in seven parts defined by their cities. On
v. 7, see commentary on 13:8–14. As usual, the
tribal territories were divided through lot casting. It was actually Eleazar who would cast the
lots in the Lord's presence at the entrance of
the tabernacle in Shiloh (19:51). For lots, see
commentary on 13:1–7.

Benjamin was strategically located towards
the Jordan between northeastern Judah
and southeastern Ephraim (18:11–28). Benjamin bordered Dan to the west. In this list
we note, among other things, that Jerusalem/
Jebus was shared between Benjamin (vv. 16,
28) and Judah (cf. commentary on 15:1–12,
20–63). Simeon (19:1–9) was located within
the southern territory of Judah. In his parting
blessings, Jacob prophesied that Simeon and
Levi would be scattered in Israel (Gen. 49:5–7).
According to Joshua 19:9, Judah's territory was
too large for them, and so a part of it was given
to Simeon. Soon, Simeon would be assimilated
by Judah. Zebulun (vv. 10–16) shared borders
with Asher (west), Naphtali (northeast), Manasseh (south), and Issachar (southeast). Their
territory mainly covered the forested mountain
rim north of Jezreel. Prophetic blessings suggest Zebulun might have had access to the seas
(Gen. 49:13; Deut. 33:18–19).

Issachar's territory covered the land between
Jezreel and the Jordan. Issachar shared borders
with Naphtali (north), Zebulun (northwest),
Manasseh (south), and the Jordan (east) (vv.
17–23). Asher bordered Naphtali (east), Zebulun (southeast), and the Great Sea (west),
thus adjoining the Phoenician coast. It covered the western Galilee highland (vv. 24–31).
Naphtali's territory covered the western shore
of the Sea of Galilee and extended to the north.
It bordered Asher (west), Zebulun (southwest),
Issachar (south), and extended over the Jordan,

thereby sharing a boundary with one half of
Manasseh in the Transjordan (vv. 32–39).
Dan's territory (vv. 40–48) was bordered by the
Great Sea (west) and Manasseh (northwest);
the rest of Dan's territory was sandwiched together with Benjamin (east), between Judah
(south) and Ephraim (northeast). Some of the
towns of Judah were reassigned to Dan (15:33;
19:41–43). The Danites failed to subdue the
inhabitants of the land (Judg. 1:34–35; 18:1).
Some of the Danites migrated to the extreme
north and took Leshem, which they renamed
Dan (Josh. 19:47). As if the rejection of their
original territory was not enough, the Danite
migrants also clung to idolatry (Judg. 18). Perhaps because they established idolatry in this
region, it later became a major center of formalized idolatrous worship during the time of
Jeroboam (1 Kin. 12:28–29).

19:49–51. Joshua. The Israelites gave an inheritance to Joshua. He had been a faithful spy
(Num. 13–14) and a great leader before the
Lord. Verse 50 implies that the Lord had promised to give him as inheritance whichever city he
would ask for. As an Ephraimite, he requested
Timnath Serah in the mountains of Ephraim.
Notice that he was the last to receive his inheritance. He did not select a place for himself
before dividing the land. As a good leader, he
served others first. There are several indications
that the division of the land was a religious
activity. First, as elsewhere (Josh. 14:1; 17:4;
21:1), Eleazar the priest is named before Joshua
and the tribal leaders. Second, these verses reiterate that the division was done through casting
lots in the Lord's presence at the entrance of the
tabernacle at Shiloh. The division of the land
was not only carried out unanimously by the
leadership of Israel but was done under divine
sanction and supervision. Now that the division
of the land was complete, it was time to designate the cities of refuge (chap. 20) and the cities
of the Levites (chap. 21).

20:1–9
Cities of Refuge

In Numbers 35:9–34, the Lord commanded
through Moses the establishment of six cities
of refuge from among the Levitical cities—three
on each side of the Jordan—where anyone who
unintentionally killed a person might seek asylum (cf. Ex. 21:12–13; Deut. 4:41–43; 19:1–13).
Joshua 20 contains the fulfillment of the promise
in Numbers 35 and related passages. Joshua

20:1–6 states the reasons for the appointment of the cities, and vv. 7–9 enumerate them. The establishment of the cities of refuge obviously served to limit and control the practice of blood vengeance and to avoid polluting the land with innocent blood. Such a provision was unparalleled in the ANE. It was a way of teaching respect for life and justice to the Israelites.

20:1–6. The Rationale. The person who killed another person unintentionally would flee to a city of refuge from the "avenger of blood." This refers to a close male relative of the deceased whose responsibility was to avenge the dead by killing the murderer. A city of refuge provided both protection and a trial for those who killed someone accidentally. Such people would explain their situation before the council of elders at the entrance to the city gate, who upon hearing would take the person in and provide asylum, including a place to live (v. 4). The city gate was usually a complex structure that both controlled traffic and facilitated the defense of a city. The council of elders normally judged cases at the gate. It was the responsibility of the elders of the city of refuge not to deliver the manslayer into the hands of an avenger of blood who pursued the slayer into the city. After the initial hearing by the elders, person who killed someone accidentally would be tried before the assembly (vv. 6, 9). A guilty slayer was handed over to the avenger of blood (v. 9; Deut. 19:12). For having caused the accidental loss of a human life, an innocent slayer would have to remain in the city of refuge until the ruling high priest died, at which time the people who killed someone accidentally could return to their original city (Josh. 20:6). The death of the high priest—who bore the people's guilt (Ex. 28:38; Lev. 10:17)—may have provided some sort of amnesty or atonement. This aspect of the high priest's death would point obliquely to the death of Christ, the High Priest, whose death provided atonement for sin (1 Pet. 2:24; Heb. 9:11–15).

20:7–9. The Cities. Cities east of the Jordan included Bezer (Reuben), Ramoth in Gilead (Gad), and Golan in Bashan (Manasseh; cf. Deut. 4:43), while those west of the Jordan comprised Kedesh in Galilee (Naphtali), Shechem (Ephraim), and Hebron (Judah). The cities of refuge provided asylum for both the native and the stranger in Israel who unintentionally slew a person. The Lord was the God of Israel and of foreigners living in Israel. The cities of refuge were also Levitical cities (Josh. 21:13–38).

21:1–42
Levitical Cities

The tribe of Levi did not receive a tribal allotment because the priesthood was their inheritance (see commentary on 13:8–14). Joshua 21:1–42 records the allocation of cities throughout the nation as dwellings for the Levites. The Levitical cities would serve as centers for religious instruction.

21:1–3. The Directive. The Lord had commanded that forty-eight cities and their common lands be given to the Levites to settle in (Num. 35:1–8). In Joshua 21:1–2 the Levites reminded Eleazar, Joshua, and the tribal leaders to fulfill the Lord's directive regarding the Levitical cities. Since the Levites represented the nation in their sanctuary service, it was the responsibility of all the other tribes to donate the cities.

21:4–42. The Distribution. The cities were determined through the casting of lots. Verses 4–8 summarize the tribal distribution of the cities, while vv. 9–40 list the cities. Levi had three sons, Kohath, Gershon, and Merari. The priestly sons of Aaron (also the Kohathites) received thirteen cities from the tribes of Judah, Simeon, and Benjamin (vv. 9–19). The priests were thus providentially settled in the vicinity of the future temple of Solomon in Jerusalem. The rest of the Kohathites received ten cities from Ephraim, Dan, and one half of Manasseh (west; vv. 20–26). The Gershonites received thirteen cities from Issachar, Asher, Naphtali, and one half of Manasseh (east; vv. 27–33). Finally, the Merarites received twelve cities from Reuben, Gad, and Zebulun (vv. 34–40). Verses 41–42 conclude the distribution of the Levitical cities. The cities were forty-eight in number, each with its common lands for the livestock of the Levites.

21:43–45
Faithfulness of the Lord

Joshua 21:43–45 accentuates the Lord's faithfulness in delivering His covenantal promises. These verses elegantly summarize the purpose of the book and the Exodus from Egypt. The Lord had taken Israel out of Egypt and led them through the wilderness in order to give them "rest" in the land of Canaan (see on 1:12–18). The text asserts that God's oath to the fathers had now been fulfilled (see Gen. 22:16–18). God's promises are reliable and fill the heart with hope. Israel obeyed the Lord and engaged the enemy in battle, but the land remained a covenant gift from the sovereign God. The use of *natan* ("give"), *yarash* ("possess"), and *nakhal* ("inherit") indicates throughout the book that Israel's occupation of Canaan occurred through a legal transaction in which the Lord, being God of all the earth, transferred the land as a covenantal gift to Israel. While Israel thus owned the legal title to the land, it would experience true "rest" only by keeping the covenant.

22:1-34
Unity and Loyalty

Joshua 22 records how the warriors of the tribes of Reuben, Gad, and one half of Manasseh, who had crossed over the Jordan to help the other tribes take possession of Canaan, returned to their land.

22:1-6. Loyalty of the Two and a Half Tribes. Now that the Lord had given rest to the nine and a half tribes in the land of Canaan, it was time for the warriors of the two and a half tribes (Reuben, Gad, and half of Manasseh) to return to their inheritance in the Transjordan. In his farewell address, Joshua commended their loyalty and obedience to the Lord's command to join the other tribes in the conquest of Canaan (1:12-15; Num. 32:20-22). He then charged them to remain true and loyal to the Lord; that is, to love the Lord, walk in all His ways, keep His commandments, hold fast to Him, and serve Him wholeheartedly (Josh. 22:5). Obedience to the Lord was the key to blessings and perpetual occupancy of the land. True success has always depended on wholehearted devotion and obedience to the Lord. Joshua's address contained a charge and a blessing, in the manner of patriarchal parting words (see Gen. 49:28-29).

22:7-9. Returning Home. The warriors of the two and a half tribes returned with both material and spiritual blessings. Joshua pronounced spiritual blessings upon the people, but he also gave them material blessings. The returning warriors divided the spoils that had been accumulated during the conquest with the other tribes, but they would have to share the booty with their brothers who had stayed behind in the Transjordan (cf. Num. 31:27). Technically, the land of Canaan was the land west of the Jordan. The lands east of the Jordan were known as Gilead and Bashan, though sometimes the area was simply called Gilead (see Josh. 22:9). By emphasizing that the land of Gilead was given by divine command to the two and a half tribes, v. 9

suggests that crossing the Jordan back to Gilead did not mean these people no longer had a share in the Lord.

22:10-12. The Altar and Its Crisis. The returning warriors built a large, imposing altar by the Jordan in the land of Canaan before crossing to their territory. Moses had instructed Israel to build an altar only at the place that the Lord would choose (Deut. 12:11), which was temporarily at Shiloh (Josh. 18:1). The construction of any alternative altar for sacrifices—even if offered in the Lord's name—constituted egregious rebellion. It was the responsibility of the congregation to punish such rebellion (Lev. 17:8-9; Deut. 13:12-15). This explains why the whole community gathered at Shiloh to prepare for war (Josh. 22:12). There is a contrast in Joshua 22 between the people of Israel and the people of Reuben, Gad, and half of Manasseh. Often, the expression *bene yisra'el* ("sons," "children," or "people" of Israel, or simply "Israelites") designates a majority of the Israelites against a minority (see 18:10; 19:49; 21:3, 41). Notwithstanding this, there is a clear distinction between the land of Canaan (i.e., the side of the people of "Israel") and the land of Gilead (i.e., where the two and a half tribes settled).

22:13-20. The Accusation. Moses had commanded Israel to carefully investigate acts of apostasy before punishing them (Deut. 13:14-15). Therefore before the intended war, the tribes west of the Jordan sent a delegation of tribal heads together with Phinehas (son of Eleazar the priest) to the Transjordan. This was a religious matter, so a priest had to lead the delegation. The delegation assumed—without asking for the rationale—that the altar was built for sacrifices and as such would signify a turning away from and rebelling against the Lord. On this basis, they reminded the two and a half tribes of Israel's iniquity at Peor and the sin of Achan, both of which brought the Lord's wrath against the whole congregation (Josh. 7; Num. 25). Included is a suggestion given to the two and a half tribes. If they thought that their own land was unclean, they could cross over to the place where the Lord and His sanctuary stood and take possession of some of that land (22:19; cf. vv. 9-12). There was no need to rebel in order to make a point.

In their accusation, the delegation signaled their fear of the Lord's anger befalling the whole congregation on account of the rebellion of the Transjordan tribes, since the covenant community shared a corporate responsibility. This is why they rehearsed the incidents of Peor and Achan. The comment that Israel was not yet cleansed of the iniquity of Peor is intriguing. Although the Lord had destroyed the offenders with a plague, Israel felt that the Lord still held this iniquity against His people. While this might not be a wholesome theology, it certainly served to warn Israel of any further rebellion against the Lord. The building of an alternative altar constituted covenantal unfaithfulness, and Israel could no longer afford the price that came with such rebellion.

22:21–29. Response to the Accusation. The delegation of the nine and a half tribes wrongly interpreted the rationale for the altar and had thereby unjustifiably accused the builders of rebellion. By the twofold invocation of the solemn title of the Lord (*'el 'elohim yahweh*—"The Mighty One, God, the LORD" or "The LORD God of gods"; v. 22), the two and a half tribes sought to prove their innocence of the accusation. The Lord, being omniscient, already knew the rationale for the altar. But in case they were found guilty, they were prepared to accept full responsibility for the altar, as punishment either from their fellow Israelites or from the Lord Himself. Rather than an act of rebellion, the altar by the Jordan was built out of fear that the future descendants of the two and a half tribes would be denied the right to worship at God's tabernacle. This replica of the Lord's altar (v. 28) at Shiloh was built not for sacrifices but as a witness, especially as future generations of the two and a half tribes could cite it as evidence that they were part of the Lord's people since their ancestors built it. The impressiveness of the altar would thus agree with its function as a witness. Verse 29 carefully debunks all the charges pressed forward by the delegation from the west. As it turned out, the altar signified commitment to the Lord and unity with the other tribes in His service. The returning warriors had been loyal to the Lord's command throughout the conquest; there was no reason they should rebel against the Lord or His chosen leader now that the conquest was over.

22:30–34. Conflict Resolved. A good response will always turn away anger and prevent tragedy (cf. Prov. 15:1). Because of the heartwarming response of the two and a half tribes, Phinehas ended up commending their loyalty to the Lord. The nine and a half tribes were obviously waiting for the results of the delegation's investigation before engaging the two and a half tribes in war. Upon receiving the pleasing report, however, they praised God (lit. "blessed" Him) and refrained from the attack. Through confrontation and dialogue, conflicts are resolved and tragedies are averted. Among other things, Joshua 22 touches on the role of communication in conflict resolution. Unity among believers is evidence of the Lord's presence. The two and a half tribes probably named the altar "witness"—a witness to their loyalty to the Lord and their right, even if they lived outside of the land of Canaan, to share with the other tribes in the Lord's worship at His tabernacle.

23:1–16
Farewell Exhortation

Chapter 23 contains Joshua's parting message to all Israel, represented by elders, heads of tribes, judges, and military officers. This was a time when he was old and nearing death, well after the end of the conquest. By outlining both the benefits of obedience (vv. 1–11) and the consequences of disobedience (vv. 12–16), Joshua's exhortation emphasized faithfulness to the Lord and obedience of His Word.

23:1–11. Benefits of Obedience. It was the Lord who fought for Israel and gave them the land of Canaan as an inheritance. It was also He who would continue to drive out the remaining inhabitants of the land. Joshua then exhorted the people to be courageous and to resolve to do everything recorded in the book of the law of Moses, being careful not to deviate either to the right or to the left (v. 6). Keeping this law would mean that Israel would not swear by the Canaanite gods, serve them, or worship them, for such would constitute rebellion against the Lord and a rejection of His covenant. The reason Israel was required to continue to "hold fast to the LORD" (v. 8) was two-fold. On the one hand, Israel had to keep the law of the Lord because He had been faithful in fulfilling His covenant promises. No nation in Canaan, though greater and stronger, was able to stand against Israel because the Lord fought for His people. But Israel would be blessed even more through obedience to the divine law. For example, the Lord would terrify the rest of the Canaanites, so that one Israelite would chase a thousand of them and thus expel them from the land. As a response, the Israelites would love the Lord and keep His commandments.

23:12–16. Consequences of Disobedience. Should Israel turn away from following the Lord to cling to the Canaanites—mingling with them in marriage and in worship—He certainly would not drive out these Canaanites but would use them as an instrument to destroy His own people (cf. Ex. 34:12–16; Deut. 7:1–6). In Joshua 32:14–16, Joshua repeated himself by highlighting the two sides of the Lord's faithfulness. The Lord was going to be faithful in fulfilling the promises of the covenant, so that none of them would fail. But in case of rebellion, He would be faithful in plaguing them with the covenantal curses (Lev. 26; see Deut. 27–28). These words of Joshua, some of which would be repeated in chapter 24, were prophetic. The rehearsal of covenantal blessings and curses was necessary to try to avoid the people's loss of faith (cf. Judg. 2).

24:1–28
Renewal of the Covenant

Chapter 24 is a covenant renewal ceremony. Unlike chapter 23, in which a location is not given, the covenant ceremony of chapter 24 took place at Shechem. Abram had built an altar at Shechem (Gen. 12:6–7). It was here that Jacob challenged his household to get rid of foreign gods (Gen. 35:1–5). Joshua's renewal of the covenant in Joshua 8 also took place in the vicinity of Shechem. The covenant between God and Israel is the foundation of the book of Joshua. Chapter 24 concludes the book by emphasizing the centrality of the covenant in God's dealings with Israel.

24:1–13. Retelling the History of Israel. All the tribes of Israel, particularly the elders, heads, judges, and officers, were gathered for the covenant renewal ceremony. That the people presented themselves "before God" probably means that the incident took place in front of the tabernacle. It is possible that at that time—if not for that occasion—the sanctuary was at Shechem rather than Shiloh (cf. Josh. 18:1; 22:12; 24:26). In vv. 2–13 the Lord, through Joshua, retold the history of Israel, starting with the call of Abraham. These verses summarize the stories of the patriarchs (vv. 2–4), the Exodus and wandering (vv. 5–10), and the conquest and settlement in Canaan (vv. 11–13). The references to the Abrahamic covenant, the deliverance from Egypt, the crossing of the Red Sea, the desert wanderings, the Balaam episode, the crossing of the Jordan, and the terrorization of the enemy

leading to the conquest and subsequent settlement in the land all combine to emphasize the sovereignty of the Lord over Israel. Israel appeared in Canaan not by chance but by divine design. (For references to the "hornet," see Ex. 23:28 and Deut. 7:20.) If the Lord had promised to defeat the nations of Canaan before Israel (Josh. 3:10; Deut. 7:1), Joshua 24:11 indicates that He fulfilled this promise (cf. 12:7–8). The Lord is as good as His word.

24:14–15. Command to Serve the Lord. On the basis of the Lord's sovereignty and faithfulness (vv. 2–13), Joshua commanded Israel to fear the Lord and serve Him faithfully in sincerity and in truth and thus take away the false gods which their ancestors served on the other side of the river (i.e., the Euphrates) and in Egypt (vv. 14–15). In commanding the people not to worship the gods of the ancestors, Joshua meant that since the Lord now owned them (vv. 1–13), they were not to turn back from following Him. It is possible that some of the Israelites served other gods during their sojourn in Egypt (cf. Ex. 32; Ezek. 20). Joshua's injunction to serve the Lord faithfully in sincerity and truth meant to completely sever any idolatrous, ancestral practices. Joshua 24:14 ends with a command to serve the Lord. But in v. 15 Joshua seems to give the option to Israel to decide whom to serve—whether the ancestral gods in Mesopotamia or the gods in the land of Canaan—if they deemed it unprofitable (lit. ra' means "evil, bad") to serve the Lord. The Lord detests forced or insincere worship. His salvific purpose for Israel depended on its choice to serve Him. Notice, however, that Joshua's words in vv. 2–14 and 23:12–16 carefully narrow Israel's choice in favor of the Lord. If Israel was required to sever their ties to the ancestral gods in Mesopotamia, how much more would they need to repudiate Canaanite gods! Verse 15 concludes with Joshua's personal resolution: he and his family would serve the Lord. By this declaration of allegiance, he sought to challenge others to ensure that their families too remained loyal to the Lord. If the Lord is worshiped, He must be worshiped with undivided loyalty and singleness of heart.

24:16–18. Commitment to Serve the Lord. If vv. 14–15 constitute Joshua's command to serve the Lord, then vv. 16–18 constitute the people's commitment to serve Him. In view of all the things He had done for them, they swore never to forsake the Lord and serve other gods. Thus, the basis on which Israel was commanded to serve the Lord (vv. 2–13) constituted the basis on which they promised to serve Him (vv. 17–18). The Lord must be worshiped in recognition of His ownership of and goodness toward His people.

24:19–24. Repeating the Commitment. The responsive speeches between Joshua and the people would serve to ensure and affirm the people's commitment to the Lord and His covenant. In vv. 19–20, Joshua tested the genuineness of their declaration of allegiance (v. 18) by insisting that they could not serve the Lord because He is holy, jealous, and would not forgive their transgressions and sins if they forsook Him and followed foreign gods. Joshua's statement does not contradict Exodus 34:6–7; it simply brings home the fact that the Lord would not let idolatry go unpunished. Israel was thus reminded to expect not only bountiful blessings from the Lord if they remained faithful to the covenant but also deleterious covenantal curses should they be unfaithful. This should motivate them to be loyal. Once Israel entered into covenant with Him, they were either for Him or against Him. They sealed their determination to follow the Lord (Josh. 24:22), and He would not share the allegiance due Him with other gods. Israel was commanded to take away (*sur*) the foreign gods and follow the biddings of only the Lord (v. 23; cf. v. 14). The Hebrew verb *sur* means "clear away," "get rid of," or "remove." It is possible that the reference to foreign gods here refers to the Canaanite gods who would soon ensnare Israel, rather than gods already in the possession of the Israelites. Verse 23 would thus be a command to get rid of the Canaanite gods in the land (cf. Deut. 31:16; Judg. 2:2). The final response of the people (Josh. 24:24) genuinely satisfied Joshua's charge to serve the Lord and obey His voice (v. 23).

24:25–28. Sealing the Covenant. Based on the people's resolution to serve the Lord (vv. 16–24), Joshua renewed the covenant with them and made a covenant transaction (*khoq*—"statute" or "rule," and *mishpat*—"judgment," "ordinance," or "decree"), which included the words of the Lord and the response of Israel. Joshua subsequently wrote the words or an account of the transaction, adding it to the "Book of the Law of God" (see 1:8; 8:31; 22:5; 23:6). A new canonical portion is produced in addition to what Moses had written. As a significant ceremony, the covenant renewal at Shechem needed to be memorialized for future generations. A large stone was set up to serve such purpose (v. 26). Through personification, the stone is said to have heard all the words the Lord spoke to the people (v. 27).

As a legal witness, the stone would remind Israel that continual possession of the land depended on their faithfulness to the Lord's covenant.

24:29–33
Three Burials

Verses 29–33 record the burials of Joshua, Eleazar, and the bones of Joseph. These burials testify to the faithfulness of the Lord in firmly establishing Israel in the land of Canaan in accordance with His promise to the fathers.

24:29–31. Joshua. Joshua was buried in his own inheritance. He had been a *sharat* (an "aide," "assistant," or "minister") to Moses, the "servant of the LORD" (see 1:1; Ex. 24:13). Only at death is Joshua accorded the prestigious title "servant of the LORD" (Jos. 24:29). It is a great honor to serve the Lord. Verse 31 states that Israel served the Lord throughout the days of Joshua and the elders who had witnessed the Lord's mighty acts. This verse anticipates a negative situation after the deaths of the elders, as can be seen in the book of Judges. Meanwhile, the book of Joshua closes with two more burials.

24:32. Joseph's Bones. Joseph's bones were buried in the very portion of land that Jacob had acquired from the Shechemites (Gen. 33:19). The transportation of Joseph's bones from Egypt and their subsequent burial in Canaan fulfilled his deathbed wish and his brothers' oath (Gen. 50:25; Ex. 13:19). In the division of the land, Ephraim, Joseph's legal firstborn, inherited the city of Shechem. Joseph was thus buried in his own tribal inheritance.

24:33. Eleazar. Eleazar, the high priest, was buried in a plot of land belonging to his son Phinehas in the territory of Ephraim. According to 21:9–19, the priestly sons of Aaron were given cities within the tribes of Judah, Simeon, and Benjamin, but not in Ephraim. The reason Phinehas received a plot in Ephraim was probably because the sanctuary was in Ephraim at that time and the high priest had to settle close to the sanctuary.

These leaders and those who followed them lived looking forward to the final fulfillment of God's promises. They saw and enjoyed the partial fulfillment of the promises but died looking forward to their full realization in a better country, the heavenly one (Heb. 11:13–16, 39–40). Promise, faith, and hope remain inseparable in the hearts of God's people.

JUDGES

INTRODUCTION

Title and Authorship. The book takes its title from its leading characters, the "judges" (Judg. 2:16–18). It describes in some detail the rule of the six major judges: Othniel (3:7–11), Ehud (3:12–30), Deborah (4:1—5:31), Gideon (6:1—8:35), Jephthah (10:6—12:7), and Samson (13:1—16:31). The six minor judges are mentioned only in passing: Shamgar (3:31), Tola, Jair (10:1–5), Ibzan, Elon, and Abdon (12:8–15). These judges were more than judicial administrators; they also were divinely appointed deliverers of God's people (2:16; 3:9, 15).

The verb "to judge" describes the activity of most of them (Othniel [3:10], Deborah [4:4], Tola [10:2], Jair [10:3], Jephthah [12:7], Ibzan [12:8], Elon [12:11], Abdon [12:13], Samson [15:20]). After a judge delivered God's people from their oppressors, he or she ruled over them for the rest of his or her life, maintaining political order and social justice in Israel. However, it was acknowledged that God Himself was the chief judge (11:27).

The author of the book of Judges is not named in the book itself, nor is there any hint in any other part of the Bible. According to Jewish tradition, the prophet Samuel wrote 1 and 2 Samuel, Judges, and Ruth. Critical scholarship holds that the book was composed by different authors over a long period.

Date. A number of historical statements in the book provide some guidance as to the time when the book was written.

1. We find the phrase "to this day" six times (1:21, 26; 6:24; 10:4; 15:19; 18:12). Most of these refer to place-names that were still in use when the book was written; hence, they are not of much help. Judges 1:21, however, tells us that the children of Benjamin did not drive out the Jebusites from Jerusalem, so the Jebusites still occupied Jerusalem in the time of the author.

This means that this text must have been written before David's conquest of Jerusalem (2 Sam. 5:6–9), shortly after he became king over all Israel in Hebron (2 Sam. 5:1–5).

2. In Judges 1:29, we read that Ephraim did not drive out the Canaanites who dwelt in Gezer. The town of Gezer, one of the cities assigned to the Levites (Josh. 21:21), lay in Ephraim's territory, but it was still a Canaanite town. This situation continued until one of the Egyptian pharaohs—possibly Siamun (986–967 B.C.)—conquered Gezer and presented it as a wedding gift (dowry) to his daughter, the wife of Solomon (1 Kin. 9:16). Judges 1:29, therefore, could not have been written later than the early part of Solomon's reign, which was before he married Pharaoh's daughter.

3. The observation that there was no king in Israel at the time of the events recorded in Judges appears four times in the book (17:6; 18:1; 19:1; 21:25). It appears to draw a contrast between the prosperous times of the monarchy (which the writer may have experienced) and the necessitous time of the judges (but see 21:23–25). If that is the case, it would fit in the early reign of Saul, before he was rejected by God, or in the time of David and the early part of Solomon.

4. The reference in 18:30–31 to the carved image that the children of Dan set up for themselves at the time that the house of God was in Shiloh (v. 31) seems to indicate that when the book was written Shiloh was no longer the religious center of Israel (see "Shiloh," p. 920). When the ark was taken by the Philistines and Eli died (1 Sam. 4:10–18), God abandoned the sanctuary at Shiloh (Ps. 78:60). Most likely, the Philistines destroyed Shiloh because when the ark was given back, it was not returned to Shiloh but stayed in Kirjath Jearim for twenty years (1 Sam. 7:2).

In summary, the internal evidence of the book of Judges seems to indicate that it was written during the early period of Saul's or

David's reign, perhaps by Samuel, as held by Jewish tradition. Samuel consistently condemned idolatry and called upon the people to live in accordance with God's commandments (2 Sam. 7:3–6; 12:14–15, 20–25).

Backgrounds. The time of the Judges was a period comparable to the Dark Ages in church history—all people did as they pleased, according to their own subjective standards (Judg. 17:6). This period extended from the time of the death of all the elders who had seen the great miracles God had done for His people Israel (2:7) until the time of Samuel and the beginning of the monarchy, from about 1350 to 1050 B.C.

During this time, we find periods of oppression, brought on by apostasies, alternating with peaceful times under the leadership of the judges whom God raised up to deliver Israel. Because the Israelites failed to drive out all of the Canaanites from the land God had promised them, some Canaanite city-states existed whose culture was advanced over that of the Israelites, who had spent hundreds of years in slavery in Egypt. Not surprisingly, there was a tendency among the Israelites to adopt some elements of Canaanite culture and to combine the worship of Yahweh with the worship of the Canaanite deities Baal and Ashtoreth (2:13).

Internationally, the monotheistic reforms of Pharaoh Akhenaten (ca. 1374–1358 B.C.) were taking place in Egypt. The letters from Canaanite city-states to Pharaoh Akhenaten in his new capital city of Akhetaten ("The Horizon of the [sun disk] Aten") at modern tal al-Amarna contain pleas for help against the Habiru, a possible reference to some of the Hebrew tribes (see *"Habiru,"* p. 365). Later, around 1200 B.C., a group of people living in Crete were driven out by the Greeks and attempted to invade Egypt, but Pharaoh Ramesses III (ca. 1198–1166 B.C.) drove them back. According to a credible theory, they settled along the coast in the south of Canaan and assimilated with, or perhaps annihilated or replaced, the existing Philistine culture of Abraham's day. Their continuing existence and interaction with the Israelites is an important part of the story of the book of Judges.

Chronology. The question of the chronology of the judges is related to the date of the Exodus event and the entry of Israel into Canaan forty years later. According to Scripture, Solomon began the construction of the temple in 967 B.C., 480 years after the Exodus (1 Kin. 6:1).

Solomon reigned for forty years (971–931 B.C.). Therefore, the Exodus event took place in about 1447 B.C. and the beginning of the conquest of Canaan in about 1407 B.C.

Jephthah, in Judges 11:26, reminded the king of Ammon that Israel had already dwelt in Heshbon and its villages for three hundred years. Israel had conquered Heshbon under Moses's leadership (Deut. 2:26–37) just before his death. Hence, there were about three hundred years between the time of Moses's conquest of Heshbon and the judgeship of Jephthah, the eighth of the twelve judges.

Israel was oppressed by foreign powers for various lengths of time and then freed by the judges. Most of the lengths of these periods are carefully preserved in the text. When these time periods are added together and then combined with the forty years wandering under Moses, the conquest under Joshua, and reigns of Saul and David, the total time is too long to fit into the 480 years of 1 Kings 6:1. In fact, even the judgeships add up to more than Jephthah's three hundred years. Thus, it is likely that some of these judgeships overlapped with each other and with some of the periods of oppression. For example, Samson judged Israel for twenty years in the days of the Philistines (Judg. 15:20); that is, he judged Israel for twenty years sometime during the forty years of oppression by the Philistines.

The tribes of Israel and their judges were widely scattered geographically. For example, Othniel was from Judah, Deborah from Ephraim, Samson from Dan, and so on. The biblical record shows that even in times of crisis, when a deliverer was fighting an oppressor, not all the tribes rallied to the cause. For example, when Barak fought Jabin, only the tribes of Zebulun and Naphtali joined him (4:10). And when Gideon defeated the Midianites, he called on only the tribes of Asher, Manasseh, Naphtali, and Zebulun (6:35). The reason could be that not all the tribes were oppressed at any one time, and that some of the judges were local rather than national deliverers. This understanding allows for the time frame to be reduced in order to fit into the three-hundred-year period mentioned by Jephthah.

Theology and Purpose. The book of Judges describes the interaction between God and His people after they entered the land of Canaan. A new chapter in the history of the nation was being written, and what we find is disturbing. We move from some elements of social order to almost total chaos. At the center of the book is the covenant relation that God established with the twelve tribes and that would have ensured safety and security. The book is about the God of the covenant and the disruption of the covenant relationship and its results.

1. Blessings of Faithfulness. The book begins with a people who existed in union with God and with each other. Before deciding what to do after the death of Joshua, they consulted the Lord, and He identified Judah as the leading tribe (1:1–2). They were ready to finish the task of conquering the land of Canaan. Yahweh and His covenant created a deep bond of unity among the tribes, which was perhaps even stronger than blood relations. Faithfulness to the covenant relationship brought with it a peaceful social interaction among the tribes. They supported Judah's lead and moved as one person to accomplish the Lord's plan for them. God had repeatedly promised to protect and bless them (Lev. 26:3–13; Deut. 7:12–24), and the people took the divine promise seriously, knowing that the God who brought them out of Egypt would also fulfill His promises to the new generation. He was powerful enough to defeat all their enemies dwelling in the land. Therefore, they had nothing to fear from the gods of Canaan. When the Lord confronted the idols of the Canaanites, they became totally ineffective. Indeed, the union with the redeeming God manifested itself in social cohesion and oneness and in the defeat of the enemy. This book will show that Israel would continue to enjoy the blessings of the covenant as long as they remained faithful to the covenant Lord.

2. Unfaithfulness and Apostasy. The positive picture of Israel's obedience and faithfulness to the Lord in the opening verses of the book is soon undone by portrayals of marked disobedience and apostasy. The people not only forgot the Lord but worshiped and served the Baals and Asherahs (Judg. 3:7), thus blatantly rejecting the God of their fathers and of Moses and Joshua, who brought them out of Egypt. Some may have chosen to worship God using the Canaanite style of worship, thereby making the Lord (Yahweh) a Canaanite "Baal" (a term which meant "lord"). This illustrates the doleful principle that the spirit of rebellion often blinds human beings and makes them believe that they are in union with God even when their actions are totally against His will.

Others among the tribes simply decided to worship the Canaanite gods, thinking they were in charge of the fertility of the land. In sum, the covenant relationship was openly violated. When the human heart breaks away from the Lord, its true nature is manifested. There is a natural spirit of rebellion in the human heart that can be subdued only in union with the Savior (Ps. 51:5; Jer. 17:9). This corrupted condition of the human heart is repeatedly illustrated in the narratives of the book of Judges. The result was spiritual, social, and moral corruption and chaos.

The spiritual collapse brought social disruption with it. The social cohesiveness of the tribal confederation was drastically damaged. There were serious conflicts among the tribes. The first judges acted on behalf of the people against their external enemies, but some of the later judges killed their own brothers in battles that should never have taken place. Although the book begins with an emphasis on Israel as a united people who have the worship of God and trust in His promises at the center of their lives, it ends with a description of a fragmented people. All of them were doing what they considered to be good in their own eyes or opinion. The internal division was so intense that it was more damaging to the nation than the oppression inflicted on them by their common enemies. Judges clearly indicates that unfaithfulness to the Lord manifested itself in a veiled or open spirit of rebellion. This type of rebellion takes humans to unexpected depths of spiritual, social, and moral chaos.

3. Divine Wrath and Compassion. Judges makes clear that God is not indifferent to human conduct; He reacts to it through covenant blessings or curses. Israel's violation of the covenant provoked the wrath of the Lord, and consequently He sold them into the hands of their enemies (2:14). Love is God's fundamental attribute (1 John 4:8, 16), but love is not indifferent to sin and rebellion. What we call divine wrath is nothing else but God's love expressing itself in opposition to sin (see "The Wrath of God," p. 918). Every time Israel turned to idol worship, God delivered them into the hands of their enemies (Judg. 2:11–14; 3:7–8; 10:6), not simply to punish them but as an act of discipline aimed at curing them of idolatry. In the process, God revealed His power and glory over the pagan gods that Israel served by demonstrating that the idols were unable to deliver His people from oppression, suffering, and evil.

The book of Judges reveals a God full of compassion and mercy toward sinners. In the OT, divine mercy or compassion is a central theological theme. In Judges, even foreign oppression served as an instrument of God's grace to bring Israel back to Him (3:1–4). Whenever they cried out to the Lord, He heard them and sent a deliverer as a sign of His grace. In other words, what Israel experienced was not the uncontrollable power of their enemies but the response of a loving God seeking to preserve His covenant relationship with them. The hand of the Lord was actively present in the historical events that took place during the period of the Judges, and He used these events not only to discipline but also to manifest His deep love for Israel. The constant falling of Israel into idolatry was never more powerful than God's grace. God's grace always abounds over sin (Rom. 5:20).

4. *Hope and Deliverance.* While the word "hope" does not appear in the book of Judges, the concept is present throughout. Each time the Israelites suffered under an oppressor, they prayed to the Lord, hoping that He would hear and deliver them. And He always delivered His people. Hope here is inseparable from the conviction that God will fulfill His promise by coming as a Deliverer. The period of the Judges was depressing but not empty of hope. It showed that God was still in control and that He always preserves some individuals who remain faithful to Him (i.e., a remnant). Whenever there is a remnant, there is hope. In fact, the book anticipates the time when the true King shall arise in Israel, One who will deliver and rule in righteousness, the messianic King. Therefore, the book speaks to us who also live at a time when everyone is doing what seems good in his or her own eyes. It speaks of a hope that continues to give meaning to the life of believers who are still anticipating, longing, and praying for the coming of the King in order to experience ultimate deliverance.

COMMENTARY

1:1—3:6

INTRODUCTION

The first major section of the book of Judges tells the story of Israel's partial conquest of Canaan (1:1–26) and the unfaithfulness of Israel in leaving some nations in the land (1:27—2:5). This section also provides a theological summary of the experience of Israel during the period of the Judges after the death of Joshua, which will be developed throughout the rest of the book (2:6—3:6). While there seems to be a contrast between this story and the record of the conquest of the land of Canaan in the book of Joshua (Josh. 11:23), we must remember that the books of Joshua and Judges speak of two phases in the process of conquering the land. Under Joshua, in the first phase, the Israelites defeated the Canaanite *armies* without immediately occupying the whole land. The second phase of completely clearing out the *inhabitants* of Canaan after the land was divided was accomplished only partially by the individual tribes (cf. chap. 13). They failed to decisively follow through to completion what Joshua had begun; a failure that was regarded as a breach of the covenant they had made with God and a cause of permanent spiritual weakness (Judg. 2:1–3). A weak faith produces weak actions. Christians whose faith is weak do not always walk closely with the Lord but are content with a generally accepted standard of the Christian life and miss out on the full blessing of the gospel of Christ.

1:1–26
Conquest of the Land

Judges 1:1–21 recounts the success of the tribes of Judah and Simeon in conquering the southern part of Canaan. In this conquest of the hill country, Judah and Simeon were joined by the Kenites, relatives of Jethro, Moses's father-in-law, who were connected with the Midianites (v. 16; Num. 10:29). This was followed by the capture of central Canaan (Judg. 1:22–26).

1:1–21. Conquest of South Canaan. With God's help and following His directions, which were most likely given through the Urim and Thummim (v. 2), the tribes of Judah and Simeon defeated the Canaanites and Perizzites,

Chariots

Depictions of chariots have been found in Mesopotamia dating from the earliest periods. In Egypt, Joseph rode in the second chariot of the pharaoh (Gen. 41:43). The two-wheeled chariot became a war machine of great importance in the history of the ancient world. While the Iron Age in the Holy Land is generally dated from 1200 B.C. onwards, the use of iron was known in the ANE before that time (e.g., by the Hittites in the eighteenth to twelfth centuries B.C.). Their technology could easily have found its way to Canaan in the south.

a minor branch of the pre-Israelite population of Canaan, in the hill country of Judea. The mutilation of Adoni-Bezek ("Lord of Bezek") was a common fate of prisoners (v. 7) that both incapacitated them to shoot arrows and damaged their balance. Although Israel captured Jerusalem and destroyed it by fire (v. 8), it was rebuilt by the Jebusites (v. 21), who lived in it until the time of David (2 Sam. 5:6–7). Judah captured the cities in the hill country, but they were unable to drive out the inhabitants of the lowlands because they had chariots of iron (Judg. 1:19).

We can detect here a lack of faith on the part of Judah, because for God, iron chariots would not have presented a problem (cf. Josh. 11:6–9). Had He not specifically promised them success against the Canaanites (Num. 33:51–53; Deut. 9:3; 11:23) regardless of whether they had iron chariots (Josh. 17:17–18)? Judah, who had been chosen to confront the enemy first, failed to provide the example the other tribes needed for their conquest of the land. Their lack of faith led them to overestimate the difficulties, just as our lack of faith may prevent us from standing firm in the face of adverse opinions, the loss of worldly advantages or friendships, and the sacrifice of personal interests.

1:22–26. Conquest of Bethel in Central Canaan. The account of the conquest of central Canaan follows that of southern Canaan. The reference to the tribe/house of Joseph (v. 22) refers to the tribe of Ephraim and half of the tribe of Manasseh, the sons of Joseph (Gen. 41:50–52), who had received their inheritance in central Canaan (the other half of Manasseh had remained in the Transjordan; Num. 32:33). They attacked Bethel ("house of God"), where God gave to Jacob the dream of the ladder reaching into heaven (Gen. 28:10–19). It was one of the sanctuaries during the period of the Judges. After the death of Solomon and the division of the kingdom into the Southern and Northern Kingdoms, Bethel became one of the two national shrines of the Northern Kingdom (1 Kin. 12:28–29). The Israelites captured the city because God was with them (Judg. 1:22), not because of their own prowess. As in the case of Judah (vv. 2–4), the presence of the Lord was a guarantee of victory. When the spies asked a man leaving the city how to gain access to it (v. 24), they were most likely not inquiring in regard to the main city gate, which would have been visible to all, but to another entrance through which they could surprise the inhabitants and capture the city.

1:27—2:5
Unconquered Cities

The last part of chapter 1 is a record of failures on the part of the Israelites, emphasizing how remiss they were in completing the conquest of the land. The text gives two main reasons that for this state of affairs. First, the Canaanites were committed to retaining their land by fighting for it (v. 27), making it more difficult for the Israelites to possess the land. Second, the Israelites apparently concluded that they could gain some financial benefits by not exterminating them. They decided to impose a tribute on the Canaanites in exchange for keeping them alive. As a result, they did not completely drive them out or destroy them (vv. 28, 33, 35). Consequently, Israelites and Canaanites lived side by side in many parts of the land, contrary to what God had planned for His people (Deut. 20:16–17).

The Angel of the Lord

This name is never used for a human messenger or prophet but always for a celestial, supernatural being who first appeared in the Bible in the story of Hagar (Gen. 16:7–13). Although in some cases He seems to be differentiated from Yahweh (see Judg. 6:12), in a good number of cases the Angel of the Lord is identified with the Lord/Yahweh Himself. For instance, the Angel of God spoke to Jacob in a dream (Gen. 31:11) and immediately referred to Himself as "God" (Gen. 31:13). The Angel of the Lord appeared to Moses in the burning bush and identified Himself as the God of Abraham, Isaac, and Jacob (Ex. 3:2–6). In Judges 2:1–2, God's deliverance of Israel from Egypt is credited to the Angel of the Lord. This Angel also appeared to Gideon under the name "Angel of the LORD" (the Angel of Yahweh; 6:12, 14, 16). Interestingly, this Angel never described Himself as a messenger bringing a message to someone from the Lord. In Him, God was speaking directly to human beings; He was His own messenger. Many Christian believers have identified the Angel of the Lord as the preincarnate Christ—equal and yet distinct from God the Father. In this case, the term "Angel" refers to the function of God as His own "Messenger," and not to His nature as God.

It is obvious that the Israelites were careless in carrying out their God-given duty to cleanse the land of idolatry. The unbelief that had kept the former generation for forty years in the wilderness kept this generation from taking possession of the whole land. Similarly, we may have experienced deliverance from the dominion of Satan and the joy of salvation, yet a weak spiritual life may keep us from progressing further on the path of sanctification.

God responded to the unfaithfulness of Israel through a strong rebuke (Judg. 2:1–5). The Angel of the Lord appeared to them with two primary purposes. First, God made a covenant with the nation, and He had remained faithful to it while the Israelites violated it by making a covenant with the Canaanites. The contrast is between the faithfulness of God and the unfaithfulness of the people. Second, since the people had intentionally preserved the life of their enemy, the Lord granted His people what they had chosen to do—He would not drive the Canaanites out of the land as He had originally intended (Ex. 33:2; Deut. 11:23; Josh. 13:6). Rather, the Canaanites would constantly be irritants, scourges, and problems, and their gods would become a snare for the Israelites (Judg. 2:3; cf. Num. 33:55; Josh. 23:13).

The Angel of the Lord came from Gilgal, which means "a rolling away" because, upon entering the promised land at Gilgal, the Israelites had dedicated themselves to the Lord through circumcision and the celebration of the Passover (Josh. 5:9–10). In response to the Lord's rebuke, the people broke out in loud weeping, which gave that place its name—Bochim ("weepers"). Here, weeping symbolizes regret and repentance.

2:6—3:6
From Faithfulness to Sin

Judges 2:6–10 is a recapitulation of events connected with Joshua's death and briefly fills in the history from that time until the experience at Bochim, emphasizing the unfaithfulness of the people (vv. 11–23). The final passage of this introductory section to the book (3:1–6) lists the names of the Canaanite nations left in the land. The reason for their being left in the land is repeated and an additional reason is added. The Israelites' apostasy is shown to have led to their intermarriage with the Canaanites.

2:6–10. Death of Joshua. The events at Bochim narrated in 2:1–5 happened after the death of Joshua. Verse 6 is a repetition of Joshua

24:28 and refers to Joshua sending off the people after the covenant ceremony at Shechem (Josh. 24:25–27). After narrating the first efforts of the tribes to consolidate their position in the land and the divine rebuke at Bochim, the author explains why it was necessary for God to raise up judges. In the rest of the chapter, he proceeds to show how God, through periods of oppression followed by times of deliverance, sought to turn Israel from their idolatry to obedience to His law.

The elders mentioned in Judges 2:7 were the tribal leaders also mentioned in Joshua 23:2 and 24:1. The emphasis of Judges 2:6–10 is on the importance of knowing the Lord through a personal experience. Most of these elders outlived Joshua because they were all younger than him. His and Caleb's contemporaries all died in the desert (Num. 14:29–30). The elders had been young when they witnessed all the mighty deeds God performed during Israel's journey from Egypt to the promised land and were well acquainted with the saving power of God in their personal experience. During their leadership, they inspired the Israelites to obey and remain loyal to Him. Once the loyal elders died, the new generation did not know the Lord. They did not remember what God had done for them in the past and did not identify themselves with the faith of their forefathers. They chose to serve the Canaanite gods. Through the work of the judges, God tried to reveal to the new generation His identity and His power to save, hoping that they would come to know and serve Him.

2:11–23. Israel's Unfaithfulness. Choosing to ignore who the Lord was led the children of Israel to serve the Baals, which was evil in God's sight (v. 11). Baal, in the singular, was the name of the Canaanite storm and weather god—the plural form refers to the many local manifestations of the weather god (see "Baal Worship," p. 493). By disregarding the Lord's requirement to destroy the pagan altars (Ex. 34:11–16) and to not make a covenant with the Canaanites, the Israelites violated the covenant and the covenant Lord abandoned them. The result was that they could no longer withstand their enemies (Judg. 2:14). The language of delivering and selling His people to His enemies makes it clear that the oppression of the people was not the result of God's absence of power to protect them. This language places the responsibility on the covenant violators. The enemy did not take them from God's hands by force. He simply abandoned them, and they fell into the hands of their enemies (v. 14).

Nevertheless, when the Israelites showed signs of repentance and remorse and cried to the Lord, He raised up judges who delivered them (v. 16). He might have abandoned them in justice, but God in His mercy took pity on them. The abandonment was not final, and therefore His anger was set aside. His mercy knows no limits if the human heart, moved by the Spirit, seeks for it. Unfortunately, as soon as the God-given judge was dead and the oppression of their enemies was a distant memory, the Israelites again acted like a prostitute with other gods (v. 17). Harlotry is a frequent metaphor in the Bible for spiritual apostasy (Ex. 34:15; Deut. 31:16; 1 Chr. 5:25; Jer. 3:6). In the prophetic books, God is at times depicted as the husband of Israel (Is. 54:5; Jer. 31:32; Hos. 2:2), and Israel and Judah are presented as faithless sisters who play the harlot, being unfaithful to their beloved (Ezek. 23). Yet, harlotry in Judges is not just a metaphor; the worship of heathen deities in the ANE was frequently accompanied by sexual immorality. God decided to use the people left in the land to test the fidelity of the Israelites (Judg. 2:22; 3:1, 4) and show them that the way of apostasy does not pay. God tested the Israelites to strengthen their character.

The sin of the people was in sparing the Canaanites, and their punishment was that God did not drive out the Canaanites; in a sense they were beaten with their own rod, as a child is disciplined for his or her own good (Prov. 13:24). Through this testing, God was endeavoring to bring His people back to Him. Throughout human history, God has "tested" His people in order for them to reveal the depth of their faith or to help them grow in grace and love.

3:1-6. The Nations Remaining in the Land. While in 2:22 and 3:4 the purpose of having the Canaanite nations in the land is to test character, faith, and obedience, in 3:2 the purpose is to train or accustom them to war. Thus, the additional reason given in this passage for God not driving out the nations was to teach the new generation of Israelites how to conduct war (vv. 1-2). God is able to transform our mistakes into something good for us. Following Joshua's conquest of Canaan, a considerable period of rest must have followed, during which the younger generations lived in relative comfort. Since Israel was to be a nation living among many others and seeking to conquer and expand, it would have to learn to war against them in order for

God to fulfill His plan for all of them (Gen. 12:1-3). The Israelite hope included the expectation of a time when no one will train for war under the leadership of the Messiah (Is. 2:4).

This passage concludes by saying that the Israelites lived among the various people groups in the land (Judg. 3:5). One sad result of this situation was mixed marriages, something expressly forbidden by God (v. 6; Ex. 34:15-16; Deut. 7:3; Josh. 23:12). Marriage contracts in those days included a mutual recognition of the religions of the two parties. Thus, it was impossible for an Israelite to marry a Canaanite and maintain the purity of his or her faith. This was illustrated graphically in the life of Solomon, whose wives led him into idol worship (1 Kin. 11:4). Today, some tragic results could be avoided if Paul's counsel in 2 Corinthians 6:14-17 against marriages between believers and unbelievers were heeded.

3:7—8:35

RULE OF THE EARLY JUDGES

The second major section of Judges introduces us to the actual narrative of the book. It describes the rule of the first four major judges in some detail (Othniel, Ehud, Deborah, and Gideon), with Shamgar mentioned only briefly. We will follow their stories, noting the repeated refrain of Israel's return to evil (Judg. 3:7, 12; 4:1; 6:1) and how upon their repentance God in His mercy raised up a deliverer. The details vary from case to case, but the basic outline is always the same.

3:7-11
Othniel

The account of the first judge provides the formula for the repeated pattern in which the main episodes of the judges are set: the apostasy of the people, the time of their servitude under the oppressor, their cry of distress and repentance, their deliverance by the judge appointed by God, and the length of rest that followed their deliverance.

The sin of Israel is described in three ways: Israel did evil in God's sight, they forgot the Lord, and they served the Baals (3:7). The idea that Israel was doing evil in the Lord's estimation runs throughout the book as an indictment against the people, meaning that in the judgment of the Lord—after He examined and evaluated their lives—their religious and moral life was atrocious (2:11; 3:12; 4:1; 6:1; 10:6; 13:1). Surprisingly, the Israelites did what was right in their own eyes—that is, as they saw fit and according to their own subjective estimation (17:6; 21:25)—rather than doing what was right in the sight of the Lord—that is, according to His estimation. The opinion they had of their own behavior was radically different from God's opinion. Indeed, they forgot the Lord (3:7). This is a willful act by which God is no longer taken into consideration in one's life; His will is ignored. The same idea is expressed with the phrase "forsook the Lord" (10:6). Israel, the wife of the Lord, abandoned Him and served the Baals. They abandoned or forgot their God and Redeemer. Consequently, God abandoned them into the hands of their enemies. His judgment against them corresponded to the spiritual and moral crime they committed—because they abandoned Him, He also abandoned them (cf. v. 13).

Because of Israel's apostasy, the Lord sold them into the hands of Cushan-Rishathaim, king of *'aram-naharayim* ("Aram between the rivers"; i.e., the Tigris and Euphrates) or Mesopotamia (v. 8) for eight years. The identity of this king is unknown. His name, most likely corrupted by his victims, means something like "Cushan-of-double-wickedness." The specific nature of the oppression is not mentioned, but, as indicated by the use of the verb "to serve," it would have included paying heavy tributes that deprived the Israelites of enjoying the fruit of their work. Toward the end of their eight years of distress, the Israelites turned to Yahweh, their God, asking for help and hoping for a deliverer. Affliction often causes those who may have cared little about God to cry out to Him for help (v. 9). This is an agonizing cry emitted by a person who is in deep distress. And God in His mercy heard their cry and raised up Othniel, Caleb's nephew (1:13; 3:9). Caleb's daughter Achsah was given to him as wife for capturing the town of Debir (Josh. 15:15–19). The spirit of the Lord came on him (Judg. 3:10); the same is said of Gideon (6:34), Jephthah (11:29), and Samson (13:25; 14:6, 19; 15:14). These judges were empowered by God to fulfill their responsibilities; otherwise, deliverance would not have been possible.

Othniel was one of the older Israelites who had seen the works of the Lord during the conquest of Canaan. Now, endowed with the spirit of God, he became the leader who first judged Israel; that is, he reproved and reformed them, and then, under God's command, he went out and defeated the oppressors (3:10). Humans and God worked together to overcome the enemy in a literal and spiritual battle. The worst enemy is sin in the camp; when it is conquered, the enemy on the outside is easier to deal with. For forty years, as long as Othniel lived, there was peace in the land (v. 11). It could have lasted forever had they kept close to God and done their duty.

3:12–30
Ehud

Humans tend to easily forget God's goodness toward them. After the death of faithful Othniel, the Israelites apostatized again and returned to what is natural to humans—doing evil in God's sight (v. 12). The Lord, who is depicted in Judges as the Sovereign Lord over the nations, strengthened Eglon king of Moab and gave him power over Israel (v. 12). In this particular case, God provided for Eglon the military superiority he needed to overcome Israel. Eglon probably credited such superiority not to God but to his ability to form a coalition with the Ammonites and the Amalekites against God's people. But Eglon's oppression of God's people was not God's last word. Deliverance would come at the appropriate time through a God-chosen instrument.

Eglon ("little bull"), the king of Moab, and Ehud the Benjamite were both used by God (Judg. 3:12, 15): one to punish Israel, the other to deliver them. Eglon took possession of the City of Palms (i.e., Jericho), which lay within the territory of the tribe of Benjamin, from which Ehud came. Jericho at that time was probably no more than an occupied oasis. The city of Jericho was destroyed by the Israelites under Joshua around 1410 B.C. (Josh. 6) and according to 1 Kings 16:34 it was not rebuilt until the time of Ahab (874–853 B.C.).

The assassination of Eglon (Judg. 3:16–26) was well planned by Ehud. He brought to Eglon the required tribute (Heb. *minkhah*, also used to refer to an offering to God; 13:23; Lev. 9:4) and then left. The stone images mentioned in 3:19 were idols (Heb. *pesil* always refers to carved pagan cult images; cf. Deut. 7:5; 2 Kin. 17:41; 2 Chr. 33:19). The reason for mentioning this place where he dismissed his helpers and returned to visit Eglon is not obvious in the text. We perhaps can infer from the story itself that the two mentions of these pagan images serve to emphasize their impotence before Ehud, God's instrument. The gods should have protected the king, but they could not. Firstly, they could have prevented the assassination when Ehud, in front of them, dismissed his servants and returned to Eglon. And secondly, these idols could have punished Ehud when he walked by them after the assassination. The message was clear that these idols were useless and incapable of derailing God's purpose. The God of Israel was superior to them. Ehud's ostensible reason for returning to see Eglon was that he had a secret message from the Lord for the king. The "message" was simply the assassination itself, a message of judgment against Eglon and the Moabites. After Ehud led a short war, with a great slaughter of the Moabites, the land of Israel had peace and rest for eighty years (Judg. 3:30). Thus, the experience of true rest is found only in the Lord.

3:31
Shamgar

Not much is known of Shamgar, the son of Anath. He is connected to the story of Ehud by the author's comments that he came after Ehud and performed the same function of saving Israel from their enemies. Anath is the name of a Canaanite goddess, well known from the ancient tablets from Ugarit in Syria. Thus, Shamgar's mother may have been a Canaanite woman who was named after the goddess. Even if he was a Canaanite, his victory over the Philistines delivered Israel. There is no indication of how long he ruled, but the phrase "in the days of Shamgar" (5:6) suggests that it must have been for a lengthy time. His activity and influence seem to have been limited to the south of Israel, where the Philistines made repeated incursions, because the only exploit we hear about involves them. He killed six hundred Philistines with an ox goad (3:31), which is a long stick with an iron point at one end and a flat chisel-like iron at the other. It was not this unusual weapon but God's power that gave him the victory.

4:1—5:31
Deborah

At the end of chapter 3, we read that the land had peace and rest for eighty years (v. 30). We do not know when Ehud died, but a later generation no longer remembered what God had done through him. The long years of peace and prosperity should have confirmed the Israelites in the way of the Lord. Instead, it made them secure and indulgent. They did evil in the eyes of God (4:1), as their ancestors had done. The result was the Canaanite oppression (vv. 1–3) and the deliverance through Deborah (vv. 4–16). We also find a vivid description of the death of Sisera (vv. 7–24) and Deborah's song of victory (5:1–31).

4:1–3. Canaanite Oppression. The natural human tendency is to give in to evil desires that are difficult to restrain unless the heart is governed by a love for God. This time, the Lord sold the Israelites into the hand of Jabin, king of Canaan, who reigned in Hazor (4:2; see commentary on 2:11–23). The chief city in Galilee, Hazor was one of only three cities that were recorded as

---

Eglon's Coalition Against God's People

The Moabites were descendants of Lot (Gen. 19:30–38). They inhabited the plateau east of the Dead Sea (4,300 ft. [1,310 m] above it) between the river Arnon and the brook Zered in the south. At the time of the Exodus, they refused to allow the Israelites to pass through their territory (Judg. 11:17–18). During the period of the Judges and in the time of the monarchy, the Israelites repeatedly fought with the Moabites (3:14; 2 Sam. 8:2; 2 Kin. 3:24).

The Ammonites were also descendants of Lot (Gen. 19:30–38) and lived to the north of the Moabites between the rivers Arnon and Jabbok. At the Exodus, God did not give the land of the Ammonites to Israel (Deut. 2:19), but there was fighting repeatedly between Israel and Ammon (Judg. 3:13; 11:32; 1 Sam. 11:1–2, 11; 2 Sam. 10:6–14).

The Amalekites, a nomadic desert tribe, were descendants of Amalek, a grandson of Esau (Gen. 36:15–16). They dwelled in the area of the Negeb, south of the Dead Sea as far as Mount Sinai. The Israelites first encountered the Amalekites during their journey from Egypt to Canaan (Num. 14:25, 45; Deut. 25:17–18). They fought with Israel in the time of the Judges and later with Saul (1 Sam. 15:2–3) and David (30:11–20).

being burned by Joshua during the conquest of the promised land. The other two were Jericho and Ai (Josh. 6:24; 8:28). In time, however, Hazor was rebuilt and its king, Jabin, terrorized the Israelites in northern Canaan. This Jabin should not be confused with the Jabin of Joshua's time, a hundred years earlier (Josh. 11). Jabin was probably a popular family name like Amenhotep, Thutmose, and Ramesses in Egypt. His general, Sisera, lived in Harosheth of the Gentiles. A great number of Gentiles, it seems, had lived in this particular place, the location of which is unknown today. The fact that he had nine hundred chariots points to a place in the Valley of Jezreel rather than in the hills or mountains.

4:4–16. Deborah and Barak's Victory over Sisera. Deborah is unique among the judges not only because she was a woman but particularly for her unique role within Israel: she was a prophetess with juridical functions. There are only two other persons in the OT who were both prophets and judges: Moses (Ex. 18:16) and Samuel (1 Sam. 7:6, 15–17). This indicates that Deborah was the primary leader of Israel. As prophetess and judge, she resided in a centralized location that made it easier for Israelites all over Israel to come to her. As a prophet, she called Barak to be the military leader of the people and muster the troops (Judg. 4:6) and assured him victory. If Barak was unwilling to go on his own, it was because he understood that Deborah was, as prophetess and judge, the leader of Israel, and he wanted her by his side. She, as the leader of Israel and like Moses (see Ex. 17:8–9), was not personally involved in the fight, but her leadership in battle, based on cultural convictions, would take away the glory of the victory from Barak because a woman would defeat Sisera and another woman, Jael, would kill him.

Jael and her husband belonged to the house of Heber the Kenite, which at that time enjoyed peaceful relations with Jabin, the king of Hazor. The Kenites were a Canaanite tribe that was in some way related to the Moabites. Moses's father-in-law is called a Kenite and a Moabite (Judg. 1:16; Num. 10:29). The Kenite family joined the Israelites, and they settled in the land of Judah after the conquest. Perhaps this connection with the Israelites moved Jael to break the peace covenant with Jabin by killing Sisera in a dramatic way.

4:17–24. The Death of Sisera. Further evidence of Deborah's close connection with God is that her prophecy came true when the Israelite army defeated the armies of Jabin and when his military leader was killed by Jael. Since there were peaceful relations between the Kenites and Jabin, Sisera probably felt safe in the tent of Jael, who treated him very well at first. She seemed to have treated him like a child by giving him milk and covering him with a blanket to put him to sleep. He would not wake up from his sleep. When Barak found Sisera, he was lying dead on the floor of the tent. God uses whomever He wants to accomplish His purpose—Deborah: a woman, a judge, and a prophetess; Barak: a man who would go to war under the leadership of a woman, breaking cultural barriers; and Jael: a woman who was not an Israelite.

5:1–31. The Song of Deborah. Israel's triumph was celebrated with a victory song composed by Deborah and Barak in a standard literary form of the time. The wonderful deliverance by the hand of God from Jabin's oppression would be better and longer remembered through song than narrative prose; in this case we have both. The song divides itself into different stanzas, according to the subject matter addressed:

5:2–3 Introduction—The song begins with a general call to praise the Lord. God is praised because the leaders and the people worked together under His leadership and were victorious in battle. The unity of the people was the result of the grace of God and should have moved them to praise Him. This unity was a manifestation of God's blessing and was recognized as such.

5:4–5 The Coming of Yahweh—Deborah describes the majestic appearance of God from Edom in the east, coming to deliver His people. God manifested His presence through natural phenomena that contributed to the victory of His people. Deborah draws on the historical memory of the Exodus story, when God manifested Himself on Mount Sinai with thunder, lightning, and earthquake. With powerful poetic expressions she recounts that the rainstorm which broke over Sisera and his army was not an ordinary storm but was unleashed by Yahweh. This description of the coming of the Lord with power to deliver His people is an intrinsic element of the biblical hope and projects itself into the time of the end when deliverance from evil will be consummated.

5:6–8 Conditions Prior to the Battle—Deborah describes the sad conditions that prevailed in the country during the time of oppression before she arose as a mother in Israel. She mentions Shamgar and Jael as exceptions who left their mark during those dark days, when the highways were untraveled because there was no trade and commerce (v. 6). The fields were laid waste and the villagers (the meaning of this Hebrew word is uncertain) were inactive (v. 7). Because they worshiped pagan idols, the Lord deprived them of a peaceful life. Instead of the administration of justice in the city gates, there was war. The enemy appeared in their city gates, and the Israelites had neither arms nor the spirit to help themselves.

5:9–11 A Call to Participate—As a good leader, Deborah praised God for the unity of the leaders and the people to fight against the enemy. Under her there were also other princes, rulers of Israel whose example influenced the people, making them willing to support her call to war. She called on those who rode on white donkeys (i.e., those of rank and authority) and those who walked along the road (i.e., the rest of the people) to offer thanks to God for this great deliverance. They were encouraged to draw water in peace and rehearse the acts of the Lord in gratefulness when they returned to their city gates to resume a normal life.

5:12–18 The Mustering of the Tribes—The mobilization of the people began with a challenge to Israel's leaders to arise and prepare for war. The tribes from which people willingly came were Ephraim, Benjamin, Machir (the western half of Manasseh), Zebulun, and Issachar. Reuben, Gilead (the eastern half of Manasseh), Dan, and Asher are criticized for neglecting their fraternal duty. Zebulun and Naphtali receive special mention because their troops constituted the main body of Barak's army.

5:19–23 The Battle at the Waters of Megiddo—This stanza is about the battle itself, especially about God's decisive intervention. In this poem, the battle is no longer between Barak and Sisera but between Yahweh and the kings of Canaan and between heaven and earth. The waters of Megiddo most likely refer to the River Kishon, which apparently played an important role in the battle. The God who controlled nature was not Baal but Yahweh. The stars in their courses, which the Canaanites credited with controlling the weather, were directed by Yahweh to fight against Sisera by causing a mighty storm that swept away his chariots. The Angel of the Lord said to "curse Meroz" (v. 23). Meroz was probably a city near the field of battle that refused to get involved in the battle and in the pursuit of the fleeing enemy.

5:24–27 The Death of Sisera—The slaying of Sisera is vividly recounted. In contrast to the curse on Meroz, Jael is blessed for her deed.

Though not an Israelite, she preferred the friendship of Yahweh's people to that of their enemies. Her treachery is described in heroic terms.

5:28–30 Sisera's Mother—At the end of the poem, there are some ironic contrasts: the anxious wait of Sisera's mother and her ladies is contrasted with Jael's victory and honor. The mother's dark forebodings are contrasted with the cheerful explanations for the delay by her wisest ladies (v. 29). Finally, there is the contrast between the expectations of the women and the cruel reality the reader already knows.

5:31 Epilogue—Deborah concludes with a prayer for the destruction of all God's enemies and the exaltation of all His friends. The consequences of this victory were such that the land had peace and rest for forty years. In this victory over Jabin, God, as we already indicated, used different instruments. He raised Deborah, who as a judge led the people and gathered the troops. He selected Barak as the leader of the troops and also used Jael, a member of a foreign and weak tribe.

6:1—8:35
Gideon

As a result of renewed apostasy, Israel's troubles were repeated. This time they were oppressed by the Midianites (6:1-6). God rebuked His people (vv. 7–10) and sent an angel to Gideon (vv. 11–24), who destroyed Baal's altar (vv. 25–32), gathered an army (6:33—7:8), and found victory in God (7:9—8:21). Unfortunately, before he died his imperfections emerged (vv. 22–35).

6:1–6. Midianite Oppression. After forty years, the spirit of Deborah was a distant memory and the generation that had grown up during those forty years fell back into the sin of idolatry. This time God delivered them into the hands of the Midianites, who oppressed them for seven years (v. 1; cf. Lev. 26:21). Sadly, sin is always accompanied by its evil consequences. The plight of the Israelites under the Midianites and their allies, the people of the east, was worse than under their previous oppressors. The Israelites hid in dens and caves and barely had enough food to survive because of the devastation the Midianites inflicted on the Israelites by plundering their fields and storehouses and carrying off their animals. This was a military tactic that forced the Israelites to think mainly about how to obtain food and not about war. It was a way of breaking up the willingness of the people to plan and execute an act of insurrection.

6:7–10. Israel Rebuked by a Prophet. Before God sent a deliverer, He sent a prophet to reprove Israel for their sins, lead them to repentance, and get them ready for their deliverance. The unknown prophet reminded them of God's saving power as manifested in His work of delivering them from Egypt and saving them from those who oppressed them in the land of Canaan. The prophet refreshed the memory of the Israelites in order for them to trust and come to know God. Forgetting how the Lord had delivered them in the past weakened their knowledge of God, their dependence on His power, and their understanding of His great mercy, thus making them more vulnerable to idolatry. They had forgotten that God was able to fulfill His promises as manifested when He gave them the land. Now as they prepared to face the Amorites and their gods, the prophet appealed to the Israelites to trust and obey the Lord based on what He had done for them in the past. The prophet did not ignore the sin of the people; he charged them with idolatry because they worshiped the gods of the Amorites. Although this prophet did not explicitly promise a deliverer, his message from the Lord was the preamble for the coming deliverance; the Lord had not forsaken them.

6:11–24. The Angel of the Lord Visits Gideon. The person chosen to deliver Israel was Gideon, the son of Joash the Abiezrite, a descendant of Manasseh (Josh. 17:2). Joash was a worshiper of Baal. Gideon was commissioned by the Angel of Yahweh (v. 11; see "The Angel of the Lord," p. 395), identified in v. 14 with Yahweh Himself. The Angel of the Lord came to a particular tree (identified variously as a terebinth or oak) that apparently was a landmark in the local area. There are several places in Scripture where significant events are associated with trees (4:5; Gen. 18:1; Josh. 24:26; Mark 11:13–14, 20–23), but no particular reason is given for this practice. One can perhaps guess that in a land that was very hot during the summer, the shade of a tree would be an appealing place for a meeting. The Angel found Gideon threshing wheat, not on a threshing floor, which would have been the usual place, but in the winepress where no one would suspect to find wheat. Fear of the Midianites had crippled the economy and the daily lives of the Israelites.

Gideon's commissioning is similar to the call of Moses in Exodus 3. Both were hiding from the enemy, both were working for their father figures (father and father-in-law), and both received the same word of authorization (Judg. 6:14; Ex. 3:12). Like Moses, Gideon claimed that he was not qualified for the task (Judg. 6:15; Ex. 3:11); but again, like Moses, he received the assurance of divine aid and a sign affirming the call (Judg. 6:16–21; Ex. 3:12). The Lord equipped him with all the necessary qualifications for the execution of his commission. If the Lord calls someone to perform a task, He also provides the means to do it.

Israel's Oppressors During the Time of Gideon

The Midianites, seminomadic Bedouin, were the descendants of Abraham and Keturah (Gen. 25:1–6). Jethro, Moses's father-in-law, was a Midianite priest (Ex. 2:16–21). The elders of Moab and Midian hired Balaam to curse Israel on their way to Canaan (Num. 22–24), so the Lord gave the Midianites into the hands of the Israelites, who defeated them (31:1–11). In Isaiah 9:4 and 10:26, the victory of Gideon over Midian in Judges 6–8 is cited as a precedent for the coming defeat of the enemies of the kingdom of Judah.

People of the east (cf. Gen. 25:6) were nomadic groups that migrated from the Arabian Desert, often raiding settled communities on both sides of the river Jordan. Any of the people living to the east of the Israelites could be included in this designation.

The Amorites (Amurru in extra-biblical sources) appear very early in secular history. In Scripture they denote the pre-Israelite inhabitants of Canaan whom the Israelites were to destroy (Gen. 15:16; Deut. 20:17). In Joshua 10, five kings of the Amorites were defeated by Joshua, and one of those five was the king of Jerusalem (v. 5). Thus, Ezekiel 16:3 states that Jerusalem had an Amorite father and a Hittite mother. According to 2 Samuel 21, the remaining Amorites were the Gibeonites (v. 2), on whom Saul inflicted a great slaughter for which David later made atonement (vv. 3–14).

6:25–32. Gideon Destroys the Altar of Baal. Before Gideon could deliver Israel from the Midianites, he had to be a reformer. That same night, God commanded Gideon to destroy the cult of Baal and restore the worship of Yahweh in Israel (vv. 25–26). Both Baal and Asherah were fertility gods worshiped through sexual union with male and female temple prostitutes. Asherah was often represented by a pole-shaped image, which, in this story, Gideon was explicitly instructed to destroy. The story points to the impotence of Baal to defend himself against the attack of a person commission by the Lord to destroy his altar and replace it with an altar dedicated to the Lord (vv. 31–32).

6:33—7:8. Gideon Gathers an Army. While Gideon restored the worship of Yahweh, the Midianites and the eastern people made another raid into Israel and camped in the fertile Valley of Jezreel. We do not know whether it was the vast army of the enemy in the Valley of Jezreel or the burden of the enormous responsibility that made Gideon's faith falter, but he needed again the assurance that God was with him. His two-fold test with the fleece, progressing from the unusual (the dry ground around a wet fleece) to the inexplicable (the dry fleece on the wet ground), is a reminder that God is patient with our weak faith and that He is even willing to go along with our sometimes trivial and arbitrary "tests" in our search for assurance as we follow His call.

Gideon and his army encamped by the spring of Harod at the foot of Mount Gilead (7:1). The land of Gilead is on the eastern side of the Jordan river; however, a strong spring that was named "the well of Harod" has been found on the northern slope of Mt. Gilboa on the western side of the Jordan river, leading most Bible scholars to consider Mount Gilead to be the same as Mount Gilboa, where Saul later died at the eastern end of the Valley of Jezreel (1 Sam. 31). The army of the Midianites would have been on the north side of the range. Before Gideon was able to march out of the camp to meet the enemy, the Lord reduced the number of Israelites in two stages from 32,000 to 300. The first stage allowed those who were fearful and *khared* ("trembling"; Judg. 7:3) to go home. The spring seems to have taken its Hebrew name, *kharod* (v. 1), from this event. Perhaps their lack of faith in the Lord would have made them ineffective warriors. The true reason for reducing the size of the army was to clearly indicate that the victory would be from the Lord. The second stage in reducing the size of the army involved separating from the rest the three hundred who lapped water like dogs (v. 6). The three hundred used their hands as a dog uses its tongue to scoop up the water while they remained on their feet, perhaps watchful and prepared for any emergency, while the rest knelt down to drink; that is, they were mainly interested in their thirst. Nothing prevents the Lord from saving by "many or by few" (1 Sam. 14:6).

7:9—8:3. Gideon's Victory. Having watched his army dwindle to almost nothing, Gideon may have had more doubts about defeating the enemy. God encouraged him to move ahead anyway, despite his doubts, for He was going to be with him. But God understood the inner feelings of Gideon and allowed, without condemnation, for events to develop that would help him overcome his fears. By arranging for Gideon to witness, through the soldiers' dreams and conversation, the fear and terror in the Midianite camp, God strengthened Gideon's faith and reassured him of victory. This is a remarkable insight into the way that God patiently waits for us, even while He urges us to take Him at His word and move ahead.

Gideon divided the army into three companies and provided them with trumpets (ram's horns) and pitchers containing unlit torches. The reason for the pitcher is not given, but it could be that its function was to increase the level of noise when broken. Apparently, none of the soldiers had a sword or at least none were provided for them. The reason for this most strange phenomenon was that the Lord Himself would fight for Israel, using the enemies' swords as they killed each other. Certainly, the military strategy was uncommon but, in this case, highly effective. The Israelites were required only to make a disturbance by shouting and breaking the pitchers and lighting the torches, giving the impression of being a huge army, but it would be the Lord who would instill fear in the enemy, defeating them from within.

Intertribal relationships were a major challenge for Israel during the time of the Judges. The Ephraimites' jealousy of Gideon's leadership and stunning success showed that they were less interested in God's miraculous deliverance than in sharing the glory and the spoils that God's deliverance brought. Fortunately, as the text indicates, they limited their reaction to a sharp rebuke rather than an actual fight, which might, in those times, have been expected. This is the first time in Judges that the threat of a civil war emerges, but it is not the last. Although invited at the last moment to help pursue the Midianites, the Ephraimites went out and assisted Gideon. It was after their involvement in the war that they argued with Gideon, whose answer is a great example of excellent leadership and self-denial and shows that envy is best handled by humility; as Scripture says, a gentle response defuses anger (Prov. 15:1).

8:4–21. Pursing the Enemy. Gideon's pursuit of the fleeing Midianites had two purposes. First, he wanted to complete the defeat of the enemy. While 120,000 had been killed, 15,000 had escaped (v. 10). Second, he was determined to avenge the murder of his brothers (v. 19). Believing that God was still on his side, he took only the three hundred men with him who had witnessed the miracle of the Midianite defeat. Having limited resources is not a problem for a God who can use the few and the many to accomplish His purposes.

The arrogance and rudeness of the men of Succoth/Sukkoth and Penuel/Peniel in refusing to provide food to Gideon may have been based on craven self-interest. Penuel (initially spelled "Peniel" in Gen. 32:31; the term means "the face of God") is an Israelite town five miles (8 km) east of Succoth along the River Jabbok. It was in this place that Jacob had his life-changing encounter with God when he wrestled with God "face to face" (Gen. 32:22–32). Because Gideon had not yet caught two of the kings of Midian, the leaders of the two towns cynically ignored God's obvious presence in Gideon's campaign and cast their lot with those they thought likely to win the contest. They chose to join the ones who would be totally defeated. Gideon showed his continuing dependence on God by withholding judgment on their arrogance until God, not his own military prowess, vindicated him in the capture of the Midianite kings.

According to Judges 8:4, Gideon's triumph over the remaining 15,000 Midianites who fled further east was again accomplished by God using only the 300 men. The strategy was similar: surprise and rout. We are not told whether Gideon's small army had to engage in physical fighting on this occasion or whether the rout occurred in the same way as the first one: confusion and self-destruction. Either way, it completely vindicated Gideon's faith, and his return to Penuel doubtlessly struck terror into the men of that town. Gideon kept his word and tore down the tower but also killed the men of the town. Israelites were now killing Israelites,

suggesting that Gideon saw himself now as a military leader ready to inflict punishment as he saw fit. We are not told why the judgement was harsher than what Gideon would soon execute on the men of Succoth. It is not unreasonable to surmise that at least some of the men decided to protect the tower, and in destroying the tower Gideon had to dispose of them. The men of Succoth, on the other hand, received exactly the punishment, unusual as it was, that Gideon had promised.

The judgment on the Midianites was completed with the execution of the two kings. They had murdered Gideon's large family and would receive the just reward for their heinous act. Perhaps, in his righteous anger, Gideon wanted to further humiliate the kings at the moment of their death by having them killed by a boy. If that was his purpose, he was disappointed, and the two prisoners, to their credit, honorably reminded Gideon that conducting an execution is not a job for a boy. Gideon killed the kings and took the spoils of war.

8:22–35. Gideon's Wisdom and Weaknesses. The words of the kings describing Gideon's appearance as that of the son of a king, as well as the recognition he had received by delivering Israel from the Midianites, may have moved some Israelite leaders to ask him to rule over them. This request possibly meant that he would become their king and establish a dynasty or hereditary kingship. Gideon's refusal was based on a theological conviction: God was the king of Israel. Gideon's refusal of the offered crown is an excellent indication of his noble intent in following the Lord and of Gideon's strength of character. It takes a strong person to resist flattery from a crowd that wishes to confer power. However, at the very moment of his greatest, God-given achievement, Gideon made what seemed a small concession to vanity by asking for some of the plunder to make an ephod, a priestly garment used to consult the Lord through the Urim and Thummim (Ex. 28:6–14). Gideon's beautiful ephod became an idol probably because it appeared as a way of access to God. While the text is vague, Gideon's desire to make an ephod led to idolatry.

Even if Gideon himself didn't take that step, his community eventually treated the ephod as an idol. Gideon's unwise action had dire consequences for the people of Israel. It became a snare to Gideon and his family (lit. "house"; Judg. 8:27). Because it caused the people to abandon the legitimate sanctuary and worship his ephod, it proved to be damaging to his family and to the nation. This illustrates what happens when a great leader uses his influence to take others down a wrong path. It should alert us to keep our eyes on the One who is above any human leader and who will never mislead us. We can only put our ultimate trust in God and not on imperfect human beings. Spiritual leaders should always abide by the will of God.

8:29–35. The Collapse of the Reformation.

After Gideon's death, the new generation who had not experienced the miraculous deliverance from the oppression by the Midianites returned to the worship of Baal, even making Baal-Berith ("Baal of the covenant") their god (8:33). By regarding Baal as a god who had made a covenant with Israel, they had substituted him for Yahweh, the real covenant God (Deut. 4:23), resulting in a false system of worship. No one can live on the religious experience of one's ancestors. Each one must have a living relationship with God. In the case of the newer generation of Israelites, they forgot not only God but also what Gideon had done for them. It is often the sad case that those who turn away from God also mistreat other human beings; their humanness is damaged because only God can renew His image in us.

9:1–57
ISRAEL'S EXPERIMENT WITH MONARCHY

Chapter 9 further develops the story of Gideon and his family. Abimelech, son of Gideon, became king after murdering his brothers (vv. 1–6). Jotham's fable doomed Abimelech and Shechem (vv. 7–21), and it was soon fulfilled (vv. 22–57).

9:1–6
Abimelech's Conspiracy

The apostasy of Israel after the death of Gideon was not punished by the invasion of some neighboring people, as previously, but by a bloody civil strife. God did not call Abimelech (sometimes transliterated as "Abimelek," meaning "my father is king") to deliver Israel from any oppression. He was Gideon's son by a concubine in Shechem, about fifty miles (80.5 km) north of Jerusalem. Shechem was the place where Abram first built an altar to Yahweh after arriving in Canaan (Gen. 12:6–7). With support from his mother's family and the leaders in Shechem and with money from the pagan temple, Abimelech conspired

against Gideon's family. His appeal revolved around the natural assumption that some individual from Gideon's dynasty would rule over the people of Shechem, and since that was inevitable, it should at least be someone from the families of Shechem. Consequently, he murdered all but one of his half-brothers, Gideon's other sons. Following Abimelech's utterly wicked deed, the people of Shechem and Beth-Millo crowned him king beside the terebinth tree (thought to be an oak) at the pillar in Shechem (Judg. 9:6). The pillar most likely was the witness stone that Joshua set up in Shechem (Josh. 24:26–27).

9:7–21
Jotham's Fable

Jotham, the only survivor among the sons of Gideon, confronted the people of Shechem with the nature of their choice and warned them of their fate by telling a fable about the trees of the forest seeking to appoint a king over them. According to the parable, the trees began their search by asking other trees, based on their size, to be king over all them. They began with the olive tree and then went to the fig tree. Finally, they went to the vine. The trees' response was always the same: each of them was pleased with its God-given role in nature—something that Abimelech was not willing to be. Finally, the trees went to the thorny bush, which is commonly found on the hills of the land. The fable becomes ironical when the bramble asked the tall trees to come and find protection under its shadow—things that the thorny bramble could not provide. This bush was good only for igniting a fire that could extend over the land. It would easily destroy the trees.

Through the fable, Jotham charged the inhabitants of Shechem with not acting in good faith when choosing Abimelech as king. They were the trees of the forest in the fable, and the king was the bramble, which was a source of fire. They were not thinking about the best for Israel but for what they thought was good for them. The message of the fable was that their experiment with kingship in Israel in the person of Abimelech would fail. There would be internal dissension and self-destruction, bringing kinship to an end.

9:22–57
Abimelech's Decline and Fall

Little is said about Abimelech's reign, except that it lasted three years and that his people rebelled against him. They grew uneasy with his government and chose a man by the name of Gaal to lead the rebellion. Judges does not mention whether Gaal was an Israelite or a Canaanite, but v. 23 tells us that God stirred up animosity or ill will between the people of Shechem and Abimelech by sending them a spirit of conflict (Heb. *ra'*—the word often used for "evil"). This is similar to the "evil [sometimes translated as "harmful" or "distressing"] spirit from God" that came upon Saul (1 Sam. 16:15) and the "lying spirit" that the Lord put into the mouths of Ahab's prophets (1 Kin. 22:23). In each case, when human beings turn away from God, they open themselves to the influence of the adversary, and God allows evil spirits to interfere in their lives.

As anticipated by Jotham, there was war between the inhabitants of Shechem and Abimelech. He destroyed the city and mercilessly killed common people and their leaders. The narrative depicts Abimelech as a mad, irrational man aiming at destruction, like a wildfire. His final fate occurred during his senseless attack against the town of Thebez. Millstones were made from two circular stones, usually basalt, one or two feet (30 to 60 cm) in diameter and two to four inches (5 to 10 cm) thick. An unknown woman transformed an ordinary kitchen utensil into a weapon that mortally wounded the king. At the last moment of life, Abimelech was concerned about dying with a damaged reputation based on the cultural conviction that being killed by a woman was shameful; he asked his armor-bearer to kill him. The record explicitly affirms that God's hand was in all of these events as a specific punishment against Abimelech for the treatment of his father's family and as a punishment of the various groups that had directly or indirectly allied themselves with him (Judg. 9:56–57).

10:1—16:31
RULE OF THE LATER JUDGES

This section of the book of Judges deals with two major leaders—Jephthah and Samson, whose activities are recounted in some detail—and five minor judges about whose work we hear very little: Tola, Jair, Ibzan, Elon, and Abdon. The oppressors during this time period were the Ammonites and the Philistines.

10:1–5
Tola and Jair

Chapter 10 begins by describing the rise of Tola ("worm"), the son of Puah, to save Israel (v. 1).

Perhaps, similarly to Abimelech, Tola was raised up to save Israel from the corruption in Israel's religious and social life and to provide a period of stable administration. Although he was from the tribe of Issachar, he lived in the hill country of Ephraim and judged Israel for twenty-three years.

Tola was followed by Jair ("may [God] enlighten") of Gilead, who lived east of the Jordan River. He judged Israel during twenty-two peaceful years. His only claim to fame was his thirty sons, who ruled over thirty towns and rode on donkeys, a sign of wealth and prominence (see 5:10; 1 Sam. 25:20). Thirty sons also meant he had several wives, another sign of wealth, but not in harmony with God's will for His people.

10:6—12:7
Jephthah

The story of Jephthah follows a vivid description of the Ammonites' oppression of the people (10:6–16). He was appointed as the instrument of liberation (10:17—11:11) and at first tried diplomacy, but it failed (11:12–28). He made a vow, went to war, and returned victorious (12:29–40). Unfortunately, there was a conflict between him and the Ephraimites (vv. 1–7).

10:6–16. Israel Oppressed Again. Idolatry, which seemed to have been contained during the rules of Tola and Jair, flourished again after their demise. Not only did the worship of Baal and Asherah prosper, but the gods of all the surrounding nations (Syria [Aram], Sidon, Moab, Ammon, and Philistia) were venerated. Therefore, the Lord gave His people into the hands of the Ammonites and the Philistines.

It is likely that the eighteen years of oppression by the Ammonites—primarily in the Transjordan but also in the territory of Judah and Benjamin—and the forty years of the Philistine harassment west of the Jordan began at the same time. The Ammonite oppression is recounted first (chaps. 10–12), followed by the story of the Philistines and their harassment of the Israelites (chaps. 13–16).

After eighteen years of oppression, the Israelites finally realized that their misery was the result of their own sinful actions: the rejection of Yahweh and the worship of foreign gods (10:10). As in the case of the Midianite oppression, the Lord did not immediately respond positively (6:7–10). First, He issued a stern reprimand by reminding them how many times

He had rescued them in the past (10:11–12), beginning with the Exodus and ending with the unknown Maonites, possibly another name for the Midianites because they are missing in the catalogue of past deliverances. In the Greek translation of the OT, the Midianites are listed in place of the Maonites.

As in Judges 1:2, the text does not mention how this dialogue between Yahweh and the Israelites was conducted, whether through an itinerant prophet or through the tabernacle. Yet Yahweh's message was clear in both instances. Since every time He saved them, they forsook Him and went back to idol worship, now God was not interested in rescuing them (10:13). In fact, He sarcastically told them to go and cry out to the idols they had been worshiping to save them (v. 14). Yet, the Israelites did not give up. They repeated their confession of guilt and initiated a reform by cleansing the land of idols and serving the Lord (v. 16). The Lord could no longer bear Israel's misery (v. 16); that is, He accepted their repentance and helped them. Anger is not God's last word to sinners. There is always hope for sinners who turn from their sins and humbly submit themselves to the mercy of God.

10:17—11:11. Jephthah and the Gileadites. When the Ammonites mobilized for one of their

The Philistines

According to Scripture, the Philistines (the meaning of the name is uncertain) originally came from Caphtor, or Crete (Jer. 47:4; Amos 9:7), and were descendants of Ham from the same line as the Egyptians (Gen. 10:6, 14). They first appear in Scripture during the patriarchal period (see Gen. 21:32; 26:1). They were later blended with a group of people that migrated from the Aegean to various places in the eastern Mediterranean in the thirteenth century. Known in history as the Sea Peoples, these migrants caused the downfall of the Hittite Empire but were repulsed by the armies of Ramesses III when they attempted to invade Egypt. Denied entrance to Egypt, they settled on the southern coast of the Holy Land, where they assimilated with the local population, retaining the name (Philistines) of the locals, and were a threat to the Israelites until the time of David, when he made them his subjects (1 Chr. 18:1–2).

annual campaigns, the Gileadites decided to make a stand at Mizpah in Gilead (the location of which is unknown). However, they discovered that they had no one to lead them. It was then that Jephthah ("he [God?] has opened [the womb?]") the Gileadite—cast out by his family because his mother was a prostitute—appears in the narrative (11:1–3). According to Deuteronomy 23:2, such persons could not enter the congregation of the Lord, probably referring to the governing assembly of the people. Rejected by his family, Jephthah lived on the edges of society in the land of Tob, probably southern Syria. Gathering like-minded people around him, he made a name for himself as a strong leader by raiding villages.

This seems to be the first time that a judge in Israel was chosen by the people and not by God (Judg. 3:9, 15; 4:4; 6:14). But Jephthah certainly had the approval of God, as indicated by the spirit of the Lord coming upon him (11:29). The story of Jephthah teaches us to be careful in how we treat those on the edges of society because they also are children of God whom He can use in moments of need. And those who are slighted and ill-treated should leave it to God to let their light shine.

11:12–28. Jephthah and the Ammonites. By misrepresenting history, the king of Ammon tried to justify his invasion of Gilead (v. 13). Jephthah corrected the king's misrepresentation by letting history speak for itself. It is notable that Jephthah, the outcast, without the advantages of cultural approbation, was able to present such an eloquent appeal to the history of his people. In a way that the feckless leaders in Gilead apparently could not do, Jephthah inspired his community with a declaration of their identity as God's people. He knew who he was and who his people were. This is a lesson for us today. God's people must know that they *are* His people, and that requires a solid understanding of how God has led them and taught them in past history. Jephthah appealed to Yahweh to render judgment between the Israelite and the Ammonite peoples. Certainly, Jephthah preferred a peaceful resolution, but God provided judgment another way.

Because the king of Ammon was not interested in a settlement, war seemed inevitable (v. 28). The reference to Moab and the god Chemosh (vv. 24–25) seems to indicate that in the time of Jephthah, the Ammonites had occupied the land of Moab, south of the Arnon river, before marching against Israel. Jephthah, therefore, spoke to the king of Ammon as the successor of the king of Moab. The three hundred years (v. 26) represent the time from Israel's conquest of Heshbon under Moses (Num. 21:25–26) until the time of Jephthah.

11:29–40. Jephthah's Vow and Victory. In spite of Jephthah's attempt to come to a peaceful resolution of the conflict, the king of the Ammonites chose to fight. Before going to war, Jephthah made a vow to Yahweh, promising to offer as a burnt offering to Him whatever would come through the doors of his house to meet him upon his return (v. 31) if the Lord would give the Ammonites into his hands. Did Jephthah plan to sacrifice a human being? (See "Jephthah's Vow," p. 408). In those days, animals and human beings lived together in one house. In hindsight, we know that this vow was wrong, but for him it was an expression of his dependence on and faith in God. He knew he was utterly dependent on Yahweh, as the God of Israel's history, for his victory over the Ammonites. It is this faith that caused him to be mentioned in the list of the faithful in Hebrews 11:32.

12:1–7. Jephthah's Conflict with Ephraim. Jealousy and pride are a dangerous combination. In 8:1, the Ephraimites, the largest of the tribes in the north, were upset with Gideon because he had not called them to battle the Midianites. In chapter 12, they were angry with Jephthah, threatening to burn down his house because he had not called them to fight against the Ammonites, so they claimed (v. 1). This was a powerful challenge to Jephthah's leadership.

Jephthah's Vow

Much has been written about Jephthah's sacrifice. The two major positions are that (a) he did literally sacrifice his daughter as a burnt offering or (b) he did not sacrifice her but dedicated her to service in the sanctuary of the Lord as a perpetual virgin.

1. *She Was a Sacrifice.* These are some of the arguments for the first position: (1) Jephthah vowed to offer a burnt offering (Heb. *'olah*), and the text clearly says that he did to her as he had vowed (Judg. 11:39). (2) There is no indication in the text that she was dedicated to the service of the Lord as was Samuel (1 Sam. 1:28). (3) Why would a custom be established to bewail her fate if she was going to serve the Lord? To belong to the Lord was a position of honor, not a fate to be lamented. (4) Jephthah's and her grief indicate that she met a pitiable fate, not a position of honor. (5) This has been the position of most church fathers and commentators throughout history.

2. *She was Not a Sacrifice.* These are some of the arguments for the second position: (1) Scripture expressly forbids human sacrifice (Lev. 18:21; 20:2–5; Deut. 12:31). Jephthah must have been acquainted with these laws of Moses. (2) The Hebrew conjunction *waw* in Judges 11:31 ("and") should be taken as a disjunctive particle and translated as "or." The text would then read, "it shall be the LORD's, or I will offer it up as a burnt offering." (3) The text does not say he sacrificed her, but that he did to her according to his vow (v. 39). (4) She wept over her unmarried state, not about being condemned to die (vv. 37–38). (5) That he literally sacrificed her does not harmonize with what we know from other texts about Jephthah. The Bible portrays him as a man of high principles. Samuel accords him a place of honor (1 Sam. 12:11) and Hebrews 11:32 lists him among the heroes of faith.

3. *Lessons to Learn.* Throughout this story, God is silent. We know God gave Jephthah His Spirit and the victory over the Ammonites, but did He accept the child sacrifice, if such it was? While the first view has the strong support of the text, the second view remains a possibility. Whatever the case, some important lessons can be learned from this story. First, even the greatest heroes of faith may have weak moments, as did Jephthah prior to going into battle. We look forward to the moment when sinful human nature will be transformed at the coming of our Lord. Second, our vows to God should not be bargains to purchase the favor of God because His favor cannot be purchased with good works, money, or special vows. Third, we should make sure that our vows correspond to God's revealed will, and once we make them, we should keep them. Vows should be carefully thought through and not made rashly.

He rejected their complaint. First, he had to act at once because they were attacked, and second, he did call them but received no help. Chapter 11 neither confirms nor denies that he sent for the Ephraimites. And third, it was the Lord who gave him the victory over the Ammonites (12:3). Therefore, there was no need to proudly feel that his prowess had defeated the enemy; it was the Lord's doing. Why should they feel slighted because the Lord used him to His glory?

It may seem inconceivable to us that a civil war that resulted in the death of forty-two thousand Ephraimites was provoked simply by their leaders' petty jealousy of Jephthah. Some of those deaths certainly occurred in the actual fighting, and some occurred when Ephraimites were caught and executed in their attempt to escape back across the Jordan. The text makes it clear that the Gileadites were inspired in the slaughter by the arrogant bigotry of the Ephraimites, who viewed the Gileadites as inferiors. Differences in pronunciation are known to have also existed along the Nile so that the Egyptians in the delta pronounced words slightly differently than those along the Nile River Valley, causing those who lived upriver to mock the delta dwellers. This account confirms (vv. 6–7) that pronunciation was a basis for prejudice in other parts of the ancient world. The word *shibbolet* means "torrent" or "stream." Scripture makes no overt judgment against the Gileadites for the clever dialect trap they set to capture and execute escaping Ephraimites. But this sad and completely unnecessary civil war is a reminder of the damage caused by letting jealousy divide families and churches, and it is an admonition regarding the consequences of setting little "tests" to identify the "other" and exact retribution. The civil war was a clear sign that Israel was losing the sense of oneness and was in the process of collapsing from within. The back-and-forth from serving God to abandoning Him was beginning to have a major impact on the people and would climax with a final civil war (chap. 20).

12:8–15
Ibzan, Elon, and Abdon

Three of the six minor judges followed Jephthah. Ibzan came from Bethlehem. Scholars suspect that this was the Bethlehem in Zebulun (Josh. 19:15), not the Bethlehem in Judah (Judg. 17:7) where Jesus was later born. This suspicion is based on the tribal identity of the next judge (Elon) and the fact that Zebulun was a prominent tribe at this time. This identification, however, is not certain. Ibzan judged Israel for seven years and was remembered for his large family of sons and daughters (12:8–10).

His successor, Elon, who judged Israel for ten years, came from Zebulun. The location of the town of Aijalon (v. 12), where he was buried, is unknown. However, the city is to be distinguished from the Aijalon mentioned in Joshua 10:12, where the sun stood still, and from the Aijalon in Joshua 19:42, which was in the south, in the territory of Dan.

Pirathon, the town of Abdon (Judg. 12:13), who judged Israel eight years, was in the hill country of Ephraim, the heartland of northern Israel. The mountains/hill country of the Amalekites (v. 15) probably refers to an Amalekite settlement in this place before Israel entered Canaan. Abdon also had forty sons and thirty grandsons. The fact that nothing important is referred to during the rule of these three judges may indicate a happy state of affairs, without apostasies, but as we see in the next chapter, that did not last long.

13:1—16:31
Samson

Samson is an exceptional figure in the OT. Two things stand out in regard to Samson's life. First, he was the only judge who was chosen by God before he was born to be a judge. Second, by divine fiat he was born a Nazirite, set apart for God, like John the Baptist (Luke 1:15). In contrast to Barak, Gideon, and Jephthah, Samson never went into battle at the head of an Israelite army. His lot was to fight the Philistines alone. Therefore, his battles look like personal quarrels and acts of revenge, but he was led by the Spirit of the Lord and did what the judges were called to do—fight the oppressor. Although the Philistines continued to oppress Israel after Samson's death, he began to deliver Israel from the power (lit. "hand") of the Philistines (Judg. 13:5).

13:1–25. Birth of Samson. The background to the story of Samson is the oppression by the Philistines because the children of Israel had again done what was evil in the Lord's sight (v. 1). This time no cry was heard for deliverance, but God in His mercy raised up a deliverer for them. Twice the Angel of the Lord (see 2:1–5) appeared to Manoah's wife and not to Manoah. Since she would have to live with a particular attention to lifestyle choices during pregnancy and would be the primary caregiver to the child after he was born, God spoke directly to her, as He had to Hagar (Gen. 16:17–14). God gave her the instructions directly—directions that He would not fully repeat to Manoah, even though He would appear to Manoah in answer to his prayer (Judg. 13:8–14). God told Manoah's wife that her barrenness would come to an end and that her son would be a Nazirite from birth (cf. Luke 1:13–17, 26–38).

When she told her husband what had happened, she called the Angel a "man of God" (*'elohim*; v. 6). The same expression appears elsewhere in Scripture to describe Moses and Samuel (Deut. 33:1; 1 Sam. 9:6). Yet, she also said that His appearance was like that of an angel of God (Judg. 13:6), perhaps realizing that this was not just another human being. When asked for His name, the Angel of the Lord responded evasively with "*pil'i*," which can be understood in two ways: (1) the name "Wonderful," as in Isaiah 9:6, or (2) an expression of His nature, which is beyond human comprehension (cf. Ps. 139:6). There are secret things that do not belong to us (Deut. 29:29).

Manoah's reaction was natural for sinful beings. Ever since the Garden of Eden, sinners have been terrified in the presence of God (Is. 6:5). The final verses of chapter 13 describe the fulfillment of God's promise: the barren womb is revived and a son is born. Where there was sadness, there is now joy. Where there was despair, there is now thankfulness, evidence that with God no situation is hopeless, not in Israel nor in our lives today.

The name Samson derives from the Hebrew word *shemesh* ("sun"). Thus "sunny" or "child of the sun" are possible translations, expressing the hope of the parents for his life. How different it turned out to be once his childhood was over. In fact, his career revolved around two Philistine women: the woman of Timnah, whom he married (chaps. 14–15), and then Delilah, with whom he had an affair (chap. 16). Both betrayed him to his enemies by revealing his secrets. Sandwiched between the two stories is a brief encounter with a third woman (vv. 1–3). And yet, during the twenty years he judged Israel, Samson was a hero whom the Lord blessed and used to punish Israel's oppressors.

14:1–20. Samson's Wedding. Samson's marriage to the Philistine girl is a typical case of passion dominating reason. To his parents' serious objection, he simply said that she pleased him (lit. "she is right in my own eyes"; 14:3). He was not willing to do what was right in God's eyes and in that sense his life illustrated the condition of the Israelites. Despite the fact that God had specifically forbidden marriages with the inhabitants of Canaan (Deut. 7:3–4), she pleased him well and that, for him, was more important. No matter that as a Nazirite he had to remain ceremonially clean; reason and the fear of God were set aside and passion and stubborn determination controlled him. It is not difficult for humans even today to go down the same road, ruining their service for God and their lives.

Verse 4 raises an important question. Did the spirit of God purposely guide him into this marriage or did God use Samson's mistake to confront Israel's enemies in a way that was different from what He had done through previous judges and their armies? James 1:13 states that God does not tempt anyone to do evil; He simply *allows* human beings to do evil actions. In other words, He does not instigate them. Nevertheless, in Hebrew thinking what God allows is credited to Him; it is as if He has done it (Is. 45:7). Hence, it is said that He hardened Pharaoh's heart (Ex. 7:3), yet at the same time we are told that Pharaoh hardened his own heart (8:15, 32). The same applies to Samson's activities. God allowed him to follow his own passions but used the occasion to achieve something good for Israel.

The episode with the lion served as a sign for Samson that the Lord was with him and would enable him to defeat the Philistines (Judg. 14:6). At the wedding, Samson proposed a riddle and a wager (v. 12). It was not uncommon in ancient times to ask difficult questions or propose riddles at entertainments or weddings. However, it was somewhat reckless of Samson to make a game about possibly giving away the secret to the strength that God had given him; he should have better kept it a secret. In v. 15, the Hebrew text says that the Philistines threatened his bride on the seventh day (as appearing in some translations), but this does not fit with the three days mentioned in v. 14. Other translations follow the Septuagint and the Syriac translation that read "on the fourth day." The Hebrew words for "seventh" (*shebi'i*) and "fourth" (*rebi'i*) differ only by one Hebrew consonant (*sh* to *r*), suggesting a copying error. Furthermore, Samson's confession is easier to understand if she badgered him for several days and not only on the seventh day. In fact, v. 17 indicates that she had wept all seven days of the feast. This would mean she was unhappy from the start that he had not told her the secret.

Samson's reaction to the betrayal of his wife is the first of his spirit-directed actions against the Philistines. This unusual affair provided an obvious lesson to the Philistines that Samson was no ordinary Israelite and an obvious lesson to Samson that his romance with the Philistine woman had been a very bad idea. From God's point of view, the immediate breakup of Samson's marriage was in Samson's best interest. True friendship could not exist between the Israelites and Philistines. Marriages between believers and unbelievers are rarely successful.

15:1-8. Growing Conflict with the Philistines.
The two incidents narrated in this passage illustrate how the relationship between Samson and the Philistines quickly deteriorated on account of his marriage to a Philistine woman. In the first one, he announced that this time what he would do to the Philistines would be well deserved. According to him, the fact that his wife was given to someone else justified his act of retaliation, which consisted of burning the grain fields, vineyards, and olive trees of the Philistines. Using foxes sounds cruel; but for Samson, seemingly oblivious to such a concern, the foxes served to do much damage in a short period of time. The second incident was motivated by the execution of Samson's wife and father-in-law once the Philistines understood why Samson had destroyed their fields. As revenge, Samson attacked the Philistines, slaughtering many of them, and promised after this last attack to stop his rampage against them.

15:9-20. Victory at Ramath Lehi.
The circle of violence continued, and this time the Philistines prepared to go against the tribe of Judah. What seems to be surprising is the fact that the Israelites were not willing to attack their oppressors. They had resigned themselves to their condition to the point that they were willing to betray Samson. At no point in the Samson narrative is it said that the Israelites prayed to the Lord to deliver them from the oppression of the Philistines. God of His own initiative raised Samson to begin delivering Israel from them (13:5). It was therefore almost natural for the Israelites to tell the Philistines that what Samson was doing was his own business; he did not have their support. Nevertheless, the Lord used Samson's arrest to inflict a significant defeat on the Philistines. His victory was credited to the Spirit of the Lord, which fell on him with great power.

Samson's song of victory (15:16) contains a wordplay. In Hebrew, the words "donkey" and "heap" are homonyms (they have the same spelling). Hence some translate the line as "with a donkey's jawbone I have made donkeys out of them." Another possible translation is "with the jawbone of a donkey, heaps upon heaps," referring to the many people he killed.

God performed a miracle and created a spring in that place which still existed in the time of the author of the book. Samson called that place En Hakkore, meaning "caller's spring" (v. 19). The epilogue in v. 20 highlights the fact that, after his great victory, Samson was finally identified as judge in Israel, a position to which God had called him and which he held for twenty years.

16:1-3. Samson and the Prostitute.
In Hebrews 11:32, Samson is a man of faith; in the book of Judges, we primarily see his other side—Samson, a man of strong passions. At the beginning of his judgeship, Samson went to Timnah and saw a woman (16:1). He desired her and made her his wife, at least for a short time. Toward the end of his judgeship, he went to Gaza and saw a prostitute and slept with her (v. 1). Like David, Samson's sin began in his eyes, his look gave birth to his desire, and his desire brought forth the sinful act. Indeed, the human heart *is* deceitful above all things and desperately sick and wicked (Jer. 17:9), and Satan knows our weaknesses better than we do. There may be a connection between Samson's action and the spiritual condition of the people. The man chosen by God to be His instrument engaged in literal harlotry while the people of God engaged in spiritual harlotry. Samson embodied the despicable condition of God's people.

By giving in to his sinful passions, Samson placed his life in danger. We do not know whether somebody tipped him off or whether his guilty conscience was the cause, but he left at midnight and no one dared approach him. He tore the gate out by its foundations and carried it about 40 miles (64.4 km) to a hill facing Hebron (Judg. 16:4), the leading city of Judah at that time, where he left it as a tangible war trophy. This was a superhuman feat, considering that the gate must have weighed several hundred pounds. Furthermore, Gaza was close to the Mediterranean coast while Hebron was more than 3,000 feet (914.4 m) above sea level in the Judean mountains. By removing the gate of the city, Samson was sending a message to the Philistines. When facing him, the Philistines were as vulnerable as a city without a gate.

16:4-31. Samson and Delilah.
Not long after the Gaza episode, Samson found another Philistine woman in the Valley of Sorek (v. 4), about 13 miles (21 km) southwest of Jerusalem. It was the border between the territories of the Philistines and the Israelites. More than once, the

love of women had resulted in physical and spiritual danger for Samson. Once the relationship between Samson and Delilah became known, the rulers of the Philistines offered Delilah 5,500 pieces (shekels) of silver if she could find out the secret of his strength and how he could be overcome. This was an enormous amount of silver when we consider that David bought the threshing floor and the oxen of Araunah for fifty shekels (2 Sam. 24:24) and that the wages offered to the Levite were only ten shekels a year (Judg. 17:10).

The story unfolds in four episodes. Three times Samson played a hazardous game of brinkmanship with her but refused to give up his secret (16:6–9, 10–14). The fourth time, worn out by her constant demand for mutual trust, he revealed to her that he was a Nazirite and that the secret was his long hair (vv. 16–17). He was quickly captured by the Philistines, and the eyes that saw the woman (14:1) and the prostitute (16:1) were blinded and could see no more. What is amazing is that in the first three episodes the Spirit of God did not leave him. Only when he revealed the secret of his power and his head was shaved—after the Nazirite vow was totally broken—did the Spirit of God depart from him. The condition of Samson was now like the condition of the oppressed people of Israel. The Lord departed from him, and he was to be oppressed by the Philistines. The fact that God bears His wayward children long is a great comfort to Christians today and should lead all to repentance (Rom. 2:4).

The Philistines took Samson to Gaza and set him to work grinding grain in prison like an animal. Weak, blind, imprisoned, degraded to the most menial service, Samson found his way back to God. As a sign that God had not completely forsaken him, his hair grew again and with it his strength gradually returned. God restored him so he could at last do what he was destined to do—to begin to deliver Israel from the Philistines.

At a feast in honor of Dagon, the grain god, all the lords of the Philistines were assembled in the temple of Dagon, rejoicing in the capture of Samson. He was hauled out of prison to entertain them (16:25). We are not told what kind of entertainment he performed. The Hebrew word used here means to "laugh," "joke," or "amuse." Just seeing him blind and bound like an animal may have amused them. Standing between two main pillars that supported the roof of the temple crowded with people,

Samson prayed to Yahweh to strengthen him one more time so he could have revenge against the Philistines (v. 28). According to most translations, Samson's prayer was for one act of vengeance (or vengeance "at once" or "with one blow") for his "two eyes" being blinded. But it is also possible to read the Hebrew text as saying, "for one of my two eyes," as if vengeance for two eyes would have demanded more of God. The Lord in His great mercy heard him, and Samson, by the power of God, pulled the temple down on his enemies. The strength that he had lost through sin, he recovered through prayer. He killed more people in his death than during his life (v. 30). Thus, God defeated the Philistines and their god in a humiliating manner through a seemingly powerless man. Despite his many weaknesses, Samson finally gave his life in the fulfillment of his divine calling. He died for the well-being of others.

According to v. 31, Samson in the end received the respect of his father's house and an honorable burial in the tomb of his father. He had judged Israel twenty years. He began his work as a judge with his victory at Ramath Lehi (15:14–17) and ended it with his victory and death in Gaza, twenty years later.

Throughout the history of the Judges, we see human depravity at work in the repeated apostasy of the Israelites but particularly in the life of Samson, the last judge. In response, God displayed His wrath against sin and iniquity through pagan nations whom He used to discipline the children of Israel. And when they repented, confessed, and cried out for a deliverer, hoping that God would hear their cry once more, Yahweh, in His mercy, sent a Spirit-endowed judge to deliver them from their oppressors. So today, God is ready and willing to come to the aid of any of His children who are "oppressed" by Satan or their own sinful nature and who reach out to Him for help. God's grace and mercy are always available to repentant sinners.

17:1—21:25

RELIGIOUS AND MORAL DEGENERATION OF ISRAEL

With Samson's death, the record of the Israelite judges comes to an end. Nothing is said about two other judges, Eli and Samuel. Instead, the last five chapters of the book present two stories. Both stories feature a Levite: the first one traveled from Bethlehem to the hill country of Ephraim to find a place to live (chaps. 17–18);

the second one traveled from the hill country of Ephraim to Bethlehem to bring back his concubine, who had left him and had gone back to her father's house (chaps. 19–21). Both stories shed light on the religious and moral standards during the period of the Judges. In these chapters, there are no foreign oppressors or liberating heroes. We are taken into the daily life of the Israelites in the land of Canaan, and the conclusion is that they were hardly better than the former inhabitants of the land. What we see is a society in spiritual, social, and moral chaos. The picture of a united Israel found in the first two chapters of the book is gone, and now everyone is unquestionably doing whatever seems right according to subjective perceptions (17:6; 21:25). There was no centralized worship at the Israelite sanctuary or a centralized system of governance. Everyone was on his or her own.

17:1—18:31
Micah and His Idol

The first story is about a man, his mother, and a Levite (17:1–13). These were visited by a group of Danites (18:1–13), resulting in a conflict that closes the story (vv. 14–31).

17:1–13. Micah's Idolatry. The story could be called the Canaanite naturalization of Yahweh; that is to say, the Israelites had transformed Yahweh into a Canaanite god by worshiping Him in a Canaanite way. The discussion about what to do with the silver that was stolen, returned, and consecrated moved to using it to make an idol that represented the Lord. The ease with which the narrative shifts to idolatry is amazing in that none of the protagonists took a moment to examine the implications of their decision. Worshiping Yahweh à la Canaanite fashion seemed to have been a very natural thing to do.

There is some question as to whether there were one or two idols. Some translations render the phrase to mean one carved "image overlaid with silver." The Hebrew verbs seem to indicate that it may have been only one. It has been suggested that the idol consisted of two parts (e.g., a wooden idol enclosed in a casing of silver). When the idol was finished, Micah ("who is like Yahweh?") put it in a shrine in his house together with an ephod (see 8:22–28) and some household gods (Heb. *terapim*); that is, small images of human shape believed to represent the gods and to be endowed with divine attributes. Micah consecrated one of his sons to serve as

priest (17:5). In doing this, he used the standard expression for the consecration of priests, "fill the hand," probably with an offering (see Ex. 28:41; 29:9). We do not know exactly when this event took place. In the next chapter, the Danites are in search of a home, and this may suggest that the event took place in the early period of the Judges when the tribes were still finding their places in the country. However, the level of social and spiritual corruption in Israel described in chapters 17–21 points to a later period of the Judges. Micah and his mother thought they were serving and worshiping Yahweh (17:3), when in reality they had transgressed the second commandment, which forbade the making of idols. Throughout history, people have adapted God to their own ideas in an attempt to manage Him as they pleased.

Since the Levites had not been given any tribal territory, only cities, they lived among the other tribes (Num. 35:2; Josh. 21:3). A young Levite who had been living with the tribe of Judah came to a group of houses in the hill country of Ephraim, one of which belonged to Micah. When Micah learned that the young man was a Levite, he invited him to stay with him and become his priest. Micah, who was not a priest, consecrated the Levite by "filling his hands" (Judg. 17:12), contrary to God's instructions that only Aaron's descendants should be priests (Ex. 29:9). The Levites were to be assistants of the priests (Num. 8:19–22). Micah seemed to have only a dim understanding of God's will. He practiced a syncretistic religion, mixing the worship of Yahweh with the worship of the local gods. This type of spiritual and moral compromise continues to be a threat for believers today who try to live the Christian life in a culture that does not support Christian values.

18:1–13. The Danites' Search for an Inheritance. The statement concerning the lack of a king in Israel (v. 1) prepares the way for the illicit deeds of the Danites. The tribe of Dan had been allotted their inheritance between the territories of Judah and Ephraim, from the western border of the Benjamites to the Mediterranean Sea (Josh. 19:40–46). It included fertile land in the valleys and the coastal plain. However, the Danites were not able to occupy all the land allotted to them because the Amorites drove them back into the hill country (Judg. 1:34). Therefore, they sent five spies north to find some additional land for their families.

The five spies arrived at the house of Micah and lodged there long enough to realize that there was a Levite residing in the house who also officiated as a priest. At this point in the narrative, the spies simply gather information that would later determine the future of the shrine in the house of Micah. Again, the perverted religious practices of Micah and the Levite were not considered by them to be unfaithfulness to the Lord, suggesting that such practices were common throughout the land of Israel. It is intriguing that the spies asked the Levite to consult God with respect to the success of their journey. Nothing is said about how the Levite consulted the Lord. In fact, one gets the impression that he immediately uttered an oracle before the scouts, and they interpreted it to be a positive one. The phrase used by the Levite is ambiguous. He literally said, "Go in peace!" (a common expression and wish) and stated that the way in which they would go would be before or in front of the Lord. This could be interpreted to mean that God was carefully watching what they are doing in a positive way (to bless them) or in a negative way (to condemn them). The Levite did not risk his life. In any case, the rest of the narrative shows that the Danites were successful not because the Lord was necessarily with them but because of their military superiority. After spying on the people living in Laish, they knew that it would be easy to possess that beautiful land that would play an important role in the Northern Kingdom.

18:14–26. The Danites Rob Micah's House.
The five spies had told their brethren what they would find in Micah's house. And while the six hundred men stood at the gate to the compound, the five spies stole the contents of the shrine and persuaded the Levite to come with them. Micah, it seems, was not at home at that time. If the Danites had taken the idols and destroyed them and punished the Levite, they would have acted in accordance with God's will, but by taking the idols for their own use, they participated in the apostasy, showing that they feared neither God nor men. They left, putting their families and goods in front of them, in case they were pursued. Not long after their departure, Micah came home and found he had been robbed. He who robbed his mother was now robbed. He gathered his neighbors together and caught up with the Danites. The Danites cared little about how Micah felt; operating according to the principle of "might makes right," they chased him away with a threat (v. 25). If the loss of his idols had driven him back to rely only on Yahweh, he would have received great benefit from it, but

we hear nothing more about him. The idol that supposedly represented the Lord was in fact like the Canaanite idols, unable to defend itself.

18:27–31. The Danites Settle in Laish.
Based on the report given by the five spies, the Danites continued their journey north and came to Laish, which they attacked, destroyed, and burned (v. 27). This was a luxurious land with great vegetation and abundant water flowing from Mount Hermon. Out of the ashes of Laish rose a new city, which they named Dan, after the first head of the tribe, and which would become one of the centers of idolatry in the Northern Kingdom of Israel. It became the northernmost city in Israel. "From Dan to Beersheba" became a common idiom for all of Israel (see Judg. 20:1; 1 Sam. 3:20; 2 Sam. 3:10).

The last two verses of this chapter record the idolatry of the Danites. Jonathan, which was probably the name of Micah's Levite, who was further identified as the son of Gershom, and his sons were set up as priests. It is possible that this is Gershom the son of Moses. Originally, the Hebrew text of the OT did not have vowels. The name in the text for the father of Gershom is *m-sh-h* (the consonants for Moses—*mosheh*). The consonantal difference between Moses and Manasseh is the consonant *n*. In some manuscripts, one finds written above the name a small *nun* (n) that would read *m-n-sh-h* (the consonants for Manasseh). Rabbinic explanations justify the change as an attempt to avoid tarnishing the memory of Moses. If the original text read "Moses," as it appears, it is sadly possible that Jonathan was a descendent of Moses's son.

The phrase referring to the priests that were in Dan until the captivity of the land (18:30) is problematic. If this is referring to the captivity under Tiglath-Pileser in 732 B.C., we have to assume that neither Samuel nor David nor Solomon stopped the idol worship in Dan. Yet, 1 Samuel 7:3–4 indicates that under Samuel's reform the Israelites discarded other gods and served only the Lord (v. 4). Furthermore, when Jeroboam set up the golden calves at Dan, he appointed priests from among all kinds of people, not only the Levites (1 Kin. 12:31) because all the Levites and priests had left the Northern Kingdom and moved south to Judah (2 Chr. 11:13–14). Thus, the descendants of Gershom, the Levite, could not have served until the Assyrian captivity in the city of Dan.

Rather, the statement that Micah's idol was in Dan all the time that the house of God was in Shiloh (Judg. 18:31) suggests that this captivity of the land (v. 30) took place earlier in connection with the Philistines, possibly in the time of Eli (1 Sam. 4:1–11) or during the reign of Saul's son, Ishbosheth, who reigned over Israel from Mahanaim, which was east of the Jordan. The Philistines presumably controlled some portions of the Northern Kingdom, including Dan (2 Sam. 2:8–10). Archaeological evidence suggests that the temple at Dan was destroyed about 1050 B.C., around the time the ark of the covenant was captured by the Philistines (1 Sam. 4).

19:1—21:25
The Levite and His Concubine

The story of the Levite and his concubine, illustrating the moral chaos during the period of the Judges, begins and ends with the statement that there was no king in Israel (Judg. 19:1; 21:25). The absence of a king does not necessarily mean there must be chaos in the land; the comment about everyone doing as desired in the last part of v. 25, however, does. One wonders whether the absence of a king may be referring to the people's unwillingness to recognize God as their king. We are not told when this story took place, but the reference to Phinehas, the grandson of Aaron (20:28), and the fact that the tribal league was still functioning and able to take combined action points to an early date.

19:1–21. The Levite Searches for His Concubine. A Levite from Ephraim took a concubine (a second-rank wife) from Bethlehem. Most versions say that she committed adultery against him (19:2) and went back to her father's house. The penalty for adultery was death (Lev. 20:10), but nothing in the text indicates that she faced death. Some wonder if there is another explanation. A few ancient versions have "his concubine became angry with him, and she went away from him to her father's house." As Israelite law did not provide for divorce by the wife, leaving the husband was considered an act of adultery. A heated argument between them could explain why the Levite sought reconciliation. Perhaps tempers had cooled.

His journey seemed to be crowned with success. He was lavishly entertained by his father-in-law, and his concubine seemed to have agreed to go back with him. They left on the fifth day of his visit, but because they left in the afternoon, they did not get as far as he had hoped. They were forced to seek shelter in Gibeah of Benjamin (Judg. 19:15), where nobody took them in except an old man from the mountains of Ephraim who lived in Gibeah (identified with modern Tel el-Ful, about 3 miles [4.8 km] north of Jerusalem). The hospitality of this man was a ray of hope in the midst of a narrative where people care only for themselves.

19:22–30. Gibeah's Crime. During the night, the men of the city surrounded the house and demanded that the traveler be surrendered to them for homosexual abuse. There are a number of parallels to Genesis 19, but this story has a different outcome. The men are called "sons of belial" in Hebrew (Judg. 19:22)—variously translated as "wicked," "perverted," or "worthless." In the OT, the word "belial" ("not worthy" or "worthless") occurs twenty-seven times and always refers to people of bad character (see Deut. 13:13; 1 Sam. 2:12; 1 Kin. 21:10).

Hospitality played an important part in the ANE society. By it a stranger found rest, food, shelter, and asylum. The old man in Gibeah took the law of hospitality so seriously that he was willing to surrender his virgin daughter and the Levite's concubine instead of his guest, who had a sacred right to his hospitality. However horrified the modern reader may be, we need to remember that the old man was acting within the confines of his culture. Women were generally only lightly esteemed in the ancient world. It was common to sacrifice a woman's honor to save the life of a man (Gen. 12:10–16; 20:2; 26:6–9). World history shows that women have been greatly abused, and similar psychological, physical, and sexual abuse continues to be a reality in many places today. The voice of the church should be one of the first voices to speak against such evil cultural practices anyplace in the world.

This story illustrates how quickly and how low some of the people in Israel had fallen morally since the death of Joshua. Sodom was reenacted, and ever since Sodom has been reenacted many times (Rom. 1:26–27), particularly in the acceptance of homosexual practices and behavior. The reaction of the Levite to the brutal rape and murder of his concubine was overdramatic. In the narrative he was not totally innocent, for he treated the woman poorly. He handed her to the men to be raped and early in the morning, when he was leaving, found her lying down by the threshold of the door of the house and treated her with disrespect. One wonders whether she was still alive. Cutting her body into twelve parts and sending them to the twelve tribes of Israel constituted a call to the people to come together for war. Saul did something similar, but he instead cut up a pair of oxen into twelve pieces and sent them to the tribes (1 Sam. 11:7).

20:1–48. War with Benjamin. All the tribes, except Benjamin, assembled in Mizpah (meaning "watchtower"), possibly modern Tel en-Nasbeh, 6 miles (9.6 km) north of Jerusalem, to decide what to do with Gibeah. The fact that the intertribal organization was still functioning normally points to an early date for these events. In addition to the tribal leaders and elders, 400,000 foot soldiers were present. The Levite recounted his story, stating that the rulers of Gibeah came against him. Most translations render the term *ba'al* here as "men," but this word can and often does mean "ruler." Thus, some translations have "leaders" or "leading citizens" (v. 5); as noted above, in 19:22 they are called (lit.) "sons of Belial." To further enhance his story, the Levite said they wanted to kill him. Considering what happened to the concubine, he may not have been far off the mark.

The response of the assembly was unanimous. They vowed not to go home until Gibeah was punished. There is a textual difficulty in v. 9 because part of the Hebrew text seems to be missing. According to most translations, the text dealing with their decision says only that they will attack Gibeah "by lot." This probably means that ten percent of the soldiers had to get supplies and the rest would move against Gibeah. Lots would choose who performed which task. Some translations understand this differently. They convey the idea that they would go up against the city "in the order decided by casting lots," or that they would "march up against it as the lot determines." Whatever the case, in complete unity they prepared for war against their own people and were willing to destroy one of their own tribes, something that none of the heathen oppressors ever attempted to do.

Through the Urim and Thumim they had asked the Lord twice before without receiving the assurance that He would give them the victory. The third time, however, they received the promise of victory. It is not clear in the text why the other tribes were defeated twice after the Lord had, on both occasions, sanctioned the battle against Benjamin (vv. 18, 23). Was it only that the Lord wanted to teach them a lesson not to trust in their superior numbers and self-confidence? From time to time, we all have to learn humility through life's lessons. But perhaps the Lord wanted them to realize that the sin of Gibeah and the Levite's behavior were only symptoms of the overall low state of morals among them and that, therefore, they all bore responsibility for what had happened. Instead of rushing to battle and being more interested in vengeance than justice, it would probably have been better to humble themselves before God, acknowledge their share of guilt in this matter, and lament over the terrible state of wickedness amongst them. Thus, they would have been better prepared and more in harmony with God's will to punish the evildoers. As Christians, we need to watch and pray to be kept from an unholy zeal in the Lord's work. Power and knowledge have to be accompanied by divine wisdom and good judgment in order to be properly used. Only God can provide us with what we need. We need to walk humbly before the Lord, constantly depending on the atonement He provided for the forgiveness of our sins.

21:1–25. Restoration of the Tribe of Benjamin. The last episode in this story of horror shows how the Israelites, after their bloody rampage through the cities of Benjamin, came to their senses and realized that they had gone too far. In their misplaced zeal for vengeance, they had nearly wiped out a whole tribe. Now they sought ways to circumvent their rash decision not to give their daughters as wives to the Benjamites (v. 1). Without wives, the six hundred men at the rock of Rimmon were destined for extinction and with them the whole tribe of Benjamin. Instead of asking God for forgiveness for their rash vow, they continued in their hypocrisy and wiped out the inhabitants of Jabesh Gilead, save for four hundred virgins, because the people of Jabesh Gilead had not come up to the Lord at the assembly in Mizpah (v. 8). The Gileadites were descended from Manasseh, the nephew of Benjamin; thus, there was a blood bond with the descendants of Benjamin.

Following the capture of the four hundred virgins, a delegation was sent to the six hundred men at the rock of Rimmon to invite them back and make peace with them, which they did (v. 14). But because four hundred virgins were not enough for six hundred Benjamite men, the leaders of Israel came up with another plan; they advised the Benjamites to snatch the daughters of Shiloh when they came out to dance at a particular festival (v. 21). This was probably a harvest festival. All this was done to avoid the guilt of perjury by equally detestable actions. However, the arrangement worked, and the Benjamites with their new wives were able to return to a normal life and to begin restoring their devastated cities. That the elders of Israel could advise acts of treachery and violence out of a sense of duty is indicative of their spiritual blindness and shows the effects of an erroneous conscience.

The book closes with the reflection of the author that the absence of a king was largely responsible for the chaotic conditions in Israel in the time of the Judges. The breakdown in God's purposes for Israel illustrates graphically the depravity of human beings, God's wrath against sin, and His mercy and longsuffering with repentant sinners. On the one hand, it is a sad picture of how low God's children can fall; on the other hand, it highlights God's love for even the most depraved of His creatures. It does not surprise us that, for the biblical writer, the solution to the condition of Israel during the period of the Judges was a coming king. Later, kings would arise in Israel, some to instill the fear of Yahweh and others to lead the people away from Him. Yet, the ultimate solution has always been the coming of a messianic King who will establish peace, justice, and righteousness in the land. For the Christian, this Messiah has come in the person of Jesus Christ. He is the only One who can truly liberate us from the oppressive power of sin and from the daily temptation of doing what is right in our own eyes. The partial victories of the judges over the enemies of Israel are almost meaningless compared to what Christ accomplished on the cross and to what will take place at the future consummation of such a victory. The book closes in expectation, waiting for the king.

RUTH

INTRODUCTION

Title and Authorship. The book of Ruth, like various biblical books, does not mention its author. Jewish tradition attributes it to Samuel.

Date. The first verse links the narrative to the time of the Judges, Israel's premonarch era when divinely summoned "judges" delivered Yahweh's people from foreign oppressors. This time frame is supported by Boaz being born of Rahab, who received the spies in Joshua's time (Josh. 2; Matt. 1:5). The record of David's lineage, including Boaz and Ruth (4:17–22), could only have been written after David had become important enough to make such details meaningful to a reader or hearer. Thus, if the entire book was written at one time, then it could not have been written earlier than David's anointing (2 Sam. 16) during the reign of Saul.

Backgrounds. The experience of Israel described in the book of Judges provides the background for the story of Naomi and Ruth. The mention of a famine in Bethlehem, normally a fruitful land, suggests that Israel had again departed from Yahweh (see Lev. 26:18–20). But the narrative is not primarily interested in apostasy, since the book indicates that many Israelites were committed to the Lord. It is a beautiful story of profound loving loyalty to God as reflected in loyalty to other human beings. It is an account that explains how Moab (and Canaan, through Boaz's mother, Rahab) became a part of David's family line. On one occasion, David left his parents in Moab for safekeeping (1 Sam. 22:3–4). As a result, this book also shows that not all Moabites were evil.

Literary Features. The book of Ruth is a literary masterpiece. We find references to legal practices (4:1–12), a poem (1:16–17), and a genealogy

(4:18–22). However, the book is fundamentally a narrative characterized by dialogues.

Theology and Purpose. Ruth is a dramatic narrative through which deep theological issues are addressed. The beginning and ending of the story indicate that it deals with the preservation of life, the divine activity in preserving it, and the role of the redeemer (Heb. *go'el*).

1. Life and Death. As the book opens, the threat of death is immediately introduced. There was a famine in the land of Bethlehem. Confronted with this danger, people searched for a way to survive. The story is about a family's concern for life and the possibility of their total extinction. The actions of practically all characters in the story revolved around the question of survival. In the absence of food in Bethlehem, Elimelech and his family went to Moab to preserve their lives. But Moab could not preserve life. In fact, there the family faced the destructive power of death and meaninglessness, even the apparent absence of the Lord from their lives. At first things seemed to go well. Then the father of the family died, leaving his two sons and wife in a strange land. Things appeared to improve again when the two sons married, thus increasing the potential for preserving the family.

Unfortunately for his two sons, the family did not grow. Their wives bore no children. The threat of extinction for this family reached a point of no return when the two sons of Naomi died. Suddenly time stopped; there was no future for her. She was ready to return to Bethlehem, not to search for life but to quietly die, leaving behind no trace of the existence of her family.

When the narrative is placed within its canonical context, we realize that this family belonged to the genealogical line from which the Messiah, typified by David, would come to preserve human life on this earth. Through a seemingly lifeless family, the Lord would eventually bring eternal life to humanity.

2. *God and Life.* The God of Naomi was beyond her comprehension. In the first part of the story, He seemed to be absent and she felt the pain of His absence. When death occurs, we may experience His silence, but it is not His absence. There are no miracles in the narrative because, like in the book of Esther, God was working from within history and through the characters of the story. He is a gracious and faithful God. The Hebrew term *khesed* is used several times in the story to designate an essential characteristic of God. It refers to His gracious, merciful, and faithful commitment to humans. This divine grace was accessible to Israelites and non-Israelites (1:8; 2:20). It is a divine concern for the needs of humans that leads people to show *khesed* ("mercy," "kindness," "loving loyalty") to others, as Naomi was about to discover.

Discouraged and frustrated with life, Naomi asked her daughters-in-law to abandon her. If God had already abandoned her, there was nothing they could do to change her fate. She had no future. It was at this point in the story that divine grace and love (*khesed*) flowed from God to Naomi through Orpah and Ruth. In the midst of her pain, the Lord was showing His loving loyalty and kindness through other human beings. Their unwillingness to abandon her indicates that God was still with her. The dramatic commitment of Ruth, not only to Naomi but to Naomi's people and her God, is the most powerful manifestation of divine compassion in the narrative. Through this decision, the potential for the divine preservation of life would become a reality in spite of Naomi's hopelessness.

Divine *khesed* is the force that drives the plot of the story. It takes the reader from death to life. Although the story begins with death experienced in such a dramatic way that hope dies, it ends with the blossoming of a new life that would preserve the family line from which David would come. The Lord was not allowing death to alter His plan for His people. Life overcomes death and fills the human heart with joy and hope.

3. *Redemption.* In the narrative, God preserved life through a redeemer. It was through His providential leading that a redeemer was found who was willing to preserve the genealogical line from which the Messiah would come. Naomi knew about a relative of her husband who was still alive and could become her redeemer. Apparently she did not know how to locate him, because when Ruth went out to glean in the fields, it was by chance—a happenstance—that she gleaned in the field of Boaz,

Elimelech's relative (2:3). Behind this historical "accident," we find the hand of the Lord leading the narrative to a resolution and to the preservation of the life of this family. Boaz, the redeemer, had the material wealth the two women lacked. He also had a wealth of character and integrity that would be used by the Lord to accomplish His purposes. In this divine plan there was no room for a selfish redeemer. The irresponsible redeemer soon disappeared from the narrative, leaving no trace of his life behind him.

The work of the redeemer was not motivated by selfishness, nor was it the result of an outburst of irrational emotion. Boaz's self-appointment as redeemer took place in the court of law, by the city gate, and before witnesses (Ruth 4:5-11; Deut. 25:5-10; cf. Rev. 5:9-10). The city acknowledged that he had the legal right to redeem, and he joyfully did so. From this point on, the story's emotional tone radically changed because a redeemer had been found. The Lord created for Naomi and Ruth a wonderful future well beyond what they would have anticipated. Through them the true Redeemer would come to redeem the human family.

COMMENTARY

1:1–22
From Moab to Bethlehem

The narrative begins in Bethlehem (1:1), moves to Moab where its plot is significantly developed (vv. 1-18), and closes with the return of Naomi and Ruth to Bethlehem (vv. 19-22).

1:1–5. Elimelech's Family in Moab. The story is about the family of Elimelech and Naomi. They had two sons, Mahlon and Chilion, and were identified as Ephrathites, meaning they were from the region around Bethlehem called Ephrath (Gen. 35:16-19; 48:7). The clan name might derive from Ephrath, the wife of Caleb, whose descendants are described as settling in Bethlehem (1 Chr. 2:19, 50-51; 4:4). The narrator is thus connecting Elimelech's family to its founders, making the subsequent tragedy more poignant. The name Elimelech ("my God [Yahweh] is king" or "God is king") suggests parental religious convictions. Naomi's name could mean "my sweetness" or "sweet, pleasant one," indicative of a parent's joy over a baby girl.

The book of Ruth opens and closes in Bethlehem, a very fertile area about six miles south of Jerusalem. As the book opens, there was no food in the "house of bread" (Bethlehem). In their search for safety and sustenance, Elimelech's family traveled to Moab, east of the Dead Sea, suggesting that this famine was localized in Israel. The Moabites originated in the incestuous relationship of Lot with his eldest daughter (Gen. 19:30–38) and were often enemies of the Israelites. Elimelech's family sought refuge among a people who had been hostile to Israel, which might also suggest their dire condition, accentuating the kindness extended to Ruth by Naomi, Boaz, and the people of Bethlehem.

Mahlon and Chilion are first presented as "his two sons." After Elimelech dies, the text indicates that Naomi was left with her sons (v. 3), a poignant allusion to the calamity. These two sons married Moabite women (v. 4). After about ten years, the two sons of Naomi also died. The writer notes that the woman was left without her two sons and her husband (v. 5), underscoring Naomi's total loss. In the absence of hope, she simply said that the hand of the Lord had turned against her (v. 13). Her age and poverty eclipsed any hope of marrying again and having more children (vv. 11–13). Naomi and her two daughters-in-law faced a bleak future.

1:6–18. Naomi's Plans.

Never intending Moab to be a permanent home, Naomi made plans to return to Israel. She was returning because she heard that the Lord was giving attention to His people's needs by providing them with food (lit. "bread"; v. 6). The "house of bread" now had bread. She had gone to Moab with much but was leaving empty.

With nothing to offer her two young daughters-in-law, Naomi first urged each one to return to her own mother's home (vv. 8–10). References to the mother's house occur rarely in the OT (Gen. 24:28, 67; cf. Song 3:4; 8:2). She prayed for a happy future for both of them, a future that the Lord was not providing through her. Naomi expressed concern only for the welfare of her daughters-in-law. "Go, return"/"go back" (the Hebrew has double imperatives) suggests urgency, freeing her daughters-in-law from any further responsibility.

Her tenderness is expressed by her prayer that Yahweh would grant them the same *khesed* ("kindness/mercy") they had given to her and her family (v. 8b). Though in deep sorrow, her faith in Yahweh was apparent as she commended her Moabite daughters-in-law to Him and His kindness (v. 8). Naomi believed that God's providential care extended beyond Israel. The Moabites were distant relatives through Lot (Gen. 19:36–37). Although as a nation they worshiped false gods, Naomi's words and the fact that Mahlon and Chilion had found acceptable wives among the Moabites may indicate that there was some openness to the God of Abraham. The concept that God was not just a God for the Hebrews but for all nations is seen elsewhere in the OT (Gen. 18:18; 22:18; 26:4; Is. 56:7; Zech.14:16). In the NT, this concept becomes vital to understanding the scope of the Gospel Commission and ultimate restoration at the end of time (Matt. 28:19; Acts 10:34, 45; 11:18; Rom. 16:26; Rev. 15:4).

Then there were kisses and tears. The Hebrew idiom literally translated "to lift up the voice and weep" (e.g., "weep loudly") occurs often in contexts of lamentation and mourning, suggesting loud sobbing and, in this context, evidence of affectionate bonds (v. 14). Naomi's daughters-in-law did not want to leave her, exhibiting a warm and loving attachment. The long dialogue points to the significance of the scene (vv. 8–17). With tearful responses, the two younger widows declared their intention to stay with Naomi and her people (v. 10).

In the second interchange (vv. 11–14), Naomi spoke tenderly to her "daughters," telling them to return home (v. 11) as she was too old to marry again (v. 12). Even if she would marry and bear sons, it would be too much of a sacrifice for her daughters-in-law to wait until those sons were grown up. The dialogue aims at persuasion. Naomi closed by wailing that the hand of the Lord had gone against her (v. 13). She was experiencing the apparent absence of God, overlooking for a moment that the love of her two daughters-in-law was an expression of God's loving mercy toward her. Again there were kisses and tears. This time the weeping led to Orpah's farewell kiss. She returned to Moab, doing what Naomi suggested and bearing Naomi's blessing of Yahweh. Orpah exits from the narrative.

In the third interchange (vv. 15–18), Naomi turned to Ruth and encouraged her to go back as Orpah did—to her people and her gods (v. 15). The biblical text does not criticize Orpah's decision, nor does it contrast her negatively with Ruth. Orpah has been commended for her loving kindness and entrusted to the blessing of the Lord. But her decision highlights Ruth's sacrifice in her decision to "cling to" an aged, widowed mother-in-law. The Hebrew word *dabaq* ("cling," "cleave"; v. 14), suggests loyalty or deep affection (Ruth 2:23; cf. Gen. 2:24; 2 Sam. 20:2).

Naomi finally stopped protesting as Ruth reaffirmed her intention, expressed in one of the most sublime statements in Scripture. This is the first time we hear Ruth's voice. Before her three-part commitment to Naomi, her people, and her God, she insisted that Naomi not attempt to dissuade her and invoked Yahweh as witness (v. 16). Her devotion would extend beyond Naomi's life ("where you die, I will die"). Renouncing burial in her homeland, Ruth determined to permanently live out the rest of her life in a foreign country: "Your people will be my people, and your God my God" (v. 16). Rejecting the gods of Moab, Ruth declared Yahweh to be her God, using His covenantal name. She was not seeking a husband but was seeking to serve the true God. This was affirmed with a solemn irreversible oath of her lifelong commitment to her mother-in-law, in which she called a curse from God upon herself if she failed to keep her promise (v. 17).

This decision is unparalleled in Scripture. The exchange between the three women (vv. 8–17) began with the use of Yahweh's name in a blessing from Naomi and ended with Ruth's absolute commitment to Him. Naomi had left Bethlehem with a husband and two sons, but returned with a committed daughter-in-law, whom the women of Bethlehem recognized as being better to her "than seven sons" (4:15).

1:19–22. Arriving in Bethlehem. Omitting any travel details, the journey to Bethlehem is briefly mentioned (v. 19). The narrative then shifts to a scene of happy celebration. The Bethlehemites responded joyously to Naomi's unexpected return. She described her distress with powerful emotions and insisted that they call her Mara ("bitter"). She referred to God with both His covenantal names, *yahweh* and *shadday*. Like Job, she questioned God's inscrutable justice because, in her mind, the Almighty had made her bitter (in words very similar to Job 27:2). Naomi—along with Job, the psalmists, and Jeremiah—was honest when suffering. And God accepted her complaints. She rejected the compliments because she had left "full," but now she said that the Almighty (*shadday*) had afflicted (lit. "to cause distress," "inflict misery," "do harm") her. Her life was always in the hand of the Lord, even during difficult moments.

The narrative is briefly summarized (v. 22), providing a helpful base for the next section. For the first time in the narrative, Naomi's daughter-in-law is identified by her name and ethnic heritage. She is described as one returning from the country of Moab, even though it was her country (1:7, 16, 22; 2:6). The narrative closes with a time frame as they arrived in Bethlehem at the beginning of the barley harvest (v. 22). They arrived when grain was gathered (March or April), barley being the first crop (Ex. 9:31–32; 2 Sam. 21:9). The beginning and end of the chapter have corresponding elements which envelop the narrative. Verse 1 anchors timing and location; v. 22 closes with corresponding details. The chapter begins with famine and departure and then ends with harvest and return.

2:1–23
A Meeting in the Field

This segment of the narrative consists mainly of five dialogues. It opens (v. 2) and closes (vv. 19–22) with conversations between Naomi and Ruth. Boaz talked to his servants (vv. 4–7), with Ruth (vv. 8–14), and again with his servants (vv. 15–16). During the dialogue, the character of those involved was manifested. Ruth's Moabite origin was mentioned several times, and the connection between Boaz and Naomi was restated. Both Ruth and Boaz displayed extraordinary lovingkindness (*khesed*). Ruth risked ostracism and physical harm as a Moabitess to provide for Naomi. Boaz showed great generosity toward both widows. Boaz's concern for Ruth's well-being, mentioned four times (vv. 8, 15, 16, 22), suggests the possibility of verbal and physical abuse, which occurred in some places and among some people in Israel during the period of the Judges (see Judg. 19; 21).

2:1–7. The Plan of Ruth. Since Boaz plays an important role in the narrative, he is introduced first. He was a relative of Elimelech, deceased husband of Naomi (v. 1). This detail would provide the legal right for Boaz to marry Ruth. He was a wealthy and influential citizen in Bethlehem, a godly man of gracious generosity and uprightness. Ruth unselfishly volunteered to find food by gleaning in the field (v. 2). Although Naomi's son had died, Ruth still honored her mother-in-law, showing courage three times (1:22; 2:2, 21) when her gender, race, and social status put her in danger. Mosaic law commanded compassion for aliens, orphans, and widows, requiring harvesters to deliberately leave grain in the fields for them to glean (Lev. 19:9–10; 23:22; Deut. 24:19). The field scene, like many in the book, includes three conversations involving Boaz and the harvesters or Ruth (vv. 4–16). Ruth went to glean in the field belonging to Boaz, Elimelech's relative (v. 3). The narrative indicates that this "happenstance" (Heb. *miqreh*; v. 3) was under the guidance of the Lord.

2:8–16. Boaz Meets Ruth. Boaz came to the field and greeted the reapers by saying, "The LORD be with you" (v. 4). He was a devout religious person who showed respect to his employees. He also noticed a stranger in his field. After inquiring, he was informed that this person was Ruth, a young Moabite woman (v. 6). She had asked for permission to glean after the reapers and had been working diligently since early in the morning. Male harvesters likely would have noticed her as well, suggesting her vulnerability.

Boaz graciously addressed Ruth as "daughter" (v. 8), suggesting that Boaz was older than Ruth. His offer of help and protection to the Moabitess revealed the absence of racial prejudice (his mother being Rahab, a Canaanite). He instructed his employees to be respectful of her and allowed her to glean among the regular sheaves where gleaners were not permitted—a generous gesture exceeding Israelite law. Ruth was also offered the water that Boaz provided for regular employees (v. 9). She responded with few words, respectful of her social status. She recognized the social disparity between them and bowed before him as a sign of respect, asking why he was so kind as to notice her, a foreigner (v. 10). Boaz knew the story about Ruth and Naomi and the lovingkindness (*khesed*) Ruth had manifested toward her mother-in-law. He referred to everything she had done for Naomi, also mentioning the fact that Ruth had left her father, mother, and land of her birth. Thus, like Abram and Sarah (Gen. 12:1–5), Ruth also abandoned the security of her homeland, choosing the life of an alien in order to follow Naomi and her God.

Boaz's request to the Lord to protect Ruth uses the metaphor of a mother bird protecting her young. God is referred to as the One under whose "wings" Ruth had come for refuge (v. 12; see also Deut. 32:11–12; cf. Matt. 23:37). Boaz blessed her—asking the Lord to reward her work—without knowing that he would be God's instrument in the realization of the blessing (v. 12). Boaz also invited Ruth to lunch. A land owner eating with his workers was notable, but Boaz's generosity and compassion toward this poor Moabite widow was specifically noticeable. *Qali* ("parched," "roasted" grain; v. 14) was a staple food at the time, and Boaz presented Ruth with a surplus amount.

After a generous meal, Ruth got up to glean again. Boaz now emphatically ordered his employees to let her glean among the bundles (or sheaves), to deliberately leave some extra for her, and to not humiliate or rebuke her (vv. 15–16).

The lovingkindness of Ruth moved others to show kindness to her. In his treatment of Ruth, Boaz displayed divine generosity and care for others.

The narrative summarizes Ruth's long day of work. She gleaned in the field until evening and then beat out what amounted to an "ephah" of barley (v. 17; see below, "Ephah"). Beating out the grain would separate the husks from kernels, eliminating extra weight when carrying the kernels home.

2:17–23. Ruth Informs Naomi. When Ruth returned to Naomi, she informed her mother-in-law that the man she worked with that day was named Boaz (v. 19). Naomi spontaneously pronounced a blessing, mentioning that he was their close relative: a *go'el* ("redeemer"). Naomi knew that Israelite family law invested near relatives with certain duties, particularly the obligation of an unmarried brother-in-law (Heb. *yabam*) to marry his brother's widow to prevent the name of a deceased man from dying out (Deut. 25:5–10). Although the situation of Naomi and Ruth did not correspond fully, it reflected the general intent of the "levirate" (from the Latin for brother-in-law, *levir*) system. That said, Obed is never in Scripture called the son of anyone other than Boaz (Ruth 4:21; 1 Chron. 2:12; Matt. 1:5; Luke 3:32).

The term *go'el* occurs for the first time in the narrative (v. 20) and becomes a key word connected to Boaz. Naomi again mentioned the lovingkindness (*khesed*) of God, manifested in Ruth "accidentally" arriving at Boaz's field (vv. 20–21). Ruth followed the counsel of both Boaz (v. 8) and Naomi (v. 22) throughout both harvests of barley and wheat, a period of seven to eight weeks (late April to June). The harvest

---

Ephah

The word "ephah," probably meaning "basket" or a basket's capacity, is borrowed from Egypt (Zech. 5:5–11). The exact weight of an ephah is debated—in any case, it was a heavy load. In the OT, it was a standard dry grain measure (Ex. 16:36; Lev. 19:36; Amos 8:5). Gideon prepared bread for the angel of Yahweh using an ephah of flour (Judg. 6:19), and Jesse sent his son David with an ephah to his elder brothers (1 Sam. 17:17). For Ruth to harvest an ephah in one day suggests long hours of diligent work, assisted by Boaz's generosity.

time provided the opportunity for Boaz and Ruth to see each other over several weeks (v. 23). The end of the grain harvest suggests that Ruth and Boaz would not see each other anymore. But the main plot of the story has not yet reached its resolution, since Ruth was still dwelling in the house of Naomi.

3:1–18
On the Threshing Floor

Significant space is given to a narrative that took place during one night, indicating that the story is reaching a resolution. Naomi gave detailed instructions to Ruth (vv. 1–4), which she followed when she and Boaz met again (vv. 6–13). Ruth then returned to Naomi and reported what happened (vv. 16–17). A new future was rising before them. Their lives were about to change in significant ways.

3:1–6. The Plan of Naomi. Seeking a better future for Ruth, Naomi directed her on a mission (vv. 1–4), addressing her again as "daughter." Ruth had previously pledged to care for Naomi; now Naomi wanted to find security for her. Realizing that she would not be able to provide for Ruth much longer, she desired to provide Ruth with the security that marriage could bring. Her rhetorical question about Boaz (v. 2) again highlighted their kinship, a key element of her plan.

Boaz apparently had not indicated any interest in Ruth. Perhaps Ruth still wore the garments of widowhood and Boaz did not want to interfere with mourning her husband's death. Naomi decided to tweak the situation with an audacious plan. As the grain harvest finished

---

Threshing Grain

After the grain was harvested, it was bundled in the field and carried manually or by cart to the threshing floor (Amos 2:13) to be beaten or trampled under animal hooves (Mic. 4:13). Sometimes the grain was crushed under the wheel of a cart to remove husks from the kernels (Is. 28:28). Threshed grain was tossed into the air, kernels separated from the husks (Amos 9:9), wind dispersed the chaff (Hos. 13:3), and kernels fell to the ground. It was then sifted and collected in piles (Matt. 3:12). The straw was used to feed animals. Threshing floors were strategically placed to take advantage of breeze patterns.

(2:23), Naomi knew that Boaz would be on the threshing floor.

Ruth was instructed to bathe, anoint herself, put on her best clothes (v. 3), and go to the threshing floor. This does not need to imply that Ruth was staging a seductive situation. She was going out at night and was to dress appropriately, needing clothing for warmth at the threshing floor where Boaz spent the night guarding harvested grain. Naomi told Ruth not to make herself known until Boaz had gone to sleep (v. 3). Boaz would likely be in a contented mood and thus more likely to acquiesce to the request.

While Boaz was sleeping, Ruth was to uncover his feet and lie down. This expression has caused much discussion. The Hebrew terms for "feet" (*margelah*) and "lie down" (*shakab*) can be taken literally. As such, the phrase "uncover his feet" means to expose them to the night's cooler temperatures so as to awaken him. Some have pointed out that both of these terms are also associated with the genitals and sexual activity respectively. Notice, for example, how *regel* (a word closely related to *margelah*; Deut. 28:57; 2 Kin. 18:27; Ezek. 16:25) and *shakab* (e.g., Gen. 30:16; 39:12; Ex. 22:16) are used. The narrative indicates that "feet" is used in a literal sense (v. 14) because it clearly speaks about the place or area where his feet are lying (*margelah* designates the place of the feet of a person who is lying down).

Since Ruth was known to be virtuous (v. 11) and this story was obviously shared without embarrassment, there is no reason to understand the narrative as describing immoral behavior. Naomi mentioned nothing about seduction, speaking only of her concern to provide security for Ruth. Neither does she say anything about Ruth lying next to Boaz. Ruth was simply to lie down and wait for Boaz to wake up and tell her what to do (v. 4).

3:7–13. Ruth and Boaz. Boaz had enjoyed his dinner and was in good spirits. The Hebrew literally says "his heart was cheerful" (v. 7). The idiom expresses the contentment and well-being accompanying a pleasant experience. When Boaz awoke suddenly in the middle of the night and learned of Ruth's identity, she took the initiative and (through symbolic language) proposed marriage in accordance with the levirate system.

Ruth invited Boaz to cover her, symbolically confirming his obligation to her. Whether this was a covering of a garment or a metaphor of being taken under his wing, the concept was clearly one of protection and redemption, foreshadowing the ultimate redemption provided by

Christ (Matt. 23:37; Rom. 3:24). God uses the same phrase in Ezekiel 16:8 for His relationship with Israel. Boaz was required to do so because he was a close relative (*go'el*). Ruth obviously understood the duties of the *go'el* and that Boaz should fulfill them. It is at this point that the nobility of Boaz is revealed. Rather than taking advantage of the situation, he praised Ruth for her family loyalty and bold action. Earlier, Boaz had praised Ruth's care for her mother-in-law (2:11) and now he praised her as a noble, virtuous woman (vv. 10–11). She had shown even more kindness than at first (v. 10). Perhaps she had been shy or nervous, for Boaz told Ruth to not be afraid, promising to fulfill her petition and noting that everyone in Bethlehem knew she was a noble woman (v. 11).

Boaz acknowledged a complication in honoring her request, reassuring her that he would work things out. A closer kinsman in the family line complicated the situation, perhaps explaining why Boaz had not exercised his *go'el* duties previously. He also lauded Ruth for not pursuing younger men, either poor or rich (v. 10), suggesting that Ruth might have had other marriage suitors. Ruth was a young woman and could have attracted younger men. Instead she was devoted to Naomi and this impressed Boaz. Boaz commended Ruth for being a woman "of noble character"/"a virtuous woman" (v. 11). This matched Ruth's character with the description of Boaz in chapter 2.

Boaz advised Ruth to remain for the rest of the night (v. 13), using the identical word she had used in 1:16 when she promised to lodge wherever Naomi did. To "lodge" has no sexual overtones in the Hebrew Bible. It was too late to leave the threshing floor in the middle of the night, but she guarded her (and his) reputation by not being recognized or seen leaving. Any negative innuendo could hamper legal transactions at the city gate in the morning.

3:14–18. Ruth Returns to Naomi. When Boaz assured Ruth that he would do what he could, he used the word *go'el* four times—sealing his determination in a strong oath with an emphatic pronoun (lit. "[by] the life of Yahweh"). Boaz would settle the matter through proper procedure, not denying another man's right to act responsibly. Blessings formed an envelope around the speech of Boaz. He sent Ruth home with threshed grain, loading one of her garments, perhaps some kind of outer mantle.

Ruth presented Naomi with the unusually large amount of threshed grain from Boaz, mentioning

his statement that the narrator did not record earlier—that Ruth should not go home to her mother-in-law empty-handed. These are Ruth's last recorded words in the book (v. 17). Naomi, who declared herself "empty" when returning from Moab (1:21), was empty no longer. She had suffered two tragedies of emptiness: famine and childlessness. The generosity of Boaz replaced famine with food, and his *go'el* promise suggested that her childlessness might soon end. The narrative next moves toward the climax.

4:1–22
At the City Gate

The question as to whether there was a *go'el* for Elimelech was already settled in chapter 3. Now the question is whether the close relative would perform the duty of the *go'el*. The chapter opens with Boaz going to the city gate that morning (v. 1) and closes with him taking the responsibility of a *go'el*, bringing hope to the poor widows and sustaining the posterity of Elimelech through Obed, whom Naomi treated as her own son (v. 17).

4:1–4. The Nameless Redeemer. Civil and legal matters were handled at the city gate (Deut. 21:19; 22:15; 25:7). Ready for business, Boaz beckoned Elimelech's close relative without naming him. Ironically, the man who refused to preserve the name of his deceased kin was not named (vv. 6, 8).

The elders of the town joined the two men. These elders governed the community's civil and legal affairs (Deut. 25:7–8; Judg. 8:14, 16; 1 Sam. 11:3). Perhaps Boaz, a wealthy land owner, was one of the elders. Verses 3–10 record the legal proceeding, with one explanatory verse (v. 7). In the legal proceedings, Elimelech was called "our brother"/"our relative" (v. 3). Clan property was never to be taken permanently from the family. In Leviticus, the *go'el* was to solve property issues (25:23–25). Since Naomi possessed land, a *go'el* could redeem her property. Perhaps someone had annexed Elimelech's land while she was in Moab. Boaz spoke on behalf of Naomi, using proper legal terminology. The legal rights of the other kinsman were recognized as Boaz informed him in the presence of the elders (4:4). Acknowledging kinship order in the family, he wanted to know the other kinsman's intention (cf. Jer. 32:7–9). The other kinsman replied that he would redeem the property. Boaz added the pivotal stipulation (4:5), informing the other kinsman that Ruth would come with Elimelech's property because he had no sons—only two widows remained. Naomi's widowhood is not mentioned, probably because her advanced age prevented her from bearing children.

Boaz argued that Elimelech's family line was precarious; Naomi was past child-bearing age and her two sons had died. Ruth was her daughter-in-law. The kinsman marrying Ruth would guard Elimelech's name by fathering an heir through her. The main issue was not simply to retain the land or to care for Ruth but to ensure that Elimelech's family line would survive. The other kinsman declined the *go'el* duties. He changed his mind, perhaps previously calculating that the widow associated with the land was aged Naomi, who would pose no complication. His own land holdings would increase, and being loyal to the family name would enhance his reputation. Future profits from the land could offset expenses in caring for the elderly Naomi. But Ruth, a much younger widow, was able to bear a child—a rightful heir to Elimelech's property. He thereby waived his redemption rights (4:6), saying that he could not do it and that Boaz should act as redeemer instead, leaving no doubt regarding his decision.

4:5-12. Boaz the Redeemer. Without any hesitation, Boaz accepted the kinsman duties. Bethlehem's elders accepted the legality of the nearer kinsman's decision and Boaz's proposal. The biblical writer comments on a binding custom utilized with property transfers and redemptions (v. 7). The sandal symbolized the legal transfer of the right of redemption from one relative to another (see Deut. 25:5-10). Boaz then exercised the redemption right he had just acquired (v. 9). He spoke to the elders and to everyone listening to the proceedings. "You are witnesses today" was apparently an OT "notarizing" action (see Josh. 24:22; 1 Sam. 12:5; Is. 43:9-10, 12; 44:8). Boaz specified the issues involved in the transaction, including everything which belonged to Elimelech, Chilion, and Mahlon. He then added that Ruth had been married to Mahlon, perhaps necessary for the formal, legal declaration. This is the only time that the narrative mentions which son of Elimelech Ruth had married.

After the transfer of responsibilities, Boaz enumerated the specific details of what had happened. His speech was framed with identical phrases, "You are witnesses today" and "today," highlighting his promptness in fulfilling his promises to Ruth (3:13) and honoring Naomi's confidence in him (3:17). This family's tragic situation ended as Boaz stated emphatically that he had acquired Ruth the Moabite, Mahlon's widow, as his wife. The marriage itself would occur later (v. 13). The elders and the people at the gate responded by saying, "We are witnesses" (v. 11). With the transaction complete, a blessing was pronounced on Boaz and Ruth that Yahweh would establish a place for Ruth among Rachel and Leah, the foundational matriarchs of Israel. Like Rachel and Leah, Ruth would become an ancestress of the covenant line (vv. 11-12).

The witnesses also mentioned Judah's prominent family line, comparing Ruth with Tamar. Both were foreigners who perpetuated Judah's family line when threatened with extinction. Comparing Tamar and Ruth does not disparage their characters or ethnicity but equates the levirate nature of their situations. The blessings knit together several themes—as Rachel and Leah built up the house of Israel, so Ruth might build up the house of Boaz (see Deut. 25:9; see also 1 Sam. 2:35; 1 Kin. 1:38; 1 Chr. 17:10). The blessing of fertility was emphasized by referring to Ruth as a "young woman" (v. 12). The closing line invoked Yahweh's blessing upon her descendants (lit. "seed"; Gen. 12:7; 13:15; 2 Sam. 7:12) whom the Lord would give her. Yahweh is exalted as the true source of offspring.

4:13-22. A Genealogy. Having married Ruth, Boaz consummated the marriage. Employing a unique grammatical construction, the narrator shows that Yahweh "enabled her to conceive"/"gave her conception." Yahweh's action opens and closes the book (1:6; 4:13). While married to Mahlon, Ruth was not able to bear a child. Now Yahweh blessed her, and she gave birth to a son to preserve the family line. In the final scene, the women of Bethlehem prayed for the baby, bursting into praise to Yahweh for His kindness and goodness (vv. 14-15).

When the book opened, Naomi spoke of her life as being emptied, but after the birth of Obed she was full of joy. Ruth was declared to be better to Naomi than seven sons. A Moabite foreigner revealed true *khesed* in Bethlehem. In a sense, death was overcome. Baby Obed would be a restorer/renewer of life for Naomi (v. 15a), assuring that the family line would continue. He would also nourish and sustain her in her old age, a reversing of Naomi's suffering from serious famine earlier and providing in some sense a joyous antidote for her childlessness (1:11-13, 20-21). Naomi's bitter outburst closed chapter 1; these exuberant comments bring reversal. The inclusio, opening in 1:5 where Naomi is bereft of her two sons, closes with baby Obed in Naomi's bosom and reversing her tragic emptiness (v. 16). Surprisingly, the women give the child his name (v. 17), which means "servant." It could be that the women were confirming the name chosen by his parents, underscoring a jubilant moment.

Although nothing more is known about Obed, his birth is significant because his grandson would be David. God built the royal line through a Moabite widow. The genealogical heading (v. 18) referring to Perez is followed by nine entries in the "A-generated-B" pattern, the form appearing several times in Genesis. The genealogy in Ruth traces David's descent from Perez, the son of another foreign widow, Tamar. The promise of blessing to all people through Abraham finds partial fulfillment in the story of Ruth (Gen. 12:1–3). This promise pushes history forward and fills it with expectation and hope.

1 SAMUEL

Title. The two books known today as First and Second Samuel were originally considered one book in the Hebrew Bible, called the "book of Samuel." The division into two books in modern translations was due to the combined length of fifty-five chapters. Following the pattern of some biblical books that end with the death of the main character (Gen. 50, Deut. 34, Josh. 24, etc.), the division between the two books of Samuel was made with King Saul at the point of death.

The practice of dividing Samuel's book into two volumes originates with the Septuagint (LXX), the earliest translation of the Hebrew Bible into Greek. In this ancient version, 1 Samuel is called "First Kingdoms" (*Basileion Alpha*). The division into two books has been followed by later translations of the Bible. The opening chapters of 1 Samuel set the prophetic tone by telling the story of Samuel's birth and his early ministry for the Lord at the sanctuary in Shiloh.

Date and Authorship. Although the book does not explicitly name its author, the title of 1 Samuel reflects the dominant role the prophet Samuel played in the first volume. Samuel was the last of the charismatic judges in Israel prior to the rise of kings. He also functioned as prophet and priest. In such a capacity, this leader anointed Saul and David, Israel's first two kings, whose personal lives and activities occupy the major part of the narrative. Jewish tradition assigns authorship of the first volume to Samuel and the second volume to Nathan and Gad. This seems to find some support in 1 Chronicles 29:29, which states that information concerning David's reign could be found in books by Samuel, Nathan the prophet, and Gad the seer. If this hypothesis regarding authorship is correct, the final book of Samuel was probably produced

shortly before or soon after the death of David. They cover the history of Israel from about 1100 B.C. to 971 B.C.

Linguistic and literary/critical approaches to the Bible have proposed a number of theories for the book's anonymous composition. Many of those theories have proven to be too hypothetical to be taken seriously. Clearly, a periodic updating of the language of 1 Samuel is evidenced in 1 Samuel 27:6, which states that time has elapsed since the recorded narrative occurred. At the same time, the author(s) of the books of Samuel explicitly claim to have used authentic source documents (2 Sam. 1:18) mentioned elsewhere in the Bible. In this commentary, biblical passages are treated as they stand. Their unity, as well as their historical and literary quality, is highly affirmed. Ultimately, the authority of the Bible rests on its divine origin.

Backgrounds. First Samuel is the sequel to the book of Judges. Together with 2 Samuel, it presents the story of Israel's first two kings, Saul and David. First Samuel begins by presenting the delicate transition of leadership in Israel from tribal judges to the first widely accepted monarch, King Saul. In fact, the author of the book of Judges repeatedly attributed the prevailing chaos and anarchy in the land to the absence of a king who could give the people a sense of national identity and security (Judg. 17:6; 18:1; 21:25). The transfer of power could be peaceful (from Eli to Samuel), problematic (from Samuel to Saul), or even difficult and openly hostile (from Saul to David).

Theology and Purpose. Due to its location within the canon, the books of Samuel are popularly viewed as primarily "historical" in character. However, they belong to a section of the Hebrew Bible known as "Early/Former Prophets." The books of Samuel offer us a significant number of theological themes for analysis, making it difficult to choose one as central.

Among the most important themes is the topic of divine leadership versus human interference.

1. *Leadership in Transition.* In the books of Samuel, we are confronted with one of the most serious crises in the history of the people of Israel. It was an attempt to redefine the nature of the relationship between God and Israel. The leaders were rejecting an old administrative structure and style—namely, theocracy—in order to introduce a new one, a monarchy with a human king. The relationship between God and Israel was properly defined and established at Mount Sinai. There Israel had an awesome encounter with God. This encounter transformed the twelve tribes into "a kingdom of priests" among the nations, a "holy nation" to the Lord (Ex. 19:6). God was recognized and accepted by the people as their only true King (Ex. 19:8; 15:18), dwelling among them while blessing, instructing, and protecting them. Thus, the theocracy was born.

The new model was, in many respects, incompatible with Israel's faith. The new system, if accepted, had to be transformed or reformulated in order for it to properly fit into the Israelite faith. The books of Samuel describe the process by which God was transforming, reformulating, and redefining kingship as known in the ANE, and Israel's demand for an earthly king was a threat to His leadership.

The books of Samuel open during the old system of judges but close with a new system in place. The first book introduces Samuel, the last judge of Israel. He is the link between the old system and the new one. He was located at a critical juncture in the history of the nation and was indispensable for a proper theological, historical, and spiritual transition. Samuel was a true giant among the prophets of the OT.

2. *Redefining Human Kingship.* Samuel begins redefining the nature of kingship in Israel based on God's instructions given in Deuteronomy 17:14–20. The king was to be an Israelite and was not to imitate the absolute monarchs of the surrounding nations by accumulating emblems of power and worldly grandeur. Instead, he was told to focus on the reading and practice of the Torah, God's revelation of truth and justice. Moreover, the king was to think of himself as a fellow Israelite brother. According to the Bible, kings in Israel were not allowed to do as they pleased. They were subject to a higher power and to the rule of law and morality, which was upheld by the prophets. In other words, they were to function as vassals of the true King of Israel, the Lord.

The success of the redefinition of kingship would depend to some extent on the attitude and self-perception of the early kings of Israel. The appointments of Saul and his successor were of critical importance. Herein lies the reason for the significant amount of space dedicated to the lives of Saul and David in the book. The contrasts between the two are very marked and deal with their own understanding of their role as king. It is soon apparent that Saul wanted to be king and not so much a vassal of the Lord. He acted on his own, independent of God, and the result is his rejection. God was redefining the nature of kingship in Israel, and Saul was not the model. The true model was David. He thought and acted as a vassal of the Lord—the servant of the Lord, under whose authority he functioned. He became the ideal king who was used to evaluate the performance of all later kings. He would also become a type of the future Messiah, Christ Jesus. In Christ, the divine King and the earthly king become one to rule over a kingdom that will last forever.

3. *God's Presence and Purpose in History.* The books of Samuel are not just historical but also prophetic in nature, teaching that the Lord cared for the people of Israel in spite of their repeated failures. The sanctuary with the ark of the covenant in the midst of the community was a constant reminder of God's abiding presence among His people. But His presence should not be taken for granted. The destruction of the sanctuary at Shiloh happened because of sin and rebellion (Ps. 78:60). Later prophets taught the people not to place their trust in the physical presence of the temple but instead to place their hope in the living God, obeying the covenant stipulations and showing mercy and justice to others (Jer. 7:4–7).

In spite of the constant failures of the nation's leaders, the Lord never completely abandoned His people. Even when human leaders fell short of the divine ideal, God promised that the coming Messiah from the house of David would fulfill His promises. Biblical narratives make it clear that God's providence directed the course of both Israel's history and that of the nations, infusing them with everlasting hope.

Literary Features. Historical narrative is certainly dominant, but it is not the only literary form used in 1 Samuel. Songs and lists are scattered throughout the book. Conversations are usually brief and include only what is essential for the reader to know. Three characters stand prominently in the stories: Samuel, the godly prophet; Saul, Israel's first king; and David, son of Jesse, the young king-elect.

The personal life of each leader is portrayed realistically, filled with their passions and aspirations. Both negative and positive qualities are placed side by side in the text. Samuel, for example, is depicted as a deeply spiritual person, whose sons unfortunately fell short of their father's outstanding example. King Saul, on the other hand, was a brave warrior who failed to heed the divine instruction given through the prophet. Young David was a very talented person with a deep sense of justice, yet he had difficulties managing his passions as well as his family's affairs. In terms of content, the book deals with the ministry of Samuel (chaps. 1–8), the reign of Saul (chaps. 9–15), and the relationship between Saul and David (chaps. 16–31).

COMMENTARY

1:1—8:22
THE MINISTRY OF SAMUEL

The opening chapters of the book focus on Samuel's early years, and they are cast in contrast with the failures of the two sons of the high priest Eli, who would normally inherit their father's position. Samuel and the two young men were reared in the same house, yet his dedication to the Lord differed from that of these two priests, who were evil and disconnected from the Lord (2:12). Samuel grew in favor with the Lord and with the people (2:26). This section discusses the birth and call of Samuel (chaps. 1–3), struggles with the Philistines (chaps. 4–7), and the call for a king (8:1–22).

1:1—3:21
Samuel's Birth and Call

The book begins with the story of the family of Elkanah and his two wives. Elkanah belonged to a distinguished Levitical family line in Israel. Samuel was born into that family and his unusual birth led to the dedication of his life to the Lord.

1:1–7. The Family of Elkanah. Although monogamy was the ideal form of marriage in Israel, some men had more than one wife (Deut. 21:15–17). Old Testament narratives describe the dangers and evil results of this practice, as is the case in 1 Samuel. Elkanah's

family lived in Ramah (1 Sam. 1:19) in the territory of Ephraim, but he belonged to the tribe of Levi (1 Chr. 6:26, 33–43). The phrase "an Ephraimite" in Elkanah's genealogy (1:1) should be understood to mean that they lived among the Ephraimites. This is further supported by the fact that Samuel wore a linen ephod (2:18) and ministered in the sanctuary.

They worshiped no other gods but the Lord of hosts, who cannot be "defied" by an enemy (1 Sam. 17:45). They lived a good life. The focus of the story is on Samuel's mother, Hannah, whose name means "grace." Hannah's inability to have children spoiled the happiness of her marriage to Elkanah, whose name ironically means "God creates" or "God possesses." It is likely that Elkanah married Peninnah because Hannah was barren.

To not have children in that culture was viewed as a disgrace or a sign of God's disapproval (Gen. 30:1, 22–23). Yet Scripture includes several stories about formerly childless women who, after being visited by God, gave birth to outstanding leaders such as Isaac (Gen. 21:1–8), Jacob (Gen. 25:19–26), Joseph (Gen. 30:1–4, 22–24), and Samson (Judg. 13:2–3, 24). Elkanah's double portion of gifts to Hannah was a sign of his great affection (cf. Gen. 43:34). Peninnah seemed jealous and intentionally hurt Hannah, who did not reciprocate but chose to weep in silence.

1:8–18. Hannah's Vow. Elkanah's reference to his devotion as more important than ten sons links this story with the previous book in the Bible (Ruth 4:15 refers to seven sons). Like Naomi, Hannah in her despair decided to turn to the God of Israel for help. Neither of these two ladies was disappointed in the end. Samuel's parents went on annual pilgrimages to the sanctuary at Shiloh to present themselves and their offerings before the Lord. This statement links the books of Samuel with the end of the book of Judges, where it is explained how an annual festival to the Lord was established in Israel (Judg. 21:19; cf. Ex. 23:17).

During the pilgrimages Hannah did not eat, yet she sat politely with her family until the end of the meals. There in God's presence at Shiloh, Hannah poured her heart out and asked the Lord to give her a son. She made a sacred vow (cf. Num. 30) to dedicate him to lifelong service in the sanctuary. Hannah's vow begins and ends with the mention of God's name. She also solemnly promised to raise her child as a Nazirite. The Nazirites were persons whose appearance and behavior showed a special dedication to God (see Num. 6; Judg. 13). After receiving a blessing from Eli, Hannah returned home in full confidence that the Lord had heard her supplication.

1:19–28. Samuel is Born and Dedicated. Whenever a Bible passage states that the Lord "remembers" an individual or group, it means that He plans to bring an end to their distress (cf. Gen. 8:1; Ex. 2:24—3:10). God's providence overrode Hannah's inability to have children. Although Samuel's birth was natural, it was remarkable because the divine power was at work in a special way at his conception. This is why Hannah named her son Samuel, which can mean "His name is God" or "[the one] heard by God." Both meanings demonstrate how in biblical times names commemorated significant experiences with the living God. The verb "to ask" dominates this passage in the original Hebrew (especially vv. 26 and 27). Hannah's experience anticipates Jesus's words, "Ask and it will be given to you..." (Matt. 7:7).

Hannah knew that her child was a special gift from God. After she stopped nursing him, she kept her vow and dedicated him to serve the Lord at the sanctuary in Shiloh under Eli's care. This was in spite of Samuel's young age. According to the custom in those days, a special ceremony was held for the child at the age of two or three years to mark the end of the weaning period. Abraham did this for his son Isaac (Gen. 21:8).

Hannah's act of faith received support from her husband, whose words sounded as reassuring as the blessing she had previously received from the high priest Eli (v. 17). The couple's special offering to the Lord also included "a three-year-old bull" (v. 25), as well as a measure of flour and grape juice. Yet the best part of the offering was Samuel, their "living sacrifice," who was dedicated to the Lord all his life (v. 28). Hannah's dedicatory words remind us of Eli's blessing (v. 17) and underline the complete fulfillment of the promised blessing.

2:1–10. Hannah's Prayer. Since this prayer takes a poetic form, it has also been called a song or psalm. In fact, many prayers found in the Bible are praise hymns, just like the one composed by Daniel in Babylon (Dan. 2:20–23). Hannah's prayer can be best described as a thanksgiving psalm of victory. Some interpreters call Hannah's prayer the "*Magnificat* of the Old Testament" due to its similarity with Mary's song of praise found in Luke 1.

This prayer celebrates God's righteousness and sovereignty as it brings down the proud and lifts up the humble. It praises God because He is powerful enough to reverse the fortunes of human beings. In a situation filled with hostility and despair, the Lord has provided a way out. He who is perfectly holy has exalted Hannah's horn, a common biblical symbol of power (see Ps. 92:10). The word "horn" in the original Hebrew is found at the beginning and end of this prayer, forming brackets around it. The reference to God guarding the feet of His children is a metaphor of divine providence (v. 9).

The Lord also upsets human schemes and causes reversals in individual lives and societies. Poor and rich, weak and mighty, living and dead are all subject to the One who is all powerful. To bring up from the grave (Heb. *she'ol*; v. 6) means to deliver from the power of death (see Ps. 30:3–4). God alone controls the rise and fall of nations on the face of all the earth. Divine security and stability are comparable to a rock, a metaphor for God's never-failing support and protection.

As Hannah said, God is all-knowing and examines the actions of human beings (cf. Prov. 24:12). Her prayer begins with a personal experience, but it ends with a far and wide proclamation of God's goodness and power. He has promised to take an active role in the events of human history in order to save the righteous and punish the wicked. Even the remotest people on earth (v. 10) would see God's involvement in the events of history through His appointed agent, who would be anointed to fulfill His great plan of salvation. God's "anointed one" is *mashiakh* in Hebrew, the word from which "Messiah" is derived. Here the term refers to the future king of Israel, who would be chosen by God. The psalm looks forward to the reign of David, the man after God's own heart, but it equally anticipates the future Son of David, the Savior of the world. His life and work will bring about God's ultimate victory over cosmic evil.

2:12–17. The Wicked Sons of Eli. It is tragic that the two priests who ministered before the Lord did not acknowledge His holy presence in the sanctuary. Their high calling should have been to exalt the holiness of God before all who came to worship. They had been called to be a light to Israel, but these two sons of Eli practiced evil and wickedness in God's very presence in the sanctuary.

Priests in Israel were entitled to a portion of the animal offering only after the fat had been burned as a sacrifice to the Lord. But the sons of Eli put themselves in first place and their servant threatened to use force to take whatever the priests wanted, showing contempt for God and His holy place. Individuals in leadership positions who dare to abuse their privileged status and take advantage of others cannot escape divine retribution.

2:18-21. Samuel's Childhood Ministry.

The sons of Eli set a very negative example for young Samuel, who ministered before the Lord under Eli's supervision. But Samuel's character shows the opposite of what he saw in the behavior of Hophni and Phinehas. His spiritual ascent is contrasted with the moral descent of the house of Eli. In the same sanctuary of God where an obedient person prospers, the proud and the arrogant are condemned.

The narrative demonstrates the radical change in the life of Hannah and her husband as they went to the sanctuary every year. Yes, they went full of joy and gratitude to worship the Lord but also to visit their son who was already ministering before the Lord. He was the concrete expression of an answered prayer, growing now before the Lord to become one of the most important leaders of God's people. This time Hannah did not ask for a child, but Eli blessed her, asking the Lord to give her more children. He appropriated her prayer, perhaps with a poignant recognition and regret for his own failings.

The contrast between Samuel, a growing boy of integrity and promise, and Eli's own decadent sons was readily apparent. The blessing was more than a simple pronouncement of gracious words and hopes. It conveyed the direct and rewarding interaction by God in the lives of the faithful parents, as evidenced by the children born to them year by year. Thus, the divine blessing Eli was prompted to give carried an implied rebuke for his own inexcusable failings to confront the problems in his own family. Eli is presented to us as a pathetic figure, one who knew what was right and perhaps earnestly wished things to be different, but who lacked the will to act and weakly settled for events to play out with terrible consequences.

2:22-36. Prophecy Against Eli's Household.

Ironically, the Tent of Meeting between the holy God and His worshiping people (Ex. 29-40) became a meeting point between corrupt priests and women who served at the entrance of the tabernacle (cf. Ex. 38:8). The morally weak father could only rebuke his sons (1 Sam. 2:24) instead of finding courage to remove them from the priestly office.

The two men had gone so far in their sins that they were affecting the spiritual lives of others. They represented God in the eyes of the people. As such there was no remedy for their transgressions, and nothing less than death was their deserved punishment (cf. Lev. 10:1-3); God had pronounced a death penalty against them. They sinned greatly against both God and their fellow Israelites by defeating the very purpose for which the Lord had appointed them to the priestly ministry (Deut. 33:8-10). As for young Samuel, he grew in good reputation with God and other people, as the boy Jesus would do many years later (cf. Luke 2:52).

Eli's desperate warnings to his sons were reinforced by a prophetic voice. A man of God not only rebuked the sins committed in Eli's household but also predicted the end to his priestly dynasty. Of particular note was the prediction that Eli's male descendants would die young. The presence of old persons in one's household was a visible sign of God's blessings in biblical times. The Hebrew word for "house" can refer to family or dynasty, and it occurs no less than ten times in this passage. The harsh verdict pronounced here applied primarily to the death of Eli's sons, who both died a violent death in a single day (1 Sam. 4:11), showing that they did not represent God, for He was not with them in battle. That same verdict applies later to the sad story of the massacre of the priests of Nob (chap. 22).

The text does not reveal who was appointed by God to take the place of Eli and his family. The later biblical narrative informs us that the line of Zadok, the priest who replaced Eli's descendant Abiathar, served the Lord faithfully during the time of God's "anointed" leader (v. 36), King David (2 Sam. 8:17; 1 Kin. 2:26-27). The words referring to God's anointed in vv. 10 and 35 bracket a passage in which the story of Samuel's ascent and the descent of the sons of Eli is located. Moreover, the same Hebrew word ('aman; "to be reliable, faithful") can refer to both the priest and his house. As for Samuel, he was destined to become a faithful prophet of the Lord, which is the topic of the next passage.

3:1-21. Samuel's First Prophecy.

Chapter 3 presents the story of Samuel's call to prophetic ministry. The revelation that God gave to Samuel marked him as a prophet. Samuel was not the only person in the Bible who was qualified to minister as both priest and prophet. Some later prophets like Jeremiah and Ezekiel, though born into priestly families, were called by God to prophetic ministry. The Levites were not given a territory to live in but rather were spread throughout the tribes. Phinehas, grandson of Aaron, was given territory in the mountains of Ephraim (Josh. 24:33), although Samuel's family came through the line of Korah and not Aaron (1 Chr. 6:33–38). It seems then that a few Levite families lived in that area.

God's call to Samuel came in the context of the young man's faithful ministry under the officiating high priest, who affectionately called him "my son." The golden lamp of God located in the Holy Place provided light from evening till morning (Ex. 27:20–21; Lev. 24:1–4). Together with God's ark, the lamp symbolized God's presence in the tabernacle. The mention of the Lord's voice (Ex. 25:22; Num. 7:89), combined with the words "the LORD came and stood" (1 Sam. 3:10), is reminiscent of Moses's experience with God on Mount Sinai (Ex. 33:20—34:8). Yet the divine voice was not recognized by young Samuel or the aged priest. Revelation through a prophetic word was rare at that time and never before had Samuel received a direct revelation from God. Following the third call, Eli instructed Samuel on how he should answer the Lord. Being in a state of awe, Samuel omitted the word "Lord." By asking that important question, Samuel was becoming a servant of the Lord.

This chapter also reports another message of calamity that was to come on Eli's family. The tragic judgment was inevitable because the sins of the people had reached a full measure (cf. Gen. 15:16; 2 Chr. 36:16). These words only confirmed that which the man of God had predicted before (1 Sam. 2:27–36). In agreement with Hebrew thought, God first informed Samuel of what would happen and then gave the reason why. Eli's sons were committing a grave sacrilege against God. Tingling of both ears (3:11) is a figure of speech that describes the shock felt by all who heard the report about the disaster (2 Kin. 21:12; Jer. 19:3). Although Eli had rebuked his sons (1 Sam. 2:23–25), he was not able to restrain them.

The revelation sent by God did not make Samuel arrogant. He continued his daily duties as before, much like David, who went back to his flock after being anointed as the next king. Samuel also kept quiet about the message he had received in order to spare Eli from grief. An affectionate relationship had formed between the two, and the words "my son" could indicate Eli's informal adoption of Samuel. The old priest made Samuel swear that he would tell him the whole truth. The oath formula referring to God's punishment (v. 17; cf. Ruth 1:17) omits an explicit mention of harmful consequences involved.

Publicly, Samuel was recognized as a faithful and trustworthy prophet of God. He paid careful attention to God's messages and faithfully delivered them to the people, even a message of rebuke concerning Eli's family, even though Eli was like a father to him. True prophets delivered messages of hope *and* rebuke. Moreover, the words that God spoke through them did come to pass (Deut. 18:22), and this was true of Samuel. From then on, the word of the Lord and prophetic visions would no longer be rare (cf. v. 1) at the sanctuary in Shiloh or in all of Israel.

4:1—8:22
Battles with the Philistines

As was the case in the book of Judges, 1 Samuel reports that God's punishment for Israel's sins came in the form of foreign oppression. The first to be judged was Eli's family, followed by the whole nation when the Philistines captured the sacred ark of the covenant. Although Samuel is not mentioned in 4:1—7:1, everything revolves around his ministry and the coming challenge to the theocracy by the people. First, the prophecy of the unknown prophet and Samuel was now fulfilled with the death of Eli's sons and his own death. The capture of the ark would demonstrate that the Lord was able to overcome His enemies without the presence of a human king. The narrative is a display of God's sovereignty, although it would first appear that He was defeated by the Philistines. He defeated them in their own territories, in the presence of their own gods, and He was the one who returned the ark to Israel. Two important affirmations of Samuel are offered here to the reader. One is the fulfillment of his prophetic voice, demonstrating that he was a prophet of the Lord. The other points to the future when Samuel would tell the people that they did not need a king because the Lord had already demonstrated that He could defeat their enemies (the story of the ark's capture).

4:1–11. The Ark of God Captured. The next three chapters of 1 Samuel focus on the ark of the covenant, as if to reinforce the sad condition of the priesthood but particularly to highlight God's sovereignty. The author also gives a report about the death of several members of Eli's family in a single day, as foretold by a man of God (1 Sam. 2:34) and by Samuel (3:11–14). This certainly is a very dark chapter in the book, comparable with chapter 31, which reports the death of Saul and Jonathan. The first part of the chapter tells about the Philistine victory over Israel, while the second describes the impact of the defeat on Eli's family.

The Philistines at this time were a mix of people by the same name who had lived along the coast of the Holy Land during the time of Abraham. They were probably migrants from the Greek island of Crete (biblical Caphtor, according to the prophets; Jer. 47:4; Amos 9:7). These long time enemies of Israel were descendants of Ham (Gen. 10:6, 14). They settled the southeastern coast of the Mediterranean and formed a confederation of five cities (pentapolis): Ashdod, Ashkelon, Gaza, Ekron, and Gath. For a long time, they were at war with the Israelites and controlled them militarily. The first reported battle took place at Ebenezer, which means "the stone of Help(er)" (cf. 1 Sam. 7:12). The battle's outcome made a major impact on Israel's worship, resulting in the celebration of God's abiding presence in the midst of His people.

By the order of the elders, who were replacing the aged priest Eli, the ark was brought onto the battlefield. This was done with the hope that the ark's presence would ensure the Israelite victory as it did at the conquest of Jericho (Josh. 6). The ark was a wooden chest containing the two stone tablets that represented the covenant between the Lord and Israel (Deut. 9:11; 10:5).

Israel treated the ark as almost an idol instead of opening their hearts to the living "LORD of hosts." The Philistine knowledge of Israel's religion was very limited and even incorrect. They thought that the Hebrews worshiped idols because the Hebrews brought a sacred object to the battlefield (v. 8). The Philistines had heard about the ten plagues the Lord had sent against Egypt (Josh. 2:10–11), but they thought those events had taken place in the wilderness.

In the parlance of the ANE at that time, the term "Hebrews" was a common designation for the people of Israel. The first person recorded in the Bible to be called a Hebrew was Abram (Gen. 14:13). It is uncertain where the name came from, but most likely it was the plural form of a term used to identify the descendants of Eber (Gen. 11:16–17). Eber, the great grandson of Shem, died just 16 years before Abraham (see "A Chronology Following the Internal Timeline of the Bible," p. 111).

When the Israelites uttered a loud shout (vv. 5–6), its effect was felt far and wide. In response to it, the Philistine cry was prompted by a great fear, yet they were still able to gather courage to fight with full strength as "men" (v. 9). In a military context the word "man/men" stands for strength and courage (1 Kin. 2:2). But not only were the Hebrews utterly defeated, the holy ark was captured by the enemy as a symbol of a defeated God. The statues of gods were customarily carried away by the conquering army as war trophies. All the Israelites could do was run for their lives and grieve over their great loss.

4:12–18. Death of Eli. A soldier from the tribe of Benjamin brought the bad news about the defeat. External signs of mourning included rending of clothes and throwing dirt or ashes on the head (2 Sam. 1:2). The report he gave to Eli increased in intensity (1 Sam. 4:17) and climaxed with the capture of the ark, news which the old priest had greatly feared (v. 13). The impact of losing the ark and his sons in battle led to Eli's death. His leadership had lasted four decades, just like the careers of some of Israel's famous earlier judges (Othniel and Gideon; Judg. 3:11; 8:28) and future kings (David and Solomon; 1 Chr. 29:27; 2 Chr. 9:30). The deaths of Eli and his sons on the same day brought the end to this priestly line, as predicted by a man of God (1 Sam. 2:27–36) and by Samuel (3:15 14).

4:19–22. Ichabod. The last in the series of disasters on that fateful day was the death of Phinehas's wife during her childbirth. We do not know much about Eli's daughters-in-law, but it is clear from the narrative that although Eli's sons were married, they still committed immoral acts (2:22). Overcome with pain, Phinehas's wife managed to name her child before dying (cf. Rachel; Gen. 35:18). Names often commemorated important events that took place at the child's birth. The name Ichabod, which means "no [more] glory," was to remind all Israelites of the tragic loss of the sacred ark. The word "glory" is here a substitute name for the ark of the covenant.

5:1–12. The Philistines and the Ark. The defeat of the Israelites implied that the stronger people prevailed over the gods of the weaker one. This is why war trophies, such as images of gods (idols), sacred articles, and pieces of armament such as swords, were deposited as trophies in the temples (21:9; 31:10; Dan. 1:2). The capture of the ark of the covenant by the Philistines teaches us that the Lord is stronger than any other being. Far from being defeated by the Philistines, the God of Israel still ruled over people and their gods, since both proved powerless in His very presence. The narrative prepares the way for the opposition of God and Samuel to the establishment of a monarchy in Israel. This may be the reason why the text refers to God's "hand," symbolizing His active role in the events reported. This word is found at least seven times in chapters 5 and 6.

The ark of God was captured and carried by the Philistines to the temple in Ashdod, a town located near the coast and a member of the five-city confederation ruled by the Philistine "lords." In addition to Ashdod, two more cities (Gath and Ekron) are mentioned in this chapter. The five principal cities of Philistia are listed in 1 Samuel 6:17. Dagon was a god of fertility and the chief god to the Philistines. Another temple to the same deity was located in Gaza, but Samson had destroyed it earlier (Judg. 16:30).

In the morning, Dagon was found prostrate before the sacred ark as a sign of reverence and total submission. This position showed the Lord's superior power over other gods. But Dagon was not the only target of the Lord's hand or the manifestation of His power. Many of the people were struck by a plague of tumors, reminiscent of bubonic plague, that was most likely spread by mice (mentioned in the Septuagint, the Greek translation of the Hebrew Bible). The plague was life threatening (cf. covenant curses in Deut. 28).

This story may remind us of the Lord's plagues on the gods of Egypt (Ex. 12:12) and the readiness of the Egyptian magicians to admit that "the finger of God" was at work and nothing could match such a power (Ex. 8:19). The cry of the Philistines "went up to heaven" (v. 12), meaning it was heard by the merciful Lord. The next chapter tells about the resolution of this problem.

6:1—7:1. The Ark Returned to Israel. In Ekron, one of the five main cities in Philistia, the religious leaders responded to pressure from the Lord and decided to return the ark to the territory of Israel. The second half of this chapter tells how the people of Beth Shemesh reacted when the ark reached their city. Since handling the ark correctly was a serious matter, the plan for its safe return to Israel came from the Philistine priests, assisted by diviners, whose function was similar to that of prophets. These two classes of religious personnel made important decisions for rituals and the future. This is why they were consulted regarding the details about where and how the ark should be returned. It needed to be sent back with a guilt offering that would acknowledge the superior power of Israel's God and recognize the wrong done by the Philistines.

In v. 3 of the Greek translation (Septuagint) and a manuscript from Qumran, the text reads "and atonement will be made for you," in contrast with the Hebrew text, which refers to a "trespass"/"guilt" offering required for a sacrilege. The number of golden tumors and golden rats matched the number of the cities affected by the plagues. The Philistines believed that when the symbolic objects departed from their territory their troubles would go also. The rats did the opposite of the activities attributed to Dagon, the god of fertility—they devoured the food that people believed their god provided. From a modern medical perspective, the rats were most likely responsible for carrying the disease.

The Bible often connects giving glory to God with making confession of a sin (Josh. 7:19; cf. Rev. 14:7). Some Philistines were unwilling to part with the holy ark, which they believed possessed magical power. The priests and diviners reminded the people of the plagues, which had brought great destruction on Egypt, and called on them to learn lessons from past history. It is remarkable to see how much respect the Philistine priests and diviners had for the God of Israel.

At this time, sacred objects were kept in special chests. The cart carrying the ark and the chest should be pulled by cows. In this story, the cows lowed continuously as they went because they were steered to go in a direction opposite to their instincts. This was done without human agency. It is implied that God's angels were leading the cows in the direction of the land of Israel. The phenomenon was witnessed by the rulers and the people from each of the five city-states of Philistia.

The name Beth Shemesh means the house/temple of the sun-god Shamash. It was the nearest Israelite town located on the border with the Philistine territory. It also was a town in Israel where priests lived (Josh. 21:13–16). When the people saw the ark, they offered thanksgiving sacrifices to God, whose power and grace were at work in bringing the sacred ark home. The handling of the ark was the work of the male descendants of Levi (i.e., the Levites; Deut. 10:8). No other persons were allowed to perform this duty (Num. 4:19–20).

It appears that the ark became as dangerous to the Israelites as it had been to the Philistines. The people who looked into the ark committed the sin of irreverent curiosity and many died as a result.

The people's reaction was similar to that of the Philistines when they were struck earlier by the plague of tumors. There was much they did not understand about how God's holy presence was manifested in the ark and how to stand before Him. In the end, the ark was sent to Kiriath Jearim, a city located west of Jerusalem. It could not be returned to Shiloh because the sanctuary had been abandoned by the Lord and most probably was destroyed by the Philistines (see Jer. 7:12–15; cf. Ps. 78:60–61; see "Shiloh," p. 920). The new home of the sacred object was that of a priestly family, with whom it resided until the days of King David (2 Sam. 6).

7:2–17. Samuel Judges Israel. The death of the irreverent persons reported in the previous chapter caused the people to be fearful and the ark to remain in one place for decades. While many of Israel's earlier judges had functioned, perhaps primarily, as military leaders, Samuel's primary role was spiritual and administrative. As judge, priest, and prophet, he was faithful in his ministry to God and to the people of Israel.

Israel was oppressed by enemies during most of Samuel's time as judge. The precondition to peace and freedom was the rejection of idols, just as in the times of the patriarchs (Gen. 35:2–4), Joshua (24:16–23), and the Judges (10:16). The text refers to "Ashtoreths" (Heb. 'ashtarot), images of the Canaanite goddess of love and fertility. Her Babylonian name was Ishtar. It also mentions habbe'alim, which were images of the storm god Baal, sometimes called Haddad. Samuel urged the people to turn away from idols and to serve God wholeheartedly. The heart was considered the thinking organ in biblical times and here it stands for one's whole being.

In this period of Israel's history, Mizpah was the place for national assemblies (1 Sam. 10:17; Judg. 20:1). The city was situated north of Jerusalem in the territory of Benjamin, whose people were famous warriors. Samuel was a leader known as a man of prayer, and he was urged by the people to never stop praying for them. Biblical prophets were known as persons who prayed on behalf of others (Gen. 20:7; Ex. 32:31–32; Jer. 15:1; Amos 7:2). Even in the later books of the Bible, Samuel is remembered as a man of prayer (Ps. 99:6; Jer. 15:1). The ritual of pouring out water before the Lord is attested only here in the Bible. Taken in context, it could be a ritual expression of the pouring out of one's life in prayer to God for spiritual cleansing (cf. 1 Sam. 1:15).

The second half of chapter 7 echoes the pattern known from the book of Judges about Israel's sin, repentance, and then salvation. Judgment on Israel's sins would usually come in the form of a foreign invasion. Verses 7 and 8 describe Philistine aggression and Israel's fear. The people turned to Samuel for help; he then offered prayer and a sacrifice to the Lord. As in the times of the patriarchs, the prophet selected a place and built an altar to offer sacrifices to the Lord, which has implications if the sanctuary was not destroyed in Shiloh.

Through the forces of nature, such as thunder and lightning, God caused panic among the Philistines and thus helped Israel (cf. Judg. 5:20–21). Such a reaction by the Lord reflects the divine covenant promises (Ex. 23:22). A stone named Ebenezer was erected to serve as a memorial of deliverance. Stone or rock is a common metaphor for God in the Bible. The place where Israel had earlier been defeated (1 Sam. 4:1) became the place of victory.

This victory, though small, was important. Unfortunately, it put only a temporary stop to the Philistine oppression. The Israelites also lived in peace with the Amorites. Their name literally meant "westerners" and was used in Mesopotamia to describe the people who lived on the western side of the river Euphrates. The Amorites at this time lived in the cities and towns of the Israelites.

Samuel's base was now his hometown of Ramah (1:19), the base from which he made yearly rounds to administer justice in towns of the heartland. He was born in this place and lived there until placed in service at Shiloh. Bethel, Gilgal, and Mizpah (v. 16) were important centers in central Israel. The name Bethel means "house of God," and the place was located north of Jerusalem. The patriarchal stories describe how this town held religious significance from early times. Abram worshiped there, while Jacob later changed its name from Luz to Bethel (Gen. 28:19). Samuel's regular trips and the building of altars remind one of Abram's journeys through the land of promise (Gen. 12). Throughout his life, the prophet Samuel was a man of prayer, following in the footsteps of his mother. His close communion with God was the ultimate source of power for his outstanding political and religious career.

8:1–22. Israel Demands a King. From the beginning, the idea of an earthly monarch posed a huge problem for the prophetic view of Israel's government. The establishment of the monarchy necessitated many changes at both national and local levels. The divine kingship, known as theocracy, would be at odds with human kingship. The disadvantages of Israel's monarchy easily outweighed its advantages.

Disappointed with the behavior of Eli's two sons and the character of Samuel's sons, the elders asked for a new form of leadership that would conform with the customs of the surrounding nations (Deut. 17:14). It is ironic that Samuel's sons were judges entrusted with the execution of justice in Israel (Ex. 23:8), yet they perverted justice. At this time, positions of power were often assigned based on hereditary rights. This ensured stability in society. The downside of this custom was it sometimes created a platform for nepotism and corruption.

There were other reasons for the elders' request. One concern was the ever-present threat posed by the Philistines, the enemy whose military actions appeared to put Israel's very existence at risk. According to Samuel's view, the people asked for a king because they lacked faith in God and had lost sight of His power as manifested in the story of the ark. They were rejecting Him as King (8:7). This is why the prophet was so reluctant to listen to them. He knew very well that a strong centralized government could lead to abuse of power.

God respects the freedom He granted to humans, so He was willing to yield to the people's desire for a king. This was the same Lord who had saved them from oppressive slavery in Egypt and whom the people had proclaimed as their only King (Ex. 15:18; Judg. 8:23). For centuries, He had fought Israel's battles and given them many victories. This is why, prior to the institution of monarchy, Israel was a theocracy, meaning that God was their King. Gideon, one of the judges, knew this very well. When asked to be king, he refused and told them that the Lord ruled over His people (Judg. 8:23). Now the people were rejecting God as their King. In spite of this, the Lord was ready to take an active part in the selection of their earthly king.

Samuel informed the people that the future king would behave like the kings of the surrounding nations. His actions would be in conformity with the standard practices of ANE monarchs. Judging by their speech, the elders expected to get something from their future king. Yet Samuel described the king as one who would take from them and not give. Like the Lord, the future king would receive ten percent of all the material increase in the land (Lev. 27:30–32).

The king would take the best fields and estates for himself (1 Kin. 21). He would also collect heavy taxes. He would take young men and women into the army and press them into forced labor. Some would become his army commanders and administrative officers in the likeness of Egypt. Biblical mention of chariots and horses is often negative because they reminded people of Egypt's opposition to God during Israel's Exodus (Deut. 17:16). All this would clash with the personal freedom of individuals and families in Israelite society. The cry to God against foreign oppressors would soon be replaced with cries about their king's exploitations.

Samuel's prophecy about the oppression and hardships that would come with a monarch would be most obviously fulfilled by the fourth-generation monarch. While the scriptural record does not emphasize these kinds of hardships during the reigns of Saul and David, we get a glimpse of such kingly excesses in the reign of Solomon (1 Kin. 4:7, 22–23, 26–28; 5:13–17; 11:3). Those excesses are explicitly highlighted in the story of the protests of the people at the beginning of Rehoboam's reign (1 Kin. 12:4). Even as God acquiesced to their demands for a monarchy, He descriptively warned His people of the very things that ultimately would undermine that monarchy and result in civil war and a divided kingdom.

Sometimes God allows people to make choices contrary to His warnings and then suffer the consequences of those choices. The people and their elders rejected not only Samuel as their leader but also God Himself. Samuel was so upset that he sent the elders home without an answer. The people's desire to be like the other nations represented a flat denial of God's call of the patriarchs and also of Israel's unique status in the world.

9:1—15:35

THE REIGN OF SAUL

This narrative covers the appointment of Saul as king (9:1—12:25) and his kingship (13:1–35), which bridges the gap between the time of the judges (Samuel being the last) and the anointing of David. The reign of Israel's first king had a promising beginning, but Saul turned out to be a very different leader from Samuel in his lack of obedience to the Lord. This resulted in God's rejection of Saul and the end of his dynasty, similar to the outcome of the priestly line of Eli.

9:1—12:25
Saul Becomes King

The fact that at least five chapters in 1 Samuel (8–12) are devoted to the establishment of Israel's kingship shows how important this event was in Israel's history. The narrative in chapters 9–12 is dominated by two leaders, the prophet Samuel and King Saul.

9:1–26. Saul Chosen to Be King. The story in this chapter describes the circumstances under which the aged Samuel and the young Saul met, most likely for the first time. It is the story of a young man who searched for lost donkeys and found a kingdom. Donkeys were beasts of burden used for short distance transportation, while camels were used for long caravan trips, especially across deserts.

The text makes it clear that Saul, whose name means "asked of the Lord," was not seeking to become someone of high importance. In this sense, Saul's beginnings were like David's. If it were not for God's providence, Saul would have never become king in Israel. In this way, the reader is shown that the choice of Saul to be Israel's first king was God's will. As Hannah had said in her prayer, God raises the humble to the throne of honor and glory among princes (2:8). Kish, Saul's father, was a man of standing in Benjamin. This was a small tribe (cf. Judg. 20) that was sandwiched between Ephraim in the north and Judah in the south. The men of Benjamin were known to be excellent warriors. Saul was a very handsome man, partly due to his unusual height.

The author narrates the details of Saul's search in order to show how God Himself directed the course of events in Saul's life. A lengthy search for lost donkeys was followed by an unusual persistence of the servant who "happened" to have some money that could be used as a gift for the prophet, as was customary in Bible times (1 Kin. 14:3; 2 Kin. 8:8–9; Ezek. 13:19). The servant insisted that Saul ask the man of God for help in their search for the lost donkeys. The title "man of God" (1 Sam. 9:6) was used to refer to a spiritual leader of the people. A prophet was one whom God used to bring messages to His people. A seer was a person who received visions from God. God used His "seer" to find the person He chose to be anointed as king.

None of the things reported in this story happened by accident. When Samuel returned to Ramah (vv. 16–17), the Lord told him about Saul. The aged prophet was told by God to anoint the young man to become a "commander," "ruler," or "prince" (Heb. *nagid*) over Israel and subject to the supreme authority of the Lord, Israel's true King. In the context of the anointing of Saul, the word "king" is not used, only the title "prince." The king of Israel would be a vassal under the true King of Israel. When speaking of Israel, God used the affectionate term, "My people." The language used by God to describe His people's distress under the oppression by their future kings reminds one of Israel's outcry in Egypt (Ex. 3:9).

The old prophet and the young man met at the city gate, which was an important place used for business transactions in the town. Saul's modesty reminds the Bible reader of Gideon's response to the heavenly messenger (Judg. 6:15). Yet Samuel's duty was to treat Saul as the guest of honor. First, he gave the young man a seat in a prominent position at the table. Samuel then gave him the best portion of the food. Later, the prophet emptied a flask of fragrant olive oil on Saul's head.

Israel's "desire" (1 Sam. 9:20) was to have a king, and God's answer was the choice of Saul. "The desire of nations," on the other hand, has always been to have a universal king of peace, and God's choice is Jesus the Messiah (Hag. 2:7; see "The Desire of All Nations," p. 1136). The task before Saul was to deliver Israel from the Philistines (1 Sam. 9:16), but the task of Jesus is to save His people from their sins (Matt. 1:21). Saul was to rule over one nation, whereas Christ is King of kings and Lord of lords. His kingdom has no boundaries, nor will it ever end.

9:27—10:16. Saul Anointed King. Due to the Philistine threat and possible jealousy from some ambitious persons in Israel, Saul's anointing was done in secret. This would also be true of Samuel's future anointing of David (1 Sam. 16:1–13). So Israel's first two kings were both secretly anointed by Samuel. The ceremony consisted of pouring fragrant oil on the head of the person designated to be king or priest (Ex. 30:22–33). The anointed person was set apart for a special task before God. Because of this custom, Israel's king became known as the Lord's "anointed" or messiah (Heb. *mashakh*). In this way, the anointing pointed to the future Messiah, who would be set apart by God to save His people from their sins.

The future king was anointed by the prophet and expected to follow his instructions. The text says that Samuel also kissed Saul as a sign of affection between the old prophet and the young man. Like Moses going down to Egypt, Saul was in need of assurance that the Lord would be with him. Just as God had given Moses three signs, which pointed to His power (Ex. 3), so now Samuel gave Saul three signs to assure him that he was chosen by the Lord to be king and lead God's people.

The first sign was the good news that the lost donkeys had been found (v. 20). God assured Saul that He would care for his needs. The second sign was connected with God's appearance to Jacob at Bethel, where He assured the patriarch of the divine plan for his life. In that same place, Saul was given two loaves of bread that were intended for the sanctuary of Bethel. This demonstrated that his future office was sacred in God's eyes.

The last sign was related to a group of "prophets." At this time, they belonged to small communities of individuals who together sought mutual spiritual support. These communities later flourished during the time of the Greater Prophetic Movement started by Elijah and Elisha (1 Kin. 20:35). The group was led by the leader, called "father" in this text (10:12; cf. 2 Kin. 2:12). Accompanied by various musical instruments, they praised God as they were moved by the Spirit. One important consequence of these signs was that Saul was changed. He became a different person, filled with God's Spirit, thus confirming his appointment as king.

Saul's hometown was Gibeah, which means "hill." It was located in the territory of Benjamin, north of Jerusalem, and became known as Gibeah of God, Gibeah of Saul, and Gibeah of Benjamin. The presence of a Philistine post in that town attested to the Philistine military superiority over Israel at that time. After Saul became king, he made Gibeah the capital city of Israel. As Saul returned to his hometown, some people were curious to know more about his whereabouts. So far only he and Samuel knew about his anointing to be Israel's first king. This secret was kept even from close relatives.

10:17–27. Saul Proclaimed King. The national assemblies of Israel were held in the city of Mizpah, which had become an important spiritual center after Israel's victory over the Philistines (7:15–16). In his speech to that city, Samuel reminded the people that the Lord was the only Warrior against Egypt during their Exodus. This was the reason why He was Israel's true King (Ex. 15:18). Samuel did not have any problem with Saul as a person and thought that Saul was the best candidate for this lofty position. The prophet's issue was with Israel for seeking an earthly king in the likeness of the nations.

The right person was chosen through the casting of lots. This was done by the use of two special stones, called the Urim and Thummim, located on the high priest's breastplate. Lots were cast to single out the tribe, clan, family, and finally the individual (Josh. 7:14). When Saul was selected and called by God, he appeared timid. Samuel's introduction of Saul to the assembly was welcomed by the people. The shout "Long live the king" was part of the coronation ceremony (1 Kin. 1:25, 39; 2 Kin. 11:12).

After the royal acclamation, Samuel reiterated the regulations of kingship (cf. 8:11) and wrote them in a book for future generations. The detailed instructions were probably an expansion of the instructions found in Deuteronomy 17:14–20. A few persons, described as "rebels" or "scoundrels" ("sons of worthlessness" in Hebrew), looked down on Saul and seemed not ready to recognize him as their king (v. 27). They refused to call him king, but rather called him "this person." Saul was aware of their resistance, and at this stage in his life, he was able to hold his temper. In his later career, he seemed incapable of controlling his anger.

11:1–15. Saul Saves Jabesh Gilead. This story shows Saul's excellent ability to take charge of the top leadership position to help his fellow Israelites. Israel's first king is described in terms of the judges who ruled before. The Holy Spirit came upon Saul as in times past with Gideon (Judg. 6:34), Jephthah (Judg. 11:29), and Samson (Judg. 14:6; 15:14). The chapter begins and ends with the report of events that took place east of the Jordan. Sandwiched between these two references is a story about Saul in his hometown of Gibeah, west of the Jordan.

Josephus Flavius and a manuscript from Qumran (4QSam^a) both supply noncanonical background information to this story. They tell how the Ammonite king Nahash oppressed the people from the tribes of Gad and Reuben. This cruel ruler plucked out his subjects' right eyes, a deeply humiliating act (Judg. 16:21). Seven thousand people were able to escape and make their way to Jabesh Gilead. The name Nahash in Hebrew means "a serpent." His people, the Ammonites, were the descendants of Lot (Gen. 19:28); their small state lay northeast of the Dead Sea. Since two and a half of Israel's tribes had settled east of the Jordan (Judg. 10:6—11:33), they had clashes with the Ammonites, who lived east of Israel.

Jabesh Gilead was a town located east of the Jordan. People who lived in that town were related to the tribe of Benjamin (Judg. 21:14), in whose territory Gibeah was located. The leaders of Jabesh seemed to have forgotten God's saving power when they doubted whether anyone would help them (1 Sam. 11:3). It is also surprising that they did not ask Saul for help. Though anointed as king, Saul's kingship had not yet been inaugurated, and he resumed his ordinary farming activities. On a previous occasion, Saul had been moved by the Spirit and prophesied (10:10). Here, he forcefully recruited people by using the threats rooted in a covenant-making ceremony (cf. Jer. 34:18).

The unity of Israel's kingdom was always a very delicate matter. It was strongest during David's and Solomon's reigns. When united, Israel's army was stronger than the Ammonites. In their second message to the enemy, the people of Jabesh said, literally in the Hebrew, "we will go out to you" (v. 3). This could be interpreted in two different ways: "we will surrender to you" or "we will come out to fight." This war was not intended to add foreign territory to Israel but to fight against oppression and injustice.

The surprise attack was carried out before dawn, at the time when sleep was deepest. Like Gideon's soldiers, Saul's army attacked from three different directions (cf. Judg. 7). In the end, the credit for victory was given to the Lord, Israel's great Deliverer. Following the victory over the Ammonites, a ceremony was held in Gilgal, a town east of Jericho where the Israelites had earlier celebrated the Passover under Joshua (Josh. 5). During this ceremony, Saul was publically recognized as king over the whole nation. This great celebration included a peace offering and great rejoicing. In biblical times, the greater the sacrifice, the greater was the rejoicing. This occasion was perfect for a renewal of the covenant and for Saul's inauguration. Samuel's farewell speech is found in the next chapter.

12:1–25. Samuel's Address at Saul's Coronation. Samuel opened his speech by declaring that he did not use his power for personal gain (see Num. 16:15) and did not *take* anything from the people. This stands in contrast to Samuel's sons, Joel and Abijah, who had been appointed as judges yet practiced corruption. It also applied to the future king who, according to the prophet's words, would *take* from his subjects one thing after another (1 Sam. 8:11–18). The old prophet

also reiterated his position toward the people's request for a king. Since he did not abuse his office and the Lord had always saved them, he could see no reason for Israel's request for a king.

Samuel mentioned some of the important judges (v. 11), such as Gideon (also called Jerubbaal; cf. Judg. 7:1) and Jephthah. The third name is *bedan* in Hebrew. It could be "Barak" (Judg. 4–5), while it has been suggested that "Samuel" should be read as "Samson" due to the similarity of consonants in the original text. During Saul's inauguration, Samuel invited the people to fear and show respect for the Lord. The future of Israel did not depend so much on the king's ability as it did on the Lord's power and the nation's loyalty to Him.

In closing his speech, Samuel prayed to God for a miraculous manifestation of divine power. In the land of Israel, it rains only from late autumn to early spring. Rain in summer is extremely rare. This miracle performed by God through his prophet demonstrated the power of prayer and the Lord's commitment never to abandon Israel. After all, they were *His* people, and all the nations around them knew this (see Ex. 32:12; Num. 14:15–16). Samuel would continue to pray for them and teach them God's way.

13:1—15:35
Saul's Wars and Conflicts

Saul's reign was characterized by military conflict with the Philistines. The beginning of this king's reign was very successful. Yet the author also records the divine displeasure every time Saul failed to obey God.

13:1–15. Saul's Unlawful Sacrifice. This story contrasts Saul's great fear of the Philistines with Jonathan's courage, summed up in his declaration that the Lord is able to save "by many or by few" (14:6). In the original Hebrew, the first half of v. 1 is incomplete because the first number has accidentally dropped out ("Saul was ___ years old when he began to reign, and he reigned over Israel [forty] two years"). The statement follows the usual biblical formula for a king's age (2 Sam. 2:10; 1 Kin. 14:21; 22:42), but it does not give the age of Saul. Based on the evidence from Acts 13:21, it is probable that Saul reigned over Israel for about forty years. This is far more likely than to say that Saul reigned over Israel for only two years.

It was customary for a king to set up a standing army. Saul did this very thing in anticipation of a war against the Philistines who had gathered in Michmash, located between Bethel and Gibeah. Israel's new king feared the well-organized Philistine army. Yet his son Jonathan, the crown prince, who is mentioned here for the first time, had no fear. He took action against the enemy and triggered the revolt. The ram's horn (*shopar*) was sounded in order to mobilize all Israelite men above twenty years. This brave act on Jonathan's part is credited to his father the king. Israel faced an army much larger and far better equipped for the battle. Some manuscripts say that "thirty thousand chariots" (v. 5) came against them. This could be a scribal error since the difference between the Hebrew words for "three" and "thirty" is rather small. Other manuscripts say "three thousand," which seems more likely.

Samuel had told Saul to wait for him to offer a sacrifice and give some specific instructions for the battle (10:8), and Saul waited for seven days in Gilgal. Because of Samuel's delay, and seeing his army diminish, Saul proceeded to offer a sacrifice. Saul was Israel's political leader, not its religious/priestly leader, and he disobeyed the instructions when he offered the sacrifice. The prophet rebuked him for this. By providing a long answer to a short question, Saul tried to defend himself. The king's disobedience would have serious consequences. He would lose his kingdom in favor of a person whose heart God loved, which alluded to the anointing of David reported later in the book. By disobeying Samuel, Saul rejected God's own instructions. There is a wordplay in v. 14—because Saul failed to heed God's *command*, the Lord would issue a *command* about a new leader. In this story Saul was again called a "prince" (*nagid*), which means that he was subject to the authority of Israel's supreme King.

13:16–23. No Weapons for the Army. After Samuel's departure, Saul moved his army from Gilgal to Gibeah in order to move geographically closer to his son Jonathan. The goal of this move was to form a single army in Geba, the place separated by a valley from Michmash, where the Philistine army was positioned. The enemy's raiders went out regularly and inflicted much damage on the population. By grouping together, Israel's army became more united, while the Philistine army became more and more divided.

The Philistines held the monopoly in that area on iron tools and weapons, so the Israelites lacked the necessary instruments of war. The Israelites also depended on their enemies for the expensive maintenance of their agricultural tools. The high price is expressed by the Hebrew word *pim*, which occurs only here in the Bible and refers to two-thirds of a shekel. Due to the lack of proper armament, most Israelite soldiers fought with bows, arrows, and slingshots.

14:1–23. Jonathan Defeats the Philistines. Chapter 14 presents a story from Saul's career characterized by a mixture of military successes and personal conflicts with other Israelites, including his eldest son Jonathan. The remarkable details found in the narrative, such as the names of the two rocks, Bozez and Seneh (v. 4), place this story in a geographic location the ancient readers would have immediately recognized.

In spite of the fact that the Hebrews used inferior weapons and were fewer in number, Jonathan bravely attacked the Philistine soldiers, whom he identified in a derogatory way as the "uncircumcised" (v. 4). Although the practice of circumcision was not limited to the land of Israel, in this context the term used by Jonathan describes the Philistines, who were not a part of the Abrahamic covenant (cf. Gen. 34:14). Jonathan's courageous action, combined with a supernatural intervention from God in the earthquake, demonstrates that Jonathan was someone who was in close connection with the Lord. His prediction is given in the past tense to stress its certainty: the coming victory is as good as done.

Saul seized the opportunity to start the battle against his bitter enemies. He was accompanied by the priest Ahijah from Shiloh, who, according to some ancient versions, brought the ephod, a garment used by priests for consulting the Lord. Probably the decisions were made based on the "yes" or "no" answers from the use of two stones, Urim for "yes" and Thummim for "no." However, the Hebrew text does not read "ephod," but "ark of the God," and it is better to retain this reading. The ark was a symbol of God's presence among His army. It was brought from Kiriath Jearim for this military event and later returned there.

Saul's soldiers were joined by the Hebrews who were serving in the Philistine army, along with those who had been in hiding (14:21; 13:6). The battle resulted in a great victory for Israel that only Jonathan had expected. The text makes it clear that this success should be credited to the Lord. Later the soldiers pointed to the role that Jonathan played in this battle.

14:24–46. Saul's Rash Oath. In his pride, Saul made a series of impulsive vows that exposed his people and his oldest son to danger. The Bible presents stories such as Jephthah's vow to show how making rash promises can afflict close family members (Judg. 11:30–31). Swearing in the Lord's name is particularly binding (Deut. 23:22–23). It appears that Jonathan had a great concern for the well-being and safety of the soldiers, and in this he was different from Saul. Jonathan's attitude served him well because when his father's irrational behavior threatened his life, the soldiers refused to carry out the execution that came from Saul's impulsive order. After all, Jonathan had only tasted a bit of wild honey, so why such a harsh punishment? What was this in comparison with the great victory granted by the Lord through the bravery of the crown prince?

Exhausted and hungry, the soldiers ate meat with blood in it (vv. 32–33). Eating meat with blood was forbidden in Israel because blood symbolizes life as belonging to God (Gen. 9:4; Lev. 19:26; Deut. 12:23). Saul took action and attempted to solve the problem he had created. When an animal was slaughtered on a stone, the blood could be drained out of its flesh before it was cooked and eaten. But despite his efforts at conformity to God's instructions, it was becoming clear that under Saul's command, the connection between the Lord and Israel's king was growing weaker. Saul would consult the Lord most of the time when he was urged by others to do so (e.g., v. 36), and sometimes the Lord did not answer him. The reason for this must have been his half-hearted devotion to God. Even when people responded to him with silence, he did not realize that the problem was with him and not with others.

14:47—15:9. Saul's Continuing Wars. Throughout Saul's reign, there were battles with surrounding nations, especially the Philistines. Moab, Ammon, and Edom were Israel's three neighbors on the eastern side of the Jordan. All three people groups were related to Israel through the patriarchs. Mention is specifically made of a battle against Amalek. The importance of obedience to God is the topic that dominates the story of God's rejection of Saul as king. Chapter 15 opens with Samuel's firm statement to Saul about the importance of following God's instructions. The people of Amalek were nomadic raiders and bitter enemies of Israel to the south. Samuel called them "wicked" and "sinners" (v. 18). Their attacks against Israel came at the most critical moments of Israel's survival in the wilderness and were aimed at the total destruction of God's people

(Ex. 17:8–16; Deut. 25:17–19). This attitude was in sharp contrast with the Kenites, who showed kindness to Israel, especially through Moses's father-in-law. The command here is in the form of a ban (Heb. *kherem*, "to exterminate") to be carried out on the main Amalekite settlement (v. 5). All the spoils of war were to be dedicated to the Lord.

Saul's decision to spare King Agag and the best part of the spoils stood in direct and flagrant defiance to God's clear command. In the book of Esther, the enemy of the Jewish people was called Haman the Agagite (Esth. 3:1), whose ancestry was Amalekite. Saul may have intended to use Agag as a negotiating tool with the rest of the Amalekite people. But Agag's punishment was intended to correspond with the crimes he had committed (1 Sam. 15:33). While the author states twice that the Lord was sorry for having chosen Saul to be king over Israel (vv. 11, 35), Saul's self-centeredness led him to build a monument to honor himself at Carmel (v. 12).

15:10–35. Saul Rejected as King. When questioned by Samuel, Saul put the blame for disobedience to God on his soldiers' greed, though later he included himself ("we" in v. 15) in his report. He would not admit that he had done anything wrong. For Saul, the end justified the means, and he claimed to want the best animals to offer as sacrifices to the Lord.

Samuel's words from vv. 22–23 read as poetry. In God's eyes, to do what is right is more important than rituals. Obedience takes precedence over the best sacrifices. This same teaching would be proclaimed down through centuries by prophets like Amos, Isaiah, Micah, and Jeremiah. Rebellion and arrogance, on the other hand, are forms of idolatry. Such sins cannot be removed through the performance of religious rites but require true repentance in order for God's forgiving grace to reach us. The Lord grieves when people make wrong choices.

Saul was afraid of the consequences of his disobedience, particularly of his public humiliation, and asked Samuel for forgiveness. He was forgiven, yet his rejection as leader of Israel still stood. He was reaping what he had sown. Saul had rejected God's command, so the Lord rejected him as king. When this happened, Samuel wept bitterly and stopped supporting Saul as king (vv. 7–11). The Lord's previous rejection of Saul had to do with his dynastic succession (13:8–24). In this case, the rejection applies to

Saul himself. The way was now prepared for God's choice of David reported in the chapter that follows.

16:1—31:13
SAUL AND DAVID

The second half of 1 Samuel narrates the interaction between Saul and David. It tells about the rise of David (16:1—17:58), David joining Saul's family (18:1—20:42), Saul's antagonism against David (21:1—26:25), David in Philistia (27:1—30:31), and the deaths of Saul and Jonathan (31:1–13). Samuel, who years before had anointed Saul to be Israel's first king, was now commissioned by the Lord to anoint David to replace Saul. Needless to say, Saul became increasingly jealous of David, who was very gifted and also a man after God's own heart.

16:1—17:58
The Rise of David

The choice of David as the future king of Israel follows the biblical pattern of electing the younger child over the elder. Although not related, this was also the case with Abel, Isaac, Jacob, Rachel, Joseph, Ephraim, Moses, etc. Outside the Bible, the custom was to favor the eldest child or son in the family. The reason given for the reversal in the story of David's anointing is that the Lord looks at the heart of a person.

16:1–13. David Anointed King. The Lord told Samuel to go to the house of Jesse. In order to disguise his true mission, the prophet used the pretext of offering a sacrifice in Bethlehem, the town located just south of Jerusalem. In this way he could not be accused of attempting a conspiracy against Saul. Discretion may have been particularly necessary because the road from Ramah to Bethlehem took Samuel through Saul's city of Gibeah. When Samuel arrives in Jesse's house, an element of suspense is introduced in the narrative as one son after the other is rejected. David's name shows up at the last moment when the prophet, not God, seemed to have run out of options. The unanticipated had happened and God's choice surprised all. Eliab's appearance reminds one of Saul, whose height was unusual (9:2; 10:23). Another biblical text lists the names of Jesse's seven sons and two daughters as follows: Eliab, Abinadab, Shimea, Nethanel, Raddai, Ozem, and David, and the daughters, Zeruiah and Abigail (1 Chr. 2:13–15).

David's occupation as shepherd prepared him to lead God's people (Ps. 78:70–71), as was also the case with Moses (Ex. 3:1). Some ANE kings called themselves shepherds of their people. The author makes it clear that David was the Lord's choice as the next king. He was filled with the power of God's Spirit (1 Sam. 16:13), which came on him as it did on Saul after his anointing (10:6). After Samuel's anointing of David, the old prophet fades away from the book. His privilege was to anoint Saul, Israel's first king, and now he had anointed David, Israel's greatest king and the ancestor of the Messiah. The remaining narrative will focus on the relationship between Saul and David until the day Saul takes his own life. In choosing David, God was about to reshape the concept of the monarchy according to His will.

16:14–23. A Distressing Spirit Troubles Saul. Since Saul had repeatedly disobeyed the Lord's voice, God's Spirit withdrew from him, and in its place an evil spirit began to disturb him. The Bible teaches that evil spirits are subject to God's control (1 Kin. 22:19–23). God's Spirit came on David, while Saul began experiencing serious mental disorders under the influence of an evil spirit. Faced with a permanent threat from the militarily superior Philistines and without God's protection, Saul became increasingly fearful and depressed. His attendants searched for a musician to sooth the king's trouble, based on a widespread belief that musical therapy could help relieve mental distress. They found David, and this is how he entered into the service of the king.

Since the Lord was with David, two of his talents gave him direct access to the court. In addition to being a skilled musician, David, whose experience consisted of fighting off wildlife up to that point, would become an able warrior. In some biblical passages, he is described as a sweet singer in Israel who composed psalms (2 Sam. 23:1; Amos 6:5). The author shows that David, from the beginning of his service, was well disposed and loyal to the king. This is why Saul liked him and began treating him as his own son. Moreover, David's father, Jesse, sent gifts to the king as a pledge of support, loyalty, and also as a means to secure the king's favor toward David. Later on, when David married Saul's daughter Michal, he became a member of the royal family. All of this was possible because of divine providence in the life of the young shepherd who was destined to become the next king of Israel.

17:1–58. David and Goliath. This famous biblical story portrays the triumph of a shepherd boy's faith over the physical strength of a giant who trusted in his arms and his idols. The setting of this event is the war that followed the Philistine invasion of a portion of Israel's territory. The two armies were stationed west of Bethlehem, near Philistine territory. Duels between two opposing champions prior to a full-scale battle were customary in ancient times (see 2 Sam. 2:14–16). The detailed description of Goliath's armor explains why the Israelites were so terrified.

About forty days later, David was sent by his father to bring food provisions to his older brothers, who had been drafted into Saul's army. Jesse also sent a gift to the army commander. The Valley of Elah was not far from the town of Bethlehem. When David saw Goliath and heard him speak, the young shepherd reacted to his words that brought dishonor to God's name. The surprise in the story comes from the fact that David was the youngest and least esteemed child in Jesse's family, yet he became a hero. Others referred to his youth (1 Sam. 17:33), pointing out that he was not of fighting age (which was twenty; Num. 1:3, 20).

David did not fight for his own popularity or gain but solely for God's glory. His dialogue with Saul shows his strong faith in the living God. While the king of Israel put stress on the importance of weapons, David focused on trust in God, who gives victory. Saul's unusual height in Israel was not enough to give him courage to fight this giant. Much like the rest of Israel's fighting men, he was afraid to fight Goliath (v. 11). The people of Israel, together with their leader, seemed to have forgotten God's covenant promise that He would fight their battles (Deut. 20:1–4).

In David's view, Goliath's challenge suggested that his god was superior to the God of Israel. The duel between two unequal soldiers shows the contrasts between an experienced military champion and an experienced champion of faith in the true God. Moreover, this was a clash of instruments of death versus confidence in the Lord of life. Curses by lifeless idols in order to demoralize and intimidate are contrasted with a statement about the living God. The whole world needs to know the saving power of the Lord, who determines the outcome of battles.

David was very confident that God would use his skill with a sling rather than depending on conventional fighting tactics and armor with which David was unfamiliar. The giant underestimated God's chosen instrument and with self-sufficiency went after David, not anticipating that the little shepherd-king would defeat him. David's victory over the giant was complete and became the catalyst of a great victory for the Israelite army.

After the battle, the king inquired of Abner, his chief army commander, about David's family, which apparently did not have a high social standing in Israel. This shows that David's service at the court was not yet permanent (16:17–23). While his musical talents had been known to the king, this time Saul also learned of David's military skills. Because Saul had promised to give his daughter in marriage to the soldier who would defeat Goliath (17:25), he was now obliged to reward David with the fulfillment of his pledge. Understandably, Saul wanted more information about the family standing of his future son-in-law. Now David had officially reached the royal palace—his future home.

18:1—20:42
David, Jonathan, and Saul

Saul's eldest son, Jonathan, who was the crown prince, became David's best friend. The two young men never viewed each other as a rival for the throne. Jonathan, his father's legitimate successor, with time would recognize David as the future king of Israel (1 Sam. 23:16–18).

18:1–16. Saul Resents David. Chapter 18 combines two different topics about David and Saul. David's success is mentioned three times in the text (vv. 5, 14, 30), and the people's love for David, contrasted with Saul's jealousy of him, is also mentioned three times in the chapter (vv. 12, 14–15, 28–29). David was successful because the Lord was with him, as He had been with Joseph in Egypt (Gen. 39:2). It became clear to more and more people that he would become Israel's next king.

David's victory over Goliath brought him much admiration from all the people and especially from Saul's family members. Jonathan made a formal pledge of loyalty to David, which included gifts of great value. When David assumed a high military rank in Saul's army, women in Israel would frequently welcome him after his battles with a song praising the accomplishments of both David and Saul. This way of celebrating victories was an established practice in those times (Judg. 11:34; 2 Sam. 1:20). The author of Exodus describes a similar way by which the Israelites celebrated the Lord's victory over the Egyptians in the Song of the Sea (Ex. 15:20–21).

Saul also liked David, but at the same time he was jealous of the young man's outstanding success. Because the song of the women was based on a numerical progression from thousand to ten thousand (cf. Deut. 32:30; Ps. 91:7; Mic. 6:7), Saul took this to mean that David was more popular. Yet the intention of the words shouted by women was to emphasize the magnitude of the victory and not necessarily to compare and contrast the two military leaders. Even so, the king's interpretation of the words made him very angry, and he began to fear for his throne. On occasion, Saul tried to kill David by throwing a spear at him. When that did not work, Saul schemed to harm him indirectly by appointing David to be in charge of very dangerous military operations so that an enemy would kill him.

18:17–30. David Marries Michal. While Saul's hostility increased, David was not hostile toward him or his family but instead showed great humility. In fact, he was so modest that he seemed willing to give up his claim to marry Saul's oldest daughter. Saul took advantage of that modesty, reneged on his promise, and gave that daughter to another man. This worked to David's favor because Michal, the younger royal princess, was in love with David.

Saul doubtless hoped that a marriage to Michal would make David more subject to his control or that an additional dowry requirement might be imposed, the fulfillment of which might result in David's death (v. 25). Michal is the only woman in the OT about whom it is said directly that she loved a man.

Although David had earned the full right to marry a daughter of the king (17:25), Saul imposed additional conditions for such a marriage. He sent word to David, who was poor and could not afford to pay the bride-price, that he should kill a hundred Philistines and deliver their foreskins to the king. David not only did as Saul demanded, but he doubled the prescribed bride-price. Saul's scheme failed in that David's victory over the Philistines showed again that he was a very capable military leader. In the end, David was fully qualified to become the king's son-in-law. Unfortunately, these successes made Saul even more afraid of David, whom he now considered to be his greatest rival.

19:1–24. Saul Persecutes David. The chapter describes Saul's increasing hatred toward David, based on his own low self-perception, as shown when Samuel found him. He openly showed that he wanted David dead on three different occasions. Under this duress, David found a temporary refuge in the company of the prophet Samuel, who lived in Ramah. Although David's family lived in the south, he fled to the north for safety. He felt that he needed support from the man who had anointed him to be the future king of Israel (chap. 16). The two men stayed in Naioth, which probably means "a camp" or "a habitation." Both were saved from bloodthirsty Saul by a manifestation of God's grace.

We are informed about Saul's ecstatic experience without details. Many people in Bible times believed that a trancelike state made a person receptive to divine revelations. Beyond the borders of Israel, ecstatic experiences were closely connected with prophesying. Saul's act of prophesying did not result in prophetic messages from the Lord but in a display or sign of God's power. Saul spent all day and night lying "naked," or without the outer garment, in front of Samuel. The Lord had humiliated him. Laying aside the royal regalia confirmed God's rejection of Saul as Israel's king.

20:1–42. Jonathan's Loyalty to David. This chapter is composed of four episodes (vv. 1–23; 24–26; 27–34; 35–42), with the first and last occurring in the open field where the young men could talk in private (Gen. 31:4). King Saul's son Jonathan was David's best friend and is one of the most positive characters in the Bible. He was loyal to David, even though he knew that David's success came at his expense. He also recognized that he would never be king of Israel because the Lord had chosen David to replace his father. David, on the other hand, respected Saul and had difficulty understanding why the king hated him.

The two young men made a pledge before the Lord by saying, "as the Lord lives." They promised to protect each other's lives and families (1 Sam. 20:12–17). The pledge was significant because its purpose was to prevent any possible future rivalry between the house of Saul and the house of David. It was not uncommon in ancient times for a new king to kill the family members of his predecessor (1 Kin. 15:29; 16:11).

The extended conversation between David and Jonathan in vv. 1–16 raises some interesting questions and presents a glimpse of Jonathan's character. He is shown as a goodhearted young man who seemed incapable of believing anything bad about anyone. He was loyal both to David and to his father. Earlier, Saul had been willing to kill Jonathan himself over the trifling matter of the honeycomb (13:44). Later (19:1–5), Saul had been explicit in his desire that Jonathan kill David. Yet in this conversation in the field, Jonathan seemed to have forgotten all this, or perhaps believed that with the passage of time Saul's attitude and unpredictable personality had changed. He was a man whose apparent innocence of heart made him either unable, or at least unwilling, to recognize what appears to us as the obvious conflict between his honor of and love for David and his filial duty to his father. He was not cynical or suspicious in nature, and Scripture doubtlessly does not want us to miss the significance of this honorable and stark contrast to his father.

David was absent from the Festival of the New Moon (cf. Num. 28:11–15; Is. 1:13) without a prior excuse from the king. Ritual impurity would prevent a person from participating in a festive meal. David's excuse shows that he was humble and submissive, yet his absence raised suspicion and enraged Saul. Because Jonathan tried to defend David, Saul accused his son of treason and wanted to harm him. With contempt Saul avoided saying "David," but instead referred to "the son of Jesse" and insulted Jonathan in the presence of family members and friends.

At the festival, Jonathan's eyes were fully opened to his father's true character and shameful treatment of David, and he made good on his loyalty to David by helping him escape. The narrative of this chapter is all about Jonathan and his remarkable, self-sacrificing commitment to justice, honor, and God's way of doing things, even at the expense of his own worldly advantage. By ensuring David's escape, the prince knew that he would never be king. A tragic and honorable figure in Scripture, Jonathan came to his end by loyally dying beside his ungrateful father.

21:1—26:25
Saul Persecutes David

Jonathan had accepted the fact that David would succeed his father as king (1 Sam. 20:31), but Saul could not agree to this and instead looked for ways to kill David. He intended to do this despite the fact that he had no proof of any wrongdoings on David's part. Saul's paranoia may have been motivated by the fear that David would kill him and take the throne by force, something that David was not planning to do.

21:1–9. David and the Holy Bread. There are two stories in this short chapter and they both show David's desperate situation stemming from a great fear. After the Philistines destroyed Shiloh and captured the ark, Israel's sanctuary moved to the town of Nob. David went there and lied to the chief priest in order to get some food and the sword of Goliath. The chief priest was Ahimelech, a descendant of Eli, who had been the priest at Shiloh and Samuel's mentor. Ahimelech was the leader of eighty-five priests (22:18). He gave to David, who was a highly ranked commander in Saul's army, the holy bread that was reserved for the priests (Lev. 24:5–9). David's lie to the priest resulted in a tragedy and the loss of many innocent lives (1 Sam. 22:18–19). He later readily acknowledged that he had been wrong (22:22). As with many problematic episodes in 1 Samuel, the biblical writer lets the story stand without any evaluation of David's actions and reports what seem to be the negative consequences that followed.

21:10–15. David Flees to Gath. Searching for safety, David attempted to find refuge as a mercenary soldier in the city of Gath, which belonged to the Philistines. Gath was the home city of Goliath, the giant he had killed. David hoped that he would not be recognized by the population. But his plan failed. Even the song sung by the Israelite women had reached Philistia. When King Achish of Gath learned this was the same soldier who had previously fought against the Philistines, David played a madman in order to save his life. Had he told the truth, some think the Philistines would have still welcomed him because they were at war with Saul, who was pursuing him. The heading of Psalm 34 connects that psalm with this story about David.

22:1–5. David's Four Hundred Men. After he escaped from the city of Gath, David hid in the barren region of Adullam, located at the border with Philistia not far from Gath. Here he was joined by a number of social outcasts who were outlaws like himself. David cared for the safety of his family and made arrangements for their stay across the Jordan in the land of Moab, the original home of Ruth, one of his great-grandmothers (Ruth 4:18–22). At that time the Moabites, like the Philistines, were Saul's enemies (cf. 1 Sam. 14:47). This passage and the story of Ruth provide two exceptions to hostile relationships between Israel and Moab. While his family found safety in Moab, David stayed in the forests of Judah at the advice of the prophet Gad.

Since David came from Bethlehem in Judah, he felt safer among his countrymen. Saul's supporters were the people from his tribe of Benjamin (v. 7). The author makes it clear that David's situation was extremely difficult, but God was still with him.

22:6–23. Saul Murders the Priests. In the narrative presented here we see the fullest, most hideous outworking of Saul's character and personality. The opening verses show him in the midst of his raging paranoia, charging his closest associates and defenders with treason. In framing his question to them in terms of being rewarded materially for their loyalty, he unwittingly based his right to rule not on principle or his God-ordained authority but on whether he could provide better material rewards than David. Such is the last desperate measure of a leader who has completely lost his way. Doeg the Edomite apparently took the hint. It is not unreasonable to believe that his treachery against the priests was based on his expectation that he would be richly rewarded in the manner that Saul had just implied.

The chief priest's reply to Saul's accusation (v. 13) of treason indicates both his simple honesty and naiveté about the malevolence of Saul. The priest flatly rejected the king's characterization of David as an enemy and sealed his own fate by candidly acknowledging that he had other ministry interactions with David, on the assumption that David was the king's friend. The priest's openness on this point leads the reader to accept his protest that he knew nothing about Saul's suspicion of David. In a way, David had protected the priest on this point by not being open about his own situation. And Doeg, who had witnessed the interaction between the priest and David, must have known of the priest's innocence. Yet he was the one who personally carried out Saul's outrageous order, which Saul's own soldiers refused to follow. Such was the degeneracy of Saul's leadership that it would find service in men like Doeg. The suspicion that the priests were conspiring with David against him was too much for Saul.

Innocent of the conspiracy charge as the priests of Nob certainly were, their death was a tragic way of partially fulfilling a prediction concerning Eli's family given in chapters 2–3 in the book. From 2 Kings 2:27, it is clear that Ahimelech was of the house of Eli, since Abiathar, Ahimelech's son, was of the house of Eli, and his removal was also a fulfillment of the prophecy. Saul was responsible for this atrocious criminal act. Careful readers have noted the ironic depravity into which Saul had sunk. His downfall began when he had failed to completely destroy the Amalekites (15:3). Now, what he had failed to do to mortal enemies at the instruction of God he apparently condoned doing to his own people through the actions of Doeg. Saul activated the law of extermination and enforced it in a way that God would have never done. The king was now acting on his own, motivated by irrational paranoia.

23:1–13. David saves the city of Keilah. Dangerous life situations taught David to depend on the Lord for safety, especially as he tried to escape from Saul. The town of Keilah was located northwest of Hebron, near the Philistine border, and this position made it vulnerable to the attacks. The Philistine raiders came with their cattle at the end of the harvest to plunder the crops and carry them to their cities. They particularly targeted the unprotected threshing floors, which lay outside the city walls.

The people of Keilah preferred to ask David instead of Saul for help. Perhaps the massacre at Nob influenced this decision. In his attempts to save this town from the Philistine invaders, David turned to Abiathar the priest (22:20), who carried with him the sacred priestly vestment with the two stones Urim and Thummim for consulting the Lord. This is another example of David's total dependence on the Lord early in his life. A positive answer from the Lord instilled courage in David's fighting men.

Despite the fact that David helped them, the citizens of Keilah were so afraid of Saul that they were ready to hand David over. He learned about this after consulting the priest. Staying in touch with the Lord again helped David to know what to do next. As for the Lord, He did not forget His servant but blessed him with an increasing number of soldiers.

23:14–29. David in Wilderness Strongholds. From Keilah, David fled further southward to the wilderness of Ziph. In that sparsely inhabited region, he hid in the small outposts built by herdsmen and villagers as signaling stations. Jonathan seemed to have had no problems locating David. This was most likely the last meeting of the two men. The passage presents the last words of Jonathan recorded in the Bible.

Supplying food to David's company of 600 men was a major challenge. This is most likely why the people from this region informed Saul of David's whereabouts. They feared for their own food supplies, and like the people of Ke-ilah, they remembered Saul's massacre at Nob and feared him. Saul gladly welcomed their readiness to hand David over and pronounced blessings on the leaders of the town. David was forced to move immediately further south, along the Dead Sea. His capture was almost certain, but in the last moment God intervened.

It was providential that due to an imme-diate threat from the Philistines, Saul was dis-tracted and forced to give up his pursuit of David. God's direct intervention saved David's life, so the place became known as *sela' ham-makhleqot*, meaning "the Rock of Escape." In the Bible, names were customarily given to per-sons and places to commemorate unusual life experiences with God. From *sela' hammakhleqot*, David moved to the oasis of En Gedi, renowned for its springs and vineyards (Song 1:14). In this way, David and his men were assured of a dependable water supply.

24:1–22. David Spares Saul. This chapter is divided into three parts. First, there is the story of how David had an opportunity to kill Saul, but refrained from doing so. This is followed by David's speech and then Saul's speech. The Hebrew word for hand (*yad*), which symbolizes power, occurs a number of times in this narra-tive (e.g., vv. 6, 11). The incident in the cave shows David's respect for proper authority, even while cutting Saul's robe demonstrated his will-ingness to take risks in trying to restore the re-lationship. At the same time, whether David intended it or not, it would have reminded Saul of the symbolism Samuel had used to show that the kingdom had been cut from Saul (15:27–28; 1 Kin. 11:29–32). David still considered Saul to be the Lord's anointed (2 Sam. 1:16) and was determined to remain loyal to him. Assassina-tions would lead only to more bloodshed. David respected Saul as Israel's legitimate king, per-haps hoping that when he became king, others would show the same respect toward him.

While Saul's kingdom was fast drawing to an end, David's reign would endure. Though Saul wept and temporarily gave up the pursuit, David did not fully trust him and remained in the wilder-ness strongholds. At least Saul should have clearly seen that David was not interested in taking the kingdom from him through a military coup.

25:1–44. David and the Wife of Nabal. The long story narrated in the middle of the chap-ter is bracketed by David's two losses. Samuel died, a great loss of moral support, and Michal,

the wife who loved him, was given to another man (v. 44). Wedged in between is the story of David's conflict with Nabal, which ended in David's marriage to Abigail.

The mention of Samuel's death appears as an-other marker of Saul's downward spiral. Samuel had been Saul's original promoter, and now he was gone. At the same time, Samuel's death certainly must have been a blow to David, who depended on Samuel as a symbol of God's direc-tion in his life. Both men, enemies as they were, had reason to feel the loss of Samuel. With the death of Samuel the historical transition from the theocracy to the monarchy was final; the last judge had died. The only problem left was that Saul had not been willing to be God's vassal and the Lord was still shaping David to become His ideal king.

Meanwhile, David and his men protected the flocks of a man whose name or more likely nick-name was Nabal. This Hebrew name means "a fool" or a person who is morally and spiritually deficient (v. 25). The first thing the reader learns about this man is that he was very wealthy. This is stated in the narrative even before his name is disclosed, suggesting that fools could be quite capable when it comes to material wealth. The time of shearing the sheep was a festive occa-sion, when wealthy people loved to show their generosity to other community members (2 Sam. 13:23). Since none of Nabal's animals was missing in the attacks by wild beasts or raiders, David sent greetings of peace with a request to re-turn kindness by providing some food for David's group, thus giving him the opportunity to be gen-erous. To show his humility, David described him-self to Nabal as "your son David" (1 Sam. 25:8). Ten of David's men were sent with an expectation that there would be a generous gift.

Nabal was probably loyal to Saul, so he re-sponded to David's polite message with con-tempt and threats. Isaiah 32:6 defines "a fool" (Heb. *nabal*) as someone selfish who keeps the hungry unsatisfied and withholds water from the thirsty. Abigail, on the other hand, showed clear signs of wisdom.

In spite of her high social status, Abigail addressed David as "my lord" (vv. 24–31) while describing herself as his servant. She took all the blame upon herself and agreed with David about Nabal's poor character, while at the same time pleading for mercy at David's feet (cf. Esth. 8:3). David's life, she says, although threatened by his enemies, would be bound "in the bundle of the living" with the Lord—which probably means that it has been recorded or sealed in God's book of life—while the lives of his enemies would be removed from there. Unnecessary bloodshed would bring only harm to David's future career. After Nabal's sudden and timely death, David took this wise woman of high status as a wife. To further demonstrate her humility, Abigail declared herself ready to wash the feet of David's servants. An amazing feature of this story is that David was willing to listen to and accept the advice of a woman who was pleading with him on behalf of a man who had insulted him. Seeking counsel from others and particularly from the Lord characterized David's leadership, with a few important exceptions.

In the meantime, Saul's daughter Michal, who was David's legal wife, had been given to another man. This suggests that Saul wanted to hurt David and tried his best to keep him away from the throne for as long as possible. David had another wife from Judah, and together with his marriage to Abigail, these connections strengthened his position in the south. David's kinship ensured the support of the elders and communities in central and southern Judah. This territory would become his future power base.

26:1–25. David Spares Saul a Second Time.

This is the second story of David's kindness in sparing Saul's life. It has both similarities and differences with the first story in chapter 24. Both stories show that benevolence was a constant trait of David's character. For the second time, the people of Ziph informed Saul (23:19) about David's movements and urged him to pursue David in their territory. David had already spared Saul's life, yet in spite of it, Saul again decided to pursue the one whom he considered as competitor to the throne. Due to his paranoia, Saul did not appear to understand that David was not seeking to take the throne from him by force. He was waiting for the Lord to hand it to him at the appropriate moment.

The king came into the remote region from his residence in Gibeah, surrounded by a great number of his troops. Under cover of night, David slipped into Saul's camp accompanied by his nephew Abishai, the son of David's sister Zeruiah and the brother of Joab. The two men discovered the place where the king slept, protected by his general, Abner, who was also Saul's cousin. Abishai urged David to kill Saul, but David refused and rebuked the young man by saying that he would not lift his hand against the Lord's anointed. David took only Saul's spear and water jug. The spear represented a symbol of Saul's kingship because he seldom

separated himself from it (18:10; 19:10; 2 Sam. 1:6), and it could have been used by David to kill him. Instead David spared Saul's life.

David's act of mercy in again preserving the king's life impressed Saul so much that once again he predicted the Lord would protect David from all danger and make him triumph in the end. Indeed one could say that the words spoken here by Saul regarding his own folly (v. 21) summarized his life, while the words spoken much later by the Apostle Paul, "I have kept the faith" (2 Tim. 4:7), could summarize David's life of faith.

27:1—30:31
David in Philistia

Following Saul's persecution of David in the Wilderness of Ziph, it became clear that David could no longer trust the king's promises. So he decided to again seek refuge in Philistia (cf. 21:11–16). This was the most difficult period in David's life, more difficult than when he faced the giant Goliath in the Valley of Elah. This time he had to convince his enemies that Saul and his soldiers were his worst enemies, although he had no intention of fighting them. How could he fight the army of the nation whose king he would soon become?

27:1—28:2. David Allied with the Philistines.

David now commanded an army of 600 men and was received favorably by Achish, king of Gath, the hometown of Goliath. David became his vassal and received an estate in return for his services and loyalty. During this time, David's soldiers were stationed in Ziklag, on the border with Israel. David would stay in this city until the death of Saul. His army regularly raided the enemies of Judah and Philistia who lived in the area. Some of the names of the tribes that are given in the text are Geshurites, Girzites, and Amalekites. Achish thought that David's army was attacking the towns in the Negev, which is in southern Israel. He could see the spoils brought back by the soldiers but could not tell where they came from.

These raids helped David in a variety of ways: to secure provisions for the survival of his army, escape dangers from Saul, eliminate some of Israel's enemies, and secure his position among the leaders of the clans of Judah. The author only reports David's acts of deception and cruelty. He does not condone them nor try to justify them. The lesson to draw from this passage is similar to the lesson found in the story of Abram in Egypt in Genesis 12. Even when God's servants lack trust in God and use questionable means of survival, God is still with them and working to transform them. The Lord used David to protect the people of Judah from bitter enemies who often raided their towns and villages.

28:3–25. Saul Consults a Medium. While God consistently answered David's questions, Saul's line of communication with the Lord grew weaker and was eventually broken. Saul had shut off the sources of divine revelations, and now he was desperate to learn God's will. But who could he turn to for help? He had killed God's priests, and the divine Warrior was no longer present by his side. Samuel was dead, while the priestly ephod was with David's priest, Abiathar. It is possible that Saul's priest had fabricated an ephod in place of the original one.

In great fear, Saul turned to a spiritual medium. This was despite the fact that he had previously condemned such practices (1 Chr.

10:13–14; cf. Lev. 19:31; Deut. 18:9–14). So the king who had banned mediums now consulted one himself. There is little doubt that this was the lowest point in Saul's life, which would lead to his defeat and death. While going to the witch in En Dor, Saul traveled at night and in disguise to conceal his identity. Later in the story, the woman did discover his true identity. En Dor was located about six miles (10 km) from Shunem. The woman must have established a reputation as one who could successfully consult the spirits of ancestors. Her ritual pit was believed to be a magical portal through which ghosts could pass to communicate with the living (see below, "Saul, the Medium, and the Spirit of Samuel").

The message given to Saul was the same he had repeatedly heard from Samuel while the prophet was still living. In summary, Saul was told that his disobedience to God had led to his downfall and David would succeed him as king (15:26–28). The only new element was that he would die in the impending battle against the

Saul, the Medium, and the Spirit of Samuel

The narrative recorded in 1 Samuel 28:3–19 is the only place in the Bible where we find a detailed account about a consultation with a medium and the appearance of a spirit of the dead. Such activity is proscribed in the strongest terms in Deuteronomy 18:9–14. We need to look at the story carefully to identify what it is, and is not, saying.

1. *A Medium.* The necromancer is called "a woman who is a medium" (1 Sam. 28:7); that is, she had the ability to communicate with the dead, seeking oracles from them. This type of person was called "one who calls up the dead" (Deut. 18:11). Apparently, they were possessed by the spirit they consulted and functioned as a medium (see Lev. 20:27: "A man or a woman *in whom* there is a spirit…" [literal translation]). In a sense, this was a counterfeit of the gift of prophecy.

2. *The Spirit.* The Hebrew word translated "spirit" in the narrative is *'ob*, not *ruakh* ("spirit"), which is the one used to refer to the Spirit of God, and designates the necromancer (1 Sam. 28:3) as well as the spirit of the dead itself (Lev. 20:27). It is believed by some that originally it could have

meant "pit, hole on the ground." Consulting the dead required that a hole be made on the ground in which food and blood were placed with the clear purpose of enticing the spirit to come up from the underworld. The underworld was also thought to be the place where demons were located (cf. Lev. 17:7). Others believe that *'ob* comes from the Hebrew word *'ab* ("father") and that it designates the spirits of the ancestors. Apparently the spirit spoke to or through the necromancer in undertones, whispering the oracle, chirping, and muttering (Is. 8:19).

3. *Communicating with the Spirit.* The spirit probably communicated with Saul through the medium, rather than directly. It should be noted that the "spirit" did not say anything new to him. It simply repeated the message given by God through Samuel. But even the prediction of the death of his children (28:19) was incorrect; not all of them died. The narrative seems to be rejecting the common idea that the spirits of the dead could function as spiritual guides for the living.

4. *Identifying the Spirit.* The necromancer did not really bring up the spirit of Samuel.

She was the only one who saw anything and then reported to Saul "that she saw a spirit ['*elohim*, 'gods, divine beings'] rising out of the earth" (v. 13). Unable to see the spirit, Saul asked what he looked like. She answered that he was old and covered with a cloth. It was Saul who concluded that this was Samuel (v. 14). So the biblical writer does not tell us who the spirit was. It tells us only what the protagonists of the story—the medium and Saul—believed him to be.

In reviewing this passage, we should take into consideration the larger context of the story, the Bible. We know that the Lord condemned any attempt to communicate with the dead (Deut. 18:10–11). We also know that the realm of death, as a place where the spirits of the dead dwell, does not exist but that death, as the end of life, is the result of sin (Heb. 2:14). In addition, we also know that demons desire to communicate with humans and at times can possess them as their instruments (e.g., Acts 19:13–16). And finally, we are told that Satan can transform himself into what seems to be an angel of light to deceive humans (2 Cor. 11:14). Based on the overall teachings of the Bible, we can conclude that it was not Samuel who spoke to Saul but some other spiritual/"divine" power not from God.

Philistines. This last statement was colored by firm determinism. The negative message brought him to a state of depression and despondency. All hope of defeating the Philistines was now lost.

Saul refused to eat, and only after strong urgings by the woman and his men did he take some food, consisting of roasted calf and unleavened bread prepared in a hurry. Saul departed from this place more frightened than when he came. Such a discouraging experience could only be the result of the deceptive work of the enemy in disguise, who was leading Saul into destruction. Thus, the objective of this experience "was not to lead Saul to repentance, but to urge him on to ruin; and this is not the work of God, but of Satan" (PP 683).

29:1–11. The Philistines Reject David.
The story of David and Achish continues, presenting the solution to David's serious problem (28:1–2). It is likely that the events reported in this chapter precede those from chapter 28, because this chapter states that the Philistines were gathered in Aphek (located just north of Mt. Carmel; v. 1) before they decided to move southeastward into the Valley of Jezreel proper (v. 11). The arrangement of the material in these chapters is more thematic than chronological.

The Philistines decided not to involve David in their battle against the people of Israel, who they consistently referred to as "Hebrews." Instead, Achish sent him back to Ziklag. It is remarkable that in his dialogue with David, Achish demonstrated such high regard for the Lord God of David, in whose name he took an oath (v. 6). Moreover, this Philistine ruler trusted David so much and praised him for his loyalty, not knowing that David had repeatedly deceived him. Truly, Achish is portrayed in much better light than David, whom he called "an angel of God" (v. 9; cf. 2 Sam. 14:17; 19:28). Although the author does not state this explicitly, he implies that the Lord helped His anointed one in the midst of an impossible situation. Clearly, the Lord was still with David, not because of what he was doing but sometimes in spite of it.

30:1–31. David's Conflict with the Amalekites.
The last two chapters in 1 Samuel describe a battle between David and the Amalekites. A separate battle between Saul and the Philistines would tragically cost Saul his life. The Philistines assembled up north in the famous Valley of Jezreel. This location differed from that of previous battles, which took place in the south. Gath was one of the five Philistine city-states forming a confederation referred to as *Pentapolis* ("five cities), and its people were expected to participate in the war. Shunem and Mount Gilboa are located on the opposite sides of this valley. It is clear that King Achish wanted David to fight on the Philistine side and even assume the role of his personal bodyguard. But it is not clear in the narrative what course of action David took in this war.

The battle between David and the Amalekites occurred soon after he returned from the battlefield. David and his men arrived just in time to pursue the Amalekites who had raided and burned the town of his residence, Ziklag. If they had returned a day or two later, it would have been too late to recover what was lost. This chapter tells how, with the Lord's help, David's defeat turned into a victory, in contrast to Saul's defeat reported in the next chapter. Both battles took place at approximately the same time. In this way, the author assures the reader that David had no part in the Philistine battle and victory over Saul and his army. Helping the enemy destroy God's people would have permanently prevented him from becoming king in Israel.

The Amalekites were Israel's enemies since the time of Israel's Exodus from Egypt (Ex. 17:8–16), and they would cleverly launch their attacks in the most opportune situations. This time, they attacked Ziklag when only women and children were in the town. They must have done this in retaliation for David's raids (27:6). In the beginning of his reign, Saul disobeyed God's word that came through Samuel and failed to destroy Amalek (15:1–9). Now David had to face them again. But before he could pursue the Amalekites, David faced the prospect of his own death at the hands of his frustrated people. At that moment, he did the right thing by turning to the Lord. God assured David (through the officiating priest) of His presence and victory, which unified his soldiers. When David pursued the raiders, God would grant him a complete victory.

The march from Aphek to Ziklag could take up to three full days. One third of David's fighting men were too exhausted to go further, so they stayed behind while the others pressed on. They achieved a complete victory, effectively completing the job that Saul had failed to do (15:1–9). David warmed the hearts of his men and the elders of Judah, from Hebron down to Beersheba, by distributing gifts to everyone, including the exhausted soldiers who had stayed behind. They had guarded the baggage, allowing others to move quickly in pursuit of the Amalekites, and were entitled to some of the spoil. David refused to listen to certain troublemakers who were selfish and wanted him to treat some of his men differently than others. Instead, David made sure that all the men benefitted equally from this victory and its spoils (cf. Deut. 20:10–15). After all, the victory came from the Lord. Distribution of wealth in Bible times was a sign of power and generosity. David also rewarded the elders of Judah who had provided hospitality during the time he was pursued by Saul. The city of Hebron figures prominently in this narrative and was destined to become the first capital city of David's future kingdom.

31:1-13
Death of Saul and Jonathan

The closing chapters of 1 Samuel present a series of contrasts between Israel's first two kings, Saul and David. Both were fighting important battles against Israel's bitter enemies—Saul against the Philistines and David against Amalek. While David was successful in consulting the Lord, Saul was fearful and decided to consult a medium. David's warfare resulted in a victory over the enemy, while Saul suffered total defeat. David successfully rescued family members, while all but one of Saul's sons perished alongside him in the battle. Lastly, Saul had failed to destroy Amalek; David had accomplished this very thing and thus fulfilled the command given through Samuel.

31:1-13. The Tragic End of Saul and His Sons. The book's last chapter reports the end of the war between Saul and the Philistines. The final battle began on the plain, giving an advantage to the Philistines, and soon the Israelites were pushed up the slopes of the hillside, where many of them died. Israel's army suffered a tragic defeat, and many were killed on Mount Gilboa, located at the southeastern end of the plain of Jezreel. The outcome of this battle appears more important to the author than any of the details. Following this victory, the Philistines invaded several Israelite towns because the people who lived near the battlefield fled to their homes.

Fearful of torture if captured alive by the enemy, Saul shamefully took his life. Elsewhere the Bible records a few other cases of suicide by individuals who did not want to be captured and tortured by the enemy (e.g., Judg. 9:54; 16:30; 2 Sam. 17:23; 1 Kin. 16:18). It is ironic that Saul, who was anointed to liberate Israel from Philistine oppression (9:16), was in essence killed by them. His dead body was publicly disgraced by the enemy in order to show their contempt for him. The head and armor of the defeated king were treasured prizes, so they were usually carried away and displayed in public by the victorious army (cf. 17:38, 54). These were sometimes placed in the temple to show the superiority of the local gods over those of the enemy. Dismembered and impaled bodies instilled terror among the local population. Three of Saul's sons also died in the battle. It appears that only the youngest son, called Ishbosheth, survived. It is ironic that David's best friend in life, Jonathan, died in the same battle and on the same day as David's worst enemy, King Saul.

The people of Jabesh Gilead had never forgotten how Saul delivered them from the Ammonite oppression (chap. 11). They travelled all night to Beth Shan to steal his body away and then gave him a decent burial. They mourned over his death for seven days, as was customary in those times (Gen. 50:10; Job 2:13). Since the bodies were in a state of decay, they were cremated while the bones were gathered and buried. In the beginning of his reign, Saul rescued these people from the enemy. Now, at the end of his reign, the same people rescued his dead body and gave him an honorable burial.

First Samuel begins with the miraculous birth of the child Samuel, but it ends with the tragic deaths of Saul and Jonathan. The book looks forward to the reign of David, the king who was not perfect but whom the Bible calls a man after God's heart. Through him the Lord would bring about a complete and permanent victory over the Philistines. This is why the book presents God as the true Leader of His people, One who was primarily interested in their hearts (16:7). The word of God states boldly that the Lord on high reigns supreme and no earthly leader is above His word. The book closes looking forward to the interaction between David and the Lord.

2 SAMUEL

INTRODUCTION

Title. Like 1 Samuel, the book of 2 Samuel was also named after the prophet who anointed Saul, and later David, to rule over Israel. Together 1 and 2 Samuel originally formed one book in the Hebrew Bible. The Greek version of the OT referred to 2 Samuel as "Second Kingdoms" (*Basileion Beta*). The English title comes from the Latin *Liber II Samuelis*. Fragments of about four different manuscripts of Samuel have been discovered among the Dead Sea Scrolls from Qumran.

Date and Authorship. For details regarding the writing of 2 Samuel, see 1 Samuel: Introduction.

Backgrounds. Second Samuel continues the story of Israel's monarchy that was begun in 1 Samuel. According to the Bible, kingship in Israel had to be radically different from the absolute kingship prevalent in the ANE. Kings in Israel were not allowed to do whatever they wished. They were subject to a higher power and to the rule of law and morality as taught by God's prophets. The beginning of the book depicts the transfer of royal power from the house of Saul to David. In ancient times the nonhereditary transfers of power often triggered civil wars based on intrigue, murder, and treachery.

The book highlights David's reign, first over the territory of Judah and then over the whole nation of Israel. Israel's second and greatest king unified the nation, conquered Israel's enemies, and received God's covenantal promises of an enduring dynasty and kingdom (7:15–16). David captured the city of Jerusalem and made it Israel's capital, as well as its administrative and religious center. This city became the symbol of national unity based on trust in God. The ark of the covenant was brought to Jerusalem to publicly acknowledge God's kingship and rule over the nation. David's plan was to build a temple to God, but he was not allowed to because he fought many wars and shed much blood.

The author recorded the history of David's life and kingship with all its triumphs and troubles. David's ascension to the throne is presented, followed by his sins of adultery and murder and their devastating consequences on his family and the nation. David himself underwent great sufferings, especially in the last years of his reign. Thus the book does not conceal the dark times of David's life. Israel's greatest king appeared weak in dealing with his children and committed grave sins of adultery and murder. Toward the end of his reign, he tended to rely on the strength of his army more than on God. Yet the author of the book consistently observes that, in spite of his failures, David was always willing to recognize his sin and repent before the Lord. He faithfully worshiped only the Lord and inspired his people to do the same.

Theology and Purpose. See 1 Samuel: Introduction. There is no doubt that 2 Samuel offers information that contributes to a better understanding of God's relationship with human beings. The following are among its dominant themes:

1. Divine Providence and Grace. God loved and cared for David long before he became king. Speaking through the prophet Nathan, God reminded David that He had taken him from being a shepherd of sheep to being ruler of His people Israel (7:8). God took him from where he was and then providentially led and shaped him to become the leader of His people. In the process David faced many challenges, conflicts, and suffering, but they helped to develop the character needed in order for God to use David for His glory and the benefit of His people. Solomon, the second son Bathsheba bore to him, was named by the prophet "Beloved of the Lord." When David sinned and repented, God's grace proved greater than his sin.

He suffered some of the consequences of his mistakes, but God always sustained him. The life of David illustrates the fact that the Lord is patient and is constantly seeking to restore us to fellowship with Him. As a result of David's wholehearted service to God, he was honored to become an ancestor of Jesus Christ, the Messiah. The NT begins Christ's genealogy with a reference to Jesus as the Son of David (Matt. 1:1). Lives placed in the hands of the Lord are in good hands.

2. God's Eternal Covenant with David. Central to the book is the covenant that God made with David (2 Sam. 7). David's life and career are contrasted with those of his predecessor, Saul. Unlike Saul, David was a successful leader in war and peace time, as well as a gifted musician. While deeply spiritual, he had a strong sense of justice. David showed himself respectful toward King Saul and his whole family, in spite of the fact that Saul wanted to kill him. Unlike King Saul, when David was rebuked by the prophet he sincerely repented. Toward the end of David's life, Israel's borders extended from Egypt to the Euphrates in fulfillment of the promises God made to the patriarchs (Gen. 15:18–21). David's reign became a standard by which the reigns of subsequent kings were measured (2 Kin. 18:3; 22:2). After his reign, God blessed Israel with the reign of his son Solomon. In spite of the later division of the kingdom, the prophets promised a future restoration under the new David, Ruler of all of God's people (Is. 9:1–7; 11:1–12; Amos 9:11–15; Zech. 9:9–13).

Such messianic passages instilled in God's people hope in the coming Messiah, the future Son of David, who was destined to rule the nations of the earth and not only Israel. In the Gospels, Jesus is often called the "Son of David." This title expressed earnest expectations that the glorious promises given in the beginning of Israel's monarchy would someday come to pass by the power of a loving and merciful God.

Literary Features. Second Samuel consists mostly of narratives, but a few songs and lists are scattered throughout the text. The long narrative section of the book is bracketed by two poetic passages, namely, the lament for Saul and Jonathan (1:17–27) and psalms of praise to God's greatness (22:1—23:7). Dispersed throughout the book are lists of David's officials, prayers, and a short lament over the death of Absalom. Finally the so-called last words of David are introduced as "the words/oracle of David son of Jesse" (23:1–7).

COMMENTARY

1:1—10:19
DAVID'S KINGDOM ESTABLISHED

In 1011 B.C. David's time in the wilderness of Judea came to an end. His most important task would be to unite a much divided nation. As Israel's king he would have to lead, unify, and inspire his people. David was successful like no other king of Israel. Under his leadership, the kingdom was consolidated, enemies were conquered, and he received promises of a lasting kingdom. David acted with wisdom and discernment under the true King of Israel. The book begins with David mourning the deaths of Saul and Jonathan (1:1–27). This is followed by David becoming king of Judah (2:1–4:12), king of Israel (5:1–6:23), the perpetuity of his dynasty (7:1–29), his military victories (8:1–18), and his dealings with Mephibosheth, the Ammonites, and the Syrians (9:1—10:19).

1:1–27
Lament over Saul and Jonathan

The author affirms that it was the Lord who made it possible for David to sit on Israel's throne. David honored the office of king as a position established solely by God. As long as Saul was alive, he refused to take the throne for himself, even though God had promised that it would come to him. Thus, the quick execution of Saul's alleged killer and David's heartfelt public mourning of Saul and Jonathan underlined his reputation as an honorable and patient leader.

1:1–16. Report of Saul's Death. The introductory words of the book, "after the death of Saul," constitute a fitting place for the division of Samuel into two parts. At about the same time that the Philistines defeated Saul, David defeated the Amalekites. Then an Amalekite dressed like a person in distress came to David in Ziklag. The dust on his head and the torn clothes suggested that he was mourning. The man reported that he had killed Saul on Mount Gilboa. In the absence of any human witnesses, he brought Saul's diadem and armlet and presented them to David. Both objects were symbols of kingship. If any part of the man's story was true, it is likely that he had been taking spoils from the fallen soldiers on the battlefield.

The account of Saul's death in this passage differs from the story in 1 Samuel 31. Some commentators propose that the Amalekite messenger told lies in order to get favors from David. However, it is possible to view the two stories as complementing each other so that the reconstructed events would have happened in this way: Saul fell upon his sword, as in the first story, but he was still alive when the Amalekite approached and, with or without Saul's request, killed the king.

David believed the story about Saul's death, but his reaction to the messenger's news was very negative. David tore his own clothes as an expression of sorrow and mourning. After a long day of mourning, he rebuked the man for raising his hand against the Lord's anointed. The guilt for the man's death was entirely his own. This swift and decisive act of David was consistent with his positive attitude toward Saul as the Lord's anointed, as he had expressed on more than one occasion (1 Sam. 24:6-7; 26:8-12). In fact, David had never treated Saul as an enemy. The execution of the Amalekite demonstrated both David's sense of justice, or righteousness, and his love for Saul and respect for the office.

1:17-27. An Elegy for Saul and Jonathan.

David's poem on the death of Saul and Jonathan was profoundly personal. It lacked religious and national elements, so no mention was made of God's name or of Israel's defeat. David expressed tribute to the fallen mighty warriors in Israel, whom he loved and respected. This elegy became a national poem as it eloquently expressed Israel's great loss of its beauty, glory, or splendor—sometimes translated as comparable to the grace and beauty of a gazelle (v. 19). The song was preserved in an ancient source (now extinct) called the Book of Jashar (cf. Josh. 10:13), where its title was "Song of the Bow." Verse 22 makes mention of Jonathan's bow, which symbolized his many victories over enemies.

The lament lists Saul's major accomplishments as king. He united the kingdom, defended Israel from the Philistines, and brought prosperity to his people. A large portion of these accomplishments is also credited to Jonathan and his bravery. Gath and Ashkelon are named as two of the five principal cities of Philistia (v. 20). The song contrasts the daughters of Philistia with the daughters of Israel. In that period, women celebrated victories with music and songs, but they also led in the singing of laments (Jer. 9:17-19). David ends his lament by devoting a whole verse to Jonathan. He describes his personal loss of one who was his best friend (1 Sam. 20). David's words, including the reference to "my brother" (2 Sam. 1:26), underline a deep fraternal love and echo covenantal terminology.

2:1—4:12
David Is Proclaimed King over Judah

Saul's death opened the way for David to assume kingship after having experienced much hardship. But before David's coronation, there were obstacles to overcome. The most serious was that Saul's defeat and death on Gilboa had resulted in national disaster and widespread chaos.

2:1-7. David Is Anointed King of Judah.

While David was still stationed in Ziklag, he sought God's guidance on how to proceed. Nothing less than a direct revelation from the Lord could help him. The answer to his question came through the stones called the Urim and Thummim (Ex. 28:30; Num. 27:21; 1 Sam. 28:6) that were kept in the pouch of the sacred ephod. David was sent to the southern city of Hebron, where the elders of Judah publicly anointed him king. His first anointing by Samuel when he was just a lad had been private. Hebron became David's capital and remained such for seven years before the conquest of Jerusalem. It was centrally located in Judah and had several springs of water. Under David's rule this city was improved and expanded.

Before his coronation David had established a solid military reputation recognized even by the Philistine lords and generals. Through his two marriages and also the distribution of gifts (1 Sam. 30:26-31), he had created strong ties with some influential families in Judah. One of his first actions as new king was to commend and bless the people of Jabesh Gilead for rescuing Saul's dead body and giving it a proper burial (2 Sam. 2:4-7; 1 Sam. 31:8-13). He promised them the same protection they had enjoyed under Saul. By doing all these things, David demonstrated to the people that he was Saul's legitimate successor. David also hoped that these men would recognize him as king. Yet in spite of this, David's authority included only the tribe of Judah, to which he belonged, and the smaller tribe of Simeon, which was likely considered part of the same kingdom.

2:8–11. Ishbosheth Is Made King of Israel. Saul's son Ishbosheth was not killed in the battle like the other three sons. So Abner, Saul's cousin (1 Sam. 14:50) and army general, proclaimed Ishbosheth king over the tribes of Israel. Ishbosheth's name in Hebrew means "man of shame," but originally the name was Ishbaal, meaning "man of Baal." Ishbosheth's residence was in Mahanaim of Gilead on the eastern side of the Jordan, a place remembered from the story of the patriarch Jacob (Gen. 32:1–3). Since Ishbosheth was not a strong king, Abner was really in charge of the kingdom. Following the battle on Gilboa, most of Israel's territory on the western side of the Jordan was under the control of the Philistines, seriously limiting the extent of Ishbosheth's kingdom.

2:12–32. Israel and Judah Are at War. The author makes it clear that the leaders of Judah favored David. This situation soon resulted in civil war, since Abner wanted the tribe of Judah to recognize Ishbosheth as king and bring their territory under his control. The two armies clashed at Gibeon, a town in Benjamin belonging to Saul's tribe. This town is known from the Bible by its large pool, whose existence has been confirmed by archaeological excavations. Each side selected twelve of their best soldiers, all of whom died because none could prevail over their opponents.

With no apparent winners, a full-scale battle followed in which Abner killed Asahel, Joab's brother and David's nephew. The battle ended with a temporary truce, although the conflict between the two armies continued. Asahel's dead body first lay on the battlefield, then was later buried in his family tomb. Joab never forgave Abner for this act of violence and looked for the first opportunity to avenge his brother's death.

3:1–5. Sons of David. Although details about Abner dominate this chapter, the author shows that as time passed, David's kingship grew stronger, while Ishbosheth's power steadily declined. The fact that many children were born to David was a sure sign of the Lord's blessing (e.g., Ps. 127:3–5). Only one son from each marriage is mentioned by name. David's marriage to Maacah was a royal one, and it strengthened his alliance with the king of Geshur, who ruled east of the Sea of Galilee (2 Sam. 15:8; 1 Chr. 3:2). The writer makes no mention of Ishbosheth's family, implying he had none left.

3:6–21. Abner Joins Forces with David. Israel's army general Abner appears to have been a very ambitious man. He suddenly made an intrusion into the harem that previously belonged to Saul, and Ishbosheth interpreted this act as a threat to his throne (2 Sam. 3:7; cf. 16:21–22; 1 Kin. 2:22). A quarrel between the two men followed this incident and ended with Abner's decision to defect to David. He promised to bring the whole kingdom of Israel with him from north to south, beginning with the tribe of Benjamin, to whom Saul and his son Ishbosheth belonged. Abner claimed that both the people and God wanted David to be king and that he would deliver the people of Israel from their enemies. This statement about David was true even during Saul's reign (1 Sam. 18:16), and it could be that Abner heard it from Saul himself.

David asked Abner to restore his legitimate wife Michal to him because she had been unlawfully taken away from him (1 Sam. 25:44). In this way David's status as Saul's son-in-law would be restored and all would see that he was the rightful successor to the throne of Israel. In other words, David's right to succeed Saul as king was closely linked with his marriage to Saul's daughter. The ANE laws included provisions indicating that a man who had been driven from home by force might claim his wife when he returned. But above all, David and Michal had been in love at the beginning of their relationship (1 Sam. 18:20). So thanks to Abner, Michal was restored to David. As was customary in those times, the alliance between David and Abner was sealed by a feast. The word "peace" is repeatedly found in this passage to show David's sincere intentions in dealing with Abner. Yet this agreement between the two of them did not last long.

3:22–30. Joab Murders Abner. Without consulting David, Joab (David's nephew and army general) proceeded to murder Abner in a treacherous way. Unlike David, Joab did not think that Abner could be trusted. He also felt obliged to avenge his brother's death. Joab struck Abner in the belly, the same way in which Abner had struck his brother Asahel. Yet for David there was a difference between the two murders. Asahel was killed in a battle, while Abner was assassinated in times of peace. It is also likely that Joab feared Abner's power in Israel and his ambitions to take Joab's commanding position over the army.

3:31–39. David's Mourning for Abner. David was first embarrassed, then angry because of what Joab did. This infamous act could raise suspicions about the king's integrity in dealing with Abner. To distance himself from Abner's murder, David declared a national day of mourning in which Joab had to take part. When all the people heard that the king wore the garments of mourning and abstained from food to grieve over Abner's death, they concluded that their king was innocent of bloodshed and their respect for him increased. It is important to understand that Abner died in the process of making David king over all Israel. David's resentment for Joab's murder of Abner lasted for a number of years (1 Kin. 2:5–6). He was aware that Joab was helped in the plot by his brother Abishai, who was also a military man. For the time being, David could only entrust the punishment of his two nephews into the Lord's hands (2 Sam. 3:29).

4:1–12. Ishbosheth Is Murdered. This short chapter narrates the death of Ishbosheth and David's reaction to the news. His response was the same as to Saul's and Abner's deaths. By telling this story, the narrator shows that David was not involved in the death of Saul's family members. After Abner's defection to David, the popular support for Saul's son began to dwindle. This situation eventually led to Ishbosheth's murder and decapitation at the hands of his two army captains. This took place during the king's midday rest ("siesta"). No reason is given for this sudden act of violence, although the two captains probably hoped that David would reward them for such an act. The two men belonged to the tribe of Benjamin, to which Saul and Ishbosheth also belonged.

Ishbosheth left no surviving son to succeed him. His death meant that David no longer had serious rivals for the throne. Jonathan's son Mephibosheth was crippled and unfit to be king, so he posed no threat to David. Ishbosheth's assassins presented the head of their king to David to prove their involvement in the assassination. They explained their act of murder as the Lord's vengeance on Saul's house. Even though Ishbosheth's death advanced David's kingdom, he once again publicly distanced himself from it. Instead of rewarding the two generals, he executed them, and their bodies were dismembered. To dismember the bodies of the assassins was an act of extreme disgrace for the victim and shame for the family. Moreover, David spoke well of Ishbosheth by calling him an innocent, righteous person (v. 11). Thus was David cleared of any suspicions of complicity. These actions were consistent with his promise to Saul that he would show mercy on his posterity. A guiding principle in David's life and reign was that violence leads to more bloodshed, in line with Jesus' teaching that all who live by the sword will die by it as well (Matt. 26:52).

5:1—6:23
David Is Made King over All Israel

Chapter 5 of 2 Samuel presents three of David's great achievements during his reign. First, there was a nationwide recognition that he was the king of all Israel (5:1–5). Second, David conquered the city of Jerusalem (5:6–16). And third, he accomplished the decisive and final victory over the Philistines (5:17–25).

5:1–5. David Reigns over All Israel. Not long after the death of Saul's last surviving son, Ishbosheth, the tribal elders of Israel took the initiative to join Judah in making David their king. In the Lord's presence, all the people of Israel and Judah, from Dan to Beersheba, anointed him to be their "shepherd" and "king" (v. 2) in Hebron, the first capital city of David's kingdom. This was David's third and final anointing as king. In Hebron and later in Jerusalem David would reign for a total of forty years (1011–971 B.C.). His long reign stands in contrast to Ishbosheth's reign that lasted for only two years.

5:6–16. Conquest of Jerusalem. The strategic position of Jerusalem (earlier called Salem and Jebus) in the center of the land was much more suitable to David's needs than Hebron in southern Judah. Jerusalem's name means "city of peace" and it would link the territory of Judah with the northern tribes of Israel. But the city was still in the hands of the Jebusites, who were descendants of Canaan (Gen. 10:16). In earlier times the tribes of Judah and Benjamin had captured it (Judg. 1:8) but failed to completely settle it (Judg. 1:21).

The Jebusites' boastful words show overconfidence in their control of the fortress. Their statement implied that even a blind and lame army could defend it from David's attack. Yet when David and his army marched against the fortress (acropolis) of Zion, they were able to capture it. This is the first mention in the Bible of the name Zion (2 Sam. 5:7), which later became synonymous with the name Jerusalem.

The city's main water supply came from a spring located outside the city walls. Instead of launching a direct attack, David's soldiers entered the city through a secret water tunnel and thus surprised the enemy.

After the conquest, Jerusalem became the city of David. From this time on, it was Israel's capital and the location of David's palace. The cordial message sent by Hiram, king of Tyre, representing the most important Phoenician city, showed the extent of respect that David enjoyed internationally. It also demonstrated that the Lord's blessings on His chosen people and their leader were now evident for all to see. Artists from Phoenicia came to build a palace for David made of cedar wood, which was a choice building material used for building royal palaces and temples in ancient times. The royal palace provided more room for David's large family, including new wives and concubines from Jerusalem.

5:17-25. The Philistines Are Defeated. David's throne was now well established and the Lord gave him important victories over Israel's bitter enemies, the Philistines. Two decisive battles took place in the Valley of Rephaim, located southwest of Jerusalem. Recognizing himself as God's vassal, David consulted the Lord before going to war, something that Saul had repeatedly neglected to do. In this way Israel's second king succeeded in doing what the first one had often failed to accomplish. The Philistines were finally driven out of Israel's territory and never again posed a serious threat to the people of Israel.

The new name Baal Perazim ("Lord of the breaking through") was given to the place of victory to ascribe this important success to God, who came to fight with the armies of heaven. During this battle David succeeded in capturing the idols the Philistines had brought along to ensure their victory, then left behind in their panic. An army would abandon its idols on the battlefield only under the most critical circumstances. The Philistine gesture marked a reversal of their capture of the ark of the covenant at the battle of Ebenezer (1 Sam. 4:11).

6:1-23. Ark of God Is Brought to Jerusalem. The narrative in this chapter is dominated by the sacred ark of God that David brought to Israel's new capital city. The ark had been stored for a considerable time in the house of Abinadab (1 Sam. 7:1-2) in Kiriath Jearim/Baalah (1 Chr. 13:6). David wanted to bring this object that symbolized God's presence into Jerusalem.

Only then could the nation be truly unified in the religious and political sense. Caring for the ark was another great accomplishment of David's reign. With the arrival of the holy ark, Jerusalem became a holy city and Israel's religious center. A large military parade was a part of the program. This testified to the importance of this event, which celebrated the glory of God sitting on His heavenly throne and commanding the armies of heaven. The appropriate music was also played for the occasion. Since the ark was particularly holy, only the priests and Levites who were descendants of Aaron were commissioned to handle it. It was not to be touched by any other individual (Ex. 25:12-15; Num. 4:15; Deut. 10:8). Instead of carrying it on poles, the two sons of Abinadab set the ark on a new cart like the Philistines did (1 Sam. 6:7) and guided it to the new destination.

When the ark shifted, Abinadab's son Uzzah reached out to steady it and was struck dead. The only reason for the punishment given in the text is that Uzzah committed an irreverent error. This is the only occurrence of the Hebrew word for irreverence in the OT. The place was named "Perez Uzzah" (v. 8), which means "outbreak of wrath against Uzzah." On an earlier occasion, some people from Beth Shemesh had suffered because of irreverent handling of the ark (1 Sam. 6:19).

King David was greatly distressed because Uzzah was punished only for wanting to make sure that the ark would not slip. For three months the ark was kept in the house of Obed-Edom the Gittite. This man may have been a member of the company of David's personal bodyguards who came with him from Gath. David now learned that the presence of the ark could be a blessing if handled with care by the priests and the Levites (Num. 7:9; 1 Chr. 15:2). So again the ark was on its way to Jerusalem.

The ark entered the capital city carried by the priests. There was a big celebration, and David offered a sacrifice to the Lord. He was not acting in a priestly role but as an ordinary worshiper because he did not belong to the tribe of Levi. In addition, countless burnt offerings were offered and completely consumed on the altar. Fellowship offerings were part of a communal meal during important celebrations such as coronations or temple dedications. In this case the Lord's enthronement in Jerusalem was the reason for celebration. The ceremony also reaffirmed David's election to kingship. The ark remained in a special tent (cf. Josh. 18:1) until the reign of Solomon, when the temple was built in Jerusalem (1 Kin. 6).

Being in a festive mood, the king distributed food and gifts to the people and chose to humble himself in the Lord's presence. Instead of being dressed in his kingly robe, he wore a priestly garment used for consulting the Lord and joyfully "danced" to the sound of the music (v. 14). The Hebrew term translated with "dance" appears only here in the OT. Comparative data from other Semitic languages suggest that its use reflects the ritual procession that accompanied the return of the ark, including the six-pace advance followed by a sacrifice (2 Sam. 6:13). This is not comparable to the modern concept of dancing, but was part of the larger ritual construct expressing reverence, joy, and the recognition that the object symbolizing God's presence was finally "coming home."

The chapter ends on another sad note, this time involving a quarrel between David and Michal, who despised David's way of rejoicing before the Lord. This caused a lasting breach between the two. In the beginning of their relationship, Michal loved David and was his only spouse, but now she was only one among his many wives and concubines. Michal never bore any children to David. Thus, no royal child was qualified to bridge the divide between the house of Saul and the house of David.

7:1–29
Promise of a Lasting Dynasty

According to this narrative, God objected to David's plan to build Him a house (temple), and instead promised to build David a lasting house (dynasty). There was a considerable time gap between the events described in chapter 6 and this chapter. The events recorded in this chapter belonged to a later period of David's reign. The two topics presented here—Israel's sanctuary and David's kingship—are vital for the entire OT.

7:1–17. God's Covenant with David. At this point in David's life the Lord had blessed him with prosperity and peace from all sides, including the hostile Philistines. God's covenant with David is presented in the context of the king's concern for the Lord's reputation. The king resided comfortably in his palace because the Lord had given him rest. In turn, David planned to provide rest for his God. David was bothered by the thought that the King of kings, whom he worshiped, instead of dwelling in an impressive temple structure, resided in a portable wilderness tent known as the sanctuary. But before David began with his plans for a temple construction, he made sure that his desire was in accordance with God's will.

The narrative in this whole section makes interesting use of the word "house," which in the original Hebrew is used here no less than fifteen times. David was relaxing in his "house" or "palace" and desired to build a decent "house" or a resting place for the Lord. Instead, God promised to build a "house" for David as a lasting dynasty. In a sense, space and location met time. God's intention for David was to provide a secure future, ultimately leading to the arrival of the other "Son of David," whose kingship would be truly "forever" and whose salvation would guarantee eternity. Instead of answering David through a priest, the Lord used the prophet Nathan to reveal His will to His servant. Although prophets spoke for God, they were not devoid of their individuality. Some of their personal opinions and feelings could differ from God's intentions. Nathan's personal opinion was that David should build a temple, but the Lord objected. This case reminds one of Samuel, who opposed the idea of setting up earthly kings over Israel, while the Lord consented to the people's demand (1 Sam. 8:6–7). In Nathan's case, the difference between the prophet's personal opinion and a divine revelation is marked by the fact that the next message he gave to David was from "the LORD" (2 Sam. 7:5), indicating the expressed will of God.

God revealed His plans for David through Nathan. He would make David's name great, just as He did for Abram by saying, "I will make you a great nation; I will bless you and make your name great; and you shall be a blessing" (Gen. 12:2). David indeed became Israel's greatest king. At the end of his life, he would peacefully die and be respectfully buried in his family tomb. God Himself would act as father to David's son. Divine parenthood implies care, protection, and even discipline when necessary, yet not rejection. God also indicated that the temple would be built not by David but by one of his sons (Solomon). The reason given involved David's tremendous military success. Too much bloodshed had disqualified him as the builder of God's temple. This privilege would be Solomon's (1 Kin. 5:3–5; 1 Chr. 22:8–10).

The story suggests that God is not primarily interested in the building of elaborate and luxurious temples. Instead, God is more interested in people, especially those who will accomplish His plans for the salvation of humanity. Throughout salvation history the permanence of the Davidic covenant strengthened the messianic hope. Whenever David's descendants failed, the hope of the people was directed toward the future David, also called the Son of David. In announcing the birth of Jesus Christ, the angel Gabriel referred to Him as the great Son of God—the Most High—and as having the throne of His "father David" with an everlasting kingdom (Luke 1:32–33).

7:18–29. David's Thanksgiving to God. David now humbled himself before God as Moses (Ex. 3:11) and Gideon (Judg. 6:15) had done. In response to the divine promises about a lasting covenant, he offered a thanksgiving prayer while standing beside the ark that represented the divine presence on earth. He praised the Lord's greatness and grace, far exceeding anything a human being can offer. Truly, God's ways are seen as incomparably higher when placed next to human standards.

In the Bible the uniqueness of God is one of the most important themes and provided a reason for the uniqueness of the nation of Israel. David thanked God for the promise of a lasting dynasty and recognized that the impact of His promises would be felt not only by the people of Israel but also by the nations of the world. This was God's intention from the beginning (Gen. 12:1–3). The divine assurances given here would bring comfort and hope to many faithful people.

8:1–18
Victories over Israel's Enemies

Chapter 8 shows how some of the divine promises (cf. chap. 7) made to David were realized through his victories. The order of the events reported here is topical rather than chronological, so many of the victories recorded in the chapter took place before the events of chapter 7. David's conquests extended the territory of Israel from the border of Egypt in the southwest to the Euphrates in the northeast, a fulfillment of God's promises to Abram (Gen. 15:18–21).

8:1–14. David's Further Conquests. David's rule was very successful in the military and administrative areas. Israel's power and influence extended in all directions. In the west he conquered Philistia, which included the city of Gath according to the parallel text from 1 Chronicles 18:1. This time the Philistines were

not only expelled from Israel's territory (2 Sam. 5:25) but also subjugated in their land. In the east David conquered Moab, the land inhabited by relatives of the Hebrews through Abraham's nephew Lot. The friendly relationship between David and the Moabites must have been spoiled by their treachery, so David treated them harshly after the battle. The author gives no other reason for David's cruel treatment of the conquered population. A later Jewish tradition claims that the king of Moab had killed David's parents, who were refugees in his country (cf. 1 Sam. 22:4).

In the north David's kingdom extended to the cities of Damascus and Zobah, which were inhabited by the Arameans, also known as Syrians. They were related to the Israelites through the patriarchs, such as Jacob. Several Aramean city-states from the north of Israel stretching as far as the Euphrates were paying tribute to David. King Hadadezer ruled over Zobah and proved hostile toward David. The military ambitions of this king also targeted Assyrian territories. In contrast to this ruler, King Toi (or Tou) acknowledged David's superiority and sent him a present. In the south David controlled the land of the Edomites.

The concluding statement asserts that God gave victories to David wherever he went. He hamstrung the horses of the enemies, thus making them unfit for battle, because at that time Israel did not use war chariots. Garrisons were put in place to maintain control over the conquered regions. The consecration of spoils from wars, consisting mostly of silver and gold or objects coated in gold, showed that David ascribed all his victories to God.

8:15–18. David's Administration. The end of this chapter tells of David's domestic organization. The king himself was the chief executor of justice in Israel (1 Kin. 10:9; Jer. 22:2–3). Joab's name heads the list of the administrators because he was the army general and also the son of David's sister Zeruiah. David's personal bodyguards included hired soldiers led by Beniah. This commander later played an important role in Solomon's accession as king (1 Kin. 1). While the Kerethites originated from the island of Crete, the Perethites (or Pelethites) were associated with the Philistines (Ezek. 25:16; Zeph. 2:5). Later in the text the reader learns about the Gittites, soldiers from the city of Gath under the command of Ittai, who was very committed to protecting David (2 Sam. 15:18–22).

Abiathar was joined by Zadok as priest, while Nathan the prophet joined Gad. Civil advisers included a recorder and a secretary. Some of David's sons and close relatives were his royal advisers and worship leaders. The original Hebrew says that they performed the duties of the "priests," which means that they served in the sanctuary (cf. Ps. 110:4).

9:1—10:19
Mephibosheth, the Ammonites, and the Syrians

Chapters 9–20 have often been called "the succession narrative," since they relate the events about David's successor to the throne (cf. 1 Kin. 1–2). In the beginning, it was not clear even to David who would be the next king, so his sons other than Solomon pursued their ambitions to seize the throne. The author also relates David's sin and punishment and thus conveys the message that kings in Israel were not above moral laws.

9:1–13. David's Kindness to Mephibosheth.
Jonathan and David were best friends, so while Jonathan was still alive David made a pledge to be kind to his descendants (1 Sam. 20:14–15). David never forgot the promises made to his friend. When he was finally well established on his throne, David desired to honor that pledge by showing loving-kindness (Heb. *khesed*) to Jonathan's only surviving son, who was also Saul's grandson.

The servant in Saul's household whose name was Ziba told David about Jonathan's son Mephibosheth (formerly called Mephi-baal), who was already mentioned in chapter 4. In the aftermath of the battle on Gilboa, where Saul and Jonathan died, the Philistines sacked Saul's capital at Gibeah. During this attack, members of Saul's household were frantically fleeing, thus causing the accident that left the child crippled for life. Mephibosheth fell on the ground and sustained a serious neck or spine injury that made him paraplegic.

The biblical text mentions twice that Mephibosheth had crippled feet. As such he was unfit to be king and posed no threat to David. When brought before the king, he was submissive and compared himself to "a dead dog," which was an expression of self-contempt (9:4). He greatly feared that David might consider him a potential rival to the throne and execute him. In ancient times, all rival claimants to the throne were systematically eliminated (1 Kin. 15:29). David calmed his fear and declared that

Saul's property be returned to Mephibosheth, who as a son of Jonathan was also Saul's legitimate grandson. As the only surviving male member of the royal family, Mephibosheth was the rightful heir of Saul's estates.

This man lived in the town called Lo-Debar in the Transjordan territory of Gilead, which had been the power base of Saul's son Ishbosheth. As a cripple, Mephibosheth had lived in obscurity. David allowed him to move to Jerusalem and eat at the king's table. The king showed the same attitude of kindness toward Mephibosheth's son Mica, who was Jonathan's grandson. To be allowed to eat at the king's table was considered a special favor (1 Kin. 2:7; 2 Kin. 25:27–30). Out of his great love for Jonathan, David gave Mephibosheth honor and privileges like one of own his sons (2 Sam. 9:11).

10:1–19. Ammonites and Syrians Are Defeated.
After the report on David's kindness to Jonathan's son and grandson, David sought to show kindness to Hanun, who reigned over the Ammonites. This happened in response to the news about the death of the Ammonite King Nahash, who had been kind to David. David sent an official delegation from Jerusalem to Rabbah with a message of sympathy. Ammon was a small kingdom on the eastern side of the Jordan. During Saul's reign the Ammonite king was hostile toward Israel and Saul defeated him. When David was hiding from Saul, he found refuge in the territories of Philistia and Ammon. The text does not provide the details about the kind of treaty that existed between David and the Ammonites. Although David was in alliance with Nahash, the Ammonite nobles feared that as king of all Israel, David could change his attitude toward them.

David's delegation was charged with espionage and publicly humiliated by order of Hanun, Nahash's son. As a consequence, Israel's ambassadors returned looking more like a group of captives in mourning (Is. 15:2; 20:4). They were instructed to stay in Jericho until their appearance improved. To grow long hair in Israel was a sign of dignity and honor. The shaming of David's delegation by the Ammonites appeared to be an act of shaming the king of Israel. Jericho was a border town between Israel and Ammon and had been poorly populated ever since Joshua's destruction and conquest.

The Ammonite leaders hired twenty large army divisions of Aramean mercenaries and readied themselves for a battle. (The Greeks later referred to the Aramean people as "Syrians.") In military terms, these two enemy armies appeared far superior to Israel's army, which was commanded by two of David's nephews. The Ammonites focused their defense on the city gate of their capital Rabbah. The Arameans were hired soldiers, so Joab made sure they were confronted by Israel's best men. The forces of Israel defeated Hanun's army and the Aramean troops as well.

Following this defeat, Hadadezer of Damascus gathered a vast army, which included troops that came from beyond the Euphrates. Joab delivered a speech before the battle, outlining the strategic plan and exhorting the soldiers to put their trust in the God of Israel. As an experienced man of war, he entrusted the outcome of the battle into God's hands. Once again the Israelites triumphed and so David's realm expanded further to the east. The victories over the Arameans were previously mentioned in the book's summary of David's military accomplishments (8:3–8). This was David's last military campaign against a coalition of foreign armies.

In the end, many of the Aramean city-states swore their allegiance to David rather than to Hadadezer. They also pledged to stop helping the Ammonites, who continued the war against Israel until they were completely defeated and their capital city sacked. The next chapter begins with that story. Even though David did not initiate the wars against the Ammonites and Arameans (cf. Deut. 20:12), this victory assured Israel's political supremacy in the region.

11:1—20:26
DAVID'S SINS AND FAMILY PROBLEMS

The report on David's sin changes the tenor of his life story from triumphs to troubles and from promises to punishments. His adultery and subsequent murder of Bathsheba's husband (11:1—12:31) show how easy it is for humans to corrupt themselves and misuse the power God entrusted to them. The monarchy was not yet what God intended it to be and will never be until the arrival of the King, who will eventually sit on the throne of David and whose kingdom will be eternal. Although David repented of his sins, the consequences of his actions were inevitable. God does not excuse the sin of His servants. We should be careful not to use this story to lightly deal with the sins of those to whom God entrusted great responsibilities. The story carries a stern warning not to follow David's example but to learn from the family problems he faced (13:1—20:26).

11:1—12:31
David's Sin of Adultery and Murder

Chapter 11 presents the less glorious side of David's wars and victories against the neighbors from the east. The king of Israel became guilty of two serious crimes. Fortunately, after his sins David repented and asked the Lord for forgiveness.

11:1–27. David, Bathsheba, and Uriah. David's sins of adultery and murder took place in the context of a war with the country of Ammon. Military operations normally ceased in the winter months due to rains and impassable roads. They resumed in the spring (March-May) before the harvest period when strong men were needed to work in the fields. David's earlier military successes gave him a sense of security. Thus, instead of going out to war with his army, the king remained behind. Roofs were flat in the lands of the Bible, so David relaxed on the roof of his palace and enjoyed the evening breeze. Sadly, sometimes a sense of ease and security is often the prelude to spiritual failure.

In the Hebrew, the description of David's temptation and sin is condensed and presented through a series of three action verbs: he "saw" (from the verb *ra'ah*) Bathsheba, enquired (from the verb *darash*) about her, and took (from the verb *laqakh*) her. All this he did despite the fact that he knew Bathsheba was a married woman. Her husband was Uriah the Hittite, originally from the ancient region of Anatolia (today's Turkey). He was a non-Hebrew soldier whose outstanding loyalty in this story stands in stark contrast with the infidelity of Israel's king. The name of Bathsheba's father, Eliam, is also given in the text as one of David's "mighty men" (2 Sam. 23:34). In short, the king was well acquainted with Bathsheba and her family.

The author makes it clear that Bathsheba's pregnancy was the result of David's adultery. When Bathsheba learned of her pregnancy, David did all he could to hide his sin because the punishment for adultery in Israel was death. So David sent for her husband Uriah the Hittite, who was on the battlefield as one of the king's best soldiers. However, Uriah refused to go home and sleep with his wife in spite of David's insistence that he do so. David sent gifts to Uriah and even made him drunk, hoping that in such a state he would sleep with Bathsheba and David's act of adultery would be covered up. But Uriah rejected all amenities that were not available to fellow soldiers who, as he reminded the king, were sleeping in tents in open fields (1 Sam. 21:4–5).

Uriah was a loyal soldier and a member of David's royal guard (2 Sam. 23:39). His exemplary behavior put the king of Israel in a very bad light. One is not surprised that his name in Hebrew means "the Lord is my light." In his desperation David devised a plot to have Uriah murdered by the hands of the enemy. Since Uriah "killed" David's hope to hide his sin, David was now determined to kill Uriah. This exceptionally honest man carried his death warrant in a letter, which he did not open. Ironically, David had a great trust in Uriah's integrity. Joab assisted the king in his secret plot against Uriah. A few other innocent soldiers also died in the schemed attack. David knew well that he was responsible for all these deaths. Yet he was calmed when he learned of Uriah's death.

With Uriah now dead, David took Bathsheba to be his wife. She mourned for her husband for at least seven days. The inspired author says that David's behavior did not go unnoticed by God. David sinned by abusing his power and position, but the Lord's authority was above that of the king. Moreover, nothing could be hidden from the One who sees everything (cf. 2 Chr. 16:9).

12:1–14. Nathan's Parable and David's Confession. The Lord seems completely absent from the story of David and Bathsheba. He is only briefly mentioned in the very last verse of chapter 11. The recurring verb in the original Hebrew version of that story is *shalakh* ("to send") when referring to David and other people as its subjects (vv. 1, 3, 6, 14, 27). Then about a year later, the Lord took the initiative and "sent" Nathan to confront David.

Nathan told the king a parable about a poor man's only lamb taken by a rich man for his pleasure. The rich man pitied his own lambs but showed no pity to the poor man and his family, despite the fact that the poor man's family loved the lamb and treated it as a family member. The parable built on emotions and made David burn with anger against the act of injustice. Without realizing it, David sentenced himself by swearing in the name of the Lord.

As king, David was the supreme dispenser of justice in the land (1 Sam. 15:4; 1 Kin. 3:4–28). He acted wisely in condemning the rich man, but he was not wise enough to understand that by doing so he was condemning himself. The penalty for a theft was fourfold repayment (Ex. 22:1), but David overacted and pronounced a death sentence on the criminal. The parable vividly portrayed the realities of David's sin and induced him to condemn himself.

The prophet confronted David with the words "You are the man!" (v. 7). Nathan then explained to the king his crime, which was abuse of power. He despised the commandment of the Lord that says to love one's neighbor as oneself (Lev. 19:18). David's greed was rooted in the attitude of ungratefulness to the Lord, who gave him Saul's throne and everything he had. Ironically, this included a wife by the same name as that of his predecessor, as if he truly replaced Saul. David's wife was Ahinoam from Jezreel (1 Sam. 25:43), the same name as Saul's wife, who was the daughter of Ahimaaz (1 Sam. 14:50).

Nathan also spelled out the consequences of David's sin. The punishment would be measure for measure in correspondence with the crime. Innocent Uriah had died by the sword. David's household would also experience the sword in the near future. Uriah was deprived of his wife, so David's wives would be taken from him before all Israel (cf. 2 Sam. 16:21–22). Although David's acts of violence and moral misconduct were done in secret, his humiliation would be public. Even the heavenly bodies, the sun and the moon, would witness God's justice (Eccl. 2:17; Is. 1:2).

Nathan's final prediction concerned the baby born to Bathsheba. Uriah died as an innocent man, and so would this child fathered by David. The chapters which follow show how these predictions were fulfilled in David's life. Three of his sons died violent deaths: Amnon, Absalom, and Adonijah. But the first to die was the child born to Bathsheba. In spite of this, David did not take Nathan's sayings in a fatalistic way. When confronted by a clear word from the Lord, he did not try to justify his sin or to blame someone else. Instead he humbled himself before God (Ps. 69:10). In this sense his attitude was very different from Saul's (1 Sam. 13, 15). He confessed his guilt openly and felt remorse for his crime (Ps. 51).

12:15–23. Death of David's Son. David fasted and prayed earnestly for the life of the baby whom Bathsheba bore to him. As he focused on God, his physical necessities faded into the background. He was seeking God's grace as he lay prostrate before a holy God in whose presence he felt as only the dust of the earth. Sadly, the child's life was not spared. The punishment for adultery and premeditated murder was death. David admitted that he would join the child in the tomb after his death and burial. These words remind one of Jacob's lament over the loss of Joseph (cf. Gen. 37:35).

12:24–25. Solomon Is Born. After the child's death, David's mood changed. His grieving ceased and he put on what the Bible calls the "oil of gladness" (Ps. 45:7). Then he went to worship the Lord before the sacred ark. God in His mercy gave David another son, who was called by the Lord "Jedidiah" ("beloved of the Lord"). The child's other name was Solomon, a Hebrew name related to the word *shalom* or "peace." This promised child was destined to become an agent of peace and also the builder of the temple to the Lord's name (cf. 7:12–13). Bathsheba became David's legitimate wife, and after his death she would become the next queen mother.

12:26–31. Rabbah Is Captured. Another evidence of God's forgiveness of David's sin was Israel's victory over the Ammonites. This victory put an end to a long war between Israel and Ammon, also mentioned in chapters 10 and 11. This time David joined his army on the battlefield. Joab had taken control of the water supply of the capital city of Rabbah, and David's soldiers were soon in control of the citadel with the palace. David had used similar strategy during the conquest of Jebus, which was renamed Jerusalem (2 Sam. 5:8). Joab wanted David to get the credit for the conquest of Rabbah.

The royal headdress of the Ammonite king weighed 75 pounds (34 kilos) and was made of solid gold. One of its jewels was placed on David's head, making him the ruler of this newly conquered territory. The war captives from the city were set to forced labor to repair damages caused by the war, as was customary in the ancient world. Eventually these people integrated and became citizens in Israel, working on farms or serving in the military.

13:1—20:26
The Loss of Two Royal Sons

Although the Lord forgave David's sin, there were sad consequences that almost destroyed his entire household. Absalom was David's third son (2 Sam. 3:2–3) and is the central figure in the next several chapters.

13:1–22. Amnon and Tamar. The events following the story of David and Bathsheba are described as punishments for David's sins. The story in this chapter combines the sin of lust leading to the sin of murder. David had serious problems in raising his sons, just as did Eli the priest and the prophet Samuel. His firstborn son, Amnon (3:2), was feeling a strong desire for his half sister Tamar, who was a chaste virgin and under the protection of her father David. Amnon lured her into a private room (lit. "house"; v. 8), raped her, and then cast her out. Tamar's long pleading with her brother, her alternative proposal, and her emphatic use of "no" all attest to her strong moral character.

As a princess, Tamar appealed to Amnon's honor as crown prince in Israel not to become a fool in his father's kingdom. She purposely contrasted the roles of a prince in Israel with the "fools in Israel." Her last resort was to consent to marry Amnon, but only with their father's approval. Even though marriage with a half sister was prohibited in Israel (Lev. 18:11; Deut. 27:22), Tamar tried to persuade Amnon that, if he wanted to marry her, David would allow it (v. 13; cf. Gen. 20:12). But Amnon was not interested in her proposal. He was ready to sacrifice his potential status of heir to the throne for a moment of lust. There was no true love for Tamar in his heart but only sensual desire and selfishness.

For Tamar, rape by a half brother meant that she would be despised and desolate for life. Tamar had worn a special robe described by a term used only here and in the story of Joseph, who also wore a special coat (Gen. 37:23). In Tamar's case the robe signified virginity. She tore this precious dress and placed ashes on her head to show her deep mourning (Esth. 4:3; Jer. 6:26). No longer a virgin, Tamar lost her status in her father's house. She found refuge in the house of her full brother Absalom, who named one of his daughters Tamar after her (14:27).

Amnon's character was just the opposite of Tamar's. He is presented as someone who could not control his lust. His command to get up and leave after the rape reversed the previous invitation for her to lie with him (v. 11). He appears purposely offensive when he called her "this woman" (v. 17). His guilt made him despise her afterwards. Biblical (Deut. 22:28–29) and extrabiblical (Assyrian) laws mandated that the rapist must marry the raped woman in order to provide for her needs and her status in society. But this irresponsible young man did not care about Tamar's future. David was angry, and yet he failed to punish Amnon for his wrongdoing. This passive attitude by a parent reminds one of Jacob's reaction to the rape of Dinah (Gen. 34:5).

13:23–33. Absalom Murders Amnon. Time passed, and Amnon did nothing to show regret for what he had done to his half sister. Meanwhile, Tamar's brother Absalom harbored anger that turned to hatred for his older brother. Absalom waited two years for Amnon's suspicions to abate. Finally, during a sheep-shearing festival in early summer (1 Sam. 25:4), Absalom invited the king to a celebration. He expected that David would decline the invitation but would make sure that Amnon, the crown prince, would be there to represent him.

Absalom also invited the rest of his siblings and half siblings to this celebration. At the agreed command, his servants rose up and killed Amnon to avenge his sister's rape. To make bad things worse, this tragic event was immediately followed by a false rumor that Absalom had killed all his brothers. This was not true because the other princes, fearing for their lives, fled on the mules that were used to transport royal family members (2 Sam. 18:9). Now Israel's king grieved for his eldest son.

13:34–39. Absalom Flees to Geshur. Absalom fled and found refuge with Talmai, his maternal grandfather (3:3), who was king of Geshur. This small kingdom was located across the Jordan and east of the Sea of Galilee. While David mourned for Amnon, he also missed Absalom. Three years passed before he had a change of heart and longed to be reunited with his eldest surviving son. Then Absalom showed his strong aspirations to replace David on his throne. Sadly, Absalom's character was not so different from Amnon's. In the narrative that follows, he appears equally deceitful and violent.

14:1–24. Absalom Returns to Jerusalem. Joab did all he could to convince David to allow Absalom to come back to Jerusalem. The first part of the chapter describes how a ruse was used to permit Absalom's return from exile. The second part records a lengthy dialogue, after which David consented to meet his son. The major player in the story was Joab.

Being a close relative of David, Joab tried to persuade David to forgive Absalom and let Joab bring him back to the royal court. It is likely that Joab was also concerned for the future of the kingdom, since this prince was a potential successor to the throne. When everything else failed Joab used a ruse in the interests of all Israel. He was helped in the scheme by a clever woman who used a trick and flattery to win David's heart.

Joab sent for a wise woman of Tekoa (cf. 2 Sam. 20:16–19) to go and speak to the king. Wisdom in the Bible is personified as a lady, and the word for "wisdom" is of feminine gender. This woman appropriately demonstrated that she possessed wisdom. The woman pretended to be a desperate widow in mourning who needed the king to help her in his role as chief judge (cf. 2 Sam. 8:15). She was very respectful toward the king and fell prostrate before him. She was also very articulate and used flattery, twice comparing David to an angel of God (cf. 1 Sam. 29:9). She sought the king's mercy on her only surviving son, who had murdered his brother. The conversation between the woman and David is one of the longest reported in the Bible. It was full of wisdom, rhetorical devices, metaphors, and similes.

Without her only surviving son, the woman would be left without support in her old age and also without an heir (Deut. 25:6; Ruth 4:10). So David ruled that her son should be spared because his act of murder was unintentional (Deut. 19:4–6). David agreed with the point of her story that the well-being of a whole family was more important than the punishment of an individual member. He guaranteed the young man's safety and sealed it with an oath in the Lord's name.

The woman now challenged the king to reconsider the banishment of his son Absalom. When the king's verdict was applied to Absalom's case, the well-being of the nation seemed more important than the prolonged exile of the crown prince. Her punch line was clear: death is irreversible, so Absalom's death will not bring Amnon back to life. Divine mercy will rather preserve the sinner's life than take it.

After the woman's appeal, Joab entered the stage. He was polite and submissive, fearing he might be punished for using deception. As the army general, he knew that if David died while Absalom was in exile, political chaos would prevail in the kingdom. The tribes from the north were not always fully committed to their union with the south, as would be evidenced by the rebellion of Sheba (2 Sam. 20). David understood the point of the story and sent Joab to bring Absalom back to Jerusalem, although refusing to fully restore him. According to the author, no conversation took place between father and son.

14:25–33. David Forgives Absalom. It is not clear from the text whether the king ever forgave Absalom completely. David made a mistake in that he allowed Absalom to return to Jerusalem while he refused to restore him to his position as crown prince. Had Absalom remained in exile, he could have done little to harm the king. Had David restored him, Absalom might have wished the king no harm. By failing to take a side between these two possibilities, David angered Absalom deeply, and this anger turned into a determination to conspire against his father.

Like Saul, Absalom was a very good-looking man. His growing and weighing of hair showed him to be self-centered and narcissistic. At times he also acted like a spoiled child. Although Joab was good to him, Absalom used violent means to compel him to intervene with the king. Moreover, Absalom never felt remorse about his murder. On the contrary, he considered himself free of guilt because killing his brother was an act of vengeance. It appears that his reconciliation with the king was enforced and did not last long.

15:1–12. Absalom's Treason. After his return to Jerusalem, Absalom spent several years preparing a rebellion against his father's rule. He used his good looks and charisma to mount an insurrection that almost resulted in a collapse of his father's kingdom. This time the pressure came from the divisions within the royal family and proved to be more devastating than any of the external threats to David's rule. If Absalom had possessed a different character, he might have been an excellent successor to King David's throne.

Absalom began to play the role of king by showing off before people with his chariots and horses in the style of an Egyptian ruler surrounded by his bodyguards (1 Kin. 10:28–29). He also tried to undermine the people's confidence in the king by casting doubts on David's ability to manage the government. He did this at the city gate, where most business and legal transactions took place (Ruth 4:1). As crown prince he desired to show how he could be a much better arbiter of justice than his father. Administering justice was one of the king's main functions (cf. 12:1–6; 1 Kin. 3:16–28; 2 Kin. 8:1–15), especially in times of peace.

Absalom exploited his father's weakness in failing to appoint regional and local judges, especially outside of Jerusalem. He was very skilled at building support for himself and achieved a large-scale conspiracy without any rumors reaching the royal palace. He also played a "common man" by not allowing people to bow to him but instead giving them a kiss of solidarity and kinship (v. 5; Gen. 33:4; Ex. 18:7). In this way, he "stole the hearts" of the people (15:6) and then proceeded to steal the kingdom.

At the appointed time, Absalom asked David for permission to leave Jerusalem so he could attend a sacrificial meal. This type of occasion with many guests could be an important part of the royal inaugural ceremony. The meal would also create an alliance between Absalom and the invited guests. Being unaware of his son's true intentions, David sent him with the words "Go in peace" (v. 9), though it is clear that Absalom was going to war. In Hebron, David's former capital city, the ram's horn (Heb. *shopar*) was blown and Absalom was proclaimed king. The choice of Hebron was a very clever move, because that was where his father's reign began and continued for seven years.

Hebron was located about twenty miles (30 km) south of Jerusalem. It is very likely that David's later decision to make Jerusalem Israel's capital made some of his kinsmen unhappy. Absalom was born in Hebron, and he exploited this feeling of discontentment. Like David when pursued by Saul, Absalom gained a great number of supporters in that region of Judah. This gave his rebellion greater legitimacy. Within a short time Absalom had significant support from influential people from north and south. Even Ahithophel, the chief royal adviser and Bathsheba's grandfather (11:3; cf. 23:34), joined the rebellion.

15:13–37. David Escapes from Jerusalem. As the support for Absalom steadily grew, David was forced to act. Fortunately, many of his trusted servants remained loyal to him. In order to spare Jerusalem a siege and destruction, the king decided to leave the city and raise an army against Absalom. Accompanied by his personal regiment (cf. 2 Sam. 8:16–18), he escaped across the Kidron Valley in the direction of the Mount of Olives and on toward the desert. He encamped on the western side of the Jordan.

Ittai, the commander of six hundred Philistine soldiers from Gath, was with David. The loyalty of David's personal regiment, as voiced by this captain, played a key role in David's ultimate victory. This non-Hebrew made a double oath in the name of the Lord and thus reinforced his troops' declaration of unlimited loyalty to the legitimate king of the land. Ittai's expression of personal loyalty to David implied a long-standing friendship that transcended monetary gains. The Philistine soldiers apparently lived in Israel with their families, since the text makes mention of their little ones (v. 22).

David left Jerusalem in a state of mourning and shame. As such he humbled himself before the Lord. Along the way there was an open-air altar where people worshiped God. His prayer for help was answered, and Hushai suddenly appeared (vv. 30–32). This wise man was a member of the royal council and personal adviser to the king. David sent him back to counter the wisdom of Ahithophel, whose support for Absalom caused David much anxiety. In the end, Hushai was successful in neutralizing Ahithophel's advice to Absalom.

The two high priests, Zadok and Abiathar, were also sent back to Jerusalem with the ark of God to serve as David's informers. But David left the royal harem behind. He strongly believed that the Lord would open the way for him to return, rejoin the remaining members of the family, and worship again in Jerusalem. This is probably why he sent the ark back. He did not believe that its presence could magically bring him victory. David knew that God's favor is not dependent on the veneration of religious objects. Regardless of where the king might go, God still remained the ruler of the nation.

16:1–4. Mephibosheth's Servant. The outcome of this struggle between Absalom and David would help decide which of the two men would get the support of Saul's family. Some of the incidents recorded in this chapter seem to imply that a number of Saul's relatives sided with Absalom. Ziba, who was Saul's servant and the manager of Mephibosheth's estate, came to support David and brought food supplies for the king and his entourage. His gesture of bringing a gift was similar to but smaller in size than Abigail's (1 Sam. 25). Ziba maliciously defamed his master, Mephibosheth, in order to better himself before the king (2 Sam. 19:24–28). David believed what Ziba said and granted Saul's property to Ziba, the same property he had previously given to Mephibosheth, Saul's grandson who was crippled in both feet (9:13). Ziba's accusation may have been fabricated because it is difficult to see how David's conflict with his son could result in Mephibosheth's gaining the kingdom. In this case, David made a rash decision, which later he would have to revoke (19:29).

16:5–14. Shimei Curses David. When the king crossed into the territory of Benjamin and was passing by an enclave of Saul's loyalists, a man who was a member of Saul's extended family was openly hostile. He cursed David by calling him a man of blood, a murderer, or a bloodthirsty man (v. 7). These offensive words falsely imply that David was guilty of murdering Abner and Ishbosheth in order to grab Saul's throne. This charge likely expressed the enmity that some surviving relatives of Saul felt toward David. However, the stories recorded in the initial chapters of 2 Samuel deny this accusation.

Shimei declared that David's present afflictions were the Lord's punishment. Some of the king's companions suggested that this contemptible person should be executed. David refused and instead entrusted vengeance to the Lord. Ultimately, God's justice and mercy alone determine people's fate. What the king's own son Absalom was doing to him was much worse than the Benjamite's abuse. David knew that discipline is always unpleasant as it is happening but that it later yields peace and righteousness (Heb. 12:11). While his group was waiting near the Jordan, the subject of the narrative shifts to the events in Jerusalem.

16:15–23. Advice of Ahithophel. Immediately after his unopposed entry to Jerusalem, Absalom consulted his advisors. Hushai was already in Jerusalem and did his best to win Absalom's favor. He greeted Absalom with "Long live the king!" (16:16), although readers know who was the legitimate king in Israel. A careful reading of Hushai's words shows that all of his statements were equivocal. The ambiguous language such as the titles "king" and "chosen one" could be applied to either David or Absalom. He purposely omitted personal names in favor of titles. In Hushai's mind, David was still the king supported by God and the people. Absalom assumed that Hushai referred to him as Israel's king.

The outcome of the contest between the two counselors, Ahithophel and Hushai, would determine the outcome of the pending battle between David and Absalom. The rebellious crown prince believed in Hushai, but Ahithophel's advice still mattered the most to him. So he welcomed the idea of a symbolic takeover of the kingdom by sleeping with his father's concubines (cf. 1 Kin. 2:17–25). Hushai wisely kept quiet over this advice given by Ahithophel. He knew that Absalom's immoral act would reverse the public support of his cause. Hushai's purpose was to deceive Absalom and thus help David's cause (2 Sam. 15:34).

On the same palace roof where David had secretly lusted after Bathsheba, Absalom committed public acts of immorality. There was no doubt that when David heard about this shameful act he was reminded of the prophecy concerning the results of his own sin of adultery (12:11–12). In biblical times the royal harem was considered the exclusive property of the reigning king. Any attempts to obtain women from there was seen as a sign of rebellion (3:6–11; 1 Kin. 2:20–21). The loss of the harem to another king was a sign of being deposed. By giving this advice to Absalom, Ahithophel's intention was to create a lasting breach between father and son.

17:1–14. Hushai's Success. The contest between Absalom's two counselors is paramount to the author because it would ultimately decide the outcome of the war between David and Absalom. Ahithophel's earlier advice concerned the moral aspect of the rebellion, while the second part involved the military. As the chief royal adviser, he counseled that Absalom should attack David while his troops were still in disarray. There is no doubt that this was the most logical thing to do. Speed and surprise would work against David's men, while Absalom's side would suffer very few casualties. Ahithophel concluded by reasoning that once David was dead, executed by his own hand, all Israel would support Absalom.

Absalom and all members of his entourage accepted Ahithophel's plan. Yet this time, most likely due to divine providence, Absalom also wanted to know Hushai's opinion. He was not aware that this wise man secretly worked for David (2 Sam. 15:32–36). Hushai's task was a formidable one. All odds seemed to be against him on several accounts. First, Ahithophel's advice made perfect sense. Second, it was an established fact that the opponent's suggestions were highly esteemed by Absalom and the elders. Third, Hushai was suspected of allegiance to David. In spite of all these obstacles, Hushai proved to be a brave man who eloquently expressed his opinion.

Hushai countered Ahithophel's strategy by proposing an alternative plan. He argued that Ahithophel's tactic of a quick attack would fail because of David's rich experience in warfare. All Israel from north to south knew how capable David was in hiding, so it would be impossible to find him. Hushai assured Absalom that in a short time his army would be much bigger than David's, and thus he could count on a complete victory, even if he did rush into a full-scale battle.

Hushai intended to buy time for David with this advice. If Absalom delayed his attack, the king would have enough time to cross the Jordan into safety. Ahithophel's advice was logically the best, but in the use of rhetorical devices such as metaphor, hyperbole, and persuasion, Hushai's speech excelled. He wisely played on Absalom's fear by reminding Absalom that his father had the heart of a lion and was as fierce as a "bear robbed of her cubs" (17:8).

While Ahithophel's self-centered speech abounded with "I" statements, Hushai's speech gave prominence to Absalom's leadership. Hushai skillfully built his case on Absalom's pride and painted a colorful picture of a new leader in command of an army without number. The prince's imagination was captivated, and he decided to heed Hushai's directives rather than Ahithophel's. So Absalom postponed his attack and this gave the opportunity for David to distance himself further from Jerusalem.

The biblical writer makes it plain that this course of events was the work of the Lord, who was answering David's earnest prayers. God had a plan to frustrate the good advice of Ahithophel, a wise man by human standards, but one acting as an enemy of the Lord's anointed servant. Fully aware of the disastrous consequences of Absalom's move and fearing a future execution by David, Ahithophel decided to take his own life.

The triumph of Hushai's advice paved the way for David's future victory. Since this is the turning point in the narrative, from now on all developments would go in David's favor. This is confirmed by the following detail: in the same place where Shimei previously cursed the king, a woman now helped David's agents (vv. 18–20), as Rahab had once helped Joshua's spies (Josh. 2:3–7).

17:15–29. Hushai Warns David. Jonathan and Ahimaaz, the sons of Zadok and Abiathar, relayed Absalom's strategy to David. Based on this news, the king established his base across the Jordan in Mahanaim, which was previously Ishbosheth's refuge and capital city (2 Sam. 2:9). David appeared to have many supporters in this area. From the historical perspective, Mahanaim was the location where Jacob had experienced the protection of the armies of the Lord and named the place "two camps" (Heb. *makhanayim*). Jacob's small camp here on earth was strengthened by the presence of a powerful heavenly camp that was sent by God to defend His servant (Gen. 32:1).

Following the departure of Absalom's chief adviser, Ahithophel, Absalom appointed Amasa to be his army general. This man was a relative of Joab, as well as David's nephew and Absalom's cousin. But as commander he did not have the skill and experience of Joab. In the meantime, David's friends Shobi, Makir, and Barzillai refreshed the king's exhausted army and displayed their firm belief in David's kingship. Along with other members of the royal houses of Saul and Ammon, they brought gifts to show their great support for David's cause. This was the third time in David's life and career that supportive people brought gifts and words of encouragement (Abigail in 1 Sam. 25:18 and Ziba in 2 Sam. 16:2).

18:1–18. Absalom's Defeat and Death. In the decisive battle between Absalom's army and David's men, Absalom was defeated and killed. This story provides us with a view of David as a father rather than as a king. At the urging of his soldiers, David remained behind the battle lines. His troops did all they could to make sure the life of the king was not endangered. They understood that David was the rebels' only target and his death would decide the battle. Ahithophel had rightly argued that David's death would result in Absalom's cheap and easy victory (17:1–4). In contrast with David's men, who were so protective of their king, Absalom's soldiers let their leader join the battle in which he would lose his life.

David dispatched his troops in three fighting units under the command of Ittai and his two nephews, Joab and Abishai. He then gave the instructions to care for Absalom's life. The decisive battle took place in the forests of Ephraim (more precisely, in Gilead), where the terrain was very precarious. More people died from the hostile environment than by the sword. Casualties on that day were great on both sides, even though David's army benefitted from the situation. Absalom, who had entered the raging battle as suggested by Hushai (17:11), was caught by the head in a tree and left hanging in midair. Various translations support the understanding that Absalom's long hair had something to do with this accident. If this is true, then the hair that had been a source of his pride became the means of his undoing.

The author says that Joab deliberately violated David's repeated instructions not to harm the prince and killed him instead. In fact, Absalom's death was so important to Joab that he offered a bonus of one year's pay to the soldier who accomplished it. He had done so much for Absalom, only to be disappointed by his ingratitude

and rebellion. Joab's main concern was the safety of the kingdom and David's life. However, the king loved Absalom and did not view him as an enemy. This was in spite of the fact that Absalom wanted to kill him.

Absalom died without an heir. His three sons mentioned earlier in the narrative (14:27) must have died before him. The name of his daughter was Tamar. The manner in which Absalom was killed and buried showed the soldiers' contempt toward this rebellious prince (cf. Josh. 7:26; 8:29). The description of his death is full of symbolism as the royal mule deserted the would-be king and left him hanging in a tree as a person cursed by God (Deut. 21:23). His hasty burial under a pile of stones in the woods stood in contrast with the imposing monument he had set for himself in the King's Valley. When Absalom's life ended, the war instigated by greed and arrogance also came to an end. The blowing of the ram's horn signaled the end of the hostilities.

18:19–33. David Hears of Absalom's Death. The joy over the victory soon turned into David's sadness. The king was still in Mahanaim, across the Jordan, stationed between the two city gates, which were connected by a passageway. He was in great anguish as he awaited the news about the battle and Absalom. All hopes of his son's survival were dashed by the news brought by the two messengers. The choice of the messenger depended on the content of the news about the outcome of the battle (1 Kin. 1:42). One of the messengers, called Ahimaz, was confident that the news would be welcomed by David. But Joab, knowing that Absalom's well-being was more important to the king, sent a foreign soldier to inform David about the situation. The king grieved over the death of his son and wished he could give himself to bring him back to life. This was not the only lament of David recorded in the Bible, although this one is different. While his laments for Saul, Jonathan, and Abner were public, his mourning for Absalom was personal and private.

19:1–15. David Returns to Jerusalem. The state of the kingdom was more important to Joab than David's feelings toward Absalom. He urged David to rise up and fulfill his public duties as king. The post-war situation in the land required strong leadership. Instead of mourning the loss of a rebellious son, the king needed to greet his victorious troops. So David went to the city gate, the gathering place for the elders and other important people of a city. There he welcomed his soldiers, who had been willing to sacrifice their lives to ensure the safety of their king.

In the beginning of David's reign, the people of Judah were the first to unite under his leadership. This time the northern tribes of Israel were the first to reinstall David as their king. Consequently, David had to remind the people of Judah that he was one of their own. He tried to win their solid support for him because for a time they had supported Absalom. The reason for this switch of loyalty was probably their unhappiness with the transfer of David's capital from Hebron to Jerusalem (cf. 2 Sam. 15:7). This is why they first responded to David's call with hesitation. Afterwards, they welcomed him back based on his ability to rule and not for personal gain.

As a gesture of national reconciliation in the southern tribe of Judah, David appointed Amasa, Absalom's former army commander (17:25), to the post of his general. Amasa was David's nephew and exercised a great influence on the people of Judah. Another reason for this change was because the king considered Joab to be responsible for the deaths of Abner and Absalom. It is assumed that some of the elite and mercenary troops remained under Joab's command. David's difficult task at this point in his career was to keep the balance between generosity and forgiveness toward former rebels, while expressing deep appreciation for his loyal supporters.

19:16–39. David's Acts of Mercy and Kindness. The events recorded in this passage are a dramatic reversal of David's flight from Jerusalem recorded in 2 Samuel 16:1–14. Instead of humiliation and weeping, there was joy and celebration. Sackcloth and ashes were replaced by the oil of gladness. In the spirit of this glorious occasion the king proclaimed a day of general amnesty in Israel. He also decided to show an attitude of forgiveness toward hostile individuals, such as Shimei from the tribe of Benjamin, who cursed David on the way out of Jerusalem (16:5–13).

Mephibosheth also came out to welcome the king. His mournful appearance (2 Sam. 19:24) indicated that during the uprising he had no ambition to be king. It appeared that he spoke the truth but had been falsely accused by Ziba. David found it difficult to know which of the two men was speaking the truth. In the end the king had to change his previous rash oath to Ziba and divide Saul's former estate between Ziba and Mephibosheth. As Jonathan's

son, Mephibosheth was still honored to sit at the royal table. David's treatment of his friend Barzillai's son continued David's pattern of magnanimity and generosity.

19:40—20:26. Unity and the Rebellion of Sheba. In spite of David's great efforts to keep the nation united, some divisions became evident as the men from the northern tribes were not invited to the welcoming party for the king. They were seriously offended by this omission. Complaints about favoritism and discrimination would continue to plague David's rule. They foreshadowed Sheba's revolt and the eventual breakup of the kingdom under Solomon's son Rehoboam.

Wars give rise to many problems even when they appear to have achieved their aims. Although Absalom's rebellion ended with a victory for David, the kingdom lost its sense of unity. God was faithful to David and preserved his throne, but his last years were not happy ones. This chapter presents yet another threat to David's rule and the unity of Israel's kingdom. As mentioned at the end of the previous chapter, suspicions of favoritism and discrimination gradually led to an intertribal argument and the threat of another civil war. David's quick and decisive action resulted in the rebel's death and prevented a division of the kingdom.

Sheba, from Saul's tribe of Benjamin, led an insurrection against David. He took advantage of the delicate situation that followed Absalom's rebellion, which was marked by divisions between Judah and the northern tribes. Fortunately, this conflict was a relatively minor affair and ended without a battle. During this crisis the men of Judah remained loyal to David. In the beginning of Sheba's rebellion, all eyes were on Amasa, who was now David's army general. But Amasa's reaction to the attempted coup was very slow. The king was forced to appoint his nephew Abishai to deal with the situation. Acting together with his brother Joab, he dealt swiftly with Sheba's challenge to David's rule. Joab used this opportunity to murder Amasa in a treacherous way, just like he had killed Abner. Amasa was Joab's relative, but he considered him to be his rival. While completely committed to David, Joab's character was brutal and ruthless.

Sheba retreated and took refuge in Israel's northernmost town called Abel Beth Maacah. This prompted David's soldiers to lay siege to the city walls. With this the people of Israel lost confidence in Sheba's chances to grab the throne from David. A wise woman from the town negotiated with Joab a resolution to the conflict, resulting in a minimal number of casualties. She was able to convince fellow citizens to offer Sheba's head to avoid the destruction of the town that, as a part of Israel, was the Lord's inheritance. The citizens of this peace-loving city were loyal to the king. They acted swiftly, and Sheba's death, like Absalom's, brought an end to the hostilities.

After this victory, Joab appears to have reclaimed his position of army general. David was not successful in his attempts to remove him from that position. The chapter ends with a short list of David's officials, similar to the one in 2 Samuel 8:15-18. This time the names of David's sons are omitted. Also, for the first time there is mention of revenue from forced labor (20:24). This novelty in David's rule would arouse popular opposition, especially later during the reign of Solomon. It would reach a climax in the murder of Adoram, chief of forced labor or revenue (1 Kin. 12:18). The list of David's officials was placed in this narrative to confirm the fact that political order in the kingdom was finally restored.

21:1—24:25
DAVID'S KINGDOM IS PRESERVED

The arrangement of the material found in the closing chapters of 2 Samuel is topical, rather than chronological. For example, the story from chapter 21 most likely took place before David's act of kindness to Mephibosheth as recorded in chapter 9. This last section of the book demonstrates how God preserved David's kingdom and opened prospects of a better future. The first narrative (21:1-22) looks back to the time when David's reign began, while the closing points toward the future of Israel's kingdom (23:1—24:25). In between, we find David praising God for His deliverance (22:1-51) and the king's farewell, along with a recognition of his valiant soldiers (23:1-39).

21:1-22
The Gibeonites Are Avenged

In this passage, the revenge by the people of Gibeon contrasts with the acts of charity to the dead done by David and the concubine of Saul. It is about the search for justice in order to restore peace to society.

21:1-14. David Avenges the Gibeonites. Early during David's reign there was a famine that lasted for three years (cf. 24:12-13). This famine was caused by a drought, and it forced the king to ask the Lord what caused such a calamity. Rains and droughts in Israel are explained in the Bible as God's way of blessing or punishing His people for the keeping or the breaking of their covenant (Deut. 11:13-17). The answer was that the famine was caused by King Saul's breaking of the long-standing covenant between Israel and the people of Gibeon (Josh. 9:25-27). These people lived in the land of Canaan before the conquest of the land by Israel. They occupied the area just north of Jerusalem in the territory of Benjamin. The covenant that Joshua made with them was confirmed by an oath taken in the Lord's name. The text says that Saul violated this treaty.

Saul's hostilities toward this minority in Israel is not mentioned anywhere in 1 Samuel. Moreover, it is unclear why Saul would attack a people who posed no threat to him or to the nation. He apparently planned to exterminate them completely, although his plan did not succeed. The author makes it clear that David was not responsible for Saul's mistakes or for the consequences of these mistakes. A blessing pronounced on Israel by the people of Gibeon would cancel the curse, but first justice had to be done. At the request of the Gibeonites, David turned over seven descendants of Saul's household to avenge the loss which these people had suffered from the hand of Israel's first king. But David spared Mephibosheth in agreement with the promise made to his best friend Jonathan to show kindness to his descendants.

After the execution of the seven men on a high hill, their remains were honorably buried and gathered with the ashes of the bones of Saul and Jonathan (1 Sam. 31:11-13). Some scholars have proposed that this execution was the reason for which Shimei accused David of bloodshed (2 Sam. 16:7-8). From a modern perspective, this passage is not easily understood. It should be kept in mind that the concept of community was very strong in the ancient world. This meant that both privileges and responsibilities were shared by all members of the community.

The big picture painted in this chapter illustrates both the Gibeonites' desire for justice over past wrongs and the acts of kindness shown toward the bodies of those executed. The latter were performed by Rizpah, Saul's concubine, and King David. All during the hot summer this exemplary lady guarded the seven corpses from scavengers until winter came. The rains put an end to the drought that caused the famine. The king then made sure that the members of Saul's family were accorded decent burials. In biblical times, burying the bones of the dead was considered an act of charity, especially if they were placed in the ancestors' grave (2 Sam. 7:12).

21:15–22. Philistine Giants Are Destroyed. This passage reports about heroic acts of David's strong men. Each one defeated a Philistine giant in a single combat. These incidents took place at various times during David's reign. This chapter ends with a catalog of wars against the Philistines, with whom David had long-standing hostilities. It also includes a list of giants, the sons of another famous giant, who were killed by David or his associates. The Hebrew indicates that Elhanen killed Goliath, while a parallel passage indicates it was a brother of Goliath (1 Chr. 20:5). For this reason, most translations say "brother of Goliath" in this passage. The short report of David's officers and their heroic deeds lays a foundation for the psalm of praise found in the next chapter. The psalm was composed by David and emphasizes the military successes of Israel. King David's rule functioned as "the lamp of Israel," which was kindled by the Lord and as such should not be quenched but should remain as the symbol of hope in God (1 Kin. 11:36).

22:1–51
David's Song of Praise

One of the best ways to celebrate victories and make such experiences memorable is to compose songs. In biblical times, it was common to compose and sing a song in response to God's help in overcoming the enemy. This is what Hannah, Samuel's mother, did after she had experienced God's saving power (1 Sam. 1–2). Seventy-two songs in the book of Psalms (about half) are credited to David.

22:1–6. God's Presence. This song is also found in the book of Psalms (Ps. 18) with minor differences. It was a thanksgiving song offered to God for David's deliverance, especially from King Saul. When facing a difficulty, David would cry out to the Lord to deliver him from mortal dangers. The narrative form of David's troubles is presented in 1 Samuel 18—2 Samuel 20. The word "Deliverer" is the key title given to God in this song. The Lord's intervention is described here in the language of the theophany at Mount Sinai (Ex. 19). The Lord came down from His dwelling place in heaven (from His heavenly temple; cf. 2 Sam. 22:7; Ps. 11:4) to rescue His faithful servant. He is a faithful God who keeps His covenant. The Lord's coming is accompanied by terrifying signs and wonders, such as earthquakes, volcanic eruptions, and thunderstorms.

The song abounds in metaphors that describe God's unlimited strength. The Lord is the psalmist's Lamp, Rock, Horn, and Shield of Salvation. Light is the metaphor of salvation and deliverance (Ps. 27:1). God gives victory over the enemy and delivers His children by leading them from darkness into light. Thunder and lightning accompany Him when He goes into battle. Some Gentile nations pictured their gods going into battles in similar ways, yet David's psalm says that none can compare to the supreme Lord of the nations. An appropriate doxology (2 Sam. 22:47–51) concludes this song.

Standing in contrast to the rock metaphor representing safety and refuge that can be found only in God is the metaphor of waves of death. Those deadly waves threaten to snatch people from the divine arms. Swirling waters in the Bible can be chaotic and destructive. Large bodies of water symbolize hostile powers that threaten to destroy God's creation. Similarly, the metaphor of the cords of the grave represents the realm of death called in Hebrew Sheol.

22:7–51. David's Safety. When the psalm is applied to David, one can see that much of his life and career was filled with struggles coming from various enemies. Yet in the end, God made His servant triumph and gave him peace. The Lord opened the way and set His child free in a broad place—a place of salvation (v. 20). David used metaphor to describe the details of the Lord's intervention in his life. Thus, David describes the Lord rushing to his aid riding on a swift angel, called a cherub. In material terms, David was delivered by a Philistine raid (1 Sam. 23) or by the wildness of the terrain (1 Sam. 24). But above these apparently material explanations, David saw the greater reality of the Lord of Sinai acting with power on his behalf.

The meaning of all this poetic imagery is that God supernaturally works through life's circumstances. Behind dark veils, the Lord works from His throne in the interest of His child. Although in the shadow, He is still in control. The psalm forms a fine commentary on David's daily walk with his Lord. As an outstanding piece of poetry, it looks forward with the eyes of faith to God's future faithfulness toward David's many descendants. The Lord promises to reward those who earnestly seek Him.

23:1–39
The King's Farewell and His Mighty Men

David's lasting legacy in Israel consisted of a firm commitment to the service of the Lord and a peaceful, prosperous dwelling in the promised land. The chapter includes David's last words in the form of a poem and lists several heroic acts of his bravest men.

23:1–7. Righteous Ruler. This short psalm was also composed by David. Other biblical personalities who uttered praises to God at the end of their lives included Jacob (Gen. 49) and Moses (Deut. 33). In this poem David compares a righteous ruler to a gentle rain, while the wicked oppressor is like thorns. The opening words of the chapter state that David was moved by the Holy Spirit to utter an oracle (ne'um, "an announcement"). This term, sometimes translated as "oracle," commonly introduces a prophetic speech (Num. 23:7; 24:3; Is. 14:28; Mal. 1:1) It can also introduce wise sayings (Prov. 30:1; 31:1). As far as the evidence goes, this is the only explicit reference in the OT to David's prophetic gift. In the NT he is plainly called a "prophet" (Acts 2:30). The passage looks back to the time when God acted as David's shield and protection. God protected him in the same way that He guarded Jacob in all his ways and delivered him from harm (Gen. 48:15, 16). The song also looks forward to the future Son of David, the promised Messiah, who will establish justice on earth.

The psalm is David's last formal reflection on life and his covenant with the Lord. The topic of God's relationship with His people is far more prominent in this song than the topic of Israel's enemies (cf. chap. 22). God has promised to cast aside those who oppose His plans as harmful thorns are cast into the fire. Fire is used in the Bible as a symbol of both God's presence and His judgment. The wicked will come to an end, while God's covenant with His anointed servant will never cease (7:16). The just ruler is compared to light. David was called by God to rule over Israel in righteousness and respect for the Lord ("fear of God").

23:8–39. Courageous Soldiers. This catalog of David's heroes is another tribute to God's goodness. The two songs that precede it ascribe all of David's victories to the Lord. The mention of mighty men testifies to the human help the king received from his outstanding soldiers. The list is ordered hierarchically and begins with the top three heroes. The first part of the catalog presents short stories about heroic acts, most of which were performed in the early period of David's reign. Many of the heroes came from Judah, particularly from David's hometown of Bethlehem. Others came from Benjamin and Ephraim, while at least two were of foreign origin.

David had two elite groups of champions who served as his bodyguards, along with a special fighting force. The first three accomplished significant exploits against the Philistines. The second group included thirty brave warriors whose names were listed in the royal annals of distinction. Some of the heroes died while performing their extraordinary duties. Two names that stand out in that regard are Asahel and Uriah (chap. 11). Surprisingly, Joab is not mentioned, although his name previously headed the list of David's officials (2 Sam. 8:15–18). Most commentators agree that he was counted in the total of thirty-seven mighty men.

Acts of bravery were performed during hot summers and cold winters. During one hot summer, three soldiers broke through the enemy camp to bring David some water from a well in his hometown of Bethlehem. But when they brought the water, David refused to drink and instead poured it on the ground. Drinking this water would have been like drinking the blood of the soldiers who risked their lives. On a snowy day, one of David's soldiers killed a lion in the midst of a pit. Hunting lions was a favorite sport of kings and heroes in the ANE and testified to their courage. The common technique used was a pit. The lion was pursued into a pit where a net was used to entangle it. The hunter would use a spear to finish the kill. To catch a lion in winter was more difficult because wild beasts had trouble finding food and became more dangerous.

24:1–25
David's Pride and Repentance

The closing chapter of the book deals with three dominant topics, namely the census, the plague, and the altar. Figuratively they stand for pride, punishment, and forgiveness. Thus, the book closes with a message of forgiveness in the context of worship.

24:1–9. David's Census of Israel and Judah. The parallel passage from 1 Chronicles 21:1 is helpful in understanding this story because it mentions the involvement of "an enemy" (Heb. satan). Although modern translations have the word "Satan" (the devil) in this parallel text, the original Hebrew has no definite article in front of the noun "enemy." There are other OT passages, such as Job 1–2 and Zechariah 3, that speak of Satan or "the enemy" (the Hebrew *hassatan*). But this is not the case in 1 Chronicles (see "Satan and David," p. 536). Nevertheless, the absence of the article does not automatically mean that the reference is not to Satan. In this case we are dealing with Satan.

The author of Samuel puts emphasis on God's control of history. The plague and its cessation resulted from David's actions, yet both were also determined by God. Since the Hebrew narrative style is such that the summary (or conclusion) is given first, we should read the statement from 24:1 as saying that the anger of the Lord burned against Israel *because* "someone" incited David to act against his subjects. According to 1 Chronicles, this someone was "Satan." The authors of 2 Samuel and 1 Chronicles seem to say that the king decided to number his fighting men in response to the threat of a military confrontation.

David usually consulted the Lord or His prophet in a time of crisis. Sadly, this time he failed to do so (1 Sam. 22:5). The Lord's prophet, Gad, appeared only later in the narrative (2 Sam. 24:11). David's decision to take the census of all men in Israel from north to south for a military purpose betrayed his pride and a growing tendency toward self-reliance. Joab's warning to the king did no good. It is true David was conscience-stricken later (v. 10), but by then it was too late to change the decision.

24:10–17. Judgment on David's Sin. God gave David a choice of three types of punishment: famine, plague, or war. All three are described as curses, which are caused by breaking the covenant (Deut. 28). David decided that the plague was the least of the three possible evils. The famous covenant chapter from Deuteronomy speaks of the three types of curses (Deut. 28:15–25). David publicly confessed that he was guilty of the deaths of many people in Israel. The nation's shepherd caused harm to his poor sheep (1 Chr. 21:17). History demonstrates that the mistakes of leaders cause suffering for ordinary people. This is a lesson that leaders often forget.

24:18–25. Altar on the Threshing Floor. The prophet came to instruct the king to build an altar on the very site where he saw the destroying angel (cf. Ex. 9:3; 12:23). Yet, the author made it clear that this angel was under the Lord's absolute control. The threshing floor of Araunah the Jebusite was located on Mount Moriah. The site where God's presence was revealed to Israel's king was to become the site of the future temple (1 Chr. 22:1; 2 Chr. 3:1). It is possible that the word Araunah in the language of the Jebusites was not a personal name but a title meaning "governor." Threshing floors were usually located outside of the city and near the gate. There, on the flat ground, the grain was separated from the chaff. This large, flat, open area was a popular gathering place for the townspeople, especially during ceremonies and festivals.

David was offered the piece of land as a gift by a local landowner who lived in the area even before David's conquest of Jerusalem. In purchasing the site, David did not neglect to pay a price. In this way the future temple site became the property of David's house. There he built an altar, offered sacrifices, and prayed on behalf of the people.

Thus, 2 Samuel ends on a hopeful note. David was always ready to confess his transgressions before God and devote himself to the proper worship of the Lord. In spite of his sin, David remained the Lord's vassal. The piece of the land promised long ago to the ancestors was now dedicated to the Lord. This represented a rededication of the whole country and nation to the holy calling that originated with God. The book closes by looking forward in expectation of what would soon happen—the building of Solomon's temple to the Lord. It also closes with the people living in a land free from plagues. This local and temporal freedom from evil anticipated one at a cosmic level and filled the heart of God's people with hope.

1 KINGS

INTRODUCTION

Title and Authorship. In the Hebrew Bible the books of Kings are simply labelled "Kings 1 and 2." They conclude the section of the Hebrew Bible known as the "Former Prophets" that also includes Joshua, Judges, and the two books of Samuel. Greek tradition saw Samuel and Kings as unified and labelled the books of Samuel as "Of the Kingdoms 1 and 2" and Kings as "Of the Kingdoms 3 and 4." It is possible that the early Greek translation of the OT, the Septuagint, was the first to divide the book of Kings into two. Christian tradition considered Kings a single book until scholars divided them in the sixteenth century.

The unified style of writing points to one primary author rather than many—one who used various records available to him, including written accounts of Solomon (1 Kin. 11:41), kings of Israel (14:19), and kings of Judah (14:29). Hebrew tradition suggests that the author may have been Jeremiah, but another prophet is just as likely since prophets play such a prominent role in the book.

Date. The events described in the books of Kings cover about 400 years and date from approximately 971 B.C., the start of Solomon's reign, to 562 B.C., when Jehoiachin was released from prison and was invited to eat at the king's table (2 Kin. 25:27–30). It is generally understood that most of the material for the book was in existence before the destruction of Jerusalem in 586 B.C.

Backgrounds. The book opens with the dying days of King David and ends with the death of Ahab. Solomon succeeded his father, David, but because of his multiplied idolatry (to cater to his foreign brides), the kingdom was subsequently divided into two (in 931 B.C.). The capital of the Northern Kingdom of Israel was Tirzah for the first fifty years, but Omri moved it to Samaria (about 12 miles [20 km] to the west). The capital of the Southern Kingdom of Judah was Jerusalem. The first northern king, Jeroboam I, afraid that his people's loyalty would remain with the temple at Jerusalem, introduced a golden calf in both Bethel and Dan and introduced a priesthood that anyone could join in order to staff the shrines. This blatant disregard of God's command regarding worship led to the downfall of the Northern Kingdom.

Each successive Israelite king maintained and embellished idolatrous worship, and all are noted for doing evil according to the Lord's evaluation. There were twenty northern kings altogether (eight in 1 Kings) from nine different dynasties: nine died by assassination, one in battle, one by injury, and nine by natural causes. During the same time there were twelve kings of Judah, all from the Davidic line except for Queen Athaliah, who was a granddaughter of the Israelite king Omri. By the time Judah went into its Babylonian Exile, they too had twenty monarchs, eleven of whom are noted for doing evil according to the Lord's evaluation.

Theology and Purpose. The books of Kings contain a unified description and evaluation of events that led to the Exile of God's people. They uncover the reasons for the loss of the land, its kings, and the temple. Its carefully constructed narrative communicates a vital message: although earthly dynasties may fail, God has bound Himself to His people through His word with covenantal promises that will not fail. He will fulfill His word within history, shaping it with His blessings or condemnation. As 2 Kings ends with the loss of land, temple, and king, readers receive a faint glimmer of hope: God, in fulfillment of His promises, would one day bring about restoration. As the books unfold, so too do a number of key theological themes: the land, the temple, the prophetic voice, sin and judgment, and hope. It is significant that each of these themes have their roots in the Pentateuch, particularly in the account of the Exodus.

1. Land. God promised His people a land to dwell in (Deut. 1:8), asked them to build Him a sanctuary to dwell among them (Ex. 25:8), and spoke through the prophetic voice of Moses (Deut. 34:10). God's action gave hope for a human-divine harmony that would benefit not only His people and their land but all peoples (Deut. 32:43). These themes are developed in the stories of the kings of Judah and Israel.

2. Temple. Solomon inherited a large domain from his warrior-father; but as a result of the idolatry he introduced for the sake of his wives, large segments of the kingdom were lost in subsequent years to increasingly emboldened enemies. Eventually this led to the destruction of the Northern Kingdom in 722 B.C., with its people scattered across foreign lands. One hundred and thirty-six years later, Jerusalem and its temple were destroyed, and the people of Judah were exiled in Babylon.

It seems that most of the Judean kings added various features to the temple to honor foreign deities (e.g., a shrine, altar, or idol), or they neglected the temple altogether to focus on a multitude of high places and attractively ornamented glades. Instead of the temple being a focal point of God's presence with His people and a constant reminder of His work of forgiveness and restoration, it was turned into a contrived monument to religious compromise and self-determination (see "The Temple in Chronicles," p. 541).

3. Prophets. In this context, the text introduces the prophets—spokespeople for God who thundered against the injustice and apostasy of idolatry. Prophets featured throughout the books of Kings include Nathan (1 Kin. 1:8–45), Ahijah the Shilonite (11:29–39; 14:1–18), an unnamed man of God (chap. 13), Jehu (not to be confused with the king who reigned about eighty years later; 16:1–7), Elijah (17:1—19:19; 21:17–29), one or more unnamed prophets (20:13–14, 22–28; 35–41), Micaiah (22:8–9, 13–28), Elisha (2 Kin. 2:1—7:2; 8:7–13; 9:1–3; 13:14–21), and Isaiah (2 Kin. 19:6–7, 20–36; 20:1–19). Other prophets also living at this time included Jeremiah, Daniel, and Ezekiel. The presence of such a large number of prophets clearly demonstrates the important role that they played throughout the books and during this period.

These prophets proclaimed the word of the Lord to the people. It is through the fulfillment of this prophetic word that the Lord controlled and guided history. Prophecy and fulfillment play an important role in the message of the books. The Lord shapes history through the word of judgment and salvation. Unfortunately, the kings and their people largely ignored the prophets, choosing instead to follow the lifestyle and cultic practices of the gods of Canaan. The word of judgment came against them and was fulfilled in the destruction of the city and the temple. But there was also the word of hope that would shape the future.

4. Hope. Destruction and exile are not the end of the story. Usually the assurance of hope, restoration, and renewal follows a prophetic word of judgment, and that is how the books of Kings end. After a description of the thorough dismantling of the realm and the complete destruction of the temple and monarchy, the story declares the release of an imprisoned king in exile (from the line of David) from his dungeon and recounts his being allowed to dine at another king's table. This indicates that the process of restoration had begun and that what had been a faint hope now ignited the assurance that by the grace of God, one day all things would be made new (cf. Rev. 21:5).

Literary Features. The books of 1 and 2 Kings probably should never have been divided—they are essentially one book. There is a definite sense of hindsight, rather than a mechanical fragmentation where the writer attempts to describe events as they happen. The style of writing is historical narrative—stories artistically crafted and told by a narrator who develops the plot and characters of each story, who repeats key words, phrases, and sounds, and who sometimes uses dialogue and the perspectives of others to communicate a lesson.

COMMENTARY

1:1—11:43

THE UNITED MONARCHY

The glorious days of David's reign were over, and a harsh reality dawned. The book opens with an aged and enervated King David who had not yet appointed his successor. Not only did this threaten the peace of the realm, but it also meant there was no new king to build the temple, complete the process of uniting the nation, build up its infrastructure, and secure its borders. David's successor would set the course, either for the success and long-term viability of the nation or for its eventual downfall. Therein lies the drama that unfolds in the book: Would the people of promise, residing in the land of promise, be guided by the conditions of the covenant, or would they instead adopt the gods, the hopes, the inspiration, the lifestyle, and the fate of their neighbors?

1:1—2:11
David's Last Days

The narrative of Kings opens by introducing a number of key characters. Abishag played a key role in the final stages of David's reign. Adonijah, sensing the impotence of his father, seized the opportunity to declare himself king before his brother Solomon could. Bathsheba, urged by Nathan the prophet, ensured that David kept his promise to make Solomon the next king. Bathsheba's plea rekindled some of David's old fire, and he called for his trusted advisors to inaugurate Solomon as his successor.

1:1–10. Abishag and Adonijah. The short story of Abishag placed at the beginning of the book alerts the reader to the fact that a new king should be immediately appointed to succeed David. David had reached a point where he had to totally rely on others, thus risking the security of the kingdom through potential palace intrigues and disputes for power. Abishag was from the town of Sunnem, and since she had a very specific task with respect to the aged king, she was not considered to be part of the king's harem.

Realizing that his father was weakened with age, Prince Adonijah (whose name means "the Lord is my God") feared that his brother Solomon would soon take the throne. He concluded that he had to move fast in order to take over the kingdom. He was David's fourth and probably his oldest surviving son (2 Sam. 3:2–4; 13:28; 18:14–15). Possibly he considered himself rightful heir apparent on that basis. He exalted himself and let those in the right places know that he would be the next king. He acquired a chariot and appointed fifty men to run before him (1 Kin. 1:5). His tactics reflect those of Absalom (2 Sam. 15:1) and suggest a similar demise.

The text describes Adonijah as handsome (1 Kin. 1:6), as in the case of Absalom (2 Sam. 14:25) and David (1 Sam. 16:12). He managed to attract some significant supporters, especially Joab and Abiathar. Joab, Adonijah's cousin, played a key role during David's reign (e.g., 2 Sam. 14; 18:14; 1 Chr. 11:6). However,

a rift developed between David and Joab from the time Joab murdered Abner (2 Sam. 3:12–39). Abiathar, the priest who had joined the fugitive David after escaping the slaughter of the priests by King Saul (1 Sam. 22:17–23), may also have fallen from the king's favor. Abiathar was being eclipsed by Zadok and Joab by Benaiah (the captain of the king's guard), so the prospect of supporting a new king may have been a very attractive option for the two old campaigners.

1:11–31. Succession Crisis. The venue for Adonijah's coronation celebration was near a well-known spring, easily visible across the Kidron Valley from Jerusalem and David's citadel valleys (v. 9). While David, in his apparent feeble condition, was unaware of what was happening, others would have understood the significance and the threat of the events unfolding. Nathan the prophet became aware of what was taking place and decided to alter the course of history initiated by Adonijah since it was not according to God's will. So immediately, together with Bathsheba, he set up a plan to approach King David, the center of power, to ensure the king's legal and proper succession. Otherwise the people of Jerusalem might assume Adonijah's rise to the throne as official (v. 20). Nathan and Bathsheba focused their coordinated speeches on the reliability of the king's word (vv. 17, 24). He had promised that Solomon would succeed him, and now the fulfillment of his word was to shape history. But the king knew that it is really the Lord who was shaping history (vv. 29–30).

This short vignette underlines the significance of the prophets of God in several of the dramas in the book. They appear suddenly on the scene at critical moments. If Nathan had done nothing, Bathsheba would not have acted; and without her impassioned plea, David would have failed to secure the throne for the divinely approved successor, and the temple might not have been built. This is an example of the crucial role of the prophets throughout the books of Kings in regard to safeguarding the future of the kingdom.

1:32–40. David's Transfer of Power to Solomon. David's vigorous and positive reaction to Bathsheba and Nathan's petition contrasts sharply with his feeble demeanor portrayed in the opening lines of the book. David ordered three trusted friends to accompany Solomon in a big procession to the Gihon Spring. The fact that Solomon sat on a mule in his inauguration demonstrates the ancient conception of mules as honored animals worthy of royalty. These animals were highly priced in that period because they had to be imported. Hebrew law did not allow the breeding of hybrid animals (Lev. 19:19).

It will be noticed that the rival ceremonies were staged at springs, doubtless because these were public places frequented by people who were constantly in need of water to carry home. Events taking place in such locations would be quickly known throughout the city. En-Rogel, on the opposite side of the valley from the city, was a well-known spring and public landmark. Gihon, down the slope from the main city, was the main water supply for Jerusalem, and while perhaps it was not as directly visible to the majority of the population in the city, it was of more immediate significance to their daily lives. A coronation procession down through the city from the palace to the Gihon Spring at the bottom of the hill would have been easily visible to Adonijah's party on the other side of the valley. Additionally, the symbolism of the place, as a counterpoint to Adonijah's location, would have been easily recognized by the people. The joyous procession, which included music, was so loud that it is described metaphorically in terms of an earthquake (1 Kin. 1:38–40).

It is significant that the security of this operation was entrusted to the Cherethites (Kerethites) and Pelethites who comprised the royal bodyguard (v. 31). They were most likely from Philistine tribes who had pledged loyalty to David in his early years. Soldiers from the Philistine city of Gath—Goliath's hometown—also formed part of David's loyal troops (2 Sam. 15:18–23). Possibly the Cherethites originated (a century or two earlier) from Crete, and the Pelethites were trusted royal couriers who also doubled as guards. While Israelite heroes like Joab supported the pretender to the throne, former enemies and worshipers of pagan deities celebrated, protected, and supported the legitimate king. God has His instruments everywhere.

2:1–11. Solomon Enthroned. Despite the repeated and more intense reminder of the nearness of David's end, the revitalized king continued his cogent instruction. He charged his son to be strong, be a man (v. 2), walk in God's ways, and abide by His instructions (v. 3). These words are similar to those used by Moses when passing on his "mantle" to Joshua (Josh. 1:7–9). David also drew on the language of Nathan the prophet when establishing a covenant between

God and David (2 Sam. 12–16). In that covenant, God promised David an everlasting dynasty, the success of which would be due (in part) to the faithfulness of his descendants (1 Kin. 2:4). David wanted to ensure Solomon's personalization of this requirement of God's covenant with him. The promises of God to David, His word, would be fulfilled as long as Solomon, the new king, was loyal to Him.

The speech concluded and the aged warrior-king subsequently died. The phrase "rested with his fathers/ancestors" (v. 10) refers to the practice of burying family members in the same tomb that was used for family members who had died previously, with the bones of various generations "resting" together. The summary of David's reign informs us that it lasted forty years—placing it from 1011 to 971 B.C.

2:12—4:34
Solomon Established

After caring for his father's unfinished business (2:13–46), Solomon married an Egyptian princess (3:1–3). In a dream the Lord promised him wisdom (3:4–15), and this was fulfilled (3:16–28). He then set out to establish his civic infrastructure (4:1–19). The biblical text highlights Solomon's prosperity (4:20–28) and includes a final statement about his wisdom (4:29–34).

2:12–46. Completing David's Unfinished Business. The reason for commencing this section at v. 12 rather than at v. 13 (as some commentaries do) is the use of a Hebrew literary devise called an *inclusio*, where a repeated statement frames a literary passage. Such is the case between v. 12 and v. 46, which repeat the statement that Solomon's kingdom was "firmly established." Solomon's rival, Adonijah, unwittingly sealed his own fate and confirmed Solomon's place on the throne when he asked Bathsheba to negotiate in order to have Abishag as his wife. Solomon interpreted Adonijah's request as an attempt to legitimize his ambitions to take over the realm (vv. 15–17) and found here a way to solve a problem once and for all. He used the widely accepted practice that a new king would take over the harem of the previous king (cf. Absalom in 2 Sam. 16:21–22) to condemn Adonijah for still seeking to take over the rest of David's harem and kingdom. Solomon ordered Adonijah's execution and then followed through with the other requests of his father (1 Kin. 2:5–9). Abiathar was effectively banned from the king's court and from the sanctuary, thus fulfilling the word of the prophet that the influence of Eli's line would come to an end (v. 27; 1 Sam. 2:31–35).

This action probably signaled to Joab that his time had come too. Although Joab was David's nephew, his kinship to the king had not stopped David from demoting him for killing Absalom (2 Sam. 19:13). Joab had also murdered Abner and Amasa, and their blood still stained his belt and sandals (1 Kin. 2:5). He fled to the sanctuary and clasped the horns of the altar in an attempt to receive asylum and amnesty. Joab thought that since Adonijah had received mercy by clinging to the horns of the altar (1:50–53), he too could receive mercy. But this Mosaic law applied to only accidental killing, not premeditated murder (Ex. 21:12–14). Joab's defiant refusal to leave the altar brought about his execution there (1 Kin. 2:28–34). Despite his shameful end, he was given an honorable burial on his home estate near Bethlehem (v. 34; cf. 2 Sam. 2:18, 32).

Shimei had cursed David during his escape from Jerusalem, but David had showed him mercy (2 Sam. 16:5–13). The time had come to set matters straight. Solomon confined Shimei to Jerusalem and forbade him to cross the Kidron Brook or to go anywhere else (1 Kin. 2:36–38). The Kidron Valley formed the boundary between Judah and Benjamin, so this restriction prevented Shimei from either working his own land at Bahurim (on the eastern slopes of Mt. Scopus) or inciting a revolt against the king among his kinsmen. The way Solomon dealt with Shimei when he disobeyed demonstrates Solomon's wisdom as a ruler, successfully walking a very fine line between just and fair leadership and alienating the key tribe of Benjamin.

3:1–15. Making the Nation Great. Now that the immediate threats to the throne had been resolved, Solomon turned to wider matters of state. Before taking the throne, he had already been married to at least one wife, Naamah (the Ammonitess; 1 Kin. 14:21), perhaps for at least two years. Naamah's son Rehoboam was forty-one when he became king (14:21), and Solomon reigned for forty years (11:42), which indicates that Rehoboam was born while Solomon was still a prince. As the new king, Solomon's next action meant to bring lasting peace by taking more wives, and his first marriage constituted a remarkable political achievement. Solomon did something that few other kings of any nation had done before: he married an Egyptian princess, becoming the son-in-law of the Egyptian pharaoh. At this time, the king of Egypt was

probably Siamun of the Twenty-First Dynasty, who came to the throne a few generations into the Third Intermediate Period (eleventh through eighth century B.C.; a time when multiple people claimed to be king simultaneously). Siamun would have seen this marriage as a way to strengthen his position as king in Egypt by aligning himself with a strong ruler. The city of Gezer served as dowry for the wedding (9:16), evidence that even by this time not all cities in the land were controlled by Israel. It also demonstrates the mutual benefits enjoyed by the two kings and of the long-standing interdependence that lasted right up to the time of the Babylonian Exile. From the outset Solomon showed his diplomatic skills. Political alliances were one way to make the nation great by protecting against invasion from the south.

At the end of 3:1 is a quick sketch of some of the civil projects that Solomon initiated: a palace for himself, the temple, and the completion of a city wall around Jerusalem. Meanwhile, the hint of future disaster is revealed—the people sacrificed at the high places (v. 2), as did Solomon. This becomes a major issue for the nation in the years ahead.

After Solomon's politically expedient marriage (which was followed by many more), the second step for making the nation great was to reinforce the importance of religious ritual (he was about to build a temple for God as He and David his father had stipulated). Solomon went to the most significant high place at Gibeon,

High Place—*Bamah*

A *bamah* or "high place" was a shrine or worship site and not strictly speaking a "high" place. The term comes from Jerome's Bible (fourth century A.D.), which translates the Hebrew word *bamah* as *excelsus* ("high" or "eminent"). The *bamah* was typically a flat platform carved in bedrock, found not just on hills and mountains (e.g., Num. 22:41; 1 Sam. 9:14) but also in towns (2 Kin. 17:29; 23:5) and in valleys (Jer. 7:31; 32:35). Although they were initially considered legitimate places of worship (e.g., 1 Chr. 21:29), they were banned after the temple's completion to prevent the Israelites from copying the ritual practices of the surrounding nations, whose "high places" included an altar for sacrifice and various stands or alcoves to display an idol or other cultic objects.

about 6 miles (9.7 km) northwest of Jerusalem, where the remnants of Moses's wilderness sanctuary resided (2 Chr. 1:3)—the ark of the covenant was in a tent at Jerusalem (2 Sam. 6:12, 15, 17). Gibeon, the largest and most important place for worship in the land prior to the construction of the temple, was in the heartland of Saul's support base. Solomon's visit to Gibeon not only sought God's blessing on his reign but also may have been an attempt to reconcile with Saul's loyal followers.

While he was still at Gibeon, God appeared to Solomon in a dream (1 Kin. 3:5–15). Not only did this unique experience (no other Israelite king received this privilege) demonstrate divine willingness to bless the new king, but it also reinforced the covenant that God had made with David (see 2 Sam. 7). On that occasion God had promised David that He would establish the kingdom of his son (2 Sam. 7:12–13), that this son would build the temple, and that God would be his Father and chastise him if he committed iniquity. God concluded His covenant speech with David by assuring him of His *khesed* ("covenant faithfulness") to bind Him and Solomon together—in contrast to the divine rejection experienced by King Saul.

When God asked Solomon to choose a gift, Solomon's four-part answer was couched in covenant language, including *khesed* (1 Kin. 3:6). Solomon recalled God's past faithfulness, pled for His continued help, demonstrated his humility, and prayed for an understanding heart in order to be a wise ruler. This became the third step for Solomon to make his kingdom great. If he truly chose wisdom over riches and fame, then every blessing would become available to him. Usually a king received wealth and honor as a result of a wise reign, but God gave Solomon all three from the beginning, and he quickly became internationally recognized as a leader of note. God assured Solomon that there would be no king like him before or after (v. 12) and that he would be preeminent among reigning contemporary monarchs as well. Unfortunately, the promise of long life was not fulfilled due to Solomon's later unfaithfulness, and he probably did not live beyond the age of sixty (11:42).

3:16–28. Solomon's Wisdom Revealed. The reality of God's promise of wisdom was publically demonstrated by the visit of two prostitutes. This remarkable drama spotlighted some very promising features for the kingdom. First, it showed that the king was approachable by all his subjects; justice was accessible to all. The struggle between the two disputing women was an impossible dialogue of "my son"—"your son," "your son"—"my son." There were no witnesses, so it was one woman's word against the other's. There was no human way through this legal impasse.

Second, it also showed that the Lord had fulfilled His promise by giving Solomon great wisdom. His immediate solution was both unexpected and seemingly brutal. Instead of analyzing the words or asking for more details, his solution revealed a deep understanding of human nature and cut through to the deepest feelings of the true mother. This story could have ended very differently if the biological mother had been as coldhearted as her companion or if she had as bad a reputation as her "profession" would suggest. Not only did Solomon expose the false claims of the false accuser, but he gave the true mother confirmation and legitimacy, encouraging her to give this child the hope of a successful and productive life in the community, despite his dubious origins.

The outcome was electric. The news traveled very quickly, and all Israel soon heard about the brilliance of their new king. They had a new respect for him and recognized God at work in their midst (v. 28).

4:1–19. Social Order. While Saul's government structure had been fairly rudimentary (mainly military), David's was a little more ordered. David had organized the basic utilities of army, public records, priesthood, secretariat, and royal bodyguards (2 Sam. 18:16–18), and later he established a department of labor or revenue (2 Sam. 20:23–25). Solomon established a more sophisticated system. He appointed chief officials with specific government functions and governors of designated districts. Solomon kept the first four basic organizational units of his father but added offices to oversee the district governors, a royal advisor (1 Kin. 4:5), an officer to manage the royal estate, and a manager to oversee the labor force necessary to accomplish the king's projects (v. 6).

Next, the governors of the districts were named (vv. 7–19). Solomon assigned twelve districts to feed the royal household—one per month. Their boundaries were not entirely consistent with the territories of the twelve tribes, which perhaps demonstrates that Solomon became more concerned with overall national unity than the preservation of tribal units. This may have caused a backlash, contributing to the unravelling of the kingdom after Solomon's death. It is interesting that no governor for Judah appears in the list of governors. It is also obvious that this system took a while to establish, since one of the governors married Solomon's daughter (v. 15), and Solomon did not seem to have had a daughter of marriageable age when he ascended the throne.

4:20–28. Extent of Palace and Realm. The description of the extent of the realm indicates fulfillment of the promise made to Abraham— from the Great River (Euphrates) to the River of Egypt (not the Nile but a wadi at the northeastern extremity of Egypt; Gen. 15:18; see 2 Kin. 24:7). The Lord was shaping history according to His word. Solomon did not have to resort to military campaigns to maintain control over the nations subdued by his father. Because God gave him "rest on every side," there were no adversaries or crises (*ra'*, "evil," "disastrous occurrence"). This gift of peace is referenced by the well-known description of each person dwelling safely under a vine and fig tree (1 Kin. 4:25)—a status that became the benchmark for peace and security that later generations longed for (2 Kin. 18:31; Mic. 4:4; Zech. 3:10).

Further evidence of the economically stable times can be found in the size of Solomon's household—estimates vary between 10,000 and 60,000. This required a carefully orchestrated administrative structure to manage it and provide enough food for it. Daily food provisions included both stall-fattened and pasture-fed animals, birds, wild game, fine flour, and meal (1 Kin. 4:22–23, 27).

In addition to the daily provision of food was the supply of fodder for the king's stables (v. 28), but it is not clear how many horses there actually were. The account in v. 26 speaks of 40,000 stalls for chariot horses, and 12,000 horsemen, but the parallel passage in Chronicles (2 Chr. 9:25) specifies 4,000 horses for the 12,000 horsemen. Considering the 1,400 chariots mentioned later in Kings (1 Kin. 10:26), 4,000 stalls seems more likely if each chariot had two horses plus a spare. The number specified in Kings is probably a scribal error. The impressive nature of the stables could be a further indication of how much Solomon relied on Egypt—if this was where he obtained his horses (10:28).

4:29–34. Solomon's Wisdom. The narrative of Kings returns again to the theme of God-given wisdom to reinforce the notion that this is the best option for the future of the nation. A large harem and many foreign alliances, huge religious ceremonies, a civil service patterned on the best political system around—none of these could compete with the effectiveness of a people guided by God's gift of wisdom. The superlatives describing Solomon's wisdom and breadth of understanding are contrasted with natural phenomena (like the "sand on the seashore"; v. 29) and with the sayings of other known wise men of the day. Neither the wise men of the East (presumably Mesopotamia; cf. the wise men in the birth story of Jesus) nor the sages in Pharaoh's court could match this (v. 30). The names mentioned in v. 31 are neither Hebrew nor Canaanite, so their identity is uncertain. Were Heman and Ethan the same people who each wrote a psalm (Pss. 88, 89)? The expression "sons of Mahol" does not tell us the name of their father—*makhol* literally means "dance" or "dancer," so they could have been from a class of musicians known for their exceptional skill. This would be in harmony with the Hebrew idea of wisdom being practical giftedness that results from being filled with the Spirit of God (see Ex. 31:2–5).

Evidently Solomon was an astute observer of nature, and he drew profound and practical lessons from it to assist especially the young to live well (1 Kin. 4:33; cf. Job 12:7–8). His many proverbs and songs were widely known, and he became so accomplished that his reputation became legendary in his own time, and foreign rulers sought him out (1 Kin. 10).

5:1—8:66
Solomon Builds and Dedicates the Temple

Solomon revealed his wisdom in the construction of the temple and the palace. He began by making preparation for the construction (5:1–18), and then he built the temple (6:1–38) and his palace (7:1–12). He also prepared everything needed for the proper function of the temple (7:13–51). Solomon brought the ark to the temple and dedicated the temple to the Lord (8:1–66). Apparently both temple and palace were considered part of the same complex, and its construction took about 200,000 workers (5:14–16) and twenty years to complete (19:10). The two buildings were structurally joined, which made it easy for the king to access the temple through his own private entrance. Solomon largely depended on Hiram, king of Tyre (c. 969–936 B.C.), for the technical details of the project, which potentially gave a Phoenician architectural touch to the buildings.

5:1–18. Workers and Supplies. Hiram was one of the first foreign kings to seek out Solomon. David's defeat of the Philistines had greatly enhanced the economic status of the Phoenicians, and a friendship had developed between the Tyrian king and David. Hiram had assisted David in building his palace (2 Sam. 5:11) and had already provided abundant materials for the temple (1 Chr. 22:4). The visit of Hiram's emissaries both affirmed Solomon as the new king and assured the continuing goodwill between the two nations.

In response to this visit, Solomon sent a diplomatic letter to Hiram (1 Kin. 5:2–6) in which he reiterated the Davidic covenant and affirmed that he would soon build a temple (2 Sam. 7:12–13). He requested not only cedar but also tradesmen to direct the local workforce. Solomon negotiated for the payment of workers and supplies, and Hiram set the rate at 20,000 kors (donkey loads) of wheat and 20 kors of first-grade olive oil per year (implying that Hiram would pay his men from this after keeping a portion for himself). This list was evidently not complete, as the Chronicles account includes an extra 120,000 gallons (440,000 L) of wine and the same amount of regular olive oil—the latter presumably in addition to the smaller quantity of first-grade oil (2 Chr. 2:10). This was almost double the quota that Solomon received for his own household, and it may be that the national production capacity struggled to keep up, which led to a national debt to Hiram. This was repaid in part by Solomon giving him twenty cities in the region of Galilee (1 Kin. 9:11). This may have also caused dissatisfaction among the populace for the increased tax burden—something alluded to by the delegation that approached Rehoboam after Solomon's death (12:4).

The narrative of 5:13–18 describes the labor force (4:6). Solomon conscripted 30,000 Israelites and rostered them in three shifts lasting a month each, so that at any one time there were 10,000 of them in Lebanon and 20,000 working at the temple site in Jerusalem. From resident foreigners he raised 70,000 to transport construction materials and 80,000 to rough cut blocks from the quarries, and he appointed 3,300 supervisors to oversee them. All stone blocks (including the foundation stones that would be hidden underground) were dressed at the quarry to a high standard (v. 17; cf. 6:7) by Solomon's and Hiram's skilled workers (v. 18).

6:1–38. Building the Temple. It is significant that the date for the construction of the temple is linked to the Exodus (v. 1). The author of the biblical text was very careful to precisely record the time—the fourth year of Solomon and the second month (Ziv/Ziph was its old Phoenician/Canaanite name), which was the spring of 967 B.C. More importantly, the prominence given to the Exodus in the context of the temple suggests the ideological linkage of the two. The temple was the permanent dwelling of God manifested among His people in Canaan. They had both found a place of rest.

The temple dimensions are impressive: sixty cubits long (90 ft. or 27.4 m), twenty cubits wide (30 ft. or 9 m), and thirty cubits high (45 ft. or 13.7 m)—double the size of the wilderness tabernacle in some regards and three times higher

Phoenicia

Tyre was a major city in the Phoenician nation of seafaring people who were descended from the displaced Canaanites with colonies throughout the Mediterranean. Although we may refer to Hiram's "domain" as Phoenicia, the cities in that geographical area were not forged into one political entity in Solomon's time but were a collection of loosely aligned city-states—perhaps Hiram was recognized as the leading monarch among them. Their main cities in the northern Levant were Tyre, Sidon, Gebal (Byblos), and Arvad, and they occupied the narrow coastal strip of land (in modern Lebanon) between the Lebanon Mountains and the Mediterranean Sea. Because of lack of arable land, they were renowned merchants and seamen, specializing in cedar and also popularizing an expensive purple dye (extracted from the murex snail). They were also experts in masonry, metalwork, fine pottery, and glassware.

Cedar from the Lebanon Mountains grew to 100 feet (30 m), and the Phoenicians were famous for their skills in working with it. The Egyptians and Mesopotamians favored cedar for the roof beams of their large civic buildings. It was a long-lasting hardwood that resisted both insects and dry rot.

in others (Ex. 26:16, 18), but only half the height of the second temple (Ezra 6:3). The early cubit (probably used here) is about 17.5 inches (about 44.5 cm; see 2 Kin. 20:20) compared with the cubit adopted by later kings that is a handbreadth longer, or about 20 inches (about 50 cm; see 2 Chr. 3:13).

At the entrance of the temple building was a platform across its width and extending out ten cubits (15 ft. or 4.6 m) in front. Surrounding the building on three sides were three floors of small rooms built against the perimeter wall (1 Kin. 6:5-10). These were used for storage and possibly for the priests to stay in when rostered for duty. The description in v. 9 of the completion sounds a bit premature, but the same phrase is repeated in v. 14. This indicates that this passage is a literary unit—a parenthesis—that breaks the flow of the narrative in order to bring an important announcement (vv. 11-13). Here, the word of the Lord came to Solomon, and this drew the focus away from the impressive architecture and engineering marvels to the covenant God made with his father (2 Sam. 7:8-16). The word of promise God had given to David takes center stage, announcing that its fulfillment was directly related to a firm commitment to Him. This brief divine speech was the key to the divine presence: it was not extensive religious exercises or a magnificent building that guaranteed the continuing presence of God among His chosen people; rather, it was the covenant God had made with His people and their willingness to maintain it. While a magnificent building was under construction, God said He would dwell among the children of Israel rather than in a building (see 2 Kin. 25:1-21).

The magnificence of the temple's internal features is described in 1 Kings 6:15-36. The walls and the ceiling were lined with cedar while the floor was covered with cypress pine (v. 15). Ornamental buds, open flowers, cherubim, and palm trees were carved into the wall panels (vv. 18, 29). All of the wood, including the floor, was overlaid with gold (vv. 22, 30). This ornamentation was reminiscent of both past and future—the flora and cherubim of the Garden of Eden, and the gold-covered "floor" of the streets of gold in the new Jerusalem (Rev. 21:21).

Partitioning the main building with a cedar wall from floor to ceiling created the holy of holies (1 Kin. 6:16). Its internal height was twenty cubits (30 ft. or 9.1 m; v. 20)—compared with the main building, whose ceiling height was thirty cubits (45 ft. or 13.7 m; v. 2) —and its walls were also carved and covered with gold.

As well as housing the ark of the covenant, the inner sanctum was also graced with two freestanding cherubim, each ten cubits tall (15 ft. or 4.6 m), carved from olive wood (v. 23) and covered with gold. They stood with wings outstretched, wing tip touching wing tip, stretching out to the opposite walls (v. 27) and overshadowing the ark (8:7). The two cherubim on the back wall together with the two on the top of the ark more closely reflected descriptions of the throne room of heaven, which was depicted with four cherubim surrounding the throne of God (see Ezek. 1; 10).

The final temple element in the description was the doors. The language is not clear, but it seems that the doorposts for the doors into the holy of holies may have been five-sided and both doors were made of olive wood (6:31-32). The doorposts into the Holy Place may have been four-sided and also of olive wood, with the outer doors of cypress (vv. 33-34). All were intricately carved and covered with gold (vv. 32, 35). In the account in Chronicles there is no mention of a curtain dividing the rooms (cf. 2 Chr. 3:14), although there is a reference to a gold chain at the entrance into the holy of holies that may have been used for a curtain suspended in front of the door (1 Kin. 6:21).

At the conclusion of chapter 6 the time reference given in v. 1 is repeated, adding just as precisely the date of the temple's completion (v. 38). In addition to forming a literary unit (an *inclusio*), the repetition underscores the importance of the dates involved and the connection between the temple and the Exodus.

7:1-51. Palace and Temple Furnished. One of the harbingers of Solomon's later apostasy was the fact that he took nearly twice as long to build the palace complex as it took to build the temple. The first one was described as the Palace (lit. "house") of the Forest of Lebanon (vv. 2-5), which was presumably named for its many internal cedar pillars that looked like a forest. At one hundred cubits long (150 ft. or 45.7 m), fifty cubits wide (75 ft. or 23 m), and thirty cubits high (45 ft. or 13.7 m), it covered more than four times the floor space as the temple building. Apparently, this building served as the royal armory (10:17; Is. 22:8), so it would have had storage rooms around its perimeter as the temple complex did. Other buildings in the complex included the Hall of Pillars or colonnade (1 Kin. 7:6) at fifty by thirty cubits (75 by 45 ft. or 23 by 13.7 m)—it, too, was larger than the temple—and the throne room or Hall of Judgment or Justice (Heb. *mishpat*; v. 7), as well as a residence for the king and another for his Egyptian wife. Each of these buildings followed the same architectural style with three rows of large, costly stones and a row of cedar beams (vv. 8–12).

The work of Hiram (Huram in some Bible versions), a bronze worker from Tyre, is featured in vv. 14–47. The name Hiram was obviously a common name (spelled the same in Hebrew as King Hiram), and this particular man was the son of a woman of Naphtali and a man of Tyre. He cast all the bronze items in the fine-grained clay of the Jordan Valley (v. 46), the combined weight of his handiwork being undetermined. The two pillars for the front of the temple, Jachin (Jakin) and Boaz (v. 21), were eighteen cubits high (27 ft. or 8.2 m), twelve cubits around (18 ft. or 5.5 m), and a span or handbreadth thick (cf. Jer. 52:21). On top of each pillar was a separate lily-shaped feature (1 Kin. 7:22) embellished with two rows of pomegranates and a chain lattice (vv. 17–18, 20, 41–42). The function of the pillars is uncertain, but their names (Jachin, "he is strong," and Boaz, "in strength") suggest that they served as visual reminders that the strength and stability of the king and the people were possible only with God's presence among them.

The laver, or sea, was a hemisphere ten cubits across (15 ft. or 4.6 ft), five cubits high (7.5 ft. or 2.3 m), and a handbreadth thick (v. 26). It was surrounded by two rows of ornamental buds on the outside of its brim (v. 24), and it was placed upon twelve bronze oxen, with groups of three oxen standing together and facing each of the four compass points (v. 25). Its capacity was between 11,500 to 12,000 gallons (43,500–45,500 L), about the capacity of a swimming pool that is 12 feet (3.6 m) by 25 feet (7.6 m) and has an average depth of 5 feet (1.5 m). However, it served as a reservoir for water, not for bathing or washing (cf. Ex. 30:19). For these functions, Solomon made ten smaller lavers, each holding about 230 gallons (870 L) and each resting on a bronze cart (1 Kin. 7:27–38). Half of these stood along the northern side of the temple court and half along the southern side. The side panels on the carts were embossed with cherubim, lions, and palm trees (v. 36).

The text in vv. 40–46 summarizes the bronze creations of Hiram: the pillars, their capitals, and all their special features; ten carts and the lavers to go on them; the sea and the twelve oxen to support it; and the pots, basins, and bowls. It is significant to note that each of the large items displayed numerous reminders of the Garden of Eden: cherubim, lilies, buds, pomegranates, palm trees, oxen, and lions, reflecting similar portrayals within the sacred golden precincts of the inner rooms. These constant visual reminders pointed to the purpose of the temple: not only for God to live in their midst (Ex. 25:8) but also for the eventual restoration of the face-to-face communion with God that Adam and Eve enjoyed in Eden. Worshiping there was in a sense a return to the original harmony between God and humans.

The chapter ends with a description of the items of gold, including ten seven-branched lamp stands (five along the north wall and five along the south side), wick trimmers, basins, bowls, ladles, censers, and hinges (1 Kin. 7:49–50). Since gold is not strong enough to hold a heavy wooden door, presumably this was some sort of embellishment or covering for the hinges to ensure that every surface within the inner rooms was covered with gold.

8:1–66. Dedicating the Temple. After the temple was complete, Solomon gathered all the key people—the elders and the tribal chiefs—to bring the ark and all other sacred items to their new resting place. The temple was completed in the eighth month of Solomon's eleventh year (6:38), and the furnishing and dedication happened in the seventh month—presumably eleven months later. Perhaps the delay was to coincide with the Festival of Tabernacles, so that while the people celebrated the Exodus by camping out in temporary shelters (Lev. 23:42–43), their attention also turned to God's promise through Moses to "camp" with His people if they built Him a temporary dwelling (Ex. 25:8).

Huge numbers of sheep and oxen were sacrificed outside as the priests put the ark in its place (1 Kin. 8:4–5) under the outstretched wings of the large cherubim. The ark contained only the two stone tablets of the Law—there is no mention of Aaron's rod or the golden pot of manna (Ex. 16:33–34; Num. 17:10; Heb. 9:4). It could be that these latter items had at some point been removed from the ark before the time of Solomon. Then the inner rooms were filled with smoke, making it impossible for the priests to stay there, as if God was claiming that domain for Himself (1 Kin. 8:11). Solomon responded by saying that God dwells in thick darkness (the Most Holy Place) but that he built Him a house/temple (vv. 12–13). Even though no temple could contain the omnipresent God (v. 27), He manifested His presence there as a God near to His people.

Solomon then turned to face the assembled crowd for a prayer of dedication (vv. 14–53). He began by honoring his father and quickly sketching the outlines of the Davidic covenant, and then he explained that his part in the covenant was to build the temple (vv. 15–20) and to properly house the ark. This signifies an interrelationship between the Davidic and Mosaic covenants (v. 21): the ark of the covenant spotlighting the Exodus and the temple having been initiated in God's covenant with David. As Solomon spread out his hands toward heaven (an act signifying "clean" motives and actions; Ps. 24:4), he again mentioned the importance of the word of God. God fulfilled the word He had spoken to David to place his son on the throne and for his son to build Him a house (1 Kin. 8:18–26).

There are a number of significant themes included in Solomon's prayer: sin, salvation, covenant, worship, loyalty, the sanctuary in heaven, the character of God, and the nature of humans. When Solomon made a general plea for God to "hear," he suggested seven situations in which people may find themselves and asked God specifically at those times to hear, act, forgive, or maintain their cause (vv. 32, 34, 36, 39, 43, 45, 49). Here was clear recognition that although the temple was a poignant symbol of God's presence among His people, it is from His heavenly temple that God actually administers justice and vindicates those calling on Him (vv. 30, 39, 43, 49).

Another dominant theme in the prayer is the way Solomon described sin and how God deals with it. The word that he used for sin signifies missing a target, failing in one's duty, failing to live up to expectations, or falling short of spiritual wholeness (vv. 16, 31, 34–36, 46–47, 50). Solomon suggested that if the people were taught the good way (v. 36), they would be more inclined to follow God. But he explained that the problem of sin resides like a plague within every human heart (v. 46). Only God really knows a heart's condition, and it is only the forbearance and forgiveness of God that can meet the challenge. The verb "forgive" appears in five verses (vv. 30, 34, 36, 39, 50) and leads to the conclusion of the prayer by connecting forgiveness and the covenant with the deliverance from Egypt.

Although Solomon commenced his prayer standing before the altar (v. 22), at its end he was kneeling (v. 54). The occasion must have been awe-inspiring—the numbers of sacrifices were so unthinkably large that the altar of sacrifice could not cope, so special provision was made to sacrifice on the ground in the middle of the court. These sacrifices were peace or fellowship ones, so it was only the fat that was burned and the rest of the animal was food to be shared between worshipers and priests (Lev. 7:11–15, 30–36). The atmosphere was so charged that the people did not want the occasion to end, so festivities were extended for a further week (1 Kin. 8:65–66) and the temple celebrations were combined with the communal joy of the Festival of Tabernacles.

9:1—11:43
The Remainder of Solomon's Reign

After twenty years, the great building projects were complete and the temple-palace complex had become the envy of surrounding nations. God appeared to Solomon a second time in response to the temple's dedicatory prayer and reminded the king of the importance of the covenant that David had entered into with God and the covenant loyalty expected from Solomon (9:1–9). The word of the Lord was also about judgment for rebellion against Him. This word was as certainly to be fulfilled as the word of blessing and salvation. The rumblings of disaster and judgment continued with the souring of relations between Solomon and King Hiram of Tyre over an unappreciated gift (9:10–14), the building costs, and other activities of Solomon (vv. 15–28). The narrative shifts back to the positive when describing the Queen of Sheba's visit and the gathering wealth coming into Solomon's coffers (10:1–29). Although times were good, subtle warnings of future crisis were in the background (11:1–43).

9:1–9. Challenge to Covenant Faithfulness. In response to Solomon's prayer, God appeared to him a second time. The context places this at the completion of Solomon's building program that had lasted twenty years. Does this mean that the completed temple stood unused for thirteen years, waiting for the completion of the palace complex, after which the temple was dedicated (see 6:38; 7:1)? The data is ambiguous, but the fact that temples were dedicated to be immediately used for the service of God rules out the idea that it was inactive for thirteen years. It is also unlikely that there would have been a large time gap between the dedicatory prayer and God's response assuring Solomon that the prayer had been heard. The answer must have come soon after the prayer (cf. PK 45).

God responded to Solomon (vv. 3–9) and assured him that his prayer of dedication had been heard and the temple had been consecrated. Furthermore, not only would God's name reside there, but also His "eyes" and "heart" (v. 3). This is an interesting response to Solomon's insistence throughout his dedicatory prayer that God resides in heaven. Rather than staying on the temple/abode of God theme, God challenged Solomon to remain faithful to the Davidic covenant in integrity of heart and uprightness by upholding the terms of the covenant like his father David, which would ensure the long-term viability of the dynasty (vv. 4–5).

Then God warned Solomon: if he or his successor sons worshiped other gods, the result would be loss of land, destruction of the temple, and ridicule by other nations. They would question why such disaster had befallen a people who had previously been so blessed by their God (vv. 6–8). The answer would be that since they abandoned their God, the word of judgment reached them. This was an ominous signal and hinted at coming disaster for both the monarchy and the nation, in shocking contrast to the spiritual high of the recent celebrations. It also served as a reality check affirming that magnificent architecture and fervent religious celebration do not necessarily define a life of faith. Without being true to the covenant-keeping God, these things mean nothing.

9:10–14. An Unappreciated Gift. The repetition of the statement announcing the completion of the temple closes the previous literary unit (9:1–9) and opens another. At the completion of the twenty-year building projects, Solomon still felt obligated and in debt to the king of Tyre for all the cedar, cypress, and gold he had supplied. Either Israel could not keep up with the original payment schedule (5:11) or what Hiram supplied far surpassed what Solomon had originally asked for. To settle the apparent debt, Solomon gave Hiram twenty cities around their common border (9:11), perhaps as collateral. Hiram was not happy with this and gave the region an insulting name—*kabul*. This word is related to a verb meaning "bound" or "restricted," but it could also be related to the Hebrew phrase "like nothing"—which would thus show his disdain for the cities (v. 13). This may have been the catalyst to sour relations between Tyre and Israel to the point of Tyre joining Israel's enemies a number of generations later (Amos 1:9–10; cf. Is. 23:1–18; Ezek. 28:1–23). Despite this inadequate gesture from Solomon, Hiram gave him a further twenty talents of gold, possibly to remove any sense of obligation that may have

been imposed on Tyre for the "gift" of all those unappreciated cities. (See commentary on 2 Chr. 8:1–11 for further clarification of the narrative.)

9:15–24. Summary of Completed Projects. This section summarizes the labor force required for not only the temple and palace building projects but also the city walls and the Millo—a heavily-fortified citadel on Mt. Zion—and other cities built at that time (vv. 15, 17–19). The forced labor providing all the heavy work came from the subjugated peoples that Israel had displaced (v. 21; cf. Judg. 1:19, 21, 27–35). Solomon appointed his compatriots to be their overseers (1 Kin. 9:22–23). The repetition of these details suggests the end of a literary unit (cf. 5:13–16) with new information inserted: after pharaoh's daughter took up residence in her new home, work began on the construction of the Millo.

9:25–28. Life after the Big Projects. For a fifth time the statement is made that the temple was finished (see also 3:1; 6:38; 7:51; 9:1). This time all the main aspects seem to have been dealt with, and it appears that this really was the end of the process. However, there was a subtext present: What would happen from that time forward? The implication is that the completion of something major (the temple, palace, or even creation itself) marks not the end but the beginning. How the main players would act from this point on was crucial.

Life for Solomon now assumed a routine, and the text provides an example of the sacrifices he offered three times a year—presumably during the Passover (Festival of Unleavened Bread), Festival of Weeks, and Festival of Tabernacles, the festivals that every Hebrew male was expected to attend at the temple (Deut. 16:16).

A further development was the fleet of trading boats that Solomon built (with Hiram's help), based at the southern port of Elath on the Red Sea. It is unclear what later happened to this fleet—Uzziah is said to have restored Elath to Judah (2 Kin. 14:22) and the Arameans retook it a decade or two later (2 Kin. 16:6). Solomon's maritime adventures did not seem to be very long lasting.

10:1–13. The Queen of Sheba. Sheba's location is uncertain. Most likely it was in southwestern Arabia. Another possibility is the Horn of Africa (modern Somalia), or it may have been an empire that included both of those places. The narrative connects the Queen of Sheba's visit and the gifts she brought with ships of Hiram, who brought gifts from Ophir as well. Some commentators suggest that the timber mentioned here is from the Horn of Africa, others suggest it is juniper from Lebanon. The queen had heard so many unbelievable reports she just had to see for herself, and she became overwhelmed with what she saw (vv. 6–9). After proclaiming the blessed state of Solomon's kingdom and praising his God, she presented Solomon with generous gifts. The narrative suggests that further gifts came by ship (v. 11), and this apparently was matched by gifts that Solomon gave her in return.

10:14–29. Solomon's Wealth. The exchange of gifts led into a description of the wealth Solomon accumulated each year through trade, taxes, possibly tribute from other dependent nations, and other royal visits. The total was enormous—about 50,000 pounds (22,679 kg) of gold, not to mention silver, ivory, and other luxury goods (v. 22). The text mentions that Solomon was involved in one type of trade, military equipment (vv. 28–29), but that he also generated an income from answering the questions that many from all over the world brought to him (vv. 24–25).

With his wealth, Solomon embellished the temple, supplied instruments to the temple musicians, provided golden shields for ceremonial occasions (vv. 16–17), built an ivory throne and lions to stand by the throne (vv. 18–20), and made golden drinking vessels (v. 21). The net effect of all this was that Solomon surpassed all the kings of the earth in both wealth and wisdom (v. 23), and he made items that were once considered valuable as nothing compared to all the gold and luxury items he accumulated (v. 27). In all this one is left wondering about his spiritual integrity—had Solomon retained his faith, or was his amassing wealth beginning to corrupt him? God is mentioned only once in passing in all this display—people flocked to hear Solomon's wisdom, but it was God who had put the wisdom in his heart (v. 24).

11:1–43. The Beginning of the End. As well as accumulating great wealth, Solomon married many women. Astonishingly, these practices were the very things Moses had warned future kings of Israel to avoid (Deut. 17:14–20), but Solomon proceeded anyway and multiplied for himself horses from Egypt, wives, and silver and gold. Additionally, his wives were from the nations that God had warned the Israelites not to associate with because of their ingrained idolatry and the nations that the Israelites were specifically told to displace (Ex. 34:12–16; Deut.

12:30–31; 20:17–18). Moreover, the 700 wives were specifically called princesses, so Solomon appeared to be more interested in human alliances than in his covenant with God. Additionally, Solomon had 300 concubines, who were perhaps women of lower rank who may have doubled as household servants.

The Hebrew word asserting Solomon's devotion to his wives is the same word used in Genesis 2:24 for the closeness that marriage was intended to bring. However tender the relationships may have been, the women turned his heart to their own gods (1 Kin. 11:4). The verb used here is the same used to describe the action of Balaam's donkey turning aside from the angel of the Lord (Num. 22:23, 33). The text says this happened when he was old. The contrast between when Solomon was a young man who loved God (1 Kin. 3:3) and when he was an elder statesman who loved women (11:1) is stark, and it is perceptively summed up in the expression of Solomon's heart not being at peace with God (v. 4).

The result was that Solomon followed after the gods of his wives, which was evil in the Lord's estimation (v. 6). The text implies that Solomon participated in their degrading, idolatrous rites. The first foreign god mentioned is Ashtoreth, the Phoenician goddess of sexuality and war that King Hiram worshiped (v. 5). There seems to be a play on words here—in Canaanite literature she is known as Ashtart (Ishtar in Mesopotamian tradition), but by inserting the vowels from the word *boshet* ("shame"), the name Ashtoreth appears. Similarly, for the Ammonite god Milcom, transposing the vowels from *boshet* produces the derogatory name Molek (Molech)—which, translated literally, could mean "king of shame" or "shameful king." This was the god that demanded the sacrifice of human babies by fire. It appears that Chemosh, god of the Moabites (v. 7), demanded the same (2 Kin. 3:27). So to honor these gods and to keep his wives happy, Solomon constructed shrines for them on the Mount of Olives (1 Kin. 11:7). The construction of shrines where the foreign wives could worship their gods was required in politically motivated marriages.

By doing these things, Solomon was essentially nullifying the covenant with the Lord. Legally speaking, God had every right to walk away from this covenant. Instead, God became angry—an indication of the passion He has for His people—and acted with a combination of justice and mercy. He informed Solomon that the kingdom would be torn from him and given to a lesser man (v. 11). That was the justice part. In mercy, God assured Solomon it would not happen in his lifetime (which was drawing to a close anyway) and that for the sake of the Davidic covenant, one tribe would remain loyal to the throne in Jerusalem (vv. 12–13). The divine word of judgment had been pronounced, and it would be fulfilled in history.

A further consequence would be adversaries that would rise against Solomon. Hadad, an Edomite who had escaped a vicious battle in David's time (vv. 14–17) and had been given refuge in the palace of the pharaoh, returned after David's death to cause Solomon much trouble. Similarly, Rezon, a Syrian who also had passed through tragedy at the hands of David, caused continual conflict with Israel (vv. 23–25).

The main adversary for Solomon, and even for his successors (v. 39), however, was Jeroboam. He initially impressed Solomon so much that the king promoted him to be chief officer over the labor force of the tribe of Ephraim, tasked with reconstructing the Millo and refurbishing various civic structures in the city. It is not clear whether there was some deeply felt grudge against Solomon for some reason or whether it was the encounter with the prophet Ahijah that turned Jeroboam on a course against the king (v. 26).

That encounter followed the pattern we see in other prophetic interventions: a sudden but calculated appearance to deliver a short but very specific, and even shocking, message (1 Kin. 17:1; 21:17; 2 Sam. 12:1–14). Through an acted-out parable the prophet tore his cloak and explained its meaning. It represented God's adjustment of His covenant with Israel and Jeroboam's role in the new plan. The kingdom would be divided. The reason given for the dramatic change was that the people of God preferred to worship the gods of the surrounding nations. Despite that fact, the prophetic assurance was that God would maintain a remnant to keep His part of the covenant He had made with David (1 Kin. 11:34).

Remarkably, God offered to Jeroboam the same covenant as He had offered to David and Solomon (v. 38). In other words, in a sense there are not many covenants but one—offered repeatedly to successive generations—a showcase of God's persistence in redeeming the human race. Jeroboam became the start of a new line, just as David had been. As David was hunted by the reigning king (Saul), so was Jeroboam (by Solomon; v. 40). Just as David sought refuge with a foreign king—Achish of Gath (1 Sam. 21:10–15; 27:2–4)—so did Jeroboam, seeking asylum with Shishak (Shoshenq I), king of Egypt (1 Kin. 11:40). Shishak, a Libyan and former commander of the Egyptian army, had just commenced a new dynasty in Egypt, so the political alliance that Solomon had previously forged with Egypt no longer held. In fact, the narrative records that Shishak, allied with Jeroboam of Israel, would later invade Judah (14:25).

The era of King Solomon was over. The narrative says that further information about his reign may be found in another record—one that no longer exists. His reign of forty years—the same length as his father's—came to an end, he was buried with his fathers, and his son Rehoboam ascended the throne (11:43).

12:1—16:34

EARLY DIVIDED MONARCHY

After Solomon's death Israel split into two kingdoms: the Northern Kingdom of Israel and the Southern Kingdom of Judah. In order to secure his new kingdom, Jeroboam, the first northern king, built a new place of worship, made two golden calves (idols), replaced the Levitical priesthood with volunteers, and instituted new festival days. From there, the nation spiraled down into an idolatry worse than that of the surrounding nations.

At first Israel and Judah fought each other, but they came together for a time through intermarriage. For three generations, kings of Judah married daughters of the Israelite kings, which opened the floodgates of idolatry into Judah. The tragedy was that a good king started this trend—Jehoshaphat.

12:1—14:31

The Kingdoms Split: Jeroboam and Rehoboam

Rehoboam (931–913 B.C.), successor to Solomon, tried to impress the leaders of his new kingdom, but his attempts backfired, and Jeroboam (931–910 B.C.) led a revolt that divided the kingdom. He took ten of the tribes with him. Rehoboam tried from then on to regain his lost realms, and the result was great losses on both sides.

12:1–24. Rehoboam Splits the Kingdom. Rehoboam's decision to hold his coronation celebrations at Shechem (which lies about halfway between Mt. Ebal and Mt. Gerizim) was significant. It was here that God promised to give the land to Abraham's descendants (Gen. 12:6–7); Jacob purchased the first parcel of land here (Gen. 33:18–19); it was here that the tribes gave their commitment to follow God when they established themselves in their new land (Deut. 11:29–32; 27:2–26); it was one of the cities of refuge (Josh. 20:1–8); it was here that Joshua gained the commitment of the nation to forsake idolatry and serve only God (Josh. 24:1, 13–18); and it was the location where Joseph's remains were buried (Josh. 24:32). If there was a best place to seek a commitment for national solidarity, this was it.

Jeroboam's arrival at Shechem may have introduced a cloud to the festivities of welcoming the new king. The apparent humility of the negotiators, which doubtlessly included Jeroboam either directly or behind the scenes, also carried a threat. Rather than simply asking that Rehoboam lighten their load, as humble servants might do, they said that if he did, they would serve him. Thus, they obviously implied that if he didn't, they wouldn't. Rehoboam certainly understood the ultimatum.

It is not surprising that Rehoboam wanted time to consider the matter. There was much at risk. He would have to either grant their request in order to keep them loyal, and thereby accept a loss of revenue and diminished kingly glory, or deny their request and see them walk away at even greater loss to his dominion.

The account of the different advice given by the two groups may be emphasizing the difference not so much between youth and age as between foolishness and wisdom. Rehoboam was forty-one years old when he became king, so while his contemporaries were obviously younger than Solomon's counselors, they were definitely into middle age. The point may be that they were foolish not so much because they were young as because, as the text says, they had grown up with Rehoboam and were the pampered offspring of the privileged class who had no knowledge of the life of the common people. As many Bible examples demonstrate (Joseph, David, Solomon, and Daniel), wisdom is determined not necessarily by age but by character. Rehoboam and his friends had been raised in a dissolute and degenerate court. Their suggested reply was arrogant and cynical, and it may contain a ribald euphemism for the private parts (v. 10), which Rehoboam wisely chose not to repeat. But he did warn the delegation that he would be using "scorpions" rather than the usual whips (1 Kin. 12:14). This may refer to a type of scourging whip with a piece of metal or bone in the end, which would feel like a scorpion's sting.

The exclamation of the people (v. 16) reveals a long-standing, bitter rivalry between Judah and the northern tribes dating back to the time of David, when the rebel Sheba uttered the same words (2 Sam. 20:1). This dramatic exit is explained in the text: added to the fact that Rehoboam ignored advice, God had His hand in this. The word of the Lord through Ahijah was being fulfilled, changing the course of the history of the kingdom (1 Kin. 12:15).

12:25—14:20. The Sin of Jeroboam. With the threat of war over for the moment, Jeroboam devoted his energies to building projects in Shechem and Penuel (v. 25). Although the verb in Hebrew is *banah* ("to build"), these cities already existed, so his activity refers to fortifying and refurbishing them (as some translations indicate). Shechem's importance was outlined above. Penuel was where Jacob had wrestled with the angel one night before meeting his estranged brother Esau (Gen. 32:30). Why did Jeroboam choose to put his fingerprints on these important places? Was it to confirm divine legitimacy for his rulership? He already had prophetic assurance of God's role for him (1 Kin. 11:31–39), and yet he was not satisfied.

Jeroboam was concerned that if the people continued traveling to Jerusalem for the three compulsory annual festivals (Deut. 16:16), it would result in them renewing their allegiance to the house of David (1 Kin. 12:26–27). This was despite being told the opposite by the prophet Ahijah (11:31) and despite the covenant God made with him: He had promised to bless his reign and give him a lasting dynasty.

Jeroboam decided to develop a new, substitute religion that would appeal to the majority. Perverting the Israelite faith, he had golden calves made and proclaimed them as the God who delivered Israel from Egypt (using exactly the same words in Hebrew as the rebellious people had used in Ex. 32:4). Perhaps the fact that the ark of the covenant, a symbol of God's presence, remained in Jerusalem led Jeroboam to construct the two images as a visual representation of the God of Israel—a clear violation of the law. The possible connection between what he did and the incident of the golden calf in Exodus is not clear, but perhaps the biblical writer, by quoting the words of Jeroboam, was indicating that what he did was as evil as what Aaron had done. The coming judgment against the Northern Kingdom is being justified on the basis of this act of idolatry. One has to wonder to what extent the priests and Levites had failed in instructing the common people about the law of Moses. Jeroboam placed one golden calf at Bethel (in the heart of the tribal land of Ephraim) and the other at Dan (vv. 28–29). The city of Dan was an enclave of Danites (Judg. 18:1, 2, 7–11, 27–29), about 12 miles (19.3 km) north of the Sea of Galilee. From there flows a powerful spring whose copious waters replenish the Sea of Galilee and in turn empty into the Jordan River to this day. As far back as human history records, Dan had always been the place where the gods and goddesses of fertility were worshiped and the God of creation ignored.

Jeroboam advanced his idea by arguing that this was for the benefit of the people, saying that it was too much for them to go to Jerusalem (1 Kin. 12:28). The lush surroundings lent themselves to pagan notions of fertility. In the symbolic list of tribes present in the new Jerusalem (Rev. 7:5–8), Ephraim and Dan are missing—the idolatry introduced by Jeroboam has eternal consequences.

Jeroboam was persistent and methodical in building a new order. He established a replacement priesthood and replacement shrines. More significantly, he introduced a new festival for the eighth month—presumably to rival the Festival of Tabernacles in the seventh month, Israel's long-standing highlight of the religious year since Sinai. That he placed it in the eighth month might have signaled that he did not want to be seen as directly competing. He could claim that his people were free to attend both festivals. But it gave his people an easy excuse not to attend the festival ordained by God. Such is often the devil's technique: create an attractive and convenient illegal substitute.

The unfaithfulness of Jeroboam became proverbial. Later in the book, when the reign of each king of Israel is evaluated, they are compared to him (e.g., 1 Kin. 15:30, 34; 16:2–3, 7; 22:52; 2 Kin. 3:3; 10:29; 13:2; 15:9, 18, 24). In the case of Omri (1 Kin. 16:25) and Ahab (16:33), their sins are declared to be even worse than Jeroboam's.

Jeroboam dedicated the religious facilities (12:32–33), which completed the rebellion and set the stage for the consequences. However, God sent him three warnings, giving him opportunity to turn around (13:1–6, 11–34; 14:7–16). The first warning was the prophecy of the man of God, in which he specifically mentioned king Josiah by name (over three hundred years in advance) as the one who would destroy the idolatrous altar at Bethel at which Jeroboam was burning incense.

The second warning was the disturbing account of the disobedience of the man of God who accepted the lie of the old prophet at the cost of his life (vv. 8–18). The text does not say what motivated the old man to lie and thus be instrumental in the temptation and ultimately the death of the man of God (vv. 26–32).

When the man of God who brought the first warning later disobeyed and died, the message should have been clear: ignore the word of the Lord at your peril. But this did not deter Jeroboam from continuing in his course of covenant violation. He appointed and consecrated anyone who desired to become a priest (13:33).

The third warning was a response to Jeroboam's misguided attempt to deceive the prophet Ahijah to try to help his sick son Abijah (14:1–6). God revealed the deception and prophesied that Abijah would die and that He would completely wipe out Jeroboam's posterity and eventually the whole kingdom of Israel (vv. 7–16).

God offered Jeroboam a measure of mercy in this prophecy against Israel (14:15–16). The destruction would be some time in the future; but for now, so God informed Jeroboam, a new king would replace him (v. 14), which would give the nation time to rethink their direction and would allow them to repent and recommit to God. Unfortunately, Israel never did.

The account of Jeroboam's reign of twenty-two years (931–910 B.C.) ended with the observation that he rested with his ancestors (or fathers) and was replaced by his son Nadab. Yet the sinful legacy of Jeroboam lived on in the lives of successive kings and became part of the life of Israel for almost 200 more years.

14:21–31. Judah Is Weakened. The impact of Rehoboam's reign in Judah was not that different from Jeroboam's in Israel, as evaluated by Ahijah (11:29–39; cf. 14:7–11). The summary statement notes that Judah's evil had become worse than that of their ancestors (14:22). The specifics include the construction of shrines and the incorporation of sacred stones or pillars and wooden Asherah poles placed in the hills under trees (v. 23).

Even more blatant was the presence of perverted persons (the Hebrew cryptically calls them "holy ones") at the shrines (v. 24). It is commonly thought that these were cultic male and female prostitutes (some translations limit the term to "male shrine prostitutes"), who engaged in fertility rites and were involved in the confusion of genuine and false worship. The fact that these were everywhere despite being specifically forbidden (Deut. 23:17) demonstrates that the nation copied the religion of the very peoples whom God in judgment had dispossessed from the land (Deut. 20:17–18).

As a consequence of the nation's interest in idolatry, Pharaoh Shoshenq (945–924 B.C.; the Hebrews call him Shishak) invaded Judah in Rehoboam's fifth year (about 926/925 B.C.). The record of this invasion is inscribed on the walls of the temple of Amon at Karnak (Egypt), which listed 150 cites that Shoshenq conquered. The Kings narrative describes him emptying the treasuries of palace and temple, including the golden ceremonial shields that Solomon had made, and taking all the booty back to Egypt (1 Kin. 14:26). This impoverished the once proud and wealthy nation of Judah overnight. In an attempt to regain some measure of dignity, Rehoboam made bronze shields to replace the gold ones (v. 27), but instead of storing them in the House of the Forest of Lebanon (10:16–17), he placed them into the care of captains of the royal bodyguard (14:27), which demonstrated their much-reduced value—a reflection of the state of the nation under Rehoboam's rulership.

Just as Jeroboam's reign ended in an anticlimax, so too did Rehoboam's. The readers are again referred to the chronicles of the kings (court records) if they want to know more (v. 29). One further piece of information is offered:

Judah's Idolatry

The sacred pillars (*matsebot*) were stone objects, sometimes occurring in clusters, that were either abstract representations of deities or phallic symbols—in harmony with the focus on fertility by the religions of the surrounding nations. The wooden images or poles (*'asherim*) were wooden representations of the goddess Asherah (or Athirat)—either in the form of a carving or of a stylized sacred tree—that may have depicted the tree of life.

At the center of the issue of worship is the question of loyalty and allegiance. Who is the Ultimate and Supreme Being? Who is the Provider and Protector of life? By choosing to follow the idolatrous practices of surrounding nations, God's people were rejecting the God of Creation and Redemption. Instead they substituted the most degrading practices in their attempts to activate the nature gods into sending rain, thus ensuring good crops, herds, and wealth.

Rehoboam and Jeroboam fought all their days (v. 30). Rehoboam was finally replaced by his son (v. 31). The repetition of his Ammonite mother's name indicates that she may have been the influence that turned the nation against their covenant relationship with God.

15:1—16:34
Judah and Israel at War

Bloodshed and intrigue characterize the four or so decades covered in this section. North and South were continually at war, and the instability of the Northern Kingdom occasioned the assassination of four kings in palace plots. The kings of Israel (not included in the Chronicles account) are either described as walking in the ways of Jeroboam or sinning more than all those before them. With the introduction of the dynasty of Omri, the level of idolatry in both kingdoms increased to their highest level yet.

15:1–8. Abijah of Judah (913–911 B.C.).
Abijah replaced Rehoboam. Though some translations use the name "Abijam" for him, "Abijah" is more likely to be his actual name and means "the Lord is my Father." Abijam means "Yam is my father"—Yam was the Canaanite sea god—and was possibly a derogatory name given to the king by those opposed to his idolatry. His mother was the daughter of Uriel of Gibeah (2 Chr. 13:2) and Absalom's only daughter, Tamar (2 Sam. 14:27). Evidence of her later idolatry (1 Kin. 15:13) suggests that her influence over her young son was a negative one. Meanwhile, Rehoboam groomed Abijah as his successor and prepared some of his twenty-eight sons for civil service and gave them experience over various responsibilities of state (2 Chr. 11:21–23).

It is no surprise then that Abijah walked in all the sins of his father (1 Kin. 15:3); but despite this, God kept him in order to preserve "a lamp in Jerusalem" for the sake of the covenant made with David (v. 4). This meant special protection for him. As a boy he grew up when his father and Jeroboam were at war, and this continued during his own reign. The Kings narrative is quite minimalistic compared to Chronicles, which describes a battle between Israel and Judah in which 500,000 Israelites were killed (2 Chr. 13:17), effectively ending Jeroboam's ability to wage war. The Kings narrative cuts Abijah's account short and continues with the ascension of his son Asa to the throne.

15:9–24. Asa of Judah (911–870 B.C.). In contrast to the brief, negative reign of his father, Asa

reigned for as long as David and Solomon. He did what was right by getting rid of the male and female cultic prostitutes, removing the idols his father had made, and deposing his grandmother Maachah from her privileged position as Queen Mother (vv. 12–13). She had carved a detestable image of Asherah into a stylized sacred tree at a high place (v. 13). Asa cut it down and burned it by the Kidron Brook. Yet he did not destroy the high places (v. 14). This is one aspect of the slavish following of heathen practices that seems to have been too ingrained to eradicate.

Then he placed silver and gold items that both he and his father had dedicated into the temple treasury (v. 15). But war with the Northern Kingdom loomed again—almost like a refrain—for the fifth time (14:30; 15:6, 7, 16, 32). Details of war are glossed over, with more attention given to either increasing idolatry or dependence on other nations for military security. So Asa followed previous kings in emptying the palace and temple treasuries (with treasure he had just placed there) as payment for Syria ('aram in Hebrew) to attack the Northern Kingdom (15:18–21). It appears that Asa attempted to prevent the completion of a northern garrison city that the northern King Baasha was constructing at Ramah, only 6 miles (9.7 km) north of Jerusalem. The Chronicles narrative suggests the city was built to prevent the flow of northerners to the annual festivals in Jerusalem (cf. 2 Chr. 16:1). Asa conscripted every able-bodied person to strip the building site of all stonework and timber, and used the materials to build rival cities—Mizpah, about a mile (about 1.6 km) north of the Ramah site, and Geba, about a mile to the east.

The end of Asa's reign is a sad question mark. The Kings narrative simply states that in his old age he was diseased in the feet (1 Kin. 15:23). Although some commentators think this is gout, in some places in the Bible the feet are a euphemism for the private parts. For example, when Saul relieved himself in a cave, he literally, in Hebrew, "covers his feet" (1 Sam. 24:3). Isaiah speaks of a coming time of humiliation when all hair, including the hair of the feet (pubic hair), would be shaved (Is. 7:20). So there is a strong possibility Asa died of a sexually transmitted disease. Here the narrative comes to an abrupt halt, and a new king ascends the throne.

15:25—16:7. Nadab (910–909 B.C.) and Baasha of Israel (909–886 B.C.).
The Kings narrative spends very little time with Nadab—just enough to say that he did evil in the Lord's estimation and

that he acted similarly to his father (v. 26). This seems to be the pattern of the Northern Kingdom. Baasha ended the dynasty of Jeroboam by killing Nadab while the latter was involved in a siege of the Philistine city of Gibbethon, which was in the tribal land of Dan, west of Jerusalem (v. 27).

After Baasha installed himself as king, he then killed the entire household of Jeroboam (v. 29). This happened in fulfillment of the prophetic word of Ahijah, the old prophet from Shiloh (14:10–11, 14). Once more the dynamic word of the Lord proved to be invincible in shaping the history of God's people.

For the remainder of his twenty-four-year reign, Baasha warred against Judah (15:32) and continued the deep involvement of the kings before him in the fertility cult of the Canaanites. In later years, both his and Jeroboam's reigns would be the benchmark of Israel's apostasy (1 Kin. 21:22; 2 Kin. 9:9). As expected, the word of the Lord came to Baasha through a prophet to warn him of his course of action (1 Kin. 16:1–4, 7). Jehu, son of Hanani (not to be confused with King Jehu who appears forty or fifty years later), gave him a message similar to that received by Solomon (11:11–13) and Jeroboam (14:7–11): God raised Baasha up to be king, but he made God's people Israel sin; therefore Baasha's household would come to an end. Not one of them would receive a decent burial (16:4), as with Jeroboam's family. Almost as an afterthought, one of the reasons given for Baasha's judgment is the slaughter of Jeroboam's family (v. 7). Although a prophet foretold the fulfillment of the divine purpose of judgment in the destruction of Jeroboam's line, that did not excuse the one who later carried out that action.

16:8–20. Elah (886–885 B.C.) and Zimri of Israel (885 B.C.).
Baasha's son, Elah, ascended the throne, but his reign was short-lived, marked by its promotion of the fertility cult, just as his father's reign had been (v. 13). One of his senior military officers took over the throne after assassinating the drunken Elah at a party in Tirzah (vv. 9–10), the early capital city of the Northern Kingdom. The death of Elah marked the end of Baasha's dynasty, which lasted only two generations—the same as Jeroboam's.

Zimri did to Elah (and Baasha's line) what Baasha had done to Nadab (and Jeroboam's line), with the added atrocity of killing all of Baasha's friends as well (vv. 11–12). Seeing that he reigned for only seven days, the coup he led must of necessity have been savage and violent. In reaction to his atrocities the people appointed

Omri, the senior military figure for the nation, as king instead (v. 16). When Zimri saw Omri's military prowess and his successful siege against Gibbethon—which a previous Israelite king, Nadab, had been unable to take about twenty-five years previously (15:25–27)—Zimri gave up the struggle, went into the palace in Tirzah, set it ablaze, and died in the flames (v. 18). Even in his short reign he encouraged idolatrous worship (v. 19). It is significant that the Kings narrative highlights this as the main feature for each reign.

16:21–28. Omri of Israel (885–874 B.C.). With Zimri dead there was a power struggle as two factions tried to get their champion on the throne. This was a somewhat protracted saga: Zimri ascended the throne in the twenty-seventh year of Judah's king Asa (16:10), but it was not until Asa's thirty-first year that Omri prevailed over his rival, Tibni, to ascend the throne. This means that the throne was uncertain for about five years.

With the palace destroyed by fire, Omri set out to build a new one but decided to relocate it on a hill that he bought from Shemer, renaming it Samaria after its original owner (vv. 23–24). This process took up about half of his reign of twelve years, but meanwhile, Omri proved himself to be far more devoted to the fertility cult than any of his predecessors (v. 25). The Kings account concludes by saying about him that the rest of his acts were being recorded in the chronicles of the kings of Israel—not the biblical books of the same name but the royal court records of the time.

16:29–34. Ahab of Israel (874–853 B.C.). Ahab was the son of Omri and reigned over Israel for twenty-two years. He married Jezebel, the daughter of Ethbaal, king of the Sidonians (v. 31). He joined her in worshiping Baal and built a temple to him in Samaria (v. 32). Ahab's rebellion against the Lord was more intense than that of all the kings of Israel who were before him (vv. 30, 33). This level of rebellion will become evident in the narratives that follow. The brief but penetrating evaluation of Ahab's reign concludes with a reference to Hiel, who built Jericho and fulfilled the word of the Lord spoken through Joshua (Josh. 6:26). According to it, whoever would rebuild Jericho would do it at the cost of the life of his firstborn and youngest sons. This was the experience of Hiel, whose two sons died in the construction project. The word of the Lord is so potent that it finds fulfillment long after its utterance by the prophet. It

never fails. Jericho was the place where the last king of Judah, Zedekiah, would be captured by the Babylonian armies (2 Kin. 25:1–7).

17:1—22:53
ELIJAH AND THE KINGS

At about the midpoint of the two books of Kings, attention turns away from the kings and focuses on two prophetic giants: Elijah and Elisha. The various accounts of their activities reveal how involved God really was, not only in the lives of the monarchy and of the nation but also in the events in the surrounding nations as well. Interwoven among the stories of Elijah and Elisha, the reigns of the various kings of Israel and Judah unfold. With the prominence of the ministry of these two key prophets, relations between the Northern and Southern Kingdoms enjoyed a time of peace. A widespread drought in Israel became the backdrop for a major show-down between God and Baal on Mount Carmel.

17:1–7. Elijah's Prophecy. Elijah grew up in the mountains of Gilead in the village of Tishbe on the eastern side of the Jordan River. The expression Tishbite may describe a quality (some suggest "stranger") as well as the village he was from. His powerful persona challenged the nation to choose either God or Baal.

Elijah's appearance before King Ahab to announce that there would not be rain for three years shows His trust in the word of the Lord revealed to him (17:1). Apparently fearless in

---

Baal Worship

The word "baal" simply means "lord." The name serves as a generic term for the fertility gods of Canaan, the main one being Hadad, the god of dew, rain, and storm. Hadad is responsible for the wealth that comes from verdant crops and fields and abundant herds. If "Baal" and his consorts were fertile, then the farmers would be wealthy, therefore his followers practiced fertility rites to encourage the gods in their fertility. The worship of the fertility cult promoted gross immorality and greed, and the vulnerable in society were exploited to satisfy the financial and sexual lust of the privileged classes. The net effect was that money and sex were the key social values, and human-rights abuses were the norm.

his willingness to confront leadership for its failings, Elijah suddenly appeared before the king. Ahab's marriage to Jezebel, a Phoenician princess (16:31), had ensured the proliferation of the fertility cult in Israel. Hence the confrontation between prophet and king was inevitable. Having delivered God's message to the patron of Baal worship, Elijah retreated to a mountain ravine in his home area—the Brook Cherith (Kerith), or according to some, the Kerith Ravine (the Heb. *nakhal* can mean either a ravine or a brook). This was an area with a small stream in rugged yet lush surroundings about 30 miles (48 km) east of Samaria, identified today as Wadi al-Yabis. There he was kept alive by the waters of the brook and with food brought to him morning and evening by ravens (v. 6).

17:8–24. The Widow of Zarephath. When the brook dried up, God instructed Elijah to go to Zarephath, a village about 80 or 90 miles (129 or 145 km) away, just south of Sidon. It is ironic that while a Phoenician woman (Jezebel) was greatly influencing the demise of the nation, another Phoenician woman (the widow) was the means of preserving the life of the prophet whom God appointed to counter Ahab and Jezebel in order to preserve the life of the nation.

When Elijah first asked the woman for a little water and some bread, she informed him of her precarious social status (vv. 12–13). That the prophetic word could help in a household like that clearly demonstrates that the whole nation of Israel would be far better off if they would heed the words of the prophet as well. Further, this humble home saw the first resurrection of a person from the dead that is recorded in Scripture (v. 22).

18:1–15. Elijah and Obadiah. The story of Obadiah and Elijah's interactions with him demonstrates several important things. First, it helps us understand the severity of the famine and the magnitude of the national crisis. The fact that the king had to involve himself personally in such a menial task as finding grass for horses indicates the desperate nature of the situation. All other kingly responsibilities or preoccupations were preempted by this most basic need. This shows how far God was willing to push his point to bring about repentance.

Second, the story shows God's willingness to affirm and encourage a faithful believer during a genuine time of trouble. God sent Elijah out of his way to meet Obadiah. This certainly must have given the faithful man an assurance that God was still in control through Elijah's ministry.

Third, the story establishes a basis for God's later rebuke of Elijah's self-pity (19:18). In some respects, Obadiah's faithfulness to God had put him under more stress than Elijah had to endure. While Elijah had been hidden away in remote places, Obadiah remained at court, at the very heart of this great controversy. Despite all the pressures to the contrary, Obadiah (whose name means "servant/worshiper of Yahweh") had the special skill of maintaining his connection and influence with the royal family. While doing so, he had done God's work by directly undermining the machinations of Jezebel. Albeit on a smaller scale, he was playing a role very similar to that of Daniel and his companions in the court of Babylon.

Fourth, the story demonstrates, in almost a humorous way, God's willingness to accept our questionings of His commands and our emotional frustrations and outbursts based on our human experience. Obadiah openly challenged the wisdom of doing what Elijah asked, and no divine rebuke came from the prophet. Obadiah was in fact concerned about unnecessarily risking his life. He had been risking it by hiding and providing food to God's servants, but this time he wanted to be certain that things would go as the prophet said. He was reassured that the prophet would do as he had said, with the implicit understanding that all would be well for Obadiah. His heartfelt, honest questions and disputations, accepted by God, remind us of those of similar Bible characters like Moses, Gideon, and Thomas.

18:16–46. Elijah, Ahab, and Mount Carmel. Ahab's initial reaction upon meeting Elijah demonstrates his seemingly willful blindness to reality. The crisis had begun with Elijah's dramatic prophecy of the drought. But Elijah had made it clear that the prophecy was made on God's authority, not his own. Thus, Ahab certainly had every opportunity to consider that the crisis was instigated by God rather than Elijah. Yet Ahab, obtuse in the extreme, decided to ignore the obvious and identify Elijah as the "troubler of Israel" (v. 17). This expression was first used in reference to Simeon and Levi, who caused their father Jacob trouble after they killed the men of Shechem in revenge for their prince raping their sister (Gen. 34). It was also used to refer to Achan (whose name is based on the word for "trouble") and the curse that his actions brought upon the people of the Exodus (Josh. 7:24–26; 1 Chr. 2:7). However, Ahab had also brought a curse on the land—as demonstrated by the three years of drought that was still in effect. So Elijah was quite justified in throwing the accusation back at the king—Ahab and his father's family were the troublers of Israel (1 Kin. 18:18). It was the action of forsaking God and following Baal that had resulted in this trouble.

Elijah's question in v. 21 expresses the idea of being halfhearted. The expression also applies in the Psalms to "double-minded" people (Ps. 119:113). The picture is of someone limping between two options but not being convinced of either. The idea is that of a "double-minded" person who is tossed about like a wave in the wind (James 1:8) or who is neither cold nor hot (Rev. 3:15–16).

Given the challenge to call upon their god, the prophets of Baal pled for hours, slashing themselves with weapons to show their devotion. It was a common belief among the followers of Baal that during times of drought, Baal was held prisoner by death in the underworld. Therefore, Elijah's comments about Baal going on a trip or taking a vacation (1 Kin. 18:27) were a bit too close for comfort for the highly offended, and increasingly bloodied, prophets (v. 28).

It is ironic that the word describing the action of the prophets, sometimes translated as "leaped" or "danced" in v. 26, is the same Hebrew verb (*pasakh*) translated as "limping" in Elijah's challenge in v. 21. This suggests that no matter the extremes of their actions, nothing was going to work. The narrative contrasts Baal, the totally powerless storm god, with Yahweh, the Creator and Redeemer and alone the Provider of rain in its season (Lev. 26:4). It is reasonable to suppose that all this time, Elijah kept diligent watch on any attempt to smuggle in some fire from elsewhere. The impotence of Baal was patently obvious.

The text does not mention where Elijah found the water he used, but a perpetual spring is located today not too far from the traditional site of this event. Elijah used the water to drench his altar, making it nearly impossible for anyone but God to be able to ignite the soggy offering. The prophet then prayed, and in obvious contrast to the prophets' frenzied activity his words were calm and reasoned. He stressed that God could be known. The dramatic burst of fire at the prayer's conclusion consumed not only the sacrifice and water but the altar of twelve large stones as well. After the people's spontaneous and awed reaction of affirming the Lord as God (1 Kin. 18:39), Elijah commanded them to seize all the fertility cult prophets and have

them executed down in the valley at the base of the mountain (v. 40). This was about the same place Deborah and Barak won victory against a vastly superior force of Canaanites—devotees of Baal—about 300 years earlier (Judg. 5:19).

After the emotional highs of the day, Elijah suggested to the king that he should quickly eat and drink because a storm was on its way (1 Kin. 18:41). This was really an invitation to partake in a covenant meal with the Lord and echoes the experience of Moses, Aaron, Nadab, Abihu, and the seventy elders of Israel as they ate and drank in God's presence at Mount Sinai (Ex. 24:9–11).

It is not only God's power as Lord over nature that is recognized in this chapter, but the authority of the prophet as well. All those to whom Elijah spoke in this narrative listened and followed his instructions: the king (1 Kin. 18:20, 42, 44), the prophets of Baal (vv. 26, 28), the crowd (vv. 30, 34, 40), and his assistant (vv. 43–44). This fact highlights the significant role that prophets played among God's people and the security that attended them if they listened. This narrative forms a significant contrast with events in the rest of the book, in which the prophets were ignored and vilified.

19:1–21. Running from Jezebel. Paradoxically, the iron-willed prophet lost his nerve when Queen Jezebel found out about the execution of her prophets and threatened Elijah with the same fate. But the Lord did not condemn Elijah for running away or for his wish to die. He knew that what Elijah needed was food and rest, and He provided both for him. With renewed strength Elijah went to Mount Horeb, taking "forty days and forty nights" to travel a distance of at least 100 miles (161 km) and possibly double that, depending on the route he took.

When he arrived at Horeb, the mountain of God, he spent the night in a cave to shelter from the frigid night temperatures there. It was at this same place Moses first met God in the burning bush (at the base of the mountain; Ex. 3:1–5), where he struck a rock and water flowed (Ex. 17:6), and where he received the Ten Commandments. The next day God asked Elijah what he was doing there (1 Kin. 19:9). Elijah's answer revealed how depressed he was. He reaffirmed his commitment to the Lord and argued that everyone else had deserted God, destroyed His altars, and murdered His prophets, and that now they wanted to kill him as well (v. 10).

The Lord asked Elijah to go outside and observe what was going to happen (as He did

Moses; Ex. 33:22; 34:6). First there was a strong wind that tore rocks out of the mountainside, then an earthquake that shook the place violently, then a fire that burned vigorously in a place where there was little or nothing to burn. The narrative states that the Lord was not in any of these phenomena (1 Kin. 19:11–12). Then there was silence—the text describes it in Hebrew as "the voice of thin silence." In contrast to the just-witnessed spectacular events, God's presence was in something small and insignificant—which must have been how Elijah felt at this moment. God does not normally express Himself with fire flashing from heaven (as on Carmel), or in violent storms, earthquakes or fire (also seen during the Exodus on the same mountain; Ex. 24:11), but He makes Himself known in times of silence when nothing seems to be happening.

God told Elijah that there were still 7,000 people in the apostate Northern Kingdom—a remnant who had kept their faith in God and had not been seduced by Baal (1 Kin. 19:18; the reference to kissing Baal refers either to actually kissing his image in the shrines as an act of worship and devotion or blowing kisses if the image was too tall). Just because Elijah was deeply discouraged did not mean that God was inactive or that Elijah was the only person still faithful in a culture of apparent total apostasy. God always preserves for Himself a faithful remnant through whom He realizes His purpose.

No details are given of Elijah's return journey, but he found Elisha ploughing a field on his family land at Abel-Meholah (v. 16). This may have been near what is now the village of Mehola on the West Bank close to the Jordan River; if so, it is only about 12 miles (19.3 km) due east of Elijah's hometown. The fact that there were twelve teams of oxen (v. 19) suggests that Elisha's family was prosperous and that the ploughing of the large field must have been a community event. Consequently, everyone in the village knew that Elijah was there and probably witnessed and understood the prophet's symbolic gesture of throwing his cloak over Elisha's shoulders. Elisha also knew the significance of this action and asked to first go home and say farewell to his parents. Elijah's response indicated he was not convinced that the young man really wanted to devote his career to the prophetic ministry (see Luke 9:61–62).

Instead of kissing his parents goodbye, the narrative speaks of Elisha slaughtering a pair of oxen, offering parts of them up as a sacrifice, and sharing a sacrificial meal with the entire village as an act of commitment. He offered peace or communion sacrifices in which selected portions were burned, while the meat was cooked and shared between the one sacrificing and his family or community (Lev. 3:3–5; 22:29–30). This special event demonstrated Elisha's commitment to the prophetic call and also gave an opportunity for Elisha to bid farewell to his family and friends.

20:1–43. Ben-Hadad of Syria. The name Ben-Hadad literally means "the son of (the god) Hadad," and it may have been a popular name applied to the kings of Aram (Syria). Hadad was the popular god also referred to as Baal and was depicted holding a bolt of lightning to illustrate his role as the storm god bringing rain and thus fertility. Ben-Hadad threatened to destroy Samaria so thoroughly that there would not be enough dust for his soldiers to have a handful each (v. 10). Jezebel had used the same oath that Ben-Hadad used in swearing this action (cf. 19:2). Old priest Eli (1 Sam. 3:17), King David (2 Sam. 3:35; 19:13), Solomon (1 Kin. 2:23), and later also Ahab (2 Kin. 6:31) used this oath formula. It seems to be the strongest possible way of committing oneself to a desired outcome.

Ben-Hadad and his confederacy convinced themselves that the God of Israel was powerful only in the hills and weak on the plains, echoing the widespread notion in ANE texts of local deities (1 Kin. 20:23). They had not yet understood that Yahweh was the Creator of heaven and earth—almighty, all-knowing, all-powerful, and inviting all to come to Him and find salvation.

21:1–29. Naboth's Vineyard. Next to Ahab's second palace at Jezreel, there was a vineyard owned by Naboth (whose name means "prophecies"). Moses had specified that land was not to change hands from one tribe to another but that the inheritance of the fathers must be kept (Num. 36:7). Naboth's refusal to the king's offer for his vineyard simply involved his being true to this command of God. Ahab's guilt in destroying Naboth and confiscating his property may have a metaphorical relationship to the very reason Naboth had refused to yield. Naboth was determined to keep the land for the purpose God intended it. Here we see that Ahab had given the land over to other gods. He maintained the idolatry of the Amorites, whom God had ejected from the land for their horrendous practices. Thus, God's judgments on the

Amorites would, in effect, fall upon those who, without repentance, embraced the same sins (Gen. 15:16; Deut. 7:1–10; 20:17–18).

In another example of a prophet of God suddenly showing up and creating a dramatic scene, Elijah confronted Ahab on the very ground he had stolen. The purpose of the confrontation was to pronounce judgment. But as in the case of Jonah at Nineveh (Jon. 3) announcing judgment, however severe, almost always includes an implicit appeal for repentance. Ahab realized the gravity of his situation and had a remarkable change of heart (1 Kin. 21:27). God accepted Ahab's contrition, informed Elijah of this, and postponed a portion of the judgment for two generations. Ahab's dynasty would end with his grandson (2 Kin. 10:1–2, 6–7) rather than him. But the prophecy of the indignity of Ahab's own death remained and was fulfilled.

22:1–40. The Death of Ahab. The visit by Jehoshaphat to Ahab may have been for family reasons. Jehoshaphat had married one of Ahab's relatives to form an alliance (2 Chr. 18:1), and that alliance was apparently strengthened in the next generation when Jehoshaphat's son Jehoram married Ahab's daughter Athaliah (2 Kin. 8:16–18). Ahab shared with Jehoshaphat his concern over Ramoth Gilead (1 Kin. 22:3) and asserted that the promise of Ben-Hadad to return all Israelite cities under Syrian control (20:34) had not been fulfilled (22:3). Ahab then asked Jehoshaphat for military assistance to reclaim Ramoth Gilead. But Jehoshaphat's pledge

of loyalty (v. 4), although an echo of the pledge that Ruth gave Naomi (Ruth 1:16–17), sounded a little hollow. Perhaps it revealed an uneasy peace between the Northern and Southern Kingdoms, which lasted for only another fifteen years or so.

A further indication of the tenuous relationship between the two kings occurred when Jehoshaphat asked for Ahab's prophets to reveal the word of the Lord to them (22:5–6). Perhaps Jehoshaphat was feeling uncomfortable about prophets of Baal speaking on behalf of God, so he asked if there was a prophet of the Lord anywhere. This begged the question of where Ahab's prophets came from. We know that 450 prophets of Baal were executed after the Carmel theophany (18:19, 40). Were the 400 prophets of the Asherim spared? Or was this group of 400 prophets (22:6) a group of new individuals whom Jezebel had recruited? It is disturbing that Baal would have had so many prophets in Israel.

Micaiah was identified as a prophet of God, but he was hated by Ahab because of his negative messages (v. 8). This suggests that the 400 prophets would say only what would please the king, whether true or not.

The interchange between Ahab and Micaiah, the report of Micaiah's vision, and the record of Ahab's death—all recorded in fascinating narrative detail—provide some theological insight into how God accomplishes His purposes in the realm of human free will. The two kings were enthroned in an outdoor pavilion and dressed in their finery. As expected, the false prophets

Divine Judgment

The harshness of the sentence on Ahab and his family answers the questions that most probably were in the mind of Naboth's wife and children and countless others since then: "Why did this happen?" "If God is good, why did He allow this?" These are questions for which we do not yet have satisfactory answers, but the sentence announced by Elijah gives an indication of how God views gross injustice: those who oppress the innocent will get what they deserve, and those on the receiving end of oppression will receive complete restoration and generous compensation (see Matt. 5:5). Justice will finally prevail. In other words, God does not step in immediately to prevent

evil in a society even when that is what the vast majority wants—as was the case in the Northern Kingdom. In those circumstances, there will be innocent victims killed in the crossfire of a raging battle between the powers of darkness and the Kingdom of God. Nothing in the immediate situation will answer the crimes against humanity that the powers of evil perpetrate, but that situation will not continue indefinitely. God has appointed a day on which He will judge the world (Acts 17:31)—a day when the oppressors of God's people will lose their power (Dan. 7:11, 21, 22, 26) and the people of God will inherit the kingdom (Dan. 7:18, 22, 27). This is part of the Christian hope.

spoke what the king wanted to hear, providing for him a false hope and security. Surprisingly Micaiah initially supported the false message, but the king was able to detect the sarcasm in the voice of the prophet and insisted on hearing the true message. And the message was clear: there was no hope for Ahab. Micaiah's prophecy of judgment was fulfilled. The narrative highlights the apparent random chance of Ahab's death, but we are to understand that there was nothing random about it. It is obvious from this story that there was no coincidence at play but rather that the battle, and that "random" arrow, was a part of a bigger plan that God had outlined in the heavenly council. The divine verdict against the king, as indicated in Micaiah's vision, was revealed to the people in the course of time. God used a lying spirit, which always is associated with Satan and his forces, to accomplish this. That God allowed Satan's minions to deceive, within boundaries, shows how far Ahab had fallen. God in His mercy granted Ahab the freedom of will, allowing him to deliberately and knowingly choose to be deceived. God does the same for all humanity. Those who wish to be deceived will have their wish granted.

22:41–50. Jehoshaphat of Judah (872–848 B.C.). Compared to the four chapters devoted to Jehoshaphat in 1 Chronicles 17–20, Kings provides only ten verses. His reign almost overlapped with Ahab's (874–853 B.C.). He came to the throne in Ahab's fourth year at the age of thirty-five, and reigned for twenty-five years. His reign was characterized by a positive relationship with God. He brought about a measure of religious reform, removing the cult of male and female prostitutes that Asa, his father, had not eradicated. But he failed to remove the high places (1 Kin. 22:43). No doubt his wife—a near relative of the idolatrous Ahab—had some influence in this, just as Solomon's wives had influenced him.

Another action that seems to be spiritually negative was Jehoshaphat's alliance with the Northern Kingdom (again, due to the influence of both his wife and Ahab). This alliance, although initiated as a marriage between royal families, also involved their close cooperation in battles against common enemies and in a shipping venture that came to nothing when all their ships sank (v. 48). The Chronicles account adds that a prophet chided Jehoshaphat for his political alliance with Ahab as well as for the shipping venture because Judah cooperated too closely with the wicked Northern Kingdom (2 Chr. 20:35–37). Although Kings says nothing about this, it does say that when he was invited to include some of the Northern Kingdom's sailors in the fleet, Jehoshaphat refused (1 Kin. 22:49).

22:51–53. Ahaziah of Israel (853–852 B.C.). Ahab's son Ahaziah became king in Jehoshaphat's seventeenth year and reigned only two years. He did as his father had done before him, serving Baal and provoking God to anger. The fact that he followed the pattern set by Jeroboam, as all his predecessors had done before him, shows the deep-seated nature of public sympathy for the fertility cult. The narrative of 1 Kings ends on that sad note.

2 KINGS

INTRODUCTION

Title and Authorship. The earlier manuscripts of the Hebrew Bible simply have two books named Samuel and Kings. When this was translated into Greek to be part of the Library of Alexandria, it was recognized that these two books were really one narrative, so the Septuagint (the Greek translation of the Hebrew Bible) retitled these two books "Of the Kingdoms" and separated it into four sections. What we call today 2 Kings was called "Of the Kingdoms 4," because it was the last of these four sections. The Latin translation in the fourth century (called the Vulgate) retained the same four sections (although it called all four sections Kings rather than Kingdoms). In 1517, Bibles used by both Protestants and Catholics began to use the Hebrew names while keeping the same four sections, thus giving us the 1 and 2 Samuel and 1 and 2 Kings that we use today.

We do not know who wrote the books of Kings. The Jewish Talmud has a statement that claims Jeremiah as the author. A comparison of the last chapter of both books (2 Kin. 25 and Jer. 52) shows that there are similarities. However, there are statements in Kings that indicate that at least some of it was written before Jeremiah was alive and some was written after he was dead. Throughout both books (1 and 2 Kin.), the authors reveal their sources as the books of the written accounts of Solomon, the kings of Israel, and the kings of Judah. These statements (e.g., 1 Kin. 11:41; 14:19, 29; 2 Kin. 1:18; 8:23) also make plain that there was much more written about these kings than is recorded here, indicating that the selections that survive in 1 and 2 Kings were compiled to teach particular spiritual lessons (see section on Theology and Purpose in 1 Kings: Introduction).

Date. A statement in 1 Kings 12:19 indicates that the tribes that formed the Northern Kingdom of Israel after the split from Judah in the south

were still in rebellion against the house of David when that part of the book was written. Since the Northern Kingdom was dissolved in 722 B.C. when Assyria conquered them, at least that part of the book was written before 722 B.C. It is likely that all of 2 Kings was written after 1 Kings, and since 2 Kings begins just after the death of Ahab, it must have been written at a time later than 853 B.C. The book of 2 Kings ends with Nebuchadnezzar's son and heir, Evil-Merodach (known in Babylonian accounts as Amel-Marduk or Awel-Marduk), releasing Jehoiachin from prison in the year Evil-Merodach became king. As a result, this part had to have been written after 560 B.C., when Jehoiachin was released from prison (see "Old Testament Timeline," p. 94). That passage (2 Kin. 25:27–30) indicates that Jehoiachin ate with the king for the rest of his life, which pushes the date even later. It is likely, however, that most of 2 Kings was written before the destruction of Jerusalem in 586 B.C. and that this last section of chapter 25 was appended later.

Backgrounds. By the opening chapter of 2 Kings, the kingdom had already been split for seventy-eight years and was thus generationally established. Eight kings had ruled the Northern Kingdom of Israel and four kings had ruled the Southern Kingdom of Judah. There would still be twelve kings in Israel before its end in 722 B.C. and sixteen rulers (mostly all kings) in Judah before its end in 586 B.C.

In 853 B.C. (where 1 Kin. ends and 2 Kin. begins) both kingdoms had a new king ascend to the throne, making the split in the book at this point reasonable. Following Ahab's death (1 Kin. 22:29–40), his son Ahaziah took the throne. He ruled for only two years because of a fatal accident (2 Kin. 1:1–18), and his brother Jehoram took over. In Judah, the good king Jehoshaphat was near the end of his reign and brought his son to the throne to co-rule with him in the same year Ahab died (853 B.C.). Jehoshaphat lived for about five more years after this.

Politically, to their north, Shalmaneser III was ruling in Assyria. About six years earlier, he had attacked Syria and Israel, and just prior to Israel and Judah's battle with Syria (which resulted in the death of Ahab), they had fought with Syria against Assyria. So while Assyria was the major threat, Syria was the more immediate threat.

To the south, Egypt was in disarray. The Libyans had been living in Egypt as mercenaries for some time but had finally wrested control from the Egyptians beginning in the Third Intermediate Period. However, in 853 B.C. more than one man claimed to be king. As a result, Egypt was weak and does not figure much into the narrative at the beginning of 2 Kings, but it will appear in the latter portions of the book during the Late Period, when Egypt was once again unified.

Theology and Purpose. The role of the prophet is prominent in both books of Kings. Elijah's ministry is the focus of the latter parts of 1 Kings, and Elisha's ministry is the focus in the initial parts of 2 Kings. The narrative in 1 Kings spends five chapters on all of the kings before Ahab (1 Kin. 12–16) and six chapters on Ahab (1 Kin. 17–22), so it is clear that God was trying to reach this major northern king who had married a Sidonian princess/high-priestess of Baal (1 Kin. 16:31–33). The narrative in 2 Kings focuses on God trying to reach the people of Israel (as well as a few foreigners and a couple of kings) through the ministry and miracles of Elisha (2 Kin. 2–13), which covers half of the book of 2 Kings. Two chapters after the death of Elisha, the narrative describes the fall of the Northern Kingdom. The focus of the last half of the book is entirely on the Southern Kingdom of Judah as God tried to reach them through a few good kings in spite of a few very bad kings. (For more, see 1 Kings: Introduction.)

COMMENTARY

1:1—17:41
THE DIVIDED MONARCHY

The second book of Kings continues the narrative of the experience of God's people during the divided monarchy, which was introduced in 1 Kings 17:1. It concludes with the collapse of the Northern (2 Kin. 15:8—17:41) and Southern Kingdoms (18:1—25:30). The book commences with a parenthetical note about Moab's rebellion against Israel after Ahab's

death (2 Kin. 1:1; see 1 Kings: Introduction) and then continues describing the reign of Ahaziah of Israel. Nothing more is said of Moab until chapter 3. Some commentators have suggested that the purpose of 2 Kings 1:1 is to form a bridge that joins the two books together.

1:1—2:11
Elijah and the Kings

This section concludes the interaction between Elijah and the kings that was initiated in 1 Kings 17:1. God's ideal for the monarchy was that the kings would always listen to His prophets in order to make clear that He was the true king of Israel. But with a few exceptions, most of the kings did not listen to God's messengers.

1:1–18. Elijah and Ahaziah. Ahaziah's choice to send messengers to Ekron says much about God's place on the list of Israel's priorities. Ahaziah did not choose to go to Jerusalem even though there was peace between the two kingdoms. He did not even choose to go to Bethel or Dan, the two Israelite places of Baal worship. Instead, a Philistine city was the most attractive to him as the place with the most healing spiritual power. Elijah's question to the officers sent by Ahaziah carried an obvious tone of sarcasm, or at least irony. Ekron was about fifty-five miles (88.5 km) southwest of Samaria, compared to Jerusalem, which was only forty miles (64.4 km) due south. Thus, the implication that they were simply out to consult the most convenient god could not be serious. To make it worse, Ekron was just inside the northern border of the territory of Judah on another highway, west of the one to Jerusalem. It was obvious that the temple and God were being avoided.

The narrative highlights in an unusual way the conflict between the prophets of the Lord and the kings of Israel. It was a conflict between the will of God and the will of the king, and between the word of God and the word of the king. There was a deep clash between the authority of the king and that of Elijah. Ahaziah obviously disliked the message of death and was willing to do whatever was necessary to avert it. The reason behind sending for Elijah is not explicitly stated, but the fact that the king sent the army to get the prophet clearly suggests that his intentions were not good. Perhaps Ahaziah thought that he would be free of the message of death if he brought the prophet under control, or even killed him. Subduing the prophet would be, according to the king, a way of neutralizing the evil omen.

The basic question seems to be, Who is able to shape the movements of history? Ahaziah believed that the god of Ekron could reveal to him the future in order for him to act accordingly, but he soon realized that only the Lord, through His word, shapes the future and fills it with hope or judgment. The military arrived at the house of Elijah and demanded that he *descend* as an act of submission to the king, but Elijah responded with a divine judgment that served to legitimize him as a prophet of the Lord. On Mount Carmel the fire that *descended* from heaven had vindicated God; now fire, not Elijah, *descended* from heaven showing that he was the messenger of the Lord. The captain of the third military unit did not ask for the submission of Elijah but rather submitted himself and his soldiers to Elijah to avoid divine judgment; lives were preserved only in submission to the will of God delivered by the prophet.

Elijah *descended* not in obedience to the king but in obedience to the divine mandate, and he went with the soldiers as the ambassador of the Lord. By now the king had realized that opposition to the word of the Lord results in judgment, and he quietly listened to Elijah as he delivered to him the original message of divine judgment. In the conflict between the authority of Ahaziah and the prophetic authority of Elijah, the powerful word of the Lord prevailed. The pattern of prediction and fulfillment, so common in the books of Kings, reveals who is the Lord of history. The narrative closes with the statement that Ahaziah died in fulfillment of the word of the Lord that Elijah had delivered to him.

2:1–11. Elijah's Departure in a Fiery Chariot. The intriguing thing about this passage is that it takes for granted that Elijah was about to depart into the heavens. Everybody in the story seems to have known about it before it happened. When two groups of students at Bethel and at Jericho asked Elisha about it, it apparently caused him distress. The narrative focuses on Elisha's determination to stay with Elijah to the very end. The unspoken expectation, and yet uncertainty, of what was in store for Elijah is what gives a sense of drama to the story. The three requests from Elijah for Elisha to turn back and Elisha's determination to continue (vv. 2–6) were probably a test intended to reveal Elisha's commitment to the prophetic ministry as the successor of Elijah.

Elijah's mantle had been introduced earlier (1 Kin. 19:19) as a symbol of the prophetic calling, but in this passage it becomes significant as a symbol of spiritual authority. The use of the mantle to divide the river (2 Kin. 2:8) brings to mind the miraculous use of Moses's rod at the Red Sea. The crossing of the Jordan itself "on dry ground," here and in Elisha's return a few verses later, would remind any Hebrew of the earlier and more famous crossing. This episode marks the last time in Scripture that a body of water is miraculously dried up to allow passage on dry ground. In the final moments of their relationship, Elijah asked Elisha a question that is reminiscent of the question God asked Solomon at the beginning of his reign: What would he like to receive? Elisha's answer carried special meaning because a double portion was, in the practice of the time, what the firstborn would legally inherit from the father to establish the firstborn as the leader of the family (Deut. 21:17). The request and the imminent fulfillment of the answer publicly legitimized the leading prophetic role Elisha would fill in Israel. While miracles are not by any means the full measure of the work of a prophet, there was a strong emphasis on them in the stories of Elisha. So commentators who have studied the matter carefully have noted that the number of miracles wrought by Elisha as listed in Scripture is exactly double the number performed by Elijah—a clear, if symbolic, indication of the fulfillment of Elisha's request for a double portion of Elijah's spirit.

The closest parallels to the phenomenon of being taken away in a chariot of fire associated with a whirlwind occur in Ezekiel and Job. Ezekiel saw a whirlwind coming from the north with fire (Ezek. 1:4) and God's throne in its midst (1:5, 22, 25–26). Similarly, Job saw a whirlwind coming, and God spoke to him from it (Job 38:1; 40:6). Other uses of the term "whirlwind" refer to God coming in judgment (e.g., Zech. 9:14). In all these biblical references, the whirlwind or powerful storm (the same word is often used in Hebrew) came toward the one describing it, but with Elijah, the whirlwind went away from the viewer. This unique and special revelation of God's presence and its description in the biblical text can be difficult for the modern reader to understand.

Nevertheless, the story teaches important truths. First, Elisha was being tested for his persistence. Perhaps he was a little reticent to bid farewell to his master, but he needed to be able to keep up with the mundane and ordinary as well as to stand up to the blatant evils that would face him. That meant simply plodding along, even if it meant doubling back a few times to where he had been. Second, Elijah visited the schools of the prophets to tie up loose ends before his departure. The students of those schools knew what was happening, thus providing a good precedent for youth today to be informed so that they can at least observe God's action among His people. Third, the only other times that water parted was during the Exodus—at the Red Sea for the first generation leaving Egypt and at the Jordan for the second generation entering the promised land. What Elijah did in dividing the Jordan with his rolled-up mantle signified a new beginning. The end of one era had come and a new day of opportunity and salvation was dawning. Finally, the translation of a living human being to heaven speaks about the reality of heaven as a place accessible to human beings. There is an element of hope present in the narrative in the sense that if one human being was taken to heaven, then others could also enjoy this privilege. The Christian hope points to the moment when the resurrected righteous will ascend to meet the Lord and be with Him forever.

2:12—9:37
Elisha and the Kings

In the record of Elijah and Elisha, the books of Kings register a wide and rich portfolio of prophetic ministry. In addition to working for national repentance and revival, their ministry also demonstrated God's care for the needs of individuals that the apostate kings of their time failed to have. The prophets provided food, helped eliminate debt, facilitated God's blessing for childless parents to have a child, cared for widows and orphans, and raised the only sons of women from the dead. Both prophets were closely associated with the schools of the prophets.

2:12–25. Elisha's Ministry Commences. Elisha's reaction to Elijah's disappearance was rather dramatic. He cried out, tore his robe in two (v. 12), picked up Elijah's mantle (cloak) that had fallen from him—a detail mentioned twice in vv. 13–14—and headed back to the Jordan (v. 13). This repetition emphatically reinforces the nature of Elijah's dramatic departure and the mantle falling down from above in the process as part of the sign that was promised to Elisha for receiving a double portion of Elijah's spirit. The waters of the Jordan were then divided in order for him to cross over (v. 14).

Back in Jericho, the men of the city told Elisha about their desperate water situation (v. 19). As a response, the prophet asked for a new bowl full of salt and tossed it into the water supply. The biblical author stated that the water remained healed until his own day, and that is still the case. This was Elisha's first miracle and was performed for the benefit of God's people. The Lord supplied for them drinkable water, which was a vital need. The God who defeated powerful armies is the same who cares for the daily needs of His servants.

Those who mocked Elisha (v. 23) were small or young (Heb. qatan) ne'arim—a term that can mean "boys," "lads," "youths," or "servants." Accordingly, Bible translations differ in regard to what they are called. Ultimately, we do not know exactly how old they were, but they were acting like a gang of juvenile delinquents. Their actions were clearly reprehensible (cf. Deut. 21:18–21). The fate they met parallels what happened to the soldiers who attempted to arrest Elijah (2 Kin. 1:10, 12). It was also a judgment against the inhabitants of Bethel and their worship of the golden calf placed there by Jeroboam. This judgment echoed the account of the serpents in the wilderness during the Exodus (Num. 21:5–9)—when God's people turned their backs on Him and mocked Him, He withdrew His protection from them, and they suffered the consequences of facing their ever-present dangers without God's protection. The youths who mocked Elisha were in reality mocking God, and they too reaped the consequences. Their action stands in marked contrast to those of the students who honored Elisha.

3:1–25. Moab Rebels. While the book opens with the statement that Moab rebelled (1:1), it is only in chapter 3 that more is said about this. The rebellion came when a new king (Jehoram or Joram, 852–841 B.C.) ascended the throne of the Northern Kingdom of Israel. This means that both kingdoms had a king of the same name at the same time: Jehoram of Judah reigned from about 853 until 841 B.C. Jehoram of Israel was the brother of the previous king, Ahaziah, whose brief reign ended after falling from a high window.

Although Jehoram of Israel did evil in God's sight, he did curb some of the idolatrous practices of his forebears by removing a sacred pillar that his father had made to honor Baal (3:2; see also 1 Kin. 14:23). But he continued the worship practices that Jeroboam introduced (2 Kin. 3:3). Although the record of events during his reign continues through 8:15, Jehoram of Israel was not the main player; it was Elisha. The king is almost incidental to all else that was happening.

It is clear that regardless of its many other problems, the Northern Kingdom had significant political influence in the region, enough to be able to exact a significant tribute from Moab, across the Jordan and to the south along the east side of the Dead Sea. Moab first fell under the control of Israel during the reign of David (2 Sam. 8:2)—control that continued in the Northern Kingdom after the split since at least two tribes (Rueben and Gad) dwelt in the area.

The amount of the tribute gives us some idea of the livestock production of Moab, now part of the modern country of Jordan and a region roughly equivalent in size to the Dead Sea. A tribute usually was understood as a token tax to acknowledge subservience to another authority—in this case Israel. An adult ram produces as much as thirty pounds (13.6 kg) of wool yearly. Thus, 100,000 rams could potentially produce 1,500 tons (about three million pounds) of wool each year. If this was only a token, the amount of wool produced yearly in Moab alone was staggering, illustrating how lush the land east of the Dead Sea was at that time.

This story illustrates Jehosophat's puzzling relationship with God and with the Northern Kingdom. The chronology of his various military alliances with Ahab and his son may be difficult to reconstruct from the various accounts in Kings and Chronicles, but almost all of the alliances ended in disaster, and in most of them he was directly or implicitly rebuked by the Lord (2 Kin. 22:32, 48; cf. 2 Chr. 19:1–3, 36–37). Worst of all for its long-term consequences, Jehosophat, a scripturally honored "good" king of Judah, had allowed his son to marry a daughter of Ahab, which corrupted Judah for generations (2 Kin. 8:18; see also 1 Kin. 22:44; 2 Chr. 18:1). About this alliance with Jehoram, Elisha made it explicit again that the Lord decried the bad company Jehosophat kept with the king of Israel (2 Kin. 3:14).

The roundabout route of the allies' attack is interesting. It would have been much more efficient for Israel and Judah to attack from the north and Edom from the south. Instead, they all apparently traveled together around the south end of the Dead Sea to attack Moab from that direction. It can only be assumed that Moab had fewer defenses on its southern border, making it a more attractive place to invade.

As noted earlier, at times of crisis the Lord's prophet was nearby (v. 11) to pronounce judgment or, in this case, to rescue his wayward people. Why Elisha was nearby, when all of his previous miracles took place north of the Dead Sea, is not stated. It is possible that the Lord sent him there in advance, as He directed Philip to meet the Ethiopian on the road to Gaza (Acts 8:26). Even though Jehosophat was the king of Judah (the Southern Kingdom) and almost all of Elisha's ministry was in Israel (the Northern Kingdom), Jehosophat knew enough about Elisha to know that he truly was a man of God. This could have been either from Elisha's own reputation or simply because Jehoshaphat learned that Elisha had been a servant of Elijah, as indicated by the saying about pouring water on Elijah's hands (2 Kin. 3:11).

The reference to music (v. 15) is one of the few places in Scripture where the association is made between music and prophetic utterance (see 1 Sam. 10:5). Why Elisha called for a musician is not stated, but it seems likely that the music was not to induce a trance, as commonly understood, but simply to put the moment in a setting of meditative and reflective communion with God on noble themes.

The destruction ordered on Moab—including commands to spoil fields, stop up wells, and cut down good trees (2 Kin. 3:19)—indicates the Lord's intent for stark judgment on Moab. Such complete destruction contrasts with the style of conquest commanded in Deuteronomy 20, where the Israelites were instructed to preserve resources, particularly fruit trees, in areas they intended to inhabit. The purpose here was not to conquer and settle new territory but to inflict lasting damage on a long-standing enemy. Indeed, the land is arid today largely because of deforestation.

The writer relates the miracle of the water (vv. 16–24) to the time of the morning sacrifice. It would be unusual to state the matter in this way unless the writer wished to convey a spiritual, salvific significance to the timing of the event. God's salvation here is presented with the imagery of both water and sacrifice. Understood in this way, it is not surprising that to the Moabites, the water had the appearance of blood, even if they misunderstood its meaning.

The particular Hebrew word *qetsap* used in v. 27, sometimes translated as "fury" or "indignation," refers in the majority of cases to the wrath of God that comes in judgment. How this wrath is to be understood here is not made plain. In one view, this wrath may not be emanating from the Moabites but from God, who brought an end to the battle and put a limit on Israel's further success. It has also been suggested that this wrath refers to the fury of the Moabites against Israel, as indicated by the horrific lengths to which the king went in sacrificing his son in order to attempt to defend his city. In this reading, we understand that the Israelites were so appalled at this action that they withdrew from the siege (v. 27).

Without Elisha, the Israelite confederation had no chance of surviving their long desert trek. Had Jehosophat not asked for God's direction, Elisha would not have been able to act. While the story ostensibly follows Jehoram, Jehosophat becomes the key character, despite his repeated, dubious relationships with Israel. He was the one who followed God, asked to consult His true prophet, and lived to witness a victory. Certainly, it was a lesson for him, and it also should have been for Jehoram.

4:1–7. The Widow's Oil. The story of the widow afraid for her future after her husband's death gives us a view of the social structure of the times. A widow was easy prey for anyone who desired to extort her dead husband's wealth, and if she could not meet her dead husband's financial obligations, she could lose her home, her children, or both to pay the debt. This particular widow was in danger of losing her two sons, whom the creditor claimed as his slaves in order to pay a debt. The sons would have to work for the creditor until such time as he considered the debt paid (a situation ripe for abuse) or until the next Jubilee year when all such workers were to be released (Lev. 25:39–41). This arrangement was not supposed to be as restrictive or as severe as slavery—Israelites were not to be bought and sold as slaves, as was permitted with foreigners, and their servitude was not permanent (Lev. 25:39–46).

The widow did not want this for her sons, so she pleaded with Elisha for help. Her husband had been one of the sons, or students, of the prophets (2 Kin. 4:1), and she thought this piece of information might help her case. But Elisha looked past that detail to what she had in her hands—a little oil—and that was what he worked with (v. 2).

This miracle parallels that of Elijah when he went to stay with the Phoenician widow during three years of drought (1 Kin. 17:14–16). Both widows were able to support and maintain their families because of a prophet in their midst. Their acceptance of and respect for the prophet indicated their dependence and reliance on God, and God honored them at a time when the majority of the people around them had rejected God and given their allegiance to Baal instead.

4:8–37. The Woman from Shunem. The small town of Shunem, now known as Sulam on the eastern outskirts of the modern city of Afula, was in the Jezreel Valley about sixteen miles (25.7 km) southwest of the southern tip of the Sea of Galilee and about the same distance from Mount Carmel to the northwest. The town must have been along a route traveled regularly by Elisha for his ministry in the region.

Elisha's question in v. 13 is unusual in that he was apparently anticipating using his political influence to help her rather than performing a miracle. The idea of what should be done for her is recorded as having come from Elisha's servant Gehazi, rather than being an original prophetic insight from the prophet himself. This may give us a glimpse into the role of the prophet, at least in Elisha's case, who sometimes lived in the moment and, through the Spirit of God, reacted to outside information and circumstances as they occurred rather than always from anticipatory insight.

The narrative of the promised son (vv. 14–17) easily brings to mind another such promise, also given in the context of hospitality provided to travelers, with an initial, similarly incredulous reaction from the mother-to-be (Gen. 18). This story is different because the promised son is not later recorded as playing a major role in the history of God's people, as did other promised sons like Isaac, Samson (Judg. 13:3–5), and Samuel (1 Sam. 1:17). However, with this miracle, Elisha demonstrated that he indeed had the spirit that Elijah had, who had also raised a boy back to life (1 Kin. 17:22). The prophetic announcement was fulfilled as Elisha had spoken—the word of God impacted the life of the woman and her husband in a unique way.

The boy's death is commonly attributed to sunstroke (2 Kin. 4:18–20). We are not told why the mother concealed the death from the boy's father. The mother is the major character in how the story is told, and the father's role is incidental. It may be that this was also true in the actual life of the family, at least in relation to raising the son. The father was understandably puzzled at the request for a service animal during the busy harvest, which probably would have caused some inconvenience. The woman's determination to save her son caused her to engage in a demanding thirty-two-mile (51.5 km) round trip to Carmel and rested entirely on the desperate hope that the prophet could be found there. Her desperation and grief also compelled her to engage in an intimate gesture of importunity toward

Elisha that his servant considered inappropriate or offensive (v. 27). Elisha, as Christ did later with many who approached him familiarly, resonated with the woman's grief, whatever the cause, and welcomed her approach and honored her faith.

The story of the boy's resurrection is notable for the process by which Elisha was involved in its accomplishment. As with some other miracles recorded in Scripture, there was a process involved. Elijah prayed seven times at Mount Carmel before the rain came (1 Kin. 18:36–37); Naaman washed seven times in the Jordan before his leprosy was healed (2 Kin. 5:10, 14); Jesus used a two-stage process to heal a man's blindness (Mark 8:23–25). Elisha's instruction for his servant to go on ahead and place his staff on the child raises in the mind of the reader the expectation that that will be the means of the boy's resuscitation (2 Kin. 4:29). But it is only Elisha's direct involvement, and that through a repeated ritual, that resulted in the intended effect (vv. 32–35). It may be that even though Elisha was the intended agent of a profound miracle (the boy had been dead for a considerable period of time), the Lord was using it as a faith-building experience for Elisha as well as the others who witnessed or became aware of the miracle.

The incident of the promised son who then became sick, died, and was resurrected illustrates that the prophetic word had again restored life and wholeness, not nationally, as was so desperately needed, but to an individual as a token of what God can do for all the faithful and willing.

4:38–44. Death in the Pot. Elisha retraced his steps back to Gilgal (near Jericho) and its school of the prophets. A famine had struck the land as a reminder of the broken covenant (Deut. 28:15, 24) and as an echo of the encounter between Elijah and King Ahab (1 Kin. 17:1). The famine showed that Baal, the storm god, was totally powerless and that it was the God of Israel alone who provides rain in its season (Lev. 26:4). When a poisonous plant found its way into the students' stew, Elisha worked a miracle. Elijah had done something similar during a famine when the meager food supplies of a widow were hardly enough to provide for her household (1 Kin. 17:10–16). This time again the Lord provided more than needed (2 Kin. 4:42–44), something echoed later in one of the miracles of Jesus (Matt. 14:13–21). That Elisha supervised the feeding of more than one hundred persons indicates that his prophetic ministry had a greater effect than that of his mentor Elijah.

The miracles performed by Elisha reveal a particular interest in the needy condition of women and reveal a God for whom gender is no barrier to personal, social, and spiritual fulfillment. But the miracles cut deeper. They were about providing food and making the infertile fertile. They were an attack against the claims of Baal to be in charge of the fertility of the land and the people. The one who could make humans and the earth fertile and who could provide food for His servants was the God of Israel. But sadly, the nation was placing its hope on the false claims of Baal and was heading toward disaster.

5:1–27. Naaman the Leper. Naaman was a senior commanding officer of the Syrian army (the nation was called Aram at the time), whose military successes were attributed directly to God (v. 1). It was unclear what his skin condition actually was since the Hebrew word (*tsara'*) used is a generic term that includes rashes, fungal infections, leprosy, psoriasis, and other conditions. The fact that he was still able to associate with people may indicate that the Syrians did not consider the disease to be contagious.

That he had a young girl working in his home was evidence of his success in raids across Israel's border (v. 2). Even though Ahab and Ben-Hadad had formalized a treaty (1 Kin. 20:34), it did not hold and there had been various skirmishes between them. In the narrative, the strong faith of the servant girl from Israel in Naaman's house was also an example of what God had told Elijah on Mount Horeb about the 7,000 who had still not bowed to Baal (1 Kin. 19:18).

The faith of the servant girl is remarkable. That she would honor her captor by suggesting, in good faith, that he visit the prophet of the Lord in Israel (2 Kin. 5:3) indicates that even in the distress and distraction of her captivity, she knew who she was. Despite the apparent benevolent treatment by her captors, she had not lost her identity, and she exemplified what was evident and later reiterated as an important teaching of Scripture: servants and slaves and the otherwise oppressed, even under adverse circumstances, are called to serve their persecutors and captors with good deeds (Prov. 25:21–22; Matt. 5:38–48; Rom. 12:19–21; 1 Pet. 2:20–25).

The response of the king of Israel to Naaman's visit indicates the obtuseness of his mind (2 Kin. 5:7). The request was for a miracle. Obviously, the king had no confidence in his own ability perform miracles, but it did not occur to him to see the possibilities for glory to

God by sending Naaman to the one person in the Northern Kingdom who had the widespread reputation of doing so. The king viewed the matter only in the political arena rather than the spiritual realm. Elisha, apparently through prophetic insight, had to intervene in order rescue the opportunity for good. It is a lesson for any leader, who should always look beyond the immediate reflexive interpretation of a situation to consider what possibilities God might have in mind.

The instruction to wash seven times (v. 10) appears to have been intended to demonstrate to Naaman that one must be diligent and exact in following God's commands. Six times was not enough to ensure the healing nor to test the full measure of Naaman's faith.

Naaman's gift, first offered to the king and then to Elisha, was an enormous sum: 750 pounds (340 kg) of silver (worth today over $150,000), and 150 pounds (68 kg) of gold (worth today over $3 million). It was common in the ancient world to pay the priests of the deity in advance to secure future blessings. That Naaman waited until after the miracle to offer gifts shows two things: first, that he was not inclined to believe that a foreign god would help him (vv. 11–12), and second, that he recognized the different character of Israel's God after the miracle (v. 15). The gift offer came from a grateful heart. Elisha's refusal was intended to convince Naaman that it is not wealth that makes a person whole but his faith in and reliance on God. Naaman obviously had an inaccurate concept of the God of Israel. With this in mind, he had assumed that God and His prophet needed gifts in payment. When he could give nothing, his sense of honor caused him to ask for something that would itself demonstrate his honor and gratitude—two muleloads of soil (v. 17). His explanation for what seems to us an unusual request was that from that time forward he would only sacrifice to the Lord God. The relationship between his request and his explanation may be interpreted in at least two ways. First, it was commonly thought in the ancient Near East that a god's influence was confined to a geographical location (e.g., 1 Kin. 20:23). Thus, Naaman may have believed that if he took some of the ground where God had displayed His power back to his home, he would be able to worship Him at that new place too. Alternatively, Naaman's strong affirmation of faith may indicate that he considered himself now to be an Israelite and was symbolically claiming his inheritance by taking with him a portion of the land.

Naaman had become a worshiper of the true God. His request for a dispensation when appearing to genuflect to another god presents an interesting use of language. Naaman called that god "Rimmon" (2 Kin. 5:18). There are several occasions in Scripture where the Hebrew language makes a joke or an ironic statement about the meaning of names by employing wordplay—where the same or similar words are used with different meanings (see Gen. 17:17; 18:12–15; 21:6, 9; 26:8 and notes; Dan. 1:7). The actual name of the god is "Ramanu," which means "the thunderer" and is, of course, a reference to Baal, the storm god. Altering the vowels to "Rimmon" changes its meaning to "pomegranate." So the thunderer was turned into a pomegranate. When Naaman used this term, he was probably intentionally confessing faith in the God of Israel while renouncing his former faith in Baal.

The wonderful story turns sour at this point with Gehazi's betrayal (2 Kin. 5:20–27). He dishonored the Lord by taking money from Naaman. Elisha knew what Gehazi had done and told him that Naaman's skin disease would now cling to him and to his descendants forever. That effectively ended Gehazi's career. Although he now had money for olive groves, vineyards, flocks, herds, and servants, he also had what Naaman was prepared to pay a much larger fortune to be rid of. The very thing that made Baal worship attractive—wealth—was now Gehazi's, but at what cost? He had lost his wholeness and his future and became an example of a nation insistent on divorcing itself from God. The story is indeed about two men. One was a non-Israelite who came to know the God of Israel and concluded that there was no god like Him. The other was an Israelite whose association with the prophet gave him high spiritual leadership advantages yet who, like the leaders of the nation, had no respect for the Lord of Israel. The literal leprosy of Naaman would cling to Gehazi, and the metaphorical leprosy of other nations would cling to Israel and would permanently separate them from the Lord. The word of the Lord, spoken through the prophet, healed Naaman and brought judgment on Gehazi and the nation represented by him.

6:1–7. The Lost Ax Head. The story of the lost ax head gives fascinating insights into the person of Elisha and his interpersonal skills. He was obviously very closely involved in the development of a new generation of prophets.

A group of students at the school of the prophets near Jericho shared with Elisha their plan to enlarge the place where he and the students lived. He is portrayed as a loved and respected mentor who provided not only for their education but for their lodging and even for their food as well (4:38–44). It is interesting that the students made the plans and he empowered their vision, rather than Elisha being the one to dictate and micromanage (6:1–2). The presence of this master-teacher was highly valued, and when his students invited him to join their physical labor, he accepted, grateful for every available teaching moment (v. 3).

When one of the students lost a borrowed ax head, Elisha focused on the solution rather than on the cause (v. 6). The retrieval of the ax head was also left to the student—Elisha did not reach out and pick it up, but he asked the student to do it (v. 7). This story illustrates not only what it means to be a successful mentor but also the success of a group trusting in God and heeding the prophetic word in their midst. It also reveals that the prophetic ministry seeks to build up faith among those who, in the midst of national apostasy, are still serving the Lord.

6:8–23. A Banquet for the Enemy.

The uneasy peace between Syria (Aram) and Israel was further weakened by the continuing cross-border skirmishes with the Syrian king (see 1 Kin. 20:34). The story of the capture of the Syrian army teaches us several things. First, God can intervene in the most private counsels of His opponents to foil their plans and accomplish His purposes. He knows everything, down to the smallest detail.

Second, and related to the first, God is in complete control of events, even in what appears to us to be the direst crises. The prophetic assertion "Those who are with us are more than those who are with them" (v. 16) has comforted God's people for millennia. The mental image of the host of the Lord surrounding and protecting his faithful servants gives us a glimpse of the protecting role of the heavenly army in the cosmic battle on earth.

Third, the prophets may sometimes, without blame, use benevolent misdirection to ultimately accomplish goodwill among enemies. Elisha was comically artful in his message to the blinded besiegers at Dothan. They sought him, without success because of their blindness, at Dothan, which was where he really was. But they would find him (when their eyes were opened) in another city (Samaria), which was also correct.

Fourth, God desires His apparent enemies to come to a knowledge of Him and experience His grace. Elisha's insistence that the captives be treated with kindness and allowed to return home unharmed explicitly anticipated the teaching of Jesus in the Sermon on the Mount when he told his followers to do good to their enemies (Matt. 5:44).

6:24—7:20. Siege of Samaria.

We do not know the exact time sequence, but the Syrian army was again on the offensive against Israel. Ben-Hadad continued to fulfill the words of the young prophet who had rebuked Ahab for not killing the Syrian king (1 Kin. 20:34, 42). Now he set out to besiege Samaria—about 120 miles (193.1 km) south of the Syrian capital, Damascus. Jehoram's army had not been able to stop the Syrians or break their siege, and a severe famine was afflicting the besieged city. Famine is one of the covenant curses, and therefore one of the main indicators of the broken covenant (Lev. 26:18–20, 25). The inhabitants of Samaria were compelled by hunger to eat their own (unclean) donkeys (2 Kin. 6:25; see Lev. 11:3) that had presumably died of starvation. The fact that they paid eighty shekels (about two lbs or nearly one kg of silver) for a donkey's head reveals their desperate situation. To give some idea of that cost, the average income at the time was about one shekel a month. Added to that, fuel for cooking was also at a premium, and all that was left to burn was dove dung, worth five shekels (five months' wages) for about cup.

More evidence that Israel was experiencing the specific curses of breaking the covenant is provided in the story of Jehoram's interaction with the two women (2 Kin. 6:26–30). The famine had become so great that mothers were willing to eat their own children, just as had been foretold (Lev. 26:27–29). Jehoram's reaction to the revolting encounter was similar to his father Ahab's reaction to an earlier famine: he blamed the prophet of God (1 Kin. 18:17), and the formulation of his intention was similar to Jezebel's oath to kill Elijah. It exhibited the very kind of stubborn rejection of God that the covenant curses, so clearly evidenced here, were intended to punish. The messenger Jehoram sent to Elisha was a senior army general whose position was similar to Naaman's in the previous story; he was someone on whom the king depended. The military situation was a far cry from the days when the Syrians were offering David tribute (2 Sam. 8:6). It was a sorrowful reminder of how far Israel had fallen in its rejection of God.

Through prophetic insight, Elisha anticipated the arrival of the messenger, who was refused an audience but to whom Elisha announced both a promise for Samaria and a curse on the unbelieving messenger (2 Kin. 6:32—7:1). The mockery of the messenger was serious because while he was apparently acknowledging the existence of Israel's God, he was denigrating His power. What he did not know or chose to ignore was that the prophetic word defeats the enemies of His people as it is fulfilled within history (7:17–20).

The account of the four lepers carries an element of dark humor and ultimate comedy (vv. 3–11). Their situation was desperate. Upon deciding they had nothing to lose by going to the enemy, they discovered the Lord's deliverance and became the messengers of salvation to those who treated them as outcasts. God's best news is sometimes given first to those who may be viewed by society as of little account. The shepherds of Bethlehem (Luke 2:8–20) and Mary Magdalene in the garden of the resurrection (Luke 24:1–12; John 20:11–18) are similar examples.

The listing of the spoils they found in the Syrian camp is similar to the goods Naaman the Syrian had brought to Elisha to be free of his leprosy. These resources gave this group of lepers a new start in life. The riches of this life are God's to distribute for His purposes, and we are called to share the good news He bestows on us. Those who reject that good news may be crushed by the results of it, as was the officer at the gate (2 Kin. 7:17).

As Elisha had said, the messenger who had disbelieved saw the large quantities of food greatly reduced in value but did not benefit from it because he was killed (vv. 18–20). The word of the Lord spoken through the prophet found fulfillment in judgment against a leader who had forsaken and challenged the Lord. This officer represented a nation that had largely given up on God and had given its allegiance instead to other gods. And yet, when trouble came as a direct result of breaking the covenant with God, they could not cope with the crisis.

The nation had forgotten that the Lord can be trusted in good times and in bad times. Instead, they blamed God for their troubles, charging Him with being inaccessible and venting their wrath on those they knew had a close relationship with Him. But God is good, and He provided not only for the faithful ones but for all those around. They all benefited from a great feast of good things supplied by God's saving love.

8:1–6. The Woman of Shunem Escapes Famine. It appears that the narrative of vv. 1–2 is retrospective, recalling a number of years previous, when Elisha advised the woman of Shunem to leave the country to escape a famine. The implication seems to be that the famine during the siege of Samaria was only part of that longer famine lasting seven years. This story continues the theme of Elisha's prophetic ministry in the lives of ordinary people. While the stories of his predecessor's ministry focus more on the national spiritual condition of Israel, the stories recorded about Elisha's ministry have a strong focus on the health and well-being of individuals. In this case, it was Elisha's reputation, as reported by Gehazi, that helped the woman, rather than Elisha's direct intervention to solve her problem. Doubtless, when the king learned from Gehazi of the great things Elisha had done for her, it helped him decide that he needed to help her too. While the order of the narratives here is not clear, it seems likely that this story occurred after Gehazi's disgrace in the Naaman incident. If so, we learn that Gehazi still admired his old master and that God was still willing to use Gehazi, greedy and disgraced as he was, as an agent to accomplish His purposes and restore the woman's land. The same can be said of the king, who himself had rejected God. The Lord had not totally abandoned these men. He is not willing that any should die but that all should repent and live (2 Pet. 3:9). God was willing to use them as much as He could to help this woman bring glory to Himself. No one is beyond redemption as long as they live, and God can use anyone as an agent to accomplish His purpose of blessing those who trust in Him.

8:7–15. A New King for Syria. No time frame is given between the fleeing of the Syrian army at the siege at Samaria and the time that Elisha went up to see the sick King Ben-Hadad. The king loaded forty camels with presents and sent one of his senior officers, Hazael, to ask Elisha if he would recover from this illness. It is ironic that when Israel's King Ahaziah was ill, he sent emissaries to the prophets of Baal at Ekron to see whether or not he would recover (2 Kin. 1:1–2). Similarly, Naaman came to Israel with great gifts so that he too might be healed. While God's people ran to pagan prophets, idolaters were seeking out the one true God.

In restoring Elijah after his flight from Jezebel, God commissioned him to anoint a new king for Syria (1 Kin. 19:15–16). The text does not say whether Elijah ever managed to see Hazael, but

Elisha got the chance to meet him (2 Kin. 8:9). God predicted that Hazael would be king. This does not mean that God intended Hazael to assassinate the previous king, but just that Hazael was impatient to carry out what he knew to be God's will. His violent action was a denial of the meaning of his own name, "the one who sees God." Instead of seeing or understanding how God would bring about his ascension to the throne, Hazael followed his own ambition and took matters into his own hands.

8:16–24. Jehoram or Joram of Judah (853–841 B.C.). Jehoram of Judah was the son of "good" King Jehoshaphat, but his marriage to Athaliah, the daughter of Ahab and Jezebel, did not bode well for his reign (v. 18). He is described as one who followed the kings of Israel, especially the house of Ahab, in doing evil in the sight of the Lord. God preserved Judah in order to leave a light burning there and for the sake of the covenant made with David (v. 19). This is an important theme, and one that is repeated on other occasions, for instance, when Jeroboam split the kingdom (1 Kin. 11:36), and when Abijam was preserved despite his apostasy (1 Kin. 15:4). God was not yet ready to give up Judah.

With the weakened ties to God, it was easier for the subdued nations paying tribute to Judah to rebel, and this was exactly what Edom did (2 Kin. 8:20). Jehoram tried to defeat the Edomite army but failed, and his army deserted and fled to their own homes. Edom was never again under the control of Judah, and when the Babylonians conquered Judah and took them into captivity the Edomites were cruel with the Judeans—for which later prophets condemned them (e.g., Obadiah 1:10–14). Emboldened by this rebellion, another vassal state, Libnah, also rebelled (1 Kin. 8:22). The summary statement for Jehoram's reign again refers the reader to the court chronicles of the kings of Judah and indicates that he was buried with his fathers in the city of David (2 Kin. 8:23–24). His son, Ahaziah, replaced him.

8:25–29. Ahaziah of Judah (841 B.C.). The narrative of Ahaziah can be divided into two parts, with this as the first and the second being in 9:27–29. The first part mentions his relationship to Ahab's dynasty. The Hebrew word *khatan* in 8:27 essentially refers to any relationship by marriage. It has been translated and understood by some to mean specifically "son-in-law" (in which case Ahaziah would have followed in his father's and grandfather's footsteps by marrying into Ahab's family), but the word here could simply mean that he was connected to Ahab's family through his father's marriage into it (v. 27). It is true that since Jehoshaphat's reign there had been peace between Israel and Judah, but at the same time Ahaziah's reign paralleled the idolatrous excesses of the house of Omri, especially of Ahab, in doing evil in the sight of the Lord.

The narrative next describes a battle in which both kings joined forces against the Syrians at Ramoth Gilead (v. 28). A similar battle had been fought a generation earlier, when Ahab and Jehoshaphat were soundly beaten and Ahab was mortally wounded (1 Kin. 22:1–4, 34–35). With this latest battle, the king of Israel (now Jehoram) was wounded, and Ahaziah visited him (2 Kin. 8:29). History seems to have been going around in a circle—as it often does when people cast themselves away from God. It is only in following God that history progresses toward a grand and glorious climax.

9:1–37. Jehu and the End of Jezebel. The anointing of Jehu as king is unique in that the prophet sent his messenger to anoint him and to define Jehu's mission to him. The fact that Jehu was anointed in secret parallels the anointing of David. The significant difference is that Jehu proclaimed himself king immediately after the anointing and did not wait for the Lord to do things at the appropriate time. This may account for the ruthlessness of his action.

Although Jehu may have exceeded God's intentions (see Hos. 1:4), he was God's instrument in bringing the dynasty of Ahab to an end. That the dead body of Joram, Ahab's son, was thrown on the very ground that Ahab had stolen from Naboth (2 Kin. 9:24–26) is a stirring reminder to us that the word of the Lord, whether affirming His deliverance or promising His judgment, will be fulfilled. Jehu's recitation of the prophecy recognized, as God told Elijah (1 Kin. 21), that some of it would be fulfilled, not in Ahab's time, but in that of his son.

Ahaziah did not escape, despite his best efforts. He was shot some distance away, along the road near Ibleam (2 Kin. 9:27). Ibleam is about nine miles (14.5 km) south of Jezreel, and Ramoth Gilead is about forty-five miles (72 km) east of Jezreel. The pursuit of Ahaziah was protracted and deliberate. The narrative in Chronicles states that Jehu's men found Ahaziah hiding in Samaria, and they took him to Jehu, who had him executed (2 Chr. 22:9). The account in Kings says that Ahaziah died in Megiddo, and his body was then returned to Jerusalem to be buried with his fathers (2 Kin. 9:27–28). It has been suggested that the two accounts can be reconciled by acknowledging the possibility that Ahaziah was wounded in Samaria, pursued by Jehu to Megiddo, captured by Jehu's soldiers in Samaria after having fled back there, and brought to Jehu, who had remained in Megiddo, for execution.

When Jezebel heard of Jehu's return, she prepared herself to look her finest and waited for him while watching from an upper-level window. Dressed like a queen and adorned with religious jewelry that would assure her the protection of her gods, she was ready to face her enemy. When she saw Jehu, she mockingly asked if he had come in peace, and called him Zimri, murderer of his master (v. 31). Zimri had killed King Elah, son of Baasha, and had destroyed Baasha's entire household, but his reign had only lasted seven days (1 Kin. 16:15–20). Jezebel was implying that Jehu would not last any longer. The section closes with a reminder of the words of Elijah regarding the details of Jezebel's death and the disposition of her body, carefully noting that the matter was resolved in just the way God said it would be. The word of the Lord was working within the arena of history, accomplishing the divine intent.

10:1—15:7
The Kingdoms' Renewed Hostilities

During the time the dynasty of Jehu ruled over Israel for four generations, the royal line in Judah had almost been snuffed out by Athaliah, daughter of Ahab and Jezebel, and the prophet Elisha died after a ministry lasting about sixty years. Despite the state of war resuming between the Northern and Southern Kingdoms, both became richer as a succession of kings brought greater prosperity (and idolatry) to their respective nations.

10:1–36. Jehu of Israel (841–814 B.C.). This chapter is a straightforward recounting of the expeditious and excessive way Jehu began to fulfill his divine mandate for the destruction of Ahab's dynasty. He cleverly arranged that the caretakers of Ahab's sons, who lived in Samaria, be the very ones responsible for the deaths of those in their care. His use of threatening political pressure and brute force quickly won the support of the people of Jezreel in the slaughter of any member of Ahab's family or court in that city. He then moved on to Samaria to complete his work as he saw it. But it appears that he had already exceeded the limits of his God-given authority to wreak judgment on Ahab.

Jehu's meeting with Jehonadab, son of Rechab (vv. 14–16), on the way to Jezreel is important to note. Jehonadab was quite a significant figure in Israelite history and is featured in a later account by Jeremiah. Jeremiah referred to Jehonadab's ("Jonadab" in some versions) group as desert dwellers living in tents and refusing to build houses, plant vineyards or crops, or drink wine (Jer. 35:6–10). It appears that Jehonadab responded positively to the purging of the Baal cult that Jehu was undertaking. He had apparently come to see for himself.

Jehu's cunning was again at work in the slaughter of the prophets of Baal. Under the ruse of zeal for the worship of Baal, he identified all the leaders of the cult and promptly slaughtered them. The temple was then demolished, and the site was desecrated by turning it into a refuse dump or public toilet (2 Kin. 10:27). The specific word used can refer to a latrine or a cesspool. In this way Jehu eliminated Baal in Israel (v. 28).

However, Jehu's zeal against the fertility cult of Baal did not extend to the worship of the golden calves Jeroboam had set up at Bethel and Dan (1 Kin. 12:28–29). That worship, though it used forbidden idols in the conduct of its rituals, still had pretensions of being directed to Yahweh, the true God of Israel, because the nation had strayed so far in their understanding of what true worship was. Thus, despite Jehu's vigorous and violent actions to cleanse Israel of the worship of false gods, he failed in his obligation to end false worship of the true God. The spiritual lesson we can learn from this applies both personally and corporately. Our zeal for reform against obvious wrong can create false confidence and self-satisfaction that blind us to other commonly accepted, and equally dangerous, impediments to our relationship with God. Despite Jehu's failings in this regard, God commended him for bringing the house of Ahab to an end and promised him a son on the throne to the fourth generation. Jehu's was the most enduring dynasty of the Northern Kingdom, and Jehu was the only northern king who is described as having made any attempt to fulfill God's purposes. For him, that purpose was to bring justice to the family of Naboth for the atrocious way in which Ahab and Jezebel had confiscated Naboth's property after arranging for his death (1 Kin. 21:13–16). Jehu's destruction of Ahab's dynasty was a judgment of God and a reminder that God ultimately settles the score of all the injustices that the innocent have suffered throughout history.

However, it was also the case that through Hosea, the word of the Lord made it clear that the bloodshed at Jezreel was much more than God had asked for, so there would be a price to pay (Hos. 1:4). Jehu's dynasty ended in bloodshed, just like Omri's. Zechariah, the fourth and last member of Jehu's dynasty, was murdered in Samaria after only a six-month reign (2 Kin. 15:8–10) This was similar to Jehu's assassination of the last reigning monarch of Omri's line (9:24).

The final description of Jehu's reign outlines the territories that he lost to Hazael of Aram (Syria) because Jehu disregarded God's covenant and slavishly followed in the footsteps of Jeroboam's apostasy (10:31). This was also a fulfillment of Elisha's prophecy concerning Hazael (8:12). As a result, Jehu lost all the territory on the east side of the Jordan (10:32–33)—one of the covenant curses was loss of land (Deut. 28:25, 33, 63). The account of the twenty-eight-year reign of Jehu comes to an end with the usual concluding formula of his burial in Samaria, a reference to the chronicles of the kings for more information, and the naming of the son who replaced him (2 Kin. 10:34–36).

11:1–16. Athaliah of Judah (841–835 B.C.). It is not only the Northern Kingdom that suffered the wholesale loss of its leaders; the kingdom of Judah suffered the same fate under Athaliah, who was the daughter of Ahab and Jezebel, widow of Jehoram (son of Jehosophat, king of Judah), and mother of Ahaziah, whom Jehu had killed.

Though Athaliah is the antagonist in this story, another woman plays a history-changing, positive role. Jehosheba was the sister of Azariah. Whether she herself was also a daughter of Athaliah is not made clear. Athaliah's wickedness, worthy of her parents, was evident in her attempted assassination of all the heirs to the throne. We are left to wonder how Jehosheba was able to hide Joash at the time of the slaughter. One can only admire her resourcefulness in maintaining the secret for so long (vv. 2–3). It seems likely that Jehosheba's standing as a king's daughter, a king's sister, and the wife of the priest Jehoiada gave her more connections and resources to accomplish her ruse than would have been available to the dead king's widow and actual mother of the child. Jehosheba's action reminds us of the resourcefulness of another woman of Scripture who worked to save a future leader from death by hiding him in the rushes of the Nile (Ex. 2:1–3). Whether by familial reflex, political

judgment, or spiritual conviction, or perhaps all three, Jehosheba managed, in a moment of desperate national crisis, to preserve the Davidic line against the invasive machinations of the one remaining individual element of Ahab's dynasty whom Jehu had not killed—Athaliah. It is interesting to reflect on the role of these two women in the lineage of Christ. One, Athaliah, as the mother of Ahaziah, became, in spite of her attempts to destroy that lineage, a direct ancestor of Christ. The other, Jehosheba, who was not directly of the same lineage, worked courageously to preserve it.

The narrative does not explain why Jehoiada waited until Joash was seven years old before staging a coup against Athaliah. Possible reasons include: (1) the presumption that it is easier for a populace to imagine as king a seven-year-old boy than an infant or toddler; or (2) it took time for the baleful effects of Athaliah's oppressive rule to become apparent to the military leaders whose support would be necessary to make the coup successful. In any event, the people and the military leadership were ready, and Jehoiada's detailed organization worked exactly as planned. Some experts have explained that the military contingent was supplied with weapons from the temple to avoid rousing the premature interest or expectation that was likely to occur if other weapons were brought to the event. The narrative doesn't explain why a Sabbath was chosen, but we can assume that it was also to further reduce suspicion that anything momentous was about to occur. It could also be that having the coronation on a Sabbath would add, in retrospect, to the significance of the event. Restoring the Davidic line gave promise of a restoration of the Mosaic covenant, and the Sabbath itself was perhaps the most notable sign of that covenant. It would be a perfect combination of salvific symbolism.

The inauguration process was in fact divided into two parts: first, the coronation, which took place in the inner temple court, and then the enthronement, which took place in the palace. More symbolism was invoked by having the new king stand by one of the pillars of the temple. This act, the significance of which was apparently understood well enough by the people to be considered a royal custom, is seen again in the story of Josiah (2 Kin. 23:3), when he called the nation to renew the covenant after the long, dark years of Manasseh's rule. Jehoiada's success in bringing about this reform, made possible by his wife's earlier wise and courageous act, brought a final end to the dynastic degradation of Ahab and gave Judah one more chance to fulfill the Davidic promise.

The fact that there is no summary statement about the reign of Athaliah suggests that she was not accepted as one of the "kings" in the line of David—which of course she was not.

11:17—12:21. Joash or Jehoash of Judah (835–796 B.C.). Little is said about Joash in his early years apart from his desire to refurbish the temple. Under the influence of Jehoiada, the high priest, he did what was right in the Lord's estimation (12:2). Joash began his reign at the age of only seven (11:21), so it was to some degree inevitable that he would follow someone much older, such as Jehoiada. But when Jehoiada died, the leaders of Judah convinced Joash to go back to the worship of the fertility cult; and Baal worship was reintroduced (2 Chr. 24:17–18). The fact that the high places were not taken away sent a bad signal (2 Kin. 12:3). The same was said of Asa four generations earlier (1 Kin. 15:14). Asa gathered up all the treasures of his kingdom and sent them to the king of Syria (Aram) to pay him to fight against the Northern Kingdom. That opened up the floodgates of unwanted attention from the warlike Arameans, who would continue to plague both Israel and Judah for the next one hundred years until the Assyrians gained the ascendancy. Joash did the same as Asa by using the palace and temple treasuries to persuade the Syrians not to attack Jerusalem (2 Kin. 12:18).

An example of Joash's inexperience in his early years is the way he organized the reparation of the temple. He made the priests responsible for collecting the money and using it for repairs (v. 5). Years later, in his twenty-third year, he realized that the temple had not yet been repaired. So he called the priests together and asked about this problem. Since they did not answer, one can presume there had been a culture of misappropriation, apathy, and compromise among them. At the king's insistence, the priests agreed to collect no further money and not to be involved in the work of repairing the temple (vv. 7–8). Joash's suggestion of a wooden chest to collect public contributions, together with the careful way in which it was counted, bagged, and paid to the tradesmen (vv. 9–16), showed that Joash had matured as a leader.

He also made clear that financial resources would only be used for the work of repairing the temple (vv. 13–14). After the work was complete, the money left over could then be used to obtain vessels of gold and silver for the temple (2 Chr. 24:14). The persons involved in the work of repairing the temple were so trustworthy that no account was required from them (2 Kin. 12:15). This was in obvious contrast to the behavior of the priests.

As noted above, Joash apostatized into idolatry after Jehoiada died, and 2 Chronicles 24:25 indicates that Joash was assassinated by his servants because of his murder of Zechariah, the son of Jehoiada (as well as possibly his brothers—the Hebrew refers to Jehoiada's "sons," but some consider this to be a copyist's error—cf. the LXX), because Zechariah prophesied against Joash.

13:1–9. Jehoahaz of Israel (814–798 B.C.). When Joash was collecting money in a wooden chest to repair the temple, a new king was coming to the throne in the Northern Kingdom: Jehoahaz, son of Jehu. He, like all his predecessors, supported the state religion established by Jeroboam I (v. 2). Consequently, God sent Hazael and later his son Ben-Hadad, kings of Syria, to oppress Israel (v. 3). The oppression was so comprehensive that the northern army was decimated, leaving only fifty in the cavalry, ten chariots, and 10,000 infantry (v. 7), compared to the 2,000 chariots and 10,000 soldiers the Assyrian King Shalmaneser III captured in the battle of Qarqar (854/853 B.C.).

The oppression that the Arameans (Syrians) inflicted upon Israel sent Jehoahaz pleading to God for relief (vv. 4–5). The narrative in Kings follows the pattern that is found in the accounts in the book of Judges: when the people descended into idolatry, God sent an oppressor; when the people repented and prayed for relief, God sent a deliverer. The text does not specify the identity of the deliverer. It could have been the Assyrian King Adad-nirari III, whose conquests into Syria rendered it powerless, or, after the pattern set in the book of Judges, the deliverer could have been a prophet like Elisha or one of his students.

13:10–25. Jehoash or Joash of Israel (798–782 B.C.). The reign of Joash is briefly summarized by the observation that he did evil in the Lord's estimation (v. 11). There was little to say about a life wasted in rebellion against the Lord. It was during the reign of Joash that Elisha died. King Joash visited the aged and sick Elisha and recited the statement Elisha made to Elijah before the latter was taken into the heavens in a "chariot of fire" (v. 14; cf. 2:11–12). It would appear that the king was expecting a chariot to come for Elisha too.

His interaction with the aged prophet may be read with irony and pathos. He came to pay his respects to a man whose leadership he had obviously rejected. We do not know the motivation for the visit. It could have been genuine guilt, or a facile and desperate effort for some kind of deliverance from the Syrians. But even then, the Lord was willing to show His continuing love and concern for a people who had so steadfastly rejected Him. The exercise of shooting the arrows was apparently intended to show Joash God's willingness to favor Israel but also to symbolically demonstrate their leader's characteristic weakness to follow through until the Lord's work was finished. Joash's limited striking of the arrows, strongly rebuked by Elisha (13:18–19), was an effective parable to show his own weakness in accepting the help of the Lord to do what was necessary to achieve ultimate victory.

Probably soon after that conversation, Elisha died and was buried. Sometime later his bones were disturbed when a squad of Moabite raiders interrupted a funeral. The alarmed locals quickly pushed the body into the closest tomb, Elisha's, and before they could escape from the raiders, the corpse of the man came into contact with Elisha's remains and came back to life (vv. 20–21). The story serves to reaffirm the ministry of Elisha as a man of God. But perhaps it also suggests that the God who can raise the dead is also able to revive a dead nation if only they would listen to the message of His dead prophet.

The hardship that followed came from the Syrians (v. 22), but it was tempered by God's compassion and His faithfulness to the covenant made with Abraham, Isaac, and Jacob (v. 23). This divine compassion and faithfulness was manifest when Joash won three significant military victories against the new king of Syria, just as Elisha had prophesied before his death (v. 25). The word of the Lord remained active among His people in spite of their sin.

14:1–22. Amaziah of Judah (796–767 B.C.).

Amaziah came to the throne when he was twenty-five years old, following the assassination of his father Joash (not to be confused with Jehoash/Joash of Israel). Evidently he had a character similar to that of his father: doing the right things but lacking a deep, inner conviction (v. 3). That the right he did was not as his ancestor David had done comports well with the parallel description in the account in 2 Chronicles 25, which says he was not wholehearted in his right doing. These two descriptions, when combined, give us a scriptural understanding of the Davidic ideal of a strong, unhesitating, wholehearted commitment to the Lord. Joash's unfaithfulness is seen in the continuation of the very popular high places and in the worship of the gods he captured from the Edomites (2 Chr. 25:14). The rationale for only executing those directly involved in the assassination and not their families (2 Kin. 14:5–6) was the stipulation in the Mosaic law that fathers were not to be put to death for the wrongs of their children, and children were not to be put to death for the wrongs of their fathers (Deut. 24:16).

Amaziah then attempted to regain some of the territories that used to be part of the kingdom but had been lost to various raiders as divine judgments against a protracted series of apostasies. He successfully won back Sela, a small city on the northern border of Edom, about eighteen miles (29 km) southeast of the southern end of the Dead Sea (2 Kin. 14:7).

The events of Amaziah's reign are described in more detail in 2 Chronicles 25. Of those mentioned in this passage, it should be noted that some interpreters suspect that Amaziah had proposed a marriage alliance between his son and the daughter of Jehoash, king of Israel. When that proposal was rejected, this theory holds, Amaziah prepared for war and Jehoash sent his mocking message to Amaziah in response to the proposed alliance and his overconfidence after having just defeated the Edomites. As the Chronicles account details, that overconfidence was on full display in Amaziah's inexplicable and stupidly brazen (by our logic) honoring of the very gods of the people he had just destroyed.

A defeat in the war with Israel resulted in yet another plunder of Jerusalem, major damage to the wall, and Amaziah's capture and long-term imprisonment. While he was away, the people of Judah chose his son Azariah (Uzziah) as his replacement in a technical, if not meaningful, coregency. When Amaziah was released upon the death of the king of Israel, his return to Judah and his apparent resumption of kingly duties alongside, or instead of, the son who had been selected in his place, was not well received, leading to his assassination. Thus ends the sad saga of a king who, nevertheless, is to be remembered as one who did what was right in the eyes of the Lord.

Both Amaziah and his father started well but were spiritually weak, bowing to the pressures of popular culture and worshiping gods who were unable to protect them.

14:23–29. Jeroboam II of Israel (793–753 B.C.). The rise of Jeroboam II was a new day for Israel. His long and fruitful reign was due in part to the presence of Assyria that kept Syria occupied and away from Israelite territory. But behind the historical events was the hand of the Lord, who appointed Jeroboam II to save Israel from the long-term affliction they had been suffering (vv. 26–27). This was despite the fact that Jeroboam II did not do anything to change the course of evil that Jeroboam I had institutionalized in Israel. His reign was only characterized as evil (v. 24). The Lord was still fighting for the affection of His people.

One impressive accomplishment of Jeroboam II was that he restored to Israel the entire territory east of the Jordan River (v. 25). The prophet Jonah was a great supporter of Jeroboam II, which probably explains why the prophet did not want to go to Nineveh. He may have thought that assisting the Assyrians would hinder the great work Jeroboam was doing in restoring the former glory of Israel. Jeroboam's capture of the territories of the Syrian cities of Damascus and Hamath, which were previously under the control of Judah, was a reminder of the glorious days of Solomon, sadly eroded by the unfaithfulness of the nation. The admission in the narrative that God did not want to blot out the name of Israel from under heaven (vv. 27) adds a very distinct flavor to this particular era. Although the nation was not interested in the Lord and would rather worship Baal, God was not interested in destroying it. God had not yet given up on His people.

15:1–7. Azariah or Uzziah of Judah (792–740 B.C.). The fact that the narrative of Kings devotes only seven verses to Uzziah is not a reflection on his ability and effectiveness as a king but on his spiritual shallowness. He did the right things, but he was not brave enough to touch the entrenched traditions of the syncretistic high places (v. 4). No other king reigned as long as Uzziah—fifty-two years (v. 2). With a weakened Syria and a weakening Assyria, both Northern and Southern Kingdoms enjoyed a period of prosperity not seen since the time of Solomon. Uzziah won back all the land of which the Philistines had regained control (2 Chr. 26:6–7); he accepted tribute from a number of foreign lands; he fortified Jerusalem; he fortified and provided new water supplies for the main areas of agriculture; and he modernized the army and cultivated new military technologies. He was admired and respected throughout the entire region.

However, when he was the strongest, his weaknesses appeared. In line with the normal practice of ANE royalty, he elevated himself to the point that he felt justified going into the temple and offering incense on the altar in the Holy Place (2 Chron. 26:16). It is notable, and perhaps a credit to Uzziah's heretofore faithful leadership, that a large contingent of priests had the courage to confront him for his wrong action. It is easy to imagine that in other times, thoroughly wayward kings would have so completely intimidated the priesthood that such an action would not have been challenged. But like David, who numbered the people against the counsel of Joab (2 Sam. 24:3–4), Uzziah was too proud to back down. It should also be noted that the Lord was obviously still active in the temple and jealous of His prerogatives. In other words, the generally good leadership of Uzziah up to this point had created an environment where God was actively present, and he was furious when he was confronted by this large group of priests and told that he had overstepped the limits of his authority. In the moment of his rage, leprosy broke out on his face and he was taken out of the temple by eighty very determined priests (2 Chron. 26:17–20). The fact that he was in isolation for the rest of his life (2 Kings 15:5) suggests that this form of skin disease was indeed the dreaded disease now known as Hansen's Disease. Consequently, his son Jotham served as coregent until his death.

15:8—17:41
Last Days of the Northern Kingdom

There were only six more kings of Israel before the nation came to an end, and four of them were assassinated. Jehu's dynasty ended when Zechariah was assassinated, and the kings that followed each had single-reign dynasties except for Menahem, whose son succeeded him. The nation finally met its end when the Assyrians defeated them, took the people into exile, and repopulated the land with subjugated peoples from other regions.

15:8–15. Zechariah of Israel (753–752 B.C.) and Shallum of Israel (752 B.C.). Zechariah was from the fourth generation of Jehu's sons. According to the word of the Lord, he would be the last one (10:28–31). Zechariah's reign lasted only six months before he was assassinated in a palace plot (15:10). His reign is summarized like all the others: he did what was evil in the Lord's estimation, and he practiced the sins of

Jeroboam. His sad end is yet another indication of the intimate connection there seems to be between a people's faith and their success. A bad king appears to be a reflection of the bad society from which he comes, and the short reign of a king is usually indicative of social upheaval. After a few decades of prosperity, it now appears that Israel was entering a period of turmoil and hardship. In the death of Zechariah, the biblical writer recognized the fulfillment of the word of the Lord that He spoke to Jehu (v. 12).

Shallum may have been one of Zechariah's generals who probably did not have the full support of his colleagues when he assassinated the king. It is uncertain whether Jabesh was his father or his hometown; but either way, Shallum probably was from Gilead in the tribal lands of Gad if Shallum and Menahem were from the same tribe, and Menahem's father's name is a reflection of the tribe's name. His reign only lasted one month (v. 13). There is no value judgment on his reign, perhaps because it was too short. More space is given to the one who plotted against him: Menahem.

15:16–22. Menahem of Israel (752–742 B.C.).
It appears that Menahem was from the same tribe as Shallum, and he probably eliminated Shallum because he was working against his own clan. Menahem's father was Gadi, which is possibly an indication of a link to the tribe of Gad. Menahem was much more successful and enjoyed more support than Shallum. It is not clear from the text whether Menahem attacked Tiphsah (v. 16) just before or just after he ascended the throne. Tiphsah was the northernmost point of Solomon's realm (1 Kin. 4:24) and was the site of a major crossing of the Euphrates River. Its modern name is Dibseh, and it is located in modern Syria. The fact that Israel's army was so far from home suggests that the prosperity and expansion brought in by Jeroboam II still inspired their nationalistic hopes.

During Menahem's reign the Assyrian king attacked, devastating the Northern Kingdom financially. The king who attacked was Tiglath-Pileser III, also known as Pul. Assyrian kings usually had two names: their Assyrian name and a Babylonian one. Tiglath-Pileser III was also known by his Babylonian name, Pulu, and the author of Kings shortened it to Pul (cf. 1 Chr. 5:26).

Menahem took the required money from the wealthy. Each of the super-rich (literally in Hebrew, "the mighty of wealth") were taxed 50 shekels of silver (2 Kin. 15:20), about 1.25 pounds (0.5 kg), which means there were nearly 57,000 of them in Israel—an indication of the financial strength that was reached under Jeroboam II. But this desperate measure also hints at the nation's approaching end. The summary of Menachem's reign characterizes it as evil and not departing from the sins of Jeroboam I (v. 18). It refers to further records of his accomplishments elsewhere and that he was buried with his fathers. His son Pekahiah replaced him on the throne.

15:23–31. Pekahiah (742–740 B.C.) and Pekah of Israel (752–732 B.C.).
Pekahiah only reigned two years before being killed in the citadel of the palace by another influential Gileadite, Pekah.

Pekah's reign seems to have been quite long and stable, lasting twenty years—an indication that he had more popular support than his predecessors. However, he too followed his predecessors in maintaining the evil of Jeroboam's idolatry.

In his days the imperial ambitions of Assyria's Tiglath-Pileser III led to the capture of large areas of Israel (v. 29). First Ijon was captured, a city at the far north of the country, about thirty-five miles (56.3 km) north of the Sea of Galilee, then Abel-Beth-Maachah fell, about twenty-six miles (41.8 km) south of that. Hazor was the next city to fall. It was an important military outpost about nine miles (14.5 km) north of the Sea of Galilee, set on a ridge with a commanding view of the entire area. This was a major blow to Israel's military. The Assyrians kept pressing south to Kedesh, on the southwestern shores of the Sea of Galilee, effectively securing control of the entire region of Galilee. They then secured the region of Gilead (the home region of Pekah). Mentioned in the list of captured towns and regions (v. 29) is Janoah, in the territory of Samaria and only about twelve miles (19.3 km) southeast of Samaria. Janoah was on the west side of the Jordan River and the newly captured region of Gilead was on the eastern side. Israel was becoming increasingly hemmed in.

Part of the imperial policy of Assyria was to uproot a people and scatter them in other areas of its empire, replacing them with foreigners gathered from across the empire. This seems to have been intended to break national and tribal identity and solidarity. It meant that the tie between the tribes of Israel and their inheritance in the promised land was now severed—they were exiled and replaced by foreigners. Israel had less than ten more years before this process was completed and the Northern Kingdom ceased to exist. In 722 B.C. the Assyrians would return and complete what had just begun.

15:32—16:20. Jotham (750–732 B.C.) and Ahaz of Judah (735–716 B.C.). Jotham came to the throne just two years after his northern counterpart Pekah. Jotham was another Judean king who did what was expedient in following God, even to the point of embellishing the temple complex, but he did not remove the high places (v. 35). The major event during his reign was the buildup of military tensions with the Northern Kingdom, which had renewed its ties with Syria (v. 37). This tension reached its climax in the reign of Jotham's son Ahaz, who probably reigned for a few years as coregent with his father before his death (v. 38).

Whereas Jotham tried to make things look good, Ahaz cut the ties to God and went the way of the kings of the Northern Kingdom. In former times, when the people's corruption sank to a lower level, God sent judgment on them in the form of foreign invaders. The same pattern followed Ahaz's apostasy—this time the invaders were an alliance between Israel and Aram (Syria; 16:5).

The text makes clear that the primary motivation for Ahaz's promotion of the worship of other gods, despite the "good king" legacy of his father and grandfather, was of his own apostate volition and in admiration of the degenerate worship practices in the Northern Kingdom. More of his open disdain for the faith of his fathers is recorded in Isaiah 7. That narrative describes how he disdained the promises of God to rescue him from the invasion and instead chose to rely on an alliance with Assyria. Thus, some of his actions in changing the rituals at the temple and some of its architecture, as recorded in 2 Kings 16:10–18, may also have been politically motivated. His apparent appreciation for the design of the altar he saw in Damascus, where he met the Assyrian king, and his arrangements for erecting a copy in the temple in Jerusalem may have been part of his plan to show obeisance to Tiglath-Pileser for his help against the Arameans. The text clearly states that his change of the royal entryway to the temple was done for that purpose (v. 18). Historians have noted that Assyria made it a matter of policy to require subordinate peoples to pay homage to their overlord's favorite deities. Whether that was exactly the dynamic operating here is not explicit, but certainly Ahaz was not resisting the pattern.

The brazen nature of Ahaz's apostasy is evident in his personal involvement in the offering of sacrifices (vv. 12–13). That was the very act that God had punished by striking his grandfather, Uzziah, with leprosy (2 Chron. 26:17–20).

The narrative books of the Bible present many cases such as this where God's professed people seem willfully indifferent to the explicit lessons from the past about reward and punishment, and blessings and curses. It is a stark and sobering reminder to readers of today, having no claim to evident moral superiority, to beware of engaging in the same folly. Ahaz's reign proved to be very costly—it drew the attention of Assyria to Israel and Syria, resulting in the death of the Syrian king and the scattering of the inhabitants of Damascus. This was a stark indication of what would happen not just to Israel but to Judah as well. Assyrian worship practices were now imposed upon the kingdom of Judah, which not only reduced their faith to the level of the dominant culture, but also put the entire nation, and its messianic future, in jeopardy.

17:1–6. Hoshea of Israel (732–722 B.C.). Hoshea was the last of the kings of the Northern Kingdom of Israel. His reign was characterized by the intriguing description of him doing evil, but not like his predecessors (v. 2). The narrative follows with a description of the incursions of Shalmaneser V, successor to Tiglath-Pileser III of Assyria. Hoshea used the opportunity of Assyrian political transition and instability to ally himself with Egypt, hoping for the Egyptians to reassert some of their former glory and free the Israelites from the Assyrian yoke. In the ANE the transition of power from one king to the next often spurred attempts by a number of vassal nations to try to regain independence from their overlords, but this backfired for Hoshea.

The account in Kings mentions the name So, the Hebrew version of an Egyptian name that is difficult to connect with any specific pharaoh. It may possibly be Osorkon IV (730 to c.a. 715 B.C.), who ruled from his capital at Tanis over the eastern delta region bordering the promised land, or it may be a high official of that time. Isaiah's condemnation of Israel's reliance on Tanis (using the Hebrew version of its name, Zoan; Is. 19:11–13; 30:1–5), which was the northern capital of Egypt at this time, supports either of these options. However, Hoshea miscalculated the resolve and military capacity of both the powerful Assyrians and the weakened Egyptians. The new Assyrian king was greatly angered when he discovered Hoshea's plot. Shalmaneser V reacted swiftly, both to punish Israel and to minimize Egypt's influence in the region. Hoshea was taken prisoner (2 Kin. 17:4).

Shalmaneser V now swept through Israel besieging Samaria (v. 5). The narrative in Kings recounts that the siege took three years, which is testament either to the very effective fortifications of the city or that Shalmaneser V died and was replaced by another, which caused another period of instability. Records of the time state that both Shalmaneser V and Sargon II (his successor) were responsible for deporting the inhabitants of Samaria. But it was Sargon who claimed that he broke the siege. When Samaria fell, its people were scattered across the northwestern reaches of the Assyrian empire—Halah, by the Habor River, Gazan, and the cities of the Medes (v. 6). These were towns and territories located in what are now the Kurdish regions of eastern Turkey and Armenia.

17:7–23. Rationale for the Destruction of Israel.

Following the description of the windup of the nation of Israel, there is an extended explanation why such a drastic action occurred. The people sinned against the Lord, who had freed them from the bondage of Egypt, by giving their allegiance to other gods (v. 7). Following this brief introductory statement, the narrative unpacks a litany of wrongs. First, they patterned their life after other nations (v. 8). The Hebrew word *khuqqah*—variously rendered as "statutes," "practices," or "customs"—refers to appropriate behaviors that respected the boundaries of personal conduct, and it has a religious rather than a legal focus. The term also contains an element of divine promise—the undergirding principle that sustains the covenant. Instead of being in harmony with the covenant, the Israelites were more concerned about being in conformity with the surrounding cultures, even if that meant violating their corporate conscience and identity and abandoning their God. This was rendered even more distasteful since it was the very nations that God drove out of the promised land—because of their crimes against humanity—that the covenant people were trying to emulate.

Next, they secretly did things against the Lord that were not right (v. 9). The text specifies these behaviors as their construction of numerous shrines in forests, fields, cities, and hilltops, setting up the trappings of worship borrowed from the surrounding nations. These included ritual stone slabs or columns (both have been found by archaeologists), wooden representations of the fertility goddess (the Asherah poles or pillars; v. 10), offering sacrifices and incense (it seems that anybody could do this without the need of specially consecrated priests), and serving idols—all of which God had warned them not to do (vv. 11–12).

But above all, the nation of Israel spurned the appeals and warnings from numerous prophets and seers. The word of the Lord came to the people through these prophets, but they did not listen. The prophets' common theme had been warnings to turn from their evil ways and to observe God's prescribed principles (v. 13). These stipulations cover the code of moral behavior and the obligations of the covenant, both couched in a relationship with God. However, the people persistently refused to cooperate, and each succeeding generation chose to remain committed to the rebellion of the previous generations. They rejected all that God tried to offer them and became instead firm followers of the idols of the nations that God had specifically charged them to drive from the land because of their idolatry and crimes against humanity (vv. 15–16). One of these crimes was the practice of burning their babies in the fire as sacrifices. Together with this, they also became involved in witchcraft and taking notice of omens, selling themselves (like prostitutes) to do evil and provoke God (v. 17).

Since Israel was so intent on copying the nations in every aspect, God gave them the same fate. None of the surrounding nations of that time exist today as a nation, and their gods are only found in history books. The ten tribes of the Northern Kingdom were to have a similar end (vv. 18, 20). However, Judah was not left out of this. They too copied Israel (v. 19). Their "lamp" (1 Kin. 11:36; 15:4; 2 Kin. 8:19) was kept burning so that God could keep His promise of the coming Messiah. If Judah at least was not preserved, there could not be the Messiah as God had promised His people.

Because of a deep-seated rebellion in the houses of both Judah and Israel, the original united kingdom was torn apart. Israel's first king, Jeroboam I, drove Israel away from God (17:21). Each successive generation of Israelites followed the pattern set by Jeroboam, until Israel was removed from its land and scattered across Assyrian lands. God's response to Israel's apostasy is summarized in v. 20. Moses foretold this and described the land as vomiting out its inhabitants if they rejected God (Lev. 18:24–28). The summary of the sins of the nation closes by saying that the Lord removed Israel away from Him just as He had foretold by His prophets (2 Kin. 17:23). Their exile was not the result of the religious or military superiority of their enemies. It was the powerful fulfillment of the word of the Lord in judgment against a rebellious people.

17:24-41. Israel's Repopulation. True to Assyrian tradition, people were uprooted from a number of Babylonian cities and transplanted in the land of Israel (v. 24). This helped to break the resolve of the two subdued people-groups (Assyria controlled both Babylon and Israel) and to foster greater cohesion and loyalty for the Assyrian regime. The narrative specifically mentions the towns of Cuthah (Kutha), which was about twenty-five miles (40.2 km) northeast of Babylon, Ava (Ivah) and Sepharvaim, which were close together (near the ancient city of Accad and the modern city of Fallujah)—all of which were on or near the Euphrates River. Hamath, about 130 miles (209.2 km) north of Damascus, was on the Orontes River in modern Syria. The inhabitants of these cities were then transplanted into Israel's deserted cities and the nation was renamed Samaria, becoming one of the provinces of Assyria (v. 24).

The people sent to repopulate Israel did not know God's *mishpat* (v. 26)—variously rendered in this context as "custom," "rituals," "what the god of the land requires," and so forth. The most basic meaning is "judgments," and in Israel's case refers to issues of social justice and the way they needed to care for the needy (orphans and widows) and destitute (Deut. 10:18; Is. 1:17; Jer. 22:3). Without that religious background, the foreigners would not be able to please God.

One priest was allowed to return home to teach the new inhabitants. He established his base in Bethel, the site of one of the golden calves that Jeroboam established (1 Kin. 12:28-33) and the former location of the wilderness sanctuary (2 Kin. 17:28). It is nearly certain that he taught the new inhabitants the hybrid religion of Israel that saw God represented as a golden calf. Each people group brought their own gods with them and their traditional worship forms as well (v. 29). They served both their own idols and the God of Israel.

In commenting on these aberrations, the narrative points to the genuine form of worship that God intends His people to follow. Rituals are fine as long as they are not disjointed from a life grounded on God's principles (v. 34). True religion impacts the whole person and the whole of life's experience; God's version of religion was based on a commitment to the covenant (v. 35). However, being in a covenant relationship brings responsibilities. The human part was to avoid worshiping other gods and worshiping with thanksgiving the One who freed His people from slavery and oppression. If God is kept as a close and precious companion, there is no need to fear any evil (v. 39).

Right up to the time of the writing of Kings, the new people of the province of Samaria also served their idols and passed on the rituals to each successive generation (v. 41).

18:1—25:30
THE SOUTHERN KINGDOM

The book of 2 Kings concentrates now on the last eight kings of the Southern Kingdom of Judah. Only Hezekiah and Josiah are described as doing what was right in the sight of the Lord, while the other six kings followed the idolatrous pattern set for them by the northern kings.

18:1—20:21
Hezekiah Reigns

Hezekiah had the courage to break a national tradition of tolerating the high places and the custom of venerating Moses's bronze serpent. He reclaimed territory lost to the Philistines and, facing the threat of a vast Assyrian army, placed his trust in God. His spectacular successes were blunted by two moments of weakness. First, he used gold and silver from the temple and palace to bribe the Assyrians into a peace deal. Second, when visited by Babylonian dignitaries in response to his miraculous healing, he chose self-glorification.

18:1-12. Hezekiah Ascends the Throne (716-687 B.C.). Verses 3-5 state that there was no other king like Hezekiah, who alone acted like his ancestor David. A similar statement is made concerning Josiah, but there are different emphases: Hezekiah's trust is highlighted in the former, and Josiah's adherence to the law in the latter. He was the first king to do something about the shrines and high places that Solomon had first popularized at the end of his reign. Hezekiah wasted no time in breaking and burning the stone and wooden objects of the fertility cult that cluttered each of the shrines and high places, effectively destroying them. He broke into pieces the bronze serpent made by Moses (v. 4; Num. 21:5-9). Its name, *nekhushtan*, is a play on the words for "serpent" and "bronze" and would have been understood by some as the healing serpent god of the ancient world and by others in a derogatory way as "that bronze thing."

Hezekiah is praised above all of the kings of Judah for the level of his trust in God and his faithfulness to the covenant (2 Kin. 18:5-6). He was not hampered by the curses of the covenant as other kings were. Hezekiah was therefore able to free himself from Assyrian control and to regain control of both the cities and the agricultural lands of Philistia (v. 8). The next narrative (vv. 9–11) recaps the last days of the Northern Kingdom (cf. 17:5–6), providing a rationale for the drastic measures that God took (18:12; cf. 17:7–23, 33–40).

18:13–16. Assyria Invades Judah. As noted earlier, Ahaz's unwise interactions with the Assyrians inevitably attracted their attention to the possibilities of profitable conquest in the broader regions of the Holy Land, particularly in Judah. About twenty years later, the armies of Sennacherib, the Assyrian king, were outside the walls of Jerusalem after decimating the rest of the country.

Hezekiah's first tactic, like that of his unwise father, was to pay a tribute by stripping the temple of much of its valuable property. The temple walls, floor, and doors had all been stripped of their gold when Pharaoh Shishak invaded during the time of Rehoboam (1 Kin. 14:25–26). It appears that Hezekiah had tried to reverse this (2 Kin. 18:16) at least in part; but when Sennacherib invaded, Hezekiah chose to take the gold back off of the doors and pillars and offer it as tribute rather than turn to God for help.

18:17—19:37. Siege of Jerusalem. Unfortunately, instead of satisfying the Assyrian king, this generous gift had the opposite effect. He concluded that perhaps there were more treasures locked up in the city and sent three senior officers with an army to Jerusalem. They stood beside the same pool that Isaiah stood by when assuring King Ahaz of divine victory (v. 17; cf. Is. 7:3–4). The Tartan was the senior military officer, the Rabsaris was the chief eunuch or court official (cf. Dan 1:3), and the Rabshakeh was the king's chief advisor.

The story of the confrontation at the wall of Jerusalem and its aftermath is remarkable for its dramatic interest, and that may be why it is one of the few narratives that is recorded in varying detail in three separate passages in Scripture (2 Kin. 18:17–37; 2 Chr. 32; Is. 36). This is a case in which the conflict is explicitly described as one between the armies of God's people and the Assyrians and between the Assyrian gods and Yahweh. The Lord is directly contrasted with the pagan gods and declared by the Assyrians to be incompetent to save. Therefore the resolution of the narrative is extremely important in that it typifies the ultimate resolution of the cosmic conflict when the Lord permanently defeats all spiritual powers and rescues His people.

In the first message, the Assyrian emissaries offered objective evidence to support their convictions. They pointed to their unquestionable military superiority and to the superiority of their gods by insinuating that since the Hebrew God had not saved other Hebrew cities He could not, or would not, save Jerusalem. The gods of other nations had not been able to deliver their cities from the Assyrians (2 Kin. 18:33–35). The emissaries also made some daring claims. They argued that Hezekiah could not rely on His own God because the destruction of the high places where the people worshiped Him had most probably angered his God (v. 22). In order to provide a religious foundation to their attack against Jerusalem, the Assyrians claimed that the Hebrews' own God had authorized the invasion (v. 23). To what extent this might have been true cannot be known from the record. But there are other places where Scripture indicates that God instructed (2 Chr. 35:21) or goaded (Ex. 4:21; 9:16; 12:12) otherwise evil powers to act as His agents for purposes of judgment. If the claim was truthful, then God had moved them to go against Jerusalem to defeat and humiliate them by displaying His majesty and power over humans and false gods.

The Assyrian emissaries were not interested in diplomacy but in breaking the spiritual backbone of the people and the king. This is made clear in the spurned request that the Assyrians speak in Aramaic, the common language of diplomacy at the time. The Assyrian emissaries instead engaged in vigorous military and religious propaganda to undermine any confidence the Hebrews might have had in their own God or in Hezekiah's leadership.

The response of the people was not to respond to the arguments of the Assyrians. They did not utter a word. Their silence indicated that Hezekiah still had their full confidence because it was on his specific orders that they chose not to respond (2 Kin. 18:36). How tempting it would have been to try to defend Hezekiah, his reforms, or their God with vigorous, noble, and defiant speeches. But this was one of those many times in institutional or personal conflict when considered silence is the most effective defensive weapon.

Nevertheless, the presence of the Assyrian emissaries created distress among God's people. In his message to Isaiah (19:3–4), Hezekiah described the day with three specific and meaningful terms: *tsarah* ("trouble" or "distress"), *tokekhah* ("rebuke"), and *ne'atsah* ("contempt," "disgrace," or "blasphemy"). In other biblical passages, *tsarah* is described as the consequence of gross injustice (Gen. 42:21) or of the absence of God (Deut. 31:17). In most cases it is something from which God delivers His people (e.g., Gen. 35:3; 1 Kin. 1:29; Jer. 30:7; Pss. 34:18; 50:15). It is the anguish caused by a threat to human existence that only God can resolve.

This experience was viewed as a rebuke in the sense of feeling that the people were under God's condemnation, as insinuated by the Assyrians. But it was also a day of humiliation, contempt, and even blasphemy against God. Isaiah's response to Hezekiah's message filled the hearts of the people and the king with hope: God Himself was to fight for His people by causing the Assyrian king to return to his land where he would die (2 Kin. 19:6-7). Would the people listen to the word of the Lord or to the threats of the Assyrian emissaries? Faith must learn to take a simple promise from the Lord for what it is—absolute assurance—because nothing can be more assured than the word of the Lord.

Sennacherib's second message to Hezekiah, delivered by letter (vv. 8-13), simply put the arrogance and blasphemy of the first message in writing. Hezekiah took the letter to the very presence of God—the One who had been maligned by the Assyrians—in His temple to express his trust in the Lord (vv. 15-19). The primary concern of the king was God's honor, reputation, and power. Hezekiah wanted all the earth to acknowledge that Yahweh alone is God.

The Lord's response to Hezekiah came through Isaiah in three parts (vv. 21-34). The first part of this reply was a taunting song directly addressed to Sennacherib for the enjoyment of the Hebrews, describing, among other things, Jerusalem's ultimate victory, the folly of Sennacherib's blasphemy against God, and the stark if unrecognized reality of his complete subservience to the will of God (vv. 21-28).

The second part was addressed directly to Hezekiah (vv. 29-31), promising in specific detail a timeline for the restoration of the fortunes of his people as illustrated by a schedule of their food supply. The wording used was the very language of the sabbatical year (Lev. 25:20-22), even of the Jubilee year, a reference that thus signified the coming of a time of freedom and restoration.

The third part filled out in more specific detail what the future of Sennacherib's military campaign would be and what would happen to Sennacherib himself (2 Kin. 19:32-34). While the exact details were not given, it didn't take long to see the evidence. The deliverance came in a stunning manner that has no parallel anywhere in Scripture (v. 35) and that would have brought to mind among the faithful a remembrance of the death and deliverance on the Passover night of the Exodus.

20:1-11. Hezekiah's Illness and Recovery. This narrative does not follow chronologically from the previous chapter and most likely describes what happened about three years earlier. Several factors lead to this conclusion: it better fits the historical context of the Babylonian characters involved (v. 12), it describes much treasure being shown off (v. 13), and Assyria was still seen as a major threat to Jerusalem (v. 6).

The sickness that afflicted Hezekiah was probably an ulcerated sore or boil (v. 7) that gave him a raging infection that was about to overwhelm his life (v. 1). Isaiah's visit, with the doleful message of Hezekiah's impending and premature death (he was only thirty-nine) provoked a natural response from one who obviously saw himself as a faithful servant of God. The image of turning his face to the wall (v. 2) should probably be understood as an act of intense devotion, of shutting himself immediately off from the world for deep, earnest communion with God. The immediacy of God's response to Hezekiah's desperate plea is amazing because Isaiah was still on his way out of the palace when the Lord instructed him to return with a different message for Hezekiah. This must rank among the quickest direct answers to specific prayer recorded in Scripture. Isaiah's message doubtlessly brought great joy to Hezekiah. While there are examples in Scripture when God informed people of their *imminent* death, such as the stories concerning Aaron (Num. 20:24), Moses (Deut. 32:48-52), the false prophet Hananiah (Jer. 28:16), and the wicked king Ahaziah (2 Kings 1:16-17), there is no other case except that of Christ (Dan. 9:26-27) where the very year of a person's death is predicted so long in advance.

To what extent Isaiah's prescription of a fig poultice had any direct therapeutic role in Hezekiah's healing cannot be known. The exercise may have been yet another example in Scripture where one is instructed to perform some apparently arbitrary physical action as a sign of faith in the Lord's miraculous work (Ex. 14:16; 17:16; 2 Kin. 4:1-7; 5:9-15; John 9:1-7). Hezekiah's request for a sign is not condemned as a lack of unquestioning faith. Asking God for a specific sign of assurance of what He will do is different from ignoring or denying what He has done for us in the past as evidence of His care.

The fulfillment of Hezekiah's wise choice for a sign leaves much room for contemplation of the miracle. The turning back of the shadow on the sundial was noted in Babylon (cf. PK 344.3), which assures us that this was not an isolated miracle for Hezekiah's benefit but was a sign to the world that God is in complete control of the creation He has made. How He accomplished it, aside from simply rotating the earth in the wrong direction for the allotted time, is not known.

20:12–21. Visitors from Babylon. Berodach-Baladan (v. 12) was a distortion of a foreign ruler's name. Isaiah's spelling of the name, Merodach-Baladan (Is. 39:1), is closer to the Babylonian equivalent: Marduk-apal-idinna. Accordingly, some translations have "Marduk-Baladan" in both places. He ruled over Babylon in two terms from 721 to 710 B.C. and again for a brief time from 704 to 703 B.C. It is not certain why he sent envoys and gifts to Hezekiah. Unquestionably, reports of the miraculous sign and healing reached Babylon, and the king wanted to know more about the God who would do this.

The record of Hezekiah's naivete in dealing with the Babylonian emissaries is a sad but potent reminder of the consequences of doing things in our own way and forgetting to ask God for guidance in the fulfillment of our duties and the nature of our witness. How much different might the result have been if Hezekiah had thought to consult with Isaiah, or had just prayed earnestly to God, before the arrival of the guests.

The story of Hezekiah, a good king like no other except David, is a stark caution to those who profess faith in God and who may have a stellar reputation for all the positive things they have accomplished. Unrestrained pride or momentary carelessness can undo it all in a moment. Past accomplishments do not protect a person from making unwise decisions that could have a negative impact on their future. While under the spotlight of honor and glory, Hezekiah gloated in self-importance and directed the Babylonian emissaries to his own treasures (2 Kin. 20:13). Instead, he should have shared with them the goodness of a life lived in a covenant relationship with the God of Israel.

In spite of this mistake at the end of his life, Hezekiah was remembered as a good king who accomplished much for God and His people, including, most importantly, bringing people back to a right worship of God. Aside from the religious reforms, he expanded the city of Jerusalem and had a massive tunnel constructed to bring water from a spring outside the city walls into a pool inside, which allowed the city to endure a much longer siege in times of war (for more on Hezekiah's Tunnel, see "Archaeology and the Bible," p. 77).

21:1–26
Manasseh and Amon and the Sealing of Judah's Doom

Manasseh was born after Hezekiah had been healed. Seemingly all that Hezekiah had worked for was reversed by his son and later by his grandson. The extent of this moral degradation is described as surpassing that of the Canaanites whom God evicted from the land. To be consistent, God now had to evict this nation from the land as well.

21:1–18. Manasseh (697–643 B.C.). The name of Manasseh's mother, Hephzibah, means "my delight is in her" (cf. Is. 62:4). It ironically expresses God's desire for His covenant people. Manasseh was only twelve years old when he became king, so presumably his mother's influence was still quite strong. Yet there is no indication that Manasseh took God seriously. The first thing he did was to rebuild all the high places and reinstall altars and images both in the shrines and in the temple (2 Kin. 21:3–4).

Manasseh set up altars (and their accompanying shrines) for the astral cult in both the priests' court and the outer court (v. 5). He also placed a carved image for Asherah in the temple building itself (v. 7). With a sense of outrage, the narrative states that this latter action was a direct affront to God and His desire to place His name in the temple. The contrast is rather startling—God, who asked not to be represented by any human-made object, had now been sidelined by a piece of wood, carved according to the fancy of some artisan, which was now being worshiped by a people who seemed oblivious to their own spiritual history, heritage, and future.

Just as Samaria had been destroyed because of its rejection of the Lord, so too would Jerusalem be wiped clean because of its filth (v. 13). This means that God would bring the covenant relationship to an end, delivering His people into the hands of their enemies (vv. 14–15). This would in fact be a temporary but necessary measure to ensure that a remnant would survive and that the Messiah would come from them. This harsh judgment on the remnant of God's inheritance (v. 14) needs to be balanced with what Micah recorded about the same remnant: God would one day pardon them (Mic. 7:18). The prophet Zechariah announced that God was determined to restore the remnant (Zech. 8:11–15). Without strong discipline, the remnant would have no future. Only God's word of judgment could reverse their course toward annihilation. The purpose of God's judgments is always for the salvation of His people, not for their destruction.

The fertility cult of Canaan, which was founded on blatant sex and financial greed, was also suffused with a lack of respect for human life. Hence it is not surprising that Manasseh filled Jerusalem with blood (2 Kin. 21:16). This was directly related to his idolatry. It is possible that the garden in which he was finally buried (vv. 17–18) was one dedicated to a Canaanite astral deity (v. 3). Intriguingly, 2 Kings does not report Manasseh's repentance during his captivity in Assyria, where he was led to recognize that the Lord was God (2 Chr. 33:10–13). Ultimately, even this did not save Jerusalem from the coming judgment described in Kings.

21:19–26. Amon (643–641 B.C.). Amon followed his father to continue the worst corruption that Judah had seen. He forsook the Lord and continued promoting and practicing the idolatry of his father (vv. 20–22). Amon only reigned two years (v. 19) before he was killed in a palace plot (v. 23). Evidently this was not a popular move, and the perpetrators were hunted down and killed in a popular backlash. They put Amon's eight-year-old son, Josiah, on the throne to replace him (v. 24). Amon was buried with his father in the garden tomb, which was possibly a last act of worship to an astral deity (v. 26).

22:1—23:30
Josiah's Reforms Delay the End

Josiah's activities as a young man paralleled much of what his forbearer Joash did eight generations, or about two hundred years, before. His enthusiasm in restoring the temple, the use of a wooden chest to collect money, his trust in the workmen who did their work faithfully and well, plus the godly influence of his mother—all of these factors slowed down the progress of the nation toward an inevitable disaster.

22:1–2. Josiah Ascends the Throne (641–609 B.C.). Josiah was only eight years old when he became king. His mother's name means "well beloved," and her father's name means "witness of the Lord." They were God-fearing people from the Judean heartland, and their son took their godly influence to heart. Fortunately, Josiah's mother and her family had more influence on the boy than his father. The description of Josiah walking in all the ways of David was a positive one that few kings received. The statement that he did not turn aside to the left or to the right (v. 2) is an expression that shows Josiah's faithfulness in every detail.

22:3–20. The Book of the Law. Josiah was stung by what he had learned from an old scroll found in the temple and wanted to know how to deal with the divine consequences of all the depravity of his people (vv. 11–13). It is likely that the scroll they found was Deuteronomy, which describes the results of breaking the covenant with God. The text underlines the confusion of Josiah's leadership circle as they asked themselves why such a calamity befell the land. They would then understand, according to the book, that this was the result of abandoning God and worshiping idols (Deut. 29:23–28). What the book said perfectly mirrored the condition of Judah. The word of God spoken to Moses anticipated the future condition of the people.

23:1–24. Josiah's Reforms. The gathering of the elders attracted the attention of the entire city, and they all made their way to the temple where they heard Josiah read from the old scroll as he stood by one of the two pillars outside the entrance to the Holy Place (v. 3). This was a significant gesture that repeated what Joash had done when he was installed as king—and which followed the tradition for all kings (11:14).

There Josiah committed himself to covenant loyalty to the Lord, pledging compliance to His commandments. The narrative says that everyone assembled there followed the king's lead (23:3). This paralleled the challenge Joshua gave to the people at the end of his life to choose which God they would serve, after which he affirmed that he and his household would serve the Lord (Josh. 24:15). Elijah did much the same on Mount Carmel (1 Kin. 18:21–22). Josiah's profession of faith is an example for spiritual leaders of God's people throughout the ages.

Josiah inspired the most far-reaching reform the nation had ever seen, beginning in the temple, then throughout Jerusalem, in all Judea, and the province of Samaria (cf. Acts 1:8). As a part of this reform, he ensured that all priests throughout Judah participated in the desecration of the illicit worship sites (2 Kin. 23:8). This implies that they were unable to participate in legitimate priestly rituals until they had been cleansed of ritual defilement. The intriguing reference to the gates that were a part of this ground-shaking reform is illustrated by the many podium-like cultic structures associated with city gates that have been excavated in Israel (e.g., at Bethsaida and Dan). Idolatry did not require hills and mountains but was facilitated by regular city architecture.

One of the most significant high places they desecrated was in the valley of Topheth (v. 10), which had been dedicated to Molech for the fiery sacrifice of babies (see Jer. 7:31). Defiling Topheth effectively ended its cultic use, and from this point on it just served as the city rubbish dump, where trash rather than babies fueled its never-ending fires. The place took on eschatological symbolism when Jesus used it to describe hellfire (Matt. 5:22; 10:28; 23:15, 33).

The narrative gives extensive details of Josiah's work to rid Judah and the territory of the now-defunct Northern Kingdom of the symbols, the structures, and even the personnel of all false and idolatrous worship. It was the most thorough physical deconstruction of false worship in the history of Judah, clearing out worship places from as far back as the time of Solomon, three hundred years before.

Once this work was completed, Josiah returned to Jerusalem and organized the most extensive and impressive Passover held since the time of the judges (2 Kin. 23:21–23). To complete the reforms, Josiah literally swept away spirit mediums and practitioners of the occult together with all types of fertility idols. All these actions were done in obedience to the law of Moses found in the scroll that Hilkiah the priest had discovered (v. 24).

23:25–30. Josiah Meets His End.
Despite Josiah's unique zeal for getting the nation back on track, it was not enough to prevent the impending judgment brought on by generations of apathy toward God and especially by the excesses of Manasseh's reign (vv. 25–26). Judah would end up like Israel, despite God's intention to permanently dwell there (v. 27). But God would find a way to fulfill His saving word, namely, through the coming Messiah. God always preserves a remnant of His people.

Following the concluding statement of Josiah's reign (vv. 25–28), there is a description of how he met his end. He took it upon himself to halt the advance of Pharaoh Necho, who was on his way to join the Assyrians in battle against the new rising superpower, Babylon. But Josiah was killed by the Egyptians at Megiddo (v. 29). His body was taken back to Jerusalem, and his son Jehoahaz replaced him on the throne (v. 30).

23:31—25:30
Judah's Last Days

The remaining four kings of Judah are all characterized as doers of evil. In their days the Babylonians had become the superpower, but in its death throes Egypt made some last excursions into Judah. The Egyptians took Jehoahaz, the son of Josiah, to Egypt, where he died in prison. His three successors were each subjected to Babylon and met the compounding wrath of the Babylonian army when they tried to rebel.

23:31–37. Jehoahaz (609 B.C.) and Jehoiakim (609–598 B.C.).
Shallum was Josiah's fourth son (1 Chr. 3:15), and his royal name was Jehoahaz. It seems unusual that he was chosen before his three older brothers. Josiah's firstborn son was overlooked (unless he died in childhood) and so were the next two older brothers, Jehoiakim and Zedekiah. Jehoahaz's brief three-month reign was characterized as evil (2 Kin. 23:31–32). Necho took Jehoahaz prisoner and cut his reign short, sending him to Egypt where he eventually died (v. 34). Necho appointed Josiah's second son, Eliakim, as a puppet king and changed his name to Jehoiakim (v. 34). Jehoiakim's first duty was to pay the tribute imposed by Necho (v. 33), and consequently he imposed a heavy tax on the land to meet the obligation (v. 35).

24:1–7. The Exile (605 B.C.).
The regional politics worsened for Judah when Babylon gained supremacy in the region by defeating the Assyrians and sweeping away the Egyptians. Because it was a vassal of Egypt, Judah was swallowed up in the Babylonian expansion, and Jehoiakim became a vassal of Babylon instead (v. 1). It was at this time that Daniel and his friends were taken into exile to Babylon (Dan. 1:1–3). At first Jehoiakim cooperated with the Babylonians, but three years later he rebelled. Judah became the object of attack by raiding parties inspired by Babylon that inflicted much damage in fulfillment of the word of the Lord spoken by the prophets (2 Kin. 24:2). When Nebuchadnezzar

arrived at Jerusalem to begin the suppression of Jehoiakim's rebellion, Jehoiakim was already dead or had died during the siege, and his young son Jehoiachin replaced him (v. 6). This was the end of the reign of another king described as evil (23:36–37). Egypt no longer rated as a regional power, and Babylon assumed all its territory from the eastern border of Egypt right up to the Euphrates River (24:7)—a territory that was once under the control of King Solomon (see 1 Kin. 4:21, 24).

24:8–16. Jehoiachin (598–597 B.C.) and the Second Deportation (598 B.C.). Jehoiachin followed the tradition of most of his forebears and did evil in the sight of God—his reign lasted only three months (vv. 8–9). When Nebuchadnezzar arrived outside the besieged Jerusalem, Jehoiachin went out to him, accompanied by his mother, his chief officers, and his courtiers, and surrendered to him. He was taken prisoner (vv. 10–12), and Nebuchadnezzar emptied the treasures of the palace and the temple treasuries. He cut in pieces the gold objects still remaining in the temple from Solomon's time and deported ten thousand of Jerusalem's leaders, artisans, metallurgists, and potential military personnel. Ezekiel was one of them (Ezek. 1:2). This tactic effectively removed from Jerusalem all those capable of leading a revolt or manufacturing supplies for an army. (The book of 2 Kings does not mention the lengthy siege of Jerusalem by the Babylonians in 605 B.C. that resulted in the first deportation of Jews to Babylon.)

24:17–20. Zedekiah (597–586 B.C.). Mattaniah and Jehoahaz were full blood brothers, so Mattaniah—given the royal name of Zedekiah—was Jehoiachin's uncle even though he was only about three years older (2 Kin. 24:17–18). Zedekiah also reigned for eleven years (v. 18), the same as Jehoiakim. He too did evil in the eyes of the Lord (v. 19). Although he initially cooperated with Babylon, he also rebelled, following Jehoiakim's example (v. 20).

25:1–21. Jerusalem Destroyed (586 B.C.). The inevitable siege commenced in the ninth year of Zedekiah's reign and lasted two years (vv. 1–2). The narrative notes that Judah, the people group, was taken away from its own land (v. 21). This is a tragic admission. The divine gift of the land was withdrawn from the people because of their rebellion against the Lord who had redeemed them from Egypt and who had entered into a loving covenant relationship with

them. After the nation's first generation of leaders had died, the land descended into a state of anarchy (the time of the judges) and then of entrenched idolatry during the time of the kings. Despite the few kings who really turned to God with their reforms and the prophets who made it clear that only God is worthy of worship, the nation seemed determined to head in the direction of their own destruction. The Canaanite religion enticed them by providing a fatal, false sense of security. Both the Northern Kingdom of Israel and the Southern Kingdom of Judah were cast out of the land and taken into exile. The destruction of their temple was a sad reminder of the fact that they had now lost the national identity and the privilege of having God living among them, cleansing them from sin. The loss was devastating and left the nation in chaos.

25:22–26. Judah in Exile. A few weeks after the start of the Exile, Ishmael, from the royal line, returned with a group of activists and killed Gedaliah, whom Nebuchadnezzar had appointed as governor, his associates, and the Babylonian military personnel garrisoned there (v. 25). At this, they, and many frightened locals, fled to Egypt, their political savior (v. 26). The prophet Jeremiah was forced to go with them (Jer. 43:5–7), even though he had warned them not to go to Egypt (42:19). They went back to the place from which the Lord had liberated them.

25:27–30. Jehoiachin Released. In the year 560 B.C., thirty-seven years after Jehoiachin was taken from Jerusalem, a new king ascended Babylon's throne. As a measure of goodwill, he released Jehoiachin (now about fifty-five) from his prison (v. 27; for more, see "Old Testament Timeline," p. 94). For some reason Jehoiachin became the favorite among the captive kings and was not only provided regular clothes rather than his prison uniform, but also given a prominent place at the king's table (vv. 28–29). Furthermore, he received regular food supplies for the rest of his days (v. 30).

This dramatic finale to the book is an indication of hope that the nation of Israel and its kingly line still had a future. The judgment against them would not be permanent or final; they would be restored. The covenant God made with Abraham would still come to pass. The covenant God made with David would still be able to climax in the Messiah. The kingdom of God would have a future, and the meek would one day inherit the earth (Matt. 5:5).

1 CHRONICLES

INTRODUCTION

Title and Authorship. First and Second Chronicles were originally one book, as indicated by a scribal note found in the Hebrew copies, placing the "middle verse" at 1 Chronicles 27:25. Its Hebrew title, *dibre hayyamim* ("matters/events of the days"), refers to records that were kept of activities usually associated with the king. These sources were mainly courtly journals recording salient events. The two books of Chronicles are cited thirty-two times in Kings and two times in Esther. The books of Chronicles appeared separately for the first time in the early Greek version, the Septuagint (LXX), with the name *paraleipomenon*, "a thing left aside (for the moment)," as if they were an appendix for the sake of completeness. The author does assume that the reader knows the content of the former historical books when presenting genealogies and administrative lists in a more complete form than could be compiled from them. But that is not the main function of the Chronicles. Jerome, the author of the Vulgate Latin translation, does more justice to its character as "a chronicle of the whole of sacred history," thus recovering the sense of the Hebrew name and originating the modern title.

Many have believed that the author of the Chronicles also wrote Ezra and Nehemiah, which were originally a single book. But the Chronicles differ in the implicit assessment of the reign of Solomon (contrast Neh. 13:26, partly echoed in 2 Chr. 1:12), as well as its emphasis on swift retribution for sin. The author of Chronicles is thus unknown, but his emphasis on Levite choristers (mentioned about one hundred times in the books of Chronicles, but only one time in the books of Kings and two times in the books of Samuel) has led some to surmise that he was also a Levite.

Date. The books of Chronicles are addressed primarily to the Judeans who returned to their land following the decree of Cyrus in 537 B.C.

The books were probably composed during the latter part of the fifth century B.C. and, if so, could be the last of the OT books to be written. Clearly, part of the genealogical information (e.g., 1 Chr. 3:19–24) reaches into the second half of the Persian period (539–331 B.C.). The position of the books of Chronicles in the Hebrew Bible, at the very end of Scripture, agrees well with a late date. Matthew 23:35 refers to the sweep of biblical history by alluding to the time comprised by Genesis 4:8 and 2 Chronicles 24:20–21, much as "from Genesis to Revelation" would be used today (see "Formation of the Biblical Canon," p. 21).

Backgrounds. Though often seen as dull today, the books of Chronicles were written, just as the Pentateuch and the rest of the historical books of the OT, in order to guide God's people through momentous transitions in their history. The Pentateuch had inspired a group of impoverished family clans after they had escaped from the oppressive power of Egypt into less developed but freer lands, there to become a nation under God, while the other historical books mapped the transformation of this new nation into kingdoms of note in the ancient world, showing how faithfulness to God's covenant did result in the blessings promised therein.

Once those blessings had been lost through disobedience, those who returned from the Exile in Babylon found themselves as a minor district in an outlying province of the Persian Empire. Research in dusty archives was necessary in order to convince the Persian government that in times past there had been kings in Jerusalem: nobody thought of those Judeans as a nation any longer (Ezra 4:19–20), but only as a cultic group huddling around a few sacred objects (Ezra 1:7–11). The books of Chronicles served to show them how to remain God's people even without national independence or a king of their own.

Theology and Purpose. The books of Chronicles do not overtly discuss theology, except in short statements by way of explaining the success or failure of people of the past. Its main purpose was pastoral in nature: the book aimed to save the Judean community from a complete loss of heart that would only facilitate their absorption into the surrounding culture. Such a process had already begun in other Palestinian communities that also treasured the Pentateuch, as the books of Ezra and Nehemiah report about the Samaritans. This danger was averted in Judah thanks, to a great extent, to reflection on the history of the people of God such as is expounded in the Chronicles. The books also provide an answer to the question of the fall of the city and the destruction of the temple. It establishes a clear connection between the behavior of the kings and the people, and the corruption of the temple services (2 Chr. 28:22—29:36; 36:14–20; see "The Temple in Chronicles," p. 541).

1. The Glorious Past of the Covenant People. In order to understand the present situation of the people after the Exile, the books of Chronicles focus on the past history of Jerusalem and the temple and its services. It takes us back to the moment when David began to make preparations for the construction of the temple that would occur under the leadership of Solomon. The one link of the postexilic community with a glorious past that would not raise the hackles of Persian authorities too much— provided it was handled with much care, and a generous amount of providential guidance— was the temple. It had been a marvel of the ancient world before its destruction by the Babylonians. Now Cyrus, the founder of the Persian Empire, authorized its reconstruction (2 Chr. 36:23). The continuity of the covenant is underlined through an emphasis on the covenant of God with David. His lineage is given a special place in the genealogical lists (1 Chr. 3), and God's promises for him are repeated (1 Chr. 17, from 2 Sam. 7). But in the Chronicles the generic "seed" or "offspring" of the dynasty (2 Sam. 7:12) is specified as one "of your sons," namely Solomon, the temple builder (1 Chr. 17:11–12). David and Solomon were not only the glorious past but also the root from which God would make Israel to sprout again. Their throne was "the throne of the Lord" (1 Chr. 29:23; 2 Chr. 9:8). Their reigns are presented in idealized form: none of the grave sins of David or Solomon are remembered in the Chronicles except David's census, for those kings are models to be followed by future leaders. The same, to a certain extent, is true of Hezekiah and Josiah.

2. The Rise and Fall of the Nation. The glorious past of Israel poses an immediate question: What went wrong? Why were the people of God in such a wretched state? Systematically, the books of Chronicles relate the fate of kings, and the people subject to them, to their obedience or disobedience to the provisions of God's covenant and to the temple services. The author underlines the principles of David transmitted to Solomon in 1 Chronicles 28:9: Their goal was to know God intimately and serve Him loyally and willingly, keeping in mind that He is found by all who seek Him, but rejects those who reject Him, which meant He would ultimately destroy them forever if they persisted in this rejection. This is no mere formal obedience, but one that arose from the heart in true humility (see 2 Chr. 7:14, 22 a passage with a clear message for us today).

Emphasis on obedience to the law of God as a key to success is pervasive in the OT, and the blessings associated with faithfulness to the covenant are already specified in the Pentateuch (most prominently in Lev. 26 and Deut. 28). The books of Chronicles do not hesitate to identify the actions of the people or the monarchs that created well-being or disaster. The author usually includes an evaluation of the religious character of each reign together with statistics. In practice, however, things were not so clear-cut: punishment might be delayed by amends (2 Chr. 34:27– 28), with the unintended consequence that some people might get it absolutely backward: they might attribute their misfortune to the renewed obedience and godly reforms of their kings, and their former prosperity to the evil deeds of previous times (Jer. 44:15–19). Thus, the just judgment of God is a tenet of faith, not an obvious conclusion to be drawn from the experiences of daily life. But even if the "obey and live, disobey and die" theology is limited in its explanatory power for the vicissitudes of this life, that very fact opens an opportunity for the doctrine of the future and righteous judgment of God.

3. God's Sovereign Elections. God made clear He had chosen the tribe of Levi alone for priesthood and temple service (e.g., 1 Chr. 15:2; 23:24–32); the lineage of David to rule the nation (e.g., 1 Chr. 28:4; 2 Chr. 6:6); the reign of Solomon in order to build the temple (1 Chr. 28–29); the city of Jerusalem as the residence of His name (e.g., 2 Chr. 6:6, 34, 38; 12:13); and even the specific site for the temple inside its limits (2 Chr. 7:12; cf. 1 Chr. 21–22). Though these choices were not a guarantee of salvation for the persons involved, neither could those who disrespected them have attained the favor of God. The corruption of the chosen leaders and their institutions led to the collapse of both. Although the Chronicler believes that the people from both the Southern and Northern Kingdoms were still the elect people of God (e.g., 2 Chr. 30:5–9; 2 Chr. 11:4), he also understands that the northern tribes have "been in rebellion against the house of David to this day" (2 Chr. 10:19). Outside Judea there was no valid priesthood, since the priests and Levites who once resided in the north had moved around Jerusalem (2 Chr. 11:13–14). However, people from the ten rebellious tribes were not to be excluded from the covenant provided they repented and returned to worship in Jerusalem (2 Chr. 30:9–10).

4. *Listening to the Law and the Prophets.* The Chronicler narrates the reigns of the kings of Judah, not of rebellious Israel, and then only briefly except for those of the "good" kings, singled out because of their compliance with the law of God: David (e.g., 2 Chron. 6:16; 23:18), Jehoshaphat (2 Chr. 17:3–9), Joash (24:6), Hezekiah (29:10–11), and Josiah (34:19–21). These kings also sought and respected the word of God through the prophets: Nathan and Gad in the times of David and Solomon (1 Chr. 29:29; 2 Chr. 29:25) and Ahijah and Iddo later (9:29), as well as the prophetess Huldah in the times of Josiah (34:20–28), among others. Of special note is the prophecy of Jahaziel, the Levite who led Jehoshaphat to confront the armies of the enemies of Judah by singing praises to God (2 Chr. 20:14–17), and the admonition of the king to trust in the messages of God's prophets in order to thrive (v. 20). The stories of these kings are used to establish that if the kings had remained faithful to the Lord, the destruction of the city and the hopeless experience of the Exile could have been avoided.

Yet, out of the chaos of the Exile God provided for His people a future and a hope (Jer. 29:11).

Literary Features. In order to preserve hope and awaken a sense of national pride, the Chronicles contain narratives that review the history of God's dealings with His people since the remote past. Part of this history is merely alluded to in genealogical and administrative lists, since the author presupposes the reader is well acquainted with the former historical books, but a modicum of new information is added. Other historical narratives are retold by quoting extensively from Samuel and Kings but are given a different perspective and new emphases. However, more is left out, in accordance with the purpose of the author, than is repeated or supplemented. The records of the glorious reigns of David and Solomon are especially singled out, both because of their value in buoying the spirits of the community of returned exiles and because of the connection of those kings with the temple, the center of community life. Sermons and addresses of those kings to the people are added as an aid to the purpose of the author (see "The Temple in Chronicles," p. 541).

COMMENTARY

1:1—9:44

THE ANCESTORS: GENERATIONS OF GOD'S PEOPLE

Reviewing past history is a means to establish roots and, consequently, identity. To us, history is a parade of centuries; to the ancients, it was a parade of ancestors. Some names may remind

---

The Genealogies of 1 Chronicles 1—9

The genealogies recorded in 1 Chronicles 1—9 are the longest in the Bible and require some attention. The fact that they are part of the book and that they are placed at the beginning of the book indicates that they have a very specific purpose. We should explore some of the theological value of the genealogies within the book itself.

1. *Genealogical Details.* These genealogies begin with the pre-Israelite history from Adam or Creation (1:1–3) to the Flood (v. 4), and from the post-Flood nations (vv. 5–26) to Abraham (v. 27). From this point on, the list of names is restricted to the sons of Abraham through Hagar (vv. 29–31), Keturah (vv. 32–33), and Sarah (v. 34). The genealogy narrows down even more by listing only the descendants of Isaac (Esau [vv. 35–54] and Israel [2:1–2]). At this point we reach what seems to be one of

the main genealogical interests of the biblical writer: Israel as the people of God. The tribes that came from Jacob/Israel are listed beginning with Judah (2:3—4:23). The intention of this section is to take the reader to David and his descendants (3:1–24). Other descendants of Judah are also listed (4:1–23). Then the descendants of the other tribes are given. It has been suggested that the list of the tribes follows a general geographical pattern. Judah is at the center, and the next one mentioned is Simeon (vv. 24–43), one of its closest neighbors. The movement is from south to north, east of Jordan (Reuben, 5:1–10; Gad, 5:11–22; the half tribe of Manasseh, 5:23–26; and Levi, 6:1–80). This is followed by the northern tribes of Issachar (7:1–5), Benjamin (vv. 6–12), and Naphtali (v. 13), and concludes with a movement from the north to the south (Manasseh, vv. 14–19; Ephraim, vv. 20–29; Asher, vv. 30–40; and Benjamin/Saul, 8:1–40). In chapter 9 we find a genealogical list of those who returned from Exile, with a primary emphasis on the Levites (9:1–34). At the end, we return to the genealogy of Saul, thus preparing the way for the reign of David (9:35–44).

2. *Purpose of the Genealogies. First*, it is obvious that these genealogies contain a compressed history of global dimensions. They begin affirming the historical facts of the Creation and the Flood and close with the beginning of the reign of David. But they also include the Exile and the return from the Exile, thus providing an element of hope. At a time when the people of God were discouraged as a result of the destruction of Jerusalem and the temple, and a return from a devastating exile, God assured them that they were part of a world history over which He is Lord. This history had not come to an end but remained open to His guiding hand as it had been in the past.

Second, history is depicted here as a result of the human capacity, given to them by God, to procreate. This begetting traces the human race to a common ancestor created by God in His image: Adam. This particular genealogy binds the people of God to the human race in a bond of existential solidarity that should exclude prejudices of any kind. In the list, the birth of Abraham takes us back to his election in order to be used by God to bless all the nations of the earth.

Third, based on the amount of space assigned to them, these genealogies place the emphasis on David and the priesthood (Levites). Genealogies were sometimes instrumental in the divine assignment of specific religious and social responsibilities and privileges to some, but every individual had a role to play in the arena of history simply because he or she had been begotten. In the Bible, the roles of king and priest played an important function as instruments used by God to represent the saving work and ministry of Jesus in whom the kingly and priestly offices coalesced. He was not simply the son of Mary. He was the Son of God, in a unique way, and to Him His Father assigned a unique responsibility, which He willingly accepted, namely, the redemption of the human race. The genealogies of the books of Chronicles are open-ended, pointing to the future son of David and to His priestly work—two ideas that pervade these books.

the reader of specific stories in other parts of the Bible, and in the case of the original readers, also of family stories transmitted orally. The genealogy begins with Genesis and the patriarchs (1:1–27), then moves to Abraham and his descendants (1:28–53), the tribe of Judah (2:1—4:23), the eastern tribes (4:24—5:26), the tribe of Levi (6:1–81), and the remaining tribes (7:1—9:44).

1:1–54
From Adam to Jacob

By beginning with Creation, the history of God's people, through the record of the genealogies in the Chronicles and earlier books, is incorporated into universal history and highlights the divine purpose for them.

1:1–27. The Patriarchs. In a sense the author rushes through Genesis, for he is only reminding the reader, by means of genealogical lists, of the foundational times of Creation, the Flood, the dispersion from Babel, and the story of Abraham. Family branches furthest away from Israel are dealt with first before concentrating on those of primary concern. Thus, both Japheth and Ham precede Shem. Nimrod (v. 10) appears only as a mighty warrior, no longer in the enigmatic character of a "hunter before the LORD" (Gen. 10:9). The family branch of Aram (1 Chr. 1:17) is worthy of a passing mention among the Semites, as is that of Joktan (v. 20), being the more remote branch of Eber. After these digressions, the genealogy of Shem (v. 17) is repeated (vv. 24–27), so the reader is not sidetracked from the more immediate branch of Peleg, from which Abraham arose.

1:28–54. The Descendants of Abraham. Ishmael (vv. 29–31), the son of Hagar, seems of less interest to the genealogist than the sons of Keturah (vv. 32–33). Genesis 25:1 leaves the impression that Keturah was a new wife after the death of Sarah. Our passage, therefore, explains that she was a concubine, not (as in modern usage) a kept mistress, but an actual spouse (Judg. 19:3–5), albeit one with incomplete inheritance rights (Gen. 25:6). The line of Esau/Edom/Seir is also dealt with in some detail (1 Chr. 1:35–54), not only as neighbors of Judah but also as brothers of Israel. The long list of Edomite chiefs and kings emphasizes that kingship arose in Edom before Israel (v. 43).

In 1:36 the Hebrew text ends the list of descendants of Eliphaz with "and Timna and Amalek." This is not always reflected in the English translations. The first five sons of Eliphaz in this verse are not joined by "and," except as supplied by translators. The "and" before Timna originally seems to have introduced an explanatory clause, "and by Timna, Amalek," as in the LXX. This is in agreement with Genesis 36:12, where Timna is the mother of Amalek. Most modern translations try to represent this more accurate understanding.

2:1—7:40
The Tribes

This section begins with a list of the twelve sons of Jacob (2:1–2) but immediately concentrates on Judah. The order of the names, given in various ways in the OT, here follows loosely Genesis 35:22–26, where they are listed according to their respective mothers.

2:3—4:23. The Descendants of Judah. They are given the pride of place (because Judah is the cradle of rulers, 1 Chr. 5:1–2) with emphasis on the genealogy of David (2:9–55) and his descendants (chap. 3). His tribe then receives much more space in the text (102 vv.) than the other tribes (Levi, 81 vv.; all others combined, just 126 vv.). We can divide the list into several

groups. First is the list from Judah to Chelubai (2:2–9). Ram (2:9), who does not appear in Numbers 26:20–21, is taken from the genealogy of David in Ruth 4:18–22. The Hebrew *kelubay* (1 Chr. 2:9) is an alternate form of Caleb (2:42); the latter spelling configures the word for "dog" in Hebrew.

Second, we find the family of David. The Chronicler reports that David was the seventh and last son of Jesse (2:15), while 1 Samuel 16:10–13 makes him the eighth, giving also some of their names. Perhaps a fifth son (Elihu in 1 Chr. 27:18) later died without children, leaving Jesse with just seven sons for genealogical purposes.

Third, we have the family of Caleb son of Hezron. His family (2:18–24) appears next to David's, perhaps because it furnished Israel with the talent of Bezalel (2:20), the master craftsman of the sanctuary. He should not be confused with Caleb the son of Jephunneh (4:15), one of the twelve spies who, together with Joshua, showed an attitude that differed from that of the other ten (Num. 14:24, 30). This incident happened one year after the erection of the sanctuary, when the spy Caleb was only forty years old, so he could hardly have been the grandfather of Bezalel, the sanctuary builder.

Fourth, the families of Jerahmeel and Caleb are listed (1 Chr. 2:25–55). The Chelubai of v. 9 resurfaces as "Caleb" (vv. 42–48), with another list of his descendants, where the emphasis is on place-names.

The fifth group is formed by the family of David (3:1–9). He is here on record as having reigned in Hebron over Judah as their native prince for seven and a half years before his reign of thirty-three years in Jerusalem as an elected king of all Israel (v. 4), in conformity with the report in 2 Samuel 2:11 and 5:4–5. In 1 Chronicles 10–11, however, his reign in Hebron, which partially overlapped with the claim of Esh-Baal/Ishbosheth, the son of Saul, is omitted, as the reign of the latter is not detailed either. Daniel, here in v. 1, is another name of Chileab (2 Sam. 3:3). The name Daniel means "God is my judge," while Chileab means "like unto the father," perhaps in affirmation that David was the baby's father, not Nabal, the former husband of Abigail from Carmel.

The sixth group is that of the royal line from Solomon to the kings of Judah (1 Chr. 3:10–24). The names in this line appear in the Bible in diverse forms; some may be throne names. Zerubbabel (v. 19) is here the nephew of Shealtiel, while elsewhere he is his son (e.g., Hag. 1:1; Matt. 1:12). Probably Pedaiah was his biological father, while Shealtiel was the juridical father, having died without offspring. However this may be, the lists of Zerubbabel's descendants here, in Matthew, and in Luke, are all different. In 1 Chronicles 3:22 we read of Shemaiah and six sons, though only five are named after him. We should probably read "The *sons* [as in v. 21] of Shecaniah were Shemaiah and the sons of Shemaiah, Hattush, Igal, Bariah, Neariah and Shaphat—six in all."

Finally we have the clans of Judah (4:1–23). These families included that of Jabez (v. 9), a clan leader who made a simple but eloquent request of God, which was, in a variation from the literary style of the genealogy, recorded for posterity. Jabez requested an extension of his land—God's loving hand of providence, protection, and avoidance of causing (or according to some, receiving) pain. There were families of scribes who lived at a place called Jabez (2:55), which was perhaps named after the person. Some have even suggested that these scribes were somehow related to Jabez or connected with him in some other way (such that his prayer had relevance to their work), but the text does not indicate anything specific. These scribes, the Tirathites, Shimeathites, and Sucathites, may be interpreted either as sub-family names deriving from the names of the respective heads (cf. 2:53) or as sub-specializations of scribes, namely, those who read aloud the words to be written, those who took them down in writing, and those who checked the final copy. Other clans of Judah specialized as skilled craftsmen (4:14) and potters (4:23).

4:24—5:26. The Eastern Tribes. The eastern tribes were those of Simeon (4:24–43), Reuben, Gad, and Manasseh (5:1–26). The tribe of Simeon was originally surrounded by territories of Judah. Part of the tribe was later incorporated into those territories, while the rest migrated eastward. Reuben lost his birthright, which entailed a double portion of inheritance, to Joseph (5:1–2). This was accomplished *de facto* when Jacob adopted both sons of Joseph, Manasseh and Ephraim, as his own (Gen. 48:12–16). Thus Joseph disappears from most lists of the twelve tribes in the Bible, while Manasseh and Ephraim now had rights to inheritance equal to those of their uncles. The wilderness (desert) by the river Euphrates (1 Chr. 5:9) was a result of gradually diminishing rainfall from Gilead (the territory of the Reubenites) toward the east. The Hagrites conquered by them (5:10) were descendants of Ishmael and his mother Hagar (cf. the Hagrites Jethur and Naphish in 1:31; 5:19).

The members of the tribe of Gad (5:11–22) are listed differently than in Genesis 46:16 or Numbers 26:15–18; here the tribe seems organized, not by ancestor, but by military chief (5:12). The same applies to the half tribe of Manasseh (vv. 23–26). This suggests that the source was a military census, perhaps related to the warfare of Saul in the region (1 Sam. 14:47). The figures of 50,000 camels, 250,000 sheep, and 100,000 men seem strangely high, compared to just 2,000 donkeys (1 Chr. 5:21). Since the Chronicles used archives from a bygone era, the author may have misunderstood some of the numeral symbols used in preexilic Israel, which, as archaeology shows, constituted an incipient, complex, and unstable system. We should probably read this verse as listing 1,050 camels, 1,250 sheep and 1,100 men. The same problem reappears often in the work (e.g., 1 Chr. 22:14). The eastern tribes, like the northern ones, acted like a prostitute (5:25) spiritually, by being unfaithful to the Lord, who was the legitimate husband of Israel. The Assyrian deportation was the consequence of this harlotry. Pul, the king of Assyria, (5:26) was not, as in some older versions, different from Tiglath-Pileser; the latter was his throne name (2 Kin. 15:19, 29).

6:1–80. The Tribe of Levi. This genealogy is based on the three sons of Levi: Kohath (vv. 2–15), Gershon (vv. 16–28), and Merari (vv. 29–30). Two specific roles of the Levitical tribe are mentioned: the musicians in the temple (vv. 31–48) and those in charge of the priesthood (the family of Aaron; vv. 49–53). The section closes with a discussion of the Levitical cities as the dwellings of the Levites (vv. 54–81). The Zadokites (vv. 2–15) replaced the lineage of Ithamar (6:3), which had held the high priesthood (1 Sam. 3:27–30) until Abiathar became embroiled in the royal pretensions of Adonijah and was deposed by Solomon (1 Kin. 2:20–23). The present passage aims to demonstrate the legitimacy of the Zadokite line through Eleazar, the brother of Ithamar. The other Levitical branches included the family of Samuel (1 Chr. 6:28), here placed in the clan of Kohath (6:33–38), probably by adoption into the family of Ebiasaph, Assir, and Tahath (cf. vv. 23, 37) after being dedicated by his mother Hannah to the temple (1 Sam. 1:19–28). The original organization of the musicians for the house of the Lord is traced back to David (v. 31). Even though Samuel, raised as a priest assistant, was eventually able to offer sacrifice, the distinction between the musical Levites (1 Chr. 6:31–48) and the altar-going Aaronites (6:49–52) is upheld. The family of Aaron is specifically mentioned because it constituted the priestly family (vv. 49–53). The genealogy of Zadokite priests is repeated from vv. 3–8, bringing it up to the times of David and Solomon only (cf. v. 10). As elsewhere, the main concern of the list is to show the legitimacy of the Eleazar-Zadok line. But it also reminds us of the Aaronite/Levite distinction, and in this way, it also serves as an introduction to the next section, the Levitical cities (vv. 54–81). The list includes the cities of refuge (Josh. 21), where Levites acted as judges in capital cases, but it goes on to cover every major city in the kingdom of David. This expansion of the original listing may reflect an attempt to establish a wider and more accessible judicial system by assigning special sections in the larger cities to Levitical judges. In this sense alone they become also "Levitical cities."

7:1–40. The Rest of the Tribes. The first one is the tribe of Issachar (7:1–5). In contrast to Gad or Manasseh, the names of the sons of Issachar here do match in general terms with Genesis 46:13 and Numbers 26:23–24, but the numbers given for the two main branches and others, totaling 87,000, correspond to the time of David (1 Chr. 7:2) and may reflect the ill-conceived census of chapter 21. The tribe of Benjamin (vv. 6–12) is also reported in military terms. In v. 12 the Hushim are said to be descendants of "Aher" (lit. "another one"), a term sometimes used in Hebrew to avoid mentioning a name with unpleasant associations. This might refer to Dan (Gen. 46:23; Num. 26:42), whose descendants are not otherwise listed and who are also absent from 1 Chronicles 6:68–69, where they would be expected (cf. Josh. 21:23; Rev. 7:5–8). This is probably related to the idolatrous apostasy of the tribe (Judg. 18–19). Together with Dan, the tribe of Naphtali (1 Chr. 7:13) constituted the only descendants of Bilhah, so after the disappearance of Dan from the scene there were no others; this is perhaps the significance of Bilhah's mention here.

The tribe of west Manasseh is discussed in vv. 14–19. Verse 14 is difficult to translate; the LXX makes Asriel a brother of Machir, the firstborn (Josh. 17:1). The exact relationship of Huppim and Shuppim to other family members is also unclear. As for Zelophehad (v. 15), Numbers 26:33 and Joshua 17:3 indicate that his father was Hepher, a son of Gilead, and was therefore his grandson.

The family history of the tribe of Ephraim (1 Chr. 7:20–29) opens with a tragic incident of patriarchal times, before the Israelites went to Egypt. The report on the tribe of Asher (vv. 30–40) agrees in general terms with Genesis 46:17 while adding a wealth of detail that demonstrates the access of the Chronicler to other ancient sources.

8:1–40. The Ancestry of Saul. Here the report differs from the account already given in 7:6–12. Besides different names, the list is also unique in often employing the term *yalad*, "begot" or "was the father of" or "bore" (vv. 1, 8, 9, 11, 33–37), perhaps because it originated from a different archive. Some differences may be due to alternate names; in other cases the names may be links omitted by some lists which use "son" in the sense of "descendant." Gera (v. 3) may have been in fact the ancestor of Ehud the judge (Judg. 3:15); the migration to the lands of Moab (1 Chr. 8:8) may explain why Ehud tangled with King Eglon there. The names Esh-Baal (v. 33) and Merib-Baal (v. 34) do not imply that Saul and/or Jonathan were worshipers of Baal. The term only means "owner" or "master"; it could be applied to the true God and is the regular Hebrew word for "husband." In its religious use, it later became identified with the Syrian god Hadad, who was invoked by his followers as their lord or "baal" (Hos. 2:16–17). For this reason scribes later replaced those names with Ish-boshet and Mephiboshet (2 Sam. 2:8; 4:4; 9:6), where "boshet" ("shame") parodies such invocation.

9:1–44. The Dwellers in Jerusalem. This list of returnees from the Exile includes some from the northern tribes and Benjamin (9:1–9), but its primary emphasis is on the tribes of Judah and Levi. The Aaronite (priestly) branch of the latter is specified first (vv. 10–13), then the others in charge of security (vv. 17–27) and equipment (vv. 28–34). The list then repeats in vv. 35–44 essentially the same information as 8:29–40. This repetition serves to focus on King Saul, whose last battle and death follow (10:1–14). Overall, the brief highlighting of Saul in 9:35—10:14 is an appropriate transition to what seems to be the primary concern of the Chronicler: the reigns of David and Solomon.

10:1—29:30

DAVID'S REIGN AND THE DEVELOPMENT OF THE TEMPLE

After a discussion of the death of Saul (10:1–14), this long section concentrates on the rise of David to power (11:1—12:40), his decision to bring the ark of the covenant to Jerusalem (13:1—16:43), his covenant with God (17:1-27), and his military success (18:1—20:8). The rest deals with matters related to the future temple, beginning with the selection of the site (20:1-30), interrupted by the military census (21:1-6), and followed by specific preparations for the building of the temple (22:1-19) and the organization of the temple services (23:1—26:32) and the kingdom (27:1-34). Since David would not build the temple, he left for his successor instructions for the building project (28:1—29:30). After parading the broad sweep of Israelite history through comprehensive genealogies, the books of Chronicles focus on the story of the temple, which was central to the identity of the community of those who returned from Babylon. The topic is close to the center of the theology of the books (see "The Temple in Chronicles," p. 541).

10:1–14
The Death of Saul

Since David was not a crown prince, an account of the change of dynasty was necessary. The end of the house of Saul (vv. 1–7) was no mere accidental overthrow of a king by foreigners. God had in Israel a kingdom and a throne (note the emphasis on these concepts in 1 Chr. 17:14, an emphasis absent in 2 Sam. 7:16), and He had already chosen David. It was only because of the godly men of Jabesh, in Transjordan, that Saul escaped the ultimate indignity: his remains unburied (1 Chr. 10:8–12). He did not, however, escape the profanation of his corpse by enemies (his head in one place, [v. 10] and his body in another, [1 Sam. 31:10]). The well-known Philistine god Dagon (1 Chr. 10:10) does not appear in the extant copies of the Hebrew text of 1 Samuel 31:10, the source of the present account, but only in copies of the LXX. The seven-day fast (1 Chr. 10:12) was customary among the bereaved; it was limited to certain types of food or times of the day (the opposite is presented as an exception to the rule in Matt. 4:2; Luke 4:2). A theological evaluation of the tragic death of Saul is given (1 Chr. 10:13): it was the result of his unfaithfulness. Two reasons are specified: he did not keep the word of the Lord, and he consulted a medium (v. 13). Here the Chronicler elaborates on 1 Samuel 28:7–20; 31:1–3. The Lord had strictly forbidden the practice of consulting the spirits in Israel (Deut. 18:11).

11:1—12:40
David's Rise to Power

The Philistines were able to eliminate Saul and his three sons and all his official "house" (1 Chr. 10:6). Another son, Esh-Baal/Ishbosheth, survived, but he lacked preparation and/or talent for the throne (see his turning against his own power base in 2 Sam. 3). Even among Saul's intimate circle, the promises of God to David were known and weighed heavily on the outcome of the ensuing civil war (2 Sam. 3:9–10). In consequence, 1 Chronicles skips this civil war entirely, instead focusing immediately on the rise of David's star.

11:1–9. The Capture of Jerusalem. This conquest was not merely a mop-up operation that eliminated the Canaanite strongholds still present in the land, centuries after the Exodus. Rather, it was crucial for the success of David as the king of a united monarchy. The reader has already been informed in 3:4 of the reign of David in Hebron over the tribe of Judah alone (2 Sam. 2:4, 7), so the Chronicler does not repeat it here. The emphasis is rather on "all Israel" (1 Chr. 11:4), perhaps indicating either that David and his men in 2 Samuel 5:6 represented the whole nation or that there was a special force under David in addition to a larger national army. The implication was that this city, hitherto in foreign hands and therefore not in any particular tribe, was to become the capital of the whole nation. At the same time, the capture granted David the aura of a conqueror. This was how he became increasingly renowned and powerful (1 Chr. 11:9).

11:10–47. The Mighty Men of David. These were the men who had taken a firm stand in support of David's rule over all Israel (11:10). The three great warriors, the mighty men (vv. 11–12), were the innermost circle of David's supporters in the armed forces. In our copies of Chronicles two are named: Jashobeam and Eleazar, and in 2 Samuel 23:9–12 Shammah is also mentioned. These three men seem to have been different from the three of the thirty chief men (1 Chr. 11:15), two of whom are named (vv. 20–26), who in turn were different from the mighty warriors named in vv. 26–47.

Despite the mighty acts of David's men, it was the Lord who always brought about a great victory (v. 14). The cave of Adullam (v. 15) was not a specific cavern, but a collective term for an area riddled with hollows of all sizes. We are not given the exact location of the incident with the water of the well of Bethlehem, David's native town, but the stronghold of v. 16 was probably one of those hollows particularly well suited to his purposes (1 Sam. 23:29). The names after Uriah the Hittite in 1 Chronicles 11:41 do not appear in the account of 2 Samuel 23, neither is their geographical provenance provided as is the case with the preceding names. This illustrates how the Chronicler was able to supplement the information of Samuel and Kings with other sources.

12:1-22. The Growth of David's Army. This section shows how David was able to quickly confront the army of Abner after the death of Saul. Many of the best men came to him while he was still a refugee in the Philistine town of Ziklag (v. 1), affirming that his God was the One who helped him (v. 18). David was wary of the Benjamites (v. 17), relatives of Saul, who had betrayed him before (1 Sam. 23:12, 19-20). But Amasai (1 Chr. 12:18) put him at ease with a speech as he was moved by the Spirit.

12:23-40. David's Army at Hebron. The numbers recorded here attest to the fact that David had the support of all Israel, having a great army, like the "army of God" (v. 22). It was not only the sons of Issachar who understood the times and what Israel should do (v. 32); they all were of one mind to make David king (v. 38).

13:1 16:43
The Ark Brought to Jerusalem

Not only did the ark contain the tablets of the covenant, the Ten Commandments, but its cover, or "mercy seat," was associated with the throne of God (flanked by its guards, the cherubim). This was the very center of God's presence and communication with Israel (Num. 7:89; 1 Chr. 13:6). Lost to the Philistines and returned by God's miraculous intervention, it had been in a private house for a long time (1 Sam. 4:1—7:1), and Saul had done nothing to restore it to its rightful place (1 Chr. 13:3). It was now time for David to show not only how different he was from Saul but also to demonstrate his religious and spiritual leadership.

13:1-14. The First Attempt. David gathered all Israel (v. 5) from the Shihor (Egyptian term meaning "pond of Horus," probably one of the Bitter Lakes in the Suez area) up to the entrance of Hamath (sometimes translated as "Lebo Hamath"; *lebo'*—"entrance" would in that case be

viewed as a town in Hamath). These locations were the God-given ideal boundaries of the promised land (e.g., Num. 34:8). Since the ark had arrived from Philistia in a cart, the family keeping it may have thought that such a vehicle was an appropriate method for its transport. But as a result of handling the ark as if it were any other load, Uzza(h), one of the members of this family, was killed, and David deposited the sacred object in the house of Obed-Edom (see 2 Sam. 6). This man was a Levite and specifically a Kohathite (1 Chr. 13:13; cf. 15:24; 16:38; 26:5; Num. 16:1; hence probably a Gittite from Gath-Rimmon; 1 Chr. 6:69). David was determined that henceforth proper procedure be followed for the transportation of the ark (chap. 16). But before the necessary preparations could be completed, he had to confront the Philistines, enemies of both the Israelites and the Tyrians.

14:1-17. The Philistine Wars. Hiram, king of Tyre (Phoenicia), was also an enemy of the Philistines. This explains the association of the topics here. Hiram sent David, his ally, a gift of palatial timber, for which his nation was famous. David interpreted this to mean that the Lord had established him as king over Israel (vv. 1-2). The Chronicler takes this opportunity to record David's palaces and new wives in Jerusalem (v. 3; 15:1). Even though displeased with the careless handling of the most sacred symbol of His presence, God was pleased with the intentions of David and provided him with the intelligence and strategy needed in order to defeat his enemies (14:8-16). His military victories gained through the Lord's help caused all nations to fear him (v. 17)—the fulfillment of God's covenantal promises (Deut. 2:25)—and his power was greatly enhanced.

15:1-24. Preparations for Moving the Ark. The account of 2 Samuel 6 is here enriched with much detail, emphasizing the care of David and the priests in preparing a place for the ark (v. 1; Heb. *maqom*, "a sacred site"). First, only the persons and transportation methods authorized by the law were to be used (1 Chr. 15:1-10; cf. Ex. 37:4-5; Deut. 10:8). Second, those approaching the ark had to be purified (1 Chr. 15:11-15). Separating sacred objects from ordinary ones helped the people to place supreme importance on God's word, so different from changeable, erring human words and concepts. Third, sacred music was to be used (vv. 16-24). The perspective and peculiar concern of the Chronicler is clear here: this sacred ministry was placed in the care of the Levites (vv. 16–24), even before their official appointment (16:37–43). Sanctuary music included singing and instruments. Levites played strings and percussion; the priests blew the trumpets (15:24).

15:25—16:3. The Procession with the Ark. First, there was a convocation (v. 25). The importance of the occasion required not only sacred personnel but also representatives from the people: the king, the elders of Israel, and the captains over thousands. The procession was, second, characterized by joy (v. 26). Bringing the ark was an especially joyous occasion (cf. v. 25), so music and a ceremony of sacrificed bulls and rams were provided. Third, proper attire was required (v. 27). None were allowed to approach the ark without sacred garments; even the king had to put on linen and an ephod (lit. "panel," placed on the chest). This was required only of high priests who had to approach the ark in the course of their yearly ministry in the inner sanctum. Now the symbol of God's presence was outdoors. Fourth, there was acclamation (v. 28). Popular shouting expressed the feelings of the people for their national religious symbol. All of this contrasted with the attitude of Michal (v. 29), Saul's daughter and David's wife (1 Sam. 18:17–30), who apparently believed that David's personal behavior, amid all the music and dance (1 Chr. 15:29) in honor of a single sacred object, was unnecessary and undignified, at least for the king. Such an attitude on the part of a member of Saul's family toward the religious past of Israel and the new king revealed her discomfort with David as king and with what he was doing.

David had erected a tent or tabernacle (16:1) to house the ark in Jerusalem (16:1–3). This differed from the sacred tabernacle of the wilderness, which had somehow survived the destruction of the temple of Shiloh by the Philistines (Jer. 7:12; cf. Josh. 18:1; 1 Sam. 1:3, 7, 24) and was now functioning as the focal point of sacrifice in Gibeon (1 Chr. 16:39; cf. 2 Chr. 1:3–6).

Because of the double-shrine situation, only some priests and Levites were assigned to Jerusalem (1 Chr. 16:4–6); the rest were left in Gibeon for the time being (16:38–39). It may be surprising that David did not bring the tabernacle from Gibeon to Jerusalem, but such a move would have been easily understood as a rejection of Gibeon as a place of worship. Instead, he was to eventually provide an awe-inspiring temple, surpassing the house of the Lord lost in Shiloh, which would silence any

possible critics. The religious act concluded with a hymn of praise composed by David for this most important occasion (16:7–36). This composition includes material also found in Psalms 105:1–15; 96:1–13; and 106:47–48.

16:37–43. Arrangements for Regular Worship. The worship program in Jerusalem was intended to invoke, thank, and praise God in Jerusalem with prayer, song, and musical instruments (16:4). The burnt offerings of the daily service (16:40) were offered on the altar located in Gibeon. Just as in the early Davidic reign, those who returned from the Exile kept sacrifices together with verbal worship in the synagogue. The role of Zadok (v. 39) in the Gibeon worship center foreshadowed the future importance of his lineage (see commentary on 6:1–81).

17:1–27
Covenant of God with David

While the Chronicler does not explicitly elaborate the foundational concept of God's covenant, this section sets forth the promises given to David that imply an eternal commitment of God toward His people.

17:1–15. David's Desire to Build a Temple and God's Promises. In contrast to Saul, David's godliness was deep and sincere. Israel was no longer a group of tribes wandering in the desert or suffering the harassment of enemies. David felt that the newly found comfort needed to be correlated with the quality of the structures erected by Israel for worship (v. 1). His pious desire was met with the enthusiastic initial approval of Nathan (v. 2), who was immediately overridden by the Lord, in whose name the prophet was speaking (vv. 4–6). God had not dwelt in one and the same place since the Exodus (v. 5), nor was He concerned with having a luxurious palace of cedar (v. 6). But He did take note of David's intention. Instead of David building for Him, God Himself would build a "house" for the faithful king (v. 10), a perpetual dynasty. As for David himself, his role was that of a warrior (vv. 8–9; cf. 1 Kin. 5:3), so it would fall to one of David's sons (1 Chr. 17:11) to actually construct the temple (v. 11). Though the emphasis of the Chronicler is on Solomon, he does record divine promises to establish the Davidic king forever (v. 12) as God's "son" (v. 13; Pss. 2; 110). For the Chronicler this means indeed forever, as is strongly emphasized in the text (1 Chr. 17:14;

Ps. 45:6–7). Such perpetual sonship was to provide an important foundation for the conception of the Messiah in the NT (Rom. 1:3–4; 8:29; Heb. 1:8).

17:16–27. The Response of the King. The story now shows the humility and godliness of David. He perceived that this was indeed the word of God, not of Nathan (cf. 17:2), so he sat before the Lord (i.e., before the ark that represented Him; v. 16) and acknowledged the greatness of God and His grace toward Israel (vv. 19–22) in contrast to his own unworthiness (vv. 16–17). At the same time he accepted the promises with faith (vv. 23–26), convinced that God had indeed made Israel His own people forever (v. 22), which is the central concept in the covenant (e.g., Gen. 17:7; Lev. 11:45; Jer. 31:33; Rev. 21:3).

18:1—20:8
The Military Glory of David

This section underlines David's role as a warrior, which prevented the realization of his dream to construct the temple. But the narrative illustrates what God was willing to do for His people when they and their king were totally committed to Him. David is depicted as the ideal king to whom God gave victories over their enemies. These enemies included the Philistines (18:1; 20:4–8), Moab and Zobah (18:2–11), Edom (vv. 12–13), and the Ammonites and the Syrians (19:1—20:3).

18:1–13. Victories over the Philistines, Moab, Zobah, and Edom. While the previous Philistine wars had been largely defensive (14:8–17), David now decided to eliminate their threat definitively (18:1), but he would have to face them again (20:4–8). The parallel in 2 Samuel 8 contains an unusual expression; modern versions tend to translate "Metheg Ammah" (lit. "the bridle of the capital") in the light of the present passage in Chronicles, as meaning that David took the control, until then exercised by Gath, of smaller towns of the area. Next fell the kingdoms of Moab (v. 2) and Zobah (in Syria, vv. 3–8). Their booty and/or tribute were dedicated or set aside (v. 11) for the future temple (vv. 2, 9–11; regarding other large numbers, see 1 Chronicles 5:21–26). Horses were admired and feared by ancient peoples as war equipment (Job 39:19–25; Is. 31:1; Jer. 4:13), but they were not to take up too much of the nation's budget (Deut. 17:16; Josh. 11:6, 9), at least until the flourishing

times of Solomon (2 Chr. 9:25). David, however, was already able to establish a small chariot corps; the rest of the horses were hamstrung (1 Chr. 18:4), perhaps in order to sell them to other peoples for their meat but to disable them as war equipment.

The successful campaign against Edom (vv. 12–13) was led by one of the generals of David's kingdom, Abishai (v. 12), a brother and lieutenant of Joab (19:11). This piece of information is not recorded in 2 Samuel 8:13 or in the superscript to Psalm 60, again underlining the access of the Chronicler to records that supplement other accounts in the Bible. Although the Lord was giving David victories, he was well-organized for the task (1 Chr. 18:14–17). He administered his kingdom wisely (v. 14), following mainly an Egyptian model of organization. Abimelech the son of Abiathar (v. 16) remained in charge of the liturgy for the ark, close to the king. The Cherethites and the Pelethites (v. 17; perhaps Cretans and Pelasgians) were bodyguards from other countries, without local ties, as an added security measure. David's sons (v. 17) were administrative officers or chief officials for the king. Second Samuel 8:18 refers to them using a Hebrew word usually employed for "priests"—*kohanim*—suggesting that they may have performed some priestly functions, unless the term was also used to designate a secular administrative responsibility as suggested by the term used in the Chronicles.

19:1—20:8. Victories over Ammon, Syria, and the Philistine Giants. Since the Ammonite king resorted to the aid of Syrian mercenaries (19:6–7), the conquest of Ammon seems to have taken place at an earlier time, before the occupation of Syrian lands by Israel (18:5–8). These were the first to flee (v. 14), as did their compatriots from beyond the Euphrates (v. 18; on other large numbers, see 1 Chronicles 5:21–26). The crown of the "king" in Rabbah (20:1–2; present day Amman), which was taken from his head (suggesting the latter was immobile), probably refers to the Ammonite idol Milcom (1 Kin. 11:5) as read by the LXX and other ancient versions (the Hebrew letters of the name "their king" spell precisely the name of the god). This explains how such a crown might have reached the unwieldy weight of one talent (75 lb or 34 kg); David probably made use of a part of this crown with only a precious stone (singular in the Hebrew text). The king had stayed at Jerusalem (1 Chr. 20:1) where the scandalous affair with Bathsheba took place (2 Sam. 11:1–5) as well as his order to have Uriah killed by the Ammonites (2 Sam. 11:16). The Chronicler omits these incidents, probably because he is concerned only with official acts of government and institutions that emphasize the glory of David's reign.

The destruction of the Philistine giants was not a definite campaign, but a collection of incidents that took place at different times (1 Chr. 20:4–8). In one of them we read about the death of Lahmi, the brother of Goliath the Gittite, by the hand of Elhanan the Bethlehemite (v. 5). By a mechanical mistake, our present copies of 2 Samuel 21:9 misread the two Hebrew letters meaning "brother of" and have Elhanan killing Goliath himself, thus appearing to contradict 1 Samuel 17. This again underlines the value of the Chronicles for comparison with other sources.

21:1–30
The Choice of a Site for the Temple

As we have seen, the Chronicler usually omits the mistakes of David in order to emphasize his role as king and his connection with the temple. But here we find a narrative about a serious mistake made by him, namely, the story of the census. This narrative is likely included here precisely because its resolution led to finding a place for the building of the temple.

21:1–6. The Military Census. Taking a census was abominable (v. 6) because a complete list of men of military age and fitness indicated reliance on human power rather than on divine intervention since in this case it does not appear that anyone paid a ransom (see Ex. 30:11, 16). The Chronicler has Satan inciting David to take the census (1 Chr. 21:1), while 2 Samuel 24:1 attributes this incitement to the "anger of the LORD" (see below, "Satan and David"). Checks and balances in international power are, of course, fully in the hand of the Lord (Dan. 4:34–35). There is also a disagreement in terms of quantities with 2 Samuel 24:9, which may be explained by supposing that in our passage the tribe of Judah, mentioned separately (1 Chr. 21:5), is included in the total, while in 2 Samuel it is an additional five hundred thousand. In any case, David did not count the tribe of Levi (v. 6), which was exempted from mandatory military service in order to guard the temple and maintain public worship (Num. 1:47–49). Probably for the same reason he did not count the tribe of

---

Satan and David

The mention of Satan in 1 Chronicles 21:1 has been a point of debate among scholars. There are two main reasons for this. First, the parallel account in 2 Samuel 24:1 does not mention Satan but speaks about God's wrath against David that incited him to take the census. Second, it is debated whether the Hebrew *satan* in 1 Chronicles is a proper name (Satan) or a function (an adversary).

1. Usage of the Term "Satan." The Hebrew word *satan* means "adversary, opponent" and is used to designate human beings who functioned as adversaries or opponents of other persons, be they military or personal (e.g., 1 Kin. 11:14, 23). It also designates the heavenly being who opposed Balaam's conduct (Num. 22:22). Concerning the absence or presence of the definitive article, some scholars have argued that in Hebrew grammar when a noun is accompanied by the definite article ("the") the noun is not a proper name but rather refers to a particular function. In the case of the Hebrew word *satan*, it would simply designate a person or being who functions as the adversary/the opponent. They believe that this is the meaning of the term in Job (1:6; 2:1) and Zechariah (3:1) where the article is used. But other scholars have argued that it is precisely when the noun is accompanied by the definite article that it functions as a proper name. The prevailing view is that in 1 Chronicles 21:1, where the article is omitted, *satan* is a proper name and designates a being called Satan, the adversary, as is the case in the NT (e.g., Mark 4:15).

2. Linguistic Connections. There are clear linguistic connections among Job 2:1, Zechariah 3:1, and 1 Chronicles 21:1. In Chronicles Satan stood (*'amad*, "to stand") against Israel and incited (*sut*, "to incite") David to sin. The use of the verb "to stand" (*'amad*) together with the noun *satan* is found in

Zechariah 3:1, establishing a connection between the two passages. In both cases he was opposing the people of God. The verb "to incite" (*sut*) appears in conjunction with the noun *satan* in Job 2:3, also establishing a connection between these two passages. In Job, he incited God against Job, and in Chronicles he incited David against God. It could be suggested that since the author of the Chronicles is aware of the other two passages his understanding of the term *satan* reflects the meaning of the term in the other two books. For him, *satan* in his two other sources designates a proper name. In other words, he is not contrasting his usage with that of the other two passages; the presence or absence of the article is irrelevant. The connection shared by the three passages makes it highly unlikely that what we have here is part of the evolution of a term from a function to the proper name of God's archenemy. The OT indicates that there is a being who opposes God and His plans for His people (e.g., Gen. 3:1–5; Lev. 16:8–10, 20–22; Job 1–2; Is. 14:12–14; cf. Rev. 12:9).

3. *The Narratives in Chronicles and Samuel.* As we have seen, the role of Satan is quite clear in the three previous passages. First, he opposed God's plan for His followers, thus becoming His adversary. This is particularly the case in Job where he opposed the way God dealt with Job. Second, he incited people to disobey God and break away from Him. Third, he wanted evil things for God's people. According to Chronicles, Satan was standing against Israel; that is to say, he was an enemy who opposed Israel, and in order to damage Israel he incited David to take a census, fully knowing that the people would suffer as a result. In the narrative, the opponent of Satan was Joab, who advised David not to do this because it would bring guilt upon the people. But Satan had blinded David, and he was unwilling to listen. The nature of the sin is not clear in 1 Chronicles. Why was taking a census a national sin? Censuses where a ransom price was paid were taken in Israel without any penalty (e.g., Ex. 30:11–16). Perhaps, as some scholars have suggested, the difference here is that this was a military census taken without divine approval, and therefore it expressed reliance on human military power. It was a breach of the covenant relation with the Lord.

If this is the case, then the difference with the account of the event in 2 Samuel 24:1 is not of major significance. The wrath of the Lord, mentioned in that verse as the cause for the census, is now clarified as God having allowed Satan to incite David to take the census. In His anger God did not intervene to protect David. Nevertheless, God was still the Sovereign Lord who brought the plague to an end and used the experience to lead David to find a place for the building of the temple. He did not give Satan complete control over His followers (see Job 1:12; 2:6). In the process, we see David acting as the ideal king who, after sinning, repented and sought forgiveness from the Lord.

Benjamin, in whose territory the worship center of Gibeon was located.

Once David recognized his sin, there was confession followed by divine punishment (1 Chr. 21:7–15). In contrast to Saul, David seemed always willing to accept his sin and make amends. He said to God, "I have sinned greatly" (v. 8), a confession motivated by the ministry of Gad, David's seer (v. 9; cf. 1 Sam. 22:3–5; 1 Chr. 29:29). While God grants forgiveness, a forgiven sin may still have consequences during earthly history. David was granted, however, the privilege of choosing between three divine judgments (vv. 11–13). They were to last either three years, three months, or three days (v. 12). This consistent "threeness" of divine judgments indicates that the Chronicles preserve the best reading in contrast to 2 Samuel 24:13, which reads "seven years" (although some translations follow the LXX, which has "three years"). In the course of the ensuing pestilence, the Lord looked and relented (v. 15).

21:16–30. Divine Choice for the Site of an Altar. A heavenly vision showed David the presence of the Angel of the Lord (v. 16) in terms reminiscent of the experience of Balaam (Num. 22:31). As a response to the intercessory prayer of David and the elders (representatives of the threatened city), he was commanded to build an altar at the place where the angel had received the order to stop the slaughter (1 Chr. 21:18; cf. v. 15). Approaching God must always remind us of both His mercy and His judgment. It is the divine intention that judgment would lead to salvation. The private property rights of an Israelite were inviolable: if sold, land would eventually revert to the family. David availed himself of this unique opportunity to buy from a non-Israelite, a Jebusite, so that the site for the temple would be completely independent from any particular tribe or Israelite family. While Ornan ("Araunah" in 2 Sam. 24:16), mindful of the high investiture of David (1 Chr. 21:21), wanted to donate it for such a sacred use, David insisted on paying full price (v. 24). Its amount varies between here and 2 Samuel 24. In 2 Samuel 24:20, fifty shekels of silver was the means of payment, but it refers only to the floor of the threshing place, while according to 1 Chronicles 21:25, David paid six hundred pieces of gold for the whole sanctuary mount plus the animals for the burnt offering.

The erection of the altar (21:26–30) was a sensitive act because God had authorized only one altar at a time (Deut. 12:8–14), and the altar at Gibeon was still functioning (1 Chr. 21:29). However, God had also made provision for moving the altar site, through a special revelation, to any place where He would cause His Name to be remembered (Ex. 20:24). Hence 1 Chronicles takes pains to show such revelation by means of the fire from heaven (the usual Hebrew idiom for lightning) which ignited the offering, as well as the success of the entreaty to stop the pestilence (1 Chr. 21:26–28; not found in 2 Sam.) and to make clear that the Gibeon altar was not accessible to David (1 Chr. 21:30).

22:1–19
Preparations for the Temple

David acknowledged that God had chosen this particular site for the house of the Lord God (v. 1) and started preparations to build the temple. He began to accumulate materials for the structure, to organize the work of construction (chap. 22) and the services in the future temple (chaps. 23–26). He even defined the overall organization of the kingdom with an eye on responsibilities related to public worship (chap. 27). Indeed, the whole period of David's reign is told from the viewpoint of the conception of God's temple (chaps. 10–29). Chapter 22 lists the gathering of workers and materials for the construction of the temple (vv. 2–5) and contains David's speeches to Solomon (vv. 6–16) and to the elders (vv. 17–19).

22:2–5. David Gathers Workmen and Materials. David resorted to recruiting foreigners (v. 2), the defeated original inhabitants of Canaan still living on the land, or landless immigrants. Stones are the ubiquitous building material in the Holy Land, usually in their natural state, but for monumental constructions like the temple they were shaped (v. 2) into regular blocks. Iron joints would reinforce the solidity of such walls (v. 3). Bronze and cedar (vv. 3–4) would also contribute to a temple which had to be exceedingly magnificent, famous, and glorious throughout all countries (vv. 4–5).

22:6–19. David's Speech to Solomon and the Leaders. David charged Solomon with the sacred task of building the temple (vv. 6–10), with an induction formula that Moses had used with Joshua (Josh. 1:6–9), and that David would later use again (1 Chr. 28:20). This included encouragement (v. 13), description of the task (v. 10), and invocation of God's assistance (v. 9). There is a reference to the reason for denying David the privilege of building the temple. It was not just that David could not build it because of the wars surrounding him (1 Kin. 5:3), but it was also because he had made himself unfit because he shed much blood (1 Chr. 22:8). A temple should not be a monument to the victories of a conqueror, nor a reminder of the spoils plundered from many lands (as was the case in Egypt and other ancient cultures), but a "house of prayer for all nations" (Is. 56:7). The figures in 1 Chronicles 22:14 may seem very high. They indicate about 3,600 tons of gold (3,265,865 kg; 220 cubic yards) or the equivalent of a wall of solid gold 3 feet high (0.9 m), 3 feet wide (0.9 m), and 660 feet long (201.2 m). However, we have no particular evidence to suggest that these figures are unreliable.

Joshua had established the sanctuary at Shiloh (Josh. 18:1), which was to function as the temple of the Lord once the land was *kabash* ("subdued," "brought under control," or "conquered") by the defeat of the Canaanites and Israel was at rest (e.g., Josh. 22:4; 23:1). In a similar way, after David defeated the Philistines and other enemies who surrounded Israel, the land was *kabash* ("subdued," "brought under control," or "conquered") and brought to rest (1 Chr. 22:18). Now he was ready to promote the construction of the temple. Leaders, therefore, were exhorted to collaborate with the project. The actual dwelling of God is in heaven, as this text and many others indicate (e.g., 2 Chr. 7), yet His name resided in this temple (1 Chr. 22:19; 2 Chr. 2:1); it was there that He revealed Himself to them.

23:1—26:32
Organization of Temple Services

The actual organization of the temple services took place in David's old age, soon after he made his son Solomon king (v. 1). Though using very ancient records, the Chronicler deals with the clergy following the order of Ezekiel (Ezek. 44), who had predicted, during the Exile in Babylon, a future ideal temple. The Chronicler identifies the Levites based on their genealogy; their responsibilities were assigned (1 Chr. 12:1-32). The divisions of the priests were organized (24:1-19), and the Chronicler identifies other Levites (24:20-31). The musicians were organized (25:1-30) as well as the gatekeepers, the treasurers (26:1-28), and the officials and judges (26:29-33).

23:1—24:31. Levites and Priests. Since they had not been included in the military census, their numbers were now determined (21:6). Following the prescriptions of Numbers 4:3, those who were thirty years old or older were to do the work in the sanctuary (1 Chr. 23:3), but in view of the fact that they would no longer have to carry heavy objects the minimum age was later reduced to twenty years (23:24; Ezra 3:8). They would assist the priests in working on the temple of the Lord (1 Chr. 23:4, 28-31), as musicians (vv. 23:5, 30) and temple guards (gatekeepers; v. 5). They would also help the Israelites during sacrifices (v. 31). They were organized according to the three branches of the tribe (v. 6).

A new list of priestly lineages is provided in this passage (cf. 6:49-53; 9:10-12). Ahimelech (or Ahimelek), the high priest from the line of Ithamar and Zadok from Eleazar's, aided David in forming their appointed offices of service (24:3). While Ithamarites contributed eight lineages, and Eleazarites sixteen, the resulting twenty-four orders of priests are not classified as belonging to one or the other line. One may suppose that even numbers up to sixteen correspond to Ithamarites, and all others to Eleazarites (v. 6). Their exalted status as officials of the sanctuary and officials of God is noted (v. 5). The list of Levites in vv. 20-31 mostly parallels that of chapter 23, except in two cases. In the line of Merari, the branch of Jaaziah is added (v. 26), and in the line of Gershon, the son of Levi is missing (but not the lineage of Gershon the son of Moses; v. 20; cf. 23:16). One further generation is usually added to each lineage, again illustrating the use of different records.

25:1-31. The Musicians. These were selected by David and the commanders (v. 1) or chiefs of the temple service (24:6). Most translations read "army commanders," but the Hebrew word *tsaba'* can be translated in various ways, including in reference to the sanctuary service (Num. 4:3). Apparently three main lines of Levites were represented among these singers and players of stringed instruments and cymbals (1 Chr. 25:1): (1) Asaph (v. 2) from the line of Gershon (6:39, 43; see 15:19; 16:4, 7); (2) Jeduthun (v. 3), also called Ethan, from the line of Merari (6:44; 15:17, 19); and Heman (vv. 4-5) from Korah's line (6:33; 15:17, 19; 16:41-42). They were to "prophesy" with music (25:1-2), which probably means that they were to sing temple hymns that were originally written under divine inspiration (see 29:30). The distribution of names of family heads among the lineages is not totally random (25:9-31). It seems as if they decided by drawing lots that the lineage of Asaph should appear first, and then, alternately (every other item), names were drawn from his line until all were assigned. The second lot fell to Jeduthun, and henceforward every other item was from that line until all its names were drawn. After finishing with the sons of Asaph, the names alternated between the lines of Jeduthun and Heman, and once the names from Jeduthun were exhausted, the remainder came from the line of Heman.

26:1-32. Gatekeepers, Treasurers, and Officials and Judges. The tribe of Levi was peculiarly warlike (Gen. 49:5-7; Ex. 32:25-29), and this skill was given expression in their temple guards. If Levites did not regularly participate in war, it was not because they were not supposed to be involved in defense activities but because the temple itself needed permanent defenders (in antiquity, temples concentrated a large amount of riches, coveted by robbers and raiders) and crowd control personnel. Those assigned to this task had duties to fulfill in the Lord's temple (1 Chr. 26:12). The treasurers (vv. 20-28) appear immediately after the "gatekeepers" probably because they needed the support of those guards. Some were in charge of the treasuries of the house (or temple) of the Lord (v. 22) and received regular tithe and offerings (23:28-29), while others kept track of items like dedicated things (26:26), such as treasure collected in wars since the times of Samuel, Saul, David, and their respective generals (v. 28). In Israel, Levitical cities and city sections served as the judiciary (see 6:54-81). Special officials served also as judges over Israel outside the Jerusalem temple area (26:29), perhaps in rural areas, and others on the west side of the Jordan, away from Israel's heartland, both for all the Lord's work and in the service of the king (26:30). This shows the wide spectrum of duties that fell to the Levites once they did not have to carry the sanctuary any longer.

27:1–34
Administration of the Kingdom

As explained previously (see chap. 22), the institutions created by David did not just support the needs of the crown but also the religious needs of the people; they all contributed to the development of the temple. The administration of the kingdom involved military divisions (vv. 1–15), tribal leaders (vv. 16–23), administrators of the properties of the king (vv. 25–31), and a royal council (vv. 32–34).

27:1–24. Military Divisions and Tribal Leaders. Some of the names of the mighty men of David (11:10–47) reappear here, but as captains of monthly relays of army/military divisions (27:1). In this way the king did not need to pay a standing army, and while not all the men needed to serve in full-time active duty roles during their turn, the kingdom enjoyed some measure of protection. Though hereditary divisions such as tribes can be dangerous in a united monarchy, it is clear that David could not do without the traditional tribal structure of the nation, if for no other reason than to supply him with the "thousands" needed for the military divisions (vv. 16–23). But that structure was altered: some tribes (Asher, Gad) had no leaders, while other tribes were subdivided (Manasseh: east and west; Levi: Aaronites and the rest of the clans). The functions of these leaders were clearly related to furnishing men for the royal service. Notice that vv. 23–24 justify the absence of concrete figures for each tribe. David now trusted the promise of the God of countless Israelites, no doubt with the help of the pestilence that interrupted his census (v. 24 and chap. 21). The manifestation of God's wrath made it impossible for Joab to complete the census; consequently, official figures were not available.

27:25–34. Managers of Crown Properties and the Royal Council. There is no indication that Israelites paid taxes under David. His expenses seem to have been defrayed from the product of royal lands: grains (v. 26), vineyards (v. 27), olive and sycamore trees (v. 28), cattle and other herds (v. 29), beasts of burden (v. 30), and various flocks (v. 31). Such production required skillful management, so David brought specialists from abroad when necessary, such as Ishmaelites to manage

the camels and sheep (vv. 30–31). Part of these lands may have been acquired through conquests.

A small cabinet of five members seems to have helped David make important decisions. Verse 34 refers to Jehoiada, who succeeded Ahithophel, David's adviser, after his suicide; this is the closest the Chronicler comes to reporting the rebellion of Absalom (2 Sam. 15–19), to whom a counselor had given intelligent advice, but which was fortunately undone by the disinformation of another counselor, Hushai (1 Chr. 27:34).

28:1—29:30
Successor and Temple Readiness

David is reported to have made his son Solomon king (i.e., designated him officially as an heir) in 23:1, though he was already thinking of him as such in 22:5. In this last speech, David gave specific instructions concerning the construction of the temple to the leaders and to his son. He handed to Solomon the plans for the construction of the temple and financial resources (28:1–8), exhorted the young king to be courageous (vv. 9–10; cf. 29:1), and provided offerings for the temple (28:11—29:5). The leaders of the people also provided offerings for sacrifices and for the building (29:6–9). First Chronicles concludes with a hymn of praise and a prayer by David (vv. 10–20), the anointing of Solomon as king (vv. 21–25), and a summary of the reign of David (vv. 26–30).

28:1–21. The Speech. The public speech was in general similar to the one given in the palace (22:6–16). The first part had the purpose of providing a smooth transition between the reigns of David and Solomon. Just as there was no direct mention of the rebellion of Absalom (see commentary on 27:25–34), so was no mention made of Adonijah's, or the intrigues of Nathan and Bathsheba in order to secure the throne for Solomon (1 Kin. 1–2). Overall, the picture in the Chronicles is that of a peaceful transition, supported by "all Israel" (1 Chr. 29:24–25). This is not because the author wants to hide facts (he assumes many of his readers know the stories in Samuel and Kings, and refers all readers to them) but because he wants to underline the essential facts from a religious point of view.

29:1–20. The Offerings, the Hymn, and the Prayer. A key to a successful collection appeal is to show that those promoting it are also sacrificing in order to contribute. David showed that he had dedicated not only the treasure taken in wars but his own property (v. 3). Things he dedicated included not only precious metals but also quality woods and materials for flooring and mosaics (v. 2). David then offered a prayer, which began with thanksgiving for the God-given opportunity of contributing to His cause (vv. 10–15). This thanksgiving in turn started with reflection on the majesty of God: His kingdom (v. 11e) and power and glory (v. 11b). This composition was, indeed, the source of the liturgical conclusion of the Lord's Prayer (Matt. 6:13). It ends contrasting such majesty with the transitory nature of humanity, a passing shadow and without hope (1 Chr. 29:15). Hopelessness seems to be the natural condition of humans. After acknowledging that in giving offerings the people of God were only returning to Him what He had given them (vv. 16–17), David interceded for Israel and Solomon. What was needed, above anything else, was a heart that was *shalem* (an adjectival form of the noun *shalom*—"peacefulness," "wholeness"), that is, a completely loyal or wholehearted commitment to trust in God and obey His instructions (vv. 18–19). This being a public prayer, it was followed by the response of the entire assembly, who bowed and prostrated themselves (29:20).

29:21–30. Solomon and Zadok Anointed: Succession of the Monarchy. The next day,

the assembly confirmed (or proclaimed for a second time; v. 22) Solomon as heir to the throne (which he temporarily occupied as part of the designation ceremony; 29:22–23) and Zadok as acting high priest (Abiathar, though still alive, had fallen in disgrace after the rebellion of Adonijah; 1 Kin. 1:25). The anointing was accompanied by sacrifices for all Israel (1 Chr. 29:21). The Chronicler recognizes again a reign of David in Hebron, which he does not detail (see commentary on 3:1–9); he subsumes these seven years under the forty years of his reign over all Israel (29:26–27). Actually, the reign in Hebron had been only "over Judah" (2 Sam. 5:5), but the Chronicler is here emphasizing David's long life of riches and honor. The civil war in times of Esh-Baal/Ishbosheth was only a minor detour in that long and glorious march. Recognition is also given to sources in the books of Samuel, Nathan, and Gad (1 Chr. 29:29), authors who may indeed have had a hand in the composition of the history in our present books of Samuel and Kings, which have a definite prophetic perspective. The kingdoms of the lands (v. 30) may be a reference to those conquered by David (see chaps. 18–20). First Chronicles, like every book in the OT, closes leaving the reader with the expectation of more divine activity in the history of God's people. In this case, the people expectantly looked forward to the building of the temple as a center of worship and atonement.

The Temple in Chronicles

The topic of the temple in Chronicles runs from the beginning to the end of the book. In the genealogies we find a significant amount of material dedicated to the tribe of Levi and the work of priests and Levites (1 Chr. 6:1–80; 9:10–34). At the close of the book, Cyrus states that the Lord God of heaven commanded him to build a temple (lit. "house") for Him in Jerusalem (2 Chr. 36:23). In between these two textual segments, we find the history of the interaction of the kings of Judah, the people, and the temple. The genealogies also assign a significant amount of attention to King David. The tribe whose genealogy is, arguably, more carefully described than others is that of Judah (1 Chr. 2:3–55; 4:1–23), from which David came, and within it the family of David receives

significant attention (3:1–24). The genealogy of King Saul and his death are mainly a foil to prepare the way for the rise of the ideal king of Israel, David (10:1–14). The theology of the temple in the books of Chronicles is worth exploring because of its connections with the kings and the people of Israel and their final fate.

1. David and the Temple. After the conquest of the city of Jerusalem, David manifested his personal devotion to the Lord by bringing the ark of the covenant to the city (1 Chr. 13:1–14). He recognized that the success of his role as king was determined by his commitment to the Lord manifested in his concern for properly handling the symbols of His presence and by obedience to the laws that regulated proper worship. Early in his career David realized that following the laws related to the sanctuary services was of supreme importance. The drastic failure of his first attempt to move the ark taught him that success was related to obedience to the divine will. In the second attempt, David followed the biblical directives and was successful (15:1–29). This pattern of success determined by submission to the cult is used throughout Chronicles to evaluate the reign of the different kings. David's practice would become the model.

The capture of the city of Jerusalem instilled in David the desire to build a temple to the Lord—a responsibility of kings throughout the ANE. He wanted for God the best house he could build (17:1; 22:5). But God surprised him by promising David that God would build a house (dynasty) for him that would last forever; one of his sons would always sit on the throne of Israel (17:10–14). David would not build the temple, but his son, Solomon, would do it (17:4, 12; 22:5). However, David would prepare everything needed for the construction, but the Lord Himself would choose the place and provide the *tabnit* (see Ex. 25:8–9) or model to be used in the construction. The first He did by manifesting Himself to David on Mount Moriah (1 Chr. 21:16, 18; 2 Chr. 3:1; 7:12; 12:13) and the second by revealing the plans for the building (1 Chr. 28:19; 2 Chr. 29:25). Thus, the temple and its services were invested with unquestionable divine authority.

David bought the land where the temple would be built (1 Chr. 21:18–30) and gathered everything Solomon would need for the building (22:1–4, 14–16; 29:2–9). He also organized the work of the priests (24:1–19) and Levites (23:1–32; 24:20–31) as musicians (25:1–31), gatekeepers (26:1–19), and treasurers (26:20–32). David encouraged his son to build the temple and to obey the laws of God (22:13). The reference here to these decrees, statutes, or judgments is not only to the moral law but more specifically to the law related to the sanctuary services (1 Chr. 16:40; 2 Chr. 23:18; 31:2–3). David established the foundation for the proper worship of the Lord in the place the Lord had chosen for this purpose. The future of the nation and of the Davidic dynasty would depend on their submission to the worship of the Lord in His temple according to the instructions He gave them. Temple, king, and nation had been permanently united.

2. Solomon and the Temple. The responsibility for the actual construction of the temple fell to Solomon, and he performed the task in perfect obedience to the instructions God gave to David. His first recorded action was to go to Gibeon, where the sanctuary was located, to worship the Lord and seek His guidance (2 Chr. 1:3–6). He then proceeded to build the temple on Mount Moriah (3:1—5:1). Finally the ark of the covenant was brought into the Most Holy Place of the new temple (5:2–12) and, as the Levites played their musical instruments praising the Lord for His goodness, mercy, and faithful love (v. 13), the glory of the Lord filled the house, thus sanctifying the temple (v. 14). The Lord was again residing among His people as His kingdom.

Solomon's prayer of dedication is theologically rich and closes with an invitation to God to arise and come to His resting place (6:41; 1 Chr. 17:5–6). At that moment fire came down from heaven and consumed the burnt offering and the sacrifices, and the glory of the Lord filled the temple (2 Chr. 7:1). The people bowed down to their majestic and powerful God and worshiped and praised Him. In a sense the experience of the people at Sinai was being repeated, but this time the Lord was moving from the tent of meeting to a temple made of stone: a permanent dwelling. Soon after this, God appeared to Solomon once more in answer to the dedicatory prayer.

God promised Solomon that He would establish his throne and kingdom, as He had promised David (7:18). But this promise was always conditional. Solomon was expected to obey God's laws (v. 17), with an emphasis primarily on obedience to the laws related to the temple services. God explained to him that if he disregarded His commands and worshiped other gods, Israel would be deported and the temple destroyed (7:19). This was an explicit statement regarding the theological, political, and social centrality of the temple in the life of God's people. As a result of disregarding proper worship in the temple, the gifts of the dynasty of David, the land, and the temple would be withdrawn from the people. The future of all was dependent on serving the Lord according to His will in His holy temple (v. 28). What made Israel the people of God was the presence of the Lord in His temple.

3. *Temple and Kings.* Through David the Lord made clear that the primary responsibility of the king was to promote and care for the temple and its services, and to lead the people in the exclusive worship of the resident deity, the Lord. The success of the king and the nation were contingent on it. Solomon obeyed the Lord, and, like David, he and the nation prospered. Rehoboam abandoned the Lord (2 Chr. 12:1), and He handed the king over into the hands of the king of Egypt (v. 5). He was preserved because he humbled himself. The Northern Kingdom is considered by the Chronicler to be without hope because they built their own place of worship and appointed their own non-Levitical priests to serve on the high places in the worship of demons and the calf idols made by Jeroboam (11:15). It became like "the peoples of other lands" (13:9).

Second Chronicles identifies good kings, such as Abiyah (13:10–12), Asa (14:2–15), Jehoshapat (17:6–9), Jotham (27:2, 5–6), Hezekiah (29:35; 30:11–19), and Josiah, as those who undividedly served the Lord in His temple. Their fate was directly related to the temple worship. Some of the others had divided loyalties, including Joash (23:18), Amaziah (25:14–16), Uzzaiah (26:16–21), and Mannaseh (33:3–9, 12–17); they were ultimately abandoned by the Lord. Jehoram (20:33; 21:9–11), Ahaziah (22:2–4), Ahaz (28:2–4, 22–25), Amon (33:23–24), and Zedechiah (36:13–14) were unfaithful to the Lord and corrupted the temple services and/or ignored the worship of the Lord in His temple. The sin of these kings was not just idolatry but an idolatry that in Chronicles is explicitly connected to the temple of the Lord.

In the long run, most of the kings of Judah showed no respect for the temple of the Lord and sought other gods and built other places for worship. During all of this the Lord sent them warnings through the prophets because He had compassion for His people and His temple (36:15). But this was to no avail because they mocked God's messengers, despised His words, and laughed at His prophets until the Lord's anger arose against His people—"there was no remedy" (v. 16).

The defilement of the temple reached such a condition that God abandoned it, and since it was directly related to the survival of the Davidic monarchy and the nation, all three—monarchy, kingdom, and temple—came to an end. God handed them to the king of Babylon, who killed King Zedechiah, took to Babylon the articles of the house of the Lord and the treasuries of the kings, and finally burned the house of the Lord and all the palaces (2 Chr. 36:17–19).

The collapse of the temple, the monarchy, and the nation was a most disturbing occurrence for the people of God. It was not a return to the pre-monarchy period and experience but rather a return to their time of enslavement in Egypt when they were not a nation and did not have a king or a temple. The covenant had come to an end primarily because of the failure of the kings to support and seek the Lord in His temple. Why was the survival of the monarchy and of the nation so deeply connected to the temple services? Chronicles provides its own answer.

4. *Temple and Theology.* We have described how important the temple was for the future of the monarchy and the nation. Now we should examine what the Chronicler has to say about the theological foundation of that significance.

First, the temple was a unique space. There could not be another place like this because there is no other God like the Lord, who in fulfillment of His covenant promise to Israel chose to dwell among them (2 Chr. 6:14). But perhaps more important, what made the temple unique was that God selected the place and sanctified it with His presence (7:16); it is *His* "house" or temple (e.g., 1 Chr. 9:26–27; 23:28; 2 Chr. 3:3; 22:12). The biblical God localized Himself within the space of His creatures, thus indicating that He was a personal being who wanted, for a variety of reasons, to interact with His people. But the localized presence of God in His temple created a theological problem for Solomon: He could be confused with another creature. Solomon clarifies that this is not the case because if heaven itself cannot contain God, how much less an earthly temple (2 Chr. 6:18).

Created space is not sufficient to be a house for God, and yet He chose to dwell in heaven (e.g., vv. 21, 30) and in an earthly temple (v. 2). Solomon's prayer makes clear that the true dwelling of God is in heaven but that He has established a close connection between both dwellings. In the earthly temple resided the name of the Lord (v. 6; 20:8); that is to say, this is the place where the Lord revealed Himself to His people—the name stands for the Lord as the One who could be invoked and who would answer (20:9). This explains why it is said that the temple was built for the ark of the covenant (1 Chr. 17:1; 28:2; 2 Chr. 6:41), which was the visible symbol of God's presence by which He guided His people (1 Chr. 13:3–4).

The uniqueness of the temple as God's dwelling place also lies in the fact that it was the center that unified the people of Israel and the monarchy. The king and the people found in it a common nucleus around which they together sought and worshiped the Lord as one nation. Setting it aside would result in chaos and the disintegration of the nation. As a unifying center, the name of the God who resided there had power over the nations and when necessary defeated them or gave them victories (e.g., 2 Chr. 12:5; 14:12); He used them according to His purpose. The presence of God in the unique place had a universal impact that no other space could have. Any other place of worship in Israel that would dare to compete with the dwelling of God was to be destroyed. The kings were to destroy the high places that occasionally were built to worship God (20:33; 33:17) but that most of the time had been built to worship other deities (14:3, 5; 17:6; 31:1; 32:12). When other temples were built for Baal, the Lord reacted with anger and called for the destruction of such places (23:16–17). In Israel the very core of worship and service was centralized in the temple because the name of the Lord dwelt there.

Second, the temple was a place of prayer for all people. This is one of the most fundamental characteristics of the temple in Chronicles, as found in the prayer of Solomon. God put His name in the temple in order to hear the prayer that the king and the people would make "toward this place" (2 Chr. 6:20–21). These were mainly prayers of supplication coming from hearts that sincerely sought the Lord in times of oppression as a result of their sin (vv. 24–25) or when they simply needed His help (v. 34). It was through prayer that the deep connection between the heavenly and earthly dwellings of God was expressed. Solomon asked the Lord to listen from His dwelling in heaven when the people prayed to Him in the earthly temple and to answer their prayers and forgive them. The temple connected worshipers with the God whose ultimate residence is in the heavens and who made efficacious whatever took place in the earthly temple. Heaven and earth found a very particular point of contact in the temple (cf. John 1:14). It was from His dwelling in heaven that God granted forgiveness to His repentant people and delivered them from oppression (2 Chr. 7:14). In other words, the Name of the Lord, who resided in the temple, connected worshipers to the true dwelling of God in heaven. This privilege was also given to the aliens in Israel who came to the temple to pray. Solomon prayed for them specifically for the purpose that all peoples of the earth might come to reverence God and His name, recognizing this temple as belonging to Him (6:33).

Third, the temple was a place to offer sacrifices to God (7:12). The first human ritual act at the end of the dedication of the temple was placing sacrifices on the altar of the temple, and then as a divine response, "fire came down from heaven and consumed the burnt offering and the sacrifices" (2 Chr. 7:1). Sacrifices such as the burnt and peace offerings were offered primarily to express joy and gratitude and to thank the Lord for the many blessings received from Him (7:7–9). But in the case of sin, an atoning sacrifice was needed. It was the responsibility of the priests to make atonement for the sins of the people on the altar of burnt offerings and the altar of incense (1 Chr. 6:49). During his dedicatory prayer, Solomon asked God to listen to His people and to forgive their sins, but nothing was said about how that forgiveness was possible. The reformation initiated by Hezekiah indicates that this was related to atonement through the sin offering (2 Chr. 29:24). Here the Chronicler is unquestionably supported by the Levitical law regulating the services in the temple.

Fourth, the temple was a place of hope. Prayer presupposes the presence of hope in the human heart. In Chronicles, prayer was not taking the place of the sacrificial system, but it was emphasized in order to underline that genuine repentance should precede the sacrificial act. Nevertheless, since forgiveness was not the automatic result of sacrifices or prayers (6:39), the Lord was still ready to forgive His people under almost any circumstance. Even during the Exile and in the absence of the temple, if there was true repentance, the Lord would be willing to forgive His people from His heavenly temple (see 6:36–39). There was here a word of hope for the exiled returnees addressed by the Chronicler. They now knew that the Exile was the result of the desecration of the temple—the rejection of the Lord—but they also knew that the Exile was not the end of hope. Their return to the land was filled with hope because it showed that the Lord listened to their prayers. The temple needed to be built, and the Lord, in the absence of a Davidic king, had raised Cyrus, His servant, to initiate the process of reconstructing the temple as the first step in the reconstitution of His people. Perhaps in a veiled way the Chronicler is suggesting that the next thing was the coming of a Davidic king. The Lord was guiding His people from His heavenly dwelling. The past tragedy occasioned by the unwillingness of the kings and the people to seek the Lord in His temple resulted in the collapse of the nation, but now God was offering a new hope by locating Himself again in a new temple in the midst of His people (cf. Rev. 21:1–4). David recognized that all things in heaven and earth belonged to God—He is the great King, and He is exalted as head over all (1 Chr. 29:11).

2 CHRONICLES

INTRODUCTION

Title and Authorship. If 1 and 2 Chronicles represent a single volume (as they originally were) and are thus the same book that is referenced thirty-four times in 1 and 2 Kings and Esther, then the original title was the *Chronicles [or Record] of the Kings of Judah* (see 1 Kin. 14:29), and this would mean that the *Chronicles [or Record] of the Kings of Israel* (see 1 Kin. 14:19) has been lost. In the Hebrew Bible the title is *Matters [or Events] of the Days [or Times]*. The LXX called it *Things Omitted [or Left Aside]* and split it into two books. In the fourth century A.D., the title in the Latin translation (Vulgate) appeared as *Chronicles of the Whole of Sacred History*. During the early years of the reformation, Bibles used by both Protestants and Catholics included a shortened version of the Vulgate's title and retained the split of the LXX, resulting in the 1 and 2 Chronicles that we use today.

The books of Chronicles do not indicate who wrote them, though the Jewish Talmud has a statement suggesting that Ezra wrote a part of them. In 2 Chronicles the narrative essentially begins with Solomon's construction and dedication of the temple, and the book ends with the command to rebuild it (36:23). The incomplete thought at the end of 2 Chronicles (36:22–23) is repeated and completed at the beginning of Ezra (1:1–2) using an ancient composition technique that appears in other non-biblical documents. This technique (called "catch-lines") helped readers know that the two scrolls (tablets) were meant to be read together; but since the scroll (tablet) was not long enough, the narrative had to be continued on a new one. Thus, it seems that Ezra at least had a hand in the closing statement of the book of 2 Chronicles, if not much more. It is also clear that the author(s) relied on historical documents since it is impossible for anyone to have lived through the entire period.

These documents are named as the books of the records of the kings of Israel (1 Chr. 9:1), King David (1 Chr. 27:24), Samuel the seer (1 Chr. 29:29), Nathan the prophet (1 Chr. 29:29), Gad the seer (1 Chr. 29:29), Shemaiah the prophet (2 Chr. 12:15), Jehu the son of Hanani (2 Chr. 20:34), the kings of Judah (2 Chr. 25:26), and perhaps even the Chronicles (or record) of the kings of Judah. These statements regarding references make it plain that much more was written about the kings of Judah than is recorded here, indicating that the selections that survive in 1 and 2 Chronicles were likely compiled to teach spiritual lessons.

Date. The closing statement of the book (the decree of Cyrus) can be dated to 537 B.C. Chronicles was designed to review Jewish history (the kingdom of Judah), which is why the kings of the Northern Kingdom of Israel are not recorded. Chronicles is the last book in the Hebrew Bible (coming after Ezra and Nehemiah), which suggests that it was written late. Also, in the genealogical section at the beginning of 1 Chronicles, information traces a family well into the Persian period (1 Chr. 3:19–24). Thus, the date for the composition of the final version of Chronicles must be after 537 B.C. with an understanding that some portions may have been written earlier.

Backgrounds. By the opening chapter of 2 Chronicles, David had died and Solomon had just been anointed king. The political struggle for the throne that is described in 1 Kings 1–2 is skipped in the narrative of 2 Chronicles 1, and instead the story of Solomon picks up where 1 Kings 3 begins—with Solomon's request for wisdom.

In 971 B.C. (the year that David died), there were no immediate threats to his kingdom from outside entities. To the north, Mesopotamia was entering a dark age. Assyria would not begin to become the strong empire that would dominate the political landscape in this region for almost sixty years. To the south, Egypt was at the beginning of the Third Intermediate period, with a king in the north (Siaman) and the high priest of Amun ruling the south, and thus it was not a threat to the outside world.

Theology and Purpose. If 2 Chronicles (along with 1 Chronicles) was written for the postexilic Jews, the purpose seems clearly to establish the kingdom of Judah in the land. To support this, the Hebrews are shown to be able to trace their ancestors back to Adam (1 Chr. 1:1). The genealogical section, in which the tribe of Judah is the first tribe presented (1 Chr. 4:1), ends with a review of those who lived in Jerusalem and those of the tribe of Levi who had responsibilities there (1 Chr. 9:2–34). Saul's reign is covered in a brief twenty-four verses (1 Chr. 9:35—10:14) in order to move quickly to David, who rose to the throne at that time (1 Chr. 10:14). From that point to the end of 2 Chronicles, the entire record is a history of David and his ruling descendents. By tracing this history (the good and the bad), the Jews would be able to demonstrate that the land was theirs and explain why they were captives returning (for more on this, see 1 Chronicles: Introduction).

COMMENTARY

1:1—9:31

SOLOMON'S REIGN

Second Chronicles concentrates on the lives of the kings who followed the model of David in terms of commitment to the Lord and to His temple. It begins with the realizations of the dream of David: building a temple for the God of Israel. The task had fallen, under divine guidance, into the hands of Solomon. The first nine chapters of this book narrate the life and accomplishments of the new king. In order for him to accomplish this most important task, God gave him wisdom (1:1–17). He then went on to build the temple (2:1—4:22) and to dedicate it to the service of the Lord (5:1–22). Finally, the main achievements of Solomon are narrated (8:1—9:31).

1:1–17
The Gift of Wisdom

Solomon inherited a kingdom appointed by God to accomplish great things for Him and His people. Guided by the Lord, David had unified it

and organized its administration and its religious character. The next king, Solomon, would need wisdom and God's Spirit to lead the nation.

1:1–6. The Assembly at Gibeon. As soon as Solomon felt strengthened (i.e., secure) in his throne (in part after eliminating the enemies of David; cf. 1 Kin. 2), he organized a religious convocation for the nation at Gibeon (2 Chr. 1–3). This was the place where the only authorized altar remained (that of Bezalel, v. 5; Deut. 12; 16:2; 26:2; 31:11), even though the ark was now housed in Jerusalem. David had, in fact, used the latter altar site. The thousand burnt offerings (2 Chr. 1: 6) suggest that the Gibeon assembly was not only an inaugural celebration but also a means of assuring the people that the new king was fully devoted to the God of his father David. The people were represented by their leaders, including leaders of groups of thousands and those of hundreds (v. 2; for the significance of these units in order to understand the large numbers in Chronicles, see commentary on 1 Chr. 5:21–26; 12:23–40).

1:7–17. The Vision and the Power of Solomon. The prophetic dream reported in 1 Kings 3:5 is presented here as an appearance of the Lord in a night vision (2 Chr. 1:7). In antiquity, requests from the worshipers at the time of sacrifice were universally expected. In this case God Himself invited Solomon to express them. The wisdom granted to Solomon was multifaceted. First Kings 3:16–28 underlines his investigative acumen, while here it is connected with the design of the temple, as was the wisdom of Bezalel (Ex. 35:31). But the first expression of the wisdom of Solomon takes the form of financial and military powers. The Holy Land is the sole bridge connecting three land masses: Africa to the south, with Egypt then as a superpower; Asia Minor and lands further north in the Caucasus and Europe; and finally Syria and lands beyond it in Western Asia. The northern lands, with their vast steppes, were the cradle of the domestic horse, while Egypt was home to the best engineers of the times (notice the high price of the chariots; 2 Chr. 1:17). Solomon, thanks to David's conquests in the Holy Land and neighboring lands, was able to monopolize the trade of horses from the north and chariots from the south. Besides supplementing the equipment of Egyptians and Hittites with each other's production, he sold the complete outfits to the many Syrian (or Aramaean) kinglets (v. 17), which were in need of both horses and chariots.

2:1—4:22
Erection of the Temple

The brief introduction to this section states that Solomon was determined to construct the temple and his royal palace (v. 1). In the rest of the narrative, practically nothing is said about the construction of the royal palace, mainly because the Chronicler is interested in the temple. In order to begin the work, Solomon requested from Hiram, king of Tyre, construction materials and skillful workers (vv. 2–15). The rest of this section is concerned with the construction of the temple and its furnishings (3:1—4:22).

2:1–18. Correspondence with Hiram of Tyre. The conscription of laborers for the temple is a starting point for the narrative (vv. 1–2), though it actually took place later (vv. 17–18). Chronicles (unlike 1 Kin. 5:15–16) adds that they were aliens or foreigners, perhaps captives taken by David in neighboring lands (now "servants"; 1 Chr. 18:2, 6, 13, and esp. v. 4). Solomon requested materials and qualified workers for the temple from David's friend and ally in Tyre. He may have used as couriers the ambassadors sent to wish him well at his inauguration (1 Kin. 5:1–2). He detailed for Hiram the offerings and sacrifices to be performed in the temple (2 Chr. 2:4), mainly the daily services, and the theological reasons for the monumental scale of the construction (v. 5). Hiram obliged (v. 13) and sent Huram (or Huram-Abi or Huram, "my master" or "of my father"—*'abi* means "my father" and could be part of Huram's name or could refer to his position as "master craftsman," as some translations have it), the son of a woman from Dan (or Naphtali; 1 Kin. 7:14—there called Hiram).

3:1–17. General Layout of the Temple. Among Bible writers, only the Chronicler tells us that the temple was located on Mount Moriah. The term appears elsewhere only in Genesis 22:2, "the land of Moriah." The Hebrew root may be related to the action of "seeing." But here the term appears with an article (lit. "to build… on the Mount of the Moriah where the Lord had appeared [or let Himself be seen] to his father David"). One might even translate, "on the mountain view, where the Lord had been viewed by…David." In any case, the term connects the place with salvation, not only from the pestilence that was stopped abruptly in David's time but from Abraham's knife, which also was abruptly stopped by a command from the Angel

of the Lord. The Chronicler does not date the start of the construction of the temple based on the era of the Exodus; he uses only the regnal date of the glorious King Solomon (2 Chr. 3:2; cf. 1 Kin. 6:1).

The foundation mentioned is that on which the Holy and Most Holy Places were to be erected. From this moment on, the temple of God would not be a portable house but a permanent one built on a foundation (e.g., 2 Chr. 6:5–10). The lavish finishing of the Holy Place was second only to that of the Most Holy Place (3:8–14). In antiquity, gold was used primarily for the sacred; this is why temples were often targeted by raiders. The cherubim were carved in relief on the walls (v. 7), and two of them were placed in the Most Holy Place (vv. 11–13), under whose wings the ark would be placed (chap. 5). The quantity of gold, though large (some 40 lbs [18 kg], close to an entire year of Solomon's revenue; 2 Chr. 9:13), is consistent with the gold-plated area (the walls of the temple alone amounted to about 9,687 ft. [900 m^2] or 44 lb. [20 kg] of gold per square meter, implying a very reasonable plate thickness, about .039 of an inch [1 mm]). The front pillars (3:15–17) are usually understood as freestanding fire cressets. The Jach(k)in and Boaz (lit. "May He establish" and "with strength") were typical ornamental features of Canaanite architecture also visible in the Hazor temple excavated in the 1950s.

4:1–8. The Temple Furnishings. Though the original altar of Bezalel was still available, it was too small for the proportions of the new temple. The new altar, more than fifteen feet (5 m) high, was probably accessed through steps. The Sea of bronze or cast metal (vv. 2–5) was probably so named because it was a large basin. Small bull-head pictures, three hundred in number (vv. 2–4), decorated the rim. The word *baths* is not the English word "baths" but refers to Hebrew units of liquid measure. The volume of 3,000 baths is equivalent to about 18,000 gallons (68,137 L). The difference in the number given here and that in 1 Kings 7:26 (2,000 baths) could be attributed to one of the following: (1) a simple copyist error; (2) a different value for the volume of a *bath* during the years between the writing of 1 Kings and 2 Chronicles; or (3) a different understanding of the shape of the Sea (hemispherical or cylindrical), which could affect how the volume was estimated. The shape of the Sea was probably both hemispherical and cylindrical, with vertical upper sides and a convex bottom. The twelve bull forms which emerged from the basin and supported it (or rather half-bulls; the hind legs were not needed; v. 4) may have represented the strength of the united twelve tribes, whose numbers would become "like the sand of the seashore" (Gen. 22:17; 32:12).

The description of the lavers or wash basins in 2 Chronicles 4:6 is more succinct than in 1 Kings 7:27–39 (see commentary on 2 Chr. 4:9–22). The rest of the sacred furnishings here often intrigue students of the passage: Solomon made ten lampstands of gold according to biblical specifications (v. 7; 1 Chr. 28:15; Jer. 52:19; contrast the single menorah of the tabernacle; Ex. 25:31–40) as well as ten tables to be distributed along the long sides of the Holy Place (2 Chr. 4:8). But then in 13:11 we read of a single lampstand and a single table for showbread in Solomon's temple. Note, however, that the passage speaks of furnishings *made* for the temple, not of articles later *present* there. This distinction is important, because 5:5 records that when the ark was brought from Gibeon to Solomon's temple it was accompanied by "all the holy furnishings that were in the tabernacle" of that place. Other than the bronze altar, which was outside, these "holy furnishings" were none other than the single lampstand (menorah), the single table for the showbread, and the incense altar. The latter is not mentioned here with things *made* by Solomon, but in the summary of 4:19–22, it does appear among furnishings of gold. The picture that is conveyed by this comparison is that Solomon added ten tables and ten lampstands to the Most Holy Place and put them along the walls (perhaps one table supporting each new lampstand), a reasonable addition in view of the much larger space in this temple. The original single table for showbread and the singular old menorah should have been kept in the middle, directly in front of the ark.

4:9–22. The Court, Bronze, and Gold.

This section summarizes the articles made for the service of the outside altar and surrounding courts, including the decoration of the pillars described in 3:15–17. In contrast to articles for the temple proper, which were made of pure gold, the articles for outside use were made mostly of bronze and cast in the clayish earth of Succ(kk) oth and Zeredah/Zarethan (4:17; 1 Kin. 7:46) in the plain of Jordan. The emphasis on the use of pure gold is not about the opulence of the temple but about the willingness of the people, the king, and his leaders to joyfully provide the very best they had for the building of the temple

(cf. 1 Chr. 29:3–9). The gold inside the temple was a display before the Lord of the generosity and gratitude of His people on the account of His loving-kindness.

5:1—7:22
Dedication of the Temple

The task was accomplished (5:1); it was now time to dedicate the temple to the Lord and to call the people to use it as their new place for worship (see "The Temple in Chronicles," p. 541). The ceremony began with bringing the ark from the city of David and the holy furnishings from Gibeon (2 Chr. 5:20—6:11). Then Solomon blessed the Lord and the people (6:3–11) and offered a dedicatory prayer (6:12–42) and solemn sacrifices (7:1–10). This section concludes with another vision of Solomon (7:11–22).

5:2–10. The Transfer of the Ark and Furnishings. The elders (v. 4), or extended family heads (v. 2), represented the entire nation. They came together for the Festival of Tabernacles in the seventh month (5:3; cf. 7:8–10; Lev. 23:33–36). While the ark was already in Jerusalem, the tabernacle and the rest of the sacred objects came from Gibeon (2 Chr. 5:5; 1:3). It is surprising that the ancient tabernacle was still in existence more than 480 years after the Exodus (1 Kin. 6:1). The tabernacle was now stowed inside Solomon's temple, which indicates that it must have also been sheltered in the temple in Shiloh (1 Sam. 1:9; 3:3). After the destruction of the temple in Shiloh (1 Sam. 4; Jer. 7:14), the tabernacle probably served again as a tent in Gibeon.

The carrying poles of the ark (2 Chr. 5:9) were more than thirty feet (9 m) long and could be seen from the entrance to the Holy Place. The writer then mentions that they are still there "today," in his time—"to this day." This latter expression is often seen as a mechanical transcription from 1 Kings 8:8. But there was no ark in the second temple after the Exile known by the Chronicler. The Jews believed that Jeremiah and his "companions" hid the ark and the tabernacle in a cave just before the Exile (2 Maccabees 2:4–5). The great length of the poles was related to the ceremonial carrying of the ark by many Levites. It is thus possible that the poles were left on the floor of the temple during the stealthy hiding operation, then carried away to Babylon and back, together with other golden objects (Ex. 25:14; Ezra 1:7), to be finally kept where they belonged, as a poignant memory of the missing ark.

5:11—6:11. God's Presence and Solomon's Blessing. In keeping with the character of the Chronicles, the role of the Levites and the priests is emphasized in these verses. During such a solemn occasion, all of them, not only the division on duty, were present and set themselves apart devotedly for the sacred events (5:11). When they praised God in perfect unison, His cloud of glory filled the building (v. 13). This thick or dark cloud (6:1) was not itself the glory but the shield that protected people from God's "unapproachable light" (v. 13; 1 Tim. 6:16). The presence of God sanctified the temple (2 Chr. 5:11—6:2). Blessing God's name for keeping His promises to Israel implied that the nation had been blessed by God and that Solomon anticipated God's blessings in the future (6:16–17). God had not expressed a preference for a particular tribe or family line before (vv. 5–6). Even though the sanctuary of Shiloh had also been a settled place for God's "name" (Jer. 7:12), as was now the temple (here 2 Chr. 6:6–10), it was in the territory of Ephraim, while the Gibeon sanctuary was on land belonging to the tribe of Benjamin. The present temple was a wholly new possession and so too was God's choice of the dynasty of David (v. 6). Thus the viewpoint of Chronicles, though focused on the past, also conveys clear hopes for the future, in spite of the loss of national independence.

6:12—7:10. Dedicatory Prayer and Sacrifices. Second Chronicles follows here 1 Kings 8:22–53 closely. One added detail is the platform that allowed Solomon to be seen and heard by the congregation, even when he knelt down in humility (2 Chr. 6:13). In the prayer the temple was basically defined as a place of prayer for God's people and for foreigners (vv. 24, 32). God's dwelling place is in heaven, and from there He listens to the prayers of His people made in the earthly temple. Solomon emphasized the divine disposition to listen to prayer and to answer it (see "The Temple in Chronicles," p. 541). The answer came in the form of forgiveness (2 Chr. 6:25, 27), protection (vv. 34–35), and restoration (vv. 36–39). Solomon recognized that the heaven of heavens cannot contain God (v. 18; 2:5), yet he prayed that His presence might come to dwell in the new temple (v. 41). The prayer closed with two statements: first, the temple is God's resting place, and, second, a request for God to be always with His Anointed (vv. 41–42). The king and the temple stood closely together. God's glorious presence, visible to the entire congregation (since the "dark cloud" inside the building, 5:11—6:2, was visible only to priests) came directly in response to this invocation (see 7:1–10). God manifested His approval of the new worship facilities in a spectacular way by sending fire from heaven (v. 1) as He had done during the inauguration of the sanctuary (Lev. 9:23–24) and when choosing the environs of Jerusalem as the new altar site (1 Chr. 21:26). In addition to the regular burnt offering already prepared on the altar (7:1), an astounding number of sacrificial victims were used to celebrate the dedication of the temple (vv. 4–5, 7), This celebration was shared by priests and the people in a sacred fellowship meal made possible through the peace offerings (v. 7). The celebration was enhanced by the music and liturgy performed by the priests, the Levites, and the congregation (vv. 3, 6) and lasted for the seven days of the Festival of Tabernacles (vv. 8–10). The temple was a place where sacrifices were offered to the Lord (see 2:4) and where the people rejoiced in His presence.

7:11–22. God's Response in a Night Vision. The signs of the cloud of glory in the temple and the fire lighted miraculously on the altar (5:3–14; 7:1) had been spectacular, but inarticulate. Miracles need to be complemented by God's revealed word. Hence, the Lord appeared again to Solomon in a night vision (as in 1:7) to deliver promises for obedience and a warning against disobedience. Here the Chronicler adds (cf. 1 Kin. 9:1–9) the famous words: "If my people… will humble themselves, and pray and seek my face…then I will hear from heaven" (2 Chr. 7:14). This is in keeping with the emphasis of Chronicles on immediate retribution (see 1 Chronicles: Introduction).

8:1—9:31
Grandeur of Solomon

In accordance with the general purpose of Chronicles, a backward look to the glorious reigns of David and Solomon was intended to instill a sense of national pride, much needed at the time. In this section we read about Solomon's achievements in the fortification of some cities (8:1–6), the wise use of human labor (vv. 7–11), his support of the temple (vv. 12–16), search for gold (vv. 17–18), the visit of the Queen of Sheba (9:1–12), and his wealth and death (vv. 13–31).

8:1–11. Urban Improvements. Since this passage begins similarly to 1 Kings 9:10–13, it has been assumed by some that they are describing the same event. If so, a question would arise:

Were these cities given by Hiram of Tyre to Solomon (2 Chr. 8:2), or was it the other way around (1 Kin. 9:10–12)? According to 1 Kings 9:12-13, Hiram was not pleased with the cities which Solomon "gave" him and called them "the land of Cabul." This word is related to a verb meaning "bound" or "restricted," but it could also be related to the Hebrew phrase "like nothing"—which would thus show his disdain for the cities. Nonetheless, the king of Tyre sent 120 talents (9,000 lb) of gold to Solomon (2 Chr. 8:14). Clearly, this gesture of Hiram went beyond the initial contract for cedar wood and qualified labor that Solomon was to pay for with agricultural products (2 Chr. 2). Solomon did not sell those cities to Hiram, so all that gold needed to be repaid. One logical explanation to harmonize the two accounts, if they are referring to related events, is that Solomon borrowed those 120 talents of gold by using the twenty border towns as collateral. In such a case, the precise value of those cities did not need to be ascertained immediately, even if they left a poor impression. According to this explanation, when Solomon repaid the loan (perhaps from the gold which Huram's servants helped collect [see 1 Kin. 9:26-28]), he would have recovered the collateral from Hiram and then, as this account says, beautified those underestimated cities (2 Chr. 8:2).

He first fortified northern cities (8:3-4). The Syrian city of Zobah, which in the times of the Chronicler belonged to the Persian province of Hamath, had provided Ammon with mercenaries in the times of David (2 Sam. 10:6). Apparently it had also recently refused to pay the tribute due Israel (2 Sam. 8:9-10), so Solomon defeated and captured it (2 Chr. 8:3). Tadmor is Palmyra, an oasis in the desert of Syria, fortified by Solomon in connection with a chain of storage cities, or military units related to chariot warfare (v. 4; cf. v. 6). Solomon also fortified some cities. He fortified cities with walls, gates, and bars, and he outfitted all the cities such as Megiddo and Gezer with chariots and cavalry (1 Kin. 9:15-16), a fact that archaeology has documented (see commentary on 2 Chr. 9:13-31). Beth Horon and Baalath are in western Israel and were strengthened against a possible Philistine resurgence. For such an ambitious construction program, Solomon resorted to the conscription of forced labor among non-Israelites (2 Chr. 8:7-8). Ethnic Israelites served only as soldiers or overseers (vv. 9-10). He also took care to maintain his foreign queen and her retinue away from the holy city (v. 11; this detail is found only in this passage).

8:12–16. Support of Temple Worship. The king not only fulfilled the instructions of David, his father, regarding the organization of temple worship (v. 14), but he also himself provided an abundance of sacrifices for the required daily, weekly, and yearly rituals (v. 12). In this way his duty to the temple was completed (v. 16). First Kings 9:25 mentions a detail that the Chronicler does not, that is, that Soloman burned incense in the temple three times a year. This ritual, while legitimate in the temple area, was later moved to the unauthorized "high places" with schismatic and/or pagan worship (1 Kin. 13:2; 2 Kin. 16:2-4; 2 Chr. 34:25).

8:17–18. The Expeditions to Ophir. In addition to a conscripted labor force, Solomon's constructions required cash. A possible explanation for Solomon's interest in Eloth is that it was an important port in the heavy trade of copper out of Edom. Since there was a glut of bronze (which contains copper) in Israel (4:18), new markets were needed for this metal. Ophir was a good candidate: they were a Semitic people (1 Chr. 1:23) whose land was rich in gold (1 Chr. 29:4; Job 22:24; Ps. 45:9; Is. 13:12), and they were possibly located in Arabia or East Africa. In Africa, copper has always been used for personal adornment, so its rate of exchange for gold was more favorable than in the Mediterranean world. Solomon's agents were thus able to acquire 450 talents (15,309 lb) of gold from there (2 Chr. 8:18). Perhaps he used some of this to redeem the cities he had given as collateral to Phoenicia (see commentary on 8:1-11). Such trade required a port on the Red Sea close to the Edomite copper mines. Ezion Geber and Elath (v. 17) fit the description, located at the end of the Gulf of Aqaba. As in the case of the temple, the Phoenician friends of Solomon provided both equipment and technical skill (v. 18). They were at the time the foremost naval power of the Mediterranean world, and their ships dominated the metal trade from tin refineries in Spain and other distant lands.

9:1–12. The Praise of the Queen of Sheba. After David, a new star was rising in the commercial sky of the Middle East. Not only was Israel, the new power, controlling the land bridge between the continents (see commentary on 1:7-17), but it was also beginning to bypass the traditional Sabean spice route by using the Red Sea (see 8:16-17). As descendants of Sheba, the Sabeans were a Semitic people (Gen. 10:28) in the southwest of the Arabian Peninsula (Yemen), which receives some rain (this is the "happy Arabia," *Arabia felix,* of classical authors); they also built large dams and irrigation systems. In addition, their caravans of camels carried spices, incense, and other luxury products, both from their land and from other coasts of the Indian Ocean, to the Mediterranean world via Syria and Phoenicia.

The visit of their queen to Solomon, using one of those caravans over more than 1,500 miles (2,414 km), no doubt aimed to assess not only the new king but also Israel as a whole. She was very much impressed (2 Chr. 9:5–8), especially with Solomon's wisdom (v. 5), which she could appreciate in the areas of administration and organization (vv. 3–4). The Chronicler records her conveying the concept that God had made of Israel His throne: the king reigned there by divine election (v. 8; 1 Kin. 10:9). The exchange of gifts (2 Chr. 9:9, 12) implies some kind of trade agreement.

9:13–31. Solomon's Wealth and Death. More than twenty tons of gold (18 metric tons) entered annually the coffers of Solomon (v. 13), not counting the toll paid by merchants or local taxes raised by the governors of the land, here designated with a Persian word *pekhah* for the benefit of postexilic readers (v. 14; the term is the source of English word *pasha*). The shields of gold were made in two sizes and were treasury reserves under the close custody of one soldier each. The House (or Palace) of the forest of Lebanon refers to the palace of Solomon, which took him thirteen years to build, using a large amount of cedar from the Forest of Lebanon. Then there was the throne of the king (vv. 17–19). This was a large throne (which was white, as remembered in Rev. 20:11)—a great throne of ivory overlaid with pure gold—aimed at impressing foreign dignitaries. Its carved animal figures included lions (2 Chr. 9:17–19). Solomon's gold may have come from other sources besides Ophir (see 8:17–18). It was transported in *tarshish* ships (strong ships able to travel into the deep sea; cf. 1 Kin. 10:22; the term can also refer to a destination; 2 Chr. 9:21). The return trip brought silver, ivory, apes, and monkeys (some translations render the final term as "peacocks," some as "monkeys," and others as "baboons"; v. 21). "All the kings of the earth" (v. 23) who sought Solomon were those within Israel's sphere of influence (v. 26); the present (Heb. *minkhah*) that was brought every year (vv. 23–24) was a vassal due. Military bases (the chariot cities; vv. 25–28), which included ample facilities that have left traces for the archaeologists today

(esp. in Hazor, Megiddo, and Gezer), reminded subject peoples (see vv. 23–24) that they could not easily throw off the yoke that Israel had imposed on them in the form of tribute and trade restrictions. In this way Israel enjoyed its heyday of splendor (vv. 26–28).

In accordance with its purpose, 2 Chronicles refrains from relating the apostasy of Solomon in the latter part of his life and the consequent divine displeasure (1 Kin. 11:1–25). The Chronicler is more interested in the public life of the king than in his private life. However, it does refer the reader interested in these aspects to other sources that detail them: the prophetic history of Israel composed by Nathan the prophet, Ahijah the Shilonite, and Iddo the seer (2 Chr. 9:29). These prophets are also mentioned as sources in the book of Kings, so this bibliographical reference in 2 Chronicles is either to our present book of Kings or to a common source of both.

10:1—36:23
KINGS OF JUDAH: VICISSITUDES OF GOD'S PEOPLE

The reigns of David and Solomon should have made the original readers justly proud. Those readers were also very much aware that disaster eventually struck the nation, but not before a series of ups and downs which, as 2 Chronicles shows next, are directly related to obedience or disobedience to God's covenant and in particular to how the temple was treated (see 1 Chronicles: Introduction). The life of the kings is analyzed beginning with Rehoboam and the division of the kingdom (chaps. 10–12). The other kings are Abijah (chap. 13), Asa (chaps. 14–16), Jehoshaphat (17:1—21:3), Jehoram and Ahaziah (21:4—22:9), Joash (22:10—24:27), Amaziah (chap. 25), Uzziah (chap. 26), Jotham (chap. 27), Ahaz (chap. 28), Hezekiah (chaps. 29–32), Manasseh and Amon (chap. 33), Josiah (chaps. 34–35), and the successors of Josiah and the Exile (chap. 36).

10:1—12:16
The Secession of the North

The division of the monarchy of Israel into a northern kingdom (which retained the name of Israel for ten of the tribes) and a southern one in Judah (together with part of the tribe of Benjamin) eventually, though unnecessarily, resulted in the fall of the nation. The story makes it clear that the division was the result of political intrigues motivated by pride and the human thirst for power. But even in such a case the Lord's hand was mysteriously at work to accomplish His ultimate design for His people through judgment and salvation. Not only did those kingdoms fight each other, but they also fell into the temptation of seeking foreign help to shore up their internecine war effort. The outsiders were very much happy to oblige out of self-interest. In 1 Kings 11:29–39 the Prophet Ahijah pointed out that the division of the kingdom was the result of the apostasy of Solomon later in life. But since the Chronicler chose not to dwell on the apostasy of Solomon, he only alludes to such divine judgment indirectly by reminding the reader of the prophecy of Ahijah (2 Chr. 9:29).

10:1–19. Revolt against Rehoboam (931–913 B.C.).

Apparently at first there was no interest in a revolt but sincere interest in pressuring Rehoboam to deal with the common people in a fair way. The unity of the kingdom was still fragile. Even though David was a native prince of Judah, he was only an elected king for the rest of Israel, requiring a double coronation (in Hebron and in Jerusalem). Such double process was not necessary in the case of Solomon since David had him sitting on the throne while he still reigned (1 Chr. 23:1; 29:23). For Rehoboam it was important to be recognized or elected by the "elders" of the other tribes as king (2 Sam. 5:3). This took place in Shechem (2 Chr. 10:1) in the territory of Ephraim. The situation required tact: if Rehoboam gave away too much, he might lose too much authority, perhaps becoming a reigning, but not ruling, king. Hence the hot-headed young people (actually in their forties; 10:10; 12:13) were all for an iron fist (10:10–11). On the other hand, as the more experienced advisors perceived (vv. 6–7), an impolitic answer could make the situation explode. People knew the prophecy of Ahijah of Shiloh about Jeroboam (1 Kin. 11; 2 Chr. 9:29). Singling out Jeroboam as the spokesman of the tribal elders (10:2–3) was a not-too-subtle means of applying strong pressure on Rehoboam.

The rift happened (vv. 12–19) as the experienced advisors had foreseen. The heartfelt cry of the people (v. 16) had already been sounded in David's times by Sheba, who could not reconcile himself to the loss of the power his tribe had enjoyed under their fellow Benjamite, King Saul, and saw an opportunity in the civil war between David and his son Absalom (2 Sam. 20:1). The attempt of Sheba was aborted (2 Sam. 20:4–22),

but it did expose strong undercurrents against the Davidic dynasty outside Judah (2 Sam. 20:2), no doubt still present in Rehoboam's time. The Chronicler states that Israel "has been in rebellion against the house of David to this day" (2 Chr. 10:19).

11:1—12:16. The Reign of Rehoboam and the Apostasy of Israel.

In Kings the reign of each king of Judah is reported in relation to a contemporary king of Israel, the Northern Kingdom. The Chronicler reports only on Judah (see commentary on 13:1), but the Kings narrative on Israel still influences 2 Chronicles. Prophets had great influence on Israel; just as Ahijah's prophecy boosted the rebellion against Rehoboam among the ten northern tribes, so Shemaiah prevented Judah from embarking on a bloody civil war to suppress the rebellion (vv. 1–5) even though the forces of Rehoboam seemed adequate—180,000 men (cf. 14:8; 25:5; but see commentary on 1 Chr. 12:23–40). Barred by the reluctance of the people from engaging in an all-out war against the north (2 Chr. 11:2–4), Rehoboam used his resources in fortifying fifteen sites (vv. 5–12). But they were not aligned along the northern border of Judah: the king did not want to consolidate the division of the Hebrew monarchy. They rather presupposed a conflict with Egypt. Since fortifications in so many places must have taken quite a number of years to complete, this section should be seen from a thematic, not chronological, viewpoint. Rehoboam was right to fear Egypt, as later events would prove (see chap. 12).

The ungodliness of Jeroboam, recorded also in 1 Kings 12:28–33, is here emphasized (2 Chr. 11:13–14). He not only installed priests from tribes other than Levi, but he had in fact rejected the latter from serving as priests, thus openly opposing the law of Moses which gave them exclusive rights to the ministry (vv. 13–14). The picture of apostasy is reinforced by noting that the illegitimate priests of Jeroboam served in schismatic high places where the God of Israel was worshiped with the help of images of calves (v. 15) as in Sinai at the time of Aaron. In reality, these high places were openly pagan shrines for the *sa'ir* ("goats," "demons," or "goat-demons"), a symbol of masculine potency in nature worship, and so a general term for pagan religion (Lev. 17:7; cf. 1 Cor. 10:20). The calves or young bulls, a symbol of force, may have represented the mount or footstool of God or an abstract icon for Deity itself, as the highest Force.

While priests and Levites left the north for good, other Israelites came as pilgrims to sacrifice in Jerusalem—presumably at least during the annual festivals—thus rejecting the sanctuaries of Jeroboam in their own tribal lands (2 Chr. 11:16–17). This strengthened Rehoboam, for the kingdom enjoyed the blessings promised for faithfulness, which unfortunately only lasted three years (v. 17). This fidelity, referred to as the way of "David and Solomon," refers to David's lifelong commitment, while in the case of Solomon it can be applied only to his early reign (contrast 1 Kin. 11:1–8).

At this point in the narrative, information is provided about Rehoboam's family (2 Chr. 11: 18–22). This account about his family is likely not tied to this particular point in time; it probably covers all seventeen years of the reign of Rehoboam, not just the interval between his third (v. 17) and fifth years (12:2). For an empire such as Solomon's (see commentary on 9:13–31), a large royal harem (vv. 18–21) might have been a political necessity for both foreign and domestic affairs since covenants and pacts were often sealed through marriages. For Rehoboam, it was a case of keeping up appearances after the glory of the kingdom had already disappeared (cf. 12:9–11). The Chronicler recognizes that he acted wisely in dispersing some of his twenty-eight sons, the royal princes, throughout all the regions of Judah and Benjamin (v. 23). The palatial intrigues of his uncles Absalom and Adonijah in their attempt to succeed his grandfather David must have provided him with a lesson.

The sins of Rehoboam are not igonored by the Chronicler (12:1). The invasion by Shishak, founder of the Twenty-Second Egyptian Dynasty, is directly connected by 2 Chronicles to the backsliding of Judah. It happened because God's people had been unfaithful to Him and rebelled against Him (v. 2). The language of v. 1 suggests that the kingdom of Rehoboam (Judah) was still considered "Israel" or, at any rate, Israel's faithful remnant (v.1; see 11:16). But this remnant joined the rebellion against God. The nation abandoned God's law—His *torah* (v. 1). The use of *torah* here implies the existence of a canonical Scripture. The Pentateuch had been long in existence and in force (Josh. 1:7–8; 1 Kin. 2:3; 2 Kin. 10:31); it was not an innovation of the postexilic community. Though the transgressions are not specified in Chronicles, they refer to idolatry (1 Kin. 14:22). This idolatry may have had something to do with the presence of a large harem of pagan women (see 2 Chr. 11:18–22), as was the case of Solomon (1 Kin. 11:1–8).

Shishak, an energetic pharaoh, wanted to reassert Egyptian control over a large part of the Middle East, not only the Holy Land. He left in a temple of Karnak the record of 150 towns captured in that campaign. But he would not have dared to attack Israel in the times of Solomon, when he contented himself with harboring Israelite rebels and promoting discontent against that monarch (1 Kin. 11:14–40). The strength of the united Israelite army no doubt dissuaded him (1 Chr. 21:5). Now, with ten of the twelve tribes under a king who had been his protégé and probably remained his vassal (1 Kin. 11:26–40), success against the southern remainder of the Hebrew nation was entirely possible and even likely. The forces of the pharaoh included not only native Egyptians, but also auxiliary troops, Ethiopians, Lybians (Lubim), and Sukkiim (Sukkites; v. 3). The latter, a people from the oasis of western Lybia, are not mentioned in the account of 1 Kings, but they appear as *tjukten* in the Egyptian records, showing once again the access of the Chronicler to other reliable ancient records.

In spite of all these forces, Shishak was not to include Jerusalem in his Karnak record of destroyed cities. Repentance and confession, prompted by the prophetic message of Shemaiah, earned Rehoboam a commuted sentence in God's historical judgment (vv. 5–7). The Israelites would again be subject to the pharaoh (the same term often translated "slaves" is used in v. 8). Humility on the part of Rehoboam turned away the Lord's anger, and conditions improved in Judah (v. 12). But Rehoboam had to relinquish the royal treasury, including the gold shields (v. 9; see 9:15–16), as part of his new vassal status though he would continue the pomp of his visits to the temple (v. 11), keeping up appearances with less expensive bronze shields (v. 10). As usual in the biblical history of Hebrew kings, life span, family, and regnal statistics are recorded (vv. 13–16). Second Chronicles adds an assessment of the religious quality of the king: he was evil because he did not determine in his heart to seek the Lord (v. 14). Some bibliographical notes are also added. The wars between Rehoboam and Jeroboam, during all their days (v. 15), refer to low-intensity conflicts; thanks to the intervention of Shemaiah (11:2–4) they did not turn into a major civil war.

13:1–22
The Reign of Abijah (913–911 B.C.)

The reign of Abijah was short, lasting only three years, and is characterized as a time of war with the Northern Kingdom. In his battle against Jeroboam, the commitment of Abijah to the Lord and to the temple services is accentuated in a particular way. His image in 2 Chronicles seems to differ in a significant way from what is written in 1 Kings (see below, "Abijah in Kings and Chronicles").

13:1. Correlation with a Northern King. Statistics of the reigns of Judah are regularly provided by the books of Kings to correlate with a contemporary king of Israel, the Northern Kingdom. Here, for the first and last time, such a synchronic note is recorded in 2 Chronicles: Abijah ("Abijam" in Kings) started his reign in the eighteenth year of King Jeroboam (v. 1). Abijah's reign was to be marked by conflict with Jeroboam, and that explains the correlation. But beyond this point, the reign of northern kings is largely ignored in 2 Chronicles (cf. the introductory note for chaps. 11–12), due to considerations related to both audience and perspective. The Chronicles were written for the exiles who returned from Babylon, now conceptualized as "all Israel" (see commentary on 11:1—12:16) since they also included some people from all the tribes (1 Chr. 9:3–5; 2 Chr. 11:16), but mainly from Judah. Besides, the Chronicler sees God's covenant with Israel as being implemented through the promises given to David (1 Chr. 17). Therefore, the secession of the north, a "rebellion against the house of David" (2 Chr. 10:19), was also a rebellion against God. People from the north were welcome in Judah, but only when they worshiped in the temple in Jerusalem (11:16; 30:1–12). Even the reign of the kings of Judah is abridged from the preexilic source in Chronicles, except in the case of the "good" kings (Asa, Joash, Jehoshaphat, Hezekiah, Josiah), where it is supplemented with material not found in the books of Kings.

13:2. Family Lineage. Here the name of Abijah's mother is given as Michaiah, but "Maachah" (or Maakah) elsewhere (11:20–21; 1 Kin. 15:2). She was identified in 1 Kings as the daughter or granddaughter of Absalom (translations vary), but here (2 Chr. 13:2) she is the daughter of Uriel of Gibeah. This could be explained by remembering that, just as "son" can sometimes metaphorically mean "grandson" (or other lineal descendant) in the Hebrew Bible, so too "daughter" may mean granddaughter. We know that Absalom had a beautiful daughter, Tamar (2 Sam. 14:27). Tamar, the daughter of Absalom, may have married Uriel of Gibeah, thus becoming the mother of Maachah, who was therefore the "daughter" (actual granddaughter) of Absalom and also the literal daughter of Uriel, as well as the mother of Abijah and grandmother of Asa.

13:3–22. Confrontation with Jeroboam. The 400,000 men of Abijah and the 800,000 of Jeroboam are obviously round numbers. This time the civil war could not be avoided (cf. 2 Chr. 11:1–5). Commanding inferior forces, Abijah tried to discourage the attack of the enemy with a forceful speech (2 Chr. 13:4–12). Its wording may also reflect the viewpoint of the Chronicler: Judah was the kingdom of the Lord (v. 8)—they worshiped in the temple in Jerusalem (vv. 10–11), while the kingdom of the north was in rebellion against God because they worshiped idols, had a center of worship other than Jerusalem, had driven out the true priests (descendants of Aaron), and consecrated as priests anyone who came with a sacrifice. Hence the north could not possibly prosper (v. 12).

In spite of the artful military strategy of Jeroboam (vv. 13–14), God defeated Jeroboam (v. 15), and Judah won the battle because they relied on

Abijah in Kings and Chronicles

When we compare the portrait of Abijah in 2 Chronicles with the one in 1 Kings, we find a major difference. In 1 Kings, Abijah seems to be assessed as an evil monarch (15:3–6). Some have seen Abijah as a hypocrite, preaching one thing and doing another; others think that the bad behavior mentioned in 1 Kings refers to a different period of Abijah's reign. But it is unclear why

Chronicles would echo the words of a notorious hypocrite, or why 1 Kings would not say a word about egregious flip-flops during the three short years of Abijah's reign. Note, however, that in the Hebrew text the name of Abijah does not actually appear in 1 Kings 15:3–6, while Rehoboam does.

One possible way of solving the problem is by suggesting that perhaps 1 Kings 15:3–6 has been accidentally transposed and should be restored between 1 Kings 14:21 and 22, where they would refer to Rehoboam. In this way the end of the passage, "and there was war between *Rehoboam* and Jeroboam all the days of his life" (not between *Abijah* and Jeroboam) would make perfect sense. If restored after 1 Kings 14:21, these verses, together with 21–24, would offer an account of the evil behavior of both Rehoboam *and* Judah (as in 2 Chr. 12:1), not of Judah alone as 1 Kings 14:21–24 now appear to record. Also, in that connection the explanation of 1 Kings 15:4–5, on why God did not put an end to the Davidic dynasty at that time, would follow immediately the account in v. 3 of a king who walked "in all the sins of his father," meaning Solomon, instead of being postponed, as in our copies of 1 Kings, for a later and much shorter reign. So, if Abijah was, in fact, a good king, this would also explain why Chronicles deals with his short reign in a rather lengthy way (see commentary on 2 Chr. 13:1), including an account of the blessings of children he enjoyed (see commentary on 13:3–22). This suggestion remains a possibility.

The other option is simply to argue that 2 Chronicles is describing Abijah at a time when he was still fully committed to the Lord in order to indicate that when the kings remained loyal to God and in full support of the temple services (2 Chr. 13:10–12; see "The Temple in Chronicles," p. 541), He did wonders for them and the people. The evaluation of his reign leaves open the possibility that at some point in his life Abijah may have been unfaithful to the Lord (2 Chr. 13:21—14:1).

the Lord, the God of their ancestors (v. 18). In the absence of any mention of natural resources such as the hail used by God on another occasion (Josh. 10:11) or confusion within the enemy camp (Judg. 7:22), we may suppose that God struck down Israel by means of the sword of Abijah and the people with him in his army (2 Chr. 13:17).

The evaluation of the reign of Abijah is brief (vv. 21–22), emphasizing that he became powerful, married fourteen wives, and had twenty-two sons and sixteen daughters (v. 21). Nothing is said about his constant commitment to the Lord. Though not strictly impossible, there is no need to suppose that those fourteen women bore all thirty-eight children within the three years of the reign of their husband. Hebrew royal family statistics are cumulative for the total life span of the monarch (see commentary on 11:1—12:16).

14:1—16:14
The Reign of Asa (911–870 B.C.)

Asa is described in Chronicles as a good king who did much to purify the Israelite faith by calling the people to the exclusive worship of Yahweh. He gathered the leaders of the people in Jerusalem and offered sacrifices to the Lord in a covenant renewal ceremony. His only weakness was relying on the king of Syria rather than on the Lord in a battle against Baasha, king of Israel.

14:1–8. The Early Years. Abijah's three-year reign, partly occupied with war, may have been insufficient to erase the remnants of Judah's idolatrous past under Solomon and Rehoboam. In contrast, Asa had leisure to do it since in his time the land had peace and quiet for ten years (vv. 1, 5). Every city in the realm was purged from the altars of the foreign gods and related stone pillars of Baal (the Father-Sky god) and the wooden pole images of Asherah (the Mother-Earth goddess) of the Canaanite religion (v. 3). These years of peace made defensive preparations possible, both by means of fortifications (vv. 6–7) and a ready army (v. 8). Perhaps Asa anticipated the Egyptian invasion, especially if he was withholding tribute.

14:9–15. The Attack of Zerah. As under Pharaoh Shishak (12:2–3), the Egyptian army continued employing auxiliary troops from subject lands bordering on their country. Here the "Cushites" or "Ethiopians" were from Nubia (modern Sudan) in the south. The Cushite commander, Zerah, had a Semitic name and answered probably to Pharaoh Osorkon I. We are not told what prompted the attack, but we may assume that in the eyes of Osorkon the new occupants of the throne of Judah (Abijah and/or Asa) were not keeping the promise of Rehoboam to behave in a proper subservient manner to Egypt (see commentary on 11:1—12:16). The invading army had the advantage of numbers, a very large army, *'elep 'ala-pim* (lit. "a thousand thousands"), translated variously as "a million" or "thousands upon thousands" (see commentary on 1 Chr. 4:24—5:26). In any case it seems that the Chronicler did not have at his disposal precise figures because the invaders are described as a fearsome "vast army" or "multitude" (see 2 Chr. 14:11). The three hundred chariots (v. 9) sound like a reasonable number for such an invasion. But Asa had the advantage of knowing the terrain better, and he decided to wait for the invaders at Mareshah, a southern city fortified by Rehoboam (11:8) in order to guard the road linking Judah with Egypt.

The "Valley of Zephathah" has not been identified, but Mareshah is in the Shephelah, where the invading army had to pass between closely spaced hills. Here the multitudinous camel cavalry would lose its advantage of speed and ability to perform enveloping manoeuvers. The bowmen and slingers of Asa, posted on the steep slopes of the hills, would decimate them continuously until they were forced to retreat (14:12). It is clear, however, that the result was by no means assured beforehand: Asa called out and cried to the Lord his God and was heard (v. 11). In the end, the failure of Zerah's invasion was to make Judah free from Egypt's yoke again. In the short run it would also allow treasure to be taken from the Egyptians as war reparations. Asa pursued them to Gerar (v. 13), between the southern Judean town of Beersheba and Gaza, seen at the time as the upper northern reach of the Egyptian army. The spoil included many sheep and camels, once the *'ahole* were attacked and taken. This term literally reads "tents of the cattle or livestock" in Hebrew and has been translated as "livestock enclosures"—where the animals were—or alternatively as "the camps of the herders," a reference to where the shepherds were staying (v. 15).

15:1–19. Asa's Religious Reform. The seer Azariah is called in v. 1 the son of Oded. In v. 8 there are differences among the ancient versions, and thus differences in the modern translations dependent on them. The Hebrew mentions only "Oded" and not Azariah, but the Syriac and Vulgate have "Azariah the son of Oded," assuming that v. 8 was referring to the same person mentioned in v. 1. Some translations follow the Hebrew, and others the Syriac and Vulgate. In any case, the message drove home the lesson already taught by the victory at Mareshah: the Lord is with you while you are with Him (v. 2).

Not as clear is the allusion to the long time of v. 3 and the deprivation for Israel, without the true God, without a priest teaching, and without law. Some intepret this verse as referring to the period of the judges, others to a more recent time, such as the apostasy under Solomon or Rehoboam, or to the situation of Israel in the Northern Kingdom. Still others would suggest that it describes what would happen in the future if Judah did not adhere strictly to the covenant. There is no easy solution to this matter, but perhaps it would be better to interpret the time reference as designating the time of the judges, when there was no king in Israel—a situation which motivated Asa to initiate a reform in his kingdom.

The purge of pagan centers of worship had been initiated before the invasion (14:2–5) and was now completed (15:8), even if the high places were not removed from Israel (15:17). This latter statement seems to contradict 14:5. Some explain that paganism was resilient; it sprouted back time and again, and Asa left part of its later regrowth standing (17:6). But in view of vv. 12–13, it is more likely that the statement refers specifically to Israel, that is, to the cities that he had taken in the mountains of Ephraim (15:8).

As part of his religious reform, Asa called a convocation of the leaders on the third month, probably during the Festival of Weeks (Pentecost, *shabu'im*—Ex. 34:22). While the worship of any god other than Yahweh had been forbidden under pain of death (Deut. 13:6–11), Asa threatened whoever would not seek the Lord God of Israel (2 Chr. 15:13). Asa's warning was addressed to men and women, thus closing any loophole that might have been exploited in the past by the foreign wives of Solomon or Rehoboam. The latter's favorite wife, Maachah (11:21), the king's grandmother, was accordingly deposed from her position as the queen mother or "mistress of the palace" because of her involvement with a detestable and obscene image of Asherah (15:16). This kind of image was wooden (14:3), so none have survived, but if gold earrings and pendants from ancient Israel are any indication, it depicted, in stylized form, female genitalia, as a way to attract good luck (*'asherah*, "bliss," "happiness") and fertility. As a leader who sought to follow the Lord with all his heart, Asa could not afford to retain his grandmother in that position of honor—not when true worship was at stake.

As a good king, Asa supported the temple services. In antiquity, metals taken as spoils (here in Abijah's war against the north [13:19] and his own raid on Gerar [14:13–15]) were deposited in the temple as an expression of gratitude for the victory and the long peace enjoyed by the nation. War did not come until the thirty-fifth year of the reign of Asa (v. 19), when Baasha attacked (16:1). If this is taken at face value, there is a conflict with 1 Kings (15:33; 16:8), according to which Baasha died in the twenty-sixth year of the reign of Asa. There is no final solution to this problem, but it is possible that the thirty-fifth and thirty-sixth (15:19; 16:1) correspond to an era starting in Judah with Rehoboam, as a kingdom separate from Israel. After ten years of peace (14:1), Asa would have defeated Zerah in the fifteenth year of his reign. He then celebrated his victory with a feast (15:10–17) the following year. The attack of the Northern Kingdom would have come soon after, as a reaction to the intervention of Asa in the northern cities (v. 8).

16:1–14. Asa's Reliance on Foreign Help. The dynasty of Jeroboam came to a violent end at the hands of Baasha (v. 1), an upstart from Issachar (1 Kin. 15:27), who renewed hostilities with Judah. He blocked the road coming into Jerusalem from the north through Ramah in order to prevent visits to the temple of Jerusalem by his people. In a military context, this prevention of people leaving or entering conveys an attack (cf. 2 Chr. 16:1), and Asa accordingly sought ways that would force Baasha to withdraw from him (v. 3). By this time it was clear that the confrontation between the Hebrew kingdoms was more or less at a stalemate. Neither side was willing to stake everything on a great battle, such as the one in Zemaraim (13:13–20). Asa thought that the situation called for a regionalization of the conflict and reached out to Benhadad, king of Aram (or Syria; 16:2–3). The mention here of a treaty between Judah and Syria, and another between Israel and Syria (v. 3), does not necessarily mean overt alliances but the implicit peaceful status quo, or the establishment of "diplomatic relations" as we would say today. What Asa requested, and was granted, was for Syria to apply military pressure on the north of Baasha's kingdom, forcing him to relieve its pressure on Ramah. In the short run, this was successful: Asa liberated Ramah and used the building materials of Baasha for his own fortifications (v. 6). But, in the long run, regionalization attracted the interest of the great empires of that day (Assyria, Egypt, and Babylon) and gave them an excuse to intervene later in the Hebrew kingdoms.

Hanani the seer (v. 7) boldly confronted Asa, stating that, instead of seeking help from Syria, he should have learned the lesson of Mareshah and trusted in the Lord (v. 8; 14:10–12): the Lord is always searching throughout the world for those who are wholeheartedly loyal to Him—and He will strengthen them (v. 9; cf. Zech. 1:7–11; 4:10). The prophet minced no words and referred to Asa's actions as foolish (2 Chr. 16: 9). Revolting against the prodding of his conscience, Asa threw the prophet in prison (v. 10), but time would vindicate the words of God's messenger. Together with the usual regnal statistics, we learn that the old king died from a disease in his "feet." This disease, which lasted for for two years, may have been referring to a disease which resulted in symptoms in his feet, such as gout or diabetes, but it could also have been something of a urological nature (vv. 12–13). In Hebrew idiom, the "feet," conceptualized as the lower limbs from the crotch down, can sometimes stand for private parts (e.g., the Hebrew expressions involving "feet" in Judg. 3:24; 1 Sam. 24:3; Ezek. 16:25). The "water of the feet" is a euphemistic idiom for urine, explicit in the margin of the Hebrew text of 2 Kings 18:27. If it was a urological disease, it may have been treated by means of a flexible catheter made from a feather. There is no evidence that ancient Hebrew physicians used spells or other pagan procedures, as is sometimes suggested. The Chronicler criticizes the king for consulting *only* physicians (2 Chr. 16:12). Diseases are best dealt with by a combination of human effort and reliance on God, just like other enemies (13:18). In spite of this lapse in Asa's reliance on God, the judgment of 2 Chronicles on his reign is favorable (14:2), as was that of the people (16:14).

17:1—21:1
The Reign of Jehoshaphat (872–848 B.C.)

Jehoshaphat is considered by the Chronicler to have done what was good in the sight of the Lord. He knew that the spiritual and social renewal of the people was directly related to their knowledge of the law of God. Consequently, he sent Levites and priests throughout the land to teach them. He also revamped the legal system. But the Chronicler is also aware of the errors committed by this man of God.

17:1–19. Overview of the Reign. Second Chronicles devotes four chapters to Jehoshaphat's reign because of its favorable judgment on him (20:32; see 17:1–4): the Lord was with Jehoshaphat because he sought the God of his father (17:3–4). Most of the material is not found in the books of Kings. He fortified Judah and the cities and towns of Ephraim recovered by Asa (vv. 1–2), and he had abundant wealth and honor (v. 5). The term *yigbah lebo*— literally "his heart [mind] was high"—has been translated variously as "his heart took delight in the ways of the Lord," "his heart was devoted to the ways of the Lord," "his heart was courageous in the ways of the Lord," or he "took pride in the Lord's ways." This latter option is interesting in light of the description of Uzziah (26:16), whose "heart was high" or proud, not in the Lord's ways but to his destruction and downfall. Jehoshaphat's mind or heart took pride in the Lord—not in himself. The king did not content himself with the periodical cleansing of idols necessary even in Judah (17:6); instead, he promoted the religious education of the people by a team of laymen, Levites, and priests. The phrase referring to the laymen, his leading officials and Ben-Hail (v. 7), may also be read "his leaders, outstanding men" as in the LXX. The name "Ben-Hail" is otherwise unknown. The presence of outstanding laypeople is critical in any mass religious education effort since a professional team of ministers alone might be seen by some as self-serving. For this task the team relied not on disjointed oral traditions or brief Pentateuch extracts, as is sometimes suggested today, but on the entire book of the law of the Lord (v. 9). This was a hefty volume which, handwritten on skins, required physical effort to handle, as may be appreciated today in traditional synagogue scrolls.

The result of the teaching of the law was that the fear of the Lord fell on all the kingdoms (v. 10). The reverential obedience of Jehoshaphat was rewarded by God with the respect and submission of neighboring lands (vv. 10–11). He became increasingly powerful in terms of military and economic power (vv. 12–13). The Chronicler had at his disposal detailed information on the Judean and Benjamite regiments based in Jerusalem (vv. 14–18); others were based in the fortified cities throughout all of Judah (v. 19).

18:1—19:3. Improper Alliance with Ahab.
The shrewd king of the northern Hebrew state, Ahab, realized that an alliance with Judah was more advantageous than perpetual war and, as usual, the alliance was sealed by marriage (vv. 1–2): Ahab's daughter married Jehoshaphat's son (21:6). Jehoshaphat, in contrast, was foolish in accepting such an uneven yoke. He did not

need any alliance, for he had military and economic power in abundance (see 17:1–6). The consequences were quick in coming. When visiting the father-in-law of his son, Jehoshaphat was obligated to honor the alliance with Ahab, and thus he could not refuse Ahab's invitation to join him in battle against the Syrians. Ramoth Gilead (18:3) was, after all, part of the territories of the promised land, a Levitical city of refuge (Deut. 4:43; Josh. 21:38) and residence of one of Solomon's governors (1 Kin. 4:13). At some point the Syrians had taken possession of the city, perhaps at the secret prodding of Judah itself (1 Kin. 15:18–20). Ahab had been fighting the Syrians three years earlier, but he missed the opportunity to decimate them (1 Kin. 20).

The request of Jehoshaphat to consult a prophet of the Lord (2 Chr. 18:4–6) before proceeding was quite in character (see chap. 20, esp. 20:20). Four hundred prophets were summoned (v. 5). They enjoyed some kind of official protection and felt that they should support the noble cause of recovering an Israelite city (vv. 5, 11), as Nathan once thought he should support David in building the temple (1 Chr. 17:2). They all forgot that preachers should proclaim God's word, not the well-meaning ideas of human beings. Jehoshaphat somehow suspected as much since he requested a "second opinion" (2 Chr. 18:6). Micaiah, who had not been summoned before, was able to withstand the tacit and overt pressures of the moment (vv. 12–13). He was willing to repeat the complacent messages of the other prophets, perhaps with a sarcastic tone, if that was what was expected of him (v. 14). But when pressed for what he had really seen in vision, he conveyed the sad consequences of the endeavor of the kings, even hinting at the death of Ahab: Micaiah referred to the Lord's depiction of Israel after the battle, scattered like sheep without a shepherd—they would then have "no master" and would return home in peace (v. 16; cf. v. 27; for the lying spirit of v. 21, see commentary on 1 Kings 22:1–40). As usual, the prophet of doom was blamed for his message: by his colleagues first, once the emptiness of their message was unmasked (2 Chr. 18: 18–24), then by the main beneficiary of the warning (vv. 25–27).

It may seem strange that such a godly man as Jehoshaphat ignored the warning of Micaiah, thus endangering his life (vv. 30–31). In fact, through that battle God was freeing him from this improper alliance. The account of the death of Ahab is much more detailed in 1 Kings 22:29–40 than here because 2 Chronicles is concerned mainly with Jehoshaphat. But the Lord sent a message to Jehoshaphat through the Prophet Jehu (19:2), perhaps the son of the same Hanani who had rebuked Asa (16:7–10). He reminded the king not to "love those who hate the Lord." The message recognized, however, that there was some good in the king because of his dedication to God (19:3).

19:4–11. The Reforms of Jehoshaphat. In contrast to Asa, Jehoshaphat seems to have taken the rebuke with humility since he then went out again in a mission to bring the people back to the Lord, the God their ancestors worshiped (v. 4; cf. 17:7–9). At the time of the conquest of Canaan, a rudimentary trial system had been established for capital cases (Num. 35:6–34; Deut. 4:41–43; 19:1–14; Josh. 20:1–9). With the development of state institutions under the united monarchy, a better judiciary was long overdue. Abuse of kingly power such as under Ahab in the north (1 Kin. 21) was not to be the practice in Judah (2 Chr. 19:5–7). The ideal judge was to strive to implement righteous, divine justice throughout all the cities of the land, particularly the fortified ones (v. 5). In addition to the general judiciary, a system was put in place in Jerusalem to adjudicate controversies, settling disputes arising from the interpretation of divine law (v. 8) and as an appellate court (vv. 9–10). At the apex of the system stood the high priest, who settled religious matters, and the prince of the tribe of Judah, who oversaw civil matters (v. 11).

20:1–30. The Moabite War. Moab, just across the thin river Jordan in front of southern Judah, had been subjugated by David (1 Chr. 18:2), but the people of Moab attempted to regain independence after the division of the monarchy. This came in two stages: first by asserting independence from Israel, then from "the house of David" (i.e., Judah). For such an endeavor they enlisted the help of Ammon, also in Transjordan, in front of northern Judah and Samaria, together with others—the '*mnm* is vocalized in the Hebrew as '*ammonim*, "Ammonites," but this term is read by the LXX as *Minaion*, or Meunites (*me'unim*, as in a number of translations; cf. 2 Chr. 26:7) from south Arabia. In the narrative, however, the coalition army comprises Moab, Ammon, and Mount Seir (20:10, 22–23), suggesting that the others besides the Ammonites (v. 1) refers to Mount Seir or Edom. With this coalition, in a surprise attack (2 Chr. 20:2), the Moabites expected a victory over the southern half of their former oppressor. There is no mention of the attack in 1 Kings,

but it was of interest to the Chronicler, whose community faced conflicts with some of those same people. The vast army, a great multitude (v. 2), sneaking in by the southern end of the Dead Sea, had already reached En Gedi, midway on the Judean side of its shore, before they were detected. Jehoshaphat was alarmed, but he had the right response to fear: he proclaimed a fast and the people gathered together, seeking help from the Lord (vv. 3–4).

The main elements of his prayer were: (a) God rules over all the kingdoms of the nations, not only over Israel (vv. 5–6); (b) He had placed His people on the Holy Land, where they built a temple in order to entreat His help in times of need (vv. 7–9); (c) at the time of the conquest of this land, Moab, Ammon, and Edom were not dispossessed, following God's instructions, but they now wanted to repay evil for good with this invasion (vv. 10–11); (d) Yahweh should intervene with His righteous judgment (v. 12).

The Chronicler is interested in all manifestations of prophecy but especially in those related to the temple services through a Levite, here Jahaziel, one of the sons of Asaph, a "seer" (29:30; cf. the titles to Pss. 50, 73–83). Judah was to meet the invaders, but instead of fighting, they would only need to stand firm, waiting in stillness for the saving deliverance of the Lord, as at the time of the Exodus (2 Chr. 20:17; Ex. 14:13). Jehoshaphat exhorted the people to receive the message of the Lord with faith, trusting in the messages of His prophets—this is what leads to true success and prosperity (2 Chr. 20:18–20). Faith in the Lord and trust in His prophets will always mean victory for the people of God. Apparently the Moabites and Ammonites held a grudge against the Edomites (Mount Seir; vv. 10, 22) and mistrusted their army, which had not yet openly rebelled against Judah (21:8; 1 Kin. 22:47). Whatever the reason, they attacked each other. The people of Judah, who all the while were singing praises to God (2 Chr. 20:21–22), were soon able to verify that no one had escaped (v. 24) and proceeded to take the spoil (vv. 25). Indeed, the Lord is always faithful to His promises. Here, He fulfilled His promise to fight the battles of His people (Deut. 20:1–4). Heartfelt gratitude rose from God's people for this deliverance in a special service organized at the temple (2 Chr. 20:26–28). After this they enjoyed peace for the rest of the reign of Jehoshaphat (v. 30).

20:31—21:1. End of Jehoshaphat's Reign. The statistical and bibliographic information found in 2 Chronicles differs little from that found in 1 Kings 22:41-45, except to note that the people were not fully committed to God (2 Chr. 20:33), in spite of the efforts of the king. It is also indicated that Jehoshaphat made a trade alliance with Israel. This appears here, as in 1 Kings 22, almost as an afterthought. Perhaps Jehoshaphat thought that since God had blessed the cooperative enterprise of Solomon with the Phoenicians, he might obtain the same result with his fellow Hebrews in the north, who were not more pagan than the latter. But the Prophet Eliezer told the Davidic king that God could not bless this alliance (2 Chr. 20:37). There was indeed a difference between an ancestral pagan, who might not know better and was sympathetic toward the religion of David (such as Hiram; chap. 2), and an Israelite in open apostasy against the Lord. The ships were wrecked (v. 37) in the Ezion Geber port itself (1 Kin. 22:48), probably in an awful storm, lacking adequate harbor facilities. The northerners were insistent and proposed joint ventures, but Jehoshaphat had learned his lesson (1 Kin. 22:49). The reference to his death is brief: he rested with his ancestors and was buried in David's city (2 Chr. 21:1).

21:1-20
The Reign of Jehoram (853-841 B.C.)

Jehoram was greatly influenced by his wife, the daughter of Ahab, king of Israel. Jeroham led the people away from worship in the temple of the Lord to worship on the high places. The Lord reacted to this rebellion by weakening his military power and finally by striking him with a deadly disease. God gave him a great privilege, but he chose not to honor the Lord.

21:1-11. Character and Behavior. The account of this reign is brief probably because Jehoram was "evil" (v. 6). Jehoshaphat had followed the wise example of Rehoboam (11:23) in spreading his six younger sons throughout the kingdom as luxury pensioners, in order to prevent them from jockeying for the throne (v. 3). But Jehoram, the firstborn, mistrusted his brothers and had them killed together with other outstanding personalities of the realm (v. 4). By this time reality had surpassed even the worst nightmares of Samuel (1 Sam. 8:4-18): the Hebrews had become "like all the nations" in their pragmatic, opportunistic, and amoral power politics.

21:5-7. Regnal Statistics. The daughter of Ahab mentioned here (v. 6) was Athaliah (22:2),

who was just as bad an influence on Jehoram as on their son Ahaziah (21:6; 22:3). Even so, because of the Davidic covenant, the Lord was not willing to destroy the house of David; He had promised to keep a lamp shining for him and his offspring forever (21:7). Data on the king are summarized and supplemented in v. 20.

During his reign, the Edomites, at the time dwelling to the southeast of the Dead Sea, revolted and gained their independence (v. 8; cf. 20:10). The account, whether here or in 2 Kings 8:21, is not entirely clear, but it seems that in attempting to put down the rebellion, Jehoram barely escaped with his life (2 Chr. 21:9). Libnah, a town named for its white (*laban*) cliffs, had been historically within Israelite territory (Josh. 15:42; 21:13) and returned to it before the time of Hezekiah (Is. 37:8). At the time of Jehoram it may have fallen into the hands of the neighboring Philistines (2 Chr. 21:16).

21:12-20. Elijah's Prophecy. This northern prophet, so prominent in the book of Kings, is only mentioned here in 2 Chronicles, which is focused on Judah. Conversely, the cycle of Elijah stories in Kings does not mention this letter sent to a southern king. The present passage is also the only extant written prophecy of Elijah. He was still in the Holy Land at the time of Jehoram of Israel, an uncle and contemporary of Jehoram of Judah (2 Kin. 1:2—2:1). The exact time of his ascension is not given, nor is the letter dated. Elijah implies that the six brothers of Jehoram of Judah were not as ungodly as their murderous sibling: they were "better" than he (2 Chr. 21:13). As a punishment for impiety and murder, the family of Jehoram and his possessions would be almost completely wiped out, and the king's end would be even more painful: he would be afflicted with a severe illness of his bowels or intestines (v. 15). This all came to pass: Philistines from the west and south Arabians from the east raided Judah and carried away most of Jehoram's family and goods (vv. 16-17). He died as predicted, apparently to no one's sorrow or regret (vv. 18-20).

22:1-9
The Reign of Ahaziah (841 B.C.)

Ahaziah was the only son of Jehoram left alive by his enemies. Under the influence of his mother, Athaliah, he followed the politics of his father. Judah had become, from the religious point of view, an extension of the Northern Kingdom.

22:1–2. The Accession of Ahaziah. The raiders, mentioned in 21:16–17, had taken captive the sons of Jehoram present in the camp of Judah's defenders (v. 1). The king himself might have been too ill to be there (21:19) and Ahaziah, his youngest son, too inexperienced. In the Hebrew text, 2 Chronicles states that he was forty-two years old at the time (v. 2), but a man, in this case, Jehoram, dying at the age of forty (21:20) cannot leave behind a "youngest son" of forty-two. According to 2 Kings 8:26, Ahaziah was twenty-two years old, so the figure "forty-two" might be a transcriptional mistake or, like the years thirty-five and thirty-six in the reign of Asa (see commentary on 2 Chr. 15:1–19; 16:1–14), it might be based on a new era, this time starting not with Rehoboam but with Omri. Ahaziah would have been regarded as a "son" of Omri through Athaliah and Ahab (22:2).

22:3–9. The End of Ahaziah. The account in 2 Chronicles is much briefer than in 2 Kings 9:27–29 since this was an evil king (see commentary on 11:1—12:16). Ahaziah first tried to flee from Jehu, but he was wounded (2 Kin. 9:27), later captured, and brought before him (2 Chr. 22:8). Jehu was an enemy of the Canaanite religion, though his methods left much to be desired (2 Kin. 9:18–24; cf. Hos. 1:4), and as a northerner he would not, of course, recognize the exclusive rights of the Jerusalem altar (2 Kin. 10:29–31). However, the house of Judah then reigning was related to Ahab and followed in his steps, so it had to be exterminated as per orders of God through Elisha (2 Kin. 9:1, 8). Consequently Ahaziah was finally executed in Samaria (2 Chr. 22:9), and permission was given to move his body to Jerusalem for burial (2 Kin. 9:28). With this execution the reconciliation of the Hebrew royal houses in the north and the south, which had started with Ahab and Jehoshaphat, came to an end.

22:10–12
The Reign of Athaliah (841–835 B.C.)

The queen mother, Athaliah, saw a unique opportunity to grab power once most of the males in the family of Jehoshaphat had been killed by Jehoram (21:4), the raiders (21:16), or Jehu (22:9). She destroyed some more (v. 10), making sure that nobody could dispute her position as the ruling queen (not as the regent queen while Joash was a minor since she tried to kill him too; 2 Kin. 11:2). But Jehoshabeath (called "Jehosheba" in 2 Kin. 11:2), the daughter of King Jehoram and wife of Jehoiada

the priest (2 Chr. 22:11), was able to hide her baby nephew within the temple facilities (v. 11). The temple functioned as a place of refuge for the future king. We are told that Athaliah reigned over the land for six years, but not with the usual formula or regnal years.

23:1—24:27
The Reign of Joash (835–796 B.C.)

Here the story follows 2 Kings 11–12 quite closely, but as usual the role of the Levites is highlighted (see 2 Chr. 23:1–2), as is the need for the purity of the temple (vv. 6–7). Joash was an excellent king as long as he was under the influence of Jehoiada, the high priest. Jehoiada was the mentor of the king, highly respected by the people, and very influential. It was under the leadership of these two men that the temple was repaired. Unfortunately, after the death of Jehoiada, the king fell under the influence of spiritually corrupted advisors, and Joash did what was evil in the eyes of the Lord.

23:1–11. The Coup of Jehoiada. In order to return the kingdom to the dynasty of David, Jehoiada first contacted the captains, probably the leaders of the royal bodyguards (cf. v. 13), and showed them the royal child (2 Kin. 11:4). They in turn gathered the Levites of the realm for additional manpower, as well as clan elders for political support (2 Chr. 23:2). As noted previously, the tribe of Levi was peculiarly warlike (see 1 Chr. 26:1–19). A gathering of soldiers in Jerusalem would have looked suspicious to Athaliah, but a Levitical assembly was easier to justify because of their concern for the temple—and just as effective from a military viewpoint. Jehoiada reminded the assembly that the covenant of God with David required that his descendant, not the daughter of Ahab, be on the throne (2 Chr. 23:3).

The operative instructions were simple: the change of priestly and Levitical divisions came on the Sabbath, and both those who should be leaving the temple area and those who should be entering it would remain together with weapons in hand, but laymen had to remain in their proper place. The seven-year-old king, Joash, was anointed by Jehoiada and his sons (v. 11; not specified in 2 Kin.) and received, in addition to the crown, the Testimony (in the sense of "document") or covenant, which normally refers to the Law; here it may be some kind of coronation deed or a pledge of the people's loyalty (2 Chr. 23:11; cf. Ps. 2:7).

23:12-21. The Purge of Baalists. This account differs little from that of 2 Kings 11:13-17, though the Chronicler emphasizes again the role of the Levitical music (here in 2 Chr. 23:13). Also, here Jehoiada took care not to pollute the temple area with a corpse (v. 14)—Athaliah was killed outside (v. 15). At this point there was a renewal of the covenant in which the people pledged to be the Lord's people (v. 16). This implies several things. First the pagan religion had to be stamped out (v. 17). Here we learn that at that time there was a temple of Baal in Jerusalem, presided over by the pagan priest Mattan ("gift"). Since this is a typically Phoenician name, he must have entered the city hand in hand with Athaliah during the reign of Jehoram (21:6). Second, the temple service returned to the proper procedures established under David, with singing (23:18-19). The triumphal enthronement ceremony required the presence of all the notable persons in the realm (v. 20), while all the people of the land rejoiced (v. 21).

24:1-14. Virtual Regency of Jehoiada. Since the king was only seven years old, the real power behind the throne was his rescuer, the elderly Jehoiada, more than ninety years old at the time (v. 15; cf. v. 1). Not surprisingly, the king decided to (lit. "was with a heart to") repair the temple, the house of the Lord (v. 4). Chronicles adds the note that much of the disrepair was due to vandalism and theft on the part of the sons of Athaliah (v. 7), presumably the older brothers of Ahaziah killed by the Philistine/south Arabian raiders (21:16-17). The virtual regency of Jehoiada was recognized by the people, who buried him among the kings (v. 16; note that the name "Israel" is applied here to Judah alone).

24:15-18. Apostasy of Joash. Soon after Jehoiada's death, the leaders or officials of Judah (v. 17)—no doubt contaminated by paganism under the reigns of Jehoram, Ahaziah, and Athaliah—demanded a return to idolatry, which brought God's wrath (anger) upon the nation (v. 18). This was not merely an emotional reaction on the part of God but the consequence of the clash of His holiness with the wanton transgression of those who suppress the truth in unrighteousness or wickedness (Rom. 1:18). As on all former occasions, starting with the reign of Solomon, paganism entered Israel from the higher classes, which were subject to foreign influences, but eventually trickled down to the common people.

24:19-22. Testimony of Prophets. God forewarned the leaders about His coming wrath through prophets who testified against idolatry (v. 19). A foremost example is that of Zechariah, here called the son of Jehoiada the priest (vv. 20-22). Since Jehoiada had been born more than 130 years earlier (v. 15), we should understand the term "son" in its frequent Hebrew sense of "grandson." His actual father was Berechiah, as mentioned by Jesus in Matthew 23:35, when alluding to Bible history from the beginning of Genesis to near the end of Chronicles, which closes the Hebrew Scriptures. This, said Jesus, is the Zechariah who was stoned "between the temple and the altar." Indeed the murder took place in the courtyard of the temple (2 Chr. 24:21). The ingratitude of Joash is appalling (v. 22) and reveals a weak character. He decided to chart his own course of action independent of the principles taught him by the high priest. He chose death rather than life.

24:23-27. The Aramaean Raid and the End of Joash. Spring was the season of the year when kings went to battle in war (2 Sam. 11:1; the lull in farm work after planting the crops made more men available). In this particular spring (lit. in Hebrew—"the turn of the year"—some translations have "the end of the year"—the Hebrew year began in the spring; 2 Chr. 24:23), a small company of men from Syria was able to successfully raid Judah because they had forsaken the Lord God (v. 24). When God's people forsake Him, He may not only forsake them but also deliver them into the hands of the enemy (vv. 20, 24). But Syria did not aim at conquering Jerusalem. This would have required major war preparations that could not have been kept secret and would certainly have been matched in Judah. Instead, the raid, carried out by a small force based far away from Damascus (v. 23), was able to maintain pressure on the Hebrews, probably in order to protect Syrian interests in Gilead (see 18:1-3). If so, the promotion of religious pluralism on the part of the "leaders" of Judah (2 Chr. 24:17) may have been fueled by ulterior motives. The Canaanite religion had not only vulgar appeal but also traditional status among the mixed population of Gilead. Its toleration along with the religion of the God of Israel seemed to provide a better chance of gaining their support for the Hebrew recovery of control. Religion was also a handy excuse for murder, here perpetrated to avenge the blood of Jehoiada's son (or grandson), whom Joash had murdered (v. 25). One may wonder, however, what the sons of Ammonite and Moabite women, respectively, were doing among the officials or servants of the king in Jerusalem (vv. 25–26). The answer is probably to be found in the royal harem, where foreign women were routinely imported. In that case, the murder may have also had obscure political motives.

25:1–28
The Reign of Amaziah (796–767 B.C.)

Amaziah was an ambivalent character with double loyalties. He tried to do what was pleasing to the Lord but not with a loyal heart. He clearly gave priority to his own interest rather than to the Lord's. Consequently, God's prophets condemned his conduct, and his life ended in failure.

25:1–13. Initial Righteousness of Amaziah. Whatever led to the murder of Joash (see 24:25–27), Amaziah does not seem to have had a hand in it. He started his reign with respect for the law of God above political expediency (25:3–4). The text notes, however, that he did what was right in the sight of the Lord but not with a *shalem* (Heb.) heart (v. 2). This term literally means "whole," and is variously translated as "perfect," "loyal," "wholeheartedly." This description is in contrast to that of David (2 Kin. 14:3). The narratives that follow illustrate this strange phenomenon.

The first is the campaign in Edom (2 Chr. 25:5–13). Edom was important to Judah mainly because of its copper mines, which provided such an important part of Solomon's wealth (8:17–18). The territory had been lost under Jehoram (21:8–11), but the campaign of Amaziah was able to reconquer it (25:11–12). This provided the foundation for renewed shipping trade from the Elath port under his son Uzziah (26:2; cf. 2 Kin. 14:7). The capital of Edom, Sela ("rock") or Petra (the Greek equivalent), was probably the site of the massacre of the Edomites (2 Chr. 25:11–12; 2 Kin. 14:7). They were thrown down from the high vertical sandstone cliffs for which the place is named.

25:14–16. The Idolatry of Amaziah. The next actions of Amaziah are hard to understand, let alone explain or justify: he brought back the gods of the people of Seir (Edom) after defeating them, and he worshiped them (v. 14). Assyria and Babylon would carry away and honor the idols together with the intelligentsia of conquered nations, so that the intellectual and religious capital of

their subjects was physically moved to the central capital of the empire, as a further instrument of domination. Amaziah may have attempted something similar with Edom. After the massacre of Edomite combatants, perhaps Amaziah tried to ingratiate himself to the remainder of the population by honoring this image. But even in his day and age the king's actions were seen as absurd. The Lord sent an unnamed prophet with a message: he asked the king why he would seek the gods who could not rescue their own people from his hands. When the king told the prophet to stop speaking on pain of death, the prophet responded by telling the king that God was determined to destroy him as a result of his rebellion and recalcitrance (vv. 15–16). The king would soon learn that God has power to save and to overthrow (v. 8).

25:17–28. Israel Defeats Amaziah, and His Death. Full of self-importance after his victory in Edom, Amaziah reacted to the raid of the northern mercenaries (v. 13) with a punitive expedition against their country, Israel. King Joash of Israel tried in vain to warn Amaziah about the folly of this action (vv. 18–19) and finally inflicted upon him a sound defeat (vv. 20–22). Joash did not try to eliminate the Davidic dynasty, however, which was native of Judah and enjoyed there too much popular support, but instead he made Jerusalem defenseless and took hostages as a warning against further military ventures (vv. 23–24). He also plundered the temple treasury, which had been in the care of the family of Obed-Edom since David's times (see 1 Chr. 13:13). The Chronicler's account differs from that of 2 Kings 14 (which does not mention the idolatry of Amaziah) mainly by emphasizing that the defeat of Judah was accomplished by the providence of God—He was punishing Amaziah and Judah because they were worshiping the gods of Edom (2 Chr. 25:20). The biographical information here is not entirely clear, but it seems that when Amaziah was brought to Jerusalem in disgrace (v. 23), the people of Judah immediately conspired against him (v. 27). They decided to place his son Uzziah on the throne (26:1), which was a logical reaction to the national humiliation. Amaziah was able to maintain himself in the Lachish fortress for fifteen years, hoping for a restoration of his power, but he was eventually murdered. Nevertheless, he was given military honors at his burial (he was brought in by horses; 2 Chr.

25:28). This information implies that there was a coregency of fifteen years between Amaziah and his son Uzziah, though in fact Uzziah was the only ruler in Judah.

26:1–23
The Reign of Uzziah (792–740 B.C.)

Uzziah was a king who was unquestionably committed to the Lord but who was not totally willing to recognize the limits of his power. In Israel the three centers of power were the king, the high priest, and the prophet. Uzziah tried to usurp priestly powers, and this resulted in his downfall (see "The Temple in Chronicles," p. 541).

26:1–15. The Power of Uzziah. It is clear that Uzziah was for a time faithful to the covenant and willing to listen to the Prophet Zechariah (perhaps the "son of Jeberekiah" of Is. 8:2). He was given understanding by God (2 Chr. 26:5). There are differing manuscript traditions in regard to this verse's description of what Zechariah understood: some Hebrew manuscripts, the LXX, Vulgate, and Syriac have "fear of God," while others have "visions of God"; thus some Bible translations follow one or the other of the text traditions. Either way, Zechariah had special understanding and used this to support and instruct King Uzziah. Though after the death of Amaziah Judah had been virtually reduced to the status of a tribal princedom (25:23), obviously Uzziah came to an understanding with Samaria because he was able to fortify the wall again (26:9, 15). Though we do not know the details, such arrangements precluded further warfare between the Hebrew kingdoms. In this way both the success of Amaziah in Edom and his folly in confronting Israel ultimately resulted in peace, wealth, and military might for a largely restored Israel (2 Kin. 14:25–27). As sole monarch, Uzziah reestablished the refinery trade from Elath (2 Chr. 26:2) and no doubt used the proceeds to reestablish the authority of Jerusalem over the peoples made subject by David (vv. 6–8). In this he was aided by a standing army of 2,600 officers (v. 12) and a reserve of 307,500 soldiers who were issued standard offensive and defensive weapons (vv. 13–14), a novelty for the times. His progressive outlook was also manifested in his love for the soil (v. 10). In Judah, where there is a long dry season, this implied sinking many wells (cisterns) in the watertight limestone underlying most of the country. Plants fended for themselves in such an environment and fed the abundant royal livestock (v. 10), but those animals could not survive without a continuous supply of drinking water, which those cisterns provided. During his reign Uzziah became very strong and powerful (v. 8).

26:16–23. Pride and Punishment of Uzziah. This passage expands the statement found in 2 Kings 15:5 regarding Uzziah's divinely inflicted leprosy. Uzziah acted unfaithfully and transgressed by rebelliously entering the temple and attempting to burn incense on the altar in front of the Most Holy Place (2 Chr. 26:16). This was the result of his inordinate pride and also perhaps because of a desire to impress all those nations recently dominated militarily. In Mesopotamia and Egypt the kings were high priests. Uzziah may have envisioned a similar role for himself, on the basis of the priesthood of kings in Salem/Jerusalem (Gen. 14:18; Ps. 110:4). The eighty courageous and valiant priests of the Lord commanded by the high priest to expel the king from the temple (2 Chr. 26:17) were necessary because the king otherwise could have resisted the expulsion (v. 18) with the help of his bodyguards. The leprosy (v. 19) was most probably Hansen's disease. The king was able to observe the outbreak in his own skin and hurried to leave the temple. While nothing prevented him, from that time on, from continuing to make important decisions of government, he could not, as an unclean leper (v. 23), attend the temple or court of judgment, kingly functions he had to delegate to his son Jotham (v. 21). After he died, he was accordingly buried in a special cemetery (v. 23).

27:1–9
The Reign of Jotham (750–732 B.C.)

Nothing bad is reported about Jotham. As a king he did what was right in the eyes of the Lord. Unfotunately, the people did not follow his example. But the Lord blessed him and gave him victories over his enemies.

27:1–2. Regnal Statistics and Evaluation. A careful study of the sometimes confusing chronological data of the Hebrew kings has led to the conclusion that Jotham reigned as coregent with Uzziah for about twelve years (see 26:21), plus four years as sole king (thus making the sixteen years—vv. 1, 8). He also reigned four years in another coregency, this time with his son Ahaz (thus explaining the "twentieth year of Jotham the son of Uzziah" in 2 Kin. 15:30). The brevity of his period as sole king may account for the paucity of items reported about him. He did what was right in the Lord's estimation (2 Chr. 27: 2), but the people acted corruptly by offering illicit sacrifices outside the temple (cf. 2 Kin. 15:35).

27:3–9. The Deeds of Jotham. The Upper Gate of the temple was probably the northern one, where it opened to an upward slope. The Ophel was a landfill in the south of the city, dominating the Kidron valley (v. 3). Jotham also continued the defensive construction plan of his father, with cities (fortresses) in the hill country of Judah, which were connected visually by a chain of observation towers (v. 4). He was also able to obtain a handsome tribute from the Ammonites, after a punitive expedition probably made to recover the tribute that was past due (v. 5). Because Jotham established and ordered his ways according to the Lord his God, he became very strong and powerful (v. 6).

28:1–27
The Reign of Ahaz (735–716 B.C.)

Ahaz was one of the most Caananized kings of Judah. During his reign he followed the ways of the rebellious kings of Israel, the Northern Kingdom. He even offered his children as human sacrifices. This was a dark period in the history of the kingdom of Judah.

28:1–4. Regnal Statistics and Evaluation. In spite of the efforts of the Prophet Isaiah to provide divine guidance for Ahaz, he turned into one of the worst kings of Judah. He lived (or "walked") in the same ways as the kings of Israel (v. 2). As noted previously, paganism entered Hebrew lands usually through the royal court (see 24:15–18). Worship of common deities seems to have been a precondition either for alliances, such as that of Ahab with Phoenicia (eventually resulting in the temple of Baal in Jerusalem; see 23:16–19), or for the annexation of other lands, such as Edom (see 25:14–16). However, the horrendous abominations here mentioned, such as child sacrifice in the Valley of the Son of Hinnom (Heb. "Ben Hinnom"; 28:3), do not seem motivated by diplomatic needs but by utter lack of faith in the God of his fathers. We do not know the conditions under which Ahaz committed such abominations, but he must have acted out of political or personal desperation (cf. 2 Kin. 3:27).

28:5–15. The Syro-Ephraimite War. The north was not completely devoid of prophets of the Lord, such as Oded (v. 9), who reminded Israel of the prohibition against enslaving fellow Hebrews (v. 11; Lev. 25:39). The captives gained the support of the tribal leaders or heads (2 Chr. 28:12–13), and they were finally returned via Jericho, well fed, clothed, and in some cases even helped to ride on donkeys (v. 15).

28:16–21. Treaty of Ahaz with Assyria. Completely surrounded by enemies in the area, Ahaz then resorted to an alliance further afield with Assyria, which did alleviate the pressure of Syria and Israel upon Judah (2 Kin. 16:7–9). However, there was a religious price to pay: Ahaz reformed the altar of sacrifice in the temple of Jerusalem in order to please the king of Assyria (2 Kin. 16:10–18). It soon became clear that Assyria had come to the Levant only for its own purposes. When its aid was requested against renewed Edomite and Philistine raids, the Assyrian king Tiglath-Pileser demanded further payments from Ahaz but did not help (2 Chr. 28:20). Judah had been brought low in humility on account of Ahaz, a king who had encouraged moral decline, wickedness, and lack of restraint (the Heb. *para'* can and has been translated as all these), as well as unfaithfulness to the living God (v. 19).

28:22–27. Further Apostasy and Death of Ahaz. Instead of repenting and seeking refuge in the Lord amid the alarming circumstances, Ahaz only deepened his unfaithfulness, experimenting with the worship of foreign idols (vv. 22–23). He actively promoted religious pluralism in every corner in Jerusalem (v. 24) and closed the doors to the temple. The dwelling place of the God who redeemed Israel from Egypt became irrelevant and unnecessary. The temple, where atonement took place, was rejected and shut up. At his death, the judgment of the people on his reign was revealed by the fact that he was not buried in the tombs of the kings of Israel (v. 27).

29:1—32:33
The Reign of Hezekiah (716–687 B.C.)

Hezekiah was one of the greatest kings of Judah. Everything he did for the Lord and the people he did with all his heart—with undivided loyalty. He repaired and cleansed the temple, reorganized its services, and celebrated the Passover. He was an effective religious, military, and administrative leader. Unfortunately, his pride cast a shadow on his character, but it was not powerful enough to permanently damage his relationship with the Lord.

29:1–36. Restoration of the Temple. At the beginning of the sanctuary ritual year, in the first month of spring, the new king opened the doors of the temple (v. 3), gathered the priests and Levites (vv. 4–5), and apprised them of his intentions to make a covenant with the God of Israel (v. 10). In order to accomplish this latter purpose it was necessary to clean up the temple that had been shut up by his father. The Levites and the temple were to be sanctified (vv. 1–17). Everything was ready by the sixteenth day of the month, theoretically in time for the Festival of Unleavened Bread (vv. 18–19; but see commentary on 30:1–27). Proper sanctuary service was then restored, with appropriate sacrifices, contributed by the representatives of the nation (vv. 20–24, 31–36), and the sacred music of the Levites (vv. 25–30). God was once more at the center of the life of the His people. Here we learn that David's instruction regarding the orchestra was based on the Lord's instruction through His prophets (v. 25).

30:1–27. The Passover of Hezekiah. The Passover victim had to be sacrificed on the evening of the fourteenth day of the lunar month. But since the temple was not yet ready, the festival was postponed for the next lunar cycle (which was permitted under the law; Num. 9:6–11), giving everybody time to prepare, even northern believers (2 Chr. 30:1–9). By this time, the latter were a minority in Israel, but some did accept the invitation of their southern brethren and came (vv. 10–12). On this occasion the Levites acted as intermediaries of the people and slaughtered the Passover victims (vv. 13–17). Those who came from the Northern Kingdom had not had time to cleanse themselves and yet ate the Passover. The king interceded for them, asking the Lord to atone for and pardon anyone who had sincerely sought Him, even if they had not been cleansed according to the sanctuary guidelines (vv. 18–20). The Lord listened to the king (v. 20). Moreover, by common consent, they kept the festival for fourteen days, instead of the seven prescribed, so as to give time for the Levites to instruct them on the finer points of the law (vv. 21–22). The king provided victuals for the multitude in view of this unexpected prolongation of the festival (vv. 23–26), reminding people of the bountiful times of Solomon (v. 26; cf. 7:7). Notice that the real holy

dwelling place of God is not the earthly but the heavenly sanctuary (v. 27), just as the heart of religion is found not in cold ritual correctness but in atonement and spontaneous confession, praise (v. 22), and joy (v. 26).

31:1–21. The Reforms of Hezekiah. Revival of faith should always be followed by reformation and changes in behavior. All the Israelites who had been present at the festival participated in the removal of cultic images and illicit altars from Judah and from some parts of Israel (v. 1). Obviously in the north this would not have enjoyed official support. The priestly and Levitical divisions were restored (v. 2), provision was made for the regular support of the sacrificial worship from the royal lands (v. 3), as well as support for the Levites dwelling in Jerusalem, so that they could devote themselves to the law (v. 4). The people resumed the delivery of tithes and firstfruits to the temple (vv. 5–10) and to special storehouses, and proper accounting procedures were added (vv. 11–15). From these financial resources a stipend was paid to everybody in Levitical and Aaronite genealogy (vv. 16–19). Hezekiah sought God in everything he did, and he did it all with diligence—with all his heart (v. 21).

32:1–23. The Defeat of Sennacherib. Second Chronicles is mainly interested in the prosperity of Hezekiah, not in his problems, which may be supplied from other sources. The alliance with Judah had given Assyria an excuse to extend its dominion in the Levant; the Northern Kingdom fell to Assyria in 722 B.C. As a vassal of Assyria, Hezekiah was not disturbed for some time, but around 701 B.C. the Egyptians began encouraging nations within their traditional sphere of influence to rebel against Assyria. Hezekiah participated in an Egyptian-led anti-Assyrian league with Sidon (Phoenicia), Ascalon, and Ekron (Philistia; cf. 2 Kin. 18:7), cities which fell to Sennacherib once he defeated the supporting Egyptian army. He then marched into Judah and took forty-six of its towns, including the fortress of Lachish. Hezekiah bought him off with heavy tribute (2 Kin. 18:13–16), but later, still worried about the pro-Egyptian party in Judah (2 Kin. 19:8–13), Sennacherib returned. This return probably took place years later (note the time-consuming intervening preparations in Jerusalem; 2 Chr. 32:2–8). A division of the Assyrian army besieged Jerusalem under the command of the chief military officers or servants of the empire while Sennacherib himself remained in Lachish (v. 9). The Assyrians realized that the morale of the people of Judah was held high because of their religion, so they tried to discourage them by deriding Hezekiah's command to worship on one altar only (v. 12) and, for that matter, his trust in Yahweh (v. 11). As well, Sennacherib's officials touted the record of Assyria's conquests—no god of any nation or kingdom had been able to protect their people from Sennacherib or those before him (v. 15). The propaganda went as far as to revile and ridicule the Lord (v. 17). Hezekiah and Isaiah pled with the Lord (v. 20) in the temple (2 Kin. 19:14–19) to vindicate His holy name. Isaiah had accurately predicted that other military needs would soon remove Sennacherib from Judah (2 Kin. 19:7).

As for the soldiers besieging Jerusalem, the Lord sent an angel who destroyed all the warriors, captains, and officers of the army (2 Chr. 32:21). We are not told how this happened, but Herodotus records that the army of Sennacherib, near the Egyptian border, was plagued by mice who had infested their supplies. Mice are well-known vectors of bubonic plague, some forms of which kill in just twenty-four hours. In any case, Sennacherib returned in disgrace to his own land, having shamefully learned the hard way that Yahweh was able to deliver His people (cf. v. 15). Although Sennacherib boasted in the Assyrian records that he "shut Hezekiah in as a bird in a cage," in fact the Lord saved Hezekiah and Jerusalem (v. 22). But Hezekiah had more to fear from the Assyrians, who were no doubt bent on a regime change. Vassals who betrayed their trust were routinely executed and replaced by pro-Assyrian relatives on the throne.

32:24–26. Illness and Recovery of Hezekiah. The root of Hezekiah's trials, including the Assyrian attack and his illness, was that he did not respond appropriately to the Lord according to the favor and kindness shown to him (32:25) during the years in which "he prospered" (31:21), or after God's healing him from his illness. While he did offer a prayer of thanksgiving for his recovery (2 Kin. 20:1–11; Is. 38), he neglected to emphasize God's greatness when the Babylonians came, for his heart was lifted up in pride (2 Chr. 32:25). Both Isaiah and Kings provide further detail regarding Hezekiah's illness and recovery. After a message of Isaiah warning of impending death (2 Kin. 20:1; Is. 38:1), Hezekiah humbled himself (2 Chr. 32:26) and "wept bitterly" (2 Kin. 20:2–3; Is. 38:2–3). The sign and recovery then followed, fifteen years before the end of his twenty-nine-year-long reign (2 Chr. 29:1; 2 Kin. 20:6; Is. 38:5), and

therefore very close to the Assyrian attack on his fourteenth year (2 Kin. 18:13). His illness is diagnosed in 2 Kings 20:7 and Isaiah 38:21 as "a boil" or ulcer (cf. the plagues in Ex. 9:9; Rev. 16:2). Perhaps this was the result of diabetes. The very high sugar content of a lump of dried figs (2 Kin. 20:7; Is. 38:21) is an effective treatment that may prevent infection in such ulcers, and the subsequent deadly gangrene. As for the sign (2 Chr. 32:24), the Chronicler assumes that readers remember it well: the Lord moved the shadow backward (2 Kin. 20:11). Though some type of natural explanation could be conjectured for this phonenemon, the biblical text records it as divine intervention.

32:27–33. Final Evaluation and Death of Hezekiah. As in the times of Uzziah, Judah's control of the southern lands brought riches (vv. 27–29) and engineering feats (v. 30). However, foolish pride is a more stubborn disease than diabetic ulcers or whatever it was that ailed Hezekiah (see vv. 24–26). When God put him to the test regarding all that was in his heart, Hezekiah failed (v. 31). The ambassadors from Babylon claimed to have humanitarian (2 Kin. 20:12) and scientific aims (2 Chr. 32:31), but in fact their main purpose was political. Babylon was, at the time, organizing its own anti-Assyrian league, which was to bring the downfall of Nineveh in 612 B.C., so they may have been sounding out Hezekiah. But no matter what the foreign powers claimed, their only constant compass was self-interest. Childish pride led Hezekiah to forget this reality and to show this "friendly" power the wealth of his realm (Is. 39), thereby exciting covetousness on the part of his visitors. Even so, the Chronicler recognizes Hezekiah's life overall as one of *khesed*—the rich Hebrew word rendered variously as "devotion," "love," "kindness," "loyalty," and "goodness" (2 Chr. 32:32). The mention of Isaiah in his bibliography shows that this prophet also had a hand in composing the sources on which the books of Kings drew.

33:1–25
The Reigns of Manasseh (697–643 B.C.) and Amon (643–641 B.C.)

The case of Manasseh will remain forever one of the most moving stories of divine forgiveness in the OT. He was a totally corrupt king who, while under oppression, repented of his sins and asked for forgiveness, and the Lord forgave him and restored his kingdom to him. Not so with his son, Amon, who decided to imitate his father in sin and rebellion but not in repentance. From the divine perspective, personal history is always open to God's love and mercy.

33:1–9. The Awful Sins of Manasseh. As seen previously, the purpose of the Assyrian invasion was probably to produce a regime change with a new king favorable to Assyrian interests (32:22). This implied, to a certain extent, a demand of recognition for the suzerain's religion, which they must have expected from a pliable twelve-year-old such as Manasseh. Indeed, the astrolatry of Manasseh (the worship of the stars—all the host of heaven; 33:3, 5) is typical of Mesopotamian religion, and the building of additional altars in the temple, the house of the Lord, clearly indicates acts of idolatry (v. 4). But the total devotion of this king to unfettered idolatry surpassed all political concerns. A carved image in the temple itself (v. 7), a blatant violation of the second commandment of the Decalogue (Ex. 20:4), only emphasized his complete denial of the covenant. The shocking evil practice of child sacrifice (2 Chr. 33:6; see 28:1–4) seems to be a residue of ancestral Canaanite practices for which the Lord had expelled such nations (2 Chr. 33:2). The Canaanites themselves resorted to such horrors only in the most extreme circumstances, and then not as a sacrifice to their chief gods, such as Father Sky Hadad (Baal), but to dark underground deities of death. These were always maligned and had to be appeased by those means in order to bring to an end an inexplicable spate of bad luck. We are not told how many sons of Manasseh suffered this fate, but his heir, Amon, was not born until Manasseh was forty-five years old. In the same order of abominations we learn of divination (fortune-telling—sometimes called "soothsaying") as well as witchcraft and sorcery. He also consulted mediums and necromancers (or "spiritists"; v. 6). The long reign of Manasseh (fifty-five years) probably includes ten years as coregent of Hezekiah plus another forty-five as sole king, during which he apostatized.

33:10–20. Punishment and Repentance of Manasseh. While 2 Kings does not mention the repentance and restoration of Manasseh, the Chronicler records this story that stands forever as a sign and testimony of God's unbounded forgiveness. We are not told on what occasion the army of the king of Assyria swooped down on Manasseh and took him to Babylon (2 Chr. 33:11). One possibility is the induction

of Asshurbanipal ("Osnapper"; Ezra 4:10) as the apparent heir of Esarhaddon in 672 B.C. Vassal princes, such as Pharaoh Necho I, were made to attend and swear loyalty to the prince as future king of Assyria. Though the capital of Assyria was Nineveh, Babylon, the ancient religious capital of the Akkadians (i.e., Assyrians and Babylonians), was used for some ceremonies (it may also stand here as a general term for the Mesopotamian region). Asshurbanipal was the last of the great Assyrian kings. The empire suffered from overexpansion, and after his death in 627 B.C., it descended into chaos. Niniveh was destroyed by an alliance between the Babylonians and the Medes in 612 B.C. It may be that the difficulties of Asshurbanipal with the Medes kept him occupied in the north, facilitating the return of Manasseh to God.

The fact is that the Lord received his plea, listened to his petition, and brought him back to Jerusalem and his kingdom (2 Chr. 33:13). Idolatry was quietly eliminated (vv. 14–19), as recorded in the book of *khozay*. This word is sometimes taken as a proper name, "Hozai," and translated as such in some versions. However, it is also sometimes translated as "the seers" (from the Heb. word *khezu*—"vision"), as it is rendered in the LXX. This could be a reference to a succession of literary prophets from which the book of Kings was able to draw.

33:21–25. Amon's Reign and Death. The return of Manasseh to the Lord was not accompanied by a high-profile festival, such as Hezekiah's, which the Assyrians would have taken as an intolerable snub. Amon only continued the pagan practices of the first part of his father's reign or was too much corrupted by them to return to the living God. Thus, he did as his father Manasseh had done at first (v. 22). The people that put an end to his life (v. 24) may have invoked religious concerns, as in the case of Joash (see 24:25–27), or nationalistic, anti-Assyrian ones, or even a mixture of both, since Egyptians, in contrast to Assyrians, did not try to impose their religion on anybody else. The gods of the Egyptians were for them alone. In any case, the population of Judah did not condone the murder of Amon (33:25) since he was "the anointed of the LORD" (1 Sam. 24:6).

34:1—35:27
The Reign of Josiah (641–609 B.C.)

Josiah did not follow the example of his father Amon but decided to restore the true Israelite faith. He initiated an energetic reform movement that included the restoration of the temple, the eradication of idolatry, and the instruction of the people about what God expected from them. Unfortunately, his reform did not take root due to the fact that he died young while trying to intercept an Egyptian army heading to help the Assyrians against the Babylonians. By then the fate of the kingdom of Judah was cast (see "The Temple in Chronicles," p. 541).

34:1–8a. Regnal Statistics and Overview. Both the Chronicler and the writer of 2 Kings evaluate the reign of Josiah positively. Second Kings 22 highlights the finding of the book (or one of the five books) of the law, displaying it as a motor of reform; the Chronicler also recounts this event as well as other episodes in the process (2 Chr. 34:15–21). The Pentateuch was by this time well known and had already been in force for a long time (see 12:1). Josiah went gradually about his reforms. At the age of sixteen he was already totally committed to the living God (2 Chr. 34:3), but since he was probably still under some form of regency, he had to tread carefully. His successive campaigns, first in the south (vv. 3–5), then in the north of the country (vv. 6–7), purified the religion of the country. The term *khereb* in v. 6, taken from the margin of the Hebrew text, may be translated literally "swords," which could have been used to hack at the idols. It could also mean "ruins" (the general sense is "wasters") and would then be understood "as far as Naphthali, with their ruins all about it." We should keep in mind that much of the territory of the Northern Kingdom lay in ruins after the Assyrian invasion. Josiah's twelfth year (v. 3; 627 B.C.) coincided with the death of Asshurbanipal and the call of Jeremiah the prophet. The rapid dissolution of Assyrian power afforded the twenty-year-old monarch an opportunity to safely purge Judah and Jerusalem of idolatry (v. 8a), whether in the form of remnants from the early reign of Manasseh or from the pagan revival of Amon. The momentous discovery of a book of the law in the temple took place later, in his eighteenth year.

34:8b–21. Rediscovery of the Book of the Law. Historical-critical reconstructions of biblical history point out that many of the reforms of Josiah seem inspired by Deuteronomy (34:2; see Deut. 7:25–26; 27:3, 26; 28:58–61; 29:9, 21–27). Then they conclude that the book had recently been composed in the north of the country under the name of Moses, in order to purify its religion and that at this point in history it reached Judah. But the purging of the idolatry took place before the discovery of the book (see 2 Chr. 34:1–8a), so the role of the latter was to reinforce, not to initiate, reform. Though passages from Deuteronomy could be and were eventually used as ammunition against a sanctuary in Jerusalem, they are not the center of its powerful message (note its effect in vv. 19–22). A better reconstruction, from a conservative viewpoint, is that Deuteronomy had been for a long time neglected in the south, even during times of faithfulness to the covenant. Now, a century after the fall of Samaria, any potential arguments against Jerusalem based on Deuteronomy were largely moot and could be forgotten, so the book was given its rightful place (vv. 19–22). Josiah sought then to have the people of Judah fully comply with the instructions of the Lord as found in this book of the law.

34:22–28. Prophecy of Huldah. Some readers may find it strange that while Manasseh was personally forgiven by God (33:13), the prophetess announced that Judah was still to suffer for his sins (2 Kin. 21:10–15; 22:15–20; cf. 2 Chr. 34:24–25). Those who violate the covenant may be forgiven through sincere repentance and restored to God's favor, but the effects of their sin on the affairs of this life often cannot be avoided. Also, the evil influence of the sins of Manasseh and Amon reverberated among the people, who committed sins of their own (33:9; 34:25).

34:29–33. Public Reading of the Law. Firmly established on his throne, Josiah gathered all the elders of Judah and Jerusalem as representatives of the nation who could pass on to their families and clans the religious education provided by him (v. 29). The venue was the temple (v. 30), and the instructors were the "priests and the prophets" (2 Kin. 23:2) or, with the characteristic emphasis of 2 Chronicles, "the priests and the Levites" (2 Chr. 34:30). Since the latter regularly addressed the people in the temple, the Chronicler may have considered them to be prophets too, and they also taught Israel (35:3). The textbook of this public education effort, the book of the covenant (34:30), is normally interpreted as a section of Exodus, which presupposes the Decalogue (Ex. 20) and extends it in the immediately following chapters (Ex. 21–23), as suggested by Exodus 24:7. Such passages of the Pentateuch might be alluded to here (2 Chr. 34:31) through the mention of commandments as well as the testimonies (or "decrees") and statutes which follow the Decalogue in Exodus, either directly or by means of the parallel passages in Deuteronomy (e.g., chaps. 5, 10–26). The covenant with the God of Israel was renewed by the king and the representatives of the whole nation (2 Chr. 34:31–32). This commitment was integral to the effort to inspire all who were present in Israel to diligently serve the Lord their God (v. 33).

35:1–19. Josiah's Passover. Much of the language of this section echoes other famous sacred occasions, such as Hezekiah's Passover (chap. 30) or the inaugural festival of Solomon (chap. 7). In contrast to the Passover of Hezekiah, however, this celebration was held at the proper time, on the fourteenth day of the first month (35:1), and at the proper venue for Israel under the Davidic dynasty, the temple. Sacrificing Passover lambs in the central sanctuary alone is commanded in Deuteronomy 16:15–16. Hezekiah, however, had organized the festival in the same way, even for the people of the north (2 Chr. 30:11, 18). Josiah's instruction to the Levites, to put the ark in the temple (v. 3), seems to imply that it was no longer there, but nothing is known about it leaving the temple at a prior time. It could be that the ark was removed from the temple by one of the evil kings. The parallel words of David in 1 Chronicles 23:26 clearly refer to the recent transfer from Gibeon (1 Chr. 15–16). The text here is probably to be read as in the LXX: "they have [already] put the holy ark" (in the temple), referring to David's times. This made it unnecessary for the Levites to occasionally carry the ark (2 Chr. 35:3). Josiah also expected the Levites to teach all Israel (vv. 3–6).

35:20–27. Death of Josiah. The new power on the horizon, since the fall of Nineveh in 612 B.C., was Babylon. Pharaoh Necho, who had sworn allegiance to the Assyrians, was as good as his word and came to their aid against the Babylonians in Carchemish by the Euphrates (v. 20). On his way there, in the valley or plain of Megiddo (v. 22), he was intercepted by Josiah, who probably thought he should help give a final shove to the tottering, hated Assyrian Empire that year (609 B.C.). Necho, on his part, felt he was on a divine mission (v. 21). The invocation of God by Necho (even if tainted by Egyptian conceptions) should have given Josiah pause for reflection (as noted in v. 22), but he stubbornly forged ahead and was fatally wounded

in the battle (vv. 23–24). The book of Laments here mentioned, however, is not the biblical book of Lamentations. Jeremiah, whose ministry prospered during Josiah's reign, wept until God specifically instructed him to stop weeping for Josiah (Jer. 22:10). The Egyptians were able to maintain themselves in Carchemish until 605 B.C., "the fourth year of Jehoiakim the son of Josiah" (Jer. 46:2), when the Assyrian army was definitively defeated.

36:1–23
The End of the Kingdom of Judah

The death of Josiah was a significant spiritual and political blow to the nation. The religious reform was soon forgotten, and the political independence of the nation was lost. From this moment on, the kings of Judah would be vassals either to Egypt or to Babylon.

36:1–8. The Loss of Political Independence. Returning from Carchemish, Necho felt that a regime change was indispensable in Jerusalem, so he deposed and carried away the recently inaugurated Jehoahaz (609 B.C.), substituting an older brother, Eliakim, in his stead, with the throne name Jehoiakim (609–598 B.C.). We are not told in what ways he did evil in the sight of the Lord his God (v. 5). This phrase usually refers to idolatry, but 2 Kings 24:4 mentions the unjust killing of his own subjects, which may be related to struggles between pro-Egyptian and pro-Babylonian parties in Jerusalem. Egyptians, as noted previously, gave ample freedom of worship, but they taxed the land heavily (2 Chr. 36:3). Jehoiakim began his reign as an Egyptian vassal, but in 605 B.C., after the final defeat of Assyria, he swore loyalty to Babylon, only to renege three years later when the Egyptians managed to temporarily contain Babylonian power (2 Kin. 24:1). But the latter was merely strengthening its army, which invaded Judah in 597 B.C. and took Jehoiakim as a prisoner. Then Jehoiachin his son took his place on the throne (2 Chr. 36:8).

36:9–14. Jehoiachin (598–597 B.C.) and Zedekiah (597–586 B.C.). As is indicated in most translations, "eight years old" (v. 9) should probably be corrected to "eighteen." Cuneiform records in Babylon show that five years later, as a prisoner in Babylon, Jehoiachin already had five sons. Zedekiah, a son of Josiah (v. 10), was a weak monarch and changed sides constantly. He ignored the warnings of Jeremiah, who sought to maintain his submission to Babylon (v. 12), and rebelled together with Judah one time too many (vv. 13, 15–23). By this time political passions and evil precedents from the time of Manasseh, or even earlier, combined to make idolatry rampant again (v. 14).

36:15–23. Destruction and Desolation of Judah. By 586 B.C., Babylon had lost patience with the country; so, following the methods of Assyria in Israel (2 Kin. 17:5–6), all the urban population of Judah was taken captive, and the city and its temple were plundered (2 Chr. 36:17–20; 2 Kin. 25:1–21). For seventy years, as predicted by Jeremiah (v. 21; Jer. 25:11–12; 29:10), the land would lie unplowed. The text suggests that for about 420 years of prior existence as an independent and politically organized nation, the Hebrews had essentially ignored the sabbatical-year regulation (Lev. 25:1–7). The default now had to be made up with seventy years of desolation until 539 B.C., when Cyrus, king of Persia, gave them freedom to return and recover their ancestral possessions (2 Chr. 36:22–23). Special mention is made of the articles from the temple, the house of God (v. 18), taken to Babylon and of the destruction of the temple itself. In this way, the marvelous history of the people of God in the promised land, worshiping Him in His holy temple, which was carefully detailed in 1 and 2 Chronicles, seems to have come to a tragic end.

But then, in the midst of this bleak panorama, just as a pine seedling might sprout up after a fearsome fire that has consumed the forest, the new king Cyrus reported in his decree that the God of heaven had appointed and commanded him to build a temple (house) for Him in Jerusalem in Judah. He then invited all among God's people to go up to Jerusalem and even proclaimed a promised blessing for all who would go, saying that the Lord their God would be with them (v. 23). Hope was ignited, and the possibility of a new future began to take shape. The Bible is, indeed, the book of hope and new beginnings (see "The Temple in Chronicles," p. 541).

EZRA

INTRODUCTION

Title and Authorship. The book bearing the name of its main protagonist is situated historically in the second half of the fifth century B.C., during the postexilic period. Jewish scholars throughout the centuries have considered Nehemiah to be a continuation of the book of Ezra and treated them as a single unit, even though the opening caption of Nehemiah (1:1) seems to indicate that they originally were separate works. Nehemiah 3:22 was marked by the Masoretes in the seventh through tenth centuries A.D. as the center of this unified book (Ezra-Nehemiah) and included a final summary note only after Nehemiah 13:31 but did not include one at the end of Ezra. Ezra and Nehemiah have appeared as separate books since A.D. 1448 in Hebrew manuscripts and still appear that way today in modern versions of the OT. Regardless, there are very good reasons to suspect that they were indeed originally one book.

Ezra's influence during the formative period of Judaism should not be underestimated, since it was his leadership that facilitated the reestablishment of worship in Jerusalem following the rebuilding of the temple. Later the rebuilding of the wall was successfully accomplished under Nehemiah's leadership. Because the last few verses of 2 Chronicles (36:22–23) and the first few verses of Ezra (1:1–3) are nearly identical, some scholars have argued that Ezra was also the author of Chronicles. It seems highly likely that the author of, at minimum, the closing portion of 2 Chronicles could have been Ezra. Repetition is common in ancient writing when a scroll (or tablet) was not long enough and the scribe had to continue on a new scroll (or tablet). The modern term for this technique is "catch-lines" (see 2 Chronicles: Introduction). What is also clear is that both books share common terminology and a significant number of theological themes. The same is true for Nehemiah. While it is true that the two men (Ezra and Nehemiah) were contemporaries (Neh. 8:9; 12:26, 36), which may explain the similarities, it is likely that the two books were originally one.

Date. The seven official documents found in Ezra were all written in Aramaic except for the first one, which was written in Hebrew. These documents correspond both in writing style and language used to non-biblical official documents from the Persian period, which is strong evidence that this book was written sometime during that era. According to Ezra 7:1, 8, Ezra was in Jerusalem in the seventh year of the reign of Artaxerxes I, which was 457 B.C. It took Ezra about four months to travel from Babylon to Jerusalem (7:9). While the events in the first six chapters took place before Ezra arrived in Jerusalem, the last four chapters took place after 457 B.C. Nehemiah is not mentioned in the book of Ezra (see commentary on Ezra 2:1–35). Nehemiah began his ministry in 444 B.C. (Neh. 2:1). Thus, the date for the composition of this book in its final version would have been after 457 B.C., but likely most of it was written before 444 B.C. (see Nehemiah: Introduction").

Backgrounds. Artaxerxes was the third son of Xerxes I (the Ahasuerus of Esther). The Greeks called him "long-handed" (Lat. *longimanus*). His father was murdered by the royal bodyguard Artabanus. Artaxerxes then killed Artabanus, but it is unclear who killed the older brothers of Artaxerxes. In the end, Artaxerxes ended up with the throne. It seems that shortly after taking the throne, Artaxerxes gave asylum to Themistocles, the Greek who had beaten his father at the Battle of Marathon and again in the naval battle of Salamis years before. He advised Artaxerxes in matters dealing with the Greeks until his death in 459 B.C. A few years before Ezra traveled to Jerusalem (in 457 B.C.), the Persians were drawn into a fight with an Egyptian-Greek alliance seeking to gain control of Egypt. In 454 B.C. the Persians won that war. A few years later (450 B.C.) Persia was at war with Greece again at Cyprus. A year later, in 449 B.C., the Persians reached a peace with the Athenians. Thus, the world that Ezra entered was one with war on its borders both before and after his arrival in Jerusalem. It was a troubled and uncertain time.

Two major sections of Ezra (4:8—6:18; 7:12–26) containing references to official letters were written in Aramaic. Aramaic (as well as the closely related Syriac) functioned as the language of choice in literature and communication at least starting in the Babylonian Empire, which is why portions of Daniel (2:4—7:28) also were written in Aramaic. These passages in Aramaic represent the only major sections of the Bible written in what was the primary international language of the second half of the first millennium B.C., even though a few Aramaic phrases occur also in Genesis (31:47) and Jeremiah (10:11). It was not uncommon to find texts written in multiple languages in the ancient world, all written by the same person. Thus, this characteristic in Ezra is not an argument that the same scribe could not have written the entire book. In fact, it supports the underlying historicity of the book as being written in the time of its assumed historical context.

Theology and Purpose. The books of Ezra and Nehemiah describe times of struggles and victories for God's people. From the vantage point of these biblical books, these struggles were God's struggles too since it was God who ultimately returned a remnant to Jerusalem and oversaw the reconstruction of the temple and the reestablishment of its sacrificial service. God's commitment to His people is easily observable in Ezra and Nehemiah—in spite of moments of disobedience, twisted priorities, or subversive rebellion. While we cannot fathom God's commitment to a sinful world, we can accept His sustaining and amazing grace and learn from the theological themes that crisscross the book.

1. *A Biblical Philosophy of History.* Human history in Ezra and Nehemiah is clearly the arena of God's activities. This account challenges readers living in the twenty-first century to look beyond the often simplistic link between cause and effect that characterizes a secular outlook on life—there is more to humanity than we can see and measure.

The two books describe three historical returns from exile for the remnant of Judah. In 537 B.C. Sheshbazzar led a group that returned and began rebuilding the temple under the leadership of Zerubbabel and Jeshua (or Joshua) (Ezra 3:8–13) in fulfillment of God's prophecy through Jeremiah that the land would be empty for seventy years (Jer. 25:11–12; 29:10; cf. Ezra 1:1; Dan. 9:2). In 457 B.C. (Ezra 7:6–9), Ezra led another group of exiles in a return to the Holy Land and began teaching them the law (Ezra 7:10), in keeping with the command of Artaxerxes I that Jerusalem and its religious system should be rebuilt and restored (Ezra 7:11–26). This command fulfilled the starting point for the seventy weeks of years (Dan. 9:25), exactly 483 years before the baptism and beginning of the Messiah's ministry (Luke 3:1–22) in A.D. 27, even though the actual building did not start for another thirteen years. Then in 444 B.C. (Neh. 2:1–10) Nehemiah led a third group and, in spite of strong opposition, began rebuilding the wall around the city (Neh. 2:17—6:16), fulfilling the prophecy that the wall would be built during times of trouble (Dan. 9:25). Each of these historic events is clearly attributed in the text to the direct intervention of God working through willing humans. And each shows the foreknowledge of God in predicting the precise time and circumstance in which each event would take place.

2. *God Is Sovereign.* God, as portrayed in the book of Ezra, is not a local or regional deity. Ezra depicts God as bigger than Jerusalem—even though He had chosen Jerusalem (and postexilic Israel) as His manifested dwelling place and base camp to fulfill His mission of saving a lost world (see John 1:14; 3:16). In this sense, Ezra and Nehemiah continue to anticipate the fulfillment of innumerable messianic promises that ultimately point to the completion of salvation history in Jesus Christ. The sovereignty of God is highlighted in the text (Ezra 1:1–5; 7:6, 9) as He is credited with moving the hearts of rulers. This sovereignty is also manifested in the fulfillment of prophecy, something that the gods of the surrounding nations clearly could not do.

3. *God's Remnant Will Prevail.* The concept of a remnant as God's instrument in the fulfillment of His saving purpose in a fallen world (Ezra 9:8) is explicitly stated in this book. Another topic is God's activity in filling the hearts of His worshiping remnant with joy (6:22) regardless of the hardships of life. This echoes Israel's wilderness experience following the

Exodus. The hope of salvation was embodied in the life of the remnant and in the promises God gave them.

4. *Holiness Is Intrinsic to the Covenant.* Ezra highlights the flawed perspectives of the remnant, who, even so, were courageous and faithful enough to make the journey back to the Holy Land to undertake the rebuilding of God's temple. When Ezra arrived, regardless of what they had accomplished with God's clear guidance, they still needed purification through changes in their lifestyle in accordance with God's law. The people already living in the land before the remnant arrived had a distorted concept of God (doubtless introduced by Assyrians brought in to repopulate the Northern Kingdom [2 Kin. 17:28], who came to be called Samaritans). The remnant needed to emphasize separation to maintain purity in those early, fragile years of resettlement. Ezra's description of these struggles echoes on a corporate level Jacob's personal struggle with God at Jabbok (Gen. 32:22–31). The reader is left with uncertainty as to whether God's people would hang on to God as Jacob did and be blessed and transformed nationally. This transformation needed to take place on an individual level so it could be reflected on a corporate scale. Eventually it resulted in factions (e.g., Pharisees, Sadducees, Essenes, Zealots, Yakhads) as groups (sects) responded to the change.

5. *Centrality of God's Word and Worship.* God's word moved the people to action (Ezra 9:4; 10:3). Particularly it was His law (9:6–15) that, when they heard it, brought about their desire to change their actions and repent of their errors. Ezra had studied God's law in earnest (7:6, 10) and was ideally suited to reveal it to the people. This again underscores the centrality of the revealed word of God.

Word and worship are two concepts that are inseparably connected in Ezra and Nehemiah. Worship is expressed in words and deeds. Worship had been the natural result after the successful laying of the foundation for the new temple (3:10–13). And worship remains the natural activity upon its completion (6:16–22). A saved and restored community acknowledged their God through worship. This reminds us that worship is intimately linked to our response to the experience of salvation, the recognition of who we really are, and the realization of how God has led us through trials and tribulations. Ezra keeps us looking at the bigger picture of salvation history and into a future where God's kingdom will finally break into human history with glory and power, leading to the eternal worship of the Lord.

COMMENTARY

1:1—6:22

FIRST RETURN FROM EXILE AND REBUILDING OF THE TEMPLE

Ezra 1:1—6:22 describes the first return from exile under Sheshbazzar (1:1–11), a list of the returnees (2:1–70), the initiation of temple worship (3:1–13), the opposition to Jerusalem (4:1–24), and the completion of the temple (5:1—6:22). It provides the template for the later returns led by Ezra and Nehemiah and introduces the struggles of the returnees.

1:1–11

Edict and Return

The introductory chapter establishes the historical and narrative framework of the entire book. The exiles, God's remnant, lived in a world where kings and princes determined the destinies of peoples, families, and individuals. Yet, as becomes evident, in spite of kingly powers and imperial grandeur, it was really God stirring and moving hearts and minds.

1:1–4. The Edict of Cyrus. The author locates this chapter in the first year of the Medo-Persian king Cyrus, circa 538/537 B.C. Several key themes are introduced in the first four verses of the book. The word of the Lord (v. 1) emphasizes the continued presence of divine revelation or the prophetic gift. The reference to Jeremiah underlines Ezra's rootedness in Scripture (Jer. 25:11–12; 29:1–23) and refers to the prophecy of the seventy years in Jeremiah 29:10. The seventy-year countdown started in 605 B.C. when Nebuchadnezzar conquered Jerusalem for the first time and took hostages to Babylon (including also Daniel, cf. Dan. 1:1–4). The exiles returned to Jerusalem in 537 B.C. The reference to God influencing Cyrus directly (lit. "raised or stirred his spirit") to issue his decree reveals an important philosophy of history also reflected in other biblical books (Dan. 1:2; cf. Is. 44:28; 45:1). Earlier, Isaiah had prophesied this divine stirring of Cyrus, eventual founder of the Achaemenid Dynasty, in his bid to conquer Babylon (Is. 44:28—45:25). Ultimately, God moved hearts and governed the great affairs of history regarding His people (Ezra 1:5) and their relationship with foreign leaders (1:1). The first part of the edict itself (vv. 2–4) contains near-identical wording as the last verse of 2 Chronicles. This represents a conscious link to a volume providing an overview of Israel's earlier history. However, there are significant additions in the second part which detail the order to rebuild God's temple in Jerusalem (Ezra 1:3b) as well as the call to financially support those staying behind (v. 4). The edict contains typical Achaemenid phrasing that locates the city and its temple in space, such as Jerusalem in Judah (v. 2) or the temple of God in Jerusalem (v. 4). Similarly, Cyrus's reference to the God of heaven (v. 2) is typical Persian parlance, appearing only three times outside postexilic books (Gen. 24:3, 7; Jon. 1:9).

1:5–11. Preparation for the Return to Jerusalem. Following the reproduction of the royal edict, the text includes the description of Jewish compliance. Verse 5 in the Hebrew refers to the "heads of the fathers/ancestors," which is a short version of a well-known phrase describing an important subunit of Israelite society (cf. Ex. 6:14; Num. 7:2; 1 Chr. 7:40). The phrase describes generally the extended family (or clan), yet the unit is smaller than a tribe. Both religious and civil leadership of Judah and Benjamin (Ezra 1:5) responded to the royal decree. The main purpose of the return was to rebuild the temple of the Lord in order to offer sacrifices (both individually and communally) for atonement. The

Ezra and the Cyrus Cylinder

The purpose of Cyrus's edict allowing Jews living in exile in Babylon to return to Jerusalem and rebuild Yahweh's temple is in line with other historical documents. The well-known Cyrus Cylinder, discovered in Babylon in 1879, provides a helpful window into Persian imperial policy toward people groups who had been exiled during the Neo-Babylonian Empire. In it, Cyrus issued a decree calling for the restoration of temples in and around Babylon and is portrayed as a gracious and considerate master. While the document was undoubtedly intended to communicate royal propaganda and ideology, the similar edict in Scripture suggests its historicity. Other examples of Persian sponsorship of temple constructions in occupied territories are known from the ANE (e.g., the Syrian city of Neirab) and were part of a larger political strategy. Prayer for the royal family was part of why the Persian ruler did this (6:10) as well as generating goodwill for the new empire.

goodwill provision to the Jews of gold, silver, and other goods strongly echoes the Exodus experience (Ex. 12:35–36). In the mind of the author of the book, this is Israel's second exodus.

The reference to the articles of the temple (Ezra 1:7) links Ezra to Daniel. Following the final fall of Jerusalem, Nebuchadnezzar, a pagan king, had carried off the temple vessels (2 Kin. 24:12–13; 2 Chr. 36:18; Jer. 52:17–19; Dan. 1:2); yet another pagan king, Cyrus, returned them to their rightful location. The Hebrew term usually translated as "treasurer" (Ezra 1:8) is a word borrowed from Old Persian and is also used in the Aramaic section in 7:21. Sheshbazzar, the prince of Judah (v. 8), was most likely the Babylonian name for "Zerubbabel" (see 1:8; 2:1, 2; 3:2–8; 5:16; Hag. 1:14–15). Sheshbazzar's designation as *nashi'* (usually translated as "prince") does not necessarily suggest royalty (cf. Ex. 16:22; Num. 1:16, 44), but may only point to leadership.

2:1–70
List of Those Going Home

For a modern reader this chapter represents tedious repetition and dozens of difficult-to-pronounce names of people and places. However, the list plays an important role in the overall structure of the book. Similar to the census list of Numbers, it gives names, places, and, ultimately, faces to those who were willing to take the risk to return home. In a sense, beyond its administrative function, it represents a veritable list of faith, comparable to Hebrews 11 in the NT.

2:1–35. The Lay Members That Returned Home. This list also appears in Nehemiah 7:2–72. The variations between the lists could have been the result of copying mistakes that confused some of the numbers and names. Verses 1 and 2 represent the heading of the section. Ezra has only eleven names here, while Nehemiah 7:7 includes twelve. It is possible that the missing name in Ezra was dropped due to a scribal error. The number twelve is significant in Israelite history and represents the totality of Israel and thus represents another link to Israel's past. The list of returnees places particular emphasis on the priests and Levites to assure that those serving at the temple were properly qualified.

The section opens with a reference to the people of the province (lit. "the sons of the province"). The plural Hebrew form *bene*—lit. "sons," which is sometimes translated as "children" or "people"—often takes on a collective meaning in the OT referring to descendants (2 Chr. 13:10). This is the usage found throughout the entire section. The "province" most likely refers to the Persian province of Yehud, the administrative Persian unit surrounding Jerusalem. The first mention of Israel in Ezra 2:2 is important. Israel appears numerous times in Ezra and Nehemiah. While most returnees were apparently descendants of Judah and Benjamin (1:5), they understood themselves as God's Israel and were thus linked to the glorious past of the divine promises involving Israel.

It is possible that this first section refers to families who had been exiled from Jerusalem, while the second section, which focuses upon locations (2:21–35), involves lay members who had come from cities in Judah. Both groups were lay members of the community and represent approximately 80 percent of the total returnees listed, while the temple personnel represent the remaining 20 percent. People were at the heart of Israel's return. Their struggles, falls, and victories are highlighted in Ezra and Nehemiah against the backdrop of the reconstruction of the temple and city.

2:36–63. The Religious Leadership That Returned Home. Priests, Levites, temple servants, and servants of Solomon, as well as those families who could not prove their priestly descent, are included in this section. The order of the list represents the Torah order of proximity to the holy of holies (or Most Holy Place) and underlines different grades of holiness. Priests (v. 36) generally served at the altar and could enter the temple proper in order to accomplish the blood manipulations needed in the Israelite sacrificial system. Once a year, the high priest entered the holy of holies during Yom Kippur (Lev. 16:32–34; cf. Heb. 9:7). The role of Levites (Ezra 2:40) involved supportive activities (including the transport of the ark prior to the construction of the temple, gatekeeping, choir work, and instruction), and they usually did not participate in the priestly duties associated with the altar and offerings. However, under specific circumstances, namely, when an insufficient number of priests were available, they could help with the sacrifices, as happened during Hezekiah's reform (2 Chr. 29:34; 30:3, 15).

Temple servants (Ezra 2:43–54) represent a lesser-known group of religious personnel. The term *natin* ("servants") appears only once outside Ezra and Nehemiah (1 Chr. 9:2) and is based on the common verb *natan*, "to give," highlighting David's appointment (and dedication) of this order of temple personnel (Ezra 8:20). Nehemiah 3:26, 31 suggest that they received special quarters in Jerusalem's Ophel. They were distinguished from the descendants of Solomon's servants (Ezra 2:55–58; Neh. 10:28). The exact nature of their service in the temple is unclear, but considering the clear hierarchical structure of the current list, they may have taken care of the menial labor needed in the temple.

The descendants of Solomon's servants (Ezra 2:55–58) are considered part of the temple servants as suggested by v. 58, which lists the total for both groups. While the Levites were "given" to the priests (Num. 3:9; 8:19), the temple servants and Solomon's servants were given to the Levites (Ezra 8:20), underlining a clear tripartite hierarchical structure. Scholars have noted the surprising fact that many names in this group are foreign, suggesting that originally the temple servants may have come to Israel as prisoners of war or resident aliens who escaped natural disaster in their home region (cf. Ruth 1). Their separate listing here, however, underlines their significance for the temple and the worshiping community. They are also a good reminder of the fact that the portrayal of God in the OT is as inclusive and transcendent, crossing ethnic and national boundaries, as the portrayal of God in the NT (Gal. 3:26–29; Eph. 2:14–22).

The last group in this section involves those whose priestly origins could not be ascertained (Ezra 2:59–63). Purity was a major concern in the community of the returnees. Since both the destruction of Jerusalem and the Exile in Babylon had been connected to the lack of obedience to God's commandments (Jer. 6:6–15; 7:1–11; 10:1–16), special attention was paid to these issues by the political leadership of the Yehud community. The governor (Ezra 2:63; possibly Zerubbabel/Sheshbazzar), designated by an official Persian title (rendered as *tirshata'* in the Hebrew), issued a decree that the missing genealogical information required the use of Urim and Thummim, or sacred lots, that had been used to know God's will prior to the Exile (Num. 27:21; 1 Sam. 14:37–42). This decree highlights the importance of political leadership in questions of religious matters.

2:64–70. The Final Tally. The total given sum of 42,360 for the entire group (v. 64) is significantly higher than the mathematical total of the list (29,818 for Ezra 2; 31,089 for Neh. 7). It is highly unlikely that scribal errors are responsible for the different numbers. The number listed here in Ezra may have included other people that did not originally live in the former Southern Kingdom of Judah. The term *qahal*, "assembly" or "company," generally includes everyone, not just the male descendants (Ezra 10:1; Neh. 8:2). The listing of servants or slaves and animals underlines prosperity. Note particularly the relatively high number of mules (Ezra 2:66), animals that had been closely associated with royalty before the Exile (2 Sam. 13:29; 18:9; 1 Kin. 1:33). Due to their hybrid nature (i.e., crossbreeding of horses and donkeys), the breeding of mules was extremely difficult, and forbidden in Israel (Lev. 19:19). They thus represented a significant monetary value.

Another important echo of the Exodus experience of Israel in the return from Babylon is the list of the special freewill offerings for the temple by Israelite leadership (cf. Ex. 25:1–9; 35:4–9; Num. 7). The translation of the currency *darkemin* in Ezra 2:69 is tentative. Some versions translate here "darics," a Persian gold coin, weighing about 8.4 grams (0.3 oz.) and equaling a soldier's monthly pay. Other versions have "drachmas." Greek drachmas were generally made of silver and less valuable. The final verse of Ezra 2 represents a concluding summary that forms a frame with 2:1. The settling of the Israelites in their own towns and cities was a tacit reminder of the fulfillment of God's promises. Israel was home again, the faithful had been listed publicly, and the second exodus generation was in place to build the new temple.

3:1–13
Reestablishment of Temple Worship

Once the returnees had settled in their cities, the focus shifted to the reconstruction of the temple and the reestablishment of temple worship. Both required the right location, utensils, and personnel—elements all introduced in chapters 1 and 2. Nothing could stop this movement, it seems, and yet more conflict and struggles lay ahead.

3:1–7. Let's Worship. The movement to reestablish temple worship began in the seventh month (v. 1), corresponding to Tishri (September/October), the most sacred month of the Israelite cultic calendar (Lev. 23:23–43; Num. 29). Israel's festival calendar included the celebration of the Festival of Trumpets (Lev. 23:23–25), the Day of Atonement (Lev. 16), and the Festival of Tabernacles (Lev. 23:34–43; Num. 29:12–38) during the seventh month. The time reference signals the important themes of worship and cultic celebrations, even though it

is not entirely clear if it refers to the calendar month or to the time since the arrival of the exiles from Babylon. The gathering of the people "as one" (Ezra 3:1) highlights the unity of the people (see Judg. 20:1; 1 Sam. 11:7). Jerusalem's central role is further emphasized by the move from the cities to Jerusalem. Interestingly, Ezra does not include any information regarding the driving force of this movement. The work was done under the leadership of Jeshua (or Joshua) and Zerubbabel (Ezra 3:2), yet the people appear to have been self-motivated.

In the building of the altar of burnt offerings, the spiritual (Jeshua) and civil (Zerubbabel) leaders acted together following the instructions given by Moses (v. 2). If Sheshbazzar and Zerubbabel are the same person, the use of the Hebrew name underlines the rejection of Babylonian influence—the Exile had ended. The concept of building with focused activity occurs repeatedly in Ezra and Nehemiah with verbal pairs of *qum*—"rise," "stand," or (in some translations) "begin"—and *banah*, "to build" (Ezra 1:5; 3:2; Neh. 2:20; cf. 1 Chr. 22:19). The work was undertaken in accordance with the requirements of the law of Moses (Ezra 3:2; Ex. 20:24–26). The presence of fear (Ezra 3:3) in the hearts of the people anticipated conflicts between them and those residing on the land. Yet, in spite of their fear, the altar was set on its foundation. The definitive article reminds the readers that this is not any altar but *the* altar in the courtyard of the temple, the only authorized location for offering a sacrifice. The reason for the construction of the altar was simple: without the altar, no regular morning and evening offerings could be made on behalf of Israel.

The next verses (vv. 4–6) offer a glimpse into the reestablished life of worship of the returnees. The list includes the Festival of Tabernacles that reminded the Israelites of their wilderness wanderings (Lev. 23:43) en route to the promised land. Note the absence of a reference to the Day of Atonement, which required the presence of a temple. Compliance with the requirements of the law is noted at every turn by referencing the fact that they were following the written instructions in the law (Ezra 3:2, 4). The community of the returnees took great pains at avoiding discrepancies with the law, as this had been one of the reasons for the Exile. However, this attention to the law did not necessarily include personal commitment to the Lawgiver, as later episodes involving mixed marriages (chaps. 9–10; Neh. 13:23–28), misplaced personal priorities (cf. Hag. 1), and inappropriate Sabbath activities (Neh. 13:15–22) demonstrate. We cannot love and keep the law without knowing and loving the Lawgiver.

3:8–13. Restoration of the Temple. The description of the preparations made for building the temple are to some extent similar to those made by David and Solomon (Ezra 3:7; 1 Chr. 22:4, 15; 2 Chr. 2:10, 15–16). The reference to the cedars from Sidon and Tyre (including also the specific note that the wood had to be shipped along the coast via Joppa) links this temple to the first temple built when Israel was independent. The activities of David and Solomon associated with the construction of the first temple represent the backdrop of Ezra 3. The work on the foundation began seven months after the construction of the altar (3:8), which again mimicked Solomon who also began construction of the first temple in the second month (1 Kin. 6:1). Since this building had significant spiritual ramifications, the supervision of its construction was entrusted to the Levites. The Hebrew text does not include here a specific term for "foundation" but rather a verbal form meaning "to lay a foundation" (Ezra 3:6, 10). The emphasis is on the "founding" activity of the second temple community.

The unity of the community is highlighted in the list of participants of the founding activities (including Zerubbabel [the civic, political leader], Je[o]shua [the high priest], the priests, the Levites, and all those who had returned from captivity; v. 8). Levites age twenty years and older (v. 8) were to supervise the construction. The Mosaic regulations indicated that Levites would only serve between the ages of thirty and fifty (Num. 4:2–3; 1 Chr. 23:2–3). However, their scarcity and the literary and thematic link to David's and Solomon's activities related to the temple apparently required this adjustment. First Chronicles 23:24–28 credits David with having lowered the age of service for Levites.

The laying of the foundations was celebrated with singing and worship, as well as an acknowledgment that the Lord is good and that His *khesed*—a rich Hebrew word variously rendered as "love," "covenant faithfulness," "mercy," "loving-kindness"—rests upon Israel forever. This word appears also in Jeremiah 33:10–11 and thus creates a link between the beginning of temple worship and God's prophetic timetable referenced in Ezra 1:1 (cf. the same refrain in 2 Chr. 7:6 during the inauguration of the first temple). We are here because of God's stirring

and moving (cf. John 6:44). We can sing because of His promises and protection.

Yet, the chapter concludes on an ambiguous note. While all the people rejoiced with a great shout (Ezra 3:11), others wept loudly (v. 12). The mixture of joy and sorrow illustrates the increasingly difficult balance between the glories of the past and the possibilities of the future. This was not the glorious temple built by an Israelite king in a time of independence and freedom (cf. Hag. 2:3). At the same time, God opened new vistas for a future following the Exile. The ambiguity of the weeping is reflected in Ezra 3:13—the people could not tell the difference between the sound of the shouts of joy and that of the loud weeping. However, the loud noise was from far away. The next chapter will take the reader to those listening and watching from afar.

4:1–24
Opposition to Jerusalem

This chapter provides a nonchronological summary of the opposition the people faced under several Persian kings (Cyrus [559–530 B.C.], Darius I [522–486 B.C.], Xerxes I [486–465 B.C.], and Artaxerxes I [465–424 B.C.]).

4:1–5. Anatomy of Opposition. The transition from the celebration of the foundation-laying ceremony to the confrontation with Jerusalem's enemies (Ezra 4:1) is stark and shocking. These people were most likely identical to the people causing fear in 3:3. The issue of contention involves participation in the rebuilding of the temple.

The offer to help with building may have seemed generous at first (4:2). The additional information provided by the enemies, however, put this seemingly generous offer in a different light. Their declaration that they were seeking Judah's God and had sacrificed to Him (v. 2) provides a window into the possible identity of these people (v. 4). While seeking God could be done in any location, legitimate sacrifices could only happen on the altar of Jerusalem's temple. Thus, the sacrifices offered by the people of the land represented idolatrous offerings. The ancestry of these people went back to the time after the fall of Samaria when Esarhaddon brought them to live on the land (2 Kin. 17:24–41). The result was a faith that mixed their pagan religious ideas with some of the Israelite beliefs. The returnees rejected their help probably because they were not sure of the intentions of these people but more likely because this was the work that God had entrusted into the hands of the returnees (Ezra 4:3).

The reaction of the surrounding people seems to confirm the strong reaction of the returnees. The intent to discourage and frighten (v. 4) suggests needle-like irritation and opposition. Literally, the Hebrew reads here "the people of the land kept making the hands of the people of Judah hang limp" (v. 4). Constant low-level opposition can often be more disheartening than major roadblocks. Jerusalem's opposition hired counselors or officials to work against them (v. 5). This suggests an organized, coordinated commitment against the city, similar to the modern practice of hiring consultants or lobbyists to achieve a desired political end. The Aramaic form of the term appears in 7:14–15, 28 and again in Hebrew in 8:25.

4:6–24. Opposition under Xerxes I and Artaxerxes I. The nature of the accusation by the enemies is not clearly stated. The Hebrew term for "opposition" occurs only here and is related to *satan*, "accuser," "adversary," which is also at times used as a personal designation of Satan. During the time of Artaxerxes I (465–424 B.C.), Jerusalem's opposition was associated with the local leadership of the Persian administration in Samaria. Verse 7 functions as an introduction and historical anchoring of the following Aramaic letters crisscrossing the Persian Empire between the Holy Land and the Persian court. The text does not make it entirely clear whether the letter written by Bishlam and his companions (v. 7) was the same as the one introduced in v. 8 and written by Rehum and Shimshai. If it was the same letter, v. 7 functions as a heading, perhaps suggesting that Bishlam and his companions were the superiors of Rehum, the commanding official, and Shimshai, the scribe or secretary (v. 8). Persian governors of the satrap beyond the River Euphrates (v. 10) by the name *bēlšunu* (a similar name to Bishlam) are known from other fifth century B.C. documents. The Aramaic term *te'em* (v. 9) used in regard to Rehum does not necessarily indicate a military office as some translations suggest, but it can refer also to a high civilian official.

Beginning in v. 8, the language of Ezra changes to Aramaic. The letter follows the general format of an ancient letter, including the names of the senders, a formal greeting, and the content, but lacks a final greeting, which suggests that the biblical author only included the relevant sections of the original document. The list of the people in v. 9 refers to groups that were resettled

in the province of Samaria by the Neo-Assyrian king Ashurbanipal (Heb. *'osnappar*; 669–631 B.C.). While there are no biblical references for these relocations during Ashurbanipal's reign, other Assyrian kings followed this practice (2 Kin. 17:24–41). The description of this king as great and honorable is a rhetorical device set in contrast with the supposed rebellious and evil city of Jerusalem (Ezra 4:12). The heading in v. 11, referring to a copy (also 4:23; 5:6; 7:11), may just indicate the content of the letter.

The essence of the accusations in Ezra 4:12–16 is this: if Jerusalem were allowed to rebuild its walls, it would again rebel against the great king and refuse to pay taxes to the Persian treasury. This carefully crafted message insinuated rebellion without providing direct evidence, and it had the desired effect. During the first years of the reign of Artaxerxes I (465–464 B.C.), the new king had to deal with an Egyptian rebellion, and he was not willing to face even a potential one. The king's answer was not only based on the information provided by Rehum and Shimshai but also included a search of the royal archives about the history of Jerusalem (vv. 19–20). This letter is important because it makes clear that Artaxerxes originally authorized Ezra to rebuild the city (see "The Decree of Artaxerxes I as Fulfillment of Daniel 9:25," p. 584). However, in spite of the unequivocal order to cease work, the king indicated that a further decree could allow for the rebuilding to resume (v. 21). This anticipates the narrative of Nehemiah 2:4–8.

The building stop was immediately implemented by the Samarian provincial government, using military force (Ezra 4:23). Rehum, Shimshai, and their cohorts went immediately to Jerusalem to carry out the king's order. The military force may have involved actual destruction (cf. Neh. 1:3–4). Verse 24 serves to introduce the conflict during the time of Darius (which is developed in chapter 5), but at the same time it returns to the concern for the temple mentioned in 4:1–5.

5:1–6:22
Prophecy Fulfilled: The Temple Completed

Following the topical list of opposition to Jerusalem in Ezra 4, covering a period of about one hundred years, the author returns to his main concern: the rebuilding of the temple, which had not been completed by the second year of Darius I (520 B.C.; cf. 4:24). The section focuses on this crucial topic and concludes with the completion of the Lord's temple.

5:1-2. God Is on the Move Again. Prophecy was not dead after the Exile. God was still speaking to His people. Haggai and Zechariah (v. 1) had been divinely called. The fact that they "prophesied to the Jews" underlines an important function of biblical prophets. While they communicated God's perspective on the future, more often than not they spoke to a particular situation currently affecting God's people. Haggai's ministry was focused on moving God's people to complete the construction of the second temple and lasted less than four months in 520 B.C. (Hag. 1:1 [Aug. 29, 520 B.C.] and Hag. 2:1, 10, 20 [Dec. 18, 520 B.C.]). Haggai's critique of the Yehud community reveals that the construction stop was not only due to external pressures but also the result of selfish priorities (Hag. 1:4). Selfishness made it impossible to receive God's blessings (Hag. 1:6, 9). Both prophets remind their audience that God was still watching "over them" (Ezra 5:1). The recognition of divine presence in the midst of severe struggles has been known to ignite hope. Again, the sequence of names, that is, Zerubbabel and Je[o]shua (v. 2), combines civil and religious leadership (see 2:2; 3:8; 4:3) working together. The biblical text explicitly states that God's prophets were supporting the temple construction work (5:2).

5:3-5. Another Challenge. Tattenai, the Persian governor of Trans-Euphrates, challenged the authorization for the reconstruction of the temple when he visited Jerusalem (v. 3). The report to the Persian king listed the names of those responsible for the reconstruction. The concern involved the rebuilding of the temple and the *'ushsharna'* (vv. 3, 9). This rare Aramaic term has been translated as "wall," but its exact meaning is uncertain, and some translators suggest that it refers to "material," "wooden structure," "paneling," or "roof scaffolding." Note that Tattenai's visit happened during the early reign of King Darius I, who had only recently overcome a rebellion led by Gaumata and was not of the royal line of Cyrus. Officials tended to be very cautious when a new king was on the throne. However, as the text indicates, God was watching over the Jewish elders. This reality underlines an important biblical motif. God is looking out for the interests of His people (see Deut. 11:12; Job 36:7; Pss. 32:8; 33:18; 34:15). One can note a curious contrast: while Tattenai and his associates functioned as the "eye" of the Persian king, God's watching "eye" (and providence) was upon His people.

5:6-17. Tattenai's Letter to Darius I. Tattenai's credentials as Persian governor are corroborated by a Babylonian document naming a certain *Tattannu* as governor of the Trans-Euphrates province during the reign of Darius I. The letter describes the visit to Jerusalem and the temple building activities of the Jews (vv. 7-10). It then quotes the justification of the Jewish leadership verbatim (vv. 11-16). The anonymous builders described themselves as "servants of the God of heaven and earth" (v. 11). This seems to contrast with the legitimate title of the "great God," which in the mouth of a Persian administrator could have implied that this God was one among others (5:8; cf. Neh. 8:6; Ps. 95:3; Titus 2:13). However, in Daniel 2:45 the phrase "great God" is used to describe God's foreknowledge of the future. It also is linked to God's creative acts (Ps. 95:3-6). The phrase appears in the Persepolis fortification tablets as well.

The reference to "a great king of Israel" (Ezra 5:11) implies Solomon. The response of the builders appealed to the ANE custom of respecting traditions and established sacred spaces. The reference to God having given His people into Nebuchadnezzar's hands in v. 12 is a good reminder of Scripture's philosophy of history: God moves people (1:1, 5), God gives His people into the hand of their enemies (Dan. 1:2), and God appoints and demotes kings and empires (Dan. 2). Following this confession, reference is made to the decree of Cyrus (Ezra 5:13; cf. 1:2-4), as well as to the return of the cultic vessels of the Jerusalem temple (v. 14; cf. 1:7-11). The order to rebuild the temple and to return the vessels is couched in a verbatim quote of the Persian king (5:15). This links the current building activity to the storied founder of the Medo-Persian Empire. Verse 16 suggests continued construction has followed the laying of the temple's foundation.

The final verse of chapter 5 includes the phrase "if it seems good to [or "if it pleases"] the king." This represents a conventional feature of official Aramaic letter writing also known from the papyri found at Elephantine in Egypt. The search of the king's *bayit nenzaya'*—Aramaic for "house of treasure"—reflects already known Persian administrative procedure (4:15, 19; 6:1). The reference to the archives (lit. "scrolls") in 6:1 clarifies the fact that there were also scrolls (Aram. *sipherayya'*) in the same place where the treasures of Babylon were stored. Accordingly, some translations render "treasure house" as "royal archives" in 5:17.

6:1–12. Decree of Darius I. Following the record of the search, the important decree of Darius is reported at length (albeit missing typical letter elements such as superscription, sender, recipient, and greeting). This vindicated the loyalty, faith, and commitment of the builders. Even a powerful Medo-Persian king was ultimately moved and used by the unseen God who is heavily invested in this world. Following an extensive search, the original decree of Cyrus was located in Achmeta (or Ectabana), one of the four capitals of the Persian Empire (together with Babylon, Persepolis, and Susa). Achmeta corresponds to the modern-day Iranian city of Hamadan. Archaeological research in the city of Persepolis has verified the close physical link between the treasury and the archives, as the previous discussion of 5:17 and 6:1 also suggests. The Aramaic *dikhron* (v. 2) is a technical term denoting an official document. Verses 3 to 5 quote Cyrus's decree in a condensed form with a few added details. It is difficult to establish the specific dimensions of the temple because the length is not provided. This temple was smaller and inferior with respect to quality, and this suggests that the reference to sixty cubits (cf. 1 Kin. 6:2) may have been a scribal mistake.

Note the important additional information involving the costs of the temple construction (Ezra 6:4), payment of which was to come from the king's treasury. This is clarified in 6:8, which indicates that the payment was to come from the taxes of the province. The decree may be emphasizing the importance of the traditional location of the temple reconstruction, the place where they offered sacrifices (v. 3), though some translations render the Aramaic in such a way as to emphasize that the sacrifices were an essential part of the function of the temple ("a place to present sacrifices" or "the place where sacrifices are offered"), rather than its location.

The royal instructions (vv. 6–12) were addressed directly to Tattenai and his colleagues, introduced by a typical "now therefore" or "now then," which marks a new section. King Darius I ratified the previous royal decree and thus suggested a political continuity (which in reality was absent since he was not a descendent of Cyrus). Furthermore, the financial arrangements of the construction as well as the costs of the daily sacrifices were clarified (vv. 8–10). Royal sponsorship of local cults is well established as having occurred during the Medo-Persian Empire and can be found in many texts of that period. The reference in Jeremiah 29:7 to pray for political leadership of a city (or a country) could be understood in this way (Ezra 6:10). The final verses of this section (vv. 11–12) describe vividly the dire consequences that would befall anyone opposing this decree (cf. Dan. 2:5; 3:29). The command to Tattenai and his associates to stay away from the temple (Ezra 6:6) clearly set the tone and transferred the responsibility of this project to the governor of the Jews and the elders (v. 7).

6:13–22. Temple Finished. The governor's response was immediate. A theme of acting diligently (v. 13) and following orders is repeatedly apparent in the Aramaic section of Ezra, often in official communication (5:8; 6:8, 12; 7:17, 21, 26)—and they denote an obedient and timely response. The description of the progress is headed by reference to the elders of the Jews (6:14). This reference would remind readers of the importance of that leadership group, which worked together with the prophets Haggai and Zechariah. In their work they honored God above the kings of Persia, as the sequence of the commands in v. 14 suggests. The construction of the temple was finished in the sixth year of the reign of King Darius (around March of 515 B.C.).

The completion of the temple was celebrated joyously by the people of Israel (6:16–18) with celebratory sacrifices. The emphasis on twelve male goats for the twelve tribes of Israel in the sin offering (v. 17) underlines the fact that this was God's Israel—even though most of the returnees belonged to the tribes of Judah and Benjamin. The temple was the residence of the Lord and the center of holiness and life for Israel. The work performed there foreshadowed the high priestly ministry of the Messiah, and as such the temple was a center of hope. The mention of the celebration of the Passover reminds us of the first Passover of the Israelites after they were liberated from Egypt. Then later, after their liberation from Babylon and the completion of the rebuilding of the temple, the people celebrated the Passover.

The biblical text highlights the fact that the Levites purified themselves and were thus ritually clean (Ezra 6:20). Ritual purity is set in opposition to the *tum'ah*—"uncleanness" or "impurity" of the nations—the practices of their Gentile neighbors (v. 21). The term is repeatedly used in cultic contexts and denotes animals or people who could not be presented to a Holy God (e.g., Lev. 5:3; 7:20; 14:19). Ritual purification was often connected to major religious celebrations (cf. Neh. 12:30), involving washing rites (of clothing and people), ritual sprinkling of water, special offerings, and possibly also sexual abstinence (Ex. 19:10, 14–15; Lev. 16:28; 22:4–7; Num. 8:5–8). The celebration of the Passover happened on the fourteenth day of the first month (Ezra 6:19), in harmony with established pentateuchal laws (Ex. 12:1–6).

Ezra 6:21 emphasizes fellowship between those who had returned from exile and those who had separated themselves from the impurity of the nations around them. Those who truly sought the Lord God of Israel were welcome in the new Israel. This represented another echo of the original Passover celebration (cf. Ex. 12:44, 48). Earnest heart searching and commitment transcend ethnic boundaries. The celebration of the Festival of Unleavened Bread is characterized by joyfulness, a topic common in Ezra and Nehemiah (e.g., Ezra 3:12–13; Neh. 8:12; 12:43).

The surprising reference to "the king of Assyria" rather than the king of Persia (Ezra 6:22) has a deliberate literary purpose. It points to the quintessential enemy of God's people (cf. Ezra 4:2; Neh. 9:32). The Assyrians first exiled Israel and Judah, followed by the Babylonians and Medo-Persians who "inherited" and often increased the empire. Then God changed the thinking (lit. "turned the heart") of the prototype of Israel's enemy. Thus, this reference to Assyria is not a scribal error or a mistaken historical reference. Rather, it is a metaphorical device underlining the fact that what had been the beginning of Israel's end God wondrously transformed into a new beginning.

7:1–10:44
SECOND RETURN UNDER EZRA AND EZRA'S REFORMS

Ezra 7:1—10:44 finally introduces the protagonist whose name functions as the title of the biblical book. Following the description of the historical backstory involving the first return under Sheshbazzar and the rebuilding of the temple, the text then moves on to discuss the rebuilding, as it were, of the people. The second return under Ezra was not so much characterized by mortar, stones, and buildings (even though they do appear!), but by a focus upon the quality of the remnant living in Jerusalem and Yehud.

7:1–8:36
Going Home—Again

This section introduces to us Ezra and his mission (7:1—8:36), but the emphasis is on God's power that brought the people back to the promised land and made them prosperous. This is followed by the consecration and purification of the people (9:1—10:44).

7:1–10. Ezra's Arrival in Jerusalem. Nearly sixty years lie between 6:22 and 7:1. The fifth month of the seventh year of Artaxerxes I (v. 8) corresponds to 457 B.C. (7:8). However, the section does not begin with time but with a person. Ezra's genealogy is detailed and includes sixteen generations, finally concluding with Aaron, the chief priest (v. 5). The Aaronic genealogy in 1 Chronicles 6:3–15 includes six more names, which suggests that Ezra used an abbreviated version of the list. The list sought to establish, beyond any doubt, Ezra's priestly credentials. Priestly leadership in the second return illustrates the increasingly important role of religious leadership in the postexilic period, as the whole book demonstrates.

Ezra is described as a *soper mahir betorat moshe*—an expert teacher or scribe of the law of Moses (Ezra 7:6). The Hebrew phrase referring to an expert teacher or scribe (*soper mahir*) is also found in Psalm 45:1. The reference to the king's granting of Ezra's request suggests that it is probable that Ezra had some influence in the Persian court. What was most important, however, was that the hand of the Lord his God was upon him (Ezra 7:6). The reference to the law of Moses emphasizes Ezra's role in establishing a special people. This reference to God's "hand" (cf. v. 9) highlights God's protection over His people.

The journey of four months was taken during the seventh year of Artaxerxes I (457 B.C.). Ezra did not travel alone, even though no specific numbers are supplied. However, the biblical text mentions predominantly religious personnel that accompany Ezra (v. 7). The explanatory note introducing v. 10 links God's blessings to Ezra's desire to study (lit. "seek") "the Law of the LORD" and to observe and teach God's rules and principles. This is the only place in the OT that links the verb *darash* ("to seek") to the *torah*—the law. There are, however, many references to seeking God (e.g., Ezra 4:2; 6:21; Deut. 4:29; Is. 55:6; Hos. 10:12). Isaiah 34:16 invites readers to search (Heb. *darash*) from the book (lit. "scroll") of the Lord (cf. Acts 17:11). The importance of Scripture as the revealed will of God was increasing in times of change and transition. If we want to meet the God of Scripture, we need to spend time with His revealed word.

7:11–28. Artaxerxes I's Decree Authorizing Ezra's Return and Mission. Ezra includes a copy of the royal decree containing two main elements. First, it authorizes Ezra's return (7:12–16); second, it confirms Ezra's supervisory role in Jerusalem and the Persian province of Yehud (7:17–26). The copy of the letter was given by the king to the emissary (7:11). In line with Ezra's reform efforts, his expertise in God's commands and statutes or decrees (shorthand for Scripture) are emphasized. The letter, in Aramaic, includes the name of the sender, position, and the customary greeting. The final exhortation to disseminate the royal order and comply with it includes also the customary penalty clause (7:25–26; cf. 6:12).

The opening lines of Artaxerxes's I decree are similar to Cyrus's first decree and provide an important historical anchor. Among those willing to return, priests and Levites in particular are named (7:13). Historical evidence suggests that a majority of Jews remained in the region around Babylon even after the first and second return. The seven counselors or advisors (7:14) are mentioned in Esther 1:14 and in extrabiblical literature as well and seem to have reflected fifth century B.C. realities at the Persian court. Ezra was being sent to *beqar* ("seek" or "inquire") concerning Judah and Jerusalem (Ezra 7:14). It is possible, as some translators have recognized, to render *beqar* as referring to evaluation or oversight. This is not only possible linguistically but also seems to fit better in the overall context. Ezra's supervisory function was based on the law of his God in his hand. Both contextual translations make better sense and are solidly based on appropriate translations of the two prepositional phrases. An important part of Ezra's mission was to establish that the Jews in Jerusalem were living in accordance with the law of Moses. Furthermore, he had to convey the financial gift of the Persian court to the temple of the Lord (vv. 15–16).

Artaxerxes I considered Ezra's God another local deity, as suggested by the phrase "whose dwelling is in Jerusalem" (v. 15). The reference to the "God of heaven and earth" (5:11) reflects the Jewish understanding of a universal God by highlighting the sovereignty of the Lord who transcends all local deities, but it probably does not reflect the king's personal belief. Ezra 7:17 allows for the use of royal funds to purchase sacrificial animals for the temple. However, v. 18 indicates that there was significant financial freedom for Ezra and opens the possibility that some of the resources were later used to rebuild the city wall.

The Decree of Artaxerxes I as Fulfillment of Daniel 9:25

The fulfillment of the prophecy of the seventy weeks, registered in Daniel 9:25, was to start during the Medo-Persian Empire and would be initiated by a decree to restore and rebuild Jerusalem (see Dan. 9). This prophecy was fulfilled through the decree of Artaxerxes I recorded in Ezra 7.

1. Restoration of the City. The decree included several important elements: (1) it granted permission to the exiles to return to Jerusalem; (2) funds were assigned for the support of the temple; (3) the temple and temple personnel were tax exempted; (4) and it established a Jewish legal system based on the Torah, which included magistrates and judges to enforce the law (Ezra 7:25–26). The Persian king made the Mosaic law part of the imperial law. The Jews could now use it freely to regulate their lives and to administrate justice in Jerusalem. The Jews were to govern themselves on the basis of the law of God. Daniel 9:25 was referring to this type of restoration. The authorization to rebuild the city was implicit in the authorization to set up a judicial system, based on the law of God, at a central place. Besides, we find clear evidence in Ezra and Nehemiah to the effect that the Jews were authorized to rebuild the city.

2. Nehemiah and the Wall. The first line of evidence is found in Nehemiah 1. About thirteen years after Ezra arrived at Jerusalem, Nehemiah was informed that those who returned had great misery and shame and that the wall of Jerusalem was broken down and the gates destroyed by fire (1:3). Nehemiah was obviously referring to a recent event and indicates that the rebuilding of the city had been in progress until it was stopped and much of the work done had been damaged and/or destroyed. This rebuilding project took place before 444 B.C.

but was unfinished. The question is, when did the rebuilding of the wall begin? The biblical text provides a clear answer. According to Ezra 4:7–23, it took place during the reign of Artaxerxes.

3. The Building of the Wall Stopped. Ezra 4:7–23 states that a group of Persian officers wrote a letter to Artaxerxes recording their opposition to the rebuilding of Jerusalem by the Jews. In the letter they mentioned, first, that the city was being rebuilt, the walls were being finished, and the foundations were being repaired. Second, this rebuilding was being done by the Jews who had returned to Jerusalem (4:12). The reference to the people coming from Artaxerxes indicates that the rebuilding was being done by a group of exiles who had been recently authorized by Artaxerxes to return to Jerusalem. According to Ezra 7, the king authorized Ezra and the exiles in 457 B.C. to return to Jerusalem.

The Persian officers were trying to persuade the king to stop the project by arguing that Jerusalem had consistently been a rebellious city (Ezra 4:13, 15), that if the Jews were permitted to finish their project they would take control of the Trans-Euphrates province, and that consequently they would stop paying taxes and tribute to the king (vv. 13, 16). This may have been based on the fact that Artaxerxes authorized Ezra to teach and to enforce the law of God throughout the province and not just in Jerusalem (7:25–26). Notice that the letter does not suggest in any way that the rebuilding of the city and its walls was being done without royal consent. Had the Jews begun to rebuild the city illegally their enemies would have charged them with rebellion against the king. The arguments they used presupposed that the rebuilding was authorized by the king. They wanted the project stopped, not because it was not supported by Artaxerxes but because of the potential danger of insurrection.

A careful reading of the answer of the king suggests that the Jews had, indeed, been authorized by Artaxerxes to rebuild the city. Once the complaint was received, the king ordered an investigation and found that the only reason he had to stop the rebuilding project was that the possibility of a rebellion appeared to him to be real. Otherwise the

charges against the Jews would have been much more serious. In other words, he could only stop the project on the basis of a potential insurrection—a suspicion supported by the fact that Jerusalem had been a rebellious city (4:19). The decree allowing for the rebuilding of the city was not canceled, but its execution was postponed by the king to a future time determined by him (and which in fact occurred during the time of Nehemiah, as indicated in Neh. 2).

The Persian officers took the letter of the king and went back to Jerusalem to forcibly stop the project (Ezra 4:23). This phrase certainly indicates that the officers employed military force to stop the project and that at least some sections of the wall were destroyed. This explains why it took Nehemiah only fifty-two days to rebuild the wall of the city (Neh. 6:15). It is to this attack on the Jews and the city that Nehemiah 1 refers.

4. A Wall in Jerusalem. The next line of evidence is found in Ezra 9:9. In one of his prayers, Ezra states that God authorized the people through the Persian kings to repair God's house, restore its ruins, and give them a wall in Judah and Jerusalem. Some scholars interpret the reference to the wall in Judah and Jerusalem to be metaphorical. They argue that there was never a literal wall around Judea and consequently the wall is to be interpreted as a symbol of divine protection. But this is not a persuasive argument. First, the phrase could simply mean that a wall in Jerusalem (cf. Ezra 4:12) was a wall in Judah because Jerusalem was located there. Second, since the same verse mentions the literal house of God, the temple, it follows that the wall is also literal. Third, although the word *gader* is not the common word used to designate a city wall, it is also used in the OT to designate such a wall (Mic. 7:11). The metaphorical interpretation is difficult to support.

The beginning of the fulfillment of the prophecy of the seventy weeks (Dan. 9:25) was initiated in 457 B.C. when Artaxerxes authorized Ezra through a royal decree to go to Jerusalem accompanied by a group of exiles to restore and rebuild the city. The books of Ezra and Nehemiah show clearly that this was exactly what took place and that the rebuilding of the city was finished under the leadership of Ezra and Nehemiah.

The king's promise of up to one hundred talents of silver (Ezra 7:22), that is, nearly 7,500 pounds (approximately 3,400 kg), was referring to a huge number. The total amount of yearly tribute of the Trans-Euphrates satrapy was only 350 talents. Instead of arguing for a textual error, this should be understood in light of the wide freedoms (vv. 18, 25) that the royal order gave to Ezra. The quantities of wheat (about 650 bushels or 22,900 liters), wine (about 600 gallons or 2,300 liters), oil (about 600 gallons or 2,300 liters), and unlimited salt showcase Artaxerxes I's commitment to this project. The command to proceed diligently emphasizes the importance of the financial element of the decree and was set in the king's letter in direct relation to possible (divine) wrath against the royal house (v. 23).

The final three verses of the decree cover administrative issues. Tax exception for temple personnel is also known from other sources from the Medo-Persian Empire (v. 24). According to the Gadatas inscription of Darius I, the priests of Apollo were exempt from paying tax. The mention of tax, tribute, and custom/duty represent different types of officially levied payments. The reforms to be undertaken by Ezra were not only religious in nature but also involved political structures. The authority to appoint magistrates and judges (v. 25) fits the particular historical context. The appointment of judges links Ezra to Moses (Ex. 18). Both the law of God and the Persian law were to be fully enforced (Ezra 7:26).

Ezra's doxology (vv. 27–28), written in Hebrew, concludes this important chapter. Written in first-person singular, it reflects a very intimate and personal expression of praise for divine guidance and blessings. God's *khesed* ("mercy," "love," "covenant faithfulness") was extended before kings, counselors, and princes. In this sense it became a testimony of divine grace pointing to the King of kings and encouraging frail human beings. Only when we recognize God's amazing grace and mercy in our own lives can we become faithful leaders.

8:1–32. List of Returnees and the Journey.

The list of returnees traveling with Ezra from Babylon to Jerusalem includes priestly families (8:2a), the royal line (8:2b–3a; cf. 1 Chr. 3:22), and, finally, lay members (Ezra 8:3b–14). Beginning with the sons of Parosh, there are twelve families listed. The list of returnees indicated that 5,000 to 6,000 returned to the land. The prospective returnees were assembled by the river that flows to Ahava (v. 15). The exact location is unclear but presumably was close to Babylon (7:9). Scholars have suggested that the reference is to a canal, not a river, since the Mesopotamian heartland was full of irrigation canals (similarly referenced in Ezek. 1:3) and was large enough to provide space for such a large group of travelers. In reviewing the assembled group Ezra realized that no Levites and temple servants could be found in the group and sent an invitation to Iddo and his brethren in Casiphia (Ezra 8:16–17). God's good and gracious hand (see commentary on 6:1–12) finally led thirty-eight Levites to join the returnees, together with 220 temple servants (8:18–20). The fact that all of them were identified by name (v. 20) would mark the precise registration in bona fide priestly lists and assure future eligibility to serve in the temple. The full list is not included in the book of Ezra.

The returning group's fasting and prayer underlines the religious character of this journey (8:21–23). The reference to their humbling themselves before God was a more comprehensive way of referring to fasting (also in Lev. 16:29, 31; cf. Acts 27:9 where the Day of Atonement is called "the Fast"). Ezra's purpose was to seek a literal "straight way" from God, and, considering Ezra 8:22, refers most likely to a safe journey (cf. Is. 40:3; 52:12). Ezra's decision not to ask for an escort of soldiers and horsemen to protect them may be explained by the important cultural value of shame: Ezra had testified before the king about the Lord's protection of His people, and so armed guards would have suggested a lack of faith.

Ezra needed the priests and Levites in order to carry the offering and donated articles for the temple (Ezra 8:24–27, 30). Pentateuchal legislation divided the work of carrying different parts of the sanctuary between priests and Levites (Num. 3–4). While Ezra's group did not return temple vessels, the successful collaboration between priests and Levites provided the matrix for another exodus. Furthermore, the link to the temple made the offerings as well as the priests and Levites holy (Ezra 8:28). Holiness and purity are important concerns in the rest of the book, and they emphasize the religious nature of Ezra's mission. Another reference to God's hand (v. 31) reminds the reader of previous references to this motif (vv. 18, 22; see 7:6). It was because of His presence with them, as in the original Exodus from Egypt, that no military escort was needed.

The safe arrival notice contains references to deliverance and ambushes (8:31). The journey took about four months (7:8–9) and covered the roughly 900 miles (1,450 km) between Babylon and Jerusalem. They used the major road system that connected Mesopotamia and the Holy Land. The three-day rest following their arrival (8:32) may suggest that they arrived on Friday and then delivered the precious articles on Monday. Another list documents the delivered articles and offerings. Twelve bulls were offered for all Israel (v. 35) as a burnt offering, another reminder of the self-perception of the returnees as being Israel. The sacrificial list abounds with multiples of twelve. We need to remember the emotions involved in offering a sacrifice in the temple, considering the fact that the Jews in Babylon were unable to offer sacrifices. The religious celebrations were similar to the two festivals recorded in chapters 3 and 6. The concluding verse indicates that the king's orders had been delivered to the king's satraps and the governors of Trans-Euphrates. This probably occurred late in the summer or early in the fall of 457 B.C. (see 9:1-5). In turn these leaders gave support to the people and the temple. Ezra's meticulous planning and his complete reliance on God showcase the delicate balance of God's children living in a world that often challenges faith. While we rely absolutely and completely on God's good hand, at the same time we are called to give our best for the glory of God.

9:1–10:44
Consecration and Purification

Prayers are important in Ezra and Nehemiah (e.g., Ezra 8:21-23; 9; Neh. 1:5-11; 2:4; 9:5-37), and in chapter 9 Ezra prays with respect to his role as teacher of the law. Following the prayer, we are informed about the people's resolution and commitment to make things right (chap. 10). Prayer without consequences is cheap talk.

9:1–5. Diagnosis: No Difference. Once Ezra had turned over the silver and gold that had been donated by the royal court and the remaining Jewish community in Babylon (7:15-16), he was ready to confront Jerusalem's real problems. Ezra 7:9 (first day of fifth month) suggests that Ezra's group arrived in Jerusalem late in July of 457 B.C., after they had begun the journey in the spring. The fact that long journeys were usually initiated in spring further supports this chronology. The events narrated in Ezra chapters 9 and 10 seem to have occurred about four months later (cf. 10:6-9), in November/December of the same year, soon after the events mentioned in 8:36 (see 9:1). In

line with Ezra's characterization in 7:10 as one who was dedicated to studying, observing, and teaching God's law, it was now time for a diagnosis. Local leadership informed Ezra that the Jews (including also priests and Levites) had not remained separate from the surrounding nations (9:1). The list of nations reflects earlier lists before the period of the conquest (Ex. 3:8; 33:2; Deut. 7:1) but also includes new groups (e.g., Ammonites, Moabites, and Egyptians), whose wrong practices the Hebrews had adopted (even if some of these people groups may not have remained as clearly defined ethnic groups by this period). Postexilic Jerusalem and the Persian province of Yehud faced challenges similar to those of Israel during the original Exodus and conquest. The abominations or detestable practices of the nations probably refer to religious and moral aberrations. The Hebrew term appears also in Genesis 43:32, where it describes the Egyptian's abhorrence of eating with Hebrews because they worked in close proximity with livestock (cf. Gen. 46:34). Leviticus 18:30 uses this word in describing sexual perversions of the Canaanites. In Malachi 2:11 it describes idolatry in terms of a perverted marriage.

The concern of the leaders involved separation. The verb is often used in cultic and ritual contexts (e.g., Ex. 26:33, Lev. 1:17; 5:8; 10:10; 11:47) to emphasize the separation between holy and profane and between pure and impure. The term also appears in the context of Creation (Gen. 1:4, 6–7, 14, 18). This lack of separation found its expression in mixed marriages, including also the leaders and rulers who had been the most egregious offenders in this matter (Ezra 9:2). The danger was that the holy people were being mixed with the peoples of those lands. The reference to the holy people (lit. "holy seed") echoes Isaiah 6:13 and is a description of the remnant. Holiness, part and parcel of Israel's DNA (Ex. 19:6; 1 Pet. 2:9), involves commitment to the Lord in life and in mission.

Ezra's reaction to this situation was very strong and involved mourning rites (2 Sam. 13:19; 2 Kin. 19:1; Job 1:20; 2:12–13). The word *shamem* in Ezra 9:3 means "astonished," "appalled," or "in severe shock." The crowd that saw their leader sitting on the ground, his hair in upheaval, and his clothes torn, was a sympathetic crowd since they trembled at the words of God. This indicated a high regard for divine revelation (Is. 66:2, 5; cf. Ezra 10:3). Finally, at the time of the evening sacrifice, silence turned to confession and prayer. The language was intimate, Ezra referring to God as "my God" (Ezra 9:5). Prayer challenges us individually to relate to our Creator and Savior personally and corporately.

9:6–15. The Prayer: "Here We Are." Ezra's prayer is a wonderful example of intercessory prayer (cf. Neh. 1; Dan. 9). It contains confession of past sins (Ezra 9: 6–7), a historical review (vv. 8–9), confession of present sins (vv. 10–12), and a heartfelt plea for God's incomparable grace (vv. 13–15). Ezra's reflection that he was "ashamed" (v. 6) underlines the importance of shame and honor in biblical times. Sin affronts God and disrupts human relationships. Ezra also described graphically a history of overwhelming guilt—it was higher than their heads and higher than the heavens (an echo of the Tower of Babel narrative; cf. Gen. 11:4). Israel's sin and guilt had reached heaven and God's presence. Ezra's point was that due to the flagrant nature of Israel's sin, he needed to respond unequivocally. The Exile represented that response.

The Hebrew of Ezra 9:8 utilizes a unique metaphor. The text refers to a *yated*—a pin or tent peg—in the sanctuary or "holy place." A tent peg provides strength and anchors a larger structure and gives it a firm hold. God's holy place could refer to either the earthly sanctuary or the heavenly sanctuary. God's provisions are not only sufficient but also secure and encompass a location and a means of communication between God and His people (Is. 33:20; 54:2).

Ezra admitted that they did not know what to say (Ezra 9:10). This was a clear recognition and confession of guilt. Following Ezra's logic, Israel had forgotten God's commandments regarding intermarriage. The reference to the unclean or polluted land (v. 11) echoes conceptually Leviticus 18:25–28 and utilizes terminology that is elsewhere linked to menstrual bleeding (Lev. 18:19) or bodily discharges (Lev. 15:19–33). The lack of ritual purity prohibited the affected person from appearing before the Lord in the temple. Due to its nonchalance regarding mixed marriages, the Yehud community was threatened by the same fate. The emphasis on purity in marriage relations does not suggest ethnic superiority but rather obedience to God's law. As was the case in Solomon's life, a spouse was either a strong help in maintaining loyalty to God or a great hindrance. Thus, religious loyalty ultimately superseded ethnic relations. This religious commitment lies at the heart of the concern about mixed marriages.

However, Ezra's prayer reminds us of God's radical grace, highlighting the fact that God did not punish Israel as much as their sins deserved (Ezra 9:13) and had given deliverance (see 2 Tim. 2:13). The prayer ends with confession of sin and a recognition of the righteousness of God. Ezra was functioning as a true mediator between the people and God, identifying himself with the condition of the people (cf. Ex. 32:10–13, 30).

10:1–4. The People's Response. Ezra's prayer and dynamic display of emotions helped to move the people to confession and led to covenant renewal. In this chapter there is a change from first to third person, which makes it easier to distinguish the I's in Ezra's autobiographical section in Ezra 9 and Nehemiah's memoirs in Nehemiah 1. The people's admission of their sin and guilt opened the possibility of a covenant renewal, which would also include the dissolution of the unlawful marriages with the foreign women and separation from their children. Shechaniah (Ezra 10:2; his name means "Yahweh dwells [near]") belonged to Elam's family that had returned with Sheshbazzar (2:7). Based on the list in 10:26, it may be possible that even his father had married outside Israel. Since the mixed marriage problem involved descendants of the earlier returnees, Shechaniah was well qualified to respond as a representative of the local community. He also recognized Ezra's leadership and authority (10:4), particularly considering Ezra's job description given by the Persian king (7:23, 25).

10:5–17. Covenant Renewal. The covenant renewal ritual included calling an assembly (vv. 7–8), confession (vv. 9–12), and forming a tribunal to investigate specific cases (vv. 13–17). Although only four persons publicly opposed the decision, there were possibly others who did as well without indicating it because ten years later Nehemiah would have to face the same problem (though it is also possible that the later opposition was unrelated; Neh. 13:23–29).

Ezra's inclusion of Yehud leadership in this reform effort, which involved priests and Levites (10:5), is highly significant. True and lasting change can only be accomplished in unity and not by coercion. Ezra's mourning rites (including fasting; Ezra 9:3) were not necessarily a public relations stunt. Even following the commitment of Yehud's leadership in 10:5, when Ezra entered Jehohanan's room, he continued his fast privately (v. 6). The identity of Jehohanan is not entirely clear since no title is included. Some have linked the name to Nehemiah 12:22–23, which contains an (abbreviated) list of high priests, especially considering the fact that the same name is referred to as a high priest in the extrabiblical Elephantine papyri from Egypt dated to 408 B.C. However, this identification is not very convincing—especially in light of the fact that both Jehohanan (and its variant Johanan) and his father's name, Eliashib, were common in the postexilic community.

The mandatory gathering assembled three days after the announcement in the open square near or in the house of God (Ezra 10:9). Commentators and translators differ in regard to whether this place was the court of the temple or a place near it. The location of the covenant renewal is significant. This was not just a matter of decrees and quick paperwork. It happened "before God" and reminded the participants of other important meetings "before God" in Israel's history. The trembling and distress of the people was because of the sad situation and because of the heavy rain. The ninth month (or Kislev) of the Hebrew calendar falls into December. Due to Jerusalem's altitude of nearly 2,600 feet (or ca. 800 m) above sea level and average highs of only about fifty degrees Fahrenheit (or ca. ten degrees Celsius) during this time of year, the meeting was not a pleasant picnic-style gathering. Ezra indicted the people directly and affirmed their sinfulness (Ezra 10:10; cf. 9:2). The Hebrew verb is in an emphatic verbal form, which emphasized the element of personal responsibility. This could not rightly be blamed on the ancestors. Ezra's priestly credentials are referred to twice here (vv. 10, 16; see Mal. 1:6—2:16). Prophetic and priestly leadership were to work in harmony. The reference to the guilt of Israel picks up an earlier motif (Ezra 9:6, 13, 15; cf. Josh. 7:1 using the same Hebrew term). Conscious (and even unconscious) sin results in guilt requiring confession and commitment to change. The people were called upon to confess (lit. "give thanks to") to the Lord. Our confessions are part of showing God's justice and mercy within the context of the Great Controversy, as we publicly recognize our sin and throw ourselves upon our Redeemer's grace.

The people's affirmative response (Ezra 10:12) is, however, balanced by the inclusion of a list of four men (v. 15) who did not support this initiative. The text is not entirely clear if the opposition involved the procedure or the actual recognition of guilt of mixed marriages. The agreed-upon process delegated the review of individual cases to the leadership (v. 14). Verses 16 and 17 suggest that the process took three months.

10:18-44. The Final Report. The final verses of Ezra lists those implicated in mixed marriages. The sequence of implicated families follows the earlier lists in Ezra, detailing first religious leadership (priests [10:18b-22], Levites [10:23], musicians [10:24a], and gatekeepers [10:24b]), followed by others—literally "from Israel" (10:25-43). A total of 113 men are mentioned, a number which corresponds to 0.38 percent of the 29,818 returnees that are listed in Ezra 2. While less than half a percent appears to be a low incident number, God was not interested primarily in quantity but quality. The existence of mixed marriages at different levels put into question Israel's commitment to the Lawgiver. Verse 19 includes a unique reference for the important resolution of the communal guilt. The implicated priestly leaders first gave their promise (lit. "gave their hand"; cf. 1 Chr. 29:24; Ezek. 17:18) to divorce their wives, followed by a reference to a ram as their trespass or guilt offering. The reference to the special sacrificial ritual underlines the importance and responsibility of spiritual leadership and the seriousness of the trespass (or "unfaithfulness") that required divine atonement.

Contemporary Bible readers will understandably ask important questions regarding the ethics of 113 named men, many of high standing in the community, sending away their foreign wives, and the implications for any children born to those marriages. It seems evident from the text that these marriages were not viewed as legitimate; thus these were essentially dissolutions of unlawful marriages rather than divorces. It is also quite likely that the children and women who were sent away were cared for in some way, though the text does not indicate what specifically happened to them. According to the law, foreigners, widows, and the fatherless (the women and children were in an essentially analogous situation in Ezra) were to be loved and cared for (Lev. 19:34; Deut. 10:18; 14:29; 24:19-21; 26:12-13). We have suggested, based on the text, that Ezra was not driven by ancient racism or religious bigotry. Ezra focused on Israel's (or Jerusalem's) relation to the God who broke the chains of their slavery, returned them from exile, and manifested love for the orphan, the widow, and the foreigner. Religious identity and commitment lay at the heart of the issue of mixed marriages—not racial superiority or nationalistic ideas. The God of Scripture is the God who searches for the lost and calls a people (or church) to obedient commitment and faithful service as they look forward in hope to a new city.

NEHEMIAH

INTRODUCTION

Title and Authorship. Nehemiah 1:1 indicates that the words that follow are from Nehemiah himself. However, for linguistic and thematic reasons, the books of Ezra and Nehemiah were combined for the greater part of history, leading some to suggest that Ezra penned both. Not until A.D. 1448 did the two books appear in the Hebrew Bible separately. These books were so much considered a single volume that the Septuagint (LXX) calls this book "Second Ezra." The Latin Vulgate follows this title.

Since Ezra was a scribe, scholars have suggested that he (who lived contemporaneously with Nehemiah; 8:9; 12:26, 36) had a hand in the final version of this book and (very likely) in the composition of 1 and 2 Chronicles (see 2 Chronicles: Introduction). The similarities in vocabulary and style between the books of Ezra and Nehemiah may be due to them having been written in roughly the same time period by two men in roughly the same social class, or by one scribe (i.e., Ezra himself).

The so-called Ezra and Nehemiah memoirs (a modern label) are offered as an additional argument for the original intended unity of the two books (see Ezra: Introduction). The term "memoir" refers to a text that is written in an autobiographic style, using the first person singular or plural ("I" or "we"). We would expect that Ezra would contain the Ezra memoirs, while Nehemiah would include his memoirs. However, the locations of the memoirs are used to suggest a more integrated literary plan. Ezra's memoir, part I (Ezra 7–10), is followed by Nehemiah's memoir, part I (Neh. 1:11—7:73a), which in turn is followed by what scholars call the second part of the Ezra memoir (Neh. 7:73b—10:39) and the second part of the Nehemiah memoir (Neh. 11–13). Some are not comfortable with identifying these as memoirs or convinced that the second part of the Ezra memoir is actually that at all since the use of the personal pronoun when referring to Ezra is directly absent. When referring to Ezra, the third person pronoun "he" (i.e., Neh. 8:3, ff.) is used with the antecedent name "Ezra" (i.e., Neh. 8:2, ff.) as if someone other than Ezra is writing.

Date. The book of Nehemiah begins in the twentieth year of Artaxerxes I (Neh. 1:1; 2:1), which was 444 B.C. The book could not have been written before this date. Nehemiah was appointed governor for twelve years, ending in 432 B.C. (5:14), at which point he returned to Babylon (13:6). Sometime after this, he traveled again to Jerusalem following what amounted to a visit to Babylon. It is not known if he ever returned to Babylon again. As a result, the final portions of the book had to have been written sometime after 432 B.C. If Darius II is the Darius mentioned in the book (Neh. 12:22), then that portion could not have been written before 423 B.C. (since Darius II reigned from 423–404 B.C.).

Backgrounds. Esther's husband, Xerxes I (also called Ahasuerus), was murdered by the royal bodyguard. Although not the eldest son, Artaxerxes, after a short period of turmoil, ended up on the throne. He was probably born during his grandfather's reign (Darius I), when his father was just a prince, making it unlikely that he would have been related by blood to Esther. About five years before Nehemiah went to Jerusalem to rebuild the walls (in 444 B.C.), Persia entered into peace with Greece (449 B.C.). Thus, the Holy Land had relative peace with local rulers jockeying for position in the new, more stable political environment when Nehemiah entered it. This is reflected in the story.

Archaeological evidence for the wall built by Nehemiah is sparse, primarily because the city has been built and rebuilt many times since. However, portions of it have been identified and are still visible for visitors today. In fact, one portion (part of the Northern Tower and its city wall) has been dated (from pottery and burials associated with it) to almost immediately after the mid-fifth century B.C. (ca. 444 B.C.)—the same year that Nehemiah arrived in Jerusalem.

Theology and Purpose. A number of theological themes appearing in both Ezra and Nehemiah have already been discussed in the introduction to Ezra. The following themes have particular significance for the book of Nehemiah:

1. *Covenant Thinking.* The covenant is an important topic in Nehemiah. The scattered remnant's only hope for restoration could be found in the Lord as the keeper of the covenant (9:32). This covenant depended entirely upon God's gracious covenant love (9:17; Ezra 7:28; 9:9), a concept also echoed in contemporary postexilic prophets (Zech. 1:3; Mal. 1:2). Ezra and Nehemiah mark the end of the OT period and anticipate already important NT developments. Nehemiah also emphasizes the renewal of the covenant, anticipating the ultimate renewal of God's covenant with humanity in Jesus. This covenant, originally made in the Garden of Eden (Gen. 3:15) and later renewed with Abraham (Gen. 12:1–3; cf. Gal. 3:16–18), had been prophesied through a vision to Daniel (Dan. 9:25–7) and was later recognized as being fulfilled in Jesus (Heb. 13:20).

2. *From King to Community.* Kings or prophets played only a limited role in events chronicled by Nehemiah, with individual leadership replaced by a focus on the community as the center of shared authority. Both Ezra and Nehemiah received help from the elders and family leaders who took up the leadership role in the community. As a result of the absence of rulers, the priests filled the vacuum, in a way, returning to the model of the early Israelites. The Messiah would combine these roles by being both King and Priest. This hopeful expectation undergirds the book.

3. *The Importance of the Written Word.* Just as in Ezra, the book of Nehemiah emphasizes the role of God's word as authority (Neh. 8:1–8; 9:3; 10:29). The oral reading of the law before the people moved them to repent. This reminds us of the importance of hearing God's word read as authority over His people and the positive response that is possible as a result.

COMMENTARY

1:1—7:72
THIRD RETURN FROM EXILE AND REBUILDING OF THE WALL

The first seven chapters of Nehemiah echo Ezra 1–6 and focus on Israel's third return from exile, this time to rebuild the wall under Nehemiah's leadership. The wall became a rallying point, a contentious issue, and a symbol of God's watch and care over His covenant people. The wall project, however, could not be completed without first filling Jerusalem (Neh. 7:4–5). Similar to the Creation account of Genesis 1, in the book of Nehemiah filling follows forming. Nehemiah's inclusion of the list of the original returnees under Sheshbazzar (cf. Ezra 2) demonstrates a straight line from liberation and return to filling and securing a safe future for God's people in Jerusalem.

1:1–11
Jerusalem in Crisis: Nehemiah's Prayer

God's remnant was in crisis and one man, Nehemiah, responded to the disheartening news of destruction and disdain. His response, however, did not involve feverish activity and politically expedient strategizing. Just as prayer is the foundation of every true change and reform, prayer is also foundational in Nehemiah's account (cf. 1:5–11; 2:4; 4:4–5; 5:19; 6:9, 14; 11:17).

1:1–4. Bad News from Jerusalem. Several important details are provided for us in these few verses. The chief human character of the book is introduced—Nehemiah, who worked at the royal palace in Shushan (or Susa). The year was 445/444 B.C. Artaxerxes I is mentioned as the king, as indicated by the reference to Sanballat and Hanani (cf. 7:2), the latter of whom was probably a relative (lit. a "brother") of Nehemiah. Hanani and his group brought news to Nehemiah that concerned Jerusalem and the current state of affairs in the province. The people were described as being in a state of *bera'ah* ("misery," "distress") and *kherpah* ("disgrace," "reproach"). These terms describe the inner and social condition of the people in Jerusalem as a result of the broken-down walls and burned gates of the city (1:3). The reference to the condition of the city and its walls supports the view that in Ezra 7:18 the king had authorized them to do whatever seemed good to them, which naturally included rebuilding the city.

Nehemiah's reaction ("he sat down and wept") reflects typical OT mourning rites, often associated with bad news or distressing and shameful situations (Gen. 21:16; Deut. 21:13; Judg. 20:26; Ezra 9:3–5). When confronted with difficulties and existential challenges, biblical characters often reacted with fasting and praying (Neh. 1:4). The text indicates that Nehemiah wept and mourned for "days." It appears that this situation must have been a matter of prayer for Nehemiah for at least four months since Chislev (December/January) in Nehemiah 1:1 and Nisan (April/May) in 2:1 are given as key time markers in the book. These passages also suggest that Nehemiah used a fall-to-fall calendar.

1:5–11. Prayer of Nehemiah. This prayer is an excellent example of a penitential prayer in which the mediator identifies with the sins of the community (cf. Ezra 9; Neh. 9; Dan. 9). In the Bible we often find personal and communal prayers, something that may appear strange in societies that emphasize individuality over collectivity. There are five important elements in this specific prayer in Nehemiah 1: the addressee (v. 5), a request for a hearing (v. 6a), confession (vv. 6b–7), recalling God's promises (vv. 8–9), and supplication (vv.10–11a). Nehemiah 1:6 in Hebrew contains a unique expression in which Nehemiah requests that God's ears be attentive and His eyes open. This is a metaphorical way of asking God to see the condition of the city and to hear the prayer by acting on behalf of His people. God was being asked to perform a new act of creation. The word "remember" in Nehemiah 1:8 introduces previous divine promises and is in line with the reference to Moses,

God's servant. God's remembering leads to divine action (cf. Gen. 8:1)—often in favor of His covenant people.

"Unfaithful" in Nehemiah 1:8 appears elsewhere in Ezra and Nehemiah's account to describe the problem of mixed marriages (Ezra 9:2, 6; 10:2, 6, 10; Neh. 13:27). The language of this section echoes the covenant language found in Deuteronomy 30:1–4. Nehemiah realized that the only way forward for God's people, identified simply in 1:10 as those whom God had redeemed, involved recognition and commitment to God's covenant established long ago. Ultimately, however, it was only God's great power and strong hand that would result in deliverance (v. 10). The language used reminds us of the Exodus (cf. Ex. 6:1; 32:11).

2:1–20
Return to Jerusalem: Let's Build a Wall

The chapter describes Nehemiah's audience with the king, his return to Jerusalem, and his clandestine inspection of Jerusalem's walls. The narrative moves from dialogue to action and then returns to dialogue, resulting in the united decision to build (Neh. 2:18).

2:1–9. Nehemiah Is Appointed by the Persian King. Four months after having received the devastating news about Jerusalem, Nehemiah did not continue his business as usual. Prayer was followed by a time of expectant waiting—and then action. Timing is always crucial when dealing with royalty (cf. Esth. 5:1–8), so the urgency should not always involve haste. We often struggle with God's timing that is not always easily understandable but is always right on target (Dan. 9:24–27). Nehemiah's strong fear upon hearing the king's question highlights the difficulty of relating to an absolute monarch whose word could have meant life or death. Nehemiah's quick prayer is a testimony of his close walk with God.

The king's question regarding how long he would be away contained tacit approval of Nehemiah's request (Neh. 2:6). The approval was recognized by Nehemiah as the good and gracious hand of his God upon him (cf. Ezra 7:6). The description of the journey is very brief. The text says only that the king sent captains of the army and horsemen with Nehemiah. Unlike Ezra (Neh. 8:22), Nehemiah did not refuse an armed guard—most likely due to the fact that he was the official governor of the Persian province and thus also commanded military personnel.

Nehemiah and the Pentateuch

Part of Nehemiah's prayer (Neh. 1:8–9) is rooted in the Pentateuch, especially Deuteronomy. "If you are unfaithful" echoes Leviticus 26:40. "I will scatter you among the nations" reflects Deuteronomy 4:27, while "but if you return" is most likely based on Deuteronomy 30:2. The mention of those exiled in distant regions is a reference to Deuteronomy 30:4. Finally, Nehemiah's reference to the place God chose as a dwelling for His name repeats Deuteronomy 12:11 and 12:5.

2:10. Introduction of the Opposition. Two individuals who appear to have been in constant opposition to Jerusalem are specifically mentioned right from the outset: Sanballat and Tobiah (v. 10). Sanballat the Horonite was the governor of Samaria (4:1–2). His name appears in a fifth century B.C. papyrus from Elephantine, Egypt. The name also appears in the later Samarian Wadi ed-Daliyeh papyri from the fourth century B.C., probably referring to his descendant. The name "Tobiah" means "the Lord is good." It is possible that he worshiped God. His son Jehohanan ("the Lord is gracious") also had a Hebrew name. Based on Ezra 2:60–62, some scholars have theorized that Tobiah belonged to a family of the same name whose Israelite origins could not be clearly established and in consequence was rejected. If this were the case, it would explain his severe antagonism. Geshem the Arab was another enemy of the people (Neh. 2:19). He was probably a leader of Arab groups perhaps operating almost independently of the Medo-Persian Empire. The situation of Jerusalem was quite precarious since it was surrounded by enemies: Sanballat/Samaria to the north, Tobiah/Ammon to the east, and Geshem/Arabs to the south. Nehemiah's arrival deeply disturbed Judah's enemies.

2:11–18. It's Time to Move. Nehemiah's inspection of the wall occurred three days after his arrival (v. 11). The third day is often a decisive moment in biblical narratives (e.g., Gen. 22:4; 31.22, Ex. 19:11; Judg. 20:30; Esth. 5:1). Nehemiah made it very clear that this operation was God driven since it was God who had put it into Nehemiah's heart (Neh. 2:12). Nehemiah's covert operation aimed at obtaining information needed to establish and develop his plan. The Valley Gate (v. 13) was probably located on the western side of the city. The description of Jerusalem's walls confirms the original report (1:3). The situation on the ground was as catastrophic as had been anticipated in the earlier report. The reference to the unsuspecting officials (2:16) may indicate local Persian-appointed leadership. The Hebrew term (*sagan*) refers to a "ruler" or "prefect" and appears mostly in exilic or postexilic literature.

After verification of the exact condition of Jerusalem's defenses, it was time to become active. Action, however, begins with leadership buy-in. But prior to action comes recognition. Verse 17 uses again the keyword "to see" (see 1:5–11). The first-person plural pronoun ("us") highlights the inclusive nature of the action. He presented himself as a visionary leader capable of communicating his vision and involving others in the action. Nehemiah gave a personal testimony of God's gracious hand in all aspects of his mission (2:18). The response of the people of Jerusalem was a unanimous commitment to engage in the building project. We can learn from Nehemiah's example: people around us will better relate to personal testimonies than to argumentation or sermonizing.

2:19–20. Reaction of the Opposition. Similar to Nehemiah's hearing in 1:4, Sanballat, Tobiah, and Geshem listened to what he had to say, but then they ridiculed him. Instead of shedding tears and initiating mourning rites, Jerusalem's enemies taunted the postexilic community and disdained them. The Hebrew term (*bazah*) for "despised" or "ridiculed" appears repeatedly in contexts where divine precepts have been consciously ignored (Num. 15:31; 2 Sam. 12:9; Prov. 14:2). This provides a hint to the reader that this conflict concerned more than two groups fervently disagreeing about a particular point. It echoed the larger cosmic conflict involving God and Satan.

The rhetorical questions of Nehemiah's opponents suggest rebellion against the king (Neh. 2:19)—a serious accusation already hinted at in Ezra 4:12–16. Nehemiah told the enemies that they had no *khcleq* ("heritage," "share"). This meant that they had no legal right over Jerusalem and no *zikkaron* ("memorial," "historic right") there either. This latter term often has cultic connotations (Ex. 12:14; 13:9; 28:29) and underlines the fact that neither Sanballat nor Tobiah shared in the authentic worship of the Lord.

3:1–32
The List of Wall Builders

The chapter details those who did have a "heritage" or "share" (cf. 2:20) in Jerusalem. The list of wall builders is divided into forty different sections. It seems to begin in the northern section of Jerusalem with the Sheep Gate (3:1), moving southward down the western side and then describing the work on the eastern side of the wall, ultimately returning to the Sheep Gate (v. 32).

Each section was built by its own work crew, even though some groups did work on more than one section (cf. the men of Tekoa; 3:5, 27). The importance of the religious leadership in the postexilic community is highlighted by the place of Eliashib, the high priest, at the head of the list (v. 1). The key verbal form of the entire chapter is *khaziq* (occurring 34 times in the chapter; e.g., vv. 4–6), a causative form of a verb meaning "to be strong." The rendering given in most translations, "made repairs," is an appropriate rendering and emphasizes the restoration of something to its previous condition. This is an important indication that Nehemiah's construction project presupposes an earlier wall-building project (see "The Decree of Artaxerxes I as Fulfillment of Daniel 9:25," p. 584).

There is a close connection between chapters 3 and 4. While chapter 3 delineates the result of the project, chapters 4 and 6 emphasize the process itself, which includes the opposition faced by the builders during the reconstruction process. In this sense, the list reflects typical Hebrew thinking, in which the outcome is considered and presented before the process of achieving it. The first entry of the list includes a reference to consecration. Eliashib and the priests consecrated the Sheep Gate and put its doors in place (3:1). The use of the important verb denoting consecration (*qadash*) underlines the fact that the work of reconstructing the walls and gates was related to the Lord, the Holy One.

The reconstruction of the wall was a communal project. However, it was not a forced or obligatory project; as a result, some leaders did not support it (3:5, 27). Commentators have suggested that due to Tekoa's southeastern location, abutting the region controlled by Geshem the Arab, the town's leaders were possibly unwilling to antagonize their closest neighbor. The voluntary nature of the project highlights a character trait of God, who offers freedom to His creation and prefers willing submission to forced compliance. Verse 10 (cf. v. 23) suggests that some sections were assigned to those living closest to the particular wall section, providing significant motivation for finishing the project.

The majority of names and families listed in chapter 3 identify male participants, reflecting the common practice of biblical times. Families were known by the father's (or grandfather's) name. However, v. 12 specifically mentions the daughters of Shallum. Shallum was probably a person who did not have sons to help him. The whole community was dedicated to this important project, which eventually came to the place where it started by the Sheep Gate (v. 32). Chapter 4 shows that the work was done under great challenges.

4:1–23
External Opposition to the Building of the Wall

The chapter echoes previous references to opposition (2:10, 19) and describes the reconstruction of the walls and gates of Jerusalem. The opposition, led by Sanballat and Tobiah, mocked Jerusalem and the Yehud community with a barrage of rhetorical questions that aimed at pointing to the futility of the effort (4:2). Sanballat and Tobiah mounted a propaganda campaign that sought to intimidate the builders in Jerusalem. Sanballat's five questions are followed (v. 3) by Tobiah's ironic statement, suggesting that even a light fox could climb up the wall and break it down. Some interpreters have suggested that the reference to the fox may actually be a reference to an ancient siege machine, transforming an ironic or sarcastic statement into a plainly threatening one.

As is always the case in crucial moments in the book, Nehemiah prayed first before responding to the external challenges (v. 4; cf. Is. 37:14–35). The belligerency of Sanballat and Tobiah was not simply an opposition to Nehemiah but also an affront to the Lord.

Nehemiah and the builders continued their efforts tirelessly. Nehemiah 4:6 introduces two important facts: the entire wall had been joined and been built to half its height. This was due to the fact that the people were highly motivated (lit. "the heart of the people was to work"). However, what was good news to Nehemiah and the inhabitants of Jerusalem had a different significance for their opponents who heard and became very angry (including here, for the first time, Ashdodites, who were most likely the inhabitants of Ashdod, located on the Mediterranean coast of Israel; v. 7). In turn, the members of the opposition conspired together and plotted serious action, involving military options (v. 8). Another prayer (v. 9) was accompanied by active guard duty. The one did not exclude the other.

Disinformation and rumors are often more damaging than concrete military action. The people began to feel their strength failing as they saw an overabundance of rubble—they began to feel weak (v. 10). Nehemiah's response to this dilemma involved careful military planning while continuing relentlessly with his rebuilding effort. The call to not be afraid (v. 14) is a formula of comfort and a call to trust in the Lord. The next call to remember the great and awesome Lord reminds readers of Deuteronomy 7:21, when Israel faced powerful cities with numerous people in Canaan. These calls to courage and remembering God's power preceded a quintessential characteristic of the theocracy: God would fight for them (Neh. 4:20).

Nehemiah's leadership involved the example of his own household. The reference to half of his workers in 4:16 (also in v. 23) uses a Hebrew term often denoting "young men" (see 5:10, 16; 13:19). This group may have included members of Nehemiah's own household or his bodyguard (cf. 2:9). Half of this group was consigned to military duties while the other half worked at construction. The next verses (4:17–18) provide a visual glimpse of military preparedness: workers, building on the wall, kept their arms and shields close by to respond to enemy action communicated by the one who, shadowing Nehemiah, sounded the trumpet. However, in spite of human preparedness and contingency plans, Nehemiah tells us that it was ultimately God who would fight for them (v. 20). The final indication of extreme caution and alertness is expressed in v. 23. There is a suggestion of ever-increasing circles of inclusion starting with Nehemiah and his brothers (possibly members of Nehemiah's clan or "father's house"), his workers (lit. "young men"), and the guards, who remained fully dressed as they slept. The NT echoes this theme of preparedness for spiritual warfare in many places (Rom. 13:12; 2 Cor. 10:4; Eph. 6:10–18).

5:1–19
Internal Tension Threatening the Building of the Wall

At first glance this chapter appears to be out of place since it does not overtly continue the story of the building of Jerusalem's walls and gates. However, looking more carefully, the narrative shows that conflict is not always external. Internal tension involving social injustice impacts not only individuals and groups but also challenges the larger building effort. Justice thus becomes an extension of unity.

The great outcry of 5:1 is a cry of protest that involved great financial difficulties. The Hebrew term appears in legal contexts when justice needs to be administered (e.g., 1 Kin. 20:39; 2 Kin. 6:26; 8:3, 5; Is. 5:7). It seems that this great outcry involved debt slavery following a famine (or other calamity) where people had to mortgage even their children in order to get grain for food (Neh. 5:2), seed (v. 3), and to pay the king's tax (v. 4). The reference to the famine (v. 3) suggests a reality that must have been well known in the region. This was not just *a* famine but *the* famine. Greek sources tell us that the satrapy that included Yehud had a tax burden of 350 talents annually, which represented a significant financial burden for the local population.

The lament-like outcry paints a dismal picture: the cycle of increasing debt resulted in the enslavement of the sons and daughters of those lamenting. Since land represents the foundation of prosperity in any agricultural-based society, the great outcry is fully understandable. The social fabric of society was at stake. Without land, the men and their wives (v. 1) stated that they were powerless to help their family members (v. 5). Some translations insert "to redeem them" in order to clarify a difficult Hebrew expression that is possibly referring to the powerlessness of the people to redeem their family members by paying their debts.

Nehemiah's angry reaction echoes earlier prophetic critiques of the abuse of debt slavery (Amos 2:6; 8:4, 6). His anger was expressed in rebuke only after careful thinking and analysis (Neh. 5:6–7). The first step to resolve this issue was to call a large meeting since the solution to problems affecting a community can only be found by working in community. Nehemiah's rebuke of the leadership of Yehud refers to usury, or charging interest (v. 7). Following the unsuccessful private rebuke of Yehud's leadership, Nehemiah addressed the entire assembly, which had been called for the purpose of dealing with these creditors, and he exhorted them that because their fellow Israelites (lit. their "brothers") had been redeemed from the nations, they should not be returned to debt slavery. Nehemiah's admonition to "walk in the fear of our God" (5:9; cf. v. 15) emphasizes an important biblical concept prevalent in the wisdom literature of the OT. Fear can be an emotional response. However, in most cases it suggests reverence and a personal relationship. We "fear" (or respect) someone whom we know as trustworthy and strive to please her or him (cf. Prov. 8:13). Nehemiah puts the fear of God in an even more compelling context. Walking in the fear of God, he suggests, involves the larger issue of theodicy, that is, God's justice before the nations and the reproach of Jerusalem before the nations (Neh. 5:9).

Verse 10 again underlines Nehemiah's selfless service that involved lending grain and money (lit. "silver") to the needy. This indicates that lending was not the problem but the usury (or interest) that ultimately led to debt slavery. The next verse, while not explicitly employing the technical term, represents a Jubilee call (Lev. 25:8–17). In the Mosaic law every fiftieth year was considered a Jubilee, which involved the return of land, property, and the liberation of slaves. The creditors' response was unanimous: they would restore the possessions and money that they had been extracting (Neh. 5:12). The issue of debt slavery and the proclamation of liberty were well anchored in Judah's memory. In fact, it was disobedience to a divinely established covenant involving God, Jerusalem's leadership, and Jewish debt slaves that had led to divine judgment during the time of Judah's last king, Zedekiah, prior to the final destruction of the city (Jer. 34:8–22).

By symbolically shaking the fold of his garment, Nehemiah indicated that the violators of the pledge would be shaken out of their possessions by the Lord (Neh. 5:13). The assembly's "amen" suggests unanimity and is further emphasized by the indication that they did what they had promised.

The following section (vv. 14–19) highlights Nehemiah's leadership during his tenure as governor, which covered twelve years. During this time, he did not use tax income to support his household or levy other tariffs on the local population (vv. 14–15). Nehemiah's commitment to the well-being of Jerusalem and its inhabitants was also marked by his hospitality and refusal to enter the lucrative real-estate market (v. 16). The final verse of this section is the first of a series of "remember me" interjections (13:14, 22, 31). These statements highlight the fact that when God remembers, He acts on behalf of His people (Gen. 8:1; 19:29; Ex. 2:24).

6:1–19
Further Intimidation

Chapter 6 is about intimidation and single-mindedness. In the midst of conflict, we find a praying leader (Neh. 6:9, 14) who refused to be distracted from his God-given task. Nehemiah allowed God to do what He had placed in his heart. Finally, following three chapters detailing obstacles, intimidation, and distraction, God came through again. The One who had given the land to Israel blessed the wall reconstruction project with success, and consequently all the nations surrounding Yehud recognized that it was God who had prospered the work (v. 16).

Nehemiah 6:1 seems to continue seamlessly the narrative of chapter 4—a fact that is underlined by the use of the autobiographic "I." The first fourteen verses of the chapter are rife with dialogue and written communications but lack specific action. Verse 4 highlights the fact that Yehud's enemies had sent a threatening personal message to Nehemiah four times. This reminds the reader that important action always originates with ideas and words. Nehemiah's response is highly significant. He affirmed that he was working on a major enterprise and could not go down to them (v. 3). This was both courteous and definitive. Distraction would not work.

After realizing that direct threats were ineffective, Nehemiah's enemies tried to attack his moral integrity by spreading the false rumor that the Jews were planning a rebellion and Nehemiah was planning to make himself king (v. 6). The reference to the open or unsealed letter in v. 5 underlines the public nature of these accusations. Sanballat's messenger possibly read the letter aloud as he traveled toward Jerusalem. Verse 7 clearly implies blackmail, yet Nehemiah did not succumb to the increasing pressure. Rather, he attempted to clear his name (v. 8) and decided to pray (v. 9).

The next section (vv. 10–14) focuses on internal challenges. The Hebrew participle 'atsar used in v. 10 is sometimes translated as "secret informer." The basic meaning of the word is "restrain," so other translations have "shut in at his home" or "confined at home." This was perhaps suggesting that Shemaiah's confinement represented what was coming to Nehemiah. The prophecy of Shemaiah was not from the Lord, which suggests that he may have been a hired prophet (cf. Num. 22–24; Deut. 13:1–5; Jer. 23:9–32; Ezek. 13; 1 John 4:1). Other prophets were also involved in the attack against Nehemiah (Neh. 6:14). The section concludes with another call for God to remember (v. 14), used here in a negative way to express divine judgment (cf. 5:19).

Finally, and in spite of constant threats, distraction, and internal challenges, the reconstruction of the wall was finished in fifty-two days (6:15). This limited time window strongly indicates that the walls had been previously reconstructed, in keeping with the broad limits of the instruction, in the time of Ezra (see Ezra 7:18). The month of Elul (Neh. 6:15) is the beginning of October. The Hebrew term for work is used in Genesis 2:2–3 for the divine work of creation and in Exodus 40:33 for the construction of the sanctuary. The implication is that the work performed in Jerusalem was a divine act of creation. The biblical author makes two important explicit statements that support this idea. First, all of Yehud's enemies lost their confidence (lit. "fell greatly in their own eyes"; Neh. 6:16). Second, they somehow knew that it was God who had prospered the work. Similar to the conquest narrative in Joshua, nations surrounding the covenant people heard and understood (cf. Josh. 9). The focus of the last few verses of this chapter moves from Sanballat to Tobiah (cf. Neh. 2:10). This is evidenced in the many letters that named leaders of the city (cf. also 13:4 which states that Tobiah was related by marriage to a priest named Eliashib).

7:1–72
An Empty City: The List of Returnees

The chapter is divided into two main sections. Nehemiah 7:1–3 contains a description of the reorganization of religious and civic life in postexilic Jerusalem, while vv. 4–72 contains a copy of the list of original returnees, already known from Ezra 2. The key reason for including a second copy of this long list can be found in 7:4: there were few people in the city. Following the reconstruction effort (or the "forming," if using creation language; cf. Gen. 1:2), the city needed to be filled.

7:1–3. Reorganization. Nehemiah's efforts did not end with the reconstruction of the wall. Verse 1 refers to the building of the wall, which was a point in the recent past. This reference serves to move the narrative forward. The appointment of gatekeepers and singers was presupposed and happened earlier (cf. Ezra 6:18). Nehemiah needed leadership that required administrative skills and interpersonal acumen, but ultimately he needed faithfulness in those appointed and for them to have a true understanding of their standing before God. Following the appointment of leaders, Nehemiah established basic guard duties, suggesting that he still considered Jerusalem to be at risk (Neh. 7:3).

7:4–5. The Empty City. The two verses introducing the already known list of the returnees (cf. Ezra 2) point to the real crux of the problem: Jerusalem was only sparsely populated and thus difficult to defend. This comment underlines the temple-city nature of Jerusalem. Archaeological research has suggested that Ramat Rahel, located about three and a half miles (6 km) south of Jerusalem, could have functioned as the de facto administrative center of Yehud. The site boasts an elaborate palace with a very complex water system. Hundreds of stamped storage jars, which had been used as containers for agricultural produce tax payments from the eighth century B.C. through the Persian period, have been found there. Furthermore, the site was never destroyed during the final Babylonian conquest of Judah.

Nehemiah's solution was God driven (Neh. 7:5). This highlights the divine initiative in the following census, which had caused divine indignation on another occasion (2 Sam. 24; 1 Chr. 21; cf. Ex. 30:11–16). Many, however, have wondered why Nehemiah included a register of the genealogy of those who had first returned from exile (Neh. 7:5). Possibly Nehemiah wanted to ascertain ancestral roots in the city; furthermore, the original register included many of the locations outside Jerusalem where the original returnees had settled.

7:6–72. The Register. For the differences in the totals (29,818 for Ezra 2 and 31,089 for Neh. 7), see commentary on Ezra 2:1–35, 65–70. The final catalogue of donations in Nehemiah 7:70–72 also contains numbers distinct from those found in Ezra 2. While the object of the donations referred to in Ezra 2:68 was the house of the Lord, Nehemiah 7:70–72 refers to "the work" and the treasury for the work. It is thus possible that Nehemiah employed a similar structure (i.e., list, followed by a registry of donations) but focused rather upon the specific needs of the postexilic community in his time, including the wall and the gates of the city, which had been described in 6:16 as "this work." This would also explain the distinct numbers included in the list and the reference to "the governor" in v. 70.

7:73—13:31
COVENANT, REVIVAL, AND THE COVENANT COMMUNITY

Beginning with the important topic of "filling" Jerusalem in 7:73, the second half of Nehemiah—echoing the second half of Ezra—focuses upon another important aspect of Jerusalem's revival: lasting growth can only be achieved by considering the spiritual dimensions of new beginnings. However, new beginnings are not always clean-cut and easy; the reality of God's postexilic covenant community was characterized by continued neglect of divine orders, including Sabbath observance (13:15–22), tithing (13:10–13), and intermarriages (13:23–28).

7:73—8:18
Between Word and Worship

Following the final verse of chapter 7 and introducing the important theme of empty Jerusalem, chapter 8 focuses upon two key elements of communal worship: the recognition of the power of the word and the response of God-inspired worship.

The summary statement in the first half of 7:73 connects to 7:4–5 and anticipates 11:1–3 and the problem of an "empty" city. The observation that the people of Israel settled into their own towns and cities was a recognition of God's blessings (i.e., God had returned the exiles to their ancestral lands; cf. Jer. 16:15; 30:3), but it was also a description of the problem, namely, too few people lived within the city limits, thus making Jerusalem less viable as Yehud's de-facto capital and difficult to defend. The seventh month (Neh. 7:73b) is a very important month in the Jewish religious system (see Ezra 3:1). The reference to "all the people" (Neh. 8:1) echoes what is described in Hebrew as "all Israel" in 7:73, and this description included men and women (8:2–3). The religious assembly focused on the law of Moses and appears to have been a grassroots movement since no specific convener of the assembly is mentioned; rather, the people gathered together as one. Unity and worshipful activities were two key ingredients of this revival, highlighted by the fact that the people asked Ezra to bring the law of Moses. The importance of this "back to basics" approach has already been noted several times in Ezra. The reference to the first day of the seventh month (8:2) suggests the Festival of Trumpets (Lev. 23:24).

The clear liturgical elements involved in the description of the public reading of the law in Nehemiah 8:4–8 should be noted: the people *stood* when Ezra began his reading (v. 5), *responded* in unison with a resounding and repeated "amen," *raised* their hands, and *fell* to the ground in worship (v. 6). The twofold "amen" occurs elsewhere in Scripture and marks complete agreement and commitment (Pss. 41:13; 72:19). Ezra, surrounded by members of the priestly leadership, however, was not leading out alone. He read (Neh. 8:3), he blessed or praised the Lord (v. 6), and then, together with other Levites, he helped the people to understand (vv. 7–8). The divine epithet "the great God" (8:6; cf. 1:5; 9:32) is used in other parts of the Bible (e.g., Deut. 10:17; Jer. 32:18; Dan. 9:4). Nehemiah 8:8 includes a verbal form that means "to break up" and has been understood as providing a running translation, considering the reality that most returnees coming from Mesopotamia (or Babylon) would have spoken Aramaic, the language of international commerce and diplomacy of the Persian period, and not Hebrew. However, Ezra and the Levites did not only translate but they also provided meaning and helped the audience to understand the law of Moses. This is a good reminder of the fact that translation (and proclamation) always involves interpretation. Later Targums, Aramaic paraphrases of the Hebrew text of the OT, further illustrated this process.

As the people were listening to the reading of the law, they were moved and wept, but the leaders encouraged them to rejoice (vv. 9–10). The narrative provides an important piece of historical information by placing Ezra and Nehemiah together in the same event (v. 9). The Persian title "governor" is found only in Ezra and Nehemiah (Ezra 2:63; Neh. 7:65, 70; 10:1) and helps to anchor the historical context. The reference in Nehemiah 8:10 to "the joy of the LORD" as the source of strength (or, "refuge," "fortress," "stronghold," or "protection"; cf. Is. 17:10; Nah. 1:7) echoes Ezra 6:22. The motivation for personal and collective joy is that God is the Lawgiver and Savior.

The following section describes the celebration of the Festival of Tabernacles (Neh. 8:13–18). The reference to the lack of celebration of this festival since the days of the settlement period in 8:17 refers to the particular motivation, worshipful spirit, and possibly the important element of remembering the "wilderness" experience (instead of only the harvest connotations), and not to the actual celebration, since Ezra 3:4 already recorded an instance of celebration prior to Neh. 8:17 (cf. also 2 Chr. 8:13; 31:3; 35:18). Hence some translations imply that they had not celebrated this festival "like this" since the days of Joshua. The actual construction of shelters (or tents) from tree branches (Neh. 8:15–16) is not mentioned in Ezra 3:4. These shelters were vivid reminders of Israel's past—both the distant past during the wilderness experience and the more recent past of the Babylonian Exile—and were built on roofs, in courtyards, in the temple court, and in public open spaces (v. 16). The link between obedience to God's explicit commands and abundant joy (v. 8:17) echoes Deuteronomy 16:13–15, which concludes with a reference to rejoicing. The continuous reading of the law of God represented a significant component of the worship experience (Neh. 8:18; cf. Deut. 31:12–13). Familiarity with Scripture leads to familiarity with the living Word. Israel's experience described in Nehemiah 8 highlights the deep hunger for the word, community, and the joy that came from obedient recognition of a personal Savior. The same is true today.

9:1–38
God's Past Acts and the People's Present Confession

Some days after the celebration of the Festival of Tabernacles, on the twenty-fourth day of the same month, the postexilic community was assembled once again. No reason is given for the assembly, yet the basic tone of confession and mourning connects to the earlier response to the reading of the word (cf. 8:9). The separation from foreigners underlines the sense of shared history—and failure. The participants stood and read (or perhaps, "heard the reading") from the law for about three hours (a fourth of a day), followed by another fourth of the day spent confessing and worshiping (9:3). The public prayer was led by eight Levites (v. 5). Perhaps they took turns leading the confessional prayer—this is the longest prayer in Ezra or Nehemiah. The text mentions two groups of eight named religious leaders, with five names overlapping (vv. 4–5). The first group cried out strongly (v. 4), echoing the lament of those who had seen the earlier temple (Ezra 3:12) and the confession of the people in Ezra 10:12, while the second led the actual prayer (Neh. 9:5).

The prayer is steeped in language from the Psalms and echoes or quotes numerous texts. The introduction in Nehemiah 9:5 echoes Psalms 41:13 and 106:48. Nevertheless, the phrase "exalted above all blessing and praise" is unique to this prayer. This situation is a reminder that each generation needs to find "new" words that communicate the essence of worship. The prayer contains a review of the relationship between God and Israel to demonstrate the pattern of divine blessings and the people's rebellion against God (cf. Pss. 105, 106, 135). It begins with Creation (Neh. 9:6), moves to God's covenant (vv. 7–8), includes the experience of Israel in Egypt and the Exodus (vv. 9–12), and

climaxes with Sinai and the giving of the Law (9:13–14). There is a special reference to God's holy Sabbath (9:14), which was not introduced at Sinai (Gen. 2:1–3; Ex. 16) but declared again at that time.

The next section in Nehemiah—and one of the longest—deals with Israel's wilderness experience (9:16–21) and includes references to God's bread from heaven (or manna; cf. Ex. 16:4–5) and water out of the rock (9:15; Ex. 17:1–7). The antithetical "but" of Nehemiah 9:16, however, introduces the reality of wilderness living, which involved repeated rebellions (the Hebrew states that they "hardened their necks"). Yet the God of the wilderness—similar to the God of the second exodus—is the same yesterday, today, and tomorrow (Heb. 13:8 applies these characteristics to Christ). God's attributes in Nehemiah 9:17 are clear echoes of Exodus 34:6; Numbers 14:18–20; and Daniel 9:9. God's compassion and grace are the basis of the covenant (Neh. 9:19, 31–32), completely unmerited and utterly transforming. Following the canonical sequence, Nehemiah 9:22–25 captures Israel's conquest of the promised land and then leads straight into the period of the judges (vv. 26–31) or deliverers (v. 27; cf. Judg. 3:9, 15). The Hebrew term used here is theologically significant, coming from the root *yasha'*, which is also the root of the Hebrew name "Joshua" or "Jesus" in Greek. Also, the "rest" of Nehemiah 9:28, literally, "as they rested," echoes God's rest in the Sabbath commandment (Ex. 20:11). Since Israel did not really enter God's final Sabbath rest, it remained a future expectation (Heb. 4:1–10).

Nehemiah 9:32 marks an important theological change introduced by "now therefore," which was used to bridge the distance between the past and its application to the present. They were at this time the rebellious people. The great, mighty, and awesome God (cf. Deut. 10:17) was not just the God of the past. He, keeper of His covenant of *khesed*—"mercy," "love," "kindness" (Deut. 7:9; 1 Kin. 8:23)—and He who had been faithful (Neh. 9:33) with Israel in the past was once again called upon to intervene on behalf of His people. The people's prayer in v. 36—which called upon God to consider them—echoes Isaiah's prayer (Is. 6:8) and indicates covenant commitment (officially ratified in Nehemiah chap. 10 and already introduced in 9:38), which some translations render as a "binding agreement." This term appears only here and in 11:23 where it is related to the king's command.

Nehemiah 9:25 and the Conquest of Canaan

The intriguing reference to possessing houses full of goods, wells already dug, vineyards, olive groves, and fruit trees (v. 25) sheds light on the historicity of the conquest that has been challenged repeatedly in modern scholarship: a close reading of the biblical text of Joshua highlights the important fact that Israel completely destroyed only three cities in Canaan (i.e., Jericho [Josh. 6]; Ai [Josh. 8]; and Hazor [Josh. 11]) and took most other city-states in less destructive ways. This was God's means of providing for His people and explains the lack of radical changes in the archaeology of Late Bronze Age Canaan.

10:1–39
Covenant Commitment

The first part of the chapter contains a list of the names of those who committed themselves to God's covenant law. It was basically a covenant renewal that included attaching to the document the seals with their names. They were the religious and civil leaders of the people and, as such, represented all of them. The specific description of the covenant stipulations can be found in vv. 28–39. These shared a common characteristic with other ANE covenant rituals, in that they included blessings and curses (cf. Deut. 28:1–14; 27:11–26) and specific covenant stipulations. Some of these appear explicitly in Nehemiah 10:30–39, such as (1) a law against mixed marriages (10:30); (2) a reminder of proper Sabbath observance (10:31a; cf. Ex. 20:8–11; 34:21; Deut. 5:12–15); (3) the cancelation of debt and celebrating a Sabbath year (Neh. 10:31b; cf. Deut. 15:1–3); (4) the temple tax (cf. Neh. 10:32–33; cf. Ex. 30:13, where half a shekel was required, while here a third of a shekel is mentioned, perhaps because the Persian monetary system was different); (5) firewood for use in the temple (Neh. 10:34); (6) firstfruit offerings and tithes (Neh. 10:35–39; cf. Ex. 23:19; 34:26; Deut. 26:1–11).

11:1–36
The Filling of Jerusalem

The list found in this chapter contains the names of people who freely offered to live in Jerusalem, and it provides a direct link to 7:4, 73. In 11:1, the use of "lots" echoes earlier uses. For example, following the conquest of Canaan, lots were cast to determine tribal lands (Josh. 14:2; see also 1 Sam. 14:41–42; Jon. 1:7; Acts 1:24–26). Lots presuppose God's active engagement in human history—a notion that is omnipresent in Ezra and Nehemiah. Those who were selected by lot to live in Jerusalem comprised only 10 percent of those who lived in the surrounding area (a trend quite different from the exploding urbanization of the twenty-first century). This number is based on the biblical tithing principle and is accompanied by sacrificial/worship language that is usually reserved for temple- or altar-related activities. Expressions such as the "holy city" (also in Neh. 11:18; Is. 48:2; 52:1; Dan. 9:24; cf. the "holy people" [lit. "holy seed/offspring," "race"] in Ezra 9:2) and the references to *barak* ("blessing," "praise," "commendation") and freely offering (Neh. 11:2; cf. 1 Chr. 29:5–6; 2 Chr. 17:16; Ezra 2:68; 3:5) point

to the religious nature of Jerusalem's "filling" or repopulation (Neh. 11:1–2). The sequence of consecration and offerings in Ezra and Nehemiah begins at the altar (Ezra 3:2) and proceeds via the temple (Ezra 6:13–18), the walls (Neh. 6:15–19; 12:27–43), and finally to the people, resulting in "the holy city" (v. 1).

The list includes priests and Levites (11:10–18), gatekeepers (11:19), and tribal groups from Judah (11:4–6) and Benjamin (11:7–9). Finally, the chapter concludes with another list of people dwelling outside Jerusalem (11:25–30). The many geographic references echo lists in the tribal division following the conquest. For example, the mention of Kiriath (Kirjath) Arba in 11:25 is a clear reference to Joshua 15:13–14 since the name used during the monarchy and later periods was "Hebron." In this sense geography becomes part of theology. God not only extended Israel's grip on the land during the conquest but also during the return from Babylon. The reference to Dibon is difficult since elsewhere in Scripture it represents a city in Moab (Num. 21:30; Is. 15:9; Dimon, which is assumed to be the same place). Here it may refer to another town located in what was formerly Judah's territory.

12:1–26
Those Who Serve

This section includes another list of priests and Levites, beginning with Zerubbabel's return and ending with Nehemiah's. Since worship is a major theme in chapter 12, it is important to retrace the genealogy of worship leaders. The first part (vv. 1–7) lists in greater detail those who returned with Zerubbabel (cf. Ezra 2:36–40), followed by a list of Levites (Neh. 12: 8–10) and of high priests beginning with Jeshua/Joshua (vv. 10–11). Verse 12 offers more details of the priestly lines (vv. 12–21) beginning with Joiakim, the son of Jeshua/Joshua who had been high priest during the return under Zerubbabel (Ezra 2:2; 3:2). Twenty-one priestly clans in total are listed.

The reference to the reign of Darius the Persian in Nehemiah 12:22 is not entirely clear since we know of at least three Persian kings with the name "Darius." Both Darius II (423–405 B.C.) and Darius III (335–331 B.C.) are possible candidates, though Darius II fits better the chronology of Nehemiah. The inclusion of an additional list of Levites and priests during the time of this Darius (vv. 22–23) underlines the importance of these lists for the priesthood and Judaism in general. Finally, the list of the leaders (lit. "heads") of the Levites in vv. 24–25 includes additional information regarding antiphonic choirs and singing, thus anticipating the processions that would be held during the dedication of the wall (vv. 27–43).

12:27–47
The Dedication of the Wall

What had been anticipated for a long time finally became a reality. The long-overdue dedication of the wall represented the grand finale of Nehemiah's ministry—yet more was to come. The dedication of the wall of Jerusalem was marked by a huge celebration. The Hebrew term used in 12:27, *khanukkah*, is also used to describe the dedication of the temple (Ezra 6:16–17). Centuries later, following the desecration of the temple by Antiochus Epiphanes, it became the name of the Jewish festival of reconsecration of the temple. The sacred significance of this ritual activity is emphasized by the purification of priests and Levites, the people, the gates, and the wall (Neh. 12:30). Purification prior to major religious festivals was commonplace in the OT (Ex. 19:10, 14–15; Lev. 8:6; 16:28; Num. 8:5–8; 19:12, 19), highlighting the fact that holiness is a major component of God's character. When we want to approach a holy God, we need to allow Him to cleanse us first.

The choreography of the event involved a lot of planning, which included two large thanksgiving choirs (Neh. 12:31) accompanied by instruments (v. 27) that moved procession-like around Jerusalem, either close to the wall or on top of the wall. One group was led by Ezra, the scribe, the teacher of the law (v. 36), while the "I" in v. 38 must refer to Nehemiah himself. This would put both leaders once again in the same location at the same time. Following the entrance of these two groups into the temple precinct, great sacrifices (which possibly refers to "many" of them) were offered (v. 43). The presence and participation of rejoicing women and children underlined the secure status of the city. Joy, once again, filled the postexilic community (Ezra 3:13) and could be heard from a distance.

Chapter 12 concludes with a description of how the offerings, firstfruits, and tithe were collected and stored in the temple for distribution to Levites and priests. There was unity and order because the leaders and the people were obeying the law of the Lord. The Levites primarily benefitted from the tithe of the people and the priests from the tithe of the Levites (see "Covenant Renewal and Tithing," p. 602).

13:1–31
Nehemiah's Second Administration: Problems and Reforms

The final chapter of Nehemiah underlines the fact that unrealistically blissful endings on this side of Eden are mostly artificial, wishful thinking. While we wish for an "and they lived faithfully ever after," we know that our hearts are "deceitful above all things" (Jer. 17:9).

The beginning of chapter 13 marks a new section that is not directly linked to the previous narrative. The text describes another moment of the reading from the book of Moses, an event that was perhaps linked to a regular festival that involved the reading of God's word (cf. Deut. 31:10–13). The "assembly of God" (sometimes translated as "congregation" or "community," esp. in other passages) is shorthand for God's covenant people in the Pentateuch (e.g., Ex. 12:6; 16:3; Lev. 4:13; Num. 10:7; Deut. 23:1–3, 8). The most likely reference alluded to here is Deuteronomy 23:4–5. Ammonites and Moabites, while related to Israel (Gen. 19:36–38), often represented the prototype of Israel's enemy (Num. 22–24). As on previous occasions, the critical issue involved mixed marriages (Ezra 9.2, 6, 10.2, 6). The people's hearing of the word moved them, once again, to action, and they separated all the foreigners (Heb. *'ereb*—lit. "the mixed company") from Israel (Neh. 13:3). The verb *badal* used here can mean "separate" or "divide." It is used in Genesis 1 when God separated things that could not go together (cf. Gen. 1:4, 6–7, 18). Here it refers to the exclusion of the pagan foreigners. Boundaries also played an important role in the sanctuary/temple involving different levels of holiness. The *'ereb*, on the other hand, echoes the Exodus (Ex. 12:38), where the same Hebrew word is used). Both the Creation and the Exodus remind us of boundaries. God called a people (that is still called "Israel" here) to attract the world around them by their unique relationship with Him. Israel was supposed to be different from the world—and yet they seldom were.

The reform initiated by Nehemiah included ousting Tobiah from the temple room (Neh. 13:7–9) and calling the people to spiritual renewal by returning their tithe and offerings to the Lord (see "Covenant Renewal and Tithing," p. 602).

Covenant Renewal and Tithing

The renewal of the covenant by those who returned from Babylon included faithfulness to the laws pertaining to tithe.

1. Sources of Tithe: The Israelites committed themselves to giving a tithe from the crops (10:39). Although the tithe from herds and flocks (Lev. 27:32-33) is not specifically mentioned, it was most probably included because the people were apparently familiar with and diligent regarding what was required by the law (Neh. 12:44).

2. The System: The system set in place by Nehemiah required that those living around Jerusalem would bring the tithe to the storehouse in the temple and those outside Jerusalem would take it to the Levites in their Levitical cities (10:37). A priest would accompany the Levites when receiving the tithe from the people in order to preserve the integrity of the system (10:38). From the cities, the Levites would send the tithe of the tithe for the priests to the storehouse in the temple and the tithe left after they received their portion of the tithe for other Levites (12:44). Following the laws related to the collection and distribution of tithe, the system was centralized in order to benefit the totality of Levites and priests serving the Lord.

3. Nature of Tithe: When Nehemiah returned to Persia, the priesthood and the people became corrupt. Eliashib, who was the priest in charge of the storerooms in the temple, allowed Tobiah, an Ammonite, to reside in one of the storerooms of the temple. Influenced by the corruption of the priesthood, the people stopped tithing. When Nehemiah returned, he dealt with the corruption of the priesthood (13:6-9). He also spoke strongly to the people for not giving their tithe. It was their responsibility to return the tithe to the Lord and not to use the corruption of the priesthood as an excuse for not tithing (13:10-12). The tithe legislation in Nehemiah assumes the holiness of tithe, its ownership by the Lord (Lev. 27:30), and that He gave it to the Levites and priests (Num. 18:21, 26-28). Consequently, the people were expected to return it to Him in fulfillment of the covenant law.

This section concludes again with a "remember me" plea (Neh. 13:14). This plea—not a self-serving request for special treatment, divine favor, or recognition of impressive accomplishments—represents the conviction of God's people throughout the ages that God knows and remembers. It clearly recognizes that God is intricately involved in all aspects of human life. Finally, Nehemiah restored true Sabbath worship, which included the Sabbath rest for foreigners (Ex. 20:10).

The issue of mixed marriages (Neh. 13:23-29) has appeared repeatedly in Ezra and Nehemiah. Apparently, Nehemiah had to tackle it once again. The reference to the inability of half of the children of these marriages to speak "the language of Judah" (v. 24) is noteworthy. The verbal and physical reactions of Nehemiah to the language limitations of the people are only intelligible if we keep in mind that a mother tongue is directly connected to the identity and culture of a people and of great assistance in the transmission of religious values. He saw in this problem a threat to the faith of Israel.

The inclusion of Solomon as a negative example of mixed marriages (v. 26; cf. 1 Kin. 11:1-13) is astonishing since Solomon was of the Davidic line and the builder of the first temple. Yet Nehemiah was willing to put the matter clearly, even if it reflected poorly on Solomon. The gist of Nehemiah's argument was that mixed marriages lead to sin! Nehemiah recognized the model function of leadership—even the high priestly family had married outside Israel and had aligned itself with Sanballat, the archetype of opposition in Ezra and Nehemiah (Neh. 13:28).

The book concludes with a summary of Nehemiah's reforms (vv. 30-31), once again using ritual terminology and contrasting two types of remembrance: "remember them" (v. 29) is pointing to divine judgment, while Nehemiah's plea for God to remember him favorably ("for good"; v. 31) represents his complete reliance on God's grace (cf. v. 22). The God who saw (and heard) Nehemiah's initial prayer (1:5-11) and opened doors at the royal court would remember—nothing more and nothing less. The request for remembrance is here connected with hope.

ESTHER

INTRODUCTION

Title and Authorship. The book of Esther is named after the female protagonist Esther (whose name is likely derived from the Babylonian goddess Ishtar; could also mean "star"), but it could have as easily been titled "Mordecai" since the two cousins worked as a team to save the Jewish people from utter annihilation. The unknown author of Esther was clearly familiar with Persian customs, laws, history, and even palace decorations in Susa during the reign of Xerxes I (Ahasuerus in Hebrew). Although unknown, the author may have even personally viewed these items, given that the details of the account suggest the recording of an eyewitness (perhaps Esther herself, or Mordecai)—one whose descriptions reflect the opulence of the royal court described by other historians.

Date. In Hebrew, the first words match the introduction to Joshua, Judges, and other historical books. In addition, the Hebrew verb "to write" is used seventeen times in Esther, implying that Esther was not only intended to be read as a book of historical records but that it also describes the recording of historical records and was likely written by someone with access to such records. The book was most likely written in the Persian period, as suggested by the many Persian loan words and a few Greek words found in it. The Hebrew is similar to that of 1 and 2 Chronicles. The third year of Xerxes I (1:3) corresponded with the great war council of Persia in 483 B.C., before the invasion of Greece, and this date could have also coincided with the 180-day banquet described in Esther 1. Given the presence and accuracy of these chronological details, the book was apparently written after this date.

Backgrounds. Xerxes I was the son of Darius I, who gave the decree for the exiled Jews to re-turn to Jerusalem. Described by other historical sources as a king of excess, Xerxes's focus on wealth and sensual pleasures is confirmed by the book of Esther. The Persian Empire consisted of various satrapies, with smaller provinces making up each satrapy. The author of Esther uses the number of the latter to emphasize opulence and prosperity.

Esther and Mordecai lived in Persia after many of the exiles had returned to Jerusalem to rebuild the temple. On first glance, it appears that there is no mention of Esther or Vashti outside the Bible, but careful analysis by several scholars of the details of Xerxes's harem do not rule out equating Vashti with Amestris (even linguistically), the main queen mentioned by Herodotus. Even if this is not the case, the book of Esther does not necessitate Esther being the queen that bore the heir to the throne, so Amestris could have remained the queen mother of Xerxes's heir, Artaxerxes. Clearly, Persian kings had multitudes of women in their harem and probably several queens as well. This may explain why the search for this queen (Esther) took about four years; she may not have been replacing the only queen (2:16–17).

Haman is called an Agagite, identifying him as a descendant of the Amalekite king Agag (1 Sam. 15:8) who represents the ultimate enemy of God's people. If Mordecai's ancestor Kish can be equated to or even related to Saul's father, the rivalry between Haman and Mordecai becomes more than petty and personal, with each standing instead for an entire nation and a continuing feud. In addition to heightening the tension of the story, this connection makes the miraculous deliverance of the Jews even more meaningful.

The entire book of Esther is written in chiastic form, with the last half of the book paralleling in reverse order (and in reversal of roles) the events and situations in the first half of the book. The center hinge is in chapter 6, where the seemingly insignificant event of the king's insomnia brings about the monumental shift in the narrative. In addition, the irony, satire, and humor in Esther showcase the incredible literary skill of the author. Esther is well worth reading slowly, carefully, and repeatedly in order to fully appreciate the drama and the comedy and to saturate the mind's eye with the colorful and sensual descriptions of excess, pomp, and posterity.

Theology and Purpose. The most unique characteristic of the book of Esther is the complete lack of the mention of God's name or even anything overtly religious beyond the act of fasting (not praying) during a time of crisis. While some might see this as a reason to discount any theological message of this book, God's hiddenness is actually the foundation of its theology. God is powerfully though silently active in the narrative.

1. Divine Providence. Woven deeply into this superficially secular book is a passionate and decisive theology of the providence of God: He acted through apparently unrelated and chaotic events to carry out His ultimate purpose. God definitely works through mighty and awesome miracles like that of the Exodus, but these are rare and unusual. Most of the time, God works through circumstances, providentially ordering and orchestrating events and lives to bring people closer to Him and execute His ultimate plan. God is everywhere when we look for Him, and the book of Esther reminds us that seemingly ordinary life events are actually tools in the hands of our sovereign and gracious God, who delivers us out of impossible situations for His glory. Apparent coincidences abound in Esther, but in such dramatic fashion and with such spectacular results as to almost force the reader to consider them miraculous. In addition, total reversals dominate the book, as well as a focus on the overall end result, even by relatively obscure characters like Haman's wife, Zeresh. The book portrays the pride and arrogance of Haman as well as his downfall, especially since he seems to set himself up as a god-like figure. Similarities to the stories of Joseph and Ruth abound, where God's providence is clear and all-powerful. Various allusions to other narratives by word clusters or phrases connect many portions of Esther with religious and God-oriented themes. Thus, as many scholars have noted, upon a careful comparison with the rest of Scripture, and a close reading of the narrative, God's presence shines out of the book of Esther from almost every angle in a veiled form.

For us today, God's presence may also seem far away at times, and yet when we open our eyes, we begin to see God's providence everywhere, through events that initially seem coincidental and random. Unlike the prophets, through whom God spoke all the time, Esther portrays a time more like today, when God does not always seem to give clear direction and humans make choices that seem to range from bad to worse. Instead, we can trust that God is working behind the scenes to care for His people, even in the darkest times.

2. God's Special Care for His People. The book of Esther contains remarkable links to the book of Exodus. In both biblical books God's people face annihilation; in both narratives God sends a human intercessor who intervenes on behalf of God's people; in both instances, the delivery is celebrated by the establishment of a new festival (Passover and Purim) that is closely associated with Israel's identity. The God who is working through human agents behind the scenes of history is committed to care for "the apple of his eye" (Zech. 2:8).

3. God's Instruments. The book of Esther portrays a battle between good and evil, which is a microcosm of the Great Controversy between Christ and Satan. God desires to save everyone who is willing, and salvation was always available (cf. Josh. 2). Sometimes, especially in cases in which the *lex talionis,* or law of retribution, applied, God allowed the people to defend themselves against attack by their enemies, as was the case with Esther. The book of Esther recounts many opportunities for the enemies of the Jews to repent and avoid death, but some still did not. God respects the choice of those who turn away from Him.

Many have noted that the actions of Mordecai and Esther suggested a set of moral values that may in some respects seem questionable, especially when compared to those of Joseph and Daniel in foreign lands, even though the narrative does not draw attention to the problem. Thus, it does not follow that the biblical description of these actions indicates that they should be considered morally acceptable (there are many similar examples in Scripture). Indeed, for both Esther and Mordecai, as they took increasingly risky stands for God in identifying more fully with His people, their concept of right and wrong became more visible and in line with the people of God. Ultimately, God is able to use fallen and faulty people to His glory.

For readers today, this should be very comforting. God is able to use imperfect human agents. If Christians are willing, God will use them right where they are, fallen and faulty. And yet He will also continue to change them into His image, to live more and more faithful lives, as He did for Esther and Mordecai.

4. *A Message of Hope.* Hope abounds in the book of Esther, as well as reminders that God delivers His people even when it seems impossible. Esther is a great book for those who need hope because there is salvation in the midst of hopelessness. It often seems that history itself is under the control of humans and that their own plans for the future will become reality. Esther tells us that, ultimately, it is God who maps out a future for His people—a future of peace and harmony. In Esther the idea of reversal as the manifestation or actualization of hope is very important and may even point to the cosmic reversal at the close of the cosmic conflict. The book of Revelation portrays a similar attempt to exterminate God's people at the end of time (Rev. 13:15), and yet God will work again in a mighty way to bring ultimate deliverance. The great cosmic controversy between Christ and Satan will conclude with a mighty and awesome deliverance of God's people from certain death and a final destruction of sin and the enemies of God and His people (Rev. 19–22).

COMMENTARY

1:1—2:23
Setting the Stage for Change

The first two chapters of Esther move from exaltation to humiliation and back to exaltation. The king was being humiliated by Vashti, the queen, who was soon deposed. This decision resulted in the loss of respect of the king in the eyes of his people. But the scene also moves to the exaltation of Esther, who is selected as queen.

1:1–9. Setting the Scene. The book of Esther opens with a rich and descriptive look into the Persian court, particularly the opulence that characterized a lengthy royal banquet. The king showed the attendees the significant wealth of his glorious kingdom and the splendor and honor of his greatness (1:4). The long strings of nouns in 1:6–7 echo the incredible amount of wealth belonging to Xerxes I and serve almost as a video panorama around the palace. This first feast was all for show in order to bring honor and glory to the king as a result of the awe and speechless wonder engendered

by the ridiculous amount of splendor. This sets up the reader to expect a reversal or downfall, especially when compared with other drunken feasts preceding downfalls in Scripture, like that of Belshazzar in Daniel 5. In addition, although Vashti's name means "best" in Persian, the paucity of description concerning her feast in comparison to Xerxes's (Esth. 1:9) hints at the insignificance to which she, as a person, would soon be relegated.

1:10–22. Vashti's Disobedience and the Aftermath. The language used to describe the king's command for the appearance of the queen classifies her as a subset of the king's honor rather than as her own person (1:10–11). However, highlighting sexism is not the point here. Xerxes is really the one who is portrayed in a negative light. He appears more and more excessive, more and more superficial and petty, and more and more weak as the chapter progresses. Many scholars note his quick changes of mood, his seeming inability to have any clue as to how to deal with his own wife, and his willingness to go along with anything suggested by his officials. This sets the pattern for his characterization as a pushover throughout the rest of the book. He may appear to have been in control, but he was really only reacting to events as they came upon him. It is almost as if the narrator is inviting and expecting the reader to make a mental shift, to see between the lines and discern the divine purpose working through the erratic and unpredictable actions and reactions of the king. Similarly, God is at work today, even in the corrupt and unpredictable actions of current political leaders in the world. What seem to be coincidences are actually God's providences.

The aftereffects of Vashti's refusal to come before Xerxes end up increasing the comical impotence of this initially powerful king. The resulting law was supposed to provide security for the empire, but it actually reflected chaos, revealing the king's impulsive and irrational reactions based on the counsel of his paranoid officials (1:16–20). Almost impossible to enforce, the law universalized the Vashti incident so that it encompassed all wives (1:20), serving to foreshadow what Haman would decree for all Jews out of spite for one Jew, Mordecai. The multilingual character of the decree also set the stage for future issues regarding ethnicity and ancestry. In addition, this decree was intended to hush up the Vashti incident, but instead her deed became known to everyone. The king began by showing his power but ended by being played a fool, both by his wife and his own officials.

2:1–18. Choosing a New Queen. After the king remembered Vashti (2:1), the description of the gathering of the virgins is ambiguous in regard to whether they were brought or came of their own volition. However, one of the primary criteria was beauty, with a focus on what pleased the king (2:4). The description of the virgins as beautiful (2:3) is also used for Vashti in 1:11. We should keep in mind that in the Bible beauty is not only external but that it also includes the qualities of a character that corresponds with the function given to the person. A beautiful queen was one who was attractive but who also embodied the demeanor that was expected of such a person. Even if the virgins were gathered and did not come voluntarily, it was, nevertheless, essentially a beauty contest; although sex was involved, the king probably was not looking primarily for a sexual partner, since he had many, but for a person with the qualities expected from a queen—most importantly, the ability to command the respect and admiration of the court (2:15). Even if this situation was not something that Esther could have avoided, one wishes that she could have been more like Daniel. But the biblical text does not pass any judgment on her; it simply describes what happened and explains how God used imperfect human beings to His glory and finally brought them to a higher spiritual plane. In the same way, God is willing to use us while still working to transform us into His likeness.

Mordecai's ancestry from the tribe of Benjamin may have been intended to hint at his connection to King Saul (2:5). Scholars debate whether it was Mordecai himself or his ancestor Kish who came to Jerusalem. If it were Mordecai, he would be 110 at the beginning of this narrative, so it seems that it must have been his Benjamite ancestor who had the same name as the father of King Saul. However, the connection to Saul's line nevertheless seems intended by the author (cf. 1 Sam. 9:1) since Haman is connected to Agag's line (cf. Deut. 25:17–19; 1 Sam. 15:8). According to 2 Chronicles 36:22–23, Mordecai and his family should have returned with the other exiles rather than staying in the luxury of Persia. In addition, it seems that though they should have publicly identified with God's covenant people, they initially did not (Esth. 2:10). Their names give further evidence of backsliding. Esther's name is very similar to that of the Mesopotamian goddess of love, Ishtar, who supposedly had great sexual powers, and Mordecai's name is related to Marduk, the supreme deity of Babylon.

And yet, Esther received favor (2:15; "grace" in Hebrew), similar to Joseph in Genesis 39:4 (also in a foreign land). Esther sought to do everything she could to make herself a suitable match for the king, asking advice from Hegai, the king's eunuch, who was in charge of the women (Esth. 2:15). Esther became associated with loyalty, obedience, restraint, compliance, and receptiveness. Nothing is said about whether or not she observed Jewish dietary laws. Neither is it clear whether not identifying herself as a Jew was good or not. Clearly, she and Mordecai were concerned about anti-Semitic prejudice.

The comment that Xerxes loved Esther more than all the other women (2:17) refers to the royal selection process—the search for a new queen. However, she also obtained *khen*, meaning "grace" or "favor," and *khesed*, an important word in the OT, variously translated as "mercy," "kindness," "love" from the king—words which imply an emotional bond as well. Even though Esther ended up marrying a pagan, a Gentile, God would work through her disobedience to the law in order to preserve His people.

This took place four years after Vashti was ousted (v. 17)—this is one of the important reversals in the book. The narrator provides no vindication or condemnation of Mordecai and Esther because the point is not to focus on their shortcomings but on the miraculous power of God to deliver His people.

2:19–23. Salvation of the King. Verse 19 does not describe a second gathering of virgins. Instead it notes the time when Mordecai began to sit at the king's gate in an administrative position and saved the king from assassination (2:21). After this, more commands are promulgated by Mordecai and Esther than by the king. The book of Esther is really about Mordecai just as much as Esther. At this point, Esther still did not openly identify with God's people, and she still followed orders (2:20, 22). And yet God was already able to use her to save others—in this case, saving the king by informing him of the assassination attempt. Esther could have taken the credit here, but she was honest and identified Mordecai as her source of information. This incident becomes a key detail in the narrative because the king was negligent to reward Mordecai (2:23). All these events were written in the book of the chronicles or annals of the Persian kingdom.

3:1—5:14
A Plot against the Jews

The story moves to a new level, placing the emphasis on developments within the palace and their impact on the Jews and the nation. At this point there is a strong element of suspense in the plot of the story as evil plans were developed against God's people.

3:1–15. Haman's Ascendency and Plot. The reader would expect Mordecai to be rewarded, but instead it was Haman, a new character in the story, who received the king's favor, and we are not told how or why. The narrator makes clear Haman's connection with Agag the Amalekite king (cf. Ex. 17:8–16; Num. 24:7; Deut. 25:17–19; 1 Sam. 15:8). Israel was to utterly destroy Amalek because of their horrific slaughter of the vulnerable and weak. Indeed, according to 1 Chronicles 4:42–43 many Amalekites were killed, so perhaps the remnant represented here by Haman was a result of a diaspora similar to the Jews in Persia. Often today, the wicked and evil are promoted unfairly, in contrast to the righteous, and we are not usually allowed to know why. However, God works even through these uncertainties and difficulties to bring about His purpose and plan.

While each word can be used to refer to respect given to humans, the combination of the Hebrew words *kara'* and *khawah*—both meaning "to bow down" or "to do obeisance" (Esth. 3:2) is otherwise used only for God (2 Chr. 7:3; 29:29; Pss. 22:29; 95:6). So this action was not about Mordecai disrespecting Haman's authority but implies that Haman was asking for more than the mere respect that the king commanded. The text does not portray Mordecai as arrogant, given to tribal enmity, caring only for monotheism, or even caring for God's dignity. Even today, respect for authority is appropriate, unless that authority is commanding the deference due only to God. Although those who worked with Mordecai knew that he was a Jew, implying that his noncompliance had other motives than disrespect (Esth. 3:4), they were nevertheless bothered by his disobedience and finally reported him to Haman.

Haman's furious response (3:13–14) was similar to the king's (1:20), in that it went beyond what would be reasonable and extended to all the people (similar to how the king went beyond simply shaming Vashti and deposing her). Haman made plans even before he talked to the king and cast lots, which ironically involved

some sort of divination, a belief in divine providence (3:7). The Hebrew word "fall" (usually translated as "cast") for the selection of the day is also used for what ultimately happened to Haman in 6:13. The *pur* ("lot") introduced fate and chance (3:7), as well as links to the Passover and Exodus, which were also in the month of Nisan. The center of divine hiddenness is found in the omission of God's name and the invisible yet powerful providences of God.

Haman's speech to the king was carefully constructed rhetoric, beginning with truth, then proceeding to half lies, and finally ending with flat-out lies. He was full of slanderous and shaming insinuations that would feed into the king's paranoia about rebellious uprisings, as well as his desperate need for money. The king had suffered a major defeat at the hands of the Greeks and was near bankruptcy; therefore the amount of the bribe, corresponding to two-thirds of Persia's total annual income, was attractive to him. Perhaps it would come from the plunder of the Jews. There are many similarities between the speeches of Memucan (1:16–20) and Haman. Both based their arguments on the misappropriation of what belonged to a single other, even though Persians usually loved and encouraged ethnic diversity (see 3:12). This was ironic since Haman was also an outsider, a minority, so he had to create prejudice, using generalities and abstractions such as suggesting that it would be inappropriate and not in the king's best interest to allow the Jews' presence to continue to be tolerated (3:8).

The plot gave no sense of respite until the solution had begun, just like in chapter 1. And yet, in contrast to the previous public decree and banquet of the king, this decree was adopted privately and ended with a private banquet; all the while the city was perplexed and in uproar, confusion, and chaos (3:15). Perhaps the irony of the law (3:12) to all nations was a large part of the confusion. Each person may have been wondering if he or she would be next.

The king carried on his tradition of never rejecting a proposal from one of his advisors. Many connections to Genesis 41:42 can be noted: Pharaoh gave his signet ring to Joseph; also in the Joseph story were false accusations, a decree against the innocent, the rescue of endangered people, and the exaltation of a Jew to prime minister. While this initially may seem to have represented the king's desire to refuse to be responsible for the genocide, he clearly sold the Jews to Haman because he would receive payment (Esth. 7:4). He used his signet ring

(3:10), his scribes or royal secretaries (3:12), and his name (3:12). In addition, the decree was ratified in his presence. Xerxes shows that an uncontrolled need for honor and respect, coupled with absolute power, leads to oppression and injustice.

4:1–17. Esther and Mordecai's Counterplot. This chapter consists of a series of exchanges between Mordecai and Esther. Until this chapter, Esther acted as a proper woman and queen. Once Mordecai asked her to reveal her Jewish identity, her first reaction was to hide it. This stemmed from the reality that Mordecai was commanding Esther to go against the king's direct orders and against the law (4:16). While Vashti was unwilling to appear before the king, Esther had to be ready to appear before him without being requested to come. As a result of Mordecai's pleas, Esther shifted into a new and commanding role as queen, and Mordecai did what she said (4:17). One wonders if the king had lost interest in Esther, which would have heightened the drama and danger since he had not called for her for thirty days (4:11). Esther had already once communicated with the king against the law (2:22), but that was for his protection, whereas this was her own request. Medo-Persian law was very clear that this would mean death for her since it could be considered a threat to the life of the king.

And yet Esther was really part of the solution to the king's dilemma regarding the Jews because she was both a Jew and in power. She wondered whether she would be able to hold to both her heritage and her position. Yet it became clear that God had chosen her for a moment like this and at the same time enabled her to fulfill her role. The story shows that she was ready to fulfill God's purpose at the risk of her life. Verses 9–10 record a short and concise dialogue, showing the speed and intensity of the communication, as well as how ignorant those in the palace were of what was happening in the outside world and how Mordecai knew nothing of what was happening in the palace. Hatach traveled back and forth between Esther and Mordecai, reporting their messages to each other (4:9).

Mordecai had faith that God would take care of His people because he told Esther that if she did not disclose her identity and bring deliverance, relief and deliverance would arise for the Jews from another place (4:14). The presence of God and His plan for deliverance is so clear here that some rabbis call Him "the Place," implying that God would deliver the Jews another way,

no matter what. The text introduces in a veiled form the need for prayer to God. "Fasting, weeping, and wailing" (4:3) are the same words used elsewhere for grief over sin (e.g., Joel 2:12). Even the non-Jews referred to in the book of Esther were religious, so the narrative seems to assume it here. The phrase "who knows" (Esth. 4:14) is used elsewhere by sinners to call upon God for help (2 Sam. 12:22; Joel 2:14; Jon. 3:9), and implies that God may relent as He has in the other cases. Mordecai's genuine grief and agitation make clear that expressing our fears and concerns is sometimes necessary and good.

Esther also called for a fast, which is associated with prayer as well as mourning in Scripture (Esth. 4:16). She continued to remain loyal to the king in how she appeared, even as she prepared to break a law, which could cause her personal harm and complete loss of status and identity. Esther did not hear a word from God, so how did she know what to do? We often think that we must ask for a specific sign or have clear direction from God before proceeding. But although we should seek wisdom from God before acting, God does not always tell us exactly what to do. Many times, He asks us to make a choice, to exercise our free will, use our reasoning powers, and reflect His image. Whatever we choose, we can continue to follow Him in our hearts even when other things are not clear, and He will make His ultimate will happen. God would have made a way for the Jews to be delivered if Esther had not chosen to go before the king, similar to how He raised up David when Saul chose to turn away from God. But Esther did choose to follow the advice of Mordecai, to risk her life for her people, even though we have no record that God told her to do so. Ultimately, God worked mightily through her because of her faith and choice to serve others.

Esther could not avoid disobedience to the king. Yet she did not do at all what Mordecai suggested or the law demanded. As a result, she ended up commanding both the king and Mordecai. This was where she really stepped into her role as queen—and into her place in God's plan of salvation. She initially obeyed Mordecai, but then she took matters into her own hands, identifying with God's people in her own time and way.

5:1–14. Esther's Invitation. The time of Esther's approach was during Passover, which was significant for it recalled God's overlooking the sins of His people, as well as sparing them from judgment and giving it instead to their enemies. Once again the king was pleased with her, and she obtained his favor (5:2). This was another possible implication of God's action behind the scenes (cf. Ex. 12:36). Esther's clothes are mentioned to compare her royalty to that of the king. She stood before him to show royal status, but she waited for the king to invite her to approach out of the inner court of the king's palace (Esth. 5:1). The king realized she must be very troubled to risk her life.

At the feast while drinking wine, Xerxes renewed his request since he realized her invitation to eat did not reveal what she really wanted (5:6). The king made an excessive promise, showing his impulsive and naive nature yet again—or perhaps his respect for the queen. Esther then acted to create a situation that would enable her to ask without having to rely on the king's promise, noting how the banquet was for him, and played on his arrogance by not mentioning Haman at that point. Esther's actions here were politically shrewd and even calculating. God enabled her to exercise the power He gave her. After this moment she is always referred to as "queen" in the book of Esther.

Esther's actions here build tension and suspense, which is further heightened by the lack of windows into her motives. In contrast to the readers' ability to see into Haman's thoughts and insecurities, Esther is portrayed as mysterious and confident, implying that she would win out in the end. She also likely waited because Xerxes was malleable and erratic, and Haman might try to change the mind of the king once again. She chose to set a trap for Haman so she could defeat him quickly and not risk his colluding with the king behind her back. She was also trying to arouse suspicion in the king, illustrating that there is nothing wrong per se with shrewdness and political awareness—they are tools that can be used to accomplish good or evil ends.

This scene plays on the irony of the king's proclamation that all men should rule their homes (1:22) because Esther was in control here, feeding them and getting them drunk. And yet the narrator clues in the readers to the emotions of Haman so that he appears needy and unstable. It becomes clear that his lack of self-control would ultimately be his downfall. Zeresh undermined Haman's role at home as well by talking of deterministic actions, just as Esther did. Haman had boasted about being honored, promoted, and lifted up (Heb. *nasa'*) above others by the king (Esth. 5:11), but in the end he would only be lifted up on a stake. Pride and greed were more important than human life in Persia, as they often are today. But God does not forget His promises, and He can overrule human pride and greed to deliver His people when they seek Him.

6:1—7:10
The Fall of the Enemy

The resolution of the plot of the narrative is filled with suspense. The powerful appeared to have in his hand the future of God's people, and there was no majestic and visible manifestation of the power of God to save them. But the Lord was working from within the narrative as the main protagonist in charge of its course and ending.

6:1–14. The King's Insomnia and Mordecai's Ascendancy. This chapter documents events emphasizing how it was on that very night when God intervened and the reversal began (6:1). The Hebrew verb in the phrase referring to the king's insomnia (lit. "sleep fled the king") shows that the king was not the one acting—this again hints at divine involvement. This is especially true when considering the accumulation of circumstances: no sleep for the king (6:1), nothing had been done to honor Mordecai (6:3), the records of the chronicles that were read to the king (6:1), and the fact that Haman happened to be outside in the outer court (6:4). The juxtaposition of all of these events further confirms that the insomnia had some cause other than the king. Even the reference to the account of Mordecai being found suggests a search was ordered, perhaps a recollection of unrewarded action or a divine appointment (6:2).

God works through ordinary events, even through things that are full of humor and irony, with a motif of concealment. In the book of Esther, chapter 6 is the narrative center, apparently Mordecai's lowest point, but also Haman's because of his pride. This exhibits a connection with eschatology, a reversal of fortunes, when all seems to be lost for God's people. At the last possible moment, when there seems to be no other way of escape, and when destruction is certain, God intervenes and brings a mighty deliverance. In v. 6, the king asked for advice, his impulsivity characteristic of one who was easily moved to honor others. It appears that Haman was standing in the court like Esther had been, coming to make a request, highlighting his vulnerability, insecurity, and egocentric nature. Haman's response should have been perceived as odd, even signaling a coup attempt with designs on the throne (see 1 Kin. 1:33–40).

The ensuing scene in Esther 6:8–9 is almost ludicrous, with a massive reversal between Mordecai and Haman, as well as between Mordecai and the king. The narrator does not give clues as to whether the king had forgotten he had decreed Jewish destruction, and the silence heightens the dramatic tension. Haman's hurried return to his house was another sign of the reversal of his decree, with which the couriers had hurried (6:12; cf. 3:15). Zeresh and Haman's friends seem to have known of commands and promises that predicted the fall of Amalek and Israel's triumph (v. 13; cf. Ex. 17:16; Num. 24:15–20; Deut. 25:17–19; 1 Sam. 15); even seeing Haman's humiliation as the first step. Indeed, Haman was hastened again (Esth. 6:14), this time to face ultimate humiliation, while Mordecai now looked more like the king than the king.

7:1–10. Haman's Fall. Both Esther and Haman pled for their lives, but ultimately Haman fell before the Persian queen, a Jew, though she triumphed over him with her shrewdness and not a sword. She began by hosting another banquet with the drinking of wine (7:2), implying security, victory, and the opposite of fasting, and the narrative is more gripping since her request has still not be made. Esther had the very delicate task of accusing Haman, but not the king (v. 3), since in a way the king was equally responsible for the planned genocide of the Jews. To do this, she used the phrase, "If I have found favor with you" (lit. "in your eyes"), which suggests intimacy and personal favor (v. 3). She also used the king's own terms—*she'elah,* meaning "petition," and *baqqashah,* meaning "request"—and reconnected with her people (v. 3). Esther's rhetorical skill matched that of Haman's masterful speeches. She intimated that to kill her people was to kill her because she realized that the king would show less vigor to save others than to save her. She may also have hinted (v. 4) at the king's decree. She used the same words as he did (3:13; cf. Judg. 2:14, 3:8). The queen tried to persuade the king that she had his best interests at heart, using the same words as Haman in Esther 3:8, 13 in regard to the destruction of the Jews.

This chapter is full of irony. Esther implied that the king was so important that the queen would rather be sold as a slave than bring this matter to his attention (7:4), and yet Esther's pose as a weak and helpless woman does not fool the reader. Esther also hinted at the money

involved with her reference to her people being sold as male and female slaves. She may have been arguing (at least according to some translations of the last part of the verse) that Haman was not actually interested in the king's welfare or Haman would have sold the Jews (v. 4). She realized that the king's convenience was the primary factor in his decisions, and he would lose labor if he lost the Jews. Likely, Esther's meekness and caution here were tactical, not manifestations of her personality, similar to Nathan's waiting to give David's name in his accusatory parable in 2 Samuel 12. In Esther 7:6 she used the balanced and resonant Hebrew sentence "*haman hara' hazzeh*" (meaning "this wicked/vile Haman"), which parallels the king's question in structure and gives the sense of a couple verbally dancing back and forth. The accusation came with force like Nathan's to David.

The king then redrew lines of personal allegiance according to criteria of royalty even though it seems it took the king a while to realize what had happened because his selling of the Jews had been so offhand. The king and queen were now working together against a common enemy. Haman was startled and disturbed, terrified before the king and queen because Esther's wit and charm effectively disassociated the king from the evil deed (7:6). Haman's panic led to misconduct that the king would use to justify his condemnation. The rage of the king followed a similar pattern as in previous incidents: instigation, rage, recommendation, implementation, return of pleasure.

Haman violated royal Persian protocol: only the king could be alone with any of his wives, so Haman should have left. Nevertheless, his departure would have suggested guilt or invited pursuit, so he was left in a very difficult position. Verse 8 contains a play on words, truly a humorous scene, as the king could now misinterpret Haman's intention: Haman is portrayed as falling on the couch, upon Esther, or both (the Hebrew is rather ambiguous). While this can also be interpreted as supplication (cf. 8:3; 1 Sam. 25:24), the ambiguity appears intentional. Haman was rendered speechless for once, and the word "fall" sealed his fate—while others cast (lit."caused to fall") the lot before him in Esther 3:7, he began to "fall" before Mordecai in 6:13.

The king looked for a convenient excuse to eliminate Haman, being now more concerned with the royal dignity (yet wives were easier to come by than prime ministers). In 7:9, it becomes clear that the palace staff favored Esther, and the king could not even formulate a coherent response. Esther did not show mercy here because Haman was an Amalekite and was not contrite. It was also not hers to offer; his fate had been devised by his own handiwork. In v. 10, the king's anger subsided when Haman suffered a fate planned for another, but for a crime he did not commit, and yet he deserved the punishment (cf. Ps. 7:16; Prov. 26:27). This turn of events shows how God's deliverance reverses impossible situations. Believers must ask for open eyes to see how God is working in their lives, especially when He seems most hidden.

8:1—10:3
The Triumph of God's People

The threat of extinction caused anguish to the people of God because the threat was universal. It moved from the palace to the whole kingdom. God was going to be left without a witness on earth, and this was not acceptable to Him. He would give wisdom and power to His human instruments to overcome and, at the end, to joyfully celebrate the victory.

8:1–17. The Salvation of the Jews and the Choosing of a New Prime Minister. This chapter begins with the comment that the events in the previous verses took place on that very day (cf. 3:13). The reversal was complete. Esther assumed Haman's position and took his wealth to give to the Jews. Mordecai received the signet ring from the king, and Esther put him in charge of Haman's house—that is, his estate (8:2). However, Esther had one more request for the king, and the scenario proceeds in a very similar way as in chapter 5 when she came before the king. Esther fell down before the king, but in this instance, she sought her own good and that of her people (8:3). The graphic description of her begging with tears (8:3) connotes intensity and importunity often used only for God.

Esther was clearly unsure of her reception since this exceeded her original petition, and so she used four elements of deference: she expressed her request in terms of whether it pleased the king, if she was regarded with favor by him, if her request seemed right to him, and if she was pleasing to him (8:5). Her request bundled approval and love together so Xerxes would find it difficult to separate the two. To the king, Esther was queen first, Jewish second, so she concluded with a lament aimed to avert destruction (v. 6; cf. Lam. 2:11; Esth. 4:1). This was not a mere request but a challenge against the administration, legal axioms, and kingdom

organization that were so convoluted and bureaucratic. Esther appealed to the king's pity, knowing she would be overcome with anguish if her people were to suffer.

Verse 8 notes a quirk of Persian law: even the king could not withdraw the first set of documents because decrees made in the king's name and set with his seal could not be revoked. So the king, in a sense, appears to have abdicated the throne—he allowed Esther to write a counter decree. The decree closely mimics Esther 3:12–15: written with the king's name (8:10), sealed with his signet ring (v. 10), and sent to all provinces and in their own language (v. 9). This underscored the new safety and security accorded Jews. Even their language was given official status.

Verse 11 uses the same three verbs that were used to describe Haman's attempted genocide. According to some translations, the decree specifically mentioned the protection of the Jewish women and children; according to others, it mentioned the right of the Jews to destroy any women and children of the people involved in an assault against them. The main point in the latter case would be primarily to mirror the original decree (cf. 3:13). In confirmation of this, the Jews actually did not take spoil, but they were given permission to do so if they wished. The decree emphasized the defensive counteraction that Jews could take, in the reversal of national fortune through a preemptive strike. The allowance for avenging (8:13) does not refer to personal vengeance but to a punitive action based on the law, assuming a prior wrong (Haman's edict) and a guaranteed right to defend themselves.

The mood in the citadel was very different from that of 3:15. The city was joyful at this decree (8:15) rather than being in turmoil. Mordecai departed from the king clothed in royal robes (8:15), in contrast to Haman in chapter 3, who was inside the palace and oblivious to what was happening in the city. These garments of Mordecai symbolized the highest degree of royal recognition. These same materials are all mentioned in Xerxes's feast in chapter 1. The reference to light (or happiness), gladness, joy, and honor (8:16) reverses the fasting, weeping, and wailing of 4:3. Gladness and joy are often used to describe delight in response to divine presence and deliverance (8:16).

In light of this, many non-Jews became Jews (8:17). A similar situation is recorded in Nehemiah 10:29, where Gentiles separated from the nations to follow God's law. Even though the change was ethnic, it also involved religious awe.

Similarly, Genesis 31:53 notes that God is the "Fear of Isaac," so there could be a veiled reference to God here in the phrase "fear of the Jews," showcasing God's presence or intervention in history (Esth. 8:17). Similarly, 2 Chronicles 17:10 states that the "fear of Yahweh fell on the nations" and resulted in the protection of Israel from her enemies.

The resolution was a complete reversal: Mordecai came with royal garb, Jews experienced joy and gladness, and others became Jews. While some argue that this was not a heartfelt conversion, when Esther 8:17 is connected with 9:27, the conversion was clearly genuine. Fear or awe that leads to conversion is the work of God. No one was forced to convert because the decree only allowed self-defense by the Jews. But Haman and his gods were defeated, so this revelation of the work of the Jewish God moved their hearts. For us today, when decisions are made to live for God, others are moved, especially those who are searching for more than materialistic goods and fleeting pleasures. It may seem that there are very few souls ripe for the harvest, but a choice to follow God under great duress can lead many others to follow Him as well.

9:1—10:3. The Last Feasts and Purim. This last section is very different in narration, style, vocabulary, and content, with less story and more history and legal counsel. Mordecai is portrayed as similar to Moses. The fear of the Jews (v. 2) and the fear of Mordecai (v. 3) are noted even though the fear of God would fit perfectly, designating God's presence and intervention in history (cf. Ex. 15:14–16; Josh. 2:8–11). All gave honor to Mordecai, showing Jewish attainment of complete political mastery. Mordecai became more famous, prominent, and powerful (Esth. 9:4) than Haman had been (3:1). Mordecai's standing at court prompted government officials to help the Jews (9:3), who were now in a similar situation as Esther had been when she gained favor in the eyes of the king. The focus here is on dominion and honor, not slaughter.

The names of the ten sons of Haman are ancient Persian names associated with demonic powers (9:10). It seems probable that they organized active hostility during the months following the issuing of the decree. In contrast, the Jews followed the rules of Deuteronomy 13:6–18, and they took no plunder even though Mordecai's decree allowed them to take spoil. This reprisal was necessary because their enemies gloated and the king seemed indifferent to their suffering (Esth. 3:11, 15). However, the Festival of Purim celebrated getting rest or relief from their enemies (9:16), which implied that the ultimate victory over enemies is due to a transcendental power, not human strength. The people responded collectively to establish the days of Purim (9:26), a spontaneous response to God's faithfulness. And in yet another play on words, the reference to the presents that the people were to send to each other uses the same Hebrew word that is used for Esther's portion in 2:9. This word also refers to the gifts or choice food morsels that are given to the poor to celebrate God giving them a portion (9:22).

Purim thus celebrated relief (not killing), with an emphasis on deliverance (not overpowering or domination). Anyone was free to join them, including future converts (cf. Is. 14:1; 56:3, 6). It was a religious celebration that sought no political advantage. In the edict to inaugurate the Festival of Purim, Esther wrote with full authority, and Mordecai sent letters to the Jews (Esth. 9:29–30), continuing to integrate their Persian and Jewish identities (vv. 31–32). Mordecai was respected and well loved by all, and he sought their good and their welfare (10:3)—the literal Hebrew here refers to speaking peace. This was an action that is otherwise attributed only to God and His speaking promises to His people (cf. Ps. 85:8). Throughout Scripture, the secular roles of God's people are significant, but they give us a challenge to act in the face of oppression, even when risks seem imminent. The hope of God's deliverance will not be frustrated because He is the ultimate Deliverer, yet He works behind the scenes through faulty yet courageous humans to bring about His sovereign and providential plan.

POETRY AND
WISDOM BOOKS

INTRODUCTION TO HEBREW POETRY AND WISDOM BOOKS

The beauty of poetry and its characteristics are difficult to transfer from an unfamiliar original language to a second one. The fullness of the beauty of Hebrew poetry can be totally enjoyed only through the original Hebrew language. Yet there is much that we can learn about it and its function through the study of the English translations of the Bible. These translations have done all that is possible to preserve the nature of Hebrew poetry.

POETIC BOOKS OF THE OLD TESTAMENT

Traditionally Job, Psalms, Proverbs, Ecclesiastes, Song of Songs, and Lamentations are considered to be the poetic books of the OT. The Hebrew Bible locates these poetic books among the *ketubim* (Writings), the third section within the threefold division of the Hebrew canon (Law, Prophets, and Writings). The first three books (Job, Psalms, and Proverbs) are grouped together as the *sipre 'emet* (books of truth), or just poetic books, whereas the second three books (Ecclesiastes, Songs of Songs, and Lamentations) form part of the *megillot*—the five scrolls (including also the books of Ruth and Esther) that are traditionally read during the Jewish holidays. In addition to the poetic books and the *megillot*, the *ketubim* also include a short list of historical books, namely, Daniel (placed among the prophets in the Protestant canon), Ezra and Nehemiah (originally combined into a single book in the Hebrew Bible), and both Chronicles (also originally a single book). The Protestant canon includes these books in the section of the poetic books except for Lamentations, which is placed with Jeremiah among the prophetic books of the OT.

POETRY VERSUS PROSE

Thinking of Hebrew poetry, one usually focuses on the six books mentioned above that are composed entirely or mostly of verse. Nevertheless, within the remainder of the Hebrew Bible, poetry appears so frequently that scholars have asked how much of the OT is poetry and how much is prose. Suggestions range from the traditional one third to the assertion that most of the OT was written as poetry. Furthermore, the claim of an artificial distinction between prose and poetry has become a widely discussed topic in the literary study of the OT and has been examined within narrative criticism. Beyond the six poetic books, the central role of poetry in the prophetic literature of the OT and even within the Pentateuch (which contains several highly significant poetic passages) has been recognized.

Beginning in the 1980s, the study of Hebrew poetry has undergone a revival that has to be understood within the context of literary criticism, which, in turn, was an expression of the growing discontent with the results—or lack of results—of historical criticism. While earlier introductions to Hebrew poetry focused on technique and style, more recent studies have addressed poetic theory, namely, the questions of how to distinguish between poetry and prose and if such a distinction can be made anyway. It became clear that it is not possible to apply modern literary notions about poetry and prose to ancient Hebrew poetry and prose. One important issue in the debate is the question of the parallelism of poetic phrases, a feature that the Anglican Bishop Robert Lowth identified in 1753 as the foremost principle of Hebrew poetry.

Moving far beyond Lowth's early and somewhat mechanistic definitions of parallelism, scholars have now recognized the linguistic complexities of parallelism and its sophisticated workings on grammatical, lexical, semantic, and phonological levels. Thus, scholars have been able to move toward a list of characteristics that, through their relative frequency, distinguish poetry from prose in the Hebrew Bible: (1) terseness or conciseness; (2) ellipses or omission of verbal forms; (3) parallelism; (4) word pairs; (5) imagery; (6) less predictable tense sequence and word order; (7) lack of syntactical markers; (8) fronting (i.e., placing elements before the main verb); and (9) decontextualization (i.e., isolating poetic discourse from its context). This list is by no means comprehensive, and other scholars have approached the subject from a linguistic, statistical perspective, indicating that the three prose particles (i.e., the definite article *he* ["the"], the relative pronoun *'asher* ["that," "which," "whom"], and the marker of the definite object *'et* [not translated into English]) are conspicuously absent in Hebrew poetry, so that a count lower than five would indicate poetry, while those above fifteen would point toward prose. For the middle range (five to fifteen), they propose a new category—prophetic discourse, which mixes prose and poetry. The general tendency appears to be that the difference between prose and poetry is more a matter of degree than one of kind, and scholars are looking for methods that will make the distinction more objectively.

Variations of prose and poetry are not only a matter of different books containing primarily poetry or primarily prose, but the variations are also to be found throughout the entire Hebrew Bible. Generally, the Pentateuch has not been the preferred terrain for the study of Hebrew poetry since its style is mainly descriptive and prescriptive narrative with some personal discourse. However, there are four major poems in the Pentateuch (Gen. 49; Ex. 15; Num. 23–24; Deut. 32–33) that are found at theologically important places, aside from numerous other smaller poetic units (beginning with Gen. 2:23; 3:14–19). This trend continues throughout the remainder of the Hebrew Bible so that scholars have started to speak of inset poetry (i.e., poetry that has been deliberately and strategically placed within prose to underline or highlight an important theological point).

Another good example, outside of the Pentateuch, is Jonah 2, also known as Jonah's psalm, which some scholars in the past identified as a later addition. It has now become apparent that this inset poem serves an important role in the narrative structure of the whole prophetic book.

There are two chapters in the OT (Judg. 4–5) that illustrate the subtle differences between Hebrew poetry and prose in a fascinating way because they reference the same event, once in prose (Judg. 4) and then again in poetry (Judg. 5). The story is the courageous killing of Sisera, commander of the Canaanite army of Jabin, king of Hazor, by Jael, the wife of Heber. For the sake of this discussion, only one verse from each chapter is selected to highlight these differences:

Judges 4:19	**Judges 5:25**
Then he said to her, "Please give me some water. I am thirsty." So she opened a container of milk, gave him a drink, and covered him. (author's translation)	For water he asked, Milk she gave; In a bowl fit for lords, She brought curdled milk. (author's translation)

The original Hebrew counts fourteen words in prose versus eight words in poetry. The prose version tells a linear story, giving heightened attention to what Jael provided to Sisera when he entered her tent, in order to lure him into a false sense of safety (he asked for a bit of water, but she gave him milk and then covered him with a blanket). The poetic account of the same moment works with parallel and simultaneous contrasts, juxtaposing "water" and "milk" and placing (fronting) them before the two contrastive verbs ("ask" and "give"). The third and fourth lines (called *cola*) then intensify the initial contrast by describing the bowl as a special vessel designed for lords and the milk as curdled, probably a type of rich, creamy yogurt that is fit for nobles. While both texts complement each other, there is no feeling of redundancy, and the poetry even tells a slightly different and more profound story with significantly fewer words. Consequently, Hebrew poetry is not a literary embellishment or poetic reformulation of narrative content.

CHARACTERISTICS OF HEBREW POETRY

The reader must recognize the limitations of understanding Hebrew poetry through the lens of modern Bible versions. However, modern translators have an increasing understanding of the workings of Hebrew poetry so that the complexities of the original language are not lost altogether. While it is difficult to translate assonances, the most important aspect of Hebrew poetry—the usage of parallelism—is usually well preserved in modern translations. The following characteristics of Hebrew poetry are mostly based on the modern English translations and provide an adequate panorama to the modern reader of the richness of God's word in its original language.

Layout in Poetic Lines (Colography)

The oldest complete Hebrew manuscripts of the OT, dated to the tenth century A.D., set the poetic sections into lines of poetry, called *cola* (plural of *colon*), by either punctuation or spacing (or both), thus differentiating it from prose. This is called colography. When the text of the Hebrew Bible was vocalized (vowels were added to the words, because written Hebrew originally consisted of only consonants) between the sixth and eleventh centuries A.D. by generations of Jewish scholars called the Masoretes, they used a system of disjunctive accents that mark the boundary of a colon (i.e., a poetic line). However, the accents were not primarily made to differentiate between prose and poetry but to facilitate recitation, and thus, colography serves as only one criterion for determining poetry. Furthermore, the Talmud indicates that in the manuscripts the delimitations of a bicolon (i.e., a verse in poetry consisting of two lines or cola) are indicated by aligning one colon to the right and the other to the left margin of the text, leaving a blank space in between. Most ancient manuscripts follow this layout, and colographic layouts are found in the oldest complete manuscripts of the Hebrew Bible. Ancient translations like the LXX follow this colographic layout of the Hebrew manuscripts, and most modern versions indicate the difference between prose and poetry based on ancient manuscript colography by changing between a justified layout and indented, broken-up lines.

Meter

Meter in Hebrew poetry arranges phonological events in a pattern that repeat themselves in successive lines. The question of meter in Hebrew verse has been a major point of contention among scholars throughout history. The biggest hindrance in determining Hebrew poetic meter is modern ignorance of the original pronunciation of ancient Hebrew, as only consonants were used. Modern theories of meter put emphasis on the similarities between lines, instead of superimposing a metric system that is derived from non-Semitic or modern languages. That does not mean that Hebrew poetry lacks rhythm; parallelism produces a certain rhythm because each colon usually consists of three words and each poetic line usually has two (*bicolon*), sometimes three (*tricolon*), and rarely four cola (*quadrocolon*).

Syntax

The sentence structure of Hebrew poetry is different from that of prose, and it shows a certain terseness or compactness. Poetic lines are shorter and more concise than sentences in prose. Furthermore, poems in the OT outside the Psalms rarely exceed thirty verses, and there are no epic poems in the Hebrew Bible. Transitions between poetic lines often are not expressed and connecting words (conjunctions) are missing. Often there is omission of the verb (i.e., there is no verb in the second line and the action of the verb in the first line is implied). Psalm 49:3 offers a good illustration:

> My mouth shall speak wisdom,
> And the meditation of my heart shall be understanding. (ESV)

The verb *speak* from the first line is omitted in the second line but really constitutes the implied action of both parallel lines. Nevertheless, *meditation* in English does not speak, so translators opt to provide alternatives—in the case above, "shall be." In Hebrew, however, it does speak because the noun *hagut* ("meditation") refers to the audible recitation or uttering of God's word and thus references "speaking" as well (cf. Pss. 1:2; 143:5).

Parallelism

As mentioned before, the most important feature of Hebrew poetry is parallelism, first identified by Robert Lowth in 1753 in his *Lectures on the Sacred Poetry of the Hebrews*. His classic definition in his *Isaiah: A New Translation with a Preliminary Dissertation and Notes, Critical, Philological, and Explanatory* still holds: "The correspondence of one verse, or line with another, I call parallelism." Lowth initially established three categories for parallelism in Hebrew poetry, which, however, have proven to be limited in scope and somewhat mechanistic.

1. *Synonymous parallelism*: The second line provides a restatement of the first:

> Praise the LORD, all you Gentiles!
> Laud Him, all you peoples! (Ps. 117:1; NKJV)

2. *Antithetical parallelism*: The second line is the opposite of the first:

> A wise son makes a glad father,
> But a foolish son is the grief of his mother. (Prov. 10:1; NKJV)

3. *Synthetic parallelism*: The second line completes, complements, or expands the first:

> Let him lead me to the banquet hall,
> and let his banner over me be love. (Song 2:4; NIV)

From this first definition, the concept of parallelism has constantly evolved, and it has become apparent that parallelism in Hebrew poetry is much more complex and can occur on various levels. The result is a more current definition: parallelism is the recurrence of grammatical, lexical, semantic, and phonological aspects in two adjacent lines. Rarely, the recurrence is identical and the correspondence between lines serves not only to equate two lines of Hebrew text but also to enhance, support, or intensify line A through line B. Thus, in the following examples, a range of linguistic features and aspects that constitute parallelism in Hebrew poetry is considered.

4. *Word pairs*: These are terms that are frequently grouped together. The discovery of Ugaritic poetry (Ugarit or Ras Shamra was an ancient port city in Northern Syria boasting an alphabetic Semitic language containing many similarities to biblical Hebrew) has promoted the study of word pairs in Hebrew poetry, which primarily takes place on a lexical level. Isaiah 1:2 (NIV) says:

> Hear me, you heavens!
> Listen, earth!

The word pair *heavens-earth* is used throughout the OT as the predominant descriptor of the created world. It is used to denote either the totality of the created cosmos or the contrasted parts of the cosmos. Word pairs also occur outside of poetic texts, as in Genesis 1 where *heaven-earth* is used as a *merism* (two contrasting words referring to a totality) pointing to the cosmological dimension of the Creation account.

5. *Grammatical parallelism*: This form of parallelism exhibits corresponding syntactic grammatical structures that are rarely identical. In Psalm 6:5 (NKJV), a declaration is set in parallel to a question:

> For in death there *is* no remembrance of You;
> In the grave who will give You thanks?

6. *Semantic parallelism*: The emphasis here is on the meaning of words and can either be paradigmatic (belonging to a certain class, like *man* and *woman*) or syntagmatic (creating similar sequential structures) associations of words. Psalm 111:6 (NKJV) says:

> He has declared to His people the power of His works,
> In giving them the heritage of the nations.

The correspondence between *people* and *nations* is paradigmatic in that they belong to the same semantic domain of *groups and classes of persons*. Nevertheless, the terms are also syntagmatically related, as there is a sequential progression from "His people" (Israel) to the nations, underlining the special election of Israel among the other nations in this verse.

7. *Phonetic parallelism*: Alliteration (repetition of same or similar consonantal sounds) and assonance (repetition of same or similar vocalic sounds) are the two most common phonetic parallelisms, which, unfortunately, are largely lost in any translation from one language to another. For example, the Hebrew text of Isaiah 22:5a uses a phrase that is full of alliteration and assonance: *mehumah—mebusah—mebukah*. In an attempt to preserve the original phonetic parallelism, this has been translated as "a day of tumult and trampling and terror" (NIV).

It is evident that there are many ways to activate linguistic equivalence and, with that, parallelism. The concentration or density of these phenomena indicates the presence of a parallelism and, thus, of Hebrew poetry.

Repetition and Recurrence

This poetic device points specifically to the repeated use of words and phrases that can be employed in a variety of ways that go beyond the parallelism of two (*bicolon*) or three (*tricolon*) lines. Psalm 122 serves as a good example, as it includes a number of poetic devices that are based on repetition and recurrence.

1. *Keywords*: The recurrence of the same word or words in the original Hebrew creates a focus on the message of the poem. In Psalm 122, three times "Jerusalem" is mentioned (Ps. 122:2, 3, 6; Heb. *yerushalaim*) and three times the word "peace" (Ps. 122:6, 7, 8; Heb. *shalom*), which in Hebrew are both derived from the same root (*shlm*). This immediately

brings the message of Psalm 122 to the forefront, namely, the peace of Jerusalem, which emanates from the temple.

2. *Inclusio*: A correspondence between the beginning and end of the poem creates a framing device or bookend, which often serves as a thematic framework. The "house of the Lord" in v. 1 and v. 9 frames Psalm 122 and points to its thematic focus.

3. *Anaphora*: Sequential lines begin with the same word or phrase. Verses 4 and 5 begin with the same Hebrew adverb of place (*sham*), which creates a movement toward the temple as the pilgrims ascend to Jerusalem, whereas vv. 8 and 9 begin with the conjunction *lema'an*, which points to the results of what has taken place in the sanctuary.

4. *Anadiplosis*: This is a rhetorical device in which the last word of the line is repeated as the first word in the next line. Verse 2 ends and verse 3 begins with "Jerusalem"; v. 4a ends and v. 4b begins with "tribes."

5. *Cataphora*: These are sequential lines that end with the same word or phrase—e.g., Isaiah 40:13–14, where both verses end with *yodi'enu* ("he made known to Him").

6. *Immediate repetition*: In Isaiah 40:1 the word "comfort" is repeated twice in order to introduce the consolation of Zion in the second part of the book.

7. *Refrain*: A phrase is repeated at the end of each subdivision. In Psalm 136, the phrase "for His mercy/love [Heb. *khesed*] endures forever" is repeated twenty-six times at the end of each verse as a liturgically composed antiphonal refrain, most probably sung as a response from the congregation when this psalm was performed.

8. *Chiasm*: This device involves lines being arranged in a cross-like pattern (ABB'A' or ABCB'A') with correspondence between the outer lines by which a focus on the center is created. A chiastic structure can even go beyond the boundaries of an individual poem; for example, Psalms 15–24 create a chiasm around the second *torah* psalm, Psalm 19. This points to the composition of the Psalms as a whole book with complex interconnections between its 150 poems. Chiastic structures are not limited to poetic texts only.

9. *Acrostic*: In an acrostic poem, each sequential line or stanza begins with the next letter of the Hebrew alphabet. In the most famous acrostic poem, Psalm 119, each stanza consists of eight verses, which each begin with the same letter of the Hebrew alphabet, followed by the next stanza of eight lines with the next letter of the Hebrew alphabet.

Imagery

An integral part of Hebrew poetry is the usage of imagery. In employing imagery, the poet creates a picture in the hearer's (or reader's) mind using a variety of devices, of which simile and metaphor are the most widely represented.

1. *Simile*: A simile compares one thing to another, and it makes the comparison explicit by using the formula *like* or *as*. An example appears in Proverbs 25:25, which states that "cold water to a weary soul" is like good news received from far away.

2. *Metaphor*: Metaphor is a deliberate form of figurative speech that works on both word and sentence level. A simplified definition of metaphor describes it as an implied comparison.

Hebrew poetry lends itself to imagery because its most prevalent literary device, parallelism, implies comparison between two lines. Psalm 23 describes God as a Shepherd in the first part of the poem and as a royal Host in the second part, whereas v. 4 creates a seam between both metaphors, overlapping both images in adjacent poetic lines in the center of the poem. It is interesting to note that language about God is often metaphorical in nature, pointing to the fact that the unknown reality of the divine is best expressed by way of known and familiar imagery.

POETRY AND WISDOM

Within the body of poetic texts in the OT, wisdom literature takes a prominent place. The principal wisdom books of the Hebrew Bible are Job, Proverbs, and Ecclesiastes. A number of scholars also include Songs of Songs in this group, although there appears to be a lack of explicit concern for wisdom in the poetic book since the word *wisdom* is not used at all. Beyond these texts, there are a number of wisdom psalms in the Psalms (e.g., Pss. 1; 34; 37; 49; 73; 111; 112) and further passages containing wisdom concepts and ideas throughout the OT (e.g., Gen. 37–50; 1 Sam. 25:2–42; Isa. 26; Amos 3:3–8).

Terminology

The Hebrew word *khokmah*, which occurs eighteen times in Job, thirty-nine times in Proverbs, and twenty-eight times in Ecclesiastes, represents the lexical term around which wisdom literature is organized in the OT. It can be translated as "wisdom," "aptitude," "skill," "experience," "good sense," and a variety of other terms. Further words that relate to wisdom are *binah* ("understanding"; e.g., Prov. 1:2) and *tushiyyah* ("sound wisdom" or "success"; e.g., Prov. 2:7). Semantically, *khokmah* does not belong to the realm of theoretical knowledge or philosophy but rather refers to a proper understanding of the basic realities of life and of God's dealings with humanity and the human role as moral agents. It is often found through observation and analysis and by drawing conclusions that help to understand the social, spiritual, and natural order of the world.

Themes

There is a close connection between "the fear of the LORD" and wisdom as epitomized in Proverbs 1:7: "The fear of the LORD is the beginning of knowledge" (cf. Job 28:28; Ps. 111:10; Prov. 9:10; 15:33). Thus, a relationship with Yahweh is the thematic point of departure for wisdom, as much as He is also wisdom's destination. The intimate correlation between God and wisdom is indicative of its mystery as well as the importance of its pursuit as a lifelong endeavor, in which choices are governed by divine perspectives. However, further themes of wisdom touch on all spheres of life.

Prosperity and suffering constitute a second grand theme of wisdom literature, touching on the question of theodicy (i.e., divine goodness and the existence of evil) and the fallacies of a rigid and unnuanced retribution theology (Job; cf. Ps. 73; Eccl. 7:15).

A third major theme of wisdom poetry can be found in the evaluation of human conduct and moral action. The first chapters of Proverbs lay out the ideals of human conduct by means of an instructional father-son conversation (Prov. 1–9), culminating with the personification of wisdom in Proverbs 8 where it is related to Creation (Prov. 8:22–31).

Historical and Social Context

Considering the date and authorship of the three principal wisdom books, it becomes apparent that wisdom sayings constituted an early element in the oral and literary traditions of the ANE and Israel itself. Moses's authorship of the book of Job can be established on various grounds, and Ellen White connects its writing to the forty years that Moses spent in the Midian desert during the first half of the fifteenth century B.C., before leading the Israelites out of Egypt (ST, February 19, 1880, Art. A, par. 14). His early education in Egypt brought him into close contact with Egyptian wisdom literature and concepts of wisdom (e.g., the cosmological principle of *ma'at*—representing truth and world order), which date as far back as the third millennium B.C. Furthermore, wisdom literature in Egypt was closely connected to the royal court, which is also reflected in the Solomonic authorship of Proverbs and Ecclesiastes. A major portion of the *Instruction of Amenemopet*, an Egyptian wisdom text with didactic features dating to 1150 B.C., has parallels in Proverbs 22:17—24:34 (see Proverbs: Introduction), and Solomon's connections to Egypt through his marriage to a daughter of the pharaoh (1 Kin. 3:1) are evident in literature and history. A number of Mesopotamian wisdom works have been connected to the theme of theodicy in Job, like the Old Babylonian *Poem of the Righteous Sufferer*, dated 1500–1200 B.C. However, as in all matters of comparison, one has to carefully evaluate similarities and differences and not assume immediately that the biblical documents were influenced by the extrabiblical ones. In Hebrew culture, wisdom was used to instruct royalty (Dan. 1:4), judges (1 Kin. 3:28), teachers/sages (Jer. 18:18), and children (Prov. 1:8), moving far beyond the royal court.

Literary Forms

Wisdom poetry in the OT employs a variety of literary forms to communicate its instructions.

1. *Sayings*: The Hebrew term *mashal* ("saying") is the technical term for a proverb or wisdom saying.

2. *Admonition*: An admonition can appear as a command (Prov. 16:3) or as a prohibition (Prov. 30:10).

3. *Numerical saying*: This usually follows a numerical pattern (Prov. 30:18–19) reminiscent of a riddle that, once resolved, provides a benefit to the person who solved it (cf. Judg. 14:14). The numerical saying seems to suggest that there are more cases than those listed, motivating the reader to look for them.

4. *Rhetorical question*: Such a question has an implied and obvious answer (Prov. 30:4).

5. *Exhortation*: This occurs often in the context of parental instruction and tends to be more extensive (Prov. 1:8–19).

6. *Personification*: Wisdom is personified as in the woman Wisdom and woman Folly of Proverbs 1–9.

7. *Dialogue*: A dialogue states and counterstates the human conceptions of wisdom and theodicy, eventually with correction by the wisdom of God Himself (Job 3–41).

8. *Parable, fable, allegory*: These literary devices often take on narrative forms to communicate wisdom truths (2 Sam. 12; Prov. 7:6–27).

THEOLOGICAL DIMENSION OF HEBREW POETRY

Hebrew poetry, in both its distribution and preeminence throughout the OT, represents more than an artistic embellishment of prose. The four major poems of the Pentateuch may be taken as an example: Genesis 49 (Jacob's blessing), Exodus 15 (Song of the Sea), Numbers 23–24 (Balaam's oracles), and Deuteronomy 32–33 (Song of Moses). The intriguing change from prose to poetry in these four sections has been noted and often interpreted from a critical perspective, identifying the poetic passages as interpolations, glosses, or later additions. However, an increasing number of interpreters recognize the strategic position of these poetic passages and their linguistic integration into the overall literary macrostructure of the Pentateuch. It can be shown that they form an essential building block in the microstructure of their respective books and the macrostructure of the overall Pentateuch. (For a more detailed discussion of the role of these passages in the overall structure of the Pentateuch, see "Introduction to the Pentateuch," p. 120.)

Scholars have noted that holiness and solemnity are often expressed through poetry. What is particularly holy and solemn in the OT is expressed in poetry. The Psalms, which, like the Pentateuch, are structured into five books, continuously recount God's actions in history (Creation, Exodus, and conquest), again with eschatological and messianic overtones throughout. Hebrew poetry, through parallelism and all its other literary devices, accomplishes what prose at times is not able to achieve: a heightening of the message. Thus, some of the most important themes in the OT are written in Hebrew poetry.

The fact that the central messages were preserved in poetry also point to the divine concern for the wide distribution of the message. It was shared with the people through the reading of the poetic portions of the OT. The terseness or compactness of poetry as well as the repetition of ideas, sounds, and words made it easier for the listeners to memorize the divine instruction and to pass it on to their children. Poetry facilitated the didactic role of priests, prophets, teachers, and parents as they made sure that the new generations would never forget God's wondrous acts of love toward His people.

JOB

INTRODUCTION

Title and Authorship. Though the book of Job pays no specific attention to authorial claims, many students of the book have long claimed that it is the work of Moses, considered to be author of the Bible's founding documents. There is ample reason to associate the book with Moses, as it seems to belong to the earliest stages of biblical composition. That Job names no author is normal rather than exceptional since many nonprophetic books have no explicitly named author. Only three of them (Proverbs, Ecclesiastes, Song of Solomon) are identified as a specific writer's work. Whether in the Hebrew Bible (MT), the LXX, or the modern versions, the book of Job is named after its great protagonist whose name occurs fifty-six times in the book, from the story's very first verse to its very last (1:1; 42:17).

Date. Proposed dates of composition range across a span of more than a millennium, from the second millennium B.C. to the times of the postexilic temple. Despite competing recommendations, internal evidence supports an early date for the setting of the story: the fact that Job offered his own sacrifices implies that the priesthood had not yet been established and the temple/tabernacle had not been built (1:5); his possessions were measured in terms of sheep, camels, oxen, donkeys, and servants (1:3), similar to what we find in the case of Abraham (Gen. 12:16); and Job's life span of 140 years fits very well with what was common during the patriarchal period (42:16). The story was a very old one. It may have been transmitted in oral form for many years before it was written down.

Backgrounds. Job's backstory is the long-standing human discomfort with suffering in general, but particularly, with the suffering of the innocent—innocent oxen, donkeys, sheep, camels, servants, children, but particularly, the righteous innocent, the servant of Yahweh named Job. The book rolls back a veil to grant to humans some insight into the workings of the Great Controversy between good and evil. Geographically speaking, the events took place in the land of Uz. In the Bible, this term is used five times as a personal name and three times as a territorial location. Jeremiah's Uz, like the land of the Philistines, was a place of foreign people (Jer. 25:20), the Edomites, according to Lamentations 4:21. The Bible's first Uz was Semitic (Gen. 10:23). Another, Uz the son of Dishan, resided in Seir (Gen. 36:28), which the Edomites later took over from the Horites. The land of Uz may have been named after him, just as the land of Israel came to be named after a man named Israel.

Theology and Purpose. Integrity is the book's major focus, whether the speakers are young or old, male or female, human or supernatural, Machiavellian or benevolent. Despite its clear focus on one individual named Job, the book really discusses the integrity of all of God's intelligent creation. In it, God's adversary argues that the relationship between God and His people is not based on disinterested love and that, therefore, it lacks integrity. The adversary's role is highly significant both to the book of Job and to the scriptural theme of the cosmic war between good and evil. The book of Job is one of the Bible's most explicit exposés of the adversary's character and role.

1. Relationship between God and the Adversary. Some have claimed that the prologue, specifically Job 1:6—2:7, shows God cooperating with the adversary, Satan, rather than being hostile toward him. Satan (*satan*), they say, was actually God's employee, His prosecuting attorney, and should not be thought of as the origin or cause of evil. The subject of Satan as God's adversary, particularly in early OT times, continues to require the attention of Bible students.

Those who think that Israel was influenced by Zoroastrianism, the Persian religion, point to the difference between 1 Chronicles 21:1 and 2 Samuel 24:1. The difference, they say, proves that dualism—the conflict between two powers—became part of Jewish thinking in the sixth century B.C. after the Persians conquered the Babylonian Empire. First Chronicles, accepted as postexilic, shows Satan doing what preexilic 2 Samuel attributes to God. In 1 Chronicles, Satan tempts David to do what God is said to push him to do in 2 Samuel. Certain scholars claim that this is evidence that before the Exile Israel knew of no conflict between Yahweh and a personal archenemy called Satan (see "Satan and David," p. 536).

Sixth and fifth century B.C. biblical books, however, provide the strongest challenge to the theory of Zoroastrian influence because the ones expected to show the most influence are the ones that lack evidence of any such influence. Postexilic historical works like Nehemiah, Ezra, and Esther do not exhibit dualistic sentiments. Zechariah's third chapter is the only postexilic prophetic material that makes any reference to Satan. Even intertestamental Qumran texts depicting a confrontation between sons of light and darkness, between the Prince of Light and the Angel of Darkness, do not use Satan as a personal name.

Extrabiblical texts, even those as old as the oldest Zoroastrian material, may or may not help with dating the book of Job. And comparative linguistics may not help either, because few, if any, cognate occurrences of the Hebrew term *satan* appear among ancient Semitic languages. This, as much as anything else, shows how distinctive the Bible's theological insights are in relation to the books and religious ideas of its time and environment. When specifically exposed, in comparison with other biblical adversaries, Satan is seen to be both malicious and secretive, a mystery to many a reader and interpreter.

2. *The Role of Satan/Adversary.* The book of Job calls the one who opposes God and Job "Satan/the adversary." While this Hebrew term is used in various places in the OT (e.g., 1 Sam. 29:4; 1 Kin. 11:14, 23), the use of the definite article here (*hassatan*) makes him "the Satan," entitling him more than any other being to be called Satan. Four things in Job's prologue that most promptly identify him are (1) his name *hassatan*; (2) those whom he opposed, that is, Yahweh and people like Job whom God wanted to protect—such as Joshua the high priest (Zech. 3:1, 2); (3) an account of his vicious-

ness (i.e., his unwarranted and destructive assaults on animals and humans); and (4) his callous presumption in his return to argue that God cheated by protecting Job. But the one who had arbitrarily destroyed Job's animals, servants, and children seems hardly qualified to discuss fairness. His presence is also found in the speeches of Job's friends and specifically introduced by Eliphaz during his first speech (4:12–16). He tells about his experience of a supernatural revelation, accepted by his other friends, received through the visit of a spiritual being. The content of this revelation contradicts the content of the voice of God in the prologue and the epilogue and aligns this spirit with the adversary of the prologue (see "The Vision/Dream of Eliphaz," p. 630).

Passages in the NT, including 1 Peter 5:8, Revelation 12:9, and 20:2, leave little doubt about who Satan is or what he does. He is the devil, the ancient serpent, accuser of God's people, the beginner and chief agent of trouble in the universe and misery on earth. Job's Satan is simply the proper name and identification for the trouble-making serpent in Genesis. Zechariah's Satan is readily recognizable because of Job. And his identification in the NT as the great adversary of heaven (Rev. 12:7–9) makes it more appropriate to wonder how he hides so well in OT times, instead of arguing that he was not present there at all. In short, it may be misleading to speak of Satan as unknown in or absent from either pre- or postexilic OT Scriptures.

3. *Origin of the Conflict.* The message of Scripture is that Adam and Eve originally lived in a flawless world, which only became subject to corruption through their yielding to temptation and the lie of the serpent. Romans 5:12 teaches that their sin in heeding his invitation brought death to earth, as evidenced in all forms of its material decay. God's own words directly link earth's physical and humanity's spiritual degradation to that same tragic error (Gen. 3:14–24). In passages such as Isaiah 14 and Ezekiel 28, the Bible also gives the backstory on Satan as the force for ill that led humanity into rebellion against God (Gen. 3:1–6; see "Evil and the Fallen Cherub," p. 1008). It is essential that we recognize the evil one for who God in Scripture tells us he is in order to have a proper understanding of why sin exists, how it came to earth, and why God is doing what He is to rid the universe of it. Moreover, in the context of the book of Job, it is indispensable for a balanced reading of the book and for beginning any biblically based Christian theodicy.

It is very difficult to exaggerate the value of the book of Job's contribution to understanding the Great Controversy between good and evil through its exposé of a personal Satan.

Without proper understanding of Satan's boldness and callous brilliance, great enough to challenge the Lord in His own court and viciously attack His creatures, many people have awkwardly charged God with Satan's actions and developed theologies that justify their thinking. These ideas tend to obscure the biblical truth that Satan is specifically responsible for all the pain and suffering in God's universe. God's punishments, Jesus's death, the sacrificial system that points to it, the process of sanctification and character development—none of this would ever have been necessary without Satan's rebellion against divine government and all the moral and physical dislocation that it introduced.

4. God's Victory and Job's Vindication. By exposing the truth about Satan, and the consequence of his way of thinking, the book of Job leaves the believer in no doubt as to the outcome of the conflict between the Lord and His enemy. At no point in the drama is God ever sympathetic to Satan's evil scheme for depriving an innocent man of life and limb. He knew from the beginning of the trial that Satan's aim with regard to Job was to have Job curse God (1:11; 2:4-5). He was not beguiled by Satan's claim to be searching for integrity. At the end of Job's trial, a God of love and fairness could do no less than restore all things to their divine order of blessedness. Job's experience wonderfully pictures the final triumph of the saints of the Most High who will receive the kingdom, dominion, and greatness of all the kingdoms in the world at the end of their trial, humiliation, and abuse at the hands of the little horn power (Dan. 7:27). There may be no cross of Calvary or lake of fire in the book of Job. But Satan's head is still crushed through the defeat of his ideas and the silencing of his arguments. And just as God will crown His saints at the end, so it is right for Him to acknowledge the faithfulness of His good and faithful servant.

Job certainly defends his integrity and loyalty to God in the midst of his trial and even speaks strong words concerning the way he perceived God was treating him. For a man who knows God very well, his deep suffering is not comprehensible unless he postulates that God is now, for reasons unknown to him, treating him like an enemy. While his friends speak about who God is and how he governs His creation, Job speaks not about God in Himself but about how God is relating to Job in his present situation. Just as Job's material possessions were not at first a divine bribe, so his material restoration in the end is not represented as a reward for piety though it may also be rewarding. It was, in the first instance, simply evidence that his trial was over. Job's restoration was simple evidence of God's mercy and justice. He was finally and completely vindicated and restored. Any reward element in God's final affirmation of Job was no less or more a function of divine grace than it will be for all the saints at the end of time (Rev. 22:12). James refers to the blessedness of those who endure testing; they will receive the "crown of life" that the Lord has promised to those who love Him (James 1:12). Job's complete vindication and restoration at the end of the story is an appropriate metaphor for the final reward of the saints who, having come through great tribulation and gained victory over the beast and his image, will be crowned with glory and honor. For them as well as for Job serving God is determined by their experience of God's grace that moves them to love Him without regard for their present trials.

5. Suffering and Hope. By appreciating God's sustaining grace, we may better appreciate the critical theological purpose of the book of Job, the book of books on suffering. That purpose would be to (a) demonstrate the utter injustice of some suffering; (b) expose the malevolent supernatural agent behind such pain; (c) highlight God's categorical opposition to the person and activities of that agent; (d) show the complexity of the issues involved, to counter inaccurate theological presuppositions; and (e) point forward to the triumph guaranteed even to those unjustly tormented and tortured because the God they insist on trusting will prove Himself worthy of their trust.

Job's existence is framed within a state of constant hope. It is clear that for him hope did not come from human sources; his friends did not offer it to him but instead gave him hopelessness in the form of guilt. And the Lord would remind him that he should never hope to defeat Leviathan by himself (41:9). Although losing everything brought Job close to losing hope, he never got to that point. Instead he fell to the ground and worshiped (1:20). When the misery of his life of sickness was intense, he wished to not have been born and simply waited for death (3:21); there was no attempt on his part to bring his life to an end. He resisted death as a final solution because to embrace it was to abandon hope (17:15). He knew very well that suffering could destroy hope in the Lord (14:19) and agreed with his friends that there was no hope for the wicked (27:7–8). But Job's emphasis on his integrity was nurtured by hope. Eliphaz understood this and tried to destroy hope when he asked Job whether his fear of God was his confidence and his honesty his hope (4:6). These provided grounds for his hope. While his friends would continue to tell Job that his only hope was in confessing his sin (8:13; 11:18, 20), Job would insist on his integrity even though he recognized that there was no immediate hope of healing for him (7:6).

For Job, hope was certainly stronger than his sufferings, though he did not deny the intensity of his pain. When he concluded that God was treating him like His enemy, he confessed that there was no hope for him (19:10). He was persuaded that God was somehow involved in what he was going through and anxiously looked forward to his vindication. He firmly stated that even if God were to kill him, he would still trust (i.e., wait, hope for) Him (13:15). He knew the Lord, and therefore he could trust Him and wait for His intervention (14:14–15). This was a strong affirmation of hope in the Lord in the midst of intense suffering. But he would go further than that. His hope for restoration looked beyond the grave to the resurrection (19:25–27). Job may have concluded that his condition would take him to the grave, but he was ready to take his hope with him, anticipating with great yearning that his body would be restored and he would see his Redeemer. He would then vindicate him. In a book where human pain is extremely intense, we find a hope that holds on to God and looks forward to a final restoration beyond the grave through the resurrecting power of the Redeemer.

COMMENTARY

1:1—2:13

THE PROLOGUE:
JOB'S INITIAL TESTING

Job 1:1—2:13 introduces the patriarch Job as well as all principal characters of the book except Elihu. The material is organized in scenes that took place on earth (1:1–5, 13–22; 2:7–13) and scenes that occurred in the heavenly realm (1:6–12; 2:1–6). There is a historical setting at the beginning of the prologue (1:1–5) and one

at its end (2:11–13), and we find sandwiched between the two dialogues that contribute to the development of the narrative. The prologue basically consists of two trials.

1:1–22
Job's First Trial

The prologue consists of a double challenge from Satan against God's character and against the integrity of Job. These challenges set the stage for what follows in the book. Chapter 1 introduces the first trial, about which Job did not know anything, and concludes with Job's first response to his experience of pain.

1:1–5. Job Introduced. Verses 1–3 provide a description of the character and social status of Job. The introduction includes four elements that will be reprised in reverse order at the end of the book: character, children, possessions, and status. Job is introduced as a wealthy person, listing first his spiritual wealth, followed by the richness of having a family, and finally, a list of all his material possessions. Job feared God and shunned evil. He was *tam* and *yashar*. The term *tam*—rendered variously as "blameless," "complete," or "perfect"—highlights his reliance on God for his righteousness. It expresses the ideas of completeness and flawlessness and is used to describe the paschal lamb (Ex. 12:5) and every burnt offering, peace or fellowship offering, and sin offering brought to the Lord (e.g., Lev. 1:3; 3:6; 4:23). These offerings were a type of Jesus, the spotless Lamb of God "who takes away sin of the world" (John 1:29). Only through His perfectly flawless offering on our behalf can we ever be made right with God. Job was also a *yashar*—"right" or "upright"—person, meaning that he acted according to moral principles when dealing with others. He feared the Lord in the sense of respecting and reverencing Him, greatly valuing his relationship with Him. Consequently, he avoided sin by not exposing himself to it—rather, he walked away from it.

His piety found expression in his concern for the spiritual life of his children (vv. 4–5). The incident demonstrates that the description of his character is not without foundation. His intercession and solicitude for his children's spiritual state was as customary as their parties. Verse 5 comments on the integrity of v. 1 and shows that Job's righteousness was a commitment to the salvation of others, not a holier-than-thou self-centeredness. Also, Job's humble, obedient offering of sacrifice expressed his faith in a substitutionary atonement.

1:6–12. God's Court and Cosmic Conflict. This new scene took place in the divine assembly. Other OT divine council scenes include Micaiah's vision in 1 Kings 22:19 and Psalm 82:1. In v. 6, it is indicated that Satan joined them (lit. "*the* Satan also came"). The use of the definite article identifies him as the archetypal adversary, as is also the case in Zechariah 3. The text gives triple markers on Satan as an intruder through the conjunction "and," the adverb "also," and the prepositional phrase "among them" or "with them" as follows: the court assembled, *and* Satan *also* came *among them*. His place of activity and concern was the earth, where he was apparently observing how God interacted with humans, in this case with Job. No reason is given for Satan's presence in the heavenly assembly, but he was not there to speak on behalf of human beings or to testify on behalf of God's integrity.

When given the opportunity to speak, Satan accused God of feeding selfishness in his creatures by rewarding good behavior—or rather by paying for it. Satan was suggesting that God's way of governing simply bought the services of humans. God's people knew that as long as they served Him, God would keep providing for them. Therefore, their love for Him was not pure but motivated by greed that was fed by God Himself. For Satan, God and Job were not honorable but self-serving. Each reinforced the other's pretense of goodness by paying for it. God paid Job with extravagant bounties, and Job paid Him back with apparent piety. If God would stop buying human service, the true character of humans would be manifested by rejecting Him (when the text mentions "curse," it literally says that "he will surely bless you," which is a delicate and codified way of saying "curse" [see 1 Kin. 21:10, 13]). In the mouth of Satan, the demand that God stretch out His hand (v. 11) implied that havoc and chaos would come from the Lord since "hand" refers to power. Though it was never humanly apparent, and though one reporting servant spoke of destruction by the "fire of God" from heaven (v. 16), God's words showed that it was Satan, not God, who was the source and means of Job's torture.

1:13–22. Satan's First Blows: Four Disasters and Job's Response. Horror built up to its climax. Job was not allowed to recover as the rhythm went from lesser to greater, from lesser

sorrow to most unbearable grief. The pattern was up, down, up, seesaw—first oxen and donkeys, numbered in the hundreds (vv. 14–15), then sheep (7,000; v. 16), followed by camels (3,000; v. 17). The rhythm also comments on the fluctuation and instability of Job's emotions and his total devastation at the climax. Reports that began with loss of oxen and donkeys, creating an element of suspense, reached their climax of pain with the death of all of Job's children (v. 19). Job prostrated himself but did not curse God. He knew that God was sovereign and transcendent, and he granted Him the freedom to do as He willed (vv. 20–22). No human is capable of knowing on his or her own the difference between Satan's direct initiatives and God's; neither was Job. The narrator's comment addresses Satan's claim: Satan's view was found wanting.

2:1–12
Job's Second Trial

The first trial was introduced by an earthly scene (1:1–5); the second trial began after an earthly scene (1:13–22) and would conclude with occurrences on earth (2:7–10). Job was victorious in both trials.

2:1–6. The Heavenly Court: Presumption's Persistence. This time the Lord rebuked Satan (vv. 1–3), whose charge was baseless. Whereupon Satan relaunched his challenge (vv. 4–5), wishing this time to damage Job's body ("skin for skin"). People will give everything they have to stay alive. Satan sought to make the case that grave sickness, perhaps perceived as a mortal threat, would be sufficient to expose Job's insincerity and separate him from his God. This presented God with a dilemma: if He denied the evil one access to His faithful children, they and He might be easily accused of collusion in bribery, with saints being paid off to be good. Providence is the natural function of His love, as well as His paternal duty. Allowing the adversary to torment His children would require Him to take the blame for whatever cruelties would result from the adversary's aggression. Nevertheless, God made clear that Job's pain was inflicted by a hand other than His.

2:7–10. Satan's Second Series: Sores and Spouse. Satan is plainly named as the agent of the cruelty inflicted on Job. The humiliating and painful condition of the patriarch is such that it provoked in Mrs. Job an outburst (v. 9), a comprehensible frustration, from one who had at this point lost as much as her husband had and was ready to give vent to her feelings, unaware of the cosmic import of her words. Her cry and its moral echoes bring to mind James's comment that whoever does not stumble in speech is perfect in being able to control his or her whole body (James 3:2). Her words came unquestionably from a heart that loved much.

Job's reaction (v. 10a, b) was not because he was any more aware than his wife of the supernatural goings on. Rather, as much as anything else, it was a shaming of the accuser and a vindication of God's confidence in His servant. Mrs. Job apparently reasoned that life with God should consist of nothing but prosperity. Her husband judged her comment as born of folly rather than wisdom. Job spoke here according to the value system of biblical wisdom that ranges mostly from what is wise to what is foolish. Job's wife echoed Satan's taunts, and they were decried as folly. The fact that Job referred to her comment as being one that was like the "foolish" women, not that she *was* a foolish woman, implies that she was speaking out of character. Her silence suggests that she received Job's rebuke well.

2:10c–12. Verdict on Job and the Arrival of His Friends. As with 1:22, the narrator's comment reflects negatively on Satan's claim that Job would sin with his lips if God removed His hedge. Job was willing to administer for the Lord not only the good things He gave him but also the pain and suffering that had come his way. His relationship with the Lord was based on disinterested love. Then friends arrived. Their names and places of origin showed that the friends were true friends. Their coming was a statement of emotional connection with and affection for Job. Their first reactions demonstrated this emotional connection: their mourning rituals expressed more than mere cultural conformity. They expressed shock. And it was not merely disfigurement that made Job unrecognizable. It was because the greatest of the men of the east who had once lived like a king among his troops (29:25) now sat on an ash heap.

3:1—37:24
DIALOGUE:
JOB AND HIS COUNSELORS

The main portion of the book is a dialogue or debate that seeks to explore the significance of Job's experience. It is introduced by Job's soliloquy (3:1–26) and then followed by three cycles of speeches (4:1—14:22; 15:1—21:34; 22:1—27:23). At the end of the dialogue there is a hymn to wisdom (28:1–28), after which we listen to Job's final speech (29:1—31:40). Then we encounter the final human speech, that of Elihu (32:1—37:24). In the book, the human dialogue ultimately sets the stage for God's intervention.

3:1–26
Job's Opening Soliloquy

In this personal reflection Job opened up his heart to his friends (and to the readers), sharing with us the intensity of his physical and emotional pain. He longed for oblivion (vv. 1–10) and saw death at birth as better than his present sufferings (vv. 11–26).

3:1–10. Longing for Oblivion. Job's speech began with a curse, not upon the God who gives and takes away but against the day he was born. Job sighed for the day of his birth to disappear into its original nothingness—to be erased from the calendar. His unrealistic longing for reversal (v. 7) indicates the depth of his frustration with existence. If his birthdate could not be erased from the calendar, then it should be a night of no deliveries; if none of its births count, Job would never have been—and he would not now be suffering. In Job's speaking of the night as mother of the day, we see an echo of the Genesis order in which evening preceded morning.

3:11–26. Death Idealized. Job lamented that he was not stillborn (vv. 11–12), and he coveted death's serenity. He knew that it is an oblivion where there are no varying levels of human status: the righteous, wicked, slave, free, wealthy rulers, and weary laborers are all equal. By contrast with the peace of death, life in the midst of suffering is both burdensome and inexorable (vv. 20–26). Although Job would have welcomed death, there is no indication that he ever considered ending his life by his own hand.

4:1—14:22
First Cycle of Speeches

The first cycle is formed by the speeches of the friends and Job's response to each one of them: Eliphaz (4:1—5:27) and Job (6:1—7:21); Bildad (8:1–22) and Job (9:1—10:22); Zophar (11:1–22) and Job (12:1—14:22).

4:1—5:27. Eliphaz's Logic and Deceptive Revelation. Eliphaz's opening (4:1-5) was cautious but accusing. He seemed conflicted—apparently sensitive to Job's distress but uncomfortable about what he labeled Job's impatience. Since Job had helped others through such times as this, he should have been able to handle it himself. Verses 6-11 already betray his critical spirit. The implicit answer to his rhetorical questions (4:7) is "no one." For Eliphaz, Job may not necessarily have been doomed, but if he were, he had earned it. The revelatory experience of Eliphaz (4:12-21) appears to play an important role in the views of Job's friends (see below, "The Vision/Dream of Eliphaz"). The account never clarifies whether Eliphaz received a dream or a vision, nor from whence or when it came. The message of the spirit who communicated with him began with a rhetorical question about the possibility of humans being more righteous than God. The question can also be translated "be righteous before" or be considered righteous "by God." The translation "more" righteous than God makes no sense in the context because Job never argued for such a view. The spirit was not speaking about a mortal being (*'enosh*, "man," "human being"), for in the following part of the verse *geber* ("man") is used—a term that usually refers to a person who is in a proper relationship with God. Job claimed to be such a *geber*/man or righteous person (3:23; 16:21), and God also affirmed it (40:7), but the friends rejected Job's claim (15:7-10; 34:7). The question is not about sinful human beings but about a radical divine transcendence and the human condition. In this passage the verb "to be righteous" (*tsadaq*) stands in parallel with the verb *taher* ("to be regarded as clean, pure") and expresses the idea of moral purity. The spirit argued that all creatures are by divine design imperfect and unable to be blameless before God. This contradicts what God indicated in the prologue to the book. Besides, it is difficult to see how Eliphaz could reconcile 4:7-8 with a God who distrusts His angels (4:18) and particularly despises His human creation—those who dwell in houses of clay (4:19). While his account of the revelation is meant to urge Job to humble himself before God (5:8), it is difficult to see where he would situate himself within such a characterization of all humanity.

The Vision/Dream of Eliphaz

From Job 4:12 onward, the entire dialogue between Job and his friends hinges on, circles around, and eventually climaxes—at least for the three friends—on the story of Eliphaz's numinous experience narrated in 4:12-21. A discussion of the impact and nature of this experience will be helpful.

1. A Personal Revelatory Experience. There are a couple of important aspects in the experience of Eliphaz that we should notice. First, he argued that the trustworthiness of his wisdom is unquestionable because it was grounded on a personal supernatural experience he had with a spiritual being who spoke to him. The revelation given to Eliphaz came from a spiritual being. Second, the identity of the spirit whose voice he heard is never stated; it remains shrouded in mystery. He heard a voice from someone that remained faceless, nameless. Elijah also heard a voice but he identified it as the voice of the Lord (1 Kin. 19:12-15). The content of the revelation will establish the identity of this being.

2. The Question. The message the spirit delivered to Eliphaz was introduced by a rhetorical question: Can a man [*'enosh*; not "a mortal"] be more righteous [*tsadaq*] before/by/than God? Can a man [*geber*] be more pure [*taher*] before/than his Maker? The expected answer is no. To be righteous (*tsadaq*) here means to be blameless or pure, for it is in parallel to *taher* ("to be regarded as pure"), suggesting that this is about being perfect or morally pure before God (see 9:2). The Creator and the creature are being contrasted: Can a human be considered to be righteous/pure and morally upright before/by the Lord? According to the spirit that spoke to Eliphaz, the natural distance between God and humans is such that this is impossible. The spirit applied this judgment even to heavenly beings: God does not even trust His heavenly messengers, the angels, and considers them to be imperfect (v. 18). This is the natural condition of their existence and of humans in particular, for they were made of clay—fragile and ephemeral beings who are here today and gone tomorrow and no one seems to notice. Consequently, suffering is the natural condition of humans as created by God. All humans suffer, and Job is no exception. The discussion is not about the need for justification by faith.

3. *The Identity of the Spirit.* Based on the previous discussion, we suggest that Eliphaz is echoing the voice of the adversary from the prologue. First, while Satan claimed there that it was impossible for a human being to be righteous before the Lord unless prompted by selfish motives (1:9), God identified for him a human being who was blameless and upright and who feared Him—Job (v. 8). The spirit that spoke to Eliphaz was contradicting what God revealed to the reader in the prologue to the book concerning Job. Second, it also contradicted God by arguing that humans suffer by divine design. The prologue demonstrates that human suffering finds its origin not in the Creator but in the adversary/Satan. Third, it is clear that the message of the spirit projects a low view of humanity before God that contrasts with other biblical pictures of humanity as created in the image of God for dominion over all creation (Gen. 1:26-29), a view that is still highly esteemed even after Eden's moral fall (Ps. 8). Although Eliphaz did not say anything about the nature of the spirit that spoke to him, we can now ascertain without doubt that it was a messenger of the adversary.

4. *Influence of the Revelation and God's Reaction.* Continuing the dialogue, Eliphaz's second speech insisted on the truthfulness of the content of his revelatory experience (15:14-16), an insistence that appears again at the start of his final intervention (22:2-3). Zophar's first speech alluded to this revelation (11:2-3). Bildad, the second friend, never accepted this perspective until his brief third speech, which is a total surrender to the revelation that Eliphaz first reported

(25:4-6). There he virtually repeated the falsehood, signaling the dialogue's total collapse, and the cycles end. Whether under strong delusion or, in Bildad's case, having apparently given up on rational argument, all three friends end up subscribing to and advocating a word about God that is false and allegedly based on revelation. But the voice of God that initiated the book will also be heard at the end, addressing the false revelation introduced in the dialogue. The epilogue shows that this sustained distortion of God's character left Him angry—not merely concerned, or disturbed, or offended, but furiously angry (42:7). God revealed that only their penitence and Job's intercession stood between them and unseemly treatment from God Himself (v. 8).

5. *Job's Resoluteness.* Initial attacks on Job's material wealth of herds, flocks, and servants, and even the unthinkable loss of all his children in a single blow, all failed to reduce him to blasphemy. Disease that made Job repugnant to family (19:17), as well as scorned and loathed by acquaintances (19:13-19; 30:9-10), also failed to accomplish the enemy's purpose. The dialogue then reveals the enemy reverting to the tactic of obscurity employed in chapter 1. There the mischief of an unseen but lethal hand led servants to blame God's fire for destruction of thousands of sheep and servants (1:16). Eliphaz's statement shows that the adversary, though unseen, continues to be present and to prosecute his goal of pressing Job to curse God. Eliphaz's revelation devalued humans and advanced a slander of God calculated to move Job to abandon his claim of integrity. But the strategy of a lying spirit is no more successful than that of widespread havoc in convincing faithful Job that God is not worth his confidence. Lying spirits work with those who choose to be deceived. Job does not so choose.

The verses that frame Eliphaz's fantastic revelation (4:7; 5:1) each include an imperative and a rhetorical question whose implied answer is "no one." Job 5:1 records an imperative, designed to point out Job's desperate need of repentance; but initially, at least, it was a command of somewhat harsh import. Just as Eliphaz had asserted

that there was no innocent suffering, so now there was no "holy one" (probably angel) who could help Job in his physical or moral distress, perhaps emphasizing that only God could help (5:8). Verses 2-7 emphasize his point regarding human inadequacy. Note that labels for the culpable one, such as foolish and simple (5:2), are typical of wisdom literature. Observe as well the vigor of Eliphaz's opposition to those he labeled. At least eighteen verses of this speech depend on his subjective authority versus only three (vv. 2, 6, 7) where the truth of his words did not depend on the speaker.

Eliphaz was in a sense correct in affirming that human beings were "born to trouble" (v. 7); but if the *natural* lot of humanity were trouble, how could he argue that Job's trouble was the proof of specific wickedness? But then in 5:8–16, Eliphaz proffered an exceptional change in tone after his categorical denunciations. Job might yet have hope. He should turn to God because God is powerful beyond human understanding, He rules nature and is able to reverse anyone's circumstances. In an opening speech that had included reproof, revelation, and harsh contempt, Eliphaz moved on to soothing consolation in 5:17–27. Problematic for the whole was not the general truth of divine chastening but his specific judgment that God was punishing Job (5:13–14, 17–19).

6:1—7:21. Job: Pity for Himself, Dismay at His Friends. Frequently through the dialogue, Job longed to know he was appreciated. Though he could refuse unpalatable food, going through his recent experience was like being forced to consume a totally unsavory meal. Living in uninterrupted agony, Job insisted that he had been faithful to God. But Job was not superhuman (6:11–13). He saw no sense in going on; staying alive was to suffer. Here (6:14) is the only occurrence of the expression "the fear of the Almighty" in Job, paralleled by "the fear of the Lord" in 28:28, itself unique. Job believed the loyalty of friends should survive spiritual crises.

The reference to the brooks and streams (6:15) expresses Job's dismay at the treachery of his friends (6:14–21). In the spring, wadis in the Middle East were flooded with water from periodic rains. They dried up in the heat of summer. Desert travelers made hopeful by the evidence of waterways were disappointed to find the gullies entirely dry (vv. 16–19). Job's friends had treacherously disappointed him in their pretense of refreshing his spirit. Verse 20 is evidently descriptive of Job's own feelings as a parallel to those of the travelers; Job refers to his friends' attitude with the similar verbs *bosh*—"to be ashamed" or "distress" or "disappoint"—and *khaper*—"to be ashamed" or "to be confounded." The first phrase of v. 21 has been rendered variously as "you are nothing," "you

are it," or (interpretively) "you have proved to be no help" (i.e., you are just like those dried up wadis whose water evaporates in the heat; you cower before a challenge).

Job dared them to silence him if they could (6:22–30), becoming more assertive in his challenge to his friends to show him his wrong. They should simply speak the truth rather than try to cajole or coerce. They could not constrain him to make any deals since he owed none of them anything. By referring to the words of desperate people such as himself as "wind" (v. 26), Job preempted any rebuke for irresponsible language, justifying whatever came from his lips as he vented his frustrations. He would welcome no reprimand on that account. The friends also lacked integrity; they were willing to cause the fatherless to *nepal*—a word which has the basic meaning of "fall." Accordingly, some translations refer to the attack, overwhelming, or fall of the fatherless. The word can also mean "cast lots"—"cause the lot to fall" (i.e., "roll dice" or gamble)—for society's most helpless (v. 27). Job accused them of mercenary and exploitative conduct, a readiness to do the same to a friend, to one they should, instead, loyally support.

Chapter 7 introduces the theme of Job's burdensome life. Job longed for some respite from days of stress and nights of tossing (7:1–6). But he had to confront the finality of the grave (7:7–10), anticipated though not idealized as in chapter 3. While vv. 9–10 might seem to imply that Job did not believe in a resurrection, this is not demonstrable from the text, especially in light of his later affirmation (19:23–27). He was simply affirming in poetically evocative language that the dead would not go back to their former earthly lives, for example, their homes (v. 10). He would not hold back (7:11–15). Given the immanence of death, he would speak his mind. He preferred death to his current *'etsem*—variously translated as "body," "bones," or "pains" (v. 15); moreover, given the torments of life, Job preferred death. "Let me alone" is the initial line of a unit (vv. 16–21) that pled for the peace of abandonment. Satan contended (1:10) that God had a hedge of protection all around Job. But God now felt to Job more like a vigilante than a watchful Father. Verse 21 suggests that Job recognized his need for forgiveness of sin, but he was unaware of any specific sin (v. 20) that would have caused God to punish him so severely. He wished to die in peace knowing he was right with God.

8:1–22. Bildad: Typical and Limited Wisdom.

Bildad believed that fate showed a reasonable God (vv. 1–7). Of the three friends he is most faithful to radical wisdom traditions and most loyal to an orthodox theology (i.e., reward for good and retribution for evil). The human condition is one or the other—a radical view of retribution that Job rejects or questions. Bildad also seems most disposed to believe that there was hope for a repentant Job. Bildad's speeches were not characterized by Zophar's cruelty or Eliphaz's self-centeredness; he held to the tenets of wisdom. He argued that Job, like a stiff wind (v. 2), had been spouting verbiage—which Job himself had tacitly conceded, using the same metaphor of wind (6:26). He took the argument to the level of the family and suggested that God killed Job's children because of their sin (v. 4; cf. Deut. 24:16). Unlike Eliphaz, Bildad is grounded in reason rather than revelation, using the principle of retribution to establish that each one pays for his or her own sins, and this includes children paying for their own sins (cf. Deut. 24:16; Jer. 31:29–30).

Bildad suggested that God would restore Job if he was or became "pure and upright" (Job 8:6). He used further conditional expressions (vv. 4–5) to appeal to him with the promise of restoration. He emphasized the wisdom of previous generations (v. 8). Bildad's appeal to the elders would lead Eliphaz also to appeal to their authority (15:7–10), though he would also rely on his vision-dream. The idea that we were "born yesterday" is a hyperbolic way of stating that we are indebted to ancient wisdom (v. 9).

Bildad employed (vv. 11–19) multiple metaphors, including papyrus, a spider's web, and a plant. As papyrus reeds perish without moisture, so the impious perish without God (vv. 11–13). What they trust will not last because they rely on things that are as fragile as spider webs (v. 14): Job would use Bildad's own terms for confidence and reliance (*kesel*, *mibtakh*) to argue that his security had never been his wealth (31:24). The spider's web was the "spider's house," which would not stand up to anyone's weight—another image of fragility (v. 15).

This is followed by another analogy of fragility and instability: plants rooted in good soil are much harder to uproot than those that hold on to rocks (v. 18). The roots of the large plant torn from a rock heap leave a much lighter footprint than those sunk in the soil; plants holding on to rocks for support will not even be missed when removed. The first part of v. 19 has been interpreted as either referring to a new section

describing God's joy or (quite differently) as the fleeting pleasure of the poorly planted and uprooted plants that were described in the previous section—symbolic of those "who forget God" (v. 13). A godless life has little profit. Verses 20–22 conclude Bildad's speech. He suggested that God does not reject (or cast away) the *tam*—a word variously translated as "blameless," "perfect," or "person/man of integrity" (v. 20; cf. 1:1, 8). He was correct in the assertion that since God does not cast away the *tam*, He would not cast away Job.

9:1—10:22. Job: Awe of God, Frustration with Him.

Job highlighted God's unmatched prowess in nature in the opening lines of this second speech (9:1–12). The question of how a person could be righteous before God (9:2) is similar to the one raised by Eliphaz's vision-dream (4:17), but the concern is a different one. Job is using a different preposition, not "before God" but "with God"; that is to say, Job is asking whether it is possible for anyone to engage God in a legal dispute and win the case (i.e., be declared righteous; v. 3). The implication is that in such a legal controversy, Job would lose the case even though he was righteous (9:15, 20). Verses 13–19 describe Job's sense of inadequacy before the divine assaults. The final part of v. 13 can be rendered as "allies of the proud" or as "Rahab's helpers"—*rahab* can refer to pride or to a proper name. God's mastery over nature is sometimes personified in ANE mythology as His victory over chaos monsters with names such as Rahab and Leviathan (Ps. 74:13–14; Is. 30:7; 51:9–10). In this case Job portrayed the Lord as victorious over them.

At the end of v. 18, the word *saba'* is used. This has been rendered as "fill" or "saturate" or "overwhelm." The literal sense is that of "satisfy" or "satiate." God was feeding Job until he was stuffed full—with bitterness. Job found no evidence that God cared enough to give him a fair hearing. He was the victim of an internal conflict (9:20–24). Intense torment made him susceptible to accusations of guilt, though conscience recalled no errant deed. To him, when it came to suffering, there was no difference between guilty and innocent (v. 22). This was a momentous statement containing truth to which Job was not necessarily committed, particularly because it was only a half-truth. It was half true because destruction had befallen Job who knew he was *tam* ("blameless"). It was only half true because the "He" Job blamed (vv. 22–24) for that destruction was God. In his pain he spoke to God freely, as a friend, sharing with Him his confusion. He even concluded that he would never again live without pain and suffering (vv. 27–28).

Job was fearful of his sufferings (v. 28)—he feared to be optimistic lest he be proved wrong by suffering. By saying that God was not human like he was (v. 32), Job was acknowledging the great distance separating him and all humans from God. He doubted that God would even listen to his voice (9:16) or that his condition could be arbitrated because he lacked a mediator (9:33). But there was a possible solution (vv. 34–35): the withdrawal of His rod. The rod, the agent of discipline, may have stood for the discipline itself. If God would relent in His aggression, Job would find the courage to speak up and to make his case before Him.

But Job chose to complain and express how he felt as he continued to speak to God (10:1–7). He was not describing how God is but seeking to understand why he was experiencing so much pain. Hence, Job challenged God to justify what he was experiencing (10:2) and accused Him, through a series of rhetorical questions, of seemingly behaving like a flawed human (10:3–5), finding guilt where there was none (10:6–7). Then Job contrasted God's previous protection and support with what appeared to Job as wrath and condemnation (vv. 8–17). God, who formed his embryo (10:10), brought it to maturity (10:11), and providentially cared for him (10:12), seems to Job to have harbored ill intent against him all along (10:13–17).

Job asked whether God was trying to destroy him (v. 8). The Hebrew word used here (*bala'*— "swallow up") echoes 2:3 where Satan had been inciting the Lord to do this to Job. Job said that God was marking, watching, or guarding him (Heb. *shamar*; v. 14), another echo of the prologue. There the Lord commanded Satan to preserve Job's life (*shamar*; 2:6). Job had just celebrated God's care that had preserved (*shamar*) his spirit (10:12), but now it seemed as though the purpose of God's *shamar* was for the sake of finding fault. Job spoke of being full of shame or disgrace (v. 15), stating that God was overwhelming him (cf. 9:18) with bitterness. Job now listed manifestations of that bitterness, such as disgrace and misery, with which he was full.

The end of v. 17 has been translated variously as "changes and war," "wave upon wave" of "forces," "fresh troops," or "hardship after hardship." The Hebrew word *tsaba'* can be taken literally as "army," "warfare," or metaphorically as hardship. These terms are also employed in

14:14, where *tsaba'* is sometimes translated as "hard service." In v. 17 Job seemed to be saying that he was constantly being called upon to render more hard service. His guard duty would not end. He renewed his old lament (10:18–22). He sighed, longing to be stillborn (10:18–19)! But while he emphasized the rest that comes with death (recorded in chap. 3), he underscored here the disorder of pitch blackness (10:21–22) and again referred to the grave as a place from which he would not return—in the sense of returning to life as it had been previously.

11:1–20. Zophar: Apparent Grace. Zophar was the least sensitive of the friends and least deferential to Job. He launched a brutal attack on Job (vv. 1–6) and returned to the question of 4:17 and 9:2: Can a human being be righteous? Zophar argued that a revelation from God would condemn Job (v. 5), for when God passes by (*khalap*) He imprisons humans and condemns them (v. 10). The verb *khalap* was used by Eliphaz to refer to the apparition of the spirit that spoke to him (4:15), and now it is used by Zophar to state that when God approaches humans He brings a message of condemnation. God, for Zophar, can only condemn humans as Eliphaz's spirit argued. Zophar had continued insisting that empty talk would not vindicate anybody. He said that Job had mocked, but it is not clear when such a thing took place. Other speakers had leveled no such accusation. Since Bildad, Job had spoken of God's power and Job's impotence before it, lamented his life, and longed again for death. The book of Job also does not support Zophar's accusation that Job had claimed that his teaching was pure. It seems improbable that Job had made such an assertion. Misattribution on Zophar's part seems more likely since someone had spoken, hypothetically, of Job being pure (Bildad, in 8:6).

In contrast with Zophar's claim, the reader may consider Job's recent attitude of humility before God (10:15). Zophar's accusation, significantly uncharacteristic of Job's language, mood, and tone, is more illustrative of the passion and blunder of human arguments in the name of God. In the first part of v. 6, the Hebrew word *kepel*— "the double"—has been variously rendered in context as "they would double your prudence," "true wisdom has two sides," or "He is manifold in understanding." The last part of the verse literally refers to the idea that God had forgotten some of Job's iniquity and has been rendered as Zophar saying that Job had received less punishment than he deserved from God. Zophar claimed that God might properly be punishing Job more severely. In vv. 7–12 he expounded on God's greatness and also the wickedness and deceit of some humans. His language soared as he extolled God. He used a proverb to describe the difficulty of those who were foolish to become wise—it was less likely than a donkey's colt being born as a human (v. 12).

Zophar spoke of hope in repentance in his final segment (vv. 13–20). Like Eliphaz and Bildad, he assured Job that repentance would bring him deliverance from his present suffering. His guilt had brought him divine wrath, but his case was not hopeless. The admonition that Job should stretch out his hands toward God described an act of adoration and supplication and is a frequent OT expression (e.g., Pss. 44:20; 143:6). Wickedness or evil (v. 14) is here personified as a conscious being that should not be a welcome occupant in Job's home.

Zophar then suggested that Job could return to his former life if he were humble and repentant (vv. 14–15). Then Job would be able to forget his troubles—they would be like water that had passed by (v. 16). Zophar sought to make a positive application of Job's pessimistic simile of vanishing water (6:15–21). He suggested that Job's misery would disappear as completely as water does when a wadi dries up. He would then be able to *khapar*—"dig" or "search"—followed by rest in safety. This suggests searching or checking and finding everything in order—this would mean the end of Job's tormented nights (see 3:26; 7:13–14). Failing eyes (v. 20) are listed among the curses of Deuteronomy (28:65) that would befall God's unfaithful people.

12:1—14:22. Job: Divine Power, Creaturely Finitude. This final speech of the first cycle opens on a note of indignation at Job's friends (12:1–6). Job's sarcastic answer revealed his irritation at their doctrinaire condemnation of his character. Job was scornful of the idea that his friends' point of view was the only one that mattered (v. 2). Job seems to have emphasized (v. 5) the friends' self-righteous attitude of complacency because danger can only befall people who are doomed to trouble anyway. Job continued to be preoccupied by life's injustice and observed that criminals prosper undisturbed (v. 6). His friends joined in ridicule of the righteous person, Job himself, missing the fact that wickedness thrives in the world. The wicked thrive on power that comes from the same God whom the wicked defy.

Job's taunt lines (12:7–12) have become famous for extolling the wisdom of God as known through nature. In the context of the book they contrast with what Job had been saying thus far and are introduced with a very strong adversative conjunction ("but"). The friends find it obvious that God blesses the good and punishes the wicked. So obvious, Job now said, that any creature can tell you that "the hand of the LORD [Yahweh] has done this" (12:9). This is the only time the name of Yahweh appears in the dialogue between Job and his friends.

Job suggested that ears evaluate words, palates evaluate foods, and the aged evaluate knowledge (vv. 11–12). Bildad had referred to the wisdom of the aged (8:8–9), and Eliphaz would also seize upon it (15:7–10). Having mocked his friends' naive claim that the wicked always suffer and the righteous always prosper, Job now depicted a God entirely more unpredictable in His power than their reasoning allowed (12:13–25). Job's experience had no specific moral implication because God's power rules over all areas of our lives (v. 16). God also rules over the nations (v. 23).

Beginning with 13:1, Job's refuting of his friends' arguments included a protest that he did have wisdom, that he preferred an audience with God, and that his friends should be silent since God Himself would repudiate their fraudulent characterizations of His person. Job recognized the risks of daring to discuss his case with the Almighty (vv. 14–15). The alternate Hebrew reading "I have no hope" is not supported by vv. 15b, 16: Job viewed God as his salvation—and he was not a hypocrite. Job had certainly not given up God. At this point Job's confidence in God's salvation and his integrity still assured him of vindication before God.

Job then launched into his most extended address to God (13:20—14:22). But his optimism would not remain constant, and gradually he focused less and less on speaking directly to God. His hope of swift physical restoration also seems to have faded. He may have clamored less for God's personal attention because he no longer expected that God would promptly alleviate his suffering. As he lost hope of early physical restoration, there was less direct engagement between him and the God he spoke of but could not find.

He spoke much less to God in the second and third cycles. And though he never abandoned his insistence on personal integrity or his clamor for vindication, he seems obliged to conceive of it in terms that were different both temporally and legally. By the second cycle his hope rested in seeing his Redeemer in the future (19:25). And by his oath at the end of the third cycle, he was apparently resigned to his black and flaking skin and burning body (30:30). No allusion was made to any form of physical restoration. Job was reduced to arguing with himself, his friends having surrendered (32:1), and clinging to the ironclad certitude that acquittal in court would grant him the moral and legal vindication he deserved—and which it seems was the only thing for which he could still hope.

"Hand" here means "oppression" (13:21). Job did not wish to be far from God. In fact, he continued to demand an audience with Him. Job was confused as to why God would pursue a weakling such as he—like a leaf or dry stubble/chaff (v. 25). Job referred to "bitter things" (v. 26; cf. Ex. 15:23), meaning that while God's accusations were hard to stomach, they reminded Job of his indiscreet youth. The reference to the decay, or wasting away of human beings (Job 13:28), expressed a sentiment more clearly connected with what follows in chapter 14 and should be thought of as introducing a new section that ends at 14:22.

Chapter 14 is the second part of Job's third address to God, introduced in 13:28, as Job turned from defending his integrity against his friends to reflections on the finality of death. Job's reference to people's lives being "full of trouble" (v. 1) takes us back to Eliphaz who said that humans are born to trouble (5:7). Job more than agreed. By saying that human beings are like shadows, Job applied to humanity the fleeting days he applied to his own life (9:25). He wondered why God pays attention to finite humanity (14:3), something that may only increase their stress. He longed for God to let humanity rest (v. 6). Humanity's fate is almost the most hopeless one within creation. Plants can spring up again, but death is the end for humans (14:10, 12)—at least "till the heavens are no more" (v. 12).

Here in this verse is a hint (confirmed in other parts of Scripture; e.g., 2 Pet. 3:13; Rev. 21:1) that the righteous dead would live again. The verses that follow (14:13–17) contain further hints of resurrection: Job spoke of being hidden in the grave *until* God's anger passed, when he would be remembered (v. 13). He asked whether people would come back to life and then spoke of relief and being called (vv. 14–15). These incipient questions and longing, tentative affirmations would become a strong expression of confidence in 19:23–27. Nevertheless, the metaphors of undoing (14:18–19)

show Job returning to poetically sorrowful descriptions of the tragedy and seeming finality of death (14:20–21).

Within the overall argument about Job's integrity, he and Bildad engaged in the topic of sons. According to Bildad they had paid for their guilt (8:4). Job retorted that the doom he faced made the discussion of sons irrelevant (14:21). But in the next speech Bildad would argue that it was Job's attitude that would determine his memory and that of his offspring (18:16–19).

15:1—21:34
Second Cycle of Speeches

As in the previous cycle, in this one we listen to conversations between Eliphaz (15:1–35) and Job (16:1—17:16); Bildad (18:1–21) and Job (19:1–29); and Zophar (20:1–29) and Job (21:1–34). His friends continue to press on him their peculiar theology, and Job continues to express his pain and wish for vindication.

15:1–35. Eliphaz: Learning and Not Learning.
Eliphaz was first indignant (15:1–6), then a borrower (vv. 7–10), and a little later an echo of himself (vv. 14–16), and finally he sought again to assert that the wicked always suffer (vv. 17–35). To begin with, he suggested that Job should be silenced rather than increase his guilt by dishonest speech. He even asserted that Job was hindering piety by his words (v. 4). He accused Job of speaking from the perspective of his sinfulness and thus was expressing his lack of integrity. Bildad had used the wisdom of the forefathers (8:8–9). The consolations of God (v. 11) might refer to the counsel of himself and the others. Eliphaz also implied that Job's show of emotion was misleading and alarming (v. 12).

Eliphaz decided to return to his revelation (vv. 14–16). He reiterated the point that human beings are sinful (v. 14). Verse 16 has been interpreted and translated to mean either that all human beings are *ta'ab* ("abominable," "vile," or "detestable") and *'alakh* ("filthy" or "corrupt") or that Job himself was a particularly despicable example of human sinfulness. Verse 20 refers to the idea that the wicked or ruthless suffer according to the years appointed "for" them. This happens because they raise a rebellious hand against God (v. 25). The wicked are described as having fat faces (a symbol of prosperity); they appear to be thriving, but it ultimately proves futile.

16:1—17:16. Job: Despair and Appeal. Job expressed his bitter despair, first in addressing the friends (16:2–6), then God (vv. 7–14). He protested that he actually had prostrated himself (v. 15). His cry to the earth (v. 18) suggests his imminent demise, borrowing the terms *dam* ("blood") and *za'aq* ("cry out") from the murder of Abel narrative (Gen. 4:10). This cry lifts us up to the summit of this speech (Job 16:19) in which the God who was Abel's witness was necessarily to be Job's own. The similar words *'ed* and *sahed* can mean "witness" and even "advocate." This was a hopeful peak whose contrasting dark valley concluded the speech (17:13–16). Job still longed for a mediator to arbitrate the case between him and God (16:21). The mention of "no return" (v. 22) expressed the seeming finality of death but also made his next speech (chap. 19) all the more poignant, particularly vv. 23–27.

Job longed for God to pledge or put up security for him—an idea criticized in the human sphere three times in Proverbs (6:1; 17:18; 22:26). Job doubted that God would be surety for him. It was difficult for him to understand the attitude of his friends, and he concluded that it was God, in some sense, who kept them from grasping the true nature of his dilemma (17:4). Therefore, the drama would not conclude with any sense of triumph on their part. Job saw himself as a person whose face people spit at (v. 6), as one rejected and unclean (see Num. 12:14; Deut. 25:9). Later, Job spoke literally, not metaphorically, about people spitting in his face (Job 30:10). He then introduced a note of despair again by saying that his days were passed (17:11). Job repudiated his friends' exhortations to repent and prosper as a distortion of reality (v. 12).

18:1–21. Bildad: A Graphic Terror Story. In terms of harshness, Bildad's second speech resembles language we associate with Zophar. But Bildad's rationale continued to depend on standard wisdom thinking. His focus here continued to be Job's restoration to the community of sages. Of all the negative consequences to befall the wicked man, Bildad found no physical pain more climactic than the psychological argument of oblivion. Having dramatized the horror of his physical encounters with net, snare, mesh, noose, trap, death's firstborn, and the king of terrors (vv. 8–14), Bildad sealed his discourse on the fate of the wicked by citing four particular elements: (1) perishing of human memory or remembrance (v. 17a; cf. Eccl. 9:5); (2) the loss of name or fame (v. 17b); (3) being left without

children (v. 19a); and (4) having no survivors (v. 19b). For Bildad death was loss of remembrance, fame, son or posterity, and any survivor. In Ecclesiastes it is reward, remembrance, love, hate, envy, portion (Eccl. 9:5–6). But the similar treatment of the subject of death shows Bildad's interest in wisdom. Since Job had already lost his children, the argument based on childlessness seems at first incongruous as a basis for appeal to Job. But this view ignores that at the end Job was restored, though not on Bildad's terms, and blessed again with a quiverful of children (42:12–16).

When Bildad asked whether the earth would be deserted and rocks would be moved from their places, he implied that Job's logic went against creation's order. Everything would have to be turned upside down for him to be right. The "firstborn" (18:13) is a Semitic superlative of significance equivalent to "the greatest" (Gen. 49:3; Ex. 4:22–23; Ps. 89:20–29). Here Bildad meant "the worst kind of death." Bildad had already warned that the hope of the godless hypocrite would perish and that what they trusted in (*mibtakh*) was like a spider's web (8:13–14). It would not be difficult for the wicked to be torn from the shelter of his tent, that is, "his trust/shelter" (*mibtakh*). Job was the only other speaker to use the term *mibtakh* to deny that he had ever oppressed the poor as the wicked do (31:16–23) and put his confidence in gold (31:24). In 18:20, Bildad used two opposite points on the compass to express the total and dramatic collapse of the wicked, astonishing to them.

19:1–29. Job's Rebuke, Plight, and Vision of Vindication. This chapter records the briefest of Job's speeches and the spiritual and emotional zenith of the book. From the depths of despair at God's treatment of him (vv. 6–13), and the abandonment of servants, intimate friends, and family (vv. 14–22), Job would soar to a testimony of confidence in his final vindication (vv. 23–27). "Ten times" (v. 3) probably stood as a superlative of intensity equivalent to "the maximum" or "the ultimate" (Gen. 31:7, 41; Num. 14:22; Neh. 4:12; Dan. 1:20). Job suggested that his error was his own problem, not a basis for his friends' conceit, gloating, or denunciation (Job 19: 4). In his opening salvo, Bildad, Job's principal interlocutor, asked whether God "subverts ['*awat*, 'to pervert,' 'to wrong']" judgment or justice (8:3). Eleven chapters later Job counters with explicit usage of the same form of the verb saying that God wronged (*'awat*) him (v. 6). He had some idea of what justice should look like but argued that in his case something went wrong.

Job expressed devastation and hopelessness (v. 10). Joshua and David spoke of death as going "the way of all the earth" (Josh. 23:14; 1 Kin. 2:2), and Job was concerned about death's seeming finality (Job 10:21), like the psalmist (Ps. 39:13). Job referred also to the fact that God's afflictions of him had caused his family, friends, and acquaintances to be alienated from him (Job 19:13–19). Job's relatives had "failed" or "gone away" (lit. "my relatives have ceased")—which makes it sound as though all of Job's relatives were dead (cf. 3:17; 14:7) and shows how lonely he felt because not even his loved ones supported him. Job said that he had escaped by "the skin of my teeth" (19:20), meaning that he felt like he was barely alive and emotionally desolate. He wanted his friends' sympathy because he felt struck by God's hand. He wondered why they were adding to God's already very difficult treatment (vv. 21–22). Job again refers to God as directly striking him. His soul is very conflicted, for he cannot expect his friends' sympathy while accusing their God of violence or accusing them of not being satisfied or sated with Job's flesh (v. 22), a phrase that suggests the idea of animals eating the carcass of another beast. Obviously the usage here was not intended to be taken literally, in the sense of cannibalism, but as suggesting that the attacks of Job's friends were so intense that Job felt that they were eating him alive. The phrase could then be an idiomatic expression meaning "to slander/abuse," emphasizing the brutality of the verbal attacks (cf. Dan. 3:8).

Job longed for a permanent record that would in the end vindicate him (Job 19:23). The reference to iron, lead, and engraving (v. 24) may refer to the practice of filling the letters traced into the rock by the iron pen with lead (see Jer. 17:1). The emphasis is here on preserving the record rather than on Job's vindication. In the Hebrew text of Job 19:25, the "I" is emphatic. Job was certain about his future because he trusted in the faithfulness of his Redeemer. He looked to a time beyond death when he would share a personal encounter with the God who is the First and the Last and who was his Redeemer (see Is. 44:6).

Job's words here (19:25–27) are one of the book's great rhetorical and spiritual mysteries. They cannot be explained as following logically or emotionally from what he had been saying thus far. They stand at a crucial point in his dialogue with his friends and are the spiritual climax of his response to Eliphaz's and Bildad's false accusations. But according to Job's inspired answer, God's loyalty to His faithful children is more powerful than death and physical decay (v. 26). Job's friends still wanted to fix him, thinking of him as the real problem. He reminded them that God, the righteous Judge, would fix them instead (vv. 28–29).

20:1–29. Zophar: Insistence on Terror. In this speech Zophar tried his hardest to frighten Job into repentance by showing him the horrible fate of the wicked. His reasoning seems to be that Job would experience even more dreadful things than what he had already experienced. In his first speech Zophar suggested that Job was not suffering as much as he might because God was not treating him as he really deserved (11:6). Job's faith and fervor about his innocence left Zophar agitated (20:2). In order to sound authentic, Zophar spoke like a true sage about ancient wisdom. Bildad, Job, and Eliphaz had already spoken of the ancient wisdom (8:8–10; 12:12) because they represented this wisdom.

Zophar described the arrogance of the wicked well but apparently applied it poorly if he thought it was true of Job (20:6). This verse is a good portrait of proud rebellion (Gen. 11:4; Is. 14:14), but the portrait did not apply to Job. Zophar spoke (Job 20:7–9) of the wicked vanishing, but Job, too, knew he would vanish because of death (7:8–10). Zophar may have been evoking Bildad's first speech to refer to the evanescence of the wicked (20:7; cf. 8:18). The reference to the sweet taste of evil (20:12), while

The Redeemer

Old Testament redeemers had a comprehensive role. They could salvage a relative's property (Lev. 25:25) or buy him out of slavery (vv. 47–49). Their duty reached beyond the grave. Even after a relative's death, the redeemer could avenge his blood by killing the person who murdered his relative (Num. 35:19, 21) or preserve his name and inheritance through a special form of marriage called levirate marriage (Deut. 25:5–6; Ruth 3–4). Jacob's words about the redeeming angel, who delivered him from all evil (Gen. 48:16), show how all embracing the redeemer's work could be. In Job's case, his undoing had been so complete that he needed total redemption, much more than just someone to clear his name.

rue of the wicked in general in many cases, cannot be applied to Job because he had neither partaken of evil nor tasted anything sweet. He had tasted the unpalatable (6:6-7, 30) or bitter misery (9:18), his soul had been bitter (7:11; 10:1), and God had written bitter things against him (13:26). There was no "sweetness" in Job's life. But after Zophar's speech Job did speak of sweetness—the sweetness of oblivion at the end of a wicked person's life (21:33).

Zophar also referred to the evil of oppressing the poor (20:19). If he was attempting to apply this to Job, this would contrast with what Eliphaz first said about Job, namely, that he strengthened the weak (4:3-4). God is right to punish the wicked who purvey social injustice, and he could have been implying that Job was guilty of such (22:6-11). Zophar believed that the wicked cannot escape God's wrath (20:24). His lesson on divine retribution is vivid. Both Bildad and Zophar concluded using the image of inheritance (v. 29). While Bildad mentioned what people stand to lose by rejecting God (fame, name, survivors), Zophar mentioned what wicked people gain—a graphically horrible end. And its horror, for Zophar, is not by chance. It is what God Himself bequeaths.

21:1-34. Job's Response to Terror Stories.

Job next painted his own very different picture of the life of the wicked as long, prosperous, and secure. He asked rhetorically if his complaint was with other human beings—and a negative answer was implied (v. 4). This offered reassurance to Job's companions and also clarified his focus. He was attempting to maintain friendship, but they infuriated and mocked him (15:12; 19:3; 21:3); they never called him friend. But he repeatedly identified them as friends—whether directly or implicitly (6:27; 16:20; 19:19, 21), and even brothers (6:15). His question implied that, whether irritated by them or not, his quarrel was ultimately not with humans. For no one but God could answer his questions about the injustice of his experience. Just calling them to mind made him shudder (21:6).

The description that follows about how wicked people live and die goes against everything that seems fair; it contradicted everything about the popular, cause-and-effect doctrine of retribution promoted by his friends. In effect, Job found his thoughts to be frighteningly true. When he stated that their descendants were established (21:8), he indicated the opposite of Bildad's claim that the wicked have no posterity, progeny, or survivor (18:19). He also observed that their bulls breed (21:10)—this signified high yielding stocks. The wealth of the wicked multiplies. Job's comment about the death of the wicked in v. 13 implies that they die without suffering. Elsewhere, Deuteronomy 7:4 refers to sudden death as God's punishment, and Job himself spoke of it as proof that life is fickle (Job 9:23). The prosperity of the wicked is not in their hands (21:16). Some read it as a question: "Behold is not their prosperity in their hand?" This would imply that their success is of their own making. Taken as a negative statement, the sentence means that the wicked are not in charge of their success. Job would then be rejecting the presumption of living so self-centeredly with breath that comes from God.

The rhetorical questions in v. 17 effectively argued against the claim that wickedness automatically brings misery. The translation and interpretation of v. 19 is difficult. According to some translations, Job was saying that instead of children being punished for their parents' wrongdoing, God should pay back the wicked directly. According to others, Job was refuting what his friends had said—that children are punished for their parents' wrongdoing. According to yet others, Job was saying that both children and parents should be punished, but that even if the children are, the parents often do not know about it. It appears that Job was saying (as he had throughout this section) that the wicked do not always receive their punishment in this life, even though their children might suffer as a result of their wrongdoing (vv. 20-21; cf. 27:14-15). In other words, Job wondered what difference punishing their children would make to dead people. The rhetorical question "Can anyone teach God knowledge?" suggests that the God who rules the *ramim*—"the exalted ones," "those on high," or "the highest"—surely knows what He is doing with humanity.

Job then observed that some people die in prosperity and others in misery. The first word of 21:24 in the Hebrew is *'atin*—a word that appears only once in Scripture, and its translation is uncertain. It is usually rendered as "breasts" because Job said that it is full of *khalab*—literally "milk." The phrase could metaphorically mean "well nourished" or "well fed," which conveys the basic meaning of the verse. The particular Hebrew word for thoughts or thinking (v. 27) here refers to assessment, and the word for schemes also often refers to evil plans. Job knew that his friends had concluded that he was receiving the punishments of God reserved for the wicked. Job suggested that his friends should learn from the testimony of those who travel and who have experienced life fully (v. 29). They would support Job's position. Some translations have the idea in v. 30 that the wicked are "reserved" for the day of trouble, others that they are "spared" from it. Job argued that the wicked do very well; they are (at least for now) spared from doom and wrath.

22:1—27:23
Third Cycle of Speeches

In this last cycle of speeches we hear only the voice of Eliphaz (22:1-30) and Job's response to him (23:1—24:25) and that of Bildad (25:1-6) followed by Job (26:1—27:23). Eliphaz's use of strong words includes some positive elements. The speech of Bildad was short and reaffirmed the first speech of Eliphaz.

22:1-30. Eliphaz's Final Manipulative Effort. In this his final speech, Eliphaz spoke both his angriest and his most positive words to Job. His denunciations were fiercer, while his invitation was more promising. He followed the stern criticism of social justice with eleven verses that mostly describe the glowing relationship Job would enjoy with God if he would only return to Him. The irony of Eliphaz's closing exhortation is that the book affirms Job's intimacy with God at its beginning and at the end. With his initial questions (vv. 2-3), Eliphaz alludes to his first speech, where he stated that God considers humans and angels by nature to be unworthy of standing before Him (4:21-21). That supernatural visitation forms the spine of the arguments of the friends in the book, running from Eliphaz's first through Bildad's last intervention. But their repetition does not make it true.

Eliphaz wanted to strip Job of his self-conceit, suggesting that it was his sin, not his fear or reverence for God, that had brought him his hardships (v. 4). In the Hebrew text the phrase regarding the charges brought against Job in the judgment is the same used by Job in 9:32 and 14:3. In the first, Job spoke of the impossibility of going to court together with God. Then in chapter 14 he voiced frustration over God's bringing a feeble mortal into judgment. As the reader knows, Job was wrong, and Eliphaz even more completely so. God was not hauling Job into court or punishing him. It was Satan who was abusing him. And it was precisely because of the devotion that Eliphaz once praised (4:6) and now mocked that Satan poured out his spite upon him. Verses 5-9 in chapter 22

record inventions of Eliphaz's desperation, all false accusations against Job.

Eliphaz accused Job of using brute force to exploit society's vulnerable (vv. 5-7). The powerful, honorable man (v. 8) was the one to whom people deferred. This person is described in a Hebrew idiom as one whose face is lifted up. Job, and later Elihu, used the same idiom in 13:8, 10 and 32:21 to refer to showing partiality. It is difficult to connect the charge in 22:13 to any of Job's previous words. It was a sheer distortion of his words. He now quoted Job (v. 17), citing Job's previous criticism of the wicked (21:14)—and perhaps implying that it applied to Job himself. Then Eliphaz appealed to Job to have a relationship with God that would bring wholeness (22:21). But his twisted judgment on Job made it difficult for Job to draw real hope from his optimistic-sounding language. Verses 21-30 close Eliphaz's body of speeches that began in 4:2-6. His words here included the sympathy absent from the rest of the speech. They reflected a sensitivity that was last heard from Eliphaz in the introductory words of his first speech (4:3-4). They were the enticement of the carrot after the rhetorical beating with the stick. Affirming as they may have been, they did not correct his false statements or undo the damage done to his relationship with his friend or to the character of the God he had claimed to speak for.

23:1—24:25. Job: Longing and Contradiction. This speech may be remembered for three things: (1) Job's dismay at God's inscrutability—he could not understand what He was doing, nor could he locate Him in order to find out (chap. 23); (2) his sense of God's knowledge of his integrity, even through this trial (23:10); and (3) his extended portrayal of the fate of the vulnerable at the hand of their exploiters (chap. 24). At the conclusion he dared anyone to disprove his account of the prosperity and fate of the wicked (24:25).

Job was confident of being acquitted, both because he was innocent and because his judge was fair (23:7). Job averred that he had kept God's ways and not turned away from his loyalty to Him. He treasured His words even more than food (v. 12). Job said that God does as He pleases (v. 13), and He would carry out what He had determined in regard to Job (v. 14). Job had anxiety as well as confidence since he did not know what God would do (vv. 13-17). Though terrified, Job was not silenced by the darkness and gloom that covered his face (v. 17). He posed a question (24:1) concerning the obscurity of God's "times"—His judgment schedule—a reality ignored by the powerful in their abuse of the desperately poor, as Job observed. Job described the wretchedness of the victims of exploitation (vv. 5-8) and narrated the violence of the strong (vv. 2-4, 9-11).

To all appearances the wicked are allowed to act with impunity (v. 12). Job showed (vv. 13-17) how their rejection of light enshrouds them in the darkness of their own criminality until the morning is the same to them as the terrors of deep darkness (v. 17). Some translate v. 18 as Job's expression of what "should be." Other translations consider vv. 18-25 as quoting the words of the friends: "You [the friends] say...." But the idea of a quote from the friends does not fit the context. Job's point was that evildoers do not last forever, that the grave will consume them, and that wickedness not merely "should" but will be broken (vv. 19-20). In other words, the wicked will eventually receive punishment, although that does not happen in all cases in this life, as his friends had claimed.

25:1-6. Bildad: Dialogue's Collapse. This is Bildad's final speech in which he finally surrenders to the lie of Eliphaz's opening speech (4:12-21), which he alone had originally refused to endorse. Scholars worry about Bildad's brevity here and the absence of a third speech by Zophar. But the book of Job is the documentation of a furious quarrel and not simply a theoretical treatise. Indeed, the greater perplexity may well be that Bildad, after long independence, so suddenly surrenders to ideas and language he has thus far not used. His unmodified falling into line with Eliphaz's distortion means that the friends' defense has collapsed, with no more hope of any new or helpful argument. Bildad argued that God is matchlessly great and all humans are simply flawed and as worms before Him (25:5-6). This was an emphatic echo of the sentiments of 4:19-20. There Eliphaz, by revelation, pronounces that if God does not even trust His angels, it is impossible for humans to enjoy His esteem (4:19-20). The friends' arguments concluded on this note regarding God's view of humanity.

26:1—27:23. Job: Emphatic Defense. Job continued to be contemptuous of the friends' elaborate speeches (26:2-4), but his most emphatic arguments in this section combined his familiar avowals of innocence (27:2-6) with arguments that sound very much like those of his friends in regard to the eventual fate of the wicked (27:7-23). The imagery of the trembling dead (26:5) does not contradict the fact that the dead know nothing (Eccl. 9:5). The Hebrew word for the "dead" here is *repa'im*, sometimes also translated "shades" or even "departed spirits"—a term that might have the unfortunate connotation of "ghosts" and thus contradicts the biblical teaching of sleep in death (cf. Ps. 6:5; 115:17; Dan. 12:2; John 11:11-12; 1 Cor. 15:51; 1 Thess. 4:13-14). This term (*repa'im*) is found in poetic texts to refer to those who died as totally lacking strength in the depth of the tomb (Sheol), the place of destruction (Job 26:6). The presence of God causes the impossible to happen: the dead react with trembling/deep anguish. Job stated that all things and beings, whether human or other, are subject to the absolute mastery of the God of life and creation (see also Pss. 74:12-17; 89:10; Is. 30:7; 51:9-10).

The reference to the pillars of heaven (Job 26:11) is imagery used to describe the earth as a building having columns supporting the sky. This is probably a reference to the mountains. Job's way of expressing the intensity of his commitment to integrity was by swearing in God's name (27:2). Verse 18 refers to the flimsy constructions of wickedness: the moth's house is its cocoon; the word for "booth" or "hut" (Heb. *sukkah*) is the term used for temporary shelters constructed for a few days. Stability and permanence are not features of wickedness.

The negations of v. 19 have been translated as referring to the transitoriness of life, but they have also been understood as expressing the transitoriness of human riches. They are there, but when people awaken, when they open their eyes, the riches are no more. Wealth vanishes and so does a person (v. 21). The east wind, known for its ferocity (Ex. 14:21; Ps. 48:7), eliminates the person. Thus, Job's complete rejection of his friends' arguments was a rational and emotional reaction provoked by their assaults on his integrity and not necessarily a rejection of their characterizations of the fate of the wicked. But even this speech, so much in sympathy with arguments they themselves had made, did not move them to change. They remained entrenched in their opposing camps.

28:1-28

Interlude: Ode to Wisdom

Within the dialogues between Job and his friends, this poem stands apart. Though it includes no introductory note to the effect, its dispassionate tone and lack of invective and personal attack mark its singularity within its context. And the unique way that Job's words are reintroduced in the chapter that follows also emphasizes the independence of Job 28 from the flow of personal arguments that makes up the dialogue. Scholars debate whether Job or the author of the book wrote the chapter. Divided into three sections, it focuses on human accomplishment (vv. 1–11), highlights human inadequacy (vv. 12–22), and honors divine omniscience, ending with God's definition of wisdom (vv. 23–28).

Thematically speaking, Job 28 documents a soliloquy on the phenomenon of wisdom that reviews the course of nature and human ingenuity, exploration, and discovery.Job sought for a satisfactory answer on the source, location, and definition of true wisdom. He began his soliloquy by pointing out that people put an end to darkness (v. 3) by exposing and exploring earth's remote regions and depths and bringing light and knowledge where before there were darkness, concealment, and ignorance. Job referred (v. 4) to places (lit. "forgotten by feet"), that is, forgotten in the sense of neglected—some translations have "untouched by human feet" or "unknown to those who walk." The poet described regions as forgotten because they were unfamiliar and rarely, if ever, trodden.

A miner's work can be precarious (v. 4). Job's mention of fire (v. 5) may have referred to the hot conditions in which mining must sometimes be done in contrast to the relative calm on earth's surface. Miners set to work on the flinty rock, accomplishing in the process what Job said God in His anger does, overturning mountains (v. 9; cf. 9:5).

People do not know the value and worth of wisdom (v. 13): value and worth are translations of a Hebrew word, *'erek*, that also means order. It is not that humans lack appreciation for wisdom but that it is beyond their control and manipulation (vv. 13–22). This is the point of vv. 13–22. Verses 23–27 indicate that it is a spiritual matter that only the all-knowing God may properly assess. The fear of the "Lord" here (v. 28) is *'adonai*, the only appearance of this word in the book of Job. By shunning evil, Job reveals understanding and wisdom (cf. Prov. 9:10). Thus, at the climax of this independent poem, set apart from the hostilities of the argument's partisanship, we learn again of Job's true standing before the God with whom he still longed to have an audience. Through the verse's synonymous parallelism, the reader is told that Job, in God's definition, is a person of wisdom.

29:1—31:40
Job's Final Speech

The seemingly independent character of Job's final speech is detached from the thrust and parry of the friends' sustained confrontation, suggesting that it may not be part of the main dialogue or that there was a break in the discourse for some period of time and Job began again with another thought. The singular phrasing that opens chapter 29, which refers to the resumption of Job's speaking, seems to support such a view. In chapter 29 Job described divine ministrations (vv. 2–6), human reactions to him (vv. 7–12), reasons why he commanded respect (vv. 13–17), his now surrendered expectations of his final days (vv. 18–20), and his earlier days of honor (vv. 21–25).

29:1–25. Reminiscence: Yesterday's Dignity.
In v. 2, "months" is in parallel with "days." This does not in itself tell us how long Job's trial had continued thus far. On balance Job may have fretted much more than savored God's "watching" him (7:12; 10:14; 13:27). But he still longed for such times (v. 2). Verse 4 records one of Job's few and most direct answers to Eliphaz, whose challenge may be recalled from 15:8. Eliphaz asked rhetorically (expecting a negative answer) if Job had access to knowledge from God. The author through narrative and in Job's own sayings repeatedly commented on Job's integrity and godliness. Beyond this, Job's counter to Eliphaz, recalling times when he was close to and sheltered by God's counsel, seems all the more credible because it was far removed from the heat and confrontation of the dialogue recorded in earlier chapters. It is not to be dismissed as the mere look backward through rose-tinted lenses.

Job's mention of his children (v. 5) expressed deep emotion as it related events that the reader knows are directly connected, that is, Job's sense of the loss of intimate fellowship and friendship with God and the tragedy of his lost children. The mention of cream (not really "cream" but a fermented product of milk, similar to yogurt) and oil flowing from the rock (the olive press) provides a metaphor for Job's previous economic standing. These commodities were luxuries in a nomadic life and thus indicated the wealth that Job had enjoyed. They were so available to Job that he could speak of his life being washed with cream and pouring rivers of oil (v. 6).

Job's reference to his going out to the "gate" refers to the gate of the city as the place of political and civil deliberation; the city courts assembled there (Gen. 23:10, 18). Job was a significant personage in these deliberations. The square was an opening in the gate area. Both the deference (lit. "hiding") of the young men and the rising of the old reflected the high regard Job enjoyed (Job 29:8). "Hid" is hyperbole since the youth were not necessarily afraid but simply showing deference, while the act of standing until the great one, Job, took his seat was a precursor to a widely recognizable practice today.

The silence of the princes and nobles emphasized that everyone deferred to his presence and words. The language of the tongue being stuck to the roof of the mouth (v. 10) is graphic language used to conjure up, mainly for his own consolation, the awe in which he remembered being held by society's two categories then acknowledged, that is, age (young, old) and class (princes, nobles).

Verse 11 contains a manner of speaking that attributed to the ear and eye (in the Hebrew) what properly belonged to the person hearing or seeing. Those who saw and heard Job pronounced blessings upon him and approved of his actions. Verse 13 refers to two commendable meanings: Job received blessings from those he delivered from perishing, as well as the blessing of helping people. Verse 16 has been translated and understood as referring to Job looking into unfamiliar issues in order to help those who needed it, investigating matters before making a judicial decision, or to his taking up the cases of strangers.

Job said that he broke the fangs of the wicked and snatched the victims from their teeth (v. 17). Joel 1:6 uses the word "fangs" for lion's teeth, which provides both a frightful depiction of the wicked person in Job 29:17 and an all the more compelling sense of Job's courageous intervention. Bible readers may hear echoes of the David story (1 Sam. 17:34–35) though the second part of Job 29:17 can be understood and translated as "I made him cast prey from his teeth."

Verse 18 indicates that Job was reflecting on the expectations of one who had lived a God-fearing life as he had. He was not in complete disagreement with his friends' thoughts regarding the prosperity of the righteous and the destruction of the wicked—their retribution theology. But he recognized, as they apparently did not, that this is not a formulaic or axiomatic description of how things always work in life.

For having lived a life of care for and service to others, particularly the needy of society, he had expected to enjoy a long life—days like the sand (v. 18), a standard metaphor of multiplicity (Gen. 22:17; 41:49; Josh. 11:4); he also expected to be able to live out his days in peace and die in his (lit.) nest, that is, his home. This line almost defies the truth of death, so snug and cozy is the security of home ("my nest"). This was the prevailing concept across cultures at this time.

In Job 29:19 he employed a metaphor expressing the same idea found in the psalmist's figure of the righteous as a tree planted by the rivers of water (Ps. 1:3). It contrasts with the planting of the wicked, easily removed and not even missed by the ground from which they are uprooted (Job 8:15–18). Job expected to savor the dew (29:19), a major gift of heaven particularly valued in the desert lands of the Middle East. The dew was a constituent of the birthright, one of the OT's most significant blessings. Jacob received it from Isaac (Gen. 27:28), and the outmaneuvered Esau, when he pled for some paternal legacy too, was consoled with the promise of dew (v. 39). The bow (v. 20) reminds us that Jacob's benediction of Joseph celebrates his bow as abiding in physical and spiritual strength (Gen. 49:24; Ps. 127:3–5). Job had expected to be physically, mentally, and spiritually viable for a long time yet.

Job 29:22 refers to the previous effect of his words. The second portion of the verse could be rendered also, "My speech dropped on them"—like the dew. Among other uses, the verb "drop" refers to the preaching of the prophets (Amos 7:16; Mic. 2:6, 11). Job's audiences attached great significance to his words. In v. 24, the word *sakhaq* can be translated as "mocked," but it may also be rendered as "played," "smiled," or "laughed." Job, while complimenting himself, had already shown the awe in which he was held. In context he may have been saying that people considered it an almost unbelievable honor to be the object of Job's smile. In other words, it was easier to believe he was mocking them than that he was affirming them. Job's approving smile (lit. the light from his countenance/face) was thoroughly appreciated (see Pss. 4:6; 44:3). Job's words here also suggest that no one would do anything to lose his look of approval or to provoke its opposite, a dark countenance ("fallen" or "downcast" [Gen. 4:5, 6]; "sad" [Neh. 2:2, 3]; or "angry"/"horrified" [Prov. 25:23]). Verse 25 refers to Job's decision, which determined what everyone else would do. He was their leader.

30:1–31. Present Reality: Today's Disgrace.
Job proceeded to narrate the dramatic changes his life had undergone through his unexpected trial. He delineated (vv. 1–8) the small view he held of those who were now his tormentors. Their insults and life's torments (vv. 9–18) were possible because God had turned against him (vv. 19–26). Five more verses of personal lament (vv. 27–31) conclude the chapter. Job commented that the people mocking him were younger than he was and that he would not have even allowed their fathers to watch his dogs/sheepdogs (v. 1). Elihu's classic confession is illustrative of the status of youth in Job's traditional society (32:6). Dogs were a popular derogation in most periods of the ancient world—a fact reflected in Scripture (Ex. 11:7; 1 Sam. 17:43; 2 Kin. 8:13; Mark 7:27–28).

The Hebrew of v. 3 is unclear. The basic sense is that the people mocking Job were like hungry scavengers in the wilderness. They gathered mallow, a plant of the salt marshes (v. 4). The end of v. 4 refers to the broom tree or juniper tree, also known as the white broom tree, or white weeping broom tree; it was more a shrub than a tree but had a broad canopy, under which Elijah, for example, could sit in the shade when he fled from Jezebel (see 1 Kin. 19:4). It was used for kindling, but Job's tormentors used to gnaw on its roots for food. Job compared these unfortunate men to wild donkeys (v. 7). Despised and expelled by society, they huddled together for company and protection among the thorns of the desert. The expression of a song that taunts or mocks (v. 9) is later used to describe what Jerusalem had become to everyone after the Babylonian devastation of 586 B.C. (Lam. 3:14). Job described a topsy-turvy world in which the despised had become the despisers, and those who were society's outcasts might now pour scorn on one who had so recently stood at the apex of society.

Spitting in the face (v. 10) describes an action that was usually directed at individuals who refused to perform the levirate duty (see Deut. 25:5–9). But there is no indication that Job was being accused of such failure. He may simply have been the victim of an act that would be contemptuous, vile, in any culture. Jesus's tormentors spat in His face (Matt. 26:67).

The translation of Job 30:11 is problematic because the Hebrew manuscripts are divided between "His" and "my" before "bow" or "bowstring." This latter word can also be rendered as "rope" or "cord." In this reading ("my"), God deprived Job of his viability. The reading "His" would probably require "His cord," indicating that God unleashed an assault on Job.

Some translations interpret v. 13 to mean that those attacking Job had no helper—they practiced this violence all on their own. Others translate it as their saying "no one can help him." Job sensed that his nobility was under assault and *tirdop* (from *radap*), which can mean "pursued" or "driven away" (v. 15). But if Job had lost his dignity, as indeed he had lost his prosperity, he never lost his integrity.

Job expressed his feelings that his end was approaching (v. 16). His assailants had been, in turn, a human rabble (vv. 1–13), impersonal terrors (v. 15), and, from v. 18 onward, God Himself (notice the third person referent of vv. 19, 24 and "You" in vv. 20–23). Verse 24 could refer to either God or a human; the verse's second line is also obscure. If God was the intended subject, the first line implies the idea of hitting one who is already down. If a human being was the intended subject, then the line indicates abject misery: someone pleading from—or even being likened to—a heap of ruins. Job seems to have been wondering how anyone could be so cruel as to strike down a person who in distress cries out to him or her for help. Verse 26 indicates more than just disappointment. It was the profound despair of thwarted expectations. How could God thus deal with one who had lived as conscientiously as he, weeping for those in trouble, grieving for the poor (v. 25)?

The alleged contradiction between hoping for good and fearing evil was more imagined than real. Thus it may be quite inappropriate to set Job's hope of good in contrast to his fear of ill. Jesus instructed His followers to daily pray for deliverance from evil—both the person of the evil one and the disruptions his power inflicts (Matt. 6:13). Job's eschewing evil signifies his consciousness of what to avoid. His hope for good (the Hebrew verb translated "looked for" means "hoped for") rested on his awareness that he had lived a God-fearing life. Based on this he expected to die in his nest/house (29:18). His understanding of a life of faithfulness to God is apparent in the narrative and in the divine comment about him (1:1, 8; 2:3), as well as in his actions on behalf of his children. Those actions revealed his constant awareness of human finitude and sinfulness. They also constantly acknowledged his dependence on substitutionary atonement by an innocent victim. Job showed that he knew that his only hope for forgiveness and cleansing from sin came through the vicarious sacrifice whose virtue he claimed by faith

(1:5). Those who seek for contradictions in the Job story may grant that his condition through the dialogue is itself a grand and inherently traumatic contradiction, as his own words establish (9:20–21). But it is admirable that even through this new and miserable turn of life he may have consistently contended that God knew of his loyalty, faithfulness to His commands, and treasuring of God's words—even more than his daily food (23:10–12). The pathos of Job 30:19–26, most clearly heard against this background, points to Job's strong feelings that now, in his suffering, God appeared to be unfaithful to His unerringly faithful servant.

Verse 28 has been taken to mean that Job was mourning but not "in the sun" or that he was "blackened, but not by the sun." This is because *qadar* means "darkened" but is also associated with mourning (Jer. 8:21). Job was reduced to begging from the very ones who once looked up to him as a king (29:25). His pleas were probably unrelated to his sores or lost children. Job's great burden was his besmirched reputation and his inaccessible God whom he longed to have vindicate him.

Verse 29 refers to "ostriches," also translated "owls." Job's cries called to mind the shrieks of jackals and owls. Multiple biblical references to their dwelling among ruins, particularly jackals (Is. 34:13; Jer. 9:11; 10:22), show that he may also have equated himself with them in terms of his own status as an outcast. The music of his life had been transposed into grief (v. 31).

31:1–40. Constant Commitment: An Oath of Integrity.

In this chapter, Job unleashed his most powerful denunciation of his friends' unwarranted accusations by describing, in detail, the course of life he was known to have followed before unspeakable tragedy struck. He invoked multiple curses on himself for any forthcoming contradiction of any of his declarations about his personal, social, and economic morality. The strength of his avowals lay in more than the fervor he exhibited or the courtroom imagery with God as Judge (see vv. 35–36; also, vv. 14, 28). The moral vindication that Job could not find from the God who continued to be silent, he found in the inability of any human being—neighbor, alien/stranger, orphan, or widow—to speak in opposition to his testimony of personal integrity. Job spoke (vv. 1–12) of the inner workings of his soul to which God alone is privy; addressed (vv. 13–23) his treatment of his slaves and of society's needy (e.g., widow, orphan), conduct for which he would be equally culpable before

God but that would be apparent to his fellow humans; spoke (vv. 24–28) of idolatry—whether of the worship of gold or of sun or moon—and declared his freedom from it; extolled (vv. 29–32) his charity to enemy, neighbor, and alien alike; asserted (vv. 33–34) his freedom from hypocrisy—behavior based on what others might say; dared (in the bold invocation of vv. 35–37) God Himself and his enemy—perhaps a parallel reference to God again—to answer him (i.e., to prove him wrong). Surprisingly, his closing appeal was not before God Himself but before the land: he would have it actively demonstrate its disapproval if he had not related responsibly to these elements of his environment (vv. 38–40). With this the narrator announces the conclusion of Job's self-defense.

Job had made a covenant with his eyes to not *'etbonen* a young woman (v. 1). This is from the verb *bin*—"to understand," "to consider." Some translators render the verb "to look" or "to look lustfully" in accordance with the reference to the eyes. Job had determined to not even consider committing adultery. The language of Job's morality was as elevated as the principles it described. It is difficult to find a more solemn OT ritual than covenant making (lit. "cutting"). Cutting a covenant, or making an agreement, implied a willingness to be cut asunder if one violated the terms of the agreement. Job's agreement with his eyes was no more stern than Jesus's own words concerning plucking out an eye if it were causing sin (Matt. 5:29). Job had fretted at the obsessive closeness of God's supervision that counted his steps (Job 7:19; 14:16). He knew that God saw him. But he also valued this very guardianship (31:4). It helped him to eschew evil. Also, the fact that God saw him was a solid basis for assurance of vindication. God knew his way (Job 23:10). He was confident that he could be weighed in "honest"—"just" or "righteous"—scales. Subjected to righteous judgment, Job's integrity would shine forth before God.

Job could swear that no blemish defiled his hands (31:7). He vowed that if he had been unfaithful, then it should be that others should eat what he had sown. God predicted this consequence for Israel if they chose the path of rebellion: others would eat what they planted (Deut. 28:30, 33). Verses 9–10 exemplify *lex talionis*—the law of eye for eye and tooth for tooth—the principle that the punishment must fit the crime (see Ex. 21:23–32). Job's adultery would be an offense against another man (Lev. 18:8, 16); he would have to pay for it by being equivalently shamed.

Job 31:14 indicates the rising up of God the Judge for a decision regarding Job's guilt or innocence (Deut. 19:15–17; Is. 33:10; Dan. 12:1). The word *peqad* (Job 31:14) literally means "to visit" (Gen. 21:1; 50:25; Ex. 4:31; Ps. 106:4), but this word is also used in the OT to mean "to punish" (e.g., Isa. 26:21; 29:6; Jer. 44:29) or "to care for" or "to come to aid" (Zech. 10:3). Some translators render the word neutrally—that is, "visit" or "examine" or "call me to account"—and others as "punish." No matter which meaning is meant, Job was probably not thinking of punishment, but he knew that God would show up to scrutinize his conduct and that any divine verdict would be preceded by a divine investigation (e.g., Gen. 3:8–24; 18:20—19:29; Dan. 7:19–22, 23–27).

In Job 31:15, he stated the rationale that framed all his human relationships, a Creation principle that dictated the ethics of both commercial and noncommercial interaction, whether with people accountable to him or among society's poor for whose needs he felt a sense of personal responsibility (vv. 13–20). Job's membership among the ranks of the privileged of his society did not alienate him from the community's poverty stricken. His Creation principle, and the ethics it constrained, always works to remedy societal inequities such as slavery and human exploitation of all sorts that demean children or youth, women or men formed in the image and after the likeness of the Creator God.

Job affirmed that he had not raised his hand against the fatherless (v. 21). In the Bible the gesture of raising the hand generally expresses hostility; here it was something that Job had avoided. The verb *nup*, often translated as "raised," could be more explicitly rendered as "waved" or "wielded my hand against." Isaiah predicted terror to the Egyptians when the Lord of Hosts performed this action (Is. 19:16). Job refrained from hostility against the undefended even when he had support from the politically powerful, those in the gate (see commentary on Job 29:1–25). Based on 31:22, he understood and appreciated the significance of *lex talionis*; indeed, he considered the punishment of "eye for an eye" to be from God (v. 23).

The end of v. 27 has been rendered variously ("my mouth has kissed my hand," "my hand offered them a kiss," "threw a kiss with my hand"). It reads, literally, "my hand has kissed my mouth." The action would be a gesture of veneration to stellar objects (sun, moon) deified in many ANE cultures and countries. But for Job, neither astral deities nor the temptation to adore material wealth, personal abilities, and success would distract him from worshiping the true God (vv. 24–27). He would have no other gods before the Lord of heaven (v. 28).

Job averred that he did not rejoice at the destruction of his enemies by pridefully gloating over them (v. 29). Having progressed from his focus on inner integrity before God to his relations with society's vulnerable, thence to the issue of false gods, Job now spoke with equal clarity of conscience on the subject of enemies and aliens. They, as surely as his own people, had been the objects of his charity. Job here also denied asking for a curse upon his enemy's "soul/life" (v. 30). He did not rejoice when his enemies received what they deserved. The thought is similar to Jesus's words in the Sermon on the Mount. Job does seem to have been committed to doing good to them, if v. 31 (on providing food for all and sundry) is to be read in the context of v. 30.

Job also denied covering his transgressions as Adam had and as many people still did and do (v. 33): "*adam*" is the Hebrew term for "man," "human." Job was repudiating the charge, so typical of human beings, of concealing guilt to preserve their dignity before others or even resorting to avoiding contact with the public by staying indoors (v. 34). Zophar had implied that Job may have been hiding wickedness under his tongue (20:12), and Eliphaz had accused him of claiming that God could not see through the dark cloud (22:13–14). Job was denying any such behavior but did not, as before (31:6, 8, 10, 22), propose any negative consequence to himself should what he denied actually be true. Instead he passed on to the most daring of all his implied self-imprecations, challenging God or whoever might be his prosecutor to contradict or, in any particular, falsify his testimony. He presented his *taw*, that is, his "mark," in this case meaning his "signature" (v. 35). Job had, in effect, volunteered his own affidavit, sworn to and signed off on it, ready to plead his innocence against any indictment.

Job's attitude was the direct opposite of the cowering culprit who hides indoors. Rather, he would decorate himself with the accusations against him, totally confident of vindication. The more conspicuous the charges of the prosecutor, the more glorious would be his exoneration (v. 36). He could not go wrong, for he would be declaring the number of his steps (v. 37) to the very One who had watched over and counted them Himself. He would do it like a prince or ruler (v. 37).

In vv. 38-40 Job expressed his ecological sensitivity. Long before it was in vogue to care about the environment, the voice of Scripture was audible in solicitude for the earth and its produce. Job's inheritance in this regard was bequeathed from earth's first man and woman, and thence from the Creator Himself, to tend and care for the perfect garden (Gen. 2:8, 15). Israel's agrarian economy was to run on rhythms of work and rest for people and for land (Ex. 23:10-11; 25:8-12). Job's sensitivity to the needs of his land led him to invoke once more the law of an eye for an eye, though on this final occasion it was the earth itself that would wreak vengeance on him (Job 31:40).

The narrator's statement of the conclusion of Job's words employs a provocative word-play by resorting to the same root (*tamam*, "to complete," "to be blameless") that opened, and has fueled, the whole drama of the book. From the opening verse, readers are introduced to Job as blameless (*tam*). The narrator chose to conclude the interlocution between Job and his three friends by stating that Job's words are completed (*tammu*). The statement obliquely reminds us of Job's last affirmation before the dialogue's start. There, despite his sudden devastation and personal affliction, and the urging of his wife to do otherwise, he did not misspeak (2:10). Job also spoke (31:30) about not allowing his mouth to sin. At the book's denouement God twice ruled in Job's favor with a startling rebuke of his friends because they had not spoken correctly about Him as Job had (42:7-8). Whatever the human judgment on Job, by his friends and by generations of readers, God and the narrator establish that there is more to his conclusion than simply an end. His words may be said to be complete. His declaration of innocence ended, Job now expected God to show the evidence against him.

32:1—37:24
A New Voice

The next speaker, Elihu, seems unexpected since there was no earlier indication of his presence (2:11-13). His genealogical record is given and also his emotional state (32:1-5). After his own introduction (vv. 6-22), he would, in his speech, attempt to answer Job's arguments addressing divine chastening (33:1-33) and freedom (34:1-37), Job's culpability (35:1-16), and God's justice and power (36:1—37:24).

32:1-5. Righteous Indignation: Introduction of Elihu. The three most significant bits of information that introduce Elihu are his identity, his relative age, and his current feelings. Much of this is stated elaborately. Job and his mature friends who appear in the book of Job's dialogue as its major personalities come to the story with rather basic information—their names and where they lived. By contrast, Elihu is introduced with an elaborate genealogy and an emphatic word on his disturbed emotional state. And all of this is set in the context of his youth, which is given as the reason why he was not worthy to speak before. It is difficult to ignore the irony that the one least established in society and in this conversation is the one with the grander genealogy. Further, the quadruple statement that his anger was aroused (vv. 2-3, 5) helps prepare the reader for the ambitious exposition that is about to follow from a sincere and insecure young man.

As his final declaration of innocence (chap. 31) makes most clear, Job continued to believe that he was an honest, decent person. The Hebrew construction in 32:2 has been rendered as "justified himself rather than God," "justified himself before God," or "justified himself more than God" comes from Eliphaz's visionary experience (4:17) and should not be given a comparative translation ("more than") either here or in 4:17 because Job has not been in competition with God for righteousness. Eliphaz has said, by revelation, that God despises His intelligent creation, even His angels. But God has stated that He is proud of Job. This becomes the issue of the dialogue (see "The Vision/Dream of Eliphaz," p. 630). And on this question, the message that emerges from the book of Job is that Job's consciousness of his failings, finitude, and sinfulness did not disqualify him from the assurance of salvation and security and righteousness by faith. Job was not justified "rather than" God, but he was justified before God on the grounds of his constant dependence on God's grace (cf. 1:5), manifested in his faithfulness to Him.

Elihu showed a sense of justice: it was unsound for the friends to condemn Job while lacking proper arguments (32:3). Elihu himself would follow the social practice of the young deferring to their elders. Not only had he acted properly, but he was anxious to make this clear once he did speak up (vv. 6-7, 11-12, 16).

32:6-22. Elihu's Self-Introduction. In his eagerness to express the urgency of his words being heard, Elihu likened himself to a wind-bag about to burst. The point of his protracted self-introduction was that he had listened, as was proper, for a long time, and now he had a right to speak. Elihu claimed to have felt shy. He thought that "age should speak" (v. 7), literally, "days should speak" (i.e., more experienced people should be given preference). "Days" is sometimes used in place of "years," as is clear from the second part of the verse, since the focus is on how many of them someone has lived. But God can give wisdom to anyone, not just those who have lived a greater number of days (v. 8). Elihu emphatically states, "I, even I" (v. 10; cf. v. 17), either nervously, arrogantly, or with nervous arrogance. His mention of the wind within him literally means "the wind in my belly." The idea of words as wind (or windy words) has already been so mocked (8:2; 15:2; 16:2–4) that Elihu only exposes himself to ridicule by speaking thus of himself. But he felt forced to speak, fearing that otherwise God would punish him (32:22).

33:1–33. Elihu's First Speech: Self-Validation and the Value of Chastening. This speech combined discussions about Elihu's appropriateness as speaker and arguments on the spiritual value of chastening. Elihu's challenge (v. 5) anticipated God's own to Job in 38:1–3 and 40:1–2, 6–7. Some interpreters find that Elihu spoke for God, while others think that his challenge was a parody of God's justified demand that Job face up and answer His questions. Elihu was just as insistent as the others that Job had done something specifically to warrant a punishment from God in the form of his afflictions (which could be implied from 34:36–37). It would appear that Elihu was paraphrasing Job's words insisting on his innocence (33:9; cf. 9:21; 10:7; 16:17), at least his innocence in regard to specific sins for which he was being punished, as his other friends had asserted. Job had been clear (repeatedly) that he knew he was a sinner (7:21; 13:23, 26; 14:17; 31:33). Although Elihu's words (33:10–11) come from Job (cf. 13:24, 27), Job had not said anywhere in this dialogue the exact words that Elihu claims (33:9) to have heard him say. The basic meaning of v. 12 is that Elihu was saying that Job was incorrect.

Elihu sensed God's transcendence—God did not have to give an account for His works and made a sympathetic allusion (vv. 14–18) to Eliphaz's revelatory experience. The reference to "pit" (v. 18) here means death (17:16; Ps. 30:3). Elihu took up a familiar theme and image in 33:21: Job had spoken of the suffering of the bones of his body (4:14; 30:17, 30), in contrast with the prosperity of the bones of the wicked (21:24), yet Zophar for his part had tried to describe the misery of the wicked person's bones (20:11).

Perhaps Elihu mentioned a messenger/angel, a mediator (33:23), because Job had wished for an arbitrator (9:33). But according to Elihu, who speaks in favor of the question, God's answer would be a rebuke to both him and Job (40:1–2). The word usually rendered as "ransom" in 33:24 is related to the verb which means "to make atonement." Though he did not elaborate on the idea, Elihu's unclear thoughts nevertheless seem to suggest something of deep theological value: that the ransom (or the atonement) may be effected through the mediator he had mentioned. The mention of two or three times (v. 29) means that God tries repeatedly to save His children from disaster, without any specific numeric value. In v. 32, Elihu suggested that he was working hard to persuade Job that he had his best interest at heart. Like Eliphaz (5:27), Elihu spoke as if he were very secure in the role of instructor (33:33).

34:1–37. Elihu's Second Speech: Job's Impertinence and God's Freedom. Elihu expanded on the theme of God's freedom to do what He wills. Job had already spoken of the ear (12:11); Elihu describes it as the agent of wisdom, analyzing and critiquing words (34:3). Then, following his alleged quotation of Job's words (vv. 5–6; cf. 27:2), he rebuked Job for saying that there was no profit to delighting in God. Job had not said this precisely though he said something similar in 9:22. Job had actually attributed the more exact phraseology used by Elihu here to the wicked in 21:15. Perhaps Elihu was saying that Job was sounding too much like the wicked that he himself had denounced (34:8). The thrust of Elihu's argument, consistent with the theology of Job's three friends, was that God is too great to be wrong—an idea that Job probably supported but that made his suffering more intense because in his case God did appear to be doing him wrong. Elihu was suggesting that Job, in his questionings, was coming too close to accusing God. All flesh would perish if God took back His breath (vv. 14–15). God would not be governing if He hated justice (v. 17).

Verse 18 has been rendered in different ways. According to some translators, Elihu was using rhetorical questions to show by analogy the lack of wisdom in questioning God too much: "Is it fitting to say to a king, 'You are worthless'?" According to others, perhaps closer to the meaning of the text, Elihu was saying that God condemns whomever He wills, even if they are kings or nobles: "Is He [God] not the One who says to kings, 'You are worthless'?"

Elihu finished his explanation of why Job was wrong by pointing out that God sees everything (vv. 21–22) and as a result does not need to have anyone appear before Him for judgement (v. 23). Those who are wicked, He punishes (vv. 24–27), particularly those who oppress others (v. 28). He is in control for the good of the people (v. 30), and no person or nation can stop Him (v. 29). Ultimately Elihu wanted Job to understand that simply denying that he did something wrong did not make it so (vv. 32–33). And saying that he had had enough punishment would not lift the punishment (v. 31). As a result, the words Job said sounded like foolishness (vv. 34–35) and worse, rebellion (v. 37). Job had clapped at his friends. During the time of Jeremiah this was a way to show contempt (Lam. 2:15). Because of this Elihu judged that Job deserved punishment without mercy (34:36).

35:1–16. Elihu's Third Speech: Job's Flagrant Culpability.
In this speech Elihu was more consistently negative than ever. He drew out the implications of Eliphaz's revealed message: neither humans' wickedness nor their goodness makes any difference to or impression on God (vv. 4–8). He quoted Job as saying that his righteousness was more than God's (v. 2), an idea introduced in the argument by Eliphaz as a revelation from a spirit (4:17). They are both on the wrong side because the revelation is a deception. Elihu was angry that Job's companions had not been able to silence him (32:3, 5). He now meant to set them all straight. The truth is, Elihu argues, that when evil is overwhelming, people cry out (v. 9). Cries of desperation may be evidence that sufferers still need to learn the lesson God wishes to teach them (v. 12); they are still proud. He concluded that Job's speeches were useless in that they did not accomplish anything (v. 16). This callous theology most probably infuriated and insulted both Job and God.

36:1—37:24. Elihu's Fourth Speech: Divine Justice and Power.
In this last speech, Elihu argued that the order of the cosmos validates the law of divine retribution according to which doing what is right brings blessings from the Lord and doing wrong results in divine judgment against the wicked. Within such a theology, there is no way to justify Job's argument. His only way out is to turn away from iniquity (36:21). He spoke of himself as one who

had knowledge "from afar" (v. 3) and set out to vindicate God (vv. 2–3). Some suggest that Elihu referred to himself as the one with "perfect knowledge" of what he was about to discuss, while others suggest that the knowledge from "afar" meant knowledge from God (v. 4). When Elihu referred to (in the Hebrew) the opening (or "uncovering") of the ear (vv. 10, 15), he probably meant that God helps them to hear—listen and learn—sometimes through suffering.

Elihu's depiction of retribution is preserved in 36:5–12, where he argued that God does not preserve the wicked alive but vindicates the oppressed (v. 6) and greatly blesses the righteous (v. 7). Elihu alluded to the experience of Job when he considered the possibility that a righteous person may experience affliction. But according to him, in such cases God was disciplining the righteous. God wanted them to acknowledge their transgression and pride and to turn from iniquity (vv. 8–10). Were they to return to God, they would prosper; otherwise they would "perish by the sword" (vv. 11–15). Job's servants had died by the sword (1:15, 17).

Elihu addressed Job directly to apply the results of his previous discussion about God's power to him. He argued that had Job turned to God, He would have delivered him from his distress. Salvation is often described in the Bible as being placed by the Lord in a broad place (v. 16)—free from emotional or physical confinement. Various translations and scholars differ on the words and meaning of v. 18. Some translations express the idea that Job should beware of God's wrath and that a large ransom could not help him to escape it. Others suggest that Job should not let wrath lead him to scoffing and that he should not let the greatness of the ransom turn him aside. Still others read the verse as a warning against being enticed by riches. In Job's case, he received from the Lord the punishment deserved by the wicked (v. 18). It would be impossible for him to provide a ransom that would free him from God's wrath (vv. 18–20). Since Job did not turn from iniquity, he was being afflicted (v. 21). God had been trying to teach him something, but he chose not to learn.

The last section of Elihu's speech is a description of God's power over the natural world, more specifically over meteorological phenomena such as rain, clouds, thunder, and lightning (vv. 27–33). These God uses to judge people, which in context means to give abundant food to some and punish others.

These ideas are further developed in chapter 37, where Elihu speaks again directly to Job (v.

2). The main emphasis was on the lightning and thunder (vv. 3–5), interpreted by him as God's voice, although the snow is mentioned as well as ice storms. They are all under the power of God, and consequently, they do whatever He commands them to perform (vv. 6–12). The reason for the discussion of God's power over nature is clearly stated by Elihu: to correct the wicked or to show His mercy to others (v. 13)—the law of radical retribution. He confronted Job with a list of rhetorical questions on the topic of God's works of creation to demonstrate, as in the previous passages, that God is righteous in whatever He does (vv. 14–22). Elihu felt that because nature spoke so strongly about God's goodness and wisdom, God could not be questioned regarding the punishment that Job was clearly enduring. Consequently, the real topic was not the natural world but the fact that God is abundant in justice and that He does not oppress the innocent (v. 23), implying that Job was not as innocent as he claimed. God gives to humans what each one deserves because He is absolutely impartial. The only thing expected from Job was to revere God (v. 24).

It is clear that Elihu's last speech is from beginning to end about his personal understanding of divine retribution. It is particularly interesting that his discussion of God's power over nature is exclusively about meteorology, in which God is described as a storm god who controls thunder, rain, wind, and lightning. The servants of Job were killed by lightning, and his sons and daughters by a strong wind (1:16, 18–19). The implication is that since God controls storms, He used them to discipline or punish Job. According to Elihu, Job stood condemned before the Lord. But one more voice is about to be heard in the dialogue.

38:1—42:6
THE THEOPHANY:
GOD CONFRONTS JOB

The transition between chapters 37 and 38 appears to be a little abrupt. Unlike all other times, here Job did not respond when Elihu finished speaking. The reason is that in his last speech Job presented before God the evidence of his innocence (an oath of integrity) and then waited for the Lord to speak and present evidence against him. However, God cannot be forced to speak whenever a human being wants Him to speak; He is the one who decides when to answer. Meanwhile the time between Job's last speech and the divine response was filled

by the unexpected speech of Elihu. When God finally appeared on the scene to address Job, He ignored Elihu's speech, given after Job's dialogue with his friends had ended. The Lord entered in a whirlwind that seemingly brushed aside the speaking Elihu, whom God does not even mention when He later rebuked the three friends (42:6–9). Some have suggested that God seems to have continued the theme of Elihu on God's power over nature and that, consequently, what Elihu stated was basically right. As we have seen, this is hardly the case because Elihu's theological agenda was radically different from God's.

It was from the whirlwind that God delivered two monologues, each followed by short dialogues: first divine monologue (38:1—39:30), dialogue between God and Job (40:1–5), second divine monologue (40:6—41:34), and dialogue between God and Job (42:1–6). Terrifying natural displays (v. 1) are a standard feature of the self-revelations of the God who is Creator and Lord of all nature (Ex. 19:16–20; Ps. 50:3–4; Ezek. 1:4; Nah. 1:3; Hab. 3:3–15; Zech. 9:14).

38:1—39:30
Yahweh's First Monologue:
God's Omnipotence

In the first divine monologue God appeared and summoned Job to enter into a dialogue with Him (38:1–3), something Job had been asking for (13:22; 23:5). God questioned Job about inanimate objects (38:4–38) and providence and the fauna (38:39—39:30). These were rhetorical questions that God did not expect Job to answer and that, in any case, he would not have been able to answer.

38:1–3. Job's Surprise: Yahweh's Appearance and Summons. Though Job had long clamored for a hearing before God, he was totally unprepared when it took place. He did not even speak when God challenged him to the confrontation. Then God unleashed a torrent of questions upon him. According to God's initial challenge, Job's uninformed words obscured the issue (v. 2). Yet God would say at the end that no one had spoken as rightly concerning Him as Job had (42:7, 9). Evidently, neither Job nor any of the other speakers fully grasped the issues at stake—none of them knew of Satan's cynical demand. Nevertheless, God did find something to honor in both Job's words and spirit during the stormy dialogue with his friends. Verse 3 reads literally, "Gird up your loins," which originally referred to pulling up one's long robe between one's legs and tucking it into the belt to prepare one to move more freely—or to be ready to perform a difficult task (1 Kin. 18:46; Jer. 1:17).

38:4—39:30. Yahweh's Transcendence: Rhetorical Questions to Job. God next subjected Job to a series of questions that first covered inanimate elements (38:4–38) and the fauna (38:39—39:30). Through a speech overflowing with attractive metaphors, God emphasized His awareness of both animate and inanimate creation and His care for a fallen creation: the fierce lion, scavenging vulture, gentle mountain goat, and vulnerable ostrich, as well as the man on the war horse. God's questions and survey show Him as very much aware of it all—the implication being that He was not simply aware but running, managing, controlling all life and nature, something Job was not unaware of (12:9–10).

The parallel reference to morning stars and sons of God, sometime rendered "angels" (38:7), indicates that they designate the intelligent, non-divine members of God's court first mentioned in Job 1:6. Doors, womb, and wrapping in darkness (38:8–9) are all metaphors for shorelines that keep the sea in bounds. The imageries highlight both the sea's almost irrepressible nature and the Lord's creative authority and control. Commanding the morning amounts to ordering the sun to rise and the light to reach out to the earth (v. 13). In v. 13, God is alluding to Job's own concern with criminal activity being covered by darkness (24:13–17) and reminds him that commanding the light would enable God to control such activity. Light gives and reveals the earth's character and contours, shape, and beauty. Since light is withheld (38:15) from the wicked, their wickedness is cemented, which will ultimately result in their final collapse. Job is ignorant of the storehouse of the snow, thus pointing to his inability to rule over it (v. 22). While the identity of some of the terms used to refer to heavenly bodies remains uncertain, Job is not unaware of these starry elements (vv. 31–32). He has already cited their testimony to God's power as seen in their creation (9:9). God then proceeded to question whether Job knew the rules of astronomy that are related to things on earth (38:33).

Concerning v. 36, interpreters are divided between those who render "mind" and "heart" in this verse and those who consider these rare terms as references to some creature of nature such as an "ibis" and "cock." Verse 39 seems to open a new series of questions, this time on faunal references (lion), suggesting that "ibis" and "rooster" would be out of place in vv. 4–38. But whether put into a human heart or a rooster brain, wisdom always has its source in God. According to God, the chicks cry to Him for food, and He provides for them (v. 41).

The Hebrew term *pere'*, translated sometimes as "onager" (39:5), designates the wild donkey that prefers the open countryside to the crowded population centers. Concerning the ostrich, it is said literally that "God caused her to forget wisdom." This does not mean that she lost something she once had (v. 17). She simply lacks what others may possess. The stork is both more elegant in motion (ostriches cannot fly) and respected for its intelligence (cf. Jer. 8:7). But whatever her lack, the ostrich too possesses her strength. God has made her a great runner (39:18). The bird's size warrants the expression "on high." The Hebrew word *ra'mah* (v. 19) has an uncertain meaning. It could be from the word *ra'am*—"to thunder." Others have suggested that it refers to the "mane" of the horse. But it is also read as "quivering" or "vibration" and as such in this context could refer to a horse in battle when it moves with speed and passion.

The Lord's first monologue ranged widely through the mysteries of earth's founding and the sea's boundaries to light and rain, young lion, wild ox and donkey, ostrich and bloodsucking eaglet. No doubt there are countless more examples that God could have given. It is likely that He chose these because they were significant to Job and a familiar aspect of life in that part of the world. One who does not properly credit the story's integrity and its principal character's intelligence may conclude that this sequence makes no sense, whether as resolution of Job's dilemma or even confirmation of the theology of the friends or Elihu.

In order to gain a better understanding of the speech, it is necessary to return to the prologue, where Satan questioned God's integrity in relation to how He governs the world. Thus in this context, God's speeches provide testimony regarding how He runs the universe that He created, revealing that in the midst of conflicts and struggles He continues to care and to provide for all of His creation. There are not ulterior motives for providing for His creation, as Satan argued, except that He by nature cares for what is His. Unquestionably the speeches reaffirm the conviction that God is greater than Job, but their ultimate intention was to show that God freely provides and cares for His creation because that is who He is. The experience of Job, who never abandoned the Lord, shows that the relationship between humans and God is grounded in disinterested love.

40:1–5
Dialogue between God and Man: Job's First Concession

God's first monologue had sufficiently exposed Job to the limits of his knowledge and pointed not only to his position in relation to God but also to God's loving concern and care for His creation. Now God rightly demanded an answer from one who had brought a lawsuit against Him (v. 2). He had stated His case. Job must react.

Job averred that he was *qalloti*—"insignificant" (some translations have "vile"; v. 4). In fact, the nature and content of the answer may be even more striking than the fact that he spoke. He acknowledged that it was impossible for him to answer God's questions, but he was not yet ready to surrender his claim. This explains the need for a second divine speech.

40:6—42:6
Yahweh's Second Monologue: God's Supremacy

In this second monologue God confronted Job with the question of whether he would actually be willing to challenge or refute God's judgment (v. 8). If Job wanted to challenge God, he would first have to challenge the mightiest creatures God had supremacy over. God as a God of order controls Behemoth (40:15–24) and Leviathan (41:1–34), and if there is any need He restores order.

40:6–14. Challenge Renewed: Offer of Divine Prerogatives. While Job had conceded that he was not able to answer God's questions, the lesson was still not over. Heaven's purposes are not served simply because creatures acknowledge their finitude. Indeed, that would wonderfully justify the taunts of the adversary whose cynicism initiated Job's drama. It would support his claim that the relationship between God and His intelligent creation is servile—that creaturely loyalty is apparent rather than real. God is both all-knowing and all-wise. But He is also all-caring. Because Job grasped this foundational truth of His character, God, in the end, would strongly affirm him. Because the three friends both missed and denounced it, God, in the end, would fiercely denounce them. Thus, it was necessary for God to continue.

God's terseness in repeating His challenge to Job was followed by a grand elaboration on the idea of girding up one's loins. God explained the nature of the task to which He was summoning Job. In effect, He wished Job to see that it was his adversarial manner, and not his sense of questioning the meaning and justice of his lot, that God rejected. God did not have to be guilty for Job to be right (v. 8).

Nothing in the theophany is more crucial for interpreting the second divine monologue, and particularly the Leviathan phenomenon, than the topic of pride directly associate with the attitude of the wicked (vv. 11–14). The discussion is now about who is powerful enough to humiliate the proud and defeat the wicked. If Job could do such a thing (resolve the problem of evil in the world), then God would acknowledge the saving power of Job. Obviously, Job could not accomplish such a task. It was too much for him, and God would make this absolutely clear to Job through the introduction in His speech of two formidable beasts: the Behemoth and the Leviathan. Indeed, there was none but God Himself who could dare to trifle with such beasts—even Leviathan, the king over all the proud (lit. "sons of pride"; 41:34).

40:15–24. Managing the Created Order: Behemoth. The first beast mentioned in the second divine speech was the Behemoth (v. 15; see below, "Behemoth"). The word is feminine

Behemoth

The identity of the Behemoth has created much discussion, and three primary explanations have been suggested. The first seeks to match the description with a known living creature. The second seeks to identify an extinct creature. The third relegates it to the realm of mythology or poetic invention. Those in the first group generally identify Behemoth as a hippopotamus. Those in the second group typically suggest a dinosaur (generally one of the sauropods [four-legged herbivore] or ornithopods [two-legged herbivore]). But this is extremely difficult to demonstrate. The Behemoth is not mentioned in the literature of the ANE at all, which makes the mythical interpretation highly unlikely. It is also difficult to imagine why God would point to an imaginary creature as the penultimate illustration of His supremacy. Finally, the Behemoth is mentioned in the Hebrew text of the Creation account (Gen. 1:24) as created by God. As a result, the third suggestion seems fundamentally flawed. There are several things that we can say about this beast.

1. Description of the Beast. The final identity of the Behemoth remains unclear, but the biblical description of this beast, found in 40:15–24, fits quite well that of the hippopotamus, with the exception of its tail (which is described as being like a cedar; v. 17). The tail of the hippopotamus is short, while the cedars are tall trees. But it has been suggested that perhaps the comparison is not in terms of size but in terms of firmness or stiffness, and in that case the comparison with the tail of the hippopotamus fits. Unquestionably, in the description of the physical features of the animal, poetic hyperbolic language is employed to emphasize its uniqueness and strength.

2. Absence of Violence. God did not emphasize the violence of the animal at all, but it was certainly not a friendly beast. It hid but was self-confident and powerful (v. 23)—so powerful that humans were unable to subdue it, including more precisely Job (v. 24). God was the only one powerful enough to approach it, and He did so with His sword at hand (v. 19) to keep it under control. This implies that only through a struggle would the beast finally be defeated by the Lord.

3. Created by the Lord. Perhaps more importantly, Behemoth was created by the Lord as one of His most important creatures (v. 19; first in the sense of preeminent). Although created by God, it appears that for some unknown reason it opposed God, and He had to control it by using His sword. One could suggest that the contrast is between how it was created—*re'shit* (v. 19), "beginning" or "chief"—and what it has become now. In that case it was somewhat similar to Satan in 1:6. He was among the sons of God, challenged God, and was defeated by the Lord. Over such an enemy Job had no power, but the Lord did. Using creatures as metaphors for an evil power was a common practice attested to in ANE cultures.

More specifically, the hippopotamus was a symbol of evil powers in ancient Egypt. The hunting of the hippopotamus in Egypt was associated with a religious ritual in which the pharaoh, representing Horus, killed the hippopotamus, representing Seth, thus symbolically defeating evil. Since in the second divine speech God raised the question of who was able to bring to an end the proud wicked, thus resolving the problem of evil (40:11–13), God was clarifying that He is the only One who can control evil in the world. Whatever evil Job was experiencing, it was not undefeatable because the Lord had power over it and controlled its damaging effects (cf. 2:6).

plural from *behemah* ("beast," "cattle"), evidently functioning as a name or title since the creature was spoken of as masculine. By poetic intention, the identity of this creature remains somewhat vague, but God spoke of it as a creature of preeminence (v. 19), subject only to His own control. The main point of this description is the creature's power and fearlessness (v. 23). Verse 24 is difficult to interpret, but it is better to read it as a rhetorical question: "Can anyone catch him with [or in] his eyes?" "With [or in] his eyes" may mean "while he is alert" or, possibly, by poking something into his eyes, which would parallel the verse's second strophe, putting a hook into his nose.

41:1–34. Beyond Behemoth: Leviathan. While Behemoth was unknown in ANE literature, Leviathan was a known mythic creature. Behemoth

was introduced with an invitation to look at it and was identified as a creature of God. Both of these elements point to the reality of the Behemoth, an identifiable object of God's creation, as Job was. But Leviathan, who followed, was both better known and less concrete in the ANE, a many-headed dragon also known as Lotan, who ruled the chaos of the deep and was attacked and defeated by other Canaanite deities (see "Leviathan," p. 654). Much of his description in Job 41 evokes the image of the crocodile, which, like the hippopotamus, was a constant and menacing feature of Egyptian Nile waters. Still, attempts to limit his identity to that of the crocodile do not seem to be that productive.

The fishing methods mentioned in vv. 1–2 were useless in the case of the Leviathan. In Job 41 the horrible might of the description

Leviathan

Certainly, the image of Leviathan is much more complex than that of the Behemoth and would require a little more analysis. The Bible provides a more detailed description of it, and we do have some pertinent ANE literature that need to be taken into consideration.

1. ANE Background. In the ancient Canaanite literature, Lotan, or Litanu, is a mythological, snake-like creature that threatened the order of the world, making it necessary for Baal or his sister to attack and defeat him. Its name means "the fleeing serpent." Lotan, together with Mot, the god of death, and Yamm, the god of the sea, represented the forces of chaos. Similar ideas are found in the mythology of Mesopotamia, where a seven-headed monster was defeated by Nabu (a wisdom god). Scholars tend to associate the mythological conflict among the gods with the creation of the cosmos. In such mythological ideas the motif of the conflict-with-chaos describes the rise of a hostile monster, a god who defeats him, and the creation of the world. It is possible that Leviathan was the creature behind these ANE ideas, and thus they could be useful when exploring biblical passages where Leviathan is mentioned. They should not determine the meaning of the text but can certainly help to clarify its message.

2. Leviathan as God's Creature and Enemy. The Bible describes Leviathan as one of God's creatures. According to Psalm 104:26, God formed it, and it dwelt in the sea together with many other creatures, large and small, which means that it was not a mythological creature. The text does not provide enough information for us to identify it with any known animal still living today; we can only say that it is described as a large sea creature. In His dialogue with Job, God asked him a series of questions about Leviathan (41:10). Some of the characteristics of the beast provided by the text are applicable to the crocodile (vv. 13–17, 30), and some of them to a whale (vv. 19–20), but others do not fit any known creature. Confronted by it, humans and their weapons of war were impotent and ineffective (vv. 7, 26–29). It was a threat to them that they could not subdue or stand against (v. 9), which means it could not have been a crocodile. Only God was able to subdue and control it. The description of the violent nature of this beast suggests that, although it was originally created by God as part of a very good creation (Gen. 1:31), its nature became corrupted. It could now be a useful symbol of corruption and violence.

3. Leviathan as a Defeated Power. The image of Leviathan as a many-headed monster is used in the Bible as a symbol of the historical and spiritual powers that God has defeated on behalf of His people. In a passage that points to the crossing of the Red Sea by the Israelites, the psalmist proclaims God's defeat of the sea monster and the breaking of Leviathan's heads (Ps. 74:13–14). The imagery from the ANE of a conflict with the sea monster is used here as a symbol of the Egyptian armies, the enemy of God and His people, defeated by the Lord. The biblical writer seems to acknowledge that behind the pagan mythology lies an element of truth: there is in the world an evil spiritual power that opposes God and His people, and only Yahweh can overcome him. This idea is explicitly stated in the prologue to the book of Job when Satan challenged and opposed God's actions.

4. Leviathan as a Power That God Will Destroy. The language of Isaiah 27:1 is very similar to the language of a Canaanite text in which Lotan is called "the fleeing/gliding serpent," "the twisted/coiling" one. This does not mean that the prophet was copying from that text but that this was common language used to designate an evil power. The biblical message is that the power represented by a snake-like animal will be destroyed forever, not by Baal but by the Lord. Thus in the Bible, Leviathan became a symbol of God's apocalyptic enemies whom He will confront at the end, just as He did Satan in the book of Job, before His people will settle down peacefully by their vineyards (27:1–5). The final defeat of the serpent is announced in the book of Revelation, and as a result humans will be finally liberated from suffering and death (Rev. 20:1–3, 7–10; 21:4).

There was a primeval enemy of God whom He confronted and defeated before the creation of humans. That power was not a god but one of God's creatures, now a demon (see "Evil and the Fallen Cherub," p. 1008). History is the arena where that evil power displays his hatred toward God and His people, in this case against Job; yet in history, he has been defeated again and again, and one day he will be finally destroyed by the Lord. God was telling Job that even though he did not understand how these evil powers operate, He, the Lord, knows and has power over them. Consequently, Job should acknowledge Yahweh as the wise, supreme Lord of the universe who will bring to an end the work of evil powers who are the true oppressors of the human race.

of Leviathan reached even beyond the Behemoth's. Leviathan was unconquerable by means of harpoons or fishing spears (v. 7); he was a creature not to be tampered with (vv. 5–8) or trusted in any agreement (v. 4). None who remembered their encounter with him ever attempted another (v. 8). Leviathan's awe provided the deity with His clearest statement on ascendancy. The unmistakable message of the rhetorical question found in v. 10, and of the entire second speech, is that in spite of the awesomeness of this beast, God is the greatest, the One who transcends the terrible might and power of Leviathan. Even in the midst of His intimidating description of Leviathan, it is appropriate for God to insist that He is Lord of all, a reassuring counter to the Leviathan picture (v. 11). With v. 18, the description veered away from anything natural by mentioning his smoke-breathing, coal-kindling, and flame-throwing mouth (vv. 19–21). By representing Behemoth as a grass-eating beast and Leviathan as a fire-spitting terror, God transferred Job from the natural realm in which he lived, suffered, and disputed with friends to the supernatural realm where the whole drama began and where alone the full answer to his crisis could be found.

There is nothing unnatural about Behemoth's description, but there is something indeterminate about it. And there is nothing natural about the fire-emitting Leviathan who, according to God, had no equal on earth (v. 33). Scripture shows that this supernatural Leviathan, unequaled on earth (v. 33), king of pride (v. 34), uncontrollable except by God Himself (vv. 10–11), was, like Behemoth, an object of God's creation (Ps. 104:26). Job put all this together. And Bible students may put it all together too. We may see Leviathan as an actual being created by God who now represents the embodiment of all that is evil: a real and insidious force, working in realms beyond the natural senses—a being exalted by pride and lord of all the proud but one who knows that God is Lord and cringes in His presence (cf. Job 9:13). He is a force so mighty as to have no equal and yet, for all his evil and power, is inferior to God—one whom God will at last destroy (Is. 27:1).

The evil power represented by Leviathan may not have been fully disclosed in God's revelation to Job, yet Job's responses make it clear that he understood. Through the images of strange animals, he looked into realities that exist beyond and behind what is apprehended by the physical senses. He came to better appreciate both the astonishing turmoil that rages in nature and the supernatural realm, as well as God's ultimate and unerring power and supremacy over the wildest forces contending in these realms. Without naming names, God shared with Job, in his suffering, something of the truth of the book's prologue. Many readers have claimed that Job received no answer from God. But Job's own testimony does not seem to agree with these frustrations. We may not see what he did, and now we may know more than he did. But Job, who so often clamored for an audience with his God, ended the dialogue in awe and gratitude at the encounter he was granted and at what he gained from that audience with the Almighty.

42:1–6
Dialogue between God and Man: Job's Surrender

The dialogue documented through twenty-eight chapters with Job's friends (chaps. 4–31), in Elihu's monologue (chaps. 32–37), and in God's confrontation (chaps. 38–41), concluded with a second abasement by Job (40:3–5). But it was an abasement of awe-filled gratitude, not one of shame. His first submission offered no comment of appreciation for his experience and Yahweh's intervention—only surrender. But now, something more that he had learned moved him to gratitude. Job had always known that God could do everything. But this acknowledgment was distinct from Job's spoken thoughts throughout the dialogue. This acknowledgment was a word of respect and deference rather than one of rage and desperation. At this point, Job could express belief that what God wishes to accomplish will be accomplished (v. 2). His friends had long insisted on this. On the surface Job's words could well be heard as capitulating to their side.

Only God's clarifications in the epilogue preserve us from such a misunderstanding (which also reminds us that no segment of the book of Job may be dismissed as superfluous). His plaguing doubts had given way to insight: he realized that he had uttered what he did not understand and attempted to dabble in things too wonderful for him that he did not know (v. 3). He knew better, now, how wonderful they are and how awesome his God is. Job expressed repentance and either (according to some translations) a retraction of (at least some of) his words about the things he could not understand or (according to others) an abhorrence or rejection of himself. Job's "therefore" at the outset of v. 6 should remove misunderstanding of his reason for self-abasement. He himself explained that it is because he now saw what he had not before seen, both conceptually ("wonderful" things), and physically, in the theophany. God had revealed Himself to him. Job was humbled. His was the reaction of godly persons throughout the ages in the presence of Almighty God: Moses hid his face (Ex. 3:6), Isaiah cried "woe is/to me" (Is. 6:5), and Daniel turned to a deathly pallor (Dan. 10:8). Theophanies are not shaming. They are honor. And Job was not shamed. He was overwhelmed.

42:7–17

EPILOGUE: FINAL RESOLUTION

The poetic dialogues have ended, and the narrative with which the book opened is now continued in order to bring about a resolution of the plot. God was upset at Job's friends (42:7–8), and Job interceded for them (v. 9). All that remained was the restoration of Job (vv. 10–17).

42:7–9
God and Graceless Theology

The epilogue confirms, should there be any need, that God was still pleased with Job. God's rage at Job's friends comes next.

42:7–8. God's Rebuke of Job's Friends. The brief dialogue between God and Eliphaz featured an expression of divine fury scarcely equaled anywhere else in the book. God's words represent a category distinction between God's revelation to Job and His new engagement with Job's friends. The first was both chiding and sympathetic, while this, the second, was hostile.

That God addressed Eliphaz shows that he was considered the leader of the group (v. 7). God's very first word to Eliphaz was that He was furious at him and his friends. He twice stated the nature of the offense: His character had been misrepresented, distorted in fact, as callous and arbitrary. The argument for His transcendence and omnipotence had been used to justify Satan's brutality as unassailable divine integrity; God gave three successive imperatives to Eliphaz and company (take, go, sacrifice), in order for them to escape the full force of His vengeance (v. 8). Four times in the span of two verses God called Job His servant. His language exposes, in God's mind, a yawning gap of separation between Job and his friends. It was only Job's intercession that would save them this time (v. 8). On a subsequent occasion God underlined both the value and limits of intercession. He advised Ezekiel that in his time and place it would not be enough to rescue doomed Jerusalem (Ezek. 14:13–20). God gave Eliphaz an ominous threat. Apart from Job's intercession, God was inclined to deal with the friends according to their folly. When humans, in God's name, justify satanic cruelty as integrity and justice, then God is highly incensed. It is folly.

42:9. Job and Grace: Intercession. God could trust Job just as surely at the end of this long and contorted drama as He did at the beginning. God trusted him to pray for those who had maligned him, and He honored that intercession on their behalf. It may have taken a divine order to have them humble themselves before a man whom they had so insulted and against whom they had fabricated lies in order to win their theological argument. But faced with the options of Job's intercession and God's wrath, they chose to obediently receive Job's prayers on their behalf. The Hebrew idiom for God's acceptance at the end of v. 9 is "the Lord lifted up Job's face," meaning that He treated him with respect. In this instance, treating Job with respect meant heeding his plea to pardon his friends. Job's prayer on behalf of his friends was a function of his grace-filled spirit. He would not have been able to ask God's mercy on them if he himself were not prepared to be merciful. Jesus promised that those who are merciful will receive mercy (Matt. 5:7). Job's prayers for, and deliverance of, his friends are metaphors that recall another intercession, that of the only perfectly righteous One, through whose intervention we too are preserved from the penalty of divine wrath that we deserve (Rom. 5:9; 1 Thess. 1:10).

42:10-17. Job's Material Vindication. Job's physical and material restoration were no more contrived than was his loyalty to God. He had not remained faithful or prayed for his friends in exchange for any promises. The adversary's opening claim that Job served God in exchange for wealth was as unfounded as his cruelty to Job, his children, his servants, and his animals was unwarranted. And when he had been banished from the scene of action and torment, God was free to deal with His child, His servant, as God's own nature willed. It is His nature to care and to give—He opens His hand and satisfies His creatures' desires (Pss. 104:28; 145:16). And it is His will to honor faithfulness (Rev. 2:10). Job had been faithful to his God.

The idiom of restoration in 42:10 says that God "turned Job's captivity" and belongs to the language of liberation and restoration after exile (Pss. 14:7; 53:6). Job's restoration brought him back from a long and horrible exile. He has been exiled from family and society, and, to some extent, from constant communion with his God. In his season of distress Job listed his family, friends, and acquaintances as those who had abandoned him (19:13). His restoration was as complete as his abandonment had been (42:11).

Eating together—the idiom is "they ate bread with him"—is one of the strongest signs of full acceptance, trust, and mutuality (v. 11). His putrid sores were a thing of the past, as was the fear that he was cursed of God. There is significance in the Hebrew term used to describe the piece of silver that each of Job's children presented to him. The term *qesitah* is only used during the patriarchal period. This provides some internal evidence in favor of the antiquity not just of the story but of the writing of the book of Job. The unusual inclusion of the names of Job's three daughters (distinct from the anonymous sons) and the specific reference to their inclusion in his will (vv. 13-15) highlights Job's recognition of human equality before God. Male or female, servant or master, we recognize that before Him we have nothing to commend ourselves—except for His grace (cf. vv. 2-6).

Job died at an old age (v. 17). Job's vindication was as complete as his restoration had been, contradicting the predictions of Bildad, the most insistent of his accusing friends. His memory was celebrated in the earth (contra 18:17), and he died surrounded by his children and posterity (contra 18:19).

In a world as chaotic as Job's personal life turned out to be, Job's end rebukes a host of judgments that establish guilt by circumstance and majority vote. The story of his singular faithfulness is a standing complement to the divine grace which alone makes our faithfulness acceptable to God and our trust in His goodness possible. The ending is a mixture of the good and the bad. Good in that Job had a long life but bad in that it says that Job died (42:17). The true ending is found in the hope of Job that reached beyond the grave to a resurrection that would make seeing the Redeemer possible (19:25-27). That is where Job's hope and the Christian hope merge.

PSALMS

INTRODUCTION

Title and Authorship. The Hebrew title of this collection of hymns and prayers is *tehillim* ("praises"), which is also the central theological theme in the book. The phrase "praise the LORD" (Heb. *halelu-yah*) occurs twenty-three times, especially toward the end of the psalms and particularly in Psalms 146–150. The title "Psalms" is derived from the Greek *psalmoi,* which is used in the Septuagint (LXX) to translate the Hebrew word *mizmor* ("psalm"; see Pss. 3:1; 4:1; 5:1).

Seventy-three psalms are attributed to David using the Hebrew phrase *ledawid* ("to/for/of David"). This Hebrew phrase denotes authorship (e.g., Hab. 3:1). Other composers of psalms are the sons of Korah (Pss. 42–49; 84–85; 87–88), Asaph (Pss. 50; 73–83), Solomon (Pss. 72; 127), Heman the Ezrahite (Ps. 88), Ethan the Ezrahite (Ps. 89), and Moses (Ps. 90). Fourteen psalms mention historical circumstances associated with the person who wrote them (e.g., Ps. 57:1). There are thirty-four psalms that lack any form of superscription. These orphan psalms are mainly found in the latter part of the psalms, beginning with Psalm 91. While critical scholarship dismisses these psalm titles as late editorial additions, biblical evidence from outside the psalms in both the OT (2 Sam. 1:17–27; 3:33–34; 1 Chr. 16:7–36) and NT (Mark 12:35–37; Acts 2:24–36; 4:25; 13:35; Rom. 4:6–8) points toward their credibility.

Date. The dating of the psalms has been the object of much debate, but comparisons with extrabiblical material as well as linguistic features used in the psalms show that the majority of them were originally composed during the Israelite monarchy (e.g., 2 Sam. 22 and Ps. 18 are almost identical) and some even before this period (e.g., Pss. 19; 29; and possibly 90). Furthermore, references to personal names and historical circumstances mentioned in the titles help us to date the respective psalms. Thus, the psalms were written over a period that spans the history of Israel, and conceivably scribes like Ezra after the exile produced the final compilation and editing of the psalms (see "Formation of the Biblical Canon," p. 21).

Backgrounds. In the case of the Psalms, we have to assume a multiplicity of historical backgrounds reflecting the history of ancient Israel between the Exodus and Exile. The majority of the psalms are associated with the time of King David and the early monarchy (tenth century B.C.), but the body of hymns and prayers continued to grow during the divided monarchy (ninth to seventh centuries B.C.), the Exile (sixth century B.C.), and the postexilic period (fifth century B.C.). Annotations in the book itself suggest a variety of communal settings with a gradual growth of the collection and a purposeful grouping of the psalms.

Traditionally the psalms have been divided into five books, echoing the fivefold division of the Pentateuch (Pss. 1–41; 42–72; 73–89; 90–106; 107–150), each section concluding with a doxology (e.g., Ps. 41:13). These divisions were already present in the ancient Greek translations, but a closer look at the different books points toward a gradual growth of the Psalms based on earlier smaller collections (e.g., the collection of the prayers of David [Ps. 72:20], the pilgrim psalms [Pss. 120–134], the Asaph psalms [Pss. 73–83]). In the final editing, some of the psalms belonging to earlier collections were moved to other sections (e.g., the eighteen Davidic psalms that are found outside Book 1 and 2 [cf. Pss. 86; 89; 101; 103; 108–110; 122; 124; 131; 133; 138–145]). The compositional connections between psalms (e.g., between 42 and 43; between 18 and 144) demonstrate that there was an intentional theological structuring in the final compilation of the Psalms reflecting the history of Israel: from the Davidic monarchy as a period of harmony with God and His law (Books 1 and 2), to the failure of the monarchy as a result of disobedience, followed by the Exile (Book 3), to the restoration of Israel under a divine King after the Exile (Books 4 and 5). This suggests that the ordering of the psalms followed a rough chronological framework with some exceptions to that pattern (e.g., Pss. 90; 105; 106).

Theology and Purpose. The book of Psalms has been the prayer book of Jews and Christians alike, providing meaningful theological insights into the OT view of God from an individual and communal perspective. It contains an OT theology in a nutshell.

1. Diversity of Themes. The theology of the Psalms is not systematically or explicitly developed but emerges from the spirituality, piety, doubts, and protests of the psalmists. Through these prayers, written in poetic language, the psalms express a theological cross section of the theocentric content of the Israelite faith from the perspective of God's covenant with Israel. Some of the overarching theological themes are the conflicting experience of God's presence and absence (e.g., Pss. 13–14; 16; 88; 95); God as Creator (e.g., Pss. 8; 19; 29; 65; 104; 139), God as Judge (e.g., Pss. 7; 51; 75) and Lord of life over death (e.g., Pss. 30; 49); God as Protector of the poor (e.g., Pss. 12; 72; 82) and Healer of the sick (e.g., Pss. 6; 41); and His sovereignty in history and His kingship over the earth (e.g., Pss. 5; 47; 105; 136). The sheer number of references to the book of Psalms found in the NT (ca. A.D. 150) demonstrates its importance in the formulation of NT theology.

2. Praising the Lord. Praise lies at the center of the book of Psalms and unlocks its theology. God is presented as the absolute and exclusive object of praises (e.g., Pss. 145–150). The worshipers came before Him to praise His name with thanksgivings for all the blessings they had received from Him. Others came with their troubles, their sickness, their doubts and fears, and their complaints concerning their oppression at the hands of their enemies. These they presented to God. But even these individuals finally thanked and praised the Lord in anticipation of the acts of salvation that He was about to perform on their behalf in answer to their prayers. Meanwhile they could feel abandoned by God in the darkness of loneliness and fear and totally unable to free themselves from such desperate condition. Yet, they always found in God a safe refuge, and this led them to praise Him in the context of hopeful expectation. At times the

individual or the community offered to the Lord a prayer for the forgiveness of their sins. In such cases they praised the Lord for His mercy and for His constant willingness to forgive their sins.

Praising the Lord brought the Israelites close to their very Source of life, the only One who could preserve and renew life and who could deliver them from the constant threat of death. The connection between praise and life is unambiguously stated in the psalms. At the close of the book we hear the voice of the psalmist saying, "Let everything that has breath praise the LORD" (150:6). Human existence expresses itself in a magnificent way through words and actions that praise the Lord. To praise Him is not simply a verbal expression—even though words are spoken only by those who are alive. We praise the Lord through actions, attitudes, and every aspect of our deportment. For the psalmists, everything we think, speak, and do should result in praises to the Lord for His goodness and mercies toward us. Only those who are dead are unable to praise the Lord.

Besides the personal and collective expressions of praises in the book of Psalms, there is a cosmic dimension. Again and again we hear the psalmists calling the cosmos to praise the Lord. In fact, the final overcoming of evil, the psalmists seem to suggest, will take place when the totality of creation with one voice will sing a song of praises to the Lord. God's intelligent creatures on this planet will set aside their selfishness and pride, and everyone—kings, princes, judges, men and women, and old and young—will find in the Lord the center of his or her existence (Ps. 148:11–12). The psalmists anticipate a glorious future when everyone in heaven and on earth will praise God for His mercy, justice, and love. Singing praise to God leads to eschatological expectation—God's people coming together to praise Him is a foreshadowing of the moment when the whole cosmos, including His children, will praise the Lord.

3. God Is Our Hope. God is portrayed in Psalms as not only the Source of hope but Hope itself. Humans may hope to be victorious in battle because of the strength of their horses, but horses are a false hope for victory (33:17). No one should place his or her hope in humans, because they are liars (116:11). There are some who want to be wealthy and who hope that through extortion and robbery their goals will be achieved. Such a hope, says the psalmists, is a vain hope (62:10). Instead of seeking hope at the horizontal level, the psalmists looked up and found hope in God. When oppressed by the enemy or threatened by death, they hoped only in God. The psalmists can affirm that their hope is in God (39:7). This is hope based on trust in the Lord (71:5; cf. Rom. 15:13).

In the Psalms the world is a place where humans face the forces of evil and chaos that seek to oppress humans through the attacks of enemies, sickness, suffering, sin, and the threat of death. The solution is deliverance, freedom, and redemption that can come only from God. Consequently, God's people place their hope in Him. This is not blind hope but rather a hope grounded in a deep and personal knowledge of the Lord, who in the past did wonderful deeds for His people and for those who waited on Him (40:1). The people trust such a wonderful God and know that He will be able to deliver His people from any situation that could diminish the quality of their personal or collective life. His promises of future deliverance are reliable. In the midst of anguish and suffering the psalmists were able to affirm that God was their refuge, shield, and hope through His word (119:114). Such a hope impacts the present life: those who have the God of Jacob as their hope and help will be blessed (146:5).

God has universal dominion over chaos and death and can therefore offer hope to every human being (65:5). One of the very peculiar ways in which this hope is to be actualized, according to the psalmists, is through praises to the Lord. As indicated above, hope is connected with praising the Lord and, as such, it looks forward to a time when humans will join the cosmic heavenly choir in praising God as Creator and Redeemer. This will be the ultimate deliverance from sin, death, and all forms of oppression perpetrated by God's enemies. The hope offered to us is one of perfect harmony between heaven and earth (Ps. 148; see commentary on Ps. 150:3–6). The psalmists eagerly waited for the full realization of this hope and encouraged Israel to also hope in the Lord—now and forever (131:3).

4. *The Coming Messiah.* The theology of the Psalms can be summarized as Israel's response to God's presence in their individual lives and His intervention in the history of the nation. Biblical history points first and foremost to salvation history, and the messianic psalms (Pss. 2; 18; 22; 40–41; 45; 68; 72; 89; 110; 118), as well as the role of these psalms in the NT (e.g., the usage of Pss. 2; 45; and 110 in Hebrews), illustrate this prophetic and typological dimension of the Psalms. In these psalms the experiences of David are often described in language that goes beyond what a human king could ever achieve.

Accordingly, there was an expectation of the coming of an eschatological Messiah through whom all divine promises would be fulfilled. David was therefore a type of this Messiah. The anticipated hope of the psalmists was to become a reality through the work of the Messiah. The Lord would give to Him the nations as His inheritance and the ends of the earth as His possession (2:8).

5. *Temple Theology.* The temple plays a central role in the theology of the Psalms as the dwelling place of God (e.g., 26:8; 43:3; 46:4). All prayers mentioned in the psalms were addressed to God in His temple and it was from there that He answered them (3:4; 28:2). The temple was the center of life because the God who dwelled there is "the fountain of life" (36:8–9; 52:8). He dwelled there as King of the earth (99:1–2; 103:19) and the kings of the earth would bring gifts to Him as tokens of submission. It was from this center of power that God sent the help and support needed to strengthen those who suffered in the midst of their affliction (20:2). The temple was the place from which the Lord defended the weak (68:5) and delivered His people from all kinds of oppression and affliction (18:6; 102:19–20).

From His dwelling place God blessed His people and declared them righteous by forgiving their sins (24:5; 32:1–3, 5, 11; 51:1, 11; 118:26). This was possible through the sacrificial system. When God accepted the sacrificial offering, He was in that act accepting the repentance of the sinner (20:3; cf. Lev. 1:4; 7:18). The Israelites and the priests had plenty of reasons to praise the Lord in His temple (135:2; 138:2). It was also in the temple that the psalmists were able to understand the fate of the wicked (73:17), probably in the sense that their lack of repentance would not make it possible for them to obtain forgiveness through a sacrificial victim. In that case their fate was represented by the fate of the sacrifice.

The book of Psalms also speaks about the heavenly temple. It is the cosmic dwelling of God, where the angelic host worship and serve Him (148:1–2; 150:1), and the ultimate source of help for God's people (20:2, 6; cf. Heb. 4:14–16). It is in that heavenly temple that Christ is now ministering for us through a work of mediation and judgment (Heb. 8:1–3; 9:23). Like the earthly sanctuary, the heavenly sanctuary is a place of judgment (76:8–9; 82:1–8). The judgment includes an investigation of the evidence (11:4–5) and the execution of the legal verdict (11:6–7; 102:19–20). The righteous will be involved in the judgment of the wicked (149:9; 1

Cor. 6:2; Rev. 20:4). It is the heavenly temple as the center of cosmic worship and judgment that brings together praises and eschatology. It is from there that the whole cosmos is called to praise God in order to restore harmony to it. The condemnation of the wicked and the salvation of the righteous will restore harmony to the universe when both groups will praise God, recognizing Him as a God of justice and love who granted to each one what they have chosen for their lives (see comments on Ps. 150).

Literary Features. The musical annotations found throughout the psalms suggest that they were mostly sung as hymns in the context of temple worship. Besides the superscriptions that refer to the use of specific instruments (e.g., "stringed instruments"; 4:1), tunes (e.g., "set to 'Lily of the Testimony'"; 60:1), or performers (e.g., "to the Chief Musician"; 88:1) for singing the psalms, there are also annotations in the texts that indicate their liturgical usage. *Selah* is the most common Hebrew annotation in the psalms (seventy-one times) but also the most enigmatic one. It seems to be a command and has been interpreted as a pausal sign (translated as such in the LXX), perhaps for a musical interlude or to read Scripture, as a sign to indicate that worshipers should lift up their voices at this specific point, or as a signal to the congregation to prostrate in prayer. There are also other worship-oriented terms woven into the content of the psalms such as "bow"/"worship" (5:7), "confess"/"proclaim" (30:9), "kneel" (95:6), and "come near" (95:2). Interestingly, *selah* occurs 67 times equally distributed in the first three books of the Psalms and four times in last two books (140:3, 5, 8; 143:6) which belong to the fifth group of Davidic psalms. This indicates that the annotation *selah* was particularly associated with the psalms of King David.

The question of classification of the psalms has overshadowed the study of the psalms for the last hundred and twenty years. It has been suggested that the historical setting for almost the entirety of the psalms is connected to cultic events in the worship service from the time of the Babylonian Exile. This has resulted in a rigid classification of the psalms according to a limited number of types (usually five main categories are listed), trying to fit each psalm into one of these categories. Thus historical names and events mentioned and alluded to in the psalms were ignored and the postexilic cultic setting became the determining factor for the message of the psalm. While it is important to try to organize a body of one hundred and fifty hymns into categories, it is more important to look at and listen to the texts themselves and not superimpose a system that is built on questionable premises. It is better to look for indicators in the text that point to a type and its function, which in turn can provide a basis for classification. Such pointers can be found in expressions like *tepillah* ("prayer"; 17:1), *tehillah* ("praise"; 145:1), or *shiggayon* ("lamentation"; 7:1).

Metaphors of God in the Psalms

The theocentric focus of the book of Psalms provides the reader with important insights into the character of God. This is often accomplished poetically through imagery and metaphorical language. A metaphor helps us to understand an unknown reality (God) by means of a more familiar reality (e.g., a shepherd). Interestingly, our theological thinking (our thinking about God) is largely informed by these metaphors. Metaphors of God are common in the Psalms and describe Him as King, Judge, Shepherd, Host, and Father. At the same time we also learn how human kings, judges, shepherds, hosts, and fathers should be more like the heavenly One. Some metaphors come from the natural realm or refer to innate objects: God as Rock, Fortress, Shield, and Refuge. There are metaphors that make us pause and look again: God as a Warrior who is fighting on behalf of His people. These metaphors are an integral part of the authors' attempt to communicate their messages.

COMMENTARY

PSALMS 1—41
BOOK I

Psalms 1–41 constitute Book 1 of the traditional division of the Hebrew Psalms. They focus on the assurance of God's protection and deliverance for the psalmist, mostly identified as King David. Book 1 begins with a psalm that extols God's law as the path of the righteous. This theme is reiterated in the center of Book 1. In fact, we can perceive a concentric structure from Psalm 15 to Psalm 24 accentuating the *torah* in Psalm 19.

Psalm 41, at the end of Book 1, outlines the responsibilities of the king to protect his people. This theme is also reiterated at the end of Book 2, which concludes the collection of the Psalms of David (72:20). There is a personal tone throughout Book 1 expressed through the usage of first-person speech vividly conveying the struggles and complaints of the psalmist turning to God for answers.

1:1-6
Torah as the Way of Life

While Psalm 1 is not a typical prayer or song of praise, the poem introduces the Psalms with a reference to the importance of the law. *Torah* ("law") should not be understood as an antithesis to grace, which is a misconception without foundation in the Scriptures. *Torah* is the story of God's actions in the human sphere communicated through history and instruction. Thus the beginning of the Psalms points back to the beginning of the OT, the instruction of Moses, and its fivefold division echoes that of the Pentateuch.

Without any type of superscription, we have no indication as to the authorship or date of this psalm. Nevertheless, its literary and thematic connections with the wisdom literature (e.g., Prov. 3:13; 8:32; 20:7) suggest a possible early (Solomonic?) date for the poem. The lack of superscription provides the psalm with a generic tone that fits its universal, introductory character to the Psalms.

1:1-3. Blessings for the Righteous. The first psalm begins with a description of the way of the righteous person set in stark contrast to the way of the many *resha'im* ("wicked" or "ungodly"), *khatta'im* ("sinners"), and *letsim* ("mockers" or "scornful") people (v. 1). The beatitude in the first word, *'asher* ("blessed" or "happy"), is juxtaposed with the destruction of the wicked expressed in the last word of the psalm, *to'bed* ("to be destroyed" or "to perish"). These words begin with the first and last letter of the Hebrew alphabet respectively. The contrast is heightened by a threefold description of the life opposed to God's law and that moves increasingly away from the divine path: first walking, then standing, and finally sitting. This suggests a progressive engagement and identification with sin that intensifies in a threefold way.

The positive alternative to this lifestyle is described in v. 2 by two parallel expressions

centered on the word *torah* ("instruction"). Instruction and delight do not often go together, at least not in modern thought, but in the biblical worldview God's instruction is as delightful as the relationship between man and woman, often described using the same Hebrew term employed here (e.g., Ruth 3:13; Esth. 2:14; Song 8:4). The parallel action in this verse refers to an ongoing "meditation" on God's instruction. The verb *hagah* ("to meditate," "to mutter") designates a continuous audible "uttering" of God's word. Such continuous immersion in the word leads to a life that can be adequately described only through imagery.

Tree and plant metaphors, as powerful images, connect the listeners and readers of the psalm to the physical world. The tree imagery at the beginning of the psalms creates another strong link to the beginning of the book of Genesis: the tree of life found next to the rivers that water the Garden of Eden (Gen. 2:9-10). In a predominantly dry climate, a tree is to be planted in a promising location—that is, close to a water source—in order to thrive and be fruitful (see Jer. 17:5-8). A threefold description of the positive results counters the threefold description of the wicked in v. 1: it produces fruit, not continuously but according to its season (possibly indicating the ups and downs of a godly life), its leaves remain green, and finally, it flourishes. The last sentence appears to be intentionally ambiguous by referring to either the tree or, most probably, the righteous.

1:4-5. What the Wicked are Like. The corresponding description of the wicked is introduced by this very abrupt statement, which creates a counter reality to the preceding abundant tree imagery. The simile of the wind-blown chaff underlines the lifeless futility of the ungodly using a well-known image that is connected to judgment terminology (e.g., Job 21:18; Is. 17:13; Zeph. 2:2). Their way is doomed to total failure, from both the legal perspective and religious perspective (Ps. 1:5).

1:6. For the Lord Knows. This final sentence underscores that the eventual separation of the two paths is dependent on God's judgment based on His knowledge of the way of the righteous. This is an ongoing knowledge expressed by the Hebrew participle of the verb *yada'* and designates much more than a mental awareness. It refers to a living, intimate relationship sustained by love—a saving knowledge that leads to abundant life and prosperity. Accordingly, some translations render this verb here as "watch over." In contrast, the wicked perish (cf. Luke 13:27) for lack of that type of knowledge. Both destinies are connected to their respective ways, which represent one's movement toward or away from God. Psalm 1 introduces so much of what is later developed in the Psalms by reducing it to an "either/or" answer centered on the relational knowledge of God and His instruction.

2:1–12
The Crowning of Yahweh's Anointed One

Psalms 1 and 2 are like two portals opening the gate into the world of the Psalms. There are a number of connections linking the two psalms. For example, whereas Psalm 1 ends with the vision of the wicked perishing (1:6), Psalm 2 ends with a vision of warning to a nation of destruction, expanding the image of the "way" from the individual to the community. This is followed by a final beatitude (2:12), connecting it to the initial beatitude in Psalm 1, thus concluding the introduction to the Psalms.

Like Psalm 1, this psalm also lacks a superscription, which further underlines its generic and introductory character. The psalm's mention of the coronation of the king on Mount Zion, surrounded by raging nations, creates an environment that is compatible with the historical situation during the early united monarchy. Yahweh's kingship becomes the ideal paradigm for earthly kingship and would find its utmost expression in the coronation of the Messiah as King.

2:1–3. The Foolishness of the Nations. The psalm is divided into four equal stanzas, beginning with a description of the wicked nations' plotting, which connects antithetically to the description of the righteous in Psalm 1. While the righteous meditates (Heb. *hagah*) on God's law (Ps. 1:2), the ungodly nations meditate (Heb. *hagah*) on emptiness (2:2), and their plots are in vain and useless (v. 1). As in Psalm 1, there is again a progression of evilness expressed by the four verbs found in vv. 1–2 and directed against the Lord and His Anointed. The psalmist refers to a rebellion instigated by the kings of the earth (v. 2), indicating a global insurgence against the authority of God and against the authority of His Anointed. The incredulous and rhetorical "why?" at the beginning of v. 1 points to the utter foolishness and futility of this endeavor. Verse 3 spells out the nature of the rebellion, saying that the nations are trying to break free from Israel's control. Literally, the

text refers to God's fetters and ropes, which may be a reference to His guiding instructions for Israel. Though these were loving commands (Hos. 11:4), the nations viewed them as restrictive and oppressive. They were, in effect, fighting against God's law (cf. Hos. 11:4).

2:4–6. God Laughs from Heaven. The next stanza underlines the foolishness of the nations' attempt to throw off God's rule. While the dominion of kings is limited to the earth, in contrast, God's dominion extends from the heavens, where He sits enthroned as the heavenly King. From that perspective He is dismayed at their self-destructive efforts in a way that conjured up, in the mind of the psalmist, laughter.

However, the psalmist describes God's amusement turning into a blazing fury (v. 5): two Hebrew words used to describe God's anger here—*'ap* and *kharon*—are often found together (cf. Ps. 69:24; 78:49) and indicate the impending action that results from God's anger. Whereas the first stanza ends with the speech of the nations, the second concludes with a divine speech contrasting His action to that of the earthly kings (v. 6), saying God has set up the king Himself, through dependence on His election and not on human intrigues.

2:7–9. The Reign of Messiah. The psalm continues with the king declaring the legitimation of his reign—that is, he will reign by divine decree—echoing the language of the Davidic covenant (2 Sam. 7:14). "Yahweh's decree" (as translated in the LXX) is a covenant of adoption (v. 7). This

Anthropomorphic Descriptions of God in the Psalms

The Psalms often describe God in anthropomorphic (human) terms, assigning to Him the full range of human emotions, both positive ("laughter") and negative ("anger"). One needs to be careful not to ascribe to God the same connotations that these emotions have in the human realm. The anger of God is different from human anger. Similarly, the term "repentance," as anthropomorphically assigned to God, is "not like man's repentance. 'The Strength of Israel will not lie nor repent: for He is not a man that He should repent.' Man's repentance implies a change of mind. God's repentance implies a change of circumstances and relations" (PP 630).

is foremost the metaphor of God as a Father and appears in various places throughout the psalms (68:5; 89:26–27). The coronation of the king has coincided with his adoption into the royal covenant. The verse introduces the strong messianic overtones of Psalm 2, which are echoed almost verbatim in Hebrews 1:5. The coronation of the Christ (Messiah) was to be the ultimate fulfillment of the Davidic covenant.

Verse 8 spells out the promises of kingship establishing the dominion of the king to the ends of the earth, which had formerly been part of the dominion of the kings of the earth (2:2). The means by which the king would establish his rule are mentioned in v. 9. The rod of iron is applied in a messianic way in Revelation 2:27 and 12:5, indicating the absolute and permanent nature of the messianic kingship.

2:10–12. Kiss the Son. The last stanza of the psalm serves as an admonition and, in this sense, as an extension of grace to the nations not recognizing the Davidic kingship. It is prudent to serve the Lord with fear, which connotes worship (cf. Ps. 134:1). The call to rejoice and celebrate with trembling is paradoxical but points to the ingredients of true worship (cf. 95:1–2).

The peculiar usage of the Aramaic *bar* for "son" (v. 12) has motivated a number of suggested changes to the text (e.g., "Do homage in purity," JPS). Taking into consideration the international context and audience in this coronation psalm, it is an appropriate term here. The phrase designates an act of homage to the victorious king by his submissive vassals.

The psalm concludes with a beatitude (see 1:1) describing those who *khasah* ("take refuge" or "trust") in Him. It is an invitation to the hostile kings to find refuge in Yahweh by submitting to His Anointed One. The first two introductory psalms contain a personal and a communal invitation to follow God's instruction, and strongly focus on the typology of the Messiah.

3:1–8
Deliverance in Adversity

Psalm 3 begins with a historic annotation that connects this poem to the moment when David and his royal court fled from Absalom, his son, rendering the nation ungovernable for some time (2 Sam. 15:12–17). The content of the psalm coincides with the experience of David when his relationship with his son crumbled. Yet the psalm repeatedly returns to the motif of salvation.

3:1–2. Adversity and Many Adversaries. The repeated word "many" in these introductory verses of lament expresses the increasing adversity faced by David as he was avoiding the military conflict with his son. There are a number of verbal links at the beginning and the end of this psalm: there are many who rise up (3:1; Heb. *qum*) taunting that there is no *yeshu'ah* ("salvation," "help," "deliverance") for David (3:2), but it is the Lord who ultimately is called upon to "arise" (3:7; Heb. *qum*) and to bring salvation and deliverance (3:8; Heb. *yeshu'ah*).

3:3–6. But God Is My Shield. The contrastive "but" (v. 3) introduces the metaphor of God as a shield that is found throughout the psalms (3:3; 5:12; 7:10; 18:2; 18:30; 59:11). It is part of an imagery that describes God as a Warrior and expresses David's trust in God in a situation where he could not shield himself. God's glory serves as a second line of protection often understood as a physical phenomenon indicating His presence and saving protection (e.g., Ex. 24:15–17; 1 Kin. 8:10–11). Finally, David speaks of God as Lifter of his head, a metaphor pointing to the future restoration and vindication of the king.

Verses 4–6 each begin with a first-person statement indicating David's trusting response in prayer for Yahweh's protection and enumerate the occasions when God sustained him during difficult times: God answered him from "His holy mountain/hill" even if David himself was no longer physically present in Jerusalem (v. 4). David also mentions that the Lord sustained him when sleeping and awakening. This is language which could connect this psalm with a morning prayer. This leads to a declaration of faith that extinguishes all fear even when surrounded by many thousands of hostile people (v. 6).

3:7–8. Petition for Deliverance. There are two imperatives in this section that connect the petition to the initial lament (vv. 1–2): "arise" and "save/deliver." This is an expression of deep faith in God in circumstances with no salvation in sight. The Hebrew perfect verb tenses used for God's striking David's enemies and breaking their teeth in v. 7 have been variously rendered: some take them as past ("you have struck," "you have broken"), others take it as another imperative ("strike," "break"), and others view them as having a kind of gnomic (expressing a general truth) connotation ("you strike," "you break"). In any case, David speaks with certainty of his deliverance, and this is expressed well by any of these renderings of the Hebrew perfect. The image of the smiting on the cheekbone and the breaking of the teeth of the ungodly refers to the silencing of the enemy who spoke against the psalmist (v. 2). The enemy was not just a political adversary but was also evil on a moral level because he had attacked God's anointed one. The language used develops the Warrior language in a more active and defensive way.

The psalm concludes with a significant theological statement (v. 8). This is the third time that the key term *yeshu'ah* ("salvation"/"deliverance") is used in the psalm. It is a final statement of trust that extends the blessing from the individual to the community. The concluding beatitude, in which David solicits/declares God's blessing upon His people, is a recognition that salvation is not only for the dethroned king, but also for all of God's people.

4:1–8
A Night Prayer

There are various literary connections between Psalms 3 and 4 (e.g., call/cry, v. 1 // 3:4; lying down and sleeping, v. 8 // 3:5; many people, v. 2 // 3:6), which have led some to suggest that they represent morning and evening prayers, respectively, uttered by David when escaping from Jerusalem. The mention of Davidic authorship in the superscription would fit this historical scenario. The musical annotations may suggest that the psalm was subsequently used on different occasions.

4:1. Hear My Call. This short prayer of petition at the beginning of the psalm is an appeal for vindication. David speaks to Yahweh, the righteous God and source of his righteousness, seeking for justice from Him. In his distress (Heb. *tsar* lit. refers to a tight place), he is praying about relief. God listens *when* we call and not *after* we call (Is. 58:9), and David pleads in this psalm for His immediate response.

4:2–5. Addressing the Adversary. In this extended section of the psalm, David directly addresses his enemies, whom he identifies as *bene 'ish* ("sons of men" or "people"), possibly indicating their ephemeral existence. He confronts them with two rhetorical questions introduced by the phrase "How long?" The question in itself serves as a delimiter to evil, followed by seven imperatives that increasingly invite the ungodly to return to God. He exhorts them to leave false accusations and *riq* ("emptiness,"

"worthlessness," "delusions") behind (v. 2; cf. Ps. 2:1) and to recognize God's election of him. God had set apart the faithful, godly ones for Himself and would listen to the prayers of His chosen one (v. 3).

In vv. 4–5, David admonishes the enemy away from his wrong ways toward fearful contemplation and reflection, searching their hearts in the stillness of the night (see 1:1–3). This act of introspection could lead them to turn to God with acts of true worship and sacrifices of righteousness as a result of a new trust in the Lord. This trust is often expressed throughout the psalms as an assured reliance upon God and security in His promises (e.g., 32:10; 56:4; 125:1–2).

4:6–8. True Gladness in the Heart. The concluding verses of the psalm underline the richness of such a life of trust in God. Although many ask what benefit such a lifestyle has, the psalmist recounts the blessings of God in an allusion to the priestly blessings, asking for the light of God's face to shine on us (v. 6; cf. Num. 6:24–26).

This might be a polemic against idolatrous practices connected to fertility cults and their celebrations of harvest time, which was the climactic moment of joy during the year. David suggests that true joy can be found only in a relationship with Yahweh. Some translations have rendered the Hebrew *me'et* in v. 7 as "when" or "in the time" and thus describe David's joy *when* the "many" would have received grain and new wine. In this case, the text would be saying that trusting in God brings gladness to those who respond to the exhortations given in the psalm to repent and trust God. Others have understood the term to mean "more than," in which case the text would be referring to the idea that David's joy in God is more significant than the celebration time of grain and new wine, when some used the occasion to worship other gods hedonistically in fertility cults. In either case, David's point is that God is the ultimate source of joy, harvest, and new wine.

The final statement of faith which concludes the psalm (v. 8) begins with peace (Heb. *shalom*), which again echoes Aaron's blessing. Trust in the Lord leads David to sleep in peace in the midst of trouble, resulting in true joy that could not be impacted by wrong accusations and opposition. It is this joy that David wants his enemies to experience. This is indeed a wonderful way of making friends out of our enemies.

5:1–12
A Morning Prayer

If Psalm 3 is possibly a morning prayer, Psalm 5 is much more explicitly a morning prayer for deliverance from slanderous people. The psalm is organized around the contrast between the psalmist and the wicked and their respective access to God and His temple.

Aside from the superscription indicating Davidic authorship, there is no other historical annotation. The reference to "flutes" or "pipes" possibly refers to reed instruments and indicates the performance instructions for the music director associated with this psalm. It has been suggested that this was performed as an antiphonal reading at the temple gate, as it moves back and forth between the righteous and their access to the house of God versus the wicked who cannot enter into the temple.

5:1–3. Lord, in the Morning Hear My Cry. As the psalm opens, a threefold appeal for God's attention—David implores God to hear, consider, and listen (vv. 1–2)—underlines the seriousness of the psalmist's cry for help. This is a crescendo of despair, and it includes the psalmist's *hagig*, a word sometimes translated as "meditation" which here can be understood as a lament or an audible groan for help (cf. 2:1; 39:4). It is affirmed that God will hear this prayer (v. 3) as He hears all our prayers, particularly those expressed in loud shouts in moments of great pain. At the same time there is a confident expectation expressed in the verb *'arak*, which could be translated "direct," "set in order," or "lay out before" (reminiscent of the laying out of the morning sacrifice on the altar; e.g., Lev. 6:5; Num. 28:4). The introduction of sanctuary language indicates a close connection between our prayers and the sanctuary (cf. Rev. 8:4). The response to the psalmist's prayer would come only from God's presence in the sanctuary.

5:4–6. No Room for the Wicked in God's Temple. The next three verses describe the incompatibility between God and the wicked. They are unable to stand before Him (v. 5) or dwell or be welcomed into His presence (i.e., they do not have access to the temple; v. 4). Those who are liars and who are bloodthirsty and deceitful will perish (v. 6).

5:7–8. But I Will Come into Your House. This is an almost antiphonic response to the previous lines. In contrast to the wicked, the righteous have access to the temple because they are in harmony with God and rely on His abundant loving-kindness (v. 7). The term *bayit* ("house") was used as a designation for the temple or tabernacle (and some translations consistently render this Hebrew word by these terms, depending on the context) since the time of the Exodus (Josh. 6:24; 2 Sam. 12:20). From the sanctuary God's way is made straight before him and life is restored.

5:9–12. Judgment and Joy. The next counterpoint enlarges on the multiple reasons for the destruction of the wicked, listing the deeds of wickedness, which in their final analysis are acts of rebellion against God (v. 10). The last antiphonal declaration (vv. 11–12) returns to the audible expression of the psalmist. This time it is a crescendo of rejoicing as the righteous are to always shout and sing for joy. Yet, the cause for joy is not the destruction of the wicked but the fact of the righteous' trusting the Lord as their refuge and His defense of them (lit. God "covers" them with His protection like a bird covers its chicks under its wings; cf. Ps. 91:4).

The psalm concludes with another beatitude (v. 12) concerning God's blessing the righteous. Here once more God is presented as a protecting shield—not the small handheld shield of Psalm 3:3, but a large shield covering the whole person. There may be another connection with the sanctuary since the shield is a place of true refuge and protection for those who seek the Lord.

6:1–10
A Prayer for Healing

This is an intense prayer for healing from physical illness. In the Israelite worldview illness was often considered to be a rebuke from God, accompanied by the fear that enemies would take advantage of this moment of weakness. In this psalm, there is a penitential tone as the psalmist expresses the desire to be right with God during the physical affliction. The psalm is one of the seven penitential psalms that some Christian denominations read during the time of Lent (cf. 32; 38; 51; 102; 130; 143). It is a psalm of David and nothing in its content denies this. The *sheminit*, an eight-stringed harp (lit. "with eighth"), seems to be related to the psalm's performance.

6:1–7. Cry for Deliverance from Anguish and Pain. The psalm is divided into two main sections (vv. 1–7; 8–10). The first section expresses the same sentiments in two consecutive subsections (vv. 1–3; 4–7). David appeals to God not to rebuke, chasten, or discipline him any longer (v. 1). Both imperatives are associated with God, indicating that David considers his illness to be God's fatherly discipline in reaction to a sin in his life (cf. Prov. 19:18). Nevertheless, he intensely requests God to be merciful to him (v. 2). This corresponds to David's reaction after his adultery with Bathsheba (2 Sam. 11–12) and after conducting the census in Israel (2 Sam. 24).

David is 'umlal ("feeble," "weak," "languishing"). His bones are bahal ("troubled" or "shuddering"; lit. his whole body is "shaking" and "trembling"; vv. 2–3). This section climaxes with the question "How long?" The sentence is incomplete and expresses David's utter despair in his condition when writing this. The Lord is invoked five times in the first section of this psalm, emphasizing the psalmist's anxious search for God. When experiencing God's silence and apparent absence, we must continue to cry out to Him for an answer. The condition of the psalmist affects the whole person: David's "soul" is greatly disturbed. The Hebrew nepesh, translated "soul," usually refers in the OT to the whole person as a unity.

The psalm proceeds to repeat a plea for healing using different expressions (vv. 4–7). If God would not deliver, then death was to be expected (v. 5). Death is a state where the Lord is not remembered or proclaimed (cf. Eccl. 9:5), an unconscious state where communication between humans and God is ended.

The extremity of the psalmist's despair is expressed through a repeated hyperbole—his bed is flooded and swimming with tears, and his couch is drenched (v. 6). In that condition he is unable to see God's acts; he is experiencing only the ongoing attacks from his enemies. The focus has now shifted to the psalmist's adversaries who contribute to his pain (v. 7).

6:8–10. Vindication and Healing. In the midst of despair and the attack of adversaries, the psalmist twice declares that the Lord has heard him (vv. 8–9), and he expresses the assurance of His receiving and accepting his prayer. Faith breaks through the darkness of personal despair and affirms God's intervention. There is no report of immediate healing, but the psalmist anticipates the vindication of the faithful and proclaims that the enemies will be shamed and disturbed. Previously the psalmist was vexed, but now he writes of shame for those who anticipated his death (v. 10, cf. vv. 2–3). Their shaming is mentioned twice and follows the double hearing of God.

Psalm 6 is reminiscent of the story of Job, whose vindication from a wrong theology of retribution as the cause for his suffering also came at the end. However, the psalm clearly connects the psalmist's sickness with sin—a balanced understanding of human suffering. While suffering should not be too easily connected to sin, neither by the sufferer nor, much less, by the observer, part of the healing process could include a personal search for a sin that might have contributed to the current condition. However, in both possible scenarios there is the assurance that God hears our prayers and vindicates us before the enemy.

7:1–17
An Appeal for Innocence

The psalm is centered on the metaphor of God as Judge, a common metaphor in the psalms. In Psalms He is referred to as seated for judgment on His throne (9:4), as probing the heart (17:3), and as defending widows (68:5). The reference to Cush, a Benjamite, has no parallel in the historical books, but the psalm probably originated during the time when David was persecuted by Saul and his men. Verses 3–4 may be connected to the events recorded in 1 Samuel 24:11 or to the Cushite ("Ethiopian," "Sudanese") who reported Absalom's death (2 Sam. 18:20–32). The psalm is classified as a meditation (Heb. shiggayon, "lament"), a genre mentioned in the psalms themselves (cf. Hab. 3:1; see Psalms: Introduction).

7:1–9. Appeal for Deliverance and the Innocence of the Righteous. In the face of persecution, the psalmist affirms his trust in God and asks for deliverance from those trying to tear him apart like a lion would. This simile is intensified by the image of a lion ripping its prey apart in pieces. The following section legitimizes the psalmist's appeal for deliverance using the language of an oath formula. This is done by three consecutive conditional clauses (vv. 3–4; protasis) which are followed by a consequential clause (v. 5; apodosis), underlining the innocence of the psalmist. The penultimate conditional clause identifies the false charge that has been brought against the psalmist: he is accused of having dealt unjustly with somebody who was at peace with him (v. 4). He is so sure of his innocence that he invites the enemy to trample him to the ground (i.e., if found guilty, he should be put to death).

The psalmist appeals to the divine Judge to establish his innocence. The anthropomorphic appellations for God to "arise" (v. 6) are urging God to stand up and pronounce a favorable verdict. The Judge assembles witnesses from the assembled peoples around Him and then rules on high, where the judgment throne is located (v. 7). The next line is central to the judgment motif of the psalm: the Lord will judge the peoples, and David prays that God will judge him and vindicate him against the false accusations he has endured. God's judgment is both universal and individual, and the psalmist invokes both, indicating his righteousness as based on a legal principle and not on a personal, preferential treatment by Yahweh.

7:10–17. Confidence in the Righteousness of God. Appellations now turn to propositional descriptions of God's righteousness. God is a defense or "shield" for the upright (v. 10), but He is angry with the wicked every day, especially if they do not turn back and repent. God will not turn back from His anger against them. The psalmist portrays God's treatment of the wicked by employing the metaphor of God as a Warrior with sword, bow, and arrows to use against those who brought the false charges (vv. 12–13).

A proverbial statement describes what would happen to those who brought false and mischievous accusations against the righteous: they dig a pit and then fall into it (vv. 14–16; cf. 9:15; 57:6; Prov. 26:27). Verse 16 describes the situation in which the persecutor's trouble recoils and falls on their own heads. The psalm concludes with a testimony of God's righteousness, not the psalmist's. This is to be expected in the legal case described in the form of a psalm that ultimately seeks to praise the Lord. It is a testimony to the integrity of the legal process and that of the person who waits for God's vindication.

8:1–9
God's Glory in Creation

This is the first actual praise song of the Psalms, and its theme is creation, a topic frequently found throughout the psalms (e.g., 19; 29; 65; 104; 139). The psalm is bracketed by the use of the same refrain in vv. 1 and 9 about the excellence or majesty of God's name. It is attributed to David and is addressed to God using a second-person speech. The musical annotation *gittit* in the ascription may either refer to an instrument of Gath (cf. Pss. 81; 84) or a melody. It has also been interpreted as pointing to Obed-Edom the Gittite, a Levitical singer (1 Chr. 13:13–14; 16:4–5).

8:1–2. Exaltation and God's Glory. The psalmist directs his praise to God, recognizing His sovereignty, which is encapsulated in the phrase "How excellent" (*'addir*, "majestic," "mighty" or "splendid") is your name in all the earth. This links Psalm 8 to the last words of Psalm 7, expressing the psalmist's decision to sing praise to the "name of the LORD Most High" (7:17). The terms used here, "heaven(s)" and "earth," describe the magnitude of God's dominion. From this high and elevated chorus, the psalm descends to the weakest and defenseless of creation, referring to the infants and children to whom God has given strength to, with their praises, silence the enemy and the avenger. God uses the weak to confound the mighty.

8:3–9. God's Glory in Humankind. God's glory (i.e., His presence and magnificence) is visible in the dominion He has given to humans. After contemplating the majesty of God's creative power displayed in creation (v. 3), the psalmist asks in amazement, "What is *'enosh*?" (This term can be translated as "man," "mankind," or "human beings.") Why does this majestic God pay attention to humans? He pays close attention to them and is actively involved in their lives.

Verse 5 is the center of the psalm, pointing to the status of humans within creation: they have been made "a little lower than the angels" and crowned with "glory and honor." Yet, they could exercise the divinely assigned role of dominion only by acknowledging God's creative glory. Beyond its immediate implications for the understanding of humans, v. 5 is used in the NT to refer to the humanity of Jesus Christ (1 Cor. 15:27; Heb. 2:6–8), thus pointing to the messianic dimension of the psalm. The human dominion over creation (vv. 6–8) reminds us of the Creation story in Genesis 1. The dominion over all things is itemized and includes both domestic and wild animals. The psalm concludes as it began, refocusing on God. The greatness of the psalm lies in the connection between God's majesty and its bestowal on humanity, showcasing a God who is worthy of praise because, in His sovereignty, He works with the most frail in His creation.

9:1–20
Praise for Vindication

There is some evidence that Psalms 9 and 10 were originally one psalm that was divided into two. They together form an alphabetical psalm that is taken by the LXX to be one unit.

Besides, Psalm 10 does not have a superscription, something unusual within Book 1. Finally, Psalm 9 ends with *selah* (see Psalms: Introduction). The division seems to be based on content. Whereas Psalm 9 is mostly thanksgiving, Psalm 10 is a prayer for protection against wickedness and violence. Besides claiming Davidic authorship, the superscription annotates that the psalm should be sung to the tune of "Death of the Son." This could be a specific musical tune or may point to a historic situation. Suggestions have included the death of Absalom or the unnamed child of Bathsheba.

9:1–12. Praising the Eternal Judge. The praise in Psalm 9 begins where Psalm 8 ended, praising God for His marvelous, wonderful works. The section is centered on the praise of God as the eternal Judge who has upheld David's just cause (v. 4) by completely destroying the wicked (v. 6). But He is, at the same time, a refuge in times of trouble (v. 10; cf. Ps. 10:1) to those who trust in Him (vv. 9–10). His judgment is in favor of the *dak* (the "oppressed" or "crushed"; v. 9). The section concludes with a renewed invitation to praise God (v. 11). Legal language is used in v. 12: God avenges blood (i.e., He holds the oppressor legally accountable for tyranny) and does not forget or ignore the cry of the *'anawim* ("the humble," "the poor," or "the afflicted"). The reason for praises is stated in concrete terms.

9:13–20. Prayer for Help. Praise is followed by prayer, which suggests that doxology could lead to petition. The prayer is personal, asking God to have mercy upon him (cf. 4:1), but it is based confidently on the experience described in the previous section. The "gates of death" (v. 13) are city gates that lead into a figurative city of death. In contrast, the gates of the daughter (of) Zion (v. 14) signify a city of abundance of life that leads to rejoicing in God's salvation. Verses 15–16 recount once more God's saving acts in the past in order to show the reliability of the promises of His future saving acts through judgment (vv. 17–18): the wicked shall be sent down or turned to *she'ol* (v. 17; preferred term for the grave), while the needy will not be forgotten by God (v. 18). The psalm concludes using imperatives to ask for God's immediate intervention. He asks God to rise up and terrify the wicked nations (vv. 19-20; cf. 3:1). By placing the fear of God into the nations, they will recognize their own mortality versus God's sovereignty.

10:1–18
Continued Prayer of the Helpless

Psalm 10 almost seamlessly continues after Psalm 9, although the tone is more intensified and personal and there are more petitions than praises. The lack of any superscription supports

---

Acrostic Psalms

An acrostic ("the tip of the verse") poem demonstrates a literary technique that emphasizes the first letter, syllable, or word of a line or verse to create a specific pattern. In an alphabetic acrostic each successive line or verse begins with the following letter of the Hebrew alphabet, which consists of twenty-two letters. In the Hebrew Psalms there are a number of acrostic psalms that use different acrostic styles: Psalms 9, 10, and 37 are *strophic* alphabetic acrostics, in which the first line of each strophe (four lines) begins with the successive letter of the Hebrew alphabet; in Psalms 25, 34, and 145 each *verse* begins with the next letter of the alphabet; Psalms 111 and 112 are *line* alphabetic acrostics, both consisting of twenty-two lines beginning with the sequential letters of the alphabet.

The largest and most complex acrostic poem is Psalm 119, which consists of twenty-two *strophes* with each strophe having eight lines and each line beginning with the corresponding letter of the Hebrew alphabet. Interestingly, Psalm 1, the first *torah* psalm, begins with the letter *aleph,* and its last word begins with the final letter of the Hebrew alphabet, *taw,* alluding to the great *torah* Psalm 119, possibly to indicate that it is a short version of 119. The acrostic technique makes it easier to memorize the poems and shows the high level of literary artistry that accompanied their composition from the earliest times of the kingdom of Israel, suggesting that literacy was widespread in Israel from an early period (see "Introduction to Hebrew Poetry and Wisdom Books," p. 614).

the suggestion that the psalm originally formed a compositional unit with Psalm 9.

10:1–11. Frightening Description of the Wicked. Two rhetorical questions express the intensification of the situation of the psalmist: "Why does God stand far away?" and "Why does He hide Himself in times of trouble?" God's hiddenness is a motif that runs through the psalms (cf. 13:1; 27:9; 30:7; 44:24; 55:1; 69:17; 88:14; 89:46; 102:2; 104:29; 143:7) and expresses in human language the psalmist's desperate sense of God's distance while hoping that He will soon draw close. The wicked are characterized as insolent and their opposition to God is stressed: pride, arrogance (v. 2), deception, curses, threats, trouble, malice, and iniquity (v. 7). The ruthless attacks of the insolent wicked are described (vv. 8–11): they lie in ambush (v. 8) and secretively plot the destruction of the helpless poor (v. 9). This idea is mentioned three times in vv. 8–9 using the mixed metaphor of a lurking lion waiting for a victim in order to catch it in a net like a hunter catches prey. While the psalmist laments the hiddenness of God, the wicked falsely count on His apparent absence or indifference (v. 11).

10:12–18. Arise, Lord! The provocation of v. 11 necessitates an immediate reaction and, in parallel fashion to Psalm 9:19, the psalmist appeals to God to "arise." But in contrast to the preceding claim by the wicked, he urges God to not forget the humble, afflicted ones (v. 12). This appeal is based on God's honor (v. 13) and the assurance that God intervenes on behalf of His people: He helps the orphans (v. 14). The prayer intensifies with a request to "break the arm" of the wicked (v. 15) and to finally do away with their wickedness. The phrase "the LORD is King" occurs for the first time in the Bible here (Ps. 5:2 makes a different point). It is one of the great images used in the psalms to describe the unknown in terms of the known (cf. 47:2, 6–8; 74:12; 84:3; 93:1; 96:10; 97:1; 98:6; 99:1; 145:1; 149:2). God's divine kingship serves as an ideal for Israel's monarchy and legitimizes it because it is God who installs His king on earth. The images of God as King and Judge are often combined, and they serve here to describe His absolute sovereignty in judging the wicked. He remains forever and ever, whereas the wicked perish (v. 16). The faithful in this psalm are described in terms of social conventions as the poor, humble, fatherless/orphan, and oppressed. This is reminiscent of the ethical

ideals found in the Pentateuch (cf. Deut. 10:18; 24:17–21; 27:19). God as King is especially concerned about justice for the defenseless groups, thus providing a paradigm for Israel's king.

11:1–7
Flee or Stay

The psalm starts with the image of a fluttering bird threatened by the hunter's bow and ready to flee to the mountains. It points to the threat the righteous are experiencing at the hands of the wicked. The threat is resolved by the central image of God in His temple enthroned in heaven.

11:1–3. Temptation to Flee. The psalm begins with a programmatic affirmation of faith, saying David puts His trust in the Lord, his Shelter. This provides at the outset an answer to the rhetorical question that follows. The simile of a bird that flees from the hunter's bow and arrow to the protecting underbrush covering the mountain seems incompatible with the psalmist's faith. The imagery is clarified in v. 2, where the bird and the hunter become the upright and the wicked respectively. As in Psalm 10 there is a secret assault: the wicked are shooting secretly from the shadows. The threat is intensified when the foundations are destroyed (v. 3). These "foundations" refer figuratively to the laws, customs, and ethical norms which hold up society (cf. Is. 19:10), which David presents as being thrown down, with the righteous apparently unable to do anything about it.

11:4–7. Reason to Stay. The center of the psalm (v. 4) is focused on a vision of Yahweh in His heavenly temple assuring us He is in control—so there is no need to flee. From His elevated position in the heavenly sanctuary, God is watching all people, testing and examining them. The heavenly sanctuary is a place of judgment. God righteously judges both righteous and wicked (v. 5). It is through judgment that God tests/examines the innermost motives of humans (cf. Ps. 139:23; Ezek. 22:18). The "testing" of the wicked leads to their rejection because God hates the wicked and those who love violence (v. 5).

This type of language indicates God's absolute opposition to evil. As a result of God's judgment, He will rain coals on the wicked (*pakhim*, "bird traps of fire"). There may be here an ironic reference to the image of the bird hunter in v. 2, suggesting that the hunter will become the hunted one. The destruction of the wicked described here is reminiscent of the destruction of Sodom and Gomorrah (v. 6; Gen. 19). The psalm concludes with an emphasis on God's righteousness and His absolute incompatibility with evil. While He hates (v. 5) the wicked, He loves (v. 7) righteousness, and the righteous will see His face (i.e., an image of God's continuous pleasure; cf. 17:15; Job 19:26). Psalm 11 is a beautiful affirmation of God's faithfulness in the midst of a morally disintegrating and crumbling society. He provides stability and judgment on behalf of His righteous from His heavenly sanctuary. While it might be tempting to flee, God's faithfulness provides enough reason to stay.

12:1–8
Words of Silver

This is a psalm about the power of words, expressed through the use of several related terms like "speak"/"say," "lips," "tongue," and "words." The force of falsities is contrasted with the purity of God's words. The superscription is almost identical to that of Psalm 6, declaring Davidic authorship and mentioning the eight-stringed instrument for the musical performance of this poem. The theme of wrong accusations would fit David's experience as expressed in previous psalms (chaps. 4; 7).

12:1–4. Blasphemous Words. The psalm begins with a cry to God for deliverance because of the vanishing of faithful and loyal people—people who are truthful and speak truth. In Psalm 15:2 the one who has access to the tabernacle is the one who speaks the truth from the heart. The psalmist refers to an increase in people who speak *shaw'* ("vanity" or "lies"), a noun found in the Decalogue (Ex. 20:7). Truth is contrasted with emptiness, which is equivalent to a violation of the law, even more so as they speak it with flattering lips and a double or duplicitous heart, which refers to the false flattery of their speech (v. 2). Verses 3–4 arrange the agents of speaking—lips and tongues—in a chiastic ABBA structure. This underlines the potentially devastating power of these organs, which are the actual means of rebellion against God in asking the arrogant and blasphemous question: "Who is lord over us?" This is an excellent illustration of the third commandment of the Decalogue.

12:5–8. God Speaks. The phrase "says the Lord" (v. 5) is the center of the psalm and is the only time in the poem where God speaks. It is framed by two negative statements that comment on the seemingly overwhelming power of the wicked. God's speech in the middle clearly indicates that He is in control and that He will deliver the faithful. His words connect again to the social groups mentioned in Psalm 10, assuring them that He is "arising" to action. The psalmist elaborates on the character of God's words: they are *tahor* ("pure," "flawless"). This is a term indicating ceremonial purity familiar from the legal sections of the Pentateuch (e.g., Lev. 6:4; 10:10). The process of purification is described as taking place seven times. There is some ambiguity in v. 7, as translations differ in regard to the question of who or what is being kept. The closest previous referent would be the "words" (v. 6), but it could also refer to the "wicked" (v. 8) or the needy of v. 5. In any case, the main point of the text is that God will protect and guard the poor and needy and will protect us from the wicked of this generation (cf. v. 5). The psalm concludes as it began (v. 1), describing the pervasiveness of wickedness in society. Nevertheless, God's word is still at the center.

13:1–6
How Long?

The fourfold "How long?" of this lament psalm arises from a sense of divine abandonment. The hiddenness of God is at the center of the lament (cf. 10:11), and while there is no specific historical situation connected to this psalm, a number of events from David's life would be compatible with this deep feeling of being deserted by everybody, including God.

13:1–2. Lament. The psalm moves symmetrically from lament (vv. 1–2) to petition (vv. 3–4) and ends with praise (vv. 5–6), constituting a model prayer psalm. Four times the psalmist raises the question "How long?" It occurs in this identical form only once more in the psalms (62:3), but can be found in alternative forms throughout the Psalms (4:2; 6:4; 35:17; 74:9–10; 79:5; 80:4; 82:2; 89:46; 90:13; 94:3). It is one of the central questions in the relationship between the psalmist and God. It is a rhetorical question that grows out of sustained pain and the feeling of abandonment. Here, it is paired with the ensuing question that includes a time element: he wonders if he will be forgotten "forever."

This sense of a seemingly endless time of sorrow wears down the psalmist's faith but, at the same time, expresses a faint hope for a limit to the pain. God's "forgetting" is the opposite of

His "remembering." It does not refer to a loss of mental recollection but to the apparent falling out of God's favor and inaccessibility to His presence and help. This is reinforced in the parallel question "How long will God hide His face from him?" The psalmist moves from the religious (his relationship with God) to the psychological aspect of his sense of abandonment. He has been pondering and anxiously ruminating in his *nepesh* ("soul," "heart," or "mind"). This is a continuous emotional pain, a constant state of depression. There is also a sociological aspect as he asks, "How long will his enemy be putting him down?" The enemy remains anonymous in the singular but is someone who exalts himself over the psalmist. The question of how long expresses pain, loneliness, and fear yet also expresses the hope of deliverance.

13:3–4. Petition. The prayer moves now from lament to petition, beginning with an appeal to the Lord God to *nabat* ("consider," "look upon") him and to break His silence. The request to light up his eyes refers to renewing the weakened life-forces, reminiscent of the story of Jonathan eating honey, after which his eyes were enlightened (1 Sam. 14:27–29). Two reasons are supplied for God to answer David's prayer: the threat of death, likened to a sleep, and the rejoicing of the enemy, who will think that he has finally defeated him.

13:5–6. Praise. There is a strong contrastive "but" at the beginning of v. 5 that introduces the last section of the prayer and provides the motivation for the psalmist's confidence: his trust in God's *khesed* ("mercy," "unfailing love," "lovingkindness," "steadfast love"). David expresses trust in God's loyal love (cf. 23:6) that will hold onto God's faithfulness, being persuaded that God will prevail over evil. This is an occasion for praises anticipating divine deliverance. David's confidence in this future deliverance is absolute and sufficient to reverse the abandonment mentioned at the beginning of the psalm. With God there is an abundance of blessings.

14:1–7
Foolishness

The instructional tone of Psalm 14 reminds us of Psalm 1. It focuses on the lifestyle of the godless and the pervasive corruption that stems out of a deep-rooted denial of God's existence. This psalm is almost identical to Psalm 53 and has led some to suggest that Book 1 and 2 of the Psalms were initially independent collections. There are other psalms that occur twice in the OT (cf. 1 Sam. 22; Ps. 18), making it necessary to look beyond the similarities and notice nuances such as the preference for *'elohim* ("God") as the name of God in Psalm 53. It is conceivable that Psalm 53 was adapted to a different historical reality and audience. The authorship of the psalm is attributed to David.

14:1–4. The Fool's Denial of God. Psalm 1 describes the blessed life of the righteous, but Psalm 14 describes the foolishness of a life without God. The term "fool" (v. 1) lacks a definite article, giving a generic and universal tone to the statement. The remainder of v. 1 and the following lines present a sustained negative description of the "fool," which climaxes in the repeated observation that there is none who does good (vv. 1, 3). The universal corruption becomes even more apparent when God searches the whole world in vain to see if there are any who understand and seek Him or who recognize His sovereignty. God's rhetorical question in v. 4 illustrates His astonishment at the extent of spiritual blindness. The foolish eat God's people as they eat bread, indicating that the denial of God leads to the persecution of His people.

14:5–7. From Foolishness to Salvation. The turning point in the psalm is found in vv. 5–6 with the change in perspective introduced by the use of an adverb of place (i.e., "there"). As God is gazing from heaven, He sees the foolish huddled together in fear and dread. Foolishness and rejection of God turn into terror, and their oppression of the poor is thwarted. They did not count on the fact that the Lord is a refuge (v. 6). There was to be a final day of accounting for those rejecting God's existence, and it would be a day of reversal of fortunes—Israel's restoration would result in rejoicing and gladness. The restoration of Israel is not referring to their return from exile but is used in preexilic passages to denote a time of misery followed by restoration (cf. Job 42:10; Hos. 6:11; Amos 9:14). In the NT, Revelation predicts terror and shame for the foolish and ungodly (Rev. 6:16), caused by the eventual recognition of God's existence and His care for His people.

15:1–5
The Gatekeeper I

Psalm 15 introduces a group of ten psalms that are organized in chiastic form around the second *torah* psalm (Ps. 19), ending with

Psalm 24. Both the beginning and end of this group serve as gatekeepers asking liturgical questions at the gate of the sanctuary. It is conceivable that these questions served to gain entrance to the Holy Place. In response the psalm lists ten characteristics of the person who is eligible to be admitted into the court of the sanctuary, reminiscent of the Ten Commandments. David is mentioned as the author of this psalm.

There is a rhetorical component in the questions that are asked at the gate concerning who may enter into and remain in God's tabernacle. The implication is that no one is worthy of close communion with God on their own merits. The "tabernacle" refers to a tent structure (Heb. *'ohel*) and not to the temple, which had not yet been built. The verbal forms used in v. 1 refer as well to temporary "sojourning" (Heb. *gur*) and to "settling down" (Heb. *shakan*). The remainder of the psalm answers the two questions. Inner qualities that reflect the character of God (righteousness and truth, v. 2) are emphasized, followed by characteristics which flow out of them in words and deeds (v. 3). The righteous are those who differentiate between good and evil and side with the good even if it is to their disadvantage (v. 4). They also refrain from dishonest economic practices and the exploitation of the socially disadvantaged (v. 5).

The list goes deep into all aspects of life, serving as a practical application of the Ten Commandments. They describe a life of integrity that assures that the person will never be moved or shaken (v. 5). The faith of the righteous is unshakable! From a human perspective, one may shrink back from such a high standard, yet Jesus upholds it (cf. Matt. 5:48). The second gatekeeper psalm answers the question as to how we can attain such a life: blessing, righteousness, and salvation are gifts from the Lord (Ps. 24:5).

16:1-11
The Lord Is My Cup

God's everlasting provisions for His children are at the center of this psalm, which continues the chiastic structure outlined above. It should be read together with Psalm 23, which uses similar imagery of the cup (16:5; 23:5), a term that is related to both salvation (e.g., 116:13) and judgment (e.g., 75:8). The superscription identifies the psalm as a *miktam* of David. The LXX understands this term to refer to an "inscription" (Gr. *stelographia*).

From comparison with ANE images, such a prayer could have been inscribed on a stele as a permanent and public commemoration of God's goodness. There is a group of other "inscription" psalms (Pss. 56-60). The connection with Psalm 23 underscores the Davidic ascription (cf. Acts 2:25).

16:1-4. Trusting in God and Not in Idols. Psalm 16 begins with a plea for continued protection, which turns into an affirmation of David's trust in God, in whom he takes refuge. This affirmation is underlined with the statement that he has no good apart from God (v. 2; lit. "my good is not beyond you"), indicating that outside of God there is no other source of well-being. The psalmist strongly identifies himself with the *qedoshim* ("saints" or "holy people") and sharply disassociates himself from those who go after other gods (vv. 3-4). The verb *mahar* here can have a secondary meaning as in "barter" or "acquire" in the sense of paying a dowry for a wife (cf. Ex. 22:16). David shows his disgust for idolaters who have "gotten" themselves a new god. He will not follow their practices nor invoke their god's name.

16:5-7. You Are My Cup. David uses two metaphors to emphasize his trust in God's provision (v. 5). God is his *kheleq* ("Portion" or "Inheritance"), a term associated with the allocation of land during the conquest of Canaan (cf. Josh. 19:9), and his Cup, which is representative of both positive and negative destinies. This imagery connects Psalm 16 with Psalm 23. The allotment motif is further developed in v. 6. The boundary "lines" mentioned refer to cords used in the surveying and measuring of property. This is followed by a response of praise (v. 7). The biggest blessings are not material but rather God's instructions received at night. These instructions come to David via his *kilyah* ("heart," "mind"; lit. "kidneys"). The "kidneys" are used in the OT to refer to the conscience through which God can communicate with humans (cf. Job 19:27; Pss. 7:9; 26:2; Jer. 11:20).

16:8-11. Future Hope. God is at the center of the life of the psalmist and therefore he can affirm, even in the face of death, that he shall not be moved or shaken (v. 10). The soul (*nepesh*) refers to the person as a whole. The threat of *she'ol* ("the grave") and *shakhat* ("corruption," "decay"; lit. "pit") leads David to think about death and beyond. The language of the passage points beyond the immediate historical context to the coming of God's holy and faithful One, which is interpreted in the NT as a prophetic reference to the resurrection of Jesus Christ (Acts 2:25–28; 13:35). Christ's resurrection is the first fruit of the defeat of death. The life-threatening experience of David foreshadowed the ultimate experience of the Messiah, who would experience resurrection instead of corruption in the tomb. He is our true refuge.

17:1–15
A Prayer for Deliverance

David is urgently praying for deliverance from a threatening situation, which is more severe than the one in Psalm 16. The two psalms are terminologically linked and both look forward to God's vindication in a legal context (cf. 7:9; 11:5–6). The poem is framed by vv. 1–2 and 15, connected by various terms, such as *tsedeq* ("righteousness," "justice," "vindication"), *panim* ("Your face," "Your presence," sometimes translated as simply "You"), and *khazah* ("to look" or "to see"). The psalm moves from God looking at the psalmist and examining his case to the psalmist looking at God for vindication. The psalm is called "A Prayer of David," but no information is given about the historical context.

17:1–5. Oath of Personal Innocence. This psalm is replete with anthropomorphic descriptions of God, such as His face (sometimes translated "presence" or simply "You"), eyes (v. 2), and hand (v. 14), as well as the image of the shadow of His wings (v. 8). These body parts are contrasted with the body parts of the wicked (vv. 10–14). The psalmist is appealing to the divine Judge as he affirms his innocence and pleads to God that vindication will come from His presence. David employs legal terminology (testing, trying, examining; v. 3) to present his case and argue for his faithfulness.

17:6–12. Liberation from Enemies. The second plea for deliverance is based on his own righteousness. Interestingly, the language of v. 7 is strongly allusive to the "Song of Moses" (Ex. 15:7, 11–13); thus there is a parallel between his deliverance and the Exodus. Two further images, the "apple" or pupil of God's "eye" (i.e., the miniature image of what the eye sees as reflected in the pupil) and the shadow of His wings (v. 8), demonstrate God's care for His children. They also underline the psalmist's urgent plea for protection from the wicked, who are like young lions lying in wait for their prey (v. 12).

17:13–15. Assurance of Future Deliverance. The series of familiar imperatives in v. 13 (cf. 7:6; 9:19) call for God's immediate action and the destruction of the wicked. The request is for deliverance from the people of the world who live only for this earthly life (v. 14). Some interpreters understand the second part of v. 14 as referring to the righteous, but the strong contrast that is created at the beginning of v. 15 suggests that it describes the wicked. They are satisfied with the immediate and will finally reap what God has stored up for them—sometimes rendered as "treasure"—an expression often used to designate God's judgment (cf. Job 20:26). In contrast to such a futile life, the psalmist will be satisfied by beholding God's face (v. 15). This is not necessarily in conflict with Exodus 33:20, which warns that no one may see God and live. It rather means that the psalmist will witness God's favor and intervention on his behalf. It might also refer to the resurrection and when humanity will behold God's face. The term "face" depicts God in a very real and tangible way.

18:1–50
Yahweh Fighting from Heaven

Psalm 18, a thanksgiving psalm celebrating God's deliverance of David in battle, is the third largest psalm in the Hebrew Psalms (after Pss. 78; 119). It describes God as a Warrior, one of the more frequently used divine images in the psalms (e.g., 21; 46; 68). The metaphor occurs mostly at the beginning of the Psalms throughout Books 1 to 3. It can be correlated to the historical situation during the early part of the monarchy and characterized by the military consolidation of the emerging kingdom (see Psalms: Introduction).

Psalm 18 and 2 Samuel 22 are almost identical, and this further supports Davidic authorship. Psalm 18 appears to have undergone some modifications in line with its liturgical usage. The liturgically modified but otherwise identical heading—the longest in the psalms—reflects this tendency. When the two psalms are compared, we find a number of cases where there are spelling variations and places where the available manuscripts and translations differ. For example, the Masoretic Hebrew text in Ps. 18:7 mentions the foundations of the mountains, whereas 2 Sam. 22:8 refers to the foundations of the heavens.

Some translations have the words matching in both places. This situation occurs several times in these parallel passages.

18:1–3. Invocation. The psalm begins with a strong commitment to God through an expression of love to God. What is unusual is that the verb used here (*rakham*) normally refers to God's compassion for humans (cf. Ex. 33:19). Nevertheless, it expresses David's strong commitment to his Lord, a concept that will be developed using nine divine epithets based on geographic and military metaphors. They are introduced by the possessive pronoun "my," expressing a deeply personal relationship between the psalmist and Yahweh. For David, the Lord is his Rock, Fortress, and Deliverer. The Hebrew word for "fortress" (*metsudah*) was applied to the later rock fortress of Masada on the western shores of the Dead Sea. This site is dated much later than David's reign but illustrates the images the psalmist had in mind when he penned his words of confidence in God, his Shield and Horn, which are terms for military strength. The invocation closes with a statement of faith in the form of praise (v. 3). The one who prays will experience salvation.

18:4–30. Affliction, Theophany, and Deliverance. The psalm now describes the life-threatening experience David is facing (vv. 4–6). There is a fourfold poetic description of death that, for the psalmist, seems to be imminent. This causes him to cry out toward God's temple for divine help. God's intervention is described as a divine appearance (a theophany; vv. 7–15), reminiscent of the Exodus experience at the Red Sea and at Sinai (cf. Ex. 15; 19). There is an earthquake, and the description of God's anger uses natural phenomena in connection with God's body (v. 8). There is a spatial movement from above to below: Yahweh rode upon a cherub with darkness and clouds surrounding Him (vv. 9–12); His voice thundered from heaven (v. 13), and He sent His arrows, which are likened to the accompanying lightning of the divine thunderstorm. This meteorological arsenal is directed against the enemies of the psalmist (v. 14). The violent descent of Yahweh as a Warrior concludes with another earthquake and the foundations of the earth being exposed. He rescues David from his enemy, drawing him out of the waters, which represent chaotic and evil forces (vv. 15–19).

Deliverance turns into praise as the psalmist exalts God's faithfulness to those who are faithful to Him (vv. 20–30). At the center of the praise is David's threefold affirmation of his own faithfulness: he is merciful or faithful (*khasid*; v. 25), blameless (*tamim*; vv. 23, 25), and pure (*nabar*; v. 26). These three words point not to the psalmist's merits or achievements but to divine characteristics that God bestows on His faithful ones. The last one could also be translated as "purified," indicating a relationship of forgiveness through ritual cleansing (cf. Is. 52:11). The section concludes with the use of some military metaphors: advancing against troops and scaling walls (i.e., in the attack of a fortified city; v. 29).

18:31–45. Yahweh Trains the King. After a short description of the character of God in which the psalmist theologically clarifies the relationship between God (His way is *tamim*— "perfect," "sound," "complete"; v. 30) and human perfection (God makes our way *tamim*; v. 33), Yahweh equips David with strength (v. 32), training his hands for battle so that his arms can bend a bronze bow. From v. 36 onward, the king remembers God's instructions that helped him to win wars with other nations (v. 43) and foreigners (vv. 44–45). The records of David's wars provide a realistic historical backdrop for this section (cf. 2 Sam. 8–21; 1 Chr. 18–20).

18:46–50. Doxology. The psalm closes with praises that begin by affirming God's power as revealed through His acts. After describing his military successes, David affirms that it is Yahweh who delivers him from his enemies (v. 48). This recognition leads into a final high note of praise to God, who shows *khesed* ("mercy," "loyal love") to His anointed, David, and his posterity forever (v. 50). Yahweh, the divine Warrior, is not necessarily a comfortable image of God for modern Christianity, but it nevertheless forms an important part of the many metaphors found in the psalms. In a period where physical warfare has moved to a spiritual one (Eph. 6:10–18), it is still comforting to know that Yahweh, the divine Warrior, is fighting on behalf of His children.

19:1–14
Torah in Creation

Psalm 19 is the center of the subgroup of psalms that are structured in a chiastic form. It is also one of the four *torah* psalms (cf. Pss. 1; 111; and 119) and relates God's law to creation. It moves from the general revelation of God in nature to the special revelation of God in Scripture and more specifically in His law. The contemplation of both necessitates a response from humans. Some commentators have suggested that the first part (vv. 1-6), which is distinct from the remainder of the psalm (vv. 7-14), was initially an old Canaanite hymn to the sun-god. However, there is an elaborate complementarity between the two parts that is reminiscent of the complementarity between Genesis 1 and 2. The divine name *'el* (short for *'elohim*) is used in the first part of the psalm, as in Genesis 1, while Yahweh is used in the second part, as in Genesis 2. According to the superscription, the psalm was composed by David.

19:1-6. Natural Revelation. All creation—represented by the heavens and the sky (or firmament)—declares the glory of God in a united chorus (v. 1). Translators differ in regard to how v. 3 is rendered. Some understand it to mean that the message of God's glory through His works is universally displayed in all languages—that is, "there is no speech nor language where their voice is not heard." Others believe that it refers to a silent yet evident declaration—that is, "there is no speech, nor are there words; their voice is not heard." The strongly personified description of nature (v. 2) connects repeatedly to the Creation account in Genesis 1. From vv. 4-6 the focus shifts to the sun as the central light in creation. Its daily journey through the sky begins as if in a tent or tabernacle that God has provided, and then it is described like a strong man or champion running its race through the circuit which God has ordained for it. The language can be associated with the Egyptian notion that the sun was reborn each morning, fresh and strong, or with Mesopotamian mythology, in which the sun-god Shamash (cf. the Heb. *shemesh*) is described as a "bridegroom." On the famous Hammurabi stele, the sun-god is shown as giving the law to the Old Babylonian King Hammurabi. However, there is a certain polemical element in the psalm since the sun is clearly part of God's handiwork and it runs the divinely ordained circuit in obedience to Him. This becomes even clearer in the next section.

19:7-14. Special Revelation. Instead of the sun-god providing the law, v. 7 emphatically and almost abruptly states that it is the law of the Lord. The psalmist moves on from natural revelation to special revelation. In Hebrew thought, there is often a movement from effect to cause or from the secondary to the primary. While natural revelation provides us with a glimpse of God, it is *torah*, His written revelation that contains a far superior knowledge and far-reaching effect on humans. The divine name of God appears only once in vv. 1-6, whereas there is a sevenfold mention of Yahweh in vv. 7-14. Special revelation through God's word points much more directly at God than natural revelation does.

The law has power to *shub*, a word that essentially means "to return" but has been rendered variously in its participial form as "converting," "refreshing," "restoring," etc. Its nature and effects are further explained as a perfect revelation of Yahweh's deeds, making the simple wise as right precepts or statues that bring joy to the heart and as pure and radiant commands that enlighten one's eyes (vv. 7-8). The effects of the law on human beings are so valuable that they surpass the value of gold and are more enjoyable than honey (v. 10). There is great reward (v. 11) in keeping the *torah*. This deep view of the law elicits a response in the form of a prayer for cleansing from sin that has been committed inadvertently, as well as for protection from willful or presumptuous sins (vv. 12-14). The concluding formulaic line is one of the most widely used prayers (v. 14), and its language connects it to sanctuary terminology linking it to the acceptability of sacrifices (Lev. 1:3). It is by beholding that we are changed. The contemplation of nature in union with God's word has a life-changing impact on our hearts.

20:1-9
Victory in Battle I

Both Psalms 20 and 21 are prayers for protection in battle and are linked through their content to Psalm 18. Since Psalm 21 has a liturgical

---

The Great Reward of Psalm 19:11

David used seven distinct words to describe six aspects of God's written word (Ps 19:7-9). He claimed that the keepers of these six would obtain a great reward (v. 11). The nature of that reward, however, is not just in the clean life that results in keeping the six. Rather, the inner thoughts of such a given voice makes God happy and thus brings such a one into harmony with God. Living in the presence of God is the greatest reward of all.

change of speaker, it may have been used in a dedication ceremony at the sanctuary before King David and his army went out into battle (cf. 2 Chr. 20). It could be read as a report of what God accomplished in battle on behalf of His king and people.

20:1–5. Prayer for Protection. The psalm begins with the people's intercessory prayer on behalf of the king. It is an urgent prayer offered in times of trouble and distress for God to send help from the sanctuary (vv. 1–2). The reference to the name of the God of Jacob (v. 1) is a powerful invocation of the experience of the patriarch. But it is now the Name that will defend the king (lit. "to set on high;" i.e., make him unreachable). The name of the Lord is closely linked to His character (see Ex. 34:5–7). Thus, God's name has saving power as it invokes past experiences of divine deliverance during the patriarchal and the Exodus periods. It is also a prayer that God will remember and accept one's offerings and sacrifices (v. 3; the Hebrew verb *dashen* here implies the fat of the sacrifices). These may have accompanied the ritual at the sanctuary, stressing the total submission of the king to God and His blessing of the king's purposes and plans (v. 4). The intercession turns into a confident affirmation of salvation, deliverance, and victory, and using military language, the people proclaim the lifting of their banners in the name of God.

20:6. David's Response. There is a shift in speaker to the first person, and it is David who now expresses his confidence in divine deliverance, introducing his statement of faith with a contrastive and very strong affirmation of what he knows (v. 6). God deeply cares about His Anointed One (the Messiah). But deliverance comes not only from the earthly sanctuary but also from His holy heavenly sanctuary. This description is reminiscent of the image of Yahweh descending from heaven in a theophany, as described in Psalm 18:7–15.

20:7–9. Trust in the Name of the Lord. The psalm returns to the "we" of vv. 1–5 and concludes with a final appeal by the people for the Lord to save. The passage is sometimes translated as a general reference for God to save, "Save, Lord," and a final petition to the King (God) to answer. It could also be translated as, "Oh Lord, save the king! May He answer us on the day when we call." The final "He" would then refer to God. Although the Lord had trained the king for battle (Ps. 18:31–45), it is He who gives victory. Psalm 20 is a beautiful demonstration of the power of communal intercessory prayer on behalf of the king as he prepares for battle. God's people should always lift up their leaders in prayer, asking God to give them victories in the spiritual battle.

21:1–13
Victory in Battle II

The deliverance of the king in battle is now an experience of the past, and the resulting prayer of thanksgiving complements the pleas of the preceding psalm. The poem is consistently addressing God in the second person. The speaker might have been a temple singer or a priest who led the congregation in praises to God as David returned from battle. Davidic authorship is indicated, and the proximity of this psalm to Psalm 21 provides the background information needed.

21:1–7. Rejoicing in the Strength of the Lord. The psalm starts out with the note of praise as the king rejoices in the Lord's strength. This idea is echoed at the end of the psalm with a similar expression of praise—the Lord is exalted in His own strength (v. 13). It is God's strength that has delivered the king and answered the urgent plea that concluded the previous psalm.

Verses 2–5 list various blessings that God has bestowed upon the king. The verses move back and forth between past answered prayers (vv. 2, 4) and present ongoing blessings (vv. 3, 5), as the Hebrew verbal forms indicate. The blessings include goodness (or "good/rich/best blessings"), a crown of gold, length of days, salvation, victory, splendor, glory, and majesty. These eternal blessings are bestowed because the king trusts in the LORD. This acknowledgment forms the center of the psalm (v. 7; cf. 13:5).

21:8–13. Future Victories. The focus shifts from the king to God's (and the king's) enemies. The final defeat and destruction of the wicked is depicted (vv. 8–12), but it is Yahweh the Warrior who will fight on behalf of His king: the Lord will swallow them up in His wrath (v. 9). Their destruction is imminent because they planned evil against "you." This "you" is ambiguous, possibly intentionally, pointing to either God or His king. Ultimately it is God who, through His king (or sometimes without him), will gain victories for His people. The psalm ends on the same note it began (as in Ps. 20), praising and expressing confidence in God's power.

22:1–31
Desperate Prayer for Deliverance

Psalm 22 is a moving lament of personal suffering and affliction that typologically epitomizes the suffering of Jesus on the cross. But it moves beyond despair to deliverance and finally to praises. One cannot read the psalm without thinking of Christ's last words on Calvary. Yet, we need to consider the historical dimension to the poem. Christ's antitypical appropriation of the psalmist's words validates the typology. This Davidic psalm is "set to 'The Deer of the Dawn,'" which possibly indicates a musical tune, although the "deer" (*'ayyalah*) could also be translated as "help" (cf. v. 19). According to the LXX, which prefers this translation, help comes at dawn.

22:1–21. Why Have You Forsaken Me? The psalm starts with a double question introduced by a twofold cry of *'eli*, which appears as a personalized appellation of God elsewhere in the psalms (cf. 18:2; 63:1; 68:24; 89:26; 102:24; 118:28; 140:6) and as a positive declaration in v. 10. Yet while David feels forsaken, God is still his God and he turns to Him in the hour of despair and forsakenness. Jesus's Aramaic appropriation of these words demonstrates the messianic dimension of the psalm and demarcates the moment of redemption in which the Son of God experienced the ultimate separation from His Father through the weight of sin (Matt. 27:46).

Facing God's silence, the faithful one recalls Yahweh's deeds on behalf of the forefathers (vv. 3–5) and invokes God's holiness (vv. 3–5). But not even this resolves the sense of abandonment (v. 6) accompanied by the mockery of the wicked (vv. 6–8). The psalmist recalls God's creative power in his birth (vv. 9–10), turning the question of v. 1 into an affirmation of faith: from his mother's womb, Yahweh has been his God. The lament is found in vv. 11–18, alternating between the third-person description of the wicked and the first-person declarations of the psalmist. The wicked are compared to bulls, lions, and dogs. Such frightening animal imagery, often used in ANE iconography to describe the realm of demons, points to the demonic dimension of the imposing company of the wicked threatening the king. They pierced his hands and his feet (v. 16), divided his articles of clothing, and cast lots over them (v. 18). The section is full of prophecies and explicitly describes Jesus's suffering on the cross (cf. John 19:24). It ends with a protracted plea for deliverance (vv. 19–21), which returns to the three animal metaphors.

22:22–31. Deliverance and Praise. Pleas move to praises that emphasize the communal character of the praise (v. 22). Praise focuses on a God who has not hidden His face (v. 24) but who hears and answers prayers. This praise increases exponentially and echoes from the individual to the assembly (v. 25) and finally to the ends of the earth and all nations (v. 27). Even the future generations will come to proclaim His righteousness (v. 31). The praises of those who experienced God's silence and deliverance are a powerful witness. Beyond the historical dimension, the messianic language of Psalm 22 illustrates how David was inspired to go far beyond his own suffering to point prophetically to the Messiah, whose death would resolve suffering forever (Ps. 22:1 // Matt. 27:46; Ps. 22:7 // Matt. 27:39; Ps. 22:8 // Matt. 27:43; Ps. 22:15 // John 19:28; Ps. 22:18 // John 19:23–24; Ps. 22:22 // Heb. 2:12).

23:1–6
Shepherd and Royal Host

This is most likely the best-known psalm. However, this familiarity does not necessarily imply a full understanding of its meaning. Psalm 23 is driven by two metaphors—God as a Shepherd and Royal Host—both of which express a deep trust in God's provisions and are intimately connected to the life of David, to whom the psalm has been ascribed.

23:1–3. My Shepherd. Psalm 22 opened with a personal appellation to God ("my God"); this psalm opens with "The LORD is my shepherd." It introduces a metaphor that runs through the Bible as a beautiful image of God's care and provision with messianic overtones (cf. John 10:11–14). Sometimes it is also applied to ungodly leaders (cf. Ezek. 34:2). The image of the king as a shepherd was known throughout the ANE and served as a paradigm for just kingship. Egyptian kings held a flail and a shepherd's crook to demonstrate their might and protective responsibilities. The Babylonian King Hammurabi (1792–1750 BC) called himself "the shepherd of the oppressed and of the slaves." The second part of v. 1 functions as a result clause to the first part. Because the Lord is the Shepherd, His sheep will not be in want or lack anything.

God's perfect provisions are further developed in vv. 2–3 using images that were familiar to a shepherd in ancient Israel and terms that go beyond the shepherd metaphor. There are green pastures, evoking vistas of abundant fresh grass on which the morning dew has fallen (cf. Deut.

32:2), and still, quiet waters (lit. "waters of rest"). Interestingly, *menukhah* ("rest," "resting place") is used elsewhere to denote the rest from war that God provided after the conquest of Canaan (cf. Deut. 12:9; 1 Kin. 8:56). God also *shub* ("returns," "restores," "refreshes") the soul/life (v. 3). This theologically significant verb *shub* is often used for forgiveness and spiritual renewal (1 Kin. 8:33). Finally, He leads in the paths of righteousness (or "the right paths"). This means that God's ways always lead home; they are righteous because God is doing this for His name's sake (i.e., He is acting according to His character).

23:4. Death Valley. The image of rich abundance and bliss changes abruptly to a valley of the shadow of death (v. 4). It threatens the psalmist, who is now speaking not *about* God but *to* Him. The somewhat odd expression can also be translated as "valley of deathly darkness," expressing a life-threatening experience (cf. Job 10:21; Jer. 13:16). It is alleviated only through the immediate presence of the Lord. Verse 4 is also the center of the psalm, where the psalmist shifts from the Shepherd metaphor to the metaphor of a Royal Host. This is done through the juxtaposition of two seemingly redundant terms: the "rod" refers to a short scepter, the insignia of a king (cf. Ps. 2:9; Is. 10:5), and the "staff"/"cane" is the longer shepherd's rod used to provide support for sheep (Zech. 8:4). God is depicted here as Lord of the sheep and the One who cares for and rescues them.

23:5–6. Royal Host. As the shepherd provides for his sheep, the royal host does the same in ways that reflect ANE hospitality. The first image is that of a royal banquet (cf. 2 Sam. 9:7–13) prepared in the presence of the guest's enemies. According to the rules of many ANE hospitality cultures, the enemy could not touch the guest because he or she was under the protection of the host (cf. Gen. 19). The royal treatment continues as oil is poured onto the guest's head, a treatment reserved only for royal guests (cf. Luke 7:46). Finally, there is a cup that overflows and satisfies all possible thirst and which, according to hospitality rules, was continuously refilled.

The conclusion of the psalm again shifts toward a theological reading of the imagery: goodness and mercy will follow. While righteousness was the theological keyword in the first image ("paths of righteousness"), now it

is *khesed*, that rich, covenantal word previously encountered and difficult to convey in one English word. Here it is sometimes translated as "mercy," but its range of meanings includes such terms as "love," "faithfulness," "lovingkindness," and "loyalty." The covenant term *khesed* does not only follow, it "pursues" and makes one "return" to the house of the Lord. *Shub*, the same verbal root used in v. 3, can be read as "return" here. The house of the Lord is both palace and temple, merging the religious and royal sphere in the image of the Shepherd and King.

24:1–10
The Gatekeeper II

Psalm 24 concludes a group of psalms and returns to a question-and-answer liturgy performed by the Levites at the gates of the temple. It is well known from its musical arrangement in Handel's Messiah (Movement 33), which connects it thematically to Christ's ascension. The psalm was possibly sung as a song of triumph after victory in battle over the Canaanites at the conquest of Jerusalem or as the ark was brought to Jerusalem by King David, the author of the poem.

24:1–2. Doxology. Using creation terminology, the psalmist acclaims God's sovereignty and proclaims that the earth is the Lord's, indirectly requesting a response in worship from its inhabitants (v. 1). The verse expresses in poetic form the OT cosmology indicating that God established the earth upon the waters (v. 2). Most probably the psalmist is criticizing Canaanite cosmology, where creation was the result of a battle between the Canaanite gods Baal and Yam. In the psalm God is depicted as the sovereign Creator.

24:3–6. Approaching Worshiper. As the worshipers respond to the doxology, the question is raised concerning the qualifications of those who are allowed to enter God's mountain and His holy place (v. 3). These qualifications of the worshipers who are worthy of approaching the temple gates are a list of standards that reflect OT ethics found in the legal parts of the Pentateuch. These are based on an inward disposition of righteousness, a pure heart, as well as on the result of just action, clean hands. They refrain from idolatry and blasphemy (v. 4; cf. Ex. 20:7), and consequently Yahweh blesses them (v. 5). The abrupt mention of Jacob at the end of v. 6

is used to designate Israel and epitomizes the experience of the patriarch as the receptor of Yahweh's blessings.

24:7-10. Gate Liturgy. The question-and-answer liturgy continues as the worshipers stand by the temple gates. The gates, which are personified (v. 7), are the *'olam* ("ancient" or "everlasting") doors of the temple, but by extension they represent the city and people that are ready for the coming King (cf. Ps. 118:20). The King is described as the Lord mighty in battle, returning victorious from war (v. 8), and as the King of glory (vv. 7-10). The refrains found in vv. 7-8 are repeated in vv. 9-10, adding new ones. The opening of the personified gates of the temple to welcome the sovereign and victorious God, invites us to also acknowledge Him as our sovereign Lord and open up the gates of our hearts to receive the King of glory.

25:1-22
An Acrostic Prayer

Psalms 25-28 bring together a group of prayers for a variety of situations. Psalm 25 initiates this with an alphabetic composition (two lines beginning with *r* instead of the expected *q*). The psalm is clearly organized around prayer and wisdom, making it a model prayer that can be easily remembered via its acrostic pattern. David is mentioned as the author and there is nothing in the psalm that could not be lined up with the events of his life.

25:1-7. Initial Invocation. The "lifting up" of the soul or life is translated idiomatically in some versions (e.g., "I put my trust" or "I turn to You"). There is a correspondence between the initial invocation and the concluding request through repetition of terminology—for example, *nepesh* ("soul" or "life"; vv. 1, 20), *'oybai* ("my enemies"; vv. 2, 19), and *bosh* ("to be ashamed"; vv. 2, 3, 20). This creates a concentric emphasis on the second section on wisdom (vv. 8-15). An initial affirmation of trust is followed by a plea not to be ashamed (i.e., not to be humiliated and ruined by enemies' victories over him) but rather to have the shame fall on them instead, since they have been treacherous with him for no reason (v. 3). Those who have dealt deceitfully with David are inexcusable and are traitors to God's cause (cf. 78:57). The plea continues by asking for God's instruction and daily guidance in His ways and paths. These two synonyms

are repeated throughout the psalm (vv. 4, 8, 9, 10, 12) and introduce the wisdom motif. The section concludes with a plea for God's forgiveness according to His mercy and love (v. 6). God's eternal (Heb. *'olam*) attributes are stressed as the basis for divine forgiveness.

25:8-15. Reflection on Wisdom. The central section consists of a series of declarative statements about the character of God and His guidance. He teaches His way, which is *mishpat* ("justice," "right," "judgment"; v. 9), *khesed* ("mercy," "lovingkindness," "loyal love"; v. 10), and *'emet* ("truth," "faithfulness"; v. 10). In the middle of the wisdom section and in the middle of the Hebrew alphabet (*lamed*), there is a supplication for forgiveness (v. 11). Then the psalm continues with a description of God's way (v. 12), focusing on the benefits experienced by those who fear Him (v. 14) and expressed in terms of the covenant promise of inheriting the land (v. 13; cf. Deut. 4:1).

25:16-22. Concluding Request. The change from third- to first-person viewpoint introduces a plea in the final section that echoes the plea of vv. 1-7. The psalmist uses the imagery of sight and asks God to look on his affliction (v. 18) and intervene. God should recognize how numerous his enemies are (v. 19) and deliver him from them (v. 20). God's seeing means action (Ps. 142:4-7). The psalm concludes with an expansion of the plea to include the people of Israel—a prayer for their *padah* ("ransom," "redemption," or "deliverance"; v. 22). This multi-themed poem is foremost an intense prayer for guidance and instruction in "the way." This term is used in the NT as the earliest self-description of Christians (cf. Acts 9:2; 11:26) based on the radical claim of Jesus as "the Way" (John 14:6-7).

26:1-12
Integrity and Vindication

Psalm 26 continues the tone set in the previous psalm by providing a model prayer for different situations in life. While Psalm 25 asked for guidance, Psalm 26 is a prayer of vindication based on a strong affirmation of the psalmist's own integrity. There are a number of links between the two psalms (e.g., v. 1 // 25:2, 21) and there is also a similar framing in the beginning and end of the psalm, centered on the theme of integrity. It has been suggested that Psalms 25-28 originated together during a specific time in the life of David, possibly during the rebellion of Absalom. They probably reflect prayers that arose from the pressing circumstances David experienced during that dark period in his life.

26:1–2. Plea for Vindication. The psalm begins with the forensic imperative, "vindicate me," followed in v. 2 by three further imperatives that use legal terminology: *bakhan* ("test," "examine," "prove"), *nasah* ("test," "try," "prove"), and *tsarap* ("try," "examine," "refine"), all intensifying the request. The petition is based on the psalmist's integrity because he trusted in the Lord (v. 1; cf. 7:8–9). This is not an expression of self-righteousness but an affirmation of faith based on his relationship with God that trustingly invites divine scrutiny (cf. 139:23–24).

26:3–8. Affirmation of Integrity. Following the invitation for divine trial, the psalmist affirms his own integrity through invoking the guiding principles of his life: he has always looked at God's *khesed* ("lovingkindness," "unfailing love") and has lived (lit. "walked") by trusting in God's *'emet* ("truth" or "faithfulness"), which refers to a lifelong commitment to God's way (cf. Ps. 25, which also uses the metaphors of *seeing* and *walking*). This implies a clear separation from the wicked, who are described as *shaw'* (lit. "empty" or "vain"), sometimes used to refer to deceit (e.g., 12:2; 41:6; 144:8) or idolatry (e.g., Jer. 18:15). They are hypocrites and evildoers (vv. 4–5). The psalmist also acclaims his ritual purity; he will wash his hands in innocence, an action that grants access to the altar in the sanctuary (v. 6; cf. Deut. 21:1–9). This is done in order to join the congregation in praise (vv. 6–8). The temple, as the place David loved (v. 8) contrasts with the assembly of evildoers that he loathed (v. 5).

26:9–12. Plea for Deliverance. The contrast is further developed in the final plea of the psalm. The description of the sinners continues and the psalmist asks not to be included among them in death (v. 9). This is followed by a final reiteration of personal integrity, which leads into public praise. Moral integrity implies a clear separation from wickedness and is foremost grounded in God's redemption and vindication.

27:1–14
Praise and Plea

Psalm 27 begins with a prayer of trust (vv. 1–6) followed by a lament in the second part of the psalm (vv. 7–14), rather than with a lament followed by praise as in most psalms. It recalls Psalms 9–10, which together form an acrostic poem following the same sequence (cf. also Ps. 40). From a theological and didactic perspective, praise should precede plea. The group of psalms that bring together prayers for different occasions demonstrates that one should present thanksgiving before requests. David's life provides the backdrop to the poem and the LXX dates it prior to his anointing.

27:1–6. Praise. At the outset the psalmist acknowledges the power of Yahweh through the metaphors of *ma'oz* ("mountain stronghold," "refuge") and *'or* ("light"; cf. Is. 60:1; Mic. 7:8–9) and asks the rhetorical question "Of whom shall I be afraid?" He then recounts how God has protected him in the past (v. 2) and how He will protect him as well in the future, even if an army were to besiege him (v. 3). Verses 4–6 enhance the image of refuge by connecting it to the sanctuary. The psalmist wants to dwell in the house of the Lord all the days of his life (v. 4; cf. Ps. 23:6) in order to be in God's continuous presence and behold the beauty of the Lord (i.e., to contemplate His wonderful works; cf. 90:16). He is looking for a hiding place in the shelter of God's tabernacle/tent and offers sacrifices with joy because God has saved him from his enemies (v. 6).

27:7–14. Plea. Now the psalmist turns to his plea, requesting that God hear and answer (v. 7). In Hebrew, it is not clear who is speaking in v. 8. Some translate as if God is speaking, while others claim it is the conscience of the psalmist (his heart; cf. v. 3, 14), which seems to speak on God's behalf as the means of communication between God and humankind. Either way, the psalmist responds affirmatively that he will seek God's face (v. 8). Seeking God's face is equivalent to longing for His presence (105:4) and trusting in His miraculous intervention (31:16). The petition is then concretized by petitioning God to not hide His face, which is a request to not be abandoned by God.

The request for instruction in God's way (v. 11) connects this psalm to the two preceding prayers (Pss. 25–26) by expressing the desire to follow God's will and be led in a smooth or straight path, even in the face of his oppressive enemies who have risen against him as false witnesses (vv. 11–12). A final exhortation of trust encourages the audience beyond the psalmist with a twofold "wait on the Lord," at the beginning and end of v. 14. The prayer of Psalm

27 follows the positive confidence of the two preceding psalms, but it adds an emphasis on the sanctuary (vv. 4–6). It is the sanctuary that provides a safe haven, God's pleasant presence and future guidance for the psalmist. In Jewish tradition the psalm is recited during the sixth month in preparation for the Day of Atonement.

28:1–9
Plea and Praise

This poem concludes the group of prayers (Pss. 25–28) dealing with various pressing situations in the life of David. As in Psalm 27, the structure is twofold and help comes from the sanctuary, in this case the holy of holies (v. 2), but the sequence is reversed and plea is followed by praise.

28:1–5. Plea. The psalmist asks the Lord to hear his cry of despair and not be silent (vv. 1–2). God's silence would mean death; he would become like "those who go down to the pit." The cry intensifies as David lifts up his hands toward the tabernacle, a physical gesture that often expresses an urgent appeal (v. 2). He seems to be standing in the courtyard of the tabernacle facing the *debir qodesh* ("the holy inner room" or "the holiest of holies"). This is the only occurrence of this phrase in the Psalms (see 1 Kin. 6:19–31; 2 Chr. 4:20 for others). The psalmist next concretizes the request. He does not want to be "dragged off" like a criminal for judgment along with the ungodly, who speak cordially and peacefully but have malice and evil in their hearts (v. 4). God can deal with them in only one way: they will be destroyed and torn down rather than built up (v. 5). Notice the contrast between the endeavors of hands of the wicked (v. 4) and those of God's hands (v. 5). One leads to destruction and the other to salvation, which is the content of the following praise.

28:6–9. Praise. The praise begins with the familiar formula, *baruk yahweh* ("praised" or "blessed be the Lord"; cf. 31:21; 41:13; 72:18; 89:52; 106:48; 124:6; 135:21; 144:1), because He has answered the supplication of the psalmist. A number of metaphors for divine refuge follow that are first applied to the individual and then extended to the community. God is the psalmist's Strength (v. 7), but also the Strength of His people (v. 8). Some translations render the phrase literally "their strength" without a referent. That "His people" is the implied referent is suggested by both the LXX and other manuscripts, as well as

by the final appeal for God to save His people and shepherd them. This invokes once more the image of the divine Shepherd (v. 9; cf. 23:1–4) who serves as the ideal paradigm for the earthly king. Psalm 28 is a prayer for separation from the wicked and from the judgment against them. While the prayer is just, we must recognize, as David did, that it is God who judges and executes that judgment.

29:1–11
Yahweh's Seven Thunders

The sevenfold *qol yahweh* ("the voice of the Lord") that runs through the center of this beautiful hymn (vv. 3–9) resounds like a thunder in a storm that rages above the interior of northern Israel, which provides the geographical locale for this psalm. The psalm has repeatedly been likened to a Canaanite hymn dedicated to the weather and storm god Baal. However, the exposition will show that it rather serves as a well-aimed polemic against Canaanite mythology, demonstrating the monotheistic supremacy of Yahweh over all the gods of Canaan. Davidic authorship provides a good link to the historical background during a time in which the Israelite king established the monarchy among its Canaanite enemies.

29:1–2. Glory in Heaven. There is a parallel between vv. 1–2 and vv. 10–11 (more specifically, v. 9c) that brackets the thoughts of the psalmist. This is done through the use of the word "glory" and the fourfold mention of the name "Lord." While the introduction serves as a call to angelic worship in heaven, the final invitation to worship extends the blessings to earth. We attribute greatness to God (vv. 1–2), and God gives us strength and peace. This represents a spatial movement from above to below that runs throughout the psalm. The term *bene 'elim* has been interpreted and translated in various ways. It is literally "sons of God" but has also been translated as "sons of the mighty." The term *'el* is sometimes understood as indicative of power, might, or "heavenly beings," understood as angelic beings that serve before God's throne (cf. 89:6; Job 2:1), or as those who are "godly." Being the "son" of something or someone conveys the idea of having their characteristics (Judg. 19:22; 1 Sam. 2:12; John 5:18; 8:44; Acts 4:36). Whichever is intended, they are invited to worship God and, by contrast, not to be worshiped by humankind as in Canaanite mythology.

29:3–9. The Divine Storm. Seven times the "voice of the LORD" is mentioned, and every time it is not only audible but also active, impacting fauna and flora. The divine manifestation through the thunderstorm begins over *rab* ("many" or "mighty") waters, an expression that often designates the Mediterranean. The natural event of a storm forming over the sea and traveling inland is an observable phenomenon in the Holy Land. There is an implied polemic here as the "waters" in Canaanite mythology represent the forces of chaos with which the gods have to fight.

However, Yahweh is over the waters and sits enthroned over the flood (v. 10). As the storm moves over the Lebanon and Sirion (i.e., the Sidonian/Canaanite name for Mt. Hermon) and finally subsides in the Syrian desert/the Wilderness of Kadesh (vv. 6–8), it breaks and splinters trees (v. 5), makes mountains skip like a calf (v. 6), shakes the wilderness (v. 8), and strips the forests bare (v. 9). The Hebrew text in v. 9 literally refers to God causing deer to writhe in birth pains, but some have suggested an emendation to the text in order to strengthen the parallel with the stripping of the forest. In this case, the plural Hebrew word for deer (*'ayyalot*—the singular is *'ayyalah*) should be replaced by one of the words for oaks (*'elot*—from the singular *'ayil* or *'elah*) instead, and accordingly the phrase would be referring to the convulsion of the oaks. Lightning and earthquakes accompany the thunderstorm, and trees and mountains—both of which are normally symbols of divine strength in Canaanite mythology—are subject to the majesty and power of Yahweh's thunderstorm. Even the wilderness, normally the habitation of demons, and the reproductive cycle of nature are subject to the power of Yahweh. One cannot but notice the continuous polemics here.

29:10–11. And Peace on Earth. The final call to worship in the heavenly sanctuary with a shout of "glory" (v. 9) introduces an almost tangible change of tone. In contrast to the dynamic verbal action forms of vv. 3–9, there is a static quality to v. 10 as Yahweh sits enthroned as King forever (v. 10). From the heavenly sanctuary He bestows blessings on earth on His people (v. 11). While in vv. 1–2 God was the object of worship, now He is the subject who blesses His people. The Psalm closes with peace after the storm. Worship of God in the heavenly sanctuary returns to earth as a blessing of peace.

30:1–12
From Weeping to Joy

This thanksgiving psalm represents a masterpiece of Hebrew poetry, playing on contrasts and reversals from negative to positive: e.g., "brought...up" and "go down" (v. 3), "weeping...for a night" and "joy in the morning" (v. 5), "mourning" and "dancing" (v. 11), all pointing to a drastic experience in the life of the poet based on a self-sufficiency that eclipsed God (v. 7). The superscription has been parsed in different ways, leading to different understandings. There are four Hebrew word groupings: "a psalm," "a song of dedication," "the house," and "of David."

There is universal agreement that the first two word groupings are meant to be separate. The relationship of the last three are debated. Some translations read, "A song at the dedication of the house of David." Others read, "A song. For the dedication of the temple/palace. Of David" (indicating Davidic authorship as in other psalms). In this way, some have understood the "house" (*bayit*) as referring to the house of God (i.e., the temple), which would then render the title anachronistic because David did not dedicate the temple. It is more likely a reference to a song David wrote in preparation for the future dedication of the temple, even though there is no indication that it was sung at the dedication (1 Kings 8:62–66). He may have composed it soon after the experience of the census he conducted (cf. 2 Sam. 24:1). On the other hand, David did complete his palace in Jerusalem (2 Sam. 5:11–12), which may be what is referred to here (though Scripture does not record a dedication event). For whichever event this psalm was composed, David gave God the glory.

30:1–3. Praise for Deliverance. The psalm commences with praise for healing from a potentially fatal illness, when God brought him up from *she'ol*, the realm of death and the grave (v. 3). The healing (v. 2) may be not just physical but also spiritual in nature, and both go hand in hand in the OT (cf. 147:3). If one takes David's census (2 Sam. 24; 1 Chr. 21) as the historical backdrop for the psalm, both aspects are relevant.

30:4–5. God's Discipline and Favor. The praise is extended to the congregational level, to the *khasidim* ("faithful ones" or "saints"; v. 4). The subject of their thanksgiving hymn is identified through striking contrasts. God's anger lasts for only a moment (lit. "twinkling of the eye"), while His favor is for a lifetime, contrasting the proportion between God's wrath and His pleasure. This is then further enhanced by the contrast between the night and the morning, when joy replaces weeping.

30:6–10. Self-Sufficiency. The psalmist now confesses in more detail what lies at the heart of his alienation from God. The *shalu* mentioned in v. 6 can be translated as "prosperity" or as "careless security" (cf. Ezek. 16:49), denoting a self-sufficiency that leads to the moment when David realizes that God had hidden His face. Then he was terrified (v. 7). The sobering realization of God's absence leads to a request to God for Him to hear him once more and show him mercy (vv. 8–10).

30:11–12. Mourning into Dancing. The final section replicates vv. 4–5 in returning to the contrasts and reversals that mark this psalm. The emblems of death (weeping and sackcloth) have been replaced by the emblems of life (dancing and rejoicing). It is an outward expression of joy over restoration (cf. Jer. 31:13), which leads to a final vow to give thanks to God forever. Psalm 30 is a striking image of a God who disciplines, but only for a moment if compared with life and eternity, and who is able to reverse and transform our darkness into light in a moment.

31:1–24
A Repeated Prayer of Distress

The two movements of Psalm 31 (vv. 1–8 and 9–24) are parallel in that they move from plea to expressions of trust and from deliverance to praise. Because of its repetitive content, it has been suggested that this psalm is a conflation of two originally individual poems. However, repetition is an important rhetoric and didactic device that goes through the same "story" twice, a phenomenon which can be found in various places throughout the psalms (cf. Pss. 30; 42–43; 95; 100). The two sections are furthermore connected by recurring expressions (e.g., "trust"; *khasah*, lit. "seek refuge"; vv. 1 and 19; "into Your hand"; vv. 5 and 15). Besides the Davidic authorship, the LXX adds "of alarm" to the superscription, an expression related to the Hebrew verb *khapaz* ("to be alarmed" or "to hurry in alarm") in v. 22. This has motivated commentators to link it with 1 Samuel 23:26, where this same verb is used in regard to David's reaction to Saul's pursuing him.

31:1–8. Prayer I. The psalm goes straight into a plea for deliverance, underlined by an affirmation of faith: David trusts and takes refuge in God. The divine metaphors of Rock and Fortress are used twice (vv. 2–3), and this could remind the listener/reader of Psalm 18. The request for deliverance is linked to a deceptive net or trap laid for him (v. 4), drawing on the imagery of hunting. The flight of David from Saul as he tried to pull his net closer and closer comes to mind here. Verse 5 commences with a statement of trust, which Christ appropriated just before His death (Luke 23:46)—the psalmist will commit his spirit into God's hands. This encapsulates the experience of all those who completely entrust their lives to God and praise Him for deliverance. Such people are contrasted with those who give homage to vain idols (v. 6). The psalmist can rejoice in God's mercy, because He has set his feet in an open place. With this image of wide space the psalm returns to the plea.

31:9–24. Prayer II. The psalmist pleads for mercy and then lists a number of physical and emotional consequences of his trouble: his eyes are weakened by his distress, his strength fails, he is despised by his enemies, and he is even dreaded by his acquaintances (vv. 9–11). He has become a *persona non grata*, somebody who is forgotten as if dead (v. 12). In v. 13, he mentions whispering slander as the cause and states that fear is on every side (or, alternatively, that his enemies are saying, "fear/terror on every side" as a plan for their attack), a phrase that occurs also in Jeremiah's sentencing of Pashhur (Jer. 20:2–3; cf. Is. 31:9). Jeremiah probably took the phrase from this psalm and used it to summarize his message of judgment.

The affirmation of trust and petition for deliverance (vv. 14–16) is linked to the high priestly benediction (Num. 6:25) that God shine His face on him. He is requesting a renewal of God's favor and the silencing of his enemies (vv. 17–18). This second prayer (vv. 19–24) concludes the psalm and serves as an extended praise of God's goodness that protects those who trust in Him. There is an exhortation for all of God's people to be encouraged (vv. 23–24). David, persecuted by Saul, becomes a type for Christ, who is the ultimate persecuted One, even unto death. Jesus used the words of Psalm 31:5 to express His ultimate trust in His Father as He breathed His last for the forgiveness of our sins.

32:1-11
A Prayer for Forgiveness

Psalm 32 is a penitential poem closely associated with Psalm 51. Both express sorrow over sin and the joy that comes with the forgiveness of sins (cf. also Pss. 6; 38; 102; 130; 143). Traditionally, the Davidic authorship of the psalm and its similarity with Psalm 51 have led to its connection with the aftermath of David's sin with Bathsheba. The superscription *maskil* (sometimes rendered as "contemplation") occurs here for the first time and can also be rendered as "instruction." The term is based on the verbal form *sakal*, "to instruct," which also occurs in v. 8. There is an instructive element here in that the psalmist encourages others to follow not the way he has taken but God's way.

32:1-5. Praise for Forgiveness. Similar to Psalm 1, this psalm opens with a beatitude, this time for those who are forgiven. This opening summarizes the content of the remainder of the psalm. Sin is described as "rebellion" (*pesha'*) and "missing the mark" (*khata'ah*), both of which can refer to a deliberate act. Theologically and legally, the Lord does not impute iniquity to the sinner. Rather, the Lord imputes (*khashab*) righteousness to those who have faith in Him (Gen. 15:6; cf. Paul's usage of Ps. 32:2 in Rom. 4:8). Verses 3-5 describe the agony of unconfessed sin, which is described in the strongest physical terms, indicating the far-reaching consequences of hidden iniquity and divine discipline (vv. 3-4). This is relieved only after David acknowledged his sin (v. 5). One needs to be careful not to relate sin and discipline too dogmatically (as Job's friends do), but the psalmist is here recognizing God's attempt to correct him in his sin. Note the immediacy of forgiveness following the confession, "and You forgave." This is expressed emphatically in the Hebrew by the placement of the personal pronoun "you" in the front position. This is not grammatically required but is done for the purpose of emphasis.

32:6-11. Encouragement and Instruction. David immediately feels the need to extend his experience to others as the burden has been lifted off his shoulders. He concludes by noting that God's faithful and godly ones should pray to Him while He may be found, leading to deliverance and protection (v. 6). In v. 7, the psalmist returns to the personal dimension. The final section (vv. 8-11) is the formal instruction, in which the speaker appears to be God first addressing the psalmist (v. 8; singular) but then extending His instructions to others as well (v. 9). He uses the metaphor of the horse and mule, which must be harnessed. This is the style of wisdom language. In v. 10, we find a proverb (cf. Prov. 28:25). The final line of the psalm returns to psalmodic praise with a resounding invitation for the upright in heart to sing and shout for joy (v. 11). The contrast between the effects of unconfessed sin and the experience of forgiveness marks this psalm as one of the great penitential psalms that should encourage sinners to seek forgiveness.

33:1-22
God in Creation and History

Besides the two portals to the Psalms (Pss. 1 and 2) and Psalm 10 (a continuation of Ps. 9), Psalm 33 is the only other psalm in Book 1 that lacks a superscription (cf. the LXX and a ms. from Qumran, which add Davidic authorship). Psalm 33 is a hymn of praise, describing God as Creator and Lord of history. Verse 1 responds to 32:11 with a similar bidding of the righteous to rejoice.

33:1-3. Call to Praise. Psalm 33 is introduced by an extended call to praise that includes song and instrument. The motivation is that the praise of the upright is *na'weh* ("beautiful," "comely," "fitting"). Praise is a natural outflow of a heart that has experienced the redeeming power of God.

33:4-19. Cause for Praise. The fundamental cause for praise is God and His character: He loves righteousness and justice (v. 5), together with *'emunah* ("truth," "faithfulness"; v. 4) and *khesed* ("mercy," "goodness," "unfailing love"; v. 5). These are the perfections of Yahweh that run through the Psalms (cf. 25:8-16). Verses 6-9 move from a description of God's character to a description of His work of Creation, which was accomplished by His word (v. 6). This should inspire all people to revere Him. There is a strong affirmation of Genesis 1 and 2 as a literal Creation account (v. 9). Based on John 1 and on Christ as the *logos*, we can find here a messianic perspective.

From Creation the psalm moves to history, declaring the supremacy of God among the nations. His purposes and plans supersede those of the nations (cf. Dan. 2). No king is saved by the great size of his army (v. 16), but by his relationship to God (v. 12). Yahweh's salvific actions are manifested throughout history, and He is ready to deliver those who fear and hope in Him. History in the OT is always linked to God's interventions and is focused on the salvation of His people and beyond.

33:20–22. Declaration of Trust. An affirmation of trust in Yahweh concludes the psalm, its final climax being a congregational invocation for the Lord's *khesed* ("mercy," "unfailing love") to be upon His people who hope in Him. Trust provides a solid foundation for hope. Yahweh as Creator and Lord of history provides a historical basis for the work of salvation, which finds its supreme expression in Christ.

34:1–22
An Acrostic Testimony

Psalm 34 continues the instruction of the previous psalm in the form of an alphabetic poem, with some small irregularities (cf. Ps. 25) that testify about the goodness of Yahweh. The psalm is continuously *about* God, but none of the lines are directly addressed to Him. It covers a variety of life situations together, with the corresponding deliverance by Yahweh. The form is that of a didactic poem, which one may easily recall under a pressing situation. It was composed by David, and the historic superscription connects the psalm with a time when he feigned insanity before Achish (here called Abimelech, likely because that was a title for Philistine kings). That event (1 Sam. 21:10–15) is connected to the psalm in a number of ways, such as the emphasis on fear and the usage of the rare term *ta'am* ("taste, good sense"), which occurs in both passages (1 Sam. 21:13 // Ps. 34:1, 8).

34:1–10. Declarative Praise. Praise as a continuous and iterative attitude, both on individual and communal levels, dominates vv. 1–3. The motivation for unceasing praise is Yahweh's deliverance, mentioned in the next lines. He delivers from fears (v. 4), hears, and saves (v. 6). The often quoted v. 7 emphasizes the ministry of angels but goes beyond as the "angel of the Lord," or "messenger of the Lord" (*mal'ak yahweh*) is used as a divine title and has attributes that belong only to God (cf. Gen. 16:7; Josh. 5:14; Judg. 6:11–22; Zech. 3:1–6; see "The Angel of the Lord," p. 395). It points to the presence of Jesus in the OT, the One who as the Son of God and supreme Commander of all angels cares for our well-being. With such protection one can only taste and see that the Lord is good (v. 8). God's goodness is like tasting delicious food and wanting more of it (cf. 1 Pet. 2:3).

34:11–22. Instruction. The "fear of the Lord" is something that can be taught (Ps. 32:8; see Excursus, "Wisdom and the Fear of the Lord," p. 764). The didactic section of the psalm is introduced in v. 11 and continues to the end as the fear of the Lord is being taught. This fear is further explained through five statements: govern both words and deeds (vv. 13–14), live the life of the righteous (vv. 15–16), search God in prayer with a broken heart (vv. 17–18), depend on God's protection in affliction because He delivers (vv. 19–20), and be confident in the judgment because no one who trusts God and takes refuge in Him will be condemned. As we can see, Psalm 34 continues the instructional tone of the previous psalms, providing practical lessons to be memorized for times of distress and connecting them to praise.

35:1–28
The Angel of the Lord

Psalms 34–35 are the only psalms that mention the "angel of the Lord." Psalm 35 does so in more detail by drawing more extensively on the divine Warrior metaphor. While Psalm 34 was more focused on protection, in Psalm 35 the request is for the "angel of the Lord" to stop the enemies who are attacking the psalmist. Three times the psalm goes through lament, plea, and praise for future deliverance, with emphasis on one of them in each of the stanzas (cf. Ps. 31). Davidic authorship is mentioned without any further superscription, but the period of his life when he was persecuted by Saul would fit this prayer well.

35:1–10. Prayer I. The first stanza emphasizes a plea for the destruction of the enemy, who is scheming without reason to take the life of the innocent psalmist (vv. 7–8). The "Lord" (v. 6) is called upon in military terms to put on his armor, to take both his *magen* ("shield") and his *tsinnah* ("large shield"; v. 2), and to draw his spear (v. 3), indicating both protection and aggression. When David requests that the Angel of the Lord chase them, the persecutors become the persecuted (vv. 1–6). By asking for the Angel of the Lord to act, David was recognizing that God often carries out these acts through these means. The section ends with a prospect of rejoicing in deliverance (vv. 9–10). The language is reminiscent of the Exodus (cf. Ex. 14–15).

35:11–18. Prayer II. In the second stanza, the focus is on the lament as it describes how the psalmist is suffering unjustly and how his enemies render him evil for good. They are false, malicious witnesses of *khamas* ("violence"), indicating that they are more interested in bloodshed than reconciliation. The psalmist even recalls that he prayed and fasted for his enemies when they were sick, as a friend or brother would (vv. 13–14). Obviously, there was a good personal relationship between the psalmist and his enemies that was now broken. His incredulity and disappointment at their hostility is summarized with a short plea in a question that echoes through the Psalms (v. 17), "How long?" The section concludes with a brief praise for future deliverance in the great assembly (v. 18).

35:19–28. Prayer III. The final stanza returns mostly to petition, requesting that God not let the enemies rejoice over him (v. 19). It is constructed by a series of calls for a divine intervention to end the slander that is aimed not only at the psalmist but also at those who live quietly in the land (v. 20). David uses legal terminology (cf. 9:4) as he invokes Yahweh to *'awar* and *qits* (stir and awaken Himself) for his *mishpat* ("vindication," "judgment") and *rib* ("dispute") and appeals to God as Judge (vv. 22–26). The final praise concludes the psalm along the same legal lines (vv. 27–28). A psalm bearing a threefold request for the destruction of the wicked, even though they persecute the just, makes some uncomfortable. However, one should not forget that it is a prayer to God (i.e., the appropriate channeling of justified anger against injustice). God prefers to take charge of our vindication instead of us taking charge of it ourselves (Deut. 32:35; Rom. 12:19).

36:1–12

A Stark Contrast

Psalm 36 is built around a stark contrast between human wickedness and divine faithfulness (*khesed* in vv. 5, 7, 10) which is developed in three movements (vv. 1–4; 5–9; 10–12). The title identifies David as the author and qualifies him as "the servant of the LORD." The title occurs only here and in 18:1.

36:1–4. Description of the Wicked. The description of the wicked moves from the inward (thoughts) to the outward (words and actions). Verse 1 should be understood as the revelation the psalmist receives from God concerning their wickedness. This is about the motivation of evil that takes place in the heart and then outflows in words and actions. At the bottom of evil motivation lies the denial of God's authority, because they do not fear Him. The denial of divine authority leads to the elevation of self and the rationalization of sin. Most translations refer to the wicked person "flattering himself" in v. 2. This expression can also be translated, "for he deals smoothly with himself" with regard to his sin. The glossing over of sin produces wicked words (v. 3), the person ceases to act with wisdom and goodness, and evil becomes an all-consuming occupation.

36:5–9. Divine Faithfulness. Without any transition, the poem moves to address Yahweh through a description of His faithful deeds. God's characteristics of mercy or constant love (*khesed*), faithfulness (*'emunah*), righteousness (*tsedaqah*), and judgments or justice (*mishpat*) (vv. 5–6) are mentioned. These characteristics, which are often linked together in covenant language (cf. Gen. 15; Ex. 34; 1 Kin. 3), are lofty, enormous, and deep, providing the safest place for humans to put their trust and take refuge under the shadow of God's wings (v. 7). This image is connected to the sanctuary and the cherubim above the ark, where all these divine attributes were at work. This is further developed through the provisions of the temple, where people ate from the fullness or abundance (lit. "the fat") or God's house and drank from the river of His pleasures, alluding to the rivers of Eden (v. 8; cf. Ps. 23 where eating and drinking is also connected to the temple). In that sense the sanctuary and its services are a reminder of paradise (see "Creation, Sabbath, and the Sanctuary," p. 231). Ultimately, it is Yahweh who is the fountain of life and He is light (v. 9), divine attributes which are appropriated by Jesus (John 4; 8:12).

36:10–12. Preservation of the Just. The final plea of the psalm returns to the themes of love and righteousness (cf. vv. 5–6) to be bestowed on the upright in heart (v. 10). There is also a request for protection from the wicked (v. 11). The psalmist describes the future downfall of the wicked, while acknowledging that for now they could be a threat to him. For him good and evil coexist often in astonishing proximity, until the day comes when God's judgment elevates the one and destroys the other (cf. Matt. 13:24–30, 36–40).

37:1–40

The Inheritance of the Land

Psalm 37 is another acrostic psalm creating a didactic poem almost at the end of Book 1 that is modeled along the lines of wisdom literature. A number of thematic parallels can be established with the book of Proverbs (e.g., v. 5 // Prov. 16:3; v. 24 // Prov. 24:16) and also with the beginning of the Psalms (especially the *torah* instruction of Psalm 1). There is a marked contrast between the way of the righteous and the way of the wicked, likened to the image of a tree (cf. v. 35; in Ps. 1:3 the just person is the tree). This contrast also links it to Psalm 73, which stands at the beginning of Book 3 (cf. also Pss. 91; 119). All these psalms create an ideal paradigm of how things should be, even if the psalms in between show how often things are not as they should be. Theologically, the psalm focuses on the possession of the land (vv. 3, 9, 11, 22, 29, 34), but not on returning to the land after the Exile. We find here both righteous and wicked living alongside each other and the righteous being under attack. This would fit well the historical situation at the beginning of the monarchy, to which the psalm has been connected through its Davidic authorship.

37:1-6. Commitment. The focus of vv. 1-6 is perseverance in faith connected to dwelling in the land. In a way this section outlines the theme of the psalm (vv. 7-40). The exhortation to not fret in v. 1 is paralleled in vv. 7 and 8 at the beginning of the next section. Refraining from anxiety in the face of adversity is possible by trusting that the wicked are like grass that withers and is cut down (v. 2). Furthermore, one should trust in the Lord and find delight in Him, the clear opposite to fretting (vv. 3-4; cf. 1:2). Using the metaphor of righteousness as light, verses 5-6 emphasize the commitment of the faithful one to God and the future promise that is connected with it.

37:7-33. Instruction. This section contains the main didactic instruction of the psalm and is a development of vv. 1-6, as indicated by the repeated exhortation to not fret (vv. 7-8). It is again a call to perseverance, to wait patiently for Him (v. 7), because the wicked will perish but the meek will inherit the earth or land (vv. 9-11). Land possession is a covenant promise and a keyword from Deuteronomy to Judges. Jesus contextualized v. 11 in the Beatitudes, extending the promise beyond Israel (Matt. 5:5). The contrast between the wicked and the just is elaborated in vv. 12-22. These contrasts often demonstrate true biblical wisdom and a worldview that transcends the here and now: the few possessions of the righteous are preferable to the wealth of many wicked people (v. 16). In reaction to the evil plotting and scheming, the Lord laughs at the wicked (v. 13) because they will perish and fade away (v. 20). This worldview also extends to ethical behavior, as the wicked borrow and do not repay but the righteous show mercy and give generously. The section ends with a summative statement that returns, by way of contrast, to the theme of inheritance. Those blessed by the Lord will inherit the land, but those cursed by Him will be *karat* ("cut off" or "destroyed").

The psalm shifts now to the blessings of the righteous (vv. 22-26), adding the voice of experience to the instruction: from his youth to his old age, the psalmist has never seen the righteous forsaken or begging for food (v. 25). The comportment of the righteous is linked to generosity, in contrast to the wicked who borrows and does not repay (v. 26; cf. v. 21). Generosity in the OT was an expression of righteousness and lending without interest, an ethical norm (cf. Ex. 22:25; Ps. 15:5). Because of this ethical lifestyle, God preserves the just from judgment and reiterates the refrain-like promise—the righteous shall inherit the land (v. 29). Ethics is described as wisdom and consequently the righteous speak wisely and the law of God is in their hearts (v. 31). This is an internalization of *torah* that projects itself into the NT (cf. Jer. 31:33; Heb. 8:10).

37:34-40. Future Perspective. Psalm 37 ends with an exhortation for the righteous to *qawah* ("wait" or "hope for") the Lord and keep His way, connecting it to previous reflections on "the way" (cf. 25:8-15). A final contrast, now located in the future, is created between the destiny of the wicked (they will have no future; it will be *karat*, "cut off"; v. 38) and the just (they will have a future). Some translations understand the future of the upright to be one of peace, while others suggest that peace is the characteristic of the upright person who has the future. The guarantor of this future is Yahweh, who will deliver the righteous from the wicked and save them (v. 40). Psalm 37 provides an ideal paradigm for a life based on God's instruction, a life of wisdom, *torah*, and eternal peace, based on the conviction that eventually and ultimately there will be peace.

38:1-22
Sin and Suffering

The physical illness described at the outset of this psalm connects it closely not only to Psalm 6 but also to the story of Job and the extended discourses with his friends on sin and suffering. Psalm 38 is also linked to Psalm 37 through a number of literary connections, such as the usage of the unusual *teshu'ah* ("salvation"; 38:22 // 37:39). It is not an acrostic, but its twenty-two verses connect it further to the preceding alphabetic poem. The psalm is ascribed to David. While physical suffering on the part of David is not recorded specifically in the historical books, the connection between sin and illness is familiar from the Davidic psalms (cf. Pss. 32; 51). The additional superscription, "to bring to remembrance" or "a petition," is also found in Psalm 70 and can be connected to the *memorial* offering, which acknowledged God's provisions as part of the sacrificial system (Lev. 2:2, 9, 16).

38:1–14. Initial Prayer and Lament. The psalmist begins by asking God not to rebuke and discipline him in His anger. The psalmist accepts divine discipline as a result of personal sin through the usage of *yasar* ("correct, discipline, chasten"; cf. 94:10), but at the same time he asks for a delimitation of divine displeasure. The first line of the psalm is almost identical to 6:1. The psalmist repeatedly expresses his physical suffering as a result of personal sin in vv. 2–4, and vv. 5–10 provide a detailed description of the sickness: his wounds are festering (v. 5), his *kesel* (translated variously as "loins," "back," or "insides") is/are burning (lit. "burning with shame"; v. 7), and his strength fails (v. 10). All this recalls the suffering of Job, yet with recognition of culpability. It is conceivable that David modeled his experience on Job as indicated by a number of linguistic and thematic connections between this lament section and the book of Job (see Job 6–7).

The lament now moves from the personal to a social dimension describing how loved ones, friends, and even relatives and neighbors stand afar off, avoiding and ostracizing the sick person—a common human reaction to suffering. The feeling of abandonment by the people closest to him worsens through the triumphant stance of his enemies, who exploit his weakness and speak of destroying him (v. 12). His reaction is a contrastive silence to all the enemies' hurtful words: he is like a mute who does not open his mouth (v. 13).

38:15–20. Faith in God's Salvation. The turning point away from lament to an expression of faith is introduced by the contrastive conjunction (*ki*), which also begins each of the next

three verses. It underlines the appropriateness of the silence with which the lament concluded: he waits for and hopes in the Lord, trusting that He will hear and answer (v. 15). He is silent so that God may answer. The emphatic personal pronoun (lit. "you, you will answer") indicates that he has handed over to God the question of personal vindication. The psalmist himself is not capable of responding because he is close to falling and his pain and sorrow are continuous (v. 17). His emotional condition is beyond the physical dimension of his suffering. Verse 18 is climactic in that it uses the contrastive *ki* for the last time, introducing the psalmist's public acknowledgment of his sin. This forms the basis for God's vindication.

38:21–22. Final Prayer. The psalm ends with an echo of its beginning, pleading for God to intervene. It concludes by invoking Yahweh as his salvation (v. 22), as Psalm 37 did. Sin and suffering are not necessarily linked to each other, but this penitential psalm expresses the sober reality of sin as the cause of suffering. What is required from all is confession of sin and a request for forgiveness.

39:1–13
Life's Brevity

Psalm 39 continues the theme of prayer for deliverance from sickness and sin found in Psalm 38, but focuses more on the final result of sin, death, and the experience of life's brevity. The two psalms are connected through verbal links such as "mute" or "silent" (vv. 2, 9 // 38:13), "rebuke" (v. 11 // 38:1), "mouth" (vv. 1, 9 // 38:13, 14), "hope" (v. 7 // 38:15). A number of repetitious phrases emphasize the transitoriness of life (e.g., everyone is vapor/breath; vv. 5, 11). The theme recalls the experience of Job (cf. vv. 12–13 // Job 10:20–21) as well as the book of Ecclesiastes (e.g. 1:2; 12:8). "Jeduthun" was a music leader in the temple during the reigns of David and Solomon (cf. 1 Chr. 16:41–42). The verbal connections with 1 Chronicles 29:15 strengthen the Davidic authorship.

39:1–3. Unbearable Silence. At the outset of the poem, the psalmist commits himself to silence (cf. 38:13) so that he will not sin with his words. Verses 8–13 (esp. v. 9) give the motivation for his silence as he wants to refrain from complaining about God's discipline in his life. He does not want to bring reproach upon Yahweh in the eyes of the ungodly. The following statement, that he did not even say anything good (lit. "I showed silence from good"), is difficult to understand. Combined with the following line, it could be interpreted as a comparative construction: "I was silent more than was good for me," therefore his sorrow increased (v. 2). The inner pressure of unconfessed sin (his heart became "hot") finally gives way to speech (he spoke with his tongue; v. 3).

39:4–6. Everyone is but Vapor. Before he confesses his sins (vv. 7–13), the psalmist directs his words only to Yahweh in a contemplation of life's brevity and the certainty of his own mortality. Verse 5 uses *hebel* ("breath" or "vapor") for describing the brevity of human life even at its best, and v. 6 repeats twice the adverb of degree, *'ak* ("surely"; translated differently or omitted the second time in some translations), followed by further descriptions of the inevitability of death. How much more fragile is life without God?

39:7–13. Hope Through Forgiveness. The turning point in the psalm is introduced by a contrastive conjunction with "now," transitioning to an expression of faith that acknowledges God's discipline yet confesses and asks for deliverance (v. 7). The plea for saving deliverance from transgressions (v. 8) refers to the forgiveness of the psalmist's rebellious acts (*pesha'*), which are the cause of his current misery. David asks God to remove His *nega'* ("plague," "scourge," "stroke"; cf. Ex. 11:1) and refers again to the motif of human mortality (v. 11). The psalm ends with a prayer in which David likens himself to a *ger* ("foreigner," "stranger"). This terminology is reminiscent of the sojourners of the patriarchic period who had no permanent dwelling place (v. 12; cf. Deut. 10:18–19; 1 Chr. 29:15).

The final petition, for God to turn His gaze away from him (lit. "blind yourself from me"), must be understood as an appeal for God not to look at the psalmist to punish him (cf. Job 7:19; 14:6). He wants to *balag* ("smile"; some translations follow the LXX and the Greek *anaphuxō* and thus have "regain strength") before he departs and is no more. The brevity of life described in this psalm serves as a sober reminder of the emotional and physical pressure that unconfessed sin creates in the life of the believer—it touches the physical, emotional, and spiritual aspects of the person. Only confession and forgiveness deliver us from this pressure, making it possible for us to smile again, even in the face of transient life.

40:1–17
Sacrificial Service

The central theme of Psalm 40 is a dedication to God's service that flows out of deliverance from a near-death experience. Psalm 39:13 ends with the idea of death and 40:1–2 follows on with a song of praise because God brought the psalmist up from the pit. The psalm moves from praise (vv. 1–12) to plea (vv. 13–17) in similar fashion as Psalm 27. It has been suggested that the two parts of the psalm were originally separate psalms, particularly because the second part is almost identical to Psalm 70. However, there are verbal links between these two parts and praise can naturally precede plea (cf. Pss. 9–10; 27; 89). It is conceivable that Psalm 70 represents a liturgical adaptation of the latter part of Psalm 40. David is mentioned as the author, and through its connection to the previous psalm it continues the theme of deliverance from sin. This psalm also has been seen as having three parts (vv. 1–5; vv. 6–10; and vv. 11–17).

40:1–12. From Deliverance to Service. The psalmist has waited patiently for the Lord, an extended time of extreme suffering that is followed by deliverance out of a horrible pit of destruction (v. 2). This is poetic language often used to describe death and the grave (cf. 28:1; 30:3; see also Jer. 38 for a literal experience). Having returned from a deadly experience, he praises God with a new song and reaffirms his faith in Him as a man who makes the Lord his trust (v. 4). Praise turns to a contemplation of God's wonderful works (v. 5) and as consequence to a personal dedication to service (vv. 6–8). That service moves beyond empty rituals (v. 6; cf. 1 Sam. 15:22–23) to commitment based on a changed understanding (opening his ears) and a new heart (where the law is).

This is not an undoing of the OT sacrificial service but a shifting of priorities to the correct motivation for service (cf. Jer. 31:33). The psalmist's dedication to service finds its typological and messianic echo in Hebrews 10:5–7 as it describes Christ's ultimate dedication to service. Verses 9–10 make personal praise a public witness and vv. 11–12 appeal to God to continue to show His love to the psalmist, as the threat of innumerable difficulties is still very present in his life. This sets the tone for the next section of the psalm.

40:13–17. A Final Plea. The final petition of the psalm begins with an appeal to God to deliver (v. 13). It is followed by a plea for divine vindication against those who seek to kill him (vv. 14–15). Then, as in the first part of the psalm, the psalmist turns from the individual to the community, asking for blessings on those whose lives are at the service of God (v. 16). Verse 17 returns to the needs of the psalmist for divine intervention as he pleads with God to not delay. The messianic dimension heightens the true motivation for service. Our dedication for service (cf. Rom. 12:1) only makes sense in the ultimate sacrificial service of the Son of God on the cross (cf. Heb. 10:5–7).

41:1–13
Healing

The last psalm of Book 1 starts, like Psalm 1, with a beatitude, thus connecting the end to the beginning and reinforcing the idea of *torah* ("instruction") once more. The central theme of the psalm is healing (vv. 4–10), which connects it well with Psalms 38–40. While there is no direct record of David being ill, there was certainly occasion in his life for him to have written this poem.

41:1–3. Beatitude. Like Psalm 1:1, Psalm 41 begins with a beatitude for those who consider the poor and needy. The focus is on ethical conduct, connecting it, through the use of the participle *masktl* ("look at," "act with insight"), to wisdom literature (cf. Prov. 16:20; 21:12). We find a list of all the fortunes that will come to those who do good to the needy. In v. 3, the blessing of right doing is recovery from sickness.

41:4–10. Healing. The section contains the psalmist's prayer for recovery. As in Psalm 38, it connects sickness with sin (v. 4; cf. also 51:2). It also includes an extended reference to the enemies who are just waiting for David to die (vv. 5–9). But it is not only his enemies who are exploiting his illness; it is even one of his close, trusted friends. The betrayal is brought to its cruel completion by the friend (some suggest Ahithophel; cf. 2 Sam. 15:31) who turned against him (lit. "lifted up his heel"). The image alludes to Jacob, who became known as the "heel-grabber" or "deceiver" (Gen. 27:36). The passage is appropriated by Jesus with reference to His betrayal by Judas (John 13:18). Yet, even if betrayed by his closest friends, the psalmist finds refuge and healing in Yahweh, who in His mercy will raise him up (v. 10).

41:11–13. Thanksgiving for Deliverance and Doxology. The psalm concludes with a short prayer of thanksgiving relating how God answered and healed him so that his integrity is reestablished and, using sanctuary imagery, he stands in the presence of the Lord once more (v. 12). The final verse (v. 13) is not part of the psalm but serves as a doxology for Book 1 (the doxologies of the other books are in 72:18–20; 89:52; 106:48; 146–150). The twofold "Amen and Amen" affirms the reality that the psalms are as much theology as they are doxology. Declarations about God call for a response in worship.

PSALMS 42—72
BOOK II

Book 2 of the Psalms continues the association with the period of the Davidic monarchy through authorship and historical notes. The book contains most of the psalms from the Korah collection (Pss. 42–49), while the remainder of this collection is in Book 3 (Pss. 84–85; 87–88). Korah and his descendants served as gatekeepers and musicians in the sanctuary from David's reign onward (cf. 1 Chr. 9:19; 26:19). This explains the thematic focus of the Korahite psalms on the nations and their pilgrimage to the temple. Beyond this group, there are Davidic psalms that end with Psalm 72:20, marking the end of an earlier collection of psalms.

The beginning of Book 2 also marks the beginning of another group of psalms that displays a preference for *'elohim* ("God") instead of *yahweh* as a designation of God (Pss. 42–83). This has motivated scholars to speak of so-called Elohistic Psalms, even though there are 45 occurrences of *yahweh* in those psalms. The divine name preference is also indicated by the fact that there are only nineteen occurrences of *'elohim* in the rest of the Psalms. However, both names often occur in poetic parallelism (e.g., 46:11), each name indicating a specific aspect of God's character; *yahweh* expresses His closeness and immanence, and *'elohim*, His distance and transcendence. It is also interesting to note that a single Asaph psalm (Ps. 50) is sandwiched between the Korah psalms (Pss. 42–49) and the Davidic psalms (Pss. 51–72), which make up the sub-collections of Book 2 (see commentary on Ps. 50:1–23).

42:1—43:5
Longing for God's Presence

A number of literary connections between Psalms 42 and 43 allow a unified reading of the two poems: (1) Psalm 43 is the only psalm in the Korahite collection without a superscription (cf.

Pss. 9–10); (2) there is a recurring refrain that is repeated thrice throughout the two psalms (vv. 42:5, 11; 43:5); (3) some Hebrew manuscripts combine the two psalms; and (4) there is a thematic continuation from lament to plea between the two poems. The superscription *maskil* ("instruction"; sometimes translated as "contemplation") occurs with thirteen psalms designated as instructional or didactic psalms (cf. Pss. 32, 42, 44–45, 52–55, 74, 78, 88–89, and 142).

42:1–5. Longing for God. The simile in v. 1 of the deer that pants for water effectively introduces the theme of longing for God. It is applied to the psalmist, whose soul (*nepesh*, refers to the whole being; v. 2) thirsts for God. More specifically, he wants to appear before God and meet with Him, an expression that is linked to the sanctuary (cf. Deut. 31:11). The deer is a familiar image found on seal impressions from OT times and communicates the intense longing for God's presence. Verse 2 repeats *nepesh,* and v. 3 introduces the mocking enemies who repeatedly ask throughout the psalm, "Where is your God?" (cf. v. 10), indicating that the psalmist is far from the temple. He reminisces the time when he had access to the temple, when he joined the thronging multitude and went *dadah* ("to walk slowly in procession") with them to the house of God. The section concludes with the first occurrence of the introspective question "Why are you downcast?" It is also an expression used in mourning (cf. Ps. 35:14). The positive answer comes with a resounding encouragement to hope in God (lit. "wait upon God"). Inner dialogues of the faithful often include God and the inner voice speaks to our conscience. Jesus appropriates the words of vv. 5–6 during His experience in Gethsemane (cf. Mark 14:34; John 12:27).

42:6–11. More Longing. After a short glimmer of hope expressed in the first refrain, the psalmist returns to the despair of separation from God's presence, using the geography of northern Israel to underline his argument. Continuing with the initial image of the deer panting for water, the psalmist now refers to the land of the Jordan, which has its headwaters at the foot of the heights of Hermon, the multi-peaked mountain on the northeastern border of Israel (v. 6). The Hill or Mount Mizar is an unknown locale, but the waterfalls in v. 7 bring to mind the cascading river Jordan at Baniyas. However, thundering nature and water imagery speak of despair and life-threatening experiences as

God's waves and billows sweep over him. There is a ray of hope in the middle of despair—the Lord's love by day and His song by night (v. 8). This is the only mention of *yahweh* among the twelve occurrences of *'elohim* in Psalms 42–43, expressing God's closeness in the middle of divine absence and in response to the psalmist's longing for His presence. The scornful question of the enemies is repeated, "Where is your God?" (v. 10). The refrain of v. 5 is also repeated. Some translations follow the LXX in which vv. 5 and 10 are identical, both affirming the Lord as the psalmist's personal Savior and God. The Masoretic Hebrew text renders v. 11 with slight modifications from v. 5, making it more affirmative. Whereas deliverance in the first refrain (v. 5) came from God's presence or countenance, now the God who delivers is his personal God and Savior.

43:1–5. Plea for Vindication. Taking both psalms together, the poem now moves into petition, requesting God in legal language to plead his cause against a faithless nation, placing the prayer in the national arena. Verse 2 connects well with Psalm 42:9, asking the almost identical rhetorical question: Why must he go mourning because of the enemy's oppression? The appeal for God's deliverance follows in v. 3 and restoration is connected to the return to God's holy *har* ("hill" or "mountain") and to His *mishkan* ("dwelling place" or "tabernacle").

Return to the sanctuary is further developed in v. 4, climatically fulfilling the longing of the psalmist to stand once more in the temple (see 42:2–4). The third repetition of the refrain in v. 5 completes the fulfilled longing, and within the context of the third section it becomes now a shout of joy, sung with rejoicing (v. 4). Longing for God's presence is often accompanied by a despaired feeling of His absence. However, His perceived absence is not necessarily real absence. Jesus used the words of Psalms 42–43 in the garden of Gethsemane, but His Father and the angelic host were at His side: "God suffered with His Son. Angels beheld the Savior's agony" (DA, 693).

44:1–26
National Defeat

The psalm is a communal psalm, using mostly "we" instead of the individual "I" that has characterized the Davidic psalms. It connects verbally to Psalms 42–43 in looking for deliverance (v. 4 // 42:5, 11), mentioning oppression (v. 24 // 42:9; 43:2), and noting the fear of being cast off by God (vv. 9, 23 // 43:2). The historical background of the psalm appears to be a national defeat (vv. 9–16), which is difficult to date. The Assyrian invasions recorded in 2 Kings 15 and 18 provide possible occasions for the poem. The superscriptions of Psalms 42:1 and 44:1 are identical (though the order is slightly changed) and unique in the Korahite group in Book 2. It identifies this psalm also as instruction.

44:1–8. Past Glories and God as King. The psalm commences with a recollection of the conquest when God drove out the nations (v. 2) and settled Israel in the promised land. This event is clearly viewed by the psalmist as a historical event, namely, the invasion of the Holy Land under the direction of God. Building on the historicity of the conquest, vv. 4–8 didactically extol Yahweh's kingship, asking Him to once more ordain victories for Jacob (v. 4). Victory, as in days past, was possible only through Him when He saved them from their enemies (vv. 4, 7). A chiastic structure for vv. 1–8 is perceivable, placing an emphasis on v. 4 as the central declaration of trust in the section.

44:9–16. National Defeat. After the historical praise of vv. 1–8, the psalmist next introduces a major contrast using the disjunctive 'ap ("yet," "even," but"). God's defeating of the other nations for the sake of Israel (v. 2) appears to have ended. He seems to have rejected them, no longer accompanying and helping their armies in battle (v. 9). This results in national defeat and exile (vv. 10–12), making Israel a byword among the nations (v. 14). All this has resulted in dishonor, disgrace, and shame for Israel (v. 15), which ultimately reflects on Yahweh.

44:17–22. Claim of Innocence. The psalmist speaks collectively, affirming faithfulness to God and to His covenant (vv. 17–18). This is not a defeat brought about by the sins of the people but rather the suffering of the innocent, and they are accounted as sheep to be slaughtered (v. 22). Romans 8:36 quotes this passage and applies it to the suffering of Christians for the sake of Christ.

44:23–26. Plea for Deliverance. The psalm concludes with four imperatives directed to God as a plea for deliverance: 'awar ("awake," "raise Yourself"; v. 23), qits ("awaken," "rise up"; v. 23), qum ("awake," "rise up"; v. 26), and padah ("redeem"; v. 26). The final appeal is to Yahweh's khesed ("mercy"). Innocent suffering has been

the experience of God's children throughout the ages, but we can appeal to God because faith knows that the moment comes when He arises again to redeem.

45:1–17
A Wedding Song

Somewhat surprising is this *shir yedidot* among the Korahite psalms. A *shir* is a song and the term *yedidot*, which occurs only here in the Hebrew Bible, is closely related to the adjective *yadid*, "beloved." The phrase has thus been translated as "a love song" or "a wedding song"—the latter primarily because of the content of the Psalm. It seems to be more in tune with the Song of Solomon (cf. Song 3:6–11; 5:10–16). It is conceivable that the psalm was composed for a royal wedding, possibly during the early monarchy. There are seven references to the king and royal regalia (throne, scepter, garments). There is a messianic dimension underlying the psalm, as characteristics which are attributed to the king seem to move beyond the human sphere (especially in v. 6, where the King is referred to as "God"). Thus the psalm has been interpreted as messianic from earliest times (supported by Ellen White, MB 49). The portrayal of military activity fits with the time of David. The poem is set to the tune of "Lilies," which is also referenced in Psalm 60.

45:1–9. Dedication and Groom. The psalmist describes himself as one whose tongue is that of a skillful scribe and who is ready to recite his poetic work for the King while his heart is *rakhash* ("stirred," "moved," or "overflowing"), a verb used only here in the OT. The psalmist is stirred by his vision as he clads a messianic prophecy within the beautiful garment of love poetry. The description of the groom begins with his outer appearance (v. 2): he is superlatively "handsome"/"fair," a description reminiscent of David's introduction in 1 Samuel 16:12. The comparative expression then moves beyond the human sphere. Beyond the physical, there is also grace that characterizes the words of the royal groom.

The king is described in terms of his military role as commander in chief, mentioning his sword and arrows (vv. 3, 5) and his enduring throne and scepter (v. 6). The expression "Your throne, O God" (v. 6) has been rendered in various versions to make it applicable to an earthly royal wedding (e.g., "Your throne is from God," NJB). However, the original text points beyond the immediate historical context to a prophetic messianic reading of the psalm. The inspired commentary on vv. 6–7, as found in Hebrews 1:8–9, confirms this by identifying Jesus as the Anointed (v. 7), the Messiah. Verses 8–9 switch back to the immediate historical context in describing the clothing of the royal groom. They are scented with myrrh and aloes and cassia (v. 8) as he awaits his queen (v. 9). The Hebrew word used here, *shegal* ("royal consort"), occurs in its noun form only here and in Nehemiah 2:6.

45:10–16. Bride. The psalm turns now to address the bride using marriage terminology reminiscent of Genesis 2–3. The emphasis is on the physical and emotional relationship between husband and wife. The king is enamored with the queen's beauty, and she is to bow down and honor him because he is her lord. The verb *'awah* ("desire, crave") does not always have positive connotations, and the description accurately reflects the marriage relationship after the Fall (Gen. 3:16). As the groom's garments were described at the end of the previous section, now the bride's attire is also described (vv. 13–14) as she is led in procession to the king (v. 15). Her dress identifies her as the queen. The wedding poem concludes with a blessing for procreation, wishing that the sons will succeed the fathers so that the royal line will continue.

45:17. Blessing. Psalm 45 concludes with a blessing for the king that he be remembered throughout all generations. The language moves once more beyond the human sphere when it is said that the people will praise the king forever. Bride/groom is an important metaphor for the relationship between Christ and His church (John 3:29; Eph. 5:25–27; Rev. 19:7–9). While it is important not to overlook the historical aspect of this psalm, the prophetic dimension is clearly indicated in the NT.

46:1–11
A Mighty Fortress

The poem is a declaration of trust in a God who, in the midst of turmoil, provides peace from His city to the whole earth. At the center of this declaration are the references to God as "our refuge," which is found three times in the psalm (vv. 1, 7, 11). The first stanza begins with the refrain, whereas the second and third stanzas are concluded by it. *Selah* marks the end of each section. The heading identifies the psalm as Korahite. The musical annotation *'alamut* occurs here and, in a modified form, *'almut*, in Psalm 9:1 (where it means something different. In comparison with

1 Chronicles 15:20, it has been suggested to translate it here as "according to maidens," possibly meaning that the instruments were tuned to a high (soprano) key.

46:1–3. Even Though. Following the programmatic refrain "God is our refuge" at the outset of the psalm, a series of four enormous upheavals in nature creates a striking contrast with the safety that the faithful find in God. Verses 2–3 describe an earthquake accompanied by roaring waters and shaking mountains that fall into the sea. These are the accompanying natural phenomena of theophany (cf. 18:7–15).

46:4–7. Peace in the City of God. From a cataclysmic nature the psalm changes its tone and moves to a peaceful description of the city of God (v. 5) that enjoys divine protection because God is in it, especially in the *mishkan* ("the holy place" or "tabernacle"; v. 4). Instead of roaring waters, there is a peaceful river whose streams make the city glad (v. 4), an image that is taken from the Garden of Eden (Gen. 2:10–14; Rev. 22:1–2). The remainder of the stanza returns to the upheaval coming from nations instead of nature, again connected to theophanic language (the earth melts at God's voice; v. 6). The refrain is now repeated with two modifications. First, instead of the more abstract *makhaseh* ("refuge;" v. 1) we find the more concrete *misgab* ("secure height," "a stronghold," "a retreat"), denoting a physical structure. Second, the phrase "God of Jacob" is added, which recalls the experience of the patriarch under the protection of Yahweh.

46:8–11. Peace on Earth. The final stanza is a surprising one. While the description of God in the previous sections has been dominated by terminology that draws on the Warrior metaphor (e.g., *yahweh tseba'ot*, "LORD of hosts" or "LORD Almighty"; v. 7), the psalm suddenly creates a striking contrast by stating that God makes wars cease (v. 9) and extends peace from the city to the ends of the earth. He destroys the implements of war (i.e., bow and spear). The destruction of warfare is completed as He burns the chariot (or shields; LXX) in the fire. This irenic departure from the expected Warrior metaphor enlarges our understanding of it and demonstrates that the ultimate objective of divine warfare is peace. The physical connotation of the refuge as a stronghold in Psalm 46 motivated Martin Luther to compose the hymn "A Mighty Fortress is Our God." The hymn recalls not only the towering fortresses of Germany but also how God will finally make all wars cease.

47:1–9
God Reigns

The divine epithet of God as Most High (*'elyon*) is used in Psalm 47:2 as well as in the previous psalm (46:4) connecting the two psalms to each other. Further connections include the universal perspective of "nations" and "peoples" (vv. 3, 8; 46:10) and the mention of Jacob (v. 4; 46:7, 11). Psalm 46 ended with a universal extension of divine peace to all the earth, and Psalm 47 invites all to acknowledge God's universal kingship as the foundation of peace. Critical scholarship has called this an *enthronement* psalm, describing Yahweh's coronation ritual, which was supposed to be an annual festival comparable to similar occasions in other ANE cultures. However, a close reading of the psalm reveals that it is an acknowledgment of eternal divine kingship rather than the initiation of God's reign. The psalm belongs to the collection of the sons of Korah.

47:1–5. Yahweh Subdued Nations. The psalm begins with a universal invitation for all people and nations to clap their hands. This is an expression of joy that acknowledges God as the universal and triumphal King. "For" or "because" (*ki*) provides the first reason for the praise of Yahweh Most High: He is a majestic and sovereign God (cf. Gen. 14:18–22; Ps. 57:2). He has also subdued the peoples. Some translations understand this to occur in the future ("will subdue") while others see it as a current situation ("subdues"). The verbal context of vv. 1–5 and the reference to the past experience of Jacob in v. 4 suggest that the section can also be understood as a reference to the past election of Israel when Yahweh subdued the nations during the Exodus and the conquest of Canaan. This is confirmed by the use of the expression *ga'on* ("height," "loftiness"; translated variously as "pride," "excellence," or "glory"), which can be a literal reference to the hill country of Israel. As Israel occupied the heights of Canaan, so God ascended with a shout and the sound of a trumpet. These expressions are associated with the conquest (cf. Josh. 6). Theologically, the exaltation of God is the reason for Israel's exaltation.

47:6–9. Yahweh Is King. The correspondence between the two sections of Psalm 47 provides a blueprint for its interpretation. The invitation to praise in v. 1 is repeated four times in v. 6, occurring as a framing device at the beginning and end of the two lines that make up the verse. The motivational clause of v. 7 (introduced by *ki*) offers God's kingship as the second reason for praise, repeating the invitation once more (lit. "sing a *maskil* praise"). God's universal sovereignty is stressed again in v. 8, and v. 9 concludes the psalm with another reference to Israel and the nations. The last motivational sentence has a Hebrew reference to the shields of earth belonging to God. This has been translated by some as a possible reference to the kings or rulers (cf. Hos. 4:18). The psalm ends with a final exaltation of God. The universal proclamation of God's kingship in Psalm 47 and the offer of peace to all the earth in Psalm 46 remind us that the healing of the human race is found in humble submission to Him.

48:1–14
The City of God

The focus of Psalm 48 is on Zion as the city of our God, linking it to the two previous psalms. This is done through its reference to the Exodus and conquest, the universal nature of divine deliverance, and other literary connections (e.g., *misgab* "fortress"; v. 3; 46:7, 11). Both psalms 46 and 48 could have been performed as victory songs, and the superscriptions on both assign them to the sons of Korah.

48:1–3. City of God. The psalm begins with an extended invitation to praise God from Zion as the great King (v. 2) who lives in Zion's citadels or palaces (v. 3). God is recognized as Zion's refuge and as the fortress (cf. 46:7, 11) that provides refuge for the whole earth (v. 2). The mention of the *tsapon* ("north"; v. 2) stresses the importance of the city, since the "north" is where the abode of God is located (cf. Is. 14:13). It could also be a polemic against Canaanite religion, for which Mt. Zaphon (Heb. *tsapon* in v. 2 can be translated as either "north" or "Zaphon") was the abode of its main deity, Baal. Thus, Zion is occupying the most important position among all mountains, and Yahweh—not Baal—is the sovereign God above all other gods.

48:4–8. Victory over Foreign Forces. The next section provides the motivation for the statements in the first section. The image is that of an attacking army that melts away in fear as they behold the fortress of Zion. The extent of their terror is likened to birth pains of a woman in labor (v. 6), and the destructive power of the *yahweh tseba'ot* ("Lord of hosts" or "Lord Almighty"; v. 8) is compared to the east wind that breaks the strongest of all seafaring vessels. The ships of Tarshish refers to ships that were capable of making the long journey to southern Spain on the other side of the known world (cf. 1 Kin. 10:22; 2 Chr. 9:21).

48:9–11. Human Response. Worship is the adequate human response to divine acts of deliverance. The language used draws on the Song of the Sea in Exodus 15 (e.g., God's right hand, v. 10 // Ex. 15:6, 12). In His temple, people meditate on God's *khesed* ("kindness," "unfailing love," "faithfulness") as the driving force that has brought deliverance from Zion. The daughters of Judah most probably designate the cities or towns of Judah (cf. Josh. 15:45).

48:12–14. Victory Procession. There is an invitation to walk throughout Zion and all around her (v. 12). A victory procession circumnavigates the city of God from all angles, marking all its architectural features and defense systems. The purpose is to tell the next generation all about the city and keep alive the memory of God's deliverance in order to sustain future generations. God has promised to always guide us, even to the end. The peace that the earthly Jerusalem has never been able to experience will be a reality when the New Jerusalem descends from heaven (Rev. 21:2, 10) as the eternal habitation of God's people.

49:1–20
Trust in Riches

The final Korahite psalm of Book 2 deals with, in the tradition of wisdom literature (cf. Pss. 1; 37), the question of where to put one's trust in the face of death and its inevitability. In line with the remainder of the collection, it maintains a universal scope by appealing to the peoples of the earth. There is a refrain that concludes both main sections (vv. 12, 20), contemplating the transience of human life apart from an understanding of God—a human being is "like the beasts that perish" (v. 12).

49:1–4. Call to Listen to Wisdom. The introduction to the poem is reminiscent of Proverbs 1–2, emphasizing the need to reflect on wisdom as it applies to everyone—low and high, rich and poor (v. 2). It draws on all sensatory faculties (the poet's mouth provides wisdom, and his heart, understanding).

49:5–12. Futility of Human Wealth. The psalmist now explores the futility of those who trust in their wealth (vv. 5–9). Since death is inevitable, wealth cannot save us or our relatives. Similarly, names, land, and wealth are subject to fading away since human beings do not remain (v. 12). The section ends with the sobering refrain that people are like "the beasts that perish." The lifestyle of those who trust in richness does not much differentiate humankind from animals.

49:13–20. Futility of Humankind. The psalm moves from the wealthy to those who pursue a beast-like lifestyle. Death is the final destiny for them, in contrast to the upright who will rule over them in the morning (v. 14). This is a reference to the concept of resurrection, which is reinforced by the reference to being redeemed from *she'ol* ("the grave"; v. 15). The rich person was not able to redeem (*padah*) him or herself or any relative (v. 7), but God will redeem the whole being (*nepesh*) of the faithful on resurrection morning. Verses 15–19 once more review the futility of humans who, separated from God, pursue riches; their final destiny is death. The repeated refrain of v. 12 in v. 20 has a variation that underlines the final message of the psalm. While v. 12 emphasizes the finality of death, in v. 20 the emphasis is on discernment. It is of existential importance to understand at some point in our lives that the riches of this world are nothing in the face of death and eternity. Only God can redeem us from the inevitability of the grave, and He has done this through the death of His Son.

50:1–23
Trust in True Sacrifice

Psalm 50 connects to Psalm 49 through numerous verbal links. Twenty-two significant terms appear in both psalms that are otherwise rare in the rest of Book 2 (e.g., *ratsah*, "to be pleased with," "to join"; v. 18; 49:13). This psalm provides a counterpoint in focusing on the sacrificial system and its life-giving effects when approached in true worship. Again, the connecting theme is trust in God (Ps. 50), not in riches (Ps. 49). There is a prophetic dimension to the psalm (esp. vv. 1–6), which is in line with its authorial superscription, "of Asaph," who was a seer and musician in David's days (1 Chr. 15:17, 19; 2 Chr. 29:30). It will become evident below that the psalm has connections not only with the first collection of the Korah psalms (Pss. 42–49) but also with the second group of Davidic psalms (Pss. 51–72). The Asaph psalm is thus sandwiched between the two groups and serves as a hinge between them. The rest of the Asaph psalms are found in Psalms 73–83 in Book 3.

50:1–6. Covenant Lawsuit. The introduction to this psalm is the proclamation of a covenant lawsuit which has its roots in Genesis 3:8–19 and the legal material of the Pentateuch (cf. Lev. 26; Deut. 27–28), and which is also common in the prophetic literature (cf. Is. 1; Mic. 6:6–8). God calls upon heaven and earth as witnesses (v. 4) as He appears from Zion (v. 2; this establishes a link with Ps. 48). The theophany is accompanied by fire and tempest (cf. 18:7–15) as He gathers together those who made a covenant with Him by sacrifice. The reference to the making of the covenant echoes the ritual of Genesis 15:7–21 but also clarifies that the covenant was ratified by sacrifice (Ex. 24:5–8), pointing typologically to the new covenant in Christ (Heb. 9:18–23).

50:7–15. First Accusation. While the previous section does not identify the parties of the lawsuit, v. 7 indicates that the accused are God's people, and it does so by modeling the charge on the Shema (Deut. 6:4). The Shema is the most explicit monotheistic confession of the covenant in ancient and modern Israel. It begins with the command to *shim'ah*, imperative of the verb *shama'* ("to hear" or "to listen"), and ends with the allusive expression "I am God, your God!" The substance of the accusation goes along the lines of 1 Samuel 15:22. While there is an abundance of sacrifices and external ceremonies, there is a lack of personal commitment and true obedience, which contradicts the original covenant conditions. The center of the section clarifies that God is not dependent on our sacrifices: all the animals in the forest and the cattle on a thousand hills belong to Him (v. 10). God rather looks for a heart full of true thanksgiving, true commitment, and a sincere prayer life (v. 15).

50:16–23. Second Accusation. The accusation intensifies against those who speak of God's covenant (i.e., those who claim to be part of the covenant people) and are now identified as being wicked (v. 16). Verses 17–20 list the ethical infractions through which the covenant has been broken (i.e., injustice, deceit, and slander). God patiently kept silent for a time, but now it is time to arraign them, rebuke them, and help them to consider this (lit. "understand"; v. 22) before it is too late, lest God tear them in pieces.

This is the same understanding (Heb. *bin*) that concluded the previous psalm (49:20), creating a further link between the two poems. The psalm concludes with an invitation to salvation for the person who directs his/her conduct well, namely, the one who responds positively to God's charges, repents, and returns to covenant faithfulness.

51:1–19
Repentance

As a truthful reaction to the indictment of Psalm 50, Psalm 51 is a penitential poem, emphasizing heartfelt repentance as the only way to return to God. Psalms 31, 38, and 51 focus on the confession of sin. Psalm 51 makes an explicit historical connection in its superscription to the life of David when he committed adultery with Bathsheba (cf. 2 Sam. 12). As in the previous psalm, God is looking not for external forms and sacrifices but for a broken and contrite heart (v. 17; 50:9–13). The psalm introduces the second group of Davidic psalms, which continues until the end of Book 2.

51:1–9. Confession of Sin. The psalmist begins with a plea for God's grace, appealing to mercy (*khanan*, "to have mercy"), faithfulness (*khesed*), and compassion (*rakhamim*) as the foundation of divine grace. All three theological terms are an integral part of Yahweh's self-revelation in Exodus 34:6. The psalmist is asking God to deal with him in accordance with His character. The three mercies of God are juxtaposed with the three offences of the psalmist that are the subject of this psalm: transgressions, iniquity, and sin (vv. 1–2). The true character of evil is identified in the acknowledgment that all our sins are committed against God (v. 4). Sin, while tragically and destructively impacting other people, is foremost a rupture of our relationship with God (vv. 3–4). Further, all of humanity is systemically affected by sin from conception. This is not an implicit reference to David's birth but a sobering affirmation of the pervasiveness of sin on this planet; it is about humanity's inherently sinful nature (v. 5). It is exactly in the *tukhot* ("the inner being") that God wants to effectuate change (v. 6). Verses 7–9 constitute a desperate cry for forgiveness and cleansing from sin. It takes us back to vv. 1–2, thus effectively framing the section.

51:10–15. Personal Restoration. Beyond forgiveness, the psalmist now moves to restoration: he asks God to give him a clean, pure heart and a steadfast spirit (v. 10). The verb *bara'* is reserved for divine creative power (cf. Gen. 1:1), which is needed to effectuate a change of heart. Such re-creation leads to the restoration of the joy of God's salvation and enables us to witness to others (v. 13). Such persons proclaim praise to God (v. 15).

51:16–19. True Sacrifice. The psalm could have ended with such high note of praise, but it returns once more to the question of true sacrifice: a broken spirit and a broken, contrite heart are just as (if not more) important to God than the sacrificial rituals themselves (vv. 16–17). However, personal transformation has a national impact because through it the walls of Jerusalem are built (i.e., the moral safety of the city depends on the integrity of its citizens). As a result, they shall offer bulls on God's altar that are acceptable to Him (v. 19). The external form of worship will finally coincide with the internal motives of the heart. Interestingly, words for sin predominate (twelve times) in vv. 1–9 and God is mentioned only once, whereas in vv. 10–19 sin (mentioned only twice) is pushed out by God's grace and God is referred to six times.

52:1–9
The Boasting of the Wicked

The psalm picks up on the theme of Psalm 49 in the form of an instructive wisdom poem, annotated in the superscription as a *maskil* ("instruction"). The idolatrous dependence of the wicked on riches and their accompanying boasting is contrasted with the righteous, who are content to dwell in the presence of God. The historical note connects this psalm with "Doeg the Edomite," who divulged to Saul that David had visited the priest Ahimelech while fleeing from the king. In the ensuing massacre, it was Doeg who killed the priest and his family because none of Saul's servants were willing to be part of the hideous act (cf. 1 Sam. 21–22).

52:1–5. Wicked Arrogance. The central rhetorical question involves the challenge to the mighty warrior, asking why he is trying to boast in evil. Doeg, as a mighty man in Saul's service, creates a credible historical backdrop for the wicked in this psalm. He was someone whose tongue devised and plotted destruction and who loved evil more than good (vv. 2–3). There is a repeated emphasis on the deceitful tongue (v. 4), and its destructive force finally leads God to take action and uproot him from the land of the living (v. 5).

52:6–9. Righteous Perspective. In contrast to the wicked, the righteous person looks at the arrogance of the wicked and, surprisingly, laughs at him. Laughter (*sakhaq*) in the Psalms is often reserved for God when He sees the futility of the wicked (cf. Ps. 37:13). The reason for the laughter of the righteous is that the wicked, instead of depending on God, trusted in wealth. Using the metaphor of vegetation, the righteous (in contrast to being uprooted; v. 5) are like a green olive tree in the house of God (v. 8). They are safely rooted in the presence of God, enjoying longevity and fruitfulness (cf. Jer. 11:16; 17:8; Hos. 14:6), which echoes the first poem of the Psalms (cf. 1:3). The psalm concludes by praising God for His intervention and reiterating His goodness. The destructive boasting of the wicked fades away as a result of his foolish self-sufficiency that leads only to his being uprooted. This is in marked contrast to the permanency of the righteous person, who is deeply rooted in God.

53:1–6
Foolishness—Once More

Psalm 53 is almost identical to Psalm 14. However, this similarity should not obstruct its exposition in this part of the Psalms. It is important to look at the poem in its context; that is, in juxtaposition to the previous psalm, which confronted the wicked and unmasked the senselessness of life without God. Psalm 53 enlarges on the theme of foolishness, which finds its ultimate climax in the denial of God's existence. The superscription adds that the psalm is related to *makhalat*. This term has been variously defined as being related to sickness/persecution or being a musical term for a tune or an instrument. It is also called a *maskil* ("a contemplation" or "instruction"), which integrates the psalm well within the current context of instructive poems. Jewish interpretation connects the fool (*nabal*) of v. 1 with the story of Nabal (1 Sam. 25).

53:1–4. The Fool. As in Psalm 14, in this psalm the fool is a person who has said that there is no God (v. 1). Whereas Psalm 14 uses *yahweh* and *'elohim* interchangeably, Psalm 53 does not use *yahweh* at all, creating a more universal tone for this wisdom psalm. The rest of this section describes the foolish from God's perspective, reaching the general conclusion that no one does good (v. 1; repeated in v. 3). Those who fashion evil lack knowledge as they ignore God and turn against His people (v. 4).

53:5-6. God's Reaction. In v. 5, we find the clearest divergence between the two almost identical poems (v. 5; corresponds to 14:5-6). Whereas Psalm 14 placed an emphasis on God's protection of the righteous using the metaphor of *refuge*, Psalm 53 concentrates exclusively on the destruction of the wicked in v. 5. It is only in v. 6 that their destruction is contrasted with the salvation of Israel when God returns His people from captivity. Thus, Psalm 53 is less concerned with the fate of the righteous than with the dire destiny of the fool. It is reassuring to know that judgment and salvation come out of Zion, from a righteous God who sees deep into the motivation of the human heart.

54:1-7
The Name that Saves

This psalm is a plea for deliverance connected through its superscription to the historical experience of David when the Ziphites betrayed him to Saul by revealing the fact that he was hiding among them (see 1 Sam. 26; cf. 1 Sam. 23:19). The sequence of Psalms 52-54 aligns with the sequence of events from the life of David (1 Sam. 21-26), illustrating human foolishness and a life without God from different angles (Doeg, Nabal, and the Ziphites).

54:1-3. Calling on Your Name. God's name serves as a framing device of the psalm. It is mentioned in v. 1 as the means by which David is saved and then praised in v. 6. Interestingly, *'elohim* and *yahweh*, together with *'adonai*, are used in this psalm in connection with the theology of God's name that emphasizes His character and authority. Verse 3 provides the rationale for the plea. The people who are rising up to attack can be connected to the Ziphites who lived in a town southeast of Hebron where David escaped from Saul. They decided to betray David because they disregarded God's authority like the fool in Psalm 53 who denied His existence. The Ziphites were part of David's own people, and while they knew God, they did not follow Him.

54:4-5. Vindication. The central message of the psalm is in v. 4, which states that God is David's help and He supports those who uphold and sustain his life. This is in contrast to those who have sought his life (v. 3). Consequently, God will cut them off or annihilate them (v. 5).

54:6-7. Praising Your Name. Beyond the crisis, the psalmist will express his praise to God in an act of worship and will sacrifice a freewill offering to Him (cf. Ex. 35:29; Lev. 7:16). A final praise for deliverance concludes the psalm and gives the psalmist an opportunity to look down on his enemies (v. 7; cf. Ps. 37:34). In the Bible, calling upon God's name is a transferral of authority to Him, a willingness to follow His will versus our own.

55:1-23
Betrayed by a Friend

As in the previous psalm, there is a strong plea for deliverance from an enemy or enemies, with a constant shift from the singular to the plural (e.g., vv. 9-10, plural; vv. 12-13, singular; v. 15, plural). There is also a progression in the usage of the divine name from *'elohim* (v. 1) to *'adonai* (v. 10) and then to *yahweh* (v. 16). There are two pleas that follow each other (vv. 1-8 and 9-14) with some correspondence between them, and then a statement of hope concludes the psalm. The psalm is a didactic poem or contemplation (*maskil*) of David, accompanied by "stringed instruments."

55:1-8. First Plea. The fourfold plea for God to hear underlines the urgency of the psalmist's need for deliverance from the enemy who is first introduced in v. 3, in both the singular and the plural. The agony of the psalmist in v. 4 is described as his *khul* ("pain," "agony"), which is used elsewhere to describe a woman giving birth (e.g., Is. 26:18). He also experiences the terrors of death (v. 4); horror has overwhelmed him (v. 5) like the Flood covered the earth (Gen. 7:19). He longs to escape this situation and wishes for the wings of a dove to fly away and remain in the desert (vv. 6-7). David's escape into the wilderness may well serve as the historical backdrop for this psalm. Some commentators have identified Ahithophel, David's counselor who deserted to Absalom, with the betrayer mentioned in the psalm (cf. 2 Sam. 15-17).

55:9-15. Second Plea. Whereas the first plea was for God to listen, the second asks Him to act by confusing their words (lit. "divide their tongues"; v. 9), which echoes the confusion of tongues in Genesis 11. This effectively puts a stop to the plans of the wicked. The motivation for this request is the presence of violence and strife in the city, caused by someone who is not an enemy but his peer, companion, and friend (vv. 12-13). It is a person that belonged to David's immediate circle, a friend with whom he had had close (Heb. *mataq*, "sweet") fellowship and walked to the house of God in procession. The enormity of this personal betrayal leads the psalmist to God for deliverance, requesting that He let death come suddenly upon his enemies (v. 15). Interestingly, the psalm switches here again to the plural, indicating how the person who betrayed him is part of a larger conspiracy. He serves as an agent of a larger evil scheme.

55:16–23. Expression of Trust. A transition is introduced in the psalm ("as for me") that reveals the psalmist's reaction to the threat: he will pray, crying out in distress—in the evening, in the morning, and at noon (vv. 16–17; cf. Dan. 6). He also expresses his confidence that God will act on his behalf and by faith states that He will rescue him unharmed from the battle (Heb. "redeem my soul in *shalom* ("peace," "soundness," "completeness"; vv. 16–18). The prophetic perfect in the Hebrew ("He *has* redeemed") here indicates that the psalmist considers his redemption as certain as if it had happened already. Accordingly, some translations place the verbs in the present ("He rescues") or future ("He will redeem"). In vv. 19–21, there is another shift from the plural to the singular, focusing on the faithless friend who betrayed the psalmist using smooth words that contrast with his violent actions (v. 21). But the psalmist reaffirms his trust in God, who will never allow the righteous to be shaken (vv. 22–23). He extends a general invitation to others, encouraging his listeners to cast their burdens and cares on the Lord, for He will sustain them. The noun *yehab* ("burden") occurs only here in the OT and is rendered in the LXX as *merimna* ("anxiety," "worry," "care"). Some personal disappointments in life are difficult to bear, but the psalmist extends the invitation across the millennia to throw onto God what life has thrown onto us.

56:1–13
Continued Persecution

Psalms 56–60 are each titled as "A Michtam/ *miktam* of David," a designation that already occurs in Psalm 16. Psalm 56 connects thematically with the previous two psalms, issuing a plea for deliverance from persecution combined with imprecations against the enemies (56:7; cf. 54:5; 55:9, 15, 23). The psalm also displays close ties with Psalm 57, starting with the identical plea for God to be merciful and

describing deliverance from similar situations. The historical note concerning his capture by the Philistines in Gath may allude to one of two experiences of David with the Philistines (1 Sam. 21:10—22:1; 27:1—29:11). The wistful musical note about the silent, distant dove occurs only here and creates a further link to Psalm 55, where the psalmist longs to fly away like a dove. In some ANE cultures, doves were messengers that carried communications to and from the gods.

56:1–4. Complaint and Trust. The request of the psalmist is introduced with a cry for God to be merciful. The verbal form *khanan* ("to be merciful") combined with the divine name occurs throughout the Davidic psalms as an appeal to God's grace for deliverance (cf. 6:2; 31:9; 41:4, 10; 51:1; 56:1; 86:3). The psalmist experiences oppression, and he feels continuously (lit. "all day") *sha'ap* by his enemies. This word can mean either to "gasp" or "pant after"; that is, he is pursued by the wicked like dogs chasing a hunted animal (or in some translations, to "trample" or "crush"; i.e., he feels crushed by his enemies). However, the section concludes with an affirmation of trust in God, ending with the rhetorical question "What can human beings do to me?" (v. 4). This puts the threat into perspective, and ultimately the enemy is only *basar* ("flesh").

56:5–13. Complaint, Imprecation, and Vow. The psalm now returns with greater detail to the initial complaint, describing the ongoing (lit. "all day") attempts of the enemies to look for an opportunity to bring him down (v. 5). The psalmist now turns to God, asking Him to act and throw down the nations (v. 7). This is followed by a request to record his lament permanently, to count his difficult experiences, and to put his tears into God's bottle (lit. "wineskin") and on His scroll or book (v. 8). Some translations follow manuscript variants which have text that reads that the psalmist's tears are on God's scroll and (with parallelism) in His record and thus omit the reference to the "bottle." But the basic meaning is the same— he wants the Lord to collect his suffering as one would collect precious liquids and place them in a leather bottle.

The idea of recording David's sorrows fits well with the idea of the *miktam* in the superscription as a commemorative inscription. God's record of human actions and experiences is mentioned throughout Scripture (e.g.,

Ps. 69:28; Mal. 3:16). "In the book of God's remembrance...every act of sacrifice, every suffering and sorrow endured for Christ's sake, is recorded" (GC, 481). The section is completed with a threefold expression of trust in God (vv. 10–11) that echoes v. 4 in a refrain-like manner. The psalm concludes with vows (v. 12) and their legally binding character (cf. Ps. 22:25). The psalmist promises to render praises to God (cf. Gen. 28:20–22) for His deliverance. Human fear can be effectively countered only with a continuous confession of trust in God.

57:1–11
Deliverance from Persecution

Psalms 56 and 57 have been called twin psalms as they coincide with each other in theme and structure and begin with the identical plea for mercy. Psalm 57 moves the emphasis to deliverance and has a more triumphant tone than Psalm 56. There is a twofold refrain (vv. 5, 11) that concludes the two parts of the poem. There are similarities in the superscriptions of the two psalms (except the tune, "the words were set to 'Do Not Destroy,'" also found in Pss. 58–59, 75; cf. Is. 65:8) and the historical background of both are connected to 1 Samuel 21–22. It is possible that David wrote the poem in the cave of Adullam, which is traditionally located on the eastern side of the Elah Valley.

57:1–5. First Plea and Deliverance. The psalm begins with a plea identical to the previous psalm, followed by the imagery of a hen gathering chicks under her wings and the cherubim throne above the ark of the covenant to express the idea of refuge in the "shadow" of God's "wings" (cf. 17:8; 36:7; 57:1). The psalmist is totally sure that God will send from heaven and save him (v. 3). David compares the experience he and his companions had as they made their nightly resting place in the wilderness among wild animals to that of a potential prey surrounded by lions. There are threats on every side, particularly that of destructive words used like a sharp sword (v. 4). A refrain concludes the first section, exalting God's sovereignty above the heavens (v. 5), creating a sharp contrast with the surrounding threats.

57:6–11. Second Plea and Deliverance. The second plea returns to the plotting of the enemies who are hunting the psalmist like a wild beast and have dug a pit for him. But this time the enemies' purposes are thwarted and consequently they have fallen into their own trap (v. 6). In reaction

to this surprising turn of events, the remainder of the psalm breaks out into a sustained song of praise (vv. 7–10), closing with the repetition of the refrain in v. 11. The mention of the dawn in v. 8 brings to mind how David might have arisen after a dark night of impending threat to a new morning of hope. The reference to God's unlimited *khesed* ("mercy," "unfailing love," "grace") connects v. 10 to the initial plea of vv. 1 and 3. The historical scenes from David's life that underlie these psalms illustrate how God can surprisingly turn a dark, life-threatening situation into a bright new hope.

58:1–11
Judgment on Unjust Judges

Psalm 58 is replete with violent imagery that vividly portrays God's judgment on unjust judges. The unjust judges are asked if they are speaking and acting justly (v. 1). This question is answered in v. 11, affirming that God is the One "who judges the earth." The psalm follows the same tune of the previous psalm, and David is identified as the author.

58:1–5. Unjust Judges. The psalm opens with an address to the *'elem*. This term has been interpreted in various ways: it might be referring to leaders (changing the Heb. text to *'elim*, "rams," "men of power") or even gods (changing the Heb. text to *'elohim*). The parallel expression *bene 'adam* ("sons of men") at the end of v. 1, connected with the verb *shapat* ("to judge"), indicates that the psalm is directed against powerful human judges who, through their corruption, have elevated themselves to the level of gods (cf. 89:6). The violence and lies of the wicked (vv. 2–3) are likened to a deaf cobra that no longer heeds the charmers (vv. 4–5), not even the most skillful.

58:6–11. Plea for Divine Judgment. The request for God to intervene changes the imagery from cobra to lions (v. 6) and connects this psalm to the previous one (57:4). Human violence meets divine judgment and God reduces all evil intentions to nothing. This is communicated through the use of fast-paced images, such as cut arrows, a dried up slug or snail, a stillborn child, or a pot that is blown over by the wind before the food is cooked (vv. 7–9). What remains is the rejoicing of the righteous (v. 10) as they see wickedness being destroyed and the confession of all human beings acknowledging that there surely is a God who judges the earth (vv. 10–11). Corruption abounds and no one is exempt from its damaging impact, not even God's children. But God is the Judge who will eventually and permanently set things right.

59:1–17
Deliverance from Violence

As in Psalm 57 there is a refrain that concludes each of the two sections of this psalm, in which David refers to God as his *misgab* ("defense," "fortress," "strong tower"; vv. 9–10a, 17). There is another repetitive phrase in each section that provides the background imagery for the psalm: the wicked traitors return at evening, growl like dogs, and go all around the city (vv. 6, 14). The imagery is that of a pack of stray dogs that are viciously dangerous, running their deadly attacks during the night (cf. 1 Kin. 14:11; 21:23; 2 Kin. 9:34–37; Ps. 22:16). Like the preceding two psalms, Psalm 59 follows the tune "Do Not Destroy" and is a *miktam* of David. The historical note connects this psalm directly with 1 Samuel 19:11 and Saul's intention to kill David in the morning. Instead, he escapes and praises God the next morning (v. 16).

59:1–10a. Attack of the Enemy. The psalm begins with a request for deliverance from the enemies, identified as those who practice evil, are bloodthirsty, and lie in wait like a prowling animal (vv. 2–3). Affirming his innocence, the psalmist now implores God to intervene with a series of imperatives in which he asks God to rise up to help him and rise up to punish the nations (vv. 5–6). He invokes punishment without mercy on all the nations and any wicked people who *bagad* ("to act treacherously"), thus raising his request to a universal level. Personal deliverance is merged here with national protection (vv. 4–5). The simile of the threatening dogs (v. 6) is followed by a sudden turn of events, as Yahweh will laugh at them (v. 8), showing that under God's protection the deathly threat amounts to nothing. David refers to God as his *misgab* ("defense," "fortress," "stronghold"). This refers to an elevated place of refuge out of reach from the attack of the enemies (cf. Ps. 46:7, 11; 48:3). God is referred to as being One of *khesed* ("mercy," "faithful love") in vv. 10 and 17.

59:10b–17. Defeat of the Enemy. The second part of v. 10 moves the focus from the psalmist's deliverance to the enemies' defeat. He asks for God not to kill them but to *noa'* ("scatter" or "uproot") them and ultimately consume them

in wrath (vv. 11–13), leading them to acknowledge Yahweh and know that He rules over Jacob (v. 13). Once more the simile of prowling dogs is repeated, but now they wander around looking for food and are not satisfied (vv. 14–15). This reversal of fates based on the same imagery provides a powerful antecedent to the final praise (vv. 16–17) in which the psalmist once more invokes the refuge metaphor of the *misgab* ("strong tower"; cf. v. 9) and God's *khesed* ("mercy" or "faithful love"). It is encouraging to understand that God laughs at what we perceive as snarling dogs and deathly threats to our lives. He laughs because He can reverse threats into blessings.

60:1–12
Military Defeat

This is the last psalm that, like Psalms 56–60, is introduced in the superscription as a *miktam*, a commemorative inscription. The language of violence that permeated Psalm 59 becomes even more pronounced in this psalm. The background seems to be a military defeat suffered by David against the Edomites (2 Sam. 8; 1 Chr. 18). There are some differences between the superscription of the psalm and the other passages (e.g., the number of Edomites slain and who did the deed), possibly pointing to variant text forms. There is an additional note, "for teaching", which occurs only here in the Psalms and recalls David's instruction to teach his song of lament about Saul's death to the people of Judah (2 Sam. 1:18).

60:1–5. Communal Lament. Verses 1–3 voice Israel's communal lament after they have been defeated by an enemy that is not further identified, unless the question at the end of v. 9 ("Who will lead me to Edom?") is understood as pointing to Edom in accordance with the historical superscription. However, within a Hebrew theocentric worldview, God is viewed as responsible for the hardships of His people. Consequently we find a series of laments directed to God, all beginning with descriptions of His actions, including their negative effects. Verse 4 continues along the same syntax, but this time a positive statement is introduced. There is a banner raised by God as a final stand against the advancing enemy and around which those who fear Him rally (cf. Is. 5:26; 11:12). It is a banner *mippene qoshet*. This has been translated as either "against/from the bow" or "because of the truth." *Mippene* can mean "in front of" or "because of." *Qoshet* can mean either "bow" or "truth," and it occurs in only one other place in the Hebrew Bible (Prov. 22:21), where it seems to mean "certainty." Here the translation "bow" would fit the military context, but it is most probably referring to the valuing of the truth by those who fear *Yahweh*. Whichever the case, the banner is displayed in order that God's beloved people may be delivered (vv. 4–5). In the narrative in Exodus, it is God Himself who is this banner (cf. Ex. 17:15), and here the psalm invokes the Exodus imagery through usage of *nes* ("banner, standard"). The section ends with a request for God to save.

60:6–8. God Responds. The following lines contain God's direct response to the allegations and appeals of the previous section. As the experience in Exodus was invoked, the psalmist now calls on the experience of the conquest of Canaan and the division of the land among the twelve tribes, covering the geographic areas east (e.g., Gilead) and west (e.g., Judah) of the Jordan River. But the conquest moves beyond the initial conquest under Joshua and includes more recent victories over Moab, Edom, and Philistia that are associated with David's conquests and battles. As much as the defeat of the nations has been God's responsibility, so is the victory that has made the nations God's washbowl.

60:9–12. Lead Me On. The question is now directed to God and the focus returns to Edom as the current enemy: "Who will bring me to the strong, fortified city? Who will lead me to Edom?" (v. 9). This is a reference to the rock fortress of Sela, the capital of Edom. In v. 10 God is asked whether it was not He who did not go out with the armies. In response, vv. 11–12 conclude the psalm with a request for God to lead on once more, to give them help against the trouble caused by their enemies and to trample them down. Overall, one can perceive an intensification of threats in this group of *miktam* psalms of David (Pss. 56–60). This has led some commentators to call this group of psalms the "passion of David," likening it to Christ's passion, as they describe moments of persecution, betrayal, and apparent defeat, which are reversed into divine victories.

61:1–8
The King's Prayer

The psalm has been associated with the time that David was exiled from Jerusalem while fleeing from his son Absalom (cf. 2 Sam. 16–19). It is a royal prayer expressing his desire to return to the sanctuary. It is mostly in first-person speech (vv. 1–5, 8) but that changes to third person in vv. 6–7. The prayer for the king is framed in vv. 5 and 8 by the expression "my vows," which may indicate that vv. 6–7 are a wish echoing the king's vows, possibly pronounced by a court official. The psalm is to be performed on a stringed instrument and is ascribed to David.

61:1–5. Plea and Vows. The prayer is introduced by a petition (v. 1) that echoes Psalm 17:1; both verses emphasize the psalmist's request to be heard by repetition with intensification. Verse 2 expresses the circumstances under which David lifts up his petition as he cries to God "from the end(s) of the earth," which hyperbolically describes his distance from Jerusalem and his emotional exhaustion from running away from Absalom. A series of three familiar refuge metaphors follow (rock, refuge/shelter, and tower), which alludes to elevated places that could be associated with Mahanaim, the fortified city along the Jabbok River to which David fled and where he regrouped before attacking the pursuing Absalom (vv. 2–3; cf. 2 Sam. 17). Verse 4 expresses the psalmist's desire to be in God's tabernacle/tent under the protection of the shelter of His wings (i.e., under the cherubim that stand above the ark of the covenant). The section concludes with an affirmation of vows that David has made toward God during his exile.

61:6–7. May the King Live Forever. The shift to a third person speech in vv. 6–7 makes it possible to understand this section as a responsive prayer on behalf of the king by one of his officials. Based on the royal vows, he reaffirms the king and prays for his longevity.

61:8. Final Vow. The final lines of the psalm return to the first-person speech and reconnect to v. 5 by mentioning "my vows" once more, indicating that it is David who now speaks. It is a final praise and a desire to *shalam* ("fulfill," "complete," "repay") these vows. This was accomplished at a special dedicatory offering publicly performed in the sanctuary (cf. Num. 6:13–21). David's prayer from exile and his longing for the sanctuary can cause us only to renew our longing to be with the Lord in the house of the Father (John 14:1–3) and pray for the end of our exile.

62:1–12
Trust in God

Psalm 62 continues the refuge imagery of the previous poems by referring to God as "Rock" (vv. 2, 6–7 // 61:2) and *misgab* ("Defense" or "Fortress"; vv. 2, 6 // 59:9, 16–17). The context of the psalm is a threatening military conflict, possibly an attack on the rock fortress of Mahanaim, which created the historical backdrop for the previous psalm. This creates a sustained affirmation of trust in God, although it is only in the last line that the psalmist addresses God directly. In the Hebrew text, there is a sixfold repetition of the adverb '*ak* at the beginning of vv. 1, 2, 4, 5, 6, and 9. This term can have either an emphatic ("surely," "truly") or a restrictive sense ("only"). In the former case, it would serve to increase the certainty of God's protection (or, in v. 4, the certainty of his enemies' plots) and set this psalm apart from the previous ones (cf. 39:5–6, where '*ak* occurs in three consecutive lines). If the word is taken as restrictive ("only"), it would serve to emphasize the uniqueness of God's capacity to save; in v. 5, it would indicate the singularity of the enemies' intentions, despite their false posture of friendliness.

In v. 9, the Hebrew word *hebel* ("breath" or "vapor") is used. The word *ak* could refer to either the certainty of the vapor/breath-like state of human beings or to the idea that they are "only" breath/vapor. There is a refrain-like repetition which frames the first section of the psalm (vv. 1–2, 5–7). The association in the superscription with "Jeduthun," one of David's music leaders in the temple, possibly points to one of his musical arrangements (cf. 39:1; 77:1).

62:1–7. Trust and Plea. The affirmation that introduces the psalm in the indicative ("my soul" or "I") *damam* ("wait" or "find rest") for/ in God is repeated as a self-directed imperative desire in v. 5, "my soul, wait/find rest." Verse 2 expresses trust in God's protection, drawing on the imagery of refuge used in previous psalms. At the center of the plea, the attitude of the attackers is described. They bless with their mouths but curse in their hearts and plot to topple him from his high position. This is possibly referring to David when he found refuge in the rock fortress of Mahanaim. Verses 5–7 expand on vv. 1–2 with repetitions and additions clarifying that God is the Refuge.

62:8–12. Trust and Advice. The second section of the psalm takes on a more universal and didactic tone in addressing the people encouraging them to trust in Him at all times and reaffirming that God is a Refuge. The psalm then turns to wisdom literature and draws heavily on Proverbs and Lamentations (vv. 9–11). The likening of humans, both low and high, to *hebel* ("vapor" or "breath") approximates the poem to Psalm 39:5–6, but it also creates a strong link with Ecclesiastes, in which this same term ("breath," "nothingness") is a central motif. The numerical saying in v. 11 is comparable with Proverbs 6:16–19 and others. The message here is clear: trust not in riches, violence, oppression, or robbery but only in God. Appropriately, the final line addresses God directly and ascribes both *khesed* ("mercy," "unfailing love") and justice to Him in His dealings with humanity. It is difficult to remain silent and wait on God in the midst of oppression, but Psalm 62 encourages us to do just that and to trust God in the midst of the storms of life.

63:1–11
Longing for God

In contrast to the previous poem, Psalm 63 continuously addresses God in a personal way. The last line shifts from the first-person viewpoint to the third. The psalm is annotated as written by David from the wilderness of Judah and consequently expresses a deep longing for closeness to God and His sanctuary.

63:1–2. Longing. The psalmist's longing for God is expressed by the vivid metaphor of someone anxious for water in a dry, parched, and weary land, a description very much in tune with the conditions of the Judean desert. In his search, he has seen God in the sanctuary, a place from which the psalmist is physically separated. The verb "to look/see" (*khazah*) could also refer to a prophetic vision. The visionary character is furthermore underlined by his desire to see God's glory (*kabod*), which is associated with God's presence in the Most Holy Place (cf. 2 Chr. 7:1–3).

63:3–8. Joy in Communion. In response to David's vision of God's glory, the psalm breaks into an extended praise, emphasizing the satisfaction the psalmist receives from communing with God. In this experience, the psalmist is satisfied as with *kheleb* ("fat") and *deshen* ("fatness"); the imagery is of rich foods in abundance within the context of an ANE banquet scene (cf. 23:5–6). In v. 6, reference is made to the spiritual experience introduced in v. 2 by clarifying how the king contemplates God's glory during the night. He meditates on Him in the night watches and finds refuge, protection, and joy in the shadow of God's wings. This is possibly another reference to the sanctuary (i.e., the cherubim above the ark; see commentary on 36:5–9; 57:1–5). He is determined to totally rely on God and encourages others to do the same (v. 8).

63:9–11. Long Live the King. David has turned his thoughts to God during a sleepless night in the wilderness of Judah. Away from the immediate threats of his pursuers, his mind now returns to his enemies and concludes that since he is under God's protective wings, those who are trying to kill him will go down into the depths of the earth. The psalm closes by contrasting the fate of the wicked with that of the king. While the wicked will be destroyed, the king will rejoice in God and together with his people will glory in Him (cf. 61:6–7). Longing for God and meditating on His goodness will strengthen the soul. Turning our thoughts to Him when the night hours are dark and long nurtures hope.

64:1–10
Deliverance from Evil Tongues

Psalm 64 concludes a group of Davidic psalms (Pss. 52–64) that addresses war and persecution combined with prayers for deliverance from violence and scheming enemies. This psalm focuses on the last motif, that of the attackers, followed by a statement of trust in God's deliverance from them. All this is done using military language in which the destructive power of the tongue is compared to swords or razors (cf. 52:2, 4; 55:9; 57:4; 64:3, 8). The superscription of the psalm points to David but lacks any further historical annotations.

64:1–6. Evil Plotting. After the initial plea for God to hear him, the psalmist describes the verbal attacks of the wicked (v. 2). They move from conspiratorial plots to open attack as they sharpen their tongues like swords and shoot cruel and bitter words like arrows. Military attacks were often accompanied by verbal assaults, as in the case of David's conflict with Absalom. It started with the young prince's sharpened words spoken at the city gate that turned away the hearts of the people from his father, the king (2 Sam. 15:1–6). This led to the open rebellion and civil war portrayed throughout this group of

psalms. The section concludes with a comment about the deep corruption of the inner being of rebellious humanity.

64:7–10. Deliverance. Deliverance begins with an ironic reversal of action. As the enemies shot their verbal arrows at the psalmist, God will now shoot an arrow at them. In this section, God's deliverance is described as something that has already taken place. David has seen how God made his enemies fall, turning their own words against them (vv. 7–8), which constitutes another ironic reversal (vv. 1–6). Verses 9–10 anticipate the time when all people will acknowledge God's work as they consider what He has done. At the end of the previous psalm the king rejoiced, and now the righteous will rejoice in the Lord. In both psalms they are said to "glory" in the Lord (cf. 63:11). The psalm affirms a biblical truth related to the cosmic conflict, namely, that the attacks of the enemy will finally come to an end through divine intervention.

65:1–13
God Waters the Earth

This Davidic thanksgiving hymn sets a different tone from the preceding psalms, although it shares some of the universal perspectives that have characterized previous psalms. It also introduces a series of four "songs" (Pss. 65–68) that provides an interlude of praises in the laments that surround the group. The psalm is characterized by praises to God for all His provisions in nature. It starts by depicting a scene of praises in the sanctuary, then moves into all of creation, concluding with a picture of God as the One who fertilizes the land. All three sections use *'elohim* ("God") only in their opening lines, and each section closes with a description of the effects of God's provision for the congregation (v. 4), for creation as a whole (v. 8), and for the land in particular (v. 13).

65:1–4. God in the Sanctuary. The congregation gathers in Zion to praise God in His sanctuary, a place where vows will be kept (v. 1; cf. 61:8), where all people (lit. "all flesh") will come, and where God will forgive their transgressions by providing atonement for them Himself (vv. 2–3). A beatitude concludes this section, describing the blessing of the atonement God provides for His congregation from His holy temple (v. 4). The *hekal* ("temple") most probably refers to the tabernacle that David erected in Jerusalem to house the ark of the covenant (cf. 2 Sam. 6:17). The same term was also used to describe the tabernacle at Shiloh during the time of Samuel (1 Sam. 1:9).

65:5–8. God in Creation. This section recalls the awesome deeds of God in Creation when He formed and established the mountains by His power and might (vv. 5–6). But it also affirms that He is able to still the noise of the roaring seas, keeping the forces of nature as well as the people who dwell throughout the earth (vv. 7–8) under control. The usage of *le'om* ("people," "ethnic group") is a more inclusive term than the usual *goyim* ("peoples," "nations") that one would expect here. It points to the universal manifestation of the power of God.

65:9–13. God's Provisions for the Land. There is a third shift in the poem with the coming of God to *paqad* ("visit" or "care for") the earth. The term *'erets* ("earth") could also be translated "land," as indicated by the reference to local geographic features, specifically the semi-desert grasslands and pastures of the wilderness (v. 12). The central hills and valleys (vv. 12–13) of the Shephelah are covered (lit. "clothed") with flocks and wrapped (*'atap*) in grain. It is God who waters the earth through the river of God (lit. the "canal of God"; v. 9), saturating its furrows with water and creating abundance (v. 10). This image of agricultural richness leads to a shout for joy (v. 13) that echoes through the valleys. The song of praise which goes out from Zion to creation in general, and to the land in particular, reflects the joyful reality that the blessings of God are dependent on His work of atonement on behalf of repentant sinners.

66:1–20
Communal and Individual Praise

This "song" divides into two parts, a communal hymn praising God for His "awesome" deeds in the past history of Israel (cf. 65:5) and an individual thanksgiving for deliverance. The latter could have been antiphonally presented at the sanctuary by the king in response to the first part of the psalm. The psalm is not explicitly associated with David in its superscription.

66:1–12. Deliverance during Israel's History. The psalm begins with a summons to shout joyfully to God and praise Him for His awesome acts (vv. 1–4), thus creating a universal perspective. This is followed by another invitation (vv. 5–7)

to come and see the works of God (v. 5), namely, His acts of salvation when He turned the sea into dry land and His people went through the *nahar* ("river," "water") on foot. There are verbal links that connect this psalm to the Song of the Sea in Exodus 15 (e.g., the reference to God ruling forever by His power clearly echoes Ex. 15:18). A final summons (vv. 8–12) invites the peoples to praise God for constantly preserving them from death. He is specifically thanked for bringing them to *rewayah* ("overflow," "superabundance") after going through fire and water (v. 12).

66:13–20. Deliverance Now. There is a change from "we" to "I" that introduces the individual thanksgiving in the second part of the psalm. The one speaking is most probably the king as representative of the people before God in the sanctuary. He sacrifices burnt offerings and fulfills his vows made when he was in trouble, thus creating a strong verbal link with the preceding psalm (cf. 65:1). The sacrificial ritual is concluded in v. 15, listing an extensive offering of rams, bulls, and goats (similar to Solomon's sacrifices at the inauguration of the temple, 1 Kin. 8:62–64). It is an offering fit for a king, which suggests that the individual in the psalm could be David. Verses 16–20 are a final invitation to all who fear God to listen to the testimony of the king that God has answered his prayer and did not turn away His *khesed* ("mercy," "steadfast love," "kindness"). The awesome deeds of God on behalf of Israel still echo through the millennia, assuring God's children today of salvation and deliverance.

67:1–7
From Israel to the Nations

It is impossible to overlook the similarity between v. 1 and the Aaronic blessing in Numbers 6:24–26. It has been suggested that this hymn was sung as a congregational response to the reading of the Aaronic blessing in the sanctuary. The Ketef Himnon silver scrolls, found in a burial cave near Jerusalem and dating to the late seventh century B.C., attest to the popularity of the blessing during OT times. The superscription of the psalm does not connect it to David, but there is nothing that disqualifies him from being its author. Both Psalms 66 and 67 could have been moved to this place in the Psalms in order to complement David's hymns (Pss. 65 and 68) that surround them on each side. There are two refrains repeated in vv. 3 and 5 that divide the psalm into three sections.

67:1–2. Blessings for the World. The previous psalm ended with *barak* ("praise" or "blessing") expressed toward God and continued in v. 1 as an invocation for God to bless (*barak*). The psalm also ends on the same note—God's blessing— making the concept of blessings the main theme of the poem. The psalm moves immediately from "us" to "all nations," who are to acknowledge God's blessings on Israel and His salvation beyond their borders throughout the world (v. 2).

67:3–5. God is Just. The outer frame of blessing is followed by an inner frame of praise as vv. 3 and 5 repeat the refrain inviting all people to praise God. This creates a concentric emphasis on v. 4, which describes God as the One who will justly rule and lead the nations. He has become the universal King.

67:6–7. Blessings for the Land. As in Psalm 65, the result of God's blessings is seen in nature as the earth yields its harvest (v. 6). The psalm concludes with a return to the initial invocation of God's blessing, which again leads to the recognition by all the ends of the earth that God is the One who blesses all. The psalm has given to the Aaronic blessing a universal theological content by connecting it to the promise given to Abraham that through him all the nations of the earth will be blessed (Gen. 12:3; 18:18; 22:18).

68:1–35
God in History

As the last of the four songs (Pss. 65–68), Psalm 68 provides a grand finale that expands on themes found in the other three hymns and includes a procession of Israelite tribes to the temple, accompanied by other nations to testify about Yahweh's power from a universal perspective. Commentators have noticed a certain disjointedness in the poem, but a thematic unity runs throughout it. The psalm could be divided into three major sections. David is once again associated with the composition of this "song."

68:1–10. Exodus and Conquest. The first lines (vv. 1–4) portray Yahweh in terms of a Warrior and invite people to extol Him. God is referred to here as "YAH," often rendered as "LORD." This shortened form of Yahweh appears from here onwards more frequently in the Psalms (e.g., v. 18; 89:8; 115:18; 118:19), and it was also used in the Song of the Sea (Ex. 15:2). The image of the divine Cloud Rider is reminiscent of Psalm 18:7– 15, which indicates that it is an ancient poetic

expression connected to the Exodus experience. The geographic terms "wilderness" and "Sinai" (vv. 7–10) recall the days of the desert wanderings, while "inheritance" connects to the time of the conquest.

68:11–23. From Sinai to Zion. This section begins with a victory song (vv. 11–13) celebrating the conquest and occupation of the land as the kings of armies flee (some translations imply that their armies flee with them; v. 12). The mention of the dove's wings plated with silver refers to the ancient custom of decorating the wings of doves after a victory and letting them fly as messengers of good news. The Transjordan geography of Zalmon (v. 14) and the mountain of Bashan (vv. 14–16) describes the battles east of the River Jordan during the Conquest. The mountains, as the abodes of the gods, are polemically set in contrast to God's mountain. These other mountains look with envy as God proceeds toward the sanctuary. His return to Jerusalem was like that of a king returning victoriously from war with captives and tributes. He "led captivity captive" (according to some translations) or "took many captives" (according to others; v. 18), and He provides escapes from death (v. 20). Paul applies this passage to the ascension of Christ and His ultimate victory over death (Eph. 4:8). The final lines of the section (vv. 21–23) return to the Warrior imagery to speak about the destruction of enemies who are unable to hide from the Lord, for He will bring them back even from the depths of the sea (v. 22; cf. Rev. 20:13).

68:24–35. Procession to the Temple. The third section of the poem begins with a detailed description of a procession as God moves into the sanctuary (v. 24). There are singers and musicians (v. 25) and the leaders of the tribes of Israel, limiting the list to Benjamin (the tribe of Israel's first king), Judah (the tribe of David), as well as Zebulun and Naphtali, representing the tribes furthest to the north of Israel (vv. 24–27). Verses 28–31 highlight God's localized presence at the temple in Jerusalem (v. 29), and God is implored to rebuke Egypt (the beast in the reeds; v. 30). Then Egyptian ambassadors would come, and Ethiopia (or Cush) would stretch out her hands in submission to God. The image of God as a heavenly Warrior who rides on the clouds is invoked in vv. 33–34, and the psalm concludes with a resounding praise of God that is universally sung by the kingdoms of the earth. God always deserves our praises for His marvelous acts of salvation on our behalf. This makes the cross of Jesus the supreme reason to praise and serve Him.

69:1–36
Zeal for God's House

Following the glorious hymns of the previous psalms, this poem returns to familiar laments and introduces the last group of Davidic psalms (Pss. 69–72) in Book 2. The complexity of its imagery has motivated commentators to suggest that the psalm was composed using two originally different psalms. However, the sequence from lament (vv. 1–12) to plea (vv. 13–28) and finally to praise (vv. 29–36) is a familiar one (cf. Ps. 28). This is evidence for the unity of the psalm, something which is also underlined by a contrastive *wa'ani* ("but I" or "but as for me"; vv. 13, 29) used to introduce the second and third sections. Thematically, the poem is a lament and prayer of an individual who is suffering under the persecution of those who hate him for no reason (v. 4). The poem is associated with David, whose authorship is confirmed by Paul (cf. Rom. 11:9). Its tune is set to the tune of "Lilies" (cf. Ps. 45).

69:1–12. Lament. After the psalmist's initial plea for God to save him, the first lines of the poem (vv. 1–3) introduce the lament describing the situation of the psalmist using the imagery of water. The threat of the enemy is like *shibbolet* ("a flowing stream" or "flood") that overwhelms the psalmist and takes him into deep mire (v. 2). From there he cries to God for deliverance as his strength fails (v. 3). Affirming his innocence, David identifies his enemies as many (more than the hairs on his head), and they hate him without cause (v. 4; cf. John 15:25 for a messianic application). Verses 5–12 describe the reason for the adversity the psalmist is experiencing and centers on his zeal for God's house (v. 9). David's intense zeal for the sanctuary has made him a reproach and alienated him from his family (v. 8). The misinterpretation of his pious actions reminds us of the moment when David was transferring the ark of the covenant to Jerusalem and Michal's reaction to his rejoicing (2 Sam. 6:16–23). When Jesus cleansed the temple, His disciples applied this psalm to Him (John 2:17).

69:13–28. Plea. The plea is introduced by a contrastive *wa'ani* ("but I" or "but as for me") and returns to the initial water imagery, asking God to deliver him out of the mire and from the deep waters (v. 14). What began as a lament now becomes a prayer for deliverance, using the identical expressions as in vv. 1–12.

The messianic dimension becomes more pronounced in vv. 20–21 as the psalmist looks for someone to show sympathy, but there was none. This situation foreshadowed the Savior's loneliness in the Garden of Gethsemane (cf. Matt. 26:56; 27:34, 48; Mark 14:50; John 15:25), as well as the gall and vinegar (v. 21) that was offered to Jesus on the cross (John 19:28–29). The remainder of the section (vv. 22–28) is a prayer for vindication that climaxes in a final request for the eternal punishment of the wicked—for them to be blotted out of the Book of Life. Within the messianic context of the psalm the request is especially meaningful as it outlines the final destiny of those who opposed the Messiah (cf. Dan. 12:2; Rev. 1:7).

69:29–36. Praise. The final *wa'ani* ("but I" or "but as for me"; v. 13) accomplishes a further change in tone from request to praise, similar to the change in another messianic poem (Ps. 22:22–31). This is a response to God's acts of deliverance, which involves all of creation (v. 34). God's saving acts extend from Zion to the cities of Judah and to all descendants of His servants who will dwell in it forever. David's personal experience, which underlies this psalm, prophetically foreshadowed the suffering of the Messiah, His loneliness, and His physical pain on the cross. The agony of the Messiah assures us of the end of all pain and suffering.

70:1–5
A Temple Plea

One of the longest psalms in Books 1 and 2 is followed by one of the shortest in the Psalms, reproducing the final plea of Psalm 40:13–17 almost verbatim. It is an adaptation of the passage for use during the memorial offering alluded to in its superscription: "to bring to remembrance" or "a petition" (cf. Ps. 38:1). Many ancient manuscripts combine Psalms 70 with 71, pointing to the possibility that the two once were a single composition. This seems to be supported by the fact that Psalm 71 does not have a separate heading and by a number of verbal and thematic links between the two poems (e.g., the unusual *khushah*, "hasten," which serves as an *inclusio* in vv. 1 and 5, appears twice in 71:12 at an important place but rarely throughout the rest of the Psalms).

Furthermore, the temple plea of Psalm 70 is answered in the concluding statements of Psalm 71. Thus, Psalm 70 becomes the invocation for the overall composition of both psalms.

70:1–5. Invocation. The combined poem of Psalms 70–71 begins with an invocation from the psalmist that serves as a plea for deliverance from those who are seeking to kill him. Verses 1 and 5 stress the theme of deliverance by using the term *khushah* ("hasten"). There is an urgent request to punish the attacker, asking repeatedly for them to be ashamed and turned back. This is contrasted with the experience of those who seek the Lord, rejoice, and are glad in Him. While the wicked say *he'akh* ("aha!") as a public expression of contempt and derision (v. 3), the righteous magnify the greatness of God.

71:1–24
Old Age

Psalm 71 directly continues with the plea that was introduced in Psalm 70. However, there is an additional concern over the difficulties that come with old age (vv. 9, 18) accompanied by a statement affirming the psalmist's trust in the Lord from his youth (vv. 5, 17). The three sections (vv. 1–8, 9–16, 17–24) are each concluded with a verbal praise. "David was deeply moved; he was distressed as he looked forward to the time when he should be aged…David felt the necessity of guarding against the evils which attend old age" (1T 423).

71:1–8. Looking Back. An initial plea asks for God's deliverance from being put to shame. The idea of being shamed serves as a connection to the previous psalm (cf. 70:2) and is a key one in the current poem (cf. vv. 13, 24). At the center of this section is a reflection on how God has led the psalmist in the past, moving backward from youth (v. 5) to birth (v. 6) and finally to his mother's womb (vv. 5–6). This leads to a verbal expression of trust and hope in the Lord.

71:9–16. Old Age. After the psalmist reviews how God has led him in the past, his thoughts turn to the impending difficulties of old age when strength fails (v. 9). The waning power of the monarch is accompanied by the increased pursuit of his adversaries who want to capture him so that no one can deliver him (vv. 10–11). With an accumulation of volitional forms, David pleads for God's protection and is ready to testify about God's righteousness.

71:17–24. Youth and Old Age. The final section of the psalm combines the two previous themes to reaffirm once more that God has taught the psalmist from his youth. Now he asks for God's continuous guidance when he is old and gray (v. 18). This suggests that David composed the psalm in his old age. The section moves between praises for the past and prayers for the present and future, concluding with praise accompanied by musical instruments (v. 22). God's deliverance is described as an already accomplished fact. God never abandons us, particularly during the time when we are perhaps more fragile. He is always trustworthy.

72:1–20
A Prayer for My Son

The final psalm of Book 2 represents David's prayer for Solomon, either as remembered and recorded by Solomon when he ascended to the throne or written by David himself. This is not clear because of the tension between the superscription referring to Solomon (cf. Ps. 127:1) and the subscript referring to the completion of the prayers of David at the end of the psalm, which closes book 2. However, if one reads the heading in the light of the ending, then *lishlomoh* could also be translated "for Solomon," identifying it as a poem written by David in old age for his son (cf. Ps. 71). It is also recognized to be a messianic psalm.

72:1–7. A Prayer for Justice. The psalm opens with a request for the new king to judge God's people with righteousness. It is a prayer for the king to exercise his authority in accordance with God's will, which anticipates Solomon's prayer in 1 Kings 3. The mountains and hills represent the geography of Israel and the blessings that come as a result of a righteous king, which are likened to showers that water the earth, an image of fruitful abundance in the land.

72:8–14. A Prayer for Dominion. The prayer continues, asking for dominion also from sea to sea. The geography could refer to the Red Sea and the Mediterranean in a north-south direction and east-west from the Euphrates River to the Aegean islands and as far as Spain. While some of the geographic dimensions reflect the extent of Solomon's reign and his international recognition, there is an element of hyperbole in his idealized prayer at the beginning of his government. More importantly, the rationale for dominion is grounded in ethical concerns (vv. 12–14). Whereas righteousness was the keyword for the first section, now it is the needy, poor, and afflicted.

72:15–17. A Prayer for Longevity. Recognition from foreign rulers and fruitful abundance of the land will characterize Solomon's reign and his name will endure forever as he is blessed and others are blessed in him (v. 17). A prayer for longevity of his reign and a final blessing concludes the psalm and at the same time creates the transition to the doxology.

72:18–20. Doxology for Book 2 and Subscript. The doxology largely corresponds to the one at the end of Book 1, except that it expands it in mentioning the splendorous things God is doing by filling the earth with His glory. The subscript ends Book 2 as well as the first two Davidic psalms, concluding with a hopeful description of not only Solomon's future kingdom but also an ideal kingdom that finds its realization only in the kingdom of the Messiah.

PSALMS 73—89
BOOK III

Book 3 begins with a group of Asaph psalms (Pss. 73–83), which is the largest collection in this part of the Psalms. Thematically they concentrate on the question "God, where are you?" which is introduced in Psalm 73. This collection also includes the second and last group of Korahite psalms (Pss. 84–85; 87–88), which largely deal with Zion theology (cf. Pss. 42–49). It is interrupted and followed by two psalms of David (Pss. 86 and 89) that were not included in the main collection of the Davidic psalms.

73:1–28
The Prosperity of the Wicked

Psalm 73 provides an answer to the question of theodicy, more specifically, why the righteous suffer and the wicked prosper. It is a didactic poem in the tradition of Psalms 1 and 2 and is framed by vv. 1 and 28 with the repetition of *tob* ("good"), emphasizing God's goodness. In this way the question of theodicy is answered right from the beginning: God is good! There is also a reversal of fates where the psalmist finds himself on slippery ground (vv. 1–3) and the wicked are secure (vv. 4–12). Then it is the wicked who are slipping (vv. 18–20) and the psalmist is on firm

ground in God's presence (vv. 21–28). This first Asaph psalm in the present collection introduces the question of God's absence and presence that will characterize the remainder of this group.

73:1–12. The Wicked Prosper. Following the preemptive declaration of God's goodness, the psalmist recalls how the question of the wicked person's prosperity (v. 3) vexed him to the point that he nearly slipped and stumbled (vv. 1–3). The psalmist is confused by the observation that everything seems to go well for the wicked while practicing their wickedness. They speak arrogantly about heaven and earth (vv. 8–9), and there is an increase in their accumulated wealth (vv. 4–12). How could this be?

73:13–16. Why Should I Remain Pure? This is the crucial but ill-directed question by the psalmist, who has kept his heart pure seemingly in vain (v. 13) and is trying to live a life of integrity in the face of adversity and successful adversaries. This question continues to haunt us even today.

73:17–20. Understanding from the Sanctuary. The turning point of the psalm is reached when the psalmist goes into the sanctuary of God. He recognizes that human reasoning by itself lacks understanding (v. 16), but that understanding comes only from the sanctuary. Like Elijah (1 Kin. 19:14), he turns to the only source of true knowledge, and there in the sanctuary he suddenly discerns the end of that generation (i.e., their ultimate destiny; v. 17). He then realizes that it is the wicked, not the righteous, who are set in slippery places and facing eternal judgment (vv. 18–20).

73:21–28. I was Wrong. As a result of his new insight, the psalmist realizes that his previous reasoning was *ba'ar* ("brutish" or "foolish") and ignorant. His foolishness is contrasted with God's faithfulness (v. 23) and guidance that accompanies him from here into eternity (v. 24). The psalm ends with a recognition that all the things that happen to us in this life can draw us closer to God, and He is the One we should desire most of all (v. 25). Thus, it is good to be near to God (v. 28; cf. v. 1). God's goodness is reiterated as the ultimate answer to the question posed in the psalm.

74:1–23
The Sanctuary in Ruins

As in the previous psalm, the sanctuary lies at the center of the psalmist's *maskil* ("instruction" or "contemplation"). The two poems are connected by verbal links—the only two occurrences of *mashu'ah* ("destruction," "desolation," "ruins") in the Hebrew Bible (Pss. 73:18; 74:3). But whereas Psalm 73 provided spiritual insight through the perspective of the sanctuary, Psalm 74 laments the desolation of the sanctuary. This is probably connected to the destruction of the temple by Nebuchadnezzar in 586 B.C. With this historical background, the superscription "of Asaph" can be understood not as designating an individual but as a reference to a category of temple singers, as was the case after the Exile (cf. Neh. 11:22).

74:1-8. Destruction of the Sanctuary. The psalm begins abruptly with the question of why God has abandoned Israel forever. The question refers to God's apparent rejection of Israel that resulted in the destruction of the temple. The Lord is invited to lift His steps toward the perpetual ruins; that is, to direct His attention to the temple and to see what is happening to Mount Zion, where He had dwelt (vv. 2–3) and which is now desolated. Verses 4–9 describe the destruction in detail as the Babylonians set up their military standards or banners (*'ot*), which usually bore the sacrilegious symbols of foreign gods. This is set in striking contrast to the Judeans who do not see signs (*'ot*) anymore, for there are no more prophets (v. 9). Not only has God abandoned His people, He is not sending them prophetic messages. The Babylonians break, smash, and burn God's sanctuary, destroying all the places of worship (lit. "appointed places of God"). This indicates that other places of congregational gatherings (Heb. *mo'ed*, "meeting-place"), existed in Judah at this time.

74:9-17. How Long? The second section of the psalm is also introduced by a series of questions. Since there is not a prophet to answer the question of how long the situation will continue (v. 9), the questions are directed to God (v. 10). They are not only a request for God to look at the destruction but also a call for Him to act and destroy the enemy (v. 11) as He had done in the past. References are made to the experience of the Exodus, the crossing of the Red Sea, and Leviathan, which is an allusion to the power of Egypt (cf. Is. 30:7 which uses another name for the sea monster, "Rahab," and connects it to Egypt; see "Behemoth," p. 652, and "Leviathan," p. 654). The psalmist goes as far back as Creation to underline God's power (vv. 16–17).

74:18-23. Final Plea. The psalm concludes with an urgent plea for Yahweh to act, suggesting that those who destroyed the sanctuary have ultimately reviled and blasphemed His name. The image of God's people is that of a helpless dove that is about to be devoured by wild beasts. Most English translations follow the LXX *theriois* ("wild beasts") here as a clarification of the Hebrew MT, which has *khayyat* ("living thing," "companies," or "animals," but not necessarily "wild"). This image is used to depict their frailty and their need for divine action (v. 19). There will be moments in history when the forces of evil seem to be triumphant and we experience God's silence, but the message remains clear: God's justice will prevail.

75:1-10
Deliverance

The "proper time" (*mo'ed*, "appointed time" or "meeting place") serves to answer the questions of "how long" and "why" in the previous two psalms where the word was used to describe the meeting places destroyed by the attackers (cf. 74:4, 8). The psalm praises God for His deliverance through judgments that come at the appropriate time. While it is possible to connect the impending destruction of Babylon at the end of the Exile with the writing of the psalm, especially based on its connections to the book of Jeremiah (cf. Jer. 25:15-29; 48:25-26), there are other occasions in the history of Israel (e.g., the deliverance from the Assyrians in 701 or 689/8 B.C.) that would fit the tone of the poem. The tune "Do Not Destroy" has also been used for Psalms 57–59.

75:1-6. Doxology and Judgment. A congregational praise at the beginning of the poem expresses thanks to God for His wonderful works and the nearness of His Name. This declaration contrasts with the emphasis of the preceding psalm on the question of God's absence. The change to first-person speech affirms that God's judgment comes at His appointed proper time (v. 2), which does not always coincide with human expectations (cf. Hab. 2:3). The effects of Yahweh's judgment are felt by the earth and its people (v. 3). Twice the arrogant and wicked people are warned to not lift up their horns (vv. 4–5). The horn is here a symbol of human strength (cf. Ps. 18:2) accompanied by arrogant defiance (lit. an "arrogant" or "stiff" neck). This self-exaltation lacks a real foundation (v. 6) and was the cause for the fall of Nebuchadnezzar (Dan. 4).

75:7–10. God is Judge. This is a didactic reflection about God as Judge (v. 7) written in the third person. God's wrath is represented by the image of a cup (cf. Ps. 60:3; Is. 51:17, 22) that is poured out on all the wicked of the earth (vv. 7–8; see "The Wrath of God," p. 918). This leads to praises expressed in the first person (v. 9), followed by another first person statement, this time by God, that picks up the symbol of the horn (v. 10). The constant change of perspectives may point to the liturgical usage of this psalm. God's timetable is always perfect, and what may appear to be delayed judgments are opportunities for grace.

76:1–12
Zion Saved

Psalm 76 has been associated with the deliverance of Jerusalem during the Assyrian attack under Sennacherib in 701 B.C. (or on his second campaign to Judah in 689/8 B.C., as some scholars have suggested; cf. 2 Kin. 19; Is. 36–39). The LXX makes that explicit by adding "to the Assyrians" in the superscription of the poem. It is a victory song for Zion that echoes Psalms 46–48 and describes God in His dwelling place in Zion, which is the focus of the Asaph psalms.

76:1–3. God in Zion. The usage of "Salem" (v. 2) as the ancient name for Jerusalem (cf. Gen. 14:18) before its conquest by David recalls the past saving acts of God that made Judah, Israel, His tabernacle/tent in Jerusalem into a place where He could be known (v. 1). It is the place where Yahweh as a Warrior broke arrows, shields, and swords (v. 3). This thought provides a smooth transition to the next section.

76:4–9. Deliverance. Yahweh's sovereignty and majesty are described in this section by recounting His deliverance from valiant, mighty warriors. Verse 4 mentions mountains filled with game or prey. The reference is to the result of the victory that precedes this verse and that left the hills around Jerusalem replenished with spoils of war that were ready to be plundered (v. 5). In line with the historical occasion, v. 6 portrays how the Assyrian army, with their chariots and horses, were caused to lie still as though sleeping. (The terminology and mention of Jacob echo the deliverance from Egypt; cf. Ex. 15). God rendered judgment from heaven (v. 8), delivering not only Jerusalem but all the 'anaw (poor," "afflicted," "humble," "meek"; vv. 8–9).

76:10–12. Praise. Victory leads to praises to the point that God's wrath directed against human rage and rebellion results in His praise—even Assyria needs to recognize that God is awesome and to be feared (vv. 11–12). At the ultimate manifestation of God on the arena of human history the superpowers of this world will indeed melt away.

77:1–20
God of Ages Past

In similar fashion to Psalm 73, the problem the psalmist is experiencing is resolved once he acquires a divine perspective from the sanctuary (v. 13). This takes place when he looks back at the wondrous deeds of God when He led His people out of Egypt. In looking back, the distress that the poet is experiencing is put into proper perspective and he can once more believe in God's guidance for his life. Psalms 77–80 recall God's historical deeds on behalf of Israel.

77:1–9. Lament and Questions. The psalmist finds himself in deep sorrow. He cries to God qoli. Some translations have rendered this as "[with] my voice" and some as "aloud," while others leave the word untranslated, as it might seem to create a redundancy. What else would one cry out with? This poetic idiom is clearly an audible expression of distress. The reference to "voice" or "sound" is also mentioned in v. 18, thus forming an inclusio. Verses 2–6 describe the trouble the psalmist is experiencing. It is an existential trouble so intense that his spirit became weak and overwhelmed (v. 3). He does not find sleep during the night (v. 4), and he meditates, earnestly trying to understand (v. 6). In his distress he raises six questions to God (vv. 7–9), climaxing in a question concerning whether God has shut out His khesed ("mercy," "faithful love," "compassion"; v. 10).

77:10–12. Reflections. These questions are interrupted by a contrastive section, which introduces some reflections that are centered on the root zakar ("to remember"), used twice in v. 11. By remembering Yahweh's wondrous actions, displayed from ancient times, the psalmist tries to find answers to his anguished questions.

77:13–20. God's Way. Understanding God's way begins in His sanctuary (cf. Ps. 73:17). Verse 13 says that God's way is baqqodesh. This has been translated as "holy" (i.e., God's way is "holy"; lit. "in holiness") but can also be translated as conveying the idea that God's way is "in the sanctuary" (*qodesh* can mean "holiness" or "sanctuary"). The psalm has now turned to a second-person speech, addressing God directly and recounting His deliverance of Israel (v. 15) from Egypt. The language and imagery strongly resemble that of the Song of the Sea (Ex. 15). After the description of Yahweh's theophany, the psalm abruptly moves to an image of the divine Shepherd leading His people like a flock by the hand of Moses and Aaron (v. 20). God in this psalm is One who listens to our most desperate cries screamed out in anguish during the long hours of a sleepless and threatening night, and He is able to lead us on through the darkness as He has powerfully done in the past.

78:1–72
God in History

This epic psalm is the second largest poem in the Psalms after Psalm 119. As its predecessor, it records God's miraculous interventions in the history of Israel, covering in more detail the period from the Exodus to the time of David. There are verbal and thematic links between Psalm 77 and 78 (e.g., "Most High"; vv. 17, 35, 56 // 77:10; as well as the Exodus motif). It is a historical psalm that reviews the history of Israel to provide a rationale for the current situation of the people (cf. Pss. 105–106; 135–136 for other historical psalms). The failure of Ephraim (vv. 9–11) at the outset of the poem (following the introduction in vv. 1–8), his rejection, and the election of Judah and David at the conclusion of the psalm (vv. 65–72) indicate how the psalm is legitimizing the Davidic monarchy. The *maskil* ("contemplation" or "instruction") in the title underlines the didactic nature of the psalm.

78:1–8. Wisdom Introduction. The psalmist invites the people to listen to his *torah* ("law" or "instruction"). Verses 2–7 go back to Deuteronomy 6:7: God gave the *torah* to Israel and commanded the ancestors to teach their children (v. 5). The instruction has multiple purposes—that the children would remember God's works, keep His commands, and not be stubborn and rebellious like their ancestors (vv. 7–8). The motif of rebellion follows throughout the whole psalm, contrasting God's wondrous deeds with Israel's repeated rebellion.

78:9–11. Ephraim's Failure. Ephraim's unwillingness to participate in a military battle (cf. Judg. 1; 12:2; 1 Chr. 7:20–24) might provide the background to this section. It is also possible that the "day of battle" (v. 9) refers to the Assyrian conquest of northern Israel (Ephraim; see Hos. 10:11–14). Whatever the occasion it might have been, Ephraim's failure is connected to his rejection and the election of Judah (vv. 65–72). The central part of the psalm (vv. 12–64) moves back and forth between God's deeds and Israel's rebellion.

78:12–32. Exodus and Rebellion in the Wilderness. This section begins with the wonders God accomplished during the Exodus as He divided the sea and led them with the cloud (vv. 12–14). However, they continued to sin and rebel against the Most High in the wilderness (v. 17) in spite of all the provisions God gave them: water (v. 20), "manna" (v. 24), and meat (v. 27).

78:33–43. God's Grace. At the center of the psalm, the psalmist recalls how God disciplined Israel until they finally sought and diligently returned to Him The section goes back and forth between a halfhearted return and rebellion, underlining the fact that God repeatedly turned His anger away because He was merciful and compassionate and He forgave their iniquities (v. 38). As in the previous psalm (77:11), the verb *zakar* ("remember") plays an important role in this section, occurring three times. First, they remembered that God was their Rock (v. 35), then God remembered that they were but flesh (v. 39), and finally they forgot His power (v. 42) and returned to their own ways.

78:44–64. Ten Plagues and Rebellion in the Promised Land. In order to counteract the lack of memory on Israel's part, the psalmist returns once more to the time of the Exodus, listing the plagues that preceded it. The list is neither complete (plagues 3, 6, and 9 are missing) nor in sequence (plague 5 [livestock in v. 48] follows plague 8 [hail in v. 47]). The point here is neither chronology nor completeness but bringing back to memory the wondrous acts of Yahweh as He guided them in the wilderness like a flock of sheep (v. 52; cf. 77:20). The remainder of the section (vv. 54–64) returns again to the topic of rebellion, condensing Israel's history from the conquest of the promised land to Shiloh (v. 60), where the sanctuary was located for about 300 years during the time of the Judges (cf. Josh. 18:10; Judg. 18:31; 1 Sam. 4:3). In reaction to Israel's renewed rebellion (vv. 56–58), God abandoned the sanctuary of Shiloh and handed

His glory into the hands of the enemy—a reference to the capture of the ark of the covenant by the Philistines (1 Sam. 4; see "Shiloh," p. 920).

78:65–72. David's Election. As the psalm ends with the continuous rebellion of Israel, God begins to react like a man awaking from sleep (v. 65). He rejects the tribe of Ephraim (v. 67), but chooses the tribe of Judah, Mount Zion (v. 68), and David, His servant (v. 70), to shepherd His people (v. 71). The previous psalm concluded with the peaceful image of Moses and Aaron shepherding Israel, while this one closes with David shepherding God's people. After centuries of turmoil and rebellion, there is peace once more through the shepherd-king. There is spiritual safety in remembering how God has led His people in the past.

79:1–13
The Temple in Ruins

The content of this Asaph psalm aligns itself with Psalm 74 by referring to the destruction of the temple during the Babylonian attack under Nebuchadnezzar in 586 B.C. It also connects with Psalm 78 in that the previous psalm ends with the election of David and Jerusalem, whereas Psalm 79 begins with the destruction of the city. All three psalms are linked by the otherwise infrequently used *nakhalah* ("inheritance"; 74:2; 78:55, 62, 71; 79:1).

79:1–9. Destruction and Confession of Sin. Jerusalem and the holy temple have been destroyed by the nations (*goyim*; v. 1). The reference to the heaps of ruins in Jerusalem echoes Jeremiah's description of its capture (Jer. 26:18; Mic. 3:12). A triple question concerning the extent of God's punishment (v. 5; cf. 89:46) introduces a section that climaxes in a petition for atonement for sins (v. 9). The verb *kipper*, as the technical term for expiation in the OT, has also been at the center of the previous psalm (78:38; cf. 49:7; 65:3; see Leviticus: Introduction).

79:10–13. Vengeance on the Oppressor. The psalmist asks for a sevenfold return of calamity on the aggressors (v. 12); and as in the two previous psalms, he uses the peaceful imagery of the shepherd in an expression of praises (v. 13). While Psalm 78 dealt with the divine rejection of leaders from the northern tribes, Psalm 79 deals with God's punishment of Judah that ended the Davidic dynasty elected by God. Divine election does not preclude the possibility of rebellion or rejection.

80:1–19
A Prayer for Ephraim

The divine rejection of Ephraim in Psalm 78 still echoes through the reading of this psalm, which connects through the use of terminology similar to the previous psalm. The "Shepherd of Israel" is requested to once more lead his flock, identified as Joseph, Ephraim, Benjamin, and Manasseh (vv. 1–2). After the rejection of Israel (Ps. 78) and the destruction of Judah (Ps. 79), this prayer asks for restoration as expressed in three refrains that irregularly intersect the poem (vv. 3, 7, 19). The expression referring to God's shining face is reminiscent of the Aaronic Benediction (Num. 6:24–26) and expresses the need for God's blessings. This psalm "of Asaph" is set to the tune of "The Lilies of the Covenant."

80:1–7. Shepherd: How Long? The initial section of this psalm describes God as the divine Shepherd who is requested to restore His people, in this case the northern tribes. The reference to God's residing between the cherubim (v. 1) is in line with the theological focus of the Asaph psalms on the sanctuary as God's dwelling place. The section concludes with the refrain asking God to restore Israel, make His face shine on them, and save them (v. 3). The invocation is followed by the same question—regarding how long God's anger will last—that marked the confessional section of the previous psalm (cf. Ps. 79:5). Israel has become a source of derision for their neighbors; contention with them leads to ridicule (v. 6). The second refrain is slightly longer than the first one, adding another divine appellation: *'elohim tseba'ot* ("God Almighty" or "God of hosts/armies"), which alludes to the image of Yahweh as a Warrior.

80:8–19. Israel as Vineyard. The familiar image of Israel as a vineyard (cf. Is. 5:1–7; Hos. 10:1) serves as the theme for the final section of the psalm. God brought a vine out of Egypt (v. 8). This alludes (as in Psalm 78) to the experience of the Exodus, and He caused it to take deep root in the land during the conquest (v. 9). As in the Song of the Vineyard (Is. 5), its hedges are broken down (v. 12) and damaged by wild animals, so the vine is burned and cut down (v. 16)—all imagery which reflects the devastating situation of the nation. The psalm concludes with an appeal for restoration and the promise of future faithfulness, followed by the third refrain adding to the divine name (v. 19).

The irregular stanzas of the poem grow longer as the increasingly longer refrain reflects the growing intensity of the anguish and prayer for restoration. It is good to read Psalms 78 and 80 together and to understand that God's rejection at one point does not prevent the possibility of future restoration. Hope is always present with the God of hope (cf. Rom. 15:13; cf. Jer. 29:11).

81:1–16
Listen!

As in the previous psalm, Joseph's experience in Egypt is singled out in this festival hymn, still recited today during the Jewish New Year's festival. Repeatedly the poem urges the people to "listen" (*shama'*; vv. 5, 8[2x], 11, 13) to what God has to say. This is a psalm of Asaph (see commentary on 50:1–23).

81:1–5. Festive Summons. The psalm begins with an invitation to worship accompanied by timbrel, harp, and trumpet (vv. 2–3). The specific time for worship is connected to the New Moon, perhaps the reference is to the Festival of Trumpets that introduced the ten-day period of repentance up to Yom Kippur, the Day of Atonement. The reason for celebrating this festival goes back to the time of Joseph (v. 5), when God went against the land of Egypt.

81:6–16. God Speaks. The change in person at the end of the v. 5 indicates that this line should be read as part of the next section, in which God speaks (lit. "I heard lips I did not know"). The statement refers to God listening to a cry for deliverance from a people (Israel) who did not have a relationship with Him. Verses 6–10 describe how God delivered Israel from the burden of slavery and the testing experience at the waters of Meribah (v. 7; cf. Ex. 17:1–7; Num. 20:13; Ps. 78:20). The giving of the law at Sinai with thunder (v. 7) is mentioned and followed by an allusion to the *shema'* ("hear") from Deuteronomy 6:4. The first two commandments of the Decalogue are also mentioned (vv. 8–10). The historical reality is that Israel did not listen, and now the Lord expresses His own pain (vv. 13–14). If Israel had listened, they would have had victory and well-being (vv. 14–16). The Lord would have provided for them, not just water from the rock, as in Meribah, but the best and purest food that can be imagined. God's yearning desire for His people to listen and walk in His ways continues to ring through the ages down to His children at the time of the end. It reminds us that listening to Him is also serving Him.

82:1–8
Judging the Judges

This Asaph psalm turns the focus from a nation that does not listen to its leaders and judges who rule unjustly. Crucial for understanding the psalm is the usage of *'elohim* ("gods") at the end of v. 1, which can designate human "judges" holding positions of divinely ordained authority among the people of Israel (Ex. 21:6; 22:8–9; cf. 7:1). Verses 1 and 8 serve as an *inclusio* for the poem, describing God as the supreme Judge over the earth.

82:1. God Judging the Judges. The psalm begins with a description of God standing in the *ba'adat 'el*. This term can be understood as God's divine council or alternatively as a superlative expression ("the highest assembly"); see 36:6. In either case, the phrase would refer to the highest council where God presides as the divine Judge.

82:2–7. Unjust Judges. Following this ideal perspective, an appeal is made to those who judge unjustly (v. 2). This is explained in terms of defending the poor and fatherless as well as the disadvantaged (vv. 3–4), whose rights have been violated by corrupt judgments (cf. Lev. 19:15; Deut. 24:17). As a result of the unjust legal decisions the foundations of the earth are tottering (v. 5). The expression "you are gods" (v. 6) should be interpreted in terms of v. 1 as referring to human judges who will eventually fall from their supreme height when God judges them. Jesus supported this understanding of the phrase (John 10:34–36).

82:8. God Judging the Earth. The final line of the poem connects to its beginning by asking God to judge the earth in the absence of just earthly judges (v. 8). It is most unfortunate that those appointed by God to care for the needy in the political and religious arena have often used their positions to abuse and exploit them. The world would be a better place if we cared for each other as God cares for all.

83:1–18
The Conspiracy of Nations

A unique conspiracy of ten surrounding nations against Israel (vv. 6–8) is at the center of this last

Asaph psalm. The number represents not necessarily a specific historical alliance but the totality of the threat under which God's people lived for most of the OT period. The mention of Assyria, which concludes the list, could point to the volatile events of the late eighth century B.C., resulting in the deportation and end of the northern tribes.

83:1–8. The Crisis. Following a plea for God to not keep silent any longer (v. 1), His silence is contrasted with the noise of Israel's enemies (v. 2) who formed a shrewd confederacy of conspiracy (vv. 2–5). The list in vv. 6–8 consists mainly of relatives. Ammon, Moab, Edom, the Ishmaelites, the Hagrites, Gebal (Byblos or a mountainous territory in Edom), the Amalekites, and Israel's immediate neighbors (Philistia and Tyre) were all aggressors at different stages in history (though never all at the same time). The superpower of Assyria completes the list and serves as a climax of the anti-Israelite coalition. The closer hostile relatives, the descendants of Lot, were actually strengthened by this archenemy.

83:9–12. God's Interventions in the Past. The psalmist now mentions famous events from the history of Israel, mainly from the time of the Judges (Judg. 4–5; 7:25; 8:5–21), to describe how God acted in the past in comparable situations. Interestingly, the seven names that are mentioned in connection with God's past victories (Midian, Sisera, Jabin, Oreb, Zeeb, Zebah, Zalmunna; vv. 9–11) anticipate the failure of the ten nation coalition.

83:13–18. God, Please Do It Again! Based on these victorious experiences, the psalm now moves to a plea. Using metaphors from nature (vv. 13–15), God is asked to punish the enemies so that they will be disgraced and terrified forever and will finally acknowledge the supremacy of God as "the Most High over all the earth" (v. 18). This divine epithet has been an important part of the vocabulary of the Asaph psalms (cf. Pss. 73:11; 77:11; 78:17, 35, 56; 82:6; 83:18) and answers the theological question found throughout them concerning the location of God in the tumult of history: He is still the Most High over all the earth.

84:1–12
Just to Be in Your House!

This is the first poem of the four Korah psalms in Book 3. In terms of content it is close to Psalms 42–43, also Korahite, expressing an existential longing for the tabernacle and its altars. We also read about pilgrimage, as in the pilgrim psalms (Pss. 120–134), and a longing for the temple, suggesting that the author was temporarily removed from access to the temple, as was the case during David's exile from Jerusalem. On the superscription *gittit*, or "instrument of Gath," see Psalm 8:1.

84:1–7. Longing for the Temple. The psalm opens with an existential longing for the temple as the psalmist faints for the courts of the Lord (v. 2). The image of the sparrow that has found a home in the temple precincts (v. 3) is most likely a metaphor for the psalmist that likens him to a defenseless bird that is hunted as prey and longs for a safe haven (cf. Ps. 11). In like manner, the altars mentioned represent a safe haven (vv. 3–4). The psalm moves to the image of a person in whose heart are the pilgrim highways to Zion (v. 5) approaching the temple through the valley of *baka'*, a place otherwise unknown in the OT. Some versions translate it as "valley of balsam" because *baka'* is used as a plural noun for what are variously referred to in translation as "balsam," "poplar," or "mulberry trees" (cf. 2 Sam. 5:23–24; 1 Chr. 14:15–16). It could also be understood as a verbal form, the "valley of weeping," since the term is related to the verb for "weeping." This would coincide with the experience of David making his way back to Jerusalem and the temple with tears but trusting in the promise that each one will appear before God in Zion (vv. 5–7).

84:8–12. Prayer. The poem turns into a prayer asking God to look upon the face of His anointed (i.e., look upon the king with favor; v. 9). The desire to be in the temple is expressed through two striking comparisons: a day in God's courts is better than a thousand anywhere else. It is also better for the king to be a doorkeeper in the house of God than to live in the tents of the wicked (v. 10). The final metaphor of God as a sun and shield (v. 11) is evocative of God's life-sustaining and protective characteristics and does not necessarily connect with ANE worship of sun-deities (e.g., the Assyrian sun-god Shamash). The Messiah is called the Sun of Righteousness in Malachi 4:2. The sevenfold mention of both divine names, *'elohim* and *yahweh*, in this short psalm demonstrates the deep longing of the psalmist to be in the presence of God.

85:1–13
Shalom

A common theme running through this Korah psalm is expressed through five occurrences of the verbal root *shub* ("return," "repent," "bring back"; vv. 1, 3, 4, 6, and 8). The psalm moves from thanksgiving (vv. 1–3) to plea (vv. 4–7) and finally to a prophetic vision of restoration. The restoring of Jacob (v. 1) could be connected to the return from the Babylonian Exile but also to other historical situations in the OT that involved restoration.

85:1–7. Return and Restoration. The psalm begins with a recollection of Yahweh's deeds in the past as He restored Jacob. The noun *shebut* ("captivity"), preceded by the verb *shub* ("bring back," "return") has been translated by some as referring to God bringing back captives from Babylon. However, it is possible to render the phrase idiomatically (as some translations have) as "restoring the fortunes" or "restoring the prosperity" of Jacob (cf. 14:7; Job 42:10 where the same phrase appears and which did not involve literal captivity). The return is based on the divine forgiveness of the people's sins, which had led to their difficulties. While God has made a return possible, the psalmist still asks for complete restoration and revival, bringing an end to God's anger (v. 4). In contrast to divine wrath, a specific request for Yahweh's *khesed* ("mercy" or "unfailing love") and salvation concludes this section.

85:8–13. Peace. The final section of the psalm turns the psalmist's attention to what God is saying (v. 8). In this way, God's utterances take on a prophetic element. The first thing God speaks is *shalom* ("peace") to His people. In the Bible, this word for peace designates a state of well-being that encompasses our relationship with God, fellow humans, and the natural environment. The following lines contain a list of theological keywords with surprising metaphors: *khesed* ("mercy," "faithful love," or "grace") and *'emet* ("truth" or "faithfulness") have met together; righteousness and peace have kissed as loving companions (v. 10). Further, *'emet* ("truth" or "faithfulness") shall spring out of the earth, like a tree that grows and flourishes. These are key characteristics of God that occur together in Yahweh's self-revelation recorded in Exodus 34:6–7. The result of the restorative process is that the land will yield its produce. The psalm ends with the beautiful image of righteousness

walking before God to prepare a way for His footsteps. Full restoration includes all spheres of human life and we can experience it when God's footsteps become our pathways.

86:1–17
A Model Prayer

The only psalm in Book 3 that is explicitly associated with David is basically an anthology of other prayers (e.g., v. 1 // 40:17; 31:2; 102:1; v. 4 // 25:1) and verses found throughout the OT (e.g., Ex. 34). The psalm has been likened to the Lord's Prayer, which put together a variety of requests to form a model prayer. The poem is punctuated by the causal conjunction *ki* ("for," "because"; vv. 1–4, 7, 10, 13, 17), which provides the rationale for David's requests.

86:1–7. Invocation. The first section of the psalm is framed by a plea for God to listen and answer (vv. 1, 6–7), including further pleas to save and be merciful to him (vv. 2–3). Every plea is motivated by a different rationale that focuses on the psalmist's needs or, by way of contrast, on God's characteristics as found in Exodus 34:6–7 (e.g., vv. 1 and 5).

86:8–10. Central Praise. The central section of the psalm breaks out into universal praise, which also has an *inclusio* structure like the previous section. Verses 8 and 10 describe the exclusivity and superiority of God and His deeds (cf. Ex. 15:11). This doctrinal proposition is most accurately expressed in the context of worship and doxology when all the nations will come and worship before the Lord (v. 9).

86:11–13. Change Me! As a response to the preceding universal praise, the psalmist moves to the individual and inward realm, asking God to teach him (cf. 27:11; 119:33) and give him a sincere, undivided heart to fear His name. A divided heart cannot serve God completely (cf. Deut. 6:5; Jer. 32:39), but a united heart praises God (v. 12), echoing the universal praises of the previous section.

86:14–17. Protect Me! A plea for protection from a group of ruthless, violent men concludes the psalm, although it is punctuated by expressions of trust in God, which involve more explicit references to Yahweh's self-revelation at Mount Sinai (v. 15) than the one used in v. 5. It echoes the exact wording of Exodus 34:6, although the original *yahweh* is replaced with 'adonai ("my Lord"), which reflects the liturgical reading of the divine name in worship. The final request is for a sign, a visible manifestation of Yahweh's power, like the signs that preceded the Exodus (cf. Ps. 78:48). The sequence of this model prayer is instructive, as only the changed heart that calls on Yahweh in worship and praise is ready to bring requests before God.

87:1-7
Born in Zion

The choice of Zion as God's dwelling place (vv. 1-3) and its future role as the exalted birthplace of nations (vv. 4-6) provides structure to this short Korah Psalm; its somewhat terse language takes on the form of prophetic speech. The psalm aligns itself with utterances found in the prophetic books about the messianic kingdom conditioned by the faithfulness of Israel to the covenant (e.g., Is. 60-62). The universal character of this psalm connects well with the universal praise of the previous psalm.

87:1-3. God's Election of Zion. God has founded Zion (cf. Is. 14:29-32; note the mention of the Philistines in Isaiah's message) and loves the gates of Zion more than all the other dwellings of Jacob (v. 2). God's preference for Zion is expressed through the "glorious things" that God speaks about it.

87:4-7. Glorious Things. These verses present three sayings of Yahweh about the city, each stating that "this one was born (in Zion)." It is thus a divine birth register that records Zion as the aspired birthplace not only for Israel but for the surrounding nations. They include Rahab, (a name for Egypt; v. 4; cf. Is. 30:7) and Babylon, covering both the hostile superpowers south and north of Israel, plus other enemies: Philistia, Tyre (already mentioned in the conspiracy of the nations in Psalm 83:2-5) and Ethiopia or Cush (modern Sudan). These nations are also mentioned in Isaiah's oracles (Is. 13-23).

The psalmist makes it clear that this is a matter of divine election, as the Most High Himself will establish Zion and record the inhabitants in His register (vv. 5-6). Verse 7 contains an instruction for the musical performers of this psalm to sing about all their springs being found in "you." This "you" ending the line can be understood as referring to Zion, which then compares the birth of peoples to springs of water that gush forth from Zion. While Zion, on account of Israel's unfaithfulness, never became

what this psalm envisions, the Israel of faith can claim a citizenship in the heavenly Jerusalem (Phil. 3:20).

88:1-18
Utter Darkness

The last of the Korah Psalms does not end on a high note; on the contrary, it appears to express utter darkness reflecting a time of physical and mental pain in the life of the psalmist. Death is ever present. A plethora of words appear throughout the poem that can be associated with the experience of a fading life (e.g. "grave," "pit," "dead," "slain," "depths," "destruction."). The last word of the psalm in Hebrew is *makhshak* ("darkness"), which provides a woeful climax to this sad poem. It is a meaningful psalm for those moments in life when the darkness surrounding us seems to be impenetrable. The tune *"makhalat le'annot"* was also used in the title of Psalm 53. "Heman the Ezrahite" was a Korahite (1 Chr. 6:33) and is mentioned among the temple singers appointed by David (1 Chr. 15:16-19). The chronological proximity of David and Heman could indicate that the temple poet wrote this psalm while contemplating the experience of the old and dying king.

88:1-9. Affliction. The psalm begins with a plea for God to turn/incline His ear—a metaphorical image of listening closely. It is clear that we are dealing with a life-threatening situation that will be laid out in detail in the following verses. In his physical and mental affliction, the psalmist finds himself near to death and the grave (v. 3). It is replete with morbid imagery as he experiences his situation as God's wrath rolling over him like waves (v. 7). The psalmist finds himself in a pit, in darkness (v. 6), from which he is unable to escape (v. 8). He can only call and stretch out his hand in despair. Job's description of his experience bears a close similarity to these dark lines (cf. Job 10:21-22).

88:10-12. Questions and More Questions. Several rhetorical questions punctuate the center of this psalm and emphasize a common topic—being among the dead (*repa'im;* v. 10). This clearly refers to the lifeless human form and not to "ghosts" or "departed spirits" (as some versions translate). There is no recognition of God's wonders (v. 10); it reflects the belief that when a person dies, all physical, mental, and spiritual activities come to an end (cf. Eccl. 9:5-6). Interestingly, the question mentions divine characteristics such as love (*khesed*), faithfulness, and righteousness (vv. 11-12) that seem to penetrate the darkness with the light of hope.

88:13-18. In the Morning. The phrase "in the morning" (v. 13) introduces the last section of the psalm, but instead of referring to God's favor that so often comes in the morning (cf. Pss. 5:3; 30:5; 46:5), there is only a return to suffering. God's terrors (v. 15) are surrounding the psalmist all day long like a flood of water (v. 17). The psalm ends in darkness (v. 18). There is not always a bright morning after the darkness, not then and not now. However, one can find encouragement in the fact that this prayer is part of the Psalms and God hears this type of prayer as much as the hymns of praises surrounding this psalm. In fact, the psalmist affirms from the outset that the Lord is the God who provides salvation for him (v. 1). Indirectly, the believer is invited to continue to hope in the Lord in every situation of life.

89:1-52
A Covenant Psalm

This is the third longest psalm (after Psalms 119 and 78) and concludes Book 3. Its repeated focus on "Your anointed" (vv. 20, 38, 51) echoes the portal of the Psalms (i.e., Ps. 2), which describes the anointed as God's answer to the plotting of the hostile nations. While the Davidic covenant stands at the beginning of this psalm, it ends with an uncertain outlook into the future of David's descendants, especially in view of the national disaster at the beginning of the Exile and the destruction of Jerusalem in 586 B.C. This event has been associated with the writing of this poem and agrees with the approximate chronological setting of Book 3, which concludes the monarchic period of Israel and Judah.

The sevenfold mention of God's *khesed* ("lovingkindness," "mercy," "faithfulness") found throughout this psalm (vv. 1, 2, 14, 24, 28, 33, 49) not only unifies the poem but also points to the underlying eternal basis of the covenant, namely, God's continuous faithfulness. As a frame, the poem mentions God's mercy and covenant with David at the beginning and end (vv. 2-3, 49). "Ethan the Ezrahite" is mentioned only here in the Psalms; as with Heman in the previous psalm, he was a temple sage and musician (1 Kin. 4:31).

89:1-4. Introduction. The introduction to the psalm is an invitation to sing of the *khasde* ("mercies," "faithful love," "kindnesses") of the Lord based on two historical deeds of God: Creation (alluded to in the mention of the heavens in v. 2) and God's covenant with His servant David (v. 3). There is an antiphonal change of speaker between vv. 2 and 3, moving from worshiper to God. Other psalms have connected David's election with the Exodus (e.g., Ps. 78), but here the psalmist concludes Book 3 with a grand historical sweep from Creation, to David, and to the time after the Babylonian Exile.

89:5-14. God of Creation. Nature lifts up praise to God in the heavens for His faithfulness, emphasizing His sovereignty and wonders (v. 5) manifested in creation and the Exodus (cf. the reference to Rahab in v. 10; 87:4). God created the north, south, east, and west, represented by Tabor and Hermon, mountains in the north of Israel that demarcate the eastern and western extension of the land (v. 12). The section is concluded with the mention of Yahweh's attributes (v. 14; cf. 25:10), which serve as the foundation of the covenant and transition to the next section.

89:15-37. God of Covenant. Verses 15-19 begin this section with a beatitude for those who walk in the light of the Lord's *paneh* ("face," "presence," "countenance"); i.e., they live according to the stipulations of the covenant. Then God speaks and announces the election of His servant David (vv. 20-29), with whom His covenant will be confirmed (v. 28). The blessings of the Davidic covenant also include the permanence of the Davidic line, even if his sons forsake God's law. God will punish them but will remain faithful to His covenant (vv. 30-37).

89:38-51. God's Judgment and Mercy. There is an abrupt change in the poem, introduced by a change in speaker and a contrastive description of God's rejection of and anger with His anointed (v. 38). The final section replaces praises and rejoicing with complaint and mourning, describing the ultimate failure of the monarchy, which contrasts with the permanence of the Davidic covenant and lineage described in the previous section (vv. 38-45). Consequently, the psalm ends with a series of questions elaborating the familiar "How long, LORD?" (v. 46). A plea for God to "remember" the ridicule against His servants (v. 50) provides a glimpse into the desperate historical situation in which Israel found itself at the end of its monarchic period.

89:52. Doxology. The doxology that ends Book 3 stands in sharp contrast to the content of the psalm. It concludes the first macrocollection of Psalms 2–89, which reflects the monarchical period of Israel. The anointed one in Psalm 2 presented God's counterprogram to the machinations of nations, climaxing in David's election as king of Israel. Its failure created the urgent need for a new firm foundation, as well as the Messiah, who has repeatedly come to the fore throughout the first three books of the Psalms. A twofold "amen" confirms that God's plans will continue forever (v. 52).

PSALMS 90—106
BOOK IV

The question of "How long?" near the end of the previous book still rings in the mind of the reader (cf. Ps. 89:46), and Book 4 appears to pick up the question (Ps. 90:13). This book begins its sequence with the only psalm ascribed to Moses. The name of Moses occurs seven times in Book 4, most notably at the end (90:1; 99:6; 103:7; 105:26; 106:16, 23, 32), in comparison to only two occurrences outside of Book 4 (18:17; 77:20). This has led commentators to call it the "Moses book." Thematically, Book 4 begins with a confession of Israel's guilt, a fitting counterpoint to the complaints that mark the end of Psalm 89. After the failure of the monarchy, the search for a rationale for Israel's existence takes us back to the beginning of the nation, when the *torah* was given. Psalms 93–100 provide a central collection within this group that stresses divine kingship as a further basis for the future of Israel. The final psalms of Book 4 (Pss. 103–106) return to Moses and God's blessings in the history of Israel. This effectively underlines the theme of Yahweh as King, creating a positive outlook for the future with a hope centered on the Messiah. There is hope for the Davidic lineage, which seemed to have collapsed by the end of Book 3.

90:1–17
God's Word Remains

This "prayer of Moses the man of God" deliberately returns to the origin of God's people and connects its content to Moses' final speech in Deuteronomy 32–33 (cf. esp. Deut.

33:1, which also uses "Moses the man of God" in the introduction). The poem creates a contrast between God's eternal nature and human brevity, an adequate response in a time of national disaster when socio-political structures are disappearing. Its place and chronological function in the Psalms do not necessarily coincide with the date of composition, yet its content is timeless. Psalms 90–92 form a thematic unit that moves from lament (Ps. 90) to divine promise (Ps. 91) and thanksgiving (Ps. 92) around the topic of long-lasting life under Yahweh's protection.

90:1–12. Past and Present. The poem begins with a wisdom meditation on the eternity of God (vv. 1–2; cf. 93:2) versus the finite nature of human life—God is from everlasting to everlasting (v. 2). The realization that a thousand years in His sight are like yesterday (v. 4) puts into perspective the immediate, but temporary, threat of the Babylonian Exile. Imagery of withering grass (v. 5; cf. 37:2; 103:15; 129:6) completes the idea of God's permanence and human transience. The poem changes now to first-person speech (vv. 7–12), taking the withering grass imagery and applying it to the current situation of God's people (His servants; v. 13) as they are consumed by His anger (v. 7). In contrast to God's thousand years, the brevity of a normal life-span is seventy years (v. 10), a life-span that is shortened by God's anger (v. 11). This can be understood only by a heart of wisdom (v. 12). In a subtle way, Moses (who lived to 120 years; Deut. 34:7) recognized that the extra forty years he lived beyond age eighty were a gift from God. By calling Moses into service at age eighty (Ex. 7:7), when his life should have ended (Ps. 90:10), God was essentially reclaiming him from death.

90:13–17. Future. The call for God to *shubah* (from *shub*, "return," "relent") followed by the question "How long?" connects this psalm to the previous one and to the historical situation of the Exile. God can warn humans to "turn/ return" and then relent from His judgments if they repent and return to Him (cf. Jer. 18:1–8). The constant reference to time units in this psalm (days and years; cf. also the seventy years that coincide with the prophesied time of the Exile) makes one wonder if this psalm describes the ongoing agony of the Exile and an enduring concern for its duration (cf. Dan. 9:2). Meanwhile, the psalm ends with a request to "establish the work of our hands," granting some degree of permanence based on the presence of God's *hadar* ("honor," "glory," "splendor"; v. 16) with His people. The recognition of the fleetingness of our lives invites us to hope for permanency and eternity in the presence of God.

91:1–16
Long Life

The fleetingness of human life in the previous psalm is contrasted here with the promise of "long life" (v. 16) for those who rest in "the shadow of the Almighty" (v. 1). An individual speaks in the first-person viewpoint to affirm his trust in God at the beginning (vv. 1–2), followed by promises of divine protection in third person (vv. 3–13). The psalm finally returns to first person, but as a direct discourse with Yahweh answering the initial petition (vv. 14–16). The change in speakers and roles points to a possible antiphonal use of this psalm in the temple liturgy.

91:1–2. Trust in God. The individual emphasizes from the outset that he trusts in God every day. The shadow of the Almighty and the appellation of God as the Most High (v. 1) introduce temple terminology (cf. 17:8; 36:7; 57:1; 63:7). The psalmist's chief desire is to be in the presence of God to find refuge in Him (v. 2).

91:3–13. Divine Protection. The central section of the psalm is replete with vivid imagery expressing God's protection of those who trust in Him when passing through dangerous situations (vv. 3–8). The situations are increasingly dangerous, including the terrors of the night, arrows (war) of the day, stalking pestilence, and ultimately the destructive plague (vv. 5–6). The repeated movement between night and day expresses the ongoing dimension of the threats, which take on anti-godly or even demonic dimensions. This day/night alternation provides a fourfold contrast to the fourfold mention of God's name in vv. 1–2. The threat climaxes in a beautiful promise of protection, which has carried innumerable readers of this psalm through perils of war and persecution (v. 7). The large numbers amplify God's protecting power in the middle of an overwhelming and dangerous situation. Verses 9–13 return to the initial refuge metaphor and detail how God will protect the individual from all of these perils. Verses 11–12 stand out dramatically for their partial use by Satan during the temptation of Jesus (Matt. 4:6). Satan is the ultimate personification of the anti-godly threats in vv. 5–6. But here the psalmist enlists the ministry of angels, who protect him even from mortally dangerous beasts.

91:14–16. God Promises. The last section of this psalm abruptly changes to God as the subject. Through direct divine discourse, He confirms the protection requested and described in the two previous sections. In addition to that, He provides an answer to the question of the transience of human life raised in the previous psalm. God will give the psalmist a long life (v. 16) and his salvation. Jesus's response to Satan's temptation demonstrates that the intention of this psalm is not to encourage presumptuous gambling with physical and spiritual dangers, but rather to promise true protection for those who continually abide in God. Note also Jesus's implied quotation of v. 13 in Luke 10:19, where He bestows on His disciples authority over demonic forces.

92:1–15
Sabbath Praises

The title of the psalm identifies it as one used on the Sabbath day. It is a unique title within the Psalms that points to its use in the temple. It connects to Psalm 91 by giving thanks for what has been promised in that psalm. It also connects to Psalm 90 in its wise, didactic tone and usage of contrastive imagery.

92:1–3. Invitation to Praise. The poem begins with an invitation for continuous praises on the Sabbath. In Psalm 91, the deathly and demonic threats were felt day and night, but now the psalmist describes the goodness of declaring God's *khesed* ("lovingkindness" or "mercy") in the morning and His faithfulness at night (vv. 1–2). This creates a positive contrast by alluding to the evening and morning sacrifices that marked the Sabbath day. Praises are also expressed through instruments and music. A *nebel* (a ten-stringed instrument, possibly a lute) and the *higgayon* ("resounding music," "harmonious sound," "melody" of the lyre) combined in a kind of "orchestra."

92:4–9. The Wicked Are Like Grass. The psalm's wisdom section begins with repeated references to God's works (vv. 5–6) and their subsequent association with Creation (cf. vv. 12–14). This provides an apt beginning for a poem about the Sabbath. The connection to the Creation narrative is further strengthened by the sevenfold mention of Yahweh in the psalm (vv. 1, 4, 5, 8, 9, 13, 15), which links it to the seven days of Creation. It then moves from the works of Yahweh to the destruction of the wicked. In Psalm 91, humanity was likened to withering grass, but here the wicked spring up like grass that will ultimately be scattered by God (vv. 6–9). This presents an answer to the question "How long?" introduced in Psalm 90:13.

92:10–15. The Righteous Are Like Trees. In contrast to the destruction of the wicked is the exaltation of the righteous, who will flourish as a palm tree and grow as a cedar (v. 12). Instead of dry grass, they bear fruit in old age (v. 14). It is interesting to note the association between tree imagery, the house of the Lord (the temple; v. 13; cf. 52:9), and a description of the fruitful longevity of the righteous in the presence of God (cf. Ps. 1). A further association with Creation might be present here through the imagery of the tree of life as it stood in the middle of Eden. The psalm ends with a reference to Deuteronomy 32:4 and God's righteousness, which provides an adequate rationale for the blessing of longevity the righteous enjoy under the protection of His righteousness. Rootedness in God versus the transiency of human life concludes this group of three psalms and prepares us for the permanence of divine kingship that characterizes the next section of Book 3 (Pss. 93–100).

93:1–5
Yahweh Is King

The divine kingship psalms in Book 4 (Pss. 93–100) are aptly introduced by the programmatic statement "the LORD reigns," which may be translated as "Yahweh is King" (cf. also 97:1; 99:1). The psalm does not have a Hebrew heading, although the LXX connects it liturgically to the "day before the Sabbath" and associates it with David.

93:1–2. Throne Scene. The declaration of Yahweh as King describes Him as dressed with majesty and strength, which denotes His divine splendor, appearance, and readiness to engage in battle. The verb *'azar* ("to gird oneself"), is usually found in a context of preparation for warfare (cf. 2 Sam. 22:40; Ps. 18:39; Is. 8:9). The question of when Yahweh's kingship began is answered in v. 2 by describing His throne as being established from the earliest times (*'az*). He is from *'olam* ("everlasting," "eternity").

93:3–4. Subduing the Nations. Some have suggested that the background for this part of the psalm borrows from the Canaanite mythological battle between the storm-god Baal and Yam, who represented the waters of chaos. A more biblically informed reading recognizes the threefold mention of *nahar* ("rivers," "streams") as referring to nations (see Is. 8:7).

93:5. Palace and Temple. The psalm concludes with a description of God's house adorned with holiness and supported by Yahweh's *'edot* ("statutes," "testimonies"; synonymous to His law; cf. 19:7). The house of the Lord is both palace and temple (cf. 5:7; 26:8). The combination of a reference to God's house and "rivers" is also found in Psalm 36:8, where the imagery connects to the rivers of Eden and sets God's eternal kingship in the context of Creation. While Yahweh as King might not be an easily accessible image in modern times, the sovereignty of God and acknowledgment of His majesty are important matters for Christian believers, who anticipate with hope the consummation of their manifestation in history.

94:1–23
Royal Judge

Psalm 94 provides further information about divine kingship, identifying God as a Judge of justice, who is ready to render punishment (v. 2) and bring onto the wicked the consequences of their sin (v. 23). The psalm lacks any superscription.

94:1–8. The Foolish. The poem begins with the twofold divine epithet *'el neqamot* ("God of vengeance"), followed by a request for Him to rise up as Judge of the earth. The question of how long the wicked will exult creates a strong verbal link to the preceding psalms, especially the beginning of Book 4 (90:13). Verses 4–8 describe the foolishness of the wicked when they break and crush God's people. The mention of the widow, stranger, and fatherless recalls Psalm 10:16–18 and its strong ethical overtones drawing on legal literature from the Pentateuch (cf. Deut. 10:18; 24:17–21; 27:19). It is unclear if the wicked represent oppressing nations or senseless people who think the Lord does not see their sin (vv. 7–8). In v. 7, a shortened form of the divine name (*yah*) is used, which becomes more prevalent in the last two books of the Psalms. The section ends by asking the fools when they will become wise (v. 8).

94:9–15. Wisdom. This didactic wisdom contemplation, similar to Psalms 90 and 92, is a response to the question of v. 8; the mention of nations in v. 10 gives the psalm a universal tone. At the center of this section is a beatitude of wisdom about instruction in God's law (v. 12) followed by a promise of restoration when judgment will return and again be established in righteousness (v. 15).

94:16–23. Personal Petition. Two questions reflect a troubled individual's need for justice and divide this section (vv. 16 and 20), each followed by answers that affirm Yahweh's role in defending the righteous. The reference to the throne of corrupt iniquity in the second question (v. 20) contrasts with Yahweh's throne of the previous psalm. The throne of iniquity gives judgments that are against the law and condemn innocent blood (i.e., condemn the innocent to death; v. 21). Here, Yahweh as Judge is contrasted with a wicked form of justice. The throne of God is also the seat of judgment. For the psalmist, Yahweh is a *misgab* ("fortress," "stronghold," "defense") in this context, perhaps connoting the idea of God as the psalmist's legal defender. The psalm comes full circle with the announcement of the punishment of the wicked (v. 23; cf. vv. 1–2). God as King and Judge are two images found in Daniel 7 in the description of the judgment scene in the heavenly sanctuary. "Thrones" are set up there and the investigative judgment begins. This psalm reminds us that Yahweh is our defense.

95:1–11
Invitation to Praise

This royal thanksgiving psalm invites God's people to sing to the Lord as a response to His wonderful works (vv. 1–7c). It then exhorts the people to listen to God's word and learn from the negative experiences of the heart-hardened generation in the desert after the Exodus (vv. 7d–11). The contrasting content of these two sections has caused questions about its original unity, but other festal psalms (e.g., Pss. 50 and 81) exhibit a similar twofold structure, whereas the second part is also a direct discourse of Yahweh. Hebrews 4:7 quotes from this psalm and mentions David in connection with the authorship of the poem, although the NT sometimes associates all of Psalms with David.

95:1–7c. Exhortation. The first part of the psalm alternates between exhortation to worship (vv. 1–2, 6) and reasons for worship (vv. 3–5, 7a-c). The exhortations give rare insight into OT worship services. There is an invitation to shout joyfully to Him with *zamir* ("songs," "psalms"; v. 2) but also to bow down and kneel before the "LORD our Maker" (v. 6). The rationale for worship is found in God's work of Creation. We also find two divine metaphors that are familiar in the psalms and are often combined (cf. e.g., Ps. 23), Yahweh as King (v. 3) and Shepherd (v. 7).

95:7d–11. Yahweh Responds. Yahweh's direct discourse picks up where the previous section left off, with the image of God as Shepherd, which connects well with the Exodus experience. Interestingly, the verb *nahal* ("to lead"), appears in both the Shepherd Psalm (Ps. 23:2) and the Exodus poem (Ex. 15:13), describing God as Shepherd during the Exodus. The psalm's unity is indicated through the image of God trying to lead them as a shepherd while they hardened their hearts. Such was the case at Meribah (Ex. 17:7; Num. 20:13), a name that means "contention" or "rebellion." Their attitudes in the latter incident led to forty years (v. 10) of wandering in the wilderness, and that generation did not enter God's rest (v. 11). While in exile years later, Israel looked forward to returning to the promised land and was called to learn from its remote past experiences. Hebrews 4 uses this psalm and issues a similar warning to hear His voice "today" (v. 7c; cf. Heb. 4:7 8). The promise of the Sabbath rest still remains today.

96:1–13
A Universal Call to Worship

This psalm, also called a missionary psalm, expands the invitation to praise found in the previous psalm and broadens it to a universal dimension by including "the nations" (vv. 3, 10) and "peoples" (see vv. 3, 10, 13). It also connects to previous psalms by a reference to divine kingship (cf. 93:1; 95:3; 97:1; 99:1) and the invitation to praise. It is parallel to the psalm recorded in 1 Chronicles 16:23–33, which David composed when the ark of the covenant was brought to Jerusalem. The differences between the two versions can be explained by the liturgical use of the poem in the Psalms.

96:1–6. First Call. Three universal calls to worship run through this poem; the first is issued to all the earth (v. 1). It is a proclamation of God's sovereignty over the natural world. God's people are invited to sing, to proclaim, and to *basar* ("proclaim the good news") of His salvation to the inhabited world (vv. 2–3). The rationale for praise is found in God's sovereignty above all gods (v. 4) manifested through His work of Creation and presence in the sanctuary (v. 6).

96:7–10. Second Call. The second call is directed to the families/tribes of the peoples/ nations (v. 7), and it serves as a response to the proclamation shared in the previous section. Verses 7–8 are a quotation from Psalm 29:1–2, although here the *bene 'elim* ("sons of God," "mighty ones," "heavenly beings") have been replaced with *mishpekhot* ("families," "tribes," "clans"). The response of the people also includes bringing an offering and coming into His courts (v. 8); that is to say, they come to worship God in His temple in Jerusalem and become part of His people. The recognition of universal divine kingship stands behind the central phrase of this group of psalms (Pss. 93–100)—the Lord reigns (v. 10).

96:11–13. Third Call. The call to worship rolls back into the uninhabited world that has witnessed the conversion of the nations. Heavens, earth, sea, and trees all lift up their voices in praises (vv. 11–12). The psalm concludes with the eschatological hope of the coming of the Lord to judge the earth (v. 13). The reference is to the coming of the Messiah and the beginning of His reign of justice (cf. John 5:22; Acts 17:31). The inclusion of creation in the act of worship and its relationship to the conversion of nations are vivid reminders of the role of humanity in the preservation of the natural environment, as the creation also eagerly waits for the revealing of the children/sons of God (Rom. 8:19).

97:1–12
Yahweh Is King

This psalm is similar to Psalms 93 and 99 as it is introduced by the phrase *yahweh malak* ("Yahweh reigns," "Yahweh is King"). The psalm describes the theophany (i.e., the appearance of God's glory) that is often accompanied by dramatic events in nature (cf. Ex. 19:18; Ps. 18:8–16; 77:17–19). Psalm 97 continues where Psalm 96 left off, describing the arrival of the King as He descends from heaven to execute the judgment announced at the end of the previous psalm. The poem is framed by the invitation to rejoice (vv. 1 and 12), first directed to the earth and the righteous, who have been

justified. There is no title for this psalm and no further indication as to the date of composition, except for its thematic connection with the surrounding psalms.

97:1–6. Invitation to Praise and Theophany. Following the universal invitation to praise in v. 1, a theophanic event is described. God's appearance is accompanied by a cloud cover that surrounds Him and serves to protect the human observer (v. 2; cf. Ex. 19:9). Fire, lightning, and intense heat melt the mountains in the presence of the Lord of the earth (v. 5). The usual elements of a thunderstorm are absent (cf. Ps. 77:17–19) and the fire imagery is emphasized, communicating the idea of judgment. The theophany climaxes in a universal declaration of God's righteousness as all the peoples see His glory (v. 6). God's appearance evokes a declarative response because it is impossible to remain indifferent to His coming.

97:7–9. Effects of God's Appearance. The positive effects of the theophany are now contrasted with its consequences on those who worship and serve carved images, emphasizing the sovereignty of God over the other gods (vv. 7 and 9). At the center of this section, the poet quotes Psalm 48:12 but transposes it into an indicative, describing the effects of God's judgments on Zion and Judah as already accomplished. The psalm is less future-oriented but views God's appearance as if it had already happened.

97:10–12. Application and Renewed Invitation. The final section begins with an admonition for those who love the Lord to hate evil. This is followed by deliverance, joy, and gladness for the upright in heart (cf. v. 8). The root *samakh* ("to rejoice") is found four times in the psalm (vv. 1, 8, 11 [as the noun *simkhah*], and v. 12). While a theophany is a dramatic event whose effects are felt negatively by the unrighteous, it is also a moment of intense rejoicing for the righteous, foreshadowing the realization of the Christian hope, the final appearing of God and the eternal joy that will accompany it.

98:1–9
A Second Universal Call to Worship

Psalm 98 has been described as an echo of Psalm 96 as it substantially repeats both beginning and end. In three similar calls to worship (vv. 1–3; 4–6; 7–9), the text moves back and forth between "Israel," the "nations," and the natural "world," focusing on the "salvation of our God" and His judgments as the central reasons for worship.

98:1–3. Invitation to Israel. The first invitation to worship is directed at Israel in the sight of all nations. The combination of the terms *khesed* ("mercy," "grace," "steadfast love") and *'emunah* ("fidelity," "faithfulness") in the psalms is used to demonstrate God's covenantal commitment to His people (cf. 36:5; 40:10; 88:11; esp. 89:2, 3, 24, 33, 49).

98:4–6. Invitation to the Earth. The implications of Yahweh's salvation for all the earth (v. 4) are expressed in a symphonic hymn of praise that recognizes God as King. The instruments of the harp, *khatsotsrah* (a metal trumpet for signaling), and *shopar* ("ram's horn") are associated with temple service (cf. 2 Kin. 12:13; 1 Chr. 16:42) and point to the liturgical dimension of the psalm. The center of praise is thus to be found in the temple.

98:7–9. Invitation to Nature. As the praises grow in concentric movements, the third invitation is directed to the natural world, which joins the singing and instrumental praises. The whole of creation praises God and (like Psalm 96) the psalm climaxes with a universal acknowledgment of Yahweh, who will judge the earth in righteousness (v. 9). The good news of God's salvation concentrically expands, reaching to the end of the world with the hope that everyone would finally praise the Lord (see Ps. 148).

99:1–9
Holy, Holy, Holy!

Like Psalms 93 and 97, this poem is introduced by the phrase *yahweh malak* ("Yahweh reigns," "Yahweh is King"), celebrating once more the divine kingship, this time from the perspective of God's holiness. The threefold refrain referring to God as holy (vv. 3, 5, and 9), which is amplified in each occurrence, divides the psalm into sections. Its historical imagery connects it to the Exodus experience ("Moses and Aaron;" cf. Ex. 15:1–18) as well as the early monarchy represented by the reference to "Samuel."

99:1–3. Yahweh Is King. The first section of the psalm is a song about Yahweh on His throne, dwelling between the cherubim in the holiest of holies (cf. Ps. 80:1). As in Psalm 97, there are elements of theophany present, but this time they are only hinted at (v. 1 reference to trembling of the earth). A universal invitation to praise God for "He is holy" (echoed in v. 5) concludes the section.

99:4–5. Yahweh's Strength. In contrast to ANE god-kings, whose strength was founded on their military power, Yahweh's strength is in His law, with which He has established equity, justice, and righteousness (v. 4). The ideas of king and judge are combined as in the concluding theme of the previous psalm (cf. 98:9). The invitation to worship at His footstool (v. 5) stands in parallel imagery to the cherubim throne of the first section and once more introduces the idea of holiness. The second refrain ("He is holy") is now amplified by the invitation to exalt and worship Him.

99:6–9. Historical Witnesses. There is a sudden change in the psalm, listing three historical personalities from the early history of Israel. The mention of Moses and Aaron (v. 6), both of whom are called priests (Moses is not called a priest outside this psalm, but he ordained Aaron; Lev. 8), associates the poem with the Exodus. The mention of Samuel (v. 6) connects it to the early monarchic period. Both are important key moments of election that form the basis for the future establishment of Israel after the Exile. Moses, Aaron, and Samuel all kept God's *'edot* ("testimonies," "statutes") and the *khoq* ("ordinance") He gave them; thus they shared a common foundation— the law of God. These individuals had to rely on the mercy of Yahweh, who is a forgiving God (v. 8; lit. the "God who lifts up," "who carries"; cf. Ex. 34:7); the verb *nasa'* is also used to denote forgiveness. The final refrain expands the concept of the holiness of God by adding a third and final refrain, "the LORD our God is holy." God's holiness is grounded in His sovereignty (vv. 1–3), His Law (vv. 4–6), and His being experientially known as the forgiving God.

100:1–5
Final Doxology to the King

Psalm 100 concludes the divine kingship psalms (Pss. 93–100) and is similar to the first psalm in this group. The psalm serves as a concluding doxology to this collection even though the word "king" is not used. In its absence there is an abundance of royal terminology (e.g., "serve"; some translate *'abad* as "worship," "gates," "courts"), as well as references to the other psalms in this group. It is a final universal hymn that invites people to worship in the temple of

Yahweh through a series of *seven* imperatives that are concentrically arranged around v. 3b and which describe God as Creator and Sustainer using the metaphor of the shepherd. The superscription marks the psalm as a psalm of thanksgiving, which points to its liturgical usage within the temple service. The psalm has found its way into Christian liturgy as the basis for the widely used doxology "Praise God, from whom all blessings flow."

100:1–3a. First Call. The first call to worship, which comprises the first group of four imperatives, is directed to all the earth. The thankful need to shout joyfully and rejoice in the presence of the enthroned king (cf. 1 Sam. 10:24; Ps. 47:2–3). The nations are to acknowledge that the Lord is God, the universal sovereign.

100:3b. Covenant. The center of the psalm is framed by imperatives on each side and emphasizes the covenant relationship between Yahweh and Israel through creation (God made them) and election using the metaphor of the shepherd—they are His people and the sheep of His pasture (cf. Deut. 26:16–19).

100:4–5. Second Call. A second call to worship using three imperatives invites the universal congregation to enter His gates and His courts (i.e., the temple, which serves as Yahweh's palace where His throne of grace is symbolically represented by the ark of the covenant; v. 4). The inclusiveness of the call is highly significant; it invites the whole world into the temple precincts, a place usually reserved for Israel only. The psalm concludes with a contemplation of Yahweh's goodness, reminiscent of His self-revelation at Sinai (cf. Ex. 34:6). The psalm anticipates the moment when the redeemed ones will enter through the portals of the eternal city to worship their Creator and Redeemer with eternal joy.

101:1–8
How to Rule

Following the group of psalms emphasizing divine kingship (Pss. 93–100), this poem serves as a response of commitment to the principles of divine governance laid out in the previous psalms. This commitment is made by the ruler on behalf of the people. It is the first poem since Psalm 86 that is associated with David in its superscription. Psalms 101–103 have been reognized as the third group of Davidic psalms. While the original authorship fits David's commitment to God, its placement in the Psalms and the absence of any explicit reference to a king may point to its use as a foundation for the governing of a new nation after the Babylonian Exile under God as King.

101:1–4. Personal Commitment. The principles of *khesed* ("steadfast love," "mercy," "grace") and justice are related at the end of the previous psalm. These divine characteristics and guiding principles of the covenant mentioned in this section form the theological basis for governance (cf. Mic. 6:8). The commitment is expressed in the form of a song of praise (v. 1), which provides insight into the use of this psalm during an inauguration ceremony for leadership. The personal commitment of the king is centered on an inner attitude, a heart that is *tamim* (v. 2), a word expressing the idea of completeness, integrity, and straightness (cf. Ps. 15:2). This is contrasted with the psalmist's resolution to abstain from a perverse heart, which is crooked or twisted (v. 4). The realization that sin often enters through visual perception is interesting to note (v. 3). This becomes especially meaningful in connection to David's initial look at Bathsheba from his palace roof (2 Sam. 11:2).

101:5–8. Public Commitment. The resolve for a pure inner attitude translates now into a public commitment to act against the wicked and support the righteous. The psalmist (i.e., the king) will oppose anyone who is slanderous, proud, or deceitful (vv. 5, 7). He will even destroy all the wicked in the land (v. 8). On the other hand, the faithful (v. 6) and the one who walks in the way of *tamim* ("integrity" or "completeness," see above on v. 2) shall be part of the future government. The heart of *tamim* in the leader translates itself into the *tamim* way in which his servants will walk. This psalm not only provides a good road map for a renewed nation under God after the Babylonian Exile but also describes a model of timeless commitment for anyone called and appointed to lead God's people.

102:1–28
It Is Time for God's Mercy

This is the fifth of the seven penitential psalms found in the Psalms (cf. Ps. 6; 32; 38; 51; 130; 143) and describes the hope of God's people in Exile for divine intervention and deliverance. A complaint (vv. 1–11) is followed by a statement of confidence (vv. 12–22), which concludes the psalm with praises to the eternal God. The psalm is permeated by references to different units of time that climax with a contemplation of God's eternity: "day(s)" (vv. 3, 8, 11, 23, 24), "years" (vv. 24, 27), "generations" (vv. 12, 18, 24), "time" (v. 13 [2]), "endure/remain" (vv. 12, 26), and so on. All this identifies the main theme of the poem: the time has come for God to have mercy and compassion for Zion (v. 13). The superscription is unique in the Psalms, although a similarity to headings of some Babylonian prayers has been noted. This could underscore a date for its composition during the Exile in Babylon.

102:1–11. Bad Days. A plea for God to hear and answer (vv. 1–2) introduces a complaint framed by the image of human life that will wither away like grass (vv. 4, 11). Other images underline the fact that these are bad days (v. 3). There are three similes of birds (vv. 6–7), whose species are difficult to determine. They are each connected to the ideas of loneliness and abandonment. These images are used to express Israel's experience of God's wrath when He threw them down or away (Heb. *shalak*) into exile. The section concludes with the image of withering grass, emphasizing the shortness of human life. It is like a lengthening evening shadow, which eventually disappears into a night of oblivion. The idea is that the nation may fade away and disappear in exile.

102:12–28. The Time Has Come. A strong affirmation of God's eternal nature and character (v. 12) contrasts with the experience of the people. There is a similar description of God's eternity at the end of the psalm, creating another frame around the second section (v. 27). Verse 13 stands out as a long line in the poetic arrangement of the psalm and is the center of the poem. There is merciful compassion for Zion and a doubly emphasized rationale—the *mo'ed* has arrived. This term, meaning "appointed time," is used for some of Israel's annual gatherings (Ex. 23:15; Lev. 23) and by the prophets as a reference to a prophetic time (e.g., Dan. 8:19; 12:7). In this psalm, it may indicate Jeremiah's prophecy about the length of the Exile (cf. Jer. 29:10).

Like Daniel (Dan. 9:1–2), the psalmist eagerly anticipates the end of the Exile. The section looks forward to the rebuilding of Jerusalem (v. 16) and the nation (v. 18). In v. 19 we find an interesting reference to the heavenly sanctuary describing the Lord as looking down from His sanctuary, and viewing the earth from heaven. Verse 23 briefly returns to the shortness of life in exile.

The psalm concludes with a prospect of God's eternity, which serves as a guarantee for a future Israel whose descendants will be established before the Lord (v. 28). The divine plan is fulfilled within the flow of history and specific moments are identified by God as particularly significant in reminding His people that He is still guiding them.

103:1–22
Yahweh's *khesed*

Psalm 103 expands on the topic of God's *khesed* (variously rendered as "mercy," "faithful love," "lovingkindness," "covenant loyalty"; vv. 4, 8, 11, 17), raising a chorus of praises that grows concentrically from the individual (vv. 1–5) to Israel in the past (vv. 6–10), Israel at present (vv. 11–14), humanity at large (vv. 15–18), and finally the whole universe (vv. 19–22). A repeated beatitude begins and concludes the poem, creating an *inclusio*. Throughout the psalm are found numerous references to the divine self-revelation at Sinai, focusing on the attributes of God (cf. Ex. 33–34). There is a timelessness about this psalm. However, the image of withering grass as a simile for the brevity of human life (vv. 15–16), in contrast to God's eternity, reminds us of the previous psalm. This psalm has been ascribed to David, but its location in the Psalms points to an application to the historical situation of the Babylonian Exile.

103:1–10. *Khesed* on the Individual and Israel. The invitation to bless (or praise) the Lord begins this psalm and is echoed at the end. The verb *barak* ("to bless"), with God as the object, can refer to the act of worshiping and praising Him. Five relative clauses in vv. 3–5 describe the characteristics of God centered on His *khesed* ("mercy," "steadfast love") and *rakhamim* ("compassion," "tender mercies"; v. 4) and their effects of forgiveness, restoration, and healing the individual so that one's youth is renewed like the eagle's (v. 5; cf. Is. 40:31). The psalm now turns to God's deeds of mercy in the past, specifically during the time of Moses, invoking in v. 8 the experience of the Exodus through a quotation from Exodus 34:6. Verse 8 forms the theological center of the psalm and has become a formulaic point of theological reference throughout the Psalms (cf. also 25:10; 86:15; 99:8). Verses 9–10 provide a commentary on v. 8.

103:11–22. *Khesed* on Humanity and the Universe. The scope of the psalm and of God's mercies gets broader now with the invocation of both heaven and earth (v. 11) and the poetic description of God's forgiveness: He has removed our transgressions from us as far as the east is from the west (v. 12). In effect, this is a further comment on v. 8. Similar to Psalm 102, this psalm also deals with the fleetingness of humanity versus God's eternity (vv. 13-17). The shortness of human life is contrasted with God's mercies, which are "from everlasting to everlasting" (v. 17). These mercies are extended to those who keep His covenant (v. 18). The conclusion of the psalm returns to the blessing at the beginning, where heavenly beings lift up their voices in praises within the heavenly realm (vv. 20-21). The impact of a person's experience of God's mercies and forgiveness can reach into the universe (cf. Luke 15:10).

104:1-35
Old Testament Cosmology

Both Psalms 102 and 103 share a common concern for humanity based on the view that humans are like withering grass. Psalm 104 moves from humans to the cosmos, shifting the focus to the way in which creation and the cosmos are held together by the Creator. As in the previous psalm, there is an *inclusio* on the topic of personal worship (vv. 1, 35): the psalm concludes with the first Hallelujah chorus of the Psalms ("Praise the LORD"). From this point on, it is found at the beginning or end of the remaining psalms in which it occurs (2x at the beginning [Pss. 111-112]; 5x at the end [Pss. 104-105, 115-117]; and 8x at both beginning and end [Pss. 106, 113, 135, 146-150]). It becomes especially prominent in the final doxology of the Psalms (Pss. 146-150).

The author of the psalm is not identified. The poem has been likened to the Egyptian Aten Hymn (fourteenth century B.C.), which originated during the reign of Amenhotep IV (who renamed himself as Akhenaten in honor of the sun-god Aten). This period was characterized by a fairly short-lived monotheistic reform focusing exclusively on the worship of Aten. Unquestionably, there is some resemblance in the imagery used. For example, v. 21 describes lions lurking during the night roaring after their prey, comparable with line ii 8 of the Aten Hymn, which mentions the lion coming from its den at night. However, the psalm constantly relates the sun to God as its Creator and the sun is not considered divine. In the Aten Hymn, the sun is divine. One could even suggest that Psalm 104 is a polemic, contrasting

the superiority of Yahweh with the inferiority of the gods of the ANE. The psalm can be divided into seven sections, echoing the seven days of Creation (vv. 1-4, 5-9, 10-18, 19-23, 24-26, 27-30, 31-35).

104:1-4. God in Heaven. As in Psalm 103, the personal acclamation of the Lord opens and closes this psalm (cf. v. 35), framing the hymn with an invitation to worship (cf. 103:1, 22). In five relative clauses (vv. 2-4) the psalm describes the activity of God as He begins to create (stretching out the heavens; v. 2) and makes close verbal links to the Creation account in Genesis (e.g., light, heavens, waters, winds/spirits [the Heb. *ruakh* can mean either]; Gen. 1:1-5).

104:5-9. Establishing the Earth. The second section uses poetic language to describe the establishment of the earth and its atmosphere, focusing on the division between the waters above and those below the firmament, creating a boundary between water and dry land (vv. 6-9). The foundations of the earth (v. 5) do not necessarily refer to pillars that stand on an underworld ocean, as has often been suggested in the discussion of this psalm; rather, these are images taken from the field of architecture (cf. 1 Kin. 8:13). Overall, while the language is poetic, there is no mythological overtone in the description of God establishing the earth. The link is with the second day of Creation (cf. Gen. 1:6-8).

104:10-18. Creator and Sustainer. The next section continues with water imagery but focuses on its effect on plants and other vegetation and recognizes its role in the sustenance of animals and plants. God is not only the Creator but also the Sustainer who preserves creation on a daily basis that it may bring forth food from the earth (v. 14). A geographical description of Israel's fauna and flora (e.g., cedars of Lebanon; v. 16) links this section with the third day of Creation (cf. Gen. 1:9-13). There are also connections with the fifth and sixth days (cf. Gen. 1:20-25).

104:19-23. Night and Day. The fourth day of Creation (cf. Gen. 1:14-19) comes into focus in the next section as it describes God appointing the moon and sun to their assigned activities. The sequence of darkness followed by light reflects the evening/morning sequence found in Genesis 1:19. There is a strong demythologizing tendency in the wording here, as moon and sun, both worshiped as deities within religions of the ANE, have clearly set limits: the moon has its seasons and the sun "knows" to go down (v. 19). The section concludes with a description of human activity (Heb. *'adam*; "man," "humanity") and alludes to the sixth day of Creation (cf. Gen. 1:26–31). It also connects humans with the daily labor of life on earth after the fall.

104:24–30. Wonder of Creation. At the end of the Creation week God contemplates His work (cf. Gen. 1:31). Within the psalm is a moment when the psalmist looks at creation and declares the bounteous plenty of God's works (v. 24). All living things are under the caring dominion of Yahweh. All nature and humans are dependent on God for sustenance (vv. 27–30). Once more the language of creation is used, as God's *ruakh* ("spirit," "breath") is identified as the source of life for all living creatures, and when it is taken away they die.

104:31–35. Final Praise and Exhortation. The psalm concludes with an invitation to praise and recognize God's majesty and its negative effects on sinners (v. 35). A contemplation of God's creative power should lead to worship. Psalm 104 moves between God's initial creation and His constant preservation of it. At a time when science seeks to explain everything in terms of cause and effect within a closed system, we must remember that God is the Creator in whom we find the purpose for our existence.

105:1–45
Yahweh in History

This praise psalm shifts the focus to Yahweh's saving activities in the history of Israel. It does so by concentrating on important historical events, beginning with the Abrahamic covenant, the Exodus, and the entrance into the promised land. Verses 1–15 are almost identical to the psalm recorded in 1 Chronicles 16:8–36, which commemorates the bringing of the ark to Jerusalem by David and may represent the incorporation of material from that composition for a liturgical purpose.

105:1–6. Invitation to Remember. The psalmist uses ten imperatives (vv. 1–5) to exhort the congregation of Israel—offspring of Abraham and Jacob, His chosen ones (v. 6)—to praise the Lord. The praises move from outward expressions (e.g., make known, sing, speak; vv. 1–2) to an inward attitude (e.g., seeking the Lord with the heart; v. 3) culminating in the command to remember His wondrous works (v. 5). The verb *zakar* ("to remember") plays an important role here by concluding this section and framing the next section, moving from human to divine remembrance.

105:7–45. God Remembers. The verb *zakar* at the beginning and end of this section (cf. vv. 8, 42) serves to frame the historical review that makes up the major part of this poem. God's remembrance involves His concrete acts of salvation in history. The psalm begins with Israel's election through the covenant He made with Abraham, including the covenant renewals with Isaac and Jacob, and culminating in an everlasting covenant (vv. 8–10). Israel's election and accompanying promise of the land characterize the next section, which focuses on the time of the patriarchal wanderings (vv. 11–15).

The patriarchs are described as anointed ones and prophets (v. 15; cf. Gen. 20:7 for Abraham as prophet), creating a historical lineage of salvation that ultimately points away from the patriarch to the Messiah. Joseph and the preservation of Israel is the next historical event in the memory of God (vv. 16–25). The experience of Joseph is summarized and followed by that of Moses and Aaron, the story of the plagues (only eight plagues are selected [vv. 26–36]; cf. Ps. 78:44–53 where seven plagues are mentioned), and the Exodus (vv. 37–41). Only the positive aspects of the Exodus experience are listed—silver and gold (v. 37), quail, bread of heaven (v. 40), and water (v. 41). Consequently, no mention is made of Israel's rebellion in the wilderness. The psalm concludes with another reference to God's remembrance and ends with entrance to the promised land (vv. 42–45). That generation and the one returning from the Babylonian Exile were called to observe God's precepts (*huqqim*) and instructions (*torot*; v. 45). Another Hallelujah ("Praise the LORD") shout concludes the psalm. A surprising element in this psalm is that God does not remember the sins of His people, probably because at the end of the conflict our sins will be no more.

106:1–48
Israel's Confession

The final psalm of Book 4 aptly presents an extended confession of Israel's wrongdoings throughout the history of the nation. Thus, it serves as a mirror image of the historical account in the previous psalm. The psalm focuses not on God's goodness and faithfulness but on the failures of Israel that finally led to the Babylonian Exile. All this is framed by a summons to praise (vv. 1–3) as individuals (vv. 4–5) and as a community (vv. 47), followed by the doxology that concludes Book 4 (v. 48). The twofold Hallelujah ("Praise the LORD") appears for the first time, both at the beginning and the end of the poem (vv. 1, 48). As one moves toward the end of the Psalms, the Hallelujahs ("Praise the LORD") become more frequent and intense until they reach the great final Hallelujah doxology at the end (Pss. 146–150). Historically, the Babylonian Exile provides the occasion for confession, and this leads to return from exile, which is thematically at the center of Book 5.

106:1–5. Introduction. In an almost identical fashion to the previous psalm, the short introduction to this psalm uses a number of imperatives to invite the congregation to praise and worship God. His goodness (v. 1), emphasized in the previous psalm, is now set into sharp contrast with Israel's sinfulness. Again the root *zakar* ("remember") appears in the introduction (v. 4) and toward the end, framing the main section (vv. 7, 45) and emphasizing God's salvific remembrance (cf. 105:5, 8, 42). The section concludes with the hope of a future restoration and communal praise for God's inheritance (v. 5).

106:6–46. Confession. The tone abruptly changes, focusing on the main theme of the psalm, that is, confession of Israel's sins (v. 6). It is a communal confession (cf. 1 Kin. 8:47; Dan. 9:5) pointing to a long history of guilt. The historical review of Israel's sins begins in Egypt at the time of the Exodus (vv. 7–12) when Israel rebelled by the sea (v. 7). Yahweh saved them for His name's sake (v. 8), thus establishing a pattern for the conduct of Israel. Next comes the rebellion in the wilderness and God's provision of manna (vv. 13–15), followed by the Korahite rebellion against Moses and Aaron (vv. 16–18; cf. Num. 16). The events at Mount Sinai are recalled (vv. 19–23), in particular the worship of the golden calf (cf. Ex. 32:4), which theologically exchanged their glory (God) for the image of an ox (v. 20). Verses 24–27 point to the rebellion instigated by the spies at the borders of Canaan (cf. Num. 13–14) and provide the first glimpse

of the Exile, as God intended to scatter them through the lands (v. 27). This is followed by the apostasy to Baal of Peor (v. 28) and Phinehas's courageous intervention (v. 30), which in terms of results was the same as Abraham's faith—it was credited or accounted to him as righteousness forever (v. 31; cf. Gen. 15:6).

The rebellion at the waters of strife (Meribah, vv. 32–33) precedes a list of wrongdoings committed in the promised land (vv. 34–39), which spans the time from the conquest to the Babylonian Exile; idolatry and child sacrifice are identified as the major abominations during this period (cf. 2 Kin. 16:3; Jer. 7:30–31). Consequently, the Exile came as God gave them into the hands of the Gentile nations (vv. 40–43). At this point the confession turns to Yahweh's *khesed* ("mercy," "steadfast love") as He remembers His covenant (v. 45), thus closing the circle of remembrance (or lack thereof) that introduced this section (cf. v. 7).

106:47–48. Final Plea and Doxology. A communal plea for salvation and return from exile concludes the psalm, connecting it to the introduction with the words "thanks" and "praise" (vv. 1, 47). The final doxology of Book 4 is slightly more expanded than the conclusion of Book 3 but is almost identical to the doxology of Book 1, adding the divine epithet "God of Israel." This title is appropriate for the end of collected confessions that tried to come to terms with the reality of the Exile, seeking a foundation for hope in Yahweh's saving deeds on behalf of Israel in the past. The confessional anti-history of Israel demonstrates the greatness of God's mercies toward His children.

PSALMS 107—150
BOOK V

The final book of the Psalms begins with another historical psalm that almost seamlessly connects to the end of Book 4, thus providing a response to the final plea for the return from exile (106:47). The compositional theme of Book 5 is the restoration of Israel during the postexilic period. Before the final doxology of the Psalms, which spreads over five psalms (Pss. 146–150), there is a last group of Davidic psalms (Pss. 138–145). Some have been adjusted to the historical realities of the postexilic Jewish communities (e.g., Ps. 144 and its dependence on Pss. 18 and 104). The importance of David as an ideal paradigm for a postexilic state formation is underlined by the insertion of this group at the end of the Psalms. The pilgrim psalms (Pss. 120–134) constitute the largest subcollection in Book 5. The expression *shir hamma'alot* ("A Song of Ascent"), found in the superscriptions of this group, may refer to the Babylonian exiles returning from captivity and "going up" to Jerusalem or possibly the annual Israelite pilgrimage to one of the main festivals. It is also possible that both meanings merged in the late exilic and post-exilic periods, emphasizing the central role of Jerusalem and the temple for the national reconstruction.

107:1–43
Israel Restored

The links between this and the previous psalm are plentiful. Both psalms begin with the same thanksgiving formula and form historical narratives of God's salvation deeds (Ps. 106:44 is taken up as a refrain in 107:6, 13, 19, 28), demonstrating that the division between Books 4 and 5 is to some extent artificial. Psalm 107 serves as a bridge between the two books. However, the negative tone of Psalm 106 gives way to thanksgiving and the topic of Yahweh's redemption. The return from the Babylonian Exile is no longer something hoped for but instead is an accomplished historical fact that leads to the restoration of Israel as a nation.

107:1–3. Invitation to Praise and Thanksgiving. The invitation to praise at the beginning of the poem is almost the same as the one in the previous psalm (106:1) and vv. 2–3 connect to the ending of the previous psalm. The request in 106:47 (to be gathered from the Gentile nations) is now a reality. God has redeemed His people from the hands of the enemy and gathered them from the lands. Yahweh's redemption brings Israel back from all four directions of the compass (cf. Is. 49:12).

107:4–32. Four Experiences that Motivate Thanksgiving. As a rationale for thanksgiving, the psalmist now lists four experiences of deliverance. They are primarily metaphorical in language and all end in a refrain followed by a short exhortation (vv. 4–9; 10–16; 17–22; 23–32). The refrain of praise and thanksgiving (vv. 8, 15, 21, 31) refers repeatedly back to the introduction and possibly serves as a liturgical response by the congregation during congregational singing of the psalm. The first experience

(vv. 4–9) recounts that Israel wandered in the desolate wilderness wastelands (v. 4). The description is vague and could be a reference to the experience of the Exile rather than to the wilderness wanderings after the Exodus. The return from the Babylonian Exile is depicted as a second Exodus. At the end of the experience Yahweh provides a straight path to a city where they may reside (v. 7).

The second experience (vv. 10–16) is even more abstract as it describes liberation from darkness (v. 10), which came as a consequence of rebellion against God's instruction (v. 11). The breaking of bronze gates and cutting of iron bars echo the promise of Cyrus's liberation in Isaiah 45:2, making the reference to the Babylonian Exile explicit. Verses 17–22 describe the rescue from the gates of death (v. 18; cf. Job 38:17; Ps. 9:13), which poetically refers to proximity to the grave (cf. Ps. 28:1; 30:3). In this case, it designates the Exile as a threat to the existence of Israel. The final experience recounts a storm at sea (vv. 22–32), which reminds us of Jonah 1–2. The metaphor of God rescuing Israel from a storm may point to the diaspora of Israel that took them to a number of foreign shores beyond Babylon (Egypt and the rest of the Mediterranean ancient world). All narratives end with the refrain to give thanks to the Lord for His *khesed* ("goodness," "mercy," "steadfast love").

107:33–41. Yahweh's Transforming Power. The psalm next moves into a contemplation of Yahweh's acts that change the destiny of both humanity and nature, characterized by a reversal of fortunes. Through His creative powers He turns dry, parched ground into flowing springs of water (v. 35). Again there is mention of a city where they could reside (v. 36; cf. vv. 4, 7), pointing to the return from exile and rebuilding of Jerusalem. Yet there is also punishment for the powerful (He pours contempt on leaders; v. 40) but deliverance for the poor and needy, who are like a flock led by the divine Shepherd (v. 41; cf. Ps. 95:7).

107:42–43. Wisdom Exhortation. The experiences of Israel in exile have a didactic function expressed in the final appeal of the psalm: the wise should pay close attention to all of these things (v. 43). All this leads to an understanding of God's *khesed* ("lovingkindness," "mercy," "faithful love"), which creates another strong linguistic link with the previous psalm (cf. 106:7, 45). Looking back at how God led us through darkness and in the wilderness can increase our faith and move us to sing about His mercies as we anticipate in hope the fulfillment of His promise of a future city for us.

108:1–13
Déjà Vu

Psalm 108 combines material from earlier psalms (vv. 1–5 // 57:7–11 and vv. 6–13 // 60:5–12) in a new way, a phenomenon that also occurs in other places of Book 5 (cf. Ps. 144 and its dependence on Pss. 18 and 104). Subtle changes take place that shift the focus from David's personal experience of musical praise (v. 2 // 57:8) to a more theocentric approach stressing Yahweh's sovereignty. Thus, it is no longer the king that is the principal actor; he is used only as a historical backdrop for a theocentric form of government, which creates a new foundation for postexilic Israel. Psalm 108 is the first of three poems that refer back to Davidic authorship (Pss. 108–110) at the beginning of Book 5.

108:1–5. Praise for Yahweh's Mercy. A hymnic praise to Yahweh introduces the poem. Some have taken *kebodi* (lit. "my glory") at the end of the verse as a reference to God (cf. Ps. 3:3), whereas others think it refers to "my soul" or "my whole being" (cf. Pss. 16:9; 57:8). Contextually, either could apply here. The praise echoes with a universal tone, combining with musical instruments to call peoples and nations to "awaken the dawn" (v. 2). This expression alludes to the Day of the Lord when Yahweh will intervene (cf. Joel 2:2; Amos 4:13); the intervention is further developed in the second section of the psalm.

108:6–13. Plea for Yahweh's Military Intervention. The petition for deliverance invoking Yahweh's right hand (v. 6; cf. Ex. 15:6, 12) is followed by the quote of a divine oracle (vv. 8–10). It is a declaration of God's rule over Israel's ancient territories on both sides of the Jordan, such as Shechem and Succoth, Jacob's first dwelling places in the land (v. 7; cf. Gen. 33:17–18), as well the neighboring countries of Moab, Edom, and Philistia. References to the tribes in v. 8 echo Jacob's blessings in Genesis 49. Following the oracle, the psalmist recalls God's abandonment of Israel in the Exile (cf. 44:9). For the psalmist, salvation is the exclusive work of God, who stands by and defends His people like a Warrior. He is always present in our battles.

109:1–31
Deliverance from False Accusations

Psalm 109 is permeated by legal terminology, turning the psalm into a court case in which the petitioner (the accused) is asking for vindication from God as the universal Judge. The long list of curses in vv. 6–19 are pronounced by the psalmist's enemies as they express the charges against him. In the second section, the psalmist does not defend himself but instead turns to God with an appeal for justice (vv. 20–29) that climaxes in a praise of thanksgiving for deliverance (vv. 30–31). The psalm has been attributed to David and can certainly reflect a dramatic situation in his life. However, its strategic placement in the Psalms and connections with Psalm 107, which portrays Israel's deliverance from the Babylonian Exile, suggest a reuse of the psalm. The legal conflicts and false charges raised against the Jews during the time of Ezra and Nehemiah could serve as a historical background for the use of the psalm.

109:1–5. Appeal to God as the Highest Judge. Following an appeal to God to not keep silent (v. 1), the psalmist repeatedly refers to the verbal accusations of his enemies and their words of hatred (v. 3). This description of the attitudes of the enemies is followed by the psalmist's reaction.

109:6–19. Accusations. As in court proceedings, the psalm now turns to the accusers' list of accusations and curses that reflect the words of hatred mentioned in the previous section, ultimately asking for a death penalty (v. 9). Most interpreters have understood this section as curses the psalmist utters against his accusers, as is the case in other psalms traditionally called imprecatory psalms. This is a viable interpretation. Nevertheless, the legal framework of the psalm, as well as the next section, which strongly contrasts the psalmist's position with that of the accusers, suggests that this section is the direct discourse of the accusing party, who are his enemies (cf. especially the contrast in v. 28 below; see "Imprecatory Passages in the Psalms," p. 733).

109:20–31. They Curse, You Bless. David asks God to help him for His name's sake, appealing to God's *khesed* ("mercy," "steadfast love"; v. 21), which culminates in the contrast of v. 28: the enemies will curse, but God will bless. Eventually, wrong accusations will return to their originators

Imprecatory Passages in the Psalms

There are a number of psalms in which the psalmist uses such strong language (referred to as imprecations) against his enemies that, according to some, it reveals an attitude that is incompatible with Christian love. For instance, when oppressed by the wicked, the psalmist prays that they be disgraced (35:4), destroyed (54:5), or descend to the grave alive (55:15). He also asks for God's wrath to consume them (59:13) and considers happy those who dash Babylonian children against the rocks (137:8–9). We will examine this type of language and explore its purpose and the theological significance.

1. *Origin of the Language.* First, there is significant evidence that the imprecations in the Psalms have theological and linguistic connections with previous revelation. The primary background for the language is the covenant curses against covenant breakers (cf. Ps. 37:22 and Deut. 30:1; Ps. 69:23 and Deut. 28:22, 28). In other cases, there are connections with previous descriptions of God's judgments in historical narratives (cf. Ps. 140:10 and Gen. 19:24; Ps. 83:9–18 and Judg. 4–5, 7–8; Ps. 55:9, 15 and Num. 16:30).

One of the significant and consistent themes is that of divine retribution. This principle is evident in the context of the court as well as that of war. There is often an implication that God's defeat of the enemies of His people in the past is a harbinger of His future judgment as well. Accordingly, it can be legitimately claimed that the imprecatory Psalms are not unique in their descriptions of God's roles of retributive Judge and Sovereign over the wars of the nations (Ps. 35:4–9; 70:2). These psalms thus often employ the language God Himself had previously used to indicate His evaluation and punishment of evil, and the suppliant was calling upon God to do again what He had done before (cf. 55:9, 15).

2. *Concern for God's Honor.* When praying for the punishment of the wicked, the psalmist is ultimately interested in God's honor (e.g., 58:6–11). Were the wicked to decisively triumph over the righteous in the contexts involved, it could convey the impression of divine indifference. God was thus implored to demonstrate His righteous character and vindicate His Name and the loyalty of His people. In some cases, there are implications that the divine punishment called for involves persons who might see the error of their conduct and repent (e.g., 9:19–20; 83:16–18). In most cases, however, the implication is that the persons are irredeemably recalcitrant and will thus be destroyed (e.g., 68:1–3; 69:25). In both circumstances, God's justice and sovereignty would be manifested to His people as well as their enemies (59:11–13).

3. *Imprecations and Revenge.* The call for vengeance is found in some of the imprecatory passages in the Psalms (e.g., 58:10). Concerning vengeance, it should first be pointed out that the English term does not exactly correspond with the biblical term. The Hebrew term *naqam* is primarily employed in two ways. It is (1) the declaration of a proper punishment against the wicked or (2) the vindication of the innocent who were oppressed by evildoers. The verb form connotes "to avenge" or "to repay," while the noun means "vengeance" or "retribution." *Naqam* appears in legal or covenant settings where the punishment is retributive (e.g., Ex. 21:20; Lev. 26:25; 2 Kin. 9:7; Esth. 8:13).

Second, extremely important for a proper understanding of the imprecatory passages is their affirmation that God is the One who is ultimately responsible for applying vengeance (18:47; 79:10; Deut. 32:43). Even when the psalmist prays to God to help him defeat his enemies and avenge him involving war or other human means (or refers to this situation in the past), it is clear that his victories were impossible without God's own righteous judgment and aid (e.g., Ps. 18:32–50; 44:1–8; 118:1–12; 144:1–10). The cries for vengeance were a request to God for the triumph of His justice and mercy, bringing redemption, restoration, and healing to the oppressed and judgment on the oppressors.

Third, personal, selfish revenge is prohibited in a number of biblical passages (e.g., Lev. 19:18; Deut. 32:35; Prov. 25:21–22// Rom. 12:19–20). It is true that provisions were made in the Mosaic theocracy for avenging the murder of a relative (Num. 35:19–21), but this type of vengeance or justice was controlled under the law of retaliation (*lex talionis*), a principle that the punishment should correspond to the crime committed (a tooth for a tooth; an eye for an eye). The imprecatory prayers were requests that God render a just verdict and punishment upon the rebellious in proper proportion to their crimes. This kind of prayer and affirmation of God's vengeance is not unique to the OT (see Rom. 12:19; 1 Thess. 4:6; Heb. 10:30; Rev. 6:10; 18:4–8, 20; 19:1–3).

3. *Imprecation and Retribution.* First, while some have evaluated the *lex talionis* to be morally primitive and determined that its association with imprecatory prayers confirms the psalmists' reprehensible stance toward wicked people, scholars have rightly pointed out that this law is found in contexts of legal settings that ensured the proper implementation of justice and compassion, including for those who were foreigners or women (Ex. 21:22–25; Lev. 24:17–22; Deut. 19:16–21). It has accordingly been suggested that a better name for this law might be the "law of equivalence"—the "eye for eye" passages use standardized language (e.g., "life for life" in Lev. 24 could refer to equal compensation for losses sustained) to convey the idea of just dealings in legal settings, not those of personal revenge.

Second, in the psalms the principle of retribution provides a legal background for the punishment of the enemy (Ps. 28:4; 54:5). This is important because through retribution the justice of divine vengeance is manifested. In other words, the judgment against the wicked is not arbitrarily imposed or unnecessarily cruel, but rather it is based on the principles that a punishment should coincide with the magnitude of the crime and that it should be restricted to the criminal. God judges individuals and nations on the basis of their deeds, and that is what the psalmist is requesting through his imprecatory language.

Third, the magistrates were responsible for ensuring law and order in society, and the implementation of the *lex talionis* was under God's purview. The individual had to learn to trust God and His judgment. As noted above, justice throughout Scripture is God's ultimate responsibility (cf. Rom. 12:17–19). He will judge, punish, and reward everyone according to their deeds (e.g., Rom. 2:6; 1 Pet. 1:17; Rev. 22:12).

4. *Imprecations and Hatred.* Sometimes the idea of hatred is used in imprecatory passages (Ps. 139:21–22). A few comments are in order. First, it should be noted that the Hebrew verb *sane'* does not have all the same connotations as "hate" in English. *Sane'* can mean "disregard," "despise," "dislike," "love less," as well as to hate maliciously. Hatred in this sense of continual hostility and antagonism is condemned (Lev. 19:17–18). The Israelites were called to love their neighbors as themselves (Lev. 19:18) as well as to extend love to strangers (Lev. 19:34; Deut. 10:19).

Second, the use of *sane'* in the context of the imprecations implies a strong disassociation of the psalmist with evil and those who are given over to the practice of it. "Hating" the assembly of evildoers (Ps. 26:5) means a rejection of their ways and loyalty to God's. A similar idea is expressed when the psalmist says that he hates those who worship idols (31:6). This is a unique way of affirming that he is not an idolater. In other passages (e.g., 101:3), the psalmist refers to his hatred—in this case referring to strong disapproval—for the actions of evil people.

Third, the hatred in these passages is not irrational or indicative of a self-inflated or fragile ego. It is referring to those who hate God and are His enemies—God's enemies are the psalmists also. He is refusing to be identified with their evil actions and hatred of God. Accordingly, this hatred is not an evil emotion but rather a rejection of evil and the evil one who exists in opposition to God. Fourth, in the Psalms this type of hatred is implied to be something that must be learned and which is not natural to fallen human beings. The psalmist exhorts those who love the Lord to hate what is evil (97:10; cf. 45:7). The natural human heart does not hate what is evil but rather loves it instead (e.g., Gen. 8:21; Jer. 17:9; Matt. 15:19; Eph. 2:1–3). Hating evil comes from a study of God's word (e.g., 119:104). Loving the law of God is associated with hating double-minded people (119:113) as well as falsehood (119:163) because the psalmist could not support any evil dispositions and actions.

Finally, none of the above findings clash with those of the NT. Jesus's reference to loving the neighbor and hating the enemy was referring not to an OT command but to a misunderstanding of some of the rabbis. However, it is significant to note that He affirmed the necessity of "hating" our immediate family as well as ourselves (Luke 14:26). Consistent with one of the connotations of the OT *sane'*, this use of the Greek verb *miseō* is not a call to harbor hostility toward relatives but rather a call not to allow any natural ties to hinder our dedication to Jesus as Savior and Lord. This "hate," as we saw above in the Psalms, actually stems from love: love for God above all else with dedicated loyalty. We could suggest that hatred in the imprecatory Psalms is not a repudiation of the law of love but actually presupposes a strong allegiance to it. Indeed, David's imprecations in the Psalms should not be read without considering how he often treated his personal enemies: Saul (1 Sam. 24; 26); Abner and Ish-bosheth (2 Sam. 3–4), Absalom (2 Sam. 18:5, 33), and Shimei (2 Sam. 16:5–14; 19:19–23). While he recognized the need for eventual punishment and justice (1 Kin. 2:8–9), he allowed for the possibility of forgiveness and did not take vengeance into his own hands unilaterally or impulsively.

6. The Psalmist and Us. While the psalmist asked God to conquer, chastise, and even kill his enemies, he renounced personal or private vengeance and requested that God would judge and execute vengeance for him. The question inevitably arises as to whether we should pray the imprecations of the Psalms at times. The answer is affirmative if we pray them with the same rejection of personal pride or vindictiveness, concern above all for God's glory and His justice, longing for the eventual eradication of all sin and rebellion, and firm faith in God as the One who saves. The problem we have with these prayers is not that they are incompatible with Christian love (as is often supposed) but rather that we are not loving enough and need the Lord to help us to find the dedicated love and commitment to Christ and His cause that the psalmists exhibited.

and they will be clothed with disgrace (v. 29). The psalm concludes by praising God for His righteous judgments and defense of the poor and needy. The NT quotes from this psalm (v. 8) in Acts 1:20, connecting it to the betrayal of Judas and the election of Matthias. Church tradition refers to this psalm as the *Psalmus Ischarioticus*, reflecting the above interpretation of the curses. It provides an inspiring example of how to react when false accusations come our way, even if it means betrayal by a close friend.

110:1–7
King and Priest

This Davidic poem points far beyond itself as one of the most prominent messianic psalms in the Psalms. It presents Christ in His twofold role as King and High Priest, in the order of Melchizedek. Outside of Genesis 14 and the book of Hebrews, it is the only mention of the typological figure of Melchizedek in the Bible. The psalm divides into two parts (vv. 1–3 and 4–7), each introduced by a divine speech. One uses the imagery of the king and the other uses the imagery of the high priest, while both parts describe the subjugation of the enemies. In the context of Book 5, it introduces an ideal form of theocratic governance for a restored Israel.

110:1–3. Christ as King. The psalm is introduced by a direct address from Yahweh to David's *'adonai* (his "Lord"). In the NT this is considered to be a conversation between God the Father and God the Son (cf. Matt. 22:41–45; Mark 12:35–37; Luke 20:41–43). It describes the king as sitting metaphorically at God's right hand, a position of honor (Mark 10:35–37). The imagery of footstool and rod or scepter (vv. 1–2) points beyond the historical and represents the universal power of the Messiah. References to the womb and youth in v. 3 mark a sudden change from the Warrior imagery and are probably an allusion to the bringing forth of the Messiah King by Yahweh (cf. Col. 1:15).

110:4–7. Christ as High Priest. Another oracle by Yahweh introduces the second messianic imagery of Christ as High Priest (cf. Heb. 7:21). The reference to Melchizedek illustrates the convergence of both kingly and priestly function into one person. Christ's supremacy as Judge of the nations (v. 6) and His strong rule are emphasized once more through warrior terminology. The section ends in a more peaceful image of the Messiah; His drinking from a brook by the road evokes the story of Gideon (cf. Judg. 7:4–6) and his army as they prepared for battle. The hopes of a postexilic Israel were directed toward a kingly priest or priestly king, yet the psalm prophetically goes beyond those immediate hopes and points to the Messiah, who fulfills the hopes of all people.

111:1-10
Torah and Wisdom

This praise psalm focuses on God's law and wisdom within the structure of an acrostic poem, as each line begins with the next letter of the Hebrew alphabet. Psalm 112 has been considered a twin of Psalm 111, as it follows the same pattern with similar content. Both psalms begin a group of psalms (Pss. 111–119) that concludes with the most extensive wisdom contemplation of *torah*, also in acrostic form. While Psalms 111–112 do not mention the word *torah*, their terminology (e.g., "precepts" in 111:7) is clearly geared toward *torah*. The initial "Praise the Lord" stands outside of the acrostic structure and functions as a title (cf. Pss. 112:1; 113:1). While an acrostic poem has an inherent structure, there are some content-based divisions in the poem.

111:1–6. Thanksgiving. The praise of Psalm 111 is congregational and in response to Yahweh's works, which should be considered carefully by all who delight or take pleasure in them (cf. 119:35). Yahweh's wondrous acts are described in terms of covenant (v. 5) terminology, identifying Him as gracious and compassionate (v. 4; cf. Ex. 34:6–7), sustaining those who fear Him (v. 5), and giving them the *nakhalah* ("inheritance") of the nations. Verse 6 has been translated to mean that the nations have become part of Israel's inheritance ("the nations as their heritage") or that the other nations' inheritances now belong to Israel ("giving them the lands of other nations"). In either case, the basic meaning is the same. The historical references are to experiences during the Exodus and conquest of the land.

111:7–9. God's Greatest Work: His Law. The gift of the Lord's precepts are described in v. 7. The noun *piqqudim* ("directions," "orders") occurs only in the psalms (cf. Ps. 19:9 and throughout Ps. 119) and expresses God's concern (*paqad*; "be concerned for," "be mindful of") for the well-being of His people. The giving of God's law to His people is part of His plan for their redemption (v. 9).

111:10. Wisdom Contemplation. The statement "the fear of the Lord is the beginning of wisdom" at the end of the psalm is associated with God's people as those who, according to the Hebrew text, "do them." "Them" probably refers back to the "precepts" of v. 7, which have been described. The psalm is a beautiful hymn about God's tender concern for His children as particularly manifested by giving them His law.

112:1-10
Beatitude

As a companion psalm to the previous one, Psalm 112 employs the same acrostic structure and contains similar expressions (e.g., God's "righteousness endures forever" in v. 112:3b // 111:3b). However, while both psalms focus on the blessings of *torah*, Psalm 112 picks up where the previous poem ended, emphasizing the didactic aspect of wisdom and how it plays out in the life of one who follows the Lord's commandments. Its introductory beatitude connects closely to Psalm 1.

112:1–3. Beatitude. Following the initial title ("Praise the Lord") the beatitude introduces the one who fears the Lord and is greatly delighted by His commandments. The blessing is for that person's family, both the current generation and the descendants. The blessing of wealth is balanced with righteousness (v. 3), which is always connected to correct ethical behavior in the psalms.

112:4–6. Representing Yahweh's Character. Correct behavior is further described in this section, listing the attributes of the God-fearer as being gracious, compassionate, and righteous (v. 4). The characteristics of a person of God are used to describe the character of His people, who also become eternally memorable (v. 6).

112:7–9. Even in Bad Times. Even in adversity, when there is news of calamity and confrontation with enemies (v. 8), the psalmist twice underlines that he will not fear because he is trusting in the Lord (vv. 7–8). The metaphor of the exalted horn (v. 9), representing strength (cf. Deut. 33:17; Pss. 75:10; 89:17), concludes this section.

112:10. Fate of the Wicked. In contrast to the righteous, the wicked have their desires come to naught. This creates a further literary link with Psalm 1. It also ends with the identical two Hebrew words, *resha'im to'bed*—the evil will come to an end (cf. 1:6; there it is the "way" of the wicked that will perish, not specifically their desires). The twin Psalms 111–112 connect well with each other; one (Ps. 111) presents theology (God's law) and the other (Ps. 112) presents anthropology, namely, the playing out of God's law in the righteous life of humans.

113:1–9
Hallel Psalms

Psalms 113–118 constitute the Passover Hallel, a group of psalms recited during the *pesakh* (Passover) which commemorates the Exodus. Jesus and His disciples most likely sang from these psalms during the Last Supper (cf. Matt. 26:30; Mark 14:26). They are bracketed by two acrostic *torah* wisdom psalms at the beginning (Pss. 111–112) and the most extensive *torah* psalm, also in acrostic form, at the end (Ps. 119). Replicating the relationship between Psalms 111 and 112, the first three Hallel psalms (Pss. 113–115) have a theological perspective on the Exodus, whereas the second three Hallel psalms (Pss. 116–118) are more anthropologically oriented. Psalm 113 serves as a hymnic introduction to the group, framed by a Hallelujah ("praise the LORD") at its beginning and end.

113:1–6. Praise and Reason. A threefold exhortation to praise the Lord introduces the psalm. This praise is not limited by time ("forevermore") and space (reference to the rising of the sun to its setting serves to refer to the totality of creation; vv. 2–3; cf. Ps. 50:1). The reason for praise is found in another set of spatial observations, namely, that God is exalted high above all nations as He dwells and reigns on high (vv. 4–6). A rhetorical question concludes the section, including another expression of totality (the heavens and the earth; v. 6), which invites a contemplation of creation.

113:7–9. God on Earth. The spatial dimension of God concretizes itself in His intervention on earth as He raises the poor from the dust and lifts the needy from the ash heap (v. 7). These descriptions, including the childless woman in v. 9 (cf. 1 Sam. 2:5, 8), are focused on lifting up the socially disadvantaged, elevating them to a position of power (cf. 112:9). It is this majestic God who is able to restore Israel after the Exile and who is still able to elevate the oppressed. Those whom God restores, He also elevates.

114:1–8
God of the Exodus

Foregoing an introduction, this poem immediately launches into a historical account of God's miraculous interventions during the time of the Exodus. Some ancient versions (e.g., LXX, Vg.) and a few Hebrew manuscripts consider Psalm 114 and 115 to be a single psalm. However, the literary independence of Psalm 114 is supported by its intricate structure and artistically composed four stanzas (vv. 1–2, 3–4, 5–6, 7–8). They are chiastically arranged (e.g., "Jacob" in stanzas 1 and 4 [vv. 1, 7]; "sea" and "Jordan" in stanzas 2 and 3 [vv. 3, 5]). The preference for Jacob throughout the psalm serves as a possible indicator for the postexilic date of the poem (cf. Is. 48:20).

114:1–2. Election of Israel through the Exodus. The first stanza of the poem describes the Exodus in terms of the election of Israel. The reference to Judah becoming God's sanctuary points to the fact that the parallel pairs of Judah/Israel and sanctuary/dominion (v. 2) describe the origins of Israel as a nation and God's dominion over the earth from His sanctuary. This theocentric perspective was illustrated by the arrangement of the camp during the desert wanderings when the sanctuary was in the center of the camp (cf. Num. 2).

114:3–4. Nature Reacts. Psalm 114 addresses nature in the second stanza, describing the reactions of sea, Jordan, mountains, and hills (vv. 3–4). The imagery is reminiscent of Psalm 29, where nature reacted in similar fashion to the "voice of the Lord." The miraculous passage through the Red Sea during the Exodus and crossing of the Jordan at the end of the desert wanderings caused reactions in nature that could be associated with the theophany at Mount Sinai (cf. Ex. 19:18). One can also interpret the mountains and hills as referring to the promised land and its joyful reaction at the arrival of God's people. Interestingly, Isaiah promises a rejoicing of mountains at the return of the exiles (cf. Is. 44:23), an idea that fits the general context of Book 5.

114:5–8. Questions and Answers. Nature is addressed through a series of four questions, which appear to move the focus from past to present. The questions recall the different reactions of nature in the previous stanza: Why do the sea and Jordan flee while mountains and hills leap and skip? The problem in this psalm is the translation of the verbal form *khul* in v. 7. While it is translated in most modern English versions with a negative connotation (i.e., "tremble"), another possible meaning of this verb is "dance," "whirl," "twist" (e.g., Judg. 21:21). This would involve the earth dancing as a sign of rejoicing. The psalm concludes with further water imagery that dominates the remainder of the fourth stanza in v. 8. The Exodus, both first and second (i.e., the return from the Babylonian Exile), is cause for solemn joy for His people because Yahweh is the One who has led the way. The next psalm reveals that the nations who have rejected Him tremble because their gods are useless.

115:1–18
God Alone

God's supremacy in history during the Exodus is followed by a liturgical poem that is characterized by polemics against idolatry and, conversely, by its strong monotheistic theology. As nature acknowledges God's sovereignty (Ps. 114), humanity needs to follow (Ps. 115). Within a postexilic context, Israel had to come to terms with the problem of idolatry that constituted one of the main reasons for the Babylonian Exile (cf. Ezek. 5–8). The message is clear: this should never happen again in the restored Israel. As a liturgical reading for the Passover, the poem constitutes a communal response to Yahweh's sovereignty in the cosmos.

115:1–8. The Idols. A brief invocation to give glory to God culminates in a question raised by the Gentile nations: "Where is their [Israel's] God?" In response to this mocking question, the first section of the poem offers an extended polemic against their idols by focusing on the contrast between the impotence of their gods against the superiority of Yahweh. One can perceive the historical context of the postexilic community that is faced with similar questions during the reconstruction of the temple and Jerusalem (cf. Ezra 4).

115:9–18. Israel's Response. In contrast to the idols of the Gentiles, Israel is exhorted by the speaker—perhaps the priest officiating at the temple—to trust in the Lord (v. 9). Following this exhortation, the priest bestows blessings on the congregation, while the change in person in the following section indicates that both the priest and congregation stand as a community before Yahweh, with the priest functioning as a mediator. The verb *barak* ("to bless") occurs six times throughout this section (vv. 12 [3x], 13, 15, 18). This verb is sometimes translated as "praise" or "extol" when directed toward God, as is the case here in the last blessing, which is a thankful response to Him. The blessings are in the form of land, descendants, and prosperity (vv. 13–15) and are rooted in God's sovereignty as Creator of heaven and earth (v. 15) who has given the earth to humankind (v. 16). The psalm concludes with another Hallelujah ("praise the LORD").

116:1–19
Thanksgiving

Psalm 116 moves from theology to anthropology (cf. introduction to Ps. 113), focusing on the human response to divine deliverance. This personal thanksgiving psalm presents the psalmist as an individual rescued by Yahweh from a life-threatening situation, which is not further clarified ("death" occurs 3x in vv. 3, 8, 15). As in Psalm 30, there is a double structure in the psalm (vv. 1–9, 10–19), repeating the thanksgiving in parallel fashion. The first section expresses the thanksgiving verbally, whereas the second section expresses thanksgiving by means of a ritual.

116:1–9. Expression of Thanksgiving. Verses 1–2 introduce the psalm with a beautiful manifestation of the psalmist's love for God (cf. 18:2) grounded in his experiences with Yahweh throughout his life. In vv. 3–6 Yahweh rescues the psalmist from the torments of Sheol. The emphasis is not so much on the exact nature of the threat but on God's characteristics (cf. Ex. 34:6). The self-characterization *peti* ("simple," "unwary," "inexperienced") in v. 6 is found elsewhere in the Psalms. Only in Psalms 19:7 and 119:130 is it used as an expression of a person who needs to grow in wisdom (cf. Mat. 11:25). As a result of the rescue, the psalmist has found rest and returns to "the land of the living" (vv. 7–9).

116:10–19. Demonstration of Thanksgiving. There is a transition in vv. 10–11 to the repetition of the thanksgiving. The conjunction *ki* ("therefore") in v. 10 could also be translated as "even though" (i.e., "I believe, even though I spoke"), similar to the confession of faith in Yahweh found at the beginning of the poem. What follows, as in the previous section, is the negative experience of affliction and a judgment that indicates that truth is found only in

Yahweh. The cup of salvation (v. 13) is a festal cup of abundance (cf. 23:5) that the psalmist takes up as a libation ritual, which connects it to the fulfillment of vows (v. 14; e.g., Num. 15). The action is repeated once more in vv. 17–19 with the addition of the place where the offering will take place (i.e., in the courts of the Lord's house). The reference to being freed from bonds or chains, which is sandwiched between the two thanks offerings (v. 16), can be understood as a reference to the Exile. Taken within the context of the postexilic community, this section expresses the hope and confidence that the psalmist will one day be able to offer his sacrifices within the precincts of a rebuilt temple. Psalm 116 is quoted by Paul (v. 10 in 2 Cor. 4:13 and v. 11 in Rom. 3:4), both within the context of faith and human response, reflecting the spirit of thanksgiving.

117:1–2
Praise the Lord

The shortest of the psalms finds itself in close proximity to the longest (Ps. 119) and is framed by a hymnic invitation to praise. It is universal in character and links to Psalm 115:1–2, inviting the nations to participate in worship to Yahweh. It forms the center of the triad of psalms (116–118) emphasizing human praises before the Lord.

117:1. Praise the Lord. The beginning and end of the psalm is an imperative directed at the nations/Gentiles and all people to praise God. With the return of Israel and the reconstruction of the temple that is envisaged in the previous psalms, Jerusalem becomes the center of universal praise. The nations that subjugated God's people in the past (106:41), who have mocked a defenseless Israel (115:2) and who have been the subject of divine judgment (110:6), are now invited to join God's people in praises.

117:2. Because God Is Good. Verse 2 provides the rationale for praises and thus constitutes the principal theme of the hymn. Exodus 34:6 is invoked once more through the mention of *khesed* ("faithful love," "kindness," "mercy") and *'emet* ("faithfulness," "truth") as eternal characteristics of Yahweh. Although most translations render the verb *gabar* in the present tense ("is great"), the Hebrew perfect tense here could also be translated as "was great" or "was mighty," in which case this could be a reference to the completed first and second exodus, from Egypt and Babylonia respectively. The psalm concludes with the second and final Hallelujah ("praise the LORD").

118:1–29
Entrance into the Temple

As the last psalm of the Passover Hallel, Psalm 118 is a thanksgiving psalm that takes its audience to the gates by means of a liturgical procession, which is reflected in the twofold division of the poem (vv. 1–18, 19–29). Verses 1–4 and 29 create an *inclusio* around this procession with the repeated phrase, "His *khesed* ("mercy," "lovingkindness," "faithful love") endures forever." The psalm has been associated with the temple dedication after the Exile, recorded in Ezra 6, or with the first celebration of the Festival of Tabernacles described in Nehemiah 8–9. Psalm 118 also contains a number of quotations from Exodus 15 (e.g., vv. 14, 16 // Ex. 15:2), applying the Song of the Sea to the return from the Babylonian exile.

118:1–18. Rescue from Exile. The exhortation to give thanks to the Lord is motivated by His goodness and the fourfold repeated formula; His *khesed* ("mercy," "lovingkindness," "faithful love") endures forever (vv. 1–4) is echoed once more in v. 29. Three groups are invited to praise (i.e., Israel, the house of Aaron, and those who fear the Lord). The last group opens up a universal dimension to the psalm, a feature that also characterizes the previous psalm. Verses 5–18 describe a crisis and the rescue Yahweh provided, using the experience of an individual who recounts the various threats he faced and the divine interventions that occurred. The literary connections to Exodus 15 in vv. 14–19 (see above) call on Yahweh's rescue during the Exodus from Egypt, but also contextualize it to the second exodus by mentioning a seeming paradox—the Lord has *yasar* ("chastened," "disciplined") him severely but has not given him over to death (v. 18).

118:19–29. Festival in the Temple. The ritual of the gatekeepers at the temple doors (vv. 19–21) has already appeared in Psalms 15 and 24. As access is provided to the righteous (v. 20), the postexilic community marvels at the rebuilt temple, looking at its stonework and masonry. The imagery of the selection of appropriate stones for building lies behind the proverbial statement in v. 22: the stone rejected by the builders has become the cornerstone. The reuse of stones from the temple ruins for rebuilding after the Exile is a familiar sight in archaeological excavations. Theologically, it signifies Israel's re-election and takes on messianic dimensions through repeated quotations and allusions in the NT (Matt. 21:24; Mark 12:10; Luke 20:17; Acts 4:11; Eph. 2:20; 1 Pet. 2:6–7). Rejoicing and blessing accompany the festive procession as it enters into the house of the Lord (v. 26). In v. 27 the altar comes into focus. The Hebrew term *khag* has been translated here as a festival (its usual meaning) or a festival sacrifice (see Ex. 23:18). Thus, this verse refers either to the binding of the sacrifice to the horns of the altar or joining of the festival procession with branches (Heb. *'abot*) waving. The twofold monotheistic confession ("You are my God") cites once more from the Song of the Sea (v. 28; Ex. 15:2), leading into the final invitation to "give thanks to the LORD" in v. 29, which is identical to v. 1 and closes the frame. While some people cried when they saw the second temple (cf. Ezra 3:12), it was this temple that greeted the Messiah.

119:1–176
The Great *Torah* Psalm

This is the greatest (and longest) of the four *torah* psalms (Pss. 1, 19, 111, and 119), presented as an intricate acrostic structure that divides the poem into twenty-two strophes of eight lines each. Each strophe, and each verse in it, begins with the subsequent letter of the Hebrew alphabet. The central theme of the psalm is *torah*, although no single commandment from the law of Moses is quoted. It is rather a constant recital of the relationship between the "I" of the psalm and God's *torah*. Thus, it serves as a personal meditation on *torah*, which has a much broader scope in biblical thought than just the Ten Commandments given at Mount Sinai. It represents a life in close relationship with God, and therefore meditation on *torah* is always a contemplation of its Giver. *Torah* is thus the complete revelation of His will, and Psalm 119 seeks a deeper understanding of it (cf. v. 18).

The psalm's location in the Psalms and its composition in eight verses for each strophe could point to its use during the Festival of Tabernacles that was celebrated for eight days at the inauguration of the temple under Solomon (cf. 1 Kin. 8:2) and again under Nehemiah following the Exile (cf. Neh. 8). *Torah* is thus the foundation of the first and second temple periods, and the reading of this poem serves as a charter for public governance and personal piety. Psalm 119 is framed in similar fashion as the whole Psalms:

a beatitude begins the psalm (strophes 1 and 2; cf. Ps. 1), and it ends with an extended praise (strophes 21 and 22; cf. Pss. 146–150). There is a center (strophes 11–12), which elaborates on the power of *torah*.

119:1–8. Aleph. Blessings are designated for those (plural, not singular as in the beatitude of Psalm 1) who are *tamim* ("complete," "sound") in their ways; they have a life in harmony with *torah* (cf. Ps. 25:10; Prov. 11:20). Verses 5–8 respond to the beatitude with the individual's desire to be steadfast in following God's instructions (v. 5).

119:9–16. Beth. In typical wisdom style, the section begins with a question that refers back to the theme of the Aleph section (v. 9)—how can young people keep their ways pure? The answer provides a comprehensive list of synonymous expressions which focus on *torah*: word, commands, *huqqim* ("decrees," "statutes"), *mishpatim* ("judgments," "ordinances," "laws"), *'edot* ("statutes," "testimonies") precepts, and ways (vv. 9–15). Throughout Psalm 119, the psalmist varies these expressions in order to demonstrate the meaning of *torah* as well as to avoid monotony. While *torah* needs to be internalized in the heart (v. 11), it also must be expressed outwardly and audibly through the lips (v. 13).

119:17–24. Gimel. The focus moves beyond the psalmist to external threats that may interfere in the relationship between *torah* and the individual. When the psalmist says that he is a stranger on the earth (v. 19), a phrase drawing on patriarchal imagery, he probably refers to the situation of the returning exiles who were surrounded by Samaritans and Edomites (cf. Neh. 2) and estranged in their own country. Within this context of personal insecurity, the psalmist, in contrast, meditates on God's *huqqim* ("decrees," "statutes"; v. 23).

119:25–32. Daleth. The negative situation intensifies in this section, and the psalmist finds himself in a deathlike situation as he is in the dust (v. 25; cf. 22:15). The Hebrew word used here, *dabaq* ("to cling"; i.e., he is "clinging to the dust"), is also used at the end of the section, where he is clinging instead to God's *'edot* ("statutes," "testimonies"; v. 31) and is totally persuaded that Yahweh will (literally in the Hebrew) make his heart larger (v. 32). This metaphor could refer to God's giving him freedom from death, or it could mean that God broadened the psalmist's understanding (*leb* can refer to the mind), and this metaphor has been translated accordingly by some scholars.

119:33–40. *He.* All eight verses in this section begin with an imperative directed at Yahweh, and the first request—to be taught—is complemented by the last, to *khayah* ("preserve," "revive") him. Instruction in *torah* leads to a renewed life.

119:41–48. *Waw.* The psalmist is longing for God's *khesed* ("mercy," "kindness," "faithful love") and salvation, which come through *torah*. The twofold profession of love for the law (vv. 47–48) is accompanied by the psalmist lifting his hands (*nasa' kap*) toward God's commandments. This has been interpreted (and translated) as either a gesture of homage or an expression of desire—he is reaching out for God's precepts as he meditates on *torah*, audibly recites it, and contemplates it (v. 48; cf. 1:2).

119:49–56. *Zayin.* The strophe is arranged around the verb *zakar* ("to remember"), which occurs three times in this section (vv. 49, 52, 55) and only here in Psalm 119. The psalmist prays for God's remembrance (i.e., His concern; cf. Gen. 8:1 and commentary), but the psalmist also remembers both God's *mishpat* ("judgments," "laws," "ordinances"; v. 52) and His name and appeals to them for deliverance from the wicked (v. 53).

119:57–64. *Heth.* There is a subtle appeal to Yahweh in the usage of the noun *khelqi* ("my portion") at the beginning of this section. It connects to the land distribution at the beginning of the conquest (cf. Josh. 14:5) but is also applicable to the repossession of Israel following the Exile. The Exile is indirectly mentioned as being bound with the cords or ropes of the wicked (v. 61).

119:65–72. *Teth.* The first and last lines of the section begin with *tob* ("good"), thus creating a frame that communicates the main theme of the passage, namely, the goodness of God. This theme permeates the remainder of the section (cf. vv. 66, 68, 71) and goes hand in hand with the psalmist's request for God to teach him (vv. 66, 68) so that he would learn (v. 71).

119:73–80. *Yod.* God as Creator introduces the section (v. 73) and forms the rationale for the psalmist's petition for Yahweh's *rakham*

("compassions," "tender mercies"; v. 77). This request connects to the deliverance from the proud, who should be ashamed (v. 78). The psalmist wants to completely follow God's statutes and decrees so that he would not be shamed (v. 80).

119:81–88. *Kaph.* The central two strophes of the psalm are juxtaposed to each other and begin with distress that is counteracted through *torah* as Yahweh's saving power. At the beginning of the Kaph section, the psalmist's soul faints (v. 81) and he asks God to *khayah* ("preserve," "revive") him. The intensity of the distress is underlined by reuse of the root *radap* ("to persecute"; v. 86), the imagery of a dried wineskin (v. 83) that can no longer hold liquids, and the pits (v. 85) dug by enemies.

119:89–96. *Lamed.* The cry for help that ended the previous section is answered at the beginning of this section with the assurance of God's faithfulness that endures through all generations (v. 89). Central to the passage is the idea that *torah* gives life (v. 93), probably referring to the role of the sacrificial system in the law. In v. 96, the psalmist says that he has seen the *qets* ("end") of all *tiklah* ("perfection"). This has been understood as "consummation of perfection" in the greatness of the law or as the "limit of all perfection," referring to human limitations over the *rekhabah mitswateka me'od* ("exceedingly broad," "boundless," "unlimited") nature of God's commandments (v. 96).

119:97–104. *Mem.* The tone of the psalm becomes more positive as it focuses on the psalmist's love for *torah*, which is the appropriate response of humankind to God (cf. Deut. 6:5; Rom. 13:10). The simile of honey (v. 103) is reflective of another *torah* psalm (cf. 19:10). The love for *torah* produces wisdom, understanding (v. 104), and a life in harmony with Yahweh.

119:105–112. *Nun.* The section begins with the most widely used line from Psalm 119, which likens *torah* to a light that illuminates the believer's path, a familiar metaphor in the wisdom literature (cf. Prov. 6:23). OT lamps were made of clay, filled with oil, and carried through the darkness as a source of light to illuminate the path ahead. *Torah* is a light that provides safe passage in the midst of darkness.

119:113–120. *Samek.* The Samek and Ayin sections are linked chiastically; the Samek section begins by contrasting hate and love (v. 113), whereas the Ayin section concludes with the reversed contrast love–hate (vv. 127–128). Strong emotions toward God and *torah* generate equally strong opposite emotions against the double-minded (v. 113), namely, people that reject God's Law.

119:121-128. *Ayin.* The psalmist realizes that the abhorrence of evildoers does not exempt him from a sinful attitude in his own heart. Consequently, this section deals with an internalization of *torah* with the accompanying request that God will give him understanding and discernment for the purpose of knowing His *'edot* ("testimonies," "statutes"). Categorically, the psalmist ends the section by expressing hatred for every deceptive path.

119:129-136. *Pe.* From a positive metaphor of a cave entrance that illuminates the darkness (v. 130), the psalm moves once more to a petition asking God for redemption from oppression (v. 134). The psalmist experiences pain and sorrow because people do not follow God's law (v. 136).

119:137-144. *Tsade.* The keyword in this section is the root *tsedeq* ("to be righteous," "righteousness") occurring five times in various forms in the Hebrew text (vv. 137, 138, 142 [2x], 144) and always associated with Yahweh. In contrast, the psalmist is insignificant and despised (v. 141), and he can live only through an understanding of *torah* (v. 144).

119:145-152. *Qoph.* The section takes the form of a repeated cry for help with an interesting contrast between near and far. While the wicked draw near, they are far from God's law (v. 150). However, Yahweh is near through His commandments (v. 151).

119:153-160. *Resh.* The verbal sequence *ra'ah* ("see/look," "consider") and *khayah* ("preserve," "revive") frames this section (vv. 153–154, 159), indicating God's response to the cry of the previous section. When God sees, as in the Exodus story (cf. Ex. 3:7–8), He acts and revitalizes.

119:161-168. *Sin/Shin.* Following a final negative allusion to persecution at the beginning of the section, the psalm now turns to a final praise of *torah* in its last two strophes, including a double expression of love for it (vv. 163, 167).

The statement about praising God "seven times a day" (v. 164) emphasizes the completeness or fullness of praises.

119:169-176. *Taw.* The final lines of the psalm once more intonate praises (vv. 171–172) and end with a number of requests. The last appeal (v. 176) uses the familiar metaphor of a shepherd and affirms that the psalmist does not forget God's commandments. The psalm describes a type of personal piety that is grounded on the divine *torah* and framed by love toward God. This is truly the good and happy life.

120:1-7
War and Peace

The contrast between "war" and "peace" characterizes this psalm and expresses the psalmist's petition to be delivered from "distress," identified as living side by side with those who hate peace (v. 6).

120:1-2. Call and Petition. The song is introduced by a call to God for help in distress, followed by a statement of trust: God heard and answered the prayer (cf. 81:8; 99:6–8). God's hearing is His acting as well. Consequently, the psalmist clarifies his petition, asking God to act and deliver him from people who speak deceitfully (v. 2).

120:3-4. Retribution. The next lines turn to the consequences that those who speak dishonestly will experience (vv. 3–4). Since the words from a false tongue can serve as arrows and weapons (cf. 57:4; 64:3), they will receive sharp arrows and burning coals. This evokes the imagery of Yahweh as a Warrior. The "broom" is a desert bush still used by Bedouins today to make charcoal. The roots burn for a long time and can be used as fiery arrows to set houses and tents ablaze in warfare.

120:5-7. Protection among Enemies. The negative mention of Meshech and Kedar could refer symbolically to threats that surround the psalmist. Meshech has been identified as a warrior people in Asia Minor (cf. Ezek. 32:26) and Kedar as a reference to Bedouin tribes in the Arabian desert (cf. Ezek. 27:21). One can understand these topographic names as referring to the extreme north and east directions and thus as a metaphorical or proverbial allusion to life-threatening forces from the far ends of the world. The final line of the psalm reaches a climax by contrasting the desire of the psalmist for *shalom* ("peace") with his current situation in the midst of war. The persistent threat is resolved only in the following psalm. David's desire for the peace of long ago is a good starting point for the postexilic pilgrims as they make their way to Jerusalem, once more surrounded by enemies from every side.

121:1–8
I Lift Up My Eyes

This beautiful poem about Yahweh's protection on the journey to Jerusalem begins with an introductory question, which is answered throughout the remainder of the psalm. The psalm is a liturgical dialogue between the pilgrim (or David in its original setting) and the congregation or officiating priest at the temple. There is a small variation in its title with the addition of a preposition that could literally be translated as "a song *for* ascents" (*shir lamma'alot*) instead of "a song of ascents" (*shir hamma'alot*), although it is grammatically ambiguous. Some have suggested that it marks the beginning of pilgrimage as this psalm is the only one in the group with the variation.

121:1–2. Help from the Lord. As the pilgrims set out on their journey, they lift their eyes to the hills/mountains. The "hills/mountains" should not be understood metaphorically (for danger) in this case but are used positively to denote the protective function of Mount Zion and reflect the actual topography of Israel (cf. 133:3). The ensuing question concerning the source of the psalmist's help is used rhetorically to set up the answer in v. 2. The last word of the line is repeated as the first word of the next line, here *'ezri* ("my help"). Yahweh helps from His abode in Mount Zion, and He is further identified as the One who made heaven and earth. The same formula concludes the Song of Ascents in Psalm 134:3, indicating that God's continuous creative power sustains Israel (cf. also 124:8).

121:3–8. Confirmation of Help. In response to the initial question and answer, the remainder of the psalm describes Yahweh's protection with verbal links to the Aaronic blessing (Num. 4:24–26). Yahweh protects Israel and neither slumbers nor sleeps, in contrast to other gods of the ANE who claim the right for undisturbed sleep. Verses 5–6 change the metaphor of protection to Yahweh providing shade at the right hand (i.e., right next to the individual or king), and His shade continues day and night. The mention of the Lord's power over the sun and moon can be understood as a further polemic reference to the deities of the surrounding nations. As a second motif from Aaron's blessing, the psalm concludes with a more concrete description of God as He will *shamar* ("preserve," "keep"; see Num. 6:24). The formulaic ending of the psalm from *'attah* to *'olam* ("from now till forever") is also found in Psalms 125:2 and 131:3. It expresses the forward and upward movement of the Pilgrim psalms, thus initiating the journey to Jerusalem.

122:1–9
Prayer for Jerusalem

The poem is accentuated by keywords creating sound pictures, which transmit the main focus

---

Pilgrim Psalms

The Pilgrim psalms (120–134) constitute an important subgroup sharing the title *shir hamma'alot*, translated as "song of stairs" (referring to the steps leading up to a city, temple, or altar; cf. Ex. 20:26; Neh. 3:15; Ezek. 40:20, 26) or "song of ascents" (referring to the return from exile or pilgrimage to Jerusalem for the annual festivals; cf. resp. 1 Kin. 12:28; 2 Chr. 36:23). Metaphorically, they are also characterized by an upward movement, describing Israel's elevation from degradation to new spiritual heights after the Exile.

Some of the songs are further associated with Davidic authorship (122, 124, 131, 133), but their grouping together and location in the psalms demonstrate their application to the historical situation following the Babylonian exile. Their short length and liturgical character made them suitable to be sung at the temple, and it has been suggested that their number of fifteen corresponds to the number of words in the Aaronic blessing (Num. 6:24–26). The keywords of the blessing ("peace," "bless," "gracious," and "keep") are frequently found throughout the collection.

of the psalm. The recurring and similarly sounding terms "Jerusalem" (*yerushalaim* 3x; vv. 2, 3, 6) and "peace" (*shalom* 3x; vv. 6, 7, 8) come together in v. 6 as the climax of the poem— "pray for the peace of Jerusalem." The psalm is ascribed to David and continues the ascent toward Jerusalem to the annual festival.

122:1–4. Ascent and Expectation. The psalm begins and ends with mention of the house of the Lord (vv. 1 and 9), a structure which communicates the function of the temple as a conceptual frame for Jerusalem's peace. This term ("house of the LORD") is echoed by the reference to the house of David in the center of the psalm (v. 5). The verbal forms of the first section are indicative, describing the ascent of the pilgrims as they approach Jerusalem. They also portray the city with its gates (v. 2) and other features that provide security, such as its being built compactly (v. 3). It is a place where the tribes of the Lord (v. 4) come together once more, a situation which is reminiscent of the early origins of Israel. The purpose of the pilgrimage is to give thanks and praise the name of the Lord for all His wondrous saving deeds (v. 4; cf. 106:1; 136:1–3).

122:5. Judgment Scene. The preposition *ki* ("for") introduces v. 5 as the center and relates it to the preceding lines. A judgment scene is described that is allusive to Daniel 7:9–10 and 13–14. It is set in the house of David, and the connection with the "house of the LORD" in v. 9 establishes a connection between sacred and governance. Israel's reign needs to be framed by Yahweh's reign. The fact that the Hebrew word for temple (*hekal*) is one of the words also used for palace is another detail which implies the overlapping of the religious and secular spheres. The Day of Atonement provides a feasible historical backdrop for the occasion of the psalm.

122:6–9. Prayer of the Changed. The ascent to Jerusalem for the festivals is not a mere ritual requirement, but it effectuates changes in the pilgrims who attend. Thus, the verbal forms of the final section of the psalm change to volitional ones, a prayer that expresses the desires of the pilgrims, who enjoy the life-changing effects of the Day of Atonement. It is a prayer for *shalom* ("peace," "wholeness") within the walls and *shalwah* ("quietness," "rest," "security") within the palaces of Jerusalem (vv. 6–7). This prayer includes the concept of *shalom,*

which is an all-encompassing concept of well-being that includes physical, emotional, and spiritual aspects. Jerusalem thus becomes the eternal city of peace, and the prayer echoes the wish of the postexilic community.

At His triumphal entry into Jerusalem, Christ alluded to the LXX of Psalm 122:8 (Luke 19:42). The text in Luke 19 reflects the progression of this Song of Ascents in a dramatic way. As in the times of Psalm 122, Jesus and His disciples approached Jerusalem as pilgrims, but this time Jesus wept over Jerusalem with the realization that the time of peace for Jerusalem was coming to an end (Luke 19:35–42). This is followed by a judgment scene (Luke 19:43–44), which is acted out in the ensuing cleansing of the temple (Luke 19:45–46). Then there is *shalom* when Jesus taught (Luke 19:47) and healed (cf. Matt. 21:12–14). The peace of Jerusalem begins with those who pray for it.

123:1–4
From the Mountain to the Master

As the psalmist looked up to the mountains in Psalm 121 and to Mount Zion in Psalm 122, the poet in Psalm 123 looks up to God as the Master (v. 2). This expresses once more the upward movement of the Pilgrim psalms. The "proud" (v. 4) could indicate the resistance manifested by the enemies of the exiles when they returned from Babylon to Jerusalem.

123:1–2. Looking Up to Yahweh. The hopeful look of servants/slaves up to their masters and a maid/female slave to her mistress is used as a metaphor for the relationship between Israel and God. While clarifying the sovereignty of God on one hand, it also expresses Israel's expectation on the other. There is a chiastic arrangement in vv. 1–2, beginning and ending with the expectant look at God (vv. 1b–c and 2c–d), which frames the inclusive metaphor of the male and female servants (vv. 2a–b). The hand of the master is the location from which blessings or favors are to be expected (cf. 145:15).

123:3–4. Petition for Mercy. The hopeful expectation of the first section is verbalized in vv. 3–4 through a twofold petition for mercy (v. 3). Among the reasons for the petition are contempt and scorn (vv. 3–4), things which occurred in Jerusalem during the rebuilding of the temple and city (cf. Neh. 2:19; 4:1, 4). We can look hopefully and expectantly to God in times of ridicule by lifting our eyes from our circumstances to the source of life.

124:1–8
True Help

A national calamity, which is not further identified, underlies this thanksgiving psalm. It is ascribed to David but can easily be contextualized to the situation of national threat following the Exile. This is also underlined by its liturgical tone.

124:1–5. Crisis. The national crisis is viewed in retrospect, preceded by Israel's liturgical repetition of a conditional clause. Verses 1–2 constitute the first part ("If...") and vv. 3–5 the second ("... then"). The contingent description ("if") of the situation, wherein the Lord was not on their side, implies that Yahweh has been faithful showing Himself as a God who delivers. The language points back not only to the Exodus (cf. Ex. 3:14) but also to the postexilic experience of Nehemiah (cf. Neh. 4:20). Verses 3–5 use water imagery to express the overwhelming threat of attack (cf. Ps. 42:7). The waters are likened to floods that would have overwhelmed them (i.e., threatened their lives).

124:6–8. Rescue. This section begins with the formula familiar from previous psalms, the verb *barak* ("bless," "praise") applied to Yahweh as "Praise/bless the LORD." This is always connected to Yahweh's marvelous deeds of deliverance (cf. 28:6; 31:21; 72:18; 144:1). It is followed by a metaphor of wild animals with sharp teeth (v. 6), introduced already in v. 3 but developed further in v. 6 and then modified once more in v. 7, where there is a switch to the metaphor of a hunter who traps prey. This overlapping of metaphors creates a fast-paced imagery, which effectively dramatizes Yahweh's rescue of Israel. Verse 8 concludes with an expression of trust that refers to the name of the Lord and His role as sovereign Creator, emphasized in the Pilgrim psalms (cf. Pss. 121:2; 134:3). The psalm's imagery foreshadows Paul's confident statement in Romans 8:31, "If God is for us, who can be against us?"

125:1–5
Mount Zion

Once again, mountain imagery and upward movement are used (cf. Pss. 121–123) to describe "those who trust in the LORD" as immovable like "Mount Zion" and its surrounding mountains.

The negative threats of the preceding psalms give way to a sense of security based on the reestablishment of Israel in Jerusalem by Yahweh. It climaxes in the final blessing, which invokes peace for Israel (v. 5). The subgroup of Psalms 125–129 within the Pilgrim psalms is marked by an *inclusio* (e.g., wicked scepter in 125:3; parallels of the cords of the wicked in 129:4) and a center (Pss. 126–128), which describes the daily life of a returned and redeemed Israel.

125:1–3. Mountains and Freedom. Two related but slightly varied similes introduce the psalm. The first one is Mount Zion, which points to the immovability of God's people (v. 1), and the second finds Yahweh protectively surrounding Israel as the mountains surround Jerusalem (v. 2). The center of the psalm introduces Israel's newfound freedom from the wicked scepter—a powerful metonymy for unjust foreign rule. Here it serves as an admonition to discourage the righteous from reaching with their hands to act wickedly. This freedom charter encompasses the allotted land, a term which references the time of the conquest (e.g., Josh. 14:2). This allusion serves to portray the return from exile as the second exodus.

125:4–5. A New Rule. God's new order of righteousness will create a contrast between those who are upright in their hearts and those who turn aside and follow their own crooked ways. For this last group there is no room in the land; the Lord will lead them away and banish them as He led Israel into captivity. The righteous will receive their allotment, as in the times of Joshua (cf. Deut. 30:5). The psalm ends with the blessing of *shalom* over Israel, which is further developed in a practical way throughout the following psalms.

126:1–6
Return to Zion

Psalm 126 celebrates Israel's return from Babylonia and recalls the "great things" (vv. 2–3) Yahweh has accomplished on behalf of Israel, which ultimately signify God's return to His people. The practical effects of freedom in daily life are recounted using agricultural imagery. The poem is a jubilant song that celebrates the reversal of fortunes for Israel at the end of the Exile.

126:1–3. Return. God brought Israel back from exile, and at the same time He again returned to Zion. The verbal form of *shub* used here and the reading of "again" (*shibah*, "turning," "return") instead of "captivity" (*shebi* "war captivity") make it possible to render v. 1a alternatively as "When Yahweh returned again to Zion." Another possible reading found in some translations is to view *shibat* as a variant of *shebut* (both from *shub*), which can mean either "fortunes" or "captivity." Thus, God has "restored the fortunes" or "the captivity" of Zion, a reading which would imply that God was restoring their land and possessions. Israel's return from Babylon implied a return of Yahweh to His city. The dreamlike character of this experience refers not necessarily to its lack of reality but to a wondrous realization that they were once more favored by Yahweh like those who receive dreams in divine revelation; that is, God once more was in communication with His people (cf. Gen. 41:15; Jer. 23:25). The result is laughter and singing as the nations recognize that the Lord had done great things for them. This is confirmed by Israel as they affirm that indeed the Lord had done great things for them (vv. 2–3). These were the same nations that mocked Israel when Jerusalem was destroyed, asking, "Where is their God?" (79:10).

126:4–6. Joy after Sorrow. The second section echoes the beginning of the first and, in line with the observations in v. 1a, could be rendered, "Return to us again, O LORD" or alternatively (as noted above) as a plea to "restore our fortunes" or "bring back our captivity." This returning is as the streams in the South or "Negev." The reference is to the riverbeds of the Negev that dry up during the summer but return in winter filled by the rains. This reversal of fortunes is further expressed in vv. 5–6, which picture the dramatic change from tears to joy through agricultural imagery familiar to its audience and often recited in the prophetic literature (cf. Jer. 31:23–25; Amos 9:13–15; Hag. 2:19). The psalm is about the reunion of God and His people in Zion and the deep joy that will accompany that experience. We also anticipate this most glorious moment at the return of the Lord.

127:1–5
God's Gift

The practical blessings of a restored Israel move from agriculture in the previous psalms to the building of houses and the blessings of children in the present poem. In Hebrew thinking the term "house" (*bayit*) denotes both a physical structure and a family unit (cf. 2 Sam. 7:5, 11–12). The association of the psalm with Solomon reminds us of his building projects, which provided important foundation stones for the postexilic community. Furthermore, there are also important links between Psalm 127 and the book of Proverbs (cf. Prov. 5:10; 10:22; 14:1).

127:1–2. Building Houses. The psalm begins with the twofold emphatic statement that all human activity is in vain unless God is the author and partakes in it. This thought is applied not only to the building of houses but to the guarding of cities (v. 1) and the daily routine of work and sleep (v. 2). Work after the Fall is characterized by the bread of *'etseb* ("sorrow," "toil"; cf. Gen. 3:17–19). This is stated as a reality and not so much as a critique (cf. the positive description of the fruits of labor in Ps. 128), especially in view of the last line of v. 2, which describes sleep as God's blessing for a fulfilled life.

127:3–5. Building Families. A further important aspect of OT daily life is the family, which is dealt with in the second section of the psalm: children are a heritage from the Lord (v. 3). This is a further extension of God's blessings (cf. Gen. 30:2; 1 Sam. 1:27). The heritage (or "portion") is reminiscent of the language of the conquest (cf. Jos. 13). The following war imagery of a quiver full of children (vv. 4–5) denotes future social and political stability that depends on Yahweh. As a result, Israel is ready to confront their enemies, meet them on par in legal or economic disputes, and not be at a disadvantage (cf. Prov. 22:22). According to this psalm, a life permeated by God's constant companionship is a truly fulfilled life. Its foundations are built on a strong family and a strong community.

128:1–6
The Fruit of Labor

This poem further develops the ideal of the Israelite family after the return from exile. It relates happiness to work, family, and society.

128:1–4. Beatitude. Psalm 128 begins with the same beatitude formula (*'ashre*, "happy," "blessed") with which the previous psalm ended, continuing the theme of daily living and family blessing bestowed on those who fear the Lord and walk obediently in His ways. As a consequence, the reward will be happiness and prosperity—the fruit of what is worked for (v. 2). This represents a significant promise in the context of postexilic Israel under the Persian administration. The Persians implemented a system of taxation that left small farmers often unable to provide for themselves and their families. Further happiness comes through the relationship between husband and wife, who is likened to a fruitful vine (v. 3). They are visibly blessed by children who are like growing olive plants (v. 3). This is a more peaceful metaphor than the quiver in Psalm 127 and more in line with the agricultural imagery that permeates this psalm. Interestingly, the olive tree in Hebrew is masculine and the vine is feminine, thus describing the complementary relationship between husband and wife as the prerequisite for a blessed family. Verse 4 resumes the beatitude of v. 1 and concludes with the same thought.

128:5–6. Blessing. In vv. 5–6, a divine blessing comes from Zion, which once more connects the Pilgrim psalms to the Aaronic blessing (Num. 4:24–26). The blessing reaches out from Zion to Jerusalem, to one's life, and further to one's progeny. This is a truly fulfilled life that is an expression of the desire that there will be peace on Israel. This conclusion points back to Psalm 125:5 and once more illustrates how *shalom* for Israel is worked out in the daily life of its citizens.

129:1–8
Liberation from Exploitation

This poem continues to use imagery from the world of agriculture, though this time it is in a negative context. The metaphor of plowing (vv. 1–4) points to Israel's exploitation by their enemies while the metaphor of a frustrated harvest (vv. 5–8) serves as a petition for Yahweh to punish and withdraw His blessings from the enemies. The postexilic context brings to mind the socio-economic realities of the Persian Empire with a heavy taxation system that made life difficult for the common Israelite peasant. Another possible scenario is the experience of the Babylonian Exile, during which the farmers were not able to sustain themselves, in contrast to the previous psalm where the farmers where able to enjoy the results of their own labor (cf. 128:2). However, the psalm makes it clear that the negative experience is already in the past.

129:1–4. Plowing. The psalm is introduced in similar fashion to Psalm 124 by a liturgical

double statement affirming the *rab* ("many," "great") hostilities suffered by Israel since its "youth." It is first introduced by the speaker/minister and then repeated by the congregation (vv. 1–2). Israel's "youth" is sometimes used as a reference to the time in Egypt (e.g., Hos. 2:17). However, the emphasis here is not on the beginning but rather on the duration of Israel's suffering, and the current situation is just another period of distress. The metaphor of plowing in vv. 3–4 presupposes that Israel is under a yoke, the preferred metaphor for bondage in the OT (cf. Deut. 28:48; Is. 9:4), and the image is cruelly intensified as Israel's back is plowed (v. 3; cf. Is. 51:23). This refers to Israel being exploited to the fullest by oppressors who make their furrows long by plowing to the edges of the field. God delivered Israel when He cut the cords of the wicked (v. 4; cf. Ps. 125:3). Yahweh has put an end to this suffering.

129:5–8. Harvest. Consequently, the psalmist shifts his focus by invoking God's wrath on those who hate Zion—he requests that they be shamed and turned back (v. 5). They are further likened to grass on the housetops, which withers quickly for lack of soil and is not even fit for harvest (vv. 6–7). The psalmist concludes with the observation that the traditional blessing usually given during the time of harvest (cf. Ruth 2:4) does not apply to the haters of Zion (v. 8). The paradox in the psalm is that those who exploit the poor to become wealthy will become poor because they lack the blessing of the Lord.

130:1–8
Out of the Depths

While Psalms 125–129 dealt with the daily life of the returned exiles, who are now in their own land, this last subgroup of the Pilgrim psalms (Pss. 130–134) portrays the restoration of the inner person after the Exile. It culminates in the blessings of righteousness and justice that proceed from Zion. Psalm 130 deals with the forgiveness of iniquity for the individual (vv. 1–6) and the community (vv. 7–8).

130:1–6. Forgive Me. Using water imagery ("out of the depths"; cf. 69:2), the psalmist implores Yahweh to let His ears be attentive to the sound of his cry for help (vv. 1–2). This is followed by an indirect acknowledgment of personal guilt by means of a rhetorical question—who could stand if God dealt with us according to our sinful records? (v. 3). The description of

God as having ears is characteristic of the language of prayers in the psalms (cf. 17:6; 31:2; 71:2; etc.). It is also common throughout the ANE (e.g., some Egyptian steles show oversized ears to which the petitioner raises hands in prayer). Verse 4 resolves the tension with an affirmation of Yahweh's willingness to forgive. The psalmist has placed his hope in this forgiveness and watches for it with more intensity than the night watchmen who wait for the morning (vv. 5–6). The morning is the time for Yahweh to save (cf. Ex. 14:24; Ps. 46:5) and to judge (cf. Jer. 21:12; Zeph. 3:5). Through divine forgiveness the psalmist has moved from the depths of darkness (first Hebrew word in v. 1) to the brightness of the morning (last Hebrew word in this section, v. 6).

130:7–8. Forgive Israel. The speaker of the psalm now turns to the congregation and extends his hope to Israel, who can also trust in God's *khesed* ("mercy," "unfailing love," "redemption"; v. 7). This is the foundation of the relationship between Yahweh and Israel, and the psalmist emphatically affirms it: God will redeem the people of Israel from all their sins and iniquities (v. 8). When the angel appeared to Joseph for the naming of Mary's baby, he alluded to Psalm 130:8 and stated that He would save His people from their sins (Matt. 1:21). The saving relationship between Yahweh and Israel is personified in Jesus, who saves us from the depths of sin and will lead us to the morning of redemption.

131:1–3
Hope in the Lord

Although this short psalm is attributed to David, it is frequently interpreted as a woman's prayer based on v. 2. The wording itself does not give any clues as to the gender of the speaker (the first person in Hebrew is not gender specific). While it is conceivable that David used this tender imagery as much as a prophet might use female metaphors (e.g., Is. 1:2; 42:14; 45:10; 46:3; 49:15; 66:9), it is also possible to see him appropriating a mother's song and applying it to Israel.

131:1. Humility. The psalm begins with a series of four negative statements that contrasts the speaker's life of humility with the lives of the arrogant and proud (cf. Prov. 16:5). The heart stands for thinking and internal attitudes, while the eyes represent sight. The distancing from

things too *pala'* ("wonderful," "profound") for him is not reluctance to think deeply but should be understood along the lines of Job 42:1–6, as an act of submission to God's knowledge versus human hubris.

131:2. Mother and Child. The metaphor of the "weaned child" builds on the calming influence of a mother toward her child (weaning usually took place at about three years of age in ancient Israel). The image here is not so much about separating the child from the mother as about fulfilling all the needs of the child and the resulting calm (i.e., God provides for all human needs; cf. 23:1).

131:3. Hope for Israel. Similar to the end of the previous psalm (cf. 130:7), hope moves from the individual to Israel. The focus is once again on hope. Within the context of this psalm, not only forgiveness is hoped for but also divine provision for all human needs without resorting to an arrogant and proud way of life. True humility is always based on forgiveness and the acknowledgment of God as the source of all human hope.

132:1–18
Remember David

From forgiveness to humility, the inward journey of this last group of Pilgrim psalms now moves to David as a role model for these qualities as manifested in his desire to build a temple for the Lord and bring the ark of the covenant to Jerusalem. As the longest of the Pilgrim psalms, it also has strong verbal links with the dedication of the temple of Solomon (2 Chr. 6:41–42, closely quoted in vv. 8–10). The emphasis has shifted toward David as the original initiator of the project to build the temple. It adds the inner attitude of commitment to God, based on the Davidic ideal, to the list of desired attitudes for a postexilic Israel.

132:1–10. David's Prayer. With an emphatic plea for the Lord to remember David, vv. 1–2 introduce David's prayer in the form of an oath directed to the Mighty One of Jacob. The reference is to Jacob's oath while fleeing Esau and seems to include a promise to build a sanctuary to Yahweh in Bethel (cf. Gen. 28:10–20). David's oath follows in vv. 3–5, and it emphasizes his humility before God (v. 3), as well as his determination and commitment for the building of the temple (vv. 4–5). Verses 6–10 retell the story of bringing the ark to Jerusalem, beginning with its return from the Philistines, which was announced in Ephrathah (the ancient name of Bethlehem), the home of David and birthplace of the Messiah (cf. Mic. 5:2). It was found in the fields of the woods (or "fields of Jaar"; v. 6), which is possibly a reference to Kirjath Jearim from where the ark was brought to Jerusalem. The psalm then describes the procession of priests and God's *khasidim* ("the faithful ones," "pious ones," "saints") as they rejoiced when the ark was brought to Jerusalem to the temple (v. 9; cf. v. 16). The section closes as it began, with a request for God to remember David and with an added future dimension—a reference to God's Anointed (v. 10), a successor in the line (and spirit) of David and ultimately the Messiah.

132:11–18. Yahweh's Response. In response to David's oath, Yahweh Himself has sworn a true oath that there will always be a descendant on David's throne if his children will keep God's covenant (vv. 11–12) because the Lord has chosen Zion (vv. 13–14). God's election of Jerusalem results in blessings on the poor, priests, and *khasid* ("kind," "saints"; vv. 15–16; cf. v. 9). Thus, the temple is not only a place to which the people bring their offerings and gifts to the Lord but also a place from which He generously distributes His gifts to them (cf. 23:5–6).

The internal theme of the psalm is further enhanced as these gifts are identified as salvation and joy (v. 16). Verses 17–18 use two images, the horn as a metonymy of power (cf. 89:17) and David's lamp (cf. 1 Kin. 11:36). The mention of God's Anointed (v. 17) points again to a future perspective, just as it does in v. 10. In contrast, God will clothe the Anointed One's enemies with shame, but His crown will flourish and shine radiantly (v. 18). The psalm uses Israel's past as a motivation for the present and guarantee for its future. "We have nothing to fear for the future, except as we shall forget the way the Lord has led us, and his teaching in our past history" (3SM, 162).

133:1–3
Living Together

The practical outworking of Yahweh's presence on Mount Zion in the life of Israel is expressed by the use of two similes (vv. 2–3). Living peacefully together as a community is linked to the imagery of Aaron's anointing, once more invoking the Aaronic blessing (Num. 6:24–26), an important theme throughout the Pilgrim psalms.

Davidic authorship is mentioned in the title and following Psalm 132, which portrays David as the originator of the plan for the temple, this psalm associates David with the institution of the priesthood and festal liturgies.

133:1. Brothers in Harmony. The wisdom statement at the beginning of this short psalm introduces the theme of the poem—the blessings of living together in unity. The two adjectives *tob* ("good") and *na'im* ("pleasant") are used together to describe the life of the righteous (Job 36:11); they are also applied to God and His Name (Ps. 135:3). The term *'akhim* ("brothers") in this psalm is ambivalent and can refer to the community of Israel but may also refer to the old sibling quarrel between Jacob and Esau. The placement of the psalm in its present context suggests that dwelling together has to do with the postexilic community. Furthermore, if the verb *yashab* ("to dwell," "live") is understood as "to sit," the scene is that of a festive gathering, a religious banquet along the lines of Psalm 23:5–6.

133:2. Like Oil. The anointing of Aaron and his sons included pouring aromatic oil on their heads, which would then drip on their garments (cf. Ex. 29; Lev. 8). The ritual inaugurated the temple service and provides a historical rationale for the gathering of the postexilic community. The repeated mention of Aaron's beard (v. 2) focuses attention on the oil as it drips down and naturally flows onto the clothing of the priest, which includes the ephod and breastplate containing the names of the twelve tribes. Thus, the blessing extends once more onto Israel as a whole.

133:3. Like Dew. The imagery shifts now to the dew on Mount Hermon (v. 3), described as a substance that descends in order to illustrate that the blessings of the Lord are continuously flowing to His people. Geographically speaking, it is impossible for the dew from Mount Hermon in northern Israel to descend upon the mountains of Zion. The imagery is not attempting to describe things as they really are, but instead it depicts a theological topography. Hermon is the highest peak in Israel, closest to the heavenly realm than any other, while Mount Zion is the highest of all and the true spiritual dew flows from it (cf. Ps. 126). The concluding line of the psalm serves as a final blessing from Zion and seems to be an introduction to the Aaronic blessing in the next psalm (cf. 134:3).

The blessing is given directly by Yahweh to the people: life forevermore (v. 3). As a Christian community under God's blessings, life can be characterized only by harmony. Where it is lacking reveals a need to reorient ourselves to the Giver of these blessings.

134:1-3
Night Service

The final poem of the Pilgrim psalms is a farewell psalm that is set against the background of a night liturgy at the temple. This ceremony could have been the culmination of the festal activities on which the Pilgrim psalms were focused. Verse 3 begins with the exact words of the Aaronic blessing in Numbers 6:24 (*yebarekeka yahweh*; "May the LORD bless you").

134:1-2. Praise God. The congregation is exhorted to bless/praise the Lord. The "servants of the LORD" can refer to the whole nation (cf. 113:1; 135:1). Considering the qualifying subclause, which describes those who are serving in the house of the Lord at night, the term may point to the priests and temple singers officiating during the night service at the conclusion of one of the annual festivals (cf. 1 Chr. 9:27-33). The praise is expressed by a gesture of adoration as they are invited to lift up their hands in the sanctuary, a movement which expresses the upward direction of the Pilgrim psalms. The end of the section includes a repetition of the first phrase (bless/praise the Lord). Blessing/praising God is an act of worship and an acknowledgment of His sovereignty (cf. Ps. 63:4).

134:3. Blessing. There is now a change of direction within the psalm. The blessings of the people have gone up to Yahweh, and now He gives His blessing to them in the form of the first line of the Aaronic blessing. He who blesses them is the One who made heaven and earth. The Creator blesses them from Zion. This identifies the specific locale from which He will bless and reestablish His people after the exile.

135:1-21
Praise and History

Psalms 135 and 136 constitute another set of twin psalms (cf. Pss. 56 and 57; 111 and 112), both of which review the history of Israel and Yahweh's divine kingship. It has been suggested that both psalms constitute the Great Hallel (in contrast to only Ps. 136 as the Great Hallel), one of the three Hallels in Book 5 (Pss. 113-118 as Passover Hallel and Pss. 146-150 as Final Hallel). The Hallelujah ("Praise the LORD") frame of this psalm and similar content of the two psalms seem to further support this suggestion.

135:1-4. Invitation to Praise. The psalm begins and ends with a Hallelujah shout of "Praise the LORD!" (cf. the Passover Hallel; Pss. 113-118). The "servants of the LORD" who stand ministering in the house of the Lord refer back to the previous psalm and not only to the priests and Levites who are lifting up their praise. The corresponding section at the end of the psalm demonstrates that all of Israel is included (vv. 19-20). The word pair "good" and "pleasant" (v. 3) as descriptions for Yahweh recurs in 133:1, while the term *tob* ("good") may also connect the psalm to the beginning line of Book 5 (107:1). It employs the concept of God's goodness as an important theological pillar for the postexilic community. A further rationale for praise is God's election of Israel (v. 4).

135:5-18. God in History. The section is introduced by an emphatic *ki* ("indeed," "yes," "for"). Verses 5-7 emphasize God's sovereign uniqueness among all gods and His omnipotence within the universe as Creator. The review of God's deeds in history begins in v. 8 with the plagues of Egypt (cf. 78:44-64; 105:26-36) and continues to the beginning of the conquest (Ps. 135 stops at approximately the same place), and He is portrayed as King and Judge (vv. 12-14). In concentric parallelism, vv. 15-18 correspond to vv. 5-7, taking up the theme of the idols. The emphasis here is not so much on God's omnipotence as on the impotence of idols. God was described as Creator in vv. 6-7, while the idols of the ANE have no creative power (there is no breath in their mouths; v. 17), a fact that epitomizes the life-creating capabilities of Yahweh (cf. 115:4-8). The final observation—that those who make them are like them—shows that humans emulate what they worship; therefore, the idol worshiper becomes like a lifeless replica of the idol (cf. Jer. 51:17).

135:19-21. Exhortation. In contrast to this lifeless imagery, the final exhortation of the psalm invites various representative groups of people—Israel as a nation with its priests (Aaron) and other temple officials (Levi)—to bless/praise the Lord. All who fear the Lord are invited to bless/praise Him from Zion, His dwelling place. The old truth that we will become like what we worship is still relevant for God's children today.

136:1–26
His Mercy Endures Forever

The second account of Israel's history in the Great Hallel is liturgically composed with an antiphonal refrain line that concludes each of its twenty-six verses: His *khesed* ("mercy," "love," "lovingkindness") "endures forever." Between the introduction (vv. 1–3) and conclusion (v. 26) are twenty-two verses, which is similar to the acrostic structure, although it is not alphabetic. In terms of its threefold structure and content there is a close correspondence to its twin psalm, taking up the themes of Creation, Exodus, and conquest, as well as a final universal note. The refrain makes it clear that Yahweh's *khesed* is the sustaining principle that underlies both history and the present.

136:1–3. Introduction. A threefold summons to give thanks to the Lord introduces the psalm using His goodness as the rationale. This is followed by an allusion to His sovereignty (He is the "God of gods") as well as His divine kingship ("Lord of lords").

136:4–25. God in History. As in the previous psalm, the section begins with a description of Yahweh as Creator (vv. 4–9), although the references to Genesis 1–2 are more explicit and direct. For example, God creates the heavens, earth, and waters (vv. 5–7) and then He fills them with content (great lights, sun, moon and stars; vv. 7–9). The Exodus with its plagues (vv. 10–16) and the conquest with the subjugation of the Canaanite kings (vv. 17–22) serve as the historical highlights of Yahweh's wondrous deeds. These are applied to Israel's situation in vv. 23–24 and commemorate their return from Exile—Yahweh has rescued them from their enemies (v. 24). A final reference to God's provision of food for all His creatures (lit. "all flesh") expands the scope of His work beyond Israel and serves as a conclusion for this section (v. 25).

136:26. Exhortation. The final exhortation repeats the first line of the psalm. God's mercy and love, which continuously echo through this psalm in its antiphonal liturgical setting, still serve as the guiding principle of our lives today.

137:1–9
By the Rivers of Babylon

While the historical context of the psalm is clearly the Babylonian Exile, the text does not clarify if it was written from an exilic or post-exilic perspective. When we take into consideration the position of the poem within Book 5, the second option seems more plausible; the exile is mentioned as a traumatic memory. Psalm 137 is a transitional psalm between the historical twin Psalms 135–136 and the group of Davidic psalms (Pss. 138–145), which appropriate themes from the monarchy and adapt them to a postexilic setting. Thus, the poem transfers Yahweh's historical deeds from the Exodus and conquest (Pss. 135–136) to the return from the Babylonian Exile.

137:1–6. Babylonian Memories. The psalm commences with a description of Babylonian topography: rivers of Babylon (v. 1), willows/poplars (v. 2), and foreign land (v. 4). The Euphrates poplar would qualify for this description, and Ezekiel 3:15 refers to a Jewish community living by the Chebar River. It is possible that Jewish captives were settled along these waterways to work in the waterworks or mud brick production of the Babylonian empire. The hanging of *kinnor* ("harps," "lyres") in the trees was in resistance to the taunting question of the captors who required them to sing a song of Zion, indicating that there was no more reason for praise (cf. the connection between harp and praise in e.g., Ps. 92:3; 98:5; 150:3). The rhetorical question in v. 4 about singing songs of the Lord in a foreign land is retrospective and could be translated as, "How could we have sung the LORD's song…?" The noun *nekar* ("foreign land") is often used in cultic contexts to contrast God with foreign gods (e.g., Deut. 32:12; Jer. 5:19), so it seems that the mocking request was bordering on blasphemy. The painful past memory of Babylon is contrasted with commitment to Jerusalem in the present through the use of two oath formulas that pledge allegiance to a restored Jerusalem (vv. 5–6).

137:7–9. Edom and Babylon. During the turmoil surrounding the fall of Jerusalem in 586 B.C., the Edomites formed an alliance with Babylon and provided mercenaries who were involved in the final destruction of Zion (Jer. 27:1–7; Obad. 10–11). These traumatic memories of war form the backdrop for the wishes of retaliation in vv. 8–9 (see "Imprecatory Passages in the Psalms," p. 733). They provide a glimpse into the atrocities of ANE warfare, often including the killing of innocent women and children, that Judah certainly experienced during the fall of Jerusalem at the hands of the Babylonians (cf. Is. 13:16; Jer. 6:11; 51:56). In the announcement of the fall of Babylon, Isaiah predicted that the children will be dashed against the rocks by the enemies of Babylon (13:16; cf. Jer. 51:20–25, 33, 48). In this psalm, it is a wish that is delimited by the law of retribution as expressed in v. 8. It is a wish not for disproportional punishment but for justified repayment—happy will be the one who repays Babylon for what was done to Israel. This war-torn world is filled with atrocities that far surpass the imagery at the end of this psalm. The poem invites us to deal with the trauma of the past by focusing on the present and future coming of the heavenly city, where injustice and warfare will come to an end.

138:1–8
Yahweh Delivers

The group of eight prayer psalms (Pss. 138–145) before the Final Hallel (Pss. 146–150) is called the fifth group of Davidic psalms as each one bears the king's name in the superscriptions, pointing to Davidic authorship. They begin with an allusion to Yahweh as King (Ps. 138) and move progressively toward a celebration of His kingship, climaxing in Psalm 145. The central Davidic themes of personal righteousness and relationship with God (Pss. 139; 141), social justice (Ps. 140), death (Pss. 142–143), and human kingship (Ps. 144) are again reviewed and at times adjusted to the needs of the postexilic community (see esp. Ps. 144).

138:1–3. Praise before Kings. The group begins and ends with a psalm of praise (cf. Ps. 145) that is introduced by a self-exhortation to praise. This praise is performed before the "gods" (the LXX translates the expression as "before angels"). As previously noted in Psalm 82:1, *'elohim* ("gods") was translated as "judges" or persons of authority ("mighty ones"). Most translations render it "before the gods," finding here a possible polemic expressed by the preposition *neged* ("before"), which can also mean "opposite" or "against." The praise is directed toward Yahweh's name (i.e., His character; v. 2). The reason for praise is His *khesed* ("mercy," "lovingkindness," "faithful love") and truth, which exemplify His character (cf. Ex. 34:6). Verse 3 speaks about deliverance without any specific definition of its nature.

138:4–6. Praise of Kings. In similar fashion to the beginning of the first section, all kings of the earth respond now in praise to Yahweh. This might support the interpretation of *'elohim* ("gods") in v. 1 as "mighty ones" or "rulers." The terms high (or exalted) and lowly (v. 6) illustrate both the transcendence and immanence of Yahweh. He specifically distances Himself from the proud.

138:7–8. Trust in Yahweh. The psalm ends with an affirmation of trust in Yahweh that resembles the syntax and tone of Psalm 23 in several places (e.g., "though I walk" in v. 7 // 23:4; God's *khesed*, "faithful love," "mercy," in v. 8 // 23:6). This promises that the Lord will *gamar* on our behalf. The verb has been rendered variously as "perfect," "complete," "fulfill," or "vindicate" and (especially if the first two nuances are emphasized) is a concept continued in the NT in Philippians 1:6.

139:1–24
You Know Me

Following the transcendent loftiness of Yahweh as heavenly King in the previous poem, Psalm 139 reveals that God comes intimately close to humanity in His omniscience and omnipresence. At the beginning and end of the psalm (vv. 1, 23–24) God is described as one who has searched and known David (in v. 23 as imperatives). The phrase portrays God as both Judge and Creator, who is personally interested in the psalmist's life and destiny. In terms of language, there is an affinity between this psalm and the book of Job, which would point to an early date for the writing of this Davidic psalm.

139:1–6. God Searches and Knows Me. The depiction of God as one examining and probing the life of the psalmist is a familiar theme (e.g., Ps. 7:9; 26:2). His omniscience encompasses the totality of human existence (vv. 1–4). The statement that God has *tsur* ("confine," "shut in") behind and before (v. 5) is ambiguous, since it can negatively refer to the encircling of a city during a siege (1 Kin. 15:27) or an act of protection as one binds up money (Deut. 14:25). Only for the wicked is Yahweh's omniscience a fearful thought, while for the righteous it is "too wonderful" (v. 6).

139:7–12. Where Can I Go? From God's omniscience the psalm moves now to His omnipresence, which is expressed by the vertical, heaven and hell (*she'ol*, "grave"; v. 8), and the horizontal, "wings of the morning" or dawn (v. 9), the remotest part of the sea (v. 9), and darkness and light (vv. 11–12). These extremes comprised the known limits of the ancient world. The reference to being held (lit. "grasp") by God's right hand creates an ambiguity between Yahweh's protection and restraining control (cf. Job 12:23; Ps. 119:53; 137:9). Nonetheless, the psalmist affirms that the abiding presence of the Lord is comforting to the believer.

139:13–18. Wonderfully Made. The pervasiveness of God's presence also transcends time, and the next section contemplates the miracle of human birth. It is a beautiful description of creation through reproduction as the embryo is intricately woven by God (v. 15). The verb used here is the same technical term used for the workmanship in the construction of the sanctuary (cf. Ex. 26:36; 28:39; 35:35). It continues with powerful statements about the value of human life before birth (e.g., God saw the unformed substance of the body in the womb; v. 16). The psalmist reacts to these wonderful thoughts with the insight that God's thoughts are countless in sum, yet this does not prevent closeness to Him (vv. 17–18).

139:19–24. Final Wish. The psalm takes a sudden turn as the psalmist asks God to slay the wicked (v. 19), who maliciously speak against Him and disregard the Ten Commandments as they misuse God's name (v. 20). The psalm concludes with a return to the initial thought as the psalmist asks God to search him and know his heart (v. 23). With confidence as to the outcome of His judgment, the psalmist can request that God will lead him in the everlasting way (v. 24). The realization that God knows the most intimate thoughts and is always present can be comforting for the believer and damaging to the wicked. Romans 8:27 takes this relationship one step further by quoting from vv. 1–2 and 23 of the psalm to introduce Christ as our intercessor.

140:1–13
Preserve Me from the Wicked

Psalm 140 begins where the previous psalm left off (namely, with a strong contrast between the righteous and wicked) while asking for deliverance from evil people. There are a number of references back to Book 2 (esp. Pss. 52; 55–59; 62; 64).

140:1–5. Description of the Wicked. The initial section of the poem uses a number of violent images to describe (in general terms and

through the use of plural) the enemies (e.g., violent men). They look for war (v. 2), are likened to a poisonous serpent (v. 3; cf. 58:4), and resemble hunters who have set traps (v. 5; cf. 64:5). These metaphors depict the wicked as being completely removed from Yahweh's sphere and belonging to the sphere of other gods (cf. Ex. 34:12; Ps. 106:36).

140:6–11. Prayer for Protection. The language mode of the psalm changes to volitional forms as David asks God to hear his prayer for protection (v. 6) while at the same time expressing thankfulness for the protection already received (v. 7). In contrast, the heads of those who surround David will be covered by their own evil mischief (v. 9). Eventually, the evil that the wicked have accomplished will return to them. *Ra'* ("evil," "disaster") will hunt the violent man (v. 11); this reverses the hunter metaphor that concluded the previous section.

140:12–13. Expression of Trust. Following the reversal of fate for the wicked, the psalm concludes with an expression of trust in Yahweh. He will ensure that justice is done for the poor and needy, whose fates are also reversed. The righteous will give thanks and praise God's name, and the upright will abide in His presence (v. 14). Paul quotes v. 3 to describe human depravity without God and create a similar contrast between the wicked and God's righteousness (Rom. 3:13), which He has revealed through Christ (Rom. 3:21–24).

141:1–10
Protect Me from Being Wicked

This prayer appears similar to the previous one as it speaks about snares, traps, nets (vv. 9–10), and protection from the wicked. But here the psalmist is taking a critical look at himself, considering the ever-present possibility of wickedness entering his own heart.

141:1–5b. Prayer for Protection. The prayer is introduced by sanctuary terminology, taking the evening sacrifice as a liturgical occasion for the supplication (v. 2). The idea of prayer as incense, which was part of the daily morning and evening sacrifice (cf. Ex. 30:7–8), is continued in Revelation 8:3–4. The psalmist continues by describing the danger of wickedness manifested through the door of the lips (v. 3) and a heart enticed to evil (v. 4). Participating in iniquity is likened to eating delicacies of the wicked. There is a progression of engagement with wickedness here that is reminiscent of Psalm 1:1. In contrast, righteous and corrective discipline are likened to oil on the head (v. 5; cf. Prov. 9:8; 27:5–6).

141:5c-7. Contrast. The last line of v. 5 shifts the focus back to the evil acts from which the psalmist intends to distance himself. Verse 6 mentions their *shopetehem* ("judges," "rulers") in a derogatory way—the unjust judges or leaders (cf. 58:1–5) will be thrown over the cliff. The expression is difficult and has been translated in a variety of ways (e.g., "their judges have fallen into a crevasse [lit. 'side of a rock']"), but the idea is that unjust judges would receive their just punishment and the rock could serve as a possible reference to God (cf. 18:3). However, the psalmist tries to convince the wicked of their mortal danger by speaking to them words that are *na'em* ("pleasant," "sweet"; i.e., the words are well spoken). The danger is underlined with imagery of bones scattered by a plowing farmer at the entrance of a grave (*she'ol*; v. 7), possibly a burial cave.

141:8–10. Resolution. Shrinking away from this morbid imagery, the psalmist confirms his commitment to Yahweh (his eyes are looking to Him; v. 8), and he asks to be kept safe from the snares or traps that have been set for him by the wicked. This can refer to either the persecution (as in Ps. 140) or the temptation of falling into wickedness himself. He is certain that he will escape safely (v. 10). A wise rebuke given in love to a friend who may be wandering onto the wrong path may preserve him or her in the path of righteousness.

142:1–7
Deliver Me!

The superscription identifies this Davidic psalm as a *maskil* ("contemplation," "instruction"; cf. 32:1) and "prayer" (*tepillah*; cf. 17:1; 86:1; 102:1). A historical annotation is also included, the first since Psalm 63: "when he was in the cave." It could refer to the cave at En-gedi, based on links between the poem and the narrative in 1 Samuel 24. For example, *qol* ("voice"; v. 1) parallels 1 Samuel 24:16 and *nepesh* ("soul," "life"; v. 4) parallels 1 Samuel 24:11. The psalm might then represent the poetic recollection of Yahweh's deliverance of David from Saul, which could have later been adapted to the life of the postexilic community.

142:1–4. Situation of Distress. The two sections of this psalm are introduced by a loud cry (cf. 107:6) to Yahweh for deliverance. The first section mainly describes the distressing situation in which the psalmist finds himself. As in the previous two psalms, there is mention of snares or traps (v. 3); an expression of utter abandonment is repeated three times and leads to the final conclusion that no one cares for him (v. 4).

142:5–7. Cry for Deliverance. The tone of the psalm becomes more personal as David addresses God directly and appeals to the ancient divine promise of a portion in the land. But the psalmist is talking about the land of the living (v. 5), indicating that he is facing a life-threatening situation. The Portion is an epithet for Yahweh Himself (cf. 16:5; 73:26), suggesting that the promise has been internalized into a life-saving relationship with God. A number of pleas appeal to Yahweh for deliverance (vv. 6–7), climaxing in the plea for God to bring him (lit. his "soul" or "life") out of prison. The infrequent noun *masger* ("prison," "dungeon") is used in connection with the return from exile (v. 7; cf. Is. 42:7; Jer. 29:2) and suggests that the prayer of David is being adapted to the experience of the postexilic Israelite community. The psalm concludes with a final note of confidence in Yahweh's deliverance. When we make the Lord our Portion, the search for self-satisfaction comes to an end because we find in Him the center of our existence.

143:1–12
Close to Death

The distress the psalmist experienced in Psalm 142 is now intensified. Both psalms are connected by verbal links (e.g., the faint/overwhelmed spirit in v. 4 // 142:3). Beyond that similarity, Psalm 143 seems to be a collection of quotations from other Davidic psalms (Pss. 25; 69; 77; 86). Perhaps it is an anthology of prayers that David collected. This psalm was later appropriated by the postexilic community for their situations of distress.

143:1–6. Distress. The psalm begins with three imperatives of intensified urgency, asking God to hear and answer (v. 1). As he appeals to Yahweh's faithfulness and righteousness (cf. Ex. 34:6–7), the psalmist contrasts his own lack of righteousness; indeed, no one living is righteous before God (v. 2). Verses 3–4 describe the situation of distress caused by persecution: the enemy crushes him to the ground (lit. "grinding my life against the ground"—an image which evokes a millstone that grinds out the psalmist's life). The imagery is used in other contexts for the oppression of the poor (cf. Is. 3:15). This section ends with a remembrance of Yahweh's historical works in past days, a reference to both the Creation and the Exodus (cf. Ps. 77:11–12; 139:14). The poet spreads out his hands in supplication and expresses his longing for deliverance (v. 6).

143:7–12. Petition. The petition is concretized in the second section, which begins with a renewed and more intensified plea for Yahweh to answer (v. 7). The next lines read like an anthology, collecting prayer lines from other psalms. The death metaphor in v. 7 comes from 28:1, the morning motif (v. 8) is similar to 30:5 (cf. also 59:16), and the plea for deliverance (v. 9) is also found in 59:1. In vv. 10–11, the focus shifts from deliverance from enemies to the future of the psalmist. He asks for instruction, guidance, and revival, and concludes with the request to bring him (lit. his "soul") out of trouble. This is concretized in a final request for deliverance from the enemies (v. 12). Paul quotes v. 2 in Romans 3:20 and Galatians 2:16, building the argument for the doctrine of justification by faith around these quotations.

144:1–15
A New Government

Psalm 144 takes up the theme of human monarchy by drawing from older psalms, mainly from Psalms 18 and 104 (e.g., v. 1 // 18:34; v. 2 // 18:47; v. 5 // 18:9, 104:32; v. 6 // 18:14; v. 7 // 18:16). The material apparently was reworked by David and may have been adapted later to the needs of the postexilic community. After the exile, a new type of leadership is needed, based on the Davidic ideal and Yahweh's kingship.

144:1–4. Divine Epithets and Humans. The introduction employs a long list of divine epithets (e.g., Rock, Fortress/Stronghold, Tower, Shield) that are reminiscent of Psalm 18:2 and 46. They are all related to war imagery used to depict Yahweh as Warrior. In contrast to the divine omnipotence, there is the fleetingness of human nature (cf. 8:4; 102:11). Humans cannot provide permanent refuge in times of conflict.

144:5–8. Theophany. The section is modeled after Psalms 18 and 104 and describes Yahweh

descending from heaven. However, a number of important changes take place. One significant change is the switch from indicative to mostly imperatives (e.g., in v. 6). This corresponds to Psalm 18:14, which describes God's activities of sending arrows and lightning to destroy enemies. Possibly the most important change is that Psalm 144 contextualizes the old theophanic realities by a new request that fits the postexilic circumstances. Yahweh must again come down from heaven and rescue, but this time from the hands of foreigners (v. 7).

144:9–15. A New Song and Blessings. In this new song (v. 9), the rescue of David from the deadly sword (v. 10) becomes a model for Yahweh's rescue of Israel from the hand of foreigners (v. 11). The final section of the psalm makes reference to the Mosaic blessings (vv. 12–15), and it follows the sequencing of Deuteronomy 28:4–5 and 11 (v. 12, sons and daughters; v. 13, agricultural produce; vv. 13–14, sheep and oxen). Some conclude that the tone of the psalm is directed not toward an individual new king but toward postexilic Israel as a whole. Two beatitudes that emphasize the relationship between Yahweh and Israel as a nation conclude the psalm (cf. Ps. 33:22). It is important to build a new community and a new life around the old historical truths and promises of salvation, claiming them anew.

145:1–21
Alphabetic Praise

The concluding psalm of the fifth group of Davidic psalms is an acrostic poem that praises God through the psalmist (vv. 1–9), through the congregation, and through nature (vv. 10–20). The psalm is framed by a blessing to Yahweh's name (vv. 1–2, 21), a common feature in this group (cf. 138:2; 140:13; 142:7). One letter of the Hebrew alphabet, *nun* ("n"), is missing in the acrostic sequence, although a psalm manuscript from Qumran (11QPsª) and the LXX provide the missing line. The psalm presents Yahweh as King as a logical consequence of Psalm 144, which searches for a new form of government after the Babylonian Exile. Psalm 145 also serves as the last psalm before the final Hallel doxology and thus provides a theological climax to the Psalms with its focus on divine kingship.

145:1–9. Individual Praise. The psalm is introduced by a promise or commitment to praise God's name forever and ever, which is also mentioned in v. 21. This future outlook is further developed by the statement that one generation extols God's works to the next and passes on the knowledge of Yahweh's saving acts in history (vv. 5–7; cf. 143:5). The grace formula from Exodus 34:6, slightly shortened and adapted to the requirements of the acrostic, is used in v. 8 and reaches a universal dimension when it states that the Lord is good to all (v. 9).

145:10–21. Creation and Community Praise.

The universal dimension in v. 9 is continued in v. 10 as it introduces a wider praise choir. All of creation and the community of Israel are invited to raise their voices. They praise God for His mighty acts and His everlasting kingdom and focus on the image of Yahweh as King, whose dominion endures throughout all generations (vv. 11–13). Yet, God still cares for the poor (v. 14) and sustains the natural world (vv. 15–16; cf. 104:27–28). God is righteous and gracious in everything He does (v. 17) and is near to all who call upon Him and follow His way (v. 18). This implies the preservation of all who love Him and, by logical implication, destruction of all the wicked (v. 20). Verse 21 closes the frame by again mentioning the extoling of God's holy name. It is astonishing how this acrostic psalm of David weaves the most important themes of the Davidic psalms into a continuous fabric that is held together by praises. Doxology truly is the key to theology.

146:1–10
Individual Praise

The last five psalms are characterized by the dominance of the verbal root *halal* ("to praise"). It occurs thirty-five times in Psalms 146–150 and ten times as an imperative to which a shortened form of the divine name is attached (*halelu yah*). The phrase is found at the beginning and ending of each psalm. The circle of worshipers who "praise the LORD" gets progressively larger, beginning with the individual (Ps. 146) and growing to include Jerusalem/Zion (Ps. 147), the created world (Ps. 148), Israel within the cosmos (Ps. 149), and finally the cosmos through time and space (Ps. 150). This creates an ever-increasing cosmic symphony that rings through the ages and carries the theological themes of Creation, *torah*, and Zion toward an eschatological end. Psalm 146 has a number of parallels with other psalms, especially with Psalms 103–104. These are not mere quotations but rather form a condensed theological summary of the Psalms in its final doxology.

146:1–2. Frame.

After the initial Hallelujah ("Praise the LORD"; v. 1), which is replicated at the end of the poem (v. 10), the psalmist commits himself to a lifelong melody of praise. This type of life is a guarantee for a full life (v. 2; cf. 104:33).

146:3–9. Yahweh Reigns.

The psalm contrasts a false trust in earthly princes and the fleetingness of their rule (vv. 3–4) with the true hope that only the God of Jacob (v. 5) provides. This hope is introduced through a beatitude; He is our hope not only because He blessed Jacob (Gen. 28) but also because He is the Creator (cf. Ps. 75:9; 76:7). From the God of history the psalm moves to the God of creation (v. 6) and His rule as the heavenly King (vv. 7–9). The ethical dimension of the theology of the psalms surfaces when God is described as caring for the socially disadvantaged groups—those who are oppressed, hungry, prisoners, fatherless, strangers/foreigners, and widows. The liberation of Israel from the Babylonian Exile is echoed in these lines (cf. Is. 42:7).

146:10. Frame.

The final "praise the LORD" of the psalm is preceded by a summary of the poem's contents. The reign of God is to be praised from Zion and throughout eternity (cf. 147:12). The contrast between human and divine rule is also found at the outset of the Psalms in Psalm 2. Thus, the end of this Psalm closes another theological circle.

147:1–20
Praise from Zion

The horizon of praises expands from the individual to the inhabitants of Jerusalem/Zion (v. 12). The LXX reproduces Psalm 147 as two separate poems (vv. 1–11 and vv. 12–20). However, the division of the poem in three sections (vv. 1–6, 7–11, 12–20), each beginning with an invitation to praise, supports the structural unity of the psalm. Each invitation to praise is followed by divine predications describing Yahweh as the Restorer of Jerusalem, Sustainer of the world, and Giver of the *torah*. The constant change of speakers points to the poem's liturgical use.

147:1–6. Restorer of Jerusalem.

The psalm begins and ends with Hallelujahs ("Praise the LORD"). The first section describes Yahweh as the One who builds up Jerusalem (v. 2) and who deals kindly with the *nidekhe* ("exiled," "banished ones," "outcasts"; the latter translation would echo the end of the previous psalm). As the divine Shepherd, He heals the brokenhearted and binds up their wounds (v. 3; cf. Ezek. 34). As Creator, He *manah* ("counts," "appoints/determines") the number of the stars (v. 4; cf. Is. 40:24–26). As King, He takes care of the humble but "casts the wicked to the ground" (v. 6; cf. Ps. 113:7). Yahweh is accomplishing an outward and inward restoration of Jerusalem.

147:7–11. Sustainer of the World. After the second exhortation to praise (v. 7), the next section describes Yahweh as the Sustainer of creation (cf. Ps. 104), who provides rain for the earth and gives food to the animals (vv. 8–9). The negative references to the strength of the horse and the power of a soldier's legs (v. 10) point to the reversal of power under the rule of Yahweh as King (cf. Ps. 143:3–4) and to the total reliance humans have on Him.

147:12–20. Giver of Torah. The psalm then turns to Jerusalem and Zion as the sources of praise. In addition to security and fruitfulness (v. 13), the main reason to praise is given in v. 14 as peace. Jerusalem has finally become the city of *shalom*. Verses 15–18 return to the topic of Yahweh's power as the Creator, who sends out His command to the earth and utters things into existence (see Gen. 1). It was this powerful and life-giving divine word that gave His ordinances and rulings to Israel (i.e., the blessing of *torah*). This creates a further connection to Psalm 1, the first *torah* psalm. Psalm 147 celebrates God as the One who even today can restore peace, provide sustenance, and give a rule of life.

148:1–14
Worldwide Praise

The choir that sings Yahweh's praise expands now to the whole of creation. The twofold cosmology of the psalm is centered on the totality of heavens and earth, which are used to divide the psalm into two parts (vv. 1–7 and 8–14). Psalm 148 occupies the center of the final Hallel and is linked to the previous two psalms by the recurring Creation motif and its emphasis on Israel's preeminent role in the cosmos.

148:1–7. From the Heavens. Yahweh's praise begins "from the heavens" with His angels (v. 2) and then moves through sun, moon, and stars (v. 3). Mention of these entities praising God clarifies their position within the created order, in contrast to their function as deities in other ANE religions. The mention of the waters above the heavens or skies refers back to the cosmology of the Creation account (cf. Gen. 1:7). The verb *bara'* ("to create"), used in Genesis 1:1, is also employed here in v. 5.

148:8–14. From the Earth. In the second section, praise is now requested "from the earth" (v. 7). The great sea creatures are connected to the waters below the firmament (Gen. 1:6–8), and they join the praise song in submission to Yahweh (in contrast to the ANE forces of chaos often portrayed as sea monsters). The psalmist then presents a list of earthly praise choir members, always in pairs. This echoes the order of creation in Genesis 1 and ends with humankind as the crown of creation, again in pairs that cover the whole spectrum of humanity by age, gender, and socio-political status (vv. 11–12). All these pairs reflect the differentiated but complimenting created order. Yahweh's glorious majesty and splendor are above the earth and heaven (v. 13) and above the created sphere that lifts up its praise in unison. Within this worldwide choir, v. 14 zooms in on Israel as a people near to Him and close to His heart. The reference to His people connects this psalm to the two preceding psalms and prepares the way for the next praise song. The whole psalm is a narrowing down from the broadest heavenly scope, climaxing with the people closest to Yahweh.

149:1–9
Israel's Praise within the Cosmos

Psalm 149 picks up the theme of the preeminence of Israel among the nations but with an increasing emphasis on the eschatological perspective of Yahweh's reign. This is expressed through a movement from imperatives in the first section (vv. 1–4) to future-oriented volitional verbal forms in the second section (vv. 5–9). According to Isaiah 42:5, Israel's "new song" is a song of liberation from exile and from the power of all "nations" and "peoples" (vv. 7; cf. also Ps. 96:1; 98:1). This psalm replicates the message at the beginning of Psalm 2 and follows the same sequence of nations, peoples, kings, and nobles (vv. 7–8; replacing the "rulers" of 2:2 here with "nobles"). The initial raging of the nations against Yahweh's "Anointed" is finally resolved eschatologically in Yahweh's eternal reign at the end of the Psalms.

149:1–4. A New Song. The Hallelujah ("Praise the LORD") frame now provides an invitation to praise that focuses on the assembly of the *khasidim* ("faithful," "godly," "pious," "saints"). The parallelism between Maker and King (v. 2) makes it clear that Yahweh's divine kingship is meant here. The expressions of praise include dance, as well as the use of timbrel and harp (v. 3). The word *makhol* could either refer to "dance" or a musical instrument; the latter would seem to be the case in vv. 3–4, where *makhol* is listed in parallelism with musical instruments (see also 150:3–5). In any case, dance was an expression of joy, but it was never performed in the temple. That joy is the result of deliverance from Israel's enemies (cf. Pss. 30:11; 150:4; Jer. 31:4, 13). Consequently, Yahweh will *pa'ar* ("beautify," "glorify," "crown") the *'anawim* ("poor," "humble," "afflicted," "meek") with salvation (v. 4). This expresses the divine concern for the oppressed and reveals the ethical dimension of the psalms.

149:5–9. Judgment for the Saints. The joyful song projects itself here into the future through a change from imperatives to volitional verbal forms, elaborating how the crowning of Israel will play out eschatologically. Praising God on beds (v. 5) recalls Deuteronomy 6:7 and the reciting of *torah* in all life situations (cf. also Ps. 1:2). The surprising metaphorical connection between praise and a two-edged sword (v. 6) alludes to the power of words (Ps. 52:2; 57:4; 59:7; 64:3), a theme that can also be found in the NT (cf. Heb. 4:12). Verses 7–9 portray the *khasidim* ("faithful," "kind," "pious," "saints") as having the glory or honor of performing the judgment written against the nations. Within the eschatological framework of the psalm, this could be understood as the participation of the righteous in the executive judgment of the nations based on the heavenly written records (cf. Dan. 7:9–14; 26–28). The overall imagery of binding with chains and fetters (v. 8) provides surprising links to Revelation 20:1–2 (cf. also Jude 1:6). Psalm 149 opens a wide vista into the glorious future of God's people, characterized by praise, ultimately leading to eternal victory and the end of sin.

150:1–6
Praise Eternal

The grand finale of the Psalms consists of ten exhortations (the imperative *halelu*, "praise," occurs ten times) to praise Yahweh, framed by the two Hallelujah shouts at its beginning and end. They all build in a crescendo to a final cosmic invitation for everything that has breath to "praise the LORD." This is an impressive conclusion to the book of Psalms in which doxology touches eternity. The number ten can be biblically associated with totality but also with the Decalogue and the ten utterances of God in Genesis 1. Thus, the beginning and end of the Psalms bring the theological motifs of Creation and *torah* into view once more. Consistent with the numerical schemes, the seven musical instruments mentioned in vv. 3–5 represent the perfection of praise.

150:1–2. From the Heavenly Sanctuary. In the last Hallelujah ("Praise the LORD") psalm, praises occur in two places, namely, in God's sanctuary and His mighty firmament in the heavens. While *qodesh* could also refer to the earthly sanctuary, the parallelism with the mighty firmament opens up a cosmic dimension and at the same time looks back to Creation. In Genesis 1:8, the firmament is called "heaven," a meaning that would fit well in this passage. The acts of God are referred to as *geburah* ("powerful," "mighty"), and they describe the historical deeds of God from Creation to re-creation.

150:3–6. Into the Cosmos. There is an interesting sequencing of musical instruments in vv. 3–5. They move from instruments used predominantly in a sanctuary context—*shopar* (trumpet), *nebel* (lute or harp), and *kinnor* (harp or lyre; e.g., Lev. 25:9; 1 Chr. 15:16)—to other instruments that were used in both cultic and non-cultic contexts, especially for the celebration of victories and deliverances (timbrel, string instruments, flutes [or pipes], and cymbals; e.g., Ex. 15:20; 1 Sam. 18:6; 2 Sam. 6:5). The dance (cf. observations to Ps. 149:3) is likewise associated with these manifestations of festive joy that go out from the heavenly sanctuary into the cosmic courts. The twofold repetition of the cymbals with the additional qualification *teru'ah* ("resounding," "clashing") cymbals announces an audible climax in the final symphony of the Psalms. The call is universal for everything that has breath to praise the Lord (v. 6) and manifests an eschatological expectation. The Hebrew *neshamah* ("blowing," "breath") refers primarily to humankind (cf. Gen. 2:7; 7:22). The final Hallelujah ("Praise the LORD") concludes the doxology of Book 5 and with that all of the Psalms.

The cosmic and eschatological perspective that concludes the psalm points to a final doxology of cosmic dimensions that will accompany a procession out of the heavenly sanctuary and fill the universe with praises. The whole cosmos will praise the Lord; the dissonance of sin has come to an end. The cosmic conflict will end in a doxology of praises to the Lord. The Christian still looks forward in hope to the moment when everyone will acknowledge Christ as the supreme Lord of all (Phil. 2:10–11).

"The great controversy is ended. Sin and sinners are no more. The entire universe is clean. One pulse of harmony and gladness beats through the vast creation. From Him who created all, flow life and light and gladness, throughout the realms of illimitable space. From the minutest atom to the greatest world, all things, animate and inanimate, in their unshadowed beauty and perfect joy, declare that God is love" (GC, 678). In the book of Psalms, praise is directly connected to soteriology and eschatology, and as a consequence, it nurtures hope.

PROVERBS

INTRODUCTION

Title and Authorship. The Hebrew title of the book of Proverbs consists of the first word in the book (*mishle*, a form of the word *mashal*), whose meaning is similar to but broader than the English word "proverb." It refers to not only proverbial sayings but also to various other types of sayings (see Num. 23:7; Job 13:12; Is. 14:4; Ezek. 18:2). Therefore, *mishle* (commonly translated as "proverbs") is best understood as "wisdom sayings." In this commentary, the two expressions will be used interchangeably.

According to a Jewish tradition, Hezekiah and his associates wrote Proverbs. This would mean they compiled the sayings rather than authoring them (Prov. 25:1). The book itself ascribes the authorship of most of its contents to Solomon (1:1; 10:1), Agur (30:1), Lemuel (31:1), and other sages (22:17). The repetition of identical or virtually identical proverbs in the book (6:10–11 and 24:33–34; 14:12 and 16:25; 18:8 and 26:22; 21:9 and 25:24; 22:3 and 27:12; possibly also 20:16 and 27:13) suggests that parts of the book may have existed as separate collections that were eventually brought together as one book. Other proverbs are not identical but are very similar (see 10:9 and 28:18; 16:2 and 21:2; 19:5 and 19:9; 19:24 and 26:15; 20:10 and 20:23; 20:18 and 24:6; 22:13 and 26:13). Furthermore, there are instances where the exact wording of part of a proverb is repeated in another wisdom saying (see 10:6 and 10:11; 10:8 and 10:10; 10:15 and 18:11) Sometimes, the repetition is similar but not exact (see 16:28 and 17:9; 19:12 and 20:2). This suggests that some parts of some proverbs were reused in the creation of new wisdom sayings (it is, of course, impossible now to determine which saying preceded which). Thus, it is probably better to say that the book of Proverbs consists of collections of wisdom sayings that were compiled by Hezekiah and his associates from the writings of Solomon, Agur, Lemuel, and other sages (see 25:1).

Date. Following the Jewish tradition, the collections of wisdom sayings in Proverbs were gathered and compiled in their final form around 700 B.C. However, Solomon would have written his portion (the majority of the book) in the tenth century B.C.

Backgrounds. The reign of Solomon, which was the golden age (in terms of wisdom, wealth, and power) of the united monarchy, provides the appropriate setting for the collection of his wisdom sayings. The word "wisdom" is used in reference to both a concept and a type of literature. The concept of wisdom in Proverbs (and in the Bible) has a wider range of meaning than it does in English. Whereas the English word "wisdom" means good judgment and the ability to use knowledge, the biblical concept of wisdom encompasses a wide spectrum, including simple factual knowledge (e.g., Solomon's knowledge of trees, animals, birds, fish, etc.; 1 Kin. 4:29, 33), various types of professional skills (see Ex. 35:35; 36:2, 8; 1 Chr. 22:15–16), good judgment and common sense (e.g., Solomon's understanding of human nature; 1 Kin. 3:16–28), and righteous living (e.g., in Prov. 10–13 the contrast between the righteous and the wicked is interwoven with the contrast between the wise and the fool). Proverbs never speaks of a God-fearing person lacking wisdom or of an unrighteous person who is wise (see 1:1–7). Though the biblical concept of wisdom is difficult to define, it can be described as the attempt to understand the order of the world through observation and analysis, appropriate its principles, and successfully live by them.

Theology and Purpose. A number of theological observations can be made regarding the book of Proverbs. The observations below are selective and do not cover the entire theological significance of the book.

1. Proverbs and Inspiration. The book of Proverbs presents important insights concerning inspiration, especially for those who hold a high view of Scripture. First, some have suggested that there are similarities between Proverbs 22:17—24:22 and the Egyptian *Wisdom of Amenemope*. Were some of Solomon's wisdom sayings copied from Egyptian wisdom? And if so, can these sayings still be considered inspired? Or did *Amenemope* copy from Proverbs? Or did they both borrow from common sources of ancient Near Eastern wisdom? The common opinion among scholars is that *Amenemope* is older than Proverbs. and consequently Proverbs was in some way influenced by it. The relationship between Proverbs and Egyptian wisdom should not bring into question the inspiration of the book of Proverbs. Inspiration does not always claim originality. Inspired NT writers, under the guidance of the Spirit, sometimes gathered material from uninspired sources (Luke 1:1–4) and even quoted them (Acts 17:28; Titus 1:12–13; see "Revelation and Inspiration of the Bible," p. 11).

The book of Proverbs does not claim to be based on direct visions and dreams. In fact, sometimes it draws lessons from nature (Prov. 6:6–11) or personal observation (24:32). It offers a broader understanding of how inspiration works. This aspect of the book of Proverbs may have relevance to Seventh-day Adventists since the inspiration of Ellen White has been challenged because of her alleged literary borrowings. It is important to consider not only what was borrowed but also how it was modified in order to achieve the purpose of the inspired biblical writer. It would also be useful to consider what was rejected and not borrowed in order to better understand the process of selection followed by the inspired writer. Further, the fact that 25:1 states that Hezekiah's scribes collected Solomon's wisdom sayings suggests that a high view of Scripture does not preclude later scribal rearrangement or compilation.

2. Central Theological Message of Proverbs. Though the book makes significant theological contributions, there is no consensus on its central theological message. Besides the ubiquitous theme of wisdom, a number of other themes are prominent. One recurring theme is the proper upbringing of children (see 13:24; 22:6, 15; 23:13–14; see also 3:11–12), which is also reflected in the frequently used introductory formula admonishing children to listen to parental instruction (see 1:8–9; 4:1–4; 6:20). Another prominent theme is wise speech (see 10:6, 10–11, 13–14; 16:20–30; 18:2–8; 25:12; 26:23–26), which is also reflected in the frequent occurrence of words such as "lips," "mouth," and "tongue." Another theme is righteousness in contrast with wickedness (see 1:3; 2:8–9; 10:1—11:31; 12:5–7; 21:3; 24:15–16; 28:1; 29:27), including references to just scales (see 16:11), integrity, justice, uprightness (see 17:26; 18:5), and so on.

Also prominent in Proverbs are the themes of fidelity and infidelity (see 2:16–19; 5:1–23; 6:20—7:27; 22:14; 30:20), diligence and laziness (see 6:6–11; 12:27; 16:5; 19:24; 21:17, 25; 24:30–34; 26:15), riches and poverty (see 18:11; 19:6–7; 23:4–5; 30:8–9), proper behavior by or toward a king (see 16:10–15; 24:21–22; 25:2–7; 31:1–9), and dealing with conflicts (see 25:8, 21–24; 26:17–22), including warnings against anger (see 25:28). Of course, this list could be expanded. However, it is questionable whether any of these themes could be considered the central theme of the book of Proverbs. The fact that so many of the wisdom sayings are self-contained units may mean that there is no one overarching theme or theology. In addition to the apparent lack of an overarching theme, Proverbs also seems to lack a clear sequence or arrangement of its themes. Hence, some scholars prefer to summarize the book as a collection of miscellaneous wisdom sayings without a central theme. This position seems to be strengthened by the fact that scholars who do propose a central theological message cannot agree on what that message is.

Perhaps the concept that could function as the theological center of the book of Proverbs is wisdom. It pervades the book from beginning to end. In addition to the frequent occurrence of terms from a Hebrew root related to wisdom (the adjective *khakam*, "wise," forty-seven times; *khokmah*, "wisdom," thirty-nine times; various conjugations of the verb *khakam*, "to be wise," thirteen times), there are also related words that occur frequently (e.g., *da'at*, "knowledge," forty times). The word *leb* ("heart," "mind," "understanding") occurs ninety-seven times. Many words related to instruction also occur frequently (e.g., *musar*, "discipline," "instruction," "correction," thirty times; *tokakhat*, "reproof," sixteen times; *torah*, "instruction," "law," thirteen times). To these could be added words that contrast with wisdom (e.g., "fool," "folly," "scoffer"). Since wisdom is, among other things, the correct application of knowledge and understanding, it can be expanded to include the various qualities promoted in the book (e.g., righteousness, diligence, the fear of the Lord). Hence, the theme of wisdom seems to be a good candidate for the central theme of the book.

Since wisdom attempts to apply a correct understanding of the order of the world by appropriating its principles in order to successfully live by them, there is a sense in which wisdom and life are related. Therefore, while the issue of the theological center of the book is still debated, this commentary adopts the working hypothesis that the central message is how to enjoy a meaningful and productive life. "In the proverbs of Solomon are outlined principles of holy living and high endeavor, principles that are heaven-born and that lead to godliness, principles that should govern every act of life" (PK 33–34).

3. *Wisdom and Faith.* An interesting aspect of the book of Proverbs is its apparent universal application. It does not mention the details of Israelite religious history, such as the Exodus from Egypt. There is no discussion of the temple or of the significance of the sacrifices. Further, many of the stated consequences of following or not following wisdom concern earthly, not spiritual, life (e.g., long life, riches, and honor; Prov. 3:16; cf. 22:4). The righteous are repaid on earth (11:31).

Although details particular to Israelite religion are not discussed, the book mentions different religious aspects of life. These include prayer (15:8, 29; 28:9), offerings and sacrifices (7:14; 15:8), firstfruits (3:9), and vows (7:14; 20:25). Proverbs also mentions God's involvement in human affairs (see 15:25; 20:22; 22:22–23; 23:10–11) and the sovereignty of God (see 16:33; 19:21; 20:24; 21:30–31). The book also states that "the fear of the LORD" is the foundation of wisdom (1:7; 9:10) and exhorts trust in Him (3:5). "The LORD gives wisdom" (2:6), and "those who seek the LORD understand" (28:5; see "Wisdom and the Fear of the Lord," p. 764).

Thus, though the book's counsel applies to the secular details of life and its benefits are not limited to any national group, Proverbs is a deeply religious book. It could be said that the historical facts concerning the religion of Israel are assumed as background knowledge. Further, the book's focus on this earthly life shows that the fear of the Lord is not limited to religious contexts. God is the God of the secular as well as the sacred. Indeed, it is hard to separate the two in the ancient world, where all life was tied to the sacred. Hence, all of life, including what are today considered secular activities, should be lived in relationship to the Lord.

4. *Wisdom and Hope.* As already mentioned, except for the Creation, the book of Proverbs does not discuss God's intervention in history, such as the Flood, the Exodus, or the future messianic age. Since the book is not prophetic or apocalyptic, not much is said about God's future direct intervention in human history. This does not mean that Proverbs is exclusively interested in everyday life. The book is also interested in a transcendental life, a life beyond the confines or limitations of an earthly existence. True life must be grounded in hope in God and requires a deep fellowship with the Lord. Therefore, Proverbs unambiguously asserts that there is no hope for the wicked beyond the grave (11:7). They know only the present, and when it is gone, their hope perishes with them. But the experience of the righteous is different: the righteous have a refuge in God even in death (14:32). This seems to imply that, for the righteous, death is not the end.

Another passage that seems to point to a life beyond the grave is 12:28, according to which there is no death in the pathway of righteousness and life. A literal translation would be "and the way of a path no death." The meaning seems to be that true life does not lead to death but transcends it. If this interpretation is right, then wisdom is associated with eternal life. It points to a life that transcends the limited nature of human existence.

The emphasis of Proverbs on earthly life offers a balancing perspective for Christians living in hope of the Second Coming of Christ. Though the ultimate Christian hope has an eschatological focus (i.e., the coming of fullness of life through Christ), which Proverbs points to, the present life should not be ignored. There is hope in the present as well as the future. Our fallen, sinful world does not always function as it should, yet God's justice and mercy are not completely absent because the law of cause and effect is still at work. Wisdom and folly still have predictable, though not unfailingly consistent, results. "To Adam and Eve in their Eden home, nature was full of the knowledge of God, teeming with divine instruction. To their attentive ears it was vocal with the voice of wisdom. Wisdom spoke to the eye and was received into the heart, for they communed with God in His created works....Nature is now marred and defiled by sin. But God's object lessons are not obliterated; even now, rightly studied and interpreted, she speaks of her Creator" (CT 186).

Further, Paul's statement in 1 Corinthians 15:19 about hope beyond this life must be balanced by John's statement that hope purifies us (1 John 3:3). That is, our eschatological hope results in changes in our present life. Proverbs also reminds us that true biblical hope impacts the way God's people live and treat others in this life. There are many wise sayings about living righteously (see Prov. 2:9; 8:20; 14:34; 16:8; 29:4); being honest (see 3:27–28; 11:1; 16:11; 20:10, 23); being generous (see 11:24; 14:21, 31; 19:17); not taking advantage of the helpless/defenseless (see 15:25; 23:10–11; 30:10); speaking with wisdom, honesty, and kindness (see 8:7–8; 15:1–2; 20:15; 25:11–12; 31:26); and even showing compassion to animals (12:10). Thus, Proverbs reminds Christians that eschatological hope should lead to choosing the path of wisdom in this present life.

5. *Wisdom Acquired and Transmitted.* Wisdom is not primarily obtained through supernatural revelations, such as visions and dreams (though these are not necessarily excluded). Rather, it is acquired by observation and experience followed by analysis and application (see 6:6). Wisdom is also acquired by accepting wise counsel, a fact emphasized throughout Proverbs. Thus, the value of wise counsel is highlighted (see 11:14; 15:22; 20:18; 24:6). The sayings are often addressed to a child urged to receive parental instruction (see 1:8; 5:1; 6:1; 7:1; 31:1).

Proverbs emphasizes the need to not only acquire wisdom but also transmit it. One of its frequent themes is the education of youth, which may have been the original setting of many of its wisdom sayings. Hebrew words for parents and children are used very frequently. In the first nine chapters, each lecture is addressed to a son (see also 23:19, 22; 24:13–14, 21; 31:2). It contains instruction concerning the responsibilities of children (see 10:1; 13:1; 15:5, 20; 17:25; 19:13, 26; 20:20; 23:24–25; 28:7; 29:3; 30:17) as well as of parents (see "Child Discipline in Proverbs," p. 776).

We can also draw some inferences from Proverbs concerning the content of education. Since God is the God of all aspects of life, including both what we consider sacred and what we consider secular, education in the context of biblical wisdom is not limited to theological reflection. A careful reading of Proverbs, as well as wisdom literature in general, suggests a positive attitude towards all kinds of learning, including practical and scientific knowledge. Nevertheless, true wisdom, hence true education, has its foundation in "the fear of the LORD."

Literary Features. On this, see "Introduction to Hebrew Poetry and Wisdom Books" (p. 614). The book of Proverbs is rich in descriptive and prescriptive sayings. With the exception of the first nine chapters and portions of the last few, most wisdom sayings in Proverbs are short, often consisting of one or two lines with parallel, opposite, or related thoughts. Many of these can be characterized as aphorisms, maxims, or pithy sayings. Since biblical proverbs are poetic in form, they use poetic parallelism. In most cases, these short wisdom sayings are self-contained units (i.e., each saying is contextually unrelated to the sayings before and after it) and the interpretation of each passage is not related to other passages in the context.

This commentary will not discuss every single wisdom saying in Proverbs individually since most of them are transparent and do not need comment or explanation. Instead, in sections where larger themes can be discerned, the discussion will focus on the larger context rather than on specific verses. Some individual verses that require special comment or explanation will also be discussed.

COMMENTARY

1:1—9:18

PROVERBS OF SOLOMON THE SON OF DAVID THE KING OF ISRAEL

The first nine chapters of Proverbs contain longer poetic sections than most of the rest of the book. Whereas much of the book consists of specific counsel for practical living, the poems in the first nine chapters interweave instructional poems with poems that praise or commend wisdom. Hence, even the admonitions against infidelity occur in the context of a contrast between choosing wisdom or the adulterous woman (see 7:4–5).

As some scholars have suggested, the material in this first major section consists of ten lectures or didactic speeches (1:8–19; 2:1–22; 3:1–12, 21–35; 4:1–9, 10–19, 20–27; 5:1–23; 6:20–35; 7:1–27) with four intervening interludes (1:20–33; 3:13–20; 6:1–19; 8:1–36), in addition to a prologue (1:1–7) and an epilogue (chap. 9). The lectures typically consist of three parts: the introduction, the body of the lecture, and some type of conclusion. The introduction usually begins with a formula expressed in the format of parental instructions. That is, the lecture is addressed to a child who is advised to listen to parental instruction (see 1:8–9; 3:1–2; 4:1–4; 6:20). This is followed by a statement of the benefits that heeding these instructions can bring. This may reflect parental instruction as the original setting of these sayings (see also 31:1). However, given the fact that the book of Proverbs is addressed to a wider audience (see 1:1–7), the imagery of parental instruction must be seen as a literary formula employed in the genre of didactic wisdom. This type of introductory formula also occurs elsewhere in the book of Proverbs (see 10:1; 23:19, 22).

1:1–7
Prologue

The title introduces the book and indicates that the following section is a compilation of proverbs written by Solomon, who was the son of David and king of Israel (1:2—9:18). Although the first seven verses of Proverbs function as a prologue to the first major section, they are also a fitting introduction to the entire book. These verses establish the book's purpose and audience.

The prologue clearly states the book's purposes: (a) To gain (lit. "know") wisdom and instruction means to obtain and apply principles of behavior that will regulate a disciplined life (1:2). (b) To perceive/understand words of understanding/insight means to separate or distinguish what is right from what is wrong in order to appropriate what is insightful or meaningful. Wisdom, discipline, and understanding are to be acquired for practical purposes. (c) To receive instruction regarding wisdom/prudent behavior means to live a life characterized by justice/righteousness (the preservation of proper relationships), integrity, and fairness (lit. what is "smooth," "straight," "free from any obstacle") and to do what is right/treat others justly (v. 3). (d) To give prudence to the

simple means to enable them to avoid being misled (v. 4). Someone who is "simple" (Heb. *peti*) is naïve and, consequently, open to enticement. The Hebrew word is related to the verbal root *patah* ("to be gullible," "to be open to enticement," "to persuade," "to entice"; v. 10; Ex. 22:15; Judg. 14:15). In some contexts, the word "simple" has a neutral connotation, referring to one who is inexperienced and needs instruction in regard to what is prudent. Such a person could either learn wisdom or be enticed to sin (Prov. 1:4; 7:7; 9:4, 6, 16; 19:25; 21:11). In other contexts, "simple" has a negative connotation. The simple are contrasted with the prudent (14:15, 18; 22:3; 27:12) and compared to fools (1:22, 32; 8:5).

Young people need knowledge and discretion that will enable them to plan (i.e., to wisely decide their own course of action in life). But Proverbs addresses not only the simple and the young but also the wise, who can increase their knowledge (1:5). Wisdom is a way of life, but it is also a way of expressing ideas and teachings through proverbs, parables, and riddles (v. 6). Although the meaning of most wisdom sayings is clear and easy to understand, the fact that they are called "riddles" encourages the reader to go beyond a casual surface reading to carefully ponder their meaning. According to v. 7, the fear of the Lord is the foundation of true wisdom. Those who want to experience true knowledge and wisdom must "fear the LORD" (i.e., be in the right relationship with God). This "fear" does not mean being afraid of God but denotes an awe-inspired respect for and obedience to Him (see below, "Wisdom and the Fear of the Lord").

Wisdom and the Fear of the Lord

The expression "the fear of the LORD" occurs quite often in Proverbs and is usually connected to wisdom. In fact, it provides a proper starting point for the search for wisdom, making it indispensable to the wise. Therefore, it is important to have a clear understanding of the expression.

1. *Terminology*. The expression may employ the Hebrew noun *yir'ah* ("fear"; 1:7, 29; 2:5; 8:13; 9:10; 10:27; 14:26, 27; 15:16, 33; 16:6; 19:23; 22:4; 23:17), the adjective *yare'* ("fearing"; 14:2; 31:30), or the verb

yara' ("to fear"; 3:7; 24:21), all from the same root. Though the basic meaning of this root is "to fear" in the sense of "to be afraid" (see Gen. 32:11; Deut. 2:25; 20:8), it can also express the idea of "respect" (e.g., toward parents; Lev. 19:3; cf. Prov. 13:13) or "reverence" (e.g., for God and His word; Lev. 26:2; Ps. 112:1). Further, the word "fear" can also refer to the "worship" of a deity (see 2 Kin. 17:32–34). There is also a sense in which fear of the Lord includes trust in God (Prov. 3:5–8). In Proverbs, the fear of humans is contrasted with trust in the Lord (29:25). The book exhorts trusting in the Lord (3:5; 16:20; 28:25) and waiting for Him (20:22).

2. *Fear as Behavior.* What is perhaps more important is the fact that the expression "the fear of the LORD" highlights not an attitude or emotion but a type of behavior. The fear of the Lord is often synonymous with righteous living (see Job 1:1; Ps. 128:1; 2 Sam. 23:3). In Proverbs, it characterizes those who walk in uprightness (Prov. 14:2). The expression means to hate evil (8:13) and to depart from it (3:7; 16:6). The parallelism in Psalm 111:10 matches the fear of the Lord with obeying His commandments (see Ps. 111:7–9; see also Deut. 6:2; Eccl. 12:13). Notice also that the commandments are to be feared/respected as well (Prov. 13:13). Thus, in the context of Proverbs, the fear of the Lord includes an awe and reverence manifested in good behavior and implies a right relationship with God. It ultimately means walking according to God's will (i.e., keeping His commandments). A life lived according to God's will is the beginning of wisdom (1:7; 9:10).

3. *Fear and Wisdom.* The book of Proverbs highlights the relationship between the fear of the Lord and wisdom. The fear of the Lord is described as the beginning of wisdom (1:7; 9:10) and the instruction of wisdom (15:33). In 2:5 the expression parallels "the knowledge of God," and 2:6 explains that the Lord gives wisdom. In 1:29, the fear of the Lord is contrasted with hatred of knowledge. According to 28:5, it is those who seek the Lord who have understanding. Further, the fear of the Lord is described in terms of its benefits, which are similar to the benefits of wisdom. These include health (3:7–8), safety (14:26), riches, honor, and life (22:4). Of these, long life seems to be more prominent (10:27; 14:27; 19:23). Thus, the fear of God, which includes living according to His will, is the foundation that leads to true wisdom and its rewards. The sages presupposed that there was a God whose wisdom was manifested in the order of His creation, and that living according to His will would place them on the path of wisdom and life that would be in harmony with His creation.

1:8–19
First Didactic Speech:
Avoid Evil Companions

The first didactic speech consists of a warning to avoid evil associates. Like most lectures in this part of the book, there is an introduction (1:8–9), the body of the lecture (vv. 10–16), and a conclusion, which here consists of an explanation of the admonition (vv. 17–19).

As is typical of the introductory formula, the lecture is addressed to "my son," who is encouraged to pay attention to parental instruction (v. 8). The benefit of following this parental instruction is compared to an elegant garland on the son's head and to a chain of honor, probably made out of gold, around his neck (v. 9). This metaphor emphasizes the beauty and value of wisdom.

Verses 10–11 introduce a long quotation (vv. 11–14). The first part (the "if" clause) in v. 10 is resumed in the second (the "then" clause), beginning in v. 15. The admonition may be summarized thus: if sinners invite you to join them in evildoing, do not join them. Although the warning involves an evil and violent gang that violates social order through violent robbery, the principle (i.e., resisting peer pressure) also

applies to less extreme temptations to do what is evil. In v. 12, "Sheol" (the grave) is personified as swallowing those who enter it. Verse 16 is missing from some early translations, including some manuscripts of the Septuagint. However, it fits perfectly with the sentiment in the preceding verses. The conclusion of this lecture consists of an explanation of the admonition: the plans of those who do evil are futile because they result in their own destruction.

1:20–33
Interlude 1: The Call of Wisdom

In this interlude, wisdom is personified (which also occurs elsewhere in Proverbs; see 8:1–36; 9:1–6) as a messenger proclaiming her instruction to large audiences in the public areas of a city. Wisdom is anthropomorphically depicted as a prophetess delivering a message to the people. The implicit idea is that no one could claim that wisdom was inaccessible.

The message consists of two parts—an invitation/call and the announcement of judgment. The invitation calls to the simple/naïve to pay attention to the rebuke of Wisdom. If they would turn and listen, Wisdom would enlighten them with true knowledge. She would pour out her thoughts/spirit on them (1:22–23). The message of judgment is based on the fact that the simple reject wisdom. The judgment reflects the law of retribution: because the simple laugh at and mock Wisdom, Wisdom announces that when they face misfortune, she will laugh at and mock them (vv. 26–27). Verses 28–31 use the third person ("they") to address those who spurn Wisdom. The element of retribution is more visible in this case. When she called and sought them, they did not answer. So Wisdom announces that when they call on and seek her, she will not answer and they will not find her. They had the chance of gaining knowledge from her, but they hated true knowledge, defined here as fearing the Lord.

Living according to divine wisdom should constantly characterize the life of God's people. Wisdom is not something to access in times of trouble; in fact, wisdom will help avoid some misfortunes. The conclusion contrasts the fate of the simple and the righteous (vv. 32–33). The simple should understand that their present decisions determine their ultimate fate. The rejection of the Lord's counsel, given through divine wisdom, will result in the destruction of the wicked. The ultimate fate of those who listen to Wisdom (i.e., those who appropriate and live according to her instructions) will be a life under divine protection, free from the fear of calamities. In the context of the cosmic conflict, such promises now find partial fulfillment in the lives of God's people, but they anticipate a future when evil will never again touch them.

2:1–22
Second Didactic Speech: The Path of Wisdom

The instruction of this lecture consists of a call to seek wisdom and to learn to follow her path. It could be subdivided into two parts. The first is a call to seek wisdom (vv. 1–10), and the second describes deliverance from the enticements of the wicked (vv. 11–22). Each of these consists of smaller blocks of verses. The first part of the lecture consists of three stanzas. The first stanza contains three "if" clauses (vv. 1–4). The following two stanzas each begin with a "then" clause (vv. 5–8, 9–11). The second part of the lecture also consists of three stanzas (vv. 12–15, 16–19, 20–22), each beginning with the same preposition.

2:1–9. If You Seek Wisdom. The speaker is the teacher, and the addressee is, as usual, called "my son" (v. 1). The instruction is identified

with that of Wisdom, indicating that Wisdom shares a deposit of instruction that can be the object of analysis—one may apply the heart (one's rational abilities) in seeking to understand it. The exhortation to listen to Wisdom takes up the rest of this first part of the poem.

Three "if" clauses suggest that the attainment of wisdom requires effort and discipline on the part of the seeker, including accepting/receiving instruction (v. 1), calling/crying out for it (v. 3), and seeking/looking for it (v. 4). But the ultimate purpose of such efforts is to gain a better understanding of the fear of the Lord, resulting in knowing Him better and developing a deeper relationship with Him (v. 5). Wisdom does not exist for her own sake but offers a deeper fellowship with the Lord. The source of wisdom is God Himself, indicating that wisdom, often personified in Proverbs, is one of His attributes. Therefore seeking wisdom is in fact seeking God. He has wisdom in abundance and is willing to give it to His children. Through this divine instruction, God keeps His people in the path/way of life characterized by justice and righteousness. Only in seeking God can His people come to understand how to relate both to Him and to others (v. 9).

2:10–22. Deliverance from the Wicked. This section describes the practical benefits received by those who embrace and appropriate God's wisdom. It is a pleasant experience that enables them to act according to their values and what they have found to be good (vv. 9–10). It prepares them to resist temptations to do evil (v. 11). The clauses regarding deliverance in vv. 12 and 16 express either purpose (i.e., wisdom preserves in order to deliver) or specification (i.e., wisdom preserves by delivering from certain kinds of people). This distinction is one of nuance, since the general substance of the passage remains the same. Three examples of deliverance are given. First, those who embrace Wisdom will not identify with those whose words entice others to do what is evil (v. 12). Second, they will not join those who abandon the way of life and choose the way of death/darkness, who find their joy not in wisdom but in crookedness (vv. 13–15). Third, they will not be trapped by the immoral/adulterous woman (vv. 16–19).

According to v. 17 the immoral/adulterous woman in this poem is a married woman who is willing to forsake the marriage covenant made before God. The word *'allup* ("companion," "partner") is not the regular word for "friend" but refers to someone very close (see 16:28; 17:9). Here the Hebrew expression *'allup ne'urim* ("companion of [one's] youth") is best understood as the masculine counterpart to the expression *'eshet ne'urim* ("wife of [one's] youth"; 5:18). The expression *'allup ne'urim* also occurs in Jeremiah 3:4, where it possibly means "husband." The motivation for following Wisdom and not the immoral woman is that the immoral woman's path leads to the dead (Prov. 2:18; the Hebrew term *repa'im* is a poetic term used to designate the dead; see Job 26:5; Is. 14:9). She promotes death while Wisdom promotes life.

Proverbs 2:20 begins with the Hebrew expression *lema'an* (see vv. 12, 16), which can express either purpose ("in order to") or consequence ("so that"). Hence, the message of the second part of the poem is that Wisdom will preserve those who follow her (v. 11), delivering them from wicked men (vv. 12–15) and wicked women (vv. 16–19) so they may walk in the right paths (v. 20). This parallels the end of the first section (v. 10). In Proverbs, as in many other places in the Bible, there are two ways/paths to walk on—the way of life or the way of death. Verses 21–22 contrast the results of walking on the two different paths: the righteous, who follow the way of life, are preserved by Wisdom and receive a promise of life. The wicked, who follow the way of death, have their lives come to an end. These verses conclude the second part of the lecture.

3:1–12
Third Didactic Speech: Trust in the Lord

This lecture contains the typical three parts: introduction (vv. 1–4), body (vv. 5–10), and conclusion (vv. 11–12). The message of these wisdom sayings is that God must be put first. This chapter contains three lectures about wisdom (vv. 1–10, 11–20, 21–35), each beginning with an appeal to the son.

3:1–4. Introduction. On the introductory formula, see remarks above on the organization of chapters 1–9. The word *torah* ("instruction," "teaching," "law") forms a fitting parallel with *mitsvot* ("commands"; 3:1). The structure of vv. 1–2 is very similar to that of vv. 3–4. The second-person negative command in v. 1 parallels the third-person negative wish in v. 3. Both are followed by affirmative commands and a statement of the results of heeding the injunctions. The concept of memory surfaces in the exhortation not to forget the father's instructions. They bring healing/wholeness and lengthen the lives of those who keep them in

their hearts. When interacting with others, mercy and honesty are important (v. 3). Those who follow these instructions find grace in the eyes of God and others (v. 4).

3:5–12. Trust in the Lord. The lecture itself can be considered to begin in v. 5. A number of commands are given in vv. 5–10. Most are affirmative: God's people should trust in Him (v. 5), acknowledge and submit to Him (v. 6), fear Him, reject evil (v. 7), and honor Him with their abundance, including the firstfruits of their produce (v. 9). A couple of the commands are negative: God's people should not rely/lean on their own understanding (v. 5) or be wise in their own eyes (v. 7). Also, a few blessings are mentioned that result from heeding the commands (vv. 6b, 8, 10). In light of the parallelism, the various commands should be understood as related facets of a proper relationship with God. Hence, this wisdom saying expands the meaning of the phrase "the fear of the LORD," which occurs throughout the book. That is, to fear the Lord does not mean to be afraid of God but rather to trust, honor, and acknowledge Him in everything and to depart from evil. Likewise, though those who trust in the Lord feel confident and safe (cf. v. 23), as opposed to afraid (see 14:16; 29:25), they should also depart from evil and honor the Lord in His rightful claims to their possessions.

Proverbs 3:5–8 affirms the human need for divine guidance, suggesting that human wisdom is not enough to lead to ultimate success. This passage exhorts fully trusting in God, meaning acknowledging Him in all activities and decisions and living in humble submission to Him and His will. The implication is that there is something wrong with humanity and that a meaningful life is achieved only by fearing God in the sense of turning away from what is evil. The promise of v. 6 uses the Hebrew word *yashar,* which does not primarily mean "to guide" but rather "to make [the path] straight/smooth." Though "to make straight" one's own path can mean "to behave righteously" (see 9:15), to make another person's path straight means to remove obstacles and difficulties from the way (see Is. 40:3). However, since trusting in the Lord involves departing from evil (Prov. 3:7), the notion of straightening/smoothing out a path that leads to righteousness could be included. Trusting the Lord has a physical impact on the life of those who do so; there is a psychosomatic component in trusting Him. Trust will impact the physical body and the bones, considered in the Bible to be the seat of a person's inner life and emotions (v. 8).

It is not only the body and the bones of the wise but also their possessions that are blessed (vv. 9-10). This passage clarifies that God is honored by those who place their possessions at His service and give Him offerings from the best they have. Since it is good for God's people to honor Him, God promises to bless them in order for them to have enough to honor Him. Although the temple is not mentioned, it is obvious that the gifts were brought there.

Verses 11-12 change the topic to a degree, but they seem to function as a conclusion to this lecture. After the emphasis on God's blessings upon the wise in the previous verses, it is surprising to find the topic of suffering at the end of the lecture. Things do not always go well for God's children. In such cases it would be tempting to despise God, but the passage exhorts those who suffer to see in their painful experience the discipline of a loving Father, who is helping them grow in His wisdom.

3:13-20
Interlude 2: Praising Wisdom

This section consists of a poem that extols the value of wisdom, both to humans and to God. The poem can be subdivided into two parts: the value of wisdom to humans (vv. 13-18) and the value of wisdom to God (vv. 19-20).

3:13-18. The Value of Wisdom to Humans. The introductory formula of this interlude is clearly different from the way the other lectures in chapters 1-9 begin. The Hebrew expression *ashre* ("happy," "blessed") is a type of beatitude (i.e., "blessed is..."). Here it emphasizes the value of wisdom by calling attention to how fortunate are those who obtain it. The enjoyment of life is directly related to the possession of God's wisdom. The benefits received from wisdom far exceed those from material valuables, such as silver, gold, and pearls (3:14-15). Searching for and finding wisdom is more rewarding than working hard to obtain material wealth. The passage proceeds to list some of the benefits of wisdom (vv. 16-18): it frees from premature death and provides true wealth and wholeness of life. The reference to the tree of life recalls the Creation narrative (Gen. 2:9). Access to the tree of life is possible now by following divine wisdom. The direct connection between wisdom and life runs throughout Proverbs as one of its unifying themes. This part of the poem ends with a Hebrew verb that comes from the same root as the first word of the poem, *'ashar* ("to be blessed/happy/fortunate"; Prov. 3:18).

3:19-20. The Value of Wisdom to God. These verses connect wisdom to God's activity in Creation and make it clear that it was God who created everything by/in wisdom. Creation is not the result of natural, irrational forces but the outworking of the divine mind configuring all of it. To speak of God "using" wisdom in Creation does not imply that wisdom is some entity that could exist without a wise God. Rather, saying that God employed wisdom in Creation is a figure of speech that is equivalent to saying that God created the world in His wisdom. Hence, the Creation reveals the wisdom of God. Verse 20 is probably a reference to Genesis 1:9 and 2:6.

3:21-35
Fourth Didactic Speech: How Not to Treat Others

This section consists of an introduction (vv. 21-26), a body (vv. 27-31), and a conclusion (vv. 32-35). The message of this wisdom saying, to deal honestly and fairly with others, is given in the form of a series of negative commands.

3:21-26. Introduction. Some consider this section to be a continuation of vv. 13-20. The reason for the uncertainty is that in Hebrew the first line has only a verb without its object. To fit English usage, some translations insert "them" or reiterate "wisdom and understanding" from v. 13. Other translations resolve the problem by reversing the lines. But it is more likely that the second line of the proverb contains the objects of the verb: sound wisdom/judgment and discretion. The Hebrew word *tushiyyah* ("sound wisdom/judgment") points to practical wisdom/ability, hence to "competence." The word *mezimmar* refers to private thoughts that people keep to themselves and could mean "discretion." These qualities are indispensable for proper social interaction. Those who keep their eyes fixed on them will enjoy a favorable, safe, and long journey in life (vv. 22-23). Notice that such virtues do not themselves create safety, protection, and inner peace (vv. 24-25). It is the Lord who does that for those who keep their eyes fixed on wisdom (v. 26).

3:27-35. Message of the Lecture. The didactic speech itself (vv. 27-31) consists of five prohibitions that, when rephrased in positive terms, exhort giving what is good (payment for work, property, etc.) to those to whom it is due (v. 27); promptly giving neighbors what belongs to them (v. 28); planning to do only good to neighbors,

knowing their services may be needed in the future (v. 29); going to court only with a just case (v. 30); caring for the well-being of others; and promoting peace (v. 31). The conclusion is that those who defy the prohibitions are an abomination/repulsive to God (v. 32). Verses 32-35 contain a series of four antitheses, which convey the message that God blesses the upright and curses the unjust. This provides good reasons for avoiding the evil actions forbidden in vv. 27-31.

4:1-9
Fifth Didactic Speech: Seek Wisdom

This lecture is slightly different from the others. It has only two parts, the introduction (vv. 1-2) and the body of the lecture (vv. 3-9). A father recalls his own father's advice and repeats it to his son. The message itself can be summarized as an exhortation to get wisdom.

As in the typical introductory formula, vv. 1-2 address children, urge them to heed parental instruction, and explain the benefit of heeding the instruction (see remarks above on the organization of chaps. 1-9). However, though most of the previous exhortations are addressed to a "son," this one is addressed to "children" or "sons." The benefit of heeding instruction is simply that the instruction is *tob* ("good," "sound," "correct"). It corresponds to God's good will for all. The body of this exhortation (4:3-9) contains the words of a grandfather and is almost autobiographical (vv. 3-4). His father instructed him to take his instruction seriously because it directly related to the quality of his life (v. 3). The exhortations are about getting/acquiring the most important thing in life, namely, wisdom and understanding (vv. 5, 7). Verse 7 is ambiguous. The Hebrew word *re'shit* connotes "beginning" (cf. Gen. 1:1), but it can also be translated as "principal" or "foremost." Thus the verse can be translated as "The beginning of wisdom is this: get wisdom" or "Wisdom is the principal/supreme thing: therefore acquire wisdom." Wisdom is described as a wife who is not to be forsaken but loved (Prov. 4:6) and highly valued (v. 8; *salal*, "raise," "lift up," "exalt," "praise"). Wisdom will also honor and exalt those who embrace her (vv. 8-9).

4:10-19
Sixth Didactic Speech: The Two Paths

This section advises choosing the path of wisdom rather than the path of wickedness. It may be outlined as an introduction (v. 10), a

body (vv. 11-17), and a conclusion (vv. 18-19). The introduction follows the typical introductory formula (see remarks above on the organization of chaps. 1-9): a son is urged to listen to and take firm hold of parental instruction (equated with wisdom; 4:10, 13) and promised that this will result in a long and stable life, a key theme in Proverbs (vv. 11-12). The passage exhorts staying/turning away from the way/lifestyle of the wicked (vv. 14-15), whose whole life, day and night, is characterized by their obsession with doing evil. Their actions reveal what nurtures them (vv. 16-17). The passage closes with a description of the ultimate fates of the righteous and the wicked. There are some eschatological overtones in the description of the path of the righteous (v. 18). In contrast, the way of the wicked is described as darkness, suggesting that is a way of ignorance or foolishness (v. 19).

4:20-27
Seventh Didactic Speech: Guard Your Heart

An interesting feature of this group of Proverbs is the figurative reference to various parts of the body, namely, the ear (v. 20), eyes (v. 21), heart (vv. 21, 23), flesh/body (v. 22), mouth (v. 24), lips (v. 24), and feet (vv. 26-27); wisdom impacts the whole person. In addition to the typical introductory call for the son to listen to his father's advice, these verses add the command to keep his words before his eyes and in his heart (v. 21). These same two body parts are used again in reverse order in the body and at the end the passage (the heart in v. 23 and the eyes in v. 25).

Since, in the biblical understanding, the heart is the seat of thinking and intentions, to keep/guard one's heart means to guard one's thoughts and will (v. 23). The Hebrew word *tots'ot* ("springs," "issues," "flows"; v. 23) refers to the place from which something or someone goes out (e.g., city exits or border limits; see Ezek. 48:30). What comes from the heart or mind is that which guides the course of life's river, as it were. In other words, the heart must be guarded because that is where life begins its journey. The thoughts of the mind determine how a person lives. The admonition to guard the heart is followed by advice against deceptive speech (Prov. 4:24). Jesus also noted the relationship between the heart and the mouth when He stated that the mouth speaks out of the abundance of the heart (Matt. 12:34).

In a sense, Proverbs 4:25-27 are part of the admonition that began in v. 23. However, these verses give less explicit counsel on the evils to be avoided. Instead, they admonish walking on the right path without swerving to the right or the left (v. 27) and staying focused on what is most important in life—divine wisdom—without being distracted by what is on the side of the path (see Heb. 12:2).

5:1–23
Eighth Didactic Speech: Warning against Infidelity

This speech is the first of three that deal with infidelity. An interesting feature of this lecture is that vv. 15–20 forms the only passage in Proverbs that celebrates marital sex. It contrasts marital sex with sex outside of marriage, endorsing the former and disapproving the latter. The introductory formula is typical, urging a son to heed advice (v. 1), followed by a statement of the benefit (v. 2). The passage exhorts preserving/maintaining discretion (i.e., behaving with discretion). The word "lips" here refers not to the physical lips but to the act of speaking. Hence, the idea that the lips will guard/preserve knowledge means that those who accept wisdom will speak knowledge, just as the priest keeps/guards knowledge in the sense that he speaks it when teaching (Mal. 2:7). The word "lips" also serves as a transition since it occurs again in Proverbs 5:3, which begins the main body of the speech.

The speech can be subdivided into three parts. Verses 3–6 state the deadliness of the immoral woman. Like the sweetness of honey and the pleasantness of oil, she appeals to the sensory dimensions of men (v. 3), but what she really offers is bitterness and death (vv. 4–5); she is deceptive (v. 6). The passage exhorts young men to keep their distance from her. Otherwise their lives would be ruined (vv. 7–14). In the end, those who listen to the words of this woman will be left with nothing of value in the midst of remorse. The metaphor of a fountain of water involves an exhortation to enjoy marital life instead of joining the immoral woman (vv. 15–20). The wife is like a cistern, and she provides streams of water to the husband. The couple is also compared to a doe and a deer in beauty and strength (v. 19). They are encouraged to sexually enjoy each other. In v. 18, "the wife of your youth" may mean either "the wife you married when you were young" or "your youthful wife." Since marital sex is such a beautiful and enjoyable relation, going to the immoral/wayward woman is foolishness/irrational (v. 20). The passage concludes by stating that

the Lord is the Judge and wickedness will be punished by the outworking of the sinner's own actions (i.e., the wicked will be ensnared and held in the cords of their own sins, vv. 21–23).

6:1–19
Interlude 3: Various Topics

Although this interlude begins with the words "my son" (v. 1), it does not contain all the elements of the typical introductory formula of other speeches in Proverbs. This interlude consists of three or four wisdom sayings placed together because of related topics or themes.

6:1–5. Loans. The book of Proverbs counsels against guaranteeing someone else's loan (see 11:15; 22:26–27). This passage gives instructions on what those who have already made that mistake with a friend or a stranger should do (6:1). Some have suggested that the loan is not given to aid the needy but is a business transaction for a fee or for profit. However, the passage does not give such details. The Hebrew verb *taqa'* literally means "to clap" or "to strike" but is sometimes translated idiomatically, in terms of Western culture, as "shake hands." Contextually it refers to sealing an agreement in order to guarantee someone a loan (see also 17:18; 22:26). Verses 3–5 advise those caught in such an agreement to humble themselves before the lender and ask for mercy. Though Proverbs is against loan guarantees, it also encourages generosity in giving to the needy (22:9; 31:20).

6:6–11. Laziness. This wisdom saying draws a lesson from the diligence of the ant (vv. 6–8) and is used to rebuke the lazy (vv. 9–11). This saying resembles 24:30–34. In fact, 24:33–34 repeats 6:10–11. Although the saying in vv. 6–11 is separate from that of vv. 1–5, it is possible that they are placed next to each other because both sayings call for diligence. The counsel to the loan guarantor not to sleep (v. 4) parallels the warning against the sleep of the lazy (v. 10). Notice that wisdom is acquired by observing the natural world, learning from it, and then applying to life the lessons drawn from the acquired knowledge.

6:12–15. The Worthless Person. Proverbs refers to wisdom as acquired by observing human behavior. These verses describe a person who is *beliyya'al* ("worthless," "useless"), a word usually applied to those with some type of serious character defect (see 1 Sam. 1:16; 2:12; 25:25). It often, though not always, refers to the wicked (see Judg. 20:13; Job 34:18). Proverbs 6:12–14 describes the gestures the worthless make with different parts of their bodies. Though the cultural significance of the gestures is not fully understood in each case, the mention of the various body parts (the mouth, eyes, feet, fingers, and heart) seems to imply that the whole person is involved in wickedness. The collapse of the wicked will arrive unexpectantly and without a remedy (v. 15; *marfe'*, "remedy," "healing"; cf. 1 Thess. 5:3).

6:16–19. What the Lord Hates. The formula "six things…seven" (v. 16) is called a numerical saying. Sometimes the climax of a numerical sequence comes at the end. For a discussion of this formula, see commentary on 30:10–33. The list of body parts in 6:17–18 is similar, though not identical, to the list in vv. 12–14. This leads some to interpret vv. 12–19 as a single saying. Alternatively, however, these lists of body parts may simply be the reason why these two sayings are placed next to each other. Verse 19 departs from the list of body parts. The common element in the list is that God hates all these personal traits of the wicked; He even abominates/abhors them. The list is about personal traits or ethical behavior that upset the social order established by the Lord. If the climax of this numerical sequence is the last item, then the focus of this wisdom saying is on those who stir up conflict and discord in a family or community. This is similar to the expression about conflict and discord created by those who are disruptive (v. 14).

If vv. 12–19 are viewed as one wisdom saying, then sowing discord can be interpreted as the chief characteristic of the worthless. However, if vv. 12–15 and vv. 16–19 are seen as separate wisdom sayings, then the first saying is simply a depiction of various actions of the worthless and their final fate, whereas the second saying focuses on how the spreading of discord is abominable to the Lord.

6:20–35
Ninth Didactic Speech:
The Consequences of Adultery

Although the speeches found in 5:1–23 and 6:20–35 are independent wisdom sayings separated by the interlude in vv. 1–19, they share the common topic of infidelity. Whereas the previous passage contrasted marital relations with extramarital relations, this time the focus is on the consequences of adultery. This lecture consists of an introduction (vv. 20–24), a body (vv. 25–29), and a conclusion (vv. 30–35).

6:20–24. Introduction. As in the typical introductory formula of lectures, the addressee is "my son." The exhortation to accept parental instruction (vv. 20–21) is followed by a statement of the benefits of receiving it, which in this case involves wisdom's guidance in life (vv. 22–23). The words for "command," "law"/"teaching"/"instruction," and "bind" (vv. 20–21), as well as the references to traveling (Heb. *halak*, "walking," "roaming") and sleeping (v. 22), echo the instruction in Deuteronomy 6:4–9 concerning God's commandments. The light of divine instruction protects the wise from stumbling and falling from the way of life. Proverbs 6:24 can be considered either part of the introduction or the body. The term *ishah ra'* in this verse is unusual in Hebrew and has been understood as a "married [adulterous] woman," "woman of evil," or "woman/wife of a neighbor." The latter is the expression used in v. 29.

6:25–35. Avoid Adultery. This passage admonishes the "son" to neither nurture sexual thoughts about a seductress in his heart/mind nor allow himself to be allured by her (v. 25). Immoral behavior has a financial impact on anyone who pays for sexual favors (v. 26). Those who sexually engage another's spouse will unquestionably reap the consequences of their action (vv. 27–29). The Hebrew of v. 26 is difficult to translate. The expression *be'ad* can be translated as "by means of," "through," or "on account of." Some translations add "a man is reduced to" in order to make sense of the Hebrew sentence. Others have suggested translating the sentence as "the price of a harlot is as much as a loaf of bread," but this is uncertain. Either way, here is a comparison between going to a prostitute and committing adultery. Following the first translation means that going to a prostitute brings poverty but adultery results in death. Following the second means that going to a prostitute costs a loaf of bread but adultery costs one's life.

In terms of application, it is important to keep in mind the context of this wisdom saying. The ancient world considered adultery a more serious crime than prostitution. But the book of Proverbs (and the rest of the Bible, for that matter) never condones prostitution (23:27; 29:3). In this particular case, it simply points out that the results of adultery are more serious than the results of prostitution. The fundamental teaching is that sexual immorality in any form has serious consequences. Proverbs 6:30–33 compares adultery with stealing food. In contrast to stealing, which can be resolved, adultery does not arouse any sympathy in the eyes of others. Consequently, the honor of the adulterer will be permanently damaged. According to the passage, the ultimate reason for not committing adultery is that the husband will take vengeance against the adulterer (vv. 34–35). The grounds for the exhortation are based on an observation and an analysis of the social consequences of adultery. Nothing is said about the commandment against adultery, but reasons are provided to support its value in preserving social harmony.

7:1–27
Tenth Didactic Speech: Warning against the Adulteress

This instruction continues the series on infidelity. The three lectures are independent sayings placed in sequence because of their common theme. This one again contains an introduction (vv. 1–5), a body (vv. 6–23), and a conclusion (vv. 24–27). The body of the lecture is a narrative of a first-person observation, similar to 24:30–34. The warnings of this and similar wisdom sayings are addressed to a son. Therefore, it is important not to read too much into the fact that they picture the woman as the temptress. In terms of application, the roles could just as easily be reversed. The warning against infidelity applies equally to both genders.

7:1–5. Introduction. As in the preceding lecture, expressions such as "words" (v. 1), "commands" (vv. 1–2), *torah* ("law," "teachings," "instruction"; v. 2), "bind," "write," and "tablet of your heart" (v. 3) echo instructions elsewhere concerning God's commandments. In addition to the typical lecture introduction, the "son" is also exhorted to choose wisdom in order to be kept from the seductress. Whereas chapter 5 pictures marital relations as the alternative to infidelity, 7:4–5 pictures the woman called "Wisdom" as the alternative to the seductress.

7:6–27. An Illustration. The wise observe human behavior and its consequences. Here the author of this passage first tells what he saw: a young man who was simple, who lacked wisdom and was unable to distinguish right from wrong, walking on the street where the harlot met her clients as the sun was setting and darkness was approaching (vv. 6–9). Then the author describes the woman's attire (perhaps referring to a particular type of veil; cf. Gen. 38:14) and demeanor, which was similar to that of a wild beast seeking its prey. Once she found the young man, she attached herself to him through a kiss, a foretaste of what she would offer him (Prov. 7:10–13). The author also reports her seductive speech (vv. 14–20). She tells the young man that he should not worry about becoming ritually impure because she had offered a peace offering in fulfillment of a vow (see Lev. 3:1–17; 7:11–21), implying that she was ritually pure. Her luxurious home indicates that she was a wealthy woman, an observation confirmed by the fact that her husband was a merchant. Even though she was dressed like a harlot, she was not a prostitute but a married woman seeking an affair. She told the young man not to worry about her husband because he was away on a business trip. Finally, the wise author reports the conduct of the simple young man. Unable to resist the seductive speech of the woman, he was led by her, like a dumb animal, to the slaughter (Prov. 7:21–23).

The author observed and analyzed human behavior and finally used it to exhort his children (vv. 24–27). He depicts those who tempt others to commit adultery as murderers to emphasize the serious risks to those who succumb. An adulterer's house is indeed the gate to Sheol/the tomb.

8:1–36
Interlude 4: Wisdom's Offer

Chapter 8 seems to be an interlude consisting of an extended call to gain wisdom. It is also a poem exalting wisdom. As in the first interlude (1:20–33), wisdom is here personified and depicted as calling out. The passage can be outlined as follows: the setting (8:1–3), Wisdom's introductory call (vv. 4–11), Wisdom's self-description (vv. 12–21), Wisdom's origin (vv. 22–31), and the conclusion (vv. 32–36).

8:1–21. Setting, Call, and Wisdom. This interlude begins with a rhetorical question by an anonymous speaker. As in 1:20–21, Wisdom's words are here preceded and introduced by a description of Wisdom calling. Though Wisdom's words here are not addressed to a son, they are similar to other introductions in that, like the prophets, she appeals to her audience to listen to her words (8:4–6) because they are truthful, righteous, and easy to comprehend (vv. 7–9). Verses 10–11 repeat the same structure: wisdom again urges people to receive her teaching and not place their trust in financial security because the value of her teaching is incomparable (v. 10).

In this passage, Wisdom describes her attributes and virtues (vv. 12–14), states her value to kings and rulers (vv. 15–16), and indicates the benefits/rewards for those who love her (vv. 17–21). In v. 12, Wisdom, prudence, knowledge, and discretion comprise four personified virtues. In contrast, v. 13 lists four vices that characterize the way of the wicked: pride, arrogance, evil, and perversity. Then v. 14 again lists four virtues that Wisdom possesses: counsel, sound wisdom/judgment, understanding/insight, and strength/power.

The activity of Wisdom in the latter part of v. 12 has been translated variously to mean that Wisdom finds out knowledge and discretion, Wisdom has found/possesses them, or Wisdom shows the way for people to find them. In any case, Wisdom is personified here and, hence, is portrayed in human terms (i.e., anthropomorphically). Human beings are not naturally endowed with wisdom or knowledge but must find them through the process of learning. Wisdom will show the way. Some regard the first poetic line in v. 13, which equates fearing the Lord with hating evil, as a later addition because it disrupts the meter of the poem and could have been influenced by similar statements in Proverbs and elsewhere (cf. 3:7; 16:6; Job 28:28). That is, whereas most verses contain two lines (i.e., two parallel statements), Proverbs 8:13 contains three, and this line seems to break the continuity of Wisdom's words. Nevertheless, the line is part of the final form of the Hebrew text and fits the general message of the book of Proverbs. The poetic lines in vv. 15–16 are addressed to kings, princes, and judges, but they apply to all leaders. Wisdom is indispensable to those who lead if they are going to do it well.

8:22–36. Wisdom's Origin. These verses could be described as a history of Wisdom. They can be divided topically into Wisdom before Creation (vv. 22–26) and Wisdom during Creation (vv. 27–31). Whereas the previous part of the poem began with Wisdom (v. 12), this part begins

with the Lord (v. 22) and ends with a reference to humanity (v. 31). This part of the poem ends with an almost personal touch. The word *sha'ashu'im* ("delight") occurs twice. Verse 30 portrays Wisdom as the Creator's delight, and v. 31 portrays humankind as Wisdom's delight.

The statement regarding the Lord's relationship to Wisdom (v. 22) has been variously interpreted. The Hebrew verb used is *qanah*, the basic meaning of which is "to acquire." However, the specific translation depends on whether God acquired Wisdom already in existence or whether God acquired her by bringing her into existence. The first would best be translated as "to get," "to possess," or even "to purchase" (see 17:16), and the latter as "to beget," "to create." Some have suggested that these are actually two different words with identical spelling in Hebrew (i.e., homographs), but the evidence seems to support the view that these are simply two different shades of meaning of the same word. Since the context describes the beginning of Wisdom (i.e., when it was born or brought forth; 8:24–25), the translation "created" is a possibility. In this case God did not acquire an already existing entity called "Wisdom," but He created it. On the other hand, there was never a time that God was not in possession of Wisdom. It has also been suggested that the word in this context means "to beget" (which is probably the meaning in Gen. 4:1) because the language of conception and birth is used. The idea is that Wisdom came from God. But the main point of the passage is that Wisdom came into existence before the Creation of the world (Prov. 8:22–26; see below, "Proverbs 8:22 and Christ"). In vv. 32–36, Wisdom repeats her invitation. The addressees are "my children" (lit. "my sons"). There are two calls to listen to Wisdom accompanied by two statements of the blessing to be received (vv. 32–35). This is followed by a statement contrasting benefits for those who receive Wisdom with the consequences for those who reject her.

Proverbs 8:22 and Christ

In the early centuries of Christianity, there were some Christians who believed that the Son of God was not eternal but had a beginning. The most prominent among them, though certainly not the originator of this idea, was the church father Arius (A.D. 256–336),

and the doctrinal debate over the Trinity came to be known as the Arian controversy. Arian Christians cited Proverbs 8, especially v. 22, as evidence that Christ had a beginning and, therefore, was not eternal. Their interpretation was based on the parallel between wisdom and Christ both existing before Creation and having a part in it (cf. John 1:1–3).

1. Wisdom as a Divine Attribute. Some scholars have viewed this passage as being directly related to Christ and His installation (cf. the birth language of Ps. 2) as Creator and eventual Mediator (due to God's foreknowledge of sin). Others have viewed the passage as being primarily related to the preeminence of Wisdom over Creation as a personified attribute of God, related to Christ only by a secondary typological application (see below).

The NT stresses the religious significance of wisdom by referring to Christ as God's Wisdom. Paul says, "Christ the power of God and the wisdom of God" (1 Cor. 1:24). While in the OT divine wisdom was to some extent accessible through the created world, the NT presents God's wisdom as being revealed in the person and work of Christ. In Him "are hidden all the treasures of wisdom and knowledge" (Col. 2:3). He in Himself is the Wisdom of God. In this case Wisdom is not a personified divine attribute but God Himself in human flesh. This wonderful Wisdom was God's hidden Wisdom, which was ordained for our glory before time began (1 Cor. 2:7). By becoming flesh, He brought life to repentant sinners. Such individuals are in Christ Jesus, who has become Wisdom from God for us—our Righteousness, Holiness, and Redemption (1 Cor. 1:30). We appropriate that Wisdom of God in submission to Him—in the fear of the Lord.

2. Wisdom as a Type. The personified attribute of God's wisdom in the OT seems to point, almost like a prophetic type, to the incarnated Wisdom of God in the person of His eternal Son. Without Him it is impossible to acquire true salvific wisdom. The most glorious revelation of God's wisdom is now located in the incarnation, death, resurrection, and mediation of our Lord. The revelation of divine wisdom is now uniquely present in a Person and not only in the objects of the natural world. Proverbs 8:22 should not be cited to support the notion that Christ had a beginning. Instead, both the Father and the Son claim, "I am the Alpha and the Omega, the Beginning and the End" (Rev. 21:6; see also 1:8; 22:13). And the NT teaches that both the Father and the Son are eternal.

9:1–18
Epilogue: Two Banquets

Chapter 9 is the last wisdom saying in the first major section of the book. It is possible that the poem is placed here not as an epilogue but simply because the interlude that immediately precedes it (chap. 8) contains an invitation by wisdom. Nevertheless, the contrasting invitations of Wisdom and Folly in chapter 9 make it a fitting climax to the section. It seems, therefore, just as likely that the placement of chapter 8 would have been influenced by chapter 9 as the other way around. The epilogue may be outlined in three parts: the invitation of Wisdom (vv. 1–6), the scoffers and the wise (vv. 7–12), and the invitation of Folly (vv. 13–18). The message of these contrasting invitations is a call to choose a way of life.

9:1–6. Wisdom's Invitation. These verses consist of the invitation/call of Wisdom. Wisdom is described as having built her house (v. 1), prepared her banquet (v. 2), and sent out the invitation (v. 3). Verses 4–6 contain her words of invitation. The seven pillars/columns (v. 1) suggest a large building. Some of the houses of rich families in ancient Israel did indeed have columns facing a courtyard; some even had seven columns. The number seven conveys the notion of completeness. Thus, both the columns and the number seven convey a picture of the greatness of the house. The size of the house shows how much Wisdom has to offer. Accepting the invitation and partaking of her food and drink (wine mixed with water) in her house means learning wisdom—and there is enough to last a lifetime.

9:7–12. The Scoffers and the Wise. Some scholars suggest that these verses constitute a later insertion because they seem out of place. But it should suffice to say that, in their present context, these verses offer a contrast between those who accept Wisdom's invitation (the wise) and those who accept Folly's invitation (the scoffers). Verses 7–9 discourage correcting scoffers because nothing good could come out of it but encourage correcting the wise because they will respond positively. Verse 10 repeats a common theme in Proverbs, the fear of the Lord.

In v. 11 Wisdom seems to refer to herself again in the first person, promising long life to those who possess and follow her. Verse 12 returns to the topic of vv. 7–9 and contrasts the wise with scoffers. The point is that they must bear the consequences of their own response to Wisdom.

9:13–18. Folly's Invitation. Folly is personified as a foolish woman. Like Wisdom, Folly is pictured as giving a loud invitation (vv. 13–15). There is, however, no description of her building a house or preparing her banquet. Verses 16–17 contain the words of her invitation to the simple/naïve, the same group that is addressed by Wisdom (v. 4). Interestingly, Folly herself is described as simple (v. 13). Although the stolen water in v. 17 may be an allusion to illicit sexual enjoyment (see 5:15–20), the imagery of stolen drink and secret food probably applies to all illicit activities (see 1:10–14). The words *lekhem setarim* ("bread of secrecy") can mean either that the bread was secretly obtained or that it was eaten secretly. The words in 9:18 are not Folly's words but state that death is the result of following Folly. Proverbs offers only two options: following Madam Wisdom or Madam Folly. The choice is a matter of life or death.

10:1—22:16
PROVERBS OF SOLOMON

This section contains wisdom sayings that are short and less closely connected. Some sayings are placed next to each other not because they address the same topic but because a word occurs in both sayings (see 22:5–6). Therefore, these proverbs are harder to group, and it is not always possible to discern thematic subsections. There is no overarching theme running through the entire section. Each proverb generally provides its own context, and the proverbs occurring before and after are not necessarily related to it. Hence, each wisdom saying in this section is a separate saying and should generally be individually interpreted.

Nevertheless, this section can be roughly divided into two major subdivisions, though neither the twofold division nor the exact boundary between the subsections is precise. The subdivision in 10:2—15:33 contains more antitheses and sayings about the righteous and the wicked than 16:1—22:16, which in turn has a greater variety in terms of structure and topics. Although the sayings in this section cannot be thematically organized, there are a few clusters of

sayings where some themes are prominent. Yet, even within those clusters, there are sayings that are not related to their prominent themes. Since most of the individual sayings in chapters 10–22 are clear and easy to understand, the ensuing discussion will not comment on every proverb but will focus on words or expressions that require clarification or whose relevance needs to be highlighted.

10:1—15:33
Introduction and First Subdivision

Proverbs 10:1 introduces the section and includes a title and an introduction. The first part of the verse consists of the title or heading of the section. The section is a collection of different proverbs of Solomon. He may have intended them for his children, but they speak to a wider audience as well.

Although there is no overarching theme in either the first or second subdivision of this section, chapters 10–15 contain a significant number of wisdom sayings about the righteous. They also consist mostly of antitheses, with only a few exceptions (see 11:29–30; 12:14; 13:14, 19; 14:7, 13, 26–27; 15:3, 10–12, 30–31). Further, many of the sayings in this section are chiastic in structure. It is worth noting that the righteous/upright are contrasted not only with the wicked but occasionally with fools (10:21), those who trust in riches (11:28), and the lazy (15:19). Also, the wicked seem to be contrasted with those who fear the Lord (10:27). Hence, there is a sense in which righteousness is equivalent to wisdom and all its good attributes (including the fear of the Lord), whereas wickedness is equivalent to folly and all its bad attributes. Chapters 10–15 most clearly bring out that wisdom entails righteousness. To be wise means to be righteous, and it is impossible to be wise without living righteously.

10:2—11:31. The Righteous and the Wicked. Although the whole subdivision (chaps. 10–15) contains many sayings about the righteous and the wicked, chapters 10–11 contain the densest group of such sayings (10:2–3, 6–7, 9–11, 16–21, 23–25, 27–32; 11:1, 3–11, 18–21, 23, 28–31). A number of sayings focus on the speech of the righteous or the wicked (see 10:6, 11; 11:9). A few of the sayings that do not explicitly mention the righteous or the wicked also focus on speech (see 10:8, 10, 13–14; 11:13).

The wording of many wisdom sayings allows them to be classified under more than one topic, and a few sayings are clustered together by common themes. The result is an interweaving of many themes. In addition to clusters of sayings whose main common topic is the contrast between the righteous and the wicked (as noted already), this group of sayings also contains single proverbs and clusters of proverbs that deal with wealth and righteousness (10:2–3), diligence and laziness (vv. 4–5, 26), speech (vv. 6, 8, 10–14, 18–21; 11:9, 13), the wise and fools (10:8, 13–14; 11:12), hatred and love (10:12), the rich and the poor (vv. 15, 22), pride and humility (11:2), the talebearer or gossip (v. 13), counsel and guidance (v. 14), being a surety/security (v. 15), honor and riches (v. 16), mercy and cruelty (v. 17), the beautiful and unwise woman (v. 22), generosity (vv. 24–26), and seeking good and evil (v. 27).

In a few instances, verses are placed next to each other not because they share the same topic but because they both contain the same word. For example, both 10:6 and 7 contain the Hebrew word *berakah* ("blessing"), while both vv. 11 and 12 contain the verb "to cover." Since the meaning of most wisdom sayings in these verses is clear, only a few isolated verses deserve further comment. That the rich find safety in their wealth but poverty brings ruin to the poor should be understood as descriptive rather than prescriptive (v. 15). That is, it is not advice, but simply an observation. In the second part of 11:7, some translations follow the Septuagint, which uses the Greek word *asebōn* ("ungodly"). The Hebrew text has the word *'onim* ("wealth," "riches"). The meanings are similar: hope based on wealth will perish, and the hopes of the ungodly will also perish.

In 11:21, the expression *yad leyad* (lit. "hand in hand"), a Hebrew expression that could mean "be assured" or "certainly," is sometimes translated as referring to the wicked "joining forces" (i.e., joining hands; see 16:5). Hence, 11:21 states the certainty of the rewards of the wicked and the righteous. Verse 30 also deserves some comment. The meaning of its first part is clear (i.e., righteousness results in a long life). The beautiful metaphor does not refer to the fruit of the tree but states that the tree is the fruit. However, the meaning of its second part is not as clear. Some translations render *loqeakh nepshot* as "he who wins souls." Some have associated this verse with the modern expression that refers to evangelism or the proclamation of the gospel. But the Hebrew word *nepesh* can mean "life" rather than "soul." In fact, the Hebrew verb *laqakh* ("to take"), coupled with *nepesh* ("soul," "life"), normally means "to kill" or "to take life" (see 1:19; Ezek. 33:6; Jon. 4:3). In Proverbs 11:30, however, it could be that the Hebrew verb *laqakh* is being used in a positive sense. That is, just as righteousness results in a long life, so the wisdom of the wise, if listened to, gathers/saves life, both that of the wise themselves and of others (see 13:14 for a proverb with a similar message).

12:1—15:33. Miscellaneous Sayings. In addition to clusters of sayings whose common topic is primarily the contrast between the righteous and the wicked (12:5–7, 12–13; 13:5–6; 15:28–29), there are verses and clusters of verses that address topics such as wisdom and folly (see 12:1, 15–16; 13:1, 13–16; 14:1, 6–8; 15:5, 7), diligence and laziness (see 12:11, 24, 27; 13:4; 15:19), wise speech (see 12:14, 17–20, 25; 13:2–3; 15:1–2, 4, 23), wealth and poverty (see 13:7–8, 22–23; 14:20–21, 31), pride (see 13:10), the discipline of children (see v. 24), the fear of the Lord (14:26–27; 15:25–26, 29), strife (vv. 16–18), and the need for counsel/guidance (see v. 22).

Child Discipline in Proverbs

Some passages in Proverbs deserve to be briefly discussed because they have been understood as commanding corporal punishment. For example, 13:24 says that parents who spare the rod hate their children but those who discipline them demonstrate their love for them. Most of these passages use the word "rod" (Heb. *shebet*; 10:13; 13:24; 22:8, 15; 23:13–14; 26:3; 29:15). There are other passages that do not use the word rod but that may also refer to corporal punishment (see 19:18).

1. *Contextual Considerations.* Such passages must be read in the larger context of Proverbs and of the ancient Near East in general, where the use of corporal punishment was not only a parenting technique but a general form of punishment. For example, Proverbs also mentions corporal punishment applied to adults (see 10:13; 17:26; 19:29;

20:30; 26:3), which, incidentally, was sometimes administered with anger (22:8). In fact, corporal punishment was also applied to slaves even in NT times (see Luke 12:47–48). Though it may have been acceptable to beat or whip an adult wrongdoer in the ancient Near East, that does not justify continuing such a practice today (slavery was also common in the ancient Near East). Thus, a proper contextual application of passages concerning the rod teaches the need for age-appropriate discipline but does not prescribe the specific form of discipline.

2. *Hebrew Terminology for Discipline.* It is instructive to understand some of the Hebrew words used in combination with the rod. One of these is the word *musar* ("instruction"), which occurs thirty times in the book (see 1:8; 3:11; 13:1, 24; 15:5, 33; 19:20, 27; 22:15; 23:12–14; 24:32). This term is not limited to contexts referring to raising children (23:12) and may be used in contexts where physical punishment is involved (see Jer. 2:30; 30:14), but it primarily refers to oral instructions (see Jer. 17:23; 32:33; 35:13). It is accompanied by the verb "to listen" in Proverbs 19:27 (cf. 23:12), and it parallels Hebrew words such as *torah* ("teaching," "law"; 1:8), *'etsah* ("counsel," "advice"; 19:20), and *da'at* ("knowledge"). The word "rod" (*shebet*) also occurs in combination with the Hebrew *tokakhat* ("reproof," "reprimand," "correction"; 29:15). The two words

tokakhat and *musar* also occur in combination with each other (cf. 3:11; 15:5). Further, *musar* is a noun formed from the root *yasar*, which is also used in the context of parenting (see 19:18; 29:17; 31:1) and can mean either "to instruct" or "to discipline." On the one hand, *yasar* in the sense of "to discipline" can refer to punishment (see Deut. 22:18) and can be translated as "chasten," "discipline" (Prov. 19:18), "correct," or "reprove" (9:7; 29:17, 19). Alternatively, however, *yasar* in the sense of "to instruct" can refer to teaching rather than punishment, such as the proverbs that King Lemuel's mother "taught" him (31:1; see also Is. 28:26). Therefore, the passages in Proverbs that are relevant to parenting do not always deal with discipline or punishment (see Prov. 22:6), and what the book emphasizes more than discipline is the need for parental teaching and instruction. Thus, the application of "the rod" must always be accompanied by a loving explanation of what the parents are trying to teach the child. And happy is the wise child who accepts instruction without the need for discipline (19:25; 21:11).

In summary, Proverbs, read in its proper context, neither requires nor forbids corporal punishment in the upbringing of children but rather teaches the need for parental instruction, which on occasion may need to be accompanied by age-appropriate discipline.

In a few instances, sayings are placed next to each other because they both contain the same word or expression. For example, the Hebrew word *tob* ("good") is the last word in 13:21 and the first word in v. 22. The word *leb* ("heart") occurs at the beginning of both 15:13 and 14, and *tob* (here usually translated as "better") again occurs at the beginning of both vv. 16 and 17. These two verse pairs are connected by v. 15, which contains both words in the Hebrew expression *tob leb* ("good of heart"), meaning "a happy mind" or "a cheerful/merry heart." It is also possible that vv. 8 and 9 are placed next to each other because both verses contain the expression *to'ebat Yahweh* ("an abomination to the Lord," "the Lord detests").

A few sayings are related by both thematic and verbal links. For example, *dabar* ("word," "instruction") and *mitsvah* ("command") occur in 13:13, and *torah* ("law," "instruction") occurs

in v. 14. Thus, in addition to the fact that both verses share the common theme of the importance of listening to advice—a theme that is also reflected in some other sayings in this section (see vv. 10, 18)—they are also connected by the use of words with similar meanings.

A number of wisdom sayings are purely descriptive. For example, v. 12 states that delay in the fulfillment of a desire discourages the heart, but its fulfillment is like a tree of life. This is not an admonition but a psychological observation. It is possible that v. 12 is placed here because v. 11 speaks of gathering by slow labor. However, v. 12 deals with fulfillment versus nonfulfillment rather than gradual fulfillment. Other examples of descriptive sayings are found in vv. 7, 21, 23; 14:5, 10; 15:13. It is important to read 13:21 in the context of wisdom literature: the statement that evil pursues sinners but the righteous are repaid with good is not an inviolable rule but a general description of truth (i.e., it tends to happen this way, but exceptions do occur).

Though the meaning of most sayings is clear and needs no comment, it is appropriate to make some remarks concerning a few specific verses. In 12:4, the expression *eshet hayil* ("excellent wife," "wife of noble character," "virtuous wife") is the same Hebrew expression as in 31:10. The saying in 12:12 presents difficulties in interpretation, as can be seen in the various ways modern versions have translated it. Notwithstanding the technical problems, the verse states that the righteous will prosper. In v. 14, the word *gemul* can mean "recompense," or it can also mean "deed" or "work." The message is that both the fruit of the mouth and the deed of the hands (i.e., speech and actions) will bring their own consequences.

Another difficult passage is v. 26. Various suggestions have been made to read the Hebrew text differently. In its present form, the Hebrew word *tur* can be translated in such a way as to imply either the idea of the cautiousness of the righteous in choosing friends or the ability of the righteous to guide others well. The text contrasts being on the right path with being on the wrong one.

The saying in 13:8 has been variously interpreted since the Hebrew word at the end of the verse (*ge'arah*) can mean either "rebuke" or "threat." Accordingly, some suggest that the verse teaches that whereas the rich can pay their way out of trouble, the poor do not heed threats because they have nothing to lose.

The two lines in v. 19 seem unrelated and have been variously interpreted. One interpretation is that they provide the context for each other. In other words, since a fulfilled desire is sweet to the soul (first line), fools do not want to depart from evil (second line). If this interpretation is correct, v. 19 is descriptive rather than prescriptive.

The expression sometimes translated as "the wise woman" in 14:1 is similar to an expression found in Judges 5:29 that refers to the wisest ladies and, hence, could mean "the wisest women." However, because the rest of the sentence is in the singular, some have suggested correcting the Hebrew text to read "wisdom" instead of "wise ones" (i.e., "the wisdom of women"), but this is unnecessary since the contrast in Proverbs 14:1 is between wisdom and folly.

In v. 14, some translate *me'alayv* (lit. "from upon him") as "from above," but others suggest correcting the Hebrew text to read *mimma'alalayw* ("by his deeds"). Again, such changes are unnecessary. The text is making a clear point, namely, that both the backslider and the good receive the consequences of their own actions.

Proverbs 15:19 contrasts the lazy with the righteous rather than the lazy with the diligent or the righteous with the wicked. The contrast between the lazy and the righteous also occurs in 21:25–26.

16:1—22:16
Second Subdivision

The exact place where the first subdivision of this section ends and the second one begins is not completely clear though, as already mentioned, there seems to be a difference between the two subdivisions in terms of the structure of the sayings. This second subdivision contains a few groups of sayings clustered around common themes. However, most of its sayings are best read individually rather than as part of a cluster. In addition to the few clusters of sayings, there are also individual sayings concerning good and bad speech (17:4, 9, 27–28; 18:4; 20:15, 19; 21:23; 22:11), false testimony (19:5, 9, 28; 21:28), riches and poverty (17:1, 5; 19:17; 21:17, 20; 22:1–2, 7, 16) being a surety/security (17:18; 20:16), disciplining children (19:18; 22:6, 15), honoring parents (19:26; 20:20), conflict (17:1, 14; 20:3; 21:9, 19; 22:10), anger (16:32; 19:11), friendship (18:19), diligence and laziness (v. 9; 19:24; 20:4, 13; 21:5, 25; 22:13), wisdom and folly (17:2; 21:22; 22:3), divine sovereignty (16:33; 19:21; 20:24; 21:30–31), the fear of the Lord (22:4), righteousness/honesty and wickedness (20:7, 10; 21:3–4; 22:5), justice (17:26; 18:5), kings (19:12; 20:2, 8, 26, 28; 22:11), the blessing of a good wife (18:22; 19:14), the grief of a contentious wife (19:13; 21:9, 19), drunkenness (20:1), vows (v. 25), adultery (22:14), and other topics.

16:1–9. Wisdom Sayings about Divine Sovereignty. This cluster of wisdom sayings consists of a group of independent sayings that share the theme of divine sovereignty. It is possible that this cluster actually begins in 15:33 since that verse also mentions the Lord (cf. 16:9). In 16:1, the heart stands for the internal processes, such as thoughts and plans, whereas the tongue stands for speech or, more broadly, that which eventually comes out. Hence, people may plan, but it is God who controls the outcome. The message of v. 2 is similar to 21:2; that is, we may think ourselves pure, but it is God who is the ultimate judge.

The saying in 16:3 states that God will honor and establish the plans of those who submit their lives to Him. Next, in v. 4, the text discusses the fact that the Lord has made everything for His *ma'aneh*. This word means "answer" or "purpose," but some translate it as "for Himself," which might convey some of both nuances. Most commentators prefer the idea of "purpose." Thus, the statement that God made the wicked for the day of doom not only implies that they will not escape the judgment but also serves as an illustration of His sovereignty. The Lord uses all things, even the wicked, to accomplish His purposes (cf. Rom. 8:28).

The saying in Proverbs 16:5 condemns pride (on the expression translated as "joining forces" or "being assured," see commentary on 10:2—11:31). The parallelism in 16:6 is interesting: the words *khesed* ("mercy," "love," "loyalty," "steadfast love") and *'emet* ("faithfulness," "truth," "trust") usually refer to attributes of God (see Gen. 24:27; Ex. 34:6–7; Deut. 7:9; Pss. 25:10; 26:3; 40:11), which Proverbs exhorts people to emulate (Prov. 3:3). If those terms refer to God's character, then the basis for atonement is His mercy and truth. The second part of the proverb would describe the human response to divine atonement. The fear of the Lord is powerful enough to turn us away from evil. Proverbs 16:6 would remind us that forgiveness and atonement must coexist with a life lived according to God's will. Though forgiveness comes through God's grace and not through our good works, a changed life is evidence of that grace. An alternative interpretation, although perhaps less likely, would be based on the fact that the Hebrew word for "atone" (*kipper*) occurs only twice in Proverbs, here and in v. 14, where it refers to appeasing the king's anger. It is possible that v. 6 may refer not to atonement in the sight of God but to reconciliation among people (i.e., acts of kindness help others forgive previous wrongs).

Verses 7–8 provide a contrast with v. 5. Instead of what is detestable/an abomination to the Lord (v. 5), vv. 7–8 describe the results of pleasing God.

Verse 9 is similar to v. 1, though the contrast here is between heart and steps rather than heart and tongue. Together, vv. 1 and 9 provide an envelope structure surrounding wisdom sayings focusing on God's sovereignty.

16:10–19. Wisdom Sayings about the King. These sayings are grouped together around the theme of the king. The placement of v. 10 may be due to the word *qesem*, which refers to

some kind of a supernatural statement (see Jer. 14:14) that usually involves forbidden occult practices (Deut. 18:10). In this context, it does not refer to the occult but compares the king's words to a divinely inspired verdict, which then becomes the reason why he is urged to pronounce just sentences. Thus, *qesem* connects the two clusters of sayings on divine sovereignty and on the king.

Proverbs 16:11 is not directly related to the previous verse but is placed here probably because honest weights/balances and scales are relevant to the king's duty to carry out justice (vv. 10, 12). The placement of v. 11 may also be due to the fact that *mishpat* ("justice," "judgment") occurs in both v. 10 and v. 11 (there conveying the idea of "honest" or "just").

Verses 12–13 use two words from the Hebrew root *tsadaq* ("to be right"): righteousness (v. 12) and righteous, implying honest speech (v. 13). A king who seeks righteousness detests wickedness (v. 12) but delights in words that are upright and honest (v. 13). Just as vv. 12–13 contrast what the king detests and what he delights in, so vv. 14–15 contrast the king's wrath with his favor. In fact, the same Hebrew word (*ratson*, "pleasure," "acceptance," "favor," "will") occurs in both vv. 13 and 15. Verse 14 compares the king's anger, which only the wise can appease, to a death sentence (cf. v. 6). In v. 15, the king's favor is compared to the latter/spring rain. The early/autumn rain (around October/November) and the latter/spring rain (around March/April) mark the beginning and end of the winter rainy season. Both are important for the growth of crops (Deut. 11:14). The proper timing of the rainy season was seen as God's blessing (Joel 2:23; Zech. 10:1), and the withholding of rain as His displeasure (Jer. 3:13; Amos 4:7). This section closes with a few miscellaneous wisdom sayings addressing the topics of wisdom's surpassing value (Prov. 16:16), the upright path (v. 17), and pride and humility (vv. 18–19).

16:20–30. Wisdom and Speech. This cluster of sayings connects wisdom and wise speech. Verses 20 to 23 describe some of the benefits of wisdom. In v. 20, the Hebrew word *dabar* can mean "word," "matter," or "thing," so alternative readings are "the one who heeds the word" or "he who is prudent [Heb. *sakal*, "to act with insight"] in a matter." Either way, this parallels trusting in the Lord and results in finding that which is good and in being happy. Verse 21 states that those who are wise in heart are recognized by others as prudent/discerning, and from their lips flows a sweet increase of knowledge. Such *sekel* ("prudence," "insight," "understanding") is like a wellspring of life for those who possess it. It enriches the quality of their lives (v. 22). This is contrasted with the correction of fools, which has been interpreted and translated as referring to the discipline that fools receive what they give. In the first sense, the proverb says either that it is foolish to discipline fools or that fools will be disciplined because of their folly. In the second sense, it means that the discipline/instruction that fools give amounts to foolishness. The understanding found in the heart of the wise teaches their mouths what to say and adds learning/instruction to their lips (v. 23).

True wisdom determines what will come out of a person's mouth. The pleasant or gracious words coming from the mouth/lips of the wise are like honeycomb in that they make life (lit. "the soul") enjoyable and the body ("the bones") healthy (v. 24). That is, they enrich the whole being, not only the mind. Verse 25 is a repetition of 14:12 and deals with the way people choose to live their lives and the need of wisdom to avoid death. The thought of death leads almost naturally to the idea of self-preservation. In 16:26, the Hebrew word *nepesh* (lit. "soul") is used in the sense of "appetite," as it is sometimes translated. That is, a person's hunger serves as motivation to work.

Verse 27 returns to the topic of speech. The ungodly are interested in searching for what is evil, and once they find it, it becomes like a burning, scorching fire on their lips, damaging both the speaker and the listener. The image worsens in v. 28, which describes a perverse person, a whisperer/gossip (from the Heb. *ragan* "to slander") who spreads strife and damages friendships. The next proverb then turns from those who spread strife to the violent who entice others and lead them into an evil way of life (v. 29). This group of proverbs concludes with a reference to those who express evil intentions through body language, like winking or pursing/compressing their lips (v. 30).

16:31—21:2. Miscellaneous Sayings. These verses include wisdom sayings on a variety of topics (see commentary on 16:1—22:16). Since the meaning of most sayings is clear, the comments below focus primarily on verses that need clarification or explanation. As elsewhere in the book, some wisdom sayings are only descriptive rather than prescriptive. For example, 17:8 describes the effectiveness of a *shokhad* ("gift," "present," "bribe"). This is not an encouragement to resort to bribes but only an observation from the perspective of the giver. Other possible short-term benefits of bribes or gifts are mentioned in 21:14 (if referring to a bribe, this would also be descriptive rather than prescriptive), but bribes are also condemned directly because they are used to pervert justice (see 15:27; 17:23). Similarly, the "gift" in 18:16 could be understood as a "bribe" (see 21:14), in which case this is also a descriptive rather than prescriptive proverb.

Other descriptive sayings include the comparison between gossip and delicious food (18:8), the contrast between the rich and the poor (v. 23; 19:4, 6–7; 22:7), and the description of a buyer's attitude (20:14). The word "heart" in 17:16 refers to "mind," "sense," "intention," or "understanding," and it is often so translated. Thus, the meaning of the verse is that there is no point in fools having money to buy wisdom since they have no understanding.

The sayings in 18:4–8 are loosely related. Verse 5 condemns improper verdicts in the context of court proceedings. Verse 6 is placed after v. 5 because of the Hebrew word *rib* ("argument," "strife," "contention"), which is often used in the context of litigation. Verses 6–7 convey similar messages (i.e., fools bring trouble on themselves by their words). They also have a chiastic relationship: v. 6 has the sequence of lips then mouth, and v. 7 has the reverse sequence, mouth then lips. In addition, though vv. 4 and 8 are not directly related, both concern speech, namely, the speech of the wise (v. 4) and the words of a talebearer/gossip (v. 8). Since vv. 10 and 11 are placed next to each other, it is possible to read them in contrast to each other to say that the rich consider their wealth as their safety (v. 11), but it is the Lord who is the safety of the righteous (v. 10). However, it is best to see v. 11 as a descriptive proverb (see 10:15). Probably the main reason why 18:10 and 11 are juxtaposed is that the Hebrew verb *sagab* ("to be inaccessible/protected") occurs in both verses, implying safety in v. 10 and height in v. 11.

The practice of casting lots was common in the ancient world (18:18; Lev. 16:8; Num. 26:55; 1 Sam. 14:41–42; Jonah 1:7; Acts 1:22–26). Since the Hebrew word *goral* also expresses the idea of destiny or fate (Is. 17:14; Dan. 12:13), casting lots was believed to be a supernaturally guided way of determining God's will (Prov. 16:33). It was also used in secular settings as a way of making decisions (Joel 3:3; Obad. 11; John 19:22–24), similar to the modern-day practice of tossing a coin. This proverb suggests that some issues cannot be resolved without resorting to casting lots.

The sayings in 18:20–21 both figuratively describe a person's speech as the fruit of the mouth, which in turn is eaten by the speaker. Both proverbs teach the importance of wise speech. The exact meaning of v. 24 is not clear. In Hebrew, there is a play on the words *re'im* and *hitro'ea'*, which some translate as "A man who has friends must himself be friendly." However, the second verb can be understood as "to smash together" or "break in pieces." Hence, some interpret it negatively to mean that those who have many friends may "come to ruin" or "be harmed" (by the friends). Others have suggested a slight change in the Hebrew text to read "to associate with." If so, the message of this proverb may be that there are different kinds of friends; that is, there are friends who simply "associate" with you, and there are friends who are closer than brothers.

The interpretation of 19:2 depends primarily on the meaning of the Hebrew word *nepesh* (lit. "soul"), which can have several possible meanings, at least two of which could fit this context. If the word is used in the sense of a "living being" (i.e., "person"), the proverb speaks of those who lack knowledge, whose haste results in sin. If the word simply means "desire," "craving," "zeal," or "passion," the proverb warns against ignorant passion. If so, the Hebrew word *khata'* (usually translated as "to sin") could be understood in the sense of "to miss the mark" or "to err." The idea then is that ignorant passion and haste result in making mistakes. In other words, "haste makes waste." The sayings in vv. 13–14 are not related but are juxtaposed because both verses mention father and wife. The proverb in v. 18 can be understood in different ways. It is possible to read it as advice to correct children but not so harshly as to cause their death. On the other hand, in light of similar passages in the book (see 13:24; 23:14), it is more likely that this proverb asserts that failing to correct children is like wishing for their destruction (cf. comments on vv. 12–14).

The Hebrew word *khesed* ("goodness," "love," "mercy"), used in 20:6, often has the connotation of "covenant loyalty." The contrast in this verse is between the large number who claim to be loyal and the few who are truly faithful. In v. 19, the last clause has been variously translated because the Hebrew verb *patah* could mean "to be simple/naïve" or "to be wide/open." Whether it refers to those who are naïve with their lips or those who are open with their lips, both possibilities fit the context and express the idea of avoiding either those who

flatter or those who say too much. The message of v. 21 is very similar to that of 13:11, though the wording of the two proverbs is different. Both warn against the danger of wealth gained without honest labor.

The sayings in 21:1–3 all mention the Lord. Verse 1 asserts the Lord's sovereignty over kings. Verse 2, which is similar to 16:2, states that the Lord is the ultimate judge of the heart. Verse 3 says the Lord loves righteousness and justice more than sacrifice (cf. 1 Sam. 15:22; Mic. 6:6–8). This, in turn, initiates a cluster of wisdom sayings in which the contrast between the righteous and the wicked is very frequent.

21:3–29. The Righteous and the Wicked. This cluster of proverbs is similar to the first cluster in the first subdivision of this section (10:2—11:31) in that it contains a larger than usual concentration of sayings about the righteous and/or the wicked (21:3–4, 7–8, 10, 12, 15, 18, 21, 25–27, 29). However, as in the earlier cluster, there are also many sayings that do not directly mention the righteous or the wicked (vv. 5–6, 9, 11, 13–14, 16–17, 19, 20, 22–24, 28). The sayings in vv. 11 and 12 probably occur next to each other because both use the Hebrew verb *sakal* ("to have insight"). In v. 11, it refers to the instruction that the wise receive (or, according to some renderings, it refers to paying attention to the wise); in v. 12, it refers to observing/considering the house of the wicked. "The righteous one" is probably a reference to God (some translations imply this by either inserting the word "God" or by capitalizing "One"). If this is a reference to God, it is the only instance in Proverbs where God is called righteous.

The sayings in vv. 25–26 can be read either as two separate sayings or one long saying. Verse 25 describes the lazy, who have intense desires but refuse to work to achieve them, whereas v. 26 contrasts greedy desire with the generosity of the righteous. It is also possible to read the two verses as one wisdom saying, in which case there is a contrast between the lazy and the righteous (see also 15:19). The claim in the first line of 21:28 that a false witness will perish is clear, but there is some difficulty with the second line. The one who hears could be understood as hearing the false witness or simply as being a good listener, which is a trait of the wise (see 18:13). The word *lanetsakh* can mean "forever," "successfully," or "victoriously."

21:30—22:16. Miscellaneous Sayings. These verses include wisdom sayings on a variety of topics (see commentary on 16:1—22:16).

Though these sayings are independent units, some are placed next to each other because of common themes or words. The sayings in 21:30–31 both deal with divine sovereignty. Similarly, the sayings in 22:5–6 are probably placed next to each other because both verses speak of a "way" or "path": the way of the wicked, those who are *'iqqesh* ("crooked," "perverse"; v. 5), and the way that a child should go (v. 6). Some verses deserve a brief comment. The saying in v. 2 is similar to 29:13. Whereas 22:2 compares the rich and the poor, 29:13 compares the poor and the oppressor. Both passages teach that all are equal in the sight of God, and both may serve as a warning to the rich and powerful not to exploit the poor. In 22:6, the Hebrew word *khanak* ("train," "start off," "dedicate") could also mean "to initiate" (Deut. 20:5; 1 Kin. 8:63). The proverb teaches that if parents "initiate" children

in the way they should go (Heb. *'al pi darko*, lit. "upon the mouth of his way"), they will not depart from it even in old age.

22:17—24:22
THIRTY SAYINGS OF THE WISE

The wisdom sayings in this section consist of a mix of short sayings and slightly longer sayings. They are also miscellaneous in nature with no discernible overarching theme. The Hebrew expression used in 22:20 can mean "excellent things" or may, alternatively, mean "thirty sayings" (see below, "Excellent Things or Thirty Sayings?"). There is a general consensus that there are thirty sayings in this section, though there is some disagreement on how to divide them.

Excellent Things or Thirty Sayings?

1. *Textual Problem.* There is a Hebrew expression in 22:20 which has been translated as "excellent things" or "thirty sayings." This may be explained as follows. First, the Hebrew word *dabar* (v. 17, assumed to be the referent in v. 20) can mean not only a "thing" but also a "word" or "saying." Second, there is some uncertainty concerning another word which has occasioned both textual and translational questions. The main text of the Hebrew Bible reads *shilshom*, which has been translated by some as "the day before yesterday," but *shilshom* carries that meaning only in the phrase *temol shilshom* ("yesterday and the previous day"; see Ex. 5:8). Besides, it does not seem to fit the context. There is a scribal reading tradition (preserved in the margin of the manuscripts) that assumes that the text is misspelled and corrects it to *shalishim* (lit. "the third man"), which designates "a military officer." The translation "excellent" has been derived from this without any linguistic basis. In any case, this suggestion does not fit the context.

2. *Possible Solution.* Scholars usually modify the Hebrew text (changing only the vowels, not the original consonants) from *shilshom* to *sheloshim* ("thirty"). They argue that this is contextually supported because there are thirty sayings in this section of

Proverbs. This modification of the Hebrew text was to some extent suggested by the discovery and publication of an Egyptian wisdom document called *Instructions of Amenemope* in 1922. Scholars began to notice similarities between Proverbs and the Egyptian document. Since the latter consists of thirty chapters and this section of Proverbs also consists of thirty sayings, most scholars conclude that the best reading of the Hebrew text is *sheloshim*, "thirty."

Moreover, it is important to note that the translation "thirty sayings" is not completely dependent on the supposed similarities between Proverbs and *Amenemope*. First, the similarities between the two occur mostly in the sayings in Proverbs 22:17—23:11. There are fewer similarities in 23:12—24:22, though these may have similarities to other documents from ancient Near Eastern wisdom literature. In some cases the similarities are not convincing. Second, this solution was first proposed by Felix Perles in 1906, a decade and a half before the publication of *Amenemope*. However, Perles had in mind the thirty(-one) chapters of the book of Proverbs. In the final analysis, the suggestion to read "thirty" instead of "excellent" remains hypothetical, but it does clarify the contextual meaning of a difficult Hebrew phrase.

22:17—23:9
Sayings One through Ten

Proverbs 22:17–21 contains the *first* of the so-called thirty sayings and also serves as an introduction to them. The message of these verses consists of an exhortation to listen/pay attention (lit. "incline your ear") to wisdom, meaning not only to pay close attention to it but to organize life accordingly. The end result of embracing wisdom is being able to trust in the Lord, whose wisdom is unfathomable, and gaining a clear understanding of the certain and reliable truth for the purpose of teaching others (v. 21).

The *second* saying calls for caring for and protecting the poor and afflicted by defending their legal rights (vv. 22–23). The primary motivation is that God cares for them and will take up their cause. Similar statements depicting the Lord as the defender of the defenseless can be found in 15:25 and 23:10–11.

The *third* proverb points to the danger of being friends with a person who is controlled by anger, lacks self-control, and is hot-tempered (22:24–25). Friendship with them would imply support for their behavior. Their influence ruins the lives of those who learn to behave like them.

According to the *fourth* saying, it is not wise to assume responsibility for the debts of others (vv. 26–27). If debtors do not pay, whose who guarantee their debts have to pay for them. As a result, what they have will be taken from them. The warning of this saying is similar to that of 6:15; 11:15; and 17:18.

The *fifth* saying is about respecting the landmarks/boundary stones that served as property markers (22:28). It was illegal to move these boundary markers, which would have been equivalent to stealing land (Deut. 19:14; 27:17; see also Prov. 15:25; 23:10–11).

Instead of stealing, the *sixth* saying commends diligence in work that enables the wise to serve/stand before those in the highest places in the land (i.e., kings; Prov. 22:29). Self-development is encouraged as a tool for effective service.

Proper behavior in the presence of those who rule is an expression of true wisdom, according to the *seventh* saying (23:1–3). Those who eat with rulers should control their appetite because the food is deceptive food (v. 3); that is, the person offering it may have some hidden agenda.

The *eighth* saying raises the topic of wealth and warns against making its acquisition a goal (vv. 4–5). Riches are like a mirage, seen one moment and then suddenly disappearing. They are like a bird that is here now and then flies away.

The *ninth* saying returns to the topic of food, counseling against accepting an invitation to eat with a person who is stingy or selfish (vv. 6–8). Such a host speaks hypocritically, causing the guest's stomach to reject the ingested food. Even the good words expressed during the meal are wasted.

The *tenth* saying unpacks what is insinuated in the previous one (v. 9). It stresses the futility of giving counsel to fools, who despise words of wisdom and insightful thoughts (cf. 9:7, 8; Matt. 7:6).

23:10—24:4
Sayings Eleven to Twenty-One

The *eleventh* saying is similar to that of 22:28. Both proverbs encourage respect for the property of others, but the emphasis here is on taking the land of the fatherless/orphan (23:10). The reason given is that there is a mighty Redeemer/Defender who will take up their case in court (cf. 15:25; 22:22–23). The Redeemer/Defender probably refers to the Lord.

Similar to vv. 17–18 and 23:19, the *twelfth* saying is an exhortation to listen to the instruction that follows (v. 12). There is an interesting wordplay here. The Hebrew word *musar* ("discipline," "instruction," "correction") is used in both vv. 12 and 13, which has caused some scholars to join v. 12 with vv. 13 and 14. But the use of the same word in the two verses justifies locating the proverbs one after the other.

The *thirteenth* saying, counsels giving correction, is presumably based on the instruction received in v. 12 (vv. 13–14). In light of the parallelism with v. 14, v. 13 does not mean that punishing children will not kill them. It means that it will rescue them (Heb. *nepesh*, "soul," "life") from the grave (see also 19:18).

Wisdom positively impacts not only those seeking it but also, as the *fourteenth* saying indicates, the parents or instructors (23:15–16). Wise children make their parents rejoice. Joy enriches the totality of a person. Nothing brings more joy to parents than to hear their children speaking what is right.

The *fifteenth* proverb teaches against envying sinners and assures a future reward for those who live in reverent submission to the Lord (vv. 17–18). This is one of the few places where Proverbs reveals a reality beyond the present, a future eternal life. The sinner may seem to prosper, but the time will come when those who hope in the Lord will triumph and the wicked will perish.

Verse 19 can be considered an exhortation introducing the *sixteenth* saying (vv. 19-21), which exhorts temperance when eating and drinking. Drunkenness and gluttony lead to poverty (cf. Deut. 21:20).

The *seventeenth* saying also begins with an exhortation to pay attention to the words that follow (Prov. 23:22-25). These words describe the joy that righteous and wise children bring to their parents (vv. 24-25). The motivation to listen to and appropriate truth, wisdom, and instruction is found in the joy that it brings to parents. Children are responsible for making the life of their parents as enjoyable as possible in the present life (see vv. 15-16).

As in the previous wisdom saying, the *eighteenth* begins with an introduction (vv. 26). The phrase "my son, give me your heart" renders the Hebrew expression *tenah beni libbeka*, which does not occur frequently. It is probably equivalent to the similar expression *sim leb* (lit. "to place the heart"), which means "to consider," or "to pay attention" (see Deut. 32:46; Is. 41:22). In this case, an alternative translation would be "pay attention to me." After the introduction, the main part of this saying warns against the potentially fatal temptation of prostitutes and adulterous women (Prov. 23:27-28; cf. 22:14).

The *nineteenth* saying contains a vivid description of the harmful effects of alcohol (23:29-35). It describes its negative social, physical, and psychological impact on the lives of those who drink it. The exhortation is so strong that it discourages even looking at it. Alcohol may appear attractive, but it is like a poisonous serpent. The condition of those under the influence of alcohol is described as pitiful. They hallucinate, and like a ship at sea or a person sitting at the top of the mast, they cannot control the movement of their own bodies. Such individuals are out of contact with reality and yet are ready to go out and drink again—a miserable life!

The *twentieth* saying exhorts against envying and wanting to be with evil people who seem to be doing well in life (24:1-2). The reason given is that they justify violence in their inner beings and then express their desire for violent behavior that disrupts proper social order (cf. 3:31).

Wisdom, according to the *twenty-first* saying, supports order (24:3-4). The example given is that of a house that is built with wisdom and that, consequently, is firmly established. In it will dwell pleasant richness. Here the house stands for the family that is guided by divine wisdom, understanding, and knowledge, which contribute to the development of the characters of its members in the fear of the Lord.

24:5-22
Sayings Twenty-Two to Thirty

The *twenty-second* saying describes the inner strength of those who have wisdom (vv. 5-6). Verse 5 does not exhort the wise to be strong but states that it is the wise who are strong (i.e., wisdom is more important than physical strength; cf. 21:22). The imagery of war in 24:6 could be understood as military advice, but it is more likely simply an illustration of wisdom's superiority over physical strength. The emphasis on the importance of many counselors is similar to 11:14 and 20:18 and applies particularly to those in leadership positions.

The *twenty-third* saying states what was observable at the city gate, where the elders met to discuss issues of importance in the community (24:7). People assembled to listen to the wise talk, to conduct public transactions (see Ruth 4:1-12), and to have judicial decisions made (see 2 Sam. 15:2; Amos 5:15; Zech. 8:16). This proverb does not mean that fools remain completely quiet at the city gate (see Prov. 15:2) but that they cannot contribute anything of value in such a setting.

The main subject of the *twenty-fourth* saying is the reputation of fools (24:8-9). By describing their poor reputation, Proverbs discourages others from following their way of life. They are social schemers/troublemakers, abominations to others/detested by all.

The *twenty-fifth* saying encourages diligence in the face of adversity (vv. 10-12). The word "if" is not in the Hebrew but is supplied for the sake of clarity. The verb *rapah* (rendered as "faint," "slack," "weak," or "falter") expresses the idea of being lax in contrast to being diligent (see 18:9). The implicit call is to become strong through wisdom (see 24:5). The saying also admonishes rescuing those in mortal danger. In the context, the One "who weighs the hearts" (i.e., God) knows that the excuse of ignorance is not an honest one. When the moral fabric of society is failing, the wise should speak for those who cannot speak for themselves. The passage also affirms that the divine judgment will be based on our deeds. Although some scholars see a break between v. 10 and vv. 11-12, resulting in a divide that creates separate sayings, the content of the verses, as we have seen, holds them together.

The *twenty-sixth* saying emphasizes the exquisite nature of wisdom (vv. 13–14). It begins with an observable phenomenon: honey is sweet and delicious, so it should be enjoyed. This is then applied to wisdom, which is as sweet as honey. It is enjoyable and enriches life to such an extent that the hope for a better future is nurtured through it. Hope will prevail over disruption.

The *twenty-seventh* saying is a warning against doing violence to the innocent and is addressed to the wicked (vv. 15–16). The righteous may fall in the sense of experiencing disaster or calamity, but there is hope that they will prevail. The righteous will recover even if they fall seven times, but the situation of the wicked is hopeless.

The placement of the *twenty-eighth* saying here may be due to word association (vv. 17–18). That is, though the two sayings are not thematically related, the verb "to fall" occurs both at the end of the previous saying and at the beginning of this one. Although the wicked will fall, the righteous are exhorted not to rejoice in that fall because it will displease the Lord, and, consequently, He will turn His wrath away from those who deserve it.

The topic of envying the wicked is raised again in the *twenty-ninth* saying (vv. 19–20). The reason given is that there is no future for the wicked. Since they exist in hopelessness, why envy them?

The *thirtieth* and final saying of the so-called thirty sayings admonishes respect for the Lord and the king (vv. 21–22). Rebellion against them will result in calamity/disaster. The principle can be applied to having respect not only for the king but for all authority established by God (8:15–16; cf. Ex. 22:28). At this point, the Greek translation of the Old Testament (the Septuagint) adds a few extra lines and then skips to Proverbs 30 (see below, "The Organization of Proverbs in the Septuagint").

The Organization of Proverbs in the Septuagint

1. Discrepancies. The Septuagint (LXX) is the Greek translation of the Hebrew Old Testament. Its translation of the book of Proverbs dates to around 200 to 150 B.C. In general, both the Hebrew and the Septuagint have the same order for the first three sections of the book (1:1—24:22). After that, the order of the passages in the Septuagint departs from the Hebrew as follows:

IV. My Son, Fear My Words (30:1–14)
V. Words to the Wise (24:23–34)
VI. Things That Come in Fours (30:15–33)
VII. Words Spoken by God (31:1–9)
VIII. Sayings Copied by Hezekiah's Men (chaps. 25–29)
IX. The Virtuous Wife (31:10–31)

Though the order of the contents is different in the Septuagint, the individual wisdom sayings and their messages are not affected. However, the different organization does affect the section titles and their ascription of authorship. In the Hebrew text, the placement of the words of Agur and Lemuel (chaps. 30–31) at the end of the book results in their functioning as an appendix of sorts, whereas the Septuagint weaves those passages among the Solomonic proverbs.

2. Reasons for the Discrepancies. It has been suggested that the organization of the Septuagint may be due to the desire of the scribe/translator to maintain Solomonic authorship of the entire content of Proverbs. This may be supported by the translation of some of the section titles. The names of Agur and Lemuel are omitted. Instead of the title for Agur's words, the Septuagint reads "My son, fear my words..." (30:1, LXX), and instead of the title for Lemuel's words, it reads "My words have been spoken by God..." (31:1, LXX). Further, in 24:23, instead of additional words belonging to (i.e., "by") the wise, the Septuagint has the words spoken to the wise (i.e., "These things I say to you who are wise that you may know them," 24:33, LXX). The assumption of a single author (i.e., Solomon) for the entire book may also be the reason for the Septuagint's omission of the title "Proverbs of Solomon" in 10:1. Hence, though the different order of the contents of Proverbs 24:33—31:31 in the Septuagint does not alter the message of the individual wisdom sayings, it may have been motivated by the desire to ascribe all of them to Solomon.

24:23–34
MORE SAYINGS OF THE WISE

This small collection consists of five wisdom sayings that may function as an appendix to the previous section (22:17—24:22). The title does not identify the author but simply says that they were written or collected by the wise. In the Septuagint translation, this section of the book is placed after 30:14 (see "The Organization of Proverbs in the Septuagint," p. 785).

24:23–26
Verdicts and Honest Speech

The setting of the first of these proverbs is a court of law. Showing partiality in court is characterized as "not good" not only because of the moral outrage is raises but also because it disrupts the social order and damages the legal system. The basic issue is that making partial or biased legal decisions that cannot be supported by the evidence presented results in the court not operating the way it should. The saying contrasts illegal decisions and their results with proper, legal decisions and their results. The wicked/guilty should not be declared righteous/innocent. Whenever that happens the legal system will be hated by the people and the judge will be discredited. But when the judges convict/rebuke the guilty/wicked, they will be blessed and will enjoy the peace of knowing that they did what was right. Notice the shift from the singular to the plural. The implication seems to be that there are more judges doing what is right than those doing what is wrong. A *nacoakh* ("straightforward," "right," "honest") answer implies a willingness to tell the truth (v. 26). This attitude is compared to a kiss, which in many cultures of the time was a sign of true friendship. The implication is that true friendship (or, for that matter, any type of social relationship) has to be based on transparency and not deceptiveness.

24:27–29
Plans, Witnesses, and Revenge

Enjoying life requires making plans for the future and prioritizing matters. Living is not just breathing but being in charge of one's life. Having a home requires making plans and then following them. This passage admonishes preparing a field outside before building a house. This could mean obtaining the field and then preparing it for the building project. It could also mean making sure that the land is good enough to farm. The wise are those who do not leave things to themselves but who work with what they have at hand to achieve what is good.

Although vv. 28 and 29 may originally have been two separate sayings, placing them together implies that they should be read as one. Verse 28 warns that those who give false testimony against someone in court damage their moral fabric. Verse 29 admonishes against revenge. Coming after v. 28, it can also mean that God's people should not seek revenge against those who give false testimony against them. They are not to render unto others according to their work. Only God should do that (v. 12).

24:30–34
The Lazy

These verses provide insights about how the mind of the wise functions. They observe a situation, analyze what they observe, and finally draw some objective conclusions that would benefit others. Here observing and analyzing the experience of the lazy leads to the conclusion that slumbering and inactivity results in poverty. The land needs the activity or involvement of a human agent in order to be fully fruitful. Otherwise, its future will be unproductive, and poverty will prevail (see 6:6–11).

25:1—29:27
HEZEKIAH'S COLLECTION
OF SOLOMON'S PROVERBS

This section is a compilation of proverbs written by Solomon that were collected by the men of King Hezekiah and preserved here in the book of Proverbs (25:1). It shows Hezekiah's interest in wisdom literature and thinking. The wisdom sayings in chapters 25–29 consist mostly of short, single-verse units. Although scholars have proposed a number of suggestions for a thematic or theological organization to this section, there is no consensus, and it is probably best to accept that the sayings in this section have no particular organizational center. Nevertheless, there is some agreement on the stylistic differences between chapters 25–26 and 27–29. One of these differences is the fact that there is a greater tendency for the sayings to occur in thematic groups in the first subdivision than in the second. Especially in the first subdivision, the wisdom sayings are often arranged in groups of sayings containing some type of verbal link.

These groups do not necessarily have a common message (see 26:4–5), but they are brought together because they mention a common word or topic. There are also some longer sayings that stand alone (see 27:23–27). In the Septuagint translation, this section of the book is placed between vv. 9 and 10 of chapter 31 (see "The Organization of Proverbs in the Septuagint," p. 785).

25:2—26:28
First Subdivision

The wisdom sayings in this subdivision may be thematically grouped into proverbs about kings (25:2–7), judicial conflict (vv. 8–10), the value of wise words (vv. 11–15), dealing with others (vv. 16–28), fools (26:1–12), laziness (vv. 13–16), provocations that incite conflict (vv. 17–22), and deception (vv. 23–28). However, these clusters of sayings have no common overarching theme.

25:2–7. Kings. These proverbs are grouped together because they concern matters that relate to the king and the court. The king makes matters clear (v. 2), but those who stand before him must remember that they cannot read his mind (v. 3). The king must remove wicked advisors if he is to rule righteously (vv. 4–5). The wise do not promote themselves before the king but wait for the king to do so (v. 6). By extension, these wisdom sayings apply not only to kings but to all human authority by showing how to properly relate to authority in order to avoid conflict (8:15–16).

25:8–15. Judicial Conflicts and Words to the Wise. Verses 8 to 10 consist of two sayings that occur in the setting of a judicial lawsuit. Verse 8 counsels against being too quick to bring matters to court for fear of losing the case. In other words, it is important to evaluate the situation and the possible results of an action before making a decision. The second saying advises those already involved in a legal case to show restraint and willingness to resolve the conflict between those involved without creating more animosity (e.g., revealing another person's secret). The application of these principles goes beyond lawsuits, encouraging restraint in interpersonal conflicts and respect for privacy in all settings.

The wisdom sayings in vv. 11–15 consist of a group of proverbs that advocate the value of wise words. Though vv. 11 and 12 are separate sayings, they are probably placed next to each other because the word "gold" occurs in both. Verse 12 states that a listening ear values reproof as much as gold, whereas v. 11 is more general, comparing words that are appropriate and fitting in various circumstances with apples of gold in silver settings (i.e., something very valuable and precious). Verses 13 and 25 are similar descriptive proverbs expressing the refreshing experience that comes from receiving good news. It revives the spirit of those who were probably depressed. Verse 14 is a warning against false claims and promises. Since rain is very important in the semiarid climate of the Holy Land, such boasting claims are compared with rainless clouds and wind. The proverb in v. 15 promotes the power of gentle, patient speech. The tongue (i.e., words) correctly used is harder than a bone.

25:16–28. Dealing with Others. The section in vv. 16–20 consists of a series of self-contained sayings that mostly relate to getting along well with others. The wise understand that social life can enrich personal life or make it miserable. Hence, this section contains instructions on how to correctly relate to others. Verses 21–22 teach the wisdom of forbearance (see Rom. 12:20). Proverbs 25:23–28 contains miscellaneous sayings on human relationships.

A few of the verses deserve brief comments. It is possible that the sayings in vv. 16 and 17 were originally separate (i.e., v. 16 advises moderation in eating and v. 17 not to visit friends too often). These sayings were then placed next to each other because the Hebrew verb *saba'* ("to be sated," "to be full") occurs in both (though the word is usually translated differently in each verse because of the differing contexts). Their adjacent placement also possibly, though not necessarily, makes an interpretation that connects the honey of v. 16 with the friendship of v. 17. Verse 24 repeats 21:9 (see also v. 19). In spite of statements elsewhere that the righteous will never be *mot* ("shaken," "removed," "uprooted"; 10:30; see also 12:3), the proverb in 25:26 acknowledges that the righteous may falter. What should have been clean becomes polluted through bad influence.

26:1–12. Fools. Almost all the verses in this group of sayings share a common mention of fools. One exception occurs in v. 2, which is not about fools, though its structure is similar to v. 1. Hence, just as honor is not fitting for a fool (v. 1), so a curse without cause (i.e., that is undeserved) will not take effect (v. 2). Also, the last saying in this group is not about fools—though it does mention a fool—but is a warning against being wise in one's own eyes (v. 12; see also 29:20).

Some brief comments on 26:4–5 are appropriate. The sayings in these two verses seem contradictory at first. Does Proverbs advise answering fools according to their folly or not? The two sayings may originally have been independent but were brought together because of their common topic and vocabulary, as is the case with the rest of the sayings in this section. There are various approaches to harmonizing the two sayings. For example, one approach is to suggest that the expression "according to" has different meanings in vv. 4 and 5. But the simplest way to harmonize the two is to acknowledge that Proverbs requires contextual application; that is, it is necessary to take the situation and circumstances into consideration in determining how each proverb is applicable. In addition, the fact that the saying in v. 5 is placed after v. 4 makes v. 5 a response to v. 4. Hence, the two verses in combination teach that, though in principle the wise should not lower their speech to the level of fools, there are times when that becomes necessary.

26:13–28
Laziness, Provocation, and Deception

Verses 13–16 contain four short proverbs that focus on the lazy, who seek reasons to justify their inactivity. They are so lazy that after placing their hands on their food, they will not perform the simple task of bringing their hands to their mouths. The saying in v. 13 is similar to 22:13, and the one in 26:15 is similar to 19:24. The lazy live in self-deception (26:16).

The wisdom sayings in vv. 17–22 warn against actions that provoke/incite conflict. Verse 17 warns against meddling in other people's quarrels, vv. 18–19 warn against deception, and the three proverbs in vv. 20–22 warn against gossip and slander. In addition to the thematic link, these verses also share verbal links. The Hebrew word *rib* ("quarrel," "fight") is used in both vv. 17 and 21. The word *madon* ("strife," "quarrel") in v. 20 might also be used in v. 21. Textual variants indicate that it may be either the same Hebrew word (*madon*) or a closely related word from the same root (*midyan*, "contention"). All the proverbs in vv. 18–21 mention fire, vv. 20 and 21 contain the word "wood," and vv. 20 and 22 mention *nirgan* ("gossip," "talebearer," "whisperer"). The saying in v. 22 is a repetition of 18:8.

The wisdom sayings contained in 26:23–28 are self-contained units that share the common theme of deceptive speech or false friendship. The apparent exception occurs in v. 27, which mentions someone digging a pit. However, since a pit is a type of trap/ambush, this saying fits with the others that deal with deception. Further, digging a pit semantically parallels the act of deceptively covering hatred/malice in v. 26.

27:1—29:27
Second Subdivision

Except for 27:23–27, the wisdom sayings in this subdivision consist of short, self-contained units. There appears to be no clear unifying theme in them, though some are thematically connected.

27:1–27. Miscellaneous Sayings. Verse 1 warns those who would boast about what they could accomplish tomorrow that they have no control over the future. Those who have a reason for boasting should let others compliment and praise them (v. 2). The topic of wrath unifies vv. 3–4. The uncontrolled anger of fools is a heavy load, probably for those around them (v. 3). While anger is almost impossible to control, a jealous person is even worse (v. 4). What good is love if it is not expressed? At least rebuke shows some level of concern, but how much better it would be to simply express love (v. 5). In fact, the wounds inflicted by a friend are useful and much better than the deceitful kisses of an enemy (v. 6).

Many of the sayings are based on observable facts. For the hungry, even what is bitter tastes sweet (v. 7). Those who abandon their homes are like birds that abandon their nest (v. 8). Friendship is emphasized in vv. 9–10 because it enriches life and provides needed support. But blessing a friend loudly at the wrong time will offend others (v. 14). That people sharpen each other (lit. "a man sharpens the face of his friend") signifies that constructive criticism helps sharpen the character of a friend (v. 17).

Wise children bring joy to their parents and enhance their reputation (v. 11). Verse 12 contrasts the prudent and the simple in terms of how they relate to evil: the prudent avoid it, but the simple become its victims. The relationship between spouses could be as annoying as the continual dripping from a leaking roof on a very rainy day, suggesting that it is much better to learn to live in peace (v. 15). However, achieving this end could be difficult (v. 16). Verse 18 applies the observable reality that those who protect their fig tree will eat of its fruit to the relationship of servants with their master. In order to be honored by their master, they need to care for and protect him or her (v. 18).

Human identity is a matter of concern for the wise. A person's true image is located in the heart—the thoughts and desires are found there (v. 19). Like death, a person's desires are never satisfied. Everyone always wants more and more (v. 20). As the quality of gold is revealed by the refining pot, a person's value is established by the opinions of others (v. 21). Fools have foolishness so deeply intertwined within their very being that it is impossible to remove it from them (v. 22).

The wisdom sayings in vv. 23–27 emphasize the rewards of caring for livestock. When other riches come to an end, livestock will provide for the needs of a family (v. 24). Therefore, it is important to provide for the well-being of livestock every day. The message of this saying can be extended in principle and applied to the need to prepare for life's uncertainties.

28:1—29:27. More Miscellaneous Sayings. Chapters 28 and 29 consist of many short, self-contained wisdom sayings on various topics. Some have suggested that these chapters contain royal proverbs with instructions especially addressed to a prince or king. However, unlike typical ancient Near Eastern royal proverbs, an example of which may be found in 31:1–9, this section is not addressed to a king. Further, although many of these sayings mention kings and rulers, their teachings are appropriate for not only monarchs and others in authority but also for those in other situations. The various wisdom sayings in this section intertwine advice to kings and rulers (28:2, 15–16, 28; 29:2, 4, 12, 14, 26) with themes such as the contrast between righteousness and wickedness (28:1–2, 5–6, 10, 12–13, 15, 17–18, 28; 29:2, 4–6, 7, 10, 13, 16, 27), wisdom and folly (vv. 1, 3, 5, 8–9, 11, 15, 20), riches and poverty (28:3, 6, 8, 11, 19–22, 27; 29:13–14), and various other topics. Thus, it is best to characterize the wisdom sayings in these chapters not as royal proverbs but as miscellaneous proverbs.

The references to *torah* are especially interesting (28:4, 7, 9; 29:18). Since this Hebrew word means "law" or "instruction," it may here refer to God's law or to instruction in general. It is used in the latter sense elsewhere in Proverbs (see 1:8; 3:1; 4:2; 6:20; 13:13; 31:26). In the context of the verses in question, while the rendering "instruction" is appropriate, the word can also be translated as "law" because it occurs

in the expression "to keep the law" (28:4, 9; 29:18) and because there is a parallel in v. 18 between *torah* and revelation (Heb. *khazon*, "prophetic vision"), which may allude to the Hebrew Scriptures (i.e., the law and the prophets). The word *khazon* occurs in a similar expression in 1 Samuel 3:1, which refers to the rarity or absence of prophetic activity.

A few of the wisdom sayings in this subdivision are placed adjacent to each other likely because they share some common Hebrew vocabulary. The sayings in Proverbs 28:16–17 are probably two independent sayings that both use words from the root *'ashaq* ("to oppress," "burden," "torment," "exploit"). Likewise, vv. 25–26 consist of independent sayings that both use the word *batakh* ("to trust"). Similarly, the sayings in 29:19–20 address different topics but both use the term *dabar*, which in this context refers to speech or words.

The sayings in 28:19–22 seem to cluster around the theme of prosperity (i.e., riches and poverty). This is apparent from the occurrence of words and expressions referring to food/bread (vv. 19, 21), riches/wealth (vv. 20, 22), and poverty (vv. 19, 22). Also of interest are the proverbs that refer to discipline in 29:15–21. These verses teach that both children and slaves must be disciplined and corrected. Verses 15 and 17 advise using the rod and words of rebuke/reprimand to discipline a child. Similarly, v. 21 warns against requiring too little of slaves. Though the meaning of the first clause is relatively straightforward, involving a slave pampered from childhood, the meaning of the word *manon* in the second part of the verse is not completely certain, as is evident by the renderings provided by translators that range from the slave becoming a son/heir to the slave becoming insolent/arrogant/ungrateful. The basic idea of this proverb is that a slave that is pampered from youth and not taught to work cannot function well as a slave. Further, v. 19 teaches that words are not sufficient to correct a slave; the rod may also be necessary (v. 15; see also 10:13; 19:29; 26:3). Though slaves are not part of modern society, the principles of these sayings apply to management and leadership in general. That is, managers who expect productivity from their employees must use appropriate rewards and consequences. However, the connection between the treatment of slaves and the treatment of children is important (29:15, 17). Just as corporal punishment for slaves was acceptable in the ancient Near East but not in today's society, the application of the rod in the education of children may not necessarily involve a literal beating, but it does require age-appropriate discipline of other kinds.

An additional observation on the proverbs concerning the treatment of slaves in vv. 19 and 21 is that they serve as examples of how the counsels of this book are adapted to a fallen world. The word in these verses is the Hebrew *'ebed*, which means "servant" or "slave." But slavery was never God's ideal, and the counsel of these verses on what is necessary to make slaves work does not reflect God's ideal. In the NT, Paul instructs slaves to serve their masters in the fear of the Lord, as slaves of Christ (Eph. 6:5–8; Col. 3:22–23). He also instructs slave owners not to threaten their slaves (Eph. 6:9) but to treat them as fellow slaves of God (Col. 4:1), that is, as brothers (Philem. 15–16). Thus, God's ideal is for His people to serve each other out of love, not out of fear of punishment or greed for rewards. That also means that God-fearing employers should treat their employees differently from the way other employers do. God Himself wants to be served out of love, not fear (John 15:12–17).

30:1–33
THE WORDS OF AGUR

Some have suggested that the last two chapters of Proverbs consist of a four-part appendix to the book, namely, the reflections of Agur (vv. 1–9), things that come in fours (vv. 10–33), the counsels of Lemuel's mother (31:1–9), and the virtuous wife (vv. 10–31). This is especially possible since the content and organization of these units differ from one another. However, since 30:10–33 does not have a title, and since the poem in 31:10–31 is not introduced by a line ascribing authorship, this commentary adopts the traditional outline, which takes 30:1a as the title for chapters 30 and 31:1 as the title for chapter 31.

30:1–9
The Reflections of Agur

Some interpret the word *massa'* ("burden," "oracle," "inspired utterance") as the proper noun "Massa," a place located in northern Arabia (Gen. 25:14; 1 Chr. 1:30). However, since the form of the Hebrew word would have to be modified to read "from Massa" or "Massaite," it is best to understand it as the common Hebrew word for a prophetic oracle. Agur expresses inspired personal reflections. The identity of Agur

and the other individuals named in Proverbs 30:1 is unknown. The Septuagint resolves this problem by translating all the names as regular words. It reads "Fear my words, my son. And when you receive them, repent. This says the man to those who believe in God. And I stop." That is, Agur is translated as "fear," Jakeh as "when you receive," Ithiel as "those who believe in God," and Ucal as "I stop." However, the Septuagint presupposes a few changes to the letters in the Hebrew original. Besides, as explained above, the Septuagint reading may be influenced by its attempt to ascribe all of the proverbs to Solomon.

In these verses, Agur confesses his ignorance. The questions in v. 4 are rhetorical, since no human being could have claimed to have performed these actions. They may be compared to the rhetorical questions in Job 38. In contrast to human ignorance, God's word is perfect. Though no one can bring knowledge from heaven, God does speak to human beings, and His revelation is reliable. Agur makes two requests of God: to be kept from practicing/speaking deception and to be kept from both poverty and riches. In effect, he prays to be kept from temptation in order to live a balanced life.

30:10–33
Things That Come in Fours

The sayings in this section seem to be grouped by the use of the number four, though they are interspersed with shorter sayings in between. The first saying condemns any malicious report against a slave (v. 10). Since slaves in the ancient Near East were defenseless, their only recourse would be to curse the wrongdoer before the Lord. Verses 11–14 contain four sayings about the wicked generation. The number four is not used, but the saying consists of four lines that each begin with the Hebrew word *dor* ("generation," "period," "dwelling"). Some translate this term as referring to some group of people in general; others, as a "generation."

Verse 15 portrays a leech as the epitome of greed, and this is followed by a reference to four greedy things (vv. 15b–16). This is the first of several sayings that use the formula "three things...four." The pattern of a graded numerical sequence is also found elsewhere, especially in wisdom literature (see 6:16–19; Job 5:19–22). The exact rhetorical purpose of the formula is not clear. In many instances the fourth item is the climax of the list (see Prov. 30:18–19), but this is probably not the case in the context of

vv. 15b-16. The list could also mean that there are many more than four and that these are examples. Since some of the sayings in this section contain four items but do not use the formula (vv. 11-14, 24-28), it is possible that the formula calls attention to the number rather than the last item on the list. The purpose is to highlight a list of things that can never consume enough or be satisfied. It seems that the idea is to learn to be satisfied because dissatisfaction is mainly associated with negative things.

Verse 17, like other proverbs, condemns contempt for parents. The first three items in vv. 18-19 refer to natural phenomena, whereas the fourth item refers to human relationships. Hence, the climax of this saying is the fourth item, the way of a man with a young woman/virgin (the Hebrew word means a young woman, whether married or unmarried). Some have explained this passage as referring to the wonder of human procreation, though it may also simply refer to love and courtship between a man and a woman. Verse 10 introduces another way: the way of an adulterous woman. The adulteress commits adultery and then denies having done wrong. One sin leads to another—an attempt to conceal the first.

The list in vv. 21-23 consists of events that violate the common order of society and that are disturbing to common sense. It is not clear whether or not there is a climax in this list. Verses 24-28 contain another numerical saying. Though not introduced by the formula "three things...four," there are four things in the list. This wisdom saying consists of a list of small creatures that display wisdom: ants, *shepannim* ("rock badgers," "hyraxes," "conies"), locusts, and the *semamit* ("spider," "lizard"). The verse does not specify how people should apply the behavior of these creatures to their own lives. In contrast to the previous list, the list in vv. 29-31 includes large creatures that display a stately, fearless stride (i.e., they walk with style): a lion, a *zarzir* ("strutting rooster," "greyhound"), and a male goat. The fourth item of the list, a king, is undoubtedly the climax. Although there is some uncertainty concerning the exact translation of this clause, this proverb seems to focus on the impressive personality of the king.

The wisdom saying on folly in vv. 32-33 does not consist of a list of four items. Instead, a double "if" clause introduces the counsel for those who are proud and who plot/devise evil to put their hands on their mouths (v. 32). This is explained through three clauses that all contain

the Hebrew word *mits* ("churning," "pressing," "twisting," "squeezing"; v. 33). The point here is that foolish words and actions produce strife.

31:1-31
THE WORDS OF LEMUEL

Proverbs 31 consists of two main sections: instructions related to the behavior of a king (vv. 2-9) and a description of a virtuous woman (vv. 10-31). This commentary takes the title in v. 1, which attributes the sayings to King Lemuel's mother, as the title for the content of the whole chapter.

31:1-9
The Counsels of Lemuel's Mother

Although Proverbs elsewhere mentions the teachings of both mothers and fathers (see 6:20), this is the only passage that actually ascribes a wisdom saying to a mother. This wisdom saying contains a title (31:1), counsel on what a king should not do (vv. 2-7), and counsel on what a king should do (vv. 8-9). The message is that a king should use his power not to gratify his own desires but to serve the needs of those who are powerless. By extension, the principle also applies to anyone in a position of authority.

Proverbs 31:1 could serve as the title of only the first section, in which case the words that Lemuel's mother taught him end in v. 9, or it could attribute the entire chapter to these words. As in 30:1 the Hebrew word *massa'* can be understood as the word for a prophetic burden/oracle or as a proper name (i.e., "king of Massa"). The word *mah* in 31:2 can also be variously understood. It is usually a simple interrogative particle ("what?," "why?," "how?"). In some cases, it is an interrogative that implies an emphatic negation (Gen. 37:26; 1 Kin. 12:16; 2 Kin. 9:18-19), and in others it could serve as a negation (e.g., Song 8:4). Hence, the three occurrences of *mah* can be understood as an emphatic negation ("No...! No...! No...!") introducing the counsel that follows. Alternatively, they could simply be a form of address ("O my son," "Listen, my son!") calling attention to the counsel that follows.

The passage admonishes the king not to waste his strength on women (Prov. 31:3) or on wine (vv. 4-7). The admonition is especially applicable to most ancient kings, who were proud of their virility (see Deut. 17:17). However, the second part of Proverbs 31:3 may indicate that the warning does not mean that the king should never love a woman, as if all women were bad, but rather that it is a warning against the kind of woman who ruins and destroys kings. Instead of wasting his strength on wine and women, a king should defend the cause of the powerless (vv. 8–9). He should open his mouth not to drink wine or beer but to speak on behalf of the helpless.

31:10–31
The Virtuous Wife

It is fitting that the book of Proverbs concludes with a portrait of a wise woman. Although wisdom is portrayed in the book as a woman and is often contrasted with an immoral woman, this passage presents the clearest, if not the only, portrayal of a wise woman. There are several ways to apply the message of this poem. The virtuous wife is the opposite of the immoral woman. Hence, this is the description of the ideal woman. On the other hand, it is noteworthy that this poem repeats some of the themes of the book. That is, the virtuous wife exhibits diligence (31:13–19, 24, 27), foresight (vv. 21, 25), wise speech (v. 26), generosity (v. 20), and the fear of the Lord (v. 30). At the same time, her actions bring to herself and her family the wealth (vv. 11–12, 24) and honor (vv. 23, 28–31) that wisdom promises. Thus, there is a sense in which the description of a virtuous wife is more than simply a portrait of the ideal woman.

Since wisdom is personified as a woman in Proverbs, the virtuous wife can also be viewed as the personification of wisdom, in contrast to the immoral woman, who is the personification of folly. By extension, then, the picture of the virtuous wife is a depiction of not only a wise wife but also a wise person (man or woman, married or unmarried). It should be noted in passing that the various levels of application do not deny the possibility that this poem may have been originally written to praise a specific individual (i.e., it could have been a praise poem composed by an unnamed husband for his wife).

The description of the virtuous wife is given in the form of a poem. However, the statements in the poem are not thematically organized. Instead, they are aesthetically organized to form an acrostic poem (i.e., the verses are arranged in alphabetical order, each verse beginning with the next letter of the Hebrew alphabet). Hence, apart from the first verse (v. 10), which introduces the topic of the poem, and perhaps the last few verses, the message of the poem is best understood in terms of the sum of its totality rather than by the way it is organized.

Some of the features of this poem, such as the characterization of this woman as a woman of strength (the Heb. word *khayil* can have several meanings and nuances; though it is usually translated variously as "virtuous," "noble," "excellent," etc., it can also mean "power," "wealth," and "army"), have led some to suggest that the poem could be a heroic hymn, which was often written for military heroes. However, since not all aspects of the poem fit that type of poem, others suggest that it is better classified as an encomium). If so, it is not an encomium in terms of the classical rhetorical type (which includes a prologue, a narration of the person's birth and upbringing, etc.) but in the general sense of a speech given in praise of a person, a type of person, or a character quality. Other examples of encomia in the Bible include Psalms 1 and 15 (see also Ps. 112; Is. 52:13—53:12; 1 Cor. 13).

There are several words or expressions in Proverbs 31:10 that deserve comment. The poem begins with the central character, an *'eshet khayil*. The expression is also found in 12:4 and Ruth 3:11. As noted above, the word *khayil* means "strength" and can refer not only to physical strength but also to character. Boaz is also referred to as *khayil* (Ruth 2:1). As various translations indicate, there the expression could mean wealth, prominence, or noble character. Though the virtuous wife is not depicted in terms of military prowess (though there is a military metaphor in Prov. 31:11), she does possess physical strength (vv. 17, 25). Though she is not depicted as wealthy, she is a resourceful woman with business abilities that bring wealth to her family (vv. 11, 14, 16, 18, 24). Her greatest strength is her character, which displays diligence (vv. 15, 18, 27), foresight in providing for the future (vv. 21, 25), wise speech (v. 26), and generosity (v. 20). She is valuable to her husband (vv. 11, 23), her children (vv. 21, 27), and even her servants (v. 15). "Who can find?" in v. 10 is a rhetorical question that expects the answer "no one" (cf. 30:4). However, in contrast to the rhetorical question in Ecclesiastes 7:28, this question does not mean that such a woman does not exist but rather that she is precious because she is rare and difficult to find. Indeed, her value is far above rubies.

Another word in Proverbs 31:10 that deserves a brief comment is the word *meker* ("sale price," "merchandise," "value"). According to some, it refers to a dowry price. Although this interpretation is possible, it is probably better to understand it metaphorically in the sense of "value" or "worth." A few remarks can be added to some of the remaining verses. In v. 23, the husband of the virtuous wife is described as a man of prominent status who meets with other leaders at the gate. The implication is that it is because of her virtuous character and behavior that he can achieve such success. The word *khayil* is used again in v. 10, where it is translated in a variety of ways that demonstrate the richness and range of meanings possible in the word: "done well," "excelled," "are capable," "done virtuously," "act competently," or "done nobly." It is not clear whether or not v. 30 continues the husband's words begun in v. 29, but this does not affect the message of the poem.

Verse 30 contrasts physical beauty with wisdom. That does not mean that the virtuous wife is ugly or that beauty is bad, but simply that the beauty of character is far more important than physical beauty. By extension, the principle applies to both men and women in the sense that their relationship with the Lord is more important than looks, strength, or any other asset. Since the fear of the Lord is the beginning of wisdom (1:7; 9:10), it is fitting that this picture of the virtuous wife includes the fact that she is a woman who fears the Lord. The final verse (31:31) is an exhortation to praise the virtuous wife but also functions as a restatement of the theme of the poem.

The journey through the book of Proverbs has been a search for wisdom. The search is in many ways never-ending. Wisdom speaks to all, the simple as well as the wise, challenging them to embrace her values and to keep on learning from her. The book communicates the importance of constantly looking forward for new and deeper expressions of God's wisdom. The wise live in hope of the constant enjoyment of a never-ending life.

ECCLESIASTES

INTRODUCTION

Title and Authorship. The name "Ecclesiastes" is derived from the Greek word *ekklesia*, which means "assembly" or "church." It is the Greek translation of the Hebrew word *qahal*, which refers to the "assembly of worshippers." The word *qohelet*, "Ecclesiastes," seems to allude to 1 Kings 8, where the word *qahal* occurs seven times to designate the assembly of worshippers who were gathered to be instructed and exhorted by Solomon. In a parallel manner, the word *qohelet* occurs seven times in the book of *qohelet* (Ecclesiastes) and thus refers to the one who instructs and preaches to the *qahal*, Solomon himself, hence the translation "the Preacher" in some Bible versions. This subtle allusion to the Solomonic authorship of Ecclesiastes in the title of the book is explicitly affirmed in the introduction of the book itself (Eccl. 1:1, 12, 16; cf. 2:7, 9) and is implied in the numerous reminiscences of the life and personality of King Solomon (2:1-2; 5:1-7).

Date. A number of Egyptianisms (in ideas, expressions, and literary features) suggest the antiquity of the book and support its association with Solomon, who was very much immersed in ancient Egyptian culture and wisdom (1 Kin. 4:30; 10:28-29; 11:1). Furthermore, the language of the teacher who often refers to himself in the past ("I was," "I acquired," and "I was king") and his profound concern with death suggest that the author was old and approaching death, an idea that was also entertained in Jewish tradition. Therefore, the book may have been written in Solomon's last years and before 931 B.C., the date of Solomon's death.

Backgrounds. The historical setting of the book is well indicated, pointing to the time of Solomon (1:2), when the temple was still present (5:1-7) and Israel was still united under the same king (1:12). There are even specific allusions to particular critical moments in Solomon's reign when he abused his power (4:1, cf. 1 Kin. 9:21; 12:4) or when his future was threatened by a potential successor (4:13-16; cf. 1 Kin. 11:26-40). Yet, the existential issues discussed in this book and its warnings and lessons transcend times and cultures.

Theology and Purpose. The keyword of the book is the Hebrew word *hebel*—"futile," "meaningless," or "vanity"—which appears thirty-eight times. This word refers to the ephemeral character of "vapor" or the emptiness of chaos and death, or it evokes the tragic fate of the frail Abel (in Hebrew, *hebel*), who came and disappeared like a vapor in contrast to his dominating brother Cain. Because this word is rendered in various ways by Bible translators ("pointless," "meaningless," "futile," "vapor," or "vanity"), this commentary will often use the single word "futile" unless there is a discussion of the particular significance of the Hebrew word *hebel* or its superlative form *habel habalim* ("vanity of vanities," "absolute futility," or "utterly meaningless"). The lesson that is emphasized throughout the book embraces all aspects and values of human existence. The book of Ecclesiastes questions the value of common activities or qualities such as work (2:4-11), joy (vv. 1-3), wealth (5:10—6:12), power (5:8-9), wisdom (2:14-15; 9:15), and even religion (5:1-6). They are denounced as futile insofar as they are the result of human achievements. Challenging questions and disturbing paradoxes can upset our easy serenity. Yet, instead of Ecclesiastes promoting skepticism or pessimism, as it has often been interpreted, the book confronts us with the tough reality of life and ourselves, inviting us to reassess our values and reorient our existence. We are thus called to be responsible before God in the heart of a complex world, where we encounter both the good and the bad. All is futile unless all is received as the gift of God. Only God's grace will save us from the vanity, futility, or meaninglessness of this world. The message of Ecclesiastes draws intensely from the early pages of the book of Genesis: the fall of humankind, the curse, sin, evil, death, the destinies of Abel and Cain, the reference to the angel/messenger of God. The book is thus universal and concerns everyone, as indicated in expressions such as "under the sun," "under [the] heaven[s]," "on [the] earth," "man/human (Adam)," and the use of the generic divine term *'elohim* rather than the particular name of the God of Israel, *YHWH*. The book addresses a number of great universal theological issues, such as the Creation, judgment, righteousness by works, grace, sin, hope, inspiration and revelation, the state of the dead, prophecy, and the apocalyptic destiny of the world. In its own peculiar way, it speaks of hope in the context of a disoriented world. Amazingly, the book of Ecclesiastes confronts us with existential issues and even speaks to secular, nonreligious people, using philosophical language, and appealing to logic and existential reflections rather than to religious considerations. References to God are rare or implicit, as are references to the cult or to the temple. The discourse of the book resonates, then, with our postmodern times, as we have begun to realize that naive optimism and what appear to be coherent systems do not fit anymore. Shaking all our shallow securities, the book of Ecclesiastes obliges us to face the desperate condition of the world and to only hope in its cosmic and eschatological salvation. The final message of the book, which summarizes all its lessons (12:13–14), is concerned not only with the totality of human existence and wise counsels for the present life but also with a great warning of judgment and good news for the redemption of the world.

Literary Features. Although the structure of the book is not clearly delineated, the regular and symmetric distribution of the two Hebrew keywords, *hebel*, "vanity," "meaningless," "futility," and *qohelet*, "Preacher" or "Teacher," play a role in the structuring of the book. The use of the word *hebel* marks the two sections of the book: *hebel* appears mostly in chapters 1–6, rarely in chapters 7–12, and can be found in the expression referring to *hebel* and chasing the wind, which appears only in chapters 1–6. Likewise, the word *qohelet*, "Preacher" or "Teacher," appears in the beginning (1:1, 2,

12), in the middle (7:27), and in the end (12:8–10), thus paralleling the design in two sections suggested by the other keyword. The first half of the book is concerned with the problem of vanity, futility, or meaninglessness. It is characterized by a refrain (1:14; 2:11, 17, 26; 4:4, 16; 6:9) that refers to *hebel*, "vanity," "meaningless," or "futility," and chasing the wind, and it is characterized by the greatest concentration of the word *hebel* (twenty-four times out of the thirty-eight times in the book). The second half of the book is concerned with the problem of wisdom and is characterized by the greatest concentration of the word "wisdom" (*khokmah*), which occurs sixteen times in this section (versus eleven times in the first section). In addition, the beginning and the end of the book echo each other (a so-called *inclusio*) with the expression *habel habalim*—"vanity of vanities," "absolute futility," "utterly meaningless" (1:2; cf. 12:8) and with the same cosmic perspective linking the prologue (1:1–11) to the epilogue (12:9–14). All these literary features suggest a particular literary structure: Prologue: The Nonsense of Creation (1:1–11); The Problem of Futility (1:12—6:12); The Problem of Wisdom (7:1—12:8); Epilogue: The Sense of Creation (12:9–14).

COMMENTARY

1:1–11
PROLOGUE:
THE NONSENSE OF CREATION

Following the superscription (v. 1), which identifies the author of the book as Solomon, the only son of David who was king in Jerusalem, the prologue is introduced by the phrase *habel habalim* ("vanity of vanities," "absolute futility," or "utterly meaningless"), which serves as the motto of the book (vv. 2–3). This is followed by a discussion and analysis of the absence of the new from God's creation (vv. 4–11).

1:2–3
Futility and Profit

The word *hebel*—"meaningless," "vanity," or "futility"—is used five times in v. 2. This repetition emphasizes the importance of the concept. The phrase *habel habalim* is a superlative suggesting the maximum of *hebel*. The word *hebel* designates the "vapor," what is passing and has no substance, and may be identified as the unformed state of creation before the Creation week (Gen. 1:2; cf. Is. 49:4). If all is futile, it is pertinent to ask if there is any profit or gain under the sun (Eccl. 1:3). The word *yitron* literally means "the plus, the supplement" and is often translated as "profit" or "gain." To the question "What is the plus; what has been gained under the sun?" the answer is already implied in the motto: it is *hebel*, meaning "nothing." The expression "under the sun," unique to the book of Ecclesiastes, echoes an Egyptian idiom and evokes the solar cycle, which refers to what is repeated on a "regular" and "daily" basis without producing any new thing.

1:2–11. Cosmic Movements. As the prologue appears to parallel Creation, the stage of formlessness and emptiness (Gen. 1:2) seems to be identified in Ecclesiastes as futility (Eccl. 1:2), after which cosmic movements are described. Generations of humans come and go, in contrast to the abiding earth (v. 4). The sun rises and sets and then goes back to its original place (v. 5). The wind goes to the south, then to the north, and then returns to its starting point (v. 6). The rivers go to the sea from where they originate, but the sea does not benefit from them and thus is never full (v. 7). Likewise, humans speak, see, and hear but are never satisfied (v. 8). From these observations Solomon concludes that there is no progress. In response to the question earlier raised of what profits, he proposes that there is no profit. "There is nothing new under the sun" (v. 9) implicitly suggests that there is no remembrance from one generation to another (v. 11), as if no one ever existed. All these vain movements of creation attest that creation has not gone beyond the stage of formlessness, the stage of futility, thus confirming the introductory programmatic statement: all is futility (v. 2).

1:12—6:12
THE PROBLEM OF FUTILITY

1:12–18
All is Futile, Utterly Futile

The first application of this truth concerns the search for wisdom. Solomon shifts from the third person in the prologue to the first person (vv. 12, 14, 16, 17). He will draw his lessons from his own thinking and personal experience of wisdom, and no longer from the objective movements of creation. Solomon verified the futility of wisdom both objectively in the object of wisdom itself and subjectively in the task of searching for wisdom.

1:12–15. The Object of Wisdom. The object of wisdom, the state of the earth, was so tragic that even wisdom would not improve its vain condition. Indeed, all these works done under the sun (v. 14) were in fact God's works. The phrase "under the sun" alludes to the work of creation that had already been observed in the prologue and thus refers to God the Creator as the subject, an idea implicit in the passive form of the verb "done." This principle is reaffirmed in v. 15— what is crooked cannot be straightened—which also implies God as the subject (v. 13). No one would be able to change a world that was under the curse of God (Gen. 3:17, 18).

1:16–18. The Search for Wisdom. The search for wisdom, even though a gift of God (v. 13), would not resolve the problems of the world.

Prologue and Creation Story Parallels

Note the parallels between the prologue (Eccl. 1:2–11) and the Creation story (Gen. 1:1—2:4a):

Ecclesiastes	Genesis
All is futile (1:2)	Shapeless and empty earth (1:1–2)
Under the sun (1:3)	Light; under the sky (days 1 and 2: vv. 3–8)
The earth (1:4)	Dry land/ground (day 3: vv. 9–13)
Sunrise and sunset (1:5–6)	Lights for days and seasons (day 4: vv. 14–19)
Rivers and sea (1:7)	Waters and seas (day 5: vv. 20–23)
Humans speak, see, and hear (1:8)	Creation of humans (day 6: vv. 26–31)
Past and future generations (1:9–11)	Historical record of generations (summary of Creation: v. 4a)

Solomon observes that the acquisition of wisdom, which he ironically could boast about (v. 16), increases the troubles of the world.

2:1–26
The Futility of Happiness

Solomon urges us to test his observation in the domain of life. The purpose of the test was to see what was good for people (lit. the "sons of *adam*"—Adam or "humanity"; v. 3). The word "good" is another allusion to the text of Creation, where it occurs seven times, and is also associated with the verb "see" (Gen. 1:4, 10, 12, 18, 21, 25, 31). Solomon's test was to check whether there was something left from the "good" of creation. Echoing the Creation story, he repeats seven times the word *hebel*—"vanity," "meaningless," or "futility" (Eccl. 2:1, 11, 15, 19, 21, 23, 26). In other words, the good of creation had turned into *hebel*, the stage of pre-Creation emptiness and formlessness. It was as if Creation in its fullest sense did not happen; good had not yet been created. Solomon included all aspects of happiness in this test (joy, work, and even wisdom).

2:1–3. Joy. Looking at his own experience, Solomon proposes now to search for the meaning and the effect of these values (v. 1). These pleasures are qualified from the outset as futile (v. 1). The kind of joy Solomon describes is not external. It was Solomon himself who produced this joy and gave himself these pleasures. With the help of his wisdom, in all lucidity (v. 3), Solomon explains the mechanism of these pleasures and provides three reasons why he considers them futile. First, they are "madness" and do not make sense, just like laughter (v. 2), which is irrational and is triggered by a person who stumbles or by a stupid joke. Second, they are inefficient; they accomplish nothing (v. 2), just like the game or the movie that entertains us. They will leave no trace, like the vapor (*hebel*) in the air. Third, they are artificial, just like wine or a drug that creates a false sense of happiness in a world of illusion.

2:4–11. Work. Solomon refers to his own works of achievement: to building projects (v. 4), clearly pointing to himself as a great builder (1 Kin. 7:1–12; 9:15–28), to his wealth (Eccl. 2:7, 8; cf. 1 Kin. 10:23), to his acquisition of cattle (Eccl. 2:7), to his silver and gold (v. 8; 1 Kin. 10:14–29), and to his many women (Eccl. 2:8; cf. 1 Kin. 11:1). The sevenfold repetition of

the verb "make" (*'asah*) in this paragraph (Eccl. 2:4, 5, 6, 8, 11) may be another pointer to the Creation narrative where "make" is a keyword (Gen. 1:11, 12, 16, 25, 26, 31). The idea is that Solomon was acting as the Creator. Likewise, when he refers to his building projects, he seems to allude to the building of the temple by using the verb "build" seven times (1 Kin. 8:8–13), referring to himself as building for God, while in our context Solomon speaks of building for himself. These allusions to the building of the temple intended for God unveil the true intention of the builder. Even in building for God, Solomon was in fact working for himself and to his own glory. This is why he concludes that all of these works, acquisitions, and achievements, including the pious ones, are futile (Eccl. 2:11).

2:12–23. Wisdom. Then Solomon turns to what he considers the most valuable quality, namely, wisdom (v. 12), which refers to intelligence, science, and practical discernment in daily behavior (7:1–12; Prov. 24:3). He acknowledges the positive value of wisdom. It is better than folly (Eccl. 2:13) and thus allows one to see clearly and to walk in the light, while folly takes one into darkness (vv. 13–14). The language is reminiscent of ancient Egyptian beliefs according to which the wise walks in the light and is alive, while the fool walks in darkness and will die. For Solomon, however, both the wise and the fool have the same destiny: they will die (vv. 15–16). Therefore, he concludes that since all will die, the possession of all the works of wisdom amounts to nothing and life is not worth living (vv. 17–23).

2:24–26. Conclusion: The Gift of God. The discourse about the futility of joy, work, and wisdom is upsetting. Solomon puts these values in the right perspective. Although we are entitled to joy, work, and wisdom, these qualities are all futile insofar as they are the product of our doing. The only way to make these values fulfill their purpose and not become futile is to receive them as the gift of God. This idea is underscored four times in different ways. The first time is through an image that evokes creation as the good (or "enjoyment," "satisfaction") from the hand of God (v. 24), and three times through the use of the verb "give" (v. 26), a verb that also belongs to the language of creation (Gen. 1:29). To make his point even more acute, Solomon concludes with a paradox. God gives to whom he wants, that is to the man who is good or pleasing in His sight

(Eccl. 2:26). This is another way of saying that who we are or what we do does not justify our beneficial reception of God's gifts, but that they are the gift of God. Only a life oriented by this perspective of God's grace is worth living and is not futile.

3:1–11
The Gift of Time

The first observation of grace is found in time. Unlike Greek philosophers, who saw time as a destructive power, the ancient Hebrews saw life in time. Thus, when Solomon says that there is a time for every event (v. 1), he does not mean that there is an appropriate moment for humans to act; neither does he mean that events happen without our control in a deterministic manner. The use of the preposition *le* ("to"), attached to the word "all," (to everything...) suggests instead that all these time-events, the times of human existence, are to be received as grace from God. This truth is then shaped in a poem balancing the opposites:

1. Birth/death; plant/pluck (v. 2)
2. Kill/heal; break down/build up (v. 3)
3. Weep/laugh; mourn/dance (v. 4)
4. Cast away stones/gather stones; embrace/ refrain from embracing (v. 5)
5. Search (or "gain")/cease searching (or "lose"—lit. "destroy"); keep/throw away (v. 6)
6. Tear/sew (or mend); silence/speak (v. 7)
7. Love/hate; war/peace (v. 8)

The lesson of this poem is that all times, positive and negative, are God's gifts. He is the One who made everything (good and bad) beautiful (or "appropriate" or "fitting") in its time (v. 11). This idea is repeated to emphasize that God is always in control. It also affirms the monotheistic principle that there is only one God (Deut. 32:39; Is. 45:6–7). Even when things are bad, all will work out for good (Gen. 50:20; Esth. 4:14; Rom. 8:28). The seesaw movement between the two poles also contains a lesson of hope: when bad things happen, the good is around the corner.

3:11–14
The Gift of Eternity

In Hebrew thought, eternity is not the absence of time but the intensification of time that will last forever. God has put eternity in the hearts of human beings (v. 11). Just like time, eternity is God's gift. The verb "give" (*natan*) that

is used here is variously translated as "set," "placed," or "put." Yet this gift is only in the heart. Humans have not been created eternal; they only have a sense of eternity. This gift of eternity, which humans have as an intuition, affirms the grace of God in time. This hope in eternal life helps us to see in our time, embedded in pain and under the constant threat of death, the presence of the Invisible. On the other hand, we are urged to enjoy the good we receive in our life (vv. 12–13). These good moments are the evidence we have now of this eternity. They are, like eternity, the gift of God (v. 13), and as such they are perfect; nothing can be added to them, and nothing can be taken from them (v. 14). This is a way of inculcating reverence in the human soul (v. 14). In passing, Solomon appeals for a life oriented by the fear of God, which is the sense that God sees everything and that we are accountable to Him for everything we do (v. 15).

3:16–22
The Gift of Judgment

Yet, Solomon's theology, which invites us to see "good" in everything, poses problems. Indeed, he observes that reality is otherwise, and things are not what they are supposed to be: instead of justice, righteousness, and judgment, there is only wickedness (v. 16). Faith is not blind. It has to confront evil in the world.

3:17. God Shall Judge the Righteous and the Wicked. The only solution to the problem of the world was in the future judgment of God, an event with a cosmic scope that concerns all. The Hebrew word *kol*, "all" or "every," occurs seven times in this passage (vv. 17–20). We have to face reality: *all* this crooked and absurd world is irreparable (1:15).

3:18–22. The Estate of the Sons of Men. To prove his point about the tragic condition of our human condition, Solomon refers to humanity's mortal nature, which is absolute and cannot be repaired. In regard to death, humans are like animals (v. 19), just as the wise is like the fool (2:16). All have the same breath, which is the vapor-breath (*hebel*; 3:19). All will die. From this hopeless description, Solomon concludes that the only and ultimate lesson for humans is to enjoy the gift of God (v. 22) and live in the perspective of His grace. As far as the future is concerned, Solomon simply encourages trust because we cannot control it. The cosmic scope of the passage, which embraces humans and animals, the wise and the fool—that is to say, everything—suggests an eschatological perspective.

4:1–16
The Case of the Other Person

Still preoccupied with the problem of human wickedness, Solomon discusses its manifestation in human relationships. Four cases are considered: the oppressed, the envious, the companion, and the usurper. Each case is introduced by the same formula in the first person, alternating between what he "returned" to consider (or considered "again") and what he "saw," referring to Solomon's initiative to investigate.

4:1–3. The Oppressed. Solomon saw the tears of the oppressed, which are those who are lacking power and suffering injustice. The nature of the oppression is not explained. What primarily disturbed him was that these victims had no comforter (v. 1), which is another way of referring to God (Lam. 1:2, 9; Is. 51:12). This absence of God in the midst of unjust persecution is indeed troubling and challenges faith. Solomon, like Job (Job 3:11, 20), questions the sense of existence. He even goes so far as to "praise" (*shabakh*) the dead (Eccl. 4:2), using a verb that normally applies to God (Ps. 117:1; 147:12; 1 Chr. 16:35), as if God is no longer worthy of praises and is absent. Yet, the repetition of the phrase referring to the lack of a comforter, which alludes to God (Is. 51:12; 66:13), contrasts with the phrase referring to wickedness in the place of justice (Eccl. 3:16). This suggests by analogy that the divine Judge is here on the horizon. There is hope despite pain. Solomon shakes the traditional logic of success religion, which provides the automatic assurance of immediate gratifications. He knew otherwise and therefore promoted the true religion, which does not deny the reality of evil but perseveres in faith despite suffering.

4:4–6. The Envious. This time Solomon did not see the human face but only the hands or arms (v. 5) and the fists (v. 6). The one turning against us is our neighbor, who is comparable to us and thus can envy what we have. This attitude will ultimately lead to wickedness, stealing, and murder (2 Sam. 12:1–15). Solomon proposes that in such conditions it is better to be alone (Eccl. 4:6). A handful of "rest," "tranquility," or "peace" is better than production

that chases the wind. All these hands and fists without faces convey a warning against the race for wealth and achievement at the expense of seeing the human face. It is better to stay alone.

4:7–12. The Companion. And yet, it is not good to be alone. Two arguments support this advice. First, it is simply not good to be alone (v. 8), for work is not gratifying. We are not satisfied (v. 8), for we do not use and enjoy what we have gained. If we have no one to give to, what we have amounts to nothing. Second, it is good to be with someone. In the Hebrew, the word "good" is repeated twice ("better" uses the root "good"; v. 9). We need the other when stumbling (v. 10), cold (v. 11), and fighting (v. 12). In conclusion, Solomon refers to a proverb that enunciates in paradoxical language the value of being two: if we are two, we end up being three. The proverb may refer to God, to the coming of a friend of our friend, or to the birth of a child to a human couple.

4:13–16. The Usurper. The fourth person is not described as a physical person. While the other three collectively have a face, hands, and eyes, this one is described simply as a poor, wise youth (v. 13) coming out of prison (v. 14), who would become king and thus take the place of the former king (v. 15). The scenario fits the sad story of Solomon's succession. Like this fourth person, Jeroboam, Solomon's successor, was poor (v. 13; cf. 1 Kin. 11:26), young, wise (Eccl. 4:13; cf. 1 Kin. 11:28), and very popular (Eccl. 4:15; cf. 1 Kin. 11:35). Solomon describes himself as old and foolish (Eccl. 4:13; cf. 1:17; 2:3, 9, 10), which is an indication of his repentance at the end of his life. The story, predicting that those who would follow the new king would not be pleased with (or "rejoice") in him (4:16), also fits the case of Jeroboam (1 Kin. 15:34; 16:2, 19, 26; 22:52). The ending shows that Solomon was right. Even the young wise man, who succeeded the old fool, would grow old and foolish and finish in futility (Eccl. 4:16). Here we find a universal and paradoxical lesson to free us from the illusion of our own wisdom. Only the awareness of our own futility will save us from futility.

5:1–7
The Futility of Religion

Suddenly, the tone changes and becomes imperative. Until this point, Solomon had merely shared his reflections about the futility of life. Now, he speaks about religion in the first person and addresses his pupil in the second person, using ten imperative verbs that end with the command to fear God (v. 7).

Verse 1 begins with the admonition to "walk prudently" or "guard your steps." The Hebrew text literally means "keep your feet." The first imperative verb *shemor*, "keep," belongs to religious language and generally indicates obedience to God's commandments (Ex. 20:6; Lev. 18:26; Deut. 5:12). Solomon refers here to conduct in the house of God and to the way we worship. Our prayers, our singing, our moving around in church should be controlled and guided by a deep sense of reverence toward God. This command also applies to the way we live our religion and keep God's commandments. We may stumble not merely in the refusal to observe God's laws but also while attempting to keep them. The greatest profanations of religion are often performed in the very practice of religion. They offer the sacrifice of fools (Eccl. 5:1).

Religion is more about hearing, obeying, and receiving from God than about giving or speaking to Him (v. 1b). Two examples illustrate this aspect of the futility of religion. The first case concerns our words (vv. 2–3) uttered before God. We should not pronounce them hastily, for we may lose the sense of the distance of God: He is in heaven and we are on earth (v. 2). Solomon urges us, then, to use few words, for many words are, like dreams, futile (v. 7). The second case concerns our vows and our commitment to God. What is implied here is not so much our failure to fulfill our pious promises. Solomon has in mind the lies religious people tell in relation to religious matters. Such behavior shows that God is not taken seriously and may generate the annihilation of the very pious goal (v. 6). With this dramatic warning, Solomon concludes with the general principle of the fear of God (v. 7), which is another way of reminding the religious person of God's capacity to see our motivations and judge the futility of our religion.

5:8–9
The Futility of Power

Solomon knew by experience the futility of power. The first illusion entertained by those in power is that they can do whatever they wish. This is based on the naive belief that there is no power above them. This futility is unveiled by Solomon by taking the reader down step by step until finally reaching the land/the earth, which represents the last and highest authority. The language of the parable is reminiscent of two

other biblical passages. The first is the curse of Genesis (common words: "earth," "land," and "serve"), which enslaves humans to the earth (Gen. 3:17–18). The second text is found in David's prayer (common words: "over all" and "earth"), which underlines God's sovereignty (1 Chr. 29:11–14). While these two parallel passages emphasize the futility of power, they both contain a perspective of hope. In Genesis we find the promise of redemption, and in David's prayer we find the assurance of the God who even controls and rules over all wicked powers.

5:10–17
The Futility of Wealth

What we observed in regard to power is similarly observed in regard to wealth. In both cases we experience futility and we end with nothing. Wealth, which begins with the positive account, ends systematically with a negative evaluation (vv. 9, 11, 13, 14). We always want more money (v. 10). Second, wealth will be taken from us (v. 11). Third, the value of wealth is denied; the rich are always worried and hurting (vv. 12–13). Fourth, we will end up as we came, which was with nothing (vv. 15–16). The lesson is that there is no profit in accumulating wealth (vv. 16–17).

5:18–20
The Gift of God

Solomon was not against wealth. His critique essentially concerns the way we see these material blessings. His message is that they should not be taken as inherently valuable. In fact, he insists that we should enjoy them. They are to be enjoyed because they are the gift of God. He affirms this lesson explicitly: God gives wealth and possessions (v. 19). This idea is reinforced by the use of the term *kheleq* ("heritage," "portion," "lot," or "reward") twice (vv. 18, 19) to signify God's effective presence (Ps. 73:26; Deut. 7:9). The lesson is the same: all is futility except if it is taken as the gift of God. Only the gift of God is not futility.

6:1–12
The Futility of the Gift of God

This is the shortest chapter in the book and may function as the conclusion of the first part of the book. After having systematically demonstrated that all is futility except the gift of God, Solomon now finds the ferment of futility even in the gift of God. He calls this "great evil" (some translations read "common" or "prevalent"—the Heb. *rab* can mean "great" or also "much"; the latter leading to the rendering of "common").

6:1–2. Lack of Satisfaction. Solomon next considers the case of a person to whom God does not provide the opportunity to enjoy all of His gifts. The thought was expressed in a positive way in 5:19. Now the negative alternative expresses the personal experience of Solomon. Like the person in the example, Solomon did receive riches, wealth, and honor (2 Chr. 1:12). Yet, the enjoyment of these gifts was limited to Solomon's life (1 Kin. 3:13). Like the man in his parable, Solomon saw that they are consumed by a foreigner. This autobiographical allusion illustrates the point of Ecclesiastes, namely, that even the gifts of God, if we are no longer present to enjoy them, qualify as futility.

6:3–6. If a Man Begets a Hundred Children. While in the previous observation the quality of futility was drawn from the experience of death, now it is inferred from the experience of birth. Another autobiographical reference is implied here. Solomon had an ambivalent experience of birth: a positive one, for Solomon had many wives and must have begotten many children, and a negative one, since his birth was associated with the birth of David and Bathsheba's child, who died not long after birth (2 Sam. 12:24). Looking at his long life (1 Kin. 3:14) and at the stillborn, Solomon reaches the conclusion that they both are futile. This hyperbolic presentation intends to prove that even without death things are bad. For the more we live, the more intense will be our experience of the futility of life, even if life is God's gift.

6:7–12. The Wandering of Desire. This last paragraph resonates with the prologue concerning the longing (*nepesh*) that is never satisfied (v. 7; cf. 1:7). The Hebrew word *nepesh* (6:9), rendered here as "desire" or "appetite," is often rendered in other contexts as "soul." This "soul" (*nepesh*) is not a separate spiritual entity distinct from the body. The term refers to a living person who has spiritual (vv. 2, 3) as well as physical aspirations (vv. 7, 9). Every part of the person is involved in desire: the mouth (metaphor for the stomach, or appetite; v. 7), the eyes (metaphor for vision; v. 9), the foot ("walk"—metaphor for conduct; v. 8), and the full person (v. 2). To express this longing of the soul, Solomon uses an idiomatic expression: the

wandering of *nepesh* (v. 9). It figuratively suggests the journey of a person (our own journey) to another place (2 Kin. 5:26). The soul, the whole person, longs for another place; it yearns for something that it does not have and cannot grasp. What is missing belongs to another order. In this connection, the wise is not more than the fool (v. 8). We are all visited by the same nostalgia and frustration; it is a thirst that will never be quenched (John 4:13–14). Solomon warns, then, that it is vain to try to explain it and systematize it. This thirst is beyond comprehension, and the more words we may utter to dissert on this mystery, the more vapor there will be and the foggier the result will be. Words are the many things that increase futility (Eccl. 6:11). The word *debarim*, translated here as "things," also means "words," which fits well here since the context implies the exercise of speech (v. 10 refers to naming and contending). Ecclesiastes concludes with a rhetorical question that implies a negative answer: who knows what is good for people (Heb. *'adam*—"man" or "humanity") in life (v. 12)? Solomon acknowledges his failure. The lost good of creation will always lie beyond human reach. He is alluding to Genesis 3:22, with which this passage shares common wording ("know," "good," "man" [*'adam*], and "life"). This allusion suggests that Adam's loss of the good was really the loss of wisdom (1 Kin. 3:12). Yet, a second rhetorical question reveals that the answer belongs to the future: who can tell a man (*'adam*, "humanity") what will happen after him, or them (Eccl. 6:12)? The second question parallels the first one and is related to it. Both questions are concerned with human destiny. The scope of these questions embraces human civilization. Similar to Gen. 3:22, Ecclesiastes ends (cf. Eccl. 6:12; 12:13–14) on a note of cosmic hope in an eschatological perspective.

7:1—12:8
THE PROBLEM OF WISDOM

7:1–18
The Ambiguity of Wisdom

This chapter begins the second half of the book. While the first half is concerned with futility, the second half is more concerned with wisdom. Solomon just concluded that no one knows what is good (6:12). Now, he focuses on the nature of this good (*tob*), a keyword in this passage (it occurs twelve times).

7:1–10. A Good Name Is Better (tob) than Precious Ointment (or Perfume). This statement parallels the observation that death is better than birth (v. 1). The following statements convey a similar lesson: mourning is better than feasting (v. 2), rebuke is better than song (v. 5), end is better than beginning (v. 8), patience is better than pride (vv. 8–9), and present is better than past (v. 10). Solomon's point is that often the "good" is found in places where one expects the bad.

7:11–18. Wisdom Is Good with an Inheritance. Wisdom works in the present only for those who have already received it and for those who have inherited it from the past (vv. 11–12). The preceding lesson was that good was found in the present. Now, the lesson is that good is also found in the past. Good is here but was also there. You cannot change a world that is made of both good and bad. Therefore, one will have to receive them both; there is good in both. The day of adversity will make one think, and the day of prosperity will make one happy (v. 14). This confirms Solomon: God has made (or appointed) the one as well as the other (v. 14). The corollary of this principle is that a fanatical obsession with righteousness is fatal. Solomon saw that (sometimes) righteous people perish in their righteousness, and wicked people prolong their lives in wickedness (v. 15). Consequently, he recommends that we not be excessively righteous, otherwise we will destroy ourselves (v. 16), and that we not be overly wicked, otherwise we will die prematurely (vv. 16–17). Instead, the good way is to grasp this and also that (v. 18). He is not promoting a compromise. This paradoxical statement means that balance is needed when applied to the good (Rom. 16:19). What justifies this unusual advice is that sometimes what we consider good or bad is not necessarily good or bad. We may not understand all of the ramifications or have enough knowledge to evaluate correctly.

7:19–8:1
The Elusiveness of Wisdom

It is not surprising, then, that wisdom is so difficult to find. The verb *matsa'* ("to find" or "discover") occurs seven times in this passage, indicating the struggle of Solomon in his search for wisdom. Two reasons are given to explain this trouble. The first has to do with the nature of wisdom itself, which is far beyond reach and is deep, mysterious, and profound (vv. 23–24).

The second has to do with the ambiguity of wisdom and its complex association with folly (vv. 25–26). The mingling of wisdom with folly makes it difficult to sort out the one from the other—to seek and find wisdom and the reasoned explanation of the scheme of things (v. 25). The word translated here as "reason," "explanation," or "scheme" (*kheshbon*) belongs in the realm of accounting and refers to the difficulty of sorting out the good from the bad and wisdom from folly. It is in the context of Solomon's frustration at not finding wisdom that we should understand his parable about a woman he could not find (vv. 27–28). He is not defending the idea of the superiority of men over women. The use of the word *'adam* for "man" suggests that Solomon had in mind the generic idea of humankind (v. 29). The woman he speaks about represents wisdom (Prov. 8). He uses hyperbolic language to demonstrate that it is impossible to find wisdom. Let's assume that it would be possible to find one human among a thousand; it would still be impossible to find a woman (wisdom) among all these, meaning all humankind. This reference to adding one thing to the other to find out the reason (*kheshbon*; Eccl. 7:27) points back to the accounting that characterized the search for wisdom (v. 25). The conclusion of this essay on wisdom (8:1), which belongs more to what precedes than to what follows, is an ironic allusion to the priestly blessing—makes his face shine (Num. 6:25)—that is directed toward those who would claim to have found wisdom.

8:2–17
The Ambivalence of the World

The impossibility to know wisdom, hence the incapacity to distinguish between good and evil, leads to a world where the borders between right and wrong are not clear. The world is both right and wrong. Solomon finds symptoms of the ambivalence of the world in the exercise of authority and in the unfairness of retribution, and he proposes an ambivalent solution.

8:2–9. The Ambivalence of Authority. The preceding discussion could lead to anarchy. For if the king is not wiser than others, why should they submit to him? The first argument to support submission to authority, even though this authority is not intrinsically superior, is its connection with God: an oath to Him (v. 2). The language of Solomon is reminiscent of the story of

Shimei, who was known for his lack of respect to the king (2 Sam. 16:5–13) and with whom Solomon had made a covenant under the "oath of God" (1 Kin. 2:43–44). The second argument is that submission to authority is in our own interest. He who obeys will not be harmed (Eccl. 8:5), which is also verified in the case of Shimei (2 Sam. 19:20). And even if the misery of a person increases, faith in God's grace is still the answer, for there is judgment for every action, just as there is a time for everything (Eccl. 8:5; cf. 3:1). In addition to this transcendent judgment, Solomon warns that judgment already works here and now. As powerful as the wicked rulers may be, they will not have power over their own breath; they will die (8:8). For surely, continues Solomon, the king's power will not save him from suffering from his own abuse of power (v. 8), just as the case was for Solomon in regard to Shimei (1 Kin. 2:46). In fact, ruling abusively is at the abuser's own expense (Eccl. 8:9).

8:10–14. The Ambivalence of Retribution. The honors that the wicked received at the funeral (v. 10) and their long life (v. 12) are not evidence of God's blessing. This is deemed as futile (v. 10). The life of the wicked, no matter how long it may be, is insignificant and comparable to a shadow (v. 13). On the other hand, promises Solomon, the righteous remain in touch with the "good" (*tob*) of creation: it will be better (*tob*) for those who fear God (v. 12). The logic is, however, upset by the observation that the wicked seem to be rewarded while the righteous seem to be punished.

8:15–17. The Ambivalent Solution. Solomon reacts to the observation of this futility (v. 14) in two ways. On the one hand, he recommends the enjoyment of the good (*tob*) of creation and remaining grateful for the gift of God (v. 15). On the other hand, he is puzzled and seeks to find the wisdom that will help him understand (v. 16). Solomon does not try to make sense of the absurd condition of the world. He knows that he cannot find the wisdom to explain it. The section ends as in the preceding chapter, with the same acknowledgment of failure and the same unanswered question. Yet, Solomon insists that he has to strive to find the answer. The solution of the wise is then ambivalent. The wise will enjoy life even though he knows that he will never be happy, and he will search for wisdom even though he knows he will not be able to fully find it (v. 17).

9:1–18
Totality of Life

The ambivalent condition of the world was the basis for Solomon's reflection. He considered all this (v. 1), referring back to all the preceding perspective. The word *kol*, "all," is a keyword in the chapter (occurring fourteen times in the Hebrew). The perspective of Solomon was comprehensive, covering the totality of humankind, the totality of life, the totality of chance, and, in conclusion, the totality of wisdom.

9:1–6. Totality of Humankind. All human categories are included in Solomon's analysis. The righteous and the wise, along with their actions, love, and hatred, are all in the hand of God (v. 1). They will all die. The list, referring to opposites, the good and the bad (v. 2), acknowledges that there is no privileged party. Death is total; it will affect the totality of humankind and will embrace the totality of the human person. No one and nothing will survive death. This description leaves no room for the idea that someone, the good one, will not die or that something of ourselves, our soul, will continue to live. Therefore, a living dog is better than a dead lion (v. 4). The unconscious state of the dead is explicitly affirmed: in contrast to the living who know, the dead know nothing (v. 5). All the spiritual faculties (memory, love, hatred, envy) have *'abad* ("perish," "vanish," or "disappear"; v. 6). This verb implies total annihilation (Ex. 10:7; Deut. 4:10). The condition of the world is hopeless. Yet Solomon assures us that there is hope (Eccl. 9:4), a unique emphasis in the book. The Hebrew word for "hope" (*bittakhon*) implies trust in God's action within a desperate situation (2 Kin. 18:19; cf. Ps. 22:4). This hope is connected to those righteous who are still alive (Eccl. 9:4; cf. Deut. 30:19).

9:7–10. Totality of Life. For this hopelessness of the human condition, Solomon recommends enjoying life. A series of imperatives describe the steps of this move.

Go (v. 7): This first verb introduces and contains all the others. The Hebrew verb *halak* is reminiscent of God's order to Abraham (Gen. 12:1; cf. 22:1), which was a call to move from his place to live a life of faith and enjoy God's gifts.

Eat and drink: Bread and wine are two basic products associated with the blessings of "grain and new wine" in the land (Deut. 33:28; Gen. 14:18). The wine Solomon refers to is "new wine" and is therefore nonalcoholic wine. This identification better fits the context of our passage, which uses the language of creation (*tob*, "good"; *ma'aseh*, "work").

Feast (Eccl. 9:8): White garments and oil are the visible signs of feasting (2 Sam. 14:2; Ps. 23:5).

Live (Eccl. 9:9): The expression "live joyfully" or "enjoy life" literally means "see life," implying that to see life with another woman (or man) is not an option. This attention, which concerns all the days of the life of futility, does not only mean faithfulness; it also helps in the endurance of the human condition.

Work with all your strength (v. 10): life with God is not passive. Humans are invited to be creative, like God. This phrase shares a common wording with the passage on the Sabbath in Genesis 2:1–3 and conveys a double lesson about work. First, it affirms the value of work; it is a sign of life. Second, it warns against abuse. Work should be controlled in proportion to our strength. The Sabbath, alluded to in this passage, puts work in the right perspective.

9:11–12. Totality of Chance. This poem confronts us with the unfair blindness of chance; time and chance happen to them all (v. 11). What we may interpret to be the result of our work—the race, the battle, the bread, the riches, the favor—is in fact undeserved. Chance is unfair, as is death; it strikes unexpectedly and unjustly, like a snare or trap for an animal (v. 12). This universal experience of the unfairness of chance paradoxically contains a universal lesson of grace: no one deserves what he or she gets.

9:13–18. Totality of Wisdom. The parable of the poor wise man, whose wisdom saved the little city and yet was forgotten (vv. 13–15), conveys an important lesson on the total value of wisdom. This is the conclusion of Solomon's meditation on the unfairness of life: wisdom is better than strength (v. 16). Despite the rule of fools, wisdom remains sovereign. Yet, he regrets that one fool may ruin much of it (v. 18), thus anticipating the following section.

10:1–20
Fools Are Everywhere

Just as dead flies putrefy perfume (v. 1), fools may penetrate wisdom and affect its identity. The perfume loses its odor and wisdom is not wise anymore. Like fleas, fools are found everywhere: in schools, in the workplace, in public life, and even in government.

10:1–7. In Schools. Solomon begins with the last place where a fool should be found, the place of instruction. This syndrome of dead flies in perfume first affects the very institution respected for its wisdom (v. 1), the so-called academic authority that teaches a corrupt lesson (falsehood, racism, evolution, etc.). Unlike the wise, whose heart is on the right side and who can therefore think clearly and rightly, the fool teaches from the left side (v. 2), the side of deception (Judg. 3:15; 21:2). The fool lacks wisdom and yet accuses the others of being foolish (Eccl. 10:3). It is therefore expected that the fool is intolerant and abuses his power. Solomon recommends self-control and a conciliatory spirit, without compromising integrity (v. 4). For the fool is dignified by authorities (v. 6). Society reflects this lack of discernment since servants ride on horses and princes walk on the ground, an image showing the same value crisis as noted before (9:11).

10:8–10. In the Workplace. Fools who are placed in their positions not because of their skills will sooner or later be unmasked by the poor quality of their performance. They will fall in the pit they have dug (v. 8). The bad mason will be bitten by the serpent (v. 8). The bad quarryman will be hurt because of his clumsiness (v. 9). The bad woodcutter will waste his energies because he does not know how to use his ax (v. 10).

10:11–15. In Public Life. The fool's foolishness will be revealed by his words. Thus, the fool is comparable to an amateur snake charmer who, for lack of knowledge, is bitten by the snake. He is unmasked as a fraud (v. 11). Their many words compromise them, and their lips will swallow them (v. 12). Fools are thoroughly fools (v. 13). Thus, they have no contribution to make. Their effect is limited to the present (v. 14). Solomon concludes his satire on the talkative fool by referring to the fool who was walking along the way, lacking wisdom, and calling everyone a fool. The fool is lost in the way and does not even know how to get to the city (v. 15). He cannot find help because he considers everyone else a fool. The mention of a city that cannot be found points to the earlier city, saved by the poor wise man (9:13–15). Yet this time, there is no wise man to save it.

10:16–20. In the Government. Wise men are no longer around. Only fools are left, and the result is catastrophic. An immature child is sitting on the throne (v. 16) and officers are continually feasting. While this situation is under the curse ("woe to you"), for a moment Solomon recounts the blessing of good leadership (v. 17). He describes a time of crisis when "the house" (the temple or the palace) is neglected because of laziness and the lack of responsible leadership (v. 18). The leaders are only interested in immediate pleasures, and they only value money, which they identify as their god; money answers everything (v. 19). The verb *'anah* ("answer") applies normally to God (Ps. 3:5; 13:4). Solomon then turns to another group of people, which was implied before in the blessing (Eccl. 10:17), and he addresses them discreetly. Considering the pervasive presence of the fools, he urges this other camp to keep quiet and behave with great prudence: even their thoughts and words in their bedrooms must be guarded—the king and the rich have ways of finding out (v. 20). Against the rule of iniquity and foolishness, Solomon does not call for a revolution. Against the talkative and noisy fools, he only recommends the silence of faith.

11:1–10
The Life of Faith

The last words of prudence do not mean cowardice and passivity. The faith Solomon has in mind implies running risks. Each risk is promoted with a specific admonition: the risk of generosity toward others, the risk of hope in the future when there is no prospect, and the risk of enjoying life in the midst of troubles.

11:1–2. The Risk of Generosity. From words against people, Solomon moves to actions on behalf of people. It is interesting that the first admonition calling for the first act of faith is not directed toward God but toward the poor. The message is based on a proverb (v. 1). Casting bread upon waters means to risk losing bread. Similarly, giving to the poor is giving without the expectation of reward and giving out of grace (9:11). This act of generosity is therefore an act of faith. It is precisely this expectation of loss that will bring the bread back. The expression *al pene hammayim* ("on the surface of the waters," "across the sea," or "on the face of the waters") is reminiscent of Gen. 1:2, when the spirit was "upon the waters." The language therefore implies the promise of God's act of creation, which will turn the futility, represented by waters, into existence and significance. In Ecclesiastes, the image of waters is also associated with the idea of return (Eccl. 1:7). There is therefore wisdom in the apparent folly of losing bread, an idea in

tune with Solomon's paradox that wisdom may be found in folly (see also Matt. 10:39).

The numerical parallelism of seven and eight (Eccl. 11:2), where the first number is followed by a higher number, is intended to express the idea of intensification (Prov. 30:29). An act of generosity should expand beyond a single act of charity. Liberality is encouraged here. The reason why we should give is not only justified with the promise that the bread will return; this act is also needed because we do not know what calamity will fall on the earth (Eccl. 11:2). Paradoxically, humanitarian activities will save us from a potential evil. Giving to the hungry will save the world from political and economic crisis.

11:3–6. The Risk of Hope. The second admonition is to sow seed. Here again the idea of not knowing is repeated three times (vv. 5 [twice], 6), but now the phrase is pregnant with hope. Instead of evil (v. 2), what is expected is the miraculous work of God. Our act of faithful "sowing" is motivated by the fact that "we do not know" how the clouds will produce rain (v. 3), where a tree will fall (v. 3), how (if) the wind will blow (vv. 4–5), or how human bones grow in the womb of a woman (v. 5). This is the faith of creation: we cannot know or understand the work of God who is the Creator of everything (v. 5). In parallel to the previous admonition, the call to sow is intensified; both morning and evening work is encouraged (v. 6). We should always sow because we do not know which seed will prosper. The last word (*tob*, "good" or "well") reminds us of God's grace. Our acts of grace are acts of creation, responding to the Creator's acts of grace.

11:7–10. The Risk of Life. The third admonition is a call to rejoice in and enjoy life (vv. 8–9). The word *tob* is used again here (v. 7), evoking the context of creation. The idiom of seeing the sun means "to be alive." This section is saturated with the language of creation (good, sun, light, living, man ['*adam*]). The call to rejoice is based on our remembrance of both life, when light is sweet (v. 7), and death, the days of darkness (v. 8). This enjoyment applies to all sorts of things (11:8). It means that we have to enjoy everything of creation. The paradigm of youth implies the intensity of enjoyment. Solomon encourages us to take all the risks of life, and walk or live according to all our desires (according to all our thoughts, emotions), and according to the sight of our eyes—all that is proposed to us. This comprehensive grace reminds us of God speaking to Adam in the Garden of Eden (Gen. 2:16). The key conjunction in Ecclesiastes 11:9 may be better understood as "and" instead of "but," conveying not so much an implicit warning as a simple statement of fact, or even an assurance. All this enjoyment is thus reinforced, not discouraged, by the knowledge of the judgment of God, which points to the good news of God's gift of salvation that is prepared for the righteous (3:17; 8:6; cf. Dan. 7:22). However, this grace is associated with a commandment just as the grace of God's permission to eat of every tree in the Garden of Eden was associated with the commandment not to eat of one tree (Gen. 2:17). Solomon's commandment is a call to remove *ca'as* ("anxiety," "sorrow," or "vexation") from the mind and *ra'* ("evil," "pain," or "trouble") from the body—he is concerned with the inside as well as the outside. Solomon's exhortation to refrain from sin is not a response to the fear of judgment but is instead a response to the grace of God.

12:1–8
Cosmic Catastrophe

Surprisingly, the Preacher/Teacher now places the emphasis on the future judgment, introducing an eschatological dimension in his discourse. Wisdom and eschatology stand side by side here.

12:1–4. The End of the World. The last message of Solomon concludes with an evocation of creation (11:7–9a) and the perspective of the future day of judgment (vv. 9b–10). The same association recurs in chapter 12, which begins with creation (v. 1) and ends with judgment (v. 14). However, the perspective has shifted from the limited scope of personal life (11:7, 10) to the cosmic scope of the world and human history (12:2–7, 14). From an allusion to old age (v. 1), Solomon moves to the description of a cosmic catastrophe. The eschatological language of the passage ("in that day," "darkening of the sun," "blossoming of the almond tree," etc.) suggests that he is referring to an apocalyptic vision of the end of the world.

12:5–7. The End of Humankind. From an allusion to the death of a man (*'adam*) going to his grave (v. 5), Solomon moves to the broader scene of the death of all humankind: the return to dust. This evokes the miracle of creation (Gen. 1:2; 2:7). In fact, creation (Eccl. 12:1) is related to the two cosmic eschatological events. The end of the

world and the end of humankind are both introduced by the same expression "before" (vv. 1, 6).

12:8. The Motto Again. In the introduction, Ecclesiastes begins with the motto of *habel habalim* ("vanity of vanities," "absolute futility," or "utterly meaningless"; 1:2) followed by creation (vv. 2–11); the conclusion echoes in a chiastic parallel the introduction of the book (AB // BA): the motto follows the reference to creation. At the end, the world returns, then, to the same state it was in before it started.

12:9–14
EPILOGUE: THE SENSE OF CREATION

12:9–12
The Words of Truth

In parallel to the destiny of the world, the book ends as it began, with an autobiographical note (1:1), but this time it focuses on the words of Solomon (vv. 9–12). His task was not only to teach the people but also to seek and sort out his heritage of wisdom (v. 9) and to find the true taste of the words (v. 10) in order to make sense of creation. The description of the written words as upright and true underlines their association with God (2 Sam. 7:28; Ps. 119:43), which is implied in the expression "One Shepherd" (Ps. 23:1). This short lecture on wisdom has a double function. First, it establishes the divine inspiration of this difficult message (it is like firmly set nails). There is a warning against anything beyond or in addition to this message that admonishes (Eccl. 12:12), which is therefore to be honored and received as holy Scriptures (Deut. 4:2; Rev. 22:18–19). It also prepares for the reception of the last and most important message (Eccl. 3:14).

12:13–14
The Day of Judgment

This is the conclusion and therefore the climax and goal of the book (v. 13). All humankind (*kal ha'adam*) is urged to make sense of life: fear God and keep His commandments. The reason for this call is the cosmic judgment, which covers everything, good and evil (v. 14). Note that this association of creation, judgment, and the fear of God reappears in the apocalyptic message of John (Rev. 14:7). This hope, which is part of the agenda of Ecclesiastes, is also shared and nurtured by those who wait on the Lord during the final judgment.

SONG OF SONGS

INTRODUCTION

Title. The title "Song of Solomon," as known to centuries of English readers, is more technically understood to be "Song of Songs." This title expresses the superlative, just like the parallel phrase "Holy of Holies" (for Most Holy Place), and thus may be translated as "The Most Sublime Song."

Authorship. The first verse of this book not only provides the title "Song of Songs" but also adds the qualifier "of Solomon." This is how authorship is expressed in other books in the Hebrew OT. In this way, then, Solomon is identified as the author of the Song. Numerous lines of external and internal evidence support the book's self-assertion that the Song was composed by King Solomon: (1) 1 Kings 4:32 mentions Solomon's 1,005 songs; (2) the name "Solomon" appears seven times in the book (Song 1:1, 5; 3:7, 9, 11; 8:11, 12); (3) all five "king" references (1:4, 12; 3:9, 11; 7:5) portray him in a manner consistent with the written account of Solomon; (4) terminology associated with a wedding (3:7–11) has been identified with Solomon's wedding to the Egyptian princess (1 Kin. 3:1); (5) the profusion of flora (twenty-one varieties) and fauna (fifteen species) mentioned in the Song parallel the account of Solomon's knowledge (1 Kin. 4:23, 33; 10:2, 10, 25); (6) an association can be made between the chariots of Pharaoh (Song 1:9) and the acquisition of horses from Egypt (1 Kin. 10:28) during Solomon's reign; (7) throughout the Song a number of luxury goods are described (e.g., Song 1:12, 13; 3:6, 9), comporting with the written description of the wealth of Solomon (1 Kin. 10:14–23) and associated with the extensive trading that took place at that time (9:26–28); (8) references to Tirzah and Heshbon fit the time period of the united monarchy; (9) there are extensive linguistic parallels

between this book and others (Proverbs and Ecclesiastes) that are traditionally attributed to Solomon; (10) contrary to scholars who posit a late date after the time of Solomon, the use of archaic grammatical and poetic features point to an early date for the book; and (11) numerous allusions to the Solomonic temple and palace can be found in the Song (e.g., Song 1:5, 16–17; 2:4; 5:15; 8:7, 9).

Date and Backgrounds. The weight of the evidence favors the traditional view that the couple in the Song are not merely literary figures existing in the author's imagination but a historical married couple. Solomon is clearly the male lover in the Song. Besides the points mentioned above in which the book refers to King Solomon, he is explicitly identified several times as the groom in the wedding of the couple (3:7, 9, 11). The Song was probably written early in Solomon's reign, circa 950 B.C., before he apostatized into idolatry and polygamy (1 Kin. 11:1–8).

The identity of the female lover in this book is a mystery that has yet to find a satisfactory solution that is widely accepted in scholarship. The various views posit, among other possibilities, that she may have been (1) Pharaoh's daughter (the traditional view in the history of interpretation until the rise of critical scholarship; 3:1; 9:24); (2) Abishag the Shulamite (1:3, 15; 2:17, 21–22); (3) both Pharaoh's daughter *and* Abishag; or (4) an unidentified woman from the village of Shulam (Shunam), an Israelite and not a foreigner (cf. 11:1–3). In light of the monogamous nature of the marriage relationship revealed in the Song viewed against the historical background of Solomon's life (see below, Theology: number 3. Monogamy) and the reference to "Shulamite" (see commentary on Song 6:13—7:10), this commentary could favor either the first or the third option above, but the verse-by-verse commentary that follows does not depend upon accepting one of these options above the other.

Theology and Purpose. The Song of Songs is a return to Eden. It presents an inspired reflection and elucidation of the divine ideal for human sexual love within the context of courtship and marriage. This theology of sexuality may be summarized under ten subheadings.

1. Creation Order. Underlying the entire Song is the same high doctrine of Creation that is found in Genesis 1–2. Sexuality is assumed to be a Creation ordinance, given by God for humans to enjoy (see commentary on 8:5–14). At the same time, sexuality and divinity are radically separated; sexuality belongs to the Creation order, not the divine realm.

2. Heterosexual Marital Form. In the Song of Songs, consistent with the divine pattern in Genesis 2:18–23, we find a heterosexual love relationship described in the context of courtship and marriage.

3. Monogamy. In harmony with the monogamy set forth as the divine pattern for marriage in Genesis 2:23, the marriage relationship depicted in the Song is a monogamous one (see e.g., Song 1:7; 2:2, 3, 16; 5:1, 10; 6:3; 7:10; 8:6–7). The historical record also implies a monogamous marital relationship between Solomon and the wife of his youth (1 Kin. 3:1; 7:8; 9:16). According to this historical record, Solomon was married early in his reign to Pharaoh's daughter, and some twenty years later he brought her to the palace he had built for her in Jerusalem. No other wives or palaces for them are mentioned during this time period. This seems to imply that Pharaoh's daughter (who became a faithful follower of the true God, Song 8:6; cf. PK 53) was Solomon's sole wife during the time when he composed this Song in the early years of his reign. The biblical record indicates that Solomon remained faithful to God during this twenty-year period (1 Kin. 9:1–5; cf. 3:3–15). Ellen White writes that "for many years he [Solomon] walked uprightly, his life marked with strict obedience to God's commands" (PK 27).

Some have pointed to the record that Solomon reigned for forty years and that his son Rehoboam took over the throne at the age of forty-one (11:42–43; 14:21), implying that Rehoboam was born the year before Solomon became king. From such data it is inferred that Solomon had other wives before the Shulamite and was therefore polygamous at the time when the Song was written. But the LXX records in 1 Kings 12:24a (in an extended section not found in the MT) that Rehoboam was sixteen years of age when he began to reign (not forty-one), and that he reigned twelve years. The LXX may well

preserve the correct chronological data since this data makes more sense of the statement in v. 8 that Rehoboam "consulted the young men who had grown up with him." The Hebrew term used for the "young men" means "boy," "[male] child," "youth." If those who grew up with him were called "boys"/"youths," then Rehoboam himself was a "boy"/"youth" when he became king, and this would not easily apply to a forty-one-year-old. But if Rehoboam was only sixteen when he ascended to Solomon's throne, there is ample chronological space for the twenty-plus years of Solomon's monogamous marriage to the Shulamite before he married Rehoboam's mother, and she gave birth to Rehoboam. As an alternate interpretation, one may note that according to 14:21 Rehoboam's mother was Naamah, an Ammonite. It is possible that Naamah had already given birth to Rehoboam by an Ammonite father before her political marriage to Solomon, and Solomon simply adopted Rehoboam as his own (eldest) son (a practice hinted at from around this very time in Ps. 2:7). David's bloodline in this case was to be passed on through Rehoboam's wife Maachah (the granddaughter of Absalom, David's son), who gave birth to Rehoboam's successor, Abijam (1 Kin. 15:1, 2; 2 Chr. 11:21).

Although later in life (after he composed the Song of Songs) Solomon fell into polygamy (1 Kin. 11:1–8), his later, dark history must not detract from the reality depicted in the narrative frame of the sublime Song. The Song has a happy, monogamous literary ending.

4. Equality within the Love Relationship. In parallel with Genesis 1–2, the lovers in the Song are presented as full equals in every way. The keynote of egalitarianism in mutual love is struck in Song of Songs 2:16: "My beloved is mine, and I am his." The Song of Songs begins and closes with the woman speaking; she carries the majority of the dialogue; she initiates most of the meetings and is just as active in the lovemaking as the husband; she is just as eloquent about the beauty of her lover as he is about her; she is as gainfully employed as he is. In short, throughout the Song the woman is fully the equal of the man.

5. Wholeness. The concept of wholeness in sexuality is highlighted in the Song of Songs by one of its key themes—the presence and/or absence of the lovers with/from each other (3:1–5; 5:2–8). Wholeness in the Song includes the holistic view of the human person as a sexual being. Sexuality in the Song is not just the sex act; it involves the whole indivisible human being: physical, sensual, emotional, and spiritual. Physical attraction includes the whole body—not just the sexual organs (vv. 10–16; 7:1–9)—and the expressions of praise often refer to inner (character) qualities of the one praised and not just physical beauty.

6. *Exclusivity.* As in Genesis 2:24 man is to "leave"—be free from all outside interferences in the sexual relationship—so in the Song of Songs the lovers are unfettered by parental prearrangements and are in love for love's sake alone. The exclusivity of the couple's relationship is apparent from numerous references in the Song (e.g., Song 2:2, 16; 6:3, 9; 7:10).

7. *Permanence.* As in the Genesis model (Gen. 2:24), man and woman are to "cleave" to each other in a marriage covenant so the Song of Songs climaxes in the wedding procession, ceremony, and wedding night (Song 3:6—5:1; see Literary Features below). As in Genesis 2:24, the fidelity, loyalty, and devotion of the partners and the steadfastness and permanence of their love is revealed in the Song (see esp. Song 2:16; 6:3; 8:6–7).

8. *Intimacy.* The Song of Songs as a whole may be considered as nothing less than an ode to intimacy. As in Genesis 2:24, where the "one-flesh" union follows the "cleaving," so in the Song of Songs sexual intercourse occurs only within the context of the marriage covenant. At the time of the wedding, the Shulamite is a garden "locked" or "enclosed" (Song 4:12), which refers to her virginity. The lyrics of Solomon in the Song also seem to indicate his virginity at the time of the wedding (2:2; 6:9; 8:5). The Song moves sequentially through the entire historical scope of the relationship between Solomon and the Shulamite. There is a consistent pattern of maturing intimacy, appropriate to each stage of their relationship.

9. *Sexuality and Procreation.* The Song contains no reference to the procreative function of sexuality. As in the Creation account of Genesis 2, the sexual experience within marriage is not linked with the utilitarian intent to propagate children. Lovemaking for the sake of love, not procreation, is the message of the Song. In the Song sexual union is given value on its own, without the need to justify it as a means to some superior (procreative) end.

10. *The Wholesome Beauty and Joy of Sexuality.* In the Song of Songs, as in Genesis 1–2, sexuality (along with the rest of God's creation) is portrayed as "very good [beautiful]" and is to be celebrated and enjoyed without fear or embarrassment (cf. Gen 2:25). A plenitude of intertwining themes and motifs in the Song highlight this wholesome beauty and goodness of paradisal sexual love. Paradisal love is presented as stunningly beautiful (e.g., Song 1:15, 16); wonderfully sensuous (e.g., 4:16; 5:1); an exuberant celebration (e.g., 3:6–11); a thrilling adventure (e.g., 1:4; 2:8, 10); an exquisite delight (e.g., vv. 3–4); marked by strong sexual desire (e.g., 5:1–6); unashamed and uninhibited (e.g., 7:2, 8–9, 11–13; 8:2); yet also restrained and in good taste (e.g., 2:7; 3:5; 5:8; 8:4); light-hearted play (e.g., 1:7–8; 7:9); romantic love (e.g., vv. 10–13; 8:5–7); powerfully passionate (e.g., 6:12; 7:4); and an awe-inspiring mystery (e.g., 6:4, 10).

A whole book of the Bible is devoted to celebrating the wholesome beauty and enjoyment of human sexual love. The Song of Songs in its literal sense is not merely a "secular" love song but is already fraught with deep theological significance. God reveals His love for humanity in the enjoyment and pleasure that He designed for lovers to find in each other in the marriage context.

The echo of God's names resonates in the dominant recurring refrain of the Song (see commentary on 2:6–7), and the actual voice of God resounds from the Song's central literary summit (see commentary on 4:16—5:1). But when one moves to the Song's thematic climax and conclusion, the great paean to love (8:6), the actual name of Yahweh makes its single explicit appearance in the book, and His flaming presence encapsulates the entire theological message of the Song: "Its [Love's] flames are flames of fire"—the very flame of Yahweh (see commentary on 8:5–14 regarding this translation).

Since human love is described as a gift from God, a flame of Yahweh, the love displayed between Solomon and the Shulamite not only depicts wholesome human sexuality but points beyond to the love of Yahweh Himself. The various characteristics and qualities of holy human love that have emerged from the Song—selfless mutuality and reciprocity, joy of presence, pain of absence, exclusivity (yet inclusiveness), intimate oneness, disinterested and enduring covenant loyalty, wholesomeness, beauty, goodness, and so on—all reflect the divine love within the very nature of God's being. Furthermore, the Song is not only a love song about human lovers but ultimately points (typologically) to the love relationship between God and His people. Far different from the allegorical approach, which regards the literal, historical meaning as the husk to be discarded in favor of a fanciful interpretation that is alien to the text, the typological approach upholds the literal sense by acknowledging what the Song already indicates—that human love typifies the divine.

In the Song of Songs, we have come to the supreme OT statement on the theology of human sexual love and the divine-human love relationship, even (as Rabbi Akiba put it) to "the Holy of Holies"!

Literary Features. For fifteen centuries the allegorical method for interpreting the Song of Songs was predominant in the Christian church. Influenced by pagan Greek philosophers, Christian allegorists posited a dichotomy between things of the flesh and things of the spirit, and all expressions of bodily pleasure—including sexual expression—were considered evil. The literal sense of the Song—the human love relationship between Solomon and the Shulamite—constituted the literal reading to be stripped away allegorically to find the intended spiritual meaning, which was the love relationship between God and His church or the individual soul. The reformer John Calvin moved away from this interpretation and interpreted the Song of Songs as an inspired song of human love. In modern scholarship, the plain-reading approach has become the consensus method for understanding the Song.

The Song of Solomon is a literary masterpiece. It is set within nature, which provides a backdrop of sensuous beauty portrayed through exquisite poetic language laced with figures of speech. The lovers in the Song celebrate the beauty of married sexual love. There are numerous parallels between the Song of Songs and Egyptian love poetry. But unlike the lengthy monologues of the Egyptian songs, the two lovers in Solomon's Song of Songs are continually interacting in speech. The Song also frequently employs the literary form of the *wasf* (Arab., "description"), a term used to describe the extravagant praise of the physical charms of the bride and groom in modern, rural Syrian wedding customs.

The basic building block of the Song, in common with other Hebrew poetry, is poetic parallelism, including chiasm (reverse parallelism, ABB'A' pattern) and block parallelism (or panel writing, ABCA'B'C'). The macrostructure of the Song contains twelve sections (demarcated by refrains) comprised of both chiasm and block parallelism, forming a double-seven pattern (including the two-verse central climax) as follows:

A 1:2—2:7 Mutual love
B 2:8–17 Coming and going
  C 3:1–5 Dream I: Lost and found
    D 3:6–11 Praise of groom, I
      E 4:1–7 Praise of bride, I
        F 4:8–15 Praise of bride, II
          G 4:16 Invitation by bride
          G' 5:1 Acceptance of invitation by groom and divine approbation
        C' 5:2–8 Dream II: Found and lost
      D' 5:9—6:3 Praise of groom, II
      E' 6:4–10 Praise of bride, III
    F' 6:11—7:10 Praise of bride, IV
  B' 7:11—8:4 Going and coming
A' 8:5–14 Mutual love

Although the Song of Solomon is not a full-blown drama, a basic story line emerges from the dialogues involving Solomon, the Shulamite, her brothers, and her female companions (the daughters of Jerusalem). Numerous recent literary analyses have pointed out the presence of narrative progression or plot throughout various sections of the Song. A three-part historical progression of the Song has been suggested: the courtship (1:2—3:5), the bridal procession and wedding (3:6—5:1), and the life of love after marriage (5:2—8:7). In this commentary the analysis is further refined, suggesting seven acts. These acts are interlinked with members of the symmetrical macrostructure (as presented above), which often subdivide these acts into separate scenes. The basic story line of acts is as follows:

I. Mutual love: Courtship (1:2—2:7) = Member A

II. Betrothal and dream of lost and found (2:8—3:5) = Members B and C

III. Wedding procession and wedding service (3:6—4:7) = Members D and E

IV. Wedding night in the bridal chamber (4:8—5:1) = Members F, G, and H

V. Marital conflict and resolution (5:2—6:10) = Members C', D', and E'

VI. Maturation of marriage (6:11—8:4) = Members F' and B'

VII. Mutual love: Mature reflections on love's meaning (8:5–14) = Member A'

This narrative structure does not consist of a detailed plotline but rather presents a collage or kaleidoscope of scenes encompassing the historical scope of the relationship between Solomon and the Shulamite. There is a consistent pattern of more restrained sexual imagery (without reference to sexual intercourse) in the scenes before the wedding, and an intensification of sexual imagery (with frequent allusions to sexual intercourse) after the wedding. The Song provides practical theological insights pertaining to each stage of the love relationship.

COMMENTARY

1:2—2:7
Act I. Courtship/Mutual Love

As noted in the introduction, the superscription of the Song indicates that it is "the most sublime Song" among the 1,005 songs written by Solomon (1 Kin. 4:32), or it may even suggest that this is the "most sublime Song" (about love) of all time. The first act is formed by eight different scenes and opens with the statement "Let him kiss me with the kisses of his mouth" (Song 1:2). This poetic line strikes the keynote of the entire Song—intimate romantic love. The sublime Song begins with the lovers already well into what we today may term a courtship relationship. This first act presents a collage of scenes from the courtship of Solomon and the Shulamite, involving both northern Israel (the home of the Shulamite, where Solomon comes to visit her) and Jerusalem (the home of Solomon, where the Shulamite comes to visit him). A close look at the clues of each scene provides hints that the seven major scenes of this act alternate symmetrically between northern Israel and Jerusalem:

Scene 1. Song 1:2–4	Jerusalem
Scene 2. Song 1:5–6	Northern Israel
Scene 3. Song 1:7–8	Northern Israel
Scene 4. Song 1:9–11	Jerusalem
Scene 5. Song 1:12–14	Jerusalem
Scene 6. Song 1:15–17	Northern Israel
Scene 7. Song 2:1–3	Northern Israel
Scene 8. Song 2:4–5	Jerusalem
Refrain. Song 2:6–7	

1:2–4. Scene 1. The Shulamite unabashedly expresses her longing for romantic kisses from Solomon (v. 2). The first poetic line of the Song begins in a third-person address (perhaps more distantly to draw the audience into the scene) but then segues to the more intimate second-person direct address to Solomon in the next line: "For your love...." The Hebrew word for "love" here (see also v. 4; 4:10; 5:1) describes physical display of affection or lovemaking without specifying the level of intimacy. In context, here it is Solomon's kisses that are sweeter than the sweetest wine!

In her expression of love for Solomon (1:3), the Shulamite compares Solomon's external desirability (his kisses and his fragrant oils) with his inner being—his name, which stands for his character (cf. Ex. 34:5–7). The Song upholds the importance of wholistic love, encompassing the entire person, and especially emphasizes one's character qualities and good reputation. After telling Solomon that her unmarried female companions admire him, she energetically invites her lover to come draw her away (Song 1:4). The maidens (probably part of a group called the "daughters of Jerusalem" later in the Song), respond spontaneously that they will hasten after her. Solomon brings the Shulamite and her female companions into his palace chambers in Jerusalem (vv. 4–5; cf. Ps. 45:13–15). The plural "chambers" refers to the whole palace of the king, and not just his bedchamber. Sexual union is not described in this courtship scene.

1:5–6. Scene 2. The scene changes, probably to northern Israel in the surroundings of the Shulamite's home (Shulam), where King Solomon has come with shepherds to examine his royal flocks, bringing with him some daughters of Jerusalem (who had perhaps become acquainted with the Shulamite earlier while she was in Jerusalem). From the Shulamite's conversation with her female companions from Jerusalem (vv. 5–6), it seems that she was not a native of Jerusalem, but grew up working outside in the hot sun, taking care of the vineyards, by order of her overbearing brothers (lit. "her mother's sons," perhaps implying a second marriage and stepbrothers). There is no mention of her father here or elsewhere in the Song.

1:7–8. Scene 3. Still in northern Israel, the Shulamite speaks to her beloved Solomon, and for the first time in the Song, Solomon replies. She learns about the king's occupation as a shepherd (probably to be taken literally as overseeing his flocks of sheep or possibly also figuratively as the king tending to his business as shepherd of the people of Israel), and a connection is made because she is also a shepherd. The Shulamite is worried about being regarded as a prostitute as she wanders around looking for Solomon among Solomon's shepherds, and Solomon wisely advises her to follow the footsteps of his flock, implying that then she will find him.

1:9–11. Scene 4. In still another scene in the collage of courtship, Solomon's voice is heard expressing words of endearment likening her to his mare among Pharaoh's chariot horses, which were beautifully decorated (see Song of Songs: Introduction). Solomon's mare and the war chariots imported from Egypt were probably located in Jerusalem; and the young women's offer to make ornaments for the Shulamite give us another hint that this scene is back in Jerusalem where the young women would have access to materials with which to make the ornaments (v. 11).

1:12–14. Scene 5. In this fast-changing collage of scenes, the courtship now highlights the meal fellowship of Solomon and the Shulamite at the king's table (in Jerusalem), with her perfumes giving forth their fragrance and causing her to imagine him like a pouch containing a bundle of myrrh lying between her breasts all night and like a cluster of henna blossoms in the vineyards of En Gedi. The henna, not the king, is in the vineyards of En Gedi, and likewise it is the pouch, not the king, that is literally between her breasts all night.

1:15–17. Scene 6. Another vignette depicts Solomon and the Shulamite exchanging short expressions of praise for each other's beauty (vv. 15–16) as they walk in the forest, an idyllic outdoor setting (probably in northern Israel) with tree branches serving as rafters or a roof. They sit down under the forest canopy on a couch or bed of green with fir and cedar trees as the roof or beams of their forest house (v. 17).

2:1–3. Scene 7. Still in northern Israel, the Shulamite acknowledges her singular, special status like a *shushan*—variously interpreted as "lily," "crocus," or "lotus flower"—among the others in the valleys (2:1), and Solomon confirms that she is indeed like a lily among thorns (v. 2). Then the Shulamite compares Solomon to an apple tree among the other (non-fruit-bearing) trees of the forest and expresses her delight in sitting (not lying, no sexual intercourse implied) under his shade (v. 3). The Hebrew verb for "take delight" is in the intensive form, which may be translated as "take great delight over

and over." This description involves not just a pause for a moment in her beloved's presence but personal contact such as sitting down in joyful companionship with him. Such intimate communion between human lovers typifies the blessed fellowship Christians may have with Christ in their times of personal devotions.

2:4–5. Scene 8. In the final scene of this courtship collage, which is back in Jerusalem, the intimate communion is intensified as the Shulamite is brought to Solomon's banqueting house with his banner of love over her (2:4). The tasting of his "fruit," when viewed in context with what precedes, is a metaphorical reference to the sweet and sustained fellowship, just as the "love banner" is metaphorical, and not an allusion to sexual intercourse. In v. 5 the Shulamite asks the daughters of Jerusalem to sustain her with cakes of raisins and apples, for she is lovesick—or faint/weak with love.

2:6–7. Refrain. The first act ends with a refrain (2:6–7) that appears again (with slight modifications) in 8:3–4. Verse 6 may be taken as either in the indicative mood, expressing reality, as rendered by most versions, or in the optative, expressing a wish. The word for "embrace" in these passages has been interpreted by some as "fondle" or "stimulate [the genitals]." However, this Hebrew word in all of its other OT occurrences outside of the Song never carries these meanings but consistently denotes the act of embracing, and there is no contextual reason to suggest a different meaning in the Song. Since the narrative approach considers v. 6 to be during the courtship period, in the context of growing intimacy but not sexual intercourse, the term implies intimate affection and loving support even though these same phrases indicate the opposite after marriage (8:3–4). In other words, in this model this could be understood as a wish, whereas vv. 3–4 is the fulfillment of that wish.

The refrain concludes (2:7) with the Shulamite adjuring her unmarried female companions not to stir up love "until *shettekhpatz*." This has been variously translated as "until it pleases," "until it so desires," "until she pleases," or "until the appropriate time" (3:5). Using the language of the formal oath, the Shulamite "swears" by animals whose names not only refer to beauty (the same word is used for "gazelle" and "beauty") but sound similar to the names of God ("gazelle" sounds like "[Lord of] hosts," and "does of the field" sounds like "El Shaddai [Almighty God]") thus bringing together the beauty of their love relationship (symbolized by the animals) with the blessing of God Himself.

In the collage of courtship, there is a period for the development of various kinds of intimacy, all at the appropriate stages of the relationship: romantic (1:2, 13; 2:6); recreational (1:4, 16–17; 2:3–4); occupational/work (1:6–8); aesthetic (vv. 8, 12, 15–16); intellectual (v. 9; 2:2); creative (1:11); meal (v. 12; 2:4); communion (v. 3); celebrative (v. 4); emotional (v. 5); and communication (1:9–10, 15–16).

2:8—3:5
Act II. Proposal of Marriage (Betrothal) and Dream of Lost and Found

This second section is frequently taken as a continuation of the deepening relationship between Solomon and the Shulamite during the courtship, with visits to the countryside illustrating a healthy dating relationship. However, a closer look at the clues in this section strongly suggest that this is no casual countryside date on the part of the couple.

2:8–17. Scene 1. Coming and Going: Betrothal/Engagement. The cumulative effect of the various lines of evidence emerging from vv. 8–17 can be seen as pointing toward a covenant-making (betrothal) setting for this stanza of the Song. Sublime Hebrew poetry forms the "musical" backdrop for a beautiful springtime betrothal between Solomon and the Shulamite. Some of the major lines of evidence supporting this conclusion are the following:

(1) "Behold/Look" (vv. 8–9) calls attention to something special to come, giving the aura of eager and breathtaking excitement.

(2) Solomon comes to the Shulamite's house (v. 9), as was the biblical custom in arranging for a betrothal or marriage.

(3) The expression "come for yourself" or "come away," which by repetition brackets Solomon's poetic song to the Shulamite (vv. 10, 13), is in Hebrew the same expression (except in the masculine), which occurs elsewhere only where it brackets God's covenant with Abraham (Gen. 12:1; 22:2), and implies a break from outside interferences so as to enter into or maintain a covenant relationship.

(4) Various kinds of imagery (Song 2:10–13) describe that winter is over and spring has come. The ripening of the figs and blossoming of vineyards are metaphors for the maturation of the Shulamite and her readiness for marriage.

(5) In the inaccessible places (rock clefts and cliff) Solomon invites his dove the Shulamite to respond to his proposal (v. 14). He calls her out of her inaccessibility in the sense of inviting her to accept his proposal of betrothal. The imperative "let me see" or "show me" is an allusion to the same construction in Hebrew (except in feminine) used by Moses when he asks Yahweh for the opportunity to see His glory (Ex. 33:18) immediately before Yahweh reveals Himself and enters into a covenant with him (34:10–28).

(6) The reference to the foxes that ruin or spoil the vineyards (Song 2:15) no doubt alludes to Samson's experience in connection with obstacles to his wedding covenant (Judg. 15:1–5) and is probably a statement of mutual agreement by the couple to count the cost and determine to belong exclusively to each other, undistracted by things that might jeopardize their covenant faithfulness and intimacy.

(7) The Shulamite uses explicit covenant language as she proclaims, "My beloved is mine, and I am his" (Song 2:16). This wording is similar to covenant formulas of God with His people (e.g., Gen. 17:8; Lev. 26:12; Hos. 2:23). This may reflect the Shulamite's acceptance of Solomon's marriage proposal, and thus she eagerly proclaims the reality of their covenant relationship in betrothal.

(8) "Until the day breaks" (lit. "breathes"; Song 2:17) is a phrase that not only refers to the beginning or ending of a regular day but in this context echoes covenantal and eschatological figurative language. "The day" can sometimes refer to times of trouble and judgment; this usage is found already in the time of Job (Job 20:28; 21:30; 38:23) and is also used this way by David (Ps. 20:1; 59:16) and Solomon (Prov. 6:34; 11:4; 16:4). The Hebrew verb for "breathe" (*puakh*) not only refers to the arrival of the morning or afternoon cool breeze (cf. Gen. 3:8 for usage in a covenant lawsuit setting) but can also denote the testimony of a witness in a legal (or covenant-making) setting (Ps. 27:12; Prov. 6:19; 12:17; 14:5, 25; 19:5, 9). In the Song this phrase probably alludes to the future eschatological legal assize—the day of judgment.

(9) The reference to the fleeing shadows (Song 2:17) not only alludes to the end of a day filled with the loving relationship between the betrothed couple but ultimately has connotations of the eschatological end of time or the end of a human's existence when life departs as a "shadow" (Job 14:2), the equivalent to our modern vow or promise to love "till death do us part." The Shulamite is vowing to be forever faithful to her covenant with Solomon.

(10) The covenant-making (betrothal) setting is suggested by the Shulamite's reference to the mountains of *bether*. In Hebrew the word *bether* denotes "cleavage/separation" and probably has several layers of meaning in this verse. While the phrase may refer both to a literal mountain cleft named *bether* and to the cleavage of her breasts, it ultimately refers to the "mountains of the covenant," as some translations recognize. The Hebrew word *bether* is used to describe the separation of the covenant-making animals in Genesis 15:17 when God made a covenant with Abraham, and Isaiah 53:8 uses this term (alluding back to Gen. 15) in predicting the covenant-sealing death of the suffering Servant. The Shulamite alludes to this covenant ceremony in Abraham's history (foreshadowing the new covenant) and applies it to her covenant relationship with Solomon, in other words their betrothal or formal engagement, which will be consummated in the marriage that is described in the next stanzas of the Song. The Song affirms the important stage of a love relationship in which the couple makes a life commitment to each other in betrothal/engagement.

3:1–5. Scene 2. Dream 1, Before the Wedding. This scene occurs sometime after the previous scene depicting the betrothal, with which it is connected by numerous terminological links. In its position in the Song just before the wedding procession (vv. 6–11), the scene may portray a situation very near the time of the wedding. The Shulamite is apparently in the city of Jerusalem visiting Solomon, perhaps to plan their wedding now that they have become betrothed.

The Shulamite had what might be a recurring night dream (v. 1; the word "night" is in the plural), either on different nights or during different parts of the night's watches. Anticipating her imminent wedding, the Shulamite had lost her lover and searched anxiously for him. The theme of seeking and finding—absence and presence—highlights the need for mutuality and wholeness, as with the first couple in Eden. As in the Garden of Eden, the lovers in the Song need each other so as to be whole.

The Shulamite went about the city (probably Jerusalem) looking for Solomon, especially in the market streets and town squares where townspeople gathered. The night watchmen who were patrolling the city found her. The Hebrew order of the sentence in v. 3 heightens the sense of drama and urgency: "The one whom I love—have you seen?" With no introductory phrase such as "I asked the guards…" the pace of the narrative poetry is quickened.

No sooner had she left the watchmen than she found her lover (v. 4). She held him in her embrace; the shift in the Hebrew tense implies her continuing to hold on to him in her present time and on into the future. In this verse the Shulamite transitions from her dream to a statement of the present situation. She announces to the daughters of Jerusalem (likely at a time other than during the night) her intention to bring her lover to her mother's home, which is still also her own home until she gets married. She may be alluding to the time of the imminent wedding, when Solomon would come to take her in his royal palanquin (i.e., his enclosed litter, suspended by poles and carried on the shoulders of several men) to the wedding ceremony in Jerusalem.

This account captures some of the conflicting emotions as the wedding approaches: eager expectation mixed with reservations and thoughts of life in her mother's house up to this time. She finds herself poised on the threshold of a new married life with her lover, yet she experiences reluctance to leave home and family. It has been suggested that she only dreamed of bringing her lost lover into her mother's room (v. 4), which would anticipate the consummation of the marriage in the near future, rather than describing a real experience of sexual intimacy with him before the marriage, as would be understood by a cursory reading of the text. The refrain (see 2:7) admonishes the daughters of Jerusalem (and by extension, the readers) not to stir up love until *shettekhpatz*. As noted in the comment for v. 7, this has been variously translated as "until it pleases," "until it so desires," "until she pleases," or "until the appropriate time" (3:5). The scene ends with the same refrain that ends the first section of the Song (2:7) and is the refrain in 8:4, except that there is no mention of the intimate embrace of the Shulamite and Solomon (cf. 2:6 and 8:3). This could be explained if the Shulamite was not actually present with Solomon but only in a dream, which she related to her female companions.

3:6—4:7
Act III. Wedding Procession and Wedding Service

The symmetrical structure of the unified Song finds its apex in the central sections, which appear to describe the royal wedding of Solomon to his bride and their wedding night.

3:6–11. Scene 1. Wedding Procession: Praise of Groom I. It has been suggested that scene 1 portrays the wedding procession of Solomon "on the day of his wedding" (3:11). The description of this lavish wedding procession is strong evidence that what is taking place is not just a simple wedding between commoners who take on the title of "king" and "queen" for a day, as some scholars have suggested, but rather a description of the royal marriage of Solomon. Commentaries are divided over *who* is riding in Solomon's palanquin. Is it Solomon, the Shulamite, or both? In light of v. 11—where the daughters of Jerusalem are admonished to observe King Solomon—it seems clear that at least Solomon is in the palanquin and that the focus in this section is upon him. At the same time, evidence within the passage, contextual indicators, and intratextual parallels with 8:5, appear to indicate that the Shulamite is also involved in the procession. In this commentary we suggest that this scene portrays Solomon bringing his bride from her home in northern Israel to Jerusalem by way of the Jordan Valley, up through the wilderness of Judea to Jerusalem for the wedding ceremony. In fact, in ancient times the bringing of the bride from her house to the house of the groom may have been part of the wedding ceremony (cf. Gen. 24:67; Ps. 45). Solomon may have traveled all the way to Shulem in northern Israel to escort his bride throughout the entire journey of several days, or he may have sent the armed guard and royal entourage to Shulem to escort the bride and then come down from Jerusalem himself on the day of the wedding to meet the Shulamite and join the formal procession up from the wilderness to Jerusalem.

The word for crown in Song 3:11 can refer to a "garland," "crown," or "diadem." Later Jewish weddings may illuminate this verse, as both groom and bride wore wedding crowns on their wedding day, a practice continued until the fall of Jerusalem in 70 A.D. The crown that Bathsheba, Solomon's mother, placed upon Solomon's head was not for the occasion of his coronation as king (predating his wedding to the Shulamite) but for a special crowning on the occasion of his wedding.

4:1–7. Scene 2. Wedding Ceremony: Praise of Bride I. This scene appears to encompass the wedding ceremony itself. The groom sings a wedding *wasf* (song describing the beauty of his bride) in which he lauds the Shulamite's beauty. In light of our analysis of Song of 2:17, where the statement "until the day breaks and the shadows flee" was seen to constitute the Shulamite's covenant vow at the time of her betrothal to be faithful "till death do them

part," the use of precisely the same covenant language at the end of this section (4:6) appears to serve a similar function in the groom's marriage vow to love and cherish his bride "as long as they both shall live." The wedding ends with the groom repeating (v. 7, as an *inclusio* with v. 1) his summary admiration of the beauty of his bride.

Allusions to the sanctuary and its services and setting are more concentrated in this passage than in any other stanza of the Song. Note the references to dove (v. 1), goats (v. 1), sheep (v. 2), scarlet (v. 3), mouth (v. 3, a Hebrew word that elsewhere in the Hebrew Bible means wilderness, and a cognate word that refers to the Holy of Holies), veil (vv. 1, 3), pomegranate (v. 3), lilies (v. 5), myrrh and incense (v. 6), and being without blemish or flaw (v. 7)—all of these are related to the sanctuary elsewhere in Scripture! An aura of sanctuary holiness is thereby drawn over the bride, who is extolled in the wedding service by the groom. The wedding service, and yes, marriage itself as an institution, are cast as sacred, as made holy (see 5:1) by the presence of God's presiding over the service, as in the Garden of Eden (Gen. 2:22–23).

4:8—5:1

Act IV. Wedding Night in the Bridal Chamber

Only in Song of Songs 4:8—5:1 does Solomon address the Shulamite as his bride (4:8, 9, 10, 11, 12; 5:1). The wedding has taken place and now it is the wedding night. This section encompasses the foreplay of the couple in the bridal chamber on their wedding night.

4:8–15. Scene 1. Wedding Night in the Bridal Chamber: Praise of Bride II. In 4:8 Solomon invites his bride to come with him from Lebanon, Amana, Senir, and Hermon. These mountain peaks were some distance away to the north and thus might serve as symbols of her character (cf. 2:14). Solomon is inviting her to come with him, to descend from this inaccessible state to one of accessibility and intimacy. He is inviting her to make love. She has kept herself pure as a virgin (a locked garden, an enclosed spring, and a sealed fountain, 4:12), inaccessible to any sexual advances, but now following the wedding, Solomon and the Shulamite are free to engage in foreplay in the wedding chamber, leading up to sexual intercourse, all the while as Solomon describes her ravishing beauty (vv. 9–15).

4:16—5:1. Scene 2. Consummation of the Marriage in Sexual Union. These two parallel verses appear in the exact middle of the Song (111 lines or 60 verses on either side), thus clearly designed by the Song's artistic composer to form the central, climactic verses of the entire symmetrical structure of the Song. These verses represent the consummation of the marriage in the marriage bed. The groom has compared his bride to a garden (4:12, 15), and now the bride invites her groom to come and partake of the fruits of her (now his) garden (v. 16) and the groom indicates that he has accepted her invitation (5:1). The identity of the speaker for the last portion of v. 1 is unclear. It may be best to understand that the marriage covenant having been solemnized, the authoritative Voice—Yahweh Himself—extends the divine approbation, while the bride and groom drink deeply in the consummate experience of sexual union (v. 1).

5:2—6:12
Act V. Marital Conflict and Resolution

After the wedding night, the remainder of the Song describes the life of love between Solomon and the Shulamite during their marriage. Act V portrays marital conflicts that arise after the wedding and models of how the resolution of such conflicts may take place.

5:2–8. Scene 1. Dream 2, After the Wedding: Marital Conflict. It is possible that there are nocturnal dream scenes (3:1–5 and 5:2–8), one coming before and one after the wedding. If so, they reveal a historical progression in the relationship by intensification in sexual intimacy. In what has been proposed as Dream 1, the woman wanted to hold him and not let him go (3:4), while in this proposed Dream 2, the husband comes by night to her boudoir, clearly for the purpose of making love (5:2), possibly with the double entendre of lovemaking embedded in the dream description.

Verses 2–8 utilize some of the same literary techniques as employed in 3:1–4, but here the eagerness is further underscored by recording the man's bold actions and words and the woman's inner feelings of desire for the presence of the beloved. In 5:2, the man "knocks repeatedly" (this is the force of the Hebrew grammar). Solomon is not just timidly tapping on the door! And he calls out—using the imperative—for her to open for him. He then addresses her with one of the longest strings of

endearment terms anywhere in the Song: "my sister, my love/darling, my dove, my perfect/flawless one!" (v. 2). His heart is overflowing with eagerness for her.

She, in turn, is reluctant to respond, making excuses to herself (v. 3). But when he perseveres in his expressions of desire for intimacy, her deep emotional desire to be with him is stirred (vv. 4, 6, 8). But by the time she responds, her husband has already turned away (vv. 5–6). What follows appears to take place in a dream. She is so intense and even frantic in her search for her lover that apparently the watchmen mistake her for a harlot and try to physically restrain her (v. 7). But she manages to adjure her female companions to tell her lover how lovesick she is for him, should they find him (v. 8).

It may be inferred from this account that adjustments need to be made in their newly married life together. Two issues seem to come to the fore: the husband's late-night arrival home from work (v. 2, describing his head as covered with dew of the late night), and the wife's indifference or lack of interest in sexual intimacy (v. 3). She realizes anew how much she loves Solomon and wants him to know her deep feelings for him. The Song is realistic; every marriage relationship will inevitably involve challenges, calling for action on the part of husband and wife to face them together.

5:9—6:3. Scene 2. Resolution of Marital Conflict: Praise of Groom II. After the Shulamite adjures her female companions to tell her lover, should they find him, how lovesick she is for him (5:8), the daughters of Jerusalem question her concerning what sets him apart (v. 9), and this query calls forth from the Shulamite a flowery song (*wasf*) expressing praise of his handsomeness and sterling character qualities (vv. 10–16). Her attitude and action change as she focuses her attention on his many wonderful attributes. There is also an intensification of intimacy in this description of Solomon compared to the matching praise of the groom earlier in the Song of Songs (3:6–11). This section ends with a double entendre that intensifies similar language used earlier in the Song before the wedding: before, Solomon had "grazed" among the lilies (2:16; cf. vv. 1–2 where she herself is a lily), but here the married Solomon not only grazes but actually gathers the lilies (6:2–3, NJPS), that is, experiences sexual activity with his wife.

6:4–12. Scene 3. Resolution of Marital Conflict: Praise of Bride III. In this scene Solomon shows no resentment for his wife's earlier indifference to sexual intimacy and for her insensitivity as he extols her exquisite and awesome beauty, highlighting her unique inner qualities (vv. 4–10), which may indicate that part of that was indeed a dream. He avoids sexual imagery here, perhaps because he does not want to give her the impression that he only desires her in a sexual way. The Shulamite and Solomon enjoy quiet fellowship together after their conflict resolution (vv. 11–12).

When Solomon looks at the Shulamite, he sees such an awesomeness revealed that he likens her to two awesome cities in Israel (v. 4). Not content with one such statement about the impressiveness of her appearance that likens her to soldiers on parade, he repeats it a few verses later (v. 10). In these passages, the term for "awesome" has the connotations of "fear/dread/awe" and "majesty."

Solomon also describes his wife as perfect and unique (v. 9) compared to the sixty queens, eighty concubines, and virgins without number. The mention of sixty queens and eighty concubines need not necessarily refer to Solomon's harem (1 Kin. 11:3), as many have supposed. Solomon does not say *"I have..."* but *"There are...* [queens, concubines, and virgins without number],...and my beloved is the only one [for me]" (Song 6:8–9). Furthermore, the Hebrew word for "queen(s)" in this passage is never used elsewhere in the Hebrew Bible for the wife of a Hebrew king, but only for the wife of a non-Hebrew king. In light of the evidence shown elsewhere in the Song that the relationship between Solomon and the Shulamite was a monogamous one (see Song of Songs: Introduction), it can be concluded that Solomon seems to have been proclaiming that however many other women of whatever status there may be around (at their wedding or in general), his beloved wife is his one and only. This interpretation is consistent with the typological meaning of the Song in which God enters into an exclusive covenant relationship with His people.

The final verse of this scene depicts the Shulamite as one who looks like the dawn of the morning, is as fair as the moon, is as bright and clear as the sun, and is as awesome and majestic as a procession (interpreted and translated variously as being one of "stars" or "banners"; v. 10), a description that John seems to allude to in Revelation 12:1 when describing in symbolism the pure woman representing God's true church.

6:13—8:4
Act VI. Maturation of Marriage

6:13—7:10. Scene 1. Praise of Bride IV Followed by Lovemaking. In this section the Shulamite went down to her garden and vineyard to see what was ripe, and while lost in contemplation, her mind seems to have wandered back to her roots, and there is an enigmatic reference that is best rendered as "chariots of my noble/royal people" or "chariots of Amminadib" (6:12). If the wife of Solomon in the Song is Pharaoh's daughter, as suggested as a possibility in the Introduction, this phrase could be linked to the Shulamite's royal Egyptian lineage and the famous chariots of Egypt (cf. 1:9).

The women of Jerusalem interrupt her contemplative experience, apparently inviting her to join a special dance, called the dance of the two camps (Mahanaim; v. 13), perhaps alluding to a group of dancers that dance in a formation of two lines and/or alluding to the historical experience of Mahanaim (see Gen. 32:1–3).

In Song of Songs 6:13, the daughters of Jerusalem use a name for Solomon's wife that only appears here in the Song: "the Shulamite." The grammatical form of this term usually refers to a person's place of origin and thus probably denotes a woman "from [the village of] Shulam." Shulam is an alternate spelling for the city of Shunem in northern Israel, the town from which Abishag the Shunamite came (1 Kin. 1:3, 15; 2:17, 21–22). Those positing the views that "the Shulamite" of the Song is either Abishag or another (unnamed) woman from the village of Shunem in northern Israel find support for their view in this verse. The alternate spelling may have been used because "Shulamite" allows a play on words with the name "Solomon" and may serve as the functional equivalent of "Mrs. Solomon" or "the Solomoness." The use of this name with this spelling also makes possible a three-way play on words with the word *shalom*, meaning peace/contentment (see Song 8:10–11).

Song of Songs 7:1 seems to transition from a public dance to a private one in the (exclusive) presence of Solomon while he sings to her of her stunning beauty. He expresses his desire for intimacy with her (vv. 7–8), and the scene climaxes with an allusion to their making love together, involving deep kissing and/or other intimate sexual activity (v. 9). As the scene comes to a close, the Shulamite expresses the egalitarian nature of their relationship: she belongs to her beloved, and his desire is toward her (v. 10). This is an allusion to Genesis 3:16, but the "curse" is reversed. Whereas in Genesis 3:16 the "desire" of the woman was for her husband, the Song announces that God longs for couples to return to the Edenic ideal before sin (Gen. 2:24), where there was full equality and mutual desire between husband and wife.

7:10—8:4. Scene 2. Going and Coming: Married Sexual Adventure in the Countryside. After the resolution of marital issues, with renewed confidence and comfort in their relationship, the Shulamite invites Solomon to make love to her, as she did on the wedding night (4:16). At her suggestion, they go for a vacation into the countryside. They continue to enjoy an ever-deepening intimacy as their marriage matures. The paired pictures of going and coming to the countryside (2:8–17 and 7:10—8:4) present another example of intensified intimacy including sexual intercourse after the couple is married. The various kinds of fruits (7:12–13; 8:2) denote the delicious aspects of the lovemaking process, including old and new sexual explorations and delights between the lovers.

The scene (and stanza) ends with the same refrain as found in 2:6–7. In its usage in the parallel stanza of 1:2—2:6, the context can be understood as one of a restrained physical relationship during courtship and wishing for fulfillment, whereas in this context of marriage (8:3–4) the same words can be understood as a reference to lovemaking culminating in intercourse.

8:5–14

Act VII. Mutual Love: Mature Reflections on the Meaning of Love

In this concluding stanza of the Song, the Shulamite reflects on her love relationship with Solomon from its beginning to the present. Her wisdom statements reveal that she is a believer in the true God of Israel. She describes the enduring quality of love that comes from Yahweh (v. 6). Love is nothing less than a *shalhebetyah.*

This term has often been translated as either expressing a superlative construction using the divine name—"a most vehement flame"—or as referring directly to *Yah*—a shortened form of *Yahweh*—the divine name, in which case the term would be referring to the very "flame of Yahweh." There is substantial evidence indicating that this expression is best translated as "flame of Yah[weh]." Coming at the thematic climax of the entire Song, this verse reveals that Yahweh is the Source of human love, and thus provides the basis for the typological interpretation of the Song (see Song of Songs: Introduction).

The Shulamite also reviews her life from the time of her puberty (v. 8), when her brothers protected her from sexual predators (v. 9), and she determined to remain a pure virgin, thus finding *shalom*, "peace," in her husband's eyes (v. 10). She then describes the current ongoing and growing love relationship with her husband Solomon (vv. 11–12). The final stanza (and the entire Song) ends as it begins, with the couple exuberantly in love. In fact, the final refrain that concludes the Song (v. 14) parallels almost exactly the refrain that concludes the courtship/betrothal part of the Song (2:17). The man longs to hear her voice (8:13; cf. 2:14), and she invites him to a thrilling adventure (8:14; cf. 2:17). The Song ends with the same sensual and tantalizing ambiguity that we see so often elsewhere in its stanzas: the Hebrew word used in v. 14, *barakh*—"to hurry," "to flee," "to come away"—may also mean to "penetrate." The passionate, romantic love of Solomon and the Shulamite does not lessen in intensity as they continue to enjoy married life together. The conclusion of the Song instructs us that a marriage filled with divine love will only become more joyous and beautiful as the years go by. Typologically, in the deepest dimension of our hope, the love relationship between God and His people will grow more intimate and glorious throughout eternity—ablaze with the flame of Yahweh!

PROPHETIC BOOKS

INTRODUCTION
TO THE PROPHETIC BOOKS

The writing prophets, whose messages are preserved in the biblical canon, ministered from the eighth century B.C. to around the middle of the fifth century B.C. The work of these canonical prophets occurred during the divided Israelite monarchy, during the Exile of both Israel and Judah, and during the period after the Exile when God's remnant returned from Babylon (2 Kin. 14:25; Jon. 1:1; Mal. 3:1). The messages of the prophets contain inspired evaluations of Israel's responses to God's revelation of His love, holiness, justice, and hope for all humanity through the promised Messiah. The prophets functioned within the historical shift of nations and spoke to (and beyond) the concerns of their time.

PROPHETIC VOCATION

True biblical prophets were never self-appointed but were considered mouthpieces of God. Their messages at times disrupted, affirmed, challenged, engaged, and even enraged their audiences. The preclassical prophets (e.g., Elijah and Elisha; ca. tenth and ninth centuries B.C.) provide examples of how prophets operated in and outside Israel. In those settings, several terms were used, often interchangeably, to refer to the prophet. The terms *seer* (Heb. *ro'eh*; Is. 30:10) and *visionary* (Heb. *khozeh,* from *khazah* "to see a vision"; Amos 7:12) imply that the prophets received divine insight into their present circumstances that was unknown to others. In 1 Samuel 9:1–10, Samuel the "seer" was expected to know where the lost donkeys had gone. The "man of God" (Heb. *'ish ha'elohim*; Deut. 33:1; 1 Kin. 13:1; 17:18; 2 Kin. 1:9) was God's special servant who proclaimed His will. Similarly, the prophet/prophetess (Heb. *nabi'*; Is. 38:1) was one who was called to proclaim God's message.

A brief profile of the prophets allows readers to see parallel motifs that recur from time to time in the descriptions of their prophetic ministries. The prophetic call of Moses (Ex. 3–4) is paradigmatic for other call narratives. God called persons of varied backgrounds and life experiences (e.g., Amos 7:14). Many times, the prophets include autobiographical information as they respond to the divine call. They respond with anxiety from being overwhelmed by the sheer magnitude of God's presence; at times they protest their inadequacy or reticence for their mission (cf. Isaiah [Is. 6:5], Jeremiah [Jer. 1:6], and Ezekiel [Ezek. 1:28; 3:16; 3:23–27]). This is often followed by the divine reassurance of empowerment and fitness for the task (cf. Is. 6:6–13; Jer. 1:7–10; Ezek. 2:1–3:15). Prophetic calls often come unexpectedly, and the person feels overwhelmed by it and by the magnitude of the task. Ultimately, the prophets realized that the One who called them would also empower them to complete the task.

A variety of life experiences shaped the ministry of biblical prophets. Their background, previous vocation, education, and most importantly, their relationship with God all influenced how their interactions with kings, leaders, and the general populace occurred. Amos informed Amaziah, the officially sanctioned priest serving at Bethel, about his prophetic call and appointment and pointed out that he was not a prophet or the "son of a prophet" (possibly a reference to the school/company of the prophets; cf. 1 Kin. 20:35; 2 Kin. 2:3–4; 4:1, 6:1; Amos 7:14–15). God uses an intriguing story about Hosea's life and marriage to express Israel's unfaithfulness. Micah came from a small town but was soon seen as an authoritative prophet (Jer. 26:18). Isaiah, a member of the royal family, had easy access to kings Ahaz and Hezekiah. Jeremiah and Ezekiel were priests, but apparently they did not minister in the temple in Jerusalem in the typical and expected way. As they received the divine messages, the language and imagery that each prophet used to communicate them were drawn from their familiar surroundings, vocations, and life experiences. Though persons of deep theological conviction, the prophets were subservient to God's directives no matter what.

God often called the prophets to engage in symbolic actions that, in some cases, exposed them to ridicule: Isaiah's required nakedness (Is. 20:2); Hosea's marriage to a harlot (Hos. 1–3); Jeremiah's donning of an ox's yoke (Jer. 27); and Ezekiel's miniature models, haircut, cooking forays, and extended repose (Ezek. 4). Through these means, God was attempting to awaken His people out of their spiritual stupor. As Judah moved closer to the Exile, the critique of the state apparatus (kingship, priesthood, prophets) became bolder and often brought the prophet into conflict with the ruling administration. By the time Ezekiel described Israel's history and crises of leadership, the imagery was extremely graphic, somber, and seemingly hopeless.

The prophets operated in Israel within a covenant relationship between God and the people. The heartbeat of God's covenant relationship with Israel is expressed through variations of the fundamental covenant promise that He would be their God and they His people (Gen. 17:7; Jer. 7:23; 11:4; 30:22; Ezek. 36:28). Springing out of this relationship, God's plan for Israel to be a light to the nations was to teach them to live out His selfless character (Is. 60:1–4). This plan necessitated Israel's restoration from sin in all its forms and a revitalization that would ultimately lead to mission (Ps. 96:1–6). The needs of the community of faith were met by the prophetic guidance of God's Spirit (Num. 24:2; 1 Sam. 10:10; 2 Sam. 23:2). Imbued with His presence as servants of the Lord of history, the prophets continually pointed to God's acts of mercy and grace in Israel's past as well as the instructions He had given to sustain them on their journey of faith.

Within this framework the prophet's role included at least five functions: (1) God's *preachers* of His revealed will in line with the revealed law of Moses (Is. 2:3; 42:21; 51:4; Mic. 4:2; Mal. 4:4); (2) God's *messengers* to summon the people to repentance (Is. 31:6; 44:22; 55:7; Jer. 3:12; 15:19; 18:11; Ezek. 14:6; Hos. 14:2); (3) God's social (covenant) *reformers* pointing to God's desire for justice and righteousness in the covenant community (Is. 1:17; Jer. 7:5–7;

Amos 5:24; Zech. 7:9–10); (4) God's *representatives* to the nations (Is. 42:1; 49:22; Jer. 1:5; Zech. 2:8; 9:10); and (5) God's *announcers* of a judgment and a future hope (Is. 40:31; Jer. 14:7–9; 17:13; Hos. 12:6).

PROPHECY FROM CREATION TO THE MONARCHY

After the Fall, God called for Himself a special people (election) with whom He would have a special relationship (covenant) to make His will known to humanity. This required that His people reflect His holiness within their community and to their neighbors. This special relationship with His people also meant that they were not to take up the "prophetic" (often occult) practices of the nations surrounding them in order to understand the past, present, or future (Deut. 18:9–14). As the Creator of all, God identified Himself as the source of true prophecy (Is. 46:10; cf. 41:22–23; 44:7; 45:21). Thus, eschatology (the study of the end of all things) is intimately connected to protology (the study of the origin of all things; cf. Is. 65:17; 66:22–23). For the prophets, Israel's eschatological hope was grounded in Creation, covenant, and redemption. The very language of the opening book of the Pentateuch, Genesis, suggests that God's plan for His people was embedded in the revelation given to Moses, God's prophet (Deut. 34:10).

First, time played a significant role in biblical prophecy. The phrase *be'akharit hayyamim* ("in the last days" or "in days to come"; Gen. 49:1), used by Jacob concerning the future of Joseph's sons, is a prophetic expression designating the last days or the end of time, the coming of the messianic King, and eschatological salvation (cf. Is. 2:2; Jer. 23:20; 30:24; 48:47; Ezek. 38:16; Dan. 10:14; Hos. 3:5; Mic. 4:1). This phrase has been recognized as a key structural indicator for the entire Pentateuch. It is found in the introduction to messianic poems (Gen. 49:1; Num. 24:14; Deut. 31:29; see "Introduction to the Pentateuch," p. 120). The forward-looking character of the Pentateuch serves as a prophetic eschatological precursor of God's divine design for humanity. Its eschatological structure and ethos would be proclaimed by the prophets in light of God's additional revelation and historical developments.

Second, the major themes of the prophetic messages are already operative in the period under discussion. The storyline seen throughout Genesis (Creation–Fall–judgment–redemption) is paradigmatic for the prophets in light of God's lordship over all creation. The prophet's *messianic hope* stems from the original promise to our ancestors (Gen. 3:15; cf. Dan. 9:25–26). This hope was continually expressed through a promised Seed (Gen. 12:7; 16:11–12; 18:9–10; Gal. 3:16). The notion of *universal judgment* is first found in the Flood narrative (Gen. 4–7; Jer. 25:33; Ezek. 38–39; Zeph. 1:7–18; cf. Matt. 24:37–38; 2 Pet. 2:4–10). The hope of a remnant who were saved from worldwide destruction is found in speeches that request God's providential leading (Ex. 33:13; Judg. 6:17; Acts 7:46). The subsequent *hope of restoration* or re-creation sprang forth from God's renewal of the earth after a worldwide destruction (Gen. 8:21; 9:11). The promise of a *renewed earth* was strongly connected with the renewal of the people's relationship with God (Is. 11:3–5; 35:1–2; 41:18–20; Ezek. 34:25; Hos. 2:16–23). Abraham, Isaac, and Jacob's election contained a promise of *land*

(Gen. 12–24; 50:22–26). This correlation of the gift of land as an inheritance from God played a key role in the prophets' calls to faithfulness (Jer. 3:18–19; Ezek. 47:13–14).

The *covenant* is a bond established by God with human beings that is (1) given by grace; (2) described in explicit promises; and (3) conditioned on the human response of faith, love, and loyalty (Ex. 20:1; Lev. 19:18; Deut. 6:4–6). The basis upon which the prophets give their stinging rebukes stems from Israel's penchant for breaking the bond of love that God established as well as following after their lustful desires and selfish ways. God's judgments against His people were both retributive and restorative and came in the form of covenant curses (Lev. 26:14–39; Deut. 28:15–68). The people of God were initially made up of the direct descendants of Abraham, Isaac, and Jacob (Gen. 49:1–27; Ex. 1:1–4), yet God's plan was always to reach out and include those from all nations who yielded to His lordship (cf. Josh. 2; Ruth 1:15–18; Is. 2:1–5; 19:16–25). The people of God were addressed as people with responsibilities based on their covenant relationship with God (Jer. 2–6; Hos. 1–3; Amos 2:6—3:8). The *nations* (Gen. 10–11; 25:23) are often mentioned, and several of the prophetic books contain a collection of oracles of judgment against them (cf. Is. 13–23; Jer. 46–51; Ezek. 25–32; Amos 1–2), indicating God's concern for them as well as His judgment.

Third, there is the dynamic of the Spirit and prophecy. From the initial promise to Abram to establish a people set apart through whom the promised Messiah would come (Gen. 12:1–7; Gal. 3:16), God's plan was to bring a knowledge of His name to the world through the indwelling of His Spirit in His chosen instruments (prophet, priest, and king) as well as in the construction of the sanctuary, the place where He would make His name and presence known (Ex. 31:1–11). The expression of Israel's status as God's elect, the people among whom He would dwell, was enlarged, enriched, and made more explicit from the time of the patriarchs to Israel's entrance into the land of Canaan (Ex. 25:8, 40). The Spirit of prophecy moved among His people to lead, guide, and correct. We see God's purposes and the Spirit of prophecy working through Abraham (Gen. 20:7), Aaron (Ex. 7:1), Miriam (Ex. 15:1), Eldad and Medad (Num. 11:27–29), Moses (Deut. 34:10), and a future prophet like Moses—Christ (Deut. 18; Acts 3:20–26).

As Israel transitioned into the promised land, God revealed His standards for the prophetic witness. Not only was the fulfillment of a prophecy important but so too was its effect in leading to trust in the Creator, Yahweh, and faithfulness to His lordship (Deut. 13:1–11). The spirit of God would give the needed divine guidance while Israel's dependence was to rest in God's wisdom and not the spiritualistic activities of the nations. As Israel transitioned from a unified tribal group to a monarchy under the Lord's kingship (Judg. 8:23; 13:9), they were to depend on His revealed will found in His Torah (Genesis through Deuteronomy) as well as the prophetic leading of His Spirit.

PROPHECY FROM THE MONARCHY TO THE EXILE

The theology of the historical books (Joshua through 2 Chronicles) reflects God's revealed will for Israel's mission on the international scene and is expressed during the centralization of the Israelite monarchy, the division of the kingdom, and the dissolution of both king-doms. These books contain a prophetic evaluation of Israel's history from the conquest of the promised land to Judah's Exile in Babylon. The endings of both the Pentateuch and the historical books close with hope. The Pentateuch ends as they anticipated entering the land with the expectation of a prophet like Moses. The historical books end with the anticipation of returning to the land with the release of the exiled king, Jehoiachin, as a visible reminder of the Davidic promise. In both instances, a figure of hope sustained Israel as it transitioned from the land to exile and back to the land.

The place of kingship and prophecy appears after Samuel's prophetic ministry during Saul's failed kingship. Nathan, God's spokesman, delivered God's dynastic promises to David (2 Sam. 7), confronted David dramatically with his gross violation of God's covenant (2 Sam. 12), and served in the expanding role of prophets who were involved in the transition of dynastic succession (1 Kin. 1:11–40). According to the author of Chronicles, Nathan also assisted, in tandem with Gad the prophet, in David's arrangements for ritual worship and music (2 Chr. 29:25). Though Nathan served the king, his primary responsibility was to express God's authority through words of encouragement and criticism. This expansion of the prophetic role during the monarchy served as a pattern for the involvement of the classical prophets (ca. eighth through sixth centuries B.C.) in Israel's political, cultic, and social affairs.

The appearance of the classical prophets (all the OT canonical prophets pointed to the Babylonian captivity) was prompted by God's providential dealings with Israel and the broader historical and political events of the ANE. The period of the classical prophets covered more than three centuries (ca. 760–460 B.C.) and underscored two catastrophic events. The first writing canonical prophets appeared about fifty to sixty years before the fall of northern Israel (722 B.C.) and after the conclusion of a century-long entanglement with the Arameans—a conflict whose results can be correlated with the vast societal division between the economically destitute masses and the wealthy few. In a little more than a century, all would experience the ravages of deprivation following the destruction of Jerusalem (586 B.C.). Within this period, three major empires successively dominated the world scene: Assyria, Babylon, and Persia.

Foundational for understanding the context in which the prophets ministered is the centralization of Israel's united monarchy under David. He continued the model of listening to the guidance of the Spirit through the prophetic office that was particularly operative during significant transitions in God's plan for His people: Moses during the establishment of the national sanctuary service, Samuel during Israel's transition to kingship, and then Nathan during the centralization of the temple, ritual worship, and kingship in Jerusalem. Sadly, even with such great promises given to David and the prosperous reign of Solomon, God's plan to work through the united Israelite monarchy was frustrated after the reign of these two kings. In the momentous time of the fracturing of the kingdom, the prophet Ahijah delivered God's message, and subsequent events eventually led to the Exile and dissolution of the Northern Kingdom, which had an impact even up to Jesus's day (1 Kin. 11:29–39; Luke 10:25–37).

From Jeroboam I to Jeroboam II (1 Kin. 12:16—2 Kin. 14:23) references to prophets are restricted to the Northern Kingdom. The events that eventually led to its dissolution and Exile began during the time of the first major nonwriting prophet, Elijah, who ministered in the Northern Kingdom during the Omride dynasty (Omri, Ahab, Ahaziah, Jehoram; 1 Kin. 15:21—2 Kin. 10:17). During this period, Israel devolved into state-sponsored idol worship (1 Kin. 18). The authoritative prophetic revelation was often introduced by the phrase, "The word of the Lord came to…," indicating God's direct revelation expressed in the prophetic proclamation (1 Kin. 17:2).

Another well-known nonwriting prophet, Elisha, ministered with Elijah and then further into Jehu's dynasty. This prophetic period of Israel's history focused on the polemic of the Lord's superiority over Baal. Elijah and Elisha's personal miracle experiences emphasized God's care for His people (1 Kin. 17:1–7, 8–16; 2 Kin. 4:1–7, 38–44), His control over nature and fertility (2 Kin. 4:8–17), His healing power (2 Kin. 5), and His power over death (1 Kin. 17:17–24; 2 Kin. 4:18–37). Shortly after the death of Elisha, the first writing prophet appears in the historical books. The prophet Jonah continued to minister to the Northern Kingdom (1 Kin. 14:23–29) during a time of prosperity for Israel. Jeroboam II (ca. 786–746 B.C.) success-fully reestablished the northern borders as they were in the days of David's rule and fulfilled a prophecy of Jonah at a time of great economic and agricultural prosperity (2 Kin. 14:25, 28).

Material prosperity and enlarged borders did not translate into a more profound faith. As Israel's fortunes rose, her moral core continued to crumble (e.g., the apostasy amid prosperity described in the books of Hosea and Amos). Israel's territorial expansion and agricultural production attracted the attention of the surrounding nations. Israel's prosperity should have been used as an opportunity to glorify God before the nations, but selfishness and unconverted hearts misused power and exploited the weak and vulnerable. Even in light of God's previous prophetic warnings (2 Kin. 10:30; 15:12), the kings of Israel did not repent. Instead they sank further into rebellion and murder, and worst of all, they turned away from God's providential wisdom to make covenants with foreign nations to protect them or to establish unauthorized coalitions to reduce the threat of external aggression (2 Kin. 15:8—17:6). The prophets warned Israel and Judah to turn from their wickedness back to God's principles in the Torah (2 Kin. 17:12–13).

Classical prophecy arose and reached its pinnacle during the rise and fall of world empires. Daniel prophesied of world empires up to the coming of Christ (Dan. 2; 7–12). The age in which these great empires rose bears witness to the providence and foreknowl-edge of God declared through the prophets. The prophets foretold of the rise and fall of each nation up to the period of Israel's restoration to the land and interpreted world-sig-nificant events in the light of God's continued preparation for the advent of the Messiah. As the Lord of history, He is the director of the theater of world history. His changing cast included renowned historical figures: Sargon, Sennacherib, Nebuchadnezzar, and Cyrus. However, His attention was constantly focused on Israel. In Scripture, figures find their importance only insofar as God sought to reveal Himself to them and through them to others even as agents of judgment for and against His people.

In addition to calling for surrender to God's redemptive purposes and lordship, the prophets supplied answers to the why of destruction and the how of future restoration, and they offered future generations the hope of One to come who would restore all that had been broken and would rule in justice and righteousness. A common notion in the ANE was that the defeat of a nation meant the defeat of its deity. However, classical prophecy teaches that Israel's defeats did not show the Lord's weakness but His strength, wisdom, and especially His foreknowledge. The play and interplay of God's predictive pronouncements, Israel's response, and world affairs are revealed through the prophets.

One of the initial examples of a long-range prophecy is the one made by a "man of God" from Judah to King Jeroboam I concerning the work of reformation that King Josiah would undertake. A special sign was given to confirm the accuracy and authenticity of the prophetic word (1 Kin. 13:1–3; 2 Kin. 23:15–20). God's sovereignty, foreknowledge, and providential acts directed affairs toward the fulfillment of this prophecy. From sustaining young Josiah on the throne with godly aides (2 Kin. 22:1–2), to the discovery of a scroll containing the Torah by the high priest Hilkiah (2 Kin. 22:8–13), to the prophetic guidance of the prophetess Huldah (2 Kin. 22:14–20), which led to the reforms that included the breaking down of the altar at Bethel (2 Kin. 23:1–25), God was fulfilling His prophetic word (see 2 Samuel: Introduction). God also continued working on the international scene. The death of Assyrian King Ashurbanipal (627 B.C.) and the ensuing civil war and general strife in Assyria provided a respite from Assyrian hegemony over and aggression against Israel. Several of Assyria's vassal states openly asserted their independence—Judah under King Josiah, Babylon under its new Chaldean dynasty, as well as the Medes.

PROPHETIC LITERARY FEATURES

Three major characteristics of prophetic poetry and narrative emerge from Scripture. They include the use of different types of literature, literary styles, and structure. These are important features insofar as they express the dynamism and beauty of God's message and serve to control speculative and fanciful interpretations.

Types of Literature

Distinct literary categories express a mode of communication that can generate an emotion, a set of expectations, and a general context for hearing the message. Among them we find laments (i.e., funeral dirges; Amos 5:1), oaths (Is. 5:9; 14:24), lawsuits (i.e., legal controversy; Is. 3:13–15; Mic. 6:1–16), salvation and judgment speeches or oracles (Mic. 3:9–12), and hymns of praise (Is. 12). Prophetic oracles largely occur in two major types: (1) salvation oracles, which are pronouncements of the Lord's intent and power to save, redeem, and restore His people or, in some cases, the nations (Is. 41:8–16), and (2) judgment oracles, which are pronouncements of the Lord's judgment against the people of God or other nations on account of their sin and rebellion (against God's people: Is. 2:6–4:1; 28:14–18; Jer. 2–10; against the nations: Is. 13–23; Jer. 46–51; Ezek. 25–32; Amos 1–2; see "God's Judgment in the Prophets," p. 981).

Other genre types include messenger speeches and vision reports. Messenger speeches are oral messages delivered by a messenger in which the words uttered by God are proclaimed by the prophet to the recipients. The prophet serves as the Lord's messenger relaying authentic messages sent from God to Israel (Is. 6:9; 43:1). Springing out of the messenger speeches are messenger formulas, standard expressions that introduce or conclude sayings, such as oracles, identifying them as words of the Lord for various purposes, such as evoking God's authority or certainty for what is said. These include the *'amar* formulas, which refer to what the Lord says (e.g., Is. 49:5); the *ne'um* formulas, which refer to the proclamation of the Lord (e.g., Ezek. 5:11); and the *dibber* formulas, which refer to the word that the Lord had spoken (e.g., Joel 3:8). Vision reports are autobiographical accounts of a prophet's revelatory experience received by seeing objects or events, often involving images that require explanations (Is. 1:1; Jer. 1:11–19; 24:1–10; Amos 7:1–8:3; Zech. 1–6).

Literary Styles

The literary style is expressed in prophetic narratives and prophetic poetry. Prophetic narratives are engaging and dramatic portrayals of the prophet's interaction with God, God's people, or the nations. They typically offer background information to prophetic oracles and reports. Time applications of prophecies typically can be broken up into three states: present, future, and distant future. The time of the application of prophecies that occur during the prophet's lifetime or shortly after that are usually found in the descriptions of the prophet's mission (call narratives: Is. 6:1–8; Jer. 1; Ezek. 1:1—3:27; prophetic encounters: Is. 39:1–8; Jer. 28; Amos 7:11–17; Jon. 2–4; or phrases that accentuate the nearness of God's action: Is. 38:5; Hab. 1:6). The time of the application of prophecies that were to occur in the people's future regarding the nearness of the Exile or the return to the land is marked by temporal expressions referring to the day, days, or time when the prophecies would be fulfilled. The last and more distant eschatological future tended to focus on the messianic reign over the nations or the distant future (Is. 24–27; Zech. 7–12).

Prophetic poetry is similar in structure, imagery, and meter and rhythm to poetry found in other parts of the Bible (including the Psalms). Its most significant characteristic involves parallelism (see "Introduction to Hebrew Poetry and Wisdom Books," p. 614).

Literary Structure

Literary structure is the most significant guide to discover the main point of any passage. This requires careful attention to a larger section defined by patterns and parallelism. This necessitates that the reader pays close attention to the text to understand how its content is organized.

Almost every biblical book in the OT exhibits chiastic structures (i.e., a concentric structure patterned ABCB'A', with C being the central thought) or parallel symmetric patterns (ABCA'B'C'). Many of these are identified and discussed in the relevant commentaries.

FACING FALSE PROPHETS

In the prophetic books, it is as crucial to receive the divinely inspired message as it is to recognize the toxic and devastating effect of false prophets. God's prophets were chosen to proclaim His word faithfully. Sometimes that meant words of comfort and sometimes words of rebuke. Unfortunately, Judah's fascination with false prophets is well documented in the Hebrew Bible (cf. Jer. 6:13–14; 8:11; 14:13–14; 23:17; Ezek. 13:10–16; Mic. 2:6–11; 3:5, 11). While most of the Minor Prophets rebuke false leaders and prophets (see especially Amos 7:10–17; see also the story of Micaiah in 1 Kin. 22 as an illustration of the conflict between true and false prophets), the Major Prophets of Isaiah, Jeremiah, and Ezekiel give a sustained refutation of this practice and its practitioners.

In Isaiah, God's rebuke was more generalized and applicable to nations beyond Israel's borders. It dealt with the problems of (1) *the source of knowledge of the future* (i.e., occultism; Is. 8:19; 19:3); (2) *equating creation with the Creator* (Is. 40:18–31; 41:21–29; 44:6–8); and (3) *unbelief in God's clear message* (Is. 6:9–8:22). During Jeremiah's ministry God was very specific about false prophecy and warned against its deceptive and inauthentic nature (Jer. 29:8–9). Judah's last kings rebelled against God's counsel and accepted messages from false prophets, such as Hananiah (Jer. 28:1–17) and Shemaiah (Jer. 29:24–32), that encouraged them to think that geopolitics was the answer to their problems. The influence of these false prophets and their messages was so pervasive, both in Judah and among the exiles in Babylon, that Jeremiah sent a letter to Babylon containing God's condemnation of the false prophets in the exiled community in Babylon (Jer. 29:1–23).

In Ezekiel, the words that characterize these false prophets' visionary experiences (Ezek. 13:1–16; Heb. *shaw'*, "false"; *qesem*, "divination"; *kazab*, "lie") describe the type of messages that come from private and, in this case, pernicious interpretations of events (Heb. *millibbam*, "from their own heart/imagination," Ezek. 13:2; cf. 2 Pet. 1:20–21). Having an understanding of the times (1 Chr. 12:32) is crucial to know how God is leading in order to encourage the faithful. Yet two different reactions emerged against a faithful prophet's messages: (1) he was seen as a doomsayer and alarmist—some people were saying that Ezekiel's words would come to nothing since nothing had happened yet (Ezek. 12:22; cf. 2 Pet. 3:3–4); and (2) people intimated that prophecy was irrelevant for them since they claimed that his messages were only for the far distant future and not for them (Ezek. 12:27). This second class of naysayers does not doubt biblical prophecy is real but rather decides that its fulfillment is so far away that it is of little consequence to their immediate lives. However, God vindicated His prophets, and the historical fulfillment of their predictions demonstrated their veracity. At times God gave, through His prophets, short-term prophecies that were soon fulfilled in order to demonstrate who was speaking for Him (Jer. 28:15–17).

READING THE PROPHETS CHRONOLOGICALLY

Reading the prophets in their *chronological* sequence helps to focus on three notable historical eras that highlight Israel's relation to the nations.

Preexilic Prophets—Main Goals of Their Message

The first historical era during which the classical prophets functioned was the Neo-Assyrian (745–612 B.C.). During this period there were strong calls to repentance with the threat and promise of exile as a restorative measure. The prophets who ministered during this period include Hosea, Amos, Isaiah, Jonah, Micah, Nahum, Habakkuk, Zephaniah, and probably Joel.

The prophets addressed their message to their contemporary situation. In Israel Amos ministered during the time of Jeroboam II before the rise of Tiglath-Pileser III and the Neo-Assyrian Empire (745 B.C.). His warnings foretold the eventual Exile and destruction of Israel without specifying that it would be Assyria who would be God's agent of judgment. Hosea, a contemporary, also ministered to Israel and foresaw its destruction. His book shows an awareness of both pro-Egyptian and pro-Assyrian factions (Amos 7:11). Turning to Judah, Isaiah's call came at the time of the crowning of Assyrian dominance. Isaiah called Assyria the rod of God's anger (Is. 10:5) and preached his message in the context of the choice between the Lord's help and Assyria's (Is. 7:1–9). Isaiah filled out more of the prophetic picture by describing the fall of Assyria as well as the nations who would follow it: Babylon and Persia (Is. 13; 36–39; 45). Isaiah's contemporary Micah also pointed to the Assyrian menace and addressed the lethargic spiritual atmosphere stemming from Uzziah's material gains in Judah. Nahum prophesied the eventual fall of Assyria. Contemporaries Zephaniah and Habakkuk both ministered after the fall of the Northern Kingdom, during the reign of King Josiah (640–609 B.C.), when Hilkiah found the book of the law (622 B.C.), and the rise of Babylon up to the fall of Assyria (626–612 B.C.).

Exilic Prophets—Main Goals of Their Message

The second historical era involved the period of the Neo-Babylonian Empire (606–539 B.C.). The primary prophetic emphasis during this period was the calls to accept God's plan and the threat of destruction and exile. The prophets Jeremiah, Ezekiel, Daniel, and Obadiah ministered to God's people with these messages in Judah and Babylon. Jeremiah received his call to ministry in the year the Assyrian king Ashurbanipal died (ca. 627/626 B.C.), and he confirmed what Isaiah had prophesied, equating the enemy described as a nation from the north with Babylon. While Jeremiah does not specifically mention Persia as the successor to Babylon, he portrays the eventual defeat of Babylon and affirms the word of Isaiah as he utilizes his earlier image of a nation from the north. Jeremiah's call to accept the Exile was intended to be encouraging as he prophesied that it would last only a short time of seventy years, after which the people would be brought back to Jerusalem (Jer. 29:10). The majority of the leaders of God's people failed to heed Jeremiah's word. Ezekiel ministered during the reign of Nebuchadnezzar, and he too announced the fall of Babylon. Jeremiah and Ezekiel bore witness to the fall of Judah and, along with Daniel and Obadiah, are the last voices to the people of God before the first exiles returned to Jerusalem in 538 B.C.

Postexilic Prophets—Main Goals of Their Message

The third historical era within which the biblical prophets proclaimed God's message of hope was the Persian period (539–331 B.C.), at the beginning of which the people of God returned from exile. During this time there were prophetic calls to reestablish God's temple and His Torah as well as the announcement of the coming Davidic kingship. The prophets who guided the people of God in this time of high expectations included Haggai, Zechariah, and Malachi. Almost two centuries before, Isaiah had prophesied that it would be Cyrus, king of Persia, the Lord's anointed, who would help restore the people back to the land (Ezra 1:1–4; Is. 44:28; 45:1).

COMMON THEMES AND PERSPECTIVES

The prophetic books are marked by a unity that brings to light a number of shared themes and perspectives. For example, Isaiah through Malachi shine a light on the various nuances of the theme of the Day of the Lord in its positive and negative contexts (Is. 13:6, 9; Jer. 46:10; Ezek. 13:5; 30:3; Joel 1:15; 2:1, 11, 31; 3:14; Amos 5:18–20; Obad. 15; Zeph. 1:7, 14; Mal. 4:5). The Major Prophets (Isaiah, Jeremiah, Ezekiel) and the twelve called Minor Prophets (Hosea-Malachi) all express a theological concept pointing to a time of great hope. The key themes that connect the message of the prophets include (1) the Day of the Lord, (2) the destiny of the wicked, (3) the hope of the remnant, (4) God's control over the succession of the nations (from Assyria to Babylon to Persia), and (5) the promise of the hoped-for Davidic King.

A structural reading emphasizes the cohesive nature of revelation, salvation, and hope in the prophets from which NT writers drew. Hearing the prophets together makes God's comprehensive message of hope ever relevant, for it exposes an aspect of God's grace that is typically overlooked. The God of the OT is often thought of as vengeful and full of wrath. On the contrary, His love, grace, pity, and mercy are clearly visible in all three major categories of the OT (Law, Prophets, and Psalms). He desired the restoration of land and people and the reestablishment of the faithful Davidic kingship, which would help to set things right through His restored rule over the nations. This was the hope of Israel into which Jesus was born; this was the hope that was more fully expressed in cosmic terms in the apocalyptic visions of Daniel and Revelation.

Finally, tracing God's prophetic word to His people *historically and geographically* is a fruitful method of hearing the message of the prophets. Comparing the prophetic books' descriptions of what was happening in the Northern Kingdom (Israel) and the Southern Kingdom (Judah) allows us to see the interplay of prophecy and history, and the information in the books of the Kings helps us in that task. All but three of these prophetic books indicate the king who was reigning at the time. Of the prophets who ministered to Israel, Jonah was from the north while Amos and Hosea were from the south, and though they were from divided kingdoms, their messages were similar and displayed conceptual unity (Jer. 30:3; 33:14–16; 50:4; Ezek. 37:15–28). These prophets wrote from the time of Jeroboam II to the destruction of Israel, which was exiled to Assyria in 722 B.C. (2 Kin. 14:23—17:41; Hos. 1:1; Jon. 1:1), and detailed the conditions that led up to Israel's demise (2 Kin. 17:6–23). Special mention is even made of the prophetic ministry to God's people in the Northern Kingdom, offering a direct connection between history and prophecy (2 Kin. 17:13).

The prophets who ministered to Judah (Joel, Isaiah, Micah, Zephaniah, Habakkuk, Jeremiah) wrote from the days of Jotham to Judah's Exile in Babylon, including also a special note on the release of Jehoiachin, king of Judah, from prison (Jer. 52:31–34; Mic. 1:1). As a collective group, their emphasis focused more toward the nations, mainly because of Judah's dependence on the nations rather than on the Lord. Two books address nations other than Judah: Obadiah was a messenger of the Lord to Edom (Obad. 1), and Nahum wrote concerning Nineveh (Nah. 1:1). Both books gave hope and comfort to Judah that her enemies and, in fact, all of God's enemies would be judged (Obad. 10; Nah. 2:2). The prophets who ministered to God's people in the Babylonian Exile—namely, Ezekiel and Daniel—use imagery and descriptions familiar to their exilic overlords, presumably as a way to minister to them as well as to God's people.

The postexilic prophets Haggai, Zechariah, and Malachi paint a clear picture that because of the response of the people and the nations to God's sovereignty, many of the beautiful pictures of restoration for Israel and the nations were not going to be fulfilled in their lifetime or in the way they expected. Hope still reigned as Malachi closed out the prophetic voice with a beautiful picture of renewal (Moses and Elijah) until John the Baptist would reignite that prophetic hope.

CONDITIONALITY OF PROPHECY

Although God's final intention for humans is salvific, He respects human freedom, and consequently many of the prophecies found in the OT contain an element of conditionality. While the faithful have always constituted the true people of God, within the larger body of professed believers the call to faithfulness was always tied to God's blessings or curses (Deut. 27–28). In biblical prophecy, there are two types of God's communicative activity in relation to the more immediate and the distant future: classical and apocalyptic prophecy. In their own way, these types of prophecy reveal important characteristics that help the reader recognize them and establish their differences.

Classical prophecies are generally (1) local in space and time, referring to Israel's contemporary situation during the monarchy, Exile, and return to the land; (2) eschatologically focused on Israel's national, geopolitical, and ethnic framework; and (3) connected, in most cases, to the covenant response of the people. Classical prophecy expresses three major categories of prediction: (1) messianic prophecies, (2) oracles for/against the nations, and (3) covenant-centered kingdom prophecies. The messianic predictions were unconditional in the sense that the Messiah would come because God determined from the beginning that the hope of humankind rested upon the coming of the Seed of the woman to defeat the enemy of righteousness (Gen. 3:15; Deut. 18:15, 18; Pss. 2; 110; Is. 53). The other two categories of prediction are primarily conditional because their specific fulfillment required a human response to the Lord's threats and promises (typically seen in calls to repent; Is. 44:22; Jer. 3:12, 14, 22; 18:11; Ezek. 18:30; Hos. 14:2). In the case of Israel, most of the promises and judgments were determined by their commitment to or lack of covenant faithfulness. The specific fulfillment was determined by the human response. In such cases God announced the judgment in terms of covenant curses while calling the people to repent, return to Him, and renew their covenant commitment. Prophecies against the nations were in some cases conditional on their response to the Lord (see Jonah), but in other cases they were unconditional. God in His sovereignty and foreknowledge announced the final collapse of nations and the rise of others. These nations fall in order for God to fulfill His plan for the human race.

Comparing classical and apocalyptic prophecy, one typical distinction between them is that the apocalyptic prophecies of Daniel and the apocalyptic sections found in Isaiah 24–27, Ezekiel 38–39, Joel 2–3, and Zechariah 9–14 reflect God's plan for humanity, but they are not contingent on human response; that is to say, they are not conditional. In these prophecies, God's word is decisive.

Nevertheless, the relationship between classical and apocalyptic prophecy reflects the same goal: God's redemptive purposes and the vindication of His justice and righteousness. Briefly, taking Isaiah as a case study, while the features among the local-immediate/historical judgment of the nations (Is. 13–23; 28–33) and the universal-eschatological judgment of the world (Is. 24–27) differ in their relationship to their temporary fulfillment, they both express how the principles of God's kingdom cohesively operate, whether referring to the immediate circumstances of the biblical text or to the future eschatological hope of the people of God. The justice of God works to right the wrongs of sin in its personal, public, and cosmic dimensions. The relationship between Isaiah 13–23 and 24–27 is akin to the relationship between Isaiah 44:24—45:4 and Daniel 2:39; 7:5; 8:3, 20. Isaiah's proclamation of hope was set within the context of Israel's return from exile as God worked through Cyrus. Daniel's proclamations were in the context of God's sovereignty and foreknowledge over history that pointed to the end of earth's history as we know it when Jesus comes for the second time. The fulfillment of these two texts, the former understood as classical and the latter as apocalyptic, is seen in Ezra 1:1–2.

The plan for God's people during the time of the classical prophets is seen in the kingdom prophecies. The promise of the land given to Abraham and the promise of the perpetuity of the kingdom of David are fundamentally nonconditional. They were part of God's eternal covenant with His people. Yet it is paradoxical that their fulfillment was related to the faithfulness of the people to God. However, their unfaithfulness did not bring to an end God's faithfulness to His promises. God always remained faithful to all of His promises (see Josh. 21:41; Rom. 3:1–4). He had determined to fulfill them through a faithful remnant within Israel and, more specifically, through His future faithful King, the Messiah. It is in and through Christ as the Messiah that the kingdom prophecies will now be fulfilled in a powerful and magnificent way (Dan. 7:13–14, 27; Matt. 28:18). In the NT this future hope is clearly spelled out as transcending geographical and ethnic limitations and finds in the book of Revelation its ultimate proclamation in cosmic dimensions. God was always able to preserve a faithful remnant who became the carriers of all of His election promises—promises that will be fulfilled through His Anointed One.

ISAIAH

INTRODUCTION

Title and Authorship. As far we know, Isaiah 1:1 served as a title for the original scroll of Isaiah. Some Bible translators translate it as "the book of Isaiah" or "Isaiah" for practical purposes. The author of Chronicles refers to it as the "vision" of Isaiah the prophet, who was the son of Amoz (2 Chr. 32:32). Each component in Isaiah 1:1 is found among other superscriptions of prophetic books. As a whole, however, it has a vital distinctiveness, implying that it is not a late addition to the book, as believed by some, but part of several features that make the book of Isaiah a literary whole.

The superscription in Isaiah 1:1 gives the identity of the seer (Isaiah, son of Amoz), the mode of revelation (vision), the main topic of the book (Judah and Jerusalem), and the approximate time in which the revelations were received (during the reigns of Uzziah, Jotham, Ahaz, and Hezekiah, kings of Judah). Isaiah's name (*yesha'yahu*), whose form is attested on ancient seals, means "the Lord's salvation," "the Lord is [my] salvation," or even "the Lord has given salvation" (cf. 12:2–3; 49:26; 60:16). The meaning of the name confirms the central message of the book.

Isaiah, the son of Amoz of Jerusalem, received the book's foundational divine revelations (1:1; 2:1; 7:3; 13:1; 20:2–3; 37:2, 6–7; 38:1; 39:3). His father, Amoz, is otherwise unknown. The book assigns no occupation or official function to Isaiah except for the epithet "the prophet" in chapters 37–39. The Lord referred to Isaiah as His "servant" or "messenger" (20:3). His wife was a "prophetess" (see 8:3). They had at least two sons, Shear-Jashub (7:3) and Maher-Shalal-Hash-Baz (8:3). Their names have symbolic meanings, "a remnant shall return" and "speed the spoil, hasten the plunder," relating to both salvation and judgment. Isaiah's own name may have a similar symbolic function.

An OT prophetic book is normally the fruit of a process of revelation, memorization, oral or literary communication (i.e., speech or public reading), and preservation. Five steps may be implied in the process that has given us the book of Isaiah: (1) God's message was *made known* to Isaiah (e.g., 6:1–13; 7:3; 8:1, 5, 11). God was the Author-Originator, and Isaiah the recipient. (2) As *author-mediator*, Isaiah expressed divine insight in a language known to the intended audience; God was speaking through the inspired prophet, whether in explicit quotations or in implied paraphrases (e.g., 7:10–17). (3) In a *dialogue* between God and the prophet, God's words are distinguished from the prophet's words (e.g., 6:1–13). but both were recorded by the prophet-narrator; (4) *Borrowed* material was previously written by other authors but *selected* by the prophet (e.g., 36:1–22; 37:8–14; 38:9–20). (5) Prophetic messages were *delivered orally*—either by speech or by being read aloud in a public or private setting. *Written* prophecy preserved the message, and Isaiah made a point to preserve predictions that would be fulfilled in a distant future, which compelled the audience to *wait* and *see* the fulfillment in real events (e.g., 29:11–12, 18; 30:8–11; 34:16). Isaiah undoubtedly wrote some prophecies himself (8:1–2; 30:8–11), but he may have used scribal assistance, which was the usual way of producing books (cf. Jer. 36:1–4).

Isaiah subordinated himself to the will and power of the Lord. Dwelling on himself was not part of his mission. However, some information on his social role in the environment of Jerusalem may be inferred from the book:

1. Family Head. Isaiah's family had a "prophetic" function. He and his wife were prophets, and both Isaiah's name and the names of his sons communicated prophetic messages (Is. 7:3; 8:1–4). In keeping with common practice, he passed on prophetic wisdom and scribal skills to his sons (cf. 38:19b). A part of this was commonly accomplished by reading and learning to write (copy) Scripture.

2. *Counselor.* As a prophet, Isaiah belonged to the circle of royal counselors. The wisdom and counsel of the Lord is occasionally contrasted with that of His human opponents (e.g., 3:2–3; 8:9–10; 14:24–27; 19:1–4). In fact, the Lord announces that the wisdom of those who consider themselves wise will come to an end (29:14). The prophet opposed the wise because his counsel was based on prophetic revelations from the Lord and differed from the empirical observations of the wise (cf. 5:19). What Isaiah said required faith and trust in the Lord, not human and political schemes. His concern was not to eliminate the wisdom-oriented theology itself but to remind the wise of God's standards for their work.

3. *Teacher.* Isaiah brought the Lord's instruction to His people in Israel and Judah. Following the Assyrian destruction of Israel (733 and 722 B.C.) and Judah (701 B.C.), the temple was the only remaining institution of religious teaching with legitimacy and credibility. Priests and prophets were particularly linked to the temple (Lam. 2:20), and teaching and counseling were their main functions (Deut. 33:10; cf. Jer. 18:18; Ezek. 7:26; 44:23; Hos. 4:6; Mic. 3:11). God had Isaiah use the Torah for instruction concerning the sacrifices in the temple (Is. 1:10–17). His emphasis on the revealed prophetic word as "instruction" (*torah*) from the Lord implies a teacher's typical concern with what students hear (cf. 50:4). Isaiah had interactions with priests (8:2; 37:1–4), discussing priesthood (61:6; 66:21) and the temple (6:1; 44:28), and some have even suggested that he may have been a priest like Jeremiah (1:1) and Ezekiel (1:3) though there is not enough evidence to know this with any degree of certainty.

4. *The Mouthpiece and Servant of the Lord.* The book indicates that there were "prophets" (*nebi'im*) in Jerusalem and Judah (3:1–2; 29:1, 10; 30:10). However, only Isaiah bears the title "prophet" (*nabi'*) in the narrative section of chapters 36–39, a section which is almost the same as 2 Kings 18:13—19:37. He never calls himself "prophet." The book gives the impression that his ministry was not determined by a prophetic office but by what the Lord had said to him: it was *the word of God* that mattered.

5. *Scribe.* Books had become common in Isaiah's time. They were read by scribes or by persons with scribal education. A mass audience such as the children of Israel would have heard the word being read. Thus, Isaiah knew that the words of his book would be heard and seen (Is. 29:18). He was an educated person who had the ability to write and edit his book, but scribal assistance is not to be ruled out. His book is fundamentally a record of the words of the Lord waiting for future fulfillment, which makes it dependent on the future work of the Lord, who in His time would confirm His counsel or plan as revealed to Isaiah. In this book, the writer's identity is not the most important thing; what matters is the word of the Lord.

Date. His commission in "the year that King Uzziah died" (6:1) occurred sometime in 740 B.C. King Ahaz ruled (735–716 B.C.) during the Syro-Ephraimite crisis, when Isaiah had revelations from the Lord and functioned as a prophetic counselor (7:1–17). At the time that he was commissioned, he may have been a very young man, like Samuel and Jeremiah (1 Sam. 3; Jer. 1:6–7).

Isaiah likely survived Hezekiah and continued his ministry in the days of Manasseh, who was king from 697 to 643 B.C. (2 Kin. 21:1). It is not known how far into Manasseh's reign Isaiah continued his ministry. A tradition attested in the apocryphal book of the Martyrdom of Isaiah claims that Isaiah was killed by Manasseh, who opposed his prophetic ministry. Ellen White accepted this tradition, which is possibly reflected in Hebrews 11:37 (see ST, Feb. 17, 1898). Scattered signs in the book make it plausible that Isaiah continued his ministry up to the first half of Manasseh's reign.

Following the practice of OT prophetic books, Isaiah did not date all of his prophecies. Establishing the dates, therefore, depends on the literary unity and historical setting of the book and on the relationship between prophetic predictions and historical fulfillments. The view taken in this commentary is summarized as follows:

1. *No Indications of Different Authors.* Recent studies have shown that chapters 40–66 never existed independently of chapters 1–39 and that the book has a remarkable internal unity.

2. *The Editor and the Author Are One.* The book of Isaiah is a planned composition. The thought in the small units corresponds with that of the larger blocks of material, suggesting that the prophet handled the overall editing of the text.

3. *Use of the Name Isaiah.* "Isaiah" is used only sixteen times, in three superscriptions (1:1; 2:1; 13:1) and in three third person narratives (7:3; twice in 20:2–3; ten times in chaps. 37–39). In comparison, the name "Jeremiah" occurs 131 times in his own book. The existing name references provide a central role in the book to the person of Isaiah. Thus, being mentioned in 1:1,

he speaks in 1:2–31 without any other introduction. The text merely implies that the prophetic voice is his. This technique is consistent in the book. Governed by v. 1, the other references to his name mark Isaiah as the *implied* speaker in the following sections: 2:1 marks Isaiah as the prophetic speaker in 2:2—6:13; 7:3 in 7:1—12:6; 13:1 in 13:2—27:13; 20:1–6 in 20:1—35:10; and 36:1—39:8 in 40:1—66:24. This feature suggests that the book we have today was written for people who knew Isaiah as prophet and author, with the Lord as the primary speaker (cf. 40:8; 55:10-11). The use of his name indicates that Isaiah was the recipient of a divine communication addressed to a particular initial audience. Only the seer of the vision was personally involved in shaping the text. Only Isaiah son of Amoz had the authority, knowledge, and skills to produce the final form of the text.

4. *The Book's View of Itself.* The book of Isaiah claims to be a reliable witness to the Lord's salvation of Zion and Israel, an idea which strengthens the conviction that the Lord's promises can be trusted. It is therefore our conviction that Isaiah—who had "seen" the things of the Lord—committed his vision to writing.

5. *Final Product in Manasseh's Reign.* During Isaiah's ministry, and increasingly toward the end of his life, the destiny of God's people became a burning issue. Assyria's grip on Jerusalem tightened, and the persecution of the prophets and the gross apostasy under Manasseh's reign confirmed that Israel's judgment would continue (cf. 1:2–31). The faithful remnant needed hope to find the strength to wait on the Lord. This is a plausible setting for the consolation and messages of restoration in the second part of the book of Isaiah (chaps. 40–66). Hypothetically, the final form of the book may be assigned to the first half of Manasseh's reign.

Backgrounds. Isaiah's commission as prophet coincided with Assyria's rise to sovereignty over the ANE. The reign of Tiglath-Pileser III (745–727 B.C.) began a century of the greatest expansion of the Assyrian Empire. It brought disorder and upheavals through fear and hopelessness, it brought the destruction of nations and peoples, and it forced the mixing of peoples and their cultural practices. The resultant religious syncretism and lack of faith in the God of their ancestors was especially problematic for Israel and Judah (cf. 2 Kin. 17:24–41). Isaiah addressed these threats, teaching faith in the Lord by revealing His plan for Israel, His elected people, and for Zion-Jerusalem, His elect city.

The word of the Lord to Isaiah regarding Assyria was complex. Assyria was to be God's instrument for punishing Israel and Judah for their unfaithfulness to Him. But Assyria was also made the object of God's punishment in order to maintain His sovereignty and to deliver His people from oppression.

1. *The Role of Babylon.* In the time of Tiglath-Pileser III (745–727 B.C.), Babylon was the religious and cultural center of Mesopotamia. It was the source and center of civilization and a religious shrine of the highest sanctity. Assyria therefore needed Babylon's prestige to keep its power over its conquered kingdoms. Tiglath-Pileser, therefore, created in 729 B.C. a close bond between Assyria and Babylon. He captured the king of Babylon, gave himself the title "king of Babylon," and turned Assyria into a dual monarchy. Babylon constantly sought to gain the upper hand in the empire and finally succeeded when Nabopolassar (Nebuchadnezzar's father) conquered Nineveh with the aid of the Medes in 612 B.C. Consequently, Isaiah referred to the Assyrian power not only as "Ashur" but also as "Babylon" and to the "king of Ashur" as the "king of Babylon" (cf. e.g., Is. 14:4, 22–23, 24–27). Thus, not all of Isaiah's sayings concerning Babylon refer to the Babylon of the Judaean Exile in the sixth century B.C.

2. *The Syro-Ephraimite War (734–732 B.C.) and Judah's Assyrian Vassalage.* The initial incident that brought Isaiah into confrontation with Assyria was the Syro-Ephraimite war. A coalition of vassal states including Syria and the Northern Kingdom of Israel coerced Jotham's son Ahaz (ca. 735–716 B.C.) to join them against Assyria. Although Ahaz did not join the coalition, he failed to heed Isaiah's warnings (7:10–13) and instead sought help from Assyria (2 Kin. 16:7–9). In 733 B.C. the Assyrian king annexed Galilee and the area east of the Jordan, establishing these regions as the Assyrian provinces of Megiddo and Gilead. The Northern Kingdom of Israel was restricted to the remnant state of Ephraim. In keeping with Assyrian practice, the urban upper classes were deported to Assyria.

3. *The Destruction of Israel in 722 B.C.* When King Hoshea of Israel renounced his allegiance to Assyria while conspiring with Egypt (2 Kin. 17:3–4), Shalmaneser V (727–722 B.C.) took immediate action and besieged Samaria. Shortly before his death and the reign of Sargon II (722–705 B.C.), Samaria succumbed and Israel was made into the Assyrian province of Samerina (722 B.C.). The first major consequence was the deportation of the people of Israel from the

promised land (2 Kings 17:6). The land was lost, and the "seed of Abraham" was scattered far and wide. Another consequence was that, following the Assyrian practice, non-Israelites were brought into the land of Israel from Babylonia and Syria, which led to widespread idolatry and foreign cult practices in the promised land (2 Kin. 17:24–41). A third consequence was that numerous refugees from the north took refuge in Jerusalem. As Isaiah therefore addressed the inhabitants of Judah and Jerusalem, he also included references to the Northern Kingdom (Is. 8:14; 28:1–29; "Ephraim" was the appellation for Israel as a whole) and to the remnant of Israel and those of the house of Jacob who had escaped (8:14; 10:20–22; 28:1–29; 46:3).

4. Sargon II (722–705 B.C.) Proclaimed King of Babylon. The Chaldean Merodach/Marduk-Baladan (known outside the Bible as Marduk-apla-iddina II) secured a formal alliance with the kings of Susa and Anshan and seized the kingship in Babylon in 721 B.C., which he kept for about ten years. The military support of Elam (i.e., Anshan and Susa) held the Assyrians back for a decade, and the dual monarchy was suspended. Sargon later came against Babylon and deposed Merodach-Baladan. Like his predecessors, Sargon held the kingship of Babylon in 709–705 B.C. and restored the dual Assyro-Babylonian monarchy.

5. Sennacherib (705–681 B.C.), Babylon, and Elam. Under Sennacherib, the dual Assyro-Babylonian monarchy continued as a demonstration of power and prestige aimed at securing the loyalty of the vassals. When Sargon died in 705 B.C., however, Merodach-Baladan raised Babylon in rebellion and took back the title of king of Babylon. The title returned to Sennacherib when he forced his opponent to escape in 703 B.C. Merodach-Baladan resumed his subversive activities in southern Mesopotamia, but Sennacherib forced him to escape to Elam with his idols and even the bones of his ancestors (cf. 43:14–15).

For several years, the kingdom of Elam attempted expansion and proved a well-organized enemy of the dual monarchy of Ashur-Babel. Elam was initially a dual kingdom comprising Anshan in the highlands and Susa in the lowlands. When Susa was destroyed by the Assyrians in 646 B.C., Anshan had been independent and growing since the 690s under a powerful new dynasty founded by King Teispes. The son of Teispes was Cyrus I, and his great grandson Cyrus II. In 689 B.C. Sennacherib captured Babylon, killed the recent usurper of the throne, and ruthlessly destroyed the city. Some passages in Isaiah may be referring to this attack against Babylon (e.g., 13:6–9, 12–19; 14:22–23; 21:1–10). The capture of Babylon by Cyrus II in 539 B.C. was "peaceful."

6. Sennacherib, Judah, and Siege of Jerusalem in 701 B.C. King Hezekiah of Judah (716–687 B.C.) broke with the syncretism of his father, Ahaz, and initiated a complete reform of religious life (2 Kin. 18:1–16). But against Isaiah's prophetic warning, he joined an insurrection of coastal cities in 701 B.C., which was backed by Egypt. His purpose was to restore the kingdom of David. However, Sennacherib defeated all the allies and, turning to Hezekiah, subdued forty-six cities and deported over two hundred thousand people. A large part of Judah was given to obedient Philistine kings. Hezekiah himself was besieged in Jerusalem, and his annual tribute was increased (2 Kin. 18:13–16). Jerusalem was miraculously spared, and Hezekiah, despite his central role in the rebellion, continued to rule. Isaiah had twice conveyed the word of the Lord that the king in Jerusalem had no reason to fear because Sennacherib would not enter Jerusalem but would return home where he would fall by the sword (Is. 37:6–7, 21–38).

7. Esarhaddon (681–669 B.C.) and the Divided Kingship of Ashur and Babylon. Sennacherib's son Esarhaddon restored Babylon and assumed the titles of king and priest of Babylon in 680 B.C. He deported King Manasseh of Judah to Babylon (2 Chr. 33:10–13) and recognized the growing power of the Medes and Elamite Anshan. Babylonians and Elamites were settled in the territories near Samaria (2 Kin. 17:24; Ezra 4:9–10), and the Israelites were settled in the cities of the Medes (2 Kin. 17:6; 18:11) and Elam (Is. 11:11). Elamite Anshan was therefore not unknown in Jerusalem in Isaiah's days.

8. Elamite Anshan, the Medes, and the Persians. Isaiah saw that the powers of the nations from the mountains east of Mesopotamia, the Medes and the Elamites (esp. Anshan), would be used as the Lord's tools to punish Babylon (13:1–5, 17–19; 21:2). He was shown that the rise to power of the Medes and Elamite Anshan would coincide with the decline and fall of the Assyro-Babylonian Empire. The Medes seized Ashur (614 B.C.) and Nineveh (612 B.C., in alliance with the Chaldeans of Babylon), and Cyrus II (a Persian), king of Anshan, captured Babylon in 539 B.C.

The Medes and Persians were associated tribes settled in the Zagros Mountains to the east of Assyria and Babylon. Many of them migrated to the southern and central areas of Zagros, where they became integrated in the Elamite kingdom of Anshan in the seventh and sixth centuries B.C. Anshan was therefore a growing kingdom in Isaiah's time. Elam was divided into lowland Susa (also called Susiana; modern Khuzestan) and highland Anshan in the Zagros Mountains to the east and southeast. The title of the king of Elam was "king of Anshan and Susa." As a name imposed by Assyrians and Babylonians, "Elam" could have been used for highland Anshan. Thus, when Isaiah speaks of "Elam" (11:11; 21:2; 22:6), he may be including the kingdom of Anshan, the home of Cyrus I and Cyrus II.

Theology and Purpose. In times of extraordinary crises and change in the kingdoms of Israel and Judah, Isaiah's purpose was to convey God's plan, which he had "seen." This plan is the unifying and structuring feature in the book and is conveyed by instruction, warning, exhortation, and comfort. Israel had apostatized, and the Lord used the Assyro-Babylonian Empire as an agent to chastise and purify them until (1) a faithful remnant of Israel would survive (i.e., Abrahamic and Sinai covenants restored), (2) royal Zion-Jerusalem would be glorified (i.e., Davidic covenant restored), and (3) the nations would acknowledge the Lord as Ruler of the world (i.e., the everlasting covenant with humanity at Creation and with Noah would be restored). As this program is laid out in the book, some key theological perspectives may be considered.

1. *The Lord is Sovereign, the God of Truth and Faithfulness*. Against mounting doubts in the Lord's power and will to save His people (cf. 20:6; 40:27-31; 49:14—50:4), the book of Isaiah points to His sovereignty as Creator and Lord of history and of nations and kings (40:12-31). He is the true God (65:16), just, reliable, and trustworthy (cf. 9:7; 10:20; 16:5; 25:1; 26:3; 42:3; 43:9; 61:8), whose word accomplishes His will (40:6-8; 55:8-11), whose plan cannot be obstructed or changed (14:24-27; 46:10-11), and whose faithfulness to His covenant promises is firm and reliable (cf. 1:26; 11:5; 25:1; 40:27-31; 49:7; 64:4-5). His plan is implemented by His word. It predicts judgment and future salvation, which He has the power to make happen, unlike the false gods and idols (e.g., 5:12, 19; 41:22; 42:9; 43:9, 44:26; 46:9). One of the greatest sins that Isaiah mentions, therefore, is contempt for the word of God (5:24; cf. 8:16, 20), for only the word of God brings salvation to the world

(2:3). In the short term, God's word and purpose should be believed because of who He is and because of His past acts of salvation (6:1-13; 7:4-9; 41:2-4, 25-26; 51:9-11). In the long term, the evidence of the continuing fulfillment of the written prophetic word proves that the word of God abides forever (40:8). God's faithful people must wait on Him as an expression of faith (8:17; 25:9; 26:8; 30:18; 42:4; 51:5; 64:4-5).

2. *God Is Holy*. God is the Other, completely different from any human or other part of His creation (57:15). His thoughts and ways are higher than those of humans (2:22; 55:8-9). He is exalted (2:11) and pure (6:5-7), and the earth is full of His glory (v. 3). His holiness is marked by the epithet "the Holy One of Israel," which is first and predominantly attested in Isaiah and is used throughout the book (e.g., 1:4; 5:19; 37:23; 41:14; 54:5; 60:14). Worshiping Him requires respect for His holiness, which makes humans feel unworthy or unclean (cf. 6:5-7). God's holiness is an *ethical* holiness (5:16). His holiness is integrated with justice, righteousness, and love (1:16-17; 5:16; 45:19-25; 58:6-7; 61:1-3). His salvation of penitent Israel expressed a love for His people that was rooted in the covenant and the election (cf. 41:8-14; 43:1-4). Although Israel had not fully repented, the Lord still offered salvation and forgiveness to His people (33:24; 43:25-26; 48:1-11; 54:6-7). His love and acceptance were extended to the nations (2:2-4; 18:1-7; 53:6; 55:6-8) because as Creator He is the God of the whole earth (54:5). The message of the Lord's mercy and abundant pardon is central in chapter 55, one of the high points of the book. God's holiness implies that He is passionate in judgment as well as in salvation. His passion in anger against sin and criminal offenses is reflected in an array of terms for anger, fury, and wrath (see "The Wrath of God," p. 918). The Lord's compassion is compared to that of a mother for her children (Is. 49:14-15; 66:13).

3. *The God of Israel, Zion, and David*. Isaiah's prophetic messages about Israel's apostasy and restoration are founded on the covenant (cf. "Covenant," p. 905). Israel's election, the covenant with Abraham, the Exodus and Sinai, and the promise of the land of Canaan to Abraham and Jacob are all referenced in this book. There are frequent appeals to covenant laws as models of righteous behavior. Israel's God was intimately connected with Zion, which was His dwelling and resting place, His throne, and His place of worship (e.g., 1:11-12; 2:2-4; 6:1-3). Historical circumstances associated with King

David linked the temple with the king and the royal palace. The covenant with David and his dynasty (9:7; 16:5; 29:1; 55:3; cf. 2 Sam. 7; 23:5) was neglected under apostate kings like Ahaz and Manasseh. This Davidic covenant was the ground for Isaiah's predictions of an ideal royal Savior: Immanuel (Is. 7:14—8:10), the Davidic Prince (9:2–7), and the Rod/Shoot from the stem/stump of Jesse (11:1–10). It was also the ground for the promise of a future glorification of David's dynasty in an everlasting covenant (55:3–5).

4. *The Lord Is Creator and the God of the Nations.* In Isaiah, the theological foundation for seeing God as the God of the nations is the "everlasting covenant" between the Creator and human beings (24:5; 54:9–10), which established the fundamental order of the world of creation (Gen. 9:16). This covenant implies that the Creator has granted life and sustenance to every being on the earth (Is. 9:11, 15–17). God is the Creator and, compared to Him, the nations and their idols are worthless (40:12–26). It is part of God's plan, however, to gather not only Israel but also those who worship Him from the nations (2:2–4; 56:6–8). This is part of His claim to world sovereignty, which means that He, as Creator of all peoples, would restore the everlasting covenant.

5. *A Message of Hope.* The hope proclaimed by Isaiah was based on God's claim that there is no other god besides Him, a thought developed in 44:6—46:13 (cf. 45:5, 14–25; 46:5) and through the work of the Holy Spirit (63:10–11, 14), who is identical with the Lord (11:2; 30:1; 34:16; 40:13; 42:1; 48:16; 59:19, 21; 61:1; 63:10–14). He cooperates with the Lord God and with the promised Davidic King (11:2). The coming salvation of Israel through this King is associated with the outpouring of the Spirit (42:1–9; 48:16; 59:20–21; 61:1–3). God had a plan, and Isaiah was the first prophetic book that emphasized it through the use of the term *'etsah,* which not only meant "counsel" but also "[determined] plan." This word constitutes a central concept in Isaiah's prophetic ministry (5:18–19; 19:17; 28:29; 40:14; 44:26; 46:10–11; cf. 30:1). God's plan would not fail in spite of the sins of His people because He would preserve for Himself a remnant. In the book of Isaiah, the concept of "remnant" represents the faithful among God's people who would enjoy His blessing when He fulfilled His promises. A remnant from the nations would also join them (see "The Remnant," p. 843). This shows that the hope of salvation was not exclusively for Israel and Judah but was also offered to all nations. As Creator, God cares for the nations and desires to be their God (e.g., 2:2–4; 52:13—53:12; 56:6–8; 66:19–24). It is a universal salvation in that it is offered to all.

God's plan would reach deep into the future and would include the resurrection of the dead, announced by the prophet in no uncertain terms (26:19; cf. v. 14), and even the destruction of death (25:8). Isaiah announced the coming of a future world; the creation of a new heaven and a new earth by the power of God. In this new everlasting creation there would be neither sin nor suffering (65:17; 66:22–23; cf. Rev. 21:1–4).

But it would be through the work of the Messiah that hope would reach its theological summit. The passage in Isaiah 52:13—53:12 speaks about a suffering and righteous individual who would atone for the sins of the nations of the world. Only Jesus Christ has fulfilled this prophecy by His life, teaching, suffering, death, and resurrection. God's plan and control of history mean that Isaiah provided a prophetic timeline of future events, beginning with his time and leading up to the full consummation of the Lord's plan (see commentary on 6:5–13; 10:5–19; 11:1–16).

6. *The Sacred, Prophetic Writing.* Beyond the revelation to the prophet and its subsequent communication to readers and hearers, Isaiah assigned a distinct value to the preserved, written prophecy as evidence of the power of the word of the Lord. It was to be a preserved record that could be seen and verified by its historical fulfillment (30:8; cf. 8:16–17). The predictive word of the Lord would necessarily wait for fulfillment because of its testimony to the truth of God's sovereign knowledge of history. Isaiah's authorship of the text, therefore, has important theological implications because it proves the issuing of God's predictions before His fulfillment of them. In fact, one of the ways in which the Lord demonstrates that there is no other God like Him is by announcing from the beginning what will take place even in the distant future. And His predictions happen (see 34:11—35:2; cf. 29:11–12, 18; 45:1–8; 46:8–11). The command to search the book/scroll of the Lord and read it (34:16) was most probably given so that readers would confirm the veracity of God's prophecy (cf. 46:10–11; 48:3). They were then invited to be His witnesses by hearing and seeing the prophecy's fulfillment (43:9–12; 44:6–8; 66:19). Thus, Isaiah's book has an eschatological function connected with the fulfillment of the Lord's plan of salvation: it predicted a time when faithful Israel would "hear" the prophetic

word and "see" its fulfillment (29:18); that is, the book would prove its relevance even in the distant future.

Literary Features. The book of Isaiah took shape in a literary setting where writing and books experienced a significant revival. Its literary genre may be defined as *prophetic book* (i.e., the literary presentation of the words of the Prophet Isaiah). The book is also in a sense a long sermon or a didactic-hortatory speech designed to persuade its hearers and readers to remain faithful, or repent and return, to the Lord. Thus, the book of Isaiah may be defined as a divine revelation functioning as a persuasive discourse. It contains literary features that imply an advanced level of learning and literary skills. Within a unit of speech, Isaiah has a wide range of literary forms associated with a lawsuit: accusation, witness statements, verdict, judgment, and argumentation. It also has lamentation, instructions, hymns, and didactic material like proverbs. There is a rich variety of metaphorical imagery, plays on words, artistic arrangements, chiastic structures, repetitions, and so on.

The book is a carefully planned composition as indicated by the prophet's continuing insights from "seeing" and "hearing" the Lord's messages. The material is fitted into a grandiose vision of the Lord's world sovereignty, which is based on prophetic predictions and divine fulfillments that provide the arguments for instruction, paraenesis (advice or counsel), and exhortation. It opens with a title (1:1) and a prologue (vv. 2–31). The rest is divided into two major parts, chapters 2—33 and 34—66. This division is marked in the oldest complete manuscript of the book, which dates to the early part of the second century B.C. In one of the complete Dead Sea Scrolls copies of Isaiah (1QIsª), there is a space of two lines after chapter 33.

The prologue in 1:2–31 describes the fundamental issue of the whole book. The covenant people of Israel—here exemplified by Judah after the Assyrian destruction in 701 B.C.—continued to disobey the covenant despite their severe punishment (vv. 4–9). This implies that Israel would face a long time of punishment until a purified remnant remained in Zion because the Lord would act with justice and righteousness (v. 27).

Chapters 2–33 outline the Lord's plan to establish His worldwide sovereignty at Zion-Jerusalem (its fulfillment is described in 2:2–4). Chapters 2–4 summarize the thematic structure of the book of Isaiah. They announce the Day of the Lord (2:10–21), to which chapters 2–66 repeatedly refer, and describe the Lord's purification of Israel for their role in His plan—by predicted judgment (3:1—4:6), by words of hortatory instruction (2:5–10, 22; 3:10–12), and by a prediction of the deliverance of His remnant people (4:2–6). This core message is then developed in chapters 5–12, 13–23, 24–27, and 28–33.

The second part, chapters 34–66, begins announcing judgment to the nations (34:1–4) and the day of recompense for the cause of Zion (v. 8). This new phase in the Lord's plan meant that He had ended the purification or chastisement process of His people by foreign powers (chaps. 2–33) and would prepare His faithful remnant for the restoration of Zion and His everlasting covenant with Israel (chaps. 34–66). However, this aim involved the salvation of the nations (52:13—53:12; 56:6–8; 60:1–22; 66:19–24) and the gathering of scattered Israel and the nations to worship the Lord at Zion (60:1—62:12; 66:5–24). The intimate tone of the Lord's appeals to His people in chapters 40–55 suggests that He was beginning to implement His plan by persuading them to become the restored covenant community in Zion. Chapters 34–54 form the foundation of the central invitation in chapter 55, which is further developed by instructions concerning a restored Zion and her citizens, and is marked by the chiastic *inclusio* in chapters 56–59 (A), 60–62 (B), and 63–66 (A'). The details of this compositional structure are provided in the commentary.

COMMENTARY

1:1–31
TITLE AND PROLOGUE

1:1
Title

The title consists of several parts. The type of text stands first and is determined by what follows:

1. Type of Text. The book of Isaiah records the "vision" (*khazon*) from God that Isaiah "saw" (*khazah*). The technical term *khazon* affirms the supernatural nature of the vision (cf. Num. 24:3–4, 15–17; Job 4:12–16; 33:14–16; Hos. 12:10). Isaiah emphasizes the divine source of his message by repeatedly using nouns derived from the same Hebrew root (Is. 21:2; 22:1, 5; 28:18 [here *khazut* is rendered as "agreement" in most translations]; 29:7, 11). The term belonged to the circle of seers, where it was associated with the supernatural revelation of divine words.

2. Identity of the Seer. The vision was given to Isaiah the son of Amoz. The Hebrew form of Isaiah's name is *yesha'yahu*, which involves *yahu* as the Lord's name. The later and abbreviated form *yesha'yah* is used as a book title in early codices. The name is attested on ancient seals and means "the Lord's salvation," "the Lord is [my] salvation," or even "the Lord has given salvation" (cf. 12:1–3; 49:6; 51:6).

3. Mode of Revelation. The vision was determined by what Isaiah saw. To "see [*khazah*] a vision [*khazon*]" is a rare, technical expression that implies a visionary experience involving the reception of God's words (cf. 2:1), as exemplified in Isaiah's commission account (6:1–13). It is rooted in the *prophetic* experience of the Lord speaking through visions (cf. Num. 24:3–4, 15–17; Job 4:12–16; 33:14–16; Hos. 12:10). Ezekiel uses a similar Hebrew phrasing (Ezek. 12:27; cf. 13:7, 16) to speak about prophecies for a distant future. Isaiah's use of the same terminology implies the presence of predictions of events in a distant future.

4. Topic of the Book. Isaiah 1:1 also indicates that Isaiah's vision would impact Judah and Jerusalem. The book's intended recipient is not specifically mentioned in the title; only the city and those in power, who would be involved with and impacted by the vision, are mentioned. Thus, the title announces its relevance to any recipient but keeps Israel, the people of God, and especially Zion-Jerusalem close to the heart of the message (see 66:10–14).

The designation "Judah and Jerusalem" (cf. 2:1) may function as a synecdoche or *pars pro toto*, namely, a figure of speech in which the *part* "Judah and Jerusalem" represents the *whole* of "Israel" as the people of God. The designation had certain political connotations. Jeroboam's rebellion in the tenth century B.C. led to the secession of the Northern Kingdom of Israel with ten of Israel's twelve tribes. Judah and Benjamin became the Southern Kingdom of Judah when Israel broke off (7:17). "Judah" therefore alludes to the *separation of* the kingdom of Israel from the kingdom of Judah (e.g., 11:12–13), while "Jerusalem" symbolizes the *unification* of the two kindred peoples by the common God worshiped there (note "the house/temple of the God of Jacob" in 2:3; cf. 10:20–23; 59:20; 65:9).

5. Time of Isaiah's Vision. Isaiah's vision was seen during the approximate time span of the days of Uzziah, Jotham, Ahaz, and Hezekiah, kings of Judah. However, his predictions about the future of Judah and Jerusalem went far beyond the time of those reigns. "Kings of Judah" brings to mind the dead rulers of Judah and Jerusalem. They are contrasted with the King of Zion-Jerusalem (2:2–4; 6:1–5), that is, the Lord. References to the reigns of kings in the superscriptions of prophetic books provide approximate dates (cf. Jer. 1:1–3; Hos. 1:1; Amos 1:1). Thus, the wording of Isaiah's title does not preclude the possibility that his ministry continued until the reign of Manasseh.

1:2–31
Prologue: Restoration of Jerusalem/Zion

This well-defined passage functions as a prologue to the book of Isaiah. It reflects the Lord's plan to chastise and purify Israel and redeem the remnant of Zion. This grand work of restoration characterizes the whole book. The unity of the passage emerges when the whole is taken as an extended lawsuit: a calling of witnesses (v. 2); a complaint against Israel for covenant crimes by the plaintiff (vv. 2–3); a complaint supported by a witness statement (v. 4); a review of the nation's moral status to ascertain the necessity or nonnecessity of further judgment (vv. 5–8); a witness statement regarding the remnant of Zion (v. 9); a further complaint against Jerusalem concerning false worship and a divine instruction offering a remedy (vv. 10–17); an offer of settlement by an arbitrator (vv. 18–20); a further complaint against Jerusalem's leaders (vv. 21–23); a predicted judgment followed by a purge and a restoration of Jerusalem; and a redemption of Zion with justice and righteousness (vv. 24–31). This summary of chapter 1 provides the essence of the Lord's plan, which is further developed in the whole book.

Chapters 1 and 65–66 form an *inclusio* that unites the book of Isaiah. Twenty-five Hebrew words or phrases in 1:2–31 are repeated in 65:1—66:24, and some of the less common ones in English are "ox," "bull" (1:3; 66:3); "sacrifices" (1:11; 66:3); "hear the word of the Lord" (1:10; 66:5); "not delight"/"displease" (1:11; 66:4); "burned incense"/"burned sacrifices" (1:13; 65:7); "New Moons, Sabbaths" (1:13; 66:23); "sword" (1:20; 66:16); "rebellious/obstinate," "rebels" (1:23; 65:2); "my enemies/foes," "his enemies/foes" (1:24; 66:14); those who "forsake the Lord" (1:28; 65:11); "chosen" (1:29; 66:3); "gardens" (1:29; 66:17); and "quench" (1:31; 66:24).

Several themes are also common to chapters 1 and 65–66: the nation, the people, and the offspring/descendants (1:2–6; 65:1–9); the destruction and the saving of a remnant (1:7, 9; 65:8–16); the survivors of Zion and the restoration of Jerusalem (1:8–9; 65:8–10, 18–19); the disapproval of worship that is not matched by righteousness (1:10–20; 66:1–4); the apostates having chosen that in which they, and not the Lord, delighted (1:11, 29; 66:3); the punishment of Jerusalem and the Lord's enemies (1:21–26; 66:5–6); the liberation of Zion and the faithful, and the destruction of Zion and the Lord's enemies (1:27–28; 66:7–16); the apostate cult in the gardens (1:29–31; 65:3; 66:17); the apostates being "ashamed" (1:29; 65:13); the judgment of the apostates by fire (1:31; 66:15–16); the apostates destroyed together (1:31; 66:17); and the unquenchable fire consuming the apostates (1:31; 66:24).

1:2–9. Rebellious Children and the Remnant. Isaiah appealed to the heavens and the earth as witnesses to verify the truth of what he said (Deut. 30:19; 31:28; 32:1; cf. Job 20:27). This belonged to the lawsuit genre (cf. Mic. 6:1–2), where those who witnessed the making of a covenant were called to witness the settlement of covenant crimes. Using two metaphors, God brought His complaint against Israel. The first used the case of a parent who had raised children (lit. "sons"; Is. 1:2c; cf. 38:19; Job 31:18). Parents instruct their children so that they "know" and "consider"/"understand" (Is. 1:3). Children's rebellion against their parents was regulated in the covenant law and led to a court proceeding involving the elders at the city gate (Deut. 21:18–21). God's claim in Isaiah 1:2 that His children had rebelled against Him means that they had abandoned their covenant loyalty (cf. 2 Kin. 1:1; 3:5, 7).

The second metaphor was that the ox knows its owner and the donkey its owner's feeding (Is. 1:3), which echoes a proverbial wisdom saying. The animals' faithfulness to their owners should have been a model for Israel's attitude to the Lord, but the people lacked knowledge and understanding. Both metaphors adduced commonsense arguments from social life.

The Lord's complaint in vv. 2–3 is supported by the prophet's witness statement (v. 4). The statement is followed by a review of Israel's moral status and past judgment to ascertain the necessity or nonnecessity of further judgment (vv. 5–8). The interjection *hoy*, "alas" or "woe," in 1:4 is associated with laments for the dead.

In this context it was used to call attention to the people's reprehensible conduct toward the Lord—in support of the complaint in vv. 2–3. The people were addressed as a sinful nation, a people weighed down with iniquity/guilt (v. 4a–b). "To sin" (*khata'*) literally means to "miss the way," that is, overstep divine laws. The term for *'awon*, "iniquity" or "rebellion," expresses the idea of a wrong mindset that is opposed to God's will. Both of these terms are used in Isaiah for the wrong *action* (e.g., 5:18; 31:7; 43:24), the *guilt* caused by the wrong (e.g., 1:18; 59:3), or the *punishment* for the wrong (53:12).

The vocabulary used in describing Israel's crimes is rooted in covenant texts (1:4; cf. Deut. 31:20; 32:16). The reference to Israel turning away (Is. 1:4) implies that when the covenant was made, Israel was loyal to their Lord. This thought returns in v. 26: the promise was that God would restore the city's rulers as they were in former times. Israel had offended "the Holy One of Israel" (v. 4). This divine epithet is used with particular frequency by Isaiah. It occurs throughout the whole book and supports its unity. It is particularly common in passages describing a violation of divine majesty (e.g., v. 4; 5:19; 31:1) or a turning to the Lord as a powerful Savior (e.g., 10:20; 17:7; 29:19; 41:14; 45:11; 55:5), which is closely associated with the idea of creation (e.g., 43:15; 45:12; 54:5). The epithet identifies the Lord as the God of Israel, the people of the two kingdoms (cf. 5:7).

The image of Israel as a sick body (1:5–8) reflects both their moral deficiencies and their punishment for disloyalty. The ruined nation is symbolized by a body covered with wounds, bruises, welts, and open, putrefying sores that had not healed for want of care. Both Israel and Judah were broken by sin and judgment, but this had not led to humility and repentance. A further witness statement testifies to the Lord's salvation of the remnant of Zion (v. 9), designated as "Daughter Zion" or "the daughter of Zion" (v. 8). The representation of a city or a people by the figure of a woman is common OT poetical imagery (cf. 3:16—4:1). The statement indicates that Zion's survival was the work of the Lord (see 36:1—37:38; note the concept of "remnant" in 37:4, 32). In the lawsuit context of 1:2–9, however, v. 9 confirms Israel's guilt *and* punishment (like Sodom and Gomorrah; cf. Gen. 19:24–29) but with the caveat (as in Gen. 19:29) that *yahweh tseba'ot*, the Almighty, Sovereign Lord of armies, had left a surviving remnant (see "The Remnant," p. 843). This title is linked to the Jerusalem temple in the OT (as well as here in chap. 1); it also alludes to the Lord's role as a Warrior and the Defender of His people (see "*Yahweh Tseba'ot*," p. 912).

The speakers in Isaiah 1:9 are a community of survivors created by the Lord of Hosts. Isaiah associates himself with them by using the first person plural (vv. 9–10) The speech in v. 9 is therefore the climactic point of vv. 2–9 and shows that in the midst of apostasy and judgment, God's plan of salvation had been (and would be) accomplished through the remnant of Zion.

1:10–17. Worship, Justice, and Righteousness. This passage is a complaint against Jerusalem concerning false worship, but with an added divine instruction offering a remedy. This "word of the LORD" and "law [or instruction, Heb. *torah*] of our God" zooms in on a central part of Israel's covenant crimes in Isaiah 1:2–4: their impure and blasphemous worship of the Lord in the temple of Jerusalem (see "The Temple in Chronicles," p. 541). The passage involves charges particularly against Jerusalem, which had committed crimes that defiled both temple and city. The crimes of rulers and people are described figuratively as involving hands full of blood, a description that points toward the need for purification (Is. 1:15–17).

The designations of Sodom and Gomorrah in v. 10 indicate that the people were corrupt and deserving of judgment (cf. Gen. 19:1–29). The Lord's initial rhetorical questions (Is. 1:11–12) pave the way for His ethical instructions (vv. 16–17). If the God who was worshiped in the temple was asking such questions, it could only mean that the worshipers did not know Him. What the Lord wanted was primarily an ethical purity of the heart to turn the religious practices into true sacrifices given with a contrite heart.

The people were told to stop bringing empty sacrifices and holding meaningless assemblies (vv. 13–14). The religious observances were not to be abolished. The repeated references to "your sacrifices," "your hands," "your festivals," and "your gatherings" (vv. 11–16) indicate that what God was rejecting was the hypocrisy of the worshipers. He turned against the multiplication of sacrifices, rituals, and festivals because they reflected the idea that "the more you offer, the more you get." The instruction does not indicate that the Lord was abolishing the weekly Sabbath, which has an important function in Isaiah (56:2, 4, 6; 58:13; 66:23). In fact, 66:23 indicates that the Sabbath was to be kept after the return from captivity and beyond. What the Lord was inveighing against was the combination of rebellion and sacred assemblies, in other words, the people's wickedness and their attempts to hide it behind a sanctimonious attitude. The Lord would not hear the prayers of such persons (1:15).

Injustice is symbolized by a reference to hands filled with blood—the blood of people who had been victimized by the community (v. 15). "Blood" denotes the blood guilt that the people had incurred by their actions. Verses 16–17 are a profound criticism of a type of worship that satisfies itself with formal and temporary cultic rituals and rites but is blind to justice. "Justice" (Heb. *mishpat*) in this context refers to the right judgment that would give what was legally right to all—especially the poor, the needy, and widows. This justice is one of the Lord's characteristics (Deut. 32:4). Justice should express itself in the life of the worshipers, who are exhorted to seek it

The Remnant

The terms *sarid* (used here in 1:9) and *she'ar* (elsewhere in Isaiah), both meaning "remnant"/"survivors," originally referred to the physical survival of any group of people after disasters, such as floods, famines, and war, but in Isaiah they are used in a theological sense with reference to the community of Israel, following the Assyrian disasters in the eighth century B.C. The remnant became the purified and faithful community, the Israel of faith. Isaiah used this concept in reference to Judah (7:3), Israel (10:20–23), a group in Jerusalem and on Mt. Zion (4:3; 28:5; 37:4, 32; cf. 14:32), or all the scattered communities of Israel once deported or having escaped to foreign nations (11:11, 16; 24:6, 12; 46:3). Of the faithful remnant of Israel, God's plan was to build a new nation through the return of scattered Israel (cf. 49:8—50:3) and the restoration of Jerusalem (cf. 52:1–12) and culminate with the glorification of Zion (cf. 59:21—62:12). In the book of Revelation, the concept of "remnant" or "rest" is used to designate the faithful people of God at the end of time (Rev. 12:17).

(Is. 1:17). Closely linked to this admonition is the demand to remove evil deeds, desist from doing evil, and learn to do what is right (vv. 16–17). Thus, the basic principles of the Lord's judgment and salvation are justice and righteousness (cf. vv. 21, 26–27). "Righteousness" is the fulfillment of the demands of goodwill in a relationship and may be associated with faithfulness, justification, and salvation, which also characterize the Lord (Deut. 32:4). This word pair is central in the whole book of Isaiah (e.g., Is. 1:21; 5:7; 9:7; 51:4–5; 56:1; 59:14).

The instruction in 1:16–17 implies that the people had ethically defiled themselves and needed cleansing (cf. v. 25). This admonition was rooted in the Lord's holiness, and as an offer to settle the dispute, it implies an offer of forgiveness to the penitent. The point in this *torah*/instruction is that true worshipers must reflect the essence of the will and nature of the God they seek. Jesus made the same point in the Sermon on the Mount (Matt. 5:21–26, 43–48).

1:18–20. Call to Settle the Lord's Complaint. The Lord's formal offer to settle the dispute was to *yakakh,* "argue" or "settle"/"decide," sometimes translated as "reason," with the people. The word conveys the idea of arguing in court in order to settle a dispute (cf. Job 23:7); the Lord as the plaintiff and Israel as the accused could argue against each other. The Lord expressed the desire to purify His people from their sins (Is. 1:18). His settlement offer was the blotting out of the blood guilt of which their hands were full (v. 15). The result of making themselves clean would be that even if their sins were like scarlet, they would be as white as snow, and even if they were red like crimson, they would be like wool (vv. 16, 18). This offer was, however, conditioned by the people's choice between two ways: either they would obey the instruction (vv. 16–17), which meant that they would eat the good produce of the land, or they would continue in rebellion, which meant that they would be "devoured by the sword" (vv. 19–20). The offer would lead to a separation between righteous and unrighteous (vv. 27–31), which was needed in the purifying judgment and the redemption announced in vv. 25–27. This theme is picked up again in 2:1—4:6 and at the end of the book. The gift of salvation comes with a choice that everyone has to make, but those who accept this gift will repent of their old way of life and depend completely on the Lord through the enabling of the Spirit.

1:21–31. Restoration and Redemption. The people's choice is implied in vv. 21–31. It resulted in a division of the people into Zion's faithful penitents (v. 27) and Jerusalem's apostate leaders (vv. 21–26) and their followers (vv. 28–31). The faithful would be redeemed and delivered (v. 27), but the apostates would be destroyed. The penitents of Zion would eat the good produce of the land (v. 19), but the apostates would be "devoured by the sword" (v. 20). The epithets *yahweh tseba'ot,* "Lord of Armies," "Lord Almighty," "Sovereign Lord," or "the Mighty One of Israel," are used in Isaiah to emphasize the Lord's power in defeating enemies and protecting His faithful people (v. 24). In order to have justice and righteousness in Jerusalem, the apostate leaders had to be replaced by faithful judges (vv. 26–27). This would restore the city to what it was in the beginning.

The apostate religion included trees (alternatively understood and translated as either "oak" or "terebinth") and gardens (v. 29). The strength and vitality of these trees made them symbols of fertility gods, and rites of fertility were carried out under them (see 57:5; Jer. 2:20, 23–27; 3:6; Hos. 4:13). In gardens with such trees, sacrifices were offered (Is. 65:3) and various rites of purification were used to prepare the worshipers for cultic activities (66:17). The seductive attraction of this cult is implied by the verbs "desire"/"delight" and "choose," but the Lord's judgment would change this admiration to disgrace (1:29). The apostates would themselves become like the oaks (or terebinths) and gardens where they worshiped, but they would be without water (v. 30). The restoration of the city by faithful officials (v. 26) and the redemption of the penitents of Zion (v. 27) form the climax of the prologue. The Lord's actions, described in vv. 24–31, would resolve His complaints mentioned earlier in the chapter.

2:1—4:6

PREPARATIONS OF ZION-JERUSALEM FOR GOD'S UNIVERSAL KINGDOM

This literary block concerns God's preparations for His universal kingdom by purifying His people Israel and His city Zion-Jerusalem and by demonstrating His sovereignty over the nations, particularly Assyria. This section of the book outlines the essence of God's plan for His universal sovereignty. It is defined by its internally coherent ring structure, in which the end is announced at the beginning—the events in 2:2–4 were to follow those of 4:2–6. The beginning is marked by the title in 2:1–2, and the end by the new unit in 5:1–30. The passage contains many links with the rest of the book, some of which are noted in the commentary. Major connections exist with the prologue in 1:2–31.

2:1–4
The Word, the End, the Nations

When associated with a prophet, the term *dabar*, "word"/"thing"/"matter" (some translations leave it untranslated here; v. 1) designates the conventional genre of "prophecy" (cf. Jer. 18:18; Ezek. 7:26). The formula "in the latter/last days" is best understood here as referring to the remote future or the end of a certain but indefinite period of time: "at the end of the days." The subtitle in Isaiah 2:1–2a could be translated in such a way as to connect the end of v. 1 with the beginning of v. 2 ("The word that…which shall come to pass at the end of the days"). It establishes a large time span between Isaiah's time and "the end of the days." This time span applies to all "the days" in chapters 2–66, which will lead to the *ultimate* events in 2:2b–4. Therefore, vv. 1–2a announce the temporal framework of the great plan of "the God of Jacob" to assume universal sovereignty.

The nations would acknowledge the Lord's sovereign kingship. The "mountain of the Lord's house/temple" refers to the throne of the Lord (cf. 6:1; 66:1; Pss. 9:4; 47:8), and the verb "established" refers to the unchallenged confirmation of a royal reign, kingship, or throne (e.g., 2 Sam. 7:16–26). The term *ro'sh* may be translated "head"/"highest"/"chief"/"top"—here related to the mountains. The language here may imply God's sovereignty over the nations and their gods. The actions by all nations will affirm God's royal kingship (cf. Is. 33:17–22; 52:7). The translation "shall flow/stream to it" builds on the term *nahar* I ("to flow"/"stream"). Another option would be to build on *nahar* II, which means "to make the face shine," "be radiant with joy," or "rejoice." This fits Isaiah's own usage in 60:5 (see also Ps. 34:6; Jer. 31:12; 51:44). On this premise, the text may be translated "And all nations will shine with joy toward Him." Such an act of joy by a king's subjects was traditionally part of the acclamation of a king.

Many peoples would decide to accept God's rule, follow His ways, and encourage each other to go up to the Lord's temple mountain, a description which signifies a pilgrimage to

the temple (see Ps. 122:4); this was usually done to bring gifts, fulfill vows, participate in festivals, pray to the Lord, praise the Lord, or "seek the Lord." The peoples would encourage each other to obey the Lord (i.e., to "walk in His paths"). The temple is called the house/temple of the God of Jacob. "Jacob"/"Israel" is the ancient name of God's elected people as a whole and includes both Israel and Judah (cf. Is. 5:7; 8:14). The phrase "the God of Jacob" occurs only here in Isaiah, but it was used in the temple worship (e.g., Ps. 46:7, 11). References to the descendants of Jacob (lit. "house of Jacob") are rather frequent in Isaiah (e.g., 2:5–6; 8:17; 14:1; 46:3; 58:1).

The law (or instruction) or the word of the Lord would go out from Zion-Jerusalem because His kingship would be acknowledged by the nations, which would result in world peace. The Lord as King would judge and decide cases (2:4), something also characteristic of the prophesied messianic righteous King (11:4). In both passages the outcome would be world peace. In view of 9:2–7 and 11:1–10, "Wonderful Counselor" and "Prince of Peace" refer to the work of the Lord's messianic agent through whom the law/instruction would go out from Zion and the Lord's word from Jerusalem (2:3).

2:5–10
Idols Removed

This hortatory passage addressed the people of Jacob (lit. "house," meaning descendants). Its purpose was to persuade them to end their widespread devotion to foreign gods and turn to the God of Jacob (v. 3). The Lord showed Isaiah what the future pilgrims to Zion would say, and this is followed by an invitation to the contemporary house of Jacob from a speaker in their midst. The invitation is to join him in walking in "the light of the LORD." The phrase "the light of the LORD" is a unique expression. "Light" is a symbol of the Lord's saving and merciful presence in the temple (Pss. 27:1; 37:6; 97:11; 112:4; Mic. 7:8). The Lord's people "walk in the light" (Is. 2:5) of His presence because "righteousness and justice are the foundation" of His throne, and *khesed*, "mercy," "love," or "covenant faithfulness," and *'emet*, "truth" or "faithfulness," go before Him (Ps. 89:14–15). Verse 6 could be also translated "For you [house of Jacob] have forsaken your people, O House of Jacob!" In other words, through its unfaithfulness the house of Jacob is no longer part of the true people of God, identified here as "your people."

The rest of the passage provides the evidence needed to support the charge.

The accumulation of objects, practices, and idol worshipers listed in 2:6–9 is contrasted with their removal on the Day of the Lord (v. 18–21; 3:1–7; 3:16—4:1). The people had adopted foreign idolatrous practices from the east and west, including (in the latter case) divination in the manner of the Philistines. The people were too closely connected with foreign, pagan influences. The silver, gold, and treasures (2:7) may reflect an accumulation of riches or material for making idols (cf. vv. 8, 18–21), or it may reflect human pride. Horses and chariots may refer to military power, the symbols of sun-worship at the entrance to the house of the Lord in Manasseh's time (2 Kin. 23:11), or both. The house of Jacob was full of idols of silver and gold. The people worshiped and bowed down to the work of their own hands (Is. 2:8–9b; cf. 17:7–8; 31:7).

The people were being exhorted to turn away from idols and humble themselves before the Lord's powerful glory (2:11–21). This served as a warning in view of the coming of the Day of the Lord.

2:11–22
The Day of the Lord

In Isaiah's time, the Day of the Lord was understood to be the day when God would come to save His people and defeat their enemies—the title *yahweh tseba'ot*, "Lord of Hosts," "Lord of armies," or "Lord Almighty" (v. 12), was specifically linked with Zion-Jerusalem and God's royal power. The Day of the Lord is a point of reference for the phrase "in that day/time," which occurs about forty-five times between 2:11 and 31:7. The description of God's judgment during the Day of the Lord moves from a local situation to a universal one (cf. 2:21). The central Day of the Lord in vv. 12–16 is framed by an *inclusio* in vv. 11 and 17. This arrangement draws attention to the fundamental contrast between God and the human idol makers. By His terrifying power and holy majesty, the Lord would supersede all and would humble humanity (v. 12). The enumeration of symbols of human pride (vv. 13–16) involves a movement from north to south and expresses totality: from the cedars of Lebanon and the oaks of Bashan, through mountains, hills, and cities with towers and walls, to the trading ships of Tarshish in the Gulf of Aqaba in the south.

In the light of how "Lebanon" is used in Isaiah, the "cedars of Lebanon" and the "oaks of Bashan" (v. 13) may metaphorically refer to the proud people of the house of Jacob, who saw themselves as living in the fruitful and protected garden/mountain of God (i.e., Zion). But as a result of a humiliating encounter with the Lord (vv. 11–17), the idolaters would end up in holes, rocks, and caves (vv. 18–19). They would cast away their idols to moles and bats as they desperately hid themselves in caverns and rocks before the frightening revelation of the Lord's power and majesty (vv. 20–21; cf. v. 10).

An idol was the work of human hands/fingers (vv. 8, 20), beautifully crafted in order to attract the admiration of human eyes (vv. 9, 11). Humans would prostrate themselves to the ground to worship the idols (v. 9). But on the Day of the Lord, people would be bowed down and humbled because of the fear of the Lord, and they would reject their idols (vv. 11, 17); only the Lord would be exalted (vv. 10–11, 17, 19, 21). Based on his condemnation of idolatry, Isaiah admonished the house of Jacob to cease trusting in human beings (esp. idolaters), and he reminded them that human life depends on the breath in the nostrils, given by God (v. 22; 42:5; Gen. 2:7). The exhortation in Isaiah 2:22 prepares the way for 3:1—4:1 that predicts the removal of three things: (1) all bread/food and water, exposing human neediness (3:1); (2) all human officials in Jerusalem and Judah (vv. 2–7) who oppress the poor and needy (vv. 8–9, 12–15); and (3) the insignia of high office, symbols of the abuse of power and foreign practices (3:16—4:6). Idolatry, pride, and injustice have no place with the Lord.

3:1—4:6
Cleansing and Restoration

The prologue in 1:2–31 predicts that the Lord would purge the apostate leaders of Jerusalem and restore it as a faithful and righteous city (vv. 24–26). In this section the purification of Jerusalem and Judah is dealt with in further detail.

3:1–7. God Removes Leaders. The reminder of human neediness in 2:22 is the foundation of 3:1–7. God was going to remove all means of support for Jerusalem and Judah and would send a famine, removing all traces of bread and water (v. 1). The cause of the famine is not stated, but the references to warriors and the mighty (v. 2a), as well as their men, falling by the sword in battle (v. 25) suggest that the cause would be a siege. The reference to the captain of fifty (v. 3a), which is possibly a figure of speech (synecdoche) for the whole army, points in the same direction.

Once the wicked leaders had been removed, children would be princes and rulers, which would result in an upheaval of the social order (vv. 4–7). The utter lack of human leadership is illustrated in vv. 6–7. Having a piece of clothing (lit. "mantle" or "cloak") would be enough for one to be asked to lead the clan, which implies that leadership requires some kind of insignia of authority, in this case a mantle. This idea is fully developed in the removal of the finery of the women (lit. "daughters") of Zion in vv. 16–23.

3:8–15. Oppression of the Poor. The reference to the stumbling and falling of Jerusalem and Judah summarizes the effect of the judgment and describes the coming disaster as having already taken place. The mention of the look (the noun *hakkarah*) on their faces (v. 9) is related to an expression using a similar verbal form (*nakar*, "to regard") that is used in an idiomatic expression ("to regard faces"), which means to "show partiality" (Deut. 1:17; 16:19; Prov. 24:23–24; 28:21). In this context it could be referring especially to judges making unjust verdicts in return for bribes (cf. Is. 1:23; 5:23). The ruin of Jerusalem and Judah would be the working out of the fundamental law of retribution—the righteous are rewarded and the wicked punished (3:9–11; cf. 1:19–20).

Two legal processes are merged here: the oppression of the poor in the courts by wicked judges and elders and the Lord's future lawsuit against them, which would restore justice to God's people (3:13–15; cf. 1:23). In the context of the implied law of retribution, crimes would be punished according to the actions suffered by the victims. The crimes of the wicked judges, princes, and elders included (1) partiality in judgment (vv. 17, 23); (2) false teaching that had mislead the people and caused them to veer from the correct paths (v. 12); (3) gleaning and eating up their vineyards without leaving some produce for the poor (v. 14); (4) keeping the plunder of the poor in their houses; and (5) crushing God's people (v. 15). The punishment of the judges, princes, and elders stands in proportion to their crimes: loss of the Lord's support and all supply of sustenance for life (v. 1d), loss of authority and honor as leaders (3:2–7), loss of pride and tokens of honor and dignity (3:16—4:1), and loss of human life, which would make the city desolate (3:25–26).

The first "woe" (v. 9; cf. v. 11a) flows from the description of the indisputable evidence against the wicked (v. 8–9c). The exhortation to tell the righteous (v. 10) stands between two woes

against wicked judges. According to Proverbs 24:23–25, the verdict pronounced by judges and elders was central in legal proceedings. Judges were admonished to speak the right verdict, as they are also here. The second "woe" (Is. 3:11) repeats the point of v. 9. In v. 12 the Lord was addressing His people and acting both as prosecutor and defender (cf. vv. 8–9, 14–15). Verse 12 has been understood in different ways. Some suggest that "children" is not the best translation for the Hebrew *me'olel* and that it should rather be translated as "gleaners" (cf. "graze the vineyard" in v. 14) or "those who inflict or maltreat" (as in Lam. 1:22; 2:20). In this case the basic meaning of the text would be "the oppressors of My people are gleaners/exactors"—oppressors who share nothing with the poor (see Lev. 19:9–10; Deut. 24:18–22; cf. Jer. 6:9). However, if the majority of translators are correct that the meaning is "children," the text would be conveying the idea that the people were so weak that they were allowing those who were acting like children to oppress them.

The word *nashim* has also been debated. The LXX takes it to be pointed with different vowels as *noshim*, which means "usurers, extortioners," and on this reading it would parallel the first part of the verse according to the first interpretation given above, as well as introduce a topic that is resumed in Isaiah 3:14 (cf. Ex. 22:25; Lev. 25:36–37; Deut. 23:19–20). Based on these observations, Isaiah 3:12 may be translated as "My people's oppressors are gleaners/exactors, and extortioners rule over them." It could also be that the MT is correct in regard to the word *nashim*, which means "women." In this case, the parallel would be with the second reading mentioned above, in other words, "Children oppress them, and women rule over them." In this case, the meaning would be that the people of Israel were so weak that they were allowing men who were acting like women and children to oppress and rule them.

The mention of those who were leading the people refers to teachers and counselors who were failing to reproach or warn the people concerning their ways (cf. Prov. 24:25). On the evidence of open wrongdoings and according to the law of retribution (Is. 3:8–12), the Lord was (as it were) rising to plead His case in court and to judge the peoples. The legal proceedings were against the elders and leaders/princes of God's people (vv. 14–15). The action is literally described as "the Lord will come before the court of justice" (cf. Job 9:32). The elders (cf. Is. 3:2) were local rulers and dignitaries who could also be called leaders/princes (cf. Job

29:8–10). The accusations are summarized in Isaiah 3:8–15: the vineyard in v. 14 is meant to feed the poor, but the elders and princes had "grazed" it, revealing a lack of compassion for the poor by not leaving behind any gleanings of their fruit trees. Such compassionate acts were stipulated in the covenant (Lev. 19:9–10; Deut. 24:18–22; cf. Jer. 6:9). The plunder of the poor (Is. 3:14) had been obtained by usury or extortion (v. 12a) and bribery in the court proceedings (cf. 1:23; 5:8, 23). The verbs "crush" and "grind" have almost the same sense, suggesting an oppression that destroys the poor (cf. Prov. 22:22–23). The latter word, "grind," is a very strong expression that conveys the idea of afflicting the poor by bribery and the perversion of justice (Is. 1:23; 3:8–15; 5:23).

3:16–23. From Pride to Humiliation. The Lord's accusation against the women (lit. "daughters") of Zion (vv. 16–17) is explained (v. 16) and would result in a complete reversal from pride to humiliation (vv. 18–24). The daughters of Zion are often taken to be the women of Jerusalem (as in Song 3:11). Another possibility would be to take the expression as a figurative reference to Jerusalem and the cities of Judah (see Is. 3:26; 4:1, 4). One could take the list of the leading classes in 3:2–3 as corresponding to the list of the daughters' finery in vv. 18–23, the scene of the people seeking a ruler (vv. 6–7) could parallel the seven women seeking a husband (4:1), and the references to food and clothing in 3:7 and 4:1 both function as the minimum tokens of authority. The combination of "daughters" and the name of a city usually referred to daughter cities. In administrative contexts, the entire territory of Judah contained about 115 cities with their villages under the capital Jerusalem (e.g., Josh. 15:20–63). It could be that the reference here to daughters of Zion refers to the dependent cities, towns, and villages of Zion-Jerusalem in Judah. Obviously, the message was for the leaders.

The list of items in Isaiah 3:18–23 is constituted of *insignia of authority* for the officials in Jerusalem and Judah (cf. vv. 1–7), *luxury items* linked to pride and wealth obtained by the abuse of power and the oppression of the poor (cf. vv. 8–15), and *magical items*, implying crimes against the covenant (cf. 2:6–22). Thus, the leading officials of the cities of Jerusalem and Judah, fittingly symbolized by the finery of the high class ladies of the city (the daughters of Zion), are described as proud, self-seeking, rebellious, and abusing their authority (as already indicated in detail in 2:6—3:15). The

accusation in 3:16 implies their figurative behavior as harlots or unfaithful wives (cf. 1:21; Ezek. 16:15–43). The *punishment* would consist of disgrace and shame in proportion to their crimes (Is. 3:17, 24).

The Hebrew word for finery (*tip'eret*) in v. 18 does not refer only to women's adornment but indicates that which brings glory and honor to a person, including dress and ornaments functioning as insignia of office or marking rank (e.g., 28:1, 4–5; 52:1; 62:3; 63:12, 14–15). The meaning of some items in 3:18–23 is uncertain, but a wealth of archaeological material now gives us a better understanding. At least several of the items were exclusively used by women, and others had magical associations: jingling anklets or bangles for protection against evil (v. 18); crescents, in the shape of the waxing or waning moon (v. 18); perfume boxes and amulets in the shape of the sun that were related to the cult of the dead (v. 19); and charms or amulets for religious purposes (v. 20). All can be classified as luxurious tokens of pride, idolatry, or riches unfairly obtained.

3:24—4:1. Lament and Mourning. The leaders' authority, pride, and beauty would be turned into slavery, shame, and ugliness (3:24), illustrating God's sovereignty, justice, and righteousness. The historical fulfillment of this prophecy was possibly the Assyrian destruction of forty-six cities in Judah and the siege of Jerusalem in 701 B.C. (see Isaiah: Introduction). The references to stench, rope, baldness, sackcloth, and branding may all be associated with captivity, mourning, and disgrace.

The woman who would sit desolate on the ground while her gates lamented and mourned represents Zion-Jerusalem. Her garb of pride and beauty would be exchanged for the garb of mourning and sorrow (see 61:3). The mourning of the mother city would be caused by the death of her men at war (3:25–26). Such a loss of men in war (v. 25) would result in humiliation and lack of people. Since Zion-Jerusalem would lose her men in war, seven women (4:1) would marry one man with the sole request of being called by his name (i.e., to belong to him). They would dispense with the husband's customary duty to provide his wife with food and clothing (Ex. 21:10) because their main desire would be to remove their disgrace as *desolate* (and barren) women (cf. the disgrace of widowhood in Is. 54:4).

4:2–6. The Branch and the People. The climax in the chain of events in that day (2:11—4:6) would be the reward of the faithful remnant, namely, those Israelites who would escape and remain in Jerusalem (4:2–3). The reference to all who were recorded among the living in Jerusalem refers to those who were inscribed on the register of the citizens of Zion (cf. 63:1—66:24). The apostate leaders of 2:6—4:1 were to be re placed by the Branch of the Lord, the promised King (for "Branch" as a messianic term, see 11:1; Jer. 23:5; 33:15; Zech. 3:8; 6:12). His reign would be beautiful and glorious—in contrast to that of the apostates. The marvelous fertility of the soil in the messianic age is a favorite theme in Isaiah (Is. 30:23; 32:1, 16–19). The fertile land would yield fruit and life, and the Branch of the Lord would bring justice, righteousness, and peace.

The summary in 4:2 is explained in more detail in vv. 3–6, with an emphasis on God's *purification* of people, land, and city (vv. 3–4) and on His *protection* of the worshipers against cold, heat, and storms (vv. 5–6). The emphasis in vv. 2–6 is on the *holiness* to be restored to God's people and on the anticipated permanent *peace* and *protection* of the faithful. It is an appropriate preparation for the fulfillment of the vision of many nations ascending to the temple to walk in permanent peace in the Lord's paths (2:2–4). The Lord would ultimately accomplish this through the Branch, the Davidic Prince of Peace, whose work would bring hope to the nations.

5:1—12:6

ISRAEL, ZION, AND THE DAVIDIC KING RESTORED

This section of Isaiah explains in more detail the Lord's plan to establish His universal sovereignty as outlined in chapters 2–4. Chapter 5 contains the vineyard song and its interpretation. The plan of God is set in the context of the commission of the prophet (6:1–13), who announced the coming of Immanuel as a sign (7:1—8:15). The prophet characterizes his family as also being a sign for the people (8:16—9:7). The judgment against Israel is described as a warning to Judah (9:8; 10:4), and the section includes announcements of the defeat of Syria, the coming of the second David, and the restoration of Israel (10:5—12:6).

5:1–30
The Song of the Vineyard

The song itself is found in vv. 1–7; it is followed by woes against the upper classes (vv. 8–23) and judgment by a foreign nation (vv. 24–30).

5:1–7. The Song. The Song of the Beloved is a parable in which the bride, in keeping with ANE customs, is compared to a vineyard. In reality, however, the song is an *accusation* in the name of a disappointed and betrayed lover. Isaiah speaks, at first, as the friend of the bridegroom who acted as an intermediary in wedding arrangements and who could have presented any complaint on behalf of the bridegroom. From v. 3, Isaiah presents God as calling upon the inhabitants of Jerusalem and Judah to recognize His justice and announcing His verdict against them.

Isaiah presents his song on behalf of the one he loved (v. 1), followed by the Lord's response about His vineyard, whose identity is not revealed until v. 7. The Hebrew preposition *le* in 5:1 has been variously translated as "to" or "for." These have some linguistic basis, but "concerning" may better fit the context. Isaiah sings a song concerning the One he loves with regard to His vineyard. The Lord complained that He had done everything possible to receive good grapes, but His vineyard had brought Him only "wild," "bad," or "worthless" ones (v. 2). The inhabitants of Jerusalem and Judah were being asked to judge between the Lord and His vineyard (v. 3). Since the answer to the Lord's question was self-evident, He proceeded to the judgment announcement: the protection of the vineyard would be removed (vv. 5–6).

5:8–23. Proclamation of Woes. Isaiah finally and clearly identifies the vineyard as the house of Israel and the people of Judah (v. 7) who had violated the principles of justice and righteousness (cf. 1:10–27; 3:8–15; 5:8–23). The statement of woes follows. The first reproaches the rich for accumulating houses and land while ignoring the coming judgment when many impressive houses would be desolate, and vineyards and fields would yield meager fruit (vv. 8–10). The second woe concerns those who drink wine and dance from early until late (v. 11) while disregarding the Lord's doing (v. 12; cf. v. 19). The third woe touches on Isaiah's conflict with the wise teachers (vv. 18–19). They were metaphorically pulling evil with cords of *shav'*, "deceit," "dishonesty," or "falsehood," which often referred to a false witness (Ex. 23:1; Deut. 5:20; Job 15:31; cf. Ps. 24:4). The parallel metaphor goes even further and refers to their sin as being so massive that a cart rope was needed to pull it.

The rebellious people mocked the Lord and Isaiah's prophetic ministry by sarcastically implying that there was no reason to believe that the Lord would hasten to fulfill His predictions (i.e., "His work") or that His purpose could be known.

The fourth woe is directed against those who remove justice and righteousness by distorting the truth (Is. 5:20). The fifth pleads for humility and rebukes those who are wise in their own eyes. This is a common negative assessment in the wisdom circles (e.g., Prov. 3:7; 26:5, 12; 28:11). The last denunciation is directed against judges and elders with minds so affected by intoxicating drinks that they justify the wicked for a bribe and deny justice to the righteous (Is. 5:23; cf. 3:9d–15).

5:24–30. Judgment by a Foreign Nation.

Because of the rejection of Isaiah's instruction, the Lord's anger was aroused against His people. He had already struck them with His hand (i.e., power) with disastrous effects, but a still greater disaster was to come (vv. 26–30). The words for the Lord's anger are metaphorical expressions of His attitude toward sin, injustice, unrighteousness, and pride. They are closely connected with the holiness of God, which is a central concept in Isaiah. The OT uses at least ten different terms for anger, and Isaiah uses eight of these.

The description of an invading army, which the Lord would call as an agent of His punishment from a distant nation, underlines their speed (v. 26), the preparation of the soldiers (v. 27), the efficiency of their weapons (v. 28), and their frightful roaring like young lions (v. 29) when the prey would be taken. It would be like the roaring of the sea (vv. 30; cf. 17:12). The people of Israel would be carried away with nobody to save them (5:29), and there would be darkness and anguish (v. 30). The banner that would be lifted up for the nations would be set up on a hill to call the warriors to assemble either for attack or defense (v. 26; see 11:10).

6:1–13
The Lord's Plan and Isaiah's Commission

This chapter reveals the Lord's plan for apostate Israel and reaffirms Isaiah's prophetic ministry (PK 307–308). In this intimate dialogue between God and His prophet (cf. Gen. 18:22–33; Amos 3:7) the prophet saw or perceived (Heb. *ra'ah*) and heard God's word (Jer. 23:18). According to his commission account, Israel would refuse to be converted (vv. 9–10), and judgment would come. In the end only a holy remnant would emerge (vv. 11–13).

6:1–4. The Lord in His Temple.

Isaiah's commission account is connected with the first king mentioned in 1:1, which states, "in the year that King Uzziah died" (around 736 B.C.). At this time the Assyrian threat under Tiglath-Pileser III was already evident. The scene of the vision was the earthly temple. Isaiah was standing at the entrance to the temple building, perhaps in the vestibule looking into the Holy Place. In the vision the doors to the holy of holies were opened, and he saw the Lord enthroned "between the cherubim" (1 Sam. 4:4; 2 Kin. 19:15; Ps. 80:1; Is. 37:16). The ark of the covenant in the Most Holy Place was probably understood as a throne with golden images of cherubim.

The occasion of Isaiah's vision may have been the Day of Atonement, when God passed judgment on Israel and atonement was made for their sins, thus cleansing them (Lev. 16:1–34; 23:36–42; Num. 29:7–11). It was the time of the year when God appeared in a cloud above the cover of the ark, often called the "mercy seat," in the holy of holies (Lev. 16:2). Only the high priest was allowed to go into the holy of holies with the appropriate offerings on behalf of the people. Thus, Isaiah functioned as a priest, perhaps as an assistant of the high priest, who stood in attendance at the entrance to the temple. The Lord's enthronement in judgment is essential in the context of Isaiah 6:9–13, and the concept of a judgment that purifies Jerusalem and Judah is meaningful in view of 1:21–26 and 3:1—4:6.

The robe is an insignia of the Lord's royal dignity. He is clothed with honor and majesty and covers Himself with a garment of light (Pss. 93:1; 104:1–2). That the train of His robe filled the temple shows the limitless character of His glory and majesty (cf. 1 Kin. 8:27). The Jerusalem temple was usually called "house" (*bayit*), but here the word is *hekal*, which could refer to a "fine building" or "temple." It was separated from the Most Holy (*debir* or *qodesh qodashim*) by a wall with doors of olive wood (1 Kin. 6:31–32). Isaiah saw the Lord sitting on His throne in the Most Holy Place, the train of His robe spilling through the open doors and filling the Holy Place. The Lord's heavenly council was comprised of a multitude of beings singing His praise and ready to serve Him. The seraphim (Is. 6:2) probably represented all the heavenly beings (1 Kin. 22:19). The seraphim hovered above the Lord's robe on both sides of the throne, flying with two of their six wings and covering their eyes and feet with the other four as an expression of humility and respect (Is. 6:2; cf. Ezek. 1:11).

The Bible mentions the seraphim only here. Their name and nature are unclear. They are represented as winged human beings with faces, voices, hands, and feet. This makes them entirely different from the winged serpent figures around the throne of Pharaoh, which may have been known at least by name to Isaiah (Is. 14:29; 30:6). Another point of contact with "seraph" is the *sarap* (lit. "fiery"; contextually translated as "poisonous" or "venomous"), the serpent of bronze that Moses made in the desert (Num. 21:6–9; Deut. 8:15) and that remained in the Jerusalem temple until the time of King Hezekiah (2 Kin. 18:4). Thus, Isaiah possibly knew the term "seraphim" in the sense of "fiery ones with wings" and applied it to heavenly beings that he had not seen before. They were closely connected with the concept of the Lord's *holiness* (Is. 6:3), which is central in Isaiah and intimately associated with fire and burning (e.g., 5:16–24; 10:17; 30:27–29).

The threefold proclamation of the Lord's holiness by the seraphim results in the temple being filled with smoke from the incense altar (v. 4). The reference to the seraphim calling to each other may imply that they were two in number, but the phrase may also have a collective sense. The emphatic threefold repetition of the word "holy" (v. 3) conveys the sense of "most holy," but it also reflects a fixed formula in the temple cult (Ps. 99:3, 5, 9). The holiness of the Lord of Hosts (or Lord Almighty) means that He is transcendent, powerful, and sovereign beyond what any human can imagine. He is perfectly pure and genuine in His very being.

That the whole earth is full of God's glory (Is. 6:3) is a central statement in the Lord's plan for universal sovereignty (cf. 11:9). The Lord's "glory" is the manifestation of His person, especially of His holiness, light, and majesty. As the train of His robe filled the temple, His glory fills the whole earth. Since His glory represents His presence, it may be said to fill the temple (6:1; cf. Ps. 63:2). It is then depicted as a cloud (1 Kin. 8:10–11; 2 Chr. 5:13–14; cf. Is. 4:5–6; 6:4). Zion-Jerusalem was considered the "center of the land/earth" (Ezek. 38:12). The localized holy presence of God in the temple anticipated the moment when the whole earth would be conquered through His holiness.

6:5–13. The Prophetic Commission. The threefold emphasis on the holiness of the Lord of Hosts, the implied relationship between temple and earth, and the need for a ritual cleansing of human sin (vv. 3–7) are all central concepts linked to the temple. Isaiah exclaimed

that he had seen the King, the Lord Almighty (v. 5). After he was purified from sin (vv. 6–7), he dialogued with the Lord and expressed a deep sense of unworthiness and fear (v. 5). Israel's apostasy and sinfulness had rendered them unclean before God's holiness. With unclean lips, their prayers for mercy would not be heard (cf. 1:15; Ps. 17:1), but the purification of Isaiah's lips removed his guilt and sin and enabled him to speak to the Holy One. Human messengers of the Lord are not without sin: He forgives, cleanses, and empowers.

The Lord's plan had been decided, and He asked whom to send to announce it. Isaiah's reply indicated his readiness to serve the Lord. His mission was part of the Lord's plan concerning "this people" (Is. 6:9)—an expression implying contempt and disfavor (8:6, 12; 9:16; 28:11, 14). Israel is described, in proverbial style, as a people who heard and saw but chose not to understand and know because they had rejected the Lord as their God (6:9–10). God's words in v. 9 allude to 5:12, 19 where Israel is accused of ignoring His counsel and disregarding His work. The Lord's commission is stated as a command (6:10). The verbal links with the characterization of the people in v. 9 are picked up, but now there is an emphasis on the human organs of hearing, seeing, and understanding. This is arranged as a chiasm: heart, ears, eyes//eyes, ears, heart (v. 10).

The people would not return to God to be healed. There was no longer any mercy for Israel; what remained was judgment. Isaiah's mission was to continue instructing Israel with warnings and predictions of judgment, but God knew that they would continue to reject Him. The command was not a denial of their freedom of choice but a way of saying that the more Isaiah would plead for conversion, the more they would choose to remain disobedient, and the judgment would therefore no longer be averted. Isaiah's question "How long?" belongs to the laments of the people (6:11; e.g., Pss. 74:10; 79:5; 89:46; 90:13; 94:3), in the hope that the judgment would not be God's final work but that in view of His loving-kindness, there was salvation in sight. The question comes from the faithful ones who wait for the Lord and trust/hope in Him (Is. 8:17). These ideas are key themes in the whole book.

The Lord's answer (6:11–13) described a series of future events for Israel. There would be destruction and deportation (vv. 11–12), comparable to the downfall of the Northern Kingdom of Israel caused by the Assyrians in 722 B.C. The holy seed (cf. 4:2–3; 11:1), which would eventually grow out of the stump or stem of Jesse, would be the remnant in Jerusalem, namely, those who would patiently wait for the Lord. Based on His loving-kindness, the Lord would not completely destroy His people: a restored Israel would be established from the remnant (cf. chaps. 60–62).

7:1—8:15
The Immanuel Sign

A sign from the Lord may (1) impart knowledge (e.g., 19:20), (2) produce faith (e.g., 7:9c, 11–16), (3) confirm a prophet's authority (e.g., 38:7, 22; cf. 2 Kings 20:8–11), or (4) reinforce the message by a symbolic act (e.g., Is. 7:3; 8:1–4, 8, 18; 20:3). It may be a *miracle* (38:7–8) or an *event* that fulfills a prediction (55:13). The Immanuel sign is a mixture of these functions. The setting of chapter 9 is the Syro-Ephraimite crisis in 734–732 B.C. (see Isaiah: Introduction). King Ahaz of Judah and his people were stricken with fear due to an imminent attack by Syria and Israel.

7:1–12. Isaiah and the King. God told Isaiah to bring his son Shear-Jashub (meaning "a remnant shall return") and give a message to the king. He encouraged Ahaz not to fear because the schemes of Syria and Israel would fail. The admonition to not fear was often used to reassure someone in trouble and was intended to alleviate fear (of death) and to strengthen resolve (vv. 8–9). The meaning of the elliptic formulation of vv. 8–9, substantiated in 8:5–10 (cf. 7:4, 8), is that Syria and Ephraim/Israel were at the time intact and their kings secure, but very soon Syria would be ruined and Ephraim diminished, and within sixty-five years Ephraim would be so broken and shattered that it would not be a people. Ephraim/Israel was destroyed by a massive Assyrian deportation in 722 B.C., but the prophecy of ceasing to be a people was fulfilled when Esarhaddon (680–669 B.C.) repopulated Israel and Samaria with many foreign colonists (Ezra 4:2; cf. 2 Kin. 17:24–41).

Ahaz was warned that if he did not firmly trust in God's promises, he would not be established (Is. 7:9). This concluding message to Ahaz implied that Judah, too, would be broken unless he and his house trusted the Lord (cf. 10:20; 26:3–4; 30:15–18; 31:1). There is a Hebrew wordplay in 7:9. The Lord told Ahaz that if he did not *'aman*, the *hiphil* form of the verb, meaning to "believe" or "trust," he would not *'aman*, the *niphal* of the same verb, meaning "to stand," "be confirmed," or "be established." Faith in the Lord, which implies trusting and relying on Him,

is all that He requires from His people. Ahaz failed to trust the Lord and contacted the Assyrians with a request for help against the Syro-Ephraimite coalition, resulting in foreign cult practices in Judah and disastrous consequences resulting from the Assyrian "protection" (2 Kin. 16:10–18).

The Lord invited Ahaz to ask for a sign—from the depths or the heights (7:11). It would be *miraculous* because it would affect anything in the realm of creation. It would *produce faith* (v. 9), and it would *confirm* that the Lord's promise of salvation would be fulfilled (vv. 3–9). But Ahaz refused the offer (v. 12). His pretentiously pious reason, that he did not want to test the Lord, followed the covenant principle in Deuteronomy 6:16, but in reality he had already decided to rely on the power of Assyria. Isaiah then reproached the house of David (Is. 7:13), which implies that the disobedience of the Davidic kings to the Lord was a major reason for the Assyrian judgment. God promised David that He would establish his house forever (2 Sam. 7:11–16). It was founded on the Lord being "with" David (2 Sam. 7:3, 9). This implied God's *protection* of David and *peace* for Israel (2 Sam. 7:9–10). The relationship between the Lord and the Davidic king was defined as a father-son relationship (2 Sam. 7:14). This Davidic covenant also contained the idea of mercy in the context of judgment (2 Sam. 7:14–15). This covenant is implied in the sign of Immanuel: *'im* ("with") and *'anu* ("us") and *'el* ("God"; Is. 7:14–16).

7:13–25. Promise of Immanuel. The translation "the virgin" is based on the LXX (cf. Matt. 1:23), but the Hebrew *'almah* designates a young woman of marriageable age. To mean "virgin," Hebrew uses the word *betulah*. However, *'almah* is flexible in meaning and can refer to a virgin. It is usually suggested that *'almah* probably referred to the unknown mother of Immanuel in the time of Ahaz. The NT would identify the fulfillment of this prophecy with the miraculous birth of Jesus, the true Immanuel (Matt. 1:25).

Immanuel means "with us God" and alludes to the ideological foundation of the house of David (2 Sam. 7:3, 9). Immanuel implies the Lord's presence, blessing, and protection and functions as a guarantee of peace. Even if God chastised the Davidic kings with the rod, His mercy would not depart from them. But the sign would not function without the king's faith in God. It is connected to the Davidic, messianic Prince of Peace in Isaiah 9:6–7 and to the righteous Branch of the stem/stump of Jesse in 11:1–10 (cf. 4:2).

The simple diet of curds and honey would be eaten in times of hardship by those remaining in the land (7:22), implying survival in humble conditions. Like the "stump" or "stem" in 11:1, the diet figuratively describes the lowly state to which the house of David would be reduced as a result of Ahaz's disobedience.

Before the age of knowing to refuse evil and choose good, the child would eat curds and honey. This refers to the time when the Assyrians would turn Judah into briars and thorns (7:18–25). However, Syria and Israel would fall before that time (vv. 1–9; 8:1–10). Thus, Isaiah drew a timeline: (1) his crisis at the time of writing (7:1–9; in 734–733 B.C.); (2) the Assyrian punishment of rebellious Syria and Israel, as the Lord predicted (v. 16b; in 732 B.C.); and (3) an Assyrian invasion of Judah, which would humiliate the house of David but not completely destroy the country (vv. 10–25; in 701 B.C.; cf. 6:11–13).

Ahaz's rejection of the Immanuel sign would have disastrous consequences over a long time. The Lord would bring the king of Assyria upon Ahaz, his people, and his family (v. 17). Ahaz's subjection of Judah to Assyrian protection brought the Assyrian army into Judah, resulting in the subjugation of Jerusalem to Assyrian overlords. Isaiah states that this would bring back the days when Ephraim departed from Judah, which resulted in the Davidic dynasty suffering a significant loss of land and people. Assyria and Egypt would be called upon to execute judgment against Judah (vv. 18–20). The mention of all those who would be left in the land refers to a remnant after death and deportation, when the available food would be curds and honey. This is a figurative reference to the humble circumstances of Judah and the Davidic dynasty in the future as a consequence of Ahaz's rejection of the Immanuel sign. God commanded Isaiah to write Maher-Shalal-Hash-Baz on a scroll. The name literally means "speed, spoil, hasten, plunder" or "quick to the plunder, swift to the spoil." The Hebrew word *gillayon* can mean "scroll" or "tablet" (of wood, stone, or leather). The reference to the *kheret 'enosh*, literally meaning "human engraving tool," presumably meant writing in a script that was legible to the people (cf. Hab. 2:2). That it was to be a large scroll or tablet may mean that it was fixed in a public place where it could be seen by all or that the text was extensive. Isaiah took faithful, reliable witnesses (Is. 7:2) to prove the authority and time of the prediction (cf. comments on 8:16). Notice that Isaiah's wife was a "prophetess" (*nebi'ah*). It was not a practice in ancient Israel to refer to a wife by the profession of her husband. No other biblical prophet named his wife "prophetess." Thus, Isaiah's wife was likely an active prophetess. The name Maher-Shalal-Hash-Baz means that the wealth of Damascus and the plunder of Samaria would be taken by the king of Assyria, confirming the prophecy in 7:3–9.

8:1–15. Assyria Captures Israel and Judah. The prediction of Assyria's capture of Syria and Israel in v. 4 continues in vv. 6–10, but with Syria replaced by Judah, making Israel and Judah the targets of the Assyrian attack. Two contrasting metaphors relating to "water" are used: the gentle, flowing waters of Shiloah (i.e., the Davidic dynasty under the Lord's protection of Zion) are contrasted with the torrents of the Euphrates (lit. "the River")—the king of Assyria in all his splendor (vv. 6–7). Isaiah quotes the Lord saying that because "this people" (i.e., the Northern Kingdom of Israel) had refused the waters of Shiloah and had instead rejoiced in Rezin and Remaliah's son, the Lord would bring the king of Assyria against them.

Assyria would first capture Israel (8:4; 2 Kin. 15:29; 17:5–6), but would then pass through Judah and overwhelm it (Is. 8:8). Here the Lord addressed Immanuel and said that the outstretched wings of the king of Assyria would cover the whole land. This is a way of saying that although Assyria would overwhelm Judah, Jerusalem would be spared because Immanuel was the Lord's sign confirming His faithfulness to His covenant with David. The prediction may, therefore, concern Sennacherib's destruction of Judah in 701 B.C., when the Lord spared Jerusalem and the Davidic king (cf. 1:4–9). The judgment against Judah turns here to salvation (8:9–10), for the Lord issued orders against the aggressors, and the people could say, "God is with us"—Immanuel. The Lord instructed Isaiah concerning "this people," including both Israel and Judah (vv. 11–15). As confirmed by the sign of Immanuel, the faithful needed to hold on to the Lord (v. 13). He would be a sanctuary or holy place (i.e., a refuge and place of rest) for the faithful but a stone of stumbling for the apostates (vv. 14–15).

8:16—9:7
Isaiah's Family: A Sign

In this section, Isaiah's predictions concerning the defeat of Syria and Israel were confirmed (cf. 7:1—8:15). The dark aftermath for Israel and Judah (8:21—9:1) would be changed by the messianic Prince of Peace (9:2-7).

8:16—9:1. Law and Testimony. The "testimony" and the "law" (or instruction) have been taken by some as two words expressing one thought, which in this case is another way of designating the word of God written on a large scroll or tablet (8:1-2) containing the Lord's judgment against Syria and Israel (v. 4). But their use in v. 20 indicates that we are dealing with two different things. The "law" refers to the written revelation of God and the "testimony" to the prophetic word as the standard by which falsehood is distinguished from truth. In Isaiah, the Hebrew word *torah* often means not only the "law" but especially "instruction," which is at times in parallel with the "word of the Lord" (1:10; 2:3; 5:24; 8:16, 20; 30:9; 51:4, 7). But it can also refer to God's law as preserved in the Pentateuch (5:24; 24:5). The sign of the testimony and the law indicates that God's word, both in His law and in the prophetic voice, is true, and yet Israel and Judah rejected both.

Literally, a "sealed" scroll was one that had been signed and witnessed legally. Metaphorically, however, it was "sealed" in the sense that its content was inviolable and to be preserved. What the people rejected—the law and the testimony—was as valid as if it had been sealed. It was also to be "sealed" or "preserved" in the sense that it was to be written in the heart of the "disciples"—those who accepted and practiced the law and the testimony (see Prov. 3:3; 6:20-21; 7:2-3; cf. 2 Cor. 3:2). In the case of Isaiah, the sealing of the testimony could refer to the validity of his prophecy that had been proven true by real events, thus confirming the reliability of God's word through him. The Hebrew verbs usually translated as "bind up" and "seal" could also be translated as "the testimony is bound up, and the instruction is sealed." The phrase "among my disciples" would then keep its literal sense "in my disciples." The house of Jacob was already under judgment (Is. 8:17). Isaiah continued to wait for the Lord and hope in Him, expecting the promise of salvation through Immanuel to be fulfilled. He would totally depend on God's revealed will.

Isaiah affirms the Lord's call (cf. 6:8). He speaks of his literal children, for children as "a gift of God" had deep roots in ancient Israel (Pss. 113:9; 127:3-5; 128:1-6; 144:12). Isaiah and his children were God's signs and wonders (or symbols) for Israel. They, and their names in particular, were evidence that God was still active within His people to move them to believe in Him.

The tragic fate of Israel served as a warning to Judah (Is. 8:19—9:1). Ahaz thought he could save his kingdom by seeking help from the Assyrian overlords, but as a result of his lack of faith in God, Judah would suffer the same fate as Israel. The law and the testimony (8:16) and the children of Isaiah (v. 18) invited the people to seek God and reject deception. But instead of listening to the written law of God and to the prophetic word, some of the people were asking mediums and wizards/spiritists for help (Deut. 18:9-14; 1 Kin. 22:5). Verse 20 contains an important hermeneutical principle: the law and the prophets are to be used to establish what is from the Lord and what is not (cf. Matt. 5:17). "They" refers to any false counselor who led the people away from their God and His word. The rejection of God's revelation would leave them in total darkness (Is. 8:21-22).

In v. 21, "they" refers to the people of v. 19 who were not seeking the Lord for help. Afflicted by hunger and oppression, the people would be enraged, cursing their king and their God (v. 21c). In desperation the people would look upward and to the earth (i.e., everywhere; v. 22a) for help, but they would be disappointed. However, there is something better (9:1a): the condition of the land would change because the state of darkness would not be permanent.

Although 9:1b is difficult, the general meaning is quite clear. There is a contrast between the former condition of the land on account of the sin of the people and what God would do to it in the future. The "land of Zebulun and the land of Naphtali" are the Israelite names for northern Israel, while the second set of names refers to the three provinces that the Assyrians created when Tiglath-Pileser annexed northern Israel in 732 B.C.: "the way of the sea" refers to Dulru (Dor), the land "beyond the Jordan" to Gal'azu (Gilead), and "Galilee of the Gentiles" or "nations" to Magidu (Megiddo). Thus, the two enumerations refer to the same areas of land but with Israelite and Assyrian names— one refers to the time before the Syro-Ephraimite war, and the other to the time thereafter.

9:2-7. Prince of Peace. In the future the Lord would bring the Davidic Prince of Peace, Immanuel, to the land to reunite the two houses of Israel. The promise of Immanuel (7:14-16; 8:8-10) reaches its climax in the promise of the Davidic Prince (9:2-7; see Matt. 4:12-16). The light of the Lord's salvation would replace the darkness (9:2) of the Assyrian occupations, which resulted from the people abandoning the

Lord (8:21—9:1) by following the instructions of mediums and wizards/spiritists (8:19–20). However, the Lord's future plan was to break the yoke of the people's burden, the staff or bar on their shoulder, and the rod of their oppressor (9:4; cf. 10:24–27) and bring war to an end (9:5; cf. 2:4). The "great light" (9:2) is a symbol of life, joy, and salvation (cf. 42:6; 49:6; Num. 6:24–26; Job 3:20; Ps. 36:9). They rejoice because God would be victorious over the oppressor, grant them everlasting peace (vv. 3–5), increase the nation (v. 3), and give it a secure future (note the contrast between the joy of harvest in v. 3 and the hunger and curses in 8:21). But more specifically, the joy derives from the announced birth of a Davidic Prince and Savior (9:6–7).

The passage in vv. 6–7 is an announcement of the birth of a unique child who would be officially elevated to the status of Crown Prince and proclaimed as the future Ruler. He would rule with just judgment and righteousness on the throne of David and over his kingdom (v. 7). War and strife would be no more, for He would end oppression from without and injustice from within (cf. 2:2–4; 4:2; 29:18–20; 30:20–22; 32:16). The statement that the government would be upon the King's shoulder alludes to the symbol of a scepter borne on the shoulder (cf. staff and rod/bar in 9:4; and cf. 14:5; Gen. 49:10; Ps. 110:2; Ezek. 19:14) as sign of power (Num. 24:17; cf. Ps. 125:3). It is contrasted with the oppressive shoulder yoke and staff mentioned in Isaiah 9:4 and indicates a shift from the oppressors to the Davidic Prince. In Israel the scepter implied that the king was a "son" of God—he was a vassal of the Divine Overlord (cf. 2 Sam. 7:14)—suggesting a very intimate relationship between the Lord and His earthly representative, the king. However, the list of names found in Isaiah 9:6 was never applied to the kings of God's people. We are dealing here with a unique king. The first two names concern the King's attributes, the second pair the character of His rule. The two words "wonderful" and "counselor" are one component (lit. "wonder of a counselor"). Counselor applies to a Ruler who, like the Lord, plans wonderful and amazing things (cf. 28:29).

"Mighty God" (*'el gibbor*; 9:6) could literally be translated "God of a Warrior," "God is a Warrior," or "Warrior God." Although this name does not by itself demonstrate that this messianic king is divine, in light of 10:21 we can claim that He is divine. There the title "Mighty God" (*'el gibbor*) is used to identify God. This qualification enables the King to overcome all

enemies (cf. 11:1–10). The Child is revealed as both divine and human (the Mighty God born of a woman).

Everlasting Father (*'abi 'ad*) literally means "Father of Eternity." Although the dynasty and kingdom of a faithful king were thought to continue forever (2 Sam. 7:16; Pss. 21:1–4; 72:5, 17; 132:11–14), no king in Israel was called by this name. The reference to the messianic "son" as also being the "eternal Father" is not a confusion of the persons of the Trinity. The language of fatherhood could be applied to the Messiah because He brought His people into existence, redeemed them, and has treated them as a loving father would, with care and mercy (cf. Is. 22:21; John 1:1–3; 1 John 2:29). The passage also bears witness to the fact that the Messiah has always been—He is eternal.

The "Prince of Peace" (*sar shalom*) is a surprising title in the context of titles that imply the power of this King. This new name shows that His power expresses itself in peace. He protects and safeguards peace by His wisdom, justice, and righteousness (cf. Is. 11:1–3; Ps. 72:3, 7). Isaiah's prediction of a royal Savior in Isaiah 9:6–7 remained unfulfilled until the coming of Jesus of Nazareth. He is called the Light (John 1:4–9), and His coming to Capernaum in Galilee, in the regions of Zebulun and Naphtali, in order to preach the imminence of the kingdom of God, was a literal fulfillment of Isaiah 9:1–2 (Matt. 4:12–17).

9:8—10:4
Israel's Chastisement: A Warning to Judah

This passage adds further background to the judgments against Israel and Judah (cf. 5:1–30; 7:17–25; 8:1–10), a review of past cases, and a warning to Judah.

The first case under review is that of the Northern Kingdom of Israel. It had been punished because of its "pride and arrogance of heart." The "heart" in Hebrew was the seat of the will and intentions, where decisions were made and the word of God was heard (i.e., understood and obeyed). A proud and arrogant heart (6:10) is often associated with idol worship (cf. 2:6–22; 3:16–23). As a whole, the proverbial saying in 9:10 expresses the pride that led to Israel's secession in the tenth century B.C. (cf. 7:17; 1 Kin. 12). References to building refer metaphorically to the people. Bricks of clay and beams of sycamore (Is. 9:10) were used by people in general, whereas hewn stones and cedar wood were used by the upper classes for palaces. The refrain in v. 12 applies the lesson of history to Judah: God's anger had not been appeased, and more disasters were to come (cf. 5:25). "For all this" summarizes the people's crime and the punishment resulting from the Lord's anger, yet His anger was still not turned away.

The second case concerns false rulers and teachers (9:15–17). The consequences for Israel and Judah would be the suffering of the innocent and great loss of life. If all Israel would have turned back to the Lord (v. 13; cf. 8:19–20), His anger would have been turned away (9:17). But since they rejected Him (v. 13), He would cut off both head and tail in Israel in one day (v. 14). In the metaphor, the head (v. 15; cf. 19:15; Deut. 28:13, 44) refers to the elders and honorable dignitaries (i.e., the political rulers), and the tail signifies the prophets who were teaching lies, in other words, the religious teachers (9:15). As representatives of two extremes, they signified totality (cf. 3:1–3). The rulers led the people astray (9:16; cf. 3:12), and every one of them was profane and evil (9:17).

The third case under review is about evil that destroys fraternal bonds and breeds its own punishment (vv. 18–20; cf. 3:9–11). The metaphor of wickedness as a consumer of the briars, thorns, and forest thickets (i.e., the apostates themselves; cf. 5:6) is explained in 9:18–19. The people's wickedness had elicited the Lord's wrath, leading to the Assyrian invasions that burned up the land and the people. The invasions would cause social chaos and civil strife (9:19d–20d). People would not spare each other, and there would be tribal warfare between the tribes of Israel (vv. 20–21). To eat the flesh of someone is a figure of speech for a bitter hostility toward them (Ps. 27:2; cf. Job 19:22). The historical background for Isaiah 9:21 was the ongoing power struggle between Manasseh and Ephraim. Roughly between 750 and 722 B.C., the struggle for the throne was mainly between these two tribes. In the Syro-Ephraimite war, Ephraim and Manasseh turned against Judah (2 Kin. 15:37; Is. 7:1—8:15). In summary, Isaiah 9:18–21 warns that if Judah were to continue in apostasy, the same fate that befell Israel would fall on Judah.

The fourth case addresses the royal officials of Judah, holding them accountable for the past and present conditions (10:1–4). Isaiah speaks regarding enactors of evil statutes and oppressive laws, who have the authority to produce documents that legalize their social injustices. The protection of the rights of the poor, the needy, widows, and orphans was the special responsibility of the

king (e.g., Ps. 72:1–4; Prov. 29:14). Compliance with this responsibility revealed the king's willingness to be loyal to the Lord. The crimes mentioned (Is. 1:17, 23; 3:14–15) elicited God's anger and judgment (10:3–4; cf. 9:17). Three rhetorical questions in 10:3 describe the judgment. For the refrain in v. 4, see 9:12.

10:5—12:6
Assyria Defeated, a Second David, and Israel

Within the frame of God's plan for Zion, He had chastised and cleansed His people through Assyria's invasions (5:1—10:4), but now He would restore His universal kingdom through a remnant of Israel and a righteous Davidic King (10:5—12:6).

10:5–19. Assyria Is Judged. The Lord chose Assyria as His agent to chastise Israel, but the woe had become directed against Assyria because of its arrogance. Isaiah quotes the Lord's decision to commission the king of Assyria as His instrument. Assyria's task was to remove Israel's pride in material goods and to humble them. But the Assyrian king distorted his task and, instead of chastising and purifying Israel, sought to destroy nations as he strove for power (vv. 7–14). God rejected the imperial goals of the Assyrian king, accusing him of excessive destruction, robbery, arrogance, and claiming world power for himself.

The king expressed arrogance in two ways. First, it was his plan to destroy Jerusalem as he had destroyed Samaria, but this was not God's intention (vv. 8–12). Second, through his arrogance and claim to world power, the Assyrian king (vv. 13–14) challenged the Lord's sovereignty. In all his self-praise in vv. 7–14, the Assyrian king never mentioned the Lord. The Lord's announcement of the punishment of Assyria opens with a set of four metaphors (v. 15). The ax, saw, rod, and staff/club are merely instruments in the hands of power. Some of these metaphors may be related to the royal insignia of rod and staff/club (v. 5), implying that Assyria's royal power was granted by God, who alone sets kings and removes them.

Another set of metaphors occurs in vv. 16–19. First, the Lord would send emaciation on the well-fed people (i.e., the people of Assyria would lack food, and the well-grown vegetation of the land would fade away; v. 16). Second, under his (the king's) glory/pomp the Lord would literally "burn a burning like burning of fire." The Light of Israel and his Holy One are terms for the Lord Himself. The fire would burn and destroy Assyria's thorns and briars in one day, as a retribution for what Assyria had done to Israel (9:18–19). The Lord would avenge His people.

10:20–34. The Remnant of Israel. Assyria at this point stands as a symbol of the fall of God's enemies, and the prophecy moves from the time of Assyria to the coming of the Messiah and the final restoration of the earth. The *first consequence* of the fall of Assyria—representing the fall of God's enemies—is that a remnant of Israel would be converted (vv. 20–22) when God inflicted His punishment upon Israel (vv. 23–27). The people in Zion were encouraged not to fear Assyria (v. 24). Although it would strike Israel as God's rod and staff/club (cf. vv. 5–6), God's wrath would eventually turn against Assyria (v. 25). He would save His people through signs and wonders as He had done when He destroyed Midian and delivered His people from Egypt (v. 26).

The *second consequence* of Assyria's fall would be the replacement of the proud human king by a righteous Davidic King (10:27—11:10). Assyria stands for the fall of the kingdoms of the earth at the coming of the Messiah. The destruction of Assyria's yoke (10:27) and the Lord's humbling of proud, mighty Assyria (vv. 33–34) frame the central passage on the arrogance and threat of the Assyrian king (vv. 28–32). The phrase *mipne shamen* (lit. "because"/"before"/"by the face of the oil"/"fat") has been understood in various ways. Some take it to refer to the *shemen*, "fat" or "oil" (i.e., "fertile," "fruitful," "plenteous"; cf. 5:1; 25:6; 28:1, 4, where the same Hebrew word is used) which indicated the prideful wealth of Assyria. Others understand it as a reference to the anointed king—Hezekiah or David (for whose sake God would defeat Assyria [37:35]), and by extension the Messiah (Heb. the "anointed One"), who was associated with the breaking of the yoke in 9:4–7. The focus is on the destruction of the yoke itself, Assyria, which stands for all of God's enemies.

During his western campaign of 720 B.C., Sargon moved quickly south to deal with the Egyptians, who supported the rebellious Philistine city of Gaza (10:28–34). By marching by Jerusalem, he intended to discourage Judah from joining the rebellious states. However, Sargon would shake his fist against Jerusalem (v. 32). This would be an act of blasphemy against the Lord comparable to the later threat by Sennacherib in 701 B.C. Jerusalem survived on both occasions. The predicted punishment of the Assyrian king and his people is recorded in vv. 33–34.

11:1–16. The Stem of Jesse. Isaiah's announcement of a Davidic King follows rather abruptly after the account of the downfall of the Assyrian king (10:33–34), which might suggest the downfall of Assyria as a microcosm of the fall of all of God's enemies. Chapter 11:1–10 resumes and elaborates the announced coming Savior as the "Branch of the LORD" (4:2), the sign of Immanuel (7:10–16; 8:5–10), and the Davidic Prince (9:2–7). The stem of Jesse refers to the father of David (1 Sam. 16:1). The future Davidic King would not be subordinated to David but would be, in typological terms, a second David (cf. Is. 9:7; 16:5; Jer. 23:5–6; 30:9; Ezek. 34:23–24; 37:24–25). The point of the image is that the royal Savior would come from humble beginnings after the disappearance of the royal house in Jerusalem (cf. Is. 39:5–7), just as it happened with Jesus of Nazareth.

"The Spirit of the LORD" (11:2) equipped leaders with divine power (e.g., Judg. 6:34; 1 Sam. 11:6), wisdom, and knowledge (Ex. 31:1–5; Is. 42:1–4; 59:21; 61:1–3; 63:10–14). Three pairs of words describe the gifts of the Spirit bestowed on the ideal messianic King (11:2): (1) wisdom and understanding refer to His judicial office (cf. vv. 3–4); (2) counsel and might refer to His role as a military leader (cf. vv. 4–5); and (3) knowledge and fear of the Lord indicate His relationship with the Lord (cf. vv. 6–9). He would delight in the fear of the Lord (v. 3), which would be necessary for making righteous judgments (v. 4). His attributes and divine values of righteousness and faithfulness are pictured as His military armor (cf. 59:17; Eph. 6:14). This description of peace among the inhabitants of Zion would impact the nations of the earth: they would come to have knowledge of the Lord (Is. 11:9). The rule of the promised messianic King would be established on "the fear of the LORD" (v. 3a) and "the knowledge of the LORD" (v. 9b). This would certainly be the ultimate result of the work of Christ.

The *third consequence* of Assyria's fall (see 10:20) would be the future recognition of the Davidic King and Savior by the nations (11:10). The peaceful reign of the coming King, with righteousness, faithfulness, and justice, would bring the nations to Him (v. 10). Verse 10 can be literally translated "A Root of Jesse who is standing as a banner of the peoples—to him will the nations turn" (see John 12:32). The "banner" or "standard" was a sign indicating a point of assembly in a military setting. The peoples' attention would be drawn to the Davidic King by His ethical attributes (v. 2), quality of government (vv. 3–5), and the peace of His reign. Finally, the earth would be full of the knowledge of the Lord (vv. 6–9). The implication is that this King, identified in the NT as Jesus Christ, would not depend on military might, executive power, or material glory.

The Gentiles would seek Him (v. 10). The act of the nations would be a religious activity. They would turn to the Davidic King (gather around Him), the Savior and Lord, to obtain His teaching and blessings (cf. 2:2–4). The "resting place" is associated in the ANE with the temples that functioned as the resting places of the gods. Similarly, the Jerusalem temple is portrayed as God's resting place in Isaiah (18:4; 66:1; cf. 28:12; 30:15; 32:18; Ps. 132:14).

The *fourth consequence* of Assyria's fall (see Is. 10:22) would be the future restoration of Israel under the messianic King (11:11–16). As the Lord had once delivered Israel from Egypt (vv. 15–16), He would now also save the remnant of His people (cf. 43:3–7, 16–21; 48:21). The countries listed in 11:11 reflect the idea of "the four sections of the earth" (v. 12; cf. 43:5; 49:12). The "banner" (11:12) has been identified as the messianic King (v. 10). The "nations" either include the remnant of the Lord's people from foreign lands or those who would be summoned to escort or bring the exiles back to Israel and Judah (cf. 49:22; 60:9; 66:18–21). The background for 11:13–14 seems to be the schism and secession of Israel from Judah, which was a severe blow to the Davidic dynasty. In 7:17 it is suggested that the split was mainly blamed on Ephraim's envy, which made them hostile to Judah. As the tribes of all Israel reunited, their archenemies would be subdued by the glory of the messianic kingdom.

The concluding passage describes the future return from exile as a new exodus from Egypt (11:15–16; cf. 42:15–17). The first part of v. 15 alludes to the Red Sea, where it is called (lit.) the "tongue" (i.e., the gulf) of the sea of Egypt, which the Lord miraculously parted so that the Israelites could cross (Ex. 14). Here it is a symbol of the power that God would display during the new exodus. The expression "seven streams" may refer to passageways through the river that God's wind, *'ayam*, variously translated as "mighty," "scorching," "powerful," or

literally "glowing," would make for the returning remnant (cf. Ex. 14:22, 29).

12:1–6. Hymn of Praise. The downfall of God's enemies would move the remnant to sing a hymn of praise to God (vv. 1–6), a hymn serving as a conclusion to chapters 2–12. The reference to what they would say on "that day" is repeated in v. 4 to introduce another hymn of praise (cf. 11:10–11). The hymn opens with words that reflect the faithful attitude of the speaker. It consists of thanksgiving, prayer, confession, and affirmation of salvation (cf. Pss. 6:9; 22:19–24; 56:13). God's last word is not of anger, and consequently the petitioners would testify of God comforting them. There is no complaint against the Lord, only faith and thankfulness. Isaiah's text contains a message of comfort, telling them that they would "draw water from the wells of salvation" (Is. 12:3), that is, there would come a day when they would experience God's salvation and draw the water of life with joy from the wells of salvation. Indeed, the messianic King, Jesus, is the water of salvation (John 4:13–14).

The second hymn of praise (Is. 12:4–6) announces that "in that day" the redeemed would burst into collective praises to the Lord for His acts. The Lord's wonders for His people would be made known to the nations so that they would turn to the "Root of Jesse" (11:10) and to the word of the Lord and His law/instruction (2:2–4). The vision of the coming messianic kingdom of peace is saturated with a hope that has sustained and continues to sustain God's people in the midst of the unrest of the nations of the earth.

13:1—23:18

PREPARATION OF THE NATIONS FOR THE LORD'S KINGDOM

This block of prophecies against twelve nations (13:1—23:18) describes the future removal of those opposed to God's sovereignty and prepares the readers for the establishment of the Lord's reign as the King of the world in 24:1—27:13.

13:1—14:27
Utterance Concerning Babylon

The superscription mentions only "Babylon," but the utterance itself concerns Babylon *and* Assyria (13:19; 14:4, 22, 25) because the Assyrian emperor had dual kingship (see Isaiah: Introduction).

13:1-5. Preparation for Battle. The Hebrew *massa'* has been variously translated as "burden," "prophecy," or "oracle." It could also mean something like "utterance" (as in Prov. 30:1; 31:1; cf. Is. 14:4). Babylon is placed first in chapters 13-23 because it is the primary representative of the evil, wickedness, iniquity, arrogance, and pride of the earth, which the Lord would punish on the day of His wrath. Assyria was also "Babylon" in the sense that it relied on Babylon's enormous prestige and power, its unique and leading role in religion, and its learning and culture. The Assyrian kings were kings of both Ashur and Babel.

"Babylon" is associated in Isaiah with human arrogance and rebellion against God (13:1— 14:23; 47:7-8; cf. Gen. 11:1-9) and with divination, sorcery, astrology, and idolatry (Is. 21:9; 47:9, 12-13; cf. 41:21-29). Babylon was widely thought to be the "gate of God." In the Lord's plan for world sovereignty, therefore, the removal of Babylon was of first importance. God commands the army leaders to summon their warriors using a banner, a vocal summons, and a gesture. The Lord musters the troops, formed by soldiers from far away countries, that will attack Babylon. They are the weapons of God's wrath to destroy all the land (13:5).

13:6-22. The Day of the Lord for Babylon. The fall of Babylon is described using the images and language of the Day of the Lord. What the Lord would do to Babylon would cause upheavals of cosmic dimensions, and there is accordingly an eschatological flavor to the prophecy. The people were commanded to wail for the coming of the Day of the Lord, which would bring destruction, fear, pain, and sorrow. The Lord's holy anger would destroy His enemies. It would be a cruel day of wrath, and it would create great commotion, for it would desolate the land and destroy the sinners in it (v. 9). The cosmic order would also be upset when the cosmic lights would go dark and leave the land in obscurity (v. 10). The Lord would punish the world and human evil and arrogance (v. 11).

The massive military attack would almost exterminate humans from the land. The reference to fine or pure gold illustrates precious value. Only a few human survivors would be left in the land—and they would be rarer than precious gold (v. 12). The prophet returns to the cosmic upheaval that would shake the heavens and the earth, giving to the prophecy a universal perspective that would reach beyond the experience of Babylon to the time when God would overcome all His enemies. The war against Babylon would include the extermination of men, women, children, and houses (vv. 14-16).

Finally, the prophet identifies the enemy that would destroy Babylon: the Medes. There would be no way to escape the Medes because they would reject gold as a ransom for human life (v. 17). They would mercilessly kill the young, the unborn, and children. They would reduce Babylon to the condition of Sodom and Gomorrah. The city and its land would be desolated, and never again would it be inhabited; it would become a wild land (vv. 20-22).

14:1-4. Mercy for Jacob. Right in the middle of the message against Assyria-Babylon we find a message of comfort for Jacob. God would have mercy on Jacob, choose Israel again, and settle them in their own land (v. 1). Amazingly, foreigners would join them and become attached to the "house" (or descendants) of Jacob. The name "Israel" implies a reunited Israel as in the times of David (cf. 11:11-16) that would also include the nations turning to the Lord (e.g., 2:2-4; 11:10; 49:8; 54:5; 55:5; 56:6-8). The nations would help in the Lord's mission of gathering the dispersed Israelites back to the promised land (cf. 11:10, 12; 49:22; 56:6-8; 60:1-16; 66:19-24).

But there would be a role reversal: they would make captives of those who had held them in captivity (14:1-2). And finally, Israel would be guaranteed peace and well-being, and the nations would join them in worshiping the Lord (cf. 56:6-8). Then they would all enjoy rest from their pain, sorrow, turmoil, and hard labor (14:3), which was caused by being separated from the promised land, and would worship the Lord in His dwelling place in Zion-Jerusalem.

14:4-11. Taunt Song and Babylon. This taunt song illustrates the disastrous fate of the wicked (cf. Job 15:20-35; 20:4-29; Pss. 7:14-16; 37:1-40). Specific details may be connected historically with Sargon II (14:8, 18-20), who was both king of Assyria and king of Babylon. The term *mashal*, which is sometimes translated as "proverb," refers here to a taunt song. After finding rest (vv. 1-4), Israel would look back at the past pride and death of the king of Assyria-Babylon to deride it. The dirge accuses the dead tyrant of wickedness and tauntingly pictures his punishment (vv. 5-6). The Lord has broken the staff or rod of the wicked and the scepter of the rulers (v. 5; cf. 9:4, 6). The king had ruled peoples and nations in anger (14:6). The last part of v. 6 has been understood in differing ways. Some translations imply that the description is still referring to what the king of Babylon had done in persecuting the nations, others imply that the king was now himself the object of persecution or aggression. This last suggestion is contextually more appropriate. The cypress or juniper trees and the cedars of Lebanon (v. 8) symbolize people, particularly kings and the rich. The whole land (or earth) is at rest and in peaceful quietness when the tyrant is dead (v. 7), but the trees celebrate since the woodsman is no longer coming (cf. the metaphor of trees in 10:17–19, 33–34).

The prophet sarcastically describes how the dead kings of the nations receive the tyrant in Sheol, the realm of the dead (14:9). Sheol is a poetic term used for the tomb, the realm of the dead, but here it is personified. It is astir and excited to meet the dead king, and the *repa'im* are agitated (v. 9). The term *repa'im* (perhaps meaning "the fallen ones") is used in the Bible to designate an ethnic group (Gen. 14:5), a geographical location (Josh. 15:8), and the dead in poetic texts (Is. 26:14, 19; Ps. 88:2). In v. 9, it is often translated as "the dead" or "spirits of the departed" who lack the vitality of life (v. 10). The language of the passage is highly poetical. The trees are personified and rejoice at the death of the king. The grave is also personified and rises up to meet the new dead king and to wake up the dead, the *repa'im*, to greet him. In an ironic tone they tell the king that he is now one of them, weak and covered by maggots and worms. The language is metaphorical, not literal. The poem is an excellent piece of literature in which a powerful person is mocked by a figurative description of what happens when he reaches the grave. It presupposes that the dead are in the grave in total unconsciousness. It is not describing the shadowy existence of human beings in the tomb. There is much biblical evidence that death is an unconscious, sleep-like state (e.g., 1 Kin. 2:10; Ps. 13:3; Eccl. 9:5; Acts 7:60; 1 Thess. 4:13–18).

The metaphorical description continues as the dead kings of the nations (such as Og, king of Bashan; Deut. 3:11) tauntingly address the tyrant (14:10b–15). In death, he will be as weak as all the other dead kings and his former glory will be gone. Death eliminates social distinctions, and the king is, like all of those in the tomb, covered by maggots. At long last, the enemy of God's people, represented by Assyria-Babylon, comes to his end.

14:12–17. King of Assyria-Babylon and Lucifer. The king lying on maggots is contrasted with his desire to ascend into heaven, elevate

his throne above the stars of God, sit enthroned on the mount of assembly (i.e., the heavenly temple), and make himself like the Most High (vv. 13–14). His humiliation is illustrated by the contrast between his desire to reach the heights of the north (*zapon*) and his final abode in the lowest depths of the pit (vv. 13, 15). The passage uses the language of the origin of evil in heaven through a fallen cherub to describe the human aspirations of the king (embodying the intentions and feelings of the fallen cherub). This angel or cherub became proud and sought to put himself in God's place but was cast down (cf. Ezek. 28:12–19). The book of Revelation expands this theme of the cosmic conflict (Rev. 12:7–9) and identifies the fallen cherub as Satan, the enemy of God and the cause of all evil on earth (17:1—18:24; 19:11—20:10; see Job: Introduction and "Evil and the Fallen Cherub," p. 1008).

The Hebrew name of the tyrant is *helel ben shakhar*, which literally means "shining one, son of the dawn," referring to the morning star, the planet Venus. The name "Lucifer" does not occur in the Hebrew text. It was introduced by the church father Jerome in his translation of the Bible into Latin (i.e., the Vg.) as a name for the morning star, literally meaning "light bearer." The naming of the tyrant as "the shining one, son of the dawn" mocks his desire to elevate his throne above the "stars of God" (Is. 14:13). It names him after the star known for rising up in the early morning sky, but this is followed by the star's sudden descent without completing its orbit. The OT refers to "morning stars" as "sons of God" or angels (Job 1:6; 2:1; 38:7). They belong to the heavenly council (Job 1:6; 2:1; Ps. 82:1), and Satan was prominent among them. Isaiah described the pride of the king of Babylon and his disastrous end in terms of what other biblical passages relate regarding the fall of the cherub who became Satan (see commentary on Ezek. 28:11–19). Isaiah 14:16–17 pictures living beings gazing in unbelieving amazement on the tyrant at his death (in the pit of Sheol), bringing to mind the final destruction of Satan (Rev. 20:10).

14:18–27. Final Fate of the King. The emperor's fate is, however, worse than that of other kings. Each of them rests in glory in his own tomb, literally "house" (v. 18), but the oppressor is thrown out of (Heb. *min*) his grave—the preposition *min* indicates that "he was thrown out without his own grave" (i.e., there was no tomb for him). To be unburied was the ultimate fate of the wicked. The tyrant's corpse would not even be buried with the dead warriors because he had destroyed his land and killed his people (i.e., he had betrayed the principles of God's government; v. 20).

The traditional fate of the wicked was that their descendants would never be named (v. 20d; cf. Job 18:16–19; Ps. 37:28, 35–36, 38; Prov. 10:7). The tyrant's children would perish, and no member of his dynasty would rise to inherit the land and populate the world with cities. The mocking dirge for the dead king of Assyria-Babylon is followed by the fall of Babylon (Is. 14:22–23) and Assyria (vv. 24–27). The Lord would eliminate their survivors, their name, and their descendants (v. 22). The city would become desolate and given to porcupines and marshes (cf. 13:17–22).

Isaiah 14:24–27 is a summary-appraisal of 13:1—14:23 that is formed by two parts: the Lord's oath concerning Assyria (14:24–25) and its application to all nations (vv. 26–27). The oath literally says, "I will break *'ashur*" (v. 25), which includes the god, city, and nation. God's land and His mountains refer to the promised land (cf. 49:11; 65:9). God would trample Assyria, thereby humiliating them and demonstrating His sovereignty. His ultimate purpose is the removal of Israel's yoke/burden (14:25). God intended the removal of Assyria's yoke to benefit the whole earth and all the nations (v. 26). The Lord delivers His people from the enemy, and this ultimately means the destruction of the enemy.

14:28—16:14
Messages against Philistia and Moab

This section is composed of two messages unveiling the destruction of Philistia (14:28–32) and Moab (15:1—16:14) and the reason for it.

14:28–32. Utterance concerning Philistia. The Philistines were the traditional enemies of Israel in Canaan. In this brief utterance, Isaiah warned Philistia and gave an assurance of salvation to the remnant of Judah. This particular message is dated to the year when Ahaz died, around 715 B.C. The Lord advised Philistia not to rejoice because of the downfall of Assyria— the rod that struck them. In the arena of international politics, another oppressor, a fiery (or poisonous) flying/darting serpent would follow the first (v. 29). He would besiege Philistia's cities with famine and leave no surviving remnant (v. 30). Therefore, Philistia was summoned to wail because smoke would come from the

north, and all Philistia would melt (v. 31). The end of v. 31 has been translated variously. The literal Hebrew is essentially "no one is separated from his appointed place," and this probably refers to the army approaching in closed, organized ranks with no one missing. Meanwhile, the royal court in Jerusalem must provide an answer for the messengers (ambassadors) from a nation seeking alliance with Judah because the Lord had founded Zion and His people, and *'ani*, "poor" or "afflicted," would find refuge there (v. 32; cf. v. 30).

15:1—16:14. Utterance Concerning Moab. This lamentation over the destruction of Moab concerns one of Israel's archenemies across the Jordan River. On the term *massa'*, "burden," "oracle," or "prophecy," see 13:1. The cause for the lament was a devastating foreign invasion. The description of the events moves from the north (15:2–4) to the south (vv. 5–7) to include all of Moab by mentioning its borders and including Eglaim and Beer Elim to the south and north of the River Arnon (vv. 8–9). The section concerning the north mentions the armed soldiers of Moab (v. 4), while the section on the southern locations mentions Moab's refugees (vv. 5, 7). The main Assyrian attack in 733 B.C. was north of Arnon, which agrees with vv. 4–7. The practices mentioned in vv. 2–3 were customary signs of mourning. Verse 6 pictures a famine brought on by drought and pictures mourning after an enemy invasion.

Isaiah advised Moab's "ruler of the land" (16:1) to send a peace offering to the mount of Daughter Zion (or Daughter of Zion). The reason was the fleeing of the daughters (perhaps a reference to the cities) of Moab across the Arnon, like birds scattered from their nests, apparently looking for refuge in Zion. Translations and commentators differ in regard to who is being addressed in vv. 3–5. Some suggest that Isaiah was advising the Moabites to be a shelter for God's outcasts (i.e., the people from Israel), while others suggest that either God or Moab's messengers were telling Israel to accept the refugees from Moab. Another issue is the unique word *pelilah*. Though usually translated as "judgment," "decision," or something similar, it is thought by some to be derived from *tepillah*, "prayer," and thus this would convey the idea of making a petition. If this is the case, and the text is referring to Moab's words to Israel, the meaning would be that Moab was to petition Zion to hide its refugees, allow them to live in Zion, and shelter them from the destroyer (or devastator). This advice was motivated by God breaking Assyria's power in the world (v. 4; cf. 10:5–34; 14:24–27) and would lead to the Messiah's kingdom when He would sit on the throne in the tabernacle of David (16:5). Once more the prophet has taken us from the local situation to the eschatological consummation in the messianic kingdom. Nations, as seekers of refuge in Judah and her God, would receive blessings.

The prophet acknowledges the news of Moab's downfall (vv. 6–8). Moab's pride, self-exaltation, and insolence were proverbial in Judah (cf. Jer. 48:29–30). The final clause of Isaiah 16:6 literally means "[we have heard of] the errors of his boastings." Proud Moab was to wail for itself (vv. 6–7), for it was like a vine with branches that stretched out and went over the sea (v. 8). This might be a reference to the export trade in wine or to the opulence of Moab's vineyards (cf. Jer. 48:31–33).

In 16:9–12 the prophet wails because the shouts of joy over Moab's summer fruit and harvests have ceased (some render *hedad* as "battle cries" rather than "shouting" or "shouting for joy"). Gladness and joy are removed from the plentiful field or orchard: the singing and shouting in the vineyards at the time of the harvest and the treading of grapes in winepresses have ceased. Praying at the sanctuary will not help. Then a new word of the Lord is added (vv. 13–14). In three years—not one moment more (time counted as in the situation of a slave who wants to leave once the debt is paid)—an enemy attack or famine would heavily reduce Moab's population.

17:1—18:7
Syria and Israel

The title includes only Damascus, and the passage provides a warning example of how the Lord punishes a proud and disobedient nation. Damascus was allied with the kingdom of Israel in the Syro-Ephraimite war (734–732 B.C.) and was ruined by Assyria.

17:1–14. Desolated Cities. Israel lost the city of Aroer to the Syrians and then to the Moabites, and it was finally destroyed by the Assyrians. This loss was a sign of the consequences of Israel's disobedience, which is the theme in vv. 4–6. Verse 2 has a common image of flocks of sheep grazing or resting in a ruined city to symbolize abandoned cities. The reference to the remnant of Syria (Aram) being like the glory of Israel

means that they would perish in the same way that the political glory of Israel perished because of their sin. According to vv. 4–6, the glory of Israel would decrease and weaken as a result of punishment. The mention of gleaning refers to the very poor remnant of the people who would survive the punishment (v. 6).

Isaiah says that a time would come, after the punishment, when humanity would recognize the Holy One of Israel (v. 7). Consequently, they would reject their idols and altars because they were the work of their hands (v. 8; cf. 2:8, 20; 5:12). But at that present time there was judgment because Israel had abandoned God, their Savior and Stronghold (17:10). The planting (end of v. 10) of foreign seedlings or imported vines may refer to fertility cults (cf. 1:29–30; 65:3). Such rebellion would make the harvest—not blessed by the Lord—into a heap of ruins on the day of grief. The woe to the multitude of many nations or peoples marks the beginning of their rebuke (v. 12). The peoples are first compared to the roar of the seas and the rushing of mighty waters. They would flee away like the chaff that is chased away by the wind during the harvest grain threshing (v. 13).

18:1–7. Distant Nations. The prophet announced that distant nations would recognize the Lord of Hosts on Mount Zion (v. 7), while Israel would reject the Lord and seek alliances with Egypt (17:1–11; 18:1–2). Israel would, therefore, be "trimmed" by the Lord (vv. 4–6). Ethiopia, or Cush (territory of modern Sudan), maintained diplomatic relations with the Near East by sea, or perhaps the Nile (v. 2). Israel and Judah occasionally considered the option of striking deals with Egypt when Cushite dynasties ruled. The speech in v. 2 seems to have been made by a king of Judah or Israel who sought to establish diplomatic relations with the nation south of Egypt. But at some point in the future, the nations of the earth would recognize the Lord. All the people in the world would see and hear the Lord's rallying signs (v. 3). As Lord of the world, He would review all nations from His heavenly temple (v. 4). Before the harvest the Lord would "trim" the buds and grapes and cut off the shoots and take away the branches (v. 5). Like the wasted parts of the vines, Israel would be cut off because of its apostasy (vv. 7–8). It would become like Damascus (17:1–3), which is what happened to Israel in 722 B.C. However, in contrast to Israel, the nation of Cush would represent all the nations from afar who would turn to the Lord (18:7).

19:1—20:6

Egypt

The message poetically describes the Lord's manifestation in the land of Egypt and its damaging effects on the nation. He would stir up civil conflicts (19:2) and destroy Egypt's spiritual guidance that was obtained through idols, charmers, mediums, and sorcerers (v. 3). He would hand them over to Assyria (v. 4). Pharaoh's counselors would not know what the Lord had devised against Egypt (v. 12). Therefore, they would give foolish counsel and make their princes into fools. Human wisdom does not save, and it would not save Egypt. The judgment of God would have five consequences (vv. 16–25). First, Egypt would fear what the Lord had determined against it, and it would also fear Judah (vv. 16–17). Second, five cities in Egypt would speak the language of Canaan (probably because they would be inhabited by Israelites who speak Hebrew), swear by (or pledge allegiance to) the Lord of Hosts, and honor Him as the true God (v. 18). Third, there would be an altar to the Lord in the land of Egypt and a pillar or monument to Him at its border as a sign and witness to the Lord. These would remind the Egyptians of the Lord's punishment, their suffering under oppressors, and the Lord's healing. The punishment would cause Egypt to turn to the Lord; they would pray to Him, and He would heal them. His healing consists in sending them a mighty Savior to deliver them (vv. 19–22). Fourth, a highway would unite Egypt and Assyria, and Egypt would serve or worship with Assyria (v. 23). Fifth, the Lord would bless the three nations: Egypt would be called God's people, Assyria the work of His hands, and Israel His inheritance. They would all belong to the Lord when He would rule the world (vv. 24–25). In this and other oracles, the prophet offered the nations an eschatological hope that could only be realized by the coming Messiah. The consequences listed in vv. 18–25 suggest that the Lord's plan not only exposed the weaknesses of Egypt but also included healing and salvation for the nations.

Isaiah 20:1–6 is a brief narrative dealing with events that occurred in 713–711 B.C., when the Assyrians conquered the Philistine city of Ashdod (for Tartan, or Sargon, see 2 Kin. 18:17). The Lord's command to Isaiah (Is. 20:2) and His explanation (vv. 3–6) tell of a symbolic action that would be a sign and a witness to Egypt and their neighbors to the south (cf. 18:1b–2, 7; 19:1b–25). Isaiah had walked naked and

barefoot (i.e., the condition of those taken into exile, which probably conveys the idea of being without adequate clothing [Is. 58:7]) for three years. This act symbolized the coming captivity of the Egyptians and those to the south who had been subdued by Assyria (19:3–4).

21:1–17

The Wilderness, Dumah, and Arabia

The three utterances on Babylon, Dumah, and Arabia belong together. When Babylon rebelled against Assyria, it often had Arabian allies.

21:1–10. The Wilderness of the Sea. This expression designates the tribal borderland ruled by Merodach/Marduk-Baladan, king of Babylon (cf. 39:1–2). In a disturbing vision, Isaiah saw an enemy from a terrifying land approaching like a whirlwind through the desert. He heard of treachery and destruction. The poetic Hebrew construction used here is also found in similar forms in 24:16 and 33:1. The Lord would make Babylon's lamentation cease by the coming event revealed in the vision. There would be no hope for the attackers' victims (21:3–4).

There is a sarcastic command urging Elam and Media to defend their ally Babylon by attacking the approaching Assyrian army (v. 2). Merodach/Marduk-Baladan's primary allies in the defense of Babylon were Elamite Susa and Anshan. Isaiah's reference to Elam and Media likely meant Elam and allies from the Zagros mountains, including Anshan. The vision predicted Babylon's fall (vv. 6–9). The prophet heard a command to the military officers to prepare for battle (v. 5)—an oiled shield would resist arrows better and would therefore be used on the walls of a fortified city.

A watchman, carefully watching and listening (v. 8), saw a charioteer shouting that Babylon had fallen and the images of her gods lay destroyed on the ground (v. 9; cf. Rev. 14:8; 18:2). This news is the focal point of Isaiah 21:1–10, indicating the loss of the power of Babylon and her gods. The passage ends with an address to those being threshed like grain, that is, the people in Judah who had put their hope in an alliance with Babylon but who would suffer the wrath not only of Assyria but later of the Medo-Persians (v. 10).

21:11–12. Utterance Concerning Dumah. This passage records a watchman's report that there was no news from Dumah, implying that it had fallen and that there were no survivors. If Dumah was an ally of fallen Babylon, the passage may be taken as a warning against foreign alliances. Dumah refers to the fortified religious center of Adummatu (i.e., Dumat al-Jandal in the Wadi Sirhan), which controlled the major Arab trade routes between Syria and Babylonia. The reference to "Seir" (v. 11b) indicates the eastern direction from which one would inquire concerning news about Dumah. In the passage, Isaiah is both the implied speaker of the text and the watchman ("He calls to *me* out of Seir"). The repeated question for news from Seir was put to him (v. 11). The answer was that the morning would come and also the night (v. 12), but no news had come. The person asking the question is told to inquire again later and to return.

21:13–17. Utterance Concerning Arabia. The intention of Isaiah's message is, as in vv. 1–10 and 11–12, to warn against reliance on foreign allies and to confirm that the Lord is in command of events. The Dedanites and Temanites are asked to assist the refugees in Arabia, who were fleeing to them from battle, by giving water to the thirsty and offering food to the hungry (vv. 14–15). The Lord had spoken to Isaiah concerning the decimation of Kedar's people and its destruction within a year. Kedar was the second son of Ishmael (Gen. 25:13; 1 Chr. 1:29) and the eponym of an important Arab tribe.

22:1–25

Utterance Concerning the Valley of Vision

"The Valley of Vision" is a unique name. It may signify the Kidron Valley to the east of Jerusalem, which could be seen both from the city walls and from the slopes of the Mount of Olives, where the Assyrian army had taken its stand in the siege of 701 B.C. Shebna's magnificent tomb was located on the eastern side of the Kidron Valley where high officials were buried during the reigns of the Davidic kings (vv. 15–16). During the Assyrian siege, Shebna's tomb—a symbol of his pride—was in Assyrian hands. The Kidron Valley therefore visually represented the fate of Jerusalem's disobedient people (i.e., the yoke of Assyria).

22:1–14. Message Against Jerusalem. There was noise in the city, but not of rejoicing. Warriors had died, not in battle but while trying to escape. Sennacherib's records confirm that many of Hezekiah's troops deserted him. The city was under siege, the people were weeping, and there was no reason for comfort. What they were facing was chaos and destruction, the safety of the city determined by the people's faithfulness to the Lord and not by the inviolability of Zion as the dwelling of God. There would be trampling and terror and people crying to the mountains (v. 5). There has been some discussion over the translation of the latter part of the verse, but most have rendered the text as "breaking down of walls." The approach of the Assyrian army is illustrated by the troops provided by Elam and Kir (vv. 6–7). After his defeat of Merodach/Marduk-Baladan and his Elamite allies, Sennacherib reported taking thousands of Elamite captives and a great deal of military equipment, such as chariots and horses.

The Assyrian army would spread out across the valleys of Judah. Before besieging Jerusalem, Sennacherib conquered forty-six cities and countless villages in Judah and deported around 200,000 people. Isaiah states that the Lord eliminated Judah's defenses (lit. "uncovered the covering of Judah"; v. 8). When Jerusalem got the news of Judah's destruction, the people looked to the armor and weapons of the Forest Palace (v. 8; lit. "House of the Forest") and to Hezekiah's efforts to fortify Jerusalem and secure the water supply, but they disregarded the Lord. This palace was one of the buildings erected by Solomon near the temple (1 Kin. 7:2; 10:17) and may have been used as an armory. Here it refers to the house of David. Hezekiah's fortifications caused great damage to the city of David, and he broke down houses to fortify the wall (Is. 22:9–10). The mention of the lower pool seems to refer to the tunnel Hezekiah made under the city to gather water from the spring of Gihon in the Pool of Siloam (2 Chr. 32:2–4).

When Judah was destroyed and Jerusalem besieged, the Lord called for mourning, baldness, and sackcloth (Is. 22:12). However, the people failed to understand the significance of the Assyrian siege. God wanted them to repent and return to Him (v. 4). Instead they celebrated and said, "Let us eat and drink, for tomorrow we die!" (v. 13; cf. 1 Cor. 15:32). There would be no atonement for such iniquity (Is. 22:14). Atonement can be given only when humans repent of their sins and humble themselves.

22:15–19. Servant Shebna. Before the Assyrian siege, Shebna was the king's master of the house. The Lord's message about him was derogatory, in contrast with His acknowledgement of Eliakim as His servant (v. 20). Isaiah's description of the status and function of the master of the house (vv. 20–24) reflects the Lord's designation of Eliakim and summarizes his investiture. Isaiah's question to Shebna implies that they had met at the tomb before the Assyrian siege. In the accusation, Shebna's tomb represents pride linked to a high office. He was self-sufficient and concerned with preserving the future honor of his name and the security and honor of his descendants (v. 25), thereby ignoring Isaiah's warnings that the Lord would punish pride (cf. 2:11-16; 3:1-3, 16-18). He had sought security by making a place for his burial in a rock (22:16) rather than seeking refuge in the Lord.

The predicted punishment of Shebna was that the Lord would hurl him away violently by seizing him, wrapping him firmly, and throwing him like a ball (vv. 17-19; lit. "winding He will wind you up [with] a winding like a ball"). Shebna would end up dying in obscurity in a large, foreign country. Thus, he would not be buried in his magnificent tomb in Jerusalem. His magnificent chariots—the sign of his high position and honor—would become the shame of his master's house. Shebna may have been deported to Nineveh as a captive, either as Sennacherib's prisoner or as part of Hezekiah's generous tribute (see 2 Kin. 18:13-16).

22:20-25. Servant Eliakim. This remarkable passage focuses on Eliakim the son of Hilkiah. His office was related to the following: (1) God who appointed him (vv. 20-21); (2) the people of Jerusalem and Judah to whom he would be a father (v. 21; "father" is an honorific title or term of respect; e.g., 2 Kin. 2:12; 6:21; 13:14); (3) the household of the king (he would receive the key of the house of David, symbolizing his administrative authority to make decisions; v. 22); (4) his own posterity (Eliakim's position would be secure, that is, he would have an enduring name; vv. 23-24). The simile of the peg involves one fixed in the wall with vessels hanging on it (v. 24; cf. Ezek. 15:3). The fact that it could be unfastened forewarned that Eliakim's security, like that of every other human, depended on his faithfulness to the Lord. Eliakim would also be honored by his descendants, for he would elevate them to a position of glorious distinction. Isaiah 22:25 is difficult: some have taken it to refer to Shebna as being a different "peg" from Eliakim—Shebna and all who depended on him for support would fall. Since v. 25 continues the metaphor as well as the description of the glorious descendants of the previous verses, others have viewed it as referring to Eliakim. The phrase "in that day," used in v. 20 to designate the exaltation of Eliakim, is now used to designate the moment of his or Shebna's fall.

23:1-18
Utterance Concerning Tyre

This lamentation over Tyre and Phoenicia relates to Sennacherib's capture of Tyre's mainland settlement in 701 B.C. Tyre was a neighboring trading partner with Judah situated in the southern part of Phoenicia on a small island.

The passage presents six appeals by the prophet for a communal lamentation over Tyre and Phoenicia (vv. 1-14). The first call addressed the ships of Tarshish. The luxurious cargos of these large ships made them symbols of wealth and luxury (cf. 2:16; 1 Kin. 10:22; Jer. 10:9). The motivation for the lament was the destruction of the home harbor. The second call addressed the coastal inhabitants and the merchants of Sidon (Is. 23:2-3). The reason was the loss of Sidon's commerce, which was the marketplace of the nations. The third call addressed Sidon. The reason was that the sea no longer provided sustenance (vv. 4-5). The report on the condition of Tyre would cause agony in Egypt, an important trading partner. The fourth call addressed the coastal inhabitants, who were told to cross over to Tarshish, a distant but unidentified port (vv. 6-9). Amazement is expressed at the downfall of the joyous, ancient, and far-reaching Tyre. The Lord had determined to humble the proud and honorable (cf. 2:11-17).

The fifth call addressed the daughter (of) Tarshish, the distant Phoenician colony (cf. vv. 1, 6). Verse 10 has been translated and interpreted in various ways: some read the verb 'abar, "to pass over," as meaning "to till" or "cultivate." The LXX has "cultivate your land; for ships will no more come out of Carthage"—that is, their supply source would be removed. Others understand 'abar to mean that the people of Tarshish should go through their land and look for another harbor since Tyre would no longer be available. Still others read 'abar as "leave," "abandon" (see 29:5; 31:9; 40:27; Job 6:15; 30:15). It seems better to understand it to mean that at that time Tarshish would be as free as the river (the Nile). There was no longer any restraint (lit. "belt," mezakh) upon Tarshish (v. 10). *Mezakh*, "belt," is sometimes rendered as "strength" (an image of restraint; cf. Ps. 109:19)—the motherland had fallen, and the colony was now free to leave Phoenicia. Some render the term here as referring to the "harbor" of Tarshish. The downfall of Tyre was part of the Lord's plan (Is. 23:11). He had granted Assyria sovereignty over many kingdoms, commanding the Assyrians to destroy the fortresses of Canaan, including Phoenicia. The

Lord's command to Sidon to cross over to Cyprus (v. 12) happened when King Luli of Sidon escaped from the Assyrian army. Phoenicia's downfall paralleled that of Babylon/Chaldea (v. 13)—both were part of the anti-Assyrian rebellion with Judah and Philistia. The sixth call to wail addressed the ships of Tarshish (v. 14; cf. v. 1b) because they could not any longer rely on Tyre's *ma'oz*, "place of refuge" or "fortress," sometimes rendered as "strength" (i.e., military and financial power).

Tyre would be forgotten for seventy years (vv. 15–18)—corresponding to a normal lifespan (v. 15). The mortal wound of Tyre would be healed, and it would behave like a harlot. Since Tyre's chief deity was the fertility goddess Astarte, which was related to temple prostitution, the city's trade is metaphorically described as a return to her hire as she prostituted herself with all the kingdoms of the world (v. 17; cf. Rev. 17:2). At the end, however, her financial success would benefit Judah—it would be set apart for the Lord and would provide His people with food and clothes (Is. 23:18). The implication appears to be that Tyre would join God's people and would thus be blessed.

24:1—27:13

THE LORD'S NEW WORLD ORDER: THE NATIONS AND ISRAEL

The message of the Lord's sovereignty over the nations (13:1—23:18) culminates with a prediction of His new world order and His blessing on Israel and the nations.

24:1–23
Law and Rule of God over the World

Having established His world sovereignty (vv. 1–22), God proclaimed that He would reign on Mount Zion and in Jerusalem (v. 23). In the process, He would devastate the earth and scatter all its inhabitants (vv. 1–2) because the earth was defiled by crimes against the laws of the Holy One (v. 5). The punishment would remove the contaminants, and the earth was to be entirely emptied or laid waste (v. 3). The "everlasting covenant"—expressed in the laws and the ordinances or statutes (v. 5)—refers to the agreement between the Creator and humans (cf. Gen. 9:16–17), and its violation disrupts the divine world order. The coming judgment would end rejoicing in the city of *tohu*, "formlessness" or "emptiness," sometimes translated here in

Isaiah 24:10 as "ruined" (*tohu* is the same word used for the primordial state of earth before it was filled with life; Gen. 1:2). The unidentified, nameless city would be broken down, and all its houses closed (Is. 24:7–13).

At the announcement of the fall of the evil city, people from different parts of the world would erupt in praises to God, acclaiming Him to be righteous (vv. 14–16). But the prophet spoke, knowing that the end had not yet arrived, and he exclaimed that he was ruined and wasting away. He knew that evil was coming upon the earth because of the violation of the Creator's world order (vv. 17–18). His word heralded an eschatological judgment of cosmic proportions (vv. 18–20). At that time the Lord would punish the powerful ones in heaven and the kings of the earth (v. 21) because He is Ruler of all—the moon and the sun were deities worshiped by the nations (vv. 22–23b). The significance of vv. 1–23 is captured by the conclusion that the Lord of Hosts would gloriously reign on Mount Zion and in Jerusalem (v. 23; cf. 2:2–4; 60:1—62:12).

25:1–12
The Lord's Blessing

The restoration of the Lord's world order through judgment (24:1–23) would result in universal blessings (25:1–12), which would include the restoration of Israel (26:1—27:13). The collapse of the universal, evil city would be followed by the praises of the people and the blessing of the Lord. This communal song of praise is grounded, first, in the fact that the Lord had done "wonderful things," proving that He had been faithful and sure in His purposes from long ago (v. 1). Second, the song notes the Lord's ruin of a mighty city that symbolized resistance to God's sovereignty (note its various names in 24:10; 25:2–3; 26:5). Third, the song recognizes the Lord, a good king, as the protector of the poor and the needy (i.e., Jerusalem; 25:4–5).

The Lord would respond to the nations' acknowledgment (v. 3) by making a feast on Mount Zion for all the peoples (v. 6). He would destroy or remove the covering or veil over the nations (v. 7). This symbolizes the Lord's revelation of Himself to the peoples. Among the Lord's blessings for the peoples of the earth is the extraordinary announcement that He would "swallow up death forever" and wipe away tears from all faces (25:8a; cf. 26:19; 1 Cor. 15:54–55; Rev. 21:4). As reigning Lord, He would remove the curse of death that resulted from the rebellion in the Garden of Eden. This hope is central to the Christian faith.

Another blessing is directed particularly to Israel: He would remove the disgrace of His people from all the earth (25:8). Israel's response would express (1) loyalty: they had waited for God and trusted in Him (v. 9; cf. 8:17; 12:1-6); (2) confession: "this is our God" and "this is the LORD"; and (3) acknowledgment: as Savior and as the source of joy (25:9). What a wonderful description of the Second Coming of Christ!

The prophet asserted that the hand of the Lord would rest on "this mountain" (i.e., He would protect Zion from harm; v. 10; cf. 4:6; 31:5-7; 33:20-24; 51:16). The prediction of the demise of Moab was a contrast and a warning. Here Moab represents nations that were invited to seek refuge in Zion but did not accept (16:1-4). Their notorious pride would be turned into utter humiliation (cf. 2:6-21; 16:6).

26:1-21
Song of Thanksgiving

In this song of thanksgiving, as Judah asks the Lord to deliver them from their enemies, the singers express joy in their strong city (v. 1), made secure by the power of the Lord. This is the righteous city. Their praises mingle with admonitions to trust in the Lord forever (v. 4) and praise Him for having defeated and humiliated the lofty city and those dwelling on high (vv. 5-6). Jerusalem's gatekeepers were commanded to open the gates to let the righteous nation (i.e., the redeemed Israel) that is true and faithful enter (v. 2). A faithful one is the person who is constant and trusts in the Lord. The Lord keeps the faithful in "perfect peace" (v. 3). They had waited for the Lord by keeping His principles and had confessed that their deep desire was for the Lord (vv. 8-9). The believer knows that when the Lord's judgments are upon the earth, the world will learn righteousness, but the wicked do not learn righteousness or see the majesty of the Lord (v. 10).

Pointing to the unwillingness of the wicked to see and learn (v. 10), the petitioners ask that they be ashamed and destroyed by fire of the Lord (v. 11). The Lord is asked to establish peace for the people because everything they had accomplished was actually done for them by the Lord and His power (v. 12). This preliminary request is extended through reflections on the past (vv. 13-15). The Lord had acted against lords or masters who, alongside Him, governed

the people (v. 13). Because of their removal, the Lord increased the nation and expanded all the borders of the land. By these actions, He was glorified (v. 15). The petition ends with the Lord's comforting answer announcing the resurrection of the dead (v. 19). This verse literally translates as "They shall live, your dead, my corpse; they shall arise." Since it is the Lord who is speaking, "my corpse" refers to the corpses of those who trusted in Him (the singular is collective). The Lord's dew gives life like the dew of the morning gives to herbs, and therefore the earth would *repa'im tapil*, literally "cause the fallen ones to fall"; the verb *napal* ("to fall") expresses here the idea of "to cause to cast out" (on the word *repa'im*, see commentary on 14:4-11)—a poetic way of stating (as most translations indicate) that the dead would rise (cf. 25:8).

Meanwhile, the people are admonished to enter their quarters, shut their doors, and wait for the Lord to bring about what He had promised (26:20-21; cf. 10:25). They are to wait patiently for ultimate deliverance during the Lord's punishment of the earth (cf. 24:1-23). The promised resurrection would bring justice: as the faithful would be raised from the dead, the bloodguilt of past atrocities and murders would be disclosed.

27:1-13
Restoration of Israel

The destruction of the city will happen on the same day that the Lord destroys all the spiritual powers that have opposed Him, powers used by the fallen cherub (14:12-15) and represented by the figure of the Leviathan (27:1; see "Leviathan," p. 654). By destroying Leviathan, the Lord will restore order and justice in the world. This victory is followed by a song about the restoration of Israel. The new vineyard allegory (27:2-6) is interpreted in vv. 7-13 (cf. 5:1-7). On that eschatological day, God will announce that His anger has passed and will offer Israel peace (27:4-5). If they accept, His people will take root, blossom, bud, and fill the surface of the earth with fruit (v. 6). The vineyard song is explained in an exhortation to the Lord's dejected people. They are asked whether they are not better off than their completely destroyed oppressors (v. 7). The meaning of v. 8 is not clear. The first word appears to be a repetition of the unit of measure, *se'ah*. So, it is taken by some to mean that God's judgment of Israel was "measured"—it was not overwhelming. Others read the first part of the verse as referring to warfare and exile. Still others see a continuation of the tree metaphor in the verb *shalakh*, "to send away," and thus translate it as "shooting forth." The basic sense is that God disciplined His people in the Exile but not to the extent of completely destroying them; Israel will spring back to life again.

The effect of scattered Israel's suffering is stated in v. 9: Jacob's sins would be atoned for— the experience of the Exile has a redemptive goal, but repentance, manifested in the rejection of idolatry, is required from the people. There would be fruit from this taking away of sin: the purification of the land through the destruction of idol worship. Ultimately, the suffering of scattered Israel would not atone for their sins and purify the land and the nations, but the Suffering Servant of the Lord would (cf. 52:13—53:12).

Because He is a God of justice and righteousness, the Lord carried away those Israelites who did not know Him (27:10–11). However, in the day of salvation, the Lord would thresh (i.e., separate the wheat from the chaff) and gather scattered Israel from the flowing channel of the river (i.e., Assyria) to the brook/wadi of Egypt (v. 12). The great trumpet would be blown as a signal to those who were about to perish in Assyria and those who were exiles in Egypt to come and worship the Lord on the holy mountain in Jerusalem (v. 13).

28:1—33:24
THE LORD'S PLAN FOR JERUSALEM

Isaiah has been showing Israel that the nations are unreliable and will come to an end under the power of God. The prophet continues to encourage God's people to trust in Him as their only dependable refuge. This section concludes the first part of the book that began in chapter 2. We find here five passages concerning the Lord's plan for Jerusalem, culminating in the vision of the Lord as King (33:17–24).

28:1–29
The Lord's Purpose for Sending Assyria

In this passage, Isaiah admonishes the leaders of Jerusalem to seek to comprehend God's plan. Otherwise, they would fall like the leaders of Ephraim.

28:1–13. Learning from Ephraim. The Ephraimite leaders are described as having had a prideful wreath or crown and as having been drunkards—note the contrast with the Lord as a glorious crown and a beautiful diadem in v. 5. Isaiah says their prestige as leaders of the fertile land is like a fading flower (v. 1). Their intoxication was a sign of their lack of the knowledge of justice (cf. 5:11–13, 20–23). The Lord had sent Assyria to punish Ephraim's leaders, and they would be trampled underfoot (v. 3). But to the remnant of His people, the Lord would bring glory and beauty. He would be a spirit of justice to the judges and strength to those defending the city (vv. 5–6).

The transgressions of Ephraim's leaders should have been a lesson to Jerusalem (vv. 7–13). Their spiritual leaders were corrupt; the priest and the prophet erred in vision and stumbled in their judgments. The image of drinking bouts and orgies at a banquet may be associated with the original Canaanite practices of contractual celebrations that often led to orgiastic excesses. Isaiah's description in vv. 7–8 is not an exaggeration. The refusal of Ephraim's leaders to hear and understand the word of the Lord is illustrated by a didactic comparison: (1) they are like ignorant babies (v. 9), and (2) they lack knowledge and understanding (v. 10). Isaiah quotes a peculiar sequence of single-syllable words that may have been a school exercise for learning to read and write. The first two parts of the sequence may be divided up to say "[the letter] *tsade* [and the letter] *waw* [unite] into *tsaw* [meaning 'rule']" and "[the letter] *qop* [and the letter] *waw* [unite] into *qaw* [meaning 'line']" (i.e., a reading exercise). The last part, in Hebrew *ze'er sham*, may then refer to the small space that separates each word "here and there." The point is that the leaders were children learning elementary things. (3) They also rejected the comforting word of the Lord (v. 12). He therefore spoke to them with *la'eg*, "mocking," "foreign," or "stammering" lips and a foreign (lit. "another") tongue (v. 11) By rejecting God's invitation to find rest and refreshment in Him (v. 12), the Ephraimite leaders brought judgment upon themselves (v. 13).

28:14–29. Warning to Judah's Rulers. This passage is a warning to the rulers of Judah. The Hebrew term for mockers (v. 14) and the concluding admonition not to be mockers (v. 22) contain the same Hebrew root, meaning "to scorn." The Assyrian punishment was caused by Jerusalem's covenant with death or the agreement with Sheol—the grave. Some suggest that this refers to some kind of anti-Assyrian alliance; others, that it refers more generally to the complacent, proud, and deceptive (as the rest of the verse mentions) attitude of the rulers. They evidently conceived of themselves as impervious to the threat of death and had come to believe that the deceptions which they had inculcated would protect them. They proudly assumed that they could not even be reached by God's providence and punishment. The lies and falsehoods that served as the leaders' refuge were the mistaken beliefs that the Lord's punishment could be avoided by political alliances and fortifications.

Instead, the Lord said that He laid a cornerstone for a sure foundation in Zion. The Lord—not the establishment in Jerusalem—would set the measuring line for true security in justice and righteousness (vv. 16-17, 21). The metaphor of God as a Rock or Stone occurs frequently in the OT, especially in the context of salvation (e.g., Gen. 49:24; Deut. 32:4, 15, 18; Pss. 18:2, 31, 46; 28:1; 31:2-3; 62; 95:1; Is. 17:10; 51:1). The NT writers found references to Christ as the Rock in these verses. He was the Rock of Israel (1 Cor. 10:1-4), the rejected (Ps. 118:22; cf. Is. 53) and tried Stone upon which God would build the foundation of His church (Eph. 2:20; 1 Pet. 2:1-6). Placing one's faith and trust in God as the Rock became an important indication that faith, not meritorious works, is the instrument by which God's salvation can be grasped (Rom. 9:30-33). Pride is the opposite of the humble trust admonished here. Thus, the proud deceptions of the leaders would not avail because the covenant with death would be swept away (Is. 28:17c-19). The people were warned not to mock God's prophecy, or else their fetters would be made stronger (v. 22). Wise persons see the whole picture, as illustrated by the farmer who gets his food by working in various stages for various complementary needs according to correct principles taught by God (v. 26). Although the farmer's work is initially destructive, it does not result in the destruction of the crop but in its survival. Israel was chastised to prepare it for the time when the Lord would restore righteous leaders to the land (vv. 5-6). The temporary judgment would be followed by comfort and salvation. The Lord is wonderful in His plan and magnificent in His wisdom (v. 29; cf. 9:6).

29:1-24
The Lord's Purpose for Ariel/Zion

The Lord would cause the threat of Assyria against Ariel (vv. 2-8), but its dissolution would have a positive outcome for Israel (vv. 22-24).

29:1-10. Message for Ariel. This threat was to be directed against Ariel, the city where David lived and a symbol of Mount Zion and Jerusalem, the city of David (vv. 1, 7-8).

The Lord announced His intention to lay siege to Jerusalem and bring it down (vv. 3-4). Its people would lie prostate on the ground before their conqueror, like one dying and, figuratively speaking, would whisper from the dust like an 'ob—"necromancer" (some translations have "ghostlike" or "spirit"; v. 4)—this simile does not endorse spiritistic beliefs, for Isaiah condemns the practice of necromancy (8:19; 19:3), as did the covenantal law (Lev. 19:31; 20:27; Deut. 18:10-11).

The scene of the punishment of Jerusalem is immediately moderated by the description of the destruction of those who had attacked Jerusalem. They would not enjoy their success for very long. They would not be satisfied but would have their short-lived dream of victory interrupted by the reality of their defeat (Is. 29:5-8). The addressee is instructed to reflect upon the significance of the assault on Jerusalem. How could it happen when God had promised to protect Zion from the attacks of the nations? The prophet's answer raises the people's unwillingness to understand the message in vv. 2-8. They were not understanding because the Lord, on account of their sins, wanted first to chasten them and then to open their eyes.

29:11-24. The Need to Understand. The vision of the Lord's plan is compared to the words of a book that cannot be read because it is sealed or because the reader is illiterate (v. 12). In this illustration, the "whole vision" refers primarily to the revelation concerning Ariel in vv. 1-8, but it could also include the whole vision of the prophet (1:1). It would be heard and seen "in that day" when the Lord would fulfill His plan (29:17-21). The Lord would deal with Jerusalem's inability to understand His plan by removing the wisdom of the wise (v. 14; cf. 5:18-19). But the Lord's plan would soon be implemented (29:17). The oppressor would be brought down, and the oppressed would flourish. This is expressed metaphorically: Lebanon—known for its dense forests and therefore a common symbol of mighty Assyria (10:18-19, 33-34)—would be turned into a fruitful field (karmel) that would appear like a forest. Lofty Lebanon-Assyria would be humbled, and the humble Israel (karmel) exalted.

"In that day" the Lord's wisdom, counsel, and plan would be seen and understood by the deaf and blind (29:18–19). Those who had waited for the Lord would be saved, but the unfaithful would be cut off, especially the unjust and unrighteous officials and judges condemned by Isaiah (vv. 20–21; cf. 1:16–23; 3:1–3, 12–23; 10:1–4). Those who ensnared defenders in court, literally the one who "decides in the gate," were appointed, impartial participants in a court setting who were supposed to put things right between contenders (cf. 1:18–20). In vv. 22–24 we find a concluding assurance from the covenant God, who redeemed Abraham, concerning the house or descendants of Jacob (i.e., all the children of Israel). Assyria's assault on Ariel would be a temporary, short-lived threat, for the Lord would resist the attackers and punish the abusive leaders. He would restore the house of Jacob, and all Israel would eventually worship the Lord in His temple at Zion. The faithful followers of the Lord would have their fate reversed when He visited them in due course.

30:1–33
The Lord's Delay

This chapter opens with a serious charge against the rebellious, obstinate children who were executing plans of their own, not of God's Spirit (v. 1). The problem was that ambassadors were going down to Egypt (v. 2; i.e., reversing the Exodus when God delivered them) without consulting the Lord (lit. "without asking My mouth"). They were seeking their strength and protection in Pharaoh and placing their trust in the shadow or shade of Egypt (v. 2). But Pharaoh would be Israel's shame, and their trust in Egypt their humiliation (v. 3). Egypt would not be of help against Assyria (vv. 6–7).

Since the people were rebellious, the Lord commanded the prophet to write His word or message (vv. 12b, 15) on a tablet or a scroll, so that it might be remembered for the times to come, forever. The people were rebellious and wanted the prophets to tell them only "smooth" or "pleasant" things (vv. 8–12). Consequently, the Holy One of Israel announced judgment against them (vv. 12–17). Their punishment would come "suddenly, in an instant"—illustrated by several similes in vv. 13–14. The Lord's word of salvation was clear: they could be saved in repentance or returning to Him and in resting in Him (v. 15). But since the people had declined the Lord's invitation, Assyria would punish them. The reliance

on horses would prove futile (v. 16), and the promise made to Israel at the Exodus would be reversed (v. 17; cf. Lev. 26:8; Deut. 32:30; Josh. 23:10). Israel would be decimated until they would be left as a pole or flagstaff on the top of a mountain, or as a banner upon a hill (Is. 30:17). A small remnant would endure further suffering until the Lord's justice would be fulfilled (v. 20).

The Lord would indeed deliver a purified remnant of Israel because He is a God of justice and grace (v. 18). He would be patient with them (lit. "the Lord waits") and be exalted in the display of His justice and mercy. Since the Lord was "waiting," or "longing," from *khakah* to deliver the remnant of Israel, the prophet blesses all those who wait for (or hope/trust in, from *khakah*) Him (v. 18; cf. 8:17; 25:9; 33:2; 40:28–31; 49:23). It is a blessing to patiently wait on the Lord; waiting encourages the faithful to remain hopeful that the Lord will reverse their fate and turn their mourning into a dance, according to His plans. The Lord would ultimately defeat Assyria. He would approach her from afar in anger, with His lips full of indignation, His tongue like a destroying fire, and His breath like an overflowing torrent that would reach to the neck (30:27–28). His intervention would mean deliverance for Israel and joy for the remnant.

31:1–9
Egyptian Support Against Assyria

The people were instructed to trust in the Lord because He would protect Zion and defeat Assyria. The prophet directed a woe against those trusting in foreign alliances and military force (Egypt) but failing to seek the Holy One of Israel (v. 1) in whom is wisdom (v. 2) and divine power (v. 3). God promised that He would descend to fight for, protect, and deliver Jerusalem (vv. 4–5). Two similes are used: the Lord would fight for Jerusalem like a lion, and He would protect the city like a mother bird protects its young in their nest. But the people were to return to God, against whom they had revolted (v. 6; cf. 30:1–11, 13–17). On the Day of the Lord, the people would throw away their idols of silver and gold and reject them (31:7; cf. 2:7–9, 18–21; 30:22)—the sin made by their own hands. The return of Judah to their God was to trigger the ultimate defeat of Assyria (31:8–9). The sword of the Lord would devour him (cf. 30:30–33); God would summon the armies that would cause Assyria's downfall.

32:1—33:24
The Lord as King and Savior

Judah's hope was not to be found in Egypt but in the Lord. The instruction is about the nature of the righteous versus the wicked ruler (32:1–20) in order to indicate that only in the Lord would there be a future for His people. This is followed by a prayer (33:1–24).

32:1–20. The Righteous King. This passage is a reflection concerning the king and his officials in Jerusalem, and it prepares the way for the account of the Lord's kingship in chapter 33. It is about ruling in justice and righteousness, the fundamental ethical basis for kings and leaders, rooted in the Lord Himself. The initial *hen*, which can mean "behold," "see," "indeed," or introduce an "if" or "when" construction, is common in the reflections of the wise (e.g., 54:15; Job 9:11–12; Hag. 2:12). If Isaiah 32:1 is the *condition*, it is followed by the *effect* (vv. 2–4), clarifying the meaning of the passage (vv. 1–2; cf. 4:5–6). Attention is given to the people who would be ruled in justice and righteousness. The example of the righteous ruler is then contrasted with that of the wicked. The full range of the wickedness of the Lord's opponents was to be exposed, while the righteous would stand (32:5–8).

A righteous ruler was to contribute to the land's fertility and peace, which were essential for survival. A righteous ruler would bring the Lord's blessing upon the people and their land, while a wicked ruler would bring a curse. In the absence of righteous leaders, complacent women (v. 9) are summoned to mourn because the harvest would fail (v. 10). The land and the cities were desolate and showed signs of a curse (thorns and briars; vv. 13–14; cf. 5:6; 7:23–25; 27:4). Such are the conditions under a wicked ruler. However, the Spirit would be poured out upon the people through a righteous ruler from on high (32:15; cf. 11:2), and the wilderness would become a fertile field (32:15). Justice and righteousness being upheld, fertility would be joined with peace (vv. 16–19). Those sowing their seed beside all places of water and allowing their oxen and donkeys to roam freely are those who faithfully wait for the Lord and hope in Him (v. 20).

33:1–9. A Prayer of Distress. A prayer for salvation stands at the center of the passage (vv. 2–6), framed by a word of woe against a foreign enemy (v. 1) and a description of the tyrannical rule (vv. 7–9). The enemy is not named, but certain code words in the passage point to Assyria. Isaiah portrays the oppressed community of Israel praying that the Lord may be gracious to them because they have waited for Him. In Isaiah, patiently waiting for the Lord's intervention characterizes the faithful (cf. 8:17; 25:9; 26:8; 40:28–31; 49:23). The next part of the prayer is a petition for God to be the strength of the people (lit. "their arm"; 33:2). The motivation for the supplication was the Lord's power and past victories. The prophet instructed the people concerning their relationship to the Lord as a condition for receiving His salvation. They were reminded that the Lord is exalted (v. 5; cf. 2:11, 17; 12:4) and that although He dwells on high, He is the One who filled Zion with justice and righteousness, that is, with His personal presence (cf. 32:1, 15–17). The prophet admonished them that God and His wisdom and knowledge would provide a stable foundation for their times and that reverence for Him is a great treasure (33:5–6).

33:10–16. Fall of the Oppressor. The Lord told the oppressor Assyria that He would destroy him. His victory meant that He would be exalted among all the nations—when they heard about His actions, they would acknowledge His might. Assyria is mocked as a nation that is like chaff and stubble; it would be annihilated (vv. 10–13). The prophet presents the Lord creating fear among the sinners and hypocrites in Zion through their recognition of the eternal results they would experience in the destroying fire or everlasting burnings (v. 14). The Lord's plan was to purify Zion by removing the sinners (1:28; 4:4). Out of the purified remnant, the Lord would create citizens of the new Zion (cf. vv. 2–6). The reward of the righteous is that they would enjoy security from attack (cf. 4:6; 31:5; 32:17–19) and freedom from want (30:23–26; 32:17). They would dwell in the elevated places with the Lord (33:14–16).

33:17–24. Triumph of God and Zion. Those left in Zion and those seeing from afar (i.e., scattered Israel) would see the King in His beauty (v. 17). With the establishment of the kingdom of God, He is recognized as Judge, Lawgiver, and King. Israel's salvation comes from Him (v. 22).

There is an underlying joy over the disappearance of the oppressor who wrote letters of blasphemy (cf. 37:8–20), weighed the tribute (cf. 2 Kin. 18:14–16), and sought out their tower defenses (Is. 33:18; cf. 2:15; 23:13). Zion would again be a secure and peaceful place with the Lord enthroned there as King. It is called the city of our festivals, or our appointed festivals (Heb. *mo'adenu*—from *mo'ed*)—all Israel would gather at the temple to worship the Lord. It would be a secure residence for scattered Israel returning from the nations (33:20). The Lord would forever dwell with His people in Zion. According to some translations and interpreters, it is the city of Jerusalem that would be like a "place of broad rivers and streams," or a place where these would flow. According to others, this metaphor applies to God Himself. Unlike the rivers in Assyria, no powerful ships or galleys with oars would pass by.

The concluding vision is of Zion's deliverance from pain and suffering and of its impregnability. Since the Hebrew word *khebel* does not only mean "cord" but can also be related to "pain," another possible translation of v. 23a is "Your [Zion's] pains are gone; they [the oppressors] shall not seize the socket of the flagstaff; a banner shall not be spread out." This translation better fits v. 23b, which describes the people in Zion taking much spoil from the oppressors. Besides, there would be no illness in Zion, and the sins of its inhabitants would be forgiven. The Lord is the Savior of His people. His actions express His wisdom, justice, righteousness (vv. 5–6), power (vv. 10–13), forgiveness, and love for His people (v. 24). The victory of the Lord over the enemy is an assurance that the believer will share in this victory.

34:1—66:24
THE LORD'S PLAN TO RESTORE ISRAEL AND RULE THE NATIONS

Chapters 34–66 aim at moving Israel to seek the Lord by *understanding* His prophetic word and *seeing* its ongoing realization in history. The nations would witness the divine salvific power on behalf of God's people (34:1—35:10) and His defeat of the threat of Babylon (36:1—39:8). God would reveal His faithfulness to Israel, Zion, and the nations (40:1—55:13). The word of exhortation is centered on chapter 55, a summons to Israel to become citizens of restored Zion. This invitation is complemented by the requirements for citizenship (chaps. 56–59), the vision of restored Zion (chaps. 60–62), and the selection of citizens (chaps. 63–66). Thus, a new phase of Isaiah's presentation of the Lord's plan is opened. It develops the theme found in

chapters 1–33 that the Lord's anger would cease and that He would act as the Restorer of Zion and as the wonderful Savior of His people. This work would involve saving the nations (52:13—53:12; 56:6–8; 60:1–22; 66:19–24) and gathering scattered Israel on Zion (60:1—62:12; 66:5–24).

34:1—35:10
The Nations, the Lord's Power, and the Return of Israel

The purpose of this section is to convince the audience of the Lord's sovereign power over *all* nations (vv. 2–4) and provide the setting of a court proceeding (v. 8) for dealing with Edom's crimes and Zion's recompense.

34:1–7. Calling the Nations as Witnesses. Isaiah sets the scene as a universal "hearing" in which the Sovereign Lord of the world would act. The witnesses are summoned to come near, hear/listen, and give attention (v. 1), due to the Lord's anger or fury against the nations (vv. 2–4). In particular, the summons is caused by the Lord's judgment against Edom, which represents the rebellious nations devoted to destruction (v. 5). The Lord's sword symbolizes His tool of punishment (vv. 5–6; cf. 1:20; 27:1; 31:8). It would be drenched in heaven (v. 5), probably caused by the overthrow of the hosts of heaven or the pagan gods (34:3–4; cf. 24:21). The Lord's punishment is described as a sacrifice in Bozrah (the capital city of Edom) and a great slaughter in Edom. The clean sacrificial animals would be lambs, goats, rams, wild oxen, bull calves, and strong bulls. These would represent the inhabitants of Edom that would perish with their leaders (34:6–7).

34:8—35:10. Day of the Lord's Vengeance. The court proceeding would be the Lord's day of vengeance against Edom and the year of retribution or recompense for the cause of Zion. The proceeding, aiming for Zion's deliverance (35:1–10), was to include witnesses (v. 1), punishment (vv. 5–17), and recompense for the victims (vv. 1–2). No specific offense by Edom is mentioned, but it symbolized arrogant and oppressive nations because of its opposition to the sovereignty of the God of Zion and its lack of compassion toward Israel and Judah (see Obadiah: Introduction). It would be filled, not with people but with unclean animals (34:11, 13–15). The result would be confusion, the breakdown of social order, and the overthrow of Edom's palaces and fortresses (vv. 11–13). Verse 10 is alluded to in Revelation 14:11 in regard to the final punishment of the wicked worshipers of the beast and its image. Isaiah 34:10 shows that the language of smoke rising forever poetically conveys the idea of total and eternal destruction, not eternal torment.

The nations (including Israel), witnesses to the Lord's power (v. 1), are instructed in Isaiah to search the book/scroll of the Lord and read (v. 16). Twelve desert animals would occupy Edom after the Lord's punishment (i.e., everything prophesied in the book would happen). The nature of this book or scroll is a matter of debate. It could designate the prophetic writings or refer to God's workings and plans that would be fully comprehended someday. It would then be clear that everything occurred according to the will of God—what He had commanded (i.e., His *word*) and what His Spirit had gathered (i.e., His *work*). The call to "search" changes the role of the nations from being mere *witnesses* to actually *knowing* who the Lord is, namely, seeing the glory of the Lord, the majestic splendor of God (35:2).

In vv. 3–10 the idea of the recompense of Israel, announced in the court proceeding (34:8), is further developed with the intention of instilling hope. It begins with an instruction to comfort the weak and the fearful (35:3–4). The weak would be restored, the land would be watered and become fertile (vv. 6c–7), none of the redeemed would go astray, and Israel would no longer be threatened by foreign nations—symbolized by the lion and the ravenous beast (vv. 8–9). The ones the Lord had saved and redeemed would return with singing and everlasting joy; there would be no more sorrow or sighing (v. 10; cf. 51:11). These words have been of great hope and comfort to God's people over the centuries, and they provide hope during times of doubt, persecution, and loss (cf. Rev. 21:1–4).

36:1—39:8
The Lord's Power and the Threat of Babylon

This section will demonstrate that Isaiah's prophetic word is true, that the Lord has sovereign power over the kings of the nations (even over the Assyrian emperor), that He is able and willing to save those who seek Him, and that, following Hezekiah's reign, a time would come when the treasures and descendants of the Davidic house would be carried to Babylon.

36:1—37:38. The Lord and Assyria. This narrative reflects events in 701 and 681 B.C. Hezekiah had rebelled against Assyria, and

Sennacherib had devastated Judah as punishment and was threatening Jerusalem from the captured fortress of Lachish. As usual, the Assyrian attack was preceded by negotiations for surrender. The participants on the Assyrian side were Sennacherib, the Rabshakeh, a high royal official, and some messengers. On Judah's side were Hezekiah, Eliakim the master of the house, Shebna the scribe, Joah the recorder or herald, and Isaiah the prophet. They met by the aqueduct from the upper pool on the highway to the Washer's Field (36:2), which was where Isaiah met King Ahaz (7:3).

In his first speech (36:4–10), the Rabshakeh, or field commander, quoted Sennacherib. The fundamental argument was that the Lord had no power to save the Israelites because He was just like the gods of the other nations who could not save them from Assyria (vv. 18–20). Hezekiah sent a message full of regret and remorse to Isaiah, asking for his counsel (37:2–5). His request was not one that normally would have been directed to a prophet but rather to a priest.

The word of God concerning Sennacherib, as proclaimed to Hezekiah, appears in vv. 21–35: (1) The *accusation* in vv. 23–25 describes Sennacherib's reproach and blasphemy of the Holy One of Israel. Sennacherib had forgotten that it was the Lord who appointed Assyria as a conqueror of cities and peoples (vv. 26–28). (2) The *judgment* against Sennacherib appears in v. 29. The Lord would turn him back by the way he had come (cf. v. 34). (3) A *sign* related to the coming harvests was given to Hezekiah to guarantee that the prophecy would be fulfilled (vv. 30–32). And (4) the passage ends with a word of *salvation* for Jerusalem: Sennacherib would return to Assyria by the same way that he had come (vv. 33–35).

The fulfillment of Isaiah's prophecy against Sennacherib is summarized in 37:36–38. An angel of the Lord killed many men in the Assyrian camp. The miraculous event has some resemblance to the tenth plague of the Exodus from Egypt (Ex. 12:23, 29) and to the Philistine capture of the ark (1 Sam. 5–6). Assyriologists have estimated that in a general call-up across the Assyrian Empire, a mustering of troops in the hundreds of thousands was possible. The record of Sennacherib's death in Isaiah 37:37–38 refers to events in 681 B.C., twenty years after Isaiah's prophecies.

38:1—39:8. The Sickness of the King. Faced with a life-threatening illness, Hezekiah turned to the Lord in prayer (vv. 2–3; cf. 37:15), pointing to his faithfulness and obedience. The Lord had compassion on the king and granted him another fifteen years to live. In this time the Lord would defend Jerusalem and deliver the king and the city from the Assyrians (38:4–8). A sign was given to guarantee this promise (v. 8). It consisted in bringing the shadow of the sun ten steps backward on the sundial of Ahaz—alluding to Ahaz's disobedience (7:10–13).

The events recorded in 38:1–10 followed the healing and recovery of Hezekiah but preceded the confrontation with Sennacherib in 36:1—37:38. These events took place before 701 B.C. (date of Sennacherib's invasion of Judah), when Merodach/Marduk-Baladan was still king of Babylon after his rebellion in 705 B.C.

Hezekiah committed two errors leading to Isaiah's ominous prophecy. He proudly boasted of his treasures to the Babylonian envoys (39:2–4). The unwise display of his riches and armory to the Babylonians functioned as a foreboding of the mistakes of his descendants that would be punished by the future plundering of Jerusalem and the deportation of the Davidic dynasty to Babylon (vv. 5–7). A postponement of the disaster was all Hezekiah could hope for, but the fate of the Davidic dynasty (and the kingdom) was left in jeopardy.

40:1—55:13
The Lord's Faithfulness to Israel, Zion, and the Nations

The Lord's plan to save and restore originated in His heavenly council, and He commissioned Isaiah to proclaim comfort (40:1–11). Chapters 40–55 answer the implied questions in 39:1–8. Would the Davidic dynasty end with the future Babylonian oppression? Would the Lord remain faithful to His covenants with Zion, Israel, and the nations? These questions are answered in the *present* for scattered Israel under Assyrian dominion as well as in the *future* for Judah during the Babylonian exile.

40:1–11. Commission to Proclaim the Restoration of Israel. The mission of hardening people's hearts by announcing judgment had been completed (6:9–13). God spoke through Isaiah as Zion's Restorer and Israel's Savior because His anger had ceased (cf. 12:1–6). He commissioned His servants to proclaim His irrevocable decision concerning Israel's comfort (40:1–2, 9–11) and announced His appearance as King (vv. 3–5, 10–11). The decision would be heralded to the cities of Judah (v. 9) and witnessed by the nations (v. 5).

The act of "comforting" (cf. vv. 9–11, 27–31) implies the conclusion of the judgment because the people had received "double" punishment for all their sins. The idiom of "double" often implies "fullness" or "completeness" (see Jer. 16:18; 17:18; Rev. 18:6), but it could also have a positive connotation (i.e., "double" grace; cf. Is. 61:7; Zech. 9:12). The speaking of comfort or tenderness to Jerusalem literally means "speak to the heart of Jerusalem," which is the language of loving care (cf. Gen. 50:21; Ruth 2:13). The term for *tsaba'*, "army" or "warfare," could refer to the ending of Jerusalem's forced labor. The Hebrew verb *ratsah*, often translated as "pardoned," means "to be accepted, to be pleased with, to be paid." Since the verb is in the passive form, it is God who is pleased or who accepted or considered the debt as paid. The term *'awon*, "sin" or "iniquity," could also be rendered "punishment for iniquity." It may be better to understand the phrase here to mean that God had accepted and acknowledged that the punishment they received was enough and that their sin was paid for. The question of how their sins could be fully atoned for so the people could be restored to fellowship would be addressed later (Is. 53).

The command to prepare "a highway for our God" (40:3) in the desert is intended to hasten His coming and enable all humans to see His glory. The "highway" was a raised road that connected major cities. "In the wilderness" should be read together with preparing the way of/for the Lord (i.e., prepare the way...in the wilderness), which forms a parallelism with the rest of the verse. Wilderness/desert is contrasted with God's glory, symbolizing Israel's desolate and dry land in the time of judgment. Glory (v. 5) is associated with the splendor, majesty, sovereignty, light, revelation, and presence of God. Humans perish but the word of God stands/endures forever (v. 8). A voice says that all human beings (lit. "flesh") are like grass that withers and flowers that fade when the breath of the Lord blows upon them (i.e., when He speaks His word [cf. v. 24], though the Heb. *ruakh*, "breath," also means "wind"), but the word of God stands/endures forever. No one can resist God's purpose (vv. 6–8). Humans are weak and frail and completely dependent upon God's power for life (2:22). The decision of Israel's God could not be changed. His plan of salvation would be implemented.

The message to the cities of Judah from Zion and Jerusalem (or from those proclaiming the message to them as well—translations differ) was that they would see their God. The meaning of this message in 40:10–11 is connected with the coming of God in vv. 3–5, which relates the Lord to the nations (v. 5; cf. vv. 15–24). He was to come with strength and power (28:2; 42:13). In Isaiah, God's "arm" is an image of strength that accomplishes righteousness, salvation, and justice (see 51:1—52:10). God's reward and *pe'ullah*, "work" or "recompense" (cf. 62:11), speaks to the coming of the Lord to judge, save, and rule. God's work of judgment and salvation anticipates the revelation of His personal glory. Isaiah was familiar with the designation of a king as "shepherd" (31:4; 44:28; 56:11). The king's role as shepherd is applied here to the Lord's care for His people (cf. Ps. 23:1–4).

40:12–31. The Lord's Sovereignty in the World.
This instruction backs up vv. 1–11 in the form of a disputation speech (i.e., an argumentation that attempts to prove a disputed point). By a set of rhetorical questions, the prophet declares the incomparable power and wisdom of the Lord (vv. 13–14). Some of the prophet's audience considered the Lord as merely one of numerous gods and not the most powerful. This objection is refuted by the argument that the nations are worthless compared to the Lord and by an appeal to Israel's traditional faith, which is based on God's past acts (vv. 15–20).

Considering the history of humans and nations, no one can fail to see that the Lord of the universe brings princes and judges/rulers to nothing (vv. 21–24). The phrase about God's reigning above "the circle of the earth" refers to God's dominion and power over all that is encompassed by the term "earth" (Gen. 1:6; cf. Job 22:14; Prov. 8:27). This leads to the topic of the incomparability of God (Is. 40:25–26). Creator of the stars and planets in heaven, He calls each one by name (v. 26). This is an implied polemic against the view that the stars and the planets were divine and deserved worship. It would have been foolishness for Israel to conclude that their way is hidden from such a Lord. He possesses endless power, lasting strength, unsearchable understanding, and loving care for the weak (vv. 28–29). Therefore, Israel must wait for (or "trust in," "hope for") the Lord. This is a key exhortation in the whole book of Isaiah (8:17; 25:9; 26:8; 30:18; 33:2; 40:31; 49:23). Like Israel's remnant, it is important for us to remember that those who wait with hope and trust will renew their strength (40:31).

41:1–29. Israel: To Reveal the Lord to the Nations.
This passage has the form of a speech before the council of nations in which the Lord, in a dispute with (the gods of) the nations, proves that He is the true God. The speech in Isaiah begins with God formally calling the council to order. The reference to the renewal of the peoples' strength favors their coming together to find the truth about the true God (cf. 40:31). The truth is His sovereignty over the events of history. The one raised or stirred up from the east who had nations given to him (41:2) has been identified with Abraham, Cyrus, or the Messiah (of whom Cyrus was a type). In any of these cases, it could be said that the Lord gave nations to him, subdued kings before him (v. 2), and helped him to pursue these kings, remaining unharmed (v. 3). The more common view is that it refers to Cyrus, king over the Medo-Persians. Then the Lord answered the question of who had done all of these things (v. 4). Thus, He proved that He is the first and the last (i.e., He is constantly in control of human history). Seeing what the Lord had done, the people reacted with fear but also encouraged each other (vv. 5–7).

Israel was God's servant (vv. 8a, 9c; cf. 44:1–2). A "servant" (*'ebed*) could be a "slave" who serves a master, usually in exchange for protection. The term may also express the relationship of the weaker to the stronger party in a "covenant" (cf. 42:6; 49:8). Israel was collectively the "servant" of the Lord in the sense that He was their God and they worshiped Him (cf. Ps. 136:22). Isaiah applies the title "servant" to both Israel as a nation and to the Messiah. Israel was a servant in the sense of being "chosen" (41:8–9) as one who belonged to the Lord (44:1–5), who was not forgotten by Him (vv. 21), whose sins were removed (vv. 22), who was redeemed by the Lord (vv. 22–23; 45:4; 48:20), and in whom the Lord revealed His glory (44:23).

God chose Jacob (41:8, 9; cf. 44:1), a reality that reminds us that Israel's servanthood was based on the Lord's election (cf. Ex. 19:3–6). The mention of Abraham enlarges that election to include all the families of the earth (Is. 41:8; cf. vv. 2–4, 25–26; Gen. 12:1–3). The Lord also had a plan for Israel and the nations. He would gather His servants, scattered Israel, who were deported and had become refugees. He also gave them an assurance of protection, an admonition to not fear, and a promise of strength and endurance (Is. 41:10). "I am your God" is the formula that maintains the covenant (cf. 42:8; 43:3). The promise of the removal of Israel's enemies fits into the history of God's people under Assyrian-Babylonian dominion (41:11–13). No particular oppressor is mentioned, and the setting of the promise is Israel's condition as a "worm" among the nations (v. 14).

The derogatory "worm" is contrasted with "the Holy One of Israel," here called "your Redeemer" (*go'el*), which Isaiah often uses (e.g., 43:14; 49:7; 59:20). The "redeemer" or "next-of-kin" had both power and obligations, especially (1) to redeem family land that was sold by a relative due to financial difficulties (see Lev. 25:23–28); (2) to redeem a family member sold into slavery in payment of a debt (Lev. 25:47–49); (3) to provide an heir for a dead, childless brother (Deut. 25:5–10; cf. Is. 49:20–21; 54:1, 4–5); and (4) to avenge the murder of a kinsman (Num. 35:6–34; the "avenger" in this passage is from the Heb. *go'el*, "redeemer"). As "Redeemer" the Lord would forgive their sins (i.e., release them from their debt), restore the land to Israel, free the deported and the refugees, provide new children to Israel, and avenge the injustices against His people (cf. Is. 34:8).

Israel's commission as the Lord's servant was that God would set them as a sharp threshing sledge for the mountains and hills (41:15). A "threshing sledge" was an instrument for separating the grain from the chaff. Israel may have been a "worm," but the Lord would strengthen His people and return them to their land, and the nations would not be able to stand in their way. There would be rejoicing in Israel because of the Lord's salvation (v. 16). He would relieve their suffering and thirst (vv. 17–18). Trees of all kinds would be planted in the arid land (v. 19). God's work would be seen by Israel, and the surrounding nations would know that it had all been done by the power of the Holy One of Israel (v. 20).

The Lord had stated His case (vv. 2–20), and at this point He challenged the idols of the nations to "present your case" (vv. 21–24). They were invited to recount the past, tell the future, and prove their knowledge. This evidence would enable the council of nations to decide if the idols were gods. But the evidence was not there. The opening rhetorical question in v. 26 is worded as a quotation. It is acknowledged that no one—except the Lord—is able to predict the future. The Lord then addressed the idols and their worshipers, concluding that the idols were silent and could not predict coming events. The Lord then announced a wonderful event: good news for Jerusalem (v. 27). The Lord was referring to His promise of liberation. The idols were incapable of announcing the

end from the beginning (vv. 28–29), and their worshipers had no counselor who could answer a word: they were all worthless and false. Verse 29 summarizes vv. 1–28 and prepares for the continuation in 42:1–13.

42:1–13. The Servant and Justice. Verses 1–4 constitute the first of the so-called Servant Songs in Isaiah (cf. 49:1–6; 50:4–9; 52:13—53:12). However, there is no reason for treating these passages as independent units because they are deeply integrated into their contexts. First, the close relationship between the Servant and the Lord is established (42:1). Second, the Lord empowers the Servant for mission with the Spirit. Third, a specific mission is given to the Servant: He would bring *mishpat*, "judgment," or in this context, "what is right and proper, what is truth and righteousness." This could refer to a society organized around fundamental legal and moral principles. Fourth, the ministerial style of the Servant is established: He would not be ostentatiously loud, and He would be gentle with the weak (vv. 2–3). He would finally establish true or real justice in the world. Fifth, the success of the Servant is affirmed (v. 4). Sixth, as a new Moses He would give to the nations the *torah*, the divine law as instruction and as exemplified in His life. In fact, the islands or coastlands would wait for (or trust in) His *torah*, "law" or "instruction." The Servant's mission to "establish justice" alludes to the righteous messianic King in 11:1–10 and the universal reign of the Lord in 2:2–4. The identity of this Servant has been a matter of dispute. It would be difficult to identify Him with Cyrus. The NT finds in this prophetic announcement a messianic prophecy describing the work of Jesus of Nazareth (Matt. 12:18–21; see "The Servant of the Lord in Isaiah," p. 885).

In 42:5–9 the Lord seems to address the Servant, elaborating a little more on His mission. The section is introduced by a description of the exclusive creative power of God (v. 5) and concludes with His unique power to announce new things before they happen (v. 9). By giving the Servant as a covenant to/for the people and as a light to the Gentiles, God reaffirmed His call and His divine guidance (v. 6). The Servant appears as the embodiment of God's covenant relationship; as such, He is representative of God's ideal for Israel (49:8) and the nations (cf. 42:5). They would indeed walk in the light or the new revelation that the Servant would bring. This light frees humans from the darkness of an existence separated from the Lord (v. 7).

The Servant would reveal to all who the Lord truly is (cf. 29:18–19; 35:5–6; 42:16) and liberate them from idol worship. Only God could announce the coming of a new world order of such a magnitude (v. 9). The disputation initiated in 41:1 closes with an admonition to the nations to praise the Lord. He is to be praised as a great Warrior who would defeat His enemies (42:10–13).

42:14—43:21. Israel and the New Exodus. The purpose of this section is to show the certainty of the coming deliverance by comparing God's past actions with His promises for future deliverance. The Lord would deliver faithful Israel by a new exodus (42:14–22). He had been quiet during Israel's oppression, but now He would act (v. 14) because He would not forsake them (v. 16). The negative description of the mountains and hills and the drying up of all their vegetation may figuratively describe the defeat of Israel's enemies (v. 15). The Lord would lead blind Israel by an unfamiliar way (v. 16), the way of the new exodus. The reference to turning darkness into light may allude to the pillar of fire that gave Israel light (Ex. 13:21). The display of God's power in the Egyptian Exodus miracle should have convinced Israel that He is the only true God. And yet, they abandoned Him and turned to idolatry (Is. 42:17).

The Lord's servant Israel had been deaf to His word and blind to His acts (vv. 18–20). And yet God called them to conversion (43:10). Israel had failed to walk in the Lord's ways and obey His law (42:24), and therefore they were given to robbers as His anger was poured on them (vv. 24–25). For Israel, now oppressed and in darkness (v. 22), the Lord had a plan to show the greatness and glory of the law (v. 21). They were still His people because He had created and formed them (43:1, 7). Thus, His plan for Israel was as firm as the created world order. The assurance given by the admonition to not be afraid is motivated by the Lord's *past* actions of the election and Exodus (v. 1) and by His *future* actions (vv. 2–3). Both sets of actions reveal His identity as the Holy One and Savior of Israel (v. 3). The Lord's love for Israel made them precious in His sight, and they had been honored (v. 4). Therefore, He would give again, in a new exodus, people and nations in exchange for them. The second assurance, to not be afraid, is motivated by the Lord's presence and His promise to return scattered Israel (v. 5; cf. 11:11–12; 49:12–13).

Another phase in the disputation with the nations commences in 43:8–13. The Lord said that only He could promise salvation and grant it. The supportive evidence is Israel's election through Abraham and the Exodus. In the present situation, the Lord had appointed Israel as His witnesses and had chosen Israel to be His servant (v. 10; cf. 41:8–9; 42:1), and consequently they would, through personal experience, know and believe Him and understand that He is God. They were to testify that, in contrast to idols made by humans, the Lord is eternal (43:10, 13). Only He could save (v. 11). He had declared His plan in advance and then saved His people; there was no foreign god that could do the same (v. 12). Therefore, the Lord declared that Israel had the knowledge of the true God and were His witnesses (v. 12), announced His plans to restore and bless His people to the shame of the foreign idols, and asserted that no power could prevent His plans (v. 13).

In order to show that the Lord controls the future, He announced a new future saving act: the destruction of Babylon (v. 14). It was a most daring prophecy, announcing the fall of the proud Babylonians long before they became a powerful empire. God would send a message to Babylon, a message that is not quoted because the argument lies in its fulfilment, which would benefit God's people. In vv. 16–21 the prophet describes the liberation of Israel from Babylon as a new exodus.

43:22—44:5. Pleading with Israel. Isaiah records the Lord pleading with unfaithful Israel, who are pictured as living in a spiritual desert. They had failed to truly worship Him, and they had burdened Him with their sins (43:23–24). The Lord's plan was to restore Israel by mercifully forgiving them (v. 25; cf. 44:22; 55:7). He would not remember their sins but would ask them to remember Him. The Lord's declaration of the approaching restoration of Israel is announced. The Lord repeated that He had made and formed His people (43:1, 7), and since He would help them, they should not fear (vv. 1–2; cf. 41:10; 43:1, 5). "Jeshurun" is a rare poetic name which designates Israel as "upright one," according to its ideal character. The coming deliverance is described metaphorically as water for thirsty people and for dry ground, symbolizing the pouring out of the Lord's Spirit and His blessing on the children of Israel. The Lord promised that they would spring up among the grass (cf. 40:6–8) like willows or poplars by the streams (44:4). This metaphor implies strength, prosperity, and the continuity of God's people.

44:6–23. God Is Israel's King and Redeemer. Several subordinate themes are integrated here under the notion that Israel's King and Redeemer, the Lord, is the only God in the world and would be recognized as such by the nations. The people of Israel were reminded about their role as God's witnesses (vv. 6–8). The central declaration—that there is no God besides the Lord (v. 6d)—is reinforced by the question and answer in v. 8: His people would testify that there is no God besides Him, no other Rock (cf. 17:10; 26:4; 32:2; 33:16)—their testimony founded on their experience of His salvation. For any god to compare with the Lord, evidence must be given that he has predicted an event that came to pass (44:7).

God contrasted Himself with the gods of the nations. He described the makers of idols (vv. 9–13), the idols themselves (vv. 9, 14–18), and the idol worshipers (vv. 9, 19–20). The repeated conclusion is that the idols cannot see or understand and that the idol worshipers will be ashamed (vv. 9, 11, 18). The passage contains an appeal to Israel to return to the Lord because of the assurance of His salvation. Isaiah presents Israel as the servant of the Lord, who was formed by Him, which implies that He would not forget them and that He had blotted out their sins (vv. 21–22; cf. 43:25). This reminder is followed by a summons to the world to praise the Lord for having redeemed Jacob and revealed His glory in Israel (44:23; cf. 52:9).

44:24–28. The Lord and the Future. The phrase "I am the LORD" (v. 24) may allude to the Lord's appearance to Moses, which preceded the Exodus (cf. Ex. 3:6–7, 14–15). A new exodus was announced in Isaiah 42:14–16 and 43:3–4. A summary in hymnic style mentions the Lord's actions in the past (Creation), present (verifying the words of His servant), and future (Jerusalem and Judah rebuilt). The point is that the future events predicted by the Lord and His prophet would come to pass because as Sovereign Lord His word is reliable. Jerusalem and Judah would be rebuilt, and Cyrus would be His appointed agent. Cyrus is partially portrayed as a second Moses, and as such (Deut. 18:17–18; Acts 3:22), he is a type of the Messiah (cf. 45:1, where he is in fact called a *mashiakh*, a "messiah"). Cyrus would free Israel from captivity; so also would the Messiah free His people from the captivity of sin (61:1; Matt. 1:21). The reference to the drying up of the deep and rivers/streams may be an allusion to the Exodus and Moses (Is. 44:27; cf. 63:11–13), as well as to the means

by which Babylon was invaded and fell—that is, the accounts of some historians that Cyrus diverted the Euphrates River and entered the city through the dry channels. Isaiah calls Moses the shepherd of His flock (v. 11) and Cyrus His shepherd (44:28). The Lord would hold the right hand of Cyrus to lead His people out of Babylonia (45:1), just as He led Israel out of Egypt by the right hand of Moses (63:12). In 45:1–13 Cyrus is depicted as a conqueror of the nations. By destroying the power of the nations through Cyrus's predicted victories, the Lord would turn Israel and the nations to Himself (vv. 3–7).

The Lord first promised that through Cyrus Jerusalem would be inhabited and the destroyed cities of Judah would be rebuilt (44:26). The reference to Cyrus performing everything that God had desired (vv. 28b) does not mean that under Cyrus Jerusalem and the cities of Judah would be actually rebuilt but that he would initiate the process that would ultimately bring this about. Since the Lord Himself was Israel's Shepherd (40:11), Cyrus was His vassal. The Hebrew term *hekal* that is used in 44:28 can mean "temple" or "palace." But contextually the palaces are included in the rebuilding of the city. According to Ezra 1:2–4, the decree issued by Cyrus authorized only the rebuilding of the temple.

45:1–8. God's Appointment of Cyrus. The divine appointment of Cyrus (vv. 1–3) was turned into an argument (vv. 3c–8) that proves that the God of Israel is the only true God. Thus, by His appointment of Cyrus—announced long before he appeared in history and even though he did not know the Lord (vv. 4–5)—God proved that *only He is God,* and therefore all nations would acknowledge that only He rules over light and darkness, peace and calamity (vv. 7–8). An extended messenger formula in v. 1 indicates that the Lord's commission appointment speech to Cyrus follows; it is found in vv. 2–8. It has the character of a covenant stipulated by the Overlord, "the God of Israel" (v. 3), and obediently accepted by the vassal, "Cyrus." Cyrus would be His anointed (v. 1), which is used figuratively, as in 61:1 (there used in regard to the Messiah), and signifies his consecration to the Lord's plan (cf. Ps. 105:15; Jer. 1:5). The Lord would subdue the nations before him (Is. 45:1) and give him the treasures of the vanquished nations (v. 3). The Lord calling him by name (vv. 3–4) indicates that He knows Cyrus in advance and has titles of honor for him— His shepherd (44:28) and His anointed (45:1).

That Cyrus was a type of Christ is supported by the fact that both of these titles (in addition to being used for priests and kings in general—who were also types of Christ) are used for Christ in both the OT and NT (Shepherd: Ezek. 34:23-24; Mic. 5:2-5; Zech. 13:7; John 10; Heb. 13:20; 1 Pet. 2:25; Anointed/Messiah/ Christ: Ps. 2:2; Is. 61:1; Dan. 9:25; Matt. 1:16; 16:16; Mark 14:61-62; Luke 9:20; 24:26; John 1:41; 20:31; Acts 10:38; Rev. 12:10).

Cyrus is promised victory over nations and kings, but this will be the Lord's work (45:1-3). The purpose of his victories involves not only liberating the Israelites and rebuilding Jerusalem and the temple but converting the nations (vv. 3, 5-7). The covenant with Cyrus was to have the purpose of bringing to him and to all nations the knowledge that the God of Israel is the only true God and that He would bring to the earth righteousness and salvation (vv. 3-8; cf. 2:2-4).

The naming of Cyrus is a sign of the Lord's divine power and foreknowledge (45:4-5). As He emerges in the book of Isaiah, the Lord certainly has the predictive power to reveal such a name in advance. The Lord is sovereign over all nations; He gives dominion to whomever He chooses and accomplishes His mission through any He deems fit.

45:9-25. Doubt and Assurance. This passage begins with a disputation against doubting the Lord's word (vv. 9-10) and turns into an assurance regarding His prediction of future events concerning Israel and His sovereignty over human history as based on His power as Creator (vv. 11-12). These points confirm the Lord's appointment of Cyrus in righteousness (i.e., in accordance with God's plan of salvation) and that He would direct all his ways or make them straight (v. 13). The reference to the idea that Cyrus would not receive a price or reward for freeing Israel is rooted in the concept that a slave could be redeemed by the payment of a ransom to his master. But, by the law of the covenant, a slave in Israel could be set free without payment on the seventh year (cf. 50:1; 58:6; Deut. 15:12-18).

The concluding statement that Cyrus would build God's city and let His exiles go free (Is. 45:13) summarizes the outcome of his victory over nations and kings (vv. 1-3). His actions meant that Jerusalem could be rebuilt and Israel would worship the Lord at Zion. Besides, the nations would submit to Israel (cf. 14:1-2) when they realized that God was with Israel and there was no other God (45:14-15; cf. 1 Cor.

14:25). The idol makers would be ashamed and disgraced, but Israel would be saved by the Lord with an everlasting salvation (45:16-17, 24-25).

Firstly, God is the only God because He created heaven and earth for a *purpose* (i.e., not in vain, to be empty, but to be inhabited; v. 18; Gen. 1:2ff.). Secondly, He had demonstrated that He alone is God by declaring true things for the *purpose* of saving the descendants of Jacob, His covenant people (45:19). But God would convince the surviving refugees from the nations that He is a just, righteous God and a Savior and that there is no other (vv. 20-21). God invited all the ends of the earth to find salvation in Him (v. 22). Many would recognize that only in the Lord could they have righteousness, deliverance, and strength, that those who were angry with God would be disgraced, and that every knee would bow before Him (vv. 23-24; cf. 2:2-4).

46:1-13. The God of Israel and the Gods of Babylon. Isaiah compares the Lord with Babylon's two main gods. The gods of Babylon were unable to save their worshipers, but the Lord had demonstrated that He could indeed save Israel. Bel (v. 1) is Bel Marduk, the chief god of the Babylonian pantheon, who was also manifested as the god Ashur. Bel was the supreme god of the nations, the head of the gods, and the creator of the world. Nebo was the son of Marduk/ Ashur and was worshiped both in Babylon and Assyria. He was the god of destiny. Keeping the Tablets of Destiny, which were thought to predict and govern the fate of humans, he was seen as the (scribal) god of history.

One way to understand the metaphor of vv. 1-2 is that Bel and Nebo are compared to beasts of burden (cf. the Lord in vv. 3-4), carrying their burdens, in other words, the people worshiping them (cf. Israel as a burden of the Lord in vv. 3-4). The two gods could not deliver the burden. Instead, they had themselves gone into captivity (i.e., when their images were taken by conquerors; v. 2). Another way to understand this is that the images of Bel and Nebo were placed onto beasts of burden (v. 1) because they couldn't move about on their own. These supposed gods could not even rescue their own images that supposedly represented them—the gods (as it were) and their images would be carried into captivity. The Lord, however, had successfully carried His people from the womb and would continue to do so in their old age (vv. 3-4). He declared (lit. "I am He," i.e., Israel's God) that He had made them, and He would carry and save them (v. 4). Some of the same vocabulary is used here as in the description of Bel and Nebo—God was able to carry his people, but the false gods had to have people carry their idols. The comparison in vv. 1–4 between Bel/Nebo and the Lord leads to a general comparison between the idols and the Lord in vv. 5–7 (cf. 40:18–26). The Lord is incomparable (v. 5). The Lord is the Giver of life, but the idols were lifeless, made of gold and silver by a hired goldsmith and then worshiped as gods. It is only the God of Israel, the Creator-God, who deserves worship, not human-made idols.

Israel is encouraged to remember that the Lord had fulfilled His word and that He would do so again in the future. The Lord says, "I am God, and there is no other" (Is. 46:9). He had predicted actions in the past, such as those related to Abraham, the Exodus, and the conquest of Canaan, which He then fulfilled (v. 9), knowing and revealing the end from the beginning (v. 10). He predicted that He would call a bird of prey from a distant land in the east—the man to execute His plan. He had spoken it and would cause it to happen. He had planned it and would accomplish it (v. 11). Contextually, this is the prophecy concerning Cyrus. The point is that God's prediction of future events would surely come to pass because He is the Lord of history. In conclusion, the Lord admonished obstinate Israel to listen to Him (v. 12). Being scattered among the nations, Israel would still be blind to the real identity of the Lord (cf. 40:27; 42:16–25; 43:22–28). God's righteousness in 46:13 is closely related to His salvation or deliverance—they are placed in a parallel relationship. The contrast between "far" and "near" indicates that here "righteousness" has the same meaning as in v. 12b. The only way for sinful people who are far from God's righteousness to be saved is for God to give them His own righteousness as a gift. The ultimate display of God's righteousness for salvation is in the life, death, resurrection, and intercession of Christ (chap. 53). His salvation would be placed on Zion for Israel, who would be a display of His glory (i.e., the gathering of Israel on Zion would mean that the Lord would redeem and restore a wretched Israel so that they would reflect and be witness to His own splendor; cf. chaps. 60–62).

47:1–15. Humiliation of Babylon. Babylon is addressed as a queen (notice the mention of "virgin daughter" and "throne" in v. 1) who would be humiliated by the Lord's vengeance (v. 3). This is followed by Israel's collective acknowledgment of the Lord as "Redeemer" and

the "Holy One of Israel" (v. 4). The silence referred to in v. 5 is the silence of grief or humiliation (cf. Lam. 2:10; Amos 8:3), and darkness is often used as a symbol for sorrow (Is. 9:2; 42:7; 50:10). The Lord explains that, being angry with His people, He had profaned or desecrated His inheritance (i.e., Israel) by giving them into the hands of Babylon (47:6). Punished and humiliated, Babylon would no longer be called the lady or queen of kingdoms (vv. 5, 7). The accusations against Babylon are of different kinds. Firstly, she had oppressed Israel without mercy while caring only about her own power and glory (vv. 6d–7; cf. 10:5–15). Secondly, she did not think of the One who had authorized her to punish His people and who would call her to account for her actions (47:7).

Babylon's crime was especially her pride: she was addicted to pleasure (i.e., the Babylonians were prosperous and ignored their duties toward the Creator), she lived in security (i.e., they trusted in their power to maintain their own security), she thought that she was the "I am" and there was no one else like her (i.e., they were self-centered and claimed to be divine [cf. God's words about Himself in 45:6; 46:9], amounting to blasphemy against the only God), and she thought that she would never know any loss or defeat (i.e., ignoring the Lord's justice and control of history). The punishment would include widowhood and loss of children, and this would take place in a moment, in one day, and in fullness (47:9). These predictions were particularly fulfilled in the destruction of the city by the Medo-Persians.

Babylon was also guilty of sorcery (v. 9) and of being deluded by the misuse of their knowledge and wisdom, which resulted in blasphemous pride. Believing that misfortune came from demons or the anger of the gods, Babylon still felt secure because she was able to thwart the demons by sorcery, spells, and enchantments, and she did not know of any god who would punish her for her crimes. The result was that she trusted in her wickedness (v. 10). In the announcement of judgment (v. 11), Babylon is firmly placed under the jurisdiction of the Lord. Her enchanters and astrologers are summoned to demonstrate whether they can save her from what would come against her (vv. 12–13). The term usually translated as "astrologers" means literally in Hebrew "dividers of the heavens," who seek to predict the future by studying the changing constellations of the stars. Those who look at the stars (sometimes translated as "stargazers") may refer to some kind of astrological occupation or simply to worshipers of the stars.

There were also those who made monthly predictions, which involved lists of lucky and unlucky days and important events that ruled the lives of their followers. The astrologers would perish like stubble in the flames (v. 14). The fire may symbolize the anger of God on the day of judgment, but it could also refer to the destruction of conquered cities, which was usually by fire. The word *sakhar* in its participial form in v. 15 means literally "those who go around." It has been translated as "merchants" or as those "who have trafficked," "traded," or "dealt with." Some have understood the "merchants" to be representative of the practitioners of magic arts described in the previous verses. In Babylon, each astrologer-counselor offered a different prediction of the future (cf. v. 9), and each of them was in error. This is completely reversed when the Lord's plan of salvation for Israel is offered in chapter 48.

48:1-11. God's Plan for Israel. The prophet resumes the theme found in chapters 1–33 that Israel's King would redeem Israel as an act of purification, enabling them to assume the task of a servant and to reveal Him as the true God to the nations (chaps. 49–54). Israel's apostasy is described as a superficial, formal ritual faith or even hypocrisy. Isaiah says they claim to rely upon (lit. "lean upon") the God of Israel (48:2), while in reality trusting in other gods. "The holy city" alludes to the Lord as "the Holy One of Israel"—the purified Jerusalem is ideally called the righteous and faithful city (1:25-26), and the purged remnant would be called "holy" (4:2-3).

Israel's chastisement came as foretold because the Lord's word accomplishes what He sends it to do (48:3-5; cf. 55:10-11). The point is to convince Israel of the certainty of the prophetic word and to confirm that the Lord gave them an opportunity to avoid their punishment. The Lord conceded (48:4) that He knew that Israel was obstinate, a state symbolized by an iron neck and a bronze forehead. His predictions were made to prove that He, as the Lord of history, and not the idols, brought the judgment.

The Lord would make them hear new, previously unknown things regarding the future (vv. 5-6). Israel had not heard or understood, for they were unable or unwilling to know their Lord (v. 8; cf. 6:9-10; 29:9-13; 43:8-13, 22-28). But through the vision of Isaiah, Israel was being admonished to notice what God was telling them (48:6) and to recognize that God would delay or defer His anger and not completely destroy them (v. 9). The chastisement of

apostate Israel had been going on long enough (cf. 40:1-2). The Lord's plan was to discipline them so that they would repent. His plan was not to annihilate them because He remained faithful to His covenant with them. Therefore, although Israel was not yet fully converted, He had forgiven them and would restore them by His love and mercy and not because of their merit (cf. 43:25; 44:21-22).

God had refined them, though not like silver. He had tested them in the "furnace of affliction," the Exile (v. 10). The implementation of the Lord's plan had so far resulted in the purification of Israel—the term translated "refine" has the literal sense of "smelt" (48:10; cf. 1:25). In the refining process, the "affliction" that had fallen upon Israel served as a smelting "furnace," which alludes to the deliverance from Egypt (as in 48:20-21). As the Lord took Israel out of the iron-smelting furnace (i.e., Egypt) to be His people (Deut. 4:20), He had chosen Israel "in the furnace of affliction" (Is. 48:10; i.e., under Babylonian oppression) to restore them as His people (cf. 41:8-9; 44:1-2; 48:9-11; 49:7).

48:12-22. The Lord Predicts Redemption for Israel. The disputation here serves to establish that the redemption of Israel was part of the divine plan. At the passage's beginning, Isaiah relates that the Speaker confirmed Himself as the only God, the First and the Last (vv. 12-13); then He called all nations together (v. 14).

A prophecy is announced concerning the future prosperity of Israel (vv. 14-15), which ties in with vv. 9-11, 20-21. The one whom the Lord had loved (some translations have "chosen"; v. 14) has been understood to refer to either Israel (who is referred to elsewhere in Isaiah as beloved of the Lord—43:4) or most probably to Cyrus, who would be instrumental in accomplishing God's purposes against Babylon. The climax of the prophecy in 48:15 is the Lord's words "I have called Him."

The Lord urged the nations, including Israel, to come near to Him and listen (v. 16). It is a little difficult to identify the speaker in this verse. In the first part of v. 16, the speaker is clearly God, but it is not clear who is speaking in the last part of the verse as having been sent by Yahweh (lit. "and now the Lord Yahweh has sent me and His Spirit"). It could be Israel responding to God's call. It could be the Messiah, representing His people, who would be sent and empowered by the Spirit (11:2; 42:1; 61:1), or it could be the prophet who would then proceed to deliver the message the Lord gave him (48:17-19). This last possibility is most likely. As Israel's Redeemer, God lamented their disobedience to His commandments (i.e., the core of the covenant), reminding them of all the benefits that would have come to them—instead of the furnace of affliction (v. 10)—if they had heeded His instructions.

The section ends with a prediction of the future salvation of Israel (vv. 20–21) and a caveat concerning the lack of peace for the wicked (v. 22). The command to Israel to flee from the Chaldeans in Babylon is in v. 20. The parallel "Babylon"/"Chaldeans" represents the home of the supreme idols among the nations (46:1–13) and the enemy that the Lord would humiliate by destruction and desolation (47:1–15). The command to leave or flee (i.e., to leave in haste; v. 20) is a reminder of the Exodus from Egypt (cf. Ex. 12:11, 31–34, 39; 14:5). Other allusions to the Exodus are Israel's song of praises to the Lord their Redeemer (Is. 48:20; cf. Ex. 14:31—15:21) and the Lord's sustenance of His people as illustrated by the provision of water (Is. 48:21; cf. Ex. 15:22–25; Num. 20:11; Ps. 78:15–16). The act of going forth from Babylon would enable Israel to proclaim to the ends of the earth that the Lord had redeemed His servant Jacob (Is. 48:20).

49:1–13. The Lord's Servant: A Light to the Nations. This passage is considered by some to be one of the so-called Servant Songs that supposedly originated independently of the present context, but since it is so well integrated in the context it is to be considered as originating in Isaiah for this specific context. The passage focuses on how the Lord commissioned His Servant to bring the knowledge of God to the nations. Scholars have debated the identity of this Servant without reaching a consensus. We will suggest that since the Servant's mission is to Israel, He cannot be Israel (see commentary on 42:4). In this passage Israel is embodied in this figure called the Servant, and the name functions as a messianic designation fulfilled in Jesus Christ (see "The Servant of the Lord in Isaiah," p. 885). The passage focuses on how the Lord commissioned His Servant to bring the knowledge of God to the nations. The Servant first acknowledged that the Lord had appointed and equipped Him as His Servant: the Lord's plan would be glorified in Him (49:3). But in the realization of His mission, He faced disappointment. However, the Servant anticipated success (v. 4).

Verse 5 begins with "and now," which indicates the arrival of a new situation that would result in the ultimate success of the work of the Servant of the Lord. His mission, which began with disappointment, would consist in bringing Jacob back to Him to gather Israel. However, His mission would also embrace the nations to whom the Servant would be given as a light (cf. 42:6–7). Through the Servant, the Lord's salvation would be given to "the ends of the earth" (49:6; cf. v. 8; 42:1–9; 44:5; 45:6–8, 14–25). This aim reveals the Lord's faithfulness to His covenant with Abraham and Israel (Gen. 22:18; cf. 12:3) and to the everlasting covenant with humanity (Is. 24:5; Gen. 9:12–17).

In Isaiah 49:7, Isaiah relates the Lord's announcement to the Servant that even though He would be despised and abhorred by His people, kings would see and stand (as a sign of homage) and princes would also worship (lit. "prostrate oneself"). This would be possible because of the faithfulness of the Lord to His commitment to save sinners. In v. 8, we find a description of the close connection between the Lord and the Servant. The references to the acceptable or favorable time are rooted in the genre of the individual lament. The troubled speaker waits for and hopes in the Lord (e.g., Ps. 69:3) and prays for salvation in a situation of unjust suffering, while the acceptable/favorable time (Ps. 69:13) would occur later when the prayer met with the Lord's favor. Isaiah 49 reveals a temporal structure that follows this pattern: (1) the Servant suffering unjustly while praying and waiting for the Lord (vv. 4, 7, 9); (2) the Lord hearing and helping Him (v. 8); (3) the Lord preserving Him and appointing Him as a covenant to restore the nations (v. 8d–g); and (4) the nations restored (vv. 9–12).

The meaning of the covenantal Servant (49:8; cf. 42:6) emerges in chapters 49–54: somehow the Servant reestablished the covenant in Himself after it was violated by the people. The people mentioned are primarily the people of Israel, though the context mentions the Gentiles as well. Through the Servant, the Lord would establish peace on earth (49:8; cf. 2:2–4; 54:1–17). Specifically, He would restore the earth/land and cause its inhabitants to live in the previously desolate areas (49:8), and the prisoners and those in darkness would emerge and see the light (v. 9; cf. 9:2; 42:7; 61:1). The proclamation of the prisoners' release is associated with the Jubilee (Lev. 25:8–17; see 2 Cor. 6:2). Under the leadership of the Servant Messiah, God would provide for the needs of His people as they gathered from the four corners of the world (Is. 49:10–12). The whole cosmos is called to rejoice in the Lord's comforting of His people and His merciful compassion to the afflicted.

49:14–23. God Remembers Zion. In spite of the rebellion of Zion, the Lord had not forgotten her. In fact, Zion reproached the Lord because she felt forsaken and forgotten by Him, implying that He did not have the will to save His people (v. 14). The Lord responded with words of assurance (vv. 15–16) and a promise (vv. 17–23). Surely, He had the will to restore His people. He had formed and created Israel (cf. 43:1; 44:1–2), and therefore He declared, "I will not forget you" (49:15; cf. 44:21). He had inscribed or engraved her name on the palms of His hands; His attention was continually directed toward her walls (49:16). Zion would be the Lord's standard or banner for the peoples (v. 22).

The reference to the children (lit. "sons") hastening (v. 17) reminds us of the Exodus from Egypt that took place hurriedly (see commentary on 48:12–22). In the second part of the verse, the rare Hebrew word *haras* is used. It has been translated as "destroyers" or "those who have laid you waste," but it can also mean "those who have overthrown or overtaken you." The Hebrew word *kharab* in the parallel expression that follows normally means "those who made you desolate," a term referring to the removal of inhabitants from the cities and the land (37:18; 42:15; Judg. 16:24; Ezra 19:7; Zeph. 3:6; cf. the reference to those who had swallowed or devoured them in Is. 49:19). The survivors in Zion were admonished to look around and see the sons gathering together and coming to mother Zion (v. 18; cf. 60:4). "As I live" is the Lord's oath (49:18; cf. 45:23) that Zion would ornament herself as a bride with the returning children of Israel (cf. Rev. 21:2). Zion, which had been desolated, would be rendered too small for all the many people returning to it (Is. 49:19–20). Zion would only wonder and marvel at what had happened (v. 21).

The gathering of scattered Israel is based on two actions communicating to Zion the reality of Yahweh and that those who wait obediently for the Lord would not be ashamed (v. 23). First, God would lift His beckoning hand to the nations (v. 22). The Servant of the Lord would be given as a light and a covenant to the nations (vv. 6, 8), and Isaiah presents the Lord affirming a covenant with them through His oath (v. 22). Second, the Lord would lift up a standard, or banner, for the peoples (v. 22). This "standard" or "banner" figuratively functions as the rallying point of scattered Israel and the peoples (cf. the figure of a light to the nations in v. 6), and this role would be fulfilled by Zion, the dwelling place of the Lord.

The kings, who would see and arise, and the princes (or "officials"), who would bow down in homage (v. 7), would come to Zion, bringing Israel's sons and daughters. The scenes of the past deportations would be reversed.

49:24—50:3. The Lord's Power to Save Israel. This passage complements 49:14–23, answering the question raised in v. 24 and presenting the Lord as indeed able to save Zion-Israel from the mighty. The Lord's answer is that scattered Israel would be saved even from mighty armies and terrible nations. He was committed to contend with those contending with Zion in order to save her children. He would punish Israel's oppressors with internal strife or extreme situations of famine. The salvation of Zion-Israel is linked to a defeat of powerful nations. Therefore, all people would come to know of the Lord as the Savior, Redeemer, and Mighty One of Jacob (v. 26; cf. 60:16).

Isaiah presents Israel's doubts about the Lord's willingness and power to save them, which are finally summarized by the Lord (50:1–3) with answers to a series of questions. The first set of questions concerns the Lord's willingness to save (cf. 49:14–23). Asking where the certificate of divorce was involved a metaphor of marriage for the relationship between the Lord and His people (50:1; cf. 54:6–8; 61:10). The covenant law stipulated that a permanent divorce was not valid unless the husband had issued a document of divorce and that, if his former wife remarried, the first husband could never take her back again (Deut. 24:1–4; Jer. 3:1, 8). However, in Israel's case, there was no letter of divorce, which indicates that the Lord's plan was to take her back again after a time of separation and chastisement (cf. Is. 54:6–8).

The second question applies the metaphor of selling children as slaves in payment of a debt (50:1). The rhetorical question in this verse is ironic, for the Lord had no creditors and would restore His children without money and without price (45:13; 52:3); namely, He would take back what rightfully belonged to Him. The nature of the metaphorical questions confirms the Lord's certain willingness to save His people. The Israelites themselves must carry the blame for their disgrace (50:1).

The Lord's *power* to save is raised in the second set of questions (vv. 2–3; cf. 49:24–26). First, He questioned Israel's reluctance to trust His promises. In the second pair of questions, the Lord raised questions regarding His power (50:2). His answer invited the people to consider His power over both the earth and the heavens.

50:4–11. The Servant and Hope. This passage probes further into the work of the Servant (vv. 4–9). Verses 4–9 are usually considered another Servant Song with a call to listen to the Servant (50:10—51:8). The speaker in the text is not defined until the mention of His Servant in 50:10. The Lord had empowered the Servant to be an efficient teacher. His patient endurance under opposition and suffering illustrates His humble trust in God (cf. 54:6–10). This may be taken as a literal description of opposition to His instruction by fellow Israelites. The giving of the Servant's back to those striking it speaks of humility and willing submission (50:6). Plucking out the beard was an extreme form of insult (cf. 2 Sam. 10:5; Ezra 9:3; Neh. 13:25), and spitting was a sign of contempt (cf. Job 30:10). The Servant passed through a humiliating experience in the hands of fellow humans (Is. 50:6). This was fulfilled in the experience of Jesus.

The Lord God's help is mentioned in both vv. 7 and 9. Setting one's face like flint (v. 7) is a figure of resolute endurance in the face of opposition (cf. Jer. 1:18; 20:11; Ezek. 3:8–9). In Isaiah 50:8–9, the Servant's confidence in God is illustrated by the dual image of the Lord as a fair judge, who would pronounce judgment in His favor, and the Lord as His advocate, who would invalidate the charges against Him. Verses 10–11 present addresses to a wide group ("you" is in the plural), probably Israel as a whole, with different counsels to two opposite groups. First is a call for the attention of those who "fear the Lord" but who are despondent, reminding them to keep trusting in God. Second is an address to disobedient Israel. The metaphor of fire may be understood as a reference to the wicked and their actions (cf. 9:18; Job 31:11–12; Prov. 26:18). Isaiah records the mocking advice for them to walk in the light of their fire and among the torches or sparks that they had ignited (Is. 50:11); that is, they were sarcastically told to continue living in their wickedness, which would be their own ruin.

51:1–16. Comforting the Faithful. The Lord would comfort and restore Zion by making it like the garden of the Lord (v. 3). As a reason for believing this promise, He admonished His people to remember where they had come from and the covenant with Abraham. The Lord announced that His law, or instruction (Heb. *torah*), and justice would be set as a light for the nations (cf. 42:6; 49:6, 8) and that Israel would soon experience His salvation through the defeat of their oppressors. God's righteousness is His faithfulness to the covenant,

manifesting itself in acts of salvation (51:5–6). In metaphorical poetry, the "arm" of God is summoned to "awake" (v. 9). The Lord is asked to intervene as of old when He delivered His people from Egypt (vv. 9–10). The sorrow and sighing of the Lord's redeemed people would be replaced by everlasting joy (cf. 35:10; Rev. 21:1–4). God Himself comforts His people and reminds us not to be afraid of other human beings (cf. Ps. 27; Rom. 8:31–39).

The Lord's plan was to expose the oppressor's lack of power. He contrasted the (powerless) fury of the oppressor with His own promise to relieve and sustain the oppressed. Thus, the verbal expressions in v. 14 are in the future tense. The Hebrew verb *tsa'ah* (sometimes translated here in its participial form as "exile") can convey the idea of being bowed down (under a burden; cf. 51:14; Jer. 2:20). Accordingly, it is also translated as "the oppressed" or "cowering prisoners." The foundation of the assurance of deliverance (Is. 51:12–14) is expressed in vv. 15–16: Israel's God is the powerful Creator and loving Savior of His people. The mention of being covered in the shadow of God's hand is a repetition of the promise to the Lord's Servant (49:2). In 51:16, the Lord reaffirmed the promise to deliver His people and return them to the promised land.

51:17–23. Jerusalem Is Summoned. The Lord calls on Jerusalem to awake and rise up from the state of hopelessness in which it finds itself (vv. 17–20). Drinking from the cup of God's wrath (v. 17) means to experience God's judgment. The ensuing intoxication is a figure of fear, desperation, shame, and suffering (cf. Jer. 25:15–29; Lam. 4:21–22). Jerusalem is pictured in Isaiah 51:18–20 as a mother staggering under the effects of the drink, suffering especially by a decimation of her population. The Lord addressed the afflicted staggering under the weight of their affliction (vv. 21–23). He was contending for His people in a court of justice where the sins of Jerusalem had been condemned and the length of the punishment discussed (cf. Job 1:6—2:10). The Lord announced that He had removed His cup of wrath from Jerusalem and that she would no longer drink from it (cf. Is. 40:1–2). Instead, He would give the cup to those who had afflicted His people.

52:1–12. Zion-Jerusalem Is Summoned. In this case Zion-Jerusalem is summoned to dress herself for celebration. Jerusalem would again be called the holy city—the time of disgrace is now over, and the city is restored (cf. 1:21–26). The people of Zion-Jerusalem were told to remove their bonds themselves by believing in the Lord's plan of deliverance. In 50:1 the Lord told His people that they had sold themselves into slavery because of their sins and, in 52:3, that they had sold themselves for nothing (cf. 45:13); therefore, they would be redeemed without money (i.e., the Lord would take back what he rightfully possessed).

The motif of redemption without price is further explored in 52:4–6, in the context of Israel's slavery in Egypt (in the past) and in the Assyrian Empire (at present). The Lord delivered Israel from Egypt although they had willingly moved there. In the case of Assyria, however, the certainty of Israel's deliverance by the Lord is even greater because Assyria oppresses them for no reason (i.e., Assyria did not pay a price for them—it took them by force—and, therefore, has no right to Israel now that the Lord is reclaiming His people). At the moment the Lord would take action, Israel would learn that He has both the power and the will to fulfill His promises, for His people would know His Name (i.e., they would witness His boundless power; v. 6).

The future deliverance of Zion and Israel is announced with absolute certainty (vv. 7–12). The feet of the heralds were already treading the mountains of Judah with the good news for Zion that there would be peace (i.e., deliverance, well-being, security, and harmony; cf. 54:10, 13) and salvation from God who reigns (52:7). The watchmen on the walls of Jerusalem (cf. 21:6–9; 40:9; 62:6–7) would sing and praise the Lord when they saw Him bringing back Zion

(i.e., scattered Israel; 52:8)—or, according to some renderings, when the Lord would return to Zion. Their hymn of praise is recorded in vv. 9–10. The promise was that God would bare His holy arm (i.e., He would throw back the folds of His garment in order to use His sword; cf. Ps. 74:11), a metaphorical description of a display of His power, deliverance, judgment, and care (cf. Is. 30:30; 33:2; 40:10–11; 51:9). Then all the earth would see God's salvation (52:10). These clauses are vital for the understanding of 52:13—53:12.

Isaiah 52:11–12 describes the deliverance of the priestly servants of the temple as a new exodus. They were holy because their God was the Holy One of Israel. The return would be a new exodus under the Lord's command: just as He had done then, He would go in front of and behind them (cf. Ex. 13:21–22; 14:19–20). But while the first Exodus was carried out with haste and flight, the new one would be peaceful and orderly because the oppressor's power had already been broken (52:12).

52:13—53:12. The Suffering Servant of the Lord. This passage brings the mission of the Servant of the Lord to a climax (cf. 42:1–9; 49:1–9; 50:4–11). It is followed by the everlasting covenant of peace (chaps. 54–55) and the acknowledgment of the nations that the Lord is the only God (chaps. 56, 60, 66). As previously indicated, a number of attempts have been made to identify the Servant, but it is better to identify Him, as the NT does, with the Messiah, Jesus Christ (see below, "The Servant of the Lord in Isaiah"). The passage provides a glorious prophecy concerning the experience, ministry, and results of the Servant's work.

The Servant of the Lord in Isaiah

The identity of the Servant of the Lord in Isaiah has been explored by scholars throughout history. In the NT, the Ethiopian, while reading Isaiah 53, raised the question but was unable to answer it and asked Phillip about the identity of the person described in the passage (Acts 8:34). Scholars have struggled with the question, but there is no consensus among them. As we look at the question, we will begin with what appears to be clearly stated in the text and try to draw some conclusions from that information.

1. Israel Is the Servant. No one would question that in some passages Isaiah indisputably identifies Israel as the servant of God. While announcing His work of gathering Israel from among the nations, the Lord states this clearly (41:8). Israel was the servant by divine election, and therefore God would not reject them (v. 9). Some of these ideas are repeated in 44:1–5. The promise of restoration is introduced with a message of encouragement (v. 1). The Lord had bound Israel to Him through election and creation, and in faithfulness to that commitment He would restore them (vv. 2–5), be with them, and become their Redeemer (vv. 6, 22; 48:20). It is even stated that the Lord would raise Cyrus as His anointed for the sake of His servant Jacob and His chosen Israel (45:4).

2. *The Failure of Israel as Servant.* It is also clear that, according to Isaiah, Israel often failed in their task as servant of God. In a disputation between God and His people, evidence is presented against them. Israel, the servant of God, is described as deaf and blind (42:18–19) because even though they saw many things, they did not obey the Lord (v. 20). They went into exile but were unwilling to learn from that experience and to understand that it happened because of their sins and their lack of obedience to the law of God (v. 24). But Israel as a servant was also a messenger (v. 19). The servant had a mission to the nations but was often unable to fulfill it because they were deaf and blind. God's plan to display His great and glorious law could not always be fulfilled through His people (vv. 21–22). Because of their spiritual corruption, they should not have even claimed to be Israel (48:1). Their actions did not correspond to their claim of being Israel. Of course, God did not give up on them, as the next two chapters indicate. Some have suggested that the faithful Israelites (the remnant) are the Servant in Isaiah 53. However, according to Isaiah, the faithful ones—the remnant—should obey God's Servant (50:10), and it is the Servant who causes Jacob to return to God and gathers Israel to the Lord (49:5). He is the One who will restore those of Israel that the Lord has preserved—the remnant—v. 6. Clearly, the remnant (52:8–12) is distinguished from the Servant of the Lord (52:13—53:12).

3. *The Mission of the Anonymous Servant.* There are some similarities between the anonymous Servant of the Lord and Israel as servant of the Lord. Both were chosen by the Lord (41:8; 42:1; 44:1–2; 49:1), called by Him (41:9; 42:6), and entrusted with a mission (42:1, 6–7; 43:10). But there are major differences indicating that the prophet is describing two different servants although both are closely related. The mission of the Servant of the Lord was different in that He had a mission to Israel. It consisted of the restoration of Israel and Jacob through the preservation of a remnant (49:5–6). Besides, the Lord gave the Servant as a covenant to the people, to restore the earth and set free the prisoners and those in darkness (vv. 8–9). This mission assigned to the Servant could not have been fulfilled by the nation of Israel.

The mission of the Servant is also universal (v. 6). The Servant would not simply proclaim salvation to the nations but would be their light and salvation, a task that would be impossible to assign to Israel or even to the prophet himself (cf. 56:1). He would also provide justice and truth to the nations (42:1–3) and would not stop until His justice and the law were established throughout the world (v. 4). The Lord gave the Servant as a covenant to the people and as a light to the Gentiles (v. 6). The new covenant mediated to Israel by the Servant who embodies it (49:8) would also include the Gentiles. He was called by the Lord to heal the blind and to free the prisoners and those in darkness (42:7). The blindness is universal, but it particularly applies to Israel (vv. 18–20). The *means* by which this most powerful act of salvation would be accomplished is not stated until 52:13—53:12.

4. *The Experience of the Servant of the Lord.* In the fulfillment of His mission, Isaiah presents the Servant as going through two main stages: humiliation and victory. From the very beginning, it is stated that the Servant would not lose strength or be discouraged (42:4), a description which implies that He would face serious challenges. In the so-called second Servant Song (49:1–9) we find a sequence of the trials and victories of the Servant. He testified that His work seemed to be in vain (v. 4). In the first stage of His experience, the work of the Servant appears unsuccessful, but He is not discouraged because His reward would be with the Lord (v. 4). By using the word "now," the Lord announced a new task for His Servant (v. 5), namely, to bring salvation to Israel and to the nations (v. 6). Then we are taken back to the humiliating experience of the Servant being despised by the people and abhorred by the nation (v. 7). This is followed by the announcement of His victory: kings and princes would worship Him. He would be acknowledged as King of kings. This would be possible because at the proper moment the Lord would hear the prayer of His Servant, preserve Him, and give Him as a covenant to the people (v. 8).

The third so-called Servant Song (50:4–11) is more explicit concerning the humiliating experience of the Servant. He is described as struck and spat upon, and His beard is plucked (v. 6). In this passage He is willing to go through this physical assault, knowing that the Lord would help Him. He accordingly set His face "like a flint" (v. 7), persuaded that the Lord would vindicate Him (v. 8). The depth of the humiliation of the Servant of the Lord is more fully described in the fourth Servant Song (52:13—53:12.

5. *The Identity of the Servant.* The Servant is described as a person to whom the Lord had spoken (42:6–7) and who spoke about Himself (50:4–9). He is not a personification or a metaphor for Israel because His description in 49:1–9 is strongly individualistic, describing the Servant as a historical figure with a particular biography. Perhaps what is surprising is that the anonymous Servant in vv. 1–9 is specifically called Israel (v. 3). This is important in that although He could be differentiated from Israel, He still carried the name, thus indicating a deep connection between both. Here we should recall that behind the people of Israel lies an individual, namely, Jacob/Israel. What Isaiah seems to be saying is that now, in front of the people of Israel and related to their future, lies a single person, namely, Israel/the Servant of the Lord. Embodying Israel, He would accomplish for the people what they could not accomplish for themselves and much less for the nations of the earth. While not making the people of Israel irrelevant, He to the contrary appears in Isaiah bringing salvation to them and gathering them back as the people of God. He would accomplish what no human being could—God's personal work of salvation for humanity. Isaiah only announces His future coming in humility (suffering) and glory. His identity is fully disclosed in the NT in the person of Jesus Christ, the Son of God.

6. *The Suffering Servant.* It is in Isaiah 52:13—53:12 that the work of the Servant of the Lord is finally unveiled with penetrating detail. The passage begins and ends with a summary of the humiliation of the Servant (52:14; 53:12) as well as an announcement of His exaltation (52:13, 15; 53:11–12), and in between there is a vivid description of the attitude of the people, the humiliating experience of the Servant, and the Lord's interpretation of the work of the Servant (vv. 1–10).

(a) The Experience of the Servant. *First,* we read about the appearance of the Servant. Isaiah presents Him as coming from humble beginnings like a plant growing in dry ground, hardly surviving the absence of water (53:2). The prophet says that people are not naturally attracted to Him. *Second,* He is described as sorrowful and familiar with *kholi,* literally "sickness," which is sometimes translated as "pain" or "grief" (v. 3), and his appearance at some point would be disfigured or marred beyond recognition (52:14). In fact, He would be oppressed, afflicted (53:7), placed in confinement, and condemned as a wicked person (v. 8). He would finally die (v. 8), having been treated like a criminal, but would be with the rich in His death (v. 9). *Third,* the people would reject Him and argue that He had no beauty to make Him desirable (v. 2). They would despise and abandon Him and would not value Him (v. 3). They would see in the Servant a person under a divine curse who was struck by God and afflicted (v 4), a person abandoned by God.

(b) Repentance of the People. There is a moment when the people finally understand the significance of the experience of the Suffering Servant. *First,* they acknowledge their sins and confess that all of them had been like straying, lost sheep who followed their own ways (v. 6). *Second,* they realize that the Servant did not deserve what He went through because He had done no violence and had not been deceitful (v. 9). Although innocent, He did not open His mouth but was led like a lamb to the slaughter (v. 7). *Third,* they give deep theological significance to the sufferings of the Servant: He was bearing their sins and taking on what they deserved. He died as their substitute. They would recognize that He had borne their sicknesses and sorrows (v. 4), that He was wounded for their transgressions and crushed for their iniquities (v. 5), and that He was chastised in order for them to have peace with and healing from God. This was possible because the Lord would lay upon Him the iniquity of all (v. 6).

(c) God and the Servant. The biblical text also provides for us the divine perspective of the experience of the Suffering Servant. *First*, the Lord provides through Isaiah a theological interpretation that coincides with that of the people and goes deeper. The Lord states that the Servant would be struck for the transgression of His people (v. 8), but this is part of the divine plan for their salvation. It was God's will that the Servant be bruised and experience grief. This is interpreted as a sacrificial act (v. 10) by which the Servant would bear the iniquities of the people (v. 11). God had provided the Sacrifice that would finally resolve the problem of sin. As a sacrifice, the Suffering Servant poured out His life, was numbered with the transgressors, and bore the sin of many (v. 12). As a result of His substitutionary death, the Servant would now function as their intercessor (v. 12) and would justify many (v. 11). *Second*, the Lord announces the exaltation of the Servant, which is firmly grounded on His sacrificial death as a substitute for sinners. His death would be followed by His return to life to see the satisfying result of His sacrifice (v. 11). He would come out victorious over His enemies and would get the spoils of victory (v. 12). Kings would submit to Him, and He would be highly exalted (v. 13).

(d) The Servant and the Nations. The atoning work of the Suffering Servant that emerges in 52:13—53:12 becomes the foundation for the establishment of peace on earth in 54:1–17. He would restore the earth and cause the people to dwell in previously desolate areas (49:8). The prisoners and those in darkness would be freed (v. 9; cf. 42:7). The exaltation of the Servant (52:13; 53:10–12) would include the restoration of His people and Zion's Davidic glory, which would bring the nations together to worship the Lord (49:5–6; 55:3–5; 56:6–8; 60:1–22; 66:18–24). The Lord's covenant with Israel would be embraced by the nations, and worldwide peace would follow (2:2–4; 51:4–5; 54:1—56:8). The establishment of God's worldwide rule through the Servant would not be through violent means but in humility (42:1–4; 50:4–9), in righteousness (45:22–25; 51:4–5), and by His Spirit (42:1; 61:1–3). The Servant's atoning suffering would make it possible for the nations to participate in Israel's glorification and victory (53:12; 60:1—62:12). Thus, Israel's descendants would inherit the nations (54:3; cf. Gen. 12:1–3).

7. *The Suffering Servant and Jesus.* The description of the experience and work of the Suffering Servant places Him in a unique category incomparable to that of any other human being or that of Israel. Here the Israelite sacrificial system reaches and transcends its deepest significance. Its symbolic or typological function is implicitly recognized as the Servant of the Lord is identified as the ultimate substitutionary sacrifice for sin, provided by the Lord Himself. The NT announces that the Suffering Servant of the Lord had come in the person and ministry of Jesus Christ and bears ample witness to it. He is the true Servant of the Lord who fulfilled in every detail the prophetic word of Isaiah (e.g., Matt. 8:14–17; Mark 10:45; 15:28; Luke 22:35–38; John 12:37–41; Acts 8:32–35; Phil. 2:5–9; 1 Pet. 2:19–25). When the Ethiopian asked Philip about the identity of this anonymous Servant, Philip took the opportunity to show him all the places in the Hebrew Bible where the coming of this messianic figure was predicted. He then presented to the eunuch the fulfillment of these prophecies in the life, ministry, death, and resurrection of Jesus the Christ/Messiah (Acts 8:35).

Isaiah 52:13—53:12 is quoted or alluded to in the NT more than any other OT passage (e.g., Matt. 8:14–17; Mark 10:45; 15:28; Luke 22:35–38; John 12:37–41; Acts 8:32–35; Phil. 2:5–9; 1 Pet. 2:19–25). The earliest Christians regarded Isaiah 52:13—53:12 as a prophecy of the expiating suffering, death, and exaltation of Jesus (e.g., Acts 8:32–35; cf. Is. 42:1–4 and Matt. 12:18–21; Is. 61:1–2a and Luke 4:16–21). It is clear that Jesus thought of His sufferings as having been written about in certain passages of the Scriptures (Matt. 26:24, 54, 56; Mark 9:12; Luke 18:31; 24:25–27, 46) and that Isaiah 52:13—53:12 belonged to them. He must have had Isaiah 53 in mind when He spoke of coming to be a Servant who would give His life as a ransom for many (Mark 10:45).

The identification of Jesus as the Suffering Servant of Isaiah is established on several grounds. *First*, a messianic understanding of the Servant in 52:13—53:12 is facilitated by the pronounced individual character of the Suffering Servant as the agent of peace in an everlasting covenant (53:5; 54:10; 55:4). The recurring features associated with David in the passage (see 52:13–14; 53:2, 6, 10–12), and Isaiah's prophecies in 9:2–7 and 11:1–10, further invite the reader to a messianic understanding. *Second*, as indicated by historical facts, Jesus's suffering, death, and resurrection match several striking details in Isaiah 52:13—53:12, like His humble beginnings (53:2), His rejection (52:14; 53:2–3, 7–9), His expiation of the human burden of sin laid upon Him by God (vv. 4–6, 10–12), His intercession for transgressors (v. 12), His being assigned a grave with the wicked and the rich at His death (v. 9), and His glorification (52:13; 53:11, 12). According to the NT, the prophecy of the Suffering Servant unquestionably found its fulfillment in Christ.

52:13–15. The Nations Are Astonished. The nations would be greatly perplexed at the Servant's success and exaltation. Notice that future events are stated as if they have already taken place. The Servant's exaltation (52:13 summarizes 53:10–12) is contrasted with His suffering and dishonor (52:14 summarizes 53:2–3). The shift from humiliation/suffering to exaltation/glory was to elicit the amazement and respect of kings (52:15—53:1). The interjection *hinneh* ("behold" or "see" in 52:13) calls attention to the Servant's future exaltation, which would be seen with amazement by the nations. The Hebrew verb *sakal* has been translated as "act wisely/insightfully," "deal prudently," or "succeed." The idea in vv 14–15 is that just as many were astonished at the Servant's suffering, so also would many be astonished at His exaltation. The Hebrew *rabbim* ("many"), used several times in Isaiah 52:13—53:12, generally has an inclusive meaning ("a multitude" or "whole assembly"), but here it may mean "all." In 52:15 "many nations" refers to all the nations that would see the Lord's power and salvation (v. 10). The "many" in 53:11 designates all, the great multitude, or the whole assembly, and includes the "we" (i.e., people of God who speak in vv. 1–6) and "they" (i.e., many nations and kings in 52:15). Finally, the *rabbim* in the first part of 53:12 seems to refer to a host of prominent and powerful nations, namely, an elite body of nations among "all nations." The second reference to *rabbim* in that same verse refers to the same group as the "many" in 53:11 (i.e., all, or the great multitude, or the whole assembly).

His disfigurement or marred appearance is probably a way of speaking about His suffering and humiliation (cf. v. 2; Pss. 22:6–8, 12–18; 38:3–14). Through His actions, the Servant would purify the nations of their guilt (Is. 52:15) and enable them to approach the Holy One of Israel. The kings would shut their mouths in amazement and wonder (cf. Job 29:9) because they would see the Lord's mighty acts that were predicted in Isaiah 52:10.

53:1–3. Humiliation and Rejection. In the previous passage, the speaker was the Lord, but now the speaker is "we," the people of God. They speak about their *shemu'ah*, literally "something heard," in other words, their "report" or "message" and what the Lord's "arm" has revealed that has amazed them. The amazement is expressed in two rhetorical questions concerning those who had believed these things (v. 1). The "we" in vv. 1–6 first *see* the Servant's suffering and despise Him (vv. 1–3) but later *consider* that He actually suffered innocently and atoned for "our" sins (vv. 4–6). They finally *hear* the Lord's words identifying all this as a fulfillment of the Lord's purpose (vv. 7–10). The Lord would exalt the Servant among the nations (vv. 10–12).

The reference to the Servant growing up (v. 2) covers His birth and earthly ministry, leading to the preparation of His tomb (vv. 2–9) and, finally, His exaltation (52:13; 53:12). The phrase "before Him" denotes being in the presence, and under the watch, of the Lord. The metaphors of the tender plant or shoot and the root from the dry ground are the opposite of the tree planted by the water (Ps. 1:3), which refers to one who enjoys the divine blessing (cf. Is. 41:17–20). The Servant would have no *hadar*, "glory" or "honor," and His appearance would not be desirable—He would not stand out by virtue of outward splendor. The people would despise and reject (or forsake) the Servant; they would think that He was under the curse of God, based on a connection between suffering and sin (53:4–5; cf. Ps. 38:11). The Hebrew words in Isaiah 53:3 are sometimes translated as "sorrows," and "grief" can also be rendered as "pain" and "sickness." The hiding of faces refers to the Servant's lack of support. He who took the sins of the world upon Himself would be rejected by the sinners for whom He came to die.

53:4–9. A Radical Change. The "we" finally recognize the reason for the Servant's suffering, that He was a righteous person and was not smitten and afflicted by God for His own sin (vv. 4–5). His suffering was caused by *their* griefs (sickness) and sorrows (pains), by *their* transgressions and iniquities. They see that the penalty that grants them peace was placed on Him and resulted in healing for them (v. 5). The Servant was God's instrument for their salvation and redemption. The reason for the people's insight is not explicitly stated but seems to be the result of the Lord's exaltation of the Servant (vv. 10–12), which brought peace and healing to them and resulted in their being declared righteous.

The Hebrew word *'aken*, "surely," in this case emphasizes a contrast: "but indeed," "but in fact." Verses 4–6 are contrasted with vv. 2–3, underlining the realization that the Servant's grief (or sickness) and sorrows (or pain) in v. 3 are in reality *our* grief, sickness, sorrows, or pain that would be borne by Him (v. 4). The Servant would suffer for our transgressions and iniquities, and this undeserved punishment would bring us peace—and we would be healed by His wounds (v. 5). The people realized that they were wrong to think that the Servant *deserved* to be chastised by God (vv. 4–5). They saw that their own transgressions and iniquities had caused His sufferings and had even brought them peace and healing. Their confession that they had lost their way appears in v. 6, along with their confirmation that the Lord had atoned for their iniquity through His Servant. Indeed, it is only through confession and faith—that the Lord Jesus is our Savior—that one can receive the gift of salvation made available through His suffering and death.

The confession that all of us have gone astray (cf. Ps. 119:176; Jer. 50:6; 1 Pet. 2:25) and have turned to our own ways (cf. Is. 56:11; 1 Sam. 8:3) is answered by an act of forgiveness from the Lord: the Lord would lay all of our iniquities upon the Suffering Servant. Through Isaiah, the Lord had repeatedly made assurances of forgiveness, but this generally had referred to Israel (Is. 33:24; 43:25; 44:21–22). In 53:6 forgiveness is extended to all people. From being mere witnesses of the Lord's salvation of Israel (52:10), the nations would be drawn into a closer relationship with the Lord through the ministry and atoning death of the Servant.

Acting as the Shepherd of His sheep (53:6), the Lord would restore the people by letting His Servant become an atoning and substitutionary sacrifice. Thus, in 52:13—53:12, the Lord is presented with a twofold purpose: to save Israel and the nations by opening their eyes to who He is and to vindicate His Suffering Servant. By exalting Him, the Lord confirms both His pleasure with the work of the Servant and that His purpose has been achieved successfully through the Servant. In the divine speech in 53:7–9, the Servant's innocence, silence, and humility are described. His undeserved sufferings are therefore presented as sufficient for the expiation of the sins of all people. The verb *'anah* is usually translated as "afflicted" here, but it could also be rendered as "He humbled himself." The clause would then mean "He was oppressed, but He humbled Himself and did not open His mouth." The Servant's silence is underlined through repetition. The Servant's silence (vv. 7–9) anticipates the Lord's intervention (vv. 10–12).

It is also stated that the Servant would be taken away by coercion or restraint (some translations have "prison"; v. 8). The Hebrew word *dor*, usually translated as "generation," could also convey here the idea of "fate" or "plight," and the word *siakh*, sometimes translated as "declare," essentially means to "consider." The translation would then be "And who [i.e., no one] will consider His plight?" (cf. 53:3). In a positive context, "the land of the living" refers to the sphere of life and shows that the Servant died—He was "cut off" for the transgressions of God's people. The innocent suffered for the guilty (cf. 1 Pet. 3:18). Assigning the Servant's grave with the wicked means that He was considered a criminal. Being buried among criminals was deeply shameful in Israel, but being buried with a rich person after a violent death would reveal innocence (Is. 53:9).

53:10–12. Exaltation of the Servant. In Isaiah's account, accomplishing the Lord's purpose through sacrificial suffering results in the Servant's exaltation. It was the purpose (lit. "be willing") of the Lord Himself to cause the suffering of the Servant (v. 10). This indicates that what the Lord was doing through the Servant was not done reluctantly but out of love. The Lord was pleased that humanity would be brought back to Himself through the Servant's suffering, and He was personally involved in the Servant's experience, reconciling the world through His death (cf. 2 Cor. 5:19). This happened when God made the Servant's soul or life an offering for sin. The Hebrew speaks about a trespass/reparation offering brought for the misappropriation of what belonged to the Lord, a very serious sin (see Lev. 5:1–13). The Servant atoned for the sin of the many.

The Servant would be raised from death and see the wonderful results of His immense sacrifice (Is. 53:10). In some manuscripts and the Greek version (LXX), the text reads: "He shall see light from the labor of His soul/life," in contrast to the Hebrew text, which refers to the Servant seeing the labor of His life (or "soul") and being satisfied (v. 11). The Lord confirms the expiating effect of the Servant's sacrifice: the Servant's knowledge (v. 11) could be the object of the preceding clause (being satisfied by His knowledge). Various suggestions have been made concerning what kind of knowledge is meant here. In Isaiah, the central knowledge is to know God, understand who He is, and consider His plan (1:3; 37:20; 43:10; 49:23, 26; 52:6; 60:16). But knowledge is also experiential, so it could here refer to the experiences leading to the Servant's death. If "by His knowledge" is a continuation of "and be satisfied," then the idea is that the Servant shall be satisfied by what He shall see after His suffering. However, if "knowledge" is the experience of suffering, then the point is that the Servant would justify many by His suffering. By stating that the Servant is "righteous," the Lord underlines the Servant's innocence (53:6, 9–11; Deut. 32:4; Ps. 145:17; on bear iniquity/sin, see Lev. 16:22).

The Servant's reward and exaltation are closely related to His justification of the people by expiating their iniquities (Is. 53:11–12), and in doing this He would accomplish the Lord's purpose (v. 10). The military expression regarding the division of plunder with the strong or mighty is associated with victory, power, and rejoicing, used figuratively here for the victory of the Servant over His enemies. The Servant would pour out His life and die (v. 12; cf. v. 8c). His life is figuratively seen as being "poured out," like the blood/life of a sacrificial victim. The term *paga'* means "entreat passionately" on behalf of someone, or "intercede for someone" (cf. 59:16). The Servant is here assigned a priestly and prophetic role of intercession.

54:1–17. Citizens of Zion. The restoration of Zion is based on the Lord's everlasting covenants with Israel (vv. 1–17), David (55:3–4), and the nations (24:5; 54:5; 55:5). Zion would expand and spread out in all directions because of the increase in population. Her people would receive the nations, and the desolate cities would become inhabited. The period of disgrace was over. The Lord declared that Zion's husband is her Maker (cf. 43:1), who is also the God of all the earth, a concept that underlines the Servant's atonement for all the earth (52:13—53:12) and

the gathering of the nations in Zion (56:3–8). The Lord's abandonment of Zion only lasted for a short while because He loved her and would reclaim her with abundant compassion, mercy, and everlasting *khesed*—a rich word with many connotations such as "love," "kindness," "covenant faithfulness," "mercy" and so forth (vv. 7–8; cf. 49:10). He had determined not to be angry again with Israel (54:9–10). The mountains and the hills might be removed (i.e., symbols of stability and permanence), but neither His *khesed* (love, mercy, and kindness) nor His covenant of peace were to be removed (v. 10; cf. Ps. 125:1). Since all their children would be taught by the Lord, Zion's inhabitants would know the Lord's *torah* ("law," "instruction"; cf. Is. 48:18–19) and do what He desires.

As is common in Isaiah, righteousness is associated with salvation or redemption (v. 14; cf. 1:26–27; 56:1). Being far from tyranny and oppression meant that they were to consider themselves free from oppression. Internal injustices (cf. e.g., 1:10–31; 3:1—4:1; 5:1–23) and foreign oppression (cf. 52:4–5) would be absent. When enemies would assemble, they would fall and surrender to them because the Lord would protect His people (v. 15). Zion would be immune to enemy attacks because weapons would fail against her, as would false accusations in court. The Lord declared that this heritage of peace belonged to the servants of the Lord (i.e., the faithful Israelites) and that their righteousness (or salvation/vindication) comes from the Lord. God's grace forgives and cleanses; the righteousness of the Servant translates into the salvation of His faithful servants because it is accounted as theirs.

55:1–13. Embracing Life. Isaiah here conveys the Lord's invitation to embrace His offer of life, which is offered without money and cost and is satisfying because it is good (v. 2). The life offered by the foreign gods requires the spending of money but yields what is not bread, what does not satisfy (v. 2). There is an appeal to listen and come to God for life made on the basis of the promised *khesed*, "mercy," "love," "kindness," "faithful love," for David. This refers to the promises that the Davidic dynasty would endure forever (2 Sam. 7:8–16) and that Israel would dwell securely and have rest from their enemies (vv. 9–11). These promises were an everlasting covenant (Is. 55:3; cf. 2 Sam. 22:51; 23:5; Pss. 18:49–50; 21:7; 89:28–49).

According to Isaiah 55:3–5, the Lord would appoint the new David as a witness to the peoples and a leader/ruler/commander for them.

David was commissioned to incorporate the nations into his kingdom (cf. 11:10–16; 14:1–3). The new David would witness to the nations about the Lord's glorious acts (cf. Ps. 18:49; Is. 11:9–10). The words in 55:3–5 allude to the promise to give the Davidic King (ultimately, the Messiah) the nations as an inheritance and the whole earth as a possession (Ps. 2:8; cf. Is. 54:3). Worshipers in the temple may have been familiar with Ps. 18:43–44, which also refers to a Davidic dominion over the nations, including a people that he had previously not known. The fact that God glorified Israel makes it possible for them to attract unknown people groups, who will come streaming to Israel (Is. 55:5); like David, they will have dominion over the nations (cf. 9:2–7; 11:1–10). The message to Israel, therefore, was that the Lord's covenant with and promises to David are everlasting. The invitation to repentance was an act of grace from God, whose love and righteousness, so deep and unsearchable, are above human imagination (55:6–9) and whose word is powerful and effects salvation (cf. 40:6–8). Repentant receivers of forgiveness would have joy and peace and would glorify the Lord's name (55:12).

56:1—66:24
The Restored Covenant Community at Zion

The invitation and call for repentance in chapter 55 is followed by an instruction concerning the restored covenant community gathering for worship at Zion. It is formed as a chiasm:

A Requirements for Becoming Citizens of Restored Zion (chaps. 56–59)
  B The Glory of the Restored Covenant Community (chaps. 60–62)
A′ Selection of Citizens for Restored Zion (chaps. 63–66)

56:1–12. Sabbath Obedience and Leaders. Justice and righteousness—shown to God and one's fellow beings (vv. 1–2)—are defined as the central principles for belonging to restored Zion. A brief instruction outlines the principle of keeping justice and doing righteousness in order to enjoy blessings. Two specific laws are mentioned in v. 2. First, to avoid profaning the Sabbath is to remember it as a sign of the covenant with the Lord (Ex. 31:12–17; Ezek. 20:12, 20). Acknowledging that a seventh of all time (the Sabbath) belongs to God symbolizes the Creator's complete lordship in the believer's life. Its

blessing consists in a deep communion with God as the Savior and is symbolized by resting from human labor. Isaiah develops his teaching on the Sabbath in 56:6–7 and 58:13–14. Second, to keep one's hand from doing any evil is to actively do acts of kindness to one's fellow humans (see vv. 6–7, 9–10). Foreigners and eunuchs represent people from "all nations" (v. 7). The restrictions against their participation in the assembly of the Lord (vv. 6–7; Deut. 23:1–8; cf. Lev. 21:16–20) would not impede them as long as they would keep the covenant and serve the Lord (Is. 56:4–6; cf. Josh. 2; Ruth).

The Lord ordained that eunuchs—who by accident or intent had lost their ability to procreate—fulfilling the covenant requirements would be given a *yad* (lit. "hand"; translated as "place" or "memorial") and a name in the temple. A eunuch was unable to have children, and his name was therefore not carried on in the community. This inability would be compensated by the better gift of having an eternal name with the Lord—spiritual blessings far outweigh material blessings. The Lord ordained that foreign proselytes be brought to His holy mountain to rejoice in His house of prayer. It was His plan that His house would be called a house of prayer for all nations (cf. 52:13—53:12; Matt. 21:13; Mark 11:17; Luke 19:46). The Lord God, gatherer of the dispersed exiles and outcasts of Israel (cf. Is. 11:12), would gather others together with them (56:8). It was necessary for Israel's failing leaders to repent in order to belong to restored Zion (vv. 9–12). Their negligence had made the flock an easy prey for wild beasts. They disregarded the Lord, became drunk, and saw no danger coming.

57:1–13. Israel and Idolatry. Something awful was happening in Israel; the righteous people were perishing, and consequently the whole nation was becoming corrupt. Those who were upright would find peace and rest in death (lit. "lying down" or "in their beds," that is to say, in their graves). The idolaters are addressed as the offspring of sorceresses, adulterers, and prostitutes. Unfaithful Zion-Jerusalem had raised unfaithful children. They seem to have been scoffing and ridiculing the prophet (57:4). The Hebrew term *khamam* can mean "warm yourself" or may refer to being sexually "heated up" or "inflamed" (cf. Gen. 30:38–39). The mention of "every green [or spreading/luxuriant] tree" (Is. 57:5) is a formulaic reference to Canaanite fertility cults and shows that Israel was involved in idolatry. Child sacrifices were condemned by the prophets (cf. Jer. 7:31; Ezek. 20:31; Mic. 6:7).

The audience in Isaiah 57:6-13 is addressed in the feminine singular as one acting like a prostitute (i.e., Zion-Jerusalem). The mention of "smooth" (most translations supply "stones" as the referent) is referring to some kind of pagan rite. "Portion" and "lot" combine the idea of choice and its consequences: as the Israelites had chosen, so would be their fate. Those to whom they had given offerings may refer to the *'ayil*, which can be rendered as the "oak," "terebinth," or "pillar" (some translations accordingly have "gods") mentioned in v. 5 or the "smooth stones" mentioned in v. 6. It seems that the Lord was among the deities worshiped by the people. This syncretism or polytheism was an abomination against the Lord. Drink offerings and grain offerings were legitimately offered to the Lord, but He was not to receive comfort in their having been given to other gods. The Lord then turned to the fertility cults, whose rituals were performed on the mountains (v. 7). The reference to a bed suggests a cult with sexual practices, as was common in Canaanite cults (cf. Ezek. 23:17).

The mention of activities behind doors and posts may refer to private homes or shrines (Is. 57:8). In view of the context, the term *zikkaron*, literally "remembrance" or "sign," may refer to a pagan cult symbol, perhaps an image of the male sexual organ, which would not have been unusual in the ANE. This term *zikkaron* may be related to a word meaning "male" (cf. Ezek. 16:17). The use of sexual imagery in Isaiah 57:8 indicates idol worship as spiritual whoredom. The last part of v. 8 literally means "you saw [or looked with satisfaction at] a hand"—the word for "hand" can be used as a euphemism for the male sexual organ. Zion the prostitute had tried to attract foreign lovers to herself (v. 9). The mention of going to the king could refer to Jerusalem's approach to a foreign king or, if the Hebrew word for king—*melek*—is pointed differently as *molek*, to a foreign false god. In either case, this resulted in idolatry and apostasy (cf. 2 Kin. 16; cf. Is. 7). The statement that unfaithful Jerusalem even descended to Sheol (the realm of the dead) may refer to the "covenant with death" mentioned in 28:14-22.

Israel's stiff-necked idolatry continued at length. The phrase "life of your hand," in the latter part of 57:10, has been understood as referring to Israel's continued commitment to their stubborn idolatry or alternatively as referring to the fruits of the soil that resulted from human work but for which Israel failed to be thankful to the Lord, as demonstrated in their idolatry (vv. 11, 19; cf. Hos. 2:8). The last view is

preferable. God reproached His people's deceit and predicted their fate. Israel had lied (57:11) by disgracing the covenant through syncretistic fertility-cult practices (v. 5) and by claiming a righteousness with requirements they failed to meet (v. 12). The Lord proceeded to address the apostates with irony (vv. 12-13), proclaiming them as doomed to rely on their useless idols for salvation. But only those trusting in the Lord would find salvation by inheriting the land and possessing God's holy mountain (v. 13).

57:14—58:14. The Need for Humility. The speaker in v. 14 is not identified. The Hebrew verb indicates "He will say" or "it will be said." Here the Lord indicated that for Israel to return/ repent, the stumbling block or obstacle had to be removed. The stumbling block was the people's lack of a contrite and humble, lowly spirit. This spirit characterizes the faithful worshiper for whom the Lord particularly cares (cf. 66:2; Pss. 34:18; 51:17). Coming to the Lord in the spirit of true worship was the implied purpose of the restoration of Zion. The Lord assured His people that His anger would not last (Is. 57:16-21; cf. 40:1-2) because He did not want them to despair. He therefore promised comfort, healing, and peace to all Israel, far and near. The Lord would heal the righteous (cf. 57:1-2), but God said there is no peace for the wicked (cf. 56:9-12; 57:3-13).

Desirous for His people to humble themselves, He instructed them on what humility really looks like (58:1-14). Although the people acknowledged the Lord as their God, worshiped Him, and daily sought Him, they failed to understand why He did not answer their prayers. The reason was that they fasted with the wrong attitude and for the wrong purpose and they transgressed against God and other human beings (vv. 2-3; cf. 56:2). The last part of 58:4 has been understood either as a command (to discontinue their contentious fasting) or more likely as a warning that they would not be heard "on high" if they continued in their error. The Lord's chosen or required fast is described as doing acts of kindness to the needy (vv. 6-7), for only then would they receive divine blessings (vv. 8-9).

The teaching on the true fast continues with an application of the two principles mentioned in 56:2: human relations (58:9-12) and the Sabbath (vv. 13-14). If the Lord's people would practice compassion, such as feeding the hungry and helping the afflicted (vv. 9-10; cf. vv. 6-7), then darkness and gloom would disappear, and

God would constantly guide His people. He would provide for them, like a shepherd, and give the flock food, drink, and protection (v. 11; cf. 40:11). He would strengthen their bones (or frame; v. 11c; cf. 66:14)—the bones were considered the seat of health and strength (cf. Job 20:11; 21:24). The comparison to water, springs, and gardens symbolizes the blessings of well-being and bliss.

The instruction concerning the Sabbath (58:13–14) is warranted because the Sabbath is a fundamental law in the covenant (56:2–7). In vv. 1–2, it expresses justice and righteousness. Here the Lord refers to the Sabbath as His holy day (cf. Ex. 20:8; Deut. 5:12), which humans should consider to be an honor and a delight. Two rewards are promised for Sabbath observance: (1) joy, restoration, and revitalization from the Lord; and (2) a triumphant ride on the high hills with abundant sustenance from the heritage of Jacob (cf. Deut. 32:13–14; Ps. 18:33; Hab. 3:19). The emphasis on Sabbath keeping as a requirement for becoming citizens of a restored Zion is central, recognizing that Judah's captivity is elsewhere blamed on their defilement of the Sabbath regulation (2 Chr. 36:21; Jer. 17:21–27). This seems to indicate that the Sabbath indeed encapsulates the moral law (cf. Ex. 20).

59:1–21. Separation, Confession, and Redemption. Isaiah acknowledges the Lord's will and power to intervene for His people (vv. 1–8), but their iniquities and sins had separated them from Him (v. 2; cf. 1:15; 50:1–3). The law of retribution is illustrated in 59:5–8: evil acts would bring evil on the perpetrators, and this was Israel's predicament. The people of Israel, who were mourning in the dark and departing from the truth, were to acknowledge their sins as the cause of their misery (59:9–15), and then the Lord would intervene on behalf of the penitent (vv. 15–21). He was displeased over the lack of justice among the leaders (vv. 15–16), for it was contrary to His own character (v. 17). The law of retribution is again stated in v. 18 as the basis for the Lord's anger and vengeance against His adversaries and enemies among the nations. The references to the Spirit of the Lord in v. 19 may indicate that the Lord will act through the righteous King foretold in 11:1–10. The Lord's intervention would result in His retributive punishment of the nations (59:18), but His coming to Zion means the redemption of the penitent in Israel (v. 20), to whom He would grant His Spirit and words forever (v. 21).

60:1–22. The Glory of God. The vision of the restored Zion-Jerusalem is a climactic point in the book of Isaiah. This passage, together with chapters 61–62, develops three themes: (1) when the glory of the Lord rises upon His temple in Zion-Jerusalem, the nations would come to her light, scattered Israel would return to her, and the nations would pay tribute to the Lord as their Ruler (60:1–20); (2) an everlasting covenant with the people of Zion-Jerusalem would bring restoration, righteousness, and praises before the eyes of the nations (60:21—61:9); and (3) the Lord would glorify Zion-Jerusalem before the witnessing nations and kings (61:10—62:12).

The passage begins with the command to Zion-Jerusalem to arise, shine (i.e. "shake yourself from the dust"), and reflect their light, the glory of the Lord, which had now come to them. Nations and kings, in darkness, were to come to Zion's light, to their glorious Lord (60:3). The passage continues with a further command to mother Zion-Jerusalem to look at her sons and daughters approaching with the nations from afar (v. 4; cf. 49:14—50:3; 54:1–17). The nations would come to pay homage and bring tribute. Peoples from afar would not only come with gold and incense but would come to proclaim the praises of the Lord (60:6; cf. Deut. 26:19) in the holy temple. In restored Zion-Jerusalem, the nations would have access to the temple, to worship the God of Israel. The phrase "the Lord's blessing of Zion with glory and splendor" is a fulfillment of God's covenant promises (Is. 60:9; cf. Deut. 26:18–19, where similar a Hebrew word is used). Zion's ornamental splendor and glory would consist of the Lord's shining glory—as expressed in the references to the Lord's glory rising upon them (60:1–2) and God being their glory (v. 19). Zion's ornamental glory, no longer determined by her ornamental jewelry (see 3:16–23), would be the beautiful garments that the Lord had commanded her to put on (52:1). They are defined in 61:10 as the "garments of salvation" and the "robe of righteousness," which are compared to the jewels with which the bride and bridegroom were adorned (61:10). The Lord would rename Zion, signifying forgiveness and restoration.

The nations and their kings would submit like vassals to their overlord (60:10–12). They were to build up the walls of "the City of the LORD" (v. 14) and serve Zion (v. 10). Zion would be ornamented by "the glory of Lebanon" (v. 13). Its fertile ground and the various trees and their shade would ornament the temple. God would make the place for His feet glorious, which means that

Zion, as God's dwelling place, would be glorified through the worship of the nations who formerly afflicted Zion (vv. 13–14; cf. v. 7d). The nations would call Zion by a new name: "The City of the LORD, Zion of the Holy One of Israel" (vv. 14d-e). Then Zion-Jerusalem would know that the Lord, the Mighty One of Jacob, was her Savior and Redeemer (v. 16) and would enjoy peace and well-being. All violence and destruction would be gone, and Zion's walls would be called "Salvation" and her gates "Praise."

The Lord would be Zion's everlasting light (vv. 19–20; cf. Rev. 21:23). Zion would no longer live in darkness because the time of her mourning would end. The symbol of the Lord as a light may be associated with His creative and reconciling power (cf. Pss. 18:28; 36:9; 104 [esp. v. 2]; John 8:12). Although the earth and all the nations were covered with darkness (i.e., lacked justice and righteousness), Zion's light (the Lord) had come, and the nations and their kings would come to Him (Is. 60:1–3). The inhabitants of Zion would be righteous and would experience the Lord's blessings (vv. 21–22). He would be glorified by the redeemed people being the work of His hand. The Lord's plan was to hasten the fulfillment (v. 22).

61:1–11. News of Restoration. Verses 1–3 summarize the mission of the righteous Servant of the Lord. Jesus applied the first part of these words to Himself in the synagogue of Nazareth (Luke 4:16–22). Isaiah presents the Servant acknowledging that He had been anointed by the Lord with His Spirit (Is. 61:1). This passage thus alludes to another messianic promise in 11:2 and to the association of the Servant with the Spirit in 42:1 and 48:16. The tasks of the Servant consist in comforting the oppressed and announcing that the Lord had heard their prayers and would grant them glory, joy, and praises. The "trees [or oaks] of righteousness" (61:3) may refer to people who had been restored by the Lord's righteousness. In this context, righteousness or vindication is connected with salvation (cf. 41:10; 45:8; 51:5; 62:1) and glory (cf. 58:8; 62:2).

The prophet proceeds to describe the future restoration of the cities of Israel that had been ruined by the enemy (61:4). Strangers would become servants of Israel as shepherds, farm laborers, and vinedressers (v. 5). The people of Israel would be called the "priests of the LORD" and the servants/ministers of God (v. 6; cf. 66:21). This probably alludes to Exodus 19:6, where Israel is referred to as "a kingdom of priests" and "a holy nation." The everlasting covenant would bring joy to the people of Israel. God would clothe His people in garments of salvation and the robe of righteousness (Is. 61:10; cf. Zech. 3; Matt. 22:1–14; Rom. 13:14; 1 Cor. 1:30; 2 Cor. 5:21; Gal. 3:27; Phil. 3:8–9; Rev. 7:14; 19:8; 21:2). These are wedding dress metaphors contrasted with a bridegroom who decks himself with ornaments or a bride who adorns herself with jewels (Is. 61:10). The wedding image points to the new covenant between God and Israel (v. 8; cf. 24:5; 54:10; 55:3; 2 Sam. 7:13, 16, 25, 29; 23:5). The blessings of the everlasting covenant would be witnessed by the nations (cf. Is. 61:9).

62:1–12. Zion Glorified. The Lord's silence (v. 1) is a recurring motif in Isaiah (42:14; 57:11; 64:12). The Lord would not be silent until He had accomplished salvation for His people. For the symbol of "light" and related images as references to the Lord when He glorifies and saves Israel, see 2:5; 9:2; 60:1–3. All nations and kings would see Zion's righteousness (or vindication and salvation; see commentary on 61:3) and glory (i.e., honor and dignity), and she would be called by a new name given to her by the Lord. His delight in His bride is expressed in her new names: Hephzibah means "my delight is in her" (62:4; cf. 2 Kin. 21:1), and Beulah means "married" (Is. 62:4). The new names indicate Zion's new status and destiny, which is further developed in 62:3, 5. The beautiful crown of splendor and glory and the royal diadem (v. 3) indicate the honor and dignity that the Lord would bestow on His people, reflecting the practices of a royal wedding. The wording in v. 3 is remarkable in that Zion, the glorious crown, would be in God's hand. The wedding and marriage metaphors hinted at in 61:10 and 62:4 highlight the honor and dignity that the husband bestows on His wife and their mutual delight. The Lord would delight in His people as the groom delights in his bride.

If in 62:6–7 the speaker is the prophet, the verses express his longing for the Lord to make Jerusalem praised throughout the earth (v. 7). The watchmen of v. 6 would be prophets invoking the Lord's saving actions for Jerusalem. But if the speaker is the Lord in v. 6a–b, and the prophet adds his comments in vv. 6c–7, the watchmen would probably be heavenly beings keeping watch over the city. As the Lord's heralds, they would keep watch in and around Jerusalem and report to the Lord. They were to continue until the Lord established Jerusalem

(v. 7). Verses 8–9 are directly connected with vv. 4–5 and assume that the future restoration had already been accomplished. The powerful image in vv. 8c–9 describes the Lord's solemn promise that Zion would never again suffer the terrors of a foreign invasion. The commanded procession into the holy city and the temple marks the end of the symbolic wedding ceremony between the Lord and His people (v. 10). The Lord's proclamation to Zion had reached to the end of the world, to scattered Israel among all the nations: Zion's Savior was coming, and His reward and recompense would be with Him (v. 11; cf. Rev. 22:12).

63:1–6. The Lord at War. The prophet describes the Messiah's victory over all His enemies (vv. 1–6; see chaps. 13–23 and 34–39). The text refers to the Lord coming from Edom and Bozrah, a possible allusion to 34:5–15. However, the central point is the defeat of the nations (59:15b–20) during the day of vengeance when God would restore His redeemed people (61:2; cf. 34:8). The passage has the form of a dramatic dialogue. A bloodstained warrior is seen returning from Edom and Bozrah. Someone— perhaps a watchman on the walls of Jerusalem—asks Him to disclose His identity, and the answer is that He is the One mighty to save (63:1). The watchman seeks an explanation of the red stains on His garments (v. 2), and the answer is that He has intervened on behalf of His people without human assistance and has annihilated the oppressive nations. The bloodstain on the Messiah Warrior signifies His victory over the enemy (symbolized here as Edom) and the redemption of His people.

63:7–14. Prayer of Remembrance. This prayer expresses the attitude which the Lord favors (see 57:14–20). A herald, on behalf of the people, recalls the Lord's khesed, "mercy," "love," "covenant faithfulness," and rakhamim, "tender mercy" or "compassion" (63:7). He made a covenant with Israel as their Savior (v. 8; cf. Lev. 26:12; Deut. 29:13; Jer. 7:23; Ezek. 11:20) because He had compassion on them. Because of the similarity of certain Hebrew words, there is some variation in regard to the Hebrew manuscripts, the LXX, and commentators with respect to Is. 63:9. Most translations have opted for the reading that God was afflicted in all of their afflictions. God carried His people as an eagle carries its young on its wings (Deut. 32:11). But the people rebelled and grieved His Holy Spirit, and consequently the Lord turned against them as an enemy (Is. 63:10). Israel remembered the days of old, when they sought the Lord who had saved them during the Exodus (vv. 11–14). They remembered Moses as the shepherd of His flock and how they sought the One who put His Holy Spirit within (or among) them (lit. "within him")—the Lord put His Spirit upon Moses (Num. 11:16–25). They remembered how the Lord led them in the wilderness. The simile of a horse in the open desert describes how the Lord led Israel with ease through the Red Sea (Is. 63:13; cf. Ps. 106:9). A second image depicts livestock given rest by the Spirit of the Lord, an image that alludes to the Lord's promise: "My Presence will go with you, and I will give you rest" (Ex. 33:14). In Isaiah 63:9–10, interesting references are made to the Lord, the Angel of His presence, and the Holy Spirit, probably pointing to the three persons of the Godhead. The three are fully involved in the work of redemption.

63:15–19. Prayer of Penitence. Based on vv. 11–14, an appeal is next made to the Lord to show His zeal, power, and compassion (v. 15). There is a phrase in the Hebrew which literally means "the sound of your inward parts," the "inward parts" being a metaphor for the seat of emotions. The Hebrew term me'eh, "inward parts," may be used in the context of a sense of pity (cf. 16:11) or compassion (cf. Jer. 31:20). The petitioners are confident that the Lord wants and has the power to save them (cf. Is. 64:1–4) because He is their Father and He has proven Himself to be their Eternal (Heb. 'olam) Redeemer (or "Redeemer from old/ancient times"; 63:16). The concept of the Lord as Israel's Father, which corresponds to Israel being His son, is defined in Deuteronomy 32:6 in the context of the Lord creating Israel as His elected people.

Isaiah, on behalf of his fellow Israelites, asks difficult and perplexing questions of God, such as "Why have You caused us to wander? Why have You hardened our hearts?" (Is. 63:17). This kind of language is similar to other passages that attribute divine involvement (in some sense) in regard to human sin and hardness of heart (e.g., 6:10; Ex. 4:21; Deut. 2:30; Rom. 9:18; 11:7–9; 2 Thess. 2:11). In the Bible God is at times described as doing that which He allows. He respects human freedom and makes humans responsible for their actions. Those who harden themselves against the Lord cannot prosper because the Lord's wisdom and strength will prevail over them (Job 9:4; Prov. 19:21). The Lord allows for the sinners' actions, but He is also ready to save them from their wrongdoings. This is what the petitioners are asking for in this passage. The appeal for the Lord to return for the sake of His servants (i.e., Israel; cf. e.g., Is. 41:8–20) and the tribes of His heritage (cf. e.g., 54:17; 58:14) is motivated by His covenant with Israel (cf. 63:15–17).

In the Hebrew, the assumed referent of what God's holy people possessed is not clear. However, an analogy may exist between the list in 64:9–11 and the content of 63:17c–19: (1) Israel as Your people (v. 17; 64:9); (2) the desolation of (lit.) "the cities of Your holiness," namely, Judah (63:18a; 64:10a); and (3) Zion-Jerusalem desolate and the temple exposed to burning (63:18b; 64:10b–11c). This analogy suggests that the implied "it" refers not to the temple but to the cities of Judah (i.e., the land). The trampling of the sanctuary may be referring either to the destruction of the temple or, figuratively, to "treating it with disdain."

64:1–12. May the Lord Come. This section is a continuation of the prayer of penitence. It begins with an appeal to the Lord to "rend the heavens" in order to show Himself (cf. 63:15). His powerful appearance is described as fire that burns brushwood and twigs and causes water to boil (64:2). The purpose of His revelation before the nations (cf. 40:3–5) was to make His power known to His adversaries (cf. 63:18b) so that the nations would tremble before Him, that is to say, in His presence. The petitioners remembered the Lord's past actions during the Exodus, the wilderness wanderings, and the conquest of Canaan. From the earliest times (Heb. 'olam), the Lord had been known as the One who helps those who wait for Him (64:3–4). They had complete confidence in the Lord because He paga', "helps" or "welcomes" (lit. "meets" or "encounters") those who rejoice in doing what is right (v. 5). But then the sad reality dawned on them: God had been angry on account of their sin. Sin causes grief in the heart of the repentant soul. Recognition and confession of one's sin result in forgiveness.

All righteous deeds are like "filthy rags." This is probably a reference to the cloths used by a woman during her menstruation or after childbirth (cf. Lev. 12), which were fit only for destruction. The people's situation was hopeless—all their acts of righteousness were so polluted that they could not be cleansed but only destroyed. Therefore, they confessed that they were withering like a leaf and being blown away by the wind (cf. Ps. 90:5–6). The hopelessness of the petitioners in Isaiah 64:6 is underlined by the reference to the lack of response to the

Lord, His punishment, and the removal of His sustaining presence from them (v. 7).

After a marked shift in the text with the Hebrew we'attah, "but now" or "yet," the petitioners expressed renewed confidence in the Lord as their Father (cf. 63:16) and Creator (64:8; cf. 57:16). The image of the potter and the clay is used here (as in Job 10:9) to remind the Lord that He made humans out of clay, and therefore they are weak and fragile beings who are fully dependent on His mercy (cf. Jer. 18:1–12). The next two requests of the Lord, namely, not to remain angry with them and not to always remember their sins, were combined with the plea to notice that they were still His people (cf. Is. 63:16–19).

The suffering and shame of the petitioners is related to the fact that the nations afflicted Judah and Jerusalem (64:10–11). The phrase "Your holy/sacred cities" is unique in the OT. That the cities belonged to the Lord, the Holy One of Israel, and therefore were holy, contains an appeal for the Lord's intervention for His name's sake. The lamentation continues: the temple referred to in v. 11 is clearly Solomon's temple, for it was where the ancestors praised the Lord. In the Hebrew it is referred to as a "house," not a "sanctuary" (see 63:18). The reference in v. 11 is most probably written from the perspective of the future Babylonian destruction of the city in 586 B.C. The reference to the makhmad, "pleasant," "desirable," or "treasured" things, may refer to valuables in, and ornaments of, the temple (cf. 2 Chr. 36:19; Lam. 1:10–11; Ezek. 24:21; Hos. 9:6). The lamentation ends with an appeal for the Lord's intervention. The question regarding whether God would continue to hold back (Is. 64:12) alludes to 63:15–16, where the Lord's intervention is expected because Israel is His covenant people. The question of whether He would remain silent is essentially the question of whether He would refuse to intervene on behalf of His covenant people. The final question of 63:12 is in regard to whether the Lord would continue to punish His people. The questions are an expression of hope and anticipate a positive response from the Lord.

65:1–16. First Answer: God Is Righteous. The Lord's answer to Israel's lamentation in 63:7— 64:12 begins with this passage. It predicts that the Lord, in His righteousness, would punish the rebellious and reward the faithful in Israel. Paul applies 65:1 in Romans 10:20 to the gospel going to the Gentiles (see 66:12, 18–20). Isaiah places the emphasis on the fact that the Lord made

Himself available to His people, but apostate Israel behaved as a nation that was not called by His name (i.e., that did not belong to Him; v. 1). A list of offenses is given (vv. 3–5) involving practices of fertility cults, divination by consulting the dead, and defilement by breaking dietary laws. The concluding offense (v. 5) is the blasphemous claim by those who had broken the covenant law and defiled themselves that they were as holy as the priests (cf. Lev. 21:6–8). Their offense lay in the blasphemy of treating defilement as holiness.

Concerning the offenders, the Lord states that they are like smoke in His nostrils and a continual fire (Is. 65:5). They had made Him angry, and their punishment is expressed in the characteristic references to the Lord's active intervention—He would not keep silent, and He would take vengeance upon them (cf. 34:8; 63:4). The image of repaying in their "bosom" or "lap" (65:7) refers to a fold of garment where money was carried, but here it is used to refer to a payment according to the law of retribution. However, God would save the faithful remnant and let them dwell in restored Zion (v. 8). The good fruit is a gift of God. As repeatedly stated by Isaiah, the righteous remnant needed to be separated from the wicked. God's chosen remnant were the people who sought Him (vv. 9–10). They affirmed the invitation to seek the Lord while He could be found (55:6) and had honestly sought the Lord (cf. 65:1). Consequently, they would inherit and possess the land (cf. 54:3; 57:13; 60:21).

Those indifferent to the peace of Zion and the worship of the Lord would be left to perish by the sword. They were preparing a table for *gad*, which refers to the worship of a Syrian god named "Fortune," and they were bringing drink offerings for *meni*, a god of fate (both Gad and Meni may have been star deities; 65:11–12). The Lord's servants would prosper in the sense that they would have food, drink, and joy. The wicked would experience only shame, pain, and a crushed spirit (vv. 13–14). The name of the wicked would function as a curse (cf. Jer. 29:22), while the name of the Lord's servants would bring blessings from the only true God who speaks truth. For those who would inherit the land, previous troubles would be forgotten and hidden from the Lord's eyes (Is. 65:16).

65:17–25. Second Answer: New Heavens and New Earth. The Lord promised to create new heavens and a new earth (cf. 66:22) and affirmed that the former things would not be remembered or come to mind. In Isaiah's setting, this verse is a reference to the new conditions that the Lord would create for Zion-Jerusalem and His people. The prophet has just indicated that the former troubles would be forgotten (v. 16) and continues to describe the joy of salvation (vv. 18–19) and the long life of all the people except sinners (vv. 20–22; see below, "The New Heavens and Earth and the Presence of Death"). Isaiah is the first prophet who explicitly announces God's future creation of an everlasting new world without sin and suffering (v. 23; cf. Rev. 21:1–4). In the new world that God would create for His faithful ones, children would be born for blessing, not for trouble, because they would be children of those blessed by the Lord. The Lord would answer before they called and hear while they were still speaking (Is. 65:24). In all of His holy mountain, the Lord says, there would be a new order of things, a state of peace and not of destruction (v. 25; cf. 11:9–10).

The New Heavens and Earth and the Presence of Death

Isaiah 65:20 has perplexed some Christian readers because it is connected to the new creation. This promise of longevity, that presupposes the presence of sin and death, is found in the context of a divine announcement of the new heavens and new earth (v. 17). The context (vv. 17–25) describes the transformation of society (vv. 18–19, 22–24), nature (v. 25), and humanity's relationship with God (vv. 19, 24). In the interpretation of the passage, we should probably examine first the concept of the "new" in Isaiah.

1. New Heavens and New Earth. The phrase "new heavens and a new earth" obviously designates a new creation (vv. 17–25; 66:22; cf. Gen. 1:1). According to Isaiah, this new creation would totally displace and bring to an end the former things. The "new" work of God would be so radical that the former would not be remembered (Is. 65:17b); absolute joy would prevail (v. 18), weeping and crying would disappear forever (v. 19), and the nature of wild animals would be transformed (v. 25). Elsewhere, the prophet even announces that God "will swallow up death forever" (25:8) by bringing it to an end when He resurrects His people (26:19). This would be the ultimate defeat of death. For the prophet, this is an end-time expectation, a return to God's paradise.

2. Israel and the "New" in Isaiah. In Isaiah God announced to His people new things before they would come into being (42:9). In fact, He was already doing a "new thing" (43:19), namely, His work of redemption for Israel, the deliverance from exile, and the return to Jerusalem. The new thing was His work of salvation within their history. This event would have an impact on nature (vv. 19–20) and would bring healing to His people (42:16). What was particularly new was that in the deliverance of Israel, the nation itself would not play any role at all (God would use the Persian king; 44:24—45:7) because it would be based on God's forgiving grace (43:25) and even the nations would benefit from it (45:22–24).

The context of this new, radical, unique work of salvation is the history of Israel, and it did not immediately bring the history of the nations to an end. The Medo-Persian kingdom would still be in power, but God was using it to bring something totally new into existence. The old oppressive powers coexisted with the new things, that is to say, the new creation that God was already bringing into existence. We could say that what the NT calls the present age and the future age (Matt. 12:32) are described in Isaiah as simultaneously present in the arena of human history.

Therefore, in Isaiah the new creation is not something totally in the future. It was to irrupt into the present of Israel through God's glorious work of redemption and forgiveness. It is within this conceptual framework that Isaiah 65:20 is to be placed. It announces that soon, in the present existence of Israel, God would begin to defeat death. This idea is expressed through the promise of longevity and the elimination of infant mortality. This promise points to a restriction imposed on the power of death, and consequently it was a prelude to the future extermination of death from the world. These promises were to be literally fulfilled in Israel had it remained faithful to God, but this was not the case. The coming of the Messiah enriched the prophecy and enlarged its fulfillment.

3. The New in the New Testament. Similarly to Isaiah and in fulfillment of his prophecy, in the NT the age of salvation was inaugurated by Christ. For now, the evil age of sin and death coexist (cf. Gal. 1:4; Heb. 6:5). The defeat of death is already a reality through the redemptive work of Christ (Heb. 2:14; Rev. 1:18). Through Him the new creation is a present reality and believers are part of it (2 Cor. 5:17; Gal. 1:4). It is already here as a promise, as a gift, as a process by which sinners are being transformed into the likeness of Christ (2 Cor. 4:16). We now wait for the consummation of that salvation (Rom. 8:19–23; Rev. 21:1).

66:1–4. Third Answer: True Worship. The true worshiper is humble, contrite, and trembles at God's word (v. 2; cf. 57:15–21). God will reject those who believe that He, the Creator of heaven and earth, could reside only in a temple built by humans (66:1–2), formally worshiped by covenant breakers (v. 3). God declared that heaven is His throne and the earth His footstool (v. 1). This alludes to Israel's ancient conviction that the Lord's favor does not depend on building a wooden building (2 Sam. 7:7) and that the highest heavens could not contain God, let alone an earthly temple (1 Kin. 8:27; cf. vv. 23, 57–61; Ps. 11:4). The Lord's footstool (see e.g., Ps. 132:7) normally represents the ark, Zion, or apparently the earthly temple (cf. Is. 60:13), but when Isaiah identifies the earth as the Lord's footstool (66:1), he is describing the Lord as the Sovereign King of the world.

Considering that the Lord's throne is heaven and earth is His footstool, these rhetorical questions belittle the presumptuous thought that humans can build a house to worship the Lord while being disloyal to Him. The Sovereign King of the universe cannot be caged in a house and manipulated through ritual formalism. The prophet describes the false worshipers as those who offer sacrifices to the Lord while committing abominable offenses (v. 3; cf. 1:10–17). The dog was a sacrificial animal in some countries but considered unclean in Israel. As the apostates—who feared their threatening enemies—had chosen what was displeasing to God, God would choose their punishment (*ta'alulim*, which could designate a severe treatment or delusion) and would bring upon them what they had feared (66:4).

66:5–13. Fourth Answer: I Will Vindicate Zion.

Verses 5–13 are addressed to the poor and contrite people of the Lord. They are clearly distinguished from their own people (lit. "brothers") who hated them and from those who excluded them because of God's name (v. 5). The latter were the apostates (vv. 3–4) who were oppressing the faithful (cf. 50:4–11; 51:7), taunting their faithful brothers and scoffing at the predictions of the Lord's intervention against the oppressors. But these would not have a part in the restored Zion: they would be ashamed (66:5), and the voice of the Lord would be heard as He took vengeance upon His enemies (v. 6). The prophet already hears the noise from the city and the voice of the Lord from the temple (v. 6).

The scoffers continued their taunt, speaking of the predicted sudden change of Israel's situation as just too miraculous to be believed (v. 8). "Zion" is treated here as a metonymy for the land of Israel and Judah, and the taunt builds on earlier passages (e.g., 49:17–26; 52:1–12; 54:1–17; 60:1–22). The Lord replied to the taunt with two rhetorical questions relating to His power and control of history and to His plan to restore Zion and return scattered Israel (66:9).

The Lord invited the faithful citizens of new Zion to rejoice and take part in the celebration of her glory (vv. 10–11; cf. chaps. 60–62). He refers to them as those who love her and mourn for her (cf. 57:18; 61:2–3). The apostates, however, were those who forsook the Lord and forgot His holy mountain (65:11). In 66:11 the restored community is depicted through the image of a child being nourished (comforted) by its mother's milk (cf. 60:16). The metaphor of glorified Zion as a mother feeding, carrying, and dandling her child (i.e., her people) continues. The Lord would extend peace to her like a river and give her the glory or wealth of the nations (or Gentiles) like an overflowing stream (66:12). Then they (the faithful citizens) would be nursed and fed (i.e., their needs would be satisfied; cf. 60:16). This portion of the passage emphatically resumes the Lord's decision in 40:1–2 to comfort Jerusalem (66:13).

66:14–24. Fifth Answer: Final Judgment. The

citizens of restored Zion were told that their hearts would rejoice and that they (or their "bones," the

Heb. word *'etsem* can mean "self" or "bone") would flourish like grass when they would see God's salvation and glory (v. 14; cf. 58:11; 60:5a). This prediction rejects the taunt of the apostates in 66:5. God would demonstrate His power and righteousness in two ways. His hand (i.e., power) would be known to His servants when they saw His plan being implemented and their oppressors being defeated (v. 14c). By contrast, His enemies would be exposed to His anger (vv. 14d–15). The apostates in Israel were among the Lord's enemies. The first clause of v. 18 does not contain a verb in the Hebrew text, and thus translators have usually supplied one. Some supply "know," in other words, "I know their works"; others have "because of their actions and thoughts" or "I can see what they are doing." These enemies are those who go to gardens to worship idols and who eat swine and mice (v. 17; cf. 65:3–4 and the prohibitions against unclean food in Lev. 7:21; 11:10–23, 29).

The Lord would rule as the King of the world: He would gather all nations and languages (lit. "tongues"; Is. 66:18). This would be the result of the atonement and intercession of the Lord's Suffering Servant on behalf of the nations (52:13—53:12). The Lord's acceptance of their sacrifices in His temple, which He had declared to be "a house of prayer for all nations" (56:6–7), implies that the nations would be citizens of the Lord's future kingdom (cf. 2:2–4). He would set a sign among the nations—probably "the banner" that is repeatedly mentioned in the book (cf. 11:10b). The survivors who would escape, that is to say, the Lord's faithful remnant that included the faithful among scattered Israel, would be saved from the fate of the apostates (cf. 66:14–17). These would be sent to the nations in order to announce God's glory among the Gentiles (or the nations; v. 19; see 11:11; Ezek. 27:10–13). They would go to Tarshish, a distant Phoenician colony; to Pul, which was probably Somaliland or Libya in Africa; to Lud, which may be Lydia in Asia Minor; to Tubal, which may refer to the people living south of the Black Sea; to Javan, which refers to the Greeks; and to the islands or coastlands, which refer to distant peoples.

The Lord told His faithful ones that those of the remnant of Israel whom He would send to distant nations (Is. 66:19) would bring their fellow Israelites to the Lord's holy mountain in Jerusalem as an offering (*minkhah*, "offering," "tribute," "gift"). The metaphor of the people being offered to the Lord in a ceremonially clean vessel describes their return as a tribute to the Lord (v.

20; cf. 52:11–12). The means of transportation are reminiscent of 60:4–9 and lend force to the multitude of people coming from distant places. Some of them would be chosen as priests and Levites (66:21). Priests and Levites were among the apostates and those who lost their lives during the Assyrian and Babylonian invasions. Consequently, faithful Israel would replace the unfaithful, and the needed numbers of temple servants would be filled (cf. 61:5–6). Thus, the Lord's plan would be accomplished—purified Israel would worship Him properly in His holy temple.

The new heavens and the new earth that the Lord would make (66:22) were to remain before Him (see commentary on 65:17–25). The new heavens and new earth would display the glory of the Lord. Israel and his descendants were to remain before Him, never to be separated. Humanity's worship of the Lord would continue eternally, from one new moon to another (i.e., monthly) and from one Sabbath to another (i.e., weekly; 66:23). The Lord's world sovereignty was to be confirmed by *worship*. The corpses of the apostates would be an abhorrent reminder of their permanent state of death and defilement. The going out referred to at the beginning of v. 24 alludes to the custom of ending the regular worship at Jerusalem with a procession from the temple. On this occasion, the worshipers would see the bodies of the dead apostates in the Valley of Hinnom (from which is derived the expression Gehenna, "hell" in the NT) at the foot of Mount Zion. Its disgrace and defilement derived from its association with human sacrifice (2 Kin. 23:10; Jer. 7:31; 32:35) and from its use as the city's rubbish dump. Unclean corpses that were denied proper burial were also deposited there

to be burned or left to decompose. The worm that would not die and the fire that would not be quenched refer to what would happen to their bodies and does not refer to the concept of an immortal soul. The verb tenses denote actions that are not yet complete and convey the sense that the worm had not yet died and the fire had not yet been quenched. The clauses simply say that no one would act to extinguish the worms or quench the fire before the consumption of their bodies, which agrees with 1:31. The fate of the corpses confirms that the apostates would permanently perish (cf. 26:14) and would be excluded from participation in the new life that the Lord would create for His people. The reference to these dead people who had rebelled or transgressed (Heb. *pasha'*) against the Lord in 66:24 echoes 1:2, where the same verb is used. The problem with God's children, announced in 1:2–3, was at last to be addressed. The many verbal and thematic connections between chapters 1 and 66 serve to mark an *inclusio* of the whole book (see commentary on 1:2–31). The nations would see the Lord's glory in Zion and the glorification of faithful Israel (61:4–11; 62:1–4, 10–12) and would choose to join the worshiping community in Zion-Jerusalem (60:1–18).

The book of Isaiah closes with a description of the final fate of the wicked, which implies the conclusion of the conflict and the transformation of hope into a visible reality through the power of God. Isaiah announces the extinction of the wicked in order to accentuate the final victory of the righteous. This hope anticipates the moment when God's people will eternally dwell in the presence of Him who is the Creator, Redeemer, and Sovereign of the universe.

JEREMIAH

INTRODUCTION

Title and Authorship. This major prophetic work is introduced as "the words of Jeremiah" (Jer. 1:1). Considering the technical sense of a prophet's "word" (*dabar*; 18:18; cf. 37:6–17), the plural "words [of Jeremiah]" signifies a collection of prophetic messages (cf. Amos 1:1). Jeremiah was the son of Hilkiah, one of the priests in the land of Benjamin (Jer. 1:1). The composition of the book of Jeremiah is best understood as a *process*. Firstly, the "word" of the Lord became the "word" of the prophet. God was the author-originator and Jeremiah the author-messenger. God placed His words in Jeremiah's mouth (v. 9; 5:14; 15:19; cf. 19:2) or commanded him to write (30:1–2; 36:2, 28), and they became "the words of Jeremiah" (1:1; 51:63). Secondly, as *mediator* of God's word, Jeremiah expressed the divine insight in his own words under the guidance of the Spirit. In this sense, Jeremiah is the author of his book, the content of which he received through divine revelation and inspiration (1:1–2). Thirdly, in some cases, Jeremiah used material that is nearly identical to that found in other books to convey his message (e.g., 2 Kin. 24:18—25:26 in Jer. 52:1–34). Arguably, this was because he either authored the other material or borrowed it because it expressed God's message to him in a particularly useful way. Finally, Jeremiah wrote some of his "words" with his own hand (29:1; 30:2; 51:60) but also used a scribe to whom he dictated his message (32:13,

---

The Two Editions of Jeremiah

There are two different editions of the book of Jeremiah. The Hebrew text, from which the Septuagint (LXX) was translated, is about 13 percent or 2,700 words shorter than the Masoretic Text (MT) of the Hebrew Bible. Certain sections in the MT are missing from the LXX, and some material is in a different order. The Dead Sea Scrolls include six fragments of Jeremiah in Hebrew, four following the MT and two following the Hebrew text used by the translators of the LXX. Since the shorter edition of Jeremiah existed in Hebrew during the second century B.C., the major differences were not introduced by the LXX translator.

However, the overall message of Jeremiah does not significantly differ. Many differences result from repetitive material found in the MT that is missing from the LXX. While two versions of Jeremiah appear to have been in circulation at least from the

second century B.C., the fact remains that the canonical edition in our Bibles was endorsed by Palestinian Judaism, associated with the Jerusalem temple, and continued in Rabbinic Judaism. These important questions remain: Which edition goes back to Jeremiah, and why do we have two editions? Various answers have been suggested, and there is no conclusive verdict.

For readers who accept the repeated claim of the book as the word of God, the same God also has the power and means to protect His word from distortions (cf. Jer. 23:28; 26:2; Ps. 119:160; Matt. 5:17–18; 1 Pet. 1:22–25). Although both editions contain, in slightly different forms, the word of God, the fact remains that the longer version in the MT was recognized as authoritative by both Judaism and Christianity as part of the biblical canon. In this we see God's providential work.

16; 36:2–4, 32; 45:1). Although the composition of the book was a process (see 36:32), the final work bears the clear imprint of Jeremiah's individual and sensitive personality, and a masterful poetical and rhetorical style.

Date. The title in 1:1–3 dates Jeremiah's ministry from King Josiah's thirteenth year (627 B.C.) until the Babylonian Exile (586 B.C.). Prophetic "words"/"messages" were dictated and/or written over a period of time (30:1–24; 36:1–32; cf. 29:1–32; 45:1–5; 51:59–64). The epilogue in chapter 52 mentions events dated to the thirty-seventh year of the exile of King Jehoiachin of Judah (vv. 31–34; cf. 2 Kin. 25:27–30), that is, the year that Evil-Merodach of Babylon succeeded Nebuchadnezzar (562 B.C.). Chapter 52 was not written by Jeremiah (see 51:64), but it demonstrates how his prophecies were fulfilled. It also indicates that the book of Jeremiah as we now have it was in existence around 562 B.C. The earliest known manuscripts of the book are among the Dead Sea Scrolls, which date to about 200 B.C., approximately when the LXX translation was initiated in Egypt. The importance of the book is attested in Daniel (9:2; cf. 2 Chr. 36:21–22), in Ezra (1:1), and in the apocryphal book of Ecclesiasticus (chaps. 44–49).

Backgrounds. Jeremiah's long prophetic ministry (627–586 B.C.) coincided with the reigns of five successive kings in Judah: Josiah (641–609 B.C.), Jehoahaz (609 B.C.), Jehoiakim (609–598 B.C.), Jehoiachin (598–597 B.C.), and Zedekiah (597–586 B.C.). Jeremiah was well acquainted with loneliness and was forbidden to marry and have children (Jer. 16:1–2). The social and political establishment opposed his messages (e.g., 1:18; 26:7–24) and put him in the stocks (20:2) and in prison (37:15–16; 38:1–13, 28). People in his hometown and family rejected him (11:18–23; 12:6), but he was sustained by his awareness of God's presence (1:8, 19; 14:8–9; 15:20) and the power of the divine word (1:9; 15:16, 19; 20:8–9; 23:29).

The most intense phase in Jeremiah's ministry occurred during the sustained historical crisis in 605–586 B.C. that climaxed in the destruction of Jerusalem (15:19; cf. 1:9; 5:14). Speaking candidly and with divine power, his relentless prophecies of judgment were intended to lead the people to repentance. Repentance was needed because the cause of the crisis was the people's desertion of the covenant God. Jeremiah's messages eventually enabled the remnant of Israel to survive Judah's fall and the Exile. Jeremiah directed them toward God's future and gave them a hope that was founded on God's grace and power (cf. 29:11).

Jeremiah's call to ministry was closely connected with Babylon's rise to supremacy. On his death, Ashurbanipal left behind a weak Assyrian Empire (627 B.C.). The same year, Nabopolassar became king in Babylon and soon subjugated Assyria. Thus, Jeremiah's appointment in 627 B.C. as a prophet to the nations (1:5) coincided with the rise of the Neo-Babylonian power that would dominate Judah politically for about seventy years. The ministry of Jeremiah covered five historical periods.

1. Before Josiah's Reform (629–622 B.C.). Jeremiah 2:1–6:30 possibly derives from these early years (cf. 3:6). The passage is characterized by (a) strong denouncements of Judah's idolatry (e.g., 2:1–3:5); (b) harsh announcements of impending punishment "from the north" (e.g., 1:13–16; 4:5–5:17); and (c) messages of hope and salvation (e.g., 3:6–4:4; 4:14).

2. Josiah's Reform (622–609 B.C.). Inspired by a book found in the temple (perhaps Deuteronomy), King Josiah launched a reform based on covenant fidelity to the Lord (2 Kin. 23:4–25). The call of Jeremiah five years earlier is congruent with this reform (Jer. 1:4–19). The messages in Jeremiah 11:1–8 (on covenant faithfulness) and 17:19–27 (on the Sabbath) were probably proclaimed to support the reform. Unfortunately, Josiah fell in a battle near Megiddo in 609 B.C. at the hands of Pharaoh Necho II (2 Kin. 23:29). A biblical record notes that Jeremiah mourned his death (1 Chr. 35:25).

3. The Reigns of Jehoahaz, Jehoiakim, and Jehoiachin (609–597 B.C.). Josiah's son Jehoahaz (or Shallum; Jer. 22:11; 32:7; 35:4) is mentioned unfavorably (22:10). After only three months as king (2 Chr. 36:2), Pharaoh Necho II put him in chains and appointed another of Josiah's sons, Eliakim, as king, renaming him Jehoiakim (2 Kin. 23:34; 2 Chr. 36:4). Jehoiakim's reign marks a turning point for Jeremiah. He now faced persecution and imprisonment, alternating with brief periods of freedom (Jer. 20:1–2; 26:8–9; 32:2–3; 33:1; 36:26; 37:12–21; 38:6–13). Jehoiakim's hostility arose from Jeremiah's repeated message that Judah was destined to fall at the hand of Babylon (36:1–32). Jeremiah attacked the syncretistic temple cult and urged the people to be faithful to Yahweh and worship Him alone. This created strong opposition from the royal establishment (e.g., 38:1–28; cf. 7:1–20:18; 22:1–30; 25:1–14).

In 605 B.C., Nabopolassar's son and successor, Nebuchadnezzar, crushed the Egyptians at Carchemish on the Euphrates (Jer. 46:2–12), and Babylon exercised authority over Western Asia for the next seventy years. The same year, Nebuchadnezzar besieged Jerusalem, humiliated Jehoiakim, and carried off Daniel and his companions to Babylon (Dan. 1:3–6). In 597 B.C., Jerusalem was defeated again, and the rebellious Jehoiakim was deported in chains to Babylon. His eight(teen?)-year-old son Jehoiachin ruled only three months (2 Chr. 36:9; cf. 2 Kin. 24:8). Jeremiah's prediction of his captivity (Jer. 22:24–30) was later fulfilled (24:1; 29:1–2; cf. 52:31–34).

4. *The Reign of Zedekiah and Jerusalem's Destruction (597–586 B.C.).* Young Mattaniah, Jehoiachin's uncle and another son of Josiah, was renamed Zedekiah and placed on Judah's throne by Nebuchadnezzar in 597 B.C. (37:1; 2 Chr. 36:9–14). Zedekiah sometimes befriended Jeremiah and sought his advice (Jer. 37:3–17) but otherwise allowed the prophet's enemies to mistreat and imprison him (38:1–28). When Nebuchadnezzar blinded and deported Zedekiah, he appointed Gedaliah as governor of Judah, and Jeremiah chose to remain in Judah (40:1–6). When Gedaliah was murdered in a conspiracy (41:1–9), his entourage feared Babylonian reprisals and fled to Egypt, taking Jeremiah and Baruch with them (43:4–7).

5. *Sojourn in Egypt (586–?).* Limited information about this period comes from 43:8–13 and 44:1–30. Because the book was not written in chronological order, Jeremiah's last recorded words are probably found in vv. 24–30. The prophecy about Nebuchadnezzar's defeat of Pharaoh Hophra was fulfilled in 568–567 B.C. (v. 30; 46:26). The circumstances of Jeremiah's death are unknown, but a Jewish tradition maintains he was stoned to death (cf. Heb. 11:36–37).

Two factors are significant for understanding the setting of the book of Jeremiah—namely, the internal conflicts between various parties in Jerusalem and Judah and the successive Babylonian deportations (cf. Jer. 52:28–30). The narration covers (a) the Sinai covenant going back to Moses; (b) the memory of earlier apostasies and prophetic judgments, at least since Amos and Hosea; (c) royal claims to power; (d) the temple theology promoted by the various groups in the priesthood; (e) pro-Babylonian and pro-Egyptian parties; (f) the influential families of nobility that were in tensions with the king; and (g) the interests of rural village elders. These contrasting voices had engaged in an ongoing dispute about

these central questions: Who had trustworthy insight regarding the nations and Judah, and who could give safe guidance regarding faith, worship, ethics, and political power? Jeremiah maintained that faithfulness to the covenant with God was the key to public well-being and that a violation of such faithfulness would bring disaster to the community. This is the position of the *prophetic movement* (e.g., Amos, Hosea, Isaiah, Micah, and Zephaniah), and Jeremiah consciously included himself in this movement (28:8–9).

Secondly, the promises of hope and salvation for the faithful, prompted by the successive Babylonian deportations, grew in importance. After the fateful destruction of Jerusalem and Solomon's temple, the book of Jeremiah was read both as an explanation of the disaster and a promise of hope for redemption and a new beginning. This influenced the central position of the so-called Book of Comfort (30:1—33:26) and the pivotal role of the prophecy of Babylon's fall (50:1—51:63).

Theology and Purpose. Jeremiah's theology is nowhere outlined or nicely articulated. Instead, the book reveals a living and moving relationship with God, a poetic mind devoted to rich and varied imagery, personal reflections, and biographical accounts. Even so, a number of theological themes are clearly emphasized.

1. *The Covenant God.* Yahweh was the God of the covenant with Israel (7:23). His faithfulness to the covenant meant that (a) He held His people accountable when they violated it and (b) He gave grace and hope to those who were faithful and to those who returned to Him. Yahweh's faithfulness to the covenant—which included blessings on the faithful and curses on the unfaithful (cf. Deut. 28)—is understood as His righteousness and loving-kindness (4:2; 9:24). The covenant provides the basis for God's messages of salvation and judgment against His people.

According to the Sinaitic covenant, God saved His people and showed them His undeserved love and mercy. The people were to faithfully respond in love, trust, and obedience. God would show mercy but would also punish rebellious lawbreaking with judgment. This belongs to God's righteous ordering of the world based on His character and will (cf. Ex. 20:4–6). In keeping with the common ANE practices of covenant making, the covenant with Israel included curses and blessings on the party that broke or kept the agreement (Deut. 28). In regard to vengeance, the principle of retribution is in view (Jer. 20:10–12; cf. Ex. 21:12–27; Deut. 19:21), especially as a reason for the judgment against Babylon (e.g., Jer. 50:15, 28; 51:11, 24, 35–36, 49, 56). However, God has the right, power, and wisdom to exercise mercy according to the circumstances. His judgment serves certain purposes and may be overruled by the same purposes if His will so requires. Thus, Jeremiah's prophecies of judgment have a sequence of purposes: (a) to declare the judgment God had in store for Judah; (b) to warn them and lead them to turn from their evil condition (25:5); (c) to instruct the people that God's judgment is a response to human behavior (i.e., judgment is a consequence of their actions); (d) to evoke a sense of inevitability since the judgment was impending; (e) to communicate God's willingness to forgive repentant sinners (36:3) and restore the covenant; and (f) to confirm the truth of the word of God. Thus, the relationship between God and His people was the central concern, not merely the approaching punishment.

The theological foundation of judgment may be summarized as follows: (a) God is the Sovereign Lord of human history; (b) God is also sovereign in the realms of nature and morality; and (c) human beings may choose a life in relationship with God or one without Him, and both history and nature will, at God's command, either reward or punish them for their choices (see "God's Judgment in the Prophets," p. 981).

Some of Jeremiah's prophecies anticipate a complete restoration of Israel (23:1–8; 30:10–11, 18–22; 31:10–14, 23–25), a gathering of the remnant from the nations (23:3–4; 30:10–11; 31:10–14), the raising up of a Davidic righteous "branch" (23:5–6), and a new exodus (vv. 7–8; 50:33–34). These promises of a blessed and hopeful future grow in importance at each deportation of Judean exiles to Babylon (see 52:28–30), especially after the disaster in 586 B.C. They are, however, coupled with realism, a demand for patience, and a fundamental appeal for faithfulness to God.

The covenant formula (i.e., God's declaration that made Him Israel's God and Israel His people) runs throughout the book (see 7:23; 11:4; 24:7; 30:22; 31:1, 33; 32:28). Since this declaration was predictive, its future realization was anticipated and experienced through the prophetic word. Such a promissory word enables the faithful to wait for God while already experiencing its future blessing. The divine promise of a lasting agreement and union between God and His people will find its ultimate fulfillment when God's mission on earth is completed (Rev. 21:1–5).

2. The Mutual Knowledge between God and Humans. Jeremiah speaks in an unparalleled manner about God's knowledge of him and his knowledge of God. Jeremiah knew that God foreknew him (Jer. 1:5). Often in his prayers, he appeals to the God who knows him (12:3; 15:15; 17:16). God's knowledge of Jeremiah presupposes a relationship. But human beings may also know God (9:24). Humans have a profound need to know God, and Jeremiah reproached Judah for not knowing Him (2:8; 4:22; 5:4; 7:9; 8:7). The nations who did not yet know God would be exhausted and fall (51:58, 64). They had not yet found the rest that life with the Lord inevitably brings (6:16; 30:10; 31:2; 46:27; 50:34). To know God is to have hope, and hope brings rest.

3. God and the Sanctuary. The covenant theology included the promise that God would dwell with His people in the land He had given them. The Jerusalem temple eventually became His dwelling place under David and Solomon. God's presence rendered the sanctuary most holy. However, according to Jeremiah, the false gods set up in Jerusalem (and in the local sanctuaries in the cities of Judah) contributed to the defilement of the sanctuary and caused God to

Covenant

The term "covenant" (Heb. *berit*) occurs twenty-three times in Jeremiah, always in the sense of a legally binding agreement between two parties (cf. e.g., 11:2–3, 6–8; 14:21; 33:20–21, 25; 34:8). Of central importance, however, is the covenant between God and Israel. This is either the Lord's covenant with the fathers after the Exodus from Egypt (e.g., 11:10; 14:21; 22:9; 31:32), which had been broken, or His new and future covenant with the remnant of Israel (e.g., 31:22, 31–33; 32:40; 50:5). A "covenant" created a legal, contractual obligation outlining requirements (usually in writing) that were to be faithfully maintained by all parties. The legal and obligatory status of the covenant explains the juridical aspect of God's just judgment against Judah. A covenant could also be promissory when the superior party Himself took on an obligation. This is exemplified in Jeremiah by God's promises of a future, everlasting covenant with His people (e.g., 31:31–34).

abandon it. This is described as Israel's abandonment of the Lord. The judgment that would destroy the sanctuary would confirm that God was no longer living among His people—in other words, Israel's disobedience had put an end to the covenant (cf. 5:19; see "The Temple in Chronicles," p. 541). However, the disappearance of the sanctuary did not end God's relationship with His people. It continued through the prophetic word.

The sanctuary plays an important role in Jeremiah's admonitions to the exiles in Babylon. The hope of restoration at the end of the seventy-year Babylonian captivity incorporates the restoration of God's honor and glory associated with His temple (Jer. 14:21; 17:12; 31:6–7; 51:50–51). God would respond to what Babylon had done in Zion (51:28) and address the shameful fact that foreign invaders had entered God's holy sanctuary (v. 51). Thus, God's punishment of Babylon (50:1—51:63) was to be God's act of vengeance for His temple (50:28; 51:11, 24). God's people would again worship Him in the temple in Zion when He would restore His honor and glory before the nations (50:4–5; 51:10; cf. 31:6–7, 12). The nations would no longer look favorably toward Babylon's chief god (51:44)—they would look favorably toward the Lord in Zion (3:17; cf. Is. 2:2–4). In essence, this theological insight continues in Daniel (cf. the little horn's pride, oppression, and desecration of the sanctuary in Dan. 8:9–14) and Revelation (cf. the appeal to the nations to give honor and glory to God in Rev. 14:6–13, turning away from "Babylon" to the true God).

4. God and the Nations. God is Lord of all nations (Jer. 1:4–10; 3:17; 4:2; 5:15; 10:7, 10; 18:7–10; 25:17–28; 46:1—51:63). The Creator gives dominion over the earth to whom He deems appropriate (1:5, 10; 27:5; cf. Dan. 2:21, 37–38, 44; 5:18–21; 7:26–27; Acts 17:24–28; Rev. 19:11–21). His power to give dominion to the nations or remove it is expressed in the central metaphor in Jeremiah's call as a prophet: to pluck up, tear down, and destroy, but also to build and plant (Jer. 1:10; cf. 18:1–11; 31:28). Thus, in the context of judgment, God made Babylon His agent in the punishment of His disobedient covenant partner, Judah (27:6–9). In the context of salvation, however, God admonished His remnant people not to fear Babylon because He was able to deliver them (42:11–12). When Babylon's allotted time would run out, God would turn against her and punish her (50:1—51:63), and world dominion would be given to another people (51:11, 28).

5. God as Creator. God's sovereignty over the nations is founded on His creation of all that exists (10:12–16; 32:17–25; 51:15–19). He is all-powerful (32:27; 48:15; 51:57) and omnipresent (23:24). Since God created the earth and all the living creatures on it (27:5), it is His to govern as He desires (vv. 5–11; cf. 18:1–11). He is in charge of the created universe with its fixed order and purpose (5:24; 8:7; 14:22; 27:1–22; 31:35–37). Therefore, those who hope in the Lord will be blessed (17:7). Under the covenant, Israel had promised to acknowledge God as Creator (Ex. 20:8–11) and care for its neighbors (Deut. 5:12–15) by keeping the Sabbath day. God called Jeremiah to remind the people of this by proclaiming in all the gates of Jerusalem to keep the Sabbath holy, just as He had commanded their ancestors (Jer. 17:22).

6. Hope and the Word. God's faithfulness includes His promise to David (33:17). The messianic hope would be fulfilled, and the King of righteousness would be Lord over God's people, bringing salvation and safety to Judah (vv. 15–16). This promise was not fulfilled immediately after the return from the Babylonian Exile, but Christian faith sees its fulfillment in Jesus Christ (Rom. 3:21; Rev. 19:11). This promise was given to Jeremiah through the divine word. Speaking the word of God was Jeremiah's destiny (e.g., Jer. 1:4, 11, 13; 2:1, 4, 31). The fact that the noun "word"/"words [of God]" occurs over 150 times in the book (besides verbal expressions like "the Lord says") underscores the introductory note to Jeremiah as one to whom the word of the Lord came (1:2). The word has God's intention and will in it. It is alive with divine energy and sovereignty, and conveys judgment at times but also, ultimately, hope. It is not only powerful and is experienced like a fire (5:14; 20:9; 23:29) or a hammer that breaks the rock in pieces (23:29), but it is also "a joy and delight" (15:16).

The word can be "seen" (2:31) because there is no distinction between the *spoken* word and the *performed* word (the Heb. *dabar* designates not only "word," but also "thing" or "matter"). Human beings have no control over the word; it cannot be conjured up by their will (17:15; 23:18). It is given, at times, even against one's own wishes (1:6–8; 15:15–21; 28:6–7). True prophets must subject themselves to God's word in obedience—listening and waiting. At certain points, Jeremiah waited for extended periods of time (42:1–7). The fulfillment of the word of God is certain (1:12; 28:9; 32:24). Many of Jeremiah's predictions were soon fulfilled (e.g., 16:15; 20:4; 25:11–14; 27:19–22; 28:15–17; 29:10; 34:4–5;

43:10–11; 44:30; 46:13; 51:41–44), while others were to be—or will yet be—fulfilled in another era (e.g., 23:5–6; 30:8–9; 31:31–34; 33:15–16).

Jeremiah was concerned with the integrity of the word of God. In conflicts with the popular prophets of the day, he was compelled to understand the nature of God's revelation to him. They too spoke in the name of the Lord, but Jeremiah denied that they had been sent (23:21, 32), that they had stood in the divine counsel (vv. 18, 22), and that God had spoken to them (v. 21). Their word lacked true hope. But Jeremiah was aware that he stood in the line of God's true prophets (7:25; 25:4; 26:5; 29:19; 35:15; 44:4) and that his word, coming from the Lord, would shape history as a beacon of hope.

7. The Prophetic Word. God's word was conveyed to Jeremiah by revelation. This term is not found in the book, and the experience is not described in any detail. Most often, the word of the Lord simply "came to" Jeremiah, and the prophet then proclaimed what the Lord "says" (e.g., 2:4; 19:2). Obviously, matters relating to the prophetic experience were widely known and accepted in Jeremiah's setting and did not need an explanation. When God reveals His message, a prophet simply "knows" the word of the Lord. Therefore, the sign of a true prophet is an intimate relationship with God and a knowledge of Him. The closest we come to Jeremiah's prophetic experience is through the reference to his standing in the council (or counsel) of the Lord (23:18, 22). This refers to an intimate dialogue between God and His prophet (cf. Gen. 18:22–33; Amos 3:7) in which the prophet listened attentively to the word (Jer. 23:18).

God's word is powerful and holy (5:14; 23:9, 29) because it carries His power and holiness. Jeremiah takes it in his mouth or writes it on a scroll with awe and trembling. Governed by this understanding, Jeremiah does not distinguish in his prophetic speeches between the linguistic elements purely from God and those from himself. God's speech is, in a sense, beyond human control and can only be accessed through the prophet. The awesome power of God's speech cannot be received and communicated by just any human being but only through mediation by a duly appointed prophet of the Lord (1:4–19; cf. Is. 6:1–13).

The prophet is called to receive God's word (cf. Jer. 23:18) and then to make it presentable in human form so that it can be efficiently communicated (i.e., spoken or written) in the language and speech forms of the intended audience. Ellen White caught this point of prophetic speech when she said, "The Bible points to God as its author; yet it was written by human hands; and in the varied style of its different books it presents the characteristics of the several writers. The truths revealed are all 'given by inspiration of God' (2 Timothy 3:16); yet they are expressed in the words of men. The Infinite One by His Holy Spirit has shed light into the minds and hearts of His servants. He has given dreams and visions, symbols and figures; and those to whom the truth was thus revealed have themselves embodied the thought in human language" (GC v. 3).

The Lord's words and Jeremiah's words are one. This explains why it is often impossible to separate them in the text. God is the originator, and Jeremiah the preacher and text producer. For example, in the call of Jeremiah, the divine word was given by God (Jer. 1:4, 11–13), then spoken (i.e., formulated) by the prophet (vv. 9–10), performed or fulfilled by God (v. 12), then recorded by the prophet. Jeremiah's message is that hope, peace, and true well-being are found only in faithfulness to God, the Creator of the world and Israel's covenant God. The book of Jeremiah revolves around God's rule and the supremacy of His kingdom (cf. 1:10; 46:1). Since any relationship between God and human beings is based on who God is and what He wants for them, His promise is therefore valid at all times: He desires to bring peace and future hope (29:11).

Literary Features. In terms of word count, Jeremiah is the longest book in OT prophetic literature. One of the extraordinary features of Jeremiah is the use of a variety of literary forms and text types with striking examples of poetry and prose at a high artistic level. Having received a priestly upbringing (1:1), Jeremiah displays an intimate familiarity with the temple literature from the book of Psalms. He also draws on passages and themes in the Pentateuch (esp. Deuteronomy) and the historical and prophetic books (e.g., 2 Kings, Isaiah, and Habakkuk). He expresses his prophetic insight through extraordinary artistic skill in speeches, prayers, and reflections.

The book of Jeremiah belongs to the literary genre of prophecy. Features of this genre found in the book include announcements of disaster with or without elements of the covenant lawsuit (Heb. *rib*): indictments, judicial sentences, and predictions of judgment (2:1–37; 29:30–32; 50:1—51:58); sermons (7:1–15); predictive prophecy (30:1—33:28); various narratives: history (39:1—44:30), biography (26:1—24), autobiography (11:18–19; 13:1–11), symbolically enacted prophecy (18:1–11), call narrative (1:4–19), and vision report (24:1–10); various kinds of instruction (11:1–17; 17:19–27; 35:12–19); letters (29:1–30); and the so-called Confessions (11:18–23; 12:1–6; 15:10–21; 17:14–18; 18:18–23; 20:7–18).

Jeremiah's Confessions contain outpourings of emotion and anguish mixed with trust and gratitude. In the midst of faithfully delivering God's word in perilous circumstances, Jeremiah remained in deep and candid dialogue with the Lord. The Confessions show the depth of honesty and forthrightness that is appropriate in prayer when the situation requires it. Although personal and original, they include conventional forms of the lament prayers found in the book of Psalms.

Jeremiah's poetry reveals great variety: the ecstatic lyricism of the war songs (4:5b–9, 13–16, 19–22), the cosmic brooding of the imminent destruction (4:23–26), the intense subjectivity of the confessional laments (15:10–11, 15–20; 20:7–18), the unsparing and withering invectives with their accompanying threats (22:13–19), the pathetic effusion of intimate grief (13:15–17), the breathtaking judgment of an entire society by "an ode to the sword" (50:35–37), and the rhetorical diversity of prophecies against the foreign nations (46:3–12; 50:35–38; 51:1–58).

Jeremiah contains examples of the effective repetition of striking phrases or ideas, such as "sword, famine, and pestilence/plague" (14:12–16; 21:7, 9; 24:10; 27:8, 13; 29:17–18; 32:24, 36; 34:17; 38:2; 42:17, 22; 44:13) and the language of plucking up, tearing down, and destroying, or building and planting (or variants thereof), which expresses God's power to destroy or prosper a nation (1:10; 12:17; 18:7–9; 24:6; 31:28; 42:10). God communicates His earnest and continuous actions through His prophets by persistently (some translations have "rising early") speaking/sending/teaching (7:13, 25; 11:7; 25:3–4; 26:5; 29:19; 32:33; 35:14–15; 44:4; cf. 11:7; 25:3; 32:33; 35:14).

To lend force and coherence to his message, Jeremiah often uses alliteration and assonance, which are not reflected in the English translation (e.g., *shaqed...shoqed*, "almond...ready," 1:11–12; *zarim wezeruah*, "foreigners to winnow her," 51:2; *pakhad wapakhat wapakh*, "fear and pit and snare," 48:43; cf. Is. 24:17). Thematically important are his plays on the Hebrew word *shub*, "turn," "return," "backsliding" (Jer. 3:1—4:4; 8:4–17; 15:1–21; 34:8–22; cf. *shub*

shebut, "restore the fortunes" or "bring back from captivity" in 29:14; 30:3, 18; 31:23; 32:44; 33:7, 11, 26). In almost every passage, we find the stylistic device of synecdoche, a partial expression referring to the whole, particularly for peoples, nations, cities, and lands (e.g., "Jerusalem" for Judah or Israel).

Like Ezekiel, Jeremiah uses powerful symbolism to highlight his messages (e.g., 13:1–11; 19:1–12; 24:1–10; 27:1–22; 43:8–13). Symbolism is also applied in the Lord's commands to perform certain actions (e.g., 16:1–4, 5–9; 32:6–15). Large portions of text are repeated throughout the book (e.g., 6:12–15 and 8:10–12; 10:12–16 and 51:15–19; 16:14–15 and 23:7–8; 23:5–6 and 33:15–16; 23:19–20 and 30:23–24; 30:10–11 and 46:27–28; 39:1–7 and 52:4–16). The purpose is pedagogical and communicative. Since books in ancient times were often read aloud to an audience due to limited reading skills and the scarcity of books, the repetition of key passages aimed at emphasis and it created bridges between different parts of the book. The technique of organizing sentences and larger units according to the principle of chiastic structures is particularly frequent (e.g., 2:1–37; 8:18—9:3; 9:4–16; 19:3–9; 31:1–40; 32:1–44).

The great variety in literary forms and styles underscores the predominant feature in the book's composition, which is the mixture of systematic order and lack of order. Some portions of the book have marked beginnings and endings, while others are lengthy sequences with little or no transition. What seems clear is that while the first half of the book deals primarily with the disobedience of Judah (chaps. 2–25), the second part focuses more on the Babylonian threat and the judgment (chaps. 26–52) with a middle point of comfort in chapters 30–33. Unlike Ezekiel, the oracles in Jeremiah are not arranged in chronological order.

COMMENTARY

1:1–19

TITLE, PROLOGUE, AND PROPHETIC CALL

The first section of the book introduces us to the Prophet Jeremiah and the historical background of his ministry (1:1–3). His prophetic call (vv. 4–19) plays a significant role throughout the book—it is a source of strength when he suffers greatly or has to confront false prophets.

1:1–3
Title and Prologue

The title is similar to that of some other prophetic books; the book contains the words of a particular prophet whose ultimate source is the Lord (cf. Amos 1:1; Is. 1:1). The "words" designate the specific messages the prophet proclaimed. Jeremiah is identified historically as emerging from the priestly circles of Anathoth, a city in Benjamin that was situated three miles (5 km) northeast of Jerusalem. Jeremiah's father, Hilkiah, may have been the Hilkiah who served Josiah (2 Kin. 22–23). Anathoth was the home of Abiathar, the priest who served David faithfully and carried the ark of the Lord before being removed from service by Solomon (1 Sam. 22:20–23; 23:6, 9–12; 2 Sam. 15:24–29, 34–36; 1 Kin. 2:26–27).

Jeremiah's Hebrew name exists in two forms, *yirmeyahu* (e.g., Jer. 1:1; 29:27; 36:4) and *yirmeyah* (e.g., 27:1; 28:5; 29:1). The literal meaning is not clear, but part of his name refers to God (cf. 15:16). The name could mean "Yahweh has exalted or appointed." God's name was written *yhwh* (cf. Ex. 3:13–15) and appeared in theophoric proper names as *yahu* or *yah*, so it is no surprise to find both name forms in Jeremiah. Hebrew *yirmeyahu* became *Ieremias* in Greek (the LXX, ca. 250–200 B.C.) and Latin (Vg., ca. A.D. 400). The English form *Jeremiah* is attested from the fourteenth century A.D. The purpose of Jeremiah 1:1–3 is obviously not to provide an exhaustive list of kings and dates (two minor kings are missing) but to indicate that Jeremiah prophesied under several kings until the Babylonian disaster (ca. 627–586 B.C.).

1:4–19
Prophetic Call

This passage cements Jeremiah's prophetic authority as established by God's commission, the details of which anticipate the content of the book as a whole. Jeremiah was called to be a prophet to the nations (v. 5), but his special task was to warn Judah and Jerusalem of the impending judgment (vv. 13–16).

1:4–10. A Prophet to the Nations. The call is a dialogue in which God declared that He was appointing Jeremiah as a prophet to the nations (vv. 5, 10). Jeremiah's immediate reply was that he was too young and unable to speak, which is a sign of humility (v. 6). God rejected the objection by repeating His decision and proceeded to assure

Jeremiah of His presence and deliverance (vv. 7–8). He then touched Jeremiah's mouth, which was a sign of placing His words in the prophet's mouth. He also explained that Jeremiah's task as prophet "over" the nations would be to announce their destruction or rise to prosperity (vv. 9–10). The motif of God's words in Jeremiah's mouth is found elsewhere in the book (5:14; 15:19; 36:18; cf. Ezra 1:1; 2 Chr. 36:12, 21–22).

The references to God knowing, sanctifying (or setting apart), and designating Jeremiah as a prophet to the nations in Jeremiah 1:5 seem influenced by formal calls to an office (cf. 49:19; 50:44). However, the technical or sacramental sense of the English term "ordain" that is found in some translations is not conveyed by the Hebrew verb. The verb *natan* used here simply means "give," "put," or "make." Jeremiah 1:4–19 describes, however, the formal commissioning of a royal priest-prophet. First, the technical Hebrew term *peqad*—"appoint," "set," or "commission"— is used in v. 10 (cf. 49:19; 50:44; 51:27). Secondly, the reference in 1:5 to God's sanctifying (*qadash*) alludes to the priestly appointment (Ex. 28:3, 41). Thirdly, Jeremiah's commissioning included the appointment (Jer. 1:5), charge/sending (vv. 6–7), assurance (v. 8), authorization to speak God's word (v. 9), acknowledgment and commission (vv. 10, 13–16), charge and exhortation (vv. 17–18), and renewed assurance (v. 19).

As the Sovereign Lord of the nations, God consecrated Jeremiah as His royal servant and messenger who would stand in His *sod*—a Hebrew word meaning "counsel" or "council" (cf. 23:21–22). God's commission (1:10) included both judgment and salvation. This dual aspect of Jeremiah's ministry is expressed in the visions of the almond branch (vv. 11–12) and the boiling pot (vv. 13–16). The duality of judgment and salvation is particularly applied to God's chosen people Israel (e.g., 2:2–3, 21; cf. Deut. 7:6). The judgment messages call the unfaithful to repentance, while the messages of salvation bring comfort and hope to the faithful in exile.

1:11–19. Commission and Assurance. The dialogue between God and Jeremiah continues with two contrasting visions. The almond branch is associated with what God would "build and plant," and the boiling pot with what He would pluck up, tear down, destroy, and overthrow (cf. v. 10). The former receives scant explanation, while the judgment on Judah and Jerusalem is detailed. The vision of the almond branch is described in terse, almost mystifying words. God's words in the Hebrew read literally, "I am *watching* my word, to carry it out" (v. 12). The striking wordplay between the branch of "almond" (*shaqed*) and God's "watching" (*shoqed*) means that God was eager and ready to accomplish His word. The almond branch is associated with "planting" (cf. v. 10), and Jeremiah often describes the harmonious relationship between God and His people as an act of "planting" (18:9–10; 24:6; 31:27–28; 32:41; 42:10; cf. 2:21; 12:10). The term "watch" (*shaqad*) is a key word in Jeremiah. In 31:27–28, God says that as He had "watched" over His people to pluck up, tear down, destroy, and overthrow, so would He "watch over them to build and to plant." Here, the theme of "watching and planting" leads directly into the prophecy about God's new covenant with His people (vv. 29–34). Thus, while the literal sense of God's explanation of the almond branch is "I am *watching* my word, to carry it out," the context (cf. vv. 4–19) allows us to understand it as an allusion to God's promissory word: as watching overseer and Lord of history, He carries out His word, which means destroying the old (vv. 13–16)—the disobedient people and the broken covenant—and planting something new (vv. 11–12)—the new covenant with His remnant people (cf. 31:27–34).

Jeremiah's office as a prophet to the nations (1:5, 10) is described with specific regard to Judah and Jerusalem (v. 18). Here, Jeremiah is contrasted with the land, the kings, the princes, the priests, and the people of the land: he was to be a stronghold against the apostate Judah and Jerusalem (cf. 15:20). It is predicted that they would fight against him, but they would not prevail. God's presence would be with him to deliver him (1:19; cf. 37:11—38:28).

2:1—25:38
JUDGMENT AND CALL FOR CONVERSION TO JUDAH AND JERUSALEM

This first half of the book of Jeremiah contains seventeen sections concerning Judah and Jerusalem. It particularly addresses the people's faithlessness to the covenant with the Lord, His judgment against them, and His repeated calls for repentance.

2:1–37
God's Case against Israel

Considering its content, internal literary features, and the number and gender of the forms of address, this section is formally structured as two chiasms. Both call attention to God's legal case against Israel as wife (marriage) and as people (covenant):

A Wife: Israel's First Love Lost: A Disaster (vv. 1–3)

   B People: God's Lawsuit against Israel (vv. 4–13)

A′ Wife: Admonition of Israel: Foreign Oppression (vv. 14–19)

A Wife: Israel Goes After Alien Gods (vv. 20–28)

   B People: God Defends His Case against Israel (vv. 29–32)

A′ Wife: Israel's Innocence Contradicted by Evidence (vv. 33–37)

The feminine singular form addresses Jerusalem (v. 1) as a "woman" or "daughter" and Israel as God's "wife" (the metaphor of marriage dominates this passage). The masculine plural form addresses "the house of Jacob"/"the house of Israel" (v. 4). As a central city and sanctuary, Jerusalem represents the people, and the people represent Jerusalem's inhabitants and worshipers in her sanctuary.

2:1–3. Israel's First Love Lost: A Disaster. Jeremiah's account of the formal address to Jerusalem (v. 1) includes the house of Jacob and all the families of the house of Israel (v. 4). The unit consists of three parts. First, the Lord said that He remembered Israel, whereas Israel had "forgotten" the Lord (v. 32). When the Lord "remembers" His people, it is generally associated with His saving actions and is expressed, for example, in prayers for God's saving intervention (Ex. 32:13; Ps. 9:12; Jer. 15:15). However, in v. 2, the Lord's positive "remembrance" of Israel concerns only the distant past, and any positive future expectations it might raise are crushed by the abrupt indictment and judgment in v. 3.

Second, the Lord remembered His people's initial relationship with Him, their *khesed* ("kindness," "devotion," "faithfulness"), their love, and their willingness to follow Him. In response, He honored them by regarding them as holy to Him and the firstfruits of His *tebo'ah*— "revenue" or "increase"; in this context, it is sometimes rendered as "harvest" (i.e., Israel specifically belonged to Him; v. 3). These references concern Israel's distant past, the Exodus, Sinai, and God's protection in the wilderness. The Lord was loved in Israel's youth, at the time of their betrothal (Sinai), in the wilderness, and in a land not sown (v. 2). This theme is expanded in more detail in vv. 5–7b.

Third, the Lord's positive remembrance of Israel is abruptly contrasted in the text by the stirring and shocking judgment announced against those who would attack them (v. 3). The reasons for such an attack are explained in vv. 4–37. The reference to "following" or "going after" describes Israel's faithfulness to God (v. 2). Following or going after God (as a husband) or gods (as lovers) binds vv. 2–37 together (vv. 2, 5, 8, 23, 25). This term is associated with an act of loyalty that may still be seen in the Near East, where the wife literally walks behind her husband in recognition of his role as her "master" (ba'al).

The end of v. 3 implies that anyone mistreating Israel would be held guilty before God. The literal Hebrew text reads, "All that *eat it* will be guilty," with "it" referring to the "firstfruits," symbolizing Israel (v. 3b). The metaphor derives from the custom of setting aside the firstfruits only for the Lord (Lev. 23:9–14). If they were put to common use, the firstfruits were "profaned." Thus, if God's firstfruits (Israel) were "eaten" like common food (i.e., treated like any other nation), God would hold the adversary accountable because the holiness of Israel would be profaned. This theme is resumed and expanded in vv. 4–37.

Israel's status as "holy" and as God's "firstfruits" among the nations was conditioned by their faithfulness to the covenant (v. 3c). If they violated the covenant stipulations, God's holy temple in Jerusalem and their special role as His servants among the nations would both come to an end. The point of the unit is that God's intimate and beautiful memory of Israel's love and faithfulness (vv. 2–3b) would be overshadowed by the breaking of the covenant.

2:4–13. God's Lawsuit against Israel. Jeremiah continues with the judgment announced as a lawsuit against Israel, with indictment (vv. 5–8) and charges (vv. 9–13), and with an assertion that Israel had abandoned their God. This indictment frames the unit as a whole (vv. 5, 13) and develops the charge against Israel mentioned in Jeremiah's call (1:16). It also explains why the harmonious betrothal of Israel and the Lord had turned into judgment.

God initiated the procedure by asking what fault or injustice Israel's ancestors had found with God (2:5a). The answer was "None." Yet unfortunately, Israel had forgotten to follow Yahweh and

had turned to other gods (vv. 5b–8). These ideas are structured in a chiastic form:

A Follow (*halak akhar*) idols (v. 5b)
　B Where is the Lord? (v. 6)
　B' Where is the Lord? (v. 8a)
A Walk after (*halak akhare*) things that do not profit (v. 8b)

The expression "walk after" was used positively to refer to the young bride Israel who faithfully followed God (v. 2). In vv. 5–8, it is applied to Israel's marital infidelity. Israel had forgotten God's faithfulness, how He had delivered them out of Egypt and led them through the wilderness (v. 6), but God remembered Israel's initial fidelity (v. 2). They had defiled the land the Lord had given them (vv. 7–8), the land made holy by His presence (v. 3a–b). All the people had defiled the land by following idols. Jeremiah holds everyone responsible for the demise of the nation: priests, those who handle the law, rulers, and prophets (v. 8).

The lawsuit, based on the indictment (vv. 5–8), is introduced by "therefore" (*lakhen*; v. 9). The formal charges follow in vv. 9–13. The substance of the lawsuit (vv. 10–11) is that Israel had changed its God. The Lord appealed to common sense: no nation changes its gods (which are not gods), but this is what Israel had done to the Sovereign Lord (v. 11). He summoned the heavens as legal witnesses (v. 12) and restated Israel's crimes (v. 13). Verses 6–7 clearly imply that when the story of the land as a divine gift was lost (i.e., when Israel failed to remember Yahweh), the loss of the land soon followed.

2:14–19. Admonition of Israel: Foreign Oppression. These verses discuss the problem of the oppression of Israel by foreign powers. First, God asks why Israel is under foreign oppression (v. 14). The initial questions regarding whether Israel was a slave, or born a slave, may be answered with yes or no. In vv. 14–19, the answer is yes, for Israel had, in reality, become a servant/slave to the foreign nations. Looking at vv. 2–37 as a whole, however, the answer is no, for Israel was meant to be a much-loved nation holy to the Lord and the firstfruits of His revenue/harvest (vv. 2–3). Some translations follow the LXX in v. 20 and describe Israel as breaking off their yoke and bonds—which could be taken to refer to their rebellion and refusal to serve God, which is described in the rest of the verse. The MT, however, states that it is God ("I") who broke their yoke and bonds, which would probably refer to the deliverance from Egypt. Thus, the answer to the final question of why Israel was plundered is implied in the first two questions: oppression and slavery were not God's plan for Israel, but they resulted from Israel's choices.

Second, we find the description of the oppression (vv. 15–16). Assyria's power in its destruction of the lands of Israel (722 B.C.) and Judah (701 B.C.) is compared to that of lions roaring at their prey. (v. 15). Egypt is referred to as the people of Noph (Memphis) and Tahpanhes. The last part of the verse uses the verb *ra'ah*, which usually means "to feed" or "to graze," but is often interpreted as referring here to either breaking or shaving Israel's head (v. 16).

Third, the foreign oppression was Israel's own fault (vv. 17–19). The answer to the initial questions in v. 14 is confirmed: Israel had brought their oppression upon themselves by forsaking their God. Israel's faith in Assyria and Egypt is referred to as drinking from the waters of these superpowers (v. 18). Israel had forsaken the Lord, the spring and fountain of living waters, and instead had dug broken cisterns that could not hold water (v. 13). For forsaking their Lord, Israel would be disciplined and rebuked. The concluding messenger formula uses the name *yahweh tseba'ot* (v. 19)—translated variously as "the Lord of Hosts," "Lord of Armies," or "the Lord Almighty." This is the first use of the term in the book of Jeremiah, where it is a frequent name for Israel's God. It is commonly associated with the concept of God as King of the world.

2:20–28. Israel Goes After Alien Gods. In an exchange between Israel's self-indictments (vv. 20, 23, 25, 27) and God's responses, the pursuit of fertility religion is denounced as a shameful criminal offense. The intention of each of these arguments is to move Israel to repentance and to return to God, the central theme of 3:1—4:4.

The first self-indictment is Israel's response to God delivering them from Egypt. There is a manuscript difference in v. 20: Some Hebrew manuscripts have *lo"e'ebod*—"I will not serve," while others have *lo"e'ebor*—"I will not transgress." If the former is correct, Israel's refusal to "serve" God is seen in their widespread apostasy to fertility cults (v. 20c). The "high hill" was a country shrine for the Canaanite deity Baal. Its altitude pointed to Baal's heavenly home from which rains fell to water the land. Shrines were located under flourishing trees (i.e., as symbols of fertility). The religious practices in these shrines were essentially sexual. Being "married" to the Lord, Israel became a prostitute when she went after other gods.

Another indictment (v. 21) is that God planted His people as a special vine and a reliable seed (cf. Ps. 80:8–11), and consequently, there was no reason for them to turn into a degenerate, wild vine. They could not claim innocence because their crimes were obvious (Jer. 2:22–25). Vivid and dynamic symbols are used: the swift dromedary (v. 23) illustrates unreliability and aimless movement; the wild donkey (v. 24) illustrates lust-debased passion and seeking a partner with whom to fulfill urgent and animal passions. Similarly, Israel had lost all sense of direction and was driven by selfish lusts.

Yahweh Tseba'ot

The solemn title *yahweh tseba'ot* was associated with the ark of the covenant in the Jerusalem temple. Jeremiah's close connection with the temple and his frequent judgment speeches in and about it would make this well-known designation of God appealing to his audience.

1. Use in the Old Testament. Of the total occurrences of the term in the OT (ca. 285), 247 are found in the prophetic books. Eighty-two of these are found in Jeremiah, thus placing the book at the top of the list of occurrences. A number of passages underscore that this is God's name (31:35;

35:18–19; 50:34; 51:19, 57), which is associated with His roles as "the God of Israel" (35:18–19; 50:18; 51:33) and Judah (v. 5) as well as the King of the nations (46:18; 51:57).

2. Meaning of the Name. The name of God (Heb. *Yahweh*) is translated "the Lord" in the LXX and in most Bible translations. The Hebrew epithet *tseba'ot* derives from *tsaba'* ("host," "army"), but its meaning is unclear. Various suggestions have been made, but the most attractive possibility is that it refers to angels or divine messengers (Gen. 1:26; 32:1–2; Josh. 5:14; 1 Kin. 22:19;

Ps. 82; Is. 6). The "hosts" or "armies" of servants surrounding the throne of God would then illustrate the royal power of God (Jer. 8:19; 10:10; 46:18; 48:15; 51:57); hence, some translations render the term as "the Lord Almighty."

3. *Cultic Significance.* The general function of the epithet *Yahweh tseba'ot* is rooted in its cultic significance. It was used in Shiloh (1 Sam. 1:3, 11) and was closely connected with the ark in the sanctuary (1 Sam. 6:4). The ark was a wooden box overlaid with gold, surmounted by the golden "mercy seat" or "atonement cover" with two golden cherubim on either end (Ex. 25:17–22). It was a symbol of God's throne, but since He is not visible, He is said to be enthroned between the cherubim. The two cherubim on the ark probably symbolized the host of God's servants (messengers, armies) forming His heavenly council. The epithet is also associated with the covenant because the ark contained the two stone tablets that Moses placed there (1 Kin. 8:9; cf. Ex. 25:16, 21). From Shiloh, the ark was eventually moved to the house of Abinadab, then to the city of David, and finally to the temple in Jerusalem (1 Sam. 7:1; 2 Sam. 6:1–15; 1 Kin. 8:1–13).

The people's attitude turned into resignation and continued rebellion (v. 25). The text presents the shameful idolatry of the nation (cf. v. 8) as ridiculed by the absence of life in the images of the gods (v. 26). What a shame to refer to a tree as father and a stone as mother while turning their backs on their Lord (v. 27; cf. Is. 44:9–20)! In the times of trouble awaiting Judah, the nation would be destroyed due to its unfaithfulness and the powerlessness of its false gods to save (v. 28).

2:29–32. God Defends His Case against Israel. After God declared His intention to bring an accusation (*rib*, "conduct a lawsuit") against Israel (v. 9), He asked why Israel was bringing an accusation (*rib*) against Him (v. 29). The foreign oppression generated accusations against God for not remaining faithful to the covenant, but such claims are refuted. All Israel had transgressed against the Lord (vv. 28–29). God had chastened Israel in vain. They accepted no correction and killed His prophets (v. 30). Jeremiah appealed to them not only to hear the word but also to see its reality and fulfillment (v. 31a).

God denied that He had been a desert or darkness to Israel (v. 31), for in reality, He had led Israel through these dangers (v. 6). The real issue was why the people declared their unwillingness to return to God and why they proclaimed "*radnu*," which could mean "We are lords," "We are free to roam," or as the LXX reads, "We will not be ruled over." The main point is clear—the people were claiming their independence from God. Israel was oppressed because they had forsaken God as their Lord and had made themselves lords by worshiping idols made by their own hands.

A virgin cannot forget her ornaments, nor a bride her attire (v. 32a). A husband's provision of ornaments and attire for his wife at their wedding ceremony represented the honor and new status of the woman. Since God had bestowed His honor upon Israel (vv. 2–3, 6–7), she should have been devoted to Him, yet she had forgotten Him (v. 32b).

2:33–37. Israel's Innocence Contradicted by Evidence. The rebuttal of Israel's claim to innocence in vv. 20–28 returns in vv. 33–37 with verbal links in the Hebrew (which are not clear in all English versions): (a) *derek*—"way," "manner" (vv. 23 [2x], 33 [2x], 36); (b) *'akhabah*—"love" (vv. 25, 33); (c) *matsa'*—"find" (vv. 24, 26 [some translations have "caught" or "discovered" here], 34 [x2—some translations have "catch" in the latter part of the verse]); and (d) *bosh*—"shame" (vv. 26, 36 [x2—some translations have "disappointed"]). Israel's claim to innocence was framed by judgment (vv. 33–37). Thus, 2:1–37 begins and ends with the theme of "love" (the love of betrothal versus the "love" of prostitution, vv. 2, 33) and the execution of judgment (vv. 3c–d, 36b–37).

Claiming innocence, Israel believed that God was not angry with them (v. 35a). However, evidence reveals that the Israelites sought love by prostitution (v. 33) and that they had oppressed the innocent, as the blood on their skirts indicated (v. 34). God's covenant protected the poor and the innocent, while the fertility cults turned "love" into sexual lust. In the face of the evidence, God would plead His case with unfaithful Israel (v. 35c–d). According to some interpretations of the Hebrew, God was reproaching His people for "taking so lightly"

(Heb. *zalal*) the need to change their ways (v. 36a). Others render the verse according to the verb *'azal* ("go about," "go away"), which results in a question regarding why Israel was going around changing their ways.

The section concludes with judgment (vv. 36b–37). Israel would be ashamed of (or disappointed in) Egypt just as much as they were of Assyria. The reference to hands placed on the head refers to captivity and death (Egyptian reliefs depicting warfare show prisoners of war or those about to be killed with arms upheld in a position of self-protection). Israel would not prosper with the support of these allies because God had rejected these nations (cf. 46:1—51:58). No ally could accomplish anything without permission from the Lord of the nations (cf. 1:10).

3:1—4:4
The Return of Unfaithful Israel

Following the indictments against God's people (2:1–37), a passionate plea for repentance and return to the Lord appears next, with a promise of restoration (3:1—4:4). It is only thereafter that judgment is declared (4:5—6:30).

3:1–5. Return to Me, Unfaithful Wife. The wife's return to her husband after belonging to another man would have raised a legal issue. The law stipulated that a divorced wife who had married another man could not return to her first husband (Deut. 24:1–4). A transgression of this law was a serious sin that polluted or defiled the land that had been made holy by God's presence. Jeremiah quotes this law in condensed form and as a popular custom, but he shifts the emphasis. The law prohibited the husband from "taking her back" as his wife, but the question in Jeremiah 3:1 is whether the husband could lawfully return to his wife whom he had divorced. The question is whether God's acceptance of Israel was proper or not. Though Israel was the estranged wife, God was asking her to return because of His loving forgiveness. Although Israel had been unfaithful, with many lovers (cf. 2:2–37), God still (3:1) wanted her back. This powerful expression of God's grace should have had a strong persuasive impact on Jeremiah's audience. The yearning of God for His people makes Him risk even the apparent dishonor of receiving His unfaithful wife back. Thus, Jeremiah echoes Hosea regarding the depth of God's love for Israel and anticipates the gospel in the NT where God's grace, not the law, is the way of salvation. The implied message is

that God assumes responsibility for our transgression of the law on the basis of His compassion. He could offer forgiveness to the people as their rejected Husband—something that many human husbands would not do.

The Lord made all Israel aware of their infidelity. His wife's unfaithfulness and wickedness had defiled the land, resulting in a sustained drought and shortage of food (vv. 2–3, 5b). She had acted like a harlot—without shame (3:3b). She ignored the outcome of her disobedience (i.e., the drought), which should have convinced her of God's power. Baal supposedly brought rain and fruitfulness, but God proved His sovereignty by withholding the rain (v. 3).

The unit ends with a summary reproach against the people for their evil words and deeds (v. 5b). Verses 2–3 describe what they had done and vv. 4–5a what they had said. Some translations suggest (v. 4) that God directs another plea for repentance to His people. However, if v. 5a continues the people's speech in v. 4, then that verse can be understood as God's way of ironically reproaching them for their treacherous way of speaking (i.e., for feigning faithfulness to the Lord while, in reality, being unfaithful). The Hebrew word *'allup* has been translated as "guide" or "friend" in v. 4. It may also be translated "Did not you then call Me: 'My Father, you are the husband of my youth?'" (cf. 2:2). The cry "My Father" characterizes the language of worship, whether of idols (2:27) or of the Lord (3:19b). Thus, God's quotation of the people's words in vv. 4–5a is a reproach for their syncretistic hypocrisy. They wanted both the old covenant promises and the new attractions of fertility worship. By saying one thing (vv. 4–5a) and doing another (vv. 2–3), they were breaking the covenant but continuing to claim the blessing of harmony with God.

3:6–11. Israel's and Judah's Past Refusals to Return. This prose unit may be dated between Jeremiah's call (627 B.C.) and the death of Josiah (609 B.C.). It develops the theme of 3:1–5 through the use of repeated terms: (a) "backsliding/faithlessness," "return," "turn" (*shub*; vv. 6, 7, 8, 10, 11; cf. v. 1); (b) *zanah*—variously rendered in translations as "to act immorally," "act like a prostitute," or "commit adultery" (vv. 6, 9; cf. vv. 1, 2, 3); (c) "divorce" (*shalakh*; v. 8; cf. v. 1); and (d) "defile" (*khanep*; v. 9; cf. vv. 1–2).

This unit starts with an account of the evil apostasy of Israel (the Hebrew word *meshubah* used to describe it derives from *shub*, "turn," "return," "repent"). The Northern Kingdom of

Israel had utterly apostatized and defiled the land (vv. 6, 9), and its destruction by Assyria in 722 B.C. was the punishment. Although God, through the prophets, invited them to return to Him, Israel refused to comply (v. 7). This ended God's covenant with the kingdom of Israel (v. 8). God then reproaches Israel's sister, the "treacherous" or "faithless" Judah (vv. 7–11). Judah failed to learn lessons from the experience of Israel and committed the same mistakes (vv. 8, 10). Therefore, Judah had less of an excuse than Israel (v. 11).

3:12–18. Israel and Judah Summoned to Return. God first turned to the Northern Kingdom (Israel) because it was "more righteous" than the Southern Kingdom (Judah), who did not learn from Israel's experience (v. 11). He commanded Jeremiah to proclaim the merciful message to Israel to return (vv. 12–13). The territory of the Northern Kingdom came under the control of Judah during the days of Josiah (2 Kin. 23:15–20), following the decline of Assyria. If 3:1—4:4 originated during Jeremiah's early ministry and in connection with Josiah's reform (see Jeremiah: Introduction), an invitation to return to the Lord would therefore have included the northerners. They were invited to respond to Josiah's call to return to the Lord.

The distinction between Israel and Judah, which was vital in vv. 6–13, is now abolished. God took a more personal and intimate approach in the invitation to return by addressing them as faithless or backsliding children (vv. 14, 22), which implied that He was their Father and God (cf. v. 19). God's call to Israel was based on the fact that He was married to them (v. 14). With the covenant in place, based on His grace and the people's repentance, God promised hope for His people. The appeal in vv. 14–18 contains a plan for the restoration of God's people. They would return to worship God in Zion; the reference to "one from a city/town" may signify the city elder, and "two from a family/clan" might refer to a married couple (v. 14). Their shepherds (kings and elders) would feed them with knowledge and understanding (v. 15), and the families were to multiply and increase (v. 16a). The ark of the covenant of the Lord would no longer be present (according to an ancient tradition, it was secreted away before the final fall of Jerusalem in 586 B.C.). Instead, God Himself was to be present. Jerusalem would be called the Throne of the Lord, and the name of the Lord was to be attached to it (vv. 16b–17a; cf. Rev. 21:22–23). God's sovereignty would be acknowledged by all

nations (cf. Rev. 21:24–26). They would gather in Jerusalem and follow His law (Jer. 3:17; cf. 4:2; Is. 2:2–4; Mic. 4:1–4). Peace and reconciliation would prevail, and Judah and Israel would reunite in the promised land (Jer. 3:18).

3:19—4:4. Implications of a Return. This unit interacts with 3:1–18 through key terms such as "children" (some translations have "people"; vv. 19, 21, 22; cf. v. 14), "heritage," "inheritance" (v. 19; cf. v. 18), "desolate [or barren] heights" (v. 21; cf. v. 2), "reproach," "shame" (v. 25; cf. v. 3), "obey"/"hear" (v. 25; cf. v. 13), and variant forms of "turn" (Heb. *shub*) throughout the entire section. The theme of the section is "turning to the Lord," and it is developed from four different angles: (a) turning to the Lord is the foundation of the covenant (v. 19); (b) Israel's adultery is healed by turning to the Lord (vv. 20–22b); (c) Israel's prayer of penitence is the path toward turning to the Lord (vv. 22b–25); (d) Israel's failure was their "turning" (*shub*) away from God and toward the fertility gods, but their healing also comes from their "turning" (*shub*) toward God. This is about the direction our lives are heading, and there are only two options: toward or away from the Lord. The consequence of returning to the Lord is that He will fulfill His promise to Abraham (4:2, cf. Gen. 12:1–3) when all the nations will pronounce blessings by God and will glory or "boast" in Him.

This unit (Jer. 4:3–4) concludes the call to repentance and return found in 3:1—4:4 and introduces a lengthy section on judgment (4:5—6:30). Two metaphors are used to illustrate the need for changing hard hearts: sowing in good, broken soil (cf. Hos. 10:12; Matt. 13:1–23) and the circumcision of the heart. Failure to do this inevitably results in judgment. God's holiness and rejection of evil are described through the symbol of an anger that would burn with such intensity that no one could quench it (see "The Wrath of God," p. 918).

4:5—6:30

The Divine Judgment

God's case against unfaithful Judah (2:1–37) is followed by repeated calls for repentance and returning to Him (3:1—4:4). Subsequently, the text develops the theme of judgment (4:5—6:30): God's reaction to the covenant violations of His people in Judah (see Jeremiah: Introduction).

4:5–10. Destruction from the North. In this unit, the language of warfare is used to warn Judah and Jerusalem about the importance of seeking shelter (vv. 5–6a). The Lord's invasion from the north would cause massive destruction: the land would become abandoned, and the cities uninhabited (vv. 6b–7). The people would lament and wail because of the fierce anger of the Lord (v. 8; cf. v. 4). The identity of the northern invader is unclear. Both Assyrian and Babylonian armies were seen as coming from the north. The metaphor of a lion (v. 7) would fit Babylon since this symbol was prominent in Nebuchadnezzar's palace. The point of the unit is that the Lord would send the invader because of the broken covenant.

The priests and the prophets had falsely promised peace to Judah (cf. 6:14; 8:11). Yet Jeremiah states that it was God who had deceived the people by promising peace (v. 10). This may be explained in various ways: (a) Jeremiah may have been interceding for the people, expressing before the Lord what they believed (even he had questions about God's judgment; cf. 12:1); (b) he may have held God responsible for allowing the deceptive prophecies to be given; or (c) he may have mocked the talk of "peace," when, in reality, what was coming was destruction by the "sword." The two best possibilities are (a) and (b); Jeremiah's point, however, is the tension he experiences between loyally delivering God's words of judgment and praying that it might be averted. In this regard, Jeremiah's attitude resembles that of Moses (cf. Ex. 32).

4:11–31. Winds of War, Woe, and Disaster. This unit opens using images of wind and winnowing to describe the harsh judgment of the invaders (vv. 11–12). The swiftness of the attackers, expressed through images of clouds, a whirlwind, and eagles, elicits a cry of woe from the people of Judah (v. 13). In response, Jeremiah announced that to be saved, Jerusalem would have to cleanse their hearts from evil (v. 14). The Lord attributed the judgment to the city herself (vv. 17b–18). This is a poignant example of Jeremiah's powerful prophetic poetry. In rapid succession, he presents multiple distinct images, hoping to persuade Judah to return to the Lord and avoid the threat of judgment. Verses 19–32 could be grouped into three subunits.

1. Destruction and Anguish—God's Lamentation over His People (vv. 19–22). The sound of the trumpet announced the alarm of war, followed by deep anguish. In the prophecy, the destruction moves closer, beginning with the whole land, then the tents, and finally the sheltering curtains (v. 20). Death is approaching in a dramatic way,

and its anticipation causes fear and anxiety—hopelessness. This personal anguish is contrasted with God's grief over His people. He laments their foolishness, their lack of understanding and knowledge of Him, their astuteness in regard to evil, and their ignorance regarding how to do good (v. 22). Knowing God and acting in harmony with God's values is a central theme in Jeremiah (see Jeremiah: Introduction).

2. Judgment as De-creation (vv. 23–28). The effects of the prophesied invasion were clearly seen by the prophet (the phrase "I beheld" or "I looked" is repeated four times). In the prophecy, judgment reinstates an absence of order: the earth was formless and void, or empty; the heavens had no light (v. 23); the mountains quaked, and all the hills moved to and fro (v. 24); there were no people (Heb. *'adam*); all the birds of the heavens had fled (v. 25); the fruitful land was deserted, and all its cities were destroyed (v. 26). A surprising statement is suddenly made: God promised that the destruction would not be complete (v. 27). This is a marked deviation from the relentless onslaught of judgment. Although the Lord announced devastation, He yearned for His people. This divine yearning was the source of hope for Judah. God had plans to create a new community through whom His mission in the world would be achieved.

3. Desolation, Contempt, and Wailing (vv. 29–31). The invaders would desolate all the cities of Judah (v. 29). After the plundering, the prostitute wife Israel/Zion would no longer be attractive, and her lovers would not only despise her but would also seek her life; she was to be like a woman wailing in labor or in fear of murderers (v. 31).

5:1–19. Indictment and Pardon. God challenged the prophet to find one person in Jerusalem executing *mishpat*—"judgment" or "justice," and seeking the truth. He would pardon the city for the sake of one person (v. 1). In the case of Sodom (Gen. 18:22–32), the condition for saving the city was to find ten righteous people. God's stated condition here to Jerusalem was less than what He required of Sodom, underscoring Jerusalem's utter depravity (cf. Jer. 23:14). Jeremiah was forewarned that even if someone swears to tell the truth, he probably swears falsely (5:2). As Jeremiah went searching, he realized that neither the poor (vv. 3–4) nor the powerful (v. 5)—the entire city—met the criteria of righteousness. This confirmed their refusal to return to the Lord.

The word "therefore" introduces the judgment (v. 6). It is described by metaphors of ferocious beasts (lion, wolf, and leopard) that would strike down, devastate, and lie in wait for the cities of Judah to tear into pieces everyone trying to escape. This judgment was a response to the increased transgressions and backslidings of the people. Verses 1-6 intensify the description of both the nation's many crimes and the cruelty of the judgment. In the midst of this, however, God spoke, still ready to pardon the repentant (v. 1). God's word in vv. 7-9 is the core of the dialogue. He asked how He could forgive the people for what they had done. The implied answer here is the impossibility of pardon. After a detailed and vivid outline of the people's violation of the covenant, God concluded by asking whether He should not punish and take vengeance upon His people (v. 9; cf. v. 29). Thus, while judgment was inevitable, God desperately looked for a way to pardon His people. But they gave Him no valid option.

The Lord's indictment of His people continues (vv. 11-13, 19), His judgment predicted in realistic and vivid terms (vv. 14-17). However, the judgment is framed by God's firm decision that He would not completely destroy Judah and Jerusalem (vv. 10, 18; cf. 4:10). Speaking of His people as a vine (cf. 2:21-22), He placed parameters on the execution of His judgment (5:10). Here, the judgment takes on the nature of pruning and removing what is alien, with the vine left to grow new branches. The grounds for this caveat to the judgment is God's love for His people and His never-ending hope that a faithful remnant would return to Him. Through them, God's plan for Israel's new future would be carried out (cf. 29:10-14; 31:1—33:26).

The Lord announced that the result of Israel's unfaithfulness would not be extermination but exile. This is underlined by connecting unfaithfulness with the coming exile (5:19b). Judah's exile would be caused by her having served other gods—a covenant term that includes loyalty, worship, moral behavior, and lifestyle—and by her forsaking the Lord—another reference to the covenant that is related to the metaphor of marriage (cf. 2:2-3). Going after alien lovers (cf. 3:1) led to an alien marriage, and this choice had brought Israel into an alien land without God's promise and provision. The hope of liberation from exile lay in returning to God, the One who would provide a future for Israel.

According to 4:10, the people were deceived not only by false prophets who promised them peace but also by the Lord, who confirmed their willingness to believe the lie. This theme is resumed in vv. 12-13. Deceived by false prophets (v. 13), all Israel concluded that God would not be the agent of the judgment and that no evil would come upon them (vv. 11-12). This mockery of the Lord completely denied His authority and right to judge His people, but it freed God from the allegation that He had deceived them.

5:20-31. The Foolish Heart of God's People. This unit develops various aspects of the people's failure, providing reasons for the inevitable judgment. The admonition to "hear" announces an instruction that Israel was to accept. But they were "without understanding" or "senseless" (lit. "without heart" or "mindless"; the Hebrew word *leb* includes intellectual as well as emotional connotations). Seeing and hearing leads to "a heart of wisdom" (e.g., Ps. 90:12; Prov. 8:5; 16:23; 21:11), while having eyes/ears but neither seeing nor hearing indicates foolishness (Jer. 5 21; cf. Prov. 16:22-23; Is. 6:9-10). God's call to Israel was to "hear" and "love their God with all their heart" (Deut. 6:4-5). The people's recalcitrant and rebellious hearts (Jer. 5:23) were challenged through a hymn that praises the power and greatness of the Creator (v. 22), using motifs found also in Isaiah (40:12-17; 44:21-28) and Job (5:8-15; 9:5-10). God rules over His creation (cf. Gen. 1:1-2, 9-10). The people foolishly did not fear the Lord, which they should have done since He, and no one else, gave them life. Only He, not the fertility gods whom the people were serving, was able to provide both rain and harvest (Jer. 5:24).

When the heart is empty of the word of God, His life-giving blessings are turned away (v. 25), there is a ruthless lack of love and care for one's neighbor (vv. 26-27), and people hoard riches while failing to show compassion to the poor and needy (vv. 27-28). Thus, Jeremiah connects the commandment to love God with all of one's heart (Deut. 6:4-5) with the commandment to love one's neighbor as oneself (Lev. 19:18; cf. Matt. 22:34-40). Jesus endorsed Jeremiah's teaching that the fear of God (Jer. 5:22, 24) unlocks divine truth and fullness of life (cf. Matt. 22:37-40). Such reverential fear is part of the eternal gospel proclaimed by the first angel to all peoples on earth (Rev. 14:6-7). The passage concludes with a question to Israel: "What will you do in the end?" (v. 31). The "end" (*'akharit*) includes the temporal sense of "future" as well as the logical sense of "outcome" (cf. Deut. 32:20; Jer. 17:11). But this term may also signify "posterity" or "remnant" (Num. 24:20; Ps. 109:13; Ezek. 23:25; Dan. 11:4).

Israel needed to hear the word of the Lord, return to Him, and be saved; if they would not listen, the outcome would be disaster (cf. Jer. 5:21).

6:1–8. Saving a Remnant. The people (lit. "children") of Benjamin were urged to flee from Jerusalem (v. 1). Benjamin represents all Israel. Since Tekoa and Beth Haccerem were located south and west of Jerusalem, and Benjamin was to the north, the warning was to be sounded around the city (v. 3). In warfare, provision could be made for some people in a city under attack to be spared from the killing and destruction (cf. Josh. 6:22–25), which would make it possible for a small remnant to survive. The faithful were warned to escape, but the vast majority (the unfaithful) would face destruction.

The record of the predicted invasion opens with an unexpected image. The daughter of Zion (Jerusalem) is presented as an attractive and delicate woman (Jer. 5:2; cf. 2:2). The foreign rulers (shepherds) she had courted would come and dwell around her with their people—though not for her pleasure but in hostility and for plunder (6:3), with the intention of destroying the city. The record communicates urgency and ruthlessness; attacking at noon and continuing into the evening and through the night was unusual (vv. 4–5). The invasion would be an act of God, for He commanded the shepherds to make preparations to besiege the city, and it is He who identified Jerusalem to the invaders. God again brings a stern indictment against the oppression and wickedness in Jerusalem's midst (vv. 6–7).

The prophet finally turns to Jerusalem. He appeals for her to be instructed, take warning, and change, lest God depart from her and she become desolate (v. 8). There was still an opportunity for repentance. Because of God's love for His people, the judgment brings Him great sorrow. Even if the judgment had to come, the passage as a whole contains subtle hints at the escape of a faithful remnant and a restored covenant. God's relentless love is always seeking to preserve humanity.

6:9–15. The Judgment Caused by Israel's Refusal to Hear. This partial dialogue between God and His prophet resembles 5:1–9. The sequence of speakers is the same: the Lord (vv. 1–2; 6:9), Jeremiah (5:3–6; 6:10), and the Lord (5:7–9; 6:11–15). The same key words and themes occur: "the streets of Jerusalem" (*khutsot*) and "outside" or "the street" (*khuts*; 5:1; 6:11); the crime of falsehood (*sheqer*; 5:2; 6:13); the "great" or "leaders" (*gadol*) among the people (5:5; 6:13); and the judgment labeled as "punishment" (*peqad*; 5:9; 6:15). The judgment in 6:12–15 also points forward to 8:10–12.

God first described the remnant of Israel as a vine to be reaped and thoroughly gleaned (6:9; cf. 2:21; 5:10). In this metaphor of judgment, God admonished the grape gatherer to relentlessly continue harvesting. Jerusalem and Judah together are called a "remnant of Israel" (6:9), which is language that recalls the destruction of the Northern Kingdom of Israel (722 B.C.). As stated in Isaiah 6:12–13, Judah and Jerusalem were then left as a remnant of God's people, Israel. A thorough gleaning of the vine does not preclude the preservation of a remnant. God sought to warn the people and to bring them to repentance, but they refused to listen. Their ears were closed (lit. "uncircumcised")—that is, they were not committed to God—and consequently, they could not receive the word of the Lord (Jer. 6:10; cf. 5:21). It was displeasing and offensive to them, for its content condemned and corrected them (6:10).

The Wrath of God

The biblical language of the wrath of God needs to be understood in its proper context. In Jeremiah, three things should be noted about such language.

1. Wrath, Infidelity, and Rejection. God's anger is rooted in the metaphor of a betrayed father and an abandoned husband. The infidelity and rejection by His beloved people wounds God's heart, and this wounded love manifests itself in anger as an expression of deep feelings. These metaphorical expressions should not be taken to mean that God's anger is exactly like human anger (cf. Is. 55:8–9; Hos. 11:9) but rather to show the similarities of His evaluative and emotional response—which is based on His eternal character—to their apostasy. Human anger usually comes from natural, sinful, and selfish motives, but God's anger comes from His loving, just, and merciful character. The law played an important function in the life of the covenant people, but they did not establish a relationship with an impersonal law. The covenant was the expression of the disposition of the heart of a redeemed people to remain in a permanent and personal relationship with the Lord. In interpersonal relationships, what a person does or does not do can hurt others. In the covenant relationship, God has a deep respect for His people, and when their actions hurt His loving heart, His love reaches them in the form of disciplinary anger. In such cases, the Lord expects them to return to Him (i.e., to repent).

2. Wrath and Covenant. God's covenant agreement with Israel was a legal contract that included certain lawful punitive measures to be applied to a disloyal partner (see "Covenant," p. 905). Thus, God's anger was part of this contract, in the context of which it represents the discipline applied by the sovereign partner to the violators of the covenant. This was done in order to maintain the spiritual and social order that was created when the covenant relationship was first established. This covenant, based on God's redemptive grace, created a sphere of safety and blessings for His people. When the covenant was violated, the individuals had abandoned the sphere of blessing and, from the legal perspective, they entered the realm of chaos and disorder. But this was not the end of the covenant. God was always ready to direct His anger against Israel's oppressors and against their pride and evil deeds. In such cases, divine wrath brought salvation to His people and destruction on their enemies (Jer. 46:1—51:58).

3. Wrath, Holiness, and Righteousness. God's holiness is like a burning fire that consumes impurity and sin. His righteousness designates His right and lawful actions that are always inseparable from His love. Love is God's faithfulness, grace, and goodness. In Jeremiah, these character traits of God are kept in balance. As an outpouring of righteousness, God's anger (judgment) deals with Israel's guilt for breaking the covenant. As an outpouring of holiness, God's anger is a burning fire that consumes sin and moral defilement. As an outpouring of His love, God's anger is His emotional reaction to the betrayal and rejection by His beloved people. However, since God's love towards the faithful remnant of Israel continues beyond His anger, love dominates His character. The revelation of the supremacy of God's love is found at the heart of the gospel of Jesus Christ, who took upon Himself our violation of the covenant and reconciled us with God (cf. John 3:16–17; 2 Cor. 5:14–21).

The judicial sentence was an expression of God's wrath, which He could not hold in any longer (v. 11). The sentence was an outpouring of His anger on all the people (vv. 11–13). The metaphor of the gleaning of the vine in v. 9 is now explained. Their houses, fields, and wives would be taken by others when God stretched out His hand against the inhabitants of Judah. The Lord said that all of them were given to greed (v. 13), coveting houses, fields, and wives (cf. Deut. 5:21). In the application of the principle of retribution, they would lose houses, fields, and wives (Jer. 6:12). Covetousness, or greed, destroys our inner peace because our trust is placed on the ephemeral instead of on the eternal.

The unit (vv. 9–15) concludes with attention to particulars (vv. 13–15), including God's condemnation of the prophets and priests for proclaiming false messages of peace to the people (cf. 4:10; 5:12–13; 8:11, 15). Because of their shameless actions, He would punish them.

6:16–30. Judgment as "the Fruit of Their Thoughts." God's efforts to save His people had been rejected (v. 16). The people had refused to listen to His prophets (v. 17; cf. v. 27). Therefore, God resumed the lawsuit and invited an assembly of the nations and the earth to be His witnesses (vv. 18–19). The coming judgment was to be the fruit of their *makhashaboh*—"thoughts," "intentions," or "schemes"—brought by their rejection of the covenant and His law/instruction (torah), which gives life (cf. Ps. 19:7–9). The people had replaced God's word with the performance of temple rituals (Jer. 6:20), but God rejected all of this. They relied on their wealth and material possessions that required no demands for obedience. According to the covenant, obedience to religious ceremonies should not be separated from total submission to the Lord and to His social and moral requirements (cf. 1 Sam. 15:22–23; Hos. 6:6; Amos 5:21–24; Matt. 9:13; 12:7).

Based on this indictment, Jeremiah conveys the Lord's pronouncement of judgment (Jer. 6:21). Instead of Israel walking in the old paths— the good way (for it would give them rest for their souls; v. 16)—God would put stumbling blocks or obstacles in their way, and they would stagger and fall. Here, Jeremiah skillfully contrasts the true covenant with idolatry. Israel was invited to an obedient walk: "old paths" and true obedience to God's word lead to life (vv. 16–19), but ritual activities linked to unfaithfulness are "stumbling blocks" that lead to death (vv. 20–21). God's judgment (4:5—6:30) ends here with a repetition of the invasion of the enemy from the north (6:22–26; cf. 4:5–10) and a reminder of His call to Jeremiah to test Israel's ways (6:27; cf. 1:17–19). The crimes of the people are confirmed, and the verdict is that God has rejected them as rejected silver (6:28–30).

7:1—8:3
Jeremiah's Temple Sermon

This section is probably the clearest statement of the basic themes of the book of Jeremiah. The Temple Sermon has been dated to 609 B.C., in the early reign of Jehoiakim (26:1). The prophet was in deep conflict with the official temple ideology on which Judah relied, and his position was regarded as treason (cf. v. 11). The king and his establishment assumed that Jerusalem could not be violated because God's promises were unconditional. In Jeremiah's day, the royal tradition linked to the temple (cf. Ps. 132:6–10; Is. 37:33–35) had become distorted. Many claimed that the presence of God's throne restricted His judgment against disobedient Israel. This was the grave error Jeremiah attacked in his sermon. The theme is worship (true and false), which necessarily involved the temple. The key word "place" (Heb.

maqom) ties the sermon together (7:3, 6, 12, 14, 20, 32 [sometimes translated as "room"]; 8:3).

7:1–15. True and False Worship. The setting for this speech was the New Gate, which connected the inner and outer temple courts (cf. 26:10). The messenger formula (7:3) names God as *yahweh tseba'ot*, which is translated variously as "Lord of Hosts," "Lord Almighty," or (perhaps most literally) "Lord of Armies," which was associated with the ark of the covenant and the temple (see *"Yahweh Tseba'ot,"* p. 912). The sermon began with an exhortation to correct their ways and actions (7:3). It targeted the deceitful royal temple ideology (v. 4). The first argument for the exhortation summarized the covenant principles: fairness in judgment, care for the poor and needy, justice in the temple court (desisting from shedding innocent blood, that is, capital punishment inflicted on innocents), and rejecting idolatry (vv. 5–6). The second argument was a promise to let Judah dwell in the land given to their fathers (v. 7). However, the promise was conditional (i.e., its fulfillment depended on faithfulness to the covenant).

The Lord indicted the people who trusted in worthless lies (vv. 8–11). He challenged his audience with two questions. The first described the perpetrators, providing a sample of Judah's violations of at least five of the Ten Commandments (v. 9). Despite their flagrant and shameful crimes, Judah had the nerve to come before God to claim the covenant promises of salvation (vv. 9–10). God's second question concerned the compatibility of the temple with God's holiness: it had become a den of thieves. The expression "den of thieves/robbers" figuratively refers to a gathering of lawbreakers (see Matt. 21:13). God testified that He had seen it (v. 11). The One worshiped in the temple was Himself the witness. God predicted judgment against Judah (vv. 12–15). It began with a lesson from Shiloh. Judah was

Shiloh

Shiloh in Ephraim was the first dwelling place for the ark of the covenant in the promised land (cf. Josh. 18:1). The ark remained in Shiloh for many years, and the sanctuary in Shiloh was considered to be "God's house" (Judg. 18:31). Following the capture of the ark by the Philistines, it was moved to Kirjath Jearim and stayed in the house of Abinadab for twenty years (1 Sam. 4:1—7:2). Then David moved it to Zion (2 Sam. 6), and finally, Solomon relocated it to the temple in Jerusalem (1 Kin. 8:1–13). It appears that the name *Yahweh tseba'ot* (see notes on 7:3; cf. 2:14–19) was first used in Shiloh (1 Sam. 1:3; 4:4; cf. notes on Jer. 2:19). In Shiloh, the Lord revealed Himself through His word (1 Sam. 3:21), but it was also a place of priestly abuse (1 Sam. 2:12–17, 22–25) and idolatry (1 Sam. 7:3–4).

Among the prophets, only Jeremiah uses Shiloh as a symbol of God's judgment, which he did when speaking to all of Judah in the temple (7:12, 14; 26:6, 9). The historical books do not directly speak about God's judgment against Shiloh, but Psalm 78 does (vv. 56–64). The psalm describes Israel's having broken the covenant after entering Canaan and how God in His anger deserted the sanctuary of Shiloh and gave His strength and His glory (the ark) into the hands of the enemy (vv. 60–61), referring to the time the Philistines took the ark (1 Sam. 4:1—7:2). The psalm's description of the event closely resembles Jeremiah's judgment speeches (Ps. 78:62–64). The psalm ends with God's rejection of Ephraim (where Shiloh was situated) and His election of the tribe of Judah and His beloved Mount Zion, where "He built His sanctuary like the heights, like the earth," which He has established forever (vv. 67–69). Thus, Shiloh was associated with God's departure from both His sanctuary and His people, His judgment against Israel, and His selection of Zion/Jerusalem for the permanent location of the temple. The symbol of Shiloh was, therefore, particularly meaningful to Jeremiah. Since Judah had turned away from God, God would turn away from the temple as He had done with Shiloh (Jer. 7:14). Instead of learning from the past, the royal establishment was infuriated by the comparison between Jerusalem and Shiloh and sought to kill Jeremiah (26:6, 9).

admonished to notice how God had punished Shiloh because of the wickedness of its people (v. 12). If Shiloh's example would not lead to repentance, the same punishment would be given to Judah (v. 14).

The indictment leading to judgment (v. 13) recalls the accusations in vv. 5–6 and 8–12. God, through His prophets, had been addressing Judah, speaking earnestly and continuously (lit. "rising early and speaking"), but Judah refused to answer His call (v. 13). The temple in Jerusalem would meet the same fate as the temple in Shiloh (v. 14). God would remove Judah from His presence, as He did with the Northern Kingdom of Israel in 722 B.C. (v. 15). God would throw Judah away from Him, as He did with all the descendants of Ephraim (cf. Gen. 48:14–16; Jer. 31:9). The temple building on which Judah had placed its trust (7:4) would be destroyed, and the glory (i.e., the Lord) would depart from Israel (cf. 1 Sam. 4:19–22). This sermon would have shocked the audience.

7:16–20. The Queen of Heaven. In the Hebrew text, this unit opens with a shift in perspective from the people to the person of Jeremiah (cf. 1:15–19). In view of the nature of Judah's crimes, Jeremiah was asked not to intercede for them because God had made up His mind and would not listen (7:16). Their worship of the "queen of heaven" (and other gods) is evidence of their utter rejection of Yahweh (vv. 17–18). The specific identity of the queen of heaven is difficult to determine, but it was most likely an astral deity (see 44:17–19, 25; cf. Amos 5:26).

The indictment in Jeremiah 7:17–18 is connected with the sermon in vv. 1–15, where breaking the Decalogue is referred to (v. 9). The cult of the queen of heaven demonstrates how the breaking of the first commandment leads to the breach of others. Children gathering sticks during the Sabbath was an illegal activity (cf. Num. 15:32–35), as was the kindling of fire (Ex. 35:3). If the pagan cult practices occurred on the Sabbath, they involved several breaches of the Decalogue (cf. Jeremiah's defense of the Sabbath in Jer. 17:19–27). Judah's crimes brought shame and the anger of the Lord upon themselves (7:18–20). The Lord's wrath would be poured out on the temple and the city: on people, animals, and crops (v. 20). Although God was bringing the judgment, the responsibility lay with the people, who were bringing shame upon themselves (v. 19).

7:21–28. Obedience Better than Sacrifice. This unit opens with a shocking command for the people to add burnt offerings to their sacrifices and to eat their meat (v. 21). The burnt offerings were to be completely consumed by fire, but for some other types of sacrifices, the worshiper could eat a portion. God's command to eat the meat of all sacrifices means that He had rejected them and their offerings. This leads to the main point of the unit. During the Exodus from Egypt, God did not command Israel to offer burnt offerings and sacrifices but to obey/hear His voice. Such submission to Him was to indicate that the Lord was Israel's God and Israel His people. In order that it might be well with Israel, they were to walk in all the ways that God commanded them (vv. 22–23). The moral and social obligations of the covenant could not be superseded by the performance of ritual acts. Religion and morality stood together. Judah's trust in the temple cult was futile if they did not hear and obey the voice of the Lord in His covenant law.

The verdict, stated four times (vv. 24, 26, 27, 28), was that Israel did not listen. It signaled four indictments against the people: (a) they were led by their evil hearts (v. 24), (b) they refused to listen to God's prophets (vv. 25–26; cf. v. 13), (c) they would not obey/hear God's word through Jeremiah (v. 27), and (d) they were a disobedient and incorrigible nation who had lost the truth (v. 28). Judah had rejected the covenant, and God was compelled to answer by rejecting them to their detriment.

7:29—8:3. Judgment on False Worship. The people were told to lament their rejection by God by cutting off their hair, which was a mourning practice (v. 29; see Job 1:20). The desolate or barren heights symbolize Judah as the object of God's wrath (cf. Jer. 7:34). An indictment (vv. 30–31) is followed by judgment and desolation (vv. 32–34). The indictment targeted the idolatry in the temple, which had polluted its holiness—*shiqquts* ("abominations" or "detestable things") refers to altars dedicated to idols in the temple area from the time of Manasseh (2 Kin. 21:1–5). These also included the high places of Tophet(h)—namely, sites for idolatry in the Valley of the Son of (*ben*) Hinnom, outside Jerusalem (referred to as "Gehennah" in NT times).

At the judgment, the Valley of Hinnom would be called "the Valley of Slaughter" (Jer. 7:32). In dishonor, the fallen of Judah would be buried

---

Tophet(h)

The Valley of Hinnom was a steep-sided valley associated with burning—both of garbage at the city dump and of children in sacrifices at the "Tophet(h)" (lit. "hearth," "fireplace"). Child sacrifices appear to have been common among the Canaanites and were sometimes practiced in Israel (2 Kin. 16:3; 21:6). Josiah's attempt to eradicate the rite (2 Kin. 23:10) was reversed under Jehoiakim. The references to child sacrifice in Ezekiel (20:25–26) indicate that it was common in Judah before Jerusalem's destruction in 586 B.C. God condemned the practice as contrary to His will (Jer. 7:31; 19:4–5).

---

there, and when graves could no longer hold the bodies, birds and beasts would consume the corpses (v. 33). The desolation of the land would bring an end to joy and gladness in the cities of Judah and the streets of Jerusalem (v. 34).

Expanding the theme of vv. 32–34, this unit also mocks the peoples' idolatrous astral worship. The bones of all the dead in Judah would be placed before the astral deities whom the people of Judah had loved, served, followed, sought for advice, and worshiped (8:2). God should have been the object of these devotions, and by applying this terminology to the people's idolatry, the seriousness of the rebellion is vividly depicted. The bones of the people would be dishonored because they would be left unburied (cf. 7:33). This drastic message paints a picture of the complete annihilation of Judah. Choosing idols instead of the Lord meant choosing death instead of life.

8:4—10:25
No Balm in Gilead

This section depicts the people of Judah and Jerusalem as an ailing community approaching death. The diverse themes in this section are worked out in rich and imaginative language.

8:4–17. Peril of False Teaching. An indictment concerning Judah's failure (vv. 4–13) is followed by the Lord's judgment through an invading army (vv. 14–17). For Judah, only faithfulness to the covenant could provide life and peace. Abandoning the Lord removes any protection against the surrounding nations and brings judgment. The first part of the indictment resumes the theme of "turning" (3:1—4:4; 15:1–21). The Hebrew word *shub*—"turn," "return"—is used six times in 8:4–6. God's deepest desire was that Judah would return to covenant loyalty. However, the prophet laments that God's people do not know His principles, contrasting Judah with birds who instinctually know the time of their migration (v. 7). Even the animals had a better sense of order and propriety than Judah.

The supposedly wise leaders who handled the instruction of the covenant and the scribes who had produced the writings were unreliable (v. 8) because they had rejected the true word of God and lacked wisdom (v. 9b). Therefore, at the judgment, they would be ashamed (loss of external honor), dismayed (loss of inner peace), and captured (loss of land; v. 9a). True discernment comes from a deep knowledge of the word of God. The statement of their judgment (vv.

10–12) is almost identical to 6:12–15. Their wives and fields would be given to others because of their unlawful desire and deceit (8:10). The false teachers could provide only temporary remedies to Judah's troubles. They taught that "all is well," but the approaching judgment would bring destruction (v. 11). The judgment speech against the wise ends with a summary of the theme of the loss of wives and fields (vv. 10, 13).

Those who were attacked sought refuge in the fortified cities and resigned themselves to God's punishment of drinking poisoned water (v. 14; the LXX and the MT [as well as the different English translations that rely on them] differ in regard to whether the people were resigning themselves to death [LXX—lit. "jumping overboard"] or being silent [MT]). Here they finally acknowledge that they have sinned against the Lord. The metaphor of drinking poison may imply a trial by ordeal (cf. Num. 5:11–31), which suits the marriage metaphor of Israel as wife and the Lord as husband. This practice was used to ascertain whether or not a man's wife had been unfaithful. If she got sick from the bitter water, she was guilty and would be rejected by the husband and become infertile. This imagery also fits the metaphor of the people's ill health, with neither a balm in Gilead nor a physician to bring them healing (8:15, 22).

The people looked for peace, but there was none. They expected healing, but there was only distress (v. 15; cf. 14:19). This was a rejection of the message of the false teachers who proclaimed peace (vv. 8–12). Jeremiah states the unfortunate fact that there would be no recovery for unfaithful Judah (v. 22). Instead, the people could already hear the snorting of horses coming from the land of the tribe of Dan (cf. 4:15), where the invading armies were first seen. The army was like a beast that had come to "devour" the land and its inhabitants, bringing death and destruction (v. 16). The invading army sent by the Lord is described as venomous vipers that cannot be charmed (i.e., they are merciless and cannot be controlled; v. 17). The snake's bites fit the theme of illness in this section; there would be no healing for the people. The devastating judgment was a way of urging God's people to confession and repentance (vv. 14–15).

8:18—9:3. Mourning for an Unfaithful People. The mixed sequence of speakers in 8:18–21 derives from Jeremiah's role as both a prophet and intercessor. The meaningful order in the sequence is supported by a chiastic structure, which forms a dialogue between the pretense of the worshiping community of Israel and the corresponding empathy of Jeremiah with his people (cf. Introduction). This may be displayed as follows:

A Sorrow (vv. 18–19a)

   B Question of the people concerning salvation relating to God's presence (v. 19b)

      C God's question of indictment and indignation (v. 19c)

   B′ Question of the people concerning salvation relating to God's timing (v. 20)

A′ Sorrow (v. 21)

The speaker in vv. 18–19a and 21 could be Jeremiah or the Lord. If Jeremiah is the speaker, he would be demonstrating his heartsickness at the fate of his fellow Israelites. If God is the speaker, He would be stating that He saw and shared in the suffering of His people. Yet the people, who had brought about their own anguish, did not know or care. Their questions in vv. 19b–20 show that they continued to misinterpret the covenant. The temple was no longer God's place, and His promises were not being fulfilled because of the people's disobedience (7:1—8:3). Therefore, God's saving presence was no longer among them (v. 19c), and consequently, His anger was provoked (cf. 6:9–15).

Continuing this line of inquiry from vv. 18–21 and using "healing" as a metaphor for salvation, God asked three questions in v. 22. Gilead was a region east of Jordan, famous for its medicinal herbs (Gen. 37:25), but even there no remedy could be found for Judah's illness! There was no immediate healing for unfaithful Judah. God's protection and care depended on Judah's relationship with Him. Idolatry placed Judah outside of the covenant relationship in a world of chaos. Jeremiah's answer to the questions in Jeremiah 8:22 expresses a mixture of feelings. He wept for their dead (9:1; cf. 8:18, 21), but he also wished to depart from them into the wilderness (9:2). God, the speaker, then accused the people of speaking lies and of not knowing Him (v. 3). The verb "to know" is a covenant term for the intimate relationship between the Lord and His people (cf. 8:7, 12).

9:4–16. Punished by Desolation. This unit addresses social and relational crimes rooted in deceitful self-seeking and the fertility cult. The outcome would be desolation of the cities through death and exile. But God's ultimate purpose was to refine and test His people. The covenant required honesty and care for one's neighbor, but the people of Judah demonstrated through their deceit that they did not know God (vv. 3, 6). "To know" in Hebrew goes beyond mere mental cognizance—it often implies a strong relationship (cf. Gen. 4:1). Accordingly, some translations render *yada'* here as "acknowledge" or "take into account." The warning against friends' and relatives' deception in 9:4 involves the Hebrew phrase *'aqob ya'qob*, which may be an allusion to Jacob's deceitful dealing with his brother Esau (cf. Gen. 27:36). None of the people were to be trusted to tell the truth; they were all living in an environment of deceit (Jer. 9:5-6). Here "deceit" consists of speaking lies and practicing wrongdoings. A loving relationship with God is deeply connected to a loving relationship with our neighbor; loving one leads to loving the other (cf. Matt. 22:34-40).

The idea that the Lord of Hosts would refine and try, or test, His people (Jer. 9:7) had been expressed before (e.g., 5:10, 6:27). The word *tsarap*—"refine"—is associated with the melting of metal (cf. v. 30). "Refine" is in parallel with "try" or "test," which may also refer to refining metal (cf. Job 23:10; Zech. 13:9). These verbs allude to the hope that God would not entirely abandon His people and that repentance was still possible. This is followed by an indictment (Jer. 9:8) that deepens the theme of the people's deceitfulness. Deceitful speech is like a arrow because what it says is denied through its actions: the tongue speaks peaceably but the heart lies in wait to destroy.

The questions in v. 9 indicate that God would punish and avenge Himself on the nation of Judah. God had to be avenged because His honor was at stake. He would not be mocked or manipulated, not even by His covenant partner. The judgment would be God's way of saying "I am God." This theme belongs to the cosmic conflict, where God's character is at stake and where His Son fully reveals His character as redeeming love. In Christ's redemptive work, judgment condemns the wicked and brings salvation to those who see God's saving power in Him.

The announcement of judgment is expressed in a lamentation (v. 10). There would be weeping and wailing for the burned-up and lifeless land—it was completely desolated. The breaking down of mutual social trust creates an atmosphere of suspicion and death. When God is left out of our social interactions, we will experience psychological and, in some cases, physical desolation. Judgment is the demonstration of God's disapproval of destructive human and social behavior.

In v. 12, the reflections on judgment are summarized in three rhetorical questions. First, it is asked, *who* has true wisdom to understand the desolation of Jerusalem and Judah? Only through the word of God, which interprets history from a divine perspective, could such wisdom be obtained (cf. vv. 13-16). Second, to *whom* had the Lord spoken who might explain or declare it? The word of God was given to His prophet (cf. e.g., 1:4-19; 6:27). Thirdly, *why* had the desolation of the land come? This question seeks the reason for the judgment, and the answer is found in an indictment (9:13-14) and the juridical sentence (vv. 15-16). The indictment is structured in terms of chiastic contrasts:

A Forsaking the law/instruction (torah) that God had given

  B Not walking according to or following God's voice

  B' Walking according to or following their own hearts

A' Walking after or following the Baals, as their fathers taught them

This is a question of choice (i.e., God, the Baals, or one's own heart), a choice directly related to the covenant law. Deuteronomy 29:14-19 defines faithfulness to the covenant in three ways, present also in Jeremiah 9:13-16: (1) not turning away from God to serve other gods (cf. v. 14); (2) avoiding the *la'anah*—"wormwood," "bitterness," or "poison" of idolatry (cf. v. 15; 8:14; 23:15; Lam. 3:15, 19; Amos 6:12); and (3) never assuming that they would be blessed despite following the dictates of their own hearts (Deut. 29:19; cf. Jer. 9:14). Now the Lord would feed His people with bitter, even poisonous, food and water (v. 15). Jeremiah had adapted the phrase to the symbol of the bitter water (see commentary on 8:4-17).

Jeremiah 9:16 alludes to Leviticus 26:32-33, which is set in the context of covenant promises of blessing and retribution (Lev. 26:1-46; cf. Deut. 7:12-24; 28:1-68). God would (a) desolate the land, (b) scatter them among the nations, and (c) pursue them with the sword of warfare (Jer. 9:11-16; Lev. 26:27, 32-33). Thus, the answers to the questions in Jeremiah 9:12, about the wisdom, the word of the Lord, and the reason for the desolation, are found in the covenant law that Jeremiah applies to Judah (vv. 13-16).

9:17-26. The People Mourn in Judgment. This section joins together several themes: (a) the previous theme of public mourning (v. 10) is further developed (vv. 17-22); (b) covenantal faith and Judah's self-sufficiency are articulated as two ways of life (vv. 23–24); and (c) God's judgment of the nations (vv. 25–26; cf. 46:1—51:58). The people were invited to imagine that the worst would happen in order to prepare for it (9:17–22). Public lamentation requires skillful experts, and specialists were summoned to mourn and teach their daughters and neighbors a lamentation for the death of their children and young men (vv. 17–21). Death would enter through the windows and take over the palaces, or fortresses, and the open streets of the entire city. The corpses would fall like refuse (v. 22; cf. 7:32–33). This would be a time of sorrowful mourning.

God set two ways of life before Judah (9: 23–24). He had created human beings with glory and honor (cf. Ps. 8:5) and wanted them to preserve this noble state. One option would be to follow the human way of wisdom, power, and riches. These are condemned as tokens of self-sufficiency. The opposite option is *khesed*— "loving-kindness," "love," "fidelity," "judgment," "justice," and "righteousness" (i.e., God's character) because He delights in these things. This way of life consists of understanding and knowing God, and it leads to humility and dependency on Him.

The unit closes by pointing to the coming days of retribution (vv. 25–26). God charged His people with being uncircumcised in their hearts (v. 26), identifying them as no different from the surrounding nations (v. 25). Being equal to the other nations meant losing their special election and covenant relationship. It also meant sharing the destiny that sooner or later reaches every nation: invasion, death, and destruction. God is indeed a God of justice.

10:1–16. Idols and the True God. The comparison between idols and the true God develops and explains the two ways of life in 9:23–24. The point is to warn against learning the way of the nations (or Gentiles) (v. 2). Verses 2–16 mock the idols and praise God's sovereignty. They present the idols as having no knowledge or power and being unable to do anything (vv. 4–5, 14). Jeremiah presents the idols made by human hands (vv. 3–4, 9) as completely stupid (v. 8), false, and futile (vv. 14–15); and, as worthless teachers (v. 8), they could not impart knowledge. They would perish at their time of punishment (v. 15; cf. v. 11). In contrast, there is none like Yahweh (vv. 6–7, 16). He is the powerful Creator of the world (vv. 12, 16), the mighty King of the nations (vv. 7, 10), and Israel belongs to Him (v. 16). He is the great, true, and living God (vv. 6, 10), the Lord of nature, rain, and wind (v. 13), worthy of being feared (v. 7; cf. v. 5). His wrath makes the earth tremble, and the nations cannot endure it (v. 10). He is Israel's God, and His name is great. He is *yahweh tseba'ot*—"Lord of Hosts," "Lord of Armies," or "Lord Almighty" (vv. 6, 16; see *"Yahweh Tseba'ot,"* p. 912).

10:17–25. The Coming Captivity of Judah. Jeremiah urged Judah to prepare for the approaching judgment (vv. 17–18). He summoned the inhabitants of the city fortress to flee or prepare for exile, for God would expel the people (suddenly and violently) from their land (v. 18).

This dramatic scene is followed by a lamentation over the invasion from the north (vv. 19–22). The exclamation of "woe" (v. 19) is an expression of anguish in the face of death and the loss of home and children (v. 20). The speaker from the countryside tells about the setting up of tents for homes (v. 20). The shepherds designate the leaders, and the scattering of the flock refers to the Exile (v. 21). The leaders had not asked the Lord for guidance. It is only in v. 22 that the invasion from the north emerges as the instrument to turn the cities of Judah into a place of jackals (cf. 9:11).

The unit concludes with a prayer of repentance (10:23–24). The prophet asks that God's anger be expressed for the purpose of correction and justice, not complete annihilation (v. 24). He also asks God to direct His wrath toward the pagan nations, who do not know Him (that is, do not appropriately acknowledge Him), and toward those who do not call upon His name (v. 25a–b). Because Judah faced the oppression of the nations (v. 25c–d), its salvation would require the destruction of their power. Later on in the book, the prayer for judgment against the nations is answered (chaps. 25, 46–51), but only after the defeat of Judah and Jerusalem. Jeremiah presents God's punishment of His people as irrevocable, but for the enduring faithful, there was hope for a return to the land. This hope was based on understanding that God directs humanity's steps (10:23–24).

11:1–17

The Broken Covenant

This section has been called a meditation on Deuteronomy 6:4 or a theological treatise on the covenant. In the treatise, God's people must "hear" and "obey" the central tenet of the covenant (i.e., to love the Lord with all their heart, with all their soul, and with all their strength).

Without this, Israel loses both its identity as a people and God's special protection, thus becoming an object of the power struggles of the nations, which leads to destruction.

11:1-5. Covenant Foundation. This unit has three parts. First, the Lord said that Judah and Jerusalem are required to listen to the content of the covenant (cf. Deut. 6:4). To listen or hear in this context means to "obey" because the covenant impacts every aspect of one's life (vv. 2-3). Second, the Israel of old obediently listened to God's voice when He articulated the covenant formula (v. 4). Contemporary Judah and Jerusalem were here invited to do the same. But in this case, the message begins with the curse against those refusing to hear/obey (v. 3). The blessings are left out because priests and prophets had blindly overemphasized them by teaching that God would grant peace despite flagrant violations of the covenant. Third, the covenant was God's way of keeping His oath to the fathers and His promise to give Israel the land of Canaan (v. 5). This promise was significant in Jeremiah's setting. Facing a threat from an invading army and the immediate prospect of extermination, exile, and loss of land, this promise gave hope to Judah. But the people at large failed to fulfill the condition of the promise, which was faith in God. It was Jeremiah's task to remind them of this conditional element.

11:6-8. Covenant Violation (Ancient). The unit is structured as a proclamation of the covenant requirements (v. 6), a summary of the history of God's instruction to Israel through the prophets (v. 7), and an indictment (v. 8a) followed by judgment (v. 8b). God recalled how He had, through His prophets, reminded Israel to obey the covenant (v. 7). Since they did not listen to Him, God would not listen to them (v. 11), and the covenant curses would be enforced (cf. Deut. 28).

11:9-17. Covenant Violation (Contemporary). God revealed to Jeremiah a conspiracy against the covenant. Judah and Jerusalem were accused of breaking the covenant and following other gods (vv. 9-10). God's response was an irrevocable judgment (v. 11) and a refusal to listen to their complaints (cf. 10:23-25). All the cities of Judah worshiped Baal, and in every street in Jerusalem, there was an altar of incense to Baal (11:13). These gods were incapable of saving Judah on the day of trouble (v. 12). Verses 14-17 expand the point in v. 11 that God would not listen to Judah when they cried out to Him

(v. 14). The judgment was final. Judah could not be saved by formal rites in the sanctuary while worshiping other gods (v. 15; cf. 2:2). Although the Lord referred to Judah as a beautiful, thriving, fruitful, and green olive tree (11: 16-17; cf. 2:21; 8:13; 11:19; 17:8), their covenant crimes had provoked His anger to such a point that He allowed the invaders to burn and break this flourishing tree (11:16b-17).

11:18—12:17
Confessions, Punishment, and Redemption

In this section we find the first two Confessions in Jeremiah (see Jeremiah: Introduction). One is linked to a plot to kill Jeremiah (11:18-23), and the other concerns Jeremiah's questioning of God's judgment (12:1-6). The section closes with a description of God's work of punishment and redemption (vv. 7-17).

11:18-23. Jeremiah's Life Threatened. Following the conventional structure of the lament prayer, the first Confession includes invocation and complaint (vv. 18-19), petition (v. 20), and divine response (vv. 21-23).

1. Invocation and Complaint (vv. 18-19). Jeremiah was initially unaware of the plot against him, but God informed him of it (cf. 12:6) and identified people from Anathoth—Jeremiah's hometown—as the ones who were trying to kill him (11:19, 21). Through the complaint, the Israelites expressed the troubles they faced, hoping for a positive divine response. In his complaint, Jeremiah accused the people from his own town of plotting against him. Drawing on the familiar language of the lament (cf. Ps. 44:11, 22), he describes himself as a lamb brought to the slaughter. God quoted the words of the conspirators who intended to destroy Jeremiah so that his name would not be remembered any more. Being unmarried and having no children (Jer. 16:2), Jeremiah would leave no descendants to continue his line or to remember him. His ministry challenged the royal temple ideology (cf. chap. 7), and his priestly family (1:1; 12:6) regarded him as a threat to their status and ambitions (v. 21).

2. Petition (v. 20). Jeremiah turns to the Lord of Hosts as the righteous Judge, praying for the Lord's vengeance on his enemies. The Hebrew *naqam* may be used as a noun ("vengeance") or a verb ("avenge") and is used to express the idea that God cares for the cause of the innocent (11:20; 15:15; 20:12) or that He deals with the adversaries of His oppressed people (46:10; 50:15, 28; 61:6, 11, 36). The term expresses justice. The plot against Jeremiah was a response to what he prophesied in the name of the Lord (11:21), so he invokes God's promised protection (cf. 1:18-19; 15:20-21).

3. *Divine Response (vv. 21-23)*. As the judge in a court, God gave His verdict and sentenced the men of Anathoth. What they had plotted against Jeremiah would now fall upon them. The divine judgment confirms the reliability of the words of His prophet.

12:1-6. Jeremiah's Question and the Lord's Answer. Jeremiah's second Confession may also be divided into invocation and complaint (vv. 1-2), petition (vv. 3-4), and divine response (vv. 5-6).

1. *Invocation and Complaint (12:1-2)*. In his prayer, Jeremiah first acknowledges that God is righteous (v. 1a). The complaint concerns God's judgments and the reliability of God to care for His faithful covenant partners. Jeremiah asks why wicked people prosper (cf. Job 21:7). Put another way, is there a gap between God's righteousness and His allowance of evil? The prayer does not seek an explanation but is rather an accusation of God that anticipates a reaction.

2. *Petition (12:3-4)*. Since God is righteous (v. 1) and knew Jeremiah's innocence, a righteous judgment is proposed against the wicked oppressors. The wicked should be set for slaughter—what his adversaries in Anathoth proposed for him, he now wishes for them (cf. 11:19; 12:6). Jeremiah's argument is that the severe drought, caused by the wicked, would damage all, righteous and wicked, faithful and unfaithful. This raises the question of how God would righteously deal with the faithful remnant in Judah and Jerusalem when the approaching judgment became reality.

3. *Divine Response (12:5-6)*. A supportive answer could be expected in light of the assurances in 1:8 and 19, but God's answer comes as a surprise—a warning that something worse was yet to come! The present ordeal compared to the tribulation to come was like becoming weary by running with people on foot (present) and then having to contend with horses (future). Or it is like feeling exhausted in a cultivated land of peace (present) and then having to dwell in the floodplain of Jordan, with its heat, humidity, wild vegetation, and animals (future). Thus, God intensified the judgment theme. Jeremiah would have to live in continued uncertainty about the issue of God's righteousness. In the

meantime, the righteous and faithful, of necessity, were to wait for and trust in the Lord. The same was taught by Jesus in His parable of the wheat and the tares (Matt. 13:24-30). The saints in the end time are admonished to have patience until the time of the harvest, even if some "die in the Lord" (Rev. 14:12-20). God's response, in sum, avoids the issue of His justice but urges the faithful to trust and obey Him. At the present time, the solution to suffering and injustice is not to be found in how the world operates but in one's relationship with God, which involves patiently waiting for His salvation.

12:7-17. Punishment and Redemption. Next, God spoke in a different tone. He pronounced a judgment that caused Him pain and grief, like a loving husband who must abandon His unfaithful and yet dearly beloved wife (v. 7; cf. 2:2). God had been compelled to give her into the hand of her enemies (12:7), despite her crying out against Him like a lion (v. 8). The Lord described her as being like a vulture under the attack of other vultures (or other birds of prey) and wild beasts (v. 9). This probably refers to the rulers' destruction and desolation of the vineyard of the Lord (vv. 10-12). God's people had sown wheat but reaped thorns because of His fierce anger (v. 13). God's righteousness requires judgment, and the faithful are asked to wait and trust in Him. Because of the faithful remnant, God would bring back the exiles and offer them a new covenant (vv. 14-17).

13:1-27
The Pride of the Chosen People

There are three units in this chapter that make the same point in strikingly different ways: the symbol of the linen garment (vv. 1-11), the symbol of the wineskins (or wine bottles; vv. 12-14), and the description of how the people's pride would be followed by captivity (vv. 15-27). All announce a verdict based on Judah's conduct and underscore the fact of God's justification in His decision.

13:1-14. The Symbols of the Linen Sash and the Wine Bottles. As the linen *'ezor*—translated variously as "sash," "loincloth" or "undergarment"—clings or is bound to the waist of a person, so God had made all Israel "cling" to Him for His renown, praise, honor, and glory (v. 11). This indictment is illustrated by three symbolic actions on the part of Jeremiah. He was to put a linen garment around his waist (vv. 1-2), go to the river Euphrates and hide it in a hole in the rock (vv. 3–5), and, after some time, return to find it ruined (vv. 6–7). In the same manner, God would ruin the pride of Judah and Jerusalem, manifested in their apostasy (vv. 10, 27). Like bottles or wineskins being filled with wine (v. 12), God would fill all Judah with drunkenness and dash them against each other. His destruction of Judah is irrevocable and will be implemented without mercy (vv. 13–14). These emphatic and harsh messages of judgment provide the background for Judah's two options in vv. 15–19.

13:15–27. Pride Precedes Captivity. Twice, the prophet asked Judah to listen in order to choose (vv. 15, 17). There was still time to hear God's word, to repent and obey, even with the looming judgment. Repentance would mean giving glory to the Lord their God (cf. Rev. 14:7) before He brought calamity (v. 16). Giving glory to God implies true worship and humility (abandoning pride)—the path to life (vv. 16, 18). There was a second option—pride or arrogance, an attitude of disobedience, which included a lack of humility and led to shame (vv. 9, 15, 17, 18, 22, 26–27). It would result in death, captivity, weeping, and the collapse of the state, the splendorous crowns (vv. 16–19, 24–27). Humility breeds glory, but pride generates shame. The shaming of Jerusalem (the unfaithful wife) through judgment (vv. 22, 26–27) would be a consequence of the shaming of the Lord (the faithful husband) through adulterous defilement (vv. 26–27). Justice in the covenant context would be brought by the curses and blessings generated by Israel's conduct (see Deut. 28; cf. Jer. 16:10—17:18), but the Lord's love and mercy would be received in humility.

14:1—15:21
Personal Experiences of the Prophet

God's relentless pursuit of righteousness and justice in the face of apostasy continues. It is mingled here, however, with the people's collective prayers of lament and the life and experiences of Jeremiah. He was both an intercessor for his people (of which he was himself a part) and a spokesperson for God (who had called him).

14:1–22. The Word Concerning the Droughts. Severe droughts in Judah had hit both farmers and nobles. Threatened by death, the people turned to God, confessing their sins and appealing to Him for His name's sake (vv. 7–9). God

was merciful, faithful, and loving (see, e.g., Ps. 136; Jer. 33:11; Lam. 3:22–26). The appeal to God's name was a request for Him to act according to His character. In a desperate prayer, the people addressed God as Israel's Hope and Savior (Jer. 14:8). The people pleaded with God to not leave or forsake them, but God's answer was one of rejection (v. 10). The nation had broken the covenant, and the consequences were inevitable.

The people's prayer of lament was interrupted by God commanding Jeremiah to stop interceding for them (vv. 11–18). God would neither listen to them (for they were not listening to Him) nor accept them, regardless of their (dishonest) offerings. Instead, He would consume them by sword, famine, and plagues (vv. 12–16). Judah had lost the covenant blessings and was experiencing the curses. God particularly condemned the false prophets prophesying peace in His name (vv. 13–18). He denied any responsibility for the *'elil* ("worthless" or "idolatrous") "words"—divinations and visions—flowing from their deceptive minds (Heb. *leb*—often translated as "heart" but also inclusive of the mind—both thinking and feeling). They all would be under the curse of the sword, famine, and pestilence (vv. 15–16). By quoting from God's previous judgment, Jeremiah reinforces it.

Verses 17–18 describe God's personal empathy for His people, expressed in a lament after the execution of judgment. The lament blames the devastation on the prophets and priests who failed to acknowledge that the land was God's gift, which could be retained only when the people remained faithful to Him. After the devastating judgment, the land would belong to strangers while God's people wandered around in an unknown land (v. 18). The people's lament continues in vv. 19–22. Three questions are asked in v. 19 regarding whether God (1) had rejected Judah fully, (2) loathed/despised Zion, and (3) had wounded them so deeply that they could not be healed. The people seem to have known the answers, for they confessed their guilt (or iniquity) as well as that of their ancestors; they had sinned against God (v. 20). They prayed for rain (v. 22), which was included in the covenant blessings (v. 21c). Two arguments provided the basis for this request. First, God was petitioned to act for His name's sake (cf. vv. 9b, 21a), to avoid disgracing His glorious throne, and to avoid breaking His covenant with them (v. 21b). Second, they acknowledged that the idols of the nations and the heavens (astral deities) were not saviors and that they could not bring rain. They recognized that only God has such power. The prayer concludes with a commitment to wait for the Lord, for He had made all the nations and the heavens (v. 22).

15:1–9. The Lord Will Not Relent. Answering the people's prayer in 14:19–22, God declared that His verdict against the people remained (15:1–9). This is followed by a reflective lament by Jeremiah (vv. 10–18) and a conditional assurance by God (vv. 19–21). The decision to punish Judah was final (vv. 1–4). Intercession for the people was pointless. If intercession was rejected by God, then only curses remained, and these are symbolized by the four destroyers: death, sword, famine, and captivity (v. 2). The phrase "let them go" (at the end of v. 1) was once God's liberating command to Pharaoh (Ex. 5:1), but now He used it to express rejection and their return to bondage (Jer. 15:1). Four forms of destruction were appointed: sword, dogs, birds, and wild animals that would slay, drag, devour, and destroy (v. 3). The nations of the earth are depicted as wild animals destroying the flock of lambs, which are identified as God's people (e.g., 13:17, 20; 23:2–3; such metaphors are possibly the root images of the "beasts" in the visions of Daniel 7–8). Largely because of Manasseh's reign of bloodshed and apostasy, Judah would become repulsive to all the nations of the earth (Jer. 15:4; cf. 2 Kin. 21; 23:26; 24:3).

Through rhetorical questions, God revealed to Jerusalem that no one would pity her, cry over her, or inquire about her (Jer. 15:5; cf. 30:14). Since Jerusalem had forsaken the Lord, no one would care about her (v. 6a). This is an implied call for her to return to the Lord. Israel's persistent refusal to change had made God weary of relenting (v. 6). The metaphor of "winnowing" (i.e., separating the grain from husks at harvest time) is used to illustrate the coming terrifying judgment (v. 7; cf. 51:2). In permitting the nations to bring down Judah, God would winnow the people (i.e., their children would die, the number of widows would increase, mothers would feel anguish and terror, and even the "remnant" [normally the survivors] would be killed by the sword, vv. 7–9). This was not what God wanted, but Judah had brought it upon themselves by their refusal to return to Him as their only safety (v. 7). Punishment in the form of chastisement had become punishment by destruction, for God's patience had come to an end.

15:10–21. Jeremiah's Dejection and Reassurance. This unit constitutes Jeremiah's third Confession (see Jeremiah: Introduction). It consists of Jeremiah's personal woe (v. 10), a response by God promising a remnant and repeating the judgment (vv. 11–14), a prayer by Jeremiah asking God to save him from his persecutors (vv. 15–18), and a reassurance by God linked to Jeremiah's call (vv. 19–21; cf. 1:17–19).

Jeremiah's woe is a bitter complaint addressed to his mother for having borne him (15:10; cf. 20:14–18). Jeremiah became a man of contention to the whole land (v. 10b) because he was called to preach unpopular messages that undermined the royal ideology and the order of the Judean state. His claim that he had not lent or received loans with interest (v. 10c) is a figure of speech (synecdoche) where a part of the covenant law represents the totality of the law. The covenant law stipulated that it was unlawful to lend money to the poor with interest (Ex. 22:25–27; Lev. 25:35–37). By mentioning this specific law, Jeremiah claimed to be obedient to the covenant law. Since his prayer of lament is sincere and just, not like that of unfaithful Judah, he knew that God would hear him.

God first assured Jeremiah (Jer. 15:11). The Hebrew text at the beginning of the verse is uncertain. Some translate it as "it will be well with your remnant" while others render it as "I will deliver [or free] you for good [or good purposes]." God then identified the coming enemy, the northern iron and bronze, as one that no one could break (v. 12). God's anger would remove personal and national wealth (e.g., the temple vessels and furnishings; v. 13; cf. 52:17–23), and the people would be exiled to a country unknown to them (15:14; cf. 6:9–15). Verses 10–14 move uncompromisingly from the land of contention (v. 10) to the land of exile (v. 14). In vv. 15–18, Jeremiah resumes his prayer, requesting God's intervention and explaining why God should hear him (vv. 15–17). He claims to be innocent and righteous and to belong to God, while being filled with words (which he "ate") of judgment and God's anger (v. 16a). This leads to a complaint which resembles an accusation against God (v. 18). Jeremiah refers to his suffering and needs as a perpetual pain and an incurable wound. From the context, Jeremiah seems to have suffered an affliction caused by his prophetic ministry and by God. Thus, in the last lines of v. 18, drawing on the well-known motif of a tree planted by a river symbolizing a righteous person (e.g., Ps. 1:3; Jer. 17:8), Jeremiah asks God why He seems to be like failing streams of water, deceptive and unreliable. His complaint, therefore, is rooted in the conviction that he had been faithful to his prophetic call and yet had not received God's promised protection and blessing (1:8, 17–19).

In His answer (vv. 19–21), God assured Jeremiah of deliverance from the wicked. God does indeed care about the faithful. However, the Lord began by putting a condition before His prophet, built on a play on the Hebrew word *shub*, "turn" (it occurs four times in v. 19; cf. 3:1—4:4; 8:4–17). The Hebrew text may be translated as "If you will return (*shub*), I will return (*shub*).... They will turn (*shub*) to you, but you shall not turn (*shub*) to them." The carefully constructed statement sets out the condition for a new covenant based on a new faithfulness. The first two occurrences of the verb *shub*, "turn," concern Jeremiah's relation to the Lord. He had accused God of being like an "unreliable stream," and the Lord wanted him to turn to Him with renewed faithfulness and to trust Him. Only then did God promise to sustain him. The second pairing of the same verb concerns Jeremiah and his persecutors. God promised that when Jeremiah turned to Him with renewed faithfulness, his opponents would yield to him, but he should never yield to them. Thus, the promises depended on Jeremiah's new obedience, which would change his relation to God and to the people. God would restore him, and his human opponents would submit to him. Jeremiah serves here as a model for God's faithful people. A foundation was laid for a covenant reorientation that would give the community hope for the future. Thus, in the dialogue between Jeremiah and God in chapter 15, steps were taken that would lead to a new covenant (see chaps. 30–33).

The exchange between Jeremiah and God may be read and understood on several levels. First, it is the prayer of a faithful person in need of God's faithful response, which he received. Secondly, it is the prayer of a prophet who had been charged to proclaim the painful and dangerous word that Jerusalem would perish, and the question was whether God, the Originator of the word, would stand by His prophet, the carrier of the word. If God did not sustain the messenger, the message would not be taken seriously because the prophet would then lose his credibility. If the message was about God's righteousness and the righteousness of His covenant that was broken by Israel/Judah, then God was also obliged, by His own righteousness, to stand by the righteous messenger proclaiming His word. In this dialogue, Jeremiah is seeking God's protection and arguing with Him on the basis of His righteousness, and God responds by assuring Jeremiah that He will be with him and save him (15:20; cf. 1:8, 19). Third, Jeremiah's personal prayer may be read as a word of assurance to the people of God after the destruction of Jerusalem. He is a paradigm, an example of God's new community. God's servants, who "find the words of God" and "eat them" and to whom His word brings joy (15:16), will be like a fortified bronze wall—despite opposition and persecution, God will be with them and save them (vv. 20–21). The passage brings hope, therefore, to God's "end-time people."

16:1–21
Symbolic Actions and Restoration

Jeremiah 16 discusses two prophetic, symbolic actions illustrating the impending doom of Judah (vv. 1–13). This is followed by a message of hope that does not ignore the sins of the people (vv. 14–18) and a concluding message of hope for the nations (vv. 19–21).

16:1–13. Symbolic Actions of Doom. The Lord first commanded Jeremiah not to take a wife or have children "in this place" (vv. 2–4). Jerusalem and Judah were under curse, and all the living—fathers, mothers, sons, and daughters—were to die. The prophet's life symbolized Judah's destiny. Second, Jeremiah was not to mourn or lament the dead (v. 5), for God had removed His peace, love, and compassion from the community. All were to die without burial or lamentation. Nobody was to cut themselves or shave their heads (these mourning rituals, though prohibited in Israel, were practiced by the covenant violators; Deut. 14:1). The radical removal of all human interaction and compassion included the preclusion of giving bread or a comforting drink to the mourners (Jer. 16:7). Jeremiah was not to take part in eating and drinking at feasts. All joy of community life had broken down, even the loving and cheerful communication between bridegroom and bride (v. 9; cf. 7:34). This stern message was intended to lead Judah to rethink its way of life and return to the Lord.

In a didactic reflection on the painful prophecies, God anticipated the reaction of the people (16:2–9). They would ask why God had announced such disasters against them—they were not aware of their sin (i.e., of violating the covenant; v. 10). Jeremiah was to tell them that the transgressions of the fathers (idolatry) were heightened in Judah at this time because no one was listening to God (v. 11–12). The covenant required that Israel listen to and obey God's word (e.g., Deut. 6:1–9) and remain in Canaan. However, since they had broken the covenant, the people were sentenced to exile in a land they did not know and where they were to serve other gods, for the Lord would show them no favor (Jer. 16:13).

16:14–21. Message of Hope and Justice. The dark and depressing picture of the future (vv. 1–13) is unexpectedly interrupted and brightened by a message of hope. God described a new future for His people. He would repeat His miraculous deliverance of the Israelites from bondage in Egypt and bring the faithful back from all the lands where He had driven them to the promised land that had been given to their fathers (vv. 14–15). However, this promise did not weaken the force of the coming judgment. God would act through mysterious agents to trap the Judeans: the fishermen and the hunters (vv. 16–19). God's eyes could not ignore what they had done (cf. Heb. 4:13). Before restoration, God would first punish Judah for "defiling" His land with idols (16:18). The Exile is here seen as a "purification" of the Holy Land preceding the restoration.

The new age for God's people was to include the future submission of the nations (vv. 19–21). Seeing God's deliverance of His people and their restoration as a nation (vv. 14–15, 21), the nations would realize that they had inherited lies from their own ancestors. They would consider their own idols to be worthless and powerless (v. 19). God would show them His hand or might—that His name is the Lord (v. 21). Jeremiah here touches on an important biblical theme: God's purpose in calling Israel was to set them as "a light to the nations" (cf. Is. 2:2–4; 51:4; 60:1–3) so the nations would recognize Him as the only true God. This is the content of "the kingdom of God" celebrated in the temple service (Ps. 93–99). It remains God's plan through Christ (Matt. 28:18–20) and acquires central importance at the end of time (Rev. 14:6–20; 15:4; 21:1–4).

17:1–18
Judah's Sin and Punishment

Jeremiah addresses again the sin of Judah through a lawsuit speech (vv. 1–4), followed by instruction regarding curses and blessings (vv. 5–13). He concludes with a prayer for deliverance (vv. 14–18), which is his fourth Confession in the book (see Jeremiah: Introduction).

17:1–4. Lawsuit Speech. The Lord proclaimed Judah's undeniable guilt as written with an iron pen and engraved with the point of a diamond on their hearts and the horns of their altars (v. 1). The horns of the altar symbolized the blessing of forgiveness, but the sacrificial blood put there for atonement engraved the people's sin due to lack of repentance. The sins of Judah had not been removed from the heart of the people or from God's temple; they had not been forgiven. Judah's sin was idolatry, especially involving the fertility cult (v. 2; cf. 10:1–16), and without God's protection, an enemy would remove the wealth and treasures from Jerusalem (17:3–4; cf. 52:17–23). The land given by the Lord would be lost and replaced by captivity in a foreign land (cf. 16:13). These punishments were to be blamed on Judah, who kindled a fire in God's anger that would burn forever, an expression signifying the intensity of God's anger or the permanence of His judgment.

17:5–13. Blessings and Curses. The reference to the two ways in vv. 5–8 was influenced by Psalm 1. Trusting in humans brings the curse of death, but trusting in God brings the blessing of life. In the year of drought, the tree planted by the waters would yield fruit (cf. 14:1–18) because it stood on the source of life. The human heart is deceitful and incurable (i.e., unfaithful; cf. 17:5), but God, from whom nothing is hidden, makes us aware of our true condition (cf. 16:17). It is useless to trust in the power and wisdom of human beings who act independently of the Lord.

A proverbial illustration of sin warns against the unrighteous gain of riches (17:11). Economic deceit was a serious issue, committed both by individuals (cf. the unrighteous practice of usury in 15:10; cf. 9:3–8) and by the royal administration (i.e., abuse of authority, 22:13–17; cf. 1 Sam. 7:10–17). Those who unjustly gain riches are, according to some translations, like a partridge that broods but does not hatch, or, according to others, like a partridge which hatches eggs it has not laid. They would not retain what they did not own; they would be shown to be fools at the end (Jer. 17:11).

The prophet praises God's majestic power—illustrated by His glorious high throne in the Jerusalem sanctuary—and addresses Him as the hope of Israel (vv. 12–13). This forms the ground for Jeremiah's conclusion: all those who had forsaken God would be ashamed. The punishment corresponds with the sin. The sins of those who depart from God are written on the tablet of their hearts and the altars (v. 1); therefore, they would be written in the earth (or dust) (v. 13); that is, they would die because they had forsaken the fountain of living waters. Abandoning God is like being a shrub in the wilderness (i.e., there is no future for it), but trusting in Him is like being a tree planted by the waters (vv. 5–8).

17:14–18. Prayer for Deliverance. Jeremiah's prayer of deliverance is his fourth Confession. It balances the lawsuit in vv. 1–4, which foretold a harsh future. As an intercessor, Jeremiah did what was needed: he turned to God. His prayer resembles the psalms of lamentation, with ongoing shifts between motivations and petitions. Jeremiah prays for salvation, defined as healing from a disease. He had served God as a shepherd (vv. 14–16). He asks God, his hope in the day of judgment, not to terrorize him (v. 17). He prays for protection from his persecutors (cf. 15:10–21) and for their destruction (17:18) because of their mockery of the word of God (v. 15). Increasingly, Jeremiah contrasts the faithful, who are in need of God's mercy and deliverance, with the persecutors, who are deserving of judgment. This distinction implies that God would justly punish the unfaithful while mercifully restoring His faithful remnant.

17:19–27
Hallow the Sabbath Day

This section has a simple structure: an admonition to remember the Sabbath (vv. 21–22), followed by a warning against repeating the disobedience of Israel's fathers (v. 23). The people were reminded of the blessing that came from following the Sabbath command (vv. 24–26) and the curse that came from not following it (v. 27).

17:19–20. Leaders, People, and the Sabbath. Jeremiah was sent by the Lord to stand in all the gates of Jerusalem, specifically where the kings of Judah went in and out, to deliver instruction regarding the Sabbath. The vital social dimension of the Sabbath made it necessary to involve the rulers. The Sabbath commandment is included in the Decalogue (Ex. 20:8–11; Deut. 5:12–15) and was considered a perpetual sign between God and Israel, reminding them that the Lord made them holy (Ex. 31:13; cf. Ex. 31:12–17). Its importance in Judah is supported by an inscription on an ostracon (a potsherd used for writing) from Jeremiah's time, in which the writer complains that as he was finishing

the reaping before the Sabbath, his garment was taken as a pledge for a debt; he was asking for its return according to the law (Ex. 22:25–27).

17:21–27. Remember the Sabbath. According to vv. 21–22, Sabbath observance consists of not doing any work. This is illustrated by the admonition not to carry burdens into Jerusalem to be sold on the Sabbath. The Sabbath was to be a day of rest and was set apart as sacred. Hallowing and resting on the Sabbath acknowledges God as the Creator of the world (Ex. 20:11) and as the Deliverer of Israel from bondage in Egypt (Deut. 5:15). Faithfully keeping the Sabbath represents covenant observance. It is singled out for its special significance as a covenant sign. Obedience to this command would ensure that descendants of David would walk through the gates to sit on the throne of David and that the leaders of the people would come to Jerusalem to offer sacrifices to the Lord (Jer. 17:24–26). If the Sabbath were desecrated, then the Lord would kindle a fire in the gates that would devour the palace and the city (vv. 27). The future of the city was directly connected to Sabbath observance.

18:1–23
The Potter and the Clay

The chapter opens with a symbolic action (vv. 1–4) and its application to the people (vv. 5–11). It continues with the rejection of the divine warning (vv. 12–17) and the persecution of Jeremiah (vv. 18–23).

18:1–17. Symbolic Action and Application. God commanded Jeremiah to visit the potter's house where he would receive His words. Jeremiah observed the potter's complete control of the clay, shaping and reshaping it in any form he wanted. Similarly, God could do with Israel as the potter did with the clay (cf. Is. 45:9–11), for He is the Sovereign Lord and Israel is His servant. The potter and the clay illustrate God's sovereignty and Israel's duty. Israel was in the hands of the Lord and was expected to submit to the will of the Lord in order for Him to accomplish His loving intentions for the people. In view of the impending judgment, God asked Judah and Jerusalem to turn/return from their evil ways and to make their doings good (Jer. 18:11).

But the people decided that they would not change (v. 12). This reaction on their part was the reason for the judgment speech immediately following (vv. 13–17). Three rhetorical questions were put to the nations as witnesses of the legal proceedings. The essential question was "Who has heard of a nation making the choices that Israel has made?" (vv. 13–14). The symbolism of water in v. 14 refers to the Lord as the water of life for Israel (2:13, 18; 17:13). What Judah had done went against common sense. God's people had forgotten their Life-Giver and resorted to idolatry (18:15a). Therefore, they had brought judgment upon themselves (vv. 15b–16). God would scatter them and show them no favor (v. 17).

18:18–23. Oppression of Jeremiah. The Judeans, who listened only to their own evil hearts (v. 12), conspired against Jeremiah and his prophecies (v. 18). They made plans to take him to court and charge him with insurrection (cf. 26:8–11). They defended their priests, sages, and false prophets but opposed the word of God from Jeremiah. The divine action (18:1–17) is compared to what Jeremiah's enemies would do to him in their resistance to God's word (v. 18). In his fifth Confession, Jeremiah appeals to God's righteousness (vv. 18–23) in not allowing the innocent to be punished (cf. 11:18–23; 12:1–4; 15:10–12, 15–21; 17:14–18; 20:7–18).

Turning to the Lord in prayer (18:19–23), Jeremiah asks for Him to pay attention to his opponents' plans. He appeals to God's sense of justice when asking whether good should be repaid with evil. The people planned to kill Jeremiah, while he was interceding on their behalf for God's wrath to be turned away (v. 20; cf. vv. 22b–23a). The unit ends with several petitions similar to the imprecatory psalms (see "Imprecatory Passages in the Psalms," p. 733) regarding the removal and punishment of adversaries opposed not only to Jeremiah but also to God Himself (Jer. 18:21–23). It should be noted that Jeremiah left vengeance in God's hands—as did the psalmists—and did not unilaterally seek vengeance. In addition, as Jeremiah mentions, he had been pleading for the people, and his decision to cease praying for them was in obedience to God's admonition to stop praying on their behalf (cf. 7:16; 11:14; 14:11). Besides, his imprecations were consonant with what God had already decreed. The Confession in 18:18–23 illustrates the irreconcilable conflict between unfaithful Israel and God, between the Judean establishment and Jeremiah, between the lies of false teachers and the truth of God's word. It argues not only for God's judgment but also for deliverance from evil and death, opening up the possibility for God's salvation of His remnant (chaps. 30–33).

19:1–15
The Sign of the Broken Flask

God announced the coming judgment (vv. 1–3) and offered evidence to justify His decision (vv. 4–9; the breaking of the flask illustrated the future of Judah [vv. 10–15]).

19:1–9. Announcing the Judgment and Punishment. Jeremiah was commanded to procure a clay water bottle (vv. 10–12) and take some elders as witnesses to the Valley of Hinnom, near the Potsherd Gate in Jerusalem (where broken pottery was thrown away). There he was to address the kings and people of Judah and Jerusalem. The first part of Jeremiah's prophecy imitates the lawsuit form and contains three units arranged as an *inclusio* (vv. 3–9):

A Punishment (v. 3)
  B Indictment (vv. 4–6)
A′ Punishment (vv. 7–9)

The coming destruction would be so terrible that all who heard of it would be stunned and shocked (v. 3; cf. Deut. 28:37).

The indictment sought to provide the needed evidence to justify the coming judgment. The evidence indicated that the people had abandoned God and treated Jerusalem as a place for foreign gods (Jer. 19:4–5). They had burned incense in Jerusalem to these gods whom neither they, their fathers, nor the kings of Judah had ever known, and they had filled their land with the blood of innocent people. God emphasized how these defiling acts had impacted Jerusalem. The place where Jeremiah delivered his prophecy intentionally oscillates between the shameful Valley of Hinnom, Tophet, and the city gate. Jerusalem had become foreign to the Lord. The blood of the innocent was associated with the high places of Baal (Tophet) where they sacrificed their children as burnt offerings (v. 5). God had never intended for this to happen.

In response, God would avenge the acts of apostasy (vv. 6–9). Those who broke the covenant by slaughtering their innocent children as sacrifices to alien gods would be slaughtered by an alien army, and the name of Tophet and the Valley of Hinnom would be changed to the Valley of Slaughter (v. 6). God's judgment is expressed by a series of verbs rooted in the covenant curses (vv. 6–9; Deut. 28:15–68). Being righteous, He was obliged to be faithful to the stipulated curses for a broken covenant.

Even the horrific sacrifice of their innocent children to Baal (Jer. 19:6) would be avenged by the desperate act of parents eating the flesh of their children (v. 9; cf. Deut. 28:53–57).

19:10–15. The Flask and the Future. Jeremiah's symbolic act of breaking the flask (v. 10) meant that God would permanently destroy the city (v. 11). In this case, the principle of justice demands retribution: the houses in Jerusalem would be defiled like Tophet, just as the people had defiled their houses by burning incense to all the host of heaven and pouring out drink offerings to other gods (vv. 12–13). Through the prediction of this judgment, God intended to bring Jerusalem to repentance. However, in a concluding scene, Jeremiah moved to the court of the temple and announced God's word to all the people. Since they had proudly and stubbornly refused to hear His words, the Lord of Hosts would surely execute the judgment (vv. 14–15).

20:1–18
Jeremiah Persecuted

This section deals with Jeremiah's struggle with his prophetic calling in the face of persecution. After recounting his confrontation with Pashhur (vv. 1–6), he describes his unpopular ministry (vv. 7–18). The reference to Babylon (vv. 4–6) suggests a date after 605 B.C., when the Babylonians defeated Egypt at Carchemish.

20:1–6. The Word of God to Pashhur. Pashhur the son of Immer, a priest and chief governor in the temple, sought to silence Jeremiah by beating him and putting him in the stocks. In response, Jeremiah delivered a prophecy linking Pashhur's fate with that of Jerusalem (vv. 3–6) and declared that the Lord had renamed him Magor-Missabib, "terror all around." This symbolic naming is linked to the first prediction in Jeremiah concerning the Babylonian disaster (vv. 4–6). The message embedded in the name was that the temple, associated with peace, would in reality bring terror.

God would make Pashhur a terror to himself and all his friends—he would see them fall by the sword. God would also give Babylon all the wealth of Jerusalem (v. 5). Pashhur and his household would be exiled to Babylon, where he would die and be buried. The reason for this punishment was that Pashhur had prophesied lies (v. 6). By falsifying the covenant law, he had made himself an agent of deception.

20:7–18. Jeremiah's Unpopular Ministry. This unit contains Jeremiah's sixth and last Confession (see Jeremiah: Introduction). Jeremiah's prayer opens with a powerful lamentation (vv. 7–10). He claims that God, at the moment of his call, persuaded (*patah*, "persuaded," "seduced," "enticed," or "deceived") him with wonderful promises (v. 7; cf. v. 10). God overpowered him. The language appears to be that of a man seducing a woman and finally forcing himself on her. Jeremiah was not able to reject his call. After the sweet moment of the divine call, Jeremiah faced the reality of a complex and difficult ministry and the hostility of the people (v. 8). Even if he wished to remain silent in order to avoid the hostility, he could not do so because the word of God was like a fire in his bones (v. 9). His oppressors mocked him, and his friends or acquaintances (lit. "all men of my peace," i.e., "all who wish me well") were trying to make him fall so that they could take their revenge on him (v. 10; cf. v. 7). This is about the cost of being God's servant at a time when God's warning of judgment against Judah was severe, though the people appeared to be enjoying peace and prosperity.

Jeremiah put his trust in God (vv. 11–12). Though his enemies attempted to make him stumble, God would make them stumble. He pleaded with God to act in his favor—the mighty, awesome One who examines the righteous. As for the conspirators, their infamy would never be forgotten. Jeremiah asked to witness God's vengeance on the persecutors who were plotting vengeance against him (vv. 10, 12). As a servant of God, Jeremiah did not take revenge into his own hands, but he asked God to act according to His will. The tone changes in v. 13, when Jeremiah offers praise to God for His salvation. The lament prayer leads to praising God for the coming deliverance (v. 13). God's favorable answer had either been given or Jeremiah knew that God would answer in the future, so he praised Him.

Surprisingly, another profound lament follows in vv. 14–18. Jeremiah seems to have moved in a circle, always coming back to the comfort of God's care but also returning to his own suffering and lamentation. The crude reality of prophetic service is that it often generates ongoing pain for the prophet, while the faith of the prophet generates ongoing comfort for the people. The lament has no explicit addressee but seems to be a personal reflection. The speaker curses the day he was born because life has brought labor and sorrow and shame (vv. 14, 18; cf. Job 3).

The lament in vv. 14-18 expresses not only Jeremiah's sense of hopelessness (v. 18) but also the hopelessness of God's people experiencing destruction and exile. This mingling of individual and collective speakers is common in some biblical texts (e.g., in the book of Psalms) and indicates that the intercessor may be identifying himself or herself with the suffering people. Jeremiah also shows a fondness for transforming a current situation into a symbol of the future situation of the people (e.g., Pashhur in 20:1-6). Thus, Jeremiah expresses his own despair in the text, but in a way his words also express his people's despair and shame after the predicted devastating judgment. His prayer for salvation from his persecutors becomes a prayer for the salvation of God's people under the hopelessness brought by the judgment (cf. 11:18-23; 12:1-6; 15:10-21; 17:14-18; 18:18-23). This theme points forward to the promise of hope and a new future (e.g., chaps. 23-25, 30-33).

21:1—25:38
Judgment and Hope

The content of this section is characterized by judgment against Judah (21:1—23:40) and is interrupted by a messianic prophesy (23:1-8), a powerful central statement of hope (24:1-10), and judgment against Babylon and the nations (25:1-38).

21:1-14. Message to King Zedekiah and Judah. Jerusalem had been left enfeebled and fearful by the Babylonian invasion in 598 B.C., when Zedekiah was on the throne. The troubled king sent servants to Jeremiah to inquire of the Lord for them. The initial question (vv. 1-2) has four answers (vv. 3-7, 8-10, 11-12, 13-14). The question aimed at averting the approaching Babylonian threat but is expressed as a wish. Zedekiah wanted to ascertain whether he could still rely on God's faithfulness in the new crisis. But he only asked because he lacked faith.

God's first answer through Jeremiah was not what the king wished to hear (vv. 3-7). Allusions are made to the Exodus (vv. 4-7; cf. Deut. 26:8; Ps. 136:12), indicating that God remained the same. But the shocking surprise was that He was now acting against Judah and in favor of Babylon. The king and all his people would be given to the Babylonians. There was no hope for Judah because of God's intense anger (Jer. 21:5).

Jeremiah's second answer addressed the people (vv. 8-10). God set before them the ways of life and death (see Deut. 30:15-20). The way

of death would be in trusting the king, his army, and Jerusalem's walls (i.e., to stay in the city and experience the sword, famine, and plague; v. 9a). The way of life and hope would be to escape from the city and defect to the Babylonians because the judgment would target the royal establishment and the temple. Surrender would be the prophet's way of survival. It may mean exile, but lives would be saved, and God might bring His faithful people back.

The third answer addressed the royal house (vv. 11-12). The evil of their past deeds was clear, but there was hope if they would change their ruling practice. The way out is expressed by imperatives to always be just and to rescue victims. This is based on the covenant duty and on what God Himself does (e.g., Ex. 22:22; Deut. 10:18; 24:14, 17-18; 27:19; cf. Jer. 22:1-30; 49:11). Jeremiah's fourth answer (vv. 13-14) addressed the self-sufficiency of people boasting that there was hardly any threat from the Babylonians. He announced that God would punish these people by fire because of their contempt for the covenant and the prophetic word.

22:1-30. Indictments of the Royal House. Jeremiah addressed the Davidic house (vv. 1-9) and the failure of the monarchy (vv. 10-30). If the king would execute justice and righteousness, safeguarding the stranger, the fatherless, and the widow, and would not shed innocent blood, then the monarchy would remain (vv. 3-9; cf. 7:5-7). But because the king did not listen to/obey, the royal house would collapse. The main concern is obedience to the covenant laws protecting the innocent and the needy (see e.g., Ex. 22:22; Deut. 10:18; 24:17; 27:19). The Davidic house was precious to God but so also was caring for the poor in accordance with the covenant (Jer. 22:16c-17).

The failure of the monarchy is addressed in vv. 10-30. It opens with an invitation to lament for the one going into exile never to return. The text then identifies the exiled as King Jehoahaz ("Shallum"), who was taken captive to Egypt, where he died (vv. 11-12; cf. 2 Kin. 23:30-34). This is followed by an indictment against the self-seeking interests of the kings (Jer. 22:13-30), illustrated by King Jehoiakim. The principles of a just ruler are outlined in vv. 13-17, and Jehoiakim's father, King Josiah, appears as an example (vv. 15-16). The basic tenet is that "knowing God" means to act justly toward the poor and needy (v. 16). But Jehoiakim is characterized in the text by covetousness, the shedding of innocent blood, and oppression and violence

(v. 17; cf. 13–14). This indictment is followed by a judgment speech (vv. 18–23). Jehoiakim's death would not be lamented, and his burial would be dishonorable (vv. 18–19). The foreign gods ("your lovers") would be destroyed (v. 20). Verse 21 is a reminder of the refusal of the king to listen to/obey God's voice. The unit concludes with a description of the shame and humiliation of the king that the judgment would bring (vv. 22–23). The leaders of God's people are expected to set aside self-interest in order to serve the people and care for those in need.

God then turned to "Coniah," also known as King Jehoiachin (598–597 B.C.). Although the king was "the signet of His right hand," God would now pull him off. Jehoiachin would be handed over to the king of Babylon and taken to exile with his mother and descendants—they all would die there (vv. 24–27). God then declared to the whole earth that the current royal house would no longer rule in Judah (vv. 26–30). This vacuum on the throne is dealt with in 23:1–8.

23:1–8. The Branch of Righteousness. The general indictment against the kings in vv. 1–2 is followed by three promises to the remnant (vv. 3–8). First, God would gather His people from all the countries where He had driven them, bring them back, and make them fruitful (v. 3). The scattering of the flock was the result of the unfaithful shepherds who did not attend to it (cf. Mark 6:34). God would, however, intervene and bring the remnant back to the land. He would set rulers over them who would show His care for them, and they would no longer be afraid (Jer. 23:4; cf. Ezek. 34:1–31).

Second, God promised the coming of the Messiah. In fulfillment of His covenant with David, God would raise a righteous Branch (i.e., a Son of David in the "tree" of David's house), a King who would reign and prosper, executing justice and righteousness on earth (cf. Is. 11:1–16). He would bring peace and reunite Judah and Israel. His name would be the Lord our Righteousness (Jer. 23:5–6), a possible play on the name Zedekiah (21:1–14), which means "the Lord is righteous." Unlike Zedekiah, the Messiah would practice God's righteousness (v. 12; 22:3), and His rule was to bring well-being to all through justice for the poor and needy.

Third, God promised a new exodus for God's people, a return from exile (23:7–8). The return was fulfilled by the command of the Persian king Cyrus in 537 B.C., but the kingdom was not restored. However, the successive foreign domination by Persia, Greece, and Rome kept alive the hope for a coming Messiah. When Jesus of Nazareth announced "the kingdom of God" and that God's people needed to "repent" (Matt. 4:17), Israel still lived in expectation of the Messiah (see e.g. Luke 2:25–37).

23:9–40. False Prophets and Empty Oracles. Jeremiah ministered in the midst of competing claims to "truth," each professing to be a revelation of God's will. In this unit, he makes his clearest argument for the truthfulness of his prophetic words. In the first part (vv. 9–22), Jeremiah brings a general indictment against the religious leaders (i.e., prophets and priests). He expresses a deep inner turmoil as he contrasts the Lord's holy words with the unfaithful words and deeds covering the land, causing it to 'abal, which can mean "mourn" or "dry up," under a curse (vv. 9–10). The profanity and wickedness practiced in the temple by both prophets and priests would be punished (vv. 11–12).

God indicted the false prophets in Samaria (Israel) and Jerusalem (Judah; vv. 13–15). They prophesied in the name of Baal and led God's people into error; they were committing adultery and practicing deception (lit. "walking in lies"). In Jerusalem, they supported the evildoers rather than calling people to turn from their wickedness. God had therefore rejected them as He had Sodom and Gomorrah and would punish them (cf. v. 15 and 9:15). As the Ruler of the world, God had laid plans and had made decisions in the council (or counsel—the Hebrew word can mean either) of His heavenly court (23:18). When a decision had been made, a messenger or a prophet was commissioned to announce it (e.g. 1 Kin. 22:19–23; Is. 6:6–8). God firmly stated that He had not sent or spoken to the false prophets (Jer. 23:21). They did not stand in God's council. If they had, as was the case with a true prophet such as Jeremiah, they would have announced God's words to His people to help them turn from their evil ways (v. 22). Unlike a false prophet, a true prophet would have led the people to faithfulness to God.

The critique of false prophets continues in vv. 23–32. God asserted His sovereignty, declaring that He would not be controlled or manipulated by humans. He is supreme, and before Him all humans must bow. God cannot be drawn into human schemes and political agendas. He could be near to His people and also distant from them. Yet He could not be avoided because He sees all and fills heaven and earth. With this in mind, God turned again to the false prophets.

Having dreams (v. 25) was no proof of divine authority. What mattered was the turning of the people to God through their messages (vv. 25–27, 30–32).

In vv. 28–29, the text provides a comparison between true and false prophets, where dreams are contrasted with God's word, like chaff and wheat. The criterion for true prophecy lies in the nature of God's word: it is like a fire and a powerful hammer that breaks rocks in pieces. Thus, the word has great power, and nothing can hinder its implementation (cf. Deut. 18:15–22; Is. 55:10–11).

God rejected the false prophets on four grounds (vv. 30–32): (a) they were stealing God's words from their neighbors (v. 30)—they were claiming for themselves others' alleged revelations (perhaps words of other genuine prophets or of other false prophets); (b) they were quoting God although He had not spoken to them (v. 31); (c) they were prophesying false dreams (v. 32a); and (d) they were causing God's people to err by their lies (v. 32b). Their uselessness to the people was based on the fact that God had not sent them (v. 32c).

The last unit (vv. 33–40) is built on a play on the word *massa'*, which is difficult to translate. It derives from the verb *nasa'* ("bear," "lift") and can mean both "that which one bears" (i.e., "burden") and "that for which one raises one's voice" (i.e., "utterance"). A prophetic utterance would be an "oracle," "message," or "prophecy." The key to the meaning of the passage is the identification of the words of the false prophets as their own words—a perversion of God's words (v. 36; cf. vv. 25–27, 30–32). Therefore, God forbade them from claiming the *massa'* ("the message," "utterance") of the Lord (six times in vv. 33–34, 36, 38). His name was not to be attached to their false prophecies. People could ask about the Lord's "burden"/"message"/"oracle" but were not to presume to know it (vv. 35–38). Such false assumptions would result in closing oneself off from the true knowledge of God's omniscience, omnipresence, and sovereignty (cf. vv. 23–24) and in being cast out into exile (v. 39). Thus, the religious leadership in Judah was accused of attempting to control God's actions through knowledge that they did not have. This is a serious matter that even Christian leaders need to recognize.

24:1–10. Two Baskets of Figs. God showed Jeremiah two baskets with figs that had been placed in front of the temple. One had good figs, but the figs in the other were so ruined

that they could not be eaten (vv. 1–2). Through this image, God revealed His plan for the faithful remnant in Babylon (i.e., the good figs) and His plan for the unfaithful people in Judah and Egypt (i.e., the bad figs). The judgment against the royal establishment in Judah included exile or death. God would send the sword, famine, and plague against them until they were consumed (vv. 8–10). The promise of hope to the faithful remnant in exile included the return to their homeland (vv. 4–7). Language found in Jeremiah's call (1:10) is used to describe their experience: God would build them up and plant them (24:6). The new covenant would be based on what God would do: He would give His people a heart to know Him, and when they returned to Him, a new covenant would be made (v. 7; cf. chaps. 30–33).

25:1–14. Seventy Years of Desolation. This unit dates to the first year of Nebuchadnezzar (605 B.C.). Babylon has now entered the scene as a new world power, becoming a threat to Judah. But God will limit Babylon's dominion to seventy years. This knowledge is central to Jeremiah, for it underscores that God is sovereign, even over Babylon, and that the possibility of Israel's return and restoration is kept open. Jeremiah accused Judah and Jerusalem of refusing to listen to God's word as given through His prophets. This had been the case not only during his own twenty-three years of ministry but also in the prophetic movement through which God had led His people for centuries (vv. 3–7). In v. 4, the Hebrew verb *shakam* (lit. "rising early") conveys the idea of "repeatedly" (see commentary on 7:13 and Jeremiah: Introduction). All of God's prophets called Israel to repentance with instructions on right conduct, warnings against apostasy provoking God's anger, and assurances of God's protection. But the people refused to hear (obey), and the Lord's anger was provoked to their own detriment (25:5–7). This is an excellent summary of Jeremiah's prophecies from chapters 2–25.

God then announced that because of their refusal to hear/obey, He would send His servant Nebuchadnezzar against Judah and the nations all around, resulting in their destruction (25:8–9). The life and joy of the community would disappear (v. 10; cf. 7:34; 16:9; 33:11). The land of Judah and its neighbors was to become desolate, and they would serve the king of Babylon seventy years (v. 11). After that, God would punish Babylon for its iniquity and make it a perpetual desolation (v. 12; cf. 50:1—51:58). Judah's liberation after seventy years came in

536 B.C. (606/5–537/6 B.C.), when the Persian king Cyrus allowed the exiles to return home. The message is that God is the Sovereign Lord of all the nations. He gives and takes away their life and dominion (1:10; cf. 18:9; 24:6; 31:28; 32:41; 42:10). God rules supreme, and His kingdom is everlasting. Therefore, despite the judgment, there is hope for God's people.

25:15–38. Judgment on the Nations. This unit announces God's judgment upon all the nations of the earth, including Judah and Babylon. His judgment on Babylon was what made the restoration of Israel possible (23:1–8; 30:1–33:28). The unit integrates two concepts: (a) God "ordained [Jeremiah] a prophet to the nations" (1:5) and "set [him] over the nations and over the kingdoms" (v. 9); and (b) the Lord is the Sovereign God and universal Ruler of the nations, and no kingdom or nation could endure His fierce anger (25:30–31, 38). The first part of the judgment outlines Jeremiah's ministry in symbolic terms (vv. 15–29). God commanded the prophet to take the cup of the wine of His fury from His hand (i.e., God's anger expressed in His word of judgment) and to cause all the nations to whom he was sent to drink it (i.e., proclaim to them God's word of judgment), with the result that they would drink, stagger, and go mad because of the sword that God would send among them (i.e., fear and chaos would rule from the day of their hearing the word until its fulfillment). The wine cup of fury is a common biblical metaphor for God's anger, which brings judgment and causes its recipients to stagger and lose control, resulting in fear and chaos (cf. Is. 51:17–22; Jer. 49:12; 51:7; Lam. 4:21; Ezek. 23:31–34; Hab. 2:15–16; Obad. 15; Zech. 12:2). Jeremiah communicated God's word to a range of nations, beginning with Judah and ending with Babylon (transliterated as "Sheshak" or "Sheshach, Jer. 25:17–26; cf. 46:1—51:58). But there is also an emphasis on all the kingdoms of the earth (25:26; cf. vv. 15, 17), linked with God's plan to bring calamity on all people (45:4–5; cf. 25:31) and which may be associated with a universal day of judgment when God's judgment, depicted by the metaphor of the sword, would fall on all the earth (v. 29).

According to vv. 30–38, God would come to hold judgment on the earth—He would bring a "lawsuit" (*rib*) against the nations (v. 31), rulers, and kings. This resembles the Day of the Lord, when God would deal with the nations and establish justice and peace (e.g., Is. 2–4; 13:6, 9; 34:8; Jer. 46:10; Ezek. 7:19; 13:5; Joel 1:15; 2:1, 11; 3:14; Amos 5:18; Obad. 15; Zeph. 1:7; Zech.

14:1; Mal. 3:23). The cause for the judgment is not clearly stated, except in Judah's case and in general reference to the wicked (Jer. 25:31). The message has more to do with God's sovereignty over the nations than with their behavior and fate. Its purpose was to strengthen Israel's faith in God as Babylon was rising to power (v. 1) and to explain why the prediction of a limit of seventy years for Babylon's dominion (vv. 3–14) was indeed to be trusted. The section closes affirming that none of the nations on earth is autonomous—they are all accountable to God.

26:1—29:32

CONFRONTATIONS WITH PRIESTS AND PROPHETS

These units cover the time of Jehoiakim's early reign (609–598 B.C.) to the reign of Zedekiah (597–586 B.C.). The chapters have been placed together between chapters 2–25 and 30–33 because of the common theme of the two perspectives on Judah's fate. On the one hand, there was the official view that Jerusalem was safe and its survival from the threat of Babylon was guaranteed by God's promises. On the other hand was the opposite view from God that Jerusalem had no guarantees of survival because the Babylonian threat was His punishment for widespread apostasy and the violation of the covenant.

26:1–24
Jeremiah Saved from Death

In this section of Jeremiah, we gain new insights into the various reactions to his sermon in the temple, recorded in chapter 7 and summarized here. In this particular case, the narrative focuses on the prophet's credibility. Was his prophetic word trustworthy? Knowing that this was going to be the heart of the debate, the Lord informed Jeremiah that He had sent the same message of judgment against the city and the temple through other prophets before him (vv. 4–6). In other words, his prophecy was in agreement with that of previous prophets.

The reaction of those who listened to Jeremiah varied. The false prophets and the priests immediately condemned Jeremiah because, based on their false sense of security, they assumed that the temple and the city would never be destroyed (vv. 7–9). Therefore, based on their preconceived ideas, Jeremiah could not be a true prophet of the Lord. Their intention was to kill Jeremiah for pronouncing judgment against the temple and the city. Years later, similar charges would be raised against Jesus (Matt. 27:61) and Stephen (Acts 6:13–14). Jeremiah knew that everything depended on the people's acceptance of his prophetic ministry. After the arrival of the princes of Judah, he proclaimed once more his message and reaffirmed that he was a true prophet of the Lord (Jer. 26:14).

The elders decided to compare the message of Jeremiah with that of previous prophets (vv. 18–28). They tested his prophetic claim. They demonstrated that there was continuity between what Jeremiah was proclaiming and the messages of judgment against the city and the temple announced by the prophets Micah and Urijah. King Hezekiah had listened to Micah, but King Jehoiakim had killed Urijah. The implicit question was whether they should react like Hezekiah or like Jehoiakim. For the moment, the continuity of Jeremiah's message with that of previous prophets indicated that he was a true prophet. The fact that the life of the prophet was preserved particularly through the intervention of Ahikam (v. 29), a supporter of Josiah's reform, suggests that the enemies of Jeremiah had not been persuaded.

This unit (vv. 1–24) also places Jeremiah within a spiritual movement in Judah that maintained the covenant—here supported by the elders of the land (vv. 16–19) and prophets like Urijah (vv. 20–23). They were in conflict with the ideology of the royal establishment that compromised the covenant by self-seeking and fertility cults. This mixed audience of the faithful and apostates explains the contrary themes of judgment and hope in Jeremiah's prophecies.

27:1–22
Symbol of the Bonds and Yokes

The purpose of the section is to show that God appointed Babylon as His servant to execute His judgment and that lives would be preserved only in submission to the Babylonians. God issued three decrees: to Judah's neighboring nations, to King Zedekiah, and to Judah and Jerusalem. God commanded Jeremiah to make a yoke of straps and bars and to put it on his neck as a symbol of Babylonian domination (v. 2; cf. 28:1–11). Envoys arriving at the Jerusalem court would take these symbols and a decree from God to the kings of Edom, Moab, Ammon, Tyre, and Sidon (27:3). The first decree has five statements (vv. 4–11): (a) God had made the world and given it to whom He deemed proper (v. 5; cf. Acts 17:24–27); (b) He had given both the land and beasts of Judah's neighboring nations to His servant, the king of Babylon (v. 6); (c) He would limit Babylon's dominion until the time of judgment against his land would come—when the nations would make Babylon serve them (v. 7; cf. the limit of the seventy years in 25:11–14); (d) therefore, God put a choice before Judah's neighbors: resisting the Babylonians would mean annihilation by the sword, famine, or pestilence (27:8), but submitting to the Babylonians and accepting their yoke would allow the Israelites to remain in their land (v. 11); and (e) the recipients were to reject the lies of the false prophets (diviners, dreamers, soothsayers, or sorcerers) advising them, for shortsighted personal gain, not to serve the Babylonians. Such false prophecies would result in exile (v. 9).

The second decree was to Zedekiah and repeated the choice offered to the kings of the neighboring nations (vv. 12–15). The third decree (vv. 16–22) was to Judah and Jerusalem. It emphasized that life and hope were connected with God's words through Jeremiah. However, a particular issue was raised. The false prophets had lied, saying that the temple vessels already taken to Babylon (597 B.C.) would be brought back shortly (v. 16). God told them that this would not be the case and that even the vessels remaining in Jerusalem would be carried to Babylon and would remain there until God's restoration of His people to Jerusalem (vv. 18–22). With irony, Jeremiah invited the false prophets to pray to God that the remaining vessels not be taken by Babylon (v. 18), which would only happen if Judah would repent and return to the Lord.

28:1–17
Hananiah's Falsehood and Doom

Hananiah appeared, claiming to be sent by the Lord (vv. 1–4). His name means "the Lord is gracious," and he asserted that God was indeed more gracious than Jeremiah's harsh judgments suggested. He confronted Jeremiah in the presence of the priests and all the people with a supposed word from the Lord (vv. 2–4). Opposing Jeremiah's message in 27:16–22, he announced that God had broken Babylon's yoke, and within two years the temple vessels and Jehoiachin ("Jeconiah"), together with other exiles, would return. Hananiah twisted the covenant promises and ignored the fact that God's promises of protection had been made void by Judah's disobedience.

Though wishing that Hananiah's prophecy were true (28:6; cf. 27:18), Jeremiah changes the topic and makes prophetic authority the central issue. Because God's prophets in the past protected the covenant, they were called to prophesy war and disaster and plagues against many nations (28:8). Their messages concerned God's covenant, not politics, and their indictments against Israel therefore resulted in judgment. Hananiah's words of peace and well-being could be tested (v. 9; cf. 6:14; 8:11). Jeremiah appealed to the covenant (Deut. 18:22), insisting that a fulfilled prophecy proved that such a messenger was one whom the Lord had truly sent. The burden of proof was on Hananiah. Only time would tell. But what if Hananiah were wrong? Did not the deportation in 597 B.C. indicate Babylon's power and intentions to rule over Judah?

Hananiah confidently broke the wooden yoke (cf. 27:2), restating his prophecy that, within two years, God would break the Babylonian dominion (28:10–11). Jeremiah withdrew from the debate. God later instructed him to tell Hananiah that he had broken the yokes of wood, but in the process, he had created unbreakable yokes of iron! The judgment, rather than being averted, would be intensified: God would put yokes of iron on all of the nations, forcing them to serve Babylon (vv. 12–14). The point is that Hananiah's prophecy was false, and he was a deceiver, not sent by the Lord. In order to show that Jeremiah was a true prophet, God announced the death of Hananiah. He died that same year, in the seventh month, because he had spoken rebellion against the Lord (vv. 15–17). The fulfillment of Jeremiah's short-term prophecy demonstrated that he was a true prophet and that, consequently, his other prophecies would be also fulfilled. He had passed another prophetic test. Hananiah's error was his unfaithfulness to the covenant and the word of God.

This episode illustrates the repeated instruction in 27:9–10 and 14–18 to reject the false prophets. But the confrontation goes deeper; it is about who God is. As Israel's God of the covenant, Yahweh loved His people and was righteous (i.e., He was faithful to Israel, as defined by the covenant, and true to His word). However, He is also the holy and powerful Sovereign Lord of the nations, who plucks up and tears down, who builds and plants (cf. 1:10). Israel's destiny, therefore, depended on their faithfulness to God.

29:1–32
Jeremiah's Letter to the Captives

Jeremiah sent a letter to the captives in Babylon through two royal messengers of King Zedekiah who had access to the court of King Nebuchadnezzar (vv. 1–3). The content confirmed the existence of at least two groups in Babylon: defectors and keepers of the covenant. The disobedient defenders of the royal establishment who trusted in the false prophets, all of whom would be punished, were admonished to repent. God's faithful remnant people, who would survive in exile and eventually be brought home, were encouraged to be patient and faithful (cf. chaps. 23–28). In the meantime, the remnant were required to (1) realistically accept the Exile as the setting where they were now required to live and where God had called them to obedience (29:5–7) and (2) continue to hope/wait for their return and restoration (vv. 10–14).

The passage (vv. 4–28) is framed by a repetition of the main admonition of hope given by God: to build houses, live in them, plant gardens, and eat their produce (vv. 5, 28). This is the letter's key pastoral advice. Another important theme is the warning against false prophets (vv. 8–9, 21–32; cf. chaps. 24–28). The most poignant part of the letter is found in 29:5–7. God's people in exile were to build and plant (cf. 1:10), to marry and have children, and to let their children marry. The promise to Abraham of a large offspring remained in place, even in Babylon. They were even to seek peace for Babylon because peace for the city would mean peace for the exiles (29:7). The purpose was to assure God's remnant of hope and a future with Him (v. 11).

Attention was given to the hope of a return from exile by reference to the seventy years (cf. 25:11–12) and God's good promise (lit. "word") for them (29:10–14). This assurance was based on God's inner thoughts toward His people: plans for peace, not harm, a future and hope i.e., hopeful future). God's plan was based on His love for Israel and His desire for communion with them. Israel would search for Him with all their heart, and they would find Him (vv. 12–14a). Then God would bring His scattered people back to the promised land.

The letter is filled with warnings against false prophets. Besides the prophets in Judah (see chaps. 23–28), there were prophets in Babylon among the exiles (29:1, 8, 15). Jeremiah deals with them in vv. 15–19, 20–23, and 24–32, particularly attacking an opponent in Babylon named Shemaiah the Nehelamite (vv. 24–28). In a letter, Shemaiah had urged Zephaniah, the priest in Jerusalem, to take advantage of his temple office and suppress any false prophets (v. 26). Shemaiah reproached Zephaniah for not having rebuked Jeremiah for prophesying that the captivity would last a long time, and that accordingly the exiles should build houses, live in them, plant gardens, and eat their produce (v. 28). Hearing what Shemaiah had said, Jeremiah sent a letter back to the community in Babylon, warning that Shemaiah was not sent by the Lord but had caused the people to trust in a lie and had taught rebellion against the Lord (vv. 31–32). Therefore, none of his family would return from the Exile.

30:1—33:26
BOOK OF COMFORT

God commanded Jeremiah to write in a book all the words He had spoken to him (v. 2). This included the assurance that Israel would repossess the land promised to their fathers. Based on the introduction (30:1–4) and the common theme of restoration, chapters 30–33 may be understood to be a single unit called "the Book of Comfort." As we have seen, both judgment and hope were part of God's plan to restore the covenant with Israel (cf. 16:14–21; 23:1–8; 24:1—25:14; 27:7, 11; 29:1–14). In this plan, judgment (destruction) and hope (reconstruction) grew out of God's will to create a new beginning (cf. v. 11). His desire to restore Israel was rooted in His character: (a) His faithfulness to His people, His promise, His honor, and His mission; (b) His power as Ruler of the nations; and (c) His forgiveness of Israel's moral and spiritual corruption. The substance of the Book of Comfort, therefore, is God's faithfulness, His power to liberate from oppression, and His compassionate forgiveness.

30:1–24
Restoration of Israel and Judah

This chapter can be divided into three units: assurance of salvation (vv. 1–11), judgment as correction (vv. 12–17), and covenant renewal (vv. 18–24).

30:1–11. God Will Save Jacob. The listener was first invited into a situation of fear and unrest but was reassured by the promissory theme of the section: Jacob was to be saved out of his trouble (v. 7; cf. Dan. 12:1). God would break Babylon's dominion over Israel; foreigners would enslave them no more; they were to serve the Lord their God and David their king, whom He would raise up for them (Jer. 30:8–9; cf. 23:1–8). Therefore, the listener was encouraged not to fear or be dismayed (vv. 10–11). God would save His servant Israel from captivity, and the people would have rest and quietness (or peace and security) because of His saving presence with them. He would wipe out all of the nations surrounding Israel (cf. 46:1—51:58), but not Israel itself (cf. 5:10, 18; 46:28). The restoration promise was balanced by a time of judgment. God would discipline His people and punish them (30:11). The reality could not be hidden—Israel was in exile as a result of a devastating judgment for their sins. But after a time, God would restore them as His servant in the world.

30:12–17. Judgment as Correction. The concept of God's punishment as "correction" (v. 11) is expanded in vv. 12–17. The Exile/restoration is described as illness/healing, which is common to both Jeremiah (e.g., 8:15, 22; 10:19; 14:19; 15:18; 30:13; 33:6) and the book of Psalms (e.g., Pss. 22; 38; 41; 74; 79; 80; 83; 90; 102; 109; 137). Israel's affliction is at first described as incurable (Jer. 30:12). At least, it could not be cured by any of the nation's erstwhile allies or by any other human means (vv. 13–16). In the end, God would cure Israel and heal the wounds (v. 17). On what grounds would God cure the incurable? The passage moves from hopelessness to hope. It begins with a portrayal of the incurable illness of Israel in exile, with no one pleading the nation's cause (v. 13), and moves to a description of the nations that had forgotten and not cared for (or sought) the chastised Israel (i.e., Israel is irrelevant to them; vv. 14–15). At that point, however, God would restore Israel (vv. 16–17) because the nations viewed Israel as a despised outcast (v. 17). Thus, God would take action against the nations that judged Israel (vv. 16–17), with the same judgment that God had brought upon Israel (v. 14), and He would release Israel from the deeply humiliating experience of being scattered and exiled before the eyes of the nations. He was moved to forgive and restore in a way similar to the petitioners who prayed in the temple, asking for salvation from "the depths," "deep waters," or "the pit" of death (e.g., Pss. 6; 30; 35; 40; 49; 57; 69; 88; 94; 109; 130; 141; 143) while their enemies gloated at their predicament. In these laments, the worshipers of the God of Zion experienced His deliverance because of His love and compassion. This would be Israel's experience.

In the book of Psalms (e.g., Pss. 46; 48; 76; 84; 87; 122; 132) and in the Prophets (e.g., Is. 2:2–4; 18:7; 60:10–12), God's deep affinity for Zion is integrated into His plan to be known as God among all the nations of the world (Pss. 47;

93; 96–99). Consequently, the nations' mocking reaction toward Zion (Jer. 30:17) undermined God's mission to the nations. Only if His glory and honor were restored could the God of Zion, the God of Israel, be acclaimed by the nations as Sovereign Ruler of the world.

Thus, the ground for God's "curing the incurable" was His love for His faithful people and His goal to be worshiped by all nations (i.e., the mission of God). God would lift up His wounded people from "the pit" (i.e., exile, contempt, death) to restore them to a new life. This new life would elicit amazement among the nations. Israel's salvation from death would become God's way of making Himself known among the nations. This message parallels the theme of the suffering servant of the Lord (Is. 52:13—53:12), who sheds light on God's redemptive intention behind the suffering and resurrection of Jesus Christ.

30:18-24. Renewed Society. God envisaged a new marriage/covenant with Israel. The gradual movement from Israel's captivity to God's final covenant declaration in vv. 18–22 begins with location and homes (v. 18), followed by a peaceful communal life (v. 19a) and the growth of the population (v. 19b–20b). All external threats and oppression were to be thwarted by God (v. 20c), and their own nobles and governors would be from among themselves (no alien rulers; v. 21). Then, God would draw Israel's ruler to Him (v. 21). The climax is God's pronouncement of the covenant formula: Israel would be His people, and He would be their God (v. 22; cf. Introduction). Finally, Israel's promised salvation assumes Babylon's defeat. No specifics are given in vv. 23–24, but the text describes God's fury moving like a whirlwind against the wicked (including Babylon) in order to perform His intentions. In due course, this would be a reality, but meanwhile God's people were to trust Him and wait for His actions (cf. chaps. 50–51).

31:1–40
The Remnant of Israel Saved

In v. 1, this section resumes the covenant formula of 30:22: God pledged to be the God of all the families of Israel, and they would be His people. This emphasis on God as father and on Israel as families and kindred people characterizes the chapter. Several promissory units follow (31:2–6, 7–14, 15–22, 23–26, 27–30, 31–34, 35–37, 38–40) that address "all Israel" as a worshiping community (vv. 2–6, 33–40) as well as

exiles from "Israel"/"Ephraim" (vv. 15–22) and "Judah" (vv. 23–30). The arrangement suggests a chiastic pattern:

A All Israel (vv. 2–14)
  B Ephraim (vv. 15–22)
  B' Judah (vv. 23–30)
A' All Israel (vv. 31–40)

31:1-14. Deliverance and Restoration. In 31:2–6, there is a movement from exile to restoration (cf. 30:18–22). We read about the people surviving the sword and finding grace (or favor) in the wilderness (31:2), the rebuilding of community life (building, celebrating, planting, eating), and the pilgrimage to Zion for the worship of God (v. 6); this movement is driven by God's everlasting love (v. 3). God's deliverance of Israel and His granting of new life are celebrated in vv. 7–14. His people, who are referred to as the chief (or foremost) of the nations (cf. Amos 6:1), are summoned to sing, shout, proclaim, give praise, and petition God to save them (Jer. 31:7). All would be brought home from the north (Assyria and Babylon) and the ends of the earth (v. 8). They would weep and pray in gratitude and joy as God their Father led them through dry lands and by the rivers of waters in a straight way where no one would stumble (v. 9).

God told the nations (vv. 10–12) that He had redeemed and ransomed Israel from the hand of those stronger than him and that He who scattered Israel would gather them and keep them as a shepherd does his flock. As a result, Israel would come singing to Zion with shining faces and rejoicing (v. 12; Heb. *nahar*, "to stream," "shine") at the goodness of the Lord and the wealth of food (see commentary on 51:36–50). Their lives would be like a well-watered garden and free from sorrow. The salvation of the Lord would lead to "rejoicing," the central theme of the unit (31:4, 7, 12–14).

31:15-22. Hope for All Israel. The next unit formally addressed Ephraim but concerned all Israel (vv. 15–22). In a scene of mourning over the dead, God declared that there was hope for the future, including their children (vv. 14–17). Ephraim's grandmother Rachel symbolized the mothers who mourned their lost children (v. 15). When her lost child Ephraim repented, God heard his lamentation and prayer for deliverance (vv. 18–19). It was His fatherly love for Ephraim that moved Him to action. This is depicted in intimate language: God still earnestly "remembered"

Ephraim as His dear son in whom He delighted and for whom He yearned and had mercy and compassion (v. 20).

The concluding appeal for repentance was motivated by God's creative act: a woman would *sabab* a man (vv. 21–22). This expression is of unknown meaning, and the verb has been variously translated in this passage as "encompass," "shelter," or "return." If it alludes to the Creation story, where man encompassed woman before they became "one flesh" (Gen. 2:21–24), it may mean that God would enhance the fertility of man and wife to greatly compensate for the previous loss of children (31:8, 15).

31:23–30. Prosperity of Judah. Judah is addressed in vv. 23–26. Its future prosperity is illustrated by farmers and shepherds dwelling in the land and its cities. The people would recognize God and bless Judah and Jerusalem. In this land of peace and blessing, God's people would experience sweet, pleasant sleep (cf. blessing in v. 23). Two promises concerning Israel and Judah are made. God would make humans and beasts fruitful (cf. vv. 22, 23–26). As He had overseen the plucking up, tearing down, destruction, overthrow, and calamity of Israel, so would He now watch over them as they built and planted (cf. 1:10). The proverb in 31:29 was often quoted and caused concern among the exiles (cf. Lam. 5:7; Ezek. 18:2–3). It expressed concepts stated in the covenant law (e.g., Ex. 20:5–6; Deut. 5:9b–10). The Lord clarifies that the current situation is not the result of the sins of the forefathers; the sins of the present generation are enough to condemn them.

31:31–40. The New Covenant. The promise of the new covenant was addressed to all Israel (vv. 31–35), renewing the old, broken covenant connected with the deliverance from Egypt. In the new covenant, God declared that He would put His law into the peoples' minds and hearts (as He had always wanted to—Deut. 6:6–9). He would be their God, and they would be His people (Jer. 31:33; cf. e.g., 30:22; 31:1; 32:28). The new covenant is based on God's forgiveness of sin, which would definitively and ultimately be accomplished by Christ (Heb. 8:8–12; 10:16–17). By this, all of His people would know Him (Jer. 31:34).

Finally, Yahweh guaranteed Israel's permanence (vv. 35–40). As long as the heavenly bodies (sun, moon, and stars) remained before the Lord, and as long as heaven remained immeasurable and the earth unsearchable, so Israel would remain before the Lord. In the rebuilding of Jerusalem (vv. 38–40), the area mapped out for the new temple was beyond the old city walls. The area of the Valley of Hinnom, with its dead bodies and ashes (cf. 7:31–32; 19:2, 6; 32:35), down to the Brook of Kidron and the corner of the Horse Gate would be holy unto the Lord. God's presence would restore the city's sanctity.

32:1–44
Jeremiah Buys a Field

Chapter 32 begins with a historical introduction (vv. 1–5), followed by Jeremiah's land purchase (vv. 6–15), his prayer for understanding (vv. 16–25), and God's assurance of Israel's return (vv. 26–44). Jeremiah's purchase of land was a symbolic act of Israel's rightful ownership of the land of Canaan, and consequently, it implied the promise of a future return from the Babylonian Exile.

32:1–15. Purchase of the Land. The context of the purchase was the predicted impending Babylonian Exile. King Zedekiah faced the siege of Jerusalem by the Babylonians (587 B.C.). Jeremiah was imprisoned for having prophesied that the city would be destroyed and that Zedekiah would be taken into exile (vv. 1–5; cf. 38:1—39:10). Jeremiah purchased the land as directed by God (32:6–7, 9–12). One of Jeremiah's relatives, Hanamel, visited him in prison and requested that the prophet buy his field because of Jeremiah's right of inheritance (i.e., redemption)—Israel's laws ensured that the possession of land remained within a tribe or a family (cf. Lev. 25:25–31; Ruth 4:1–2).

The details of the purchase process are given (Jer. 32:10–12), and the scribe Baruch, Jeremiah's assistant, is mentioned here for the first time. Before witnesses, Jeremiah gave the purchase deeds to Baruch (one sealed and one open). On the Lord's instruction, he asked Baruch to put them in a clay container so that they would last for a long time (v. 14). The significance of this act was that houses, fields, and vineyards would be purchased again after the Exile (v. 15). Jeremiah's plot of land was paradigmatic of all the land that Israel lost at this time to the Babylonians but which God would restore it to them in the future. The written deeds in the jar symbolized Israel's right to the promised land and God's commitment to restore it to them (vv. 14–15, 42–44).

32:16–44. Jeremiah's Prayerful Dialogue with God. A two-part prayer in the form of a dialogue between Jeremiah and God is next (vv. 16–44). In the dialogue, two interventions in each part of the prayer together form a chiasm that unifies the exchange:

A Jeremiah's Prayer: God's power to deliver Israel (vv. 17–22)

B Jeremiah's Prayer: Israel's disobedience and punishment (vv. 23–24)

B' God's Answer: Israel's disobedience and punishment (vv. 26–35)

A' God's Answer: God's power to deliver Israel (vv. 36–44)

There are several key elements that deserve to be noted. First, the covenant formula (v. 38; cf. 7:23; 11:4; 24:7; 30:22; 31:1, 33) underscores the deep and intimate relationship between God and His people, as in a marriage: He would be their God, and they would be His people. If stated in the present tense, it is a declaratory formula that actually makes or institutes the covenant. Here it is a prediction revealing God's plan: the future covenant being made in the present by the promissory prophetic word of God. Living in the hope of this promissory word would bring hope as a foretaste of the future reality. Second, God's gift to His people—undivided loyalty and direction—was to manifests itself in the people as the fear of God (32:39; cf. 6:16; 21:8; 24:7; 29:13; 42:3; Ezek. 11:19–20; 36:26–27). Thirdly, the promise of an everlasting covenant (Jer. 32:40) would not be broken or terminated by disobedience and divine judgment, the fear of God being forever in Israel's heart; Lastly, God promised to plant Israel in the promised land with all His "heart" and "soul" (v. 41).

These elements emphasize God's faithfulness and His transforming work in the hearts of human beings with whom He enters into a relationship. God's promises in vv. 36–44 taught Israel that hope for a future good life depended on God's loving care and their faithfulness to Him as their Redeemer Lord. Having the fear of God in one's heart enables people to experience God's love and to commune with Him (cf. Rev. 14:6–7).

33:1–26
Excellence of the Restored Nation

The word of the Lord came a second time while Jeremiah was imprisoned (v. 1; cf. 32:2). Asserting His name by reference to His creative acts (33:2), God invited the listeners to call to Him and promised that He would answer by showing them great and *batsurot* things. The Hebrew word *batsur* can mean either "unassailable" (i.e., strong, mighty) or "inaccessible" (v. 3; cf. 32:17, 27). These "things" are seven promissory announcements regarding God's decision to revert the fortunes of Judah from exile to restoration. These promises conclude the Book of Comfort.

33:1–10. Health and Healing. The historical context of these verses was the Babylonian destruction as a result of God hiding His face from Jerusalem. His anger against the wicked people had raged through the victorious Babylonians, who had desolated the cities of Judah and destroyed their houses (vv. 4–5).

God's first promise was to bring health and healing (vv. 6–10; cf. 8:15, 22; 30:17). This theme is common in the psalms of lament (cf. vv. 4–24). God would restore the conditions of old by bringing Israel and Judah back from captivity (*shub*, "return," and *shebut*, "captivity") God would restore the fortunes of Judah and Israel (33:7; cf. *shub shebut* in 29:14; 30:3, 18; 31:23; 32:44; 33:7, 11, 26). He would rebuild the city and make it inhabitable, cleanse the people, and forgive them for their sinful rebellion (vv. 7–8). All the standard Hebrew words for "sin" occur in v. 8: *'awon* ("rebellion," "iniquity"), *khata'* ("to sin"), and *pasha'* ("to transgress"). The shame and humiliation caused by Israel's sin would be replaced by joy, praise, and honor from God. The nations would be afraid and tremble because of God's goodness to Israel, and His honor among the nations would be restored (v. 9; cf. 30:12–22). The most persuasive evidence of God's kingship in the world is His power to bring the dead back to life. Jeremiah exemplifies this through the healing of Jerusalem, and the Bible revisits this theme in the resurrection of Jesus Christ.

33:11–13. Joy and Gladness and Restoration. The second promise (vv. 10–11) is of a massive restoration of fortune for Judah and Jerusalem (v. 11; cf. vv. 7, 26). The cities would be reinhabited, and there would be joy and gladness (of bridegrooms and brides) and praise to God. Three times in Jeremiah, Jerusalem's destruction is illustrated by descriptions of the disappearance of the sounds of weddings (7:34; 16:9; 25:10). As a symbol of joy and life, God would restore the joy of the bridegroom and his bride. The hymnic chorus of praise to *yahweh tseba'ot* (see *"Yahweh Tseba'ot,"* p. 912) will resound because He is good and His *khesed*—"mercy," "faithful love," "kindness"—endures forever (cf. Ps. 106:1; 107:1; 118:1-4, 29; 136:1-26).

The third promise (Jer. 33:12-13) announces that the empty cities of Judah (cf. v. 10) would be filled by shepherds and their flocks (cf. 32:44). There would be safe governance (shepherds), abundant food (pastures), and the people (the flock) would again pass under the hands of those counting them. Order, growth, and safety were to be restored.

33:14-18. New Leadership. The fourth promise (vv. 14-16) repeats 23:5-6, adding to it 33:14 and applying the name "The Lord Our Righteousness" or "The Lord Our Righteous Savior" to "her" (Jerusalem) instead of "him" (the Branch). A righteous king of Davidic descent was to arise who would execute justice and righteousness (see commentary on 23:1-8). The identity of the city was inextricably tied to that of the Davidic king.

The fifth promise (vv. 17-18) concerns Israel's governors. The hereditary offices of the Davidic king and the priests/Levites would be permanent. Since the king's tasks are not specified, but those of the priests/Levites are, this promise may imagine Israel as a worshiping community rather than a kingdom. In his judgment speeches, Jeremiah prophesied the permanent abrogation of the corrupted Davidic monarchy (22:30), but 33:14-16 (also 23:5-6) gives room for the fulfillment of the true Davidic covenant. The implied hope of a messianic king is confirmed in the following promise in 33:19-22.

33:19-26. God's Faithfulness to His People. The sixth promise (vv. 19-22) expands on 31:35-37, underscoring the permanence of God's covenants with David (cf. 2 Sam. 7:11-16; Ps. 89:24-37; Is. 55:3) and the priests and Levites (cf. e.g., Ex. 29; Lev. 8). They would remain as surely as the continuance of the created order of day and night. God would multiply their descendants like the countless stars and immeasurable sand of the sea. The final promise (vv. 23-26) is a response to the fact that the nations had despised God's chosen people (Israel and Judah) by assuming that God would no longer consider them a nation. This argument against faith in God's promises is refuted by a reference to God's ordering of night and day and heaven and earth (cf. 31:35-37; 33:20-22).

The concluding words confirm God's intention, based on chapters 30-33, to bring the captives back (or "restore their fortunes") and have

compassion on them. This promise was fulfilled in 537 B.C. when the Persian king Cyrus ordered the return of the exiles. However, if the promise of a Davidic king in Israel concerned an earthly king, it was not fulfilled. As a messianic promise, many hundred years later, Christians acclaimed Jesus as the "Christ" (Messiah), not of an earthly kingdom but of the kingdom of God (Matt. 16:16; Acts 17:7; Rev. 19:16).

34:1—35:19
CASE STUDIES:
INFIDELITY AND FIDELITY

This block contains two narrative examples of infidelity (Zedekiah: 34:1-7; treatment of slaves: vv. 8-22) and one of fidelity (the Rechabites: 35:1-11). Two case studies are discussed in the conclusion (vv. 12-19).

34:1-7
Zedekiah Warned by God

The setting for the first case study was the Babylonian invasion (vv. 1-2, 6-7; cf. 21:1-7; 37:3-10; 38:14-28). Only two fortified cities near Jerusalem continued to resist (34:6-7; cf. 2 Chr. 11:5-11). Azekah (Tell Zakariya, southwest of Jerusalem) and Lachish (Tell ed-Duweir, further north) appear in one of the letters found in the debris of Lachish's destruction in 586 B.C. ("And let [my Lord] know that we are watching for the signals of Lachish...for we cannot see Azekah"). Jeremiah's prophecy suggests a massive attack (Jer. 34:1). God's warnings through Jeremiah had been proven true (cf. 32:25).

Jeremiah warned King Zedekiah concerning Babylon's approaching victory, Jerusalem's destruction, and the king's captivity in Babylon (cf. 34:2-3; 32:3-4a). However, this is followed by a description of a different fate for Zedekiah: the king would not die by the sword but in peace. He would be honored in death and duly buried and grieved (34:4-5; cf. 52:8-11). Probably the best way to interpret this shift is to suggest that Jeremiah was telling Zedekiah what would happen to him if he surrendered to the king of Babylon instead of opposing him, as suggested in 38:17-18. Zedekiah's actual fate is evidence that he did not pay attention to the message of the Lord (53:8-11). Thus, Israel had two options for responding to God: infidelity and fidelity. This theme is developed further in 34:8—35:19.

34:8–22
Treacherous Treatment of Slaves

Infidelity was exemplified by the people and their leaders. They broke the covenant by not freeing their male and female Hebrew slaves every seventh year (vv. 8–9, 14; cf. Ex. 21:1–6; Deut. 15:1–18). Fellow Israelites became slaves because they were unable to pay their debts. The sabbatical law not only presumed that the debt would be written off but also required that a freed slave receive a liberal provision of food and drink (Deut. 15:14). Faithfulness to this law implied that Israel "remembered their slavery in Egypt and the Lord's redemption" (Deut. 15:15)—this was an act of faith that demonstrated care for one's kin in the covenant community. Zedekiah compelled the people to follow this law. However, though they initially obeyed, the princes and the people eventually changed their minds and broke the covenant (Jer. 34:8–11, 15–16), perhaps out of greed and selfishness. Such infidelity implied gross indifference to God and to the duty of sharing His gifts with people in need.

God drew a parallel (vv. 12–22) between the covenant He made with Israel's fathers (vv. 13–14) and the covenant regarding freedom for Hebrew slaves made by Zedekiah (vv. 8–9, 15–16). Both covenants concerned a proclamation of release, but God's fidelity and Judah's infidelity are contrasted. Using a wordplay on "turn" (*shub*; cf. 3:1—4:4; 8:4–6; 15:19), God asserted (34:15) that Israel turned (*tashubu*) back (or "repented") to covenant fidelity and swore to practice the commandment regarding liberty for debt slaves. But this commitment was soon abandoned: they turned around (*tashubu*) from covenant fidelity and profaned God's name by bringing the debt slaves back into subjection. Since the oath of the covenant was taken in the temple in God's name, breaking the oath meant profaning His name (v. 16). God concluded that Judah had broken their oath to the Lord, making a mockery out of Him and of their obligation to fellow members of the covenant community.

God sentenced Judah using an ironic wordplay: because of their infidelity in not proclaiming freedom to their own people, He would proclaim freedom to the sword, plague, and famine (v. 17a). He would give Judah into the hands of the Babylonians, and Judah and Jerusalem would become desolate (vv. 17–22). This sentence is based on the fact that all the people had entered the covenant with Him and cut the calf in two and passed between the parts of it (vv. 18–19). Again, a wordplay is included: the word cut (*karat*) is used both for the making of the covenant (vv. 8, 13) and for the cutting (*karat*) of the animal, which represented the fate of covenant breakers (v. 18; cf. Gen. 15:7–11, 17).

The argument in Jer. 34:8–22, then, is that covenant fidelity, exemplified in the act of releasing the debt slaves, would bring safety and well-being to Jerusalem. Breaking the covenant by economic exploitation, however, would clear the way for the invasion of Babylon. Obedience to the Lord brings peace, but disobedience brings destruction. God had entered into a covenant with His people based on His work of redemption on their behalf. Their role was to accept Him as their God and respond in gratitude and obedience. If they trusted Him, He would continue to protect and save them from their enemies. But because they rejected Him and no longer trusted Him, the covenant was violated.

35:1–19
The Obedient Rechabites and Conclusion

In contrast to Judah's disobedience, the obedience of the Rechabites is adduced as a model. God asked Jeremiah to bring the Rechabites into one of the chambers in the temple area and to test them by giving them wine to drink (vv. 1–2). They refused because their father commanded them not to drink wine or build houses, sow seed, plant vineyards, or own any of these things, but to live in tents and maintain a nomadic lifestyle (vv. 3–7). They had obeyed their father's command. Only when the Babylonians entered the land did they seek refuge in Jerusalem (vv. 8–11). God then compared the disobedience of Judah and Jerusalem with the obedience of the Rechabites (vv. 12–16). The Rechabites obeyed their human father, and Judah refused to obey their divine Father. He had tried to call Judah to repentance through His prophets. Had they obeyed, they would have dwelled in the land He had given them. But they did not. Therefore, God's sentence of doom against Judah would be executed (v. 17).

God also recognized the obedience of the Rechabites and rewarded them with the promise that their descendants would prevail and there would always be a servant of the Lord from their household. The Hebrew expression *'omed lepanay*, literally "stand before," is associated with the concept of standing before an authority ready to serve (Gen. 41:46; 1 Kin. 1:28; 17:1). Accordingly, some translations render it as "serve." A life of fidelity results in blessing and communion with God, but infidelity results in the loss of God's protection. Jeremiah 34–35, therefore, is an urgent message to the listeners to be faithful to God and His word. This faithfulness is also a mark of the end-time community of faith (Rev. 14:12).

36:1—45:5

JEREMIAH AND THE FALL OF THE CITY

This portion of the book reveals that God's will was visibly working in the shifts of international power occurring in the ANE. Refusal to accept the "pro-Babylonian" reading of the destiny of Jerusalem was seen as disobedience to God's word and will. This section is also about the experiences of Jeremiah shortly before and after the fall of Jerusalem. Baruch was Jeremiah's scribe, preserving the prophecies (36:1–32), and Jeremiah would be imprisoned during the fall of the city (37:1—40:6). The section details an insurrection against Gedaliah (40:7—41:18) and finally a flight to Egypt (42:1—44:30). It closes with an assurance to Baruch (45:1–5).

36:1–32
The Jeremiah Scroll

Jeremiah had been on trial for his life. Although acquitted, he was treated with suspicion by the Jerusalem establishment (cf. chaps. 7, 26). Thus, chapter 36 pictures him as an outsider and an unwelcome threat to prevailing policies. The confrontation between Jeremiah and King Jehoiakim (609–597 B.C.) is a classic example of "truth speaking to power." Chapter 36 is central for understanding how prophets preserved their messages for future generations and how these messages finally became part of the biblical canon. Jeremiah's scroll had come to have a life of its own and to exercise authority independently of Jeremiah. It was, at this time, the written word of God that challenged the king.

36:1–3. Purpose of the Scroll. It was in 605 B.C. (v. 1a) that God commanded Jeremiah to write His words on a *megillat seper*, "scroll of writing" (vv. 2, 4; Ps. 40:8; Ezek. 2:9; cf. the single word *megillah*, "scroll," in Jer. 36; Ezek. 3:1–3; Zech. 5:1–2). The book was not an invention of Jeremiah but of God. Jeremiah was to write down all of the words God had given to him from the beginning of his ministry regarding Israel, Judah, and the nations (Jer. 36:2). The purpose was to inform the people of Judah about the potential disasters God was threatening in order to encourage them to turn from their wicked ways so that God would forgive them of their sin and guilt (v. 3).

36:4–19. Role of Baruch. Baruch the son of Neriah wrote the scroll at Jeremiah's instruction (v. 4). A clay imprint of a seal from Jeremiah's time, which was used for sealing papyrus scrolls, has been found with the text "Belonging to Berechiah [short form of Baruch] son of Neriah." Because he was either barred from entering the temple or was imprisoned (cf. 7:2–15; 20:3), Jeremiah commissioned Baruch to read the scroll in the temple to all the people of Judah so that repentant prayer might avert the anger of the Lord (36:5–9).

Baruch's public reading was heard in the temple and repeated before the princes in the palace (vv. 10–15). The leaders reacted with fear and promised to tell the king (v. 16). They asked if Baruch wrote the scroll at Jeremiah's instruction. When Baruch affirmed this (vv. 17–18), the prophetic authenticity of the scroll was established. Anticipating the king's reaction, they warned Jeremiah and Baruch to go into hiding (v. 19; cf. v. 26).

36:20–32. Burning and Rewriting of the Scroll. Receiving a verbal summary, the king ordered the scroll to be brought to him and asked Jehudi to read it (vv. 20–21). For every three or four columns that Jehudi read, the king cut the scroll with a scribe's knife and cast it into the fire until the whole scroll was burned (vv. 21–23; a papyrus sheet normally had room for three to four columns).

Jeremiah rewrote the scroll at God's command (vv. 27–28). It was accompanied by a divine indictment and a judicial sentence against the king. Sadly, the narrative includes a brief assertion indicating that the rewritten warning did not have the desired effect (vv. 29–31). The sentence of condemnation was harsh: no leader would sit on David's throne, and the king's corpse would be dishonorably cast out into the heat of day and the frost of night. God would punish him, his family, and his servants and would bring on them and on Jerusalem and Judah all of the predicted disasters.

This narrative illustrates how God counters human pride and resistance. God's relentless resolve brings the truth back again and again to those who need to hear it. His word cannot be stopped, only ignored or accepted. Chapter 36 reveals that Jeremiah's proclamation of judgment was intended to lead Judah to change its ways. Yes, the Babylonian invasion was inescapable, but, in order to survive, it was necessary for the people to listen to God's voice. He yearned to forgive their sins (v. 3) and to grant them peace and well-being. He wanted once more to be their God and for them to be His people (cf. 30:1—33:26).

37:1—40:6
Jeremiah Imprisoned and the Fall of Jerusalem

After the final reaction of the king to the word of God, he could only wait and witness the fulfillment of the word of judgment against him and the land. Next, the events surrounding Jerusalem's fall in 586 B.C. are described. Judah's struggle for survival in the international rivalry between Babylon and Egypt impacted Jeremiah's life and ministry.

37:1–10. A King Seeking Help. King Zedekiah (597–586 B.C.) was at first a Babylonian puppet king who finally rebelled against Nebuchadnezzar. The text indicates that the king, his servants, and the people refused to accept God's words through Jeremiah (v. 2). Zedekiah had abandoned his covenant faithfulness, and by ignoring the Lord's word, he had brought about Judah's fall.

Surprisingly, he asked Jeremiah to intercede for the people (v. 3). He wanted the prophet's (God's) aid but did not want to obey the prophet's (God's) command. This type of compromise is unacceptable.

The king's request was motivated by fear and desperation rather than faith. Jerusalem was under siege by the Babylonians (v. 5; cf. vv. 7–10). Against Jeremiah's clear warning, Zedekiah had rebelled against Babylon's rule, relying on Egypt for help (cf. Ezek. 17:15; 29:1–21). The Babylonians reacted quickly and imposed a siege on Jerusalem from the beginning of 588 to August 586 B.C. (2 Kin. 25; Jer. 21:3–7; 39:1–10; 52:4–5; Ezek. 24:1–2). Under Pharaoh Hophra, Egypt supported Judah militarily (Jer. 37:5–11; cf. Lam. 4:17; Ezek. 17; 29–32), but this temporary support was insufficient to save Judah. After the Babylonians' temporary withdrawal from Jerusalem (Jer. 37:5), Jeremiah insisted that Pharaoh's army would return to Egypt and the Babylonians would come back, take Jerusalem, and burn it (vv. 6–10). This was bad news for the king and gave no warrant for interpreting the movements of the two imperial powers in Judah's favor.

37:11–21. Jeremiah's Arrest and Imprisonment. The story in this passage provides evidence for the level of fear and paranoia that had engulfed the court and the confusion regarding the loyalty of Jeremiah. The prophet had opposed the politics of the king, supporting surrender to the Babylonians instead of fighting them. Now during a moment of respite, the prophet left the city to claim his property in the land of Benjamin and was unjustly accused of defection to the Babylonians. This was a serious charge of treason. Jeremiah's enemies in the army and at court found a pretext to arrest, abuse, and imprison him. The relationship between Zedekiah and Jeremiah had been problematic. Since the charges were serious, the king probably approved of the actions taken against Jeremiah. The king's reason for seeking a word from the Lord is not stated, but one could suggest that since Jeremiah was in a precarious situation, Zedekiah may have hoped that he would deliver a positive message in exchange for deliverance from prison. But a true prophet cannot alter the word of the Lord. Zedekiah's steadfast practice of ignoring that word had already sealed his fate. God's word remained, and no last-minute and feckless courtesies to the prophet he had despised could alter the course he had chosen.

38:1–13. Back to the Dungeon. The insincerity of Zedekiah's apparent kindness to Jeremiah was evident in his decision to send him back to prison on pressure from the cabal at the court. But Jeremiah's deliverance from inevitable death depended on the compassion of Ebed-Melech the Ethiopian, one of the eunuchs in the king's palace. He informed the king about Jeremiah's condition, and the king ordered Jeremiah's release (vv. 7–13). Ebed-Melech's act was an act of faith in God and His word. Later on, Jeremiah announced to him the Lord's promise that He would deliver him from the sword at the coming destruction of Jerusalem because he had put his trust in Him (39:15–18). There is a close solidarity between God and His servant the prophet, and people's actions against the prophet are indeed actions against God and His word (cf. Matt. 25:40).

38:14–28. Once Again, the King and the Prophet. In a secret conversation, Zedekiah asked for straightforward counsel, and Jeremiah could not have been plainer: surrender and live, resist and die. In order to persuade the king, Jeremiah pointed to the outcome of a wrong decision: it would harm his wives and children (vv. 22–23a), his close friends would turn against him (v. 22b), he himself would be captured (v. 23b), and his city would be burned (v. 23c).

The king did not seem to realize the danger he was in (vv. 24–26). Rather than dealing with the larger issue, he kept God's word secret, fearing the princes in Jerusalem more than the Babylonians. The king and the princes of Judah were about to face complete destruction, but rather than accept God's word, which would allow them and their people to live, they dwelled on their petty intrigues and disputes over personal power. Jeremiah remained in prison and was still there when Jerusalem was taken (v. 28).

39:1–18. Fall of the City. The most significant event in the book is the fall of the city, mentioned in the prologue (1:1–3) and in the historical epilogue (52:1–30). It is the central topic in numerous judgment speeches of Jeremiah and is the background for the words of comfort given to the faithful. Jerusalem's fall and Zedekiah's fate, in this account, are the fulfillment of God's word, and they confirm Jeremiah's prophetic ministry (39:1–10). After penetrating the walls of Jerusalem, the princes of Babylon sat down in the Middle Gate (cf. 21:4). Zedekiah and his armed men were able to escape by night, but the Babylonians pursued and captured them in the plains of Jericho, eighteen miles (30 km) northeast of Jerusalem. They were brought to Nebuchadnezzar in his headquarters in Riblah, on the Orontes River in Hamath, Syria.

Nebuchadnezzar killed Zedekiah's sons and all the nobles of Judah. He then put out the eyes of Zedekiah, bound him, and carried him off to Babylon. Killing Zedekiah's sons may have been intended to halt future claims to the throne. The killing of the nobles may have had to do with their anti-Babylonian position, which is well documented in Jeremiah and would have been known to the pro-Babylonian faction. The torture of Zedekiah is usually understood as an example of Babylonian cruelty—the killing of his sons was the last thing he would ever see—however, inflicting blindness may also be understood in a wider context. First, blinding could be an ANE suzerain's punishment for a rebellious vassal, for Nebuchadnezzar had made a treaty with Zedekiah when he became king of Judah in 597 B.C., which Zedekiah had confirmed with an oath (cf. Ezek. 17:11–21). Second, being blinded was included among the punishments for breaking the Lord's covenant (Deut. 28:28–29, 32). Third, Jeremiah's numerous prophecies against

the kings of Judah included the punishment of no longer seeing the homeland (Jer. 22:8–12; 42:17–18) and never again seeing the good that God would do for His people (29:32). Although Zedekiah was largely responsible for the disaster, his fate was for now left open-ended (cf. 32:3–5; 34:2–5). The idea seems to be that even if Zedekiah were to survive imprisonment and return to Jerusalem, he would not be able to see the land, which was the predicted punishment for breaking the covenant. It was precisely this cruel warfare practice that the Lord had wanted the king to avoid by listening to His word.

After the destruction of Jerusalem (39:8; cf. 52:12–14), Nebuzaradan, the Babylonian captain of the guard, carried away the remnant of the people to Babylon but left the poor in Judah and gave them vineyards and fields (39:9–10). This was an initial fulfillment of God's promise to give His people "a future and a hope" (29:11). God's people were, at this time, a remnant in Judah and a remnant in exile. Both groups had to wait for the fulfillment of God's promises. Jeremiah was set free from prison by the Babylonians (39:11–18). He was not to be harmed, and his wishes were to be followed. Jeremiah was assigned to Gedaliah, who took him home to Anathoth in Benjamin to dwell among the people (for the account regarding Ebed Melech in vv. 15–18, see commentary on 38:1–13.)

40:1–6 Jeremiah and Nebuzaradan. More details are given about the future of Jeremiah. The town of Ramah, five miles (8 km) north of Jerusalem, served as a staging post for captives bound for Babylon. Jeremiah had been brought there in chains (v. 1), but Nebuzaradan liberated him and gave him two options: either to follow the captain to Babylon or remain in the land. Later, Nebuzaradan gave Jeremiah another choice: either to follow Gedaliah, the new governor over the cities of Judah, or go wherever he wanted. Jeremiah decided to stay with Gedaliah at Mizpah, among the people who were left in the land.

Nebuzaradan's speech (vv. 2–5) summarizes the fulfillment of God's judgment on Jerusalem and Judah and explains its cause: their sinfulness and disobedience. Although this was spoken by the Babylonian captain of the guard, its truth is undeniable and originated from God. The defeat of the city was not credited by this Babylonian to the superiority of his gods but to the actions of the God of Jeremiah in reaction to the sins of His people.

40:7—41:18
The Insurrection against Gedaliah

This section deals with the governorship of Gedaliah in Judah and the plot to kill him. The setting is Judah after the Babylonian conquest (39:1–10). The idea of an escape to Egypt emerges toward the end of the narrative (41:17–18; cf. 42:1—44:30).

40:7–8. New Leaders in Judea. After the fall of Jerusalem, three parties are represented under Gedaliah, Ishmael, and Johanan. A respected Judean, Gedaliah son of Ahikam, was pro-Babylonian (vv. 5, 9). His father and grandfather had been sympathetic to Jeremiah (e.g., 26:24). Ishmael fought fiercely for Judean independence, cooperating with the small neighboring nations. And Johanan eventually opted for Egypt. Jeremiah had long opposed Ishmael's goal (e.g., 38:2–3). He would also object to Johanan's belief that Egypt was the solution (42:1—44:30). However, Gedaliah, who agreed with Jeremiah's pro-Babylonian views and with whom Jeremiah was dwelling in Mizpah, would fall victim to a conspiracy. The story of Gedaliah illustrates that the political tensions and divisions that existed in Jerusalem before its fall (see commentary on 37:1—40:6) continued after it.

40:9—41:18. Gedaliah. Gedaliah spoke to the people under oath and assured them safe dwelling and income from wine, summer fruit, and olive oil (40:7–10). All Judeans who were scattered during the war returned from Moab, Ammon, Edom, and other countries (vv. 11–12). However, Gedaliah was soon killed by Ishmael and his men. The rebels killed many others and carried away as captives all the remaining people in Mizpah, including the king's daughters who had been left in Gedaliah's care. Hearing of these atrocities, Johanan and the captains of the forces pursued Ishmael and found him in Gibeon. His Judean captives escaped and joined Johanan, while Ishmael and eight men joined the Ammonites (see 40:7—41:15). Johanan gathered his people and set out for Egypt, in fear of a Babylonian retaliation for the murder of Gedaliah, who had been appointed governor by the king of Babylon. On the way, they stayed in Chimham, near Bethlehem (41:17).

42:1—45:5
Flight to and Experiences in Egypt

The flight to Egypt was characterized by fear and rebellion against the Lord. This block of material describes the prophetic ministry of Jeremiah among the survivors as they traveled to and lived in Egypt. He received five messages from the Lord: one on the way to Egypt (42:1–22), three while in Egypt (43:8–13; 44:1–19, 20–30), and one for Baruch (45:1–5).

42:1—43:7. Requesting a Message. When the leaders ran out of options, they turned to Jeremiah and sought the word of God (cf. 37:3, 17; 38:14, 24–28). Thus, Johanan's Judean remnant, who were already escaping to Egypt in disobedience (41:17–18), asked Jeremiah for divine guidance regarding what the "remnant" should do (42:1–3). The request came at a decisive moment. Johanan's people understood that they were a small and vulnerable community, encamped near Bethlehem en route to Egypt. Their choice was vital to God's plan for Israel (i.e., to reveal His glory to all the nations). They promised Jeremiah unconditional obedience to God's will (vv. 5–6; cf. Ex. 24:3, 7; Josh. 24:21, 24; 1 Sam. 7:4, 6–8; 12:19). They acknowledged that they had been "many" but were at this time "few." Israel had begun as a small group when Jacob's family went to Egypt, but they later became numerous (Deut. 10:22). When Johanan referred to his group as being the few left over from the many, it was a reminder of how God's blessing of multiplication had been reversed with a curse of diminution.

God offered two options (Jer. 42:10–22), each with a condition and its consequence. The positive option was to remain in Judah. If they did so, then God would build and plant the remnant of His people (vv. 10–12). The negative option was to go to Egypt (to avoid war and famine), which would mean disobeying God. If they chose this option, then the sword, plague, and famine, which they feared, would overtake them (vv. 16–17). The same divine fury that struck Jerusalem would reach them in Egypt, making them a public example of divine rejection (vv. 13–18). God's word was plain: do not go to Egypt (v. 19).

43:8–13. Jeremiah's Message in Tahpanhes. Jeremiah received another message from the Lord (vv. 8–13). He was commanded to take stones and secretly hide them in the brick courtyard at the entrance to Pharaoh's house. This was interpreted to mean that God would send Nebuchadnezzar of Babylon, His servant, to set his throne over these hidden stones and to spread his royal pavilion over them. Nebuchadnezzar would defeat Egypt and would bring death and exile (v. 11). He would destroy the temples of the Egyptian gods and break down the sacred stones of Beth Shemesh (lit. "house of the sun"), which was central to sun worship (cf. 46:1–28). Acting as God's servant, Babylon's destruction of Egypt and its gods would testify to the sovereignty of Israel's God (43:12). The response of the people is not stated, but a considerable group of Judeans went to Egypt (44:1).

44:1–19. Message of Judgment. In the first part of God's message through Jeremiah in this section, there is a summary of God's wrath against Judah and Jerusalem because of their disobedience (vv. 2–6). In the second part, Jeremiah announced that the Judeans in Egypt were practicing the same idolatry that had led Judah to disaster (vv. 3, 5, 8). Consequently, all of them would be cut off (vv. 7–10) or rejected by God (cf. e.g., Ex. 30:33, 38; 31:14; Lev. 7:20). The destruction of Jerusalem had not humbled them. They did not fear God and did not live according to the covenant. Therefore, the Judean remnant in Egypt would die (Jer. 44:11–14)—the standard punishment for breaking the covenant was death by the sword, famine, and plague (vv. 12–13). God's declaration that they would be destroyed in the land of Egypt was balanced by an open door of invitation for individuals who desired to dwell in Judah (v. 14). The possibility of a faithful remnant remained. God did not give up on His plan to restore His people in Judah.

Unfortunately, the people rejected God's word (vv. 15–19). They continued to burn incense to the queen of heaven and pour out drink offerings to her, as they and their forefathers and kings did in Judah (cf. 7:18), where they had plenty of food, prospered, and were safe. Their flagrant and shameless apostasy was rooted in a fundamental misunderstanding, for their past blessings did not come from the queen of heaven but from the Lord. Their hardship at this time was the result of their disobedience. It was possible for their well-being to be restored by repentance, but in their degenerate state, they were not interested in returning to the true God.

44:20–30. Message against the Apostasy of the Judeans. Jeremiah addressed the people's reliance on the queen of heaven. First, he declared Judah and the Judean remnant in Egypt to be one and the same. They had burned incense (as admitted in vv. 15–19, 24–25), sinned against the Lord, and had not obeyed His *torah* ("law," "instruction"), *khuqqah* ("decrees,"

"statutes"), and *'edot* ("testimonies," "stipulations"; i.e., they had refused to heed the words of the prophet). Second, God summarized what the Judean remnant in Egypt had said (vv. 24–25). The men and their wives had made vows and had implemented them by burning incense to the queen of heaven and pouring out drink offerings to her. So God sarcastically told them to continue performing and fulfilling these vows.

Third, the judgment in vv. 26–30 against the Judeans in Egypt repeats what is found in vv. 11–14. God disassociated Himself from the Judean community in Egypt. Just as they had sworn an oath to worship the queen of heaven (v. 25), so God swore that His great name would no longer be used by these Judeans in their oaths (v. 26). Because of their apostasy, the Judean community was alone and without God. Yet, again, there was a faithful remnant: a small number would escape the sword and return from Egypt to Judah, and all the remnant of Judah who went to Egypt would come to know whose word would endure—God's or theirs (v. 28). God announced a particular sign that would confirm that His words would surely stand against them: Pharaoh Hophra would be given into the hands of his enemies, just as King Zedekiah had been given to the Babylonians (v. 30). God was acting here in defense of His authority, His plan, the covenant with Israel, and His prophetic word, which invites repentance from idolatry and predicts judgment against the disobedient. In the midst of judgment, however, He carefully kept the door open for a faithful remnant desiring to follow His instruction.

45:1–5. Assurance to Baruch. This long section (chaps. 36–45) concludes with a message to Baruch that was given after he wrote the words of Jeremiah on the scroll, before the fall of Jerusalem. The message is motivated by a lament he expressed after writing the scroll for Jeremiah (45:2–3). Baruch complained that the Lord had added sorrow to his grief and left him without rest. Through Jeremiah, the Lord confirmed His judgment against Judah: He would tear down what He had built and uproot what He had planted (v. 4; cf. 1:10; 18:7; 24:6; 31:28; 42:10). He then reprimanded Baruch for expecting too much. He was not to seek great things for himself because the coming judgment would bring adversity onto all people. However, God would give his life to him as a prize (i.e., spoil or prize of war) everywhere he went (45:5). God knows the pain of His servants and comforts them.

There is a future with Him for those who, in faith, risk everything.

46:1—51:64

JUDGMENT AGAINST THE NATIONS

Prophecies against foreign nations are common in the prophetic books (e.g., Amos 1–2; Is. 13–23; Ezek. 25–32). The messages reveal Israel's God as Sovereign Lord over all nations, none of whom could effectively challenge His authority and power. Their rise and fall is an unmistakable witness to such universal sovereignty. Theologically, Jeremiah 46:1—51:64 presumes that the God of Israel had created the world (see Jeremiah: Introduction) and assigned it to different nations (Gen. 10; Deut. 32:8). Consequently, He was to be feared and worshiped by the nations (Ps. 96; cf. Rev. 14:6–7). He was their King, and they were His servants (Jer. 10:7, 10; 46:18; 48:15; 51:57; cf. Ps. 96), and He had the right to hold them accountable (Jer. 18:7–10). His intention was to move them to fear Him and give glory to Him, as modeled in His covenant with Israel, through whom He would accomplish His purpose (3:17; 4:2; cf. Ex. 19:5–6; Ps. 2:8; 82:8; Is. 2:2–4; 49:1–7). God acted as Israel's protector against hostile nations, provided they remained faithful to Him (cf. Num. 23:9; Ps. 2:1, 8; 46:6–7). If Israel were unfaithful, God would judge them in accordance with His judgment of all nations (as amply illustrated in Jeremiah). The prophecies against the nations in Jeremiah were designed for Israel's instruction, particularly for those in exile.

46:1–28

Against Egypt

God's massive judgment against all people (lit. "flesh") was to begin with Egypt. It was, at that time, the only power capable of resisting Babylon. In Israel's history, Egypt symbolizes those who resist God's will. The escape of the Judean remnant to Egypt caused God to issue harsh judgments against Egypt (43:10–13; 44:30).

46:1–12. Introduction and Battle. Verse 1 introduces chapters 46–51, declaring that the word of the Lord determines the future of the nations (cf. 1:10). This connection between 1:10 (the core theme of Jeremiah's call in vv. 4–19) and 46:1 suggests that the book of Jeremiah revolves around God's rule and the supremacy of His kingdom. The abrupt title found in v. 2, *lemitsrayim*—"against" or "concerning Egypt"—is meaningful only in the

context of God as Ruler and Judge of the nations. The full title mentions the battle of Carchemish (605 B.C.) where the Babylonians defeated Pharaoh Necho II. The ensuing prophecy describes Egypt under the burden of this defeat.

The battle of Carchemish proved the foolishness of relying on Egypt (vv. 3–12). God invited the audience to imagine a dramatic battle that would demonstrate the weakness and shame of Egypt (vv. 3–4). The Babylonian army was called to move into action while the Egyptian army was already in retreat, struck by fear (vv. 5–6). Playing on its intention to rise up and cover the earth, like the annual flooding of the Nile, Egypt was derisively summoned to battle with its horses, chariots, and army of allies (vv. 7–9). Egypt's real enemy was not the Babylonians; it was the Lord God (v. 10). Babylon was merely His tool. His rule required the demise of Egypt, and the shame of the defeated empire was heard among all the nations (v. 12).

46:13–28. Impotence of the Egyptian Gods. God predicted the Babylonian attack on Egypt (568 B.C.). God would assert His power by defeating Pharaoh and his gods (vv. 15–17). Verse 15 may be a reference to the sacred bull Apis that represented the god Ptah of Memphis. God's imagery belittled "powerful" Egypt. Using the metaphor of a biting fly defeating a beautiful heifer (as a sarcastic reference to Egyptian bull worship; cf. vv. 15, 21), He illustrated how the mighty empire, with all its gods, would be overcome by the sting of a small insect. From the image of something mighty and numerous being destroyed by something small and singular, the text switches to an image of something small and singular (a snake) being cut down by something mighty (an army with axes) and numerous (like locusts or grasshoppers). All that the Egyptians could do was hiss like a serpent (v. 22).

Israel's God would punish Egypt's national god, Amon of No (i.e., Amun of Thebes), and all of Egypt with its gods and its kings (vv. 25–26). The punishment of Pharaoh and those trusting in him would include the Judean remnant, who relied on Pharaoh's protection instead of obeying God's call to dwell in Judah (see chaps. 42–44). Israel's God is indeed the Sovereign King of the nations. Therefore, the word of comfort to Israel in 30:10–11 (cf. 45:4–5) is repeated here (46:27–28). God would extinguish the power of all the nations except that of Israel. He would not leave Israel without due punishment, but they were not to be afraid, for He would bring them home and give them rest.

47:1-7
Against Philistia

The Philistines were old enemies of Israel (cf. 1 Sam. 4), but by the time of Jeremiah, Philistia had been reduced to a pawn of Egypt (cf. Jer. 47:1). Consequently, this prophecy is short and follows the one against Egypt. The Philistines were under threat from the north, and the description of their peril uses formulas common in Jeremiah for invasions and war. But it was the Lord who would punish the Philistines (v. 4). The invader from the north was the sword of the Lord (vv. 6-7). No specific reason is given for this judgment against Philistia. But the defeat of this ancient enemy by the Lord was to instill in Israel the hope that God would eventually restore His people's fortunes.

48:1-47
Against Moab

This lengthy prophecy is structured as an explanatory sequence of woes (i.e., "trouble," "death," "judgment"; v. 1), which constantly shifts between admonitions to escape, indictments, judgments, and lamentations. The historical events are unknown, and many of the locations mentioned cannot be pinpointed. The section has obvious links with other OT passages (e.g., Num. 21:28-29; 24:17; Deut. 28:49, 52; Is. 15:2-5; 16:6-12; 24:17-18). It addresses a close neighbor on the other side of the Jordan River with a long history of rivalry with Israel and Judah.

48:1-13. Moab's Judgment and Complacency. The woe in 48:1-9 predicts the destruction of the cities of Moab. The judgment upon these military strongholds and centers of economic power would elicit cries of mourning and desperation throughout Moab. The inhabitants were admonished to escape and save themselves although they would be like the juniper in the wilderness—a symbol of desolation (vv. 6, 9). Chemosh (the Moabite chief god; cf. 1 Kin. 11:7) would be powerless and exiled with his priests and princes. All Moab would be attacked, and every city and the entire land would be made desolate.

Moab was accused of complacency through the metaphor of winemaking (Jer. 48:10-13). All of its life, Moab had been, like wine, at ease, prosperous, and indolent (cf. Amos 6:1; Zeph. 1:12). Moab was the wine that had been left undisturbed, not moved about or poured out, which means that it had not experienced exile/ captivity. The absence of turmoil had made Moab complacent. Now God would pour out its bottles and smash its jars (Jer. 48:12-13). This is a reference to destruction and exile. Thus, Moab would resemble Israel under judgment and would be ashamed, together with its god Chemosh, in whom it trusted.

48:14-28. Moab's Pride and Indictment. Another accusation against Moab highlighted its pride. Moab had no reason to be proud, for it would be plundered and its young men slaughtered (vv. 14-16). Its former power would be broken (vv. 17, 20). As an illustration of this fate, the inhabitants of Aroer (also north of the River Arnon) were admonished to ask the fleeing crowds what had happened; the response was that Moab had been shamed, broken, and ruined (vv. 19 20). God's case against Moab was painted in rich and varied images in a dual indictment followed by judgment (vv. 21-28). The first indictment was that Moab had arrogantly defied the Lord (v. 26). This is a peculiar statement since Moab had no covenant with Israel's God. However, it fits the theme of the Lord as Ruler of the nations. Israel celebrated this in hymns which called all nations to acknowledge the Lord as the true God (Ps. 93-99; cf. Rev. 14:7-8). Moab had offended the Lord's honor and status as Ruler of the universe by its proud self-seeking (Jer. 48:26) and its scorn of Israel (v. 27). The latter was the second indictment. The language here resembles the psalms of lament (Ps. 59:8; Jer. 20:7; Lam. 1:7). Moab's contempt for Israel had offended God because an intimate relationship existed between God and His people that could encourage Israel in exile and give them hope.

Following this dual indictment, the judgment was severe. Moab would lose its power and strength (Jer. 48:21-25). It would be made drunk by God's cup of wrath (cf. 25:15) and would wallow in its own vomit (48:26)—an image of humiliation and degradation. It would be treated with the same contempt that it had held for Israel (v. 26; cf. v. 27). The offense and its punishment corresponded, according to the principle of retribution (Ex. 21:23-24; Lev. 24:19-20; Deut. 19:21; cf. Matt. 5:38-42). Moab was admonished to flee to a remote location, hiding in caves among the rocks (Jer. 48:28)—another sign of humiliation.

48:29-39. Lawsuit and Punishment. The next unit includes a lawsuit with an indictment (vv. 29-30) and a punishment (vv. 31-33; cf. Is. 16:6-10). The indictment develops the theme of Moab's arrogance (Jer. 48:26). In a terse proverbial utterance, the verdict was made—Moab's arrogance was without substance (v. 30). The coming devastation is worded as lamentation: instead of the joy and laughter associated with wine, there would be sorrow and wailing (vv. 31-33).

The theme of Moab's punishment is expanded in vv. 34-39 (cf. vv. 21-26, 31-33). The text is clearly influenced by Isaiah (15:4-6; 16:11-12), but the lament in Isaiah 16:11 resulted from the loss of the wine trade, while the lament here followed the cessation of idolatry. This adaptation of the material borrowed from Isaiah adds to the evidence that God's power and sovereignty were central to Jeremiah. An overwhelming outpouring of grief and lamentation is described. The last lines refer to the derision and dismay of Moab's neighbors at its fate.

48:40-47. Summary of the Message to Moab. The prophecy ends with variants on previous themes: Moab was to be destroyed because it exalted itself against the Lord (v. 42; cf. v. 44). The references to dread, pit, and snare (v. 43) summarize a series of events in a movement from one danger to another, which indicate inescapability and hopelessness for Moab. The climax contains three motifs. First, Moab's destruction is illustrated by the fate of Heshbon, a center of power that was now powerless and devastated (v. 45). Second, a concluding woe (cf. v. 1) concerns the captivity of the worshipers of Chemosh (v. 46; cf. vv. 7, 13). Moab's defeat was to be, in effect, a defeat of Chemosh, who was not a god at all. Third, a promise of hope was to be fulfilled in the future (v. 47). Elsewhere, Jeremiah uses the phrase *shub shebut* for restoration after exile (cf. 29:14; 30:3, 18; 32:44; 33:11, 26). Even for Israel's enemy, there was hope, but only after exile. Thus, God's primary concern with Moab was not primarily its destruction but destruction as a means of establishing His sovereignty and turning Moab and the remnant of Israel in Moab to Himself. His response to their turning to Him would be mercy and a new life. From then on, the life of the nation would be founded on God's deliverance, as in the case of Israel's deliverance from Egypt.

God's purpose is to establish His rule over the nations as a condition for their well-being. He is the Lord of heaven and earth, and therefore, life cannot be preserved without Him, not even among the nations. Moab resisted the Lord's authority by trusting in its own works and treasures (48:7), by exalting itself at the Lord's expense (vv. 26, 42), by holding Israel up to ridicule (v.

27), and by its pride and arrogance (vv. 29-30). Such behavior was unacceptable, and Israel's God was in command of the nations and held them accountable. The prophecy sought to prove to Israel that they could trust such a God because He could reverse the fortunes of His remnant people in exile. In this regard, the prophecies against the nations in Jeremiah 46-51 were designed for the instruction of Israel.

49:1-6
Against Ammon

This prophecy consists of two units. Each unit is introduced by an indictment.

49:1-3. First Indictment. In the first indictment, which uses the metaphorical language of sons, heirs, and family rights (v. 1), Ammon was accused of taking land through military aggression. Israel had sons and heirs, so *Malkam* (also called "Milcom" or "Molek") had no right to occupy the land of Gad or dwell in the cities of Gad. As a result of the judgment for this crime (v. 2), Ammon would become a desolate mound, be burned down in a military attack, and Israel would dispossess those who had dispossessed them and reacquire their inheritance. This outcome would inspire hope that Judah's land, at this time occupied by the Babylonians, would one day be restored to its rightful owner. A call for wailing and mourning was to be made after Ammon's defeat, when *Malkam* would go into exile with his priests and princes (v. 3). *Malkam* was to have proven himself powerless at the intervention of Yahweh—again a tribute to the power of Israel's God.

49:4-6. Second Indictment. In the second indictment (v. 4), Ammon was accused of pride, boasting of her fertility, and trusting in her treasures by claiming that nobody could threaten her. But God would turn pride into fear (v. 5; cf. 48:43-44). All the people would be driven out of their land with no leader to gather them. Instead of the wailing mentioned in the first indictment, this section ends in a promise of Ammon's return to her land (49:6; cf. 48:47). Yahweh would demonstrate His sovereignty over Milcom when He punished the Ammonites for their aggressions and pride. The prophecy that the land of Gad would be restored to Israel created hope for a restoration of Judah. As the Ammonites came to understand that Israel's God ruled the nations, they would submit to Him and not to Milcom.

49:7–22
Against Edom

The Edomites, situated southeast of the Dead Sea, were descendants of Esau, the brother of Jacob/Israel (Gen. 36:1, 9). There is a verbal connection or dependence between vv. 9, 14–16 and Obadiah 1–5. Prophecies against Edom are common in the OT (Amos 1:11–12; Is. 21:11–12; 34:5–15; 63:1–6; Ezek. 25:12–14; 35:1–15; Obad. 1–21; Mal. 1:2–5). The passage in 49:19–21 is a variant of 50:44–46.

49:7–13. Images of Judgment. The judgment against Edom is presented in vivid language (vv. 7–13). First, through rhetorical questions, Edom was accused of having lost his famous sense of wisdom (cf. 1 Kin. 5:11; Obad. 5). Second, Edom was to flee the approaching disaster of Esau (Jer. 49:8; cf. 48:6–8, 28; 49:30; 50:8–10; 51:6, 45). Through synecdoche (a part representing the whole), this was addressed to the inhabitants of Dedan (an Arabian city southeast of Edom, or perhaps a settlement of Dedanites along the caravan route passing through Edom). The point was to warn Edom against the coming punishment.

Third, two images underline the rigor of the judgment (vv. 9–10). Grape gatherers would not pick the vines completely clean but would leave a portion for the gleaners (ct. Deut. 24:19–22). Thieves in the night would not take everything available—only what they needed. Both would leave something behind, but God would leave nothing in Edom because the nation would not survive. Fourth, the scene abruptly shifts to the innocent victims of the judgment, the orphans and widows (Jer. 49:11). In His mercy, God would care for them (cf. e.g., Ex. 22:22; Deut. 10:18; Ps. 68:5; Mal. 3:5). The covenant laws about caring for orphans and widows included leaving some grapes of the vineyards for them, and the reference to this law in Jeremiah 49:9 explains the content of v. 11: only the abandoned and defenseless would find rescue in the Lord.

Finally, in a prose summary of the judgment, God used the image of the cup of suffering and devastation (vv. 12–13; cf. 25:15–29). The punishment on Edom was as sure as God's oath. It was aimed first at Bozrah, the capital, which was to become a curse (cf. Deut. 28:37), and all the other cities were to become perpetual wastes.

49:14–16. The Pride of Edom. This unit contains a central indictment against Edom for trusting in his god and for his pride (v. 16), framed by judgment themes (vv. 14–16). God was mobilizing all the nations against Edom (v.

14), and they would despise him (v. 15). The people of Edom had been deceived by their god, the pride of their hearts. This god is referred to by the unusual Hebrew word *tipletset*, which seems to be a by-form of *mipletset* (1 Kin. 15:13), some type of image or symbol dedicated to Asherah. Translations have rendered this word variously as "fierceness," "terror," or "horror" (nominative terms derived from the verb *palats*, "shudder," "be horrified"). Figurines representing Astarte or some other fertility goddess have been found in Edom.

49:17–22. Metaphors of Defeat. The third and final unit returns to God's judgment against Edom, here expressed in three powerful metaphors (vv. 17–22). First, Edom's fall would be like that of Sodom and Gomorrah: no one would remain and dwell in it (vv. 17–18). Second, God was to be like a lion, attacking and devastating the flock of sheep in Edom (vv. 19–21), for no shepherd (king) in Edom could stand up to the Lord. Third, Edom's attacker would be like an eagle (v. 22), that is, threatening and terrorizing, making warriors quake like women in labor. Behind these images in Jeremiah stand God's power (v. 19) and intention (v. 20a). He would be the lion-God, sending the eagle Babylon as His agent against Edom. The purpose of vv. 7–22 was to denounce Edom's pride and idolatry (i.e., not recognizing the sovereignty of God over the nations of the world). The passage reassured exiled Israel that Yahweh was indeed the most powerful God. He could not be defeated by any other god or nation. This was to assure Judah that God's promises of delivering His remnant were trustworthy.

49:23–27
Against Damascus

Damascus, Israel's northern neighbor, is a reference to all of Syria (cf. Is. 7:8), but Jeremiah also uses Hamath and Arpad to represent Syria as a nation (Jer. 49:23). The introductory terror and paralysis inflicted by judgment (vv. 23–24) are followed in the passage by a cry of lament by the inhabitants of Damascus that can also be read as a taunt from the prophet (v. 25). This section concludes with a harsh judgment in vv. 26–27. No formal indictment explains the punishment because the intended function of the prophecy was to remove every rival claim to historical-political power. Its message brought hope to Israel because it exalted Yahweh and His sovereignty over all nations, kings, and gods.

49:28–33
Against Kedar and Hazor

Kedar refers to Arabian tribes who were descendants of Ishmael (cf. Gen. 25:13) and lived in the desert (cf. Jer. 2:10). The eastern location of Hazor (not the famous city, north of the Sea of Galilee) is unknown, but the noun may mean "unwalled villages," implying a nomadic form of life (cf. Jer. 49:31). The prophecy announced invasion and devastation (vv. 31–33) and explicitly mentioned Nebuchadnezzar as the agent (vv. 28, 30). The Lord gave a command mobilizing the enemies of Kedar and Hazor (vv. 28–29) and urged the inhabitants to escape to safety (v. 30). Nebuchadnezzar had conceived of a plan against Kedar and Hazor (v. 30), but he acted under the command of God (vv. 28, 31). Israel's God would scatter the people and bring devastation upon them from every side (v. 32). The prophecy exalts God's sovereign power over the nations, their kings, and their gods.

49:34–39
Against Elam

This prophecy against Elam, located east of Babylon, dates to Zedekiah's reign (ca. 597 B.C.). Elam was once an ally of Babylon but later came under its control. It may symbolically represent the eastern nations subjugated by Babylon who would be liberated when Babylon fell. This prophecy forms a transition to the extensive prophecy against Babylon (50:1—51:58). Threats and judgments are worded in the first person, with the Lord as agent. The climax is God's resolution to nullify the power and leaders of Elam by replacing them with His own direct rule (49:38). As in the cases of Egypt (46:26), Moab (48:47), and Ammon (49:6), God planned better days for Elam. He would bring back the captives of Elam and restore their fortunes (v. 39) when His throne was established in Elam and all other claims to power had been eradicated (v. 38). These are subtle hints to the exiled remnant of Israel that God would also bring them back home.

50:1—51:58
Against Babylon

The pattern followed in the prophecy against Babylon is the same as for other nations: the Lord called military forces against Babylon and declared her fall. While in the rest of the book Babylon is God's agent for punishing the nations, in chapters 50—51 she is the object of God's punishment. Since Babylon stood under judgment and would soon fall, trust in her as a lasting power was futile. These chapters support the promises of a return from the Babylonian Exile for the remnant of some nations (46:26; 48:47; 49:6, 39) and for Israel (e.g., 30:1—33:26), and they exhort Israel to trust God and wait for the fulfillment of His promises. The fall of Babylon had only been hinted at in previous passages (cf. 25:11–12, 26; 27:7).

The prophecy of the fall of Babylon is so certain that at times it is described as if it had already taken place (e.g., 51:8). God would intervene to punish the oppressor and to liberate His people. The danger of remaining in doomed Babylon and the necessity of avoiding complicity in Babylon's guilt are used to persuade the remnant to make the right choice. The theme of God's vengeance gains ground in this prophecy (i.e., God's judgment is founded on the principle of retributive justice). This is particularly linked to His concern for Zion and for the restoration of the sanctuary and its services.

The theme of God's vindication that runs throughout the book reaches its climax in chapters 50-51. The collapse of Babylon and her gods clearly demonstrates that the destruction of Jerusalem and the Lord's temple was not the result of God's impotence before the Babylonian gods. At this point, it was clear that He always had dominion over them. He had voluntarily, as a result of the sin of His people, handed the people, the city, and the temple into the hands of Babylon, but He—indeed, the Lord of Hosts—was now ready to take them back from her hand.

50:1–3. Introductory Message of Judgment. (See "Content of Jeremiah Chapters 50 and 51," p. 957). The introduction of this prophecy resembles the introduction in 1:1–3. In both instances, Jeremiah received the word of the Lord, and both concern the issue of the Exile in Babylon. Since the fall of Babylon had been announced, the end of the Exile was on the horizon (cf. Rev. 14:8). The content of this section of the message is very rich. There is an announcement among the nations of Babylon's fall. The accumulation of six verbs for the act of proclamation underlines its importance. The fall was to include Babylon's chief god, Bel, as well as Merodach (or Marduk). The passage refers to venerated idols that would be put to shame, terrorized, and shattered (cf. 50:38;

Content of Jeremiah Chapters 50 and 51

The structure of Jeremiah 50 and 51 has been a matter of discussion among scholars, and the result has been a significant number of organizational arrangements. The following is a useful breakdown of both chapters.

1. Content of Jeremiah 50. Jeremiah 50 has an introduction and a conclusion. The introduction (vv. 1–3) is a brief summary proclaiming the fall of Babylon and its gods, which is reiterated in vv. 45–46. The content of the rest of the chapter seems to be organized around those to whom God speaks. His messages appear here addressed to three groups: Israel, Babylon, and the enemy of Babylon. These three are clearly introduced in vv. 4–16: Israel (vv. 4–10), Babylon (vv. 11–13), and the enemy (vv. 14–16). In the next block of material, the addressees of the messages are Israel (v. 17), Babylon (v. 18), and Israel (vv. 19–20). The enemy is not mentioned, which indicates that the problem was between God, Israel, and Babylon. The messages begin and end with Israel as the addressee in order to show God's concern for His people.

The next section of the material is organized as follows: enemy (vv. 21–23), Babylon (vv. 24–25), and enemy (vv. 26–30). This time there is no message addressed to Israel because the main emphasis is on what God was doing to Babylon through the enemy from the north. The last section returns to the problem between Israel and Babylon: Babylon (vv. 31–32), Israel (vv. 33–34), and Babylon (vv. 35–46). The emphasis is on what God would do to Babylon on behalf of His people.

2. Content of Jeremiah 51. The organization of chapter 51 is difficult to establish. A helpful approach would be to focus on the speakers, namely, God and the prophet. There are five divine and four prophetic speeches. Through the interlocking of the speeches in this chapter, the destruction of Babylon is effectively announced.

The *first divine speech* (51:1–5) contains God's announcement of the coming judgment against Babylon. The *first prophetic speech* (vv. 6–19) contains two sections: one exhorting the people to leave Babylon, and another summoning the enemy of Babylon for war.

The *second divine speech* (vv. 20–26) is a confirmation of the previous prophetic one: the Lord at this time announcing that He would use the enemies of Babylon, the Medes, to punish Babylon. In the *second prophetic speech* (vv. 27–32), God's right to attack Babylon is justified based on His status as Creator and Sustainer of the world.

The *third divine speech* (v. 33) is the proclamation that the time to harvest Babylon was coming. The *third prophetic speech* (vv. 34–35) is in the form of a lament and includes a call for retribution on behalf of Israel.

The *fourth divine speech* (vv. 36–50) is God's response to the words of the people expressed by the prophet. The final *(fourth) prophetic speech* (v. 51) is a confession of the shame experienced by the people because of what Babylon had done to them.

The final *(fifth) divine speech* (vv. 52–58) is a response to the words of the prophet, culminating in the announcement of the total destruction of the city of Babylon.

51:17, 47, 52). Through the destruction of Babylon, Yahweh would assert His supremacy over the gods of Babylon, and He would completely undermine the idea that in the destruction of Jerusalem, the Babylonian gods had defeated Yahweh. The instrument of the downfall was to be a nation coming out of the north.

50:4–10. Message to Israel. The fall of Babylon was good news for all captives. God's people would return to Him and to Zion in an eternal covenant that was not to be forgotten (v. 5). This prophecy announced the unquestionable fulfillment of earlier promises (29:12–14; 31:31–33; 32:40). In the message, God's people are described as lost sheep misled by false shepherds. God laments over what the shepherds did to His people (i.e., kings or leaders; cf. 22:22; 23:1–4; Ezek. 34:1–10). Their priests and prophets had led them away from Him by encouraging them to worship other gods, thus causing them to forget their resting place (cf. Ps. 23). The indictment is against the leaders, particularly the royal establishment. As a result of being a lost sheep,

Judah was devoured by Babylon. Apparently, Babylon claimed innocence at Judah's fate, blaming it on the sins of the people against their Lord, who was their abiding place of righteousness (Jer. 50:7). The remarkable balance between God's righteous judgments and His love for Israel indicates that the Babylonians understood, better than the kings of Israel did, the price to be paid for sin and the deep roots of hope in Israel's history. However, Babylon did what was in her heart to do, and it was inexcusable. It would have to assume responsibility for its action. This speech concludes with an admonition to Israel to leave Babylon (vv. 8-10), which should have prompted leaders to take action. The metaphor of rams is used to describe the strong leaders that Israel would need. The military threat that God would cause to overtake Babylon is described as a coalition of nations from the north (vv. 9-10; cf. 51:27-28).

50:11-16. Speeches to Babylon and the Enemy. Babylon's joy would turn into shame (vv. 11-13) for having gleefully taken advantage of Judah and recklessly plundering it. The superpower is derogatorily described as being like a heifer thrashing grain and bellowing like stallions (lit. "the mighty," sometimes translated as "bulls"; cf. 46:21). Babylon's abuse and self-serving exploitation would be judged by God. Babylon would become the least of the nations, and all passing by would hiss or whistle at her in derision (50:13; cf. 49:17, 33). The deep shame of the city ("mother") and her desolation would be caused by the indignation of the Lord (50:12-13; cf. 6:9-15).

In 50:14-16, the object of the speech is the enemy of Babylon. God was summoning armies against Babylon, for she had sinned against the Lord (v. 14; cf. v. 24). Subject to His vengeance, she would be punished according to the law of retributive justice: as she had done, so would be done to her (v. 15; cf. 50:28; 51:11, 24, 35-36, 49, 56). Babylon would surrender (lit. "give her hand"; 50:15). This expression could also refer to a broken covenant, perhaps to stave off destruction (cf. 2 Kin. 10:5; 1 Chr. 29:24; 2 Chr. 30:9; Lam. 5:6; Ezek. 17:18). The sower and the harvester would be cut off from the city, resulting in famine. Then everyone would turn to his own people and flee to his own land (Jer. 50:16).

50:17-20. Messages to Israel, Babylon, and Israel. The first message here is about Israel

as a victim of political powers, and scattered throughout the nations (v. 17). But the Lord also addressed Babylon, announcing that He would punish her for her actions as He had done to Assyria. He then turned to His people and proclaimed that He would bring them back home. They are commanded to leave Babylon (vv. 17-20) and to return home (vv. 4-5, 8, 16b). This was to be the work of the Lord; He would reconcile with and forgive those whom He would preserve (v. 20; cf. 31:34). Israel's Good Shepherd would give them life, hope, and a place of rest (cf. 50:6-10).

50:21-30. Messages for the Enemy, Babylon, and the Enemy. God summoned the armies of the unidentified enemy of Babylon to attack and destroy her (vv. 21-23). The text now describes how God would deal with Babylon. Merathaim (in southern Babylon) and Pekod (Aramaean people on the eastern bank of the lower Tigris River) are used to represent the whole of Babylon. Merathaim may be linked with "the bitter river" in southern Babylonia, which was taken as a symbol of the outer edges of the earth, with Babylon at its center. Its ironic use here implies that the city, formerly the center of the world, would now be at the world's outer edges. Next, the Lord spoke about the fall of Babylon in a lament that continues this irony (vv. 23-24; cf. 49:25). Such an expression is that of Babylon as a hammer (which symbolized power and strength—cf. 23:29; 51:20-23) that has been cut down and smashed. Having fought against the Lord, Babylon was to face His judgment (50:24-25; cf. v. 14). What Babylon did against God's people was considered a sin against God Himself. The text returns to the topic of the enemies of Babylon, who were again summoned to punish and destroy her (vv. 26-27). Fugitives from Babylon (cf. vv. 8, 16, 19) would declare in Zion that God had repaid Babylon for what she did to the temple (v. 28; cf. v. 15; 51:11, 24, 35-36, 49, 56). Babylon's crime was proud defiance against the Holy One of Israel (50:29) and proven indifference to His authority, power, and status.

50:31-46. Messages for Babylon, Israel, and Babylon. The one who was to attack and punish Babylon was the Lord Himself (vv. 31-32). He would set the city on fire, and everything would be consumed. However, Israel and Judah, with Babylon's refusal to release their captives, had now a strong Redeemer defending their case who would liberate them and give rest to the land. He would disturb the inhabitants of Babylon (v. 34; cf. Rev. 14:9–11). The language in this section alludes to the deliverance from Egypt (cf. Ex. 2:23–25; 3:7–8; 6:6; 7:14; 15:13). Thus, a new exodus, this time from Babylon, was to be followed by a new covenant with the Lord (cf. Jer. 30:1—33:28; 50:4–5).

The last object of the discourse is Babylon. This section begins with an ode to a sword (vv. 35–38). The Lord's sword against Babylon (cf. v. 25) would impact every part of Babylonian society—princes, wise men, soothsayers, warriors, horses, chariots, mercenaries, and treasures. It would reduce everything to weakness, lifelessness, and instability. All of this was to happen because of their idolatry (v. 38), that is, the self-serving pride that had distanced Babylon from the God of heaven and earth.

Second, God would judge Babylon's pride (vv. 39–40). Because of her pride, Babylon would become a perennially desolate place. The symbols of human power and presence would disappear, and its inhabitants would be the wild animals of the desert. Its fate would be like Sodom and Gomorrah. God's judgment would come from the north, from a great nation allied with many kings from the ends of the earth. Verses 41–43 reiterate 6:22–24, with the essential difference being that Babylon is no longer the attacker (vv. 22–24) but the attacked (50:40–43; there is also a parallel between vv. 44–46 and 49:19–21). Again, the inversion of fates was to be complete. God (not Babylon) would rule the world, and there is none like Him (v. 44b).

51:1–19. First Divine and Prophetic Speeches.

(See "Content of Chapters Jeremiah 50 and 51," p. 957) In His first speech, God expressed His resolve to destroy Babylon (vv. 1–4). He would raise up a destroyer against Babylon, who is here called "Leb Kamai," "the heart of those who raise up against me." A destructive *ruakh*, "spirit" or "wind," would winnow and destroy the land. At the same time, He would comfort Israel and Judah (v. 5). In spite of their sins, God had not forsaken His people, and the fall of Babylon would demonstrate this. The first part of the prophetic speech is an admonition to God's people to abandon Babylon and to worship God in Zion (vv. 6–10). Thus they would save themselves from God's judgment against Babylon (v. 6). The common practice of using balm for pain and healing would be ineffective for Babylon: she could not be healed because her judgment would reach to the skies or "the heavens," literally, "the clouds" (v. 9). Here, "judgment"

(*mishpat*) may, as in other cases (Deut. 19:6; 21:22; Ezek. 7:23), refer to "guilt," and the idea of something reaching the clouds or heaven could mean that it has no end (cf. 2 Chr. 28:9; Job 20:6; Pss. 57:11; 108:5; Dan. 4:22). The remnant of Israel would realize that God had vindicated them (lit. "brought out" or "revealed" their righteousness), and therefore they were to worship Him in Zion (Jer. 51:10; cf. 50:5). The righteousness of Israel (cf. vv. 4–5) was totally dependent on the mercy and grace of God, their pardoner (cf. v. 20; 51:5). In forsaking Babylon, the people were not only to escape judgment but also to show no complicity in Babylon's crimes (cf. Rev. 18:4).

In the second part of the prophetic speech, the Medes are summoned against Babylon (51:11–14). God had taken an oath to destroy Babylon (v. 14) as vengeance for His temple (v. 11; cf. 50:15, 24, 28; 51:24, 35–36, 49, 51, 56). The prophet proceeds to contrast the Lord with Babylon's idols (vv. 15–19) in order to demonstrate His right to judge Babylon. This unit is parallel to 10:12–16. It celebrates God's power by contrasting it with the powerlessness of the idols lacking "breath" (i.e., life). The superiority of Israel's God asserted Israel's special status.

51:20–35. Second and Third Divine and Prophetic Speeches.

In His second speech, God expresses again His resolution to destroy Babylon (vv. 20–26). The structure of this unit is similar to 50:35–38. Commentators have differed over the identity of the referent in 51:20–23. According to some, it is Israel, due to the immediately preceding verses; others believe it is Babylon (in light of 50:23, 51:25, and vv. 13–14, where Babylon is addressed as "you" a few verses before this section, starting in v. 20). According to others, and most likely, it is the kingdom of the Medes (vv. 11; 41–46). Babylon's social structure would be destroyed as retribution for all the wickedness they had perpetrated in Zion (v. 24; see vv. 11, 51). The prophetic speech was a summons for the nations to come to attack Babylon (vv. 27–29), and it recorded the reaction of the Babylonians (vv. 29–32).

The third divine speech announced that the time for the harvest of Babylon would come. Babylon would become like a threshing floor—its pride and honor would be trampled (v. 33). The Judean exiles were encouraged to remain confident in God's purpose and to wait faithfully until the Lord's soon-coming harvest. In the third prophetic speech, the prophet appropriates a lament of the people concerning Babylon's abuse of Jerusalem (vv. 34–35). He accuses Nebuchadnezzar of deporting the people and swallowing the city like a *tannin* ("serpent," "dragon," "sea monster"), a symbol of chaos and evil. Bloodguilt is assigned to the Babylonian king. His state policy was regarded by the victims as murder. This is an enormous allegation that cannot go unpunished. The principle of retributive justice is therefore adduced (v. 35).

51:36–50. Fourth Divine Speech. God responded to the lament of vv. 34–35 by pleading Zion's case and taking vengeance for her (v. 36a). He would dry up Babylon's water and would make her completely desolate, a home for jackals. God would provide banquets for them and make them drunk and merry until they would sleep and not awaken (v. 39). Through the attackers, He would slaughter the Babylonians and render them helpless, like sacrificial animals (v. 40). God here introduced the topic of reversal (vv. 41–44). A complete reversal would come to the city (vv. 40, 44)—the glory of Babylon would be turned into desolation and derision (v. 41; for "Sheshach," cf. 25:26). Her devastation was to be like a violent flood (51:42). Her cities—once filled with people, bustling life, and treasures—would be deserted (v. 43). God would punish Bel, the god of Babylon, and would liberate the captives he had "swallowed" (i.e., conquered, killed, and exiled). The nations that formerly praised Babylon's glory (v. 41) would no longer *nahar 'el*. This has been translated "stream to him," which would imply the streaming of nations in their masses to Bel and his city. However, in chapters 50–51, Bel is shamed by the nations attacking Babylon (50:2–3, 9; 51:27–28). As in 31:12, *nahar* can be understood in 51:44 as "shine" (i.e., look with favor or favorably toward). The acclamation of a great ruler traditionally involved greeting him with joy or "shining faces," and v. 44 could imply that the nations would no longer "look favorably toward" Bel.

Babylon would be defenseless, and its famous and secure walls would fall (v. 44). God would demonstrate His supremacy over the Babylonian gods by punishing the city. Babylon would no longer command the respect of the nations; it would not receive tax, allegiance, or praise. Babylon was to fall (50:32; 51:44). This implies a message of hope for exiled Israel and desolate Zion. At this time, the Lord admonished Israel to abandon Babylon (vv. 45–46; see v. 6). God's anger was no longer directed toward His apostate people but toward the oppressor who was

preventing the fulfillment of His plan to bring His people to the promised land. Endless rumors of violence and intrigue could create fear, but the exiles were admonished to trust in the Lord and avoid the impending judgment by fleeing Babylon (v. 46).

Another reason to abandon Babylon was God's judgment of her false gods (v. 47). The land would be ashamed, and the people would die in her midst. While the nations had looked favorably toward Bel in Babylon (v. 44), the heavens, the earth, and all in them would at this time sing with joy at the demise of the oppressor (v. 48). Babylon's bloodguilt for killing God's people would be avenged through retributive justice. The exiled remnant was admonished again by the Lord to leave Babylon (cf. 50:8–10, 11–13, 14–16; 51:6, 45), with the instruction to keep the Lord and Jerusalem in mind (v. 50) as they were traveling.

51:51–58. Fourth Prophetic and Fifth Divine Speeches. The fourth prophetic speech is a short confession voicing the shame of Judah that had been brought on by the Babylonians (v. 51). This could have been another reason to leave Babylon and return to Jerusalem to restore the temple services. In vv. 11 and 24, Jeremiah expressed concern regarding Zion and the temple. Here, in v. 51, the reason for abandoning Babylon is that the temple had been profaned. In His final speech, the Lord responded to the shaming of Judah by announcing that the judgment against Babylon's gods was inescapable (vv. 52–53; cf. v. 47). Nothing would stop those who sought to plunder Babylon, not even if Babylon reach up to heaven (cf. Gen. 11:1–9). These prophecies seek to persuade the remnant of Israel to prepare for their return home.

The Lord announced that Babylon would be destroyed by plunderers (Jer. 51:54–58). He is a God of retribution, and He would certainly repay the nation completely (v. 56). The sovereignty of the Lord and the principle of retributive justice come together. God's resolve was to make drunk (i.e., punish; v. 39) all representatives of Babylonian society (v. 57) to cause them to fall into a perpetual sleep. This was the decision of the King, the Sovereign Lord.

Verse 58 summarizes the chapter's divine speeches against Babylon. Babylon's substantial walls would be destroyed and her high gates incinerated (v. 58). The collapse of Babylon demonstrates the futility of the peoples' labor (in building and defending their broad walls and high gates). Verse 58b parallels Habakkuk 2:12–13, though with some differences. What Habakkuk says generally about the ongoing works of the Babylonians, Jeremiah applies specifically to the future fall of Babylon. Jeremiah draws a lesson for the nations: they all labored and exhausted themselves in futility and would be destroyed by fire. Implied is a contrast between the nations and God's people, who would find "rest" for their souls (6:16). By dwelling in the land with the Lord, they would find their "resting place" (50:6; cf. 30:10; 31:2; 46:27; 50:34).

51:59–64
Jeremiah's Command to Seraiah

This short narrative dramatically underlines, by word and acted parable, the content, seriousness, and intentionality of the prophecy about the fall of Babylon (50:1—51:58). Jeremiah had written this prophecy against Babylon on a scroll and asked Seraiah son of Neriah, who was possibly Baruch's brother (cf. 45:5), to be his representative. As one of the king's staff officers, Seraiah accompanied King Zedekiah to Babylon (ca. 593 B.C.).

The life of the scroll had three parts: (1) Its *preparation* was completed by Jeremiah, who wrote it himself (51:60). (2) Its *administration* was managed by Seraiah. He was instructed to take it to Babylon, read it publicly (cf. chaps. 32, 36), and invoke the Lord's resolve to destroy Babylon (51:61–62). (3) Its *deposition* (vv. 63–64) was a formal and public act that symbolically linked the content of the prophecy against Babylon with the geography of Babylon (cf. 13:3–11). The scroll, with its prophecy describing the future of Babylon, became a symbol for the city itself. Thus, its "drowning" in the river was intended as a prophecy that Babylon would be overwhelmed. As history would reveal, the Euphrates and its engineered manipulation by Cyrus played a key role in the city's destruction.

God's word stands and will be fulfilled, but Babylon would sink to its death, and its fall would be permanent. God's sovereignty is sure. As repeatedly underscored in 50:1—51:58, this message was to bring hope and resolution to the remnant, saying, "Rely on God's plans for you. Break away from Babylon, and become a part of God's future for Israel!"

The reference to weariness or exhaustion in the last word of the prophecy (51:58; some render it as "fall") could apply literally to the walls of Babylon or to the nations that behave like her. It translates one single word in Hebrew (*ya'ap*) and resumes the theme that the nations—even the impressive historic Babylon—labor for noth-

ing if their lives are not submitted to the King, the Sovereign Lord (v. 57). This is a vital message for God's people, for unless they know God and acknowledge Him as the Lord of their lives, all their labor is in vain. The message of the fall of Babylon is a call to rely on God's plans and to break away from Babylon to become a part of God's future for Israel (cf. Rev. 14:6–12).

Chapter 51 ends with a note that Jeremiah's words end here. Thus the book essentially closes where it began, with a reference to the words of Jeremiah. (1:1; 51:64). The phrase indicates that what follows in chapter 52 was added to the book but was not written by Jeremiah.

52:1–34
HISTORICAL EPILOGUE

This chapter confirms the fulfillment of Jeremiah's prophecies regarding Judah's punishment. It also provides a necessary background for the promissory words to the exiles in Babylon, with encouragement to them to remain faithful and wait for the return to their homeland (30:1—33:28). In relation to the prophecy against Babylon in 50:1—51:58, chapter 52 balances God's opposition against Babylon and removes any doubt that He would relent in His resolve to punish Judah. The material in chapter 52 (except vv. 28–30) derives from historical biblical sources (2 Kin. 24:18—25:30) and does not mention Jeremiah. The story about Gedaliah in 2 Kings 25:22–26 is found in Jeremiah 40:7—41:18. The unit in 52:1–11 partially overlaps with 39:1–10.

52:1–23
The Fate of Zedekiah and Fall of the City

Zedekiah (597–586 B.C.) is said to have done evil in the Lord's estimation and is compared to King Jehoiakim (609–598 B.C.). The gruesome fate of Judah and Jerusalem is blamed on Zedekiah, who was thrown away from God's presence. The account of the events begins with Zedekiah's rebellion against Nebuchadnezzar (v. 3b). Nebuchadnezzar's punitive invasion (vv. 4–10) is addressed in the notes on 39:1–10 (cf. also 2 Kin. 25:1–7).

Here, the reckoning of time shifts to the chronology of Nebuchadnezzar, Judah's new ruler (12–23). The siege of Jerusalem began in January 588 B.C. and lasted eighteen months. Three things are reported from the conquest: (a) a great destruction of the temple, the walls, and many houses (vv. 13–14); (b) a massive deportation (v. 15); and (c) some people who cared for the vineyards and the fields were left in the land (v. 16). The report becomes more detailed. The taking of the vessels of the temple meant a loss of honor for the God who resided there. There are also hints at how the plunder signifies the end of the Davidic dynasty and the historical splendor of Jerusalem since Solomon (v. 20).

52:24–30
The People Taken to Babylonia

The occupation included the seizure and execution of leading citizens. The deportations from 597 to 582 B.C. are listed, with the number of exiles (vv. 28–30) totaling four thousand six hundred. The actual number may have been considerably higher since this figure may cover only the heads of households. This compact list of Nebuchadnezzar's three acts of deportation is absent from the historical source material and is found only here in the OT (for the deportation in 598 B.C., see also 2 Kin. 24:15–16). This underscores the fact that "exile" is central in the book of Jeremiah. The deportations in Jeremiah 52:28–30 give a sense of completeness and finality to the prophecies of Jeremiah. The punitive concept of being thrown out from the presence of God (v. 3a) looms over this brief unit.

52:31–34
Jehoiachin Released from Prison

This unit is chronologically removed from the fall of Jerusalem (cf. 2 Kin. 25:27–30). The last date in Jeremiah 52:30 is 582 B.C.; here in v. 31, it is 560 B.C. Jehoiachin or Coniah (22:24–30), the young king brought to Babylon in 597 B.C., was still alive and recognized as king after thirty-seven years (commentators and translators differ over whether the Heb. *shemoneh*, "eight," for Jehoiachin's age in 2 Chr. 36:9 is an error that should be corrected to *shemoneh 'esreh*, "eighteen," in light of 2 Kin. 24:8). His new Babylonian master, Nebuchadnezzar's son Evil-Merodach (562–560 B.C.), befriended him and treated him honorably. Extrabiblical records confirm that Jehoiachin and his family received regular rations of oil and barley during their captivity in Babylon.

Is this simply a report of historical events, or does it have a theological point? Although Jehoiachin ruled only a few months before his deportation (2 Chr. 36:9–10), he was a special royal exile (cf. Jer. 22:24–30; 24:1; 29:1–2). Given the threat of the extinction of the Davidic line, this paragraph may have given a feeble hope for its continuation (cf. the promises in 23:5–8; 33:15–18), even though Jehoiachin would die in Babylon (22:26–27). A note in 1 Chronicles 3:19 makes Zerubbabel ("seed of Babylon") the grandson of Jehoiachin, and according to Ezra 2:1—3:13 (cf. Neh. 7:6–73), he and the high priest Joshua led the return from Babylon and the restoration of the temple. In some of Jeremiah's prophecies, it is stated that God would not completely destroy His people (Jer. 4:27; 5:10, 18; 46:28), and the note on Jehoiachin may serve to confirm this assurance. Thus, the theme that runs throughout the book of Jeremiah—of hope in the midst of a hopeless condition—closes the book.

LAMENTATIONS

INTRODUCTION

Title and Authorship. In Hebrew, the book of Lamentations is referred to as *'ekah*, a cry of exclamation meaning "how," which is the first word in the Hebrew text. It also occurs at the beginnings of chapters 2 and 4. The book was also known among the Jews as *qinot* ("lamentations") on the basis of its contents. As in the case of many biblical books, the author is anonymous. The traditional view is that Jeremiah wrote it. This tradition is quite solid and goes back to the second century B.C., to the Greek translation (LXX), which introduces the book, saying "And it came to pass after Israel had been carried away captive and Jerusalem had become desolate that Jeremiah sat down weeping and lamented this lamentation over Jerusalem, saying...." This tradition is confirmed both by Jewish and early Christian traditions. It is also supported by biblical data. Second Chronicles 35:25 reports that Jeremiah sang lamentations for Josiah that were found in the *quinot* (the Laments). The reference may not be to the book of Lamentations, for the only king who is specifically mentioned in it is Zedekiah (4:20). It is clear, however, that Jeremiah wrote some lamentations.

The book of Lamentations uses expressions that parallel those found in Jeremiah, particularly when dealing with similar subjects (e.g., Lam. 3:14, 48–49 // Jer. 9:1; 20:7 //Lam. 5:16; 3:42 // Jer. 14:7; Lam. 3:52–56 // Jer. 12:9; 37:16; 38:6). Also, the personal sufferings described in Lamentations 3:14, 48–57, and 61–63 are similar to those of Jeremiah. There is no legitimate reason to reject the traditional view of Jeremiah as the author.

Date. It is generally agreed that Lamentations was written shortly after the fall of Jerusalem in 586 B.C., before Jeremiah was forced to join his contemporaries as they traveled to Egypt (Jer. 43:1–7). It was probably written no later than 580 B.C., while the memory of the events described was still fresh in his mind.

Backgrounds. The previous twenty years in Judah were politically turbulent. Babylon in the north and Egypt in the south competed for the control of the strategically located Judah. Upon the death of King Josiah in 609 B.C., the people of Judah placed his son Jehoahaz on the throne (2 Kin. 23:30). Three months later, the Egyptians invaded, deposed him, took him captive to Egypt, and replaced him with his older brother Eliakim, whom they renamed Jehoiakim (2 Kin. 23:34). They also imposed a heavy fine on the land.

In 605 B.C., the Babylonians took several individuals captive to Babylon, among them Daniel and his three friends. King Jehoiakim reluctantly submitted to the Babylonians. Following a confrontation between Babylon and Egypt in 601 B.C., in which Babylon was apparently defeated, Jehoiakim openly defied Babylon (2 Kin. 24:1). Jeremiah strongly advised him against rebelling and encouraged him to submit to Babylon instead. But the king and his advisers saw these messages as evidence of treason and responded accordingly by oppressing Jeremiah.

On December 19, 598 B.C., the Babylonians returned to Judah, besieged the city of Jerusalem, and captured Jehoiakim (2 Chr. 36:6). But before he could be deported, he either died or was killed (cf. Jer. 22:18–19), and his son Jehoiachin took his place on the throne. Three months later, on March 16, 597 B.C., the city fell and the king surrendered (2 Kin. 24:12). Leading citizens and ten thousand captives (including the Prophet Ezekiel) were taken to Babylon, along with the treasures of the king's house (vv. 12–13). The king of Babylon made Jehoiachin's uncle, Mattaniah, king in his place and changed Mattaniah's name to Zedekiah (v. 17). He proved to be a weak leader, unable to stand up to his nobles (Jer. 38:4–6). Even though he owed his allegiance to Nebuchadnezzar, he ventured to rebel against him at a time when fierce, but misguided, patriotism pushed Judah into open and irrevocable rebellion.

On January 15, 588 B.C., Jerusalem was again under a siege that lasted eighteen months (2 Kin. 25:1; Jer. 52:4). As the city was about to fall, Zedekiah wished to surrender but lacked the courage to do so. When the walls were breached, Zedekiah and his soldiers snuck out of the city into the night but were captured near Jericho (for more on the chronological issues with dating the fall of Jerusalem, see "Old Testament Timeline," p. 94). After seeing his sons killed before his eyes, Zedekiah was blinded, chained, and brought to Babylon (2 Kin. 25:7; Jer. 52:9–11). A month later, Nebuzaradan, one of Nebuchadnezzar's captains, set fire to the city and broke down its walls (2 Kin. 25:8–12). Most of the Jews were deported to Babylon, with only some of the poorest left behind. These events marked the end of the kingdom of Judah and form the background to the book of Lamentations.

Theology and Purpose. The book is primarily a poetic reflection precipitated by the destruction of Jerusalem in 586 B.C. It is about the experience of national disaster and the place of the nation in God's overall plan for His people. The reflection faces the pain of a loss and the possibility of hope for the future. The book opens with a sense of divine abandonment and the sense of loneliness that comes with it. The city that had been full of people became isolated and desolate (Lam. 1:1). Without God in our lives, we are indeed alone. The book ends with hope and a prayer that the divine abandonment of the city would not be final (5:21–22).

1. *A Painful Sense of Loss.* Almost everything that had characterized Israel's place among the nations was gone—the Davidic kingship, the priesthood, the temple with its services, and even the land itself. Three hundred and fifty years of the nation's independence had come to an end. For some, it was inconceivable that such a thing could happen to God's special people. More than a thousand years earlier, God had called Abraham to be the father of His people in order to make them a visual evidence of the blessings of serving Him. This election was reiterated at the time of the Exodus (Ex. 19:5–6). The blessings of obedience and the curses for failure are summarized in Deuteronomy 28 (cf. Lev. 26). The people quickly became accustomed to expecting only God's rich blessings that were promised within the covenant. They gradually lost sight of their responsibilities as covenant partners with God and of the conditional nature of the covenant promises. Consequently, they suffered the curses of the covenant. A reliance on the external aspects of their faith, without an underlying heart commitment, ultimately brought them to their ruin (cf. Jer. 7:3–7).

2. *The Cause of the Loss.* In Lamentations, the prophet expresses his understanding of the destruction of Jerusalem as the deserved consequence of Judah's sins (1:5, 8, 14–15, 18, 20, 22; 3:42; 4:3; 5:7, 16). The priests and prophets, who should have warned and guided the people, failed them. Instead of warning the nation against iniquity and transgression, they proclaimed peace and prosperity, thereby giving the people a false sense of security (see Jer. 8:8, 11; Lam. 2:14). They even took part in spilling the blood of the righteous (4:13). The temple, which represented God's presence among His people (Ex. 25:8; Lev. 26:12), had been desecrated and destroyed. This came as a shock to the people, who had assumed that God would miraculously protect His sacred meeting place (Lam. 2:15; 4:12) from their enemies. Jeremiah, however, was well aware of the fact that the disaster was a direct fulfillment of the predicted consequences of departing from God's ways, as listed in Deuteronomy 28. Given that sin was the cause for the disaster, God's decision to hand His people over to the enemy was considered to be just and right.

The poet and the faithful among God's people ultimately admitted their sinfulness and recognized God's justice. But they also appealed to God to avenge them of their enemies. This attitude can best be understood in light of the so-called imprecatory psalms, which are prayers for a curse on one's enemies, who were seen to be the enemies of God Himself (e.g., Ps. 37:20; 137; see "Imprecatory Passages in the Psalms," p. 733).

3. *Hope as the Solution to the Riddle.* Chapter 3 is the theological center of the book. It was difficult for the exiles to understand that belonging to God and being His special people meant more than having a superficial religious experience. They had lost sight of the true essence of religion: doing justice, loving mercy, and walking humbly with God (Mic. 6:8). The central section of the book (Lam. 3:21–42) gives the theological solution to the riddle of the disaster. God had warned the nation not to forget Him in times of prosperity (Deut. 8:10–20). If they failed, He would discipline them. This should not, however, be seen

as a rejection but rather as a means of bringing them back to Him. Human experience has demonstrated that it is easier to remember God in hard times than in prosperity. It is often when we are in our deepest despair that we come closest to God and remember that the Lord is the one who provides salvation (Jon. 2:9).

Thus, the author challenged the nation to remember how they had experienced the Lord's steadfast loving-kindness in the past: it had never failed but was "new every morning" (Lam. 3:23). Remembering God's loving-kindness awakens hope in the midst of despair (vv. 21–23). After declaring that all he had hoped for was gone (v. 18), the prophet found new hope in the memory of God's loving acts of salvation in the past. Hope looks forward without losing sight of the saving work of God in the past. In fact, the two are inseparable. This is particularly clear in the message of hope found in the NT. It is grounded on the cross of Jesus—the past—and yet patiently waits for the return of the Lord in glory. Since in Lamentations remembrance brings hope, Judah's punishment, far from being an indicator of final rejection, was for the purpose of restoration. God is in control, and He promises that everything will ultimately work together for the good of those who love Him (Rom. 8:28).

It has been noted that Lamentations outlines the steps for processing grief. Difficulties are not denied. The pains and grief over the destruction and ruined dreams are openly acknowledged. This is indispensable to the healing process. The detailed listing of specific events and situations, along with the confession of sins, is an important part of the process of dealing with grief. Jeremiah wrestles with the thought of God causing this disaster and at the same time sees Him as the source of comfort, hope, and help. It is comforting to have the assurance of God's unfailing compassion and faithfulness. At the end, Jeremiah felt safe turning the situation over to Him in prayer, confident that He would do what was in the best interest of everyone involved.

Literary Features. The literary structure of Lamentations is somewhat unique. It consists of five poems/chapters, each one structured on the basis of the Hebrew alphabet. The first four chapters are acrostic—that is, the first line of each stanza or verse begins with a consecutive letter of the alphabet, with a few variations. Scholars agree that this is by design, but they have debated the specific purpose of the acrostics. Some see the structure as a memory device, and others think it may be part of a liturgical ritual. Though no specific reasons are given, the choice may indicate the poet's interest in literary beauty. Unfortunately, this literary feature is lost in translation.

The book belongs to a literary type called a lament. A characteristic feature of laments is the expression of a great loss with a vivid contrast between past glory and present misery. Laments may also express the community's despair over its misfortunes and sorrow for its wrongs (Jer. 22:18; Ezek. 19:1–14; 26:17–18).

It has been proposed that the five laments that form this book follow a chiastic arrangement, also referred to as inverted parallelism (these terms refer to a literary structure arranged in an ABCBA pattern, in which the most important idea/concept is in the center; e.g., Is. 45:5–6). Accordingly, chapters 1 and 5 present a general description of the scenes of misery. Chapters 2 and 4 further illustrate the people's sufferings, their enemies, and God's wrath. The central and longest chapter (chap. 3) views the people's suffering in the context of their understanding of God. Even though He is punishing them, He is not capricious—He is acting in righteousness. Several speakers are present in these laments, one of whom is identified by various titles, such as "the daughter of Zion"/"Daughter Zion"/"Judah"/"Jerusalem"/"my people"/"the widow Jerusalem." In chapter 1, Jeremiah bemoans the disaster that struck the "daughter of Zion"/"Daughter Zion" (Lam. 1:1–11, 17) and she also expresses grief over her fate (vv. 12–16, 18–22). In chapter 2, the prophet again mourns over the city's misfortunes (2:1–9), tries to console her (vv. 10–17), and calls on her to lament (vv. 18–19), which she does (vv. 20–22). In chapter 4, Jeremiah again weeps over the city (4:1–16), and her inhabitants likewise bewail their fate (vv. 17–20). Then the poet proclaims punishment for Edom and salvation for Zion (vv. 21–22). In chapter 5, the community takes up the lament.

The identity of the speakers in chapter 3 has puzzled some scholars. Jeremiah speaks of his sufferings at the hand of the Lord (3:1–18), then expresses his hope for deliverance (vv. 19–24) and challenges the sufferer to trust in a just and compassionate Lord (vv. 25–39). Then the community breaks into lament (vv. 40–47). The speakers grieve Zion's fall (vv. 48–51) and give thanks for the Lord's deliverance (vv. 52–58). The poem comes to an end with the community's prayer for deliverance (vv. 59–66).

COMMENTARY

1:1–22
Zion: A City in Shambles

Jeremiah and the city itself reflect on the fate of Zion. The present condition of the city is described in contrast to her former glory and beauty (1:1–11). What they are experiencing is profoundly painful. The prophet expresses his deep need for comfort but acknowledges that there is none (vv. 12–17). They are experiencing the Lord's affliction. In the last section (vv. 18–22), the prophet recognizes the guilt of the people and prays for God's intervention against their enemies.

1:1–11. The City's Destruction. The city was deserted and lonely like a widow (v. 1). The same image is found on a victory medal issued by Titus when the temple was destroyed in A.D. 70: a woman weeping beneath a palm tree, with the inscription *Iudaea capta* ("Judah captured"). Once full of people (Is. 1:21; 1 Sam. 2:5), it had become empty (Lam. 1:1; cf. Jer. 4:23–26). "Her lovers" (Lam. 1:2) is a reference to those who tempted her into alliance against the Babylonians (Jer. 27:3). They had turned against her, and therefore there was no one to help or comfort her (Lam. 1:2, 7, 9, 16–17, 21). Once a prestigious hub of activity, she had been reduced to the status of a slave (v. 3; cf. Deut. 12:10). Once her roads had resounded with the songs of rejoicing as pilgrims flocked to the city for the appointed festivals (Pss. 48; 122–134), but now, the prophet said, the roads to Zion mourned (Lam. 1:4). The gates, which had regularly been the center of important activities (Deut. 21:19; Ruth 4:1, 11; 2 Sam. 19:8; 1 Kin. 22:10), were now desolate (Lam. 1:4). How incredible that this could have happened to the great city of Jerusalem!

Even God Himself seemed to have turned against her because of her rebellions (v. 5). As a result, the splendor had departed from the daughter of Zion (v. 6), and she felt like a widow, sitting alone. Throughout the book, Jeremiah refers to the city in endearing terms, such as "the (virgin) daughter (of) Zion" (e.g., "the daughter of my people"), "the (virgin) daughter (of) Judah" (e.g. v. 5; 2:5), and "the daughter (of) Jerusalem" (e.g. vv. 13, 15). Jerusalem was remembering all of its precious things from the days of old (1:7). The city had been renowned for her beauty and great treasures from the time of King Solomon (1 Kin. 6:21–35; 10:11–25), but

as a result of various invasions by foreign powers, these had been stripped away and removed (2 Kin. 18:15–16).

The relationship between God and His people is most frequently seen as a marriage (cf. Deut. 29:12–13; Jer. 31:32). Unfaithfulness to God is seen as a breach of that relationship and is, therefore, often expressed in terms which imply sexual immorality. Those who despised her saw her nakedness (Lam. 1:8), and there was filthiness or uncleanness in her skirts (v. 9). Now, other nations had come into her sanctuary (v. 10). The term *goyim*, "nations," is almost exclusively used for pagan nations. Ammonites and Moabites were not to enter the assembly, much less the temple (Deut. 23:3–4). As a result of the attack against the city, Gentiles had entered the holy precincts (2 Kin. 24:2; Ps. 70:1; 74:3–7). The siege, which lasted eighteen months, drained the city's food rations (Lam. 1:11; cf. Deut. 28:17, 38–42; Jer. 52:6). The people were forced to barter away their valuables in order to obtain bread to eat (Lam. 1:11).

1:12–17. A Plea for Comforters. In this section, Jerusalem reflects on her fate and acknowledges it as the direct result of her own rebellion (vv. 14, 20, 22). Even though she complained about her harsh treatment at the hands of the Lord through the actions of her enemies, she did not blame Him. She recognized that He is righteous (v. 18) and that she deserved her sentence though the experience was difficult to bear.

The city searched for someone to comfort her in the midst of her sorrow, but people passed by and did not show sympathy (v. 12). The only one who could comfort her was the Lord, but He felt distant (v. 16). In fact, He was inflicting the punishment. In the aftermath of the disaster, the city had time to assess the situation and its causes. She realized that the Lord had brought this upon her on the day of His fierce anger (v. 12). All of her boasting had vanished, and she was like a captive animal because of her transgressions. Divine wrath is always a response to human sin. After realizing that the Lord had called for a *mo'ed*—the word used for Israel's festivals here designates "an appointed time" (which is sometimes translated in Lamentations as "assembly" or "army")—against her (v. 15), she wondered if there were any pain or suffering like hers (v. 12). In spite of God's mercy, there comes a time when humans reap what they have sown. The winepress is a graphic picture of God's judgment (v. 15). Grapes were put into a stone trough and then trampled in order to release their juice. Neither the children (v. 16) nor the elders and priests (v. 19) escaped the destruction. The nation had been forewarned by the Prophet Jeremiah (Jer. 19:8).

1:18–22. Admission of Guilt and Plea for Revenge on Enemies. In this section, the city admits her wrongdoing three times (vv. 18, 20, 22) and pleads with the Lord not to overlook the cruelty of her enemies (vv. 20–22; cf. Deut. 32:35). She expected her lovers to help and comfort her, but they showed no interest (Lam. 1:19, 21). She now realized how pointless it is to rely on human strength. Sin brings with it a deep sense of loneliness and abandonment. She prayed that the Lord might avenge her of her enemies (cf. Ps. 37:20; 137:1–9). Instead of seeking to implement her own vengeance, she surrendered it to the Lord and asked Him to act on her behalf.

2:1–22
God, the Destroyer of Zion

Chapter 2 further clarifies the nature of the disaster that had struck Zion. It emphasizes God's anger against Zion (vv. 1–14), the suffering of the city and the attitude of her enemies (vv. 15–17), and ends with an appeal to God for compassion in the form of a lament (vv. 18–22). The main emphasis of the chapter is on the fact that the Lord Himself had caused the destruction of the city, thereby assigning no supreme power to her enemies. What happened was not their doing, but the Lord's, because of the people's unfaithfulness.

2:1–14. God's Anger against Zion. Verse 1 introduces two topics that will be further developed in the first nine verses of the chapter: God's action against the city (v. 1a; developed in vv. 2–5, 8–9) and the destruction of the temple, His footstool (v. 1b; developed in vv. 6–7). This is followed by a description of the reaction of the elders and the prophet to the fall of the city (vv. 10–13), concluding with a charge against false prophets (v. 14). God's anger against the nation is mentioned five times in vv. 1–6. In His anger, He destroyed the city by throwing down the beauty and splendor of Israel from heaven to earth (v. 1)—hyperbolic language of total defeat, most likely emphasizing the magnitude of the fall (cf. Prov. 25:3). God's footstool refers to the temple (cf. Ps. 99:5; 132:7). God had destroyed the houses, the strongholds of the city,

and the princes (Lam. 2:2). God's anger is compared to a fire that devours everything (v. 3). The Lord had also been likened to a warrior fighting against Zion (v. 4). He had become the enemy of Judah, destroying the palaces and the strongholds, and leaving behind Him increased or multiplied mourning and lamentation (v. 5). But above all, the Lord destroyed the tabernacle, His dwelling (vv. 6–7), the outward symbol of His presence among His people (cf. Jer. 22:5; Ezek. 9:3; 10:4, 18–19; 11:23; Matt. 23:38). The religious festivities associated with the temple—the appointed festivals and sabbaths—had come to an end. The king, who was responsible for protecting the temple, and the priests, who were responsible for ministering in it, had been removed (Lam 2:6). The sacred precincts had been profaned by pagans, who made a noise of victory where Jews once raised shouts of praise to God (v. 7). This was happening because the Lord had abandoned His sanctuary and had handed over the city to the enemy of His people (v. 7). They were not taken from Him by force. This was a coming of the Lord in judgment against His people as a result of their sins and rebellions.

The disaster affected the elders and the young women or virgins of Jerusalem (v. 10). But it particularly impacted the prophet when he saw children, infants, and mothers struggling to survive (vv. 11–12). He was overcome with emotion over their condition, crying his heart out in pain over the apparently hopeless situation (v. 11). He felt unable to console the city (v. 13). The catastrophe was absolutely without parallel in his eyes. The prophets who should have delivered warnings from God to the people to bring them back from their evil ways (Jer. 23:22) had failed in their duties and instead communicated false and deceptive messages (Lam. 2:14; cf. Jer. 23:9–22).

2:15–17. The Sufferings of the City and the Taunts of Enemies. This situation could have been avoided. Had the nation repented, it might have enjoyed peace and prosperity again. But as it was, passersby would hiss and shake their heads, gloat and scoff at the nation's misfortune (vv. 15–16; cf. Obad. 12–15), and wonder why this calamity had struck Jerusalem (cf. Jer. 22:8). The reason was that Judah had forsaken the Lord (cf. Jer. 22:9). The catastrophe happened in accordance with God's ancient warnings (Lev. 26:14–16ff; Deut. 28:15ff). Therefore, what the people experienced was the fulfillment of prophecy (Lam. 2:17).

2:18–22. Appeal to God for Compassion. Jeremiah appealed to the wall of the daughter of Zion to lift her hands to God and take her sorrow to the Lord. The wall is personified to represent the whole city (vv. 18–19). In her desperation, the city responded and cried out in pain to the Lord, "How could this happen to us?" The people should have learned from the earlier experience of Israel (2 Kin. 6:25–29), but they did not (Jer. 3:6–10). Therefore, due to the severity of the siege, mothers in Judah stooped to eating their own offspring (Lam. 2:20; cf. Jer. 19:9), and God's servants were killed within the holy precincts of the temple. There was no safe place for anyone in the day of the Lord's anger (v. 22).

3:1–66

Hope Amid Crisis

Chapter three is the literal center of the book, with vv. 19–39 forming the theological hub, which gives meaning to the rest of the book and provides hope in an apparently hopeless situation. At times, the speaker appears to speak as an individual, but at other times he speaks on behalf of the population in general. The chapter moves from despair (vv. 1–20) to hope (vv. 21–29), mercy (vv. 40–47), and vindication (vv. 48–66).

3:1–20. A Cry of Despair. Jeremiah moves away from the specific description of the destruction of the city to a discussion of human suffering. Usually God's leading (v. 2a) is toward salvation (Ex. 15:13) or out of captivity (Is. 40:11; 49:10; 63:13, 14), but here the Lord is a shepherd who seems to have misled, a ruler who oppresses and imprisons. The prophet says that the Lord led him to darkness (v. 2b), which represents imprisonment or even death (Ps. 88:10–12). He no longer listens to the prayers of those who suffer (Lam. 3:8) and has frustrated the intentions of the prophet (v. 9). The prophet depicts Him as a wild animal (vv. 10–11) and as a hunter performing target practice (vv. 12–13), someone who had served bitterness (lit. "poison"; v. 15). Jeremiah has been made an object of derisive laughter and ridicule (v. 14). As the prophet describes his condition, he concludes in a shout of despair that his strength/splendor and his hope are lost (v. 18). But sometimes hope can be found even in moments of extreme hopelessness.

3:21–39. A Ray of Hope. Hope flourishes when we recall the wonders of God's mercies in our past experiences with Him. Jeremiah remembered the compassions of the Lord (vv. 20–22; cf. Ex. 34:6–7). Because His boundless mercies and inexhaustible compassion are new every morning (Lam. 3:22–23), the prophet could wait for or hope in (Heb. *yakhal*) the Lord (v. 24). Even in our trials, the Lord continues to be our "portion" (v. 24). This is a probable reference to the time when the Israelites received their allotments, except for the priests, for God said to Aaron that He Himself was the portion (or allotted share) for them (Num. 18:20). Even though they were now without a homeland, God would remain with them (Ps. 73:26).

Trials can be transformed into something positive for those who wait for or hope in (Heb. *qawah*) the Lord (Lam. 3:25; cf. Rom. 8:28). He can turn sufferings and trials into gains (cf. Ps. 94:12–14). It is therefore useful for us to learn to trust the Lord in times of difficulty and silence, for there may yet be hope (Lam. 3:29). The prophet was filled with confidence, knowing that it is not God's nature (lit. "from His heart") to cause grief (vv. 31–33). Even when our troubles are due to sin (v. 39; cf. Job 2:10), God shows compassion (v. 32). This leads to a call for repentance.

3:40–47. Appeal to God's Mercy. In the midst of disaster, the prophet gave a call for the nation to examine itself and return to the Lord (vv. 40–41). It is only in Him that true refuge is found. In the absence of repentance, there was no divine forgiveness (v. 42). In the absence of forgiveness, the nation was faced with the disturbing anger of the Lord (vv. 43–47). He had forsaken them, and consequently He no longer listened to their concerns (v. 44). Enemies had overcome God's people (vv. 46–47).

3:48–66. Assurance of Vindication. Perhaps the voice here describing streams of tears like water is that of the prophet (v. 48). Those who do not rebel against the Lord may also experience pain—their struggles may not always be the result of personal sin. In such cases, like Jeremiah's, they bring their concerns to the Lord in prayer, seeking vindication (vv. 49–54). The prophet had been oppressed by his enemies, but he had not given up on the Lord. He could testify that God was close to him and had told him not to fear (v. 57). He confidently states that the Lord redeemed his life, thus vindicating him (v. 58). His enemies would receive what they deserved according to what they had done (v. 64), based on righteous judgment. He wanted the Lord to judge his case (v. 59) and to avenge his enemies for wronging him (vv. 60–66). It was not for him to avenge himself but for the Lord to do it with justice.

4:1–22
The Guilt of Zion's Leadership

Chapter 4, like chapter 2, is an eyewitness account of the contrast between Zion's former glory and present condition (vv. 1–10). The content of the two chapters is very similar although chapter 4 reiterates the Lord's part in the city's demise and emphasizes the effect of the ruin on the various classes of people rather than on the city itself. The blame is primarily laid at the feet of the religious leaders, who failed in their duties and thus became part of the problem (vv. 11–20). The chapter ends on a note of hope for the suffering people (vv. 21–22).

4:1–10. Then and Now—Contrast. The first two verses summarize the contents of the whole chapter. The fine gold referred to in v. 1 is clearly a metaphor for the precious children of Zion (v. 2), who are regarded as clay pots. The reference to the sacred stones of the sanctuary scattered all over the city points to the total destruction of the temple. The dwellers of the city had become worse than animals, neglecting their own infants (vv. 3–4). The rich were to be found among the ashes (v. 5), a symbol of humiliation and worthlessness (Gen. 18:27; Is. 44:20). The fate of the city was severer than that of Sodom due to the city's lingering condition, with no hand of compassion to help her (Lam. 4:6; cf. 1:7). The use of the term *nezireah* and its meaning here have puzzled scholars and elicited various translations: "Nazarites," "princes," "dignitaries," or "consecrated ones." It could refer to a select group who took a vow of self-discipline, such as abstaining from wine and contact with the dead—the "Nazarites" (Num. 6:2–8). It could also be a picture of an elite who was the epitome of leadership, health, and beauty, like Joseph, who was said to be a *nazir* of his brothers (Deut. 33:16). The situation had become so desperate that self-preservation had become everyone's sole focus, even if this meant cooking their own children (Lam. 4:10; cf. 2:20).

4:11–20. The Failure of Religious Leaders. Verses 11–13 summarize what had happened and why. The fall of Jerusalem was unanticipated and came as a surprise to all (v. 12). Not only was the city strategically located between two converging valleys, but it was also the holy place of the Most High (Ps. 46:4). The Assyrian army had surrounded the city in 701 B.C. but was destroyed in the night by an angel (2 Kin. 19:35). The current collapse was due to internal weakness, the sins and iniquities of those who were appointed to ensure obedience to the covenant but who had become a part of the problem and the cause of the siege. This fact is emphasized in all the poems (Lam. 1:8; 2:14; 3:42; 4:13; 5:7). The priests, the prophets, and the elders had become unclean. When the people saw them, instead of showing respect, they shouted at them to go away because they were unclean (4:13–16). In vain, the people had worn out their eyes looking for help from Egypt (v. 17; cf. Jer. 37:5–10). The siege became increasingly oppressive (Lam. 4:18–19), and King Zedekiah—"the breath in [their] nostrils"—fled but was caught by the Babylonians (v. 20; cf. Jer. 39:4–7). The king is also identified as the anointed of the Lord, and the nation had felt safe under his shadow (Lam. 4:20; cf. Ps. 17:8). In spite of Zedekiah's resistance to the message, Jeremiah still considered him to be the appointed leader.

4:21–22. Enemies Warned against Gloating. The book of Obadiah points out how the Edomites, descendants of Esau, took advantage of the chaos following the collapse of Jerusalem. Using irony, Jeremiah commanded them to rejoice while they could (v. 21), for the cup, a symbol of punishment and approaching death (cf. Is. 51:17; Jer. 25:15; Obad. 1:16; Mark 14:36), would ultimately be passed on to them. A note of hope is introduced, for the sin of Zion would ultimately be pardoned, and its punishment would end (cf. Is. 40:2).

5:1–22
Hope for the Future

This last chapter differs from the others. It is not an acrostic, but it has twenty-two lines, the number of letters in the Hebrew alphabet. It is written in the form of a prayer, beginning with a review of the situation in Jerusalem (vv. 1–14) and climaxing in a plea to the Lord for help (vv. 15–22).

5:1–14. Orphans in Their Own Land. The poet calls on the Lord to remember His people (v. 1). Biblical "remembering" is not limited to the recollection of facts but includes acting upon that remembering (cf. Gen. 8:1; Ex. 2:24ff.). The emphasis is on the people's reversal of fortune. God's promised blessings—for example, land, houses, water (Deut. 6:10–11)—had been overturned (Lam. 5:2–4). The people were as defenseless as orphans and widows (v. 3). Their economy was controlled by foreigners (v. 4). Their status as God's special people had been removed, so there was no rest for them (v. 5), and their investment in alliances with Egypt and Assyria had proven futile (v. 6; cf. Hos. 2:5). The sins of the fathers were now being visited on their children (v. 7; cf. Jer. 3:25). Instead of being "the head and not the tail," as God had wanted them to be (Deut. 28:13), they were now being ruled over by servants or slaves (Lam. 5:8; cf. Prov. 30:21–22), and their young men (lit. "choice men") were grinding at the millstones, a work commonly done by women or slaves (cf. Judg. 16:21; Is. 47:2). Their religious and social life had been turned upside down (Lam. 5:12–14).

5:15–18. Admission of Guilt. Jeremiah was overwhelmed when he realized that the destruction of Jerusalem, which could have been avoided, was the result of the people's defiance of God's covenant. He exclaimed, "Woe to us, for we have sinned" (v. 16). He identified himself with his people and prayed on their behalf. He again fearlessly declared that the present deplorable condition of Jerusalem was a result of the sinful condition of the people. They were living in fear—their hearts were faint and they were slowly dying—their eyes were growing dim (dark; v. 17). The desolation of Zion was extremely depressing.

5:19–22. Plea for Restoration. The book opens with a cry of desperation but concludes with an assurance based on the central concept of the book—the Lord is good to those who wait and hope for Him (3:25). The experience of the fall of Jerusalem and the destruction of the temple would have raised questions about divine sovereignty and effectiveness. It is therefore appropriate for the book to end with an emphasis on the everlastingness of God. Everything may collapse, but God will remain King forever (v. 19). He is the final and supreme refuge. His throne is unshakable, and His kingdom will not be replaced by any other kingdom (cf. Dan 7:27). It is to this God that Jeremiah turned as the source of hope and restoration. Though it appeared that God had forgotten His people, the prophet nevertheless requested that He reestablish them (Lam. 5:21). This is about the divine willingness and initiative in restoring repentant sinners. The miracle of grace consists in the fact that it does for us what we cannot do for ourselves. The book closes in anticipation of the full renewal of God's people. Though it ends in the context of a desolating experience that appears to be the result of God's absence, hope remains that God's anger will be set aside and His people renewed (vv. 21–22). For those who accept God's offer of salvation through Christ, God's wrath has been removed: "God did not appoint us to wrath, but to obtain salvation through our Lord Jesus Christ" (1 Thess. 5:9). The full realization of this salvation continues to be the hope of His people.

EZEKIEL

Title and Authorship. The title, "Ezekiel," appropriately designates the person and prophetic voice of the book. Ezekiel (Heb. *yekhezqe'l*, "may God strengthen") was a priest and prophet taken from Judah into exile by the Babylonians in 597 B.C. Mentioned twice in the book (1:3; 24:24), his name indicates encouragement and consolation. The book's emphasis on purity and holiness points to Ezekiel's priestly, Zadokite lineage (1:3; 40:46; 43:19; 44:15; 48:11). He writes of the Jerusalem temple with a depth of familiarity, which indicates his access to it by vocation. As a deeply devoted married man (24:15–16), he conveys the messages of Israel's husband, Yahweh, with tenderness while also bearing the message that lambasted the people's fornicating ways with a holy zeal.

The book of Ezekiel is part of the section of the OT known as the Major Prophets (Isaiah, Jeremiah, Ezekiel) and points to a time period covering more than two decades (ca. 592–571 B.C.). Several factors, which occur throughout the book, point to single authorship: (1) its consistency of thought, literary genres, ritual perspective and language, and uniform formulaic markers; (2) a clearly identifiable movement from judgment to restoration; (3) autobiographical accounts; and (4) a standardized usage of dates. Ezekiel's messages mostly address "Israel" (e.g., 2:3; 3:1–9; 4:3; 8:9–12), though at the time of his call, the Northern Kingdom of Israel had already been taken into Exile. In this book, the preferential usage of the term "Israel" instead of "Judah" probably reflects the prevalence of the term since the time of Hezekiah's reign. Hezekiah saw himself as the king of both Israel and Judah. The remnant of the Northern Kingdom had fled south to Judah after the Assyrians destroyed it. The usage of the term "Israel" also points to the promised reunification for Israel and Judah under the Davidic Shepherd (e.g., 37:18–28).

Date. Ezekiel prophesied during the reign of kings Jeconiah (Jehoiachin, 598–597 B.C.; 1 Chr. 3:16; Esth. 2:6; Jer. 24:1; 27:20; 28:4; 29:2)

and Mattaniah (Zedekiah, 597–586 B.C.; 2 Kin. 24:17–20) from the Southern Kingdom of Judah (Ezek. 1:2–3). Jehoiachin, a young man of eighteen years, was brought to Babylon by Nebuchadnezzar after reigning for only three months (2 Kin. 24:8–17; 2 Chr. 36:9–10). His uncle, Mattaniah, was installed as a puppet ruler until Israel's final deportation in 586 B.C. The dating outline of the book uses Jehoiachin's and Ezekiel's exile (Ezek. 40:1) as its reference point. Ezekiel's ministry is last dated in the twenty-seventh year after his deportation (29:17; ca. 570 B.C.). In addition, this dating plan serves a larger theological purpose: prophecies in the book serve to verify Ezekiel's prophetic calling (cf. 2:5; Deut. 18:22) as well as significant events in Israel's history. The book itself covers the period before and after the fall of Jerusalem in 586 B.C.

Backgrounds. God secured a place for His people at the crossroads of the nations. The temple was built for all nations to come to hear about Him and to worship Him as the true God. He had promised that after cutting off David's enemies, God would first establish a royal dynasty under Himself as Israel's true King and under the human king as His son; after that there would be an eternal Davidic kingdom under the Messiah, God's Son in a unique sense (2 Sam. 7; cf. Ps. 89; Matt. 21:9; Luke 1:27; Rom. 1:3). After the Northern Kingdom of Israel apostatized and was taken into exile to Assyria, Judah was the sole witness to God's glory and promises (722 B.C.; 2 Kin. 17). God graciously gave more than a century for Judah to fulfill His divine mission. However, by the time of the first Babylonian invasion (Dan. 1:1), Judah had also lost its way.

From the time of King Manasseh of Judah (ca. 697–643 B.C.; 2 Kin. 21:1–18), Israel continued to stumble along, so God sent a succession of prophets (Zephaniah, Jeremiah, Nahum, and Habakkuk) with strong messages of hope to warn Judah of its impending judgment if it did not repent and submit to God's plan. The messages of faithfulness to God, rejection of idolatry, and biblical social justice (i.e., feeding the poor, caring for widows and orphans, and dealing honestly in business matters) were God's means of showing grace and mercy by providing for and protecting the vulnerable. Sadly, the rich and powerful used God's blessings to enrich and comfort themselves (Is. 5:11–12; Amos 6:4–6). They engaged in unauthorized political alliances that compromised cultural and worship customs (Is. 30:1–5; 31:1–3; Amos 3:13–15) and engaged in dishonest business practices (Is. 5:8–10; Mic. 6:11–16). Finally, they rebelled against God's messages (Mic. 2:6; 3:11–12). Ezekiel began his ministry alongside other prophets serving the exiled community in Babylon (Daniel) as well as those who remained in Israel (Jeremiah). By the time Ezekiel was called to the prophetic ministry, Jeremiah had been laboring for God's people for over three decades (Jer. 1:1–3) and they were in the process of reaping their final harvest of rebellion. Ezekiel's message, like those of the prophets before him, focuses on the religious leaders and their failure to fulfill God's plan. Their roles encompassed the administration of a godly society as a witness to the nations: (1) the prophet would proclaim God's messages of justice and righteousness; (2) the priest would mediate God's plan for forgiveness, purity, and worship; and (3) the Davidic king would administer God's ethic of justice and righteousness in Israel and oversee diplomatic overtures to the nations. Israel's godly society collapsed when the leaders thwarted God's organizational structure through wickedness and rebellion (Ezek. 7:26–27; 12:1—14:23). Against the background of Israel's failure and Assyria's ensuing demise by the late seventh century (626 B.C.; Is. 14:15–27), Babylon emerged as the major power in the ancient Near East.

During Ezekiel's prophetic career of over twenty years, Babylon was his point of reference, both geographically and politically (Ezek. 1:1). His vision of the Jerusalem temple served as God's point of reference for judgment, but Babylon served as the place where Ezekiel carried out his prophetic calling. During Ezekiel's captivity, Babylon's control over the region of Syria-Palestine was secure. The tendency to depend on Egypt for military help against Babylon (Is. 30–31) finally proved unfruitful to Judah (2 Kin. 24:7).

There are probably two reasons why Ezekiel does not use the reign of Zedekiah (597–586 B.C.) as a date marker. First, Zedekiah was a puppet king placed on the throne by Nebuchadnezzar (2 Kin. 24:17). Second, Ezekiel's exile was connected with Jehoiachin's, so he used his experience as a reference point for the book as he associated himself with his fellow exiles. Jehoiachin's surrender and exile included the elite in Judah: the royal court, chief persons, military elite, craftspersons, and artisans (2 Kin. 24:14–16). Babylon often used this policy of removal to weaken the political and economic backbone of a nation in order to ensure that it would lack the potential for an organized revolt. The fact that many of the exiles were of the powerful and elite class of Judah is crucial to understanding God's command to Ezekiel to not fear their faces and words (Ezek. 2:6–7).

Theology and Purpose. The main character in the book of Ezekiel is the Lord, and consequently the theology of the book is developed around His words and actions. We will explore some of the concepts associated with Him.

1. Yahweh, the Lord of Glory. God's name, His character and reputation, plays a significant role in the book. The phrase "I am the Lord" appears more than one hundred times in various contexts throughout the book. Israel, as well as other nations, needed to know the true God and understand His gracious and holy ways (20:9, 14, 22; 36:20–23). These statements underpin Yahweh's sovereignty and require that humans worship Him. His character would be vindicated in the face of rampant idolatry inside and outside of Israel. God's abhorrence of idol worship stems from proud humans who ascribe glory and honor to the work of their hands rather than evincing a reverential awe for the Creator and Lord of life (6:4–13; 8:10; 14:3–7; 18:6–15; 20:7–39; 22:3, 4; 44:10–12). The glory of Yahweh was to be the central focus of Ezekiel's ministry. His condemnation of sin, portrayal of history, and messages of hope were to be understood as the outworking of God's glory. In the opening visions of the book, we find that prior to the destruction of Jerusalem, the glory of the Lord departed to Babylon (10:18–19; 11:16). In the closing visions, however, we see the return of the glory of the Lord to the temple (43:2–5). As it were, the Lord voluntarily exiled Himself and followed His people to Babylon; there He would comfort them and cause them to return to their "own land" (37:21).

2. Yahweh, the Lord of History. Ezekiel's considerable interest in the history of God's unfolding plan is expressed in the careful dating of his prophecies and in his outline of Israel's history and future (1:1–2; 3:16; 8:1; 20:1; 24:1;

26:1; 29:1, 17; 30:20; 31:1; 32:1, 17; 33:21; 40:1). Ezekiel frames three major historical reviews in the context of a marriage covenant: chapter 16 utilizes the metaphor of a bride, chapter 20 traces the history of Israel from the Exodus to the Exile, and chapter 23 utilizes the metaphor of unfaithful sisters that parallels chapter 16. History in Ezekiel is more than a cause-and-effect sequence of events. It is the unfolding of the sovereignty of God revealed in two important ways. First, through a messianic hope announcing the coming of a Shepherd-King, God would establish a messianic-centered community. Second, in this account of history God reveals His sovereignty through His promise to return to dwell in His temple. Ezekiel portrays the presence of God in His temple as central to Israel's hope (Ex. 33:15). In the context of a disaster, the Lord was ready to create a new hope for them.

3. *Yahweh, the Judge of the Wicked and Vindicator of the Righteous*. God's holiness demands justice against iniquity. Hence, the Babylonian Exile was the consequence of Israel's idolatry. Israel, as God's elect, had a high and holy mission to represent God's character of grace through just and righteous lives. They would proclaim His name and reputation to the nations through their ethical values, sanctuary system, prophetic utterances, praise and worship, and covenant faithfulness. However, Israel failed on all fronts, and God characterized them as a "rebellious house" (Ezek. 2:5–8; 3:9, 26; 12:2, 9; 17:12; 24:3; 44:6), indicating a tenacious unwillingness to yield to His authority. They often took up the cultic practices of their pagan neighbors (2 Kin. 21:10–18; 2 Chr. 28:1–4; Jer. 10:1–16). Daring to speak in the name of God, false prophets gave false messages (Jer. 28:1–17) while attempting to quench the voice of the true prophets (Amos 2:12; 7:10–13; Mic. 2:6). The people did not speak about trust in God's power to deliver, but they put their trust in foreign nations (2 Chr. 28:16; Is. 30:1–5). Finally, not only did the kings enter into unauthorized covenants and alliances with foreign rulers (2 Kin. 16:5–20; Jer. 37:1–10), but most of them also engaged in pagan practices (1 Kin. 11:1–8; 16:29–34) and thus encouraged the people to apostatize.

4. *Prophecy and Covenant*. Israel's creation, Exodus, election, and covenant are narrated in the Pentateuch and provide the background for many of the prophets' criticisms of the people. The history of the monarchy, as described in Samuel and Kings, gives the background for the ultimate failure of the people to live out God's unfolding covenant of grace. Prophets like Isaiah and Jeremiah provide chronological developments of the demise of both Israel and Judah, giving details that are not addressed in Ezekiel's book. Finally, the prophet Daniel, Ezekiel's contemporary, who also was in Babylon, provides a message that addresses the universal, apocalyptic perspective whose fulfillment reaches even to our days. Ezekiel mainly addresses the more local and immediate issues of Israel's restoration to the land of Canaan and points to the Messiah's mission. The book of Ezekiel plays a special role in the Christian's understanding of the book of Revelation, as the latter uses much of Ezekiel's imagery, themes, and language. Close attention to these parallels shows the consistency of God's plan and illustrates how the local situation of Judah in the sixth century B.C. can illuminate our understanding of the cosmic conflict in Scripture's last book.

5. *Personal Application*. We are remiss if we read Ezekiel simply as a historical record of the sins of Israel and Judah and God's pleas and punishments. The problems of Ezekiel's time are the problems of our time. We have the hindsight to look back and see the consequences of idolatrous hearts, stubbornness, and vile practices. The hope of Ezekiel's time is the hope of our time as well. For Israel, the ministry of reconciliation meted out through the earthly sanctuary was central to their relationship with God. For the church, the ministry of reconciliation is meted out through the cross and Christ's high priestly ministry in the heavenly sanctuary. In the book of Ezekiel, the church can see and learn what the book of Revelation describes and affirms—the throne room, God's heavenly sanctuary, as the vehicle through which hope and joyous worship are found (Rev. 4–5). As we listen in on Ezekiel, it behooves us to sit with the prophet and hear God's Word, to sit with the exiles and hear God's rebuke, and to sit in a foreign land and hear about a better one where the God of righteousness and purity reigns.

Literary Features. Ezekiel has been noted for its depth of descriptive imagery and the evocative prophetic indictments couched in language familiar to Israel from the Torah. This language signals Israel's unfaithfulness to God's covenant with the resulting curses uttered through a variety of prophetic speech patterns. Its wide array of depicted visions, symbolic acts, parables, and prophecies are intermingled with historical date markers, personal incidents, and prophecies.

Structure. The general survey of the book outlines a three-part structure: chapters 1–24, before Jerusalem falls; chapters 25–32, an indictment of the nations; and chapters 33–48, after Jerusalem falls. A more detailed study has revealed an intricate chiastic structure:

A God comes to His defiled temple to investigate and then departs (1–11)

  B Oracles of judgment for Israel (12–23)

    C Jerusalem besieged (24)

      D Oracles against the nations (25—28:10)

        E Judgment on the fallen cherub (28:11–19)

      D' Oracles against the nations (28:20—32:32)

    C' Jerusalem falls (33)

  B' Oracles of restoration for the restored people (34–39)

A' God comes to His restored temple to dwell with His People (40–48)

The structural emphasis of this chiasm brings into focus two complementary themes: (1) Yahweh, the Lord of history; and (2) the cosmic conflict motif (i.e., judgment on the fallen cherub). First, the storyline of the book moves historically from disaster (chaps. 4–7), judgment against Israel (chaps. 8–11), and alienation (chaps. 12–24) to joy, restoration, and communion (chaps. 34–48). The prediction of Jerusalem's Exile and final destruction in 586 B.C. is an indication of God's sovereignty over history. The dating system of the book can be broken up into three periods: (1) dates that focus on the reasons leading up to judgment and Exile (1:1; 8:1; 20:1); (2) dates that focus on the immediate circumstances of the judgment and Exile in international terms (24:1; 26:1; 29:1, 17; 30:20; 31:1; 32:1, 17; 33:21); and (3) one date concerning the postexilic plan of God for His restored people, their worship, and their land. Second, the battle between Yahweh (God's covenant name) and the false gods of the nations, through whom the anointed cherub Lucifer is working, is pervasive not only in international militaristic terms but also, as chapters 8–11 detail, in Israel's worship life and daily living.

Within the book there are smaller groupings by themes: prophecies of judgment through sign-acts (chaps. 4–5); judgment oracles against Israel (chaps. 6–7); parables of reproof and judgment (chaps. 15–17); judgment oracles against outside nations (chaps. 25–28); prophecies of a restored temple (chaps. 40–43); prophecies of restored worship (chaps. 44–46); and prophecies of a restored land (chaps. 47–48).

Literary Forms. As a prophet and trained priest, Ezekiel expresses God's message through various literary genres, prophetic formulas, and ritual expressions characteristic of his professions. The patterns of some of Ezekiel's speeches indicate that they were public proclamations that at some point were embedded into a structured literary book. A comparison of Ezekiel with the prophetic writings and speeches of the historical books (Judges through 2 Kings) and with the legal and cultic language of the Pentateuch (Genesis–Deuteronomy) reveals a similarity of literary patterns intended to guide the reader in understanding the biblical message more clearly. These literary patterns include genres, prophetic formulas, and acted parables. Among the literary genres we find:

- Narrative
- Call Narrative (Ezek. 1–3)
- Divine Abandonment and Return (8–11; 40–48)
- Poetry
- Oracles (28; 29:1–5; 31:1–9)
- Laments (19; 26:15–18; 27; 30; 32:1–21)
- Riddles, parables, allegories; for example, the parable of the vine and allegories of an eagle and cedars, a lion, and a boiling pot (15; 17; 19; 23; 24; 27).

Among the prophetic formulas we find:

- Judgment Oracles—a prophecy of calamity; a speech on behalf of God to announce disaster to individuals, groups, or nations.
- Salvation/Restoration Oracles—a prophecy of salvation; a speech on behalf of God that reverses a judgment to individuals, groups, or nations.
- Recognition Formula—a formula used to express the purpose of God's action. The main elements (with minor variations) are: (1) "and you/they shall know," (2) "that I am Yahweh," and sometimes (3) "when I...." This formula expresses God's sovereignty, revelatory purposes, and vindication of His reputation whether Israel suffered or prospered. This paradigm was

first used in Exodus (Ex. 6:7; 7:5, 17; 14:4, 18; 16:12; 29:46).

- Revelation Formula—a formula used to identify how God communicates with His messenger to reveal Himself to the people. Two basic forms are "the hand of the Lord was upon me" and "the word of the Lord came to me, saying."

Among the prophet's acted-out object lessons or prophetic signs are the following:

- Ezekiel acting out the siege and destruction of Jerusalem (Ezek. 4:1—5:17).
- Ezekiel acting out the Exile (12:1–20).
- Ezekiel being commanded not to mourn his wife as a sign of Israel's response to exile (24:15–27).
- Ezekiel using sticks to symbolize the reunification of Israel (37:15–28).

COMMENTARY

1:1—3:27

VISIONS OF GOD AND EZEKIEL'S CALL

Chapters 1–3 form a unit, an introductory collection of three visionary experiences that expose readers to the grandeur and indescribable glory of God and His mission for His servant (1:1—3:11; 3:12–21, 22–27). Each instance includes the same elements and similar or exact language. The use of similar language holds this unit together: smaller plot vignettes can be recognized by the repeated phrase "son of man" (2:1, 3, 6, 8; 3:1, 3, 4, 10, 17, 25), the characterization of Israel as rebellious (2:5, 6, 7; 3:9, 26, 27), and stylistic features such as small literary chiasms (cf. 2:6; 3:1) and parallel clauses (2:5, 7; 3:11, 27) seen best in the original Hebrew.

God's revelation, call, and commission to Ezekiel manifested His purpose for His people and the world. Judgment on Israel and the nations would be an antidote to the injustice and anguish in a world bent on living apart from God and His creation design. In that vein, Ezekiel saw God coming from the north, from where judgment typically came in the form of nations hostile to Israel (26:7; Is. 41:25; Jer. 4:6; see "God's Judgment in the Prophets," p. 981).

Ezekiel's first visionary experience sets forth the context of the book and the issues its messages express—judgment intended to turn the hearts of the rebellious and hold the unrepentant accountable. God called Ezekiel to a restorative mission that would possibly bear little fruit and would inevitably stir up animosity and dissension among the rebellious. Ezekiel's response to God's glory and His intention to pierce the hardened and disobedient hearts of His people exudes both awe and despondency. In Ezekiel's book there is a record of God having the first and the last word with this prophet, encouraging him as He put His words in the prophet's mouth and moved him from place to place. Like God's other prophets, Ezekiel was responsible for holding the people (especially the leaders) accountable for their sins, calling them to return to God in covenant faithfulness. It is crucial to understand Ezekiel's passiveness in the visionary experiences. He was picked up, transported, shown what God wanted him to see, and given the interpretation of the symbols. The book is entirely God's word to His people through Ezekiel (e.g., 2:3–5). It is noteworthy how often it is said that "the word of the Lord came" to Ezekiel (e.g., 1:3; 20:45; 30:1; 38:1). It was not his word, but the Lord's.

1:1–3
Setting, Context, and Prophetic Experience

Several years before the Babylonians' final breach of the walls of Jerusalem (2 Kin. 25:2–4) in Ezekiel's thirtieth year (Ezek. 1:1), which was the fifth year of King Jehoiachin's exile (v. 2; 592 B.C.), Ezekiel was in the strange land of Babylon by the River Kebar (alternatively spelled as Chebar), known for the large manors and date palm groves located along its course. This "thirtieth year" most likely refers to Ezekiel's age, which indicates that he was born around the year in which the book of the law was discovered in the temple (622 B.C.; 2 Kin. 22:8–20). His upbringing was filled with experiences of reformation and focused attention on the Word of God. Ezekiel and the other exiles, however, were not to enjoy the accoutrements of prosperity and blessing found in the Torah (cf. Deut. 6:10–11). They were most likely reduced to forced labor for irrigation canals in Babylon. They lived in strange settlements, not as guests but as the displaced covenant people of God (Deut. 28:45–68). Yet, what seemed catastrophic for the people was ultimately a sign of hope because the land was dormant and in a process of restoration until it was ready to receive back a purified people (Ezek. 36:24–28; Lev. 26:34; 2 Chr. 36:21). Ezekiel, in harmony with earlier prophets, warned of this impending judgment (Is. 39:6–7; Mic. 3:9–12; 4:10).

The introduction sets forth the main characters and setting of the book. The prophet was among the exiled people (Ezek. 1:1), which indicates he probably belonged to the upper class: the elite, the educated, and those skilled in various professions who were typically taken into exile (2 Kin. 24:14–16). This was the second wave of exiles taken to Babylon. The prophet Daniel was among the first wave taken in 605 B.C., during the reign of Jehoiakim, the father of Jehoiachin, when Nebuchadnezzar attacked Jerusalem and took the royal class hostage to Babylon (2 Chr. 36:6; Dan. 1:1). In Israel, God's covenant was a corporate relationship as much as it was individual. Not all of Israel individually rebelled against God, but as a nation, they failed to live up to His plan and turned their backs on Him (see Ezek. 18). Ezekiel was with them in the second deportation, and he had experienced the grueling and dehumanizing march of the faithless. It took Ezekiel and the caravan with which he was traveling many months to traverse the nearly 900 miles (1,448 km) from Jerusalem to Babylon. An army could have traveled much faster, but Ezekiel's fellow exiles probably included hungry and tired children and elderly people. This protracted march invited reflection.

When he was old enough to take up his priestly responsibilities (Num. 4:3, 23, 30), his prospects seemed hopeless outside of the temple in Jerusalem. Five years after the decimation of the Davidic kingship of Jehoiachin and the non-start of his priestly ministration, Ezekiel received his prophetic call. Though God gave a message of encouragement through the prophet Jeremiah (Jer. 29:4–7), the outlook of a true worship experience seemed a faint pipe dream (Ps. 137:1–6). In this hopeless situation, from what was basically the beginning of a seventy-year waiting period (Jer. 29:10), God's call of Ezekiel involved both hope and judgment. It was from the throne of the universe that he received his commission to serve as a mouthpiece to correct and encourage his people. His message for them embraced a universal hope, the glory of God breaking out of the confines of geographical limitations.

Ezekiel knew about the glory of God appearing after the ordination of the Aaronic priests, and he saw similar elements as they appeared in his commission. The Levitical ordination finished with a sign of divine acceptance and fitness for priestly mediation in the proper worship of God (Lev. 9:6, 22–24). So God gave Ezekiel several indications of his divine ordination for the ministry of summoning the people to return to the true and proper worship of God (Ezek. 2–3). Ezekiel's response, the only acceptable one, was to fall down in reverential awe. In the Bible a theophany (i.e., an appearance of God) usually contains portents of hope (Num. 20:6–9; 2 Chr. 7:1–3), judgment (Num. 14:10–12; 16:19–50), or both. Here the phrase "the heavens were opened" (Ezek. 1:1), as used elsewhere in Scripture, points both to the threat of judgment and the hope of re-creation according to God's grace (Gen. 7:11; cf. Is. 24:18). The word of the Lord to Ezekiel in prophetic vision was signified by God's hand upon him (Ezek. 1:3; cf. 3:14, 22; 8:1; 37:1; 40:1), which could terrify in judgment (Ex. 9:3; Deut. 2:15; Josh. 22:31) or sustain, direct, and encourage the fulfillment of God's salvific plan (1 Kin. 18:46; Acts 11:21). Ezekiel's recounting of this dual purpose draws from the enduring revelations of God and indicates that the same God of Abraham, Isaac, Jacob, Moses, and Israel was with him in exile.

1:4–28
Glory of the Lord Approaches

This section of Ezekiel's visionary experience focuses on three interconnected entities: the four living beings (vv. 5–14); the wheels (vv. 15–21); and the dais, the throne above, and God Himself (vv. 22–27).

In reverential awe, Ezekiel moves cautiously to his description of God. First, he describes a pyrotechnic storm cloud (v. 4; cf. Ex. 19:16; Job 38:1; Pss. 77:18; 107:25; 148:8) that he saw coming from the north, out of which came four living creatures. The prophetic books frequently utilize animal imagery to depict certain aspects commonly understood in historical and cultural contexts (cf. Dan. 7:1–8; 8:1–8). Ezekiel's description of these creatures is similar to ancient Near Eastern images of protectors of a deity (e.g., griffins in Persia and Greece, the sphinx in Egypt, winged bulls in Mesopotamia). His description is of a dynamic, gleaming, portable, Spirit-driven team of throne protectors or bearers. The major distinction in the Hebrew Bible is that they are not attached to mythological stories, but they appear in judgment scenes and the construction of the sanctuary as real entities (Ex. 25:17–22; 1 Kin. 6:15–30). The language and imagery is highly symbolic. The moveable chariot-throne would serve two purposes for the exiled community and for those in Jerusalem. First, it would affirm God as being not another deity confined to a temple but the Sovereign Lord. Second, it would acknowledge that the glory of the Holy One would not reside in a temple filled with abominable practices and competing idols.

Ezekiel was so overwhelmed by the awesome sight that it was not until fourteen months later that he would write a clear explanation of the powerful beings he saw and their relation to the work of God (Ezek. 10:3, 20). In Ezekiel's account, these angelic beings or cherubim are linked with God as guardian figures (28:14, 16; cf. Gen. 3:24). The Apostle John picks up on much of Ezekiel's language and description: (1) the fourfold description of the faces of a human, a lion, an ox, and an eagle (Ezek. 1:10; Rev. 4:6–8); (2) the glory throne with a rainbow over it (Ezek. 1:28; Rev. 4:2–3); (3) the brilliant and splendid appearance of God in luminous colors (Rev. 4:3); and (4) the terrifying magnificence of God's glory (Ezek. 1:26–27; Rev. 4:5; cf. Ex. 19:16). The significance of these beings in Scripture and in the ancient world comes from their association with divine majesty (the human face or image, Gen. 1:26–28; Ps. 8), royalty and ferocity (the lion, Ps. 7:2; Prov. 28:1; 30:30; Amos 3:8), speed and power (the eagle, 2 Sam. 1:23; Is. 40:31; Jer. 4:13), and strength and fertility (the ox, Deut. 33:17).

Ezekiel's account of the glory of the Lord (Ezek. 1:28) and the imagery of God as the Divine Warrior, a familiar concept in Israel's history (Deut. 33:26; Job 38:1; Pss. 18:7–14; 68:4; 104:3–4; Is. 19:1), are in harmony with the work God had come to do. Unfortunately, this time it would be not only against the enemies of His people but against His people as well. Ezekiel depicts the sound of the movement of God's throne in militaristic language. He uses language from after the Flood—God set His rainbow (lit. "bow," the same word used for the weapon— Gen. 9:13; cf. Ezek. 1:28) in the clouds as a sign of His promise. In Ezekiel's account, the God of judgment and the Lord of restoration are one and the same. Against the backdrop of a firmament, expanse, or vault (vv. 22–26; cf. Gen. 1:6–8; Ex. 24:9–10), Ezekiel can only speak in similes as he uses language from the Creation narrative. He saw something that looked like a throne and someone who looked like a (Heb. *demut*; Gen. 1:26) a human being (Heb. *'adam*; Gen. 1:26), in appearance like gleaming metal, or a bonfire.

Ezekiel's descriptions of visions of God (Ezek. 1:1; 8:3; 40:2) portray an indescribable multimedia extravaganza that serves several purposes. What begins as a storm ends with the appearance of the throne of God front and center. Hence, the throne of God, His sovereignty, is central to understanding the book. The movement of the book reveals the glory of the Lord as a terror in judgment but ends as a source of hope to the people of God. Here Ezekiel writes concerning God as the ruler of the world responsible for Israel's exile—reassuring realities to him. Despite current circumstances, God promised that their exile would be for a limited period (Jer. 25:11; 29:10), that He would judge Babylon, and that Israel would go free (Is. 14:4, 22; 44:24—45:13; Jer. 28:4). Additionally, the glory of God reveals the serious nature of Israel's covenant breach. In times past, God had come to His people through His prophets to address their sins and rebellions. Now He would come to His sanctuary to investigate and render judgment (Ezek. 8–11).

2:1–10
God Calls and Prepares Ezekiel

Transitioning from observation to dialogue, Ezekiel records the divinely empowering call for him to stand on his feet and listen. The infusion of God's Spirit points to the life-giving potency of God's presence (3:24; 37:14; cf. Gen. 1:2–3). The account here of Ezekiel's call follows the familiar pattern of God sending an emissary for a special mission (Ezek. 2:3). In other texts, God is the subject of the "sending" in contexts of judgment (Ex. 9:14; Jer. 25:9, 15–16, 27; 29:17), protection (Ex. 23:20), and restoration (Mal. 3:1–2). The central themes of hope and judgment come to light as Ezekiel's ministry would be dominated by the leading of the Spirit. This emphasis serves to highlight the distinction between Ezekiel and false prophets (Ezek. 13:8–16). He was commanded to utter what he had first experienced. His physical weakness paralleled the spiritual weakness of the people and required the same remedy: the necessity for God's Spirit to empower the people to stand faithfully in the light of His presence and hear in obedient submission (chap. 37).

In Ezekiel's call and commission, God conferred His authoritative stamp on his ministry, the content of the message appearing afterward (2:4; 3:27). The focus is on the divine word and its efficacy (2:1–2, 7–8). Forty-nine times Ezekiel uses the announcement "The word of the LORD came to me" to confirm the divine origin of his message and the basis of judgment that stemmed from a divine assessment of the people's sins as well as those of their ancestors (v. 3). The overwhelming designation of the people of Israel in the book is that they were rebellious. The Hebrew Bible uses the noun "rebellion" (Heb. *meri*) twenty-four times; sixteen of those are used by Ezekiel to indicate a central problem in Israel. God's description of Israel's rebellious mind and actions appears in various ways. Their actions (v. 3; "they rebelled," "they broke faith with") and their disposition, literally described as "hard-faced" and "strong of heart" (i.e., obstinate or impudent and stubborn; v. 4), are structurally central and the reason for God sending Ezekiel. God said:

A I am sending you to the children of Israel (v. 3a)
  B They are a rebellious house/people who rebelled against God (v. 3b)
  B' They are impudent/obstinate and stubborn children (v. 4a)
A' I am sending you to them (v. 4b)

The irony is profound: the rebellious people were exiled because they had been rebellious, but instead of surrendering to God, they continued on their present course. Verses 5–7 sharpen the focus on the obstinate, hostile reaction and dangerously aggressive response to the divine message.

A Ezekiel would convey God's messages whether they listened or not (v. 5)
  B He was not to be afraid of them or their words (v. 6a)
    C Briers and thorns were around him and he lived among scorpions (v. 6b)
  B' He was not to be afraid because of their words or presence (v. 6c)
A' He would give God's messages regardless of whether they listened or not—the people were rebellious (v. 7)

The rebellious nature of the people "to this very day" (v. 3) is further developed in chapters 16 and 23. The validity of the message is grounded in the source of its authority; people would know that the Lord had sent a prophet. The fulfillment of the prophetic word implies that by delivering his message, Ezekiel demonstrated his commission, his reception of the divine instruction, and his mission as God's authorized messenger. God's command for Ezekiel to open his mouth and eat what God was giving him (v. 8) emphasized the source of the message as well as the problem with the people. Not only were they rebellious, but they also refused to take the medicine God offered for their healing: His word and its authority. And instead of consuming the humbling divine message of rebuke, the rebellious house in Jerusalem would eat their children (5:10; cf. Deut. 28:53–57).

3:1–11
God's Preparatory Commissioning and Empowerment

God was preparing Ezekiel for his prophetic ministry in two ways: through Ezekiel's consumption of the message (vv. 1–3) and through the divine strengthening for the negative response he would receive (vv. 4–11). The divine command to "Go!" (vv. 1, 4, 11) structures Ezekiel's commission. This command focuses on his reception of the message in the form of a scroll. As can be seen throughout the book, symbolic actions follow a similar pattern of an introductory formula (2:8), a symbol or sign-act (3:1–3), and a prophetic interpretation (vv. 4–11). The scroll is described as a symbol of the message of lamentation, mourning, and woe (2:10). The symbolic action of eating the scroll is interpreted as a prophecy: as the eaten scroll contains lamentations, mourning, and woe, so too the substance of and the responses to Ezekiel's prophecies and revelations consist of lamentations, mourning, and woe from God's people. Thus, the command to eat portrays a divine enablement to absorb the prophetic word in its most hopeful, doleful, and woeful tones (Jer. 15:16). The assertion that God fed Ezekiel the scroll, or caused him to eat it, evokes the passive reception on Ezekiel's part while emphasizing that his mission encompassed divine content and carried the force of God's will. By eating the scroll, the prophet appropriated the divine message and joyfully accepted the prophetic call.

Ezekiel was not commissioned to go to a foreign nation that might show signs of receptivity (cf. Ezra 1:2–4; Jon. 3:6–10) but to those who had the benefit of the revelation and grace of God for over a millennium. The repeated references to the recipients as the *bet yisra'el* ("house" or "people of Israel") emphasize the message as being for the covenant people (cf. Deut. 30:11–20) who had participated in a persistent, self-induced spiritual coma (Ezek. 3:1, 4, 5, 7, 11). Israel's response was foretold as an unwillingness to obey and submit to God's humbling tutelage under Nebuchadnezzar, for they were hardheaded and trusted in human devices (namely, Egyptian support) to solve their crises (cf. chap. 17; 2 Kin. 24:20; Jer. 27; Hab. 1:5–11). As a sensitive and caring soul (Ezek. 24:15–18), Ezekiel was prepared by God with the strongest resolve for a head-on collision (3:7–9; cf. Jer. 1:18). In the face of corporate rebellion, God empowered Ezekiel to neither fear the aged, the powerful, or the multitude, nor become emotionally dismayed or shattered (*khatat*, "dismayed," "terrified") by Israel's abominations, acceptance of false prophecies, or recalcitrant attitude toward the true prophetic message (cf. Ezek. 2:6).

3:12–21
The Spirit's Work and Warning

Up to this point, Ezekiel has described the movement of the living creatures and his own experience in harmony with the Spirit (1:17–21; 2:2). Consequently, he describes the two together as the account of his first visionary experience closes (3:12–15). Two powerful and overwhelming experiences converged as the Spirit lifted him up while he heard the departure of the living creatures lifting up the glory of Yahweh with the sound of a great earthquake (cf. 1:24; 3:13). The creatures' wings flapped together, creating a divine panoramic perspective as he was brought back to the Chebar River (1:1; 3:15) at the village *tel 'abib* ("mound of the flood," i.e., "mound of ruins"). Back to reality, bitter with an intense anger or "heat" of spirit, he sat appalled among his fellow exiles for seven days. His reality forced him to wrestle with the certainty that many, if not most, of those he dwelled among were just described to him as the callous rebels who would fight against God's message of rebuke. So the word of the Lord came to him again to explain his role as a watchman for the house of Israel (vv. 16–17; cf. Is. 21:6–8; Jer. 6:17–21).

Ezekiel's mission and message of rebuke and judgment were so vital to the restoration of Israel that God repeated it right before the message of the fall of the city reached them (Ezek. 33:1–9). The relation between God and the prophet is clearly stated: he would give God's warning to the people (3:17). He was the messenger of the Lord in charge of delivering a clear message; the prophet must deliver a dire warning of death, or he would be held accountable for the death of the wicked

(vv. 18–19). The future of the people would be determined by their response to God's message of warning that was conveyed to them through the divine word. God described the status of His people before Him in moral terms: the "wicked" (vv. 18–19) and the "righteous" (vv. 20–21). The morally upright were the true covenant keepers (Deut. 6–9), and the morally bankrupt were the covenant breakers (Ezek. 16:8, 59–63; 17:13–19). The assent to outward religious ceremonies (cf. Is. 1:5–15), as outlined in the Pentateuch, was no evidence of true faithfulness. The main covenant breaches of the people were: (1) idolatry (Ezek. 6:13; 8:10; 14:3–7; 20:8–39; Deut. 12:29–32); (2) false leadership, including false prophecy (Ezek. 11:1–13; 14:1–11; 34; Deut. 13); (3) social injustice (Ezek. 16:49; 18:5–18; 22:29; Lev. 25:36, 37; Deut. 23:19, 20), and (4) religious syncretism (Ezek. 16:36; Deut. 17:17; 18:9–14). The divine declaration identifying the wicked and the righteous was made in the courtroom of God's heavenly sanctuary. We should keep in mind that its earthly counterpart was in a state of disrepute and impurity (Ezek. 8).

Ezekiel's own deliverance would be connected to the faithfulness he exercised toward his calling, but his culpability for neglecting his role would receive God's judgment (3:19, 21). As watchman, his vocation required wisdom and discernment to recognize danger and report it for the safety of God's people (2 Sam. 18:24; 2 Kin. 9:17). The danger ironically came from within their hearts. His proclamation of God's message was not to inspire the people to greatness but to call them to humility and surrender; they were to turn from wickedness and dwell in God's righteousness (Ezek. 3:19–20). Yesterday's good deeds provide no assurance for today's standing before God, and today's failures can be repented of as long as the doors of God's mercy are still open.

3:22–27
God's Sovereignty over Ezekiel's Ministry

In the final part of his prophetic calling, Ezekiel was taken in a visionary experience that ended where it began. Following what he saw (the glory of the Lord, 1:28), how he reacted (falling on his face, 1:28), and the work of the Spirit in him (infusing, standing, speaking; 2:2), Ezekiel was commanded to shut himself inside his house (3:24). It seems like an ironic order in light of God's earlier instruction to speak to His people (2:7; 3:4). However, Ezekiel was to be bound (v. 25) by God's sovereignty regarding how he should interact with the people. The glory of Yahweh was to be the central focus of Ezekiel's ministry. His condemnation of sin, his portrayal of history, and the messages of hope are to be understood as the outworking of God's glory. The muteness that was imposed should not be understood as Ezekiel's inability to talk. Indeed, he would speak after receiving his call (4:14; 5:5–17; 11:25). Because they were a rebellious people, the temptation for Ezekiel would be to rebuke or reprove/arbitrate (3:26) on behalf of the people. God would have none of it; a true assessment of their spiritual condition and its practical implications was necessary to prepare the people for true repentance. God would open his mouth to engage in a type of reconciliatory mission after Jerusalem's fall (33:22). Until then, only messages of God's judgment would come from Ezekiel's mouth.

4:1—7:27
JERUSALEM'S JUDGMENT

Chapters 4–7 form a unit that elaborates on Jerusalem's judgment and the devastation that would follow. This unit can be divided into two sections, namely, (1) sign-acts or acted-out object lessons (chap. 4, the siege of Jerusalem; chap. 5, Jerusalem's judgment and exile) and (2) judgment oracles (chap. 6, the mountains of Israel; chap. 7, the disaster soon to come). Chapters 5 and 6 begin with "son of man, take," while chapters 6 and 7 begin with God's word coming to Ezekiel, who is addressed as "son of man," and end with the same phrase affirming that they will know that God is Yahweh through His described judgments and actions. (On the concept of judgment, see "God's Judgment in the Prophets," p. 981.)

4:1—5:17
God's Sign-Acts

Chapter 4 records the beginning of God's prophetic show-and-tell (cf. Is. 20:2–3; Jer. 13:1–7; 19:1–5; 27:1–22; Hos. 1:1–9), followed by symbolic actions and a prophetic interpretation. Chapters 4 and 5 record symbolic actions: (1) building a model siege (Ezek. 4:1–3), (2) lying on his sides (vv. 4–8), (3) preparing a siege diet (vv. 9–17), and (4) dividing up hair (5:1–17). They follow a similar pattern: God addressing Ezekiel as "son of man" and then commanding him to engage in a sign-act.

4:1–3. Ezekiel's Street Ministry. Ezekiel was commanded to take a piece of clay and draw on it a picture of Jerusalem under siege, including the details of a siege with ramps, camps, and battering rams (cf. 2 Kin. 25:1; Jer. 39:1–7). The intricate detail indicates that the city was entrapped so that no one could get out and the besiegers would be able to intercept incoming supplies. The process would be laborious and psychologically overwhelming, yet efficient. God previously told the people that He would cut off all staples necessary for survival (Is. 3:1) and thus create a situation that implemented a covenant curse: the lack of bread (Lev. 26:26). Here in Ezekiel, it is God who proclaims through these acts that an army would besiege Jerusalem and break through the wall to take the city captive.

4:4–8. Prophetic Time and Judgment. Ezekiel has established the action to take place; now he describes the duration. He would lie on each of his sides in turn. God Himself makes clear His, not Babylon's, control of Israel's future. The time appears here as converted from years to days. The three hundred and ninety days for Israel and forty days for Judah (v. 5) are representative of the period of each kingdom's defection. The times generally refer to the starting period of the divided monarchy for Israel and the beginning of the downfall for Judah. Similarly, Numbers 14:34–35 reverses a day for a year and states that Israel would bear their punishment for forty years, a year for each day that the spies searched the land. Both texts associate one or more time periods with judgment for Israel's rebellion. Ezekiel's historical view of Israel in chapters 16 and 23 indicates that Israel's monarchical failure was one in a long line of apostasies. God commanded the prophet to roll up his sleeves for his prophetic work that, before the fall of Jerusalem, would be centered on judgment against Israel.

4:9–17. Unclean Food and People. Ezekiel's next symbolic actions involved bread, water, and dung. He was to bake bread using dung as fuel, to eat measured portions of it, and to drink measured portions of water, indicating the smallest of rations for the people of Israel during the siege. This command is connected to the previous one because God ordered Ezekiel to eat the rations during his symbolic action of lying on his side (v. 9). God described the experience of the Exile using the language of covenant curses. Ezekiel's rationed meal times (v. 10) and small portions indicated that Israel would have to eat bread and drink water in rations because God would make food and drink scarce, breaking their supply of food (v. 16; 5:16; Lev. 26:26). Also, among the Gentile nations where God would drive them, Israel would eat food defiled by the use of human waste as fuel (Ezek. 4:10–11, 13; Josh. 22:19). Human waste was unclean and had to remain outside the camp of Israel (Deut. 23:15). Ezekiel's revulsion to engage in such culinary procedures harked back to his priestly training and faithfulness to ritual cleanliness and avoidance of forbidden food (Ezek. 4:14; cf. Lev. 5:2; 7:18, 24; 17:15; 22:8). Ironically, it highlights the condition of Israel, defiled and under a covenant curse. God allowed Ezekiel to substitute human waste with cow dung and then reiterated the prophecy of Jerusalem's coming starvation (Ezek. 4:15–17).

5:1–4. God's Barbershop and Israel's Trouble. In an increasingly doleful picture of a slowly emaciating, malnourished form, Ezekiel was commanded to shave his hair and his beard, divide it into three parts, and then burn one-third, repeatedly strike one-third, and scatter one-third. After the description of the trauma of a siege, the protracted act of shaving with a sword or sharp knife indicated that one-third of Jerusalem would be a smoldering heap, destroyed by fire. One-third would suffer a military defeat that would leave an unsightly bloodbath. Finally, one-third would be scattered, exiled from the land of Judah with God pursuing them as an enemy. A small number of them or a remnant (v. 3), made up of the poor, would be left over in the land (Jer. 52:16). In addition to the escalation of catastrophes, an unavoidable experience of horror would come to the people of Jerusalem.

If one thing did not get them, something else would (cf. Amos 5:19).

5:5–17. God's Dynamic Speech. In a series of four prophetic announcements that emphasize His sovereign lordship, the messenger formula ("Thus says the *'adonai yahweh*"—"Thus says the Lord God," or "This is what the Sovereign Lord says") is used three times in vv. 5, 7, 8 (cf. v. 11). God explained why judgment was coming. First, God set Judah at the crossroads of the major nations (Mesopotamia, Egypt, and Syria) to be a light, but the people rebelled by refusing God's lordship (vv. 5–6). In their refusal to accept the divine charter for a just and holy society, the people did not even follow the customs of the pagan nations (v. 7). Second, Israel tended toward a syncretistic practice of religion (2 Kin. 16–17). Thus, the worst scenario of God's response would be their punishment: God changing His role from that of covenant Lord to that of enemy (Ezek. 5:8). Israel saw God break greater nations like Egypt, Syria, and Assyria. Now, without the empowering and life-transforming presence of God as an ally, the basest human instincts would emerge in the form of a famine-induced cannibalistic fury (v. 10). Verse 11 gives the first indication of what is described in chapters 8–11, namely, the withdrawal of God from His sanctuary. Third, Israel had been unfaithful to God. In vv. 12–15, Ezekiel's sign-acts are interpreted as covenant curses: plague, famine, sword, and exile (Lev. 26:25–39; Jer. 29:17). Fourth, its results would be revelatory and missional; the judgment would remind the people and the nations that God is the sovereign Lord (Ezek. 5:16–17). (On the concept of judgment, see below, "God's Judgment in the Prophets.")

God's Judgment in the Prophets

The messages of the prophets are in most cases announcements of judgment or salvation. In the case of prophecies of judgment, we encounter expressions and language that may sound too strong to the contemporary reader. For example, in regard to His punishments, God spoke of (1) parents eating their children (Ezek. 5:8–10); (2) cutting off food and causing famine (14:13); (3) the destruction of infants and the rape of women (Is. 13:16); and (4) destruction by cruel people in which the Israelites would become "fuel for the fire" (Ezek. 21:31–32). There are many other passages like these. We suggest that when reading the prophetic announcements of judgment, we should keep in mind a few principles or concepts that may help us understand the origin and reason for such seemingly harsh language.

1. Covenant and Judgment. When we read the messages of judgment proclaimed by the prophets against Israel, we find in practically all of them the common charge that the people had violated the covenant relationship with the Lord. The covenant between God and Israel was established after God redeemed His people from Egypt and permanently formalized the initial redemptive relationship He had established with them. God became their God, and they were constituted into His people. Within that covenant relationship, the people enjoyed God's presence and blessings. The violation of the covenant by the people was a rejection of the covenant and of the Lord of the covenant (i.e., a claim of independence from Him). In most cases this act of rebellion expressed itself in the worship of other gods and in political alliances with other nations that were intended to secure self-preservation in case of war (e.g., Hos. 7:11; 12:1). Theologically speaking, the people were in fact abandoning the sphere where divine blessings were operative and entering into the dangerous realm of sin and death (i.e., the curses of the covenant). After the violation of the covenant, the people of Israel had two alternatives: either to repent and renew their commitment to the covenant (which would mean forgiveness and healing from the Lord) or to continue the path of rebellion and separation from God (which would mean abandonment by the Lord and destruction). The prophetic word that connected covenant and judgment was used to provide a legal foundation for the announced judgment of God. Judgment was not an irrational or arbitrary decision on the part of a violent God but what the people should have legally expected from Him in response to their rebellious actions against the loving covenant Lord.

2. Prophetic Nature of the Judgment. The words of judgment proclaimed by the prophets were indeed prophecies concerning what the Lord would do soon or even in the distant future. The fact that the judgments were proclaimed before they happened served several purposes. Among these we mention a few: First, in some cases the description of the nature of the coming judgment was so intense that it could have and should have moved the people to repentance in order to avoid its damaging effects—it should have appealed not only to their emotions but also to their reason. Second, the prophetic prediction demonstrated that the

Lord knew what was going to happen and that consequently He was not surprised by the unfolding events. The implication is that the divine judgments revealed God's sovereignty over history. He, not the nations, was in ultimate control of what would happen to Israel. Third, by announcing the coming defeat of His people, the Lord was demonstrating that the nations that would attack Israel were not more powerful than He. In fact, it was the Lord who was using the nations to accomplish His own purpose, namely, disciplining His people for their sins. But in doing this, there was great pain in the heart of the covenant Lord (cf. Hos. 11:8).

3. Rejection of the Lord and Judgment. Breaking with the Lord, who was and continued to be the only reliable "place" of safety, left the people of Israel at the mercy of their enemies. The result of their rejection of the Lord blocked the only source of blessings and life, bringing with it famine and plagues. These results were not the impersonal and automatic consequences of sin but those of God's decision to abandon the city, the temple, and the land. They chose to abandon Him, and He honored their decision by abandoning them—He granted them their wish. Most of the language used in the messages of judgment against the people is of a military or political nature. What we often read about is what a military attack would look like: the siege of the city bringing famine, and often cannibalism, inside the city (Ezek. 5:8–10); the destruction of the city and the temple (Jer. 9:11; 12:10–12); the raping of women (Lam. 5:11); the killing of children, women, and men (Is. 13:16); and the leaving behind of a few survivors, many of whom would have preferred to die during the attack. The language describes the cruelty and inhumanness of war, not of God. In a sense the Lord assumes responsibility for the military fall of His people by referring to it as His response to their rebellion. Ultimately, the people are responsible for what happened to them because of their rejection of the covenant Lord (Jer. 18:16). In the destruction of Samaria or Jerusalem, the nations did not defeat the Lord nor did they defeat His people; it was the Lord who handed His people over to the nations because Israel had chosen the path leading to death rather than the one leading to life with Him (Deut. 30:15–19; Jer. 12:7; 21:8).

4. *Judgment and Cosmic Conflict*. God's people have always existed in the context of a cosmic conflict. This conflict does not take place in a mythical world but in the arena of human history. The enemies of Israel were primarily the political and military powers of the nations that surrounded them, but behind the nations were their gods and the demonic powers that in many cases influenced the people of God (see Ezek. 28:14). This often led Israel into idolatry, a rebellion against the Lord that left them vulnerable to military defeat and political oppression as the Lord handed them over to their enemies. In the context of the cosmic conflict and through the words of judgment, the Lord continued to inform His people that there was hope for them because not only was He in control of what was happening to them, but He would also be fighting for them against their enemies if His people returned to Him. Through His judgments, He would ultimately defeat the nations and their gods (Jer. 51–52). God's last word was not condemnation but salvation and victory for the remnant of His people and of the nations who would come and worship Him in His temple (Is. 2:3). Because of the righteousness of God's judgment, His people would recognize that He was righteous in what He did to them (Ezek. 14:21–23), and the nations would come to know that "I am the Lord" (36:23). The end result of the judgments would be that the nations would no longer take up the sword against each other nor train for war ever again (Is. 2:4).

6:1—7:27
The Nations Will Know That I Am Yahweh

Through a series of prophetic formulas (recognition formula—"you will know that I am *yahweh*": 6:7, 10, 13, 14; 7:4, 9, 27; messenger formula: 6:3, 11; 7:2, 5), Ezekiel proclaims God's authoritative speeches of judgment coming on the people. These prophetic formulas also serve to organize the messages. The structure of chapter 6 expresses an alternating parallel format and thus emphasizes knowing the identity of Yahweh in the face of idolatry (vv. 4–6, 13). The chapter is introduced by a messenger formula plus a "son of man" command in vv. 1–2.

A First announcement of punishment: Destruction of idolatrous worship and people (vv. 3–7)
Summary: Recognition formula

B Description of the results of rebellion: Only a remorseful remnant left (vv. 8–10)
Summary: Recognition formula

A′ Second announcement of punishment: Famine, sword, and plague (vv. 11–13a)
Summary: Recognition formula

B′ Description of the results of rebellion: The land desolate (vv. 13b–14)
Summary: Recognition formula

Picking up much of the language used in Isaiah 13:1–16, Ezekiel 7 can be divided into three sections that announce the coming judgment (vv. 2–4, 5–9, and 10–27). All three sections assert that the end is coming by using different emphases—the certitude, the experience, and the results (the end, v. 2; disaster, v. 5; doom, v. 10).

6:1–10. Judgment: Defilement and Restoration. God continued to ask Ezekiel to proclaim His message against the rebellion of His people. Anticipating His departure from the sanctuary and city, God painted a doleful picture of death, decay, and destruction while using the language of the covenant curses (Lev. 26:25–32). God would decimate the holy vessels along with the carved idols beside them (Ezek. 6:4–5). The mixture of the holy and the profane necessitated a complete eradication of the works of humans (cf. Gen. 7:23). Chapters 8 and 9 more fully depict the extent of idolatry among God's people and its requisite result of judgment, defilement, and execution. Both here and in chapter 9, the remnant are described as penitent (Ezek. 6:9; 9:4). The description of the destruction of the altars uses what is typically called a *divine passive* (the use of the passive voice of the verb to denote the hidden action of God as the agent responsible for the activity) and is used mainly in reference to the articles of worship (6:4, 6). Concerning the people, Ezekiel presents God's message with Him speaking in the first person (vv. 4–5, 8). The very presence of corpses would have the effect of defiling everything within the same enclosed space

(Num. 19:14–15). The place chosen by God to be a center of worship (Deut. 12:1–7) had become an abominable place.

So Israel's rebellion was twofold: they set up competing worship sites (cf. 1 Kin. 11:1–8), and they set up idols instead of tearing them down. Ezekiel 6:8–10 shifts the focus from the announcement of judgment to its devastation: a few survivors (Ezek. 7:16), a scattered captive nation (5:10, 12), and a self-loathing disgust and revulsion of their covenant infidelity (cf. Ps. 119:158). On the other hand, the results of judgment would elicit a faithful remnant who would remember their Lord and recognize His claims on them (Ezek. 6:8–10; cf. 20:43; 36:31). He in turn will remember His promise and restore the relationship the people had broken (Lev. 26:40–45).

6:11–14. Judgment: Death and Destruction. Verses 3–10 and 11–14 share many of the same words and parallel phrases, but the emphases are radically different. The sections that describe the results of rebellion (vv. 8–10, 13b–14) both serve as a prophetic affirmation of God being in control: He knows the future and He is directing events to those ends. The first section (vv. 8–10) ends with the hope of restoration among the exiles and with Ezekiel's word of hope to those scattered among the nations and lands. This second section (vv. 11–14) ends with an account of the despair of the wicked and with Ezekiel's word of judgment against those far/outside the city proper, those near/inside the city, and those left over (v. 12; cf. v. 14; 7:15–16). Through both restoration and judgment, all would know that God is the Lord of the covenant, the Lord of history, and the Lord of human destiny.

Ezekiel was commanded to express feelings of anger and lamentation—to stamp his feet in conjunction with clapping his hands and to say, "Alas" (v. 11). These actions would depict God's anger in response to the wickedness of the people. The destruction that would follow (sword, famine, and plague/pestilence) was known to the people as evidence of divine displeasure in the form of covenant curses. Ezekiel condemns the mountains of Israel (v. 13), which earlier referred to people (v. 2), because the people built high places or cultic platforms on them. These were often situated on the wooded heights of hills or mountains frequently used for idolatrous worship (e.g., Lev. 26:30; Num. 33:52; Deut. 12:2; 1 Kin. 14:23). The people used sweet incense (Ezek. 6:13) to cover the stench of their idolatry. God would turn their cultic groves into

a desolate wasteland all throughout the furthest reaches of Israel's territorial extent (47:17–20; Num. 34:11).

7:1–4. The End Is Coming. With a tripart blast of urgent warning (vv. 2–3, 6), God sought from His people a response of faith and a recognition of the impending danger. The two keywords in this chapter—the Hebrew verb *bo'* (contextually here, "to come," "to enter," or "to bring"; vv. 2, 5–7, 10, 12, 22, 24–26) and the noun *qets* ("end"; vv. 2–3, 6)—emphasize the imminence, certainty, and pervasiveness of judgment. God addressed the message to the land of Israel (vv. 2, 7), but contextually it was directed to the exiled community. The purpose for both communities was the same: God would punish them for their evil ways (vv. 3–4). Zedekiah's rebellion and the messages from false prophets like Hananiah (Jer. 28:1–17) and Shemaiah (Jer. 29:24–32) may have encouraged some to think that geopolitics was the answer to their circumstances. Evidently, their influence was so strong that Jeremiah had to send a letter to the exiled community in Babylon (Jer. 29:1–23).

The punishment would match the crime (Ezek. 7:3), and the picture of the coming judgment evoked the deepest feelings of abandonment (cf. 6:9). Though not the eschatological end, Ezekiel uses eschatological language ("the four corners of the land"; 7:2b) to indicate not simply a transition to another king but a cataclysmic end of the kingdom. The covenant promises that God made to David would reach fruition, not through the stratagems of a political kingship (chap. 34; cf. Pss. 89, 110) but through God's kingship (Matt. 4:17; Mark 1:14). The scope, experience, and results of judgment are associated with God's anger (Ezek. 7:3, 8), disaster (v. 5), doom (v. 7), tumult (v. 7), horror/terror (v. 18), day of wrath (v. 19), and devastation/desolation (v. 27). They would know that God is the covenant Lord because of His complete defeat of the wicked.

7:5–9. The Fury of the Lord. This section almost seems redundant in its language, yet it has, among other things, two pivotal functions: emphasis and anticipation. The certainty of the end is repeated, but now the experience of disaster and the psychological paralysis of impending doom is added (vv. 5–7). The finality of God's actions in pouring out His anger without pity would overwhelm the people (vv. 8–9; cf. Zeph. 1:14–16). Israel's wickedness had ripened, and it had borne the fruit of idolatry, social injustice, and abominable practices; the Master Harvester must come, and the people would reap the judgment that they had sown in their pride (cf. Rev. 14:14–20).

7:10–27. The Totality of Judgment. Arboreal imagery is used to describe the wickedness of Israel. Violence is pictured as growing into a *lematteh resha'* (translated as either "a rod of wickedness" or "a rod to punish the wicked"; v. 11). Aaron's staff budded under the blessing of God (Num. 17), but here Ezekiel reverses the picture with a botanical metaphor showing the result of the wickedness of the people—God's curse was coming in the form of the Babylonian invasion. This invasion would have multiple effects. In the ancient Near East there was not a clear separation of civic, religious, and economic life. Together they expressed an integrated whole of life and the consequent impact on the life of the people. Babylon's invasion was seen as (1) creating economic turmoil (Ezek. 7:12–19), (2) a profanation of the land (vv. 20–24), and (3) a devastation of political life (vv. 25–27).

As a result of God's judgment, the commercial life in Israel would come to an end (vv. 12–13a). This meant that the buyer and the seller alike would share the same fate. Their most treasured possessions—land, temple, and holy furnishings—would become the booty of the invaders (v. 21). Ezekiel uses linguistic parallels to draw out the association of God's judgment with the irrevocable outcome of the word of God given in the vision (vv. 12–13; chaps. 4–6).

Typically, a trumpet was blown in times of warfare as a call to prepare for battle (7:14; Num. 10:9). But Israel had prepared for battle in vain; they would only suffer the casualties of divine warfare against them (Ezek. 7:14–15). Even the physiological effects (v. 17) reflect a psychological paralysis created by God's judgment (v. 18). Alongside the sad conditions of a future with rationed sustenance (4:9–17), Ezekiel addresses those who may have believed they had the resources to mitigate the scarcity and economic woes of a siege. The affluence of the wealthy could not possibly assuage the wrath of God (7:19; cf. Zeph. 1:18).

The defilement (Ezek. 7:21–22, 24; cf. Lev. 20:3) of the land and sanctuary created two major problems. First, if the very system of maintaining the holiness of God placed among the people turned sour, how was Israel to abide in God's presence? Second, if the temple and its ritual activity were defiled, how was forgiveness to be mediated? Israel's world and worldview would be shattered.

The prophets, priests, and kings stood as covenant mediators and as political operatives in God's political and ritual economy. Confusion and chaos within the confines of Israel's leadership meant that access to the divine word and its corporate blessing were unavailable. As if this was not bad enough, God Himself took responsibility for the profanation of His temple and land (Ezek. 7:22; 24:21). He would bring the worst, the most despicable people, to displace them from their beloved home and take their accoutrements of covenant life with Yahweh (e.g., strangers and foreigners, the wicked of the earth, robbers, and the most evil of the Gentiles; 7:21–24; cf. 2 Kin. 25). The principle of retribution was working here. The people had committed murder (i.e., bloodguilt) and violence, so they in turn would experience the same (Ezek. 7:23, 27; cf. vv. 1, 8).

8:1—11:25
THE GLORY OF GOD WITHDRAWS FROM THE TEMPLE

The structure of chapters 8–11 is framed as a literary chiasm supported by a cadre of parallel words and themes.

A Introduction (8:1–4)
  B Abomination: the problem (8:5–18)
    C Judgment on land and leadership (chap. 9)
      D God's glory to abandon the temple (chap. 10)
    C' Judgment on land and leadership (11:1–13)
  B' Abomination: the solution (11:14–21)
A' Conclusion (11:22–25)

This second major vision details the story of the abandonment of the temple by God. Each section explains, expands, or resolves the preceding section as it moves to the central focus of the catastrophic reality: God leaving Jerusalem (D). Learning that God Himself would leave the place where all hope, forgiveness, worship, prayer, and wisdom were centered would leave a dim sense of meaning in life.

The significance of the theophany in chapter 1 now unfolds as it relates to the sanctuary, to judgment, and to God's presence. Both the introduction and conclusion (A, A') focus on the glory of God (8:4; 11:22–23), both indicate that the Spirit lifted Ezekiel up and took him somewhere in a vision (8:3; 11:24), and both focus on a previous vision (8:4b; 11:25). The account of the intervening vision paints a doleful picture of the people's condition. But there is also a note of hope: God was moving to Babylon with the exiled community! He had not totally abandoned His people. After His revival and restoration of His true people, He would return to Jerusalem (43:1–5).

God's departure (chaps. 8–11) and return (chaps. 40–48) to His restored temple indicate that judgment was not God's final word for His people. The theme of divine abandonment frequently occurs in ancient Near Eastern writings, where usually the military defeat of a people by another nation is interpreted to mean that their gods had abandoned them or that the gods of the enemy had defeated their gods. In the OT, however, Yahweh abandons His temple because of the people's moral failures, covenant breaches, and faithless compromises with pagan ideologies and rituals. In this OT context, God is not conquered; His people are conquered by sin, and the judgment against them is the Babylonian Exile (cf. Hab. 1:5–11).

The importance of Ezekiel 8–11 for the message of the Bible cannot be overemphasized. The account in these chapters of the investigation and execution of judgment on the faithless was related initially to Ezekiel's immediate audience and location, but its application has resonances for our time as well. John the Revelator presents a number of parallels with this vision in Ezekiel and shows that the work of judgment applies to the whole of creation (see "Judgment in Ezekiel and Revelation," p. 986).

8:1–18
Abominations in the Temple

After describing his visionary experience (vv. 1–4), Ezekiel utilizes a repetitive fourfold pattern that reaches its climax in a description of utter abomination (vv. 5–6, 7–13, 14–15, 16–18). The Spirit brought Ezekiel to and guided him through the temple complex (vv. 5, 7, 14, 16), addressed him as "son of man" (vv. 5–6, 8, 12, 15, 17), asked him to see what was happening (vv. 5–7, 9, 12, 15, 17), and guaranteed that the worst was yet to come (vv. 6, 13, 15).

8:1–4. Visions of God. Over a year's time, Ezekiel had performed a prophetic street ministry and had spoken what appeared to be discouraging words to the inhabitants of Jerusalem and the exiles. God's dialogues, earlier with

Judgment in Ezekiel and Revelation

A brief comparison with Revelation 14 makes clear that John's language parallels Ezekiel's account of the vision, yet the Revelation account involves the people of God from every nation, kindred, tongue, and tribe. The parallels help readers of Revelation to understand that God's plan and methods have not changed; He expects His professed people to live by His righteousness. This will lead to faithful obedience and will glorify His name. The parallels include the following:

- Judgment/vindication at the sanctuary: Ezek. 8:3 (Jerusalem); Rev. 14:1, 15 (heavenly Mount Zion).
- Six messengers of judgment: Ezek. 9:2; Rev. 14:6, 8–9, 15, 17–18.
- Seal of God/mark of the righteous/ wicked: Ezek. 9:4; Rev. 7:3; 9:4; 14:1, 9.
- The wicked are killed: Ezek. 9:6–8; Rev. 14:10, 19–20.

- The righteous are saved: Ezek. 9:4; Rev. 14:1–5, 14–16.

In Revelation, conditions have not radically changed from those of Ezekiel's time. In both accounts, the righteous exhibit the same call to faithfulness while they express sorrow for the condition of God's people (Ezek. 9:4; Rev. 6:9–11), and the wicked engage in the same sins (idolatry, Ezek. 8:3, 14; Rev. 14:10–11; defiling God's sanctuary, Ezek. 8:7–13; Rev. 11; cf. Dan. 8:9–12; sun worship, Ezek. 8:16; Rev. 14:6–10; and injustice, Ezek. 9:9; Rev. 18). As in Ezekiel's day, in our time God's activity results in judgment and in the revelation of His justice. Revelation 14 also uses imagery and language from the judgment section of Ezekiel (chaps. 4–24): the cup of wrath (Ezek. 23; Rev. 14) and the vine of the land (Ezek. 15; Rev. 14:18–20). The two books complement one another and bring out issues of present relevance for our thoughts and prayers.

Jeremiah about Israel's exile (Jer. 7:1–34) and subsequently with Ezekiel about Israel's final destruction (Ezek. 12:21–28), indicate a hard-hearted rejection of God's word by the people (3:5–7). Now God was giving the elders of Israel a final confirmation of Ezekiel's prophetic calling through a visionary experience, which they later would be told involved Jerusalem and the temple (8:4; 11:25).

8:5–18. God Who Sees. God's questions to Ezekiel and the description of Israel's apostasy appear in Ezekiel's book, depicting the activity of the people. Twice Nebuchadnezzar had come and decimated Judah's population as God had announced, but the people continued to be engaged in the very practices that called forth God's judgment. God clarified now that not only would judgment come, but these abominations were driving Him far away from His sanctuary. In the daily ministration of the sacrifices, the confessed sins of the people were forgiven as the blood was shed and the priest made atonement (Lev. 1–7). In the yearly ministration, the sanctuary itself was cleansed (Lev. 16). The only known cases of unforgiven sin were of unconfessed sin and high-handed sin (deliberate, intentional, and defiant; Num. 15:30). So, God leaving His defiled sanctuary implies that the people's sins were unconfessed and/or high-handed.

For now, God took up residence in the temple to begin His covenant lawsuit against the people (cf. Ps. 50; Amos 2:9–16) that included, per typical form, a summons (Ezek. 8:1–5a), a trial (vv. 5b–17), and a sentence (v. 18). Ezekiel specifically describes four types of abominations (vv. 4–6, 7–13, 14–15, 16–18) that God prohibited. The description of the divergences from His revealed character and will could not be more vivid. The abominations were connected in some way with Israel's misconstrued theology of God's presence and the denial of the prospect of divine abandonment. First, not only were they breaking the first commandment by making an image or idol of jealousy (or an idol arousing God's jealousy; vv. 3, 5; Ex. 20:4–6; Deut. 4:16; 2 Chr. 33:7), but it was placed in the temple precinct as a rival to the glory of God. Second, God had revealed Himself as the Creator of all things (Gen. 1–2) and as the Holy One of Israel (Is. 1:4; 12:6). His holiness was being defiled by the engravings of unclean animals and idols (Lev. 7:21) and by the unholy worship of creation. Similar things have been observed in Egyptian burial chambers, and Israel did engage in religious syncretism with

Egypt (Ezek. 16:16). As in times past, the elders of Israel probably incorporated in their worship the rituals of idol worship and the religious practices of the nations from which they sought help (cf. 11:12; 2 Kin. 16:10–20). Especially evident was their pro-Egyptian attitude (cf. Is. 30–31; Jer. 37:5–10), their proud mindset against the Lord, and their denial of His judgment and omniscience (Ezek. 8:12). Third, the worship of Tammuz (called *dumuzi*, "the good/proper son" in Sumerian), a Mesopotamian god widely honored as a god of vegetation and who was also the lover and consort of Inanna/Ishtar, was instituted most likely as a response to the scarcity of agricultural produce (cf. Is. 3:1–2). The women's lamentations (Ezek. 8:14) reveal a religious syncretism associated with an annual ritual mourning practice concerning the death of the deity. Some in Israel, besieged and exiled, interpreted God's supposed absence (v. 12) as a reason to compromise the true worship of the Lord instead of confessing and repenting of their sins in submission to God and His will. Finally, in front of the temple between the porch and the altar, there were twenty-five men worshiping the sun in the east (the Babylonian god Shamash, who was worshiped primarily as the "lord of judgment"). This was the place where they should have come before the Lord to seek forgiveness (cf. Joel 2:17).

The people had unquestionably turned their backs on the Lord physically and spiritually as they worshiped the sun (Jer. 32:33–35), and the result was rebellion and violence in the city (Ezek. 9:9). Apparently the people wanted the benefits of God's presence without accepting and yielding to God's lordship (Jer. 27:12, 17; 38:17–18).

9:1–11. Judgment on Land and Leaders. In Ezekiel's vision, God gave His verdict. The compromising religious activities of the people (8:18) were connected to God's response in judgment. Though He would later judge the nations (chaps. 25–32), God began His judgment at His house, among the leaders and at the place where the professed people of God congregated. By standing at the bronze altar (9:2), God started in the area where the twenty-five elders would have been. He specifically started with the leaders (chaps. 12–14) as His representatives. The writing angel would put a mark on the foreheads of those who would be saved (9:3–4). God always has an authentic remnant who are faithful to Him and who also show reverence to His holiness (i.e., those who are disturbed by and mourn over all the abominations done in the land, v. 4).

God's command to execute without pity and without mercy (v. 5) may seem hard-hearted to modern ears, but divine love shows divine patience for as long as God's holiness allows. God put up with numerous impenitent, rebellious, and heartless kings and with injustice, oppression, idolatry, cruelty, commandment-breaking, stubbornness, and selfishness from His people for almost four centuries. He continually sent them messages of warning and hope, but there was no consistent response of faith and trust. Sin had run its course, and the cancerous heart of rebellion had to be rooted out (cf. Gen. 15:12–16) so that God's faithful ones could continue to bear witness to His glory. Ezekiel's response of intercession (Ezek. 9:8) shows a depth of covenant care (cf. 11:13)

seen in the lives of faithful leaders like Moses (Ex. 32:30–34), Daniel (Dan. 9:1–19), and Paul (Rom. 9:1–2), and without equal in the life of our Savior, Jesus (Luke 23:34–43).

10:1—11:25
Abandonment of God's Temple

Echoing his earlier vision, Ezekiel alternates between God's movement toward and away from the entrance of the temple and the movement of the cherubim. The phrase "I looked" (10:1, 9) divides chapter 10 in two sections. Verses 1–8 focus on God's movement toward the temple and His purifying work, while vv. 9–22 depict the glory of God and the cherubim as Ezekiel describes God's departure from the

The Mark/Sign/Seal of God

In times of national importance, God has always had a sign to distinguish His faithful people from those who simply claim His name without the fruit of faith (Ezek. 9:4; cf. 20:12, 20; Exod. 12:23; Eph. 1:13; Rev. 7:2; 14:6–12). The mark (Heb. *taw*, the last letter of the Hebrew alphabet) is a divine sign of ownership, identity, and faithfulness and is placed on the forehead (Deut. 6:8).

1. *Sabbath as a Sign.* The Sabbath is a seal of God because it carries the title (Creator), territory (the world), and the authoritative name of the Lord (Yahweh, your God). In Exodus 20 the fourth commandment is the only command that relays and emphasizes these aspects of a seal (Ex. 20:8–11). It is a visible sign of faithfulness to God's authority and all of His revealed will. The Sabbath is a sign that recognizes that God is the Creator who blesses and sanctifies (Gen. 2:3), is Sovereign Lord (Mark 2:27–28) as well as Redeemer, and gives us true rest (Heb. 4:9–13). Genesis 2:3 emphasizes the sanctifying agency of the Lord, who blessed the seventh day and sanctified it—i.e. made it holy, and set it apart as special. Those who faithfully worship God in time (Sabbath) and space (holiness) belong to God by creation and redemption, and they acknowledge His lordship in their lives. The disciples' postresurrection Sabbath observance indicates that they did not understand the Sabbath to be replaced by another day, but that they had in

fact found a deeper meaning to the Sabbath in light of Christ's life, death, and resurrection (Acts 13:27, 42, 44; 15:21; 16:13; 17:2; 18:4). In this regard, the Sabbath will continue to serve as a "sign" between God and His people (Ezek. 20:20; Ex. 31:12–17).

2. *Eschatological Seal.* In Revelation 7:2–3 John uses imagery similar to that in Ezekiel 9:3–4. God's end-time people have two main identifying marks that set them apart as His covenant people: (1) they have the faith of/in Jesus (the gospel), and (2) they keep all His commands (Rev. 12:17; 14:12). In Ezekiel 9, the sealed ones are persons who are faithful and keep God's commands, mourning over all the abominations in Judah (v. 4). In the first of the three angels' messages found in Revelation 14:6–12, an allusion is made to the Sabbath in connection with worship and the time of universal judgment (Rev. 14:7). Thus, there are important parallels between the sign/seal of God in Ezekiel and John: worship/Sabbath and judgment (Ezek. 20:12, 20; cf. the linguistic parallels between Exod. 20:8–11 and Rev. 14:6). Moreover, if the Sabbath, with its call to worship, encapsulates the commandments of God—in that observing it expresses one's love for God and recognition of His ownership—then the saints with the "faith of Jesus" who "keep the commandments" (Rev. 14:12) are those who will also observe the Sabbath.

temple complex. Chapter 11 also divides into two sections: judgment on land and leadership (vv. 1–13) and the question of a remnant (vv. 14–25).

10:1–22. The Lord Departs. Ezekiel interrupts his narrative about the man in linen with a description of the presence of God, moving from a scene of destruction to a scene of God's glory (v. 1; cf. 1:26; 43:7). The glory of God and His royal prerogatives must always be kept central to our understanding of judgment and salvation. God's command to the man in linen in 10:2 reminds us that the purging of the wicked is a part of God's judgment activity (cf. Rev. 8:5; 20:7–15). In this case, the fire represents Babylon's destruction of Jerusalem and the removal of the people from the land (cf. 2 Kin. 25:9).

Ezekiel clarifies that the four living beings he saw were cherubim (Ezek. 14–17, 20; cf. 1:10; 1 Kin. 6:29–35). His understanding of God's sovereignty as displayed in the sanctuary and its rituals enabled him to appreciate God's royalty and holiness and how human sinfulness is a revolt against Him. He also began to perceive the relationship between the earthly pattern and its heavenly reality (typology; cf. Ex. 25:8, 40). It was no longer just a vision of grand proportions; Ezekiel saw that God is the King, and the significance of the vision he saw at the beginning was clarified. In language reminiscent of the inauguration of the sanctuary (Ex. 40:34–38) and the temple (1 Kin. 8:10–11), Ezekiel describes a divine de-inauguration (i.e., abandonment) of the temple. It would not function as the site of God's sovereignty and place of atonement until after the Exile (cf. Ezra 6:13–22). Israel's disobedience and idolatry had pushed away God's holy presence, and He was ready to leave, granting them what they wanted.

Describing the functional importance of his earlier vision of the wheels (Ezek. 10:9–17; cf. 1:15–21), Ezekiel focuses on the departure of God's glory from the temple (10:18–19). The people had forsaken God—His kingship, His plan of salvation, His ethical guidance, and His wisdom for social justice (cf. 2 Kin. 21; 23:31—24:20)—and now Ezekiel's vision presented God as abandoning them.

11:1–13. Judgment on Land and Leadership. The vision continued as God acquainted Ezekiel with the activity of the leaders and its influence on the people (v. 2). The leaders were expected to guide the people and teach them the will of God, but Jaazaniah ("the Lord

hears") and Pelatiah ("the Lord rescues") did not follow through on their holy calling. They are characterized as wolves destroying lives (v. 6; 22:27). The evil schemes of the powerful led them to seize the houses of those who were already exiled (cf. Is. 5:8; Mic. 2:1–2).

The rule of King Zedekiah (597–586 B.C.) and the oracles in Ezekiel 12–14 about the leaders, who apparently were mulling over their course of action in light of Babylonian oppression, provide the historical backdrop for this occasion. Vacillating Zedekiah naively believed the rebellious war party in Judah, who trusted that Egypt would help them and refused to trust in God. The sudden death of Pelatiah validated God's message (Ezek. 11:13). Through divine judgment the people would know that God is the Lord (vv. 11–12; cf. Phil 2:9–11). Ezekiel's reaction is instructive to Christians. On the one hand, our proclamation of the judgment message ought to cause us to reflect as we seek to understand and live out God's justice in the community. On the other hand, we need to understand that God is holy, just, and true to His word, and He will work out His purposes in harmony with His character. His constant attention to Israel, His overwhelming and undeserved care, and His protection and providence were, and often are, met with unbelief, disbelief, and willful rebellion. God calls humanity to Himself and appeals to us not to harden our hearts (Ps. 95:7–11; Heb. 3:7–19), for He must be true to His holy, just, and true character.

11:14–25. Solution to the Abomination; but Not Yet. In His continued dialogue with Ezekiel, God answered his question about the "remnant" (v. 13). In Isaiah the remnant are (1) a penitent group who would return to God and to the land (Is. 7:3; 10:20–22; 11:10–16; 17:5–8; 28:5; 30:17–19; 37:4, 31–32; cf. 6:13), (2) the survivors who would be the foundation of the renewed community (Is. 1:25–26), and (3) those called to a fruitful life as the people of Yahweh (Is. 4:2–6). Ezekiel was concerned about the possibility that the righteous remnant would be wiped out with the wicked (Ezek. 11:13). God responded with one of the greatest pictures of divine love: though His people were removed and scattered from the land, God would go into exile with them (cf. Ex. 25:8, 40). He also addressed what would have been a main concern for any displaced Israelite, namely, the future of the land. God promised a reversal; the faithful would be restored to the land, for He would gather His people out of exile (Ezek. 11:17), but not for a return to "things as usual." Idols would be removed, new hearts would be implanted, and the covenant would be renewed: they would be His people, and He would be their God (v. 20). This is a theme that permeates the whole book (e.g., 14:11; 36:28; 37:27).

At the end of the vision, the glory of God lifted off from within the city and exited to the east, toward what later would be known as the Mount of Olives (11:22–23). For Ezekiel, it was a vision of God's grandeur and Judah's defeat, but also a vision of hope for the remnant. Now that Ezekiel had received the message, His prophetic task would deliver all of God's messages to those in captivity (v. 25).

12:1—14:23

COUNTERFEIT LEADERSHIP REBUKED

Now that Yahweh had abandoned His temple, the people were open to the assaults of the surrounding nations. Yet the main concern of the Lord was the failure of the leaders of His people. They either tried to inculcate a false sense of security through false messages, or they encouraged the mixing of pagan ideas and rituals with the true worship of God. Ezekiel's account begins by describing the wicked leaders as the main culprits for Judah's demise: the prince (chap. 12), false prophets (chap. 13), and idolatrous elders (chap. 14).

12:1–28
Portrayal of Judah's Captivity

The storyline follows Ezekiel's sign-act (vv. 1–7), its interpretation (vv. 8–16), its effects (vv. 17–20), the leaders' foolish thinking (vv. 21–25), and God's response (vv. 26–28). Ezekiel uses a repetitive pattern to establish the certainty and implications of the Exile. Israel refused the knowledge of God that was given through His wise words and ways (Deut. 4:5–8), and now they would know who He is through judgment.

12:1–7. Ezekiel Is a Sign: The Rebellious House. Ezekiel first summarizes his prophetic drama by stating God's word that the people among whom he was living were rebellious (vv. 1–2). The emphasis on Israel as a rebellious people recapitulates the result of God's previous investigation into Israel's condition. Israel lacked the spiritual discernment of sight and

listening, though they had the physical senses to see the signs of the times and hear the message of judgment. Israel was unresponsive to God's overtures of grace—the same problem addressed by Isaiah (Is. 6:9–10) and alluded to by Jesus Himself about the majority of the people in His day (Matt. 13:13–15).

Ezekiel packed his bags and left home. The sign-act describes how the leaders (Ezek. 12:10) would try to avoid the consequences of their rebellion. It appears that it was not readily clear to his audience just what Ezekiel was doing by carrying his baggage (v. 9), but the interpretation in vv. 8–16 shows that He was acting out a direct prophecy. An exile's baggage probably included only the scantiest essentials: a skin for water, a mat for sleeping, and a container for food. The drama juxtaposes two realities: the certainty of exile and the dogged desire to escape it (vv. 5–6).

12:8–16. Prophecy and the Prince. As a sign to the people, all the prophet's acts (i.e., digging through the wall, carrying this baggage, going out at dusk, covering his face, and not seeing the land; v. 7) would meet their historical fulfillment in Nebuchadnezzar's siege of Jerusalem and Zedekiah's attempt to flee. The experience of Zedekiah is specified in that he would not be able to see Babylon (v. 12; cf. 2 Kin. 25:7). The exiles were assured of the divine agency while being depicted as beasts of prey (Ezek. 12:13–14). As a result of the experience of judgment, the people would know who Yahweh is (v. 15, cf. Ex. 6:1–2). The judgment remained the same; God would scatter His people because of their rebellion. Ezekiel had explicitly stated the destructive means in the final exile and connected his description with earlier statements (sword, famine, plague, Ezek. 12:16; cf. 5:12; 6:11; 7:15). The fulfillment of his prophetic message affirmed to the exiled community that his messages were from the Lord (cf. 2:5). But at this stage in their rebellion, they doubted the immediacy and authenticity of the message (12:21–25).

12:17–20. Fear and Trembling. Ezekiel acted out another scene of the psychological effects of judgment. To make the action prophecy realistic, we can picture Ezekiel shaking and trembling to the point that he could barely get any food or drink in his mouth (v. 18). Reminiscent of the siege rations from 4:10–11, the people of Jerusalem and the land of Israel would eat and drink with anxiety and horror (12:19). Invading armies often took the crops and livestock of the inhabitants, so the concerns of those remaining would not be focused on real estate (11:15) but on the preservation of life itself. Since the land would be desolated, it would be impossible for the people to find security in politics, economic stability, and religious history. Israel's hopes, purpose, identity, and pride were attached to the land. Not only would most of the people be exiled from it, but the remaining few would not be able to sustain the land, the traditions, or the corporate worship system; the land would lie in ruins (cf. Lev. 26:14–16).

Contrary to some popular uses of these "scattering and gathering" passages in end-time scenarios, no rapture of the church will occur secretly with the lost left behind. As in Israel's history, at the end of time God's judging of the wicked entails Him turning their fortunes into rubble (Rev. 18:9–24). In the execution of judgment at Christ's coming (Rev. 19:11–16), there will be only death for the wicked (Rev. 19:17–21). John presents the finale of God's judgment for the rebellious in the end as being not a second chance in a renewed Israel but only the second death (Rev. 20:11–15).

12:21–28. The Lord Will Speak and It Shall Happen. The validity of Ezekiel's visions and sign-acts were doubted on two counts. First, the people thought Ezekiel's words would come to nothing since nothing had happened yet (v. 22; cf. 2 Pet. 3:3–4). The prophets were often seen as doomsayers and alarmists. A few years earlier, Jeremiah had experienced the same kind of denial (Jer. 5:12), even receiving physical blows because of his perceived pessimistic message (Jer. 27:12—28:11). It had only been about six years since the exiles were deported in 597 B.C., and only a year into Ezekiel's ministry (Ezek. 1:2; 8:1), yet proverbs had already developed discounting God's warning. Even Isaiah and Micah had spoken about the coming Exile, and the people replied with cynicism and doubt (Is. 5:19; Mic. 3:11). Jeremiah indicated that the people's belief in their status as the chosen people in God's appointed place would not save them from destruction if they failed to amend their ways (Jer. 7:4). Some of the leaders in Jesus's time had the same mentality, misunderstanding His relationship to the temple as well as their own to the point that they were ready to condemn Him and commit murder (cf. Matt. 12:6, 14; Mark 14:57–58; John 2:19). Second, the people intimated that prophecy was irrelevant to them

since it was related to times far in the future (Ezek. 12:27). They did not doubt that biblical prophecy was real, only that its fulfilment was so far away that it was of little consequence to their immediate lives.

The institutions, buildings, and leadership roles were a means to an end—not a religious talisman that proved divine acceptance and protection irrespective of their relationship to God. The false vision or flattering divination (v. 24) apparently had been successful in its intended effect. Whether the cause was false prophetic proclamations or false hopes, the result was an environment of religious deception. God had given instructions on how to relate to prophetic sayings (Deut. 13:1–5) and how to avoid judgment through repentance (cf. Jer. 18:1–11; Jon. 3:4–10). God's spoken promise (Ezek. 12:25, 28) that the deceptive proclamations would cease was a response to the cynicism of the leaders and the people. He would bring judgment on the false prophets as announced in the next chapter.

13:1–23
Prophecy against the Prophets

Beginning a series of seven woes (vv. 3, 18; 16:23; 24:6, 9; 34:2), Ezekiel's message addresses male prophets who were lying about having received a divine word (13:1–16) and female prophets who were engaging in obscure magical practices (vv. 17–23). Two major problems are addressed: (1) the character of God's prophetic leading and (2) the reliability of the prophetic message. The nature of prophecy is integral to understanding the sanctuary judgment message in Ezekiel (chaps. 8–11) and the eschatological prophecy found in the book of Daniel and the NT. It was important for the people of God to have a true understanding of how God was leading His people through the prophetic message and its ethical component. Because people make moral choices based on their understanding of prophecy, false prophecy always poses an obstacle to the clarity of God's purposes and expectations.

True biblical prophecy is of upmost importance because it helps to keep holy living in a broader context (Matt. 24:4–5, 11; Rev. 10:7; 22:6). The words of some false prophets and leaders in Israel are quoted and refuted in Ezekiel's account (Ezek. 8:12; 9:9; 11:3; 12:22, 27; 18:2, 19, 25, 29) because their false messages were leading the people astray. Their influence in the community added a persuasive power to their words, especially when they introduced their messages with "Hear the word of the LORD!" (13:2). God corrected the first problem of the false prophets' claiming to represent Him to the people by clarifying that everyone would know who God is at the coming of judgment (vv. 9, 14, 21, 23). He addressed the second problem of the lies and false visions by having His own prophet, Ezekiel, state what would take place, in advance of its happening (cf. John 13:19).

13:1–16. Lies, Divination, and False Vision. The words characterizing these false prophets' visionary experiences (e.g., false, lie) describe the type of messages coming from private and, in this case, pernicious interpretations of events (v. 2; 2 Pet. 1:20–21). Instead of protecting and sealing the breaches with faithful messages from God, the false prophets' lies were making use of the breaches like sly foxes or jackals in a vineyard, running about through the ragged walls and damaging the vine shoots (Ezek. 13:4; cf. Neh. 3:35; Song 2:15). Contrast this depiction with God's command to Ezekiel to be a watchman warning of impending danger (Ezek. 3:17). The Lord specified that the deceptive nature of these prophets was expressed in two ways: (1) using the same religious language as God's true prophets (13:6–7; cf. vv. 8, 16), and (2) engaging in spiritualism— a product of supernatural intervention—to give a semblance of accurate prediction that lacked a moral component.

Deuteronomy 13:1–5 establishes a miracle, sign, or accurate prediction as being no proof of God's leading if it turns the people away from God's revealed word (cf. Ex. 7:22; Rev. 16: 13–14). God's response was threefold: (1) the false prophets would not be a part of the assembly of leaders; (2) they would not be written in the civil list (census); and (3) they were not to come back to the land of Israel (Ezek. 13:8– 9). These responses anticipated the final exile of 586 B.C. but clarified that the false leaders would not be a part of the restored community. False prophetic messages would be refuted because of their tendency either to promise things not in accordance with God's word (v. 10, cf. Jer. 14:13–16) or because of their tendency to take financial advantage of the people of God with false messages (Ezek. 13:18–19; cf. Jer. 6:13–14; Titus 1:11). Their false messages were unstable like whitewashed (limestone mixed with water), flimsy walls: initially thought to provide comfort and stability, but truly exposed by judgment striking like a hurricane, hailstorm, and tsunami all at once (Ezek. 13:11–13; Deut. 13:6–18).

13:17–23. Witches, Witchcraft, and Wickedness. Several women served as prophetesses in Israel's history: Miriam, Moses's sister (Ex. 15:20); Deborah (Judg. 4:4); and Huldah (2 Kin. 22:14; 2 Chr. 34:22). It is important that Ezekiel does not call the women he was dealing with "prophetesses" (cf. Ex. 15:20; Judg. 4:4; Is. 8:3). By taking up the pagan practices of sewing magic charms, these women are more accurately called witches. The Hebrew word *keset* (meaning "bands, cushions") in v. 18 is a term likely related to the Akkadian term for magic. Babylonian incantations involved magical knots and bonds and making veils (Heb. *mispakhah*, suggesting a special type of covering, possibly with an amulet used in magical rituals). The popular image of a dark, horned demon can be a misleading portrayal of the obviousness of the evils in witchcraft, which in fact is often presented in attractive wares, beautiful tapestry, and appealing artistic symbolism (GC 566–567). The moral purpose of prophecy is brought into view through the condemnation of wickedness and through God's message calling His people to fidelity and obedience to His revealed will (Ezek. 13:22–23). The Hebrew term *nepesh* (which is used in vv. 18, 20) can have various meanings, including "emotions," "thoughts," "mental faculties," "desires" (especially in poetic passages, e.g., 24:25; Job 24:12; Pss. 6:3; 13:2; 31:9; 42:4–6), and even sometimes "dead body" (see e.g., Num. 5:2; 9:6), and is sometimes translated as "souls." In no case can it be said to denote a bodiless entity living within the body, which is a pagan idea. In this context it refers to the whole person.

14:1–23
Matters of the Heart

The theme of false prophecy is taken up again, this time with the elders of Israel in view. Though removed from Jerusalem, the problem remained: idolatrous hearts. Ezekiel associates the idolatry of the elders ("these men," v. 3) with the deceptive message of the false prophets (vv. 4, 10). This indicates that the ones accepting the false message were not victims but were in a sense complicit in the deception because their hearts were not with God (cf. 2 Tim. 4:3–4).

14:1–11. They Shall Be My People. Ezekiel's priestly training and prophetic calling helped him understand the relationship between prophetic proclamation and holy living. There are many linguistic parallels between this chapter and Leviticus 17–26 (esp. Lev. 17). Just as Israel was instructed about the sanctity and purity of life as they were moving into the promised land, so in Ezekiel they were instructed, as those who would go back to the promised land as the remnant, to repent and renounce their idols (Ezek. 14:6). Restoration is twofold: God called His people to return to Him in faithfulness and to turn away from idolatry.

Some of the elders did not see any problem with serving idols in their heart while at the same time going to God's designated spokesperson to hear God's word. But God would have none of their religious double-mindedness. He would "set His face against" such people. (cf. Lev. 20:6), and make the wicked a negative example (Ezek. 14:8; Deut. 28:37).

God said something seemingly strange (Ezek. 14:9), which was that in the case of a false prophet, He Himself had *patah* ("persuaded," "seduced," "enticed," or "deceived") that prophet. Since God is morally pure and cannot lie (Titus 1:2; Heb. 6:8), this should probably not be taken to mean "deceived"—at least not in an overly literal sense. God's involvement consisted of both establishing and permitting circumstances in which He knew the deception of already recalcitrant and rebellious people would occur, and He used these circumstances to bring about His will in their punishment (cf. Ezek. 14:9; 1 Kin. 22:19–23; Is. 63:17; 2 Thess. 2:11). These foolish prophets, who benefit from capitalizing on the fears of people with words of peace (Ezek. 13:10), would be destroyed by God; this is an announcement of complete annihilation (see Lev. 26:30). Yet judgment was not the final word, and herein lay an instructive warning to Ezekiel. He needed spiritual discernment because he had people with idolatrous hearts coming to him and seeking a word from God. God desired to restore His people to a faithful covenant relationship with Him, and consequently, He would see to it that false leaders would not make His people wander around like lost sheep (Ezek. 13:11; cf. chap. 34; John 10).

14:12–23. A Survivor Will Be Left. Denying any notion of corporate righteousness by proxy, God told His people not to rest their spiritual laurels on their heroes of the faith. He summarized the modes of punishment described earlier (vv. 12–23; cf. chaps. 5–7): famine (14:12–14), wild beasts (vv. 15–16), the sword (vv. 17–18), and pestilence or plague (vv. 19–20), which were part of the covenant

curses (Lev. 26:22–26). Thus, He made the people's true condition clear to them. Reaffirming the terror of His just punishment (Ezek. 14:21), God then announced that He would preserve an unfaithful remnant from Jerusalem to be taken to Babylon. Their rebellious and corrupt way of life, even in exile, would demonstrate that the Lord was just in His judgment against Jerusalem. The Lord promised Ezekiel that by observing the evidence of rebellion in the former inhabitants of Jerusalem, he would be comforted knowing that the Lord did what was right (vv. 22–23).

The repetition of Noah, Daniel, and Job (vv. 14, 16, 18, 20) at the end of each section brings up two important practices in Israel's history: intercession by prayer and sacrifice, and the effect of the presence of the righteous. First, the prayers of intercession were an expression of righteousness. Job interceded for his children (Job 1:5). Daniel interceded for Jerusalem (Dan. 9). Noah also interceded for his family after the Flood, when he expressed his faith and offered a sacrifice as an act of atonement— an expiation for their sin (Gen. 8:20). But even those known for their righteous intercession could not rescue others from the judgment to come. Second, because the righteous found favor in the eyes of God, others also were delivered (Gen. 6:8; Job 1:1; Dan. 1:8, 17). But here Judah's sin was so ingrained and malignant that the intercession of the faithful would bring no healing balm (cf. Amos 7:1–9). The judgment is here stated as indeed final and, given the circumstances, unavoidable.

15:1—17:24

GOD'S PARABLES: A VINE, A SPOUSE, AND TWO EAGLES

Ezekiel uses three different parables about a useless vine, an unfaithful wife, and two eagles to show God's tender care and Israel's rebellious and ungrateful heart. Each chapter focuses on a different aspect of Israel's rebellion. The vine symbolizes what Israel should have been— full of life and fertile growth in righteousness as a witness to God's care for humanity (cf. Is. 5:1–7)—but it had become useless (cf. Jer. 2:21), ready for the fire.

The unfaithful wife depicts Israel's political and religious activities as shameless infidelity toward their covenant Lord (cf. Jer. 3:14). Ezekiel uses wisdom language from the book of Proverbs to describe the illicit lust of the adulteress woman, Folly (cf. Prov. 5; 6:20–35; 7; 9:13–18). Israel's rebellious ways reflected a rejection of the wisdom of God in establishing a faithful covenant relationship. The two divinely established institutions from Creation that are the target of Satan's ire are the Sabbath and marriage (between one man and one woman). When God's people break those vows of faith, hope, and love, His character is impugned in the sight of the nations and, more immediately, in the sight of their neighbors.

The parable of the two eagles and the vine shows the folly of rebelling against Babylon and seeking help from Egypt. Israel's history is fraught with unfaithfulness. They broke their covenant with God, and without God's grace and lordship, Israel had no reason or power to be faithful to their commitments. These three chapters are held together by a repetitive formula: "The word of the LORD came to me": "'Son of Man....'" This section shows the recalcitrance of rebellious hearts even in the face of divine grace and providence.

15:1–8
Israel, a Useless Vine

Like other writers of the Hebrew Bible, Ezekiel depicts Israel using the floral imagery of a vine, a symbol of God's care and of His plan to make Israel a blessing to the nations (Ps. 80:8–11; cf. Gen. 12:1–3). This chapter begins with a graphic depiction of God's judgment resulting in the demise of His people as worthless wood (Ps. 80:12–13; Jer. 2:21). Not only had the people failed to live up to God's expectations, but they also had flagrantly rebelled against Him and His word. As the vinedresser, God should not be blamed for moral evil. Jesus utilized this prophetic imagery multiple times: (1) a parable where pernicious weeds of rebellion would be consigned to the fires of judgment (Matt. 13:24–30); (2) a metaphor for the connection between Himself and His believers (John 15:1–8); and (3) the fruit of the vine to symbolize His blood (Matt. 26:27–29). John the Revelator also used the fruit of the vine as a metaphor for judgment (Rev. 14:18–20). God's plan was for His people to bear fruit (justice and righteousness; Is. 5:7), but when the spoiled fruit of oppression, selfishness, and idolatry was found, the vine was fit only for firewood.

16:1–63
Faithless Bride

Ezekiel continues to use different pictures to illustrate the development of Israel's apostasy. While chapter 20 describes a cyclical picture, chapters 16 and 23 describe a picture of ever-increasing apostasy. As in Hosea, the image of Israel as God's wife shows the love God has for His people. Sadly, His love was often spurned and not reciprocated. Ezekiel uses lewd and almost sexually explicit imagery to describe Israel's infidelity to Yahweh. The metaphor of whoredom expresses Israel's false worship (16:15–18), and her paramours, the pagan nations, represent the political associations Israel made instead of trusting in God's abiding presence and revealed will (vv. 26–32).

16:1–14. Israel Abandoned but Adopted. After being given a summary statement of his mission to make the capital city aware of their abominations (v. 2), Ezekiel was commanded first to show what Israel had abandoned. After calling attention to the ethnic origins of the Hebrew people (v. 3), God reminded them that their present status as God's people was an act of grace. During the time of the Exodus, the Canaanites, Amorites, and Hittites would be displaced once Israel entered into the land (Ex. 3:8, 17; 23:23; 33:2; Deut. 7:1; 20:17) in fulfillment of God's promise to Abraham (Gen. 13:14). Their displacement was also a judgment on them because of their deplorable ways, not because of ethnic inferiority (Gen. 15:15–21; 1 Kin. 21:26).

Ezekiel uses a motif common in the ancient Near East in which an abandoned child found in the open country is adopted and cared for. This serves as a rebuke and a tribute. In several societies in the ancient world, the exposure of unwanted babies, especially girls, was an alternative to birth control. This unwanted baby that God rescued reminded Ezekiel's audience of their historical deliverance from slavery to adoption and pointed toward God's ability to once again free His people from the bondage of exile and restore them to Himself as His children. Israel's adoption was a prominent marker of divine election that brought the nation into a covenant relationship with Him (Ezek. 16:8). This gracious act of the adoption of an enslaved nation was later utilized by NT authors to describe the special status of the people of God who were redeemed by the sacrificial work of Jesus (Rom. 8:14–17; Gal. 4:4–7; Eph. 1:5–6). Israel's growth from wilderness wanderers to a thriving monarchy during David's and Solomon's reigns is depicted as a young woman's development into a beautifully adorned queen (Ezek. 16:9–14).

16:15–34. Israel's Harlotry and Adultery.
But Israel became a harlot and engaged in foreign, anti-Yahweh practices: (1) false worship at shrines (vv. 16–19; cf. Prov. 7:16–17); (2) filicide (i.e., killing one's child; Ezek. 16:20–23; cf. Lev. 18:21; 1 Kin. 11:5); and (3) making illegitimate covenants with the surrounding major powers—Egypt, Assyria, and Babylon (Ezek. 16:24–30). Isaiah warned Judah repeatedly against seeking alliances with Egypt in order to resist Assyria, but his warnings went unheeded (2 Kin. 18:21–24; Is. 30–31) even though they knew such a plan had not worked for the Northern Kingdom (2 Kin. 17:1–5). Judah's alliance with Assyria refers to Ahaz's appeals to Assyria for help against the Syro-Ephraimite coalition and the Northern Kingdom of Israel in the eighth century (2 Kin. 16:1–9; Is. 7:1–9). The interaction with Babylon (Ezek. 16:29) probably refers to Hezekiah's foolish interaction with the Babylonian envoys (Is. 39:1–8) and later kings' alliances with Babylon (2 Kin. 24).

The vulgar description of the people of God acting as an insatiable prostitute (Ezek. 16:15–17, 26, 28)—engaged in idolatry, spiritualism, and covenant infidelity—provides a background for the description of the unfaithful people of God in the book of Revelation (Rev. 17:1–14). The faithful people of God are described as chaste (James 1:27; Rev. 14:4; cf. Heb. 13:4). The adulterous ways of a harlot are used to describe how God's people turn their backs on Him to serve other gods. Just as in Ezekiel's time God's people became enamored with paganism and God appealed to them to come out of that false religious system, so in Revelation the true people of God are called to turn from their spiritual adultery, come out of spiritual Babylon, and return to true worship that is centered in the Creator and covenant faithfulness (Jer. 50:8; 51:6, 45; Rev. 18:1–4).

Israel's harlotry was worse because normally prostitution resulted from economic privation, but Israel had all God's blessings, even royalty. Prostitute Israel did not take payment for their services; they gave the payment (Ezek. 16:30–34) in the form of God's material blessings for erecting idolatrous practices in defiance of their covenant Lord (cf. Deut. 23:18). The end-time harlot depicted in the book of Revelation goes one step further to become the worldwide epicenter of spiritualism (Rev. 18:1–3), arrogance and cruelty (Rev. 18:4–8), and political and economic depravity (Rev. 18:9–20). God's call is the same in Ezekiel: come out of her and cease following her ways!

16:35–43. O Prostitute, Hear the Word of the Lord. Israel's debauchery exposed them to paganism and did not lead to fruitful results. Most pagan deities were connected with nature in some fashion, and agricultural produce was a sign of the deities' blessing. Israel's self-imposed bondage to ungodly acts stemmed in large part from their confused beliefs about God. Their intention to manipulate God through rituals, like that of the surrounding nations, was met with divine wrath. Because Israel trusted in false deities, Yahweh would allow them to be returned to the state in which He found them in order to show Israel what those false deities would do for them (v. 39; cf. vv. 7, 22). Like Israel, God would mobilize those nations, but for different purposes. Because of capital offenses like adultery (Lev. 20:10) and the shedding of blood (Deut. 19:11–12), the people deserved to die, and God would bring judgment, but in all this His purposes were redemptive.

16:44–59. Samaria, Sodom, and Hypocrisy. Israel's defection from God was so thorough that there was no difference between them and the surrounding nations. The saying "Like mother, like daughter" was an appropriate one (v. 44). The mother (Hittite) represents the heathen Canaanites, and the sister (Israel) is associated with Sodom (vv. 44–46; Gen. 19:1–29; Is. 1:15). The people of Judah had surpassed the notoriously infamous and immoral Sodomites and the people of the Northern Kingdom of Israel (Ezek. 16:47). God's objection to Judah and Israel was that they strove to be like the pagan nations. The implication was that Yahweh was just another localized deity, one among others. Whenever conceptions of God are brought down to the level of human machinations, He makes it clear that He has no equal (20:9; 39:7; Is. 45:20–21; 46:5–13; 48:9–11). God's original plan was for Israel to be a light on a hill to the nations, an illustration of God's rule of justice and righteousness (Deut. 28:1–14; 1 Kin. 3:1–15). When God and His truth are disregarded, there is nowhere else to go but in a downward spiral of destruction (Ezek. 16:47–48). Spiritual rebellion has a social impact, and in Israel it took the form of the oppression of the vulnerable (poor and needy, v. 49; cf. Deut. 15:11) and spiritual pride (Ezek. 16:56–58).

16:60–63. God's Memory and Mercy. Memory plays an important role in the life of the people of God. When God said He would remember His covenant, it meant He would act in light of it

(v. 60). To establish the covenant meant to confirm and maintain something that already existed (vv. 60, 62; 34:20–31; cf. Gen. 6:18; 9:9, 11, 17; 17:7, 19, 21; 26:3). To remember their sins meant that Israel would feel ashamed and act in a way that would honor God. In both the OT and the NT—in type and antitype, in shadow and reality—restoration was made by atonement (Ezek. 16:63; Heb. 8–10).

17:1–24
Two Eagles and a Vine

Ezekiel is given a parable (vv. 1–10), its interpretation (vv. 11–21), and a parable reiteration with a statement of its consequences (vv. 22–24). A crucial question is raised throughout the chapter: "Will it thrive?" As Ezekiel brings back the metaphor of the house of Israel as the vine (cf. 15:2, 6) to comment on the political situation, he sets forth Judah's imminent demise.

17:1–10. Great Eagles and the Vine. In the Bible, animals are used to symbolize important historical events (e.g., Dan. 7–8; Rev. 12–13; 17–20). Ezekiel's symbolism points to his immediate circumstances to explain Judah's folly. The words *khidah* ("riddle" or "allegory"; cf. Judg. 14:12–16) and *mashal* ("parable" or "proverb"; cf. Prov. 1:1; Eccl. 12:9) are used in wisdom contexts, and here they serve to reinforce Judah's folly. Both words intimate a need for interpretation and introduce an allegorical story. By couching history in an enigmatic story, the people would be drawn initially into the plotline. The story, however, ends on a sour note. A beautiful eagle (or griffon vulture), known for its size and flying ability, took the top of the cedar (Ezek. 17:1–6). The irony of the eagle planting the topmost of the cedar's young twigs is already a subtle indication of the presence of foreign elements. Dissatisfied with its condition, the now finely trestled vine turned its attention to another eagle (v. 7). With deadly claws, the first eagle would not accept a swap, especially since it helped the vine to grow (vv. 9–10).

17:11–21. Prophetic Riddles and Parables Explained. The first eagle stands for Nebuchadnezzar, king of Babylon, who campaigned in Judah in 597 B.C. and took King Jehoiachin (the topmost of the cedar's shoot; vv. 4, 12b) and his officials (v. 12) into exile ("city of merchants," Babylon; v. 4). Zedekiah is probably the one referred to as the seed of the land (vv. 5, 12–13;

2 Kin. 24:15; 25:6). The planting of a vine by Nebuchadnezzar refers to his stratagem to reestablish the kingdom of Judah as a puppet client and buffer state against any Egyptian aggression. Branches turning to the eagle emphasize Judah's vassal state under Babylon's control. The second eagle most likely represents Pharaoh Psammetichus II of Egypt (595–589 B.C.). However, Judah's hope was not Egypt (Jer. 27:1–22). The faith of God's people must not rest in human wisdom and strength (cf. 1 Cor. 2:5). The prophet Daniel later made it clear that Babylon would be followed on the world stage by Media and Persia (Dan. 8:20). The wisdom of God is seen in His foreknowledge and proclaimed through prophecy, which serves to establish faith in His providence despite external circumstances (Is. 46:10).

17:22–24. Messianic Hope. God continued to show His sovereignty, entering the arena of politics and promising to set up His own royal leader. This is a messianic prophecy of a Davidic king originating from on high (v. 22). The branch, fruit, and splendor that earthly powers intended for Israel would come to naught (vv. 8–9), but the same characteristics would be fully displayed in God's promised king (v. 23). Here, God is evidently the agent instead of the eagles, indicating that His will supersedes the machinations of earthly powers in the establishment of His king and kingdom (cf. 1 Sam. 2:1–10; Dan. 2:34, 44–45). The influence of a foreign nation or king would not impede the fulfillment of this messianic promise, though Herod tried (Matt. 2).

18:1—23:49
ACCOUNTABILITY AND RETRIBUTION

Chapters 18–23 in a sense recapitulate Ezekiel's criticism against the leadership of Judah (chaps. 12–14), but in a more specific and larger historical context. Because of the corporate exile of Judah, some of the people seemed to believe that they were the unjust victims of their fellow Israelites' crimes. In several historical vignettes, God showed how all Israel benefitted from His gracious acts. At the same time, the promises of redemption and returning to the land were corporate. So the Exile was a response to the nation's faithlessness. The innocent would suffer, but the others were guilty by sins of omission or commission, in word or deed, and by faithlessness or presumption. But in

His gracious way, God would punish individuals for their own sins and save individuals by His grace as they trusted in Him.

18:1–32
The Righteous Shall Live; the Wicked Shall Die

Those in exile used a proverb to question God's fairness (vv. 2, 25). This catchy adage attempted to put the spotlight on God, and it garnered some popularity, as shown by its use in Jeremiah 31:29-30. God correctly put the spotlight back on the people, where it belonged. Like a petulant child, Judah refused to acknowledge their sins and brazenly accused God of being reckless in His execution of justice. God set the record straight by using irony to show these "righteous" people that the judgment was justified and that in His patience He had borne long with them.

18:1–18. If…Then. God, through an oath, stated that His assessment of the problem would bring clarity to the situation (v. 3). In chapter 14 it was noted that the righteous (Noah, Daniel, Job) could not mitigate the punishment of the wicked. In chapter 18, the focus is on individual responsibility, answering the question of whether children would be punished for the sins of their fathers. Three case studies are given to disprove the proverb: the righteous person (vv. 5–9); the wicked son (vv. 10–13); and the righteous son of a wicked father (vv. 14–18). The righteous person is described (vv. 5-9, 14-18) as one faithful to the covenant. Justice and righteousness show themselves in what a person avoids and by what people promote through their actions. The main issues that all three cases touch on are: (1) worship—pagan monuments, idol worship (v. 6); (2) sexual contact—sexual contact with a neighbor's spouse (v. 6; Ex. 20:14; Lev. 18:20), sexual ritual impurity (Ezek. 18:6; Lev. 18:19); (3) financial dealings—piling up bad debts, theft, exploitation of the vulnerable (Ezek. 18:7; Ex. 22:21), living by impulse and greed; and (4) legal disputes—considering one person better than another (Ezek. 18:8; Lev. 19:15). It is important to note that the passage presents the lives of the righteous son and father as in accordance with God's gracious revelation (Ezek. 18:9, 17), while the wicked son would die because of disobedience (v. 13). Notice that Ezekiel presents only the righteous as going beyond the prohibitions and promoting justice and acting with integrity (vv. 7-9, 17).

This includes feeding the hungry, clothing the naked, and executing true justice with fairness and equity as an expression of what it means to worship God (cf. Ps. 5:3-8). Not just their behavior but their character is in view (Ezek. 18:9), and the righteous do what God loves (Ps. 33:5). Habits, dispositions, and the will express the heart's condition, for out of it flow the issues of life (Prov. 4:23).

18:19–32. Turn and Live! Justice and righteousness describe and define God's character from Genesis to Revelation. God wants His people to pursue justice and righteousness as a sign of submission to His lordship. The second commandment indicates that the immoral behavior of parents often carries negative results for children and grandchildren, whether by nurture or nature. The judgment applies to those who hate God and only to the third and fourth generations. So while this command describes the consequences for the disobedient and unbelieving, it focuses on God's mercy, especially in view of His steadfast love for thousands of those who love Him (Ex. 20:6). A misunderstanding of God's justice often leads to despair and doubt about His grace, love, holiness, and wisdom in the practical spheres of life. Ezekiel addresses two interconnected problems. First, though Scripture (including elsewhere in Ezekiel itself, e.g., 21:4; 23:46-49; 24:21) mentions many examples of children being punished for their parents' sins (e.g., Gen. 9; Ex. 12:29; Lev. 26:39-40; Josh. 6:26; 2 Sam. 12:14; cf. 2 Sam. 21; 1 Kin. 14:10; 16:34; 22:19-20; 2 Kin. 5:27; 23:26-27; Matt. 23:34-39), children will not ultimately and eternally bear their parents' guilt, and parents will not bear their children's guilt. Second, any wicked person can be transformed into a righteous person, while a righteous person can turn from his or her righteousness and commit iniquity (Ezek. 18:21-27; 33:18-19). In both instances, the person who sins is culpable for his or her own actions, and one's past does not dictate one's future.

Apparently the people did not want to be treated as individuals but were wrongly using the principle of familial guilt as an excuse to be fatalistically complacent in regard to their own guilt and sin. In 18:19, 25, and 29, the people objected.

Ezekiel uses the verb *shub* ("to turn," "repent," "restore") in several passages to show the nature of hope and of rebellion (vv. 21, 23-24, 26-28, 30, 32). True repentance includes a godly sorrow for sin as well as a turning from sin and selfishness to righteousness and holiness. God's command to repent, turn, and live (vv. 30, 32) was a call to Israel to surrender to God's authority as Creator and Father. Herein lies the biblical teaching of righteousness by faith. The call to life (vv. 9, 17, 21, 28, 32) is a call to embrace God and the gift of His holiness. He gives to His children a new heart and new spirit (v. 31; 37:22–32; cf. Ps. 51:7–12). His commands are indeed His enablings, for it is His love that seeks out human beings, honestly assesses their condition, and offers forgiveness, reconciliation, and sanctification. When individuals return to God, though they have been sinful, none of their sins will be remembered (Ezek. 18:22, 24). That God will not remember their rebellions, perversions, injustices, abominations, and treachery means that He will not treat them as sinners.

The question in v. 23 and the affirmations of v. 32 point to the depths of God's love and the sickness of the human heart. God seeks to save and not to destroy. He wants sinners to live. How will His people live? By (1) honoring God in obedience (v. 21); (2) turning from wicked ways (v. 23); and (3) doing justice and righteousness (v. 27). But the rebellious are disobedient and seem only to assail God and question His motives rather than their own (vv. 25, 29). Thus, the ultimate purpose in judgment is revealed: God wants His people to see what life is like without Him. The removal of His presence can only result in calamity (chaps. 8–11), but His abiding presence with His people results in abundant life (chaps. 40–48).

19:1–14. Lament for the Princes of Israel. Ezekiel confronted his contemporaries by exposing them again to the reality of God's sovereignty over history. Two familiar images, the lion (cf. Gen. 49:8–12) and the vine (cf. Ezek. 15; 17; Is. 5:1–7), show the crisis of leadership in Judah (cf. Ezek. 17). The many literary connections with Jacob's words about Judah in Genesis 49:8–12, which are filled with the messianic promise, emphasize the failure of the Davidic kingship. Haggai and Zechariah would encourage the despairing hopes of the people to see God's promise to David realized. The coming of the messianic King would be fulfilled in Jesus (Matt. 9:27; 15:22; 20:21; 21:9; Mark 10:47; 12:35–37). Not only would this Davidic King rule over the earth, but even at this time He would reign over the hearts of His people in love and grace.

In the first section (Ezek. 19:1–9), the first lion, taken to Egypt, was Jehoahaz (vv. 3–4; 2 Kin. 23:29–33; 609 B.C.). The second lion, taken

to Babylon, was most likely Jehoiachin (Ezek. 19:5, 9; 2 Kin. 24:8–12; 598 B.C.), who is described in Ezekiel 17:2–4, 12 as one exiled to Babylon. Also, the text makes it clear that the mother lioness raised up the lion. The imagery of a mother represents Judah (19:2, 10), and the other lions are the other kingdoms of the world, the Gentile nations (vv. 2 [lions], 4 [nations], 6 [lions], 8 [nations]). The vine also represents the kingdom of Judah, which became a fruitful vine but was then uprooted in fury (vv. 10, 12). The focus on the activities of the lioness emphasizes that God was no longer being consulted about the kingship. In fact, as a result of God's judgment, foreign rulers were seemingly in control of the monarchy from 605 to 586 B.C. (cf. 2 Kin. 23:34; 24:17; Dan. 1:1). The image of the vine focuses on the Davidic dynasty and the branches represent their rulers. The parable describes how it was dismantled from its high estate and taken into exile.

The literary significance of chapter 18 is now brought into view. The placement of this chapter on individual responsibility—between chapters 17 and 19—shows God's justice and mercy being applied to the Davidic kings. Unfortunately, as the author of the book of Kings informs us, most of the kings did evil in the sight of the Lord. God's mercy and justice apply to all alike, regardless of status.

20:1–49
Rebellion, Revelation, and Redemption

As Ezekiel's timeline moves closer to the besiegement of Jerusalem, Israel's history is described as a repetition of apostasy. This reinforces the fact that God had gone above and beyond in His dealings with His people. Pivotal events in Israel's history are noted, with an assessment of that generation carrying serious implications for Judah during its exile and for us as well. The content of the chapter is organized around the ways God revealed Himself to His people ("I am the Lord," vv. 5, 7, 12, 19, 20, 26, 38, 42, 44).

20:1–17. Exodus and Sinai. During the Exodus (vv. 5–9), God elected Israel and promised them the gift of the land of Canaan. He was their Savior and Warrior (Ex. 15:1–18). Yet Israel rebelled against God and retained their vile and abominable/detestable idols (Ezek. 20:7–8; cf. Ex. 32–34; Deut. 29:16–17), defiling themselves with Egyptian idols (cf. Rom. 1:18–23; PP 315–330). God's restraint was based solely on His sovereign choice of maintaining the holiness of His name/reputation, which would be vindicated before the nations (Ezek. 20:9).

At Sinai (vv. 10–17), God gave them His regulations and His Sabbath (vv. 11–12) as a sign of the covenant, and He revealed Himself as Israel's wise Lawgiver. Sadly, Israel's first generation of the Exodus established a pattern of sin and rebellion in the wilderness (vv. 10–16). The core of the problem was that their hearts were unwilling to appropriate God's grace and holiness. The focus of worship must be the true Creator and Redeemer, whose relationship to Israel and all creation is particularly detailed in the Ten Commandments. The plural form "Sabbaths" does not necessarily include the religious festivals that required the people to go up to Jerusalem to worship God three times a year (Ex. 23:14–19; Deut. 16:1–17). The reference is to the Sabbath as a sign of the covenant. The ceremonial sabbaths served to promote the true worship of God by identifying Him as the source of Israel's temporal wealth and blessings. In the NT, these sabbaths find their deeper meaning through biblical typology in the life, death, and high priestly ministry of Jesus (cf. Acts 2:1–4; 1 Cor. 5:7; Rev. 7:9–12). Because the people desired something other than God's way,

He was justified in disciplining them. But because He is a gracious and loving God, He continually sought to bring them back to covenant faithfulness (Ezek. 20:17).

20:18–44. From the Wilderness to the Monarchy. God gave to the second generation of the Exodus the same opportunity He had given to their fathers, but they also sinned in the wilderness (vv. 18–26). The children did not learn the lessons of their forebearers and repeated the same sins. But this time God informed them that one day they would be scattered among the nations (v. 23; Deut. 28:64). The pattern of rejecting God's way of life had become a way of life for the people (Ezek. 20:24). On the idea that God gave statutes and laws that were "not good" to the Israelites, see below, "God and Bad Laws (Ezekiel 20:25)."

The people rejected the laws of the firstborn (Ex. 13:2, 13; 22:29; 34:20; Num. 18:15) and offered their children in sacrifice to the surrounding pagan idols instead. They disregarded God's law by passing their firstborn through the fire (cf. Ezek. 20:31; Deut. 12:29–31; 2 Kin. 21:6; 23:10; Jer. 7:31; 19:5; 32:35). God passed judgment on their actions and declared them defiled

God and Bad Laws (Ezekiel 20:25)

Ezekiel 20:25 is probably one of the most difficult passages in the book of Ezekiel. Some translations render it as "I gave them statutes that were not good." The commentaries offer different interpretations, but unfortunately none of them has been widely accepted. We will offer a possible way of reading the verse.

1. Stating the Problem. If Ezekiel is stating that God gave the Israelites statutes and laws that "were not good, and judgments by which they could not live," then He would be contradicting Himself. This is the basic problem we face. Nowhere else in the OT is any divine statute or law described as "not good." Rather, what we find is that God told the Israelites that His principles were ones that they should live by (Lev. 18:5; cf. Deut. 4:1). These verses are even quoted in Ezekiel 20:11, 13 and 21—all in the very same context as v. 25, where God refers to giving them what was "not good." On the surface, these statements seem to be in conflict. However, it is important to take

into account other considerations, including other aspects of the context, which will help lead to a viable harmonization.

2. Contextual Considerations. As indicated in the commentary, v. 25 belongs to a passage in which the Lord recounted His mighty acts of redemption on behalf of Israel during their departure from Egypt and their sojourns in the wilderness. But the main interest of the text is to reveal the constant spirit of rebellion manifested by God's people in acts of idolatry. It was because of His concern for His honor that God did not abandon them. It is within that review of what He had done for Israel that the Lord said, "I gave to them statutes that were not good." Therefore, He was referring to something He Himself did at a particular moment. However, the context also indicates that the laws God gave to His people were good, and they were expected to live by them. Interestingly, while Ezekiel uses the feminine form *khuqot* ("statutes") when referring to God's law (vv. 11, 13), in v. 25 the masculine *khuqqim* ("statutes") is used. This change may be a signal that in v. 25 Ezekiel is not referring to the same statutes mentioned in vv. 11 and 13. Whatever v. 25 may mean, Ezekiel himself, as well as the rest of the OT, considered God's laws to be good.

3. Suggested Solution. A possible solution is found in the next verse (v. 26), where a specific law is mentioned. The passage refers to the law of the firstborn. Every firstborn child belonged to the Lord, but since the Lord rejected child sacrifice, the Israelites would redeem their children. Unfortunately, there were times when they chose to sacrifice their children to the pagan deity Molech. This practice is explicitly mentioned in v. 31. This certainly was a bad law, but it was not from the Lord. So, the context informs us what was meant by a law that was "not good." If that is the case, then we must ask, Why would the Lord say that He gave them statutes that were not good? We should look at the text a little closer.

Most Bible versions render the first verb in v. 25 to read "I gave them." That is a good translation, but there are other possibilities. For instance, we could also translate it as "I even imposed on them" or "I also gave them over to statutes." These translations are based on the fact that when the Hebrew verb *natan* ("to give") is followed by the preposition *le* ("to"), it could mean "to deliver someone to." The translation "I also gave them up to statutes that were not good" could be correct. In that case, the text would be saying that since the Israelites determined to follow bad laws from their neighbors, the Lord confirmed their willing rebellion against Him by handing them over to obedience to laws that were not good. The idea that God confirms disobedience by handing rebellious people over to it is attested in other places in the Bible (e.g., Is. 6:9–10; 63:17; 2 Thess. 2:11–12). According to Ezekiel 20:26, even then the Lord is seeking to impress upon them the magnitude of their sins, hoping to lead them to repentance.

(Ezek. 20:31). This custom of filicide (killing one's own children) indicates that the Israelites were following the cultic practices of pagan nations (cf. v. 18). Declared defiled, they could not approach the Lord and finally had to be expelled from the land. Thus, God would show that He is God. Verse 27 summarizes the charges against the people as being related to blasphemy and disloyalty. God is blasphemed when His people take up the customs of the world and reject His grace, love, and lordship.

The experience of the people, from the times of the Judges to the monarchy (vv. 27–32), shows that God fulfilled His promise of the land (v. 28). But unfortunately, Israel blasphemed Him by worshiping the gods of the Canaanites.

Each section of the chapter reflects the same pattern: God giving undeserved grace, Israel responding with apostasy, and God withholding judgment for His name's sake. Though there were bright spots in the history of Israel, Ezekiel's long view of that history is one of false starts, calamitous outcomes, and continuous rebelliousness (cf. 2:3). God's remedy was restorative judgment (20:33–44). To remind the exiles that He was the reason for every good thing they experienced, He promised to bring them back to the place where they had experienced His grace and covenant promises.

20:45—22:31
The Drawn Sword and the Impure City

The storyline of this section is structured around fire (cf. the *inclusio* 20:45-49//21:31-32) and the sword—the riddle of the sword (21:1-7); the sword sharpened and ready (vv. 8-17); the sword in action (vv. 18-27); and the sword sheathed (vv. 28-32). (In modern translations, 20:45-49 corresponds to 21:1-5 in the Hebrew text.) Ezekiel was informed that God would execute judgment on Israel in the same way He judged the nations—through military defeat (cf. chaps. 25-32). His sword, Babylon, would be unsheathed, slicing and dicing, bringing death and destruction, yet even the sword would become an object of God's judgment (21:30-32; cf. Hab. 1:5—2:20). Because the people complained that Ezekiel was speaking in parables, the metaphor of fire is interpreted as referring to the sword (Ezek. 20:46-49; 21:3). Bad news was coming that would cause hearts to melt, hands to become feeble, spirits to faint, and knees to become weak as water (21:7).

20:45—21:7. The Flame and Sword of Judgment. Now that a historical review of Israel has been given (chap. 20), the consequences are to be meted out (21:1-5). God had made use of a multitude of images that depicted historical circumstances, and He used fire to depict judgment on the inhabitants of Jerusalem (cf. 15:5–8) and stating that Babylon was God's instrument of judgment on His own people (12:13; 17:12, 16, 20; 19:9). The apparent grievance was not due to the content of the message; it stemmed from the spiritual dullness of the people, whose attitude is elsewhere expressed as being in denial (12:21–28). God directed Ezekiel to use his present position in Babylon as his point of reference (20:46). Teman (Southland) is Jerusalem, which is considered to be south of Babylon (vv. 46–47). The land of Israel is depicted as a forest that is fuel for the unquenchable fires of judgment (v. 47; cf. 1 Kin. 5:6). Ezekiel has already described the circumstances of the besiegement of Judah (Ezek. 4–7), and here he writes about the reaction to the report of Babylon's preparation for the invasion (21:6–7). While God can distinguish between the righteous and the wicked in an investigative judgment (cf. chap. 9), an invading pagan army could not make such a distinction (21:3–5). In this regard, the few righteous persons would suffer with the wicked.

21:8–17. The Sword Is Sharpened. In a poetic utterance filled with anguish, the sword is made ready for Yahweh's use in judgment—it was sharpened and polished (v. 9). In His workshop of divine providence, He had prepared Babylon (the Neo-Babylonian Empire) for the world stage. The actions of the nations would be seen within the purview of God's sovereignty and prophetic fulfillment (Is. 44:28; Jer. 25:9). Through the prophet Jeremiah, God told His people to accept the current political regime (i.e., Babylonian rule) and focus on restoring their relationship with Him (Jer. 25:5–6; 29:1–14).

God directed Ezekiel to strike his hands together (Ezek. 21:14) as a symbol of God's use of the sword (v. 17). He would move the sword to the right and left, up and down (v. 16). The Lord would cause slaughter and destruction everywhere upon the people. However, there was a note of hope in this proclamation of judgment. The nations, subject to God, could only go as far as He would allow. God's people were not to be left wholly to the machinations of the wicked; it was God who would brandish the sword (vv. 16–17). The prophet Habakkuk (ca. 640–609 B.C.) saw the decline of the Assyrian juggernaut and the ascendancy of Babylon, and he asked about what many today are concerned with: the justice of God (theodicy).

But Ezekiel is depicting God as the Divine Warrior who restores justice and righteousness to the land (Israel), albeit through warfare.

21:18–32. The Sword in Action. Ezekiel would mark out two ways or roads and place a signpost where the two roads branched out, one to the Ammonite capital of Rabbah and the other to Jerusalem (vv. 19–20). The king of Babylon would stand at the head of the two roads with his sword, using three specific types of divination to choose one of them: (1) the selection of marked arrows; (2) consulting idols; and (3) hepatoscopy—examining the liver of slain animals to make predictions. Not only would God send Babylon to execute judgment upon Judah, but He would allow the Babylonian king to work through his religious practices to determine the way to go that would result in the fulfillment of God's purposes. Behind all of this was God's sovereignty. To the Judahite leaders, whose focus was on ritual rather than on obedience (1 Sam. 15:22–23), it seemed like a false divination, and because it was judged false, they would deny its validity. But the message to Judah was clear: God is sovereign and He works with people where they are. Nebuchadnezzar eventually came to his senses (Dan. 4:34–37), but the Davidic king, who had contact with the God of heaven, access to His revelation and abiding presence, and evidence of His faithfulness and mighty acts on the Israelites' behalf, remained in disbelief and rebellion.

The Ammonites probably assumed that since Babylon attacked Israel, they would be safe, but God assured them that their time was coming (Ezek. 21:28–29). In 25:1–7, God laid out further details in regard to Ammon's destined doom. Like Assyria (Is. 10:5–19), Babylon was used by God to bring judgment but would also receive judgment. God's engagement with Israel's neighbors in the wider landscape of history shows how, with Israel's compliance or defiance, the nations would have a witness to the Sovereign of the world.

22:1–31. The Impure City. Israel's concept of holiness included their God (Lev. 19:1–8), their bodies (Lev. 11:1—14:32; 18), their social interactions (Lev. 19:9–18; 25:35–55), their homes (Lev. 14:33–57), their land and property (Lev. 25:1–34), and their worship (Lev. 17:1–8; 23). Every area of life was set apart as belonging to God. Ezekiel now describes the reason for the judgment announced in the previous chapter. Israel had defiled herself in every area of life: religiously, politically, socially, and economically. God enumerated Judah's sins (Ezek. 22:1–16), stated His response of punishment (vv. 17–22), and identified the main culprits (vv. 23–31).

The catalog of Israel's offenses includes breaches of covenant provisions found mainly in Leviticus 18–20. God's focus was the city, a metaphor (i.e., metonymy) for those who constituted the city. The nations would mock Israel (Ezek. 22:4–5). The breakdown of the social relationships among God's people can be attributed to an unbiblical view of the image of God (Gen. 1:26). The shedding of blood (Ezek. 22:3) refers to the literal taking of life, demanding the life of the one who took it as recompense because people are made in God's image (Gen. 9:6; Num. 35:33). But the shedding of blood created another problem. It had defiled the land and had made it incompatible with holiness. Ezekiel's point is that left unresolved, such a defilement would lead to exile (Lev. 18:28). The murderers deserved just retribution. Other problems are identified: idolatry (Ezek. 22:3; cf. Ex. 20:2–7), dishonoring parents (Ezek. 22:7; cf. Ex. 20:12; Lev. 19:3), not caring for the disadvantaged classes of society (Ezek. 22:7; cf. Lev. 19:3, 10), Sabbath breaking (Ezek. 22:8; cf. Ex. 20:8–11), slander (Ezek. 22:9; cf. Ex. 20:16), pagan worship (Ezek. 22:9; cf. Lev. 18:17), sexual deviancy (Ezek. 22:10–11; cf. Lev. 18:7–20; Ex. 20:14), and financial bribery and extortion (Ezek. 22:12; cf. Deut. 16:19; 27:25). All these, in one way or another, defamed God's intention to restore His image in humans. But God would bring all of this to an end (Ezek. 22:13–16).

The God of Ezekiel and the God of Gideon are the same (cf. Judg. 7). God wanted the pure metal of faith; the dross of unbelief, doubt, and rebellion needed to be removed (Ezek. 22:18). Quality is desired over quantity. While God's desire is for everyone to be saved (1 Tim. 2:4), His rhetorical question (Ezek. 22:14) indicates that many would not be willing to have the gold of a faith that could endure to the end (Luke 18:8). Judah had become impatient with God's call for endurance and trust (Jer. 28:1–4; 29:24–28). The future "gathering" prophecies typically signify hope, restoration, and renewal (Is. 11:12; 40:9–11; 54:7; Jer. 23:3; 29:14). Unfortunately, here the people would be gathered for judgment (Ezek. 22:19). The imagery is of leftover dross, the waste material left after metals are purified by the process of smelting (vv. 17–22).

Though leaders and people alike were guilty of rebellion (cf. Hos. 4:9), the emphasis in Ezekiel is predominantly placed on the leaders who were primarily responsible for defiling the city. They were chosen as God's agents of grace who would (1) proclaim His word faithfully (prophets; Ezek. 22:25); (2) help the people distinguish the holy from the profane, mediate God's reconciliation, and lead out in true worship (priests; v. 26; Lev. 10:10); and (3) exemplify God's sovereignty before the nation through justice (princes or officials; Ezek. 22:27; Deut. 1:9–18). They turned upside down every means and method God established to guide the people in holy living: the Torah, the holy places, the purity laws, justice, etc. The leaders used their position to enrich themselves through lies, manipulation, bribes, extortion, and all forms of injustice. Among God's people, leadership is meant to protect and provide for an environment where God's grace can be made manifest and His character can be revealed.

23:1–49
Oholah and Oholibah

The evident parallels with chapter 16 display once again God's love for His people and their constant refusal to live in harmony with Him. Through the imagery of two sisters, the acts of the capital cities of Samaria (23:5–10) and Jerusalem (vv. 11–35) are described. God's judgment on the two kingdoms is reviewed in graphic detail as He again encouraged Ezekiel to get through to His people in His final word (vv. 36–49). The theme of harlotry ties together the various sections of the parable. Israel's adulterous acts describe a moral pathology, where they courted political alliances, copied foreign cultic rituals, and denied their Lord, who provided for them.

23:1–4. Two Sisters and Their Harlotry. Israel's mission would be a light to the nations as a royal priesthood and a holy nation (Ex. 19:6). Solomon's son Rehoboam foolishly misused his position of trust as a badge of autonomous rule and brought an impassable division to an already tense relationship between the Judahites and the northern Israelites (2 Sam 2–5; 1 Kin. 12). The two sisters, Oholah ("her tent") and Oholibah ("my tent is in her")—Israel and Judah—came from one mother: a common patriarchal origin and exodus experience (Ezek. 23:2; cf. Ex. 19:1–5). In the description of the sisters as the capital cities of each kingdom (Samaria and Jerusalem; Ezek. 23:4), a political context is in view. The picture of a fractured people of God (the Northern and Southern Kingdoms) is addressed by God's gracious promise of the renewing work of His Spirit (chap. 37). Before that work of grace could occur, it was necessary to address their sin. Israel's idolatrous relationship began early in Egypt and carried on throughout their political existence (23:3; cf. 16:23–26; 20:5–8; Ex. 16:1–3; 32; Is. 30–31). Samaria was ultimately forsaken by Egypt, who never had their best interests at heart like their Lord Yahweh did (2 Kin. 17:4).

23:5–10. Samaria and Her Lovers. Samaria's harlotry with Assyria is seen best in its dependence on Assyria to the point of becoming a vassal who paid tribute. The northern kings Menaham (2 Kin. 15:19) and Hoshea (2 Kin. 17:3) operated by sight and not by faith, and they assumed that placating the major world power at the time was the best way to retain their own hold on power (Hos. 5:13; 7:11; 8:9). The political influence on Israel's religious actions stemmed back to the Northern Kingdom's first king, Jeroboam, who was the prototype of covenant failure in kingship (2 Kin. 10:29; 17:21). It is interesting that he tried to connect Israel's worship to Egypt with his idolatrous acts (1 Kin. 11:40; 12:28). The Northern Kingdom's relationship with foreign nations was constantly a subject of criticism by the prophets sent to them (Hos. 8:9; Amos 1–2).

23:11–35. Judah and Her Lovers. While it is hoped that people learn from the mistakes of others, Jerusalem never took any lessons from the destruction of Samaria. In fact, Jerusalem's duplicity seems to have gone far beyond Samaria's (Ezek. 16:47–52). More attention is paid to Judah (Oholibah) for two reasons: (1) she was the only kingdom left when Ezekiel wrote, and was so for over a century; and (2) Judah was the only and last bastion of hope for God's purposes to be carried out through the Davidic dynasty. Isaiah's proclamations of the coming of the Branch from Jesse seemed a distant dream (cf. Is. 11:1). Judah's vacillations between Egypt, Assyria, and Babylon exemplified the existing confusion among the leaders. Even one of Judah's best kings, Hezekiah, was carried along with a folly typical of the northern kings. While still subject to Assyria, Hezekiah accommodated envoys from Babylon, which drew the dismay and rebuke of Isaiah (Ezek. 23:12–18; 2 Kin. 18:14–16; 20:12–13; Is. 39). Though the people of God had been liberated from Egyptian bondage, Egypt continued to be a major influence on the political scene for Judah. Even after the only king prophesied about by name (Josiah) fell to the Egyptians (2 Kin. 23:28–30),

even after Jehoahaz was taken captive to Egypt (2 Kin. 23:31–34), even after having a puppet king placed on the throne and being stripped financially (2 Kin. 23:34–35), Judah still lusted after Egypt for aid (Ezek. 23:19–21). In four oracles of judgment, God explained how Judah would be dismantled: the betrayal of their lovers (vv. 22–27), the economic devastation of agricultural life (vv. 28–31), the international disdain and exile (vv. 32–34), and the necessity for divine retribution to be rendered for their idolatrous ways (v. 35).

23:36–49. This They Have Done to Me. The presence of God departed from the sanctuary in Jerusalem because it had been polluted with Judah's abominations. Child sacrifice is mentioned several times (16:20; 23:37, 39), and it is crucial to ascertain why this was such an abomination, even beyond the murdering of their own children, which was horrifying enough. The law required that every firstborn be given to Yahweh—set apart for Him as a memorial of His redemption in bringing the people out of Egypt. Every male firstborn had to be redeemed by an animal (Ex. 13:12–16; 34:19–20). Unlike Israel, some of the surrounding pagan nations sacrificed their children to their idols (2 Kin. 3:27). It is likely, as the Moabite Stone intimates, that King Mesha used this practice to appease his national god Chemosh, who was angry with his land. The practice is also associated with Molech (Lev. 18:21; 20:2–5). The Judahites may have at times engaged in this practice in an attempt to avert the judgment of God. They may have brought this pagan practice into God's sanctuary, thus making it even more atrocious (Ezek. 23:39) as they rejected God's call to repentance and worsened their situation instead of averting disaster. Furthermore, by duplicating the practices of the nations, Judah may have been seeking to curry acceptance from the surrounding nations, thereby abandoning their distinctive role as a covenant people through whom the nations could seek Yahweh. Sadly, their sons would be killed anyway, this time not to avert a crisis but as part of the crisis (vv. 46–49).

24:1–27

SIEGE OF JERUSALEM

As a pivotal turning point in the book, Ezekiel 24 in a way foreshadows Jerusalem's ultimate destruction because of Judah's constant fracturing of their relationship with God. Yet God's ultimate purpose remained for a redeemed and purified people. While the besiegement of Judah meant the beginning of the end of the Davidic dynasty, it also marked the fulfillment of the Torah's warnings and the fulfillment of the prophecies of a series of preexilic prophets. The effect of suffering included an encouragement to go back to God's word and to ask what went wrong. In the aftermath of the siege, the postexilic prophets conveyed a deeper sense of, and hope in, God's sovereignty as they saw His promises of return and restoration come to fruition.

The siege of Jerusalem would establish trust in what the Lord, Yahweh, had said, which had permeated Ezekiel's proclamations up to that point. Ezekiel's contemporary, Daniel, proclaims an apocalyptic view of history while standing on the shoulders of Ezekiel's eschatological language and focusing on the sanctuary of God, atonement (Ezek. 8–11; 40–48; Dan. 8:14; 9:24–27), the judgment of the nations, and the vindication of the faithful people of God (Ezek. 25–32; 34–37; Dan. 2, 7–8, 10–12). Because of Israel's misplaced trust in a physical structure (Jer. 7:1–4), the destruction of the first temple in a sense paved the way for a temple of greater significance (Matt. 12:6; John 2:19). In Ezekiel's book, the last message before the beginning of the siege divides into two sections: the parable of the boiling pot (Ezek. 24:1–14) and the sign-act of a sudden death (vv. 15–27).

24:1–14
The Boiling Pot and the Siege of Jerusalem

The parable of the boiling pot is told in a poem (vv. 3–5) and is followed by its explanation (vv. 6–14). God commanded Ezekiel to write down the date when the king of Babylon began his siege against Jerusalem (i.e., January 15, 588 B.C.; vv. 1–2). The divine request to date prophetic events was not simply done to satisfy human curiosity but was an announcement of divine foreknowledge and providential sovereignty. It was implicitly a call to submit to the all-powerful and all-knowing majesty of the Creator and Redeemer. Scripture proclaims God as telling the *what* (event) and the *when* (time), but also as being intimately involved in the *how* (process) (cf. Dan. 9:20–23; 10:18–21).

The boiling pot (Ezek. 24:6; Jerusalem) in chapter 11 and the corrosive elements mentioned in 22:18–22 are now combined in a proverb of epic proportions. What was thought of as a metaphor of protection by the princes (11:3, 6–7) here (chap. 24) is turned on its head

by God becoming a purifying cauldron of judgment. In satirical fashion, the cook would put all the good and choice pieces into the pot (cf. 23:7). This is a reference to the political and social elite. Combined with sacrificial language, the unusual use of a copper cauldron (24:11) suggests both a court banquet and a cultic meal. God's interpretation of the parable is twofold. First, Judah's defilement included a disdain for the sanctity of life (vv. 6–8). Their acts of bloodshed (v. 7) are here described as a failure to observe the obligation that respects life, for which the penalty was to be "cut off" and to "bear his iniquity" (Lev. 17:10–16). Second, God is described as the master cook, whose work would bring the needed cleanness (Ezek. 24:9–14). Judah's attempts to purify itself were short-lived and ultimately failed to work the type of purity God called for (e.g., Hezekiah's reforms, 2 Kin. 18; Josiah's reforms, 2 Kin. 22–23).

24:15–27
Ezekiel's Wife a Sign

God informed the prophet Ezekiel that he was going to take away from him the desire or delight of his eyes, but He would not allow any type of visible grief on the prophet's part. There would be no ceremonial mourning rites (v. 17; cf. Lev. 13:45; Mic. 3:7). So Ezekiel's wife died, and noting Ezekiel's past unorthodox actions, the people realized that his response carried some prophetic import. Just as Ezekiel experienced suddenly the death of his wife, so would the sanctuary of God be destroyed suddenly. Just as Ezekiel would not mourn for the loss of his wife, even so the children of Israel were not to be permitted to mourn for the profanation of God's dwelling place or the loss of their spouses and children who would perish during the siege (Ezek. 24:15–24). This was not a typical situation that would elicit the typical responses to death. During the long trek to Babylon from Jerusalem, the survivors would confirm the veracity of the prophetic message.

25:1—32:32
ORACLES AGAINST THE NATIONS

The oracles against Judah's surrounding neighbors start in the upper Transjordan area in the northeast and move southward and then westward toward the coastal regions: northeast (Ammon), east (Moab), southeast (Edom), and southwest (Philistia). All nations addressed in chapter 25 denote small, local nation-states whose power and influence was typically exerted within their geographical boundaries and who in some way took advantage of Judah's misfortune. Sporadically they formed alliances and fought against God's people (2 Sam. 8; 2 Kin. 24:2). Ezekiel proclaims a series of three oracles in chapters 26–28 against Phoenicia (Tyre and Sidon, powerful city-states), Israel's neighbor situated in the northwest. He rounds out his oracles in chapters 29–32 against Egypt. The oracles against Tyre/Sidon and Egypt follow a similar pattern of prophecy (chaps. 26, 29) and lament (chaps. 27, 30), followed by another prophecy (chaps. 28, 31). The oracles against the nations have a common format that shares a varied form of four or five elements between them (here there are four):

- Messenger formula—God's declaration
- Indictment of the wrong committed
- Verdict of God's judgment
- Purpose of revealing God

It is unknown whether these oracles were actually sent to the nations they critique. For Judah, the literary placement of these oracles between the commencement of the siege (chap. 24) and its completion (chap. 33) served several instructive purposes. First, these prophecies pointed to God's sovereignty over the nations. Created in the image of God, all humans share ethical norms and are accountable to Him. The law codes of Israel's neighbors indicate that in many cases they had judicial, social, and cultural mores similar to those of Israel. So the lawsuits against the nations are based on a basic code of ethics (cf. Amos 1–2). Second, the prophecies also served as a warning to Judah: (1) not to trust in the human devices of military strength or political acumen because they too receive the judgment of God, and (2) that though Judah was His elect people, God is no respecter of persons; if Judah was acting like the surrounding nations, it would experience the same judgment. According to Jeremiah 27, with the exception of Egypt, which is mentioned later in the book, these nations would be given over to Babylonian control by God's decree.

25:1–17
Ammon, Moab, Seir, Edom, and Philistia

Typically grouped together in the prophets, the first several nations mentioned can be seen as extended familial states that engaged in unending conflicts with Israel (Ps. 60:8; Jer. 9:25–26). First, Ammon (Ezek. 25:2–7) was born to Lot, Abraham's nephew, through an incestuous encounter (Gen. 19:30–38). His ancestor's historical interaction with Abraham's descendants was marked with squabbles over land and economic interests (Judg. 10–11; 1 Sam. 11; 2 Sam. 10; Jer. 49:1–6). Ammon's pagan influence and attitude toward God's sanctuary, land, and kingship (Ezek. 25:3) were part of the reason for Josiah's efforts to remove the holy places dedicated to Ammonite idols (2 Kin. 23:13). In Ezekiel 21:19–20 a signpost marked Nebuchadnezzar's decision to move his invading army first against Judah. Ezekiel 25:1–7 expands on 21:28–29, alerting Ammon not to gloat over its assumed escape because judgment was on its way. True to his warning, God turned the capital city and center of Ammon's economic activity (Rabbah) into a pastureland; it was largely depopulated, with many of its people displaced. Nebuchadnezzar's punitive campaign, around 582 B.C., stopped Ammon from functioning as an independent polity.

The ancestors of Ammon's brother Moab (Ezek. 25:8–11) had a history of conflicts with Israel (Judg. 3:12–20; 2 Kin. 3), but also a history connected with Israel's kingship (Ruth 4:13–18; Matt. 1:5). Solomon's introduction of Moabite religion into Israel near Jerusalem (1 Kin. 11:7, 33; 2 Kin. 23:13) established a pattern of syncretism in the political activity of the kings of Judah and Israel, leading Moab and others to assume Israel was just another small nation-state (Ezek. 25:8, cf. Is. 37:8–13). However, God would show the Moabites that despite Judah's failures, their God was Lord of all (cf. Is. 15:1). Through a series of providential events, Moab would be open to invasion. All three cities, Beth Jeshimoth, Baal Meon, and Kiri[j]athaim were along Moab's western line of defense. Like Israel, Moab would be the recipient of the execution of divine judgment (Ezek. 5:15; 11:9; 16:41).

The perpetual enemy of Israel, Edom (25:12–14; Is. 34) consisted of the descendants of Jacob's brother, Esau (Gen. 25:19–30). Edom's duplicity was exposed as it initially joined the conspiracy against Nebuchadnezzar (Jer. 27:3) but then took advantage of Judah's weakened state as a result of the Babylonian invasions. In poetic justice, the vengeance that Edom took against Judah would be met with divine vengeance through Israel at some future time (Ezek. 25:14). This promise provided Israel with the hope of a restored kingdom as God's elect (God referring to them as "My people"). God declared that Edom would know His vengeance (v. 14), with a biblical principle of retribution at work (cf. Obad. 15). Since the language used in the message against the Philistines is similar to that of Edom, the inclusion of the Philistines stems from its similar interaction with Judah.

26:1–21
Tyre and the Judgment of God

The oracles against Tyre ("rock," cf. v. 4) are divided into four sections introduced by the messenger formula: the announcement of Tyre's destruction (vv. 1–6), the agent of Tyre's destruction (vv. 7–14), the impact of Tyre's destruction (vv. 15–18), and the aftermath of Tyre's destruction (vv. 19–21). As a major commercial merchant and occasional ally to Israel, Tyre's lucrative exchanges with Israel (2 Sam. 5:11–12; 1 Kin. 5:1; 9:26–28; 10:11–12) showed signs of deterioration as Egyptian, Assyrian, and Babylonian hegemony shifted throughout the ancient Near East. The anticipation of a fortuitous plundering of Israel—the gateway to the nations/peoples (Ezek. 26:2)—during the besiegement (v. 1) indicates how Tyre traded in on power politics through subterfuge that would ultimately lead to an astonishing lament (vv. 15–18). Foreshadowing later descriptions, Tyre's duplicity, indifference, and deception based on its commercial affluence portrays a historical archetype and a foreshadowing of subsequent theological use (see chap. 28).

The proclamation of judgment and its fulfillment bring to light the different emphases of the two types of prophecy. Though it uses eschatological language when it comes to the judgment of the nations, classical prophecy, unlike the apocalyptic prophecies of Daniel and Revelation, is typically focused within the immediate timeframe and circumstances of the prophet, or soon thereafter. Tyre's destruction is described as the result of the attacks of many nations (26:3, 5). However, only Nebuchadnezzar is mentioned by name (v. 7). His siege from 585 to 572 B.C. cut the major supply lines to the island and devastated Tyre's mainland satellite cities (vv. 6, 8), but not the island proper (29:17–20). Historians affirm that it was Alexander the Great in 332 B.C. who penetrated Tyre's defenses on the island and finally incapacitated it. While giving a nod to its eventual captors (26:4–5, 12–13), the focus of the prophecy is on the judgment of this commercial juggernaut and Babylon as God's agent in judgment. Elements from its final

destruction are mixed with historical elements from Nebuchadnezzar's siege.

Two important points of interpretation for classical prophecy are: (1) the literary placement and the theological description of events, and (2) the historical fulfillment within the context of God's merciful warnings, His providential acts, and a nation's response (cf. Jer. 18:1–11; Jon. 1–4). By devoting three chapters to the description of Tyre's judgment, Ezekiel sets the literary scene for the judgment of the anointed cherub in 28:10–19. Historically, when Judah was besieged and finally fell, only Tyre and Egypt still offered resistance to Babylon. Thus, it is understandable that the larger focus is on these nations in comparison with the others in chapter 25.

27:1–36
Tyre: A City Shipwrecked

Continuing the lament (Heb. *qinah*, term for a dirge sung at the death of a person or city; cf. 19:1) from 26:17–21, Ezekiel increases the metaphorical weight of Tyre's self-confidence, affluence, and excess that provides the language and themes upon which the anointed cherub will be paralleled in the next chapter. In a catalog of nations (27:12–24) couched between two laments (vv. 4–11, 25–36), the key Hebrew verb *rakal* ("to trade" or "to gossip" in its participial form; translated as "the trading ones" or "merchants" in vv. 3, 13, 15, 17, 20, 22, 23, 24)—provides the context for the litany of Tyre's international reach in commerce. Some of the nations mentioned (Greece [Javan], Tubal, Meshech [Meshek], Togarmah, Dedan, Uzal, Canneh [Kanneh], Sheba, Asshur [Ashur], vv. 12–27) appear in the Table of Nations in Genesis 10. The use of Tyre's king as an archetype is thus based on its international reach, its commercial trade among the powerful, and its connection back to a time of worldwide diffusion of nations.

The lament satirizes Tyre metaphorically as a ship (Ezek. 27:4). This is an apt metaphor for a maritime power with two major sea ports that served as a trader for the Mediterranean world and transported commodities throughout the ancient Near East. By underscoring the highest-quality materials (vv. 5–7) and the skilled crew (vv. 8–11), Tyre's commercial ability, efficiency in trade, and prominence among its peers is revealed. The impressive networking among the nations (v. 10; Persia, Lydia, and Put [or Libya]; i.e., Iran, Turkey, and Egypt) signifies the farthest parts of the known world that were within its reach. The scope of its business, ranging from the domestic (food, animals, and slaves) to the royal (precious stones, war implements, elegant palace wares) left no aspect of life untouched (vv. 12–25). In poetic style, its massive shipwreck (v. 26) is described in the most catastrophic terms. All that made its value formidable was destroyed not by war, intrigue, or a loss in vitality or skill but by the providential hand of God in the "east wind." The east wind represents a sign of judgment, and in scriptural accounts God is typically the agent who brings it (Gen. 41:6; Ex. 10:13; Ps. 48:7; Is. 27:8; Jer. 18:17). Tyre's demise would cause confusion as well as dismay (Ezek. 27:28–32). Tyre is said to have provided the accoutrements and allurements of wealth and ease, but they would be like scattered pieces of wood on the sea. What made Tyre great was what ultimately led to its demise. One more vivid picture is relayed before the central issue of the book is reached: the cosmic conflict—its actors, its plotline, and its finale.

28:1–10
Tyre and the Prince

The indictment and judgment of the human ruler (Ithbaal), the prince or ruler (Heb. *nagid*; 1 Sam. 9:16) of Tyre, is summarized here, harking back to Adam and Eve's fall—the attempt to be God (Ezek. 28:2; Gen. 3:6). The main issue of their sin was their attempt to claim divinity and independence from God. Eve took upon herself the prerogatives of God's sovereignty (cf. Gen. 1:10, 12, 18, 21, 25, 31: "and God saw that it was good"; and Gen. 3:6: "and the woman saw that the fruit [that God had forbidden] was good"). This resulted in Eve making judgments in the place of divine providence: seeing the food as (1) "good" to eat, (2) pleasing to her eyes, and (3) something desirable for wisdom (Gen. 3:6). The Lord God had already made provision for these in His gift of what He deemed good (Gen. 2:9). God intended life, but humans desired autonomy, which usually leads to unintended negative consequences (Prov. 14:12). The prince of Tyre took up the same quest and met with the same reminder of human limits (Ezek. 28:2; cf. Gen. 3:17–19). His acquisition of wealth was not in accordance with God's desire (Ezek. 28:4; Prov. 16:16; Zech. 9:2–4). Instead of seeking to reflect the image of God in obedience, mercy, love, and justice (Deut. 10:12–13), his accrual of wealth was intended to reflect his aspirations for divinity (Ezek. 28:6).

God promised to bring Babylon against Tyre (v. 7; see also 26:7; 30:10, 11; 31:12).

28:11–19
Tyre and the Judgment on the Fallen Cherub

Ezekiel shifts the focus to the king of Tyre. This subtle shift from "prince/ruler" (Heb. *nagid*) to "king" (Heb. *melek*; vv. 2, 12) perhaps suggests someone more prominent being in view beyond the earthly ruler who was just addressed. Although one can detect some linguistic parallels with the narrative of Adam and Eve, the background of the passage is more sinister. In describing the activities of the King of Tyre, the language and experience of the fall of a heavenly cherub is used in Ezekiel's account and consequently provides important information related to the origin of evil. The king/cherub is described in three ways. (1) He was the seal (Heb. *khotem* from the verb *khatam* could also mean "the one who seals") of perfection. This king is compared to a perfectly designed seal, probably in order to indicate that he possessed influence and authority (see Is.14:12; cf. Ps. 104:2). Also, (2) he was full of wisdom and (3) perfect in beauty, a description that suggests he had inner and external beauty (Ezek. 28:4, 5, 7). This being, who had a symmetry of character ("perfect" or "blameless," v. 15; cf. Gen. 6:9) and appearance, was in close proximity to God and was consequently respected by others. His beauty, wisdom, capabilities, and previous access to the heavenly abode would have made him a formidable foe. Ezekiel's description was a warning not to underestimate him (see 2 Cor. 11:14; 1 Pet. 5:8).

The precious stones in the list (Ezek. 28:13) are similar to the precious stones on the priestly vestment (Ex. 28:17–20) but not exactly the same. The primary function of the precious stones is probably to identify the person as a royal figure. The Hebrew text could be read as indicating that the cherub was wearing the stones or that the stones were part of the fence of the Garden of God. Contextually, it may be better to see them as part of the dress of the cherub. This anointed cherub (Ezek. 28:14), like the cherubim mentioned earlier in 1:4–14 and 10:1–22, was a throne guardian with a doxological function. The meaning of the Hebrew words *top* and *neqeb* (v. 13) in the context of this passage is not clear. If the reference is to musical instruments ("tambourine" [Ex. 15:20; Ps. 149:3] and "pipe" or "flute"), the implication would be that the cherub was also a musician. Other options are to see these terms as referring to "settings" and "mountings" or "sockets" for precious jewels, or "pendants" and "engravings" themselves. Moreover, the presence of this cherub in the heavenly holy mountain of God suggests a cosmic focus (Ezek. 28:14). All told, the connection of royal and religious prerogatives with his anointed status indicates that this cherub had an exalted position over the other cherubim in heaven. In the earthly sanctuary, there were two covering or guarding cherubs (Ex. 25:18–22), so this angel (Ezek. 28:14) dwelt in the very presence of God.

The moral descent of this heavenly being to wickedness is incomprehensible. One thing is clear, namely, that he was a creature (vv. 13, 15). Evil originated not in God but in a creature. Moses states that the serpent, whom NT writers later identified as Satan (Gen. 3:1; Rom. 16:20; 2 Cor. 11:14; Rev. 12:9; 20:2), was created, yet by sophistry and subtlety it deceived Eve. Like Tyre, this powerful angel was successful in trafficking (Ezek. 27:3; 28:5, 16, 18), albeit in iniquitous acts that generated violence (28:16; Heb. *khamas*, "malicious intent"; cf. Ex. 23:1) and sin. The notion of trafficking pictures a trader in wares going back and forth, plying his trade with skillful artistry to enrich himself in some way (see below, "Evil and the Fallen Cherub"). In comparison with the prince who gained wealth, the anointed cherub applied his wisdom to traffic in a pursuit of praise and worship on account of his splendor and beauty (v. 17). Yet like Israel, he corrupted himself on account of pride (cf. 16:47; 20:44; 23:11). Just as Israel's iniquity profaned (24:21) God's sanctuary, so the cherub corrupted his sanctuaries (v. 18; some manuscripts have the singular "sanctuary"), which presumably could refer to himself as the object of God's holiness or perhaps to his profanation of God's dwelling (v. 18). This was redressed by his expulsion from it. Like Tyre, all would be appalled that one so blessed of God could rebel and come to such an inglorious end (v. 19; see also 27:36).

The nature of Satan's sin can be better apprehended through the many linguistic parallels that the text has with the Flood narrative (Gen. 6). This narrative has been understood as a reversal of creation. Humanity corrupted itself in rebellion against God, so did Satan (Gen 6:11). The earth was filled with violence, so was Satan (Gen. 6:11). Noah was blameless and walked with God, at one point so did Satan (Gen. 6:9). Just as the implications of the Flood were universal, so also are the implications for the destruction of this anointed cherub.

Evil and the Fallen Cherub

It would be useful for a clearer comprehension of the topic to summarize the origin of evil in a fallen cherub as depicted in Ezekiel 28 and Isaiah 14. In both passages the activities of two earthly kings (Tyre and Babylon) are described using the experience of the fall of a majestic cherub. It is here that we find the origin of the cosmic conflict.

1. A Heavenly Creature. The cherub was not a self-existing being but a creature (Ezek. 28:15). This is important when we discuss the nature of evil itself. It first indicates that sin and evil are not eternal, parallel phenomena, coexisting with God as the source of what is good. Second, it shows that evil did not originate in God but in one of His creatures. God is not responsible for sin because free creatures are responsible for their own actions. Finally, the fact that the cherub was a created being speaks about its finitude. Its existence can and will come to an end (Rev. 21:1–4).

2. A Covering Cherub. The idea of covering cherubim is found in the setting of the sanctuary with the making of the two golden cherubim placed on each end of the cover of the ark of the covenant and looking down toward the place where the glory of God was manifested (Ex. 25:20; 37:9). They represented the heavenly beings who were worshiping God in the heavenly temple. The living cherub of Ezekiel was the one located in closest proximity to God. Therefore, he must have been influential among the angels. This position of honor had been assigned to him by God. The language of Ezekiel 28:14 could be translated as "I ordained/appointed you." He seems to have been exercising an important leadership position.

3. A Blameless Cherub. God describes this cherub as being perfect in his ways since the day he was created (Ezek. 28:15). This is about both his inner being and his outward appearance. When God created him, there was nothing wrong with him. The Hebrew noun *tamim* ("perfect") refers to someone who is as complete as God intended him or her to be. Through his actions, the cherub contributed to the preservation of order within the cosmos. This is something that God himself does because "His way is perfect" (2 Sam. 22:31). When applied to humans, *tamim* designates a person who walks according to the law of God (Ps. 119:1) and who consequently has access to God's dwelling (Ps. 15:2). This is the person who does what is right. The least we can say about the perfection of the cherub is that he lived in submission to God's will for him and the rest of His creation. In other words, there was once a perfect harmony between him and God.

4. *Wickedness in the Cherub*. The origin of evil is and will remain a mystery because it lacks a reason for its appearance. The cherub was "perfect" in his ways until sin was found in him (Ezek. 28:15). The biblical text makes clear that God created a blameless cherub, but God does not assume responsibility for his wickedness—an unexpected phenomenon was found in him. This was not the way God created him. The verb *matsa'* ("to be found") is often used in legal contexts to indicate that what was found was the result of a judicial process (e.g., Esth. 2:23; Ps. 17:3). It is implied here that the strange behavior of the cherub was legally examined—he went through a judicial process—and it was determined that his behavior did not correspond to what was expected from him but that he was disrupting the harmony of heaven. The judicial process established that there was wickedness in him. Evil became his natural disposition.

5. *A Proud Heart*. Something strange happened in the inner being of the cherub—something that was related to pride. This is the desire to be high and exalted, to see oneself as better and superior to others. He tried to justify this experience in view of his beauty and splendor (Ezek. 28:17). Because of his pride, the wisdom of the cherub was corrupted or permanently ruined. But behind all of this was a deeper yearning in the heart of the cherub: he wanted to be like God (Is. 14:13). This is what is meant when the text says that the cherub desired to be exalted. The conflict was between the cherub and God. His person was recentralized and at its center was placed hubris—his own ego. He was claiming total independence (i.e., self-sufficiency) from God. He was able to persuade a number of angels and finally Adam and Eve to join his rebellion (Gen. 3:1–8).

6. *Trade and Violence*. Ezekiel describes the cherub as involved in trade (*rekullah*) that filled him with violence and resulted in sin (Ezek. 28:16). He was a merchant who, in the context of the passage, was trading a spirit of rebellion. This suggests that other heavenly beings were listening to him. The root meaning of the term *rekullah* (related to the verb *rakil*, "to slander") designates a person who walks about like a merchant seeking to sell merchandise. The cherub was distributing what he considered to be his goods, but what he was really doing was slandering God, and the result was violence in heaven. This violence probably expressed itself in false accusations, influencing others to do likewise, and even self-aggrandizement. The cherub was upsetting God's established order and damaging the quality of life for himself and others. The conflict was now in the open, and there was war in heaven (Rev. 12:7)—a war that continued on earth after the fall of Adam and Eve and that would be resolved through the cross of Christ. (For a significant discussion of the origin of sin in the writings of Ellen White, see 1SP, 17–24; PP 33–43, and GC 492–504.)

28:20–26
Oracles against the Nations (Sidon)

The oracle against Sidon almost seems like an addendum, yet it reinforces the conviction that the cosmic judgment of the anointed cherub is the paradigm for understanding the local judgment against the wicked. It also buttresses God's sovereignty over the universe and gave Israel the hope that their King to defeat their enemies, sin, and the nations. While the format follows that of the briefer oracles against the nations in 25:1–17, Sidon's judgment is mainly framed as a reversal of Israel's fortunes (cf. 5:17). God's glory and holiness would be displayed as Sidon became a pawn in the fight of the major powers of the ancient Near East and could no longer obstruct Israel's growth (28:22–24, cf. 1 Kin. 16:29—22:40). The future "gathering" prophecies reflect not only a return to the land but a return to holiness and God's covenant relationship with Israel (Ezek. 28:25–26; cf. 11:16–17; 20:34; 34:12; Deut. 6:10–11).

29:1—32:32
The Fall of Egypt

The seventh nation, Egypt, received pronouncements of doom in a sequence of seven oracles, mainly dated to around the time of the fall of Judah (29:1, 17; 30:1, 20; 31:1; 32:1, 17). Chapters 29–32 prophesy Egypt's destruction in relation to God, Babylon, and Assyria. First, 29:1–16 describes Egypt's fall because of its hubris toward God. Second, vv. 17–20 and 30:20–26 describe Egypt's fall to Babylon with a lament (vv. 1–19). Third, 31:1–18 compares Egypt's fall to Assyria's fall and is followed by another lament (chap. 32).

29:1–21. The Great Dragon Pharaoh. Escaping Assyrian control only to face a new menace in the Babylonian Empire during the Saite Period (Twenty-Sixth Dynasty), Egypt continued to pose a formidable counterpart to the major powers east of Israel. Shortly after the ascension of the Egyptian Pharaoh Hophra (Apries, 589–570 B.C.), Ezekiel was given two oracles concerning the arrogance and pride of Egypt that mark a year into the siege of Judah (vv. 1–16; ca. 587 B.C.) and probably the end of his ministry (vv. 17–21; ca. 571 B.C.). The *tannin* (variously translated as "crocodile," "dragon," or "monster") reflects Egypt's crocodile cults that were associated with the divine ruler. For Israel, it was the embodiment of a mysterious evil (Is. 51:9–10). God showed His sovereignty over all of creation and predicted that Pharaoh Hophra would be destroyed by the "sword" (i.e., by military might; Ezek. 29:8; cf. Jer. 37:7; 44:30); this destruction is also described as a hunt (Ezek. 29:4–5).

The conventional language of forty years (i.e., a generation) reminded Judah of Israel's wilderness wanderings (v. 11; Deut. 1:6—3:29) and the time of judgment described earlier (Ezek. 4:6). Judgment for Egypt meant that there was no second option for Judah. Initially, before the siege, King Zedekiah ill-advisedly requested help from Egypt (17:11–21), and subsequently God's word came to pass and Pharaoh Hophra, in a twist of irony, had to flee Egypt when a rebellion broke out against him. He was later defeated by Amasis, his own general. After Nebuchadnezzar

despoiled Egypt's wealth, the subsequent domination of Egypt by the Persians and the Greeks affirmed God's omniscient promise (29:15). The first oracle closes on a note of hope in a restored horn (v. 21), a token of power whose symbolism likely points to the restoration of a faithful Davidic kingship through the Messiah, which is developed further along in chapter 34 (cf. Ps. 132:17). Those who lived through the Exile and its aftermath would see Zedekiah's folly in trusting in even the most promising human power, and they would realize that God indeed declares the end from the beginning and brings His word to pass (Is. 46:10–11).

30:1–26. Alas for the Day. In two more oracles, Ezekiel lays out a dateless lament with prophetic elements (vv. 1–19) followed by a dated prophecy about the weakness of Egypt on the world scene (vv. 20–26). In the first oracle, there is an announcement (vv. 1–5), its consequences (vv. 6–9), a description of God's agent (vv. 10–12), and a summary of judgment (vv. 13–19). In language similar to the Day of Yahweh motif in other prophetic books (i.e., clouds or thick darkness; Joel 2:2; Zeph. 1:15), Egypt was called on to wail (Ezek. 30:2), for God's judgment through warfare ("sword," v. 4; cf. 7:1–27) would encompass the entire land of Egypt (Migdol to Syene, 30:6) and devastate Egypt's economic and military infrastructures (vv. 4–10). Military treaties, paid mercenaries, and trade usually sustained cordial relationships between nations (Jer. 46:9), but now Egypt and its allies would no longer present an option for Israel's faithless overtures. Nebuchadnezzar would take the resources that enabled Egypt to remain a superpower for so long: land and money. After the Saite Dynasty (664–525 B.C.), Egypt was controlled by a succession of foreign empires. The country was annexed by Cambyses of Persia (525 B.C.), then by Alexander the Great (332 B.C.), and finally by Rome (30 B.C.). The litany of toponyms (place names) emphasizes how God's judgment would affect all the major links in Egyptian life, especially its geographically significant areas and well-known religious centers, and this would prevent coordinated coalitions and cultural solidarity.

In the second oracle (Ezek. 30:20–26), God proclaimed that He had broken Egypt's military might (to "break the arm" indicates the removal of power; cf. Job 38:15; Pss. 10:15; 37:17; Jer. 48:25) and thus frustrated its attempts to intervene in the affairs of Judah. In contrast to the pharaonic art of the period, which featured a strong arm with a raised sword, Ezekiel describes the pharaoh (representing Egypt's military power) with an unattended broken arm that could not hold a sword (Ezek. 30:21). Egypt's strength would atrophy and become incapacitated, limping on for about four decades, until its eventual dispersal amongst the nations (v. 23). The cascade of first-person verbs emphasizes God's providential leading over the movement of history and thus affirms the dream and its interpretation that God gave to king Nebuchadnezzar (vv. 24–25; Dan. 2:1–45). The message to Judah was clear: hope in Egypt's help was fool's gold. After the destruction of Jerusalem, God would send a catastrophe against those people of Judah who had fled to many of the cities mentioned here and were astonishingly engaging in many of the same idolatrous practices that landed them in those places to begin with. By this they would learn the lesson that God's holiness is not confined to one geographical place because He is sovereign over the world (Ezek. 30:19; Jer. 44:1–11).

31:1–18. Fall of a Great Tree. Using a familiar ANE motif of a great tree (vv. 2–9) in his fifth oracle two months later, Ezekiel points to Assyria (v. 3) as a historical lesson for Egypt and for the people of God. Assyria exercised hegemony over such a vast empire and impacted almost every nation by its power. Yet the prophet Isaiah had earlier prophesied that God would hew down Assyria (Is. 10:5–19). Egypt's fruitless attempts to help Assyria against Babylon ended in Assyria's destruction and Egypt's isolation (2 Kin. 24:1–7). Egypt's likeness can be found in Assyria (Ezek. 31:3). The message for the people of God was clear: if in prophetic fulfillment Assyria was broken by the mighty hand of God because of its pride, Egypt's fate would be assured (vv. 10–14) and Judah's folly would be exposed. For over a century, Assyria's fall (Is.10:5–19), Babylon's ascendancy and judgment (Is. 13:1–22), and finally, Persia's rise (Is. 13:17; 44:24—45:13) had been foretold. Yet Judah still trusted in Egypt's power to deliver. Isaiah, Ezekiel, and Daniel describe the rise and fall of nations to show that the prophetic word had and would come to fruition. God took responsibility for Egypt's demise (Ezek. 31:15–18), and despite human strategies and plans, His judgments carried worldwide significance (v. 16).

32:1–32. Requiem for a Funeral. This prophecy revisits many of the prophetic elements of Egypt's demise as announced two years earlier in chapter 29. Ezekiel was instructed to lift up a lament (32:1–16) over Egypt's descent to the grave with its allies (vv. 17–32). In these last two sayings, dated two months after Jerusalem's fall (vv. 1, 17; cf. 33:21), his funeral dirge blends apocalyptic language, familiar cosmic motifs, and prophetic proclamations as he details the fulfillment of God's victory over Egypt. Suffering from an apparently pride-induced identity crisis, the self-styled lion is described by the Lord as little more than a crocodile (or sea dragon, 29:3) churning up water by thrashing around (32:2). God's providential sovereignty (v. 3; 12:13; Hos. 7:12) among the nations had reduced Egypt to a feast for scavengers (Ezek. 32:3–6).

God's people would be reminded of His victory over Egypt during the Exodus through the language of judgment and the "Day of the Lord" imagery: the land covered in blood, and the darkening of the sun, stars, moon, and land (vv. 7–8; cf. Ex. 7:14–24; 10:21–23; Is. 13:9–11; Amos 8:9). John the Revelator draws together all these themes of judgment in his description of prophetic events throughout Christian history (Rev. 6:12–13; 8:12). God reminded His people that He determines the destiny of nations when He again identified Nebuchadnezzar as His agent of divine judgment (Ezek. 32:11–15; cf. 29:18–19; 30:10, 24–25). Ezekiel proceeds to show how Babylon's destruction of Egypt had shifted international relations. In highly repetitive and formulaic language, each nation is described as languishing in the grave (Heb. *she'ol*) as victims of Babylon's might. Its reach crossed the then-known world and encompassed a formidable force made up of the temperamental allies of Egypt and Judah (Assyria, Elam, Meshech-Tubal [Anatolia], Edom, the princes of the north [Syria], and Sidon [Phoenicia]). Ezekiel emphasizes that these nations are uncircumcised (32:32), which means they were not in a covenant relationship with God. Judah had failed to carry their mission to the nations. They had not demonstrated the faith of David, who trusted in the living God (1 Sam. 17:26). Instead, they trusted in failed states that were destined for judgment and death. The coming of the Davidic Shepherd would provide hope to those choosing to believe His word (Ezek. 34; Rev. 14:1–5; 22:16).

33:1–33

JERUSALEM FALLS

The interlude of the cosmic conflict between God and Satan depicted in the oracles against the nations places the announcement of the fall of Jerusalem in perspective (Ezek. 24:1–26). Behind the nations' and Israel's idolatrous ways stood a powerful angel striving to usurp the sovereignty of God by obliterating His image through various means. Israel's special status as the people of God had not made them immune to the machinations of the proud cherub. Chapter 33 goes back to events in Jerusalem that focus on the justice of God, a pivotal issue in the conflict. The evidence of God's justice had been presented by Ezekiel and the preceding prophets, yet God's people remained stubborn and rebellious. As the warnings from all the previous prophetic oracles would be fulfilled in the fall of Jerusalem, the foundation for a restored remnant is being laid.

33:1–20
The Watchman and the Justice of God

God encouraged Ezekiel to faithfully carry out his mission as a watchman for the house/people of Israel (v. 7). His role as a watchman (vv. 2–9) is a repetition and intensification of 3:17–19. The responsibility of the people is almost a repetition of 18:21–32. The recurrence of these themes points to a crucial aspect of the cosmic conflict, namely, that the God of judgment and the God of salvation are one and the same and the message is the same. There are no such things as the OT God of vengeance and judgment and the NT God of love and mercy. In fact, God reinforced His unswerving compassion, declaring that He does not take pleasure in the death of the wicked and desperately wants people to turn to Him in faith (33:11; see also 18:21–24). In chapters 3 and 18 the messages pointed toward Judah's judgment, and now the same messages point to their—and by extension to humanity's—hope.

33:21–33
Fall of Jerusalem

Though the city was captured (Heb. *hukketah*, "is struck down") in 586 B.C. and the people were dismayed at the destruction of their homes and place of worship, salvation was still available. The present orientation of a person's life is what matters to God. He desires that the wicked repent and return to faith in Him, trusting completely in Him. Yet, the people continued to question the fairness of God because of their suffering (vv. 17, 20; 18:25, 29). But the Lord clarified that they would be judged according to their ways because their works testified to their faith or lack of it (v. 20; cf. James 2:24). The people focused on the quantity of their number rather than the quality of their faith; they lived in continual disobedience to God's revealed will (Ezek. 33:24–26). They epitomized those who hear the blast of the trumpet but do not heed the warning (vv. 4, 31–33).

Two years had passed between the announcement of the siege and the actual fall, so plenty of time was given (1) to see the folly of dependence on Egypt, (2) to recognize the fulfillment of God's previous warnings, and (3) to respond to God's overtures of grace and mercy. Ezekiel's mouth was loosened to begin his pastoral ministry of restoration, focusing on the messianic hope, restoration of Israel, and judgment of the confederacy of evil. Israel might yet live a renewed life in safety. Ezekiel repeats several of Israel's abominations regarding the land, the people, the king, and the temple (see chaps. 5–24), but then he begins to shift toward how God will bring restoration in all these areas (chaps. 34–48).

34:1—39:29
ORACLES OF RESTORATION

In a series of oracles, God's messages now would convey hope—the hope of resurrection and restoration. Before the restoration of the temple and the land, Ezekiel set forth the ultimate basis of hope: the Messianic Davidic King. His rulership must be restored in the hearts of the people or else the restoration of the temple, land, and even the destruction of Israel's enemies would only be an external window dressing. God's purpose is to restore His image in human beings. The rulership of His chosen King pointed to a reign beyond a simple restored political rule. Like Hezekiah and Josiah, this new Davidic King would restore the covenant with God's people, but His reign would also reach and change the human heart.

34:1–31
Restored Covenant and Messianic Hope

Now that God had pointed out what a just society is—one governed by justice and righteousness—He began to establish how that society would come to be. First, godly leadership would reign at the heart of His ordered society. Ezekiel spent much time exposing the problem of leadership. In a language and theme similar to Jeremiah 23, Ezekiel's last woe message uses a familiar ANE metaphor of leaders as shepherds and the community as a flock (sheep). The leaders had been exploiting the people (Ezek. 34:3) through political, economic, and religious manipulation and deception. In a series of six indictments (v. 4) the leaders are exposed and shown to be preying on the people for personal benefit. They were not showing the sacrificial care for God's people that was expected from them (Deut. 15:7, 11). The announcement of the Exile due to the lack of a true shepherd (Ezek. 34:5, 6, 12, 21; Deut. 4:27) points to a string of unfaithful kings, despite the bright spots of Hezekiah and Josiah. God proclaimed through Jeremiah that because of Manasseh's wickedness, Exile would come to Judah (Jer. 15:4; cf. 2 Kin. 21:9).

God's ministry of restoration encompassed care for the vulnerable, weak sheep and judgment on the callous, selfish leaders. While judgment was often brought through the nations during Israel's long history, redemption was only brought through God's specially chosen leader. In the redemption of Israel, it was Moses; in the establishment of Israel's dynastic kingship, it was David; in Israel's return from exile, it was Ezra and then Nehemiah. The promise of the seed (Gen. 3:15) would be fulfilled, but He would not entrust His restoration project to another king of the current line of the kings of Judah. Though glimmers of hope rested on King Jehoiachin's grandson (Hag. 1:1; Ezra 3:2; cf. Matt. 1:12; Luke 3:37), and in a twist of irony even Cyrus is referred to as God's shepherd (Is. 44:28), the promise of the messianic hope found no fulfillment prior to the first century B.C. The promised shepherd is designated as the Lord's Shepherd (Ezek. 34:23–24; Is. 42:1), and He would be of Davidic lineage (Ezek. 34:23; cf. Is. 11:1). Combining language from Ezekiel 34 and Psalm 23, Jesus pointed to Himself and His ministry as the fulfillment of all of Israel's hopes (John 10:11–21). His statement in John 10:8 alludes to Ezekiel 34:2–4—those who came before Him were thieves and robbers. He stated that He would separate the nations as a shepherd separates sheep and goats in His work of judgment (v. 17; Matt. 25:32–33). Scripture presents Jesus's work as one of restoration (Ezek. 34:25, 30–31; Mark 14:22–26; Rev. 21:3–4). The prophets testified to the work of the promised shepherd, and Jesus showed in word and deed that He alone fulfilled all messianic expectations; in Him alone one flock would be gathered (Ezek. 34:23; cf. Num. 27:17; Mic. 2:12–13; Matt. 9:36; John 10:3). His establishment of

the covenant promises of a restored land, safety, and blessing reached beyond the temporal borders of Israel and, as the NT writers explain, pointed to a universal application for a new heaven and new earth, a heavenly Jerusalem, and eternal safety and blessing (2 Cor. 1:19–20; Heb. 12:18–24; Rev. 7:9–17; 21:1–5).

35:1—36:38
Two Mountains, Yahweh's Land, and Honor Restored

When read without the standard versification of most Bibles, it becomes readily apparent that 35:1–15 and 36:1–15 are parallel texts that should be read together. The reference to the mountains of Israel (35:12) provides a clue for comparing the links between these oracles. This is followed by the renewal of the people (36:18–38) and the announcement of the resurrection of the nation (37:1–28), and it concludes with the failure of the final attack of the nations against God's people (38:1—39:29).

35:1—36:15. Mountains. This is the story of two mountains, Mount Seir (Edom) and the mountains of Israel (35:2; 36:1). Ezekiel 35:1–15 proclaims judgment on Mount Seir, and Ezekiel 36:1–15 proclaims salvation to the mountains of Israel. The comparisons in these chapters resonate with the proclamations about Esau and Jacob (Gen. 25:19–28), who over time spiraled into conflict (see Ezek. 25:12–14). The prophets Amos and Obadiah, and later also Malachi, depict this tension of brothers (Amos 1:9; Obad. 10–12; Mal. 1:2–5). In these passages Edom seems to play a symbolic role as the representative of all the nations of the earth (see commentary on Obadiah). Just as in Rebekah's womb two nations struggled, the stress in Ezekiel is on the struggle between the righteous and the wicked. When Israel was unfaithful, their lot was thrown in with the noncovenant peoples. Paul picked up on God's words toward Esau (Ezek. 35:3) and toward Jacob (36:9) to discuss God's promise and divine election (Rom. 9:10–13). His point is that God's grace toward His people is not based on merit but on faith. Ezekiel's seminal expression of this can be seen in chapter 9, where a distinction is made between the righteous and the wicked within Israel. While historically Edom as a nation was ultimately defeated and God restored Israel to the promised land, these two divine oracles illustrate the character of the righteous and the wicked. Mount Seir depicts the arrogance, hostility, and covetousness of a people who wanted to take possession of what they saw as a land abandoned by God (35:10–13). Using language from the Creation narrative and covenant promises in Deuteronomy, the mountains of Israel depict the covenant recipients of God's grace, a reversal of 6:1–14 (36:8–12). Israel would be a new creation. The land is depicted in flourishing terms in preparation for the exiles' homecoming (vv. 6–12). This is an expansion on the theme of the covenant of peace in 34:25–30.

36:16–38. Internal Renewal. Against the backdrop of the restoration of the land and judgment on Judah's enemies, the renewal of the people now comes into view. As God reviewed His reasons for bringing judgment and exile (vv. 17–21; Lev. 18:24–25), He clarified that His work was done because of His holy name or reputation (Ezek. 36:20). Israel did nothing to merit a return to the land, but God is gracious, longsuffering, and merciful (Ex. 34:6–7), and it was necessary that His name be vindicated before the nations (Ezek. 36:23, 36). His sovereignty encompasses all creation, and everyone will know that He is the Lord of grace and justice (vv. 22–23; Rom. 9:14–18). Even the faithful need God's purifying grace (a new heart and a new spirit; Ezek. 36:26). The promise of renewal (a new covenant), fulfilled in the life and work of Jesus, is announced here and in Jeremiah 31:3–34. The work of redemption and regeneration would not replace God's holy law, but it would rather engrave the law on a transformed, submissive, and receptive heart. The role of the Messiah, the Davidic King, would bring this about, as confirmed in the pastoral imagery of Ezekiel 36:37–38. Chapter 34 emphasizes the royal work of the new David; here the priestly work is emphasized (v. 25; Heb. *zaraq*, "sprinkle," Num. 8:7; 19:18–19; *taher*, "cleanse," Lev. 16:30). The language of a ritual that cleanses from the impurity of corpse contamination (Ezek. 6:1–7; cf. Num. 19:13–20) signifies Israel's need of purification to atone for their idolatry and bloodshed. That regeneration would be made efficacious only by the work of the Spirit (Ezek. 36:27). The doctrine of righteousness by faith has been the keystone of God's plan from the foundation of the world (Rev. 13:8). The litany of first-person verbs in Ezekiel 36:24–30 emphasizes the providential leading of God and His role in the work of restoration. The promised divine enabling is captured in a beautiful literary chiasm in v. 27:

A God would "cause" or "move" (Heb. *'asah*, "make, do") the people

B They would "walk" or "follow" (Heb. *halak*) God's principles

B' They would observe (Heb. *shamar*, "keep, guard") God's decrees

A' They would be careful to keep (Heb. *'asah*, "make, do") God's rules

Yahweh's work of building and planting is a picture of the restored covenant community that He would establish (v. 36; see also 28:26; Is. 65:21; Jer. 24:6) and a reversal of the judgment of uninhabited houses and unfruitful vines (Deut. 28:30; cf. Zeph. 1:13). God would restore the remnant, a holy and consecrated people, as a testimony to His grace and power.

37:1–28
Valley of Dry Bones

Ezekiel relays another vivid visionary experience similar to his encounters with Yahweh in chapters 1–3, 8–11, and 40–48. The parallels with other visionary experiences indicate that here God's justice had come full circle: a similar setting (a valley, 3:22–23; 37:1; the city, 8:3; 40:1); the hand of the Lord upon him (3:22; 8:1; 37:1; 40:1); the work of the Spirit (3:24; 8:3; 37:1, 10; 40:2; the vision of God is combined with "spirit of God" in 11:24); and a divine question (8:6; 37:3). The first two visionary experiences deal with judgment and death, and the last two deal with resurrection and life. In chapter 37 we find a great message of hope for God's people. What hope of life can there be for very dry bones? God's question to Ezekiel in the vision narrative (vv. 1–10), "Can these bones live?" evokes a response of faith and points to His sovereignty. Ezekiel would have been familiar with the possibility of resurrection based on the experiences of the prophets Elijah (1 Kin. 17:17–24) and Elisha (2 Kin. 4:32–37). In the interpretation of the vision (Ezek. 37:11–14), Yahweh explained to Ezekiel that the bones represented all of Israel. Continuing the theme of ritual contamination from Numbers (Num. 19:14–16), whoever would touch Israel's bones would be defiled, but astonishingly the ritual contamination does not apply because the Life Giver is present and His life enlivens, purifies, and sanctifies—something that the blood of animal sacrifice could not do (Heb. 10:1–7). He gives life, and as in His original creation of humans, He would breathe into lifeless matter and human beings would come into existence (Ezek. 37:9; Gen. 2:7). In this chapter we see a graphic reversal of death and decay, reiterating the fact that the Lord has power over death. It presents the prophecy that the lifeless, dry bones of Israel will be brought back to life by the word of God. As at Creation, the Lord breathed into a human and he became a living being, so here the spirit (Heb. *ruakh*, "spirit," "wind," "breath") entered the lifeless bodies and they became living beings once again. The vision of the dry bones also gives an assurance of resurrection.

Ezekiel's performance of the sign-act, consisting of bringing two sticks together, depicted the reunification of Israel and Judah (Ezek. 37:15–20; cf. 33:23, 29; Jer. 3:18; 23:5–6; Hos. 1:11; Amos 9:11). This reunification must be seen in its cosmic context. Israel, like humankind, was brought to life to live in relationship with God and fulfill His will in their election. The promised Seed spoken of in Genesis 3:15 would come through the royal line of Judah (Gen. 49:8–10; Num. 24:15–17). Scripture presents God's restoration of Israel to the land as carrying the profound purpose of universal hope (Gen. 12:1–3, 7; Matt. 1; Luke 3:23–38; Gal. 3:16). The faithful kings of Judah, Hezekiah and Josiah, strove to incorporate the people within the former Northern Kingdom into a covenant hope (2 Kin. 23:15–20; 2 Chr. 30:1–12). This hope of reunion was also a mainstay among the prophets who drew from God's covenant promises to Abraham (Is. 11:12–13; Jer. 3:6–18; Hos. 1:10–11). This point is brought out in the interpretation (Ezek. 37:21–28). The two kingdoms would have one king over them—the Messiah, the new David, their Shepherd—who would establish an everlasting covenant of peace (v. 26; cf. Gen. 17:7, 13, 19; 2 Sam. 23:5; Is. 24:5; 55:3; Jer. 32:40). Righteousness would prevail under the Davidic Shepherd (Ezek. 37:23–24). The promise of the restoration of the sanctuary meant that God would reestablish His presence, covenant, salvation, and vindication in connection with the work of the Messiah (vv. 24–28). The sanctuary and its place in the plan of salvation become the main focus of the concluding chapters of the book (chaps. 40–48).

38:1—39:29
Gog and Magog

This oracle of judgment ends the section on the restoration of the people of Israel. Several features connect these two chapters: (1) both begin the same way, (2) the main antagonist is the same (Gog of Magog), (3) there is a cohesive storyline of war and judgment, and (4) the result is the same (all the nations will know that the Lord

is God; 38:16, 23; 39:6, 13, 21, 28). There are several factors to keep in mind when interpreting this prophecy. First, Ezekiel uses geographic references from the Table of Nations in Genesis 10 to give a worldwide scope to his vision. Magog is the second of the Japhethite nations (Gen. 10:2), and several of the other nations can be found in Genesis 10:2–6. Second, the use of this prophecy in the book of Revelation highlights an apocalyptic/eschatological fulfillment applied directly to Satan after the millennium (Rev. 20:1–10). Also in Ezekiel, this prophecy is one that would take place in the future (Ezek. 38:8, 16).

Indeed, 38:17 is a key verse that refers to previous prophesies about Gog. However, nowhere in Scripture is a direct prophecy about Gog ever mentioned. The intertextual biblical parallels suggest that this refers to a conglomerate of previous prophetic oracles concerning Israel's enemies and indicates a theological interpretation of the passage.

It is probably better to follow the storyline of the prophecy and comment on a few motifs that emerge from this cosmic war between good and evil. In broad terms, what is described is the summons to war (38:1–9) and the defeat of Gog (vv. 10–23), followed by the disposal of Gog (39:1–29). Gog was the commander-in-chief (Heb. *nesi' ro'sh*, "chief prince"; some translations render the Heb. *ro'sh* as a place name—"prince of Rosh") of Meshech and Tubal (38:2, 3, 5–6, 15). God would force him to assemble with all his allies, encompassing an unholy alliance of seven nations from the remotest parts of the known world: as far east as Persia (Paras), as far north as Anatolia (Gomer), and as far west as Libya (Egypt) (27:10; 30:5; 38:16–17). They would assemble against Israel (i.e., against the returnees from captivity; 38:8–9, 11–13), who is described in language reminiscent of chapters 34–37. Like the king of Assyria, Gog's ambitions would be to conquer Israel and enrich itself (38:13; cf. 27:15–22; Is. 10:5–14). In a time when the returnees of Israel would rest securely, trusting in the Lord (38:8–12, 14), Gog would proceed from the farthest parts of the north (cf. Is. 14:13). But forewarned of God's promise of judgment, Gog and his allies would be broken (Ezek. 38:14). The creation language mixed with imagery of the Divine Warrior, similar to descriptions of the cosmic upheaval in the plagues of the Exodus, and the conquering of Canaan signals Yahweh's victory and the confounding of the enemy (vv. 15–23; 39:3; Gen. 1; Ex. 9–15; Josh. 1–10). Through the defeat of Gog and his allies, the nations would know that the Lord is God (Ezek. 38:23).

Chapter 39 expands on the judgment against Gog with details of the defeat. It remains clear that when the Lord fought Gog, He would do so to protect and defend His chosen people (i.e., the house of Israel) for His name's sake. The chapter emphasizes that what would take place would be the last judgment; the tragic events of 586 B.C. would not happen again (Ezek. 39:29). Israel would have a new king, a renewed land, no foes, and a clear understanding of their guilt. The covenant promise of God's presence is in view here; He would not hide his face, meaning that His people would see Him in His glory. His Spirit would enable justice and righteousness to function without deterrent.

The destruction of these nations from the ends of the earth represents an ultimate attempt by the joint forces of evil to destroy the tranquility of God's people. Revelation's use of this text and others like it indicates that those prophecies are applied theologically in the context of the cosmic conflict between Christ and Satan. Two motifs that emerge from these chapters express this principle: the Day of the Lord and the Defeat of the Nations. (1) The Day of the Lord: Ezekiel's expressions "after many days" (38:8; Dan. 8:26), "in the latter years" (Ezek. 38:8), "in the latter days" (v. 16; Dan. 2:28; 10:14), and "on that day" (Ezek. 39:11) give a general future time framework for this prophecy. The use of phrases such as "the Day of the LORD," "in the latter days," and "in future years" is typical of eschatological passages. Thus, eschatological judgment and victory are in view here. (2) The Defeat of the Nations: in chapter 37, God's Spirit transforms a valley of dry bones into a living community, while in chapter 39 God reduces a numberless throng to a valley of bones (37:1-14; 39:11-15). Israel would spend seven months burying the corpses of Gog and his multitude in order to cleanse the land (39:12-16). By this time, the land of Israel would have been already restored, so a worldwide cleansing is in view. The defeat of the nations means a cessation of antagonism toward the people of God, and it means a restored world. The number seven (v. 12) also points toward the completeness of victory.

40:1—48:35

VISION OF GOD AND HIS REVIVED PEOPLE

Like chapters 38-39, chapters 40-48 are a vision that appears to deal with "theological geography" rather than literal geography. To be sure,

the contours of the land and the dimensions of the temple are described in realistic fashion, but the application has no literal fulfillment in human history; it was never built, and there was never an attempt to build it. Israel's hope lay in the presence of God with His people, the return of the King, and the reestablishment of the covenant apparatus of land, law, and leadership. Through Ezekiel, God was inviting His people to view their renewal and hope as being beyond the normal expectations of ritual. Ezekiel's plan for the temple is described in a language that has many parallels with the construction of the wilderness tabernacle and the temple of Jerusalem (40:1—43:27; Ex. 36-40; 1 Kin. 6:1—8:21). Coupled with the Davidic hope, the promise of a new temple inspired the returning, postexilic priests and prophets to rebuild the temple (Ezra 2-3; 5; Neh. 2-3; 6:1—7:3; Hag. 1:1—2:23; Zech. 2-3; 8). Ezekiel presents the ritual laws of the new temple as patterned after many laws found in the Pentateuch (Ezek. 44:1—46:24; Ex. 21-23; Lev. 1-7; Deut. 12-26). Finally, the allotments of the land are described similarly to the tribal allotments in Numbers 34:1-12. The visionary descriptions carry a degree of familiarity that conjures memories of the grace God expressed in the giving of the sanctuary, law, land, and leadership. Revelation's use of this section in its description of the New Jerusalem points to a NT understanding in eschatological rather than literal terms (cf. Rev. 21-22).

40:1—43:27
Temple Restored

Structurally, Ezekiel's vision revisits Israel (8:1). The vision related in chapter 8, from about twenty years previously, was of God abandoning His sanctuary, which fell, along with Jerusalem, to the Babylonians. One can imagine Ezekiel's anxiety as he now encounters another being similar to the one he interacted with as judgment commenced on Israel (8:2; 40:3). One can also imagine his hope as this new vision, according to priestly reckoning, was around the time of the Passover (Ex. 12:2-3). His experience, mediated in apocalyptic sensory form ("see" and "hear," Ezek. 40:4; cf. Rev. 1:10-12; 7:4, 9; 14:1-2), was also similar to the apocalyptic visions facilitated by a supernatural being (Dan. 10:2-9; Rev. 17:1). He saw something like a city structure on a very high mountain. He entered the city and was given a tour of a complex like a fortress with guardrooms at the entrance (Ezek. 40:5-7; cf. 1 Kin. 14:28). He began and ended at the outer court entrance of the temple. This spatial description is important because this was where God's glory would enter the temple complex; it was the same point from where He exited because of the abominations that took place in the temple before it was destroyed (Ezek. 43:1–5; cf. 10:18–22; 11:23). At the end of his tour, Ezekiel was taken out to see God's entrance from the east, where the sights and sounds evoked awe, reverence, and a sign of hope (1:24, 28). The reference to the glory of the Lord filling the temple (43:5) indicates a divine acceptance and inauguration (vv. 12–27). A similar reference also appears in connection with the inception of the wilderness tabernacle (43:5, cf. 42:15; Exod. 40:34–35) as well as the temple of Solomon (1 Kin. 8:10–11).

The key word "measure" is mentioned thirty times in this section (e.g., Ezek. 40:27; 41:1, 5, 13; 42:15, 20). The man with the measuring rod measured the wall (40:5), the temple (vv. 6–49), and the *hekal*—usually translated as "temple" but here rendered variously as "sanctuary," "main hall," or "nave" (41:1–4). The passage from 41:5 to 42:20 provides further descriptions and measurements of the temple. Not only do these measurements speak of the architectural precision of the temple, but as Zechariah also later expressed, they indicate that it would be ready to welcome its divine inhabitant and for Him to receive joyful songs of praise (Ps. 137:1–6; Zech. 1:16; 2:2). The priests would once more administer the sacrifices (Ezek. 40:39–46; 42:13–14). Ezekiel was moved closer to the inner court, into the interior of the temple, but was not taken into the Most Holy Place (41:4). Though different in some respects, the general layout is similar to Solomon's temple, which is described in 1 Kings 6:1–37. The scarcity of detail concerning the Holy and Most Holy Places suggests that Ezekiel was not being shown an architectural plan to be followed, but a vision of the gradations of the sacred space where the cherubim and palm trees evoke the hope of a new creation (Gen. 1–2; 3:24; Rev. 7:9–17). The function of the temple was finally revealed to Ezekiel—radiating from the top of the mountain, everything around it became holy ground. With no need for a royal palace like Solomon's, Israel's King would rule from His throne room in the temple (Ezek. 43:7; 1 Kin. 7:7). The return of the glory of the Lord (Ezek. 43:2–7) required that Israel put away idolatry and seek the Lord (vv. 9–11), who tabernacles among His people (vv. 12–27).

44:1—46:24
The Torah Restored and the Prince

Since Ezekiel's focus had shifted to the rules and procedures regulating the activities in the temple, he exited its complex precincts and was informed that only the Prince had entered through this entrance; His status is thus associated with the Lord (44:1–3; 43:4; 46:12). Usually, the word "prince" (Heb. *nasi'*) in Ezekiel denotes a political role, namely, the leader of the Jewish community (7:27; 12:10; 21:25; cf. 1 Kin. 11:34). Ezekiel also uses the term to refer to the Davidic Messiah (Ezek. 34:24; 37:25). His special access to the temple reflected the idea of a special processional entrance open only to the honorable (Pss. 15; 24). The focus on the glory of the Lord filling the temple (Ezek. 44:4) shows that this Davidic King would have access to the very presence of the Lord, which is reminiscent of Moses at Sinai (cf. Ex. 19–24). Yet in this case, the laws address a superior quality of sanctity and a more rigorous form of access and ritual purity (Ezek. 44:5–14). Even though Yahweh directly gave him laws, Moses could not enter into the presence of God when His glory filled the tabernacle (Ex. 34:34–35). Ezekiel presents the Prince as having a special relationship with Yahweh: not only having access to the Lord's presence but also having a deep covenant relationship with Him (Ezek. 44:3; cf. 34:23–24; 37:24–28). The book mentions the rebellions of Israel (44:6), how they brought uncircumcised foreigners who profaned the temple (vv. 7–9), and how the Levites deserted God (vv. 10–11). As far as the priests are concerned, only the Zadokite priests would approach to minister before the Lord. These priests are presented as showing sacrificial fidelity, but stricter regulations apply to them concerning ministry, including whom they could marry and how they would arbitrate among the people (vv. 15–31).

The purity required in this new temple emphasizes that the maintenance of God's holiness would be of a different order than in the past. In anticipation of the fuller account of the allotment of the land (47:13–23; 48:1–35), holiness would radiate outward from God's holy mountain to the land—the Priest and the Prince would extend the purity of the temple (45:1–9). The bulk of the material emphasizes the special status and responsibilities of the Prince as a leader (44:3; 45:7–9; 46:10, 12, 16–18), and it emphasizes the maintenance of holiness through ritual (45:1–25), through worship (Sabbath and New Moon, 46:1–15), and through equity in land inheritances (vv. 16–18). The book of Revelation picks up on this theme and expands on the faithful being closest to the presence of the Lord with the Davidic King on the mountain of God (Rev. 14:1–5; cf. 1:6).

47:1—48:29
The Land Restored

Ezekiel's temple tour concluded at the entrance of the temple proper, where he saw a stream of water coming from beneath the temple and flowing east (47:1–12). What started out as a trickle eventually became so deep that it was over Ezekiel's head, and it was going out into the land. The healing property of the water was rejuvenating the driest portion of the land (the Dead Sea area) and preparing for the description of the purified land, recalling the Edenic fertility and Zion's hope (Gen. 2:10–14; Pss. 46:4; 65:9). Revelation's portrayal of the renewed earth uses Ezekiel's description of the waters of the river of life healing the people (Rev. 22:1–2).

Ezekiel builds on his earlier picture of a restored people of God (Ezek. 47:13; cf. 37:15–28). The inheritance of the twelve tribes and the allotment of the land recall God's victory during the wilderness wanderings (Josh. 13:1—21:45). However, in Ezekiel, contrary to earlier biblical descriptions, Israel's former enemies had been destroyed (Ezek. 38–39). The account of the division of the land in chapter 48 elaborates on the brief account in chapter 45; its borders were already demarcated in chapter 47. The allotment

of sections of the land follows this order: (1) sections for the first seven tribes (48:1–7; cf. 45:6); (2) a holy district set apart for the Lord—for the priests and the temple (with the temple in the center; 48:8–12; cf. 45:1–4); (3) a section for the Levites (48:13–14; cf. 45:5); (4) the common land (48:15–20); (5) the portion for the prince (vv. 21–22; cf. 45:7–9); and (6) sections for the last five tribes (48:23–28; cf. 45:6). The foreigners or strangers, resident aliens (47:22–23) who are "grafted" into the people of God, would experience the same covenant benefits of inheritance (cf. Rom. 11:11–24). The book of Ezekiel ends on a note of hope for all people who choose to be a part of God's family.

48:30–35
The City Restored

Ezekiel's prophetic account concludes with the restoration of the people and the land, ending with a picture of hope: God reigns while the world remains at rest. The book of Revelation picks up this covenant rest when it focuses on the twelve gates named after the twelve tribes, representing the royalty of the people of God (vv. 30–35; Rev. 21:12). Revelation expands Ezekiel's picture of the ultimate covenant blessing. The Hebrew name of the city would be *yahweh shammah* ("The LORD Is There") which symbolizes Yahweh's promise to dwell among His people (Ezek. 48:35). This remains the hope of God's people (Rev. 22:4–5, 17). The book of Ezekiel closes the way it began, focusing on the God of all glory and hope.

DANIEL

INTRODUCTION

Title and Authorship. The Hebrew name of the book is *daniyye'l*, rendered in English as "Daniel," meaning "God is my judge." It appears to have been a common name in the Semitic world. The book is named after its main character, a young man from Judah called Daniel who was taken into exile in Babylon. Although there have been debates concerning the author of the book, the book itself indicates that the Prophet Daniel wrote it (e.g., Dan. 12:4). The historicity of Daniel is confirmed by Jesus (Matt. 24:15).

Date. The date for the composition of Daniel has been a topic of disagreement among scholars. Critical scholars, influenced by rationalism and its denial of divine intervention in history, have rejected predictive prophecy and therefore sought arguments to date the book to the second century B.C. They believe that Daniel's so-called predictions were written after the events had taken place, that is, after the empires of Babylon, Medo-Persia, and Greece had already disappeared from history. The book was written, they claim, to provide meaning and encouragement to the Jews in the mid-second century B.C. in their struggle with the Syrian king Antiochus IV Epiphanes, with whom the book ends. But when all evidence is taken into consideration, the liberal position is either ambiguous or lacks clear historical support. Interestingly, in the manuscripts from Qumran, written in the second century B.C., the book of Daniel was already well known and considered an authoritative prophetic book. Conservative Christians, including Seventh-day Adventists, who take into consideration the historical and chronological information found in Daniel, believe that it was written by the Prophet Daniel in the sixth century B.C.

Backgrounds. When Nabopolassar ascended to the throne of Babylon (626 B.C.), the Neo-Assyrian Empire underwent a rapid decline.

The Medes captured Assur in 614 B.C., and Nabopolassar, in alliance with the Medes, took Nineveh, the Neo-Assyrian capital, in 612 B.C. The final collapse of the Neo-Assyrian Empire occurred during the battle of Carchemish in 605 B.C. In the same year, Nabopolassar died and his son Nebuchadnezzar II became king of the Neo-Babylonian Empire. It was also the year when Daniel, as a young man, was taken to Babylon. He served at the court of Nebuchadnezzar as minister and counselor. After the Persians conquered Babylon in 539 B.C., he also served under Darius the Mede and the Persian king Cyrus. During his long and distinguished career, Daniel consistently displayed a profound trust in God, regardless of circumstances. He served God faithfully to the end of his days (sometime after 536 B.C.).

Theology and Purpose. The book of Daniel is formed by a series of historical narratives and a series of apocalyptic prophecies. The historical conflict Daniel and his friends experienced was a microcosm of the cosmic conflict depicted in the prophetic chapters. This conflict provides a theological center to the book around which other theological topics are developed.

1. God's Sovereignty. The God of Daniel is indeed the Lord of history. History is the arena in which the cosmic conflict between God and the powers of evil takes place. Throughout the book it is repeatedly demonstrated that in spite of the efforts of human instrumentalities, behind which evil powers are at work (Dan. 10:12–13) to destroy God's faithful servants, God is always able to deliver them. The acknowledgment of His sovereignty is expressed by the willingness of God's people to worship Him at any cost.

2. God's Messiah. God's most important instrument in this cosmic battle is His Messiah, the Son of Man (7:13–14). Historical narratives in Daniel record His deliverance of His servants from the attacks of their enemies

(3:19–30; 6:18–22), and the prophetic words in Daniel promise He will do the same during the last eschatological drama (12:1). The messianic prophecy of the seventy weeks points to the time when the Messiah, the hope of God's people, would come to procure salvation for them. He would be the sacrifice to bring to an end all the animal sacrifices by giving His life for the world (9:26–27).

3. *Judgment*. The book begins and ends with references to judgment: apostate Israel is judged at the beginning (1:1–2), and the king of the north is judged at the end (11:40—12:2). The middle of the book (7:9–13) portrays God as the Ancient of Days, with the books of judgment open and multitudes of angels present. On each side of this great judgment scene, we find further references to judgment. In Daniel 4 heaven judges Nebuchadnezzar, the proud boaster, and humbles him to animal status, and in chapter 5 Belshazzar, his grandson, receives the message that he has been evaluated and found wanting (v. 27). Chapters 8 and 9 indicate the beginning date of the pre-advent judgment, and chapter 12 spells out its significance concerning rewards and punishments.

4. *Vindication of God's People*. Daniel places great emphasis on the people of God on earth and on their struggles against the forces of evil. The historical chapters of the book (Dan. 1–6) illustrate how God vindicates and delivers those who remain faithful in the midst of a pagan nation. These chapters contain the motif of trial and trouble ending in elevation and glory. Thus, the good news that trials and temptations are followed by blessings for those obedient to God is continually proclaimed, anticipating the full realization of the hope that at the Second Coming of the Messiah all trials and temptations will come to an end.

Literary Features. Daniel was written in two languages, namely, Hebrew (1:1—2:4a; 8:1—12:13) and Aramaic (2:4b—7:28). The reason for this particular phenomenon is unknown, but perhaps it could be said that when dealing with the rulers of worldly empires, Daniel decided to use Aramaic (the diplomatic language of these empires), whereas the sections written in Hebrew deal primarily with matters important to the people of God.

The book is divided into two parts: the first six chapters primarily contain narrative (chaps. 1, 3–6), while the last six contain visions (chaps. 7–12). The climax in each narrative is the elevation of the worshipers of the true God,

and each vision ends with the establishment of the kingdom of God. The worshipers of the true God are associated with the kingdom of God. The first chapter tells the story of the destruction of God's earthly kingdom, Judah, while the last chapter promises the establishment of His heavenly kingdom, which will last forever. Daniel 2 and 7 contain visionary symbols and their interpretation. The first half of chapter 8 again contains a symbolic vision, but after 8:14 most of the symbolism is dropped, indicating that 8:14 is the climax of the symbolism of the book. In the next verse the explanation begins; it is continued in 9:24–27 and enlarged upon in chapters 10–12. In other words, the rest of the book seems to be a development and explanation of the symbolic vision in chapter 8 or a new revelation in the form of an audition.

Interpretation of the Book. The history of the interpretation of Daniel is quite extensive. We will only offer a brief description of the major interpretational systems used for the understanding of the book of Daniel.

1. *Historicist School*. This is the oldest school of interpretation. It accepts the authorship of Daniel in the sixth century B.C. and holds that the prophecies of Daniel cover the entire historical period from Daniel's day to the Second Advent of Christ. Seventh-day Adventists are historicists (see "Interpreting Biblical Apocalyptic Prophecies," p. 46).

2. *Futurist-Dispensational School*. Interpreters of this school also accept Danielic authorship in the sixth century B.C., but they believe that the little horn power in Daniel 7 is a future antichrist rather than apostate Christianity. This school can be divided into two groups: (a) dispensationalists, who believe that there is a gap in the fulfilment of the prophecies of Daniel from the first century until seven years before the Second Advent; and (b) futurists, who believe that from the destruction of the Roman Empire (the fourth beast) until the appearance of the antichrist (the little horn) there will be a number of kingdoms (the ten horns), which are the successors to the Roman Empire.

3. *The Historical Preterist School*. Like historicists and futurist-dispensationalists, historical preterists believe that Daniel wrote the book in the sixth century B.C., but they limit the fulfillment of its prophecies to the time period which runs from the time of Daniel to the first coming of Christ, or to the end of the Roman Empire.

4. The Historical-Critical or Modern Preterist School. Adherents of this school hold that an unknown Jew in the second century B.C. wrote the book of Daniel. They believe that all the prophecies in the book end in the time of Antiochus IV Epiphanes, in the second century B.C., and that the book is a reflection of the political and religious situation of the Jewish people during the time of persecution under that Syrian king.

COMMENTARY

1:1–21

GLIMPSES OF JUDGMENT AND RESTORATION

The first chapter of Daniel introduces a number of topics that will surface several times and in different ways throughout the rest of the book. It begins with a description of the result of God's judgment against His people (vv. 1–2) and proceeds to describe an effort to influence Daniel and his friends to adopt the Babylonian culture (vv. 3–7). The issue of diet illustrates how important it is to preserve one's identity in a setting of conflict (vv. 8–14). The chapter ends describing the results of remaining loyal to the Lord (vv. 15–21). Daniel and his friends model what it means to be faithful servants of the Lord in a context of opposition while waiting for deliverance.

1:1–2. Inevitable Results of Disobedience. The fall of Jerusalem mentioned here took place in the year 605 B.C. Daniel lived in the sixth century and was a contemporary of Nebuchadnezzar. Here he is not simply recounting casual historical incidents but also identifying the cause of the events: the Lord ensured that Jehoiakim would be defeated and given over to Nebuchadnezzar (v. 2). The biblical obituary of Jehoiakim states that he did evil in the Lord's estimation, just as those who came before him had done (2 Kin. 23:37), and Judah did the same (2 Kin. 24:3). Daniel begins his narrative describing God's judgment against His people and His sovereignty over history. He records the conflict between Babylon and Jerusalem; Jerusalem represents the rule of righteousness and Babylon the rule of evil. The first time we read of Babylon and Jerusalem in Scripture is in the book of Genesis; the last time we hear of them is in the book of Revelation. The stories

and prophecies of the book illustrate the Great Controversy between good and evil.

1:3–7. Conflicting Identities. Daniel and his three Jewish companions (Hananiah, Mishael, and Azariah) were selected to obtain the best education Babylon (Shinar) could offer them. This opportunity would make it possible for them to change their social status as prisoners of war or slaves to that of Babylonian scholars or wise men. In the process, their faith was to be seriously tested. First, they were offered a new Babylonian identity by being given Babylonian names. This was part of a larger purpose of gradually transforming their allegiance to Babylon and its gods. The new names associated Daniel and his companions with Babylonian deities (v. 7). So Daniel, which means "God is my judge," was changed to Belteshazzar, "may Bel [another name for Marduk, the principal god of Babylon] preserve his life." Hananiah ("the grace of God") was named Shadrach ("the command of Aku," a Babylonian god). Mishael ("who is like God") became Meshach ("who is like Aku"). Finally, Azariah ("God has helped") was named Abednego ("servant of Nebo," another name of Marduk).

1:8–14. Babylonian Diet. The second attempt at Babylonian indoctrination came through a new lifestyle. It was the king, not the Lord, who carefully determined what they should eat and drink. In fact, they would eat from the table of the king. The meal would have included unclean foods and food offered to the Babylonian deities. This test over eating and drinking seems insignificant, but the first test recorded in the Bible (Gen. 3) also seems to have been insignificant; it too concerned appetite. At times, the depth of love is best revealed in the little things we do. Great doors often swing on little hinges. Genesis 3 and Daniel 1 illustrate that Satan always endeavors to reach us through our senses. Successful Christian living, therefore, depends on the adequate control of the senses.

Daniel and his friends decided not to defile themselves with the king's food and wine (1:8). The request from Daniel and his companions must have seemed very strange and even foolish to the Babylonian officers. But the Lord used Daniel's kindness to gain him the respect and sympathy of the chief of the eunuchs (v. 9), a high court official, and he assented to their request and tested them for ten days (v. 14).

Daniel's diet was nothing particularly new but was based on faithfulness to God's will for him and his friends. They asked for a simple and wholesome plant-based diet and water (v. 12). The term *zero'im* (plural of *zeroa'*) used in v. 12 (usually translated as "vegetables") is related to the one used in Genesis 1:29 to designate the original diet assigned by God to humans. The Hebrew young men were going back to God's original diet.

1:15–21. Blessings of Obedience. Under God's influence, the ten days were enough to show that the diet established by God was the best. The four young men were in better health than any of the other young men who had been eating the king's food (v. 15). A battle had been won. They also excelled in their education in literature and wisdom (v. 17). However, this was not directly credited to their diet but to the Lord who gave them such capacities. In other words, God blessed their faithfulness and gave them more than they expected. When they went before the king for their final examination, he witnessed their superiority over the other students. It was ten times better, and as a result they were given jobs close to the king himself (vv. 19–20). Daniel and his three friends were able to remain faithful to God through "the right exercise of the will" (SC 48), through the recognition of the influence of the body on the mind (CD 154), and through a prayerful dependence on God (SL 20). What helped Daniel and his friends in their walk with God remains true for every follower of Christ today.

Daniel 1:21 is the epilogue of the chapter. The chapter starts describing the people of God as having been taken captive to Babylon, but it ends with a reference to Cyrus, the king who brought the captivity of the people to an end by allowing them to return to Israel. He is described by Isaiah in messianic terms as the liberator of God's people (Is. 44:28). According to Daniel, not all was dark; there was a happy ending on the horizon. At the beginning of the chapter, there is hardly any hope left for the people, but at the end there is a glimpse of hope for them. The Deliverer would be coming. The book of Daniel is designed to inspire hope in the midst of a cosmic conflict for those who put their trust in the Lord and remain loyal to Him.

2:1–49
GOD INTRODUCES NEBUCHADNEZZAR TO HIS KINGDOM

Four facts stand out in this chapter: the complete uselessness of divination to forecast the future (vv. 1–13); God as the only One who knows the future (vv. 14–30); the miracle of prophecy (vv. 31–45); and God's invitation to Nebuchadnezzar to become part of His kingdom (vv. 46–49).

2:1–13. Control over the Future. Nebuchadnezzar was worried about the future of his kingdom. The God of Israel, who cares for all peoples, listened to his concern and spoke to him in a dream. The dream captured the attention and interest of the king. He apparently could not remember all of its details but remembered enough to realize that its content was important. He needed two things, a full description of the dream and its interpretation. In the ancient Near East, the dreams of a king were extremely important, for they were considered to be messages from the gods announcing, among other things, possible misfortunes for the king or the kingdom. Therefore, it was important for the king to know about these matters in order to perform certain rituals that would protect him, his family, and the kingdom. Dreams could be a matter of national security. What Nebuchadnezzar was doing was not strange at all.

Kings had professional interpreters of dreams and people who could use different means of divination to predict the future. In the case of Nebuchadnezzar, he had a group of wise persons trained in the art of divination and in the interpretation of dreams. He decided to call a meeting of those skilled in divination. Human wisdom would be seriously tested. It was precisely the wise persons who immediately realized the limits of human wisdom. They possessed different techniques for divination, but they had not developed one that would allow them to recover a forgotten dream. They argued that no one on earth could do what the king was asking them to do and, further, that no ruler had ever asked for such a thing (v. 10). In other words, what the king was requesting was not only irrational but, since it lacked a legal antecedent, was an arbitrary demand.

The king was abruptly confronted by the limits of human wisdom, and consequently, he was frustrated. If wisdom is so useless, who needs it? Angry and frustrated, Nebuchadnezzar ordered that all the wise men of Babylon were to be executed (v. 12). Among them were Daniel and his friends (v. 13). Perhaps they had not been invited to the meeting because they were considered young and inexperienced, but their fate was the same as that of all of the others.

2:14-30. God's Lordship over the Future.
What first impacted Daniel was the urgency
of the king's command. Once properly informed, Daniel went to see the king to ask him
for time so that he could inform him of the
dream's interpretation (v. 16). The wise men
of Babylon complained about the impossibility
of the task, but this young man told the king
that what he was requesting was not impossible. All he needed was time—time to pray
that God would reveal to them the secret (or
mystery) of the interpretation in order for them
to be delivered from death. Daniel opted for
the only way out of the problem, namely, divine intervention. This possibility had been
considered by the magicians, astrologers, and
Chaldeans, but they concluded that this was
impossible because the gods do not share that
information with humans (v. 11). However, the
God of Daniel knows all mysteries and could
reveal them to His servants the prophets. And
the secret (or mystery) was revealed to Daniel
(v. 19).

After receiving the revelation, Daniel gave
thanks and glory to God. In his prayer, which
is a doxology, Daniel identified God as the
source of true wisdom (v. 20) and as the One
who has control over the flow of history (v.
21). This wonderful God is willing to provide
wisdom and knowledge, as well as to reveal
deep, hidden, secret things to humans (vv.
21-23). After talking to the King of kings, the
young man was ready to talk to the king of
Babylon. In order to highlight the limits of
human wisdom, Daniel told the king that there
were no wise men that could reveal the mystery the king had requested (v. 27). This is the
first time that Daniel is described as testifying
before the king on behalf of God. What the
king had demanded could be done by a God
he did not know but who would be introduced
to him by Daniel (v. 28). It is this God, unknown to the king, who had made known to
King Nebuchadnezzar what would be in the
future (lit. "days of the end" or "latter days").
In this case that future reached from the days
of Nebuchadnezzar to the advent of the stone
kingdom. Daniel did not take any personal
credit. It was revealed to him for the benefit
of the king and in order for the king to know
what had been in his mind (lit. "heart"; v. 30).

2:31-45. Prophecy and History. Daniel
would give the king what he had requested,
namely, the dream and its interpretation. He
dreamed about a colossal image of a man

made of different materials. This type of image
was common in the ANE. Images were made
to represent the gods (idols) or the king. In this
particular case, it was a royal image because it
would represent the king and the kingdoms. Its
head was of fine, pure gold; the arms and the
chest were made of silver; the abdomen and
thighs of bronze; the legs of iron; and the feet
were a mixture of iron and clay (vv. 32-33).
The metals decreased in value but increased
in strength, except for the feet. The feet made
the image vulnerable and anticipated its final
collapse. In the dream, the king saw a stone
or rock, which was cut without human hands
(i.e., not of human origin), hit the image on
its feet, blowing it apart. Daniel used the language of winnowing to express the effortless-
ness with which the image was destroyed. It
was as easy as separating the grain from the
chaff that is blown away by the wind. The
stone became a large mountain that filled the
whole earth (v. 35).

The interpretation is introduced by a establishing a connection between the king and the
God of Daniel. Daniel acknowledged the king
of Babylon as a king of kings (v. 37) but stated
that he was expected to function as the representative of God, who is indeed the King of
kings (cf. Rev. 19:16). It was the Lord who entrusted to Nebuchadnezzar kingly dominion,
power, strength, glory, and his rule over nature
and humans (Dan. 2:37-38). The language is
similar to Genesis 1:28, with the exception that
God did not give to Adam and Eve dominion
over other human beings. But the point is that
the king was to function under God. Daniel's
God ruled above the king.

The head of gold as a symbol represented the
king of Babylon and his kingdom (Dan. 2:38).
The king was concerned about his kingdom and
its future, and Daniel told him that his kingdom
would be succeeded by another, represented
by silver and inferior to his—stronger but less
magnificent. A third kingdom of bronze would
arise, to be followed by a fourth kingdom of
iron (vv. 39-40). The mixture of clay and iron
of the feet meant that the last kingdom would
be divided (vv. 41-43). The stone was a symbol
of the kingdom of God that would never be destroyed and that would remain forever (v. 44).
This fifth kingdom would bring to an end all
the kingdoms of the earth. Intriguingly, stone
imagery denoting divine action and power is
known in Mesopotamian religious literature. In
order to effectively communicate with the Babylonian king, God used familiar imagery that

was able to connect to Nebuchadnezzar's heart and head.

This prophetic dream represents an outline of the history of human kingdoms and was fulfilled as predicted. The kingdoms that followed the Babylonian Empire (605–538 B.C.), in the order announced, were Medo-Persia (538–332 B.C.), Greece (332–168 B.C.), and Rome (168 B.C.–A.D. 476). The kingdoms that came out of the division of the Roman Empire have never reunited into a single empire. They tried to unite by marriages between the different ruling houses of Europe, but these alliances never lasted. The European nations and the whole world have been a dramatic spectacle of divisiveness and conflicts between the weak (clay) and the strong (iron).

That the stone must symbolize the Second and not the First Advent becomes clear when we remember (a) that the stone struck the image on the feet of iron and clay, indicating that it came after the Roman Empire had been divided, not when it was united; (b) that the shattering of the image suggests a world-shaking catastrophe rather than an obscure event almost unnoticed by the world; and (c) that if the First Advent is meant, the stone kingdom had been running concurrently with the iron-leg and the feet-and-toe powers for two thousand years. The vision represented the stone destroying all the preceding kingdoms and replacing them, not coexisting with them.

This dream and its interpretation provide an excellent introduction to the nature of apocalyptic prophecy. This type of prophecy provides an outline of history usually beginning at the time of the prophet and running up to the establishment of God's eternal kingdom. Apocalyptic prophecy provides hope for those who wait on the Lord in the midst of a world fragmented by sin. But in a very particular way, apocalyptic prophecy is about God's sovereignty that assures us that love and justice will finally prevail. The fulfillment of the prophecy of Daniel 2 alone is sufficient to demonstrate the inspiration of the Bible.

2:46–49. Nebuchadnezzar and God's Kingdom. The reaction of the king was the reaction of a person who had seen the greatness and majesty of the God of Daniel. He honored the prophet by prostrating before him and ordering that an offering and incense be presented to him (v. 46). This is close to an act of worship, but the fact that Nebuchadnezzar immediately acknowledges the superiority of the God of Daniel indicates that this was not an act

of worship directed to Daniel but to his God. The king was not accepting the God of Daniel as the only God but as the God of gods, the Lord of kings, and the Revealer of secrets and mysteries (v. 47). He is superior to all other gods and rules over all kings. God used this incident to locate Daniel in a social position where he could be more useful to Him as His servant. He was placed in charge of Babylon and over all its wise men (v. 48). The prophet did not forget his three companions who went seeking wisdom together with him in prayer to the Lord and whose prayers He answered. They were delivered from death through divine wisdom. The connection with Jesus, who is the wisdom of God (1 Cor. 1:24), is appropriate. He is the One who delivers humans from death by giving His life for them (Mark 10:45). This is divine wisdom and the mystery of all mysteries.

3:1–30

THE IMAGE OF GOLD AND TRUE WORSHIP

Daniel 3 reveals the unwillingness of the king to accept God's plan for him and his kingdom. The idea that his kingdom would be followed by another made Nebuchadnezzar unhappy. He sought to alter the divine revelation to fit his own desires. In the process the king transformed the issue into one of loyalty to him and his kingdom by forcing everyone to worship his image. Daniel 3 is about false and true worship. It describes the call to worship (vv. 1–7), the challenge to the king's command (vv. 8–18), the divine deliverance (vv. 19–25), and the king's reaction (vv. 26–30).

3:1–7. Call to Worship. The question remains the same: Who is in control of history? The king was unwilling to accept that the One who has ultimate control of history was the God of Daniel. He preferred to believe that his kingdom would remain forever, applying to himself and to his kingdom the attributes of the kingdom of God. He decided to make this clear by building a colossal image of gold.

The dream image's head of gold, representing Nebuchadnezzar, now became the whole colossal image. The king anticipated the failure of the prophetic dream. What was needed to avoid the collapse of the kingdom was the absolute loyalty of those in administrative positions throughout the kingdom. The king ordered all of them to be present at the dedication of the image (v. 2).

The ceremony was not only a political one but also a religious one. At the appropriate moment, all of those standing before the image were to fall down and worship it (v. 5). The rejection of the divine plan for the human race leads to idolatry. But this was compulsory idolatry imposed through absolute royal power. The matter was so serious for the king that whoever would not fall down and worship would be cast into a furnace of blazing fire (v. 6). He, not God, seemed to have had the power to determine who would live or die. The oppressive power of the state made no allowance for dissenting minorities.

3:8–18. The King Is Challenged. On the plain of Dura (v. 1), a battle was to be fought between false and true worship. While there may have been other Hebrews in the crowd, only Daniel's friends were reported to the king for their refusal to serve the king's gods or worship the golden image (v. 12). The word "worship" indicates that true religion springs from the awareness that God is worthy to be revered. This event on the plain of Dura is a particularly notorious example, among others from the ANE and throughout history, of a government attempting to achieve conformity through a particular worship ritual. King Nebuchadnezzar attempted to enforce uniformity of worship by threatening a death decree to be administered to those who refused to worship his golden image.

In comparing Daniel 3 with Revelation 13:11–18, we notice several important parallels: (1) in both chapters the issue is worship—in Daniel 3 the people involved were only those living in the Babylonian Empire, while in Revelation 13 we are told of a universal test over worship at the climax of history; (2) in both chapters an image appears to be worshiped—one a literal image, the other a spiritual image; (3) in Daniel 3 the king of literal Babylon demanded this worship, while in John's prophetic vision in Revelation 13 spiritual Babylon requires the worship of the image to the beast; (4) the three Hebrews faced a death penalty—in the future, church and state will unite to enforce uniformity of worship, and those who refuse to conform will face economic boycotts and ultimately the death penalty; and (5) in both chapters the number *six*, as a symbol of humans under the control of evil powers, is prominent. Human beings and "the serpent" were created

on the sixth day, and in Revelation 13:18 that number is associated with satanic opposition to God. In the time of Daniel, the people in Babylon were to worship the golden image. This is mentioned six times (Dan. 3:5, 7, 10, 12, 14–15, 18). In the book of Revelation, the warning against worshiping the beast and his image is also given six times (Rev. 13:15; 14:9, 11; 16:2; 19:20; 20:4).

Following the three Hebrews' refusal to bow down to his image, King Nebuchadnezzar threw down the gauntlet and rhetorically asked which god could deliver them from his power—in other words, there was none (Dan. 3:15). The three young men knew the options very well. They knew that the God whom they served was able to deliver them from the fire (v. 17). But they also knew that sometimes God, in His wisdom and love for us, does not deliver His servants from the burning fire. Their loyalty to Him was not determined by selfish concerns but by a love that was strong enough to sustain them when facing death. When the three young men were thrown into the oven, dressed in all their regalia and with their hands tied, the heat was so intense that the flames killed the soldiers who threw them in (v. 22). This incident indicates that only the God of the young men could deliver them from certain death.

As the king watched closely, he was astonished at the fact that the three Israelites were walking around in the fire with their hands loose (v. 25). The ropes used to tie their hands had burned, but not their flesh. But what really surprised the king was that instead of three there were four men inside the furnace and that the form of the fourth was like the Son of God (v. 25), meaning a divine being—in other words, the preincarnate Christ (PK 508–9). Some translations have "son of the gods" instead, most likely to indicate that Nebuchadnezzar might not have fully understood that this figure was *the* unique Son of God. Perhaps he considered him to be a majestic supernatural being related to the gods. Fire is associated in many cases in the Bible with the presence or apparition of God (e.g., Ex. 19:18; Deut. 4:11–12). In this case, the fire prepared by the king to destroy God's servants became the fire that accompanied the saving presence of God among mortals. The young Israelites had a private audience with their God, and the king was allowed to witness it.

3:26–30. The King's Reaction. Realizing that the fire did not do any damage to the three men, the king answered his own sarcastic question (v. 15) by stating that their God had saved His servants who trusted in Him (v. 28). The mighty act of God on behalf of His servants was so impressive that the king immediately reacted to it. First, he extolled the God of Israel because He frustrated his own plans as king of Babylon against God's servants. In other words, he recognized that this God was more powerful and majestic than he was. In the presence of the God of heaven, who manifested Himself in the fire of the furnace, the king could only raise his voice in praise. He called the God of the three Hebrews "the Most High God" (v. 26). This is a title applied to God in order to emphasize His supremacy and is used several times in Daniel 4 and 7. Second, the king made a decree in the form of a threat against any person throughout the kingdom who would dare to say anything against the God of Shadrach, Meshach, and Abednego (v. 29). To speak against God meant to show disrespect or even to blaspheme Him. The penalty would be death. Finally, the king reacted to the power of God by promoting the three Hebrews to important positions within the province of Babylon (v. 30). Their loyalty and commitment to the Lord were rewarded by Him in order to make them even more effective in His service.

4:1–37

CONVERSION OF NEBUCHADNEZZAR

After his introduction (vv. 1–3), the king continued by telling his experience of a dream (vv. 4–9) and its content (vv. 10–17). This is followed by Daniel's interpretation of the dream (vv. 18–27), its fulfillment (vv. 28–33), the restoration of the king (vv. 34–36), and a conclusion (v. 37). The central topic of the chapter is God's universal dominion over the dominion of earthly kings. True kingly human dominion is only meaningful in submission to the God of heaven.

4:1–3. Introduction. The format is that of a royal letter to be sent to the nations that constituted the Babylonian Empire (cf. Ezra 7:11–13). The king wanted everybody to know about his experience with the Most High God. The language used emphasizes the universality of the proclamation (see Rev. 14:6). He was witnessing on behalf of the God of Israel. In fact, that was the purpose of the letter: God had performed miracles of signs and wonders for him, and this

had led the king to recognize and proclaim that God's kingdom is everlasting and His dominion is from generation to generation (Dan. 4:3). The signs and wonders God performed were rejected by Pharaoh but not by Nebuchadnezzar. The eternal dominion of God's heavenly kingdom was already a reality and would be fully manifested in the future among the kingdoms of the earth (Dan. 2, 7).

4:4–9. The King's Dream. The king provided the setting within which he experienced the wonders of the Most High. He was in the palace, enjoying the benefits of national peace. In the absence of war, he was interested in developing, strengthening, and beautifying the city of Babylon. It was in this setting of peace that the king had a dream that made him afraid and unsettled (v. 5). His inner peace was gone, and he could only think about this dream. This time, in contrast to the earlier dream (Dan. 2), Nebuchadnezzar remembered every detail of it and expected his wise men to interpret it for him. Once more human wisdom was unable to provide the interpretation. Finally, Daniel was summoned before the king to interpret the dream.

4:10–18. Content of the Dream. The dream was indeed very strange. The king saw a very high tree in the middle of the earth, reaching to the heavens and visible from the extremes of the earth. It was a beautiful and fruitful tree that provided food for all and shade to the animals. This was a cosmic tree, which was a common idea in the mythology of the ANE. The cosmic tree integrated the cosmos by bringing together the heavenly and the earthly realms of creation. Life flowed from it to all living creatures. The reference to its height reaching the sky (v. 11) reminds us of the Tower of Babel (Gen. 11:4), which was a symbol of human pride, arrogance, and ambition.

In the dream the king saw a heavenly being, an angel called a holy watcher or messenger, descending directly from heaven with an urgent message of judgment against the tree. The cosmic tree would be chopped down. Only a stump with a band of iron and bronze would be left.

There is some evidence for an ancient custom of putting metal bands on trees, whether to prevent them from cracking or for some other undetermined reason. Tree stumps with bands of metal have been found at Khorsabad and on cylinder seals from the palace of Ashurnasirpal (885–860 B.C.) at Nimrud.

The images used change rather quickly from the tree stump to a human being grazing among the animals of the earth (Dan. 4:15). The heart of the human being was to be changed to the heart of an animal. This mental condition would last for "seven times" (v. 16) or seven years. The reasons we do not apply the year-day principle to this time period are that (1) this is primarily a historic and not a prophetic chapter and (2) it is a period of judgment restricted to King Nebuchadnezzar.

The purpose of this judgment was to make clear to humans that the Lord rules over all the kingdoms of the earth (v. 17). The final authority in human affairs is found in God and not in political and religious institutions of human origin. There is a proper place for an earthly kingdom as long as it recognizes that God's kingdom is above all others. He gives the earthly kingdom to whomever He wants.

4:19–27. Daniel Interprets the Dream. It appears that the interpretation of the dream was given to Daniel as he was listening to the king. For a moment he was disturbed (v. 19). One of the Aramaic words used here means "to be devastated." This suggests that he respected and appreciated the king. Daniel was perhaps troubled because he could not anticipate the reaction of the king to what Daniel had to tell him. The king, sensing the emotional state of Daniel, encouraged him to speak. The prophet cautiously began to tell the king the interpretation of the dream, starting with the graceful and diplomatic wish that the import of the dream would not apply to the king but to his enemies.

The tree represented the king, not his kingdom. It illustrated the human achievements of the king who, like the tree, had become strong. His greatness reached to heaven/the sky and his dominion to the farthest parts of the earth (vv. 21–22). But like the tree, the king would lose all of his greatness and would be deprived of social interaction. For seven years he would dwell among the beasts of the field, eating grass and without shelter (v. 25). Some scholars have identified this type of behavior with a mental disease that used to be called lycanthropy (Gr. *lukos*, "wolf," and *anthrōpos*, "human being," a person behaving like an animal or a wolf). The emphasis of the text is not on natural causation but on direct divine intervention. Although the greatness of the king would be removed from him, his kingdom would be preserved—the stump and the roots

were to be left in place. There was hope for him. The dream was not about the collapse of the Babylonian kingdom (v. 26).

Daniel informed the king of a divine purpose in the experience he would go through. He had infringed on the realm of God, and this needed to be redressed. It was important for the king to understand that the Most High is the Sovereign Ruler of all human kingdoms and that He gives them to whomever He chooses (v. 25). Nebuchadnezzar had to acknowledge that Heaven rules (v. 26). This may be the first time in the Bible where the term "Heaven" stands for "God." There are limits to human power, particularly in cases when it expresses itself through human kingship. Human pride should never attempt to usurp divine sovereignty. Daniel concluded his speech with personal advice to the king. If the king ruled with justice and mercy, his prosperity would perhaps continue (v. 27). Daniel's counsel indicated that the king still had a chance to avert the necessity of learning the hard way. It was a call to repentance, to accept his role within the divine plan.

4:28–37. Fulfillment of the Dream. The Lord gave the king a year to reflect on the dream and on Daniel's advice to him. While walking about the royal palace, his pride reached up to heaven—he claimed to be able to rule over the earth by himself, in total independence from God. He ascribed to himself might, power, honor, and glory, based on his achievements (v. 30). What was left for him was a divine judgment that would reveal to him his true condition. Instead of greatness, the king had reached the level of irrational animals, and God would actually bring him down to that level. By his actions the king sealed his fate, and the heavenly messenger announced it to him. Once more it was revealed to the king that judgment aims at salvation. This happened in order for him to know that the Most High rules over earthly kingdoms. This would not be an arbitrary divine action but rather something intended for the good of the king.

At the end of the seven years, Nebuchadnezzar looked toward heaven, and his mental state was restored (v. 34). This was not a mere look to the heavens but a look that acknowledged the supremacy of the God of heaven and a willingness to be part of His plan for the king. This was a fundamental act of humility and dependence on God (cf. Ps. 123:1–2). His first recorded action was to praise and honor the

Most High (Dan. 4:34) because only His dominion and kingdom are truly everlasting (v.
35). Compared to Him, said the king, humans
are reputed as nothing and are unable to restrain
His hand. No one could call Him to account.
But this confession does not mean that humans
could not enjoy success, splendor, and honor.
Once the king found his place within the divine plan and will for him, he was restored to
even higher greatness (v. 36). He concluded his
royal missive not only praising God, the King
of heaven, but confessing that He could humble
those who live (lit. "walk") in pride (v. 37).

This is one of the most remarkable stories in
the Bible. It is a public confession by one of the
greatest kings of ancient times, telling of his arrogance, humiliation, and eventual conversion
to the God of heaven. Nebuchadnezzar's life
prior to this event was one long success story.
By military might he had subdued all the surrounding nations. At his feet bowed the representatives of all nations. But at the height of
his power, God brought him low. It is a story
of warning to us all. If we make our happiness
depend on anything less than heaven, we invite
failure.

With this chapter Daniel brings to a close the
involvement of Nebuchadnezzar in the affairs
of Babylon. The existing Mesopotamian records
do not provide detailed information about his
death. His conversion and public proclamation
of his acceptance of the authority of God was
the last act of his life recorded in Scripture. "The
once proud monarch had become a humble
child of God" (PK 521). After a long reign, he
died clearly blessed and full of glory. None of
those who succeeded him on the throne were
able to maintain the golden glory, much less follow the example of repentance and surrender
to the Almighty. The principle that Nebuchadnezzar took a long time to learn is still valid
today—God is in control of this universe and
has assigned to each individual a place and a
task in His great plan.

5:1–31
THE WRITING ON THE WALL

The events in Daniel 5 took place on the night
of the fall of Babylon in 539 B.C. Daniel at that
time had been in Babylon for more than sixty
years and was an old man. A thousand guests
were in a great banquet hall. While the king
and his guests drank from containers from the
temple in Jerusalem (v. 2), a divine hand wrote
on the wall. The king was terrified and called
for the wise men, but they were unable to deci-
pher the writing. Finally, the queen mother reminded the king about Daniel (vv. 10–12). The
aged prophet proclaimed God's judgment to the
king (vv. 25–28). The epilogue simply states
that during that very night God's judgment was
carried out.

5:1–12. Belshazzar's Feast. In the ten years
that followed the death of Nebuchadnezzar
in 562 B.C., four different rulers ascended the
throne of Babylon in quick succession. The
fourth, Nabonidus, a prince from Haran who had
served Nebuchadnezzar as a diplomatic officer,
married his daughter Nitocris. Around 550 B.C.,
while campaigning in the Holy Land, Nabonidus fell ill and went to Lebanon to recuperate.
He summoned his son Belshazzar and entrusted
the kingship to him; in other words, Nabonidus
made him coregent to safeguard the perpetuity of his royal house. After recovering from his
illness, Nabonidus began an invasion of northwestern Arabia where he conquered the oasis of
Tema, which was to become his residency and
where he built large palaces. He stayed there
until 539 B.C. while his son Belshazzar reigned
in Babylon as its king. Until 1854, critics claimed
Belshazzar was an invention of the biblical author because ancient sources available at that
time reported that Nabonidus was the last king
of Babylon and made no mention of Belshazzar.
Then in 1854 the first cuneiform cylinder with
Belshazzar's name was found in the city of Ur.
In 1882 the Nabonidus Chronicles, which state
that Nabonidus lived in Tema for several years
while his son Belshazzar was ruling in Babylon,
were translated.

In 539 B.C. Cyrus captured Babylon without
a fight. According to the Babylonian Chronicles, Nabonidus fled south prior to the attack,
while Belshazzar, who had stayed in Babylon,
remained there, trusting in the city's strong fortifications. It was here that, in a spirit of pride
and arrogance, he spent his last evening with
his friends in frivolous drinking, using the sacred drinking containers of Solomon's temple.
Then the fingers of a human hand appeared on
the wall (v. 5). Instantly, the laughter, singing,
and merrymaking stopped, and a stunned and
petrified silence filled the room. The night of
revelry became a night of revelation. The biblical text notes that four things happened to
Belshazzar: (1) a recognizable change came
over his face; (2) courage left him; (3) he lost
strength in his legs/bowels (a description of

incontinence); and (4) his knees knocked together (v. 6). In one brief moment, the boastful king became a shivering, shaking, and hopeless mortal. God is deadly serious when it comes to holy things. Belshazzar wantonly profaned the sacred drinking containers from the temple of Jerusalem, and he died by the end of the day. What God has declared holy (including the Sabbath or His tithe) should be treated with reverence and care.

The inscription was probably in Aramaic, which like Hebrew is written only in consonants, and it was so short that although they may have understood the individual words, they did not grasp the overall message. The queen mother referred to Nebuchadnezzar as Belshazzar's "father," but as already stated, according to the ancient sources, Nabonidus was the father of Belshazzar. The word "father" in Semitic languages, to which Hebrew and Aramaic belong, can also mean grandfather, ancestor, or even unrelated predecessor. There are no known terms for "grandfather" or "ancestor" in these languages.

5:13–31. The Fall of Babylon. Before Daniel read and interpreted the writing, he reviewed the experience of the king's grandfather, who was humbled by the Lord as a result of his refusal to heed God's warnings. Belshazzar was acquainted with these experiences, but he had chosen to ignore them. Daniel told Belshazzar that he had learned nothing from his grandfather's experiences and that he had now lifted himself up against the Lord of heaven by bringing the vessels of the temple in Jerusalem into the banqueting hall.

Then Daniel proceeded to read the inscription. In Aramaic the inscription consisted of four words. How they were to be read depended on what vowels were supplied. Daniel read them out as *mene', mene', teqel, (u)parsin* and then gave the interpretation. The interpretation spelled imminent doom for Belshazzar. A few hours later, the Persians under Gobryas (probably the biblical Darius the Mede, one of Cyrus's generals) entered the city and slew Belshazzar (v. 30). Gobryas established order in the city and won the people's goodwill by his respect for their temples.

How were the Persians able to penetrate the seemingly impregnable defenses of the city? The Greek historian Herodotus reports that the Medes and the Persians turned the Euphrates out of its channel and were able to march into the heart of the city through it. The Babylonians did not expect their city to fall. They thought they were safe behind its mighty walls, but there is no real peace in human achievements (cf. 1 Thess. 5:3).

Cyrus appears in Isaiah 45:1 as a type of Jesus the Messiah. As Cyrus came from the east (41:2, 25; 46:11) to overthrow ancient Babylon and deliver Israel from the Babylonian captivity, so Christ would come from the east to deliver His people from end-time Babylon at the battle of Armageddon (Rev. 16:12–16). As God's people of old left Babylon to return to Jerusalem, so God's people will leave this earthly, spiritual Babylon (18:1–4) to enter the new Jerusalem (21:2).

6:1–28

THE DELIVERANCE OF DANIEL AND DARIUS

Daniel 6 is the last historical chapter in the book. Although he was now more than eighty years of age, Daniel was placed in charge of the government of Babylon by the Persians, the conquerors of the Babylonian Empire. But this aroused the jealousy of his colleagues. They managed to deceive the king, and Daniel ended up in the lions' den, but God delivered him, and in the end the king honored God.

6:1–9. Plot against Daniel. The term "satrap" means "protector of the kingdom." According to Xenophon and other Greek historians, it referred to any rank of subordinate officials in the kingdom and should not be confused with the geographic regions of the kingdom called satrapies. According to Herodotus, the Medo-Persian Empire was divided into twenty satrapies. Since Darius the Mede in Daniel 6 ruled only over the kingdom of Babylon, the 120 satraps most likely were royal officials who ruled over smaller divisions within his realm.

Under Darius the Mede, Daniel was recalled from retirement and became one of the three chief officials. As such he had supervisory powers over all the provincial governors. The king undoubtedly acted in the best interests of the state in elevating Daniel to the highest civil office, but he failed to take into account the feelings of jealousy among his top officials. To place a Jew, a former prime minister of the defeated Babylonians, in such a high position was too much for the other officers. These politicians, therefore, ordered their legal sleuths to "dig for dirt" in Daniel's character, but they could not find any skeletons in his closet because he was loyal to the king (v. 4). Digging up dirt and slandering the other contenders has obviously been a favored method since ancient times to bring down the opposition.

Daniel's "colleagues" managed to persuade the king to make a firm decree that his people must pray for one month to no one but the king. Though in this instance aimed at Daniel, it may have been suggested by a national custom of earlier times among the Medes, according to which special honors were rendered to the king.

6:10–17. Daniel in the Lions' Den. In spite of the decree, Daniel went home and did what he was used to doing; he prayed three times to his God. Daniel neither left on pretended business nor said his prayers in secret. To rationalize such compromises to preserve his life and his position would have been easy, but he refused to compromise. Knowing very well what was going on, he was willing to risk his life to honor God, trusting his Lord to deliver him if He saw fit. Like Shadrach, Meshach, and Abednego, he chose loyalty to God over obedience to a pagan government.

Daniel's house would have been the normal flat-topped dwelling, with a room built on the roof that had large latticed windows to allow free circulation of air. The custom of turning toward Jerusalem when praying is based on Solomon's prayer (1 Kin. 8:35) and is still practiced by many Jews today. Eliezer and Solomon stood when praying (Gen. 24:12–14; 1 Kin. 8:22–23). Daniel, like Ezra (Ezra 9:5), Jesus (Luke 22:41), Stephen (Acts 7:60), and Paul (Eph. 3:14), used the more customary position of kneeling.

The king soon realized that his own officials had led him into a trap to get rid of Daniel, and Darius was greatly upset. Although he did his best to save Daniel from the den of lions to which Darius had unwittingly condemned him, Darius was unable to change the law of the Medes and Persians. At sunset he was forced to execute the sentence. What a long night he must have spent with a bad conscience!

The den of lions was probably an underground pit with perpendicular walls and an opening at the top. The condemned were lowered or thrown into it from above. In this particular case, a large stone was rolled over the opening and was sealed with the king's signet ring and that of his nobles. The seal was a guarantee to Daniel's enemies that no attempt would be made to save him but also to the king that Daniel would not be harmed in any way

if, as the king hoped, the God of Daniel should preserve him from the lions.

6:18–28. Daniel Saved and Darius's Response. As soon as the morning dawned, the king hastened to the lions' den. He called to Daniel and asked him whether his God had been able to deliver him (v. 20). Yes, God is able to deliver, but whether He does or not must be left in His hands. He did not deliver Daniel from being thrown alive into the den of lions, and neither did He deliver John the Baptist. Through the ages many martyrs who perished were comforted as they recalled that Christ Himself had been permitted to suffer.

In throwing the accusers with their wives and children into the den of lions (v. 24), the king acted in the fashion typical of the despots of his day. Herodotus testifies that consigning to death whole families along with condemned men was in accordance with Persian custom. Darius then sent out a letter in different languages across his kingdom (cf. 4:1). He commanded his people to fear and revere the God of Daniel, the living God who performed a miracle in delivering Daniel from the lions (6:26). The chapter concludes with the statement that Daniel prospered in the reigns of Darius and Cyrus (v. 28). Daniel prospered because he could give thanks to God although facing the lion's den (v. 10); he believed in prayer. He was faithful in his work and refused to do evil. Neither rank nor wealth could sway him from his faithfulness to God (2:48; 5:29; 6:3).

7:1–28
THE KINGDOM OF GOD

Daniel 7 is the last chapter written in Aramaic. This links it with the preceding chapters, while the vision of the four beasts connects it with the later chapters. It is largely parallel to the vision of the image given to King Nebuchadnezzar in chapter 2, but from here on we have the record of Daniel as the recipient of the visions and their interpretations. There are some differences between both chapters. Daniel 2 provides a general survey of the future from Nebuchadnezzar's days until the Second Advent, while Daniel 7 focuses on the time period between the end of the fourth empire and the Second Advent. Daniel 2 portrays the worldly empires from a political perspective, but Daniel 7 includes the military struggles, through the symbol of wild animals, and also the spiritual conflict, through the symbol of the little horn. Daniel 7 shows that between the fourth empire and the Second Advent, symbolized by the falling stone in Daniel 2, a religiopolitical power would grow from small beginnings to great dominion.

7:1–8. Vision of the Beasts and the Little Horn. In 550 B.C., during the first year of Belshazzar (v. 1), or about fifty years after the vision of chapter 2, Daniel saw that the four winds of heaven were breaking out upon the Great Sea, from which four beasts arose. These symbols were familiar to the prophet. In Scripture, winds represent storms of war and conquest (Jer. 25:31–33; 49:36–37; Zech. 7:14; Rev. 7:1). Flooding rivers symbolize the movements of invading armies (e.g., Is. 8:7–8; Jer. 46:6–8; Amos 8:8). According to Daniel 7:17, the four beasts represent four kings or kingdoms that would be or exist upon the earth (v. 23). In both the Scriptures and popular symbolism of ancient and modern times, wild animals are a familiar symbol for nations and empires. The symbolism of beasts that rise from a wind-torn sea points to political wars and conquests. Three of the kingdoms are identified in Daniel as the Babylonian (2:38), the Medo-Persian (5:28, 30), and the Greek (8:20–21). The fourth one was identified by Jesus as Rome (Matt. 24:15–16).

The first beast, a lion (Dan. 7:4), was a particularly appropriate symbol for Babylon. Representations of lions have been found on the walls of the great Babylonian processional way to the Ishtar Gate and on the gate itself. That its wings were taken off indicates that after Nebuchadnezzar's completion of his immense program of conquest and reconstruction, his successors settled down, in the way so typical of human complacency, to enjoy the wealth and luxury they had inherited. The second beast, a lopsided bear that was crunching three ribs, represents the empire of Medo-Persia and its conquest of Lydia (547 B.C.), Babylon (539 B.C.), and Egypt (525 B.C.) under the leadership of Cyrus and Cambyses. The third beast, a leopard, is noted for the swiftness and the agility of its movements. The four wings are a fitting symbol for the speed of movement that was characteristic of the young Alexander the Great, who set out in 334 B.C. with thirty-five thousand men and who, in ten years, established the greatest and most influential empire the world had known up to that time.

In vision, Daniel saw that the empire of Greece would be divided into four kingdoms, and this is exactly what occurred. When Alexander died, a power struggle among his generals led to the division of the empire into four kingdoms: Seleucus controlled Syria and the East all the way to India; western Asia Minor and Thrace fell to Lysimachus; Ptolemy became king of Egypt; and Cassander, already governor of Macedon, was now recognized as the sovereign of Greece. In this way they created a new political map of the Near East that was to last until the Romans conquered the whole ANE.

Based on the clear parallel structure of the visions between Daniel 2 and 7, the fourth beast, the animal with iron teeth (v. 7), appears here as evidently the counterpart of the iron legs and feet of the image in Daniel 2. By A.D. 200 it was commonly recognized among the church fathers that the fourth kingdom was Rome. World power may be said to have passed from the Greeks to the Romans at the Battle of Pydna in 168 B.C., when the Roman general Paullus won a decisive victory over Perseus of Macedonia. By 146 B.C. Macedonia was a Roman province, and in 63 B.C. Syria and Judea became Roman provinces. During the next few decades, Roman legions marched westward and conquered the countries that were to become Spain, France, and England. Finally, in 30 B.C. Egypt, the last of the great Hellenistic kingdoms, was annexed as a province, and all the then-known world was united under one government, speaking Greek in the east and Latin in the west. Notice that the Roman Empire is described as different from all the previous kingdoms (7:7, 19) and that it would do what the others could not do, namely, "devour the whole earth" (v. 23). It was to transcend geographical boundaries and become a universal phenomenon.

The ten horns (v. 24) are not treated independently from the beast but are seen as a continuation of its activities. The horns correspond to the feet and toes of the image and represent the nations that would arise from the ruins of the Roman Empire and would maintain Roman civilization to a large extent. Some interpreters have identified the ten horns as ten tribes and the European kingdoms descending from them (e.g., Vandals, Visigoths, Sueves, Anglo-Saxons, Franks, Alemannians, Burgundians, Lombards, Ostrogoths, and Heruls). Others have argued that it is best to take the number ten as a round figure (e.g., Gen. 31:7; Num. 14:22; 1 Sam. 1:8) representing a multiplicity of states in contrast to the one empire of Rome.

Among the ten horns, another horn, a small one, emerged (Dan. 7:8). Though small at the beginning, this little horn is later described as more significant than the other ones (v. 20).

Critical scholars, as well as some conservative Bible interpreters, identify the little horn in Daniel 7 and 8 as the Syrian king Antiochus IV Epiphanes (175–164 B.C.). This interpretation goes back to the Neoplatonic philosopher Porphyry (A.D. 232–305), who wrote fifteen books attacking Christianity. In one of them, he claimed that the book of Daniel was written in the second century B.C. and that the little horn is the Syrian king Antiochus IV (see "The Little Horn and Antiochus IV," p. 1039). Today, most conservative interpreters are futurists and see the little horn as a symbol of a yet future end-time antichrist or argue that the symbol has a dual application to Antiochus and the antichrist. Seventh-day Adventists, who champion historicism, agree with those church historians who believe that the only power in history that fits the description of the little horn is Christian Rome and that the three uprooted horns were Arian kingdoms (see "The Union of Church and State," p. 1033).

7:9–14. Vision of the Ancient of Days, the Beast, and the Son of Man. This passage presents three scenes: (a) a judgment in heaven (vv. 9–10); (b) an announcement of the end of the fourth beast (vv. 11–12); and (c) Christ receiving the kingdom (vv. 13–14). The whole picture is one of overwhelming grandeur, with God, the Ancient of Days, as supreme judge, seated on His throne in the heavenly court surrounded by myriads of angels. The prophet saw the Ancient of Days (v. 9), literally "one advanced in days," a symbolic description of God the Father as a wise judge, moving to where the judgment would take place. His movable throne was like a chariot of fiery flames, with wheels of burning fire, similar to the movable sapphire throne Ezekiel saw in vision (Ezek. 1). The emphasis is on the brightness of the throne.

In the vision Daniel saw that books were opened (Dan. 7:10). In Scripture the heavenly books are a record of human deeds, experiences, and words, and they are used in a judgment setting to provide objective evidence supporting the pronouncement of a just verdict. In the biblical concept, the judgment includes an examination or investigation of the information found in the books. The Bible mentions the Book of Life (or "the living"; Ps. 69:28; cf. Phil. 4:3) and the scroll or book "of remembrance" (Mal. 3:16), and John not only mentions the Book of Life but also other books (Rev. 20:12), perhaps the same as those mentioned in Daniel 7:10. The Book of Life contains the names of those who place their faith

in God (Dan. 12:1; Heb. 12:23; Rev. 17:8; 21:27) or of those who have entered the service of God. One of the purposes of the judgment is to publicly show whether a person has remained faithful to his or her commitment to God. The judgment described in Daniel is of cosmic proportions and takes place before the heavenly family (see "The Cleansing of the Sanctuary and Judgment in Daniel," p. 1043).

In the vision the judgment scene was interrupted by the proud (lit. "great") words uttered by the little horn (7:11), but when Daniel turned, he saw the ultimate destruction of the beast whose body was burnt because of its unfaithfulness (cf. Lev. 20:14; 21:9; Josh. 7:15; Rev. 17:16; 18:8). This executive judgment against the beast was to occur at the eschatological end and not at the time of the collapse of the pagan Roman Empire. The beast was to remain alive through the period of the ten horns, into which it was divided, and particularly through the period of the little horn itself (Dan. 7:25–26).

Verse 12 functions as a parenthesis that reflects on the fact that the first three beast-kingdoms, although deprived of their authority, were allowed to live for a period of time. Babylon was conquered by Persia in 539 B.C., but the city continued to exist for centuries. Greece and Persia still exist today but not with the power and glory they had in OT times. Thus, each of these powers lived on after its dominion was taken away. Elements of those ancient cultures have impacted the Western world.

In the judgment scene (vv. 13–14), Daniel saw One like the Son of Man or a humanlike being coming to the courtroom (v. 13). "Son of Man" was Jesus's favorite title for Himself (e.g., Matt. 8:20; 10:23), and it is one that can be viewed as emphasizing His connection with humanity. At the same time, it was a messianic title, based on this text in Daniel (26:63–64). Some have assumed that coming with the clouds must refer to the Second Coming of Jesus, and in fact there are passages which associate the clouds of heaven with the Second Coming of Christ (24:30; 26:64; Rev. 1:7). But in Daniel 7 this interpretation is not possible because in the vision the Ancient of Days was not on this earth but in heaven. The text says that He went before the Ancient of Days. Both of them move from one place to another—as the high priest did during the Day of Atonement. In fact, the imagery used in the vision is that of the high priest approaching God covered by a cloud of incense during the Day of Atonement—a day of judgment (see "The Theology of the Day of

The Union of Church and State

The apostles hardly could have imagined that the time would come when the church would move from the fringes of the Roman Empire to its very center of power. In fact, the church received civil power in almost unexpected ways and soon began to use it, becoming an oppressive institution. The details about how this happened are not always clear, but we have enough historical information to pinpoint the events that led to a radical transformation of the Christian church and its message.

1. Chronological Focus. As we examine the history of the first few centuries, we can identify the following events as key ones in the union of the secular and the sacred powers.

• **A.D. 303** Beginning of the last and most severe persecution of Christians in the Roman Empire under Emperor Diocletian.

• **A.D. 313** Edict of Milan. Christians were granted full religious freedom. This included the restoration of confiscated property to the previous owners. Only one year later, religious freedom was restricted through a decree that ordered that the returned church property must be given to the Catholic body of the Christians. From that time Constantine began to side with the Catholic faction of the Christian church.

• **A. D. 314** Sylvester I was named bishop of Rome. He was crowned and clad in imperial raiment as an earthly prince. For centuries persecuted by the Roman Empire, Catholic Christianity assumed an intimate relationship with secular power and quickly grew to a position of great influence over the affairs of the empire.

• **A.D. 321** Emperor Constantine issued an edict, establishing a pagan day of rest that prohibited work on "the venerable day of the sun" (Sunday), the day that has come to be substituted for the seventh-day Sabbath. (In about 364, the local Catholic Church Council of Laodicea formally prohibited the keeping of the "Jewish Sabbath" by Christians.)

• **A.D. 324** The emperor formally recognized Christianity as an official religion of the empire. The previous year, Constantine defeated the eastern emperor, Licinius, and became the sole emperor of east and west. Thus, Christianity was at this time an established religion throughout the Roman world.

• **A.D. 330** Emperor Constantine moved the capital of the empire to Byzantium (Constantinople). The result was that the bishop of Rome gradually filled the power vacuum left in Rome.

• **A.D. 380** Emperor Theodosius I (378–395) made Catholic Christianity the official religion of the empire. In 394 he formally outlawed worshiping the ancient gods in the empire.

• **A.D. 452** Attila the Hun appeared in northern Italy with a great army. The road to Rome lay open before him. Its citizens expected the worst, but Rome was spared. The bishop of Rome at this time, Leo I (440–461), traveled northward to the River Po to meet the mighty Attila. There is no record of the conversation between the two, but one fact is clear: as a fearless diplomat, Leo confronted the "Scourge of God" and won. He somehow persuaded Attila to abandon his quest for the Eternal City. Attila died shortly afterward, and the Huns troubled Europe no more.

The prestige of the medieval church was greatly enhanced by Leo's intervention on behalf of Rome. As the civil government grew increasingly incapable of keeping order, the Catholic Church began to take its place, assuming many secular responsibilities. History records that it was Leo the Great who laid the foundations for the temporal power of the popes. Leo became the leading figure in Italy, and in the religious sphere he strongly asserted the primacy of Rome's bishop over all other bishops. Earlier in the century, the illustrious Augustine (354–430), bishop of Hippo in North Africa, uttered the now-famous words, *"roma locuta, causa finite"* ("Rome has spoken, the case is closed"). At the Council of Chalcedon in 451, the assembled bishops responded to Leo's pronouncements with the words "Peter has spoken by Leo; let him be anathema who believes otherwise." The doctrine that papal power had been granted by Christ to Peter, and that that power was passed on by Peter to his successors in Rome, began to take firm root.

• **A.D. 533** Emperor Justinian in Constantinople recognized the pope in Rome as the head of the whole church, both east and west. This was incorporated in his law code, Codex Justinianus, which ensured that Catholic Christianity was the state religion of the empire. All citizens of the empire became required to belong to the Catholic Church. Through this legislation Justinian achieved the complete union of church and state.

• **A.D. 538** Belisarius, the general of the Eastern Roman emperor Justinian, delivered Rome from the siege of the Arian Ostrogoths, and the papacy was able to freely expand its power from then on. Thus, the formal appointment of the bishop of Rome as "the head of all the Holy Churches" was implemented with the liberation of Rome in 538 and the establishment of the Justinian code as the underlying philosophical and legal basis of Roman law.

2. Arian Influence. The Germanic tribes who invaded the Roman Empire were converted to the Arian form of Christianity. The Council of Nicea (325) condemned Arianism, but the movement continued to be strong in many areas of Europe. Arianism was a heresy of the fourth century A.D., named for Arius, a presbyter in Alexandria, Egypt, who denied the eternal existence of Christ and the Trinity. Arius held that Jesus was created by God as the first act of Creation. This view was condemned at the Council of Nicea in 325. However, Arianism achieved great popularity after the death of Constantine in 337 because his son and successor Constantius promoted it. The controversy came to an end at the Council of Constantinople in 381 when Arianism was again condemned.

It was probably in 508 that Clovis, pagan chieftain of the Franks who was married to a Catholic wife, converted to Roman Catholicism and was baptized (see commentary on Dan. 12:5–13). The Catholics rallied around him as the only Catholic prince in the west and assisted him in conquering the Arian princes. In turn he found it prudent to promote the church, and the Franks were called the "oldest son" of the Roman church.

Through the influence of the bishop of Rome, the emperors of the Roman Empire were instrumental in eliminating three of the ten barbarian kingdoms that had settled in the Roman Empire. In 493 the Heruli were eliminated by the Ostrogoths as one of the three "plucked out" horns. The other two Arian kingdoms were defeated by the Eastern Roman emperor Justinian's general Belisarius: the Vandals in 533 and the Ostrogoths in 553.

3. Centralization of Power. Political foresight and shrewd diplomacy are characteristic of apostate Christianity. The removal of the capital to Constantinople in A.D. 330, and the end of the Western Empire in A.D. 476, left the bishop of Rome as the one to whom the people in the Western Empire looked in place of the emperor. Thus, the pope in Rome soon became the political, as well as the spiritual, head in the west. Three events greatly enhanced the power of the church.

The first event was the *Donation of Pippin.* In 756, Pippin, king of the Franks, responded to an appeal from Pope Stephen II for help against the Lombards. Pippin went to war against the Lombards, defeated them, and presented the pope with some of their conquered territory.

The second event was the purported *Donation of Constantine.* In the eighth century, a document appeared that claimed that Emperor Constantine (306–337) had given to the pope the city of Rome, all of Italy, and the western regions as his temporal domain and that Constantine had also given him supremacy over the four principal sees of Alexandria, Antioch, Jerusalem, and Constantinople and the churches of God in the whole earth. It has been suggested that Stephen II used this document in his negotiations with Pippin to obtain the conquered Lombard territories. In 1440 Lorenzo Valla exposed the document as a fraud.

The third event was the crowning of Charlemagne by the pope. On Christmas Day A.D. 800, Pope Leo III unexpectedly placed a crown on the head of Charlemagne while the latter was kneeling before the altar of the old St. Peter's Basilica, proclaiming him ruler of the Holy Roman Empire. The pope thereby established under his own control the so-called Holy Roman Empire, in which, for a thousand years, emperors would be presumed to rule Europe by permission of the pope. The Holy Roman Empire continued until 1806 when Napoleon forced Emperor Franz II of Austria to relinquish the title "Holy Roman Emperor."

The power of the church reached its zenith under Gregory VII (1018–1085), who first promulgated the theory that the pope could depose kings, and under Innocent III (1198–1216), who made himself absolute sovereign over the Roman Catholic kings of the Holy Roman Empire and organized crusades against the Muslims in Spain and the Holy Land and the Albigenses or Cathars in southern France.

Atonement," p. 264). It is in the presence of God that the Son functions as the Mediator for sinners (Dan. 12:1; Heb. 7:25), and it is there that at the eschaton the Son receives dominion, glory, and the kingdom.

7:15–28. Interpretation of the Vision. As in chapter 2, here also the symbolic revelation is followed by its interpretation. Daniel found the vision incomprehensible and sought an interpretation from the accompanying angel, who offered a brief interpretation identifying the four beasts as four kings that would arise in human history. But the only kingdom that was to last forever was the kingdom of the Most High, and it would be given to His saints. Note that the term "kings" is used throughout this section interchangeably with "kingdoms" (7:17–18, 22–23).

Daniel was particularly concerned about the fourth beast and its little horn. In a flashback, he describes again what he saw in the vision, adding a few new insights (vv. 19–22). He saw the little horn persecuting the people of God and also that the coming of the Son of Man to the Ancient of Days would initiate the judgment that resulted in the vindication of His people (v. 22). An angel said to Daniel that the judgment would result in the destruction of their enemies (v. 26). The angel proceeded to interpret the vision and informed Daniel that the beast would not be an ordinary kingdom but one intending to control the whole earth through terror and violence. The angel explained the ten horns as a symbol of the division of the kingdom and clarified the nature and work of the little horn that would last for a time, times, and half a time (see below, "The Little Horn in Daniel 7").

The Little Horn in Daniel 7

The interpretation of the little horn is to be based on the information that the text itself provides for us and its correlation to the history of God's people. The text informs us about its origin, its nature, and its work.

1. Its Origin. The text places the origin of the little horn at a particular chronological moment in the vision. First, it appears in history after the division of the Roman Empire, that is to say, after the ten horns/ kings arise (v. 24). The Christianization of the Roman Empire prepared the way for the rise of the little horn after the fall of the kingdom. The successor of the empire was not the barbarian kingdoms but the Christian church, later to be known as the Holy Roman Empire, a kingdom without geographical boundaries. What at first may have seemed to be a good thing—the union of church and state—proved itself to be toxic to Christianity. Second, its origin is associated with the uprooting of three of the ten horns (vv. 8, 20, 24), thus confirming the fact that it was the successor of the Roman Empire. The three kingdoms that accepted an Arian understanding of the Trinity were basically exterminated (see "The Union of Church and State," p. 1033).

2. Its Nature. The little horn is described as both different from and more significant than the others (vv. 20, 24). Compared to the other horns, this one was to have an element of uniqueness. It consolidated the remainder of pagan Rome under the Christian faith and the civil power. It was a religiopolitical entity with the power needed to violate human conscience or to persecute others. In the vision, it had eyes (vv. 8, 20), probably referring to the misuse of wisdom and insight in order to achieve its purpose. Its words were to evince arrogance, pride, and the absence of the humility that characterized the Savior (Matt. 11:29). In fact, it would speak against the Most High (Dan. 7:25). By seeking political power to promote and impose its ideas, the little horn would act against God, who has the power to lead and protect His people without human political powers. This therefore would be an arrogant religiopolitical power, identified in history as Christian Rome, which, like the kings of Israel and Judah, united with other political powers to achieve its purposes.

3. Its Work. The work of this religiopolitical power is quite clearly stated. First, it would attempt to change times and law (v. 25). The term "times" plays an important role in Daniel. God changes the "times" in the sense that He, as the Lord of history, determines when kingdoms arise and fall (2:21). He is also the One who determines the time when the saints will receive the kingdom (7:22). The fulfillment of prophecy is in His hands. The little horn, by uniting political and religious powers, would believe itself to be in control of history and the establishment of the kingdom of God on earth. It was to practically take or assume the place of God on earth. The attempt to change the law is well attested in history with the change of Sabbath to Sunday as the day of worship and rest, as well as in the modification of the second commandment regarding the worship of images. In a broader sense, the law could refer to God's instructions to His people that were preserved in the Bible. Apostate Christianity has in many ways changed, ignored, or abandoned biblical truth (cf. Acts 20:28–29).

Second, the little horn would make war against God's holy people (Dan. 7:21); that is to say, it would persecute and oppress them (v. 25). This is one of the ways in which the union of church and state was to demonstrate its power. Christianity appeals to the human conscience through the persuasive power of the word of God and the power of the Spirit without violating human freedom. When the church uses civil power to enforce its positions, it is acting against God and His people. The best example of the persecuting power of the little horn is the Inquisition. During the Middle Ages, the growing threat of heretical groups led to the acceptance of the use of secular authority and an inquisitorial method by the church as a means to suppress heretics. Part of the theological justification for this practice was based on Augustine's (A.D. 354–430) understanding of Luke 14:23, where Jesus, in the parable of the Great Supper, said, "Compel them to come in." Augustine took this as a justification for the use of force if they would not come of their own free will.

Third, the oppressive power of Christian Rome was to remain unchallenged for a time, times, and half a time (Dan. 7:25). This time period is identified in the Bible as the equivalent of 1,260 days (Rev. 12:6) or 42 months (13:5 [42 x 30 = 1,260]), indicating that the "time" is 360 days (12 months of 30 days each = 360), "times" is twice as much (24 months of 30 days each = 720 days), and "half a time" is half a year (6 months of 30 days each = 180 [360 + 720 + 180 = 1,260]). This prophetic period extends from 538 to 1798 (see "The 1,260 Days/Years," p. 1037; "The Union of Church and State," p. 1033; and "Interpreting Biblical Apocalyptic Prophecies," p. 46).

The victory of the people of God and the destruction of the beast are directly related to the heavenly court and the opening of the books. For God's people this would be a moment of paramount importance, for at that moment they would be vindicated before the universe. As a result of their vindication, the dominion of the little horn would come to an end, and it would be consumed and destroyed forever.

While the destruction of the enemy was to be eternal, the kingdom of the Most High is an everlasting kingdom entrusted to the saints through their Mediator, the Son of Man (vv. 13–14, 27). The vision was about the limited power of the earthly kingdoms that were to come to an end. They would succeed each other through violence and would even oppress the people of God in an attempt to defeat God's plan, but at the end all of them would fail, and God's love and concern for His people would prevail. This reversal of history was to be determined in the divine court of law and enforced in human history through the power of God and the Son of Man.

8:1–27

GOD'S SANCTUARY UNDER ATTACK

Daniel 7:28 concludes the Aramaic section of the book of Daniel; chapter 8 resumes in Hebrew. Even the symbols employed are different from those in the Aramaic section. No longer do we have wild beasts, but the clean sacrificial animals of the sanctuary are present. On the Day of Atonement, the ram and the goat were the burnt and sin offerings used in the cleansing ritual of the sanctuary (Lev. 16:5). Beyond representing Medo-Persia and Greece, these animals imply that this chapter is interested in the sanctuary service, specifically the Day of Atonement. This chapter contains a vision (Dan. 8:1–12), an audition (vv. 13–14), and a partial interpretation (vv. 15–27).

8:1–8. Vision of a Ram and a Goat. In this vision, which Daniel received about 548 B.C., he saw a ram that had two horns (v. 3). Daniel was specifically told that the ram represents the kings of Media and Persia (v. 20). Ancient records tell us that the king of Persia, when at the head of his army, bore in the place of a crown the head of a ram. The same figure is frequently found on Persian seals. The Persian kings established an empire that stretched from Asia Minor (Turkey) in the west to the borders of India in the east. Perhaps what is surprising in this vision is that it ignores the Babylonian Empire even though it is dated to the third year of the reign of Belshazzar. The chapter itself suggests an answer: the time period mentioned in it (the 2,300 days; v. 14) is to be counted from the beginning of the vision, that is to say, from the time of the Medo-Persian kingdom.

Next, Daniel saw a goat with a notable horn between its eyes. The interpretation identifies it as the kingdom of Greece (v. 21). Alexander the Great claimed to be the offspring of the god Jupiter Ammon, whose symbol was a goat. He established an even greater empire than that of the Persians. Alexander first drove the Persians out of Asia Minor. Following these victories, he marched his armies down through Syria, Phoenicia, and the Holy Land to Egypt, taking time to destroy the kingdoms along the way, including the great sea power of the island city of Tyre (332–331). After defeating Egypt, he turned east, subdued Babylon and Medo-Persia, and did not rest until he reached India. He marched his soldiers ten thousand miles (16,093 km) in eight years.

When Alexander returned to Babylon, he was only thirty-two years old and the world was at his feet. But in 323 B.C., at the height of his glory, he died, and thus the large horn was broken (v. 8). In its place four significant horns came up. The four horns represented in the vision the four kingdoms (v. 22) that arose from Alexander's empire (see 7:6). In his explanation Gabriel stated that these four kingdoms would not be as powerful as Alexander's kingdom (8:22).

8:9–14. The Little Horn. Next, we are told that a small horn came out of one of them (lit. "one horn came from smallness"). This new horn came forth from small beginnings and developed in various directions, gaining immense strength. Most commentators have assumed that in the prophecy's fulfillment the little horn came out of one of the four horns, in other words, out of one of the four Greek kingdoms that succeeded the kingdom of Alexander the Great. They have identified this little horn with the Syrian king Antiochus IV Epiphanes (175–164 B.C.). But grammatically this is unlikely, first, because the nearest antecedent of "one of them" is the winds of heaven, not the

The 1,260 Days/Years

The time, times, and half a time mentioned in Daniel 7:25 is equivalent to 1,260 days/years (see "The Little Horn in Daniel 7," p. 1035). This period extends from A.D. 538 to 1798. In A.D. 533 Emperor Justinian recognized the bishop of Rome as head of the church of both the west and east, and in A.D. 538 General Belisarius delivered Rome from the siege of Arian Christians. Thus, the bishop of Rome as "the head of all the Holy Churches" became effective in 538 (see "The Union of Church and State," p. 1033).

On November 9, 1793, the French Revolution abolished Christianity and replaced it with the worship of reason, and on February 10, 1798, Napoleon's general Berthier entered Rome and took Pope Pius VI prisoner, ending the dominant position the church had held throughout the Middle Ages. The events that took place in 533 and 1793 prepared the way for the beginning (538) and ending (1798) of the 1,260-day prophecy.

Roman Christianity, however, began to recover after 1798, as prophecy had predicted (see Rev. 13:3). On February 11, 1929, a treaty was signed in the Lateran Palace between the See of Rome (Pope Pius XI) and the Kingdom of Italy (King Victor Emmanuel III); the Lateran Treaty, as it is known in history, was ratified on June 8 of the same year. The treaty recognized the Kingdom of Italy under the dynasty of the House of Savoy, with Rome as its capital, and Italy recognized the See of Rome, with its absolute, sole jurisdiction over the state called the Vatican, and guaranteed its freedom and independence.

four horns. Thus, from the perspective of Daniel's time, the little horn would come out from one of the four points of the compass (the winds of heaven) and grow toward other directions of the compass (east and south). Second, in the vision of Daniel 7:2, "the four winds of heaven," in conjunction with the sea, were the source from which the kingdoms arose, and from that same source the little horn originated. It designates the origin of another powerful kingdom, not the origin of an insignificant political power. Third, notice how the description of the previous kingdoms compares with that of the little horn: Medo-Persia "became great" (8:4), Greece became "very great" and strong (v. 8), and the little horn was *gadal yeter* (v. 9). *Gadal* can be translated as "to become great"/"strong" or "to grow." *Yeter* can mean "excess" or "preeminence." But the phrase itself should be translated as "it became great exceedingly." It underscores the little horn's greatness as superior to those of both Medo-Persia and Greece, something which is evident from its description in the rest of the chapter (e.g., it will reach up to the heavenly hosts; v. 10). The comparison and contrast in the vision is not between the four kingdoms that were to come out of Greece but with the two previous kingdoms. This is understandable because the little horn stands for the fourth beast of Daniel 7—the part (the horn) stands for the whole (the beast). The beast is not explicitly mentioned in order to emphasize the work of the horn (Christian Rome). Besides, the symbols for the kingdoms were clean animals, and the beast was anything but clean. Fourth, the Hebrew word *yatza'* ("set out"/"came," "go out"; v. 9) is often used in Hebrew to describe movement in reference to location (e.g., Gen. 2:10; 11:31; Ex. 16:29). It is never used to describe the growing of a horn, an activity designated by the Hebrew word *'alah* ("go up," "come up") used in Daniel 8:3, 8.

Since references to the little horn in Daniel 7 and 8 come after references to Persia and Greece, it must be, as suggested, a symbol for Rome in both chapters. In Daniel 7, both the union and the distinction between pagan and Christian Rome is pointed out by their being represented separately and yet united as beast and horn. In Daniel 8, the essential unity is taken for granted, and the horn represents Rome in both its phases. Gabriel's reference to the latter period of the Grecian kingdom (v. 23) fits the gradual rise of Rome well.

The little horn, we are told, extended itself to the south, east, and the Glorious or Beautiful Land (v. 9). Rome ruled a larger territory than any of the kingdoms before it. Persia ruled from Asia Minor to India, Greece from Macedonia to India, Rome from England to Mesopotamia. Rome also ruled for a longer period than any of the kingdoms before it. Persia and Greece each ruled for about two hundred years. As a civil power, Rome ruled for six hundred years, and adding its religious form, papal Rome, has existed for more than two thousand years. Rome also had a better organized government than Persia and Greece.

Not only did the little horn become great politically, but it grew up to the host of heaven and caused some of the host and the stars to fall (v. 10). The reference to the heavenly hosts introduces a vertical shift toward heaven. According to the interpretation given to Daniel, they would be God's people on earth (v. 24) but with citizenship in heaven (Phil. 3:20; see "The Work of the Little Horn and the Prince," p. 1040). According to Revelation 1:20, stars symbolize the leaders of the church. In Daniel 8:24, the stars are called the "mighty" among God's people. When Jerusalem was destroyed by Rome in A.D. 70, more than a million Jews perished but no Christians. In the first two centuries of the Christian era, however, the emperors Nero, Decius, and Diocletian destroyed hundreds, perhaps even thousands, of Christians who refused to offer incense to the emperor.

In v. 11, the transition to the vertical plane is total. The horizontal movement serves to identify the activities of pagan Rome, but now we see the full vertical dimension. In the vision, the little horn magnified itself even as high as the Prince of the host or the Commander of the Lord's army. This suggests that now we are dealing with Christian Rome. In Joshua, the title Prince or Commander (Heb. *sar*) of the host of God's people is used to refer to a heavenly being later identified as the Lord Himself (Josh. 5:13–15; 6:2). In Daniel that heavenly being must be the One called Michael the prince (*sar*; 10:21) and Michael, the great prince (*sar*; 12:1; i.e., Christ; see "The Work of the Little Horn and the Prince," p. 1040). In 9:25, the Messiah is called *nagid*—a similar term (ruler or prince). Since the scene in the vision took place in heaven, it is obvious that we are dealing with the heavenly sanctuary, and since it was related to the work of Christian Rome, it described Christ's work after His ascension. The vision described a conflict between the little horn and the ascended Lord. In fulfilling the vision, how was the little horn to magnify itself against Christ? By openly assuming the office of Christ as mediator between God and humans, apostate Christendom would exalt itself against the Prince of the host and would fulfill 2 Thessalonians 2:4.

In the vision, the little horn also took away the *tamid*—"continual" or "daily" (the word "sacrifice" is not in the text but is supplied in most translations). This Hebrew word is frequently used in connection with the ritual in the sanctuary, not only with the sacrifices. Various parts of the sanctuary ministration in the OT are qualified by *tamid*, such as the burnt offering (Num. 29:6), the lamp that was to burn continually (*tamid*; Ex. 27:20), the fire to be kept burning on the altar (*tamid*; Lev. 6:13), and the bread that was to be (*tamid*) on the table (Num. 4:7). The word designates cultic activities performed on a regular basis, every day or once a week, in the courtyard or inside the Holy Place of the tabernacle. The term is never used with respect to the ritual of the Day of Atonement. Daniel is providing for us a view of the priestly work of Christ in the heavenly sanctuary. He is performing the antitypical work of mediation and intercession typologically represented by the daily work of the priests in the Holy Place of the earthly sanctuary (Heb. 7:25; 8:1–2).

Furthermore, the little horn cast down God's sanctuary (lit. "the place of His sanctuary"). There are two sanctuaries in Scripture: the earthly (Ex. 25:9, 40) and the heavenly (Heb. 8:1–6). The second Jerusalem temple was destroyed in A.D. 70. Yet even at that time it was not "His sanctuary" anymore (Matt. 23:37–39; 27:50–51). The only sanctuary functioning after Christ's ascension was the heavenly one.

In fulfilling the prophecy, how did apostate Christianity take away the daily and cast down the place of its sanctuary? By placing the work of intercession into the hands of priests through the confessional and by sacrificing Christ anew in every mass, spiritual Rome removed Christ's heavenly ministry from the thinking of people. Through the absolution of sins, the Roman priests occupied the place of Jesus before believers. These teachings and practices led to the overthrowing of the ministry of Christ in the heavenly sanctuary in the minds of many

The Little Horn and Antiochus IV

Characteristics of the Little Horn	Reasons Why the Little Horn Is Not Antiochus IV
The little horn came up among ten horns (7:8).	Antiochus IV did not come up among ten Hellenistic kings.
Three horns were plucked out before it (v. 8).	There is no historical evidence that Antiochus uprooted three kingdoms.
The little horn became greater than his fellows (v. 20).	Antiochus was not greater than the other kings in his time. In fact, the presence of the Roman ambassador Popilius Laenas, without an army, was sufficient to cause Antiochus IV to withdraw from Egypt. Seleucus I and Antiochus III the Great were definitely greater Syrian kings than Antiochus IV.
The saints were to be given into his hands for three-and-a-half times/years (v. 25).	According to 1 Maccabees 1:54; 4:52–54, the desecration of the temple lasted only three years and ten days. According to 2 Maccabees 10:3–4, the desecration of the temple lasted only two years.
As indicated, there appears to be a definite progression of increasing greatness from Medo-Persia to Greece to the little horn (8:4, 8, 9, etc.).	Antiochus IV's kingdom was not greater than Medo-Persia or Greece.
It would last for 2,300 days, and then the sanctuary was to be cleansed (v. 14).	The sanctuary defiled by Antiochus was cleansed after three years and ten days, not after six years and approximately four months if the 2,300 days are taken as a literal time reference.
The little horn was to come in the latter days of their kingdom (v. 23).	Antiochus IV was the eighth king in the Seleucid kingdom. He was followed by another twenty kings.

Christians, and its place was effectively taken by human substitutes. Through the mass and the confessional, the minds of Christian believers are drawn away from a continual dependence upon the mediatorial ministry of the Savior in His sanctuary. By elaborate ceremonies, all in the name of Christ, the ministry of Christ is obscured and lost sight of. The full forgiveness that Christ offers to those who put their trust in His perfect righteousness is taken away, and its place is taken by an ineffective pardon dispensed by humans.

In v. 12, the little horn continued its attack on Christ's ministry in heaven. The beginning of v. 12 has been translated and understood differ-

ently: some take *tsaba'*—"army" or "host"—to refer to a different army from the one previously mentioned in v. 11. There the *tsaba'* referred to God's people, as it evidently does in v. 13 also. If so, this other *tsaba'* would be referring to a spiritual army, the Roman priesthood, through which the little horn would operate its counterfeit daily (see below, "The Work of the Little Horn and the Prince").

As its final action in the prophecy, the little horn threw the truth to the ground—that is, he rejected and disregarded it. The Lord Jesus said of Himself, "I am...the truth" (John 14:6). In another place, but with not greatly different meaning, He said, "Your word is truth" (John

The Work of the Little Horn and the Prince

Daniel 8 contains an apocalyptic narrative describing a conflict between the little horn and the Prince of the heavenly hosts. It is part of the cosmic conflict and will result in its closing. The narrative combines military and cultic language that helps us understand the nature of the little horn. We will summarize the findings of the previous exposition of the text.

1. Little Horn in Daniel 7 and 8. It is difficult to ignore the parallelism between the little horn in Daniel 7 and 8. A summary of the similarities may suffice: (1) both are represented by the same symbol, a horn (7:8; 8:9); (2) the title "little" or "small" applies to both (7:8; 8:9); (3) both become "great" (7:20; 8:9); (4) both are persecuting powers (7:21, 25; 8:10, 24); (5) both persecute the people or the saints (7:27; 8:24); (6) both seek self-exaltation (7:8, 11; 8:10–12); (7) both exercise a crafty intelligence (7:8; 8:23–25); (8) both represent the enemy of God at the climax of the vision (7:8–9, 25–26; 8:12–14, 25); (9) both are associated with prophetic time (7:25; 8:14); (10) both of their activities reach the time of the end (7:25–26; 8:17–19); and (11) both are finally destroyed (7:11, 26; 8:25). These similarities demonstrate that we are dealing with the same religiopolitical power—Christian Rome. The prophecy has taken us from the Medo-Persian Empire, through the Greek and Roman ones, and into the Christian era.

2. Initial Work of the Little Horn. The horn was to interact at the horizontal level with other earthly powers. The prophecy shows that it was to grow through aggressive military expansion and to become great (v. 9) like the other two kingdoms (vv. 4, 8). It was to extend itself to the south, the east, and the land of Israel with unstoppable aggression. This first stage of growth was to be fundamentally of a military and political nature. Verse 10 is transitional because, although it refers to the servants of God on earth, at the same time it points to the heavenly host (cf. 10:13). It introduces an important shift in the work of the little horn.

3. Vertical Move. By launching an attack against the people of God, the horn moved to the vertical dimension of its conquests. It was reaching out to control those belonging to the Lord. The term "host" refers in the OT to troops or an army (Deut. 20:9; 1 Kin. 2:5; Ps. 60:10), but when it is associated with God, it designates the people of Israel as God's army (Ex. 6:26; 7:4) or the army of God's angels (Ps. 103:19–21). A leader of the army of Israel is called "a commander of the hosts"/"a commander of the armies" (Deut. 20:9; 1 Sam. 14:50; 26:5; 1 Kin. 2:5). The earthly and the heavenly hosts work closely together in the realization of the Lord's plan. It could be said that an attack against one of them is an attack against the other. Interestingly, "host" is used in the context of the sanctuary to refer to the Levitical guard in charge of protecting the sanctuary from those intending to violate its holiness (Num.

4:3, 23, 30). This usage fits very well into Daniel's prophecy.

The apocalyptic narrative speaks about a military and political power that would go through a radical change in its search for power. It would intend to take the war to a new level: a celestial one associated with the heavenly temple. It would try to achieve what the fallen cherub had attempted to do (Is. 14:12–13). From this point on, the primary emphasis of the text in Daniel is on language related to the sanctuary and its services. The little horn was to become a political and religious power opposing God and His people. In this new move, the first enemy the horn was to face would be the Levitical guard/army that would protect God's dwelling (Dan. 8:10). It would be able to throw down or overcome them and then to trample or humiliate them. But the victory was not to be total because the horn would overcome only "some" of them (v. 10). Nevertheless, there would be a breach, and the horn would take advantage of it.

4. The Work of the Prince. In the vision, the first target in the attack was the heavenly host. The second was the Prince or Commander of the host—the Prince of the heavenly army, as revealed in the experience of Joshua, who as prince of the earthly army of the Lord had met the Prince of the heavenly hosts (Josh. 5:14). Daniel refers to this Prince as the Messiah and the heavenly high priest. The term prince/commander was also applied to the Israelite high priest, and in Daniel the context indicates the Prince's function as a high priest (cf. 1 Chr. 24:5; Ezra 10:5). In the prophecy, He officiated in the heavenly temple and was responsible for the daily services—the work of mediation on behalf of the people (Dan. 8:10). The parallel with the judgment scene in 7:9–10, 13–14 also shows the Prince as directly involved as high priest in the final judgment, typologically represented by the services of the Day of Atonement (see "The Theology of the Day of Atonement," p. 264, and "The Cleansing of the Sanctuary and Judgment in Daniel," p. 1043). This facet of His work is announced in v. 14: "Then the sanctuary shall be cleansed." This Prince is none other than the high priest mentioned in Hebrews who officiates in the true tent/tabernacle

set up by God, not human beings (Heb. 8:2). Through His incarnation, sacrificial death, resurrection, and ascension, He is totally qualified to be our high priest in the heavenly sanctuary.

5. The Little Horn against the Prince. Because the work of the Prince is of such importance for the redemption of humans, the horn would threaten it. In the prophecy, it removed the continual (or daily) from the Prince by usurping His priestly work. It also threw down the place of the sanctuary. The adverb "down" is an addition not found in the Hebrew text. When the verb is used without a preposition or an adverb, it means to abandon, reject, or forsake. The "place of the sanctuary"/"foundation of the sanctuary" refers metaphorically to the very essence and purpose of the sanctuary (cf. Ps. 89:14) as the place where the Prince was to perform His work of mediation, intercession, and forgiveness of sins. In the vision, the little horn rejected or forsook the true nature of the sanctuary and its services and established its own.

Once the little horn claims to be in control of the daily services, it appoints its own host/army (human priestly system) to perform its own religious services. This is considered to be an act of rebellion (Dan. 8:12). According to 11:31, the work of the little horn profaned (not "defiled," for the Heb. verb is *khalal*, "to profane"; it is not *tame'*, "to contaminate," "defile") the sanctuary by treating it as a common place. In the prophecy, the horn expressed its rejection of the order established by God and regulated through His law, acting against God's sovereignty. The horn finally threw the truth to the ground (8:12). Contextually, "truth" refers to the truth about the daily and the sanctuary and summarizes the work of the horn. But the term is broad enough to include the revelation of God's redemptive plan as well as the revelation of His will for us (see 7:25). Truth was to be despised and disregarded by this prophesied religiopolitical power. Although in the vision, the horn did what it intended to do (8:12; interpreted as being in the future in v. 24), at the end of the narrative we are informed that it "shall be broken without human means," in other words, by God Himself. The Prince would be victorious (12:1–3).

17:17). How the written truth of Scripture has been cast down by apostate Christianity is well known. From the twelfth century onward, various popes prohibited the use of the Bible in the vernacular. The Council of Trent in 1546 decreed that no one was to interpret Scripture contrary to the interpretation given by the church, the church being the judge of the true sense of Scripture.

In 1897, Pope Leo XIII, in an encyclical letter, forbade all versions of the Bible, in any vernacular language, made by non-Catholics. Today, of course, the picture has changed. In 1943, Pope Pius XII issued an encyclical letter urging priests to study and preach from Scripture, to help Catholic associations to spread Scripture in modern languages, and to encourage the laity to read the Bible daily. What has not changed is the conviction that Scripture and tradition continue to have the same authority in the life and beliefs of the church. History clearly shows that not only has the Bible been placed on the same level as tradition but that the church continues to be the final interpreter of Scripture.

8:13–14. Time Period: Cleansing of the Sanctuary. In vv. 13 and 14, Daniel heard two heavenly beings speaking to each other. One asked the other how long it would be for the events in the vision to take place. The question was not about how long the desolation would last but about the historical time period that this vision would cover. The scope of the whole vision—beginning in v. 3, which reached back to the time of the Persian ram (v. 20) and extended forward to the time of the end (vv. 17, 19, 26)—was in view. The time element encompassed all the events mentioned in the vision (see "The Cleansing of the Sanctuary and Judgment in Daniel," p. 1043).

The answer given was 2,300 evenings and mornings—some translations have "days." The phrase "evening and morning" appears in the Creation account, where it constitutes one calendar day (Gen. 1:5, 8, 13, 19, 23, 31). The 2,300 prophetic days/years would reach to the time of the end (Dan. 8:17). In 9:24–27, Gabriel explained that this long time period was connected with and included the first coming of the long-expected Messiah and extended to the year A.D. 1844 (see chap. 9).

At the end of the 2,300 evenings and mornings, the sanctuary would be *nitsdaq*, from the verb *tsadaq*. This is the only place where this particular verbal form of *tsadaq* appears in the

entire OT. This latter root word (*tsadaq*) has the basic meaning "to be just or righteous" or "to be in the right." Apart from this basic meaning, it could express the idea of being "put right," in the sense of restored to its rightful place, "to be clean"/"to be pure," "to cleanse"/"to purify," or even "to justify" or "vindicate" (for further analysis of the term, see "The Cleansing of the Sanctuary and Judgment in Daniel," p. 1043).

The cleansing of the heavenly sanctuary corresponds to the cleansing of the Mosaic tabernacle on the Day of Atonement once every year (Lev. 16:30). As the Israelites had a daily and a yearly service in the respective first and second apartments of the earthly sanctuary, so Jesus in the heavenly sanctuary performs the daily service, in other words, His intercessory ministry, and is now also performing a work of judgment equivalent to the Day of Atonement as a day of judgment.

The context of the prophecy of Daniel 8:14 shows that what was cast down—the daily sacrifice, the truth, and the sanctuary's place—was to be restored at the end of the 2,300 evenings and mornings. While the translation "shall be restored" serves well to indicate the restoration of the truth about the sanctuary, the rendering "shall be cleansed" conveys the important truth of the cleansing of the heavenly sanctuary (see Heb. 9:23).

Daniel 8 describes, in apocalyptic symbols, a deeply religious conflict between Christ, the Prince of the host, and the little horn, apostate Christianity, with each side offering a plan of salvation. During the judgment described in Daniel 7, the true plan of salvation is reestablished, God's people are vindicated, and the little horn is condemned. While this judgment is taking place in heaven, the people of God on earth continue to depend on His grace, walking humbly with Him and restoring the truth cast down to the ground by the little horn, particularly the biblical teaching of the high-priestly work of Christ in the heavenly sanctuary. In this sense they are also participating in the restoration of the sanctuary on earth (see Rev. 11:1).

8:15–27. Gabriel's Interpretation of the Vision. The vision strongly impacted Daniel intellectually and emotionally. He was trying and was unable to understand it. Since he could not understand it (cf. 1 Pet. 1:10–12), the angel Gabriel was sent to help him ascertain the import of the vision (*mar'eh*, the term used in regard to the evenings and mornings).

In the OT, the name Gabriel occurs only here and in Daniel 9:21. In the NT, he appears several times in Luke 1. He tells the prophet that the vision (*khazon*, the totality of the vision) reaches to the "time of the end" when the desolating power was to be destroyed (cf. 2 Thess. 2:8). The phrase "time of the end" is found only in the book of Daniel (Dan. 8:17; 11:35, 40; 12:4, 9) as a technical term for the final period of human history leading up to Christ's return. Based on the historicist method of interpretation, the books of Daniel and Revelation indicate that this "time of the end" began at the close of the 1,260-year period in 1798 (see 12:40; see also "The 1,260 Days/Years," p. 1037).

In vv. 20–22, Gabriel explains the symbolic details of the vision recorded in vv. 3–8 but not the vision related to the "evenings and mornings" in vv. 13 and 14. This is left for chapter 9. Gabriel said that the ram symbolizes the kings of Media and Persia and the goat symbolizes the king(dom) of Greece. This is an important passage for the interpretation of all the visions in Daniel because this is the only

The Cleansing of the Sanctuary and Judgment in Daniel

It is generally acknowledged by many scholars representing different Christian traditions that the temple/sanctuary motif plays a significant role in the book of Daniel. The services in the Israelite sanctuary were performed to preserve and strengthen the relationship of the worshipers with the covenant Lord and, whenever necessary, to restore, through atonement, a broken relationship with Him (see Leviticus: Introduction). The priestly ministry consisted of a work of mediation performed on a regular basis (the daily services) in the courtyard of the sanctuary and in the Holy Place. Once a year, during the Day of Atonement, the sanctuary was cleansed from the sins and impurities of the people of Israel (see "The Theology of the Day of Atonement," p. 264). These two services pointed typologically to the high-priestly work of Christ in the heavenly sanctuary. Daniel addresses both of them (see "The Work of the Little Horn and the Prince," p. 1040). Here we will concentrate on the cleansing of the sanctuary mentioned in Daniel 8:13–14.

1. Context of the Passage. The context employs, within a few verses (vv. 9–14), a significant number of Hebrew terms often found in the setting of the sanctuary/temple services or having sanctuary connotations. We are referring to terms like "the daily," "regular," or "continual" (*tamid*; Ex. 29:42; Num. 28:3; Lev. 6:13); "holy," (v. 2); "sanctuary" (*miqdash*; Dan. 8:11; Ex. 25:8; Lev. 26:2); "glorious"/"beautiful" (Dan. 11:45); "host"/"army"/"service" (*tsaba'*; Num. 4:3, 5); "prince"/"commander" (*sar*; 1 Chr. 24:5); "take away" (Lev. 2:9; 4:8); "horn" (v.

7); "transgression"/"rebellion" (16:16); and "truth," which could designate the true instruction given by the priests to the people (Mal. 2:6). This language is related to the sanctuary and its services in a context dealing primarily with the daily service (the *tamid*), and, as indicated, it serves to identify the Prince as a heavenly high priest. The movement to the Day of Atonement is addressed in Daniel 8:13–14.

2. "Then the Sanctuary Shall be Cleansed" (v. 14). The Hebrew verb *nitsdaq* ("to be brought to its right state"), a verbal form used only here in the OT, is from the root *tsadaq*, meaning primarily "to be righteous," "to be vindicated." It is employed in the OT in three different contexts. First, in legal contexts it designates the restoration of the legal rights of a person falsely accused of a crime. The innocent who was charged with a crime was to seek the Lord's vindication in the sanctuary (e.g., Ps. 7:8), and the Lord would vindicate him or her (9:4). When the righteous were acquitted, the accuser would be condemned by the Lord (7:8–9; Deut. 25:1). Second, it is used in the context of salvation. Since those who are vindicated by God are delivered from oppression, the terms "salvation" and "righteousness" are used as synonyms (Ps. 98:2–8; Is. 1:27; 46:13).

Third, it is used in the context of the sanctuary services. In Leviticus what is required in order to have access to the sanctuary is purity obtained through sacrificial atonement. In the book of Psalms, what is required to enter the temple is "righteousness" or "vindication" granted to the worshipers as a gift from the Lord in the sanctuary (Ps. 24:3–5). These people were righteous not only because they remained loyal to the covenant but also because their sins had been forgiven (Ps. 32:1–2, 11). In the book of Daniel, the verb *tsadaq* is connected to *kipper* ("to make atonement"), which expresses the idea of the removal of sin or impurity (Dan. 9:24). The concept of righteousness is deeply connected to the sanctuary/temple. The Israelites had access to the temple through "the gates of righteousness" (Ps. 118:19), brought a righteous sacrifice (4:5), and the priest, a mediator before the Lord who "is righteous" (11:7), officiated while clothed with righteousness (132:9). Consequently, the worshiper received blessing from the Lord and righteousness/vindication from God, the Savior (24:5). This person "has clean hands and a pure heart" (v. 4). The person was declared righteous/purified/vindicated.

The connection between the Hebrew root *tsadaq* or its noun form *tsedeq* and the sanctuary is indicated by the fact that they are used as synonyms for words related to purity, cleanness, and justification (18:20; 51:4). One of the best examples of this linguistic phenomenon is found in Isaiah 53:11. God's righteous (*tsadiq*) Servant would justify (*yatsdiq*) many, for He would bear their iniquities (by removing/cleansing them from iniquity). To be declared righteous by God is the same as to be cleansed/purified and thus forgiven from sin, and, as an act of divine salvation, it vindicates the people of God.

Since the root *tsadaq* expresses in some contexts, particularly in a sanctuary setting, the concept of cleansing, it is expected to find it used this way in Daniel 8:14. The ancient Greek translation of the OT, the LXX, as well as the first-century Greek Theodotion translation, renders the Hebrew *nitsdaq* in v. 14 by the Greek verb *katharizō*, "to cleanse" (the same Greek term used in the LXX in Lev. 16 for the cleansing of the sanctuary). Also, in the Aramaic translation of the Hebrew Bible (the Targums), *nitsdaq* is translated as "to be pure," "to be clean" in 40 percent of its occurrences. If the meaning of the Hebrew verb *nitsdaq* is "to be brought to its right state," the best interpretational option would be to find in the use of the verb in Daniel a reference to the moment

when the Israelite sanctuary was restored to its right state or condition, namely, the Day of Atonement. It is useful to observe that the word translated in Daniel 8:14 as "sanctuary" (*qodesh*) is the same Hebrew word used in Leviticus 16, the chapter dealing with the Day of Atonement, to refer to the Most Holy Place of the tabernacle (vv. 2–3, 16–17, 20, 23, 27, 33). It was during this day that all sin and uncleanliness was removed from the tabernacle and its purity and holiness were restored.

3. The Question of Time. The reference to the Day of Atonement is introduced by a question that one holy being asked another (Dan. 8:13). The question was not how long the little horn would usurp the work of the Prince of the hosts but about the time period that was to cover the fulfillment of the whole vision. A literal translation of the question makes this clear: "Until when the vision [*khazon*], the daily [*tamid*], and the rebellion/transgression [*pesha'*] that causes desolation to give both the host and the sanctuary a trampling?" The "vision" refers to v. 1 and designates the totality of the vision, the "daily" refers to the work of the Prince (v. 11), and the "rebellion" designates the work of the little horn (vv. 11–12). The question was how long the vision (vv. 3–14), including the daily and the rebellion, would last ("Until when?"). It was not about how long the little horn would be able to usurp the daily.

Within this long period of 2,300 prophetic days, the kingdoms of Medo-Persia, Greece, and Rome and its subsequent division would pass away, and the little horn would oppose the priestly work of the Prince. Then, after the 2,300 days, the antitypical Day of Atonement would begin. The question indicates that the 2,300 days/years (see "Interpreting Biblical Apocalyptic Prophecies," p. 46) would begin during the time of the Medo-Persian Empire—a more specific date is provided in Daniel 9.

4. A Day of Judgment in Daniel. The Day of Atonement was essentially a day of judgment when God and His people were vindicated and their ultimate enemy deleted from God's creation (see "The Theology of the Day of Atonement," p. 264). In Daniel, we find several important insights on the topic. First, judgment is clearly coupled with the Day of Atonement. Apart from the fact that *tsadaq* is a legal term, the parallels between Daniel 7 and 8 demonstrate the direct connection between the Day of Atonement and judgment. In both chapters the kingdoms of Medo-Persia (7:5; 8:3–4) and Greece (7:6; 8:5–8) are mentioned, as well as Rome and the little horn (7:7–8; 8:9–12). In Daniel 7, after the struggles between the little horn and the Lord and His people, we find the judgment scene and the final disposition of God's enemies (vv. 13–14, 26–27). In Daniel 8, we find at the same juncture the reference to the purification of the sanctuary and the final disposition of God's enemies (vv. 13–14, 25). The parallel between the two chapters makes clear that the cleansing of the sanctuary and the judgment in heaven refer to the same event, in other words, the Day of Atonement.

Second, the judgment described in Daniel 7 was to take place in heaven, before the Son of Man and the saints would receive the kingdom. The preparations for the initiation of the heavenly judicial inquest were to begin while the little horn would still be active in its opposition to the people of God (vv. 9–14). Therefore, the judgment was to begin before the Second Coming of Christ, and consequently it could be called a pre-advent judgment. It would also be proper to call it an investigative judgment because the heavenly books would be opened to analyze the life of God's people. Third, the reception of the kingdom was to be the divine verdict, pronounced in the judgment in heaven, on behalf of God's people (vv. 21–22). Their ultimate destiny is firmly grounded on a legal process, which is accessible to the dwellers of the cosmos (v. 10) and shows their immovable faith commitment to the covenant Lord who redeemed them. Fourth, the vindication of God's people would result in the defeat of the little horn that unjustly oppressed them (v. 26). This decision, made in heaven, would be executed within history. Through judgment, destinies were to be determined before any rewards would be given. Fifth, Daniel speaks not only about the beginning of the judgment (vv. 9–10) but also about the moment of its end (12:1–3), when the work of Michael the Prince, as the high priest of God's people, would come to an end. In the absence of a Mediator before God for wicked humanity, there would be an unparalleled time of trouble on earth, but deliverance would only come to those with names preserved in the heavenly book after the judgment (12:1). This will be followed by the resurrection of some to eternal life and others to everlasting death (vv. 2, 13). In the biblical time frame, the investigative judgment in heaven precedes the granting of rewards. Finally, the prophecy indicates that after the judgment, and as a result of it, God's cosmic order would be reestablished by His everlasting kingdom (7:27).

5. Cleansing and Cosmic Judgment. The book of Daniel and the rest of the Scriptures show that the removal or cleansing of sin from the universe is grounded in a legal process beginning in the heavenly temple of God as the center of cosmic governance. First, theodicy is at the center of the Day of Atonement as a day of judgment. The Godhead has been involved in the cleansing of God's people from sin and uncleanliness through the sacrifice of Christ (1 John 1:7) and the work of the Spirit in the human heart (Titus 3:5–6). This saving and cleansing act of God on behalf of sinners is a magnificent revelation of His love and will demonstrate that He is indeed righteous and loving (1 John 3:16; 4:10). The display of His love on the cross will have been so powerful that at the end even the evil powers will recognize the love, mercy, and justice of God (Phil. 2:9–10). Second, God's people are vindicated before the universe, for the judgment will reveal that they found justification only in Christ, in other words, in what God had done for them through His Son. Third, the judgment will therefore provide a solid legal basis for the cleansing of the universe from all evil powers, sin, and death. It will reveal that their presence in God's creation was totally unnecessary and damaging to God's established order at Creation. After the cleansing of the cosmos, the eschatological Day of Atonement will restore cosmic order through God's work of re-creation.

We can summarize the biblical understanding of the final judgment in terms of three phases, each one containing an investigation and a verdict.

(1) The Pre-Advent Judgment in Heaven. This is the judgment of those who have claimed at some point in their lives to belong to God. It involves an examination of

their lives in the divine tribunal (Rom. 14:10; 2 Cor. 5:10) and judgment according to their works (1 Cor. 3:8-15; Eph. 6:8). Works reveal where the heart is and will provide objective evidence to show that God's people have been firmly established in their faith in Jesus and are covered by His righteousness. This pre-advent judgment in heaven involves believers giving an account of themselves to God (Rom. 14:12), not in person but through Jesus, as their Mediator, speaking for them and confessing them before God and the angels in heaven (Luke 12:8-9; cf. Heb. 7:25; 1 John 2:1). At the Second Coming, they will receive the benefit of the verdict pronounced on their behalf in heaven. It will be on the day of divine wrath (the Second Coming) that God's righteous verdict (*dikaiokrisia*) will be revealed, and He will render to each person according to what he or she has done (Rom. 2:5-6). The verdicts determined in heaven will be made public on earth at the return of Christ. The judgment of God's people begins in heaven before the coming of Christ, and they will be rewarded at the Second Coming (e.g., Heb. 9:28). They will be saved while the wicked that are alive will perish (2 Thess. 1:3-10).

(2) Millennial Judgment. This judgment takes place after the Second Coming when God's people in heaven will participate in the judgment of the wicked (Rev. 20:4). Paul expressed the idea well when he stated that God's holy people will judge the world (1 Cor. 6:2). They will even judge the fallen angels (v. 3). During the Millennium they will examine the heavenly records of the deeds of the wicked, and a verdict will be pronounced against them. This decision will be revealed to them after the Millennium.

(3) Executive Judgment. After the Millennium, Satan, his fallen angels, and the wicked of the earth will stand before the throne of God to receive their final reward. The evidence for their eternal condemnation will be presented to them to clearly understand the reason for their exclusion from the company of the redeemed ones (Rev. 20:12-13). They see the records of their lives and the immensity of the love of God in saving the righteous ones and condemning the wicked. This will be the moment when the cosmic theodicy takes place and the whole cosmos, including the wicked, will acknowledge the justice and love of God (Phil. 2:9-10; see "The Theology of the Day of Atonement," p. 264). The moment has come for the cosmos to experience eternal cleansing from the presence and effect of evil. This will be the permanent return to Eden for the human race.

place where the second and third kingdoms in the four-kingdom scheme are clearly identified by the angel himself. It is one of the passages historicists can use to show that the historicist method of interpretation is found in the book of Daniel itself.

As already indicated, after the death of Alexander, his kingdom was divided into four Greek kingdoms (see 7:6). When the iniquity of these kingdoms had reached a point of no return (8:23; see Gen. 15:16), the Roman Empire would begin to rule the then-known world. Rome was the fierce king described in Daniel 8:23. This is an allusion to Deuteronomy 28:50, which was a passage long understood as applying to the Romans and their oppression of the Jews. The statement that the little horn was to be strong and mighty, but not by his own power (Dan. 8:24), suggests that Christian Rome would be mighty by means of the secular powers over which it exercised spiritual control and behind which there was an evil power (cf. Rev. 13:2, 4). The little horn would misuse intelligence and wisdom through deception to establish and enforce the convictions of this power (see "The Little Horn in Daniel 7," p. 1035).

Yet in the end, the little horn would be broken without human power. Evil may assert itself for a long time, but it will be destroyed by divine decree in the end. The metal image in the prophecy in Daniel 2 came to an end by a stone prepared without human hands (2:45), and the little horn would have its dominion taken away by the heavenly court (7:26). So, the willful king who is the main actor in Daniel's most detailed prophecy would likewise come to his end, and no one would help him (11:45).

Finally, the angel confirmed to Daniel the reliability of the vision (*mar'eh*) of the evenings and mornings, which was not interpreted for him (8:26). He was told to seal up the vision (*khazon*) because it primarily dealt with events related to the distant future (lit. "for many days," that is to say, "many years" or "the time of the end"; v. 17). Daniel had a general grasp of the meaning of the vision, except for the section dealing with the evening and mornings, the *mar'eh*. He was disturbed by it and could not understand it.

9:1–27
THE COMING OF THE MESSIAH

Ten years had passed since the vision of chapter 8, and during that time Babylon, the conqueror of Israel, had fallen to the Medo-Persians, but the Jews were still in exile in Babylon. Daniel seems to have been interested in the political changes and their significance for his people. This chapter is formed by an introduction (9:1–2), Daniel's prayer (vv. 3–19), and the prophecy of the seventy weeks (vv. 20–27). There is a clear connection between this chapter and the prophecy of the 2,300 days recorded in chapter 8.

9:1–19
Introduction and Prayer

The chapter opens with a dating statement of great importance for Daniel and his people: the Babylonian Empire had ended, and a new one had arisen. Daniel's prophecy of the four kingdoms had been partially fulfilled. The date is also important in that it implies the arrival of the moment for the liberation of God's people from exile. King Cyrus, the messianic figure announced by Isaiah (Is. 44:28—45:4), was reigning, and hope was rekindled in God's people, particularly in Daniel. Through a study of Jeremiah, Daniel understood that the prophecy of the seventy years of the desolation of the land would soon come to an end. He was most probably concerned about the relationship between the seventy years and the prophecy of the 2,300 years that he had not been able to understand. Although the longer period is related to the seventy weeks, the prophecy of the seventy years prepares the way for the other. The prophet looked forward in hope while facing deep uncertainty; he prayed.

The reason for Daniel's prayer was his misunderstanding of the vision in chapter 8. Although according to Jeremiah's prophecy (Jer. 29:10) the time for the return of the Jews to Jerusalem was close at hand, Daniel's last vision gave him

the impression that it would be a long time before the sanctuary/temple was restored to its right condition. Daniel no doubt feared that God intended to prolong the period of captivity because of Israel's sins. The prayer is one of the longest and most moving prayers recorded in Scripture. It models the nature of prophetic mediation that anticipates the role of the coming Messiah as the supreme Mediator between humans and God. As mediator, Daniel pleads for the people dispersed throughout the nations and for the leaders in Jerusalem and Judah (Dan. 9:7). First, he stands before the Lord as their representative (cf. Heb. 7:25). Second, he identifies himself with his sinful people and asks God to forgive and bless them (Dan. 9:8–9; 2 Cor. 5:21). Third, Daniel recognizes that God has shown Himself to be righteous in what He has done to His people (Dan. 9:7, 18; see Rom. 3:25–26), thus representing God before the people. Finally, Daniel appeals to God's mercy and not to human achievements as he prays for forgiveness (Dan. 9:18; see Matt. 7:11; John 16:24).

9:20–27
The Seventy Weeks

While Daniel was still praying, Gabriel appeared and delivered to him one of the most important messianic prophecies found in the OT. Daniel 9:24–27 is to a certain extent the foundation stone of the Christian religion because it predicted almost six hundred years in advance not only the time when the Messiah would appear but also the duration of His public ministry, His atoning death for humanity, and His work as Mediator in the heavenly temple. In his prayer Daniel uses three different names to address God: Yahweh (vv. 4, 8, 10, 13–14); Adonai (vv. 4, 7, 9, 15–16, 19); and Elohim (vv. 4, 9–11, 13–15, 17–20, 23).

9:20–23. Coming of Gabriel and Daniel 8. In response to Daniel's prayer, the angel Gabriel was sent again (vv. 20–21; cf. 8:16–17) to help him understand the vision (v. 23; *mar'eh*). The information Gabriel provided did not describe a new vision but was an explanation of that part of the earlier vision in chapter 8 that Daniel did not understand (8:27). What he did not understand was the time element—the 2,300 evenings and mornings. He had received an explanation for the animals, the four horns, and the little horn (vv. 20–25) but not for the 2,300 evenings and mornings.

There are some specific links between Daniel 8 and 9 that show a close connection between both chapters. First, the same angel, Gabriel, revisited Daniel (8:16; 9:21); second, Daniel makes reference to the vision of chapter 8 (9:21); third, Gabriel came to give Daniel understanding of the previous vision (v. 23); fourth, the time element not explained in Daniel 8 is now discussed in 9:24–27; fifth, in both chapters Daniel uses two words for vision, *khazon* (8:1, 2, 13, 15, 17, 26; 9:21, 24) and *mar'eh* (8:16, 26–27; 9:23). When in 8:26 Gabriel said that "the vision [*mar'eh*] of the evenings and mornings" was true, he was referring to the time prophecy of the 2,300 years. Upon returning he said that he had come to help Daniel understand the *mar'eh* vision (9:23). In other words, what Daniel did not understand was the time element in Daniel 8. In Daniel 9 Gabriel came to him again and said that he would explain the time element of the 2,300 evenings and mornings.

9:24. Goal of the Seventy Weeks. According to the year-day principle, seventy weeks are 490 years (see "Interpreting Biblical Apocalyptic Prophecies," p. 46). Gabriel told Daniel that the seventy weeks were "decreed" or "determined" for his people. The Hebrew word *khatak* used here could also mean "to cut off." This is the only occurrence of this root in the Hebrew Bible, but in postbiblical Hebrew it is used to mean "to cut," "to cut off." In the LXX, the Greek translation of the OT, the verb used is *suntemno*, which means "to cut," "to cut off," "to chop up," or "to divide." Contextually, that is to say, in view of the connections between Daniel 8 and 9, the seventy weeks or 490 years are "cut off" from the longer period of the 2,300 evenings and mornings in Daniel 8:14. The great work to be accomplished within the seventy-week period is listed using six infinitive constructions in three pairs.

To finish and *to bring* sin to an end; to eliminate (*kalah*) it. Jesus came "to put away sin by the sacrifice of Himself" (Heb. 9:26), thus providing salvation for those who place their faith in Him (Rom. 3–5; 2 Cor. 5:17–21). *To atone* (*kipper*, "to make atonement"; some translations have "make reconciliation") for wickedness and *to bring* in everlasting righteousness. This was all achieved through the atoning sacrifice of Jesus Christ on the cross (cf. 1 John 2:2). It is only through Christ's atonement that we can be declared righteous by faith (Is. 53:11–12; Rom. 3:4–5; 21–31). *To seal* means to authenticate something and to affirm its genuineness. In the context of a prophecy, it means that the prophecy is authenticated when what it has announced finds its fulfillment in history. Here the prophecy is the messianic prophecy of the seventy weeks. Its fulfillment was to establish that God spoke through Daniel and that the rest of his prophecy would also be fulfilled. The coming of Christ is considered to be the fulfillment of prophecy (e.g., Matt. 2:5–6). According to Paul, He came at the appropriate prophetic time (Gal. 4:4). Jesus Himself announced the fulfillment of this prophecy in Mark 1:14–15 when at the beginning of his ministry He said that the time was fulfilled or had come. Such an expression would have been clearly understood as referencing the prophecy of Daniel 9.

To anoint the Most Holy is not a reference to the anointing of Jesus as the Messiah because the phrase "Most Holy" is practically always used in the OT to refer to the sanctuary or something connected with it (e.g., Ex. 26:33; 29:37; 30:10, 29; Num. 4:4, 19). The best interpretation is to find a reference here to the anointing of the heavenly sanctuary, where the Messiah, Christ, began His high-priestly work after His ascension toward the end of the seventy weeks (Heb. 9:18–24: cf. Ex. 40:9–16). This echoes the anointing of the earthly sanc-

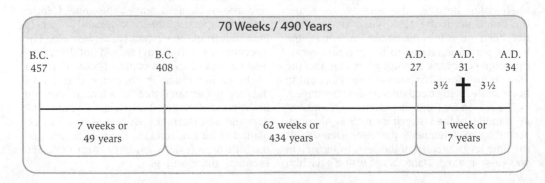

70 Weeks / 490 Years		
B.C. 457 B.C. 408	A.D. 27 A.D. 31 A.D. 34	
7 weeks or 49 years	62 weeks or 434 years	1 week or 7 years

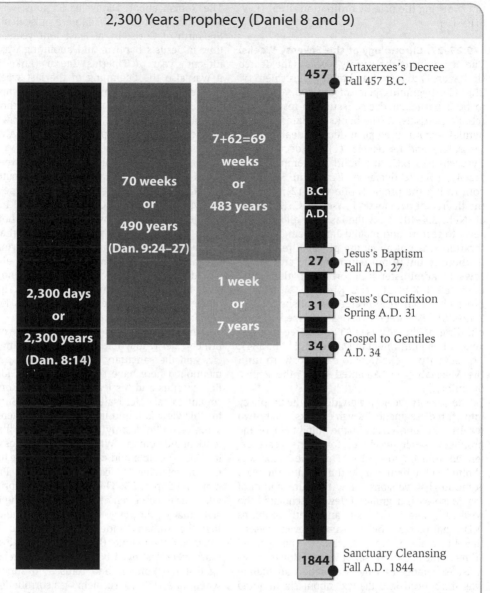

2,300 Years Prophecy (Daniel 8 and 9)

457 Artaxerxes's Decree
Fall 457 B.C.

7+62=69 weeks or 483 years

70 weeks or 490 years (Dan. 9:24–27)

B.C.
───
A.D.

1 week or 7 years

2,300 days or 2,300 years (Dan. 8:14)

27 Jesus's Baptism
Fall A.D. 27

31 Jesus's Crucifixion
Spring A.D. 31

34 Gospel to Gentiles
A.D. 34

1844 Sanctuary Cleansing
Fall A.D. 1844

457 B.C. Beginning of the 70 weeks (490 years). Marked by the command to restore and rebuild Jerusalem (9:25) issued by the Persian king Artaxerxes I in the seventh year of his reign (Ezra 7:11–26).

A.D. 27. End of the 69 weeks (483 years) predicted for the coming of Messiah the Prince (Dan. 9:25) and beginning of the last week. Fulfilled in the fifteenth year of the reign of Tiberius Caesar when Jesus was baptized and began His ministry (Luke 3:1, 21).

A.D. 31. Middle of the last week (Dan. 9:27) of the 70 weeks (490 years). After 3 1/2 years of earthly ministry, the death of Christ confirmed a covenant for the benefit of all.

A.D. 34. End of the 70 weeks (490 years). Marked by the martyrdom of Stephen and the related persecution that scattered Christians from Judea, which thus spread the gospel to the Gentiles.

A.D. 1844. End of the 2,300 days (2,300 years). Marked the beginning of the cleansing of the heavenly sanctuary and the end-time work of judgment.

tuary during the priestly ordination ritual (Lev. 8:10–12).

9:25–27. Chronology of the Seventy Weeks.

The beginning of the seventy weeks is the decree (lit. "word") to restore and rebuild Jerusalem (v. 25). The beginning point of the 490 years was to be a particular decree issued to restore and rebuild Jerusalem. The books of Ezra and Nehemiah record three main decrees dealing with Jerusalem and its temple: (1) the decree from Cyrus in 538 B.C. to rebuild the temple (Ezra 1:2–4); (2) the decree of Darius in 519 B.C., confirming the previous one (6:3–12); and (3) the decree of Artaxerxes I in 457 B.C. (7:12–26; cf. Neh. 2:4–10). Only the last one allowed the Jews to restore and rebuild Jerusalem. The restoration was not about the physical rebuilding of the city but about returning the city to the Jews to administer it according to their own laws (cf. 1 Kin. 20:34; 2 Kin. 14:22). This is precisely what this decree established (Ezra 7:12–26). The decree also authorized the rebuilding of the city (see "The Decree of Artaxerxes I as Fulfillment of Daniel 9:25," p. 584). The seventy weeks were to carry forward until the Messiah (the "Anointed One," the Prince or Ruler).

The seventy weeks are divided in the prophecy into three segments: seven weeks, sixty-two weeks, and one week. In the fulfillment of the prophecy, seven weeks or forty-nine years extended from 457 to 408 B.C. This time period was allotted to the rebuilding of the city and the wall. Some English versions follow the punctuation of the Masoretes, a group of Jewish scholars who worked between the sixth and tenth centuries A.D., that places a full stop after "seven weeks," thereby making "the Messiah," "the Prince" come at the end of the seven weeks. However, we must remember that the Masoretic punctuation was introduced into the text about six hundred years after the Christian area and is not part of the original text. Theodotion, who around A.D. 150 translated the Hebrew Bible into Greek, reads "seven weeks and sixty-two weeks." In any case, the seven weeks and sixty-two weeks are included together in the following verse, and v. 25 cannot be taken to imply that the Messiah was to come after 49 years—the next verse indicates that He was to be cut off after the 483 years.

The sixty-two weeks or 483 years extended from 408 B.C. to A.D. 27, when the Messiah was to appear. In A.D. 27, Jesus was about thirty years old (Luke 3:23) because He was born about four to five years before A.D. 1.

The Roman abbot, Dionysius Exiguus, who in 532 established the Christian era, miscalculated the birth of Christ by at least four years. The time of Jesus's baptism and anointing was the fifteenth year of Tiberius Caesar (Luke 3:1); it was also the beginning of the last week of the seventy weeks. Tiberius became emperor in A.D. 14. According to the Syrian method of computing regnal years, his fifteenth year would have commenced in September/October A.D. 27 when Jesus was baptized.

In A.D. 31, in the middle of the last week of seven years, the Messiah would be executed— literally "cut off." When Jesus died, type met antitype (Ex. 12:21; 1 Cor. 5:7), the veil in the temple was torn in two from top to bottom (Matt. 27:50–51), and this event marked the end of the earthly ceremonial system. The terminology used indicates that, abandoned by all, he would experience a violent death (lit. "no one shall be for him"). This is an apt description of the experience of Jesus on the cross (Matt. 26:56; John 1:11).

Daniel 9:26 also tells us that the people of the prince/ruler who would come would destroy the city and the sanctuary. The prince and people mentioned here have been traditionally identified as Titus and his legions when the Romans sought to take Jerusalem in A.D. 70. Support for this view is found in Daniel 8:24, where the same verb ("to destroy") is used to describe the work of the Romans. While this may be possible, it is also possible and contextually better to see this as referring to Jesus, the Messiah Prince mentioned in v. 25. The "people of the prince" who was to come refer to the people of the Messiah, that is, the Jews. History clearly indicates that the Romans under Titus destroyed Jerusalem and the temple. But the city and the sanctuary were destroyed because the Jews rebelled against the Romans and refused to surrender when, in A.D. 70, Jerusalem was surrounded by the Roman army. In this sense it could be said that the people of the Jewish Messiah caused the destruction of their city and temple. The description stating that the end would come like a "flood" fits well with the manner in which Romans penetrated the defenses of Jerusalem in the summer of A.D. 70. The comparison of military forces to a flood occurs elsewhere in the Bible (e.g., Is. 8:7–8; Jer. 46:6–8; 47:2).

The next verse (Dan. 9:27) begins with the pronoun "He," which is clearly referring to the Messiah of v. 26. If, in v. 26, the Prince/ Ruler is Christ, then the "He" mentioned here in v. 27 would refer back to the Prince or Ruler who was to come and who, as the Messiah, would be executed. If the reference in v. 26 to the prince/ruler is to Titus, then the "He" of v. 27 would be a switching of antecedents back to the Messiah. It is helpful to consider the prince/ruler who is to come as the Messiah for it is grammatically consistent and helps explain why the futurist interpretation is faulty. Futurist interpreters see the Roman general Titus as the coming prince/ruler and do not consider the "He" of v. 27 to refer back to the Messiah but to the antichrist, in its final phase, in other words, the ten-toe phase of Daniel 2 and the ten-horned-beast phase of chapter 7. They believe the final antichrist will be involved in concluding this covenant with the people of God during the final seven years before Christ's return. This view assumes a long gap of time between vv. 26 and 27, from Titus in the first century A.D. (v. 26) to a future Roman ruler, the antichrist, in the time of the end in v. 27. The text, however, does not support such a gap. Christ is the One who confirms the covenant in v. 27, and this is the best option here.

The Messiah would "confirm [strengthen] a covenant with many" in the sense of extending it to many people. The death of Christ ratified the covenant God made with His people (Matt. 26:28) and extended it to include Gentiles. This event, part of the seventy weeks, took place during the last week, in A.D. 34, at the end of which the theocracy formally came to an end and the faith of Israel was embraced by Gentile believers (see Acts 8 and 9). In the middle of the week, the death of the Messiah was to put an end to the sacrificial system (see John 4:21; Heb. 10:1, 9).

The last part of v. 27 is somewhat cryptic and has been translated variously: some indicate that a desolator was to be on "the wing of abominations," others that someone was to "set up an abomination that causes desolation," while others refer to the abominations to be placed at "a wing of the temple." In all of these cases, the text is taken to be referring back to the desolation mentioned in v. 26, in other words, to the destruction of Jerusalem and the temple (see Matt. 24:15–16; Luke 21:20–22). The phrase "on the wing" might be used to indicate that, once the abominations were present, desolation would follow. However, now a new thought appears: at the eschatological end, the final destruction determined by God would be poured out on the one causing the desolation. The desolation would not be something that would happen only to Jeru-

salem but something that would be part of the Christian experience, even to or until the occurrence of the end/destruction that God has determined against the oppressor (cf. Is. 10:23). We detect here a connection to Daniel 8. The desolating power of Rome, in its pagan and Christian expressions, is mentioned in Daniel 8:24–25. The attack of the little horn against the Prince is called the desolating transgression (v. 13; cf. 11:31; 12:11, where it is called the desolating abomination). The Lord told Daniel that at the end the little horn would be broken but not by humans (8:25). This is what the Lord determined to do to the desolating power, and now 9:27 returns to the same idea. Daniel 9 takes us from the beginning of the 2,300 days/years to the very eschatological end when the little horn would be unmasked and the enemies of God and His people would be permanently defeated. The chapter closes with the proclamation of a victorious God.

10:1—12:4
KINGS FROM THE NORTH AND THE SOUTH

The last vision in the book of Daniel contains the most detailed prophecy of future events in the OT. We do well to remember, therefore, that the great prophecies in Daniel are given according to the principle of repetition and enlargement. These prophecies begin either in the days of Babylon (Dan. 2, 7) or Medo-Persia (Dan. 8, 10–12), but they each climax in the establishment of the kingdom of God. All these prophecies deal with the same powers; Daniel 7 enlarges the outline of Daniel 2, and Daniel 8 and 9 enlarge the outline of Daniel 7. We can expect, therefore, that the vision of Daniel 10 to 12 enlarges at least the outline of Daniel 8 (see "Interpreting Biblical Apocalyptic Prophecies," p. 46).

10:1—11:2
Introduction to the Prophetic Speech

Daniel 10 to 12 form a unit with three main elements:

A **Introduction**—Daniel and Heavenly Beings (10:1—11:1)
    Vision of Heavenly Man in Linen (10:4–14)
        Dialogue—Daniel and Heavenly Being (10:15–21)
B **Prophetic Speech** (11:2—12:4)

A' **Epilogue**—Daniel and Heavenly
　　Beings (12:5–13)
　　　Vision of Heavenly Beings
　　　　(12:5–6)
　　　　　Dialogue—Daniel and Man
　　　　　　Dressed in Linen (12:7–13)

The introduction and conclusion of the book correspond to each other in terms of the visionary presence of heavenly beings and Daniel's dialogue with one of them. The man dressed in linen is presented in both chapters, which constitute a literary unit. The last vision of Daniel was given two years after the return of the Jews from Babylon. In this vision God lifted the veil of history and showed Daniel some of the realities of the unseen world—the conflict going on between the forces of good and evil. In Revelation 12:7–9, we find a similar picture: Michael and his angels fighting the prince of evil and his angels. Yet the outcome in both books is the same—Michael, the great prince, overcoming Satan and delivering His people.

10:1–9. Date and Vision of Heavenly Being.
The introduction dates the experience of Daniel to the third year of King Cyrus (536/535 B.C.). Daniel had been mourning and fasting for three weeks (v. 2). The reason for this is not given, though from v. 14 we can infer that the future of his people must have been of concern to him. Cyrus succeeded to the throne of Babylon in 538 B.C., and probably because of Daniel's witness, Cyrus had come to know the prophecies of Isaiah about himself (Is. 45:1–3, 13) and had already taken steps to fulfill them (Ezra 1:1–4; 6:3–5). At the end of the three weeks, Daniel received a vision by the Tigris River in which he was shown the Great Controversy between the spiritual forces in the universe. The conceptual connections between this description of the controversy and Daniel 8 to 9 are presented in "The Great Controversy in Daniel 8—12" (p. 1053).

In answer to Daniel's prayer, a celestial being appeared to him. A comparison of the words of Daniel 10:5–6 with Revelation 1:13–15 suggests that this divine Being was Christ, who is named Michael later in the chapter (Dan. 10:13, 21; 12:1).

Only Daniel saw the vision (10:7). This was a day vision, in contrast to night visions or prophetic dreams. The effect of this day vision on Daniel's companions is comparable to what happened when Jesus appeared to Saul on the Damascus road (Acts 9:3–7; 22:6–9). The physical effects of the vision on Daniel were similar to that of Balaam (Num. 24:2–4) and John (Rev. 1:17). Daniel, like Peter (Acts 10:9–11) and Paul (2 Cor. 12:1–3), was unconscious of his immediate surroundings. He was so fully absorbed in the things he was shown that he became a participant in the actions (Dan. 12:5–9; cf. Rev. 1:10; 5:4–5; 19:10; 21:5).

10:10–14. Behind the Scenes. At this juncture another angel came to Daniel and touched him (v. 10). Although this angel is not named, the way he addressed Daniel is similar to the way Gabriel spoke to him. It is a wonderful fact that a human being can be said to be the object of such regard by the Creator of the universe.

The heavenly being informed Daniel that he had come to respond to Daniel's words (v. 12). This gave Daniel confidence that his prayer would be answered. Gabriel then explained that while Daniel was fasting and praying, there was a struggle between the forces of good and evil to influence Cyrus's mind. God does not force, and neither does He allow Satan to force humans to act against their wills. The reference to the prince of Persia (v. 13) is primarily to Satan himself, who through his agents tried to turn the Medo-Persian ruler against Israel. Ezra 4:1–6 relates the events in the Holy Land, while in this chapter the veil is drawn back, and the supernatural powers of good and evil are seen engaging in the conflict concerning the rebuilding of the temple. Probably no other text in Scripture than Daniel 10:13 describes more clearly the struggle between the invisible powers that control and influence nations. Scripture indicates that even as God's angels carry out His purpose in the natural world (2 Sam. 24:16; Ps. 78:43–49) and in the moral world (Luke 15:10), so they also do in the political world. And just as Israel had a spiritual champion to protect her (Dan. 10:21), so the powers opposed to Israel had their demonic princes.

In order to understand the prophecy in chapter 11, Daniel 10:14 is particularly important. This text tells us that the vision is concerned with the future (lit. "days of the end" or "days afterwards"; see 2:28). Other nations are mentioned only as to their effect on the lives of God's chosen people, but the prophecy transcends geographic limitations and has cosmic dimensions.

10:15—11:1. Dialogue with Heavenly Being.
Daniel then describes his own subjective experience while in vision: he bowed with his face

to the ground (v. 15). Again, he speaks of the complete loss of physical strength and of the supernatural strength received (v. 16). He also mentions a new feature: he stopped breathing (some translations interpret the literal description "no breath left" to mean that he had difficulty breathing). Twice in these verses, we read of the strengthening of Daniel (vv. 18–19). This time Daniel became a partner in dialogue with the heavenly being—Daniel sharing the reason for his reaction to the vision, and the angel speaking words of encouragement. Gabriel then predicted the struggle with the powers of Persia and their successors in the days of the Greek Empire (v. 20). He explained that he received no help from anyone, except from "Michael your prince." "Michael" means "who is like God?" No one is like God except the

The Great Controversy in Daniel 8—12

Daniel 8		Daniel 9		Daniel 10–12	
8:2	At the river Ulai			10:4	At the great river
8:3	I raised my eyes and saw, and behold			10:5	I lifted up my eyes and looked and behold
8:8	The large horn was broken—four horns toward the four winds of heaven			11:4	His kingdom was to be broken/divided toward the four winds of heaven
8:9	The little horn grew mighty—toward the Glorious/Beautiful Land			11:23	He was to become strong with few people
				11:16	The Glorious/Beautiful Land
8:11	The daily/continual (tamid) was taken away			11:31	Was to take away the daily/continual (tamid)
8:11	God's sanctuary was overthrown	9:26	Was to destroy... the sanctuary		
8:11	The Prince/Commander of the host/army	9:25	An Anointed One, a Prince/Ruler	11:22	The prince of the covenant
8:13	The desolating transgression/rebellion	9:27	Desolating abomination	11:31	The desolating abomination
8:16	Gabriel was to explain the meaning of the vision	9:21–23	Gabriel came to help Daniel understand		
8:17	Gabriel identified the vision as being for the time of the end	9:26	Until the end	11:35	Until the time of the end
8:19	The future time of anger			11:36	Until the anger would be finished
8:24	Destruction of the holy people	9:26	Destruction of the sanctuary		
8:25	He was to oppose the Prince of princes	9:26	An Anointed One/ Messiah was to be cut off/executed	11:22	The prince of the covenant would be killed
8:25	He would be broken/ destroyed without human power (lit. "hand")	9:27	Total destruction would be poured out on the desolator	11:45	He would come to his end
8:26	The vision: true			10:1	The word/message: true

Son of God (John 10:30), who intercedes for His people (Heb. 7:25; 1 John 2:1–2). Jewish literature describes Michael as the highest of the angels and identifies him with the "Angel of Yahweh," who is frequently mentioned in the OT as a divine being (see Gen. 16:7–14; 22:11–18; 31:11–13; Ex. 3:2–6; 14:19; 23:20–23; Judg. 2:1–5; 13:2–23; Hos. 12:3–5; Mal. 3:1). This "Angel" (Ex. 23:23) was capable of pardoning or refusing to pardon transgressions, and God's name was "in Him" (Ex. 23:21). Since forgiveness of sins is the prerogative of God (Ex. 34:7; Is. 43:25; Mic. 7:18; Mark 2:7), the conclusion is inevitable that God's Angel or Messenger (Ex. 23:23) is a member of the Godhead. In this case "Angel" does not designate a creature but a function. One of the members of the Godhead is the Messenger of the Lord.

In Daniel 10:21, Michael is called "your prince," in other words, the Prince of God's people. In Isaiah 9:6, Jesus the Messiah is called the "Prince of Peace"; in Daniel 8:25, He is "the Prince of princes"; and in Daniel 9:25, He is identified as "Messiah the Prince/ Ruler." Thus, the conclusion seems justified that in the OT "Michael" is "the Angel of the Lord" or "My Angel," who is also called "My Son" (Ps. 2:7).

11:2—12:4
The Prophetic Speech

Daniel 11 is the most difficult chapter of the book, and in some cases there are different interpretations among historicist expositors dealing with the historical fulfillment of the prophecy (we will discuss various Adventist views). Modern critical scholarship views Daniel 11 as a description of the wars between the Seleucid and Ptolemaic kings, culminating in the career of the Syrian king Antiochus IV Epiphanes, who is seen as the main actor in vv. 21–45 (see "The Little Horn and Antiochus IV," p. 1039). Evangelical scholarship generally follows this outline, except that some see, starting with v. 35, the career of Antiochus IV Epiphanes foreshadowing the activities of the last-day antichrist; others have postulated a gap of many centuries between vv. 35 and 36 and interpret the last ten verses as applying only to a future antichrist. We see no need to inject such a huge time gap into the biblical text.

Although there are some differences among historicists on the interpretation of Daniel 11,

there are five events within the prophecy that are fairly clear and straightforward; these can be used for interpretations based on the principle that Scripture interprets Scripture, with one passage being the key to other passages. First, at the beginning of Daniel 11, the angel referred to Persian and Greek kings. The reference to the mighty king (v. 3), whose kingdom was to be broken up toward the four winds (v. 4), was clearly a reference to the reign of Alexander the Great (336–323 B.C.). This is supported by parallelism with Daniel 8:8, where Alexander is the large horn that was broken and in whose place four other significant ones rose up toward the four winds of heaven. The four horns symbolize the Hellenistic kingdoms that emerged after the breakup of Alexander's empire.

The next clearly identifiable event is the death of the Messiah in v. 22. The word for "prince" in this verse is *nagid*. It is used only in one other place in the book of Daniel, namely, in Daniel 9:25–26. In other places Daniel uses the similar word *sar*, "Prince"/"Commander" (8:11, 25; 10:13, 20, 21; 12:1). On linguistic grounds, therefore, the "prince of the covenant" in 11:22 is the same as the one who would confirm a covenant with many (9:25–27). Since Daniel 9:26–27 and 11:22 obviously refer to the crucifixion of Christ by the Romans, the Roman Empire is probably prophesied as entering the stage of history sometime prior to the prophecy in 11:22.

The third event is the taking away of the *tamid* ("daily"/"continual") and the setting up of the abomination of desolation (11:31). The terminology used in 11:31 for this event is also used in 8:11, where it refers to the earthly priesthood taking away the intercessory ministration of Christ in the heavenly sanctuary. And the desolating abomination refers to the vast system of beliefs and practices of spiritual Rome, which led people away from the priestly ministry of Jesus for more than a thousand years. Thus, it appears that apostate Christianity is prophesied in this chapter in either v. 31 or before.

The fourth event that provides a chronological marker in the prophecy is the "time of the end" (11:40). This phrase is found only in the book of Daniel, once in Daniel 8:17 and four times in connection with Daniel's last vision (11:35, 40; 12:4, 9). The visions of Daniel 8 and 11 both reach to "the time of the end," at which point, according to Daniel 12:2, a resurrection will take place. Thus "the time of the end" is the time prior to the Second Coming (see v. 1). At the end of the vision, Daniel was told to close the book and seal it for "the time of the end" (v. 4). At that time knowledge of these visions would increase, and their meaning would be understood (v. 10).

The fifth event that is easily understood is the resurrection at the end of the vision (v. 2). We suggest that this resurrection includes a special resurrection that will occur immediately prior to the appearance of Jesus in the clouds of heaven and will be followed by the general resurrection of the righteous (v. 13). This interpretation seems warranted by the fact that some of the wicked will be raised at this special resurrection to witness the coming of Christ (Matt. 26:64; Rev. 1:7; cf. GC 637).

These five events provide the basic chronological outline for Daniel 11. All the other historical events mentioned in the chapter must fit into this framework. That this is by no means an easy task is shown by the various interpretations.

11:2-4. Medo-Persia and Greece. Gabriel told Daniel that three more kings would arise in Persia and that the fourth would be much wealthier than the others. At the time of the vision, Cyrus (559–530 B.C.) was the ruling monarch. The next four kings were Cambyses (530–522 B.C.), Gaumata or the false Bardiya/Smerdis (522 B.C.), Darius I (522–486 B.C.), and Xerxes I (486–465 B.C.). The last one was the king who married Esther. When his fleet was destroyed by the Greeks at Salamis (480 B.C.) and his army was defeated at Plataea (479 B.C.), the Persians gave up the idea of conquering Greece. About one hundred and fifty years later, the Greeks under Alexander the Great (336–323 B.C.) conquered Persia instead. After Alexander's death the kingdom was eventually divided among four of his generals (see Dan. 7:6). Out of the divided Greek Empire arose two dynasties, the Seleucids and the Ptolemies, who became the kings of the north (the Seleucids in Asia Minor) and of the south (the Ptolemies in Egypt) in relation to their geographical proximity to the Holy Land.

11:5-39. Warring Kings of North and South. Adventist interpreters, with a few exceptions, generally identify in the first part of the chapter the king of the south as referring to the rulers of Egypt (south of Israel) and king of the north (11:5-6) as Syria (north of Israel). In Egypt, the Ptolemies ruled from 305 to 30 B.C. (Cleopatra VII, 51–30 B.C., being the last ruler of this dynasty). The kings of the Seleucid dynasty in Syria ruled from 305 to 65 B.C. Verses 5–13 and 15 describe the wars between these two countries. Both dynasties were eventually replaced by the Roman power.

Within the Seventh-day Adventist Church, a wide variety of interpretations have been applied to several details of this portion of Daniel 11. "Different Historicist Views on Rome and the Papacy in Daniel 11:5-39" (p. 1056) shows three of the interpretations, all of which are based on the historical-grammatical method used in the interpretation of prophetic chapters. The differences are based on the challenge of identifying some of the historical fulfillments of the prophecy. The differences among the various Adventist interpreters primarily concern the question, "At what points in the story do the Romans and the papacy enter the picture?" The table summarizes three views for Daniel 11:5-39.

Here we will provide a short commentary on each of the three positions summarized in "Different Historicist Views on Rome and the Papacy in Daniel 11:5-39" (p. 1056).

Position 1. According to this view, following the death of Jesus (v. 22; the fulfillment of the seventy weeks), v. 23 would take us back two hundred years to 161 B.C., when the Jews under the Maccabees made a pact with Rome against the Seleucids. Next, Rome under Augustus fought against the king of the south, the Ptolemies in Egypt (v. 25), and returned to their land with great riches (v. 28). Having incorporated Egypt into the Roman Empire, Rome turned against the holy covenant God had made with His people and destroyed Jerusalem in A.D. 70 (v. 28).

The ships from *kittim* are identified with the ships of the Vandals from Carthage who sacked Rome in A.D. 410. Although this word originally referred to Cyprus, it later was extended to include the Mediterranean Roman coastlands to the west of Israel. Verses 31 and onward contain a prophecy concerning the main actor—apostate Christianity, the spiritual king of the north—that would take away the *tamid* ("daily"/"continual"). On this view, the *tamid* refers to paganism, and the abomination of desolation refers to the power that apostate Christianity developed from A.D. 538 onward. A new power is introduced in v. 36, namely, the new king who would speak blasphemies against the God of gods. According to this view, this figure is identified with the atheistic power of France.

Position 2. This interpretation basically follows the previous one in the first section of the prophecy but has imperial Rome enter the prophecy in v. 16. The prince of the covenant who was to be broken (v. 22) is again Jesus, but from vv. 23 to 39 it sees the activities of spiritual Rome not in chronological but in topical order. This means that vv. 23–30 are about the military campaigns during the Crusades (eleventh to thirteenth centuries), followed by the subversion of the system of salvation in v. 31. The profaning of the temple/sanctuary fortress in v. 31 is interpreted as the attack of apostate Christianity on Christ's ministry in the heavenly sanctuary. Thus the *tamid*, "daily"/"continual," is not identified with paganism but with Christ's ministry that was taken away from Him and put in the hands of earthly priests (see 8:1–14). Martin Luther identified the desolating abomination in Daniel 11 with the papacy, its

	Different Historicist Views on Rome and the Papacy in Daniel 11:5–39				
Position 1		**Position 2**		**Position 3**	
11:5	King of the South: Ptolemies in Egypt	11:5	King of the South: Ptolemies in Egypt	11:5–8	Rise of Christianity and papacy
11:6	King of the North: Seleucids in Syria	11:6	King of the North: Seleucids in Syria	11:9–10	Rise of papal supremacy
11:14	Rome conquers the Holy Land	11:16	Rome conquers the Holy Land	11:11–12	Avignon captivity, Renaissance, and Rationalism
11:20	Emperor Augustus	11:20	Emperor Augustus	11:13–25	Counter-Reformation, missionary expansion, wars, and persecutions
11:21	Emperor Tiberius	11:21	Emperor Tiberius		
11:22	Prince of the covenant broken: Jesus crucified	11:22	Prince of the covenant broken: Jesus crucified	11:22	Persecution of God's people using the language of the experience of Jesus
11:23	Roman league with the Jews in 161 B.C.	11:23–30	The Crusades		
11:29	Removal of the seat of the empire to Constantinople in 330			11:25–27	French Revolution—Napoleon and the Concordat (1801)
11:30	Ships of Cyprus (*kittim*): ships of the Vandals from Carthage attacked Rome	11:30	Ships from the western coastland helped in the last Crusade	11:28–39	Nonchronological report of a theological nature—denunciation of the corruption of the church
11:31	The daily: paganism; the abomination of desolation: the papacy	11:31	The daily: Christ's ministry in heaven; the abomination: the union of church and state		
11:32–35	Papal persecution	11:32–35	Papal persecution		
11:36	Self-exaltation and blasphemy of papal Rome	11:36	Self-exaltation and blasphemy of papal Rome		
11:37–39	French Atheism				

doctrines, and practices. In view of the parallelism between 8:11, where in prophecy the little horn took away the *tamid*, and 11:31, where again the *tamid* was to be taken away but in addition the abomination of desolation was to be set up, it is concluded that the power that would take away the *tamid* is also the power that would set up the abomination of desolation. This means that spiritual Rome and its unscriptural teachings constitute the fulfillment of these prophecies in history.

That many were to fall by sword and flame (11:33) describes the persecution of the people of God during the Middle Ages. The king that would exalt and magnify himself above every god (v. 36) corresponds to the activities of the little horn in Daniel 8:11, which was fulfilled by the display of the power and blasphemy of the apostate church in history.

Because this interpretation views the historical events described in vv. 23–39 in topical and not chronological order, the events in v. 31 were to occur before those described in vv. 23–29. The same is also true of position 1, which breaks the chronological sequence in v. 23 by going back two hundred years in history to the Jewish league in 161 B.C.

Position 3. This interpretation divides Daniel 11:5–39 into three sections based on the structure of the text. (1) The first is the emergence of the little horn. Daniel 11:5–13a describes the troubled period of the rise of Christianity and the beginning of alliances between the church and the state (Constantine, Clovis—see "The Union of Church and State," p. 1033), the abuses and iniquities of Christian Rome during the Middle Ages, the Crusades, and the Inquisition. These were followed by a reaction from the other side: the Avignon captivity, the Renaissance, and the rise of Rationalism.

(2) The next section (11:13b–27), describes the process of persecution from its beginnings and development to its fall. This is the time of the wars of religion and of intensive persecution. This part of the vision can be applied to the St. Bartholomew's Day Massacre and the intrigues of Henry IV's conversion to Catholicism. This is the time of the development of foreign missions when the church, supported by the Jesuits, expanded to the whole world. This period ended with the dramatic blow of the French Revolution (the "wound"; cf. Rev. 13:12), which marked the fall of the persecuting power.

(3) In 11:28–39, the vision does not follow a chronological progression but focuses on the church's opposition to God and His people.

The iniquity of the church is denounced ("the abomination of desolation" and the taking away of the *tamid*, "daily"/"continual," from the heavenly sanctuary are mentioned). The perspective here is the eschatological Day of Atonement.

11:40–45. A Closer Look. This passage contains some unfulfilled prophecies. Christ counseled that full understanding often comes only after a prophecy's fulfillment (John 14:29). This does not mean that we should not try to interpret a prophecy, but it certainly indicates that we should not be dogmatic on a position taken. The identification of the kings of the north and south in these six final verses of chapter 11 has been a matter of debate among Adventist interpreters, some of whom look for identifications of these kings in contemporary religiopolitical events within a given period in modern history. For example, at the end of the nineteenth and the beginning of the twentieth centuries, Turkey (the Ottoman Empire) was identified as the king of the north, but the majority of Adventist interpreters now agree that the king of the north is the papacy. During the Cold War, communist Russia (the Soviet Union) was identified as either the king of the north or the south, who was in clear opposition to religion. With the fall of the Soviet Union, this interpretation is no longer viable. Israel itself was also, for a time, proposed as the king of the south. This approach is still being used by some who find in current events an anticipated fulfillment of Daniel 11:40–45. We will suggest that it would be better to connect this passage to the book of Revelation, where we seem to find a further expansion of the end-time prophecies of Daniel. Prophecy indicates that spiritual Babylon will be the final persecutor of the people of God and describes the final, deadly conflict of the church with the powers of darkness (Rev. 12–14).

The prophetic events in vv. 40–45 occur during the time of the end. The term "time of the end"—which appears five times in the book of Daniel (8:17; 11:35, 40; 12:4, 9)—is not found in any of the other OT books or in any extrabiblical Hebrew sources. The key to its meaning is found in the vision in Daniel 11. In the concluding part of this vision, a resurrection of the dead is prophesied to take place (12:2). It is this event that holds the key to the proper understanding of the expression "time of the end." In Daniel 12:4, the prophet was told to shut up the prophecies and seal the book until the time of the end. Many will then intensively search the book of Daniel, and as a result the knowledge of these prophecies will increase. The expression "time of the end" in 12:4 refers back to "the time of the end" in 11:35, 40. In view of the larger context, "the time of the end" in these texts refers to the time preceding the resurrection of the dead in 12:2 that will happen at the Second Advent. This is also the meaning of 12:4. Prior to the end of history, people will study and search out the Danielic visions just as Daniel himself searched out the seventy-year prophecy of Jeremiah (9:2). From history we know that in the nineteenth century, after the end of the 1,260 years of Daniel 7:25, knowledge of the Danielic prophecies increased dramatically. It is reasonable, therefore, to conclude that the time of the end began with the end of papal dominance in 1798. This means that the events from Daniel 11:40 onward must be sought in the time between 1798 and the resurrection at the end of time.

In what follows, we offer a possible way of reading the closing verses of Daniel 11 that takes into consideration the connection between Daniel and Revelation. In Daniel 11:40–45, the king of the south is identified with Egypt. In Exodus 5:2, Pharaoh proclaimed his independence by asking who the Lord was that he should listen to His words. He declared that he did not know the Lord. This does not mean, of course, that he was not aware of the existence of the God of the Hebrews. It simply reflects the king's views that Yahweh was irrelevant to him, implying that he was only under submission to the gods of Egypt. Revelation 11:8 uses Egypt to signify that which is opposed to true religion. Thus, in Daniel 11:42 Egypt represents the nations that put all their trust in something other than the biblical God. These would include non-Christian religions and nations where secularism and atheism prevail. The spiritual Babylon of the last days was prophesied to defeat this anti-God power and overcome it through demonic agencies and spiritual deception (Rev. 13:13–14; 16:13–14), until even the most distant powers (represented by Libya and Ethiopia) were to be brought to submission (Dan. 11:43).

Verse 40 also says that the king of the south would attack the king of the north. Which power is symbolized by the king of the north? In the OT, Babylon was the king of the north and the enemy of the kingdom of Judah (e.g., Jer. 1:14–15; 4:6; 6:1, 22). In the book of Revelation, Babylon is a code name for spiritual Rome. Thus, the king of the north stands for the end-time spiritual Rome. This harmonizes with

Daniel 11:36–39 where the king who would exalt himself also represents a spiritual Rome.

The king of the north, on his way to do battle with the king of the south, would pass through the Glorious/Beautiful Land, which represents God's people living during the time of demonic deception. While he was to overthrow many, Edom, Moab, and Ammon would escape. These nations no longer exist although their descendants do in the country of Jordan. Accordingly, we are not expected to understand this passage literally. In the OT, these nations were related to the Hebrew people but were all enemies of God's people (Edom from Esau; Moab and Ammon from Lot). God in His grace promised to save a remnant of them (cf. Is. 11:14). Through the Prophet Amos, God prophesied that all the Gentiles/nations having His name (Amos 9:12) would be part of the messianic kingdom. Thus, it could be suggested that Edom, Moab, and Ammon represent those who hear the call of Revelation 18:4 and come out of Babylon during the time of the end. The people of God are found in all Christian communities, and some are even found among the world religions. As we approach the end, the Lord is going to do a special work among those religions, and many adherents will join God's remnant people. Escape from Babylon is the same as finding refuge on Mount Zion (Joel 2:32).

The king of the north was to conquer the land of Egypt (Dan. 11:42), in other words, the king of the south, but this victory was only to be enjoyed for a short time because news from the east and the north was to frighten him (v. 44). The message troubling the king of the north could be the message of Revelation 18:1–4 that unmasks Babylon and proclaims its fall at the moment when it was apparently all-powerful. Another possibility is the announcement that the kings from the east were to march forth (Rev. 16:12) and engage in the spiritual battle at Armageddon (v. 16).

The chapter concludes with the statement that the king of the north would try to meet the challenge of the news from the east, but he would come to his end and no one would help him (Dan. 11:45); he would be defeated (see Rev. 16:17–21). In general, Seventh-day Adventists have held the fulfillment of vv. 40–45 to be yet in the future, and consequently any interpretation of this segment of the prophecy is tentative.

12:1–4. Michael Stands. The concluding portion of the vision in chapter 11 is found in 12:1–4.

It describes the final battle between the forces of God and the forces of Satan and the deliverance of the saints. When Christ appears in the clouds of heaven, the righteous dead will be delivered from their graves. Deliverance will come only to those found written in the Book of Life, the register of the redeemed, whose sins were forgiven by the blood of the Lamb and who now will enjoy the consummation of their salvation.

The chapter division between 11:45 and 12:1 is unfortunate, for the vision of chapter 11 ends in 12:4, not in 11:45. "That time," which is mentioned in 12:1, is the time period just mentioned in the preceding verse. The first three verses of chapter 12 describe the end of the conflict that is discussed at length in chapter 11. At that time God determined that Michael was to "arise" or "stand up." The word 'amad, "to stand up" or "arise," is used repeatedly in this long vision (11:2–4, 7, 16, 20–21). Each time it refers to a new king ascending to the throne or establishing himself as the new power. When Michael stands up, he will assume rulership. Jewish literature describes Michael as the angel who vindicated Israel against Satan's accusations at the heavenly tribunal. Similarly, Christ is prophesied as vindicating His people in the final showdown.

Michael will stand up after completing His work in the heavenly sanctuary and the finishing of the pre-advent judgment. Since there will be no mediator before the Father, the door of mercy will be closed, and the time of trouble will begin (12:1; cf. Rev. 22:11). We are told that many people "who sleep in the dust of the earth" will awake to either eternal life or everlasting damnation (12:2). As mentioned before, this description is inclusive of a special resurrection of some righteous and wicked (Matt. 26:64; Rev. 1:7), which will occur shortly prior to the general resurrection at the Second Advent when only the righteous will be resurrected (Dan 12:13; 1 Thess. 4:16–17). The resurrection of the wicked will occur a thousand years later (Rev. 20:4–6).

The reference to those who were to lead or turn many to righteousness (lit. "justify") and who were to shine like the stars (Dan. 12:3) is an encouragement to all who faithfully work for the Lord, often under the most difficult circumstances. There is no greater joy than seeing people change under the influence and power of the Holy Spirit. To see them in the kingdom will be a wonderful reward for God's servants.

Daniel was told to seal the book/scroll until the time of the end. This indicates that "the time of the end" begins with the unsealing of the closed portions of Daniel. Concerning the time of the end, it was prophesied that many would run or move quickly back and forth. This does not refer to the inventions of cars or planes since the end of the nineteenth century. The Hebrew word used here is sometimes associated with searching (cf. Jer. 5:1; Amos 8:12; Zech. 4:10). When the book of Daniel is unsealed after the commencement of the time of the end, the knowledge regarding its prophecies will be increased.

12:5–13
EPILOGUE

Daniel was still by the Tigris River, where he was in 10:4. Now he overheard a conversation between two heavenly figures and eventually joined in (see chap. 10 for its literary connection with the epilogue). This passage parallels Daniel 8:13–14 in several ways: both take place beside a river, involve two anonymous heavenly beings, and ask the question "How long?" (12:6). This refers back to the vision in chapter 11. Gabriel had given Daniel this long explanation to help him understand what was to happen to God's people in the future (10:14). This passage also has a number of linguistic and thematic parallels to Revelation 10.

Next, two other heavenly beings appeared, and one of them asked Michael, the man clothed in linen, a question that aimed at sharing more information with Daniel. The answer is that it would be for a time, times, and half a time and that the period would end when the power of the holy people would be broken completely. This defines the time of the end as that following the 1,260 years (three and a half times) of papal supremacy and persecution (see "Interpreting Biblical Apocalyptic Prophecies," p. 46).

A new time prophecy is introduced in v. 11. The taking away of the tamid ("daily"/"continual") is mentioned three times in the book of Daniel (8:11; 11:31; 12:11), but only in 12:11 is it connected to a time period ("From the time…1,290 days"). There are important parallels between Daniel 11:31 and 12:11. In both passages the taking away of the tamid ("daily"/"continual") is associated with the setting up of the desolating abomination.

The two texts are clearly parallel and refer to the same events in history. Since 11:31 refers to the past, so must 12:11. In Daniel 8:11, we saw that the *tamid* ("daily"/"continual") refers to Christ's intercessory ministry that was usurped by the work of the priests through the mass and the confessional. By sacrificing Christ anew in every mass, Christ's heavenly ministry has been removed from view. Since the period of 1,290 is based on the prophetic period of 1,260 days, to which another month was added (1,260 + 30 = 1,290), the year-day principle is to be used in its interpretation. The extra month points to the beginning of the prophetic events while the 1,260 years place the emphasis on the end of the period in 1798. Therefore, the process mentioned in this prophecy began in the sixth century (1798 – 1,290 = A.D. 508). Using the historicist method of interpretation, the 1,290 years would have begun in A.D. 508.

Sometime before A.D. 508 or, as some historians claim, in A.D. 508, Clovis, the king of the Franks who had married the Catholic Burgundian princess Clotilda, became a Roman Catholic. All the other Germanic tribes who had dismantled the Roman Empire were Arians (see "The Union of Church and State," p. 1033) and were therefore in opposition to the pope in Rome. After his great victory over the Visigoths in A.D. 507, Clovis went to Tours in A.D. 508 to hold a victory celebration. According to Gregory of Tours, Clovis was dressed in the uniform of imperial officials. The Franks became the first civil power to join up with the rising Church of Rome. France, therefore, is called the oldest daughter of the Roman Catholic Church.

The joining of the civil and the religious powers (the Franks and the papacy) at that time was an important step in setting up the abomination of desolation, in other words, a religiopolitical system that cast truth to the ground and used force to enforce its religious teachings. It is one of the ironies of history that France, the power that helped the papacy at the beginning of the 1,290 years, was the same power that brought about its demise at the end of this time period. From history we know that the supremacy of the medieval church came to an end in 1798 when Pope Pius VI was taken prisoner by Napoleon's army.

Another new time prophecy is introduced in v. 12. No specific event is mentioned for the beginning of the 1,335 days/years, but it is an extension of the 1,290 days (a month and a half is added to the previous prophetic period: 1,290 + 30 + 15 = 1,335). The prophecy simply promised a special blessing to those who keep on waiting. Contextually, it is most probable that this prophetic period began at the same time as the 1,290 days. Unless the 1,335 days were to begin at the same time as the 1,290 days, they would be the only time prophecy in Daniel that has no historical starting point, which would be out of character with the other time prophecies in Daniel. Therefore, the 1,335 prophetic days ended in 1843. This time period is closely connected to the 2,300-year prophecy that ended in 1844. The 1,335 days and the 2,300 evenings and mornings respond to the same question, "How long?" (8:13; 12:6), and connect the two prophetic periods, after which there are no more time prophecies (Rev. 10:5–6). Those who lived at the time of the advent expectancy when the first angel's message (Rev. 14:6–7) was proclaimed in Europe and the Americas were blessed to see the fulfillment of prophecy. This message was then followed by the full proclamation of the messages of the three angels of Revelation 14:6–12 by God's end-time remnant (Dan. 12:17).

The connections between the epilogue of Daniel and chapters 7–11 are clear. For example, (1) since the little horn in Daniel 7 and 8 designates the same historical power, the removal of the *tamid* ("daily"/"continual") in 8:11 and 12:11 must refer to the same past historical event. (2) There is a strong thematic and linguistic connection between the texts in 7:25 and 12:7. The shattering of the power of the holy people in 12:7 was to last for three and a half times, the same as the persecution of the saints in 7:25 that also was to last for three and a half times. (3) The year-day principle is operative in all the time prophecies. The 1,290 and 1,335 days are prophesied as extensions of the 1,260 days mentioned in 7:25 and 12:7 as a time, times, and half a time. Because the periods of 1,290 and 1,335 days are based on the 1,260 days, and because the 1,260 days are years, the year-day principle is also applied to the 1,290 and 1,335 days.

The book closes with two messages for Daniel. He was exhorted to go on with his life until he would rest—a euphemism for death (cf. Job 3:13, 16, 26). However, death would not be the absolute end because he would rise to receive his inheritance in the general eschatological resurrection. The book closes with a return to the topic of hope that characterizes it. The forces of evil would oppose the divine plan and oppress God's people throughout history, but at the end they would receive, together with Daniel, their inheritance. In the context of the book, the inheritance is the kingdom of God. It will be theirs through the work of the

Son of Man, the Messiah whose First Coming is clearly announced in Daniel 9, where He is described as a sacrifice and the high priest. At His Second Coming, His enemies and the corrupt kingdoms of the earth will be destroyed. This wonderful hope will be revealed in greater detail in the NT. Ultimately, it is humanity's only hope.

HOSEA

INTRODUCTION

Title and Authorship. The title of the book is the name of the author (Hos. 1:1). *Hoshea'* means "He [Yahweh] has saved" (shortened from *hosha'yah* "Yahweh has saved"; cf. Jer. 42:1; 43:2). This was also the name of Israel's last king (2 Kin. 15:30; 17:1–6), as well as of other figures in OT history (Num. 13:8, 16; 1 Chr. 27:20; Neh. 10:23). Joshua and Jesus are variations of the same name. Hosea's father was named Beeri, and his wife was named Gomer, daughter of Diblaim. He had three children: a son, Jezreel; a daughter, Lo-Ruhamah; and another son, Lo-Ammi. Nothing is known about Hosea's birthplace, but he probably came from the Northern Kingdom of Israel since he mainly addressed his prophecies to its people.

Date. Hosea addressed his message primarily to the last generation of the Northern Kingdom of Israel before its fall in 722 B.C. He prophesied during the reigns of four kings from the Southern Kingdom of Judah: Uzziah (= Azariah; ca. 792–740 B.C.), Jotham (ca. 750–732 B.C.), Ahaz (ca. 735–716 B.C.), and Hezekiah (ca. 716–687 B.C.; Hos. 1:1). The first verse mentions only one king of Israel (Jeroboam II; 793–753 B.C.), although six more kings reigned after Jeroboam II. These last six kings were probably omitted because the Lord did not appoint them (8:4). Hosea prophesied under more kings than any other prophet. His ministry probably lasted at least thirty-five years (ca. 760–725 B.C.).

Backgrounds. Hosea began his ministry during a period of great prosperity for the kingdoms of Israel and Judah. Jeroboam II, the third king in succession of the Jehu dynasty, brought Israel to the zenith of its power and enlarged its territory to the northern boundary it held under Solomon. King Uzziah likewise enlarged Judah's territory to the southern border of the united monarchy. During this time the Assyrians were preoccupied with foreign invasions to their north, while Egypt experienced a period of internal weakness. Israel and Judah were safe from their enemies and internally strong.

Commerce flourished in both Israel and Judah, bringing great wealth and luxury to the upper class. Excavations of Samaria, Israel's capital city, have revealed spacious ivory-inlaid palaces. Excavations in Judah's capital city, Jerusalem, have demonstrated great expansion and fortification. It was a time of external optimism and national pride. The people confidently expected a glorious future because they believed that God's election guaranteed their ongoing prosperity.

But it was also a time of internal sickness with a shocking disparity between the wealthy and the poor. The middle class all but disappeared, as is evidenced by excavations at towns like Tirzah (Tell-el-Farah). Those in power demonstrated heartless injustice, materialistic greed, and flagrant dishonesty. Society was rife with crime of every sort, feasting and drunkenness, gross licentiousness, debauchery, and corrupt religious practices. Jeroboam I had set up two golden calves at Dan and Bethel (1 Kin. 12:26–30), which became centers for the counterfeit and syncretistic worship of Baal (Hos. 2:8; 13:1), nominally carried out in the name of Yahweh. Baal worship involved gross immorality, including cultic prostitution, as part of worship.

After the death of Jeroboam II, the Northern Kingdom fell into chaos. They experienced a thirty-year period of political anarchy, a veritable revolving door of power (cf. 8:4). A series of political assassinations led to three different kings ruling within a period of one year. Shallum assassinated and supplanted Zechariah, and Menahem assassinated and supplanted Shallum. A decade later, Menahem's son, Pekahiah, was himself assassinated by Pekah. The political security of Israel and Judah began to crumble with the rise of the Neo-Assyrian Empire under Tiglath-Pileser III (also called Pul, 745–727 B.C.). During his first campaign into the Holy Land, he exacted a high tribute from Menahem (2 Kin. 15:19–20). He returned to the Holy Land in 734 B.C., when King Ahaz of Judah cried for help against King Pekah of Israel and King Rezin of Syria during the Syro-Ephraimite War (2 Kin. 15:37; 16:5–9; Is. 7). In 732 B.C., Tiglath-Pileser III conquered, exiled, and annexed the northern and eastern provinces of Israel, placed Hoshea on the throne, and reduced Judah to vassal status (2 Kin. 15:29–30). When Tiglath-Pileser III died, his son Shalmaneser V (727–722 B.C.) succeeded him. King Hoshea withheld tribute from Assyria, shifting his loyalty to Egypt. In response, Shalmaneser (via his general, Sargon II) besieged the city of Samaria for three years. The city finally fell in 722 B.C. Sargon II succeeded Shalmaneser, subdued the rest of the Northern Kingdom, and sent the populace into exile. The Prophet Hosea prophesied during this turbulent time in the history of Israel and Judah. His prophecies, apparently ordered in general chronological sequence from the 750s to the 720s B.C., probably allude to various details of the contemporary political chaos.

Theology and Purpose. Written in the last days before the destruction of the Northern Kingdom, the book of Hosea serves as God's "Laodicean message" (see Rev. 3:14–22) to the people. In an attempt to stop their national apostasy, God sent a personal, emotion-packed message calling for them to change their course. Hosea's wife, Gomer, was unfaithful to him, but he forgave and ransomed her out of enduring love. Their relationship became a dramatic life parable of Yahweh's steadfast love for unfaithful Israel.

1. *God as the Source of All Blessings.* Among the OT prophets, Hosea became the leading expositor of God's paradoxical outrage and heartbreak at Israel's participation in pagan fertility cults. The promiscuity/adultery motif and God's reaction to it appear repeatedly throughout the book. God, at the risk of being misunderstood, used unmistakable sexual imagery to counteract the distorted sexual theology and ritual of Baal worship. The book of Hosea describes the genuine love relationship between God and His people and affirms that the fertility of the people, the land, and the animals comes from the Lord.

The book presents a conflict between Baal and the Lord, who was unwilling to let Baal have Israel. The Lord was the exclusive source of all of Israel's blessings. He, not Baal, fertilized the land like the dew (Hos. 14:5). Although outside nature, the Lord acts within it. To a people obsessed with the fertility of the land, He presented Himself as an evergreen tree, unaffected by seasonal changes (v. 8). As Israel's Husband, He cared for His wife by bestowing upon her gifts from the land (2:5, 8).

2. *Rejection of Divine Love.* In Hosea, the history of Israel illustrates God's contemporary relationship with His people. The problem with the Northern Kingdom dated back beyond the rebellion of Saul (13:10–12) to the conquest of Canaan and Israel's first experience with Baal (9:10). Hosea uses these and other historical references (e.g., the Exodus, 2:15; 11:1; the desert wanderings, 2:3, 14; 9:10; 13:5; Jacob, 12:3–4, 12) to expose the present guilt of Israel and the Lord's struggle with His people. Throughout their history, the Lord had cared for and protected them (2:8), but they went after foreign lovers (vv. 5, 13). Israel acted like a stubborn son, who rejected the love and concern of his Father (11:1–6). Hosea also describes God as a Husband, vividly equating Israel's sin with harlotry, an image applied to both political and religious behavior (2:2–5; 3:3; 4:10–18; 8:9). The religious and political leaders had all been unfaithful to Israel's loving, divine Husband.

The priests encouraged national apostasy instead of teaching God's word (4:6, 8, 11–13). The political leaders committed intrigues and murders instead of consulting the Lord when appointing new kings (7:5–7; 8:4). They thirsted for power without any concern for the people. They also sought the assistance of Egypt and Assyria, physicians who could not heal (5:13; 7:8–11). In Hosea, sin is simply unfaithfulness. The Lord had been their loving Husband (2:2–20), their Father (11:1–6), and their healing Physician (7:1; 14:4). But the people committed adultery and abandoned Him (2:13; 4:10).

3. *Everlasting Love.* The key theme in the book is God's steadfast love (Heb. *khesed*) for His people and His passionate desire for an intimate love relationship with them. He wanted them to know (Heb. *yada'*) Him on a personal level. They had gone after other lovers, but He longed for them to return/repent (Heb. *shub*) and to seek (Heb. *baqash*) Him again. Indictments (about two-thirds of the book) and threatened covenant curses (about one-fourth of the book) fill the extended legal case (Heb. *rib*) against God's wayward wife/son. Yet seven times God extended a promise of hope

and salvation for His people in the eschatological future (1:10—2:1; 2:14–23; 3:5; 6:1–3; 11:8–11; 13:14; 14:1–8). Yes, He announced punitive judgment (1:5; 4:1–3; 5:7; 7:16; 8:3; 10:14), but that judgment constituted a loving act of a God striving for the love of His people. For change to come, the Lord would have to bring it about. He would cut off the way to the idols (2:6), bring Israel back to the wilderness (2:14), and remove all the perverted political and priestly institutions (3:4). He promised to heal their rebellious nature and love them freely if only they would return to Him (14:4). If this hope remained unrealized, it would not be because God stopped loving but because His unfaithful wife would not repent/return.

Literary Features. The book of Hosea is a literary masterpiece. Except for the narrative prose of chapters 1 and 3, it has an elegant poetic style. Hosea utilizes more figures of speech (metaphors, similes, wordplays, etc.) and makes more allusions to Israel's history than any other OT prophet. The Hebrew of Hosea's book also contains more obscure passages than that of any other prophetic book. The prophet probably spoke a distinct northern dialect of Hebrew.

The book comprises three main sections. The first section (chaps. 1–3) pictures Israel as God's wayward wife, as illustrated in the life parable of Hosea's marriage to Gomer. The matching final section (chaps. 11–14) portrays Israel as God's wayward son, whom God would finally bring home. The middle section (chaps. 4–10) forms an extended covenant lawsuit (Heb. *rib*) in which God presents the legal case against His people. The middle section contains five symmetrical subsections, forming an overall seven-part chiastic mirror-image macrostructure.

A God's Wayward Wife (chaps. 1–3)
    B Indictment for Spiritual Prostitution/
         Idolatry (4:1—5:7)
        C Indictment for Political and Cultic
             Unfaithfulness (5:8—6:11)
            D Laments over Israel's Failure to
                 Return to Yahweh (6:11b—7:16)
        C' Indictment for Political and Cultic
             Unfaithfulness (8:1—9:7b)
    B' Indictment for Spiritual Prostitution/
         Idolatry (9:7c—10:15)
A' God's Wayward Son (chaps. 11–14)

Each of the seven sections of this macrostructure also contains internal chiastic structuring, as shown in the commentary on each section. The chiasms in Hosea display traits generally true of any chiastic structure. The central member often highlights the major emphasis of the section, and the second half of the chiasm reaffirms and amplifies the major themes of the first half *in reverse order*. Sometimes the first and last chiastic members also serve to emphasize a major theme.

COMMENTARY

1:1—3:5
GOD'S WAYWARD WIFE

Chapters 1–3 use a life parable to illustrate the message of the whole book. God instructed Hosea to marry a harlot and have children. This relationship enabled the prophet to personally experience and communicate the pathos of God's relationship with His spiritually wayward wife, the people of Israel. These chapters form an ABA' pattern that alternates between narrative prose (chaps. 1, 3) and poetry (chap. 2).

1:1—2:1
Hosea's Unfaithful Wife and Their Children

Following the introductory verse of the book, the remainder of the first chapter (plus 2:1) forms a chiastic structure:

Introduction Hosea's Promiscuous Wife
     (1:2–3a).
    A Jezreel ("God Sows"; 1:3b–5)
        B Lo-Ruhamah ("Not-Shown-Mercy";
             1:6–7)
            C Lo-Ammi ("Not-My-People";
                 1:8–9)
                D Israel Multiplied (1:10a)
            C' Lo-Ammi Reversed (1:10b)
        B' Lo-Ruhamah Reversed (1:11a)
    A' The Great Day of Jezreel (1:11b)
Conclusion "Mercy" for "My People" (2:1)

1:2–3a. Hosea's Promiscuous Wife. Many have insisted that God did not actually ask Hosea to marry a harlot. But the Bible forbids only priests from marrying a harlot (Lev. 21:7), and Hosea was not a priest. The Hebrew word *zenunim* ("harlotry") normally refers to the actual status and practice of a harlot. Hosea 1:2 probably indicates that at the time Hosea married her, Gomer was either a common prostitute or one of the temple prostitutes of the fertility cult. These desperate times called for desperate measures on God's part. He involved Hosea in shocking actions as an attempt to wake up Israel before it was too late.

The reference to children of harlotry/promiscuity possibly refers to children Gomer had before marrying Hosea, but in the immediate context the phrase more likely reflects the promiscuity of the children's mother. God did not tell Hosea which harlot to marry. Hosea chose Gomer, whose name, ironically, means "perfection."

1:3b–9. Gomer's Three Children. Only the first of Gomer's children is explicitly referred to as the son of both Gomer and Hosea (1:3). The other two may have been born as a result of Gomer's prostitution (vv. 6, 8). Hosea named his first son Jezreel ("God sows") because of the bloodshed that occurred in the city of Jezreel when Jehu wiped out all the royal line of Ahab and Jezebel (v. 4; cf. 2 Kin. 9–10, esp. 9:22). Although carrying out God's behest (2 Kin. 10:30), Jehu was motivated by bloodthirsty self-interest and pride (2 Kin. 10:16, 31). The Hebrew word *paqad*, sometimes translated as "avenge" or "punish," literally means "visit" (Hos. 1:4). Jezreel may epitomize how God's "visitation" brings an end to dynasties and kingdoms. God would break the bow of Israel in the Valley of Jezreel (v. 5), the same location where He once broke the bow of Israel's enemies (see Judg. 6–7). Tiglath-Pileser III probably fulfilled this prophecy when he took away the northern and eastern territories of Israel (ca. 732 B.C.; see 2 Kin. 15:29).

Gomer's second child was a daughter. God told Hosea to name her Lo-Ruhamah ("Not-Shown-Mercy"; Hos. 1:6). Because of Israel's persistent covenant faithlessness, God would no longer show them mercy. The Hebrew word *nasa'* can mean "take away," "forgive," or "bear." The last clause may mean that God could no longer bear or forgive them. But since v. 6 matches v. 11, which prophesies the gathering of Israel and Judah, it probably means Israel would be taken away into captivity.

God commanded Hosea to name Gomer's third child, another son, Lo-Ammi ("Not-My-People") as a sign of covenant breaking. The final line of v. 9 reads literally "I am no longer 'I Am' to you." God called Himself by the name "I Am" (Heb. *'ehyeh)* in Exodus 3:14. God would withdraw His very name from Israel.

1:10—2:1. The Eschatological Restoration of Israel. In the first of seven passages addressing eschatological hope and salvation, God promised to ultimately fulfill the covenant promises by restoring Israel from exile with an innumerable posterity (1:10a; cf. Gen. 13:15; 22:17; Lev. 26:9, 45; Deut. 30:5). In the eschatological future, He would undo the curses represented by Gomer's children, listed in reverse order. "Not-My-People" would once again be His people (Hos. 1:10b). "Not-Shown-Mercy" would once again receive His mercy. He would gather them together in a new exodus from the land of their exile (v. 11a; cf. 2:15). The great day of Jezreel would once again unite both Israel and Judah under one *ro'sh* ("head," "ruler," "leader"), an allusion to the coming Davidic Messiah (1:11b; see 3:5).

This prophecy looks ahead to the last days (3:5), which according to the NT began when Jesus came to earth (Heb. 1:2). Paul claims that the faithful remnant of Israel, including believing Gentiles, fulfills Hosea 1:10 (along with 2:23) when they accept Jesus as the Messiah (Rom. 9:25–26). This section concludes with the reunion of Israel, a complete reversal of the fortunes symbolized by Gomer's children (Hos. 2:1).

2:2–23
Yahweh's Covenant Lawsuit against His Unfaithful Wife

Hosea 2:2–23 introduces the covenant lawsuit that occupies much of the book (see "Covenant Lawsuit in Hosea," p. 1066). Hosea's relationship with his promiscuous wife, Gomer, illustrates the formal trial proceedings. While this chapter applies primarily to God's case against Israel (see v. 13), it also pertains to Hosea's relationship with Gomer (and to broken marriages even today).

A The First Punishment: Removal of the Land's Fertility (vv. 2–5a)
  B The Second Punishment: Restraints on Israel (vv. 5b–7)
    C The Third Punishment: Reclaiming Gifts Attributed to Baal (vv. 8–13)
      D Wooing Israel Back (vv. 14–15)
    C' Reversal of the Third Punishment: Removal of Baal's Name (vv. 16–17)
  B' Reversal of the Second Punishment: God's Marriage to Returning Israel (vv. 18–20)
A' Reversal of the First Punishment: Restoration of the Land's Fertility (vv. 21–23)

2:2–13. Three Indictments and Punishments.

In v. 2 God calls for His wayward wife to immediately remove the outward signs of her prostitution (e.g., amulets and other jewelry worn in connection with the fertility cult; see v. 13). A broken marriage cannot mend without the offending party being held accountable and taking concrete steps to separate from promiscuous practices. If His wayward wife remained unfaithful, God would invoke the legal ultimatum—public exposure (v. 3). In a shame-based society (see v. 5), stripping a woman bare and publicly exposing her constituted the ultimate punishment (see Ezek. 16:37; 23:29). Historically, this means the land would be stripped and the people taken into exile in fulfillment of the predicted covenant curses (Lev. 26:31–33; Deut. 28:38–42). The common people would not escape either because they had also participated in the Baal cult (Hos. 2:4–5a).

Verses 5b–13 provide further evidence against Yahweh's wife, focusing on her spiritual harlotry and worship of Baal. God quotes her own words as testimony against her (v. 5b). This testimony reveals the basic theological tenets of the Baal fertility cult, which regarded the land as a female deity and Baal as the storm god who impregnated her with his semen (i.e., the rain fertilizing the land). Yahweh turned Baal theology upside down, presenting Himself as the Provider of fertility and Baal as sterile (vv. 8, 12).

God pronounced two formal sentences against His wife for her adulterous actions, each prefaced by the word "therefore" to emphasize His intention to actually mete out the sentence. The first

---

Covenant Lawsuit in Hosea

The Hebrew word *rib* (used as a verb twice in Hos. 2:2 and as a noun once in 4:1) is a technical term for "covenant lawsuit" or "investigative judgment." In the Hebrew Bible, it occurs forty-four times in reference to a divine lawsuit, either a negative judgment (condemnation) or a positive judgment (vindication) of God's people. Hosea 2 involves both. The basic structure of the covenant lawsuit mirrors the regular covenant-making procedure in Scripture and in the ancient Near East (esp. Hittite suzerain-vassal treaties). The basic structure of a covenant in the ancient Near East normally contained the following elements:

1. List of witnesses
2. Preamble (introduction of the suzerain and call to judgment)
3. Historical prologue (review of the suzerain's benevolent acts toward the vassal)
4. Indictments or charges (evidence of covenant violations investigated)
5. Verdict and sentence (either condemnation or vindication)

The complete structure of this lawsuit pattern occurs in Hosea 4:1–13 (see also Deut. 32; Josh. 24; Is. 1:2–20; 3:13–15; Jer. 2:4–13; Mic. 6:1–8). Scripture contains over three hundred references to a divine covenant lawsuit. Condemnation resulted in the pronouncement of covenant curses/punishments (cf. the twenty-seven different kinds of covenant curses/punishments summarized in Lev. 26:14–39 and Deut. 28:15–68). Vindication resulted in the pronouncement of covenant blessings (cf. Lev. 26 and Deut. 4, 28, 30, 32).

Hosea 2 contains a partial formulation of the covenant lawsuit pattern. In v. 2 the children of the adulterous wife are called as witnesses to her promiscuity. As applied to the relationship between Yahweh and Israel, the children probably represent the common people, the individual members of the nation, while the mother represents Israel's upper-class leaders who are responsible for the nation's unfaithfulness to Yahweh. Most of the lawsuit in chapter 2 involves indictments and the verdict and sentence. The covenant curses (vv. 2–13) and blessings (vv. 14–23) are taken largely from Leviticus 26 and Deuteronomy 27–28 (see "God's Judgment in the Prophets," p. 981).

The covenant lawsuit in this chapter resembles the adultery trial proceedings described in Numbers 5:12–31 and conducted by God in Ezekiel 16 and 23. In Hosea 2:2, God's statement regarding Israel probably signifies the broken relationship and not yet actual divorce. This divine lawsuit, like many others in Scripture, aims to both correct (in the immediate situation) and restore (ultimately).

sentence was a preliminary attempt to save the relationship: God would block her way with a hedge of thorn bushes to prevent her from finding her lovers (v. 6). Historically, the Assyrian domination of the northern and eastern parts of Israel (ca. 732 B.C.; see Hosea: Introduction), which thwarted Israel's participation in the Baal cult located there, probably fulfilled this prophecy.

The second sentence predicts the captivity and Exile of Israel after the fall of Samaria in 722 B.C. Yahweh's wife would refuse to return to her Husband, so He would take back His gifts that she considered to be rewards from her lovers (v. 12). He would uncover (*galah*) her lewdness (*nablot*, which probably refers to the female genitalia) in the sight of her lovers (v. 10). The Hebrew *galah* also means "go into exile." Hosea plays on the double meaning of the word to predict Israel's Exile and shameful exposure in the process. Yahweh would realize the covenant curses by making the land barren (Lev. 26:20; Deut. 28:39–40) and canceling Israel's entire cultic calendar—pilgrim festivals, new moons, and ritual sabbaths (Hos. 2:11; Lev. 26:31). Israel had forgotten Yahweh (Hos. 2:13), so the marriage was over.

2:14–23. Wooing Israel Back and Reversal of the Three Punishments. Verse 14 begins with a third "therefore." But instead of pronouncing the expected further punishment, Yahweh defies all logic by announcing that He would *patah* ("allure," "persuade," "woo," "court") Israel back to Himself. This is the second of seven passages of eschatological hope and salvation in the book. Eventually Israel would willingly choose to return to Yahweh (vv. 15–23). The Great Reversal employs language from Israel's Exodus from Egypt, recalling the joyful desert days when God tenderly spoke comfort to Israel (lit. "spoke to her heart"; v. 14). The Exodus, wilderness wandering, and settlement in the promised land prefigure the re-betrothal and remarriage of Yahweh and Israel. The Valley of Achor (lit. "trouble"; located southwest of Jericho), where Achan and his family were stoned for their sin (Josh. 7:26), would become a door of hope when the divine Groom brings His new bride home. The singing/responding (Hos. 2:15) may allude to the Song of Moses after the crossing of the Red Sea (Ex. 15). The Hebrew word *'anah* can mean "sing" as well as "answer" or even "[sexually] respond." God promised to revirginize Israel, as it were, bringing His bride back to the intimacy, ardor, and covenant relationship of her youth. Such actions toward an adulterous

wife engender hope for any marriage, even one scarred by unfaithfulness. But both parties must be willing to reconcile and start anew.

The phrase "in that day" in Hosea 2:16 looks forward to a future eschatological fulfillment. God promised to reverse the three punishments announced in vv. 2–13. First, instead of focusing on Baal and the gifts attributed to him, Israel would have his name totally removed from their vocabulary and memory. Playing on the twofold meaning of Baal—the name of the fertility god Baal and a word denoting a husband (lit. "master")—God promised that Israel would not only forget the god Baal but would also no longer call Yahweh Himself *ba'ali* ("my Master"), which implies ownership or possession. Instead, they would call Him *'ishi* ("my Husband"), which implies an intimate, personal partnership. Thus, God would take a new marriage name, a common feature in the ancient sealing of a marriage covenant.

Second, instead of restraining His wife, Yahweh would remarry her (vv. 17–20). Using language reminiscent of the peace in the Garden of Eden before sin (Gen. 1–2) and of the divine covenant made with the earth after the Flood (Gen. 9:8–17), Yahweh promised to betroth Israel to Himself forever. Instead of the normal dowry, God offered to bestow upon her His own character qualities: His righteousness (Heb. *tsedeq*), justice (*mishpat*), steadfast love (*khesed*), compassion (*rakhamim*, lit. "womb love"; derived from *rekhem*, "womb"), and covenant faithfulness (*'emunah*; related to "amen"). This language reflects God's self-revelation in Exodus 34:6–7. These marriage gifts climax with the promise that Israel would know the Lord. The Hebrew word *yada'* ("know") often refers to a deep personal relationship, even sexual intimacy.

Third, Yahweh promised to reverse the first punishment by restoring the land's fertility. Hosea 2:21–23 describes the entire agricultural cycle, which would cause the land to burst with new life. The word *'anah*, as noted above, may not only refer to various parts of the ecosystem participating in the antiphonal responding/singing during the wedding festivities. It may also have sexual connotations. Ultimately, Yahweh would sow/plant (*zara'*) Israel for Himself in the earth (v. 23). The Hebrew *zara'* alludes to the name Jezreel ("God sows") but can also have sexual connotations. Biblical and ancient Near East thought compared the insemination of a woman with a man's seed to sowing a field. Obviously, God is above the sexuality depicted among the pagan gods, and this passage does not refer to actual sexual relations. Nonetheless, God used sexually charged language to describe His intimate personal relationship with His eschatological bride!

In the end-time restoration of Israel, God would have mercy on His people, another allusion to the reversal of the name *lo-ruhamah* ("Not-Shown-Mercy"; v. 23). The wedding ceremony would end with another name change, this time the bride's. Both Paul (Rom. 9:25) and Peter (1 Pet. 2:10) point to the Israel of faith, comprising all who place their trust in Jesus the Messiah, whether Jew or Gentile, as the fulfillment of this verse.

3:1-5
Taking Back the Unfaithful Wife

A Hosea's Love for Gomer (v. 1)
  B Gomer Bought Back (v. 2)
    C Gomer Restricted from Harlotry and Sex (v. 3)
    C' Israel Restricted from Court and Cult (v. 4)
  B' Return of Israel (v. 5a)
A' Fearing Yahweh and His Goodness (v. 5b)

3:1-3. Gomer's Return to Hosea. Verses 1-3 recounts the rest of Hosea and Gomer's story. In contrast to the third person account of chapter 1, Hosea now narrates in the first person to enhance the sense of intimacy. Although some have denied that this woman was Gomer, the context clearly assumes a specific woman already known, and the description of this adulterous woman matches that of the promiscuous Gomer in chapter 1. The adverb *'od* ("yet," "again") probably does double duty in 3:1. God told Hosea to go and love "yet again." Hosea's relationship with Gomer is a life parable, as he compares his love for Gomer, despite her promiscuity, with God's love for Israel, despite her spiritual harlotry/idolatry.

Hosea bought Gomer for fifteen shekels of silver and one and a half homers (lit. "one homer and one letek") of barley (v. 2). The shekel weighed about six ounces (170 g), and a homer held about ten bushels (about 87 gal or 330 l). The *letek* probably measured half a homer. The fact that Hosea had to piece together silver and barley (the cheapest flour) may indicate how much he had to sacrifice to purchase Gomer. When Gomer came home, he insisted that she stay at home with him for many days without

sexual intercourse, neither with her former lovers nor with himself. This may represent a time of purifying and probationary deprivation.

3:4-5. Israel's Eschatological Return to God. Like Gomer, Israel would go through many days of purification, a period of exile that would deprive them of king and cult. The *matsebah* (variously translated as "sacred pillar," "pillar," "sacred stones," "image") was a phallic symbol used in the fertility cult. The ephod and *teraphim* ("household idols/gods") were used in pagan divination (see Ezek. 21:21; Zech. 10:2). Hosea 3:5 has a chiastic arrangement:

A "Afterward"
  B Returning and Seeking Yahweh
    C Seeking David, the (messianic) King
  B' Fearing Yahweh and His Goodness
A' "In the Latter/Last Days"

This verse serves as the climax of the entire first section of the book. It clarifies that Israel's promised restoration would have an eschatological fulfillment (see Deut. 4:29-30). This is the third of seven passages of eschatological hope and salvation in the book. As elsewhere, God called for His people to perform two major actions—return/repent (Heb. *shub*) and seek (Heb. *baqash*) Him. The people would respond to the Lord and His goodness/blessings with fear/awe/trembling. The center of the chiasm reveals the Christocentric focus of the book: Israel would one day seek the Messiah, the Davidic King (Is. 9:1-7; 11:1-9; Jer. 23:5-6; 30:9; Ezek. 37:15-25; Amos 9:11-12; Mic. 5:2-5). As already discussed, this began when Christ first came and will reach its consummation when Christ returns and the faithful Israel of all ages will receive the complete fulfillment of Hosea's restoration promises (Rev. 3:7-13; cf. PK 298-300).

4:1—10:15
GOD'S COVENANT LAWSUIT AGAINST ISRAEL

4:1—5:7
Indictment for Spiritual Prostitution and Idolatry

Hosea 4:1—5:7 begins Yahweh's formal covenant lawsuit (Heb. *rib*) against Israel. He summoned His people to court, examined the evidence, found them guilty of violating His covenant stipulations set forth in the Torah (esp. the Decalogue), and sentenced them to receive the covenant curses. In contrast to the sevenfold structure of most other sections of the book, this section has a fivefold structure, perhaps in conscious parallel to the five books of the Torah. It does not include a historical prologue or witnesses, possibly because these elements occur in chapter 2.

A God's Legal Case (*rib*) against Israel: Basic Indictments and Covenant Curses (4:1–3)

B Condemnation of Priests and People: A Hopeless Situation (4:4–10)

C Israel's Harlotry (4:11–14)

B' Condemnation of the People: A Hopeless Situation (4:15–19)

A' God's Legal Case against Israel: Indictments and Imminent Judgment (5:1–7)

4:1–3 (A). God's Legal Case (rib) against Israel: Basic Indictments and Covenant Curses. Hosea 4:1–3 constitutes a virtual paradigm of Hosea's whole message. In v. 1, God lists Israel's basic sins of omission. They lacked the essential character qualities of Yahweh, *'emet* ("faithfulness," "truth") and *khesed* ("mercy," "steadfast love"; see Ex. 34:6), and did not know/acknowledge (Heb. *da'at*) Him. These sins of omission broke the first four commandments. Hosea 4:2 delineates their sins of commission, which broke at least five commandments: swearing/cursing, lying, killing, stealing, and committing adultery. Verse 3 describes the destruction of the three categories of animals in the Creation account, listed in reverse order. The divine sentence constituted a reversal of Creation.

4:4–10 (B). Condemnation of Priests and People: A Hopeless Situation. Hosea 4:4–10 focuses on the priests who, along with the prophets, stumbled in their sin (v. 5; cf. 5:5). Hosea pinpoints the underlying problem of both leaders and nation: they lacked knowledge (i.e., a personal relationship with God) and forgot/ignored God's Torah (4:6; cf. 5:4). Forgetting is not amnesia but failure to act in harmony with God's covenant by obeying His law. In response, God would *shakakh* ("forget"; i.e., ignore or not act in favor of) their children (cf. chaps. 1–3, where "mother" and "children" represent Israel). The priests, chosen to make atonement for sin, instead increased sin.

They enriched themselves by encouraging the people to bring more sacrifices.

4:11–14 (C). Israel's Harlotry. The major theme of Hosea 4:11–14, the center of this section's chiasm, concerns the immorality and spiritual harlotry (idolatry) Israel committed by participating in the fertility rituals of the Baal cult. The entire section of 4:1—5:7 contains a twelvefold repetition of the Hebrew root for prostitution/harlotry (*znh*), the root of *ruakh* for *zenunim* ("[spirit of] prostitution"; 4:12; 5:4), *zanah* ("to act as a prostitute"; 4:10, 12–15, 18; 5:3), and *zonah* ("prostitute"; 4:14). Other terms referring to committing adultery, such as *na'ap* (4:2, 13–14) and *qedeshah* ("ritual or temple prostitute"; 4:14), reinforce this emphasis.

Verse 11 contains a proverb that links harlotry/prostitution to wine and new wine (cf. v. 18), which *laqakh* ("take," "seize," "take away") the *leb* ("heart," "mind," "understanding"). This means they all cause either addiction or loss of understanding/judgment. In the days of Baal-Peor, the use of wine "beclouded the senses and broke down the barriers of self-control" (PP 454; cf. Num. 25:1–3). Likewise, in Hosea's day, it led to immorality (*qalon*, "shameful lewdness"; Hos. 4:18) in the Baal cult.

Verses 13–14 describe the heart of the fertility cult rituals. According to Canaanite theology, since the sperm (rain) of Baal fertilized the land (see commentary on 2:2–13), his sexual activity must be stimulated. Worshipers engaged in ritual intercourse with the shrine devotees (male and female ritual prostitutes) in order to emulate and stimulate the sexual activities of the gods. Hence, cultic groves on the sacred mountaintops, seemingly upon every high hill and under every significant tree (Jer. 2:20; 3:6; cf. Deut. 12:2; 1 Kin. 14:23; Is. 57:5, 7), became scenes of the most degraded sexual debauchery—all under the guise of worship.

God held the fathers particularly responsible because they apparently encouraged their daughters to join them in these sexual orgies (Hos. 4:14). This verse, a landmark in moral history, insists that men are no less responsible for faithfulness to their marriage vows than women are.

4:15–19 (B'). Condemnation of the People: A Hopeless Situation. Hosea 4:15–19 matches vv. 4–10. Yahweh warned the Southern Kingdom of Judah, which did not yet completely participate in Baal worship, to avoid coming up to the Northern Kingdom's cult centers (v. 15).

"Beth Aven" is probably a slur on the name Bethel, where Jeroboam erected one of the two golden calves (1 Kin. 12:26–29). The Hebrew word 'aven ("wickedness") is substituted for el ("God").

The animal simile of Hosea 4:16 compares Israel to an obstinate heifer that forced Yahweh to let it range free. In one of the saddest verses of the entire book, God commanded that Ephraim be left alone (v. 17). He recognized that Ephraim (a synonym for the Northern Kingdom of Israel) had become addicted to (Heb. *khabar*, lit. "join") idols. This resulted in the dissolution of the marriage between Yahweh and Israel implicit in 2:9–13.

5:1–7 (A'). God's Legal Case against Israel: Indictments and Imminent Judgment. Hosea 5:1–7 matches 4:1–3. God indicted Israel, especially the political leaders, for prostitution (5:4). The leaders had not protected Israel, their intended function, but had instead hunted the people down and captured them (vv. 1–2). The *ga'on* ("pride," "exaltation," "arrogance") of Israel probably refers to Yahweh, the true Leader Israel had rejected, but some translators understand it to refer to Israel's arrogant attitude (v. 5; 7:10). The indictment declares the whole nation *tame'* ("corrupt," "defiled"; 5:3), having *bagad* ("acted treacherously", "faithlessly") against Yahweh while continuing with formalistic sacrifices. Consequently, when they sought Yahweh, they would find that He had withdrawn from them as a result of their choice (vv. 6–7a). They were children of apostasy (lit. "alien," "pagan," or "illegitimate" children), and their New Moon festivals (when the moon is dimmest) represented darkness enveloping the land (v. 7b).

5:8—6:11A
Indictment for Political and Cultic Unfaithfulness

A The Alarm Raised in Benjamin (5:8–9)
  B Social Injustice in Judah and Ephraim (5:10–11)
    C Judah and Israel Torn to Pieces by God (5:12–15)
      D Israel's Repentance and Healing/Resurrection (6:1–3)
    C' Judah and Israel Cut to Pieces by God's Prophets (6:4–6)
  B' Social Injustice in Ephraim (6:7–9)
A' The Horrible Thing in Israel (6:10–11a)

5:8–9 (A). The Alarm Raised in Benjamin. The Syro-Ephraimite War of 734–732 B.C. probably forms the background of Hosea 5:8–9 (see Hosea: Introduction). The Israelites blew a ram's horn (*shopar*) to warn of invasion by an enemy force and/or to rally troops for battle. The towns mentioned are all in the territory of the tribe of Benjamin, situated on the often-disputed border between Israel and Judah (see 1 Kin. 11:31, 35; 12:21; 2 Chr. 11:12–13). Since the towns are mentioned from south to north, these verses probably describe the attack of Judah upon Israel after the failure of the Syro-Ephraimite coalition, when Judah may have secured its northern defenses by recapturing the land of Benjamin.

5:10–11 (B). Social Injustice in Judah and Ephraim. Ultimately, both Judah and Ephraim had transgressed by committing acts of social injustice (vv. 10–11). In this context, the Hebrew *tsaw* (usually "a command" or "precept") is probably a slang expression for "excrement," "vomit," or "filth of drunkenness" (the variety of renderings in translations includes "worthless," "filth," and "idols") denoting the depths of degradation to which the two nations had sunk.

5:12–15 (C). Judah and Israel Torn to Pieces by God. Verse 12 compares the divine judgment upon Judah and Israel to *'as* (often translated as "moth," but in this context it probably refers to "putrefaction" or "pus") and to *raqab* ("rottenness," "decay"). Maggots have infected the putrefied wound (v. 13; the Hebrew word *mazor* occurs only here and in Jer. 30:13) and have begun to devour the flesh (cf. Job 13:28), probably alluding to the wounds Israel and Judah inflicted upon each other in the aftermath of the Syro-Ephraimite War. The king referred to in this verse is probably Tiglath-Pileser III. The Hebrew, sometimes translated as "King Jareb," may read *malekh rab* ("great king"). This would parallel the Akkadian *sarrurabû*, a title for the Assyrian kings that had the same meaning (cf. 2 Kin. 18:19). Any appeal to Assyria was in vain. Far from providing a cure, Assyria would become the rod of Yahweh's wrath, destroying Israel and subjugating Judah as a vassal state.

Hosea 5:14–15 describes the stages of a lion's hunt, including the lion capturing and killing the prey, tearing up the carcass, and dragging it away to his den to eat. The imagery of the lion, also used by other prophets (Is. 5:26–30; Nah. 2:12–14), fittingly describes Assyria. God declared that no one would rescue Israel and Judah. Other uses of lion imagery also indicate the impossibility of escape from divine judgment (Pss. 7:2; 50:22; cf. Is. 43:13; Mic. 5:7–8). These verses clearly depict the death (i.e., dissolution and exile) of the Northern Kingdom at the hands of the Assyrians (see Hos. 1:4; 2:3; 7:16; 8:14; 9:11–16; 10:15; 13:1, 7–9, 16) in fulfillment of the covenant curse of Deuteronomy 32:39. Judah's death would come a century later at the hands of the Babylonians. Although by this point they could not escape from lethal punishment, nonetheless hope remained in the eschatological future, when Israel and Judah, torn to pieces, would accept the consequences of their guilt and diligently seek Yahweh's face (Hos. 5:15b).

6:1–3 (D). Israel's Repentance and Healing/Resurrection.

Hosea 6:1–3 is the fourth and center of the seven eschatological messages of hope and salvation in the book. Hosea 5:13–15 describe sickness and mauling leading to death, but these verses depict healing and resurrection in response to Israel's decision to return (*shub* "return," "repent") to Yahweh. Although some commentators hesitate to acknowledge a resurrection hope in this passage, the language of resurrection is unmistakable: the two Hebrew words *qum* ("revive," "arise") and *'khayah* ("raise," "restore," "stand"; 6:2), when used together elsewhere in Scripture, clearly refer to resurrection (2 Kin. 13:21; Job 14:12–14; Is. 26:14, 19). The reference to three days may well allude to Jonah's experience. In Jonah's prayer during his three days and nights in the belly of the great fish, the prophet's language went beyond his own literal ordeal to describe a virtual death and resurrection (see Jon. 2:2, 6). Only a few years after Jonah's experience in the early eighth century, while Israel still vividly remembered his "death and resurrection," the late-eighth-century Prophet Hosea seems to have alluded to this event. Hosea reinforces this parallel to the experience of Jonah in the next chapter, where he compares Israel to a *yonah* (Jonah's name, which means "dove"; 7:11) who, like Jonah, fled from the presence of the Lord (7:13; cf. Jon. 1:3), went to Assyria (Hos. 7:11; cf. Jon. 3:1–3), and was swallowed up (Heb. *bala'*; Hos. 8:8; cf. Jon. 1:17). Hosea envisioned the Exile and subsequent return of Israel (and Judah) as recapitulating the "death and resurrection" experience of Jonah.

Also in the eighth century B.C., Isaiah clearly described the Messiah as the Representative Israel, whose life would recapitulate the experience of Israel, especially with regard to His death and resurrection (see esp. the Servant Songs of Is. 42–53). There are numerous intertextual links between Hosea 5:11—6:3 and the messianic Servant Songs; for example, the words *ratsats* ("crush" or "trample"), *kholi* ("sickness," "grief," or "pain"), *rapa'* ("heal"), *nasa'* ("carry," "bear," or "go away"), *'asham* ("guilt" or "sin"), *khabash* ("bind"), *nakah* ("strike"), and numerous additional linguistic parallels in the messianic Psalm 22.

Thus, Hosea identifies Israel as another Jonah, dying and then being resurrected on the third day, and Isaiah shows that the Messiah would be the Representative Israel, undergoing a death and resurrection like the first Israel. Jesus recognized these OT connections between God's servant Jonah (2 Kin. 14:25), the servant Israel, and the messianic Servant when He confidently proclaimed that as Jonah was in the belly of the fish for "three days and three nights," so the antitypical Jonah would be in the heart of the earth and rise after three days (Matt. 12:40). Likewise Paul can say that Christ rose on the third day "according to the Scriptures" (1 Cor. 15:4). Both Jesus and Paul accurately announced the fulfillment of the Jonah/Israel typology indicated by the prophets.

Yahweh would come to Israel like the dawn and like the rain (Hos. 6:3). The similarity in language between this description of Yahweh and the description of the messianic (Davidic) King in Psalm 72:6 gives this passage messianic connotations (cf. 2 Sam. 23:4). In the Holy Land, the rain falls throughout the grain-growing season from autumn (September and October) to early spring (sometimes translated as the "former rain"). It appears again at the end of the season (late March and April; sometimes translated as the "latter rain") and ripens the grain for harvest. In the eschatological context of Hosea 6:1–3 (cf. Joel 2:23, 28), this analogy prefigures the outpouring of the Holy Spirit at Pentecost (Acts 2) and the climactic outpouring of the Holy Spirit just before Christ's Second Coming to gather His people (Rev. 14:14–16; 18:1–4).

6:4–6 (C'). Judah and Israel Cut to Pieces by God's Prophets.

Hosea 6:4–6 matches 5:12–14, repeating the same themes in reverse order. Historical Israel and Judah had no intention of repenting. In desperation God asked them both what He should do with them (6:4). He compared their *khesed* ("covenant loyalty," "love," "faithfulness") with morning clouds and dew that dissipate when the sun rises. Verse 5 repeats the image of God cutting Israel to pieces, but here the Lord specifies that He used the pronouncements of judgment through His prophets to cut (v. 5). The next verse presents His desire for *khesed* ("covenant loyalty," "love," "mercy," "kindness") and *da'at* ("true acknowledgment"; that is, knowing Him in a personal relationship), not meaningless, formalistic sacrifices (v. 6). Jesus cited this verse when challenging the Pharisees, linking this prophetic word with His own ministry of compassion (Matt. 9:13).

6:7–9 (B'). Social Injustice in Ephraim. Hosea 6:7–9 matches 5:10–11. God compared Israel's covenant breaking to the time of Adam. Though the Heb. *'adam* has been interpreted as a place name ("at Adam") or as humankind in general ("like men"), it is best translated here as the personal name of the first human. Adam and Eve broke the covenant of Creation by their disobedience (6:7; cf. Gen. 1–3). Hosea 6:8–9, like the matching 5:10–11, describes various acts of social injustice, collectively called *zimmah* ("infamy," "monstrous crimes," "villainy," "atrocities").

6:10–11 (A'). The Horrible Thing in Israel. Hosea 6:10–11 matches 5:8–9 and decries to the cultic defilement (*tame'*) and spiritual harlotry (*zenut*) of Ephraim/Israel (see commentary on 4:11–14), called the "horrible thing" (Heb. *sha'aririyyah*). The subsection ends by warning Judah of a harvest of judgment appointed for them in the more distant future (6:11a).

6:11b—7:16
Laments over Israel's Failure to Return to Yahweh

Hosea 6:11b—7:16 is the central, climactic chiastic section of the book of Hosea. In a series of accusations, Yahweh lamented over Israel's sins and coming fate. He referred to them in the third person, as if addressing the court as a witness in the covenant lawsuit. This passage probably occurs during the unstable history of the Northern Kingdom in its final years of existence (see Hosea: Introduction).

A Lament over Failed Divine Efforts (6:11b—7:2)
  B Lament over Samaria's Domestic Policies and Practices (7:3–7)
    C Lament over Folly in Foreign Affairs (7:8–9)
      D Failure of Israel to Return and Seek God (7:10)

    C' Lament over Folly in Foreign Affairs (7:11–12)
  B' Lament over Domestic Policies and Practices (7:13–14)
A' Lament over Failed Divine Efforts (7:15–16)

The Hebrew word *shub* ("return," "restore," "repent") encapsulates the major theme of this section: Israel has sealed their fate by not returning to Yahweh. The section begins with 6:11b, best translated as a dependent clause connected to what follows in 7:1. Thus, it conveys the idea that God would cause the fortunes of His people to return (*shub*). The section ends in 7:16 with the divine lament of the fact that the people of Israel had not turned (*shub*) to the Most High (the "Most Sublime One"; cf. Deut. 3:12; 1 Sam. 2:10; Is. 59:18). Hosea 7:10, the center of this section and of the whole book, records the legal testimony of Yahweh against His people. Despite all His efforts to get their attention, they still refused to return and seek the Lord their God.

6:11b—7:2 (A). Lament over Failed Divine Efforts. Yahweh longed to restore Israel's fortunes and heal them. But despite His efforts to train and strengthen them, they had followed the way of evil, apparently oblivious of the fact that God knew all about their evil deeds (7:2).

7:3–7 (B). Lament over Samaria's Domestic Policies and Practices. Hosea 7:3–7 probably depicts the last years of Israel's history as a nation, when one king after another took the throne by means of conspiracy, lies, and/or assassination (v. 3; cf. v. 7, which refers to the fall of their kings). The text plays on the Hebrew word for "adulterers" (*na'ap*) and the similar-sounding words for "bake" (*'apah*) and "anger" (*'ap*) (v. 4, 6; 8:5; 11:9). Yahweh compares the passion of the rulers for the fertility cult and for political treachery to an oven so hot that the baker does not need to stoke the fire throughout the baking process (7:4, 7). The rulers were also inflamed with wine (v. 5; cf. the parallel v. 14). Stretching out/joining hands (v. 5) refers to sealing an agreement with a handshake, as still occurs in modern times (see Is. 42:6).

7:8–9 (C). Lament over Folly in Foreign Affairs. Two baking metaphors calling Israel mixed up and half-baked describe their disastrous policy of flip-flopping between loyalties to Egypt and to Assyria. Bakers had to turn bread dough around in the bee-shaped oven so that all parts would get exposed to the hot coals. Like a round flat bread/cake that the baker failed to turn, Israel was half-baked, a fitting description of the poor quality of Israel's political situation.

7:10 (D). Failure of Israel to Return and Seek God. Hosea presents the Pride of Israel (i.e., Yahweh; see commentary on Hos. 5:1–7—although some translations consider the text to be referring to Israel's arrogance) giving legal testimony summarizing the divine indictment: Israel pursued other alliances but would not return to Yahweh. Yahweh did not identify any particular sin that Israel needed to stop. Rather, He repeatedly pled for the people to return/repent (Heb. *shub*) and to seek Him (Heb. *baqash* or *darash*); that is, seek a personal relationship (Heb. *da'at*) with Him (see 2:7; 3:5; 5:15; 6:1, 3, 6; 10:12; 11:5, 10–12; 12:6; 14:1–2). All the other reforms would naturally follow these two essentials. But Israel persistently refused, until finally God could do nothing more. They had broken the covenant relationship, and God lamented their imminent demise.

7:11–12 (C'). Lament over Folly in Foreign Affairs. Hosea 7:11–12 matches vv. 8–9. Like a silly dove (Heb. *yonah*; see commentary on 6:1–3), Ephraim first called to Egypt, then shifted to an alliance with Assyria, only to shift back to Egypt a few years later (7:11; see Hosea: Introduction). They were mixed up indeed.

7:13–14 (B'). Lament over Domestic Policies and Practices. Hosea 7:13–14 matches vv. 3–7. Yahweh cried out in woe (Heb. *'oy*), a cry usually reserved for a funerary lament or situation of impending disaster (v. 13; cf. 1 Sam. 4:7–8; Is. 3:11; Jer. 4:13; Ezek. 24:6). Translators render the key verb in Hosea 7:14 variously as "assemble" or "slash/gash." The latter would refer to the violent practice of members of the fertility cult, who cut themselves to get the attention of Baal so he would provide rain (cf. 1 Kin. 18:28).

7:15–16 (A'). Laments over Divine Failed Efforts. Hosea 7:15–16, the closing section of the chiastic structure, repeats the same themes as the opening section in 6:11b—7:2.

8:1—9:7b
Indictment for Political and Cultic Unfaithfulness

This section (C') repeats and reinforces various themes encountered in the matching section (C) above.

A Announcement of Coming Judgment (8:1–3)

  B Political and Cultic Sins (8:4–6)

    C Alliances with Other Nations (8:7–13)

      D Israel's Maker Forgotten (8:14)

    C' Alliances with Other Nations (9:1–4)

  B' Dissolution of the Cultic Festivals (9:5–6)

A' Announcement of Coming Judgment (9:7a–b)

8:1–3 (A). Announcement of Coming Judgment. Hosea 8:1–3, probably written during the reign of Hoshea, the last king of Israel (732–722 B.C.), begins with an alarm sounded on the *shopar*, warning of imminent judgment upon Israel (as section C began in 5:8). Yahweh compared the coming judgment to an eagle/vulture swooping down upon its prey (cf. Deut. 28:49–50), which reverses the picture of Yahweh as an eagle hovering over its nest at Israel's creation (Deut. 32:10–12). Hosea 8:1–3 gives a general summary of Israel's sins: though Israel claimed to know God, they had in fact broken Yahweh's covenant and rebelled against His Torah. A series of indictments and covenant curses follows.

8:4–6 (B). Political and Cultic Sins. Verse 4 refers to the rapid succession of kings at the end of Israel's history. Most took the throne through coups, intrigues, and assassinations (see Hosea: Introduction). Yahweh also condemns the counterfeit worship of the golden calf Jeroboam I set up in Bethel, called the "calf of Samaria" (a metonymy for the entire nation; cf. 10:5; 13:2). Only one calf remained because by this time in Israel's history, Assyria had already taken the northern part of the country, where the calf in Dan was located.

8:7–13 (C). Alliances with Other Nations. Verse 7 contains a proverbial wisdom statement expressing cause and effect. Israel had sown the wind (so to speak) of strife by casting about between alliances with superpowers. As a result, they would receive a much stronger blowback, reaping a storm/gale/whirlwind of devastating destruction (cf. Is. 29:6; Amos 1:14; Nah. 1:3). Another metaphor describes Israel as a stalk that never reached maturity and thus would produce no flour. But even if it were to produce, the grain would be swallowed up by foreigners.

The Lord continued to compare Israel to something undesirable (Hos. 8:8), to a wild donkey hiring lovers (v. 9; cf. Jer. 2:24–25), and to menial servants (Hos. 8:10). These metaphors all describe Israel's shifting alliances with other nations. Israel had also committed cultic sins related to the sacrifices (see 4:8) and spurned the many important teachings of God's Torah (8:11–13a). So God announced a reversal of the Exodus: Israel would return to Egypt (v. 13b).

8:14 (D). Israel's Maker Forgotten. Verse 14 summarizes the judgment against Israel for breaking the divine covenant. It closely parallels the covenant lawsuit of Deuteronomy 32:15–18. As the only explicit reference in Hosea to the Creation motif, it also parallels Isaiah 51:13. God made Israel a nation, but instead of remembering their Maker, both Israel and Judah had trusted in the constructions of their own hands (i.e., their vast building projects of temples, royal palaces, and city fortifications/strongholds). The historical fulfillment of their punishment, the covenant curse of destruction by fire (Deut. 32:22), occurred when Assyria destroyed Samaria in 722 B.C. and when the Babylonians later destroyed Jerusalem in 586 B.C.

9:1–4 (C′). Alliances with Other Nations. Hosea 9:1–4 matches 8:7–13. Hosea again rehearses Israel's spiritual harlotry. They loved the prostitute's wages but would not receive them. They would not continue to dwell in the Lord's land (see Lev. 25:23) but would "return to Egypt" (Hos. 9:3; further developed in 9:6; 11:5, 10–11).

9:5–6 (B′). Dissolution of the Cultic Festivals. Hosea 9:5–6 matches 8:4–6, returning to the theme of the false cult. The entire cultic calendar, including the counterfeit Festival of Tabernacles (cf. 1 Kin. 12:32), would end with the destruction and exile of the nation.

9:7a–b (A′). Announcement of Coming Judgment. Hosea 9:7a–b briefly summarizes the section and matches 8:1–3. Hosea proclaims the imminent arrival of the days of punishment/recompense. The nation knew what it had done, and Yahweh would hold it responsible.

9:7c—10:15
Indictment for Spiritual Prostitution/Idolatry

Hosea 9:7c—10:15 reinforces and further elaborates on the theme of Israel's spiritual harlotry discussed above. The whole section is structured around historical and geographical allusions that show that Israel's covenant unfaithfulness (spiritual harlotry) had a long history. It stretched all the way back to the time of the Exodus and the period of the judges and involved some of Israel's most revered and sacred geographical locations.

A Sins at Bethel ("House of God"; 9:7c–8)
   B Sins at Gibeah (9:9)
      C Sins at Baal Peor (9:10–14)
         D Sins at Gilgal (9:15—10:4)
      C′ Sins at Beth Aven (10:5–8)
   B′ Sins at Gibeah (10:9–10)
A′ Sins at Bethel (10:11–15)

9:7c–8 (A). Sins at Bethel. The reference to "house of his God" (Heb. *bet-'elohayw*) probably alludes to Bethel ("house of God"; v. 8). This matches the mention of Bethel in 10:15 (subsection a′). Hosea 9:7b–8 can be understood either as God's indictment against the foolish prophets and the *ish haruakh* (lit. "man of the spirit," "inspired man"), who had become insane, or alternatively as a false evaluation of true prophets by the wicked in Israel. Hosea 10:11–15 indicts the nation's vain trust in their mighty men. Both passages indicate that the punishment was to come because of their wickedness (9:7; 10:15). Bethel, once the place where the prophets flourished (2 Kin. 2:3), had become the main center for idolatrous worship of the golden calf, and the prophets had become fools and snares to the people (Hos. 9:7–8).

9:9 (B). Sins at Gibeah. Hosea's reference to Gibeah looks back to the time of the Judges, when the rape and murder of a Levite's concubine resulted in outrage and subsequent war (Judg. 19–21). Placed at the end of the book of Judges, this incident shows the shocking depths of depravity to which Israel had sunk. Now Hosea compares that generation to his contemporary generation, which had become just as deeply corrupted (Hos. 9:9).

9:10–14 (C). Sins at Baal Peor. Continuing the historical and geographical comparisons, Hosea refers back to the period of the Exodus from Egypt (9:10). He likens God's delightful experience with Israel, His "firstborn" son (Ex. 4:22), to the taste of early figs. But at the time of Israel's tragic apostasy at Baal Peor, just before entering Canaan (Num. 25:1–5), they devoted themselves to *laboshet* (lit. "the shame"), the Baal fertility cult rituals and deities. Thus, they became an object of abhorrence themselves (Hos. 9:10). In a parody on the fertility cult, Hosea warns that the people would receive the opposite of the fertility they desired: infertility, infanticide, miscarriage, and shriveled breasts (vv. 11–14).

9:15—10:4 (D). Sins at Gilgal. Gilgal was a major cultic center in Hosea's time (see 4:15; 12:11). Because of the evil deeds Israel had done there, Yahweh said that He hated them, which He immediately explained to mean that He would no longer love them (9:15). To "hate" in this context means to reject (see commentary on Mal. 1:2–5). This was no insensitive, arbitrary abandonment of His people. Letting them go caused God deep anguish (see Hos. 11:8–9). Using a wordplay on Ephraim's name (from Heb. *para'*, "fruitful"), Hosea announced that they had dried up and would no longer bear fruit (*peri*; cf. 13:15; 14:8). God said He would cast away/reject/drive out (*garash*) Ephraim from His house (9:15), technical language that finalized the divorce between Yahweh and Israel (see Lev. 21:7; Num. 30:9).

Gilgal may have been singled out because of its historical association with King Saul's failed kingship and rejection by God (1 Sam. 11:14–15). Now God would reject His people and their princes (Heb. *sar*), who were stubborn/rebellious (Heb. *surur*) just as Saul was. As God had rent the kingdom from Saul, so would He remove the kingdom of Israel, sending the people into captivity as "wanderers among the nations" (Hos. 9:17). He would break down the cult centers with their altars and sacred pillars and remove their king (in fulfillment of the covenant curse of Deut. 28:36) because they did not revere the Lord. The people, whose hearts were divided (Heb. *khalaq*, "slippery," "deceitful"), would realize too late that their human king, far from being a blessing, was like a poisonous herb growing up in the midst of a food-producing field (Hos. 10:1–4).

10:5–8 (C'). Sins at Beth Aven. Hosea 10:5–8 matches 9:10–14. Hosea depicts the dismantling of the cult at Beth Aven ("house of iniquity," a slur for Bethel; "house of God"; see 4:15; 5:8), its glory or splendor taken away. This alludes to the naming of the child Ichabod ("the glory has departed") when the Philistines captured the ark in the time of Eli (1 Sam. 4:21). The golden calf would be given over to the great king of Assyria (see Hos. 5:12–15), the cultic high places of Ephraim destroyed, and their king cut off/destroyed. In unbearable shame the people would cry for the mountains and

hills to fall on them (cf. Luke 23:30; Rev. 6:16). In short, Assyria would wholly destroy and dissolve Israel (fulfilled in 722 B.C. and afterward).

10:9–10 (B'). Sins at Gibeah. Hosea 10:9–10 matches 9:9. The Lord charged Israel with sins that had continued since "the days of Gibeah."

10:11–15 (A'). Sins at Bethel. Hosea 10:11–15 matches 9:7c–8. In 10:11 the Lord compares Israel to a heifer that once loved to thresh grain and did not even need a goad or tight rein. But now He had to harness it along with Judah. Employing another agricultural metaphor, He encouraged His people to sow righteousness, reap love, and till the ground by seeking Him so He would come down and rain (Heb. *yarah*, which can also mean "teacher of") righteousness (v. 12). He mentioned the foundational work of tilling last. But instead they had plowed/planted wickedness and reaped injustice (v. 13). As punishment their fortresses would be decimated, as some already had been when Shalmaneser III campaigned in Israel in the time of Jehu (841 B.C.), forcing the king to capitulate (v. 14). The location of Beth Arbel is not known.

11:1—14:9

GOD'S WAYWARD SON

This third major part of the book also forms the seventh section of the book's chiastic macrostructure.

A   Israel's Ultimate Return (11:1–11)
    B   The Deceitful Son (11:12—12:8)
        C   Israel Led Up from Egypt (12:9–14)
            D   Summary of Yahweh's Case against Israel (13:1–3)
        C'   Israel Led Up from Egypt (13:4–9)
    B'   The Foolish Son (13:10–16)
A'   Yahweh's Invitation and Promise of Restoration (14:1–9)

Whereas Hosea 1–3 depicted Israel as Yahweh's wayward wife, chapters 11–14 shift the metaphor to describe the nation as Yahweh's wayward (prodigal) son.

11:1–11 (A). Israel's Ultimate Return. Hosea 11:1–4 contains the most tender depiction in all of Scripture of Yahweh's love for Israel, His own son (v. 4 extends the metaphor to God's loving care for animals). In its immediate context, the statement "out of Egypt I called My son" refers to historical Israel's Exodus from Egypt. But both in Hosea and in other eighth-century prophets, it also refers to the future eschatological exodus connected with Israel's return from exile and the coming of the Messiah (see 2:14–15; 12:9, 13; 13:4–5; Is. 11:15–16; 35; 40:3–5; 41:17–20; 51:9–11; 52:3–6, 11–12; 55:12–13; Amos 9:7–15; Mic. 7:8–20). The Latter Prophets recognized Israel's Exodus from Egypt as a type of the messianic new exodus. Matthew remains faithful to this larger context, citing Hosea 11:1 as a catchphrase for all OT passages that predict the eschatological new exodus and point to the Messiah as the Representative Israel. The life of the Messiah would recapitulate the experience of ancient Israel, but He would succeed where the historical Israel had failed (Matt. 1–5).

Instead of responding to Yahweh's tender love with respect and obedience, His prodigal son rebelled and left the Father (Hos. 11:2; cf. Luke 15:11–32). Israel spent his fortune, so to speak, on riotous living amid the licentious Baal cult. Bent on backsliding/turning away from God (Hos. 11:7), they refused to return and repent (v. 5). In the Torah the punishment for such a rebellious son was death (Deut. 21:18–21), which happened when the nation was destroyed and the people were exiled (Hos. 11:5–6).

Hosea 11:8–11 constitutes the fifth of the seven hope and salvation oracles in the book. As in the covenant lawsuit against His wayward wife (2:14–15), the verdict upon God's wayward son ends with a surprise. God could not bear to give Israel up or hand His people over to everlasting destruction, as He had the cities of the plain (Admah and Zeboiim; Gen. 19:24–25). Yahweh had overturned (Heb. *hapak*) those cities in His anger, but now His own heart was overturned/churned/disturbed (Heb. *hapak*; cf. Lam. 1:20) with passionate love, and His compassion/sympathy (Heb. *nikhumim*) was aroused/stirred (lit. "grew warm"; Hos. 11:8). Although having every right to eliminate Israel forever, the Holy One is not vindictive, arbitrary, and heartless. The Lion (Heb. *'aryeh*) of Israel would roar, calling His wayward children (cubs) home. Never again would they be destroyed. They would come back home trembling (*kharad*), a fitting attitude of humility before the great Lion (vv. 9–10). But they would also return from Egypt (= Assyria) swiftly and eagerly fluttering (the second meaning of the Heb. *kharad*) like a bird (v. 11). The prodigal son would return home, welcomed by the rejoicing Father.

11:12—12:8 (B). The Deceitful Son. Judah still roamed (*rad*, "walks," "roams," "rules," or "is unruly") with God, the faithful Holy One (11:12b), but Israel was self-deceived like a person attempting to herd the wind (12:1). Hosea might have written these verses during the mid-720s B.C., when a measure of prosperity briefly returned to Israel under its last king. Self-deceived Israel dealt deceitfully with Yahweh (11:12; 12:1), cheating on His covenant, making foreign treaties with Assyria (12:1), and using deceitful scales in commerce (v. 7; cf. Prov. 11:1). Self-deception overtook the nation: they felt secure in their riches and confident that no one could accuse them of a sinful offense (Hos. 12:8; cf. Rev. 3:17).

Yahweh included Judah in His covenant lawsuit (Heb. *rib*) against "Jacob" when He announced the verdict. According to the principle of lex talionis (retributive justice), the punishment would correspond to their deceitful ways (Hos. 12:2). Hosea reinforces the theme of deceit by reminding Israel of the experience of their forefather Jacob, whose life story and very name (*ya'aqob*, "supplanter") were linked to trickery. This is the only mention of the patriarchal period in the book. Hosea focuses on Jacob's positive experience of repentance at the Jabbok River, where with anguish and tears he struggled and prevailed against the Angel (Gen. 32:24–28), and on Jacob's night vision at Bethel (Gen. 28:12–19). Some translations bring home the message to Hosea's contemporary audience (and to us) by characterizing Jacob's experience as God speaking to *us* (Hos. 12:4). Other translations, including the LXX, read "spoke to him." Although the experience happened to Jacob, later generations could relate to it as if it had actually happened to *them*. Hosea continues his aside by appealing to the faithful remnant of Israel (and to us today) to repent/return (Heb. *shub*) with God's help, to keep the basic covenant stipulations of mercy/love (*khesed*, "covenant loyalty") and justice (*mishpat*), and to wait/hope (*qawah*) continually on their God (v. 6; cf. Mic. 6:8).

12:9–14 (C). Israel Led Up from Egypt. Yahweh reminded Israel that He was the God of the Exodus. In an ironic reversal of Israel's current prosperity, Yahweh would punish their rebellion by stripping them of their opulent luxury. Instead of dwelling in tents for just a few days during the Festival of Tabernacles (Lev. 23:42–43), they would again dwell in tents permanently (Hos. 12:9–10). In Gilead (*gil'ad*, "heap of witness"), where Jacob memorialized his covenant with Laban by erecting a heap (Heb. *gal*) of stones and making sacrifices (Gen. 31:52), Israel had erected pagan altars. The destruction of these altars would turn them into heaps (Heb. *gal*) of stones (Hos. 12:11). In vv. 12–14, Hosea compares Jacob's experience tending/keeping/guarding (Heb. *shamar*) sheep in Syria (Gen. 28–29) to that of the Prophet Moses, who kept/cared for/preserved (Heb. *shamar*) Israel at the time of the Exodus. Alluding to the covenant curses predicted by Moses (Deut. 4:25–26; 32:16), Yahweh would leave Israel in their bloodguilt and repay (Heb. *shub*, lit. "return") them for their reproach/contempt of Him and His law (Hos. 12:14).

13:1–3 (D). Summary of Yahweh's Case against Israel. In three pathos-filled verses Hosea summarizes Israel's apostasy and the fundamental indictments of Yahweh's covenant lawsuit against them. Verse 1 has been understood as either saying that before committing apostasy Ephraim spoke with trembling (Heb. *retet*)—that is, humbly and with "piety" (NJPS; cf. Is. 66:2)—and was exalted in Israel, or that he spoke with such imposing authority that people trembled (*retet*)—either way a positive evaluation. But they incurred guilt in the Baal fertility cult and (spiritually) died (Hos. 13:1). Verse 2 summarizes how Israel kept sinning "more and more" by worshiping idols. Verse 3, the final verse of this section, depicts Israel's disappearance from history, utilizing four similes from the natural world—morning mist/clouds, early dew, chaff before the wind, and smoke

13:4–9 (C'). Israel Led Up from Egypt. Verse 13:4a repeats the opening verse of the matching subsection (12:9–14) almost verbatim. Focusing on Israel's Exodus, 13:4–5 provides a synopsis of the Decalogue in Exodus 20:1–3, including the covenant preamble (lit. "I am Yahweh"); a historical prologue identifying Yahweh as the Savior who freed them from Egypt and led them in the wilderness; and a restatement of the central stipulation, the first commandment against worshiping other gods. Yahweh then indicted Israel for following the path predicted by Moses (Deut. 8:11–15; 31:2). When they were filled/satisfied, they became proud and forgot Yahweh, going after other gods (Hos. 13:6). At the conclusion of this subsection, Yahweh sentenced Israel to destruction for their polytheism using the imagery of brutal and fatal wild animal attacks (vv. 7–9). The reference to Yahweh keeping watch/lurking (*'ashur*) like a leopard may be a wordplay on the homonym Assyria

(*'ashur*), implying that God would use Assyria as the agent of Israel's destruction.

13:10–16 (B'). The Foolish Son. Ephraim was not only a deceitful son (as in 11:12—12:8) but an unwise one who lacked the sense to even present himself at the opening of the womb at the time of birth (13:13). This birthing metaphor captures a time of crisis in Israel's government, probably after Shalmaneser V took King Hoshea captive along with the royal family and high-ranking government officials (722 B.C.; see vv. 9–10). A baby in a breach position in the womb also puts the life of the mother in serious doubt. The situation seems hopeless.

Amid this context of apparent hopelessness and imminent death, the Lord presents the sixth of the seven eschatological hope and salvation oracles in the book (v. 14). There will be a resurrection from the dead. God promised to ransom/deliver His people from the grave and redeem them from death. The following two sentences are either declarative statements (MT, "I will be…") or rhetorical questions (LXX, "Where are…?"; the two phrases look similar in Hebrew) announcing victory over death and the grave (cf. 1 Cor. 15:54, 55). Yahweh assures that vengeance/revenge (sometimes translated as "pity, compassion, repentance") would end (lit. "hidden from My eyes"). In the meantime, however, Israel's fruitful prosperity would pass away before the proverbial withering east wind (Hos. 13:15), as Samaria would face a three-year siege (2 Kin. 17:5). In fulfillment of the covenant curses, the cruel and violent onslaught of the Assyrian army would slit pregnant women open (Hos. 13:16; see 2 Kin. 15:16; Amos 1:13; "God's Judgment in the Prophets," p. 981).

14:1–8 (A'). Yahweh's Invitation and Promise of Restoration. Hosea 14:1–9, the final section of the book, matches 11:1–11. It addresses a people soon to be orphaned in exile. In 14:1–3, Hosea urged Israel to return to Yahweh, even suggesting what to say to Him: words of repentance, requests for forgiveness, and vows of right actions (sacrifices/fruit "of our lips") and loyalty to/trust in only Him. He encouraged them to come boldly, with the promise that in God the fatherless/orphan finds mercy/compassion (v. 3).

The last of the seven passages of eschatological hope and salvation, vv. 4–8 present the glorious promise that God would one day heal their backsliding (Heb. *meshubah*, "turning back," "apostasy," "waywardness") and "love them freely" (Heb. *nedabah*, "unconditionally"). His anger would turn away (v. 4). In vv. 5–6 Yahweh depicts Himself as dew watering Israel. As a result Israel would grow rapidly and prolifically like a lily/crocus, with roots (stability), spreading branches/shoots (splendor), a fragrance (desirability) like the mighty cedar forests of Lebanon, and beauty like the olive tree—all in fulfillment of the promised covenant blessings (Deut. 30:9–10; 33:13–16). Shifting the metaphor, Hosea 14:7 presents God Himself as the spreading tree (for the only time in Scripture) and those who would return (*from* exile and *to* Yahweh) as sitting/dwelling under His shadow (cf. Song 2:3). They would experience abundant life comparable to new grain, a luxuriant vine, and the sweet scent of wine from Lebanon (Hos. 14:7; cf. Song 4:11–15). Again, God likens Himself to an evergreen tree with edible fruit (perhaps the stone pine, *Pinus pinea*). He, not the idolatrous fertility cult, is Israel's sole source of fruitfulness (Hos. 14:8).

14:9. Wisdom Epilogue: The Ways of Yahweh Are Right! The final lesson of Hosea is a wisdom saying inviting wise readers to understand and know (Heb. *yada'*) the contents of his message; that is, to apply it to their own lives in practical ways. The invitation opens with a question: "Who is wise?" (or "Whoever is wise..."; Heb. *mi khakam*). This parallels other such wisdom invitations (see Ps. 107:43; Jer. 9:12), as does the contrast between the righteous and wicked/rebellious (Ps. 1:6; Prov. 10:24, 29–30; 11:3; 12:3, 5, 7). However, in keeping with Israel's rebellion against Yahweh detailed in his book, Hosea uses the more specific word "rebels" for the wicked. Finally, Hosea focuses on vindicating the character of Yahweh, whose ways are right (Heb. *yashar*, "upright," "straight," "just"). He leaves the reader with a choice: walk according to the upright ways of Yahweh (i.e., the covenant stipulations) and reap the glorious blessings promised for the future of Israel or rebel and stumble in iniquity (i.e., reap the covenant curses; cf. Hos. 4:5; 5:5; 14:2; Lev. 26:37) as Israel did. In other words, the reader must either embrace the hope offered by the Lord or stagger in the hopelessness that leads to destruction.

JOEL

INTRODUCTION

Title and Authorship. The book is named after its author, the Prophet Joel, whose name means "the Lord is God." Several others bear this name in the OT, so it was not uncommon. Much of Joel's life remains unknown, yet the literary quality of his poetry and his familiarity with the temple rituals suggests that he was well educated. He may have lived in Jerusalem, since most of his message refers to Jerusalem and Judah.

Date. The book of Joel provides no direct information to determine its date of composition. Based largely on internal evidence, scholars have suggested dates ranging from the early monarchy to the postexilic period. Although evidence exists for a later date, this commentary opts for an early date, around the ninth century B.C. This date appears to be more consistent with the historical context reflected in the book, although there is evidence that it could be a little later.

Backgrounds. Joel delivered his message against the backdrop of a plague of locusts that decimated the entire agricultural production of the nation. Since the book provides no information about the time when this plague occurred or about the historical circumstances of Joel's ministry, it is difficult to determine the background of the book. Some scholars have attempted to reconstruct its background based on circumstantial information within the book itself. It makes no reference to the king, prominently mentions priests and elders, portrays active temple service, discusses captive Israelites and Jewish slaves sold to the Greeks, and alludes to Egypt, Edom, Tyre, Sidon, and Philistia as enemies. Therefore, some have argued that the prophetic activity of Joel occurred during the childhood

of King Joash, when priests and elders held power over Judah (2 Kin. 11:18–21). Therefore, Joel's invective against foreign nations may allude to the invasion of Judah by a coalition of nations in the time of Jehoram (852–841 B.C.; 2 Chr. 21:16–17). These circumstantial details, however, may have more than one interpretation, and most scholars have tended to understand the same data as indicating a later time, most likely the postexilic period after the reconstruction of the temple.

Joel is a unified composition produced during a crisis caused by a locust invasion. Although the ambiguity of the data precludes absolute certainty, the lack of any reference to the Assyrians and Babylonians may indicate that Joel ministered prior to the appearance of these nations as enemies of Israel and Judah. Joel's prophetic message begins by describing a locust invasion in his own time and follows with predictions of future judgments and blessings. This appears to place Joel's prophetic activity sometime during the early monarchy.

Theology and Purpose. The book of Joel belongs to the genre of classical prophecy and contains a prophetic message framed within God's covenant with Israel that reaches universal dimensions in the context of the Day of the Lord.

1. Day of the Lord. Joel organizes his message around the concept of the Day of the Lord, when God would intervene in history to judge and/or deliver His people and punish those who oppose His kingdom (Is. 13:6–16; Amos 5:18–20; Obad. 15–16; Zeph. 1:7–18; Mal. 4:5). Joel depicts the coming of the Day of the Lord in three stages. First, an unprecedented plague of locusts fell upon the land as an immediate judgment, which called for a response of submission and repentance (Joel 1:1–20). Joel implies that the Lord brought the current crisis because the people had neglected their covenantal responsibilities. Second, a worse judgment would follow the locust plague: an enemy invasion led by the

Lord (2:1–27). Finally, the Lord would mercifully reverse the punishment and fully restore the land and the people. In connection with the eschatological Day of the Lord, God would pour out His Spirit, accompanied by signs in the heavens, and would bring His people to their land. Subsequently, the Lord would summon the nations to gather together in the Valley of Jehoshaphat to receive God's verdict, culminating in the final establishment of God's rule from Zion (2:28—3:21).

2. *God and Evil.* The book depicts a conflict between God and evil in Israel and among the nations. In keeping with His holy character, God would bring judgment on both His people and the enemy nations. Indeed, the judgment would begin with His people, indicating the responsibilities entailed in the covenant relationship. Once His people respond with repentance and humility, God would mitigate judgment with mercy. In other words, God's rightful reaction against sin and sinners always blends with mercy and forgiveness. Through the outpouring of the Spirit, God would generously bestow immeasurable blessings upon His people to transform them into instruments of the Spirit. The theme of cosmic conflict emerges in a very particular way as God unceasingly battles the evil forces embodied in the enemy nations. On the eschatological Day of the Lord, He would reverse the chaotic circumstances of a world marked by sin and rebellion. As God's chosen city, Zion (Jerusalem) would play an important role in this conflict (Zion is mentioned seven times; 2:1, 15, 23, 32; 3:16–17, 21). The mention of Zion, the seat of God's presence and universal kingship, evokes God's covenant with His people. It appears as the place of refuge and joy for the remnant. The prophet announces the final restoration of God's people and the establishment of God's kingdom. The promises of salvation would infuse hope in the hearts of the people.

COMMENTARY

1:1–20
The Immediate Day of the Lord

Joel 1:1–12 describes a locust invasion, drought, and fire that combined to devastate the nation. In the face of such unspeakable disaster, the prophet calls the leaders and the people to lament, fast, and pray as they appeal to the Lord to reverse the crisis (vv. 13–20).

1:1–12. Description of the Judgment. The prophet commences by describing an unprecedented plague of locusts that destroyed the economy. The content of the message originated with God. He revealed it to His servant, the prophet, who proclaimed the word of the Lord (v. 1).

As described here, locust probably refers to a common edible insect (Lev. 11:22). Locust plagues are always a concern throughout the Middle East. They sometimes come from the semiarid parts of eastern Africa and southwestern Asia. They form huge swarms that migrate to distant lands, where they rapidly devour large amounts of vegetation. After the devastation, the locusts either depart or stay and reproduce themselves to continue their destructive task. The prophets often declared destructive natural phenomena, such as locusts (cf. Deut. 28:38, 42) and drought (Deut. 11:17), to be manifestations of God's judgment against His people's unfaithfulness to the covenant (cf. Deut. 28:15, 38, 42; 11:17) or against the nations (cf. Ex. 10:1–20). When He punished His people, God intended to call them back to the covenant faithfulness (Deut. 30:1–3; 1 Kin. 8:35; 2 Chr. 6:26) that would enable them to find refuge in Him. In other words, these were disciplinary actions of a loving Father who controls all natural phenomena.

Although locust invasions happened occasionally, the plague mentioned by Joel caused exceptional destruction of crops, grains, and orchards. It must have caused terrible devastation, leaving in its wake starvation, poverty, and disease. The animals had no food, and the priests had no resources to perform the ritual oblations and sacrifices in the temple.

In addition to the locusts, a severe drought caused a fire and devastated the land, likely destroying whatever had escaped the voracity of the locusts (Joel 1:19). The prophet addressed different groups within the community, the elders, the inhabitants of the land, the drunkards, the priests, and the farmers, calling attention to the impact of the disaster on each one of them. The breakdown of the economic and spiritual situation had affected all segments of society and called for an urgent response. What God had done to Egypt, He was now doing to Israel (cf. Ex. 10:4, 5). The prophet lists no sins to merit so harsh a punishment, but the reference to the drunkards may indicate that the people enjoyed sinful pleasures. Other prophets explicitly condemn drunkenness (Hos. 7:5; Amos 4:1). Joel 2:27 may also indicate a problem with idolatry, a sin which would constitute a most serious violation of the covenant bond. As a result of covenant transgression, all the trees of the field dried up and the joy of all the people (lit. "sons of Adam") withered (1:12). In the Garden of Eden, God gave the first couple the fruit of all the trees of the garden for food, but now human survival was threatened because of the unfruitfulness of the trees.

1:13–20. Response to the Judgment. In view of that devastating plague, the priests should have taken the lead and convoked the elders and the people to lament, fast, and pray. Human strategies and resources could not resolve this crisis. A crisis that has spiritual causes ought to be confronted with spiritual resources. Lamentation provides sufferers with a strategy to master a crisis. Lamenters pour out their souls before the Lord and acknowledge that only He can provide relief amidst their suffering and grief. Some psalms demonstrate how the Israelites lamented. They usually contain not only expressions of grief but also statements of confidence in God and vows to praise Him (Pss. 3; 4; 13; 22; 31; 39; 57; 69; 71; 77; 139).

In modern times, fasting (abstaining from food) has become a means of protest and a way to pressure higher authorities. In biblical times, however, fasting expressed grief over sin and a recognition of our ultimate dependence on God. The law mandated fasting only on the Day of Atonement; however, in times of crisis the leaders could call for fasting as an expression of repentance and humility to seek God's mercy (1 Sam. 7:6; 2 Chr. 20:3; Neh. 9:1–3; Jon. 3:5–8).

Crying for help seems to be one of the primary functions of prayer in the Bible. Joel summoned the people to cry out to the Lord, the proper response to the ominous crisis engulfing the land. In crying to the Lord, the suffering people expressed not only pain but the recognition that only the Lord could reverse their unbearable circumstances. By urging lamenting, fasting, and praying, the prophet acknowledged the swarm of locusts and its consequences as the Lord's work. While humans engaged in rational communication with God, the cattle, flocks of sheep, and beasts of the field groaned (their way of praying?) to the Creator for the satisfaction of their hunger (Joel 1:18). Because of human sin, both human and animal life suffered, and both depended on God for restoration.

The first section of the book describes a contemporary crisis, triggered by the locust invasion, and a prescribed response to it. However, as terrifying as that disaster may have been, an even worse judgment loomed on the horizon: the impending Day of the Lord.

2:1–27
The Impending Day of the Lord

Using the imagery of a locust plague, the prophet predicted that the Lord would raise up a foreign army to punish Judah (2:1–11). In response to the impending intensified disaster, the people should repent and turn to the Lord (vv. 12–17).

2:1–11. Description of the Judgment. Guards manned the towers on the walls of ancient cities and would sound the trumpet (*shopar*) as soon as they spotted an enemy army or a suspicious movement on the horizon. Having privileged information, the prophet demanded they sound the trumpet/horn to warn of the impending disaster. The crisis would come with thick darkness, clouds, and fire (vv. 2–3). Notably, these elements also appeared on Mount Sinai when God came down to make a covenant with His people (Deut. 5:22). Now the Lord would come to enforce the covenant curses. As He brought the darkness of the ninth plague on the land of Egypt (Ex. 10:21–23), the Lord would also bring darkness on His unfaithful people. Next, the prophet describes a powerful army marching toward Zion. Some scholars have argued that this section, like chapter 1, describes a locust invasion. However, the language and imagery of the locusts appears to metaphorically announce an imminent enemy attack. By evoking the ceaseless advance of a locust horde, the prophet describes the enemy's military prowess. They would come like an avalanche that no barricade could hold.

As that powerful army marched forward, humans would panic with terror and the cosmic order would come to the brink of collapse. This poetic description stresses the severity of God's impending judgment, which would dwarf the previous crisis triggered by the locusts. After a brief description of an invading army, this section climaxes with an astonishing observation: the enemy army belongs to the Lord, who marches forward to execute judgment upon His own people (Joel 2:11). At times, the Israelites understood the Day of the Lord as a day of deliverance and blessings for Zion. They felt secure in the promises of God and firmly believed that even though other cities like Samaria might be defeated, Zion would stand forever because it belonged to the Lord in a unique way. Indeed, no enemy could overtake Zion. But the Lord Himself could. Because they neglected their covenantal responsibilities, the people had become the Lord's enemies. He would march ahead of that destructive army to inflict due punishment upon the covenant breakers.

2:12–17. Response to the Judgment. The prophet now explicitly demands a change of heart. The external signs of contrition he called for in response to the locust invasion should reflect internal thoughts and intentions. Israelites customarily tore their clothing to express grief or repentance, but Joel tells the people to rend their hearts, not their garments (2:13). Repentance ought to accompany fasting, prayer, and weeping as the proper response to the impending Day of the Lord. God invited His people to turn to Him (v. 12), a call the prophet immediately reiterated (v. 13). God intended for the people to repent (Heb. *shub*, "turn," "repent"), turn toward Him, and completely change the direction of their lives. The prophet again lists no specific sins from which they were to turn, although, as already noted, drunkenness (1:5) and idolatry (2:27) are plausible inferences. Presumably, once they humbled themselves and turned to the Lord, they would know which sins to confess in order to mend their broken relationship with God.

As the basis for repentance, the prophet alludes to the covenantal relationship between God and His people that is implicit in the expression "your God" (v. 13). Furthermore, by listing God's gracious attributes, Joel points to God's immutable character and loyalty to the covenant in order to reinforce the hope that God would reverse the judgment. After all, God is not a vengeful judge but a gracious and merciful Lord (Ex. 34:6–7; Num. 14:18; Neh. 9:17; Pss. 86:15; 103:8; 145:8; Jon. 4:2; and Nah. 1:3). Repentance, however, does not function as a magic manipulation of God; the Lord remains sovereign to either accept or reject the penitent response of His people. All they can do is repent and leave the rest with God. As the prophet clarifies, who knows if the Lord might relent? (Joel 2:14). The phrase "who knows" expresses hope amidst uncertainty, calling people to willingly submit.

Again the prophet called for the trumpet to be blown. But instead of announcing the coming of an invading army, this time the trumpet call was to convoke a sacred assembly to plead with the Lord for mercy. Joel addressed the priests using language reminiscent of the Sinai covenant. He commanded them to sanctify the congregation in order to prepare them to appear before the Lord (see Ex. 19:10). Usually, only the elders or heads of families attended such an assembly. However, the seriousness of the impending crisis required the entire nation to attend the convocation, including children and nursing babes, who apparently had no formal worship obligations (1 Sam. 1:21–24). Even those recently married, who were usually excused from such convocations (Deut. 24:5), had to interrupt their honeymoons. Such a time of crisis required them to deny themselves a most legitimate human pleasure and come to the temple to join the sacred assembly. Such an extensive demonstration of contrition recalls the response of the Ninevites to the preaching of Jonah (Jon. 3:5–9).

Joel called the priests, as representatives of the community before God, to stand in the inner court (1 Kin. 6:36), the area between the porch (i.e., the door of the temple) and the altar of burnt offerings, where priests performed some of their cultic services. The priests wept and interceded for the nation on the same spot where Solomon had prayed to the Lord during the inauguration of the temple years before (1 Kin. 8:22). Scholars have called prayers like the one Joel composed "communal laments" (see Pss. 44; 79–80; 89; Lam. 3:40–42; 5:1–22). This prayer reveals three essential aspects of biblical prayer. First, it petitioned God to spare the people and, in doing so, acknowledged the people's sinfulness and exclusive reliance on God's mercy. Second, it appealed to the covenant. God Himself had a vested interest in the restoration of Judah because they were His people and His inheritance/heritage (Joel 2:17). The exhortation for the people to honor their covenant obligations (v. 13) matches the petition for God to remember His covenant with His people. Third, the prayer focused on protecting God's reputation among the nations, not on the material prosperity of the people.

2:18–27. Reversal of the Judgment. Joel 2:18 marks a turning point in the crisis Joel had announced. Because of His inexhaustible love, God would accept the people's repentance and answer their prayer. In turning His merciful attention to His land and His people, the Lord restored the covenant bond and set out to reverse the effects of the locust plague. He reiterated the covenant promises and pledged to give grain, wine, and oil back to His people (Deut. 11:13–15). To a people suffering the ravages of famine and other hardships, such promises must have sounded like hope for the renewal of life itself. The Lord would even go beyond their material needs by removing their reproach and restoring their dignity. Moreover, He would drive away the very enemy threatening their security (lit. "the northern one"; some translations supply "army" or "horde" because of the context; Joel 2:20). Weakened by lack of food, that enemy would drown in the eastern sea (the Dead Sea) and the western sea (the Mediterranean), provoking a rising stench. The identity of "the northern one" is debated. It may refer to either a locust swarm or an invading foreign army. Although the locusts are a plausible reference, this term most likely refers to a foreign army attacking God's people. Most invasions of Israel and Judah came from the Syrians, Assyrians, and Babylonians who penetrated the land from the north (Is. 14:31; 41:25; Jer. 1:4, 13–15; 4:6; Zeph. 2:13; cf. Ezek. 38:6, 15; 39:2).

In light of such bountiful blessings, the prophet invited those who had previously groaned and lamented to celebrate the restoration. In a complete reversal of fortunes, the prophet exhorted the personified land to rejoice because of the marvelous acts of the Lord, assured the beasts of the field that the fields and trees had received new life, and finally urged the people to rejoice in the Lord because He would send rain to reverse the drought (Joel 1:7), bringing back bountiful harvests (2:21–24). The call for celebration progresses from the inanimate land to the animals and finally to God's people. This reverses the arrangement of the first chapter, which begins by summoning the people to mourn (1:2–15) and concludes with a portrayal of the miserable state of the animals and the land (1:16–20). The former/autumn rain normally began in September and October and produced the right conditions for plowing and sowing. The latter/spring rain fell in March and April, enabling the crops to ripen fully.

The Hebrew word *hammoreh*, usually translated as "the former rain" or "the autumn rain," can also mean "the teacher." Joel 2:23 would then become a promise to send "the teacher of righteousness." The context may favor the translation "the former rain" in connection with the word *litsdaqah* ("righteously," "faithfully"). Moreover, the Bible associates rain with right teaching (1 Kin. 8:35–36; Is. 30:20–23) and compares the lack of the word of God to a drought (Amos 8:11–12). On the other hand, the translation "the teacher of righteousness" could refer to the eschatological prophet announced by Moses (Deut. 18:15–18; 34:10). This messianic figure, in contrast with the previously mentioned "northerner," would expose error and teach the truth to the people.

In an absolute reversal, the Lord promised to restore the years of devastation by reaching back into the past and recovering all that the plague had destroyed. This magnificent act of redemption would culminate in a restoration and reaffirmation of four fundamental truths: God would reaffirm His presence in the midst of His people, reiterate His covenantal relationship with them, claim their exclusive loyalty, and deliver them from shame (Joel 2:27). The destructive Day of the Lord would become the redemptive Day of the Lord. The devastated land would turn into a fertile ground teeming with lush vegetation and fruitful harvests, the starving cattle would enjoy abundant pastures, and God's suffering people would delight in the blessings of the covenant.

2:28—3:21
The Eschatological Day of the Lord

The final major section of Joel takes a clear eschatological turn. Although God's covenant with Israel remains the frame of reference, the scope of the prophetic message transcends national and ethnic boundaries to depict a universal Day of the Lord, a day of blessing and salvation. In connection with that day, God would give the Spirit to all flesh (2:28–32), judge the enemies of His people (3:1–15), and eventually establish His eternal kingdom (3:16–21).

2:28–32. Description of Promises. The opening sentence of v. 28 clearly marks the beginning of a new section. This promise harks back to Moses, who wished all of God's people would become prophets (Num. 11:29). Throughout OT times, God gave the Spirit intermittently to enable select individuals (e.g., judges, prophets, and kings) to perform specific assignments. Through Joel, God promised the Spirit to all flesh, regardless of age, gender, or social boundaries. The universal outpouring of the Spirit points back to the promise of rain in Joel 2:23. As the rain would revitalize the vegetation, so the Spirit would rejuvenate the people. The outpouring of the Spirit prophesied here specifically entails the manifestation of the prophetic gift. By turning all people into prophets, the Spirit would propel a powerful proclamation of God's message.

Joel announced wonders in heaven and on earth that would come in connection with the outpouring of the Spirit and would precede the Day of the Lord. These signs would include blood, fire, pillars of smoke, and the upheaval of the sun and the moon (vv. 30–31), some of which also accompanied the events surrounding the Exodus (Ex. 7:17–25; 9:23–29; 13:21–22; 19:16–18) and other divine apparitions (Ps. 18:7–15; Hab. 3:8–16). This short section closes with the Lord's promise to deliver whoever "calls on" His name; that is, whoever worships Him and publicly proclaims His deeds (Ps. 105:1; Is. 12:4). He promised to in turn call them among the survivors/remnant who would dwell safely in the eschatological Zion (Joel 2:32; see below, "Outpouring of the Spirit").

3:1–15. Description of the Judgment. The opening of Joel 3:1–15, "in those days and at that time," conveys the eschatological tone of this section and points to events far beyond the lifetime of the prophet. In connection with the restoration of His people and the establishment of His kingdom, the Lord would inflict upon the nations the punishment they deserve for having oppressed the chosen people. Along with other crimes, they took over the land, sold the people as slaves, and pillaged God's treasures to adorn foreign temples/palaces (vv. 5–6). The Lord would repay them by inflicting on them the same evil deeds they had inflicted on His people. While Tyre, Sidon, Philistia, Edom, and Egypt are mentioned, no reference is made to Assyria or Babylonia. The prophetic message, however,

summons all the nations (v. 11), an indication that these political and ethnic entities function as a sampling of a much larger gathering of enemy nations for the eschatological judgment.

The Valley of Jehoshaphat (vv. 2, 12) is not mentioned anywhere else in the OT, and its location, if it is a literal place, is unknown. Two observations suggest that the name may be symbolic. First, the name Jehoshaphat means "the Lord judges," making it a most appropriate designation for a place of judgment. Second, the name "Valley of Jehoshaphat" calls to mind the Valley of Berakah, where God defeated a coalition of enemy nations on behalf of Jehoshaphat, the king of Judah (2 Chr. 20:26). Regardless, the appellation "Valley of Jehoshaphat" most likely points to the universal judgment of the nations, not to the place of its occurrence. Significantly, Joel also calls the same location "the valley of decision" (Joel 3:14), which points to God's decision to punish the nations for their crimes against His people. A harvest scene also portrays the same event. The command to put in/swing the sickle and come down to trample the grapes (v. 13), which was probably addressed to the angelic host (Ps. 103:20; Zech. 14:5), portrays a frightening image of punishment (Is. 63:1–6). Again the prophet associates cosmic signs with the eschatological Day of the Lord. The darkening

Outpouring of the Spirit

According to Peter, the outpouring of the Spirit on the small group of disciples during Pentecost fulfilled Joel's prophecy (Acts 2:16–21). God poured out the Spirit even on Gentiles (Acts 10:44–45). The work of the salvation of Christ and the coming of the Spirit inaugurated a new age. But Pentecost was only a partial fulfillment that signaled the ushering in of the eschatological era. Joel pointed not only to the inauguration of the age of salvation but also to its consummation on the Day of the Lord. He described cosmic signs, which Jesus associated with His Second Coming—the ultimate Day of the Lord (Matt. 24:29; cf. Rev. 6:12). According to the NT, the judgment of the nations mentioned in Joel 3:1–2 will take place at the close of the cosmic conflict (Rev. 20:7–15). The partial fulfillment during Pentecost points to the future fulfillment of all elements of the prophecy in preparation for and

in connection with the coming of the Lord. The initial outpouring of the Spirit at Pentecost will intensify in a unique way to prepare God's people (His end-time remnant) and the world for the final events leading to the glorious return of Christ (cf. Rev. 12:17; 19:10; 22:17). At that time, God's people will find refuge on Mount Zion (Rev. 14:1). The coming of the Spirit at Pentecost was like the early rain, and His intensified and glorious manifestation at the end will be like the latter rain that matures the crops for the harvest (Joel 2:23; Rev. 14:14–20; 18:1; cf. Is. 44:3). Joel compresses a large sweep of salvation history into a short description. The outpouring of the Spirit, the cosmic signs and earthly portents, the remnant on Mount Zion, and the judgment of the nations all refer to a cluster of eschatological entities and events, covering a significant span of history leading to the end.

of the sun and moon, along with the dimming of the stars, further emphasizes the seriousness of that day (Joel 3:15). If the created order quakes before such a powerful Judge (v. 16), the enemy armies stand no chance of success.

While the enemy would receive due punishment, God would reconfirm Israel as the covenant people. The Lord reassured them that He was their God, who dwells in Zion (v. 17). God encamped among His people during the Exodus and subsequently chose Zion to be His permanent dwelling among them. The promise that by no means would any alien/foreigner pass through Zion implies the exclusion of Gentiles. It means that Zion, as a holy city, would be off-limits to unclean and rebellious people. To those who call on the name of the Lord, the city would remain shelter and home (2:32; Zech. 14:17; Heb. 12:22; Rev. 21:1-3, 27).

3:18-21. Description of the Blessings. Joel ends his book by announcing a glorious future for God's people. The blessings of "that day" (3:18), the eschatological age, would reverse all the disasters lamented in the beginning of the book. The lack of wine (1:5) would give way to vineyards that would produce rivers of grape juice. The formerly starving cattle (1:18) would

have so much pasture that copious streams of milk would flow from the hills. The dry brooks (1:17-20) would overflow with abundant water. And the temple, previously deprived of joy (1:9, 13, 16), would become a source of living water (cf. Ezek. 47:1-12) irrigating the arid Valley of Shittim/acacias. (Acacias usually grow in arid and infertile soil.) This valley was likely a continuation of the Kidron Valley that runs down to the Dead Sea; however, the emphasis does not lie on its geographical location but on the paradisiacal life-giving waters that would flow from the temple in eschatological times. This image points back to the river in the Garden of Eden and forward to the river of life flowing from the throne of God in the new Jerusalem (Rev. 22:1-2).

In contrast, Egypt—in spite of the Nile River—and Edom would become desolate places because of the crimes committed against God's people (Joel 3:19). These two nations, persistent adversaries of Israel and Judah, symbolize the enemies of God and His people. In concrete language, the prophet affirms that the restoration of God's people would entail the removal of all threats to their security. So Joel closes his book with a message of hope and deliverance: Judah and Jerusalem would stand forever because the Lord dwells in Zion (vv. 20-21).

AMOS

INTRODUCTION

Title and Authorship. The opening verse attributes the book to the Prophet Amos, whose name derives from the Hebrew verb *'amas* and means "carried," "supported," "lifted," or "saved" (i.e., by the Lord; cf. Ps. 68:19; Is. 46:3). The name alludes to the message of the book: the Lord will preserve those who repent, trust in God, and love justice and mercy. Amos was from Tekoa, a fortified city south of Bethlehem (Amos 1:1; cf. 2 Chr. 11:5). He worked primarily as a *noqed* (1:1; a term that appears elsewhere in the Hebrew Bible only in 2 Kin. 3:4), a shepherd who may have been involved with breeding sheep. God chose him as a prophet for the Northern Kingdom of Israel (Amos 7:15).

Date. Amos prophesied during the reigns of Uzziah, king of Judah (792–740 B.C.), and Jeroboam II, king of Israel (793–753 B.C.; 1:1). This would place his ministry between 792 B.C. and 753 B.C.

Backgrounds. The reign of Jeroboam II was a time of territorial expansion, peace, and prosperity. He reconquered the Transjordanian region of Israel, including Damascus, Lebo Hamath, Lo Debar, Karnaim, and the Sea/Valley of Arabah. This proved a token of divine mercy, for it secured Israel's existence a little longer (6:13–14; 2 Kin. 14:23–29). Hegemony over these lands led the kingdom to the zenith of its power and affluence (see Amos 3:10–12, 15; 4:1; 5:11, 17; 6:4–6, 11). Archaeologists have found written documents from that time that record the delivery of quality wine and fine oil as (tax) payments to the capital city (cf. 2:8), shedding light on the extensive production of wine and oil in the region. Unfortunately, however, religious syncretism marred the reign of Jeroboam II, corrupting the worship of the Lord and perverting justice and mercy. Indeed, Samaria sinned through the monumental cultic centers (i.e., sanctuaries) that Jeroboam I had set up at Dan and Bethel to house the two golden calves (7:13; 8:14; 1 Kin. 12:25–33; 2 Kin. 14:24).

Theology and Purpose. God sent Amos to the Northern Kingdom with a message of final judgment, though one not totally devoid of hope. The book has three main theological themes.

1. God's Righteousness. The book of Amos contains three beautiful doxologies describing God's power and proclaiming Him as Lord over the created world (4:13; 5:8–9; 9:5–6). This monotheistic and universalistic understanding of God explains His intervention within history. For Amos, God is Lord over nature because He created it and can therefore uncreate it (4:13). The second and third doxologies communicate the same idea (5:8–9; 9:5–6). But between the act of creation and the act of judgment comes an act of revelation. The transcendental and powerful God of Creation willingly speaks to humans. He led Israel out of Egypt, protected them in the wilderness for forty years, and guided them through His prophets (2:10–11; 3:1). But He is also Lord over all nations, overseeing and guiding their movements (9:7). The One who raises up nations (6:14) and brings them down (2:9) controls the political and military achievements of these nations. As the moral Judge of both Israel and the nations, He cares about proper interpersonal relations among human beings and reacts against the oppression of the poor and the needy. He is not indifferent to social evils but requires that His people live in righteousness (5:24).

2. Social Justice. Amos speaks against social injustices, showing the importance of proper social behavior in the eyes of the Lord. Religion cannot be divorced from respect for other human beings. He decries Israel's inability to understand what was honest and right (3:10). God expected them to let justice run down like a river of water and righteousness like an ever-flowing, mighty stream (5:24), but instead they turned justice into bitterness and threw righteousness to the ground (5:7). They transgressed through court procedures, the accumulation of wealth, and worship. Amos criticizes the court procedures at the city's gate because they abused the poor and the innocent and refused to recognize their rights (2:6–8). Those in power economically abused the poor (5:11) and hated those who stood up to defend them (5:10). They accepted bribes (5:12) and turned justice into venom and righteousness into the bitterness of wormwood (6:12). Amos condemns the lifestyle of the upper classes because the poor suffered as a result of their greed (4:1).

Chapters 1–2 also address the problem of social injustice among the nations. The Lord condemned Damascus for its treatment of prisoners of war (1:3; cf. 2 Kin. 10:32–33), Gaza and Edom for selling slaves for economic gain (Amos 1:6, 9), Ammon for ripping open the pregnant women of Gilead (1:13), and Moab for showing total disrespect for human remains (2:1). God is not indifferent to such crimes against humanity.

Amos also attacks Israel's religious practices. The upper class appeared very religious, offering many sacrifices to the Lord (4:5; 5:21–23). But the Lord rejected their sacrifices not only because the people offered them in Bethel and Gilgal (4·4) but also because they did not practice social justice (5:23–24). Social injustices, a violation of the covenant, tainted their offerings and songs. Our relationship with God should transform the way we relate to our fellow human beings. If it does not, then we are not properly relating to God, even though we may follow the external forms of religion.

3. Judgment and Hope. The Lord would put an end to the social injustices practiced in Israel. The luxurious mansions of the upper classes would be destroyed (3:15), and the proud wives of the wealthy would go into captivity (4:2–3). The Lord would raise His sword against the house of Jeroboam (7:9) and destroy the altar at Bethel (3:14), resulting in weeping and mourning (5:16–17). Amos never identifies the instrument of judgment (Assyria), but he makes it clear that a military power (3:11; 5:5; 6:14) would take the people into captivity (5:7, 27; 6:7). Amos did not doubt that Israel would be led away captive (7:17). The Lord had done all He could to bring them back to repentance, but they refused to listen (4:6–11).

Amos calls that day of destruction "the day of the LORD" (5:18, 20). The popular theology in Amos's days defined the Day of the Lord as the future punishment and destruction of Israel's enemies. The people looked forward to that day as a day of liberation. But Amos redefined it as a day when the Lord would confront Israel because of their sins, a day of darkness and destruction for His people (5:18–20; 8:3). The religious festivals would end (8:10), strange natural phenomena would occur (8:9), an earthquake would destroy many, and those who survived would be killed with the sword (9:1). God would preserve only a very small remnant, first described as the survivors of the catastrophe (historical remnant) and then as those willing to seek the Lord (faithful remnant; 5:6). But because of the severe nature of Israel's sins, the remnant who survived would not necessarily suffice to perpetuate the nation (5:14). Yet, a note of hope remained: God might have mercy on the remnant of Joseph (5:15).

This opens the door to a hopeful future. The Day of the Lord would not result in the extermination of God's people. The book of Amos ends on a positive note (9:11–15). God would restore David's kingdom, the united monarchy, and bring the nations under the rule of the future David. The true eschatological remnant embraces peoples from all nations who willingly submit to the rule of the Messiah under the new Davidic covenant. The rule of the new David would bring fertility and blessings. The exiled ones would return to their own land, never again to be removed from it (9:15). Thus, the book of Amos, which proclaims judgment, ends with a proclamation of hope that looks to the future establishment of social, moral, and religious justice once and for all.

Literary Features. Amos uses characteristic oracles, sayings, and vision reports to communicate judgment against Israel and hope for the remnant. These include features such as numerical formulas (see 1:3, 6), rhetorical questions (3:3), metaphors (4:1), taunts (4:4–5), allusions (4:10–11), and laments (5:2).

COMMENTARY

1:1—2:16

SUPERSCRIPTION AND ORACLES AGAINST THE NATIONS

After the superscription (1:1-2), the first occurrence of the messenger formula (1:3) declares the divine origin of the prophecy. The Lord is speaking. He unveils the transgressions of eight nations and passes judgment against them. These transgressions include the practice of lawlessness and violence and the violation of common social laws protecting the life of the innocent and the rights of the weak (Ex. 23:7; Deut. 24:14; Prov. 14:31; 22:16). The Lord specifically charged them with genocide, corpse desecration, brutality, and a lack of compassion (Amos 1:3—2:16; Ps. 11:5). Such transgressions brought about the Flood (Gen. 6:11, 13). As in the days of Noah, God would again decimate the wicked. The oracles against the nations contain three important elements. First, the ascending numerical sequence ("three...four") lists three despicable transgressions plus a fourth climactic condition that exceeds the limit of God's forbearance. Second, this formula of irrevocability stresses that God had determined not to avert His judgment and would inevitably pour out His wrath. Third, God would use fire to target the buildings that provided the inhabitants with a sense of power and security: temples, altars, fortresses, and palaces.

1:1–2. Superscription. The opening phrase refers to the book as "the words of Amos" instead of the more common "the word of the Lord" in other prophetic books. Only Jeremiah uses the same formula (Jer. 1:1; 36:10; 51:64). However, these words of divine revelation came to him from the Lord. Amos had no prophetic pedigree, but he willingly obeyed God. Amos 1:2 introduces the theological theme of the Day of the Lord by describing God as a lion roaring from Zion. His roar causes nature to wither, even to the top of Carmel, a place famous in Israel's history for deliverance from a drought (1 Kin. 18:41–46). From the outset, the book prophesies divine judgment (see "God's Judgment in the Prophets," p. 981).

1:3–8. Damascus and Gaza. The Aramaeans fought with the Northern Kingdom over possession of Gilead, the region to the east of the Jordan River. This continued for decades until Jeroboam II put an end to the wars (1 Kin. 15:16–22; 2 Kin. 14:28; 2 Chr. 16:1–6). In Amos, Gilead refers to the land and its inhabitants, who suffered brutal attacks. Hazael and Ben-Hadad represent two dynastic titles rather than different kings (Amos 1:4). God would directly punish the leadership and the public edifices but send most of the population into exile to Kir as a historical remnant (v. 5; 9:7).

The Philistines settled in the southwestern portion of the Holy Land, where they established a confederation of five city-states, each under a lord, mostly along the coastal plain. Among these city-states, Gaza was the leading power. Beginning in the period of the Judges, this confederation constantly fought with the Israelites. Later, David, Solomon, and Uzziah all subjugated them. In the interest of economic gain, the Philistines engaged in the slave trade and human trafficking, probably perpetrated against the people of Judah (1:6; cf. 2 Chr. 28:18; Ezek. 27:13; Joel 3:6–7). They sold the slaves to the Edomites to work in their copper mines. As with the Aramaeans, the Philistines' punishment would target mainly the structures and the ruling class. The destruction of the remaining Philistines does not refer to the whole population but to the army and leaders (Amos 1:8).

1:9–12. Tyre and Edom. Tyre was the chief city of the Phoenician city-states. God accused the Phoenicians of complicity in the slave commerce (v. 9). Together with the Philistines, they plotted against the Israelites (Ps. 83:4–6), thereby violating the covenant made with David, Solomon, and, later, Ahab (2 Sam. 5:11; 1 Kin. 5:1, 7–11; 9:13–14; 2 Chr. 2:11–16). As punishment, God would send an inferno upon the city wall and fortresses (Amos 1:10).

Edom is another name for Esau (Gen. 25:30), who lived in conflict with his brother, Jacob (Gen. 27:40). The Edomites had acted unbrotherly toward the Israelites since the time of their ancestor, and this continued in the time of Amos and beyond (cf. Obad. 10–16). The Lord indicted them for cruelty and deadly persecution of Israel (Amos 1:11). As the sentence, a blaze would consume the main fortresses of the kingdom, signaling the collapse and permanent defeat of the nation (v. 12). The fire refers to a military attack.

1:13—2:3. Ammon and Moab. The people of Ammon were the descendants of Ben-Ammi, a son of Lot (Gen. 19:30–38). During the conquest of Canaan, God explicitly ordered the Israelites not to attack them (Deut. 2:19, 37). Despite this privilege, the Ammonites often showed animosity toward the Israelites and sought to take over their territory (Judg. 11; 1 Sam. 11; 2 Sam. 10:1–19; 2 Chr. 20:1–30) until Uzziah subdued them (2 Chr. 26:8; 27:5). They committed a heinous genocide against the pregnant Israelite women from Gilead (Amos 1:13). Consequently, God's inferno would consume their military defenses and political structures. The king and his officials would go into exile as a historical remnant (vv. 14–15).

Moab was the brother of Ben-Ammi and the ancestor of the Moabites (Gen. 19:30–38). Moab and Edom were relatives through Lot and Isaac. Biblical history depicts them as a pair of powers inhospitable toward Israel (Judg. 11:17–18), but they would ultimately be defeated (Ex. 15:15; Num. 24:17; 1 Chr. 18:2). On one occasion the king of Edom joined forces with King Jehoram of Israel and King Jehoshaphat of Judah against Moab. This alliance led King Mesha of Moab to sacrifice his crown prince as a burnt offering (2 Kin. 3:26–27). The burning of the bones of the king of Edom attests to great hatred (Amos 2:1). According to the expression's common usage, the destruction of Moab may designate the army, soldiers, leaders, or strongholds (v. 2; cf. Num. 22:14; Judg. 3:28–29; 2 Kin. 3:22–24). On account of their transgressions, the Lord would burn down their fortresses and annihilate their king and his officials (Amos 2:2–3).

2:4–5. Judah. Whereas the Lord charged foreign nations with very specific transgressions against humanity, He condemned Judah because they *ma'asam* ("despised," "rejected") His law (v. 4). However, the nature of the punishment placed Judah alongside the foreign nations under the same destiny. Judah disobeyed by perverting justice and mercy. To *ma'as* ("despise," "reject") the law of God generally means reversing the values of justice, goodness, and mercy rooted in God's commandments (cf. Ex. 18:16, 20; Deut. 5:1–21). In Amos it refers to such wrongs as false oaths, deception, bribery, extortion, theft, adultery, murder, and bloodshed. The lies of false prophets, priests, and officials had superseded God's laws (Amos 2:4). These lies typify a form of speech and behavior that wears the deceptive appearances of truth (cf. Hos. 4:1–2, 6). Like the other nations, Judah's sentence included the burning of its palaces.

2:6–16. Israel. The previous oracles pave the way for a thorough indictment of the Northern Kingdom of Israel. The Lord accused Israel of crimes similar in nature to those of the foreign nations, in that they exploited the weak. But even worse, the Israelites perpetrated these crimes against their own people. Since the divine law embodied justice and mercy, these crimes should be viewed against a legal background. The guilty party, always referred to in the plural, frequently represents the government, the high social classes, and the religious elite. Amos chronicles brazen crimes, often perpetrated at the gate of the city; that is, the courthouse and center of commercial and civic activity (3:10; 5:7, 10, 12, 15). As to Israel's relationship with God, Amos records how Israel forgot and forsook their Maker (cf. Hos. 2:13; 8:14), rebelled against His law and the prophetic word, and broke His covenant (Amos 2:11–12; 7:13; 2 Kin. 17:15–16; 18:12; Hos. 7:13; 8:1; cf. Num. 12:6; Deut. 18:15). Their moral violations included sexual relations with a girl by both a man and his father (Amos 2:7; Gen. 19:30–38; Lev. 18:6, 9; 20:17) and the transgression of the law of the Nazirite (Amos 2:11–12; Num. 6:3, 21).

As to the Israelites' relationship with each other, Amos chronicles how they denied the most vulnerable people justice by favoring the ruling class and by breeding corruption through bribes and dishonest scales (Amos 2:7–8; 4:1; 5:12; 8:4–5; Hos. 12:7, 8; cf. Lev. 19:15, 36). They infringed the laws that protect the defenseless (Ex. 23:7; Deut. 24:14; Prov. 14:31; 22:16). In other words, they overturned kindness and generosity (Deut. 15:7, 11; Hos. 6:4) by selling the righteous, the needy, and the poor into slavery for a pittance; imposing levies on them; charging interest on money lent to them (Amos 2:8; 5:11; cf. Ex 22:22–24; Prov. 17:26), and keeping their pledges for loans overnight (Amos 2:8; cf. Deut. 24:12–13, 17).

Power, wealth, and security caused them to forget their roots and the way the Lord had led them in their journey from Egypt to the land of Canaan. When they were oppressed and persecuted, God saved them. When they were orphans and homeless, He gave them an inheritance (Amos 2:9–10). Now that they had become the oppressors and persecutors, God, in retribution, would bring the kingdom ruin and death on the Day of the Lord. The swift, the strong, the warrior, the archer, the fleet of foot, the rider, and the stouthearted would all fall victim. But despite the severity of the devastation, a bruised remnant would remain as Israel's hope for survival.

3:1—6:14

ORACLES AGAINST ISRAEL

3:1–15
Ruin and Survival

Amos 3:1–15 articulates divine justice and mercy, retribution for iniquities, and the preservation of a remnant torn into pieces.

3:1–8. The Revelation of Judgment. In Amos 3:1–8 the Lord speaks against Israel, whom He had brought out of Egypt. The revelation of God's grace requires fidelity on the part of those who receive it (vv. 1–2). The Exodus from Egypt, His care for His people during their wilderness travels, the covenant at Sinai, and the inheritance of the land all attest to God's mercy. Israel's election did not grant the nation an unconditional covenant relationship. The covenant required them to reciprocate God's love and behavior. As their Redeemer, God was justified in disciplining His people. Amos artfully represents retributive judgment through a list of causes and effects, moving from imagery to reality. The images of the lion, the hunter, and the trumpet portray God's refusal to continue leading Israel as their Shepherd. Because they had entangled themselves in their own paths instead of seeking Him, the unexpected would happen. God would turn against them like a hungry lion and like a hunter laying a trap. Israel would become His prey (vv. 3–5). The blowing trumpet heralds God's presence as an enemy. In the past, the personal manifestation of God served to instill the people with fear so that they might not sin (Ex. 20:20). However, another theophany in the near future would effect ruin upon the nation. Previously, the people had trembled in awe; now they would tremble in terror for their lives. But God did not leave His people in darkness, unaware of His plans. Before the execution of judgment, He sent a prophet to them to warn them about the coming disaster and to urge repentance (Amos 3:7–8; 5:4–6). Despite any opposition to prophesying (2:12), God would ultimately succeed in conveying His message.

3:9–12. The Sentence and Promise of a Remnant. Before imposing a sentence, God summoned eyewitnesses in compliance with Israelite law, which required two witnesses for a conviction for a crime (v. 9; cf. Deut. 17:6; 19:15; cf. 1 Kin. 21:10). He probably summoned the Philistines and the Egyptians because of their historical status as known oppressors. They could therefore give competent testimony to support the legality of the penalty. The Lord would execute judgment on those who stored up ill-gotten plunder in their fortresses (Amos 3:10). He would send an adversary as His instrument to invade the land, take its wealth, and plunder its palaces (v. 11).

The Lord compares the coming experience of Israel to that of a shepherd facing a voracious lion (v. 12). The passage portrays the Lord as both Shepherd and Lion, both the Condemner and the Defender of His people. In His wrath, God would decimate the sinful leaders of the kingdom to the extent that the residue of human resources would not suffice for the recovery of the nation (9:8, 10). But in His grace, He would save a historical remnant, survivors of trauma and loss, as a shepherd saves a bruised and mutilated sheep (3:12). In antiquity, when a wild beast killed a domestic animal, a hired shepherd had to present evidence of the loss. The smallest rescued pieces could serve as proof that the shepherd had not stolen the animal. Likewise, the mention of the corner of a bed and the foot of a couch indicates that an insignificant amount of the wealth of Samaria would remain. Even though God would disempower Israel's leadership and deplete their material resources, a bruised and almost useless remnant would remain. Those who remained in the land would probably comprise commoners and patricians. Thus, the land was occupied by shepherds, farmers, fugitive soldiers, war survivors, professional lamenters, palace singers, and relatives of the dead officials (1:2; 2:14–16; 5:3; 5:16; 6:9–10; 8:3; 2 Chr. 30:1, 6–12; 34:6–9). Those in the diaspora would mainly include members of the religious, military, and political aristocracy as well as their families (Amos 4:1–3; 2 Kin. 17:27–28). But God intended to transform them into a faithful eschatological remnant (see Amos 5:14–15).

3:13–15. Evidence against Israel. God continues presenting the evidence against the nation and describes in more detail the punishment that would follow. He does not identify the invaders but describes their onslaught here. The conquerors would dismantle the religious and political centers of the nation and demolish the altar and its horns, destroying the Bethel sanctuary (v. 14). The invader would also destroy the splendid residences of the aristocracy, mansions and houses adorned and decorated with ivory (v. 15; 1 Kin. 22:39). Excavations at Samaria have unearthed the opulence of these precincts with their plethora of ivory inlays. The imminent devastation combined with the preservation of a remnant (Amos 3:12) expresses the two sides of God's character: justice and mercy.

4:1–13
Refusal to Repent

This prophecy justifies the irrevocable stroke of divine retribution upon Israel. Despite various divine warnings, they refused to repent of their heinous religious and moral misconduct. God rebukes the entire population and especially the authorities of Israel, who had oppressed the needy.

4:1–3. Judgment on the Social Elite. The designation "cows of Bashan" calls to mind the fertile plain in Transjordan known as Bashan, where cows grew well-fed, plump, and healthy (v. 1; cf. Deut. 32:14; Ps. 22:12; Ezek. 39:18). The "cows" are generally understood to denote the leading women of Samaria. However, they may well represent the overindulged and defiant chiefs (cf. Hos. 4:4–6, 16; 5:1; 10:11), who fattened themselves on the poor. Bashan stands for the rich kingdom. The husbands/lords with whom they wished to feast and celebrate their ill-gotten fortune were probably their peers in the regime (Amos 4:1). The title *'adon* ("master," "lord") not only denotes the servant/master relationship but also, less frequently, refers to an esteemed and respected social equal (Gen. 23:6, 11; 32:5–6, 18; 33:8). That is probably the meaning intended here. God describes the coming punishment of the wealthy oppressors using the painful image of fishhooks, representing military defeat (Amos 4:2–3).

4:4–5. False Worship. The Lord next presented the list of transgressions requiring requital. The first transgression was their religious and moral duplicity. The panacea of ritual behavior, manifested in the presentation of animal sacrifices, tithes, and thanksgiving and freewill offerings, substituted for moral behavior. They performed these ritual enactments on a daily basis and every three days at the shrines of Bethel and Gilgal, places of religious importance throughout Israel's history (Gen. 12:8; 28:10–22; 35:1–8; Josh. 4:19–20; 5:2–12; 1 Sam. 7:15–17; 11:14–15). Out of the two, Bethel was the primary national sanctuary in the Northern Kingdom at the time of Amos (Amos 7:13; cf. 1 Kin. 12:26–33). The sarcastic invitation to sin/transgress by bringing sacrifices to the cultic centers serves as a parody of justice and mercy. The leaders apparently assumed that after performing the established rites through which they obtained forgiveness, they could still go on sinning. Ironically, they enacted these rights to compensate for their injustice and exploitation of the vulnerable. Intellectual assent to faith and devotion to religious practices may help to arouse spirituality, but they alone do not avail before God. However, if coupled with repentance, trust, and a moral life

in accordance with God's will, they become a blessing. That theoretically sound religion had so little impact on their lives is a travesty. Consequently, the prophet rails heavily against the rupture of cult and moral conduct.

However, although other prophets list idolatry as one of the causes of Israel's fall (2 Kin. 17:5–23; Hos. 2:8, 15, 19; 4:17), Amos does not stress this (but see Amos 5:26). He grapples with the core of the problem: the separation of worship and divine moral standards (i.e., formalistic ritualism devoid of the true fear of the Lord) that results in idolatry and merely human standards (5:4–6, 25–26). Idolatry replaces the image of God, whereas lawlessness and violence deface that image.

4:6–11. Human Impenitence. The second transgression requiring divine requital was willful and obstinate impenitence. Before sending Amos, God had sent seven temporary calamities against the Israelites to condemn their sins, move them to repentance, and restore them. Each calamity represented a preamble of judgment which, if abided by, would have revoked the next calamity and, ultimately, the retribution. Unfortunately, every one of them proved ineffective. First, God sent a famine that covered the entire land (v. 6). Second, He sent a tragic drought (vv. 7–8; 1 Kin. 17:1, 7; 18:5–6). Because He withheld the latter rains three months prior to the harvest in May and June, the yield of crops failed. Moreover, wells and cisterns dried up, causing some people to search for water in other places. But they could not quench their thirst. Despite the havoc, evidence exists that God cared for and protected righteous individuals, such as Elijah, the seven thousand, the widow of Zarephath, and Obadiah (1 Kin. 17:1–24; 18:3–4, 7–8, 12, 16; 19:18). The third and fourth plagues struck the cereal crops (Amos 4:9). Damaging winds of blight (scorching desert winds from the east) and mildew (humid winds from the west) caused the desiccation and withering of the crops (cf. Gen. 41:6; Hag. 2:17). Locusts devoured the most important agricultural products of the land: gardens, vineyards, and fig and olive trees. The fifth scourge, pestilence, alludes to a similar disaster that struck the livestock and the population of Egypt (Amos 4:10; Ex. 9:3–7, 15). Sixth, the Lord slew the young soldiers, together with their captive horses, in the course of battle. The direst of all the calamities occurred last (Amos 4:11). The Lord compares the devastation to that which befell Sodom and Gomorrah (Gen. 19:25, 29), emphasizing the state of ruin of some of

Israel's lands, probably resulting from war. But most of the people remained alive. Apparently, some lands and properties were destroyed, but God, as a token of divine grace, saved the leaders and the population from death's door, like a firebrand plucked from the fire (Amos 4:11). The divine characteristics of justice and mercy always give hope to God's people.

4:12-13. Meeting the Lord. Having presented the evidence for all to see, the Lord found the Israelites guilty of committing willful, brazen transgressions and of resisting His calls to return. After ignoring numerous admonitions, they had missed the opportunity to return to God. Consequently, God signed the sentence. He would not send another announcement of judgment because the final hour was at hand. This dramatic situation mirrors the plagues executed against Egypt. Pharaoh did not heed the warnings of the calamities, hardening his heart instead of relenting. Therefore, the hour came when the Lord brought the worst of the plagues, the death of the firstborn. Paradoxically, those who had once endured Egypt's oppression had now become the oppressors, the embodiment of Pharaoh. Instead of calling for repentance again, the Lord summoned them to the theophany of the "Day of the LORD," a day of divine retribution (4:12). As Creator and Warrior (v. 13), He would mobilize an enemy nation against Israel to forcibly deport the (surviving) members of the aristocracy, the historical remnant, into exile (3:11; 4:2-3). The oath formula stresses the irreversibility and finality of the Day of the Lord: God has sworn by His holiness (4:2).

5:1-27
Justice and Mercy

Amos 5:1-27 portrays God's justice and mercy through the manifestation of the "Day of the Lord" and the establishment of a righteous remnant at the end. Ancient Israel understood justice and mercy to be character traits of God (Job 37:23; Pss. 33:5; 89:14; 103:6; Is. 5:16; Jer. 9:24) that He also required of His people (Pss. 72:1; 106:3; Ezek. 18:5; Mic. 6:8; Zech. 7:9), especially a leader (king, ruler, judge, etc.). These traits served to harmoniously preserve order in society. Justice and mercy refer first and foremost to the establishment of justice, the restoration of morality, and the protection and deliverance of the weak. As Judge and Lawgiver, God used Moses and Aaron to give

His people laws that embody justice and mercy (Ps. 99:6-7; Is. 33:22). He commanded any future king to fear Him and obey His commandments, learning them by heart and reading them all the days of his life (Deut. 17:14-20). In Amos, the opposite of justice and mercy is lawlessness (*khamas*) and violence (*shod*; Amos 3:10; 6:3). The transgression of these pillars of society sets in motion God's justice and mercy in a context of judgment, condemnation, and salvation.

5:1-9. Lament and Call. In a short lament, the prophet announces that the Northern Kingdom would never rise again. Only ten percent of the population would survive the decimation of the cities and towns (vv. 2-3). Based on the lament, the Lord called the people to seek Him and not go to Bethel and Gilgal, their centers of false worship. Gilgal would go into exile and Bethel would be totally desolated (vv. 4-5). If the people wanted to live, they had to obey the Lord's urgent call. Otherwise, He would break out like fire to devour the house of Joseph (v. 6). The fire would be unquenchable on account of the people's perversion of justice and righteousness on the earth.

Seeking the Lord implies repenting, returning to God, and trusting in His salvation and providence instead of in self-sufficiency, human power, or a religious system (4:6, 8-11; 5:4-6, 22-23; 6:1, 13). It also connotes a total dedication to a moral life; that is, seeking and loving justice and mercy (5:7, 24; 6:12). Although the sinful kingdom of Israel would inevitably meet its end, God offered life to all on an individual basis. As the Creator and Sustainer of the earth, the Lord has the power to destroy the strong and accomplish His design (5:9).

5:10-15. Sin, the Lord, and the Remnant. Amos provides more specific reasons to seek the Lord—all of them based on the sins of the powerful. The gates served as places where the poor and needy could seek justice, but those in power were not interested in justice. They hated those who spoke the truth (v. 10). The powerful exploited the poor. They selfishly acquired wealth to build beautiful houses and plant wonderful vineyards. But because of the impending catastrophe, they would not live in those houses or drink wine from those vineyards. The Lord knew very well that they lacked integrity and abused the poor. Many quietly suffered under such evil circumstances (v. 13). The only way out was for the people to stop and seek good instead of evil so that they might live (v. 14).

The call to seek the Lord transitions the topic back to the remnant. The historical remnant, introduced in vv. 1-3, could become a righteous (eschatological) remnant, crediting their existence to God's grace (vv. 14-15). In this case the Hebrew term *'ulai* ("perhaps," "it may be") could mean "hopefully," denoting a hope rooted in God's generosity/mercy and, therefore, likely to happen (Gen. 16:2; 32:21; 1 Sam. 9:7; 14:6, 12-14; Zeph. 2:3). The hope of justice being restored at the gate resided with them.

5:16-27. The Day of the Lord. The Lord announces the Day of the Lord by describing the wailing that would occur throughout the land (v. 16). Those who expected its coming hoped for the light of a new day, but they would be surprised to receive absolute darkness (v. 18). God compared the terrors of that day to running from a lion only to find a bear ahead or finding safety at home only to be bitten by a snake while leaning on the wall (v. 19). He would bring military defeat (vv. 2-3, 9) and exile beyond the territory of Aram (v. 27) to destroy the oppressors in Israel, as well as their sources of power and wealth (v. 17).

The last part of Amos 5 returns to the topic of worship in the context of the Day of the Lord, as if to provide another reason for that event. Since His people had separated ritual performance from justice, the Lord rejected their celebrations of the annual festivals, their sacrifices, and their songs of praise (vv. 21-24). He posed a rhetorical question to underline the limited value of sacrifices (v. 25). During the wilderness period, the people and God enjoyed a strong relationship without an emphasis on sacrifices. Thus, a righteous life took priority over nominal, ritual practices. Verse 26 is difficult to interpret. It could refer to a "shrine," a "tabernacle," or "the pedestal for an idol," but it more likely refers to the specific names of two astral deities. On the Day of the Lord, the people and their gods would go into exile together.

6:1-14
Inwardly-Directed Attitudes

This oracle addressed the distinguished elite of Zion (cf. 2:4-5) and Samaria (cf. 3:12, 15; 4:1), who lived a carefree and secure lifestyle. Overall, Amos condemns core sentiments because they thwarted any recognition of personal sin and shut off the voice of God.

6:1-8. People at Ease. The Israelites experienced all the ease, comfort, and security that material prosperity, military strength, and systematic religion could provide. But Amos called them to reflect on what was happening around them—to go and observe Calneh (also Kalneh), Hamath, and Gath (v. 2). The Assyrians destroyed Calneh and Hamath, while Gath fell to King Uzziah of Judah (2 Chr. 26:6). The Israelites were not superior to or better off than these defeated kingdoms. They, too, would soon receive the onslaught of the Assyrian blow.

Pleasure and excess were the hallmarks of Israelite society. The selfish pursuit of luxury, idleness, gluttony, and extravagance in drinking and music hindered fellowship with God. The rich lounged on couches decorated with precious ivory, ate the best meat, and lavishly imbibed wine, all while listening to soothing music played on harps. They anointed themselves with the finest oils and used cosmetics as a sign of self-sufficiency and wealth (Amos 6:4-6). In v. 3, Amos uses the phrase *yom ra'* as another name for the Day of the Lord. The term *ra'* often means "evil," but it can also connote the idea of "calamity," "doom," or "disaster." In addition to the lack of justice and mercy (vv. 3, 12), their privileged attitudes and sheer lack of concern over the imminent calamity (v. 6) provoked the divine visitation.

Self-confidence and self-indulgence left little room for God (v. 8). The army of Samaria was alienated from God, following its own military interest. They viewed their conquest of Lo Debar and Karnaim as a testament to their military strength (v. 13). The Lord abhorred their pride (a form of idolatry; v. 8; cf. Prov. 8:13) and was ready to destroy the palace and the city (Amos 5:21-23; 6:8).

6:8-14. Demolition of Houses. Through the agency of another nation, God would bring Israel to its knees. The enemy would demolish their houses; annihilate the wicked chiefs, their wives, and their children; and deport the people into captivity (6:7-9, 11; 7:17). The oppression would reach all the way to the northern and southern boundaries of the Northern Kingdom, the entrance of Hamath/Lebo Hamath, and the Valley of the Arabah (6:14; 2 Kin. 14:25). They would lose all the land they had previously reconquered. However, as a token of divine mercy, a remnant would survive. The remnant would include relatives who would perform the burial ceremonies for the dead chiefs (cf. 1 Sam. 31:12-13; 2

Chr. 16:14; 21:19). Because of death's pollution, they would not invoke the name of the Lord in the houses of the deceased (Amos 6:9–10).

7:1—8:15
VISIONS OF DIVINE RETRIBUTION

7:1–17
Mercy for Israel and Justice for Evildoers

The visions in Amos 7:1–17 focus on God's use of the natural world and human affairs as agents to judge His people. The Lord did not expunge Israel's guilt, but He alleviated the punishment. He expressed both justice and kindness in determining to destroy property and the evildoers and to exile others. Amos trusted in the righteousness of God's judgment.

7:1–6. Locusts and Fire. The plague of locusts Amos saw would threaten the agricultural land. The late crop was the harvest after the late spring rains (v. 1; Ex. 10:15). It consisted of vegetables and other non-grain produce. A locust attack on the crop would create an agricultural disaster, potentially resulting in a famine so devastating that the entire population would die, leaving no surviving remnant. Therefore, Amos interceded for the people, and God listened to him.

Blazing fire and heat would cause the desiccation of the soil, resulting in a drought. These conditions would also lead to hunger and the extermination of the people. Consequently, Amos again interceded on behalf of the remnant, and God, in His mercy, listened to him. These visions reveal God's divine disposition to show mercy to His people.

7:7–9. The Plumb Line. Amos's third vision is difficult to interpret because the meaning of the Hebrew term *'anak*, traditionally rendered "plumb line," is uncertain. It appears only in this passage. Scholars have found a similar Akkadian term (*annaku*) that means "tin," but they debate how this meaning would fit into the context of Amos. The translation "plumb line," an item used to construct a vertically straight wall, better fits the context. A plumb line has a weight that could have been made of tin. This could make "the tin" an idiom referring to a plumb line. In the vision, it represents God examining His people to establish whether they were morally and spiritually upright. He would no longer ignore or even forgive their

sins (v. 8). The Lord would come as a Warrior with His sword against the dynasty of Jeroboam and would destroy their multiple places of worship (v. 9).

7:10–17. The Penalty. King Jeroboam and Amaziah the priest responded by opposing Amos's message. As a result, they and their offspring would receive the death penalty. Assyria would conquer the nation and exile some of the population (7:11, 17; 2 Kin. 15:29; 18:9–12).

8:1–14
Vision of the Summer Fruit

Amos's fourth vision proclaimed the end of Israel. The content of the vision itself precedes three oracles explaining its significance, each one introduced by "in that day" or a similar phrase (vv. 9, 11, 13).

8:1–8. Doomsday. The message of the vision revolves around a play on words. The Hebrew *qayits* ("summer fruit") and *qets* ("end") resemble each other in orthography and in pronunciation. Israel was like a summer fruit ready for the harvest, but that harvest symbolized its end, the collapse of the kingdom (vv. 1–3). This time Amos describes the judgment as carnage accompanied by natural phenomena and lamentation. Despite heaps of corpses strewn everywhere, the Lord would demand silence from all in recognition of their guilt and rebellion. No one would invoke the name of God, because He had brought about everything they experienced as punishment for their religious and moral duplicity (v. 3; cf. 5:13; 6:10; see commentary on 4:1–13; 5:1–9, 10–15, 16–27).

A focus on religious doctrine and ritual at the expense of God's moral demands resulted in lawlessness and violence. On the new moon (Num. 29:7; 2 Kin. 4:23; Is. 66:23; Hos. 2:11) the Israelites discontinued work and trade (Amos 8:5) as they did on the weekly Sabbath (Ex. 20:8-11; 23:12; 31:15; Lev. 23:3), but they violated the commandments requiring justice, mercy, and the use of honest scales, weights, and measures (Amos 8:5; cf. Lev. 19:35–36; Prov. 11:1; Ezek. 45:10–11). Merchants measured grain using an ephah smaller than the normal thirty-nine liters (10.3 gallons) but measured their payment using a shekel heavier than the normal eleven grams (.02 pounds or .39 ounces). Because of this fraud, the buyer received too little and paid too much. The merchants also sold the gleanings, the fallen grapes designated as food for the poor (Amos 8:6; Ex. 23:11; Lev. 19:10; 23:2; Deut. 15:9). The Lord would not forget or ignore the sins of the people and would act accordingly. The prophet's proclamation should have instilled fear in their hearts, but they apparently remained unimpressed (Amos 8:7–8).

8:9–10. Nature and Mourning. Divine retribution would take the form of an earthquake and a solar eclipse (8:9). The imagery of waters in upheaval (surging, swirling, and sinking) depicts the rise and fall of the earth's surface during an earthquake (9:5). The ancient world considered eclipses as representing the anger of the gods. These disasters would bring about a complete reversal of normal conditions. The people, possibly the professional "wailing women," would chant dirges, and survivors would perform mourning rites as an expression of sorrow, national disaster, and loss of divine protection (8:10; cf. Jer. 9:17).

8:11–15. Expectation. Beginning with the phrase "the days are coming," the oracle in Amos 8:11–15 suggests an intermediate phase of the Day of the Lord (see 5:1–3, 14–15), a time of spiritual awakening and crucial choices due to the unavailability of prophecy and shrines (8:11; cf. 1 Kin. 8:46–53). As an act of grace, the survivors would have another chance. The downfall of the political, economic, and religious powers would enable them to undergo a process of testing, shaking, and sifting (Amos 9:9), whether in the native land or in exile. Without sanctuary, ephod, teraphim, or oracle, God would be inaccessible (Hos. 3:4; 5:6), and the people would experience divine abandonment. While waiting for restoration, some would lose their hope in God, but others would repent, confess their sins, and look forward to their deliverance and the establishment of God's kingdom (cf. Dan. 9:3–19). Throughout this period, God would remain sovereign over the times and seasons, awaiting the due time to inaugurate a new action in history, reunite His people, and restore all things anew (see Amos 9:11–15).

During this time, those who engaged in the syncretistic cult at Dan and Bethel and who made pilgrimages to Beersheba would fall among the condemned (8:13–14; cf. 2:11; 4:10; 5:2; 1 Kin. 12:28–30; Hos. 8:6). Hosea compares the devastation of abandoned Israel to a parched land whose inhabitants die of thirst (Hos. 2:3; cf. Ezek.

19:12–13). Accordingly, the imagery of death by thirst in Amos 8:13 may serve as a metaphor to depict the tragic death of impenitent sinners.

9:1–15
ORACLES ON SURVIVAL AND RENEWAL

The book closes with a vivid description of judgment against the Northern Kingdom (9:1–6), followed by promises of renewal and hope (vv. 7–15). God never runs out of mercy and grace if only humans would listen to Him.

9:1–6. God's Word of Judgment. The last chapter of Amos begins by stressing the finality of God's judgment against Israel, a divine blow that He would personally inflict as Creator and Sovereign Lord over the cosmos. Amos depicts God as standing by the altar of the northern temple—not as a mediator to make atonement but as an enemy ready to annihilate the sanctuary and the religious/political culprits (v. 1; see also 7:7; Ex. 17:9). The Lord would end all contact with His people. From Sheol ("the tomb," "the depths," "hell") to the heavens and from the top of Carmel to the bottom of the sea, there is nowhere to flee to escape from His judgment (Amos 9:2–3). Divine agency is thus linked to the idea of God's cosmic presence.

9:7–10. Judgment and Survival. God's impartiality is universal. Just as God had saved Israel and the nations (the Ethiopians, Philistines, and Aramaeans) each through its own exodus, so, too, would He hold each accountable for its crimes on the "Day of the Lord." The Northern Kingdom would come to an end. In Amos, the term "Israel," also called "Jacob" (3:13; 6:8; 7:2, 5; 8:7; 9:8), "Isaac" (7:9, 16), and "My people Israel," denotes strictly the Northern Kingdom (cf. Hos. 11:12). Although Israel would suffer material and human loss and oppression, a historical remnant would survive both in exile and in the land and would undergo a sifting process of evaluation and selection (Amos 5:3; 9:8–9; cf. 8:11–12). God compared this process to a sieve that retains grain. Throughout the time of expectation for the eschatological restoration, He would remove the rubbish (i.e., the sinners) to perish but preserve the fine grain (i.e., the righteous who had recommitted to the Lord) to join the ranks of the end-time kingdom.

9:11–15. Restoration. God's final message to His people communicates a promise to save the people and give them righteous leaders (cf. Prov. 2:21–22). He would restore the palace, their property, their joy, and the abundant fertility of the land (cf. Lev. 26:5). The phrases "that day" and "the days are coming" represent not only a time of retribution but also an eschatological time of restoration. This is the only place in the OT that the tabernacle/shelter/booth of David occurs. It is unlikely that it designates a royal residence. It could mean the same as the "house of David" (that is, the Davidic dynasty; 2 Sam. 3:1, 8, 10; 1 Kin. 12:19–20; 2 Chr. 10:19), or it could refer to the kingdom, united under David but now fallen, that the Lord would restore under a messianic David. After the establishment of the kingdom, his heirs would gain authority over the righteous remnant of Edom and all the other nations. The nations that have God's name would not only belong to Him but would also embrace the religious and ethical values necessary for a covenantal relationship with Him, including care, compassion, and justice (Amos 9:12; cf. Deut. 28:8–10; Prov. 21:3; Is. 63:19; Hos. 2:19; 12:7; Joel 2:32; Zech. 7:9).

Amos specifically includes Edom in this group of *goyim* ("nations," "Gentiles"; cf. 1 Kin. 8:43). James and the early church understood this passage as evidence that Gentiles could receive full membership among God's people without first having to become Jews (Acts 15:13–21). This remnant would constitute the remnant of Joseph, that is, the eschatological people of God.

The motif of the remnant is present in every chapter of the book (Amos 1:5, 15; 2:16; 3:12; 4:2–3, 6–11; 5:3, 13–17, 27; 6:7, 9–10; 7:8–9, 11, 17; 8:3, 8, 10–12; 9:8–15). The eschatological remnant would be both exclusive, because its members would be righteous, and inclusive, because its members would comprise all ethnicities. The righteous of Israel, Judah, Edom, and all the nations would inherit God's end-time kingdom. The book of Amos, filled with prophesies of doom announcing the collapse of the Northern Kingdom, closes with a message of hope proclaiming the final victory of God's mercy in a world of social injustice, moral corruption, and rebellious sin.

OBADIAH

INTRODUCTION

Title and Authorship. Obadiah contains only twenty-one verses, making it the shortest book in the OT. The title of the book comes from the first line, *khazon 'obadjah* ("the vision of Obadiah"). The name Obadiah means "servant of the Lord," and some have suggested that it may be a generic way of referring to a prophet rather than the specific name of the author. However, Obadiah is a common name in the OT, referring to more than ten different individuals. Therefore it is most likely the actual name of the prophet, whose very name would constantly remind his listeners of the divine source of his message.

Date. Based on the content of the book and its near-parallel passage in Jeremiah 49:7–22, most interpreters place Obadiah in the first half of the sixth century, after the Babylonian army destroyed Jerusalem in 586 B.C. and before Babylon's war against Edom in 553 B.C. The vivid description of the fall of Jerusalem and the plight of its people at the hand of Edom may suggest a date shortly after the city's destruction, perhaps around 585–580 B.C. However, the ancient conflict between Israel and Edom allows for an earlier date (cf. Amos 1:11–12).

Backgrounds. Obadiah lived during one of the most traumatic periods in Israel's history, shortly after the fall of the Southern Kingdom of Judah. Centuries before, the nation had divided into two separate kingdoms, Israel in the north and Judah in the south. In 722 B.C. Assyria conquered the Northern Kingdom and exiled many of its citizens. Less than 150 years later, in 586 B.C., the Southern Kingdom of Judah met a similar fate. Babylon defeated Judah and burned Jerusalem, the capital city, and its magnificent temple to the ground (2 Kin. 25:9). The small neighboring nation of Edom, Judah's brother and longtime rival, helped sack Jerusalem and gloated over Judah's defeat. Obadiah wrote his book to bring renewed hope when all hope seemed lost.

Theology and Purpose. The theology of this short book emerges from its two central themes: the divine judgment of wicked nations and the establishment of God's kingdom.

1. Edom and the Nations. Obadiah focuses his message on Edom, a relatively unimportant nation on the world stage. Edom sided with Babylon in the war against Judah, identifying itself with those who destroy God's people (cf. Ps. 137:7–8). Obadiah decries conflict that respects no boundaries, demolishes family ties, and makes humans cruel and inhumane. This ungodly treatment of others occurs not only at a national level but also at a personal level. When humans inflict pain on others or refuse to help them, they violate a basic principle of Christianity (cf. Matt. 7:12). The phenomenon is universal, and Edom/Esau merely serves as a symbol of all who fight against the Lord and His people. They rejoice prematurely in their partial and temporary victory, unaware of the coming of a more powerful kingdom.

2. Edom's Punishment. As God works out His plan in the cosmic controversy, He humbles the proud and lifts up the humble. Pride is the root of all sin, the very essence of transgression (cf. Is. 14:12–20; Ezek. 28:11–19). It eliminates any sense of need that humans have and produces feelings of superiority, ruining their life-giving relationship with their Creator and ultimately making them insensitive and cruel toward others. Humility, on the other hand, recognizes the need for a life-giving relationship with God and results in care and concern for others. God condemned Edom's pride and how they rejoiced over the captivity of God's people (Obad. 11–12). It would lead to the undoing of the whole nation. The Day of the Lord against the nations was yet to come (v. 15).

3. Jerusalem and Judah's Restoration. God promised restoration not merely to replace one earthly nation with another but to restore the kingdom of God in the world. In a preliminary restoration, God would return His people to their home as He promised their forefathers. At that time the land would become safe, it would support life, and peace would ensue. The Savior, representing the presence of God Himself among His people, would accomplish this (v. 21). Thus, Obadiah's prophecy anticipates and symbolizes the final restoration of the earth itself, when God would establish His kingdom in the world (cf. Rev. 21). It moves from the regional (Edom) to the universal, culminating in the return of God's people, the rule of the saviors/deliverers (Heb. *moshi'im* from *moshia'*) from Mount Zion, and the restoration of the Lord's kingdom (Obad. 19–21).

Literary Features. Obadiah wrote his prophecy in poetic form. It displays a certain rhythm and cadence when read in its original language. Hebrew poetry frequently repeats thoughts for heightened effect, a feature known as parallelism. For example, in v. 8 Edom and "the mountains of Esau" (lit. "Mount Esau") refer to the same place. Hebrew also uses repetition for emphasis or dramatic effect. For example, vv. 12–14 contain the word *'al* ("not") eight times for emphasis. This builds up in a crescendo of persuasion (a similar technique is used in Prov. 30:18–31; Amos 1–2).

Additionally, familiar expressions serve as formulas to help explain what follows. For example, in the ancient world servants proclaiming an edict or proclamation of the reigning king would use a messenger formula similar to Obadiah 1. Obadiah and other prophets used this formula to indicate that their message came from the one true King, the Sovereign Lord. Moreover, they used standard expressions to indicate an important subject. For example, "the day of the Lord" (v. 15) generally introduces prophetic announcements regarding final events. Such literary devices are telltale clues to what follows.

COMMENTARY

1–4
Introduction and Message of Doom

The book of Obadiah recounts a vision (*khazon*). Of the two terms used to describe a prophetic vision, *ro'eh* and *khozeh*, the former generally refers to the visionary experience of the prophet, while the latter typically focuses on the content of a special revelation given to the prophet in vision. Obadiah, the messenger, attributes his message to God. He is not venting personal hostility toward Edom but announcing what divine revelation showed him.

The originator of the message, the Lord God, is identified by His personal name, *yahweh* (translated as "Lord"), as well as the title *'adonai* ("Lord"), indicating that God is Lord of the whole world. Some understand the recipient of the message to be Edom, but in this case *le-edom* (lit. "to Edom") probably means "concerning Edom" or "about Edom." The plural "we have heard" confirms that the recipients were the surrounding nations, including the people of Judah, called to listen to God's message. The report/message concerned all the nations in the region and the role Edom played among them. They would humiliate Edom, thereby ending its arrogance and pride. The Hebrew verb *qum* ("rise"), repeated for emphasis, expresses God's command to the nations to mobilize for a battle against Edom.

The reversal of fortunes from arrogance to humility is a familiar theme in the prophetic books (cf. Is. 14:12–23; Ezek. 28:1–19). God brings the proud low, regardless of the heights to which they have ascended (Obad. 2–3). Those who lived in the rock clefts were Edomites who inhabited the caves and crags of the massive mountains found in Edom (v. 3). The word *sela* ("rock") may specifically refer to the Edomite site by the same name, which Judah had captured much earlier (2 Kin. 14:7), or it could represent the entire territory of Edom.

The first part of Obadiah's vision concludes by comparing Edom to a soaring eagle (Obad. 4). Here the eagle represents national strength (cf. Ezek. 17:1–21) not only because of its plumage and the power of its talons but also because it builds its nest on the highest pinnacles. However, the Lord declares His intention to bring the eagle down from its lofty position. This illustrates one of the central, universal messages of the book: God will humble the proud.

5–7
Complete Destruction

Given Edom's pride and sense of security, their fall would seem stunning and almost inexplicable. But the higher the eagle soars, the further it will fall (v. 4). Obadiah prophesies Edom's total destruction using two familiar images: thieves coming to steal in the night and grape gatherers working during the day (v. 5). Edom would not be safe during either the night or the day.

God had instructed harvesters to leave some of the crop for the poor to glean (v. 5; cf. Lev. 19:9–10; Ruth 2:2–3, 7). But the destruction of Edom would leave nothing in the houses or the fields.

In commenting upon this remarkable punishment, Obadiah refers to the story of Edom's ancestor, Esau, Jacob's brother (Obad. 7; Gen. 27). Deception followed deception in the life of Jacob and his family. In the end he felt obliged to return large gifts from his flocks to appease his angry brother (Gen. 32:1–21). Obadiah hints at these stories in his prediction that Esau/Edom's former confederates (lit. "all the men of your covenant") would remove all their possessions and drive the people of Edom to its national borders (Obad. 7). The friends in whom Edom once trusted would now become enemies. Pride breeds deception, and deception leads to destruction. Eventually that fate overtakes the proud everywhere.

8–14
Edom's Offense: The Heart of the Matter

The expression *ne'um yahweh* (lit. "the declaration of the Lord"), frequently used throughout the prophets, introduces the third part of Obadiah's message, underscoring the divine authority behind the message. The passage describes the impending punishment (vv. 8, 9), the charge against Edom (vv. 10, 11), and the violations against Jacob, Edom's brother (vv. 12–14).

8–9. The Punishment. "That day" in v. 8 might refer to the "day of the Lord," when the Lord would restore Zion to its former glory (v. 15). However, here it more likely refers to the immediately preceding description of the punishment of Edom, a catastrophe caused by the absence of understanding in a land traditionally known for its wisdom (v. 8; Job 4:1; Jer. 49:7). God would destroy the wise in Edom and understanding on Mount Esau (Obad. 8; cf. 1 Cor. 1:18–30). The latter is not otherwise identified and could refer to Mount Seir or Mount Teman. However, the parallel construction shows that it refers to the entire country. The lack of Esau's understanding alludes to his foolish decision to sell his birthright for food (Gen. 25:29–34). Without understanding, they would lose the battle. First the warriors and then everyone in the city (Teman) and throughout the country would be cut down. In the OT, a lack of understanding, rather than a lack of power, frequently leads to personal or national defeat (cf. 2 Sam. 16:23; 17:14).

10–11. The Charge Against Edom. God clearly spells out the reason for punishing Edom: they had committed violence against a brother (Jacob) that reached unimaginable proportions (vv. 10–11). That is not how brothers should relate to each other. Specifically, Edom stood by or even assisted the Babylonians when they attacked Jerusalem. By taking the side of the enemy, Edom became like one of the Babylonians, a foreigner who acceded to Judah and Jerusalem's defeat. Edom helped decide Jerusalem's fate, treating it like an object to "cast lots" (i.e., gamble) over (v. 11). They had broken the bond of brotherhood.

Therefore, what Edom did to Judah would now happen to them. They would be covered with shame (v. 10). Those without clothing normally suffered shame (Gen. 3:7, 10, 21), so conquerors customarily stripped their defeated enemies naked for all to gloat over (Obad. 12). As punishment for crimes against a brother, Edom would be stripped bare.

12–14. Principles Violated. As though sensing questions about the severity of this punishment, God lays out eight prohibitions that Edom violated. The Hebrew negative *'al* ("not") indicates a strong, categorical prohibition. Here God directs these prohibitions specifically at Edom's offences at the time of the destruction of Jerusalem. The total number of eight highlights the seriousness of Edom's unbrotherly conduct: (1) They gazed on/gloated over their brother's captivity. (2) They rejoiced over the destruction of Judah. (3) They spoke proudly at the time of Judah's distress. (Boasting, always wrong, is particularly hateful when it occurs at a family member's expense.) (4) They entered Jerusalem's gates on the day of disaster. (By doing so, Edom joined the Babylonians.) (5) They gazed on/gloated over Judah's suffering, finding pleasure in harm done to others. (6) They laid hands on Judah's possessions, stealing from the defenseless on the day of their greatest need. (7) They cut off/destroyed those who escaped. (8) They delivered up/handed over the remnant of survivors, taking the escaping fugitives captive or, worse yet, selling them into slavery.

In his vision, Obadiah experienced the disastrous event of Jerusalem's destruction as though it were current, reliving its pain, and so described the prohibitions as they would have applied at the time of the offense. The family is a sacred unit, making hatred toward brothers or sisters particularly offensive. When love turns to hate, it respects no bounds.

15–18
Reversal of Fortunes

This section begins with the prophet announcing the approaching Day of the Lord for all nations (v. 15). He transitions from the previous judgment gradually, as though unable to leave behind the horrors of the eight prohibitions without a backward glance. The prophet announces judgment on the nations (vv. 15–16) and the deliverance of Zion (vv. 17–18).

15–16. Judgment on the Nations: The Day of the Lord. The Prophet Amos had first prophesied about the Day of the Lord nearly two hundred years before Obadiah (Amos 5:18–20; cf. Is. 13:6–13), so the expression was familiar to at least some of the covenant people. It refers to the day (time) of the end, when God will enter history to determine its outcome, saving His people and punishing the enemy. Unlike "that day" for Edom (Obad. 8), the Day of the Lord would be universal—the day when the Lord Himself would judge all nations and restore the whole world. This phrase connects the local conflict between Judah and Edom with the worldwide conflict between good and evil and with God's judgment upon all nations (v. 16). Obadiah compares this judgment to drinking God's cup of wrath. As Edom had drunk to celebrate victory on God's holy mountain (Zion; v. 16), so all the nations, including Edom, would continually drink the cup of defeat/wrath. For those opposed to the Lord, this cup would contain a curse (cf. Rev. 14:10) leading to drunkenness and judgment that would render them as though they had never existed (Obad. 16). However, for followers of God, drinking from the cup He provides results in blessing (cf. Ps. 23:5). The consequence of drinking from God's cup depends on whether one drinks with a heart of confession and commitment or a heart of unbelief and denial (cf. 1 Cor. 11:27–29).

17–18. Deliverance from Zion. On that day only Mount Zion would be secure, but it would make the whole world a safe and holy place (on the centrality of Zion on the Day of the Lord, see Is. 2; Ezek. 40–48; Mic. 4). From there God would teach all nations His law, and they would beat their weapons into farming tools (Is. 2:1–5; Mic. 4:1–5). Zion would be God's holy mountain—a house of worship for all (cf. Is. 56:7).

The house of Jacob refers to the family of the patriarch, the twelve tribes, and thus to the whole nation of Israel (Obad. 18). The house of Joseph would again constitute part of the house of Jacob, as when Jacob blessed his descendants (cf. Gen. 48:5). The northern and southern tribes would reunite and, like a fire, burn everything in their path, including Edom. In a reversal of fortunes, Edom would end and the land and people of Israel would be restored. This foreshadows the outcome of the final conflict between good and evil. God would banish wickedness forever and exalt His people. This section concludes with the assurance that the Lord has spoken (Obad. 18b).

19–21
Restoration of Land and People

The ultimate goal of God's judgment was not the destruction of Edom but the restoration of Judah and all Israel. The people of Israel would retake possession of areas that had fallen into the hands of others since the period of the united monarchy. The people of the Negev, the southern desert between the Arabah Valley and the Sinai Desert, would occupy the southernmost part of Transjordan (the land east of the Jordan River), including Edom (v. 19). To the west, the inhabitants of the Shephelah, the lowlands/hill country between the Judean mountains and the coastal plain, would inhabit the land of the Philistines (v. 19), including Ephraim and Samaria, areas once controlled by Philistine outposts. Benjamin, just north of Jerusalem, would possess the northern part of Transjordan, known as Gilead. Israelite exiles would return to the Holy Land and possess the northwest as far as Zarephath by Sidon (v. 20). Finally, captives from Jerusalem in faraway Sepharad, perhaps in the distant north, would return to the south. This redistribution of the promised land to displaced Israelites would once again unite land and people within Israel's original borders.

In the center of it all, saviors/deliverers would rule from Mount Zion over Edom and all the territory Israel held during the golden age of David and Solomon, from Dan to Beersheba and from the eastern desert to the western sea. This vision of Israel's future was never realized, even when Judah returned from exile and restored Jerusalem a few decades after Obadiah. Sadly, the restored Judah was just as disobedient as before. However, the vision anticipates a future end-time kingdom as promised to Abraham, Isaac, and Jacob. The destruction of Edom would merely pave the way for the restoration of the righteous in a kingdom belonging to the Lord (v. 21). This promise has become the advent hope of those who wait for the Messiah to return. The resolution of the conflict between Edom and Judah represents a future when God's eternal kingdom, populated by God's faithful children throughout the ages, will replace all the nations of this world.

JONAH

INTRODUCTION

Title and Authorship. In Hebrew this book is titled *yonah*, the name of the Prophet Jonah, which means "dove." Jonah was the son of Amittai from Gath Hepher in the territory of the tribe of Zebulun (Jon. 1:1; 2 Kin. 14:25). Unlike many other prophetic books, the book of Jonah does not specify its author. Though it tells Jonah's story, another person could have written it using material from the prophet himself. This would explain why the narrative is written in the third person.

Date. Jonah prophesied in the first half of the eighth century B.C., during the reign of King Jeroboam II of Israel (793–753 B.C.; 2 Kin. 14:23–27). Sometime during this period, God sent the prophet to Assyria, the major foreign power at the time, to prophesy in the city of Nineveh. The author states that Nineveh "was" a large city (Jon. 3:3). Some suggest that the use of "was" implies that, by the time the book was written, Nineveh was no longer large. This would point to a time after the fall of the city in 612 B.C. However, the likelihood that the book was written in the Northern Kingdom would point to a date before Israel and Samaria fell to Assyria in 722 B.C.

Backgrounds. During the reign of Jeroboam II, Israel experienced a period of territorial expansion and economic growth, developments that Jonah interpreted as God's will (2 Kin. 14:25). However, other prophets during this period of prosperity denounced the injustices and rampant materialism that arose (see Amos 2:6–8; 4:1–3). Against this background, the book of Jonah reveals a prophet willing to announce God's blessing on Israel but not His positive involvement with the nations.

No independent historical evidence exists for Jonah's ministry in Nineveh. However, some have plausibly suggested that events in Assyria during this period might reflect his ministry or provide a context for its acceptance. For example, Adad-Nirari III (ca. 810–783 B.C.) introduced religious reforms that shifted away from traditional polytheism. Also, several plagues and a solar eclipse occurred during the reign of Ashur-Dan (ca. 772–755 B.C.). These might have predisposed the Ninevites to accept Jonah's message. The title "king of Nineveh" in Jonah 3:6 may suggest a local ruler rather than an emperor since Nineveh did not become the capital of Assyria until the time of Sennacherib (705–682 B.C.). So the emperor did not live there at that time.

Theology and Purpose. The book of Jonah presents a more complex theology than its length or apparent simplicity might suggest. It covers three main areas: the sovereignty of God, God's people and the people of the world, and the compassion of God.

1. The Sovereignty of God. Jonah sums up the extent of God's sovereignty when he states that he fears/worships "the LORD, the God of heaven, who made the sea and the dry land" (1:9). As Creator, God has dominion over creation. He sent a great wind on the sea (1:4), prepared (Heb. *manah*) a great fish to swallow Jonah (1:17), commanded the fish to deposit Jonah on dry ground (2:10), prepared (*manah*) a plant to shade Jonah's head (4:6), prepared (*manah*) a worm to destroy the plant (4:7), and then prepared (*manah*) an east wind to beat on Jonah's head (4:8). Significantly, in each case creation immediately obeyed. God also showed His sovereignty in His role as Judge. He told Jonah to denounce Nineveh, a city He had judged to be wicked (1:2). When God renewed this commission, Jonah proclaimed a message of destruction against the city (3:4). Yet the sovereign Judge also saved Nineveh from destruction (3:10), just as He used the fish to save Jonah from drowning (1:17; 2:10). In the absence of hope, God creates hope for all.

2. *God's People and the People of the World.*
The heart of the book's radical message concerns how God relates to His chosen people on the one hand and to the nations on the other. The author communicates this message through a series of striking comparisons and contrasts. In chapter 1, while the pagan sailors prayed, Jonah, the Israelite prophet, slept (1:5). Using the same Hebrew verbs which God used to call Jonah at the outset—*qum* and *qara'* (1:6; cf. v. 2)—the ship's captain roused Jonah from his slumber and told him to pray to his God. The captain understood that when life is threatened and hope seems to fade away, prayer provides the most important refuge. In this respect, the pagan mariners appear more spiritually aware than Jonah. Moreover, God answered the prayers of both the Gentiles (1:14-15) and the Israelite (2:2), saving both from the storm. Jonah's rejection of God's word in chapter 1 contrasts with the positive response of Nineveh to God's word in chapter 3. In both chapters, the ship's Gentile captain (chap. 1) and the Gentile king of Nineveh (chap. 3) humbly submitted to the will of God. They did not try to dictate His actions (1:6; 3:9). By contrast, the salvation of Nineveh angered Jonah, who refused to accept God's will (4:1-3). These and other comparisons and contrasts challenge Jonah's view that only God's chosen people should receive His compassion and grace.

3. *The Compassion of God.* Jonah summed up the depth of God's compassion, affirming His attributes of grace, mercy, slowness to anger, abundant kindness, and long suffering patience before bringing judgment (4:2b). The prophet quoted Exodus 34:6-7 in confessing

Nineveh

Nineveh was a large city in Assyria, an empire with a legendary reputation for ruthlessness and barbarity. The prophets frequently prophesied about God's future judgment on Nineveh/Assyria. The entire book of Nahum addresses the issue (see also Mic. 5:6; Zeph. 2:13). Situated on the Tigris River, Nineveh exerted a strong political influence for several centuries. In Jonah's time it had not yet reached its golden age as the Assyrian capital under Sennacherib (705-682 B.C.). Nevertheless, it had already achieved considerable power. The Assyrians conquered the Northern Kingdom of Israel in 722 B.C., and Nineveh itself fell to a Babylonian and Median coalition in 612 B.C.

that he had disobeyed because of God's well-known compassion (Jon. 4:2a). The plot of the whole book revolves around the consequences of Jonah's rejection of God's compassion for others. Jonah did not want to extend the hope of life to the nations. Yet Jonah himself received God's compassion. God prepared a fish to rescue him from certain death and implicitly forgave his initial rejection of God's call by renewing it the second time (3:1). His experience parallels Nineveh's. Despite their moral offenses, the Ninevites experienced God's compassion when He responded to their repentance by explicitly forgiving them (3:10). God heard the sincere cry of sinners and relented (3:9-10). Indeed, the abounding compassion of God, an expression of His loving-kindness (Heb. *khesed*), continues to give hope to sinful human beings who repent and run to Him.

Literary Features. Jonah is one of the most accomplished literary works in the Bible. It is meticulously structured, with each part of the book preparing for or echoing another. This is most obvious when comparing chapter 1 with chapter 3 and chapter 2 with chapter 4. However, important interconnections extend beyond those pairings. The use of chiasms (see 1:4-16) achieves an accomplished balance and symmetry. Subtle repetitions of key terms (e.g., "arise" and "call"/"cry out") underline important themes. The use of wordplays and words with more than one connotation (e.g., "overthrow") keep the reader alert to deeper meaning in the text. The author artfully crafts allusions to other passages of Scripture into the narrative, suggesting numerous comparisons and contrasts to guide interpretation. Finally, the large number of questions (see 1:10; 3:9; 4:11) shows that the book is less concerned with telling readers what to do or believe and more with asking them how they might respond to its challenging message.

COMMENTARY

1:1-16
God's Word and Jonah's Response

God told Jonah to go to Nineveh, but he disobeyed and fled by ship (1:1-3). A great storm threatened to wreck the ship, and the terrified pagan sailors discovered that God had sent it to punish Jonah (vv. 4-7). Jonah confessed his faith in the Lord and requested that the sailors throw him overboard (vv. 8-15a). The sea immediately calmed down and the sailors worshiped the Lord (vv. 15b–16).

1:1–3. Jonah's Call. Jonah ministered to two evil rulers, Jeroboam II of Israel and the king of Nineveh. He was apparently willing to prophesy success for Israel (2 Kin. 14:25); but for Nineveh, only judgment. Such contrasting attitudes to Israel and the nations appear throughout the book.

Like many other prophets, Jonah is introduced by a declaration that "the word of the LORD came to" him (see also Hos. 1:1; Joel 1:1; Mic. 1:1). The same phrase introduces Elijah (1 Kin. 17:2–3, 8–9), the first of several parallels between the ministries of the two prophets. In 1 Kings 17:9, God's command to Elijah begins with the same words as His command to Jonah (Heb. *qum lekh*, "arise and go, go at once").

Despite this conventional introduction, Jonah's response contrasts not only with Elijah's but also with all other prophets. He refused to go to Nineveh to denounce its wickedness. Instead, he fled to Tarshish. Some identify Tarshish with Tartessos, on the Baetis River in modern-day Spain. If correct, then Jonah tried to flee as far west from Nineveh as possible. However, Tarshish may more likely be Tarsus in Cilicia, home of the Apostle Paul. Several texts seem to place Tarshish close to Greece (see Gen. 10:2–4; Ezek. 27:12–14). Wherever it was, Tarshish was outside of Israel and nowhere near Nineveh. Jonah intended to go there to flee from the Lord (Jon. 1:3). The only other character in the OT to do something similar was Cain, who went to the land of Nod after murdering his brother (Gen. 4:16). That connection suggests the seriousness of Jonah's disobedience. Significantly, however, the text does not immediately say why Jonah disobeyed. The author wants to reveal a little more about him first.

1:4–16. Jonah's Flight. Jonah 1:4–16 forms a chiasm:

A Beginning of the Storm: Worshiping Other Gods (vv. 4–5a)

  B Goods Thrown into the Sea (v. 5b)

    C The Captain's Hope for Deliverance (vv. 5c–6)

      D The Culprit Discussed (v. 7a)

        E Jonah Identified as the Cause (v. 7b)

          F Jonah Interrogated (v. 8)

            G God, the Creator of All Things (v. 9)

          F' Jonah Interrogated (v. 10a)

        E' Jonah Identified as the Cause (v. 10b)

      D' Punishment Discussed (v. 11)

    C' The Means of Deliverance Revealed (vv. 12–13)

  B' Jonah Thrown into the Sea (vv. 14–15)

A' End of the Storm: Worshiping the Lord (vv. 15b–16)

The structure begins and ends with pagan sailors worshiping and hinges in the center on Jonah's confession of faith in God as the Creator of all things. This highlights the main feature of this section: the contrast between pagans and God's prophet.

The series of contrasts begins with mariners worshiping their gods while the prophet, who was running away from his God, slept (v. 5). In a striking role reversal, the ship's captain had to wake Jonah up and tell him to call on God (v. 6). Normally, the prophet should call on others to seek God. Just as strikingly, the captain's words repeat God's commands to Jonah (cf. v. 2). The word of the Lord came to Jonah (v. 1), but a pagan sailor, not the Israelite prophet, spoke it. Jonah finally confessed his faith but only when the sailors discovered his guilt and forced him to answer their penetrating questions (v. 7–9). His confession of God as the Creator of all things rings very hollow considering he had boarded the ship to flee from Him (v. 3). However, it forms the basis of the rest of the book, which serves as a commentary on its implications.

The sailors then prayed to the Lord, worshiped Him, offered a sacrifice, and made vows (vv. 14, 16). This contrasts with the beginning of the section, when they worshiped their individual gods. Despite Jonah's behavior, they had come to believe in the power of his God. But Jonah did not pray, sacrifice, or make vows to the God of Israel. He mentioned God's name only when directly asked about the cause of the storm. The pagan sailors behaved more admirably than the prophet called by God. This disturbing assessment paves the way for even more radical revelations later in the book.

The ship's captain roused Jonah from his sleep because he hoped that Jonah's God might have concern for them and prevent them from perishing in the storm (v. 6). The captain wanted to save all life on board his ship but knew he could not demand it. This is the first of several expressions of hope found throughout the book (see 2:1–2; 3:9). The full significance of Jonah's willingness to be thrown overboard, essentially a death wish, does not become clear until his second expression of the same desire (1:12; 4:3, 9).

1:17—2:10
God's Salvation and Jonah's Praise

God prepared a fish to swallow Jonah (1:17). From the belly of the fish, Jonah praised God for saving him from drowning (2:1–7), denounced idol worship (2:8), and vowed to offer sacrifices to the Lord (2:9). At God's command, the fish vomited Jonah onto dry land (2:10).

1:17. Jonah Swallowed by the Fish. The book of Jonah stresses God's sovereignty, a theme that recurs several times in chapter 1. In His sovereignty, God sent Jonah to cry out against Nineveh (v. 1), sent a great wind on the sea in response to Jonah's flight to Tarshish (v. 4), and later calmed the storm (v. 15). He also prepared a large fish to swallow Jonah to rescue the prophet from drowning to death. Jonah was in the great fish for "three days and three nights" (v. 7). His experience foreshadows "the three days and three nights" Christ would spend "in the heart of the earth" (Matt. 12:40).

2:1–10. Jonah's Psalm and God's Response. Jonah offered a type of psalm known as a thanksgiving, used in Israel to thank God for specific acts of His grace, especially for saving the worshiper(s) from death or persecution. The fact that he uttered the thanksgiving from within the fish shows that Jonah recognized it as God's means of saving him from drowning. Understanding the role of the fish is essential to understanding the dynamics

of the book as a whole. Significantly, the psalm is not a lament (such as Pss. 22, 44), in which psalmists typically complained to God when they faced death or experienced persecution. A lament would mean Jonah viewed the fish as punishment rather than salvation.

Jonah used conventional language commonly found in many other psalms to describe his cry from the depths of *she'ol* ("grave," "death," or "pit"; Jon. 2:2; cf. Ps. 86:13), God's answer (Jon. 2:2; cf. Ps. 120:1), the feeling of turbulent waves sweeping over him (Jon. 2:3; cf. Ps. 42:7), and his removal from the Lord's sight (Jon. 2:4; cf. Ps. 31:22). Numerous other similarities to various psalms also occur throughout Jonah. These similarities indicate that he knew how to worship in an appropriate manner, just as his words to the sailors show he knew his theology well (Jon. 1:9). He was an orthodox Israelite. Yet he declared his faith in God, called on God to rescue him, and offered Him praise all while fleeing from Him. Jonah had an orthodox faith but struggled to live out its obvious implications. The introduction of this theme here leads to the climax at the end.

Jonah's psalm begins with a description of his thoughts and experience as he descended through the deep waters. The psychological distress/affliction caused by the real threat of death moved him to seek help from the Lord. He affirms that the Lord had answered his prayer, probably in the sense that God sent him the great fish to preserve him alive (2.2). He again describes his fearful experience, but this time he expresses his real fear that he had been permanently expelled from the presence of God (vv. 3–4). Nevertheless, Jonah looked toward the heavenly temple and prayed to the Lord. Another description of his deadly experience follows (vv. 5–6b), closing with the affirmation that God rescued him from the grave by sending the fish (v. 6c). The Lord had heard Jonah's prayer and answered it from His holy temple (v. 7). Jonah concludes the psalm by renewing his commitment to the Lord, affirming God's superiority over idols, and making a vow of thanksgiving to the Lord for saving him (vv. 7–9). The psalm demonstrates his orthodox faith, such as his belief in the efficacy of prayer and the heavenly sanctuary (v. 7; cf. Ps. 20:7).

Jonah's experience parallels that of the sailors. They faced a threat to their lives and called on the Lord (Jon. 1:14). He heard them and delivered them (1:15). Jonah also came face to face with death and called on the Lord, and God heard his voice and delivered him (2:2).

The Sign of Jonah

In Matthew 12:39, Christ responded to a request for a sign by saying that the only sign his generation would get was "the sign of the prophet Jonah" (cf. Matt. 16:4; Luke 11:29). He explained that just as Jonah was in the fish for three days and three nights, so He would be in the earth. He, like Jonah, would face death but be rescued from it after three days. But the parallel is only partial, for Christ is "greater than Jonah" (Matt. 12:41; Luke 11:32). Nonetheless, Jonah prefigures His death and resurrection (see commentary on Hos. 6:1–3).

God answered the prayers of Gentiles and Israelite alike. Unknown to Jonah down in the belly of the fish, these same mariners on board the ship also offered a sacrifice to the Lord and took vows (1:16). The prophet and the sailors reacted in identical ways because they had all seen the power and authority of Jonah's God. The rest of the book reveals how this saved Israelite would react to more Gentiles in need of salvation.

This entire section began with the fish swallowing Jonah (1:17) and ended with the fish vomiting him out. The fish's obedience to God contrasts with Jonah's disobedience and brings the first half of the book to an appropriate conclusion.

3:1–10
God's Word and Nineveh's Response

Jonah obeyed God's renewed call to go to Nineveh (3:1–3). He prophesied the city's imminent destruction. The population repented because the king hoped that their repentance would avert punishment (vv. 4–9). God accepted their repentance and did not destroy the city (v. 10).

3:1–4. Jonah Preaches God's Word. Verses 1–3 echo the language of Jonah's first call in chapter 1. For a second time the word of the Lord came to Jonah, telling him to go to Nineveh and proclaim God's message to the people. This time, however, rather than fleeing to Tarshish, he obeyed God and went to Nineveh. The contrast between Jonah's two responses to the word of God shows how his salvation from death had profoundly affected him. He had already praised God for His grace, promising to serve Him (2:9), and now he obeyed Him.

Jonah proclaimed that Nineveh would be overthrown in forty days (3:4). The same Hebrew verb, *hapak* ("overthrow"), describes the destruction of Sodom and Gomorrah, when God "overthrew the cities" (Gen. 19:29). Nineveh's destruction also seemed certain because Jonah did not invite the people to repent. It took three days to save Jonah (Jon. 1:17); it also took him three days to preach judgment (3:3). However, Nineveh was given forty days to await its destruction. Yet the city responded immediately—on the first day (vv. 4–5). Nineveh's immediate repentance contrasts with Jonah's delayed obedience.

Although Jonah ministered in the first half of the eighth century B.C. (2 Kin. 14:25), the fate of Nineveh can be compared to the later fate of two other cities. The capitals of Israel (Samaria) and Judah (Jerusalem) were destroyed as divine punishment for their sins in 722 B.C. and 586 B.C., respectively (2 Kin. 18:9–12; 25:1–10). If God did not spare His own people, surely He would not spare Nineveh, a center of pagan injustice and cruelty. The rest of Jonah gives a surprising response to this assumption.

3:5–10. Nineveh Repents and God Relents. Nineveh's startling reaction to Jonah's preaching strongly contrasts with others in the Prophets, particularly Jerusalem's reaction to Jeremiah. In Jeremiah 36, Jeremiah threatened Jerusalem with God's judgment so they might repent of their sins. Repentance would lead to God's forgiveness (Jer. 36:3), just like it did in Nineveh. However, King Jehoiakim of Judah rejected Jeremiah's preaching, so God responded by bringing about all the threatened disasters (Jer. 36:31). In contrast, the king of Nineveh commanded his people to call urgently on God (Jon. 3:8). Consequently, God relented from the threatened disaster and did not destroy Nineveh (v. 10).

Jonah 3:4 subtly conveys the possibility of Nineveh repenting. Jonah's announcement that Nineveh would be "overthrown" (*hapak*) seems to offer no hope of salvation. If he had used the verb "perish" (*'abad*), used by the captain (1:6), the sailors (1:14), the king (3:9), and finally the Lord (4:10), then this would definitely be the case. However, the verb *hapak* has two distinct meanings. It can mean "overturn," in the sense of "destroy" (Gen. 19:29), or it can mean "turn around." For example, in Jeremiah 31:13 God promises that He will turn [*hapak*] mourning into joy/gladness. In fact, all occurrences of *hapak* in the Niphal verbal stem, the form used here, mean "turn around" rather than "destroy." Before Nineveh repented, Jonah's words seemed to mean that the city would be overturned, but instead it was turned around. So, Jonah's words were in fact fulfilled, just not in the way Jonah expected. The repentance of Nineveh decided between the two possibilities.

While Nineveh's response to God contrasts with Jerusalem's later response, it resembles the reaction of the pagan sailors in chapter 1. The sailors "feared the LORD" and "offered a sacrifice" (Jon. 1:16), while the Ninevites believed God and proclaimed a fast (3:5). The ship's captain and the king of Nineveh also behaved in similar ways. The captain (unconsciously) repeated God's own words (1:6; cf. 1:2) like a prophet delivering "the word of the LORD." The king's call for Nineveh to repent and reform resembles the prophets frequent call for Israel to repent (3:8; cf. Joel 2:12–14). The king's choice of words when he admonished the people to turn from/give up their evil ways in Jonah 3:8 also occurs in God's instructions to the prophet Jeremiah (Jer. 36:3, 7; cf. 26:3), a passage already shown to be closely related to Jonah 3. The king's behavior also contrasts with Jonah's. In chapter 1 the word (*dabar*) of the Lord came to Jonah, commanding him to leave immediately (Heb. *qum lekh*, lit. "arise and go"), but instead he immediately rose and fled from the presence of the Lord (1:2–3). In 3:6, when the king heard the message/word (Heb. *dabar*) from God, he immediately rose (Heb. *qum*) from his throne and told the city to repent, reform, and call out urgently to God (v. 8). Nineveh was more responsive than Jerusalem, and the sailors and the king of Nineveh were more responsive than Jonah.

This chapter climaxes with God's response to Nineveh's repentance. The people of Nineveh turned (*shub*) from their evil (*ra'*) ways, and God relented (*nakham*) from the disaster (*ra'ah*, lit. "evil"; v. 10). The people changed their behavior, so God changed His intention. The king received precisely what he hoped for when he wondered whether God would yet turn (*shub*) and relent (*nakham*; v. 9). His hope echoes the ship captain's hope for divine deliverance (1:6). For a pagan, the king showed remarkable spiritual insight, for God often changes His intention (*nakham*) in a demonstration of His grace (see Jer. 18:8; 26:3; cf. 2 Sam. 24:16). In Exodus 32:14, a verse virtually identical with Jonah 3:10, the Lord relented (*nakham*) from the disaster (*ra'ah*, lit. "evil") which He said He would bring on His people, Israel. What God did for Israel in the past, He now did for Nineveh. In the OT God frequently relents from sending punishment on Israel. But the book of Jonah makes clear that God's mercy extends beyond His own covenant people.

The experiences of Jonah and of Nineveh parallel each other. At the beginning of the book, Jonah deserved God's judgment because he disobeyed and fled from His presence. He faced death when he was thrown overboard into a raging sea. But God, in His grace, saved him by sending the fish to swallow him. Like Jonah, Nineveh too deserved God's judgment because of its wickedness. It too faced death when Jonah prophesied its overthrow in forty days. And God, in His grace, also saved them when He "relented" from sending the punishment. God offers salvation by grace through faith to all, whether Jew or Gentile (Eph. 2:8).

4:1–11
God's Salvation and Jonah's Protest

The final chapter is structured in three parts. Each concludes with God asking Jonah a question (4:4, 9, 11). Jonah answered only the second question. The first two challenged Jonah's right to be angry. The third defends the Lord's pity for Nineveh—the main reason for Jonah's anger.

4:1–4. Jonah's Anger and God's First Question. When God saved him, Jonah was extremely thankful (2:1–9). But when God saved Nineveh, Jonah was extremely angry (4:1). In a book full of contrasts, this is the most telling of all. The repetition of the Hebrew word *ra'ah* to describe Jonah's anger recalls both Nineveh's repentance and God's relenting in order to underline that Jonah was angry about both of these.

- The king of Nineveh told the people to turn from their evil (*ra'*) ways (3:8).
- They turned from their evil (*ra'*) ways (3:10).
- God relented from the disaster (*ra'ah*) (3:10).
- But it displeased Jonah exceedingly (*ra'a' ... ra'ah*) (4:1).

Jonah responded to Nineveh's repentance and God's relenting with great displeasure and anger. Verse 4:1 literally reads, "it was evil to Jonah—a great evil—and he became angry." His anger prompted him to offer his second prayer in the book, which produces yet another contrast. In his first prayer, Jonah prayed that he might live (2:2, 6). In the second, he prayed that he might die (4:3). What could possibly explain this huge contrast between life-affirming thankfulness for his own salvation and death-seeking anger for Nineveh's salvation?

Jonah's problem was not caused by a lack of biblical knowledge or theological understanding but by an inability to accept the implications of his belief. He finally confessed why he fled to Tarshish at the outset. He disobeyed because he understood the character of God. He quoted Exodus 34:6–7, which enumerates God's loving, gracious, and patient characteristics, including His willingness to relent from His threatened punishments (Jon. 4:2b). God did precisely what Jonah had surmised He would do (v. 2): He relented (*nakham*) from the disaster (3:10). Elsewhere, the people of Israel cited Exodus 34:6-7 to praise God (see Num. 14:18; Neh. 9:17; Pss. 86:15; 103:8; 145:8; Joel 2:13), but Jonah cited it in order to condemn Him. The grace which God offered to Israel, He now offered to foreigners. Jonah had enough theological knowledge to predict that but not enough compassion to accept it. That is why he was extremely angry (see PK 271).

Jonah's confession sheds light on why he told the sailors to throw him into the sea (Jon. 1:12), which should have meant certain death. He had a death wish when running away from Nineveh, and he had one after going there. Whether fleeing or going, disobeying God's word or obeying it, he would rather die than see Nineveh saved. Jonah refused to embrace the lesson the Lord was trying to teach him.

This section ends with the first of three questions God asked Jonah in this chapter. "Is it right for you to be angry?" (4:4). The answer is surely "no!" But Jonah's answer is delayed to the end of the next section, maximizing its effect.

4:5-9. Jonah's Anger and God's Second Question. Arresting contrasts are common in Jonah, and this paragraph provides three pairs of them. The first contrasting pair comes from within the book itself. Inside the city, the king of Nineveh repented and sat (*yashab*) in dust and ashes, hoping for the city's salvation (3:6). Meanwhile, outside the city, Jonah made a shelter and sat (*yashab*) under it, wishing for the city's destruction (4:5). While Jonah sat there, God made a plant grow to shade Jonah from the heat. Jonah's response to the plant contrasts with his reaction to Nineveh's turnaround: Jonah was exceedingly glad about the plant (lit. "Jonah was glad concerning the plant—a great gladness"; v. 6) but upset about Nineveh's salvation (literally, "it was evil to Jonah—a great evil"; v. 1).

The second and third contrasts look beyond the book of Jonah. Just like Jonah, Elijah sat beneath a plant and prayed that he might die (1 Kin. 19:4). But Elijah wanted to die because the Israelite king and queen were apostate and did not listen to his message. Jonah wanted to die because the king of Nineveh had listened to his message and he and his people had repented. Formerly, Abraham argued with God about the destruction of the wicked, pagan cities of Sodom and Gomorrah because he wanted to preserve them if even a few righteous remained (Gen. 18:23-33). Jonah wanted the wicked, pagan city of Nineveh to be destroyed despite its mass repentance.

Such stark contrasts with characters within and beyond the book highlight how it ridicules Jonah for his narrow-minded bigotry. He was indeed behaving like a silly, senseless dove (*yonah*; cf. Hos. 7:11). God again asked if Jonah had a right to be angry, this time about the plant that died (Jon. 4:9a). This time Jonah responded that he had every right to be angry (v. 9b), confirming just how self-centered he was and how unwilling to rejoice in the salvation of others. In this book two things make Jonah happy: his own salvation (2:1-9) and the plant shading his head (4:6). Two things make him angry: the salvation of Nineveh (v. 1) and the death of the plant (vv. 8-9). He was glad when God saved him or provided for him, but he was angry when God saved others or withdrew His provision from him. Jonah would not accept the idea that God had any concern for anyone other than Israelites like himself.

4:10-11. Jonah's Anger and God's Final Question. The book concludes with God asking Jonah to consider a challenging point. He reminded Jonah of his pity for the plant, which Jonah neither created nor destroyed. God then asked why He should not have pity on Nineveh if Jonah had such great concern for a plant. God wanted Jonah to understand that the city of Nineveh was far more important than Jonah's plant and the shade it gave him.

The book ends on this question and, at first sight, seems incomplete, for we never hear Jonah's response. However, the book ends on an open question not to encourage speculation about Jonah's possible answer but to challenge readers to answer it for themselves. The Apostle Paul posed the same question using different words (Rom. 3:29). Is the one true God not also the God of the Gentiles? Does He extend hope to all or only to a few? The answer to these questions lies at the heart of the message of the book of Jonah.

MICAH

INTRODUCTION

Title and Authorship. The book is named after the Prophet Micah (Micah 1:1). This name, a short form of *mikayehu*, means "Who is like Yahweh?" It reflects part of the book's message: the uniqueness and incomparableness of the Lord (7:18). Micah himself authored the book, as indicated by both the first-person editorial note in 3:1 ("I said") and the personal conviction about the power of his prophetic office in 3:8. Micah hailed from Moresheth Gath (1:1, 14), probably modern Tell ej-Judeideh (Tel Goded), which is located in the lowlands near Lachish and Gath, about twenty-one miles (33 km) southwest of Jerusalem. The byname "Micah of Moresheth" shows that Micah was well known beyond his hometown. He was a contemporary of the older Prophet Hosea and the younger Isaiah. God proclaimed His message through Micah in tears (1:8), with pleading and beseeching (6:1–8). Outside his book, Micah is mentioned only in Jeremiah 26:18, in a context a hundred years later and relating to his prophecy of doom as remembered by some elders in Jerusalem. According to tradition, Micah died peacefully in his hometown during the first half of Hezekiah's reign.

While some believe that the passages about the return from exile and Israel's restoration were written at the time of the Exile or later, these messages of hope belong to the twin messages of impending divine judgment and ultimate divine mercy relentlessly proclaimed by all the prophets. Doom and salvation, blessings and curses: all play an integral part in classical prophecy (see Deut. 28). Nothing in the book conflicts with the style and theology of the eighth-century prophets.

Date. According to 1:1, Micah prophesied around 740–700 B.C., during the reigns of three kings of Judah: Jotham (750–735 B.C.), Ahaz (735–715 B.C.), and Hezekiah (716–687 B.C.). The book prominently features the Neo-Assyrian Empire. Partly due to their army of mercenaries and their deportation policy, Assyria was becoming a world power. In v. 1:6, Micah presents the fall of Samaria as still in the future. The Assyrian King Sargon V captured it in 722 B.C. Micah 1:8–16 contains prophecies against particular cities of the Southern Kingdom, which date the book before 712 B.C., when Gath no longer belonged to Judah (1:10). The Assyrians destroyed Lachish in 701 B.C. (1:13). Micah 3:12 reports an Assyrian invasion that apparently succeeded. Verses 5:4–5 refer to another invasion that would fail, most likely Sennacherib's campaign against Jerusalem in 701 B.C. (cf. 2 Kin. 19; Is. 37).

Backgrounds. The rise of Assyrian dominion put its stamp on the second half of the eighth century B.C. In its wake the Israelite double monarchy came to an end when the Northern Kingdom fell in 722 B.C. Tiglath-Pileser III (745–727 B.C.) campaigned against Philistia in 734 B.C. and came threateningly close to Israel and to Micah's hometown (2 Kin. 16; 2 Chr. 28; Is. 7–8). Rezin of Aram/Syria and Pekah of Israel formed an alliance against Assyria, but Ahaz of Judah did not join. In the ensuing Syro-Ephraimite war (734–732 B.C.), Ahaz called Assyria for help. Tiglath-Pileser conquered Damascus in 732 B.C., subjugated parts of Israel, and allowed Hosea to take the throne. However, Assyria did not settle quickly. Soon after, Shalmaneser V (727–722 B.C.) besieged Samaria, the capital of the Northern Kingdom, for three years (725–722 B.C.). In 722 B.C. Sargon II (722–705 B.C.) captured it and deported the inhabitants. His son Sennacherib (705–681 B.C.) engaged the western front in 701 B.C. and captured most of Judah. But he had to withdraw from Jerusalem empty-handed (Is. 36–37).

Like the other prophets before him, Micah announced that God would use foreign nations to castigate His covenant-breaking people. He prophesied the siege and fall of Samaria (Mic. 1:6–7) as well as the Assyrian invasion of Judah under Sennacherib (1:8–16), but this only foreshadowed a far greater disaster: the destruction of the temple and the Babylonian Exile (3:12).

Jotham "did what was right" in following the Lord, although the people continued to sacrifice on the high places (2 Kin. 15:34–35). However, his son Ahaz followed the practices of the kings of Israel, sacrificing on the high places with the common people (2 Kin. 16:1–4). He even burned his son in the fire as a sacrifice to a false god, one of the abominable practices of the Canaanites (2 Kin. 16:3). The people's hypocrisy intensified the situation. Many formally followed the religion of their fathers while simultaneously practicing idolatry. The priests and prophets did not want to lose their popularity, so they tolerated the double standard and predicted peaceful times (Mic. 3:5). Hezekiah attempted to reverse the negative effects of his father's reign and succeeded to some degree. He trusted in the Lord like no other king of Judah (2 Kin. 18:5; similar to Josiah in 2 Kin. 23:25). It seems that Micah prophesied mainly during the reign of Ahaz and the early years of Hezekiah. He certainly supported Hezekiah in his religious reformation (cf. Jer. 26:18).

The book of Micah provides enough information to sketch the internal situation in Judah. Social exploitation accompanied the religious and moral demise under Ahaz. Everyone in leadership was corrupt. They lived in wealth but ruthlessly oppressed the poor and the marginalized. Micah, often called the "prophet of the poor" by modern scholars, fought for the cause of the poor and the oppressed (Mic. 2:1–11).

Theology and Purpose. Micah oscillates between messages of judgment and doom and messages of mercy and salvation. The core of his message emphasizes that God stays true to His covenant with His people in three ways: He accuses Israel and Judah of sins and transgressions (see 3:8). He announces punishment, specifically the Exile and the destruction of Jerusalem and the temple. And in His mercy, He promises salvation to instill hope for the future.

1. *Judgment.* Micah's accusations cover all areas of society. He accuses the wealthy of economic exploitation (6:9–12); the leadership of judicial oppression, bribery, and corruption (chap. 3); and the entire people of social and moral bankruptcy (7:1–7). Micah specifically upholds the principle of representative accountability; that is, leaders are responsible for the

people. If the leaders do not walk with God, the people will also err on their path. All are guilty and will suffer punishment, but Micah holds the leaders particularly accountable for not exerting a godly influence. The prophet believed that God would inevitably judge His covenant people. Deportation and exile would come. Israel would go to Assyria (1:16) and Judah to Babylon (4:10). Even Jerusalem and the temple would be destroyed (3:12; 6:16) as the last effective means to lead the people to repent of their sins. As a result, God would save the remnant comprised of those who had returned to Him. Through judgment the Lord sought to continue using Israel to fulfill His plan to save the nations (see "God's Judgment in the Prophets," p. 981).

2. *Salvation.* God is merciful and compassionate; He loves to forgive and to bless (Micah 7:18–20). His promises of hope include the deliverance and restoration of Israel and the glory of the coming messianic kingdom (2:12–13; 4:1—5:15; 7:8–20). He does not restrict salvation to the remnant of Israel but offers hope to all. Although God would punish the nations, He would also give them a part in the promise. They would come to Zion to seek counsel from the Ruler of Israel (5:4) and to receive God's manifold blessings (4:1–3; 7:12–17) in fulfillment of the covenant promise given to Abram (Gen. 12:3).

3. *Messianic Prophecy.* The messianic reign provided the only hope for a society in which justice and mercy would prevail. With a few strokes, Micah sketches the reign of the messianic Davidic King born in Bethlehem (Micah 5:2). He would lead "in the strength of the LORD" (5:4) and His influence would encompass the entire world, making Zion the center of the nations. The world would never find peace except at the coming of the One who is peace (5:5). The NT identifies Jesus Christ as the royal Shepherd-King from Bethlehem (Matt. 2:5–6).

4. *Remnant Motif.* The term "remnant" (*she'erit*), a keyword in the message of hope, appears in each of the promises of salvation (Micah 2:12; 4:7; 5:7–8; 7:18). Although the expression itself seems to indicate that only a few would survive, the remnant would consist of many people (2:12) and become a strong nation (4:7). The term "remnant" thus serves as an honorific title for the faithful in Israel.

Literary Features. The book takes the form of oracles of judgment followed by oracles of salvation. This pattern subdivides it into three main parts (chaps. 1-2; 3-5; 6-7), each beginning with the imperative "Hear!"/"Listen!" (1:2; 3:1; 6:1).

COMMENTARY

1:1
Prophetic Formula

Like many other prophetic books, Micah begins with the prophetic formula "the word of the LORD that came" (see Hos. 1:1). Micah came from Moresheth, a small town in the south Shephelah, and prophesied in the second half of the eighth century B.C. The reference to three Judean kings—Jotham (750-735 B.C.), Ahaz (735-715 B.C.), and Hezekiah (716-687 B.C.)—indicates that Micah mainly prophesied to Judah. But his prophecies concern both Samaria, the capital of the Northern Kingdom of Israel (Mic. 1:5-6), and Jerusalem, the capital of the Southern Kingdom of Judah (see vv. 5, 9, 12), though they focus on the latter (see Micah: Introduction).

1:2—2:13
Penalty and Promise

The first cycle of judgment followed by salvation focuses on the imminent threat to Samaria (1:6-7), the threat to Judah and Jerusalem (vv. 8-16), and Judah's social, economic, and religious injustices that were deserving of divine punishment (2:1-11). Though God would war against His people (1:2-5), He would also gather the remnant of Israel and be their Shepherd-Leader (2:12-13).

1:2-5. Yahweh's Judgment. Micah repeats the imperative "Hear!"/"Listen!" at the beginning of several sections (3:1, 9; 6:1-2, 9; see also Amos 3:1, 13; 4:1; 5:1; 8:4). Elsewhere, he summons the leaders or the people of Judah to hear. But in Micah 1:2, he calls the physical earth and all its inhabitants as witnesses of God's judgment upon His covenant-breaking people (cf. 6:2). Verses 3 and 4 describe a theophany of the divine Warrior in which the Lord leaves His holy temple (i.e., the heavenly sanctuary and throne room; vv. 2-3; cf. Jon. 2:4, 7; Hab. 2:20) to come down to the earth, obviously ready to judge (cf. Gen. 11:5). As the Creator and Judge, He would trample the heights/high places of the earth, an apparent allusion to Amos 4:13. The disintegrating elements recall the theophany at Mount Sinai (Mic. 1:4; Ex. 19:18-19), except that in Micah's

time the people were not prepared to meet their God. The awe-inspiring, ominous image portrays the natural world as unable to withstand God's presence when He comes to pass judgment on both kingdoms. The Lord singles out their capitals, Samaria and Jerusalem, as centers of idolatrous practices (Mic. 1:5). Consequently, He would destroy Samaria (vv. 6-7) and devastate the towns of Judah (vv. 8-16). The historical instrument of judgment, though not explicitly mentioned, was the Assyrian army.

1:6-16. Samaria and Judah Lost. The prediction of Samaria's downfall focuses on its stone buildings and idols. The personification of Israel's capital as a harlot represents the Northern Kingdom's religious prostitution with other gods (cf. Jerusalem as a prostitute in Ezek. 16). The God of Israel would repay them accordingly. The prophet laments over the doom of Samaria.

The passage about Judah and Jerusalem also takes the form of a dirge. The prophet physically displayed his grief (Mic. 1:8). The list of eleven villages in vv. 10-16 does not appear to involve any sequence, but all the towns were located in the Shephelah, west and south of Jerusalem, and all were captured or suffered loss during the Assyrian military campaign against Jerusalem in 701 B.C.

The names of the chosen towns create assonance (similar sounds in Hebrew) and wordplays with the prophetic statement associated with them. For example, people would roll in the dust in the "house of dust" (Beth Aphrah/Ophrah); the "beautiful" (Shaphir) would be humiliated in naked shame; no one would go out of "going out" (Zaanan); support would be withdrawn from the "house of withdrawal" (possible meaning of Beth Ezel); "bitterness" (Maroth) would long for good but receive disaster; "deceit"(Achzib/Akzib) would prove a deceitful lie; and an heir/conqueror would come against "inheritance" (Mareshah; vv. 11-15). The first and last places mentioned recall the frailty of the early history of the monarchy in Israel. "Tell it not in Gath" is identical to David's words in his lamentation for Saul and Jonathan (v. 10; cf. 2 Sam. 1:20). The *kebod yisrael* (lit. "the glory of Israel"; possibly the nobility, the army, or, less likely, God Himself; cf. 1 Sam. 4:21-22; Is. 17:4) would find refuge in Adullam, the place of David's refuge (Mic. 1:15; cf. 1 Sam. 22:1). At the climax of the prophet's lament, he announces the Exile (Mic. 1:16).

2:1-11. Wealthy Oppressors and False Prophets Condemned. Micah directs his oracle of woe in 2:1-5 against the greedy rich in Judah, who acquired more property by oppressing others and hijacking their inheritance, robbing them of their socioeconomic livelihood (v. 2). Like the preflood generation, the affluent continually focused their thoughts and actions on wickedness and evil (cf. Gen. 6:5). As retributive judgment, God planned a time that would be *ra'* ("evil," "disaster") against Judah, just as He did for Israel (Mic. 2:3; cf. Amos 5:13). The judgment day for the mighty would leave them with no inheritance among "the assembly of the LORD" (Mic. 2:4-5).

Although the Hebrew of vv. 6-11 is difficult, the passage clearly recounts a dispute between Micah and his opponents. His accusation met resistance, so he pinpointed their socioeconomic crimes against their fellow men, women, and children (vv. 6, 8-9; cf. vv. 2-3). To take away God's glory and blessing from children means to despise the human dignity that God conferred on them (v. 9; cf. Ps. 8:5). Consequently, the prophet either warns the passersby to flee or pronounces judgment by ordering the violators to leave (Mic. 2:10). Micah's sarcastic mockery of his adversaries in v. 11 refers back to v. 6. The verb *natap* ("prophesy," "prattle"; lit. "drip," "dribble" words) occurs three times in v. 6 and twice in v. 11, forming an inclusio (or bracket). Micah, fueled by the Spirit of the Lord, spoke of transgression and sin (3:8), but the unrighteous deserved false prophets (2:11; cf. Is. 28:7).

2:12-13. Hope for the Remnant. God's plans for His people do not end in exile. Micah's first message of hope briefly describes God as the source of salvation. Micah 2:12 introduces the theme of the remnant using the familiar metaphor of the shepherd and his flock (cf. 4:7; 5:6-7; 7:18). God Himself, the royal Shepherd, would assemble and gather the remnant of Israel from exile (2:12; cf. Is. 40:11; Jer. 23:3; 31:8-10). He would deliver His people to safety in the sheep pen (lit. "like sheep in the fold"; cf. Jer. 23:3; Ezek. 34:14) and increase their number enormously (cf. Ezek. 36:37-38). God Himself would break through the enemies to open the way and, in a new exodus, lead His people from exile (Mic. 2:13; cf. 2 Sam. 5:20).

3:1—5:15
False Leaders and a Righteous Ruler

In the second cycle of judgment followed by salvation, the judgment on the unjust leaders of Judah, both political and religious (3:1-12), contrasts with a fantastic future outlook. The Lord will reign in Zion, and the temple will be the religious center of the world (4:1-5). He will gather His people from the Diaspora and judge Israel's enemies (vv. 6-13; 5:5b-15). The messianic King from Bethlehem will bring peace and rule justly from Jerusalem (5:1-5a).

3:1-12. False Leaders Rebuked. In chapter 3, Micah rebukes all of Israel's leadership, including the political leaders (vv. 1-4), the prophets (vv. 5-7), and the priests (vv. 9-12). Each of the three sections follows the same pattern, first naming the accused, then listing their offenses, and finally announcing the penalty. The first and the third sections start with the imperative "Hear!"/"Listen!" (vv. 1, 9; cf. 1:2).

The keyword "justice" encompasses not only judicial justice but also ethics and morality (3:1, 8-9). The rulers perverted good and promoted evil (v. 2). Returning to the shepherd metaphor, Micah uses brutal and graphic language to describe Israel's shepherds mercilessly slaughtering the flock for consumption (vv. 2-3). They should have led and protected the flock as God Himself promised to do (cf. 2:12-13). Because of their love of evil deeds, Micah declares God's sentence of divine silence. Although He had promised to help His people if they cried out to Him (see Is. 30:19), He would not listen to the rulers or answer them (Mic. 3:4). God would completely forsake them.

The prophets also misled the people (vv. 5-7). They no longer spoke for God; they made the content of their prophecies dependent on money. Bribery led to oracles of peace (v. 5). They sanctioned the behavior of the upper class, blessing the rulers who exploited the common people but declaring war on the poor and oppressed who could not pay. Therefore, God would punish them with silence as He would the rulers (vv. 6-7; cf. v. 4; Amos 8:12). They would no longer see visions. In shame, they would cover their faces/lips (lit. "mustache"; Mic. 3:7), an act required of a leper (Lev. 13:45) and practiced in mourning rituals (Ezek. 24:17, 22).

In a rare first-person speech, Micah declares that, in contrast to the false prophets, he is filled with power from the Lord's Spirit, making him God's legitimate prophet (Mic. 3:8). His virtues of justice, strength, and courage enable him to uncover the horrendous condition of the leadership and make it public. He does this in the all-encompassing final rebuke against all of Israel's leaders (vv. 9-12). Their corruption spoiled the entire society. The leadership perverted moral standards and sold "justice" to the highest bidder (v. 9). They built up Zion with bloodshed, proving their hostility toward God (v. 10). Worse, they arrogantly claimed that nothing bad could ever happen to Zion because of the Lord's presence, a blatant misapplication of Zion theology and the epitome of blasphemy (v. 11; Ps. 46:5; Zeph. 3:15, 17).

Micah 3:12 announces the divine judgment: since the leaders had built Zion (Jerusalem) through bloodshed, the city, including the temple (lit. "the house"), would be devastated. This is the first announcement of the destruction of Solomon's temple in prophetic literature, and Micah's audience must have found these words outrageous and shocking. Jeremiah's contemporaries remembered Micah's prophecy just before its fulfillment in 586 B.C. when the Babylonians conquered Jerusalem and destroyed the temple (Jer. 26:18).

4:1—5:15. A Righteous Kingdom and Ruler.

After the section on the false leaders (chap. 3), Micah describes the idyllic reign of the Lord in Zion. God's plan for obedient Israel after the Exile included the future messianic kingdom and its impact on the nations (4:1–4). God would bestow the benefits of the kingdom on all who would come to Jerusalem, including Gentiles. Everyone would worship the Lord, and in Jerusalem the Messiah would lead justly. The vision in Micah 4:1–3 also occurs in Isaiah 2:2–4, with slight variation. The question of which one is original or whether they both used another source might never be resolved beyond doubt. However, Micah 4:1–3 is closely integrated within its context. It contains references that look both backward (Zion, the temple mountain, teaching, judging; cf. 3:10–12) and forward (walking in God's ways, strong nations; cf. 4:5, 7). The phrase "in the last days"/"in the latter days" refers to the future messianic age, when Mount Zion would be the highest point on earth (4:1). The static aspect of its great height (cf. Ps. 48:2) precedes a description of dynamic movement. The nations would flow into Zion (Mic. 4:2a) and the law out of Zion (v. 2b), making it the hub of the world (cf. Ezek. 38:12).

Many peoples and nations would "go up" to Jerusalem (Mic. 4:1–2; cf. Is. 60:3; Hag. 2:7; Zech. 8:22). The same verb appears regularly in the title of the pilgrimage psalms: "A Song of Ascents" (Pss. 120–134). The imagery of many nations streaming uphill to Mount Zion represents God breaking down national and ethnic barriers. The house/temple of the God of Jacob

will truly become "a house of prayer for all nations" (Is. 56:7). All will desire the teaching and wisdom of the Lord and will walk in His paths (Mic. 4:2), making God's Torah universally effective. The Lord will "judge between many peoples" (v. 3), which refers either to imposing law and order among the nations or to peaceful conflict resolution. In Micah, peace leads to disarmament, not disarmament to peace. Instruments of destruction will become instruments of agriculture when the nations beat their swords into plowshares and their spears into pruning hooks. This line reverses the call for war in Joel 3:10. The United Nations garden in New York City contains a bronze sculpture of a powerful blacksmith beating "swords into plowshares." Then and now, Micah's imagery depicts the world's hope for an end to all wars and conflicts, but Micah insists that only through the teaching of the Lord and an adherence to His law will this hope find fulfillment.

Following God will result in agricultural blessing and peace (Mic. 4:4). Micah's reference to sitting under a vine and a fig tree evokes a tangible image of safety, a symbol of the *pax messianica* ("messianic peace"; cf. 1 Kin. 5:5; 2 Kin. 18:31; Zech. 3:10). The concluding formula affirming this as a proclamation of the Lord of Hosts impresses God's seal on this prophecy (cf. Is. 40:5; 58:14).

Micah follows up his vision of hope with a call for action. He calls the Israelites of his time to walk according to the future vision and to do what all the nations would do in the latter days: to walk in the name of the Lord their God (Micah 4:5; cf. v. 2). "In that day" in vv. 6–8 refers to the time of the glorious kingdom described in vv. 1–3. Micah portrays the Lord as both Shepherd (first-person speech; vv. 6–7a) and King (third-person account; v. 7b). The lame and the exiles/outcasts harmed by the Lord refers primarily to His people as a nation, though it could also refer to the poor classes of society oppressed by the leadership (v. 6; cf. chap. 3). God will make them a remnant, a strong nation among strong nations (4:7; cf. v. 3). The true King is the Lord, and He will reign from His temple (v. 7; cf. v. 2). The Lord will rule in Zion forever. Even at the time of this proclamation, when Israel was in danger of being corrupted by its leaders and taken by foreign nations, God was ultimately in charge. Therefore, even as the people watched God take the kingdom away from them (4:9—5:15), they could hope that He would one day reestablish the former dominion, the glorious Davidic kingdom, with Zion/Jerusalem as its capital (4:8).

Micah 4:9—5:4 is marked by the repetition of the Hebrew word *'attah* (lit. "now," or translated idiomatically as "this/that day"; 4:9, 10, 11; 5:1, 4), forming three units: the *'attah* of the crying and labor (4:9–10), the *'attah* of the assembled nations (vv. 11–13), and the *'attah* of the coming king (5:1–4). Each section moves from distress to a turn of events. The first compares Jerusalem's distress to the pain of a woman in labor. In their time of distress, both their king and ruling counselor would disappear, and they would have to go to Babylon (4:9–10; cf. Jer. 6:22–26). This is arguably the first explicit prophetic mention of the Babylonian Exile. However, Israel would experience a new exodus, for the Lord would redeem (Heb. *ga'al*) His people. Israel's deliverance from exile would correspond to their Jubilee release described in Leviticus 25:25–55, where *ga'al* occurs ten times.

The second unit describes the nations assembling against Jerusalem, either for battle or to mock them after falling to the Babylonians (Mic. 4:11–13; cf. 7:8–10; Ezek. 36:1–15; Obad. 11–14). But this would result in their undoing, for God planned to gather them for judgment (Mic. 4:12–13). God would make Zion like a threshing animal under His guidance, administering just punishment to the mocking nations (cf. the judgment against Babylon in Jer. 51:33). In the end, the God of Israel would stand as the Lord of the entire world (Mic. 4:13; cf. Ps. 97:5).

The third unit (Mic. 5:1–4) both starts with *'attah* (omitted in some translations) and ends with a final *'attah* (sometimes translated idiomatically to refer to the future of the prophecy as "at that time" or "then") that envelops all the *'attah* sections by stating a purpose: His greatness would "now" (at that time) extend throughout the world (v. 4). As with the other two units, the third starts with a grim look at a hopeless situation. Some translations interpret the Hebrew *gadad* in v. 1 to mean troops, referring to the futile mobilization of Zion's military power against its enemies. Others render this word as "slash yourself in grief," indicating a rite performed as Zion mourns her siege and fall (588–586 B.C.; cf. Jer. 16:6; 41:5; 48:37). This prediction and the humiliation of Israel's judge/ruler (Heb. *shopet*) who would be struck on the cheek with a rod (Heb. *shebet*, a wordplay on *shopet*) likely refer to the downfall of the king of Judah in 586 B.C. It is less likely that they might refer to Sennacherib's siege in 701 B.C.

The attention shifts suddenly from the large city of Jerusalem to the small village of Bethlehem Ephrathah (Micah 5:2), which demonstrates the folly of underestimating something because it is small. This otherwise insignificant place suddenly becomes important because of the One who would come from there. The Messiah, not strength or size, determines importance. The humble King originated from a small village. "House of bread" (Bethlehem) and "fruitful" (Ephrathah) characterize His rule.

Verse 2 affirms the coming One as a Davidic King. Bethlehem, Ephrathah, and Judah are closely associated with David and his father, Jesse (1 Sam. 16:18; 17:12). The Hebrew word *li* ("to," "for Me") recalls 1 Samuel 16:1, which uses the same word to describe God choosing David to replace Saul as king. The reference to the rule of the messianic King also recalls God's words to David in 2 Samuel 7:8.

The King would come as a king comes forth for victory (cf. Is. 11:1). He would stand in the service of the Lord because He would come "to"/"for" God, in marked contrast to the present rulers. The dominion of this King is from antiquity (cf. Is. 45:21; 46:10; Hab. 1:12), from the days of *'olam*, a word variously translated as "ancient times," "days long ago," "days of old," "former years," "the days of eternity," or "from everlasting" (Mic. 5:2; cf. 7:14; Is. 63:9, 11; Mal. 3:4). These time references seem to indicate the eternal existence of the Messiah. The woman in labor in Micah 5:3 might recall the young woman who would give birth to Immanuel (Is. 7:14), or it could refer back to Zion in labor (Mic. 4:9–10). In any case, God would reverse the fortunes of His people, and the faithful remnant would return from exile.

Micah 5:4 describes the inauguration of the Ruler who would shepherd His people (cf. David as shepherd-king in 2 Sam. 5:2; Ps. 78:70–72). He would stand (i.e., have authority) and reign as the Lord's Representative because He would act in the strength and majesty of the Lord His God. As a result, the flock (Israel) would abide in safety (cf. 2 Sam. 7:10). In Jesus's time the Jews considered this prophecy to refer to the Messiah (John 7:42). Matthew identifies Jesus as the Messiah from Bethlehem (Matt. 2:5–6).

At the climax of Micah 5:2–5a, Micah refers to the coming King as *shalom*, a word that encompasses peace, welfare, prosperity, friendliness, deliverance, and salvation. It is the best word to describe not only the reign of the King but the King Himself. The threat of Assyria itself was immediate, and Assyria is also a code name for Mesopotamian enemy powers (cf. 7:12; Ezra 6:22; Zech. 10:10–11). The Assyrians and the Babylonians ("the land of Nimrod"; cf.

Gen. 10:8–12) invaded between the eighth and sixth centuries B.C. (Mic. 5:5–6). However, the Messiah would strengthen Israel, rising against the invading Assyrians, a group described as seven shepherds and eight rulers, referring to a plurality of military powers (for similar numerical literary devices, see also Prov. 30:15, 18, 21, 29; Eccl. 11:2; Amos 1:3). Israel would emerge victorious because God and/or the coming King would rescue them from the Assyrians (Mic. 5:6).

The remnant would be like the dew, which brings blessings, and a majestic, invincible lion (vv. 7–9). The subject of the praise in v. 9 could refer to the coming King, to the remnant of Jacob, or to God Himself.

In vv. 10–15 the Lord declares His intention to destroy/cut off (Heb. *karat*, used four times in vv. 10–13) not just His enemies (v. 9) but also the military protection and pagan Canaanite religious activities that gave Israel a false sense of security, including witchcraft, fortune-telling (Lev. 19:26; Deut. 18:10, 14; Is. 2:6), idols, and pillars (Lev. 26:1). "In that day," when God would assemble the remnant of Jacob, He would prove the land's only real security and the only God worthy of worship (Mic. 5:10; cf. 4:6). Then Israel would set their hopes on the Lord alone. The conclusion in 5:15 reveals that God would direct His vengeance not against Israel but against the nations that have not obeyed Him. This unexpected ending shows that vv. 10–14 describe Israel's cleansing, not judgment. God would renew His covenant with a purified people. Micah's message for the nations expressed their need to understand that God would both punish Israel *and* stand by His covenant. They needed to come to Israel (4:1–3) to hear and listen (1:2), for those that disobeyed God would receive His anger and wrath.

6:1—7:20
Judah's Fault and God's Forgiveness

The third cycle of judgment followed by salvation presents God's covenant lawsuit against Judah (6:1–8), another set of accusations and the threatened punishment of Jerusalem (vv. 9–16), and a lament of the bankruptcy of moral values in society (7:1–7). But in the end, hope once again shines forth as the prophet predicts a change in Judah's attitude toward God and the reversal of their fate because of His compassion and forgiveness (vv. 8–20).

6:1—7:7. Judah's Sin and Misery. The covenant lawsuit in 6:1–8 consists of the summons (v. 1),

the call of witnesses (v. 2), the plaintiff's address reviewing benevolent acts (vv. 3–5), the defendant's response (vv. 6–7), and the indictment stating the general covenant stipulations broken (v. 8). The call to "Hear!"/"Listen!" introduces the Lord's trial against Judah (v. 1; cf. 1:2; 3:1, 9; 6:2). The Hebrew word *rib* appears as a verb in v. 1 ("plead the case") and as a noun in v. 2 ("complaint, accusation"). A common term in prophetic literature, it describes a lawsuit between God and His people (Jer. 2:4–9; cf. Is. 3:13–15; Hos. 2:4–25; 4:1–3). God called mountains and hills as witnesses, indicating the universal character of the dispute (Mic. 6:1–2; cf. Deut. 32:1). Though God tried hard to hold them back, Judah, like Balaam of old, continued to follow the wrong path. God saved His people during the Exodus and the wilderness wanderings. He protected them from enemies and an ill-minded prophet (Balak and Balaam; Num. 22–24). He led them over the Jordan from Shittim/the Acacia Grove to Gilgal (Josh. 3:1; 4:19–24). And He provided leadership through Moses, Aaron, and Miriam (Mic. 6:4; cf. Ex. 15:20).

Confronted with the past salvific acts of their covenant God, the people responded with a series of four questions that reveal their wrong attitude toward worship (Mic. 6:6–7). These would-be worshipers offered God what they believed to be increasingly more valuable sacrifices as a show of their commitment. Burnt offerings and year-old calves were common sacrifices (v. 6; Lev. 1; 9:3). Thousands of rams and ten thousand rivers of oil were part of extraordinary offerings during special occasions (Mic. 6:7; 1 Kin. 8:63; 1 Chr. 29:21; 2 Chr. 29:32–35). Micah even speaks of the abhorrent practice of offering firstborn children, though God forbade human sacrifice (Mic. 6:7; Lev. 18:21; Ps. 106:38). God required them to redeem their firstborn (Ex. 13:13; cf. Num. 3:44–51). The people gravely misunderstood God's desire for far more than sacrifices (1 Sam. 15:22). Confronted with the past salvific acts of their covenant God, the people ought to have worshiped Him in spirit and in truth rather than in outward formalism.

The climactic statement in Micah 6:8 responds to the people's lack of covenant loyalty by providing them with divine guidelines, the "golden rule" of the OT (cf. Deut. 10:12–13). To act justly forms the ethical basis of society (cf. Mic. 3:1, 9). To love mercy goes even further to restore compassion, kindness, and generosity. To walk humbly with God fully recognizes dependence upon the covenant Lord. Humans should imitate God, who loves justice and mercy (7:18, 20; cf. Ps. 33:5). This statement summarizes the message of the preexilic prophets, the essence of true worship and life within God's covenant.

The verdict of the lawsuit rules against the city of Jerusalem (Mic. 6:9–16). Because of the prevalent injustice of the wealthy oppressors and the cunning merchants ripping off innocent people, it would share Samaria's fate (vv. 10–12, 16; cf. 2:1–11; Amos 8:4–7). God would strike the country with fertility and military covenant curses (Mic. 6:13–15; cf. Lev. 26:26; Deut. 28:30, 39–41). Omri and Ahab—kings of the Northern Kingdom's most prominent dynasty—had set Samaria on a course of destruction (1 Kin. 16:15—22:40). Like Samaria, Jerusalem would also become desolate. Onlookers would hiss and scoff at the city (Mic. 6:16; cf. Jer. 19:8; Lam. 2:15–16).

Micah laments the disintegration of moral principles and solidarity in society, both in public (Mic. 7:1–4) and in private (vv. 5–6). Although the prophet again accuses the leaders specifically (cf. 3:9–11), he refers to universal corruption. No "faithful" (derived from the same Hebrew root as "mercy" in 6:8) or "upright" person remained anywhere (7:2; cf. Ps. 14:1–3). Therefore, Micah announces the approach of the day of the watchman (Mic. 7:4; cf. Ezek. 33:2–9), that is, the judgment he had proclaimed. Even in private affairs, no one could be trusted, not even friends, neighbors, leaders, or household members (Mic. 7:5–6; cf. Matt. 10:35–36). The nucleus of Israelite society, the family, had become corrupted. Everyone stood alone except those who trusted in God (Mic. 7:7). Micah refers to God as his Savior/salvation (cf. Ps. 25:5) and insists that God will hear his prayers (cf. Ps. 55:16–17). He, like the psalmist(s), hoped that God would save him from his plight. Micah uses the first person at both the beginning and the end of 7:1–7, balancing his frustration about society (v. 1) with his declaration of hope in the Lord (v. 7).

7:8–20. God's Forgiveness and Judah's Rise.

The last section completes the book's third cycle of judgment followed by salvation. It consists of four subunits. The first unit affirms that Judah would bear the just wrath of God (7:8–10). But even in such dark times, the Lord would be their light (v. 8). The confession of sin is central to Micah's message (v. 9). Judah acknowledged God's accusations as justified (cf. chaps. 1–3; 6:9—7:7), reflecting a change of attitude (cf. 6:1–8). This confession allowed God to remove Judah's iniquity and transgression (7:18) and to fulfill His promises of salvation (2:12–13; chaps. 4–5). God will justify those who ask for forgiveness, and they will see His righteousness

(7:9; cf. 2 Chr. 7:14). In Judah's case, this included seeing the final fall of its gloating enemy (Mic. 7:10).

The second unit describes the day of reversal for Judah and Jerusalem (vv. 11–13). Judah would become a large, secure country (v. 11). God would return His people from exile (v. 12) and devastate unbelievers in an apocalyptic scene (v. 13; cf. Is. 24:1, 5).

The third and fourth units concern the relationship between God's people and the nations (Mic. 7:14–17) and the relationship between the remnant and their God (vv. 18–20). God would shepherd His people (v. 14; cf. 2:12). In remembrance of the Exodus and the conquest, He would bring His people out of exile and into the promised land in full view of all the nations. As a result, the nations would fear the Lord (7:14–17; cf. Josh. 2:9–11).

The last unit is a short doxological hymn of God's grace and mercy. It starts off with the rhetorical question (v. 18; *mi-'el kamoka*), an allusion to the prophet's own name (*mikah*). It recalls the profound question from the Exodus: Could there be any among the gods like the Lord (Ex. 15:11)? Micah illustrates God's uniqueness through His attributes (Mic. 7:18) and His achievements (vv. 19–20), highlighted by His willingness to forgive. Several lexical similarities link the description of God's uniqueness in vv. 18–20 with the positive part of His self-introduction in Exodus 34:6–7. Micah apparently omits God's retributive character because God has already judged (cf. Ex. 34:7). Also, the allusion to Exodus 34:6–7 and the emphasis on judgment in Nahum 1:2–3 (cf. Joel 2:13; Jon. 4:2) balance the emphasis on forgiveness in Micah 7:18–20. Chapter 7 moves from justice to mercy, reflecting the book's main movement from judgment to salvation, from punishment to forgiveness. God would much rather forgive than punish.

Once more the remnant motif appears. God does not forgive everyone without any consideration of attitude. He forgives the faithful remnant made up of those who seek Him (v. 18; cf. 2:12; 4:7; 5:6–7). The unique picture of God hurling sins into the depths of the sea (7:19) recalls Him hurling Pharaoh's army into the sea at the Exodus (Ex. 15:5; Neh. 9:11). Micah goes even further back in time to Jacob and Abraham, showing God's covenant faithfulness throughout the entire patriarchal period (Mic. 7:20). In the end, Micah and the remnant put their confidence in the faithfulness and unchanging love and mercy of God. As long as God is involved in human affairs, there is hope.

NAHUM

INTRODUCTION

Title and Authorship. The book begins with information about its primary focus and its author (1:1). It is titled after the Prophet Nahum the Elkoshite, who wrote the oracle against Nineveh, the capital city of Assyria. The name Nahum, a shortened form of Nehemiah ("comfort of Yahweh" or "the Lord comforts"), occurs only here in the OT. It means "consolation" or "comfort," a fitting name for the prophet and the book because the message of the fall of Nineveh would bring comfort to the people of Judah.

Date. Though scholars debate the date of the book, several clues narrow it to a period in the mid to late seventh century B.C. The mention of the fall of Thebes (No Amon) to the Assyrians in 3:8–10 provides a precise historical anchor point. Assyrian cuneiform texts dated to 663 B.C. record the conquest of the city by Ashurbanipal (669–627 B.C.). The prophet portrays Assyria as a nation of strength, near the height of its power (1:12; 2:11–13; 3:1, 4), and indicates that it still controlled Judah (1:12–13, 15; 2:2). The Assyrian empire began to decline after Ashurbanipal's death in 627 B.C. Shortly prior, in 629 B.C., King Josiah of Judah (641–609 B.C.) enforced massive religious reforms that would have been impossible had Assyria still maintained tight control of the region. Therefore, Nahum probably prophesied sometime between 663 B.C. and 629 B.C., between the reigns of Manasseh and Josiah, making Nahum a contemporary of Habakkuk, Zephaniah, and the young Jeremiah.

Backgrounds. The book of Nahum is a sequel to the book of Jonah. But Nahum offers no hope for Nineveh. By 722 B.C. the Northern Kingdom of Israel had fallen to a succession of attacks led by Assyrian kings that culminated in Sargon II (721–705 B.C.) removing the last survivors from

Samaria and placing them in Babylonia, Media, and Persia. Around 700 B.C., Sennacherib (705–681 B.C.) moved the Assyrian capital city from Dur-Sharrukin (Khorsabad) to Nineveh. In 670 B.C., Esarhaddon (681–669 B.C.), son of Sennacherib, moved other conquered peoples into Samaria and Galilee (2 Kin. 17:24; Ezra 4:2), further weakening the region. Assyria's brutality reached its peak at the height of the empire, during the reign of Ashurbanipal. Nahum probably prophesied during this time period. Nahum's prophecy was fulfilled in 612 B.C., when Assyria and King Sin-shar-ishkun (623–612 B.C.) fell to a coalition of Medes under Cyaxares (625–585 B.C.) and Babylonians under Nabopolassar (626–605 B.C.). A small remnant of Assyrians escaped Nineveh in 612 B.C. and fled to Haran, where they made Ashur-uballit II (612–609 B.C.) the new king of Assyria. However, Haran also eventually fell to the Babylonians, making Babylonia the most powerful empire in the ancient Near East.

Theology and Purpose. Nahum's opening statement summarizes the message of the book: God's awesome power in wrath and in judgment. God spoke to Judah, but the message concerns Nineveh. The obvious celebration of vengeance against the Assyrians reveals the character of God, forcing the reader to ask what kind of God the book portrays. The answer lies in the two themes addressed in Nahum: judgment and salvation.

1. Judgment against Nineveh. To correctly understand God's intent here, the book of Nahum must be read after the book of Jonah, which portrays God as compassionate and patient, not wanting any to perish. God's loving-kindness frustrated Jonah in the mid-eighth century B.C., but now a hundred years later, God had seen enough suffering, not only of His chosen people but also of the surrounding nations. Nahum refers to Nineveh as the city of bloodshed, deception, and pillaging (3:1). He further describes the city as a prostitute engaged in witchcraft

(3:4). God declared that Nineveh and its gods would be *karat* (lit. "cut off"), indicating complete destruction (1:14–15). In a terrifying tirade, Nahum outlines the nature of Nineveh's military violence, painting a scene of destruction and death in one breath (3:3) and the naked exposure of Nineveh the prostitute in the next (3:5–7). As punishment, other nations would attack the Assyrians, and they would experience the cruelty of war they themselves had practiced, including the brutal destruction of their children (3:10; see "Introduction to the Prophetic Literature"; see "God's Judgment in the Prophets," p. 981). Nineveh had had a chance to repent, but the time for forgiveness was past, and the sovereign God made it clear that justice must prevail against such a wicked city. This was a nation in a state of absolute hopelessness.

2. *Salvation for God's People.* Interwoven throughout the oracles of doom against a wicked nation are promises of hope and blessing for Judah. Divine wrath and judgment fill the book of Nahum, but it also contains the consolation that ultimately God will not stand by and allow those who hurt His children to go unpunished. The magnitude of His power matches His apparent slowness to anger (1:3), and He is a shelter in times of distress/trouble (1:7). As a result of God's judgment on Nineveh (1:12), salvation would come to Judah, and once again God's people would joyously celebrate their sacred festivals (1:15). But the message also implies a forewarning that Judah might eventually share Nineveh's fate if oppression and wickedness continued there unchecked. The same message applies today: God will not tolerate oppression and corruption. The book of Nahum declares the universal sovereignty of God; He is the Lord of history, the Lord of nature, and the Lord of destinies. He alone provides a future for His people.

The connection between hope and the fall of Assyria implies at least an eschatological hope. In Nahum, God's promise that trouble and affliction would not return lies at the heart of this hope. He announces the end of evil extending beyond the evil caused by Assyria, a promise reinforced by the statement that God would finish it completely (1:9). At the end of the book, God describes the wickedness of Assyria in universal terms. Its cruelty had affected everyone (3:19). Consequently, the book constantly emphasizes the absolute extermination of Assyria (1:14–15; 2:10) followed by the resurgence of Jacob in excellence and splendor (2:2). Like Edom in Obadiah, Assyria in Nahum seems to stand for much more than an ancient empire.

It stands for the archenemy who has oppressed God's people throughout history. The power of God would permanently destroy this enemy, ushering in a new era of peace for His people (cf. 1:15). Isaiah, who also used Assyria as a symbol of God's ultimate enemy, voiced this same eschatological hope when he announced that the coming Messiah would bring Assyria to an end (Is. 10:20–34).

Literary Features. The book of Nahum contains several woe oracles against Assyria (cf. Is. 13–23; Jer. 46–51). The prophet uses poetic language with vivid, evocative imagery to convey intense moods and sights. He utilizes sound-based wordplays, metaphors (Nah. 2:11–12), similes (1:10; 2:8; 3:12), repetition (2:11–13; 3:15–17), and short, often staccato, phrases. The oracles in Nahum are war poetry with taunting motifs and imagery referencing God as the divine Warrior (1:2–11). They communicate certain judgment, with no mention of redemption for Assyria.

COMMENTARY

1:1
Introduction

The double title in the superscription introduces what follows as both a prophetic pronouncement and the "book" of Nahum's vision. No other superscription of a prophetic book refers to the contents as a *seper* ("book," "writing," "scroll"). The Hebrew word *massa'* ("burden," "prophecy," "oracle") denotes a pronouncement made about or against an entity, in this case, Nineveh. The term *khazon* ("vision") also appears in the superscriptions to Isaiah and Obadiah. The author does not mention the source of the vision, but presumably this was a divine revelation.

The location of Elkosh, Nahum's hometown, is unknown. Early tradition placed it in the territory of Simeon or in Galilee, possibly Capernaum (lit. "village of Nahum"). Later tradition suggests 'Alqush, a town near Mosul in Iraq. This mountainous site maintained by modern "Assyrian Christians" was home to a Jewish community that survived into the 1940s of the modern era.

1:2–8
A Psalm Praising the Divine Warrior

Nahum begins his oracle by describing God as jealous (1:2; Ex. 20:5; 34:14) and avenging

(Nah. 1:2; Deut. 32:35, 43; Is. 1:24), yet slow to anger (Nah. 1:3). His jealousy and vengeance arise from a justifiable sense of indignation (Ps. 94). He appears in the whirlwind and storm (Nah. 1:3; Jer. 23:19; 30:23) and rebukes the sea (Nah. 1:4; Ps. 106:9). In His presence, the mountains quake, and the hills melt (Nah. 1:5; Pss. 18:7; 46:6; Jer. 4:24; Amos 9:5).

The use of the terms 'el for God and ba'al for Lord (Nah. 1:2) may reference Canaanite religious ideas in order to show who is the true God and Lord. The association of God with seas, rivers (v. 4), storms (v. 3), and fire (v. 6) further supports this. Similar imagery of water, sea, floods, storm, and fire/lightning also appears in Psalm 29. The God of Israel, not the Canaanite Baal, controls the fertile regions and rich pasturelands of Bashan in northern Transjordan, beautiful Mount Carmel next to the Mediterranean Sea and close to Lower Galilee, and mountainous Lebanon, the source of luxuriant cedars (Nah. 1:4; Is. 33:9).

God's anger burns against His enemies; but in contrast, He is a refuge and deliverer for those who khasah ("trust," "take refuge") in Him (Nah. 1:7–8; Pss. 27:1; 37:39; Is. 17:10; Jer. 16:19).

1:9—2:2
Judgment on Nineveh and Deliverance of Judah

God's promise that tsarah ("trouble," "affliction," "distress") would not return indicates that He would not give Assyria another opportunity to torment His people (1:9). In fact, the great power of Assyria disappeared from the pages of history soon after 612 B.C. If Assyria represents God's archenemy, then this promise would also apply to the eternal destruction of evil at the end of time (cf. Mal. 4:1; Rev. 20–21). The Hebrew word tsarah means not only "trouble" or "affliction" but also "adversity," "anguish," and even "calamity." Isaiah also announced the eschatological end of all affliction/adversity (Is. 65:16). Never again would sin raise its ugly head in God's universe (cf. GC 504).

At the time of Nahum's prophecy, Assyria seemed at the height of its power (Nah. 1:12a), which historically was most likely during the reign of Ashurbanipal (669–627 B.C.). Assyria heavily oppressed both Israel and Judah (2 Kin. 16:7–8; 18:13–16; Is. 7:18–25) and did not ease up until the reign of Josiah. They attacked Judah for the last time during the reign of Manasseh

(2 Chr. 33:11) and led him away like an animal to Babylon. But God promised His people that He would no longer afflict them (Nah. 1:12). Instead, He would bring the oppressor, Assyria, to its end (1:13–14).

The fleet feet of the bearer of glad tidings are blessed because the bearer brings news of Nineveh's imminent fall and the ensuing period of peace for God's people, when they could once again celebrate the festivals (v. 15). During Josiah's eighteenth year, Judah celebrated Passover as never before (622 B.C.; 2 Kin. 23:21–25), and by the end of his reign, the Assyrian empire had been completely eradicated. The motif of feet bringing good news also appears in Isaiah 52:7, which announces deliverance from the Babylonians. In Romans 10:15 this motif again appears, but this time the bearer of good news tells of deliverance from sin.

Assyria had scattered nations through mass deportations. Israel fell victim in 722 B.C., and much of Judah was decimated in 701 B.C. However, another nation came to scatter Assyria. The Lord used Assyria as a scourge and rod (Is. 10:5, 24) against both Israel and Judah, but He would restore the majesty of Jacob (Nah. 2:2). This would culminate in spiritual restoration through the coming Messiah (cf. Rom. 9:4–5).

2:3–13
A Vision of the Coming Destruction of Nineveh

The prophecy moves from the restoration of Jacob (2:2) to a lengthy description of the fortification of the city of Nineveh against the coming attack (v. 5). The Babylonians attacked the neighboring Assyrian city of Ashur in 615 B.C. but failed to take it. In the next year, the Medes successfully conquered the city. In 612 B.C., a Median and Babylonian coalition besieged Nineveh for three months before it fell. Excavations have uncovered two preemptive, fortified narrowings of the eastern Halzi Gate, one of the fifteen gates of Nineveh. Within the same area lay the remains of numerous fallen Assyrian soldiers from the 612 B.C. battle. Nabopolassar graphically described his victory over the hated Assyrian enemy: "I slaughtered the land of Subartu (Assyria), I turned the hostile land into heaps and ruins. The Assyrian, who since distant days had ruled over all the peoples, and with his heavy yoke had brought injury to the people of the Land, his feet from Akkad [Babylonia] I turned back, his yoke I threw off."

Nahum prophesied that the city would be led away captive into exile (v. 7). This certainly refers to the inhabitants of the city of Nineveh but may also refer to the city's goddess, Ishtar, whose temple and its associated cult prostitution dominated the religious lives of Assyrians. Her attribute animal, the lion, figured prominently in Nineveh, especially during the reign of Ashurbanipal. His North Palace is replete with reliefs of lion hunts staged in the expansive grounds within the walls of the city. At the end of the hunt, the killed lions were presented to Ishtar while the king poured libations over the heads of the dead victims.

Nahum's use of lion imagery draws upon the many levels of meaning that the lion held in Assyrian ideology. Assyria had torn apart its victims as a lion tears its prey, but now Assyria itself would be torn to pieces (vv. 11–12) and the stunning wealth of the city looted (v. 9). Using powerful wording, Nahum characterizes the city as desolate, plundered, and devastated (v. 10). In the Hebrew, three words with alliterative similarity (the first two from the same root) express the idea that emptiness signals absolute desolation: *buqah* ("emptiness," "pillaged"), *mebuqah* ("void," "plundered"), and *mebullaqah* ("devastation").

3:1–19
The Sin and Destruction of Nineveh

A declaration of a curse and lament (Heb. *hui*, "woe") for the city of bloodshed (3:1) succinctly introduces the final focus of this oracle. The single word "woe" contains within it the horrors facing Assyria, while the designation of Nineveh as the city of bloodshed provides the justification for the meting out of those woes.

3:1–4. Woe against Nineveh. Three charges brought against the city justify its ruin: bloody violence (v. 1), deceitful harlotry (v. 4; cf. the Assyrians lying to Hezekiah's men; 2 Kin. 18:31–32), and lion-like plundering of the nations (Nah. 2:11–12; cf. Is. 10:13). The consequences match the crimes: Nineveh would meet a violent end. Just as Assyrian kings had boasted of erecting pyramids with the heads of their enemies, so countless corpses would fill the streets. The city would be exposed and shamed, as befits a lying prostitute (cf. Jerusalem in Jer. 13:22, 26 and Babylon in Is. 47:1–3), and that which the Assyrians had stolen would be stolen from them.

3:5–17. Taunts against Nineveh. God declared that He was against Nineveh (3:5), an idea that first occurs in 2:13, conveying the Lord's determination to destroy the city. Passersby would indeed confirm that Nineveh lay in ruins (3:7), just as the many enemy cities Assyria had destroyed. In vv. 8–10, the mention of the fall of No Amon (lit. "city of [the god] Amun"; see also Jer. 46:25; Ezek. 30:14–16) reflects Ashurbanipal's conquest of the Egyptian city in 663 B.C. Known to the Greeks as Thebes, this city housed the great Karnak temple of Amun. Their alliance with Egypt, Put (probably Libya or possibly Somalia), and Lubim (another poetic name for Libyans) would have made Thebes appear indomitable before it fell. What the Assyrians did to Thebes would now be done to Nineveh. Just as Ashurbanipal "put a dog chain on [the captured leader] and made him occupy a kennel at the eastern gate of Nineveh," so Nineveh's great men would be bound with chains. Nahum calls Nineveh's strongest men *'ishah* (lit. "women"; Nah. 3:13). This cultural insult of the time refers to their physical weakness. Isaiah uses it in reference to the Egyptians (Is. 19:16). Nahum prophesied that fire would devour the bars of Nineveh's gates, and in fact, the Halzi Gate burned in the 612 B.C. battle. Archaeologists have since uncovered the charred remains.

3:18–19. Destruction of Hopeless Nineveh. Tragically, Judah, like Nineveh, refused God's salvation. As punishment, the Babylonians also conquered them and took them into exile. Other descriptions of Judah during the Babylonian attack of 587 B.C. employ imagery very similar to that of Nineveh's final days: calamities against children (Is. 51:20; Lam. 2:19; 4:1–2), leaders as bad shepherds (Jer. 23:1–2; Ezek. 34:2–10), and passersby clapping their hands (Lam. 2:15). The book of Jonah concludes with God asking, rhetorically, whether He should have pity/concern for Nineveh (Jon. 4:11). In contrast, Nahum ends by asking whether anyone had not suffered Nineveh's relentless cruelty (Nah. 3:19). God had reached out His divine hand to save Nineveh, but they ultimately refused His salvation. The resulting loss forever serves as a lesson in the pages of human history. It also brings hope that in the experience of Nineveh, we can anticipate the ultimate collapse of the wicked.

HABAKKUK

INTRODUCTION

Title and Authorship. The book of Habakkuk is the eighth book among the Minor Prophets. Named after the prophet, its Hebrew title (*khabuqquq*) is probably derived from the root *khabak* ("to embrace"), which may serve as a key to deciphering the principal message of the book. But Habakkuk had already been expecting God to embrace humans with His love, compassion, and grace. Rather, the prophet himself, as well as all humanity, needed to wholeheartedly embrace God and His word by faith. The Greek Septuagint translation used the name *ambakoum*, possibly derived from the Akkadian word *hambaququ*, a type of exotic flower. The Latin Vulgate adopted this name (*habacuc*), which became the title of most translations.

While the book of Habakkuk does not mention its author, one can assume the prophet himself presumably wrote it since the Lord specifically commanded him to write out the vision plainly (2:2). The book gives no information about Habakkuk's family, occupation, or leadership position in his country of Judah. This is not uncommon because the prophets wrote about God, not themselves. However, Habakkuk states twice that he is a prophet (1:1; 3:1). Among the other prophetic books, only Haggai and Zechariah make this claim in the superscription (Hag. 1:1; Zech. 1:1).

Outside of his own book, nothing from historically reliable sources is known about Habakkuk. The apocryphal book *Bel and the Dragon* mentions a legend according to which he was miraculously transported to Babylon to feed Daniel in the lion's den. Jewish traditions claim that he was the son of the woman who hosted the Prophet Elisha. This is rather fanciful since Elisha ministered in the ninth century B.C., whereas Habakkuk lived in the late seventh century.

Backgrounds. Although the book does not mention a date, the internal data reveals the historical background. The Northern Kingdom of Israel came to an end when the Assyrians destroyed Samaria in 722 B.C. Nabopolassar (624–605 B.C.) established the Neo-Babylonian Empire, which Nebuchadnezzar (605–562 B.C.) then expanded and fortified. Nineveh, the ancient capital and stronghold of the Assyrian Empire, fell to the Babylonians in 612 B.C. From Judah's perspective, this event happened far to the north. However, when Pharaoh Necho tried to assist the Assyrians in May/June 605 B.C., Nebuchadnezzar, the Babylonian crown prince, defeated him at the battle of Carchemish (2 Chr. 35:20; Jer. 46:2). This unexpected victory removed the whole Syro-Palestinian territory from the strong influence of Assyria and Egypt and opened it up to Babylonian control. Nebuchadnezzar pursued the Egyptian army southward while simultaneously besieging Jerusalem in the late summer of 605 B.C. (Dan. 1:1–2).

Date. The book's prediction of the imminent Babylonian attack on Judah (Hab. 1:6) narrows down the timeframe of the writing of Habakkuk. At the time of this prophecy, Babylon had not yet threatened Judah, but they would soon unexpectedly come. Habakkuk does not write about or allude to the fall or destruction of Jerusalem; he was still waiting for God's judgment upon Judah (2:2–3; 3:16).

Considering the book's internal evidence, Habakkuk probably wrote it during the short period of time after Assyria and Egypt had lost their domination of the land to Nebuchadnezzar but before Babylon's power had grown enough to threaten Jerusalem. This would place Habakkuk after the fall of Nineveh in 612 B.C. but before the battle of Carchemish in 605 B.C. The corrupted state of God's people likely places the book after 609 B.C., when Pharaoh Necho defeated and killed Josiah, the last godly king of Judah, at Megiddo (2 Kin. 23:29; 2 Chr. 35:20–24).

After Josiah's death, it looked like Egyptian supremacy would dominate Judah's future. At that time, Judah lacked a positive figure on the throne in Jerusalem to stop, prevent, or at least slow down the avalanche of evil and violence that spread unrestrained through society. The first part of the book reflects on this unjust and corrupt situation. The prophesied shocking surprise occurred in 605 B.C., when Nebuchadnezzar gained a decisive victory over Pharaoh Necho, making the Chaldeans the new dominant force in the Middle East (Hab. 1:5).

Theology and Purpose. The book of Habakkuk, like the book of Job and Psalm 73, is a theodicy, a response to the question of God's silence in the midst of evil. The prophet expresses frustration with God's way of handling injustice and approaches Him with serious complaints regarding His character, government, judgments, and care for His people. Habakkuk does not understand why God seems to overlook the sins of His people by not doing anything to stop the flood of wickedness. The prophet's questions bring out the main theme of the book: embrace God's word by faith and wait patiently for the fulfillment of His promises because He is reliable.

1. *Opening Up to God.* Habakkuk differs from other prophetic books in that it contains a dialogue between the prophet and God. In the book, God does not so much speak *through* His prophet as *with* His prophet, addressing Habakkuk's questions. This conversation is open and honest but also tough and disturbing. Habakkuk asks hard questions because evil and rebellious people prevail. When calamity strikes, God seems far away. Why does God not intervene and do something against wickedness? Why does He not respond? Why does the holy and just God not punish the guilty when things go wrong? Is God really in control of history? No wonder one of the key themes of Habakkuk is God's justice. The book challenges His character and holiness because, despite the incompatibility between good and evil, God seems to tolerate evil (Hab. 1:3, 12–13).

Dialoguing with the Lord allows Him to provide answers to difficult questions, react to disappointments, heal emotions, and save. God welcomes open, sincere, and honest dialogue. He delights in His children as they pour out their hearts to Him expressing honest thoughts, feelings, and expectations. He reacts to problems, frustrations, and troubles by giving hope and renewed strength. The book of Psalms also contains many sincere and honest prayers full of frustration and emotion.

2. *Patiently Waiting and Hoping in the Lord.* Even after lamenting in his frustration, Habakkuk is still dissatisfied and disheartened. He needs to learn to look up to God and constantly trust His word as the source of power and courage. Strength does not come simply through crying out to God but through trusting His word. The book underlines the importance of God's promises and previous mighty acts as revealed in Scripture. The fulfillment of His promises instills hope and trust in the human heart. The Lord's past mighty acts prove the reliability of His word even in times of crisis. The prophet as well as the people needed to wait patiently, trusting God's word. Meaningful and true answers to real-life problems do not come suddenly; they come at the end. Although God's way often seems paradoxical, waiting for Him is necessary (see 2:3).

Thus, Habakkuk provides a crucial example of what it means to live by steadfast trust (2:4): trusting God's word and waiting unwearyingly on the Lord in times of crisis or prosperity. The prophet's point is clear—God's word alone provides security. Trusting in Him means believing in His word, relying on it, and living according to it. This trust brings inner peace and joy even in times of national and personal adversity. The deep undertone of the book encourages believers to cultivate God's presence in their lives through a personal relationship with Him. Trusting His word opens our eyes to see Him even though He is not visible to our naked eyes.

3. *The Wicked and the Righteous.* The book contrasts the righteous with the wicked. The key phrase that the righteous live by steadfast trust (2:4) means that the believer needs to embrace the word of God by faith and wait patiently on the fulfillment of His promises. Such promises not only reorient us but also address life's problems and empower us to go forward in hope. On the other hand, the wicked, typified by the Babylonians, have no future because they are proud, self-centered, violent, and arrogant. Habakkuk describes five woes that result in disaster for the wicked (2:6–19).

The book attests to the importance of prayer. The righteous pray. The prophet directly addresses God and recalls His past mighty acts. He wishes that God would renew them in his day (3:2). The last chapter forms a prayer or hymn culminating with a doxology where the prophet expresses His full trust and joy in the Lord (3:17–19).

4. *The Righteous God Overcomes Evil.* Habakkuk uses several different names and titles for God, including Lord, Sovereign God, and Savior. Even when God's power and presence

are invisible, He provides joy and strength, enables a victorious walk, and empowers His people to go through life singing. Thus, in the midst of life's troubles, the prophet underlines the true source of happiness and joy as the Lord who strengthens and saves (3:18-19).

The book attests that God will inevitably judge humanity and hold them accountable because He created them. Habakkuk understood that God would judge Judah and the nations for their wickedness and rebellion. But he could not comprehend how God could use the Babylonians as His agents of judgment. They were more wicked than the inhabitants of Judah! Hence he questioned whether the punishment fit the crime (1:12-13). God assured him that although He may delay His judgments, they would certainly come at the appropriate time (2:3; 3:16). This called for patience. The prophet needed to wait for the fulfillment of God's word, to learn to live with his questions while relying on the divine promises.

The prophet concludes his book by saying that he would wait patiently with the Lord as his strength (3:16, 19). In the midst of calamities, violence, disorder, evil, unanswered questions, and disappointments, believers must look up, embrace the Lord by faith, and stand firm on His promises because He is a righteous God. This trust in the Lord gives hope, courage, joy, and a renewed motivation to press on.

Literary Features. The book of Habakkuk is unique when compared to other prophetic material. Habakkuk does not simply prophesy but rather poses pertinent questions to God regarding Judah's current disturbing situation and other issues impacting himself. The dialogue between the prophet and God is an exceptional literary feature. The different discourses contain rhetorical features that require close attention in order to discover the meaning of the overall message. The book has a very straightforward literary structure divided into two main sections: Habakkuk's dialogue with the Lord (1:2—2:20) and his prayer with a concluding hymn (3:1-19). Both these sections contain several subsections.

COMMENTARY

1:1—3:19
THE LORD IS MY STRENGTH: WHEN EVIL REIGNS AND FAITH NEEDS TO WAIT

In spite of his serious questions, frustrations, and disappointments with how God treats evil

and judges the guilty, Habakkuk ultimately recalled God's past mighty acts, enabling him to trust God's promises and joyfully wait for the fulfillment of His word. Habakkuk was a prophet of hope.

1:1—2:20
Dialogue with the Lord

After a brief introduction to the book (1:1), the prophet expresses his disappointment with the Lord (vv. 2-4), and God answers (vv. 5-11). Habakkuk then complains further (1:12—2:1), prompting God's final response (2:2-20). Because God had delayed His response to evil, Habakkuk questioned His reputation, His holiness, and ultimately His ability to rule and care for His people. At the end, the prophet saw the majesty of God in His temple and was reverently silent because He understood that God, in His timeline, would bring judgment on the wicked and punish the arrogant. The Babylonians would answer for their wicked behavior.

1:1. Introduction. The introduction identifies Habakkuk as God's spokesperson. It characterizes the revelation he received as a *massa'*. This Hebrew word can mean "burden" as well as "oracle" or "prophetic utterance." The first nuance would suggest that carrying the divine message was a heavy burden. Habakkuk had a difficult role because, although he had received God's word, it required him and his listeners to wait for its fulfillment. The message he received (lit. "saw" in a vision), gave him special historical insights that helped him gain a better perspective on life. As a prophet, he spoke on behalf of God, reminding the people of God's faithfulness, care, judgments, and sovereignty.

1:2-4. The Prophet's Disappointment with the Lord. The book opens not with the expected revelation from God but with the prophet's lamenting and complaining. A tough dialogue between the prophet and the Lord ensues. In frustration, Habakkuk confronted God with forceful, pointed, and dramatic questions: Why are You silent? Why do You not intervene? Why does evil among Your people continue unpunished? How long will You not listen and save? The phrase "how long" occurs sixty-five times in the Bible (see Pss. 6:3; 13:1-2; 74:10; Rev. 6:10) and usually invites divine intervention in undesirable situations. Six keywords describe the condition of Israelite society—injustice, wrong, destruction, violence, strife, and conflict—and Habakkuk passionately detested this situation. The law was powerless/ paralyzed, meaning that God's teaching was ineffective, not respected or honored. For the first time the prophet mentions two opposite groups of people: the righteous and the wicked.

Habakkuk's questions show his bitterness and deep disappointment. He could not understand why God did not answer his prayers and intervene to punish evil. But he did right by bringing all these frustrations and negative emotions to the Lord. He invoked Him as "LORD" (Yahweh), which designated Him as a close, personal God, the God of His people, the God of the covenant.

1:5—11. God's Answer: The Babylonians will Punish Judah. God assured the prophet that He was about to do a strange and unbelievable work. He would use the Chaldeans (Babylonians) as His instrument to punish Judah. Three events fulfilled this shocking prediction: (1) In 605 B.C., the Babylonians besieged Jerusalem and took Daniel and other young nobles into captivity (Dan. 1:1–5). (2) In 597 B.C., the Babylonians deported King Jehoiachin along with ten thousand others, including Ezekiel (2 Kin. 24:10–16; Ezek. 1:1–3). (3) In 586 B.C., Judah lost its autonomy, and the Babylonians destroyed Jerusalem and the temple (2 Kin. 25:1–12). Habakkuk never mentions the fall or destruction of Jerusalem, suggesting that he wrote the book before the invasion. The Lord characterizes the Babylonians as behaving like animals, ruthless, violent, selfish, and proud. But in the end, they would also experience divine judgment according to the law of retribution. This happened in October 539 B.C., when Cyrus, the Medo-Persian king, conquered them (see Dan. 5:28–30; 6:28; Is. 45:1–4).

1:12—2:1. The Prophet's Complaint. Habakkuk struggled with the Lord's answer and became even more frustrated, leading him to question God's character. If the Lord is holy, how can He tolerate evil and wickedness? Furthermore, how can He use a more wicked people (Babylon) to punish a less wicked people (Judah)? The Babylonians played with human lives like fishermen with fish (1:14). The metaphor of catching enemies in nets symbolizes power, defeat, and judgment. The book mentions violence five times (1:2–3, 9; 2:8, 17). In the book of Genesis, the same word describes the condition of society in Noah's time (Gen. 6:11). Why is God silent when injustice prevails even among His people? The book of Psalms contains similar expressions of frustration with God's apparent silence in the face of evil (see Pss. 83:1; 109:1). But Habakkuk insisted on hearing the Lord's response (Hab. 2:1). By His powerful word, God created the world, and as the incarnated Word, He redeemed the world. When He speaks, tangible things occur because of His creative power (Ps. 33:9).

2:2–19. God's Answer: The Punishment of the Babylonians. The Lord responded that Habakkuk would have to wait patiently for Him to act. The implementation of God's revelation would take time (2:2–3; see Ezek. 18:32; 2 Pet. 3:9). At the core of the book, Habakkuk 2:4–5 contrasts the wicked with the righteous. The Lord describes the wicked as prideful, deceptive, arrogant, selfish, greedy, violent, and shallow. The wicked, modeled by the Babylonians, live without God, controlled by their own decisions and evil passions. The righteous, on the other hand, live by personal steadfast trust, not by visions, dreams, proofs, or miracles. They live by embracing God and trusting His word, patiently waiting for its fulfillment. They find their strength in His promises because His word is trustworthy. Paul says that the believer lives by faith rather than by sight (2 Cor. 5:7). A passage in the Talmud suggests that Habakkuk narrows all the commandments of the Torah down to one command: Israel must live by its faith in God.

Scholars debate both the meaning of the Hebrew word *'emunah* ("faith," "faithfulness," "trust") and the antecedent of the pronoun "his." The word *'emunah* does not mean "faith" in the sense of "belief" so much as "steadfast trust" in the sense of one's commitment to God. In Habakkuk, it means recognizing God as the only One who can preserve life and holding on to Him in the midst of uncertainty. The Septuagint, the Greek translation of the OT, reads "my faithfulness" (i.e., God's faithfulness), suggesting that it is God's faithfulness to His promises that preserves the lives of His people. The Hebrew plausibly refers to God's faithfulness. However, the contrast with the wicked (Hab. 2:4a), described as proudly relying on their own strength for survival, shows that the pronoun refers to those who rely on the Lord. In 1:12–17 the prophet contrasts the wicked with the righteous, represented by Babylon and Judah, respectively. Since 2:4 is part of God's response to the prophet's question, the righteous one who lives by faith may refer to Judah as a nation and the proud one may refer to Babylon (vv. 4–5). But the existence of both the wicked and the righteous within Judah (1:1–4) implies that in the coming disaster only those totally committed to the Lord would survive.

God promises life to the righteous but pronounces five woes against the wicked (2:6–19). The first woe condemns greediness, plundering, dishonesty, and violence (vv. 6–8) and describes the wicked as proud, selfish, violent, greedy, lacking self-control, and idolatrous. The second condemns exploitation, covetousness, and pride (vv. 9–11). The third condemns injustice and crime (v. 12).

In the middle of this list of woes God proclaims His lordship and His intention to reveal Himself and fill the earth with His glory (vv. 13–14; cf. Num. 14:21; Ps. 72:19; Is. 6:3; 11:9). Humanity will acknowledge Him as the Lord, recognize the beauty of His character, and understand His presence in human affairs. This positive message affirms God's control even though His presence may not be recognized.

After this brief interlude, the list of woes continues. The fourth woe condemns intemperance and the resulting immorality and lack of self-control (Hab. 2:15–17). And the final one condemns the constant problem of idolatry (vv. 18–19). Instead of recognizing God's benevolence in their prosperity and success, the Babylonians attributed their victories to their gods, represented by idols (cf. 1:11). This section concludes with an important theological statement affirming the Lord's presence in His temple and commanding all to remain silent. Though people on earth could not yet perceive God's holy, dazzling, and awesome presence (see Gen. 28:16–17; Is. 6:1–9), the faithful could find rest and peace in the middle of real threats because the Judge of all the earth had taken His seat and would soon pronounce judgment against the wicked.

3:1–19
The Prophet's Prayer: Talking Confidently to God

This section includes a brief introduction (3:1), a discussion of God's awesome deeds (vv. 2–15), a hymn (vv. 16–19a), and an epilogue (v. 19b). The book begins with questions but ends with a magnificent affirmation. The prophet, silent since the beginning of chapter 2, eloquently expresses his full confidence in God in a powerful prayer. After perceiving God's awesome presence, he contemplated God's past mighty acts. He stood in wonder before the Lord's miraculous interventions in the history of His people. Relying on these accounts, the prophet asked God to again intervene according to His timing. Then people would stand in astonishment before the Sovereign God, who deals with evil and saves the

---

Habakkuk 2:4 and the New Testament

Three NT epistles mention the phrase in Habakkuk 2:4 about the righteous living by faith.

1. In Romans. For the apostle Paul, this central thought demonstrated that God's righteousness comes by His grace through faith in Christ Jesus (see Rom. 1:16–17). According to his reading, the text does not simply refer to the believers' faithfulness to God but to the saving faith in Christ that makes faithfulness possible. Paul considered this key prophetic text on justification by faith as complementing texts from the Torah (Gen. 15:6) and the Writings (Ps. 32:1–2). These connections between the Pentateuch and the Prophets strongly attest to the continuity between the teaching regarding redemption in both the OT and the NT. There has always been only one way of salvation—by God's grace through faith in Him.

2. In Galatians. In Galatians, Paul underlines the fact that the law cannot save anyone, otherwise Christ would have died in vain. The law, however, continues to be an important guide for the believer (Gal. 5:6, 13–14). When Paul speaks about the misuse of the law and explains that Christ redeemed us from the curse of the law, he shows that the law cannot justify. In God's sight, the righteous live by faith (Gal. 3:11). God justifies those who place their trust/faith in Christ.

3. In Hebrews. Hebrews 10:36–38a references Habakkuk to show that only by faith can a believer confidently and victoriously persevere through trials, conflicts, and the crises of life. While Paul uses Habakkuk 2:4 to underscore justification based on a saving faith in Christ, the book of Hebrews uses the passage to encourage maintaining faith in God to endure the hardships of life. The apostles explained to the church the different theological elements all packaged in Habakkuk 2:4.

righteous. Interestingly, the Lord does not speak at all in chapter 3. The entire chapter contains Habakkuk's expression of full trust in the Lord in response to His revelation. He would look up in hope and find power and joy in the Lord.

3:1. Introduction. Recalling how God had fulfilled His promises in the past encouraged the prophet to face tomorrow and strengthened him to live in the midst of calamity. God's faithfulness to His covenant forms the background of this prayer. Two Hebrew musical terms (not always translated into English) attest to the poem's status as a psalm sung as part of the temple liturgy: *shigyonot* may designate changes in the mood and rhythm (3:1), and *selah* may indicate a change in melody (vv. 3, 9, 13). In addition, v. 19 contains a specific notation for the music leader.

3:2–19a. God's Past Awesome Deeds. In this passage, Habakkuk portrays God as a divine Warrior (cf. Ex. 15:3; Deut. 1:30; Zeph. 3:17). Using the Exodus from Egypt as background (Hab. 3:2–10), Habakkuk pleads with God to show His mighty deeds in his time (lit. "in the midst of the years"). This is the only place in which this phrase appears in the OT connected with time. The prophet wishes for God to act, to intervene, and to again reveal His mighty actions and His mercy. God does not require blind trust but trust built on His past mighty acts. Because He saved His people in the past, we can have confidence for the future.

The reference to Teman in v. 3 points to Edom in the south (Is. 43:6), and Mount Paran represents Sinai (Deut. 33:2). With poetic language and colorful imagery, the prophet recalls Israel's liberation from Egyptian slavery. God opened the Red Sea (Ex. 13:17—14:31) and led His people on dry ground across the Jordan River (Josh. 3:3–17; 4:21–24). Later, He stopped the sun during Joshua's victory at Gibeon (Josh. 10:12–14; cf. 2 Kin. 20:9–11; Is. 38:8) and gifted the promised land to His people (Hab. 3:11–12).

Habakkuk 3:13–15 recalls God's triumphant victory over the powers of evil. Habakkuk remembers some of the greatest events in the history of God's people: the Exodus, the covenant at Sinai, and the conquest of Canaan. God accomplished all these splendid and magnificent deeds. As He led Israel during that time, so will He lead His faithful ones to the final day of victory, when they will rejoice in His salvation. This eschatological perspective anticipates its ultimate realization at the Second Coming of Jesus Christ.

The Anointed One of v. 13 is the Messiah, the Representative of Israel. Because God remembered His covenant promise to send the Seed (Gen. 3:15) and to protect and preserve the ancestral line of the coming Messiah, He would intervene and save His people. When the fullness of time came, God sent His Son, Jesus Christ, the Savior of the world (John 1:12; Gal. 4:4).

In the end, Habakkuk did not respond to disaster in fear and trembling but in triumphant faith (Hab. 3:16–19a). His powerful concluding confession of faith provides a model for trusting the Lord. His total dedication is exemplary. Habakkuk went from theological crisis (chap. 1) to triumphal faith because God taught him the difference between the wicked and the righteous. Like Thomas in the NT, he grew from doubts to a full trust in the Lord. In this way, he encourages his readers to be faithful to the Lord, which gives the book a pastoral aspect. When the prophet finally looked fully to God, his joy burst forth in a prayer of trust in the Lord (3:18–19). God's past mighty acts bring peace, assurance, and new hope for the future by building trust in God and in His word.

This culminating passage presents one of the best OT confessions of trust in the Lord. These verses express full confidence in God's goodness and care in spite of disappointments, difficulties, and the tragedies of life. Despite everything going wrong, the prophet vows to stay with the Lord, not only clinging to His word but actually rejoicing in the Lord. Why could he rejoice? Because the Lord was His strength! In the past, God had proven the sufficiency of His promises by fulfilling His word, and this satisfied Habakkuk. He could go forward in full confidence knowing that God is still on His throne.

3:19b. Epilogue—Sing It! The book ends with a seemingly strange note dedicated to a musician, giving instructions to play it on "my stringed instruments" (v. 19). Habakkuk designed the whole book, or at least the prayer of chapter 3, for singing purposes in public worship (see also v. 1). The message of the book of Habakkuk needs to be part of our personal experience. Trust and joyfulness in the Lord should be our song. The cantillation of the text serves to strengthen our confidence in the Lord as a collective expression of faith, trust, and joy in Him. Singing expresses thankfulness, reminds us of God's promises, ties us together, and brings victory (see Ex. 15:1–21; Deut. 31:19, 30; 32:1–47; 2 Chr. 20:22; Rev. 15:3). Despite incomprehensible struggles, Habakkuk anticipates God's ultimate triumph.

ZEPHANIAH

INTRODUCTION

Title and Authorship. The book of Zephaniah is the ninth of the Minor Prophets and bears the name of its author. However, scholars debate the meaning of the name. The majority hold that it means *"yah[weh]* has hidden/protected," from the root *tsapan* ("to hide," "to conceal") and the shortened form of the divine name, *yahweh* (i.e., *yah*). Others suggest that it means "watchman of *yah[weh]*," from the root *tsapah* ("to watch") and *yah*. The book identifies the Prophet Zephaniah as the great-great-grandson of Hezekiah (1:1). Although not explicitly stated, the unusual length of this genealogical note seems to imply a reference to the famous King Hezekiah of Judah. No other superscription in a prophetic book traces the prophet's ancestry as far back as four generations.

Date. Zephaniah prophesied during the reign of Josiah (1:1), the son of Amon and grandson of the notorious Manasseh. Josiah ruled the kingdom of Judah from 641 to 609 B.C., so the prophet must have ministered within this timespan. More specifically, Zephaniah predicted the destruction of Nineveh (2:13–15), which occurred in 612 B.C. The repeated mention of Judah's wickedness (cf. 1:4–6, 8–12; 3:1–3, 7) probably points to the time before Josiah's reform, which picked up steam with the discovery of "the book of the law" in 622 B.C. These observations place Zephaniah's ministry in the first half of Josiah's reign, perhaps around 630–625 B.C. Yahweh likely raised him up as a prophet to further the spiritual revival during the reign of Judah's last godly king.

Backgrounds. The fall of Samaria in 722 B.C., an event that brought about the end of the Northern Kingdom of Israel, should have warned the leaders of the Southern Kingdom of Judah about the possibility of divine judgment. But wickedness and apostasy characterized the reigns of Manasseh (697–643 B.C.) and Amon (643–641 B.C.). When Josiah (641–609 B.C.) ascended the throne, the people of Judah participated in many kinds of foreign cults and worshiped various astral deities and Canaanite gods (1:4–5; cf. 2 Kin. 23:4–25). These spiritual and moral lows threatened the kingdom's very existence. Judean society was on the brink of collapse. At this critical moment for the nation, God called Zephaniah to warn the people of impending judgment.

Zephaniah's ministry overlapped with the early part of Jeremiah's ministry. Around this time, the tumultuous international scene saw Assyrian power declining, while Babylon grew in might under Nabopolassar. Babylon would soon pose a serious danger to its neighboring countries, including Judah. Egypt also periodically threatened Judah. God called Zephaniah to his prophetic ministry during a time of serious political and moral decline in Judah.

Theology and Purpose. The book of Zephaniah affirms the need for God's people to remain faithful to the covenant relationship. The prophet highlights the impending Day of the Lord, when Yahweh would judge Judah for their continued apostasy and idolatry. But He would also preserve a faithful remnant to fulfill His mission to the nations. The Day of the Lord would bring both justice and mercy.

1. The Day of the Lord. Zephaniah's message revolves around the coming of the Day of the Lord, when God would judge the whole world and vindicate a faithful remnant. Through His prophet, God describes the Day of the Lord as an imminent day of war (Zeph. 1:7, 14), a dark, cloudy day of gloom, desolation, and ruin (1:15–16). He does not take pleasure in proclaiming judgment and destruction, but He offers a warning to call His people to seek Him and to save them from destruction (3:17–20). For the wicked, the Day of the Lord would bring judgment and divine punishment (1:7—3:8); for the righteous, salvation and hope (3:9–20). It would have both a historical fulfillment (2:4–15) and an eschatological one (3:8–13), affecting both God's covenant people (1:4–13) and the nations (2:4–15). The NT refers to the same epochal event using a variety of phrases, including "the day of judgment" (Matt. 10:15; 11:22, 24; 12:36; cf. 2 Pet. 3:7), "the last day" (John 6:39–40, 44, 54; 11:24; 12:48), "the day of the Lord" (Acts 2:20; 1 Cor. 5:5; 2 Cor. 1:14; 1 Thess. 5:2; 2 Thess. 2:2; 2 Pet. 3:10), "the day of Christ (Jesus)" (Phil. 1:6, 10; 2:16), "the day of God" (2 Pet. 3:12), "the great day" (Jude 6; cf. Rev. 6:14, 17), and "the blessed hope" (Titus 2:13). All these refer to the day of Christ's Second Coming. Believers should look forward to this event and prepare the world as well as themselves for that day.

2. *Justice and Mercy.* Zephaniah describes Yahweh as a God of justice and judgment as well as love and mercy. In fact, God's wrath springs from offended love, resulting in a mixture of judgment and mercy. He promises to slaughter the wicked in His anger (Zeph. 1:2–18) but also to intervene for His people, restoring and exalting the remnant of Judah and Israel, the meek and humble who trust in His name (2:7, 9; 3:12). He would reign over them as the King of Israel, and His people would no longer fear (LXX, "see") evil (3:15).

Literary Features. Zephaniah delivers a direct and forthright message using rich and concise language that manifests powerful rhetorical skills. He vividly portrays the destructive character of the Day of the Lord through imagery of war and devastation (1:2–3, 15). The book contains three main sections: the judgment upon Judah (1:1–18), the judgment upon the nations (2:1–15), and the destruction of Judah and preservation of the faithful remnant (3:1–20).

COMMENTARY

1:1–18
JUDGMENT UPON JUDAH

Chapter 1 focuses on God's judgment of Judah. The description of the Day of the Lord reveals that continued apostasy and idolatry had made Judah's destruction inevitable (see "God's Judgment in the Prophets," p. 981).

1:1
Superscription

Verse 1:1 introduces the author and the timeframe of his message. The book begins, as some other prophetic books do, by stating that the word of the Lord came to the prophet (see Hos. 1:1; Joel 1:1; Jon. 1:1; Mic. 1:1). If the name Zephaniah means "Yahweh has hidden/protected," it is a fitting name for a prophet conveying an urgent but unwelcome message to a wicked people. Zephaniah was probably of royal descent, giving him access to Josiah, the king of Judah, during whose reign he ministered. Being a godly king, Josiah might have listened to Zephaniah and other contemporary prophets, who would have encouraged the reforms the king undertook.

1:2–6
Destruction Declared

Yahweh first directed His judgment against all living things (Zeph. 1:2–3) and then focused on His people, Judah (vv. 4–6). Verses 2–3 proclaim the Lord's devastating judgment. Because of the intensity of His wrath and indignation against all kinds of evil, God would destroy everything, including humanity, animals, birds, and fish, in a divine act of uncreation (v. 3; cf. Gen. 1). Human sin had caused all nature to groan and suffer (cf. Rom. 8:21–22).

While Zephaniah 1:2–3 portrays Yahweh's judgment as universal, vv. 4–6 focus on the judgment of Judah and its inhabitants. Judgment would begin with Judah and Jerusalem. They deserved punishment more than others because they had committed deliberate apostasy against their Lord. Their main sin—idolatry—included the worship of Baal and the stars of heaven, gods worshiped by the Canaanites and Assyrians (cf. Deut. 4:19). Led by idolatrous priests (Zeph. 1:4), they professed loyalty to God verbally but in practice swore by Milcom/Molek (Heb. *malkam*)—an Ammonite deity for whom Solomon had built a high place to please his foreign wives (1 Kin. 11:5–7).

The Lord mentions three groups of people: those who worship the host of heaven, those who swear oaths by both Yahweh and Milcom/Molek, and those who turn/have turned back from the Lord and from seeking Him. In those days, as today, it was fashionable to profess and practice syncretism (i.e., combining the worship of Yahweh with that of other gods or powers). But the worship of the true God is incompatible with the worship of other gods.

1:7-18
The Day of the Lord

This section contains two subsections that start with the imminence of the Day of the Lord. 1:7-13 describes the judgment of Judah on the Day of the Lord, and vv. 14-18 further describe the Day of the Lord in universal terms.

1:7-13. The Destruction of Judah on the Day of the Lord. Zephaniah portrays the Day of the Lord as a sacrifice prepared by Yahweh Himself. The sacrifice in 1:7 represents the destruction of the guilty nation of Judah, and the invited and consecrated guests represent the foreign nations the Lord would use as instruments of punishment (cf. Is. 13:3). The Hebrew word *qadash* ("holy," "consecrated") here seems to mean "set apart for a special purpose." Thus some translations render the word as "invited." In the context of Zephaniah, this refers to the Babylonians (cf. Hab. 1:6). The Lord would punish Judah's princes/leaders/officials as well as the king's children—the members of the royal family. They had all transgressed the law and deserved punishment. Their foreign apparel reflects their adoption of heathen values and customs, including idolatrous worship (cf. Is. 3:16-24). They would leap over the threshold, possibly pointing to the heathen practice of not stepping on the threshold when entering a temple (Zeph. 1:9; cf. 1 Sam. 5:4-5). The second part of Zephaniah 1:9 also suggests a possible reference to servants who ignored boundaries when carrying out commands to enrich their wicked masters. The Fish Gate (located on the north side), the Second/New Quarter (where the rich lived, northwest of the temple), Maktesh/Mortar (probably a market district), and the hills (including Ophel, Zion, and Moriah) were all sections or places within Jerusalem. As the capital of Judah, Jerusalem represented the whole nation (vv. 10-12). Yahweh's inevitable judgment would begin with His people, Judah, because of their deliberate apostasy. They violated the Lord's explicit commands by repeatedly worshiping the idols of surrounding nations.

1:14-18. Further Description of the Day of the Lord. Verses 1:14-18 contain the most detailed description of the Day of the Lord of any passage in Scripture. Although vv. 7-13 make Judah the immediate object of destruction, the lack of any specific reference to Judah in 1:14—2:3 and the proclamation of judgment against foreign nations in 2:4-15 seem to allow for a universal application of the Day of the Lord. Indeed, the final Day of the Lord would bring judgment not only to Judah and the surrounding nations but to the entire world. The word "day" occurs seven times in 1:15-16, reflecting the seven days of Creation (Gen. 1-2). As God created this world in seven days, He uses seven "days" to proclaim its destruction.

The prophet uses five pairs of words to describe the Day of the Lord. The first pair describes the distressing emotional pain that the day would bring; the second, the devastating physical destruction of the earth; the third, the terrible scene of darkness and gloom; the fourth, the feeling of utter helplessness before the black storm clouds; and the fifth, the sounds of battle trumpets warning of attacking enemies. On that day, people would try to save themselves with silver or gold (Zeph. 1:18), only to find them useless before the God of righteousness and justice. On this day of the Lord's wrath, He would pour out the blood of the wicked like dust and their intestines like excrement (v. 17).

Zephaniah emphasizes the imminence of the coming judgment (v. 14) as the NT emphasizes the imminence of the Second Coming of Christ (Rev. 22:12). On that day, the Lord would bring the bitterness of war against the impenitent, and His jealousy would burn like fire to devour the whole earth/land (Zeph. 1:14, 18). These "prophecies of impending judgment upon Judah apply with equal force to the judgments that are to fall upon an impenitent world at the time of the second advent of Christ" (PK 389).

2:1-15
JUDGMENT UPON THE NATIONS

Chapter 2 exhorts Judah to repent and declares judgment against five neighboring nations. The aftermath of the divine punishment would prove more disastrous for these nations than for Judah, from whom God would preserve a remnant (vv. 4-7).

2:1-3
Urgent Call to Seek Yahweh's Mercy

Because of their wickedness, Judah deserved destruction just like the heathen nations (cf. 2:4-15). However, Zephaniah offered them the hope of mercy if they repented. The meek/humble of the land refers to the righteous, and to "seek the LORD" means to seek righteousness and humility (v. 3). Zephaniah both urgently summons the wicked to repent of their ways and return to the Lord and encourages the righteous to continue to uphold His commands of justice. The threefold repetition of "before" in v. 2 emphasizes the urgency of the call to repent and seek the Lord. He might hide/shelter them from His anger on the day of judgment, but the Hebrew word *'ulai* ("it may be," "perhaps") points to the divine freedom to show mercy. Humans have no control (v. 3).

2:4–15
Geographical Oracles

Verses 2:4–15 contain oracles against the Philistines, Moabites, Ammonites, Ethiopians/Cushites, and Assyrians. The Philistines lived to the west of Israel (vv. 4–7), the Moabites and Ammonites to the east (vv. 8–11), the Ethiopians to the south (v. 12), and the Assyrians to the north (vv. 13–15). The Lord would punish them for their wickedness, including their hostility against Judah. As Creator, Yahweh rules over all nations and controls the whole world.

2:4–7. Philistia. The land of the Philistines consisted of five major cities, also called the Pentapolis: Gaza, Ashkelon, Ashdod, Ekron, and Gath (2:5; 1 Sam. 6:17). Here, as in Jeremiah 25:20, Gath is not mentioned, because it was destroyed earlier. The Cherethites/Kerethites, who originated from the island of Crete, inhabited the southern part of the Philistine seacoast (cf. 1 Sam. 30:14). God would desolate these cities and destroy the people living in them. Curiously, Zephaniah does not explain God's judgment against the Philistines. But God had already stated the reason through the Prophet Amos: the Philistines ruthlessly took people captive and sold them to Edom (Amos 1:6). Therefore, the remnant of Judah would pasture their flocks in the desolated land of the Philistines.

2:8–12. Moab, Ammon, and Ethiopia. Moab and Ammon appear together in the book of Zephaniah because of their common origin and geographical proximity. Their history dated back to the time of Abraham and Lot. Moab and Ben-Ammi (i.e., Ammon) were the sons of Lot by his two daughters after God saved them from the destruction of Sodom and Gomorrah (Gen. 19:36–38). The descendants of these brothers threatened the Israelites for many generations. About a century earlier, God had accused Ammon and Moab of cruelty (Amos 1:13; 2:1). He now condemned them for their reproaching

insults, pride, and arrogant threats against His people, Judah, and swore to destroy them like He did Sodom and Gomorrah (Zeph. 2:8–9). These nations emerged out of the destruction of those very cities but failed to treat Israel, their brother, with mercy. Once again, Yahweh would give their lands to the remnant of Judah. He would destroy all the gods of the earth, leading to the true worship of the sovereign God. Even those from distant shores would join the remnant in worshiping Him (v. 11).

The Hebrew *kushim* (lit. "Cushites"), though sometimes translated "Ethiopians," refers to the northeastern peoples of Africa in modern Sudan. God simply states that His sword would slay them too. He may have had a particular offense in mind, or He may have cited the most distant known nation to the south to show that His judgment would extend over the whole world.

2:13–15. Assyria. At the time of Zephaniah's ministry (ca. 630–625 B.C.), Assyria posed the greatest threat to Judah. Its capital city, Nineveh, was destroyed by the Medes and the Babylonians in 612 B.C., but it was still strong during the time of Zephaniah's ministry (ca. 630–625 B.C.). Nineveh consisted of an inner city surrounded by a wall eight miles (12.9 km) in circumference, plus an outer city, twelve hundred towers, and fourteen gates. Pronouncing the doom of this awesome and seemingly impregnable metropolis must have appeared a tall order and an enormous risk. But the Lord, using human instruments, would stretch out His hand and destroy Assyria (2:13). The desolation of the once proud city would leave it as dry as the wilderness. Passersby would hiss in ridicule and shake their fists in horror and amazement. Through Nahum, God accused Nineveh of idolatry, lies, robbery, harlotry, and sorcery (Nah. 1:14; 3:1–4). Zephaniah condemns this rejoicing, reveling city for pridefully considering itself greater than all others (Zeph. 2:15). In fulfillment of his prophecy, the Medes and the Babylonians destroyed Nineveh in 612 B.C. Indeed, pride goes before a fall.

3:1–20

JUDGMENT AND BLESSING

The final chapter begins with a reiteration of the judgment against Judah and the nations. It picks up the universal tone of 1:2–3 before concluding with promises of the restoration of the faithful into a glorious state of blessing.

The prophet condemns Jerusalem and its inhabitants for their flagrant sins and their persistent refusal to listen to the divine warnings. But God would not destroy His people completely. Yahweh, the jealous covenant-keeping God, would protect the faithful remnant and restore them to eternal joy and happiness.

3:1–7
Jerusalem Rebuked

Zephaniah proclaimed woe to Jerusalem because of obstinacy, impurity, and oppressiveness. In 3:2, the prophet summarizes their misdeeds with four negative sentences. Jerusalem refused to obey, accept correction, trust the Lord, or draw near to Him, all things God's chosen people should do. In vv. 3–4, God denounces the four leading social classes of that time: the princes/officials, the judges/rulers, the prophets, and the priests. He condemns them for their iniquity, injustice, impurity, idolatry, and violence to the law. The people of Judah and Jerusalem, both leaders and followers, knew no shame despite the Lord's unfailing faithfulness to His people (v. 5). Yahweh had punished them and other nations, which should have led them to fear Him and to accept His instructive correction. Yet their corruption persisted (v. 7). Judah had disregarded the righteous Lord among them and deserved destruction (v. 5).

3:8–13
Judgment upon All Nations and Restoration of the Remnant

In 3:8, Yahweh envisions the great day when He would arise in wrath and judgment in order to testify against all the inhabitants of the earth. The King and Judge of the world would gather the nations and assemble the kingdoms to punish them in His fierce anger. This universal judgment would devour all the earth, consuming it with the fire of His jealousy. The righteous, however, would join Isaiah in proclaiming that the Lord is Judge, Lawgiver, and King. He would save them (Is. 33:22).

In contrast to His roles as Judge and Lawgiver that are emphasized in Zephaniah 3:8, vv. 9–13 show Him as Savior and King. He would purify the lips/language of the peoples (cf. the cleansing of Isaiah's lips by one of the seraphim;

Is. 6:5–7). He would remove impure elements from Judah and the nations so that the faithful remnant might remain and call on the name of Yahweh, serving Him with one accord (Heb. *shekem 'ekhad*, "with one shoulder, shoulder to shoulder"; Zeph. 3:9). The meek, humble, and contrite remnant would seek to please Yahweh (v. 12). With no unrighteousness or lying among them, they would live in peace under Yahweh's care. No one would make them afraid (v. 13). What a blessed world after centuries of distress and disasters!

3:14–20
Redemption and Restoration

Zephaniah calls God's people to sing, shout, be glad, and rejoice because of Yahweh's past deeds (3:15a), His future deliverance (v. 17), and His very presence with them as their loving and gracious King (vv. 15–17). Verses 14–17 form a short, self-contained psalm with a chiastic structure. Israel rejoicing over Yahweh's deliverance at the beginning corresponds to Yahweh's joy over their return to Him at the end. Yahweh would keep His covenant of love and mercy by preserving the remnant of Judah, an assurance that certainly calls for rejoicing on the part of the faithful.

In vv. 18–20, Yahweh repeats His promise to redeem and restore His people from exile and give them renown and honor among the nations. The use of several active verbs, the emphatic interjection "behold" (Heb. *hinni*, from *hinneh*, omitted in some translations; v. 19), and the final affirmation that Yahweh Himself had spoken (v. 20) combine to emphasize this as a proclamation of Yahweh's desire to fulfill His covenant promises through Israel. Yahweh spoke as the sovereign God of punishment for the wicked but also as the covenant-keeping God of redemption for His people.

The book of Zephaniah vividly describes the Day of the Lord as a day of destruction for the wicked but also as a day of redemption, restoration, and rewards for those who trust and follow the Lord until the end (Ps. 18:20; Is. 40:10; 62:11; Acts 3:20–21; Eph. 4:30; Heb. 11:6; Rev. 11:18). This is "the blessed hope" of God's people of all ages (Titus 2:13; Rom. 10:12; 1 Cor. 12:13; Gal. 3:7–9, 28; Col. 3:11). This eschatological Day of the Lord will bring the cosmic conflict to an end.

HAGGAI

INTRODUCTION

Title and Authorship. The name Haggai is based on the Hebrew *khag* ("festival"). The ending *ai* could be an abbreviation for *yahweh* ("festival of the Lord") or a personal pronoun ("my festival"). The Prophet Haggai's name and ministry expressed hope and joy and aimed at energizing God's people to fulfill His plan for them. The book of Ezra mentions Haggai (Ezra 5:1; 6:14), and Zechariah alludes to his work (Zech. 8:9), but no information exists about his ancestry, occupation, or age. The text gives the impression that he was a dynamic, young preacher.

The book gives no indication whether Haggai had remained in Judah or returned from exile, but it twice claims he was a prophet of the Lord (Hag. 1:3; 2:1). More than two dozen times, this prophet of new beginnings used the messenger formula and variants of it to affirm his message as divine communication (see 1:13; cf. 1:2–3, 12; 2:1, 10). He themed his oracles around the Exodus and saturated them with covenantal language.

Date. Haggai was the first of the postexilic prophets who ministered in Judah. Like other prophets, he provided specific dates for his messages (see also Ezek. 8:1; Dan. 1:1; 2:1; Zech. 1:7; Ezra 1:1; Neh. 1:1; 2:1). His prophetic activity spanned a period of a little more than three months, but the effects transcend millennia. He proclaimed his first message at the celebration of the new moon on August 29, 520 B.C. (Hag. 1:1) and his last oracle a couple of months later, on December 18, 520 B.C. (2:10, 20).

Backgrounds. During the early Persian period, Jerusalem was not the political center of the province. The governor of Judah lived in Mizpah, while the religious center continued to be in Jerusalem. The Neo-Babylonians had left Jerusalem in ruins after their short hegemony over the land (cf. Jer. 40:5–8). It no longer served as the political center of the province, though it continued as the religious center and as a place of pilgrimage (see Jer. 41:4–5). Archaeological evidence shows occupation among the ruins and in some parts of the city that did not suffer the full intensity of the Neo-Babylonian destruction.

While the kings of Babylon weakened and the kingdom slowly became ineffective, the Medes and the Persians gained strength. Cyrus arose from the obscure tribes of today's southern Iran and began conquering kingdom after kingdom until he finally faced the Neo-Babylonians. When he entered the city of Babylon on October 12, 539 B.C., he did not meet serious resistance. Thus, Cyrus the Achaemenid, grandson of a Median king, consolidated an empire even larger than the one achieved by the Neo-Babylonians.

Ezra carefully documented the events that fulfilled Isaiah's and Jeremiah's prophecies (Ezra 1:1–4; cf. 2 Chr. 36:22–23; Is. 44:24—45:25; Jer. 29:10). Cyrus, "the anointed one" (Heb. *mashiakh)*, ordered the rebuilding of the temple of the Lord (ca. 538 B.C.; see 2 Chr. 36:22–23; Is. 44:24—45:3), so batches of exiles returned to Judah to resettle Jerusalem (Ezra 1:11; 7:7). After Cyrus's untimely death, his son Cambyses occupied the throne (530–522 B.C.). During his reign the reconstruction of the temple of Jerusalem stopped, due mainly to opposition from neighboring groups (Ezra 4:24). Cambyses's rule ended unexpectedly when he died on his way back to Persia to fight a usurper, the so-called "Pseudo-Smerdis."

Darius Hystaspes (522–486 B.C.) then rose to power. He was from the Achaemenid family, not a descendant of Cyrus II, the Great. He promoted and supported the rebuilding of temples that had been neglected or destroyed before his rule, and his propaganda stimulated the good will of temple administrators. His major contribution to the people of Judah came in 520 B.C. when he supported the reconstruction of the Jerusalem temple and the restoration of its services (Ezra 6).

Theology and Purpose. Haggai lived and preached hope in a time of hopelessness, during which those who had returned to Judah were stuck in survival mode.

1. *Hope for the Hopeless.* Because of their condition, the people focused only on satisfying their material needs. They had lost their kingdom and the land promised to them. Haggai called their attention to higher ground, to the covenantal promises that the Lord had made to their ancestors. He assured them that the promise made to Abram (see Gen. 15:13–14) and fulfilled in the Exodus from Egypt also applied to the exodus from Babylon. Haggai echoed Moses with prophetic authority directly from the Lord.

2. *Faithfulness to the Covenant.* Haggai succinctly summarizes the blessings and curses uttered at the dawn of Moses's ministry. He challenges his audience in a covenantal lawsuit that moves them to react as the Israelites had a millennium earlier. His oracles are a condensed version of Deuteronomy but strengthened with far-reaching promises of hope. In order to completely fulfill the promised deliverance, the Lord needed a sanctuary so He could dwell among His people to direct, protect, and atone for them. The forgiveness and cleansing of the nation came through the sacrifices. The temple would please the Lord by providing a place of hope for God's people to praise Him, and its services would point to the atoning work of the coming Davidic King, the Messiah.

3. *Messianic Hope.* Haggai's vision of the Messiah's rule and the submission of the nations to the Lord in His temple transcends the pitiful reality of his time and motivates all believers to fulfill the plans of the Almighty and hope for the fulfillment of the covenant.

Literary Features. The book of Haggai communicates its message using a simple, direct style and energetic tone mixed with rhetorical questions (Hag. 1:4, 9; 2:3, 12–13, 19), key phrases (1:5, 7), parallelism (1:4, 6, 9–10), and allusions (cf. Gen. 46:3; Ex. 3:12; Deut. 28:22–24, 38–40; Josh. 1:9; Is. 7:14). The book follows a chronological order formed by four parallel oracles. Oracles one (1:1–11; Aug. 29; followed by a response from the people, 1:12–15; Sept. 21) and three (2:10–19; Dec. 18) charge the audience with their failures, while the second (vv. 1–9; Oct. 17) and fourth (vv. 20–23; Dec. 18) promise hope to the people.

COMMENTARY

1:1–11
An Apparently Hopeless Situation

The experience of the new exodus from exile was not what the returnees expected. Unlike their ancestors' glorious deliverance from Egypt (ca. 1447 B.C.), no signs or wonders signaled their departure from Babylon. The hopes of a present-day kingdom ruled by the promised Messiah had crumbled under the weight of the Persian Empire, and they had lost their original enthusiasm to rebuild the house of the Lord. Haggai 1:1–11 rebukes the people for their failure to rebuild the symbol of God's presence among them. According to the prophet, the economic crisis they faced resulted from their unfaithfulness to the covenant.

1:1. Introduction. During the exodus from Babylon, God had not visibly displayed His divine power but had exhibited His silent presence among His people. But the word from the Lord that Haggai received interrupted the apparent divine silence, arriving precisely when the people needed it. Haggai dates his oracle to the second year of King Darius of Persia, on the first day of the sixth month (i.e., August 29, 520 B.C.; 1:1), a festival day to celebrate the new moon (cf. Num. 10:10; 28:11; 2 Kin. 4:23; Ps. 81:3).

For the first time, a prophet of Yahweh did not mention a Hebrew king as a point of reference for his ministry. They had no king when Haggai dated the messages, so he had to refer to King Darius instead. This serves as a gloomy reminder of Judah's colonial status and the degenerate times in which the prophet lived. Zerubbabel the son of Shealtiel, though a descendant of David, was only a governor (Ezra 3:2; Neh. 12:1; cf. Ezra 2:2; Zech. 4:6; Matt. 1:12; Luke 3:27). The chronicler identifies Zerubbabel as the son of Pedaiah (1 Chr. 3:17–19). Some connect him with Sheshbazzar, governor of Judah in Ezra (Ezra 1:5–11; 5:14). Regardless, he was clearly a descendant of Jehoiachin (2 Kin. 24:15; 1 Chr. 3:17) and a rightful candidate for the throne of Judah.

Joshua the son of Jehozadak (also Jozadak), the high priest, was a descendant of Aaron (1 Chr. 5:1–15). He emerged as a capable spiritual leader, listening to the words of the prophet. The Prophet Haggai is mentioned without pedigree or renowned ancestry. But as the Lord's prophet, he spoke with as much authority as the prophets during the monarchy. The phrase *dabar yahweh* (lit. "the word of Yahweh") first appears in Genesis 15:1 to describe God's revelation to Abram. It later became a common description of a divine and authoritative communication. This "word" calls us to celebrate and to hope.

1:2–4. Their Place in the Journey. The prophet introduces his message by invoking *yahweh tseba'ot* ("Lord of hosts/armies, Lord Almighty"; 1:2), a name that emphasizes the rule of Yahweh, the covenantal God of Israel, over all armies and nations. The Lord controls human affairs (cf. Dan. 4:34–35), but by not finishing the rebuilding of the temple, His people actually denied His presence among them. Joshua and Zerubbabel had laid the foundations of the temple two years after arriving in Jerusalem (Ezra 3:8–10), but almost twenty years later, they had not finished construction. Because of God's perceived absence, the people focused on their own survival and not on restoring religious structure.

The contrast between what the people said and what the Lord said could imply a covenantal lawsuit (cf. Ex. 33:12–13; Is. 1:18; 43:26; Hos. 4:1; 12:2; Mic. 6:2). The Lord accused the people of obstructing His work through indifference, neglect, and mistaken priorities. Haggai avoids discussing sociopolitical explanations for the delay, like opposition from enemies (Ezra 4:5) or a lack of resources. The people did not oppose rebuilding the temple; they simply concluded that the time had not yet come (Hag. 1:2). Meanwhile they lived in *sepunim* ("paneled," "roofed") houses, not luxurious mansions but houses with roofs, in contrast to a temple in ruins. The book of Haggai, along with archaeological findings, indicates that Judah was a poor province during the time of Haggai.

1:5–11. Considering the Past. Before the Israelites entered the promised land, Moses reminded them of the Exodus and invited them to reflect on their past experiences. Haggai used a similar approach, calling the people to consider their ways and how their covenant violations had caused a deep ecological and economic crisis (vv. 5–7; 2:15–18; Deut. 28:15; 38–39, 48; cf. Lev. 26:20). No matter how much they sowed and planted, they harvested only a little (see also Mic. 6:14–15; cf. Hag. 2:15–19).

Despite having clothing, the Israelites could not stay warm (1:6). Sheep and goats need nourishment to produce healthy wool and hair. Perhaps scarcity of green pasture affected their production.

Without water there was not enough linen, so no one was warm due to lack of sufficient clothing materials. Even their small leather bags rotted and broke apart, letting their wages fall to the ground. While most transactions at the time were in kind, the people of Judah may have used Samaritan, Philisto-Arabian, or Phoenician coins for taxes, commerce with foreigners, or wages.

Reflections on the past must lead to positive actions in the present. The Lord commanded the people to go up to the mountains to collect wood and to build the temple for His pleasure and glory (v. 8). The rebuilt temple would bring Him honor. The command did not necessarily require the people to seek timber from Lebanon, an unlikely task given their tense relationship with their neighbors. More likely they went to the surrounding hills of the Judean highlands to find trees for scaffolding to support the stone structure and roofing of the temple. Because of their proximity to a quarry of high-quality stone, they needed only wood to finish the work.

The Lord explained that He had caused the people's dire situation because they had left His house in ruins while preoccupied with their own houses (v. 9). God took responsibility for the drought and the scorching desert winds that brought about the covenant curses, including lack of grain, wine, and oil (v. 11). In an agrarian society, climate changes can mean the difference between prosperity and starvation, especially in the highlands, where irrigation requires terraces and cisterns to maximize the use of the rain. The Judean hill country needs the seasonal rains affected by the atmospheric pressure and winds coming from the sea (see Lev. 26:4; Deut. 28:12). That area has only two seasons: the dry season and the rainy season. Most of the year, moisture coming from the Mediterranean Sea falls as dew before condensing over the hill country. The Lord sent the dew from the heavens (cf. Gen. 27:28; Deut. 33:28; Zech. 8:12), so Judah's only hope for survival was to rebuild His house.

1:12–15
The People's Response

In response, the people obeyed the voice of the Lord their God as the ancient Israelites at the feet of Mount Sinai had sworn a thousand years earlier (1:12; cf. Ex. 19:8). The passage concludes by describing how the Lord stirred up the spirit of each group that constituted the Lord's community—the civic establishment, the religious leaders, and the rest of the people (Hag. 1:14). Their answer must have been unanimous.

This time everyone supported the prophet, making Haggai one of the most successful prophets in terms of community response.

Zerubbabel, Joshua, and the rest of the people obeyed the voice of the Lord (v. 12). Haggai does not differentiate between the returnees and the ones who had remained in Judah. The *she'erit* ("remnant," "rest") included *all* those affected by the experience of the Exile. Through them the Lord would fulfill His purpose. Moses had warned the Israelites about the possibility of exile (Deut. 28:36, 41, 63–68), the ultimate curse, but he also promised that the Lord their God would bring them back from captivity and have compassion on them (Deut. 30:3). The restoration of the community fulfilled this promise. As the Lord's messenger, Haggai offered the people hope and promised them God's presence (Hag. 1:13; cf. Deut. 7:21, Josh. 1:9; Ps. 23:4; Is. 43:2). Like the official messenger of the Persian Empire, he had access to the "Great King."

God's action rallied His people to action (cf. 2 Chr. 36:22–23; Ezra 1:1–4; Is. 41:2, 25; Zech. 4:6–10; Phil. 2:13). Energized by God, they cut trees for the scaffolding, removed stones, and cleared the site. Several weeks later, on the twenty-fourth day of the sixth month in the second year of King Darius (September 21, 520 B.C.; Hag. 1:15), the people began to build the temple in Jerusalem. The temple provided an unquestionable symbol of the covenant and a clear evidence of hope.

2:1–9
Hope and the Temple

Haggai presented his second message at the climax of the Festival of Tabernacles. The twenty-first of the month (Oct. 17, 520 B.C.) was the final day of the celebrations. He addressed a discouraged people who felt that the reconstructed temple did not compare to the magnificent temple of Solomon. He rejected their attitude and reminded them of the covenant the Lord established when they came out of Egypt (2:5). They needed to be strong. This passage climaxes with the announcement of the coming of the Desire of all nations.

2:1–3. Faded Glory. The Festival of Tabernacles, celebrated in the seventh month (known as Tishri), reminded the people of their experience during the wilderness wanderings (see Lev. 23:33–44; cf. Num. 29:12–40; Deut. 16:13–15). The religious calendar climaxed on the twenty-first of the month, a time of feasting and celebrating the harvest. But in the time of Haggai, the harvest was sparse, leaving little to celebrate. Hopelessness had disheartened the builders (see Ezra 3:12), so Haggai delivered a message from the Lord. He asked the people if any among them had seen the temple in its former glory, a rhetorical question since few of them would have been alive when the Babylonians destroyed Solomon's temple in 586 B.C. But even though it looked less impressive, the glory of the temple did not come from the gold and silver that once decorated it but from the presence of the Lord in His house of worship (see Hag. 2:7).

2:4–5. Covenant and Promise. The book of Haggai uses the Exodus as a type of the return from Babylon. God reminded the people that He had acted according to the covenant He made with them when they came out of Egypt (v. 5). He promised redemption to humanity (Gen. 3:15), reassured Abram of it (Gen. 12, 15, 22), formalized it with the Israelites (Ex. 19–20; cf. 34:10; 1 Kin. 8:9), and guaranteed it to David (2 Sam. 7:1–16). God is faithful to His word. The prophet echoed Moses's words to Joshua son of Nun when he encouraged Zerubbabel, Joshua son of Jehozadak, and the people of the land to be strong (Hag. 2:4; Deut. 31:7; Josh. 1:6–7, 9, 18). He uses the Hebrew verb *hazaq* ("be strong") three times to highlight the need for effort in the task at hand (cf. Zech. 8:9, 13). But success would come from the Lord, whose Spirit remained among them (see commentary on Hag. 1:12–15). The divine presence would cast out their fear of the nations and provide them with hope that was grounded in the presence of God with His people.

2:6–9. Future Glory. The Lord promised to shake the heavens and the earth, the sea and the dry land, just like He did in Egypt during the Exodus (see Heb. 12:26–29). In ancient Near Eastern literature, the deities demonstrate their power through earthquakes, eclipses, and storms. The Lord established His authority using imagery familiar to His people (cf. Judg. 5:4; Joel 2:10–11; Amos 9:1). God's rule over the natural and political worlds would shake all the nations, as the people of Judah had witnessed through the edicts of Cyrus and Darius to rebuild the temple. In a little while, God would again intervene directly in history, shaking all nations by the manifestation of His power and leading them to the Desire of all nations.

Although Haggai lifted the spirits of the people with the assurance that silver and gold belong to the Lord, his main concern was not economic prosperity but the restoration of the glory of God. After the shame of the Exile, the Lord would restore His honor and glory in the new temple. Even though Haggai encouraged the rebuilding of a physical temple, it merely served as a symbol of God's sanctifying presence among His people. And the presence of the Messiah would bring greater glory to this temple (see Mal. 3:1). In fact, He would take the functions of the earthly temple on Himself (John 2:19).

2:10–19
The Lives of Committed Believers

Before asking the Israelites to build the sanctuary, the Lord gave them the Decalogue and laws concerning purity and holiness. On the twenty-fourth day of the ninth month in the second year of Darius (December 18, 520 B.C.), several weeks after beginning the rebuilding

of the temple, God instructed His people how to live in faithfulness to the covenant (2:10). Haggai explained the importance of holiness and the need to avoid defilement (vv. 10–14). But he also reminded them of God's power to turn the curse into a blessing (vv. 15–19; see Deut. 28:1–14). The "early rains" had recently arrived in the month of October and its abundance promised a plentiful harvest, reenergizing Judah's hope.

2:10–14. Holiness and Defilement. The prophet's words demonstrated the people's need for cleansing. Moses had instructed the people concerning holiness as a prerequisite for approaching the Lord (Lev. 17–26). The priests were responsible for instructing the people on such matters (see Deut. 17:8–13; Ezek. 44:23–24; Mal. 2:1–7), and Haggai affirmed that function of the priesthood. He reminded them that although uncleanness is transferable through

The Desire of All Nations

For centuries Jewish and Christian interpreters supported the rendering "desire" for the Hebrew *khemdah*, which made "desire of all nations" a treasured messianic title (Hag. 2:7). However, modern translators have questioned and mostly abandoned that reading, preferring to render *khemdah* as "wealth." Linguistically, both translations are possible, but the context supports the traditional translation.

1. *Syntax of the Verse.* The verb "they shall come" is third-person plural, while the noun *khemdah* is feminine singular. For *khemdah* to be the subject of the sentence, it would have to agree with the verb in number. The only way to translate the phrase without changing the text would be "they [the nations] will come to the desire of all nations." The subject of the verb is the nations mentioned in the first part of v. 7, and the noun "desire" functions as the object of the verb.

2. *A Theophany.* Haggai 2:6–7 describes a theophany that would shake nature and the nations. They would witness a powerful manifestation of the Lord that would create a new order. Confronted by this majestic power, the nations would come to

the Messiah to seek refuge. Verses 21–23 also describe the shaking of nature and the nations in reference to the coming Messiah. The passage emphasizes the glory of God. The people perceived the glory of the new temple to be inferior to that of the temple of Solomon (v. 3), but the prophet immediately corrected this false perception. The glory of the temple did not stem from external appearance (v. 9) but from the presence of God within it (vv. 4–6). The power of this glory would completely fill the temple (v. 7) and would spill over the earth and the nations, shaking them up. In that temple, the nations would find the Desire of all nations, making it more glorious than the previous one (v. 9). The silver and the gold did not matter because it all belongs to the Lord (v. 8).

3. *Use of khemdah.* The word *khemdah* has a variety of uses, including references to Israelite kings. At the beginning of the monarchy, "the desire of Israel" was on Saul as the appointed king (1 Sam. 9:20). The people did not desire an evil king (2 Chr. 21:20). Therefore, Haggai logically identifies the Messiah as the Desire of all nations, including Israel.

touch, holiness is not (Lev. 22:4; Num. 19:22). Touching a dead body would make a person unclean and would contaminate anything else the unclean person touched, including offerings. To enjoy the coming of the Desire of all nations, they needed to cleanse their hearts and turn to the Lord (Hag. 2:17).

2:15–19. Blessings Strengthen Hope. The people needed radical change. Haggai reminded them that when they expected twenty units of grain, they reaped only ten, and when they expected fifty liquid units from the winepress, they received only twenty. The Lord had struck the work of their hands (the fields) with blight (scorching desert winds from the east), mildew (humid winds from the west), and hail in fulfillment of the covenantal curses (see Deut. 28:22; Amos 4:9). Through this experience, the Lord wanted them to understand their spiritual condition and turn to Him, but they had not. So He would now do something different. He would show them kindness even though they did not deserve it. He would bless them (Hag. 2:19). Love turns people around. Yes, they needed to be reminded to seek the Lord, but His mercy would change their hearts.

2:20–23
Present Promises and Future Hopes

The imagery in Haggai's last message—chariots overthrown, horses and riders hurled down, heaven and earth shaken—again recalls the Exodus (see Ex. 14:23–25). He looked at the past, applied it to the present, and then pointed to the future and God's final work of deliverance, the awaited Messiah, the Hope of His people.

2:20–22. The Shaking. In the new exodus, the Lord would shake heaven and earth. This global event looks beyond the conflicts faced by Darius to the establishment of the kingdom of the Lord (cf. Dan. 2:44). The apocalyptic language describes the climax of the cosmic conflict, when God would overcome all the kingdoms of the earth. As in Haggai 2:7, the shaking of the nations not only pertains to the temple but to the role of the Messiah as Judge and Savior.

2:23. The Signet. Zerubbabel was a governor (v. 21), a title highlighting his status as a vassal of Persia (see commentary on 1:1). But the Lord also identified him as His "servant," a title used for David and for the Messiah (Is. 42:1; 49:5–7; 52:13—53:12). Zerubbabel seems to function as a type of the Messiah. In this eschatological context, the signet (Heb. *khotam*) symbolizes God's redemptive power and the reversal of earlier curses. Haggai must have had in mind Jeremiah's warning to Coniah (Jehoiachin) that even if he were the last king of Judah, the *khotam* in the Lord's hand, God would nevertheless pluck him off (Jer. 22:24–30). But now the Lord would reverse the curse, making Zerubbabel, who was never a king, like a signet ring, a type of the One who would come as the *khotam* of the Lord. The Lord rejected Coniah as a symbol of the Davidic monarchy but would make Zerubbabel a symbol of the Messiah. The book of Haggai closes with a look forward—a hope grounded in the experience and expectations of the remnant of Judah.

ZECHARIAH

INTRODUCTION

Title and Authorship. The Hebrew title of the book, *zekaryah*, means "Yahweh remembers." The author names himself four times but provides little personal information (Zech. 1:1, 7; 7:1, 8). He is also mentioned in Ezra 5:1 and 6:14 and probably Nehemiah 12:16. Several others in the Bible bear this name (Ezra 8:11, 13, 16; 10:26; Neh. 11:4–5, 12; 12:35, 41).

Zechariah was the son of Berechiah/Berekiah and the grandson of Iddo, but we know no more of his father and grandfather than of him. The title "prophet" probably refers to Zechariah himself, not his grandfather (Zech. 1:1, 7). The Berechiah mentioned in Nehemiah, seven decades later, could not have been Zechariah's father (see Neh. 3:4, 30; 6:18). Since Zechariah's ministry began less than twenty years after the Jews returned from exile, he was probably born in Babylon and returned to Judah with Zerubbabel in 536 B.C. If Nehemiah 12:16 refers to the prophet, then he was a priest.

Some scholars argue that chapters 9–14 come from a different author than the one who wrote chapters 1–8. The two sections do have differences in form and content, but there is no concrete evidence to determine how long Zechariah's ministry lasted. He could have written chapters 9–14 later, when concerns about the temple were no longer pressing. The content of the latter chapters does not necessarily reflect a different author.

Date. Zechariah contains three dates. He received his call "in the eighth month of the second year of Darius" (1:1). Darius's second regnal year began in the spring of 520 B.C. and the eighth month fell in the autumn. Thus Zechariah's ministry began about November 520 B.C. He saw the visions "on the twenty-fourth day of the eleventh month...in the second year of Darius" (1:7). All eight of Zechariah's visions probably occurred on the same night or within a short interval during the winter of 519 B.C. Consequently, Zechariah heard from the Lord again "in the fourth year of King Darius...on the fourth day of the ninth month" (7:1). This date, near the end of 518 B.C., probably applies to chapters 7 and 8. Chapters 9 through 14 are not dated. Since they differ somewhat in subject, vocabulary, and style, Zechariah may have composed them later in his ministry.

Backgrounds. Zechariah's prophecies addressed the situation of the Jewish people shortly after their return from Babylon (for the historical background, see Haggai: Introduction). The first part of the book (chaps. 1–8) deals with the immediate issues concerning the returning exiles: resettling the people, rebuilding the temple, and reestablishing sacrificial worship and annual festivals. The second part (chaps. 9–14) deals with the postexilic community's future concerns: relations with neighboring nations, messianic expectations, and eschatology.

Theology and Purpose. The central theme of the book of Zechariah is the restoration of God's people (Israel and Judah) following captivity. The divine promises to Israel and Judah foreshadow the eschatological restoration of God's people throughout the earth.

1. Restoration and Salvation. The book of Zechariah announces the restoration of land (14:10–11), cities and towns (1:17), people (8:4–8), temple (6:12–13), and priesthood (3:1–7). Zechariah calls the people to abandon their prior sins, which led to the Exile (7:8–14), and to return not only to the land (10:6–10) but to a proper relationship with God (1:3). He assures them of God's promises to return to them (8:3). His presence would fill the rebuilt temple (1:16), and He would forgive their sins (3:9; 13:1), restore the land, deliver them from their enemies (12:2–13:1), and provide them with the hope of a glorious future that would extend to all humanity (14:6–11). God will restore not only Judah to its promised earthly homeland but all humanity to their Edenic home. The nations will turn to God (2:11; 8:22–23) and worship Him in Jerusalem (14:16). In this regard, Zechariah's message parallels that of the Bible as a whole.

The Scriptures tell how God placed humanity in a perfect home. But because of sin, they lost this home and face-to-face communication with their Creator, who exiled them into a hostile world to suffer the consequences of their misdeeds. Nevertheless, God showed them kindness by bringing them back into communion with Him and promising them a glorious eternal future in which they and their world would be consecrated to Him. Zechariah tells the same story. When exiled to Babylon, the people of God lost their home in the promised land and the privilege of close communication with God in the temple. But in His love, God forgave their sins and brought them back to their land, where the temple was rebuilt and the priesthood was reestablished. And there, through the ministry of Zechariah, God assured His people of His presence and promised them a glorious future.

In this way, the book of Zechariah communicates an overarching message of Scripture. It does not deal merely with some small aspects of God's workings with His people in antiquity but presents a microcosm of the entire plan of salvation. Judah's exile and restoration represent, in miniature, the story of humanity from paradise lost to paradise restored. Thus, Zechariah offers both a present historical hope for the people of Judah and a future eschatological hope for all nations.

2. The Coming King. In his description of the promises of restoration, Zechariah refers to a coming King and Agent of restoration called the "Angel of the Lord," the "Branch," and the "Shepherd." In the OT, the Angel of the Lord is often identified as Yahweh but is sometimes presented as a divine being distinct from Yahweh (e.g., Gen. 16:11–12; 31:11–13; Ex. 3:4, 7–18; 14:19, 24; Judg. 6:11–25). Similarly, the book of Zechariah both distinguishes between the Angel and Yahweh and presents the two as divine persons (e.g., 3:1–2, 6–9; cf. 1:8–12; 12:8). Again, in Zechariah we have the promise of Yahweh to send His "Servant the Branch," through whom the guilt of the land will be removed (3:8–9; 6:12). This is the coming King whose kingly and priestly roles are symbolized by Joshua and Zerubbabel, the kingly role being further presented through the shepherd metaphor—the "Shepherd" (the

Lord's close associate) who would be betrayed and stricken for His people (cf. 11:12–13; 12:10; 13:7–9). He would combine the kingly and priestly roles symbolized by Zerubbabel, the governor, and Joshua, the high priest. The descriptions in Zechariah recall the promise of a divine Branch who would reign on the Davidic throne in everlasting peace and righteousness (Is. 7:14; 9:6; 11:1–16; Jer. 23:5–6; 33:14–18; Dan. 7:13; 9:25–27; Mic. 5:2) and whose suffering and death would bring healing to humanity (see Is. 52–53). The book anchors the hope of God's people in this Messiah, who would come to Zion riding on a donkey, bringing salvation and joy (Zech. 9:9).

Literary Features. The book of Zechariah uses three distinct literary forms, forming the three major sections of the book. Apart from the introduction and appeal for repentance in Zechariah 1:1–6, it contains a series of vision reports (1:7—6:8) that ends with a command for a symbolic act (6:9–15), a prophetic inquiry (chaps. 7–8), and two prophetic oracles (chaps. 9–11; 12–14).

The form of the vision reports resembles those in the book of Daniel. Both present the supernatural revelation in symbolic terms, explained by an angelic interpreter. The angel may explain only the historical significance of the symbols or may expand on the spiritual implications with appeals to repentance and declarations of encouragement.

The prophetic inquiry in chapters 7–8 resembles some of the inquiries found in preexilic biblical books (see 2 Kin. 22:11–20; 1 Chr. 17:1–15; Jer. 21:1–14). In each case, someone (often a messenger) comes to the prophet with a question about some contemplated course of action. The prophet then gives an answer from God. The answer, often more complex than the question, not only specifies God's will on the matter but also includes messages of warning or encouragement that spell out the practical implications of proceeding.

The prophetic oracles of Zechariah 9–14 resemble the national oracles in many of the preexilic prophets that announced God's judgments against various nations (cf. Jer. 46–51; Amos 1:3—2:16). Zechariah formally directs the two oracles against "the land of Hadrach" (Syria; Zech. 9:1) and against Israel (12:1), though he also mentions several other nations.

Certain sections of Zechariah contain characteristics of apocalyptic literature, which normally involves symbolic visions, interpretations by angelic messengers, and messages of deliverance for God's people and judgment against other nations. The apocalyptic character of the book is most evident in the first and third sections, which discuss God's plan to restore not only the postexilic Jewish community but also the entire world.

COMMENTARY

1:1–6
INTRODUCTION

The introduction dates the beginning of Zechariah's prophecies to the second year of Darius (i.e., 520 B.C.). The eighth month of the Jewish calendar would overlap October and November. Like many other prophets, Zechariah asserted the authority of his message by claiming to speak "the word of the LORD" (1:1). All the major sections of the book of Zechariah also begin with some indication of the divine origin and authority of the message (v. 7; 7:1; 9:1). The call to repentance begins with a statement of God's anger. Because of the actions of their forebears, Judah had experienced difficulties since the Exile. Their ancestors refused to listen to the prophets (1:4). But the Lord's command to return to Him (i.e., repent; v. 3) offers the solution for the sin of disobedience.

Even after the prophets died, the potent words they spoke on the Lord's behalf came to pass and eventually led those who went into exile to confess that the Lord had treated them as their deeds deserved (v. 6). The people of Judah needed to learn from what happened to their ancestors and to act differently. After all, even their forbearers eventually returned to God and repented when they were exiled.

1:7—6:15
THE NIGHT VISIONS

Each of Zechariah's eight visions follows a similar literary pattern: the prophet describes what he saw in his own words and requests an interpretation, which an angel provides. In several cases, the interpreting angel adds an oracular statement that emphasizes the significance of the vision. The visions assured the postexilic Jewish community of God's protection as they built the temple and restored worship of the Lord.

1:7–17. The First Vision. Zechariah gives a more precise date for his vision than for his

call (cf. 1:1)—around February 15, 519 B.C. The prophet affirms the message as "the word of the LORD" even though he himself describes the vision. He presumably saw all the visions on the same day since he gives no other date. He wakes up in 4:1, suggesting he may have slept between the visions.

The prophet saw a man riding on a red horse standing among the myrtle trees (1:8). This was probably the Angel of the Lord (v. 11), not the angel who talked with Zechariah (v. 9). The designation "man" probably refers only to appearance since this messenger disclosed supernatural information. Scripture often identifies the Angel of the Lord as Yahweh but sometimes presents Him as a divine being distinct from Yahweh (cf. Gen. 16:11–12; 31:11–13; Ex. 3:4, 7–18; 14:19, 24; Judg. 6:11–25). Details such as the colors of the horses are not significant in any discernable way, and the text does not interpret them. But the series of four colored horses recalls the similar vision in Revelation 6:1–8. Symbolic horses show up again in Zechariah's eighth vision (Zech. 6:1–8) and in the latter half of the book (see 9:10; 10:3).

The horses had roamed throughout the earth and returned to inform the Angel of the Lord that everything was quiet, peaceful, at rest, and still (1:11). This could mean that the Persian Empire, including Judah, was under no threat, so the Jews could proceed to reconstruct the temple without fear. The promises of vv. 16–17 would support this interpretation. But it could also indicate that the nations around Judah were not assisting the Jews and remained hostile, an interpretation supported by the rebuke against the nations in v. 15. It seems that while Judah struggled, other nations enjoyed ease and did not care about Judah's welfare. In either case, God clearly wanted the Jews to rebuild the temple.

The Angel of the Lord responded to the message with a complaint that reflected the thoughts of the people. Although the world was at rest, Judah had still not received relief (v. 12). Apparently, the return of the small remnant did not completely fulfill the prophecies of restoration (cf. Jer. 29:10; 24:6–7). They also had to restore the city and temple. The seventy years (Zech. 1:12) may refer to the years of captivity predicted by Jeremiah (Jer. 25:11–12), from 605 to 536 B.C., or to the seventy years extending from the beginning of Nebuchadnezzar's final siege of Jerusalem to the year of Zechariah's visions, from 589/8 to 519 B.C.

Concerning the response of God to the angel, we are only told that He spoke *tobim* ("good," "pleasant," "kind,") and *nikhumim* ("comforting," "compassionate") words (v. 13). Whatever He said, He intended to encourage. Though He had been a little angry with Judah, He could not accept how the nations had treated them. Judah had not done what the Lord wanted, but their enemies had overdone what He wanted. God's anger against Judah (v. 2) had turned into extreme jealousy/zeal for Jerusalem and Zion and anger against the complacent nations (vv. 14–15).

In his vision, Zechariah explains that God had returned to Jerusalem with mercy and compassion. As a sign of His mercy, the Lord would secure the rebuilding of His house, symbolized by the line (of the surveyor or builder) stretched out over it. He would reinstate His past mercies by comforting Zion, choosing Jerusalem, and causing the cities to overflow again (v. 17).

1:18–21. The Second Vision. In the Bible, horns symbolize power and pride (cf. Deut. 33:17; Ps. 75:4–5; Dan. 8:3–9). Here, the horns which had scattered Judah, Israel, Jerusalem, and the nations that lifted up horns represent those who opposed the Jews (Zech. 1:19, 21). But craftsmen would oppose the horns by frightening them and throwing them down. The Hebrew word *kharashim* ("craftspersons," "carpenters," "metalworkers") can refer to any type of skilled worker but often indicates those who produce religious objects (see Is. 40:19; Hos. 13:2), including those who built the sanctuary (Ex. 38:23) and Solomon's temple (1 Kin. 7:14). Here, the "craftspersons" are those building and furnishing the temple. Thus, rebuilding the temple would repel Judah's enemies.

2:1–13. The Third Vision. The "measuring line" in 2:1 translates a different Hebrew term from the one used in 1:16, but both are instruments for architectural measurement used to measure Jerusalem. In Zechariah's time, they had not yet rebuilt the wall, so the man could not have measured Jerusalem's walls. But the act of measuring Jerusalem implies that the city would have a specific size. Two angels explained this vision and the two implications for Jerusalem of the absence of a wall. First, a wall would not limit the city because of its great size and population (2:4). Second, the Lord would protect the city and be the glory inside it, making a wall unnecessary. In some sense, the wall is the glory of a city and not its fortifications. God would not only surround the city to protect it but be present within it as well (i.e., in the temple). The repetition of the

verb *'ehyeh* ("I will be") seems to imply two different but complementary roles for God. The Hebrew says literally "I will be a wall...and I will be for glory" (v. 5). Zechariah did not see either of these predictions fully realized. Nearly a century later, in the time of Nehemiah, the city was still underpopulated. Not until the time of Jesus did it overflow during festivals.

A poetic explanation follows the vision. The Lord repeatedly exhorted the exiles to flee from the land of the north (i.e., from Babylon; v. 6; cf. Jer. 25:9; Ezek. 26:7) and to escape from the daughter of Babylon (Zech. 2:7). They no longer needed to cringe in Babylon. God assumed responsibility for the punishment and restoration of Judah: He had scattered them abroad to the four winds (v. 6), so they could safely return when He called them back.

Verses 8 and 9 offer additional reasons to return. God watches over Judah as the apple of His eye (v. 8). The "apple" of the eye is either the eyeball or the pupil. In either case, this is a very sensitive, easily seen body part. God was very aware of and sensitive to any offense against Judah. The Jews also needed to return because God would soon punish the nations in which they were exiled. It was no longer safe to remain in Mesopotamia. This confirms the message that Zechariah received in the first vision: either all was at peace (and it was safe to return to Judah), or the hostile nations would be punished (and it was unsafe to remain there). The fulfillment of Zechariah's prediction would prove to the people that God (*yahweh tseba'ot*, "LORD of hosts, LORD Almighty") Himself had sent Zechariah (v. 9). Unfortunately, most of the Jewish exiles never returned despite these assurances.

Two seemingly paradoxical exhortations bracket the latter part of the oracle, one to shout, sing, rejoice, and be glad because God was coming to live among them (v. 10) and another to be silent because the Lord had aroused Himself from His holy dwelling (v. 13; cf. Hab. 2:20). But the first exhortation is addressed to the daughter of Zion and the latter is addressed to all flesh/human beings. It was time for Zion to rejoice and for the rest of humanity to hold its tongue in awe because the Lord would inherit and take possession of Judah. In response, the nations had to join with the Lord (Zech. 2:11) or else face destruction (14:3, 12). Then they would know that God had indeed sent Zechariah (2:11). Thus, both the affliction of the nations and their conversion appear as signs of the truthfulness of Zechariah's message. The idea of foreigners joining with Judah recurs in 8:20–23.

3:1–10. The Fourth Vision. The next two visions address the two leaders of the Jewish community, a pivotal issue in this part of the book. The fourth vision centers on Joshua, the first high priest after the return from Babylon (see Ezra 3:2, 8; 4:3; 5:2; 10:18; Hag. 1:1, 12; 2:2, 4), and his fitness to serve. The high priest represented the people before God. Bringing Judah and the world back into order necessitated two things: the temple and the priesthood. But both had been out of commission for nearly sixty years, and only appropriately consecrated priests could renew the temple and minister in it.

In his vision, Zechariah saw a courtroom scene: Joshua stood before the Angel of the Lord with Satan at the right to oppose/accuse him. The verb "oppose" or "accuse" derives from the same Hebrew root as the name "Satan." The prospect of Judah's restoration aroused challenges from the opponents of God's people (Ezra 4:4–16; cf. Neh. 4:1–11), here epitomized by the Accuser (i.e., Satan). He based his objections on the sinfulness of the people both before and after the Exile. Strangely, however, instead of Satan rebuking Joshua, the Lord rebukes Satan. Although Joshua stands before the Angel of the Lord (Zech. 3:1), the Lord Himself speaks in his defense. Here, again, the divine Angel of the Lord is distinguished from Yahweh (see commentary on 1:7–17). In such contexts, the Angel most probably refers to the Messiah (3:1–9; cf. Ex. 14:19; 23:20–21; Mal. 3:1–3).

God Himself had grounds for accusing the people of Judah and sending them into exile. But now He had again chosen Jerusalem (Zech. 3:2; cf. 1:17; 2:12). Since God had chosen Jerusalem, the restoration of the city constituted a rebuke of Judah's enemies, including Satan. The brand rescued from the fire refers not only to the high priest Joshua but also to all of postexilic Judah. The high priest represents the people whom God had taken back from the "fire" of exile and reinstated in their holy calling.

Zechariah saw Joshua dressed in dirty clothes, representing the iniquity of Joshua and the people he represented. The defiled garments and his personal iniquity would make him unfit for his priestly functions. This presented a vicious dilemma: Joshua could not officiate because of his defilement. He could be cleansed only through a sacrifice, but he was the priest who had to offer the sacrifice to remove the defilement. Divine intervention solved Joshua's problem. God ordered Joshua's filthy garments removed and replaced them with clean garments that would enable him to serve in his capacity as high priest. He does not deny Joshua's defilement. He takes it away. Joshua's transformation symbolizes what God would do for Judah and for every person who turns to Him. By taking the side of repentant sinners, God continues to remove the iniquity of those who cannot rescue themselves.

In the vision, a series of assurances follows the change of Joshua's clothes. First, God would assure Joshua's position if he would remain obedient, walking in the Lord's ways (moral conformity to God's will) and keeping the Lord's charge (faithful performance of ritual duties). If he would do these things, Joshua would have a share in Judah's restoration and a place among the heavenly beings present in this scene (3:7).

Second, God assured Joshua that He would send His Servant, the Branch (v. 8). "The Branch" is a messianic title (cf. Jer. 23:5–6; Is. 4:2; see Zechariah: Introduction). Zechariah 6:12 indicates that the Branch would build the temple. Though Zerubbabel rebuilt the temple (4:6–10), he was not the Messiah. Rather, as the sanctuary builder, he symbolized the coming Messiah, who would inaugurate a new sanctuary, as indeed Jesus did (Heb. 8:1–2; 9:11).

Third, God assured Joshua that He would remove the iniquity of the land (Zech. 3:9). The text does not explain the stone with seven eyes placed before Joshua. Commentators have variously associated the stone with Christ, the kingdom of God (cf. Dan. 2:34–35, 44), and Zerubbabel, though none of these has been conclusively established. Since the promise of the coming Servant, the Branch, immediately precedes (Zech. 3:8), the stone may refer to the Messiah (Is. 28:16), who would come to remove iniquity (Zech. 3:9; cf. Is. 53:4–5), and the seven eyes may refer to the Holy Spirit, who accompanies and endues the Servant (cf. Is. 11:1–2; 42:1; 48:16). Elsewhere in Scripture, Revelation 5:6 mentions seven eyes, which are "the seven Spirits of God." Understood differently, "seven eyes" may refer to seven facets on the stone, though a seven-sided stone would be unusual. Since God would engrave an inscription on the stone, it likely had some commemorative purpose. Some have suggested that the stone was a cornerstone, but a cornerstone with seven sides would seem impractical. The word translated as "eyes" could also mean "water springs" or "fountains," and the expression *mepattekh pittukhah* (usually rendered as "I will engrave an engraving") could instead mean "I will open its openings." If this is correct, it would fit with the final clause of the verse, which refers to the removal of the iniquity/sin of the land in one day (Zech. 3:9), especially in view of the promise in 13:1. The idea of removing iniquity in one day probably refers to the Day of Atonement and fits well with the high priest's change of clothes on that day (Lev. 16).

Fourth, the Lord assured Joshua that after the cleansing the inhabitants of the land would dwell at peace. This also fits the Day of Atonement because after the cleansing the inhabitants of the land would dwell at peace. Zechariah 3:10 points to times of peace and prosperity when the people of Judah would invite their neighbors under their vine and fig trees (cf. 1 Kin. 4:25; Mic. 4:4).

4:1–14. The Fifth Vision. In his fifth vision, Zechariah saw a lampstand resembling those in the tabernacle and Solomon's temple. Zechariah's description of the seven lamps probably means that each of them had seven lips, or notches, to hold wicks. This single fixture would then have forty-nine flames on it, making the lamp very bright. The bowl on top may have contained oil for the lamps, though this is not specified. Unable to understand the vision or the function of the two olive trees, the prophet asked about it, but he did not receive an immediate answer (v. 4).

Before answering the prophet's question, the angel provided a spiritual interpretation: the Spirit of the Lord, not human activity, would fulfill the vision. This certainly provided hope to a people whose limited numbers and resources made the tasks at hand quite daunting. The first few visions represented God's decision to scatter Judah. But now God's power had reassembled them and purified Joshua. Here, the message encourages Zerubbabel, the governor of the postexilic community. The Spirit of God would accomplish great things, leveling obstacles that seemed like mountains before him (v. 7), and he would have the honor of placing the capstone on the completed temple.

Fifteen years after the exiles had returned from Babylon, they had still not restored the temple, the very reason for returning. Zerubbabel, who was probably already old, might have doubted whether he could complete the reconstruction. But the angel assured him that this would happen. Like the punishment of the nations (2:9) and their future conversion (v. 11), the completion of the temple would show that God had truly appointed Zechariah. Some may have despised "the day of small things" because of its seeming insignificance (4:10). Others would weep seeing how the new temple paled in comparison to Solomon's temple (cf. Ezra 3:12–13;

Hag. 2:3). But the prophets viewed this meager building as a sign of God's intervention and the promise of greater glory to come (cf. Hag. 2:7). The seven may refer to the seven lamps with seven pipes representing God's presence on the earth (cf. Rev. 4:5; 5:6), to the seven eyes of the Lord, or possibly to those who despise "the day of small things" (Zech. 4:10). The combination of the words *eben* and *bedil* in v. 10 are somewhat obscure. Conjectural translations include "plumb line" and "chosen capstone," the last stone put in place.

The angel finally answers Zechariah's question from v. 4. The seven lamps represent the eyes of the Lord, which scan back and forth through the whole earth (see Rev. 4:5). The two olive trees/branches and the two gold pipes are the two anointed ones who stand beside the Lord, serving the Sovereign of the whole earth (Zech. 4:14). As high priest, Joshua would have been anointed (cf. Ex. 28:41), and the previous vision had already depicted him standing before the Angel of the Lord (Zech. 3:1). Zerubbabel, as a descendant of David, would also have been eligible for such a rite (see 1 Sam. 9:15–16; 16:1–3). Similarly, Revelation 11:3–4 refers to two olive trees and two lampstands standing before the God of the earth.

The word *tsanterot*, usually translated as "pipes" (Zech. 4:12), does not appear elsewhere in Scripture. The symbol of the trees is not perfectly clear. Although the two anointed leaders did not have the power to reestablish Judah, they served as intermediate sources of God's power. The lampstand itself appears to represent the community, which God empowers to become "the light of the world" (Matt. 5:14). Despite the obscurity of some of the description, Zechariah 4:13–14 clearly explains the point of the vision: God's power would accomplish what Judah needed.

5:1–4. The Sixth Vision. In his sixth vision, Zechariah saw a scroll of normal length but abnormal width. Normal scrolls were much smaller than 10 cubits (15 ft or 4.6 m) wide. The size indicates the importance of the message written on it. The flying scroll must have been unrolled (and therefore readable). Zechariah did not see the content of the scroll, but the interpreting angel told him that the scroll contained the curse going out over the face of the whole earth/land (5:3). One side of the scroll announced the expulsion of thieves, the other the expulsion of perjurers. It does not mention idolatry, the sin the preexilic prophets most commonly denounced.

After the Exile, polytheism was rare among the Jews. Like the words of God, the curse worked without human agents (see also Ps. 147:15; Is. 55:11). Since the scroll and its curse would destroy the homes of thieves and perjurers, no place would remain for them among the returned exiles (Zech. 5:4). The fourth vision provided for the purification of the nation, and the sixth provided for the removal of those persisting in sin.

5:5–11. The Seventh Vision. While the sixth vision denounced sin, the seventh describes its removal. An *'epah* was either a fiber basket or a clay jar used to measure about 20 liters of grain (5.3 gal). A normal *'epah* could not hold an adult, so the basket, like the scroll in the previous vision, must have been oversized and, therefore, symbolic. Its occupant symbolizes wickedness. She apparently attempts to leave the *'epah*, but the angel throws her back in. The heavy lid prevents the woman from reopening the *'epah* and escaping.

The removal of the *'epah* to Shinar (i.e., Babylon) describes the process of Judah's purification, accomplished by the seventy-year Exile, which destroyed most of the nation and scattered most of those left (cf. Ezek. 5). Of those scattered, a few faithful ones returned home, leaving behind the idolatry of previous generations. Spiritual problems, but not idolatry, remained after the Exile. Throughout the Scriptures, Babylon symbolizes evil, even when God uses it as an instrument of punishment (as in Jer. 25:9 ff.).

The Hebrew name for the stork (*khasidah*; Zech. 5:9) derives from the adjective meaning "faithful," so "faithful ones" removed wickedness from Judah and took it to a land representing enmity toward God. They would build a house/temple for the *'epah* and permanently install it in wicked Babylon. Wickedness would no longer have a place among God's people; this is possibly connected to the removal of sin from Israel on the Day of Atonement.

6:1–8. The Eighth Vision. The eighth vision reprises the first, except that Zechariah saw chariot horses instead of riding mounts. Again the colors remain unexplained, as do the mountains of bronze (which could represent God's dwelling place; 6:1; cf. 8:3). The angel does explain that the chariots represent "four spirits of heaven." The Hebrew word *rukhot* can mean either "winds" or "spirits." The meaning "winds" (as in Dan. 8:8) would perhaps imply their destinations (the four directions), but the fact that they stand before the Lord of all the earth

allows for "spirits" (i.e., angels) as a possible translation (Zech. 6:5). The angel sent two of the chariots to the north (i.e., Mesopotamia) and one to the south (i.e., Egypt). However, some translations render the destination of the white horses as "west" rather than the more literal "after them" (i.e., north, following the black horses). The angel did not give the chariot of the red horses a destination but sent the chariots to travel throughout the earth, patrolling the nations (v. 7).

Those going toward the north gave God's Spirit rest in that region (v. 8). This differs slightly from the first vision, in which the whole earth rested quietly (1:11), but both represent peace. Assyria and Babylon always invaded Judah from the north, so the mention of rest in the north assured God's people that these invaders would not return. The postexilic community no longer needed to worry about the dangers around them (cf. Hag. 1:2). The rest for God's Spirit may refer to Darius's decree permitting the rebuilding of the temple (cf. Ezra 6:1–12). The night visions ended as they began, on a hopeful note. The whole earth was at rest, including Judah (Zech. 1:11; 2:12; 12:1–14). Even the Lord had found rest in the restoration of His people and temple.

6:9–15. The High Priest's Crown. At this point the book shifts from vision reports to an oracle commanding symbolic action. The exiles who had come from Babylon had perhaps brought the silver and gold as an offering for the temple from the Jews remaining in Mesopotamia, as Sheshbazzar had twenty years earlier (cf. Ezra 1:1–11). Since the Branch is a messianic title, this entire passage could prophesy the coming of the Messiah (see Zech. 3:8). More likely, it presents either Zerubbabel or Joshua as a historical type of the Messiah. Zerubbabel, the first governor of the postexilic Jewish community, was a descendant of King David, a "branch" from the Davidic line. He led the rebuilding of the temple (6:12). Both Matthew and Luke identify Zerubbabel as an ancestor of Jesus (cf. Matt. 1:12–13; Luke 3:27). But the Lord told Zechariah to crown Joshua the high priest, not Zerubbabel, the Davidic scion. The Hebrew word *'atarot* is plural, though many translations render it as "crown" rather than "crowns." The text indicates that Joshua was to receive both crowns. However, the command for Joshua to behold the Man named the Branch implies that Joshua should look for another messianic figure (Zech. 6:12). The crowns foreshadow the dual role of the Messiah as both priest and king (cf. Heb.

3:1; Rev. 17:14; 19:11–16). Jesus fulfilled these prophecies, for He is King (cf. Luke 19:37–38; John 18:37–39; Rev. 19:11–16), Priest (Heb. 3:1; 9:11), and the Provider of a new temple (John 2:19–21; Heb. 8:1–2; Rev. 21:22).

The crowns would remain in the temple as a memorial for those who would come from afar to rebuild it, drawing their attention not to individuals but to the temple's whole reconciliatory function (Zech. 6:14–15). Though worn by the high priest, the crowns honored the temple and the Lord. The assistance of distant people in reconstructing the Lord's temple would serve as a fourth sign that the Lord had sent Zechariah (v. 15, cf. 2:9, 11; 4:9).

7:1—8:23

QUESTIONS ABOUT RELIGIOUS PRACTICE

Chapters seven and eight form the third section of the book, containing Zechariah's response to an inquiry. Other prophetic books also contain such responses (cf. Jer. 21:1–2; Ezek. 20:1). These two chapters form an *inclusio* in which the end of Zechariah 8 echoes the beginning of chapter 7. The question (7:1–3) receives an extended answer (7:5—8:23) centered around an appeal to restore social justice and a promise of material restoration (7:8—8:17), which leads to the encouraging note within the direct response eventually granted to the inquiry (8:18–23).

7:1–7. Inquiry about Fasting. Two years after the visions of Zechariah 1–6, during the winter of Darius' fourth year (around December 7, 518 B.C.), Zechariah received an inquiry about fasting. By this time, the people had resumed work on the temple, as indicated by the presence of the priests in the house of the Lord (7:3), though they did not complete reconstruction until about March 12, 515 B.C. (cf. Ezra 6:15). Zechariah 7:2–7 describes the messengers sent to make an inquiry, but different translations understand the Hebrew *betel* ("house of God") in different ways. It could mean the place of Jacob's encounter with God (Gen. 28:19), the temple itself, or the city. In any case, they came to inquire concerning a traditional day of fasting on the ninth day of the fifth month that commemorated the destruction of the temple by the Babylonians in 586 B.C. Since the fast commemorated the Exile, which had ended, and the destruction of the temple, which was being rebuilt, they wondered whether they should still observe it. They asked this question in the ninth month, eight months before the next observation of the fast. This was not a spur-of-the-moment question; the enquirers wanted to know how their religious life should change after the return from exile.

Zechariah responded with the divine authority of the word of God (Zech. 7:4). But first he challenged the inquirers' sincerity. They fasted and feasted, motivated by personal concerns rather than a real interest in the Lord. They had ignored His instructions given by the prophets. God did not command the fast in question. It was merely a human ordinance. The other fast in the seventh month (Tishri) commemorated the murder of Gedaliah. The seventy years in v. 5 refers to the period from the destruction of Jerusalem in 587/6 B.C. until this inquiry in 518/7 B.C., seventy years by inclusive reckoning.

7:8–14. A Call to Justice. The Lord has always desired social and economic justice over meaningless rituals (see Is. 58:1–12; Mic. 6:6–8). It is therefore no surprise that God responded to an inquiry about fasting by calling for His people to practice justice and mercy and to stop oppressing the weak and plotting evil against each other (Zech. 7:9–10; see also Deut. 27:19; Is. 1:16–17; Jer. 7:5–7). The four commands mentioned—two positive (practice justice and show mercy) and two negative (do not oppress the widows and orphans or plan evil; Zech. 7:9–10)—were intended to change the way worshipers related to their fellow beings. This, rather than external ceremonies, is the essence of true religion (cf. Prov. 21:3; James 1:27). Such justice was particularly commanded toward widows, orphans, aliens, and other marginalized people (Zech. 7:10). God has expected the same behavior of humanity in all ages (cf. Matt. 23:23). When His people had obstinately refused to listen to His message, as communicated through the prophets, God had treated them the same way, refusing to listen to them when they called (Zech. 7:11–13). Finally, He scattered them with a whirlwind, the inevitable consequence of their own behavior (v. 14).

8:1–8. The Promise of Restoration. God did not desire the Exile, and the curse that followed was not His final word. God always wanted to bless His people, and when they were ready to receive blessings, He granted them abundantly. God promised to dwell again in the city (i.e., to sanctify it) and to repopulate it with His people, whom He would save from the east and the west (8:3–8). The "east" may refer to Persia, but the "west" is less identifiable. Instead, east and west may represent all directions. God plans to do the same again in the last days by bringing His people from all nations (cf. Rev. 5:9) and all directions (Luke 13:29).

8:9–15. The Promise of Prosperity. For God to restore Judah, giving them a place in the city again, the people needed to give Him a place again by rebuilding the temple. The Lord had refused to listen to those who did not listen to Him. But now He would bring Judah back to dwell in Jerusalem, and they would provide a temple for Him to dwell in among with them. The repeated exhortation to "let your hands be strong" (8:9, 13) parallels the instructions Haggai gave to Zerubbabel and Joshua, leaders of the postexilic community (cf. Hag. 2:4–5). The words of the prophets seem to refer to the preaching of Haggai, the only other prophet around this time (Zech. 8:9).

The people had previously neglected the work of rebuilding the temple. As a result, poverty, harassment, and conflict characterized the nation (v. 10; Hag. 1:3–9). Both Zechariah 7:14 and 8:10 mention God punishing His people by means of human choices and actions. Through free choice and providence, He both allowed and arranged circumstances under which He knew the nations would ravage Judah and turn against their neighbors. But now God promised to reverse Judah's desperate situation, including changes in both the natural and the social worlds. God would make the land fertile and send rain to the fields (see Deut. 7:13; 28:4; Hag. 2:18). He promised to restore both Judah and Israel, all twelve tribes (Zech. 8:13; cf. 10:6–7; Jer. 50:17–20). In return, He required Judah to both rebuild the temple and reestablish socio-economic justice (Zech. 8:16–17).

8:18–23. The Response to the Inquiry. Until this point, Zechariah had given no answer to the question about fasting. But Judah's response to the Lord's appeals would elicit a natural change in their fasting. Just as true worship and justice would replace the preexilic sins, so festivals would replace fasting. The fast on the seventeenth day of the fourth month (Tammuz) commemorated the breaching of Jerusalem's defensive wall during the last siege (2 Kin. 25:3–4). The fast on the ninth day of the fifth month (Ab) commemorated the destruction of the temple (2 Kin. 25:8–9). The fast on the third day of the seventh month (Tishri) commemorated the assassination of Gedaliah

(2 Kin. 25:22–26), and the fast on the tenth day of the tenth month (Tevet) commemorated the beginning of the final siege of Jerusalem (2 Kin. 25:1). But they would all become festival days.

The rebuilding of the temple would reverse the improper worship so common before the Exile, and justice would replace preexilic injustices. So the return of the exiles would also reverse the scattering of Judah. People from other nations would seek to join them in worshiping the Lord (cf. Is. 60:3–22). Zechariah had earlier announced God's judgment against the nations (Zech. 1:15, 21; 2:8–9), but now he foretells their attachment to His people (8:22–23; cf. 2:11). Zechariah predicted this future ingathering of foreign nations would join the ingathering of Judah that was already happening (8:9, 15).

9:1—14:21
COMING JUDGMENT AND DELIVERANCE

Zechariah 9 begins the last major section of the book. It contains two prophetic sermons (9:1—11:17; 12:1—14:21) that form a continuous, integrated message arranged as a chiasm:

A God's Acts in History, Giving Victory to Zion (9:1–17)

   B God's People Restored (10:1—11:3)

      C Leaders Appointed (11:4–17)

   B' God's People Reformed (12:1—13:9)

A' God's Acts to Culminate History on the Day of the Lord (14:1–21)

9:1—11:17
The First Prophetic Sermon

Both prophetic sermons are called *massa'* of the word of the Lord. The prophets used the Hebrew word *massa'* (9:1; 12:1) two dozen times to refer to an oracle from God, but it does not occur in the earlier sections of Zechariah. This final section of the book appears less systematic than the earlier parts, leading some commentators to suppose that it comes from a different writer. But the hypothesis is unnecessary since we do not know how long Zechariah remained active as a prophet. He possibly wrote various parts of the book at widely separated times, resulting in differences of topic and style.

9:1–8. The Punishment of the Coastal Peoples. The first part of Zechariah 9 announces the

Lord's judgment regarding Judah's neighbors. The cities mentioned were north of Judah, either in Syria (Damascus and Hadrach) or near the Syrian border (Hamath). Zechariah does not describe any particular sins of these Syrian cities or specify any particular punishments. Some translate the Hebrew preposition *be*, used in v. 1 before the land of Hadrach and possibly implied before Hamath in v. 2, as "against." However, it is unclear whether this prophecy condemned or commended. Either way, the eyes of all people (including the tribes of Israel) had turned to the Lord (vv. 1–2).

Tyre and Sidon, both located north of Jerusalem, were the principal surviving Phoenician cities. Several prophets pronounced oracles against these cities (see Is. 23:1–18; Ezek. 26–28; Joel 3:4–5; Amos 1:9–10). The word *matsor* ("tower," "stronghold," "fortress") in Zechariah 9:3 refers to fortified defensive constructions built in the time of King Hiram. The people of Tyre took great pride in these defenses, and God's judgment came against them precisely because of this pride (Is. 23:8–9).

Ashkelon, Gaza, Ekron, and Ashdod were four of the five cities of the Philistine confederacy located southwest of Jerusalem along the Mediterranean coast (the text omits Gath; see Jer. 47:1–7; Amos 1:6–8, Zeph. 2:4–7). Zechariah foresaw these cities becoming dependencies of Judah, without a king and inhabited by a mixed population (Zech. 9:5–6). Ironically, around this time Judah itself had no king, depended on the Persian Empire, and struggled with problems of ethnic and religious diversity. Despite the antagonism between Judah and Philistia, Zechariah predicted the conversion of a remnant of the Philistines, who would integrate into the covenant community, each becoming an *'allup* ("leader," "chief," "clan") in Judah (v. 7). The comparison of Ekron with a Jebusite recalls David's conquest of Jerusalem when the Jebusites were not destroyed but integrated into David's kingdom.

9:9–17. The Triumph of Zion. In contrast to the Philistine's lost king, Judah's king would come (v. 9), initiate an era of peace (v. 10a), and reign over a vast realm. No one between Zechariah and Jesus even remotely resembles the career of this coming King. Zechariah certainly did not expect Zerubbabel to exercise worldwide dominion (v. 10). He expected the coming Messiah. Jesus Christ, a descendant of Zerubbabel (Matt. 1:12–13; Luke 3:27), fulfilled the general terms of this prophecy. Jesus's triumphal entry into Jerusalem fulfilled the

prophecy that Judah's King would come riding on a donkey (Matt. 21:1–7; John 12:12–15). Although the military commonly used horses, both judges and kings rode donkeys and mules (see Judg. 10:4; 1 Kin. 1:33). Though "lowly" (Zech. 9:9), this King would exercise global authority with justice and power, and He and His people would promote peace (v. 10; cf. Is. 9:6–7; Matt. 5:9; Eph. 2:13–17; Heb. 12:14). The expressions *bat tsiyyon* and *bat yerushalam*, literally "daughter [of] Zion" and "daughter [of] Jerusalem," are personifications or poetic terms for the city and/or its inhabitants.

In another postexilic reversal of fortune, the prisoners would return from their places of captivity. The waterless pit (Zech. 9:11) may metaphorically refer to the arid climate of Mesopotamia. Captives hoping for God's deliverance (lit. "prisoners of hope"; i.e., "hopeful prisoners") would return to the stronghold/fortress, presumably Jerusalem, whose fortifications at the time were not impressive. However, God, their true stronghold, had promised to be a wall of fire around Jerusalem (2:5). The text does not explain the nature of the double restoration promised in 9:12, which may relate to the double blessing given to the firstborn (cf. Gen. 48:15), but clearly their final condition would surpass that of their former state.

The military imagery of Zechariah 9:13–15 does not propose that the Jews went to war but rather identifies the returning Jews as the weapons of the Warrior God. In the past God had used the pagan nations as instruments against His disobedient people (cf. Is. 5:24–28; 10:5–6; Jer. 5:15–17; 25:8–9; Hab. 1:5–6). After this, God would use these returning exiles to accomplish His will in a resistant world.

The Lord would punish Judah's neighboring enemies (Zech. 9:1–8), provide Judah with a king (v. 9), establish peace (v. 10), release their imprisoned compatriots (vv. 11–12), and arm Himself with the returning exiles (v. 13). Finally, He would assure their safety (vv. 14–16) and prosperity (v. 17). God Himself would advance as a Warrior to defend His people (vv. 14–15) and display them as His special treasure, a mark of His presence (v. 16). The beauty and goodness Zechariah praises is possibly God's, and he also praises His land (v. 17). As in Zechariah 8:12, God promises the bounty of the earth: grain and new wine (9:17).

10:1—11:3. Restoration of Judah and Ephraim. Canaanite religion associated rainfall with the activities of Baal. Before the Exile, pagan influences had often led the people of Judah into this belief as well. However, the prophets insisted that the Lord, not the Canaanite gods, made the farms and flocks fertile. Zechariah reasserts the teaching of the earlier prophets: idols deceive but the Lord would provide the rain (10:1-2). The "rain" contrasts with the "waterless pit" (9:11). The latter/spring rain fell around February or March, bringing grain crops to maturity.

Zechariah reprises the shepherd metaphor, commonly used in the Torah and the Prophets to describe a national leader (see Num. 27:17; Ezek. 34:1-12). Some passages portray the shepherds positively and some negatively. Zechariah uses the metaphor both ways. At the beginning of chapter 10, Judah either lacks a shepherd (v. 2) or has shepherds who displease the Lord (v. 3). The Hebrew verb *paqad* ("visit," "attend to," "care for") has both positive (see Gen. 50:24-25) and negative connotations (see Ex. 32:24). In this case, Zechariah uses it to express God's care for His people, Judah. The Lord threatened to punish the shepherds and *'attudim* ("leaders," lit. "male goats"; Zech. 10:3-4). These may have been Judeans rather than foreigners, but Zechariah portrays the Lord as warring against foreign enemies, resulting in the restoration of His people. Judah would be His flock and His royal, valiant warhorse (v.3; cf. 9:13).

For Zechariah 10:5, some translators supply the object "enemies" after the verb for treading down/trampling. Other translators, however, indicate that Judah would tramp through muddy streets to fulfill of God's commission. This is the first indication that Judah would join the fight. But their victory would depend on God's presence with them.

God promises to rescue not only Judah but also Joseph and Ephraim (vv. 6-7); that is, the Northern Kingdom of Israel, exiled nearly a century and a half before the captivity of the Southern Kingdom of Judah. In contrast to the promises to Judah, which emphasize leadership (the shepherds) for the nation and their victory, the promises to Ephraim focus on their return. The Lord would willingly restore the northern tribes, just like those of the south. Sadly, few of the exiles from the Northern Kingdom responded to God's call.

The Lord makes several promises to Ephraim. He would *zara'* ("sow," "scatter") them among the peoples, where they would remember Him. Then He would gather them, and they would return with their children. They would survive and their numbers would increase (vv. 8-9). God foretells good for Judah and Israel, not evil.

God promises twice to return the exiles from both Egypt and Assyria (vv. 10-11), conveying the wide scope of the message. Zechariah himself had not returned from either of these nations. He returned from Babylon (at that time part of the Persian Empire). Most of the exiles in Egypt had gone there voluntarily at the time of Jeremiah (cf. Jer. 41-43), and the exiles in Assyria were from Israel, not Judah, and had been taken there many years before Nebuchadnezzar began deporting the people of Judah to Babylon. The scope of the message conveyed by Zechariah is very wide, not concerned only with the exiles from Judah in Babylon but also with God gathering all the tribes of Israel, whether they had been scattered forcibly or voluntarily, and adding to them non-Israelite nations (Zech. 8:22-23). The returning exiles would reenact the Exodus, passing through the sea and the dried-up river (cf. Ex. 14:21—15:22; Josh. 3:10-17).

In chapter 11 Zechariah again addresses Judah's neighbors, Lebanon to the north and Bashan to the east. In Scripture, forests and trees, especially the cedar, symbolize pride (cf. Is. 2:12-13; Ezek. 31:3-5). The destruction of their forests may symbolize the fall of the nations themselves or of their leaders. The shepherds in Zechariah 11:3 probably refer to the leaders of the nations.

After the poetic portion that ends with v. 3, only two other short passages in Zechariah contain poetry (v. 17 and 13:7-9).

11:4-17. Good and Evil Shepherds. A reference to wailing shepherds in Zechariah 11:3 brings the discussion back to Judah's leaders. If this part of the prophecy refers to specific historical persons and events, it is the least transparent part of the book. The two staffs and three shepherds are not easily identifiable. The prophet writes as though he is actually acting out the prophecy as the Lord commands him. Since the flock (v. 4) probably refers to the inhabitants of the land of Judah (v. 6) rather than to an actual flock of sheep, the scene is symbolic, like the manufacture of the high priest's crown in 6:9-15.

The Lord commanded the prophet to feed the "flock" intended for slaughter (11:4), implying that the flock was destined for slaughter even before the prophet became responsible for it. The owners exploited the flock, and its shepherds did not pity them (v. 5). Further, the Lord warned Zechariah that he would not succeed in rescuing the flock, for even God Himself would no longer pity the people (v. 6). Despite God's warnings, Zechariah accepted his appointment and became a good shepherd, or at least an obedient one. He fed the flock, giving special attention to the poor, and selected two staffs for his work as a shepherd, symbolically named *no'am* ("Grace," "Favor," "Beauty") and *khobelim* ("Bonds," "Union," "Harmony"; v. 7). He does not identify the three dismissed shepherds or clarify the reason for the mutual hatred between himself and them—possibly based on their disdain for the flock or, according to some translations, on the enmity with the flock itself (v. 8). The frustrated prophet finally left those of the flock who were dying to perish and those remaining to eat each other (v. 9). Like the Lord in v. 6, the shepherd abandoned the flock to the consequences of their chosen way. He broke the first staff, which represented the covenant he had made with all people (v. 10). This seems to represent the prophet terminating connections between himself and the nations, perhaps represented by the false shepherds and the flock.

Zechariah then broke the second staff, ending the bond between Judah and Israel (v. 14). Of course, Israel had not existed as a nation for about two centuries at this point. Previous chapters foretell the restoration of the people of the Northern Kingdom (cf. 9:13; 10:6-8), so it is not clear why Zechariah announced that the alliance between Israel and Judah would not prevail. He seems to indicate that such prophecies were conditional. In the rest of the book, he speaks about only Judah.

Finally, the prophet asked for payment for the services he rendered as a shepherd, and he received thirty shekels. This acted-out prophecy predicts God's rejected prophet, the Messiah, who would give His life for the people. To this service, they would assign an estimated value of thirty shekels (Matt. 27:9-10).

It is not entirely clear how the foolish shepherd of Zechariah 11:15-17 differs from his predecessor in vv. 4-9, except that the rejected shepherd seems more responsible than the cruel shepherd. The former shepherd let the "dying die" and the "perishing perish" (v. 9). His successor would not care for the dying, young, ill, or healthy of the flock and would go further by exploiting the flock (v. 16). Zechariah curses both the shepherd's action (his arm) and his perception (his right eye; v. 17). Because the flock had not accepted the shepherd appointed by the Lord, they would end up with a cruel shepherd under whom they would fare even worse. They would suffer because of their own

wrongdoing. If we assume that "the flock" refers to Judah, this passage leaves the nation in a perilous state, deprived of God's pity and led by a worthless shepherd (vv. 6, 17). Judah had experienced this situation in exile, when they gravely needed the divine deliverance described in the second prophetic sermon (chaps. 12-14).

12:1—14:21
The Second Prophetic Sermon

12:1-9. Jerusalem's Rescue. Zechariah's second *massa'* ("burden," "oracle," prophecy") concerns Israel (i.e., the people of God residing in Judah; 12:1). In it he denounces all the nations of the earth who gather against Judah and Jerusalem (vv. 2-3). The prophecy contains words of hope intended to encourage the people, both historically and eschatologically. Therefore, the Hebrew preposition *'al* in v. 1 probably means "concerning" rather than "against." The passage communicates God's promise to protect Judah and Jerusalem.

This oracle often uses the imagery of war. As in 9:13, which describes Judah as a weapon in God's hands, Zechariah here prophesies that Judah would become an instrument capable of impeding or injuring the nations opposing it—a heavy, massive stone/immovable rock (12:3) and a cup causing drunken reeling/staggering (v. 2). "That day" refers to the time when God would punish His enemies, purify His people, and perform wonders (v. 3; cf. v. 8; 13:1-2; 14:4, 6). In the Hebrew, this expression (*bayyom hahu'*) occurs five times in chapters 1-11 but seventeen times in chapters 12-14, indicating a shift in Zechariah's focus from his own era to the eschaton.

The Lord's promise addresses the *'alupe*, a term sometimes rendered as "clans" and sometimes as "governors," "leaders," or "chieftains" (12:5-6). During this time Judah had no king, leaving royal appointees, like Zerubbabel, as the highest political officials. Whether leaders or clans, the *'alupe* would consume/devour all the surrounding peoples on the right and left (v. 6). Since "right" and "left" in Hebrew can equally mean "south" and "north," respectively, this may refer to the nearby nations mentioned in 9:1-7, to the more remote superpowers in Egypt and Mesopotamia (10:10-11), or most probably to all of Judah's enemies. Like a flaming torch among sheaves, Judah would completely destroy their enemies. Again, Judah's own strength would not accomplish this, but God would assure their protection and destroy all the nations coming against Jerusalem (12:9; cf. 4:6). The promises of deliverance not only extend to Jerusalem but also to the rural areas, the dwelling tents of Judah, where seminomadic shepherds moved from season to season. God promised that the glory/honor of Jerusalem would not exceed that of the less developed areas (12:7).

12:10-14. Jerusalem's Mourning. Zechariah foresaw not only material restoration for Judah but spiritual restoration as well. The same God who would defend them and cause them to rebuild their city and temple would also give them a spirit of grace and supplication (v. 10). They would not rejoice over the destruction of their enemies. Instead they would mourn as a parent mourns for an only child or a firstborn son. But they would not mourn because of their own material losses but because of the God they pierced (v. 10). Christian interpreters usually take this as a reference to the crucifixion of Jesus, when the only begotten Son of God was pierced on the cross for the sins of humanity. The listing of various families and clans who would mourn implies that God's people would mourn both universally and individually over their offenses against Him (vv. 12-14; cf. Matt. 24:30; Rev. 1:7). This passage contains several similarities with the messianic prophecy of Isaiah 52:13—53:12.

13:1-9. Spiritual Reformation. In response to Judah mourning over their offenses, a "fountain" would open in Jerusalem to deal with sin and uncleanness. Zechariah 13:1 does not state who would open this fountain, but v. 2 specifies that the Lord Himself would remove the names of the idols as well as the prophets and the unclean spirits (cf. 1 Kin. 22:22). The "names of the idols" signifies calling upon idols to invoke their help, and their removal means that the people would commit themselves exclusively to the Lord. The Lord does not explain the reason for the removal of the prophets, but Zechariah 13:4 hints that some people dressed in hairy garb resembling that of prophets in order to deliver false messages. In fact, all references to prophets in chapter 13 are negative. The prophets God would remove were likely those He had not commissioned. Not only would God remove the prophets, but their own families would reject and kill them (v. 3). These prophets would deny any pretention to prophetic function, no longer wishing to be identified as prophets (vv. 5-6). They would explain away their wounds, possibly associated with prophetic

ecstasy, as injuries suffered in "the house of my friends" (v. 6; cf. 1 Kin. 18:28). Some consider the reference to the wounds as a messianic prophecy announcing the sufferings of Christ during the crucifixion (see Zechariah: Introduction; Matt. 27:26; Mark 14:65)

Zechariah 13:7 returns to the image of the shepherd that is used eight times in chapters 10-11. The text does not explain the striking of the shepherd and the scattering of the people, nor does it identify the shepherd. But he is clearly an agent of God, who calls him His companion, someone close to Him, and His associate. Jesus quoted this verse to predict that His disciples would abandon Him at His arrest (Matt. 26:31). Some translations capitalize the words "Man" and "Shepherd," considering them divine titles referring to Christ. The death of two-thirds of the flock does not correspond precisely to any historical event in the time of Zechariah or in the ministry of Christ (cf. Matt. 26:31; Mark 14:27). But the proportions are not necessarily mathematically precise. The ratio of two-thirds to one-third means that most would be cut off. But God would bring the remaining third through the fire to refine them (Zech. 13:9). This refining process would result in their attachment to the Lord. He would call them His people, and they would call Him their God. In this way, He would purify the mourners and prepare them for the Day of the Lord.

14:1-21. The Day of the Lord. For the first time in the book, Zechariah 14:1 introduces the concept of the Day of the Lord. Eight of the other prophets also use this expression, usually to describe a day when the Lord would act on behalf of His people to correct wrongs and to establish justice. Christian interpretations often associate it with the return of Christ since the prophecy of Chapter 14 was never fulfilled in Judah. Its eschatological character suggests that its fulfillment may not follow the specific details mentioned in this chapter. The concept of the Day of the Lord in the Hebrew Bible includes the gathering of not only God's people but also His enemies for a final confrontation between good and evil (v. 2; cf. Joel 3:1-2). Zechariah depicts it in menacing terms, including the capture and looting of Jerusalem, the rape of its women, and the captivity of half of its survivors (Zech. 14:1-2). He predicts a time not of ease and delight but of conflict, calamity, and cataclysm, though not utter destruction. God would spare His people. He would not *karat* ("cut off," "remove") the remaining remnant from the city (v. 2).

In the eschatological conflict, the forces of evil would have their moment. But in the end God Himself would fight against them and defeat them (vv. 3, 5). The presence of the Lord and supernatural changes in the earth are essential elements of the concept of the Day of the Lord. In Zechariah's description, this includes the transformation of not only the land (v. 4) but also changes in the celestial realm (vv. 6–7). Enemies would capture Jerusalem (v. 2), but God would provide an escape by dividing the steep Mount of Olives (a north–south ridge) from east to west, creating a very large valley by which the inhabitants of Jerusalem could flee (vv. 4–5). The *kedoshim* ("holy ones," "saints") mentioned in v. 5 could be humans (cf. Deut. 33:3; Ps. 50:5), but here they are probably heavenly beings (cf. Job 4:18; 15:15).

The cataclysmic alteration of the earth on the Day of the Lord continues in Zechariah 14:8–10. Historically, Jerusalem owed its existence to a permanent water source, the Gihon spring. This spring provided just enough water to sustain the city in all seasons. However, the waters of Gihon all flow out into the Kidron brook, which leads to the Jordan River and the Dead Sea. Zechariah describes geographical changes in the land which would convert all of Judah, from Geba to Rimmon, south of Jerusalem, into a plain. Much of this area is mountainous, so this would require a striking transformation. In Zechariah's description, two streams originating from Jerusalem would water this vast plain. But even after the creation of the vast, well-watered plain, Jerusalem itself would remain elevated on a mountain (i.e., a defensible location), safe and inhabited (vv. 10–11). Similarly, the book of Revelation describes a transformed earth and a high-walled, holy city with gates that never close, apparently because there is no need for defense (Rev. 21:1–25).

As the spiritual consequence of His intervention, God would establish His reign. Those who have trusted Him have always regarded Him as King, but Zechariah recognizes the distinct unity and unique authority of the Lord as King over all the earth (Zech. 14:9; cf. Ps. 10:16; Is. 33:22; Jer. 10:10; Dan. 7:27). The oneness of the Lord implies that all the peoples of the earth would worship only Him. The Lord would not only intervene on behalf of His people but also send plagues to afflict those opposing Judah (Zech. 14:12). The plagues would affect even the livestock of Judah's enemies (v. 15).

Although Zechariah expected the surrounding nations to oppose the people of Judah, he also anticipated their conversion (cf. 8:22–23). The survivors of all the opposing nations would eventually go to Jerusalem to celebrate the Lord's festivals (14:16). Those failing to observe the Festival of Tabernacles would lose the seasonal rain necessary for cultivation. The possibility of disobedience and punishment suggests that this foretells what would happen if Judah remained faithful rather than serving as an unconditional eschatological prophecy.

As a result of the events of the Day of the Lord, Jerusalem would be holy. Even common vessels used for everyday purposes would be just as holy as the vessels of the temple (v. 21). A term regarding the Lord's holiness was engraved on a gold plate attached to the turban of the high priest (v. 20; cf. Ex. 28:36). On that day, every pot in Jerusalem would be holy to the Lord, and everyday utensils would be raised to sacred status (Zech. 14:21). Some versions translate the word *kena'ani* (lit. "Canaanite") as "merchant," which would indicated the end of commerce in the Lord's temple. God would accept all nations and would no longer consider anyone a foreigner.

This description of the Day of the Lord in Zechariah closes the book on a high note by proclaiming hope. The direct and personal intervention of God in human history would permanently defeat evil. Holiness would triumph over uncleanness and sin (see Lev. 16), bringing with it a glorious future in the presence of the Lord.

MALACHI

INTRODUCTION

Title. The book is named after the Prophet Malachi and contains the prophetic messages the Lord sent to Israel through him. Since the Hebrew word *mal'aki* means "my messenger," some interpreters suggest that it is not a proper name. In that case, we would not know who wrote the book. But the fact that the name has a general meaning does not signify that it is not a proper name. Obadiah, for instance, means "servant of the Lord," but it is also the name of a prophet.

Date. Malachi did not date his message, but the content of the book leaves little doubt that its author ministered during the postexilic period, possibly during middle of the 5th century B.C., which would make him a contemporary of Ezra and Nehemiah, whose books address similiar issues current at the time.

Backgrounds. After his victory over the Babylonians (539 B.C.), Cyrus the Great issued an edict to rebuild the temple of Jerusalem (Ezra 1:2), bringing Israel's captivity to an end. The first batch of returnees laid the foundation in 536 B.C. Malachi must have ministered after Haggai and Zechariah, during whose time the temple was rebuilt (Ezra 6:14). The social and religious conditions reflected in Malachi's preaching closely resemble the situation faced by Ezra and Nehemiah. Malachi condemns similar abuses, such as the exploitation of widows and orphans (Mal. 3:5; cf. Neh. 5:1–13), divorces, and mixed marriages (Mal. 2:10–16; cf. Neh. 10:30; 13:23–29). Both Malachi and Nehemiah emphasize tithing as part of religious reform (Mal. 3:7–10; Neh. 10:37–39).

Authorship. Everything known about the author comes from the book itself. This commentary shares the view of a growing number of modern scholars that Malachi is the personal name of the author of the book.

Theology and Purpose. Malachi presents his message within the framework of God's covenant with His people. God gives abundant love and undeserved grace as His part within the covenant (Mal. 1:2, 9; cf. Deut. 7:7). Malachi addresses the people's response to these gifts.

1. Obedience. God expected the people to respond to His election with love, obedience (cf. Deut. 20:12–13), faithfulness (Mal. 2:14–16), and respect (1:6). Malachi prophesied because the people were not living up to the responsibilities required by this covenant relationship. The prophet assured the people of God's unfailing love, but also held them accountable for their response. God's love is unconditional, but His blessings are not. Basing his appeal on the "oneness" of God (cf. Deut. 6:4–9), Malachi calls for not only total, undivided commitment to God but also for loyalty and faithfulness in human relations, such as social justice, equality, and marriage vows (Mal. 2:9–10, 14–16).

2. The Covenant. Malachi conveys his message using covenant language, much of it borrowed from Deuteronomy. Terms such as "love," "fear," "faithfulness," "law of Moses," and "all Israel" fit the covenant context, as does Malachi's emphasis on the Levitical priesthood, tithing, and the covenant blessings and curses (2:2; 3:8–10, 12). The Lord calls His people to "remember," a concept central to the personal relationship embedded in the covenant (4:4; cf. Deut. 4:10; 5:15; 32:7), and promises to remember those who feared Him and honored His name (Mal. 3:16).

3. Universality and Hope. Malachi contains strong elements of universality (cf. 1:5, 11, 14; 2:10; 3:12), which provide a solid basis for future hope by encouraging the reader to look back to God's original design. The universality provides a solid basis for future hope. Malachi exposes and condemns sin and warns of the fate of the unrepentant. But he also promises a better future and a faithful remnant (1:5; 2:14; 3:12, 16–18; 4:2). A future generation would experience a revival that would prepare them for the Day of the Lord (2:15; 4:5–6).

Literary Features. Malachi's style borders between prose and poetry. Following the superscription (1:1), he presents his message in a series of five disputations (i.e., oral defense of thesis using logic) between God and the people of Judah.

COMMENTARY

1:1–5
First Disputation

After a brief introduction (1:1), the book immediately moves to the first disputation, which addresses God's love for His people. The people question His love for them, and God responds (vv. 2–5).

1:1. Superscription. The superscription identifies the originator of the message (the Lord), the prophetic instrument (Malachi), the recipients (Israel), and the nature of the message (the word of the Lord). The Hebrew word *massa'* literally means "burden," but in this context it seems to carry the technical meaning of "oracle," a divine communication through a prophet (cf. Is. 19:1; 21:1; Nah. 1:1; Hab. 1:1). The prophets repeatedly use "the word of the Lord" to stress the divine authority and reliability of their messages. As commonly used during postexilic times, the name Israel designates the people of God in Judah.

1:2–5. God's Love for His Elect. The disputations in Malachi all follow the same basic structure: God's initial statement, the people's objection, and God's response to the objection. Here the people questioned God's love for them. The statement "I have loved you" could also be translated as "I love you." God's love is not based on any merit or inner quality of the people but on God's grace (Deut. 7:7). The people should have responded to such abundant grace with loving obedience (cf. Deut. 6:6; 10:12–13), but instead they questioned His love (Mal. 1:2).

In response, the Lord reminded them of His election of Jacob instead of Esau, as evidenced by the condition of Esau's land at that time. The strong statement "Esau I have hated" does not imply any animosity against Esau or his descendants (v. 3). Such hatred was actually prohibited in the law (Deut. 23:7). In context the phrase simply means, "I have chosen Jacob

rather than Esau." The nonelection of Esau was manifested in the condition of his land at that time. The description leaves no doubt that the fate of the Edomites was connected to their sins and not predetermined by God. Their ambition to return and build up what they had lost was rejected because they were a wicked land (Mal. 1:4), against whom God's indignation/wrath would last forever. During the fifth century B.C., the Nabateans expanded their power and forced Edom further south into what in NT times was named Idumea.

The notion of God's wrath is part of an important biblical pattern. Sin and apostasy lead to retribution, which results either in repentance and purification or in condemnation. This first disputation ends, however, on a positive note of hope for the future. The people of Israel would see the Lord magnified and His greatness acknowledged beyond the border of Israel. They would proclaim Him as Lord over history. This prophecy gives the disputation a universal perspective.

1:6—2:9
Second Disputation:
Honoring God's Name

The second disputation contains two dialogues in which God accuses the priests of dishonoring His name (1:6–11, 12–14), followed by a monologue affirming God's sovereignty (2:1–9).

1:6–11. First Dialogue. In this disputation, Malachi invokes the name *yahweh tseba'ot* ("the Lord of hosts," "the Lord Almighty," "the Lord of heavenly forces") eleven times to emphasize the divine origin of his message. The oracle opens with two proverbial sayings contrasting Israel's attitude toward God with a son who honors his father and a servant/slave who honors his master. As Israel's Father, God created and cared for them (cf. Is. 64:8; Hos. 11:1). As Israel's Master, He brought them out of Egypt, redeemed them, and became their Lord. God naturally expected respect, but His children despised/showed contempt for Him. They had shamed His name through disloyalty to the covenant.

The Hebrew word for "honor" (*kabod*) literally means "to be heavy." God is a person of weight, and His children should honor Him by taking what He says seriously. But the priests, who were responsible for maintaining proper worship, offered imperfect sacrifices on the Lord's table (the altar of burnt offerings). They would never have offered the Persian governor such gifts (Mal. 1:8). In this way, they despised the Lord by belittling His importance in the eyes of the people and the nations. Only a perfect sacrifice could represent the sacrifice of Christ to atone for the sins of the world. The Lord found this practice so contemptible that He wished someone would shut the doors leading to the temple complex so the priests could not offer defiled sacrifices (v. 10).

The Lord concludes by expounding on the future, when all would worship Him. His name would become great among the nations/Gentiles, a hope also reflected in the writings of previous prophets (see Is. 56:6–7). This broad, grand vision marks a stark and deliberate contrast to the petty attitude of the priests who received the message.

1:12–14. Second Dialogue. Like the first conversation, the second contains God's statement, a response, and a reference to the universal nature of the covenant. The Lord condemned the priests for treating the altar and the sacrifices as common and for complaining about their ministry, which they considered a burden instead of a privilege (Mal. 1:12–13). In response, the Lord rejected their blemished, disrespectful sacrifices. As a great King, He should be feared among the nations (vv. 13–14).

2:1–9. God's Speech. Malachi now moves from dialogue to divine monologue. "And now," introduces a judgment oracle (cf. Is. 5:5; 16:14; Jer. 18:11; Hos. 5:7). The Lord had presented evidence against the priests and would now pronounce the verdict. The word *mitswah* (lit. "commandment," "decree") underscores the certainty of God's verdict against the very priests expected to guard His commandments. God would curse the blessings of the priests, reversing the blessing He gave Aaron, unless they resolved (Heb. *tashimu al leb*, lit. "take it to heart") to honor/glorify His name (Mal. 2:2; cf. l:6; Num. 6:24–26; cf. Deut. 28–29).

God further explained two consequences of the curse. First, God would rebuke the descendants of the priests (Mal. 2:3). Scholars dispute the vocalization of this phrase (the original Hebrew text did not contain vowels). The word translated as "descendants" could actually mean "arm," implying that God would weaken, even paralyze, the priests, making them unable to perform their duties (cf. 1 Sam. 2:31; Ps. 10:15). However, the translation "descendant" or "offspring" (lit. "seed") makes better sense. In context, the use of *ga'ar* ("rebuke") suggests that God would humiliate the descendants of

the priests by withholding His blessings in order to hopefully preserve the covenant with Levi (Mal. 2:4). As the second consequence of the curse, God would spread refuse/dung from sacrificial animals on the faces of the priests. This gross act would not only humiliate them but also render them unclean. The priests normally removed and burned the feces from the sacrifices (Lev. 4:11–12). But because of this ritual pollution, those appointed by God to remove uncleanness would find themselves carried off from His presence and thrown out with the fecal matter of the sacrifices.

God issued this stern verdict to preserve His covenant with Levi (Mal. 2:4). Translations such as "abolish" or "fall to the ground" presuppose an unnecessary change of the Hebrew text. God positively recalled the time when Levi showed Him respect/fear and reverently stood in awe of His name (v. 5). As Levi taught the truth, his descendants, the priests, were tasked with sharing divine instruction as the messengers of the Lord (vv. 6–7). This wordplay on the meaning of Malachi's own name ("my messenger") identifies the failure of the priests. By failing to communicate God's message, they had corrupted/violated God's covenant with Levi.

God's retribution naturally followed. Just as the priests despised God's name by making His table contemptible (1:7), so would He make them contemptible and humiliate them before the people (2:9). They had failed to walk with God and had shown unfair partiality and favoritism in their implementation of the law (cf. 1:9).

2:10—3:6
Third Disputation:
God's Justice and Judgment

Malachi begins the third disputation with a passionate appeal to the people (2:10). The divine indictment follows, juxtaposed with two attempts by the people to defend themselves (vv. 11–13). They first protest God's judgment and then question the fairness of His justice. God responds unambiguously with the facts about the people's behavior (vv. 14b–16, 17b). The oracle ends with a pronouncement of God's judgment: He will arrive at His temple (3:1–2), and both the priesthood (vv. 3–4) and the people (vv. 5–6) will face their fate.

2:10–13. God's Lawsuit against the People. The prophet's passionate appeal to the people in v. 10 functions as a transition to this section. Malachi condemns the partiality of the priests by citing the universal implications of the nature of Yahweh as "one God" (cf. 2:9–10; Deut. 6:4). God, not Abraham, is the one Father of all because He created us (cf. Ex. 4:22; Hos. 11:1). In the OT, only God appears as the subject of the verb *bara'* ("create"). God created all humanity (Gen. 1–2), and He created His people when He delivered them from Egypt (cf. Is. 43:1, 7, 15).

Like Daniel in his prayer of penitence, Malachi includes himself among the people when he asks why "we" are treacherous/unfaithful with each other (cf. Dan. 9:4b–19). He emphasizes the brotherhood and common ancestry of the people of Israel through their collective covenant with God. Equality before God should lead to proper behavior toward each other. The Hebrew verb *bagad* ("to be treacherous," "unfaithful") occurs five times in Malachi 2:10–16, highlighting God's condemnation of faithless behavior in marriage and social relationships. The use of metaphors from family relations is expanded by a reference to their collective covenant with God, emphasizing the brotherhood of the people of Israel with a common ancestry.

In vv. 11–13, the prophet accuses the men of Judah of marrying women who worshiped foreign gods (lit. "a daughter of a god"). The Hebrew word *to'ebah* ("abomination," "detestable thing") often refers to foreign gods or the act of marrying foreigners and worshiping their gods (see also Ezra 9:14). The abomination was not the mixed marriages but the resulting corruption of worship, as the foreign women brought pagan worship into the community. The social problem arose from the religious element. The peoples of the ancient Near East (despite ethnic differences) did not divide life into sacred and secular elements. Everything had religious implications. The people of Judah had desecrated God's sanctuary by what some today might consider a secular act (Mal. 2:11). The women's ethnicity did not matter, but their religious beliefs did. The Hebrew word *qodesh* ("holy institution," "sanctuary," "holy place") may refer directly to the temple, but it may also include everything set apart for God (e.g., the temple, the city, and the people). God had expressly forbidden the Israelites from marrying foreigners because they would turn them away from God (Ex. 34:11–16; Deut. 7:3–4). Through these marriages and the pagan worship resulting from them, the people became both ceremonially and morally unclean. The prophet wished that the Lord would cut off/remove (Heb. *karat*) anyone acting this way from the tents of Jacob (Mal. 2:12). *Karat* means

to expell from the worshiping community of God by exile or, in extreme cases, by execution (Gen. 17:14; Lev. 7:20, 21; 17:10; 19:8; 20:17; cf. Dan. 9:26).

Finally, Malachi reveals the utter hypocrisy of those who, though living in violation of the covenant, bring an offering to the Lord and cover the altar with tears and laments (Mal. 2:13). Immoral behavior does not necessarily prevent expressions of strong religious emotions.

2:14–17. Objections Refuted. When Malachi declared that God would no longer favorably accept their offerings, the people demanded to know the reason. He answered that they had broken their marriage vows, which rendered their expression of religious emotions worthless. Their moral life directly conflicted with the values of the covenant (see Ezra 9–10). It appears that the men had divorced their Jewish wives, the wives of their youth, in order to marry the pagan women.

God intended marriage to reflect the covenant love and faithfulness He Himself showed His people (cf. Jer. 2:2; Hos. 2:18–20). Marriage is a permanent covenant between a man and a woman with God as the witness (Mal. 2:14; cf. Prov. 2:17). God intended close intimacy between them. The word *khaberet* means a close friend/companion/partner with whom one shares everything.

Malachi 2:15–16 is fraught with grammatical issues that make translation difficult. Some translations apply "one" to God (the "one God"). Others apply "one" to the marriage union, referring to the Creation, when God made the first couple one. In this context, the reference to the Spirit would mean that husband and wife share the same original spiritual bond of love and understanding because God continues to be part of it. Such a union results in "godly offspring," children taught to follow God because they have a mother and father who both have a right relationship with Him. Malachi reminded those men of Judah who had divorced their wives to take foreign wives that the spiritual dimension of their previous marriages remained because God remained as witness. In light of the original ideal of Eden, it is no wonder that God hates divorce (v. 16). Those who divorce their spouses engage in an act of treachery/disloyalty (Heb. *bagad*).

The people's second objection functions as a transition and introduction to the subsequent divine speech (3:1–6). The question "Where is the God of justice?" cynically casts doubt on God's moral integrity, prompting Him to answer.

3:1–6. God's Response: Judgment Will Come.
The Lord assured His people that He would suddenly and dramatically come to His temple to judge (cf. Pss. 96:13; 98:9; Dan. 7:22). Before His coming, He would send His messenger to prepare the way. In Hebrew, "my messenger" is the same as the name of the prophet, but the context seems to militate against any reference to Malachi himself. The messenger would announce God's arrival and encourage the people to pave the way (cf. Is. 40:3). He would proclaim peace, joy, and the good news of salvation (cf. Ps. 68:12, 18; Is. 52:7–8).

Judgment implies deliverance and often has a positive connotation in the OT. Given Judah's moral state in Malachi's time, however, the statement that the people seek the Lord and delight in/desire Him must be ironic (cf. Amos 5:18–20). The messenger of the covenant, a concept unique to Malachi, stands in clear parallel to "the Lord," suggesting that it is a name for God (more specifically, for the Messiah), not for the prophet. "Lord" here translates from the Hebrew *'adon*, referring to God as the heavenly King (cf. Zech. 4:14; 6:5).

"The God of justice" would come to His sanctuary to judge, beginning with the Levites (Mal. 3:3; cf. 2:17). He would purify and refine them, bringing moral and spiritual renewal that would make the sacrifices and offerings once again ceremonially pure and acceptable/pleasing to the Lord (cf. Jer. 2:2–3). After purifying the priesthood, God would judge all the people, eradicating those who practice sorcery, commit adultery, perjure themselves, treat foreigners unjustly/turn away aliens, defraud laborers of their wages, and oppress widows and orphans.

Malachi 3:6 is a transitional verse that many consider an introduction to the following section. If so, the Hebrew conjunction *ki* ("for," "because"), which some versions leave untranslated, could mean "indeed." That God does not change does not mean that He is indifferent to what happens. It emphasizes that He has always been and will always continue to be the covenant God of mercy (cf. Ex. 34:6–7). Through judgment and purification, God shows grace to the descendants of Jacob, saving them from destruction though they are wayward deceivers just like their ancestor.

3:7–12
Fourth Disputation: The Practical Benefits of Repentance

The fourth disputation plays off of the reference to Jacob in 3:6, equating the attitude and behavior of the people to that of their ancestors.

This leads into a divine call for the people of Malachi's time to return to the Lord, followed by their response (v. 7). The central part of the disputation covers the covenant curses and blessings associated with the laws of tithes and offerings. The phrase *amar yahweh tseba'ot* ("says the LORD of hosts," "says the LORD Almighty," "says the LORD of heavenly forces") highlights Malachi's prophetic authority.

3:7–9. The Past and the Present: Tithing. The people continued to turn away from God's decrees and ordinances, as they had since the time of their fathers/ancestors. The Lord begins the discussion by appealing to the people to return to Him, the typical OT expression for conversion. If the people would return to God, God would return to them. Both parties would stop walking away from each other.

The people responded immediately by asking in what way/how they should return, an apparent claim of innocence denying that they had done anything that required repentance. The Lord responded with a clear example: they had robbed Him. When they again asked in what way/how they had robbed Him, God replied that they had cheated Him "in tithes and offerings." This had brought the covenant curses on them (vv. 8–9). A tithe (lit. "a tenth") refers to the divine law requiring the Israelites to give a tenth of their income or spoil to the Lord (Gen. 14:18–20; 28:20–22; Lev. 27:30–33). An offering refers to any gift carried to the temple.

3:10–12. The Tithe and Blessings. God appealed to the people a second time, this time to supply His house with food by bringing all the tithes/the full tithe into the storehouse (i.e., the temple treasury). God set this up as a test. If the people would faithfully bring in the tithes and offerings, He would open heaven and pour out His blessings, proving that He alone supplies all His children need (see "Covenant Renewal and Tithing," p. 602). This reciprocal movement connects the earthly sanctuary with the heavenly sanctuary, the location of God's throne room.

The practice of tithing, already introduced in Genesis, relates closely to the concept of blessing (Gen. 14:18–20; 28:20–22). This sermon in Malachi reflects the theological message of these accounts from the origin of Israel. Tithing is not about paying God, and blessing is not about God automatically repaying the giver. Jacob had to learn that tithing involves more than a simple trading contract (Gen. 27:20; 32:27–30).

Like marriage, it is a covenant based on mutual grace, love, faithfulness, trust, and commitment (see Mal. 2:11–16). God's people should bring Him tithes and offerings as an expression of gratitude for His undeserved mercy, responding to His initiative by returning a portion of what He has already given them.

God's promise to bless the fertility of the land resembles the covenant blessings in Deuteronomy (Mal. 3:11–12; Deut. 28:12–13; 30:8–10). God's blessings again have universal implications, indicating that He was about to fulfill His promise to make Abraham a blessing to all people (Mal. 3:12; Gen 12:3; cf. Mal. 1:5, 12; 2:10).

3:13—4:3
Fifth Disputation: Benefits of Serving God

The fifth disputation begins by contrasting two groups with two very different attitudes concerning judgment. The Lord characterized each group by its words. The first group argued with God's assessment of them (3:13–15). God never directly replies to their objections. Instead, He turns His focus to the second group, those who feared Him and trusted His plans for them (vv. 16–17). The section ends with God explaining what would happen to these two groups in the judgment to come (3:18—4:3).

3:13–15. Speech of the People. The Lord charged the people with speaking harsh, arrogant words against Him, claiming that it is useless/futile to serve Him. They treated God's commands as a means to gain profit/benefit for themselves, so they considered serving Him a drudgery that brought only sorrow and mourning (3:14). By calling the arrogant/proud blessed, they mocked God's promise that all the nations would call His people blessed (vv. 12, 15). By proclaiming that the arrogant and wicked successfully get away with tempting/ testing (Heb. *bakhan*) God, they mocked God's plea to try/test (*bakhan*) Him through tithing (vv. 10, 15). Since God did not intervene, they stopped caring.

3:16–17. Those Who Fear God. Following the dialogue of the previous section, verse 3:16 switches to prophetic monologue. Malachi portrays those who respond favorably to God's message as people who fear the Lord (i.e., honor Him) and *khashab* His name. This Hebrew word, sometimes translated as "meditate," means to esteem and value (cf. Is. 13:17).

It contrasts with the attitude exhibited by the priests (Mal. 1:6, 11). The Lord does not accept the worship of the rebellious (1:8, 10, 13), but He listens to those who fear Him.

Malachi describes a scroll/book of remembrance written in God's presence in His heavenly sanctuary concerning the words and actions of those who fear the Lord. The Bible speaks about several heavenly books, most significantly the Book of Life, which records the names of those who believe (Ex. 32:32–33; Ps. 69:28; Dan. 12:1). The mention of a "book/ scroll of remembrance" is unique to Malachi. This may refer to the Book of Life, but it more likely refers to a book of deeds (cf. Esth. 2:23; 6:1). The word "remembrance" underlines the fact that God does not forget anyone or anything. Those who fear the Lord would become His special possession and receive their reward on the day of judgment (Mal. 3:17; cf. Ex. 19:5). Because they are so precious to Him, He will spare them.

3:18—4:3. Two Destinies. The Lord proclaimed that the fire of purification would burn on the day of judgment to destroy the arrogant and wicked, those who do not serve Him. The fire would burn them completely, leaving neither root nor branch (4:1; cf. 3:2–3, 18). There is no "soul" burning in an eternal torment. This contrasts with the fate of those who fear God's name, who would leap and jump for joy (Heb. *push*, "leap," "gallop," "frolic," sometimes translated as "grow"; cf. Hab. 1:8), like calves running free in the field, and trample the ashes of the wicked (Mal. 4:2–3; cf. 3:16).

The phrase "Sun of Righteousness" occurs only here in the OT. The authors of the Bible hesitated to associated the sun with God, mainly because of the prevalence of pagan sun worship (but see Ps. 84:11; Is. 60:1–3). Here the image portrays the dawn of a new day in which the rays/wings of the sun bring healing. "Righteousness" often describes God's merciful intervention in the life of His people to save and deliver them (Pss. 96:10–13; 97:4; 98:1–2; Is. 56:1; cf. Rom. 3:21–22). God's new day of righteousness would bring life and joy. The saved ones are compared to calves: they would *push*. The idea is that the people would leap and jump for joy like calves running freely on a field after leaving their stall. They would trample the ashes of the wicked. This image also connects to Malachi 4:1, which states that the proud would be completely burned. There is no "soul" burning in eternal torment.

4:4–6

Final Appeal

The book of Malachi concludes with the Lord's final appeal to the people. It summarizes and weaves together major themes of the previous disputations and connects them with the larger theological setting.

4:4. Remember the Law. God exhorted the people to "remember" the law. A key concept in God's covenant with Israel, remembering means more than just mentally recalling the event (Ex. 13:3; 20:8; Deut. 5:15; 24:18). It means reacting appropriately to the recollection, in this case by obeying the law (cf. Ps. 103:18). The law of Moses broadly encompasses all of God's revelation at Mount Sinai. Together with the *khuqqim* ("statutes," "decrees") and *mishpatim* ("judgments," "laws"), it designates the law in its totality (cf. Lev. 26:46). Horeb is another name for Sinai (Ex. 33:6). These repeated references to the covenant make this exhortation to remember the law a natural, final summary of God's intention for His people (Mal. 1:6; 2:6; 3:7, 14).

4:5–6. The Coming of Elijah. The Lord moves from a discussion of the law to prophecy, combining the references to the past with expectations for the future. He promised to send the prophet Elijah to prepare the way for the Day of the Lord. Elijah, as the typical prophet for spiritual renewal, represents the messenger prophesied in 3:1. Jesus applied this text to John the Baptist, who came "in the spirit and power of Elijah" (Luke 1:17) to prepare the way for Jesus (Matt. 3:1–12; 17:12–13). The announcement of the coming of the "great and dreadful day of the Lord" clearly links it to previous descriptions of God's intervention (Mal. 3:2; cf. Joel 2:31). In Malachi, by the pairing of law and prophecy, the reference to the past combines with the expectations of the future.

The prophetic messenger would turn the hearts of the parents (lit. "fathers") to the children and the hearts of the children to the parents. This description expands on the function of the messenger in 3:1 by describing how the messenger would prepare the way for the Lord. Malachi uses several family metaphors and references to fathers/ancestors (see 1:6; 2:6, 10), but God promises more than bridging generational gaps. He promises a return to His original covenant made with the fathers/ancestors at Sinai. Hence the call to remember serves as a call for His people to return to the faith of their ancestors. The mutual turning of hearts between parents and children indicates the two temporal directions of law and prophecy, both past and future. The appeal closes with a warning that God would strike the earth/land with a curse if the people rejected the message. The "earth" could refer to the land of Israel, or in view of Malachi's proclamation of the universality of the God of Israel, it could refer to the entire world.

Christians place Malachi as the last book of the OT. It fittingly ends without closure, looking to the future. The Lord promised blessings to come but also warned the impenitent. He commanded His people to remain in His family, to keep His law, to listen to His prophets, and to honor and praise Him (3:16). The book closes with the potential for either judgment or salvation, leaving the last word yet unspoken. There is still hope.